Encyclopedia of

Library and Information Sciences, Fourth Edition

Volume 4

Encyclopedias from the Taylor & Francis Group

Print	Online

Agriculture

Encyclopedia of Agricultural, Food, and Biological Engineering, 2nd Ed., 2 Vols.   Pub'd. 10/21/10
K10554 (978-1-4398-1111-5)   K11382 (978-1-4398-2806-9)

Encyclopedia of Animal Science, 2nd Ed., 2 Vols.   Pub'd. 2/1/11
K10463 (978-1-4398-0932-7)   K10528 (978-0-415-80286-4)

Encyclopedia of Biotechnology in Agriculture and Food   Pub'd. 7/16/10
DK271X (978-0-8493-5027-6)   DKE5044 (978-0-8493-5044-3)

Business and Computer Science

Encyclopedia of Computer Science & Technology, 2nd Ed., 2 Vols.   Pub'd 12/21/2016
K21573 (978-1-4822-0819-1)   K21578 (978-1-4822-0822-1)

Encyclopedia of Information Assurance, 4 Vols.   Pub'd. 12/21/10
AU6620 (978-1-4200-6620-3)   AUE6620 (978-1-4200-6622-7)

Encyclopedia of Information Systems and Technology, 2 Vols.   Pub'd. 12/29/15
K15911 (978-1-4665-6077-2)   K21745 (978-1-4822-1432-1)

Encyclopedia of Library and Information Sciences, 4th Ed.   Publishing 2017
K15223 (978-1-4665-5259-3)   K15224 (978-1-4665-5260-9)

Encyclopedia of Software Engineering, 2 Vols.   Pub'd. 11/24/10
AU5977 (978-1-4200-5977-9)   AUE5977 (978-1-4200-5978-6)

Encyclopedia of Supply Chain Management, 2 Vols.   Pub'd. 12/21/11
K12842 (978-1-4398-6148-6)   K12843 (978-1-4398-6152-3)

Encyclopedia of U.S. Intelligence, 2 Vols.   Pub'd. 12/19/14
AU8957 (978-1-4200-8957-8)   AUE8957 (978-1-4200-8958-5)

Encyclopedia of Wireless and Mobile Communications, 2nd Ed., 3 Vols.   Pub'd. 12/18/12
K14731 (978-1-4665-0956-6)   KE16352 (978-1-4665-0969-6)

Chemistry, Materials and Chemical Engineering

Encyclopedia of Chemical Processing, 5 Vols.   Pub'd. 11/1/05
DK2243 (978-0-8247-5563-8)   DKE499X (978-0-8247-5499-0)

Encyclopedia of Chromatography, 3rd Ed.   Pub'd. 10/12/09
84593 (978-1-4200-8459-7)   84836 (978-1-4200-8483-2)

Encyclopedia of Iron, Steel, and Their Alloys, 5 Vols.   Pub'd. 1/6/16
K14814 (978-1-4665-1104-0)   K14815 (978-1-4665-1105-7)

Encyclopedia of Plasma Technology, 2 Vols.   Pub'd 12/12/2016
K14378 (978-1-4665-0059-4)   K21744 (978-1-4822-1431-4)

Encyclopedia of Supramolecular Chemistry, 2 Vols.   Pub'd. 5/5/04
DK056X (978-0-8247-5056-5)   DKE7259 (978-0-8247-4725-1)

Encyclopedia of Surface & Colloid Science, 3rd Ed., 10 Vols.   Pub'd. 8/27/15
K20465 (978-1-4665-9045-8)   K20478 (978-1-4665-9061-8)

Engineering

Dekker Encyclopedia of Nanoscience and Nanotechnology, 3rd Ed., 7 Vols.   Pub'd. 3/20/14
K14119 (978-1-4398-9134-6)   K14120 (978-1-4398-9135-3)

Encyclopedia of Energy Engineering and Technology, 2nd Ed., 4 Vols.   Pub'd. 12/1/14
K14633 (978-1-4665-0673-2)   KE16142 (978-1-4665-0674-9)

Encyclopedia of Optical and Photonic Engineering, 2nd Ed., 5 Vols.   Pub'd. 9/22/15
K12323 (978-1-4398-5097-8)   K12325 (978-1-4398-5099-2)

Environment

Encyclopedia of Environmental Management, 4 Vols.   Pub'd. 12/13/12
K11434 (978-1-4398-2927-1)   K11440 (978-1-4398-2933-2)

Encyclopedia of Environmental Science and Engineering, 6th Ed., 2 Vols.   Pub'd. 6/25/12
K10243 (978-1-4398-0442-1)   KE0278 (978-1-4398-0517-6)

Encyclopedia of Natural Resources, 2 Vols.   Pub'd. 7/23/14
K12418 (978-1-4398-5258-3)   K12420 (978-1-4398-5260-6)

Medicine

Encyclopedia of Biomaterials and Biomedical Engineering, 2nd Ed.   Pub'd. 5/28/08
H7802 (978-1-4200-7802-2)   HE7803 (978-1-4200-7803-9)

Encyclopedia of Biomedical Polymers and Polymeric Biomaterials, 11 Vols.   Pub'd. 4/2/15
K14324 (978-1-4398-9879-6)   K14404 (978-1-4665-0179-9)

Concise Encyclopedia of Biomedical Polymers and Polymeric Biomaterials, 2 Vols.   Pub'd. 8/14/17
K14313 (978-1-4398-9855-0)   KE42253 (978-1-315-11644-0)

Encyclopedia of Biopharmaceutical Statistics, 3rd Ed.   Pub'd. 5/20/10
H100102 (978-1-4398-2245-6)   HE10326 (978-1-4398-2246-3)

Encyclopedia of Clinical Pharmacy   Pub'd. 11/14/02
DK7524 (978-0-8247-0752-1)   DKE6080 (978-0-8247-0608-1)

Encyclopedia of Dietary Supplements, 2nd Ed.   Pub'd. 6/25/10
H100094 (978-1-4398-1928-9)   HE10315 (978-1-4398-1929-6)

Encyclopedia of Medical Genomics and Proteomics, 2 Vols.   Pub'd. 12/29/04
DK2208 (978-0-8247-5564-5)   DK501X (978-0-8247-5501-0)

Encyclopedia of Pharmaceutical Science and Technology, 4th Ed., 6 Vols.   Pub'd. 7/1/13
H100233 (978-1-84184-819-8)   HE10420 (978-1-84184-820-4)

Routledge Encyclopedias

Encyclopedia of Public Administration and Public Policy, 3rd Ed., 5 Vols.   Pub'd. 11/6/15
K16418 (978-1-4665-6909-6)   K16434 (978-1-4665-6936-2)

Routledge Encyclopedia of Modernism   Pub'd 5/11/16
Y137844 (978-1-135-00035-6)

Routledge Encyclopedia of Philosophy Online   Pub'd. 11/1/00
RU22334 (978-0-415-24909-6)

Routledge Performance Archive   Pub'd. 11/12/12
Y148405 (978-0-203-77466-3)

Encyclopedia titles are available in print and online.
To order, visit https://www.crcpress.com
Telephone: 1-800-272-7737
Email: orders@taylorandfrancis.com

Encyclopedia of

Library and Information Sciences, Fourth Edition

Volume 4

From: *Information Retrieval Protocols: Z39.50 and Search and Retrieve via URL*
To: *Library Publishing Initiatives: North America*

Encyclopedia Edited By

John D. McDonald

and

Michael Levine-Clark

CRC Press
Taylor & Francis Group
Boca Raton   London   New York

CRC Press is an imprint of the
Taylor & Francis Group, an **informa** business

First published 2018 by CRC Press

Published 2019 by CRC Press
Taylor & Francis Group
6000 Broken Sound Parkway NW, Suite 300
Boca Raton, FL 33487-2742

First issued in paperback 2020

© 2018 by Taylor & Francis Group, LLC
CRC Press is an imprint of the Taylor & Francis Group, an informa business

No claim to original U.S. Government works

ISBN-13: 978-1-4665-5259-3 (HB Set)
ISBN-13: 978-0-8153-8623-0 (Vol. 4) (hbk)

ISBN-13: 978-0-3675-7010-1 (PB Set)
ISBN-13: 978-0-3675-7019-4 (Vol. 4) (pbk)

This book contains information obtained from authentic and highly regarded sources. Reasonable efforts have been made to publish reliable data and information, but the author and publisher cannot assume responsibility for the validity of all materials or the consequences of their use. The authors and publishers have attempted to trace the copyright holders of all material reproduced in this publication and apologize to copyright holders if permission to publish in this form has not been obtained. If any copyright material has not been acknowledged please write and let us know so we may rectify in any future reprint.

Except as permitted under U.S. Copyright Law, no part of this book may be reprinted, reproduced, transmitted, or utilized in any form by any electronic, mechanical, or other means, now known or hereafter invented, including photocopying, microfilming, and recording, or in any information storage or retrieval system, without written permission from the publishers.

For permission to photocopy or use material electronically from this work, please access www.copyright.com (http://www.copyright.com/) or contact the Copyright Clearance Center, Inc. (CCC), 222 Rosewood Drive, Danvers, MA 01923, 978-750-8400. CCC is a not-for-profit organization that provides licenses and registration for a variety of users. For organizations that have been granted a photocopy license by the CCC, a separate system of payment has been arranged.

Trademark Notice: Product or corporate names may be trademarks or registered trademarks, and are used only for identification and explanation without intent to infringe.

Visit the Taylor & Francis Web site at
http://www.taylorandfrancis.com

and the CRC Press Web site at
http://www.crcpress.com

Encyclopedia of Library and Information Sciences, Fourth Edition

Brief Contents

Volume I

Academic Libraries 1
Accessibility 14
Accreditation of Library and Information
  Studies Programs in the United States
  and Canada 18
Acquisitions Institute at Timberline Lodge ... 22
African Librarianship 33
Altmetrics 44
American Association of Law
  Libraries (AALL) 48
American Association of Museums (AAM) 56
American Association of School
  Librarians (AASL) 59
American Library Association (ALA) 67
American Medical Informatics
  Association (AMIA) 85
American National Standards
  Institute (ANSI) 87
American Society for Information Science
  and Technology (ASIST) 90
Approval Plans 96
Arab Federation for Libraries and
  Information (AFLI) 100
Archival Appraisal and Acquisition 105
Archival Arrangement and Description 115
Archival Documentation 127
Archival Finding Aids 133
Archival Management and Administration .. 141
Archival Reference and Access 149
Archival Science 166
Archives 179
Archivists and Collecting 195
Area and Interdisciplinary Studies
  Literatures and Their Users 209
ARMA International, Inc. 221
Armenia: Libraries, Archives, and
  Museums 228
Art Galleries 241
Art Librarianship 249
Art Museums 259
Artificial Intelligence 269
Artificial Neural Networks and Natural
  Language Processing 279
Arts Literatures and Their Users 293
ASLIB 301
Association for Information Science and
  Technology 311
Association for Information Systems (AIS) ... 318
Association for Library Collections and
  Technical Services 324
Association for Library Service to
  Children (ALSC) 333

Volume I (cont'd.)

Association of College and Research
  Libraries (ACRL) 338
Association of Library Trustees, Advocates,
  Friends and Foundations (ALTAFF) 361
Association of Research Libraries
  (ARL) 364
Association of Specialized and Cooperative
  Library Agencies (ASCLA) 376
Australia: Libraries, Archives, and
  Museums 379
Australian Library and Information
  Association (ALIA) 396
Authentication and Authorization 401
Automated Acquisitions 408
Automatic Abstracting and
  Summarization 418
Automatic Discourse Generation 430
Back-of-the-Book Indexing 440
Bibliographic Control [ELIS Classic] 447
Bibliographical Society (London) 456
Bibliographical Society of
  America (BSA) 463
Bibliography 468
Bibliometric Overview of Information
  Science 480
Bibliometric Research: History
  [ELIS Classic] 492
Bibliothèque Nationale de France 531
Binding [ELIS Classic] 538
Biological Information and Its Users 554
Blind and Physically Disabled: Library
  Services 563
Bliss Bibliographic Classification
  First Edition [ELIS Classic] 573
Bliss Bibliographic Classification
  Second Edition 581
Boolean Algebras [ELIS Classic] 591
Brazil: Library Science 597
Brazil: Library Science—Distance
  Education 603
Brazil: Museums 611
British Library 616
Business Informatics 630
Business Information and Its Users 635
Business Literature: History
  [ELIS Classic] 643
Canada: Libraries and Archives 654
Canadian Heritage Information
  Network (CHIN) 675
Canadian Library Association (CLA) 681
Careers and Education in Archives and
  Records Management 685

Volume I (cont'd.)

Careers and Education in Information
  Systems 693
Careers and Education in Library and
  Information Science 706
Careers and Education in Records and
  Information Management 715

Volume II

Cataloging 723
Cataloging Cultural Objects (CCO) 733
Catalogs and Cataloging: History
  [ELIS Classic] 743
Censorship and Content Regulation
  of the Internet 780
Center for Research Libraries 789
Charleston Conference 794
Chartered Institute of Library and
  Information Professionals (CILIP) 806
Chemistry Literature and Its Users
  [ELIS Classic] 814
Chemoinformatics 830
Children and Information Technology 839
Children's Literature 852
Children's Services in Libraries 876
China: Libraries, Archives, and Museums ... 886
Circulation Services 916
Citation Analysis 923
Citation Indexes and the Web of Science 940
Citer Motivations [ELIS Classic] 951
Classification Theory 958
Clinical Decision-Support Systems 974
College Libraries 983
Communication and Communication
  Studies 994
Communication Policy: United States 1007
Community Informatics 1027
Complexity and Self-Organization 1034
Computer-Mediated Communication
  (CMC) 1044
Computer-Supported Cooperative Work
  (CSCW) 1053
Conservation and Preservation of
  Museum Objects 1068
Controlled Vocabularies for Art,
  Architecture, and Material Culture ... 1076
Corporate Archives 1081
Corporate Art Collections 1086
Corporate Information Centers 1094
Corporate Records Management 1104

Volume II (cont'd.)

Credibility and Cognitive Authority of
Information 1113
Croatia: Libraries, Archives, and
Museums 1121
CrossRef Publisher Linking Network 1132
Cultural Memory 1139
Curating Archaeological Artifacts 1147
Curating Natural History Collections 1156
Custody and Chain of Custody 1164
Data and Data Quality 1171
Deaf and Hearing Impaired:
Communication in Service
Contexts [ELIS Classic] 1183
Decision Sciences 1192
Decision Support Systems 1200
Demand-Driven Acquisition/Patron-Driven
Acquisition 1209
Denmark: Libraries, Archives, and
Museums 1215
Descriptive Cataloging Principles 1229
Design Science in the Information
Sciences 1242
Dewey Decimal Classification (DDC) 1256
Digital Content Licensing 1267
Digital Divide and Inclusion 1279
Digital Humanities 1286
Digital Humanities and Academic
Libraries 1298
Digital Images 1307
Digital Millennium Copyright
Act of 1998 1316
Digital Object Identifier (DOI®) System ... 1325
Digital Preservation 1332
Diplomatics 1338
Disaster Planning and Recovery for
Cultural Institutions 1347
Document Information Systems 1360
Document Theory 1372
Document Type Definition (DTD) 1381
Dublin Core Metadata Initiative (DCMI):
A Personal History 1390
Economics Literature: History
[ELIS Classic] 1399
Electronic Records Preservation 1413
Electronic Resources & Libraries (ER&L) ... 1419
Encoded Archival Description 1423
Engineering Literatures and Their Users
[ELIS Classic] 1433

Volume III

Epistemology 1455
Ethical and Legal Aspects of Archival
Services 1463
Ethical Aspects of Library and
Information Science 1469
Ethical Issues in Information Systems 1484
Ethiopia: Libraries, Archives, and
Museums 1494
Everyday Life Information Seeking 1506
Evidence-Based Practice 1516
Exhibition Design 1523
Facet Analysis [ELIS Classic] 1534
Faceted Application of Subject
Terminology (FAST) 1539
Federal Electronic Information in the
United States 1549

Volume III (cont'd.)

Film and Broadcast Archives 1560
Film Archiving: History 1584
France: Archives, Museums, and
Libraries 1589
Functional Requirements for Subject
Authority Data (FRSAD):
Conceptual Model 1606
Fuzzy Set Theory 1618
Games and Gaming 1636
Genealogical Literature and Its Users 1644
Genre Theory and Research 1662
Geographic Information Systems (GIS) 1671
Geographical Literature: History
[ELIS Classic] 1683
Germany: Libraries, Archives, and
Museums 1693
Global Open Knowledgebase 1710
Government Documents: Collection and
Management 1715
Greece: Archives 1728
Greece: Libraries 1733
Greece: Museums 1741
Grey Literature [ELIS Classic] 1746
HathiTrust 1757
Health Science Professional Literatures
and Their Users 1763
Historical and Archaeological Sites:
Development and Preservation 1771
Historical Societies 1779
Historical Sources and Their Users 1786
History of Libraries 1796
History of Museums 1812
History of Paper 1824
History of Public Libraries
[ELIS Classic] 1836
History of Records and Information
Management 1850
History of the Book 1859
History: Three Basic Printing Processes 1865
Hospital Libraries 1870
Human–Computer Interaction Research
in Information Retrieval 1895
Humanities Literatures and Their Users 1909
Hungary: Libraries, Archives, and
Museums 1917
Hypertext and Hypercard: Early
Development [ELIS Classic] 1935
Illumination [ELIS Classic] 1945
Impact Assessment of Cultural
Institutions 1958
Incunabula [ELIS Classic] 1966
Indexing: History and Theory 1978
India: Libraries, Archives and Museums ... 1992
Indigenous Librarianship 2031
Information 2048
Information Arts 2064
Information Behavior 2074
Information Behavior Models 2086
Information Crises and Crisis Information ... 2094
Information Explosion 2101
Information Management 2106
Information Needs 2115
Information Needs and Behaviors of
Diasporic Populations 2122
Information Needs and Behaviors of
Populations in Less Developed
Regions 2130
Information Policy: European Union 2138

Volume III (cont'd.)

Information Policy: United States 2147
Information Practice 2162
Information Retrieval Experimentation
[ELIS Classic] 2172

Volume IV

Information Retrieval Protocols: Z39.50
and Search and Retrieve via URL 2181
Information Retrieval Support
Systems 2192
Information Retrieval Systems 2199
Information Scattering 2210
Information Science 2216
Information Search Process (ISP)
Model 2232
Information Searching and Search
Models 2239
Information Society 2253
Information Systems 2272
Information Systems Failure 2280
Information Technology Adoption 2290
Information Technology Literacy 2303
Information Technology Project
Implementation in Developing
Countries [ELIS Classic] 2312
Information Technology Standards for
Libraries [ELIS Classic] 2341
Information Theory 2350
Information Use for Decision Making 2359
Informetrics 2367
Institutional Records and Archives 2377
Intellectual Freedom and the American
Library Association (ALA): Historical
Overview [ELIS Classic] 2387
Intelligence and Security Informatics 2398
International and Comparative
Librarianship 2404
International Association of Sound and
Audiovisual Archives (IASA) 2413
International Association of Technological
University Libraries (IATUL) 2418
International Communication Association
(ICA) 2421
International Council of Museums
(ICOM) 2429
International Council on Archives (ICA) ... 2437
International Council on Knowledge
Management (ICKM) 2445
International Federation of Library
Associations and Institutions
(IFLA) 2451
International Federation of Television
Archives (FIAT/IFTA) 2465
International Organization for
Standardization (ISO) 2470
International Records Management
Standards ISO 15489 and 23081 2481
International Records Management Trust ... 2487
International Society for Knowledge
Organization (ISKO) 2494
Internet Genres 2503
Internet Search Tools: History to 2000 2516
InterPARES 2526
iSchools 2536
Israel: Libraries, Archives, and
Museums 2542

Volume IV (cont'd.)

Japan: Libraries, Archives, and
    Museums 2560
Kazakhstan: Libraries, Archives, and
    Museums 2578
Kenya: Libraries, Museums, and
    Archives 2592
Knowledge 2610
Knowledge Creation and Use in
    Organizations 2618
Knowledge Discovery in Data Streams 2626
Knowledge Management 2640
Knowledge Management Systems 2649
Knowledge Management: Early
    Development 2657
Knowledge Organization System
    Standards 2665
Knowledge: Tacit and Explicit 2677
Latent Semantic Indexing 2688
Latinos and U.S. Libraries: History 2698
Law Firm Librarianship 2705
Law Librarianship 2710
Law Literature and Its Users 2733
Learning and Information Seeking 2751
Libraries 2762
Library and Information Science 2768
Library and Information Technology
    Association (LITA) 2775
Library Anxiety 2782
Library Architecture and Design 2788
Library Architecture: History 2797
Library Automation: History 2810
Library Consortia in Europe 2822
Library Fundraising and Development 2832
Library Leadership and Management
    Association (LLAMA) 2841
Library of Congress Classification (LCC) 2847
Library of Congress Genre/Form Terms
    for Library and Archival Materials ... 2856
Library of Congress Subject Headings
    (LCSH) 2866
Library of Congress: History 2879
Library Portals and Gateways 2892
Library Publishing Initiatives:
    North America 2901

Volume V

Library Science in the United States:
    Early History 2909
Library Technical Services 2918
Linguistics and the Information Sciences 2927
Linked Data 2938
Lithuania: Libraries and Librarianship 2943
Louvre 2958
Machine Readable Cataloging (MARC):
    1961–1974 [ELIS Classic] 2963
Machine Readable Cataloging (MARC):
    1975–2007 2980
Makerspaces in Libraries 2990
Management of Very Large Distributed
    Shared Collections [ELIS Classic] 2997
Managing an Information Business 3004
Marketing Library and Information
    Services 3011
Mathematics Literature: History
    [ELIS Classic] 3019
Medical Library Association (MLA) 3033

Volume V (cont'd.)

Medical Literature: History
    [ELIS Classic] 3041
Metadata and Digital Information
    [ELIS Classic] 3058
Metamarkup Languages: SGML and
    XML 3072
Mexico: Libraries, Archives, and
    Museums 3082
Modeling Documents in Their Context 3105
Moldova: Archives, Museums, and
    Libraries 3117
Moving Image Indexing 3129
Multilingual Information Access 3140
Museum Accreditation Program 3146
Museum Architecture and Gallery Design ... 3148
Museum Collecting and Collections 3161
Museum Computer Network (MCN) 3170
Museum Informatics 3176
Museum Management 3185
Museum Registration and Documentation ... 3199
Museum Studies 3214
Museum Web Sites and Digital
    Collections 3222
Museums 3233
Museums and Community 3243
Museums and Their Visitors: Historic
    Relationship 3251
Museums as Place 3258
Music Information Retrieval 3267
Music Librarianship 3275
Name Authority Control 3288
National Archives 3298
National Biological Information
    Infrastructure (NBII) 3306
National Historical Publications and
    Records Commission (NHPRC) 3315
National Libraries 3320
National Library of Medicine 3334
Natural Language Processing for
    Information Retrieval 3346
Network Management 3356
Network of European Museum
    Organisations (NEMO) 3365
Networked Knowledge Organization
    Systems/Services (NKOS) 3366
New Zealand Aotearoa: Libraries 3371
Non-governmental Organizations and
    Information 3380
North American Serials Interest Group 3388
OCLC: A Worldwide Library
    Cooperative 3392
Older Adults' Information: Needs and
    Behavior 3406
One-Person Libraries 3413
Online Catalog Subject Searching 3422
Online Library Instruction 3432
Online Public Access Catalogs (OPACs)
    [ELIS Classic] 3450
Ontologies and Their Definition 3455
Open Access Scholarship and Publishing 3465
Open Archival Information System (OAIS)
    Reference Model 3477
Open Source Software 3488
Oral History in Libraries and Archives 3494
ORCID 3505
Organization Theories 3510
Organizational Culture 3520
Organizational Learning 3526

Volume V (cont'd.)

Organizational Memory 3534
Pacific Islands Association of Libraries
    and Archives (PIALA) 3541
Papyrology 3552
Patents and Patent Searching 3560
People with Disabilities 3573
Personal Information Management 3584
Peru: Libraries and Library Science 3606
Philosophy and the Information Sciences 3610
Philosophy of Science [ELIS Classic] 3623

Volume VI

Physical Sciences and Mathematics
    Literatures and Their Users 3637
Piracy in Digital Media 3649
Plagiarism of Print and Electronic
    Resources 3664
Poland: Libraries and Archives 3674
Politics of Representation in Museums 3688
Popular Literature Genres 3700
Precision and Recall [ELIS Classic] 3708
Presidential Libraries 3714
Primary Records: Future Prospects
    [ELIS Classic] 3719
Print on Demand 3733
Private Presses and Fine Printing
    [ELIS Classic] 3738
Provenance of Archival Materials 3746
Provenance of Museum Objects 3756
Provenance of Rare Books 3766
Public Librarianship [ELIS Classic] 3774
Public Libraries [ELIS Classic] 3781
Public Library Association (PLA) 3801
Qualitative Research Methods in Library
    and Information Science
    [ELIS Classic] 3806
Rare Book Collections 3820
Reading and Reading Acquisition 3830
Reading Disorders 3841
Reading Interests 3850
Recommender Systems and Expert
    Locators 3860
Records Compliance and Risk
    Management 3869
Records Continuum Model 3874
Records Organization and Access 3887
Records Retention Schedules 3892
Reference and Informational Genres 3897
Reference and User Services Association
    (RUSA) 3908
Reference Services 3912
Regional Library Networks:
    United States 3920
Relevance in Theory 3926
Relevance Judgments and Measurements ... 3940
Renaissance Libraries [ELIS Classic] 3948
Resource Description Framework (RDF) 3961
Saudi Arabia: Libraries, Archives, and
    Museums 3970
Scholarly and Trade Publishing
    [ELIS Classic] 3982
School Librarianship 3991
School Libraries 4000
Science and Engineering Librarianship 4008
Science and Technology Studies 4020
Search Engine Optimization 4029

Volume VI (cont'd.)

Search Engines 4046
Self-Publishing Online 4054
Semantic Interoperability 4062
Semantic Web 4080
Semiotics 4094
Senegal: Libraries, Archives, and
    Museums 4104
Sense-Making 4113
Serbia: Libraries, Archives, and
    Museums 4125
Serials Collection and Management
    [ELIS Classic] 4139
Serials Vendors [ELIS Classic] 4150
Shared Libraries 4158
Site Museums and Monuments 4164
Slovakia: Libraries, Archives, and
    Museums 4173
Smithsonian Institution 4188
Social Epistemology 4197
Social Influences on Classification 4204
Social Informatics 4212
Social Justice in Library and Information
    Science 4218
Social Networks and Information
    Transfer 4235
Social Science Literatures and Their
    Users [ELIS Classic] 4246
Social Science Professional Literatures
    and Their Users 4255
Society for Scholarly Publishing (SSP) 4262
Society for the History of Authorship,
    Reading and Publishing (SHARP) 4268
Society of American Archivists (SAA) 4271
Sociology of Reading 4279
Sociology of the Information Disciplines 4286
Software and Information Industry
    Association (SIIA) 4297
Sound and Audio Archives 4299
South Korea: Archives and Libraries 4307
Spain: Libraries, Archives, and Museums 4314
Special Collections 4335
Special Collections and Manuscripts 4343
Special Librarianship 4351

Volume VII

Special Libraries 4361
Special Libraries Association (SLA) 4370

Volume VII (cont'd.)

Specialty Museums 4379
State Archives 4384
State Libraries and State Library
    Agencies 4392
State-Sponsored Destruction of Books
    and Libraries 4400
Still Image Indexing 4407
Still Image Search and Retrieval 4417
Storytelling 4437
Strategic Planning in Academic Libraries 4447
Students' Information: Needs and
    Behavior 4459
Subject Cataloging Principles and
    Systems 4466
Subscription Libraries [ELIS Classic] 4478
Switzerland: Libraries, Archives, and
    Museums 4487
Tanzania: Libraries, Archives, Museums,
    and Information Systems 4497
Task-Based Information Searching:
    Research Methods 4526
Taxonomy 4537
Technical Writing 4547
Test Collections 4554
Text Encoding Initiative (TEI) 4559
Text REtrieval Conference (TREC) 4569
Theft, Vandalism, and Security in
    Libraries and Archives 4576
Theft, Vandalism, and Security in
    Museums 4593
Theological Librarianship 4604
Topic Maps 4611
Tunisia: Libraries, Archives, and
    Museums 4624
Ukraine: Libraries 4642
Undergraduate Library Collections
    [ELIS Classic] 4649
UNESCO: Communication and
    Information Sector 4656
Unicode Standard 4662
Unified Medical Language System®
    (UMLS®) Project 4672
Uniform Computer Information
    Transactions Act (UCITA) 4680
Unions in Public and Academic Libraries 4689
United Kingdom: Archives and
    Archival Science 4699
United Kingdom: Libraries and
    Librarianship 4707

Volume VII (cont'd.)

United Kingdom: Museums and
    Museology 4723
United States: Archives and
    Archival Science 4740
United States: Libraries and
    Librarianship in the 21st Century 4766
United States: Museums 4776
Universal Decimal Classification
    (UDC) 4783
University Archives 4791
Usability Testing of User Interfaces in
    Libraries 4797
User-Centered Design of Information
    Systems 4803
User-Centered Revolution: 1970–1995
    [ELIS Classic] 4812
User-Centered Revolution: 1995–2008 4847
User-Oriented and Cognitive Models of
    Information Retrieval 4872
Venezuela: Libraries and Librarianship 4886
Version Control 4896
Vietnam: Libraries, Archives, and
    Museums 4902
Visitor Studies 4917
Visual and Performing Arts Archives 4925
Visual Resources Association (VRA) 4933
Visual Resources Management in
    Cultural Institutions 4940
Volunteer Services in Cultural
    Institutions 4951
Wayfinding and Signage 4958
Web Scale Discovery Services 4978
Webometrics 4983
Word Processing: Early History
    [ELIS Classic] 4993
World Intellectual Property Organization
    (WIPO) 5000
World Summit on the Information
    Society (WSIS) 5012
World Wide Web (WWW) 5019
World Wide Web Consortium (W3C) 5034
XML Information Retrieval 5039
Young Adult Library Services Association
    (YALSA) 5052
Young Adult Services in Libraries 5058
Youth Information: Needs and
    Behavior 5067
Zoological Park and Aquarium Libraries
    and Archives 5077

Encyclopedia of Library and Information Sciences, Fourth Edition

Editors-in-Chief

John D. McDonald
Analytics and Assessment, EBSCO Information Services

Michael Levine-Clark
University of Denver Libraries, Denver, Colorado

Editorial Advisory Board

Rick AmRhein
Valparaiso
Rick Anderson
Reno
Beth Bernhardt
Greensboro
Char Booth
Claremont
Paul Bracke
Purdue
Chris Brown
Denver
Todd Carpenter
NISO
Jill Emery
Portland
John Feather
Loughborough University
Barbara Ford
University of Illinois at Urbana-Champaign
Rachel Frick
Digital Library Federation
Martin Garner
Regis
Rich Gazan
University of Hawaii
Jason Griffey
Tennessee Chattanooga
Frances Harris
University of Illinois at Urbana-Champaign

Kalervo Järvelin
University of Tampere
Robert Kieft
Occidental College
Jesús Lau
University of Veracruz
Greg Leazer
UCLA
Elena Macevičiūtė
University College of Borås
John Myers
Union
Gerald Perry
University of Colorado Denver
Jason Price
Claremont
Nancy Roderer
Johns Hopkins University
Jonathan Rose
Drew University
Adam Schiff
Washington
Sanna Talja
Uppsala University
Bonnie Tijerina
Claremont
Virginia Walter
University of California at Los Angeles
Kelvin White
University of Oklahoma

Contributors

June Abbas / *School of Library and Information Studies, University of Oklahoma, Norman, Oklahoma, U.S.A.*

Richard Abel / *Portland, Oregon, U.S.A.*

Eileen G. Abels / *College of Information Science and Technology, Drexel University, Philadelphia, Pennsylvania, U.S.A.*

Tia Abner / *American Medical Informatics Association (AMIA), Bethesda, Maryland, U.S.A.*

Donald C. Adcock / *Dominican University, River Forest, Illinois, U.S.A.*

Kendra S. Albright / *School of Library and Information Science, University of South Carolina, Columbia, South Carolina, U.S.A.*

Mikael Alexandersson / *University of Gothenburg, Gothenburg, Sweden*

Joan M. Aliprand / *Cupertino, California, U.S.A.*

Jacqueline Allen / *Dallas Museum of Art, Dallas, Texas, U.S.A.*

Romano Stephen Almagno / *International College of St. Bonaventure, Rome, Italy*

Connie J. Anderson-Cahoon / *Southern Oregon University Library, Ashland, Oregon, U.S.A.*

Karen Anderson / *Archives and Information Science, Mid Sweden University, ITM, Härnösand, Sweden*

Rick Anderson / *University of Utah, Salt Lake City, Utah, U.S.A.*

Silviu Andrieş-Tabac / *Institute of Cultural Heritage, Moldova Academy of Sciences, Chişinău, Republic of Moldova*

Peng Hwa Ang / *Wee Kim Wee School of Communication and Information, Nanyang Technological University, Singapore*

Hermina G.B. Anghelescu / *School of Library and Information Science, Wayne State University, Detroit, Michigan, U.S.A.*

Leah Arroyo / *American Association of Museums, Washington, District of Columbia, U.S.A.*

Terry Asla / *Senior Lifestyles Researcher, Seattle, U.S.A.*

Shiferaw Assefa / *University of Kansas, Lawrence, Kansas, U.S.A.*

Ilse Assmann / *Radio Broadcast Facilities, SABC, Johannesburg, South Africa*

Maija-Leena Aulikki Huotari / *University of Oulu, Oulu, Finland*

Henriette D. Avram / *Library of Congress, Washington, District of Columbia, U.S.A.*

Sven Axsäter / *Department of Industrial Management and Logistics, Lund University, Lund, Sweden*

Murtha Baca / *Getty Research Institute, Los Angeles, California, U.S.A.*

Roger S. Bagnall / *Institute for the Study of the Ancient World, New York University, New York, New York, U.S.A.*

Nestor Bamidis / *GSA-Archives of Macedonia, Thessaloniki, Greece*

Franz Barachini / *Business Innovation Consulting—Austria, Langenzersdorf, Austria*

Rebecca O. Barclay / *Rensselaer Polytechnic Institute, Troy, New York, U.S.A.*

Judit Bar-Ilan / *Department of Information Science, Bar-Ilan University, Ramat Gan, Israel*

Alex W. Barker / *Museum of Art and Archaeology, University of Missouri, Columbia, Missouri, U.S.A.*

John A. Bateman / *University of Bremen, Bremen, Germany*

Marcia J. Bates / *Department of Information Studies, Graduate School of Education and Information Studies, University of California, Los Angeles (UCLA), Los Angeles, California, U.S.A.*

Philippe Baumard / *School of Engineering, Stanford University, Stanford, California, U.S.A., and University Paul Cézanne, Aix-en-Provence, France*

David Bawden / *City, University of London, London, U.K.*

Jennifer Bawden / *Museum Studies Program, Faculty of Information Studies, University of Toronto, Toronto, Ontario, Canada*

David Bearman / *Archives & Museum Informatics, Toronto, Ontario, Canada*

William K. Beatty / *Northwestern University Medical School, Chicago, Illinois, U.S.A.*

A.R. Bednarek / *University of Florida, Gainesville, Florida, U.S.A.*

Clare Beghtol / *Faculty of Information Studies, University of Toronto, Toronto, Ontario, Canada*

Lori Bell / *Alliance Library System, East Peoria, Illinois, U.S.A.*

Danna Bell-Russel / *Library of Congress, Washington, District of Columbia, U.S.A.*

William Benedon / *Benedon & Associates, Encino, California, U.S.A.*

Anna Bergaliyeva / *Kazakhstan Institute of Management, Economics and Strategic Research (KIMEP), Almaty, Kazakhstan*

Sidney E. Berger / *Phillips Library, Peabody Essex Museum, Salem, Massachusetts, U.S.A.*

Andrew J. Berner / *University Club of New York, New York, New York, U.S.A.*

Sean F. Berrigan / *Policy, Library and Archives Canada, Ottawa, Ontario, Canada*

John W. Berry / *NILRC: Network of Illinois Learning Resources in Community Colleges, Dominican University, River Forest, Illinois, U.S.A.*

Michael W. Berry / *Department of Electrical Engineering and Computer Science, University of Tennessee, Knoxville, Tennessee, U.S.A.*

Suresh K. Bhavnani / *Center for Computational Medicine and Bioinformatics, University of Michigan, Ann Arbor, Michigan, U.S.A.*

Tamara Biggs / *Chicago History Museum, Chicago, Illinois, U.S.A.*

Frank Birkebæk / *Roskilde Museum, Roskilde, Denmark*

Ann P. Bishop / *Graduate School of Library and Information Science, University of Illinois at Urbana-Champaign, Urbana, Illinois, U.S.A.*

Julia Blixrud / *Association of Research Libraries, Washington, District of Columbia, U.S.A.*

Gloria Bordogna / *Italian National Research Council, Institute for the Dynamics of Environmental Processes, Dalmine, Italy*

Steve Bosch / *Administration Department, University of Arizona, Tucson, Arizona, U.S.A.*

Kimberly S. Bostwick / *Ecology and Evolutionary Biology, Cornell University Museum of Vertebrates, Ithaca, New York, U.S.A.*

Natalia T. Bowdoin / *University of South Carolina Aiken, Aiken, South Carolina, U.S.A.*

Patrick J. Boylan / *Department of Cultural Policy and Management, City University, London, U.K.*

Amy E. Brand / *CrossRef, Lynnfield, Massachusetts, U.S.A.*

Judy Brooker / *Australian Library and Information Association, Deakin, Australian Capital Territory, Australia*

Terrence Brooks / *iSchool, University of Washington, Seattle, Washington, U.S.A.*

Vanda Broughton / *School of Library, Archive and Information Studies, University College London, London, U.K.*

Cecelia Brown / *School of Library and Information Studies, University of Oklahoma, Norman, Oklahoma, U.S.A.*

Jos de Bruijn / *Digital Enterprise Research Institute, University of Innsbruck, Innsbruck, Austria*

Steve Bryant / *BFI National Archive, Herts, U.K.*

Alan Bryden / *International Organization for Standardization, Geneva, Switzerland*

Jeff E. Bullard / *Free Library of Philadelphia, Philadelphia, Pennsylvania, U.S.A.*

Kathleen Burns / *Beinecke Rare Book and Manuscript Library, Yale University, New Haven, Connecticut, U.S.A.*

Brenda A. Burton / *Library, Kirkland & Ellis LLP, Chicago, IL, U.S.A.*

E. Burton Swanson / *Anderson School of Management, University of California, Los Angeles, Los Angeles, California, U.S.A.*

Donald I. Butcher / *Canadian Library Association, Ottawa, Ontario, Canada*

Kevin Butterfield / *Wolf Law Library, College of William and Mary, Williamsburg, Virginia, U.S.A.*

Alex Byrne / *University of Technology, Sydney—Sydney, New South Wales, Australia*

Brian Byrne / *Discipline of Psychology, School of Behavioural, Cognitive and Social Sciences, University of New England, Armidale, New South Wales, Australia, Australian Research Council Centre of Excellence in Cognition and its Disorder, Australia, and National Health and Medical Research Council Centre of Research Excellence in Twin Research, Australia*

Bernadette G. Callery / *School of Information Sciences, University of Pittsburgh, Pittsburgh, Pennsylvania, U.S.A.*

Paul D. Callister / *Leon E. Bloch Law Library, University of Missouri-Kansas City School of Law, Kansas City, Missouri, U.S.A.*

Perrine Canavaggio / *International Council on Archives, Paris, France*

Sarah R. Canino / *Dickinson Music Library, Vassar College, Poughkeepsie, New York, U.S.A.*

Robert Capra / *School of Information and Library Science, University of North Carolina, Chapel Hill, North Carolina, U.S.A.*

Nicholas Carroll / *Hastings Research, Inc., Las Vegas, Nevada, U.S.A.*

Ben Carterette / *Department of Computer and Information Sciences, University of Delaware, Newark, Delaware, U.S.A.*

Vittorio Castelli / *T.J. Watson Research Center, IBM, Yorktown Heights, New York, U.S.A.*

Jane Rosetta Virginia Caulton / *Library of Congress, Washington, District of Columbia, U.S.A.*

Richard Cave / *Formerly at the Public Library of Science, San Francisco, California, U.S.A.*

Roderick Cave / *Loughborough University, Loughborough, U.K.*

Marcel Caya / *Department of History, University of Quebec at Montreal (UQAM), Montreal, Quebec, Canada*

Frank Cervone / *Purdue University Calumet, Hammond, Indiana, U.S.A.*

Leslie Champeny / *Alaska Resources Library and Information Services (ARLIS), Anchorage, Alaska, U.S.A.*

Lois Mai Chan / *School of Library and Information Science, University of Kentucky, Lexington, Kentucky, U.S.A.*

Sergio Chaparro-Univazo / *Graduate School of Library and Information Science, Simmons College, Boston, Massachusetts, U.S.A.*

Mary K. Chelton / *Graduate School of Library and Information Studies, Queens College Flushing, New York, U.S.A.*

Hsinchun Chen / *Department of Management Information Systems, University of Arizona, Tucson, Arizona, U.S.A.*

Jianhua Chen / *Computer Science Department, Louisiana State University, Baton Rouge, Louisiana, U.S.A.*

Eric R. Childress / *OCLC, Dublin, Ohio, U.S.A.*

Michael A. Chilton / *Department of Management, Kansas State University, Manhattan, Kansas, U.S.A.*

TzeHuey Chiou-Peng / *Spurlock Museum, University of Illinois at Urbana-Champaign, Urbana, Illinois, U.S.A.*

Hyun-Yang Cho / *Department of Library and Information Science, Kyonggi University, Suwon, South Korea*

Jae-Hwang Choi / *Department of Library and Information Science, Kyungpook National University, Daegu, South Korea*

Carol E.B. Choksy / *School of Library and Information Science, Indiana University, Bloomington, Indiana, U.S.A.*

Su Kim Chung / *University Libraries, University of Nevada–Las Vegas, Las Vegas, Nevada, U.S.A.*

James Church / *University Libraries, University of California, Berkeley, Berkeley, California, U.S.A.*

Barbara H. Clubb / *Ottawa Public Library, Ottawa, Ontario, Canada*

Arlene Cohen / *Pacific Islands Library Consultant, Seattle, Washington, U.S.A.*

Barbara Cohen-Stratyner / *New York Public Library for the Performing Arts, New York, U.S.A.*

Edward T. Cokely / *Center for Adaptive Behavior and Cognition, Max Planck Institute for Human Development, Berlin, Germany*

Arthur H. Cole / *Harvard University, Cambridge, Massachusetts, U.S.A.*

John Y. Cole / *Center for the Book, Library of Congress, Washington, District of Columbia, U.S.A.*

Patrick Tod Colegrove / *DeLaMare Science & Engineering Library, University Libraries, University of Nevada, Reno, Reno, Nevada, U.S.A.*

Edwin T. Coman, Jr. / *University of California, Riverside, California, U.S.A.*

Nora T. Corley / *Arctic Institute of North America, Montreal, Quebec, Canada*

Sheila Corrall / *Department of Information Studies, University of Sheffield, Sheffield, U.K.*

Erica Cosijn / *Department of Information Science, University of Pretoria, Pretoria, South Africa*

Richard J. Cox / *School of Computing and Information, University of Pittsburgh, Pittsburgh, Pennsylvania, U.S.A.*

Barbara M. Cross / *Records and Information Management, Sony Pictures Entertainment, Culver City, California, U.S.A.*

Kevin Crowston / *School of Information Studies, Syracuse University, Syracuse, New York, U.S.A.*

Adrian Cunningham / *National Archives of Australia (NAA), Canberra, Australian Capital Territory, Australia*

Judith N. Currano / *University of Pennsylvania, Philadelphia, Pennsylvania, U.S.A.*

Susan Curzon / *University Library, California State University–Northridge, Northridge, California, U.S.A.*

Ingetraut Dahlberg / *Bad Koenig, Germany*

Nan Christian Ploug Dahlkild / *Royal School of Library and Information Science, Copenhagen, Denmark*

Jay E. Daily / *University of Pittsburgh, Pittsburgh, Pennsylvania, U.S.A.*

Kimiz Dalkir / *Graduate School of Library and Information Studies, McGill University, Montreal, Quebec, Canada*

Prudence W. Dalrymple / *Drexel University College of Computing & Informatics, Philadelphia, Pennsylvania, U.S.A.*

Marcel Danesi / *Department of Anthropology, University of Toronto, Toronto, Ontario, Canada*

Xuan Hong Dang / *Computer Vision and Image Understanding, Institute for Infocomm, A* STAR, Singapore*

Yan Dang / *Department of Management Information Systems, University of Arizona, Tucson, Arizona, U.S.A.*

Evelyn Daniel / *School of Information and Library Science, University of North Carolina at Chapel Hill, Chapel Hill, North Carolina, U.S.A.*

Richard A. Danner / *School of Law, Duke University, Durham, North Carolina, U.S.A.*

Regina Dantas / *Museu Nacional, HCTE, Universidade Federal do Rio de Janeiro, Rio de Janeiro, Brazil*

Daniel C. Danzig / *Consultant, Pasadena, California, U.S.A.*

Robert Allen Daugherty / *University Library, University of Illinois at Chicago, Chicago, Illinois, U.S.A.*

Charles H. Davis / *Indiana University, Bloomington, IN, U.S.A., and School of Library and Information Science, Indiana University, Bloomington, Indiana, U.S.A.*

Gordon B. Davis / *Carlson School of Management, University of Minnesota, Minneapolis, Minnesota, U.S.A.*

Mary Ellen Davis / *American Library Association, Chicago, Illinois, U.S.A.*

Peter Davis / *International Centre for Cultural and Heritage Studies, Newcastle University, Newcastle upon Tyne, U.K.*

Sheryl Davis / *University Library, University of California, Riverside, Riverside, California, U.S.A.*

Ronald E. Day / *School of Library and Information Science, Indiana University, Bloomington, Indiana, U.S.A.*

Cheryl Dee / *School of Library and Information Science, University of South Florida, Tampa, Florida, U.S.A.*

Robert DeHart / *Department of History, Middle Tennessee State University, Murfreesboro, Tennessee, U.S.A.*

Brenda Dervin / *School of Communication, Ohio State University, Columbus, Ohio, U.S.A.*

Brian Detlor / *Information Systems, McMaster University, Hamilton, Ontario, Canada*

Don E. Detmer / *American Medical Informatics Association (AMIA), Bethesda, Maryland, U.S.A.*

Stella G. Dextre Clarke / *Information Consultant, Oxfordshire, U.K.*

Catherine Dhérent / *National Library of France, Paris, France*

Anne R. Diekema / *Gerald R. Sherratt Library, Southern Utah University, Cedar City, Utah, U.S.A.*

Susan S. DiMattia / *DiMattia Associates, Stamford, Connecticut, U.S.A.*

Gloria Dinerman / *The Library Co-Op, Inc., Edison, New Jersey, U.S.A.*

Jesse David Dinneen / *School of Information Studies, McGill University, Montreal, Quebec, Canada*

Bernard Dione / *School of Librarianship, Archivists Information Science (EBAD), Cheikh Anta Diop University, Dakar, Senegal*

Dieyi Diouf / *Central Library, Cheikh Anta Diop University of Dakar, Dakar, Senegal*

Keith Donohue / *National Historical Publications and Records Commission, Washington, District of Columbia, U.S.A.*

Ann Doyle / *Xwi7xwa Library, First Nations House of Learning, University of British Columbia, Vancouver, British Columbia, Canada*

Carol D. Doyle / *Government Documents Department and Map Library, California State University, Fresno, California, U.S.A.*

Marek J. Druzdzel / *School of Information Sciences and Intelligent Systems Program, University of Pittsburgh, Pittsburgh, Pennsylvania, U.S.A., and Faculty of Computer Science, Bialystok Technical University, Bialystok, Poland*

Kathel Dunn / *National Library of Medicine, Bethesda, Maryland, U.S.A.*

Luciana Duranti / *School of Library, Archival and Information Studies, University of British Columbia, Vancouver, British Columbia, Canada*

Joan C. Durrance / *School of Information, University of Michigan, Ann Arbor, Michigan, U.S.A.*

Maria Economou / *Department of Communication and Cultural Technology, University of the Aegean, Mytilini, Greece*

Gary Edson / *Center for Advanced Study in Museum Science and Heritage Management, Museum of Texas Tech University, Lubbock, Texas, U.S.A.*

Mary B. Eggert / *Library, Kirkland & Ellis LLP, Chicago, IL, U.S.A.*

Daniel Eisenberg / *Florida State University, Tallahassee, Florida, U.S.A.*

Innocent I. Ekoja / *University Library, University of Abuja, Abuja, Nigeria*

Sarah Elliott / *International Centre for Cultural and Heritage Studies, Newcastle University, Newcastle upon Tyne, U.K.*

David Ellis / *Department of Information Studies, Aberystwyth University, Wales, U.K.*

Jill Emery / *Portland State University Library, Portland, Oregon, U.S.A.*

Zorana Ercegovac / *InfoEN Associates, Los Angeles, California, U.S.A.*

Timothy L. Ericson / *School of Information Science, University of Wisconsin-Milwaukee, Milwaukee, Wisconsin, U.S.A.*

Elena Escolano Rodríguez / *National Library of Spain, Madrid, Spain*

Leigh S. Estabrook / *Graduate School of Library and Information Science, University of Illinois at Urbana- / Champaign, Champaign, Illinois, U.S.A.*

Mark E. Estes / *Alameda County Law Library, Oakland, California, U.S.A.*

Beth Evans / *Library, Brooklyn College, City University of New York, Brooklyn, New York, U.S.A.*

Joanne Evans / *Centre for Organisational and Social Informatics, Monash University, Melbourne, Victoria, Australia*

Dominic J. Farace / *Grey Literature Network Service, TextRelease/GreyNet, Amsterdam, The Netherlands*

David Farneth / *Special Collections and Institutional Records, Getty Research Institute, Los Angeles, California, U.S.A.*

Sharon Fawcett / *Office of Presidential Libraries, National Archives and Records Administration, College Park, Maryland, U.S.A.*

Dieter Fensel / *Institute of Computer Science, University of Innsbruck, Innsbruck, Austria, and National University of Ireland, Galway, Galway, Ireland*

Thomas L. Findley / *Leo A. Daly/Architects & Engineers, Omaha, Nebraska, U.S.A.*

Karen E. Fisher / *Information School, University of Washington, Seattle, Washington, U.S.A.*

Nancy Fjällbrant / *Chalmers University of Technology Library, International Association of Technological University Libraries, Gothenburg, Sweden*

Julia Flanders / *Brown University, Providence, Rhode Island, U.S.A.*

Nancy Flury Carlson / *Westinghouse Electric Corporation, Pittsburgh, Pennsylvania, U.S.A.*

Roger R. Flynn / *School of Information Sciences and Intelligent Systems Program, University of Pittsburgh, Pittsburgh, Pennsylvania, U.S.A.*

Helen Forde / *Department of Information Studies, University College London, London, U.K.*

Douglas J. Foskett / *University of London, London, U.K.*

Susan Foutz / *Institute for Learning Innovation, Edgewater, Maryland, U.S.A.*

Christopher Fox / *Department of Computer Science, James Madison University, Harrisonburg, Virginia, U.S.A.*

Carl Franklin / *Consultant, Columbus, Ohio, U.S.A.*

Jonathan A. Franklin / *Gallagher Law Library, University of Washington, Seattle, Washington, U.S.A.*

Thomas J. Froehlich / *School of Library and Information Science, Kent State University, Kent, Ohio, U.S.A.*

Steve Fuller / *Department of Sociology, University of Warwick, Coventry, U.K.*

Crystal Fulton / *School of Information and Communication Studies, University College Dublin, Dublin, Ireland*

Carla J. Funk / *Medical Library Association, Chicago, Illinois, U.S.A.*

Jonathan Furner / *Department of Information Studies University of California, Los Angeles, Los Angeles, California, U.S.A.*

Dennis Galletta / *Katz Graduate School of Business, University of Pittsburgh, Pittsburgh, Pennsylvania, U.S.A.*

D. Linda Garcia / *Communication Culture and Technology, Georgetown University, Washington, District of Columbia, U.S.A.*

Holly Gardinier / *Honnold/Mudd Library, Libraries of The Claremont Colleges, Claremont, California, U.S.A.*

Sally Gardner Reed / *Association of Library Trustees, Advocates, Friends and Foundations (ALTAFF), Philadelphia, Pennsylvania, U.S.A.*

Janifer Gatenby / *Online Computer Library Center (OCLC), Leiden, The Netherlands*

Ramesh C. Gaur / *Kalanidhi Division, Indira Gandhi National Centre for the Arts (IGNCA), New Delhi, India*

Lee Anne George / *Association of Research Libraries, Washington, District of Columbia, U.S.A.*

David E. Gerard / *College of Librarianship Wales, Cardiganshire, Wales, U.K.*

Malcolm Getz / *Department of Economics, Vanderbilt University, Nashville, Tennessee, U.S.A.*

Mary W. Ghikas / *American Library Association, Chicago, Illinois, U.S.A.*

Nicholas Gibbins / *School of Electronics and Computer Science, University of Southampton, Southampton, U.K.*

Gerd Gigerenzer / *Center for Adaptive Behavior and Cognition, Max Planck Institute for Human Development, Berlin, Germany*

Tommaso Giordano / *Library, European University Institute, Florence, Italy*

Lilian Gisesa / *Kenya National Archives, Nairobi, Kenya*

Edward A. Goedeken / *Iowa State University, Ames, Iowa, U.S.A.*

Warren R. Goldmann / *National Technical Institute for the Deaf, Rochester Institute of Technology, Rochester, New York, U.S.A.*

David Gordon / *Milwaukee Art Museum, Milwaukee, Wisconsin, U.S.A.*

David B. Gracy II / *School of Information, University of Texas at Austin, Austin, Texas, U.S.A.*

Karen F. Gracy / *School of Library and Information Science, Kent State University, Kent, Ohio, U.S.A.*

Renny Granda / *Universidad Central de Venezuela, Caracas, Venezuela*

Paul Gray / *School of Information Systems and Technology, Claremont Graduate University, Claremont, California, U.S.A.*

Jane Greenberg / *Metadata Research Center, School of Information and Library Science, University of North Carolina at Chapel Hill, Chapel Hill, North Carolina, U.S.A.*

Karen Greenwood / *American Medical Informatics Association (AMIA), Bethesda, Maryland, U.S.A.*

Jill E. Grogg / *Libraries, University of Alabama, Tuscaloosa, Alabama, U.S.A.*

Melissa Gross / *School of Information, Florida State University, Tallahassee, Florida, U.S.A.*

Andrew Grove / *Guest Faculty, Information School, University of Washington, Seattle, Washington, U.S.A.*

Dinesh K. Gupta / *Department of Library and Information Science, Vardhaman Mahaveer Open University, 3 Kota, India*

Laurel L. Haak / *Open Researcher and Contributor ID, Inc. (ORCID), U.S.A.*

Kate Hagan / *American Association of Law Libraries, Chicago, Illinois, U.S.A.*

Kathleen Hall / *Leon E. Bloch Law Library, University of Missouri-Kansas City School of Law, Kansas City, Missouri, U.S.A.*

Virginia M.G. Hall / *Center for Educational Resources, The Sheridan Libraries, Johns Hopkins University, Baltimore, Maryland, U.S.A.*

Wendy Hall / *Intelligence, Agents, Multimedia Group, University of Southampton, Southampton, U.K.*

Stuart Hamilton / *International Federation of Library Associations and Institutions, The Hague, The Netherlands*

Maureen L. Hammer / *Knowledge Management, Batelle Memorial Institute, Charlottesville, Virginia, U.S.A.*

Jong-Yup Han / *Research Information Team, KORDI, Seoul, South Korea*

Debra Gold Hansen / *School of Library and Information Science, San Jose State University, Yorba Linda, California, U.S.A.*

Derek L. Hansen / *University of Maryland, College Park, Maryland, U.S.A.*

Eugene R. Hanson / *Shippensburg State College, Shippensburg, Pennsylvania, U.S.A.*

Jane Hardy / *Australian Library and Information Association, Deakin, Australian Capital Territory, Australia*

Julie Hart / *American Association of Museums, Washington, District of Columbia, U.S.A.*

Hiroyuki Hatano / *Surugadai University, Saitama, Japan*

Robert M. Hayes / *Department of Information Studies, University of California, Los Angeles, Los Angeles, California, U.S.A.*

Caroline Haythornthwaite / *Graduate School of Library and Information Science, University of Illinois at Urbana- / Champaign, Champaign, Illinois, U.S.A.*

Penny Hazelton / *Gallagher Law Library, University of Washington, Seattle, Washington, U.S.A.*

P. Bryan Heidorn / *Graduate School of Library and Information Science, University of Illinois at Urbana-Champaign, Champaign, Illinois, U.S.A.*

Helen Heinrich / *Collection Access and Management Services, California State University– Northridge, Northridge, California, U.S.A.*

Doris S. Helfer / *Collection Access and Management Services, California State University–Northridge, Northridge, California, U.S.A.*

Markus Helfert / *School of Computing, Dublin City University, Dublin, Ireland*

Jean Henefer / *School of Information and Communication Studies, University College Dublin, Dublin, Ireland*

Steven L. Hensen / *Rare Book, Manuscript and Special Collections Library, Duke University, Durham, North Carolina, U.S.A.*

Pamela M. Henson / *Archives, Smithsonian Institution, Washington, District of Columbia, U.S.A.*

Peter Hernon / *Graduate School of Library and Information Science, Simmons College, Boston, Massachusetts, U.S.A.*

Dorothy H. Hertzel / *Case Western Reserve University, Cleveland, Ohio, U.S.A.*

Francis Heylighen / *Free University of Brussels, Brussels, Belgium*

Randolph Hock / *Online Strategies, Annapolis, Maryland, U.S.A.*

Theodora L. Hodges / *Berkeley, California, U.S.A.*

Sara S. Hodson / *Huntington Library, San Marino, California, U.S.A.*

Judy C. Holoviak / *American Geophysical Union, Washington, District of Columbia, U.S.A.*

Aleksandra Horvat / *Faculty of Philosophy, University of Zagreb, Zagreb, Croatia*

Ali Houissa / *Olin Library, Cornell University, Ithaca, New York, U.S.A.*

Pamela Howard-Reguindin / *Library of Congress Office, Nairobi, Kenya*

Han-Yin Huang / *International Centre for Cultural and Heritage Studies, Newcastle University, Newcastle upon Tyne, U.K.*

Kathleen Hughes / *American Library Association, Chicago, Illinois, U.S.A.*

Betsy L. Humphreys / *National Library of Medicine, Bethesda, Maryland, U.S.A.*

Charlene S. Hurt / *University Library, Georgia State University, Atlanta, Georgia, U.S.A.*

Sue Hutley / *Australian Library and Information Association, Deakin, Australian Capital Territory, Australia*

John P. Immroth / *University of Pittsburgh, Pittsburgh, Pennsylvania, U.S.A.*

Peter Ingwersen / *Royal School of Library and Information Science, University of Copenhagen, Copenhagen, Denmark*

Vanessa Irvin / *Library and Information Science Program, Information and Computer Sciences Department, University of Hawaii at Mānoa, Honolulu, Hawaii, U.S.A.*

Karla Irwin / *University Libraries, University of Nevada–Las Vegas, Las Vegas, Nevada, U.S.A.*

October R. Ivins / *Ivins eContent Solutions, Sharon, Massachusetts, U.S.A.*

Kalervo Järvelin / *School of Information Science, University of Tampere, Tampere, Finland*

Jean Frédéric Jauslin / *Federal Department of Home Affairs (FDHA), Swiss Federal Office of Culture, Bern, Switzerland*

V. Jeyaraj / *Hepzibah Institute of Conversion, Chennai, India*

Scott Johnston / *McPherson Library, University of Victoria, Victoria, British Columbia, Canada*

Trevor Jones / *Mountain Heritage Center, Western Carolina University, Cullowhee, North Carolina, U.S.A.*

William Jones / *Information School, University of Washington, Seattle, Washington, U.S.A.*

Jay Jordan / *OCLC Online Computer Library Center, Inc., Dublin, Ohio, U.S.A.*

Corinne Jörgensen / *School of Information Studies, Florida State University, Tallahassee, Florida, U.S.A.*

Gene Joseph / *Aboriginal Library Consultant, Langley, British Columbia, Canada*

Daniel N. Joudrey / *School of Library and Information Science, Simmons College, Boston, Massachusetts, U.S.A.*

Heidi Julien / *Library and Information Studies, State University of New York–Buffalo, Buffalo, New York, U.S.A.*

Janet Kaaya / *Department of Information Studies, University of California, Los Angeles, California, U.S.A.*

Philomena Kagwiria Mwirigi / *Kenya National Library Service (KNLS), Nairobi, Kenya*

Athanase B. Kanamugire / *Library Consultant, Dhahran, Saudi Arabia*

Paul B. Kantor / *School of Communication and Information, Rutgers University, New Brunswick, New Jersey, U.S.A.*

Sofia Kapnisi / *International Federation of Library Associations and Institutions, The Hague, the Netherlands*

Nelson Otieno Karilus / *Kenya National Library Service (KNLS), Nairobi, Kenya*

Amy M. Kautzman / *University of California, Berkeley, Berkeley, California, U.S.A.*

Karalyn Kavanaugh / *Account Services Manager, EBSCO Information Services, Birmingham, Alabama, U.S.A.*

Caroline Kayoro / *Kenya National Library Service (KNLS), Nairobi, Kenya*

Andreas Kellerhals / *Federal Department of Home Affairs (FDHA), Swiss Federal Archives, Bern, Switzerland*

John M. Kennedy / *Indiana University, Bloomington, Indiana, U.S.A.*

Kristen Kern / *Portland State University, Portland, Oregon, U.S.A.*

Christopher S.G. Khoo / *School of Communication and Information, Nanyang Technological University, Singapore*

Tapan Khopkar / *University of Michigan, Ann Arbor, Michigan, U.S.A.*

Irene Muthoni Kibandi / *Kenya National Library Service (KNLS), Nairobi, Kenya*

Ruth E. Kifer / *Dr. Martin Luther King, Jr. Library, San Jose State University, San Jose, California, U.S.A.*

Seong Hee Kim / *Department of Library and Information Science, Chung-Ang University, Seoul, South Korea*

Pancras Kimaru / *Kenya National Library Service (KNLS), Nairobi, Kenya*

Karen E. King / *Washington, District of Columbia, U.S.A.*

William R. King / *University of Pittsburgh, Pittsburgh, Pennsylvania, U.S.A.*

Susan K. Kinnell / *Consultant, Santa Barbara, California, U.S.A.*

Laurence J. Kipp / *Harvard University, Cambridge, Massachusetts, U.S.A.*

Thomas G. Kirk, Jr. / *Earlham College Libraries, Earlham College, Richmond, Indiana, U.S.A.*

Breanne A. Kirsch / *Library, Emerging Technologies, University of South Carolina Upstate, Spartanburg, South Carolina, U.S.A.*

Vernon N. Kisling, Jr. / *Marston Science Library, University of Florida, Gainesville, Florida, U.S.A.*

Adam D. Knowles / *San Diego, California, U.S.A.*

Rebecca Knuth / *Library and Information Science Program, University of Hawaii, Honolulu, Hawaii, U.S.A.*

Michael Koenig / *College of Information and Computer Science, Long Island University, Brookville, New York, U.S.A.*

Jesse Koennecke / *Cornell University Library, Cornell University College of Arts and Sciences, Ithaca, New York, U.S.A.*

Jes Koepfler / *Museum Studies Program, Faculty of Information Studies, University of Toronto, Toronto, Ontario, Canada*

Amelia Koford / *Blumberg Memorial Library, Texas Lutheran University, Seguin, Texas, U.S.A.*

Toru Koizumi / *Library, Rikkyo University, Tokyo, Japan*

Josip Kolanović / *Croatian State Archives, Zagreb, Croatia*

Sjoerd Koopman / *International Federation of Library Associations and Institutions, The Hague, the Netherlands*

Donald Kraft / *Department of Computer Science, U.S. Air Force Academy, Colorado Springs, Colorado, U.S.A.*

Allison Krebs / *University of Arizona, Tucson, Arizona, U.S.A.*

Judith F. Krug / *Office for Intellectual Freedom, American Library Association, Chicago, Illinois, U.S.A.*

D.W. Krummel / *Emeritus, Graduate School of Library and Information Science, University of Illinois at Urbana-Champaign, Champaign, Illinois, U.S.A.*

Carol Collier Kuhlthau / *Department of Library and Information Science, Rutgers University, New Brunswick, New Jersey, U.S.A.*

Krishan Kumar / *Former Head, Department of Library and Information Science, University of Delhi, New Delhi, India*

Sanna Kumpulainen / *Library, Tampere University of Technology, Tampere, Finland*

Michael J. Kurtz / *National Archives at College Park, U.S. National Archives and Records Administration, College Park, Maryland, U.S.A.*

Zhenhua Lai / *Department of Management Information Systems, University of Arizona, Tucson, Arizona, U.S.A.*

Mounia Lalmas / *Department of Computing Science, University of Glasgow, Glasgow, U.K.*

Heather M. Lamond / *Massey University Library, Palmerston North, New Zealand*

F.W. Lancaster / *Graduate School of Library and Information Science, University of Illinois at Urbana-Champaign, Urbana, Illinois, U.S.A.*

Ronald L. Larsen / *School of Information Sciences, University of Pittsburgh, Pittsburgh, Pennsylvania, U.S.A.*

Ray R. Larson / *School of Information, University of California—Berkeley, Berkeley, California, U.S.A.*

Jesús Lau / *Library Services Unit USBI Veracruz (USBI VER), University of Veracruz, Veracruz, Mexico*

Judith V. Lechner / *Department of Educational Foundations, Leadership, and Technology, Auburn University, Auburn, Alabama, U.S.A.*

Christopher A. Lee / *School of Information and Library Science, University of North Carolina at Chapel Hill, Chapel Hill, North Carolina, U.S.A.*

Janet Lee / *University of Denver, Denver, Colorado, U.S.A, and Regis University, Denver, Colorado, U.S.A.*

Catherine Leekam / *Museum Studies Program, Faculty of Information Studies, University of Toronto, Toronto, Ontario, Canada*

Kjell Lemström / *Department of Computer Science, University of Helsinki, Helsinki, Finland*

Timothy F. Leslie / *Department of Geography and Geoinformation Science, George Mason University, Fairfax, Virginia, U.S.A.*

Noémie Lesquins / *Scientific Mission (DSR), National Library of France, Paris, France*

Rosalind K. Lett / *Information-2-Knowledge, Atlanta, Georgia, U.S.A.*

Allison V. Level / *Colorado State University, Fort Collins, Colorado, U.S.A.*

Michael Levine-Clark / *Penrose Library, University of Denver, Denver, Colorado, U.S.A.*

Anany Levitin / *Department of Computing Sciences, Villanova University, Villanova, Pennsylvania, U.S.A.*

Marjorie Lewis / *Canaan, New York, U.S.A.*

Elizabeth D. Liddy / *School of Information Studies, Syracuse University, Syracuse, New York, U.S.A.*

Silje C. Lier / *Software & Information Industry Association, Washington, District of Columbia, U.S.A.*

Jane E. Light / *Dr. Martin Luther King, Jr. Library, San Jose Public Library, San Jose, California, U.S.A.*

Paul M. Lima / *Canadian Heritage Information Network (CHIN), Gatineau, Quebec, Canada*

Louise Limberg / *Swedish School of Library and Information Science, University of Borås and University of Gothenburg, Borås, Sweden*

Shin-jeng Lin / *Department of Business Administration, Le Moyne College, Syracuse, New York, U.S.A.*

Sarah Lippincott / *Educopia Institute, Atlanta, Georgia, U.S.A.*

Peter Johan Lor / *School of Information Studies, University of Wisconsin-Milwaukee, Milwaukee, Wisconsin, U.S.A., and Department of Information Science, University of Pretoria, Pretoria, South Africa*

Beth Luey / *Fairhaven, Massachusetts, U.S.A.*

Joseph Luke / *Kazakhstan Institute of Management, Economics and Strategic Research (KIMEP), Almaty, Kazakhstan*

Claudia Lux / *Central and Regional Library of Berlin (ZLB), Berlin, Germany*

Marianne Lykke / *Information Interaction and Architecture, Royal School of Library and Information Science, Aalborg, Denmark*

Elena Macevičiūtė / *Faculty of Communication, Vilnius University, Vilnius, Lithuania, and Swedish School of Library and Information Science, University of Borås, Borås, Sweden*

Juan D. Machin-Mastromatteo / *Universidad Central de Venezuela, Caracas, Venezuela*

Barbara A. Macikas / *American Library Association, Chicago, Illinois, U.S.A.*

Leslie Madsen-Brooks / *Boise State University, Boise, Idaho, U.S.A.*

William J. Maher / *Archives, University of Illinois at Urbana-Champaign, Urbana, Illinois, U.S.A.*

Thomas Mann / *Library of Congress, Washington, District of Columbia, U.S.A.*

Sylva Natalie Manoogian / *Department of Information Studies, University of California, Los Angeles, Los Angeles, California, U.S.A.*

Daniel Marcu / *Information Sciences Institute, University of Southern California, Marina del Rey, California, U.S.A.*

James W. Marcum / *Fairleigh Dickinson University, Madison, New Jersey, U.S.A.*

Francesca Marini / *School of Library, Archival and Information Studies, University of British Columbia, Vancouver, British Columbia, Canada*

Johan Marklund / *Department of Industrial Management and Logistics, Lund University, Lund, Sweden*

Dian I. Martin / *Small Bear Technical Consulting, LLC, Thorn Hill, Tennessee, U.S.A.*

Susan K. Martin / *Lauinger Library, Georgetown University, Washington, District of Columbia, U.S.A.*

Paul F. Marty / *College of Communication and Information, Florida State University, Tallahassee, Florida, U.S.A.*

Dan Marwit / *Lee H. Skolnick Architecture + Design Partnership, New York, New York, U.S.A.*

Laura Matzer / *Arizona Museum for Youth, Mesa, Arizona, U.S.A.*

Robert L. Maxwell / *Special Collections and Metadata Catalog Department, Brigham Young University, Provo, Utah, U.S.A.*

Hope Mayo / *Houghton Library, Harvard University, Cambridge, Massachusetts, U.S.A.*

Sally H. McCallum / *Network Development and MARC Standards Office, Library of Congress, Washington, District of Columbia, U.S.A.*

Gavan McCarthy / *eScholarship Research Centre, University of Melbourne, Melbourne, Victoria, Australia*

Ian McGowan / *Former Librarian, National Library of Scotland, Edinburgh, U.K.*

Roger McHaney / *Department of Management, Kansas State University, Manhattan, Kansas, U.S.A.*

I.C. McIlwaine / *University College London, School of Library, Archive and Information Studies, London, U.K.*

Sue McKemmish / *Centre for Organisational and Social Informatics, Monash University, Melbourne, Victoria, Australia*

Marie E. McVeigh / *JCR and Bibliographic Policy, Thomson Reuters - Scientific, Philadelphia, Pennsylvania, U.S.A.*

Linda Mboya / *National Museums of Kenya, Nairobi, Kenya*

Judith Adams Meadows / *State Law Library of Montana, Helena, Montana, U.S.A.*

K. van der Meer / *Faculty of Electrical Engineering, Mathematics and Computer Science, Delft University, the Netherlands; Information and Library Science, IOIW, Antwerp University, Belgium; and D-CIS, Delft, The Netherlands*

Bharat Mehra / *School of Information Sciences, University of Tennessee, Knoxville, Tennessee, U.S.A.*

Margaret Ann Mellinger / *OSU Libraries & Press, Oregon State University, Corvallis, Oregon, U.S.A.*

Elizabeth E. Merritt / *American Association of Museums, Washington, District of Columbia, U.S.A.*

David Millman / *Academic Information Systems, Columbia University, New York, U.S.A.*

Jack Mills / *North-Western Polytechnic, London, U.K.*

Kevin L. Mills / *National Institute of Standards and Technology, Gaithersburg, Maryland, U.S.A.*

Staša Milojević / *Department of Information Studies, University of California, Los Angeles, Los Angeles, California, U.S.A.*

Marla Misunas / *Collections Information and Access, San Francisco Museum of Modern Art, San Francisco, California, U.S.A.*

Joan S. Mitchell / *OCLC Online Computer Library Center, Inc., Dublin, Ohio, U.S.A.*

Yoriko Miyabe / *Rikkyo University, Tokyo, Japan*

Diane Mizrachi / *University Libraries, University of California–Los Angeles, Los Angeles, California, U.S.A.*

William Moen / *Texas Center for Digital Knowledge, University of North Texas, Denton, Texas, U.S.A.*

Abdul Moid / *University of Karachi, Karachi, Pakistan*

Hermann Moisl / *Center for Research in Linguistics, University of Newcastle upon Tyne, Newcastle upon Tyne, U.K.*

Ole Magnus Mølbak Andersen / *Danish State Archives, Copenhagen, Denmark*

Mavis B. Molto / *Utah State University, Logan, Utah, U.S.A.*

Philip Mooney / *Heritage Communications, Coca-Cola Company, Atlanta, Georgia, U.S.A.*

Reagan W. Moore / *San Diego Supercomputer Center, University of North Carolina at Chapel Hill, Chapel Hill, North Carolina, U.S.A.*

Mersini Moreleli-Cacouris / *Department of Library Science and Information Systems, Technological Educational Institute (TEI) of Thessaloniki, Sindos, Greece*

Paul K. Moser / *Department of Philosophy, Loyola University Chicago, Chicago, Illinois, U.S.A.*

Clara C. Mosquera / *Library, Kirkland & Ellis LLP, Chicago, IL, U.S.A.*

David J. Muddiman / *Leeds Metropolitan University, Leeds, U.K.*

Nancy C. Mulvany / *Bayside Indexing Service, Fort Collins, Colorado, U.S.A.*

Sue Myburgh / *School of Communication, University of South Australia, Adelaide, South Australia, Australia*

Elli Mylonas / *Brown University, Providence, Rhode Island, U.S.A.*

Jeremy Myntti / *J. Willard Marriott Library, Salt Lake City, Utah, U.S.A.*

Jacob Nadal / *ReCAP: The Research Collections and Preservation Consortium, Princeton, New Jersey, U.S.A.*

Diane Nahl / *Information and Computer Sciences Department, University of Hawaii, Honolulu, Hawaii, U.S.A.*

Robert Nardini / *Vice President, Library Services, ProQuest Books, La Vergne, Tennessee, U.S.A.*

Arnold vander Nat / *Department of Philosophy, Loyola University Chicago, Chicago, Illinois, U.S.A.*

Charles M. Naumer / *Information School, University of Washington, Seattle, Washington, U.S.A.*

Sophie Ndegwa / *Kenya National Library Service (KNLS), Nairobi, Kenya*

Dixie Neilson / *University of Florida, Gainesville, Florida, U.S.A.*

Sarah Beth Nelson / *School of Information and Library Sciences, University of North Carolina at Chapel Hill, Chapel Hill, North Carolina, U.S.A.*

Stuart J. Nelson / *National Library of Medicine, Bethesda, Maryland, U.S.A.*

Stephanie Nemcsok / *Museum Studies Program, Faculty of Information Studies, University of Toronto, Toronto, Ontario, Canada*

Ken Neveroski / *College of Information and Computer Science, Long Island University, Brookville, New York, U.S.A.*

Jennifer Ng / *Museum Studies Program, Faculty of Information Studies, University of Toronto, Toronto, Ontario, Canada*

Melissa Niiya / *Portland Public Schools, Portland, Oregon, U.S.A.*

Angela Noseworthy / *Museum Studies Program, Faculty of Information Studies, University of Toronto, Toronto, Ontario, Canada*

Barbara E. Nye / *Ictus Consulting, LLC, Pasadena, California, U.S.A.*

Charles Nzivo / *Kenya National Library Service (KNLS), Nairobi, Kenya*

Dennis O'Brien / *Maps and Wayfinding, LLC, Mystic, Connecticut, U.S.A.*

Karen Lynn O'Brien / *American Library Association, Chicago, Illinois, U.S.A.*

Kieron O'Hara / *Intelligence, Agents, Multimedia Group, University of Southampton, Southampton, U.K.*

Elizabeth O'Keefe / *Morgan Library and Museum, New York, U.S.A.*

Denise I. O'Shea / *Fairleigh Dickinson University, Teaneck, New Jersey, U.S.A.*

Douglas W. Oard / *College of Information Studies, University of Maryland, College Park, Maryland, U.S.A.*

Maria Oldal / *Morgan Library and Museum, New York, U.S.A.*

Lorne Olfman / *School of Information Systems and Technology, Claremont Graduate University, Claremont, California, U.S.A.*

Bette W. Oliver / *Austin, Texas, U.S.A.*

Annette Olson / *Biological Resources Division, U.S. Geological Survey, Reston, Virginia, U.S.A.*

Hope A. Olson / *School of Information Studies, University of Wisconsin-Milwaukee, Milwaukee, Wisconsin, U.S.A.*

Lawrence J. Olszewski / *OCLC Library, Dublin, Ohio, U.S.A.*

Kok-Leong Ong / *School of Information Technology, Deakin University, Burwood, Victoria, Australia*

Tim Owen / *Chartered Institute of Library and Information Professionals (CILIP), London, U.K.*

John C. Paolillo / *School of Informatics and School of Library and Information Science, Indiana University, Bloomington, Indiana, U.S.A.*

Eun Bong Park / *Library Service Department, National Library of Korea, Seoul, South Korea*

Soyeon Park / *Department of Library and Information Science, Duksung Womens University, Seoul, South Korea*

Gabriella Pasi / *Department of Informatics, Systems and Communication, University of Studies of Milano Bicocca, Milan, Italy*

Norman Paskin / *Tertius Ltd., Oxford, U.K.*

Christiane Paul / *Whitney Museum of American Art, New York, U.S.A.*

Ellen Pearlstein / *Information Studies and UCLA / Getty Program in the Conservation of Ethnographic and Archaeological Materials, University of California, Los Angeles, Los Angeles, California, U.S.A.*

Kathleen de la Peña McCook / *School of Library and Information Science, University of South Florida, Tampa, Florida, U.S.A.*

Steve Pepper / *Department of Linguistics, University of Oslo, Oslo, Norway*

Manuel A. Pérez-Quiñones / *Department of Software and Information Systems, University of North Carolina, Charlotte, North Carolina, U.S.A.*

Paul Evan Peters / *University of Pittsburgh, Pittsburgh, Pennsylvania, U.S.A.*

Jakob Heide Petersen / *Danish Agency for Libraries and Media, Copenhagen, Denmark*

Mary Jane Petrowski / *American Library Association, Chicago, Illinois, U.S.A.*

Katharine J. Phenix / *Northglenn Branch, Rangeview Library District, Northglenn, Colorado, U.S.A.*

Robert B. Pickering / *Gilcrease Museum, and Museum Science and Management Program, University of Tulsa, Tulsa, Oklahoma, U.S.A.*

Janice T. Pilch / *Rutgers University Libraries, Rutgers University, New Brunswick, New Jersey, U.S.A.*

Thomas E. Pinelli / *Langley Research Center, National Aeronautics and Space Administration (NASA) Hampton, Virginia, U.S.A.*

Daniel Pitti / *Alderman Library, Institute for Advanced Technology in the Humanities, University of Virginia, Charlottesville, Virginia, U.S.A.*

Elena Ploşniţă / *Science Department, National Museum of Archaeology and History of Moldova, Chisinau, Republic of Moldova*

Gabriela Podušelová / *Slovak National Museum, Bratislava, Slovak Republic*

Danny C.C. Poo / *School of Computing, Department of Information Systems, National University of Singapore, Singapore*

Martine Poulain / *Department of Libraries and Documentation, National Institute for the History of Art (INHA), Paris, France*

Tammy Powell / *National Library of Medicine, Bethesda, Maryland, U.S.A.*

Stephen Prine / *Library of Congress, Washington, District of Columbia, U.S.A.*

Mary Jo Pugh / *Editor, American Archivist, Walnut Creek, California, U.S.A.*

Ajit K. Pyati / *University of Western Ontario, London, Ontario, Canada*

Aimée C. Quinn / *Government Publications Services, Brooks Library, Central Washington University, Ellensburg, Washington, U.S.A.*

Jennie Quiñónez-Skinner / *University Library, California State University–Northridge, Northridge, California, U.S.A.*

Debbie Rabina / *School of Library and Information Science, Pratt Institute, New York, New York, U.S.A.*

Katalin Radics / *Research Library, University of California—Los Angeles, Los Angeles, California, U.S.A.*

Carl Rahkonen / *Harold S. Orendorff Music Library, Indiana University of Pennsylvania, Indiana, Pennsylvania, U.S.A.*

Jocelyn Rankin / *Centers for Disease Control and Prevention Library, Atlanta, Georgia, U.S.A.*

Samuel J. Redman / *Department of History, University of California, Berkeley, Berkeley, California, U.S.A.*

Thomas C. Redman / *Navesink Consulting Group, Little Silver, New Jersey, U.S.A.*

Barbara Reed / *Recordkeeping Innovation, Sydney, New South Wales, Australia*

Marcia Reed / *Getty Research Institute, Los Angeles, CA, U.S.A.*

CarrieLynn D. Reinhard / *Department of Communication, Business, and Information Technologies, Roskilde University, Roskilde, Denmark*

Harold C. Relyea / *Congressional Research Service, Library of Congress, Washington, District of Columbia, U.S.A.*

Steve Ricci / *Department of Information Studies/Film and Television, University of California–Los Angeles, Los Angeles, California, U.S.A.*

Ronald E. Rice / *Department of Communication, University of California–Santa Barbara, Santa Barbara, California, U.S.A.*

John V. Richardson, Jr. / *Department of Information Studies, University of California, Los Angeles, Los Angeles, California, U.S.A.*

Soo Young Rieh / *School of Information, University of Michigan, Ann Arbor, Michigan, U.S.A.*

Kevin S. Rioux / *Division of Library and Information Science, St. John's University, Queens, New York, U.S.A.*

Julian Roberts / *Wolfson College, University of Oxford, Oxford, U.K.*

Lyn Robinson / *City, University of London, London, U.K.*

Diane Robson / *University Libraries, Media Library, University of North Texas, Denton, Texas, U.S.A.*

Michael Rodriguez / *Michigan State University Libraries, East Lansin, Michigan, U.S.A.*

Juraj Roháč / *Department of Archival Science and Auxiliary Historical Sciences, Comenius University in, Bratislava, Slovak Republic*

Mark Roosa / *Pepperdine University, Malibu, California, U.S.A.*

Jonathan Rose / *Department of History, Drew University, Madison, New Jersey, U.S.A.*

Howard Rosenbaum / *School of Library and Information Science, Indiana University, Bloomington, Indiana, U.S.A.*

Catherine Sheldrick Ross / *Faculty of Information and Media Studies, University of Western Ontario, London, Ontario, Canada*

Shannon Ross / *Canadian Heritage Information Network (CHIN), Gatineau, Quebec, Canada*

Richard Rubin / *School of Library and Information Science, Kent State University, Kent, Ohio, U.S.A.*

Lynne M. Rudasill / *University of Illinois at Urbana-Champaign, Champaign, Illinois, U.S.A.*

Michael Rush / *Beinecke Rare Book and Manuscript Library, Yale University, New Haven, Connecticut, U.S.A.*

Mariza Russo / *Faculty of Administration and Accounting Sciences (FACC), Federal University of Rio de Janeiro, Rio de Janeiro, Brazil*

Athena Salaba / *Kent State University, Kent, Ohio, U.S.A.*

Romelia Salinas / *California State University, Los Angeles, Los Angeles, California, U.S.A.*

Airi Salminen / *Department of Computer Science and Information Systems, University of Jyväskylä, Jyväskylä, Finland*

Michael J. Salvo / *Department of English, Purdue University, West Lafayette, Indiana, U.S.A.*

Robert J. Sandusky / *University Library, University of Illinois at Chicago, Chicago, Illinois, U.S.A.*

Tefko Saracevic / *School of Communication and Information, Rutgers University, New Brunswick, New Jersey, U.S.A.*

Chris Sauer / *Said Business School, University of Oxford, Oxford, U.K.*

Rejéan Savard / *School of Library and Information Science, University of Montreal, Montreal, Quebec, Canada*

Reijo Savolainen / *School of Information Sciences, University of Tampere, Tampere, Finland*

Barbara Schaefer / *Geneseo, New York, U.S.A.*

Silvia Schenkolewski-Kroll / *Department of Information Science, Bar-Ilan University, Ramat Gan, Israel*

Lael J. Schooler / *Center for Adaptive Behavior and Cognition, Max Planck Institute for Human Development, Berlin, Germany*

Joachim Schöpfel / *Department of Library and Information Sciences (IDIST), GERiico Laboratory Charles de Gaulle University Lille 3, Villeneuve d'Ascq, France*

Catherine F. Schryer / *Department of English Language and Literature, University of Waterloo, Waterloo, Ontario, Canada*

Marjorie Schwarzer / *Museum Studies Department, John F. Kennedy University, Berkeley, California, U.S.A.*

Jo Ann Secor / *Lee H. Skolnick Architecture + Design Partnership, New York, New York, U.S.A.*

Sara Selwood / *Department of Cultural Policy and Management, City University, London, U.K.*

Frank B. Sessa / *University of Pittsburgh, Pittsburgh, Pennsylvania, U.S.A.*

Mark Sgambettera / *Bronx County Historical Society, Bronx, New York, U.S.A.*

Ayman Shabana / International Institute, University of California, Los Angeles, Los Angeles, California, U.S.A.

Nigel Shadbolt / *School of Electronics and Computer Science, University of Southampton, Southampton, U.K.*

Kalpana Shankar / *School of Informatics, Indiana University, Bloomington, Indiana, U.S.A.*

Debora Shaw / *School of Library and Information Science, Indiana University, Bloomington, Indiana, U.S.A.*

Conrad Shayo / *Department of Information and Decision Sciences, California State University—San Bernardino, San Bernardino, California, U.S.A.*

Elizabeth Shepherd / *Department of Information Studies, University College London, London, U.K.*

Beverly K. Sheppard / *Institute for Learning Innovation, Edgewater, Maryland, U.S.A.*

Ross Shimmon / *Faversham, U.K.*

Snunith Shoham / *Department of Information Science, Bar-Ilan University, Ramat Gan, Israel*

Lyudmila Shpilevaya / *New York Public Library, New York, New York, U.S.A.*

David Shumaker / *School of Library and Information Science, Catholic University of America, Washington, District of Columbia, U.S.A.*

Judith A. Siess / *Information Bridges International, Inc., Champaign, Illinois, U.S.A.*

John Edward Simmons / *Museologica, Bellefonte, Pennsylvania, U.S.A.*

Anestis Sitas / *Aristotle University of Thessaloniki, Thessaloniki, Greece*

Roswitha Skare / *Institute of Culture and Literature, UiT The Arctic University of Norway, Tromsø, Norway*

Katherine Skinner / *Educopia Institute, Atlanta, Georgia, U.S.A.*

Lee H. Skolnick / *Lee H. Skolnick Architecture + Design Partnership, New York, New York, U.S.A.*

Mette Skov / *Department of Communication and Psychology, Aalborg University, Aalborg, Denmark*

Bobby Smiley / *Vanderbilt University, Heard Libraries, Nashville, Tennessee, U.S.A.*

Linda C. Smith / *School of Information Sciences, University of Illinois at Urbana-Champaign, Champaign, Illinois, U.S.A.*

Lois Smith / *Human Factors and Ergonomics Society, Santa Monica, California, U.S.A.*

Lori Smith / *Linus A. Sims Memorial Library, Southeastern Louisiana University, Hammond, Louisiana, U.S.A.*

Patricia A. Smith / *Colorado State University, Fort Collins, Colorado, U.S.A.*

Scott A. Smith / *Langlois Public Library, Langlois, Oregon, U.S.A.*

A. Patricia Smith-Hunt / *Science Library, Preservation Services, University of California, Riverside, Riverside, California, U.S.A.*

Karen Smith-Yoshimura / *Online Computer Library Center (OCLC), San Mateo, California, U.S.A.*

Diane H. Sonnenwald / *University College Dublin, Dublin, Ireland*

Nour Soufi / *Library Cataloging and Metadata Center, University of California, Los Angeles, Los Angeles, California, U.S.A.*

Barbara M. Spiegelman / *Churchill Associates, Pittsburgh, Pennsylvania, U.S.A.*

Robert P. Spindler / *Department of Archives and Manuscripts, Arizona State University, Tempe, Arizona, U.S.A.*

Joie Springer / *Information Society Division, UNESCO, Paris, France*

Suresh Srinivasan / *National Library of Medicine, Bethesda, Maryland, U.S.A.*

Guy St. Clair / *Knowledge Management and Learning, SMR International, New York, New York, U.S.A.*

Cheryl L. Stadel-Bevans / *National Archives and Records Administration, College Park, Maryland, U.S.A.*

Jill Stein / *Institute for Learning Innovation, Edgewater, Maryland, U.S.A.*

Marcia K. Stein / *Museum of Fine Arts, Houston, Houston, Texas, U.S.A.*

Jela Steinerová / *Department of Library and Information Science, Comenius University in, Bratislava, Slovak Republic*

Dick Stenmark / *Department of Applied IT, IT University of Gothenburg, Gothenburg, Sweden*

Andy Stephens / *OBE, Board Secretary, Head of International Engagement, The British Library, London, U.K.*

Margaret Stieg Dalton / *School of Library and Information Studies, University of Alabama, Tuscaloosa, Alabama, U.S.A.*

Katina Strauch / *Addlestone Library, College of Charleston, Charleston, South Carolina, U.S.A.*

Robert D. Stueart / *Graduate School of Library and Information Science, Simmons College, Boston, Massachusetts, U.S.A.*

Paul F. Stuehrenberg / *Yale Divinity Library, New Haven, Connecticut, U.S.A.*

Brian William Sturm / *School of Information and Library Sciences, University of North Carolina at Chapel Hill, Chapel Hill, North Carolina, U.S.A.*

Anna Suorsa / *University of Oulu, Oulu, Finland*

Brett Sutton / *Aurora University, Aurora, Illinois, U.S.A.*

Sarah Sutton / *Mary and Jeff Bell Library, Texas A&M University-Corpus Christi, Corpus Christi, Texas, U.S.A.*

Destinee Kae Swanson / *Adams Museum & House, Inc., Deadwood, South Dakota, U.S.A.*

H.L. Swanson / *GSOE, University of California, Riverside, California, U.S.A.*

Miriam E. Sweeney / *School of Library and Information Studies, University of Alabama, Tuscaloosa, Alabama, U.S.A.*

Shelley Sweeney / *University of Manitoba, Winnipeg, Manitoba, Canada*

Jean Tague-Sutcliffe / *Graduate School of Library and Information Science, University of Western Ontario, London, Ontario, Canada*

Masaya Takayama / *National Archives of Japan, Tokyo, Japan*

Sanna Talja / *Department of Information Studies and Interactive Media, University of Tampere, Tampere, Finland*

G. Thomas Tanselle / *Vice President, John Simon Guggenheim Memorial Foundation, New York, New York, U.S.A.*

Ivan Tanzer / *Museum Studies Program, Faculty of Information Studies, University of Toronto, Toronto, Ontario, Canada*

Melissa Terras / *UCL Department of Information Studies, UCL Centre for Digital Humanities, University College London, London, U.K.*

Mike Thelwall / *School of Computing and Information Technology, University of Wolverhampton, Wolverhampton, U.K.*

Lynne M. Thomas / *Rare Books and Special Collections, Northern Illinois University, DeKalb, Illinois, U.S.A.*

Lawrence S. Thompson / *University of Kentucky, Lexington, Kentucky, U.S.A.*

Jens Thorhauge / *Danish Agency for Libraries and Media, Copenhagen, Denmark*

Anne Thurston / *International Records Management Trust, London, U.K.*

Michael Tiemann / *Open Source Initiative, Chapel Hill, North Carolina, U.S.A.*

Christinger Tomer / *School of Information Sciences, University of Pittsburgh, Pittsburgh, Pennsylvania, U.S.A.*

Elaine G. Toms / *Faculty of Management, Dalhousie University, Halifax, Nova Scotia, Canada*

Jack Toolin / *Whitney Museum of American Art, New York, U.S.A.*

Jennifer Trant / *Archives & Museum Informatics, Toronto, Ontario, Canada*

Barry Trott / *Williamsburg Regional Library, Williamsburg, Virginia, U.S.A.*

Alice Trussell / *Hale Library, Kansas State University, Manhattan, Kansas, U.S.A.*

John Mark Tucker / *Abilene Christian University, Abilene, Texas, U.S.A.*

James M. Turner / *School of Library and Information Sciences, University of Montreal, Montreal, Quebec, Canada*

Louise Tythacott / *Centre for Museology, University of Manchester, Manchester, U.K.*

George Tzanetakis / *Department of Computer Science, University of Victoria, Victoria, British Columbia, Canada*

Franklyn Herbert Upward / *Centre for Organisational and Social Informatics, Monash University, Melbourne, Victoria, Australia*

Richard Urban / *Graduate School of Library and Information Science, University of Illinois, Champaign, Illinois, U.S.A.*

Rachel E. Vacek / *University of Michigan, Ann Arbor, Michigan, U.S.A.*

Ron Van den Branden / *Centre for Scholarly Editing and Document Studies, Royal Academy of Dutch Language and Literature, Gent, Belgium*

Sydney C. Van Nort / *The City College of New York, The City University of New York, New York, U.S.A.*

Edward Vanhoutte / *Centre for Scholarly Editing and Document Studies, Royal Academy of Dutch Language and Literature, Gent, Belgium*

Rebecca Vargha / *Information and Library Science Library, University of North Carolina at Chapel Hill, Chapel Hill, North Carolina, U.S.A.*

Jana Varlejs / *School of Communication, Information and Library Studies, Rutgers University, New Brunswick, New Jersey, U.S.A.*

Jason Vaughan / *Library Technologies, University of Nevada, Las Vegas University Libraries, Las Vegas, Nevada, U.S.A.*

Dale J. Vidmar / *Southern Oregon University Library, Ashland, Oregon, U.S.A.*

Diane Vizine-Goetz / *OCLC Online Computer Library Center, Inc., Dublin, Ohio, U.S.A.*

Ellen M. Voorhees / *Information Technology Laboratory, National Institute of Standards and Technology, Gaithersburg, Maryland, U.S.A.*

Sharon L. Walbridge / *Libraries Washington State University, Pullman, Washington, U.S.A.*

Stephanie Walker / *Brooklyn College, City University of New York, Brooklyn, New York, U.S.A.*

Virginia A. Walter / *Department of Information Studies, University of California, Los Angeles, Los Angeles, California, U.S.A.*

Mark Warschauer / *School of Education, University of California, Irvine, CA, U.S.A.*

Nigel M. Waters / *Department of Geography and Geoinformation Science, George Mason University, Fairfax, Virginia, U.S.A.*

Kathryn M. Wayne / *Art History/Classics Library, University of California, Berkeley, California, U.S.A.*

Frank Webster / *City University, London, U.K.*

Jeff Weddle / *School of Library and Information Studies, University of Alabama, Tuscaloosa, Alabama, U.S.A.*

Judith Weedman / *School of Library and Information Science, San Jose State University, Fullerton, California, U.S.A.*

Stuart L. Weibel / *Office of Research and Special Projects, OCLC Research, Dublin, Ohio, U.S.A.*

Jennifer Weil Arns / *School of Library and Information Science, University of South Carolina, Columbia, South Carolina, U.S.A.*

Bella Hass Weinberg / *Division of Library and Information Science, St. John's University, Queens, New York, New York, U.S.A.*

Volker M. Welter / *Department of the History of Art and Architecture, University of California, Santa Barbara, Santa Barbara, California, U.S.A.*

Caryn Wesner-Early / *ASRC Aerospace & Defense, US Patent & Trademark Office, Alexandria, Virginia, U.S.A.*

Lynn Westbrook / *School of Information, University of Texas at Austin, Austin, Texas, U.S.A.*

Howard D. White / *College of Computing and Informatics, Drexel University, Philadelphia, PA, U.S.A., and College of Information Science and Technology, Drexel University, Philadelphia, Pennsylvania, U.S.A.*

Layna White / *San Francisco Museum of Modern Art, San Francisco, California, U.S.A.*

Michael J. White / *Engineering and Science Library, Queen's University, Kingston, Ontario, Canada*

Sarah K. Wiant / *School of Law, Washington and Lee University, Lexington, Virginia, U.S.A.*

Stephen E. Wiberley, Jr. / *University of Illinois at Chicago, Chicago, Illinois, U.S.A.*

Gunilla Widén-Wulff / *Information Studies, Åbo Akademi University, Åbo, Finland*

Bradley J. Wiles / *Hill Memorial Library, Louisiana State University, Baton Rouge, Louisiana, U.S.A.*

Mary I. Wilke / *Center for Research Libraries, Chicago, Illinois, U.S.A.*

Barratt Wilkins / *Retired State Librarian of Florida, Tallahassee, Florida, U.S.A.*

Peter Willett / *Department of Information Studies, University of Sheffield, Sheffield, U.K.*

Kate Williams / *University of Illinois at Urbana-Champaign, Champaign, Illinois, U.S.A.*

Kirsty Williamson / *Caulfield School of IT, Monash University, Caulfield, Victoria, Australia and School of Information Studies, Charles Sturt University, Wagga Wagga, New South Wales, Australia*

Concepción S. Wilson / *School of Information Systems, Technology and Management, University of New South Wales, Sydney, New South Wales, Australia*

Ian E. Wilson / *Librarian and Archivist of Canada 2004–2009, Ottawa, Ontario, Canada*

Kristen Wilson / *North Carolina State University Libraries, Raleigh, North Carolina, U.S.A.*

Thomas D. Wilson / *Publisher/Editor in Chief, Information Research, U.K.*

Catherine C. Wilt / *PALINET, Philadelphia, Pennsylvania, U.S.A.*

Charles Wilt / *Association for Library Collections and Technical Services (ALCTS), Chicago, Illinois, U.S.A.*

Niels Windfeld Lund / *Institute of Culture and Literature, UiT The Arctic University of Norway, Troms , Norway*

Michael F. Winter / *Shields Library, University of California, Davis, California, U.S.A.*

Erica Wiseman / *Graduate School of Library and Information Studies, McGill University, Montreal, Quebec, Canada*

Steve W. Witt / *University of Illinois at Urbana-Champaign, Champaign, Illinois, U.S.A.*

Blanche Woolls / *iSchool, San Jose State University, San Jose, California, U.S.A.*

Louisa Worthington / *Public Library Association, Chicago, Illinois, U.S.A.*

Jadwiga Woźniak-Kasperek / *Institute of Information and Book Studies, University of Warsaw, Warsaw, Poland*

Judith Wusteman / *School of Information and Communication Studies, University College Dublin, Dublin, Ireland*

Iris Xie / *School of Information Studies, University of Wisconsin–Milwaukee, Milwaukee, Wisconsin, U.S.A.*

Yiyu Yao / *Department of Computer Science, University of Regina, Regina, Saskatchewan, Canada, and International WIC Institute, Beijing University of Technology, Beijing, China*

Janis L. Young / *Library of Congress, Washington, District of Columbia, U.S.A.*

Priscilla C. Yu / *University Library, University of Illinois at Urbana-Champaign, Urbana, Illinois, U.S.A.*

Jana Zabinski / *American National Standards Institute, New York, New York, U.S.A.*

Lisl Zach / *iSchool, Drexel University, Philadelphia, Pennsylvania, U.S.A.*

Olga Zaitseva / *Kazakhstan Institute of Management, Economics and Strategic Research (KIMEP), Almaty, Kazakhstan*

Marcia Lei Zeng / *School of Library and Information Science, Kent State University, Kent, Ohio, U.S.A.*

Yi Zeng / *International WIC Institute, Beijing University of Technology, Beijing, China*

Višnja Zgaga / *Museum Documentation Center, Zagreb, Croatia*

Jun Zhang / *Pitney Bowes, Shelton, Connecticut, U.S.A.*

Yulei Zhang / *Department of Management Information Systems, University of Arizona, Tucson, Arizona, U.S.A.*

Kai Zheng / *Department of Health Management and Policy, University of Michigan, Ann Arbor, Michigan, U.S.A.*

Ning Zhong / *Department of Life Science and Informatics, Maebashi Institute of Technology, Maebashi-City, Japan, and International WIC Institute, Beijing University of Technology, Beijing, China*

Maja Žumer / *University of Ljubljana, Slovenia*

Vladimir Zwass / *Computer Science and Management Information Systems, Fairleigh Dickinson University, Teaneck, New Jersey, U.S.A.*

Encyclopedia of Library and Information Sciences, Fourth Edition

Contents

Volume I

Academic Libraries / *Susan Curzon and Jennie Quiñónez-Skinner* 1

Accessibility / *Lori Bell* 14

Accreditation of Library and Information Studies Programs in the United States and Canada / *Karen Lynn O'Brien* 18

Acquisitions Institute at Timberline Lodge / *Scott A. Smith* 22

African Librarianship / *Natalia T. Bowdoin and Janet Lee* 33

Altmetrics / *Richard Cave* 44

American Association of Law Libraries (AALL) / *Kate Hagan* 48

American Association of Museums (AAM) / *Elizabeth E. Merritt* 56

American Association of School Librarians (AASL) / *Donald C. Adcock* 59

American Library Association (ALA) / *Mary W. Ghikas* 67

American Medical Informatics Association (AMIA) / *Don E. Detmer, Tia Abner and Karen Greenwood* 85

American National Standards Institute (ANSI) / *Jana Zabinski* 87

American Society for Information Science and Technology (ASIST) / *Charles H. Davis and Debora Shaw* 90

Approval Plans / *Robert Nardini* 96

Arab Federation for Libraries and Information (AFLI) / *Nour Soufi* 100

Archival Appraisal and Acquisition / *Barbara Reed* 105

Archival Arrangement and Description / *Joanne Evans, Sue McKemmish and Barbara Reed* 115

Archival Documentation / *Gavan McCarthy and Joanne Evans* 127

Archival Finding Aids / *Su Kim Chung and Karla Irwin* 133

Archival Management and Administration / *Michael J. Kurtz* 141

Archival Reference and Access / *Mary Jo Pugh* 149

Archival Science / *Elizabeth Shepherd* 166

Archives / *Adrian Cunningham* 179

Archivists and Collecting / *Richard J. Cox* 195

Area and Interdisciplinary Studies Literatures and Their Users / *Lynn Westbrook* 209

ARMA International, Inc. / *Carol E. B. Choksy* 221

Armenia: Libraries, Archives, and Museums / *Sylva Natalie Manoogian* 228

Art Galleries / *Daniel C. Danzig* 241

Art Librarianship / *Kathryn M. Wayne* 249

Art Museums / *David Gordon* 259

Volume I (*cont'd.*)

Artificial Intelligence / *Jianhua Chen* 269

Artificial Neural Networks and Natural Language Processing / *Hermann Moisl* 279

Arts Literatures and Their Users / *Lisl Zach* 293

ASLIB / *David Bawden and Lyn Robinson* 301

Association for Information Science and Technology / *Diane H. Sonnenwald,*
  Charles H. Davis and Debora Shaw 311

Association for Information Systems (AIS) / *William R. King and Dennis Galletta* 318

Association for Library Collections and Technical Services / *Charles Wilt* 324

Association for Library Service to Children (ALSC) / *Virginia A. Walter* 333

Association of College and Research Libraries (ACRL) / *Mary Ellen Davis and Mary Jane Petrowski* . . . 338

Association of Library Trustees, Advocates, Friends and Foundations (ALTAFF) / *Sally Gardner Reed* . . . 361

Association of Research Libraries (ARL) / *Lee Anne George and Julia Blixrud* 364

Association of Specialized and Cooperative Library Agencies (ASCLA) / *Barbara A. Macikas* 376

Australia: Libraries, Archives, and Museums / *Alex Byrne* 379

Australian Library and Information Association (ALIA) / *Sue Hutley, Jane Hardy and*
  Judy Brooker 396

Authentication and Authorization / *David Millman* 401

Automated Acquisitions / *Patricia A. Smith and Allison V. Level* 408

Automatic Abstracting and Summarization / *Daniel Marcu* 418

Automatic Discourse Generation / *John A. Bateman* 430

Back-of-the-Book Indexing / *Nancy C. Mulvany* 440

Bibliographic Control *[ELIS Classic]* / *Robert L. Maxwell* 447

Bibliographical Society (London) / *Julian Roberts* 456

Bibliographical Society of America (BSA) / *Hope Mayo* 463

Bibliography / *D. W. Krummel* 468

Bibliometric Overview of Information Science / *Howard D. White* 480

Bibliometric Research: History *[ELIS Classic]* / *Dorothy H. Hertzel* 492

Bibliothèque Nationale de France / *Noémie Lesquins* 531

Binding *[ELIS Classic]* / *Lawrence S. Thompson* 538

Biological Information and Its Users / *Kalpana Shankar* 554

Blind and Physically Disabled: Library Services / *Jane Rosetta Virginia Caulton and Stephen Prine* 563

Bliss Bibliographic Classification First Edition *[ELIS Classic]* / *Jack Mills* 573

Bliss Bibliographic Classification Second Edition / *Vanda Broughton* 581

Boolean Algebras *[ELIS Classic]* / *A. R. Bednarek* 591

Brazil: Library Science / *Mariza Russo* 597

Brazil: Library Science—Distance Education / *Mariza Russo* 603

Brazil: Museums / *Regina Dantas and Pamela Howard-Reguindin* 611

British Library / *Andy Stephens* 616

Business Informatics / *Markus Helfert* 630

Business Information and Its Users / *Eileen G. Abels* 635

Business Literature: History *[ELIS Classic]* / *Edwin T. Coman, Jr.* 643

Canada: Libraries and Archives / *Ian E. Wilson and Sean F. Berrigan* 654

Canadian Heritage Information Network (CHIN) / *Shannon Ross and Paul M. Lima* 675

Canadian Library Association (CLA) / *Donald I. Butcher* 681

Careers and Education in Archives and Records Management / *Karen Anderson* 685

Careers and Education in Information Systems / *Paul Gray and Lorne Olfman* 693

Volume I (*cont'd.*)

Careers and Education in Library and Information Science / *Jana Varlejs* 706

Careers and Education in Records and Information Management / *Carol E. B. Choksy* 715

Volume II

Cataloging / *Daniel N. Joudrey* 723

Cataloging Cultural Objects (CCO) / *Elizabeth O'Keefe and Maria Oldal* 733

Catalogs and Cataloging: History *[ELIS Classic]* / *Eugene R. Hanson and Jay E. Daily* 743

Censorship and Content Regulation of the Internet / *Peng Hwa Ang* 780

Center for Research Libraries / *Mary I. Wilke* 789

Charleston Conference / *Katina Strauch* 794

Chartered Institute of Library and Information Professionals (CILIP) / *Tim Owen* 806

Chemistry Literature and Its Users *[ELIS Classic]* / *Judith N. Currano* 814

Chemoinformatics / *Peter Willett* 830

Children and Information Technology / *June Abbas* 839

Children's Literature / *Judith V. Lechner* 852

Children's Services in Libraries / *Virginia A. Walter and Melissa Gross* 876

China: Libraries, Archives, and Museums / *Priscilla C. Yu and TzeHuey Chiou-Peng* 886

Circulation Services / *Vanessa Irvin and Jeff E. Bullard* 916

Citation Analysis / *Howard D. White* 923

Citation Indexes and the *Web of Science* / *Marie E. McVeigh* 940

Citer Motivations *[ELIS Classic]* / *Terrence Brooks* 951

Classification Theory / *Clare Beghtol* 958

Clinical Decision-Support Systems / *Kai Zheng* 974

College Libraries / *Thomas G. Kirk, Jr.* 983

Communication and Communication Studies / *Brenda Dervin and CarrieLynn D. Reinhard* 994

Communication Policy: United States / *D. Linda Garcia* 1007

Community Informatics / *Kate Williams and Joan C. Durrance* 1027

Complexity and Self-Organization / *Francis Heylighen* 1034

Computer-Mediated Communication (CMC) / *Michael A. Chilton and Roger McHaney* 1044

Computer-Supported Cooperative Work (CSCW) / *Kevin L. Mills* 1053

Conservation and Preservation of Museum Objects / *Ellen Pearlstein* 1068

Controlled Vocabularies for Art, Architecture, and Material Culture / *Murtha Baca* 1076

Corporate Archives / *Philip Mooney* 1081

Corporate Art Collections / *Laura Matzer* 1086

Corporate Information Centers / *Barbara M. Spiegelman and Nancy Flury Carlson* 1094

Corporate Records Management / *Barbara M. Cross and Barbara E. Nye* 1104

Credibility and Cognitive Authority of Information / *Soo Young Rieh* 1113

Croatia: Libraries, Archives, and Museums / *Aleksandra Horvat, Josip Kolanović and Višnja Zgaga* . . . 1121

CrossRef Publisher Linking Network / *Amy E. Brand* 1132

Cultural Memory / *Robert DeHart* 1139

Curating Archaeological Artifacts / *Alex W. Barker* 1147

Curating Natural History Collections / *Kimberly S. Bostwick* 1156

Custody and Chain of Custody / *Bernadette G. Callery* 1164

Data and Data Quality / *Thomas C. Redman and Christopher Fox and Anany Levitin* 1171

Deaf and Hearing Impaired: Communication in Service Contexts *[ELIS Classic]* / *Warren R. Goldmann* . . . 1183

Volume II (cont'd.)

Decision Sciences / *Sven Axsäter and Johan Marklund* 1192

Decision Support Systems / *Marek J. Druzdzel and Roger R. Flynn* 1200

Demand-Driven Acquisition/Patron-Driven Acquisition / *Michael Levine-Clark* 1209

Denmark: Libraries, Archives, and Museums / *Jens Thorhauge, Jakob Heide Petersen and
  Ole Magnus Mølbak Andersen* 1215

Descriptive Cataloging Principles / *Elena Escolano Rodríguez* 1229

Design Science in the Information Sciences / *Judith Weedman* 1242

Dewey Decimal Classification (DDC) / *Joan S. Mitchell and Diane Vizine-Goetz* 1256

Digital Content Licensing / *Paul D. Callister and Kathleen Hall* 1267

Digital Divide and Inclusion / *Mark Warschauer and Melissa Niiya* 1279

Digital Humanities / *Julia Flanders and Elli Mylonas* 1286

Digital Humanities and Academic Libraries / *Bobby Smiley and Michael Rodriguez* 1298

Digital Images / *Melissa Terras* 1307

Digital Millennium Copyright Act of 1998 / *Jonathan A. Franklin* 1316

Digital Object Identifier (DOI®) System / *Norman Paskin* 1325

Digital Preservation / *Jacob Nadal* 1332

Diplomatics / *Luciana Duranti* 1338

Disaster Planning and Recovery for Cultural Institutions / *Sheryl Davis, A. Patricia Smith-Hunt and
  Kristen Kern* 1347

Document Information Systems / *K. van der Meer* 1360

Document Theory / *Niels Windfeld Lund and Roswitha Skare* 1372

Document Type Definition (DTD) / *Judith Wusteman* 1381

Dublin Core Metadata Initiative (DCMI): A Personal History / *Stuart L. Weibel* 1390

Economics Literature: History *[ELIS Classic]* / *Arthur H. Cole and Laurence J. Kipp* 1399

Electronic Records Preservation / *Robert P. Spindler* 1413

Electronic Resources & Libraries (ER&L) / *Jesse Koennecke* 1419

Encoded Archival Description / *Daniel Pitti and Michael Rush* 1423

Engineering Literatures and Their Users *[ELIS Classic]* / *Thomas E. Pinelli, Ann P. Bishop,
  Rebecca O. Barclay and John M. Kennedy* 1433

Volume III

Epistemology / *Paul K. Moser* 1455

Ethical and Legal Aspects of Archival Services / *Sara S. Hodson* 1463

Ethical Aspects of Library and Information Science / *Richard Rubin and Thomas J. Froehlich* 1469

Ethical Issues in Information Systems / *Vladimir Zwass* 1484

Ethiopia: Libraries, Archives, and Museums / *Shiferaw Assefa* 1494

Everyday Life Information Seeking / *Reijo Savolainen* 1506

Evidence-Based Practice / *Prudence W. Dalrymple* 1516

Exhibition Design / *Lee H. Skolnick, Dan Marwit and Jo Ann Secor* 1523

Facet Analysis *[ELIS Classic]* / *Douglas J. Foskett* 1534

Faceted Application of Subject Terminology (FAST) / *Eric R. Childress and Diane Vizine-Goetz* 1539

Federal Electronic Information in the United States / *Carol D. Doyle* 1549

Film and Broadcast Archives / *Karen F. Gracy and Karen E. King* 1560

Film Archiving: History / *Steve Ricci* 1584

France: Archives, Museums, and Libraries / *Martine Poulain* 1589

Volume III (*cont'd.*)

Functional Requirements for Subject Authority Data (FRSAD): Conceptual Model /
Marcia Lei Zeng, Athena Salaba and Maja Žumer 1606

Fuzzy Set Theory / *Donald Kraft, Gloria Bordogna and Gabriella Pasi* 1618

Games and Gaming / *Diane Robson and Breanne A. Kirsch* 1636

Genealogical Literature and Its Users / *Mavis B. Molto* 1644

Genre Theory and Research / *Catherine F. Schryer* 1662

Geographic Information Systems (GIS) / *Timothy F. Leslie and Nigel M. Waters* 1671

Geographical Literature: History *[ELIS Classic]* / *Nora T. Corley* 1683

Germany: Libraries, Archives, and Museums / *Claudia Lux* 1693

Global Open Knowledgebase / *Kristen Wilson* 1710

Government Documents: Collection and Management / *Aimée C. Quinn, Lori Smith and James Church* . . . 1715

Greece: Archives / *Nestor Bamidis* 1728

Greece: Libraries / *Anestis Sitas and Mersini Moreleli-Cacouris* 1733

Greece: Museums / *Maria Economou* 1741

Grey Literature *[ELIS Classic]* / *Joachim Schöpfel and Dominic J. Farace* 1746

HathiTrust / *Rick Anderson* 1757

Health Science Professional Literatures and Their Users / *Cheryl Dee and Jocelyn Rankin* 1763

Historical and Archaeological Sites: Development and Preservation / *Robert B. Pickering* 1771

Historical Societies / *Mark Sgambettera* 1779

Historical Sources and Their Users / *Margaret Stieg Dalton* 1786

History of Libraries / *John Mark Tucker and Edward A. Goedeken* 1796

History of Museums / *John Edward Simmons* 1812

History of Paper / *Sidney E. Berger* 1824

History of Public Libraries *[ELIS Classic]* / *Frank B. Sessa* 1836

History of Records and Information Management / *William Benedon* 1850

History of the Book / *Jonathan Rose* 1859

History: Three Basic Printing Processes / *Sidney E. Berger* 1865

Hospital Libraries / *Rosalind K. Lett* 1870

Human–Computer Interaction Research in Information Retrieval / *Shin-jeng Lin* 1895

Humanities Literatures and Their Users / *Stephen E. Wiberley, Jr.* 1909

Hungary: Libraries, Archives, and Museums / *Katalin Radics* 1917

Hypertext and Hypercard: Early Development *[ELIS Classic]* / *Susan K. Kinnell and Carl Franklin* . . . 1935

Illumination *[ELIS Classic]* / *Abdul Moid* 1945

Impact Assessment of Cultural Institutions / *Sara Selwood* 1958

Incunabula *[ELIS Classic]* / *John P. Immroth and Romano Stephen Almagno* 1966

Indexing: History and Theory / *Bella Hass Weinberg* 1978

India: Libraries, Archives and Museums / *Krishan Kumar, V. Jeyaraj and Ramesh C. Gaur* . . . 1992

Indigenous Librarianship / *Kathleen Burns, Ann Doyle, Gene Joseph and Allison Krebs* . . . 2031

Information / *Marcia J. Bates* 2048

Information Arts / *Christiane Paul and Jack Toolin* 2064

Information Behavior / *Marcia J. Bates* 2074

Information Behavior Models / *Thomas D. Wilson* 2086

Information Crises and Crisis Information / *Philippe Baumard* 2094

Information Explosion / *Ronald E. Day* 2101

Information Management / *Brian Detlor* 2106

Information Needs / *Charles M. Naumer and Karen E. Fisher* 2115

Volume III (*cont'd.*)

Information Needs and Behaviors of Diasporic Populations / *Ajit K. Pyati* 2122

Information Needs and Behaviors of Populations in Less Developed Regions / *Innocent I. Ekoja* 2130

Information Policy: European Union / *Debbie Rabina and Scott Johnston* 2138

Information Policy: United States / *Peter Hernon and Harold C. Relyea* 2147

Information Practice / *Crystal Fulton and Jean Henefer* 2162

Information Retrieval Experimentation *[ELIS Classic]* / *Jean Tague-Sutcliffe* 2172

Volume IV

Information Retrieval Protocols: Z39.50 and Search and Retrieve via URL / *William Moen* 2181

Information Retrieval Support Systems / *Yiyu Yao, Ning Zhong and Yi Zeng* 2192

Information Retrieval Systems / *Ray R. Larson* 2199

Information Scattering / *Suresh K. Bhavnani and Concepción S. Wilson* 2210

Information Science / *Tefko Saracevic* 2216

Information Search Process (ISP) Model / *Carol Collier Kuhlthau* 2232

Information Searching and Search Models / *Iris Xie* 2239

Information Society / *Frank Webster* 2253

Information Systems / *E. Burton Swanson* 2272

Information Systems Failure / *Chris Sauer and Gordon B. Davis* 2280

Information Technology Adoption / *Conrad Shayo* 2290

Information Technology Literacy / *James W. Marcum and Denise I. O'Shea* 2303

Information Technology Project Implementation in Developing Countries *[ELIS Classic]* /
     Athanase B. Kanamugire 2312

Information Technology Standards for Libraries *[ELIS Classic]* / *Christinger Tomer* 2341

Information Theory / *Paul B. Kantor* 2350

Information Use for Decision Making / *Edward T. Cokely, Lael J. Schooler and Gerd Gigerenzer* 2359

Informetrics / *Judit Bar-Ilan* 2367

Institutional Records and Archives / *David Farneth* 2377

Intellectual Freedom and the American Library Association (ALA):
     Historical Overview *[ELIS Classic]* / *Judith F. Krug* 2387

Intelligence and Security Informatics / *Hsinchun Chen, Zhenhua Lai, Yan Dang and Yulei Zhang* 2398

International and Comparative Librarianship / *Peter Johan Lor* 2404

International Association of Sound and Audiovisual Archives (IASA) / *Ilse Assmann* 2413

International Association of Technological University Libraries (IATUL) /
     Nancy Fjällbrant and Alice Trussell 2418

International Communication Association (ICA) / *Ronald E. Rice* 2421

International Council of Museums (ICOM) / *Patrick J. Boylan* 2429

International Council on Archives (ICA) / *Perrine Canavaggio and Marcel Caya* 2437

International Council on Knowledge Management (ICKM) / *Franz Barachini* 2445

International Federation of Library Associations and Institutions (IFLA) / *Ross Shimmon,*
     Peter Johan Lor, Sofia Kapnisi, Sjoerd Koopman and Stuart Hamilton 2451

International Federation of Television Archives (FIAT/IFTA) / *Steve Bryant* 2465

International Organization for Standardization (ISO) / *Alan Bryden and Catherine Dhérent* 2470

International Records Management Standards ISO 15489 and 23081 / *Barbara Reed* 2481

Volume IV (*cont'd.*)

International Records Management Trust / *Anne Thurston* 2487

International Society for Knowledge Organization (ISKO) / *Ingetraut Dahlberg* 2494

Internet Genres / *Kevin Crowston* 2503

Internet Search Tools: History to 2000 / *Dale J. Vidmar and Connie J. Anderson-Cahoon* 2516

InterPARES / *Luciana Duranti* 2526

iSchools / *Ronald L. Larsen* 2536

Israel: Libraries, Archives, and Museums / *Snunith Shoham and Silvia Schenkolewski-Kroll* 2542

Japan: Libraries, Archives, and Museums / *Masaya Takayama, Yoriko Miyabe,*
    Toru Koizumi and Hiroyuki Hatano 2560

Kazakhstan: Libraries, Archives, and Museums / *Leslie Champeny, Joseph Luke,*
    Anna Bergaliyeva and Olga Zaitseva 2578

Kenya: Libraries, Museums, and Archives / *Irene Muthoni Kibandi, Pancras Kimaru,*
    Caroline Kayoro, Philomena Kagwiria Mwirigi, Sophie Ndegwa, Nelson Otieno Karilus,
    Charles Nzivo, Linda Mboya and Lilian Gisesa 2592

Knowledge / *Paul K. Moser and Arnold vander Nat* 2610

Knowledge Creation and Use in Organizations / *Maija-Leena Aulikki Huotari and Anna Suorsa* 2618

Knowledge Discovery in Data Streams / *Xuan Hong Dang and Kok-Leong Ong* 2626

Knowledge Management / *Kimiz Dalkir* 2640

Knowledge Management Systems / *Dick Stenmark* 2649

Knowledge Management: Early Development / *Michael Koenig and Ken Neveroski* 2657

Knowledge Organization System Standards / *Stella G. Dextre Clarke* 2665

Knowledge: Tacit and Explicit / *Philippe Baumard* 2677

Latent Semantic Indexing / *Dian I. Martin and Michael W. Berry* 2688

Latinos and U.S. Libraries: History / *Romelia Salinas* 2698

Law Firm Librarianship / *Brenda A. Burton, Mary B. Eggert and Clara C. Mosquera* 2705

Law Librarianship / *Richard A. Danner, Mark E. Estes and Judith Adams Meadows* 2710

Law Literature and Its Users / *Penny Hazelton* 2733

Learning and Information Seeking / *Louise Limberg and Mikael Alexandersson* 2751

Libraries / *Jennifer Weil Arns* 2762

Library and Information Science / *Miriam E. Sweeney and Leigh S. Estabrook* 2768

Library and Information Technology Association (LITA) / *Rachel E. Vacek* 2775

Library Anxiety / *Diane Mizrachi* 2782

Library Architecture and Design / *Charlene S. Hurt and Thomas L. Findley* 2788

Library Architecture: History / *Nan Christian Ploug Dahlkild* 2797

Library Automation: History / *Robert M. Hayes* 2810

Library Consortia in Europe / *Tommaso Giordano* 2822

Library Fundraising and Development / *Susan K. Martin* 2832

Library Leadership and Management Association (LLAMA) / *Robert Allen Daugherty* 2841

Library of Congress Classification (LCC) / *Lois Mai Chan and Theodora L. Hodges* 2847

Library of Congress Genre/Form Terms for Library and Archival Materials /
    Janis L. Young 2856

Library of Congress Subject Headings (LCSH) / *Janis L. Young* 2866

Library of Congress: History / *John Y. Cole* 2879

Library Portals and Gateways / *Frank Cervone* 2892

Library Publishing Initiatives: North America / *Katherine Skinner and Sarah Lippincott* 2901

Volume V

Library Science in the United States: Early History / *John V. Richardson, Jr.* 2909

Library Technical Services / *Doris S. Helfer and Helen Heinrich* 2918

Linguistics and the Information Sciences / *John C. Paolillo* 2927

Linked Data / *Jeremy Myntti* 2938

Lithuania: Libraries and Librarianship / *Elena Macevičiūtė* 2943

Louvre / *Bette W. Oliver* 2958

Machine Readable Cataloging (MARC): 1961–1974 [ELIS Classic] / *Henriette D. Avram* 2963

Machine Readable Cataloging (MARC): 1975–2007 / *Sally H. McCallum* 2980

Makerspaces in Libraries / *Patrick Tod Colegrove* 2990

Management of Very Large Distributed Shared Collections [ELIS Classic] / *Reagan W. Moore* 2997

Managing an Information Business / *Gloria Dinerman* 3004

Marketing Library and Information Services / *Dinesh K. Gupta and Réjean Savard* 3011

Mathematics Literature: History [ELIS Classic] / *Barbara Schaefer* 3019

Medical Library Association (MLA) / *Carla J. Funk* 3033

Medical Literature: History [ELIS Classic] / *William K. Beatty* 3041

Metadata and Digital Information [ELIS Classic] / *Jane Greenberg* 3058

Metamarkup Languages: SGML and XML / *Airi Salminen* 3072

Mexico: Libraries, Archives, and Museums / *Jesús Lau* 3082

Modeling Documents in Their Context / *Airi Salminen* 3105

Moldova: Archives, Museums, and Libraries / *Hermina G.B. Angbelescu,*
    Silviu Andrieş-Tabac and Elena Ploşniţă 3117

Moving Image Indexing / *James M. Turner* 3129

Multilingual Information Access / *Douglas W. Oard* 3140

Museum Accreditation Program / *Leah Arroyo and Julie Hart* 3146

Museum Architecture and Gallery Design / *Volker M. Welter* 3148

Museum Collecting and Collections / *Robert B. Pickering* 3161

Museum Computer Network (MCN) / *Marla Misunas and Richard Urban* 3170

Museum Informatics / *Paul F. Marty* 3176

Museum Management / *Gary Edson* 3185

Museum Registration and Documentation / *Dixie Neilson* 3199

Museum Studies / *Marjorie Schwarzer* 3214

Museum Web Sites and Digital Collections / *David Bearman and Jennifer Trant* 3222

Museums / *Leslie Madsen-Brooks* 3233

Museums and Community / *Tamara Biggs* 3243

Museums and Their Visitors: Historic Relationship / *Samuel J. Redman* 3251

Museums as Place / *Peter Davis and Han-Yin Huang* 3258

Music Information Retrieval / *Kjell Lemström and George Tzanetakis* 3267

Music Librarianship / *Holly Gardinier, Sarah R. Canino and Carl Rahkonen* 3275

Name Authority Control / *Janifer Gatenby and Karen Smith-Yoshimura* 3288

National Archives / *Helen Forde* 3298

National Biological Information Infrastructure (NBII) / *P. Bryan Heidorn and Annette Olson* 3306

National Historical Publications and Records Commission (NHPRC) / *Keith Donohue* 3315

National Libraries / *Ian McGowan* 3320

National Library of Medicine / *Kathel Dunn* 3334

Natural Language Processing for Information Retrieval / *Elizabeth D. Liddy* 3346

Network Management / *Robert J. Sandusky* 3356

Volume V (*cont'd.*)

Network of European Museum Organisations (NEMO) / *Frank Birkebæk* 3365

Networked Knowledge Organization Systems/Services (NKOS) / *Marianne Lykke* 3366

New Zealand Aotearoa: Libraries / *Heather M. Lamond* 3371

Non-governmental Organizations and Information / *Lynne M. Rudasill and Steve W. Witt* 3380

North American Serials Interest Group / *Jill Emery* 3388

OCLC: A Worldwide Library Cooperative / *Jay Jordan* 3392

Older Adults' Information: Needs and Behavior / *Kirsty Williamson and Terry Asla* 3406

One-Person Libraries / *Judith A. Siess* 3413

Online Catalog Subject Searching / *Danny C.C. Poo and Christopher S.G. Khoo* 3422

Online Library Instruction / *Beth Evans* 3432

Online Public Access Catalogs (OPACs) *[ELIS Classic]* / *Kevin Butterfield* 3450

Ontologies and Their Definition / *Jos de Bruijn and Dieter Fensel* 3455

Open Access Scholarship and Publishing / *Malcolm Getz* 3465

Open Archival Information System (OAIS) Reference Model / *Christopher A. Lee* 3477

Open Source Software / *Michael Tiemann* 3488

Oral History in Libraries and Archives / *Debra Gold Hansen* 3494

ORCID / *Laurel L. Haak* 3505

Organization Theories / *Evelyn Daniel* 3510

Organizational Culture / *Gunilla Widén-Wulff* 3520

Organizational Learning / *Erica Wiseman* 3526

Organizational Memory / *Maureen L. Hammer* 3534

Pacific Islands Association of Libraries and Archives (PIALA) / *Arlene Cohen* 3541

Papyrology / *Roger S. Bagnall* 3552

Patents and Patent Searching / *Michael J. White* 3560

People with Disabilities / *Amelia Koford* 3573

Personal Information Management / *William Jones, Jesse David Dinneen, Robert Capra,*
    Anne R. Diekema and Manuel A. Pérez-Quiñones 3584

Peru: Libraries and Library Science / *Sergio Chaparro-Univazo* 3606

Philosophy and the Information Sciences / *Jonathan Furner* 3610

Philosophy of Science *[ELIS Classic]* / *Paul Evan Peters* 3623

Volume VI

Physical Sciences and Mathematics Literatures and Their Users / *Cecelia Brown* 3637

Piracy in Digital Media / *Stephanie Walker* 3649

Plagiarism of Print and Electronic Resources / *Zorana Ercegovac* 3664

Poland: Libraries and Archives / *Jadwiga Woźniak-Kasperek* 3674

Politics of Representation in Museums / *Louise Tythacott* 3688

Popular Literature Genres / *Barry Trott* 3700

Precision and Recall *[ELIS Classic]* / *F. W. Lancaster* 3708

Presidential Libraries / *Sharon Fawcett* 3714

Primary Records: Future Prospects *[ELIS Classic]* / *G. Thomas Tanselle* 3719

Print on Demand / *Steve Bosch* 3733

Private Presses and Fine Printing *[ELIS Classic]* / *Roderick Cave* 3738

Provenance of Archival Materials / *Shelley Sweeney* 3746

Provenance of Museum Objects / *Layna White* 3756

Volume VI (*cont'd.*)

Provenance of Rare Books / *Marcia Reed* 3766

Public Librarianship *[ELIS Classic]* / *Kathleen de la Peña McCook and Katharine J. Phenix* 3774

Public Libraries *[ELIS Classic]* / *Barbara H. Clubb* 3781

Public Library Association (PLA) / *Louisa Worthington and Kathleen Hughes* 3801

Qualitative Research Methods in Library and Information Science *[ELIS Classic]* / *Brett Sutton* 3806

Rare Book Collections / *Andrew J. Berner* 3820

Reading and Reading Acquisition / *Brian Byrne* 3830

Reading Disorders / *H.L. Swanson* 3841

Reading Interests / *Catherine Sheldrick Ross* 3850

Recommender Systems and Expert Locators / *Derek L. Hansen, Tapan Khopkar and Jun Zhang* 3860

Records Compliance and Risk Management / *Bradley J. Wiles* 3869

Records Continuum Model / *Sue McKemmish, Franklyn Herbert Upward and Barbara Reed* 3874

Records Organization and Access / *Sue Myburgh* 3887

Records Retention Schedules / *Barbara E. Nye* 3892

Reference and Informational Genres / *Thomas Mann* 3897

Reference and User Services Association (RUSA) / *Barbara A. Macikas* 3908

Reference Services / *Linda C. Smith* 3912

Regional Library Networks: United States / *Catherine C. Wilt* 3920

Relevance in Theory / *Howard D. White* 3926

Relevance Judgments and Measurements / *Erica Cosijn* 3940

Renaissance Libraries *[ELIS Classic]* / *Lawrence S. Thompson* 3948

Resource Description Framework (RDF) / *Nicholas Gibbins and Nigel Shadbolt* 3961

Saudi Arabia: Libraries, Archives, and Museums / *Ayman Shabana* 3970

Scholarly and Trade Publishing *[ELIS Classic]* / *Richard Abel* 3982

School Librarianship / *Blanche Woolls* 3991

School Libraries / *Blanche Woolls* 4000

Science and Engineering Librarianship / *Margaret Ann Mellinger* 4008

Science and Technology Studies / *Sanna Talja* 4020

Search Engine Optimization / *Nicholas Carroll* 4029

Search Engines / *Randolph Hock* 4046

Self-Publishing Online / *Caryn Wesner-Early* 4054

Semantic Interoperability / *Marcia Lei Zeng and Lois Mai Chan* 4062

Semantic Web / *Kieron O'Hara and Wendy Hall* 4080

Semiotics / *Marcel Danesi* 4094

Senegal: Libraries, Archives, and Museums / *Bernard Dione and Dieyi Diouf* 4104

Sense-Making / *Brenda Dervin and Charles M. Naumer* 4113

Serbia: Libraries, Archives, and Museums / *Staša Milojević* 4125

Serials Collection and Management *[ELIS Classic]* / *Sarah Sutton* 4139

Serials Vendors *[ELIS Classic]* / *Karalyn Kavanaugh* 4150

Shared Libraries / *Ruth E. Kifer and Jane E. Light* 4158

Site Museums and Monuments / *Destinee Kae Swanson* 4164

Slovakia: Libraries, Archives, and Museums / *Jela Steinerová, Juraj Roháč and Gabriela Podušelová* . . 4173

Smithsonian Institution / *Pamela M. Henson* 4188

Social Epistemology / *Steve Fuller* 4197

Social Influences on Classification / *Hope A. Olson* 4204

Social Informatics / *Howard Rosenbaum* 4212

Volume VI (*cont'd.*)

Social Justice in Library and Information Science / *Bharat Mehra, Kevin S. Rioux and Kendra S. Albright* 4218

Social Networks and Information Transfer / *Caroline Haythornthwaite* 4235

Social Science Literatures and Their Users *[ELIS Classic]* / *David Ellis* 4246

Social Science Professional Literatures and Their Users / *Lynn Westbrook* 4255

Society for Scholarly Publishing (SSP) / *Judy C. Holoviak, October R. Ivins and Lois Smith* 4262

Society for the History of Authorship, Reading and Publishing (SHARP) / *Beth Luey* 4268

Society of American Archivists (SAA) / *Timothy L. Ericson and Steven L. Hensen* 4271

Sociology of Reading / *Martine Poulain* 4279

Sociology of the Information Disciplines / *Michael F. Winter* 4286

Software and Information Industry Association (SIIA) / *Silje C. Lier* 4297

Sound and Audio Archives / *Mark Roosa* 4299

South Korea: Archives and Libraries / *Hyun-Yang Cho, Eun Bong Park, Soyeon Park, Jae-Hwang Choi, Seong Hee Kim and Jong-Yup Han* 4307

Spain: Libraries, Archives, and Museums / *Lawrence J. Olszewski* 4314

Special Collections / *Lynne M. Thomas* 4335

Special Collections and Manuscripts / *Lynne M. Thomas* 4343

Special Librarianship / *Susan S. DiMattia* 4351

Volume VII

Special Libraries / *David Shumaker* 4361

Special Libraries Association (SLA) / *Guy St. Clair, Andrew J. Berner and Rebecca Vargha* 4370

Specialty Museums / *Trevor Jones* 4379

State Archives / *David B. Gracy II and Adam D. Knowles* 4384

State Libraries and State Library Agencies / *Barratt Wilkins* 4392

State-Sponsored Destruction of Books and Libraries / *Rebecca Knuth* 4400

Still Image Indexing / *Corinne Jörgensen* 4407

Still Image Search and Retrieval / *Vittorio Castelli* 4417

Storytelling / *Sarah Beth Nelson and Brian William Sturm* 4437

Strategic Planning in Academic Libraries / *Sheila Corrall* 4447

Students' Information: Needs and Behavior / *Heidi Julien* 4459

Subject Cataloging Principles and Systems / *Theodora L. Hodges and Lois Mai Chan* 4466

Subscription Libraries *[ELIS Classic]* / *David E. Gerard* 4478

Switzerland: Libraries, Archives, and Museums / *Jean Frédéric Jauslin and Andreas Kellerhals* 4487

Tanzania: Libraries, Archives, Museums, and Information Systems / *Janet Kaaya* 4497

Task-Based Information Searching: Research Methods / *Sanna Kumpulainen* 4526

Taxonomy / *Andrew Grove* 4537

Technical Writing / *Michael J. Salvo* 4547

Test Collections / *Ben Carterette* 4554

Text Encoding Initiative (TEI) / *Edward Vanhoutte and Ron Van den Branden* 4559

Text REtrieval Conference (TREC) / *Ellen M. Voorhees* 4569

Theft, Vandalism, and Security in Libraries and Archives / *Sydney C. Van Nort* 4576

Theft, Vandalism, and Security in Museums / *Jes Koepfler, Ivan Tanzer, Stephanie Nemcsok, Jennifer Ng, Catherine Leekam, Angela Noseworthy and Jennifer Bawden* 4593

Theological Librarianship / *Paul F. Stuehrenberg* 4604

Volume VII (*cont'd.*)

Topic Maps / *Steve Pepper* 4611

Tunisia: Libraries, Archives, and Museums / *Ali Houissa* 4624

Ukraine: Libraries / *Lyudmila Shpilevaya* 4642

Undergraduate Library Collections *[ELIS Classic]* / *Amy M. Kautzman* 4649

UNESCO: Communication and Information Sector / *Joie Springer* 4656

Unicode Standard / *Joan M. Aliprand* 4662

Unified Medical Language System® (UMLS®) Project / *Stuart J. Nelson, Tammy Powell,*
Suresh Srinivasan and Betsy L. Humphreys 4672

Uniform Computer Information Transactions Act (UCITA) / *Sarah K. Wiant* 4680

Unions in Public and Academic Libraries / *Kathleen de la Peña McCook* 4689

United Kingdom: Archives and Archival Science / *Helen Forde* 4699

United Kingdom: Libraries and Librarianship / *David J. Muddiman* 4707

United Kingdom: Museums and Museology / *Sarah Elliott and Peter Davis* 4723

United States: Archives and Archival Science / *Cheryl L. Stadel-Bevans and Danna Bell-Russel* 4740

United States: Libraries and Librarianship in the 21st Century / *John W. Berry* 4766

United States: Museums / *Beverly K. Sheppard* 4776

Universal Decimal Classification (UDC) / *I. C. McIlwaine* 4783

University Archives / *William J. Maher* 4791

Usability Testing of User Interfaces in Libraries / *Sharon L. Walbridge* 4797

User-Centered Design of Information Systems / *Elaine G. Toms* 4803

User-Centered Revolution: 1970–1995 *[ELIS Classic]* / *Diane Nahl* 4812

User-Centered Revolution: 1995–2008 / *Diane Nahl* 4847

User-Oriented and Cognitive Models of Information Retrieval / *Mette Skov,*
Kalervo Järvelin and Peter Ingwersen 4872

Venezuela: Libraries and Librarianship / *Juan D. Machin-Mastromatteo and Renny Granda* 4886

Version Control / *Jill E. Grogg and Jeff Weddle* 4896

Vietnam: Libraries, Archives, and Museums / *Robert D. Stueart* 4902

Visitor Studies / *Susan Foutz and Jill Stein* 4917

Visual and Performing Arts Archives / *Francesca Marini* 4925

Visual Resources Association (VRA) / *Virginia M.G. Hall* 4933

Visual Resources Management in Cultural Institutions / *Jacqueline Allen and Marcia K. Stein* 4940

Volunteer Services in Cultural Institutions / *Barbara Cohen-Stratyner* 4951

Wayfinding and Signage / *Dennis O'Brien* 4958

Web Scale Discovery Services / *Jason Vaughan* 4978

Webometrics / *Mike Thelwall* 4983

Word Processing: Early History *[ELIS Classic]* / *Daniel Eisenberg* 4993

World Intellectual Property Organization (WIPO) / *Janice T. Pilch* 5000

World Summit on the Information Society (WSIS) / *Alex Byrne* 5012

World Wide Web (WWW) / *Christinger Tomer* 5019

World Wide Web Consortium (W3C) / *Terrence Brooks* 5034

XML Information Retrieval / *Mounia Lalmas* 5039

Young Adult Library Services Association (YALSA) / *Marjorie Lewis* 5052

Young Adult Services in Libraries / *Mary K. Chelton* 5058

Youth Information: Needs and Behavior / *Melissa Gross* 5067

Zoological Park and Aquarium Libraries and Archives / *Vernon N. Kisling, Jr.* 5077

Introduction to the Encyclopedia of Library and Information Sciences, Fourth Edition

How to Use This Encyclopedia

Entries are arranged alphabetically in this encyclopedia (see end papers for alphabetical list). The editors of this edition (ELIS-4) have decided to forego the Topical Table of Contents that was provided in ELIS-3 by editors Marcia Bates and Mary Niles Maack. At the time of publication of ELIS-3, the Topical TOC was crucial for readers to get a sense of how subjects were grouped and an understanding of the field or subfield through the clustering of categorical entries in the print edition. ELIS-4 is envisioned as a primarily online reference work where a Topical TOC does not serve the same purpose. The print edition is served well by the main TOC as well as the detailed index, while entries in the online version are easily discoverable through title, author, keyword, and full text searches.

In sum, relevant entries can be found by

1. Entry title (alphabetical arrangement of entries in the encyclopedia or listing in the end papers)
2. Specific name or keyword, including the index at the end of each volume

If the first name or keyword searched is not found, try several more variations—either different words or a different order of words. Most topics are described in several ways in the literature of a discipline, and the first term or phrase that comes to mind may not be the one used here.

Scope of the Encyclopedia

The title of the third edition, *Encyclopedia of Library and Information Sciences*, ended with the letter "s" because the encyclopedia was broadened to cover a spectrum of related and newly emerging information disciplines, including archival science, document theory, informatics, and records management, among others. The fourth edition continues this trend but with an extensive focus on the aspects of library and information sciences that have been heavily impacted by the adoption and reliance on online information distribution. This focus is reflected in the inclusion of numerous new entries such as digital preservation, altmetrics, web-scale discovery services, demand-driven acquisitions, and global open knowledgebases. Alongside these entries based on entirely new topics, the expanded use of the Internet for information has led to new treatment of traditional LIS topics such as resource description and access (RDA) that reflects the adoption of new standards for cataloging.

ELIS-4 also seeks to build upon the description of professional practice to round out the theoretical perspective that previous editions covered very well. Both current editors are academic research librarians and thus, focused heavily on addressing gaps in the encyclopedia related to academic research information while still relying heavily on the structure established by editors of ELIS-3. For example, ELIS-3 introduced country profiles and ELIS-4 builds upon that with new entries for New Zealand and a third on Brazil, in addition to revisions for Slovakia, Netherlands, Canada, Belarus, Kazakhstan, and Brazil among others. This edition also expands the number of entries for named cultural and information entities that did not appear in previous editions, such as the National Library of Medicine, North American Serials Interest Group (NASIG), the International Association of Scientific, Technical and Medical Publishers (STM), and ASLIB, as well as entities like the HathiTrust that have been established since the last edition was published. A number of new entries describing important information conferences such as the Acquisitions Institute at Timberline, the Charleston Conference, and Electronic Resources in Libraries (ER&L) also help round out the encyclopedia and further the description of the current state of academic research librarianship.

ELIS-4 also continues the tradition of designating important entries of historical or theoretical importance as "ELIS Classics." These are entries by major figures in the library and information sciences or those that describe core concepts in LIS theory, practice, or education that appeared in earlier editions of the encyclopedia. The current editors preserved the approximately 40 previous "ELIS Classics" and designated 13 previous entries as new "ELIS Classics."

There are more than 550 entries, of which more than 20 are new, another 93 are revisions to prior entries that have been brought up to date by their authors or by new authors, about 30 are ELIS Classics, and about 400 are reprinted from an earlier edition since they have remained relevant to the present. It is important to note that the editors also had to make some choices related to retiring entries that were no longer relevant—due to the passage of time and the development of the field, the technologies and theories described in those entries were deemed to be out of scope for the new edition and thus not revised or reprinted.

Encyclopedia Authors

As in past editions, the authors writing for the encyclopedia are major researchers, librarians and practitioners, and leaders in the fields and subfields in the disciplines in which they are writing. Noted scholars are well represented, and a number of authors are former leaders in LIS associations, including the American Library Association (ALA), the Association for College and Research Libraries (ACRL), the International Federation of Library Associations and Institutions (IFLA), the American Society for Information Science and Technology (ASIS&T), and the American Association of Library and Information Science Education (ALISE). In addition, there are many contributors who are current or former directors of major institutions. As in past editions, the editors are very proud of the range and diversity of authors who have written these entries for the encyclopedia and we thank them for sharing their expertise with the current and future readers and researchers in the field.

Finally, the editors for ELIS-4 have grappled with the challenges of entry generation that was noted by previous editors in nearly every edition: that not all ideas, topics, and potential entries were able to be completed for publication in this edition. While we made a valiant attempt to include entries identified by ELIS-3 editors but not secured for publication in that edition, we sometimes could not find authors willing to take those topics on. Similarly, we were sometimes unable to secure revisions to entries from new authors when previous authors were unable to perform that task. To the greatest extent possible, we endeavored to replace authors when entries were deemed important enough to appear in ELIS-4 but initial or previous authors had to decline or defaulted. No doubt, the editors of ELIS-5 will also pick up the mantle and attempt to round out the encyclopedia with entries for anything that ELIS-4 missed. As noted by editors Bates and Niles Maack in ELIS-3, this problem of missing topics was also acknowledged by Allen Kent, editor of the first edition of ELIS. Kent stated in 1973, "I have prepared this presentation to make sure the lessons of Diderot-d'Alembert are recalled in terms of encyclopedia-making as an exercise in the art of the possible."

Background and Development of the Encyclopedia

The first edition of ELIS, under the editorship principally of Allen Kent and Harold Lancour, was published between 1968 and 1982. The 33 volumes of the first edition were published in alphabetical sequence during those years. After the "Z" volume appeared in 1982, a number of supplements were published at roughly the rate of two per year, up to and including volume 73, which appeared in 2003. Miriam Drake was appointed editor for the second edition, which appeared in 2003, both online and in paper. The second edition came out at one time in four large-format volumes, with a supplement in 2005 [3]. Kent and Lancour covered a wide range of librarianship, information science, and some computer science topics. Drake, an academic library director, emphasized academic libraries, and the ELIS-2 volumes contained many profiles of major academic libraries and professional library associations.

The third edition, under the editorship of Marcia Bates and Mary Niles Maack, reflected a growing convergence among the several disciplines that concern themselves with information and the cultural record. As information science educators and noted researchers in the field, their focus was on growing the encyclopedia in the theoretical fields of information sciences as well as drawing together the associated information and cultural disciplines such as archival sciences and museum studies within the overall field of LIS.

For this edition, we have focused on developing the encyclopedia to reflect the changing nature of information production and consumption through online and digital forms. We have also endeavored to fill in gaps in the description of important people, places, and theories in the information sciences, and further enhanced the description of important concepts related to the provision of research information and the field's major institutions.

We continue to see the audience for the encyclopedia just as previous editors have: as principally consisting of 1) the educated lay person interested in one or more of its topics, 2) students learning about a topic, and 3) professionals and researchers in the several fields who want to learn about something new, or to be refreshed on a familiar topic.

We honored the previous editors by reengaging their superb Editorial Advisory Board with significant new additions of experts known to the current editors. (See listing in the front matter.) These leaders and experts from as many disciplines as are in the encyclopedia provided excellent guidance and feedback for the editors as they began the process of new topic generation, evaluation of previous entries, and offering to author or review numerous entries throughout the process of publication.

All new and revised entries were reviewed by one or more outside expert reviewer as well as one or more of the editors. Referees provided invaluable feedback to authors, including noting errors or omissions as well as making suggestions on additional aspects of the topic to cover. While we made every reasonable attempt through this process to check the accuracy of every entry and every fact, undoubtedly readers will find some topics explained more thoroughly or accurately than others. Indeed, due to the time frame from the beginning of the generation of the fourth edition and the time of publication, readers will reasonably note that some topics have been quickly superseded due to this passage of time, so the date of acceptance of the entry will be noted on each entry since several years may have passed since the writing of the entry and the publication of this edition.

Acknowledgments

This edition of the encyclopedia was possible only through the countless hours that the editors, John McDonald and Michael Levine-Clark, spent reviewing the previous encyclopedia entries, outlining the topics that were missing or that were newly emerging in the field, and identifying appropriate expert authors to write those new entries. In addition, the editors devoted extensive time to corresponding with previous authors encouraging them to revise their entries, and finding replacement authors for important entries that needed revisions but whose original authors were unavailable.

Both editors wish to acknowledge the expertise of each other and their knowledge of our field, their extensive network of contacts, and their ability to work closely together to ensure the success of this encyclopedia. Neither of them could have completed this project alone.

They acknowledge and thank the Taylor & Francis Group editors, Claire Miller and Rich O'Hanley, as well as Susan Lee, who passed away at the early stages of the preparation of this edition, and more recently, Alexandra Torres, who supported and kept the editors and authors on track over the course of the years of work on this edition of the encyclopedia.

The editors thank the authors who wrote and revised entries, and the huge number of reviewers who refereed the entries. Without their dedication, expertise, and willingness to share their knowledge with others, there would be no encyclopedia. They also wish to thank the Editorial Advisory Board for their advice, suggestions of topics and authors, their hours spent writing or reviewing for the final edition. They also wish to thank the previous editors, Marcia Bates and Mary Niles Maack, whose organization and structure for ELIS-3 provided an excellent blueprint for ELIS-4.

Encyclopedia of Library and Information Sciences, Fourth Edition

Volume 4

Pages 2181–2908

Information Retrieval–
Information Society

Information Systems–
Information Use

Informetrics–International
Council

International Federation–
iSchools

Israel–Knowledge Discovery

Knowledge Management–
Law Librarianship

Law Literature–Library
Architecture

Library Automation–Library
Publishing

Information Retrieval Protocols: Z39.50 and Search and Retrieve via URL

William Moen
Texas Center for Digital Knowledge, University of North Texas, Denton, Texas, U.S.A.

Abstract

Information retrieval (IR) protocols support effective and interoperable intersystem search and retrieval. Although intersystem search methods have been envisioned and under development since the 1970s, it was the Z39.50 IR protocol, first released in 1988, that demonstrated real-world possibilities for such search and retrieval. As the networked information environment changed with the emergence of the World Wide Web, the need for standard IR protocols did not disappear, and one can argue the need is even more compelling given both the visible and invisible Web. A new protocol, based on the experience from Z39.50 but simpler and more comprehensible than Z39.50, is now being used for Web search and retrieval. Search and retrieve via URL (SRU) uses Web technologies and standards resulting in a Web friendly protocol that provides standard search access to existing Z39.50 resources and a wide-range of new non-catalog digital resources. This entry provides both an overview of the two protocols and technical details to understand both. A brief discussion of IR and communications protocols provides background to the specifics of these two IR protocols. Although communication protocols are by their nature technical specifications, this entry focuses on an overview of the functions and capabilities of the protocols. It uses technical concepts and terminology from the protocols to help explain how the protocols work but limits discussion of technical details.

INTRODUCTION

In the 1970s, a number of library leaders, such as Henriette Avram at the Library of Congress and the developer of the machine-readable catalog record (MARC), envisioned the convergence of computing and telecommunications that would enable machine-to-machine communication for accessing bibliographic and other types of information. Initial work on intersystem communication focused on connecting large bibliographic databases such as those at the Library of Congress, the Online Computer Library Center (OCLC), and the Research Libraries Group (RLG). Making this vision a reality required the development of standard protocols for intersystem communication. Protocols specify rules for communication including what information can be exchanged, in what format, and in what order. Thirty years later, the networked information landscape has changed dramatically, but the need still remains for standard protocols that support information retrieval (IR) transactions (e.g., sending a query and receiving the results of the executed query) against a range of databases or systems. Standards development work through the 1980s and 1990s yielded the ANSI/NISO Z39.50 IR Protocol, developed in a historical context predating the World Wide Web. By the late 1990s, Web technologies were providing a new context for networked IR, and implementors of Z39.50 and others responded to these changes by evolving Z39.50 into Search and retrieve via URL (SRU), a protocol that uses key Web standards and technologies.

This entry addresses both Z39.50 and SRU. A brief discussion of IR and communications protocols provides background to the specifics of these two IR protocols. Although communications protocols are by their nature technical specifications, this entry focuses on an overview of the functions and capabilities of the protocols. It uses technical concepts and terminology from the protocols to help explain how the protocols work but limits discussion of technical details.

IR

IR, in the context of protocols, can be viewed very simply or quite complexly. At its simplest, IR involves issuing a query to an IR system, having the IR system execute the query, and presenting the results of the query to the user (human or machine). Web search engines such as Google provide exactly this functionality. The vision for networked IR assumes, though, an environment that contains a large number of IR systems and their databases that provide a range of search and retrieval functionality but differing in important ways (e.g., types of field searching supported).

A first step in preparing a protocol to support IR transactions requires modeling those transactions and the components of IR systems. Fig. 1 illustrates these basic components of the IR model.

The following description provides an abstract view of IR and IR systems in the context of bibliographic

Encyclopedia of Library and Information Sciences, Fourth Edition DOI: 10.1081/E-ELIS4-120043689
Copyright © 2017 by Taylor & Francis. All rights reserved.

Information Retrieval–
Information Society

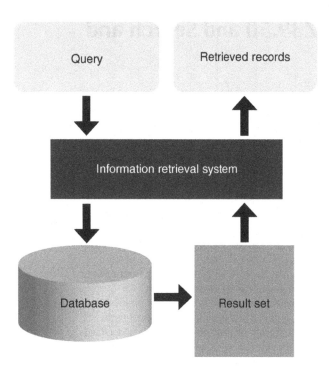

Fig. 1 Abstract model of IR.

databases (i.e., databases containing metadata records describing bibliographic items held, for example, in a library's collection). This description of an abstract model for information retrieval is derived from *ANSI/NISO Z39.89-2003. The U.S. National Z39.50 Profile for Library Applications.* The author drafted the text describing the abstract model in his capacity as chair of NISO Standards Committee AV that created this profile. Since this is an abstract view, actual implementation of these components may differ.

- *Bibliographic database:* This is the logical component that stores data representing bibliographic items. These representations can be created according to accepted standards (e.g., the Anglo-American Cataloguing Rules) and can reflect the use of various metadata element sets (e.g., MARC 21, Dublin Core, or others). Typically, the database records include information about the title, author, subject, and other salient features of bibliographic items. The physical structure of the database will be implementation specific, and no specific physical database model is assumed (e.g., relational, flat file, etc.).
- *Access points and indexes:* This is the logical component related to searching the database. This model assumes there is an index, which is a list of values with pointers to the database records that contain those values. Indexes are created for specific types of searches the IR system will support, and reflect searchable areas of the database record. A bibliographic database in an online catalog implementation typically supports title, author, subject, and other types of searches. The physical structure of an index and how it associates the

list of values with pointers to database records will be system and implementation specific.
- *IR system:* This is the logical component that manages the search of the database and retrieval of records from the database. It typically provides an interface to receive a query and then executes the query by matching the search criteria with information stored in the indexes. When values in the index(es) match the query criteria, the system retrieves the relevant records from the bibliographic database for presentation to the user.
- *Query:* This is the logical component that contains simple or complex criteria along with a search term specified by the user (human or machine). Also referred to a search criteria, the query can contain criteria related to access points to be searched (e.g., search the author access point), characterizations of the search term (e.g., treat this search term as a phrase or treat this search term as a date), and also indicate processing of the search term (e.g., perform right truncation where specified).
- *Result Set and retrieved records:* This logical component manages the results of the executed query. The result set comprises all records that the IR system identified as matching the criteria contained in the query. From this Result Set, the IR system selects one or more records to return to the user. A specific IR system may store the Result Set for later processing, but that consideration is implementation specific and not addressed by this model.

IR can include other tasks beyond what the basic model describes. For example, some IR systems allow the user to specify how the results should be sorted (e.g., by date of publication in ascending order). Protocol developers face the challenge of modeling all IR transactions and components in a way that a standard IR protocol does not privilege specific implementations or structures. Before discussing the details of Z39.50, a basic description and explanation of a protocol is needed.

COMMUNICATIONS PROTOCOLS

Protocols governing communication and behavior between two entities exist for human-to-human as well and machine-to-machine interactions. For example, diplomatic protocols guide the interaction between representatives of sovereign entities. The protocols are agreed upon rules (written or unwritten) for governing behavior. When addressing machine communication, the rules must be specific and well-documented to ensure machine-to-machine communication is successful and the machines and applications behave according to the rules.

Machine-to-machine communication typically involves the sending and receiving of messages. One machine or an application residing on the machine (referred to here as the client) initiates the communication by sending a message requesting some service or other behavior from the receiving machine or application on that machine (referred to here as the server). The server responds by returning a message to the client. The model for this communication is characterized as request and response.

A communications protocol defines the services supported and provides the rules controlling the order in which messages can be sent, the contents of those messages, allowable request and response messages, and other aspects of the communication (e.g., the character set for encoding the data in a message). Machines conforming to the protocol can conduct successful intersystem communication because they know how to send and receive protocol messages and "understand" the content of those messages.

In the networked information environment of computers and their applications, there are a range of familiar communications protocols such as File Transfer Protocol (FTP), Simple Mail Transport Protocol (SMTP), and HyperText Transfer Protocol (HTTP) to name a few. Each is distinguished by the services or functions it provides. In fact, a large number of protocols exist to support successful communication between two machines and applications. Models representing a layering approach to intersystem communication (e.g., in the Open Systems Interconnection (OSI) seven-layer model and the five-layer model from the Internet) identify specific protocols to handle communication from the lowest layer of physical connection through routing and session information to the top layer, which in both models is called the application layer. Z39.50 is an application-layer protocol as indicated by the title of the Z39.50 standard: *Information Retrieval (Z39.50): Application Service Definition and Protocol Specification.*[1]

Returning to the context of IR protocols, the following are basic aspects that such a protocol needs to accommodate:

- Providing a standard way to encode the request and response messages
- Specifying methods to transport request and response messages across a network
- Identifying a database on a server to search
- Utilizing a vocabulary and grammar for expressing search requests, search criteria, retrieval requests, etc.
- Specifying formats for records that are returned in response to a search request.

The Z39.50 protocol provides these and more, which are discussed next.

THE Z39.50 IR PROTOCOL

Z39.50 is a technical standard, developed under the auspices of the National Information Standards Organization

(NISO), a standards developer accredited by the American National Standards Institute (ANSI). At the international level, Technical Committee 46 of the International Organization for Standardization (ISO) worked concurrently on an IR protocol called Search and Retrieve. This section provides a brief history of the development of the Z39.50 standard, explains in relatively nontechnical terms what the standard addresses, and discusses sufficient details of the specifications to yield a basic understanding. Many resources are available that discuss the Z39.50 protocol, features, and implementations (see Bibliography).

A Brief Chronology of Z39.50 Development

The nearly 30-year period during which Z39.50 and SRU, its successor protocol, were developed was marked by major computing and networking technology changes that strongly influenced the character of these IR protocols. Technical standards often reflect assumptions and beliefs about existing technologies, and it is fair to say that this was true for Z39.50.

The genesis for the standard was the late 1960s and early 1970s when library leaders began envisioning a future of interconnected automated bibliographic systems and identified the need for computer communication protocols that would enable the interconnection of systems and sharing of bibliographic data. The need for an IR protocol emerged also from visions for a national bibliographic network articulated by library leaders such as Henriette Avram and organizations such as the Library of Congress and its Network Advisory Committee, the National Commission on Library and Information Science, and the Council of Library Resources. A detailed historical treatment is beyond this entry's scope, but readers interested in Z39.50 history can review chapter 4 in *The Development of ANSI/NISO Z39.50: A Case Study in Standards Evolution.*[2]

Work on the Z39.50 standard began in 1979 by a formal standards committee authorized by NISO. NISO issued the first version of the standard in 1988.[3] After 1988, work on protocol development shifted from NISO, which disbanded the standards committee, to a group of people and organizations interested in implementing the standard. This group became known as the Z39.50 Implementors Group (ZIG). NISO established the Z39.50 Maintenance Agency, located at the Library of Congress, to oversee further development of the standard. The Maintenance Agency and the ZIG worked collaboratively to produce a revision to the 1988 standard, which was submitted and approved by NISO in 1992.[4] One specific goal of the 1992 standard, known as Version 2, was to harmonize the Z39.50 specifications with those in the ISO Search and Retrieve standard. Version 2 also specified critical services lacking from the 1988 standard such as access control, and as a result it provided a solid basis for widespread pilot projects, testing, and production implementations by members of the ZIG.

Information Retrieval–
Information Society

The early versions of the protocol were particularly library-centric, in that many of the specifications addressed issues related to searching bibliographic databases in the context of library catalogs. ZIG members, however, wanted to evolve Z39.50 into a more generalized IR protocol that could be used by libraries and many other information providers. Version 3 was approved in 1995 by NISO.[5] Many new features were specified in Version 3, and it became the basis for wide-spread implementation, albeit predominantly within the library community and by information services supporting libraries. In addition, the separate ISO Search and Retrieve standard was abandoned, and in its place, ISO adopted verbatim the 1995 Z39.50 standard and labeled it ISO 23950-1998.

Part of NISO's standards development process as approved by ANSI includes regular 5 year reviews of published standards. In the late 1990s, the Maintenance Agency initiated this review and issued in 2003, a revised version of the Z39.50 standard.[6] The Maintenance Agency viewed this version as a reaffirmation version, and included clarifications, commentaries, defect reports, amendments, and implementor agreements.

Z39.50 Protocol Details

When discussing Z39.50, it is important to distinguish between: (1) the technical standard that defines the protocol; and (2) the implementation of those specifications in software. Taking the latter first, system developers (e.g., vendors of integrated library systems) implement the protocol specifications in software programs: client-side software and server-side software. The Z39.50 client initiates a communication session with the Z39.50 server. A user (human or machine) initiates a search, which is passed to the Z39.50 client for processing into standard protocol messages and sends the query to the Z39.50 server. The Z39.50 server passes the request to a local IR system, which executes the search, finds records that match the criteria, and then returns results back to the Z39.50 client via the protocol. The Z39.50 client passes the results back to the local machine for presentation to the user. Building on the IR model presented earlier, Fig. 2 illustrates where the Z39.50 client and server software logically sit in relation to the client- and server-side applications.

The Z39.50 client and Z39.50 server each have their own responsibilities, listed below in the order of a typical Z39.50 session:

- Initiate a session: client
- Send query: client
- Execute query: server
- Create result set: server
- Request records "in" result set: client
- Specify database elements to be returned: client
- Specify format in which to return records: client
- Create retrieval records and sent to client: server

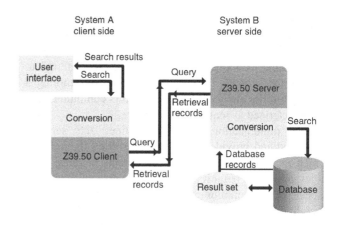

Fig. 2 Z39.50 and the abstract model of IR.

As a communications protocol, Z39.50 specifies a standard set of messages that are communicated between two systems. The initiating system's request needs to be transformed from the local language of that system into the language of Z39.50. The Z39.50 client and server both understand the meaning of the Z39.50 language, and thus provide the communication link between the two different systems. Upon receipt of the Z39.50 message, the Z39.50 server then translates it into the local language of the IR system. For example, it maps a request for a title search where the search term is a phrase into the appropriate commands, syntax, and query of the local IR system.

In the context of the protocol specifications, Z39.50 defines a set of "services." A Z39.50 service describes functionality and defines the specific protocol messages related to that service exchanged between the Z39.50 client and Z39.50 server in support of that functionality. Z39.50 defines 14 services, but for purposes here, only a few core services will be discussed: Init, Search, and Present. These services enable: (1) establishing a connection between a client and server (Init); (2) issuing a query (Search); and (3) retrieving results (Present).

Init service

The Init service provides for a Z39.50 client to initiate a connection and session with a Z39.50 server by first issuing an Init request message. Included in the structured message are a number of parameters: Version, Id/authentication, Options, Preferred-message-size, Exceptional-record-size, Implementation-id; some of these are mandatory and some are optional. The Z39.50 client sends the Init request message with values listed for each of the parameters. The Z39.50 server responds by returning to the Z39.50 client an Init response message with the following parameters (again, some of which are mandatory and some optional): Version, Id/authentication, Options, Preferred-message-size, Exceptional-record-size, Result, Implementation-id. If the server responds positively to the Init request, it returns a value of "accept" in the result parameter. Upon successful negotiation in the Init service, the client can then move to requesting the server to execute a search using the Search service.

Search service

For successful IR interoperability between two systems, there are two important considerations: a mutual understanding of the search request and a mutual understanding of the format of records retrieved. We will examine how Z39.50 addresses these two requirements, since at its core, Z39.50 was developed to support interoperable search and retrieve.

When one submits a search to a local IR system via its native interface, there is a tight linkage between the search interface offered to the user and the underlying IR system and database. Communication is not an issue. Yet, to send a search from one system to a different IR system, the search must be transformed into a language understood by both systems where information about some of the following must be clearly communicated:

- The database to search.
- The access points or searchable fields to search.
- How search terms are to be interpreted, such as treating the search term as a word, phrase, date, normalized name, etc.
- The use of Boolean operators for complex queries.
- Other search qualifications and criteria, such as limiting the search by date, language, etc.

Z39.50 defines a standard language for expressing searches. The language is very rich and precise to reduce ambiguity in the communication. A query in Z39.50 is a specified structure for expressing the search requirements; it identifies a database to search and characterizes the search term using attribute types and values. A query can also include Boolean operators.

Key to the query is the attribute types and their values; these are what allow the search to be expressed in a standardized and mutually understood vocabulary and grammar. The following is an example of part of a Z39.50 query:

(1,1003)(2,3)(3,1)(4,1)(5,100)(6,3) Twain, Mark

The pairs of number in parentheses are the attribute/ type value pairs and "Twain, Mark" is the search term. The following explains how the attribute types and values characterize the query term, "Twain, Mark."

Attributes and their permissible values are defined in attribute sets. A basic Z39.50-related attribute set goes by the label of Bib-1 (for use when searching a variety of databases).[7] The Bib-1 attribute set defines six attribute types (identified by the first number in parentheses): Use (1); Relation (2); Position (3); Structure (4); Truncation (5); and Completeness (6). The Z30.50 query contains a number representing an attribute as the first part of the

type/value pair. The use of numbers avoids problems of words in various languages and yields more universality.

Each attribute type represents a feature of the search and search term; for example the Use attribute indicates the index to be searched, while the Relation attribute indicates, for example, that the search term should match exactly an entry in the index, and the Truncation attribute indicates whether the IR system should perform some type of truncation on the search term. The Bib-1 attribute set defines the values associated for each attribute type. For example, if the Use attribute value is 1003, this means that the IR system should process this query as an author search; if the value is 4, the IR system should process the query as a title search. It is beyond the scope of this entry to give all the details on attribute types and values, but this indicates how the search term can be characterized using a standard vocabulary and grammar to result in intersystem communication for the purpose of searching.

Parsing the Z39.50 query listed earlier, which means in human terms "search for items where Mark Twain is listed as author," the use of attribute type/value pairs are understood by the server as:

(1,1003) means execute this search as an author search.
(2,3) means exactly match the search term with an entry in the index.
(3,1) means to begin matching the search term with the first term in the field.
(4,1) means to treat the search term as a phrase rather than two words.
(5,100) means to carry out no truncation on the search term.
(6,3) means that the search term should match the complete data value in the field (i.e., the entry in the index).

The Z39.50 server receives the query as expressed in the type/value pairs, parses the query, and maps the search to the local IR system and its search engine.

Present service

The other aspect of IR is the return of records to the Z39.50 client that match the query. The Z39.50 Present service is used to request records to be returned from the result set, how many to return, what syntax the records should be returned in, and what elements in the records to return. To support interoperability, Z39.50 registers a number of record syntaxes in which records can be exchanged between Z39.50 clients and servers. The original focus of Z39.50 was on bibliographic records and the retrieval of MARC records. As Z39.50 evolved into a general IR protocol, the MARC format for records became just one of a variety of record syntaxes in which records could be formatted and returned via Z39.50. Record syntaxes include HTML, Extensible Markup Language (XML), and others, including a syntax developed by the ZIG called Generic Record Syntax (GRS).[8] While accommodating more applications with this variety of record syntaxes, interoperability problems also increased.

This brief glimpse into some of the details of Z39.50 illustrates that for intersystem communication to occur, the Z39.50 client and server must not only support the defined protocol messages but also understand the language of Z39.50, its vocabulary and grammar. Most current Z39.50 implementations robustly support the protocol messages. However, implementors make choices from the options available in the standard for specific protocol messages. Also, the local IR system on the Z39.50 server side does not always provide the functionality requested by the Z39.50 client as expressed in protocol messages. These and other issues have led to interoperability problems. There has been, unfortunately, a pervasive sense that Z39.50 did not live up to the promises of providing a solution for interoperable intersystem search and retrieval across disparate databases.

INTEROPERABILITY AND INTERSYSTEM IR

Implementing a standard IR protocol on systems is intended to enable interoperability of those systems and applications. System-level interoperability can be defined as the ability of two or more systems or components to exchange information and use the exchanged information without special effort on either system. One can also define interoperability from the perspective of the end user in terms of the user's ability to successfully search and retrieve information in a meaningful way and have confidence in the results. Interoperability between two systems can be assessed from a binary perspective; they either do or do not interoperate. However, experience has demonstrated that when two systems have implemented the Z39.50 protocol, it is more likely that systems may be more or less interoperable, and interoperability is better assessed as a continuum rather than a binary decision. This raises the question of what acceptable levels of interoperability can be produced, especially from the perspective of the end user.

To understand how or why IR systems may not interoperate or not have an acceptable level of interoperability, a number of factors that threaten interoperability can be identified:

- Multiple and disparate systems, operating systems, IR systems, etc.
- Multiple protocols such as Z39.50, HTTP, SOAP, etc.
- Multiple data formats, syntax, metadata schemes such as MARC 21, UNIMARC, XML, ISBD/AACR2-based metadata, Dublin Core, etc.
- Multiple vocabularies, ontologies, disciplines such as LCSH, MESH, and AAT.

- Multiple languages, multiple character sets.
- Indexing, word normalization, and word extraction policies.

If a protocol has a range of options, implementors can choose from (e.g., what protocol services are implemented, specific values for parameters, etc.) as is the case with Z39.50, different implementations of the protocol specifications can threaten interoperability. However, the experience with Z39.50 has shown that the key threats to interoperability relate mostly to differences in local IR systems specifically the differences in search functions supported, the indexes available for searching, and the record syntaxes supported for retrieved records. Examples of these differences include whether IR systems support the searches being requested by the client, such as how to treat the search term (e.g., as word, phrase, date, etc.), the access points to be searched (e.g., author, title, subject, ISBN, etc.), and the format of records available (e.g., in MARC, MARCXML, etc.)

Optimal interoperability occurs not only if the Z39.50 client and server both implement the same protocol services and choices among options within the protocol but also when the IR system on the Z39.50 server side provides the search functions requested by the Z39.50 client, including types of searches and access points, and also is able to supply the records in the syntax requested by the Z39.50 client.

A common approach to address the threats to Z39.50 interoperability was the development of application profiles. A profile specified what Z39.50 clients and servers had to implement from the options available in the Z39.50 standard, as well as the searches supported on the local IR system. Conformance to a profile's specifications increased the level of interoperability. An example of such a profile is *The U.S. National Z39.50 Profile for Library Applications* published by the NISO as ANSI/NISO Z39.89.[1]

A NEXT GENERATION Z39.50

The development of Z39.50 and release of Version 3 in 1995 occurred in advance of the emergence of the World Wide Web in the 1990s. By the late 1990s, the ZIG was discussing how the broader Web community, and especially those involved with Web search, could be made interested in the power provided by the Z39.50 IR protocol. Yet, where the ZIG saw Z39.50's power, many in the Web community and even some in the library community—its core implementation context—perceived it as difficult and complex, heavyweight, reflecting old technology, not Web friendly, and in some cases simply broken. The ZIG recognized that the Web was quickly becoming the common implementation environment. For several years Z39.50 implementors discussed and tried out a number of initiatives as part of a Z39.50 International Next Generation (ZING) project.[9]

A pivotal meeting of the ZIG occurred in 2001 at which a discussion about the future of Z39.50 resulted in a consensus recognition that Z39.50 needed to evolve in the context of the Web. The goal for developing the next generation Z39.50 was to lower the barriers to implementation while preserving the intellectual contributions of Z39.50 and discarding those aspects no longer useful or meaningful. Part of lowering the barrier to implementation was to recast Z39.50 protocol specifications in terms of existing and emerging Web technologies, tools, and standards (e.g., HTTP, XML, and XML schemas). Part of preserving the intellectual contributions of Z39.50 was to separate the abstract and semantic models provided in Z39.50 from representation of the protocol in the arcane Abstract Syntax Notation (ASN.1) and associated Basic Encoding Rules (BER) and running it directly over TCP/IP for transport rather than HTTP.

In 2001, an international team of implementors and standards developers began work on a new IR protocol that would be simpler, more easily implemented, and more comprehensible than Z39.50 and most importantly Web compatible. The result of discussions and deliberations was the decision to develop a new Web services based protocol: SRU. The name of the new protocol has changed since its inception in 2001. Initially it was referred to as Search/Retrieve Web Service (SRW). This was later accompanied by SRU. Except for the method the client used for sending a search request to the server, the details of the protocol were the same. By 2007, the label SRW had been deprecated and the protocol is officially known as SRU. The first version of the protocol was released in late 2002; Version 1.1 was released in 2004, which was registered with NISO. The current Version 1.2 was published in 2007.[10]

The Z39.50 Maintenance Agency at the Library of Congress plays a key role in managing the development of the new protocol and now serves as the maintenance agency and managing editor for SRU, supported by a SRU Editorial Board consisting of the managing editor along with a senior editor, XML editor, and associate editors. The Board oversees the development of proposals for changes and enhancements, and a SRU Implementors Group, an open membership group, serves in an advisory capacity to the Editorial Board.

SRW

SRU addresses the same IR problems confronted by Z39.50, namely, communicating with a range of information services and servers that have their own local IR systems with different database structures, indexes, and local query structures. However, SRU adopts current standards for syntax of messages and records (i.e., XML)

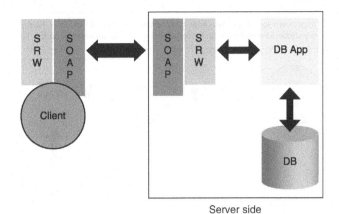

Server side

Fig. 3 SRW Communication using SOAP.

exchanged between a client and server and for transport of the messages (i.e., HTTP). It retains and builds on the abstract models, concepts, and functions developed through the experience with Z39.50 such as abstract access points, abstract record schemas, result sets, and others. The protocol defines a set of operations and associated parameters (see below) and all responses are encoded in XML. The Contextual Query Language (CQL) is used to represent queries in search requests (see below). The result is a Web friendly and standard protocol for networked IR.

At the outset of protocol development, there were two related protocols referred to as SRW and SRU. In fact, there is no real difference between SRW and SRU at the protocol parameter level but only in the way they are implemented as Web services.

The basic difference between them relate to how they issue search requests. SRW uses SOAP (originally known as Simple Object Access Protocol) and encodes messages in XML within SOAP (Fig. 3). SRU uses the Representational State Transfer (REST) approach, which encodes protocol messages from the client in the URL syntax and issues a HTTP GET request (Fig. 4). Both protocols return data encoded in XML, and both use HTTP for transport of messages.[11]

Protocol Operations and Examples

SRU uses the concept of "operation types" to describe and define what IR functions the protocol supports and defines the following operations:

- *searchRetrieve:* Expresses the query criteria and specifications for records to be returned
- *Explain:* Allows a client to retrieve a description of the facilities available at a server
- *Scan:* Allows the client to request a range of the available terms at a given point within a list of indexed terms

Information Retrieval–
Information Society

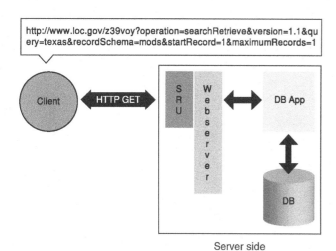

Fig. 4 SRU Communication using HTTP GET.

The searchRetrieve and explain operations are core to the protocol, and each is discussed in more detail below.

searchRetrieve operation

This operation combines the Z39.50 Search and Present services in one operation. The searchRetrieveRequest message contains the query which is expressed using CQL (see below). In addition to the query, the searchRetrieveRequest contains specifications for returning the records that match the query, such as what schema should be used to package the retrieved records.

If one uses SRW, the searchRetrieveRequest message is encoded in XML and sent via HTTP wrapped in SOAP. Fig. 5 is part of a searchRetrieveRequest (in XML) that includes a single-word query.

There are a number of parameters defined for the searchRetrieveRequest, and Fig. 5 shows two mandatory parameters (<version> to indicate the version of the protocol; <query> to express the search criteria), and several optional parameters (<maximumRecords> to indicate how many records should be returned; <startRecord> to indicate in the list of records found where to begin returning; and <recordSchema> to indicate in what format the records should be returned. In this sample case, the request is to have the records returned in the form of Dublin Core records according to a Dublin Core XML schema.

```
<searchRetrieveRequest>
  <version>1.1</version>
  <query>texas</query>
  <maximumRecords>1</maximumRecords>
  <startRecord>1</startrecord>
  <recordSchema>dc</recordSchema>
</searchRetrieveRequest>
```

Fig. 5 Sample searchRetrieveRequest expressed in XML.

If one uses SRU, the searchRetrieveRequest parameters are expressed in standard URL syntax, which includes the baseURL for the server separated from the protocol parameters with a question mark (?). Fig. 6 shows the same searchRetrieveRequest as in Fig. 5 but expressed as a URL.

Fig. 6 shows that the URL syntax can express all searchRetrieveRequest parameters without any loss of specification.

After the server receives the searchRetrieveRequest and executes the search and finds records, it returns a searchRetrieveResponse (no matter whether the searchRetrieveRequest was sent via SOAP or as HTTP GET) that indicates the number of records found and may also include the records found. Fig. 7 is a sample of a searchRetrieveResponse to the sample searchRetrieveRequest in Figs. 5 and 6.

There are a number of parameters defined for the searchRetrieveResponse, and Fig. 7 shows two mandatory parameters (<version> ; < numberOfRecords> to indicate the number of records found on the server), and several optional parameters (<records> which indicates the beginning of the records being returned; <record> which indicates the segment containing the records; <recordSchema> which indicates the XML schema according to which the records are encoded; and <recordData> that contains the actual record. In this example, the <schema> parameter indicates that the records are formatted according to the Dublin Core (i.e., DC) schema, as requested in the searchRetrieveRequest above. The <recordData> parameter in this example contains only one DC element simply to illustrate elements that might comprise the record.

In summary, the searchRequestResponse is in XML syntax and may include the actual records found in the XML schema requested by the client. Other schemas in which records can be returned (assuming the server supports those schemas) include ONIX, MODS, and MARCXML.

Explain operation

A challenge for Z39.50 in the context of interoperability was the difficulty for a Z39.50 client to discern what a Z39.50 server supported in terms of Z39.50 services and especially in terms of available access points and record formats. The development of SRU gave priority attention to ensuring a robust method for the server to tell the client what it supports. The explain operation addresses this need. A client sends an explainRequest to the server and the server responds with an explainResponse, and the response message contains a record in XML structured according to the ZeeRex schema.[12] The ZeeRex record provides several key pieces of information including:

Information Retrieval–
Information Society

http://www.loc.gov/z39voy?operation=searchRetrieve&version=1.1&query=**texas**& recordSchema=dc&startRecord=1&maximumRecords=1

Fig. 6 Sample searchRetrieveRequest expressed as URL.

- Information about the database such as title and description
- Information about how to search in the database including what indexes exist to search
- Information about the record syntaxes in which records can be returned and what record elements can be returned.

With the information contained in the explainResponse, the client is able to configure searches against the server that are likely to be more successful and request records in specific schemas (e.g., MARCXML, MODS, Dublin Core, etc.) that the server is able to supply. Interoperability can be significantly improved because of this protocol operation.

CQL

In addition to the protocol, another component for successful intersystem IR communication is a standard language to express the query. Based on the experience with Z39.50 and in keeping with the desire to build upon that experience, SRU developers created the CQL.[13] CQL is a formal language for representing queries to issue to IR systems such as Web indexes, bibliographic catalogs, and museum collection information. It is capable of expressing complex queries and yet can be used for very simple keyword searches. CQL is also human-readable, unlike the query types associated with Z39.50.

A CQL query contains one or more search clauses connected by Boolean operators. A search clause contains at a minimum the search term. A single word in a search clause comprises a perfectly legitimate instance, and this reflects the simplicity available in CQL. It has

the power of expressiveness in that the search clause can indicate a specific index to search, and CQL supports relation and proximity operators as well as masking characters (e.g., to indicate truncation) to express more complex queries.

As a general purpose query language, CQL provides a syntax for expressing the component parts of the query. The basic syntax for a CQL search clause is: [index][relation][search term]. CQL also supports searching by semantics or context and introduced the concept of context sets in relation to indexes; this begins to make the meaning of "contextual" in the name of CQL clearer.[14] For example, a SRU search to a database can indicate that the index to be searched should be in the context of the Dublin Core element semantics. Individual communities can define their own context set to indicate the semantics of the indexes available. Context sets and individual indexes supported by the server can be listed in the ZeeRex record returned through the explain operation, which assists the client in issuing queries that take advantage of what the server offers. Fig. 8 shows legitimate CQL search clauses from the simplest to more complex.

The examples in Fig. 8 show that <index> and <relation> are optional, and further that <index> can be include a prefix to the index name to indicate that the index is from a specific context set.

Current Status and Plans for SRU

A variety of projects and implementations are using SRU for networked IR.[15] In some cases, implementations provide a SRU gateway to existing Z39.50 servers, For example, the Library of Congress implemented SRU access to its Z39.50 server and can return records in MARCXML, MODS, and even DC.[16] The European Library uses SRU as a search gateway to 47 European national libraries from a single interface, thus providing metasearch functionality across those libraries' resources.[17] SRU is used in venues

```
<searchRetrieveResponse>
   <version>1.1</version>
   <numberOfRecords>10</numberOfRecords>
   <records>
    <record>
     <recordSchema>info:srw/schema/1/dc-
               v1.1</recordSchema>
     <recordData>
      <dc:record>
       <dc:title>The prediction of subsequent violent
                offenses by the inmates of the Texas
                Department of Corrections </dc:title>
      </dc:record>
     </recordData>
    </record>
   </records>
</searchRetrieveResponse>
```

Fig. 7 Sample searchRetrieveResponse.

Search Clause	Explanation
cat	Simple single word search
cat and dog	Simple two-word Boolean search
"black cat"	Simple two word phrase; quotation marks must be used to indicate that words comprise a phrase
title = cat	Search for term cat in a title index
dc.title = cat	Search for term cat in an index defined in the Dublin core context set

Fig. 8 Sample CQL search clauses.

Information Retrieval–
Information Society

beyond accessing library catalogs. For example, OCLC has developed a SRU interface to the DSpace digital repository system, allowing a standard search interface to the Lucene indexer used in DSpace repositories.[18] The NISO Metasearch Initiative has included reviewing SRU as the basis for a metasearch search and retrieval standard.[19]

In a move to gain formal standards status for SRU, the SRU Editorial Board, with support from the SRU Implementors Group, decided to pursue standardization of a specification based on SRU through the Organization for the Advancement of Structured Information Standards (OASIS) Consortium. Work on that effort began in Summer 2007. The specification has not yet been approved as an OASIS standard, and work is continuing on moving the specification through the OASIS process. Members of the SRU Editorial Board established the OASIS Search Web Services Technical Committee and the Committee's work includes the development of an Abstract Protocol Definition.[20] An important aspect of the OASIS work is to provide methods for accessing servers that support OpenSearch. The OpenSearch provides a method for describing a search engine's interface to assist clients in automating search Web forms.[21] The OASIS Committee plans to define application protocol bindings that provides the description (either human-readable or machine-actionable) of a server. A client will be able to access any server that provides such a description, if only it implements the capability to read the description file and interpret the description and based on that description to formulate a request (including a query) and interpret the response.

According to Ray Denenberg, cochair of the OASIS Technical Committee and managing editor for SRU, the plans are for the committee to produce initially two bindings: SRU 1.2 (compatible with the current SRU 1.2 specification) and OpenSearch (compatible with the current OpenSearch 1.1 specifications).[22] These will be straightforward renderings of the two existing specifications. The committee will follow with a third binding for the planned SRU 2.0, a revised version that will introduce new features into SRU. The committee will also initially produce a draft CQL 1.2 (compatible with the current CQL specifications) and will follow later with CQL 2.0, which will introduce new features into CQL.

CONCLUSION

"Information retrieval, while seemingly simple and obvious when accessing Google, is surprisingly complex."[16] IR tasks can range from simply submitting a keyword search to a search engine to issuing complex queries simultaneously to multiple and diverse information servers living on the Web. Searching a diverse set of IR systems and the data they hold, and then returning results in useful formats are made possible through the development and implementation of IR protocols. Z39.50 first explored the complexity of intersystem search and retrieval, and the attendant issues of interoperability. The widespread deployment of Z39.50 servers, primarily in the context of library catalogs, demonstrated the utility of a standard, protocol-based, search and retrieval interface to the diversity of library systems. Cross-database searching, or metasearch, was first explored by using Z39.50 for concurrent access to multiple resources, including but not limited to library catalogs.

Search in the context of the Web presented both challenges and opportunities for Z39.50. On the one hand, that protocol appeared to be both library-centric and not Web friendly, and thus there was little take up of that protocol by the wider Web search community. On the other hand, implementors and developers—primarily from the library community—have built on the experience and intellectual contributions of Z39.50 and evolved Z39.50 into a search/retrieve protocol and an associated query language more in line with the needs and expectations for the Web. SRU uses current standards and technologies to reduce the barriers to implementation and provides a robust IR protocol that effectively supports networked IR.

REFERENCES

1. National Information Standards Organization, *ANSI/NISO Z39.89-2003. The U.S. National Z39.50 Profile for Library Applications*, NISO Press: Bethesda, MD, 2003; Available at http://www.niso.org/kst/reports/standards?step=2&gid=& project_key=e1a85edddd965ac64eaefa7f3ba28d136c6c08f5 (accessed June 2008).

2. National Information Standards Organization (NISO), *ANSI Z39.50-2003, Information Retrieval (Z39.50) Application Service Definition and Protocol Specification*; NISO Press: Bethesda, MD, 2003; http://www.loc. gov/z3950/agency/Z39–50-2003.pdf (accessed June 2008).

3. Moen, W.E. *The development of ANSI/NISO Z39.50: A case study in standards evolution*, School of Information Studies, Syracuse University: Syracuse, NY, 1998; Available at http://www.unt.edu/wmoen/dissertation/Dissertation Index.htm Ph.D. Dissertation UMI Publication Number: AAT 9904698, (accessed June 2008).

4. National Information Standards Organization (NISO), *American National Standard Z39.50, Information Retrieval Service Definition and Protocol Specifications for Library Applications*; Transaction Publishers: New Brunswick, NJ, 1988.

5. National Information Standards Organization (NISO), *ANSI/NISO Z30.50-1992 (version 2) Information Retrieval Service and Protocol: American National Standard, Information Retrieval Application Service Definition and Protocol Specification for Open Systems Interconnection*; NISO Press: Bethesda, MD, 1992; http://www.cni.org/pub/NISO/ docs/Z39.50-1992/ (accessed June 2008).

6. National Information Standards Organization (NISO), *ANSI Z39.50-1995, Information Retrieval (Z39.50) Application Service Definition and Protocol Specification*; NISO Press: Bethesda, MD, 1995; http://www.loc.gov/z3950/agency/markup/markup.html (accessed June 2008).

7. http://www.loc.gov/z3950/agency/defns/bib1.html Bib-1 Attribute Set, 2007.

8. http://lcweb.loc.gov/z3950/agency/defns/oids.html#5 Registry of Z39.50 Object Identifiers. Record syntaxes. (n.d.).

9. Needleman, M. ZING—Z39.50 international next generation. Ser. Rev. **2002**, *28* (3), 248–250 doi:10.1016/S0098-7913(02)00188-0.

10. http://www.loc.gov/standards/sru/specs/ SRU Version 1.2 Specifications. 2007.

11. Morgan, E.L. An introduction to the search/retrieve URL service (SRU). Ariadne **2004**, (40), http://www.ariadne.ac.uk/issue40/morgan/intro.html (accessed June 2008).

12. The ZeeRex DTD. 2004, http://explain.z3950.org/dtd/index.html (accessed June 2008). See also, An overview of ZeeRex. 2002, http://explain.z3950.org/overview/ (accessed June 2008).

13. Contextual Query Language (SRU Version 1.2 Specifications). 2008. http://www.loc.gov/standards/sru/specs/cql.html CQL.

14. CQL Context Sets. 2008. http://www.loc.gov/standards/sru/resources/context-sets.html.

15. Implementors. 2008. http://www.loc.gov/standards/sru/resources/implementors.html.

16. McCallum, S.H. A look at new information retrieval protocols: SRU, OpenSearch/A, CQL, and XQuery World Library and Information Congress: 72nd IFLA General Conference and Council Seoul, Korea August, 20–24, 2006 http://www.ifla.org/IV/ifla72/papers/102-McCallum-en.pdf (accessed June 2008).

17. Woldering, B. The European Library: Integrated access to the national libraries of Europe. Ariadne **2004**, (38), Available at http://www.ariadne.ac.uk/issue38/woldering/intro.html (accessed June 2008).

18. OCLC. Search & retrieve web service/search & retrieve URL service. (n.d.). http://www.oclc.org/research/projects/webservices/default.htm.

19. NISO Metasearch Initiative. (n.d.). http://www.niso.org/workrooms/mi.

20. OASIS Search Web Services Technical Committee. (n.d.). http://www.oasis-open.org/committees/search-ws/charter.php.

21. OpenSearch. (n.d.). http://www.opensearch.org.

22. Personal communication, June 2, 2008.

BIBLIOGRAPHY

1. Additional information related to Z39.50 and SRU can be found at: The Z39.50 Maintenance Agency website under Z39.50 Resources. Available at http://www.loc.gov/z3950/agency/resources/ (accessed June 2008).

2. SRU Maintenance Agency, Available at http://www.loc.gov/standards/sru/index.html (accessed June 2008).

3. Z39.50: Selected list of resources, Available at http://www.unt.edu/wmoen/Z3950/BasicZReferences.htm (accessed June 2008).

Information Retrieval Support Systems

Yiyu Yao
*Department of Computer Science, University of Regina, Regina, Saskatchewan, Canada, and
International WIC Institute, Beijing University of Technology, Beijing, China*

Ning Zhong
*Department of Life Science and Informatics, Maebashi Institute of Technology, Maebashi-City,
Japan, and International WIC Institute, Beijing University of Technology, Beijing, China*

Yi Zeng
International WIC Institute, Beijing University of Technology, Beijing, China

Abstract

The study of Information Retrieval Support Systems (IRSS) focuses on the next generation retrieval systems and Web search engines. It is an emerging research field driven by the demands, challenges, and opportunities of the fast growing Web. The philosophy of IRSS requires us to go beyond the two basic tasks of browsing and searching provided by current retrieval systems. We must provide the necessary new utilities, tools, and languages that help and support a user to perform multiple tasks in finding useful information and knowledge. In the Web context, IRSS may be viewed as an important type of Web-based systems supporting Web Intelligence (WI). The main objective of this entry is to provide an overview of the study of IRSS, covering the emergence of IRSS, the architecture of IRSS, and implementation-related issues.

INTRODUCTION

With the advances of information and Web technologies, everyone faces a great challenge of information overload. One may feel lost in the overwhelming volume of information, and in many cases misinformation. For example, a scientist can have a real difficulty in keeping up with current research and figuring out what has been done by using Information Retrieval Systems (IRS) and search engines.[1,2] One is no longer satisfied with retrieval systems that provide limited supports of browsing, navigation, and retrieval. There is a great demand on retrieval systems and search engines with a great variety of new functionalities and supports.[3]

We can observe a few trends in the new, or latest versions of, retrieval systems and search engines that attempt to address the above-mentioned problems. For example, some recent retrieval systems provide better user interface that allows more user control[4] in the search process and retrieval-results refinement and reorganization. Some search engines provide more utilities that support user exploration of a collection of information items. There are more domain-specific and narrow-scope search engines that make more effective use of domain knowledge and structures of a collection of information items. In addition, results from machine learning, data mining, intelligent agents, and other fields are being incorporated into retrieval systems and search

engines to increase their performance. However, there is still lack of a commonly agreed label for those research efforts, and there seems to be a need of a framework so that we can study them systematically. The recently proposed notion of Information Retrieval Support Systems (IRSS) may serve this purpose.[5–7] IRSS may be used as a subsystem of a research support system (RSS).[7–9] They may also be considered a step toward knowledge retrieval systems (KRS).[10,11]

By introducing IRSS as a new field of study, we may be able to draw the attention of researchers working on the related topics. Many related, but isolated and scattered studies, techniques, tools, and systems can be unified under an umbrella term of IRSS. The benefits are the convergence of new generation retrieval systems, search engines, and Web services that aim to provide a variety of utilities, tools, and languages to support a user to find what they really need, including data, information, and knowledge.

Three fundamental issues are investigated in this entry. We examine the evolution process of retrieval systems, from data retrieval to information retrieval, and from information retrieval to information retrieval support. We outline the conceptual architecture of IRSS and discuss the basic concepts, characteristics, and functionalities of these types of systems. We comment on implementation issues of IRSS with reference to related fields and suggest a technical foundation based on granular computing. The materials of this entry are based on our preliminary studies.[5–7]

Encyclopedia of Library and Information Sciences, Fourth Edition DOI: 10.1081/E-ELIS4-120044533
Copyright © 2017 by Taylor & Francis. All rights reserved.

EMERGENCE OF IRSS

There are several factors that affect the evolution of retrieval systems, namely, the characteristics of information items, the characteristics and demands of users, and available technologies. It can be said that retrieval systems evolve from simple and specific task to intelligent and multiple tasks. We are now entering a stage when IRSS are necessary and technologically feasible.

From Data Retrieval to Information Retrieval

Van Rijsbergen provided a comparative study of data retrieval systems (DRS) and IRS regarding their common features and differences.[12] Both DRS and IRS focus on storage-and-retrieval functionality, with very limited support for other functionalities.

In traditional DRS, data items can be precisely described by using well-understood representation schemes, and user needs can be formally represented by query languages (e.g., SQL). The model is deterministic in the sense that the relationships between data items and user needs are well and objectively defined and consequently exact match and deductive inference can be used. The intolerance of uncertainty of data retrieval had motivated many researchers to search for generalized data retrieval models, such as fuzzy databases and extended Boolean queries.[13]

The stringent requirements of data retrieval made it unsuitable for the case of documents storage and retrieval where a collection of natural language documents is involved. Information retrieval was evolved from data retrieval by considering the following issues. Documents and user needs cannot always be precisely described, and their relationships are ill and subjectively defined. The model is nondeterministic in the sense that partial or best match and inductive inference are used. The results of an IRS are typically a list of ranked information items. They are documents or paragraphs containing keywords in queries. One needs to read those documents in order to find the required information. In other words, IRS and search engines are reference systems that indirectly meet the user requirements.

From Information Retrieval to Information Retrieval Support

The limited functionalities of IRS and search engines is insufficient to meet the demands of users in the Web age. IRSS have emerged as the next generation in the evolution of retrieval systems that focus on more supporting functionalities at a higher intelligence level.

The emergence of information retrieval support can be seen from several important trends in the search

community. One of them is the separation of vertical search and horizontal search. While traditional horizontal search deals with general purpose search needs, vertical search handles domain-specific needs. Vertical search[14] plays a daily-increasing important role on the Web.[15–18] For example, Google Scholar, CiteSeerX, DBLP, MSRA Libra, etc., are specialized retrieval systems for academic literature search; Amazon, Google product search, Microsoft Live product search, etc., are for product retrieval online; Zoominfo is a vertical search engine for company, people network, and job information. All of these vertical search systems provide various ways to better support specific groups of users in particular domains. Another trend is the study of exploratory search systems for users with insufficient domain and contextual knowledge to formulate effective retrieval queries.[10,19] Many related workshops and special issues have emerged during these years. They include HCIL SOH 2005 Workshop on Exploratory Search Interfaces, SIGIR 2006 Workshop on Evaluating Exploratory Search Systems, SIGCHI 2007 Workshop on Exploratory Search and Human Computer Interaction, a special issue on "Supporting Exploratory Search" in *Communications of the ACM* (49(4), 2006), a special issue on "Evaluating Exploratory Search Systems" in *Information Processing and Management* (44(2), 2008). Exploratory search systems support users through information visualization and multimedia presentation and allow users to browse and explore an information collection to refine queries.[20,21] The third trend is that retrieval systems and search engines start to provide more tools for users to manipulate retrieval results, so that they may make better use of retrieved items. It becomes evident that these trends have a common goal of providing more and better supports to users by increasing the functionality and flexibility of traditional IRS.

By moving beyond browsing, navigating, and retrieval, IRSS focus on a wide range of supporting functionalities, including summarization, exploration, analysis, knowledge discovery, results organization, retrieval strategy recommendation, and so on.[5–7,22] The objective of an IRSS is to support many different types of user tasks in finding and utilizing information, in a similar way that a decision support system (DSS) assists managers in decision making.[23]

Characteristics of IRSS

As the next generation retrieval systems, IRSS are extensions of IRS. In order to provide more supporting functionalities by IRSS, we need to design and implement new models, languages, utilities, and tools to assist a user in investigating, analyzing, understanding, and organizing a document collection and search results. These tools allow a user to explore both the semantic and structural

Information Retrieval–
Information Society

information of each individual document, as well as the entire collection. An IRSS is a user-oriented system in the sense that a user plays a more central role, and the system plays a supporting role. First, the system should be very flexible so that a user can perform a wide range of tasks. In some sense, an IRSS is a platform that allows a user to work on tasks in information and knowledge search. A user can make decisions at various stages. Second, instead of being a passive system waiting for user queries, the system may actively support a user by providing useful information without being explicitly asked. Third, an IRSS is adaptive to a user by collecting implicit and explicit feedback through user–system interaction. Thus, an IRSS must have learning capacity. From the performance point of view, an IRSS emphasizes accuracy and effectiveness more than efficiency and online processing. Fourth, the results from an IRSS must be more than a simple ranked list of information items. Moreover, a user should be allowed to visualize, reorganize, and compare various search results from different perspectives.

An IRSS needs to manage a large class of models of data, information, and knowledge. Three related types of models need to be considered. Documents in a document collection serve as the raw data of IRSS. The document models deal with representations and interpretations of documents and the document collection. The retrieval models deals with search. The presentation/recommendation models deal with the representation and interpretation of results from search. A single document model, retrieval model, or presentation model may not be suitable for different types of users. Therefore, IRSS must support multiple models, and provide tools for users to manage various models.

The document models allow multirepresentation of documents. Granular computing will play an important role in the construction of document models.[6,24,25] One can use hierarchical granulation for a document, namely, a layered and multiresolution representation of documents. The same document is represented in less detail at a higher level than at a lower level. With multimodel capability, a user can create different logical views of a document and logical links between documents, as well as compare and investigate various views. The resulting in-depth knowledge can help the user locate and infer useful information. The recent development of XML enables us to describe both the structural and semantic information of a document. Such information makes the construction of multirepresentation document models an achievable goal.

The retrieval models provide languages and tools to assist a user in performing tasks such as searching and browsing. IRSS should provide multistrategy retrieval. A user can choose different retrieval models with respect to different document models. The retrieval process of IRSS is no longer just keyword matching. Instead, it must consider different types of inference methodologies. Thus, an IRSS provides different inference models to meet various

needs from different users. Both deductive inference and inductive inference are considered. Recently, several models were proposed for inference on Web scale, and can be considered as possible choices for IRSS. For example, associative inference and analogical inference can help find relevant results more effectively.[26] Variable precision logic can be used to develop reasoning method based on incomplete information source and under time constraints.[27] Based on Simon's theory on rational choice,[28] combining reasoning and search on the Web scale is proposed.[29] which may also be related to the study of IRSS.

The presentation/recommendation models allow a user to view and arrange search results, as well as various document models. The same results can be viewed in different ways by using distinct presentation/recommendation models. Moreover, a user can analyze and compare results from different retrieval models.

An IRSS also needs to build various models of users to provide better and personalized support. An IRSS may actively collect user information, user–system interaction information, and various other logs to build user profiles. With deep knowledge of users, an IRSS may provide more intelligent support. For example, user models may help an IRSS to select the best combination of document, retrieval, and presentation models. The full function of an IRSS is achieved by managing these models, as well as the associated languages, tools, and utilities.

THE CONCEPTUAL ARCHITECTURE OF IRSS

Many retrieval systems are starting to provide more supporting functionalities to users. They are typically implemented by simply adding components to existing IRS. There is still a lack of conceptual framework that allows us to have a more systematic study. And one cannot expect great progress without such a framework. For this reason, we consider here a conceptual architecture of IRSS.

Our interpretation of IRSS draws extensively from the related field of Decision Support Systems (DSS).[23] While DSS focus on supporting and improving decision making, IRSS focus on supporting and improving retrieval. The philosophy, principles, and techniques from DSS are applicable to IRSS by substituting the tasks of "decision making" for the tasks of "information retrieval." This view of IRSS is particularly reasonable if one considers the fact that it is necessary to obtain useful information in order to make intelligent and rational decision.[5]

Gorry and Morton[30] define DSS as "interactive computer-based systems, which help decision makers utilize data and models to solve unstructured problems." Turban and Aronson[23] compare different definitions of DSS and suggest that DSS are "computer-based information systems that combine models and data in an attempt to solve unstructured problems with extensive user involvement through a friendly user interface." From these definitions, we want to stress two important features of DSS pertinent to our interpretation of IRSS. One feature is the combination of data and models. Data are raw and uninterpreted facts. In order to make sense of raw data, one needs to construct various models. Therefore, a DSS deals with both data and their interpretations. The other feature is the emphasis on the user involvement.[5]

A simple conceptual architecture of IRSS is shown in Fig. 1, consisting of a user interface subsystem, an information-management subsystem, a knowledge-based management subsystem, and a retrieval subsystem. Their main functionalities are summarized below:

- User interface subsystem: provides a friendly interface for user–system interaction (containing different functionalities, and tools to support retrieving and postprocessing).
- Information management subsystem: collects and manages data, information, and knowledge of a collection of information items.
- Knowledge-based management subsystem: manages various models (e.g., document models, retrieval models, presentation/recommendation models, and user models) to support other subsystem.
- Retrieval subsystem: performs the retrieval and inference tasks, and analyzes retrieval results from multiple perspectives and provides the results to users through user interface.

The four subsystems work together to provide retrieval support to users. The main concern of this architecture is based on a combination of the traditional architecture of IRS and DSS.

IMPLEMENTATION OF IRSS

In this section, we look at the implementation of IRSS by mentioning results from related fields and giving the granular computing basis of IRSS.

Fields Related to IRSS

To build a relatively new discipline, we need to draw ideas, techniques, results, and lessons from many other fields. A few related fields are summarized below, in addition to previously mentioned DSS.[5]

Expert systems

A well-established practice in expert systems is the separation of knowledge and inference engines. While the inference engine is logic-based and problem-independent, the knowledge base is domain-specific. Expert system shells that implement an inference engine can be used to build many different domain-specific expert systems. Similarly, we can build a knowledge-based IRSS by separating knowledge-base and management subsystems. An IRSS shell can be built that provides a set of domain- and user-independent tools. Another feature of expert systems is the explanation functionality. An expert system not only provides a solution, but can also give reasons to justify the solution. It is reasonable to insist on the explanation functionality of an IRSS.

Machine learning and data mining

By applying algorithms of machine learning, data mining, and especially text mining to documents stored in an IRSS, one may discover patterns and extract knowledge useful to a user. Such functionalities are particularly useful to users who are interested in exploratory searching and browsing. For example, a user can track trends in a particular area or discover emerging topics from the constantly changing document collection. A user may also discover links between different documents or research areas.

Computer graphics and information visualization

In many cases, a user may not want the details about particular documents. A user may want to have a general feeling before going to a more in-depth analysis. This can be accomplished with a granulated view, in which details are omitted. Most current IRS present search results in the form of ranked list of individual documents. In an IRSS, a user should be able to use graphics and visualization tools to view a particular document model and retrieval results. Graphics and visualization techniques may enable users

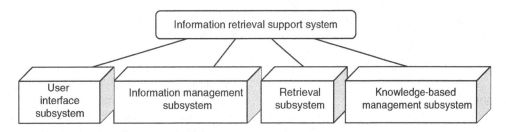

Fig. 1 The conceptual architecture of IRSS.

easily to perform qualitative inference and analysis at multiple levels.

Intelligent information agents

Intelligent information agents have been used by many IRS to collect information and interact with users. The potential of agents needs to be further explored in IRSS. In particular, a user should be allowed to construct a personalized agent to interact with an IRSS. The autonomy and learning capabilities of agents make them attractive to both IRSS and users.

Granulation in IRSS

An important task of an IRSS is the management of various models. Typically, these models provide multiview and multilevel representations of the information items and users. In order to obtain such representations, the recently proposed theory of granular computing may provide the required theoretical and technological basis.[31]

Document space, user space, term space, and retrieval-results space can be granulated respectively, to achieve multilevel and multiview representations. The four types of space granulation are related to each other. To provide retrieval results for different types of users, user space is granulated. A user granule may require a specific type of retrieval-result granule. Term space is granulated to support document-space and query-space granulations. An IRSS can recommend relevant terms to users for refining a query based on different levels of term granulation. Document space is granulated to different categories and the document granules can be retrieved based on relevant-term granules.

Document-space granulation

Traditional IRS focus more on documents, and the associated granulations are always document clusters based on the contents of documents.[1,12] This single view may not fully explore information and knowledge about a document collection. In general, a document collection can be granulated in at least three views: content view, structure view, and usage view.[32]

From the content view, document-space granulation may reveal the relationships among different documents or relationships between a specific document and a given topic. From the structure view, citations and links among different documents can be considered as implicit connections, which provide a different kind of granulation.[33] From the usage view, documents that are accessed together can be put into the same document granule.[32]

User-space granulation

Different types of users have different needs, and hence they should be classified into different user granules. User-space granulation is mainly based on user profiles and user access logs. Based on Web-usage mining, we can find interesting rules for certain types of users.[34] User-space granulation is necessary for personalized retrieval support. The granulated user space will be useful for locating relevant retrieval-results granules.

Term-space granulation

In IRSS, terms are granulated into a hierarchical structure based on relationships among them. For example, some terms may be very specific and belong to a more general term, and some terms may be synonyms, etc. Manual and automatic thesauri (such as co-occurrence analysis and grammatical analysis) are concrete methods for one-level term-space granulation.[35,36] In general, one may consider hierarchical classification methods for multiple-level granulations. A granule network of domain knowledge can be built based on term-space granulation.[7,32] Document granulation can be based on this granule network of terms, and a document can be associated with term granules. For example, gene and protein names are used for building domain-knowledge structures for biomedical literature classification.[37] In the retrieval process, if query terms are too general, an IRSS could suggest users to refine the query terms using the granulated term space. On the other hand, if user terms are too specific, the system could suggest users with synonyms, co-occurring words, or more general terms. The term-space granulation also can be used for retrieval-results granulation. Retrieval results can be organized into a granule network based on term-space granulation.

Retrieval-result-space granulation

In order to have an in-depth understanding of the retrieval results, one may granulate them to form a multilevel view. One way to achieve this is through the use of user-space granulation and term-space granulation. For example, by using term-space granulation, retrieval results may be organized to reflect different levels of generality of terms, which may meet the user needs at different level of details. Depending on user-space granulation, one may choose the right level of term-space granulation for presenting retrieval results. Retrieved documents can also be presented based on document-space granulations.

CONCLUSION

With the advance of any technology, we need to find new applications that realize its benefits. The introduction of IRSS is to take advantage of recent achievements in information and Web technologies on one hand, and to maximize the potential values of the Web on the other. A search engine equipped with more supporting functionalities will enable users to make full and wise use of the Web. The main feature of an IRSS is to expand the functions of current retrieval systems beyond search, navigation, and browsing. Such systems will play an important role in the next generation of the World Wide Web and the study of WI.

This entry briefly discusses the fundamental issues of IRSS. We demonstrate that IRSS represents the next generation in the evolution of retrieval systems, from DRS to IRS, and from IRS to IRSS. A conceptual architecture of IRSS is proposed. Regarding the implementation of IRSS, we examine a few related fields. Granular-computing theory is used to obtain multiview and multilevel representations through term-space, user-space, document-space, and retrieval-results-space granulations. These multiple representations may enable an IRSS to support users more intelligently.

REFERENCES

1. Baeza-Yates, R.; Ribeiro-Neto, B. *Modern Information Retrieval*; 1st Ed. Addison Wesley: New York, 1999.
2. Dominich, S. *Mathematical Foundations of Information Retrieval*; 1st Ed. Kluwer Academic Publishers: Dordrecht, the Netherlands 2001.
3. Solso, R.L.; MacLin, O.H.; MacLin, M.K. *Cognitive Psychology*; 8th Ed. Allyn & Bacon, Inc.: Boston, MA, 2007.
4. Bates, M.J. Where should the person stop and the information search interface start?. Inform. Process. Manage. Int. J. **1990**, *26*(5), 575–591.
5. Yao, Y.Y. Information retrieval support systems Proceedings of the 2002 IEEE World Congress on Computational Intelligence Honolulu, Hawaii May 12–17, 2002; 773–778.
6. Yao, Y.Y.; Song, K.; Saxton, L.V. Granular computing for the organization and retrieval of scientific XML documents Proceedings of the 6th Joint Conference on Information Science North Carolina March 8–13, 2002, Caulfield, H.J., Chen, S.H., Cheng, H.D., Duro, R.J., Honavar, V., Kerre, E.E., Lu, M., Romay, M.G., Shih, T.K., Ventura, D., Wang, P.P., Yang, Y.Y., Eds., 2002; 377–381.
7. Yao, Y.Y. Granular computing for the design of information retrieval support systems. *Information Retrieval and Clustering*; 1st Ed.; Wu, W., Xiong, H., Shekhar, S., Eds.; Kluwer Academic Publishers: Dordrecht, the Netherlands 2003.
8. Yao, Y.Y. A framework for web-based research support systems Proceedings of the 27th Annual International Computer Software and Applications Conference Dallas, TX November 3–6, 2003 IEEE Computer Society, 2003; 601–606.
9. Yao, J.T.; Yao, Y.Y. Web-based information retrieval support systems: Building research tools for scientists in the New Information Age Proceedings of the 2003 IEEE/WIC International Conference on Web Intelligence Halifax, Canada October 13–17, 2003 IEEE Computer Society, 2003; 570–573.
10. Yao, Y.Y.; Zeng, Y.; Zhong, N.; Huang, X.J. Knowledge retrieval (KR) Proceedings of the 2007 IEEE/WIC/ACM International Conference on Web Intelligence Silicon Valley November 2–5, 2007 IEEE Computer Society, 729–735.
11. Zeng, Y.; Yao, Y.Y.; Zhong, N. Granular structure based knowledge retrieval. Comput. Sci. **2008**, *35*(3), 194–196, 224 (in Chinese).
12. Van Rijsbergen, C.J. *Information Retrieval*; 1st Ed. Butterworths: London, U.K., 1979.
13. Takahashi, Y. Fuzzy database query languages and their relational completeness theorem. IEEE Trans. Knowl. Data Eng. **1993**, *5*(1), 122–125.
14. Chau, M.; Chen, H.C. Comparison of three vertical search spiders. IEEE Comput. **2003**, *36*, 56–62.
15. Nie, Z.Q.; Ma, Y.X.; Shi, S.M.; Wen, J.R.; Ma, W.Y. Web object retrieval Proceedings of the 16th International World Wide Web Conference Banff, AB, Canada May 8–12, 2007; 81–90.
16. Nie, Z.Q.; Wen, J.R.; Ma, W.Y. Object-level vertical search Proceedings of the 3rd Biennial Conference on Innovative Data Systems Research Asilomar, CA January 7–10, 2007; 235–246.
17. Wang, Y.; Geng, Z.H.; Huang, S.; Wang, X.L.; Zhou, A.Y. Academic web search engine: Generating a survey automatically Proceedings of the 16th International World Wide Web Conference Banff, Alberta, Canada May 8–12, 2007; 1161–1162.
18. O'Brien, P.; Abou-Assaleh, T. Focused ranking in a vertical search engine Proceedings of the 30th ACM SIGIR Conference Amsterdam, the Netherlands July 23–27, 2007; 912.
19. White, R.W.; Kules, B.; Drucker, S.M.; Schraefel, M.C. Supporting exploratory search. Commun. ACM **2006**, *49*(4), 37–39.
20. Marchionini, G. Exploratory search: From finding to understanding. Commun. ACM **2006**, *49*(4), 41–46.
21. Schraefel, M.C.; Wilson, M.L.; Russell, A.; Smith, D.A. MSPACE: Improving information access to multimedia domains with multimodal exploratory search. Commun. ACM **2006**, *49*(4), 47–49.
22. Brajnik, G.; Mizzaro, S.; Tasso, C.; Venuti, F. Strategic help in user interfaces for information retrieval. J. Am. Soc. Inform. Sci. Technol. **2002**, *53*(5), 343–358.
23. Turban, E.; Aronson, J.E. *Decision Support Systems and Intelligent System*; 1st Ed. Prentice Hall: Englewood Cliffs, NJ, 2001.
24. Wong, S.K.M.; Yao, Y.Y.; Butz, C.J. Granular information retrieval. In *Soft Computing in Information Retrieval: Techniques and Applications*; Crestani, F., Pasi, G., Eds.; Physica-Verlag: Heidelberg, Germany, 2000; 317–331.
25. Zadeh, L.A. Towards a theory of fuzzy information granulation and its centrality in human reasoning and fuzzy logic. Fuzzy Set. Syst. **1997**, *19*, 111–127.
26. Berners-Lee, T.; Hall, W.; Hendler, J.A.; O'Hara, K.; Shadbolt, N.; Weitzner, D.J. A framework for web science. Foundation. Trend Web Sci. **2006**, *1*(1), 1–130.
27. Michalski, R.S.; Winston, P.H. Variable precision logic. Artif. Intell. **1986**, *29*(2), 121–146.
28. Simon, H.A. A behavioral model of rational choice. Quart. J. Econ. **1955**, *69*(1), 99–118.

Information Retrieval–
Information Society

29. Fensel, D.; van Harmelen, F. Unifying reasoning and search to web scale. IEEE Internet Comput. **2007**, *11*(2), 94–95, 96.

30. Gorry, G.A.; Morton, M.S.S. A framework for management information systems. Soloan Manage. Rev. **1971**, *13*, 55–70.

31. Yao, Y.Y. The art of granular computing Proceedings of the International Conference on Rough Sets and Emerging Intelligent Systems Paradigms, Lecture Notes in Artificial Intelligence 4585 Warsaw, Poland 2007 Springer, 2007; 101–112.

32. Yao, Y.Y.; Zeng, Y.; Zhong, N. Supporting literature exploration with granular knowledge structures Proceedings of the 11th International Conference on Rough Sets, Fuzzy Sets, Data Mining, and Granular Computing, Lecture Notes in Artificial Intelligence 4482 Toronto, ON, Canada May 14–16, 2007 Springer, 2007; 182–189.

33. Salton, G. *Dynamic Information and Library Processing*; 1st Ed. Prentice-Hall: Englewood Cliffs, NJ, 1975.

34. Wong, S.K.M.; Yao, Y.Y. Query formulation in linear retrieval models. J. Am. Soc. Inform. Sci. **1990**, *41*(5), 334–341.

35. Morita, K.; Atlam, E.; Fuketa, M.; Tsuda, K.; Oono, M.; Aoe, J. Word classification and hierarchy using co-occurrence word information. Inform. Process. Manage. **2004**, *40*(6), 957–972.

36. Tokunaga, T.; Iwayama, M.; Tanaka, H. Automatic thesaurus construction based on grammatical relations Proceedings of the 1995 International Joint Conference on Artificial Intelligence, Montreal, QC, Canada 1995 Morgan Kaufmann, 1995; 1308–1313.

37. Hoffman, R.; Valencia, A. Implementing the iHOP concept for navigation of biomedical literature. Bioinformatics **2005**, *21*, 252–258.

BIBLIOGRAPHY

All the bibliography can be accessed online (accessed December 20, 2008).

1. 2008 International Workshop on Web Information Retrieval Support Systems. Available at http://uxlab.cs.mun.ca/wirss2008/.

2. Proceedings of the SIGIR 2006 workshop on evaluating exploratory search systems. Available at http://research.microsoft.com/en-us/um/people/ryenw/eess/EESS2006_Proceedings.pdf.

3. Proceedings of the 2008 Information Seeking Support Systems Workshop. Available at http://ils.unc.edu/ISSS/papers.

4. Special issue on supporting exploratory search. Commun. ACM **2006**, *49*(4). Available at http://portal.acm.org/citation.cfm?id=1121949.1121978.

5. Special issue on evaluating exploratory search systems. Inform. Process. Manage. **2008**, *44*(2).

6. Web-based Support Systems (WSS): http://www2.cs.uregina.ca/~wss.

7. Yiyu Yao's page on publication related to "Information Retrieval Support Systems". Available at http://www2.cs.uregina.ca/~yyao/research/IRSS.htm.

Information Retrieval Systems

Ray R. Larson
School of Information, University of California—Berkeley, Berkeley, California, U.S.A.

Abstract

Information retrieval (IR) systems aim to select relevant material from large collections of information in response to user queries. The approaches used to accomplish this have been the focus of much research and development, and have led to the algorithms underlying many commercial and Web-based search engines today.

This entry describes the common components that go into the design of IR systems (from text processing to inverted file indexes). The major classes (or models) of retrieval algorithms (Boolean, vector, and probabilistic) are described along with formal definitions of the basic form of these algorithms and some of the variations in common use in IR research. In addition, the entry examines query expansion techniques, and in particular *relevance feedback*, and how they are used in IR systems.

INTRODUCTION

Information Retrieval (IR) is concerned with the storage, organization, and searching of collections of information. It has been part of significant part human technological development since the development of writing (or even earlier, since the mnemonic systems probably developed in prehistoric times can also be considered a form of mental IR). The earliest IR systems were the organization schemes of ancient archives and libraries, such as early Sumerian archives, or the "Pinakes" developed by Callimachus for the library of Alexandria. In the twentieth century the largest impetus to development of automated IR systems was the need to manage increasing larger quantities of information in business and scientific development. Early attempts at automating search capabilities for document collections involved techniques based on punched cards, as well as machines using optical sensing of codes on microfilmed documents.[1] The concept of using machine-based systems for storage and retrieval of information was popularized by Vannevar Bush's article "As We May Think" in 1945.[2] The term "information retrieval" was coined by Mooers in 1950.[3]

The goal of any IR system is to select the informational items (texts, images, videos, etc. which we will refer to as "documents") that are expected to be relevant for a given searcher (or user) from a large collections of such items. Today these collections range from small sets of items on an individual's personal computer to the vast resources of the World Wide Web. In all cases the task is the same: to extract some set of items that searchers *wants to have* from all of those they *do not want*.

This is not a simple task, and involves not only the technical aspects of constructing a system to perform such selection, but also aspects of psychology and user behavior to understand what differentiates the desired items from the nondesired from the particular user's point of view. In this entry, we focus on the technical aspects of the system and leave the many issues of user interaction in search systems to the entry "User-Oriented and Cognitive Models of Information Retrieval." We also do not consider, except in passing, the specific aspects of collections or of measuring relevance and search effectiveness. The entries "Information Retrieval and Evaluation," "Test Collections," "Web Information Retrieval," and "TREC (Text Retrieval Evaluation Conference)" cover these aspects of IR in detail. We also note that that we will focus on computer-based IR systems and will not attempt to cover other types (indexes, catalogs, etc.), nor will we spend time discussing the related field of database management. Note also that this entry does not attempt to cover *all* of the myriad variations of approaches to IR that have been tested over the years, but only those we consider to be of interest and that have been shown to be effective in IR evaluations.

In this entry, and in much of the history of IR research, the focus has been on the system and how to obtain the best possible results using some collection of documents with predefined set of "correct" answers (known as a *test collection*). This is sometimes referred to as the laboratory model of IR, where the system and its algorithms are the primary foci of the research and user aspects of the system are considered hardly at all. There are many critiques of this laboratory approach, but it has the advantage of allowing comparability between IR systems in terms of standardized measures of effectiveness for a given collection and set of queries.

This entry describes the common components that go into the design of IR systems. The major classes (or models) of retrieval algorithms (Boolean, vector, and probabilistic) are then described along with formal definitions of the basic form of these algorithms and the

Encyclopedia of Library and Information Sciences, Fourth Edition DOI: 10.1081/E-ELIS4-120044022
Copyright © 2017 by Taylor & Francis. All rights reserved.

Information Retrieval–
Information Society

variations in common use in IR research. This section is an expansion and update of a similar description appearing in Larson.[4] We then examine query expansion techniques, and in particular *relevance feedback*, and how they are used in IR systems. Finally, we conclude with a short discussion of experimental IR systems and their relation to commercial and public IR systems.

INFORMATION RETRIEVAL SYSTEM COMPONENTS

Information retrieval systems are made of a number of software components (varying in details from system to system) that are concerned with the primary functions of the system. These are: 1) accepting input in the form of documents, extracting information from those documents and storing that information in a form that can be quickly accessed for matching to user searches; and 2) accepting user queries and converting those to a form that can be compared to the stored information about documents. These two processes are often referred to as "indexing" and "retrieval." In this section, we describe the common processes for indexing and retrieval, and indexes for matching the content of queries and documents. The retrieval models for ranking the results are discussed in the following section.

Text Processing

Fig. 1 shows an abstract representation of an IR system. All IR systems rely on two interdependent processes to make their stored items (*records*, *documents*, or *document representatives*) accessible to users: *indexing* and *retrieval*. Although IR systems need not be computer-based (e.g., printed indexes and card catalogs can also be considered forms of IR systems), this entry focuses on computer-based systems.

The indexing process in IR systems (right-hand side of Fig. 1) is concerned with deriving a representation of a document according to the rules and processes set up for the particular system. One of simplest forms would be to extract all of the words occurring in each document and store them in an index along with an indication of which document they came from. This is commonly known as *binary indexing*, that is, a given word is either associated with a document, or it is not. Alternatively, an IR system may use some form of *weighted indexing*, where words are assigned to documents with an associated numerical weight indicating the importance or significance of that term to the document.[5] Indexing will often also identify word position within a document, sometimes with enumeration of paragraph, sentence, and word position within a sentence. Such indexing can be used to determine proximity constraints for a query in a Boolean system (e.g., words in the query must occur in the same sentence or paragraph), or proximity weighting in ranked systems.

More commonly, the document normalization and index creation involve more complex text processing of the document contents than simple word extraction (the central trapezoid in Fig. 1). In the rest of this entry, we will use "terms" to indicated elements of a document

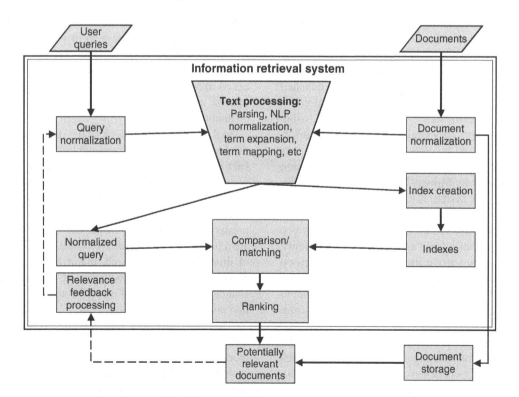

Fig. 1 Structure of an information retrieval system.

stored in the index. Terms may be words, or phrases, or some mapping of document content words to controlled vocabularies. The typical stages of text processing for document indexing may include

1. Structural identification: Recognition and selection of document elements based on document structure (e.g., selecting the title or author of the document). Because the structured document markup XML is now commonly used for the majority of documents available online, it has become relatively simple to identify and extract the significant structural elements of documents. Indexing may also store indications of the source of extracted terms in the index itself, permitting searches for both content and structure.

2. Tokenization: Individual "tokens" in the content are extracted. Tokens are portions of the content, typically sequences of alphabetic and numeric characters. Typically this involves ignoring spacing, page boundaries, and punctuation. The result is a set of tokens which may become terms in the index, or go through further processing. When individual words are extracted, their original positions in the content may also be retained in the indexes so that, for example, words near each other in the original text can be identified.

3. Token pattern recognition: Tokens may be examined to identify particularly meaningful or useful patterns. These may include such things as recognition of URLs or identifying sequences of capital letters (or capital letters with periods following them) as potential acronyms.

4. Normalization of tokens: This typically involves changing the capitalization of tokens to a single form (all lower case, for example). In some systems diacritics (accents, umlauts, etc.) may be removed and replaced with the appropriate base letter alone, or have multiple letters substituted. Some system may create duplicate tokens normalized in this fashion while retaining the original as well.

5. Part of speech tagging: Natural language processing (NLP) techniques such a part of speech tagging may be used to identify the different parts of speech in the content. Because the most common type of search is for nouns and noun phrases, this can be used to identify and extract noun phrases for special treatment.

6. Stopword processing: IR systems may have lists of words considered to be worthless in retrieval (these typically include articles like "an," "the," "a"). Some systems have different stopword lists for each of identified structural elements, or for each index. Stoplists may also specify classes of tokens (such as numbers) or parts of speech.

7. Stemming or morphological analysis: Many IR systems use some form of stemming to collapse various inflected forms of a word (e.g., cat and cats) into a single form. Stemming uses simple rule-based

processing to perform this task and often does a poor job on some words. Morphological analysis typically uses a combination of exception dictionary lookup and rules. The intent of either is to have a single form of a word used in the indexes for all forms of that word.

Systems may include various combinations and variants of these processes. For example, some systems include both the "stemmed" form and original forms of terms, generating a table of original forms for each stem encountered during indexing and then using all forms during search. One advantage of this approach is that searches may be constrained to the original forms when needed, such as when the stemmed form is too inclusive.

As indicated in Fig. 1, both document indexing and query processing require similar or identical text processing steps. This is to ensure that the tokens from the users query are comparable with the tokens extracted during document indexing.

Indexes and Query Matching

The results of text processing on incoming documents are stored in the indexes of the IR system. These indexes provide a fast lookup mechanism for each token extracted by the text processing, along with other information including some identifier for the document(s) that the token came from, and usually other information, such as statistical information about the frequency of occurrence of the token in each document, and in the collection as a whole, and possibly information about the location that each token came from in each document.

The specific file structures used for the indexes vary from system to system, but the most common are some form of "inverted file," where the data on all occurrences of a token in a collection are organized by a single instance of the token itself. This allows all of the data for resolving most queries to be fetched by a single lookup in the index for each token. The "comparison/matching" part of the processes shown in Fig. 1 is responsible for this task. This tends to be fairly common across a wide variety of IR systems, regardless of their type or "model." The result of matching (or index lookup) is an unordered set of tokens and their associated information from the indexes, that were also in the *normalized query* (i.e., the results of applying the same text processing steps to the content of query that were applied to the stored documents).

INFORMATION RETRIEVAL MODELS AND RANKING

The true differentiation between IR systems occurs in the variations in the Text Processing and Ranking portions of Fig. 1. The different approaches to deriving a ranked list of potentially relevant documents from the index matching results are often referred to as the "IR model." In this section, we will examine the main IR models and how they obtain this ranking of potentially relevant documents.

There are three main classes of retrieval models: Boolean, vector, and probabilistic. In addition there are many systems that are hybrids of two or more of these models (e.g., a vector system with Boolean result limiting features). We begin with some formal definitions of system elements that are common to all of the models, and then examine each model in turn.

In an IR system, we have a collection, $\mathbf{D}$, of N documents, indexed by a set, $\mathbf{T}$, of M unique index terms or attributes. An individual document in the collection, D_i, may be represented as a vector of index term weights:

$$D_i = (w_{i1}, w_{i2}, w_{ij}, \ldots, w_{iM})$$

The value of each w_{ij} term weight is determined by the indexing function applied. These values may represent binary indexing, (where $w_{ij} = 1$ if term T_j occurs in document D_i, and $w_{ij} = 0$ otherwise), simple term frequency weights (where each w_{ij} represents the number of times index term T_j occurs in document D_i), to more complex probabilistic weighting schemes (where w_{ij} is based on an estimation of the conditional probability that users would consider D_i to be relevant given that their query contains the term T_j).

The set of index terms, $\mathbf{T}$, consists of any searchable attribute associated with the documents in the collection. These may be word stems, words, phrases, or other elements (such as class numbers) that occur in the text of the document or derived during text processing. They may also include associated elements that are not index terms in a conventional sense, such as related terms or cross-references from a thesaurus, citation information, or references to other documents (e.g., hypertext links). These index terms may be formally represented by an *inverted file*, where each index term, T_j, has an associated vector of weights, I_j such that:

$$I_j = (w_{1j}, w_{2j}, w_{ij}, \ldots, w_{Nj})$$

The document and index term vectors can be seen as a $N \times M$ matrix of w_{ij} weights. Thus, the collection of documents can be viewed as a matrix where the rows are individual document vectors and the columns the individual term vectors. In some systems the inverted file may also include positional information on the occurrence of the terms, and even include weights for the document, paragraph, and sentence level.

In virtually all IR systems, the inverted file is commonly used in retrieval operations instead of the document vectors.

Each query Q_k from the set of queries, $\mathbf{Q}$, submitted to the system may be represented as a vector of index term weights:

$$Q_k = (y_{k1}, y_{k2}, y_{kj}, \ldots, y_{kM})$$

where y_{kj} is the weight assigned by the user or system to term T_j in the kth query.

The Boolean Model

The earliest retrieval model was the Boolean model based on Boolean logic. Systems using the Boolean model include most of the earliest commercial search services (like DIALOG or LEXUS/NEXUS), many online library catalogs, and many local search systems on individual Web sites. The Boolean model is a set-oriented model, where sets of documents are defined by the presence or absence of an individual index term. Using our formal definitions above, a single inverted file vector I_j can be considered as Boolean set, were each nonzero document weight in the vector defines a member of the set. In processing Boolean queries the sets representing the different search terms can be combined using the Boolean set operations intersection, union, and negation. These are usually expressed in a user's query as the *Boolean operators* AND, OR, and NOT.

> **AND:** Set intersection generates a new output set from two input sets where the members (documents) shared by both sets become the members of the output set.
> **OR:** Set union generates a new output set from two input sets where the members of either (or both) of the input sets are combined to become the new output set.
> **NOT:** Set negation operates on a single input set, and generates a new set that contains all members (documents) that are not in the input set.

All of these operations can be performed using a simple binary inverted file, or more complex weighted inverted files. Note, however, that the unary NOT operation can be very expensive to process in inverted files, since the result set would be all documents in the system not included in the set. As a result most Boolean IR systems restrict the use of NOT to the binary "ANDNOT" operation which excludes any members of the right-hand set from the left-hand set.

In Boolean IR systems, the user is typically responsible for formulating a combination of terms and Boolean operators that will, it is hoped, select the relevant documents for the user's information need. Boolean systems are commonly extended by inclusion of other operators usually providing additional restrictions on set intersection

Information Retrieval–
Information Society

operations. For example, term proximity operations restrict a intersection to those documents that not only have both terms, but also have those terms within a specified distance from each other.

Pure Boolean IR systems have no inherent ordering of the result of Boolean query processing. Any order presented to the searcher is applied after the final Boolean result set is obtained. Many systems use some assumed useful ordering of the result set using document information (such as the date or author name of books in a library online catalog).

Many IR researchers have pointed out the major drawbacks with Boolean IR systems. These include

1. Boolean logic requires that the users be trained in construction of queries, because it is not intuitively obvious, and differs from common natural language usage. (e.g., a user seeking books on "cats and dogs" probably wants books on either, not just those that treat both.)
2. Boolean AND operations tend to be too restrictive. A search for "A AND B AND C" will eliminate any records that do not have all these terms. Those that have one or two of the three terms are rejected along with those that have none of the terms.
3. Boolean OR operations tend to be too inclusive. A search for "A OR B OR C" will retrieve any record with at least one of the terms, but no priority is given to those that include more than one of the terms.
4. Due to steps 2 and 3, the result of AND operations is often search failure, and the result of OR operations is often information overload.
5. Boolean logic treats each term equally, giving no priority to those that may be more important to the user's need.
6. Boolean logic requires that the user's query and the document indexing use the same terminology for matching to succeed.
7. Boolean logic does not permit the retrieved documents to ranked in any significant fashion, documents are either retrieved or rejected with no "middle ground."

Various extensions to Boolean systems have been proposed and tested over the years to allow result ranking based on applying weights to the terms and/or the Boolean operations. Examples include the use of "fuzzy sets," where set membership is weighted instead of binary, and the "AND" operator returns the minimum of the two input weights, while the "OR" operator returns the maximum. The final result set is ordered by the weights.

Vector Model

The vector space model[6] considers each document vector as described above to be a vector in an M-dimensional space (i.e., one dimension for each term in the collection). Vector space IR systems base their ranking on how close together the document vectors and query vector are in this M-dimension space. This can be seen as calculation of a similarity measure based on the terms used in the query and in the documents in the collection. In practice, the inverted file is used to ensure that the processing considers only documents with at least one term in common with the query (otherwise in typical collections vast amounts of computation would be needed to process all document vectors even when they have no terms in common with the query).

In retrieval, partial match techniques based on the vector space model[7] may be used to rank the documents in the collection in decreasing order of their similarity to the query. The simplest similarity function is the *inner product* of the document and query vectors:

$$\text{INNER}(D_i, Q_k) = \sum_{j=0}^{M} w_{ij} y_{kj}$$

A variety of other vector similarity measures normalize the value of the similarity to range between 0 and 1. Probably the most commonly used is the *cosine correlation*:

$$\text{COSINE}(D_i, Q_k) = \frac{\sum_{j=0}^{M} w_{ij} y_{kj}}{\sqrt{\sum_{j=0}^{M} w_{ij}^2 \cdot \sum_{j=0}^{M} y_{kj}^2}}$$

This is angular separation of the two vectors in the M-dimensional *vector space*.

The partial match techniques based on the vector model are distinguished by the different term weights and similarity measures used in calculating the *document weight* used to rank the retrieval. Some basic vector approaches are

1. Coordination-level matching. In coordination-level matching the term weights for documents (w_{ij}) and queries (y_{kj}) are binary and the inner product similarity function is used. The document weight calculated is simply the number of terms in common between the document and the query.
2. Cosine correlation with binary weights. This approach uses binary term weights and the cosine correlation to calculate the document weight.
3. Cosine correlation with frequency weights. This approach uses the term weights consisting of simple term frequencies, f_{ij}. That is, each w_{ij} is the number of times term T_j occurs in document D_i, and each y_{kj} is the number of times term T_j occurs in query Q_k. The

cosine correlation between these weighted vectors is calculated to yield the document weight.

4. Term frequency–inverse document frequency (TFIDF) weights. In TFIDF matching, term weights are calculated as follows:

$$w_{ij} = f_{ij} \cdot \log \frac{N}{n_j}$$

where n_j is the number of documents that contain term T_j. This gives the highest weights to terms that occur frequently in a given document, but relatively infrequently in the collection as a whole, and low weights to terms that occur infrequently in a given document, but are very common throughout the collection. Query terms are weighted by simple term frequency, as above, and the document weight is calculated as the inner product of the query and document vectors.

The TFIDF approach is the most common form of vector space weighting, although there are a very large number of variants for it. Most of the variants include some form of normalization of term frequency. Well-known IR systems that use the vector space model are Salton's SMART system,[8] and more recently the open source Apache Lucene IR system originally developed by Doug Cutting.

Probabilistic Retrieval Methods

In the vector model there is an underlying assumption that documents which are similar to a query will be considered *relevant* to the information needs of the user who submits that query. Relevance is usually defined as a subjective assessment by a given user of the value or utility of a particular document in satisfying a particular need for information. We can say that for a particular search of an IR system, each of the documents in the collection either contains information that the individual wants, or it does not. If it does, then it is considered relevant, otherwise it is nonrelevant. The *document retrieval problem* is to select all of the records in the database that the user would find to be relevant, and reject all those that would be considered nonrelevant, that is, *all* and *only* the relevant documents should be retrieved.[9]

Given the individual nature of relevance judgements, we can assume that there are no purely deterministic relationships between the terms used in indexing documents and the relevance of a given document, or between the terms used in searching for a document and the relevance of that document. Instead, these relationships are *probabilistic* in nature. This suggests that there are no perfect solutions to the document retrieval problem, but there may be approximate solutions. According to a significant body of theoretical work in IR, the appropriate approach

to IR is to rank each document in the database in descending order of its *probability of relevance* for a given user and query. This has been called the *probability ranking* principle.[10]

There were originally two competing schools of thought on probability of relevance that have come to be known as Model 1[5] and Model 2.[11] These models were subsequently unified into a unified higher-level Model 3 and lower-level Model 0.[12]

In discussing these probabilistic models we will assume that the set of all (present and future) documents in the collection, **D**, and the set of all (present and future) queries, **Q**, are described by binary vectors representing the presence or absence of index terms (although it should be noted that Robertson et al. (1982) make no such assumptions regarding representation). All possible document/query pairs (D_i, Q_j), define a $\mathbf{D} \times \mathbf{Q}$ probabilistic event space. Within this event space we can define relevance as a relation which holds between certain document/query pairs:

$$R = (D_i, Q_j) | D_i \in \mathbf{D}, Q_j \in \mathbf{Q},$$

document D_i is judged to be relevant by a user submitting query; Q_j Nonrelevance, $\overline{R}$, is the complement of this relation.

We also define a subset of documents, $\mathbf{x} \subseteq \mathbf{D}$, such that all documents in x are represented by identical binary vectors i.e., those that are indexed by the same set of terms). Similarly, we have a subset, $\mathbf{y} \subseteq \mathbf{Q}$, of identical queries.

The notion of probability of relevance has a different interpretation under the four probabilistic models discussed in Robertson, Maron, and Cooper.[12] In Model 1, first formulated in a somewhat different form by Maron and Kuhns,[5] probability of relevance is seen as the relationship between a class of users (those submitting the same query) and a particular document:

$$P(R|y, D_i)$$

Model 2, on the other hand, defines probability of relevance as a relationship between a class of documents and a particular user and use (or query):

$$P(R|Q_k, x)$$

The higher-level Model 3, proposed by Robertson, Maron, and Cooper,[12] defines the probability of relevance as the relationship between an individual use (query) of the system and an individual document:

$$P(R|Q_k, D_i)$$

The lower-level Model 0, also proposed by Robertson, Maron, and Cooper[12] and expanded by Wong and

Yao,[13] defines the probability of relevance as a relationship between a class of queries and a class of documents:

$$P(R|\mathrm{y}, \mathrm{x})$$

Most experimental and operational IR systems based on probabilistic principles have used forms of Model 2 for their implementation. For retrieval in a Model 2 system, the probability of relevance is used to define a Bayesian decision function, that is, for any particular query, documents with a given description x should be retrieved if

$$P(R|Q_k, \mathrm{x}) > P(\overline{R}|Q_k, \mathrm{x})$$

That is, documents should be retrieved if the probability of relevance is greater than the probability of nonrelevance.

This decision rule commonly takes the form of a discriminant function:

$$g_{Q_k}(\mathrm{x}) = \log \frac{P(R|Q_k, \mathrm{x})}{P(\overline{R}|Q_k, \mathrm{x})}$$

These probabilities are difficult to calculate directly, but Bayes theorem can be applied to convert them to the more convenient form:

$$g_{Q_k}(\mathrm{x}) = \log \frac{P(\mathrm{x}|R, Q_k)}{P(\mathrm{x}|\overline{R}, Q_k)} + \log \frac{P(R|Q_k)}{P(\overline{R}|Q_k)}$$

where $P(\mathrm{x}|R, Q_k)$ is the probability that if, for a given query, a particular query/document pair is judged relevant, then the document would have description x. Since we are considering only a single query, we can define a subset, $\mathbf{D} \times Q_k$, of the $\mathbf{D} \times \mathbf{Q}$ event space, and the relevance relation:

$$R_{Q_k} = (D_i, Q_k)|D_i \text{ is relevant to } Q_k$$

where $R_{Q_k} \subseteq R$. If we define $P(R_{Q_k}) = P(R, Q_k)$, and $P(\overline{R}_{Q_k}) = P(\overline{R}, Q_k)$, and assume that index terms are stochastically independent with respect to the relevance or nonrelevance of a document then

$$P(\mathrm{x}|R_{Q_k}) = P(w_1|R_{Q_k})P(w_2|R_{Q_k})\ldots P(w_M|R_{Q_k})$$
$$P(\mathrm{x}|\overline{R}_{Q_k}) = P(w_1|\overline{R}_{Q_k})P(w_2|\overline{R}_{Q_k})\ldots P(w_M|\overline{R}_{Q_k})$$

where the w_i represent the individual index terms of the binary vector x. We also define the symbols, $p_i = P(w_i = 1|R_{Q_k})$, and $q_i = P(w_i = 1|\overline{R}_{Q_k})$. Under these assumptions:

$$P(\mathrm{x}|R_{Q_k}) = \prod_{i=1}^{M} p_i^{x_i}(1 - p_i)^{1-w_i}$$
$$P(\mathrm{x}|\overline{R}_{Q_k}) = \prod_{i=1}^{M} q_i^{x_i}(1 - q_i)^{1-w_i}$$

By taking logs and substituting into the discriminant function, we get

$$g_{Q_k}(\mathrm{x}) = \sum_{i=1}^{M} w_i \log \frac{p_i(1 - q_i)}{q_i(1 - p_i)} + \sum_{i=1}^{M} w_i \log \frac{1 - p_i}{1 - q_i}$$
$$+ \log \frac{P(R|Q_k)}{P(\overline{R}|Q_k)} = \sum_{i=1}^{M} a_i w_i + K_1$$

where

$$a_i = \log \frac{p_i(1 - q_i)}{q_i(1 - p_i)}$$

and K_1 is a constant for any given query.

The Model 2 probabilities p_i and q_i can be calculated, or estimated, from frequency data. If there are N documents in the database and R' of them are relevant for a given query, and the ith term occurs in n_i of the documents of which r_i are relevant, then a_i can be calculated as

$$a_i = \log \frac{r_i(N - n_i - R' + r_i)}{(n_i - r_i)(R' - r_i)}$$

Notice that this assumes that relevance is known, or can be estimated, in order to provide the frequency data that are used to estimate the probabilities. In practice, what is usually done is to estimate the frequencies based on a sample of documents evaluated by the user, or when such information is not available this formula reduces to the inverse document frequency described above. Thus Model 2 is most effective applied in a secondary search, or *relevance feedback*[14] situation, where documents retrieved in an initial search, often ranked according to a matching function based on rough estimates of the probabilities, are evaluated and the user's relevance judgments used to estimate Model 2 weights for a second search and re-ranking of the collection.

Okapi BM-25 algorithm

The most widely used form of a probabilistically based IR algorithm is known as the Okapi BM-25 algorithm developed by Robertson.[15] The basic form of the Okapi BM-25 algorithm is

$$\sum_{j=1}^{|Q_c|} w^{(1)} \frac{(k_1 + 1)tf_j}{K + tf_j} \frac{(k_3 + 1)qtf_j}{k_3 + qtf_j}$$

where (in addition to the variables already defined)
  $|Q|$ is the total number of terms in Q,
  $|Q_c|$ is the number of terms in Q that also occur in the document,

tf_j is the frequency of the jth term in a specific document,

qtf_j is the frequency of the jth term in Q,

K is $k_1((1-b)+b \cdot \mathrm{dl}/\mathrm{avdl})$,

k_1, b and k_3 are parameters (set by experimentation for a given collection),

avdl is the average document length,

$w^{(1)}$ is the Robertson–Sparck Jones weight:[11]

$$w^{(1)} = \log \frac{\left(\frac{r+0.5}{R-r+0.5}\right)}{\left(\frac{n_{t_j}-r+0.5}{N-n_{t_j}-R-r+0.5}\right)}$$

n_{t_j} is the number of documents containing the jth term,

r is the number of relevant components of a given type that contain a given term,

R is the total number of relevant components of a given type for the query.

The Robertson–Sparck Jones weights, when no relevance information is available, resolve to the inverse document frequency like the a_i measure above.

Logistic regression algorithm

Another approach to estimating probability of relevance uses the *Logistic Regression* (LR) algorithm originally developed by Cooper, Gey, and Dabney.[16] The LR model of probabilistic IR attempts to estimate the probability of relevance for each document based on a set of statistics about a document collection and a set of queries in combination with a set of weighting coefficients for those statistics. The statistics to be used and the values of the coefficients are obtained from regression analysis of a sample of a collection (or similar test collection) for some set of queries where relevance and nonrelevance has been determined. More formally, given a particular query and a particular document in a collection $P(R|Q_k,D_j)$ is calculated (or estimated) and the documents or components are presented to the user ranked in order of decreasing values of that probability. To avoid invalid probability values, the usual calculation of $P(R|Q_k,D_j)$ uses the "log odds" of relevance given a set of S statistics, s_i, derived from the query and database, such that

$$\log O(R|Q_k,D_j) = b_0 + \sum_{i=1}^{S} b_i s_i$$

where b_0 is the intercept term and the b_i are the coefficients obtained from the regression analysis of the sample collection and relevance judgements. The log odds form can be used to rank results directly or be simply converted to probabilities:

$$P(R|Q_k,D_j) = \frac{e^{\log O(R|Q_k,D_j)}}{1+e^{\log O(R|Q_k,D_j)}}$$

The form of the LR algorithm used in the Cheshire II IR system[17,18] is

$$\log O(R|Q,C) = b_0 + \left(b_1 \cdot \left(\frac{1}{|Q_d|}\sum_{j=1}^{|Q_d|} \log qtf_j\right)\right)$$

$$+ (b_2 \cdot \sqrt{|Q|}) + \left(b_3 \cdot \left(\frac{1}{|Q_d|}\sum_{j=1}^{|Q_d|} \log tf_j\right)\right)$$

$$+ (b_4 \cdot \sqrt{\mathrm{dl}}) + \left(b_5 \cdot \left(\frac{1}{|Q_d|}\sum_{j=1}^{|Q_d|} \log \frac{N-n_{t_j}}{n_{t_j}}\right)\right)$$

$$+ (b_6 \cdot \log|Q_d|)$$

where (in addition to the variables already defined above)

dl is the document length measured in bytes,

N is the number of documents in the collection,

b_i are the coefficients obtained though the regression analysis.

The LR approach to IR is one of a class of approaches that attempt to "learn" how to rank based on collected previous results. Other approaches use methods ranging from machine learning to genetic algorithms to learn the best ways of ranking results, usually for specific collections.

Language models

A rather different approach to probabilistic IR is based on language modeling originally developed for applications such as automatic speech recognition, machine translation, and OCR correction. A "language model" as used in IR systems is simply the statistical distribution of terms in documents and the collection as a whole. In language model-based IR instead of attempting to estimate probability of relevance, the system attempts to estimate the probability that a particular query was (or could have been) generated from language model for a given document. The results are then ranked according to this probability. The assumption is that if the query could have come from the document, then that document is likely to be relevant.

In the original description of language modeling, Ponte and Croft[19] define the probability estimates used to rank a document in the search results as

$$P(Q_k|M_d)$$

where Q_k is a query (as above) and M_d is the language model for a given document. A simple approach to estimating this model would calculate

$$p_{\mathrm{ml}}(T_j|M_d) = \frac{tf_j}{\mathrm{dl}_d}$$

This is simply the *Maximum likelihood estimate* of the probability of term T_j in document d where tf_j is the raw term frequency in document d and dl_d is the length of document d (in tokens). The simplest ranking function is then the product of the individual term probabilities:

$$P(Q_k|M_d) = \prod_{T_j \in Q_k} p_{ml}(T_j|M_d)$$

The obvious problem with this ranking function is that it will be zero for any document that does not contain all of the query terms. Various approaches have been taken to normalize and *smooth* this basic model to avoid both the problem of going to zero and the implicit assumption that all documents with a given term share a common language model. Most implementations use much more sophisticated smoothing and model expressions than the simple unigram language model outlined here.

Language models have been quite effective in IR evaluation exercises like TREC (q.v.). The open source Lemur toolkit[20] makes language modeling algorithms available to researchers and students.

Inference network models

Inference networks are a form of probabilistic model that uses networks of known probabilities of events (such as the a priori probability of a term occurring in a document) to infer the probability of unknown events (such as the probability of relevance for a given document and query). Inference networks were developed by Turtle and Croft,[21] and are used in the INQUERY IR system. Inference networks can include nodes that are the results of Boolean operations into the probabilistic inference network.

Similar to inference networks are the IR application of neural networks where the probabilities of relevance given particular inputs are estimated by training the network, which involves adjusting the low-level probabilities of activation from one node to any connected nodes. The major difference is that in an inference net the inferential information is pre-encoded in the model (both as structure and parameters), while in neural nets nothing is encoded a priori, but instead a "blank" network is extensively trained on data and the inferences discovered based on this training.

Hybrid models

Many IR systems combine two or more of the basic models discussed above in a single system. The most common combination is to permit some form of Boolean operations or restrictions on a ranked result set. This may involve use of explicit Boolean or extended Boolean operations (such as proximity processing) to restrict a ranked result set to those items that satisfy the Boolean constraint. Other hybrid systems may use "data fusion" methods to combine results from different retrieval algorithms.[22,23]

Combining probabilistic and (strict) Boolean elements, as well as operators to support various merging operations have been used in many systems as well. In implementation, strict Boolean operators and probabilistic searches (such as OKAPI BM-25 or LR) can be performed using the same inverted file structures, and they can be seen as two parallel *logical* search engines. Each logical search engine produces a set of retrieved documents. When a only one type of search strategy is used then the result is either a probabilistically ranked set or an unranked Boolean result set. However, both can be combined in a single query and the search results are evaluated using the assumption that the Boolean-retrieved set has an estimated $P(R|Q_{bool}, D) = 1.0$ for each document component in the set, and 0 for the rest of the collection. The final estimate for the probability of relevance used for ranking the results of a search combining strict Boolean and probabilistic strategies is simply

$$P(R|Q, D) = P(R|Q_{bool}, C) P(R|Q_{prob}, C)$$

where $P(R|Q_{prob}, C)$ is the probability of relevance estimate from the probabilistic part of the search, and $P(R|Q_{bool}, C)$ is the Boolean. In practice the combination of strict Boolean "AND" and the probabilistic approaches has the effect of restricting the results to those items that match the Boolean part, with ranking based on the probabilistic part. Boolean "NOT" provides a similar restriction of the probabilistic set by removing those document components that match the Boolean specification. When Boolean "OR" is used the probabilistic and Boolean results are merged (however, items that only occur in the Boolean result, and not both, are usually reweighted to the lower range of probabilistic results).

QUERY EXPANSION AND RELEVANCE FEEDBACK

In many IR tasks the queries submitted by a searcher are often very short and sometimes ambiguous. The goal of query expansion is to create a larger query from the searcher's initial expression and to use that to obtain (it is hoped) more relevant results. Some forms of query expansion take place in the initial text processing of the query (as discussed above) but the most effective methods involve obtaining relevance judgements on a sample of documents obtained using the initial query expression, and performing *relevance feedback* processing on those documents (shown as the dashed lines in Fig. 1).

Relevance feedback has been shown to be remarkably effective in improving the result of a query. The Vector Space and Probabilistic models take somewhat different approaches to relevance feedback. However, the main idea is to modify the existing query based on the judged relevant and nonrelevant documents, usually extracting terms from the relevant documents and adding them to the query and also adjusting the weights for terms already in the query.

The most widely used Vector Space algorithm for relevance feedback is the Rocchio Method.[24] The Rocchio method is defined by

$$Q_{\text{new}} = \alpha Q_{\text{old}} + \frac{\beta}{n_1} \sum_{i=1}^{n_1} R_i - \frac{\gamma}{n_2} \sum_{i=1}^{n_2} S_i$$

where

Q_{old} is vector for the initial query,
R_i is the vector for the judged relevant document i,
S_i is the vector for judged nonrelevant document i,
n_1 is the number of relevant documents chosen,
n_2 is the number of nonrelevant documents chosen,
α, β, and γ are parameters to tune the importance of the initial query and the relevant and nonrelevant terms. Common settings are $\beta = 0.75$ and $\gamma = 0.25$.

The probabilistic models commonly use some form of the Robertson–Sparck Jones weights for relevance feedback. This appears in the Okapi BM-25 Formula above. In relevance feedback the portions of that formula that need relevance information are filled in from the judged relevant and nonrelevant documents, and new weights are calculated for the query terms based on resulting weights. In the Cheshire II system the Robertson–Sparck Jones weights are calculated and used to select a number of most highly weighted terms from the judged relevant documents to add to the initial query and to reweight the initial query terms. This expanded query is then searched using the same LR algorithm as the initial query.

One interesting, and effective, technique that has been used in many retrieval evaluations with good results is the so-called Blind or Pseudo relevance feedback. In this approach there is no searcher involved nor actual relevance judgements made. Because many (if not most) IR systems tend to have relevant documents at the top of their rankings, this approach assumes that some arbitrary number of the top-ranked documents from the initial search are in fact relevant and applies relevance feedback processing to them (usually with a corresponding number of assumed nonrelevant documents from the bottom of the initial ranking). Even though there is no user judgement involved in this process, it has on average improved the results for systems using this method. Generally, however relevance feedback is most effective when the searcher is directing the relevance choices.

CONCLUSION

Information retrieval systems aim to select relevant material from large collections of information in response to user queries. The approaches used to accomplish this have been the focus of much research and development, and have led to the algorithms underlying many commercial and Web-based search engines today. The article on Web Search Engines goes into more detail on the approaches taken by the various Web search companies. Even though the specific algorithms of any particular search engine are considered proprietary "trade secrets," we can safely say that all existing Web search engines use some combination of the models outlined above, usually with the addition of Web-specific ranking algorithms (such as Google's PageRank that ranks Web pages based on the numbers of ingoing HTML links for that page, as well as other "reputation-based" metrics). Effective search is considered to be one of the critical requirements of the Web, and is also an essential requirement in corporate and academic databases, digital libraries, and library catalogs. Information retrieval systems, as described here, provide proven effective search capabilities to these important services of the digital age.

REFERENCES

1. Buckland, M.K. *Emanual Goldberg and His Knowledge Machine*, Libraries Unlimited: Westport, CT, 2006.
2. Bush, V. As we may think. Atlantic Mon. **1945**, *176*(1), 101–108.
3. Mooers, C.N. Information retrieval viewed as temporal signalling Proceedings of International Conference of Mathematicians Cambridge, MA August 30–September 6, 1950 AMS: Providence, RI, 1952; 572–573.
4. Larson, R.R. Evaluation of advanced retrieval techniques in an experimental online catalog. J. Am. Soc. Inform. Sci. **1992**, *43*(1), 34–53.
5. Maron, M.E.; Kuhns, J.L. On relevance, probabilistic indexing and information retrieval. J. ACM **1960**, *7*(3), 216–244.
6. Salton, G.; Wong, A.; Yang, C.S. A vector space model for information retrieval. Commun. ACM **1975**, *18*(11), 613–620.
7. Salton, G.; Buckley, C. Term weighting approaches in automatic text retrieval. Inform. Process. Manage. **1988**, *24*(5), 513–523.
8. Salton, G. *SMART Retrieval System: Experiments in Automatic Document Processing*. Prentice-Hall Series in Automatic Computation; Prentice-Hall: Upper Saddle River, NJ, 1971.
9. Maron, M.E. Probabilistic design principles for conventional and full-text retrieval systems. Inform. Process. Manage. **1988**, *24*, 249–255.
10. Robertson, S.E. The probability ranking principle in IR. J. Doc. **1977**, *33*, 294–304.
11. Robertson, S.E.; Sparck Jones, K. Relevance weighting of search terms. J. Am. Soc. Inform. Sci. May–June, **1976**, 129–146.
12. Robertson, S.E.; Maron, M.E.; Cooper, W.S. Probability of relevance: a unification of two competing models for document retrieval. Inform. Technol.: Res. Develop. **1982**, *1*, 1–21.

Information Retrieval–
Information Society

13. Wong, S.K.M.; Yao, Y.Y. A probabilistic inference model for information retrieval. Inform. Syst. **1991**, *16*(3), 301–321.

14. Salton, G.; Buckley, C. Improving retrieval performance by relevance feedback. J. Am. Soc. Inform. Sci. **1990**, *41*, 288–297.

15. Robertson, S.E. Walker, S. On relevance weights with little relevance information Proceedings of the 20th Annual International ACM SIGIR Conference on Research and Development in Information Retrieval ACM Press: New York, 1997; 16–24.

16. Cooper, W.S. Gey, F.C. Dabney, D.P. Probabilistic retrieval based on staged logistic regression 15th Annual International ACM SIGIR Conference on Research and Development in Information Retrieval Copenhagen, Denmark June, 21–24 ACM: New York, 1992; 198–210.

17. Larson, R.R.; McDonough, J.; O'Leary, P.; Kuntz, L.; Moon, R. Cheshire II: designing a next-generation online catalog. J. Am. Soc. Inform. Sci. **1996**, *47*(7), 555–567.

18. Larson, R.R. A logistic regression approach to distributed IR SIGIR 2002: Proceedings of the 25th Annual International ACM SIGIR Conference on Research and Development in Information Retrieval Tampere, Finland August, 11–15, 2002 ACM: New York, 2002; 399–400.

19. Ponte, J.M. Bruce Croft, W. A language modeling approach to information retrieval. *SIGIR '98: Proceedings of the 21ˢᵗ Annual ACM SIGIR Conference on Research and Development in Information Retrieval*, August 24–28, 1998; 275–281 Melbourne, Australia. ACM: New York.

20. The Lemur Project. The Lemur Toolkit for Language Modeling and Information Retrieval. Available at http://www.lemurproject.org.

21. Turtle, H. Bruce Croft, W. Inference networks for document retrieval Proceedings of the 13th International Conference on Research and Development in Information Retrieval; Vidick, J.-L. Ed.; Association for Computing Machinery: New York, 1990; 1–24.

22. Lee, J.H. Analyses of multiple evidence combination SIGIR '97: Proceedings of the 20th Annual International ACM SIGIR Conference on Research and Development in Information Retrieval Philadelphia, PA July 27–31, 1997 ACM: New York, 1997; 267–276.

23. Larson, R.R. A fusion approach to XML structured document retrieval. Inform. Retriev. **2005**, *8*, 601–629.

24. Harman, D. Relevance feedback and other query modification techniques. In *Information Retrieval: Data Structures & Algorithms*; Frakes, W., Baeza-Yates, R., Eds.; Prentice Hall: Upper Saddle River, NJ, 1992; 241–263.

Information Scattering

Suresh K. Bhavnani
Center for Computational Medicine and Bioinformatics, University of Michigan, Ann Arbor, Michigan, U.S.A.

Concepción S. Wilson
School of Information Systems, Technology and Management, University of New South Wales, Sydney, New South Wales, Australia

Abstract

Information scattering is an often observed phenomenon related to information collections where there are a few sources that have many items of relevant information about a topic, while most sources have only a few. This entry discusses the original discovery of the phenomenon, the types of information scattering observed across many different information collections, methods that have been used to analyze the phenomenon, explanations for why and how information scattering occurs, and how these results have informed the design of systems and search strategies. The entry concludes with future challenges related to building computational models to more precisely describe the process of information scatter, and algorithms which help users to gather highly scattered information.

INTRODUCTION

Whether one searches for research papers about a subject in journals, or for facts about a topic on the Web, a common observation is that there are very few sources (e.g., journals or Web pages) that contain many items of relevant information, while most sources have only a few. This phenomenon is referred to as *information scattering*, and has been a topic of research for over seven decades.

Although the first report on the phenomenon of information (or literature) scattering is generally attributed to Bradford,[1] it became increasingly clear by 1900 that a large part of the scientific literature on any subject seemed to be scattered across an indefinite number of generalist and specialist journals, with no direct relationship to the subject.[2] This phenomenon posed a problem for the bibliographic control of information because of the possibility of "missed literature" in any comprehensive search.

Bradford, a chemist turned librarian, helped to quantify this observation.[1] He recorded a regularity in the numbers of papers on two scientific subjects across different journals. He noticed that if the journals in each of the two scientific subjects were first ranked in order of the numbers of papers they contain on a subject, and then divided into, say, three groups with an equal number of papers, the numbers of journals in successive groups grew in the ratio of 1: k: k^2. For example, if 3000 papers on a subject were found in 800 journals, then the ratio of (ranked) journals, in successive groups of 1000 papers, is 42: 158: 600, or approximately 1: 3.8: 3.8^2.[3] The number of preselected groups can be other than three, which will result in a different number of journals in each group, but will result

in a similar regularity. This mathematical regularity, which predicts a core, middle, and peripheral groups of journals for any subject, is often referred to as *Bradford's Law of Scattering* and the resulting distribution of papers across journals as a *Bradford Distribution*.

When Bradford published the above quantitative findings, they were surprising as it suggested that the "missed literature" could be as much as two-thirds of the total for any subject. However, these results are relevant even today because current electronic databases (e.g., Web of Science or Scopus) analyze only a fraction of the world's journals leading to a similar result.

Subsequent to the publication of Bradford's[1] paper, there has been considerable debate about inconsistencies in the verbal and graphical description of the law,[4] and how to represent the law of scattering using more standard statistical measures such as frequency distributions. The latter has led to comparisons[5] with other similar laws such as Zipf's Law[6] and Lotka's Law[7] which describe skewed distributions for other kinds of information phenomena (e.g., the distribution of words across books or authors across papers). Such hyperbolic distributions are referred to as the informetric laws and are studied in the broader field of Informetrics, generally defined to include all quantifiable aspects of Information Science.[3,8] Bibliometrics, including bibliometric laws are (earlier) terms still used in the literature of information scattering.

Furthermore, there have been debates on how to define the concept of "subject"[9] or "topic"[10] (e.g., melanoma vs. melanoma treatment), which could produce different results when deriving Bradford distributions of papers across journals or studying the distributions of authors

Encyclopedia of Library and Information Sciences, Fourth Edition DOI: 10.1081/E-ELIS4-120043255

Copyright © 2017 by Taylor & Francis. All rights reserved.

Information Retrieval–
Information Society

across papers (Lotka's Law). However, despite these debates about specific details on the original formulation of Bradford's law of scattering, there is now general agreement that information scattering is a fundamental information phenomenon, and continues to be an active research area for bibliometricians, informetricians, scientometricians, webometricians, and other researchers.

This entry provides an overview of the research on information scattering based on five sections: (1) Types of information scatter; (2) Methods to analyze information scatter; (3) Explanations for the process of information scatter; (4) Implications of information scatter for search strategies and the design of search systems; and (5) Future research challenges.

TYPES OF INFORMATION SCATTER

One way to classify the different types of information scatter is based on how different granularities of *information objects* (e.g., articles, words, facts) are distributed across different granularities of *containers* (e.g., journals, books, Web pages). Several studies on information scatter have analyzed different combinations of information objects and containers, at different granularities. As discussed in the introduction, Bradford[1] analyzed the distribution of articles across journals and Zipf[6] analyzed the distribution of words within a book. More recently, research has analyzed the distribution of articles across online databases,[11–13] the distribution of images across databases,[14] and the distribution of facts about a topic across Web pages and Web sites.[15,16] In each case, while the exact fitted curves (e.g., power law, exponential, Poisson) of the distributions vary, the researchers have found strong similarity to the overall regularity originally observed by Bradford. For example, as shown in Fig. 1, the distribution of facts across Web pages is best fitted by a discrete exponential curve.[15]

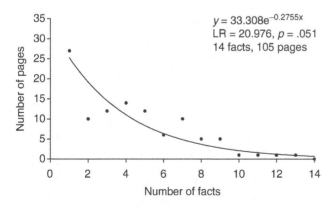

$$y = 33.308e^{-0.2755x}$$
$$LR = 20.976, p = .051$$
14 facts, 105 pages

Fig. 1 Distribution of facts about melanoma risk and prevention across high-quality healthcare pages. The distribution is best fit by a discrete exponential curve.
Source: From Bhavnani.[15]

Nicolaisen and Hjørland[9] have also classified the different types of information scatter in terms of (1) lexical scattering (words across collection of texts); (2) semantic scattering (concepts across texts); and (3) subject scattering (items useful to a given task or problem). Furthermore, the different types of information scatter constrain the relationships between object and container. For example, facts and articles about a topic can be in multiple Web pages or databases respectively. However, a particular article can be in only one journal. These constraints result in different relationships between information objects and containers.

METHODS USED TO ANALYZE INFORMATION SCATTER

There have been three principal methods used to quantitatively characterize information scatter: (1) Frequency distributions; (2) Coverage analyses; and (3) Network visualizations and analysis.

Frequency Distributions

Frequency distribution is a standard statistical method designed to show for a dataset the relationship between a ranked list of categories of observations (e.g., 1–10 journals, 11–20 journals, etc.) and the number or frequency of data items that fit into each category (e.g., 200 articles occurring in 1–10 journals). Typically the categories are placed on the *x*-axis and the number or frequency is on the *y*-axis, however, several researchers such as Zipf[6] chose to transpose them. Fig. 1 shows the frequency distribution of the number of facts about a topic across a ranked list of pages.[15] Depending on the data and the point that the researcher wishes to make, frequency distributions have been used in formats other than the above to characterize information scatter. For example, while the graph in Fig. 1 represents unique occurrences of facts in each category, a *cumulative frequency* distribution includes successive values. Furthermore, when there are a large number of categories and frequencies, the distribution are often plotted on a log–log plot which significantly reduces the length of the *x*-axis for such large datasets, while preserving the overall relationship.

Coverage Analyses

While the above distributions describe the data, they cannot reveal the minimum number of information containers to visit to get all the information objects. To reveal such details, researchers use distributions which are focused on coverage. Fig. 2 shows how many databases are needed to find all the papers related to a subject.[13] Such a distribution provides another measure for comparing the information scatter among topics or databases. Similar to Fig. 2,

Information Retrieval–
Information Society

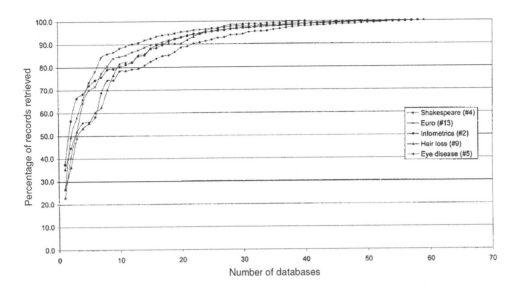

Fig. 2   Distribution of the percentage of journal articles retrieved as a function of the number of databases accessed.
Source: From Hood and Wilson.[13]

most results in information scatter studies have revealed that it takes many containers to get full coverage of information objects.

Network Visualizations and Analyses

Graphical networks are increasingly being used in a wide range of domains to analyze complex relationships such as information scatter. A network is a graph consisting of nodes and edges; nodes represent one or more types of entities (e.g., facts or Web pages), and edges between the nodes represent a specific relationship (e.g., a Web page contains a fact). Figure 3 shows a bipartite network (where edges exist only between two different types of entities) of how facts about melanoma risk and prevention, are contained in Web pages from the top 10 healthcare Web sites for melanoma information.

Networks have two advantages for analyzing information scatter: (1) They represent a particular relationship between different nodes and therefore can reveal patterns, such as how specific facts occur in different groups of Web pages and (2) They can be rapidly visualized and analyzed using a toolbox of network analysis methods and visualization algorithms. For example, Fig. 3 shows a force-directed layout algorithm which helps to visualize the relationship between Web pages and facts.[17] The algorithm simulates placing attractive forces between connected nodes and a weakly repulsive force between all nodes. The result is that facts which co-occur in many of the same pages are placed close to each other and close to the pages that mention them. The analysis revealed that there are two subgroups of pages (the top and bottom), which contain a concentration of different sets of facts, while another group of pages in the middle that contain both groups of facts. Furthermore, the visualization

reveals common and rare facts, and how they co-occur across the pages. Such visualizations (and related quantitative network measures used to verify the visual observations) therefore help to reveal new regularities about information scatter which are often concealed in aggregate measures such as frequency distributions.

EXPLANATIONS FOR INFORMATION SCATTER

While there are many studies that quantify information scatter, there are relatively few explanations for why information occurs. This scatter of articles across journals has been explained as follows: Although each field has a core set of a few journals where authors publish, there are many other journals with suitable subject scopes. Furthermore, because papers are often interdisciplinary in nature and therefore relevant to more than one field, authors may publish such papers in journals that are close to as well as distant to their main field. This results in the core journals of one field becoming the peripheral journals of another field.[18] Hood and Wilson[13] posit that information scatter could be related to the interdisciplinarity of topics: the more interdisciplinary a topic, the higher probability that the authors would choose to publish results in either a generalist journal related to the interdisciplinary topic or in a specialist journal of a field other than the authors' academic field. This publishing practice may result in the high scatter of such topics across journals and databases.

Bhavnani[15] found that facts (e.g., high UV exposure increases your risk of getting melanoma) about five healthcare topics (e.g., melanoma risk and prevention) were scattered across high-quality Web sites specializing in that topic. There were many pages which had few facts, few pages that had many facts, and no pages that had all

Information Retrieval–
Information Society

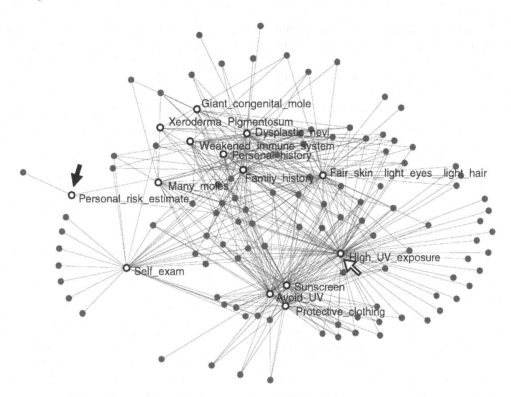

Fig. 3 The scatter network for melanoma risk/prevention showing how 14 facts (white labeled nodes) occur in 108 relevant pages (solid nodes). The white arrow points to a common fact and the black arrow points to a rare fact.
Source: From Adamic et al.[17]

the facts. Furthermore, the analysis revealed that underlying this distribution were three different page profiles that varied in fact density and role: *General pages* which contain many facts in medium amount of detail and play the role of providing an overview of the topic (e.g., What Are the Risk Factors for Melanoma?); *Specific pages* which contain few facts in a large amount of detail and play the role of providing detailed description of a few facts (e.g., Sunscreens and Prevention of Malignant Melanoma); and *Sparse pages* which contain few facts in a small amount of detail and were pages that were of broader topics (e.g., Skin Cancer) with a brief reference to the search topic.

The above observations led to the *information saturation* model[19] to explain this phenomenon. In this hypothetical model, Web page authors follow a process of *accumulation* to progressively add facts in detail to a page, until a length and detail saturation threshold is reached. At such a threshold, because the Web page becomes unwieldy and difficult to read, Web page authors heed design guidelines by removing detail about facts from these pages through the process of *abstraction* resulting in general pages. Concurrently, they also might be creating new pages to elaborate particular facts in high detail through the process of *specialization* resulting in specific pages. Finally as a topic becomes more important, the topic *permeates* otherwise irrelevant pages resulting in sparse pages. The above processes could lead to the creation of a large number of specific pages and sparse pages, while constraining the total

number of general pages. However, while there have been quantitative models that generate different informetric phenomena such as the distribution of papers per author,[20] there appears to be no research that has quantitatively modeled phenomena related to information scatter.

IMPLICATIONS OF INFORMATION SCATTER FOR SEARCH AND DESIGN

While there have been claims that Bradford's law has been useful for selecting journals for libraries or databases, there are actually no references about how it has been applied in practical library and information sciences.[9] Some researchers have explored the implications for the phenomenon of information scatter to search strategies, and the design of systems to help users find comprehensive information. Bates[21] proposed that because the core, middle, and peripheral regions of the Bradford distribution have different densities of relevant articles, they imply the use of different search strategies. For example, when searching for articles, users should identify the core set of journals for that topic. Because there is a high density of relevant articles in the core, browsing could be sufficient to find many relevant articles. In contrast, because the middle region has a lower density of relevant articles, users need to use queries that exploit systematic organizations of articles such as indexes. Finally, in the peripheral region where articles are very scattered, users need to use strategies such as *citation tracking* to quickly find the relevant articles.

While the above search strategies are implied by the density of articles *across* the different regions of the Bradford distribution, Bhavnani[15] leveraged the idea of information density *within* Web pages through the *general–specific–sparse* search strategy. This strategy recommends that users first find and read general pages about a topic to get an overview of the topic and to ensure that they do not miss any facts. Next (as often prescribed by earlier authors such as Kirk),[22] users should find specific pages that specialize in the facts they found within the general pages, to help elaborate facts of interest. Finally, they should broaden the search by finding and reading sparse pages to understand how the topic of interest relates to other topics.

The above strategy was operationalized in a Web site called the *Strategy Hub*[23] to help users find comprehensive healthcare information. In this system Web pages were organized in terms of general, specific, and sparse pages, and users were guided to read pages that followed that strategy. In a controlled experiment, users of the Strategy Hub found more comprehensive information in the same amount of time compared to equivalent users of MedlinePlus and Google.

FUTURE RESEARCH CHALLENGES

Future research challenges include: (1) building models to understand the process of information scatter; and (2) algorithms to help users gather highly scattered information. As described earlier, although a few researchers have proposed explanations for information scatter, none of these have been formalized into a model and tested to simulate the process of information scatter. Future research should therefore develop computational models to simulate information scatter over time so that the phenomenon can be precisely understood. The second area of potential future research is to leverage a precise understanding of information scatter to develop new algorithms which either automatically aggregate different types of scattered information or work interactively with users to help them find comprehensive information.

ACKNOWLEDGMENT

This research was supported by NIH grant # UL1RR024986.

REFERENCES

1. Bradford, S.C. Sources of information on specific subjects. Engineering **1934**, *137*(3550), 85–86. [Reprinted in: Bradford, S.C. (1948). Documentation. London: Crosby Lockwood.].

2. Campbell, F. *The Theory of National and International Bibliography*; Library Bureau: London, U.K., 1896.

3. Wilson, C.S. Informetrics. Ann. Rev. Inf. Sci. Technol. **1999**, *34*, 107–247.

4. Vickery, B.C. Bradford's law of scattering. J. Doc. **1948**, *4*(3), 198–203.

5. Chen, Y.; Leimkuhler, F.F. A relationship between Lotka's law, Bradford's law and Zipf's law. J. Am. Soc. Inf. Sci. **1986**, *37*(5), 307–314.

6. Zipf, G.K. *Human Behavior and the Principle of Least-Effort: An Introduction to Human Ecology*; Addison-Wesley: Cambridge, MA, 1949.

7. Lotka, A.J. The frequency distribution of scientific productivity. J. Washington Acad. Sci. **1926**, *16*(12), 317–323.

8. Bar-Ilan, J. Informetrics at the beginning of the 21st century—A review. J. Inform. **2008**, *2*(1), 1–52.

9. Nicolaisen, J.; Hjørland, B. Practical potentials of Bradford's law: A critical examination of the received view. J. Doc. **2007**, *63*(3), 359–377.

10. Wilson, C.S. *The Formation of Subject Literature Collections for Bibliometric Analysis: The Case of the Topic of Bradford's Law of Scattering*; The University of New South Wales: Sydney, New South Wales, Australia, 1995 [http://unsworks.unsw.edu.au/vital/access/manager/Repository/unsworks:412] PhD dissertation (accessed May 5, 2009).

11. Tenopir, C. Evaluation of database coverage: A comparison of two methodologies. Online Rev. **1982**, *6*, 423–441.

12. Lancaster, F.W.; Lee, J.-L. Bibliometric techniques applied to issue management: A case study. J. Am. Soc. Inform. Sci. **1985**, *36*(6), 389–397.

13. Hood, W.; Wilson, C.S. The scatter of documents over databases in different subject domains: How many databases are needed?. J. Am. Soc. Inform. Sci. **2001**, *52*(14), 1242–1254.

14. Bhavnani, S.K. The retrieval of highly scattered facts and architectural images: Strategies for search and design. Automation Construct. **2005**, *14*(6), 724–735.

15. Bhavnani, S.K. Why is it difficult to find comprehensive information? Implications of information scatter for search and design. J. Am. Soc. Inform. Sci. Technol. **2005**, *56*(9), 989–1003.

16. Over, P. TREC-6 Interactive track report. NIST Special Publication 500-242 The Seventh Text Retrieval Conference, Voorhees, E.M.; Harman, D.K., Eds.; Gaithersburg, MD, 1998; 20899–20941.

17. Adamic, L.A.; Bhavnani, S.K.; Xiaolin, S. Scatter networks: A new approach for analyzing information scatter on the web. New J. Phys. (Special Issue on Complex Systems) **2007**, *9*, 231.

18. Garfield, E. Bradford's law and related statistical patterns. Essays Inform. Sci. **1980**, *4*, 476–483.

19. Bhavnani, S.K.; Peck, F.A. Scatter Matters: Regularities and Implications for the Scatter of Healthcare Information on the Web. J. Am. Soc. Inform. Sci. Technol. (in press).

20. Goldstein, M.L.; Morris, S.A.; Yen, G.G. Group-based Yule model for bipartite author-paper networks. Phys. Rev. **2005**, *E*, 71.

Information Retrieval–
Information Society

21. Bates, M.J. Speculations on browsing, directed searching, and linking in relation to the Bradford Distribution. Emerging Frameworks and Methods Proceedings of the Fourth International Conference on Conceptions of Library and Information Science (CoLIS 4), Bruce, H., Fidel, R., Ingwersen, R., Vakkari, P., Eds.; Libraries Unlimited: Greenwood Village, CO, 2002; 137–150.

22. Kirk, T. Problems in library instruction in four-year colleges. In *Educating the Library User*; 1st Ed.; Lubans, J. Jr., Ed.; R.R. Bowker: New York, 1974; 83–103.

23. Bhavnani, S.K.; Bichakjian, C.K.; Johnson, T.M.; Little, R.J.; Peck, F.A.; Schwartz, J.L.; Strecher, V.J. Strategy hubs: Domain portals to help find comprehensive information. J. Am. Soc. Inform. Sci. Technol. **2006**, *57*(1), 4–24.

Information Science

Tefko Saracevic
*School of Communication and Information, Rutgers University, New Brunswick,
New Jersey, U.S.A.*

Abstract

The purpose of this entry is to provide an overview of information science as a field or discipline, including
a historical perspective to illustrate the events and forces that shaped it. Information science is a field of
professional practice and scientific inquiry dealing with effective communication of information and
information objects, particularly knowledge records, among humans in the context of social, organizational, and individual need for and use of information. Information science emerged in the aftermath of the
Second World War, as did a number of other fields, addressing the problem of information explosion and
using technology as a solution. Presently, information science deals with the same problems in the Web
and digital environments. This entry covers problems addressed by information science, the intellectual
structure of the field, and the description of main areas—information retrieval, human information behavior, metric studies, and digital libraries. This entry also includes an account of education related to
information science and conclusions about major characteristics.

INTRODUCTION

The purpose of this entry is to provide an overview of
information science as a field or discipline, including a
historical perspective to illustrate the events and forces
that shaped it.

Information science is the science and practice dealing
with the effective collection, storage, retrieval, and use of
information. It is concerned with recordable information
and knowledge, and the technologies and related services
that facilitate their management and use. More specifically, information science is a field of professional practice and scientific inquiry addressing the effective
communication of information and information objects,
particularly knowledge records, among humans in the
context of social, organizational, and individual need for
and use of information.[1] The domain of information science is the transmission of the universe of human knowledge in recorded form, centering on manipulation
(representation, organization, and retrieval) of information, rather than knowing information.[2]

There are two key orientations: toward the human
and social need for and use of information pertaining
to knowledge records, on the one hand, and toward
specific information techniques, systems, and technologies (covered under the name of *information retrieval*)
to satisfy that need and provide for effective organization and retrieval of information, on the other hand.
From the outset, information science had these two
orientations: one that deals with information need, or
more broadly human information behavior, and the
other that deals with information retrieval techniques
and systems.

Information science is a field that emerged in the aftermath of the Second World War, along with a number of new
fields, with computer science being but one example. While
developments and activities associated with information science already started by the end of 1940s, the very term
"information science" came into full use only at the start of
the 1960s. A significant impetus for the coalescence of the
field was the *International Conference on Scientific Information*, held in Washington, D.C., November 16–21, 1958,
sponsored by the (U.S.) National Science Foundation, the
National Academy of Sciences—National Research Council, and the American Documentation Institute, and attended
by some 1000 delegates from 25 countries. The conference
was meticulously planned for over 3 years and attracted wide
international attention. The 75 papers and lively discussions
that followed, all recorded in the *Proceedings* of over 1600
pages, affected the direction of research, development, and
professional practice in the field for at least a decade if not
longer.[3] It also affected the internationalization of the field
and the approaches used. They became global.

This entry covers problems addressed by information
science, the intellectual structure of the field, and the further description of main areas—information retrieval,
human information behavior studies, metric studies, and
digital libraries. At the end, the entry includes an account
of education related to information science and conclusions about major trends.

PROBLEMS ADDRESSED

To understand information science, as with any other field,
a description of problems addressed and methods used in

Encyclopedia of Library and Information Sciences, Fourth Edition DOI: 10.1081/E-ELIS4-120043704
Copyright © 2017 by Taylor & Francis. All rights reserved.

their solution is crucial. Generally, information science addressed the problem of information explosion and used information technology as a solution.

The rapid pace of scientific and technical advances that were accumulating since the start of the twentieth century produced by mid-century a scientific and technical revolution. A most visible manifestation of this revolution was the phenomenon of "information explosion," referring to the unabated, exponential growth of scientific and technical publications and information records of all kinds. The term "information explosion" is a metaphor (as is "population explosion") because nothing really exploded but just grew at a high rate, even exponentially at times. Simply put, information explosion is information and information objects piling up at a high rate. The problem this presents is getting to the right information as needed at a given time.

A number of scientists documented this growth, but none better and more vividly than Derek de Solla Price (1922–1983, British and American physicist, historian of science and information scientist), recognized as the father of scientometrics. In his seminal works, *Science since Babylon* followed by *Little Science, Big Science*, Price documented the exponential and logistical growth of scientific publications linking them with the growth of the number of scientists. The logistical growth started slow right after the appearance of the first scientific journals in the seventeenth century, accelerated by the start of the twentieth century and became explosive after the Second World War.[4,5]

The impetus for the development of information science, and even for its very origin and agenda, can be traced to a 1945 article, "As We May Think" by Vannevar Bush (1890–1974), a respected MIT scientist and, even more importantly, the head of the U.S. scientific effort during World War II.[6] In this influential article, Bush did two things: (1) he succinctly defined the critical and strategic problem of information explosion in science and technology that was on the minds of many, and (2) proposed a solution that was a "technological fix," and thus in tune with the spirit of the time. Both had wide appeal. Bush was neither the first nor the only one that addressed these issues, but he was listened to because of his stature. He defined the problem in almost poetic terms as "The summation of human experience is being expanded at a prodigious rate, and the means we use for threading through the consequent maze to the momentarily important item is the same as was used in the days of square-rigged ships." In other words, Bush addressed the problem of information explosion and the associated methods for finding relevant information.

As a solution, Bush proposed a machine, dubbed Memex, incorporating (in his words) a capability for "association of ideas," and the duplication of "mental processes artificially." A prescient anticipation of information science and artificial intelligence is evident. Memex,

needless to say, was never built, but to this day is considered an ideal, a wish list, an agenda, and, some think, a utopia. Information science is still challenged by the ever-worsening problem of information explosion, now universal and in a variety of digital formats, and the field is still trying to fix things technologically.

A number of scientists and professionals in many fields around the globe listened and took up Bush's challenge. Most importantly, governments listened, as well, and provided funding. The reasoning went something like this: Because science and technology are strategically important for society, efforts that help them, information activities in particular, are also important and need support. In the United States, the United Kingdom, and other countries, this led to the support of research and development related to information problems and solutions. By the end of the 1940s information science was well on its way.

Bush also participated in the establishment of the National Science Foundation (NSF) in the United States. The National Science Foundation Act of 1950 (P.L. 81-507) provided a number of mandates, among them "to foster the interchange of scientific information among scientists in the U.S. and foreign countries" [Section 3(a)3] and "to further the full dissemination of [scientific and technical] information of scientific value consistent with the national interest" [Section 11(g)]. The 1958 National Defense Education Act (P.L 85-864) (the "Sputnik act") enlarged the mandate: "The National Science Foundation shall [among others].undertake programs to develop new or improved methods, including mechanized systems, for making scientific information available" (Title IX, Section 901). By those mandates, an NSF division, which after a number of name and direction changes is now called the Division of Information and Intelligent Systems (IIS), has supported research in these areas since the 1950s. Information science evolution, at least in the United States., was greatly affected by the support of the U.S. government. In this respect it was not an exception. For instance, artificial intelligence, among others, was for decades supported by the U.S. government starting in the 1950s and ending by the 1990s.

Historically, one force affecting government support of information science, as of many other fields in the United States and a number of European countries, had to do with the cold war. Among others, one impetus was the establishment in 1952 of the All-Union Scientific and Technical Information Institute of the Academy of Sciences of the USSR (Russian acronym: VINITI). VINITI implemented a massive gathering and bibliographic control of scientific and technical information from around the world, eventually covering some 130 countries in 66 languages; it employed thousands of scientists and engineers full- and part-time. In the framework of the Cold War, VINITI was repeatedly brought up as a challenge needing a response.

At the start, information science was directed solely toward information explosion in science and technology.

However soon it expanded to other areas, including business, humanities, law, and eventually any area of human endeavor. In all areas, the phenomenon of information explosion is continuing and even accelerating to this day, particularly in the digital and Web environments. Addressing the problems of dealing with information explosion in any human area where information and knowledge records are overbearing is at the heart of information science. The approach to these problems involves a number of disciplines; in other words, information science, as many other modern fields, is interdisciplinary in nature.

In its goals and activities, information science established early, and maintains prominently, a social and human function—not only a technological one. On the social level, it participates actively, with many other fields, in the evolution of information society around the globe. Yet information science also has an individual human function. It relates to searching for and use of information as done by (or on behalf of) individuals. People individually search for and use relevant information. For information science, managing information is a global, social function, while providing and using information is an intense individual function.

INTELLECTUAL STRUCTURE

Information science, like any other field, has a dynamic intellectual structure; the objects of study and practice appear, change, disappear or are emphasized, realized, and interwoven in different ways over time. A general framework for the intellectual structure for the field can be derived from the Three Big Questions for information science as identified by Bates:[2]

1. The physical question: What are the features and laws of the recorded information universe?
2. The social question: How do people relate to, seek, and use information?
3. The design question: How can access to recorded information be made most rapid and effective?

Indeed, when looking at the literature of information science since its emergence to this day, the general structure can be discerned from these questions in both research and practice reported. While they can be approached individually, the three questions are not independent but interdependent. Effective design is highly dependent on the consideration of social and physical features. Over time, details in the answers differed greatly. But, as is seen from three examples below, the general structure stands.

Three examples illustrating the intellectual structure of information science spanning some five decades are presented here. The first one is the enumeration of topics in the proceedings of the mentioned 1959 *International Conference on Scientific Information*.[3] The second one is an author cocitation analysis mapping information science for the years 1972–1995.[7] And the third one is a similar analysis, using the same methods, mapping information science for the years 1996–2005.[8] Author cocitation analysis is a statistical and visualization method developed in information science that allows for mapping of connections between authors in a given domain and identifying clusters or oeuvres of work in that domain. The raw data reflects the number of times selected author pairs are cited together in papers, regardless of which of their work is cited.

The 1959 Proceedings had seven areas covering the research, practice, and interests of information science at the time and illustrating the intellectual structure of the field by the end of 1950s. These were

1. *Literature and reference needs of scientists*. An example of a title of a paper in the area: An Operations Research Study of the Dissemination of Scientific Information.
2. *The function and effectiveness of abstracting and indexing services*. A paper example: All-Union Institute for Scientific and Technical Information (VINITI).
3. *Effectiveness of monographs, compendia, and specialized centers. Present trends and new and proposed techniques and types of services*. A paper example: Scientific, Technical, and Economic Information in a Research Organization.
4. *Organization of information for storage and search. Comparative characteristics of existing systems*. A paper example: The Evaluation of Systems Used in Information Retrieval.
5. *Organization of information for storage and retrospective search. Intellectual problems and equipment considerations in the design of new systems*. A paper example: Linguistic Transformations for Information Retrieval.
6. *Organization of information for storage and retrospective search. Possibility for a general theory*. A paper example: The Structure of Information Retrieval Systems.
7. *Responsibilities of government, professional societies, universities, and industry for improved information services and research*. A paper example: Differences in International Arrangements for Financial Support of Information Services.

Results from the next two studies are comparable—they used the same set of basic data (major journals in information science) and the same method (author cocitation analysis and mapping).[7,8] The authors of both studies mapped clusters of authors, classifying their areas of publications in a number of categories—they labeled the categories—and showing the relation or lack thereof between

Table 1 Intellectual structure of information science as presented in studies of two time periods (labels provided by authors of respective studies).

1972–1995	1996–2006
1. Experimental retrieval (design and evaluation of IR systems)	1. User studies (information seeking/searching behavior, user-centered approach to IR, users and use)
2. Citation analysis (interconnectedness of scientific and scholarly literatures)	2. Citation analysis (scientometrics; evaluative bibliometrics)
3. Practical retrieval (applications in "real world")	3. Experimental retrieval (algorithms, models, systems, evaluation of IR)
4. Bibliometrics (statistical distributions of texts and mathematical modeling)	4. Webometrics
5. General library systems (library automation, library operations research, services)	5. Visualization of knowledge domains (author cocitation analysis)
6. Science communication (including social sciences)	6. Science communication
7. User theory (information needs and users)	7. Users' judgment of relevance (situational relevance)
8. Online Public Access Catalogs (OPACs) (design, subject searching)	8. Information seeking and context
9. Imported ideas (information theory, cognitive science, etc.)	9. Children's information searching behavior (usability, interface design)
10. Indexing theory	10. Metadata and digital resources
11. Citation theory	11. Bibliometric models and distributions
12. Communication theory	12. Structured abstracts (academic writing)

categories. The categories reflecting clusters of work in the two studies, as labeled by the authors, are shown in Table 1.

Some of the areas in the three examples remain the same over time, showing an overall stability of general interests and foci of information science from its emergence to this day. The three areas of major and continuing interest are *information retrieval, user and use studies, and metric studies*. They correspond to the Three Big Questions for information science listed at the start of this section. Naturally, the variety and type of work in these three areas has changed and evolved over time, as elaborated below, but the general thrust and emphasis stayed stable.

Some areas have disappeared. The interest in the functioning of abstracting and indexing services, specialized information centers, and the responsibilities of different agencies for improved information services, so prominent in the 1959 Proceedings, are not prominent at all in later periods. Online Public Access Catalogs (OPACs) were prominent as an area cluster in the period 1971–1995 but did not appear in the 1996–2005 period; research in this area waned. The same holds for general library systems, covering library automation; the area was prominent during 1971–1995, but not anymore. The field had a prominent area of imported ideas between 1971–1995, covering the deliberations of adaptation and the application of various theories from information theory (Shannon), sociology (Merton), and other fields, but not anymore. Theory importing is not a major area any longer in information science. However, there is a significant exception. A major trend is evident in the incorporation of ideas, theories, and methods from the social sciences into many studies related to human information behavior to such an extent that they are not considered as imported any more.

In the Web age, covering the period 1996–2005, new areas have appeared. Not surprisingly, one of them is webometrics, extending the metric studies to the Web. Another new area is the visualization of knowledge domains, providing a new method of presenting retrieval processes and results and also extending citation and metric analyses.

The intellectual structure of information science also covers two camps of authors concentrating in different areas. White and McCain called them "retrieval people" and "literature people."[7] The first group congregates in the area of information retrieval; the second in the area of human information behavior and metric studies. They represent two broad branches of information science, one system-oriented and the other user-oriented. They are relatively isolated from each other. In the words of White and McCain again: "As it turns out, information science looks rather like Australia: Heavily coastal in its development, with a sparsely settled interior." The relative isolation is conceived as unproductive for all areas. There were a number of calls for collaboration, some quite impatient, and a few efforts at actually bridging the gap, but the gap has yet to be effectively bridged.

INFORMATION RETRIEVAL

Considering the Three Big Questions for information science, stated above, this section addresses the design question: *How can access to recorded information be made most rapid and effective?* The area is concentrated on systems and technology.

Right after the Second World War a variety of projects started applying a variety of technologies to the problem of controlling information explosion, particularly in

Information Retrieval–
Information Society

science and technology. In the beginning the technologies were punched cards and microfilm, but soon after computers became available the technology shifted to, and stayed with, computers. Originally, many activities involved specific fields of application, such as chemistry. By the mid-1960s computer science joined the efforts in a big way.

Various names were applied to these efforts, such as "*machine literature searching,*" or "*mechanical organization of knowledge*" but by the mid-1950s "*information retrieval*" prevailed. Actually, the term "*information retrieval*" (IR) was coined by mathematician and physicist Calvin N. Mooers (1919–1994), a computing and IR pioneer, just as the activity started to expand from its beginnings after Second World War. He posited that

> Information retrieval is ... the finding or discovery process with respect to stored information ... useful to [a user]. Information retrieval embraces the intellectual aspects of the description of information and its specification for search, and also whatever systems, technique, or machines that are employed to carry out the operation.[9]

Over the next half century, information retrieval evolved and expanded widely. In the beginning IR was static. Now it is highly interactive. Earlier it dealt only with representations—indexes, abstracts—now it deals with full texts as well. It concentrated on print only, now it covers every medium, ..., and so on. Advances in the field are impressive, now covering the Web, and still go on. Contemporary search engines are about information retrieval. But in a basic sense, IR still continues to concentrate on the same fundamental things Mooers described. Searching was and still is about retrieval of relevant (useful) information or information objects.

It is of interest to note what made IR different, compared to many other techniques, applied to the control of information records over a long period of time. The key difference between IR and related methods and systems that long preceded it—such as classifications, subject headings, various indexing methods, or bibliographic descriptions, including the contemporary Functional Requirements for Bibliographic Records—is that IR specifically included "specification for search." The others did not. Since the days of the pioneers in bibliographic organization in the United States, Charles Ammi Cutter (1837–1903) and Melvil Dewey (1851–1931), the emphasis was on the creation of systems for bibliographic representation and control. In these long-standing techniques, what users' needs are and should be fulfilled was specified in detail. Following that, the representation of information objects was also prescribed in detail. In other words, data about information objects (books, articles, etc.) in bibliographic records are organized in a way to fulfill the specified needs. However, how the search ought to be done was not specified or addressed at all. Searching was

assumed and left to itself—it just happens. In IR, users' needs are assumed as well, but the search process is specified in algorithmic detail and data is organized to enable the search. Search engines are about searching to start with; everything else is subsumed to that function.

Relevance

The fundamental notion used in bibliographic description and in all types of classification or categorization, including those used in contemporary databases, is *aboutness*. Cataloging and classification describe what the documents were all about with an implied idea that *about*, among others, may facilitate searching. Machine Readable Cataloging (MARC) that was developed by Henriette Avram (1919–2006) at the Library of Congress beginning in the 1960s follows the same principle. Online Public Access Catalogs (OPACs) that emerged more than a decade later are based on MARC. They include various search mechanisms, but are relatively difficult and ineffective as search tools. While implying searching *aboutness* does not really facilitate it.

The fundamental notion used in IR is *relevance*. Retrieval is not about any kind of information, and there are a great many, but about *relevant* information (or as Mooers called it *useful to a user* or Bush *momentarily important*). Basically, relevant information is that which pertains to the matter or problem at hand. Fundamentally, bibliographic description and classification concentrate on describing and categorizing information objects. IR is also about that, but in addition IR is about searching, and searching is about relevance. Very often, the differences between databases and IR are discussed in terms of differences between structured and unstructured data, which is OK, but the fundamental difference is in the basic notion used: *aboutness* in the former and *relevance* in the latter. The two notions are not at all equivalent. Relevance entered as a basic notion through the specific concentration on searching. True, searching for relevant information precedes IR by centuries, if not millennia, but in IR the process was adapted as primary orientation.

By choosing relevance as a basic, underlying notion of IR, related information systems, services, and activities—and with it, the whole field of information science—went in a direction that differed from approaches taken in librarianship, documentation, and related information services, and even in expert systems and contemporary databases in computer science.

In this sense, information science is on the one hand connected to relevance and on the other hand to technologies and techniques that enhance probability of the retrieval of relevant and the suppression of nonrelevant information. Relevance, as a basic notion in information science, is a human notion, widely understood in similar ways from one end of the globe to the other. This affected the widespread acceptance of information retrieval techniques globally. However, relevance, and with it information retrieval, involves a number of complexities: linguistic, cognitive, psychological, social, and technological, requiring different solutions. But the basic idea that searching is for relevant information does not.

As mentioned, relevance is a human notion. In human applications, relevance judgments exhibit inconsistencies, situational and dynamic changes, differences in cognitive interpretations and criteria, and other untidy properties common to human notions. This stimulated theoretical and experimental investigations about the notion and applications of relevance in information science. The experiments, mostly connected to relevance judgments and clues (what affected the judgments, what are people using in judgments) started already in the 1960s and continue to this day. The idea was and still is that findings may affect development of more effective retrieval algorithms. This is still more of a goal; actual translations from research results to development and practical applications were meager, if attempted at all.

Algorithms

IR systems and techniques, no matter in what form and including contemporary search engines, are geared toward retrieval of relevant information. To achieve that they use algorithms—logical step-by-step procedures—for the organization, searching, and retrieval of information and information objects. Contemporary algorithms are complex and in a never-ending process of improvement, but they started simple and still incorporate those simple roots.

The first and simple algorithm (although at the time it was not called that) applied in the 1940s and early 1950s was aimed at searching and retrieving from edge-notched punch cards using the operation of Boolean algebra. In the early 1950s Mortimer Taube (1910–1965), another IR pioneer and entrepreneur, founded a company named Documentation Inc. devoted to the development and operation of systems for the organization and retrieval of scientific and technical information. Taube broke away from the then-standard methods of subject headings and classification, by developing Uniterms and coordinate indexing. Uniterms were keywords extracted from documents; a card for a given Uniterm listed the documents that were indexed by that Uniterm. Coordinate indexing was actually a search and retrieval method for comparing (coordinating) document numbers appearing on different Uniterm cards by using a logical AND, OR, or, NOT operation. Although at the time the algorithm was not recognized as Boolean algebra by name, the operation was in effect the first application of a Boolean algorithm for information retrieval. Uniterms and coordinate indexing were controversial for a time but soon it was recognized that the technique was a natural for use as a base for computerized search and retrieval. All IR systems built in the next few decades incorporated Boolean algebra as a search algorithm and most have it under the hood today, along with other algorithms. All search engines offer, among others, Boolean search capabilities.

At the start of IR, and for a long time to come, the input—indexes and abstracts in particular—was constructed manually. Professionals indexed, abstracted, classified, and assigned other identifiers to information objects in a variety of fields. Input was manual; output—searching—was automated. Big online systems and databases, such as Medline and Dialog, which came about respectively in 1971 and 1972 and operate to this day, were based on that paradigm. Efforts to automate input, as well, commenced in the 1950s by the development of various algorithms for handling of texts. They took much longer to be developed and adopted more operationally than searching algorithms—the problem was and still is much tougher.

Hans Peter Luhn (1896–1964) a prodigious inventor with a broad range of patents joined IBM in 1941 and became a pioneer in development of computerized methods for handling texts and other IR methods in the 1950s. Luhn pioneered many of the basic techniques now common to IR in general. Among others, he invented the automatic production of indexes from titles and texts—Key Words in Context or KWIC indexing that lead to automatic indexing from full texts; automatic abstracting that lead to summarization efforts; and Selective Dissemination of Information (SDI) to provide current awareness services that led to a number of variations, including today's RSS (Really Simple Syndication). The demonstration of automatic KWIC indexing was the sensation at the aforementioned 1959 International Conference on Scientific Information.

Luhn's basic idea to use various properties of texts, including statistical ones, was critical in opening the handling of input by computers for IR. Automatic input joined the already automated output. Of course, Luhn was not the only one who addressed the problems of deriving representations from full texts. In the same period of the 1950s for instance, Phyllis Baxendale developed methods of linguistic analysis for automatic phrase detection and syntactic manipulations and Eugene Garfield was among the first, if not even the first, to join automated input and output in an operational system, that of citation indexing and searching.

Further advances that eventually defined modern IR came about in the 1960s. Statistical properties of texts—frequency and distribution of words in individual documents and in a corpus or collection of documents—were expressed in terms of probabilities that allowed for a variety of algorithms not only to extract index terms, but also to indicate term relations, distances, and clusters. The relations are inferred by probability or degree of certainty. They are inductive not deductive. The assumption, traced to Luhn, was that frequency data can be used to extract

Information Retrieval–
Information Society

significant words to represent the content of a document and the relation among words. The goal was to find a match between queries and potentially relevant documents, based on a probability of documents being relevant. Once expressed in terms of probabilities, documents can be ranked from those that have a higher probability to those that have a lower probability of a match. There are many methods for doing this. The basic plan was to search for underlying mathematical structures to guide computation. These were powerful ideas that led to an ever-expanding array of new and improved algorithms for indexing and other information organization methods, along with the associated search and retrieval. Moreover, they lend themselves to experimentation.

A towering figure in advancing experimentation with algorithms for IR was Gerard (Gerry) Salton (1927–1995), a computer scientist and academic (Harvard and Cornell Universities) who firmly connected IR with computer science. Within a framework of a laboratory he established, (entitled the SMART project) Salton and collaborators, mostly his students, ran IR experiments from the mid-1960s to the time of his death in 1995. Many new IR algorithms and approaches were developed and tested; they inspired practical IR developments and further IR research in many countries around the world. Many of his students became leaders in the IR community. Salton was very active nationally and internationally in the promotion of IR; he is the founder of the Special Interest Group on Information Retrieval (SIGIR) of the Association of Computing Machinery (ACM). SIGIR became the preeminent international organization in IR with annual conferences that are the main event for reporting advances in IR research. As a result of global interest in IR, these conferences now alternate between continents. While Salton's research group started in the United States, today many similar groups operate in academic and commercial environments around the globe.

Contemporary IR has spread to many domains. Originally, IR concentrated on texts. This has expanded to any and all other media. Now there are research and pragmatic efforts devoted to IR in music, spoken words, video, still and moving images, and multimedia. While originally IR was monolingual, now many efforts are devoted to cross-lingual IR (CLIR). Other efforts include IR connected with Extensible Markup Language (XML), software reuse, restriction to novelty, adversarial conditions, social tagging, and a number of special applications.

With the appearance and rapid growth of the Web starting in the mid-1990s many new applications or adaptations of IR sprouted, as well. The most prominent are search engines. While a few large search engines dominate the scene globally, practically, there is no nation that does not have its own versions tailored to its own populace and interests. While practical IR was always connected with commercial concerns and information industry, the appearance, massive deployment and use of search engines pushed IR into a major role commercially, politically, and socially. It produced another effect, as well. Most, if not all, search engines use many well-known IR algorithms and techniques. But many search engines, particularly the major ones, in addition have developed and deployed their own IR algorithms and techniques, not known in detail and not shared with the IR community. They support aggressive efforts in IR research and development, mostly in-house. Contemporary IR also includes a proprietary branch, like many other industries.

Testing

Very soon after IR systems appeared, a number of claims and counterclaims were made about the superiority of various IR methods and systems, without supporting evidence. In response, the perennial questions asked of all systems were raised: *What is the effectiveness and performance of given IR approaches? How do they compare?* It is not surprising that these questions were raised in IR. At the time; most developers, funders, and users associated with IR were engineers, scientists, or worked in related areas where the question of testing was natural, even obligatory.

By the mid-1950s suggestions for two measures for evaluation of effectiveness of IR systems were made; they were precision and recall. Precision measures how many of *retrieved* items (let's say documents) were relevant or conversely how many were noise. Recall measures how many of the *potentially relevant items in a given file or system* were actually retrieved, or conversely how many were not retrieved even though they were relevant. The measures were widely adopted and used in most evaluation efforts since. Even today, the two measures, with some variation, are at the base for evaluation of the effectiveness of output using given retrieval algorithms and systems. It is significant to note that the two measures are based on the comparison of human (user or user surrogate) judgments of relevance with IR algorithms' or systems' retrieval of what it considered as relevant, where human judgment is the gold standard.

A pioneer in IR testing was Cyril Cleverdon (1914–1997), a librarian at the Cranfield Institute of Technology (now Cranfield University) in the United Kingdom. From the late-1950s until the mid-1970s Cleverdon conducted a series of IR tests under the name "Cranfield tests." Most famous were the tests sponsored by the (U.S.) National Science Foundation from 1961 to 1966 that established a model of IR systems (the so-called traditional model that concentrates on query on the one end and matched with static retrieval from an IR system or algorithm on the other end), and a methodology for testing that is still in use. One of the significant and surprising finding from Cranfield tests was that uncontrolled vocabularies based on natural language (such as keywords picked by a computer algorithm) achieve retrieval effectiveness comparable to vocabularies with elaborate controls (such as those using thesaurus, descriptors, or classification assigned by indexers). The findings, as expected, drew skepticism and strong critique, but were confirmed later by Salton and others. Not surprisingly these conclusions caused a huge controversy. But they also provided recognition of automatic indexing as an effective approach to IR.

Salton coupled development of IR algorithms and approaches with testing; he enlarged on Cranfield approaches and reaches. Everything that Salton and his group proposed and developed was mandatorily tested. The norm was established: No new algorithms or approaches were accepted without testing. In other words, testing became mandatory for any and all efforts that propose new algorithms and methods. It became synonymous with experimentation in IR.

After Salton, contemporary IR tests and experiments are conducted under the umbrella of the Text REtrieval Conference (TREC). TREC, started in 1992 and continuing to date, is a long-term effort at the (U.S.) National Institute for Standards and Technology (NIST), that brings various IR teams together annually to compare results from different IR approaches under laboratory conditions. Over the years, hundreds of teams from dozens of countries participated in TREC covering a large number of topics. TREC is dynamic: As areas of IR research change, so do the topics in TREC. Results are at the forefront of IR research.[10]

In many respects, IR is the main activity in information science. It has proved to be a dynamic and ever-growing area of research, development, and practice, with strong commercial interest and global use. Rigorous adherence to testing contributed to the maturing of information retrieval.

HUMAN INFORMATION BEHAVIOR

Considering the Three Big Questions for information science, stated above, this section addresses the social and individual question: *How do people relate to, seek and use information?* While often connected with systems, the emphasis in this area of information science is on people rather than systems.

Human information behavior refers to a wide range of processes which people employ when engaged with information and to related cognitive and social states and effects. In his book that comprehensively covers research on information behavior (with over 1100 documents cited, most since 1980), Case defines that information behavior:

> "encompasses information seeking as well as the totality of other *unintentional* or *passive* behaviors (such as glimpsing or encountering information), as well as purposive behaviors that do not involve seeking, such as actively *avoiding* information [11, p. 5]. (emphasis in the original).

As can be imagined, human information behavior, as with many other human behaviors, is complex, not fully understood, and of interest in a number of fields. A great many studies and a number of theories address various aspects related to human information behavior in psychology, cognitive science, brain sciences, communication, sociology, philosophy and related fields, at times using different terminology and classifications. Under various names, scholarly curiosity about human information behavior is longstanding, going back to antiquity.

Of particular interest in information science are processes, states, and effects that involve *information needs and use* and *information seeking and searching*. The order in which these two major areas of human information behavior studies are listed represents their historic emergence and emphasis over time.

Historically, the study of information needs and use preceded information science. Many relevant studies were done during the 1930s and 1940s in librarianship, communication, and specific fields, such as chemistry, concentrating on use of sources, media, systems, and channels. Already by the 1950s this area of study was well developed in information science—for instance, the aforementioned 1959 *Proceedings of the International Conference on Scientific Information*[3] had a whole area with a number of papers devoted to the topic. The *Annual Review of Information Science and Technology* had regular annual chapters on "information needs and use" starting with the first volume in 1966 and ongoing through 1978. Thereafter, chapters covering this area were broadened to cover in addition various aspects or contexts of information behavior, including information seeking. This change illustrates how the emphasis in topics studied significantly changed over time. Studies in human information behavior are evolving and slowly maturing.

Information Needs and Use

Over the years "information needs and use" was used as a phrase. However, while related information need and information use are distinct concepts. *Information need* refers to a cognitive or even a social state and *information use* to a process.

For decades, *information need* was used as a primitive concept on two levels: on an individual level it signified a cognitive state which underlies questions posed to information systems and requests for information in general; on a social level it signified information required for functioning and keeping abreast of a whole group, such as chemists. On the first, or cognitive, level it was assumed that individuals ask questions and request information because of a recognition that the knowledge one has is inadequate for a given problem or situation; it is subjective as represented by individuals; it is in the head of a user. On the second, or social, level it was assumed that a social group with common characteristics, goals, or tasks shares common information requirements that may be satisfied by specific information sources; it is more objective as determined by a group of individuals on the basis of some consensus or by experts based on experience. In general, information need was considered as instrumental in reaching a desired informational goal.

The concept of *information need* was entrenched until the start of the 1980s. Slowly, critiques of the concept gained ground by pointing out that it is nebulous, as are most other "need" concepts in every field where they are used; that it is often substituted for "information demand," which is a very different process and not a state; that it is associated with behaviorism, which in itself fell out of favor; that it is a subjective experience in the mind of a person and therefore not accessible for observation; and that it ignores wider social aspects and realities. Moreover, underlying assumptions were challenged. By the end of the decade information need was largely abandoned as a subject of study or explanation of underlying information processes. Instead, studies of information seeking and other aspects of information behavior gained ground. However, information need is still represented in the traditional IR model (mentioned above) as the source of questions that are submitted to retrieval systems. It is not further elaborated in that framework, just listed as a primitive concept.

The concept of *information use* is more precise and it is operationally observable. Studies of information use were done for a long time and in many fields. For instance, use of libraries or use of literature in a given area was investigated long before information science emerged and before information use became one of the major topics of information science research. In information science, information use refers to a process in which information, information objects, or information channels are drawn on by information users for whatever informational purpose. The process is goal-directed. Questions are asked: *Who are the users of a given information system or resource? What information objects do they use? What information channels are used to gather information?* Or in other words: *Who uses what? How? For what purpose?*

The studies addressing these questions were, and still are, pragmatic, retrospective, and descriptive. Historically, as they emerged in the early 1950s, they were directed toward fields and users in science and technology. This is not surprising. As mentioned, information science emerged as a response to the problem of information explosion in science and technology thus the use studies were in those areas. Regarding topics, many early studies addressed users' distribution of time and resources over different kinds of documents: scientific journals, books, patents, abstracting and indexing services, and so on. As the realm of information science expanded to cover other areas and populations, use studies expanded their coverage as well. By the 1990s, studies emerged that also covered information use in many populations and activities, including the small worlds of everyday living.

The early motivation for user studies was pragmatic: to discover guidelines for the improvement of practice. This was of great concern to practitioners, and consequently most such studies were done by practitioners. By 1970 or so there was a move toward academic studies of information use motivated by a desire to understand the process better and provide models and theories. By 2008 there are still two worlds of user studies: one more pragmatic, but now with the goal of providing the basis for designing more effective and usable contemporary IR and Web systems, including search engines, and the other more academic, still with the goal of expanding understanding and providing more plausible theories and models. The two worlds do not interact well.

Information Seeking and Searching

Information seeking refers to a set of processes and strategies dynamically employed by people in their quest for and pursuit of information. Information seeking also refers to the progression of stages in those processes. In the majority of theories and investigations about information seeking, the processes are assumed to be goal directed. In his aforementioned book, Case defines information seeking as

"a conscious effort to acquire information in response to a need or gap in your knowledge." [[11], p. 5]

Not surprisingly, information seeking is of interest in a number of fields from psychology, sociology, and political science to specific disciplines and professions, often under different names and classifications, such as information gathering or information foraging. The literature on the theme is large, spanning many decades. Historically, information-seeking concerns and studies in information science emerged by the late 1970s in academic rather than pragmatic environments. Only lately have they turned toward pragmatic concerns, as well. It was recognized that information use was the end process, preceded by quite different, elaborate, and most importantly, dynamic behavior and processes not well understood. The studies began in large part by trying to observe and explain what people do when they search and retrieve information from various retrieval systems, to expand fast to involving a number of different contexts, sources—formal and informal—and situations or tasks. The dynamic nature of information-seeking became the prime focus in observations, experiments, models, and theories. Questions are asked: *What do people actually do when they are in a quest for and pursuit of information? How are they going about and how are they changing paths as they go about? What are they going through on a personal level? What information channels are used to gather information? How?*

Information seeking, as is the case with most human information behavior, is highly dependent on context.

While context may be everything, the very concept of context is ill defined, or taken as primitive and not defined. The contexts may involve various motivations for information seeking, various cognitive and affective states, various social, cultural, or organizational environments, various demographic characteristics, values, ways of life, and so on. A number of information-seeking studies were indeed directed toward various contexts. Thus, there is a wide range of such studies regarding context, accompanied by difficulties toward generalization.

To deal with more defined contexts, and enable specific observation, task-oriented information-seeking studies emerged in the 1990s. And they are going strong up to this day. Task studies deal with specific goals, mostly related to assignments in defined circumstances, time periods, or degree of difficulty. They represent a step in the ongoing evolution, not only of information-seeking studies in particular but also in information behavior research in general. By the 2000s we also see the emergence of studies in collaborating behaviors, also related to given tasks.

Information searching is a subset of information seeking, and in the context of information science, it refers to processes used for interrogating different information systems and channels in order to retrieve information. It is the most empirical and pragmatic part of information-seeking studies. Originally, search studies concentrated on observation and modeling of processes in the interrogation of IR systems. With the advent of digital environments, the focus shifted toward Web searching by Web users. New observational and experimental methods emerged, becoming a part of exploding Web research. Such search studies have a strong pragmatic orientation in that many are oriented toward improving search engines and interfaces, and enhancing human–computer interactions.

Models and Theories

The research area and accompanying literature of information behavior in information science is strong on models and theories. It follows a tradition and direction of such research in many other disciplines, particularly psychology, communication, and philosophy. Being primarily pragmatic and retrospective, information use studies were not a great source for models and theories. In contrast, broader studies of information behavior, and particularly of information seeking, are brimming with them. Numerous models and theories emerged, some with more, others with less staying power. The extent of this work is exemplified in a compilation *Theories of Information Behavior*,"[12] where some 70 different (or differing) theories and models are synthesized. To illustrate, we should sample three well-known theories, each in one of the three areas of human information behavior described above. Each of them is widely accepted and cited, and tested, as well.

What is behind an information need? Why do people seek information in the first place? Starting in late 1970s and for the next two decades or so, Nicholas Belkin and his colleagues addressed this question by considering that the basic motivation for seeking information is what they called "anomalous state of knowledge" (ASK), thus the "ASK theory," or as they called it, "ASK hypothesis" (described among others in Belkin, Oddy, and Brooks).[13] Explicitly following a cognitive viewpoint, they suggest that the reason for initiating an information-seeking process could be best understood at the cognitive level, as a user (information seeker) recognizes that the state of his/her knowledge is in some way inadequate (anomalous) with respect to the ability to resolve a problematic situation and achieve some goal. Anomaly was used explicitly, not only to indicate inadequacy due to lack of knowledge, but also due to other problems, such as uncertainty of application to a given problem or situation. ASK theory is an attempt to provide an explicit cognitive explanation of information need or gap by proposing specific reasons why people engage in information seeking. It also suggests that anomalous states could be of different types. One of the strengths of ASK theory is that, unlike many other similar theories, it was successfully tested in a few experiments. One of the weaknesses is that it rests solely on a cognitive basis, using the problem or situation toward which the whole process is oriented as a primitive term.

What is behind the information search process? How is it constructed? Carol Collier Kuhlthau addressed these questions in a series of empirically grounded studies through a period of some 20 years starting in the early 1980s.[14] Her model and theory, called the Kuhlthau Information Search Model, provides a conceptual and relatively detailed framework of the information-seeking and search process. It is based on the personal construct theory in psychology that views learning as a process of testing constructs; consequently it views the search as a dynamic process of progressive construction. The model describes common patterns in the process of information seeking for complex tasks that have a discrete beginning and ending over time and that require construction and learning. The innovative part of the model is that it integrates thoughts, feelings, and actions in a set of stages from initiation to presentation of the search process. Not only cognitive, but also affective aspects, such as uncertainty connected with anxiety, are brought in the explanation of the process. The work started within learning context in schools, continued with a series of longitudinal studies, and moved on to a series of case studies in a number of fields. The strength of the model is that it incorporates affective factors that play a great role not only in searching but in human information behavior at large; furthermore it was extensively verified and revised over time. The weakness is that its educational roots are still recognizable—many search processes have different goals and contexts, thus the model may not fit.

What types of activities are involved in information seeking in general and information retrieval searching in particular? What is the relation between different activities? Starting in the mid-1980s and continuing for close to two decades, David Ellis and his colleagues addressed these questions in a series of empirical studies that led to the formulation and continuing refinement of a model known as Ellis's Model of Information-Seeking Behavior, primarily oriented toward behavior in information retrieval.[15] The model is based on a theoretical premise that the study of behavior presents a more tractable and observable focus for study than cognitive approaches. Consequently, its base is behavioral rather than cognitive. The model incorporates a premise that the complex process of information seeking, particularly as related to information retrieval, rests on a relatively small and finite number of different types of interacting activities, these include starting, chaining, browsing, differentiating, monitoring, and extracting. The explicit goal of studies associated with Ellis' model was pragmatic: to inform design and operations of IR systems. The strength of the model is in the reduction of a complex process to a relatively small set of distinct and dynamically interacting processes. The weakness is that it does not address cognitive and affective aspects, shown to be of importance.

The three models can be considered also as theories of information behavior. In turn, each of them is based on a different approach and theory. The first one is related to cognition as treated in cognitive science, the second to personal construct theory in psychology, and the third to behaviorism in psychology. This illustrates different approaches and multidisciplinary connections of human information behavior studies in information science. As yet, they have not found a common ground.

METRICS

Considering the Three Big Questions for information science, stated above, this section addresses the physical question: *What are the features and laws of the recorded information universe?* While often connected with systems, the emphasis in this area of information science is on information objects or artifacts rather than systems; these are the content of the systems. It is about characterizing content objects.

Metrics, such as econometrics, biometrics, sociometrics, etc., are important components in many fields; they deal with statistical properties, relations, and principles of a variety of entities in their domain. Metric studies in information science follow these by concentrating on statistical properties and the discovery of associated relations and principles of information objects, structures, and processes. The goals of metric studies in information science, as in other fields, are to characterize statistically entities under study and more ambitiously to discover regularities

and relations in their distributions and dynamics in order to observe predictive regularities and formulate laws.

The metric studies in information science concentrate on a number of different entities. To denote a given entity under study over time, these studies were labeled by different names. The oldest and most widely used is *bibliometrics*—the quantitative study of the properties of literature, or more specifically of documents, and document-related processes. Bibliometric studies in information science emerged in the 1950s right after the start of the field. *Scientometrics*, which came about in the 1960s, refers to bibliometric and other metric studies specifically concentrating on science. *Informetrics*, emerging in the 1990s, refers to the quantitative study of properties of all kinds of information entities in addition to documents, subsuming bibliometrics. *Webometrics*, which came about at the end of the 1990s, concentrates, as the name implies, on Web-related entities. *e-Metrics*, which emerged around 2000, are measures of electronic resources, particularly in libraries.

Studies that preceded bibliometrics in information science emerged in the 1920s and 1930s; they were related to authors and literature in science and technology. A number of studies went beyond reporting statistical distributions, concentrating on relations between a quantity and the related yield of entities under study. Here are two significant studies that subsequently greatly affected development of bibliometrics. In the 1920s, Alfred Lotka (1880–1949, American mathematician, chemist, and statistician) reported on the distribution of productivity of authors in chemistry and physics in terms of articles published. He found a regular pattern where a large proportion of the total literature is actually produced by a small proportion of the total number of authors, falling down in a regular pattern, where the majority of authors produce but one paper—after generalization this became known as Lotka's law. In the 1930s, Samuel Bradford (1878–1948, British mathematician and librarian), using relatively complete subject bibliographies, studied the scatter of articles relevant to a subject among journals. He found that a small number of journals produce a large proportion of articles on the subject and that the distribution falls regularly to a point where a large number of journals produce but one article on the same subject—after generalization this became known as Bradford's law or Bradford's distribution. Similar quantity-yield patterns were found in a number of fields and are generally known as Pareto distributions (after Italian economist Vilfredo Pareto, 1848–1923). Lotka's and Bradford's distributions were confirmed many times over in subsequent bibliometric studies starting in the 1950s. They inspired further study and moreover set a general approach in bibliometric studies that was followed for decades.

Data Sources

All metric studies start from and depend on data sources from which statistics can be extracted. Originally, Lotka

Information Retrieval–
Information Society

used, among others, Chemical Abstracts, and Bradford used bibliographies in applied geophysics and in lubrication. These were printed sources and analysis was manual. For a great many years, the same kind of print sources and manual analysis methods were used.

The advent of digital technology vastly changed the range of sources, as well as significantly enlarged the type and method of analysis in bibliometrics, or as Thelwall put it, in a historical synthesis of the topic, "bibliometrics has changed out of all recognition since 1958."[16] This is primarily because sources of data for bibliometric analyses proliferated (and keep proliferating), inviting new analysis methods and uses of results.

In 1960 Eugene Garfield (U.S. chemist, information scientist, and entrepreneur) established the Institute for Scientific Information (ISI), which became a major innovative company in the creation of a number of information tools and in bibliometric research. In 1964, ISI started publishing the *Science Citation Index*, created by use of computers. Citation indexes in social sciences and in art and humanities followed. While citation indexes in various subjects, law in particular, existed long before Garfield applied them in science, the way they were produced and used was innovative. Besides being a commercial product, citation indexes became a major data source for bibliometric research. They revolutionized bibliometrics.

In addition to publication sources—journal articles and citations—de Solla Price pioneered the use of a range of statistics from science records, economics, social sciences, history, international reports, and other sources to derive generalizations about the growth of science and the factors that affected information explosion.[5] Use of diverse sources became a trademark of scientometrics.

As the Web became the fastest growing and spreading technology in history it also became a new source of data for ever-growing types of bibliometric-like analyses, organized under the common name of webometrics. The Web has a number of unique entities that can be statistically analyzed, such as links, which have dynamic distributions and behavior. Thus, webometrics started covering quite different grounds.

As more and more publications, particularly journals and more recently books, became digital they also became a rich source for bibliometric analyses. Libraries and other institutions are incorporating these digital resources in their collections, providing a way for various analyses of their use and other aspects. Most recently, digital libraries became a new source of analysis for they are producing massive evidence of the usage patterns of library contents, such as journal articles, for the first time. Thus, the emergence of e-metrics.

[From now on all the metric studies in information science (bibliometrics, scientometrics, informetrics, webometrics, and e-metrics) for brevity will be collectively referred to as *bibliometrics*.]

In the digital age, sources for bibliometric analyses are becoming more diversified, complex, and richer. They have become a challenge for developing new methods and refining existing methods and types of analysis.

Types and Application of Results

Lotka showed distribution of publication regarding authors and Bradford distribution of articles regarding journals. In seeking generalization, both formulated respective numerical distributions in a mathematical form. The generalizations sought a scientific law-like predictive power, with full realization that social science laws are not at all like natural science laws. In turn, mathematical expressions of Lotka's and Bradford's laws were refined, enlarged, and corrected in numerous subsequent mathematical papers; the process is still going on. This set the stage for the development of a branch of bibliometrics that is heavily mathematical and theoretical; it is still growing and continuously encompassing new entities and relations as data becomes available. Bradford also illustrated the results graphically. This set the stage for the development of visualization methods for showing distributions and relations; the efforts evolved to become quite sophisticated using the latest methods and tools for data visualization to show patterns and structures.

Over the years bibliometric studies showed many features of the ever-growing number of entities related to information. Some were already mentioned, here is a sample of others: frequency and distribution analysis of words; cowords; citations; cocitations; emails; links; etc., and quite a few others.

Until the appearance of citation indexes, bibliometric studies in information science were geared to analysis of relations; many present studies continue with the same purpose and are geared toward relational applications. But with the appearance of citation data, a second application emerged: evaluative.[16]

Relational applications seek to explicate relationships that are results of research. Examples are emergence of research fronts; institutional, national, and international authorship productivity and patterns; intellectual structure of research fields or domains; and the like.

Evaluative applications seek to assess or evaluate the impact of research, or more broadly, scholarly work in general. Examples are use of citations in promotion and tenure deliberations; ranking or comparison of scholarly productivity; relative contribution of individuals, groups, institutions, or nations; relative standing of journals; and the like.

Evaluative indicators were developed to numerically express the impact of given entities. Here are two of the most widely used indicators. The first deals with journals, the second with authors. *Journal Impact Factor*, devised in the 1960s by Garfield and his colleagues, provides a numerical value to how often a given journal is included

Information Retrieval–
Information Society

in citations in all journals over a given period of time, normalized for the number of articles appearing in a journal. Originally, it was developed as a tool to help selection of journals in *Science Citation Index* but it morphed into a widely used tool for ranking and comparing the impact of journals. The second indicator deals with authors. A most influential new indicator of impact is the *h-index* (proposed in 2005 by Jorge Hirsh, a U.S. physicist). It quantifies and unifies both an author's scientific productivity (number of papers published by an author) and the apparent scientific impact of a scientist (number of citations received)—it unifies how much was published with how much was cited. Both of the indices are continuously discussed, mathematically elaborated, and criticized.

Evaluative studies are controversial at times. By and large, evaluative applications rest on citations. The central assumption here is that citation counts can be used as an indicator of value because the most influential works are most frequently cited. This assumption is questioned at times, thus it is at the heart of controversies and skepticism about evaluative approaches.

Evaluative applications are used at times in support of decisions related to tenure and promotion processes; academic performance evaluations of individuals and units in universities; periodic national research evaluations; grant applications; direction of research funding; support for journals; setting science policies; and other decisions involving science. Several countries have procedures in place that mandate bibliometric indicators for the evaluation of scientific activities, education, and institutions. They are also used in the search of factors influencing excellence.

The current and widening range of bibliometric studies is furthering understanding of a number of scholarly activities, structures, and communication processes. They are involved in the measuring and mapping of science. In addition, they have a serious impact on evaluation, policy formulation, and decision making in a number of areas outside of information science.

DIGITAL LIBRARIES

Long before digital libraries emerged in the mid-1990s, J. C. R. Licklider (1915–1990, U.S. computer scientist) in a prescient 1965 book *Libraries of the Future* envisioned many of the features of present digital libraries, with some still to come.[17] While Licklider was a technology enthusiast and formulated his vision of the library in a technological context, he also foresaw the handling of content in cognitive, semantic, and interactive ways.

Many of the components were in place quite some time before they were shaped and unified operationally into digital libraries. For instance, online searching of abstracting and indexing databases; a number of network information services; library automation systems; document structuring

and manipulation procedures based on metadata; digitized documents; human computer interfaces; and others. With the advent of the Web, many of these older components were refined as needed and amalgamated with a number of new ones to form digital libraries as we know them today.

From the outset, people from a number of fields and backgrounds got involved in the development of digital libraries. Thus various conceptions were derived. Two viewpoints crystallized, one more technological the other more organizational. From the first point of view, a digital library is a managed collection of digital information with associated services, accessible over a network. From the second point of view, a digital library is that, but in addition it involves organizations that provide resources to select, structure, and offer intellectual access to collections of digital works for use by defined communities, and to preserve integrity and ensure persistence of collections and services. The first viewpoint comes mostly from computer science and the second from libraries and other organizations that house and provide digital library services. Digital libraries continue this dual orientation, technological and organizational, because, yes, they are indeed completely dependent on technology but by their purpose and functions they are social systems in the first place.

Many organizations other than libraries enthusiastically started developing and operating digital libraries—museums, historical societies, academic departments, governments, professional organizations, publishers, nonprofit organizations, and so on. As a result, digital libraries take many shapes and forms. They involve a variety of contexts, media, and contents. Many are oriented toward a specific subject. Most importantly, they are used by a variety of users and for a variety of uses. Digital libraries are a highly diverse lot.

The wide and constantly increasing diversity of digital libraries and related collections and portals suggest several issues: traditional libraries are not traditional any more, but hybrid and coming in many digital library forms; many new players have entered the arena, particularly in subject areas; and many new types of uses have emerged in addition to the traditional use of libraries. Digital libraries are truly interdisciplinary. Information science was one of the fields that actively participated in digital library formation, development, and research.

Through NSF and other agencies, the U.S. government funded research in digital libraries through Digital Library Initiatives; European Union and other governments funded similar research and development programs. Governmental funding started around 1995 and lasted about a decade. Most of the funding went toward technological aspects and demonstrations. An important by-product of this funding was the creation of a strong international community of digital library researchers from a number of fields, information science included. Here is another by-product often mentioned: Google was initially developed at Stanford University under an NSF grant in the Digital Library Initiatives program.

From the outset, information science was involved with digital libraries in a number of ways. Professionally, many information scientists work in digital libraries, particularly in relation to their architecture, systems operations, and services. A diverse number of topics were addressed in research covering the whole life-cycle of digital libraries as reflected in numerous reports, journals, proceedings, and books. Here is a sample: development and testing of digital library architecture; development of appropriate metadata; digitization of a variety of media; preservation of digital objects; searching of digital library contents; evaluation of digital libraries; access to digital libraries; security and privacy issues; study of digital libraries as a place and space; study of users, use, and interactions in digital libraries; effect of digital libraries on educational and other social institutions; impact of digital libraries on scholarship and other endeavors; and policy issues. New research topics are coming along at a brisk pace.

The rapid development and widespread deployment of digital libraries became a force that is determining not only the future of libraries but also of many other organizations as social, cultural, and community institutions. It is instrumental in the development of e-science. It is also affecting the direction of information science in that the domain of problems addressed has been significantly enlarged.

EDUCATION

The fact that education is critical for any field is a truism that hardly needs to be stated. Information science education began slowly in the 1950s and 1960s. Two educational models evolved over time and were followed for decades to come: For brevity, they should be referred to as the Shera and Salton models, after those that pioneered them. Both have strengths and weaknesses. A third model is presently emerging, under the label of i-Schools.

Jesse H. Shera (1903–1982, librarian and library educator) was a library school dean at Western Reserve University (later Case Western Reserve) from 1952 to 1970. Among others, he was instrumental in starting the Center for Documentation and Communication Research at the library school there in 1955. The Center was oriented toward research and development in IR. Shortly thereafter, the library school curriculum started to include courses such as "machine literature searching" (later to become "information retrieval"), and a few other more advanced courses and laboratories on the topics of research in the Center. The basic approach was to append those courses, mostly as electives, to the existing library school curriculum, without modifications of the curriculum as a whole, and particularly not the required core courses. Information science (or information retrieval)

became one of the specialty areas of library science. The base or core courses that students were taking rested in the traditional library curriculum. Information science education was an appendage to library science. Library schools in the United States and in many other countries imitated Shera's model. They used the same approach and started incorporating information science courses in their existing curriculum as a specialty.

The strength of the Shera model is that it posits education within a service framework, connects the education to professional practice and a broader and user-oriented frame of a number of other information services, and relates it to a great diversity of information resources. The weakness is a lack of a broader theoretical framework, and a lack of teaching of formalism related to systems, such as the development and understanding of algorithms. A majority of researchers in the human information behavior and user-centered approach are associated with this educational environment. Out of this was born the current and widely used designation *library and information science.*

Shera's model, with contemporary modifications is still the prevalent approach in a majority of schools of library and information science. Some schools evolved to include a major in information science, or reoriented the curriculum toward some of the aspects of information science, or even provided a separate degree. The changes in curricula are accelerating. Dissatisfaction with the model as not in synch with contemporary developments related to information-spurred development of i-Schools discussed below.

Gerard Salton (already mentioned above) was first and foremost a scientist, and a computer scientist at that. As such, he pioneered the incorporation into IR research a whole array of formal and experimental methods from science, as modified for algorithmic and other approaches used so successfully in computer science. His primary orientation was research. For education, he took the time-honored approach of a close involvement with research. The Salton model was a laboratory and research approach to education related to IR. As Shera's model resulted in information science education being an appendage to library science education, Salton's model of IR education resulted in being a specialty of and an appendage to computer science education. Computer science students that were already well-grounded in the discipline got involved in SMART and other projects directed by Salton, worked and did research in the laboratory, completed their theses in areas related to IR, and participated in the legendary IR seminars. They also published widely with Salton and with each other and participated with high visibility in national and international conferences. From Harvard and Cornell, his students went to a number of computer science departments where they replicated Salton's model. Many other computer science departments in the United States and abroad took the same approach. The strength of Salton's model is that it: (1) starts from a base of a firm grounding in formal mathematical and other methods; and

Information Retrieval–
Information Society

(2) relates directly to research. The weakness is in that it: (1) ignores the broader aspects of information science, as well as any other disciplines and approaches dealing with the human aspects, that have great relevance to both outcomes of IR research and research itself; and (2) does not incorporate professional practice where these systems are realized and used. It loses users. Consequently, this is a successful, but narrowly concentrated education in IR as a specialty of computer science, rather than in information science. Not surprisingly, the researchers in the systems-centered approach came out of this tradition.

The two educational approaches are completely independent of each other. Neither reflects fully what is going on in the field. While in each model there is an increase in cognizance of the other, there is no educational integration of the systems- and user-centered approaches. The evident strengths that are provided by Shera's and Salton's model are not put together.

The late 1990s and early 2000s saw a movement to broaden and reorient information science education, spearheaded by a number of deans of schools with strong information science educations. Some library and information science schools were renamed into Information Schools or i-Schools. An informal i-School Caucus was formed in 2005. By 2008, the Caucus included over 20 schools quite diverse in origin. They include schools of: information; library and information science; information systems; informatics; public policy and management; information and computer sciences; and computing. The i-Schools are primarily interested in educational and research programs addressing the relationship between information, technology, and people and understanding the role of information in human endeavors. While the i-School movement was originally restricted to the United States, some schools outside the United States are joining. The movement is attracting wide international interest.

The i-Schools represent an innovative, new approach to information science education, with some true interdisciplinary connections. As the millennial decade draws toward an end, it is also signifying a new direction to information science education.

CONCLUSIONS

It was mentioned that information science has two orientations: one that deals with information retrieval techniques and systems and the other that deals with information needs and uses, or more broadly with human information behavior. One is technical and system-oriented, the other individual and social and user-oriented. In pursuing these orientations certain characteristics of the field emerged.

Information science has several general characteristics that are the leitmotif of its evolution and existence. These are shared with many modern fields.

- First, information science is interdisciplinary in nature. However, with various advances, relations with various disciplines are changing over time. The interdisciplinary evolution is far from over.
- Second, information science is inexorably connected to information technology. A technological imperative is compelling and encouraging the evolution of information science, as is the evolution of a number of other fields, and moreover, of the information society as a whole.
- Third, information science is, with many other fields, an active participant in the evolution of the information society. Information science has a strong social and human dimension, above and beyond technology.
- Fourth, while information science has a strong research component that drives advances in the field, it also has an equally strong, if not an even stronger, professional component oriented toward information services in a number of environments. Many innovations come from professionals in the field.
- Fifth, information science is also connected with information industry, a vital, highly diversified, and global branch of the economy.

With accelerating changes in all these characteristics, information science is a field in a constant flux. So are many other fields. The steady aspect is in its general orientation toward information, people, and technology.

REFERENCES

1. Saracevic, T. Information science. J. Am. Soc. Info. Sci. **1999**, *50*(12), 1051–1063.
2. Bates, M.J. The invisible substrate of information science. J. Am. Soc. Info. Sci. **1999**, *50*(12), 1043–1050.
3. National Science Foundation, National Academy of Sciences, American Documentation Institute, National Research Council, *Proceedings of the International Conference on Scientific Information*, The National Academies Press: Washington, DC, 1959; 2 volumes http://books.nap. edu/openbook.php?isbn=NI000518&page=R19 (accessed April 15, 2008).
4. Price, D.J.; de, S. *Science Since Babylon*, Yale University Press: New Haven, CT, 1961.
5. Price, D.J.; de, S. *Little Science Big Science*, Columbia University Press: New York, 1963.
6. Bush, V. As we may think. Atlantic Mon. **1945**, *176*(11), 101–108 http://www.theatlantic.com/doc/194507/bush (accessed April, 14, 2008).
7. White, H.D.; McCain, K.W. Visualizing a discipline: An author cocitation analysis of information science. 1972–1995. J. Am. Soc. Info. Sci. **1998**, *49*(4), 327–355.
8. Zhao, D.; Strotmann, A. Information science during the first decade of the Web: An enriched cocitation analysis. J. Am. Soc. Info. Sci. Technol. **2008**, *59*(6), 916–937.

9. Mooers, C.N. Zatocoding applied to mechanical organization of knowledge. Am. Doc. **1951**, *2*(1), 20–32.

10. In *TREC. Experiment and Evaluation in Information Retrieval*; Voorhees, E.M., Harman, D.K., Eds.; MIT Press: Cambridge, MA, 2005.

11. Case, D.O. *Looking for Information: A Survey of Research on Information Seeking, Needs, and Behavior*, 2nd Ed. Academic Press, Elsevier: New York, 2007.

12. Fisher, K.E.; Erdelez, S.; McKechnie, L.E.F. *Theories of Information Behavior*, American Society for Information Science and Technology: Washington DC, 2005.

13. Belkin, N.J.; Oddy, R.N.; Brooks, H.M. ASK for information retrieval. Parts 1 and 2. J. Doc. **1986**, *28*(2), 61–71 145–164.

14. Kuhlthau, C.C. *Seeking Meaning: A Process Approach to Library and Information Services*, 2nd Ed. Libraries Unlimited: Westport, CT, 2004.

15. Ellis, D. A behavioral model for information retrieval system design. J. Doc. **1989**, *45*, 171–212.

16. Thelwall, M. Bibliometrics to webometrics. J. Info. Sci. **2008**, *34*(4), 605–621.

17. Licklider, J.C.R. *Libraries of the Future*, The MIT Press: Cambridge, MA, 1965.

Information Search Process (ISP) Model

Carol Collier Kuhlthau
*Department of Library and Information Science, Rutgers University, New Brunswick,
New Jersey, U.S.A.*

Abstract

The information search process (ISP) is a six-stage model of the users' holistic experience in the process of information seeking. The ISP model, based on over two decades of empirical research, identifies three realms of experience: the affective (feelings), the cognitive (thoughts), and the physical (actions) common to each stage. These studies were among the first to investigate the affective aspects or the feelings of a person in the process of information seeking along with the cognitive and physical aspects. Central to the ISP is the notion that uncertainty, both affective and cognitive, increases and decreases in the process of information seeking. A principle of uncertainty for information seeking states that information commonly increases uncertainty in the early stages of the search process. Increased uncertainty indicates a zone of intervention for intermediaries and system designers.

INTRODUCTION

Prior to this research, most studies were constrained by the system's definition of information needs. For the most part, library and information science concentrated on the system's representation of texts rather than on the user's tasks, problems, and processes in information gathering. The classic triad of thoughts, actions, and feelings central to any constructive process had rarely been taken into consideration in study or discussion of information-seeking behavior. Although cognitive processes were increasingly recognized as significant components for understanding information behavior, affective experience continued to be overlooked. There was little or no acknowledgment that the feelings of users may have any import. In the study and understanding of information-seeking behavior, Kuhlthau's work introduced the holistic experience of information seeking from the user's perspective and stressed the important role of affect in information-seeking behavior.

The information search process (ISP) presents a view of information seeking from the user's perspective in six stages: initiation, selection, exploration, formulation, collection, and presentation. The six-stage model of the ISP incorporates three realms of experience: the affective (feelings), the cognitive (thoughts), and the physical (actions) common to each stage.[1] The ISP reveals information seeking as a process of construction influenced by Kelly's personal construct theory[2] with information increasing uncertainty in the early stages of the ISP.

The development of the ISP as a conceptual framework is the result of more than two decades of empirical research that began with a qualitative study of secondary school students and the emergence of an initial model, that was verified and refined through various quantitative and longitudinal methods of diverse library users and further

developed in case studies of people in the workplace. To summarize the findings of these studies of the user's perspective of the ISP, the affective symptoms of uncertainty, confusion, and frustration prevalent in the early stages are associated with vague, unclear thoughts about a topic or problem. As knowledge states shifted to clearer, more focused thoughts, a corresponding shift was noted in feelings of increased confidence and certainty. Affective aspects, such as uncertainty and confusion, influenced relevance judgments as much as cognitive aspects, such as personal knowledge and information content. Central in the model of the ISP is uncertainty described formally as a principle of uncertainty for information seeking. Increased uncertainty in the exploration stage of the ISP indicates a zone of intervention for intermediaries and system designers.[3]

MODEL OF THE ISP

The model of the ISP describes users' experience in the process of information seeking as a series of thoughts, feelings, and actions. Thoughts that begin as uncertain, vague, and ambiguous become clearer, more focused, and specific as the search process progresses. Feelings of anxiety and doubt become more confident and certain. Through their actions, people seek information relevant to the general topic in the beginning stages of the search process and pertinent to the focused topic toward closure. Formulation of a focus or a personal perspective of the topic is a pivotal point in the search process. At that point, feelings shift from uncertain to confident, thoughts change from vague to more clear and interest increases. The model was verified in longitudinal case studies and large-scale studies of diverse samples of library users.[4,5] Further

Encyclopedia of Library and Information Sciences, Fourth Edition DOI: 10.1081/E-EISA-120053993
Copyright © 2017 by Taylor & Francis. All rights reserved.

studies have examined the implementation of a process approach in education contexts and investigated the ISP in the workplace.[6]

The ISP describes common experiences in the process of information seeking for a complex task that has a discrete beginning and ending and that requires considerable construction and learning to be accomplished.[7] The model reveals a search process in which a person is seeking meaning in the course of seeking information. From the user's perspective, the primary objective of information seeking is to accomplish the task that initiated the search, not merely the collection of information as an end in itself. The ISP presents seeking information as a means to accomplish a goal. The model of the ISP is articulated in a holistic view of information seeking from the user's perspective in six stages (Fig. 1):

1. *Initiation*, when a person first becomes aware of a lack of knowledge or understanding and feelings of uncertainty and apprehension are common.
2. *Selection*, when a general area, topic, or problem is identified and initial uncertainty often gives way to a brief sense of optimism and a readiness to begin the search.
3. *Exploration*, when inconsistent, incompatible information is encountered and uncertainty, confusion, and doubt frequently increase and people find themselves "in the dip" of confidence.
4. *Formulation*, when a focused perspective is formed and uncertainty diminishes as confidence begins to increase.
5. *Collection*, when information pertinent to the focused perspective is gathered and uncertainty subsides as interest and involvement deepens.
6. *Presentation*, when the search is completed with a new understanding enabling the person to explain their learning to others or in some way put the learning to use.

In the first stage, *initiation*, a person becomes aware of a gap in knowledge or a lack of understanding, where feelings of uncertainty and apprehension are common. At this point, the task is merely to recognize a need for information. Thoughts center on contemplating the problem, comprehending the task, and relating the problem to prior experience and personal knowledge. Actions frequently involve discussing possible avenues of approach or topics to pursue.

In the second stage, *selection*, the task is to identify and select the general topic to be investigated and the approach to be pursued. Feelings of uncertainty often give way to optimism after the selection has been made and there is a readiness to begin the search. Thoughts center on weighing prospective topics against the criteria of task requirements, time allotted, personal interest, and information available. The outcome of the possible choices is predicted, and the topic or approach judged to have the greatest potential for success is selected. Typical actions are to confer with others or to make a preliminary search of information available and then to skim and scan for an overview of alternative topics. When, for whatever reason, selection is delayed or postponed, feelings of anxiety are likely to intensify until the choice is made.

The third stage is *exploration* characterized by feelings of confusion, uncertainty, and doubt that frequently increase during this time. The task is to investigate information on the general topic in order to extend personal understanding. Thoughts center on seeking to become oriented and sufficiently informed about the topic to form a focus or a personal point of view. At this stage in the ISP, an inability to express precisely what information is needed can make communication between the user and the system awkward. Actions involve locating information about the general topic, reading to become informed, and relating new information to what is already known. In this stage, the information encountered rarely fits smoothly with previously held constructs, and information from different sources frequently seems inconsistent and incompatible.

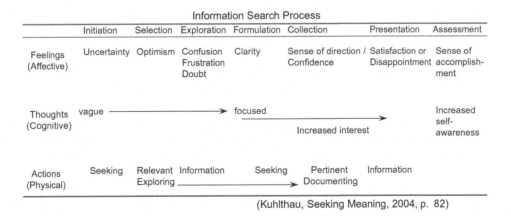

	Initiation	Selection	Exploration	Formulation	Collection	Presentation	Assessment
Feelings (Affective)	Uncertainty	Optimism	Confusion Frustration Doubt	Clarity	Sense of direction / Confidence	Satisfaction or Disappointment	Sense of accomplishment
Thoughts (Cognitive)	vague ⟶			focused	Increased interest ⟶		Increased self-awareness
Actions (Physical)	Seeking	Relevant Exploring ⟶	Information	Seeking	Pertinent Documenting	Information	

(Kuhlthau, Seeking Meaning, 2004, p. 82)

Fig. 1 Model of the information search process.
Source: From Kuhlthau.[7]

Information Retrieval–
Information Society

People may find the situation quite discouraging and even threatening, causing a sense of personal inadequacy as well as frustration with the system. Some actually may be inclined to abandon the search altogether at this stage. Exploration is considered the most difficult stage in the ISP when information encountered can increase rather than decrease uncertainty, prompting a dip in confidence.

The fourth stage in the ISP, *formulation*, is the turning point, when feelings of uncertainty diminish and confidence increases. The task is to form a focus from the information encountered. Thoughts involve identifying and selecting ideas in the information from which to form a focused perspective of the topic. A focus in the search process is comparable to a hypothesis in the process of construction. The topic becomes more personalized at this stage if construction is taking place. While a focus may be formed in a sudden moment of insight, it is more likely to emerge gradually as constructs become clearer. During this time, a change in feelings is commonly noted, with indications of increased confidence and a sense of clarity. People often express an awareness of being involved in seeking meaning, such as purposefully engaging in "focusing and narrowing," in seeking "a thread," "a story," "answers to all my questions," "a central theme," or "a guiding idea." The four criteria used to select a topic may be employed again to choose a focus: Task; What am I trying to accomplish? Time; How much time do I have? Interest; What do I find personally interesting? Availability; What information is available to me?

Collection is the fifth stage in the ISP when interaction between the user and the information system functions most effectively and efficiently. At this point, the task is to gather information related to the focused topic. Thoughts are centered on defining, extending, and supporting the focus. Actions involve selecting information relevant to the focused perspective of the topic and making detailed notes on that which pertains specifically to the focus. General information on the topic is no longer relevant after formulation. The person, with a clearer sense of direction, can specify the need for pertinent, focused information to intermediaries and to systems, thereby facilitating a comprehensive search of available resources. Feelings of confidence continue to increase as uncertainty subsides, with interest in the project deepening.

In the sixth stage, *presentation*, feelings of relief are common with a sense of satisfaction if the search has gone well or disappointment if it has not. The task is to complete the search and to prepare to present or otherwise use the findings. Thoughts concentrate on culminating the search with a personalized synthesis of the topic or problem. Actions involve a summary search in which decreasing relevance and increasing redundancy are noted in the information encountered.

ROLE OF AFFECT IN INFORMATION-SEEKING BEHAVIOR

These studies were among the first to investigate the affective aspects or feelings in the process of information seeking along with the cognitive and physical aspects. Prior to the introduction of the ISP, the affective dimension of information seeking had not been fully recognized in library and information services and systems. One of the surprising and important findings in this research was the discovery of a sharp increase in uncertainty and decrease in confidence after a search had been initiated. A person "in the dip" commonly experienced uncertainty, confusion, and anxiety until a focus or a personal perspective had been formed.

The ISP presents information seeking as a process of construction influenced by George Kelly's personal construct theory.[2] Information seeking involves construction in which the person actively pursues understanding and seeks meaning from the information encountered over a period of time. The process is commonly experienced as a series of thoughts and feelings that shift from vague and anxious to clear and confident as the search progresses.

Kelly describes the emotional experience of constructing meaning from new information. The information is assimilated in a series of phases, beginning with confusion. Confusion increases as inconsistencies and incompatibilities are confronted between the information and the constructs the person already holds. As confusion mounts, it frequently causes doubt in the ability to assimilate the new information. The disruption caused by the new ideas may become so threatening that the new information is discarded and construction abandoned. At this point, Kelly proposes another alternative to move the process of construction along. The person may form a tentative hypothesis to move toward incorporating the new construct into their existing system of personally held constructs.

The ISP is a process of seeking meaning not just finding and reproducing information. This is a process of construction involving exploration and formulation that rarely proceeds directly from selection to collection. Experience influences the decisions and choices a person makes throughout the process of information seeking.

Studies of the ISP in the workplace reveal that a person's experience of the stages in the ISP is related to how much the person knows about the problem and the degree of construction that needs to be undertaken during information seeking. In more routine tasks, where the goal is to answer a simple question or to monitor periodic change, people do not usually experience stages in their information seeking. In more complex tasks, where the goal requires considerable construction and learning, people are likely to experience a process as described in the ISP model.[6]

Focus Formulation as a Pivotal Point in the ISP

The formulation of a focus or personal perspective is a pivotal point in the ISP. Focus formulation calls for reflective thinking about the information encountered in the exploration stage of the ISP that provides a direction for the completion of the search. A focus is a guiding idea to concentrate on to complete the search and accomplish the task.

People often find the period preceding formulation of a focus the most difficult phase in the search process. Exploration is a difficult stage because uncertainty commonly increases, rather than gradually decreasing, during this time. People can experience anxiety and frustration as they encounter information from many different perspectives, much of which may not be compatible with their specific constructs and personal knowledge. The connection between feelings and formulating is evident from the rise in confidence that parallels increased clarity as formulation unfolds. Formulation, the central task in the ISP, is frequently misunderstood when the search process is thought of as merely a process of collection not a construction activity.

Exploration facilitates formulating a focus during the search process. However, people often attempt to move from selection directly to collection without the essential exploration for the formulation that gives direction to the search. Exploring uncovers information for formulating new constructs, whereas collecting gathers information for documenting established constructs. Tolerance for the mounting uncertainty in the exploration stage is important for formulation within the ISP. Using information involves interpreting and creating. No matter the amount or the quality of the information gathered, the problem is not solved or the topic understood until the information has been interpreted. Understanding develops through extending and defining a topic by reflecting on the information encountered to solidify personal understanding.

Acquiring More Information Can Increase Uncertainty

The axiom that information reduces uncertainty is not necessarily the user's experience in information seeking. In some situations, new information actually increases uncertainty. Prior to formulation, users are likely to experience heightened uncertainty in the face of unique, incompatible, inconsistent information that requires construction and interpretation. It seems helpful for users to expect uncertainty to increase during the exploration stage of the ISP rather than thinking that increased uncertainty is a symptom that something has gone wrong. The tolerance of uncertainty is introduced as enabling the early stages of the ISP, when the experience of uncertainty may overwhelm the person and deter progress in the process. Uncertainty from the user's perspective is a natural experience in the search process.

If unexpected, the presence of uncertainty and particularly any increase in uncertainty can heighten anxiety.

Central to the ISP model is the notion that uncertainty, both cognitive and affective, increases and decreases in the process of information seeking. Uncertainty, the predominant experience in the early stages of the search process, had not been sufficiently addressed in library and information services.

PRINCIPLE OF UNCERTAINTY FOR INFORMATION SEEKING

Uncertainty is a cognitive state that commonly causes affective symptoms of anxiety and lack of confidence. Uncertainty and anxiety can be expected in the early stages of the ISP. The affective symptoms of uncertainty, confusion, and frustration are associated with vague, unclear thought about a topic or question. As knowledge states shift to more clearly focused thoughts, a parallel shift occurs in feelings of increased confidence. Uncertainty due to a lack of understanding, a gap in meaning, or a limited construct initiates the process of information seeking.[8]

The principle is expanded by six corollaries: process corollary, formulation corollary, redundancy corollary, mood corollary, prediction corollary, and interest corollary.

Six Corollaries of the Principle of Uncertainty

1. *Process corollary*: The process of information seeking involves construction in which the person actively pursues understanding and meaning from the information encountered over a period of time. The process is commonly experienced in a series of thoughts and feelings that shift from vague and anxious to clear and confident, as the search progresses.
2. *Formulation corollary*: Formulation is thinking, developing and understanding, and extending and defining a topic from the information encountered in the early stages of a search. The formulation of a focus or a guiding idea is a critical, pivotal point in the ISP when a general topic becomes clearer and a particular perspective is formed as the person moves from uncertainty to understanding.
3. *Redundancy corollary*: The interplay of seeking what is expected or redundant and encountering what is unexpected or unique results in an underlying tension in the ISP. Redundant information fits into what the user already knows and is readily recognized as being relevant or not. Unique information is new and extends knowledge and does not match the person's constructs requiring reconstruction to be recognized as useful. Too much redundant information leads to boredom, whereas too much unique information causes anxiety. The lack of redundancy in the early stages of the ISP may be an

Information Retrieval–
Information Society

underlying cause of anxiety related to uncertainty. Uncertainty may decrease as redundancy increases.

4. *Mood corollary*: Mood, a stance or attitude that the person assumes, opens or closes the range of possibilities in a search. According to Kelly, an invitational mood leads to expansive, exploratory actions, whereas an indicative mood fosters conclusive actions that lead to closure. The person's mood is likely to shift during the ISP. An invitational mood may be helpful in the early stages and an indicative mood in the later stages. A person in an invitational mood would tend to take more expansive, exploratory actions, while a user in an indicative mood prefers conclusive actions that lead to closure.

5. *Prediction corollary*: The ISP is a series of personal choices based on the person's predictions of what will happen if a particular action is taken. People make predictions derived from constructs built on past experience about what sources, information, and strategies will be relevant and effective. These predictions lead to the choices they make in the stages of the ISP. People develop expectations and make predictions about the sources used or not used, the sequence of source use, and the information selected from the sources as relevant or irrelevant. Relevance is not absolute or constant but varies considerably from person to person.

6. *Interest corollary*: Interest increases as the exploratory inquiry leads to formulation in the ISP. Motivation and intellectual engagement intensify along with construction. Personal interest may be expected to increase as uncertainty decreases. The person's interest and motivation grows as the search progresses. Interest is higher in later stages after the person has formed a focus and has enough understanding of the topic to become intellectually engaged.

IMPLICATION OF ISP FOR INFORMATION SERVICES AND SYSTEMS

Information searching is traditionally portrayed as a systematic, orderly, and rational procedure rather than the uncertain, confusing process that users commonly experience. After the search is completed, the topic understood, and the problem solved, a person may look back and deny the chaos and confusion that was actually experienced in the process. A gap exists between users' expectations in information use and search design.

The ISP considers uncertainty as natural and essential for constructing personal knowledge in the process of information seeking rather than regarding the reduction of uncertainty as the primary objective of information seeking. Uncertainty is a concept that offers insight into the user's quest for meaning within the ISP. If

uncertainty is viewed as a sign of the beginning of learning and creativity, the goal of library and information services shifts from reducing uncertainty to supporting the user's constructive process.

Increased uncertainty in the ISP indicates a need for intervention that enables the person to move on to further construction and understanding. Uncertainty in the ISP indicates a zone of intervention in the ISP for information intermediaries.[9]

Zone of Intervention for Information Services and Systems

The zone of intervention is a concept modeled on Vygotsky's notion of a zone of proximal development.[10] Vygotsky, the soviet psychologist whose work has had a profound influence on learning theory, developed the concept of identifying an area or zone in which intervention would be most helpful to a learner. The zone of proximal development is the distance between the actual developmental level as determined by independent problem solving and the level of potential development as determined by problem solving under professional guidance or in collaboration with more capable peers. This concept provides a way of understanding intervention in the constructive process of another person.

The zone of intervention in information seeking may be thought of in a similar way. The zone of intervention is that area in which an information user can do with advice and assistance what the user cannot do alone or can do only with difficulty. Intervention within this zone enables individuals to progress in the accomplishment of their task. Intervention outside this zone is inefficient and unnecessary, experienced by users as intrusive, on the one hand, and overwhelming, on the other.

Taken together, the stages of the ISP, uncertainty principle, and the concept of a zone of intervention propose a conceptual framework for understanding information seeking as a process of construction from the user's perspective. In summary, the ISP model describes the experience and behavior of people involved in extensive research projects. People using libraries and information systems to learn about a particular subject or to investigate a problem or issue often have difficulty in the early stages of information seeking. Even when they begin with great enthusiasm and initial success, many become confused and uncertain as to how to proceed after a short period of time. This is particularly noticeable with students who have been assigned a research paper but is not limited to students. Initial hesitation, confusion, and uncertainty are reported by people in all types of libraries and in the workplace. In fact, we have no way of knowing just how many people give up after initiating a search because they become uncertain and feel incompetent to continue.[11] It is helpful to understand that a period of cognitive and affective uncertainty is natural and essential in the early stages of learning from a variety of sources of information.

IMPLICATIONS FOR EDUCATION

The challenge facing educators is to prepare students for learning, living, and thriving in the dynamic, cluttered, and chaotic information environment of today's world. At the core of what it means to be educated today is to know how to learn from a variety of sources of information. The ISP studies found that students need considerable guidance and intervention throughout the research process to enable a depth of learning. Without guidance, students often view research as a simple collecting and presenting assignment that can result in copying and pasting with little real learning. With guidance, students are able to concentrate on constructing new knowledge in the phases of research to gain personal understanding and transferable skills.

Based on the findings of the ISP studies, an approach called Guided Inquiry has been developed with practical strategies and tools that engage and support students in each phase of the research process.[12] The ISP model has been translated into Guided Inquiry Design, a phased design framework that can be applied by teachers to guide students through the process of learning from multiple sources of information.[13] The phases of the design framework, *open*, *immerse*, *explore*, *identify*, *gather*, *create*, *share*, *evaluate*, follow the flow of feelings, thoughts, and actions described in the ISP, as shown in Fig. 2.

Emotions play an important role in learning. Recent brain research confirms that emotions work in conjunction with thinking in the holistic process of constructing knowledge, as described in the ISP. In Guided Inquiry, a learning team of teachers and librarians concentrate on what students are feeling as well as what they are thinking and doing as they are learning throughout the research process. Students come to realize that feeling uncertain is a normal and necessary part of learning. They acquire strategies to support them during phases of uncertainty and are guided in their efforts to learn in the research process.

CONCLUSION

People engage in an information search experience holistically, with an interplay of feelings, thoughts, and actions. Common patterns of feeling, thinking, and acting are characteristic in each phase. These studies were among the first to investigate the affective aspects or the feelings of a person in the process of information seeking along with the cognitive and physical aspects. Rather than a steady increase in confidence from the beginning of a search to the conclusion, as might be expected, a dip in confidence is commonly experienced once an individual has initiated a search and begins to encounter conflicting and inconsistent information. A person "in the dip" is increasingly uncertain and confused until a focus is formed to provide a path for seeking meaning and criteria for judging relevance. Advances in information technology, which open access to a vast assortment of sources, have not helped the user's dilemma and may have intensified the sense of confusion and uncertainty. Information systems may intensify the problem particularly in the early stages of

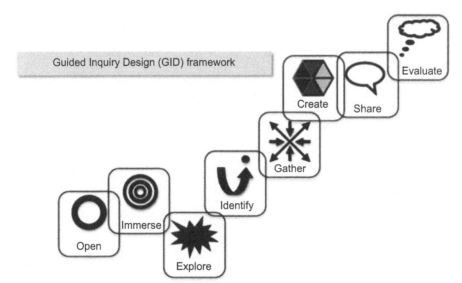

Fig. 2 Phases of the design framework.
Source: From Kuhlthau, Maniotes, and Caspari[12,13]

Information Retrieval–
Information Society

the ISP by overwhelming the user with "everything" all at once. Increased uncertainty indicates a zone of intervention in the process of information seeking for information intermediaries.

REFERENCES

1. Kuhlthau, C.C. Developing a model of the library search process: investigation of cognitive and affective aspects. Ref. Q. **1988**, *28* (2), 232–242.

2. Kelly, G.A. *A Theory of Personality: The Psychology of Personal Constructs*; Norton: New York, 1963.

3. Kuhlthau, C.C. Inside the search process: information seeking from the user's perspective. J. Am. Soc. Inf. Sci. **1991**, *42* (5), 361–371.

4. Kuhlthau, C.C. Longitudinal case studies of the information search process of users in libraries. Libr. Inf. Sci. Res. **1988**, *10*, 257–304.

5. Kuhlthau, C.C.; Turock, B.J.; George, M.W. Validating a model of the search process: a comparison of academic, public and school library users. Libr. Inf. Sci. Res. **1990**, *12* (1), 5–13.

6. Kuhlthau, C.C. The role of experience in the information search process of an early career information worker: perceptions of uncertainty, complexity, construction and sources. J. Am. Soc. Inf. Sci. **1999**, *50* (5), 399–412.

7. Kuhlthau, C.C. *Seeking Meaning: A Process Approach to Library and Information Services*, 2nd Ed.; Libraries Unlimited: Westport, CT, 2004.

8. Kuhlthau, C.C. A principle of uncertainty for information seeking. J. Doc. **1993**, *49* (4), 339–355.

9. Kuhlthau, C.C. The concept of a zone of intervention for identifying the role of intermediaries in the information search process. In *Global Complexity: Information, Chaos and Control*, Proceedings of the 59th American Society for Information Science Annual Meeting, Baltimore, MD, October, 21–24, 1996. Hardin, S., Ed.; Information Today: Medford, NJ, 91–94.

10. Vygotsky, L. *Mind in Society: The Development of Higher Psychological Processes*; Harvard University Press: Cambridge, MA, 1978.

11. Kuhlthau, C.C. Accommodating the user's information search process: challenges for information retrieval system designers. Bull. Am. Soc. Inf. Sci. **1999**, *25*, 12–16.

12. Kuhlthau, C.C.; Maniotes, L.K.; Caspari, A.K. *Guided Inquiry Design: A Framework for Inquiry in Your School*; Libraries Unlimited: Westport, CT, 2012.

13. Kuhlthau, C.C.; Maniotes, L.K.; Caspari, A.K. *Guided Inquiry: Learning in the 21st Century*, 2nd Ed.; Libraries Unlimited: Westport, CT, 2015.

Information Searching and Search Models

Iris Xie
School of Information Studies, University of Wisconsin–Milwaukee, Milwaukee,
Wisconsin, U.S.A.

Abstract
It is a critical issue to design information retrieval (IR) systems to effectively support users in their information searching. Users are naturally drawn to systems whose features make their searching easy, intuitive, efficient, and successful. However, there is a gap between user studies and the application of study results to actual system design. This entry serves as a summary of information searching and search models, and calls for the need to incorporate these user studies into system design and testing. Key terms related to information searching and search models are defined. A historic context is provided to illustrate the evolution of the four main digital environments that users interact with in their search process to offer readers background information regarding the transition from manual information systems to computer-based IR systems, as well as the transition from intermediary searching to end user searching. New emerging research areas in information searching are also discussed. Emphasis is placed on the review of different levels of information searching, including search tactics/moves, search strategies, usage patterns, factors affecting searching in relation to tasks, user knowledge structure, IR system design, social-organization context, and search models. Search models are further classified into two types, with one type illustrating information search process and the other type emphasizing the factors that influence the process. In addition, unsolved problems and future research are discussed and suggested.

INTRODUCTION

Since the emergence of the Internet, searching for information has become part of everyday activities for the general public. Successful information searching can only be achieved if information retrieval (IR) systems can effectively support users in their search processes. Users seek out and favor IR systems that make them feel like successful and accomplished searchers in addition to retrieving the information being sought. However, there is a lack of integration between findings of user studies and actual IR system design and evaluation. This entry summarizes information searching and search models, and offers the opportunity for system designers to apply user studies into IR system designs. This entry starts with the definitions of key terminologies in the Introduction, and follows by providing the overview of the historical context portraying the history of the four digital environments. The focus of the entry is on the identification of levels of search strategies ranging from search tactics/moves, types and dimensions of search strategies, and usage patterns to the factors that influence the selection and application of search strategies. More important, this entry presents 11 search models that illustrate the dynamic search process and a variety of variables that define the search process. Finally, future research for information searching and search models is discussed.

Despite their different foci, information searching can also be used as a synonymous term for IR, information seeking, and information access.[1] While information seeking refers to purposive behavior involving users' interactions with either manual or computer-based information systems in order to satisfy their information goals, information searching refers to the micro level of purposive behavior when interacting with different types of information systems.[2] IR is also a broad concept similar to information seeking but is more limited to users' interactions with computer-based information systems. Focusing on intellectual perspectives (information searching, IR, and cross-cutting) and theoretical orientations (information, people, and technology), information searching and IR were systematically compared. Based on the comparison, the authors identified 17 key constructs of information searching and retrieval. While information searching research focuses on users' interacting with specific IR systems, IR research emphasizes information representation, storage, and finding. The two areas gradually converge.[3] Since research on information seeking and IR has contributed significantly to research on information searching, some of the associated works are also reflected here.

Information searching can be characterized at different levels including tactics/moves, strategies, usage patterns, and models. Tactics or moves are the micro-level behaviors that users exhibit in their search process. Specifically, a tactic is a move that advances the search process. In some studies, a move can be defined narrowly by researchers. For example, a move is termed as any

Encyclopedia of Library and Information Sciences, Fourth Edition DOI: 10.1081/E-EISA-120053393
Copyright © 2017 by Taylor & Francis. All rights reserved.

changes made in formulating a query.[4] Searching strategies are a combination of tactics or moves. According to Bates,[5] "A search strategy is a plan for the whole search, while a tactic is a move made to further a search (p. 207)." A search strategy involves multiple dimensions, such as intentions, resources, methods, and so on. Usage patterns identify patterns of query formulation and reformulation based on analysis of transaction logs submitted to electronic IR systems. Search models are illustrations of patterns of information searching and the search process. Some of the models also identify the factors that influence the search process.

Users and online IR systems are partners in the information search process (ISP). Online IR systems can be characterized as IR systems that allow remote access with searches conducted in real time.[6] Users generally search information from four types of online IR systems: online databases, online public access catalogs (OPACs), Web search engines, and digital libraries. In recent years, users also search information in different types of social media. Information searching can be categorized into intermediary information searching and end user information searching. In intermediary searching, information professionals serve as intermediaries between users and the IR system in the search process, whereas in end user searching, users directly search for information themselves.

HISTORICAL CONTEXT

In order to discuss information searching and search models, we have to first provide a historical context, in particular, the evolution of the four major digital environments that users interact with. The emergence of online databases and OPACs indicates a new era for information searching from manual information systems to computer-based IR systems. The availability of OPACs and CD-ROM databases enabled users to search for information themselves. Later, the Web and the array of information resources to which it provided access made end user searching of IR systems much more widely available. As partners of information searching, the development and evolution of online IR systems to some extent affects how users search for information. That is why it is important to offer a historical context for information searching before presenting a discussion of information searching and search models.

OPACs hold interrelated bibliographic data of collections of a library that can be searched directly by end users. In the 1960s, library automation projects started in university libraries. Computer-based library systems were implemented in large universities by commercial vendors in the 1970s. OPAC systems designed for public access started in the 1980s. Four generations of OPACs have evolved across time, from the first generation of OPACs that followed either online card catalog models emulating the familiar card catalog or Boolean searching models

emulating online databases to the new generation of Web OPACs, which incorporate advanced search features and new designs from other types of IR systems and allow users to search for information resources generated from libraries, publishers, and online vendors.

Online databases consist of full-text documents or citations and abstracts accessible via dial-up or other Internet services. Several dial-up services were offered in the 1960s, and in 1972 commercial online services, such as Dialog and ORBIT, started. Traditionally, online searchers were information professionals who acted as intermediaries between users and online databases. After the creation of the World Wide Web, online vendors began to design Web versions of online services to help end users search for information themselves more easily. Characteristics of the new online database services include easy access, customization, and interactivity.

The emergence of the Web in early 1990 enabled millions of users to search for information without the assistance of intermediaries. Web search engines allow users to mainly search for Web materials. Four types of search engines have been developed to enable users to accomplish different types of tasks:

- Web directories with hierarchically organized indexes facilitate users' browsing for information.
- Search engines with a database of sites assist users' searching for information.
- Meta-search engines permit users to search multiple search engines simultaneously.
- Specialized search engines create a database of sites for specific topic searching.

Many of the Web search engines also offer users the opportunity to search for multimedia information and personalize their search engines. Now, Web search engines also extend their services to full-text books and articles in addition to Web materials. The popularity of Web search engines influences the way that users interact with other types of online IR systems.

Digital libraries collect, organize, store, and disseminate electronic resources in a variety of formats. The availability of online access to digital libraries began in the 1990s. Digital libraries allow users to search and use multimedia documents and can be hosted by a variety of organizations and agencies, either for the general public or for a specific user group. Digital libraries also pose challenges for end users to interact with multimedia information in different interface designs without the same support as of physical libraries.

SEARCH TACTICS AND SEARCH MOVES

Research on information searching has focused on four levels: tactics/moves, strategies, usage patterns, and

Information Retrieval–
Information Society

models. Tactics are moves that users apply in the search process. Different types of tactics play different roles in assisting users who are searching for information. Based on their functions in the ISP, information tactics can be classified into monitoring tactics, file structure tactics, search formulation tactics, and term tactics. While monitoring tactics and file structure tactics are tactics used to track the search and explore the file structure to find desired information, a source, or a file, search formulation tactics and term tactics are tactics applied to assist in the formulation and reformulation of searches as well as to help select and revise terms in search formulation.[5] In addition to search tactics, idea tactics assist users in identifying new ideas and resolutions to problems in information searching. While idea generation tactics include think, brainstorm, meditate, etc., pattern-breaking tactics consist of catch, break, breach, and others.[7] Focusing on topic management, knowledge-based search tactics are another type of tactic that broadens the topic scope, narrows the topic scope, and changes the topic scope.[8]

Similar to tactics, search moves directly illustrate how users interact with online IR systems. Search moves in general relate to query formulation and reformulations. They can be classified based on whether the meaning of a query has changed. When operational moves that keep the meaning of query components remain unchanged, conceptual moves change the meaning of query components. Conceptual moves are highly associated with search results. The objectives of these moves are to reduce the size of a retrieved set, enlarge the size of a retrieved set, or improve both precision and recall.[4] Search moves can also be grouped depending on whether the moves are related to conceptual or physical moves. Cognitive moves refer to moves that users conceptually make in order to analyze terms or documents, while physical moves refer to moves that users make in order to use system features.[9]

TYPES AND DIMENSIONS OF SEARCH STRATEGIES

Search strategies consist of combinations of tactics or moves and can be characterized by types and dimensions. In online databases and OPAC environments, search strategies can be classified by different types: concept-oriented, system-oriented, interactive, active, and reactive strategies. Concept-oriented strategies refer to strategies that manipulate concepts of search topics. The majority of the most-cited search strategies belong to this type. Building block, pearl-growing, successive-fractions, most-specific-facet-first, and lowest-postings-facet-first[10] represent concept-oriented strategies. Unlike concept-oriented strategies, system-oriented strategies focus on making good use of different system features: the known-item instantiation strategy, the search-option heuristic

strategy, the thesaurus-browsing strategy, and the screen-browsing strategy.[11]

Search strategies can also be defined by how and to what extent users interact with IR systems and information objects embedded in the systems. Search and browsing are the main strategies users employ when they interact with IR systems. Browsing strategies require more interactions than analytical search strategies.[12] Active and reactive strategies specify another approach to classifying search strategies. By applying active strategies, users make decisions about how to search for information before the first move, such as author, title, concepts, external support, system features, etc. By applying reactive strategies, users make decisions by following one move after another, such as focus shifts, search term relationships, error recovery, and so on.[13]

Search strategies in Web search engine environments have their own characteristics. Search strategies that concentrate on query reformulation were generated based on log analysis: specified, generalized, parallel, building-block, dynamic, multitasking, recurrent, and format reformulation.[14–16] Some of them are similar to search strategies in online database environments, such as specified, generalized, and building-block, but others show unique characteristics of search strategies in the Web search engine environment, such as multitasking, recurrent, dynamic, and others. In Web search engine environments, users sometimes perform different search tasks simultaneously; their searches are more dynamic, and they often apply the same search queries repeatedly. The Web environment also defines the unique design and features of the Web and Web searching. The 10 problem-solving strategies[17,18] represent search strategies in Web searching: surveying, double-checking, exploring, link-following, back- and forward-going, shortcut-seeking, engine-using, loyal engine-using, engine-seeking, and meta-searching.

In order to further analyze the structure of strategies, researchers have explored dimensions of information-seeking strategies. A multifaceted classification of information-seeking strategies was first developed based on four behavioral dimensions consisting of the goal of the interaction (learn, select), method of interaction (scan, search), mode of retrieval (recognize, specify), and types of resources interacted with (information, meta-information). Each type of information-seeking strategy corresponded to a specific prototype of dialogue structure.[19,20] The underlying common dimensions of browsing—scanning (looking, identifying, selecting, and examining), resource (meta-information, whole object, and part of object), goal (locate, confirm, evaluate, keep up, learn, curiosity, and entertain), and object (specific item, common items, defined location, general, and none)—were identified to illustrate nine patterns of browsing.[21] Integrating research and empirical studies in different digital environments, dimensions of information-seeking strategies are

Information Retrieval–
Information Society

further illustrated by intentions, methods, entities, and attributes of interactions. Twelve types of intentions include identify, learn, explore, create, modify, monitor, organize, access, keep records, evaluate, obtain, and disseminate. Eleven types of methods consist of scan, manipulate, specify, track, select, survey, extract, compare, acquire, consult, and trial-and-error. While entities refer to what users intend to acquire or work on, attributes specify the traits/elements of these entities. Entities contain knowledge, concept/term, format, item/object/site, process/status, location, system, and human. Attributes are associated with entities; for example, specific, common, general, and undefined are attributes of data/information. Different combinations of the four dimensions represent a variety of information-seeking strategies that people engage in within an ISP.[22]

Researchers further designed prototypes of IR systems consisting of different types of supportive techniques that have been identified, such as database summaries, navigable content tables, results clustering, and fielded query to support multiple types of information-seeking strategies. Moreover, a dialogue structure based on multiple types of information-seeking strategies was implemented into IR system design. The findings show that the supportive techniques and structure provide better support for multiple types of information-seeking strategies.[23–25]

USAGE PATTERNS

Web searching adds new meaning to research on search strategies, in particular, the analysis of transaction logs. Unlike studies on search strategies, usage patterns identified in Web search engine environments focus on patterns of query formulation and reformulation based on analysis of transaction logs submitted to search engines. Patterns of query formulation and reformulation in Web search environments can be characterized in five ways: 1) short queries, 2) short sessions with minimum reformulations, 3) minimum use of operators and search modifiers, not always used correctly, 4) minimum viewing results, and 5) search topics ranging from entertainment, recreation, and sex to e-commerce.[26–30] Log analysis is not limited to quantitative analysis; facets of query formulations were identified as well.

Usage patterns in different types of IR environments have also been compared. Both similarities and differences were identified. Short queries, short sessions, minimum view of search results, and similar unique queries were shown in Web search engine, Web page, and digital library environments. Search sessions vary in OPAC environments even though OPAC studies also exhibit short queries. More queries contain Boolean operators in digital library environments than in Web search engine environments.[31,32] Wolfram and Xie[33] defined the context of digital libraries as representing a hybrid of both "traditional" IR, using primarily bibliographic resources

provided by database vendors, and "popular" IR, exemplified by public search systems available on the World Wide Web. Usage of online databases in digital libraries reveals that users' search topics were close to online databases and digital libraries but their search behaviors were more similar to searching Web search engines. In general, users engage in more extensive searching in more traditional IR environments, such as OPAC and online database environments.

Usage patterns in multimedia environments is an emerging area for research. Characteristics of multimedia search can be described as follows: 1) short queries with minimal usage of Boolean operators and advanced features occur frequently. 2) Among all the metadata, media format and copyright information are most searched. User knowledge and media formats affect users' query formulation and reformulation.[34–36] Clickthrough data are important indicators of user-system interactions. In particular, they provide implicit relevance feedback by users. Although there is disagreement on the accuracy of clickthrough data, multimedia clickthrough data are much more accurate in general than traditional text search clickthrough data. They have been demonstrated to have the functions of improving searches, suggesting queries, annotating resources, and offering relevance feedback.[37–39]

More and more people use social media tools in searching and browsing information. In particular, browsing is the dominant user activity across social media. Social browsing is a unique behavior that people employ in using social media tools in which they browse their friend's updated information, especially images. As a result, browsing friends' pages increases the interactions among users.[40–43] However, new users of social media use Facebook as a social searching tool to investigate people they met offline instead of using it as a social browsing tool.[44] Among all the information in social media, factual, opinion, and recommendation information are the most frequently obtained information.[45]

FACTORS AFFECTING INFORMATION SEARCHING

Information searching is influenced by different types of factors, in which four main types determine the selection and application of different search strategies: 1) user goal and task, 2) user knowledge structure, 3) design of IR systems, and 4) the social and organizational context.

As to task, complexity of task and stages of task play major roles in influencing search strategies. Task complexity has systematic relationships with the types of information, information channels, and sources needed. As the level of task complexity increases, more information channels and resources are required.[46,47] Specifically, for a task involving less concepts, either a searching or browsing strategy is applied, although

Information Retrieval–
Information Society

searching plays a major role, and the interaction process is short; for a task involving more concepts, both browsing and searching strategies are combined, and the interaction process is long.[48] The task stages, such as initiation, selection, exploration, formulation, collection, and presentation, on the one hand, affect physical actions, cognitive thoughts, and affective feelings and appropriate tasks.[49] On the other hand, task stages such as prefocus, formulation, and postfocus decide changes in search tactics, term choices, and types of information, as well as relevance criteria.[50–53] When users move to a more focused stage, they apply more specified search terms, additional operators, and additional tactics. The types of information they search ranging from background information, theories, and models to methods, specific information, and empirical research results. In addition, the familiarity of tasks, timeframe, and types of tasks affect how users plan and apply different types of information-seeking strategies in the IR process.[54] Research has also demonstrated that different types of search tasks lead to the application of different types of information-seeking strategies.[55–57]

Three types of knowledge are required for effective information searching: 1) IR knowledge, 2) domain knowledge, and 3) system knowledge. While domain knowledge helps users to develop an in-depth understanding of the search task and what they want, IR knowledge assists users to develop conceptual and procedural strategies.[58] No doubt, experienced users apply better strategies and perform better than novice users in the ISP.[59–62] Domain expertise was proved to affect search behaviors and strategies and search performance.[63–66] Users in different disciplines have their unique characteristics in searching for information. For example, compared with scientists, humanities scholars engage in more searching for individual names, geographical and chronological terms, and unique terms in humanities.[67] There are also intertwining relationships among different types of knowledge. For example, domain knowledge only influences search tactics of experienced searchers. Simultaneously, domain knowledge of users determines whether their retrieval knowledge has an impact on their search tactics.[68]

In addition to users' knowledge structure, their cognitive abilities as part of personal information infrastructure, unavoidably, also control their search strategies.[12] Cognitive styles, learning styles, and searching styles have been demonstrated as the main personal traits that influence search behavior and search performance.[69–72] Learning styles affect users' selection of search tactics and their interaction strategies with help features of digital libraries.[73,74] Simultaneously, cognitive styles and users' knowledge structure are interrelated with search performance and search behavior. For example, cognitive styles have more impact on experienced users than on novice users in their interactions with Web search engines.[75]

The design of IR systems no doubt affects users in their selections of search strategies. Interfaces, computational mechanisms, and information objects are the main components of IR systems that guide or impede users in their application of different search strategies. As partners of users in the ISP, IR systems—in particular, the design of interfaces—could direct users to more or fewer applications of certain strategies. At the same time, the availability or unavailability of certain features determines whether users could engage in certain strategies. Finally, the information objects that users interact with and the outcomes of interactions might influence their choices of next strategy. Many studies conducted in the Text Retrieval Conferences have compared IR systems with different designs, and the results demonstrate that the design of IR systems makes significant differences in users' application of search strategies and search performances. Researchers have enhanced their IR systems based on the results of the evaluation studies.

The social-organizational context also defines the environment that user-system interactions take place. Mainly, the work environment influences how users determine their search strategies in the search process. Dimensions of a working place, such as the goals and constraints, priorities, general functions, work processes, and physical objects, in particular, priorities, constraints, and business/ work cycles, have an impact on users' choices of search strategies.[54,76] In addition, cultural dimensions shape how users interact with IR systems.[77]

SEARCH MODELS

Because it is difficult to differentiate search models and retrieval models, in particular interactive IR models as well as some of the information-seeking models that involve search components and process, 11 models in relation to information searching regardless of what terms are used by their original creators are presented here. These search models can be classified mainly into two types. The first type, which mainly illustrates ISPs, includes Ellis' model of information-seeking behaviors, Bates' berry-picking approach, Kuhlthau's model of the ISP, and Workman, Fiszman, Rindflesh, and Nahl's model of serendipitous information search. The second type, which emphasizes the factors that influence the process, consists of Fidel and Soergel's conceptual framework for online bibliographic retrieval, Vakkari's theory of the task-based IR process, Ingwersen and Järvelin's cognitive model, Belkin's episode model of interaction with texts, Saracevic's stratified interaction model, Xie's planned-situational interactive IR model, and Wang, Hawk, and Tenopir's multidimensional model of user–Web interaction. In order to avoid repetition, some of the search models are briefly discussed because they are also presented in other entries.

Ellis' Model of Information-Seeking Behaviors

Ellis[78,79] developed a behavioral model of the information-seeking behaviors of academic social scientists. This approach concentrates on the behavior instead of on cognitive activities. The six types of information-seeking characteristics are the key components of the model: 1) starting, 2) chaining, 3) browsing, 4) differencing, 5) monitoring, and 6) extracting. These characteristics cover the overall search process and indicate that users do engage in multiple types of information-seeking strategies. Ellis and Haugan[80] further modeled the information-seeking patterns of engineers and research scientists in relation to their research activities in different phases and types of projects. Similar behavior patterns were identified from this group of users: surveying, chaining, monitoring, browsing, distinguishing, extracting, filtering, and ending. Ellis' model starts a new behavior approach to identify information-seeking patterns of users and cited widely by researchers who developed other search models.

Bates' Berry-Picking Approach

Continuing her work on search tactics, Bates[81] illustrated the dynamic search process that searchers went through in the berry-picking approach (Fig. 1). It is one of the most cited approaches that not only identify the limitations of traditional IR models, but also characterize the complexity of the search process. It demonstrates that users engage in multiple information-seeking strategies in their search process. The berry-picking approach can be summarized with four characteristics: 1) searchers' queries evolve; 2) the search process is dynamic as people pick up berries instead of finding one retrieved set; 3) searchers apply multiple search strategies including footnote chasing, citation searching, examining journal runs, area scanning, performing subject and author searches in bibliographies

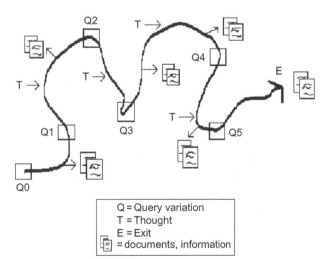

Q = Query variation
T = Thought
E = Exit
= documents, information

Fig. 1 Bates' berry-picking approach.
Source: From Bates,[81] p. 410.

and abstracting and indexing services, and they shift their strategies during the search process; and 4) searchers access resources in different formats and content. The approach also outlines how to implement new search capabilities in the design of online search interfaces. Bates[82] further developed the cascade model that describes several design layers, which have to be taken into account in the process of system implementation. Design decisions at each layer have a cascading impact on subsequent layers; therefore, the information content, its database structure, and retrievable elements are essential for effective IR. Bates' berry-picking approach sets up the foundation for interactive IR that considers search process as user–system interactions.

Kuhlthau's Model of the ISP

The ISP model was created based on a series of studies of users searching for information in different information-seeking situations.[49] The ISP model consists of six stages of ISP with affective feelings, cognitive thoughts, and physical actions taken in each stage. The six stages comprise

1. Initiation and recognition of a need to search for information
2. Selection and identification of an appropriate topic or approach
3. Exploration of relevant information on the topic
4. Formulation of a more focused topic
5. Collection of pertinent information
6. Presentation and summarization of search results

Correspondently, affective feelings common to each stage change from uncertainty, optimism, confusion/frustration/ doubt, clarity, sense of direction/confidence to satisfaction or disappointment; cognitive thoughts shift from vague to focused with increased interest; and actions range from exploring to documenting in seeking pertinent information. The ISP model has been widely tested and validated in a variety of digital environments.[50–53,83–85]

Workman, Fuszman, Rindflesh and Nahl's Model of Serendipitous Information Search

Recently, researchers (Workman, Fiszman, Rindflesh and Nahl, 2014)[86] have investigated serendipitous information seeking and information searching. A model was proposed to illustrate the interaction process occurring in serendipitous information search. It consists of four themes: the iterative process, changes or clarifications of initial information interests, user's prior knowledge, and information organization and presentations. Serendipitous information search is an interactive process including clarifying or changing a current topic, or introducing new topics, etc. The system output needs to be presented in

Information Retrieval–
Information Society

Information Retrieval–
Information Society

such a way as to associate users' new knowledge to prior knowledge. Information organization and presentation are the keys to facilitate opportunistic browsing.

Fidel and Soergel's Conceptual Framework for Online Bibliographic Retrieval

Fidel and Soergel[87] presented a conceptual framework for online bibliographic retrieval. The framework highlights the main factors that affect the search process. Eight elements of the search process and interactions were identified including the setting, the user, the request, the database, the search system, the searcher, the searcher process, and the search outcome. The variables associated with these elements were systematically collected and analyzed: 1) the setting (e.g., organization's orientation, organization affiliations, subject area of the organization, organization mission, etc.); 2) the user (behavior, education, prior experience, attitude, etc.); 3) the request (degree of specificity, degree of difficulty, etc.); 4) the database (coverage, update frequency, thesauri availability, cross-reference listings, cost, etc.); 5) the search system (search aids, search support capabilities, search capabilities, etc.); 6) the searcher (cost consciousness, personality traits, cognitive factors, demographic variables, etc.), 7) the search process (interaction with the user, database selection, query formulation, termination of the search, etc.), and 8) the search outcome (quality of retrieved results, precision, recall, etc.). This framework identifies the main factors affecting online bibliographic retrieval and suggests possible relationships among the variables related to the search process. Although it is created specifically for the online bibliographic retrieval environment, it can also be applied to other digital environments.

Vakkari's Theory of the Task-Based IR Process

Vakkari's theory of the task-based IR process (Fig. 2) considers the ISP as part of the task performance process. This theory is derived from a series of longitudinal studies that investigate students' information-seeking process in their research proposal-writing process for their master's theses.[50–52,88,89] Based on the results of a series of studies, this model illustrates how the task performance process, in particular stages of ISP, influences the information sought, search tactics applied, terms chosen, operators used, relevance judgments assessed, and documents obtained and used. It further enhances Kuhlthau's model of the ISP in terms of the relationships between stages of task and types of information searched for, changes in search tactics and terms, as well as relevance judgments. This theory systematically presents how tasks have impact on the search process.

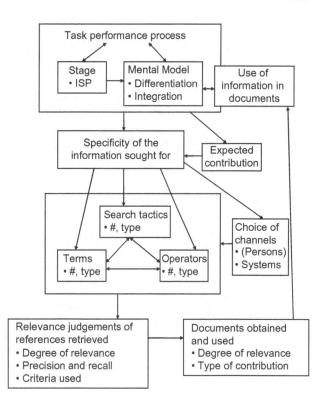

Fig. 2 Vakkari's theory of the task-based IR process.
Source: From Vakkari,[88] p. 58.

Ingwersen and Järvelin's Cognitive Model

Ingwersen and Järvelin[90] developed a cognitive framework of interactive information-seeking, retrieval, and behavioral processes (IS&R) (Fig. 3) based on Ingwersen's original work[91,92] on the process of IR interaction. The new research framework places the cognitive actors or teams which bring their organizational, cultural, and social context to the interaction as the major component of the model instead of the searcher as the center of the interaction. The cognitive actors or teams include creators of information objects, indexers, designers of interfaces, designers of retrieval mechanisms, gatekeepers, searchers, and communities representing different groups. While the first four arrows (1–4) present the interaction process, the rest of the four arrows (5–8) reflect the different types of generation and transformation of cognition or cognitive influence. An information seeker's cognitive space, interacting with both social context and IR systems, plays a central role. Interaction and perception are the central processes of the model. "Models" in each of the components reflect the perception of interpretation of their own contexts by any actor or component of the framework in a certain situation. All the participating cognitive structures are interrelated. This is one of the most comprehensive frameworks that reflect the dynamics and complexity of information seeking and the retrieval process as well as associated factors.

Information Retrieval–
Information Society

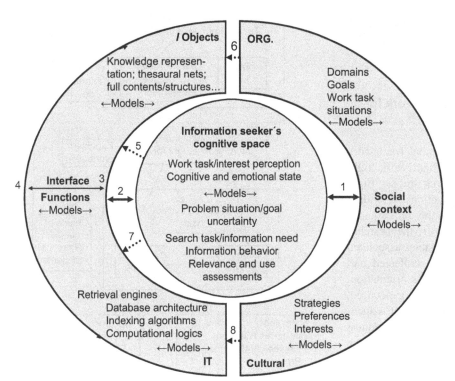

Fig. 3 Modified version of Ingwersen and Järvelin's complex cognitive framework of interactive IS&R.
Source: From Ingwersen and Järvelin,[90] p. 274, Modified by P. Ingwersen, 2007.

Belkin's Episode Model of Interaction with Texts

Contrary to the traditional view of IR that people can specify their information needs and only engage in one type of information-seeking behavior, Belkin[93] pointed out that IR is interaction with texts. He[94] proposed the episode model interaction with texts (Fig. 4), in which users' interaction with texts is the central process of IR. Belkin and his associates[19,20] further classified information-seeking strategies into four behavior dimensions

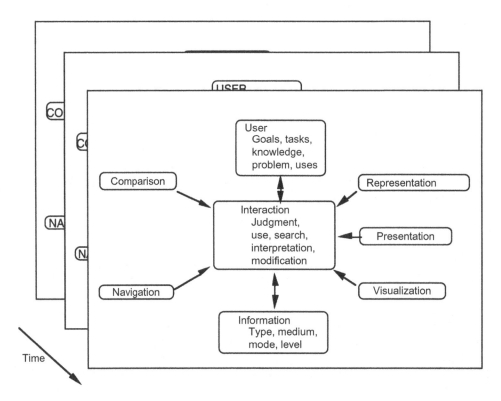

Fig. 4 Belkin's episode model of interaction with texts.
Source: From Belkin,[93] p. 29.

(the goal of the interaction, method of interaction, mode of retrieval, and type of resource interacted with) and designed a dialog-based IR system that supports different types of information-seeking strategies. In this model, users' goals and tasks are the driving force for IR whereas representation, comparison, navigation, presentation, and visualization are the processes that facilitate users' interaction with texts. This model offers a theoretical framework for understanding how users interact with texts by applying multiple information-seeking strategies, and it further suggests how to design interactive IR systems to support multiple information-seeking strategies.

Saracevic's Stratified Interaction Model

Saracevic[95,96] proposed and enhanced the stratified interaction model (Fig. 5) in which interaction of the interplay among different levels of users and systems is the central component. While users engage in cognitive, affective, and situational levels of interaction, system involvement includes engineering, processing, and content level. On the cognitive level, the interaction takes place between the cognitive structure of users and texts. On the affective level, users interact with intentions, beliefs, and motivation. On the situation level, users interact with tasks and problems that lead them to look for information. On the engineering level, the process level, and the content level, the hardware, software, and information resources are the foci for analysis, respectively. Users interact with IR systems via interfaces on the surface level by searching, browsing, navigating, organizing, and viewing search results, providing feedback, and other activities. Interactions not only take place at the surface level, but also occur at the deeper levels, which might also lead to changes at the surface level. The complexity and dynamic

interaction process requires changes and adaptations from both the user and system side. The main contribution of the stratified model is its identification of different levels of interactions from both the user and system side and their interplay.

Xie's Planned-Situational Interactive IR Model

Xie[22] enhanced her previous work[97,98] on the planned-situational interactive IR model derived from an empirical study. The planned-situational model of interactive IR (Fig. 6) is developed to illustrate how plans and situations codetermine users' applying and shifting different information-seeking strategies in their search process. User goal and task are the driving forces for people to look for information. Four levels of user goals are constructed: 1) long-term goal, 2) leading search goal, 3) current search goal, and 4) interactive intention. Dimensions of the work task (stages, timeframe, and nature) and search task (origination, type, and domain) are identified to characterize tasks. Higher levels of the goal/task impact lower levels of the goal/task. More important, levels of user goal and dimensions of tasks influence how users interact with IR systems. At the same time, information search requires users to apply different types of knowledge and skills into the search process. In addition, the social-organizational context defines the environment in which users interact with IR systems. Users and IR systems are the two partners of information searching. By interacting with the interfaces of IR systems, users interact with the information objects stored in these systems as well as with the computational mechanisms of the software and hardware of the systems.

Information-seeking strategies comprise interactive intentions and retrieval tactics, entities, and associated

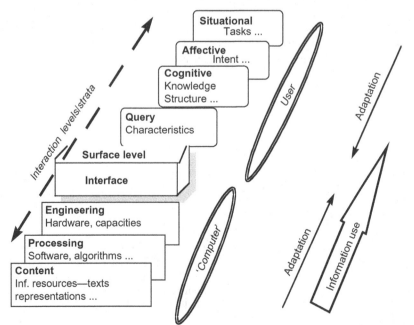

Fig. 5 Saracevic's stratified model of IR interaction.
Source: From Saracevic,[95] p. 316.

Information Retrieval–
Information Society

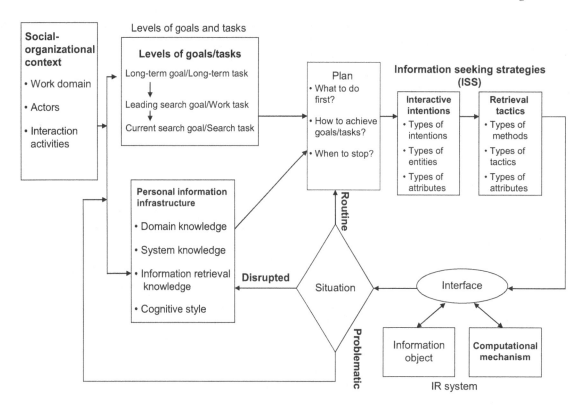

Fig. 6 Planned-situational interactive IR model.
Source: From Xie,[22] p. 216.

attributes. Planned and situational aspects codetermine the selection and shifts in information-seeking strategies. Three types of situations (routine, problematic, and disruptive) lead to different types of shifts in information-seeking strategies. In a routine situation, the situation can be determined sufficiently with the aid of habitual knowledge. In a problematic situation, after associating the elements of situations with his/her knowledge and plans, further clarification of the open elements of the situation is required. A third type of situation is a "disruptive situation," in which users do not encounter any problems, but they are distracted during the process of fulfilling their original current search goals/search tasks. The planned-

situational model was tested and validated by empirical studies.[99–101] This model not only identifies the macro-level components for search and retrieval, but also uncovers shifts in information-seeking strategies and the factors that lead to the selection and shifts in information-seeking strategies at the micro level.

Wang, Hawk, and Tenopir's Multidimensional Model of User–Web Interaction

Focusing on the Web environment, Wang et al.[18] proposed a multidimensional model of user–Web interaction (Fig. 7). The model consists of the user, the interface, and

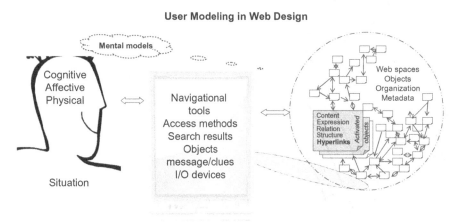

Fig. 7 Modified version of Wang, Hawk, and Tenopir's multidimensional model of user–Web interaction in IR.
Source: From Wang et al.,[18] p. 233. Modified by P. Wang, 2008.

the Web space. Among them, the user is the key component. Users are influenced by situation factors, cognitive behavior, affective state, and physical skills. The interface facilitates users' interactions with Web spaces. Access methods, navigation tools, access results/objects, messages/clues, and input/output devices are the elements of the interface. The Web elements contain objects, activated objects, Web spaces, organization schemes, and metadata. This model is further tested and validated by an exploratory study of graduate students' interaction with a university website. They identified approximately ten problem-solving strategies. The findings show that cognitive factors define how users analyze questions, construct search statements, and develop problem-solving strategies; affective factors affect how users adopt and use of strategies; and physical factors determine whether users can engage in efficient interactions. The multidimensional model of user–Web interaction defines how users search for information in the Web environment.

CONCLUSION

Information searching has evolved from searching for information using manual information systems to using electronic IR systems, as well as from intermediary search to end user search. Research has revealed the limitation of traditional IR research: the assumption that information searching is static and people only formulate queries in their search process. Furthermore, research has shown that the ISP is a dynamic one in which people apply multiple types of search strategies. Multimedia search and social media search have their own unique characteristics and challenges. Different levels of information searching, from search tactics/moves to search strategies and usage patterns, have been identified, as well as factors associated with task, user knowledge structure, system design, and the social and organizational context influencing the search process. More importantly, search models have been developed to illustrate either the dynamic search process or major elements that affect the search process. These models also offer suggestions for IR system enhancement and design.

Unsolved problems in research on information searching and search models still exist, however. First, although research on information searching helps reveal the nature of how people interact with different types of IR systems, very few findings of user studies have been applied to the design of IR systems and even less research has been done on testing the new designs. There is a big gap between user-oriented study and system-oriented design. More collaborative work is needed to incorporate and implement the design principles derived from user studies into IR system design and evaluation. Second, a variety of search models have been developed; the problem is that we may not be able to find a one-size-fits-all model to account for all of the issues in the search process. Further research needs to examine how to integrate different types of search models and identify what is still missing. Third, the newer digital environments call for the need to search for multimedia information and information in different social media. More research is needed to identify search patterns in multimedia and cross-language retrieval. Finally, in order to facilitate users' easy adaptation to different digital environments, future research also needs to compare the similarities and differences of information searching in different digital environments and transform research results into IR system design.

REFERENCES

1. Chu, H. *Information Representation and Retrieval in the Digital Age*; Information Today: Medford, NJ, 2003.
2. Wilson, T.D. Human information behaviour. Inform. Sci. **2000**, *3* (2), 49–56.
3. Jansen, B.J.; Rieh, S.Y. The seventeen theoretical constructs of information searching and information retrieval. J. Am. Soc. Inf. Sci. Technol. **2010**, *61* (8), 1517–1534.
4. Fidel, R. Moves in online searching. Online Rev. **1985**, *9* (1), 61–74.
5. Bates, M.J. Information search tactics. J. Am. Soc. Inf. Sci. **1979**, *30* (4), 205–214.
6. Walker, G.; Janes, J. *Online Retrieval: A Dialogue of Theory and Practice*, 2nd Ed.; Libraries Unlimited: Englewood, CO, 1999.
7. Bates, M.J. Idea tactics. J. Am. Soc. Inf. Sci. **1979**, *30* (5), 280–289.
8. Shute, S.J.; Smith, P.J. Knowledge-based search tactics. Inf. Process. Manag. **1993**, *29* (1), 29–45.
9. Shiri, A.A.; Revie, C. The effects of topic complexity and familiarity on cognitive and physical moves in a thesaurus-enhanced search environment. J. Inf. Sci. **2003**, *29* (6), 517–526.
10. Markey, K.; Atherton, P. *ONTAP. Online Training and Practice Manual for ERIC Database Searchers*; ERIC Clearinghouse on Information Resources: Syracuse, NY, 1978.
11. Chen, H.; Dhar, V. Cognitive processes as a basis for intelligent retrieval system design. Inf. Process. Manag. **1991**, *27* (5), 405–432.
12. Marchionini, G. *Information-Seeking in Electronic Environments*; Cambridge University Press: Cambridge, U.K., 1995.
13. Soloman, P. Children's information retrieval behavior: a case analysis of an OPAC. J. Am. Soc. Inf. Sci. **1993**, *44* (5), 245–264.
14. Bruza, P.D.; Dennis, S. Query-reformulation on the Internet: empirical data and the hyperindex search engine. In *RIAO 97: Conference Proceedings with Prototype and Operational Systems Demonstrations: Computer-Assisted Information Searching on Internet*, McGill University, Montreal, Quebec, Canada, 25th–27th June 1997; RIAO 97, Ed.; CID: Paris, France, 1997; Vol. 1, 488–499.

Information Retrieval–
Information Society

15. Lau, T.; Horvitz, E. Patterns of search: analyzing and modeling Web query refinement. In *Proceedings of the Seventh International Conference on User Modeling Banff, Canada, June 1999*; Kay, J., Ed.; Springer-Wien: New York, 1999; 119–128.

16. Rieh, S.Y.; Xie, H. Analysis of multiple query reformulations on the web: the interactive information retrieval context. Inf. Process. Manag. **2006**, *42* (3), 751–768.

17. Hawk, W.B.; Wang, P. Users' interaction with the World Wide Web; problems and problem solving. In *Proceedings of the 62nd ASIS Annual Meeting*, 1999; Vol. 36, 256–270.

18. Wang, P.; Hawk, W.B.; Tenopir, C. Users' interaction with World Wide Web resources: an exploratory study using a holistic approach. Inf. Process. Manag. **2000**, *36* (2), 229–251.

19. Belkin, N.J.; Marchetti, P.G.; Cool, C. BRAQUE: design of an interface to support user interaction in information retrieval. Inf. Process. Manag. **1993**, *29* (3), 325–344.

20. Belkin, N.J.; Cool, C.; Stein, A.; Thiel, U. Cases, scripts and information seeking strategies: on the design of interactive information retrieval systems. Expert Syst. Appl. **1995**, *9* (3), 379–395.

21. Chang, S. *Toward a multidimensional framework for understanding browsing*; Unpublished doctoral dissertation, Rutgers University: New Brunswick, NJ, 1995.

22. Xie, I. *Interactive Information Retrieval in Digital Environments*; IGI Global Inc.: Hershey, PA, 2008.

23. Yuan, X.; Belkin, N.J. Supporting multiple information-seeking strategies in a single system framework. In *Proceedings of the 30th Annual International ACM SIGIR Conference on Research and Development in Information Retrieval*, July 2007; ACM: New York, 247–254.

24. Yuan, X.; Belkin, N.J. Investigating information retrieval support techniques for different information-seeking strategies. J. Am. Soc. Inf. Sci. Technol. **2010**, *61* (8), 1543–1563.

25. Yuan, X.; Belkin, N.J. Applying an information-seeking dialogue model in an interactive information retrieval system. J. Doc. **2014**, *70* (5), 829–855.

26. Jansen, B.J.; Spink, A.; Saracevic, T. Real life, real users, and real needs: a study and analysis of user queries on the Web. Inf. Process. Manag. **2000**, *36* (2), 207–227.

27. Moukdad, H.; Large, A. Users' perceptions of the Web as revealed by transaction log analysis. Online Inf. Rev. **2001**, *25* (6), 349–359.

28. Spink, A.; Jansen, B.J. *Web Search: Public Searching of the Web*; Kluwer Academic Publishers: Boston, MA, 2004.

29. Spink, A.; Wolfram, D.; Jansen, B.J.; Saracevic, T. Searching the Web: the public and their queries. J. Am. Soc. Inf. Sci. **2001**, *52* (3), 226–234.

30. Silverstein, C.; Henzinger, M.; Marais, H.; Morica, M. Analysis of a very large Web search engine query log. SIGIR Forum **1999**, *33* (1), 6–12.

31. Jones, S.; Cunningham, S.J.; McNab, R.; Boddie, S. Human-computer interaction for digital libraries: a transaction log analysis of a digital library. Int. J. Digit. Libr. **2000**, *3* (2), 152–169.

32. Wang, P.; Berry, M.; Yang, Y. Mining longitudinal Web queries: trends and patterns. J. Am. Soc. Inf. Sci. Technol. **2003**, *54* (8), 743–758.

33. Wolfram, D.; Xie, H. Traditional IR for Web users: a context for general audience digital libraries. Inf. Process. Manag. **2002**, *38* (5), 627–648.

34. Choi, Y.; Hsieh-Yee, I. Finding images in an online public access catalogue: analysis of user queries, subject headings, and description notes. Can. J. Inf. Libr. Sci. **2010**, *34* (3), 271–295.

35. Huurnink, B.; Hollink, L.; Van Den Heuvel, W.; De Rijke, M. Search behavior of media professionals at an audiovisual archive: a transaction log analysis. J. Am. Soc. Inf. Sci. Technol. **2010**, *61* (6), 1180–1197.

36. Jörgensen, C.; Jörgensen, P. Image querying by image professionals. J. Am. Soc. Inf. Sci. Technol. **2005**, *56* (12), 1346–1359.

37. Craswell, N.; Szummer, M. Random walks on the click graph. In *Proceedings of the 30th International Conference on Research and Development in Information Retrieval (ACM SIGIR '07)*; Kraaij, W., De Vries, A., Clarke, C., Fuhr,, N., Kando, N., Eds.; ACM: New York, 2007; 239–246.

38. Ashman, H.; Antunovic, M.; Donner, C.; Frith, R.; Rebelos, E.; Schmakeit, J.F.; Truran, M. Are clickthroughs useful for image labelling? In *Proceedings of the International Joint Conference on Web Intelligence and Intelligent Agent Technology (WI-AT '09)*; IEEE: Washington, DC, 2009; 191–197.

39. Smith, G.; Brien, C.; Ashman, H. Evaluating implicit judgments from image search clickthrough data. J. Am. Soc. Inf. Sci. Technol. **2012**, *63*, 2451–2462.

40. Benevenuto, F.; Rodrigues, T.; Cha, M.; Almeida, V. Characterizing user behavior in online social networks. In *Proceedings of the Ninth ACM SIGCOMM Conference on Internet Measurement Conference*, November 2009; ACM: New York, 49–62.

41. Benevenuto, F.; Rodrigues, T.; Cha, M.; Almeida, V. Characterizing user navigation and interactions in online social networks. Inf. Sci. **2012**, *195*, 1–24.

42. Lerman, K.; Jones, L. Social browsing on flickr. arXiv. preprint cs/0612047, 2006.

43. Lerman, K. Social browsing & information filtering in social media. arXiv preprint arXiv:0710.5697, 2007.

44. Lampe, C.; Ellison, N.; Steinfield, C. A Face (book) in the crowd: social searching vs. social browsing. In *Proceedings of the 2006 20th Anniversary Conference on Computer Supported Cooperative Work*, November 2006; ACM: New York, 167–170.

45. Diakopoulos, N.; De Choudhury, M.; Naaman, M. Finding and assessing social media information sources in the context of journalism. In *Proceedings of the SIGCHI Conference on Human Factors in Computing Systems*, May 2012; ACM: New York, 2451–2460.

46. Byström, K. Information and information sources in tasks of varying complexity. J. Am. Soc. Inf. Sci. Technol. **2002**, *53* (7), 581–591.

47. Byström, K.; Järvelin, K. Task complexity affects information-seeking and use. Inf. Process. Manag. **1995**, *31* (2), 191–213.

48. Zhang, Y.; Wang, P.; Heaton, A.; Winkler, H. Health information searching behavior in MedlinePlus and the impact of tasks. In *Proceedings of the Second ACM SIGHIT International Health Informatics Symposium*, January 2012; ACM, New York, 2012; 641–650:

49. Kuhlthau, C.C. *Seeking Meaning: A Process Approach to Library and Information Services*, 2nd Ed.; Libraries Unlimited: Westport, CT, 2004.

50. Vakkari, P. eCognition and changes of search terms and tactics during task performance: a longitudinal study. In *RIAO' Conference Proceedings, Content-Based Multimedia Information, Collège de France, Paris, France, April 12–14, 2000*; RIAO, Eds.; C.I.D.: Paris, France, 2000; Vol. 1, 894–907. http://www.info.uta.fi/vakkari/Vakkari_Tactics_RIAO2000.html (accessed July 15, 2008).

51. Vakkari, P. Relevance and contributory information types of searched documents in task performance. In *Proceedings of the 23rd Annual International ACM SIGIR Conference on Research and Development in Information Retrieval*; Belkin, N.J., Ingwersen, P., Leong, M.-K., Eds.; SIGIR forum. ACM Press: New York, 2000; Vol. 34, 2–9.

52. Vakkari, P.; Hakala, N. Changes in relevance criteria and problem stages in task performance. J. Doc. **2000**, *56*, 540–562.

53. Vakkari, P.; Pennanen, M.; Serola, S. Changes of search terms and tactics while writing a research proposal. Inf. Process. Manag. **2003**, *39* (3), 445–463.

54. Xie, H. Understanding human-work domain interaction: implications for the design of a corporate digital library. J. Am. Soc. Inf. Sci. Technol. **2006**, *57* (1), 128–143.

55. Bilal, D. Perspectives on children's navigation of the World Wide Web: does the type of search task make a difference. Online Inf. Rev. **2002**, *26* (2), 108–177.

56. Ford, N.; Miller, D.; Moss, N. Web search strategies and retrieval effectiveness: an empirical study. J. Doc. **2002**, *58* (1), 30–48.

57. Schacter, J.; Chung, G.K.W.K.; Dorr, A. Children's Internet searching on complex problems: performance and process analyses. J. Am. Soc. Inf. Sci. **1998**, *49* (9), 840–849.

58. Marchionini, G.; Dwiggins, S.; Katz, A.; Lin, X. Information seeking in full-text end-user-oriented search-systems—the roles of domain and search expertise. Libr. Inf. Sci. Res. **1993**, *15* (1), 35–69.

59. Howard, H. Measures that discriminate among online users with different training and experience. Online Rev. **1982**, *6* (4), 315–326.

60. Lazonder, A.W.; Biemans, H.J.A.; Wopereis, I.G.J.H. Differences between novice and experienced users in searching information on the World Wide Web. J. Am. Soc. Inf. Sci. **2000**, *51* (6), 576–581.

61. Siegfried, S.; Bates, M.J.; Wilde, D.M. A profile of end-user searching behavior by humanities scholars: the Getty online searching project (Rep. No. 2). J. Am. Soc. Inf. Sci. **1993**, *44* (5), 273–291.

62. Sutcliffe, A.G.; Ennis, M.; Watkinson, S.J. Empirical studies of end-user information searching. J. Am. Soc. Inf. Sci. **2000**, *51* (13), 1211–1231.

63. Bhavnani, S.K. Important cognitive components of domain-specific search knowledge. In *The 10th Text REtrieval Conference, TREC-2001*; Voorhees, E.M., Harman, D.K., Eds.; Information Today: Medford, NJ, 2002; 571–578.

64. Drabenstott, K.M. Do nondomain experts enlist the strategies of domain experts? J. Am. Soc. Inf. Sci. Technol. **2003**, *54* (9), 836–854.

65. Dumais, S.T.; Belkin, N.J. The TREC interactive tracks: putting the user into search. In *TREC: Experiment and Evaluation in Information Retrieval*; Voorhees, E.M., Harman, D.K., Eds.; The MIT Press: Cambridge, MA, 2005; 123–152.

66. Wildemuth, B.M. The effect of domain knowledge on search tactic formulation. J. Am. Soc. Inf. Sci. Technol. **2004**, *55* (3), 246–258.

67. Bates, M.J.; Wilde, D.N.; Siegfried, S. An analysis of search terminology used by humanities scholars: the Getty Online Searching Project report no. 1. Libr. Q. **1993**, *63* (1), 1–39.

68. Hsieh-Yee, I. Effects of search experience and subject knowledge on the search tactics of novice and experienced searchers. J. Am. Soc. Inf. Sci. **1993**, *44* (3), 161–174.

69. Bellardo, T. What do we really know about online searchers? Online Rev. **1985**, *9* (3), 223–239.

70. Fenichel, C.H. Online searching: measures that discriminate among users with different types of experience. J. Am. Soc. Inf. Sci. **1981**, *32* (1), 23–32.

71. Fidel, R. Searchers' selection of search keys: I. The selection routine. II. Controlled vocabulary or free-text searching. III. Searching styles. J. Am. Soc. Inf. Sci. **1991**, *42* (7), 490–527.

72. Ford, N.; Wilson, T.D.; Foster, A.; Ellis, D.; Spink, A. Information seeking and mediated searching. Part 4. Cognitive styles in information seeking. J. Am. Soc. Inf. Sci. Technol. **2002**, *53* (9), 728–735.

73. Huang, C.; Joo, S.; Xie, I. Effects of learning styles on the selection of search tactics: a preliminary result. Proceedings of the 75th ASIS&T Annual Meeting **2012**, *49* (1), 1–4.

74. Huang, C. *Understanding novice users' help-seeking behavior in getting started with digital libraries: influence of learning styles*; Doctoral dissertation, University of Wisconsin: Milwaukee, WI, 2014.

75. Palmquist, R.A.; Kim, K.S. Cognitive style and online search experience on Web search performance. J. Am. Soc. Inf. Sci. Technol. **2000**, *51* (6), 558–567.

76. Fidel, R.; Pejtersen, A.M. From information behavior research to the design of information systems: the cognitive work analysis framework. Inf. Res. **2004**, *10*(1), http://informationr.net/ir/10-1/paper210.html (accessed July 10, 2008).

77. Callahan, E. Interface design and culture. Annu. Rev. Inf. Sci. Technol. **2005**, 39, 257–310.

78. Ellis, D. *The derivation of a behavioral model for information system design*; Unpublished doctoral dissertation, University of Sheffield, U.K., 1987.

79. Ellis, D. A behavioural approach to information retrieval system design. J. Doc. **1989**, *45* (3), 171–212.

80. Ellis, D.; Haugan, M. Modeling the information seeking patterns of engineers and research scientists in an industrial environment. J. Doc. **1997**, *53* (4), 384–403.

81. Bates, M.J. The design of browsing and berrypicking techniques for the online search interface. Online Rev. **1989**, *13* (5), 407–424.

82. Bates, M.M. The cascade of interactions in the digital library interface. Inf. Process. Manag. **2002**, *38* (3), 381–400.

83. Cole, C. Intelligent information retrieval: Part IV. Testing the timing of two information retrieval devices in a

Information Retrieval–
Information Society

naturalistic setting. Inf. Process. Manag. **2001**, *37* (1), 163–182.

84. Hyldegard, J. Collaborative information behaviour: exploring Kuhlthau's information search process model in a group-based educational setting. Inf. Process. Manag. **2006**, *42* (1), 276–298.

85. Kracker, J. Research anxiety and students' perceptions of research: an experiment: part 1. Effect of teaching Kuhlthau's ISP model. J. Am. Soc. Inf. Sci. Technol. **2002**, *53* (4), 282–294.

86. Workman, T.E. et al. Framing serendipitous information-seeking behavior for facilitating literature-based discovery: a proposed model. J. Am. Soc. Inf. Sci. **2014**, *65* (3), 501–512.

87. Fidel, R.; Soergel, D. Factors affecting online bibliographic retrieval: a conceptual framework for research. J. Am. Soc. Inf. Sci. **1983**, *34* (3), 163–180.

88. Pennanen, M.; Vakkari, P. Students' conceptual structure, search process and outcome while preparing a research proposal. J. Am. Soc. Inf. Sci. **2003**, *54* (8), 759–770.

89. Vakkari, P. A theory of the task-based information retrieval process. J. Doc. **2001**, *57* (1), 44–60.

90. Ingwersen, P.; Järvelin, K. *The Turn: Integration of Information Seeking and Retrieval in Context*; Springer: Heidelberg, Germany, 2005.

91. Ingwersen, P. *Information Retrieval Interaction*; Taylor Graham: London, U.K., 1992.

92. Ingwersen, P. Cognitive perspectives of information retrieval interaction: elements of a cognitive IR theory. J. Doc. **1996**, *52* (1), 3–50.

93. Belkin, N.J. Interaction with texts: information retrieval as information seeking behavior. In *Information Retrieval '93: Von der Modellierung zur Anwendung*; Knorz, G., Krause, J., Womser-Hacker, C., Eds.; Universitaetsverlag Konstanz: Konstanz, Germany, 1993; 55–66.

94. Belkin, N.J. Intelligent information retrieval: whose intelligence? In *Proceedings of the Fifth International Symposium for Information Science (ISI '96): Humboldt-Universität zu Berlin, 17–19 October 1996*; Krause, J., Herfurth, M., Marx, J., Eds.; Universitätsverlag Konstanz: Konstanz, Germany, 1996; 25–31.

95. Saracevic, T. Modeling interaction in information retrieval (IR): a review and proposal. In *Proceedings of the 59th ASIS Annual Meeting*; Information Today: Medford, NJ, 1996; Vol. 33, 3–9.

96. Saracevic, T. The stratified model of information retrieval interaction: extension and applications. In *Proceedings of the 60th ASIS Annual Meeting*; Information Today: Medford, NJ, 1997; Vol. 34, 313–327.

97. Xie, H. Shifts of interactive intentions and information-seeking strategies in interactive information retrieval. J. Am. Soc. Inf. Sci. **2000**, *51* (9), 841–857.

98. Xie, H. Patterns between interactive intentions and information-seeking strategies. Inf. Process. Manag. **2002**, *38* (1), 55–77.

99. Xie, I. Dimensions of tasks: influences on information seeking and retrieving process. J. Doc. **2009**, *65* (3), 339–366.

100. Xie, I.; Joo, S. Transitions in search tactics during the web-based search process. J. Am. Soc. Inf. Sci. Technol. **2010**, *61* (11), 2188–2205.

101. Xie, I.; Joo, S. Factors affecting the selection of search tactics during the web-based searching process. Inf. Process. Manag. **2012**, *48* (2), 254–270.

Information Society

Frank Webster
City University, London, U.K.

Abstract

The author problematizes the popular notion of "information society," and demonstrates that the concept is vague and imprecise, even of dubious value. It may be, therefore, that a good deal of policy today is premised on somewhat shaky foundations. Five different definitions of an information society are presented, each of which presents criteria for identifying the new. These criteria are technological, economic, occupational, spatial, and cultural. The concepts of information and of theoretical knowledge are also addressed within the larger discussion.

INTRODUCTION

It has been commonplace for more than a decade now to say that those of us who inhabit advanced societies such as in North America, Japan, and Western Europe live in an "information society." The claim that this is so comes routinely from politicians, educationalists, and industrialists, each of whom have concerns about how best to prepare for and compete in this information age. So familiar now is the term information society that it scarcely seems controversial: It is simply part of the accepted vocabulary of opinion leaders who currently comment on the state of the world, a taken-for-granted backcloth to more pressing issues of policy.

For the purposes of this entry, I step back from these more immediate matters deliberately to problematize the notion of the information society. I examine here more precisely than is usual what commentators actually mean when they use the term. As we shall see, when we delve a little, it becomes apparent that the concept is actually vague and imprecise, even of dubious value. Indeed, I shall argue here that the concept information society is inadequate and unhelpful when we try to establish the character of the era in which we live. This suggests, at the least, that a good deal of policy today is premised on somewhat shaky foundations.

We may proceed by distinguishing at least five different definitions of an information society, each of which presents criteria for identifying the new. These criteria are technological, economic, occupational, spatial, and cultural. Let us examine each in turn.

TECHNOLOGICAL

The most common definition of the information society lays emphasis upon spectacular technological innovation. The key idea is that breakthroughs in information processing, storage, and transmission have led to the application of information technologies (IT) in virtually all corners of society. The major concern here is the astonishing reductions in the costs of computers, their prodigious increases in power, and their consequent application any and everywhere. Because it is now economical and feasible to put computers in typewriters, cars, cookers, watches, factory machines, televisions, kids' toys... it follows that we are certain to experience social upheaval of such magnitude that we shall enter a new era. Many books, magazine articles, and television presentations have encouraged the development of a distinct genre that offers this viewpoint: the "mighty micro" will usher in an entirely new "silicon civilization."

Somewhat more sophisticated versions of this technological route to the information society pay attention to the convergence and imbrication of telecommunications and computing (now termed ICT, information and communications technology). In these instances, the argument runs along the following lines: cheap information processing and storage technologies (computers) lead to their being extensively distributed; one of the major areas thus impacted is telecommunications, notably switching centers which, in being computerized, in effect, merge with the general development of computing and impel still more dramatic improvements of information management and distribution. This unification is especially fortuitous because the widespread dissemination of computers means that, for optimum use, they require connection. In short, the computerization of telecommunications means that it is increasingly the case that computer can be linked to computer: hence, the prospect of links between terminals within and between offices, banks, homes, shops, factories, schools, and the globe itself.

This scenario of networked computers is often compared to the provision of electricity: The "information grid" is seen as analogous to the electrical supply. As the electricity grid links every home, office, factory, and shop

Information Retrieval–
Information Society

to provide energy, so the information grid offers information wherever it is needed. This is, of course, an evolutionary process, but with the spread of an ISDN (integrated services digital network), we have the foundational elements of an "information society." Once established, these information networks become the highways of the modern age, akin to the roads, railways, and canals of the Industrial Age. As the latter were crucial because they carried back and forth the materials and goods that made the Industrial Revolution, so an ISDN will provide the infrastructure supporting the key ingredient of the Postindustrial Society—information. The rapid growth of the Internet appears to bring about precisely this.

Undoubtedly, what we have here is a technological definition of an information society. Whether it is one that envisages this resulting from the impact of dramatically new technological innovations or as the outcome of a more incremental development of ISDN systems, all perceive technology to be the major distinguishing feature of the new order.

It is very tempting to dismiss technological approaches to the information society out of hand. There has been a surfeit of gee-whiz writing that, awed by the pace and magnitude of technological change, tells us that "the Computer Revolution...will have an overwhelming and comprehensive impact, affecting every human being on earth in every aspect of his or her life."[1] The genre of futurism that adopts this tone is characteristically full of "wake up" warnings, shallow analyses of the substantive realm, and the self-assurance that only the author has understood what most others have yet to comprehend. It presents but a poor case for the validity of technological measures.

Nevertheless, it is a recurrent account, one that appears in a seemingly cyclical manner. During the 1980s, amidst interest in the "microelectronics revolution," this was offered by the likes of James Martin and Christopher Evans, and it gained much media attention. For a while it went out of fashion, only to return with heady talk of an "information superhighway" in the 1990s and in the breathless prose of MIT (Massachusetts Institute of Technology) researcher Nicholas Negroponte.[2] However, if the likes of Alvin Toffler, Christopher Evans, and James Martin impel one toward rejection of technological criteria, it has to be acknowledged that very many more serious scholars adopt what is at root a similar approach. In Britain, for example, a much respected school of thought has devised a neo-Schumpeterian approach to change. Combining Schumpeter's argument that major technological innovations bring about "creative destruction" with Kondratieff's theme of "long waves" of economic development, these researchers contend that IT represents the establishment of a new epoch. This new "techno-economic paradigm"[3] constitutes the Information Age that is set to mature early in the first century of the millennium.[4,6]

Elsewhere, Piore and Sabel[7,8] have suggested that it is the new technologies that provide the foundation for a radically different way of working—"flexible specialization." Thanks to communication and computer technologies, and the information edge they give to small firms now able quickly to assess markets and adroitly respond to them, the prospect is for an end to "mass production" and its replacement with customized products made by multiskilled and adaptable craftspeople.

It has to be conceded that, commonsensically, these technological definitions of the information society do seem appropriate. After all, if it is possible to see a "series of inventions"[9]—steam power, the internal combustion engine, electricity, the flying shuttle, etc.—as key characteristics of the "industrial society," then why not accept the virtuoso developments in IT as evidence of a new type of society? As John Naisbitt puts it: "Computer technology is to the information age what mechanization was to the industrial revolution."[10] And why not?

Technological definitions of the information society must encounter a number of well-founded objections. These include:

1. If technology is the main criterion for defining a society, then why not just call the emerging era a "high-tech society" or an "automated age?" Given the variety of possible ways in which one could describe a society in which IT predominates—Silicon Society? Cybernetic Society? Robotic Age?—why choose to designate it an "information society?" If technology is the key, then it is rather hard to see why it should need the prefix information attached. But then again the "technological society" scarcely evokes the idea of a new, or even significantly different, world that an information society does.

2. When one reads the literature that tells of profound and portentous changes that new technology is bringing about, one cannot but be struck by its palpable presence. Whether it is learning about the impact of the microelectronics revolution in the home, the consequences of robotics for the factory, or the tidal force of a "third wave" of computers, telecommunications and biotechnology that announce "the death knell of industrialism and the rise of a new civilisation,"[11] there is a self-evident reality about the hereness of the new technologies. Since this is so, and each of us can see it with our own eyes, then it does seem obvious that the technologies are valid as distinguishing features of a new society.

But when one probes further, one cannot but be struck also by the astonishing vagueness of technology in most of these books. Asking for an empirical measure—In this society now, how much IT is there and how far does this take us toward qualifying for information society status? How much IT is required in order to identify an information society?—asking simply for a usable measure, one becomes aware that a good many of those who emphasize technology are not able to provide us with anything so mundanely real-worldly or testable. It begins to appear, that it is everywhere...and nowhere, too.

This problem of measurement, and the associated difficulty of stipulating the point on the technological scale at which a society is judged to have entered an information age, is surely central to any acceptable definition of a distinctively new type of society. It is ignored by popular futurists: The new technologies are announced and it is unproblematically presumed that this announcement in and of itself heralds the information society. This issue is, surprisingly, also bypassed by other scholars who yet assert that IT is the major index of an information society. They are content to describe, in general terms, technological innovations, somehow presuming that this is enough to distinguish the new society.

There are, however, serious scholars who are not content with this and find that the issue of measurement causes considerable obstacles to progress. They encounter two particularly awkward problems. First, how does one measure the rate of technological diffusion, and, second, when does a society cease being "industrial" and enter into the "information" category? These are formidably difficult questions, and ones that should make enthusiasts for the information society scenario hesitate. For instance, in Britain, a decade of social science research by PICT (Programme on Information and Communication Technologies), one charged with mapping and measuring the information society, has not as yet produced any definitive ways of meeting its objectives.[12,14] Certainly, there have been some advances, with several studies charting the diffusion of some IT into factories and offices.[15] But how is one to assess this diffusion in more general terms: by expenditure on IT (Yet, given the tumbling prices of the new technologies, how is one to differentiate the economic variable from the more central element of information handling capacity?) or by the amount and range of IT introduced? Ought one to center on IT expenditure or on takeup per head, or is it better to examine this on an institutional basis? How is one to quantify the significance of the expansion of microcomputer applications vis-à-vis mainframe systems? And, if one opts to focus on the uptake of IT, just what is to count as a relevant technology? For instance, should video games come before personal computers, networked systems before robotic applications? Further, while one may be able to imagine a time at which some measures of "informatization" will have been developed that gain widespread assent, one will still be left with the serious query: Where along that graph is the break point that separates the information society from the merely "advanced industrial?"

3. Finally, critics object to those who assert that, in a given era, technologies are first invented and then, subsequently, impact on the society, thereby impelling people to respond by adjusting to the new. Technology in these versions is privileged above all else; hence, it comes to identify an entire social world: the Steam Age, the Age of the Automobile, the Atomic Age.[16] The central objection here is not that this is unavoidably technologically determinist—in that technology is regarded as the prime social dynamic—and, as such, an oversimplification of processes of change. It most certainly is this, but more important is that it relegates into an entirely separate division social, economic, and political dimensions of technological innovation. These follow from, and are subordinate to, the premier league of technology that appears to be self-perpetuating though it leaves its impress on all aspects of society.

But, it is demonstratively the case that technology is not aloof from the social realm in this way. On the contrary, it is an integral—indeed constitutive—part of the social. For instance, research and development decisions express priorities, and, from these value judgments, particular types of technology are produced (e.g., military projects received substantially more funding than health work for much of the time in the twentieth century West—not surprisingly, a consequence is state-of-the-art weapon systems that dwarf the advances of treatment say of the common cold). Many studies have shown how technologies bear the impress of social values, whether it be in the architectural design of bridges in New York where heights were set that would prevent public transit systems accessing certain areas; the manufacture of cars that testify to the values of private ownership (as opposed to public transport), presumptions about family size (typically two adults, two children), attitudes toward the environment (profligate use of nonrenewable energy alongside pollution), and status symbols (the Porsche, the Mini, the Rover); or the construction of houses that are not just places to live but also expressions of ways of life, prestige and power relations, and preferences for a variety of lifestyles. Again, market power has an obvious influence on what gets manufactured technologically: corporations think of the customers and potential customers prior to production, so it is not surprising that there are limits to what gets made imposed by ability to pay criteria. By the same token, the corporate directors' dictum, "curb costs, increase productivity, and lose heads,"[17] has an obvious influence on what the engineers produce, thereby confounding the approach of those who presume that technology is the driving force of change.

There is an extensive literature on this issue that does not need to be labored. All that is required is to state the objection to the hypostatization of technology as applied to the issue of defining the information society. How can it be acceptable to take what is regarded as an asocial phenomenon (technology) and assert that this then comes to define the social world when it is demonstrable that the dichotomy is implausible because technology is an integral part of the social world?

ECONOMIC

There is an established subdivision of economics that concerns itself with the "economics of information." From within this, and indeed as a founder of this specialism, the late Fritz Machlup (1902–1983) devoted much of his professional life to the goal of assessing the size and growth of the information industries. Machlup's pioneering work, *The Production and Distribution of Knowledge in the United States*,[18] has been seminal in establishing measures of the information society in economic terms. Machlup attempted to trace the information industries in statistical terms. He distinguished 5 broad industry groups (broken down into 50 subbranches), namely:

1. education (e.g., schools, colleges, libraries).
2. media of communication (e.g., radio, television, advertising).
3. information machines (e.g., computer equipment).
4. information services (e.g., law, insurance, medicine).
5. other information activities (e.g., research and development).

Machlup, working with these sort of categories, then attempted to ascribe an economic value to each and to trace its contribution to gross national produce (GNP). If the trend is for these to account for an increased proportion of GNP, then one may claim to chart the emergence through time of an "information economy." This is just what Machlup proposed in this early study,[18] which calculated that 29% of the United States' GNP in 1958 came from the knowledge industries—then a remarkable rate of expansion.

As early as the 1960s, management scholar Peter Drucker was contending that knowledge "has become the foundation of the modern economy" as we have shifted "(f)rom an economy of goods (to)...a knowledge economy."[19] It is commonplace to argue that we have evolved into a society where the "distinguishing characteristic...is that knowledge and organisation are the prime creators of wealth."[20]

Probably the best known—and certainly the most cited—study of the emergence of an information economy conceived on these lines comes in a nine-volume report from Marc Porat[21,22] In allocating industries to his five categories, Machlup had adopted catholic definitions of "knowledge production," broadly including those that created new information and those that communicated it. Porat echoed much of Machlup's approach in his reliance

on government statistical sources to design a computer model of the U.S. economy in the late sixties, but divided the economy between the "primary," "secondary," and "noninformation" sectors. This tripartite schema stemmed from his identification of a weakness in Machlup's approached that failed to account for information activities that were disguised from initial examination; for example. because they are an in-house element of other industries. Porat included in the primary information sector all those industries that make available their information in established markets or elsewhere where an economic value can be readily ascribed (e.g., mass media, education, advertising, computer manufacture). Thus:

The primary information sector includes...industries that in some way produce, process, disseminate, or transmit knowledge or messages. The unifying definition is that the goods and services that make up the primary sector must be fundamentally valued for their information producing, processing, or distributing characteristics.[23]

However, Porat then sought to identify a secondary information sector that would allow him to include in his typology important informational activities such as research and development inside a pharmaceutical company, information produced by government departments for internal consumption, and the library resources of an oil corporation. Thus:

The secondary information sector includes the informational activities of the public bureaucracy and private bureaucracies. The private bureaucracy is that portion of every noninformation form that engages in purely informational activities, such as research and development, planning, control, marketing, and recordkeeping... The public bureaucracy includes all the informational functions of the federal, state, and local governments.[23]

In this way, Porat is able to distinguish the two information sectors, then to consolidate them, separate out the noninformational elements of the economy, and, by reaggregating national economic statistics, is able to conclude that over 46% of the U.S. GNP is accounted for by the information sector. Ipso facto "The United States is now an information-based economy." As such, it is an "information society (where) (t)he major arena of economic activity are the information goods and service producers, and the public and private [secondary information sector] bureaucracies."[23]

This quantification of the economic significance of information is an impressive achievement. It is not surprising that those convinced of the emergence of an information society' have routinely turned to Machlup and especially Porat as authoritative demonstrations of a rising curve of information activity, one set to lead the way to a new age.

However, there are difficulties too with the economics of information approach.[24] One is that, behind the weighty statistical tables that are resonant of objective demonstration, there is a great deal of hidden interpretation and value judgement as to how to construct categories and what to include and exclude from the information sector.

In this regard, what is particularly striking is that, in spite of their marked differences, both Machlup and Porat create encompassing categories of the information sector that exaggerate its economic worth. There are reasons to question the worth of at least some of these categories. For example, Machlup includes in his "knowledge industries" the "construction of information buildings," the basis of which presumably is that building for, say a university or a library is distinguishable from construction of warehouses meant to house tea or coffee. But how then is one to allocate the many buildings that, once constructed, change purposes (many university buildings, in the United Kingdom at least, are located in erstwhile domestic houses and stately homes, and one even in a former warehouse)?

Again, Porat is at some pains to identify the "quasi-firm" embedded within a noninformational enterprise. But is it acceptable, from the correct assumption that R&D in a petrochemical company involves informational activity, to separate this from the manufacturing element for statistical purposes? It is surely likely that the activities are blurred, with the R&D section intimately tied to production wings, and any separation for mathematical reasons is unfaithful to its role. More generally, when Porat examines his secondary information sector, he, in fact, splits every industry into the informational and noninformational domains. But such divisions between the thinking and the doing are extraordinarily hard to accept—where does one put operation of computer numerical control systems or the line management functions that are an integral element of production? To be sure, one could say that everything here involves information—and as we shall see, many writers identify the expansion of "managers" and "white collar" work tout court as reason for the coming of an information society—but that is not the point. The objection here is that Porat divides, arbitrarily, within industries, to chart the secondary information sector as opposed to the noninformational realm.

Such objections may not entirely invalidate the findings of Machlup and Porat, and they are not intended to do that, but they are a reminder of the unavoidable intrusion of value judgments in the construction of their statistical tables. As such, they lend support to a healthy skepticism toward ideas of an emergent information economy.

A second difficulty is that the aggregated data inevitably homogenize very disparate economic activities. In the round, it may be possible to say that growth in the economic worth of advertising and television is indicative of an information society, but one is left with an urge to distinguish between informational activities on qualitative grounds. In asking which economically assessed characteristics are more central, are more strategic, to the emergence of an information society, one is requesting scholars to distinguish between, say information stemming from

policy research centers, corporate think tanks, transnational finance houses, manufacturers of 35-mm cameras, software designers, and advertising copywriters.

The enthusiasm of the information economists to put a price tag on everything has the unfortunate consequence of failing to let us know the really valuable dimensions of the information sector. This search to differentiate between quantitative and qualitative indices of an information society is not pursued by Machlup and Porat, though on a commonsensical level, it is obvious that the 4 million daily sales of the *The Sun* cannot be equated with—still less, be regarded as more informational, though doubtless it is of more economic value—the 400,000 or so circulation of *The Financial Times*. It is a distinction to which we shall return, but one that suggests the possibility that we could have a society in which, as measured by GNP, informational activity is of great weight, but that in terms of the springs of economic, social, and political life, is of little consequence. A nation of couch potatoes and Disney-style pleasure seekers consuming images night and day?

Of course, these economists are concerned solely with developing quantitative measurements of the information sector, so the issue of the qualitative worth of information would be of limited relevance to them. However, even on their, own terms, there are problems. One, mentioned earlier, is the question "at which point on the economic graph does one enter an information society?" When 50% of GNP is dedicated to informational activities? This may seem to be a reasonable point, one at which, in straightforward quantitative terms, information begins to predominate. Sadly for information society theorists, however, we are some distance even from that point. Replication studies of Machlup and Porat lead one to qualify any initial sighting of the new age. In a large scale update of Machlup's study, Rubin and Huber concluded that, in the United States, the contribution of "knowledge industries" to GNP increased from 28.6% to 34.3% between 1958 and 1980, with virtually no change since 1970, this constituting an "extremely modest rate of growth relative to the average rate of growth of other components of total GNP."[25] These econometric studies scarcely trumpet the arrival of an information society.

OCCUPATIONAL

A popular measure of the emergence of an information society is the one that focuses on occupational change. Put simply, the contention is that we have achieved an information society when the predominance of occupations is found in information work. That is, the information society has arrived when clerks, teachers, lawyers, and entertainers outnumber coal miners, steelworkers, dockers, and builders. The intellectual groundwork for this conception of the information society was done by Daniel

Bell (1919–) in the 1960s, but it is worth stressing that this definition is presently enjoying much popularity as concern has shifted from a technological measure toward an occupational notion. The emphasis here is on enterprising deal makers, people who "think smart" and quickly in a fast-changing world. Reich[26,27] has called these "symbolic analysts," those who do the thinking, planning, innovation, and organization of the "new economy." They may work in the "creative industries" (media, design, arts), consultancy, or general management, but a popular idea is that such information workers are key to future prosperity. What they have in common is high-level education, and, accordingly, a priority is placed by national governments on the capability of their own education systems to produce such people.[28]

The occupational definition is frequently combined with an economic measure. Porat, for example, whose work we discussed in the previous section, calculated that by the late 1960s, a little under half the U.S. labor force was to be found in the information sector, a growth of almost 500% during a century in which agricultural employment has plummeted and information occupations have massively expanded. Porat connects the growth in economic significance of information with changing occupational patterns as follows:

In 1967, 25.1% of the U.S. GNP originated with the production, processing, and distribution of information goods and services sold on markets. In addition, the purely informational requirements of planning, coordinating, and managing the rest of the economy generated 21.1% of the GNP. These informational activities engaged more than 46% of the work force, which earned over 53% of all labor income. On the strength of these findings, we call ours an "information economy."[23]

On the surface, the changing distribution of jobs seems an appropriate measure. After all, it appears obvious that as work that demands physical strength and manual dexterity, such as hewing coal and farming the land, declines to be replaced by more and more manipulation of figures and text, such as in education and large bureaucracies, then so we are entering a new type of society. Today "(o)nly a shrinking minority of the labour force toils in factories... and (t)he labour market is now dominated by information operatives who make their living by virtue of the fact that they possess the information needed to get things done."[29]

Most identifiers of an information society draw on occupational changes as indices of the approach of a new age, as many probably as see it in the introduction of new technologies. And, a great number combine the two, regarding new technologies and new informational occupations almost as synonymous. However, it should be noted that the occupational definition is by no means the same as one that identifies an information society by the take-up of new technologies. Many information occupations (e.g., solicitors, teachers) may use little IT, while many distinctly noninformational jobs have been impacted dramatically by new technologies (e.g., factory operatives, supermarket checkout workers).

The shift in the distribution of occupations is at the heart of the most influential theory of the information society. Here Bell[30] sees, in the emergence of "white collar society" (and, hence, information work) and in the decline of industrial labor changes as profound as the end of class-based political conflict, more communal consciousness and the development of equality between the sexes.

Robins and I[31] have criticized Bell's theorization elsewhere, but here it is appropriate to raise some general objections to occupational measures of the information society. A major problem concerns the methodology for allocating workers to particular categories. The end product—a bald statistical figure giving a precise percentage of "information workers"—hides the complex processes by which researchers construct their categories and allocate people to one or another.

Porat, for instance, develops what has become an influential typology to locate occupations that are primarily engaged in the production, processing, or distribution of information. His is a three-fold scheme that encompasses over 400 occupational types that are reported by the U.S. Census and Bureau of Labor Statistics. He explains it as follows:

The first category includes those workers whose output as primary activity is producing and selling knowledge. Included here are scientists, inventors, teachers, librarians, journalists, and authors. The second major class of workers covers those who gather and disseminate information. These workers move information within firms and within markets; they search, coordinate, plan, and process market information. Included here are managers, secretaries, clerks, lawyers, brokers, and typists. The last class includes workers who operate the information machines and technologies that support the previous two activities. Included here are computer operators, telephone installers, and television repairers.[23]

Jonscher[32] simplifies this further still, discerning just two sectors of the economy: the first, an "information sector," is where people whose prime function is creating, processing, and handling information; the second, a "production sector," is where workers are found who chiefly create, process, and handle physical goods. These distinctions appear reasonable, precise, and empirically valid, but there are difficulties. Not least is something of which Porat is well aware, namely that "(s)tating precisely who is an information worker and who is not is a risky proposition."[23] Indeed, it is, since every occupation involves a significant degree of information processing and cognition. Porat acknowledges this in his attempt to distinguish noninformational from informational labor on the basis of estimating the degree to which each type is involved with information. In other words the categorization is a matter of judging the extent to which jobs are informational or not. Crude percentages of information workers thus disguise the fact that they are the outcome of the researcher's estimations. As Porat puts it: when "we assert that certain occupations are primarily engaged in the manipulation of symbols... It is a distinction of degree, not of kind."[22]

For example, the railway signalman must have a stock of knowledge about tracks and timetables, about roles and routines; he needs to communicate with other signalmen down the line, with station personnel and engine drivers; he is required to "know the block" of his own and other cabins, must keep a precise and comprehensive ledger of all traffic that moves through his area, and has little need of physical strength to pull levers since the advent of modern equipment. Yet, the railway signalman is, doubtless, a manual worker of the Industrial Age. Conversely, the person who comes to repair the photocopier may know little about products other than the one for which he has been trained; may well have to work in hot, dirty, and uncomfortable circumstances; and may need considerable strength to move heavy machinery and replace damaged parts. Yet, he will undoubtedly be classified as an information worker since his work with new age machinery suits Porat's interpretations.

The point to be made here is simple: We need to be skeptical of conclusive figures that are the outcomes of researchers' perceptions of where occupations are to be most appropriately categorized. As a matter of fact, social scientists know very little about the detail and complexity of people's jobs; there are precious few ethnographies that record the stuff of working lives.[33] And, researchers trying to label information and noninformation work are just as much in the dark as the rest of their social science colleagues.

One needs also to beware the oversimplifications that can come from allocating a wide variety of jobs to the same pigeonholes. Miles rightly observes that "(t)he categories of work subsumed under the different headings are often extremely heterogeneous."[34] When one considers, for example, that Porat's first category (information producers) lumps together opticians, library assistants, composers, paperback writers, university professors, and engineers, while his second (information distributors) subsumes journalists on quality newspapers with deliverers on the street, and when the OECD (Organization for Overseas Co-operation and Development) puts together as information producers physicists, commodity brokers, and auctioneers, then one may well have doubts about the value of this composition of occupations as a means of identifying social change. Further, what of the diversity of occupations, each with the same title? Librarian, for example, can encompass someone spending much of the day either issuing books for loan or reshelving returns, as well as someone routinely involved in advising academics on the best sources of information for progressing state-of-the-art research. Again, the title journalist covers a range from hacks specializing in the sex lives of celebrities, cub reporters

describing local weddings, to feature writers whose work can match the best analyses of university professors. Is it really sensible to lump together such diversity?

Finally, an important consequence of this homogenization is a failure to identify the more strategically central information occupations. While the methodology may provide us with a picture of greater amounts of information work taking place, it does not offer any means of differentiating the most important dimensions of information work. The pursuit of a quantitative measure of information work disguises the possibility that the growth of certain types of information occupation may have particular consequences for social life.

I alluded to this distinction when commenting on economic measures of an information society, but it is especially pertinent as regards occupational measures since some commentators seek to characterize an information society in terms of the "primacy of the professions,"[30] while still others focus on alternative sources of strategically central information occupations. It has to be said that counting the number of information workers in a society tells us nothing about the hierarchies—and associated variations in power and esteem—of these people. For example, it could be argued that the crucial issue has been the growth of computing and telecommunications engineers since these may exercise a decisive influence over the pace of technological innovation. A similar, perhaps even greater, rate of expansion in social workers to handle problems of an aging population, increased family dislocation and juvenile delinquency may have little or nothing to do with an information society, though undoubtedly social workers would be classified with IT engineers as information workers.

Or it may be argued that it is an "inner circle"[35–37] of corporate leaders, quite different from their predecessors, which is the most decisive index of the information society. These are people who are empowered by communicative skills, analytical abilities, foresight, and capacities to formulate strategic policies, who also enjoy privileged educational backgrounds, connections through shared clubs and boardroom affiliations, plus access to sophisticated information and communications technologies. All of this provides them with extraordinary leverage over social, economic, and political affairs at the national and even the international level. They are information specialists but radically different from the run-of-the-mill information workers with whom crude quantitative methodologists would lump them.

Perhaps we can better understand this need to qualitatively distinguish between groups of information workers by reflecting on a study by social historian Harold Perkin. In *The Rise of Professional Society*, Perkin argues that the history of Britain since 1880 may be written largely as the rise to preeminence of "professionals" who rule by virtue of "human capital created by education and enhanced by... the exclusion of the unqualified." Perkin contends

Information Retrieval–
Information Society

that certified expertise has been "the organising principle of post-war society,"[38] the expert displacing once-dominant groups (working class organizations, capitalist entrepreneurs, and the landed aristocracy) and their outdated ideals (of co-operation and solidarity, of property and the market, and of the paternal gentleman) with the professional's ethos of service, certification, and efficiency. To be sure, professionals within the private sector argue fiercely with those in the public, but Perkin insists that this is an internecine struggle, one within "professional society," which decisively excludes the nonexpert from serious participation and shares fundamental assumptions (notably the primacy of trained expertise and reward based on merit).

Alvin Gouldner's discussion of the "new class" provides an interesting complement to Perkin's. Gouldner identifies a new type of employee that has expanded in the twentieth century, a new class that is "composed of intellectuals and technical intelligensia,"[39] who, while in part self-seeking and often subordinate to powerful groups, can also contest the control of established business and party leaders. Despite these potential powers, the new class is itself divided in various ways. A key division is between those who are for the most part technocratic and conformist, and the humanist intellectuals who are critical and emancipatory in orientation. To a large extent, this difference is expressed in the conflicts identified by Perkin between private-and public-sector professionals. For instance, we may find that accountants in the private sector are conservative, while there is a propensity for humanistic intellectuals to be radical.

Our main point here is that both Gouldner and Perkin are identifying particular changes within the realm of information work that have especially important consequences for society as a whole. To Gouldner, the new class can provide us with vocabularies to discuss and debate the direction of social change, while to Perkin, the professionals create new ideals for organizing social affairs.

If one is searching for an index of the information society in these thinkers, one will be directed to the quality of the contribution of certain groups. Whether one agrees or not with either of these interpretations, the challenge to definitions of an information society on the basis of a count of raw numbers of information workers should be clear. To thinkers such as Perkin and Gouldner, the quantitative change is not the main issue. Indeed, as a proportion of the population, the groups they lay emphasis upon, while they have expanded, remain distinct minorities. Tiny in the case of Useem's "inner circle" and more numerous where the growth of professions is identified but never more than 20% or 25% of the workforce.

SPATIAL

This conception of the information society, while it draws on sociology and economics, has at its core the geographer's distinctive stress on space. Here, the major emphasis is on the information networks that connect locations and, in consequence, have dramatic effects on the organization of time and space. It has become an increasingly popular index of the information society, largely because of a remarkable trilogy written by Manuel Castells titled *The Information Age (1996–1998)* in which he describes a "network society."[40,41]

Goddard[42,43] identifies several interrelated elements in the transition to an information society. These include:

• Information is coming to occupy center stage as the "key strategic resource" on which the organization of a world economy is dependent.

The modern world demands the coordination of globally distributed manufacture, planning across and between sovereign states, and marketing throughout continents. What might be called the globalization of enterprise—from production, through distribution, to marketing—means that economic (and other) affairs are increasingly conducted on a world scale. As historian Eric Hobsbawm has observed, especially from the 1960s, a world economy began to come into existence "which actually has no specifiable territorial base or limits," and by the early 1970s, such a transnational economy became an effective global force. The inexorable logic of this for the participants, chiefly transnational corporations that are "the dominant forces in the world economy,"[44] is to develop global strategies and mechanisms to maximize their comparative advantages. Information, or what Peter Dicken calls the "circulation activities" that "connect the various parts of the production system together,"[44] is axial to these diverse activities, thus of heightened importance in the contemporary world. It follows too that "information management" is of exceptional pertinence and that, as a result, we witness the rapid expansion of information occupations.

• Computer and communications technologies provide the infrastructure that enables information to be processed and distributed. These technologies allow information to be handled on an historically unprecedented scale, to facilitate instantaneous and real-time trading, and to monitor economic, social, and political affairs on a global stage.
• There has been an exceptionally rapid growth of the "tradeable information sector" of the economy, by which Goddard means to highlight the explosive growth of services such as new media (satellite broadcasting, cable, video) and on-line databases providing information on a host of subjects ranging from stock market dealings, commodity prices, patent listings, currency fluctuations, to scientific and technological journal abstracts.

Complementing these developments has been the radical reorganization of the world's financial system that has resulted in the collapse of traditional boundaries that once separated banking, brokerage, financial services, credit agencies, and the like. Inside this bewildering world of high finance—which few people understand and still fewer appear able to control—circulates, in electronic form, dazzling sums of capital (one estimate suggests there are $2 trillion Eurodollars in the system, though there were none just over a generation ago[45]). It might be hard to conceptualize, but it is difficult to underestimate the import of the growth of an integrated global financial market. With sophisticated IT systems now in place, plus the deregulation of stock markets and the abolition of exchange controls, we now have facilities for the continuous and real-time flow of monetary information, for round-the-clock trading in stocks, bonds, and currencies. The scale and speed of these information flows is astonishing. Hutton,[46] for instance, observes that foreign exchange turnover dwarfs the size of national economies and makes trade flows (a traditional method of measuring national economic activity in terms of import and export levels) appear small in comparison. Thus "the total level of world merchandise trade in 1993 is two-thirds of US Gross Domestic Production; it will take turnover in the foreign exchange markets less than a fortnight to reach the same total."[46]

Courtesy of immediate and effective information processing and exchange economics has become truly global and with this has come about a reduction in the constraints of space. Companies can now develop global strategies for production, storage, and distribution of goods and services; financial interests operate continuously, respond immediately, and traverse the globe. The boundaries erected by geographical location are being pushed further and further back—and with them too the limitations once imposed by time—thanks to the virtuoso ways in which information can be managed and manipulated in the contemporary period.

Such developments emphasize the centrality of information networks linking together locations within and between towns, regions, nations, continents and, indeed, the entire world. As the electricity grid runs throughout an entire nation, extending down to the individual household, so too we may envisage now a "wired society"[47] operating at the national, international, and global level to provide an "information grid"[48] to each home, shop, or office. Increasingly, we are all connected to the network—which itself is expanding its reach and capacities. We come across it personally at many levels: in electronic point of sale terminals in shops and restaurants, in accessing data across continents, in e-mailing colleagues, or in exchanging information on the Internet. We may not personally experience it, but the 'information ring main' functions still more frantically at the level of international banks, intergovernmental agencies, and corporate relationships.

In many writings, emphasis is put on the technological bases of the information network.[49] Perhaps predictably

then with these accounts of an emerging network society considerable attention is given to advances in and obstacles to the development of an ISDN infrastructure.[50] However, notwithstanding the importance of technology and actually providing a salutary reminder of the easily neglected centrality of telecommunications to IT developments, most thinkers concerned with the emergence of a "network marketplace" place stress on ways in which networks underline the significance of the flow of information.[40]

The salient idea here is of information circulating along electronic "highways." Interestingly, no one has been able to quantify how much and at what rate information must flow along these routes to constitute an information society. In fact, no one has produced reliable figures capable of giving us an overall understanding of information traffic.[51] We have data on telephone density in relation to population, figures on the expansion of facsimile services, statistics for sales of computer systems, automated telecommunications exchanges, and so on, but lack a clear picture of the size, capacity, and use of the networks.

Nevertheless, all observers are aware of a massive increase in transborder data flows, in telecommunications facilities, in communications between computers at every level from home to transnational organization, in exchanges between stock markets and corporate segments, in access to international databases, in telex messages, and in uptake of the Internet. Similarly, there is considerable awareness of increases in the global distribution of mass mediated information: satellite television being the obvious and preeminent example, though one would also have to include news gathering and distribution services in any adequate picture. As Mulgan has it, "the networks carry an unimaginable volume of messages, conversations, images and commands"[52]

Why much greater volume and velocity of information flows should impel us to think in terms of the constitution of a new type of society returns us to the geographer's special concern with space. All things happen in particular places and at specific times, but the characteristics of space and time have been transformed with the advent of the network society. Where once trade was cumbersome and slow moving across distances, nowadays it can be effected instantaneously with computerized communications technologies; where once corporate activity had to be coordinated by slow-moving letter that took days and even weeks to cross the space that divided the interested parties, nowadays it takes place in real time courtesy of sophisticated telecommunications and video-conference facilities.

A world built on networks calls into question older conceptions of space and power. Where the early market economies grew out of the temporal and spatial regularities of city life, today's are built on the logical or "virtual" regularities of electronic communications, a new geography of nodes and hubs, processing and control centers.

The nineteenth century's physical infrastructure of railways, canals, and roads are now overshadowed by the network of computers, cables, and radio links that govern where things go, how they are paid for, and who has access to what.[52]

In short, the constraints of space have been dramatically limited, though certainly not eliminated. And, simultaneously, time has itself been "shrunk" as contact via computer communications and telecommunications is immediate. This "time/space compression," as Giddens[53] terms it, provides corporations, governments, and even individuals with hitherto unachievable options.

No one could deny that information networks are an important feature of contemporary societies: Satellites do allow instantaneous communications round the globe; databases can be accessed from Oxford to Los Angeles, Tokyo, and Paris; facsimile machines and interconnected computer systems are a routine part of modern businesses.

Yet, we may still ask: Why should the presence of networks lead analysts to categorize societies as information economies? And, when we ask this, we encounter the problem of the imprecision of definitions once again. For instance, when is a network a network? Two people speaking to one another by telephone or computer systems transmitting vast data sets through a packet switching exchange? When an office block is "wired" or when terminals in the home can communicate with local banks and shops? The question of what actually constitutes a network is a serious one and it raises problems not only of how to distinguish between different levels of networking but also of how we stipulate a point at which we have entered a network/information society.

Finally, one could argue that information networks have been around for a very long time. From, at very least, the early days of the postal service, through to telegram and telephone facilities, much economic, social, and political life is unthinkable without the establishment of such information networks. Given this long-term dependency and incremental, if accelerated, development, why should it be that in the 1980s commentators began to talk in terms of information societies?

CULTURAL

The final conception of an information society is perhaps the most easily acknowledged, yet the least measured. Each of us is aware, from the pattern of our everyday lives, that there has been an extraordinary increase in the information in social circulation. There is simply a great deal more of it about than ever before.

Television has been in extensive use for well over 40 years in Britain, but now its programming is pretty well round-the-clock, people being able to watch from breakfast time until the early morning. It has expanded from a single channel and discontinuous service to include now five broadcast channels, while digitalization of television, now well advanced, will bring a huge increase of channels within the next decade or so. This has been enhanced to incorporate video technologies, cable and satellite channels, and even computerized information services such as teletext. An avalanche of computerized games has become attached to Personal Computers and virtual reality products have begun to enter the home. There is very much more radio output available now than even a decade ago, at local, national, and international levels. And radios are no longer fixed in the front room, but spread through the home, in the car, in the office, and, with the walkman, everywhere. Movies have long been an important part of people's information environment and, indeed, attendances at cinemas have significantly declined. But movies are today very much more prevalent than ever: available still at cinema outlets, broadcast on television, readily borrowed from video rental shops, cheaply purchased from the shelves of chain stores. Walk along any street and it is almost impossible to miss the advertising displays, the billboards, and the window arrangements in shops. Visit any railway or bus station and one cannot but be struck by the widespread availability of paperback books and inexpensive magazines—their subject matter ranging from classical, pulp fiction, middlebrow, to self-therapy—a scale and scope without precedent. In addition, audiotape, compact disc and radio all offer more, and more readily available, music, poetry, drama, humor, and education to the general public. Newspapers are extensively available and a good many new titles fall on our doorsteps as free sheets. Junk mail is delivered daily.

All of this testifies to the fact that we inhabit a media-laden society, but the informational features of our world are more thoroughly penetrative than a short list of television, radio, and other media systems suggests. This sort of listing implies that new media surround us, presenting us with messages to which we may or may not respond. But, in truth, the informational environment is a great deal more intimate, more constitutive of us, than this suggests. One may consider, for example, the informational dimensions of the clothes we wear, the styling of our hair and faces, the very ways in which, nowadays, we work at our image (from body shape to speech, people are intensely aware of the messages they may be projecting and how they feel about themselves in certain clothes, with a particular hairstyle, etc.). A few moment's reflection on the complexities of fashion, the intricacy of the ways in which we design ourselves for everyday presentation, makes one well aware that social intercourse nowadays involves a greater degree of informational content than previously.

To be sure, there has long been adornment of the body, clothing, and makeup being important ways of signaling status, power, and affiliation. But, it is obvious that historically the present age has dramatically heightened the symbolic import of dress and the body. When one considers the lack of range of meaning that characterized the peasant smock that was the apparel of the majority for centuries, and the uniformity of the clothing worn by the industrial working class in and out of work up to the 1950s, then the veritable explosion of meaning in terms of dress since then is remarkable. The availability of cheap and fashionable clothing, the possibilities of affording it, and the accessibility of any amount of groups with similar—and different—lifestyles and cultures (divided by age, gender, race, ethnicity, affluence, region, etc.) all make one appreciate the informational content even of our bodies.

Homes too are informational laden in an historically singular way. Furniture, layout, and decorative design all express ideas and ideals: the G-plan style, the Laura Ashley settee, the William Morris wallpaper and the mixing of some and all of these according to choice and budget. Certainly, since the days of the Industrial Revolution, homes have signified ways of life—one thinks, for example, of the style of the "respectable" working class of the late Victorian period or the distinctive design of the professional middle classes between the wars. But, it is the explosion in variety, and the accessibility of it to a great many, that is most remarkable. With this has come an astonishing vista of signification.

This intrusion of information into the most intimate realms of home, bedroom and body is complemented by the growth of institutions dedicated to investing everyday life with symbolic significance. One thinks of the global advertising business, of publishing empires, of the fashion industry, of worldwide agencies of media production that bring to the domestic scene reflections of our own ways of life and images of other lifestyles, thereby presenting us with alternative meanings that may be absorbed, rejected, and reinterpreted by people, but all the time adding to the vocabulary of the symbolic environment.

Contemporary culture is manifestly more heavily information laden than any of its predecessors. We exist in a media-saturated environment that means that life is quintessentially about symbolization, about exchanging and receiving—or trying to exchange and resisting reception—messages about ourselves and others. It is in acknowledgment of this explosion of signification that many writers conceive of our having entered an information society. They rarely attempt to gauge this development in quantitative terms but rather start from the "obviousness" of our living in a sea of signs, one fuller than at any earlier epoch.

It is not difficult to explain why this should be so. For most of history, people would have lived in relatively fixed conditions with neighbors who would have been well-known to one another since all lived in the same location. Today, life is characteristically one of the interaction of strangers, each with a heightened sense of their individuality and the choices open to them. Nowadays, people live for only a few years in one place before moving on; daily, they make decisions about what to wear,

buy, eat, and do from a range that to their forebears would have seemed astonishingly broad; during the day, they are likely to meet others about whom they know little; urban dwelling is the norm. In a world of strangers, it is essential that people have means of communication to reach out to others, to establish their own identities, and to exchange information. Obviously, the spoken word is central to this, and this vocabulary has expanded over the years, but so too are goods, cars, clothes, and so forth because they provide us with "languages" with which to connect to a changing world.

Into this—the familiar story of a shift from community to association that appears to be accelerating—needs to be placed the spectacular expansion of media technologies[54] that help produce conditions in which much of life today is experienced symbolically rather than personally encountered: news is not passed from word of mouth by people who know one another, but electronically from around the globe; our work is very often concerned with exchanging symbols with others with whom we do not come into personal contact, but substitute for by writing or telephone communications; our entertainment is more often made by watching a screen than by personally attending a show.

Furthermore, it is easy to appreciate that this world of signification is also characterized by constant change and, accordingly, with persistent shifts and strains in the symbolic environment. Just think of the proliferation of lifestyles nowadays (among students, social classes, the young, family forms, etc.), or reflect on the rapidly changing appeal of intellectual ideas, of musical tastes, and of fashionable "looks," and consider the innovation, conflicts, misunderstandings, and tumult that this engenders.

Paradoxically, it is perhaps this very explosion of information that leads some writers to announce, as it were, the death of the sign. Blitzed by signs all around us, designing ourselves with signs, unable to escape signs wherever we may go, the result is, oddly, a collapse of meaning. As Baudrillard puts it: "there is more and more information, and less and less meaning."[55] In this view, signs once had a reference (clothes, for example, signified a given status, the political statement a distinct philosophy, the television news, "what really happened"). However, in this, the postmodern era, we are enmeshed in such a bewildering web of signs that they lose their salience. Signs come from so many directions and are so diverse, fast-changing, and contradictory, that their power to signify is dimmed. In addition, audiences are creative, self-aware, and reflective, so much so that all signs are greeted with skepticism and a quizzical eye, hence, easily inverted, reinterpreted and refracted from their intended meaning. Thus, the notion that signs represent some "reality" apart from themselves loses its credibility. Rather signs are self-referential: they—simulations—are all there is. They are, again to use Baudrillard's terminology, the "hyper-reality."

People appreciate this situation readily enough: They deride the poseur who is dressing for effect, but

Information Retrieval–
Information Society

acknowledge that it's all artifice anyway; they are skeptical of the politician who "manages" the media and his image through adroit PR (Public Relations), but accept that the whole affair is a matter of information management and manipulation. Here, it is conceded that people do not hunger for any true signs, because they recognize that there are no longer any truths. In these terms, we have entered an age of "spectacle" in which people realize the artificiality of signs they may be sent ("it's only the president at his latest photo opportunity," "it's news manufacture," "it's Jack playing the tough guy") and in which they also acknowledge the inauthenticity of the signs they use to construct themselves ("I'll just put on my face," "there I was adopting the 'worried parent' role").

As a result, signs lose their meaning and people simply take what they like from those they encounter (usually very different meanings than may have been intended at the outset). And then, in putting together signs for their homes, work, and selves, happily revel in their artificiality, "playfully" mixing different images to present no distinct meaning, but instead to derive "pleasure" in the parody or pastiche of, say, combining punk and a 1950s Marilyn Monroe facial style. In this information society we have then "a set of meanings (that) is communicated (but which) have no meaning."[56]

Experientially, this idea of an information society is easily enough recognized, but, as a definition of a new society, it is considerably more wayward than any of the notions we have considered. Given the absence of criteria we might use to measure the growth of signification, it is difficult to see how students of postmodernism such as Mark Poster can depict the present as one characterized by a novel "mode of information."[56] How can we know this other than from our sense that there is more symbolic interplay going on? And on what basis can we distinguish this society from say, that of the 1920s, other than purely as a matter of degree of difference? Those who reflect on the postmodern condition may have interesting things to say about the character of contemporary culture, but, as regards establishing a clear definition of the information society, they are glaringly deficient.

QUALITY AND QUANTITY

Reviewing these varying definitions of the information society, what comes clear is that they are either or both underdeveloped or imprecise. Whether it is a technological, economic, occupational, spatial, or cultural conception, we are left with highly problematical notions of what constitutes, and how to distinguish, an information society.

It is important that we remain aware of these difficulties. Though as a heuristic device, the term information society might have some value in helping us to explore features of the contemporary world, it is far too inexact to be acceptable as a definitive term. For this reason, though one may readily acknowledge that information plays a critical role in the present age, one has to remain suspicious as regards information society scenarios and maintain skepticism toward the view that information has become the chief distinguishing feature of our times.

Now, however, I want to raise some further difficulties with the language of the information society. The first problem concerns the quantitative versus qualitative measures to which I have already alluded. My earlier concern was chiefly that quantitative approaches failed to distinguish more strategically significant information activity from that which was routine and low-level and that this homogenization was misleading. Here I want to reraise the quality/quantity issue insofar as it bears upon the question of whether the information society marks a break with previous sorts of society.

Most definitions of the information society offer a quantitative measure (numbers of white collar workers, percentage of GNP devoted to information, etc.) and assume that, at some unspecified point, we enter an information society when this begins to predominate. But there are no clear grounds for designating as a new type of society one in which all we witness is greater quantities of information in circulation and storage. If there is just more information, then it is hard to understand why anyone should suggest that we have before us something radically new. This is a point made well by Giddens when he observes that all societies, as soon as they are formed into nation states, are information societies in so far as routine gathering, storage, and control of information about population and resources are essential to their operation.[57] On this axis, all that differentiates the present era from, say seventeenth-century England, is much greater quantities of information that are amassed, dissembled, and processed. Kumar voices much the same complaint against postindustrial theorists (and postindustrial society is currently synonymous with the concept of an information society): How can they uphold the claim to have identified a postindustrial society when the trends they single out "are extrapolations, intensifications, and clarifications of tendencies which were apparent from the very birth of industrialism?"[58]

Against this, however, it may be feasible to describe as a new sort of society, one in which it is possible to locate information of a qualitatively different order and function. Moreover, this does not even require that we discover that a majority of the workforce is engaged in information occupations or that the economy generates a specified sum from informational activity. For example, it is theoretically possible to imagine an information society where only a small minority of information experts hold decisive power. One need look only to the writings of H.G. Wells to conceive of a society in which a "knowledge elite" predominates and the majority, surplus to economic requirement, are condemned to drone-like unemployment.

On a quantitative measure, say of occupational patterns, this would not qualify for information society status, but we could feel impelled to so designate it because of the decisive role of information/knowledge to the power structure and direction of social change.

The blunt point is that quantitative measures—simply more information—cannot of themselves identify a break with previous systems, while it is at least theoretically possible to regard small but decisive qualitative changes as marking a system break. After all, just because there are many more automobiles today than 30 years ago does not qualify us to speak of a "car society." But, it is a systemic change that those who write about an information society wish to spotlight, whether it be in the form of Bell's postindustrialism, or in Castells's informational mode of development, or in Poster's mode of information.

What is especially odd is that so many of those who identify an information society as a new type of society do so by presuming that this qualitative change can be defined simply by calculating how much information is in circulation, how many people work in information jobs, and so on. What we have here is the assumption that quantitative increases transform—in unspecified ways—into qualitative changes in the social system.

It is noticeable that those scholars such as Schiller and Harvey who stress the present's continuities with the past, while they acknowledge an increasingly central role played by information, have at the forefront of their minds the need to differentiate between categories of information and the purposes to which it is put. In other words, those who insist that the "informationalized" society is not radically different from the past are at pains to differentiate information on qualitative grounds. For instance, they will examine how information availability has been affected by the application of market criteria and contend that the wealthier sectors of society gain access to particularly high quality information that consolidates their privileges and powers. Yet, while they emphasize these sort of qualitative dimensions of informatization, they do so to highlight continuities of the socioeconomic system. Conversely, those who consider that the information society is a radically different system most often recourse to quantitative indices to demonstrate a profound qualitative change.

Roszak[59] provides an interesting insight into this paradox in his critique of information society themes. His examination emphasizes the importance of qualitatively distinguishing "information," extending to it what each of us does on an everyday basis when we differentiate between phenomena such as data, knowledge, experience, and wisdom. Certainly, these are themselves slippery terms, but they are an essential part of our daily lives. In Roszak's view, the present "cult of information" functions to destroy these sort of qualitative distinctions that are the stuff of real life. It does this by insisting that information is a purely quantitative thing subject to statistical measurement. But to achieve calculations of the economic value of the information industries, of the proportion of GNP expended on information activities, of the percentage of national income going to the information professions, and so on, the qualitative dimensions of the subject (Is the information useful? Is it true or false?) are laid aside: "For the information theorist, it does not matter whether we are transmitting a fact, a judgement, a shallow cliché, a deep teaching, a sublime truth, or a nasty obscenity." These qualitative issues are overlooked as information is homogenized and made amenable to numbering: "Information comes to be a purely quantitative measure of communicative exchanges."[59]

The astonishing thing to Roszak is that along with this quantitative measure of information comes the assertion that more information is profoundly transforming social life. Having produced awesome statistics on information activity by blurring the sort of qualitative distinctions we all make in our daily lives, information society theorists then assert that these trends are set to change qualitatively our entire lives. To Roszak, this is the mythology of "information" talk: The term disguises differences, but in putting all information into one big pot, instead of admitting that what we get is an insipid soup, the perverse suggestion is that we have an elixir. As Roszak says, this may be very useful for those who wish the public to accept unprotestingly change since it seems so uncontentious.

Information smacks of safe neutrality; it is the simple, helpful heaping up of unassailable facts. In that innocent guise, it is the perfect starting point for a technocratic political agenda that wants as little exposure for its objectives as possible. After all, what can anyone say against information?[59]

Roszak vigorously contests these ways of thinking about information. A result of a diet of statistic upon statistic about the uptake of computers, the data-processing capacities of new technologies, and the creation of digitalized networks, is that people come readily to believe that information is the essential sustenance of the social system. There is so much of this food that it is tempting to agree with those information society theorists who insist that we have entered an entirely new sort of system. But against this "more-quantity-of-information-to-new-quality-of-society" argument Roszak insists that the "master ideas" that underpin our civilization are not based upon information at all.[60] Principles such as all men are created equal, my country right or wrong, live and let live, we are all God's children, and do unto others as you would be done by are central ideas of our society—but all come before information.

It is important to say that Roszak is not arguing that these and other master ideas are necessarily correct (in fact a good many are noxious—e.g., all Jews are rich, all women are submissive, blacks have natural athletic ability). But, what he is emphasizing is that ideas, and the necessarily qualitative engagement these entail, take

Information Retrieval–
Information Society

precedence over quantitative approaches to information. And, what he especially objects to is that information society theorists reverse that situation at the same time as they smuggle in the (false) idea that more information is fundamentally transforming the society in which we live.

WHAT IS INFORMATION?

Roszak's rejection of statistical measures leads us to consider perhaps the most significant feature of approaches to the information society. We are led here largely because his advocacy is to reintroduce qualitative judgment into discussions of information. Roszak asks questions like: Is more information necessarily making us a better informed citizenry? Does the availability of more information make us better informed? What sort of information is being generated and stored and what value is this to the wider society? What sort of information occupations are expanding, why, and to what ends?

What is being proposed here is that we insist on examination of the meaning of information. And, this is surely a commonsensical understanding of the term. After all, the first definition of information that springs to mind is the semantic one: Information is meaningful; it has a subject; it is intelligence or instruction about something or someone. If one were to apply this concept of information to an attempt at defining an information society, it would follow that we would be discussing these characteristics of the information. We would be saying that information about these sorts of issues, those areas, that process, are what constitutes the new age. However, it is precisely this commonsensical definition of information that the information society theorists jettison. What is, in fact, abandoned is a notion of information having a semantic content.

The definitions of the information society I have reviewed perceive information in nonmeaningful ways. That is, searching for quantitative evidence of the growth of information, a wide range of thinkers have conceived it in the classic terms of Shannon and Weaver's[61] information theory. Here, a distinctive definition is used, one that is sharply distinguished from the semantic concept in common parlance. In this theory, information is a quantity that is measured in "bits" and defined in terms of the probabilities of occurrence of symbols. It is a definition derived from and useful to the communications engineer whose interest is with the storage and transmission of symbols, the minimum index of which is on/off (yes/no or 0/1). This approach allows the otherwise vexatious concept of information to be mathematically tractable, but this is at the price of excluding the equally vexing—yet crucial—issue of meaning and, integral to meaning, the question of the information's quality. On an everyday level, when we receive or exchange information, the prime concerns are its meaning and value: Is it significant, accurate,

absurd, interesting, adequate, or helpful? But, in terms of the information theory that underpins so many measures of the explosion of information, these dimensions are irrelevant. Here, information is defined independent of its content, seen as a physical element as much as is energy or matter. As one of the foremost information society devotees puts it:

Information exists. It does not need to be perceived to exist. It does not need to be understood to exist. It requires no intelligence to interpret it. It does not have to have meaning to exist. It exists.[62]

In fact, in these terms, two messages, one that is heavily loaded with meaning and the other that is pure nonsense, can be equivalent. As Roszak says, here "information has come to denote whatever can be coded for transmission through a channel that connects a source with a receiver, regardless of semantic content."[59] This allows us to quantify information but at the cost of abandonment of its meaning and quality.

If this definition of information is the one that pertains in technological and spatial approaches to the information society (where the quantities stored, processed, and transmitted are indicative of the sort of indexes produced), we come across a similar elision of meaning from economists' definitions. Here it may not be in terms of bits, but at the same time, the semantic qualities are evacuated and replaced by the common denominator of price.[63]

To the information engineer, the prime concern is with the number of yes/no symbols, to the information economist, it is with their vendibility. But, as the economist moves from consideration of the concept of information to its measurement, what is lost is the heterogeneity that springs from its manifold meanings. The "endeavour to put dollar tags on such things as education, research, and art"[64] unavoidably abandons the semantic qualities of information. Kenneth Boulding observed thirty years ago that "The bit abstracts completely from the content of information and while it is enormously useful for telephone engineers for purposes of the social system theorist we need a measure which takes account of significance and which would weight, for instance, the gossip of a teenager rather low and the communications over the hot line between Moscow and Washington rather high."[65,66] How odd then that economists have responded to the qualitative problem that is the essence of information with a quantitative approach that, reliant on cost and price, is at best "a kind of qualitative guesswork,"[64,65] "Valuing the invaluable," to adopt Machlup's terminology, means substituting information content with the measuring rod of money. We are then able to produce impressive statistics, but in the process we have lost the notion that information is about something.[67]

Finally, though culture is quintessentially about meanings, about how and why people live as they do, it is striking that with the celebration of the nonreferential character of symbols by enthusiasts of postmodernism, we have a congruence with communications theory and the economic approach to information. Here, too, we have a fascination with the profusion of information, an expansion so prodigious that it has lost its hold semantically. Symbols are now everywhere and generated all of the time, so much so that their meanings have imploded, hence ceasing to signify.

What is most noteworthy is that information society theorists, having jettisoned meaning from their concept of information in order to produce quantitative measures of its growth, then conclude that such is its increased economic worth, the scale of its generation, or simply the amount of symbols swirling around, that society must encounter profoundly meaningful change. We have, in other words, the assessment of information in nonsocial terms—it just is—but we must adjust to its social consequences. This is a familiar situation to sociologists who often come across assertions that phenomena are aloof from society in their development (notably technology and science) but that carry within them momentous social consequences. It is demonstrably inadequate as an analysis of social change.[68]

Doubtless being able to quantify the spread of information in general terms has some uses, but it is certainly not sufficient to convince us that, in consequence of an expansion, society has profoundly changed. For any genuine appreciation of what an information society is like, and how different—or similar—it is to other social systems, we must surely examine the meaning and quality of the information. What sort of information has increased? Who has generated what kind of information, for what purposes, and with what consequences?

THEORETICAL KNOWLEDGE

It is tempting to stop this critique here, satisfied to have drawn attention to the peculiarly deracinated notion of information that plays a pivotal role in conceptions of the information society. However, there is another suggestion, intriguing if imprecise, that can contend that we are on the point of entry into a distinctly novel information society without any need to reflect on the meanings of the information involved. Furthermore, this proposition has it that we need not discover any of the quantitative measures of information expansion (information employees, tradeable information, etc.), because the suggestion is that it is a decisively qualitative change in information that can be pointed to and which marks a break with the past.

From this point of view, an information society is regarded as one in which theoretical knowledge takes on a preeminence that it has hitherto lacked. The theme that unites what is in fact rather a disparate range of thinkers is that, in this information society (though frequently the term knowledge society is preferred, for the obvious reason that it conjures much more than agglomerated bits of information), affairs are organized and arranged in such a way as to prioritize theory.

It is worth noting that Bell[30] presents this as an "axial principle" of postindustrial society and that, although the weight of his analysis leans toward quantitative increases in service—i.e., information—occupations as indicators of postindustrialism, he is emphatic that "what is radically new today is the codification of theoretical knowledge and its centrality for innovation."[69] It is easy enough to understand what Bell means by this when we contrast today's postindustrialism with its predecessor industrial society.[70] In the past, it is argued, innovations were made, on the whole, by "inspired and talented tinkerers who were indifferent to science and the fundamental laws underlying their investigations." In contrast to this decidedly practical and problem-solving orientation, it is suggested by Bell that nowadays innovations start from theoretical premises. That is, now that we have arrived at a situation in which it is possible to codify known scientific principles, then our knowledge of these becomes the starting point of action. In this way, what was once dismissed as useless—as just theory—has becomes the axis of practical innovations.

Again, it is not difficult to find illustrations of this "change in the character of knowledge itself."[30] For instance, Alan Turing's paper, "On Computable Numbers" (1937), sets out mathematical principles that underpin later applications in computer science; the development of integrated circuits that enabled the "microelectronics revolution" to get under way in the late 1970s was founded on known principles of solid-state physics; and innovations in areas as diverse as compact disc technology and nuclear energy were reliant on theoretical breakthroughs that were regarded initially as without practical consequences. It is rather difficult to think of technological applications nowadays that do not hinge on theoretical knowledge, whether it is calculating the needs of households for water supply, building a bridge, or estimating energy needs in a particular area. Not surprisingly, perhaps, we find historian Eric Hobsbawm confirming Bell's perception, concluding that during this century, "the theorists (have been) in the driving seat... telling the practitioners what they were to look for and should find in the light of their theories."[71]

Bell takes his argument for the "primacy of theoretical knowledge" considerably further, to suggest that it is preeminent not only in the realm of technological innovation, but even in social and political affairs. For instance, governments today introduce policies based on theoretical models of the economy. These may be variable—Keynesian, monetarist, supply side, and so forth—but each of them are theories that are the foundations that underpin day-to-day decisions ministers may make in response to practical exigencies. Again, we can see emerging major concerns with environmental consequences of policies. The response is, arguably, not just to respond to a particularly pressing problem (say, an oil spillage), but to act, increasingly, on the basis of theoretical models of the ecosystem's sustainability. To be sure, such models are at present inchoate and unrefined, but they and other instances help us to appreciate that, while theoretical knowledge does not have to be true in any absolute sense, it does play a decisive part in life in the late twentieth century.

Theoretical knowledge is undeniably an arresting idea, one that does, prima facie define a new type of society that hinges on the generation and use of information/ knowledge. If theory is at the point of initiation of developments, in contrast to one-time practical demands, then such knowledge could be said to herald a new sort of society. Moreover, we are not talking here merely of more white-collar workers or more bits of information being produced but of a new foundational principle of social life.

Nonetheless, a major difficulty with this notion is defining with any precision what is meant by theoretical knowledge. Theory evokes abstract and generalizable rules, laws, and procedures, and, with this, there can be agreement that advances, especially in scientific knowledge, have resulted in their codification in texts that are learned by would-be practitioners and that, in turn, become integrated into their practical work. This principle can reasonably be thought to be at the heart of research and development projects at the forefront of innovations, but it is clearly in evidence, too, in a large range of professions such as architecture, building, handling of food, and even the design of much clothing.

However, there are those who would extend the notion of theoretical knowledge to encompass a much vaster range, all of which could be cited as evidence of a knowledge-based society. Here, for example, one might include the training of many white-collar employees in law, social services, accountancy, etc., as evidence of the primacy of knowledge in the contemporary world. Indeed, one might also choose to argue that the whole of higher education, at the least, is concerned with transmitting theoretical knowledge. After all, it is a common refrain that the rapid transition to mass higher education (with about 30% of the age group attending universities) has been required by the need to equip appropriately very large numbers of people to operate successfully in the knowledge society.[72] Such knowledge as is transmitted is undoubtedly codified and generally abstracted from practical applications, and it is even generalizable, though it is surely of a different order of magnitude to the theoretical knowledge expounded in sciences such as chemistry and physics.

Stehr,[73] proposing that we now inhabit a knowledge society, does extend the definition of theory in such a way, arguing that nowadays knowledge has come to be constitutive of the way that we live. Recourse to theoretical knowledge is now central to virtually everything that we do, from designing new technologies, producing everyday artifacts,[74] to making sense of our own lives when we draw upon large repositories of knowledge to help us better understand our own location. Here, we are surely extending the idea of theoretical knowledge a very great deal, but it is helpful in so far as Stehr does echo themes in the stimulating and original work of social theorist Anthony Giddens that merit some comment. Stehr[73] proposes a three-fold typology of the development of knowledge, meaningful (the Enlightenment ideal of knowledge for better understanding), productive (knowledge applied to industry), to action (where knowledge is intimately connected to production with, for example, the inclusion of intelligent devices, and where it influences the performance of one's everyday activities). This latter form of knowledge appears close to Giddens's emphasis on what he refers to as the intensified reflexivity of "late modern" existence. What Giddens highlights here is that, and increasingly, modernity has been a story of people's release from the strictures of nature and restrictive forms of community where it appeared that one had to do what one did as it was a matter of fate, toward individuals and groups making choices about their own and collective destinies in circumstances of "manufactured uncertainty." That is, the world increasingly is not bounded by fixed and unchangeable limits, but is rather recognized as malleable and the outcome of human decisions. A requisite of this is heightened self and collective interrogation, otherwise reflexivity, though this is not to be perceived as some trend toward self-absorption. Quite the contrary, it is premised on openness to ideas, information, and theories from very diverse realms, which are examined and incorporated as circumstances and people so decide.

A key point here is that a posttraditional[75,76] society that is characterized by intensified reflexivity of actors and institutions hinges on information/knowledge. Of course, some of this is local and particular (one's biography reflected upon, a company carefully scrutinizing its customer records), but a great deal is also abstract, emanating especially from electronic media and from other, notably educational, institutions. If one accepts Giddens's argument that we do inhabit a world of "high modernity" in which reflexivity is much more pronounced than hitherto, then it is feasible to conceive of this as heightening the import of information and knowledge in contemporary life. A world of choices, for both organizations and individuals, is reliant on the availability and generation of detailed and rich information. If one follows Giddens's contention that ours is an era of intensified reflexivity on the basis of which we forge our material, as well as psychical conditions, then it follows that this will sustain and will demand a complex and deep information environment. It is perhaps not quite the same sort of theoretical knowledge as that which Bell has proposed, but, in so far as it is frequently abstract and codified, then it could find inclusion in a suitably widened category.

Nevertheless, there are reasons why we should hesitate to depict any novel information society in these terms.

Not least is that Giddens himself is reluctant to do so. While he does emphasize that a "world of intensified reflexivity is a world of clever people,"[76] he is unwilling to present this as other than an extension of long-term trends, hence as a high modern era rather than a postmodern or postindustrial epoch. Life today is certainly more information intensive, but this is not sufficient to justify projections that it represents an entirely new sort of society.

In addition, Giddens has also raised serious doubts about the novelty of theoretical knowledge. Several years ago, he observed that "there is nothing which is specifically new in the application of 'theoretical knowledge'... Indeed... rationality of technique... is the primary factor which from the beginning has distinguished industrialism from all preceding forms of social order."[77] This being so, we return to the problem of designating as novel today's society in which theoretical knowledge is prevalent. Further, Giddens's objection begs the key question: Just what, precisely, do commentators mean by theoretical knowledge? It is clear, from the quotation above, that Giddens feels that the classical sociologist Max Weber's conception of formal rationality that underpins purposive action (most famously manifested in the growth of bureaucratic structures) might apply in one definition. After all, it involves abstract and codifiable principles, rules, and regulations (the entire bureaucratic machine), as well as requiring, from participants, command of abstract knowledge (how the system works). Theoretical knowledge, in these terms, is not much more than learning the rules and procedures of how bureaucracies function. If so, then one is forced also to ask what is especially new about this.

This leads us to the wider complaint about the imprecision of the term theoretical knowledge. If, for instance, the primacy of theoretical knowledge is taken to refer to known scientific principles (the boiling point of water, the conductivity of elements, etc.) that are codified in texts, then this is one matter. However, if theoretical knowledge is taken to include hypothetical models such as the relation between inflation and unemployment or social class and educational opportunity, then this surely is quite another. Again, if theoretical knowledge is conceived as the primacy of research and development funds and teams in modern innovations, then this is another matter too. And if theoretical knowledge is perceived as the prominence in modern life of expert systems that operate services like the water and sewerage systems, airlines, and retail organizations, then this is another thing again. Alternatively, if theoretical knowledge is to be understood as a trend toward very much more intensified reflexivity among individuals and institutions, on the basis of which they then shape their future courses of action, then this is another thing again. Finally, if the rise of theoretical knowledge is to be chartered by the spread of educational certification—a common strategy—then this is to introduce still another significantly different definition.

In view of such ambiguities of definition, at best, one can conclude that theoretical knowledge may be more in evidence than hitherto, but that it is a far cry from this to conclude either that it is the preeminent force in society or that it marks a decisive turning point in history.

CONCLUSION

This entry has focused on the criteria used by those who depict an information society. Each has been found wanting, chiefly because they forward inappropriate quantitative measures that cannot, in themselves, identify a qualitative change from one type of society to another. It was further demonstrated that conceptions of the information society operated with variable—but uniformly nonsemantic—definitions of information, whether it was conceived as so many bits, or so much economic worth, or as an explosion of signs. Such notions of information, all of which ignore its meaning/content, were useful in that they facilitate quantification, but they are unacceptable when it comes to suggesting that we are witnessing the emergence of a qualitatively new information society. Finally, the distinctively qualitative notion, that the primacy of theoretical knowledge is the distinguishing feature of the information/knowledge society was considered. While it has an initial appeal, the term was too vague and imprecise to persuade that the undoubted expansion of some forms of theoretical knowledge signal a new type of society.

REFERENCES

1. Evans, C. *The Mighty Micro: The Impact of the Micro-chip Revolution*, Gollancz: London, 1979; 13.
2. Negroponte, N. *Being Digital*, Stoughton: London, 1995.
3. Freeman, C. Perez, C. Structural crises of adjustment, business cycles and investment behaviour. In *Technical Change and Economic Theory*; Dosi, G., Ed.; Frances Pinter: London, 1988; 38–66.
4. Hall, P. Preston, P. *The Carrier Wave: New Information Technology and the Geography of Innovation*, Unwin Hyman: London, 1988; 1846–2003.
5. Freeman, C. *Technology Policy and Economic Performance*, Frances Pinter: London, 1987.
6. Freeman, C. Clark, J. Soete, L. *Unemployment and Technical Innovation: A Study of Long Waves and Economic Development*, Frances Pinter: London, 1982.
7. Piore, M. Sabel, C. *The Second Industrial Divide*, Basic Books: New York, 1984.
8. Hirschhorn, L. *Beyond Mechanisation: Work and Technology in a Postindustrial Age*, MIT Press: Cambridge, MA, 1984.
9. Landes, D. *The Unbound Prometheus: Technological Change and Industrial Development in Western Europe from 1750 to the Present*, Cambridge University Press: London, 1969.

10. Naisbitt, J. *Megatrends: Ten New Directions Transforming Our Lives*, Futura: London, 1984; 28.

11. Toffler, A. *The Third Wave*, William Morrow: New York, 1980; 2.

12. MILES, I. et al. *Mapping and Measuring the Information Economy*, British Library: Boston Spa, 1990.

13. Dutton, W. H., Ed. *Information and Communication Technologies: Visions and Realities*; Oxford University Press: London, 1996.

14. Dutton, W. H., Ed. *Society on the Line: Information Politics in the Digital Age*; Oxford University Press: London, 1999.

15. Norcott, J. Walling, A. *The Impact of Microelectronics*, Frances Pinter: London, 1989.

16. Dickson, D. *Alternative Technology and the Politics of Technical Change*, Collins/Fontana: London, 1974.

17. Thomas, R. J. *What Machines Can't Do: Politics and Technology in the Industrial Enterprise*, University of California Press: Berkeley, NC, 1994; 50.

18. Machlup, F. *The Production and Distribution of Knowledge in the United States*, Princeton University Press: Princeton, NJ, 1962.

19. Drucker, P. F. *The Age of Discontinuity*, Heinemann: London, 1969; 247–249.

20. Karunaratne, N. D. Issues in measuring the information economy. J. Econ. Stud. **1986**, *13*(3), 51–68.

21. Porat, M. U. *The Information Economy: Sources and Methods for Measuring the Primary Information Sector (Detailed Industry Reports)*, OT Special Publication US Department of Commerce, Office of Telecommunications: Washington, DC, May 1977; Vol. 2, 12–77.

22. Porat, M. U. *The Information Economy: Definition and Measurement*, OT Special Publication US Department of Commerce, Office of Telecommunications(Contains Executive Summary and Major Findings of the Study): Washington, DC, May 1977; Vol. 13, 12–77.

23. Porat, M. U. Communication policy in an information society. In *Communications for Tomorrow*; Robinson, G. O., Ed.; Praeger: New York, 1978; 4–6, 8, 9, 32.

24. Monk, P. *Technological Change in the Information Economy*, Frances Pinter: London, 1989; 39–63.

25. Rubin, M. R. Taylor, M. *The Knowledge Industry in the United States, 1960–1980*, Princeton University Press: Princeton, NJ, 1986; 3.

26. Reich, R. *The Work of Nations: Preparing Ourselves for 21st Century Capitalism*, Vintage: New York, 1992.

27. Leadbeater, C. *Living on Thin Air: The New Economy*, Viking: London, 1999.

28. Brown, P. Lauder, H. *Capitalism and Social Progress: The Future of Society in a Global Economy*, Palgrave: Basingstoke, 2001.

29. Stonier, T. *The Wealth of Information: A Profile of the Post-Industrial Economy*, Thames Methuen: London, 1983; 7–8.

30. Bell, D. *The Coming of Post-Industrial Society: A Venture in Social Forecasting*, Penguin: Harmondsworth, 1973–1976.

31. Robins, K. Webster, F. Information as capital: a critique of Daniel Bell. In *The Ideology of the Information Age*; Slack, J. D., Fejes, F., Eds.; Ablex: Norwood, NJ, 1987; 95–117.

32. Jonscher, C. Information resources and economic productivity. Inf. Econ. Policy **1983**, *1*, 13–35.

33. Terkel, S. *Working: People Talk About What They Do All Day and How They Feel About What They Do*, Peregrine: Harmondsworth, 1977.

34. Miles, I. Measuring the future: Statistics and the information age. Futures. **1991**, *23*(9), 915–934.

35. Useem, M. *The Inner Circle: Large Corporations and the Rise of Business Political Activity in the US and UK*, Oxford University Press: New York, 1984.

36. Useem, M. The rise of the political manager. Sloan Manage. Rev Fall. **1985**, *27*, 15–26 .

37. Useem, M.; Karabel, J. Pathways to top corporate management. Am. Sociol. Rev April. **1986**, *51*, 184–200 .

38. Perkin, H. *The Rise of Professional Society: Britain Since 1880*, Routledge: London, 1989; Vol. 406, 2.

39. Gouldner, A. W. The new class project 1. Theory Soc. September **1978**, *6*(2); 153–203. Later published (1979) as *The Future of Intellectuals and the Rise of the New Class*. Macmillan.

40. Castells, M. *The Informational City: Information Technology, Economic Restructuring and the Urban-Regional Process*, Blackwell: Oxford, 1989.

41. Castells, M. *The Information Age*, Blackwell: Oxford, 1996–1998; 3 Volumes.

42. Goddard, J. Networks of transactions. Times High. Educ. Suppl. **1991**, *22*, VI.

43. Robins, K. Ed. *Understanding Information: Business Technology and Geography;* Belhaven Press: London, 1992; 198–201.

44. Dicken, P. *Global Shift: The Internationalization of Economic Activity*, 2nd Ed. Paul Chapman Publishing: London, 1992; 5, 49.

45. Harvey, D. *The Condition of Postmodernity*, Blackwell: Oxford, 1989; 163.

46. Hutton, W. *Markets Threaten Life and Soul of the Party, Guardian*, Frances Pinter: London, 1994; 13.

47. Martin, J. *The Wired Society*, Prentice-Hall: Englewood Cliffs, NJ, 1978.

48. Barron, I. Curnow, R. *The Future with Microelectronics: Forecasting the Effects of Information Technology*, Frances Pinter: London, 1979.

49. Hepworth, M. *Geography of the Information Economy*, Belhaven Press: London, 1989.

50. Dordick, H. S. Bradley, H. G. Nanus, B. *The Emerging Network Marketplace*, Ablex: Norwood, NJ, 1981.

51. EEC (Economic Commission for Europe). *The Telecommunications Industry: Growth and Structural Change*, United Nations: New York, 1987.

52. Mulgan, G. J. *Communication and Control: Networks and the New Economies of Communication*, Polity: Cambridge, MA, 1991; (my emphasis); 1, 64.

53. Giddens, A. *The Consequences of Modernity*, Polity: Cambridge, MA, 1990.

54. Rogers, E. M. *Communication Technology: The New Media in Society*, Free Press: New York, 1986. C 2.

55. Baudrillard. *In the Shadow of the Silent Majorities*, Semiotext(e): New York, 1983; 95.

56. Poster, M. *The Mode of Information: Poststructuralism and Social Context*, Polity Press: Cambridge, MA, 1990.

57. Giddens, A. *The Nation-State and Violence: Volume Two of a Contemporary Critique of Historical Materialism*, Polity: Cambridge, MA, 1985; 178.

58. Kumar, K. *Prophecy and Progress: The Sociology of Industrial and Post-Industrial Society*, Allen Lane: London, 1978; 252.

59. Roszak, T. *The Cult of Information: The Folklore of Computers and the True Art of Thinking*, Lutterworth Press: Cambridge, MA, 1986; 11, 13, 14, 19.

60. Roszak, T. *The Cult of Information: The Folklore of Computers and the True Art of Thinking*, Lutterworth Press: Cambridge, MA, 1986; 91.

61. Shannon, C. Weaver, W. *The Mathematical Theory of Communications*, University of Illinois Press: Urbana, IL, 1949.

62. Stonier, T. *Information and the Internal Structure of the Universe: An Exploration into Information Physics*, Springer-Verlag: London, 1990; 21.

63. Arrow, K. J. The economics of information. In *The Computer Age: A Twenty-Year View*; Dertouzos, M. L., Moses, J., Eds.; MIT Press: Cambridge, MA, 1979; 306–317 Ch.14.

64. Machlup, F. Knowledge: its creation, distribution, and economic significance. *Knowledge and Knowledge Production*; Princeton University Press: Princeton, NJ, 1980; Vol. 1, 23.

65. Boulding, K. E. The economics of knowledge and the knowledge of economics. Am. Econ. Rev. **1966**, *56*(2), 1–13.

66. Lamberton, D. M., Ed. *Economics of Information and Knowledge: Selected Readings*; Penguin: Harmondsworth, 1971; 23.

67. Maasoumi, E. Information theory. In *The New Palgrave: A Dictionary of Economics*; Eatwell, J., Ed.; Macmillan: London, 1987; Vol. 2, 846–851.

68. Woolgar, S. Why not a sociology of machines? The case of sociology and artificial intelligence. Sociology. November **1985**, *19*(4), 557–572.

69. Bell, D. The social framework of the information society. In *The Computer Age: A Twenty-Year View*; Dertouzos, M. L., Moses, J., Eds.; MIT Press: Cambridge, MA, 1979; 189, 163–211.

70. Bell, D. *The Coming of Post-Industrial Society: A Venture in Social Forecasting*, Penguin: Harmondsworth, 1976; 20.

71. Hobsbawm, E. J. *Age of Extremes*, Michael Joseph: London, 1994; 534, 535, 1914–1991.

72. Gibbons, M. Limoges, C. Nowotny, H. Schwartzman, S. Scott, P. Trow, M. *The New Production of Knowledge: The Dynamics of Science and Research in Contemporary Societies*, Sage: London, 1994.

73. Stehr, N. *Knowledge Societies*, Sage: London, 1994; 99–101.

74. Lash, S. Urry, J. *Economies of Signs and Space*, Sage: London, 1994.

75. Giddens, A. *Beyond Left and Right: The Future of Radical Politics*, Polity: Cambridge, MA, 1994.

76. Giddens, A. *Modernity and Self-Identity: Self and Society in Late Modern Age*, Polity: Cambridge, MA, 1991; 7.

77. Giddens, A. *The Class Structure of the Advanced Societies*, 2nd Ed. Hutchinson: London, 1981; 262.

BIBLIOGRAPHY

1. Beniger, J. R. *The Control Revolution: Technological and Economic Origins of the Information Society*, Harvard University Press: Cambridge, MA, 1986.

2. Gouldner, A. W. The new class project 2. Theory Soc. November **1978**, *6*(3), 343–389. Later published (1979) as The Future of Intellectuals and the Rise of the New Class. Macmillan.

3. Habermas, J. *The Structural Transformation of the Public Sphere: An Inquiry into a Category of Bourgeois Society*, Polity: Cambridge, MA, 1962. Translated by Thomas Burger with the assistance of Frederick Lawrence; 1989.

4. Lipietz, A. *Mirages and Miracles: The Crises of Global Fordism*, Verso: London, 1987.

5. Lyotard, J.-F. *The Postmodern Condition: A Report on Knowledge. Translated by Geoff Bennington and Brian Massumi*, Manchester University Press: London, 1979.

6. Machlup, F. Knowledge: Its creation, distribution, and economic significance. *The Economics of Information and Human Capital*, Princeton University Press: Princeton, NJ, 1984; Vol. III.

7. Mulgan, G. J. *Connexity*, Vintage: London, 1997.

8. Preston, P. *Reshaping Communications: Technology, Information and Social Change*, Sage: London, 2001.

9. Reich, R. B. *The Work of Nations: Preparing Ourselves for 21st Century Capitalism*, Vintage: New York, 1992.

10. Robins, K. Webster, F. *The Technical Fix: Education, Computers and Industry*, Macmillan: London, 1989.

11. Rubin, M. R.; Taylor, M. The US information sector and GNP: An input-output study. Inf. Proces. Manag. June **1981**, *17*(4), 163–194.

12. Schiller, H. I. *Who Knows: Information in the Age of the Fortune 500*, Ablex: Norwood, NJ, 1981.

13. Schiller, H. I. *Information and the Crisis Economy*, Ablex: Norwood, NJ, 1984.

14. Toffler, A. *Powershift: Knowledge, Wealth, and Violence at the Edge of the 21st Century*, Bantam: New York, 1990.

15. Webster, F. *Theories of the Information Society*, 2nd Ed. Routledge: London, 2002.

16. Webster, F. Robins, K. *Information Technology: A Luddite Analysis*, Ablex: Norwood, NJ, 1986.

Information Systems

E. Burton Swanson
Anderson School of Management, University of California, Los Angeles, Los Angeles, California, U.S.A.

Abstract

An information system provides information to help guide organizational actions. It typically features substantial human–computer interaction. Application software and a data base form the digital content around which a system is built. Among the different types are transaction-processing systems, management information systems , decision support systems, group support systems, and enterprise systems.

INTRODUCTION

An information system is commonly a computer-based system for providing information to an organization to help guide its actions.[1] The term "information system" is also sometimes used in information science to refer to information retrieval systems based more on documents than on data, an application domain familiar to libraries, in particular. The term is sometimes also used very generally and informally, without reference to either computers or organizations. People sometimes refer to their own personal information systems, for instance. In this entry, we take the organizational perspective, which has its origins in business, but applies to organizations of every kind, including libraries.

In an organization, an information system typically features people working interactively with computers to accomplish a particular task. Human–computer interaction (HCI) enables both people and their machine extensions to be informed via the system. Where decisions are routine and highly structured, they may sometimes be automated and relegated to the machine.[2] Often, the information provided serves to coordinate workers' specialized but necessarily collective efforts. The varieties of information systems are many, reflecting the diversity of organizations and tasks to be accomplished. A typical large business firm has information systems to support its accounting and finance, operations, supply chain management, sales and marketing, customer service, human resource management, and research and development. But information systems are found everywhere, in organizations of all kinds and sizes, public as well as private.

This entry discusses information systems both as a subject and as a field of study and practice. In the sections to follow, information systems are first described in terms of their: (1) origins; (2) varieties; and (3) practices. As information systems also constitute: (4) an evolving field of study and practice with; (5) attendant social issues, these aspects too are considered.

ORIGINS

Modern information systems emerged with the rise and spread of digital computing in the 1950s, although punched card tabulating equipment was in use for data processing in organizations before then. The stored-program computer itself was initially viewed as a high-powered calculating device, suitable primarily for numerical and other sophisticated analyses. Such "scientific computing" was distinguished from what was termed "electronic data processing" (EDP), which emerged about the same time to support the more prosaic work of business, such as accounting.[3] In the 1960s, computers came to be designed and marketed specifically for business purposes, eventually displacing the tabulating equipment. Notably, a high-level programming language for business applications, Common Business-Oriented Language (COBOL), was also developed, which emphasized data and file structures, and deemphasized the computational features found in FORmula TRANslation (FORTRAN), the language most commonly used in scientific computing. COBOL ultimately became the most widely used programming language for the development of application software for information systems on mainframe computers. As much of this code remains in use, the language persists even today.

Beyond business-oriented application software, the emergence of data base technology in the late 1960s was central to the rapid rise and spread of large-scale information systems among firms. A data base is an organized collection of related data files.[4] A data base management system (DBMS) is system software that enables data bases to be managed as integrated wholes, where relationships among files are clearly delineated. With a DBMS, data can be defined via a data dictionary and managed separately from the different software which access it. Finally, the articulation of the relational data model as a foundation for data bases spurred the development of relational data bases in the 1970s, which came to dominate the field.[5] Today, Oracle provides the leading relational data base

Encyclopedia of Library and Information Sciences, Fourth Edition DOI: 10.1081/E-ELIS3-120043700

Copyright © 2017 by Taylor & Francis. All rights reserved.

software for medium to large firms, while Microsoft's Access is well established among small businesses.

Together, application software and a related data base have come to form the digital content around which any modern information system is now built. Typically, the application software incorporates the "business rules" to be followed, while the data base incorporates the "business facts" that shape the data processing, for instance, in processing a business payroll, or in selling seats to a concert, or in managing the circulation of a library's holdings, or in almost any other endeavor in which carefully informed organizational actions are routinely taken. While the business facts and data base will typically be specific to the enterprise, the business rules and application software may be either specific or generic, i.e., commonly used, as with accounting systems that incorporate professionally mandated rules and principles. Where the business rules and application software is specific to the organization, it may underpin the unique capabilities of the enterprise, in which case it may be strategic.[6] Today, people in a wide variety of occupations and in organizations large and small are likely to work interactively with information systems to accomplish much of their work. Through networks and the Web and Internet, in particular, and through the use of laptops and mobile devices they engage in this HCI from wherever they happen to be and at whatever times they choose or are called upon to be available.

VARIETIES

Information systems come in a wide variety, reflecting the diversity in the organizations that employ them. Among business firms, some information systems will be characteristic of the industry, in particular, as with process control systems in chemical and refining enterprises, or electronic funds transfer (EFT) systems in banks and other financial services firms. However, certain basic types are found in enterprises of all kinds, reflecting both their historical origins based in then-new technologies and the nature of organization itself. These include transaction-processing systems; management information systems (MIS); decision support systems (DSS); group support systems; and enterprise systems. These are not pure types; actual systems may combine features of two or more basic types.

Transaction-Processing Systems

Transaction-processing systems support an enterprise in its transactions with others, such as customers, suppliers, and employees.[7] Every business transaction involves an exchange of goods, services, money, and information in some combination between the parties. Transaction-processing systems exist to ensure the integrity of these transactions. In today's world, each time a consumer makes a purchase with a credit card, withdraws cash from an account, or books an airline ticket, the consumer likely engages the other party's transaction-processing systems. Increasingly, a consumer does this directly, by swiping a bank card at a point-of-sale (POS) device or employing an automated teller machine (ATM) or initiating a purchase from the Web.

Beyond their primary function, transaction-processing systems also enable a business to coordinate its internal operations among units, especially in the making of goods, where parts are withdrawn from inventory and a manufactured item is assembled in a series of operations, and the final product eventually distributed from one location to another, for instance. Here and elsewhere, transaction-processing systems are basically event-driven, and are often engaged to authorize formal actions, such as accepting a customer order or authorizing a credit purchase. The business rules for such data processing may be quite sophisticated, as in credit authorization which incorporates rules aimed at fraud detection, for instance. The data pertaining to these events will ultimately serve to update a data base that is typically drawn upon in processing and is relied upon to give the current status of the organization's affairs. Where the data base is immediately updated as events happen, the system is said to operate in "real time." In the case of firms, basic transaction data will further feed the accounting systems that provide a formal financial picture of the ongoing business.

Where firms do business with each other, for instance, within a supply chain, their transaction-processing systems are also sometimes tied together by means of an interorganizational system that enables them to communicate directly with each other.[8] For such machine-to-machine communication, this necessitates resolution of disparities in how the data themselves are defined by the communicating parties. The interorganizational system may be based on electronic data interchange (EDI) arrangements or increasingly on eXtensible Markup Language (XML) standards for exchange over the Web. The concept of Web services envisions a world of business services and firm transactions seamlessly tied together via standards for business data of all kinds.[9]

Management Information Systems

Management information systems support an organization's hierarchical structure and are targeted to management at all levels. MIS aim to support every manager's need to know within his or her scope of responsibility, typically by extracting important performance information from data gathered from the organization's transaction-processing and operational systems and presenting it efficiently in tabular or graphical form. The concept of an MIS emerged in the 1960s and signaled an important transition in information systems, from traditional EDP to systems that served more sophisticated purposes.[10] In the United States, both practitioners and educators embraced the MIS concept and many business schools originated programs of study under this banner. Today the term continues to be widely used, although the more generic term "information systems" has become more common.

Executive information systems (EIS) were founded in the 1980s as a new form of MIS aimed at top management.[11] The early EIS featured access to news external to the business, in addition to traditional performance metrics, and further employed new graphics and communications technologies. Most recently, executive support systems have been developed which provide a personalized Web page and "executive dashboard" of up-to-the-minute information with which the manager is to engage and steer the enterprise. These systems are now also popularly referred to as "business intelligence systems," reflecting the sophisticated analytics that may lie behind the dashboard metrics.[12]

Decision Support Systems

Decision support systems emerged in the 1970s as interactive systems that supported managers and other "knowledge workers" in tasks that were semi-structured, where decisions could be aided by analytical computer-based means.[13] These systems shifted the original MIS focus from information to decisions. Early DSS featured innovative HCI employing graphics, formal models, and heuristics or algorithms as means of support. A pioneering example was IBM's Geodata Analysis and Display Systems (GADS), which supported organizational decisions related to urban geography, such as arranging police beats and assigning school district boundaries.[14] Today, the concept of geographical information systems (GIS) continues in this tradition as a major area of application supported by new technologies such as remote sensing, geographical positioning, graphical analytics, and visualization. The firm ESRI is the leading provider of GIS software.

The concept of group decision support systems (GDSS) extended the basic DSS concept in the 1980s. Substantial research led to the development of decision rooms equipped with systems that facilitated complex, interactive group decision making in a particular location.[15] The early focus was typically on largely unstructured problems, with tools provided to support collective brainstorming and idea evaluation, for instance, while further capturing a record of the group meeting. With advances in communications technologies, the GDSS concept soon evolved into one that supported group work more broadly, where group members could be at multiple locations and could also meet asynchronously as needed.

Group Support Systems

Beyond the informational and decisional needs of managers, it is well understood that communication and cooperation more broadly in the organization is required to coordinate the work undertaken within and across units. Certain of this communication and cooperation can be built into the work systems themselves; however, other organizational means such as cross-functional teams can also facilitate lateral communication, cooperation, and coordination, thus moderating the burden on the management hierarchy.[16] Not surprisingly, given the ubiquity of group work in organizations, a wide variety of systems have in recent years been originated to support group work, in particular.

The concept of computer-supported collaborative work (CSCW) originated in the 1980s to characterize designs for computer-enabled group work, understood to require substantial communication and coordination, typically over time and across locations.[17] Lotus Notes exemplified the software then deployed in these new systems and remains in wide use today. Current groupware in support of group work is diverse and includes, e.g., that which provides for electronic meetings, electronic mail and messaging, calendar management, project and document management, knowledge sharing, workflow management, and collaborative design, Today, group work can also be organized and conducted on the Web, making use of a commercially available service.

Enterprise Systems

Enterprise systems emerged in the 1990s with the rise of enterprise resource planning (ERP), a concept for integrating the major functional systems of the enterprise, in particular, the organization's financial, human resource, and operational systems around a common data base.[18] The principal means of integration was typically a software package provided by a vendor such as SAP or Oracle. Firms sought to replace their older and disparate home-grown legacy systems, which required high maintenance, with standard off-the-shelf software that promised an integrated solution to relieve them of this burden. ERP basically incorporated the firm's major transaction-processing and operational systems. Its adoption was further given a large boost by concerns related to the millennium bug and the threat it posed at the time to vulnerable legacy systems. Today, most large firms have adopted and implemented ERP in the form of packaged software provided by one or more leading suppliers.

A second type of enterprise system termed customer relationship management (CRM) has more recently also become popular, focusing on the "front office" of a firm, beyond the already heavily computerized "back office."[19] A central CRM aim is to provide the firm with a "unified view" of its customers, who might otherwise engage in separate transactions with different business units, each in the absence of full customer information. Just as it promises better customer service, CRM also typically supports a firm's sales force and enables it to be

Information Systems–
Information Use

better managed. Still another CRM aim is to help the firm assess the profitability of its different customer segments, in the interest of focusing marketing and customer retention initiatives on achieving higher overall profits.

PRACTICE

Information systems practice rests on four closely intertwined bodies of professional knowledge: (1) application knowledge; (2) technology knowledge; (3) development knowledge; and (4) management knowledge. Each is associated with job specialties in the field.

Application Knowledge

Application knowledge refers to the domain in which the information system supports work within the organization. The system's users are of course expected to be knowledgeable in this domain, first and foremost. So too are the systems analysts who aid in specifying the requirements for any new system. The required knowledge may be relatively broad or narrow, shallow or deep, according to the work supported, which often involves multiple individuals in different roles. The purpose of the information system is typically to inform its various users within such a work system, in support of their decisions and actions.[20] Beyond their domain knowledge, users are typically trained in their interactive use of any new system, such that they understand how to navigate it, interpret its displays or other output, and provide needed data or other input. Ease of use is a major issue in successful implementation.

Notwithstanding such training, research suggests that new information systems are unlikely to deliver full value to organizations and their users until they have been assimilated into the work practices they support.[21] Repeated "learning by doing" is needed before users "appropriate" a system into their preferred work practices. Moreover, with such assimilation, certain application knowledge will be tacit on the part of users, demonstrated primarily in their competently doing the needed work. Users will also typically find new uses of information systems, beyond those envisioned by system designers. Systems are thus substantially "reinvented" through their use. Importantly, then, application knowledge is ultimately inseparable from the work practice that gives it meaning.

Technology Knowledge

Technology knowledge pertains to the computer-based platforms on which applications are built. This includes the computers, communications, storage and other devices, and the system software that operates these resources. Among the jobs associated with building and maintaining these platforms are those of the system programmer, the network manager, the data base administrator, and the Web master. Technology knowledge also pertains to basic tools and resources drawn on by those engaged directly in application development; these are sometimes integrated and provided in the form of a "work bench."

The most basic aspects of a computer-based platform are its suitability, capacity, and reliability in supporting applications. Growth in firms and their information systems makes capacity planning a vital task. Also important are standards.[22] Where the platforms are in wide use by organizations, the associated technology knowledge is similarly widespread and more easily acquired in the marketplace when needed. Even more significantly, widely used platforms attract their own extensions, as vendors build new features for them roughly according to the potential market reached. This advantage extends to the application software employed in system building, where a wider variety of packaged systems will be readily available for standard platforms.

Development Knowledge

Development knowledge pertains to the application software, data model, Web or other interface, and human procedures that are specified, built or otherwise acquired, documented, tested, installed, and maintained over the life of an information system. It pertains further to the methodology used in this particular work.[23] Principal jobs include those of the systems analyst, who in collaboration with prospective users specifies the functional requirements for the system, and the applications programmer, who in consultation with the systems analyst designs and codes the software to meet these specifications. Within the user community, "lead users" often represent the interest of their peers in the development activity, helping in particular with system implementation and needed training.

Project management knowledge for guiding implementation of systems is especially important, as system development work tends to be organized as projects. Senior developers of individual systems often work as project managers. Projects are typically managed according to their associated deliverables, schedule, and budget. Because of characteristic pressures on schedule and budget, a particularly important aspect of project management is attention to the quality of the deliverables as well as the avoidance of their expensive elaboration through "feature creep." While these issues have long been well known among professionals, they continue to bedevil most of those engaged in the work.[24]

Management Knowledge

Management knowledge pertains to the management of information systems activities within the enterprise. Depending on the size of the organization, managers may

Information Systems–Information Use

include: the data center or operations manager, the network manager, the applications development manager, the applications maintenance manager, and the executive in charge of the function as a whole, who in a large organization sometimes has the title of chief information officer (CIO). A primary responsibility of the CIO is the alignment of the information systems strategy with the broader firm strategy.[25] Another is the staffing and organization of the function and the building of its expertise, as well as setting policy and contracting for external services. A third is the building of a reliable and adaptable network and technological infrastructure.[26] Still another is the management of the application systems portfolio, and the allocation of resources between maintenance of existing systems and the development of new or replacement systems.[27]

One highly visible issue in recent years has been the outsourcing of the information systems function, in whole or in part. "Off-shoring" is much discussed, in particular. Much system development work in the most developed nations is now carried out in countries with more attractive wage rates and growing technical competencies, such as India and China, and certain eastern European states. Exactly which work should be outsourced and which should not remains controversial.[28] The data center itself is a prime candidate for outsourcing. In general, programming is more easily outsourced than is systems analysis, which requires a deep grasp of the work context. The long-run implications of this shift in work are globally significant for the world economy, beyond the immediate challenges and choices faced by today's managers.

AN EVOLVING FIELD

Today, the information systems field of study and practice remains an evolving one marked by continuous change. Notwithstanding its accomplishments to date, the field faces numerous challenges. Its various professional associations, publications, and research firms and consultancies will play important roles in guiding future information systems developments.

Professional Associations

The International Federation for Information Processing (IFIP), founded by 13 national computer societies in 1960, established Technical Committee 8 (TC8) on Information Systems in 1966. TC8's aims are "to promote and encourage interactions among professionals from practice and research and advancement of investigation of concepts, methods, techniques, tools, and issues related to information systems in organizations."[29] TC8 now includes eight working groups, the first of which, WG8.1, Design and Evaluation of Information Systems, was established in 1976, and the second of which, WG8.2, The Interaction of

Information Systems and the Organization, was established in 1977.

The International Conference on Information Systems (ICIS) is the premier academic research conference in the field, held annually since 1980. The Association for Information Systems (AIS) is the leading academic association, established in 1994 to bring IS academics together from around the world. It sponsors ICIS and three regional conferences annually: the Americas Conference on Information Systems (AMCIS); the European Conference on Information Systems (ECIS); and the Pacific Asia Conference on Information Systems (PACIS). Among its other activities, AIS publishes the *Journal of AIS* and *Communications of AIS*, and sponsors AIS World, an important Web resource for IS scholars.

The IS field today also maintains its important roots in the allied fields of computer science, operations research, and management. The Association for Computing Machinery (ACM), founded in 1947, claims to be the world's oldest educational and scientific computing society and now serves professionals in more than 100 countries. Its many publications include the widely read *Communications of the ACM*, which features many articles of interest to IS professionals. Its interest groups include the Special Interest Group on Management Information Systems (SIGMIS). Among ACM's most important contributions has been its issuance since 1972–1973 of curriculum recommendations for academic programs of study in information systems.[30]

The Institute for Operations Research and Management Science (INFORMS), formed in 1995 from two earlier societies, is now an umbrella association of operations for research-oriented academics and practitioners that includes an Information Systems Society among its 10 societies. It also publishes the leading journal, *Information Systems Research*, begun in 1990.

The Academy of Management includes an Organizational Communications and Information Systems Division among its some two dozen interest groups and divisions.

Among practitioners, the Society for Information Management (SIM), originally founded as the Society for Management Information Systems (SMIS) in 1969, serves IS executives and professionals through a series of chapters located primarily in North America. In its early years, SIM was instrumental in advancing the MIS concept among executives.[31] It also established the leading journal, *MIS Quarterly*, in 1977, in cooperation with the Management Information Systems Research Center (MISRC) of the University of Minnesota, which now publishes it exclusively, while SIM members receive it as a membership option.

Publications

Today, a wide variety of publications reaching both general and specialized audiences feature articles on information systems. Business periodicals such as *The Economist*, *Business Week*, and the *Wall Street Journal* provide good coverage for the general reader. In addition to those already mentioned, other notable academic journals devoted to information systems include the *Journal of Management Information Systems*, the *Journal of Information Technology*, *Information and Organization*, and the *European Journal of Information Systems*. Practitioners in the field find the periodicals *Information Week*, *CIO Magazine*, and *Computerworld* important for following current events in the fast changing technology industry.

Research Firms and Consultancies

Practitioners are also served by a number of market research and analysis firms such as Gartner Group and Forrester Research, which offer assessments of new technologies and their markets, as well as international consultancies such as Accenture, Deloitte, Tata Consulting, and IBM Business Services, which are widely engaged in "system integration" activities, and which further help to spread "best practices" in information systems among firms. These research firms and consultancies also serve as "thought leaders" in the institutional environment within which "organizing visions" for the application of new technologies originate and serve to guide adoption and diffusion.[32]

SOCIAL ISSUES

Information systems are associated with several ethical and social issues inherent to their nature, design, and use.[33] The authors Kenneth and Jane Laudon identify five moral dimensions to the Information Age: information rights and obligations; property rights and obligations; accountability and control; system quality; and quality of life.[34] We consider each briefly.

Information Rights and Obligations

Every information system poses questions of information rights and obligations, often for both persons and organizations. Rights to individual privacy are particularly salient in an age where much organizational data are gathered about customers, employees, and others, and too where those who do business on the Internet can easily gather individual data generated through Web site visits, for subsequent use in targeted advertising, for instance. Throughout the world, businesses thus now operate under various laws intended to safeguard individual privacy. In Europe, privacy protection is stronger than in the United States, as businesses there are generally prohibited from using information about persons without their prior consent. In the United States, most businesses make their privacy policy known to their customers, who

must typically then "opt out" if they wish to avoid having certain of their data shared with others for marketing purposes. As many U.S. customers do not take this opt-out step, nor do many probably even consider it, their individual data are widely shared in marketing.

Privacy concerns are of course also inherent to surveillance schemes which employ information systems. Firms may closely monitor the work of their employees, sometimes stepping over the line into private lives. Governments of all kinds are notoriously tempted to keep more than close track of their citizens as well as others, as they seek to repel threats both real and imagined.

Property Rights and Obligations

Information systems also pose challenges to certain intellectual property, which increasingly is represented in digital form, and which a firm may seek to protect as a trade secret, or through copyright or patent. Both the software and the data associated with information systems are likely to be associated with property rights, as are other digital products such as music or video or text recordings that offer entertainment and education, and which are commonly organized, managed, and distributed via information systems. An interesting illustration today is Apple's i-Tunes business, which is entirely digital in nature, and which distributes music for download by consumers on demand, much of it under protection of Apple digital rights management (DRM) software that is itself a protected asset, with several different parties sharing in the resulting revenues.[35]

Accountability and Liability

Information systems also pose new issues of accountability as well as liability, where harm results from their employment. When things go massively wrong, e.g., when an operating error at a bank results in failure to automatically deposit customer paychecks in a timely manner, it may be difficult to disentangle the reasons behind the debacle. Often we are told that a software bug was the problem, and indeed this is often the case. But because information systems are based substantially in HCI, whether it was human error or a software bug or a problem in data exchanged or the interaction itself, or more broadly a problem in the design or execution of the work being carried out, or a failure in the oversight and management of overall system quality, blame can be difficult to fix and hence may sometimes be misplaced to avoid accountability and in some cases liability.

System Quality

As just suggested, system quality is a broader issue than one of minimizing the bugs in software. Organizations bear a responsibility to attend to the broader quality of their information systems. Research suggests that notwithstanding this responsibility, few firms systematically assess the quality of the data associated with their systems, for instance, even though data errors are known to be rather commonplace.[36] One area where attention to data quality is typically enforced is in business accounting, where external auditors provide independent oversight. However, even here, where the financial stakes may be high, system quality may be compromised through inattention or misguided cost cutting measures. The reality is that system quality is achieved only at the cost of means that ensure it.

Quality of Life

Lastly, information systems have long been associated with a variety of quality of life issues, especially as they pertain to system users.[37] Among ongoing issues are the extent to which power is centralized or decentralized through systems, the increased difficulty in maintaining a balance between individuals' working and private lives, new vulnerabilities to crime and abuse such as spam, the reengineering of work and its consequences for job skills needed, characteristic health problems such as repetitive stress injury (RSI), the problem of electronic trash disposal, and social inequities in access to technology, as illustrated by the much discussed problem of the "digital divide" in U.S. schools. In short, information systems have come to have pervasive consequences for the quality of our individual and social, and private and public lives.

CONCLUSION

In the relatively short span of several decades, information systems have emerged to be a dominant feature of modern organizational life, with broad implications for people everywhere. The future promises to extend this story. Currently, organizations throughout the world are rapidly building their presence on the Web, and moving from merely offering certain published content, sometimes disparagingly referred to as "brochure ware," to engaging in basic transactions with their customers, suppliers, and other partners. In short, more organizations are doing everyday business on the Web, popularly termed "electronic commerce," underpinned by information systems that make this possible. New businesses are at the same time originating everywhere on the Web to provide the basic infrastructure for doing this business (Google, eBay, and Amazon.com are widely known examples), as well as to offer new distribution for digital content in the realms of education and entertainment, in particular, attracting more traffic to the Web and thus broadening and deepening its user base, making it more appealing for social networking and advertising. As of this writing, the concept of "Web 2.0" as a social space that enables new forms of

organizing is the latest new vision to capture the fancy of the field.[38]

ACKNOWLEDGMENTS

I have benefited from several excellent textbooks in preparing this entry and have incorporated them in the references section. They provide good resources for additional reading. I am also grateful to Ephraim R. McLean and an anonymous reviewer for their comments on an earlier prepared version.

REFERENCES

1. Langefors, B. Information systems theory. Inform. Syst. **1977**, *2*, 207–219.
2. Simon, H. *The New Science of Management Decision*; Harper & Row: New York, 1960.
3. Canning, R. *Electronic Data Processing for Business and Industry*; Wiley: New York, 1956.
4. Date, C.J. *An Introduction to Data Base Systems*; 3rd Ed.; Addison-Wesley: Reading, MA, 1981.
5. Codd, E.F. A relational model of data for large shared banks. Commun. ACM. **1972**, *13* (6), 377–387.
6. Porter, M.E.; Millar, V.E. How information gives you competitive advantage. Harvard Bus. Rev. **1985**, *63* (4), 149–160.
7. Zwass, V. *Foundations of Information Systems*; Irwin/McGraw-Hill: Boston, MA, 1998, Chapter 9.
8. Johnston, R.; Vitale, M.J. Creating competitive advantage with interorganizational information systems. MIS Quart. **1988**, *12* (2), 153–165.
9. Hagel, J., III; Brown, J.S. Your next IT strategy. Harvard Bus. Rev. **2001**, *79* (10), 105–113.
10. Dickson, G.W. Management information systems: evolution and status. Adv. Comput. **1981**, *20*, 1–37.
11. Watson, H.J.; Rainer, K.; Koh, C. Executive information systems: a framework for development and a survey of current practice. MIS Quart. **1991**, *15* (1), 13–30.
12. Gray, P. *Manager's Guide to Making Decisions about Information Systems*; Wiley: New York, 2006, Chapter 8.
13. Keen, P.G.W.; Scott Morton, M.S. *Decision Support Systems: An Organizational Perspective*; Addison-Wesley: Reading, MA, 1978.
14. Sprague, R.H., Jr.; Carlson, E.D. *Building Effective Decision Support Systems*; Prentice-Hall: Englewood Cliffs, NJ, 1982; 41–54.
15. Dennis, A.R.; George, J.F.; Jessup, L.M.; Nunamker, J.F. Jr.; Vogel, D.R. Information technology to support meetings. MIS Quart. **1988**, *12* (4), 591–624.
16. Galbraith, J. *Designing Complex Organizations*; Addison-Wesley: Reading, MA, 1973.
17. Grudin, J. Computer-supported cooperative work: its history and participation. IEEE Comput. **1994**, *27* (5), 19–26.
18. Davenport, T.H. Putting the enterprise into enterprise systems. Harvard Bus. Rev. **1998**, *76* (4), 121–131.

Information Systems–
Information Use

19. Winer, R.S. A framework for customer relationship management. Calif. Manage. Rev. **2001**, *43* (4), 89–105.

20. Alter, S. *Information Systems*, 4th Ed.; Prentice-Hall: Upper Saddle River, NJ, 2002.

21. Orlikowski, W.J. Improvising organizational transformation over time: a situated change perspective. Inform. Syst. Res. **1996**, *7* (1), 63–92.

22. Shapiro, C.; Varian, H.R. *Information Rules*; Harvard Business School Press: Cambridge, MA, 1999.

23. Davis, G.B. Olson, M.H. *Management Information Systems*, 2nd Ed.; McGraw-Hill: New York, 1985, Chapter 18.

24. Keil, M.; Robey, D. Blowing the whistle on troubled software projects. Commun. ACM. **2001**, *44* (4), 87–93.

25. Luftman, J.N., Ed. *Competing in the Information Age: Strategic Alignment in Practice*; Oxford University Press: New York, 1996.

26. Weill, P. Broadbent, M. *Leveraging the New Infrastructure: How Market Leaders Capitalize on IT*; Harvard Business School Press: Boston, MA, 1998.

27. McFarlan, F.W. Portfolio approach to information systems. Harvard Bus. Rev. **1981**, *59* (5), 142–150.

28. Lacity, M.C.; Willcocks, L.P.; Feeny, D.F. IT outsourcing: maximize flexibility and control. Harvard Bus. Rev. **1995**, *73* (3), 84–93.

29. Information bulletin. International Federation for Information Processing, January 2007, No. 37, 82.

30. Information systems curriculum recommendations for the 80s: Undergraduate and graduate programs. In *Commun ACM*; Nunamaker, J.F., Jr., Couger, J.D., Davis, G.B., Eds.; 1982; 25, 781–805 (11).

31. Society for Management Information Systems: Chicago, IL, 1970. Society for Management Information Systems. What is a management information system? Research report no. 1.

32. Swanson, E.B.; Ramiller, N. The organizing vision in information systems innovation. Organ. Sci. **1997**, *8* (5), 458–474.

33. Mason, R.O. Four ethical issues of the information age. MIS Quart. **1986**, *10* (1), 5–12.

34. Laudon, K.C.; Laudon, J.P. *Essentials of Business Information Systems*, 7th Ed.; Prentice-Hall: Upper Saddle River, NJ, 2007; 405.

35. iTunes: How copyright, contract, and technology shape the business of digital media—A case study. The Berkman Center for Internet & Society at Harvard Law School, 2004 March Digital Media Project.

36. Strong, D.M.; Lee, Y.W.; Wang, R.Y. Data quality in context. Commun. ACM. **1997**, *40* (5), 103–110.

37. Mumford, E. Weir, M. *Computer Systems in Work Design —The ETHICS Method*, Wiley: New York, 1979.

38. McAfee, A. Enterprise 2.0: The dawn of emergent collaboration. MIT Sloan Manage. Rev. **2006**, *47* (3), 21–28.

Information Systems Failure

Chris Sauer
Said Business School, University of Oxford, Oxford, U.K.

Gordon B. Davis
Carlson School of Management, University of Minnesota, Minneapolis, Minnesota, U.S.A.

Abstract

Information systems (IS) failure is characterized as one particular form of evaluation of IS performance. It is multidimensional and relative to stakeholder interests. The objective of failure studies is to assist understanding of how to achieve success. This entry reviews recent performance data to assess the magnitude of the issue. It traces historical developments in the understanding of failure. It examines various changes that have affected perceptions of IS performance. It identifies a number of cognate subliteratures whose emergence recently signals a growing maturity of analysis. The entry proposes a framework by which to understand the historical development of academic research in this field. Finally, it offers some key conclusions for academic research and for practice.

INTRODUCTION

Information systems (IS) failure has been a focus for study and action for both practitioners and academics since the late 1960s.[1–3] Most organizations have struggled to deliver systems that work and deliver benefits. Practitioners have wrestled with these difficulties in their workplace and the public has experienced systems' shortcomings in trying to use them. Nobody seriously doubts that failure has been and continues to be a problem to be tackled.

The focus on failures does not mean that there are two classes of applications—those that succeed and those that fail. There is a continuum of results ranging from clear and utter failure to very high success. There are applications that are barely acceptable but survive, and there are applications that are mildly successful and fail.

This entry reviews only one end of the spectrum of results: applications that are failures. The meaning of "information system success" is a significant issue[4] in itself and is not the purpose of this entry. Information system failure and information system success are not simply opposites.[5] To achieve success, it is necessary to remove causes of failure, but doing so may not be sufficient for a successful outcome. More broadly, the study of failure is justified by the belief that, just as the study of cognitive malfunction can help us understand good mental functioning, it casts light on what it takes to achieve success. Understanding "information system failure," therefore, represents one but only one part of what needs to be understood for the effective design, implementation, management, and exploitation of an information system.

Where once "failure" was viewed as an almost objectively identifiable state, today there is wide recognition that it is an evaluation based on an assessment of some dimension or dimensions of performance relative to goals, targets, or expectations. Failure in one dimension, say a budget overrun, may be more than compensated for by success in another dimension, say timely implementation. And, as what is regarded as performance has itself changed, so the domain of failure studies has evolved. For this reason, it is appropriate for this entry to take an historical approach.

In this entry, the study of failure is treated as one important branch of the study of IS performance. Our overall objective is to provide a rigorous basis by which to understand what may be meant by "IS failure" and a set of signposts to appropriate analytical approaches by which to develop greater insight into the phenomenon.

We start with a review of recent performance data. We examine the various changes that have affected perceptions of IS performance. We identify a number of cognate subliteratures that have developed over recent years and which signal a growing maturity of analysis. We provide a framework by which to understand the historical development of academic research in this field.

THE SCALE OF IS FAILURE

Prior to 1995, most assessments of the scale of IS failure were informal in nature and anecdotally derived. In 1995, the Boston-based consulting group, Standish, published its findings under the banner headline, *Chaos!*[6] Based on data about more than 3000 IS projects, it reported that 31% were abandoned without being completed. These it dubbed failures. Some 53% failed to meet at least one of its budget, schedule, and scope targets. These were dubbed challenged projects. The remaining 16% that hit all three

Encyclopedia of Library and Information Sciences, Fourth Edition DOI: 10.1081/E-ELIS4-120044131

Copyright © 2017 by Taylor & Francis. All rights reserved.

targets were deemed successes. These have since become the most widely cited failure statistics.

Every 2 years since 1995, the Standish Group has released updates on these figures. Figures released for 2004 revealed 29% hit all targets, 53% were challenged in missing at least one target and 18% were classified as failures.[7] In summary according to the Standish Group figures there has been sustained improvement but there remains continuing cause for concern. While some question the Standish survey and analysis methodology,[8] raising questions about the accuracy of the detailed findings, in 1995 few doubted the broad conclusion that most IT projects seriously underperformed. Subsequent surveys reinforced the point (e.g., Taylor).[9] Likewise today, more than a decade later, the improving trend they identify is commonly acknowledged.

Less clear is the extent of the improvement and therefore the extent of the outstanding problem. To measure this, it is better to use percentage variance from targets.[10] Otherwise we cannot tell whether "challenged" projects are more or less challenged over time. Sauer et al.[10] also argue that an absolutist definition of success by which any variance however small assigns a project to the challenged category is too strict. In most cases a small budgetary or schedule overrun is of negligible significance. Using statistical clustering techniques, they show that there is a significant gap between the majority of projects that miss their targets by just a small percentage margin and those that are clearly failing on a more substantial scale and that therefore it is worth tolerating some small margin of variance. However, even on this more optimistic assessment, at least one-third of all projects fall well short of delivering on all their targets.

THE EVOLUTION OF IS PERFORMANCE

In the previous section we saw that IS performance has changed over time and that the metrics by which performance in general and failure specifically are identified are not definitively agreed. In this section we explain how the phenomenon itself has changed and explore the implications for the measurement and identification of failure.

We start with a distinction between systems and systems projects. In the 1960s and 1970s, the system and the project were often conflated. If a system failed, say because it did not deliver the functionality its users wanted, it was usually the case that the project had been troubled too and vice-versa. This was also a period in which computer malfunctions were common resulting in breakdowns ranging from the everyday experience of the computer being "down" to catastrophic loss. Such malfunctions have been extensively cataloged by Peter Neumann in his Inside Risks column in the Communications of the Association for Computing Machinery over many years.[11] While more reliable hardware and standardized and re-usable software

have removed many causes of such malfunctions, they remain a continuing hazard (e.g., Hodgson)[12] but today are rarely such as to cause abandonment of a system.

With the advent of rigorous project management disciplines it has become normal to detail precise targets, in terms of budget, schedule, quality, and scope. These are essentially internal measures that in principle are within a project manager's capacity to control. It has become apparent therefore that a project may be successful in meeting its internal targets yet not deliver beneficial business outcomes. More recently, as the role IT plays in organizations has become critical to their functioning as exemplified by the widespread adoption of e-business for front office business functions, there have been cases of projects failing to hit budget and schedule targets but nevertheless delivering highly desirable business outcomes. The distinction between the system and the project is therefore both conceptually sensible and practically relevant.

What counts as an information system and therefore what is involved in an IS project has changed over time and this has affected the measure of performance. Purpose-built systems have given way to standard packages (so-called enterprise software). Projects are therefore more about system integration than software development. This has led to two important consequences. First, it has engendered more ambitious, more complex projects that combine packaged functionality to an extent that was previously unimaginable. Second, because the software is prewritten, it has encouraged organizations to direct project managers' efforts to implementation, business process change, and value harvesting. This latter has extended project scope considerably and turned managers' attention to an external target, the business value achieved by investment in an information system.

This shift in emphasis from internal to external targets, from assessing performance against process to performance on outcomes, is appropriate from a commercial investment perspective. It is, however, problematic to measure because IT systems do not deliver value on their own, they do so through organizational and business process change.[13] Even if the value itself is measurable and measured, and it often is not, the extent to which that value derives from the information system may not be possible to determine. Further problems include the question of when to measure value outcomes. Often immediately after implementation, organizational performance suffers[14] before recovering and improving. But the longer the lag between implementation and outcome measurement, the more space there is for extraneous variables to affect the value outcome.

Thus far in this section, we have examined how IS performance has evolved in practice. We now turn to how its conceptualization has evolved academically. A significant breakthrough came with the explicit recognition that "failure" is an evaluation not an objective description. Lyytinen and Hirschheim[15] developed a

Information Systems–
Information Use

new pluralist concept of expectations failure which explicitly recognized that failure was a judgement relative to expectations and that expectations vary among stakeholders. This pluralism opened the way to the possibility that a single system or project could be a failure relative to one set of stakeholders and a success relative to others. It also triggered discussion of whether some stakeholders' expectations might weigh more in arriving at a single overarching evaluation—this is "on balance" a failure notwithstanding some less important stakeholders viewing it as a success. Several responses have emerged. Some have tried to identify apparently unequivocal failures such as abandoned projects (e.g., Johnson[6] and Ewusi-Mensah[16]) though it has been argued that even an abandoned project might be viewed by some stakeholders as a success if an objective was to learn about a new technology, test customer responses, or experiment in some other way.[17] Sauer[17] advanced an uneasy compromise that recognized the plurality of stakeholders but recognized that a distinction should be made between supporters of a project and those who were uninvolved or active opponents. Others have finessed the issue by focusing on specific dimensions of performance such as budget and schedule variance without using explicitly evaluative terminology.[18–20] In doing so, by the very nature of their choices of performance dimensions to study including the recent introduction of business value as an outcome measure, they can be argued to implicitly favor the expectations of traditional stakeholders such as the owners and managers of businesses. By contrast, others have embraced pluralism and absorbed it into new theoretical approaches such as Actor-Network Theory which we discuss below.

We can summarize this section by saying that the conceptualization of failure has evolved and matured in three ways. The first has been the distinction between systems and projects. The second has been the expansion of the legitimate scope of IS projects with consequences for what dimensions of performance are assessed. The third has been recognition of the evaluative nature of "failure." This has surfaced disagreement as to which stakeholders' expectations should receive priority. This is a political disagreement rather than one of facts or data. Those who believe that owners and manager as the agents of owner matter more will adopt a more traditional view of failure where as those who believe that employees, the public, and others have just as much right to their interests and expectations being respected will take a more egalitarian and pluralist position.

EMERGING COGNATE LITERATURES

A further manifestation of the maturation of our understanding of IS failure has been the emergence of several cognate literatures. We briefly discuss in turn risk, partial abandonment, expectation management, escalation, and drift.

Risk as discussed in the extensive IS and software engineering literatures relates to failure by seeking to identify what may be conducive to failure, how to assess its probability and impact, and how to manage it. It is about the probability of failure in some shape or form. It has typically been strongest at identifying sources of risk such as starting conditions or behaviors that give rise to failure.[21] Such studies usually result in extensive lists. The usual suspects thus identified typically include: unclear objectives, uncertain requirements, inadequate project management, too little user involvement, and shortage of top management support. The literature has been less convergent in its focus on risk assessment. While there is an in-principle agreement that risk consists of two elements (the probability of some outcome and its impact), the determination of what the actual risk amounts to has proved problematic. Some have focused on the impact of total failure as represented by abandonment,[22] while others have looked at specific dimensions of performance such as running over schedule or budget. Some studies while recognizing that impact is an element of risk focus principally on the probability of underperformance.[10] The management of risk, and therefore the prevention of failure, has principally consisted of attending to risk factors to prevent their occurring or mitigating their effect when they do occur.

A further set of cognate studies is that on partial abandonment.[23,24] This recognized that a common strategy for coping with underperformance, such as projected schedule or budget overruns, or unanticipated events is to descope, which is to say abandon, some elements of a project. It advanced our thinking by showing that what might simplistically be viewed as a symptom of failure can also be an instrument for preventing failure or further failure. Failure is not a simple cut and dried function of any single indicator.

The focus on expectations failure brought into focus the idea that success and failure are a function of the targets as well as the delivery and performance of a system. That is to say that one way of preventing failure is to manage expectations closer to what is realistically achievable. Ginzberg[25] pioneered this notion. It has received limited attention subsequently[26] although, influenced by Danish research,[27] the United Kingdom's Office of Government Commerce today mandates that all projects control for "strategic optimism," the tendency to set expectations unduly high.

A more abundant cognate literature has been that on escalating commitment to a failing course of action. It addresses the key question of why organizations do not cut their losses sooner. Inspired by a substantial corpus of work in Organizational Behavior,[28–32] and recognizing that many IS projects have been characterized by sponsors pouring in good money after bad to projects that would ultimately fail, researchers have explored the applicability of existing theory and sought to adapt it to the IS failure phenomenon.[33–35] While escalation of resourcing is indeed a common feature of projects and existing research enriches our understanding of why it occurs, its practical value is limited by the question of whether we can adequately recognize failure in advance and the extent to which escalation often genuinely sustains a project that would have collapsed without it.

Finally, the "drift" literature introduces a further recognizable phenomenon associated with project performance and which may often either result in failure or substitute for it. Instigated by Ciborra,[36] the idea is that objectives are not immutable fixtures in a project but are subject to organizational politics that often neutralizes them without radically reviewing the case for the project or system. The resultant drift leaves organizations with IS investments that do not meet their real needs but which are not subjected to the scrutiny that might lead to their redevelopment or abandonment. Empirical exploration and development of this phenomenon is in its infancy.[37,38]

So, while risk research has worked to connect failure to management practice with a view to reducing its probability, the other cognate literatures have functioned to situate failure within a more sophisticated understanding of organizational contexts and what counts as success within them. Specifically, partial abandonment recognizes that failure on one dimension of performance, namely scope, may be sacrificed to achieve better performance on another such as budget. Expectation management extends this more realistic approach to what will count as good or bad performance by recognizing that targets in the form of stakeholder expectations are legitimately subject to influence and change. Escalation theory is an inverse of partial abandonment in that it shows why larger and larger overruns on resourcing such as budget may be promoted in the interests of achieving scope and outcome expectations, and how this can be dysfunctional. The focus on drift brings a recognition that not all systems and projects are subject to clear-cut evaluations on a continuing basis and that over time objectives and expectations may be diluted through organizational political processes without any re-evaluation occurring. Failure studies if they are to embody a realistic and sympathetic understanding of the richness and complexity of organizational life must embrace the insights that these cognate studies have brought to the table.

APPROACHES TO UNDERSTANDING IS FAILURE

As our understanding of the concept of IS failure has evolved, so too have our approaches to analyzing the causes of failure. We can distinguish three broad approaches. At one extreme, we have static analyses based on the identification of factors that predispose to failure. At the other extreme, the emphasis is on dynamic analysis and the explication of processes by which failure comes about. Bridging the two is the interactionist approach.

Static Approaches

Static, factor-based approaches were at their most popular in the early days when failure was seen more as an objective phenomenon. It was easy then to ask what caused failure and to look for factors that "determined" failure. What were seen in retrospect as common features of failures rapidly became accepted as causes which if rectified would lead to improved performance and outcomes. Research was undertaken to validate this view (see Larsen[39] for a compendious review of factors identified in the research).

Within this class of approaches, several versions developed emphasizing different perspectives and therefore different failure factors. We identify three here: the technological perspective, the organizational/cultural perspective, and the political perspective.

The technological perspective

A distinguishing feature of the technological perspective has been its strong focus on the technology elements as the most important considerations for an information system (and often the only components to consider in building the system). The efficient processing of data and the efficient operating of hardware and software provide the goals around which people and procedures are to be organized. Studies in this perspective have often embodied two important assumptions. The first is that technology in all its forms (including hardware, software, and databases) is considered to be "good." The "imperative" in technological imperative refers to the inevitability of technology to "compel" acceptance, use, and conformity to it.[40] Any resistance to a given technology is regarded as merely an irrational, impermanent phenomenon. The second is that implementation of technology alone is sufficient to secure organizational benefits. Together these assumptions conspire to exclude other factors as relevant to success and failure.

The technological perspective therefore implies a dominant focus on formal development procedures for systems analysis and design, the purpose of which is to build or upgrade an information system. There are four major phases in the development cycle. The first phase consists of requirements determination to identify the output of the hardware–software system and the data to be input and processed. The second phase is conceptual design to create a "logical" or conceptual blueprint for the system. The third phase is the "physical" or implementation design for specific software and hardware needed in the information system. Building or upgrading the hardware–software system follows. All formal system development methodologies, as well as the tools of computer-aided software engineering that implement them, involve these four phases or variations of them. The technological perspective tends to underlie not only most development methodologies but

Information Systems–
Information Use

also most textbooks on programming, systems analysis, systems design, database management systems, and telecommunications.

In the technological perspective, the diagnosis of an information system failure focuses on a hardware failure, a software failure, a data failure, or any combination of these. The chosen hardware platform may have defects in its manufacture or configuration. The software may suffer from poor design or error-prone construction. The database may harbor inconsistent, incomplete, or outdated data. Since the technological perspective assumes that users can correctly and completely define processing requirements, a failure in the system may also arise because the requirements were specified incorrectly or incompletely. For instance, the information system could lack the capacity to support the processing load if this were not specified correctly.

In general, the remedy for a potential information system failure based on the technological perspective view is for people to conform to the development cycle procedures and to follow processes specified for operation of the system with its hardware, software, and database. The technological perspective requires that people (analysts, designers, managers, programmers, end users, etc.) do or redo the steps of the systems analysis and design correctly. Any failure by people to respond appropriately (e.g., users who do not willingly participate in the requirements determination step, users who resist using the installed system, designers who neglect to install adequate backup procedures, or designers who themselves resist using computerized tools) is seen as a failure of developers and users and not a failure of technological solutions to organizational problems.

The organizational/cultural perspective

By contrast with the technological perspective, in the organizational/cultural perspective it is technology that must adapt to people and to organizations. An organization, in this view, is more than a collection of people. An organization is a structure of roles and rules in which the rules delimit the aims, resources, prerogatives, actions, and behaviors allowed to the person occupying a role. The "culture" in organizational culture refers to the organizational members' shared knowledge or shared understanding of the structure of roles and rules. As successive generations of participants enter, pass through, and leave an organization, its structure of roles and rules continues to exist and to evolve slowly. Upon entering an organization, an individual becomes subject to the organization's structure of roles and rules. Different individuals, when placed in the culture, tend to display similar actions and behaviors. Thus, the culture is the ongoing realization, albeit often partial, of the formal organizational design. An information system application that reflects the desires of one person or a group of people but ignores

organizational culture is unlikely to fit the way the organization works.

Preceding the installation of a new information system or the upgrading of an existing one, the organizational/cultural perspective emphasizes the existence of beliefs and assumptions shared among the organizational members, about what computers do, how technology affects jobs, why the current information system is being upgraded or replaced, and so forth. When held by people in contemporary organizations, these beliefs and assumptions operate much like myths, metaphors, and magic among "natives" in preliterate societies.[41] In this view, an information system is but one among many artifacts crafted by organizational natives for use in their daily activities and rituals. Hence, in the organizational/cultural perspective, an information system failure is a failure of this artifact to serve and be compatible with the activities and rituals of the organizational natives.

In the organization culture of information technology, a poor fit between an information system (the hardware, software, and data) and the organizational culture is conducive to an information system failure. A framework useful for identifying a poor fit between information system and organizational culture specifies seven categories of shared beliefs and assumptions that can be violated by systems:[42,43]

1. Shared beliefs and assumptions about innovation and action (e.g., are original and creative behaviors "good?").
2. Risk taking (e.g., is the norm to be proactive and take responsibility for one's own actions, or to be reactive and avoid responsibility?)
3. Integration (e.g., how much importance is placed on communicating and cooperating with other organizational members?)
4. Top management contact (e.g., does top management customarily relate to subordinates by being affirming or openly critical?)
5. Autonomy in decision making (e.g., are organizational members allowed, encouraged, expected, or trusted to make decisions on their own?)
6. Performance orientation (e.g., are the criteria for compensation, job security, and job promotion concretely established, explicitly known, and actually used?)
7. Reward orientation (e.g., do rewards take the form of a "carrot" or "stick?")

In this framework, the failure potential for an information system increases with the number of categories of cultural assumptions with which the information system is incompatible, as well as the extent of the respective incompatibilities. For instance, consider an information system that makes an assumption that there is open sharing of data across the organization's different divisions (integration) and that new users of the system will take responsibility for the decisions that they make with the help of the information system (risk taking). If the organizational members share a norm in which each division guards its data as a valued resource and if the organizational members share, as an accepted practice, the custom of "blaming the computer" for their bad decisions, there is a significant threat of failure for the new system. Any additional incompatibilities between the information system and other shared beliefs and assumptions would increase the threat of an information system failure.

To prevent or to remedy an information system failure, the organizational/cultural perspective requires that the information system be designed and adjusted to respect the constraints that the organizational culture imposes. A strong proponent of this view will maintain that an information system is an artifact crafted to serve the activities of an organization, and therefore the information system should always conform to the organization, rather than vice versa. In other words, a proponent of the organizational culture view may take the position that altering an organizational culture to fit an information system, even if possible in the long run, is a dangerous course of action.

The organizational/cultural perspective extends the technological perspective by bringing in organizational/cultural factors. It also introduces the idea of a fit between the technology and the organization/culture. However, it continues to assume that the important challenge is to establish the right conditions in terms of getting two sets of factors aligned with each other.

The political perspective

The political perspective extends the organizational/cultural perspective by introducing power as the real basis by which organizations work. Power is the ability of a person, group, or organizational unit to overcome resistance or opposition to achievement of its ends; politics is the exercise of this ability.[44–46] In this view, activities that accompany the development, implementation, and use of an information system provide an arena in which a person, group, or organizational unit can exercise power, whether or not the ends for which the power is exercised bear any relevance to the purposes that the information system is ostensibly said to serve. Success or failure of the information system relative to these ostensible purposes is secondary to the achievement of the power objectives.

In a classic case study of an information system implementation,[47] a new information system threatened to alter the power between the corporate accounting group and divisional accounting personnel. The system was designed to allow the accounting group at corporate headquarters immediate access to data belonging to the accounting group in each of the company's different divisions. In the existing procedures, each division controlled its own data (stored in thick manual ledger books), and corporate accounting could only obtain it through reports prepared by division accountants. Built into the design of the new information system was a presumption that there should be a different distribution of power relative to the division data. This design was contrary to the existing power over the data. In the technological imperative view and the organizational culture view, resistance to the proposed system could be explained as opposition to a more efficient system or opposition to changes in the culture of corporate versus division roles. In the political perspective, the efficiency considerations or role changes were secondary; the main objective of the system for the corporate accountants was political. They wanted to disrupt the existing balance of power in the organization and introduce a new balance of power based on data access that favored the corporate group.

In the political perspective, the failure potential for an information system application increases if it violates the constraints imposed by the organizational distribution of power. In some cases, an application will be allowed to succeed only if it supports the political agenda of a powerful group within the organization. IS may be used explicitly to change the distribution of power in an organization; in such cases, the design of the system is a secondary factor in success or failure. The major issue is the effectiveness of change agents in negotiating redistribution or organizational power.

To prevent or remedy an information system failure due primarily to strong political opposition, the political considerations must be surfaced and negotiated. Political considerations may be somewhat hidden; surfacing them through high-level discussions allows the effect of the system to be dealt with in the context of high-level goals of the organization. An explicit understanding of the effect of the system on the relative power of the organizational participants may allow negotiations and compromise. In the absence of such compromise, political opposition to a system may be sufficient to cause failure.

The political perspective has sometimes been operationalized in research in terms of the fit between an information system or project and the power structure. Such operationalizations fall under the factor approach. Others however have recognized that power can be renegotiated and as such the processes by which IS are treated affect their success or failure.

Interactionist Approaches

Interactionist approaches bridge the step from factors to processes. In accepting that factors may influence each other, they implicitly introduce a temporal element to the analysis of failure. For example, a factors analysis might identify inadequate involvement of business users inrequirements specification and user resistance as critical causes of failure. The interactionist recognizes that the user resistance may be a function of the lack of involvement. In turn, perceived user resistance may deter

Information Systems–
Information Use

technologists from consulting the users. The causes of failure develop and harden over time. Implicitly, such approaches recognize that the different factor approaches embody important elements that may contribute to a comprehensive analysis of failure. We briefly describe two such approaches: the sociotechnical perspective and the exchange perspective.

The sociotechnical perspective

In the sociotechnical systems view, an information system is more than a technical system of hardware and software. An information system is a social system that uses information technology.[48,49] Failure is not a failure of the information technology alone or the organization alone, because there is a strong interaction between the two. The same information technology will exhibit different properties when used in different organizational contexts. Sociotechnical theory[50] predicts that optimizing only the technical system or optimizing only the social system will lead to information system failure. To avoid failure, neither system can be managed separately from the other.

The interactive effects between the social system and the information technology have a parallel in the chemical difference between mixtures and compounds. The properties of a mixture are simply a combined set of the respective properties of the individual elements that constitute the mixture. The reason is that the elements in a mixture do not react to one another; their respective properties remain intact. However, the properties of a chemical compound are different from the respective properties of the constituent elements. The reason is that the elements react to one another; their respective properties are replaced by the new properties of the compound entity. In this analogy, an information system is more like a compound than a mixture. Its constituent social system and information technology react to one another, so that their properties in combination are different from their properties in isolation.

In the sociotechnical view, failure potential is increased by development processes and procedures that do not integrate both social and technical considerations. In sociotechnical development, the future users of the system specify important job and work design considerations. There is a joint effort involving both users and technical personnel to consider alternative information system technical designs and select one that achieves a reasonable trade-off between job design and technical efficiency. Dominance of technical considerations increases the probability of failure due to user resistance. The sociotechnical approach recognizes the fact that user resistance can cause a technically well-designed system to fail and user enthusiasm can cause a somewhat mediocre technical design to succeed. These dynamics are the basis for a process that looks for the best combination of technical and social factors.

To prevent or remedy an information system failure, the sociotechnical view specifies a sociotechnical requirements and development process. Users are empowered with sufficient information to be effective participants in design discussions and decisions. Obtaining commitment by users to make the system succeed is an essential part of the process.

The exchange perspective

The exchange perspective[17] develops the sociotechnical perspective in one specific direction. It emphasizes one critical basis of interaction, viz. the creation and sustaining of a balanced exchange between a project team or those who manage an information system and the key supporters of that project or system. It argues that projects and systems fail if two conditions obtain:[1] there are insufficient resources to continue developing or operating the system, and[2] key supporters are dissatisfied.

This perspective sees systems and projects as needing a range of different forms of support from a range of stakeholders. Support can include material resources such as funds, equipment, space, practical support such as involvement in project processes, problem-solving, and management attention, psychic support such as publicly observable commitment, as well as organizational support in terms of politics and working the organizational system. Stakeholders who may be key supporters include senior management sponsors, operational users, end customers, the project team, and the supply chain. As supporters' levels of satisfaction may ebb and flow over time, the task of IS management and project management is one of maintaining sufficient levels of satisfaction to ensure a continuing flow of needed resources. Thus, for example, the project process can be seen as the challenge of marshalling the right resources to deliver sufficient progress and expectation of benefit that supporters will continue to provide those resources. If progress stalls, resources needed to overcome a hurdle may not be forthcoming resulting in further difficulties for the project and further damage to supporters' expectations. The project team may be able to break out of this vicious circle by actions that restore confidence such as bringing forward the delivery of some benefits or by actively managing supporters' perceptions. If on the other hand it is unable to break out of this vicious circle, the project will be set for failure. Projects can be seen as an ongoing complex interactive process where exchange is at the heart of the interactions.

Process Approaches

Since the mid-1990s failure analyses have emerged that focus more on a detailed examination of process and the search for patterns in process. They have tended to view success and failure outcomes as not determined by factors or even by interactions but as a function of a yet more complex account of the processes by which multifarious influences affect projects and systems over time. As yet no single perspective has come to dominate the field. However, we shall give special attention to Actor-Network Theory because it has been widely employed in social studies of IS including failures, and because it encompasses ideas from numerous other perspectives.

From within the IS discipline, Newman and Robey[51] enabled process analyses of failure through their more general articulation of the elements of process analysis, and Newman has applied it in his failure research.[52,53] Outside the discipline, in the broad area of social studies of technology, a number of case studies have been published that have cast light on IS failure through detailed accounts of IS processes.[54] This has then been brought back into the discipline by critical theory–oriented researchers such as Howcroft, Wilson, and Mitev adopting a social shaping of technology perspective and applying it to failures.[55,56]

Actor-network theory

Actor-Network Theory has recently become a popular tool for analyzing IS failure.[36–38,57–59] Actor Network Theory has a number of attractions. First, it is the first approach in many years to take a balanced position in relation to technology. That is, where for most researchers it has been accepted that technology is subservient to human/organizational objectives, Actor-Network Theory places technology on a par with other stakeholders. It then views the object of study, say a project failure, through the lens of the actor-network in which it is embedded. Humans, institutions, and technologies are among the stakeholders who populate the network and propagate influences through its nodes. In this manner, the complexity of the contexts within which IS failures occur is well represented. Further, one of the core ideas of the theory is that of breakdown. The essence of this insight is that when something appears to be functioning well we treat it as a black box. Only when it begins to fail do we start to unpack it to understand what is going on. Thus, for example, we can understand "drift" in these terms.

The limitations of Actor-Network Theory are that it is still evolving a set of concepts for general use. Early analyses using it have tended to be very complex and not productive of readily practical conclusions.

Conclusion: The Future of Failure

Ten years ago, the question arose as to whether the increased commodification of IT would lead to standard solutions to such an extent that the problem of failure might dissolve.[60] The alternative scenario was that the strategic benefits of IT would be such that organizations would continue to seek to differentiate themselves and

would therefore continue to pursue distinctive, non-commodity solutions. The improvements in performance are noted earlier in this entry but the continued difficulties in achieving expectations suggest that elements of both scenarios have occurred. This suggests that the issues associated with understanding and preventing failure will continue to be highly relevant for the foreseeable future.

The challenge for research is to strike a balance between analyses that embody every causal constituent in a failure but where it is difficult to see the wood for the trees, and those that are simpler but which promise too much to the practitioner because they suggest that a relatively simple intervention will be sufficient to prevent failure. Having developed a growing maturity in our understanding it is easy for research to fall into the former category. It is this trick that Actor-Network Theory or alternatives will have to master if it is to be both academically successful and practically useful.

CONCLUSION: SUMMARY OF LESSONS ABOUT FAILURE FOR PRACTITIONERS

The entry has lessons for scholars and researchers. It also has lessons for practitioners. These can be summarized as follows:

1. The evaluation of success or failure for a project is not usually a simple "success" or "failure" or identification of a single reason for the result. Success or failure depends on the criteria being used, the stakeholders being considered, and the level of expectations.
2. Organizations respond to perceptions of failure in various ways. One response is abandonment. Other possible responses include escalation and revision of expectations.
3. The ideal lessons for practitioners would be a set of simple prescriptions to prevent failure and ensure success. The analysis of the failure research provides guidance but no simple list of prescriptions. A thoughtful practitioner seeking to reduce the potential for failure should consider both static factors that predispose to failure and the interaction of factors that may lead to failure.
4. Static causes. Three types of causes that predispose to failure and therefore should be considered as part of prevention measures are:
    Technological. The focus in failure prevention and failure analysis is on correct and complete hardware, software, or data (or a combination of these technological elements). Today, these are the least common causes of failure.
    Organization/culture. The focus is on a good fit between the system and the activities, rules, roles, rituals, and culture of an organization.

Political. The focus is on incorporating the effect of political power on design, acceptance, and use of a system.

5. Interaction causes. The focus on static causes may not be sufficient. Factors may influence each other. Two approaches to understanding and analyzing failure based on interactions are:

Sociotechnical. This analysis is based on the view that an information system is a social system that uses information technology. To avoid failure, the interaction of the two systems must be considered in the designs of both.

Exchange perspective. Systems and projects need forms of support from a range of stakeholders. Critical to avoiding failure is creating and sustaining a balanced exchange between a project team and key supporters.

6. An emerging view that is perhaps not ready for widespread practitioner use is to analyze the process by which a complex set of influences affect the way projects and systems develop over time.

ACKNOWLEDGMENT

This entry adds to and develops aspects of the entry on Information Systems Failure by Gordon B. Davis, Allen S. Lee, and Kathryn Nickles in the previous edition of the Encyclopaedia of Library and Information Sciences.

REFERENCES

1. Naur, P. Randell, B. *Software Engineering: Report on a Conference Sponsored by the NATO Science Committee*, Garmisch: Germany, October 7–11, 1968. http://homepages.cs.ncl.ac.uk/brian.randell/NATO/nato1968.PDF (accessed January 11, 2007).

2. Colton, K.W. Computers and police: Patterns of success and failure. Sloan Manage. Rev. **1972**, *Winter*, 75–98.

3. Lucas, H.C., Jr. *Why Information Systems Fail*, Columbia University Press: New York, 1975.

4. DeLone, W.H.; McLean, E.R. Information systems success: The quest for the dependent variable. Inform. Syst. Res. **1992**, *3*(1), 60–95.

5. Hirschheim, R.; Smithson, S. A critical analysis of information systems evaluation. In *Information Systems Assessment: Issues and Challenges*; Bjørn-Andersen, N., Davis, G.B., Eds.; Elsevier (North-Holland): Amsterdam, the Netherlands, 1988; 17–37.

6. Johnson, J. Chaos: The dollar drain of IT project failures. Appl. Dev. Trends. January **1995**, 41–47.

7. Johnson, J. *My Life is Failure*, Standish Group International: West Yarmouth, MA, 2006.

8. Jørgensen, M.; Moløkken-Østvold, K.J. How large are software cost overruns? Critical comments on the Standish Group's CHAOS reports. Inform. Softw. Technol. **2006**, *48*(4), 297–301.

9. Taylor, A. IT projects: Sink or swim. Comput. Bull. January **2000**, *42*, 24–26.

10. Sauer, C.; Gemino, A.; Reich, B. Managing projects for success: The impact of size and volatility on IT project performance. Commun. ACM **2007**, *50*(11), 79–84.

11. Neumann, P. CACM inside risks. 2007. http://www.csl.sri.com/users/neumann/insiderisks.html#menu2 (accessed January 11, 2007).

12. Hodgson, M. Computer error keeps airport on summer time. Guardian Newspaper. October 29, **2007**, Monday.

13. Markus, M.L. Technochange management: Using IT to drive organizational change. J. Inform. Technol. **2004**, *19*(1), 4–20.

14. Ross, J.W.; Vitale, M. The ERP revolution: Surviving vs. thriving. Inform. Syst. Front. **2000**, *2*(2), 233–241.

15. Lyytinen, K.; Hirschheim, R. Information systems failures: A survey and classification of the empirical literature. Oxf. Surv. Inform. Technol. **1987**, *4*, 257–309.

16. Ewusi-Mensah, K.; Przasnyski, Z.H. On information systems project abandonment: An exploratory study of organizational practices. MIS Quart. March **1991**, 67–86.

17. Sauer, C. *Why Information Systems Fail: A Case Study Approach*, Alfred Waller: Oxfordshire, U.K., 1993.

18. Faraj, S.; Sproull, L. Coordinating expertise in software development teams. Manage. Sci. **2000**, *46*(12), 1554–1568.

19. Nidumolu, S. The effect of coordination and uncertainty on software project performance: Residual performance risk as an intervening variable. Inform. Syst. Res. **1995**, *6*(3), 191–219.

20. Gemino, A.; Reich, B.H.; Sauer, C. A temporal model of information technology project performance. J. Manage. Inform. Syst. **2008**, *24*(3), 9–44.

21. Schmidt, R.; Lyytinen, K.; Keil, M.; Cule, P. Identifying software project risks: An international delphi study. J. Manage. Inform. Syst. **2001**, *17*(4), 5–36.

22. Barki, H.; Rivard, S.; Talbot, J. An integrative contingency model of software project risk management. J. Manage. Inform. Syst. **2001**, *17*(4), 37–69.

23. Sauer, C. Partial abandonment as a strategy for avoiding failure. *Information Systems Development: Human, Social and Organizational Aspects*, Proceedings of IFIP WG8.2 Working Conference, Noordwijkerhout May, 17–19, 1993; Avison, D.E., deGross, J., Kendall, J., Eds.; Elsevier (North Holland): Amsterdam, the Netherlands, 143–167.

24. Martin, A.; Chan, M. Information systems project redefinition in New Zealand: Will we ever learn?. Aust. Comput. J. **1996**, *28*(1), 27–40.

25. Ginzberg, M.J. Early diagnosis of MIS implementation failure: Promising results and unanswered questions. Manage. Sci. **1981**, *27*(4), 459–478.

26. Sauer, C.; Willcocks, L.P. Unreasonable expectations: NHS IT, Greek choruses and the games institutions play around mega-programmes. J. Inform. Technol. **2007**, *22*(3), 195–201.

27. Flyvbjerg, B. Bruzelius, N. Rothengatter, W. *Megaprojects and Risk: An Anatomy of Ambition*, Cambridge University Press: Cambridge, U.K., 2003.

28. Brockner, J. Rubin, J.Z. *Entrapment in Escalating Conflicts: A Social Psychological Analysis*, Springer-Verlag: New York, 1985.

Information Systems–
Information Use

29. Brockner, J. The escalation of commitment to a failing course of action: Toward theoretical progress. Acad. Manage. Rev. **1992**, *17*(1), 39–61.

30. Ross, J.; Staw, B.M. Expo 86: An escalation prototype. Admin. Sci. Quart. **1986**, *31*, 274–297.

31. Ross, J.; Staw, B.M. Organizational escalation and exit: Lessons from the Shoreham nuclear power plant. Acad. Manage. J. **1993**, *36*(4), 701–732.

32. Staw, B.M.; Ross, J. Behavior in escalation situations: Antecedents, prototypes, and solutions. In *Research in Organizational Behavior*; Staw, B.M., Cummings, L.L., Eds.; JAI Press: Greenwich, CT, 1990; Vol. 9, 39–78.

33. Keil, M. Pulling the plug: Software project management and the problem of escalation. MIS Quart. December **1995**, 420–447.

34. Keil, M.; Mann, J.; Rai, A. Why software projects escalate: An empirical analysis and test of four theoretical models. MIS Quart. **2000**, *24*(4), 631–664.

35. Drummond, H. *Escalation in Decision Making: The Tragedy of Taurus*, Oxford University Press: Oxford, U.K., 1996.

36. Ciborra, C. Associates *From Control to Drift: The Dynamics of Corporate Information Iinfrasructures*, Oxford University Press: Oxford, U.K., 2000.

37. Holmstrom, J.; Stalder, F. Drifting technologies and multipurpose networks: The case of the Swedish cashcard. Inform. Organ. **2001**, *11*, 187–206.

38. Elbanna, A.R. The inertia of ERP projects: Diffusion or drift. *Organizational Dynamics of Technology Based Innovation: Diversifying the Research Agenda*, Proceedings of the IFIP TC 8 WG 8.6 International Working Conference June, 14–16, 2007; McMaster, T., Wastell, D., Ferneley, E., DeGross, J., Eds.; Manchester, U.K., 2007; 253–266.

39. Larsen, K.R.T. A taxonomy of antecedents of information systems success: Variable analysis studies. J. Manage. Inform. Syst. **2003**, *20*(2), 169–246.

40. Markus, M.L.; Robey, D. Information technology and organizational change: Causal structure in theory and research. Manage. Sci. **1988**, *34*(5), 583–598.

41. Hirschheim, R.; Newman, M. Symbolism and information systems development: Myth, metaphor and magic. Inform. Syst. Res. **1991**, *2*(1), 29–62.

42. Romm, T.; Pliskin, N.; Weber, Y.; Lee, A. Identifying organizational culture clash in MIS implementation. Inform. Manage. **1990**, *21*(2), 99–109.

43. Pliskin, N.; Romm, T.; Lee, A.; Weber, Y. Presumed versus actual organizational culture: Managerial implications for implementation of information systems. Comput. J. **1993**, *36*(2), 143–152.

44. Pfeffer, J. *Power in Organization*, Ballinger: Cambridge, MA, 1981.

45. Markus, M.L.; Pfeffer, J. Power and the design and implementation of accounting and control systems. Account. Organ. Soc. **1983**, *8*(2/3), 205–218.

46. Robey, D. Power and politics. In *Designing Organizations*; Robey, D., Irwin, H., II, Eds.; Homewood: Illinois, 1991; 347–382.

47. Markus, M.L. Power, politics and MIS implementation. Commun. ACM. June **1983**, *26*(6), 430–444.

48. Land, F.; Hirschheim, R. Participative systems design: Rationale, tools and techniques. J. Appl. Syst. Anal. **1983**, *10*, 91–107.

49. Davis, G.B.; Lee, A.S.; Nickles, K.R.; Chatterjee, S.; Hartung, R.; Wu, Y. Diagnosis of an information system failure. Inform. Manage. **1992**, *23*(5), 293–318.

50. Cherns, A. The principles of sociotechnical design. Hum. Relat. **1976**, *29*(8), 783–79.

51. Newman, M.; Robey, D. A social process model of user-analyst relationships. MIS Quart. June **1992**, *16*(2), 249–266.

52. Newman, M.; Noble, F. User involvement as an interaction process: A case study. Inform. Syst. Res. **1990**, *1*, 1.

53. Pan, S.L.; Pan, G.S.C.; Newman, M.; Flynn, D. Escalation and de-escalation of commitment to information systems projects: Insights from a project evaluation model. Eur. J. Operat. Res. **2006**, *173*(3), 1139–1160.

54. *Information Technology and Organizations: Strategies, Networks and Integration*; Bloomfield, B., Coombs, R., Knights, D., Littler, D., Eds.; Oxford University Press: Oxford, U.K., 1997.

55. Mitev, N.N. More than a failure? The computerised reservation systems at French Railways. Inform. Technol. People **1996**, *9*(4), 8–19.

56. Howcroft, D. Mitev, N. Wilson, M. What we may learn from the social shaping of technology approach. In *Social Theory and Philosophy of IS*; Mingers, J., Willcocks, L., Eds.; John Wiley & Sons: Chichester, U.K., 2004; 329–371.

57. Vidgen, R.T.; Mc Master, T. Black boxes, non-human stakeholders, and the translation of IT through mediation. *Information Technology and Changes in Organizational Work*, Proceedings of the IFIP WG 8.2 working conference on information technology and changes in organizational work Chapman and Hall, London, U.K., 1995. Orlikowski, W.J., Walsham, G., Jones, M.R., DeGross, J.I., Eds.; Chapman and Hall: London, U.K., 1995; 250–271.

58. Sarker, S.; Sarker, S.; Sidorova, A. Understanding business process change failure: An actor-network perspective. J. Manage. Inform. Syst. **2006**, *23*(1), 51–86.

59. Bartis, E. Mitev, N.N. A multiple narrative approach to information systems failure: A successful system that failed. *Relevant rigour, rigorous relevance'*, Proceedings of 15th European Conference on Information Systems. June 7–9, 2007, St. Gallen University: St. Gallen, Switzerland.

60. Sauer, C. Deciding the future for IS failures: Not the decision you might think. In *Re-Thinking Management Information Systems*; Galliers, R.D., Currie, W., Eds.; Oxford University Press: Oxford, U.K., 1999.

Information Systems– Information Use

Information Systems–
Information Use

Information Technology Adoption

Conrad Shayo
Department of Information and Decision Sciences, California State University—San Bernardino, San Bernardino, California, U.S.A.

Abstract
Since the dawn of time, humans have relentlessly continued to develop and adopt various information technologies (ITs) to thrive successfully in their environment. Generally, the rate of adoption has depended on the adopter's perceptions of the ITs' net benefits. In this entry, we draw from innovation diffusion theory, and the DeLone and McLean IS success model to discuss the literature on IT adoption by individuals and organizations. Since the proliferation of newer and more powerful ITs is apt to continue unabated for many years to come, we suggest new ways of identifying, learning, and implementing new ITs.

INTRODUCTION

This entry provides a general overview of existing literature on new information technology (IT) adoption by individuals and organizations. The terms adoption, implementation, consumption, acceptance are used interchangeably. Also the terms information technology (IT), information and communication technology (ICT), and information technology systems (ITS), are taken to be synonymous. Organizational adoption looks at adoption by aggregates: viz. work groups, departments, directorates, strategic business units, and companies or corporations including intranets and extranets. Other aggregate levels such as industries, communities, national governments, and society at large are beyond the scope of this entry. We define adoption as the process by which an IT innovation is acquired, installed, and used to perform tasks in work-related environments. The rate of successful IT adoption depends on the adopter's perceptions of the ITs' relative advantage, compatibility, and complexity, as well as its triability and observability.[1] We draw from innovation diffusion theory,[1] and the DeLone and McLean Information Systems (IS) success model[2,3] to discuss adoption at each level of analysis: individual and organization. Innovation diffusion theory uses the S-Curve to classify adopters of a new IT into innovators, early adopters, early majority, late majority, and laggards. The DeLone and McLean IS success model posits that successful IT adoption is mainly determined by: 1) the quality of the technology itself; 2) the quality of the information the technology provides; 3) the quality of the service provided by IT support staff; 4) continual usage of the IT; 5) user satisfaction from the use of the IT; and 6) the overall impact it will have on the adopting individual or organization.[2,3] The citations used are only representative of existing literature, not exhaustive. The entry starts with the premise that IT has the potential of profoundly transforming individual and organizational welfare. That IT offers both an opportunity and a challenge (i.e., opportunity to increase productivity and effectiveness and a challenge to keep the motivation of perpetually learning newer and sometimes complex disruptive ITs), and that, whether the adoption of IT occurs voluntarily, through sanctions, or by pressure from outside parties,[4] it will have to eventually help the individual user or the organization meet stipulated personal, strategic, or operational goals. One key factor is that there will always be a constant cycle of breakthrough IT innovations that will inevitably dislodge previous, now moribund, innovations. The entry describes the unavoidable role of IT discontinuities in the adoption process, and concludes by suggesting that since the proliferation of newer and more disruptive ITs is apt to continue unabated into the future; there is a real need for individuals and organizations to develop new ways of identifying, acquiring, learning, and implementing new technologies. Individual and organizational lifelong learning, and coping strategies are two recent constructs that depict the essence of survival in an increasingly interdependent IT-networked society.

BACKGROUND

Why IT Is Important

It is an accepted fact that IT "will change the world more permanently and more profoundly than any technology so far seen in history and will bring about a transformation of civilization to match."[5] It is also accepted that IT has the potential of enhancing individual and organizational performance. Individual or organizational performance is measured in terms of the tangible and intangible net benefits resulting from the using the IT innovation. Information technology is defined here as

Encyclopedia of Library and Information Sciences, Fourth Edition DOI: 10.1081/E-ELIS4-120043941
Copyright © 2017 by Taylor & Francis. All rights reserved.

any system, product, or process whose underlying technology base is composed of computers (both hardware and software), workstations, and/or computerized communication networks of all types, including Local Area Networks (LANs), Wide Area Networks (WANs), Metropolitan Area Networks (MANs), intranets, Internet, robotics, and smart chips.[6] Recognition of the potential of IT has led individuals and organizations to invest enormous amounts of time and money in IT assets. It is noteworthy that a worldwide IT expenditure of more than $4 trillion is expected in 2009 alone.[7] Information technology is now so pervasive that more than 55% of the workforce in the developed world relies on it to produce their goods and services.[8] For example, today's banks and global financial markets could not function without IT. It is now fashionable to refer to our generation as the information society.

Role of IT Discontinuities

Information technology discontinuities are breakthrough innovations that significantly change the rules of competition in terms of how data/information are captured, stored, processed, and used by individuals, organizations, and entire industries. Such IT discontinuities threaten to disturb the mode of doing business in the industry and have led to the collapse of companies and industries that do not adopt.[9] For example the current convergence of digital and telecommunication technologies such as the Internet, Peer to Peer, MP3, and cellular phone on the music industry may lead to the creation of an entirely new industry that delivers music on demand; anytime, anywhere. Companies in the CD, cassette tape, or boom box businesses will be forced to adopt before an impeding doom befalls them. According to Anderson and Tushman,[10] and

Utterback,[11] as a general rule, technological innovations tend to have a life cycle of their own.

As shown in Fig. 1, for the IT industry, the cycle begins with a new IT invention or the arrival of a newer IT (e.g., the Apple Computer) that is a substantial improvement of the prevailing technology in the industry. An era of turmoil then sets in as the new IT replaces its predecessor. In this era, innovators and early adopters identify, purchase, and learn to use the new IT. At this time, entrepreneurs and IT developers continue to experiment with alternative designs and compete for market share (e.g., Apple vs. IBM PC). Finally a dominant design emerges as the industry default standard. The industry default standard emerges by offering a combination of features and services that allow adopters to make effective use of the IT at an affordable price. We think that this is probably the time when the early and late majority adopters purchase and use the proven IT. Then the innovation cycle enters an era of incremental change where the focus is on market segmentation and lowering costs (e.g., Workstations, Laptops, PC Tablets, Internet, PC). This era continues until the arrival of the next IT discontinuity. Schumpeter[12] argues that technological discontinuities should be encouraged and that unprofitable methods, firms, and industries must be allowed to perish in order to release trapped resources for new enterprises.

Despite the evident opportunities offered by IT, such as increases in output or decreases in the cost of some inputs in specific organizations, there is no clear evidence at least in the United States that IT consumption has raised overall national productivity. For example, "profitability rates have been falling in U.S. industries in the last decade despite the new investments in information technologies."[13] As such, much of the investment in new IT may not have led to successful results after all. Some of the cited reasons for non-adoption are inability to learn "how

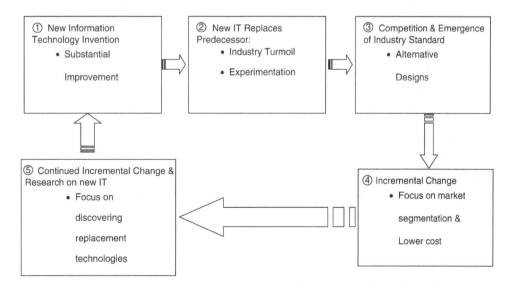

Fig. 1 Information technology innovation life cycle.

Information Systems–
Information Use

to change organizations faster than humans naturally want to change,"[13] technically deficient ITs that are threatening to its users, low user satisfaction from usage of the IT, and high knowledge burden requirement to master the technology. Others are: users getting information that is not necessary for decision making, low individual or organizational ability to recognize the value of new information and adopt it for productive ends, and lack of adequate means to realistically measure the costs/benefits of IT. In short, there is skepticism out there about how quickly one should adopt a new IT:[13]

> At the level of the individual firm, the problem will be to overcome the resistance to change, both by individuals who feel threatened by such changes and by those who doubt the potential returns available from the large investments necessary in the new technologies. At the national level, countries may become laggards if, for example, they fail to provide an IT infrastructure adequate to enable their firms to take advantage of the new ways of doing business, ways that shrink the effects of time and distance(p. vii)

This entry provides a general overview of existing literature on new IT adoption by individuals and organizations. The guiding questions are: What role do IT discontinuities play in the adoption process? Why do individuals or organizations decide to adopt or not to adopt IT? How can individuals and organizations know whether IT adoption

has been successful? Why does the adoption of IT occur at different rates?

The entry is divided into two parts. The first part identifies the general attributes of adoption of innovations and generalizes them to IT adoption. The second part discusses the rate of IT adoption based on Rogers' S-Curve.[1] A conclusion is provided at the end of each of the two parts.

PART 1: ADOPTION OF IT INNOVATIONS

According to Rogers,[1] the rate of adoption of an innovation (in this entry, any new IT is considered an innovation) depends on the perceived attributes of the innovation, the type of innovation decision, the communication channels used to advertise the technology, the nature of the social system in which the IT is implemented, and the extent of the promotional efforts of change agents (see Fig. 2).

Perceived Attributes of Innovations

According to innovation diffusion theory, the perceived attributes of innovations are *relative advantage*, *compatibility*, *complexity*, *observability*, and *triability*. *Relative advantage* is "the degree to which an innovation is perceived as better than the one it replaces" as measured by

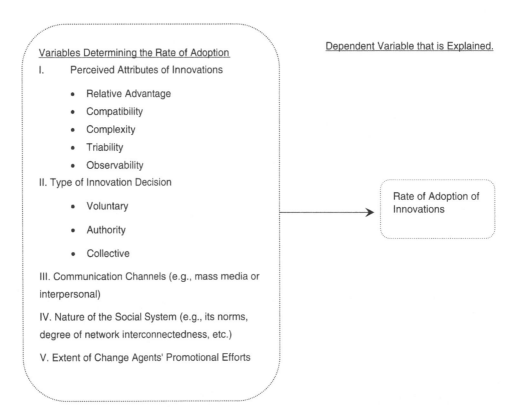

Fig. 2 Variables determining the rate of adoption of innovations.
Source: From Rogers[1] on p. 207.

actual monetary gains, convenience, enjoyment, and satisfaction derived from its use. The greater the relative advantage, the higher the perceived usefulness,[14] and the better the rate of adoption of the innovation. Constructs similar to relative advantage found in the literature include: performance expectancy, outcome expectations, job-fit, and extrinsic motivations.[15]*Compatibility* is "the degree to which an innovation is perceived as being consistent with the existing values, past experiences, and needs of adopters." For example, the implementation of a new IT in a work environment that has had previous experiences with poorly designed systems is much harder than the implementation of a new IT in an environment that has had prior good experiences with a well-designed system.

Complexity is "the degree to which an innovation is perceived as being difficult to use." The level of enjoyment one gets from using a new innovation is inversely proportional to the degree of complexity one encounters. The lower the degree of complexity; the greater the perceived ease of use of the innovation[14,15] and better the rate of adoption. Theories of cognitive absorption stipulate that low complexity leads to heightened levels of curiosity, playfulness, personal innovativeness, and rates of adoption.[16] *Observability* is "the degree to which the results of an innovation are observable to others." Individuals may adopt a specific IT in order to gain recognition or make themselves indispensable. This is what the technology acceptance model calls social influence. *Triability* is "the degree to which an innovation may be experimented with on a limited scale before adoption." Ability to pilot enables potential adopters to reduce uncertainty and become acquitted with the new innovation.

A number of research studies have investigated the efficacy of these attributes to the adoption of new IT13.[17] Moore and Benbasat[17] used the attributes as a basis of developing an overall validated research instrument to measure the various perceptions of adopting an IT innovation. All attributes had fairly high alpha coefficients: relative advantage, 0.90; compatibility, 0.86; complexity (also called ease of use), 0.84; observability (also called result demonstrability), 0.79; and triability, 0.77. An alpha coefficient measures the squared correlation between observed scores and true scores. A high score means that the observed score is strongly correlated with the true score; which was the case with the Moore and Benbasat study.[17] What follows is a discussion of each attribute in more detail.

Relative advantage

This construct captures both objective and perceived advantages of adopting the new IT. The literature shows that IT researchers have used different measures to assess the relative advantage of a new IT compared to the one it replaces. Six general interrelated and interdependent measures have been identified: *IT quality, information*

quality, service quality; *intention to use, actual usage, user satisfaction, and impact (including net benefits) to the individual and organization.*[2,3] In 1992, DeLone and McLean[3] reviewed 180 research studies on measures of information system success and drawing from the work of Shannon and Weaver[68] came up with six measures: System Quality, Information Quality, Use, User Satisfaction, Individual Impact, and Organizational Impact. In a revised model in 2003, DeLone and McLean[2] added Service Quality, Intention to Use, and generalized the Individual and Organizational impacts to one construct, namely, Net Benefits. We think these measures apply to IT adoption success as well. Given the multidimensional and interdependent nature of the IS success construct, the measures selected by researchers would depend on their research intentions. Fig. 3 shows the relationship between the various measures of the revised 2003 DeLone and McLean Model of Information Systems Success.[2]

IT Quality. At the *IT quality* level, researchers have used "more engineering-oriented performance characteristics of the [IT] in question."[2] Specifically, research studies compared the new IT with the old one by focusing on resource and investment utilization,[18] reliability,[19] online response time,[20] perceived usefulness,[14,21] and accuracy.[22] Overall, the studies found that any new IT that ranked higher in one or a combination of these factors had a higher chance of getting adopted compared to one that ranked lower. Other researchers have focused on measuring the relative advantage of the quality of the information generated by the new technology.

Information Quality. The perceived relative *quality of information* generated by a new IT in the form of reports is another determinant of successful IT adoption. Bailey and Pearson[20] identified 39 IT-related items for measuring individual satisfaction with information quality. Out of the 39 items, the most important ones were accuracy, timeliness, reliability, completeness, relevance, precision, and currency. Other researchers have used other attributes of information quality such as uniqueness, conciseness, clarity and readability;[23] and sufficiency, understandability, unbiasedness, quantitativeness.[24] Ahituv[25] summarized the relative value of information into four main multiattribute utility category measures: *timeliness, content, format,* and *cost and benefit.* Timeliness includes a class of attributes related to the time factor in information update and retrieval. These time factors are: currency/recency, response time, and frequency. If a business transaction occurs in time t_0, the related record may be updated later at time t_1, and the user of this information may get a processed report at time t_2; the *currency of the data* presented to the user is measured by the difference $t_2 - t_0$. The *currency of the file* is measured by the difference $t_1 - t_0$ and the *response time* is measured by the

Information Systems–
Information Use

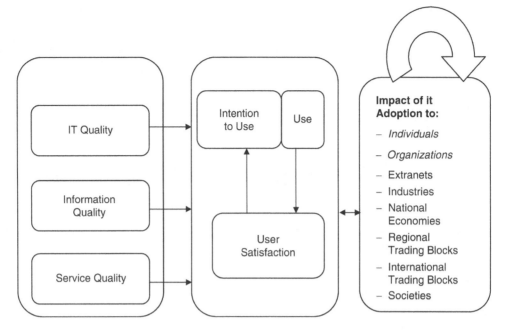

Fig. 3 DeLone and McLean IT success model.
Source: Adopted from DeLone and McLean.[2]

difference $t_2 - t_1$. The *frequency of the reports* is measured by the number of times the user retrieves updated information for decision making. For example, if you have a bank account, monthly frequency statements may be sufficient. However, if you manage your own shares you may need daily or continuous updates of information from the stock exchanges.

Content attributes relate to the meaning of the information provided to the users. The attributes of content include: *accuracy, relevance, exhaustiveness, redundancy,* and *level of detail*. Accuracy refers to the integrity of the data used to produce reports. Relevance refers to the pertinence of the information to the decision at hand. Exhaustiveness refers to completeness or comprehensiveness of the information. Often, one can have relevant but incomplete information. Redundancy is the degree of repetitiveness of the information. Level of detail refers to the aggregation level of the data. The optimal level of aggregation is obtained when any extra detailed information does not improve the decision being made, and any more aggregation would worsen the decision.

Format attributes relate to the mode of presentation of the information. The attributes of format include: medium (hard copy, visual display, plotters, graphs, microfilm), layout (order of columns and rows, sequencing of detail and totals, etc.), and graphics design (colors, letter sets, fonts, etc.). Research studies on the format attributes have relied on the IT adopter's perceptions with respect to the medium, layout, and graphics design due to the problem of obtaining objective measurements. A laboratory study by Benbasat and Dexter[26] found that whereas tabular reports led to better decision making, graphical reports led to

faster decision making by individuals under time pressure. However, they also found that reports with a combination of graphs and tables led to superior decision making when compared to tabular or graphical reports.[26] Another study by Lim and Benbasat[27] found that multimedia presentation using text, tables, video, and graphics reduced ambiguity, increased comprehension and accuracy of complex problem solving. These findings have been corroborated by studies on presenting spatial decision support information to managers when using geographical information systems.[28]

Cost and benefit refers to the economic value of the new IT relative to the old one. The focus here is on reduction in fixed or variable costs, avoiding certain costs incurred while using the previous IT (e.g., overtime, stationery); profit enhancement through increased sales volume; and customer goodwill. The problem is that some benefits and costs are intangible and cannot easily be assigned monetary values. For example, it may be difficult to justify a new IT that could be used by a police 911 emergency services system to save lives. In this case how does one trade-off between the benefits of saving a life and the cost of the IT?

Overall, research studies that compared existing ITs to newer ones found that newer ITs that ranked higher on the timeliness, content, format and cost and benefit attributes; had a higher chance of getting adopted.

Service Quality. IT *service quality* is the gap between the IT adopter expected support and the actual support provided by a designated service provider, i.e., the IT vendor, the organization's Information Systems

Department, or other appointed third party. In formal settings, service level agreements (SLAs) could be made between the IT adopter and the service provider. An SLA is an adopter-driven formal written agreement that stipulates the level of service that will be provided.[29] To evaluate an SLA, the IT adopter is asked to rate the level of service received for any number of itemized services using a rating scale, e.g., excellent (96–100%), above average (91–95%), satisfactory (86–90%), or unsatisfactory (below 86%). An unsatisfactory score may lead to non-adoption depending on the IT adoptor's zone of tolerance. The zone of tolerance is the range of IT service an IT adopter would consider satisfactory.[30] Service quality can also been measured using SERVQUAL, a 22-item instrument developed by market researchers for measuring service in general. The SERVQUAL measurement attributes are: *reliability*, *responsiveness*, *assurance*, *empathy*, and *tangibility*.[31] Reliability is "the ability to perform the promised service dependably and accurately"; responsiveness is "the willingness to help customers and provide prompt service"; assurance is "the knowledge and courtesy of the [service] employees and their ability to inspire trust and confidence [in the IT adopters]"; and empathy is the ability to provide caring and individualized attention to the IT adopters.[31] Tangibility is "the appearance of the physical facilities, equipment, and servicing personnel" including visual appeal, up-to-date service technology, and dress and neatness of the service personnel. Although some studies have praised the efficacy and robustness of the cognitive and psychometric properties of the SERVQUAL instrument,[31–33] other studies provide criticism.[34,35] Overall, such mixed results are common in most studies that solicit self-reported perceptual measures.

Behavioral Intention to Use, Actual Use, User Satisfaction. Given a relatively higher-quality new IT system that provides higher-quality information, and has high-quality service support; the other measures of successful IT adoption are: *behavioral intention to use*, *actual usage*, and *user satisfaction*. Fig. 3 shows that IT quality, information quality, and service quality have a joint impact on behavioral intention to use, actual use, and user satisfaction.

Behavioral intention to use/actual usage. Fig. 3 shows that there is a cyclical relationship between intention to use, actual usage, and user satisfaction. Behavioral intention to use is sometimes measured by a self-reported survey or by asking potential adopters their willingness to pay for the IT system.[25] Some studies have measured actual usage by collecting data through hardware monitors, i.e., connect time,[36] number of functions utilized,[37] and actual charges for IT use.[38] Other studies have measured IT use by questioning managers about their use of the IT.[39–41] In either case, the success of an IT innovation will be measured by the degree to which the adopters rely on it, their feelings of ownership of the IT, and the degree

to which the IT becomes part and parcel of the standard operating procedures in the workplace.[42] Moreover, in order to measure the actual use of a newly adopted IT, such use should be voluntary. We postpone the discussion of voluntariness to the section on type of innovation decision.

Each interaction with IT creates a certain level of *user satisfaction*. Other measures related to user satisfaction are *user enjoyment* and *user appreciation*. Increased satisfaction leads to repeated use of the IT, which in turn increases the user satisfaction level even further (hence the double arrows linking IT use to user satisfaction in Fig. 2). There is wide appeal among IT researchers to use this measure to evaluate success of new IT adoption. There is wide appeal to use of this measure to evaluate the success of a new IT adoption.[2,20] Also, a number of research studies have found that user satisfaction from using a specific IT is related to their attitudes toward that IT.[43,44] So, it is recommended that whenever user satisfaction is used as a measure of IT adoption, the users' attitudes should also be included in order to control for the biasing effects of the attitudes in the analysis—hence the arrow pointing to behavioral intention to use the IT innovation.

As shown in Fig. 2, behavioral intention to use, actual use, and user satisfaction have a joint *impact* on the *individual* or *organizations* using the IT innovation. It is generally accepted that information created by an IT is not beneficial until it is meaningful and useful to its user. Information technology benefits to the individual adopting the technology could include any of the following: a reduction in the average time to make a decision, increase in confidence in the decision made, increase in number of decisions made by a participant, increases in productivity, and increase in the number of reports requested by higher level managers. Researchers have used both quantitative and qualitative measures to evaluate the impact of IT on individual adopters. Quantitative measures include test scores, amount of performance improvement, time to make a decision, number of members participating in making a decision, and number of reports. Qualitative measures include: perceptions of improvement of decision making, perceived confidence in the decision, and the amount of money the adopters are willing to pay for the new IT.

Most managers are eventually concerned about the bottom line. It is therefore of interest to assess the *organizational* impact of new IT investments at the unit, department, or overall enterprise level. The recursive relationship on top of the "Impact of IT Adoption" box in Fig. 2 indicates that the aggregate of all individual impacts resulting from IT adoption in an organization contribute to the overall organizational impact. Several measures of IT organizational adoption impacts are available in the literature. They include overall: cost reduction,[45,46] cost avoidance, increase in sales volume,[47,48] reduction in overall operating expenses,[49] and return on IT investment.[50,51]

Information Systems–
Information Use

Current research has focused more on measuring the impact of IT on the organization structure,[52] increases in customer switching costs, erecting barriers to new firm entry into the industry, product differentiation, and increasing organizational bargaining power with buyers or suppliers.[46,53]

Summary. Relative advantage is "the degree to which an innovation is perceived as better than the one it replaces" as measured by the monetary gains, convenience, enjoyment, and satisfaction derived from its use. The greater the relative advantage, the higher the rate of adoption of the innovation. McLean and DeLone[2] reviewed the IT literature and identified seven categories that can be used to assess the relative advantage of new IT investments, namely: IT quality, information quality, service quality, behavioral intention to use, actual usage, user satisfaction, and impact on the adopting individuals, organizations, extranets, industries, etc. Fig. 2 shows the relationship between the various measures.

Compatibility

One characteristic of IT is that it requires people to think, work, and behave differently. This emanates from the ability of IT to open organizational boundaries, integrate and coordinate work, speed up work, change the way work is done, provide faster feedback systems, and change perceptions of status and power.[54] Not only should the various IT networks be compatible with each other, individuals should also adjust their work behavior to the new demands. Information technology can therefore place a significant amount of cognitive burden on users—who may not only be unsure about their job situation but also may have to invest in education and training in new skills. *Compatibility* is the degree to which the new IT is perceived as being consistent with the existing values, past experiences of adopters, and existing IT applications and networks. In Fig. 2, compatibility belongs to the behavioral intention to use, actual usage, and satisfaction category. Whenever there is lack of compatibility, passive or active resistance may occur.[55]

It is therefore recommended that users be involved in IT acquisition and implementation decisions. As recommended by Osterman:[54]

> Beyond investing in people early, through education, training in new skills and so forth, it turns out to be helpful for the organization to develop flexible human resource policies that enable and encourage the organization to capitalize on the new IT. Employees at all levels are more inclined to experiment with new ways of working if they know their standing in the organization will not be affected by their learning process. (p. 220)

Several studies have identified compatibility as an important factor in IT adoption. One classical study is the one reported by Markus.[55] In the study by Moore and Benbasat[17] a factor analysis grouped compatibility with relative advantage.

Complexity

Complexity is a relative measure of perceived cognitive burden imposed by the new IT. In Fig. 2, complexity belongs to the IT quality category. Measures of complexity include ease of use,[14,56,57] ease of learning,[58] and enjoyment.[59] The more user-friendly a particular innovation is, the greater it's potential for adoption.

Triability

The ability to try out a new IT before integrating it into the routine activities and standard operating procedures of the workplace is an important measure of IT adoption. Triability affords individuals and organizations the opportunity to investigate the relative advantages, compatibility, complexity, and observability of the new IT. The study by Moore and Benbasat[17] found that although triability had significantly less weight than other factors in an organizational context, it should be of great concern for organizations that would adopt IT at their own risk.

Observability

Observability includes the ability to demonstrate the results (benefits and costs) of using the IT to potential users, as well as making the results visible to others within and outside the organization. Users are more likely to use a new IT if they feel that using the IT will bring higher approval and recognition from management and colleagues. In Fig. 2, observability could belong to the user satisfaction category.

Summary. A new IT that is perceived to be relatively useful, compatible, easy to learn and use, has observable results, and can be used on a pilot basis will most likely be adopted than the one that is lacking in any or all of these attributes.

Type of Innovation Decision

There are three types of innovation decisions: voluntary, authoritative, and collective. Innovations requiring the adopter's voluntary decision to adopt are generally more rapidly adopted than innovations that are mandated by an organization or other external pressures.[1] Voluntariness of use is the degree to which the use of the IT is perceived as being voluntary or of free will. In Fig. 2, the type of innovation decision belongs to the behavioral intension to use, actual use, and satisfaction category.

At the individual level, management may mandate (authoritatively) the use a specific IT, or may provide incentives for those who use the specific IT. Sometimes management may even enact policies that discourage the use of a specific IT. The decision to adopt may also be made by a few IT champions in the organization and then imposed on the rest of the business unit or department.

At the organizational level, an organization may be forced to adopt specific ITs in order to survive competition in their industry. In this case, IT becomes the cost of doing business. For example, a new bank may adopt ATM machine technology as the cost of doing business, irrespective of whether the benefit of implementing ATM technology has been proven in the specific area of operation. These circumstances deny the adopter the freedom of choosing to reject the IT.

According to Ajzen and Fishbein,[60] it is often not actual voluntariness that influences behavior, but rather, the perception of voluntariness. This means the rate of adoption will be increased if the people championing the adoption of the IT (change agents) can successfully make the adopters believe that they are the ones who are choosing to adopt. To accomplish this, change agents must understand the dynamics of change. Lewin[61] and Schein[62] proposed a three-stage model for managing change (see Fig. 4).

Unfreezing is a process of removing old habits and creating a climate receptive to change. Moving is the process of learning new work methods, behaviors, and systems. Refreezing is the process of reinforcing the new changes so that the new work processes and behavior are accepted as part and parcel of job. When a new IT is introduced, IT professionals become the agents for change. An understanding of the dynamics of change can help change agents understand how to make IT implementation more successful.

The number of people involved in decision making is another factor that may affect successful IT adoption. Rogers[1] observed that the more people or institutions are involved in making an innovation adoption decision, the slower the rate of adoption. Few studies in the IT adoption literature have focused on this aspect. One notable study is the one by Keen.[63] He noted that increasing the number of people involved in the IT adoption decision could be a tactic to prevent implementation success. He called this phenomenon counterimplementation.

Communication Channels

The communication channels used to spread information about the relative advantages, compatibility, complexity, triability, and observability of the new IT can also influence the rate of adoption. Mass media is recommended when the new IT is relatively simple to use. For example in 2007, Microsoft spent more than $500 million to advertise their flagship Vista operating system because they believed the Vista interface was relatively intuitive to use. Interpersonal contacts with change agents are recommended when the new IT is perceived by potential adopters to be complex. For example, we observed that computer-assisted software engineering (CASE) tools such as AutoCAD are mainly marketed via interpersonal contacts between vendors and potential professional users in academia or industry.

Nature of the Social System

This includes the norms of the organization where the new IT is being adopted and the existence of interpersonal network influences on potential but skeptical adopters. In an organization receptive to new IT ideas, opinion leaders play a significant role in providing innovation-evaluation information critical to decreasing uncertainty about the new IT. Opinion leaders are those adopters who act as role models in influencing others opinions about innovations. As will be discussed later, these people belong to the early adopters' category.

Extent of Change Agents' Promotional Efforts

The rate of adoption is also influenced by the extent of the promotional efforts of the change agents. The more opinion leaders the change agent can convert, the greater the rate of adoption. The rate of adoption and the extent of the change agents' efforts may not be direct or linear; however, Rogers[1] observed that the rate of adoption is greatest when opinion leaders adopt, and continues to grow with little promotion by change agents after a critical mass of adopters has been established. A critical mass is defined as the point at which enough adopters have accepted the new IT to cause the perceived cost–benefit of adoption to shift from negative to positive.[55]

Summary

Left on their own volition, not all individuals, organizations, or nations are receptive to IT adoption; there is considerable skepticism about the real benefits of IT adoption. The rate of adoption of an innovation depends on the perceived attributes of the innovation, the type of innovation decision, communication channels used to advertise the technology, nature of the social system where the IT is implemented, and extent of the promotional efforts of change agents. Often, it is not the actual voluntariness of the decision to adopt a new IT that influences behavior, but rather, the perception of voluntariness. Change agents who understand the dynamics of change can play a role in influencing successful IT adoption. The stages through which a technological innovation passes are

Fig. 4 The Kurt Lewin and Edgar Schein model.

Information Systems—
Information Use

- Knowledge (exposure to its existence and understanding its functions)
- Persuasion (the forming of favorable attitudes toward using it)
- Decision (behavioral intention to invest, experiment, learn and commit to its adaptation)
- Implementation (putting it to use)
- Confirmation (reinforcement based on positive net benefits received as a result of adopting it)

PART 2: RATE OF IT ADOPTION CATEGORIES

In part 1, we discussed the important elements of successful IT adoption. We noted that despite the overwhelming opportunities offered by IT, however, not all individuals or organizations may implement a new IT at the same rate. Even when the adoption decision is mandated (authoritatively or collectively), users may not implement the full features of the new IT at the same rate.

One way to describe the rate of IT adoption or consumption is to use the "S-Curve of Adoption and Normality" developed by Rogers.[1] Although some research has found only weak support for the S-Curve,[64] many studies have supported its applicability especially in the early days of the introduction of a new IT.[1,65,66] The S-Curve is shown in Fig. 5. According to the S-Curve, the first 2.5% (i.e., minus 2 standard deviations) of individuals or organizations to adopt IT are called the innovators. The next 13.5% (i.e., between the mean minus 1 standard deviation and the mean minus 2 standard deviations) are called the early adopters. The next 34% (between the mean and the mean minus 1 standard deviation), are called the early majority. The next 34% (between the mean and the mean plus 1 standard deviation) are the late adopters, and the remaining 16% (above the mean plus 1 standard deviation) are called the laggards.

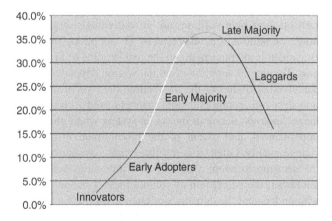

Fig. 5 The S-Curve of adoption and normality.

Individuals

Innovators are the first 2.5% of IT users. They include venturesome or cosmopolitan individuals who have enough resources to acquire and experiment with new IT or can have their organizations buy the technology for them. The value of IT to innovators is the potential return they may get for being the first to try a potentially beneficial technology. People working in beta and alpha test sites for new software applications belong to this category. Innovators command a certain amount of social prestige and peer respect for being at the cutting edge of IT. Observability and triability are the two main attributes at play here.

Early adopters are the next 13.5% of people to perceive the relative advantage, compatibility, and observability of a new IT and are willing to pioneer its use. Early adopters are valued as change agents, and as such, have high subjective norms.[60] Subjective norm is a social influence term that refers to the importance the person attaches to opinions of referent others. "The early adopter knows that [in order] to continue to earn [the] self respect of colleagues and to maintain a central position in the communication networks of the IT system, he or she must make judicious innovation decisions...".[1] As such, early adopters are motivated by the social influence and respect they obtain from their peers.

Early majority is a group of individuals who adopt IT because it has been proven to work. Comprising 34% of the IT adopter category, the early majority are the first most numerous group to implement the new IT. As such they bring in a "critical mass" of IT users. This group interacts with the early adopters to get guidance on how to use the new IT. Moreover, they provide interpersonal networks to the late majority.

Late majority comprise of skeptical individuals who adopt IT for fear of losing their jobs or due to peer pressure. Like the early majority, they comprise 34% of the new IT adopter categories. Additionally, individuals in this category may not have enough resources to spend on IT and hence have to rationalize any IT expenditure they consider risky or uncertain.

Laggards are the remaining 16% of the adopters who may fear computers, have negative attitudes toward computers, or have the fear of using poorly designed systems. Laggards tend to be suspicious of new IT and change agents. They want to be sure about the costs and benefits of adopting the new IT before accepting it. Similar to the late majority, individuals in this category may not have enough resources to spend on IT.

Summary

Individuals can be innovators, early adopters, early majority, late majority, or laggard depending on the impact of the rate of adoption variables on them. There are both intrinsic and extrinsic factors influencing how adopters perceive the rate of adoption variables. Innovators value IT for the potential returns that may accrue by being the first to try a potentially beneficial technology. They hope that by the time other groups catch on, they will be high up on the learning curve. Early adopters are motivated by the respect they obtain from their peers and their value as change agents. The early majority are risk averse individuals who join the IT bandwagon only when it has been proven to work. The late majority are skeptical individuals who adopt IT as the last resort. Finally, the laggards adopt new IT only when they can ascertain all the benefits and costs.

Organizations

Innovators are the first 2.5% of organizations which adopt a specific IT. Such organizations either have enough resources to acquire and experiment with new IT or have an influential Management Information Systems (MIS) department manager who has a secure budget for new IT. The value of IT to innovator organizations is the competitive advantage that may accrue for being the first to try a potentially beneficial technology.

Early adopters are the next 13.5% of organizations to perceive the relative advantage, compatibility, and observability of a new IT early and are willing to pioneer its use. Most organizations in volatile industries, e.g., computer hardware, computer software, telecommunications, and entertainment are forced to become early adopters of new IT. Volatile industries are ones characterized by cut throat competition and uncertainty. For example, Microsoft's late move into the Internet search engine market cost the company significant competitive advantage, albeit temporarily. Early adopters develop ways to use IT to lock in customers and lock out competitors early, and as such, tend to maintain their market share, which in turn, increases their chances for long-term survival and profitability. These early adopters are motivated by the customer loyalty they obtain due to their innovative efforts to provide higher-quality products and service.

Early majority is a group of organizations who adopt IT because it has been proven to work. Comprising 34% of the IT adopter category, the early majority are the first most numerous group of organizations to implement the new IT. As such they form part of a "critical mass" of IT using organizations. This group of organizations sometimes assigns specific individuals the role of reading the literature on the experiences of the early adopting organizations in order to get guidance on how to use the new IT. Other organizations employ people from the early adopting organizations so that they can benefit from their experiences. In other instances, organizations may acquire or enter into strategic alliances with early adopting organizations in order to learn from them. In other cases, organizations have formed a separate organizational unit

called the "emerging technology group" to oversee IT adoption into the organization.

Late majority are skeptical organizations who adopt IT for fear of being swept away by the competition. Like the early majority, they comprise 34% of the new IT adopter categories. Organizations in this category may not have enough resources to spend on IT, and hence have to rationalize the IT-related expenditure they consider risky or uncertain.

Laggards are the remaining 16% of the adopting organizations who may believe "if ain't broke, why fix it?" Laggard organizations tend to be suspicious of new IT and the hype that surrounds new ITs. They want to be sure about the costs and benefits of adopting the new IT before implementing it. Similar to the late majority, organizations in this category may not have enough resources to spend on IT. They also want tried and proven technology.

Summary

Organizations can be innovators, early adopters, early majority, late majority, or laggard depending on their mission, culture, the nature of the industry they are in, their structure, and the impact of the rate of adoption variables on the long-term profitability and survival of the organization. The decision to adopt or not to adopt is mainly driven by demands from the internal and external environment of the organization. For example, organizations with a culture that emphasizes "internal control," "creativity," and "individual autonomy" are more likely to adopt new IT than the ones that emphasize "external controls," "conformity," and "hierarchies."[67]

Innovators value IT for the potential returns that may accrue by being the first to try a potentially beneficial technology. Early adopters are motivated by the customer loyalty they create by providing better products and superior service. Such organizations hope that by the time other organizations catch on, it would be difficult for them to tap into their market share. The early majority are risk adverse organizations which are in relatively stable operating environments. Most public sector organizations fall into this category. The late majority are skeptical organizations which adopt IT as the last resort. Finally, the laggards are would adopt a new IT only when they can establish all the benefits and costs of the new IT.

CONCLUSION

We conclude by suggesting that since the proliferation of newer and more powerful ITs is apt to continue unabated for many years to come, there is a real need for individuals and organizations to device new ways of identifying, learning, and implementing new technologies. One way to do this is to have a clear understanding of the factors that influence successful adoption of IT. Specific factors that may influence IT adoption in particular industries, national states, or societies are beyond the scope of this entry. This entry used the variables that affect the rate of adoption of IT innovations (see the section "Part 1: Adoption of IT innovations"), the categories of successful IT adoption (see the section "Part 2: Rate of IT Adoption Categories"), and the S-Curve (see the section "Part 1: Adoption of IT innovations") to provide a general overview of existing literature on new IT adoption by individuals and organizations. The variables that influence successful adoption and the categories of successful IT adoption are multidimensional and interrelated. For example, one cannot discuss the relative advantage of a specific IT without considering the IT quality, information quality, usage of the information provided by the IT, user satisfaction, and benefits accruing to the individual and organizational adopters. Use of the S-Curve will allow individuals and organizations to position themselves with respect to where they fit in their rate of IT adoption. It seems individual life long learning, and organizational learning are the indispensable characteristics of the very survival of an increasingly IT dependent society: One caveat though: ". . . management can promote the acquisition of skills by creating a climate supporting continuous learning in general and by encouraging experimentation with IT tools in particular. . ."[68] (p. 275).

REFERENCES

1. Rogers, E. *Diffusion of Innovations*, 4th Ed.; The Free Press: New York, 1995.
2. DeLone, W.H.; MCLean, E.F. The DeLone and McLean model of information systems success: A ten-year update. J. Manage. Inform. Syst. Spring 2003, *19* (4), 9–302.
3. DeLone, W.H.; McLean, E.R. Information system success: The quest for the dependent variable. Inform. Syst. Res. 1992, *3* (1), 60–95.
4. Bhattacherjee, A.; Sanford, C. Influence processes for information technology acceptance: An elaboration likelihood model. MIS Quart. December 2006, *30* (4), 805–825.
5. Diebold, J. Six issues that will affect the future of information management. Data Manage. 1984, *22* (7), 10–13.
6. Scott Morton, M.S. Introduction. In *The Corporation of the 1990s: Information Technology and Organizational Transformation*; Scott Morton, M.S., Ed.; Oxford University Press: New York, 1991.
7. *The Digital Planet 2006: The Global Information Economy*, World Information Technologies and Services Alliance (WITSA) and Global Insight Inc.
8. Wolff, E.N. The growth of information workers in the U.S. economy. Commun. ACM. 2005, *48* (10), 37–42.
9. Ehrnberg, E. Jacobsson, S. Technological discontinuities and incumbents' performance: An analytical framework. In *Systems of Innovation Technologies, Institutions, and Organizations*; Edquist, C., Ed.; Pinter: London, 1997.

10. Anderson, P.C.; Tushman, M.L. Technological discontinuities and dominant designs: A cyclical model of technological change. Admin. Sci. Quart. 1990, *35*, 604–633.
11. Utterback, J.M. *Mastering the Dynamics of Innovation*, Harvard Business School: Boston, MA, 1994.
12. Schumpeter, J.A. *Capitalism, Socialism, and Democracy*. Harper and Row: New York, **1942**.
13. Thurow, L.C. Foreword. In *The Corporation of the 1990s: Information Technology and Organizational Transformation*; Scott Morton, M.S., Ed.; Oxford University Press: New York, 1991.
14. Davis, F.D. Perceived usefulness, perceived ease of use, and user acceptance of information technology. MIS Quart. **1989**, *13* (3), 319–340.
15. Venkatesh, V.; Morris, M.G.; Davis, G.B.; Davis, F.D. User acceptance of information technology: Toward a unified view. MIS Quart. **2003**, *27* (3), 425–478.
16. Agarwal, R.; Karahanna, E. Time flies when you're having fun: Cognitive absorption and beliefs about information technology usage. MIS Quart. December **2000**, *24* (4), 665–694.
17. Moore, G.C.; Benbasat, I. Development of an instrument to measure the perceptions of information technology innovation. Inform. Syst. Res. **1991**, *2* (3), 192–221.
18. Kriebel, C.A.; Raviv, A. An economics approach to modeling the productivity of computer systems. Manage. Sci. **1980**, *26* (3), 297–311.
19. Srinivasan, A. Alternative measures of system effectiveness: Associations and implications. MIS Quart. **1985**, *9* (3), 243–253.
20. Bailey, J.E.; Pearson, S.W. Development of a tools for measuring and analyzing computer user satisfaction. Manage. Sci. **1983**, *29* (5), 530–545.
21. Xiao, B.; Benbasat, I. E-commerce product recommendation agents: Use, characteristics, and impact. MIS Quart. March **2007**, *31* (1), 137–209.
22. Hamilton, S.; Chervany, N.L. Evaluating information system effectiveness. Part 1. Comparing evaluation approaches. MIS Quart. **1981**, *5* (3), 55–69.
23. Swanson, E.B. Management information systems: Appreciation and involvement. Manage. Sci. **1984**, *21* (20), 178–188.
24. King, W.R.; Epstein, B.J. Assessing information system value. Decision Sci. **1983**, *14* (1), 34–45.
25. Ahituv, N. A systematic approach toward assessing the value of an information system. MIS Quart. **1980**, *4* (4), 61–75.
26. Benbasat, I.; Dexter, A.S. An investigation of the effectiveness of color and graphical information presentation under varying time constraints. MIS Quart. March **1986**, *10* (1), 59–83.
27. Lim, K.H.; Benbasat, I. The effect of multimedia on perceived equivocality and perceived usefulness of information systems. MIS Quart. Septmeber **2000**, *24* (3), 449–471.
28. Mennecke, B.E.; Crossland, M.D.; Killingsworth, B.L. Is a map more than a picture? The role of SDSS technology, subject characteristics and problem complexity on map reading and problem solving. MIS Quart. December **2000**, *24* (4), 601–629.
29. Singleton, J.P.; McLean, E.R.; Altman, E.N. Measuring information systems performance: Experience with the

Information Systems–
Information Use

management by results system at security pacific bank. MIS Quart. June **1988**, *12* (2), 325–337.

30. Kettinger, W.J.; Lee, C.C. Zones of tolerance: Alternative scales for measuring information systems. MIS Quart. December **2005**, *29* (4), 607–623 .

31. Jiang, J.J.; Klein, G.; Carr, C.L. Measuring information systems service quality: SERVQUAL from the other side. MIS Quart. **2002**, *26* (2), 145–166.

32. Watson, R.T.; Pitt, L.F.; Kavan, C.B. Measuring information systems service quality: Lessons from two longitudinal case studies. MIS Quart. **1998**, *22*, 61–79.

33. Pitt, L.F.; Watson, R.T.; Kavan, C.B. Service quality: A measure of information systems effectiveness. MIS Quart. **1995**, *19* (2), 173–188.

34. Kettinger, W.J. Lee, C.C. Perceived service quality and user satisfaction with the information services function. Decision Sci. **1995**, *25* (5–6), 737–765.

35. Van Dyke, T.P.; Kappelman, L.A.; Prybutok, V.R. Measuring information systems service quality: Concerns on the use of the SERVQUAL questionnaire. MIS Quart. **1997**, *21* (2), 195–208.

36. Ginzberg, M.J. Finding an adequate measure of OR/MS effectiveness. Interfaces. **1978**, *8* (4), 59–62.

37. Green, G.I.; Hughes, C.T. Effects of decision support training and cognitive style on decision process attributes. J. MIS. **1986**, *3* (2), 81–93.

38. Gremillion, L.L. Organization size and information system use. J. MIS. **1984**, *1* (2), 4–17.

39. Zmud, R.W.; Boynton, A.C.; Jacobs, G.C. An examination of managerial strategies for increasing information technology penetration in organizations. Proceedings of the Eighth International Conference on Information Systems, Pittsburg, December **1987**, 24–44 .

40. Raymond, L. Organizational characteristics and MIS success in the context of small business. MIS Quart. **1985**, *9* (1), 37–52.

41. Kim, E.; Lee, J. An exploratory contingency model of user participation and MIS use. Inform. Manage. **1986**, *11* (2), 87–97.

42. Trice, A.W.; Treacy, E.M. Utilization as a dependent variable in MIS research. Proceedings of the Seventh International Conference on Information Systems, San Diego, December **1986**, 227–239.

43. Igbaria, M. User acceptance of microcomputer technology: An empirical test. Omega. **1993**, *21* (1), 73–90.

44. Igersheim, R.H. Managerial response to an information system. AFIPS Conf. Proc., National Computer Conf. **1976**, *45*, 877–882.

45. Chervany, N.L. Dickson, G.W. Kozar, K. *An Experimental Gaming Framework for Investigating the Influence of Management Information Systems on Decision Effectiveness;* MISRC, University of Minnesota: Minneapolis, MN, 1972. MISRC Working Paper No. 71-12.

46. Johnston, H.R.; Vitale, M.R. Creating competitive advantage with inter-organizational information systems. MIS Quart. **1988**, *12* (2), 153–165.

47. Rivard, S.; Huff, S.L. User developed applications: Evaluation of success from the DP department perspective. MIS Quart. **1984**, *8* (1), 39–50.

48. Chrismar, W.G.; Kriebel, C.H. A method for assessing the economic impact of information systems technology in

organizations. Proceedings of the Sixth International Conference on Information Systems, Indianapolis, IN, **1985**, 45–56.

49. Emery, J.C. *Cost/Benefit Analysis of Information Systems*, The Society for Management Information Systems: Chicago, IL, 1971. SMIS Workshop Report Number 1.

50. Weill, P. The relationship between investment in information technology and firm performance: A study of the valve manufacturing sector. Info. Syst. Res. **1992**, *3* (4), 307–333.

51. Perry, D.F. Assimilation innovative technology: A more comprehensive model. Proceedings of the Fourth International Conference on Information Systems, Houston, TX, December **1983**, 281–297.

52. Bakos, J.Y. Dependent variables for the study of firm and industry-level impacts on information technology. Proceedings of the Eighth International Conference on Information Systems, Pittsburg, PA, December **1987**, 10–23.

53. Porter, M. *Competitive Advantage*, Free Press: New York, 1985.

54. Osterman, P. Impact of IT on jobs and skills. In *The Corporation of the 1990s: Information Technology and Organizational Transformation*; Scott Morton, M.S., Ed.; Oxford University Press: New York, 1991.

55. Markus, M.L. Power, politics, and MIS implementation. Commun. ACM. **1983**, *26* (6), 430–444.

56. Adams, D.A.; Nelson, R.R.; Todd, P.A. Perceived usefulness, ease of use, and usage of information technology: A replication. MIS Quart. **1992**, *16* (2), 227–247.

57. Mathieson, K. Predicting user intentions: Comparing the technology acceptance model with the theory of planned behavior. Inform. Syst. Res. **1991**, *2* (3), 173–191.

58. Belardo, S.; Kirk, R.K.; Wallace, W.A. DSS component design through field experimentation: An application to emergency management. Proceedings of the Third International Conference on Information Systems, Ann Arbor, MI, December **1982**, 93–108.

59. Igbaria, M.; Iivari, J.; Maragahh, H. Why do individuals use computer technology? A Finnish case study. Inform. Manage. **1995**, *29*, 227–238.

60. Ajzen, I. Fishbein, M. *Understanding Attitudes and Predicting Behavior*, Prentice-Hall Inc.: Englewood Cliffs, NJ, 1980.

61. Lewin, K. Group decision and social change. In *Reading in Social Psychology*; Maccoby, E., Newcomb, T., Hartley, E., Eds.; New York: Halt, Rinehart & Winston, 1958; 197–211.

62. Schein, E. *Process Consultation: Its Role in Organizational Development*, Addison-Wesley: Reading, MA, 1969.

63. Keen, P.G.W. Information systems and organizational change. Commun. ACM January **1981**, *24* (1), 24–33 .

64. Carter, F.J., Jr.; Jambulingama, T.; Guptaa, V.K.; Melone, N. Technological innovations: A framework for communicating diffusion effects. Inform. Manage. **2001**, *38*, 277–287.

65. Gurbaxani, V. Diffusion in computing networks: The case of BITNET. Commun. ACM. **1990**, *33* (12), 65–75.

66. Gurbaxani, V. Mendelson, H. The use of secondary analysis in MIS research. In *The Information Systems Research Challenge: Survey Research Methods*; Kraemer, K.L., Ed.; Harvard Business School: Boston, MA, 1991; Vol. 3.

Information Systems–
Information Use

Information Systems–
Information Use

67. DeLisi, P.S. Lessons from the steel axe: Culture, technology, and organizational change. Sloan Manage. Rev. Fall **1990**, 83–93.

68. Mckersie, R.B. Walton, R.E. Organizational change. In *The Corporation of the 1990s: Information Technology and Organizational Transformation*; Scott Morton, M.S., Ed.; Oxford University Press: New York, 1991.

69. Shannon, C.E. Weaver, W. *The Mathematical Theory of Communication*: University of Illinois Press: Urbana, IL, 1949.

Information Technology Literacy

James W. Marcum
Fairleigh Dickinson University, Madison, New Jersey, U.S.A.

Denise I. O'Shea
Fairleigh Dickinson University, Teaneck, New Jersey, U.S.A.

Information Systems–
Information Use

Abstract

Information technology literacy is a broad, many-dimensional description of the skills and knowledge needed for effective participation in business and education in the twenty-first century. First considered to be generic, those capabilities are now understood to be contextual, social, determined by the specific situation, be it workplace, academic, or social. This becomes clear when the term is compared to information literacy (knowing when information is needed, search strategy development, accessing and managing the information, and using it legally and ethically to meet the need). Information literacy (IL) is extensively explored and discussed in a vast literature. There remains considerable disagreement about what it is and how it should be taught and assessed; yet IL is relatively simple compared to the less developed concept of IT literacy. Information technology literacy involves using the tools of information technology (hardware, software, networks) as well as the data and information (as with IL), as well as working in a specific context (which might be professional, social, industrial, or academic). Workplace, social, behavioral, and cognitive issues become, therefore, part of the complexities in play. Furthermore, complexity accelerates as new media, new communication technologies, and new collaborative capabilities combine to create a dynamic information universe of participation and interactivity. This emergent reality changes the way people learn and the very nature of knowledge. Librarianship, scholarship, research, business, and the professions are all being reformulated in the process of adapting to these new conditions. Information technology (IT) literacy provides a useful concept for tracing, exploring, and better understanding this world-changing phenomenon.

INTRODUCTION

Information technology literacy is a significant, if not fully delineated, concept of the knowledge and skills needed for effective participation in the age of information, knowledge, learning, and networks that characterize the new millennium. The term offers approaches to needed knowledge and skills and guidelines to support the development of these competencies by students and learners. Information technology (IT) literacy resides among, and overlaps in some measure, other definitions including computer literacy, visual literacy, media literacy, digital literacy, multiliteracies, information literacy, information competence, fluency with information technology, and information-communication technology literacy. In this brief discussion a broad-gauged perspective is taken of the issues, suggesting that IT literacy does not require a major campaign to distinguish it from the other, closely related definitions, but that defining and discussing IT literacy provides the opportunity to trace, develop, and illustrate the relationships and manifestations of the roles and effective uses of technology in society, the workplace, and in education. The discussion loops back toward a conclusion that IT literacy—or perhaps "information and technology literacy"—is a useful descriptor for a range of theories and practices that come together to lead to a better understanding of a complex situation.

Information technology literacy means being "information literate" (able to find, access, and use information to solve the need of the seeker) as well as "technology literate," sufficiently skilled for competent utilization of a networked, interactive, multimedia environment.[1] An outline history of the topic reveals major shifts in technology and its impact in recent decades and the resulting adaptations as professions exchange the lead position in discussing the significance of those changes.

With the rise of the personal computer (PC) in the 1980s, and the rapid expansion in the number of people using the tool, the need for "computer literacy" became apparent and IT specialists and information scientists took the lead in defining and refining the term. The PC was difficult to use—before Apple and Windows software and World Wide Web (hereafter simply Web) search engines rendered it more intuitive—and "technical" people led the way in exploring how to train others to utilize the new "machines."

In the 1990s, with the growth of the Internet, intuitive and graphic interfaces, and the number of "user friendly" databases of information available, information literacy became the focus of the discussion and librarians,

Encyclopedia of Library and Information Sciences, Fourth Edition DOI: 10.1081/E-ELIS4-120044482
Copyright © 2017 by Taylor & Francis. All rights reserved.

particularly academic librarians, moved center stage as the champions of preparing a wider public to use the new tools, resources, and technologies made available by the Internet. The work soon expanded to encompass a much broader "digital" world of communications and visual/multiple media resources.[2] As we entered a new millennium, a variety of substantive definitions of information literacy demanded consideration and competed for influence. A federal government initiative proposed Fluency with Information Technology (FIT) as the appropriate metaphor;[3] the Educational Testing Service proposed information and communication technologies (ICT) literacy as the preferred concept;[4] and academic librarians broadened their concerns to encompass "competencies" that could be measured to assure appropriate "learning outcomes."[5] The ground soon shifted toward a broader perspective, leading to serious consideration of the need for definitions and a model for IT literacy. Shapiro and Hughes[6] suggested, in a much cited article, that information literacy (IL) could be a stand-alone liberal art, that both the tools of IT and an ability to perceive emerging technologies were important elements of the model.

Getting more specific, Brandt proposed in his 2001 article[1] the need to think in terms of a broader "computer literacy" and a bridge to IL. A few years later Brandt and colleagues returned to the issue and proposed merging IT literacy with IL as the more comprehensive and proper approach.[7] By this time, roughly 2005, focus shifted away from information literacy back toward the technology side of the IT literacy equation. There are several features of this shift. The broader view was already becoming accepted. The National Research Council reported in 2002[8] that IT was clearly impacting teaching and research, compelling new collaboration and restructuring intellectual disciplines, pointing to a clear need for faculty and many others to "reskill."

During the early years of the new century, communications and education professionals—and practitioners—actively engaged in the discussion, arguing for the crucial importance of media literacy, instructional design, and related concerns. The dialogue continues. While different descriptors are preferred by various proponents of IT literacy, there is a general consensus regarding the critical importance of literacy—or fluency or competence—for effective participation in the classrooms, offices, and workplaces of the day. Each of the perspectives adds something to the larger picture, and this overview will endeavor to be inclusive.

STAGES AND LIMITATIONS OF LITERACY

Tracking the evolution of literacy and its segue into considerations of fluency and competence is a useful path for exploring the power of technology and networks to change, nay revolutionize, not only how we search for and share information, but how we learn and carry on business, polity, and entertainment. The varieties of literacy "in use" provide a connecting theme for this many-faceted development.

Basic Literacy

Literacy in the broadest sense is a process that is valued by society. The term is popularly understood, however, to mean simply the ability to read and write. By implication, basic communication skills are included. This is the social dimension to literacy in that people need others to help them learn to read and write. Literacy cannot be self-generated, as a rule, because meanings must be social and not just personal. More is involved than reading, however. Literacy is a human phenomenon, grounded in a social context. Meaning comes from interpretation and influence, both of which are social. A substantial "politics" swirls around the issue, seen by some as a means by which a society maintains control, sets priorities, and shapes cultures.[9] Bilingual people and individuals with advanced literacies enjoy special advantage; they can communicate at another level. A consideration of literacy cannot dwell long at the level of learning how to read.

Advanced Literacies

A second spoken language, a symbolic language (such as mathematics or a programming algorithm), and various other skills indicate advanced capabilities. Basic information tool literacies, such as desktop computer literacy, visual literacy, or new media skills are alternative abilities signaling advanced literacy. Navigating the Web and participating in wikis or instant messaging systems or social gaming are necessary skills in many workplaces. Communication skills are more advanced at this level, moving beyond basic signaling to greater engagement, where information is shared and can lead to improved coordination among people and between organizations. These literacies quickly become more specialized, often requiring additional media tools or different perspectives. Literacy becomes a process of making meaning out of confusion; advanced literacy involves dealing with the complexities of learning, text, and context leading to improved understanding and dynamic relationships.[10] Kuhlthau[11] puts it succinctly: literacy is the ability to construct one's own meaning from an information rich environment.

At this point, technological literacy has moved well beyond computer skills, entering the realm of working effectively in a given context which, today, is likely to have a moderate to high level of electronic devices as basic tools. Achieving technological literacy broadly across society is a great challenge and carries an enormous cost that will require involvement of the state, education, and the corporate sector.

Information Systems–
Information Use

Visual and Media Literacies

In recent decades, the impact of broadcast media and the Web requires a greater literacy, or better understanding, of how visual images are created and used. Reliance on the image, especially the moving image, in communication and the easy manipulation (morphing) of these images requires higher levels of technological competence and different ways of thinking or, more specifically, new cognitive skills.[12] What we "see" is in good part actively "constructed" by the individual mind (amidst social influences of course), not passively received through vision.[13] The fact that visual communication can bring together codified (linguistic) and uncodified (tacit or experiential) knowledge gives the technology enormous power. For example, hand-drawn sketches and lists of words and ideas are popular for planning and brainstorming sessions. Heretofore separate genres (text, graphics, audio, and video) converge into digital communication capabilities: symbols, images, and words are now mixed, replicated, and widely disseminated on Web pages, advertisements, and presentations.[13]

In the emerging information-learning culture a reversal is well underway: where the word long held sway and the image augmented, increasingly the image now dominates and the verbal augments. Today visual language is proposed as a way of integrating words, images, and shapes into a new language for communication and understanding. This "visual language" makes learning accessible to many more people.[2,14,15] Visual language warrants additional investigation and demonstration; for one thing it offers an escape route out of the gridlock of print vs. digital media arguments.

Media literacy is central to modern communication studies. It involves the ability to access, analyze, evaluate, and communicate messages in a variety of formats. Digital media literacy utilizes information digitization to perceive and present a distributed, interactive, malleable world. This is not an extension of TV, but the antithesis of it; the viewer—particularly the younger generation—is taking charge of their own information. Labeled "new media literacy," new image production tools allow *many* more people to create media and join in the great "conversation" facilitated by the Internet even if only a tiny percentage actually gain attention and achieve influence.[16]

Some of these literacies are narrow, of interest only to select disciplines. Nevertheless, a holistic concept of literacy permits escape from many limitations and allows entry into more demanding realms.

Literacy 2.0: Social and Workplace Literacies

At this point the discussion moves into the more complex dimension that can be called "Literacy 2.0," the ability to use information in whatever format to interact with others to solve problems and create new knowledge. In a sense, solving a new problem, even in a narrow field or context, can be considered the creation of new knowledge.

Literacy 2.0 or workplace IT literacies is a shorthand label for the increasing skills required in more and more lines of employment. These skills are contextual, varying with the social, professional, and intellectual practices of a given workplace. In addition to information literacy, this capacity builds competence in contexts that change frequently. Neither basic literacy skills nor higher order thinking skills are sufficient. Literacy as traditionally constructed rarely is informed by actual observations of work.[17] Workplace literacy involves participation and is something very different from traditional training or education.[18] In the varied and complex world of the workplace, different terminologies are used—such as fluency with IT—and other methods, such as relying on "masters" as mentors.[19] Additionally, other articulated literacies are valuable. For example, "learning literacy" requires learning one's own "identity" and learning style as well as learning skills.[20] Rosen[21] defines "social literacy" as the skills required for leadership; these include inspiring others to excellence, listening and communicating effectively, promoting common goals and values, and transforming conflict into creative action.

Socio-technical practice warrants mention. Tuominen and colleagues[22] emphasize that IL and IT literacy cannot remain detached and generic practices but are situated, in a given workplace, context, a community of practice, or within a disciplinary, epistemic methodology. While the Tuominen article is ostensibly about IL, its breadth of consideration renders it useful for this discussion.

Multiliteracies

The case for multiliteracies provides a culmination for the literacy discussion. A wide-ranging effort of a group of international experts in learning and language has created a pedagogy of social and multimodal learning. They bring the meaning of literacy to a new level of importance by including such work life issues as competitiveness, coping with diversity, and collaboration. Information design is essential and interface icons are important as a metalanguage to allow access for many more people.[23]

An additional note on the term, literacy: The label of illiteracy clearly implies that a fundamental skill is lacking. In situations where people are engaged in learning and willing to acknowledge their limitations, illiteracy is not deemed insulting or belittling. Indeed, each of us has our illiteracies, domains where general information and skills are lacking, and where basic instruction is appropriate. But common sense requires that additional levels, beyond the basics, provide part of the scheme for the ongoing, dynamic world of interactive communication and learning that has become central for our time. That is why a literacy–competency–expertise continuum is useful as a design for framing the process of continuous learning.

Information Systems–
Information Use

There is no simple conclusion to this discussion. We live amidst increasing complexity and the list of proposed literacies allows the seeker to select the model that best fits their situation and context. Information technology literacy will work for many of these situations, but no single definition will be found satisfying to all.

THE NECESSITY OF COMPETENCE

Today's workplace requires more than either special skills or general knowledge; it also requires competence involving personal characteristics and behaviors that can be measured or recorded. Such competence encompasses cognitive knowledge, functional experience, and interpersonal, social skills and is a recurring concern in higher education and for human resource training and development. Brief consideration is necessary to complete this overview of IT literacy.

The issue is not new; a half-century ago a proposed standard of biological factors including growth potential, maturity, and behaviors defined competence as the functional ability of humans to exercise personal independence and social responsibility.[24] Before the rise of the PC, Reisman[25] outlined society's need for competence and higher education's poor record in developing those skills among the young. More recent versions of the need for competence stress the importance of character and emotions, both managing one's own emotions and coping with the emotional behavior of others.[26,27]

At present, there are several approaches to competence, creating some confusion. One approach relies on behaviors, including cognitive behaviors (thinking; learning; and information processing); affective behaviors (managing and using emotions and feelings productively); connative behaviors (persistence and determination); and habits and experience. Competence requires participation in the process, whatever the work or assignment.[28] A second approach to competence stresses skills, including managing self (adapting, dealing with change); communicating with diverse people and groups; managing people and tasks (coordinating resources and people); mobilizing innovation and change; and taking initiative.[29] Sveiby provides a concise overview, delineating five elements: knowledge of the explicit domain ("knowing what"); appropriate skills ("knowing how"); sufficient experience in the domain; exhibiting appropriate value judgment ("knowing why"); and having a social network ("knowing who") in the domain. One cannot be an effective professional, or worker in most fields, without knowing and carrying on dialogue with others in the profession, field, or practice.[30] To repeat for emphasis, a combination of behavior, skills, and knowledge is needed to demonstrate the broad capabilities that make up competence, or an overarching meta-competence.[31]

Information Technology Competence

The ability to use IT in the workplace is obviously essential today.[18] Yet that is insufficient. A more advanced level of skills, such as fluency or expertise, is required more and more frequently as businesses and organizations adapt to the information age. A federal government expression of these advanced skills is Fluency with Information Technology (FIT). Fluency is defined as higher levels of competence. Fluency with Information Technology goes beyond skills (which are quickly obsolete) and includes problem-solving capabilities.[3] New information and communication technologies enable a new era of information and knowledge grounded in interactivity. Not media as signal, but media as action–perception cycle is the emerging reality.[32] Individuals working alone cannot be expected to master all these technologies. Teams or workgroups are required to encompass the variety of skills and knowledge needed to deal with the complexities of today's problems with the extensive range of tools and resources available.

Social competence

Today competent people must be able to collaborate with others of diverse backgrounds. The sharing of work between genders and across ethnic lines and national and cultural frontiers is essential. New standards of people skills, supervisory skills, and management skills are vital. Teams and communities of practice are frequently required for organizations to adapt to meet the challenges they face. At this level, communication becomes interactive and participatory; top-down signals are often dysfunctional. Organizational change is becoming more common, requiring cross-boundary partnerships, research, and innovation. These techniques require social competence.[33] Today's places of work and learning are more often participatory and interactive in nature.

Socio-technological information (cyber) competence

What would address all of the necessary elements of information-related competencies required today? One possibility is social–technological information competence, or cyber-competence for a shorthand definition. Cyber-competence consists of the converging technology-based interactive skills and practices required to find and utilize information in multiple formats and varied contexts to encourage knowledge sharing, foster knowledge creation, and enhance organizational effectiveness in a competitive global and networked environment. Elements of "cyber competence" include Internet research and communication; visual and media literacy; digitization, visualization, and presentation; interactive communication and networking; self-knowledge and reflection; and action research skills. Competent people will be able to find needed information, utilize and manipulate it for new purposes, know

Information Systems–
Information Use

how to use new tools, learn new skills, and assess their own progress and development.

To focus for a moment on the library-centered world, it is appropriate to insert here that there is growing attention to and consideration of the notion of "information competence." Information competence is included in the general discussion of information literacy to demonstrate that the appropriate level of literacy has been accomplished.[5] To illustrate, projects at UCLA and the California State University system have demonstrated, experimented with, and evaluated how information competence might best be implemented on the university campus.[34,35] A review of these efforts suggests, however—regardless of the value of the endeavor—that the underlying assumption regards literacy and competence as essentially equivalent, a continuum, whereas others emphasize their differences.

More technology-minded discussants might argue that "instructional systems design" (ISD) is the path to follow. On this topic the work of the American Society for Training and Development becomes significant. Instructional systems design is work-context focused and takes a systematic, logical approach to the skills needed with tracking and assessment built in. The limitation of this model is that its intent is the *transfer* of information and/or knowledge, existing knowledge, rather than the creation of new knowledge.

It is important to realize that the emphasis on competence requires a major shift beyond the data–information–knowledge transfer continuum to a more dynamic learning domain—expressed in the term Internet 2.0 or Library 2.0—demanding more comprehensive capabilities. More content knowledge does not help; it must be tested in the real world of the workplace, or the lab, or other social–economic–political domain.

Can Competence Be Taught?

Functional effectiveness in today's workplace requires social skills and emotional stability as a supplement to IT literacy; competence requires experience in practice. Competent behavior rarely depends entirely on formal knowledge.[36] Individual brilliance is not always highly prized in work situations unless it produces unique solutions to problem situations. "Learning" must be broadened to mean learning to make one's own observations, to lead, to work with others, to clarify values, to correct actions, to understand how organizations work and how to influence them. A quick look at incompetence helps define competence: Incompetence can include deficits in skills or knowledge, but the list of personal factors is longer, including unprofessional behaviors or attitudes, difficult personality traits, lack of motivation, unsafe activities, or poor communication skills.[37]

Some efforts skip over educational standards. A U.S. Department of Education conference on "Competence without Credentials"[38] considered whether new Internet-based instruction could replace traditional credentials and certificates, apparently on the assumption that assessed workplace performance and computer-based learning were inadequate for the social, interpersonal, and collaborative dimensions of effective work. The assumption in this essay is, however, that enhancing student competence increasingly will be an important challenge for the future of education. While reading and writing are basic skills that can be transferred to many situations, workplace competency often is highly specialized, grounded in the specific work context. It cannot be taught; it must be learned and demonstrated "on the job."

Beyond Competence to Expertise

If competence is the goal for workplace effectiveness, it ultimately is insufficient. In a technology-driven world, today's competence can vanish with a new software release. It is expertise that is the goal at critical times in the information-gathering, decision-making human development process. Whether we face eye surgery or planning for retirement, there are circumstances where competence is not the ideal. We require expertise, someone who has mastered the rules and understands them so completely that they can cross the lines when circumstances demand. According to one report, it is the development of relevant knowledge structures and the ability to monitor their own thinking processes and adapt them as necessary that distinguishes the work of experts.[39] It is this level of expertise that is the ultimate goal of the learning–literacy–competence continuum. Expertise requires capabilities of learning, growth, and adaptation to changes in the "ecology" of the context.[40] This point takes us, however, beyond the scope of this discussion.

A BRIEF GLOBAL PERSPECTIVE

We can generalize with confidence that IL and IT literacy are of greater concern in democratic societies than in less developed countries. Training is widespread in Europe, where searches for writings on "digital literacy" uncover more activity than "IT literacy" searches. There is great variety in skill levels and the intensity of library activities promoting the capability within the EU, as might be expected with recent incorporation of former Soviet-dominated areas. A British survey of national policies suggests that the global trend is clearly toward greater openness as a encouragement to innovation, e-commerce, and e-government and growing recognition that information is now a key driver in building social and economic prosperity. A widespread pattern of specific programs to build broad citizen activity and learning has not yet emerged.[41] The assumption that providing access to computers and the Internet is sufficient is commonly held in many parts of the world.

Information Systems–
Information Use

Henri and Asselin[42] work from a similar premise to present widespread activity on the part of the library professions to promote IL and IT literacies in the schools in many areas of the world. The articles they present suggest emergent themes including "new learning," new literacies and multiliteracies, and the potential role that teachers and librarians play in creating information literate schools and communities. This work does not focus on IT literacy but many of the points are relevant. The difficulties in distinguishing IL and IT literacy mentioned in the introduction of this discussion once again merit noting.

Information Culture Literacy

When focus shifts beyond the Western democracies, a different perspective comes into view. Global library leadership, associated with IFLA (International Federation of Library Associations) is working closely with UNESCO to promote global access to information and learning under a flag of Information for All Programme (IFAP).[43] This initiative has produced additional studies and reports making a case regarding the need to address the challenges of a comprehensive information culture. Not an information society, but information culture, requiring reading, gathering, and managing information, and ongoing learning and knowledge improvement. This dynamic process encompasses upgrading knowledge and human intellect, designing and utilizing diverse media for communication, improving understanding, and expanding the uses and socialization of information throughout human activity.[44] This perspective reveals that individuals have personal information cultures, varying widely in their world outlook and system of knowledge, seeking information narrowly or widely, competently or carelessly, thoughtfully and critically or mindlessly and without reflection. Their engagement in or neglect of the process shapes their mindset, determining whether they are open or closed-minded, learning and growing, or stagnant.[45]

The UNESCO program, seeing information and knowledge as a global public good and basic human right for improving health, advancing education, furthering creativity, and preserving diversity and the human heritage, adds enormous value to the work of IL and IT literacy advancement. The importance of reading is stressed, compared with its declining status in this country. We find that the United States is not among the top dozen countries in achieving high levels of reading competence in its students.[45] UNESCO positions reading for pleasure and learning as a vital task for libraries, museums, and information institutions; this is a sobering counter-trend to the technology-focused IT literacy movement.

CURRENT AND FUTURE ISSUES

Several issues and debates not yet addressed are important to the topic. They include the need to rethink the relationship of IT literacy and information literacy, the difficulties of assessing IT literacy; the new focus on learning and innovation, the posture libraries should consider for addressing these challenges, the changing nature of knowledge, and the consequences of growing complexity in society triggered by networks and connectivism. Brief discussions of these issues follow.

Issues with Terminology

Sharkey and Brandt[7] combine earlier arguments to make the case that both information literacy and IT literacy are required capabilities for our day. Assessment of outcomes must be part of the process. None of the pieces of the larger picture suffice. The user's access and use of the information to good effect may require an electronic presentation, or a range of papers and presentations comprising an electronic portfolio of the work done and progress achieved. Work remains to be done; greater clarity and intuitive guidelines are needed. A terminology requiring both IL and IT literacy is clumsy. Information competence, ITC literacy, socio-technical literacy, fluency with IT, and all the terms utilized to date cause confusion and hamper focused progress. Information technology literacy is probably the best label available at this time, particularly when used in the socio-technical and contextual sense presented by Talja.[46]

Technology and Academic Literacies

The new literacies require participation. The level and form of participation is determined by the competence of the participant. Several issues emerge. First, readers become less passive and more engaged as their skills develop. The reader–author distinction fades and texts become fungible, multivoiced, and increasingly unstable. Linking and hypertext—as well as visual and audio media—diminish the role of text. Boundaries fade as discontinuities and disorientation place new demands on the participant and the organization. New "literacies"— particularly IT literacies—move beyond skills and cognitive knowledge into the realm of experience.[47] Donald Norris and colleagues address the issue as creating a new "technology economy" that requires measurement and improvement. They label the process "action analytics."[48] The process they describe involves incorporating workforce factors into educational curricula, utilizing open architectures to enhance access and affordability, and adapting organizational cultures to enable greater collaboration and innovation.

It is obvious that librarians must adapt to the users of new technologies. Today's students—the Net-generation to some, "millennials" to others—are mobile (with cell phones, i-pods, and laptops), collaborative, and "game oriented." These devices facilitate learning the skills required for the new age, but librarians need to be able to better help them with that use. Students are restless in crowded lecture halls and impatient with "nonconnected" authority figures, for which a segment of the professoriate and the library profession qualify.[49]

Librarians by no means have the field to themselves. Other groups and companies are pushing into the arena. Two notable examples are the European/International Computer Driving License certification program and the P21 skills development efforts of the Partnership for 21st Century Skills. Civic and corporate organizations are joining the campaign to assure that more young people have the skills necessary for the new century.

Connectivism

We have not yet discussed adequately the importance of the network and connectivity. The power of the network is widely proclaimed and increasingly self-evident. Its importance in organizational change and development is discussed elsewhere. But how does it work for people and what sort of challenge does it present for IT literacy and libraries?

Scholars and researchers are turning their attention to "connections," their nature and importance. This is not connectivity, a technological concept that focuses on bandwidth and issues of communication and access. Connectivism is something different, an object of recent interest to select denizens of cyberspace only beginning to turn up in early 2008 searches of mainstream databases, from *Academic Search OneFile* to Elsevier's *Science Direct*. But influential bloggers promote connectivism as a theory of learning that goes beyond behaviorism, cognitivism, and constructivism to become a learner-driven approach. Not a learner-centered approach, but a learner-driven approach. The very act of joining in, of connecting, signals the engagement of the learner.

In a persuasive argument, Siemens offers connectivism as a "learning theory for the digital age," a view seconded, disseminated, and discussed from time to time by Downes on his influential *Stephen's Web* blog. Siemens' essay is spotty, with weaknesses that include his definition of the half-life of knowledge. But his description of connectivism is captivating. He asserts that connectivism integrates chaos, network, complexity, and self-organization theories. He believes that knowledge begins with a diversity of opinions, is a process connecting nodes of information, and may reside in nonhuman appliances (computers). The theory stresses the nurture of connections to enhance currency, enable the difficult perception of connections across disciplines, and regards decision-making as a learning process.[50] The learner-driven element is suggested as the distinguishing characteristic of the new decentralized learning. A complementary case is presented in an extensive Australian study. Candy[51] demonstrates that "learners" are busy collaborating and creating knowledge on their own, independent of their instructors. He suggests that students and learners are far ahead of their instructors in utilizing networks and personal connections to share and create knowledge informally. Brown[52] places this trend in a larger context: something very big is underway, a shift from "pushing" information and knowledge through our schools, systems, and media, to a system, a paradigm, whereby people seek and "pull" what they want and need. Jenkins[53] defines the situation as one of growing technological/media convergence, and points out that the process is as much social and cultural as it is "technological." It is not the existence of the tools and devices but their use by people at work and play that is transformative. This way of thinking fits nicely into a coherent argument that explains the power of the network through understanding the importance and character of connectivism. Fully comprehending this trend and participating in its development is one more challenge for librarians and information specialists.

Learning and Inquiry

This brings us directly to the process of learning. Libraries have always been places where people can learn. For centuries that is where the information was, in the well-ordered shelves of books, periodicals, documents, and newspapers. But now information is almost ambient, virtual, available at the click of a button. Now the problem is information overload and the learner has different needs, such as selection and evaluation and using the information legally in the variety of formats where it resides. So the librarian's role is now different. Libraries can still be the places where people learn, but librarians must provide different kinds of assistance. Now the crucial skills have technology components, of steadily increasing complexity.

Information literacy and IT literacy attend the questions of the information seeker. Librarians help the inquirer get from "where they are" to where they want to go. Reference librarians start with the questions of the patron and work to satisfy their information needs. Information literacy and IT literacy give the learner tools to find their own way more effectively; the skill segues directly and smoothly into inquiry methods and "learning how to learn." Judging by the extent of the literature, Commonwealth libraries are further down this path than their American counterparts in the practices of information literacy leading to inquiry learning.

Knowledge Sharing

Learning leads to knowledge, but generally accepted ideas about knowledge are proving increasingly dysfunctional. Knowledge is Janus-like, dualistic in its complexity. It is simultaneously widely dispersed and personal, articulated and emergent, tacit and codified; it can no longer be sliced definitively into neat disciplines of epistemic practice, but blends across borders into mélanges of perspectives.

Its meaning is found in its application to given problems and contexts, not from the quick recall of "facts" for a game show. How knowledge is used increasingly is the product of how knowledge is shared. The traditional "know what," "know how," and "know why" proposed by Quinn and colleagues[54] is supplemented with the networked components of "know who" (authorities, collaborators), "know where" (positioning), "know when" (context, strategy), and "know if," through scenarios and foresight. New tools and methods of better sharing and utilizing knowledge include institutional repositories, wikis, and other collaborative IT methods producing what has been described as a knowledge-sharing revolution.[55]

Assessment

There is an important—and political—need for IT literacy to be assessed; we must understand how best to promote it in our schools and across society. Talja presents an important argument that the traditional assessment of computer skills is not the best way to determine needs and capabilities. She proposes that a sociocultural *context* or *domain oriented* perspective is a better approach than the more common user-psychological *generic skills* method. This view takes into consideration the social, interactive, and context-specific dimensions of the issue, suggesting that IT literacy/competence is "dialogic, multilayered, and context-dependent."[46] This explanation enriches the literacy–competence–capability approach presented here as an important way to think about the issue.

Others take a more critical view of assessment practice. For some there is too much focus on information processing assumptions and computational-style cognition;[56] others point to weaknesses in the testing process,[57] or stress the uncertainty about what can be tested (information gathering and management) and what cannot (understanding and knowledge building).[58] The aforementioned UNESCO report[43] makes it clear that there is no agreement on the use of standards and indicators in assessing information literacy; by extension, such is even more the case for IT literacy. The complexities of remaining current amidst rapid technological change render traditional assessment methods questionable. Additional study and alternate approaches are required.

CONCLUSION

New tools can lead to new human capabilities; at that point technologies demonstrate the potential to change society, culture, and the human condition. Today information and communication technologies exercise that power, or at least their potential. To adapt to this situation requires widespread use of knowledge and skills that best can be described as IT literacy, a new fundamental capability that is necessary for effective participation in the twenty-first century. Librarians are well situated to play a central role in promoting those skills and guiding society in adapting to the new knowledge and lifelong learning requirements.

REFERENCES

1. Brandt, D.S. Information technology literacy: Task knowledge and mental models. Libr. Trends Summer **2001**, *50*(1), 73–86.
2. Marcum, J.W. Rethinking information literacy. Libr. Quarterly **2002**, *72*(1), 1–26 January.
3. Lin, H. Fluency with information technology. Government Inform. Qua. January **2000**, *17*, 69–76.
4. International ICT Literacy Panel. *Digital Transformation: A Framework for ICT Literacy*; Educational Testing Service: Princeton, NJ, 2002.
5. ACRL Task Force, Information literacy competence standards for higher education. Coll Res. Libr. News March **2000**, *61*(3), 207–215.
6. Shapiro, J.J.; Hughes, S.K. Information literacy as a liberal art. Educom Rev. **1996**, http://net.educause.edu/apps/er/reviewArticles/31231.html (accessed January 25, 2009).
7. Sharkey, J.; Brandt, D.S. Integrating technology literacy and information literacy. In *Technology Literacy: Applications in Learning Environments*; Carbonara, D., Ed.; Information Sciences: Hershey, PA, 2005.
8. National Research Council. *The Knowledge Economy and Postsecondary Education*, Report of a Workshop: Washington, DC, 2002.
9. Winterowd, W.R. *The Culture and Politics of Literacy*, Oxford University Press: New York, 1989.
10. Moje, E.B.; D.R.O.B. Dillon, D.G. Reexamining roles of learner, text, and context in secondary literacy. J. Educ. Res. January–February **2000**, *93*(3), 165–180.
11. Kulhthau, C.C. Literacy and learning in the information age. In *Learning and Libraries in an Information Age*; Stripling, B.K., Ed.; Libraries Unlimited: Englewood, CO, 1999; 3–21.
12. Hoffman, D.D. *Visual Intelligence: How We Create What We See*, Norton: New York, 1998.
13. Henderson, K. *On Line and on Paper: Visual Representations, Visual Culture, and Computer Graphics in Design Engineering*, MIT Press: Cambridge, MA, 1999.
14. Horn, R.E. *Visual Language: Global Communication for the 21st Century*, Macro VU, Inc.: Bambridge Island, WA, 1998.
15. Kozma, R.B. Learning with media. Rev. Educ. Res. Summer **1991**, *161*, 179–211.
16. Brunner, C. Tally, W. *The New Media Literacy Handbook*, Anchor/Doubleday: New York, 1999.
17. Bruce, C.S. Workplace experiences of information literacy. Int. J. Inform. Manage. **1999**, *19*, 33–47.
18. Hull, G. Hearing other voices: A critical assessment of popular views on literacy and work. In *Changing Work: Changing Workers: Critical Perspectives on Language, Literacy, and Skills*; Hull, G., Ed.; SUNY Press: Albany, NY, 1997; 3–39.

Information Systems–
Information Use

19. Spitler, V.K. Learning to use IT in the workplace: Mechanisms and masters. J. Org. End User Comput. June **2005**, *17*(2), 1–25.

20. Falk, I. The future of work and the work of the future. J. Adult Adol. Liter. **2001**, *44*(6), 566–571.

21. Rosen, R.H. *Global Literacies: Lessons on Business Leadership and National Cultures*, Simon and Schuster: New York, 2000.

22. Tuominen, K.; Savolainen, R.; Talja, S. Information literacy as a sociotechnical practice. Libr. Quart. July **2005**, *75*(3), 329–345.

23. New London Group, A pedagogy of multiliteracies: Designing social futures. Harvard Educ. Rev. Spring **1996**, *66*(1), 60–92.

24. Doll, E.A. *The Measurement of Social Competence: A Manual for the Vineland Social Maturity Scale*, Educational Test Bureau: Vineland, NJ, 1953.

25. Reisman, D. Society's demands for competence. In *On Competence: A Critical Analysis of Competence-Based Reforms in Higher Education*; Grant, G., Ed.; Jossey-Bass: San Francisco, CA, 1979; 18–65.

26. Colby, A. James, J. Hart, D. *Competence and Character through Life*, University of Chicago Press: Chicago, IL, 1998.

27. Saarni, C. *The Development of Emotional Competence*, Guilford: New York, 1999.

28. Raven, J. Stephenson, J. *Competence in the Learning Society*, Peter Lang: New York, 2001; 253–258.

29. Evers, F.T. J.C.B. Rush, I. *The Bases of Competence: Skills for Lifelong Learning and Employability*, Jossey-Bass: San Francisco, CA, 1998.

30. Sveiby, K.E. *The New Organizational Wealth*, Berrett-Koehler: San Francisco, CA, 1997.

31. Delamere Le Diest, F.; Winterton, J. What is competence?. Human Res. Develop. Int. **2005**, *8*(1), 27–46.

32. Brockerbrough, S.A. Orr, R.G. Media as lived environments: The ecological psychology of educational technology. In *Handbook of Research for Educational Communications and Technology*; Jonassen, D.H., Ed.; Macmillan: New York, 1996.

33. Brown, J.S.; Duguid, P. *The Social Life of Information*, Harvard Business School Press: Boston, MA, 2002.

34. California State University. What is Information Competence? 2002. Available at http://library.csun.edu/susan.curzon/infocmp.html (accessed February 25, 2008).

35. Rockman, I.K. Integrating information literacy into the learning outcomes of academic disciplines: A critical 21st-century issue. Coll. Res. Libr. News October **2003**, *64*(9), 612–615.

36. Raven, J.; Stephenson, J. *Competence in the Learning Society*, Peter Lang: New York, 2001; 17.

37. Raven, J.; Stephenson, J. *Competence in the Learning Society*, Peter Lang: New York, 2001; 253–258.

38. In *Competence without Credentials*; Stacey, N.G., Ed.; U.S. Department of Education: Washington, DC, 1999.

39. Schön, D.A. *Educating the Reflective Practitioner*, Jossey-Bass: San Francisco, CA, 1991.

40. Bierschenk, I. Development of competence in dynamic learning environments. Cognitive Sci. Res. **2001**, *79*, 3–25.

41. Muir, A. Oppenheim, C. *Report on Developments World-Wide on National Information Policy*, Department of Information Science: Loughborough University: Loughborough, U.K., 2001.

42. In *Leadership Issues in the Information Literate School Community*; Henri, J., Asselin, M., Eds.; Libraries Unlimited: Westport, CT, 2005.

43. UNESCO. *Toward Information Literacy Indicators*. 2008. http://www.uis.unesco.org/template/pdf/cscl/InfoLit.pdf (accessed September 8, 2008).

44. Ramirez, E. *Reading, Information Literacy, and Information Culture*. 2002. http://www.nclis.gov/libinter/inforlit.conf&meet/papers/Ramirez-fullpaper.pdf (accessed September 3, 2008).

45. Fedorov, A.; Gendina, N.I.; Petrova, V. *Russia: Information Literacy*. UNESCO/IFLA Information Literacy: An International State-of-the-Art Report. 2007. http://www.uv.mx/usbi_ver/unesco.

46. Talja, S. The social and discursive construction of computing skills. J. Am. Soc. Inform. Sci. Technol. January **2005**, *56*(1), 13–22 .

47. Crook, C. Addressing research at the intersection of academic literacies and new technology. Int. J. Educ. Res. **2005**, *43*(7–8), 509–518.

48. Norris, D.M. Action analytics. Educause Rev. January **2008**, *43*, 42–67 .

49. Breeding, M. Technology for the next generation. Comput. Libr. **2006**, *26*(10), 28–30.

50. Siemens, G. Connectivism: A learning theory for the digital age. Int. J. Instruct. Technol. Dis. Learn. **2005**, *2*(1), 3–10.

51. Candy, P.C. *Linking Thinking: Self-Directed Learning in the Digital Age*, Department of Education, Science and Training: Canberra, Australia, 2004.

52. Brown, J.S. The next frontier of innovation. McKinsey Quart. **2005**, *3*, 82–91.

53. Jenkins, H. *Convergence Culture: Where Old and New Media Collide*, New York University Press: New York, 2006.

54. Quinn, J.B.; P.F. Anderson, S. Managing professional intellect: Making the most of the best. Harvard Business Rev. March–April **1996**, *74*(2), 71–80.

55. Norris, D.M. A revolution in knowledge sharing. Educause Rev. September–October **2003**, *38*(5), 14–26.

56. Budd, J.M. Cognitive growth, instruction, and student success. Coll. Res. Libr. July **2008**, *69*(4), 319–330 .

57. Scharf, D. et al. Direct assessment of information literacy using writing portfolios. J. Acad. Librarianship **2007**, *33*(4), 462–478.

58. Gendina, N.I. *Could Learners Outcomes in Information Literacy Be Measured: Pluses and Minuses of Testing?*, 2008; (accessed September 5, 2008). http://www.ifla.org/IV/ifla74/papers/134-Gendina-en.pdf.

Information Systems–
Information Use

Information Technology Project Implementation in Developing Countries [ELIS Classic]

Athanase B. Kanamugire
Library Consultant, Dhahran, Saudi Arabia

Abstract

Kanamugire's essay is a wise and widely knowledgeable survey of the issues and problems involved in carrying out information technology projects in developing nations. While some of the technology described has been superseded, the broad range of issues addressed and helpful solutions suggested by the author are still pertinent.

—*ELIS Classic*, from 1998

INTRODUCTION

In recognition of the importance of information and information technology (IT) in development, some governments in developing countries, as well as the international community, have implemented IT projects in library and information services in developing countries. The term developing countries is used to refer to the group of countries known as developing nations, Third World, less-industrialized, least-developed, or the South. The World Bank, for example, defines developing countries as those with per capita incomes in 1992 in the range of $80 to $12,000, 5% to 64% of their productive resources devoted to agriculture, adult literacy rates of 35–90%, life expectancy for residents from 40 to 73 years, and 10–75% of their populations living in urban areas. The human development index (HDI) developed by the U.N. Development Program (UNDP) is also used to complement the World Bank gross national product (GNP). The HDI index combines life expectancy, educational attainment, and income into a composite index. According to the HDI, developing countries are those with 0.191 to 0.835.[1] The working definition in this entry, therefore, refers to the many countries in Africa, Asia, the Middle East, the Caribbean and Latin America, and Asia/Pacific, which have different degrees of scientific, technical, economic, and social developments. However, as Mahoney points out, in an immediately postcolonial world there was little argument about what constituted a developing country. Now we have the extremes of Singapore and Rwanda; enormous disparities in population wealth in individual countries, and to cap it all, the end of the Eastern bloc and all the problems of development unleashed there.[2]

Among the many international organizations that have been involved in implementing IT projects in developing countries, the U.N. Educational Scientific and Cultural Organization (UNESCO) has played a leading role through its various programs, including UNISIST (UNESCO/ICSU Program for the Development of a World Science Information System), NATIS (the National Information System), and PGI (General Information Program). For instance, UNESCO has underscored the significance of creating databases that can handle locally produced information and facilitate the exchange of information in computer-readable form. One of the objectives of UNESCO is therefore to promote the development and use of software packages for bibliographic and functionally related nonbibliographic applications that implement internationally accepted programs for the exchange of bibliographic data. The UNESCO/PGI program facilitates assistance in the selection, acquisition, and installation of appropriate software packages, training, and provision of hardware, especially microcomputer systems.[3] Other UN agencies that have supported and implemented IT projects in libraries and information centers in developing nations include the International Atomic Energy Agency, the Food and Agriculture Organization of the United Nations (FAO), the U.N. Environment Program, the U.N. Development Program (UNDP), and the U.N. Fund for population Activities through its Population Information Network (POPIN) programs.[4]

Some regional and governmental organizations have also played a major role in implementing IT projects in developing nations. Chief among them is the EEC (European Economic Community), which has sponsored the application of IT to information systems in the ACP (Africa, Caribbean, Pacific States) countries. The Technical Center for Agricultural and Rural Cooperation (CTA) has been instrumental in implementing CD-ROM technology projects.[5] Besides international and regional organizations, some national government institutions, such as IDRC (International Development Research Center) of Canada, have also played a crucial role in implementing IT projects in developing nations. In Saudi Arabia, for example, the Saudi Arabian Center for Science and Technology (SANCST), currently known as King Abdulaziz

Encyclopedia of Library and Information Sciences, Fourth Edition DOI: 10.1081/E-ELIS4-120044773
Copyright © 2017 by Taylor & Francis. All rights reserved.

City for Science and Technology (KACST), has developed IT-based national science and technology information systems.

Information, Information Technology, and Development

These international, regional, and national institutions have expended considerable effort and resources in implementing IT in information systems in developing countries hoping that their efforts would lead to information and IT transfer, and ultimately to development. UNESCO has underscored the importance of information in development in a number of documents. The *Final Report of the Intergovernmental Conference of the Planning of the National Documentation Libraries and Archives Infrastructure* underscored that the conference recognized that information has become an essential basis for the progress of civilization and society and that improving human relationships in their own societies and among peoples of different cultures and traditions contributes to better understanding and world cooperation.

The same document further reaffirms document NATIS/3's statement that "Information is not only a national resource vital for scientific and economic progress, but also the medium of social communication." NATIS declares that "access (to information) is one of our basic human rights." Recommendations 14–21 on the application of technology to documentation, library, and archives services are particularly relevant.

Some of the major pertinent recommendations include the following

- Insofar as the systematic analysis of a nation's requirements reveals the need to use modern technology, they enact special legislation or take appropriate measures in order to deploy all the technical applications of NATIS and accept the possibility of cooperation with a view to distributing resources equitably.
- UNESCO should arrange for a study on the feasibility of a file of software packages in the filed of documentation, libraries, and archives.
- With regard to the application of technology to documentation, library and archives services, no indiscriminate introduction of mechanized techniques be made into information fields in countries where the technological environment is not ready for them.[6]

The experience of many organizations involved in implementing IT projects, however, has shown that the role of information and IT might have been overestimated. Due to many problems, especially infrastructural constraints, many IT projects in developing countries have failed. There are indeed three schools of thought on this question. The first school contends that IT would help developing countries "leapfrog" the industrial age into the electronic age by means of the application of the new technology. Abid claims that "CD-ROM will help libraries in developing countries to leap ahead into the 21st century."[7] De Horowitz summed up the idealism of this school of thought:

> New technologies, it was believed, would extend the benefits of information to all, in forms tailored to individual needs and skills and, hence, would foster development and enhance the quality of life in all nations and throughout all sectors of society.[8]

While acknowledging the potential role of IT in development, many authors advocate a cautious approach to adopting IT and question the impact of IT in developing countries. Slamecka argues that IT unquestionably evolves in a general direction beneficial to the Third World with respect to both its utility and affordability. However, he concludes that the fundamental problem of the Third World, its poor standard of living of the masses, is caused by low productivity of their agricultural and industrial sectors and by their inability to compete in international markets; hence it is an economic problem. Developmental strategies that fail to address this fundamental point in the hope that developing countries may somehow circumvent it and blossom into postindustrial "knowledge" societies, are utopian unless one accepts the unlikely premises that these basic needs will be provided permanently by someone else and that the Third World can rapidly overcome the highly skewed distribution of knowledge resources.[9]

On the other hand, it has been contended that developing countries need appropriate IT; that is, IT that suits their stage of development. The proponents of the appropriate technology theory contend that IT is too advanced for developing countries and that economies of developing countries are incapable of acquiring IT, as it is too expensive. They thus recommend that developing countries should continue with manual systems or make do with affordable semiautomatic technology. They argue that technology should match the level of development of a country and must be appropriate to available resources. On the contrary, the opponents of this school of thought assert that the appropriate technology ploy is dangerous because it means that the Third World should always lag far behind in development due to its poverty. Second, the Third World cannot even keep the development pace it could attain with IT. and third, there is an imminent dichotomization of the Third World as well as the development of two worlds within the Third World because the richer among them can afford IT, leaving the poor further behind.[10]

Despite the criticisms against the role and impact of IT in development, many libraries and information centers have come to realize that the application of IT is a critical factor in their role of providing effective information

Information Systems–
Information Use

services, and thus facilitate effective transfer of information for development. Nonetheless, they have encountered numerous challenges in their endeavor to plan, implement, and manage IT projects. These challenges and possible strategies to overcome them are discussed in the following entries under management and operational concerns.

MANAGEMENT ISSUES

Most of the problems encountered in the implementation of IT projects in developing nations are intrinsically linked to their socioeconomic and political underdevelopment, and hence the existing underdeveloped information infrastructure, such as the lack of information policies. Many problems could be alleviated if there were sound information policies covering the major issues pertinent to the development and implementation of IT projects. Unfortunately, a considerable number of countries are yet to recognize information as a major sector for which policies should be developed. This could be explained by the state of the economic underdevelopment prevailing in many developing countries, whereby the majority live under the poverty line. Under these circumstances, priority goes to these sectors that are vital for meeting essential needs, such as food, clothing, health, and shelter. Since it is generally recognized that sound information policies including IT policies are crucial for successful planning and implementing IT projects, policy and decision makers should be vigorously sensitized on the important role information and IT can play in development. This may be achieved through aggressive marketing of information, especially strategic information to policy makers, planners, and decision makers. Political factors have also significantly inhibited the implementation of IT projects in developing countries. Such factors include instability which hinders the implementation of sustainable IT projects, and censorship against importing some IT equipment, such as the ban against modems during the dictatorship of Dr. Kamuzu Banda in Malawi. Thorpe summarized the political factors inhibiting IT as adopted from Eres as follows: unstable governments, desire for often excessively tight security and secrecy, constantly changing priorities, centralization of decision makers, and lack of scientific impact at the highest levels of government.[11] The planning of IT projects should normally start with needs assessment. A thorough feasibility study may be conducted to determine the actual and potential needs of the target user population as well as the systems requirements. In conducting a needs assessment study, all parties concerned with the implementation of IT projects should be involved. In fact, it may be useful to form a working group on IT project implementation during the initial phases of planning and IT project. The working group may consist of representatives of all parties that will be involved in or directly affected by the design and

implementation of the projects. The working group may include policy and decision makers or their representatives, actual and potential users, IT departments, other departments of the library/information center, and the sponsoring institution. The objective of creating the working committee is to provide an experienced group of personnel who may steer the project through all its stages and be self-sufficient in appropriate expertise. This approach is appropriate in developing nations since it provides the opportunity to impart professional skills that may not be readily available in the library; thus the project may be completed more quickly. The planning committee would be involved in the development of the vision, strategy, and action plan of implementing IT projects. At this stage it is essential to formulate realistic and attainable goals and objectives, bearing in mind the infrastructure problems, such as financial, political, policy, procedural, cultural, and above all, human resource constraints. It is important to anticipate delays in implementing IT projects. The action plan and especially the schedule should be flexible. During actual implementation many management problems and issues are likely to arise that may delay the implementation of the project.

A number of methods such as informal interviews, structured interviews, questionnaire surveys, and observation and documentary descriptive methods have been employed in needs assessment. The informal and structured interview methods may be effective, as the interviewer can explain concepts that are difficult to understand, and pertinent information may be gathered during the process of interviewing. The main problem with this method in developing nations is that the interview appointment may not be promptly fulfilled and many interruptions are likely to occur during the interview. The questionnaire method has been useful for eliciting information from a large, geographically dispersed population. The problem with the questionnaire survey is that the response rate is likely to be low because of a number of reasons, including apathy. Although documentary or descriptive methods may provide vital data, it is often difficult to get access to institutional documents. There is a tendency to protect or hide information. Relevant documents are often labeled classified. It may also be difficult to have access to documents due to the lack of a system of organizing them.

Another major problem encountered in an attempt to conduct needs assessment in developing countries is the problem of communication. The target audience may not understand the technical jargon used in conducting a needs assessment or feasibility study. Moreover, input from the respondents may not be very useful or very reliable, as many respondents may not be familiar with IT discourse, devices, and requirements. The question of communication is even more complicated when a foreign consultant who does not understand the cultural and political milieu conducts a feasibility study. Such a consultant may often end up formulating unattainable goals and objectives or issuing unworkable recommendations due to the lack of understanding of the socio-cultural, political, and economic environments. Projects implemented according to the "inappropriate" objectives and strategies prescribed by such consultants are often short-lived, nonsustainable, and doomed to failure. Dosa contends that the success of projects dealing with the design, management, and evaluation of information systems or the development of library and information science curricula are especially dependent on the consultant's sensitivity to local conditions.[12] Knowledgeable as they might be in their fields, technical advisors might become frustrated and impatient with their local counterparts if the advisors lacked practical experience with the host country's traditional approach to changes. Mustapha stresses the need to develop clear guidelines for consultancy work in developing countries to ensure the success of future consultancies in these countries. His recommendations below are based on IFLA's Standing Committee on Theory and Research Panel discussion at the IFLA general conference held in Manila in 1980.

1. The consultant should have an adequate knowledge of the politics, culture, history, manners, customs, language of the host country, and a thorough knowledge of library services and their administrative problems in the region/country.
2. The consultant must have good public relations skills to enable him to deal with high-ranking officals in the host country, thereby winning their confidence.
3. A clear definition of the problems and realistic expectations as to the goals and objectives of the project and a prior agreement between the consultant and the host country on the objectives of the consultancy is therefore deemed necessary.
4. There is a need for involvement of local librarians at all levels of activity, with emphasis on project continuation beyond the term of the consultant's tenure.
5. There is a need for more contacts between the consultants and librarians and other information specialists in the host country, rather than concentrating too much on their own meetings with government officals who are influential, but who hardly understand ambiguous, and full of jargon and highly technical phrases.
6. There is a need for multi- and interdisciplinary consultancy. Such an approach may be more productive and successful than those undertaken by specialist consultants working alone.
7. Consultants should participate in the implementation of the mission's recommendations.
8. Aid agencies should take more active roles in the implementation of consultancy rather than leaving this aspect of the outcome to the recipient countries; consultancy missions should be coordinated to avoid duplication of effort and to ensure follow-up reviews of recommendations.[13]

In order to address some of the problems related to the language barrier, simple terms familiar to the target audience may be used in designing the interview or the questionnaire. Technical jargons familiar to the information professionals but not familiar to the respondents should be avoided. Using local information professionals who understand the local environment and local languages as consultants may help to elicit more information. They would not only translate the questionnaire into local languages, but through their influence and understanding of the local politics, policies, and procedures, they may also easily have access to essential documentary sources. They may count on their personal contacts, which are quite important not only in needs assessment, but also in the whole process of implementing IT projects in developing nations. Should it be necessary to recruit an external consultant, he should then work closely with a national counterpart.

Human Resource Concerns

Apart from the question of consultants, there are other equally significant human resource challenges faced by information systems in developing nations. These challenges range from a lack of qualified and experienced information professionals to a lack of appropriate staff development opportunities. The low status, meager salary, and lack of other fringe benefits of information workers may mean that the information profession does not attract the most competent and qualified personnel. Ideally, the person responsible for the implementation of an IT project should combine IT and library or information science qualifications, skills, competencies, and experience. In some cases, subject background or qualification in the subject of interest of the parent organization is desirable. It is difficult ot recruit people with such qualifications. Even when competent personnel are recruited, it is often difficult to retain them because of unsatisfactory conditions and terms of service. Some join other institutions what offer better salaries and fringe benefits within the country, while others migrate to the so-called greener pastures.[14] Wesley underscores the scale of the brain drain of qualified and experienced manpower in the Sudan, where over 40% of the professionals, 13.5% of the paraprofessionals, 23% of the clerical workers, 11.75% of the nonlibrarian graduates and 11.75% of all others, had migrated from the Sudan in 1985.[15]

The needs assessment exercise would be useful in determining human resource requirements. There may be a need to recruit new members of staff. In such a case it is advisable to recruit computer-literate information professionals or computer professionals who are knowledgeable in library matters. Those who lack computer skills should at least have an interest in computers and the willingness and aptitude to learn and acquire computer skills. In order to avoid nepotism, corruption, and other kinds of

Information Systems–
Information Use

Information Systems–
Information Use

malpractices rampant in many developing countries, it is advisable to form a broad-based committee to deal with recruitment issues. Recruitment may involve three types of staff categories: nationals, consultants, and expatriates. One of the critical factors that should be taken into account in recruiting expatriates is their ability to adopt to local conditions. Apart from their professional/technical expertise, their experience in developing countries should be a credit. Unfortunately, it is not easy to recruit someone who combines both IT expertise and local experience. If possible, an information system may recruit both expatriates from the West as well as those from developing nations. In order to develop a sustainable IT project, it is essential that one of the major roles of expatriates be to train the local counterparts who will ultimately take over from them. A strategic plan to this effect should be developed and implemented. Many libraries and information systems may not be able to afford recruiting expatriates, but they may rely on development or humanitarian aid agencies in the recruitment of different types of experts. Some voluntary organizations, including the U.N. Volunteers, British Volunteers Overseas (VSO), and the U.S. Peace Corps provide expertise and assistance that involve training of national counterparts. Also, many NGOs, such as the British Council, the Ford Foundation, and the Rockefeller Foundation, have assisted in developing library, documentation, and information services in developing countries.

The problem of a shortage of qualified human resources may be alleviated through offering such staff development programs as in-service training, on-site training, workshops, short courses, symposia, study tours, seminars, meetings, self-instruction, distance learning, and internship or attachments to another library. Participation in seminars, symposia, conferences, and meetings are useful for providing information on the latest developments in IT. Short courses may be useful for providing basic or up-to-date information in a particular IT area. However, a major criticism of many short courses is that too much is covered within a short period. Moreover, some short courses are not tailored to a specific level of audience. Training should be an essential component throughout the various stages of project implementation. It should figure high up in the project proposal document. A comprehensive program including all categories of staff and encompassing training during the preimplementation, implementation, and postimplementation phases should be developed. Training may start with conducting a user sensitization program for policy makers and managers. This may be conducted in a center of excellence where a similar project was successfully implemented in a developing nation or a developed country. The rationale behind such sensitization programs is that policy makers would develop appreciation of the benefits of implementing IT projects and would hopefully support IT implementation projects in their own organizations. Apart from policy and

decision makers, another group needing training during the initial phase of the project comprises potential trainers, including systems librarians and/or persons from the computer services responsible for library IT projects. It is crucial to select the right person for training. In addition to appropriate aptitude and interest, the person to be trained as a trainer should also have the will to share with his colleagues the skills acquired during the training. Unfortunately, this is not always the case. In order to offer an effective IT training program, it is important to involve all the concerned parties—sponsoring agencies, international and national consultants, and institutional library and computer services department staff—in organizing and conducting the training. This strategy was adopted successfully by the University of Singapore in 1980 when it implemented a project of the MINISIS test program for an integrated system at the library of the National University of Singapore. The MINISIS project committee set up to prepare a program for staff training comprised the heads of major library departments and a systems analyst from the computer center.[16]

Other major training issues that should be borne in mind are timing, duration, venue, content, format, method, and evaluation. The timing of training should not coincide with other activities that may be going on in the organization. Some training should be offered prior to, during, and right after the implementation of an information project. Training should indeed be an ongoing activity throughout the life of the project. This is important to enable staff keep abreast of the latest developments in IT. The issue of whether training should be offered on-site, within the country, or abroad deserves serious attention. If well-planned, on-site is valuable, since many staff members are likely to benefit from it. Moreover, some of the practical problems peculiar to a particular environment may be more appropriately addressed. On-site training is particularly useful for training staff who would be directly involved in the day-to-day operation of the IT project. Training abroad, especially in industrialized countries, is useful for planners and decision makers, systems librarians, and other senior staff members who would be involved in the actual planning and implementation of the project. Training within the country or region is useful especially for new graduates who have pursued studies in developed countries in which the IT environment differs from the situation prevailing in many developing countries. Such training is desirable to help the new graduates reorient themselves and marry theory learned in library information science schools to the actual IT environment in developing nations.

By and large, the content of the training program should be determined by the level of IT literacy of the targeted staff members as well as their functional responsibilities. For example, a microcomputer training package for information workers without computer background may include: operating systems, microcomputer hardware and software (especially database management software packages), data and file management, world processing desktop publishing, generation of reports by using microcomputers, and application of microcomputers in the various functions of an information system; that is, management; acquisition; information processing such as indexing; abstracting; information retrieval, including CD-ROM searching; online searching; access to network resources, especially the Internet; and electronic information marketing. Training programs are often carried out with no significant tangible impact. It is therefore imperative to evaluate the training programs on a regular basis and to modify the objectives, content, methods, and formats in response to the feedback obtained and lessons learned.

Financial Resources

Probably the most critical management issue facing information systems in developing countries in implementing IT projects is the lack of (or inadequate allocation of) financial resources. To make matters worse, many of the materials needed for implementing IT projects in developing nations must be paid for in hard currency, which may be difficult to come by. Furthermore, information systems have to undergo cumbersome bureaucratic procedures in order to obtain the necessary financial resources. To solve this problem, information systems should strive for allocation of an adequate budget for implementing or developing IT projects. Enough financial resources must be allocated to meet (a) the initial investment cost, the purchase of equipment, and the construction of buildings, (b) the recurrent costs for personnel salaries, staff development, interlibrary loan and document delivery, and (c) the acquisition of documents. Financial assistance may be sought from international donor agencies; however such external assistance may be useful as an interim measure in implementing and developing IT projects. It is not a durable solution. Recipient institutions should therefore develop some mechanism that would lead to institutional self-reliance. In addition to seeking funds from donor agencies, library information systems should endeavor to raise funds from internal institutional or other national sources. Academic libraries may seek assistance from academic and research programs that benefit from library IT resources and services. They may also exploit the possibility of hardware and software donation to the library. Value-added information services may be provided to policy and decision makers to sensitize them to the importance of information and hopefully win their financial support. Information systems may also carry out some income-generating and fund-raising activities as well as charge for some services in order to ensure the sustainability of the project at the end of external financial assistance.[17] However, such charges may not be in the interest of the disadvantaged majority who cannot afford to pay the fees. This practice may indeed widen the gap between the minority haves and the majority have-nots. This is not desirable in most developing countries.

Hardware and Software Options

In addition to human and financial concerns, issues related to hardware and software options such as their selection, procurement, installation, and maintenance are equally important in implementing IT projects in developing nations. Results of the needs assessment study would be useful in determining hardware and software requirements. To many information systems in the Third World, mainframes and minicomputers are too expensive to purchase and maintain. A considerable number of information systems in developing countries have therefore opted for microcomputers. Not only are microcomputers relatively cheap, but they are also easy to install and use. Moreover, they are readily available in the local markets, although purchasing microcomputers locally is more expensive than ordering them from abroad. Besides, technical support, maintenance, supplies, and training are locally available.[18] Furthermore, microcomputers allow some kind of autonomy. Opting for mainframes or minicomputers may mean a bond with the computer departments. Experience has shown that libraries and information centers do not often get the necessary priority from computer services departments. Also, many powerful microcomputers have emerged, and through networking they may perform the same tasks as those performed by mainframes or minicomputers. Moreover, donor agencies are more willing to assist in developing microcomputer/mini-based information systems through the provision of hardware and software packages than to assist in developing mainframe-based information systems.

Although hardware and software options may be primarily determined by the requirements as ascertained during needs assessment and the application to which they would be used, it is advisable to opt for powerful and durable hardware as well as user-friendly software systems. Due to rapid developments in IT, and particularly in the use of software packages that demand a lot of memory such as Windows '95 and multimedia products, it is advisable to opt for a powerful and fast PC with a massive amount of memory. Cost and durability are crucial factors in selecting hardware and software packages because of the existing harsh climatic conditions in many developing countries coupled with the inexperienced hands of some staff members and the uncertainty of acquiring new equipment or upgrading the machine due to financial constraints. Compatibility is still a major factor for sharing information and IT resources in view of the lack of a standard hardware and software interface and the scarcity of resources in developing nations. As IBM is still the de facto standard in the PC world, it is advisable to opt for IBM or IBM compatibles or Macintoshes with a great

Information Systems–
Information Use

amount of memory and considerable expandability. Only computers manufactured by well-known companies such as IBM, Compaq, Apple, Power Computing, and HP should be used.

With regard to the acquisition of peripheral hardware, the options for printers should be primarily dictated by durability, quietness, and simple operation. Dot-matrix printers are relatively cheap, simple to operate, and fast; however, they are unsuitable for public access services since they produce a high-pitched noise. On the other hand, if an information system needs high-quality print, especially if the printer is to be used for desktop publishing, a laser jet printer would be more appropriate. In view of the existing IT environment, especially the Windows and multimedia environment. SVGA or XGA monitors should be purchased. As for Keyboards, bilingual, heavy-duty one's are recommended. The selection of communications hardware components should be determined by the existing communications IT. Power stabilizers and regulators such as power surges or uninterruptible power supply (UPS) are indispensable in most developing countries because of frequent power interruptions.

There are many problems related to the use of IT hardware in developing nations. These include such environmental hazards as dust and humidity, and natural disasters such as those caused by the Harmattan in Nigeria, hurricanes in the Caribbean, or typhoons in the Pacific. Dust leads to floppy disc failure as well as to the use of more ribbons than usual. To alleviate these problems, printers and floppy disk drives should be covered with polyethylene bags. The snag of voltage variation common in many developing nations, in which there are few power stations that are able to provide a continuous supply, may be partly solved by using a noninterruptible, surge filter supply, or UPS. Car batteries could be used, but as observed in Nigeria, they are subject to theft. Instead of car batteries, cadmium rechargeable batteries may be used, since they are seldom used in many developing nations and therefore not recognized by thieves.[19] Given the shortage of spare parts in developing nations, it is imperative to include a wide range of supplies, including ribbons, toner, and plugs in the project budget.

As for the application software options, designing in-house software packages may not be the most appropriate option. First, most librarians in developing nations lack the expertise to design or use in-house software. Second, developing in-house programs is rather expensive and time-consuming. Since a lot of software packages suitable for a variety of library applications are available, libraries and information systems in developing countries should opt for such packages. These include CDS/ISIS, In-Magic, D-base, Sci-mate and Knowledgeman, Microsoft Access, and Excel. Among these, CDS/ISIS is the most widely used package, primarily because nonprofit organizations of UNESCO member countries obtain it free from UNESCO. Moreover, installation can be done through

CDS/ISIS local or regional offices such as ARSO in East Africa or ALESCO in the Middle East. Besides, the package comes with very clear instructions on how to install the system and there are many users, including CDS/ISIS user groups, who can offer installation and other assistance. Micro CDS/ISIS enables information systems to define a database structure, enter new records, and modify, edit, delete, retrieve, sort, display, and print existing records. CDS/ISIS can be used for most major library functions, including library catalogs, serials holdings, union lists of periodicals, union catalogs, and bibliographic and referral databases. On the other hand, CDS/ISIS has been criticized for lack of user-friendly documentation as well as search software interface.[20] Other two software packages that have been widely used in many developing nations are In-magic and dBase. In-magic can handle catalogs, acquisitions, serials control, current awareness, and loan service systems. It also offers a password facility for file security purposes. The major shortcoming of In-magic within the context of developing nations is that it is expensive. D-base, a general-purpose database management software package, allows creation of a database with customized fields, updating, editing, sorting, indexing, printing, and a combination of concepts by using Boolean logic operators.

There is a plethora of micro-based software packages that can be used in specific library functions in developing nations. Ventura and Page Maker may be used for desktop publishing, while LOTUS can be used for statistical purposes. WordPerfect, MsWord, and Windows'95 have been widely used for word processing. Besides micro-based software packages, a number of mini- and mainframe-based automation systems are preferred in developing nations, mainly because they are supplied free to nonprofit organizations in developing countries or because they are bilingual. Such systems include MINISIS, which runs on HP minicomputers. MINISIS has been extensively utilized in Africa, Asia, the Middle East, and Latin America. DOBIS/LIBIS, a bilingual integrated library system, has also been widely used in the Middle East. Recently a new bilingual system, Horizon, which has a vendor in the Arab world, was introduced. The Arabic version was developed by Ameritech Library in cooperation with Arabian Advanced Systems. In addition to the Dynix minicomputer-based and the NOTIS LM8 mainframe-based systems, it has rich functions and features. The Horizon automated library system provides a graphical user interface standards-complaint, industry-leading database management system and a client server processing model that allows the system to operate on an unusually wide range of hardware platforms.[21]

In selecting software packages for information systems in developing nations, the application for which they would be used as well as the existing software and hardware IT environment should be taken into consideration. The *Datapro Guidelines* for software selection, which

Information Systems—
Information Use

consists of ten logical steps for selecting software for any computing systems, could be adopted. These steps are: determine the requirements, gather information on the existing systems, draw up a short list, perform a detailed evaluation, review previous users' experience, conduct a benchmark, make a final decision, negotiate a contract, install the package, and check the results. These steps need modifications, however, taking into account the unique circumstances prevailing in developing nations. The *Datapro Guidelines* have been criticized for having too little regard for the user and his or her environmental constraints. To solve this problem, Bell recommends that users should be given details of existing systems and the potential users should be allowed to reevaluate their requirements.[19]

Having selected the hardware and software platforms, library information systems may encounter numerous problems in their procurement and installation. Although the purchase of hardware and software systems from computer dealers in developing nations promises reliable technical assistance in installing, training, providing supplies, upgrading, and procuring hardware and software packages, it is more costly than purchasing them from developed nations. Any problems faced in installation and maintenance may not be easily resolved if there is no local dealer to provide technical support, and the requisite training may not be provided. Consequently, one ends up with delays in the installation of the systems, or in some cases the systems are never installed. Even if installed, breakdowns that are likely to occur may not be resolved due to the lack of spare parts and technical assistance. In the final analysis, it may be more cost-effective in the long run to purchase hardware and software systems from the local market, if available. On the other hand, procurement of such items from industrialized countries may take a long time in processing paperwork, applying for import licenses, using foreign currency, and paying for customs clearance and tax. Referring to her experience in implementing information projects in Yamen, Hutchinson refers to the lengthy bureaucratic and technical obstacles that delayed the arrival of a microcomputer and a minicomputer.[22] Johnson asserts that procurement invariably takes twice as long as purchasing agents estimate. Procedures for purchasing, tendering for suppliers, and waiting for equipment to be supplied and delivered all add up to the general time frame required. In her experience in Bangladesh, equipment procurement was estimated at 3 months, but it took over a year, as a result of both donor and host country procedures.[23]

Once acquired, a suitable siting of the hardware may be selected, taking into consideration accessibility, security, visibility, and future expansion of the facility. Some of these factors may be conflicting; for example, accessibility and visibility vis-à-vis security. In view of the difficulty of obtaining replacement hardware in case the system is damaged or stolen, many libraries, including the University of Dar es Salaam in Tanzania, the Faculty of Medicine of the University of the West Indies in Jamaica, the University of Nairobi in Kenya, and Makerere University in Uganda, have decided to locate equipment in secure offices that are not easily accessible to the public. An equally important problem regarding the location of equipment is a lack of adequate space to house the hardware, users, and staff. To solve this problem, some rearrangement by weeding out the collection and reallocating staff, equipment, and information resources may be done. The installation of IT equipment may also pose problems. In order to expose library staff to the intricacies and issues involved in the installation as well as to impart skills that may be useful in installing and troubleshooting in the future, library staff members responsible for the day-to-day operation and management of the IT system should be fully involved in the installation of hardware and software systems. Citing her experience in Pakistan, Johnson explained that there was only one electrical outlet in a room that was to house two computers and two printers, including one UPS and two stabilizers. The Department of Works staff was called in to add the necessary wiring and fabricate the required bars. The librarian realized how important it was for him to be involved in the design of the electrical plugs since the equipment would be moved in a few months to remodeled headquarters and he did not want to have to go through the same process again. Working with the electricians, the librarian designed modular power bars that would meet both current and future needs.[23]

Cultural, Organizational, and Other Barriers

Cultural barriers have also inhibited the implementation of IT in developing countries. Chief among them is the language factor, whereby the languages of the developed nations dominate IT products. These languages are not understood by the majority of the people in developing countries. The efforts that have already been made at the international, regional, and national levels to use the languages of developing countries, such as Arabic and Chinese, in documentation and information processing should be continued. Another cultural barrier is the lack of a reading culture. It is no wonder, therefore, that many IT projects have been implemented only to be underutilized. This problem may be addressed through fostering and nurturing a reading habit through the major social and educational institutions such as the family and primary, secondary, and tertiary educational institutions. The provision of adequate reading facilities such as different types of libraries can also play a major role in promoting reading. Other cultural constraints include the time concept or the general slow pace of doing things and the significant role of personal contact and influence that adversely affect the implementation of IT projects.

Information Systems–
Information Use

Other problems related to management include organizational and restrictive, protective control measures. The organizational issue is particularly a problem in documentation or information centers. Such centers are usually affiliated to parent organizations that consist of other divisions or units that are often considered more important than information centers. Indeed, information centers are often considered so unimportant that in some cases they are regarded as support units of the lowest order, and consequently they are often allocated unqualified personnel and inadequate financial and material resources. From the initial planning, efforts should be made to ensure that information centers rank high in the organizational structure of the parent institution. The head of the information center should be on par with the heads of major divisions in the organization and report directly to the chief executive officer. Restrictive control measures practiced by many information centers serve as barriers to easy and convenient access to information. As a result, the target users avoid using information services. There is therefore a need to liberalize procedures that limit access to information, such as a unnecessary filling out of forms, the need to obtain approvals prior to admittance to the library, and limited access to some essential information sources and services.

These problems cannot be changed overnight; nevertheless, they must be taken into account in planning and implementing IT projects. Flexibility, development of realistic schedules, and personal contact and influence must be taken into consideration throughout the planning and implementation of IT projects. Some of the cultural constraints may be overcome through the involvement of local or national human resources in the implementation of IT projects in developing nations. Other major problems and issues, such as the inadequate existing information infrastructure, will be discussed in detail in the entry below on operational issues.

OPERATIONAL ISSUES

Information technology has been applied to a variety of operational functions of library and information services in developing countries. These functions include information retrieval, dissemination of information, information processing, collection development, interlibrary loan and document delivery, and user training. In information retrieval, IT has been utilized in accessing remote online databases, searching CD-ROMs, searching network resources, and developing local databases.

In information processing, IT has been employed in developing bibliographic, referral, numeric, and full-text databases. In interlibrary loan and document delivery, IT has enhanced the efficiency and effectiveness of identifying and transmitting requests, along with supplying and delivering documents. Information technology has also played a major role in the dissemination of information through current awareness services and selective dissemination of information.

Online Searching

Probably the earliest application of IT to information systems in developing nations was for accessing international commercial online databases. Some developing nations in Latin America have been at the forefront in this regard. The use of DIALOG from Latin America began in September 1975, when the Seccion de Consultas en Bancos de Information (SECOBI) of the Consepcion Nacional de Ciencia y Tecnologia (CONACYT) in Mexico established an account. Besides DIALOG, Latin American institutions also used other online systems, such as SDC, ORBIT, and NLM. In 1979, the Bibliotheca Regionale de Medicina (BIREME) in Brazil established the *Index Medicus Latino-Americano*, submitting citations to NLM from regional publications for inclusion in the larger databases sponsored by the Pan American Health Organization, the World Health Organization (WHO), and the Brazilian government.[24] The late 1970s and early 1980s witnessed the development of online access in the Middle East and the Far East. Some of the developing countries that pioneered in online searching during this period include: Brazil, Mexico, the Philippines, Hong Kong, Iran, Taiwan, Singapore, the People's Republic of China, Ivory Coast, Saudi Arabia, Senegal, South Africa, Egypt, Tunisia, and Ethiopia.[25]

A number of reasons have been given for the use of online searching services in developing countries. The principal ones are to access a vast amount of relevant, up-to-date, and accurate information that may be used for development; to augment the poor local information sources; to complement other media, such as CD-ROM when retrospective information is needed; and to search multiple and diverse online databases provided by a particular or different online information service provider(s). In his case study at the Institute of Applied Science and Technology (IAST) of the Republic of Guyana, Bahaa El Hadidy concluded that CD-ROM databases alone cannot satisfy all IAST information needs adequately, and decided that an online search access to international vendors was judged necessary to supplement the use of CD-ROM searching.[26] Many institutions have opted for online searching in order to consolidate and enhance their access to science and technology activities. This was clearly stated in a document prepared by the National Science Foundation in 1979 on the establishment of the Saudi Arabia National Center for Science and Technology (SANCST). The document asserts that the single most effective thing that SANCST could do was to strengthen Saudi Arabia science and technology activities at that point in their development. It was further pointed out that the most effective way of providing science and technology information was through online searching for information that would be used for planning research programs, identifying individuals and organizations for consultancy, identifying foreign technology for application in Saudi Arabia, and identifying research designs, methods, and patents.[27] Bourne has proposed that the use of online facilities can be cheaper than trying to improve the library collection in many locations in developing countries, and adds that despite problems such as poor telecommunications facilities and the expense of direct mail, computer-based reference services could be used to augment local information resources.[28] Although the importance of online searching in developing countries has been recognized for a long time, many Third World countries are yet to take full advantage of online searching due to a number of constraints. Essential components of information infrastructure such as economic, manpower, cultural, and political, inadequate physical facilities, and poor or nonexistent information policies and plans constitute some of the major factors that have inhibited effective implementation and use of online searching. Highlighting the interdependency of the various elements of information infrastructure, Mahon asserted that without parallel development of not only documentation stores but also the skills in information service development and database and databank development and training, the simple availability of technical access is insufficient.[29] Many developing countries can hardly afford the initial cost or investment of setting up an online search service. It may also be difficult to meet recurrent costs such as connect time charges, printing and downloading costs, annual subscription fees, staff development costs, and system ungrade charges. Libraries are rarely allocated adequate online searching budgets.[30] Discussing the problems associated with initial investment and recurrent costs, Brito pointed out that the installation of an online database requires a large initial commitment of funds and must be expected to generate high recurring costs. He further argues that in developing countries a number of factors combine to make online searching highly costly: the use of public telecommunications is usually very expensive in comparison to the cost of living; the unreliability of the public telecommunication systems, frequently interrupting a call, may turn a simple remote database search into an expensive nightmare of repeated unsuccessful attempts; and the inexperience of the infrequent users results in excessive search time, thus increasing the telecommunications costs considerably.[31]

The question of human resources has also inhibited the effective development of online searching in developing nations. Many information professionals lack skills and experience in automated information retrieval. Training courses, like those offered by online information services providers, are nonexistent in many developing countries. The unavailability of funds also makes it difficult for information professionals to attend online searching training courses or to participate in pertinent staff development activities. Those who pursue course in online searching through their formal education or special training soon lose online searching skills for a number of reasons. For example, they may not have the opportunity to practice online searching or to sharpen their skills because their institutions do not have an online searching facility. Furthermore, they often lack subject background that is crucial for better understanding the information needs of the users and for formulating an appropriate information search strategy. Even when an online searching facility is available, a number of reasons may account for the under-utilization of online searching. Probably the most important factor is the fact that potential users are not aware of the existence and availability of the service. Those who are aware of the potential benefits of online searching neither appreciate its importance in their work nor know how to use online searching services. They also lack online searching information retrieval skills.

Another major reason that partly explains the underutilization of online searching in developing countries is the frustration experienced by users in accessing or using online searching services. Users are often frustrated when they do not obtain adequate, accurate, and relevant information. This is particularly the case with the users interested in literature in developing countries. The bulk of literature included in most online databases understandably has a strong coverage bias of literature from developed countries. To make matters worse, users from developing nations may not have access to desired databases because of financial constraints coupled with other barrier and control measures. For example, access to the *TULSA* database has for a long time been allowed to institutions that also subscribe to the prohibitively costly print *Petroleum Abstracts*. Other common frustrations experienced by users include document unavailability, prohibitive costs, technical difficulties of transmitting full-text or image databases electronically, and delays in receiving documents ordered through interlibrary loan. This problem of delays in interlibrary loan and document delivery services has been clearly highlighted in a recent study conducted in Saudi Arabia. A significant number of respondents complained about document unavailability and document delivery delays. One of the respondents commented that

> The citations obtained from these sources are usually not available in the library. They are reports of Laboratory/Institute or theses/dissertations or articles in some periodicals which are not available in library. The time for procurement is long and usually when it reaches the university, the need for it is over, or it is found that it is not very useful.[32]

This issue has been extensively discussed in the literature on online searching in developing countries. In his study

Information Systems–
Information Use

Information Systems–
Information Use

on delayed online searching in Egypt, Al-Hadidy showed that the elapsed time between the search requests and the output delivery was substantially high, ranging from approximately 20–83 days.[33] Munn has recognized that the introduction of computer services without library backup is counterproductive in that it raises a user's appetite, and with it the frustration in not satisfying the appetite, thus turning him or her away from information services.[34]

Although there are numerous problems that have inhibited online access to remote databases, some information systems in developing countries have carefully adopted various temporary and durable alternatives. Such options include submitting and receiving search requests by mail, telex, or fax; using a national government or commercial telecommunications service; accessing online services through telecommunications services of another country; twinning with another institution in the developed world; and establishing full direct access to online databases through such telecommunications services as Tymnet or Telenet (and recently accessing online databases via the Internet). In Egypt, the National Information and Documentation Center (NIDOC) first had access to U.S. online databases through the Georgia Institute of Technology library system. Search queries initially developed at NIDOC were transmitted via telex from Egypt to a U.S. intermediary (at Georgia Tech.), who in turn conducted the online search using the search formulation developed in Egypt, but also exercising the option of optimizing the search strategies online.[33] In Saudi Arabia, the University of Petroleum and Minerals (UPM) library started using online databases in the United States in 1979 by submitting search requests to DIALOG by telex and receiving search results by mail. Later it had access to DIALOG and ORBIT through Bahrain Telecommunications Company (BATELCO). Government institutions in Saudi Arabia without their own access to commercial online databases can benefit from the online search services of the KACST, the national institution responsible for promoting and encouraging applied scientific research and for coordinating the activities of scientific research institutions in accordance with Saudi Arabia's development requirements.[35] In China, a connection was initially made via Cable and Wireless (HK) Ltd. through the agency of the China Overseas Building Company Ltd. (COBDC) in Hong Kong in 1980. Users in China were restricted to access by postal request. In 1983 the Institute of Scientific and Technical Information (ISTIC) of China established a data communications link ESA-IRS between Beijing and Rome for access to the databases on the vendor system. This was later extended to link up with the U.S. telecommunications networks Tymnet and Telenet. The following year, ISTIC gained access to DIALOG and ORBIT, and a connection to STN in Germany was made in 1986.[36]

In spite of the significant options adopted by the various developing country regions to access online databases, only limited access has been achieved by most developing countries, mainly because of financial constraints. Some countries adopted interim measures to alleviate financial constraints. Such steps include seeking technical assistance from international, regional, and national organizations, as well as NGOs. That kind of assistance could be useful in establishing an online search service, including carrying out a feasibility study, procuring and installing hardware and software systems, and providing document delivery services, training, and evaluation. However, self-reliance should be nurtured and fostered throughout the implementation of an online search service so that the recipient institution would eventually finance the entire project.

Other measures that may be taken to solve the problems of funding online searching include income-generating activities and nominal charges. To alleviate the bottlenecks of telecommunications, transitional options such as delaying online access or using satellites for accessing online databases may be useful. In order to promote greater use of online searching, adequate publicity of the service to policy makers and planners, academics, professionals, and other potential users should be repeatedly carried out. It is particularly important to publicize the service prior to, during, and after the launching of the service. Since policy and procedural control measures account for the underutilization of online services, such restrictions on use should be avoided or minimized in order to stimulate and accelerate the use of online services. Over the past decade, information systems have tried to overcome some of the problems associated with online searching by opting for CD-ROM. Online searching is used to supplement CD-ROM when most up-to-date or comprehensive information is needed, when one needs to search multiple databases or different online systems, or when the required retrospective information is not available through CD-ROM searching.

CD-ROM Searching

To many information systems in developing countries, the advent of CD-ROM technology has been a blessing. The advantages of using CD-ROM in developing nations abound. These include access to a massive amount of bibliographic, numeric, referral, and full-text image information, broad user base, user-friendliness, convenience of use, relevance, speed of information retrieval and document delivery, portability, durability, exposure to information retrieval skills, space saving, suitability for resource sharing, image raising, added value services, and development of local CD-ROM databases.[37] On the other hand, CD-ROM has been subject to a number of problems and criticisms. Some of the major criticisms are content relevance, lack of search software interface compatibility, lack of funds or allocation of inadequate budget for CD-ROM, costly hardware and networking licensing, technical problems such as head crashes, breakdown of UPS, compatibility problems, manufacturing defects, currency, inadequate retrospective coverage, material and financial resources, document unavailability, inadequate user training and documentation, lack of awareness of what is available and how to access it, lack of computer experience, delays in implementation schedules, inadequate human resources, security problems, slow access time, lack of simultaneous access to multiple databases, ownership issues, end-user misconceptions, maintenance problems, endlessly increasing demands for quantitative and qualitative enhancements, and increasing demand for more and different types of databases.[38]

In spite of the above problems, many library information systems have implemented CD-ROM projects because the advantages of CD-ROM far outweigh the disadvantages. Prior to implementing CD-ROM projects, institutions should start with conducting a needs assessment or a feasibility study to determine whether there is a genuine need for a CD-ROM project. The feasibility study should also assess the adequacy of the existing IT infrastructure, including the IT environment and material, financial, and human resources. Access to national, regional, and international information network resources must also be assessed and taken into consideration prior to deciding whether a CD-ROM project should be implemented. The potential beneficiaries of the CD-ROM service, the staff of the information system as well as the staff of the computer center who would be involved in the implementation, maintenance, and evaluation of the CD-ROM service, should participate in the needs assessment exercise. In fact, it is important to create a planning committee consisting of representatives of all concerned parties.

Since users and representatives of the various interested parties may not understand CD-ROM technology, it is crucial to provide simple basic infomation on CD-ROM in a handout or information leaflet format, including the advantages of CD-ROMs and the different types of CD-ROM databases. Potential users may be requested to suggest some pertinent titles. However, such suggestions should be critically reviewed by the information professionals. Users tend to recommend whatever they feel may be relevant to their individual or departmental information needs without taking into account the needs of other users or departments. This may lead to developing biased CD-ROM collections or acquiring specialized databases that may not be heavily utilized.

The data and results of the needs assessment study would be useful in determining whether or not a CD-ROM project should be implemented; how it should be implemented; what hardware and software platforms including databases would be required; the type of human resources that would be needed; the necessary planning,

management, and operational functions and activities; and how the CD-ROM project would be evaluated. The results should also be useful in developing the CD-ROM project vision and project document that may include: short-term, medium-term, and long-term goals and objectives of the project, activities that would be carried out in the planning, management, operation, evaluation, and development of the project. In developing a CD-ROM project document it is quite crucial to set goals, objectives, and schedules that are attainable in light of the immense political, economic, cultural, and technical obstacles that are likely to be encountered in the planning and implementation of the project. In most developing countries, financial factors constitute the single most important factor that would determine whether a CD-ROM project would be implemented successfully. It is therefore important to develop a honed project that would be used to seek funding from the parent organization or from external donor agencies.[39] A sound methodology on how the CD-ROM project would be implemented, and how the sustainability of the project would be ensured through local institutional support, reporting, monitoring, and evaluation mechanisms should be included in the project document.

Since many information systems in developing countries cannot afford procuring, maintaining, and developing CD-ROM systems, many international, regional, and national organizations, as well as NGOs have financially assisted information systems in developing CD-ROM services. The U.N. Fund for Population Information Activities has contributed to the production and distribution of *POPLINE;* WHO and the Pan American Health Organization (PAHO) have played a key role in the development and distribution of the LILACS database. Other organizations that have contributed to the development of CD-ROM systems and services in developing nations include the World Bank, IDRC, USAID, and the British Council. The EEC (European Union), in cooperation with the Tropical Institute of Agriculture in the Netherlands, has also successfully implemented CD-ROM projects in ACP countries.[5] Some developing nations, especially the oil-rich countries in the Middle East and the Tiger economies of Southeast Asia have financed the production, implementation, and development of CD-ROM products and services. In Saudi Arabia, the National Standards Organization (SASO) has produced Saudi standards on CD-ROM in cooperation with the Arabian Advanced Systems. Also, KACST CD-NET, a national network of over eighty bibliographic, full-text image, and numeric databases held by KACST, can be accessed by Saudi government institutions.

The needs assessment results are useful in selecting a CD-ROM system. In consideration of the rapid developments in IT, it may be difficult to recommend specific CD-ROM hardware and software components; however, it is advisable to opt for IBM or IBM compatibles or

Information Systems–
Information Use

Information Systems–
Information Use

Macintoshes with a great amount of CPU memory capacity. This is of vital importance because the microcomputer will probably operate in Windows, multimedia, and network environments that demand a lot of memory. Besides memory capacity, the speed of the CPU is important, especially if the machine is to be used for remote access. The major criteria that should be taken into consideration in selecting CD-ROM drives should include reliability, price, manufacturer or vendor's technical support, security, expandability, price, and audio playback capability. Safeguards such as built-in automatic laser read head cleaners, sealed casing, and doors to cover openings are of vital importance. Most of these requirements are met in products of major CD-ROM manufacturers, including NEC, Toshiba, Sony, and Hitachi. Reliability, especially the ability to withstand extremes of temperature, humidity, shock, vibration, and contamination, should be one of the major criteria in selecting CD-ROM drives, as many developing countries face hars climatic and environmental conditions. The choice of CD-ROM drives for developing countries may pose a challenge. Compton reported that "finding manufacturers to build reliable drives was a headache as was navigating the complex maze of import-export regulations."[40] The speed criterion is particularly important in selecting CD-ROM drives. As noted above, one of the criticisms of CD-ROMs is that they are slow. If speed is very crucial in the application of CD-ROM in an organization, then fast drives may be used. In selecting CD-ROM drives, serious consideration should be given to the DVD option. DVD drives can read discs containing at least 4.7 gigabytes of data, more than seven times as much as today's CDs. Dual-sided discs would double data capacity. If the information system intends to provide access to CD-ROM databases over a network, CD-NET servers such as the Meridian Data CD-NET server may be used. It is desirable to select a CD-NET server that has substantial expandability and compatibility with most PC local area networks such as Novel, Banyan, Microsoft, and IBM. Regarding the selection of printers, dot matrix and laser jet printers are suitable because of their low cost, simple operation, high speed, and durability. Nonetheless, dot matrix printers produce a high-pitched noise and hence are not the most suitable for public services. Jet printers are quieter, but they cost more and have special requirements. Laser jet printers, though also relatively expensive, are the most suitable for full-image article printing. For routine printing work in CD-ROM systems, dot matrix printers may be the most appropriate because they are less expensive, reasonably durable, and do not have special requirements.

Special hardware may be needed in installing a full-text image database as well as multimedia products. Jukeboxes may be needed for accessing hundreds of discs easily without having to change the numerous discs manually. To provide remote access, remote searching and printing hardware and software may be required. Information

systems in developing nations cannot do much in selecting the CD-ROM retrieval systems, however, until a common CD-ROM search interface emerges, libraries and information centers may circumvent the problem of the lack of a common CD-ROM interface by subscribing to CD-ROM products from the same producer, especially the systems that are user-friendly and well known, such as Wilsondisc and Silverplatter. Moreover, information professionals in developing nations may provide feedback to CD-ROM manufacturers. Such feedback would be used to enhance information retrieval systems in future editions. It is important to select appropriate CD-ROM network software. Whatever system is selected, it should be easy to install and use, allow simultaneous multiple access to the shared CD-ROM-related resources, include E-mail, and support Windows and DOS as clients. Furthermore, the software should also have a good facility of expandability, and should be able to accommodate additional drives to support larger and more diverse sets of information and multiple systems for the network. Finally, it should work well with most popular computer local area networks. Regarding remote access to CD-ROM databases, information systems should opt for reputable communication software packages such as PROCOM or Norton PC Anywhere, and CROSSTALK.

Bearing in mind the needs of the actual and potential users as well as the actual use of the existing resources in various formats, appropriate databases could be selected for acquisition. The major consideration in selecting CD-ROM databases should include: relevance to user needs in terms of subject, geography, language, type of literature, and period coverage. The existence and availability of alternative sources of information at the library, institutional, national, regional, and international levels should also be taken in account, since those resources may be accessed through cooperative resource-sharing programs. Frequency of use of printed sources or online database versions is a useful criterion in selecting CD-ROM databases. Other factors that should be taken into consideration include vendor reliability, licensing and lease terms, alternative price arrangements, and user interface. While subject-specific databases that are not adequately covered in the core databases available in the library information system may be acquired, high usage of such databases cannot be expected. Information systems in developing nations may therefore concentrate on acquiring and maintaining a core collection of heavily used databases. Subject-specific databases may be accessed in other formats or in other institutions through resource-sharing activities. Institutions in developing nations may seriously consider acquiring major CD-ROM databases that have extensive coverage of developing countries. Such databases include CABI, TROPAG, POPLINE, AGRIS, and LILACS. Library information systems in developing countries should also endeavor to produce CD-ROM databases of their local sources of information, especially unconventional literature such as offical publications and unpublished reports.

Although the installation of CD-ROMs is not difficult, information professionals who are not computer-literate may find it perplexing; however, local resources from computer departments in the parent organization or vendors could install CD-ROM systems. It is no longer prudent to fly in consultants from developed countries to install CD-ROMs or to offer initial training.[41] Having installed the CD-ROM system, initial training may be conducted for the staff who will be directly involved in operating the system. Training should be preferably conducted on-site so that many staff members benefit from it. If training is provided outside the organization, then a person should be trained to train his colleagues. Depending on the level of the trainees, the training program content may include microcomputer basics, hardware, software, MS-DOS, MS-Windows, WordPrefect, installation of CD-ROM databases, troubleshooting, information retrieval, and information marketing.[38] At the University of Botswana, the CD-ROM training program consisted of the availability and content of CD-ROM databases within the University of Botswana library, bibliographical control of CD-ROM and the CD-ROM marketplace, how to start up CD-ROM, a few search technique basics, and how to find information and get online help. There were also plans to cover operating systems and environments, PC management, desktop publishing, and computerized communications and online searching.[42] Once the CD-ROM system is operational, it should be publicized and user training activities in groups or individually should be organized; online tutorials, library Web pages, and print materials should be utilized. Apart from utilizing the CD-ROM technology for information retrieval and technical operations, CD-ROM could be utilized to provide value-added services such as current awareness and selective dissemination of information to policy and decision makers, researchers, professionals, and other types of users.

In addition to systems-related user training and publicity concerns, complaints have been aired about document un-availability and delays in interlibrary loan and document delivery as well as staffing. Users in developing countries identify relevant sources of information through searching CD-ROM bibliographic databases only to be frustrated by the fact that their library does not own the actual physical documents. Efforts to obtain such documents through interlibrary loan are hampered by delays due to communications problems as well as personnel constraints.[43] Library staff would also be adversely affected by the introduction of a CD-ROM service. Not only would they have to deal with the user frustrations mentioned above, but they would also have to study the system and documentation and to practice CD-ROM database searching, which may entail learning different search retrieval systems. They would also have to conduct user

education, offer assistance in information retrieval, and attend to clerical and technical duties, such as fixing printers. Library services and resources have been equally affected by the introduction of CD-ROM systems. Apart from user education, assistance, and interlibrary loan, there may be a significant decline in the use of mediated international online systems. Also, the space problem, which is a perennial problem in many information systems in developing nations, may be exacerbated. The use of print indexes may decline, and consequently cancellation of subscriptions to print indexes and journals in the case of full-text or image databases may follow the introduction of a CD-ROM service.

A number of strategies may be implemented to alleviate some of the major problems arising from the implementation of CD-ROM projects. At the planning stage, some budget provision should be made available to cope with projected increasing demand for more and different types of databases, CD-ROM stations, network costs, jukeboxes, and CD-NET servers. As for system maintenance, staff with sound information technology background, competence, and experience should be recruited. Alternative, a staff member with interest and aptitude in IT should be made responsible and be trained in troubleshooting. Other issues, such as user-friendliness and system slowness, may be addressed at the stage of system selection by selecting fast CPUs and CD-ROM drives. As for document availability and delivery, efforts should be made to subscribe to highly used journals that are indexed in a CD-ROM index. If funds allow, full-text or image databases should be purchased. In the case of projects funded by donor agencies, some budget for interlibrary loan or document delivery should be allocated. Subscription to CD-ROM databases that carry substantive abstracts such as *ABI-INFORM* may be a useful alternative to information systems in developing countries, which may never have access to the physical documents. Regarding staffing problems, many libraries and information systems may not be able to provide additional staff in response to the increasing workload due to the introduction of a CD-ROM service. The existing staff may tro to cope if all concerned staff would acquire competencies and proficiencies in CD-ROM searching. Staff members may also be transferred from other library departments to CD-ROM service departments.

Since its advent in the library world a decade ago, CD-ROM has to date proven itself as one of the most appropriate technologies for information storage, processing, and retrieval, and for the dissemination of information in developing nations. Library information systems should therefore exploit the CD-ROM technology in developing appropriate relevant and indigenous CD-ROM databases; however, CD-ROM does not provide the best access to information, which is through network resources such as the Internet and intranet. Library information systems in developing nations should therefore make the best use of

Information Systems–
Information Use

CD-ROMs and at the same time they should strive to provide access to network resources to complement CD-ROM resources.[43]

Access to Network Resources

The international community and national governments have recognized the imperative of resource sharing through information networks for a long time. It has been argued that the optimal and cost-effective use of the limited resources could be achieved through resource sharing and cooperation within the context of information networks. UNESCO has spearheaded efforts to develop cooperative programs and information networks in developing nations. Recommendation 21 of the UNISIST study report proposes that UNISIST should, among other things, propose guidelines for establishing and managing information networks and help to design a few pilot projects to assess different ways of linking developing countries with UNISIST.[45] One of the major programs of GIP (General Information Program of UNESCO) is the improvement of access to information through the use of modern technologies, standardization, and interconnection of information systems. One of the subprograms is on the exchange and flow of information through regional and international cooperation among member states and within the organizations of the U.N. system.[46] Other U.N. agencies, especially the U.N. Atomic Energy Agency through its INIS project, the FAO through its AGRIS program, the WHO, and the UNFPA through its support to POPIN, have contributed to the development of information networks in developing nations. These organizations have developed global information networks with regional, national, institutional, or sectoral nodes. The IDRC through the DEVSIS programs as well as through cooperation with such other donor organizations as UNDP, UNFPA, and UNHCR, has greatly assisted developing nations in developing information networks.

The objectives of implementing information networks in developing nations include the following, as stated in the objectives of the Pan Africa Documentation Information System:

1. Identifying and collecting information resources and creating an efficient system for the utilization of information.
2. Promoting information exchange.
3. Establishing a system that would ensure access to both published and unpublished documents.
4. Providing assistance to member institutions to strengthen their information infrastructures so that they would be able to participate fully in the system by contributing as well as deriving benefits from it. These would include regional, subregional, or sectoral participating centers.

5. Establishing links (systems interconnection) with international information networks, databases, and information and documentation units.
6. Utilizing the most recent technology of data transmission, including telecommunication satellites.
7. Organizing the necessary training programs for users.
8. Establishing technical procedures and standards to ensure the system's compatibility with existing national and international information systems to facilitate information transfer and exchange between them.[47]

The main functions of information networks have been to explore the needs of information users, to define the field to be covered, to identify all information available on the field, to choose methods that allow for the transfer of information between information centers (standards and systems interconnection), to supply information and documents to users by compiling and publishing directories, union lists, newsletters, and similar publications, to provide technical assistance, and to organize training workshops for information specialists and users. Information technology has been utilized in enhancing most of the functions of information networks. It has been used in identifying and creating information resources through the use of indigenous databases, online and CD-ROM databases, the development and use of common standards and information-processing tools, information dissemination, and promotion of information exchange. Information technology has also been utilized in providing training.

The 1980s and 1990s have witnessed the development of and access to computer networks in developing nations. A few examples of such networks are: GULFNET, Internet,[48] Fidonet,[49] and BITNIS,[48] a network arising between the University of Chile and the National Library of Medicine that permits the consultation of the MEDLARS database via E-mail. In the Muslim world, the International Organization of Islamic States is in the process of developing a network on Islam (OICIS-NET) that will also serve as a gateway to the Internet.[50]

The World Bank and UNDP have also been involved in promoting the development of computer networks in developing countries. The World Bank, in collaboration with UNDP, OSS/UNITAR, and USAID/WRI-NRICG has developed AFRICA-EIS, an E-mail service provided by the program on environmental information systems in sub-Saharan Africa hosted at the Environmentally Sustainable Development Division (AFTES) of the Africa Technical Department of the World Bank. The objective of AFRICA-EIS, which is open to any interested parties, is to provide a forum for discussion and especially to promote the use of geographical information systems (GIS) and spatial information on environmental issues as a support tool for decision making for natural resource management in sub-Saharan Africa. AFRICA-EIS keeps an archive and an index of issues relevant to GIS issues and a list of EIS newsletters of the program on environment information systems in sub-Saharan Africa. Through this network, a user can contribute to a conference and request a document. Many African countries have already participated in the network in sharing information. These include Benin, Botswana, Burkina Faso, Ivory Coast, the Gambia, Ghana, Kenya, Lesotho, Madagascar, Mali, Nigeria, Senegal, Mauritania, Mozambique, South Africa, Tanzania, Uganda, Zambia, and Zimbabwe.[51] The UNDP has also recently launched a network of immense value to developing nations. The Sustainable Human Development Network Program (SDNP), a computer-mediated communication project of the UNDP, addresses issues of information flow by fostering information sharing within developing countries, empowering users, and helping decision makers on issues related to sustainable human development. The project was launched in 1992 with twelve countries in Africa, Asia, and Latin America. To date some twenty countries are or will shortly be in operation with SDNPs. These countries include Angola, Chad, Indonesia, Pakistan, Nicaragua, Honduras, Bolivia, Cameroon, Lebanon, Morocco, Tunisia, Korea, Colombia, Guatemala, Chile, Mexico, India, and Costa Rica.[52]

Another interesting development in networking is the development of networks through the cooperation of institutions in both the South and the North. A good example of such networks is the PANGIS (Pan-African Network for a Geological Information System) network. The PANGIS network was initiated by ASGA (Association of African Geological Services), with the technical support of CIFEG (International Center for Training and Exchanges in Geology). The network is currently supported by UNESCO, cooperation agencies of French-speaking countries (ACCT and BIET), and the French ministries of industry, foreign affairs, and research and technology. PANGIS uses formats and procedures compatible with the common communication format and exchange modules compatible with PADIS or AGRIS methodologies. The centers were initially equipped with 386 microcomputers and used the CDS/ISIS 2.32 software. A quarterly bibliographic bulletin and a CD-ROM database are produced by the PANGIS network.[53]

Besides information networks that have been established through international cooperation, some developing nations have developed their own information networks. A good example of such a network is Gulfnet, which was established by the Saudi government in 1985. It is a computer network of academic and research institutions in the Arab world—a store and forward network similar to BITNET. Gulfnet has two major goals: to provide an infrastructure for the exchange of data, information, and messages between scientists and researchers in the Arab Gulf countries as well as to promote informal cooperation and thus promote cooperation in research projects. The Gulfnet Academic Network consists of fourteen institutions: eight Saudi universities, KACST, King Faisal Specialist Hospital and Research Center, Cooperation Council for the Arab States of the Gulf, Ministry of Health, Islamic Research and Training Institute, Kuwaiti Institute for Scientific Research, Kuwait University, and IBM Kuwait Scientific Center. Gulfnet provides the following information services to its participating centers: accessing international databanks, providing document delivery, maintaining a union list of periodicals held by participating centers, and providing access to a bibliographic and terminology databank and the library online catalog. Other services provided through the Gulfnet communication networks include interactive messaging, file transfer, E-mail, a user directory, access to databases, conference systems, and CHAT, an organized way of providing E-mail and an answering service for answering reference queries. Gulfnet provides access to many computer and medical forums, as well as access to the KACST library information resources and databases such as the CICS DOBIS/LIBIS and dial-up or public data network access to over eighty international databases and eighty-four online CD-ROM databases.[54]

In implementing information networks, library information systems have faced numerous problems. One of the critical management concerns that has adversely inhibited the effective implementation of information networks in developing countries concerns organizational structure and approach. Most cooperative information networks consist of coordinating units at global, regional, and national levels, which consists of participating centers at a lower hierarchical level. The problem with that kind of information network structure is that the coordinating unit seems to be benefiting more from the network than the participating nodes. Coordinating units tend to be better staffed, better provided with equipment, and alienated from the practical problems prevailing in regional or national participating centers. As a result, participating centers are indifferent or apathetic, since they do not see any tangible benefit from participating in the information networks that do not provide any material, financial, or personnel support. The initial enthusiasm of participating in the network wanes in the failure of regional information networks or their governments to provide the necessary support for effectively implementing information networks at the regional or national node. In order to tackle this problem, the approach should rather be from the bottom to the top. The regional, subregional, or national participating centers should be provided with financial, human, information, and other material resources. Another organizational structure issue related to the implementation of information networks in developing nations is the fact that oftentimes inappropriate institutions are designated as national coordinating centers due to political and other nomenclature factors.

Regarding technical operations of the network, standardization and compatibility of hardware and software systems as well as information-handling tools and

Information Systems–
Information Use

methodologies pose the most significant challenges. It is thus essential that information networks examine existing standards and apply totally or partially standards that are compatible with international standards, such as UNESCO, CCF, UNIMARC, ISBDS, and AACR II. Since these standards do not adequately cover developing nations, standards should be modified to meet local requirements. Reclassification of geographical regions may be necessary. Likewise, manuals should be made as simple, self-explanatory, and accessible as possible.

Another major technical operational constraint faced by information networks is inadequate telecommunications systems. Telephone lines are inadequate, slow, and unreliable. Dial-up services are often very slow, and leased circuits are too expensive. Circuits and bandwidth are often overloaded and the network links may be saturated. A number of alternative options such as the use of microwave networks, installation of X-25, use of packet radio, use of orbiting satellites, or Fidonet technology and the use of CD-ROMs should be explored. Last but not least is the problem of establishing and developing information networks in developing countries because of the widespread lack of awareness of the existence and potential of information networks, and consequently their underutilization. Publicity and user training should therefore be essential components in the planning and implementation of information networks.

Internet Access

In addition to cooperative international and regional information networks, many information systems in developing nations are already connected to the Internet. Many library information systems started using the Internet in the early 1990s. In Latin America and the Caribbean, for example, 1994 marked the year of consolidation or integration of numerous national networks into the global Internet. However, some institutions, such as SAICYT (Sistema Automatiza Information Scientifica y Technologica, or Scientific and Technological Information Automated System), established connections to the Internet through the JVN Cnet (John Von Newman Computer Network) of Princeton University by the end of 1991. By May 1993, SAICYT was completely based upon the TCP/IP protocol.[48] In Africa, South Africa was connected to the Internet in 1991, although efforts to establish Internet connection started in 1989.[56] In the Middle East, some countries, such as Egypt, have had limited Internet access since 1993, whereas the Arabian Gulf countries such as Kuwait and the United Arab Emirates established an Internet connection in 1994/1995. A number of countries in the Asia Pacific region, such as Malaysia, Indonesia, and Taiwan, established an Internet connection in the early 1990s.

There is a wide range of potential benefits of using the Internet in developing countries. The global network may play a crucial role in tackling the book famine experienced by many libraries in developing nations. Westhuizen argues that the electronic library enables access to electronic journals and books via computer networks through the Internet and by telephone modem.[56] On the other hand, it has been recognized that due to infrastructural problems, many information systems have not taken advantage of IT, including the Internet. In fact, it has been argued that the Internet may exacerbate underdevelopment. Sanchez-Vegas contends that if accessibility obstacles—funding, ownership, and costs—are not adequately addressed and resolved, then only the elite (within and among countries) will benefit from this immensely powerful information superhighway.[55] However, it is encouraging to note that in spite of the many problems related to Internet access in developing countries, the Internet has been used for a wide range of purposes. Through Internet remote log-in, some libraries have had access to the most important data and knowledge banks. Ainsworth and Levinson underscored the use of the Internet to solve problems of access to databases and the wealth of information available through the link of information systems. Levinson contends that the Internet offers many national and international library catalogs with strong Latin American collections and that they frequently help with reference interlibrary loan, and collection development. Having established a connection to remote online catalogs, libraries can verify library holdings for interlibrary loan (ILL)/document delivery purposes and the selection of reference sources.[57,58] Through Telenet connection to bibliographic, referral, numeric, full-text, and image databases, information systems can retrieve and obtain valuable information that can be used for research, reference, document delivery, current awareness, and acquisition purposes.

Library information systems in developing nations can use the FTP (file transfer protocol) of the Internet to download files of documents for ILL or document delivery, current awareness, or the building of an electronic sources reference collection. For instance, the veterinary science library at the University of Pretoria in South Africa uses FTP to build its electronic sources collection, downloading relevant animal health information such as descriptions of various animal breeds onto disk for its students. Westhuizen indicates that through FTP they often find information difficult to obtain or unavailable in the more conventional publication forms.[56] Probably the most viable application of Internet in developing countries has been E-mail communication. Relevant Internet lists have been used for exchanging relevant and topical information or requesting hard-to-come-by articles. In Africa, for example, many libraries have an E-mail connection. These include the medical library of the Unversity of Zambia, the veterinary library of the University of Zimbabwe, the veterinary faculty of the University of Eduardo Mondlane, Mozambique, the International Livestock Research for

Animal Diseases (ILRAD) now International Livestock Research Institute (ILRI) library in Nairobi, Kenya, and Makerere University in Uganda.

One of the interesting recent developments in Africa is the project of the "African virtual university." The university is a World Bank pilot project that is linking selected African universities to European and U.S. institutions. Recognizing that most libraries are empty shelves and that broken science facilities litter most of the laboratories, the World Bank believes that with planning and commitment, these dilapidated universities could make use of the lifeline from cyberspace. As a first step, the World Bank has established a Web site for the new university. It is also encouraging private information technology bodies to provide Internet links to universities and research institutions in sub-Saharan Africa. During the first phase of the $1.2 million project, Makerere (Uganda), Haille Sellassie (Ethiopia), Dar es Salaam (Tanzania), Nairobi, Moi (Kenya), Legon, Kumasi (Ghana), and Zimbabwe universities will form an examination faculty for the African virtual university, while the University College, Salway, and the New Jersey Institute of Science will provide lectures and course materials.[59]

The Internet's conference features have also been exploited for information dissemination. Westhuisen gives a good example of such a conference on animal health. The WINROCK International Livestock Conference held in 1993 had participants in Colombia, Peru, Bolivia, India, and other developing countries as well as in the United States and Europe. The conference continued for several months, with keynote papers being commissioned and contributions being made by a wide range of participants without incurring travel costs. Also, published conference proceedings can be accessed through electronic conference.[56]

Although there is a wide recognition of the advantages of using the Internet, many developing nations have not exploited the potential of the network due to a number of complex problems. Two major interrelated bottlenecks have hampered access to the Internet resources: lack of reliable good data communications systems and the relatively prohibitive communications cost. Citing the state of communications in Latin America, Cubezas[48] pointed out the lack of a dependable communication system, while Lawrie, in reference to the situation in Africa, identified poor telecommunications infrastructure as well as prohibitive prices as some of the major factors inhibiting access to the Internet.[60] Kamaruddin points to the lack of both high-speed data communications facilities, and a direct link to the Internet as two of the obstacles that would hamper Islamic nations from fully benefiting from the services of the OICIS-Net (Organization of Islamic Countries Information Systems Network) project.[50]

Other problems related to poor communication systems include rigid, time-consuming, and difficult log-on procedures and an overloaded or saturated bandwidth. The

constraints pertinent to prohibitive costs encompass expensive leased circuits and other prohibitive prices. Other issues that inhibit the effective utilization of Internet resources in developing nations include weaknesses of library collections and hence the problems of identifying and obtaining relevant, up-to-date sources, a lack of understanding of the strategic value of information, and easy access to undesirable sources, such as pornography and seditious literature. Kamaruddin claims that OICIS-Net would ensure that its users would be protected to the extent possible from some of the difficulties that have emerged in the Internet, such as an overload of information, a lack of security, and the tendency to use the network to exchange undesirable information.[50] Some developing nations enact regulations and other control measures that inhibit or limit access to the Internet. Referring to South Africa, Lawrie points out that Internet connection was delayed in South Africa mainly because of telecom regulations that prevented any Internet activity.[60] In order to alleviate the above problems, some developing countries have adopted a number of options, such as using store and forward E-mail networks such as Bitnet and Fidonet or dial-up link until the time when they would have UUCP or TCP/IP link. Research and academic libraries in the Arabian Gulf region, for example, have been using Gulfnet/Bitnet for E-mail communication, however, such E-mail networks have basic limitations since they are not interactive. Interactive Internet tools such as Gopher, WWW, or WAIS are not available at Bitnet/Gulfnet-only sites. South Africa also used a dial-up Bitnet telelink Fidonet mailing system from 1988 until 1990, when it got a dial-up UUCP link. For institutions that can afford it, the best approach would be to install a high-capacity satellite to enhance international links to the Internet. To tackle the problem of high communication costs, libraries should negotiate with telecommunication companies for fair costs. In order to provide access to indigenous literature, some information systems have developed local databases and made them accessible through networks. The following entry discusses the development and access to indigenous databases.

Development and Access to Local Databases

One of the major shortcomings of IT-based information sources in developing countries is inadequate coverage of information on developing countries. To address this problem, efforts have been made since the 1970s to develop local databases. Highlighting this problem in the foreword of the document *International Cooperative Information Systems*, IDRC-156e, IDRC contends that developing countries need first of all to build mechanisms so that the information that they generate themselves can be retrieved when it is needed for development purposes.[4] IDRC has therefore been actively involved in assisting developing nations build databases on and in developing countries

Information Systems–
Information Use

that include considerable indigenous literature. In Africa, IDRC has significantly contributed to the development of the bibliographic and referral databases of the Pan African Development Information System (PADIS), the PIDSA (Population Information and Documentation System for Africa), and ILICA (International Livestock Information Center for Africa).

UNESCO has also been at the forefront in assisting developing nations plan and develop national bibliographic agencies and services through the provision of consultancy, equipment, software packages, and training. Examples of UNESCO participation in developing databases in developing nations abound. In Latin America, UNESCO has been instrumental in developing CRESALC—a database of UNESCO's Regional Center for Higher Education in Latin America and the Caribbean, covering Santiago, Chile, Port of Spain, Trinidad, and Caracas, Venezuela. Other U.N. agencies have participated in developing databases, including FAO, which has developed AGRINTER, a regional database located in Costa Rica covering Latin America and the Caribbean contributions to the worldwide database AGRIS; WHO, which has contributed to the development of the LILACS (Literatura de Latinamerica Sobre Ciencias de la Salud) database produced on CD-ROM in Sao Paulo, Brazil by BIREME, the Latin America Center for Information on Health; and the U.N. Environmental Program, which has developed PNUMA, which has regional offices in Mexico City and Kingston, Jamaica.[61] Besides international organizations, some national institutions have developed local databases. In Saudi Arabia, KACST has developed a number of databases on Saudi Arabia. These include: science and technology database (English), Arabic science and technology bibliographic database (Arabic), manpower database, union list of serials database, current awareness database, science and technology terminology databank (BASM), online library catalog, research project data base, and project review database.[62]

The rationale for the developing local databases has been to improve access to locally produced information for development. Such information would be useful to individuals and institutions in developing nations as well as those in the North, which are interested in information on or in developing countries. They would not only serve as selection tools, but would also enable users identify the existence and availability of relevant information. Most databases developed in developing nations have been mission-oriented, with the purpose of identifying and delivering information that can be useful in research and development planning and decision making, hence they are concerned not only with scientific and technical information that may be important in decision making, but also with economic, social, and legislative information. In their endeavor to develop indigenous databases, many information systems in developing nations have, however, encountered a number of bottlenecks. Most of the major

problems discussed earlier such as the lack of qualified and experienced staff, budgetary constraints, lack of a reading, documentation, and information culture and hence the underutilization of information systems, and language barriers have all hampered the effective development and use of local databases.

In addition to these problems, issues pertinent to information processing have also posed serious problems. The international information-processing standards, codes, rules, and guidelines do not always adequately meet the requirements of developing nations. Such information-processing tools as the *Anglo-American Cataloging Rules*, *UNISIST Reference Manual for Machine Readable Bibliographic Description, UNESCO Common Communication Format (CCF)*, and MARC and UNIMARC formats need to be modified to cater to the requirements of developing nations. This explains why many developing countries have developed their own national MARC formats formats.[62] Indonesia has developed SINGMARC, South Africa SAMARC, Taiwan CHINESE MARC, and Thailand THAIMARC. In order to overcome problems posed by information-processing tools such as guidelines to bibliographic descriptions and thesauri, many information systems have developed their own guidelines. For example, PADIS and POPIN-Africa have developed the *PADIS Manual for Document Analysis and the POPIN-Africa Guidelines for Bibliographic Description and Analysis of Population and Family Planning*, respectively. Since the preparation of information-processing tools is time-consuming, it may not be wise to expend a lot of effort, time, and human and material resources in developing tools for an individual information system. For example, the development of comprehensive information tools by POPIN-Africa based on the PADIS manual was an unnecessary duplication of efforts. Information-processing tools developed by international or regional information systems should be adopted and tailored to the specific subject or geographical requirements of an information system.

Menou contends that the barrier to the exchange of bibliographic information created by incompatibility among formats was noted from the inception of UNESCO'S UNISIST program, which led to the proliferation of standard formats, giving birth to four groups of formats, somewhat similar yet antogonistic, that were supposed to overcome this barrier. Those geared to universal bibliographic control are best represented by UNIMARC, but such formats are relatively complicated and not very suitable for the management of databases in small, specialized documentation centers. The second group of formats derived from the UNISIST reference manual is more readily usable for the design of specialized national databases. Most international information systems are in line with the UNISIST manual (e.g., RESA-DOC and AGRIS): however, they can be regarded as a third group, as they have to introduce specific features according to their particular types of operation, which do not necessarily correspond to the requirements of national databases, as well as to changes in the international systems. The last group, the common communication format, has intrinsic complications, and these formats are aligned on the basic organization of data elements found in the first group. Menou concluded that there is no format able to respond to all the constraints.[64]

Thesauri pose significant problems. Major international thesauri do not adequately cover developing nations in terms of geographical and semantic scope. This shortcoming may be rectified if information systems in developing nations pointed out these weaknesses to the institutions responsible for building and managing thesauri. In order to ensure that different geographical regions and cultures are adequately covered, the organizations responsible for developing thesauri should include representatives from the different geographical regions. For example, the U.N. High Commission for Refugees included members from Africa, Asia, Europe, and Latin America in the International Refugee Terminology Thesaurus Working Group in 1988, when they were involved in compiling the International Refugee Multilingual Thesaurus. It is also important to develop multilingual information-processing tools for developing nations, since different languages are used in the Third World (e.g., English, Spanish, and French). The language barrier is obvious in information-processing formats as well as in information-processing guidelines and thesauri. Fortunately, concerted efforts to address these issues are under way. The Arab world, for example, has been striving toward developing Arabic MARC formats and "Arabizing" other information-processing tools and systems that are crucial for the development of local databases.

Interlibrary Loan and Document Delivery

Access to relevant references identified through searching local databases, CD-ROM, online, and other electronic network resources may be frustrating because the actual documents are not locally available. Many information systems have tried to solve the problems of document unavailability through ILL and document delivery. Cornish contends that CD-ROM stimulates a demand that cannot be satisfied by making the reader aware through extensive bibliographic data of what is not available.[65] In view of the limited resources available in developing countries, ILL, document delivery, and cooperative acquisition have been recognized as vital possible solutions to the problem of collection deficiencies and document unavailability.

A wide variety of IT has been employed in ILL and document delivery, ranging from rudimentary equipment such as photocopiers to computer networks. Photocopiers have been used to provide current awareness and document delivery services, as was the case of the East Africa Literature Service and the Tanzania Literature Service.

These two services provided photocopies of tables of contents to scientists who selected relevant articles. Photocopies of the selected articles were delivered to the scientists by mail. Telex has also been used in many developing countries, mainly for requesting documents; delivery is through the mail. Requests for ILL are also often submitted by phone. Fax machines are used both for transmission of requests as well as for document delivery. E-mail has also been utilized for submitting requests. In the Arabian Gulf, E-mail requests are submitted through Gulfnet, and documents are sent by mail or through the FTP facility of Gulfnet. Other libraries in developing nations, such as the KFUPM library in Saudi Arabia, submit their requests to the British Library Lending Division through ARTTel (automated retrieval telephone). Besides utilizing IT in transmitting and receiving ILL requests, IT has been used in ILL database management.

Information technology has also played a vital role in developing and enhancing access to location tools such as online catalogs and union lists in machine-readable formats such as magnetic tapes or CD-ROMs. Guerrero points out that IT has improved availability for some of the libraries by creating union catalogs essential for identifying and locating documents. In Latin America, for example, LIBRANUM, a union catalog on CD-ROM, covers holdings in 164 departments of the National University of Mexico and included 500,000 records in 1995. The university union catalog of serial holdings also includes sixty-two other higher education institutions and research centers in the country. The National Library of Venezuela has an online union catalog containing more than 900,000 records, which contains information on monographic and serial holdings.[66]

Notwithstanding some significant achievements in utilizing information technology to enhance ILL and document delivery services, numerous barriers have impeded the optimal exploitation of IT in interlending and document delivery. Lack of adequate financial, human, and material resources, poor information policies, and inadequate information infrastructure are some of the major problems. Probably the most important problem is the nonexistence or lack of availability of adequate location tools. Ferguson suggests that librarians may overcome this problem through the development of national databases of locally published materials, and cites the example of the National Library of Jamaica whereby the development of a national database has contributed to the growth of ILL activity. Ferguson also advocates participation in sectoral information systems such as INFOTERRA, LILACS, ECLAC, and AMBIONET.[67] Cornish recommends that union catalogs that take into account uniformity of style, cataloging, practice, and formats should be combined. Since union catalogs are difficult and time-consuming to compile, Cornish suggests an alternative strategy of compiling directories of strengths of collections.[68]

Information Systems–
Information Use

An equally important issue that librarians have faced in implementing IT is the increasing demand for ILL resulting from identifying citations through searching IT-based systems for which actual documents are not owned by the local library. Barr points out this problem as follows: "It is extremely frustrating if the references are obtained but the documents to which they refer are not available." To overcome this frustration, Barr recommends that information systems in developing nations should try to obtain special funds for document delivery; measures should be taken to combine reference and document delivery of core heavily used journals; and the existing research libraries should be consolidated.[69] Kanamugire suggests that this problem may be alleviated through the production of CD-ROM products with substantive abstracts, since many libraries and information centers in developing nations do not have easy access to efficient ILL or document supply systems, and further suggests that donor agencies should allocate a budget for purchasing photocopies of references identified through CD-ROM searching.[70] In another article on the impact of CD-ROM on ILLs, Kanamugire concludes that libraries that decide to offer a CD-ROM bibliographic database search service should anticipate an increase in ILL requests and be ready to respond accordingly to the impact of CD-ROM database searching through providing more human, financial, and information resources. He also suggests that libraries offering CD-ROM index services should seriously contemplate acquiring these journals not only in hard copy, but also in CD-ROM image and microform formats.[43] Keylard suggests that information systems in developing nations use the facilities of the many CD-ROM producers that offer document delivery for references included in their databases.[38]

Many problems inhibiting document delivery and ILL in developing countries are caused by the existing poor information infrastructure. Referring to the situation in Latin America, Guerrero points out that insufficient or unreliable postal and other services lead to delays in document delivery or loss of documents.[66] To overcome the problems posed by inadequate postal services, a number of options have been advanced, but many of them are not viable. Cornish suggests that telefax could be used for requesting documents and that the requested documents could be received by normal mail since transmission of documents by fax would be prohibitively costly. This approach has been adopted by Barbados and Trinidad.[68] Similarly, Ochs recommends the use of telefax because it is efficient, cost-effective, and provides rapid delivery of documents. She further points out that some telefax machines have a feature for delayed sending, taking advantage of off-peak phone rates, and suggests that in purchasing a telefax machine, one should look for as much memory as possible in order to send a large number of pages on off-peak hours.[71] Phone lines have also been useful in requesting ILL documents as well as for receiving documents. However, they are also expensive and unreliable, and because of a lot noise and vibration, they are of low quality. Poor phone lines may lead to a distortion of image documents. Also, fax modems used for transmitting messages have to step down to lower speeds due to poor phone lines. This results in an increased communications cost and poor quality. In the short term, little can be done to improve the quality or cost of phone lines, but in the long run, librarians should continue supporting efforts to improve telecommunications infrastructure and to decrease phone charges. In addition to fax and phone media, another medium that could be used in transmitting and receiving ILL and document delivery requests are computer-based communications systems. However, many information systems have not used electronic media because online delivery is prohibitively expensive and also because of the lack of adequate data communications networks.

In addition to problems pertinent to tools of identification, document unavailability, and infrastructural problems, other key ILL/document delivery obstacles experienced by information systems in implementing IT projects include: behavioral problems, lack of equipment, secrecy and confidentiality, financial constraints, and poor collections. Oftentimes there is no budget for ILL/document delivery activities. Even when there is a budget, hard currency to pay for ILL documents is not easily available. To solve this problem, there should be a fund for document delivery. The British Council has helped many developing countries in obtaining the British Library Document Supply Center photocopy coupons by accepting payment for the coupons in local currency.

Another problem related to finance is the lack of equipment, especially photocopiers. There are insufficient and unsatisfactory photocopying machines, and even if machines are available, shortages of paper and other materials, the unavailability of spare parts, poor servicing arrangements, and frequent power failures adversely affect photocopy services in developing nations.[69] In order to solve this problem, equipment, especially photocopiers, should be one of the major components in the planning and implementation of IT projects. Also, there should be a budget for paper, toner, and other supplies. Libraries and information systems should charge for photocopy services and use the money collected for purchasing new photocopiers, for buying supplies, and for meeting other photocopy recurrent costs. Since it may be difficult in some libraries to afford a one-time purchase of a photocopier, information systems should negotiate with vendors to procure photocopiers on loan or for payment in installments. Another option of providing a photocopy service when the institution cannot afford purchasing a photocopier would be contracting a photocopier vendor/dealer to provide photocopy service in or near the library. Under such an arrangement libraries may get some discount and some other preferential benefits. The last, but

Information Systems–
Information Use

not least, major barrier to ILL/document delivery in developing nations is behavioral or attitudinal. Graham contends that information professionals are unwilling to become too involved in interlending because of fears of loss, damage, financial commitment, and inconvenience to library's home clientele.[65] Guerero argues that a major drawback in ILL/document delivery in Latin America is that a few of the larger libraries will have to deal with the great bulk of the demand, which will conflict with the needs of their own users.[66]

Although interlending has been advanced as a possible solution to the problems of inadequate collections, there are a number of obstacles that limit the effectiveness of ILL in developing nations. Mills contends that borrowing outside their own region is beyond the budgets of many libraries.[72] Allen argues that ILL is not a practical method, or even generally a legal method, for the provision of textbook material to undergraduate students. The volume of material in demand would be too large for lending libraries to handle, there would be numerous copyright hurdles to overcome, the time factor would be extremely difficult to manage, the physical format, durability, and usability of the copies so supplied would make them difficult for receiving libraries to handle, and the costs, at ruling rates of supply from the major supplying libraries, together with postal or electronic delivery charges, would almost certainly make them as expensive as purchase. He emphasized that the present ILL financial structures militate against its extensive use by developing country libraries and pessimistically concludes that the ability of librarians, however well motivated, to make any meaningful impact on the resources of developing country libraries through ILL is extremely limited.[71] Many library information systems have therefore focused their efforts on strengthening collection development activities.

Collection Development

Collection development in developing countries is fraught with many difficulties, especially financial ones. Probably no other function of libraries is so adversely affected by the lack of financial resources as that of collection development. Without adequate funds in local as well as hard currency, many libraries have failed to develop or update their information resources. This problem is compounded by the ever-skyrocketing prices of journals and books. Woolston highlighted the problems of price, foreign exchange, lengthy bureaucratic procedures, and the lack of a domestic information industry. Woolston asserts that prices that appear reasonable in, say, the United Kingdom are astronomical in Bangladesh. Worse still, it has to be paid for in hard currency, which may be difficult to come by.[74] Similarly, Kaungamno, referring to Tanzania's situation, stated that

Probably the most crucial problem facing librarians in Tanzania is the lack of foreign exchange. The local book industry faces many difficulties, and the absolute dependence on imported books threatens the existence of libraries. Libraries cannot keep their book stocks up to date. The situation has been made worse by inflationary prices all over the world, and it is difficult to get a sufficient number of suitable books.[75]

Allen clearly highlighted the problem of acquisitions in developing nations as follows:

The essential problem in the developing countries is that libraries do not have the funding to purchase the required resources in sufficient quantities from the developed world publishers. This problem is being exacerbated by the deteriorating economic situation in many developing countries, while the situation of political instability and even total collapse of civil authority in some countries, are only making an already pain situation intolerable. At a time when the librarians of major American universities are debating action to offset the escalating costs of publications, the ability of libraries in the developing countries to acquire even the most essential materials is threatening their operations with extinction.[73]

Some of the problems of inadequacy of information sources may be solved by making better use of the substantial amount of unconventional literature in the social, natural, and physical sciences produced in developing countries. However, it is extremely difficult to identify the existence of and to acquire such literature because of poor bibliographic control. Unfortunately, unconventional literature is usually produced in limited quantities and stocks are consequently used up as they are produced. Nonetheless, there have been some positive developments in bibliographic control of gray literature over the past two decades. Some donor agencies, especially the IDRC through its DEVSIS programs, has rendered assistance in developing bibliographic databases and collections to some institutions in developing countries, including the University of the West Indies in Jamaica and the PADIS in Africa. Similarly, FAO and UNFPA through their AGRIS/CARIS and POPIN programs, respectively, have significantly contributed to bibliographic control of developing country unconventional literature.

In his study on resources acquisitions and the viability of university libraries in developing countries, Allen advances one viable suggestion that IFLA could implement.

That expert subject committees be established, or the advice of specialist subject associations to select limited numbers of up-to-date text books of recommended additional readings for the support of undergraduate studies in the major disciplines taught in a majority of universities in developing countries, and that negotiations then be undertaken with the publishers of such texts for the production of special editions/printings to be made available to university libraries in developing country libraries at, or near to marginal production costs.[73]

Information Systems–
Information Use

It would demand considerable effort to convince the academic staff of university libraries in developing countries that the proposal is workable and does not imply intellectual imperialism, while publishers would also need to be persuaded that their commercial interest would not be harmed. Allen also advocated negotiations of a twin relationship between a specific library in a developing country with a specific library in a developed country. He points out that such an arrangement may do much to develop ongoing close relationships that are of cumulative value to both libraries in the partnership.

Libraries in developing nations should also take advantage of international programs that aim at addressing collection development problems. Such programs include the UNESCO coupon and twinning programs as well as the INASP project of the international Council of Scientific Unions (ICSU), which is supported by UNESCO. INASP is a cooperative network of donors and representatives of recipient institutions. It has three immediate objectives: to map, support, and strengthen existing programs involved in the distribution, local publication, exchange, and donation of books, journals, and related materials (e.g., maps and charts, audiovisual materials, software, and CD-ROM); to encourage and support new initiatives that will increase local publication and general access to quality scientific literature, and to identify methods that will permit the ongoing and sustainable exchange and distribution of scientific publications.[74]

Since it is virtually impossible for developing country governments to allocate adequate budgets for the purchase of books and journals, information systems may also benefit from the numerous institutions involved in donation programs, such as funders who provide funding for other groups to use; donors that donate books for distribution in other countries; senders and suppliers that collect books from donor and send the materials to recipients in other countries, primarily libraries; and distributors—that is, organizations in or acting on behalf of a specific country that collect or solicit donations. At times the solicited donations are in response to requests from receiving libraries for specific titles. An example of such an organization is the Asia Foundation, which distributes an average of 1 million books and journals a year to over 8,000 libraries, schools, universities, research centers, and government agencies throughout the Asia-Pacific region. The British government through its Overseas Book Development Program has played a crucial role in this respect. The British Council also accepts payment in local currency for purchasing British Library photocopy service coupons, which are then used for ordering photocopies of articles or for borrowing books from the British Library Document Supply Center. Books for Africa procures and ships books to indigenous, nongovernmental partner organizations in recipient countries that receive and distribute books to libraries and schools. It handles 500,000 books a year. Ranfurly Library Service (RLS) sends over 700,000 books overseas every year in response to urgent requests. The CTA finances a donated books program through which 44,000 of its own publications as well as an additional 10,000 non-CTA books are distributed annually. The World Bank Volunteer Book Project (WBVS) receives donations of new and used books from schools, universities, libraries, medical schools, and publishers, and ships over 120,000 books annually to several developing countries. The U.S. Information Agency (USIA) sometimes donates collections on an occasional one-time basis. The USIA book programs division also conducts programs to promote the sale and distribution of American books overseas in close collaboration with the book export efforts of the American publishing industry. The books are eventually donated to foreign institutions.

Although some libraries and information centers have benefited from gifts and exchange and other resource-sharing activities, donations and gifts and exchange programs have been criticized on a number of grounds. First, libraries are supplied with materials that are not the most desirable. As a result some key subjects may not be adequately covered, and the collection may not be updated as donations are given on an occasional one-time basis. Mills summed up the problems associated with the reliance on donations for a significant proportion, sometimes the majority, of their book stock, and pointed out that such reliance may lead to collections that are not in keeping with the needs or objectives of their users, since donations depend on what the donors are able to offer. Consequently, collection gaps, unevenness in coverage of subjects, and outdated collections may occur.[72]

Recently the concept of library twinning has been given special attention by IFLA. IFLA contends that twinning of libraries arises from the need to improve the practice of librarianship across national boundaries.[77] Nancy John listed, among other things, the following factors as being relevant to information resource sharing: exchange of information about libraries; improved access to published information in both developed and less developed countries; information about new techniques for library management and new technologies for library programs to be made available more widely in developing countries; greater awareness by libraries in developed nations of the issues facing libraries in developing countries; regular international sharing of problems at the operational level; involvement of all levels of library staff in sharing information about their problems and common concerns; and a broader view of the library profession.[78] Doyle contends that collection development seems to be the preeminent rationale for twinning arrangements with a library from another country and it leads to the acquisition of materials usually difficult or impossible to obtain using conventional methods. Moreover, twinning arrangements in resource sharing and through donation and exchange programs can help and improve delivery and collections.[79]

To tackle the immense collection development problems, a combination of traditional and innovative methods should be adopted in the acquisition of library materials. Alumni may be requested to support the library, chairs may be established, and the library may be involved in fund raising and income-generating activities. Resource-sharing efforts through ILL or cooperative acquisition have failed due to negative attitudes toward cooperation, personal conflicts, and inadequacies of human and information resources. Institutions should try to acquire U.N. and other intergovernmental publications in their areas of interest. These are often distributed free. Information systems should also acquire indigenous sources of information and use them not only for developing their own collections but also for gifts and exchange purposes. Furthermore, in cooperation with the parent organization, libraries and information centers should promote indigenous publishing, including the use of desktop publishing and online publishing tools.

User Sensitization and Training Issues

Two critical factors in successfully implementing IT projects in developing countries are user sensitization and user training. The UNESCO document Com.74/NATIS/3 highlights the issue of awareness in NATIS objective 2, which states among other things

In many parts of the world, even though information is available in the collections of documentation, library and archives services, the potential users of these facilities are unaware of their existence and the advantages they offer, or the information remains unused because it does not meet the special needs of specific sectors of the community.

The same document further recommends the following:

> In order to increase user awareness, appropriate bodies, including universities and other educational institutions should include in their progams systematic instruction in the use of the information resources available in all of the elements of NATIS. It is therefore recommended that: use of libraries should be part of instruction offered from the primary school level onwards so that seeking information becomes a normal part of daily life; the efforts of stimulation of user awareness and user education started within the educational programs should be continued in professional life, and research workers should be encouraged to seek and use the specialized literature which would help them carrying out their research and development programs.[6]

Another significant UNESCO document, *Education and Training of Users of Scientific and Technical Information: UNISIST Guide for Teachers*, clearly underscores the significance of user training.

In every country, from the least developed to the most advanced, a certainamount of scientific and technological information—locally produced or of the international origin—is processed and stored in some fashion for the benefit of users. Unless these users know how to find relevant information, the information "machinery" falls short of its main goal.[80]

Indeed, many information professionals, academics, IT experts, and regional institutions have underlined the importance of user sensitization and training in various regions of the Third World. Syed Salim Agha and Akhtar, in their study on sustaining information systems in developing countries, recommended promotion and marketing of an information system to existing and potential users in order to enhance awareness and use of its products and services.[17] Likewise, Bell asserted that information systems that are available do not always advertise themselves as well as they might, leaving the service to be discovered by those who want it. He further argued that the lack of use, or underuse of information systems, might relate to lack of user education.[19] Keylard pointed out that the bulk of users and information professionals are inexperienced.[38] In the same vein, Paez Urdaneta advocated that one of the objectives of the information implementation strategy in developing countries should be stimulating and increasing the demands.[81] The need for user sensitization and education in Africa has also been widely recognized. One of the major objectives of PADIS is to organize training courses and seminars for users of the system.[47]

In the Middle East, Alkoudasi advanced in his proposal for a structure for Arab scientific and technological information and computer networks that one of the major objectives of the envisaged IIP-ARABNET, a network linking willing S & T institutions in the Arab region, should be to enhance the national and regional capacity for information handling and use through, among other things, increasing the awareness and enhancing the capacity of potential users of information and data through the promotion of greater utilization of existing facilities (ENSTINET, KISR, RSS, SSRC, etc.), as well as orienting them toward more effective use of the available services.[82] In Saudi Arabia, one of the recommendations of the National Science Foundation (U.S.), which conducted a feasibility study in 1977 on the development plan for a national information system for science and technology for the kingdom, recommended among other things that SANCST should train users and libraries in the use of online services.[27] In the same vein, Saleh Ashoor and Zahir Khurshid conducted a study on user reaction to the online catalog at the University of Petroleum and Minerals Library (the present KFUPM library) in 1985, and identified a training program to maximize the use of the computer catalog as well as an updated manual as two of the major areas needing improvement. They subsequently recommended that there should be a help desk near the terminals staffed by librarians during specified hours to give users instructions on the use of the catalog.[83]

Information Systems–
Information Use

Information Systems–
Information Use

The objectives of user sensitization and training programs in developing countries include stimulating user awareness and use of IT-based information systems; dispelling the fear of using IT or IT phobia; dispelling misconceptions about the potential as well as limitations of IT-based systems; and imparting basic and advanced information retrieval and life-learning skills. In short, the goal of user training in developing countries should be imparting information literacy skills. The target population of user sensitization and training programs should not only include students, but must also include different types of users, ranging from policy makers, academics, researchers, professionals, and technicians to workers. Referring to online searching, Marghalani identified the need to inform the academic community about the service and recommended that an effective plan to publicize online searching service to all users should be developed.[84] Planning of user sensitization and training programs should involve all information professionals who would be directly involved in implementing the programs. Concerted efforts should be made to win the support of the organization's senior administrators. Planning and implementing awareness and training programs may be frustrating because of the lack of appreciation of the importance of information, and thus low attendance. Patience, vigilance, vigorous efforts, and flexibility are therefore vital in the planning, organization, and implementation of user sensitization and training programs. Their timing should avoid coincidence with any other major activities taking place in the organization.

In organizing a user-sensitization program, the head of the library/information center could start with enlightening the organization's management on the significance of valuable information resources and services provided by the information system. In doing so, it should be emphasized that these resources are vital for realizing the mission of the organization. This is important to win their support. The chief executive of the organization may be invited to open the event, while heads of departments may be invited to attend as well as to encourage members of their departments to attend. A combination of instructional methods and formats, including group discussions, on-the-spot demonstrations, hands-on practice, seminars, workshops, open house, videos, online tutorials, and library Web page is likely to be more effective than the lecture method. Al Hadidy, in his study on delayed online searches in Egypt, suggested that effective means of user education should include brochures, live demonstrations, and seminars in the user's departments, as well as fliers and posters. Print materials, including flip charts, simple search guides on a particular system, and handouts are useful in giving tips on effective search strategies and techniques.[33] Users cannot entirely rely on the bulky and too-detailed documentation provided by vendors; simple guides tailored to the needs of the user community are more useful.

In order to enhance user awareness about the existence and availability of information resources and services, library information systems have been involved in compiling and distributing bibliographic listings. These listings include acquisition or accession lists, bibliographies such as topical and geographic bibliographies, pathfinders, and directory information. With the application of IT, many of these bibliographic services have been computerized. For example, POPIN-Africa, a project based in the population division of the U.N. Economic Commission for Africa in Ethiopia used to produce monthly accession lists by using MINISIS CDS/ISIS software packages. POPIN-Africa also published *POPINDEX-Africa* an indexing and abstracting journal, as well as *Country Bibliographies* and the *Directory of African Demographers* out of the POPIN-Africa referral database.

In Saudi Arabia, KACST provides an electronic current awareness bulletin to researchers in the kingdom. The International Livestock Center for Africa in Ethiopia, the Tanzania Literature Service, and the Zambia Literature Service also disseminate information to their participating centers through current awareness and document delivery services based on photocopying and distributing tables of contents as well as supplying desired articles. Information systems have also used library publications such as brief information leaflets and basic guides, as well as detailed library handbooks for user sensitization. These publications are processed by using IT such as word processing and desktop publishing, such as Ventura and Page Maker. Graphic software packages have also been employed in designing publicity posters and brochures. Recently some library and information services have started disseminating information by using library home pages as well as electronic bulletins. Communications technology, especially fax machines, E-mail, and telephones are useful delivery media for disseminating information on IT systems. Special events may also be used to disseminate information. Such events may include an open house, distribution of publications, and demonstrations of IT-based resources and services.

Libraries and information centers in developing countries may take advantage of major events in the library/organization to provide awareness/user training programs. For example, the KFUMP library in Saudi Arabia uses Library Awareness Day, an annual event at which newcomers are introduced to library resources and services while the returnees are updated on the latest developments in the library to invite researchers to conduct comprehensive searches on their special areas of interest. Apart from aggressive publicity that may include the use of posters located in key important areas, announcements in the organization or library newsletter, word of mouth, and electronic bulletins, E-mail, and other electronic communication media may be effective in user sensitization. Offering free refreshments may attract a great number of children and students, while conducting comprehensive searches in users' fields of interest may lead to a positive response from researchers, faculty members, and other serious researchers. A quiz may also attract positive participation, especially if some prize is awarded. In addition to the activities mentioned above, other items that would be included in a user sensitization program would include demonstration of IT-based information services such as CD-ROM and online searching, access to network resources through national, regional, and international networks such as Bitnet nd Internet resources, and searching of online public access catalogs. Publications on IT-based systems may be distributed. Publicity information such as leaflets, fliers, or publicity jackets may be more effective than detailed documentation.

The discussion above have pointed out that for a successful implementation of user sensitization and training programs, management, marketing, communication, teaching, and evaluation skills are desirable. These skills are particularly crucial for public services information specialists who may be involved in the planning, actual implementation, and evaluation of the programs. Unfortunately, however, many public services librarians lack marketing and teaching skills. Worse still, these proficiencies are inadequately covered in many library and information science education or continuing education programs. Information professionals should therefore pursue and participate in professional development programs pertinent to information management, communication, marketing, teaching, and learning.

While the responsibility of organizing user sensitization programs may rest with the information centers or library services, user training programs may be organized and implemented in partnership with the computer services department or any other department interested in offering user training programs pertinent to IT-based information systems. It is important to evaluate user sensitization and user training programs in order to ascertain whether the programs have achieved their objectives. This may be accomplished through analyzing statistics of attendance and observing whether those who participated in user sensitization and training programs use the automated information systems and services more frequently since their participation in user training programs. A simple suggestion form may be distributed to participants during the promotion event to solicit comments and suggestions. After offering promotional events for a couple of years, an evaluation of the overall program may be conducted. A survey instrument may be used to elicit information on the magnitude, frequency, and adequacy of user-sensitization program objectives, planning and organization, content, and methods.

As for the evaluation of user training on IT-based information services, an immediate evaluation may be carried out by using a simple questionnaire instrument to elicit information on whether the patron understood the information presented in the programs—the adequacy of the information provided and the level of confidence attained in

using IT-based systems independently as a result of their participation. The simple questionnaire may be completed and submitted right after the user-training session. A more detailed questionnaire may be administered to participants or nonparticipants after a couple of months to ascertain why nonparticipants who had been identified did not attend and how useful those who attended found the programs.

CONCLUSION

This entry has discussed some major issues pertinent to planning, implementing, and managing IT projects in developing countries. It has contended that IT projects can positively contribute to socioeconomic development, but due to numerous problems, the contribution of information and IT to development has been questionable. Hardly any significant positive impact has been observed. Worse still, IT has often led to the widening of the gap between the rich and the poor within the developing world as well as between the developing and the industrialized countries. It is therefore recommended that developing countries should carefully plan for the implementation of IT projects. While the selection of hardware and software may be primarily determined by the requirements as ascertained through needs assessment, the existing IT environment, including the availability of technical support and cultural factors, should also be given serious consideration.

Although a variety of IT projects have been effectively applied to a number of operations of library information systems such as online searching, CD-ROM searching, and access to network resources, developing countries with poor information infrastructure may like to continue exploiting CD-ROM technology. Nevertheless, CD-ROM should be supplemented by access to other electronic network resources such as the Internet and intranet resources. This entry has also underscored several factors crucial for the implementation of IT projects in developing countries. Such factors include offering aggressive user sensitization, information marketing, and end-user training.

In the future, developing countries will have to apply IT to their various development activities. The question is no longer whether IT should be applied, but how it should be effectively used to solve the many diverse and complex development problems. It is strongly recommended that a strategic plan include the development and refining of new visions and adopt a partnership; a flexible and resourceful approach is vital for implementing successful and sustainable IT projects in developing countries.

REFERENCES

1. Wint, A.G. *Corporate Management in Developing Countries*, Quorum Books: London, U.K., 1995.

Information Systems–
Information Use

Information Systems–
Information Use

2. Mahoney, M. The world and sticking plasters: Or, how can we help developing countries?. Focus Int. Compar. Libr. **1996**, December *26*(3), 127–132.

3. Kaungamno, E.E.; Ilomo, C.S. Towards improving libraries, archives and documentation centers in Tanzania,. In *Libraries: Vital Factors in Development*; Kaungamno, E.E., Ilomo, C.S., Eds.; Tanzania Library Services Board: Dar-es Salaam, Tanzania, 1989; 311–397.

4. Proceedings of the International Cooperative Information Systems, Vienna, Austria, July 9–13, 1979 International Development Research Center: Ottawa, Ontario, Canada, 1980.

5. Broadbent, K.P. *Increasing Access to Scientific and Technical Information in Agriculture: An Evaluation of the CD-ROM Program for the Technical Center for Agricultural and Rural Cooperation (CTA)*, Wageningen, the Netherlands, 1994.

6. Intergovernmental Conference on the Planning of National Documentation Library and Archives Infrastructure September, 23–27, 1974. UNESCO: Paris, France.

7. Abid, A. Improving access to scientific literature in developing countries: A UNESCO program review. IFLA J. **1992**, *18*(4), 315–324.

8. De Horowitz, R.G. *Librarianship: A Third World Perspective*, Greenwood Press: New York, 1988.

9. Slameeka, V. Information technology and the third world. ASIS. **1985**, *36*(3), 178–183.

10. Mwinyimbegu, R.M. Obstacles to information technology transfer to the third world. Libr. Rev. **1993**, *42*(5), 28–37.

11. Thorpe, P. The impact of new information technology in developing countries. J. Inform. Sci. **1984**, *8*, 213–220.

12. Dosa, M.L. The consultant as information intermediary *The Challenge of Information Technology*, Proceedings of the Forty First FID Congress Hongkong September, 13–16, 1982; Brown, K.R., Ed.; North-Holland: Amsterdam, the Netherlands, 1983; 181–196.

13. Mustafa, A.S. LIS consultancy in the Arab world: The Sudanese experience. In *Information and Libraries in the Arab World*; Wise, M., Olden, A., Eds.; Library Association Publishing: London, U.K., 1994; 155–180.

14. Kanamugire, A.B. Implementing information technology in developing countries. Inform. Dev. **1993**, *9*(1\2), 56–65.

15. Wesley, C. Library and information services in the Sudan. In *Information and Libraries in the Arab World*; Wise, M., Olden, A., Eds.; Library Association Publishing: London, U.K., 1994; 181–189.

16. Hotchstadt, P.W. et al. Towards an online integrated system at the National University of Singapore Library *The Challenge of Information Technology*, Proceedings of the Forty-First FID Congress Hong Kong September, 13–16, 1982; Brown, K.R., Ed.; 1983; 41–54.

17. Agha, S.S. The responsibility and the response: Sustaining information systems in developing countries. J. Inform. Sci. **1992**, *18*, 283–292.

18. Were, J. Computerization of library services: Developments in Kenya. In *Information and Libraries in the Developing World: Sub-Saharan Africa*; Wise, M., Olden, A., Eds.; The Library Association: London, U.K., 1990, 59–82.

19. Bell, S. Issues in electronic information diffusion and information technology: The problems of diffusion, access and use in the development community. City University:

London, U.K., 1987, May A thesis submitted for the master of philosophy degree in the department of information Science.

20. L'Frantao, S. Utilization de CDS/ISIS dans les Reseaux d'Information: les Perspectives Pour l'Afrique *International Symposium on New Information Technologies in Agriculture* November, 10–12, 1993; Powell, A.P., Ed.; December 1994; 85–87 special issue Q. Bull. Agric. Inform. Spec., *XXXII*, (1–2).

21. *Horizon Hardware/Software Requirements*, Ameritech Library Services, 1994; December.

22. Hutchinson, B. Information management projects in developing countries: The challenge of working with varying levels of infrastructure. IAALD VIIIth World Congress, **1991**, *XXXVI*(1–2), 110–116.

23. Johnson, J.S. Computerizing information systems in developing countries: Keys to sustainable development. QB IAALD Q. Bull. **1992**, *XXXVII*(3), 140–143.

24. Green–Mahoney, N. The development of online information in Latin America: A perspective Proceedings of the 9th International Online Information Meeting, 1985; December 4–5, 121–130.

25. Moore, N.L. Problems of online database access in rural and isolated areas with particular attention to developing countries Proceedings of the First–West Online Information Meeting Moscow, 1989; 58–71.

26. El Hadidy, B. The breakeven point for using CD-ROM versus online: A case study for database access in a developing country. JASIS. **1994**, *45*(4), 273–283.

27. *National Science Foundation Development Plan for a National Information System for Science and Technology for the Kingdom of Saudi Arabia: Report and Appendices*, Washington, DC, 1978.

28. Bourne, C.P. Computer-based reference services as an alternative means to improve resource-poor local libraries in developing countries. Int. Libr. Rev. **1977**, *9*, 45–50.

29. Mahon, F.V. Perspectives of access to on-line information by the developing countries. UNESCO J. Inform. Sci. Libr. Arch. Admin. **1982**, *IV*(4), 239–244.

30. Woon, L.Y. Online databases and developing countries. Libri **1990**, *40*(4), 318–326.

31. Brito, J.C. The developing countries and CD-ROM. Inform. Dev. **1989**, *5*(4), 210–216.

32. Ashoor, M.S.; Kanamugire, A.B. Responding to researchers' and faculty use patterns and perceptions of CD-ROM services. Online CD-ROM Rev. **1996**, *20*(4), 172–180.

33. Al-Hadidy, B. Delayed online search: An alternative access mode for developing countries. J. Inform. Sci. **1983**, *5*, 173–185.

34. Munn, R.F. Appropriate technology and information services in developing countries. Int. Libr. Rev. **1978**, *10*, 23–27.

35. Al-Khulaifi, M. Gulfnet in Saudi Arabia: An overview. Inform. Serv. Use. **1995**, *15*(1), 53–56.

36. Song, J. International online information retrieval in China: A model for developing countries In Proceedings of the 2nd Pacific Conference on New Information Technology Singapore, 1989; May 29–31; 365–372.

37. White, W.D. CD-ROM implementation in developing countries. CD-ROM Prof. **1992**, May *5*(3).

38. Keylard, M. CD-ROM implementation in developing countries: Impacts and pitfalls. IFLA J. **1993**, *19*(1), 35–45.

39. Raseroka, K.H. The role and purpose of the university library in a rapidly changing information environment with reference to the Eastern and Southern African region. IFLA J. **1993**, *19*(1), 50–58.

40. Foullon, L. A high tech tool in developing countries. CD-ROM End-User **1990**, February, 48–51.

41. Adeniran, O.R. et al. Availability and use of CD-ROM products in Nigerian libraries and information centers. Electron. Libr. **1994**, *12*, 155–168.

42. MacLeod, R.; Chiware, E.R.T. Lessons to be learned: Information technology training in a developing country academic library. Libr. Mgmt. **1993**, *14*(6), 24–30.

43. Kanamugire, A.B. Impact of CD-ROM searching in a science and engineering library in a developing country. J. Interlibr. Loan Doc. Del. Inform. Supply Serv. **1993**, *4*(1), 25–44.

44. Kanamugire, A.B. Planning, emplementing and managing CD-ROM services in developing countries. Electron. Libr. **1997**, *15*(2), 133–141.

45. *UNISIST Study Report on the Feasibility of a World Science Information System*, UNESCO: Paris, France, 1971.

46. Neelameghan, A.; Tocatlian, J. International cooperation in information systems and services. JASIS. **1985**, *36*(3), 158–165.

47. *Pan African Documentation and Information Systems*, U.N. Economic Commission for Africa: Addis Ababa, Ethiopia, 1981.

48. Cabezas, A. Internet: Potential for services in Latin America. IFLAJ. **1995**, *21*(1), 11–14.

49. White, W.D.; Barad, B. FidoNet Technology Applications. Bull. Am. Soc. Inform. Sci. **1993**, April/May 20–21.

50. OIC Information Systems Network Project (OICIS-NET) Concept, Plans and Progress Seminar Presentation Made by Abdul Rahman Kamaruddin at KFUPM Library January, 1996 Dhahran, Saudi Arabia.

51. Environmental information systems in Sub-Saharan Africa: An Internet resource. Bull. Amer. Soc. Inform. Sci. **1995**, *30*(3), 26–27.

52. Zambrano, R. The UND sustainable development network. Bull. Am. Soc. Inform. Sci. **1995**, *30*(2), 23–24.

53. Bidet, J. The PANGIS network. Bull. Am. Soc. Inform. Sci. **1995**, *30*(2), 26–27.

54. Al-Musa, A.O. The future of GULFNET and the Internet pilot project In Paper Presented at the AGC/SLA Conference on Strengthening Resource Sharing in Libraries and Information Centers in the Arabian Gulf Region March, 15–17, 1995 UAE University: Al Ain, United Arab Emirates.

55. Sanchez Vegas, S. David meets Goliath on the information superhighway: Venezuela in the context of the electronic communications network. Inform. Tech. Libr. **1995**, March *14*(1), 32–35.

56. Westhusien, E. Electronic communication in Africa— Promotion of animal health information dissemination. Electron. Libr. **1995**, *13*(4), 299–307.

57. Ainsworth, S. Mexican information resources in electronic format. *The Bowker Annual: Library and Book Trade* Almanac, Bowker: New Providence, NJ, 1994; 70–90.

58. Levinson, A. Latin America online: Best databases for news, business and current affairs. Database **1993**, December 14–28.

59. Kigotho, W. Internet lifelines for a continent. Times Higher Ed. Suppl. **1997**, July 11.

60. Lawrie, M. Southern Africa internetworking: Where we are, where we could be. Electron. Libr. **1995**, *13*(4), 397–399.

61. Rodriguez, K. The information search in Latin American: An analysis of Latin American data-bases. Libri **1993**, *43*(3), 245–262.

62. Tasan, M.A. The role of King Abdulaziz city for science and technology in information services in the Kingdom of Saudi Arabia. J. Inform. Sci. **1992**, *18*, 491–495.

63. Kokabi, M. The internationalization of MARC Part IV: UNIMARC. Some formats based on it and some other MARC formats. Libr. Rev. **1995**, *44*(7), 8–33.

64. Menou, M.J. et al. BABINAT and the development of microcomputer-based national documentation networks in the less developed countries. Inform. Proc. Mgmt. **1991**, *27*(6), 699–712.

65. Cornish, G.P. CD-ROM: Impact on the interlending area. ABI-Technik. **1991**, *11*(1), 11–14.

66. Guerrero, E. Interlibrary loan in Latin America: Policies and practices. Interlend. Doc. Supply **1995**, *23*(3), 13–17.

67. Ferguson, S. Interlibrary lending and document delivery in the Caribbean: The perplexing reality. Interlead. Doc. Supply **1995**, *23*(2), 4–9.

68. Cornish, P.C. Interlending in the Caribbean. Int. Inform. Libr. Rev. **1989**, *21*(2), 249–261.

69. Barr, K.P. Document delivery service in developing countries. In *The Infrastructure of an Information Society*; El-Hadidy, B., Horne, E.E., Eds.; Elsevier Science Publishers B.V.: North Holland, 1984; 441–446.

70. Kanamugire, A.B. Partners in developing CD-ROM services in developing countries. Libri **1995**, *45*(2), 106–112.

71. Ochs, M. New technologies for document delivery and the barriers to their use in the developing countries. IAALD VIIth World Congress **1991**, *QXXXVI*(1–2), 118–121.

72. Mills, C. *Collection Development and Aid: Considering the Problems of Developing Collections Where Aid and Donations Are a Significant Contribution, booklet 8*, IFLA, 1993.

73. Allen, G.G. Resources, acquisition and the viability of university libraries in developing countries. Libri **1993**, *43*(3), 232–244.

74. Woolston, J.E. Information exchange in a north-south context: Is there more to gain through cooperation than in trying to establish new markets?. Aslib Proc. **1984**, *36*(1), 7–19.

75. Kaungamno, E.E. The case of Tanzania Library Services. Can. Libr. J. **1985**, *42*(4), 185–187.

76. INASP Newsletter **1995**, May *4*.

77. UNESCO. *Guidelines on Library Twinning: General Information Program and UNISIST*, U.N. Educational, Scientific and Cultural Organization: Paris, 1994.

78. John, N. IFLA projects on twinning of libraries. IFLAJ. **1991**, *27*(3), 316–317.

79. Doyle, R.P. Library twinning. IFLAJ. **1995**, *20*(4), 403–410.

Information Systems–
Information Use

Information Systems–
Information Use

80. Evans, A.J.; Kennan, S. *Education and Training of Users of Scientific and Technical Information: UNISIST Guide for Teachers*, UNESCO: Paris, France, 1977.

81. Urdenata, I.P. Information in the third world. Int. Libr. Rev. **1989**, *21*, 177–191.

82. Alkoudasi, M.T. Proposed structure for Arab scientific and technological information and computer networks Final Report Regional informatics Expert Group Meeting on "Scientific and Technological Information and Computer Networks in the Arab States." UNESCO Office for Science & Technology for Arab States: Bloodan, Syria, 1989.

83. Ashoor, M.S.; Khurshid, Z. User reactions to the online catalog at the University of Petroleum and Minerals Library. J. Acad. Libr. **1987**, *13*(4), 221–225.

84. Marghalani, M.A. Online search service at the King Abdulaziz University Library, Jeddah, Saudi Arabia. Int. Inform. Libr. Rev. **1993**, *25*(1), 27–41.

Information Technology Standards for Libraries *[ELIS Classic]*

Christinger Tomer
School of Information Sciences, University of Pittsburgh, Pittsburgh, Pennsylvania, U.S.A.

Abstract
Information technology standards, which have been an important part of librarianship in the United States for more than 70 years, are today more important than ever. The environment in which such standards arise grows increasingly complex, as the technical concerns of librarians and archivists intersect with the communities formulating technical standards for computing, networking, and digital publishing. In this entry, the nature of standards and basic aspects of the standardization process are described, key standards-making organizations are identified and their roles are assayed, and the various benefits of information-oriented technical standards are assessed.

INTRODUCTION

With the rise of digital libraries and the emergence of digital documents as the primary means of composition and publication, technical standards have become more important than ever for libraries and other information services. In fact, information technology standards may be viewed properly by librarians and archivists as blueprints for survival, because the interoperability of systems is now essential to the continuation of high-quality library and archival services.

Technical standards have been an important part of librarianship in the United States since 1939, when the American National Standards Committee Z39, the forerunner of the current National Information Standards Organization (NISO), was formed. Today, the environment in which technical standards bearing on libraries arise grows increasingly complex, as the rise of the Internet and the World Wide Web engage a wide array of organizations and interests in the development and use of technical standards, and the technical concerns of librarians and archivists have intersected with those communities formulating technical standards for computing, networking, and digital publishing. So, in the early twenty-first century, organizations like the Internet Engineering Task Force (IETF), International Organization for Standardization (ISO) and the World Wide Web Consortium (W3C) play prominent roles in the development of technical standards that have significant effects on digital libraries and archives, and on digital publishing.

Technical standards "are the basis for making many exciting and empowering things happen – like connecting one system to another, producing files on one system that can be transferred to another, and saving users money when a different manufacturer's less expensive component can be connected to their system."[1] Or, to cite another view, "[w]ithout standards no one can use intelligent machines very effectively, equipment cannot interoperate,

and all the information people are so busy creating would stay locked in files and archives, largely inaccessible."[2] Perhaps even more to the point, Lynch has written:

> We are beginning to recognize that standards documents are really a form of "public good," reflecting and recording achievements of intellectual consensus among a broad community of developers, rather than representing acts of individual creative authorship. They serve as a social construct and intellectual record.[3]

Looking ahead, it is clear that as the desire for more and more interdependence grows, technical standards will only increase in importance. It is also clear that the development of open technical standards like those developed by NISO, ISO, IETF, and W3C are critical factors in the broader advance, penetration, and benefits of information technologies.

THE NATURE OF STANDARDS

What is a standard? How are standards developed? How specifically are information technology standards developed? These are vital questions, because understanding standards and the role of standards requires an understanding of the nature of such specifications and the processes leading to their acceptance.

A number of relevant definitions are available. According to the ISO, a standard is "a document, established by consensus and approved by a recognized body, that provides, for common and repeated use, rules, guidelines or characteristics for activities or their results, aimed at the achievement of the optimum degree of order in a given context." The ISO stipulates further that standards should be based on the consolidated results of science, technology, and experience, and aimed at the promotion of optimum community benefits.[4]

Encyclopedia of Library and Information Sciences, Fourth Edition DOI: 10.1081/E-ELIS4-120044422
Copyright © 2017 by Taylor & Francis. All rights reserved.

The general view is that "a standard is the deliberate acceptance by a group of people having common interests or background of a quantifiable metric that influences their behavior and activities by permitting a common interchange." In addition, it is held that a standard represents the belief of its authors that its specifications will be "understood, accepted, and implemented by the market," and that standards are formulated with the expectations of substantial effect on the markets that they address.[5]

The British Standards Institution states that:

> . . . a standard is an agreed, repeatable way of doing something. It is a published document that contains a technical specification or other precise criteria designed to be used consistently as a rule, guideline, or definition. Standards help to make life simpler and to increase the reliability and the effectiveness of many goods and services we use. They are intended to be aspirational – a summary of good and best practice rather than general practice. Standards are created by bringing together the experience and expertise of all interested parties such as the producers, sellers, buyers, users and regulators of a particular material, product, process or service.[6]

With specific reference to information technology standards, the ISO stipulates that the "purpose of IT standardization is to ensure that products available in the marketplace have characteristics of interoperability, portability and cultural and linguistic adaptability," and that standards should therefore reflect the following "Common Strategic Characteristics": repeatability; interoperability; portability; and cultural and linguistic adaptability.[7]

TYPES OF STANDARDS

There are several types of technical standards, including conceptual and implementation standard and process and product standards. The first type of standard is the conceptual standard. Conceptual standards usually constitute the detailed articulation of a proposal to produce a new technology or induce a revolutionary change in the way in which a process is conducted. For example, the IEEE 802.3 Ethernet standard, which was conceived so that individual computer users might have access to remote facilities such as printers, is rooted in problems of effectiveness and efficiency and predicated on the idea that facilitating communications between computer users and systems resources affords a basis for maintaining high levels of both performance and service at acceptable costs. Although implementation of this conceptual standard led more or less directly to the development of the local area network and an array of technologies necessary to support specific aspects of the service envisioned in the standard, the standard itself is conceptual in nature.

The second type of standard is the implementation standard. Implementation standards are typically evolutionary as opposed to revolutionary in nature, and tend to reinforce existing industry patterns. An example of this type of standards work is efforts aimed at ensuring that a programming language, which exists in various versions, is implemented properly.

Today, the notion of the implementation standard extends to digital document formats, such as the Portable Document Format (PDF) and the OpenDocument Format (ODF). In the case of the PDF, after more than 15 years of proprietary development, Adobe Systems decided in 2007 to release the PDF specification to the Association for Information and Image Management (AIIM), with the understanding that AIIM would work with and through the ISO to establish PDF as an open standard. PDF had become a de facto global standard for information exchange and archival storage (and Adobe had already worked within the ISO process to deliver specialized subsets of PDF as standards for specific industries and functions), but the powers-that-be at Adobe decided that the most effective way to continue to advance this particular technology was to make the underlying specification an open standard, so that other developers had a readily available reference standard in implementing PDF writers, readers, and other applications. The standard, ISO 32000-1:2008, specifies "a digital form for representing electronic documents to enable users to exchange and view electronic documents independent of the environment in which they were created or the environment in which they are viewed or printed." The standard also specifies that "[i]t is intended for the developer of software that creates PDF files (conforming writers), software that reads existing PDF files and interprets their contents for display and interaction (conforming readers) and PDF products that read and/or write PDF files for a variety of other purposes (conforming products)." PDF/Archive (PDF/A) and PDF/Exchange (PDF/X) are ISO standards.

The ODF is a file format for electronic office documents, such as spreadsheets, charts, presentations, and word-processing documents. The specifications were originally developed by Sun Microsystems, in conjunction with its development of an office productivity suite called Star Office, and the standard was further developed by the Open Office Extensible Markup Language (XML) technical committee of the Organization for the Advancement of Structured Information Standards (OASIS) consortium. Based on an XML format originally created and implemented by the OpenOffice productivity suite, the open source version of Star Office, the purpose of the ODF is to establish a basis for the creation and exchange of formatted documents based on open standards and without reliance on any specific application.

The standard was published as an ISO/IEC international standard, ISO/IEC 26300:2006 Open Document Format for Office Applications (OpenDocument) v1.0.

Information Systems–
Information Use

Development of the Open Document Format continues, with the expectation that version 1.2 will approved by the ISO in 2009. Its importance was reinforced and expanded in 2007, when Microsoft announced that beginning with Microsoft Office 2007 Service Pack 2 native support for the ODF will be included.[8] Microsoft also released the specifications for the binary document formats associated with Microsoft Office, and indicated that subsequent versions of Office would also include native support for the PDF. At this writing, there is reason to believe that as a result of Microsoft's commitment to ODF, digital documents are about to enter a new and even more productive era, since the use of the ODF as the default format for documents generated under the Microsoft Office productivity suite will enhance interoperability at the document level, presumably in great measure.

A third type of standard is the product standard. Typically, a product standard described an existing product or service and establishes the characteristics of the product or service as a model for other products of the same type within a specific industry.[9] Product standards, de facto or de jure, are commonly derived from products that dominate specific markets; recent examples of de facto product standards include the file format supported by a popular computer application like Microsoft Excel or a widely used peripheral device.

Finally, there are process standards, which are concerned with the transformation of a need into a solution, but not with the products that produce the transmutation. In other words, process standards are generally device independent specifications. An example of such a standard is ISO 8879: Standard Generalized Markup Language (SGML), a meta-language providing a standard syntax for defining descriptions of classes of structured information and rules to structure information that led to the development of the Hypertext Markup Language (HTML), which is, in its various forms, an SGML document type definition (DTD). Under SGML, a set of DTDs is established, and then segments of a document (e.g., the title statement, the bibliography, or illustrations) are labeled in accord with the DTDs, thus dividing the document into named, logical elements. The advantage of using a standardized language for describing documents in structural terms is that a single source document may be processed by a wide array of applications, where those applications are capable of interpreting SGML, thus liberating the interchange of electronic documents from the realm of specific applications and proprietary document structures. Today, SGML has been superseded by the XML, which is:

> ... a simple, very flexible text format derived from SGML (ISO 8879). Originally designed to meet the challenges of large-scale electronic publishing, XML is also playing an increasingly important role in the exchange of a wide variety of data on the Web and elsewhere.[10]

HOW STANDARDS ARE MADE

The process under which standards are made varies from organization to organization, but the development process employed by NISO is, in general terms, representative. New standards are proposed by NISO's Topic Committee as a "work item," when it can be demonstrated that the proposed standard is relevant to NISO's purposes, that its development is feasible, and that it warrants the requisite investment. A proposed work item includes a working group charter, a description of the proposed standard, a suggested timeline for development, and a description of related standards. In the second phase of the process, if the work item is approved, a working group is recruited and then approved by the Topic Committee. (Approval of a work item requires that 10% of the NISO membership votes in favor of the item.) In the third phase, a work plan, timeline, and budget are created and approved by the Topic Committee. The work plan is then implemented, with the plan typically divided into a data-gathering phase and the development of the draft standard. In the fifth phase, assuming support by two-thirds of the working group, the draft standard is forwarded to the Topic Committee, with the recommendation that NISO release it as a Draft Standard for Trial Use or for ballot. If two-thirds of the Topic Committee approve, the trial use period runs from 6 to 18 months. If and when a draft standard secures the approval of the Topic Committee, the Architecture Committee, the majority of the NISO Board of Directors, and the direction of NISO's managing director or a petition from 5 or more voting members of NISO, a standard ballot is issued. Once the standard goes to ballot, there is a 60-day public review period, followed by a 45-day voting period. If a majority of the "voting pool" casts ballots and two-thirds of those votes are in the affirmative, the draft standard is approved. (Comments must be addressed and resolved before the standard is officially published.) In the next phase, the standard is submitted to American National Standards Institute (ANSI) for approval, under a nine-stage process administered by ANSI. Once ANSI approval has been secured, NISO establishes a maintenance agency or a standing committee, in either instance assuming responsibility for changes, clarification, and interpretation.[11]

THE BENEFITS OF TECHNICAL STANDARDS

Technical standards offer several important advantages. First, the process of developing technical standards affords a structured basis for exchanging relevant ideas and information. In addition, technical standards offer what has been termed a collaborative advantage, meaning that developers, particularly the developers of standards that are prospective in nature, often have a substantial amount of time in which to investigate the implications of a new

Information Systems–
Information Use

Information Systems–
Information Use

standard or a revision of an existing one. Of equal importance, open standards create a more competitive environment, and that usually provides consumers with a wider array of choices and lower prices. For organizations such as libraries and archives, standardization has been a crucial factor in making computing and networking economically feasible.

STANDARDS-MAKING BODIES

Who makes standards? The realm of standards making is a complex one, ironically lacking a high degree of standardization. Industry or interindustry groups, treaty organizations, professional organizations, government agencies, and ad hoc vendor groups each make standards.

On the international scene, the ISO is the primary standards-making body, but other organizations, such as the International Telecommunication Union (ITU) also play important, sometimes crucial, roles in the development of technical standards. The ITU has been engaged in standardization work since 1865, when the International Telegraph Union was established. The ITU became a United Nations specialized agency in 1947. It was renamed the International Telecommunications Union in 1993. An example of an ad hoc vendor group with a long-standing interest in standards making is The Open Group. Originally known as the Open Software Foundation (OSF), it was organized in 1988 for the purpose of standardizing the Unix operating system, and continues as an industry consortium to set vendor- and technology-neutral open standards for computing infrastructure. Another such group is the European Computer Manufacturers Association, which has been active in defining a framework and developing standards for Computer-Aided Software Engineering (CASE).

In the United States, the principal standards-making body is the ANSI, which charters committees and accredits other groups to formulate standards. NISO is one of the bodies that ANSI accredits for the purpose of developing standards in a specific area. Standards of the federal government, not necessarily inconsistent with the standards devised by ANSI and its allied organizations, are developed by the National Institute of Standards and Technology (NIST), with considerable influence from other federal agencies, including regulatory agencies such as the Federal Communications Commission and the nation's largest consumer of goods and services, the U.S. Department of Defense. Some unaccredited standards bodies, such as the IETF and Internet Architecture Board, are also highly influential. The IAB supports the development of documents that define standards for the Internet protocol suite. The IAB has developed these standards in order to coordinate the evolution of the Internet protocols. The majority of Internet protocol development and standardization activities takes place in the working groups of the IETF. Protocols that are to become standards in the Internet go through a series of steps: proposed standard, draft standard, and standard. Each step in this process involves increasing amounts of scrutiny and experimental testing. At each step, the Internet engineering steering group of the IETF must make a recommendation for advancement of the protocol and the IAB must ratify it for the process to move forward. If a recommendation is not ratified, the protocol is returned to the IETF for review and further development. It is a general practice of the IAB that no proposed standard can be promoted to draft standard without at least two independent implementations and the recommendation of the Internet engineering steering group. Promotion from draft standard to standard generally requires operational experience and demonstrated interoperability of two or more implementations, as well as the recommendation of the Internet engineering steering group.

THE ANSI

The ANSI is a private, nonprofit organization that approves national standards and coordinates a system for voluntary standardization. Founded in 1918, ANSI is also the U.S. representative to the ISO and the International Electrotechnical Commission (IEC). Its membership includes more than 125,000 organizations, including corporations, government agencies, and professional, technical, trade, labor, and consumer organizations.

ANSI is the official U.S. representative to the ISO and, via the U.S. National Committee, the IEC. ANSI is also a member of the International Accreditation Forum (IAF). At the regional level, ANSI is the U.S. member of the Pacific Area Standards Congress (PASC) and the Pan American Standards Commission (COPANT). It is also a member of the Pacific Accreditation Cooperation (PAC) and Inter American Accreditation Cooperation (IAAC). ANSI's mission is:

> To enhance both the global competitiveness of U.S. business and the U.S. quality of life by promoting and facilitating voluntary consensus standards and conformity assessment systems, and safeguarding their integrity.[12]

THE NISO

The NISO is accredited by the ANSI to develop voluntary technical standards for libraries, publishers, and the information industry. Its mission is to foster "the development and maintenance of standards that facilitate the creation, persistent management, and effective interchange of information so that it can be trusted for use in research and learning."[13] In addition, NISO serves as the expert technical advisory group to ANSI on international standards concerning information sciences, documentation, and libraries developed by the ISO/technical committee 46.

NISO is supported by a number of organizations, ranging from the American Library Association, the American Society for Information Science and Technology and the Modern Language Association to the Library of Congress, Online Computer Library Center (OCLC), the U.S. Government Printing Office, Reed Elsevier, and Recording Industry Association of America. At present, NISO has more than 70 voting members, who assist in the development of new standards and review all the standards developed by NISO.

In addition, the Library Standards Alliance, which has 27 members, has been established in order to provide libraries a role in NISO's activities. The members of the Library Standards Alliance include Boston College, the British Library, Columbia University, Harvard, the Library and Archives Canada, the NIST, Ohio State, Princeton, Stanford, the Universities of Chicago, Florida, Maryland, and Notre Dame, and the World Bank.

Throughout its history, NISO has been concerned with the formulation and implementation of standards that address the needs of libraries and archives, information services, publishing, and the book trade in a series of areas, including information transfer, forms and records, identification systems, publication formats, transliteration, preservation of materials, and library equipment and supplies. Today, NISO's mission includes identifying areas in which standards are needed; developing, writing, and maintaining voluntary technical standards; reviewing and updating current standards; and representing national interests in the development of international standards.

More than 35 NISO standards are currently in print, and a substantial number of other standards are being developed or revised at this writing. Standards produced to date include specifications for bibliographic information interchange, the construction and formatting of indexes, a Common Command Language (CML), interlibrary loan data elements, patron record data elements, and international standard numbering for both books and serials. Each NISO standard is reviewed as a matter of policy after five years in force.

In the past, NISO has been largely reactive in its dealings with the library community, and has not been engaged in the "incubation or early development of standardization efforts." In recent years, however, NISO has begun to work on standards-related activities that go beyond its traditional portfolio of Z39.xx standards and its relationship with ISO. According to strategic plans established in 2005, in the future NISO will be engaged in the development of other outputs, including "recommended practice documents; tools, plugins, or Web services definitions; white papers investigating and educating on new technologies; registries in support of identifiers and other processes; and creation of "living documents" such as wiki sites (with an editorial board)." Under the new framework, another goal is to accelerate the standards-making process by compressing both the incubation and testing periods for draft standards, so that the process which begins with a concept and culminates in final approval of a standard typically requires less than two years. ("Final approval" in this case is a majority vote of NISO members, not the full consensus needed for approval of an ANSI Z39-track standard.)[14] Under NISO's previous system, the initial phase of standards development in the NISO environment took two to three years. At the end of this period, a draft of the proposed standard entered into a round of comments and revisions that could take another 12–18 months, followed by a vote of the NISO membership. If the proposed standard was approved, a resolution phase followed, during which the changes necessary to achieve consensus are sought in order to finalize the standard. Finally, ANSI reviewed and approved the new standard prior to publication. It was not unusual for this process to span a period of 5–8 years. This is a formidable task, given that acceptable, useful standards must be clear and reflect consensus, neither of them being qualities that are easily achieved.[15]

CURRENT NISO STANDARDS

Some of the key NISO standards have been in place for years. Examples include the Information Interchange Format, ANSI/NISO Z39.2, which is the basis for the MARC (Machine-Readable Catalog) record and the standard for serial numbering, ANSI/NISO Z39.9. Of the newer standards, several are likely to be of critical importance, including ANSI/NISO Z39.88, the OpenURL Framework for Context-Sensitive Services, which defines an architecture for an open framework for information services in networked environments; ANSI/NISO Z39.29, which establishes rules, guidelines, and examples for bibliographic references; ANSI/NISO Z39.85, the Dublin Core Metadata Element Set, defining metadata elements for resource description in cross-disciplinary information environments; and ANSI/NISO Z39.93, the Standardized Usage Statistics Harvesting Initiative (SUSHI) Protocol, which defines an automated request and response model for the harvesting of electronic resource usage data within a Web services framework.

THE ISO

On the international scene, about 100 countries have national standards bodies that bring together experts from industry and universities to develop standards. In addition to ANSI, prominent standards-making bodies include Deutsches Institut fuer Normung (Germany), the British Standards Institution, Association francaise de normalisation (France), Ente Nazionale Italiano di Unifacatione (Italy), Nederlands Normalisatie-instituut (Netherlands), Standards Australia, the Standards

Association of New Zealand, Norges Standardiser-ingsforbund (Norway), Dansk Standard (Denmark), and the ITU. The is the organization that coordinates the activities of national standardization bodies at the international level. Together with the IEC, ISO concentrates its efforts on "harmonizing" national standards all over the world. The results of these activities are published as ISO standards.

ISO has 157 national members, out of the 195 total countries in the world. The ISO's Central Secretariat, which coordinates the system, is located at Geneva, Switzerland.

There are three categories of membership in ISO. Member bodies are national bodies that are considered to be the most representative standards body in each country. Member bodies are the only members of ISO that have voting rights. Correspondent members are countries that do not have their own standards organization. Subscriber members are countries with small economies. Correspondent and subscriber members are informed about ISO's work, but they do not participate in standards-making process.

As a matter of policy, ISO standards are developed on the basis of consensus, taking into account the interests and views of manufacturers, vendors and users, consumer groups, testing laboratories, governments, engineering professions, and research organizations. ISO standards are intended to be global solutions that address and satisfy the requirements of industries and consumers on a worldwide basis. Finally, ISO standards are voluntary, and their promulgation is based on the view that international standardization is and should be a market-driven process.

ESTABLISHING ISO STANDARDS

There are three principal phases in the ISO standards development process. In the first phase, the need for a standard is articulated, usually within an industrial sector, and then communicated to a national member body. The national member body then proposes the new work item to ISO. If the need for an international standard is recognized, the technical scope of the proposed standard is defined, usually by a working group of experts from countries interested in the subject matter of the proposed standard.

Once agreement has been reached by the working group on the technical aspects to be covered under the proposed standard, the second phase of the process begins, during which the detailed specifications of the proposed standard are reviewed and revised by representatives of the member bodies. It is during this phase of the process that the consensus building necessary for the eventual approval of the proposed standard occurs. In the final phase of the process, the draft standard is taken to ballot, with formal approval requiring affirmation by two-thirds of the ISO members that have participated actively in the standards-development process and 75% of all members voting on the draft standard. Following formal approval,

the text of the standard is published as an ISO International Standard. (Most standards require periodic revision, owing to factors such as technological evolution, new methods and materials, and new quality and safety requirements. Consequently, ISO mandates that all standards should be reviewed at least once every five years.)

At this writing, ISO has published more than 16,000 standards, including the metric system of units, international stationery sizes, rules for technical drawings, electrical connectors, security regulations, computer protocols, file formats, bicycle components, ID cards, programming languages, international standard book numbers (ISBN), barcode symbology, and RFID. Within the ISO, the ISO/IEC Joint Technical Committee 1, which is maintained in collaboration with the IEC, deals with information technology. The ISO/IEC Joint Technical Committee 1 was formed in 1987 by merging ISO/TC 97 (Information Technology) and IEC/TC 83, with IEC//SC 47B joining later, thereby establishing a single approach to information technology standardization by and for the two parent organizations. Its mandate is to develop, maintain, promote, and facilitate information technology standards in the following areas:

- Design and Development of IT Systems and Tools
- Performance and Quality of IT Products and Systems
- Security of IT Systems and Information
- Portability of Application Programs
- Interoperability of IT Products and Systems
- Unified Tools and Environments
- Harmonized IT Vocabulary, and
- User-Friendly and Ergonomically Designed User Interfaces.

Membership in the ISO/IEC Joint Technical Committee 1 is open to any national body within either of the parent organizations. Other organizations may participate as liaison members. Membership in the ISO/IEC Joint Technical Committee 1 expanded substantially in 2007, immediately prior to the initial vote on Office Open XML as DIS (Draft International Standard) 29500.

ISO STANDARDS RELEVANT TO LIBRARY AND INFORMATION SERVICES

Although the ISO is engaged in the development of standards in many different areas, most of the ISO standards that are applicable to libraries and related information services are standards addressing specific issues in computing and networking. There is, for example, the Linux Standard Base (LSB), a joint project by several Linux distributions under the organizational structure of the Linux Foundation to standardize the software system structure used with the Linux operating system. The LSB, which is based on the POSIX (Portable Operating System Interface) specification, the Single UNIX Specification,

Information Systems–
Information Use

and several other open standards, was submitted for approval as ISO/IEC 23360 in 2008. Another recent example is the PDF. Developed by Adobe Systems for document exchange and in widespread use since the mid-1990s, PDF was officially published as an open standard in 2008, as ISO 32000-1:2008. PDF encapsulates a complete description of a fixed-layout two-dimensional document (and, with Acrobat 3D, embedded 3D documents), including the text, fonts, images, and vector graphics which comprise the document. Last but not least, there is ISO 8879: 1986, which describes the SGML, a format for storing documents together with their logical structure and layout information in a standardized scheme and the basis for the HTML, and which is effectively the precursor of contemporary documents standards, such as ISO/IEC 29500-1-4:2008, which defines a set of XML vocabularies and other conventions for representing word-processing documents, spreadsheets, and presentations, based on the Microsoft Office 2008 applications, and ISO/IEC 26300:2006 Open Document Format for Office Applications (OpenDocument) v1.0, which defines an XML schema for office applications and its semantics in more expansive terms.

An ISO standard more directly relevant to the interests of libraries (and illustrative of the conditions that influence the evolution of technical standards) is ISO 23950, also known as ANSI/NISO standard Z39.50. Designed as a protocol for searching and retrieving information, usually from bibliographic records, Z39.50 specifies procedures and formats for a client to search a database provided by a server, retrieve database records, and perform related information retrieval functions.

Z39.50's design predates the World Wide Web, relying on now largely outmoded connection oriented, program-to-program communication. As a result, substantive work aimed at updating and revising the protocol has been under way since 2000, leading thus far to the development of two new protocols, SRU (Search and Retrieve via URLs) and SRW (Search/Retrieve Web Service), and a synthetic query language, the Contextual Query Language (CQL), intended to support their implementation. (The CQL is a formal language for representing queries to information retrieval systems. The language represents an effort to combine the qualities of more powerful, more expressive query languages such as SQL, PQF, and XQuery with simpler, more intuitive languages, such as the CCL and Google's search syntax.) The suite encompassing SRU, SRW, and CQL was originally called "Z39.50 Next Generation," and then later it was known as "Z39.50 International Next Generation" (ZING). Today, neither designation is used. Development of SRW/SRU/CQL began in 2000. An experimental version, 1.0, was released in 2002, and the first official version, 1.1, in 2004. A minor revision, 1.2, was released in 2007.[16]

SRU is based on Representational State Transfer (REST), a collection of network architecture principles that specify how resources are defined and addressed, and enables queries to be expressed in URL query strings. SRW uses SOAP, the Simple Object Access Protocol, a specification for exchanging structured information within the framework of Web services, as the basis for the expression of queries. SRU and SRW address the same information retrieval problems that Z39.50 confronted, each of them relying on XML as their message and results format.[17]

The OASIS Search Web Services Technical Committee is developing a unifying model for Web-based search and retrieval services that incorporates SRU/CQL and Amazon's OpenSearch, with the expectation that other protocols will be integrated into this model at a later date.[18] One of the goals of this effort is to lower the barrier to entry for developers through a reliance on existing Web services technologies.

Other, library-oriented ISO standards include: ISO 15511:2003 Information and documentation—International Standard Identifier for Libraries and Related Organizations (ISIL); ISO 9230:2007 Information and documentation—Determination of price indexes for print and electronic media purchased by libraries; ISO/TR 21449:2004 Content Delivery and Rights Management: Functional requirements for identifiers and descriptors for use in the music, film, video, sound recording, and publishing industries; and ISO 11620:2008 Library performance indicators.

W3C

The W3C was established in 1994, as an industry consortium dedicated to building consensus around Web technologies through the creation of relevant standards and guidelines. Tim Berners-Lee, who invented the World Wide Web in 1989 while working at the European Organization for Nuclear Research (CERN), was one of the founders and has served as the W3C Director since its inception.

Since 1994, W3C has published more than 110 such standards, called W3C Recommendations. The goal of the W3C is to maintain and promote "Web interoperability," which means that for the World Wide Web to reach its full potential, the basic technologies must be device and platform independent, vendor neutral, and fully compatible with one another. The W3C works to avoid the fragmentation of the Web by developing and publishing open, nonproprietary standards for Web languages and protocols. According to Berners-Lee:

W3C is where the future of the Web is made. Our Members work together to design and standardize Web technologies that build on its universality, giving the power to communicate, exchange information, and to write effective, dynamic applications—for anyone, anywhere, anytime, using any device.

Information Systems–
Information Use

In 2008, the W3C has more than 400 member organizations from more than 40 countries. As part of its dedication to the internationalization of the Web, the W3C instituted a number of changes to its fee structure in 2005 to encourage participation from organizations in developing countries.

W3C's operations are supported by a combination of dues, research grants, and other sources of public and private funding. The MIT Computer Science and Artificial Intelligence Laboratory (CSAIL), the European Research Consortium for Informatics and Mathematics (ERCIM), and Keio University in Japan, provide administration jointly. In addition, the W3C maintains regional offices around the world, to promote W3C technologies in local languages, broaden its geographical base, and encourage international participation.

A main focus of the activities of the W3C is to make the World Wide Web and its services "available to all people, whatever their hardware, software, network infrastructure, native language, culture, geographical location, or physical or mental ability." Work in areas such as Web accessibility, internationalization, device independence, and the so-called mobile Web is emphasized. (The goal of W3C's Mobile Web Initiative (MWI), which was launched in 2005, is to make Web access from any kind of device as simple, easy, and convenient as Web access from a desktop.) In addition, the W3C is committed to fostering "technologies that enable a more collaborative environment, a Web where accountability, security, confidence, and confidentiality are all possible, and where people participate according to their individual privacy requirements and preferences."

W3C ACTIVITIES

W3C activities are organized into groups: Working Groups (for technical developments), Interest Groups (for more general work), and Coordination Groups (for communication among related groups). The groups, made up of participants from Member organizations, the Team, and Invited Experts, produce technical reports, including Web standards, open source software, and services. These groups also ensure coordination with other standards bodies and technical communities. At this writing, there are currently 23 activities incorporating and managing 77 groups.[19]

MAJOR W3C ACHIEVEMENTS

W3C's most important achievements fall into four broad categories. First, there are the specifications that relate to digital documents, including Cascading Style Sheets, HTML, the Document Object Model (DOM), XML, and Compounds Document Formats. Second, there are the metadata standards, RDF and OWL. These technologies, which have been designed to support the Semantic Web by providing structured descriptions and addressing ontological issues, respectively, provide a standardized framework for asset management, enterprise integration, and the sharing and reuse of data on the Web.

Third, there are the access-oriented initiatives, including the Web Accessibility Initiative (WAI), the MWI, the Internationalization Activity, and the development of standards supporting multiple, simultaneous modes of interaction. Finally, there are the coordinating efforts aimed at providing the infrastructure necessary to realize the goals embedded in Berners-Lee's notion of the Semantic Web. An example of this sort of activity is the work done by the Technical Architecture Group and expressed in *Architecture of the World Wide Web, Volume One*.[20]

THE IMPORTANCE OF TECHNICAL STANDARDS IN LIBRARIANSHIP

Standards, which are important to any organization that proposes to connect technologies of different types and made by different manufacturers, are especially important to libraries, because neither libraries nor librarians are able to exercise great influence over the creation or design of the technologies on which so much of their future depends. With the emergence of digital libraries, the reliance on standards has expanded, including not only hardware and software, but also digital documents, metadata, network-based services, and schemes for accounting and management of related information activities. Perhaps more to the point, a generation of documentation has been built on the basis of various digital document formats, including the Microsoft Office formats and the PDF, as well as open HTML and XML, and as we look to the future, there is reason to believe that the work of the W3C in the area of compound document formats will become increasingly important, as various agencies work to make digital documents richer, more informative, and more useful.

In each instance, the key issue is and will continue to be interoperability, which is defined under ISO/IEC 2382 Information Technology Vocabulary as "the capability to communicate, execute programs, or transfer data among various functional units in a manner that requires the user to have little or no knowledge of the unique characteristics of those units." From a systematic perspective, interoperability assumes that the objects of interaction, including metadata, can be exchanged across systems, that as a result an aggregated content layer may be constructed on the basis of resources drawn from a distributed system of digital libraries, and that technological standards enabling different kinds of interoperability, including more traditional approaches geared toward librarian metadata interoperability such as Z39.50, harvesting methods based on OAI-PMH (Open Archives Initiative-Protocol for Metadata Harvesting), and/or Web service-based approaches, constitute a critical dimension in achieving and maintaining this capability.

THE FUTURE

As always, the future is uncertain. However, if recent history is a sign, it is likely that more and more standards bearing on information technology in general and libraries in particular will be formulated and promulgated. The reasons will be many and varied, but in the end the proliferation of standards (and standards-making bodies) will constitute a collective, rational response to the increasing complexity of the information environment, as well as an expression of the need for continuity, both diachronically and synchronically.

It seems reasonable to imagine, too, that the standards-making process itself will be a matter of increasing interest, particularly as the economic benefits of standards in information technology and allied areas are more clearly understood.[21,22] Such trends will intensify the longstanding debate over the speed and complexity of the standards-making process, especially when it is coupled with the growing sense that the responsibility for maintaining, information technology and library standards has become too diffuse and perhaps too chaotic.

REFERENCES

1. Campbell, N. Standards are key to information. OCLC News November/December **1992**, *17*, 200.
2. Libicki, M.C. *The Common Byte, or, Why Excellent Information Technology Standards Are Both Absolutely Essential and Utterly Impossible*; Research draft of the Program on Information Resources Policy, Center for Information Policy Research, Harvard University: Cambridge, MA, 1992.
3. Lynch, C. *The Case for New Economic Models To Support Standardization Efforts.* Information Standards Quarterly 1999, *11* (2), 5–10. (accessed April 24, 2009).
4. ISO/IEC Guide 2:2004, definition 3.2.
5. Cargill, C.F. *Information Technology Standardization: Theory, Process, and Organizations*; Digital Press: Bedford, MA, 1989.
6. http://www.bsi-global.com/en/Standards-and-Publications/About-standards/What-is-a-standard/. (accessed May 2, 2009).
7. See ISO/IEC JTC 1 Directives, Edition 5, Version 3.0, http://www.iso.org/iso/standards_development/supporting_services/information_technology_task_force.htm (accessed December 15, 2008).
8. *Microsoft Expands List of Formats Supported in Microsoft Office*, http://www.microsoft.com/Presspass/press/2008/may08/05–21ExpandedFormatsPR.mspx (accessed December 4, 2008).
9. Cargill, C.F. *Information Technology Standardization: Theory, Process, and Organizations*; Digital Press: Bedford, MA, 1989, 33.
10. Extensible Markup Language, World Wide Web Consortium, http://www.w3.org/XML/ (accessed May 2, 2009).
11. Wetzel, K. *Standards Development: An Overview*; NISO, 2008.
12. See *ANSI Overview*, http://www.ansi.org/about_ansi/overview/overview.aspx (accessed February 7, 2009).
13. *About NISO*, http://www.niso.org/about/ (accessed December 6, 2008).
14. *Notes from the LITA Standards IG meeting, June 2007*, http://dltj.org/article/lita-standards-ig/ (accessed February 7, 2009).
15. Standards 101. Inform. Stand. Quart. January **1992**, *4*, 6–7.
16. CQL: Contextual Query Language (SRU Version 1.2 Specifications). 2007. http://www.loc.gov/standards/sru/specs/cql.html (accessed February 7, 2009).
17. Morgan, E.L. An introduction to the search/retrieve URL service (SRU). Ariadne **2004**, (40), http://www.ariadne.ac.uk/issue40/morgan/intro.html (accessed June 2008).
18. Denenberg, R. Search Web Services—The OASIS SWS technical committee work the abstract protocol definition, OpenSearch binding, and SRU/CQL 2.0. D-Lib Magazine *15*(1/2), http://www.dlib.org/dlib/january09/denenberg/01denenberg.html (accessed February 7, 2009).
19. *World Wide Web Consortium Process Document*; 2005. http://www.w3.org/2005/10/Process-20051014/ (accessed February 7, 2009).
20. *Architecture of the World Wide Web, Volume One.* W3C Recommendation December 15, 2004. Latest version, http://www.w3.org/TR/webarch/ (accessed February 7, 2009).
21. Tiemann, M. An objective definition of open standards. Comput. Stand. Inter. **2006**, *28*, 495–507.
22. Neus, A.; Scherf, P. Opening minds: Cultural change with the introduction of open-source collaboration methods. IBM Syst. J. **2005**, *44* (2), 215–225.

Information Systems—
Information Use

Information Theory

Paul B. Kantor

School of Communication and Information, Rutgers University, New Brunswick, New Jersey, U.S.A.

Abstract

Information theory "measures quantity of information" and is that branch of applied mathematics that deals with the efficient transmission of messages in an encoded language. It is fundamental to modern methods of telecommunication, image compression, and security. Its relation to library information science is less direct. More relevant to the LIS conception of "quantity of information" are economic concepts related to the expected value of a decision, and the influence of imperfect information on that expected value.

THE FUNDAMENTALS OF INFORMATION THEORY

Information theory traces its origin to technical work done by Claude Shannon of Bell Laboratories, in the late 1940s.[1] Communication engineers wanted to determine the largest amount of information that could be transmitted when noise on the "channel" (which was, at the time, a cable carrying electrical waves) made the signal at the receiving end different from what was originally sent.

Shannon introduced measures of the amount of information, of the capacity of a channel and of the noisiness of the channel, and by combining them was able to prove important mathematical results relating the "rate of transmission of information" to the "capacity of the channel" and the amount of "noise."

Unpredictability, Random Variables, and Information

The capacity required to transmit a message, even through a channel which has no noise in it at all, depends on the unpredictability of the characters in the message.

The discussion of unpredictable messages requires the mathematical concept of a "random variable." An entity is represented mathematically as a random variable when it may take any one of a specified set of values, and, over the long term, the relative frequencies of those alternatives remain steady. The frequencies will then converge to numbers which represent the probabilities of the several alternatives. The choice among them is (subject to these probabilities) not controlled by any known forces, and thus is regarded as random. As an example, the result of a coin toss can be represented by a random variable. In the field of economics, the concept is extended to events that do not repeat many times, and one speaks of "the probability of a nuclear reactor accident" or similar rare events.

A random variable is completely characterized by specifying the allowed set of values, and the probability that it takes on each of its possible values. We can represent this by displaying the alternatives and the probabilities together in an array, as shown in Eq. 1:

$$FairCoin = \begin{bmatrix} .5 & .5 \\ head & tail \end{bmatrix}; \; BiasedCoin = \begin{bmatrix} .8 & .2 \\ head & tail \end{bmatrix}$$

$$(1)$$

The expression in brackets corresponding to the random variable *FairCoin* means that the event "head" occurs with probability 0.5 or 50%. So does the complementary event "tail." The second expression represents a random variable, *BiasedCoin*, which assumes the value "head" 80% of the time and the value "tail" only 20% of the time.

Equally Probable Alternatives

Shannon showed that the relation between the amount of information in a message and the number of different possible values that the message might have is a logarithmic one. This can be understood in an intuitive way by the following simple argument. Suppose that we have to send a message about which of three alternatives, let us say {A, B, or C} is true. And we also have to send a message about which of some other four alternatives, let us call them {1, 2, 3, 4} is true. For example, suppose we want to specify that we will meet for one of three meals, {breakfast, lunch, or dinner}={A,B,C}, and will do so on one of four days: {Monday, Tuesday, Wednesday, or Thursday}={1,2,3,4}.

Whatever the amount of information required to specify one out of three alternatives is, and whatever the amount of information required to specify one out of four alternatives is, taken together the amount of information that they provide is enough to specify one out of 12 alternatives, as there are $12 = 4 \times 3$ possible combinations. The only continuous

Encyclopedia of Library and Information Sciences, Fourth Edition DOI: 10.1081/E-ELIS3-120043262

Copyright © 2017 by Taylor & Francis. All rights reserved.

function which has the required property: that it be additive when its arguments are multiplied, is the logarithm.

Therefore, when there are N equally possible alternatives, the "amount of information" required to specify one of them should be related directly to the logarithm of N. Logarithms may be computed to any base. It is customary in communication to compute the logarithm to the base 2. The resulting number is measured in "bits" (binary digits). For example, $\log_2(8) = 3$ bits.

Varying Probabilities and the Entropy Measure

The situation is more complicated when the alternatives are not equally probable, which leads to the very important concept of entropy. The entropy, or amount of disorder, is a concept previously known for physical systems, which Shannon used very effectively in the discussion of messages.

Shannon showed that this unpredictability could be characterized by a numerical function which is called the entropy of the message. The higher the entropy of the message, the longer the string (or the larger the "alphabet") required to transmit it accurately, and the more "information" it carries.

The entropy is a mathematical function which represents the amount of uncertainty presented by a random variable, in terms of the set of probabilities of the outcomes. If the values of a particular random variable whose name is X are represented by the numbers $1, 2, 3, \ldots, n$, and their corresponding probabilities are represented as p_1, p_2, p_3, $\ldots$, p_n then the entire random variable can be represented, in the notation of Eq. 1 as

$$X = \begin{bmatrix} p_1 & p_2 & p_3 & & p_n \\ & & & \ldots & \\ 1 & 2 & 3 & & n \end{bmatrix}. \tag{2}$$

The entropy of this random variable, $H(X)$ is defined by the equation:

$$H(X) = - \sum_{i=1}^{n} p_i \log_2(p_i) \tag{3}$$

If a particular alternative cannot occur, the corresponding term in the sum is 0. If, for example, there are 16 alternatives, and each of them is equally likely, then each of the probabilities $p_i = 1/16 = 2^{-4}$. Thus $-\log_2(p_i) = 4$. The whole sum consists of 16 identical terms, each equal to $-p_i \log_2(p_i) = 1/16 \times 4$, and thus the sum (the entropy) is equal to 4. This is precisely the logarithm to the base 2, of the number of equally probable alternatives. It can be shown mathematically that this is the largest value that the entropy can have, when there are 16 possible alternatives. If, for example, one of them were enormously more probable than the others, one of the terms in the sum

would have the value $-(1-\delta)\log_2(1-\delta)$ (where δ is a very small positive number). This number becomes proportional to δ when δ is small, and vanishes as δ goes to zero. At the same time, all of the other terms in the sum vanish because they have vanishingly small probability. So when one of the possible outcomes is nearly certain, the entropy is nearly 0. The entropy formula can be shown to satisfy all other requirements of a "reasonable" measure of the quantity of information, and it is unique, up to a constant factor. We have, in effect, selected that constant factor by choosing to use logarithms to the base 2, rather than to the base 10, or the base of natural logarithms, e.

The Entropy of a String of Characters

The entropy can be defined for any situation in which there is a series of events or symbols, which are determined to some degree, by those that precede them. As a concrete example, we might consider an alphabet containing only the three letters a, b, c. From these 3 letters we can form 9 ($= 3 \times 3$) two letter "words": *aa, ab, ac, ba, bb, bc, ca, cb, cc*. Similarly we can form 27 ($= 3 \times 3 \times 3$) three letter "words": *aaa, aab, aac, aba, abb, abc, aca, acb, acc, baa, bab, bac, bba, bbb, bbc, bca, bcb, bcc, caa, cab, cac, cba, cbb, cbc, cca, ccb, ccc*. Thus it would appear that when we specify which one of those three-letter sequences occurs, we have specified 1 out of 27 possibilities. If they are equally likely, then the entropy, or amount of information, will be given (to three decimal places) by $\log_2(27) = 4.755$. On the other hand, if we know in advance that the three letters will *form a complete word in the English language*, there is only one possibility, and the amount of information conveyed when we see the string *cab* is, in the sense of information theory, 0. Finally, if we know only that the string will be the whole or a part of an English word, then there are several more possibilities, including *acc, bab, bac*, and perhaps others. In this case the amount of information conveyed when we see the string is greater than 0, but less than 4.755. Thus, in the sense of Information Theory, the amount of information conveyed by a message is related to the number of possible messages that might have been received.

This concept has been applied, on a character-by-character basis to compute the entropy of the English alphabet, given that the 26 letters (and the space character) are being used to form (possibly meaningless) English expressions. The result is usually given as about 1.5 bits per letter.[2] (Luenberger[2] is an excellent introduction for a reader comfortable with elementary algebra, elementary calculus, and elementary probability.)

The Mutual Information in a Pair of Random Variables

When there are two random variables that have some relation to each other, the strength of that relation can be

Information Systems–
Information Use

measured in many ways. Shannon approached this problem by considering the amount of information in the pair of random variables (observed together) and comparing that to the amount of information in observation of each of the variables separately. Specifically, using the definition of entropy as given above, we can calculate the entropy of each variable separately, and of the two variables together. This is somewhat complicated, and example calculations are shown in Table 1.

Combining the information in Table 1, we calculate the Mutual Information $M(X,Y)$ of the two random variables X and Y according to the formula of Eq. 4.

$$M(X,Y) = H(X) + H(Y) - H(X,Y)$$
$$M(meals, days) = 1.44 + 1.79 - 2.91 \qquad (4)$$
$$M(meals, days) = 0.32 \text{ bits}$$

This is a relatively weak relationship. A stronger one is shown in Table 2. The mutual information in that case is, in fact, precisely equal to the information about which meal I designate. The joint information is precisely equal to the information about the day on which I meet. This is because, when the day is specified, with these probabilities, the meal is completely determined, and knowing the meal in addition to the day, adds no information. Note that although the day determines the meal, and the meal does not determine the day, the mutual information is symmetric.

This is because, if we want to convey information about the meals, by reporting only the days, we can cleverly choose the "days" to remove the ambiguity. Note that we have moved here from describing a "real world" to a situation where we are trying to exploit the probabilistic relation between meals and days to convey information about one of the two, when it is expressed in terms of the other. So the connection to Shannon theory is to imagine that, for example, we want to tell someone about the day, but the nature of our "communication channel" is such that when we choose a day, the recipient is told the name of a meal, according to the probabilities specified.

The situation in Information Theory has some additional freedom for the sender of the message. I could choose to use the "days" as a kind of code. For example, I might represent the letter P by the code string {Monday, Thursday, Tuesday}. The situation becomes quite complex, and this entry provides only a brief introduction.

The reader may verify, by detailed calculations, that if there is a one-to-one correspondence between the two variables, the mutual information is equal to the information in either of them separately.

Communication and Mutual Information

Being employed by the telephone company, Shannon was concerned with the real-world situation in which the

Table 1 The information in joint variables and in the variables separately.

Case I
Probabilities

	Breakfast	Lunch	Dinner	Which day (1)	Logarithms ([4])
Monday	10%	30%	10%	50%	−1.00
Tuesday	0%	15%	0%	15%	−2.74
Wednesday	5%	0%	10%	15%	−2.74
Thursday	5%	10%	5%	20%	−2.32
Which meal (2)	20%	55%	25%	100%	H(days) = 1.79
Logarithms (5)	−2.32	−0.86	−2.00	*1.44* = H(meals)	

The numbers in the cells represent the probability that my lunch meeting falls on each specified meal and day. Let us say that I meet only once per week. Thus there is a 30% chance that the meeting, in a particular week is Monday lunch. There is only a 5% chance that the meeting of the week, for me, is Thursday dinner. Of course these numbers add up to 100% as shown in the lower corner of the table. We can also compute the probability that I meet on each particular day (1), or that I meet for each particular meal (2). These sets of numbers themselves each sum to 100% separately. Using an additional column (4) to record the logarithms (to the base 2) of the "by day probabilities" I have enough information to compute the entropy of the "by day" information. It is 1.79 bits. [Each logarithm is multiplied by the probability to its left, and the products are summed]. This is the amount of information conveyed, or the amount of uncertainty resolved, by determining on which of the 4 days I meet for a meal. Note that although there are four possible days, this amount of information is less than 2 = Log([4]) because the days are not equally likely. Similarly, I could work with the totals in the columns, multiplying them each by their logarithms, and summing the results to yield the entropy of the "which meal" information, which is 1.44 bits. This is less than 1.58 = Log (3), again because the meals are not equally likely.

Logarithms	Breakfast	Lunch	Dinner	
Monday	−3.32	−1.74	−3.32	
Tuesday	0.00	−2.74	0.00	
Wednesday	−4.32	0.00	−3.32	
Thursday	−4.32	−3.32	−4.32	H(meals, days) = **2.91**
Mutual Information = 1.44 +1.79 − 2.91 = 0.32				

Finally, we can calculate the information in the array of information about days and meals. To see how this works, we display the logarithms of the probabilities in this small table. Multiplying each logarithm by its corresponding probability, and summing the numbers yields the entropy of the joint distribution. This is the number, 2.91, referenced in the text.

Table 2 A stronger information relation.

Probabilities

	Breakfast	Lunch	Dinner	Which day	Logarithms
Monday	10%	0%	0%	10%	−3.32
Tuesday	0%	35%	0%	35%	−1.51
Wednesday	0%	0%	45%	45%	−1.15
Thursday	0%	10%	0%	10%	−3.32
Which meal:	10%	45%	45%	100%	H(days) = **1.71**
Logarithms	−3.32	−1.15	−1.15	*1.37* = H(meals)	

The numbers above could represent the fact that if I send a message such as "Monday" it will **definitely** arrive as "Breakfast."

Logarithms	Breakfast	Lunch	Dinner	
Monday	−3.32	0.00	0.00	
Tuesday	0.00	−1.51	0.00	
Wednesday	0.00	0.00	−1.15	
Thursday	0.00	−3.32	0.00	H(meals, days) = **1.71**
Mutual Information = 1.71 + 1.37 − 1.71 = 1.37				

signals initially sent over a telephone cable could be distorted or affected by "noise," with the result that the signal received at the other end of the cable is not precisely the one that was transmitted. To address this problem, he defined two concepts: *the rate of information transfer*, and the *capacity of the channel* (or cable) itself.

As suggested above, suppose that we wish to send information as to which specific day we have in mind. But we are constrained to do this not by naming the *day*, but by, instead "transmitting" specific information about *which meal* we ate, and asking the recipient to decode that information, and decide which *day* we mean. To be specific, in Table 3, we show a relationship in which only the day "Tuesday" corresponds to more than one meal. If we avoid "Tuesday" then the message that he receives will be unambiguous. For example, if we want to indicate "Monday" he will receive the message "Breakfast." And he will know that this corresponds only to Monday. But we have to avoid Tuesday because in that case the message could be either "Breakfast" or "Dinner" and this will introduce ambiguity into the decoding.

We can choose how often we send the message corresponding to each particular day. As we have mentioned above, balancing them equally will transmit the largest amount of information, provided that we never choose Tuesday. This is because Tuesday sends an ambiguous message: the meal might be breakfast or dinner. If we choose among the remaining days in an unbalanced way, we decrease the amount of information that we can transmit.

Using these ideas, Shannon was able to establish his Second Theorem of communication. This expresses the amount of information that can be communicated. The highest possible amount is called the capacity of the channel. In its most fundamental form this is given in terms of maximizing the mutual information, as described above.

$$
Capacity \left\{ \begin{array}{c} When\ a\ message \\ about\ X\ is\ received\ it \\ terms\ of\ signals\ Y \end{array} \right\} = \underset{all\ distributions\ of\ X}{\text{maximum}} M(X,Y)
$$

(5)

Here, the maximum means that we choose how often each message X is sent, in order to get the best possible communication. Strictly speaking, as was articulated by subsequent research, this is the limiting rate when the source of the message is "ergodic," which means, roughly, unpredictable, or having maximum entropy when viewed as a sequence of characters in whatever alphabet is being used.[3] There are many implications of this formula. Some variants deal with the specific case where the values assumed by the variables X and Y are both binary. Other variations take account of the entropy of the message to be sent.

In all real cases the difficult technical problem is to find a scheme for encoding which comes as close as possible to the theoretical limiting rate. This involves considerable ingenuity, and there are many open problems.

In addition to this mathematical and engineering focus of Information Theory, the book by Shannon and Weaver,[1] included a speculative essay by Weaver on the possible general implications of these results for behavioral sciences in general, and opened other worlds for exploration.

INFORMATION THEORY TODAY

Sixty years later the field of Information Theory, whose central professional society is the IEEE Society for Information Theory, is flourishing. The problem of finding the actual encoding which will come close to the Shannon theoretical limit is a difficult one leading into complex fields of mathematics.

The corresponding methods for the compression of information are part of our everyday lives, especially for users of the Internet. They range from the use of zipped compression to reduce the size of files, to the complex compressions involved in the jpeg and mpeg conventions for static and moving images.

Table 3 Another relation between the intended message (the day) and the code used to represent it (the meal). The entry is the probability that a given message is received, given what message is sent

Intended message	Message received				
	Breakfast	**Lunch**	**Dinner**	$P(X)$	$-\text{Log}(P)$
Monday	100.0%	0.0%	0.0%	33%	1.58
Tuesday	50.0%	50.0%	0.0%	0%	0.00
Wednesday	0.0%	0.0%	100.0%	33%	1.58
Thursday	0.0%	100.0%	0.0%	33%	1.58
$P(Y)$	33.3%	33.3%	33.3%	33%	
$-\text{Log}(P)$	1.58	1.58	1.58	100.0%	

Here we represent the fact that if I send the message "Monday" the recipient is certain (100%) to get the message "Breakfast." Alternatively, we might say that I am "encoding" "Monday" by sending the message "Breakfast." However (perhaps due to noise in the transmission process, when I encode "Tuesday" the recipient gets the message "Breakfast" 50% of the time and "Lunch" 50% of the time. This introduces ambiguity. We can think of it as noise in the transmission process. If I insist on sometimes sending the message "Tuesday" then I cannot achieve the full channel capacity.

Probabilities $P(X,Y)$

	33.33%	0.00%	0.00%	
	0.00%	0.00%	0.00%	
	0.00%	0.00%	33.33%	
	0.00%	33.33%	0.00%	
				100.00%
$E(Y)$	1.5850			
$E(X)$	1.5850			

Note: 1.05850=log$_2$3

Logarithms of $P(X, Y)$

	1.58	0.00	0.00
	0.00	0.00	0.00
	0.00	0.00	1.58
	0.00	1.58	0.00
$E(X, Y)$	1.5850		
$M=E(X)+E(Y)$			
$-E(X, Y)$	1.5850		

Progress on the social science side has also been energetic, but has not proceeded in the directions anticipated in Weaver's essay.

Human Communication

Scholars in the field called Communication (e.g., the National Communication Association, NCA, of the United States) concern themselves primarily with the social contexts and functional roles of communication. In their analysis it is never important to attempt to quantify the "amount of information" that is being communicated. Thus the approaches pioneered by Shannon have only rhetorical impact in that field.

Library and Information Science

In the field of Library and Information Science, it has seemed that one might want to know something about the relation between the "amount of information" and something else, which Brookes[4] has called the "increase in knowledge." Brookes proposed that the phenomenon of importance to information science is that the transmission of information *to a suitable recipient* results in an increase in the amount of knowledge "held by" that recipient. The idea, while often referenced, does not seem to have led to any serious attempt to provide a measurement of either the "amount of information" or the "increase in quantity of knowledge."

Economics

The third social scientific discipline which concerns itself with information is Economics. In Economics there has been an effective effort to quantify the notion of the value of information. It is clear that information has economic value, since, for example, information about tomorrow's stock prices could be immediately converted into economic gain. Economic theory has further developed, drawing upon the von Neumann and Morgenstern theory of games[5] and economic behavior, a concrete way of measuring the economic value of information which is uncertain or noisy, in precisely the way that the channels described by Shannon are.

Utility theory

However, the detailed theory works out rather differently. The essential concept is "utility," an abstract measure of worth which behaves in a very specific way with respect to uncertain situations. In particular, the utility measure of an uncertain event, or "lottery," L, such as

$$L = \begin{bmatrix} p & 1-p \\ A & B \end{bmatrix}, \tag{6}$$

which is represented by the expression $u(L)$, is required to satisfy the equation

$$u(L) = pu(A) + (1-p)u(B) \tag{7}$$

This equation will continue to be satisfied if the utility is transformed to any new scale of the form: $u_{\text{new}}(X) = b^2 u(X) + c$, for any real numbers b and c. This means that the utility is measured on an interval scale, whose zero point and unit of measure may be set at any convenient values.

Utility theory applies to decision makers, who are assumed to be able to (perhaps implicitly) assign a utility value to every situation that they might need to consider. This assignment is called the decision-maker's "utility function": $u_{\text{decision-maker}}(X)$. Utility theory is related to observable behavior by the requirement that a "rational" decision maker who values specific situations X,Y, according to a specific utility function for which $u_{\text{decision-maker}}(X) > u_{\text{decision-maker}}(Y)$ will definitely prefer to be in situation X, rather than in situation Y. It can be shown that a decision maker who does not follow Eq. 7 when making decisions about lottery can be systematically caused to make decisions which, over the long run, will reduce his cumulated utility. This is the specific sense in which Eq. 7 is interpreted as representing rationality.

A decision may depend on the current estimates of probability

The application of utility theory for measuring the value of information is made clear by a simple example of a two-fold decision involving an uncertain outcome. Suppose, for example, a decision maker must decide whether or not to carry an umbrella, and assigns the following utilities to the four possible alternative situations:

A = carry an umbrella and have it rain.
B = carry an umbrella and not have it rain.
C = not carry an umbrella and have it rain.
D = not carry an umbrella and not have it rain.

Specific values for these parameters are shown in Table 4a.

This information can be used to create a graph as shown in Fig. 1a, where the abscissa is the probability that it will in fact rain, and the ordinate is the utility value to the decision maker. The two straight lines on the graph represent the expected utility of the two possible actions, both of which depend on the probability that it will rain. The value of the choice or action "carry an umbrella" is

Table 4a Specific choices for the utility function of a decision maker.

Utilities of the decision maker		
	Action	
State	**Not carry**	**Carry**
No rain	0	2
Rain	2	−1

low when the probability of rain is low, but increases as the probability of rain increases. The value of "not carrying the umbrella" is high for low probabilities of rain, and decreases as the probability of rain increases. An important feature of this situation is the value of the probability at which the two lines cross, which we call the "critical probability" for this utility function. According to the principles of utility theory, the decision maker will not carry an umbrella if the probability is less than this value, will carry an umbrella if it is greater than this value, and is indifferent when the probability of rain is equal to the critical value.

Imperfect information can improve the expected utility of a situation

The preceding discussion describes the situation, without any information, or the "prior situation." Suppose now that the decision maker is offered an imperfect or "noisy" prediction of whether it will rain. We can calculate the expected value of "being in the situation of having this information" and compare it to the expected value in the present situation. The difference can, of course, be interpreted as the "value of the information." The mathematics is somewhat complicated. To begin with, an imperfect prediction can be imperfect in two distinct ways: failing to predict rain, on rainy days, and predicting rain on days when there is no rain. These two numbers are independent of each other, and both are needed to complete the calculation. We denote the first probability by "t" for true alarm or warning, and the second by "f" for "false warning." The information can be summarized as in Table 4b or Table 5.

The second complexity comes in interpreting a prediction which is known to be inaccurate in this way. This is accomplished using Bayes' rule,[6] which relates the probability of rain, given the imperfect information, p_1, to the prior probability of rain p_0. That equation is given in terms of odds ratios as

$$\frac{p_1}{1-p_1} = \frac{t}{1-t}\frac{p_0}{1-p_0} \quad \text{if the prediction is "rain"}$$

$$\frac{p_1}{1-p_1} = \frac{f}{1-f}\frac{p_0}{1-p_0} \quad \text{if the prediction is not "rain"}$$

$$\tag{8}$$

For a reasonable weather predictor, the first of the numbers p_1, found by solving these equations, will be higher

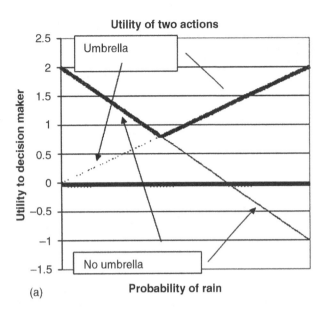

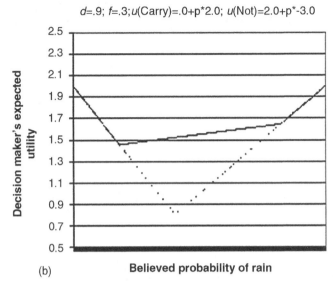

Fig. 1 (a) As the probability of rain increases, the utility of not carrying an umbrella decreases. Correspondingly, the utility of carrying an umbrella increases. In this case they cross at 40%, the critical probability. The decision maker, according to his estimate of the probability, chooses the action corresponding to the higher line. His expected utility, as a function of the probability, never falls below the crossing value. (b) With an imperfect predictor of rain, the decision maker can still improve his expectation, in some situations, but not all. The "bridge" in this diagram shows the higher utility that can be achieved if 1) his estimate is close enough to the critical point; and 2) he makes use of the prediction. The expected utility increase, due to using the prediction is the rational basis for assigning "value" to the prediction. Note that the same prediction will have higher value for a decision maker whose original estimate of the probability is closer to the critical value. This is quite different from entropy measures, which increase as the probability nears 50%.

than the second; that is, it is more likely to rain if the prediction is "rain" than if it is "not rain." Let us refer to them as p_H and p_L, respectively (H for high; L for low). Having this prediction, the decision maker will then refer to his personal utility diagram. If the result of the prediction leaves the probability below p_C, he will not carry an umbrella. If the result falls above the critical probability, he will carry an umbrella. But the results of these calculations depend on the prior probability estimate: p_0. If the prior estimate is very low, both P_H and P_L fall below p_C, and he will not carry an umbrella. If the prior estimate is very high, both P_H and P_L fall above p_C, and he will carry an umbrella, with or without the prediction. In those two situations, the information has no value to him, since he will do precisely what he would have done without the information. The value of the information is, therefore, 0.

However, for a certain range of the prior probability, spanning the critical value, the information will cause him to change his behavior. Therefore it has some potential value. The calculation of this value depends on the

principle of expected utility. In particular, it depends on the chance that the prediction is "rain." This, as we see from Eq. 8, depends on prior estimate of the probability. One might ask: "doesn't it really depend on the chance of rain?". But there is no way the decision maker can know the truth. He is restricted to choosing between his prior belief and the available imperfect prediction. In other words, if he buys the information, he will face a lottery where the outcomes are "predictions he receives" and he must compute the probability that each will occur.

$$\begin{bmatrix} \text{probabilty prediction is "rain"} & \text{probabilty prediction is not "rain"} \\ p_H & p_L \end{bmatrix}$$
(9)

Note that for any given belief about p, the probability of rain, the computed probability of the prediction "rain" contains two terms, corresponding to the true and false predictions. Thus:

$$p_H = tp + f(1-p)$$
$$p_L = (1-t)p + (1-f)(1-p)$$
(10)

Table 4b Specific performance characteristics of an imperfect predictor of rain.

Performance of the predictor

Predict	Truth	
	Rain	Not
Rain	0.9	0.3
Not	0.1	0.7

Table 5 The accuracy of a prediction of rain.

Prediction	Truth	
	Truth = rain	Truth = not rain
Rain	t	f
Not rain	$1-t$	$1-f$

Note that the sum of these two probabilities is 1, since the predictor must make *some* prediction.

The decision maker can then apply Eq. 7, carrying through the calculations. The result is a third line segment on the graph of expected utility, as shown in Fig. 1b. It forms a "bridge" above the intersection at the critical probability. The left-hand end of the bridge falls at the lowest prior probability for which the information has nonzero value. The right-hand end of the bridge falls at the highest prior probability for which the information has nonzero value. The expected value of the information, in units of the decision-maker's utility, is the vertical distance between the bridge and the higher of the original two lines, at the specific value of the prior probability. For further details see, for example, Hirshleifer and Riley.[7]

Thus we see that the expected value of the information depends not only on the unreliability of the prediction (that is, on the numbers t and f) but also on the decision maker's own prior estimate of the probability of rain. While the first two parameters represent the kind of information about uncertainty that is addressed by Information Theory, the dependence on the prior probability is quite a different matter. This complexity has prevented the development of any accepted theory that relates the expected value of information, in a decision situation, to computations of the type introduced by Shannon. Some efforts to develop an alternative to the Shannon formulation are discussed by Renyi.[8]

Behavior Beyond Expected Utility Theory

The field called Behavioral Economics addresses the many ways in which observed human behavior does not easily fit with the specific assumptions of utility theory. For example, if there is a set of possible situations, then the decision maker should be able to select one of them, or be indifferent among two or more. But experiments showed[9] that if the set is not small (i.e., contains more than six or seven alternatives) decision makers will report pair preferences that are not transitive, which is inconsistent with the notion that preferences correspond to inequalities relating real numbers (the values of the utility function). Leaders in behavioral economics include Daniel Kahnemann[10] and Amos Tversky.[11]

The question of whether the notion of utility can be broadened beyond the formulation given here, to accommodate apparently irrational human preferences, remains open. An interesting discussion, from the perspective of a philosopher, has been given by Nozick.[12] He proposes that, in addition to economic utility, dealt with as above, human decision makers base their actions on a separate property of actions, which he calls "symbolic utility." There is no conversion between these two utilities, and so, the model does not make specific predictions about behavior.

The study of behavior in the context of the theory of evolution suggests that actions that do not provide calculable utility gain for the individual decision maker may be the result of complex evolved behavior which has net utility for the genome of which the individual is a particular instance. ("A person is the gene's way of making a new gene.") This is an area of intense study, but no irrefutable demonstrations of the principle have been shown, for human behavior. It has been reported that the *Toxoplasma gondii* protozoan affects the brains of infected rodents in such a way as to decrease their innate fear of cats, enabling the parasite to progress to its next reproductive stage, which takes place in cats.[13] One possible example in humans is infection with the thirst for education, which causes young adults to sacrifice productive and child-bearing years to the pursuit of academic degrees, and thus perpetuate the academy.

SURPRISE AND IDENTIFICATION

There are some relatively new streams of research which show promise of beginning to capture the element of information that is most salient from the perspective of library information science: the degree to which the message received causes a change in what the recipient already knows or believes.

Surprise

The computer scientist Pierre Baldi[14] has proposed that messages can be judged on a scale which measures their "surprise" value. The analysis is based in part on measures related to the entropy. Specifically, he uses a measure called the Kullback-Leibler[15] measure, which assesses the difference between one probability distribution and another, when both describe the same basic set of outcomes. The analysis adds the notion of Bayesian updating, as discussed in economics section above. When information is received the recipient is presumed to alter his prior beliefs about the probability distribution, to yield a new distribution. The "distance" (the Kulback-Leibler measure is not a proper metric in the geometric sense, but could be converted to one if needed) of the new distribution from the old is a measure of the "surprise" that the information represents to the recipient.

Identification

The information scientist Rudolf Ahlswede[16] has developed a line of research that is somewhat dual to classical Shannon theory. He considers the problem of a recipient who knows in advance the list of messages that might be sent and wishes to determine, with at least a specified probability of being correct, which of the messages has, in fact, been sent to him. The capacity of channels,

Information Systems–
Information Use

measured against this criterion, becomes different (and, roughly speaking, higher). At a very superficial level, it appears that this line of thinking might eventually develop into a convergence between the Library/Information Science view of the problem (in which the possible messages are constrained by language, social roles, customs of expression, etc.), and the more rigorous theory which has produced so many striking improvements in the storage and transmission of the messages themselves.

CONCLUSION

In addition to its own practical contributions to our lives, it appears that the most concrete translation of the original hope that information theory might contribute to the social sciences is in the field of economics. However, in that setting, rigorous analysis shows that the value of information is not in any simple way functionally determined by the quantity of information as it was defined by Shannon. Very recent developments may eventuate in a convergence of the problems, but the path to solution is not yet clear.

There are excellent sources on the Web for information about these topics, from many perspectives, and this rich field is very much open for exciting future developments.

SCHOLARLY AND SCIENTIFIC ORGANIZATIONS (WEB SITES)

American Economic Association. http://www.vanderbilt.edu/AEA/

American Society for Information Science and Technology. http://www.asis.org/

IEEE Information Theory Society. http://www.itsoc.org/

Institute for Operations Research and Management Sciences. http://www.informs.org/

The National Communication Association. http://www.natcom.org/nca/

REFERENCES

1. Shannon, C.; Weaver, W. *The Mathematical Theory of Communication*; University of Illinois Press: Urbana, IL, 1949.
2. Luenberger, D. *Information Science*; Princeton University Press: Princeton, NJ, 2006.
3. http://en.wikipedia.org/wiki/Shannon_limit.
4. Brookes, B.C. The foundations of information science. Part II. Quantitative aspects: classes of things and the challenge of human individuality. J. Info. Sci. **1980**, *2*(5), 209–221.
5. von Neumann, J.; Morganstern, O. *Theory of Games and Economic Behavior with an Introduction by Harold W. Kuhn and an Afterword by Ariel Rubinstein*, 60th Anniversary Ed.; Princeton University Press: Princeton, NJ, 1944.
6. http://en.wikipedia.org/wiki/Bayes'_theoremBayes.
7. Hirshleifer, J.; Riley, J.G. *The Analytics of Uncertainty and Information (Cambridge Surveys of Economic Literature)*; Cambridge University Press: New York, **1992**, 9.
8. Rényi, A. On measures of information and entropy. Proc. 4th Berkeley Symp. Math. Stat. Probability **1960**, 547–561.
9. Luce, R.D.; Raiffa, H. Games and decisions: Introduction and critical survey. In *A Study of the Behavioral Models Project, Bureau of Applied Social Research,* Columbia University Wiley: New York, 1957.
10. Kahneman, D. Maps of bounded rationality: A perspective on intuitive judgment and choice prize lecture. 2002; December 8. http://nobelprize.org/nobel_prizes/economics/laureates/2002/kahnemann-lecture.pdf.
11. In: *Choices, Values, and Frames*; Kahneman, D.; Tversky, A., Eds,; Cambridge University Press: New York, 2000.
12. Nozick, R. *The Nature of Rationality*; Princeton University Press: Princeton, NJ, 1993.
13. Berdoy, M.; Webster, J.; Macdonald, D. Fatal attraction in rats infected with *Toxoplasma gondii*. Proc. R. Soc. Lond. **2000**, 1591–1594. *B267*.
14. Itti, L.; Baldi, P. Bayesian surprise attracts human attention. Adv. Neural Inform. Process. Syst. NIPS **2005**, *18*, http://ilab.usc.edu/publications/doc/Itti_Baldi06nips.pdf.
15. Kullback, S. The Kullback-Leibler distance. Am. Stat **1987**, *41*, 340–341.
16. Ahlswede, R. Towards a general theory of information transfer, Shannon Lecture at ISIT. Seattle, WA, 2006; July 13. http://www.itsoc.org/publications/nltr/itNL0907.pdf.

Information Use for Decision Making

Edward T. Cokely
Lael J. Schooler
Gerd Gigerenzer
Center for Adaptive Behavior and Cognition, Max Planck Institute for Human Development, Berlin, Germany

Abstract

How should we use information to make good decisions? Historically, the view has been that normatively superior decision making is the product of complex optimization processes that rationally consider and integrate all available information. Such optimization processes are well beyond the capabilities of mere mortals and in many cases are computationally intractable by any means. Fortunately, optimization processes are not always necessary: Less can be more. Simple decision processes—i.e., heuristics—used in the right environments enable fast, frugal, and adaptive decision making that can be as good as, or better than, even the most complex optimization processes. In what follows, we introduce research on ecological rationality and the science of adaptive heuristics. Our review includes 1) a brief history of the study of decision making; 2) a discussion of simple yet computationally precise heuristics, and how, when, and why they lead to superior performance; and 3) examples of how simple heuristics are starting to be used in the information sciences, such as in database literature prioritization or in the development of more user-friendly technologies. Although it may seem conventionally paradoxical, intelligent and adaptive information use often requires that information be ignored.

INFORMATION USE FOR DECISION MAKING

·In the modern world, one of the leading causes of death is heart disease. As such it is easy to imagine that many people will search for information on its causes, symptoms, and treatments. But how will they search? One candidate is a keyword search in a search engine such as Google, which as of April 2008 returned about 35,500,000 "heart disease" results in less than 2/10 of a second. This is not only a lot of information, it is too much information. Given the exponential rates of information growth in science and technology this number will likely continue to grow.[1] Can people with limited knowledge, time, and computational capacities effectively search through vast amounts of information and make good decisions under conditions of high uncertainty? Can a scientific understanding of the cognitive processes involved in human information search and decision making help us improve information technology? In short, we believe the answer to both questions is *yes*.

To begin to illustrate our perspective, consider a recent study conducted by Michael Lee and his colleagues.[2] Lee et al. compared the performance of a leading research database (i.e., PsycINFO) with the performance of two very different systems, each based on a model of human decision making. The first model was a "rational model" that attempted to combine all information in an optimal (or near-optimal) way. This model was inspired by what has traditionally been regarded as a normative theory of decision making. Relevance was determined using a Bayesian learning algorithm allowing additive weighting and integration of *all* available information from cues such as authors, journals, keywords (title and abstract), language of the publication, and others. When some cue was associated (or unassociated) with a relevant article the probability that another article with that cue would be relevant (or irrelevant) was updated. Eventually, search was prioritized by selecting articles with "optimal" cue configurations as those of the highest relevance.

The second decision model developed by Lee et al.[2] for the literature prioritization task used a rather different, perhaps even paradoxical process. In sharp contrast to a rational model, the one-reason decision-making model *ignored* a considerable amount of the available information in order to prioritize choices. This model, inspired by research on simple, adaptive heuristics[3] used cues for inferring and assigning relevance, as did the rational model. However, in this case cues were first ordered by validity from most strongly associated and relevant to least relevant. Subsequently, a literature search prioritized results by selecting articles based solely on the most relevant cue that discriminated between options (for a more detailed discussion of validity, discrimination, cue ordering, and one-reason decision-making, see *take-the-best* later in this entry). Rather than attempting to integrate and use all possible sources of information, the one-reason decision-making model made choices based on a simple heuristic process (i.e., a rule of thumb), namely it

Encyclopedia of Library and Information Sciences, Fourth Edition DOI: 10.1081/E-ELIS4-120044539
Copyright © 2017 by Taylor & Francis. All rights reserved.

prioritized results based only on the single most important cue that discriminated.

To assess prioritization performance, Lee et al.[2] compared both decision-making models (rational, one-reason) with the performance of PsycINFO. As expected, results indicated that all models returned relevant articles at above chance levels. More interestingly, and to some more surprisingly, the one-reason decision-making model consistently outperformed the rational model, which in turn outperformed PsycINFO. These results add to a growing body of evidence suggesting that more complex decision making processes do not necessarily provide superior decision-making performance. Instead, superior decision making can result from simple heuristic processes when used in the right environments.

So how is it possible that a simple heuristic was able to perform so well even when compared to a sophisticated optimization process? Part of the answer is that in our fundamentally uncertain world, simplicity often leads to robustness and efficiency. Heuristics improve performance by ignoring potentially misleading information. Heuristics also confer other benefits as this type of choice process tends be fast and efficient, relying on radically limited information search and decision rules. As well, in human, animal, and machine cognition, simple decision processes can be fine-tuned and can exploit the fit between our environmental task constraints and our available capacities, such as a human's limited attentional capacity and our adaptive ability to forget.[4–6] In these ways and others, simple heuristics tend to produce and enable effective, adaptive judgment and decision making in many situations.[3,7]

In this entry we will review a research program focused on adaptive behavior and cognition—or how simple heuristics, in the right environments, can make us smarter. Our entry will begin with a discussion of the history of decision-making theory and will then turn to issues of adaptive cognition, ecological rationality, and computational models of heuristics. Next, we will provide some examples of a few widely used heuristics. Finally, we close with a discussion of implications for the design of information-rich environments.

Perspectives on Rationality: A Brief History

The emergence of the modern debate on human rationality, or how people make decisions and what qualifies as a good decision, can be traced in large part to the Ages of Reason and Enlightenment (i.e., seventeenth and eighteenth centuries, respectively). During these times logic and careful, justifiable reasoning became highly prized by philosophers, empiricists, and political actors alike. As an example, consider the astronomer and physicist Pierre-Simon Laplace. Laplace's legacy includes seminal contributions to probability theory; however, more important for our purposes, he also provided a description of a fictional

omniscient being that captured the Zeitgeist of the times. This being, known as Laplace's superintelligence, was envisioned as one who would know all the details of past and present and with this knowledge could readily make good choices and predict the future with perfect certainty.[8]

For many people, Laplace's vision of a decision maker who is omniscient and computationally unbounded may seem like an elaborate fantasy. Yet this fantasy or some version of it is fundamental to much of the research and theory in the modern decision sciences. Some readers will find this surprising, or ironically unreasonable, but models of "rational man" and *homo economicus* are among the most central and influential models used in decision science. According to neoclassical economic theory people behave as if they were *unboundedly rational* and make optimal (but not necessarily perfect) choices as if they had solved a complicated decision calculus.[9,10] These decisions can be described by optimization processes that reflect people's maximization of their own subjective expected utilities (i.e., personal values) via multiattribute integration calculations. Such theories are at the core of dozens of models of decision making, including modern theories of motivation, attitudes, and moral judgments.[3,7] However, even if this approach has provided interesting and useful theory, these models often conflict with empirical evidence. Psychological science has clearly demonstrated that this is not how real people with limited resources (i.e., time, attention, memory) use information to make decisions.[7,10–13] Perhaps even more interestingly, these complicated and time-consuming processes are not even necessarily required for good, adaptive decision making.[3,7]

In the mid-twentieth century, Herbert Simon[14–16] introduced his notion of bounded rationality. Simon argued that, among other things, people have only limited time, knowledge, and cognitive resources, and thus human decision makers cannot carry out the types of optimization computations that were (and still are) often assumed to underlie rational decision making. In part in reaction to Simon's notion of bounded rationality, a more modern version of a rational decision maker was developed by some decision researchers. The new theory, characterized by *optimization under constraints*, was once again concerned with a complex optimization calculus that could be used to make rational choices, but in these cases the optimization processes were also subject to any one of a number of constraints.[17] To illustrate, in some models information search was necessary (i.e., no more omniscience) and so search processes were described and thus carried a cost. However, as a simplifying assumption the information search processes were often described by yet another optimization calculus wherein search was terminated according to the optimal cost–benefit ratio. As the number of constraints increases so too do the computational complexities of the search optimization functions that must be solved, even in simple decisions. In this way, optimization under constraints can be even *more* computationally demanding than what is required of the unboundedly rational agents. In efforts toward greater psychological plausibility, the optimization under constraints models created in some cases an even more psychologically unrealistic, and computationally unbounded, superintelligent decision maker.[17]

To be fair, although optimization models are not accurate process models of how real people make decisions, they do in some cases predict people's decisions or tell us about what outcomes or decisions should be favored.[18–20] For these reasons, optimization models can be valuable tools. Nevertheless, optimization models are *as-if* models of human decision making: Many decision makers behave as if they use optimization processes even though they rely on other processes.[21–23] Unfortunately, most research focusing on as-if models is essentially uninterested in and ill-equipped to understand the psychological dynamics involved in decision making. Hence, the as-if approach to modeling decision making leaves unanswered at least two crucial questions. First, how do people actually use information to make decisions? Second, given our known cognitive constraints (i.e., our bounded rationality), how is it that real decision processes can approximate and in some cases outperform optimization processes? To answer these questions, we turn to two different but related research programs that study human decision making and heuristics.

In the 1970s, Daniel Kahneman and Amos Tversky developed the *heuristics and biases* research program in cognitive psychology.[11,24,25] This program was aimed at understanding how people actually make decisions. Toward this end researchers worked to reveal cognitive processes (i.e., heuristics) by focusing on judgment errors and "biases." However, in order to identify errors one must have normative assumptions (i.e., what is the appropriate standard for an accurate or good judgment), an issue that is not without controversy.[26,27] In the case of the heuristics and bias approach, it was assumed that human cognition should be compared to a very specific set of rational, normative standards such as the outcomes of optimization processes and logic. Specifically, the heuristics and biases program searches for errors that are evidenced when people's judgments deviate from "an established fact... [or] an accepted rule of arithmetic, logic, or statistics" (p. 493).[28] Indeed, it has demonstrated rather unequivocally that people do not reason in accord with content-blind logical laws or optimization processes, and that people often use heuristic processes for judgments and decisions.[10,29] The research and findings on heuristics and biases have played key roles in shaping psychological and behavioral decision making research, contributing to the development of new research fields such as behavioral law and economics.[24,30]

In spite of its many successes, the heuristics and biases program has its limitations. One of our most serious concerns is that the program has emphasized ways in which

heuristics are associated with errors, which has led some to an interpretation that heuristic use is a problem that needs to be corrected. In this light heuristics are seen as inferior choice processes designed to be used by computationally disadvantaged individuals. In contrast, other research demonstrates that heuristics (e.g., satisficing) are often powerful tools.[16,31,32] As illustrated by the literature prioritization example in the introduction, in real-world environments these simple processes can enable adaptive decision making, matching or outperforming even the most sophisticated and time-consuming optimization processes.

Ecological Rationality: Computational Models of Heuristics

Consider for a moment a Darwinian inspired perspective on decision making. On this view, the goals and needs of organisms, such as finding food, securing mates, or protecting offspring, may or may not benefit from cognition that is logically coherent. For these organisms, fitness is best served when cognition can be tuned to ecological constraints. An organism's success will rely on the extent to which its cognition and behavior can benefit from and exploit features of its internal and external environment, regardless of how well these processes actually adhere to logical norms. An organism's ability to survive and reproduce depends on the fit between: 1) its evolved and developed capacities, 2) its cognitive processes, 3) and the structure of its natural environment. The analysis of the fit between capacities, processes, and environment is known as the study of ecological rationality.

Understanding the relationship between the mind and its environment serves as a starting point for the study of adaptive behavior and cognition.[32] This adaptive framework has deep roots in psychology. For example, Herbert Simon has argued that "Human rational behavior is shaped by a scissors whose two blades are the structure of task environments and the computational capabilities of the actor" (p. 7).[16] If one wants to understand how people make judgments and decisions, and why and when these processes work, one cannot examine only processes (as most psychologists do) or only environments (as most economists and sociologists do). Studying how one scissor blade cuts, or fails to cut, does not tell us how, why, or when the scissors will actually work.

In concert with the study of ecological rationality, a second key concept for the research program on adaptive behavior and cognition is the *adaptive toolbox*. This adaptive toolbox is conceived of as a collection of precisely defined cognitive heuristics and other adaptive processes that can be used both consciously and unconsciously (e.g., intuitively) to solve problems in the real world. Organisms use a number of specific tools that are well-suited to certain task environments, not entirely unlike specific wrenches and screwdrivers that are designed for specific chores.

Information Systems–Information Use

In this way, there is no general all-purpose heuristic (or optimization calculus) that can provide the best solution for every judgment or decision. In contrast, heuristic application is more narrow and constrained, although many heuristics can be used more or less effectively across a range of situations (e.g., a screwdriver can also be used to open a can of paint). Perhaps most critically, by defining heuristics as formal computational models, one can then identify (e.g., via simulations) exactly when, how, and why certain heuristics will succeed or fail. Theoretically, this collection of adaptive heuristics provides a precisely defined, psychologically plausible alternative to as-if optimization models of human decision making.

So how is it that these simple heuristic processes can match and outperform complex optimization processes? The answer has at least two key parts. The first part has to do with computational tractability. Regardless of the extraordinary increases in computing power that we have enjoyed in recent years, for most decisions there simply is no optimization strategy that can be computed.[3] Optimization, except in radically simplified environments, is largely computationally intractable. Even simple problems turn out to be so complex as to be impenetrable to optimization techniques. This is true of problems that are well-defined such as in games like Chess or Go, as well as for the many ill-defined problems we face in the modern world such as choosing an outfit, a dinner, a career, or a spouse. In all of these cases, heuristic processes are not only valuable but they are absolutely essential.

The second reason heuristics can perform well is that they are robust and reduce the chance of fitting noise in our environment (i.e., overfitting). Because we live in a fundamentally uncertain world, information in our environment (i.e., environmental signals) consists, of both reliable and unreliable content (i.e., noise), or in other words, information that is diagnostic and information that could lead us astray. Particularly in situations that involve high uncertainty, the trick for intelligent decision making is to *ignore* information, such as seemingly informative but ultimately irrelevant information (e.g., past performance of stocks for predicting changes in valuation). If we performed an optimization calculation for every decision that included every regularity from every previous situation, our ability to accurately predict outcomes in new environments would be crippled as it would be based on many kinds of random, non-diagnostic noise. In contrast, because heuristics are simple and exploit cognitive capacities such as our adaptive capacity for forgetting[4] we can reduce the risk that we will overfit non-diagnostic environmental signals. Moreover, because adaptive heuristics rely on a limited search of the available information there is a good chance that they will avoid most sources of the random noise while still benefiting from a focus on the most reliable sources of information.[33]

In addition to the performance benefits noted above adaptive heuristics confer at least one more set of ecologically important advantages: Heuristics can provide *fast and frugal* decision making. Because heuristics can exploit our capacities (both evolved and developed), such as our remarkable capacity for highly accurate recognition memory, the time and energy needed for these decision processes are minimized. Heuristics provide essential competitive advantages (e.g., minimizing time, search, effort invested) whether one is making decisions in the wild or in the boardroom. This frugality may benefit us physiologically as our brain, which is roughly 2% of our overall mass, commonly requires between 15% and 25% of our daily energy and oxygen budget. Even simple acts of deliberative, effortful processing can significantly influence and deplete our energy stores.[34] In these ways and others simple heuristics tend to enable adaptive decisions in ecological environments.

Heuristic Building Blocks

Advances in the science of adaptive behavior and cognition rely in large part on identifying and modeling exact heuristic processes. These processes are described by dividing heuristics into different building blocks (i.e., sub-processes), often including: 1) *search processes*, 2) *stopping rules*, and 3) *decision rules*, which are composed of either unique processes or nested combinations of other more basic heuristics. Consider the *take-the-best* heuristic.[34] Take-the-best belongs to a family of one reason decision-making heuristics and has proven itself to be a common and effective decision tool. Take-the-best can be used when one is faced with a choice between two different options. In these cases, take-the-best orders and considers different cues (reasons) for making its decision by selecting the best option with the first cue that discriminates between the options. In simpler language, consider a preference situation in which one is trying to decide which of two colleges to attend. One way you could make a decision would be to focus on only a single factor, the one that seems most important. For some people that might be prestige, and thus when considering both Harvard and say San Francisco State University (SFSU), one would likely pick Harvard. However, if the most important consideration was which school was affordable, you might then select the public school (SFSU) where tuition is far less. In either case, the process is roughly the same and requires only a very minimum amount of search and reasoning. First identify and order the most important cues that you will use to decide and then make your choice based on the first discriminating cue (i.e., the first cue in which one option is clearly better than the other). Indeed, in investigations of real world choices such as the one described above (but also including multiple-cue inference tasks where there are known correct answers such as inferring which of two cities is larger) we see that people often make decisions with simple processes like take-the-best.[36,37]

Information Systems–
Information Use

More formally, take-the-best is made of three precisely defined building blocks including:

1. *Search rule*: Search through the cues in order of their validity (correlation with criteria). Look up the cue values of the cue with the highest validity first.
2. *Stopping rule*: If one object has a positive cue value and the other does not (or is unknown), then stop search and proceed to Step 3. Otherwise, exclude the cue and return to Step 1. If no more cues are found, guess.
3. *Decision rule*: Predict that the object with the positive cue value has the higher value on the criterion.

Again, each of these rules precisely defines behavior, leads to a testable prediction, and therefore can be computationally modeled or evaluated empirically. Given this precision, researchers have also used mathematical analysis and simulations to tell us about the ecological rationality of heuristics, describing for example the environments wherein take-the-best will perform better and worse.[38] To illustrate, one can analytically prove that take-the-best is associated with superior decision making in environments that have a *non-compensatory* cue structure. Any time the sum of the cue weights does not add up to the sum of the best (remaining) cue, take-the-best will perform very well. We might imagine a task of trying to model which libraries have experienced a budget growth of at least 10%. In this example we will assume that the ecological validities (i.e., the relative frequency with which a binary cue correctly predicts the criterion) of the cues are one, one-half, one-fourth, and one-eighth, where lending rates of the library are the single most important factor (i.e., more lending is most strongly associated with strong growth), the current size of the library is one-half as important, and location is half again as important. In this case, the structure is non-compensatory because the sum of the cue weights can never add up to (or compensate for) the difference between the first cue (lending rates) and all other cues (Fig. 1).[39] Even if one finds that another library is larger and is in the perfect location, etc., these factors could not compensate if that library had low lending rates. Findings such as these can tell us both when a simple heuristic will fail and when it will work better than or at least as well as more complex decision processes. These findings also allow for insights into what decision (or inference) should be made as well as what information should actually be used and ignored in the decision-making process.

Two Memory-Based Heuristics

Many heuristics benefit by taking advantage of evolved and developed capacities. In humans, some capacities are more fundamental than others, in the sense that they

Information Systems– Information Use

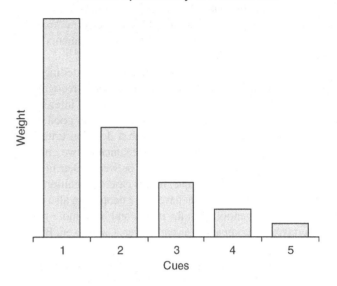

Noncompensatory environment

Weight

Cues

Fig. 1 A noncompensatory environment. In this environment one can see that the first (binary) cue will always make predictions that are always as accurate as any linear combination of all cues.

develop earlier and persist longer. Recognition memory is one such capacity. In many ways our recognition memory is much more sensitive and reliable than the vast majority of other mnemonic processes, something that becomes increasing apparent as we age. To better appreciate this capacity we invite you to try an exercise: Do your best to recall the names of the seven dwarves from the story *Snow White and the Seven Dwarves*. Although many of us will have trouble recalling these characters' names nearly everyone, or at least most Americans, will immediately recognize them (Can you recognize the seven real dwarves in this list of nine: "*Bashful*," "*Doc*," "*Sloppy*," "*Dopey*," "*Grumpy*," "*Pudgy*," "*Happy*," "*Sleepy*," and "*Sneezy*"). As noted, recognition not only reflects a fundamental aspect of memory, it also provides a powerful cue for adaptive decision making.

Considerable research now demonstrates that when facing a choice people often rely on their recognition, or lack thereof, to help inform their inferences. This heuristic process has been formalized in the *recognition heuristic*, which is modeled as follows: "if one of two objects is recognized and the other is not, then infer that the recognized object has the higher value with respect to the criterion."[40] The interesting theoretical finding is that sometimes *less is more*, such that ignorance will actually improve our decision making in a variety of environments. Imagine for instance that your task is to select which of two stocks to invest in. One company might be named Coca Cola Company and the other Ameritech. One way to decide between the two companies is simply to invest in the company that is recognized and familiar. If you do this, and thus decide according to the recognition heuristic, you'd likely select Coca Cola. Although it is a simple strategy that relies largely on one's ignorance, research shows that it can match or outperform "expert" stock portfolios, in certain common environments[41,42] (for boundary conditions see also Andersson).[43]

By way of analysis and computational modelling it is possible to understand the conditions in which recognition will be likely to provide good (and not so good) inferences. Research indicates that recognition will lead to good decisions whenever it is correlated with a decision criterion. Consider the task of trying to decide which of two cities is larger (in population), selecting between Detroit and Houghton (MI), for example. In this case, recognition may be diagnostic as cities that have more people are also more likely to be mentioned in the media and have more major sports teams, companies, airports, events, and so on. Bigger cities are therefore more likely to be recognized and not recognizing a city becomes a valuable basis for inference. Of course, recognition does not guarantee that one city is larger than another (e.g., Hollywood, CA, vs. Fresno, CA). However, when there is a strong correlation between recognition and the decision criteria, recognition will tend to provide accurate inferences.

The *fluency heuristic*[44,45] is a second fundamental memory-based inference process (for a recent review see Kelley).[46] Considerable converging evidence reveals that fluency, which is roughly defined as our subjective experience of the ease of information processing (cf. availability), often dramatically influences our confidence, judgment, and decision making.[24,25,47–49] If we again consider the real-world task of selecting stocks we find that people tend to judge that unrecognized companies with names that are easier to read (pronounce) are more likely to be profitable. This is true in laboratory studies and can also be seen in actual stock trading during initial public offerings.[50,51] Indeed, there is a long tradition of studying fluency and availability. Here we focus on more recent research done within the adaptive framework. Specifically, we have developed the *ACT-R fluency heuristic* that formalized: "If one of two objects is more fluently processed, then infer that this object has the higher value with respect to the criterion" (p. 612).[4] In this case, fluency is precisely defined as the speed with which declarative memory chunks can be retrieved in the computational cognitive architecture ACT-R. As with the recognition heuristic and take-the-best, the ACT-R fluency heuristic relies on a simple but powerful one reason decision-making process. The critical difference is not whether or not one recognizes some bit of information but how quickly and easily one recognizes it. The more easily one option is recognized the more likely it is to influence our decision, a process that is fundamental to a variety of adaptive inferences. Understanding these processes provides insight into the adaptive nature of our cognitive architecture. More generally, understanding the processes used by one of the most complex and efficient

adaptive devices known—i.e., the human mind—can help enable the design of better innovative engineering and information technology solutions.[52]

Heuristics, Usability, and Environmental Design

The work of Lee et al.[2] on search prioritization serves as an excellent example of the potential for using adaptive heuristics to improve information technology. However, this is only one side of the usability issue. Opportunities also exist to study user decision making to further understand the heuristic processes commonly relied upon in database and library type environments. Currently there is a small but growing body of work using process-oriented or otherwise ecologically grounded approaches that may be valuable for future research efforts.[53,54] For example, some research focuses on variations in human search strategies in database environments[55] such as differences in the processes of children and adults (Bilal and Kirby, 2002).[61] In these studies, key results indicate that specific information search strategies can be identified that tend to systematically vary with age. Similarly, there is a somewhat more developed tradition of studying human search behavior in general consumer choices that has begun to explore Internet or database-type environments.[57–59] These studies have also been successful in identifying search strategies, with some going a step further and identifying stopping rules and the environmental constraints that mediate heuristic selection.[60] For instance, Browne et al. have started to identify the relationships between environmental factors and search processes, suggesting that there often exists a positive relationship between task complexity, search times, and stopping rules. Similarly, other recent work has used our understanding of human decision-making heuristics to improve human–computer interface design. By eliminating non-diagnostic or highly redundant (correlated) product-attribute information researchers limit the redundant search processes of users, which allows consumers to better cope with information overload effects including the so-called *too much choice effect*.[62]

There are also a number of other connections between specific heuristics and library and information search behaviors that have yet to be explored. As noted, both recognition and fluency tend to influence everyday choices. In a library environment it is easy to imagine that these heuristics would influence decisions such as which book(s) to order or read (e.g., an author is recognized, an author is more quickly recognized); what search queries to use (e.g., do you recognize any results from these keywords); and when to stop searching (e.g., when further search yields little in the way of relevant recognizable information; stop search when information is no longer easily recognized or fluent). However, these simple connections and the review provided here can only serve as an introduction. There are many other heuristics and aspects of information use and search processes that may prove to be very influential in the design of user-friendly technology (for a more complete overview see Gigerenzer).[7,32]

CONCLUSION

There has been considerable focus on the fact that people often use heuristics to make decisions. Fortunately, in the right environment these simple heuristic processes make us smart by simplifying and speeding decisions, and by helping us ignore irrelevant information. In our complex and uncertain world simple heuristics sometimes represent the very best decision making processes available. Whether designing better information technology, better decision support systems, or better decision environments one lesson is clear: Superior decision making does not necessarily require more complex processes. Less can be much more. In these ways and others, the future holds great opportunities and promise for engineering simplicity.

REFERENCES

1. Egghe, L.; Rao, I.K.R. Classification of growth models based on growth rates and its applications. Scientometrics **1992**, *25*, 5–46.
2. Lee, M.D.; Loughlin, N.; Lundberg, I.B. Applying one reason decision-making: The prioritisation of literature searches. Aust. J. Psychol. **2002**, *54*(3), 137–143.
3. Gigerenzer, G. Todd, P.M. and the ABC Research Group. *Simple Heuristics That Make Us Smart*, Oxford University Press: Oxford, U.K., 1999.
4. Schooler, L.J.; Hertwig, R. How forgetting AIDS heuristic inference. Psychol. Rev. **2005**, *112*, 610–628.
5. Anderson, J.R.; Schooler, L.J. Reflections of the environment in memory. Psychol. Sci. **1991**, *2*, 396–408.
6. Schooler, L.J.; Anderson, J.R. The role of process in the rational analysis of memory. Cogn. Psychol. **1997**, *32*(3), 219–250.
7. Gigerenzer, G., Selten, R. Eds. *Bounded Rationality: The Adaptive Toolbox* MIT Press: Cambridge, MA, 2001.
8. Gigerenzer, G. Bounded and rational. In *Contemporary Debates in Cognitive Science (Contemporary Debates in Philosophy No. 7)*; Stainton, R.J., Ed.; Blackwell: Oxford, U.K., 2006.
9. Hastie, R. Problems for judgment and decision making. Annu. Rev. Psychol. **2001**, *52*, 652–683.
10. Shafir, E. Tversky, A. Decision making. In *Thinking*; Smith, E.E., Osherson, D.N., Eds.; MIT Press: Cambridge, MA, 1995; Vol. 3.
11. Kahneman, D.; Slovic, P.; Tversky, A. *Judgment under Uncertainty: Heuristics and Biases*, Cambridge Press: New York, 1982.
12. Payne, J.W.; Bettman, J.R.; Johnson, E.J. Behavioral decision research—A constructive processing perspective. Annu. Rev. Psychol. **1992**, *43*, 87–131.
13. Payne, J.W. Bettman, J.R. Johnson, E.J. *The Adaptive Decision Maker*, Cambridge University Press: Cambridge, U.K., 1993.
14. Simon, H.A. Rational choice and the structure of the environment. Psychol. Rev. **1956**, *63*, 129–138.
15. Simon, H.A. *Models of Man: Social and Rational*, Willey: New York, 1957.
16. Simon, H.A. Invariants of human behavior. Annu. Rev. Psychol. **1990**, *41*, 1–19.
17. Sargent, T.J. *Bounded Rationality in Macroeconomics*, Oxford University Press: New York, 1993.
18. Chater, N.; Oaksford, M. Ten years of the rational analysis of cognition. Trends Cogn. Sci. **1999**, *3*(2), 57–65.
19. Chater, N.; Oaksford, M.; Nakisa, R.; Redington, M. Fast, frugal, and rational: How rational norms explain behavior. Organ. Behav. Hum. Decis. Process. **2003**, *90*(1), 63–86.
20. Chater, N.; Tenenbaum, J.B.; Yuille, A. Probabilistic models of cognition: Conceptual foundations. Trends Cogn. Sci. **2006**, *10*, 287–291.
21. Brandstätter, E.; Gigerenzer, G.; Hertwig, R. The priority heuristic: Making choices without trade-offs. Psychol. Rev. **2006**, *113*(2), 409–432.
22. Weber, E.U.; Johnson, E.J.; Milch, K.F.; Chang, H.; Brodscholl, J.C.; Goldstein, D.G. Asymmetric discounting in intertemporal choice—A query-theory account. Psychol. Sci. **2007**, *18*, 516–523.
23. Cokely, E.T.; Kelley, C.M. Cognitive abilities and superior decision making under risk: A protocol analysis and process model evaluation. Judgem. Decis. making. **2009**, *4*, 20–33.
24. Kahneman, D.; Tversky, A. Eds. *Choices, Values and Frames*; Cambridge University Press and the Russell Sage Foundation: New York, 2000.
25. Tversky, A.; Kahneman, D. Judgment under uncertainty: Heuristics and biases. Science **1974**, *185*, 1124–1130.
26. Anderson, J.R. Is human cognition adaptive? Behav. Brain Sci. **1991**, *14*(3), 471–484.
27. Gigerenzer, G. On narrow norms and vague heuristics: Reply. Psychol. Rev. **1996**, *103*, 592–596.
28. Kahneman, D.; Tversky, A. On the study of statistical intuitions. In *Judgment under Uncertainty: Heuristics and Biases*; Kahneman, D., Slovic, P., Tversky, A., Eds.; Cambridge University Press: Cambridge, U.K., 1982.
29. Kahneman, D. A perspective on judgment and choice—Mapping bounded rationality. Am. Psychol. **2003**, *9*, 697–720.
30. Gigerenzer, G., Engel, C. Eds. *Heuristics and the Law*; MIT Press: Cambridge, MA, 2006.
31. Gigerenzer, G. Fast and frugal heuristics: The tools of bounded rationality. In *Handbook of Judgment and Decision Making*; Koehler, D., Harvey, N., Eds.; Blackwell: Oxford, U.K., 2004.
32. Gigerenzer, G.; Brighton, H. Homo heuristicus: Why biased minds make better inferences. Top. Cogn. Sci. **2009**, *1*, 107–143.
33. Brighton, H.; Gigerenzer, G. Bayesian brains and cognitive mechanisms: Harmony or dissonance?. In *The Probabilistic Mind: Prospects for Rational Models of Cognition*; Chater, N., Oaksford, M., Eds.; Oxford University Press: Oxford, U.K., 2007.
34. Gailliot, M.T.; Baumeister, R.F. The physiology of willpower: Linking blood glucose to self-control. Pers. Soc. Psychol. Rev. **2007**, *11*, 303–327.

35. Gigerenzer, G.; Goldstein, D.G. Reasoning the fast and frugal way: Models of bounded rationality. Psychol. Rev. **1996**, *103*, 650–669.

36. Galotti, K.M. Decision structuring in important real-life choices. Psychol. Sci. **2007**, *18*(4), 320–325.

37. Dhami, M.K. Psychological models of professional decision making. Psychol. Sci. **2003**, *14*, 175–180.

38. Katsikopoulos, K.V.; Martignon, L. Naive heuristics for paired comparisons: Some results on their relative accuracy. J. Math. Psychol. **2006**, *50*, 488–494.

39. Martignon, L. Hoffrage, U. Why does one-reason decision making work? A case study in ecological rationality. In *Simple Heuristics That Make Us Smart*; Gigerenzer, G., Todd, P.M., the ABC Research Group, Eds.; Oxford University Press: New York, 1999; 119–140.

40. Goldstein, D.G.; Gigerenzer, G. Models of ecological rationality: The recognition heuristic. Psychol. Rev. **2002**, *109*, 75–90.

41. Borges, B. Goldstein, D.G. Ortmann, A. Gigerenzer, G. Can ignorance beat the stock market?. In *Simple heuristics that Make Us Smart*; Gigerenzer, G., Todd, P.M., the ABC Research Group, Eds.; Oxford University Press: New York, 1999.

42. Ortmann, A. Gigerenzer, G. Borges, B. Goldstein, D.G. The recognition heuristic: A fast and frugal way to investment choice?. In *Handbook of Experimental Economics Results: Vol. 1 (Handbooks in Economics No. 28)*; Plott, C.R., Smith, V.L., Eds.; North-Holland: Amsterdam, 2008, 993–1003.

43. Andersson, P.; Rakow, T. Now you see it now you don't: The effectiveness of the recognition heuristic for selecting stocks. Judgm. Decis. Making **2007**, *2*, 29–39.

44. Jacoby, L.L.; Brooks, L.R. Nonanalytic cognition— memory, perception, and concept-learning. Psychol. Learn. Motiv. Adv. Res. Theory **1984**, *18*, 1–47.

45. Jacoby, L.L.; Dallas, M. On the relationship between autobiographical memory and perceptual learning. J. Exp. Psychol. Gen. **1981**, *3*, 306–340.

46. Kelley, C.M.; Rhodes, M.G. Making sense and nonsense of experience: Attributions in memory and judgment. In *Psychology of Learning and Motivation: Advances in Theory and Research*; Ross, B.H., Ed.; 2002; Vol. 41, 293–320.

47. Jacoby, L.L.; Kelley, C.; Brown, J.; Jasechko, J. Becoming famous overnight—Limits on the ability to avoid unconscious influences of the past. J. Pers. Soc. Psychol. **1989**, *56*, 326–338.

48. Jacoby, L.L.; Woloshyn, V.; Kelley, C. Becoming famous without being recognized—Unconscious influences of memory produced by dividing attention. J. Exp. Psychol. Gen. **1989**, *118*, 115–125.

49. Tversky, A.; Kahneman, D. Availability: A heuristic for judging frequency and probability. Cogn. Psychol. **1973**, *5*, 207–232.

50. Alter, A.L.; Oppenheimer, D.M. Predicting short-term stock fluctuations by using processing fluency. Proc. Natl. Acad. Sci. **2006**, *103*, 9369–9372.

51. Cokely, E.T., Parpart, P., Schooler, L.J. On the link between cognitive control and heuristic processes. Proceedings of the 31st Annual Conference of the Cognitive Science Society Taatgen, N.A., van Rijn, H., Eds.; Cognitive Science Society: Austin, TX, 2009; 2926–2931.

52. Pirolli, P.; Fu, W.T. SNIF-ACT: A model of information foraging on the world wide web Proceedings of the Ninth International Conference on User Modeling Johnstown, PA, 2003.

53. Marewski, J.N.; Galesic, M.; Gigerenzer, G. Fast and frugal media choices. *In Media Choice*: A Theoretical and Empirical Overview; Hartmann, T.,Ed.; Routledge: New York and London, 2009; 107–128.

54. Van Maanen, L. Marewski, J.N. Recommender systems for literature selection: A competition of decision making and memory models Proceedings of the 31st Annual Conference of the Cognitive Science Society. Taatgen, N.A., van Rijn, H., Eds. Cognitive Science Society: Austin, TX, 2009; 2914–2919.

55. Thatcher, A. Information-seeking behaviours and cognitive search strategies in different search tasks on the WWW. Int. J. Indus. Ergon. **2006**, *36*, 1055–1068.

56. Dresang, E.T. The information-seeking behavior of youth in the digital environment. Libr. Trends **2005**, *54*, 178–196.

57. Ozanne, J.L.; Brucks, M.; Grewal, D. A study of information search behavior during the categorization of new products. J. Consum. Res. **1992**, *18*, 452–463.

58. Guo, C. A review on consumer search: Amount and determinants. J. Bus. Psychol. **2001**, *51*, 505–519.

59. Zhang, J.; Fang, X.; Sheng, O.R.L. Online consumer search depth: Theories and new findings. J. Manage. Inform. Syst. **2006–2007**, *23*, 71–95.

60. Browne, G.J.; Pitts, M.G.; Wetherbe, J.C. Cognitive stopping rules for terminating information search in online tasks. Mis Quart. **2007**, *31*, 89–104.

61. Bilal, B.; Kirby, J. Differences and similarities in information seeking: Children and adults as Web users. Inform. Process. Manage. **2002**, *38*, 649–670.

62. Fasolo, B.; McClelland, G.H.; Todd, P.M. Escaping the tyranny of choice: When fewer attributes make choice easier. Marketing. **2007**, *7*(1), 13–26.

Information Systems–
Information Use

Informetrics

Judit Bar-Ilan
Department of Information Science, Bar-Ilan University, Ramat Gan, Israel

Abstract

Informetrics is a subfield of information science and it encompasses bibliometrics, scientometrics, cybermetrics, and webometrics. This encyclopedia entry provides an overview of informetrics and its subfields. In general, informetrics deals with quantitative aspects of information: its production, dissemination, evaluation, and use. Bibliometrics and scientometrics study scientific literature: papers, journals, patents, and citations; while in webometric studies the sources studied are Web pages and Web sites, and citations are replaced by hypertext links. The entry introduces major topics in informetrics: citation analysis and citation related studies, the journal impact factor, the recently defined h-index, citation databases, co-citation analysis, open access publications and its implications, informetric laws, techniques for mapping and visualization of informetric phenomena, the emerging subfields of webometrics, cybermetrics and link analysis, and research evaluation.

INTRODUCTION

In the literature, several definitions have been suggested for *informetrics* and the related fields of bibliometrics, scientometrics, cybermetrics, and webometrics. In this entry, we adopt the definitions suggested by Björneborn and Ingwersen,[1] where all the above-mentioned metrics are viewed as subfields of *informetrics*. This entry is organized as follows: first, we clarify the terminology and provide a general introduction and then we discuss the major topics of interest in the field (citation studies, theory, visualization, cybermetrics/webometrics, and research evaluation).

TERMINOLOGY AND DEFINITIONS

Informetrics was defined by Tague-Sutcliffe[2] as "the study of the quantitative aspects of information in any form, not just records or bibliographies, and in any social group, not just scientists." Brookes[3] characterized *informetrics* as "a generic term that embraces both biblio- and scientometrics." To understand Brookes' definition, we need to define *bibliometrics* and *scientometrics*. Here we use Tague-Sutcliffe's definitions again, she defined *bibliometrics* as "the study of the quantitative aspects of the production, dissemination, and use of recorded information" and *scientometrics* as "the study of the quantitative aspects of science as a discipline or economic activity."

The above definitions were published at the time the World Wide Web was just "born."[4] Although the Internet had existed for a long time already,[5] at the time the above definitions were published there were no quantitative studies of Internet-based and Web-based information to the best of our knowledge. Later the definition of *informetrics* was extended as a result of the Internet and the Web becoming major information sources, and currently *informetrics* is accepted to encompass *cybermetrics* and *webometrics* as well. *Cybermetrics* is defined in Ingwersen[1] and Björneborn[6] as "[t]he study of the quantitative aspects of the construction and use of information resources, structures and technologies on the whole Internet drawing on bibliometric and informetric approaches," and *webometrics* as "[t]he study of the quantitative aspects of the construction and use of information resources, structures and technologies on the Web drawing on bibliometric and informetric approaches." Fig. 1 illustrates the relation among the different "metrics."

There is some confusion regarding terminology. Egghe,[7] for example, provides a similar definition, but he does not differentiate between *cybermetrics* (study of information from *all* Internet applications) and *webometrics* (study of information from the World Wide Web only): *informetrics* is "the broad term comprising all-metrics studies related to information science, including bibliometrics (bibliographies, libraries,...), scientometrics (science policy, citation analysis, research evaluation,...), webometrics (metrics of the web, the Internet, or other social networks such as citation or collaboration networks),...." Glänzel and Schoeflin[8] use the term *bibliometrics* as a synonym for bibliometrics, informetrics, scientometrics, and technometrics, and at the same time claim that these subdisciplines are not interlinked. In their view, bibliometrics as a field "includes all quantitative aspects and models of science communication, storage, dissemination, and retrieval of scientific information," i.e., they limit the scope of *bibliometrics* to scientific information. The professional society of informetricians is ISSI, the International Society for Scientometrics and Informetrics, whose mission is to "to encourage communication and exchange of professional

Encyclopedia of Iron, Steel, and Their Alloys DOI: 10.1081/E-ELIS4-120045180
Copyright © 2017 by Taylor & Francis. All rights reserved.

Informetrics—International
Council

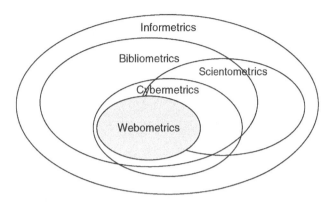

Fig. 1 The relationships between the LIS fields of infor-/
biblio-/sciento-/cyber-/webo-/metrics. Sizes of the overlapping
ellipses are made for the sake of clarity only.
Source: From Small-world link structures across an academic
web space: A library and information science approach, by L.
Björneborn. PhD dissertation, Royal School of Library and Information Science, Copenhagen, Denmark, xxxvi, 399, 2004.[6]

information in the field of scientometrics and informetrics."[9] From the mission statement we understand that
scientometrics is not considered to be a subfield of
informetrics, and there is no indication to the relation of
bibliometrics to these two fields. The society does not limit
the scope of these fields to scientific information only.

Hood and Wilson[10] provide a detailed discussion on the
use of the different terminologies, their origin and relative
popularity in the Information Science subset of databases of
DIALOG as of 2000. At that time *bibliometrics* was by far
the most popular term, followed by *scientometrics* and
informetrics. *Webometrics* and *cybermetrics* were not
included in their searches. We submitted a variant of some
of their searches on September 6, 2008 using

- ISI Web of Science (by Thomson Reuters)—searching
  for topics, which include title, abstract, author keywords, and keywords plus (keywords assigned based
  on the reference list), coverage from 1965 and onward
- Scopus (by Elsevier)—the searches were conducted in
  title and abstract. Keywords in Scopus are assigned
  both by the authors and by the database, and bibliometrics is one of the database-assigned keywords,
  therefore keywords were excluded from this search;
  coverage from 1996 and onward
- Google Scholar—a freely available bibliographic database with unspecified coverage both in terms of time

span and in terms of publications. Here the search term
can appear in any part of the publication (depending on
what is indexed by Google Scholar)
- Google—currently, the most popular Web search
  engine indexing Web pages and not necessarily scholarly publications
- Yahoo—currently, the second most popular Web
  search engine indexing Web pages and not necessarily
  scholarly publications

The results are presented in Table 1. The numbers of
course are not comparable, since the search conditions in
the different databases were not identical. Still we see that
like in 2000,[10] in each database the term *bibliometrics*
was the most frequent, but the rank order of the other
terms varied.

Hood and Wilson state that, the term *bibliometrics*
according to most sources was coined by Pritchard[11] in
1969; however, both Hood and Wilson[10] and Rousseau
(See the entry, "Informetric Laws," p. 2747) mention
a much earlier use of the French term bibliometry by
Otlet 1934. *Scientometrics* is the translation of the
Russian term "naukometriya," coined by Nalimov and
Mulchenko in 1969. The term *informetrics* comes from
the German word "informetrie" and was first proposed by
Nacke[12] in 1979. The term *webometrics* was introduced
by Almind and Ingwersen[13] in 1997. The origin of the
term *cybermetrics* is not clear. It should probably be
attributed to Isidro Aguillo, the editor of the e-journal
Cybermetrics (http://www.cindoc.csic.es/cybermetrics/
cybermetrics.html), founded in 1997.

GENERAL OVERVIEW

The literature related to informetrics is very extensive;
in this section we list some review and encyclopedia
entries and books on the topic. These references can serve
the interested readers as starting points for exploring
informetrics.

There are several reviews of *informetrics* and its subfields, including a number of review articles in the Annual
Review of Information Science and Technology: the 1989
review by White and McCain of bibliometrics;[14] a review
of informetrics by Wilson in 2001;[15] the 2001 review of
scholarly communication and informetrics by Borgman
and Furner,[16] and a review of webometrics by Thelwall,

Table 1 Relative popularity of the "informetrics family" terminology. The number in brackets in each cell is the rank order of the term
in the specific database.

Search term	Web of Science; 1965–	Scopus 1996–	Google Scholar	Google	Yahoo
Informetrics	86[3]	98[3]	3330[3]	62,300[5]	164,000[5]
Bibliometrics	360[1]	284[1]	78,000[1]	1,320,000[1]	846,000[1]
Scientometrics	164[2]	216[2]	13,100[2] (incl. the journal by this name)	164,000[3]	447,000[2]
Cybermetrics	11[5]	12[5]	1250[4] (incl. the journal by this name)	149,000[4]	200,000[4]
Webometrics	62[4]	37[4]	1160[5]	253,000[2]	414,000[3]

Vaughan and Björneborn[17] in 2005. Most recently Bar-Ilan[18] published an updated review of informetrics, covering the literature published between 2000 and 2005.

The *Encyclopedia of Library and Information Sciences* also contains several articles related to *informetrics*, please see topical contents list. Russell and Rousseau[19] discuss bibliometrics and institutional evaluation in the Encyclopedia of Life Support Systems' section on science and technology policy.

To this day there is only one textbook dedicated to informetrics, the book written by Egghe and Rousseau.[20] The full text of the book is available online at http://eprints.rclis.org/archive/00003297/. There are a number of additional monographs on informetric topics, including Garfield's book on citation indexing;[21] Cronin's book on the citation process;[22] Moed's recent book[23] on the use of citation analysis in research evaluation; and Thelwall's[24] book on link analysis, one of the major topics in webometrics.

In order to identify the major journals related broadly to *informetrics*, Wilson[15] ran the query bibliometric? OR informetric? in 11 databases using DIALOG. Here we ran the query bibliometric OR bibliometrics OR informetric OR Informetrics OR scientometric OR scientometrics OR webometric OR webometrics OR cybermetric OR cybermetrics on the currently existing two major, comprehensive commercial bibliographical databases, ISI's Web of Science (by Thomson Reuters) and Scopus (by Elsevier). Note that in Bar-Ilan,[18] a much more detailed query was executed on the same databases. The publication year in both databases was limited to 1996 and onward, because Scopus' comprehensive coverage is from 1996 and onward. The journals producing the largest number of items for both databases are displayed in Table 2. Note that there are major differences in the two databases for the ranking of some of the journals. The major reason for this is that Scopus adds keywords, and bibliometrics is one of the keywords used, while WOS indexes only author-assigned keywords and what are called "Keywords Plus": keywords generated from the titles of the references. Many of the articles indexed by Scopus as "bibliometrics" are short items (e.g., letters) in Nature. These do not have abstracts, but deal with issues like the impact factor (IF) and citation analysis in general. The query terms do not appear in the title; thus, they are not retrieved by WOS, but these publications are definitely related to informetrics, and are picked up by Scopus because the keyword bibliometrics was assigned to them. In some cases, Scopus retrieves fewer items, than WOS—a paper-by-paper comparison of the two sets reveals that there are some differences between the two sets as a result of the use of the keywords and index terms in WOS, the index keywords in Scopus and the different indexing policies between the two databases regarding book reviews.

The results show that there is a wide interest in the topic, as papers appear both in general science journals

Table 2 Top journals related to informetrics, 1996–2008 based on documents retrieved for the query "bibliometric OR bibliometrics OR informetric OR Informetrics OR scientometric OR scientometrics OR webometric OR webometrics OR cybermetric OR cybermetrics" from WOS and Scopus. For both databases, the 10 most productive journals for the query are ranked and displayed.

Journal Name	Rank in Web of Science (number of documents in journal in parenthesis)	Rank in Scopus (number of documents in journal in parenthesis)
Scientometrics	1 (522)	1 (447)
Journal of the American Society for Information Science and Technology	2 (103)	3 (80)
Information Processing & Management	3–4 (42)	5–6 (39)
Journal of Information Science	3–4 (42)	7 (38)
Research Evaluation	5 (39)	4 (46)
Journal of the American Society for Information Science	6 (35)	9 (24)
Research Policy	7 (31)	8 (26)
Journal of Documentation	8 (29)	10–12 (23)
Current Science	9–10 (18)	29–33 (13)
Medicina Clinica	9–10 (18)	10–12 (23)
Journal of Informetrics	11–12 (16)	10–12 (23)
Nature	165–519 (1)	2 (103)
Journal of the Medical Library Association	19–22 (9)	5–6 (39)

(e.g., *Nature*), in major information science journals (e.g., *JASIST*) and in specialist journals (e.g., *Scientometrics*). In addition to the specialist journals in the area; *Scientometrics*, *Journal of Informetrics*, *Research Policy*, *Research Evaluation*, and *Cybermetrics*, there are several conference series covering informetrics: the Biannual International Informetrics and Scientometrics Conferences of the International Society for Informetrics and Scientometrics (ISSI—http://www.issi-society.info/), the Biannual International Conferences on Science and Technology Indicators and the newly established International Conferences on Webometrics, Informetrics and Scientometrics of the COLLNET Research Network (http://www.collnet.de). Note that while *Scientometrics* was started in 1978, the *Journal of Informetrics* is a brand new journal; its first volume appeared in 2007.

OVERVIEW OF THE MAJOR INFORMETRIC TOPICS

Citation Studies

As Wilson[15] claims: "[p]erhaps the largest subfield of informetrics is citation analysis or citation studies." First we need to clarify the difference between citations and

Informetrics–International Council

references, because in many cases there is some confusion between the two. We use here the terminology proposed by Price:[25] "if Paper R contains a bibliographic footnote using and describing Paper C, then R contains a reference to C, and C has a citation from R. The number of references a paper has is measured by the number of items in its bibliography as endnotes, footnotes, etc., while the number of citations a paper has is found by looking it up [in a] citation index and seeing how many others papers mention it."

Until 2004 there was only a single source for conducting citation studies: ISI's citation indexes: the Science Citation Index (SCI), the Social Sciences Citation Index (SSCI) and the Arts and Humanities Citation Index (A&HCI). These three indexes are accessible now as a single index through the Web of Science tab of Thomson Reuters' Web of Knowledge (http://apps.isiknowledge. com). ISI, the Institute of Scientific Information (now owned by Thomson Reuter), was founded by Eugene Garfield. Thus an excellent starting point to understanding citation theory and citation indexing is Eugene Garfield's book[25] and his Web site (http://www.garfield.library. upenn.edu/) containing links and full texts of many works related to the topic. A detailed discussion of "citation cultures" can be found in Paul Wouters' Ph.D. thesis.[26]

Why should we study and count citations? The basic assumption is that a scientific paper refers to other items because they are relevant to the current study; for example, they provide background, the current paper uses methods described in the referred paper, the current study is comparable/superior to other studies. For a detailed discussion of citation motivations the reader is referred to (pp. 28–30).[22] To sum up, the basic assumption is that document A refers to document B for positive reasons in the vast majority of the cases and acknowledges the work reported in B. Of course, a reference can be negative as well, but this is the exception and not the rule. If one accepts the above assumption, then citation counts reflect the influence of the paper on subsequent literature. In the scholarly community usually each citation is considered equal; however, citations can be weighted based on the "importance" of the citing document.[27–29] The weighted approach was proposed by Pinski and Narin,[30] and a similar method is applied in PageRank, Google's ranking algorithm.[31]

Of course, there are opponents to the assumption that the influence of a document can be measured by the number of citations it receives. Some of the reasons for criticizing this approach include bias in choosing references, missing references to influential work, and errors in the reference lists.[32]

The impact factor

One of the most controversial issues in the area of citation analysis is the impact factor (IF). The IF was introduced by Garfield and Sher,[33] and it serves as a measure of journal importance. The Journal Citation Reports (JCR) annually publishes the IFs of journals indexed by the ISI Science and Social Sciences Citation indexes. The IF of a journal is defined as the number of citations the articles published in the journal in years $x-1$ and $x-2$, received in year x, divided by the number of articles published in the journal in years $x-1$ and $x-2$. Thus, IF measures the average number of recent citations that an article in the journal receives.

The IF is often misused when it serves as a proxy for the "importance" of articles published in the journal.[34] Sometimes, articles in a high impact journal are not cited at all, and on the other hand some articles in low impact journals are cited heavily.

Citation practices differ greatly among disciplines,[35] for example in the JCR category *Medicine, General & Internal*, the highest ranking journal in the list for 2007, *The New England Journal of Medicine* has an IF of 52.589, while the highest ranking journal in the category Information and Library Science, is *MIS Quarterly* with an IF of 5.826. The above example shows that IFs are not comparable across disciplines. In order to compare citation count and IF, the data have to be normalized.[36–38]

h-index

A newly-introduced indicator to measure scientists is the h-index[39] proposed by Hirsch. A scientist has h-index h, if he/she published h papers that have been cited h times or more, while all his/her other papers have been cited h times or less. Thus the h-index is a single measure that combines productivity and citation counts. The h-index is dependent on the data source used for collecting information on production and citations,[40] on the time span used for calculating the index, the number of years the scientist has been active (biased against young scientists), and its characteristic values are discipline dependent. In spite of this, currently there is a huge interest in understanding and modeling the indicator[41,42] and in proposing variants of the measure, e.g., the g-index proposed by Egghe.[43] The g-index is the (unique) largest number such that when the articles are ordered by the decreasing number of citations, the top g articles receive (together) at least $g^{[2]}$ citations.

Citation databases

As pointed out above, until November 2004 there was only a single comprehensive source for carrying out citation studies—the ISI Citation Indexes. In November 2004, Elsevier launched Scopus (http://www.scopus.com) and Google launched (as a beta) its free service Google Scholar.

Google Scholar enables searching for scholarly literature and also provides citation counts of the items discovered by it. Google Scholar has unspecified coverage both

Informetrics–International
Council

in terms of the indexed items and in terms of time-span. It has agreement with major publishers and also gathers information by crawling through the Web. Google Scholar was greeted by the scientific community with mixed feelings. For criticism about its performance, the reader is referred to some of the articles published by Jacso,[44,45] and for more positive impressions the reader is referred to Harzing.[46] Harzing developed an application called "Publish or Perish" (http://www.harzing.com/pop.htm) for carrying out informetric analyses based on Google Scholar data. Although the informetric community is currently quite ambivalent about Google Scholars, scientists, and students use it heavily, as can be seen from statistics provided in:[47] 73% of the academic institutions examined in the study provided link resolution from Google Scholar results to their online resources.

Scopus is a bibliographical and citation database. It covers more publication sources than the Web of Science and is not limited to indexing journals but also includes some proceedings. The citation data only goes back to 1996, whereas the Web of Science has citation data from 1900 for Sciences, from 1956 for the Social Sciences and from 1975 for Arts and Humanities.[48] As of September 2008, Scopus indexes 15,000 journal publications,[49] as compared to 8700 indexed by the Web of Science. Journal indicators based on the Web of Science data are published in the Journal Citation Reports, and other country and discipline specific statistics are provided by the Essential Science Indicators. Freely accessible country and journal indicators based on Scopus data are available from the SciMago Research Group (http://www.scimagojr.com/). In October 2008 data from the ISI Proceedings Indexes were merged into the Web of Science.

Co-citation analysis

Co-citation measures the frequency with which two documents are cited together.[50] Frequent co-citations are interpreted as similarity or co-occurrence of ideas. Co-citation analysis can reveal the core literature for a topic, and then map the structure of the topic.[50,51] Co-citation analysis was independently introduced by Small[54] and Marshakova.[52] Later co-citation analysis was extended to author,[53–55] and journal co-citation analyses.[56] Mapping based on co-citation matrices is only one of several available techniques. In the section on visualization, we mention additional data sources for visualization like citation matrices, co-authorship data, and co-word analysis.

Open access

Open access is defined as "free, immediate, permanent, full-text, online access, for any user, web-wide, to digital scientific and scholarly material."[57] An interesting question regarding open access publications is whether free access to publications increases the publication's citation impact. Several studies showed that electronic access (even if the access is not free) increases citation counts (e.g., Lawrence[58] and Harnad);[59] however, some studies (e.g., Anderson)[60] reached a different conclusion. There are several possible reasons for increased citation counts, including early access (papers are online even before the refereeing process is over), selection bias (authors prefer to publish online their "better" papers), and the ease of access, called the "open access advantage."[61] Moed[62] examined these effects on two sample data sets from Arxiv, a huge open access e-print archive containing nearly half a million e-prints as of September 2008, and found no sign of open access advantage. A similar conclusion was reached by Craig et al.[63] Harnad[64] advocates institutional repositories for self-archiving and open access, and promotes mandating archiving of publications in institutional repositories to ease access to scientific publications.

Theoretical Informetrics

There are three famous regularities or informetric laws: Lotka's law, Zipf's law, and Bradford's law.[15] Lotka's law[65] is an inverse square law between the number of authors of scientific papers and the number of publications of each author. According to this law, the number of authors producing two items is about one-fourth of the number of authors producing a single item, and the number of authors producing three items is about one-ninth of those producing a single item, and about 60% of all authors contribute a single item only.

Zipf's law[66] has a similar flavor, but instead of authors and publications, it relates to the rank order and the frequency of words in texts. The rank order of a word in a text is the placement of the word in a list sorted in decreasing order of frequency in the text. The law says that if the words in the text are listed in decreasing frequency, then the rank of the word in the list times its frequency in the text is a constant.

Bradford's law[67] is called Bradford's law of scattering, and describes the scatter of scientific literature. He listed the publication sources (e.g., journals) on a specific topic in decreasing order of productivity (productivity is assessed by the number of items on the topic published by the publication source) and partitioned the ordered list into three equal size sets in terms of the number of publications, and showed that the ratio between the number of publication sources in the three zones is about 1: n: n;[2] i.e., a small number of publication sources (called the "core") produce a considerable fraction of the publications.

Extensive discussions of informetric laws can be found in additional ELIS entries (see the Topical Table of Contents). These laws are also discussed in the informetrics textbook[20] and the ARIST review on informetrics.[15] Egghe recently published a book[68] where all informetric laws are described in terms of appropriate Lotkaian functions, thus producing a unified theory based on Lotkaian informetrics.

In addition to studying informetric laws and distributions, the theory of informetrics is also concerned with other issues including modeling growth processes. It should be noted that besides the growth of the scientific literature, older items are usually cited less—they become "aged" and sometimes even obsolete. Well-known, applicable growth models are so-called rich-get-richer models, also known as preferential attachment,[69] or cumulative advantage.[70] Examples of such models and studies include works on the evolution of coauthorship networks.[71,72] Börner, Maru, and Goldstone[73] proposed a model where both author and paper networks evolve simultaneously. Visualizations of evolving networks are discussed in the next section.

Mapping and Visualization

Many informetric results call for visualization. We have previously seen examples of co-citation analyses that model the structure of scientific topics. Collaboration networks are also best understood through visualization, and visualization techniques also help in gaining insights into evolutionary processes. Here we provide only a number of examples of visualizations. Excellent starting points for exploring the topic are the recent ARIST review on visualization[74] and Chen's book on mapping scientific frontiers.[75] Several studies of citation patterns between journals visualized the resulting structures.[76–78] Garfield[79] developed algorithmic historiography that allows studying the origins of a topic and its development over time, and the resulting visualization is called a "historiograph." Glänzel[80] studied and mapped coauthorship relations between countries. Maps can also be created based on co-word analysis, i.e., on co-occurrence of words.[81]

Cybermetrics and Webometrics

Cybermetrics and webometrics are the newest subfields of informetrics. The first webometric/cybermetric studies conducted in the late 1990s showed the applicability of informetric techniques for the Internet in general and specifically for the World Wide Web.[82–84] Ingwersen[85] defined the Web Impact Factor (WIF), which corresponds to the Journal Impact Factor, where instead of citations; links pointing to the Web site are counted. More precisely the WIF is the number of pages with links pointing to the given site divided by the number of Web pages in the site. Note that Egghe[86] warned against drawing a direct analogy between citations and links. Ingwersen used a Web search engine to collect both the number of links and the number of Web pages. However, Web search engines are not very reliable and their coverage of the World Wide Web is far from being

even.[87–90] Problems of search engine reliability are far from being solved, as can be seen in.[91]

One way to overcome the problem of search engine reliability is not to use them for data collection, but to use a Web crawler instead. Thelwall developed such a crawler (available from http://socscibot.wlv.ac.uk/) and studied extensively the link structure between U.K. universities (for a summary of this work see Thelwall).[24] He also developed several variants of the WIF that correlated better with actual research performance.

Similarly to the study of citation motivation, it is of interest to understand why academics are mentioned on Web pages[92] and why links to pages on academic Web sites are created.[93] Bar-Ilan[94] created a framework for classifying links between academic sites and applied it to links between Israeli academic Web sites.

Most studies of inlinks to academic Web sites from other academic Web sites found strong correlation between the number of inlinks and research performance. A natural question is whether there is a similar correlation between the number of inlinks to a journal Web site and its IF. Vaughan and colleagues[95,96] found such a correlation both for LIS and law journals. Link structure of commercial Web sites has been studied as well. In a number of studies carried out by Vaughan,[97,98] significant correlation was found between the business performance and the number of inlinks.

Vaughan and Shaw[99] introduced the concept of "Web citation," which is roughly an appearance of the title of a publication within a Web page (not necessarily as a link). They found good correlation between the number of "regular" citations and the number of "Web citations" in a number of disciplines. Kousha and Thelwall[100] examined so-called Web/URL citations, where a "Web/URL citation of an online journal article is a Web mention of its title, URL, or both" for a number of disciplines. For all disciplines except psychology they found good correlations between Web of Science citation counts, Google Scholar citation counts and Web/URL citation counts.

Just as the growth and evolution of scientific topics are studied, the evolution of the Web is also a topic of interest for webometrics. Several longitudinal studies were carried out in the webometric context. Scharnhorst and Wouters[101] proposed a classification of temporal changes that occur to the web graph. Koehler[102] studied the changes that occurred to a fixed set of pages over time. Bar-Ilan and Peritz[103] carried out an eight-year study following the evolution of the pages containing the search term "informetrics" on the Web. They showed that besides growth; disappearance and changes to the content of Web pages are nonnegligible processes as well. Disappearance can also be demonstrated by testing URL references in scientific publications.[104]

More recently there are also webometric studies of Web 2.0, including studies of blogs,[105] of tagging systems,[106] and of social networks like Myspace.[107] With

Informetrics–International
Council

the widespread use of Web 2.0 technologies, more studies in this direction can be expected in the future.

Research Evaluation

Scientometrics, as defined in the introduction is the study of the quantitative aspects of science. Scientometric studies serve as tools for research policy makers and also help in the evaluation process. Historical aspects of measurement and statistics of science and technology are discussed by Godin.[108] Etzkowitz and Leydesdorff[109,110] model the interaction between government, industry, and universities as the "triple helix" for explaining the research system. The recently published *Handbook of Quantitative Science and Technology Research*[111] provides a state-of-the-art survey of research in this area. What can be evaluated using scientometric techniques? Here we bring examples of evaluations of individual researchers, research units, universities, journals, and countries.

Individual researchers can be evaluated based on their productivity (number of publications), patents, funding, citation counts, the IFs of journals they publish in, and peer review. One of the more interesting questions is how much agreement there is between the quantitative, scientometric measures and peer review. There is a lively debate around this issue in the context of the U.K. Research Assessment Exercise (RAE). Until the 2008 exercise, the distribution of funding for the U.K. universities was decided based on peer review only. In the current exercise, both peer review and bibliometric indicators are considered. Norris and Oppenheim[112] found high and significant correlations between RAE rankings and rankings based on citation counts for archeology. Weingart[113] warns that when bibliometric indicators are used for research evaluation, the results can be manipulated. An interesting example of this is Australian science, where funding is mainly based on the number of publications, as a result of which Australia's share of publication increased by 25% between 1988 and 1997, while its citation impact decreased.[114]

Thus one question is whether to employ peer review or to rely on indicators. Another question is which indicators to use. To illustrate this point, Cronin and Shaw[115] compared rankings based on citation counts, Web hits, and media mentions. The resulting rankings were considerably different. The data source for computing the indicators is also of importance.[116]

Also of interest are rankings of universities. There are several rankings, the best known are the Shanghai rankings (http://www.arwu.org/) and the rankings produced for the *Times of London* Higher Education Supplement (http://www.timeshighereducation.co.uk/). Both these rankings take into account some bibliometric data, but include nonbibliometric measures as well. There are also rankings based on webometric data (http://www.webometrics.info/) and also rankings based on pure bibliometric data (http://www.cwts.nl/cwts/LeidenRankingWebSite.html). There

are several Leiden rankings demonstrating the variability of the results according to the chosen indicator(s).

When considering the world of science, policy makers are often interested in comparing countries. For example, King[117] calculated the scientific impact of nations, based on publications counts, citation counts, share of top 1% papers, GDP, normalized citation counts, and financial inputs. The findings indicate that the share of United States is declining and the EU countries are catching up. Glänzel, Schubert, and Braun[118] studied the productivity and citation impact of the 32 most prolific countries based on ISI data for the years 1990–1998. Zhou and Leydesdoff[119] concluded that China has become the fifth leading nation in terms of scientific productivity based on data from the Web of Science as of 2004.

Scientometric indicators have considerable weight in decisions regarding the funding and development of science. As can be seen from the above-mentioned studies, there does not exist one "correct" or "perfect" method or indicator for evaluation, but informetricians continue to search for better quantitative indicators for evaluating and forecasting science.

SUMMARY

In this entry, we tried to provide an overview of informetrics and its subfields. It is impossible to cover all areas of interest in the field in such an entry. However, we hope that the interested reader will consult some of the sources mentioned in the references in order to deepen his/her knowledge of the topic.

REFERENCES

1. Björneborn, L.; Ingwersen, P. Toward a basic framework for Webometrics. J. Am. Soc. Inform. Sci. Technol. **2004**, *55*(14), 1216–1227.
2. Tague-Sutcliffe, J. An introduction to informetrics. Inform. Process. Manag. **1992**, *28*(1), 1–4.
3. Brookes, B.C. Biblio-, sciento-, infor-metrics??? What are we talking about? *Informetrics 89/90*, Selection of Papers Submitted for the Second International Conference on Bibliometrics Scientometrics and Informetrics London, Ontario July 5–7, 1989; Egghe, L., Rousseau, R., Eds.; Elsevier: Amsterdam, the Netherlands, 1991.
4. Cailleau, R.; Connolly, D. A little history of the World Wide Web. Revision 1.49,. 2006. Available at http://www.w3.org/History.html (accessed September 2008).
5. Leiner, B.M.; Cerf, V.G.; Clark, D.D.; Kahn, R.E.; Kleinrock, L.; Lynch, D.C.; Postel, J.; Roberts, L.G.; Wolff, S. A brief history of the Internet, version 3.32, 2003. Available at http://www.isoc.org/internet/history/brief.shtml (accessed September 2008).
6. Björneborn, L. *Small-world link structures across an academic web space: A library and information science approach*, PhD dissertation; Royal School of Library and

Informetrics–International Council

Information Science: Copenhagen, Denmark, 2004; xxxvi, 399. Available at http://vip.db.dk/lb/phd/phd-thesis.pdf (accessed September 2004).

7. Egghe, L. Expansion of the field of informetrics: Origins and consequences. Inform. Process. Manag. **2005**, *41*(6), 1311–1316.

8. Glänzel, W.; Schoeflin, U. Little scientometrics, big scientometrics…and beyond?. Scientometrics **1994**, *30*(2–3), 375–384.

9. Davis, M.; Glänzel, W. International Society for Scientometrics and Informetrics. Mission **2004**. Available at http://www.issi-society.info/mission.html (accessed September 2008).

10. Hood, W.W.; Wilson, C.S. The literature of bibliometrics, scientometrics, and informetrics. Scientometrics **2001**, *52*(2), 291–314.

11. Pritchard, A. Statistical bibliography or bibliometrics?. J. Doc. **1969**, *25*(4), 348–349.

12. Nacke, O. Informetrie: Ein neuer name für eine neue disziplin. [Informetrics: A new name for a new discipline.] Nachrichten für Dokumentation **1979**, *30*(6), 212–226.

13. Almind, T.C.; Ingwersen, P. Informetric analyses of the World Wide Web: Methodological approaches to "webometrics". J. Doc. **1997**, *53*(4), 404–426.

14. White, H.D.; McCain, K.W. Bibliometrics. In *Annual Review of Information Science and Technology*; Williams, M.E., Ed.; Elsevier: Amsterdam, 1989; Vol. 24, 119–186.

15. Wilson, C.S. Informetrics. In *Annual Review of Information Science and Technology*; Williams, M.E., Ed.; Information Today: Medford, NJ, 1999; Vol. 34, 107–247.

16. Borgman, C.L.; Furner, J. Scholarly communication and bibliometrics. In *Annual Review of Information Science and Technology*; Cronin, B., Ed.; Information Today: Medford, NJ, 2002; Vol. 36, 3–72.

17. Thelwall, M.; Vaughan, L.; Björneborn, L. Webometrics. In *Annual Review of Information Science and Technology*; Cronin, B., Ed.; Information Today: Medford, NJ, 2005; Vol. 39, 81–135.

18. Bar-Ilan, J. Informetrics at the beginning of the 21st century – A review. J. Informet. **2008**, *2*(1), 1–52.

19. Russell, J.; Rousseau, R. Bibliometrics and institutional evaluation. In *Encyclopedia of Life Support Systems (EOLSS); Part 19.3: Science and Technology Policy*; Arvantis, R., Ed.; Eolss Publishers: Oxford, 2002.

20. Egghe, L.; Rousseau, R. *Introduction to Informetrics: Quantitative Methods in Library, Documentation and Information Science*, Elsevier: Amsterdam, 1990.

21. Garfield, E. *Citation Indexing – Its Theory and Applications in Science, Technology and the Humanities*, John Wiley and Sons: New York, 1979.

22. Cronin, B. *The Citation Process*, Taylor-Graham: London, 1984.

23. Moed, H. *Citation Analysis in Research Evaluation*, Springer: Dordrecht, 2005.

24. Thelwall, M. *Link Analysis: An Information Science Approach*, Elsevier, Academic Press: Amsterdam, 2004.

25. de Solla Price, D.J. *Little Science, Big Science and Beyond*, Columbia University Press: New York, 1986.

26. Wouters, P. *The Citation Culture*, 1999. Available at http://www.garfield.library.upenn.edu/wouters/wouters.pdf (accessed September 2008).

27. Liu, M. The complexities of citation practice: A review of citation studies. J. Doc. **1993**, *49*(4), 370–408.

28. Baird, L.M.; Oppenheim, C. Do citations matter?. J. Inform. Sci. **1994**, *20*(1), 2–15.

29. Peritz, B.C. A classification of citation roles for the social sciences. Scientometrics **1983**, *5*(5), 303–312.

30. Pinski, G.; Narin, F. Citation influence for journal aggregates of scientific publications: Theory with an application to the literature of physics. Inform. Process. Manag. **1976**, *12*(5), 297–312.

31. Brin, S.; Page, L. The anatomy of a large-scale hypertextual Web search engine. Comput. Networks ISDN **1998**, *30*(1–7), 107–117.

32. MacRoberts, M.H.; MacRoberts, B.R. Problems of citation analysis. Scientometrics **1996**, *36*(3), 435–444.

33. Garfield, E.; Sher, I. New factors in the evaluation of scientific literature through citation indexing. Am. Doc. **1963**, *14*(3), 195–201.

34. Seglen, P.O. Why the impact factor of journals should not be used for evaluating research. Brit. J. Med. **1997**, *31*(4), 498–502.

35. Bordons, M.; Fernández, M.T.; Gómez, I. Advantages and limitations in the use of impact factor measures for the assessment of research assessment in a peripheral country. Scientometrics **2002**, *53*(2), 196–205.

36. Moed, H.F.; De Bruin, R.E.; van Leeuwen, T.h.N. New bibliometric tools for the assessment of national research performance: Database description, overview of indicators and first applications. Scientometrics **1995**, *33*(3), 381–422.

37. Schubert, A.; Braun, T. Relative indicators and relational charts for comparative assessment of publication output and citation impact. Scientometrics **1986**, *9*(5–6), 281–291.

38. Braun, T.; Glänzel, W. United Germany: The new scientific superpower?. Scientometrics **1990**, *19*(5–6), 513–521.

39. Hirsch, J.E. An index to quantify an individual's scientific research output. P. Natl. Acad. Sci. U.S.A. **2005**, *102*(46), 16569–16572.

40. Bar-Ilan, J. Which h-index? — A comparison of WoS, Scopus and Google Scholar. Scientometrics **2008**, *74*(2), 254–271.

41. Glänzel, W. On the h-index – A mathematical approach to a new measure of publication activity and citation impact. Scientometrics **2006**, *67*(2), 315–321.

42. Egghe, L.; Rousseau, R. An informetric model for the Hirsch-index. Scientometrics **2006**, *69*(1), 1221–1229.

43. Egghe, L. Theory and practise of the g-index. Scientometrics **2006**, *69*(1), 131–152.

44. Jacsó, P. Google Scholar – The pros and the cons. Online Inform. Rev. **2005**, *29*(2), 208–214.

45. Jacso, P. Google Scholar revisited. Online Inform. Rev. **2008**, *29*(2), 208–214.

46. Harzing, A.K.; van der Wal, R. Google Scholar as a new source for citation analysis. ESEP **2008**, 8. Available at http://www.int-res.com/articles/esep2008/8/e008pp5.pdf (accessed September 2008).

47. Neuhaus, C.; Neuhaus, A.; Asher, A. Google scholar goes to school: The presence of Google scholar on college and university websites. J. Acad. Libr. **2008**, *34*(1), 39–51.

48. Thomson Reuters. *Web of Science*, http://scientific. thomsonreuters.com/products/wos/ (accessed September 2008).

49. *Scopus Overview*. Available at http://info.scopus.com/ overview/what/ (accessed September 2008).

50. Small, H. Co-citation in the scientific literature: A new measure of the relationship between two documents. J. Am. Soc. Inform. Sci. **1973**, *24*(4), 265–269.

51. Small, H. Visualizing science by citation mapping. J. Am. Soc. Inform. Sci. **1999**, *50*(9), 799–813.

52. Marshakova, I.V. A system of document connections based on references. Nauchno-Technicheskaia Informatsiia **1973**, *2*(6), 3–8 In Russian.

53. White, H.D.; Griffith, B.C. Author cocitation: A literature measure of intellectual structure. J. Am. Soc. Inform. Sci. **1981**, *32*(3), 163–171.

54. McCain, K.W. Mapping authors in intellectual space: A technical overview. J. Am. Soc. Inform. Sci. **1990**, *41*(6), 433–443.

55. White, H.D.; McCain, K.W. Visualizing a discipline: An author co-citation analysis of information science, 1972–1995. J. Am. Soc. Inform. Sci. **1999**, *49*(4), 327–355.

56. McCain, K.W. Mapping economics through the journal literature: An experiment in journal cocitation analysis. J. Am. Soc. Inform. Sci. **1991**, *42*(4), 290–296.

57. Wikipedia contributors, "Open access," Wikipedia, The Free Encyclopedia. Available at http://en.wikipedia.org/w/ index.php?title=Open_access&oldid=237421344.

58. Lawrence, S. Free online availability substantially increases a paper's impact. Nature **2001**, *411*(6837), 521.

59. Harnad, S.; Brody, T. Comparing the impact of Open Access (OA) vs. non-OA articles in the same journals. D-lib Mag. **2004**, *10*(6). Available at http://www.dlib.org/ dlib/june04/harnad/06harnad.html (accessed September 2008).

60. Anderson, K.; Sack, J.; Krauss, L.; O'Keefe, L. Publishing online-only peer-reviewed biomedical literature: Three years of citation, author perception, and usage experience. J. Electron. Publish. **2001**, *6*(3). Available at http://quod. lib.umich.edu/cgi/t/text/text-idx?c=jep;view=text;rgn=main; idno=3336451.0006.303 (accessed September 2008).

61. Kurtz, M.J.; Eichhorn, G.; Accomazzi, A.; Grant, C.; Demleitner, M.; Henneken, E.; Murray, S.S. The effect of use and access on citations. Inform. Process. Manag. **2005**, *41*(6), 1395–1402.

62. Moed, H.F. The effect of "open access" on citation impact: An analysis of ArXiv's condensed matter section. J. Am. Soc. Inform. Sci. technol. **2007**, *58*(13), 2047–2054.

63. Craig, I.D.; Plume, A.M.; McVeigh, M.E.; Pringle, J.; Amin, M. Do open access articles have greater citation impact? A critical review of the literature. J. Informet. **2007**, *1*(3), 239–248.

64. Harnad, S. The self-archiving initiative. Nature **2001**, *410* (6832), 1024–1025.

65. Lotka, A.J. The frequency distribution of scientific productivity. J. Wash. Acad. Sci. **1926**, *16*(12), 317–323.

66. Zipf, G.K. *Selected Studies of the Principle of Relative Frequency in Language*, Harvard University Press: Cambridge, MA, 1932.

67. Bradford, S.C. Sources of information on specific subjects. Engineering **1934**, *137*, 85–86.

68. Egghe, L. *Power Laws in the Information Production Process: Lotkaian Informetrics*, Academic Press: Amsterdam, 2005.

69. Barabási, A.L.; Albert, R. Emergence of scaling in random networks. Science **1999**, *286*(5439), 509–512.

70. Price, D.J.D.S. A general theory of bibliometric and other cumulative advantage processes. J. Am. Soc. Inform. Sci. **1976**, *27*(5–6), 292–306.

71. Barabási, A.L.; Jeong, H.; Neda, Z.; Ravasz, E.; Schubert, A.; Vicsek, T. Evolution of the social network of scientific collaborations. Physica A **2002**, *311*(3–4), 590–614.

72. Newman, M.E.J. Clustering and preferential attachment in growing networks. Phys. Rev. E **2001**, *64*(2), Art. No. 025102, Part 2.

73. Börner, K.; Maru, J.T.; Goldstone, R.L. The simultaneous evolution of author and paper networks. P. Natl. Acad. Sci. U.S.A. **2004**, *101*(1), 5266–5273.

74. Börner, K.; Chen, C.M.; Boyack, K.W. Visualizing knowledge domains. In *Annual Review of Information Science and Technology*; Cronin, B., Ed.; Information Today: Medford, NJ, 2003; Vol. 37, 179–255. Available at http://ivl. slis.indiana.edu/km/pub/2003-borner-arist.pdf (accessed September 2008).

75. Chen, C. *Mapping Scientific Frontiers*, Springer Verlag: London, 2003.

76. Bassecoulard, E.; Zitt, M. Indicators in a research institute: A multilevel classification of journals. Scientometrics **1999**, *44*(3), 323–345.

77. Leydesdorff, L. Clusters and maps of science journals based on bi-connected graphs in Journal Citation Reports. J. Doc. **2004**, *60*(4), 371–427.

78. Boyack, K.W.; Klavens, R.; Börner, K. Mapping the backbone of science. Scientometrics **2005**, *64*(3), 351–374.

79. Garfield, E. Historiographic mapping of knowledge domains literature. J. Inform. Sci. **2004**, *30*(2), 119–145.

80. Glänzel, W. National characteristics in international scientific co-authorship relations. Scientometrics **2001**, *51*(1), 69–115.

81. Noyons, E. Bibliometric mapping of science in a science policy context. Scientometrics **2001**, *50*(1), 83–98.

82. Larson, R. Bibliometrics of the World Wide Web: An exploratory analysis of the intellectual structure of Cyberspace Proceedings of ASIS96 Medford, NJ 1996; 71–78, 2002, Available at http://sherlock.berkeley.edu/ asis96/asis96.html (accessed September 2008).

83. Rousseau, R. Sitations: An exploratory study. Cybermetrics **1997**, *1*(1). Available at http://www.cindoc. csic.es/cybermetrics/articles/v1i1p1.pdf (accessed September 2008).

84. Bar-Ilan, J. The 'mad cow disease', Usenet newsgroups and bibliometric laws. Scientometrics **1997**, *39*(1), 29–35.

85. Ingwersen, P. The calculation of web impact factors. J. Doc. **1998**, *54*(2), 236–243.

86. Egghe, L. New informetric aspects of the Internet: Some reflections – Many problems. J. inform. Sci. **2000**, *26*(5), 329–335.

87. Smith, A.G. A tale of two web spaces: Comparing sites using web impact factors. J. Doc. **1999**, *55*(5), 577–592.

Informetrics–International
Council

88. Bar-Ilan, J. Search engine results over time: A case study on search engine stability. Cybermetrics **1999**, *2/3*(1), paper 1. Available at http://www.cindoc.csic.es/cybermetrics/articles/v2i1p1.html (accessed September 2008).

89. Thelwall, M. Web impact factors and search engine coverage. J. Doc. **2000**, *56*(2), 185–189.

90. Mettrop, W.; Nieuwenhuysen, P. Internet search engines – Fluctuations in document accessibility. J. Doc. **2001**, *57*(5), 623–651.

91. Bar-Ilan, J. Expectations versus reality – Search engine features needed for Web research at mid 2005. Cybermetrics **2005**, *9*(1), paper 2. Available at http://www.cindoc.csic.es/cybermetrics/articles/v9i1p2.html (accessed September 2008).

92. Cronin, B.; Snyder, H.; Rosenbaum, H.; Martinson, A.; Callahan, E. Invoked on the web. J. Am. Soc. Inform. Sci. **1998**, *49*(14), 1319–1328.

93. Thelwall, M. What is this link doing here? Beginning a fine-grained process of identifying reasons for academic hyperlink creation. Inform. Res. **2003**, *8*(3), paper 151. Available at http://informationr.net/ir/8–3/paper151.html (accessed September 2008).

94. Bar-Ilan, J. What do we know about links and linking? A framework for studying links in academic environments. Inform. Process. Manag. **2005**, *41*(3), 973–986.

95. Vaughan, L.; Hysen, K. Relationship between links to journal web sites and impact factors. Aslib Proc. **2002**, *54*(6), 356–361.

96. Vaughan, L.; Thelwall, M. Scholarly use of the web – What are the key inducers of links to journal web sites?. J. Am. Soc. Inform. Sci. Technol. **2003**, *54*(1), 29–38.

97. Vaughan, L. Web hyperlinks reflect business performance – A study of US and Chinese IT companies. Can. J. Inform. Lib. Sci. **2004**, *28*(1), 17–31.

98. Vaughan, L. Exploring website features for business information. Scientometrics **2004**, *61*(3), 467–477.

99. Vaughan, L.; Shaw, D. Web citation data for impact assessment – A comparison of four science disciplines. J. Am. Soc. Inform. Sci. Technol. **2005**, *56*(10), 1075–1087.

100. Kousha, K.; Thelwall, M. Google scholar citations and Google web/URL citations: A multi-discipline exploratory analysis. J. Am. Soc. Inform. Sci. Technol. **2007**, *58*(7), 1055–1065.

101. Scharnhorst, A.; Wouters, P. Web indicators – A new generation of S&T indicators?. Cybermetrics **2006**, *10*(1), paper 6. Available at http://www.cindoc.csic.es/cybermetrics/articles/v10i1p6.html (accessed September 2008).

102. Koehler, W. Web page change and persistence – A four-year longitudinal study. J. Am. Soc. Inform. Sci. Technol. **2002**, *53*(2), 162–171.

103. Bar-Ilan, J.; Peritz, B.C. The lifespan of "informetrics" on the Web: An eight year study (1998–2006). Scientometrics **2009**, 79(1), 7–25.

104. Lawrence, S.; Pennock, D.M.; Flake, G.W.; Krovetz, R.; Coetzee, F.M.; Glover, E.; Nielsen, F.A.; Kruger, A.; Giles, C.L. Persistence of web references in scientific research. IEEE Comput. **2000**, *34*(2), 26–31.

105. Kumar, R.; Novak, J.; Raghavan, P.; Tomkins, A. On the bursty evolution of blogspace. World Wide Web **2005**, *8*(2), 159–178.

106. Angus, E.; Stuart, D.; Thelwall, M. General patterns of tag usage in Flickr image groups. Online Inform. Rev. **2008**, *32*(1), 89–101.

107. Thelwall, M. How are social network sites embedded in the web? An exploratory link analysis. Cybermetrics **2008**, *12*(1), 1. Available at http://www.cindoc.csic.es/cybermetrics/articles/v12i1p1.html (accessed September 2008).

108. Godin, B. *Measurement and Statistics on Science and Technology: 1920 to the Present*, Routledge: London, 2005.

109. Leydesdorff, L.; Etzkowitz, H. *Universities and the Global Knowledge Economy: A Triple Helix of University-Industry-Government Relations*, Cassell Academic: London, 1997.

110. Etzkowitz, H.; Leydesdorff, L. The dynamics of innovation – From national systems and "Mode 2" to a triple helix of university-industry-government relations. Res. Policy **2000**, *29*(2), 109–123.

111. Moed, H.F.; Glänzel, W.; Schmoch, U.; Eds. *Handbook of Quantitative Science and Technology Research: The Use of Publication and Patent Statistics in Studies of S&T Systems*; Kluwer Academic: Dordrecht, 2004. London.

112. Norris, M.; Oppenheim, C. Citation counts and the Research Assessment Exercise V – Archaeology and the 2001 RAE. J. Doc. **2003**, *59*(6), 709–730.

113. Weingart, P. Impact of bibliometrics upon the science system—Inadvertent consequences?. Scientometrics **2005**, *62*(1), 117–131.

114. Butler, L. Explaining Australia's increased share of ISI publications – the effects of a funding formula based on publication counts. Res. Policy **2003**, *32*(1), 143–155.

115. Cronin, B.; Shaw, D. Banking (on) different forms of symbolic capital. J. Am. Soc. Inform. Sci. Technol. **2002**, *53*(14), 1267–1270.

116. Bar-Ilan, J. Which h-index?: A comparison of WoS, scopus and Google scholar. Scientometrics **2008**, *74*(2), 257–271.

117. King, D.A. The scientific impact of nations. Nature **2004**, *430*(6997), 311–316.

118. Glänzel, W.; Schubert, A.; Braun, T. A relational charting approach to the world of basic research in twelve science fields at the end of the second millennium. Scientometrics **2002**, *55*(3), 335–348.

119. Zhou, P.; Leydesdorff, L. The emergence of China as a leading nation in science. Res. Policy **2006**, *35*(1), 83–104.

Institutional Records and Archives

David Farneth
Special Collections and Institutional Records, Getty Research Institute, Los Angeles, California, U.S.A.

Abstract

Modern organizations are exploring holistic approaches to managing records, information, and knowledge. The value and use of institutional records are optimized when records management and archival activities are coordinated and closely aligned according to a common set of goals and principles. Integration of records management and archives functions, along with the adoption of newer conceptual models for managing the life cycle of institutional records, have led to revised methods and best practices. Archival processes for "in-house" records may diverge in some ways from those for collecting repositories. Information professionals are expanding their roles and working collaboratively to manage and preserve electronic records. Societal attitudes about transparency and free access to information are changing the ways that institutions think about their information assets.

INTRODUCTION

As modern organizations become more flexible and managed more laterally, institutions are exploring holistic approaches to managing records, information, and knowledge. Improved conceptual models for managing the life cycle of institutional records are prompting information professionals to expand their roles and to work collaboratively across their organizations. At the same time, new technology solutions designed to manage and preserve electronic records are moving from the planning phase to implementation. Most recently, changing societal attitudes about transparency and free access to information are influencing the ways that institutions think about their information assets. All of these factors are prompting institutional archivists and records managers to find new ways to collaborate and integrate their programs in ways that will better serve their institutions' goals and mission. This new form of information professional—the archivist-records manager—must develop skills that are not yet routinely covered in many graduate program curricula.

Records management and institutional archives programs are key components in managing the operational, program-specific, and administrative records of active, modern organizations. Contrary to traditional practice, many institutions now believe that the value and use of institutional records are optimized when records management and archival activities are coordinated and closely aligned according to a common set of goals and principles. Using this perspective as a point of departure, the entry provides a summary of the key concepts that inform traditional and newer approaches to managing the life cycle of modern records and highlights ways in which archival processes for "in-house" records may differ from those of collecting repositories. The focus is on managing the records themselves, rather than the administrative strategies required to establish, staff, fund, and sustain the different types of programs and repositories that fall under the general rubric of institutional or "in-house" archives, such as business archives, museum archives, hospital archives, university archives, etc. Also excluded are discussions of the types of records specific to these repositories (for example, the exhibition-related records typically found in a museum's archives, or grant-giving records found in a philanthropic organization's archives). Readers are encouraged to explore more detailed texts about the concepts and standards introduced herein.

The specific topics cover a range of concepts and activities associated with integrated management of institutional records: institutional context, the value of institutional records, conceptual models, appraisal and selection of records, archival arrangement and description, research access to institutional records, and integration of records management and archival functions. The entry concludes with a look at institutional records in the broader information environment and a gloss on some of the issues associated with managing electronic records, which arguably now comprise the most important records produced in modern organizations.

INSTITUTIONAL CONTEXT

An understanding of the nature and value of an institution's operational and administrative records may be gained through a careful and systematic analysis of the organization's mission and activities. Both records managers and institutional archivists benefit from this activity

Encyclopedia of Library and Information Sciences, Fourth Edition DOI: 10.1081/E-ELIS4-120043265
Copyright © 2017 by Taylor & Francis. All rights reserved.

Informetrics–International Council

Table 1 Techniques for organizational analysis

To gain an understanding of...	...these analytical techniques can be used
The wider world in which the organization operates, including the legal and regulatory framework	Environmental analysis
What the organization does and how it carries out its work	Systems analysis, functional analysis, process analysis
The formal structure of the organization, and its values, beliefs, and attitudes	Cultural typology, structural analysis
Existing procedures for creating, maintaining, and using records	Process analysis, records survey
The nature and extent of records	Records survey

Source: Shepherd, E.; Yeo, G. *Managing Records: A Handbook of Principles and Practice*; Facet: London, U.K., 2003; 31.[1]

because it supports the kind of functional analysis that is central to many of the current trends for managing both paper and electronic records.

Elizabeth Shepherd and Geoffrey Yeo have articulated why an organizational analysis contributes to records management objectives: "(R)ecords managers must analyze the role and responsibilities of the organization, study its structures and working methods, and discover how these have changed during its life. They also need to identify the broader issues that influence the way the organization operates, including its corporate culture and the interests and expectations of stakeholders within the organization and externally."[1] They have also compiled a list of analytical techniques for undertaking an organizational analysis (Table 1). The National Library of Australia has published a guide for undertaking an institutional analysis in its highly influential *Designing and Implementing Recordkeeping Systems (DIRKS) Manual* (part two, steps A and B).[2]

VALUE OF INSTITUTIONAL RECORDS

As a society we value the achievements of prominent and creative individuals, and, as a result, their archives are regularly acquired by special collections and manuscripts repositories. But significant cultural advancements also take place within organizational environments. Therefore, the records of organizations, too, explain and illuminate some of mankind's greatest achievements.

Value of Institutional Records

The value of institutional records to society and to the parent organization is complex and intertwined (Table 2). Active use of institutional records stimulates institutional memory, preserves knowledge and intellectual property, improves accountability, and provides the larger

Table 2 Value of institutional records

Societal benefits	Contributes to education and the creation of new knowledge
	Preserves records needed for historical and other research
	Documents contributions to society
	Protects legal rights of institutions and individuals
	Protects ownership of property
	Documents place and identity in modern society
Business uses	Strategic planning and decision-making
	Communications, both internal and external
	Accountability and compliance
	Organizational continuity
	Preservation of intellectual property and information assets
	Protection of legal rights and assets
	Public relations and advertising
	Finance
	Research and development
	Repository of corporate culture and memory
	Evidence achievements (both corporate and individual)
	Evidence of place and identity in modern society

Sources: Cox, R. *Managing Institutional Archives: Foundational Principles and Practices*; Greenwood: Westport, CT, 1992; 4–7 and Goldstein, M.G. The evolving role of in-house business archives: from tradition to flexibility. In *The Records of American Business*; O'Toole, J. M., Ed.; Society of American Archivists: Chicago, IL, 1997; 41–55.

community with a broad historical focus on the organization's evolution and role in society. The business uses are diverse, ranging from strategic planning to leveraging existing knowledge to documenting achievements. Whether institutional archives are used to document the history of a specific institution, or to enable a scholar to understand important historical trends and events, or to inform individuals of the reasons for certain occurrences in his or her local community, they are vital to a society and its inhabitants.

Categories of Records

Institutional records are often divided into two categories: administrative records and program (or operational) records. These distinctions become important for managing retention of the records and for determining archival value.

An administrative record is "a document that has been preserved because it facilitates the operations and management of an agency, but which does not relate directly to programs that help the agency achieve its mission."[3] Administrative records often have shorter retention periods governed by a specific section of the retention schedule. They typically support functions related to

Informetrics–International Council

scheduling, coordination of activities, logistics, and lower-level reporting.

Program records "relate to the substantive activities an organization undertakes to accomplish its mission or mandate."[4] They typically will have longer retention periods and longer-term value to the organization.

A subset of institutional records may also be defined as vital records that are needed to recover business operations after a disaster or those that "protect the assets, obligations, and resources of the organization, as well as its employees and customers or citizens." They may also document the delegation of authority and lines of succession.[5]

CONCEPTUAL MODELS

Institutional records are usually managed through a combination of records management and archival processes. Some of the goals and objectives of these two disciplines are shared, while others are not, leading to professional and operational tensions that may be challenging to resolve.

Life-cycle Concept

Traditionally, records management has been more oriented toward the efficient management of large quantities of records in support of current business operations, while archival programs have focused on preserving permanent records that document organizational history and memory. The records life-cycle concept first introduced by T.R. Schellenberg in 1956 reenforces this division by postulating that records go through a number of distinct phases: creation, capture, storage and maintenance, use, and disposition. When records reach the disposition phase they are either destroyed or transferred to an institutional archive for permanent retention and preservation. The various attempts at modeling this concept have shown it to be a linear or circular progression, often related to the physical location and care given to paper records. Best practices in both the records management and the archives communities developed around each of the phases of the life cycle. Records management units managed the records during their active and inactive phases, and archives units took charge of the records when their business value was diminished and they were no longer actively used by the organization.[6]

Continuum Concept

As organizations adopted new, more flexible management structures, and as the challenges of managing electronic records began to be identified and analyzed, the life-cycle concept became unworkable. The structure of electronic records is more logical than physical. Archivists and records managers agreed that records could serve many uses at the same time. The continuum concept (Fig. 1) was therefore developed in the 1980s and 1990s to show that managing records was actually a continuous process in which various elements passed "seamlessly into another."[7] Rather than being time-based, the continuum concept recognizes that there are different perspectives to managing records operating at the same time. Records that support current business operations may simultaneously be used to document organizational and collective memory.

Informetrics–International Council

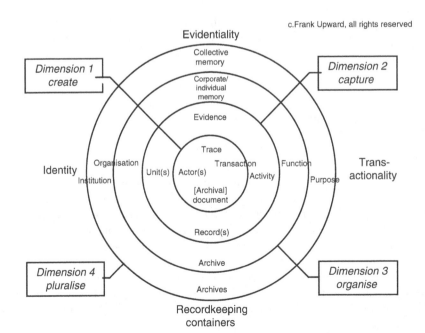

c.Frank Upward, all rights reserved

Fig. 1 Records continuum model.
Source: Courtesy of Frank Upward.

APPRAISAL AND SELECTION OF RECORDS

Appraisal is a core activity in both records management and archives management, and it is often thought of as the essence of both professions.

In records management, "appraisal is the process by which an organization identifies its requirements for maintaining records."[8] In archives management, appraisal is "the process of determining whether records and other materials have permanent (archival) value."[9] Some recent writings on archival appraisal have preferred the term "selection" over "appraisal."

Appraisal in both contexts is complex and difficult, and a large body of literature is devoted to it. This section will simply introduce concepts and issues related to appraisal that have most relevance to institutional records. Readers are encouraged to consult the sources listed in the bibliography and related entries in this encyclopedia for more comprehensive information.

Records Management Appraisal

In records management, appraisal refers to the often lengthy, complex, and reiterative three-step process required to develop and implement records retention procedures. It is comprised of:

1. Analyzing an organization's records to determine the proper retention period based on primary values (administrative, fiscal, and legal) and secondary values (evidential and informational).
2. Documenting a retention policy, usually in the form of a records retention schedule.
3. Reviewing, updating, and maintaining the policy.[10]

Records appraisal is an ongoing activity even after a retention policy is developed and adopted. Newly created records must be classified according to the policy, and new records series may be required as the organization changes. The policy may also be applied to "legacy" records that were created before the policy was adopted. Records creators and records managers continuously make decisions about which records need to be created, how they should be captured in a record-keeping system, how they should be classified for retention, and which ones need special handling for preservation or security.

Archival Appraisal and Selection

The selection of records to be preserved in an institutional archives usually flows from the mission of the individual repository. These selection activities usually focus inward, with a goal of documenting the parent organization. The mission of an institutional archive may articulate several goals, for example: to support accountability, to capture history, and/or to preserve products and intellectual property. Appraisal decisions will therefore support the defined mandates. Archivists usually also have guidelines for the level of detail desired, or may make selection decisions based on the person or business function that created the records.

Some institutional archives are also "collecting repositories" that accept materials from external sources. For instance, they may collect the family papers of the organization's founder or attempt to document the reputation and societal impact of the organization as reflected in external publications and media coverage. They may also attempt to document particular research topics related to the organization's core mission. For instance, the archives of a philanthropic organization may decide to select and acquire materials related to the history of philanthropy.

Traditional appraisal methodologies analyze the content of records, while newer methodologies focus on the context in which the records were created. The methodology selected by an individual repository will, again, be determined by its mission. Repositories with a historical, informational approach may prefer the traditional approaches. Those focused on evidence and accountability, and those that have large volumes of records to manage, will probably prefer the contextual approach. In practice, however, many institutional repositories have hybrid missions and often choose to rely on a combination of both approaches.

Value based on content

Schellenberg's seminal approach to American archival appraisal defined the primary and secondary values of records. He believed that records should be selected for archival preservation only after their operational value had ceased. Then, only those records that had evidential or informational value that would support historical and other scholarly research should be preserved. Traditional methodologies based on Schellenberg's model require the archivist to examine the content of the records to determine their value. This traditional approach is often called "bottom-up" appraisal.[11]

Value based on context

As the bulk of modern-day records increased and more records were created and stored electronically, archival theorists recognized that a new approach was needed that did not require the time-intensive task of inspecting all records. David Bearman, in particular, proposed reverting to provenance as the basis for selection and refined a method of selection based on records functions.[12] From this approach evolved selection processes based on the record continuum approach. Canadian archivists were particularly attracted by the functional approach. Terry Cook

Informetrics–International Council

defined a "macro-appraisal" (or "top-down") approach based on the function of the records creator, which, in turn led to refinements in functional analysis that emphasized context over content.[13] American archivist Helen Samuels has applied a functional analysis to university records, and her study has made a strong case for applying this methodology to the records of any type of organization.[14]

Christopher Baer has drawn on both traditional and newer approaches to develop a model for appraising business records that considers four parameters: the business strategy of the organization, the structure of the organization, the level of informational detail provided in the record, and the elemental purpose and activities (i.e., "function") supported by the records. This more hybrid approach takes into account both the context and content of records.[15]

ARCHIVAL ARRANGEMENT AND DESCRIPTION

Most national and international content standards for archival description cover both corporate records and personal papers (Table 3). Working within these frameworks, archivists in active organizations have a unique opportunity to emphasize information about the context, function, and purpose of records, which, in turn, adds inestimable layers of complexity to their meaning.[16]

- Who created the record (which department and which person of what status within the department)
- Why the record was created (for what administrative purpose)
- What form the record has (minute book, file of correspondence, etc.)
- How it can be found and accessed

Table 3 Selected standards for managing institutional records and archives

Records management, general

ISO 15489:2001 Information and Documentation—Records Management Part 1: General; Part 2: Guidelines http://www.iso.org/iso/catalogue_detail?csnumber = 31908 (accessed October 26, 2008)

Requirements for Managing Electronic Messages as Records (ARMA) http://www.arma.org/standards/ElectronicMessages.cfm (accessed October 26, 2008)

The Digital Records Conversion Process: Program Planning, Requirements, Procedures (ARMA) http://www.arma.org/standards/DigitalConversion.cfm (accessed October 26, 2008)

Vital Records Programs: Identifying, Managing, and Recovering Business Critical Records (ARMA) http://www.arma.org/standards/VitalRecords.cfm (accessed October 26, 2008)

Requirements for electronic records management systems

DoD 5015.2-STD Design Criteria Standard for Electronic Records Management Software Applications http://jitc.fhu.disa.mil/recmgt/standards.html (accessed October 26, 2008)

Model Requirements Specification for the Management of Electronic Records (MoReq2) http://www.moreq2.eu/ (accessed October 26, 2008)

Metadata content and transmission

Describing Archives: A Content Standard (DACS) http://www.archivists.org/catalog/pubDetail.asp?objectID = 1279 (accessed October 26, 2008)

Rules for Archival Description (RAD) (revised 2008)

http://www.cdncouncilarchives.ca/RAD/RADComplete_July2008.pdf (accessed January 19, 2009)

General International Standard Archival Description, 2d Edition (ISAD(G))

http://www.ica.org/sites/default/files/isad_g_2e.pdf (accessed January 19, 2009)

International Standard Archival Authority Record For Corporate Bodies, Persons and Families, 2d Edition (ISAAR(CPF)

http://www.icacds.org.uk/eng/ISAAR (CPF)2ed.pdf (accessed January 19, 2009)

ISO 23081-1:2006 Information and documentation – Records management processes – Metadata for records – Part 1: Principles http://www.iso.org/iso/catalogue_detail?csnumber = 40832 (accessed October 26, 2008)

Minnesota Recordkeeping Metadata Standard http://www.mnhs.org/preserve/records/electronicrecords/ermetadata.html (accessed October 26, 2008)

Metadata Encoding Transmission Standard (METS) http://www.loc.gov/standards/mets/ (accessed October 26, 2008)

Metadata Object Description Schema (MODS) http://www.loc.gov/standards/mods/ (accessed October 26, 2008)

Digital preservation

ISO 14721:2003 Space data and information transfer systems — Open archival information system — Reference model http://www.iso.org/iso/iso_catalogue/catalogue_tc/catalogue_detail.htm?csnumber = 24683 (accessed October 26, 2008)

PREMIS: Data Dictionary for Preservation Metadata, v.2 (March 2008)

http://www.oclc.org/research/projects/pmwg/ (accessed June 30, 2009)

PRONOM: The File Format Registry http://www.nationalarchives.gov.uk/pronom/ (accessed October 26, 2008)

ISO 19005-1:2005 Document management – Electronic document file format for long-term preservation – Part 1: Use of PDF 1.4 (PDF/A-1) http://www.iso.org/iso/catalogue_detail?csnumber = 38920 (accessed October 26, 2008)

Informetrics–International Council

- How it relates to other records (whether there are likely to be more records on the same subject somewhere else)
- When and why were related records destroyed

The arrangement of institutional records according to provenance is particularly important to the researcher for determining point of view and analyzing biases (For instance, correspondence between two mid-level managers about a particular event may be much more revealing than a press release about the same event.). It is also important to know why the records were created, how the records were kept, and what functions and activities they supported.

Arrangement and description of collections that come into collecting archives is relatively straightforward, because each new acquisition usually represents a discrete and independent unit that can be arranged, described, and stored without reference to direct or integral connections to other collections in the repository. Record groups and record series are based solely on the records themselves. Each collection is usually described by its own finding aid.

Records that enter an institutional archives have fundamentally different characteristics, both in the way that they enter the repository and how they have to be arranged and described. Even though archivists strive for the logical and orderly acquisition of new records according to the retention policy, records may also come to the repository in a less planned way, motivated by staff departures, the physical movement of offices, an upcoming anniversary, or the completion of major projects.

The record groups and record series in an institutional archives are usually based on provenance, which means that they will reflect, in part, the organizational structure of the organization. New acquisitions are usually described as additions to existing records series and groups. Many different accessions may be brought together intellectually in a single finding aid.

The systems that institutional archivists use to create and maintain descriptive information about their holdings will vary widely according to the type of organization, the degree of public access afforded to the collections, the amount of information technology support that is available, and the degree to which archivists are compelled to use existing systems rather than acquire new ones specific to archives management. The ideal systems for documenting information about archival collections accommodate many levels of hierarchy that can reflect the context and relationships of and between the records themselves. These systems might take the form of relational databases or they may use text encoding to maintain hierarchical relationships, such as with Encoded Archival Description.[17] Library bibliographic systems do not provide enough levels of hierarchy to describe archival collections. (See the related entries "Archival Appraisal and Acquisition," p. 120, and "Archival Arrangement and Description," p. 130, for more detailed coverage.)

RESEARCH ACCESS TO INSTITUTIONAL RECORDS

While government archives must follow laws and mandates governing public access to information, the policies that determine access to information in institutional archives usually reflect the business nature of the organization and the level of security that is required to protect the organization's interests. Many organizations have guidelines for handling sensitive information. Legal statutes protecting personal privacy, medical records, and student records also dictate types of information that should be kept confidential.[18] Most organizations find it necessary to protect access to records related to attorney-client privilege, human resources, and those that contain business or trade secrets. Even nonprofit organizations have sensitive records related to sustaining the organization's business.

In practice, most business and corporate archives do not exist to provide public access to their holdings. Other types of institutional archives, especially those associated with nonprofit and educational organizations, exist in large part to serve the public interest.

Most institutional archives hold records of interest to the staff of the creating organization, the general public, and the media, and attempts are made to provide the appropriate level of access to each of these groups while maintaining a suitable level of confidentiality and security.[19] Some records were created for public distribution, and these are usually made available for research as soon as they enter the archives. For the most part, however, the records held by institutional archives were created for internal use, and public research access may be restricted to varying degrees. The policies controlling access may be directives communicated by the executive management of the organization or they may be entrusted to the archivist to determine.

Effective access policies for institutional records will include "clear description of restrictions, time limits on restrictions, procedures for determining restrictions, and a statement regarding lines of administrative authority." The categories of restriction usually include "open," "restricted" to staff, and "closed" to all except the office of origin. There is often a general period of restriction (for instance, 10–20 years) and then longer periods for records of extra sensitivity or those whose confidentiality is protected by statute. The policy should state when and how restrictions are placed on records and the lines of authority and procedures for obtaining access.[20]

INTEGRATION OF RECORDS MANAGEMENT AND ARCHIVAL FUNCTIONS

Practical solutions do not always line up neatly with theoretical models. The goals and activities of records management and archival programs do not always neatly mesh, but their missions should align with the goal of

Informetrics–International Council

Informetrics–International Council

fostering efficient management of institutional records and leveraging their value. By working collaboratively, records managers and archivists identify areas of conflict and seek productive resolutions.

Records Retention and Archival Appraisal

When managing the records of an active organization, records managers must deal with records in large groups and are intent on destroying records according to policies that are designed, in part, to promote efficiency and to protect the organization. Archivists work to preserve a subset of records consistent with selection guidelines. Sometimes these two organizational goals come into conflict.

In theory, an organization's retention schedule should be a useful tool for guiding archival appraisal, but this is often not the case in practice. Modern-day retention schedules are designed with fewer categories (often called "big buckets") to promote ease of understanding and use. As a result, they usually do not provide enough detail to support archival appraisal. Function-based retention schedules are difficult to apply to unified files of correspondence, or project, case, and subject files, all of which might be of high interest to archivists. They also may not correlate easily with individual office file plans.

Retention schedules may be strongly tied to organizational structure, and retention policies are usually implemented through official departments. But the work in modern organizations is more fluid, with people and information traveling easily across departmental lines. While retention schedules may capture the official flow of documents, they often do not capture the real flow of information. In addition, compliance with retention schedules across a large organization is usually inconsistent, and often the records of the offices of senior executives are not scheduled. These situations lead to gaps in documentation and loss of records at the higher decision-making levels of the organization.[21]

Because of these inherent tensions between records management and archival appraisal, some records professionals argue that these functions should be separated organizationally. Others contend that the tensions are best resolved by an integrated approach, because the logical road to conflict resolution is through dialogue and compromise, and this happens more easily when both records managers and archivists are members of the same team.

Records Managers and Archivists Working Together

Collaboration between records managers and archivists is becoming essential as more information professionals are recognizing that the continuum model is closer to reality than the life cycle model, especially in the digital age. Archivists should be proactive in bringing their organizational and preservation skills to the process of records creation and the maintenance of active records, and capture copies of electronic records much earlier than they would paper records. Records managers should understand archival appraisal, be alert to records that meet the collecting policies of the institutional archives, and encourage the creation of authentic and reliable records that will document key organizational functions. Both groups should keep theoretical goals firmly in sight while remaining flexible in their respective areas of control and delivering a unified message to staff in the organization.

INSTITUTIONAL RECORDS IN THE BROADER INFORMATION ENVIRONMENT

The documentation of an institution exists in many forms and is cared for by many units across the organization. The value of institutional records can be leveraged though integrated access to information achieved through strong partnerships between many departments in the organization, including archives, records management, legal, communications, compliance, information technology, and business units. Institutional records can be key components of programs devoted to document management, information management, knowledge management, disaster recovery, digital asset management, intellectual property management (including institutional repositories), and preservation of electronically stored information (including trusted digital repositories).

The technological revolution is providing new opportunities for information integration and collaboration among information professionals. "In this new world of records, archivists must become more involved with records creation and maintenance. Managers, information managers, and systems managers must become more involved with records quality. Archivists, records managers, and information managers must work together to establish standards and procedures before electronic records become the primary media for maintaining the institutional memory."[22] This prescient statement was published in 1993. Now, years later, information professionals are still grappling with the challenges of capturing and preserving electronic records. Many archivists fear that 25 years of key documentary evidence has been, or will be, lost.

THE CHALLENGE OF ELECTRONIC RECORDS

The amount of electronically stored information in organizations and businesses is growing exponentially. Managing electronic records across an organization is one of the most challenging tasks facing institutional information managers, and it is also the one most easy to ignore for institutions that do not have high risks associated with poor records management, that lack technological

Informetrics–International Council

expertise and infrastructure, or whose mission is focused on more traditional functions.

Electronic records are much more fragile and at risk of deterioration and loss than are paper records. Although the concept of the paperless office has yet to reach fruition—and may never do so—the importance and criticality of electronic records has evolved substantially in recent years. At first, most electronic records were considered to be transient; desktop computers were the tools used to prepare a record that was printed on paper and filed. Now, more often than not, the electronic document is considered to be the permanent record, and the paper copies are transient, used for ease of reference and then discarded.

Records managers and archivists have attempted to apply traditional methodologies to electronic records. While this task is challenging enough, it is complicated by quickly changing technological advancements, system and format obsolescence, and the need for new resources to support technology infrastructure, software acquisition and implementation, training, and sustainability. The problem of obsolescence applies to hardware, operating systems, software, file formats, and storage media. Different processes are evolving to address each.

Thousands of people in government, industry, and the academy are working on these problems, from creating conceptual models, to writing standards, to building technology solutions for implementing them, to solving technological obsolescence. National archives programs in the United States, United Kingdom, Australia, New Zealand, Canada, and the Netherlands (to single out just a few) are developing systems and processes to identify, capture, classify, describe, preserve, and provide appropriate access to electronic records. Various international, national, and local agencies are promulgating standards and best practices related to processes, metadata, and digital preservation (Table 3). The information management sector has developed suites of applications to manage electronically stored information, all with limited or mixed success, including systems for document management, digital asset management, content management, electronic record management, and e-mail "archiving."

Records Management Context

The principal challenges of managing electronic records relate to the computer's inability to classify records and activate event-driven retention policies. Most systems developed to date require the user to classify records, most often by dragging them into folders that emulate series on a retention schedule. Records managers have therefore been moving toward simplifying retention schedules and reducing the number of records series in an attempt to create systems that can realistically be learned and applied by the entire staff of an organization. Event-driven retention policies pose larger challenges because they usually require a human to recognize that an event has happened before the retention period can be properly assigned.

Records managers working in collaboration with staff in information technology, legal, and business units have been devising new processes to manage three categories of electronic records: those created and retained in e-mail systems, those produced by enterprise database applications and managed by information technology teams (structured data), and those produced by desktop applications and managed by business units on workstations and shared network folders (unstructured data). Many records managers are experimenting with ways to leverage current technology and train staff in new procedures for managing electronic records according to established policy, including the distribution of directory structures that correspond to official records and training staff to associate more metadata with records created in desktop applications. Other more comprehensive strategies include auto-classification, applying retention rules to records in legacy systems, managing access based on privacy and security requirements, and building records management functionality into enterprise business applications.

Archives Context

Archival functions have been largely ignored by the emerging technologies developed for content management and records management, which have had difficulty appreciating the need for long-term digital preservation strategies and identifying a viable market. As a result, archivists tend to look to governments that have provided mandates and money for developing electronic records solutions, with the hope that systems designed for extraordinarily large repositories will be scalable to smaller ones.

The challenges associated with the archival management of electronic records are many and varied. Archivists are charged with preserving and providing access to authentic and reliable records over a long time (decades, if not centuries). Lacking expertise and resources to ensure long-term preservation and access, archivists have been hesitant to accept electronic records into their repositories.

Leaving aside technological and organizational cultural issues (such as lack of a pressing business need, lack of resources, and lack of motivation) the traditional functions of archival management—accession, appraisal, arrangement, description, access, and preservation—have traditionally required a large degree of human analysis. The continuum model and top-down appraisal methods have been helpful in explaining the archivist's new role during records creation and in applying appraisal decisions without having to look at the individual records, but much work remains to develop suites of applications that can automate the full range of archival functions. How should computers apply macro-appraisal rules? What new metadata schemas are required? How can computers enhance the records with value-added description? How will computers review records for appropriate access? These are just a few of the questions being explored.

Need for Collaboration

Successful institution-wide electronic records management requires close collaboration between records managers and archivists, information technology staff, legal staff, and the various business units in an organization. These people bring together the knowledge and skills required to propose institutional priorities and advocate for resources, write requirements for systems, undertake the acquisition and implementation of systems, and carry out training, compliance, data management, and long-term digital preservation.

Records managers and archivists usually control the retention policy and records classification scheme. They also understand the organization's business processes, the nature of the records created by those processes, and the metadata required to support management and access. Records managers routinely train staff in good recordkeeping and are the best equipped to monitor compliance with policies. Archivists know at the time of creation which records are likely to require long-term preservation, and they are knowledgeable about the systems, policies, processes, and results that are required for a viable digital preservation program.

Information technology staff usually controls the system architecture, software acquisition and implementation, data storage, and disaster recovery for systems. They have the knowledge to articulate system requirements in a manner that is understood by vendors and to ensure that software applications have the ability to interact and run in the corporate technology environment. Legal staff provides system requirements for managing legal discovery and for producing electronic records that will stand up in court.

Most important, however, are the business units and end users. Ultimately, if the systems and processes designed for managing electronic records are difficult to use or fail to do what the business unit requires, then they will not be used.

CONCLUSION

Institutional archivists and records managers are evolving into proactive leaders as they bring their knowledge and skills to the task of preserving and integrating access to their organization's knowledge, information, and records. In so doing, they are making adjustments to some of the traditional practices of their professions and adopting a flexible approach to collaboration, all of which require a certain amount of risk-taking. Institutional archives and records management programs are working together to

analyze the institutional context, functions, and business processes that inform the creation of records and then using this information to make informed appraisal and access decisions. Working together, archivists and records managers understand better the uses and values that characterize institutional records and then combine their skill sets to communicate requirements for records creation and management of records over their entire life cycle.

In managing institutional archives repositories, archivists adapt traditional methodologies of arrangement and description to suit the nature of the records in their repository, and they negotiate an access policy that balances open access to records with the business needs of the institution.

At the same time, institutional archivists and records managers must be knowledgeable of standards and best practices for managing electronic records and be proactive in planning and implementing institution-wide systems for managing e-mail, data in enterprise applications, and records created by desktop applications. To this process they bring knowledge of records and business processes, records creation and retention policies, training requirements, and compliance monitoring. They also bring a strong liaison with the creators of records across the institution. Archivists and records managers have an especially important role to play in communicating requirements for digital preservation programs.

The future promises to bring more challenges to institutional archivists and records managers as institutional electronic records are created, transmitted, and retained in many and varied communication devices and stored in data repositories no longer managed by the institution. In addition, many futurists are predicting a greater socialization of information in the coming years, stimulated in part by Web 2.0 technologies. These trends will challenge the ability of archivists and records managers to manage records and will test an institution's real and perceived need for control over its records and information.

ACKNOWLEDGMENTS

The author gratefully acknowledges Mahnaz Ghaznavi and Nancy Enneking, both colleagues in the Institutional Records and Archives department at the J. Paul Getty Trust, who generously shared their knowledge of the theoretical issues addressed in this entry and who have worked collaboratively to test them in practice. Special thanks go to Murtha Baca, David Gilbert, and Barbara Nye for their ideas, advice, and inspiration.

REFERENCES

1. Shepherd, E.; Yeo, G. *Managing Records: A Handbook of Principles and Practice*; Facet: London, U.K., 2003; 30.

Informetrics–International Council

2. http://www.naa.gov.au/records-management/publications/DIRKS-manual.aspx (accessed September 25, 2008).

3. Pearce-Moses, R. *A Glossary of Archival and Records Terminology*; Society of American Archivists: Chicago, IL, 2005; 11.

4. Pearce-Moses, R. *A Glossary of Archival and Records Terminology*; Society of American Archivists: Chicago, IL, 2005; 316.

5. Pearce-Moses, R. *A Glossary of Archival and Records Terminology*; Society of American Archivists: Chicago, IL, 2005; 404–405.

6. Shepherd, E.; Yeo, G. *Managing Records: A Handbook of Principles and Practice*; Facet: London, U.K., 2003; 5–7.

7. Shepherd, E.; Yeo, G. *Managing Records: A Handbook of Principles and Practice*; Facet: London, U.K., 2003; 9.

8. Shepherd, E.; Yeo, G. *Managing Records: A Handbook of Principles and Practice*; Facet: London, U.K., 2003; 146.

9. Pearce-Moses, R. *A Glossary of Archival and Records Terminology*; Society of American Archivists: Chicago, IL, 2005; 22.

10. Shepherd, E.; Yeo, G. *Managing Records: A Handbook of Principles and Practice*; Facet: London, U.K., 2003; 146–172.

11. Boles, F. *Selecting and Appraising Archives and Manuscripts*; Society of American Archivists: Chicago, IL, 2005; 13–14.

12. Boles, F. *Selecting and Appraising Archives and Manuscripts*; Society of American Archivists: Chicago, IL, 2005; 23–24.

13. Cook, T. Mind over matter: towards a new theory of archival appraisal. In *The Archival Imagination: Essays in Honour of High A. Taylor*; Craig, B., Ed.; Association of Canadian Archivists: Ottawa, Ontario, Canada, 1992; 38–70.

14. Samuels, H.W. *Varsity Letters: Documenting Modern Collections and Universities*; The Society of American Archivists and Scarecrow Press: Lanham, MD, 1998.

15. Baer, C.T. Strategy, structure, detail, functions: four parameters for the appraisal of business records. In *The Records of American Business*; O'Toole, J.M., Ed.; Society of American Archivists: Chicago, IL, 1997; 75–135.

16. Pemberton, P. Arrangement and description of business archives. In *Corporate Archives and History: Making the Past Work*; Jones, A.A., Cantelon, P.L., Eds.; Krieger: Malabar, FL, 1993; 81–82.

17. http://www.loc.gov/ead/ (accessed October 25, 2008).

18. Access to medical records in the U.S. is governed by the Health Insurance Portability and Accountability Act (HIPAA) of 1996, Public Law 104–191, and the Standards for Privacy of Individually Identifiable Health Information (the Privacy Rule), promulgated by the Department of Health and Human Services (HHS). http://www.hhs.gov/ocr/hipaa/ (accessed October 17, 2008). The Family Educational Rights and Privacy Act (FERPA) (20 U.S.C. § 1232g; 34 CFR Part 99) is a U.S. Federal law that protects the privacy of student education records. http://www.ed.gov/policy/gen/guid/fpco/ferpa/index.html (accessed October 17, 2008).

19. Jeremy, J.; Woodley, E.; Kupke, L. Access and reference services. In *Keeping Archives*; 3rd Ed.; Bettington, J., Eberhard, K., Loo, R., Smith, C., Eds.; Australian Society of Archivists: Canberra, Australian Capital Territory, Australia, 2008; 353.

20. Van Camp, A. Access policies for corporate archives. In *Corporate Archives and History: Making the Past Work*; Jones, A.A., Cantelon, P.L., Eds.; Krieger: Malabar, FL, 1993; 77–79.

21. Boles, F. *Selecting and Appraising Archives and Manuscripts*; Society of American Archivists: Chicago, IL, 2005; 55–56.

22. Merz, N.M. Archives and the one world of records. In *Corporate Archives and History: Making the Past Work*; Jones, A.A., Cantelon, P.L., Eds.; Krieger: Malabar, FL, 1993; 156.

BIBLIOGRAPHY

1. Behrnd-Klodt, M.L.; Wosh, P.J. *Privacy and Confidentiality Perspectives: Archivists and Archival Records*; Society of American Archivists: Chicago, IL, 2005.

2. Bettington, J.; Eberhard, K.; Loo, R.; Smith, C., Eds. *Keeping Archives*, 3rd Ed.; Australian Society of Archivists: Canberra, Australian Capital Territory, Australia, 2008.

3. Boles, F. *Selecting and Appraising Archives and Manuscripts*; Society of American Archivists: Chicago, IL, 2005.

4. Cox, R. *Managing Institutional Archives: Foundational Principles and Practices*; Greenwood: Westport, CT, 1992.

5. Dearstyne, B.W. *Leading and Managing Archives and Records Programs: Strategies for Success*; Neal-Schuman: New York, 2008.

6. Jones, A.A.; Cantelon, P.L., Eds. *Corporate Archives and History: Making the Past Work*; Krieger: Malabar, FL, 1993.

7. McKemmish, S.; Piggott, M.; Reed, B.; Upward, F. *Archives: Recordkeeping in Society*; Centre for Information Studies: Wagga Wagga, New South Wales, Canada, 2005.

8. McLeod, J.; Hare, C., Eds. *Managing Electronic Records*; Facet: London, U.K., 2005.

9. O'Toole, J.M., Eds. *The Records of American Business*; Society of American Archivists: Chicago, IL, 1997.

10. O'Toole, J.M.; Cox, R. *Understanding Archives and Manuscripts*; Society of American Archivists: Chicago, IL, 2006.

11. Shepherd, E.; Yeo, G. *Managing Records: A Handbook of Principles and Practice*; Facet: London, IL, U.K., 2003.

12. Stephens, D.O. *Records Management: Making the Transition from Paper to Electronic*; ARMA: Lenexa, KS, 2007.

Informetrics–International Council

Intellectual Freedom and the American Library Association (ALA): Historical Overview [ELIS Classic]

Judith F. Krug
Office for Intellectual Freedom, American Library Association, Chicago, Illinois, U.S.A.

Abstract

One of the major initiatives of the American Library Association has been to promote intellectual freedom in society. The author of this entry was one of the driving forces of this effort over many years. Though, as Krug noted, intellectual freedom has been understood in many different ways, a simplified definition can be taken as the right to freedom of thought, expression, and access to informational materials of any kind. In this entry, Krug described the long, rich history of librarians' efforts to oppose censorship and assure intellectual freedom for library users.

—ELIS Classic, from 2003

INTRODUCTION

At the outset, two myths can be dispelled: 1) intellectual freedom in libraries is a tradition; and 2) intellectual freedom has always been a major, if not the major, part of the foundation of library service in the United States. Both myths, assumed by many librarians, are grounded in the belief that librarians support a static concept of intellectual freedom. Nothing, however, could be farther from the truth.

The attitude of librarians toward intellectual freedom has undergone continual change since the late 1800s when, through the American Library Association (ALA), the profession first began to approach such issues with the semblance of a unified voice. The ALA, however, has never endorsed a uniform definition of "intellectual freedom." Instead, through the council, ALA's governing body, the Intellectual Freedom Committee (IFC), and the Office for Intellectual Freedom (OIF), ALA has promoted a variety of principles aimed at fostering a favorable climate for intellectual freedom but without the limits imposed by a rigid definition. This approach has permitted a broad definition capable of meeting the needs of librarians as they arise.

CENSORSHIP OF PUBLISHED MATERIALS

The catalyst spurring librarians to take initial steps toward supporting intellectual freedom was the censorship of specific publications. "Censorship" in this context means not only deletion or excision of parts of published materials but also efforts to ban, prohibit, suppress, proscribe, remove, label, or restrict materials. Opposition to these activities emanated from the belief that freedom of the mind is basic to the functioning and maintenance of

democracy as practiced in the United States. Such democracy assumes that educated, free individuals possess powers of discrimination and are to be trusted to determine their own actions. It assumes further that the best guarantee of effective and continuing self-government is a thoroughly informed electorate capable of making real choices. Denying the opportunity of choice, for fear it may be used unwisely, destroys freedom itself. Opposition to censorship derives naturally from the library's historic role as an educational institution providing materials that develop individuals' abilities, interests, and knowledge. Censorship denies the opportunity to choose from all possible alternatives, thereby violating intellectual freedom. The library profession has aimed to ensure every individual's freedom of the mind so that society as a whole benefits. Even in this central area, however, the professional position has fluctuated, being influenced by such factors as taste, quality, responsibility, morality, legality, and purpose.

One early incident concerning censorship, involving a substantial number of librarians, occurred in 1924 when the Librarians' Union of the American Federation of Labor reported that Carnegie Libraries fostered "a system under which only books approved in a certain manner may be placed on Carnegie Library shelves and that amounts to censorship and is so intended."[1] The ALA Executive Board considered the union's charges and offered to enlist volunteers to investigate the claims. Apparently, however, the union did not act on the offer, and the matter was not considered further by the executive board.

In 1934, the association recorded its first protest against the banning of a specific publication, *You and Machines*, a pamphlet by William Ogburn. Prepared for use in Civilian Conservation Corps camps under a grant from the American Council on Education, the pamphlet was denied circulation by the camps' director, who believed it would

Encyclopedia of Library and Information Sciences, Fourth Edition DOI: 10.1081/E-ELIS4-120008776

Copyright © 2017 by Taylor & Francis. All rights reserved.

Informetrics–International Council

induce a philosophy of despair and a desire to destroy existing economic and political structures. Initially, the ALA president and executive secretary wrote a joint letter to President Franklin D. Roosevelt, stating that "[governmental] censorship on a publication of this character written by a man of recognized authority is unthinkable."[2] Later the board discussed the banning further and appointed a committee to draft another letter for approval by the ALA Council. The result was a formal request that President Roosevelt "make it possible for the U.S. Commissioner of Education and the Education Director of the Civilian Conservation Corps to direct the educational policies to be operative in these camps and to make available the reading matter essential in a modern program of education."[2]

These examples illustrate the association's wavering position and reflect the ambivalent attitude of the profession as a whole regarding censorship. A review of library literature reveals relatively few articles on intellectual freedom prior to the 1930s, and many of the articles that did appear supported censorship and only quibbled over the degree and nature of it. Typical was the opinion of ALA President Arthur E. Bostwick, whose inaugural address at the 1908 Annual Conference included these remarks:

'Some are born great; some achieve greatness; some have greatness thrust upon them.' It is in this way that the librarian has become a censor of literature... Books that distinctly commend what is wrong, that teach how to sin and how pleasant sin is, sometimes with and sometimes without the added sauce of impropriety, are increasingly popular, tempting the author to imitate them, the publishers to produce, the bookseller to exploit. Thank Heaven they do not tempt the librarian.[3]

Given the multiplicity of professional attitudes toward censorship of print materials, it is not surprising that censorship of nonprint media was once viewed as completely outside the concerns of the profession. For example, as late as 1938, the ALA Executive Board believed it was inappropriate to protest when the Federal Communications Commission forced a radio station to defend its broadcast of Eugene O'Neill's *Beyond the Horizon*.[4]

The association's basic position in opposition to censorship finally emerged in the late 1930s, when John Steinbeck's *The Grapes of Wrath* became the target of censorship pressures around the country. It was banned from libraries in East St. Louis, Illinois; Camden, New Jersey; Bakersfield, California; and other localities. Although some objected to the "immorality" of the work, most opposed the social views advanced by the author.

The initial response of the ALA to the pressures against *The Grapes of Wrath* was the adoption in 1939 of the *Library's Bill of Rights*, the precursor of the present *Library Bill of Rights*, the profession's basic policy statement on intellectual freedom involving library materials.

In 1940, 1 year after adoption of the *Library's Bill of Rights*, the association established the Intellectual Freedom Committee (IFC). (Originally called the Committee on Intellectual Freedom to Safeguard the Rights of Library Users to Freedom of Inquiry, the Committee's name was shortened by council action in 1948 to Committee on Intellectual Freedom and inverted through usage to Intellectual Freedom Committee.) The 1940 charge to the IFC was "to recommend such steps as may be necessary to safeguard the rights of library users in accordance with the Bill of Rights and the *Library's Bill of Rights*, as adopted by Council."[5] Although the IFC's role has varied, its main function has been to recommend policies concerning intellectual freedom, especially—but not limited to—matters involving violations of the *Library Bill of Rights*. Although its original statement of authority referred only to library users, in reality the IFC became active in promoting intellectual freedom for librarians and patrons as well. Its diversified role was recognized and formalized in 1970 when the council approved a revised statement of authority:

To recommend such steps as may be necessary to safeguard the rights of library users, libraries, and librarians, in accordance with the First Amendment to the United States Constitution and the *Library Bill of Rights as adopted by the ALA Council. To work closely with the Office for Intellectual Freedom and with other units and officers of the Association in matters touching intellectual freedom and censorship.[6]

The original *Library's Bill of Rights* focused on unbiased book selection, a balanced collection, and open meeting rooms. It did not mention censorship or removal of materials at the behest of groups or individuals. Over the years, however, the document has been revised, amended, and interpreted, often in response to specific situations with general implications. The first change, a 1944 amendment against banning materials considered "factually correct," was occasioned by attacks on *Under Cover*, an expose of Nazi organizations in the United States, and *Strange Fruit*, a novel about interracial love. Reference to "factually correct" was later dropped, but the directive against removal of materials remained. Opposition to censorship of nonprint media was amended to the document in 1951 because of attacks on films alleged to promote communism. To combat suppression of communist materials or other allegedly "subversive" publications, the association issued its "Statement on Labeling," which stated that designating materials "subversive" is subtle censorship, because such a label predisposes readers against the materials. Responding to pressures against materials about civil rights activities, a 1967 amendment to the *Library Bill of Rights* warned against excluding materials because of the social views of the authors. In its 1971 "Resolution on Challenged Materials," the

Informetrics–International Council

association counseled libraries not to remove challenged materials unless, after an adversary hearing in a court of law, the materials were judged to be outside the protection of the First Amendment.

Changing circumstances necessitate constant review of the *Library Bill of Rights* and often result in position statements, called *Interpretations*, to clarify the document's application. The most recent *Interpretations* are Access to Electronic Information, Services and Networks adopted by the ALA Council in January 1996 and Intellectual Freedom Principles for Academic Libraries, approved by the ACRL Board in June 1999 and adopted by the ALA Council in July 2000.

Taken together, these documents recognize and explain that censorship of any materials, in any guise, eventually affects the library. The *Library Bill of Rights*, therefore, provides principles on which libraries may stand to oppose censorship and promote intellectual freedom. Referring directly to censorship practices, the *Library Bill of Rights* states that no library materials should be "excluded because of the origin, background, or views of those contributing to their creation" and that materials should not be "proscribed or removed because of partisan or doctrinal disapproval."

On its face, the profession's view of intellectual freedom is a pure one, based on a strict reading of the First Amendment to the U.S. Constitution, which states, "Congress shall make no law...abridging freedom of speech, or of the press." Within the limits defined by the United States Supreme Court (e.g., the legal doctrines governing obscenity, defamation, or "fighting words"), the position relies on the extension of First Amendment principles via the Fourteenth Amendment to the states and their agencies, including publicly supported libraries. (Some state constitutions actually provide greater protection for free speech than does the First Amendment as interpreted by the United States Supreme Court, but no state is permitted to provide less protection for these fundamental rights.) In actual practice, the purist position sometimes gives way to compromises by individual librarians, resulting in removal, labeling, or covert nonselection of certain materials.

If followed by librarians and governing bodies, however, the association's policy statements provide an effective means of helping to prevent library censorship. Ideally, application of these policies to materials selection, circulation practices, and complaint handling establishes the library as an indispensable information source for individuals exercising their freedom of inquiry.

FREE ACCESS TO LIBRARY MATERIALS

Access to library collections, and services is another concern of the profession. For intellectual freedom to flourish, opposition to censorship of materials is not

enough. Free access to materials for every member of the community also must be ensured. The ALA first recognized this in the 1939 *Library's Bill of Rights*, which included a proviso that library meeting rooms be available on equal terms to all groups in the community regardless of the beliefs and affiliations of their members.

Another policy on free access emerged from a study of segregation made by the association's Special Committee on Civil Liberties during the late 1950s. One result of the study was a 1961 amendment to the *Library Bill of Rights*, stating that "the rights of an individual to the use of a library should not be denied or abridged because of his race, religion, national origins, or political views." This amendment was broadened in 1967, when "social views" and "age" were incorporated to emphasize other areas of potential discrimination. "Age" was included to resolve a long-standing debate on the right of minors to have access to libraries on the same basis as adults.

In 1971, at the urging of the Task Force on Gay Liberation of the Social Responsibilities Round Table, the association recommended that libraries and ALA members strenuously combat discrimination in serving any individual from a minority, whether it be an ethnic, a sexual, a religious, or any other kind of minority. In 1980, the *Library Bill of Rights* was revised to encompass all discrimination based on "origin, age, background, or views." Interpretations of the *Library Bill of Rights* addressing specific issues that fall under these deliberately broad categories include "Access for Children and Young People to Videotapes and Other Nonprint Formats," "Access to Resources and Services in the School Library Media Program," "Free Access to Libraries for Minors," "Economic Barriers to Information Access," and "Access to Library Resources and Services Regardless of Gender or Sexual Orientation."

Another aspect of the library patron's access to materials was broached in 1970 when the Internal Revenue Service requested permission from several libraries to examine circulation records to determine the names of persons reading materials about explosives and guerilla warfare. The association responded by developing its "Policy on Confidentiality of Library Records," urging libraries to designate such records as confidential and accessible only "pursuant to such process, order, or subpoena as may be authorized under the authority of, and pursuant to, federal, state, or local law relating to civil, criminal, or administrative discovery procedures or legislative investigatory power." The rationale of the policy was that circulation records are purely circumstantial evidence that a patron has taken a book out of the library and that fear of persecution or prosecution may restrain users from borrowing any conceivably controversial materials, for whatever purpose.

The question of library records and the confidentiality of relationships between librarians and library users arose again in 1971 regarding the "use of grand jury procedure

Informetrics–International Council

Informetrics–International Council

to intimidate anti-Vietnam War activists and people seeking justice for minority communities." In response, the association asserted "the confidentiality of the professional relationships of librarians to the people they serve, that these relationships be respected in the same manner as medical doctors to their patients, lawyers to their clients, priests to the people they serve," and that "no librarian would lend himself to a role as informant, whether of voluntarily revealing circulation records or identifying patrons and their reading habits."

In late 1987, it was disclosed that FBI agents were visiting libraries in what are best described as "fishing expeditions." Agents generally first approached library clerks and solicited information on the use of various library services (e.g., interlibrary loan, database searches) by "suspicious looking foreigners" and, in some instances, asked to see the library's circulation records.

A public confrontation between the IFC and the FBI eventually ensued. The IFC stressed the inextricability of First Amendment and privacy rights, as well as the fact that the bureau was requesting that librarians violate not only a professional ethic but also the law in 38 states and the District of Columbia. (As of this writing, there are confidentiality laws in 48 states and the District of Columbia and an attorney general's opinion supporting confidentiality in two states.) The bureau refused to back away from what it characterized as a program to alert librarians to the possibility that libraries were being used by foreign agents as a place to recruit operatives, that librarians themselves were sometimes targeted for approach by foreign agents, and that valuable material was being stolen by these agents and their operatives. The IFC emphasized, in congressional testimony and in the media, the principle of open access to publicly available information and the central role of libraries in this society as providers of that access.

In the fall of 1989, through a Freedom of Information Act (FOIA) request, the ALA obtained documents from the FBI in which 266 individuals, all of whom had in some way criticized the Library Awareness Program (LAP), were identified as subjects of FBI "index checks." These documents also suggested that the Library Awareness Program covered parts of the country other than solely New York City, as previously claimed by the FBI.

Early in 1990, the ALA wrote to President George Bush, then director of the FBI William Sessions, and the relevant House and Senate committees, urging that the LAP be discontinued and that the files of the 266 individuals be released to them and expunged from FBI records. Director Sessions responded in March 1990 by defending the program and denying that any investigation of the 266 had taken place, claiming that "index checks" were administrative and not investigative in nature. Subsequently, individuals were urged to make their own FOIA requests, but only one person who filed such a request later reported receiving any information from the FBI.

In addition, the ALA filed yet another FOIA request, which was denied, as was the appeal of that denial, on the grounds that the FBI was in litigation with the National Security Archive (NSA) over the same issue. The FBI promised to give the ALA any information released to the NSA and eventually did so. Nevertheless, the ALA reserved the right to bring suit against the FBI for denying its right of appeal and obstructing a legitimate attempt to gain information under the Freedom of Information Act.

The FBI has never publicly abandoned the Library Awareness Program and may still be conducting it.

Federal agencies are not alone in attempting to make use of library patron records. Local law enforcement officials, journalists, students, parents, fund-raisers, marketing professionals, civil litigants, and politicians have been known to seek borrowing records, registration data, mailing lists, and other information about library patrons. In 1990, a library director in Decatur, Texas, challenged one such attempt in court and won an important victory for library confidentiality policies. In *Decatur Public Library v. The District Attorney's Office of Wise County*,[7] the district attorney, investigating a child abandonment case, subpoenaed the records of all libraries in Wise County, requesting the names, addresses, and telephone numbers of all individuals who had checked out books on childbirth within the previous 9 months, the titles they borrowed, and the dates the materials were checked out and returned. The police had no evidence indicating that the person who abandoned the child might have borrowed library books or otherwise used the library. They were simply conducting a "fishing expedition."

The director of the Decatur Public Library refused to comply with the subpoena and, with the help of the city attorney, filed a motion to quash it on behalf of the library's patrons. On May 9, 1990, Judge John R. Lindsey ruled in favor of the library and quashed the subpoena. His decision recognized the library's standing to assert a constitutional privilege on behalf of its unnamed patrons and clients, affirmed a constitutional right of privacy available to patrons, and held that the state was unable to demonstrate a compelling governmental objective under its police powers or other legitimate function of government to warrant intrusion of those rights.

In 1995, the issue of library user confidentiality again reached the courts in connection with a lawsuit brought by a tobacco company, Brown and Williamson, against the University of California. The company alleged that the University of California at San Francisco library possessed in its collection documents stolen from the company that purportedly showed that the tobacco industry had known of a link between smoking and cancer for many years and had failed to disclose it. The documents had previously been leaked to the press and discussed in congressional hearings at the time the lawsuit was filed. The lawsuit sought not only return of the documents but a list of all library patrons who had access to them and a description of the nature of those users' research and publications.

The ALA's sister organization, the Freedom to Read Foundation, identified the case as one of extreme importance, with potential to set positive precedent in favor of First Amendment protection for library-user privacy, and filed an amicus brief explaining the crucial link between library confidentiality and First Amendment rights. Although the case ultimately was resolved without reaching the confidentiality issue, the fact that a request for library-user records was made as part of the lawsuit indicates the breadth of circumstances in which a threat to confidentiality may arise.

Through the association's various position statements, the profession has established a code of free access to services and materials for all library users. Opposed to using the library as a means of intimidating patrons, the profession strives to enhance the intellectual freedom of the library user by providing not only all materials requested but also free and equal access to all materials without fear of recrimination for pursuing one's interests.

THE LIBRARIAN AND INTELLECTUAL FREEDOM

Although the profession, through ALA, formulates policies to help ensure a climate favorable to intellectual freedom, the individual librarian is the key to achieving the end result. Adherence to the *Library Bill of Rights* by individual librarians is the only means of effecting the profession's goals. Consequently, the concept of intellectual freedom also considers the individual librarian's intellectual freedom, both in pursuit of professional responsibilities and in personal life. Several agencies within, or closely affiliated with, ALA encourage and protect the librarian's commitment to the principles of intellectual freedom. In relation to support for intellectual freedom, the *Code of Ethics* of the American Library Association, adopted by the ALA Council in June 1995, specifically states: "We uphold the principles of intellectual freedom and resist all efforts to censor library materials."

From 1940 until 1967, most of such activities were centered in the Intellectual Freedom Committee. For many years, the IFC not only recommended policies but also directed a variety of educational efforts, including collecting and publicizing information about censorship incidents, sponsoring censorship exhibits at conferences, conducting preconferences on intellectual freedom themes, and planning complementary programs to further the association's goals regarding intellectual freedom.

One of these complementary programs is the Office for Intellectual Freedom (OIF), established in December 1967. OIF evolved from a 1965 preconference on intellectual freedom held in Washington, DC. That meeting recommended establishing an ALA headquarters unit to conduct and coordinate the association's intellectual freedom activities and to provide continuity for the total program. The goal of OIF is to educate librarians and the general public on the importance of intellectual freedom, relieving the IFC of this task and allowing it to concentrate on developing policy. The OIF serves as the administrative arm of the Intellectual Freedom Committee and bears the responsibility for implementing ALA policies on intellectual freedom, as approved by the ALA Council. The philosophy of the Office for Intellectual Freedom is based on the premise that if librarians are to appreciate the importance of intellectual freedom, they must first understand the concept as it relates to the individual, the institution, and the functioning of society. Believing that with understanding comes the ability to teach others, OIF maintains a broad program of informational publications, projects, and services.

The regular OIF publication is the bimonthly *Newsletter on Intellectual Freedom*. The Office also prepares special educational materials, (e.g., the *Banned Books Week Resource Kit* and others as need dictates). In addition, OIF works closely with ALA Publishing to develop relevant monographs. Recent titles have included *The Intellectual Freedom Manual, Sixth Edition*, by the Office for Intellectual Freedom (ALA, 2001); *Libraries, Access, and Intellectual Freedom: Developing Policies for Public and Academic Libraries*, by Barbara M. Jones (ALA, 1999); *Libraries, the First Amendment, and Cyberspace: What You Need to Know*, by Robert S. Peck (ALA, 2000); and *Speaking Out! Voices in Celebration of Intellectual Freedom* by Ann K. Symons and Sally Gardener Reed (ALA, 1999). OIF also distributes documents, articles, brochures, and all ALA policy statements concerning intellectual freedom in print and on the Web. As part of its information program, OIF maintains and distributes a banned books exhibit. The exhibit is available for display at national, state, and local conferences, workshops, seminars, and other meetings.

The Office for Intellectual Freedom advises and consults with librarians confronting potential or actual censorship problems. Telephone and letter requests about materials that have drawn the censorial efforts of an individual or group in the community prompt efforts to give appropriate assistance. Another means of assistance established in 1994 is the Intellectual Freedom Action Network, a group of concerned volunteers who have identified themselves as willing to stand up in support of intellectual freedom when controversy comes to their area and to alert OIF to the activities of censorship pressure groups in their communities. The OIF coordinates the Action Network, calling on its members when necessary to write letters, attend meetings, or provide moral support to librarians fighting censorship in their localities.

OIF also coordinates the Intellectual Freedom Committee's relations with other organizations having similar concerns. These include the intellectual freedom committees of the ALA divisions and state library association intellectual freedom committees. Close contact with

Informetrics–International Council

Informetrics–International Council

nonlibrary organizations, such as the Association of American Publishers, the American Booksellers Foundation for Free Expression, the American Civil Liberties Union, the National Coalition against Censorship, and others, is also maintained.

As ALA's intellectual freedom program developed, the need for an organizational forum through which individual ALA members could participate in intellectual freedom activities according to their varying levels of interest began to be felt. At the 1973 Annual Conference in Las Vegas, the Intellectual Freedom Round Table (IFRT) was organized as the Association's membership, activity program for intellectual freedom. The activities of the round table supplement OIF's education program and offer opportunities for ALA members to become active in the association's intellectual freedom efforts.

The IFRT sponsors three intellectual freedom awards. The annual State and Regional Achievement Award, given by the IFRT since 1984, was revised in 1991. Formerly presented to a state Intellectual Freedom Committee, the award has been expanded to include "state educational media association intellectual freedom committee[s], state intellectual freedom coalition[s], legal defense fund[s] or other such group that has implemented the most successful and creative state intellectual freedom project during the calendar year. The award also may be presented for on-going or multiyear projects." In 1975, IFRT established the John Philip Immroth Memorial Award for Intellectual Freedom, given annually in memory of the cofounder and first chairperson of the round table, "to honor notable contributions to intellectual freedom and demonstrations of personal courage in defense of freedom of expression." Biennially, the IFRT sponsors the Eli M. Oboler Award, presented for the best published work in the area of intellectual freedom.

The Intellectual Freedom Committee, the Office for Intellectual Freedom, and the Intellectual Freedom Round Table are the primary agencies for establishing and promoting the association's positions on questions involving intellectual freedom. In addition, the Intellectual Freedom Action Network supports these positions and responds to controversies on the local level. The element in the association's program in support and defense of intellectual freedom that takes the most aggressive, proactive role, however, is the Freedom to Read Foundation.

Incorporated in November 1969, the Freedom to Read Foundation was ALA's response to librarians who increasingly wanted defense machinery to protect their jobs from jeopardy when they undertook to challenge violations of intellectual freedom. Another primary objective in establishing the foundation was to have a means through which librarians and other concerned individuals and groups could begin to set legal precedents for the freedom to read. The foundation was created outside the structure of ALA and, to ensure its full freedom to act with vigor in

the legal arena, it remains legally and financially independent. But the foundation is closely affiliated with ALA through the ex officio membership of ALA officers on its board of trustees, and through its executive director, who also serves as director of the ALA Office for Intellectual Freedom.

A program of education on the importance of, and the necessity for a commitment to, the principles of intellectual freedom requires assurance that such commitment will not result in reprisals, such as legal prosecution, financial loss, or personal damage. The Freedom to Read Foundation attempts to provide that assurance through financial and legal assistance and legal challenges to restrictive legislation, thereby helping to create a favorable climate for intellectual freedom. Through the provision of financial and legal assistance, the foundation attempts to negate the necessity for librarians to make the difficult choice between practical expediency (i.e., keeping a job) and upholding principles, such as in selecting materials for library collections. Through its various projects and grants, the foundation hopes to establish those principles enunciated in the *Library Bill of Rights* as legal precedents rather than mere paper policies.

Established by the Freedom to Read Foundation, but now formally independent, the LeRoy C. Merritt Humanitarian Fund was created in 1970. The Merritt Fund was established by the foundation's board of trustees in recognition of individuals' need for subsistence and other support when their positions are jeopardized or lost as a result of defending intellectual freedom. This special fund offers short-term, immediate assistance even prior to the development of all pertinent facts in a particular case, whether or not legal action has been taken.

In the combined forces of the Intellectual Freedom Committee, the Office for Intellectual Freedom, the Intellectual Freedom Round Table, the Intellectual Freedom Action Network, and the Freedom to Read Foundation, along with the LeRoy C. Merritt Humanitarian Fund, the library profession has available a complete program to support the practice of intellectual freedom. The profession, however, has not yet achieved the same success in a closely related area, that of the librarian's personal rather than professional intellectual freedom. The question of what support should be given to librarians who suffer professionally because of personal beliefs and actions has been approached in individual cases but has not been fully resolved.

One of the first instances involving potential recriminations in a professional capacity as a result of personal beliefs occurred in the late 1940s, with the advent of "loyalty oaths" and "loyalty programs" designed to ferret out communists and "subversives." The Intellectual Freedom Committee faced the loyalty issue with its Policy on Loyalty Programs, first adopted by the council in 1948 and revised in 1951. When another case arose in Florida in 1969, the Policy on Loyalty Programs was reexamined and again revised. The last revision, adopted by the council in January 1971, states in part the following:

> The American Library Association strongly protests loyalty programs which inquire into a library employee's thoughts, reading matter, associates, or membership in organizations, unless a particular person's definite actions warrant such investigation. We condemn loyalty oaths as a condition of employment and investigations which permit the discharge of an individual without a fair hearing.[8]

In 1969, another incident arose involving a librarian who lost his position because of actions, based on personal beliefs, taken in his capacity as a private citizen. T. Ellis Hodgin was fired as city librarian of Martinsville, Virginia, shortly after he joined a lawsuit challenging the constitutionality of a religious education course taught in the city school his daughter attended. He also had been active in civil rights efforts. Hodgin's situation sparked a controversy among librarians, resulting in a recommendation from the Intellectual Freedom Subcommittee of the Activities Committee on New Directions for ALA (ACONDA):

> The scope of intellectual freedom encompasses considerably more than just the freedom to read. Support must also be rendered to the librarian who is fired for sporting a beard, for engaging in civil rights activities, etc., etc. And he should not have to claim "poverty" in order to receive it.[9]

The recommendation, however, was not approved as part of the final ACONDA report.

Some concerned librarians responded to Hodgin's plight by organizing the National Freedom Fund for Librarians (NFFL), which collected several thousand dollars to aid him. (When the NFFL disbanded in 1971, its cash balance was sent to the LeRoy C. Merritt Humanitarian Fund.)

Hodgin also appealed to the Freedom to Read Foundation for assistance to defray the financial hardship he suffered when he lost his position. In June 1970, the foundation's executive committee awarded him $500

> for having suffered in his defense of freedom of speech as a result of which he lost his position as a librarian. Inasmuch as it is the obligation of the librarian to protect free speech and a free press through his work as a librarian, it is then particularly appropriate that, when he is deprived of his job because of his own exercise of free speech, the Freedom to Read Foundation assist him in the defense of his freedom.[10]

A second grant of $500 was made to Hodgin in January 1971 for the specific purpose of perfecting an appeal of his suit for reinstatement to the U.S. Supreme Court.

The limits of intellectual freedom were again debated by the profession when the case of J. Michael McConnell arose in 1970. The Intellectual Freedom Committee found that McConnell's rights "under the First Amendment have been violated" because he met reprisals for freely expressing his sexual preference.[11] On that basis, the LeRoy C. Merritt Humanitarian Fund granted $500 to help defray financial hardship occasioned by his inability to find another job.

The question of how far librarians are willing to extend the scope of intellectual freedom for the benefit of their colleagues was raised anew in 1979 by the case of Utah librarian Jeanne Layton. In September 1979, Layton was dismissed from her position as library director in Davis County after she refused to comply with requests to remove the novel *Americana*, by Don DeLillo, from library shelves. The following month she filed suit to regain her job.

The suit was supported from the beginning by the Freedom to Read Foundation, but it soon became clear that the legal battle would be a lengthy and very costly one. Both the Intellectual Freedom Committee and the Freedom to Read Foundation designated the case a priority for 1980. The Utah Library Association rallied librarians and others statewide in support. At the 1980 ALA Annual Conference in New York, the Freedom to Read Foundation announced that it would match two dollars for every dollar contributed to Jeanne Layton's defense from June 27, 1980, to December 31, 1980, up to a limit of $10,000 in matching funds. The response was, in the words of Foundation President Florence McMullin, "nothing short of overwhelming." When the challenge expired, $6024 had been received, of which $5000 was matched "two for one" by the foundation. Moreover, Jeanne Layton won her suit and regained her job, and one of her main antagonists was defeated for reelection to the county commission.

Although the question of how far librarians will go to support colleagues in defense of intellectual freedom will always be resolvable only on a case-by-case and issue-by-issue basis, the response to Layton's courageous stand surely indicates that in general the library profession takes its responsibilities on this front seriously indeed.

THE LIBRARY AND INTELLECTUAL FREEDOM

Each aspect of intellectual freedom in libraries that has been discussed to this point has involved library users and their access to all published materials, as well as librarians and their practice of professional or personal intellectual freedom.

One aspect of intellectual freedom remains to be examined: the library as an institution and the nature of its role in social change and education. Continually debated within the profession and the American Library

Informetrics–International Council

Association, the issue has been summarized as "neutrality versus advocacy." In essence, the question is, can libraries, as institutions, advocate social or political causes and still maintain their image as providers of views representing all sides of all questions?

Whenever the question is raised, it initiates further queries. For example, what constitutes advocating a cause—biased book selection, biased displays, prejudicial assignment of library meeting rooms? Or, what constitutes a cause—peace, ecology, democracy? If a library sponsors a display of books on peace, to maintain neutrality must it also sponsor a display on war? The questions are complex, and the answers have shown no uniformity whatsoever. The American Library Association itself has vacillated on the main issue, reaching only a partial resolution in the late 1960s and the early 1970s.

At the 1969 Annual Conference in Atlantic City, the membership and the council debated whether the association should take a public stand opposing the war in Vietnam or opposing deployment of an antiballistic missile system (ABM). It was argued that because political and moral issues are so deeply entangled with education and library issues, institutions such as ALA and libraries are obligated to take such positions. Those who opposed such positions argued in favor of neutrality on questions not directly related to libraries. They argued that intellectual freedom for those librarians opposed to the majority view would be violated if the association attempted to take stands on social and political issues. They further maintained that they had tradition on their side, because the association had always declined to take a stand on issues not directly related to libraries. That argument, of course, was incorrect. The association had previously taken stands in some instances and refused to do so in others.

In June 1921, for example, the ALA Council espoused a very decided position on the question of disarmament after the First World War. In a strong resolution, the council stated the following:

> WHEREAS, The members of the American Library Association had full demonstration of the pain and pinch that belongs to war and the increased cost of all necessities, both personal and professional, caused thereby; and
>
> WHEREAS, The exigencies of international conditions brought about by the cost of war is appalling from every standpoint; and
>
> WHEREAS, We believe the example of the United States in this matter will be followed by the other nations;
>
> THEREFORE BE IT RESOLVED, That the American Library Association urge upon the president of the United States and Congress the initiative of a movement leading to a reduction of armament at the earliest possible moment; and be it further

> RESOLVED, That a request be made by the members of the American Library Association to their individual congressman for such action and that a record be made of the replies.[12]

However, in 1928, when faced by a request from the American Civil Liberties Union that ALA adopt "one or more resolutions on civil liberty," the ALA Executive Board declined, saying the association "does not take actions on questions outside the library and bibliographic field."[13] That was similar to the philosophy that prevailed in 1969, when the Vietnam and ABM resolutions failed to pass the council. The question arose again, however, at the 1970 and 1971 Midwinter Meetings and Annual Conferences. After a great deal of debate, the Council voted at its 1970 Annual Conference in Detroit to "define the broad social responsibilities of ALA in terms of the willingness of ALA to take a position on current critical issues with the relationship to libraries and library service clearly set forth in the position statements."[14]

In line with this policy, a carefully reworded resolution opposing the war in Vietnam was adopted by the council 1 year later:

> WHEREAS, The stated objective of the American Library Association is the promotion and improvement of library service and librarianship; and
>
> WHEREAS, Continued and improved library service to the American public requires sustained support from the public monies; and
>
> WHEREAS, The continuing U.S. involvement in the conflict in Southeast Asia has so distorted our national priorities as to reduce substantially the funds appropriated for educational purposes, including support for library services to the American people; and
>
> WHEREAS, Continued commitment of U.S. arms, troops, and other military support has not contributed to the solution of this conflict;
>
> BE IT THEREFORE RESOLVED, That the American Library Association calls upon the president of the United States to take immediately those steps necessary to terminate all U.S. military involvement in the present conflict in Southeast Asia by December 31, 1971, and to insure the reallocation of national resources to meet pressing domestic needs.[15]

With approval of the Vietnam resolution, the association seemed to give broader interpretation to the old "library and bibliographic field." However, this more permissive interpretation still did not resolve the more basic question of whether libraries themselves should follow the course of neutrality or advocacy.

The contradiction was further focused in July 1974, when ALA endorsed the Equal Rights Amendment.

Informetrics–International Council

ALA's support for ERA went much farther than its opposition to U.S. military involvement in Southeast Asia. In 1977, the council voted not to hold conferences in states that had not ratified the amendment. In June 1978, the council endorsed the ERA Extension Resolution and, at the 1979 Midwinter Meeting, established an ERA task force charged with assisting and consulting with "ALA Chapters in carrying out the commitment to passage of the Equal Rights Amendment in ways best suited to the individual states."[16]

The association justified this active support of the proposed amendment, first, by noting the support already expressed by other professional associations "by reason of its beneficial implications for all persons in the American society," and, more specifically, as an outgrowth of ALA's policy requiring equal employment opportunity in libraries, adopted at the 1974 Midwinter Meeting. The resolution in support of ERA noted that "women constitute 82 percent of the library profession." Hence, it was argued, "equal employment required support of equal rights for women."[17] None of the operative resolutions on ERA addressed themselves to the content of library collections. Opponents of the amendment and pro-ERA advocates of ALA neutrality, however, were quick to argue that library users "have a right to expect the library to furnish them with uncensored information on both sides of this and all other issues. Adoption of advocacy positions and participation in boycotts cannot help but strike a blow at the public's confidence in the fair-mindedness and even-handedness of librarians."[18]

Yet another aspect of the advocacy versus neutrality conundrum was addressed by the association in 1987 at its annual conference in San Francisco. David Henington, director of Houston Public Library, brought to the IFC for its response and assistance an antiapartheid ordinance passed and implemented by the City of Houston. This ordinance required that all city agencies obtain certification from suppliers of goods and services that they had no affiliates in, and did no business with, the Republic of South Africa. The Houston City Council subsequently voted to exempt both the public library and the city zoo from the requirements of the ordinance. Henington asserted that this requirement was causing serious acquisition problems for the library. Major information services, such as the New York Times Company, the *Wall Street Journal*, and leading publishers, refused to sign such certificates. Some refused because they have reporters in South Africa, one religious group because it has missionaries there, and on principle, in the belief that the free flow of information both into and out of the Republic of South Africa must be defended and enlarged for the sake of those struggling to dismantle the apartheid system there. Because it did not have a copy of the ordinance in hand and because it had received reports of similar ordinances elsewhere, the IFC voted to explore the matter further.

Two ALA members decided that the issue should be taken to the membership at that conference, and they presented a resolution at the membership meeting. The resolution stressed the intellectual freedom implications of this policy and asked that ideas and information be exempted from the laudable goal of enforcing economic sanctions against the Republic of South Africa for its abhorrent apartheid system. A heated encounter ensued between the presenters and other supporters of the resolution and those who saw it as supportive of apartheid and, therefore, racist. The resolution was resoundingly defeated.

At the 1988 Annual Conference in New Orleans, the membership adopted a resolution reaffirming its commitment to Article 19 of the Universal Declaration of Human Rights: "Everyone has the right to freedom of opinion and expression; this right includes freedom to hold opinions without interference and to seek, receive and impart information and ideas through any media regardless of frontiers."

Measuring the Profession's Response

At the present time, the profession uniformly disdains censorship of published materials, print or nonprint. The attitude toward user access is somewhat uniform but contains a great deal of dissent on the question of access for minors to all the materials in a library collection. On the question of the librarian's professional practice of intellectual freedom, there is near agreement that every effort should be made to encourage and protect this aspect of librarianship. The librarian's personal intellectual freedom, on and off the job, presents some points of agreement, but major areas of dissent still exist. The same is true in the area of institutional neutrality versus advocacy.

One conclusion from a review of the history, status, and future of intellectual freedom in libraries is that the American Library Association's positions and programs provide one of the few gauges for measuring the profession's response to the problems of defining, promoting, and defending the concept. The evolving position of the ALA reflects the steady emergence of a philosophy within the entire library community. Although that philosophy exhibits some loose ends, its core grows firmer, based on a history of trial and error and forced response to a continually changing social climate. The philosophy is young, too young to be rooted in tradition, but gradually it has gained recognition as the substance of the total philosophy shaping library service in the United States.

Challenges and Issues Today

The major issues facing libraries today continue to focus on free and open access to information. The ALA continues to support a commitment to the right of unrestricted access to information and ideas, regardless of the communications medium. This commitment was confirmed most recently in regard to the Internet.

Informetrics–International Council

Informetrics–International Council

In February 1996, the Communications Decency Act (CDA) was signed into law by President Clinton as a way to keep "indecent" material from anyone under the age of 18. The act said that if anyone under 18 was allowed to view "indecent" material, the provider was subject to a fine of up to $250,000 and/or up to 2 years in prison. The CDA placed librarians and libraries at risk because the term "indecent" was not defined, providing no guidelines for librarians. The ALA filed a lawsuit (*American Library Association v. U.S. Department of Justice*) in February 1996 challenging the CDA's constitutionality. It was later consolidated with, and decided under, a separate suit brought by the ACLU (*ACLU v. Reno*). The lawsuit argued three points: 1) Prohibiting material as "indecent" was unconstitutional because the term was vague and undefined. In addition, the act did not distinguish between the information needs of a five-year-old child and a 17-year-old in college. 2) Congress had not considered alternative ways that parents might protect their own children in their own home, for instance, by using filtering software. 3) The Internet is not a broadcast medium but is more like the print medium in that each person controls what they access.

In June 1996, a lower court declared the CDA unconstitutional. The government appealed, and in June 1997, the U.S. Supreme Court, by a 9-0 vote, held the CDA unconstitutional.

A unanimous Supreme Court decision not withstanding, Congress went back to the drawing board. The second proposal was the Child Online Protection Act (COPA). In this attempt to circumvent the Supreme Court's CDA decision, Congress made two major changes: the "harmful to minors" standard replaced the "indecency" standard, and the focus was on "commercial" speech.

COPA also established a commission to study the effects of "inappropriate" material on children.

The sponsors believed these changes would save COPA from the fate of the Communications Decency Act, but the Third Circuit Court of Appeals in Philadelphia, the same court which handed down the original CDA decision (subsequently upheld by the Supreme Court), held COPA unconstitutional. The government, of course, appealed to the U.S. Supreme Court, and the Supreme Court heard the case on Wednesday, November 28, 2001.

The government's third attempt to control the Internet is the Children's Internet Protection Act (CIPA). CIPA requires libraries receiving certain types of federal funding to establish Internet safety policies and to use technology that blocks or filters material that is obscene, child pornography, or, when a minor is using the computer, "harmful to minors." This legislation once again puts librarians in an impossible position. Even filtering companies acknowledge that "technology" is incapable of making the fine distinction between legal speech and speech, which falls into these three and is not constitutionally protected.

On March 20, 2001, the American Library Association and several coplaintiffs filed suit, challenging the Children's Internet Protection Act in the Third Circuit Court of Appeals. The case is scheduled to be heard in early 2002.

In addition to the ongoing debate over the Internet and filtering, there are a number of other issues facing libraries and librarians today. These include:

- Harassment, or a hostile work environment, produced by open access to the Internet.
- First Amendment rights of minors and their free access to information, as well as the attempt by some to mandate protection for minors from materials that may be "harmful to minors."
- Continued requests to libraries for patron records under the Freedom of Information Act. This has been of great concern to librarians in relation to new technology which can track a specific patron's Internet use.

The ALA continues to regularly develop resources to aid librarians in managing and communicating about the Internet. These include the *Libraries & The Internet Toolkit*. For the most current resources and the latest information, see the ALA Web site, which is updated and revised regularly.

CONCLUSION

Although the specific challenges will continue to evolve, the issues and principles remain the same. Librarians and libraries fulfill a unique role in our democratic society. Like no other group, we strive to preserve and protect free and open access to information for all who use our libraries. For, as James Madison explained: "A popular government, without popular information, or the mean of acquiring it, is but a prologue to a farce or a tragedy; or perhaps both. Knowledge will forever govern ignorance; and a people who mean to be their own governors must arm themselves with the power which knowledge gives."

REFERENCES

1. American Library Association, Minutes of Executive Board Meetings. **1924**, September 29 *3*, 20 mimeographed.
2. American Library Association, Minutes of Executive Board Meetings. **1934**, December 27 *7*, 48, 49, 89, mimeographed.
3. Bostwick, A. E. The librarian as censor. ALA Bull. **1908**, September *2*, 113.
4. American Library Association, Minutes of Executive Board Meetings. **1938**, October 5 *10*, 48, mimeographed.
5. Cincinnati Proceedings—Council. ALA Bull. **1940**, August *34*, P-37.
6. American Library Association, *Handbook of Organization 1971–1972*, ALA: Chicago 13 n.d.

7. No. 90-05-192, 271st Judicial District Court; Wise and Jack Counties, Texas; (Letter Opinion) Judge John R. Lindsey.

8. Resolution on loyalty investigations. Am. Libr. **1971**, March *2*, 270.

9. American Library Association Activities Committee on New Directions for ALA, *Final Report and Subcommittee Reports*, 1970; June 53 mimeographed.

10. Hodgin appeal rests with U.S. Supreme Court. Freedom Read Found. News **1971**, Fall *1*, 5.

11. Berninghausen, D. K. Report of the Intellectual Freedom Committee to Council, Dallas, June 25, 1971. Am. Libr. **1971**, September *2*, 891.

12. ALA Bull. **1921**, July *15*, 169.

13. American Library Association, Minutes of Executive Board Meetings. **1928**, May 29 *4*, 142.

14. Am. Libr. **1970**, July–August *1*, 674.

15. Resolution on Southeast Asia Conflict. Am. Libr. **1971**, September *2*, 826.

16. *News Release*, American Library Association, 1979; September.

17. *ALA Council Minutes*, 1974; P-335.

18. Day, T. L. Chairman, Neill Public Library Board of Trustees, Letter to the Editor. Chic. Trib. **1979**, January 21.

Informetrics–International Council

Intelligence and Security Informatics

Hsinchun Chen
Zhenhua Lai
Yan Dang
Yulei Zhang
Department of Management Information Systems, University of Arizona, Tucson, Arizona, U.S.A.

Informetrics–International Council

Abstract

The tragic events of September 11, 2001, have had far-reaching effects on many aspects of U.S. society. Six critical mission areas, as suggested in the "National Strategy for Homeland Security" report, have been identified where information technology can contribute to safeguarding our national security. These areas include *intelligence and warning*, *border and transportation security*, *domestic counterterrorism*, *protecting critical infrastructure*, *defending against catastrophic terrorism*, and *emergency preparedness and responses*. Intelligence and Security Informatics (ISI) encompasses the development of advanced and socially responsible information technologies, systems, algorithms, and databases for national security related applications, through an integrated technological, organizational, policy-based, and privacy-preserving approach. This entry reviews current ISI research challenges and presents a research framework with a primary focus on knowledge discovery from databases (KDD) technologies. The framework is discussed in the context of crime types and security implications. In addition to the technical discussions, caveats for data mining and civil liberties concerns are also considered.

INTRODUCTION

The tragic events of September 11 have caused far-reaching changes to many aspects of society. Terrorism is one of the most significant threats to national security due to its potential of bringing massive damage to our infrastructure, economy, and people. In response to this challenge, federal authorities are actively implementing comprehensive strategies and measures in order to achieve the three objectives identified in the "National Strategy for Homeland Security" report:[1] 1) preventing future terrorist attacks; 2) reducing the nation's vulnerability; and 3) minimizing the damage and enabling recovery from attacks that occur. State and local law enforcement agencies, likewise, are becoming more vigilant about criminal activities, which can harm public safety and threaten national security.

Academics in the fields of natural sciences, computational science, information science, social sciences, engineering, medicine, and many others have also been called upon to help enhance the government's abilities to fight terrorism and other crimes. Science and technology have been identified in the "National Strategy for Homeland Security" report as the keys to win the new counterterrorism war.[1] Especially, it is believed that information technology will play an indispensable role in making our nation safer,[2] by supporting intelligence and knowledge discovery through collecting, processing, analyzing, and utilizing terrorism- and crime-related data.[3,4] Based on the crime and intelligence knowledge discovered, federal, state, and local authorities can make timely decisions in selecting effective strategies and tactics as well as allocate the appropriate amount of resources to detect, prevent, and respond to future attacks.

PRIVACY VS. INFORMATION SHARING: A BROADER SOCIETAL ISSUE

To protect the United States from future terrorist attacks, various law enforcement and homeland security agencies must act proactively and collaboratively to thwart planned or future acts of aggression. Most government agencies involved in safeguarding national security create their own databases and other stores of information which relate to potential sources of threats. The sharing of such data stores has been widely proposed as a method for leveraging existing knowledge to better forecast possible attacks. However, these shared databases may be misused, and may violate the privacy rights and civil liberties of innocent citizens. Privacy is the ability of an individual or group to keep their lives and personal affairs out of public view, or to control the flow of information about them. It is considered by many to be one of the most fundamental rights of citizens in a modern society.

More than ever, information technologies have become more prevalent and overreaching in modern day, post-Internet society. Companies, organizations, and governments are using better databases, Internet applications, and information technologies to collect information about

Encyclopedia of Library and Information Sciences, Fourth Edition DOI: 10.1081/E-ELIS4-120043514

Copyright © 2017 by Taylor & Francis. All rights reserved.

their customers, employees, and citizens. Advanced data mining techniques have also been increasingly used by companies and governments to better understand their customers or citizens. These pervasive and powerful technologies are also beginning to adversely affect individual privacy. How can one tell what kind of data is being collected by whom, and for what purposes? How can one ensure that data are collected and used for, and only for, the intended purposes?

Many information misuses have been reported in popular news sources (e.g., identity theft reported in http://law.jrank.org/pages/7469/Identity-Theft.html). In one federal prosecution, the defendants allegedly obtained the names and social security numbers of U.S. military officers from a Web site. The defendants used more than 100 of those names and social security numbers to apply for a Delaware Bank credit card. The fraudulent credit card transaction cost the Delaware Bank millions of dollars in 2000. In another reported case in the Central District of California, a woman pleaded guilty for using a stolen social security number and filing for bankruptcy in the name of her victim. Because (digital) information can be easily collected, copied, transmitted, and (potentially) misused, information collectors' abilities to safeguard the data they collect is even more critical now.

Despite the clear need for maintaining individual privacy, governments and businesses may have reasons for accessing and sharing customer or citizen information. Many previous court cases have supported such uses. For example, in *Davis versus Freedom of Information Commission*, 259 Conn. 45 (2001) The Connecticut Supreme Court declared that the Drivers Privacy Protection Act (DPPA) does not prohibit other government agencies from receiving personal information from the State DMV in the course of their normal government functions. Similarly, in 2002, Nevada's highest court ruled that the incoming and outgoing calls on the public telephones are not considered to be protected information and may be used for other purposes. Clearly, privacy and information sharing will continue to raise serious debates for the foreseeable future.

INFORMATION TECHNOLOGIES AND NATIONAL SECURITY

As part of the post-9/11 national security programs in the United States, six critical mission areas have been identified where information technology can contribute to the accomplishment of the strategic national security objectives identified in the "National Strategy for Homeland Security" report:[1]

- *Intelligence and warning*. Although terrorism depends on surprise to bring damage to targets,[1] terrorist activities are neither random nor impossible to track. Terrorists must plan and prepare before the execution of an attack by selecting a target, recruiting and training executors, acquiring financial support, and traveling to the country where the target is located.[5] To avoid being preempted by authorities they may hide their true identities and disguise attack-related activities. Similarly, criminals may use falsified identities during police contacts.[6] Although it is difficult, detecting potential terrorist attacks or crimes is possible and feasible with the help of information technology. By analyzing the communication and activity patterns among terrorists and their contacts (i.e., terrorist networks), detecting deceptive identities, or employing other surveillance and monitoring techniques, intelligence and warning systems may issue timely, critical alerts and warnings to prevent attacks or crimes from occurring.

- *Border and transportation security*. Terrorists enter a targeted country through an air, land, or sea port of entry. Criminals in narcotics rings travel across borders to purchase, carry, distribute, and sell drugs. Information, such as travelers' identities, images, fingerprints, vehicles used, and other characteristics, is collected from customs, borders, and immigration authorities on a daily basis. The collection can greatly improve the capabilities of counterterrorism and crime-fighting capabilities by creating a "smart border" where information from multiple sources is shared and analyzed to help locate wanted terrorists or criminals. Technologies such as information sharing and integration, collaboration and communication, biometrics, and image and speech recognition will be greatly needed to create smart borders across all ports of entry.

- *Domestic counterterrorism*. Because both international and domestic terrorists may be involved in local crimes, state and local law enforcement agencies are also investigating and prosecuting terrorism-related crimes. Terrorism, like gangs and narcotics trafficking, is regarded as a type of organized crime in which multiple offenders cooperate to carry out offenses. Information technologies that help find cooperative relationships between criminals and their interactive patterns are also helpful for analyzing terrorism. Monitoring activities of domestic terrorist and extremist groups using advanced information technologies will also likely to be helpful to public safety personnel and policy makers.

- *Protecting critical infrastructure and key assets*. Roads, bridges, water suppliers, and many other physical service systems are critical infrastructure and are key assets of a nation. They may become the target of terrorist attacks because of their vulnerabilities.[1] Moreover, virtual (cyber) infrastructure such as the Internet may also be vulnerable to intrusions and inside threats.[7] Criminals and terrorists are increasingly using cyberspace to conduct illegal activities, share ideology, solicit funding, and recruit. In addition to

Informetrics–International Council

Informetrics–International
Council

physical devices such as sensors and detectors, advanced information technologies are needed to model the normal behaviors of the usage of these systems and then use the models to distinguish abnormal behaviors from normal behaviors. Protective or reactive measures can be selected based on the results to secure these assets from attacks.

- *Defending against catastrophic terrorism.* Terrorist attacks can cause devastating damage through the use of chemical, biological, or radiological weapons. Biological attacks, for example, may cause contamination, infectious disease outbreaks, and significant loss of life. Information systems that can efficiently and effectively collect, access, analyze, and report data about catastrophe-leading events can help prevent, detect, respond to, and manage these attacks.[8]

- *Emergency preparedness and responses.* In case of a national emergency, prompt and effective responses are critical to reducing the damage resulting from an attack. In addition to the systems that are prepared to defend against catastrophes, information technologies that help design and experiment optimized response plans,[9] identify experts, train response professionals, and manage consequences are beneficial for both planning and emergency response. Moreover, information systems that facilitate social and psychological support to the victims of terrorist attacks can also assist disaster recovery efforts.

PROBLEMS AND CHALLENGES

Although it is important for the critical missions of national security, the development of information technology for counterterrorism and crime-fighting applications faces many problems and challenges. Currently, intelligence and security agencies are gathering large amounts of data from various sources. Processing and analyzing such data, however, have become increasingly difficult tasks. Treating terrorism as a form of organized crime allows the categorization of these challenges into the following types:

- *Characteristics of criminals and crimes.* Crimes can be geographically diffused and temporally dispersed. In organized crimes such as transnational narcotics, the trafficking criminals often live in different cities, states, or even countries. Drug distribution and sales occur in different places at different times. Similar situations exist in other organized crimes (e.g., terrorism, armed robbery, and gang-related crime). As a result, investigations must cover multiple offenders who commit criminal activities in different places at different times. This can be fairly difficult given the limited resources that most intelligence and security

agencies have. Moreover, as computer and Internet technologies advance, criminals are utilizing cyberspace to commit various types of cyber-crimes under the disguise of ordinary online transactions and communications.

- *Characteristics of crime and intelligence related data.* A significant source of challenge is information stovepipe and overload resulting from diverse data sources, multiple data formats, and large data volumes. Unlike other domains such as marketing, finance, and medicine in which data can be collected from particular sources (e.g., sales records from companies, patient medical history from hospitals), the intelligence and security domain does not have a well-defined data source. Both authoritative information (e.g., crime incident reports, telephone records, financial statements, immigration and custom records) and open-source information (e.g., news stories, journal articles, books, Web pages) need to be gathered for investigative purposes. Data collected from these different sources often are in different formats ranging from structured database records to unstructured text, image, audio, and video files. Important information such as criminal associations may be available but contained in unstructured, multilingual texts and can therefore remain difficult to access and retrieve. Moreover, as data volumes continue to grow, extracting valuable and credible intelligence and knowledge becomes a difficult problem.

- *Characteristics of crime and intelligence analysis techniques.* Current research on the technologies for counterterrorism and crime-fighting applications lacks a consistent framework for addressing the major challenges. Some information technologies including data integration, data analysis, text mining, image and video processing, and evidence combination have been identified as being particularly helpful.[2] However, the question of how to employ them in the intelligence and security domain and use them to effectively address the critical mission areas of national security (with proper protection of privacy and civil liberties) remains unanswered and requires further research.

AN ISI RESEARCH FRAMEWORK

"Intelligence and Security Informatics" (ISI)[3,4,10] is a multidisciplinary science with its main objective being the "development of advanced and socially responsible information technologies, systems, algorithms, and databases for national security-related applications, through an integrated technological, organizational, policy-based, and privacy-preserving approach." ISI has at its core a focus on developing and employing computationally intensive techniques with the goal of increasing current levels of national security through an integrated approach that takes into account organizational considerations; national security priorities; laws, regulations, and policies; and privacy protection. This next section presents a research framework with a primary focus on knowledge discovery from databases (KDD) technologies, and is discussed in the context of crime types and security implications.

Crime is an act or the commission of an act that is forbidden, or the omission of a duty that is commanded by a public law and that makes the offender liable to punishment by that law. The more threat a crime type poses to public safety, the more likely it is to be of national security concern. Some crimes, such as traffic violations, theft, and homicide, are primarily in the jurisdiction of local law enforcement agencies. Other crimes need to be dealt with by both local law enforcement and national security authorities. Identity theft and fraud, for instance, is relevant at both the local and national levels—criminals may escape arrest by using false identities, or drug smugglers may enter the United States by holding counterfeited passports or visas. Organized crimes such as terrorism and narcotics trafficking often diffuse geographically, resulting in common security concerns across cities, states, and countries. Cyber-crimes can pose threats to public safety across multiple jurisdictional areas due to the widespread nature of computer networks. Table 1 summarizes the different types of crimes sorted by the degree of their respective public influence.[4] International and domestic terrorism, in particular, often involves multiple crime types (e.g., identity theft, money laundry, arson and bombing, organized and violent activities, and cyber-terrorism) and has the potential to cause enormous damage.

KDD techniques can play an important role in improving counterterrorism and crime-fighting capabilities of intelligence, security, and law enforcement agencies by reducing cognitive and information overload that results from dealing with massive amounts of data. Knowledge discovery refers to the nontrivial extraction of implicit, previously unknown, and potentially useful knowledge from data. Knowledge discovery techniques promise easier, more convenient, and practical exploration of very large collections of data for organizations and users, and have been applied in marketing, finance, manufacturing, biology, and many other domains (e.g., predicting consumer behaviors, detecting credit card frauds, or clustering genes that have similar biological functions).[11] Traditional knowledge discovery techniques include association rule mining, classification and prediction, cluster analysis, and outlier analysis.[12] As natural language processing (NLP) research advances, text mining approaches that automatically extract, summarize, categorize, and translate text documents have also been widely used.

Many of these KDD technologies can be applied in ISI studies.[3,4] Existing ISI technologies can be categorized into six classes: *information sharing and collaboration, crime association mining, crime classification and clustering, intelligence text mining, spatial and temporal crime mining,* and *criminal network mining.* These six classes are grounded on traditional knowledge discovery technologies, but with new approaches added, including spatial and temporal crime pattern mining and criminal network analysis, which are more relevant to counterterrorism and crime investigation. In addition, new research has begun in the areas of privacy-preserving, security-aware data integration and data mining. Although information sharing and collaboration are not data mining per se, they help prepare, normalize, warehouse, and integrate data for knowledge discovery and thus are included in the framework.

Fig. 1 presents the proposed research framework, showing crime types and the six classes of techniques useful for (or showing the promise of utility to) the investigation of the various crime types.[4] The crime data mining techniques are listed, from bottom to top, in an increasing scale of analysis capability. Note that more serious crimes—those inducing greater public harm—may require a more complete set of knowledge discovery

Table 1 Crime types and security concerns.

Crime types		
Type	**Local law enforcement level**	**National security level**
Traffic violations	Driving under influence (DUI), fatal/personal injury/property damage, traffic accident, road rage	—
Sex crime	Sexual offenses, sexual assaults, child molesting	Organized prostitution, people smuggling
Theft	Robbery, burglary, larceny, motor vehicle theft, stolen property	Theft of national secrets or weapon information
Fraud	Forgery and counterfeiting, fraud, embezzlement, identity deception	Transnational money laundering, identity fraud, transnational financial fraud
Arson	Arson on buildings, apartments	
Organized crime	Narcotic drug offenses (sales or possession), gang-related offenses	Transnational drug trafficking, terrorism (bioterrorism, bombing, hijacking, etc.)
Violent crime	Criminal homicide, armed robbery, aggravated assault, other assaults	Terrorism
Cyber crime	Internet fraud (e.g., credit card fraud, advance fee fraud, fraudulent Web sites), illegal trading, network intrusion/hacking, virus spreading, hate crimes, cyber-piracy, cyber-pornography, cyber-terrorism, theft of confidential information	

Informetrics–International Council

	Crime Types							
Crime Data Mining Techniques	Traffic Violation	Sex Offense	Theft	Fraud	Arson	Organized Crime	Violent Crime	Cyber Crime
Criminal Network Analysis						X	X	X
Spatial and Temporal Pattern Mining				X		X	X	X
Text Mining		X	X	X	X	X	X	X
Classification & Clustering	X	X	X	X	X	X	X	X
Association	X	X	X	X	X	X	X	X

Analysis Capability →

Public Harm →

Fig. 1 A knowledge discovery research framework for ISI.

techniques. For example, the investigation of organized crimes such as terrorism may depend on criminal network analysis technology, which requires the use of other knowledge discovery techniques such as association mining and clustering. An important observation about this framework is that the high-frequency occurrences and strong association patterns of severe and organized crimes such as terrorism and narcotics trafficking present a unique opportunity and potentially high rewards for adopting such a knowledge discovery framework.

Some of these classes of data mining techniques are of great relevance to ISI research. *Text mining* is critical for extracting key entities (people, places, narcotics, weapons, time, etc.) and their relationships presented in voluminous police incident reports, intelligence reports, open-source news clips, etc. Some of these techniques need to be multilingual in nature, including the abilities to employ machine translation and cross-lingual information retrieval (CLIR). *Spatial and temporal mining and visualization* is often needed for geographic information systems (GIS) and temporal analysis of criminal and terrorist events. Most crime analysts are well trained in GIS-based crime mapping tools; however, automated spatial and temporal pattern mining techniques (e.g., hotspot analysis) have not been widely adopted in intelligence and security applications. Organized criminals (e.g., gangs and narcotics) and terrorists often form interconnected covert networks to carry out illegal activities. Often referred to as "dark networks," these organizations exhibit unique structures, communication channels, and resilience to attack and disruption. New computational techniques including social network analysis, network learning, and network topological analysis (e.g., random network, small-world network, and scale-free network) are needed for the systematic study of those complex and covert networks. These techniques are classified under *criminal network analysis* in Fig. 1.

ISI, CIVIL LIBERTIES, AND DATA MINING

The U.S. Constitution and its Bill of Rights were drafted in part to define and protect the civil liberties of United States citizens and to set limits on the government's power. Important civil liberties include freedom of association, freedom of assembly, freedom of speech, and the right to privacy. In the United States, the American Civil Liberties Union (ACLU) is a powerful advocacy group that aims to ensure the protection of free speech, privacy, and other fundamental human rights.

The potential negative effects of intelligence gathering and analysis on the privacy and civil liberties of the public have been well publicized.[13] There exist many laws, regulations, and agreements governing data collection, confidentiality, and reporting, which could directly impact the development and application of ISI technologies. Intelligence and security agencies and ISI researchers must be aware of these laws and regulations in research and practice. The use of a hypothesis-guided, evidence-based approach in crime and intelligence analysis research can also help assure that privacy is appropriate respected. For example, there should be probable and reasonable causes and evidence for targeting particular individuals or data sets for analysis. Proper investigative and legal procedures need to be strictly followed. It is neither ethical nor legal to "fish" for potential criminals from diverse and mixed crime, intelligence, and civilian related data sources. The well-publicized Defense Advanced Research Program Agency (DARPA), Total Information Awareness (TIA) program, and the Multi-State Anti-Terrorism Information Exchange (MATRIX) system, for example, have been shut down by the U.S. Congress due to their potential misuse of citizen data and impairment of civil liberties.[14]

However, other initiatives have been maintained, as the catastrophic 9/11 events had a profound impact on the way the U.S. government acts on security concerns. In response to the attacks, for example, the U.S. government enacted the USA PATRIOT Act, created the Department of Homeland Security (DHS), increased security efforts and airports and other ports of call, etc.

The PATRIOT Act expands the government's ability to examine records on an individual's activity whether those records are being held by third parties or were acquired by secret searches and/or wiretap surveillance. The Act expands a narrow exception to the Fourth Amendment that

Informetrics–International Council

had been created for the collection of foreign intelligence information and also expands another Fourth Amendment exception for spying that collects "addressing" information about the origin and destination of communications. An immediate result of the events of September 11, 2001 was the extraordinarily rapid passage of the USA PATRIOT Act in late 2001. The legislation was passed by the Senate on October 11, 2001 and by the House on October 24, 2001; it was signed by the President on October 26, 2001, with some revisions following in 2005 and 2006. But the continuing legacy of the then-existing consensus and the lack of detailed debate and considerations have created an ongoing national argument as to the proper balance between national security and civil liberties.

FUTURE DIRECTIONS

National security research poses unique challenges and opportunities. Much of the established data mining and knowledge discovery literature, findings, and techniques need to be reexamined in light of the unique data and problem characteristics in the law enforcement and intelligence community. New text mining, spatial and temporal pattern mining, privacy-preserving data mining, and criminal network analysis of relevance to national security are among some of the most pressing research areas. However, researchers cannot conduct research in a vacuum. Partnerships with local, state, and federal agencies need to be formed to obtain relevant test data and necessary domain expertise and feedback for ISI research.

ACKNOWLEDGMENTS

We would like to acknowledge the funding support of NSF and other agencies:

- NSF, Knowledge Discovery and Dissemination (KDD) Program, "Detecting Identity Concealment," September 2004–August 2005.
- NSF, Digital Government Program, "COPLINK Center: Social Network Analysis and Identity Deception Detection for Law Enforcement and Homeland Security," September 2003–August 2006.
- NSF, Information Technology Research (ITR) Program, "COPLINK Center for Intelligence and Security Informatics—A Crime Data Mining Approach to Developing Border Safe Research," September 2003–August 2005.
- NSF, Community Resource Development (CRD) Program, "Developing a Dark Web Collection and Infrastructure for Computational and Social Sciences," September 2007–August 2010.

REFERENCES

1. Office of Homeland Security. *National Strategy for Homeland Security*, Office of Homeland Security: Washington, DC, 2002.
2. National Research Council. *Making the Nation Safer: The Role of Science and Technology in Countering Terrorism*, National Academies Press: Washington, DC, 2002.
3. Chen, H., Miranda, R., Zeng, D.D., Demchak, C., Schroeder, J., Madhusudan, T., Eds. *Intelligence and Security Informatics*; Springer: Berlin, 2003. Proceedings of the First NSF/NIJ Symposium on Intelligence and Security Informatics.
4. Chen, H., Moore, R., Zeng, D., Leavitt, J., Eds.; *Intelligence and Security Informatics*; Springer: Berlin, 2004. Proceedings of the Second Symposium on Intelligence and Security Informatics.
5. Sageman, M. *Understanding Terror Networks*, University of Pennsylvania Press: Philadelphia, PA, 2004.
6. Wang, G.; Chen, H.; Atabakhsh, H. Automatically detecting deceptive criminal identities. Commun. ACM **2004**, *47*(3), 71–76.
7. Lee, W. Stolfo, S. Data mining approaches for intrusion detection In Proceedings of the 7th USENIX Security Symposium San Antonio, TX January 26–29, 1998 USENIX: Berkeley, CA, 1998.
8. Damianos, L.; Ponte, J.; Wohlever, S.; Reeder, F.; Day, D.; Wilson, G.; Hirschman, L. MiTAP for bio-security: A case study. AI Mag. **2002**, *23*(4), 13–29.
9. Lu, Q. Huang, Y. Shekhar, S. Evacuation planning: A capacity constrained routing approach. Proceedings of the First NSF/NIJ Symposium on Intelligence and Security Informatics Tucson, AZ June, 2003; Chen, H., Miranda, R., Zeng, D., Demchak, C., Schroeder, J., Madhusudan, T., Eds.; Springer: Berlin, 2003; LNCS 2665.
10. Chen, H. *Intelligence and Security Informatics for International Security: Information Sharing and Data Mining*, Springer: New York, 2006.
11. Fayyad, U.; Uthurusamy, R. Evolving data mining into solutions for insights. Commun. ACM **2002**, *45*(8), 28–31.
12. Han, J. Kamber, M. *Data Mining: Concepts and Techniques*, 2nd Ed. Morgan Kaufmann: San Francisco, CA, 2005.
13. Cook, J.S. Cook, L.L. Social, ethical and legal issues of data mining. In *Data Mining: Opportunities and Challenges*; Wang, J., Ed.; Idea Group Publishing: Hershey, PA, 2003; 395–420.
14. American Civil Liberties Union. MATRIX: Myths and reality. Available at http://www.aclu.org/Privacy/Privacy.cfm?ID=14894&c=130.

Informetrics–International Council

International and Comparative Librarianship

Peter Johan Lor
*School of Information Studies, University of Wisconsin-Milwaukee, Milwaukee,
Wisconsin, U.S.A., and Department of Information Science, University of Pretoria,
Pretoria, South Africa*

Abstract

The concepts of international librarianship and comparative librarianship first appeared under their respective titles in the 1950s, when their literatures were overlapping. During the 1960s, and continuing through the 1980s, much energy was devoted to defining each of them and attempting to distinguish between them. Although clearer definitions were developed during the mid-1970s by J. Stephen Parker and J. Periam Danton respectively, some confusion has persisted. In practice the two fields are often grouped together as "international and comparative librarianship" or "international and comparative library science." Nevertheless, the two fields can and should be distinguished. This entry attempts to articulate the definition and scope of each, outlines some methodological issues, and surveys the development of the literature.

INTRODUCTION

In today's globalized knowledge society international relations and resource sharing among libraries and the exchange of knowledge among librarians are indispensable. Historically librarianship has had a significant international dimension, dating back to the ancient Library of Alexandria, which maintained a policy of attempting to collect all the world's knowledge. During that time, according to a possibly apocryphal tradition, visiting ships from foreign ports were required to surrender books for copying by the Library's scribes.[1] This method hardly serves as an example for library cooperation today, but does illustrate that librarianship has an inherently international outlook. During the late nineteenth century this international dimension took on a more meaningful shape in the form of international conferences of librarians, bibliographers, and book lovers, resulting in the establishment of the first international organizations for those groups. International librarianship and comparative librarianship first appeared under their respective names in the 1950s, and their literatures continued to overlap during the 1960s through the 1980s, during which time much energy was devoted to defining each and attempting to distinguish between them. Clearer definitions were developed during the mid-1970s by J. Stephen Parker[2] and J. Periam Danton[3] respectively. However, some confusion persists. In practice the two fields are often grouped together as "international and comparative librarianship" or "international and comparative library science." Nevertheless, the two fields can and should be distinguished. In an attempt to clarify the distinctions, this entry discusses the definition and scope of international librarianship and comparative

librarianship, outlines some methodological issues, and surveys the development of the literature.

DEFINITIONS AND SCOPE

International Librarianship

The origins and early definitions of international librarianship have been articulated by Danton,[3,4] Parker,[2] Harvey,[5] and Keresztesi.[6] Some recent contributions and further clarifications have been attempted by Sami,[7] Bliss,[8] Liu,[9] and Lor.[10] However, Parker's definition has been widely cited and it serves as an authoritative point for discussion:

> International librarianship consists of activities carried out among or between governmental or non-governmental institutions, organizations, groups or individuals of two or more nations, to promote, establish, develop, maintain and evaluate library, documentation and allied services, and librarianship and the library profession generally, in any part of the world. (p. 221)[2]

Several key points for consideration are raised by the definition:

1. International librarianship is a field of *activity*, rather than a scientific discipline. This does not, of course, prevent the activities from being studied with scientific rigor. In this case the field may be referred to as "international library science," particularly as practiced in the United States, where the term "library science" is used to refer to the field as a scientific discipline.

Encyclopedia of Library and Information Sciences, Fourth Edition DOI: 10.1081/E-ELIS4-120044658

Copyright © 2017 by Taylor & Francis. All rights reserved.

2. The activities are conducted in a *relationship* "among or between" parties at various levels, ranging from individuals to governments. Such activities, among others, include resource sharing, standardization, development aid, political and cultural influences, relations between and/or among national associations, and exchanges of staff, students, and scholars.

3. These parties are located in *two or more nations* (countries). This stipulation raises the question of what is meant by "international." Strictly speaking, relations between two countries are referred to as "bilateral" and purists would restrict the use of the term "international" to refer to relations between more than two countries,[6] but in international librarianship this distinction is seldom observed.

This last point requires some elaboration. In the United States the term "international" is often used to mean "foreign," hence the use of the term "international librarianship" to mean "librarianship in other countries." This designation is common in the literature, where books bearing titles that include the term "international librarianship" may be, in fact, collections of articles describing aspects of librarianship in countries other than the United States. Such literature has been classified by Harvey as "foreign library science," which he defined as being "the description of any aspect of library operations in one or more countries other than the author's own country."[11] The notion of "foreign" librarianship has been criticized, notably by Danton,[3,4] who points out that what is foreign depends on one's nationality. To illustrate: an article on school libraries in Tunisia written by a Tunisian might be considered by American readers—but not by Tunisian readers—to be foreign librarianship. Conversely, how would American readers classify an article on American school libraries written by a Tunisian? Therefore, the notion of foreign librarianship will always be relative to the nationalities of authors and readers and it would be impossible to delimit the corpus of writings on the subject. Lor[10] argues that to qualify as a contribution to international librarianship a book or article should not merely describe conditions in another country. There should be an international dimension in terms of relationships between countries, influences of one country on another, etc. In practice this requirement is often ignored. There is some merit in the argument that an author from one country may bring fresh insights to library conditions in another country and therefore the work qualifies to be regarded as a contribution to international librarianship. The well-known book of the Norwegian librarian, Wilhelm Munthe,[12] on American librarianship is often cited as such an example.

The activities of international organizations are also generally included within international librarianship.[6,13]

The promotion of library development by UNESCO is an example. Some writers would also include the library and information services of such bodies as part of the scope of international librarianship. However, this does not easily fit within Parker's definition.

Comparative Librarianship

During the 1960s and 1970s the origins and definitions of comparative librarianship were discussed by various writers, including Foskett,[13,14] Shores,[15,16] Simsova and MacKee,[17,18] Collings,[19] Harvey,[11] and Yayakuru.[20] Having systematically reviewed all prior attempts to define comparative librarianship and delimit its scope, J. Periam Danton in 1973 formulated what remains the most authoritative and appropriate definition of the field to date. He states that comparative librarianship is an

> area of scholarly investigation and research (that) may be defined as the analysis of libraries, library systems, some aspect of librarianship, or library problems in two or more national, cultural or societal environments, in terms of socio-political, economic, cultural, ideological, and historical contexts. This analysis is for the purpose of understanding the underlying similarities and differences and for determining explanations of the differences, with the ultimate aim of trying to arrive at valid generalizations and principles. (p. 52)[3]

Danton, later slightly amended his definition (p. 4).[4] Both of his contributions emphasize three essential aspects of comparative librarianship:

1. There has to be a "cross-societal or cross-cultural element." Often this is cross-country or international, but the comparison can be conducted within a single country, provided that the societal, cultural, or ideological differences are such that they can give rise to differences in the nature of the library as an institution. Hence a comparison of public libraries in the German, French, and Italian speaking cantons of Switzerland can legitimately be classified as comparative librarianship, but a comparison of the library use of working class and middle class Britons would not. On this point opinions diverge. While Danton, basing his position on the example of disciplines such as comparative education, comparative law, and comparative sociology, insists on the cross-societal, cross-cultural, or cross-country element, other writers such as D.J. Foskett,[13] Simsova and MacKee,[17,18] Sami,[7] and Lor[10] open the door to comparisons that are not cross-societal or cross-cultural in scope. The danger of this approach is that, since comparisons are inherent in much empirical research, the greater part of research in library science could be labeled as "comparative librarianship."

Informetrics–International Council

Informetrics–International Council

2. There have to be "actual comparisons," which go beyond mere descriptions or juxtaposition of data. Comparison implies the analysis of the similarities and differences in the sets of data collected.

3. An attempt should be made to explain the observed similarities and differences with a view to building theory.[4] Thus comparative librarianship is described as a discipline which employs a rigorous scientific methodology, on the pattern of other, older comparative disciplines such as comparative education.

Distinction between International and Comparative Librarianship

As Danton[4] pointed out, a considerable literature about the definitions of international and comparative librarianship arose more or less at the same time that Parker's definition of international librarianship and Danton's own definition of comparative librarianship appeared. The result is a literature in which there is much discussion but no clear consensus on the distinction between international librarianship and comparative librarianship. Attempts to distinguish between the two have generally taken one or more of the following approaches:

• Hierarchical: comparative librarianship is a species of the genus international librarianship or vice versa.[9] For example, Harvey subsumes "comparative library science" (along with "foreign library science" and "international institutional library science") under "international library science" (pp. 296–297).[11] Krzys, Litton, and Hewitt subsume both "international library science" and "comparative library science" under "world library science."[21] Against this it has to be pointed out that attempts to impose such hierarchical relationships are problematic if the concepts belong to different categories: "international" denotes a geographic scope, whereas "comparative" denotes a methodology.

• Study–Activity: comparative librarianship is the scientific study, while international librarianship is the field of professional activity, often conceived in a rather soft and idealistic manner as aiming to promote international understanding and cooperation.[22] A more rigorous distinction was made by Miles Jackson:

International librarianship is limited strictly to those activities that involve librarianship and all its aspects across national boundaries. It would thereby exclude comparative analysis, but include such activities as exchange of librarians, books, ideas, and the study of the library systems in different countries...comparative librarianship should lean on the tradition of comparative studies found in other fields such as political, government and legal studies.[23]

Against this it should be pointed out that the "activities" included under international librarianship can and should also be subjected to systematic and rigorous investigation.

• Subject–Methodology: international librarianship is the subject field while comparative librarianship is the methodology. Collings states that comparative librarianship is a "scholarly method of investigation."[19] Keresztesi has stated that "comparative librarianship is essentially a method of enquiry" (p. 437).[6] Against this it has to be pointed out that more than one methodology can be used to study international librarianship. Parker describes comparative librarianship as a tool, the most appropriate one, for international librarianship.[2] However, it is not the only tool.

In practice the terms "international librarianship" and "comparative librarianship" are often used interchangeably or in combination, as in "international and comparative librarianship." This combination of subject matter is also taught under this name in five of the nine U.S. library schools that offer courses related to international and/or comparative librarianship as surveyed by Liu and Cheng in a book tellingly entitled *International and comparative studies in information and library science*.[24] Nevertheless, the two can and should be clearly distinguished. Concluding a review of the discussion up until 1977, Danton challenged the profession to stop writing *about* comparative librarianship and to start *doing* it.[4] In this spirit no new definitions are offered here. Instead, the definitions of international librarianship by Parker and of comparative librarianship by Danton, cited above, are endorsed. In any case, discussions of definitional issues have become less frequent since the 1970s.

METHODOLOGY

International Librarianship

In contrast to that of comparative librarianship, much of the literature of international librarianship lacks methodological rigor. It tends to be descriptive rather than analytical. This is particularly true of the genre of "foreign librarianship," much of which is anecdotal and based on personal experience. Such publications, however, should not be overlooked as primary source material for more rigorous research, as they may be useful not only for descriptions of particular contemporary situations, but also for what it reveals of the attitudes of the writers. The literature of international librarianship as distinct from comparative librarianship is generally descriptive in nature and derives its data from sources such as

- Literature (both published and unpublished, e.g., government statistical reports, annual reports and Web sites of libraries and other organizations, project reports, autobiographical materials).
- Observation (e.g., study tours, reports by participants in exchange programs, or by aid workers assisting in library development programs).
- Interviews (including telephonic interviews).
- Questionnaire surveys (with increasing use being made of Web-based surveys).

Comparative Librarianship

The methodology of comparative librarianship has been described by a number of authors, with a strong emphasis on methodological rigor. Early contributions by Simsova and McKee[17] and Danton[3] are frequently cited, although Parker pointed out that their proposals were largely untested and untried.[2] Collings distinguished three major types of studies: area studies, cross-national or cross-cultural studies, and case studies, and outlined the primary and secondary sources for such studies.[19] Harvey put forward a "general comparative research methodology," comprising 12 stages, starting with a speculative stage and proceeding through description, analysis and comparison and interpretation, correlation and extension, to prediction, the evolution of new theories and the formulation of laws.[11] This is very much in accordance with the approach of the positivist social science and educational research methodology texts of that period, e.g., Van Dalen,[25] which emphasized the painstaking assembling of small empirical building blocks in the quest for the holy grail of science: universal scientific laws. Harvey also usefully outlines the research techniques that can be used in comparative librarianship, including "statistical comparisons, problem analyses, trend identification, factorial and analytical approaches, analysis against norms, developmental criteria identification and historical analyses" (pp. 307–308).[11] Krzys, Litton, and Hewitt put forward an impressive research program for "world librarianship."[21] Liu describes a cooperative methodology to conduct cross-country comparisons, involving the collaboration of experts in both countries.[26] Danton stressed the interdisciplinary nature of comparative librarianship.[3] This is hardly surprising, considering the cross-national, cross-cultural, or cross-societal nature of such studies.

The basic elements of the comparative method are

- The identification of a research problem. The problem should be of a significant rather than trivial nature. There is more to be learned from a study on the selection of Arabic name authorities in Egypt and Iran than from a study of the shape and size of catalog cards formerly used in these two countries.
- The selection of a suitable theoretical framework. This is important for guiding the subsequent steps.

- The formulation of research questions or hypotheses.
- The selection of two or more systems (or processes, institutions, situations, etc.) for study. There should be sufficient underlying commonality (e.g., in terms of types of libraries, materials, or processes) to make the comparison worthwhile. There is little point in comparing children's libraries in Norway with young adult services in Wales.
- The collection of data on the systems. The data may be derived from available case studies, area studies, or descriptive studies, such as are typically found in the literature of international librarianship, or they may be collected by means of surveys, interviews, observation, etc., specifically for the purpose of the comparative study.
- The processing, classification, tabulation, and juxtaposition of the collected data. An interesting example of developing a classification scheme for categorizing the data of an international comparative study is found in Rochester and Vakkari.[27]
- The analysis undertaken to search for patterns of similarities and differences in the sets of data and to reveal their causes, this process being guided by the research questions, or if hypotheses have been formulated, taking the form of the formal testing of these. This is a critical step. If it is missing, the study is not truly comparative.
- The discussion and interpretation of the findings in relation to the theoretical framework in order to further develop and generalize the theory.

LITERATURE AND THEMES

There is a considerable literature on international librarianship, which is difficult to separate from the less extensive literature of comparative librarianship. Much of the literature of international librarianship falls in the category of foreign librarianship: descriptions of library conditions in countries other than that of the author or editor. This ongoing category can be regarded as the wallpaper or background to the literature of international librarianship proper. In this section a necessarily impressionistic overview of themes is presented in a roughly chronological order.

Origins and Early Development

Interest in international librarianship is not a new phenomenon. The American Library Association (founded in 1876) and the (British) Library Association (founded in 1877) engaged in international activities at an early stage. Initially these mainly took the form of representation at each other's conferences and at those of other national associations, but in the first decade of the twentieth century cooperation between the United States and the United

Informetrics–International Council

Informetrics–International
Council

Kingdom was manifested more concretely in the adoption of the Anglo-American cataloging rules of 1908.[28] The International Institute of Bibliography, which later became the International Federation for Information and Documentation (FID), was founded in 1895, while the International Federation of Library Associations and Institutions (IFLA) was founded in 1927 in close association with the League of Nations. The early leaders of IFLA were inspired by ideals of world-wide peace and cooperation.[29] A pioneering work of this period was Wilhelm Munthe's *American Librarianship from a European Angle*, published in 1939.[12]

The first recorded use of the term "comparative librarianship" occurred in 1954, in two articles by Chase Dane.[30,31] The early literature on this new field, reviewed by Danton,[3] exhibited an idealistic and affective dimension, emphasizing its value for enhancing international understanding and also its practical value for furthering library cooperation and development, for example in Dane,[31] Shores,[16] and Collings.[19] As already noted, much energy was expended on largely inconclusive attempts to define the field and distinguish it from international librarianship. Writers on comparative librarianship drew much inspiration from writers on other comparative disciplines, such as comparative education, for example Fraser and Brickman.[32]

The term "international librarianship" also appears to date from after the Second World War, being used by Peter Havard-Williams in 1959.[33] As with comparative librarianship, much of the literature of this period reflects normative, moral, or idealistic concerns, such as internationalism, the striving for international peace and tolerance, and international cooperation.

The 1960s and 1970s

In the first decades following World War II the influence of UNESCO was strong and the *UNESCO Bulletin for Libraries*, since discontinued, was an important medium for the field. The post-war emergence of independent states in Asia and Africa aroused much interest among internationally minded librarians[34] and gave rise to idealistic and ambitious plans for developing national library services. The work of foreign cultural and aid agencies, for example the work of the British Council in developing national library services in former British colonies, featured in the literature, sometimes in descriptive accounts, at other times more critical observations. By that time professionals in developing countries, including Wijasuriya, Lim, and Nadaradha[35] were warning of the challenges facing the extension of library services to their various countries' peoples. UNESCO's own work in library development in the developing world, which emphasized the importance of libraries for education, was an important theme, as were its efforts to promote the adoption of national information policies in these

countries: primarily the UNISIST (World Science Information System) and NATIS (National Information Systems) programs.[2,33] UNESCO promoted the international exchange of publications, which was a significant activity for countries lacking foreign exchange. UNESCO's role as a partner and sponsor of IFLA programs was also important. The development of specialized international indexing and abstracting services such as MEDLARS (for medicine), AGRIS (for agriculture) and INIS (for nuclear science and technology) generated much literature of an international character.

The 1960s and 1970s were also years of theoretical reflection on the purpose, scope, and methodology of comparative librarianship; most of the sources cited in the above section on "Definitions and Scope" date from this period. A number of highly regarded comparative studies were published during this period, including a comparative study of public library development in France, Great Britain, and the United States by Jean Hassenforder[36] and Frank Gardner's comparative study of public library legislation.[37] Excellent single-country studies, while not strictly part of comparative or international librarianship, also appeared during this period, Those include Ferguson's *Libraries in France*,[38] which appeared in Clive Bingley's Comparative Library Studies series, and Maack's *Libraries in Senegal*.[39]

Throughout the post-war period, and particularly from the late 1960s, when IFLA adopted deliberate policies of reaching out to a potential membership outside Europe and North America, IFLA featured prominently in the literature of international librarianship.[40] The *IFLA Journal* remains an important source of material in the field. IFLA's work in international library cooperation, especially its programs of Universal Bibliographic Control (UBC) and Universal Access to Publications (UAP) were promoted in its publications and in the writings of leaders, such as Maurice B. Line, who wrote dozens of articles promoting UAP. As information and communication technology developed in the 1970s and 1980s "library cooperation on an international scale (p.172)"[33] became increasingly feasible, and the early notions of cooperation were progressively extended to resource sharing and networking. The MARC format, developed in the United States, soon became an international standardization phenomenon, generating national variants and international cooperation in the development of library catalogs, union catalogs, and national bibliographies. This also stimulated international cooperation in respect to cataloging rules, standards such as the international standard bibliographic descriptions (ISBDs), and the fundamental principles of cataloging, as expressed more recently in the *Functional requirements for bibliographic records* (FRBR) and related principles for authority records.

Other international nongovernmental organizations such as the FID (which was dissolved in 2002) have also provided forums for international cooperation, discussion, and reflection, adding to the literature, and themselves featuring in it. Beginning in the 1950s various specialized international associations such as IAML (International Association of Music Libraries) and IBBY (the International Board on Books for Young People) were established, as were regional bodies such as ACURIL (Association of Caribbean Research, University and Institutional Libraries), CONSAL (Congress of Southeast Asian Librarians) and SCECSAL (Standing Conference of East, Central and Southern African Library and Information Associations). The growth of international associations has been attributed to greater international awareness following the Second World War, and to the advent of regular, affordable air transportation[41]—it was no longer necessary for delegates to spend a week or more on board an ocean liner to attend an international conference.

From the 1980s to the Current Scene

In the 1980s and 1990s there was increasing emphasis on the impact of information for development.[42] In a significant number of developing countries well-intentioned, Western-inspired library development programs had begun to falter. Starting in the 1970s a critical reevaluation of these post-colonial efforts, sometimes referred to as "cultural imperialism" (p. 7]),[13] got under way, as is described, for example, in seminal works such as *The Quiet Struggle: Information and Libraries for the People of Africa*, by Sturges and Neil[43] and Gassol de Horowitz's *Librarianship: A Third World Perspective*,[44] as well as in contributions by younger African librarians such as Kingo Mchombu.[45,46] During the 1980s questions were increasingly raised about international aspects of education for librarianship. These concerns related to the appropriateness of Western, particularly the United States and British, as well as East European models of content, curricula, and qualifications in developing countries.[47] Concern was also expressed about the internationalization of library school programs, particularly in the United States.[8,48]

In spite of the critical questions, a number of governmental aid agencies, particularly those of the United States, Canada, Great Britain, and the Nordic countries, have continued to play a significant role in supporting library development in the developing countries, as have a number of foundations such as the Andrew W. Mellon Foundation, the Carnegie Corporation of New York, and the Bill and Melinda Gates Foundation in the United States, and the Open Society Institute in Europe. These donors increasingly emphasize accountability and the sustainability of projects. This has stimulated programs aimed at capacity building by providing training opportunities for future leaders of the library profession in developing countries, such as those of the

Mortenson Center for International Library Programs at the University of Illinois at Urbana-Champaign, the Goethe Institut (Germany) and the Jay Jordan IFLA/ OCLC Early Career Fellowship program of OCLC in partnership with IFLA.

Since the mid-1990s the economic, political, and ethical aspects of the international flow of information, particularly between developed countries and developing countries, have emerged as an important theme. The gap between rich and poor countries is often referred to as the "digital divide." However, it is not merely digital, as it has significant political, legal, and economic dimensions. Librarians have become increasingly aware of the impact on their institutions and users of decisions on intellectual property and related matters that are taken at international forums such as the World Summit on the Information Society (WSIS), the World Trade Organization (WTO), the World Intellectual Property Organization (WIPO), and in multilateral or bilateral trade agreements between countries.[49,50] In addition, issues of freedom of access to information and freedom of expression,[51] and vexed questions of tolerance in multicultural environments have come to prominence at the international level as a consequence of increasing globalization.[52] Advocacy has become a key activity of IFLA, which represents libraries and librarians internationally, often in partnership with other national and international organizations such as the (US) Library Copyright Alliance, the European Bureau of Library, Information and Documentation Associations (EBLIDA), and Electronic Information for Libraries (eIFL). Only through cooperation and continuous monitoring is the library profession able to ensure representation at the plethora of international meetings and to keep abreast of the huge volume of documentation generated by the international organizations. Currently, most of this documentation is disseminated through the Internet. Globalization has seen to it that the international affairs relevant to library professionals have multiplied to an extent that could not be foreseen by their predecessors. To many practicing librarians much of this may seem remote, but continuing vigilance is called for. It is therefore important to raise awareness of international issues in the profession.

It is an ongoing challenge to ensure that libraries are not taken for granted or ignored in international programs to promote the information society. In recent years the attention paid by UNESCO to libraries as such has decreased in favor of more general information society issues and the use of information technology. However, themes such as documentary preservation, access to knowledge, information literacy, and information ethics fortunately remain on the agenda of UNESCO's Sector V (Information and Communication) and its Information for All Program (IFAP), while other UNESCO sectors concern themselves with literacy and book development. In all these areas librarians need to cooperate strategically in advocating for libraries as key agencies in the information or knowledge society.

At the immediately practical level matters such as international bibliographic standardization, international document supply, collection development and services in area studies, and international aspects of human resource development (study abroad, job exchanges, working in foreign libraries, etc.) continue to form part of the literature of international librarianship.

In the 1980s a steady stream of contributions to comparative librarianship developed and this swelled as young researchers discovered a fruitful field for Ph.D. dissertation topics. The problem or thematic approach (in which library types, processes, problems, etc. in two or more countries are compared, as distinct from whole-country comparisons) is predominant. Library education and training seems to be the most popular area, followed by developing countries, school libraries, national information infrastructures (replacing the national information *policies* of the 1980s), various aspects of management (including evaluation, measurement, and statistics), and library and information science (LIS) research. General trends in LIS literature are reflected in that of international librarianship. For example, since the turn of the century the digital divide and issues of access to digital resources, and information literacy have come into prominence. Among developing regions the Far East attracts most attention;[24] here the number of comparative studies in which various library practices in the United States and China are compared reflects the relatively large number of postgraduate students from China preparing Ph.D. dissertations in the United States.

CONCLUSION

International librarianship is an extensive and growing field of activity with an extensive body of literature. However, compared with that of comparative librarianship, its literature is largely practical, discursive, and descriptive, and lacks a theoretical basis. The literature of comparative librarianship, although smaller, is also growing. Much effort was expended some decades ago on attempts to distinguish between international and comparative librarianship. Although sound definitions for both fields were put forward and logic demands that they be clearly distinguished, the result was inconclusive, and this thread appears to have been abandoned. The practice of combining these two fields in textbooks and library science courses as "international and comparative library science" is pragmatic. Regardless of how the field is conceptualized, it can be expected to remain vital, since in a globalized world all fields of human endeavor have an increasingly significant international dimension. This applies *a fortiori* to librarianship, which serves the conservation, development, and utilization of all human knowledge without regard to boundaries.

ACKNOWLEDGMENTS

I would like to thank Prof Theo Bothma and Serah Rademan of the Department of Information Science at the University of Pretoria and Jeannette C Jordan of the School of Information Studies, University of Wisconsin-Milwaukee for assistance in obtaining literature for me at a time when I was located far from a major academic library.

REFERENCES

1. Thompson, J.W. *Ancient Libraries;* Archon Books: Hamden, CT, 1962.
2. Parker, J.S. International librarianship—A reconnaissance. J. Libr. **1974**, *6*(4), 219–232.
3. Danton, J.P. *The Dimensions of Comparative Librarianship;* American Library Association: Chicago, IL, 1973.
4. Danton, J.P. Definitions of comparative and international library science. In *Comparative and International Library Science*; Harvey, J.F., Ed.; Scarecrow Press: Metuchen, NJ, 1977; 3–14.
5. Harvey, J.F., Ed.; *Comparative and International Library Science*; Scarecrow Press: Metuchen, NJ, 1977.
6. Keresztesi, M. Prolegomena to the history of international librarianship. J. Libr. Hist. **1981**, *16*(2), 435–448.
7. Sami, L.K. Comparative librarianship. CLIS Obser. **1991**, *8*(3/4), 3–6.
8. Bliss, N.J. The emergence of international librarianship as a field. Libri. **1993**, *43*(1), 39–52.
9. Liu, Y.Q. Introduction. In *International and Comparative Studies in Information and Library Science: A Focus on the United States and Asian Countries*; Liu, Y.Q., Cheng, X., Eds.; Scarecrow Press: Lanham, MD, 2008; xv–xxxvi.
10. Lor, P.J. Critical reflections on international librarianship. Mousaion **2008**, *26*(1), 1–15.
11. Harvey, J.F. Towards a definition of international and comparative library science. Int. Libr. Rev. **1973**, *5*(1), 289–319.
12. Munthe, W. *American Librarianship from a European Angle;* Shoe String Press: Hamden, CT, 1939.
13. Foskett, D.J. Comparative librarianship as a field of study: Definitions and dimensions. In *Reader in Comparative Librarianship*; Foskett, D.J., Ed.; Information Handling Services: Englewood, CO, 1976; 3–9.
14. Foskett, D.J. Comparative librarianship. *Progress in Library Science 1965*, Butterworths: London, 1965; 125–146.
15. Shores, L. Why comparative librarianship?. Wilson Libr. Bull. **1966**, *41*(2), 200–206.
16. Shores, L. Comparative librarianship: A theoretical approach. In *Comparative and International Librarianship*; Jackson, M.M., Ed.; Greenwood Press: Westport, CT, 1970; 3–27.

Informetrics–International Council

17. Simsova, S.; MacKee, M. *A Handbook of Comparative Librarianship*; Bingley: London, 1970.

18. Simsova, S.; MacKee, M. *A Handbook of Comparative Librarianship;* 2nd Ed. Bingley: London, 1975.

19. Collings, D.G. Comparative librarianship. In *Encyclopedia of Library and Information Science*; Kent, A., Lancour, H., Eds.; Marcel Dekker: New York, 1971; Vol. 5, 492–502.

20. Yayakuru, K.S. Comparative librarianship—Subject or research methods?. Libr. Assoc. Rec. **1974**, *76*, 91–92.

21. Krzys, R.; Litton, G.; Hewitt, A. *World Librarianship: A Comparative Study;* Marcel Dekker: New York, 1982.

22. Kawatra, P.S., Ed. *Comparative and International Librarianship*; Envoy Press: New York, 1987; 33.

23. Jackson, M.M., Ed. *International Handbook of Contemporary Developments in Librarianship*; Greenwood Press: Westport, CT, 1981.

24. Liu, Y.Q.; Cheng, X., Eds. *International and Comparative Studies in Information and Library Science: A Focus on the United States and Asian Countries*; Scarecrow Press: Lanham, MD, 2008; 323–326.

25. Van Dalen, D. *Understanding Educational Research: An Introduction;* McGraw-Hill: New York, 1962.

26. Liu, Y.Q. Introducing an international cooperative research method employed in cross-country studies in information and library science. Chin. Libr. Int. Electron. J. **2002**, (13), Reprinted in *International and Comparative Studies in Information and Library Science: A Focus on the United States and Asian Countries*; Liu, Y.Q., Cheng, X., Eds.; Scarecrow Press: Lanham, MD, 2008; 31–36.

27. Rochester, M.; Vakkari, P. International library and information science research: a comparison of national trends. IFLA J. **1998**, *24*(3), 166–175.

28. Munford, W.A. *History of the Library Association*; Library Association: London, 1976.

29. Wieder, J.; Campbell, H.C. IFLA's first fifty years: A reprise. Extracts from 'An outline of IFLA's history', by Joachim Wieder, selected and edited by Harry Campbell. IFLA J. **2002**, *28*(3), 107–117.

30. Dane, C. The benefits of comparative librarianship. Aust. Libr. J. **1954**, *3*(3), 89–91.

31. Dane, C. Comparative librarianship. Libr. Book World **1954**, *43*(8), 141–144.

32. Fraser, S.E.; Brickman, W.W., Eds. *A History of International and Comparative Education*; Foresman: Glenview, IL, 1968.

33. Havard-Williams, P. International librarianship. In *International Librarianship: Surveys of Recent Developments in Developing Countries and Advanced Librarianship Submitted to the 1971 Pre-Session Seminar for Developing Countries Sponsored by UNESCO*; Chandler, G., Ed.; Library Association: London, 1972; 169–180 Liverpool City Libraries, August 24–September 1, 1971.

34. Asheim, L. *Librarianship in the Developing Countries*; University of Illinois Press: Urbana, IL, 1966.

35. Wijasuriya, D.E.K.; Lim, H.T.; Nadaradha, R. *The Barefoot Librarian: Library Development in Southeast Asia with Special Reference to Malaysia*; Bingley: London, 1975.

36. Hassenforder, J. *Développement Comparé des Bibliothèques Publiques en France, Grande-Bretagne et aux États-Unis dans la Seconde Moitié du XIXe Siècle*; Cercle de la Librairie: Paris, 1967.

37. Gardner, F.M. *Public Library Legislation: a Comparative Study*; UNESCO: Paris, 1971.

38. Ferguson, J. *Libraries in France*; Bingley: London, 1971.

39. Maack, M.N. *Libraries in Senegal: Continuity and Change in an Emerging Nation;* American Library Association: Chicago, IL, 1981.

40. Campbell, H. Advancement of librarianship through IFLA. In *International Librarianship: Cooperation and Collaboration*; Carroll, F.L., Harvey, J.F., Eds.; Scarecrow press: Lanham, MD, 2001; 23–36.

41. Harrison, K.C. *International Librarianship;* Scarecrow Press: Metuchen, NJ, 1989.

42. Stone, M.B. Assessment of indicators and the impact of information on development. Can. J. Inform. Libr. Sci. **1993**, *18*(4), 50–64.

43. Sturges, P.; Neill, R. *The Quiet Struggle: Libraries and Information for Africa*; Mansell: London, 1990; (2nd edition published in 1998 under the title *The Quiet Struggle: Information and Libraries for the People of Africa*).

44. Gassol de Horowitz, R. *Librarianship: A Third World Perspective*; Greenwood Press: New York, 1988.

45. Mchombu, K.J. On the librarianship of poverty. Libri. **1982**, *32*(3), 241–250.

46. Mchombu, K.J.; Miti, K. Formulation of national information policies in Africa: some unlearnt lessons. Int. Inform. Libr. Rev. **1992**, *24*(1), 139–171.

47. Aman, M.M. Library and information science in the Muslim world. In *Library Education Across the Boundaries of Cultures: A Festschrift to Mark the Silver Jubilee Celebration of the Library Science Department*, Department of Library Science, University of Karachi: Karachi, 1981; 43–54.

48. Harvey, J.F.; Carroll, F.L. *Internationalizing Library and Information Science Education: A Handbook of Policies and Procedures in Administration and Curriculum*; Greenwood Press: New York, 1987.

49. Britz, J.J.; Lor, P.J.; Bothma, T.J.M. Global capitalism and the fair distribution of information in the marketplace: a moral reflection from the perspective of the developing world. J. Inform. Ethics **2006**, *15*(1), 60–69.

50. Lor, P.J. IFLA, the world summit on the information society, and after. Alexandria **2008**, *20*(1), 11–21.

51. Byrne, A. *The Politics of Promoting Freedom of Information and Expression in International Librarianship: The IFLA/FAIFE Project*; Scarecrow Press: Lanham, MD, 2007.

52. Sturges, P. Limits to freedom of expression? Considerations arising from the Danish cartoons affair. IFLA J. **2006**, *32*(3), 181–188.

IMPORTANT JOURNALS

1. *Focus on International Library and Information Work*. 1967 —Formerly: (*Focus on international and comparative librarianship*) Published by the International Library and Information Group of the Chartered Institute of Library and Information Professionals (CILIP). Available at http://www.cilip.org.uk/specialinterestgroups/bysubject/international/publications/focus.

Informetrics–International
Council

2. *IFLA Journal.* 1952—Published quarterly for IFLA by Sage Publications, London.

3. *Information Development: The International Journal for Librarians, Archivists and Information Specialists.* 1985—Published quarterly by Sage Publications, London.

4. *International Information and Library Review.* 1969—Formerly *International Library Review.* Published quarterly by Elsevier, Amsterdam.

5. *Libri: International Journal of Libraries and Information Services.* 1951—Published quarterly by K.G. Saur Verlag, Munich.

6. *Library Times International: World News Digest of Library and Information Science.* 1984—Published by Future World Publishing Co., Conway, PA.

7. *New Library World.* 1898—Published bi-monthly by Emerald Group Publishing, London.

8. *World Libraries: An International Journal Focusing on Libraries and Socio-Economic Development in Africa, Asia,* *and Latin America.* 1990–Published semi-annually by the Graduate School of Library and Information Science, Rosary College, River Forest, IL.

BIBLIOGRAPHY

1. Kaula, P.N.; Kumar, K.; Venkatappai, V., Eds.. *International and Comparative Librarianship and Information Systems*; B.R. Publishing Corporation: New Delhi, 1996; Vol. 2.

2. Kesselman, M.A.; Weintraub, I.; Eds. *Global Librarianship*; Marcel Dekker: New York, 2004..

3. Sharma, R.N., Ed. *The Impact of Technology on Asian, African and Middle Eastern Library Collections*; Scarecrow Press: Lanham, MD, 2006.

4. Stueart, R.D. *International Librarianship: A Basic Guide to Global Knowledge Access;* Scarecrow Press: Lanham, MD, 2007.

International Association of Sound and Audiovisual Archives (IASA)

Ilse Assmann
Radio Broadcast Facilities, SABC, Johannesburg, South Africa

Abstract

The International Association of Sound and Audiovisual Archives (IASA) was established in 1969 in Amsterdam to function as a forum for international cooperation between archives preserving recorded sound and audiovisual documents. This entry looks at the beginning years of IASA and its growth from nine founding members to an independent organization with a membership of more than 400 members, representing 64 countries.

BIRTH OF IASA

The International Association of Sound and Audiovisual Archives (IASA) was established in 1969 in Amsterdam to function as a forum for international cooperation between archives preserving recorded sound and audiovisual documents. During its 30-year anniversary celebrations, Rolf Schuursma, a founder member and former IASA President, divided its history into three periods, saying: "...Like every organization of this kind, beginning from scratch, IASA has gone through different stages, each with its own qualities and problems ...." Rolf (Schuursma, 1999) identified the stages as:

- *Getting acquainted*, when newly recruited members got to know one another and the membership was growing worldwide;
- *How did we do it*, during which time the membership studied the various ways of collecting, storing, cataloging, access, copyright, and technical matters, and during which time IASA became more professional in its management;
- *Widening the scope*, when IASA received international recognition and began to play a role in the international information field.

But a fourth stage can now be added: *digitization;* with IASA taking the lead by investigating new ways and setting standards to save sound and audiovisual collections, thereby preserving original qualities and enabling easy/easier access.

IASA was founded on August 22, 1969 after a letter of intent to establish a new international organization of sound archives was drafted the previous year and submitted to the *International Association of Music Libraries* (IAML). IASA's beginning was thus directly linked to the IAML.

IAML supported the floundering first few years when IASA lacked infrastructure and resources to host its own conferences. Harald Heckmann of IAML played an instrumental role in finding solutions that would eventually give IASA the independence it needed.

IAML had been officially founded in Paris in July 1951. Its Radio Library Commission which also had a Radio Sound Archive Subcommittee was primarily interested in music recordings. Before IASA came into existence, earlier attempts to unite sound archivists were made. The first initiative came from linguists who, in 1962, formed IALSA, *(International Association of Linguistic Sound Archives)* at a meeting in Amsterdam. Shortly thereafter, IALSA was absorbed by a newly founded organization, the *Fédération Internationale des Phonothèques* (FIP). The inactivity of FIP, however, led to the decline of the organization which practically faded away during the early 1970s.

Rolf Schuursma, at that time from the Archive at the Institute of History at Utrecht University in the Netherlands, remembers that it was Patrick Saul, the then director of the British Institute of Recorded Sound, who invited him to a meeting in Paris to participate as a representative of a spoken word recordings archive. The meeting took place in the *Département de la Musique* of the Bibliothèque Nationale in Paris on September 4, 1968. Seven members attended the meeting. They were IAML members Patrick Saul (Director of the British Institute of Recorded Sound), Vladimir Fedorov (Director of the Department and President of IAML), Dr. Kurt Dorfmuller (Bayerische Staatsbibliothek, München), Dr. Herbert Rosenberg (Director of the Nationaldiskotek in Kopenhagen), Dr. Israel Adler (Director of the Jewish Music Research Centre at the Jewish National and University Library in Jerusalem), FIP president, Roger Décollogne (Director of the Phonotèque Nationale), and oral historian, Rolf

Copyright © 2017 by Taylor & Francis. All rights reserved.

Informetrics–International Council

Schuursma, Rolf Schuursma from the Institute of History at the University of Utrecht, represented spoken word archives. Dr. Adler was the Chairperson. On September 5, a preliminary letter of intent was drafted to inform IAML of the decision by the meeting to establish a new international organization of sound archives. This letter was submitted by Dr. Adler to the IAML conference held in Washington DC and New York in 1969.

The first IASA meeting took place in Amsterdam at the *Institute of Theater Klank en Beeld (Institute for Theatre Sound and Image)* on August 18, 1969. The meeting was attended by Lou Hoefnagels (Director of the Theater Klank en Beeld), Rolf Schuursma, Patrick Saul, Donald L. Leavitt (Library of Congress), Philip Miller (Rodgers and Hammerstein Archives of Recorded Sound in New York), Dietrich Lotichius (Norddeutscher Rundfunk in Hamburg), Herbert Rosenberg, Claes Cnattingius (Swedish Radio), and Timothy Eckersley (BBC). This group of nine became known as the founding members of IASA. Earlier that year, in March, Rolf Schuursma and Lou Hoefnagels had already begun preparations for the first meeting. Don Leavitt presented the draft constitution for deliberation at the IAML conference in Amsterdam. A joint committee was formed between the Record Libraries' Commission and the newly founded IASA. In principle the roles were clear: IAML was interested only in music recordings and IASA in all recordings, But IAML also represented a branch of librarianship, whereas IASA was a response to the fact that sound recordings were more often held in an archival environment — a separate professional context at least equal to librarianship. IAML was not sufficiently hospitable to the technical challenges in the sound archives, which are most acute in the areas of unpublished recordings, held in archives, rather than published phonograms held by IAML member libraries. It would take a while before full agreement was achieved to avoid overlapping and even competing activities between IAML's Record Libraries' Commission and IASA.

The founding meeting took place on August 22, 1969 with 24 participants. The official name of the new organization was *International Association for Sound Archives.* The first Executive Board was made up by Don Leavitt (President), Patrick Saul (Vice-President), Claudie Marcel-Dubois (Vice-President), Rolf Schuursma (Secretary), and Claes Cnattingius (Treasurer). One of its primary tasks, together with the Record Libraries' Commission, was to prepare a *Directory of Sound Archives*, but this never happened. The concept was later replaced by an IASA *Directory of Member Archives*, first compiled by Ann Briegleb (Head of the Ethnomusicology Archive of the University of California at Los Angeles) in 1978, with an expanded update in 1982, and subsequently by the *Membership Directory*, which is still regularly published.

Initially IASA held joint annual conferences with IAML because of the lack of its own infrastructure and resources. During the Leipzig Conference in June 1970, a decision was taken that IASA should have its own periodical, and this led to the birth of the *Phonographic Bulletin*. The first issue was in A4 format with different shades of green for the cover and lettering and highlighting the IASA logo designed by Rob van der Elzen, a graphic designer with the Film Research Foundation. From Issue no. 16 onward the lettering on the cover was changed to black, and in 1977 the A4 format was replaced by the B5 format. In 1990, the IASA Board decided to publish a separate *Information Bulletin*, originally compiled by Vice-President Hans Bosma, in order to keep the membership more regularly informed about IASA-related activities. The publication was renamed *IASA Journal* in 1993 under the editorship of Grace Koch, with four *Information Bulletins* and two *IASA Journals* per annum being published instead of three *Phonographic Bulletins*. IASA now has its own Web site, and in 2006 the first *eBulletin* was published to keep members electronically informed. Currently, IASA publishes two Information Bulletins, two eBulletins, and two Journals per year, and maintains and updates the Web site regularly. IASA also operates a listserv to facilitate the exchange of information between members.

The joint 1971 IAML/IASA annual conference in St Gallen was a first for IASA in several respects. It was the first conference where IASA had a separate program (put together by Don Leavitt, Claes Cnattingius, and Rolf Schuursma), and the first issue of the *Phonographic Bulletin* (A4 format) (3 issues annually) was launched by Rolf Schuursma and Phita Stern (Utrecht).

By the time the 1972 joint IAML/IASA annual conference took place in Bologna, Italy, IASA had 40 institutional and 37 personal members. IASA's second Executive Board was elected with Timothy Eckersley (President), Claudie Marcel-Dubois, Herbert Rosenberg, and Ivàn Pethes (Vice-Presidents), Rolf Schuursma (Secretary), Claes Cnattingius (Treasurer), and Don Leavitt (Past-President).

Under the leadership of Timothy Eckersley, IASA further expanded its membership. It also became a fully recognized partner of the joint annual conference with IAML in London in 1973.

The election of the next IASA Executive Board in 1975 during the Montreal Conference was of particular significance. Two new members were elected that would help to take IASA decisively on a route to greater independence and recognition: Dietrich Schüller (Director of the Phonogrammarchiv in Vienna) and David Lance (Keeper of the Department of Sound Records of the Imperial War Museum in London). Dietrich Schüller was elected as President, and David Lance as Secretary, with Claudie Marcel-Dubois (Vice-President), Herbert Rosenberg (Vice-President), Rolf Schuursma (Vice-President), Léo

LaCLare (Treasurer), and Timothy Eckersley (Past-President).

The new Executive Board under the leadership of the young and dynamic Dietrich Schüller made dramatic changes to IASA. One of the first was to have midterm meetings to ensure better planning of annual conferences, and to discuss other issues and activities in which IASA had an interest.

The first midterm meeting was in April 1976 in the *Musée des Artes et Traditions Populaires*, Bois de Bologne, Paris, at which the Executive Board agreed to include the *Editor* on the Board. The first Editor was Rolf Schuursma, with Ann Briegleb replacing him as Vice-President. The Executive Board also decided to form committees to look after the specialized interests of the membership. The first committee was the Technical Committee with Dietrich Schüller as Chair, followed by the Copyright Committee under Robért Ternisien. David Lance initiated the formation of National Branches. The first national branches were established in Great Britain, the Netherlands, France and Australia. But several countries were already interested to unite audiovisual archives under one umbrella, something IASA as an association of sound archives did not cater for. Austria, therefore, never officially liaised with IASA, while the original Netherlands IASA branch broke away to form an independent Association of AudioVisual Archives. National branches also wanted to include non-IASA members, which had the potential to weaken IASA. In the early 1980s, following administrative difficulties with IASA International, the French and the Australian national branches broke away to form AFAS (Associacion française des archives sonores) and ASRA (Australasian Sound Recordings Association) as independent, but still IASA affiliated associations. This situation led to a drop in the number of IASA members, which was, however, compensated soon by the further growth. During the 1980s the IASA constitution was revised several times to reflect the changing nature of National Branches and independent organizations, known as Affiliated Organizations.

The year 1978 was nearly a watershed year for IASA.

During the 1978 mid-term meeting in Vienna, the constitution, which had originally followed the IAML model, was entirely renewed and adapted to the needs and realities of IASA. It was adopted at the Annual Conference in Lisbon. The basic structure is still in place today, with several adaptations to reflect the changing nature of the organization.

At the same conference, a new Joint IAML/IASA Committee on Music and Sound Archives was established to coordinate the activities of both organizations.

The fourth Executive Board was elected with Rolf Schuursma (President), Marie-France Calas (Vice-President), Tor Kummen (Vice-President), Ulf Scharlau (Treasurer),

Ann Briegleb (Editor), and Dietrich Schüller (Past-President). During the 1978 midterm meeting in Vienna, proposed changes to the Constitution were discussed: the election procedure needed to accommodate the entire membership as opposed to suggestions from the outgoing Executive Board, and the Council to be cancelled.

In 1983, Ulf Scharlau and Dietrich Lotichius were responsible for the formation of the Radio Sound Archives Committee for IASA while the Radio Sound Archives Subcommittee of IAML was suspended. In 1993, a name change was proposed at the Helsinki Conference, whereby the word "audiovisual" would be included in IASA to accommodate the breadth of audiovisual collections. The name change was officially accepted during the 1994 conference in Berlin-Bogensee, Germany, and IASA became known as *The International Association for Sound and Audiovisual Archives*.

In 1988, the time was ripe for IASA to hold its first solo conference in Vienna. It was attended by over 100 delegates, which proved the viability of IASA's independence. During the following years, joint conferences with IAML were replaced by solo events or joint conferences with other audiovisual associations such as ARSC (Association for Recorded Sound Collections), FIAT (International Federation of Television Archives), SEAPAVAA (Southeast Asia-Pacific Audiovisual Archive Association) and ASRA (Australasian Sound Recordings Association).

YEARS OF GROWTH

The late 1980s and 1990s were a time of tremendous expansion of IASA, especially in the establishment of cooperation with UNESCO. Helen Harrison who was a Board member for over fifteen years, was instrumental in establishing the UNESCO Round Table, which later became the CCAAA (Co-ordinating Council of Audiovisual Archives Associations) under the leadership of Crispin Jewitt. The Technical Committee of IASA joined cooperation with Technical Committees of organisations such as FIAT, FIAF (International Federation of Film Archives), IFLA (International Federation of Library Associations) and ICA (International Council on Archives) and eventually formed the UNESCO TCC (Technical Coordination Committee) with George Boston of IASA as chairperson. This body organised the Joint Technical Symposiums (JTS), which were and still are one of the most important professional meetings in audiovisual archiving. IASA also became closely involved in the UNESCO Memory of the World programme.

This period was also a fertile one for publications about audiovisual archive matters. Several 'Special Publications' were written, including An Archive Approach on

Informetrics–International Council

Informetrics–International Council

Oral History in 1978 and in 1983 Sound Archives: A Guide to their Establishment and Development by David Lance. For UNESCO Helen Harrison wrote the publication AV Archives: A Practical Reader which is still a valuable reference work and regularly accessed on the UNESCO website. This was the result of nearly five years work by a team from the Round Table and led by Gerry Gibson and Sven Allerstrand of IASA. The Glossary includes French, German and Spanish terms, as well as English terminology from both sides of the Atlantic. In 1978 Briegleb, Ann & Don Niles compiled the first Directory of Member Archives. The 2nd edition of the Directory of Member Archives was compiled in 1982 by Grace Koch.

With their excellent connections to non-governmental organizations, both Helen Harrison and Dietrich Schüller have boosted the Association's prestige by furthering its application to become a member of UNESCO. This success has enabled IASA to recruit new members from non-Western countries, i.e. countries in Asia, Africa, and South America. Since the end of the Cold War, IASA has gained many new members from the former socialist countries of Middle and Eastern Europe.

During the current decade IASA actively expanded its membership to Africa and South America with conferences held in 2003 in Pretoria, South Africa, and in México in 2006. A partnership between Dietrich Schüller and Albrecht Häfner in particular saw a series of very successful workshops across the world. The Board became truly representative of its international membership with members elected from India, Mexico, South Africa and Canada. IASA is currently respected for taking the lead by setting standards to digitally preserving sound and audiovisual collections.

IASA: THE ORGANIZATION

IASA has members from more than 60 countries, representing audiovisual archives and personal interests that are distinguished by their focus on particular subjects and areas. This includes archives for all sorts of musical recordings, historic, literary, folkloric and ethnological sound documents, theatre productions and oral history interviews, bioacoustics, environmental and medical sounds, linguistic and dialect recordings, as well as recordings for forensic purposes.

Every three years the IASA membership elects the Executive Board to oversee the business of the organization. Various committees, sections, and task forces are responsible for developing the work of IASA, and these serve as important information and discussion conduits in addition to dealing with specific areas of interest.

- The *Cataloging and Documentation Committee* looks after standards and rules, as well as with systems, automated or manual, for the documentation and cataloging of audiovisual media. The IASA Editorial Group, originally convened by Mary Miliano, compiled and edited the *IASA Cataloging Rules*, which is a manual for the description of sound recordings and related audiovisual media. An electronic version is available on the IASA Web site. It is also available in Spanish as *Reglas de Catalogación de IASA (2005 ed.)*.

- The *Discography Committee* deals with standards and recommended practices relating to collections of published recordings. The *National Discography* document provides guidelines on best practices for members who may have a responsibility for establishing national discographies in their countries, who intend to establish such a service, or who may be seeking funding.

- *The Technical Committee* devotes itself to all technical aspects of recording, storage, and reproduction, including new recordings, transfers, and storage technologies. Producing special publications that enable the audiovisual archive community to make educated decisions, is a main concern of the committee. The series *"Standards, Recommended Practices and Strategies"* includes

  — IASA-TC 03, *The Safeguarding of the Audio Heritage: Ethics, Principles and Preservation Strategy*, Version 3, December 2005, (Dietrich Schüller (Ed.)), which has been translated into German, French, Swedish, Italian, Spanish and Russian.

  — The IASA-TC 04, *Guidelines on the Production and Preservation of Digital Objects* (Kevin Bradley (Ed.)). The first edition (2004) is also available in Spanish and Italian. The revised, second edition, substantially enlarged and updated, was released in 2009.

- The *Training and Education Committee*, which had published the results in the *Phonographic Bulletin* of surveys of training for audiovisual archivists, typologies of sound archives, and existing job descriptions, became dormant in the mid-1990s. Recently it was revitalized under the leadership of Vice-President Pio Pelizzari and concerns itself with audiovisual training and education in the educational context, bibliographies of training and education-related publications, as well as concentrated actions in gaining multifunctional training and education material.

- The *National Archives Section* is where members meet to consider issues facing national archives, e.g., acquisition policies, legal deposit, and the management of large collections. Policy guidelines for the *legal deposit of sound recordings* have been published and are available on the Web site.

- The *Radio Sound Archives Section* handles the special responsibilities of audiovisual archives in broadcasting companies.
- The *Research Archives Section* concerns itself with special issues relating to audiovisual archives whose holdings include collections of recordings originally made for research purposes.

IASA's Technical Committee follows closely the progress of technology, and the association's members can call upon a pool of expertise for help and advice on all technical problems faced by AV archives including digitization and problems arising from the use of computer storage systems for heritage collections. As such IASA has published the following publications in addition to those already mentioned:

- Treatment and restoration of historical audio recordings.
- Standards for International Tape Exchange (1978).
- Role of the Compact Disc (1982).
- Automation of Archive Systems (1989).
- Analogue and Digital Technologies for Restoration and Long-term protection of endangered recorded sound collections.

IASA "Task Forces" report on specific topics of interest to the membership such as selection criteria and endangered carriers. These and other reports will be made available on the IASA Web site as they are completed. In this regard the IASA published the Task Force findings to establish *Selection Criteria of Analogue and Digital Audio Contents for Transfer to Data Formats for Preservation Purpose* (Majella Breen, Gila Flam et al. (Ed.)).

IASA enjoys international cooperation with organizations such as UNESCO and has partnered with organizations such as AFAS, ARSC, IFLA, FIAT, and FIAF. IASA is also a founding member of the CCAAA.

Current membership: 411 members representing 64 countries

- Institutions: 224
- Individual: 184
- Sustaining: 3

Honorary members: The first honorary member was Tim Eckersley in 1980. Current honorary members are Claes M. Cnattingius (Sweden), Gerald Gibson (U.S.A.), Carlo Marinelli (Italy), and R.L. Schuursma (the Netherlands).

APPENDIX

Table A.1　List of IASA Presidents and terms served.

	Term	Name	Institution
1	1969–1972	Donald Leavitt	Library of Congress, United States
2	1972–1975	Timothy Eckersley	BBC, United Kingdom
3	1975–1978	Dietrich Schüller	Phonogrammarchiv, Austrian Academy of Sciences, Austria
4	1978–1981	Rolf L. Schuursma	Foundation Film and Science, the Netherlands
5	1981–1984	David G. Lance	Imperial War Museum, United Kingdom
6	1984–1987	Ulf Scharlau	Süddeutscher Rundfunk, Germany
7	1987–1990	Helen P. Harrison	Open University, United Kingdom
8	1990–1993	Gerald D. Gibson	Library of Congress, United States
9	1993–1996	James McCarthy	National Film and Sound Archives, Australia
10	1996–1999	Sven Allerstrand	ALB, Sweden
11	1999–2002	Crispin Jewitt	British Library National Sound Archive, United Kingdom
12	2002–2005	Kurt Deggeller	MEMORIAV, Switzerland
13	2005–2008	Richard Green	National Library of Canada, Canada
14	2008–	Kevin Bradley	National Library of Australia, Australia

BIBLIOGRAPHY

1. Contributions were made by Grace Koch, Dietrich Schüller, George Boston, Crispin Jewitt, Kurt Deggeller, Eva Fønss-Jørgensen.
2. Ilse Assmann, *IASA Membership Directory*, 2007; Johannesburg, South Africa.
3. Scharlau, U. A personal review of thirty years of IASA (1969–1999). IASA Inform. Bull. (August), 9–11, **1999**, *Special Issue.*
4. Schuursma, R. IASA: The first ten years: Some personal memories. IASA J. **1994**, *3* (May), 5–15.
5. Schuursma, R. Keynote Address to the IASA annual conference, Vienna, Austria, September 18–25, 1999. IASA J. **1999**, *14* (December), 6–10.

Informetrics–International Council

International Association of Technological University Libraries (IATUL)

Nancy Fjällbrant
Chalmers University of Technology Library, International Association of Technological University Libraries, Gothenberg, Sweden

Alice Trussell
Hale Library, Kansas State University, Manhattan, Kansas, U.S.A.

Abstract

The International Association of Technological University Libraries (IATUL) was founded in Düsseldorf, Germany, in May 1955, as an international forum for the exchange of ideas relevant to librarianship in technological universities throughout the world. The IATUL is a voluntary international nongovernmental organization of a group of libraries, represented by their library directors or senior managers, who have responsibility for information services and resources management. Many of the members of IATUL provide services, not only to the teaching and research staff and students of their own university but also to industrial organizations and national research institutions, in their respective countries. The main objective of IATUL is to provide a forum where library directors and senior managers can meet to exchange views on matters of current significance and to provide an opportunity for them to develop a collaborative approach to solving problems. The IATUL is an excellent example of the development of an effective informal international network between libraries of similar type, with a common high level of professional expertise and offering a similar range of services to their users. The IATUL also welcomes into membership organizations that supply services to university libraries, if they wish to be identified with the association's activities. This entry will examine the historical development, membership, organizationalstructure, activities, and publications of IATUL.

INTRODUCTION

The International Association of Technological University Libraries (IATUL) was founded in Düsseldorf, Germany, in May 1955, as an international forum for the exchange of ideas relevant to librarianship in technological universities throughout the world. The IATUL is a voluntary international nongovernmental organization of a group of libraries, represented by their library directors or senior managers, who have responsibility for information services and resources management. Many of the members of IATUL provide services, not only to the teaching and research staff and students of their own university but also to industrial organizations and national research institutions, in their respective countries. The main objective of IATUL is to provide a forum where library directors and senior managers can meet to exchange views on matters of current significance and to provide an opportunity for them to develop a collaborative approach to solving problems. The IATUL is an excellent example of the development of an effective informal international network between libraries of similar type, with a common high level of professional expertise and offering a similar range of services to their users. The IATUL also welcomes into membership organizations that supply services to university libraries, if they wish to be identified with the association's activities.

HISTORY AND DEVELOPMENT OF IATUL

Dr. E. Hemlin from Chalmers University of Technology, Sweden was the founder of IATUL and also its first president, and, in this capacity, he did much to develop the association. In September 1955, IATUL was recognized as a subsection of the International Library Association's division of the International Federation of Library Associations and Institutions (IFLA). This division no longer exists, and IATUL, as an International Library Association member, now works in association with the IFLA Section of Science and Technology Libraries. In 1990, IATUL was formally affiliated with UNESCO. This affiliation operates now through IFLA. Since 1999, IATUL is also a member of the International Council for Scientific and Technical Information.[1–3]

In the early years, many of the members of IATUL came from Europe, where there were a number of well-established institutions for technological education. The eighteenth century had seen the founding of some of the earliest "schools" of this type in France, Germany, and Hungary. The first half of the nineteenth century was a period of considerable economic and social growth and development. This period saw the increasing use of steam power for industry, the rapid change from local craft

Encyclopedia of Library and Information Sciences, Fourth Edition DOI: 10.1081/E-ELIS4-120044711

Copyright © 2017 by Taylor & Francis. All rights reserved.

production to factory-based industries, and considerable improvements in communications. These changes led to an increased need for the provision of technical education and training, resulting in the founding of "trades and craft schools," and polytechnic institutions throughout Europe. Similar institutions were founded in the United States.[4] The early members of IATUL came mostly from European universities of technology and from some American institutions. During the last 25 years, there has been a steady growth in IATUL members coming from all parts of the world, resulting in a truly international organization.

At the 16th IATUL Conference, which was held at the University of Twente in the Netherlands in 1995, IATUL celebrated its first 40 years with a special session on the history of the organization. Several papers given at this session by previous board members provide interesting glimpses of the history of IATUL from a variety of angles.[5–8] The 50th anniversary was celebrated at the 26th IATUL Conference, which was held at the University of Laval in 2005. An extensive display of historic photographs was on display, and the speakers at the conference banquet provided a warm reflection on half a century of service.

MEMBERSHIP

Ordinary and associate membership of IATUL is open to the libraries of universities and other higher educational institutions that offer programs of science and technology. Applications for membership of IATUL shall be addressed to the Secretary of the Association. In addition to academic institutional membership, there are two other types of membership. These are the categories of membership:[9]

> *Ordinary membership*—available to libraries/information services whose institutions offer masters or doctoral degrees in engineering, science, or technology;
> *Associate Membership*—available, subject to confirmation by the Board, to libraries/information services interested in supporting the aims and objectives of IATUL
> *Honorary Membership*—which the Board may confer upon individuals who have served the Association, or international librarianship, with particular distinction; and
> *Sustaining Membership*—available, subject to confirmation by the Board, to commercial organizations interested in supporting the aims and objectives of IATUL

In an effort to recruit more members from countries and continents outside of Europe, a graduated membership fee structure was adopted at the general meeting in 2005. The new fee structure was based on the UNESCO Scale of Assessments. Libraries in those countries whose current UNESCO assessment is at 0.251 or greater pay the standard fee. Those libraries in countries whose UNESCO assessment is at 0.250 or below pay a fee of 50% of the standard membership rate.[10] In 2007, President Maria Heijne reported that there were 241 member libraries from 46 countries.[11] The IATUL is small enough to allow individual members to develop a close relationship, yet widespread enough to cover the interests of libraries operating in virtually all modern social, economic, and political situations.

ORGANIZATION AND ACTIVITIES

The association is governed by a Board of Directors consisting of the President, First Vice-President, Second Vice-President, Secretary, Treasurer, Immediate Past President, and at least three board members elected by member libraries.[9] The board meets at least two times each year. Beginning in 2005, the board organizes a regional seminar in conjunction with the fall board meeting. The goals of hosting a regional seminar are to "interact with representatives of local libraries, to share information about developments for technological university libraries, and to create interest for the activities of IATUL."[12] The current president of IATUL is Maria Heijne, University Librarian at the Delft Institute of Technology. The IATUL brings its members together by means of meetings, an e-mail list for members, and a Web site. The meetings include conferences, seminars, and regional gatherings. The conferences started as triennial meetings, which then became biennial, and finally, in 1997, annual conferences. During the period of biennial conferences, seminars were held during the year when there was no conference.

Recent conferences:

- The 28th IATUL Conference was held at the Royal Institute of Technology, Stockholm, Sweden in 2007 with the theme *Global Access to Science*.
- The 27th IATUL Conference was held at the Faculdade de Engenharia, Universidade do Porto, Portugal in 2006 with the theme *of Embedding Libraries in Learning and Research*.
- The 26th IATUL Conference was held at the Université Laval Library, Québec City, Canada in 2005 with the theme of *Information and Innovation*.
- The 25th IATUL Conference was held at the Library of Krakow University of Technology in Krakow Poland in 2004 on the theme of *Library Management in Changing Environment*.
- The 24th IATUL Conference was held at the Middle Eastern Technical University in Ankara, Turkey in 2003 on the theme of *Libraries and Education in the Networked Information Environment*.
- The 30th IATUL Conference was held at the Katholieke Universiteit Leuven Belgium in 2009 with the theme of *Just for you: Quality through innovation*.

Informetrics–International Council

Informetrics–International
Council

- The 29th IATUL Conference was held at the Auckland University of Technology, Auckland New Zealand in 2008 with the theme of *Digital Discovery: Strategies and Solutions*.

Conferences immediately prior to these most current ones were held in Greece, Norway, Australia, the United States, and South Africa. The scope of the conference themes and venues illustrate the world-wide impact of IATUL. Future plans for IATUL will take the annual conferences to Purdue University in the United States in 2010 and to Warsaw University of Technology in Poland in 2011.

PUBLICATIONS

The first IATUL publications were a series of irregular reprints and publications from 1956 (Number 1) to 1967 (Number 25).[13] The first regular publications of IATUL were the *Newsletters* (January 1963–November 1965) with about 20 more extensive contributions and innumerable brief reports about the activities of the members. In 1965, the journal *IATUL Proceedings* started publication. Publication started at Delft University of Technology in the Netherlands and was transferred first to Loughborough University of Technology in the United Kingdom during the years 1968–1973, and then from 1974 till 1986 to Chalmers University of Technology, Gothenburg, Sweden.[14]

From 1987 to 1991, the *IATUL Proceedings* and the *IATUL Conference Proceedings* were merged to form the *IATUL Quarterly* (Volumes 1–5) published by Oxford University Press. Owing to the high costs of publishing the *IATUL Quarterly*, it was decided to cease publication in 1991 and instead to publish the *IATUL News* as a quarterly newsletter, with the aim of providing a timely flow of information to members, together with the annual *IATUL Proceedings (New Series)*, which contains a selection of the papers presented at the IATUL Conferences and Seminars.

From 1996 onward, papers from *IATUL Proceedings* are available on the IATUL Web site at http://www.iatul. org. From 1997 to 2006, the *IATUL Proceedings (New Series)* is also distributed in a CD-ROM version; prior to 1997, a print version was produced. For a description of the *IATUL, Proceedings* see the article published in 1996 by Elin Törnuudd, former president of IATUL—*IATUL as a Mirror of Library Developments Since 1966 as Documented in IATUL Proceedings.*[6] *The IATUL News*, Editor Nancy Fjällbrant, was published at Chalmers University of Technology from 1992 onward, in two forms: as a print publication from 1992 to 2000, with a parallel Web version available beginning in 1994. At the 2000 General Assembly of IATUL in Brisbane, it was decided to end the printed version of the *IATUL News* at the end of 2000. Distribution of IATUL News moved to mailing lists with archived issues maintained on the organizational Web site. This transition brings about the realization of the IATUL Electronic Publishing Plan that was launched in 1997—with the aim of publishing all the IATUL publications in electronic form.

CONCLUSION

Although IATUL began as a European centric organization of technological university library managers, the scope of service and participating membership has expanded far beyond the geographical distribution of the original members. The IATUL continues to build membership and service to the engineering and technology library community around the world. The IATUL has recognized that due to variations in university organizational differences, participation by university libraries offering a wide scope of disciplines including engineering and technology needs to be cultivated. This organizational difference is most noticeably present in North America, where participation by universities is greatly encouraged. The forum provided by IATUL for the exchange of ideas relevant to engineering and technological librarianship continues to help enable the library community to meet the challenges of the twenty-first century information needs.

REFERENCES

1. Schmidmaier, D. The history of the International Association of Technological University Libraries. IATUL Proc. **1976**, *8*, 42–45.
2. Schmidmaier, D. The early history of IATUL from 1953–1962. IATUL Quart. **1990**, *4* (4), 200–204.
3. Shaw, D. IATUL and library cooperation. IATUL Quart. **1989**, *3* (3), 153–157.
4. Fjällbrant, N. The library of the Institute for the History of Electricity at Chalmers University of Technology in Göteborg. IATUL Quart. **1987**, *1* (3), 182–195.
5. Shaw, D. Whither IATUL 1986–1990? (Reflections of a former president). IATUL Proc. (new series) **1996**, *5*, 353–360.
6. Törnudd, E. IATUL as a mirror of library developments since 1966 as documented in IATUL Proceedings. IATUL Proc. (new series) **1996**, *5*, 362–365.
7. Dömötör, A. Small is beautiful. IATUL Proc. (new series) **1996**, *5*, 350–352.
8. Slajpah, M. The impact of IATUL on the development of the central technical library in the Republic of Slovenia. IATUL Proc. (new series) **1996**, *5*, 341–349.
9. IATUL Constitution. http://www.iatul.org/about/constitution.asp.
10. Minutes, IATUL General Assembly 2005. May 31, 2005, 2. http://www.iatul.org/doclibrary/public/MeetingMinutes/2005GA.pdf .
11. Heijne, M. President's Report 2006–2007. General Assembly Meet Handout **2007**, 1.
12. Heijne, M. IATUL President's Report 2007. June 12 **2007**, Available at http://www.iatul.org/about/general.asp.
13. Schmidmaier, D. The publications of IATUL from 1955 to 1965. IATUL Proc. 11(new series) **1996**, *5*, 329–340.
14. van Marle, G.A.J.S. Presidential address. IATUL Proc. (new series) **1996**, *5*, 6–10.

International Communication Association (ICA)

Ronald E. Rice
Department of Communication, University of California–Santa Barbara, Santa Barbara, California, U.S.A.

Abstract

The International Communication Association (ICA, 1500 21st Street, NW, Washington, D.C. 20036, Tel.: 202-955-1444; Fax: 202-955-1448, E-mail: icahdq@icahdq.org; http://www.icahdq.org) is an academic association for scholars interested in the study, teaching, and application of all aspects of human and mediated communication. ICA is an international association with over 4500 members. This entry summarizes its history, governance and administration, past presidents, divisions and interest groups, membership, annual conferences, fellows, awards, links with other communication associations, publications, impact factors and local citation environments of ICA, and references. Much of this material comes from ICA's website, with permission.

INTRODUCTION

ICA is an academic association for scholars interested in the study, teaching, and application of all aspects of human and mediated communication. ICA is an international association with over 4700 members from nearly 90 countries. Since 2003, ICA has been officially associated with the United Nations as a nongovernmental association. The overall purposes of the association are to advance the scholarly study of human communication and to facilitate the implementation of such study so as to be of maximum benefit to humankind. The association seeks to achieve this purpose by 1) encouraging the systematic study of theories, processes, and skills of human communication; and 2) facilitating the dissemination of research through an organizational structure responsive to communication study areas, a program of organizational affiliates, regular sponsorship of international meetings, and a commitment to a program of scholarly publication. This entry summarizes its history, governance, presidents, divisions and interest groups, membership, annual conferences, awards, and journals.

THE EARLY DAYS

The National Society for the Study of Communication (NSSC) was founded in 1950, led by such individuals as Elwood Murray, Paul Bagwell, Ralph Nichols, and Wesley Wiksell, from its parent organization the Speech Association of American (now the National Communication Association) partially to support and encourage the study of communication as a research topic instead of as primarily rhetoric. The first issue of the *Journal of Communication* appeared in 1951. In order to reflect the increasingly more diverse makeup of the society, four

initial divisions were formed in 1968: information systems, interpersonal communication, mass communication, and organizational communication. The NSSC changed its name in 1969 to the International Communication Association. During this period, membership rose from 900 members in 1967 to more than 2000 members in 1971. The first annual convention outside North America was held in West Berlin in 1977. (For a detailed history of the first quarter century of the International Communication Association, see Weaver.[1] For more detail and references, see http://www.icahdq.org/about_ica/history.asp.)

GOVERNANCE AND ADMINISTRATION

The ICA Board of Directors includes an Executive Committee (the president, president-elect, immediate past-president, and past-president, the president-select-elect, and, ex-officio, the chair of the financial committee—who is the past-past president—and ICA's executive director), the chairs of the divisions and interest groups, two student members, and board members at large representing Africa-Oceania, non-U.S. Americas, East Asia, West Asia, and Europe. This regional (based on United Nations criteria) representation was implemented in 2000 to reflect the increasingly international focus of ICA. Standing committees of ICA include membership and internationalization, student affairs, finance, publications, nominating, and sustainability, as well as committees for each award. The headquarters relocated from Austin, Texas, to Washington, D.C. in 2001, and purchased its own office building in 2006. The full-time staff includes an executive director, a member services director, a publications manager, a communication director, an executive assistant, and a member services associate.

Encyclopedia of Library and Information Sciences, Fourth Edition DOI: 10.1081/E-EISA-120053421
Copyright © 2017 by Taylor & Francis. All rights reserved.

PRESIDENTS

In the year that ICA presidents are elected, they are responsible for determining the theme of the following year's conference. In that following year, the "president-elect" is responsible, working with the executive director, staff, and the executive committee, for selecting a conference theme chair and organizing that year's annual conference, responding to a constant flow of requests, proposals, and administrative matters, and representing ICA. In the following year, the "president" presides over board meetings and that year's annual conference, reconstitutes all the committees, represents ICA, attends to policy and other matters that come before ICA, and presents the presidential address. Table 1 lists the ICA presidents.

DIVISIONS AND INTEREST GROUPS

ICA's principal areas of concern are represented by its divisions and interest groups. These currently include 20 divisions (each maintains a membership of at least 10% of all ICA members) and five interest groups (newly founded sections with at least 20 members). Table 2 lists the divisions and interest groups. Two network analyses of the joint memberships and paper titles in ICA's division and interest groups revealed three underlying dimensions of the groups: mediated/interpersonal, humanistic/scientific, and theoretical/applied.[2,3]

MEMBERSHIP

ICA's membership hovered around 500 until 1967, to 2000 by 1970, to 3000 after 2001, and by June 2014 included 4700. Some two-thirds are teaching and conducting research in colleges, universities, and schools around the world, while others work in the media, communication technology, business law, medicine, government, and other professions.

As part of ICA's continuing emphasis on increasing internationalization, about half of its committee members and about half of the board of directors are members of non-U.S. universities. Of the 80 countries represented in ICA, the greatest percentages of ICA membership include, at 58% the United States; from 8% to 2%: Germany, the United Kingdom, the Netherlands, Canada, and Australia; and from 1.5% to 1%: Switzerland, Japan, Republic of Korea, Israel, Belgium, Hong Kong, Sweden, and Singapore.

ICA has a triple-tiered dues structure following the United Nations model for A, B, and C countries. Residents of B-tier countries pay 75% of the A-tier price and residents of C-tier countries pay 50% of the A-tier price. These differing fee levels were instituted in 2002 to

Table 1 ICA presidents.

2014–2015	Peter Vorderer
2013–2014	Francois Heinderyckx
2012–2013	Cynthia Stohl
2011–2012	Larry Gross
2010–2011	Francois Cooren
2009–2010	Barbie Zelizer
2008–2009	Patrice M. Buzzanell
2007–2008	Sonia Livingstone
2006–2007	Ronald E. Rice
2005–2006	Jon F. Nussbaum
2004–2005	Wolfgang Donsbach
2003–2004	Robert T. Craig
2002–2003	Jennings Bryant
2001–2002	Cindy Gallois
2000–2001	Joseph N. Cappella
1999–2000	Linda L. Putnam
1998–1999	Howard Giles
1997–1998	Peter Monge
1996–1997	Stanley A. Deetz
1995–1996	Charles R. Berger
1994–1995	Bradley S. Greenberg
1993–1994	Akiba A. Cohen
1992–1993	Ellen Wartella
1991–1992	Mary Anne Fitzpatrick
1990–1991	Margaret L. McLaughlin
1989–1990	Jay George Blumler
1988–1989	Phillip K. Tompkins
1987–1988	L. Edna Rogers
1986–1987	B. Aubrey Fisher (deceased)
1985–1986	Brenda Dervin
1984–1985	Klaus Krippendorff
1983– 1984	James A. Anderson
1982–1983	Erwin P. Bettinghaus
1981–1982	Steve Chaffee (deceased)
1980–1981	Everett M. Rogers (deceased)
1979–1980	Gerald R. Miller (deceased)
1978–1979	Frederick D. Williams (deceased)
1977–1978	Robert J. Kibler (deceased)
1976–1977	Richard W. Budd
1975–1976	Mark L. Knapp
1974–1975	Nathan Maccoby (deceased)
1973–1974	Alfred G. Smith (deceased)
1972–1973	Malcolm S. MacLean (deceased)
1971–1972	Ronald L. Smith (deceased)
1970–1971	R. Wayne Pace
1969–1970	Robert S. Goyer
1968–1969	Darrell T. Piersol
1967–1968	Lee Thayer
1966–1967	Frank E. X. Dance
1965–1966	Harold P. Zelko (deceased)
1964–1965	Clarence J. Dover (deceased)
1962–1963	W. Charles Redding (deceased)
1961–1962	John B. Haney
1960–1961	Thorrel Fest (deceased)
1958–1959	Francis A. Cartier
1955–1956	Kenneth A. Harwood
1954–1955	Burton H. Byers (deceased)
1951–1952	Elwood Murray (deceased)
1950–1951	Ralph G. Nichols (deceased)
1949–1950	Paul D. Bagwell (deceased)

Informetrics–International
Council

Table 2 ICA divisions and interest groups (IG).

Children, adolescents, and the media:	Focuses on the production, content, uses, and reception of both print and electronic media. It strives to be a fruitful intellectual forum for academics from all over the world who study the role of media in the lives of children and young people. CAM's orientation is interdisciplinary and multimethodological.
Communication and technology:	Focuses on information and communication technology in relation to processes of human communication. Specifically it addresses new media, social media, human–computer interaction, computer-mediated communication, mobile communication, "big data," crowdsourcing, and other technologically mediated social interaction and networking in all contexts and levels of analysis. CAT is not about technology per se, but rather about the interaction with social and personal entities at the micro, meso, and macro level.
Communication history:	Promotes theory, research, and professional education in the history of communication. the notion of "communication history," in this interest group, pulls together three major areas of research: the history of communication including media history, the history of the idea of communication, and the history of the field of communication.
Communication law and policy:	Is interested in research and analysis of law, regulation, and policy that deals with information, communication, and culture. Defining policy broadly, the division includes within its purview: principles that should or do underlie law and regulation, proposals for new law and regulation, and the programs and institutions through which policy is implemented.
Environmental communication:	Advances research on the interplay of the environment with any level of communication and in any setting. Specific foci include health, risk, and science communication. Also helps members integrate sustainability issues into their teaching and research.
Ethnicity and race:	Is concerned with methodological approaches and research that apply, extend, or develop communication theory and analysis through an examination of race and ethnicity within local, international, and transnational contexts. Advocates for the improved status, representation, and opportunities for underrepresented scholars in communication.
Feminist scholarship:	Is interested in exploring the relationship of gender and communication, both mediated and nonmediated, within a context of feminist theories, methodologies, and practices. Areas include feminist teaching; international commonalities and differences by race, class, and gender; women's alternative media; and feminist cultural studies.
Game studies (IG):	The study of games and the game experience offers opportunities for the study of human communication that involve multidisciplinary approaches that merge the disciplines of conventional communication studies and research, arts and visual design, cognitive studies, computer sciences, cultural studies, engineering social sciences, health sciences, and information design.
Global communication and social change:	Encourages and debates research on issues of production, distribution, content, and reception of communications media at global, "glocal," transnational, transcultural, international, and regional levels.
Health communication:	Is primarily concerned with the role of communication theory, research, and practice in health promotion and health care. Areas of research include provider–patient interaction, social support networks, health information systems, medical ethics, health policy, and health promotion.
Information systems:	Is concerned with information, language, and cognitive systems. Its central goal is promoting the development of general theories of complex systems and quantitative methodologies for communication research in a variety of domains.
Instructional and developmental communication:	Is concerned with both communication related to any learning environment and communication that transpires across the life span. Its dual goals include promoting the study of communication variables and theory in the instructional process and promoting the study of communication as a developmental phenomenon across the complete life span.
Intercultural communication:	Is primarily concerned with theory and practice of communication between and among different cultures of the world; with comparisons of different communication systems in different cultural, national, or ethnic groups; with other aspects of international communication; and with the relationship between communication and national development.
Intergroup communication (IG):	Focuses on the ways in which communication within and between groups affects social relations. Intergroup encounters occur when social, rather than personal, identity forms the basis for communication. Intergroup communication is often characterized by power inequality, bias, competition, or conflict. Some relevant topics would include prejudice and discrimination, social identity processes, language survival and death, social influence, leadership, communicative shifts and concomitant effects on relationships, computer-mediated communication, linguistic biases, power, terrorism, collaboration, and altruism.

(Continued)

Table 2 ICA divisions and interest groups (IG). *(Continued)*

Interpersonal communication:	Emphasizes the study of communication processes between people in a variety of settings, including friendship formation, influence, relationship development, small group processes, and family relations, through face-to-face and mediated communication.
Journalism studies:	Is concerned with journalism theory, journalism research, and professional education in journalism, across temporal and geographic contexts. The division seeks to facilitate empirical research and to bring more coherence to research paradigms.
Language and social interaction:	Is concerned with exploring details of human discourse and human interaction. The division sponsors research in language theory, linguistics, pragmatics, semiotics, sociolinguistics, ethnography of speaking, conversation analysis, and related approaches to human social interaction. The primary focus is in interpersonal and group settings, through face-to-face or mediated communication.
Lesbian, gay, bisexual, transgender, and queer studies (IG):	Is concerned with the analysis and critique of sexual systems, discourses, and representations, particularly those which animate, inform, and impinge upon the lives of lesbian, gay, bisexual, and transgender people. Such systems and discourses occur in institutional, community, domestic and intimate contexts, are closely connected to other social and cultural practices (such as nationalism, education or popular entertainment), and play a critical role in the formation and communication of individual and group identity.
Mass communication:	Is primarily concerned with the differential impact of messages transmitted by various mass media, including international exchanges through mass media. Its members develop theory, examine the processes and effects of mass communication, and develop and evaluate policy relevant to mass communication.
Media industry studies (IG):	Promotes research and teaching practice on the history, organization, structure, economics, management, production processes, and cultural forms, and the societal impact of media industries from a variety of theoretical, empirical, and cultural perspectives. Among other things, our members study the relationship between government and industry, the intersection of audience and industry, audiences as consumers, the business of media, production and creative labor, ownership structure, and content diversity from a range of micro and macro-levels
Mobile communication (IG):	Studies the phenomenon of mobility in communication—the intersection of mobility, technology, and culture in human communication. Members apply a wide array of perspectives from historical perspectives to studies on future media innovations, from ethnographic to quantitative empirical approaches, from journalism studies to media effects research. The common ground is state of the art theorizing on mobile communication as well as the discussion of adequate methodology to do so.
Organizational communication:	Seeks to expand our understanding of the processes, prospects, and challenges of communicating and organizing in a global society. Its scholarship articulates concepts and theories to better understand these processes, develops the tools needed to investigate them, and helps to implement the social practices to improve them.
Philosophy, theory, and critique:	Is broadly concerned with theoretical, analytical, and political issues that cut across the various boundaries within the study of communication and its intersections with other modes of studying human interaction.
Political communication:	Is concerned with the interplay of communication and politics, including the transactions that occur among citizens, between citizens and their governments, and among officials within governments.
Popular communication:	Is concerned with providing a forum for scholarly investigation, analysis, and dialogue among communication researchers interested in a wide variety of communication symbols, forms, phenomena, and strategic systems of symbols within the context of contemporary popular culture.
Public relations:	Is concerned with the theory and practice of communication between organizations and specified publics. Research interests include target group analysis, internal/external communication integration, systems analysis, and channel effectiveness.
Public diplomacy (IG):	
Sports communication (IG):	Intends to understand human and mediated communication processes and effects within sports contexts.
Visual communication studies:	Seeks to enhance the understanding of the visual in all its forms—moving and still images and displays in television, video and film, art and design, and print and digital media. Research areas include creation, processing, function, meaning, and critical consequences of visual representation.

Infometrics–International Council

Table 3 Membership in ICA divisions and interest groups.

Division or interest group	Percent of all memberships
Children, adolescents, and the media	2.9
Communication and technology	9.8
Communication history	2.7
Communication law and policy	2.9
Environmental communication	2.2
Ethnicity and race in communication	2.3
Feminist scholarship	2.5
Game studies	2.2
Gay, lesbian, bisexual, and transgender studies (IG)	1.2
Global communication & social change	4.5
Health communication	5.6
Information systems	3.4
Instructional/developmental communication	1.9
Intercultural communication	4.3
Intergroup communication (IG)	1.6
Interpersonal communication	3.9
Journalism studies	6.0
Language and social interaction	2.3
Mass communication	10.2
Organizational communication	5.5
Philosophy, theory, and critique	4.2
Political communication	7.6
Popular communication	3.8
Public relations	4.2
Sports communication (IG)	0.0
Visual communication studies	2.5
Total	10785

Note: There are 4500 unique members, and one division or interest group is provided free with membership, but members typically belong to multiple divisions or interest groups. So, the total is the overall total of group registrations (including multiple groups for a person), and the percentage is based on that.

continue the increased emphasis on international representation. Membership categories for individuals include regular, employment exception, student, emeritus, life, and sustaining. Membership categories for groups include family, institutional, and association. Members may join one division/interest group as part of regular dues and may add additional divisions/interest groups for a few dollars.

Table 3 presents the percentage of memberships for each division and interest group. Mass communication has the greatest percentage of memberships as of 2014.

The primary benefits to members of ICA include opportunities to network with colleagues who share teaching and research interests worldwide; access to membership in the divisions and interest groups and their related websites; attendance at annual conferences at member rates with discounted air/hotel/car rates; print or online subscriptions to five professional journals; and access to the annual yearbook at a members-only discount. Other book discounts include several series: Blackwell's *Communication in the Public Interest* and *The International Encyclopedia of Communication*, Routledge's *ICA-LEA Handbook Series*, and Hampton Press's *ICA Theme Series* (highlighting the primary theme of each year's conference theme sessions), as well as discounted membership in the Communication Institute for Online Scholarship (http://www.cios.org). Finally, ICA's website contains the latest information and allows for online registration for conferences and membership renewals; provides the latest information, online access to ICA journals, and the ICA membership directory; and provides access to the ICA online newsletter, published 10 times per year, which includes job listings, association and member news, ICA officer columns, and calls for papers.

ANNUAL CONFERENCES

The ICA annual conference is generally held each year at the end of May when in North America and in June or July when outside of North America. About 1500–2000 scholars come together at this event to learn about the latest research, socialize with colleagues, visit the city, and learn about job opportunities. Submitted papers undergo a double-blind peer review process; in 2005 a record number of 2300 papers were submitted (New York); in 2006, 2000 were submitted (Dresden). Another change to expand the international identity and presence of Caws to increase the frequency of annual conferences held outside of North America from every 4 years to every 3 years, beginning in 2010. Non-U.S. conferences include Berlin (1977), Acapulco (1980), Montreal (1987), Dublin (1990), Sydney (1994), Montreal (1997), Jerusalem (1998), Acapulco (2000), Seoul (2002), Dresden (2006), Montreal (2008), Singapore (2010), London (2013), Fukuoka Japan (2016), and Prague (2018).

FELLOWS

ICA annually recognizes distinguished scholarly contributions to the broad field of communication, as well as service to ICA and other public institutions through fellow status. Currently, there are over 100 Fellows. Meyen[4] published an insightful "collective biography" based on interviews with 57 Fellows. To some extent, fellows are representatives of dominant paradigms, provide role models, are agents in field's decision-making, and influence perceptions and expectations. They are influenced by the geography of the field's founders and universities, by family background and academic socialization, a shift from the early emphasis on journalism to a more social science perspective, a commitment to field of communication and its symbolic capital, and their interest in service and mentoring and working with graduate students.

Informetrics–International Council

Informetrics–International
Council

AWARDS

ICA presents eight major awards at the annual conference to recognize significant research in and contributions to the field. ICA divisions and interest groups also offer their own awards.

Steven H. Chaffee Career Achievement Award

The award honors a scholar (or small group of collaborating scholars) for sustained work on a communication research problem over an extended period. The selection committee favors research that is original, asks conceptually rich questions, and offers empirically sound evidence. The research must have comprised multiple projects and publications and generated second-generation work among students and other scholars. Rather than recognizing general productivity in the field or contributions to ICA, the award acknowledges sustained and coherent work on a well-focused communication problem central to the communication discipline. Most recipients are members of the discipline and belong to ICA, but other scholars are eligible, regardless of current membership or department affiliation. The winner presents research at the following year's ICA conference.

James W. Carey Urban Communication Grant

This annual prize supports communication research that enhances urban social interaction and civic engagement inane age of global communication. It encourages applied research on the role of city and community at a time when communication technology alters the parameters of the urban landscape. The award is for proposals that feature innovation and creative approaches to reconciling the growing gap between tradition and modernity as suburban sprawl threatens the very nature of urban traditions. This award facilitates research in progress or in the planning stages. It gives priority to projects that study places where traditional modes of communication are being juxtaposed with the new, including the adoption of changes that may have a radical impact. Proposals from developing nations are encouraged.

Outstanding Book Award

The award honors a book published in the previous two calendar years (between January 1 and December 31). The selection committee judges each nominated book on several criteria including the importance of the problem it addresses in the fields represented in ICA and to communication studies as a whole, the quality of writing and argument, and the strength of evidence it presents. The committee will consider all the available book reviews, the reputation of the publisher, and any other submitted evidence regarding the book's quality from independent sources, along with nominating letters and their own assessment of the nominated books. Most award-winning books address a scholarly audience, but books aimed at a general readership but satisfying the criteria for the prize are also eligible—edited books are not eligible.

Applied Research Award

The Applied Research Award honors a scholar or group of scholars who has or have produced a systematic and outstanding body of research that addresses a significant communication problem of relevance to a public representing one or more groups of stakeholders relevant to a division(s) or interest group(s) of ICA. Individual or collaborative applied research programs that include community engagement, group and organizational interventions, or advocacy and/or political policy work at the local, national, international, and/or global levels are all appropriate candidates for this award. Evidence for quality and public importance can come from conventional publications but also from such materials as technical reports, news media coverage, and testimonials from those making use of the research or those it has affected.

Outstanding Article Award

The award honors an article published in a refereed journal during the previous two calendar years (between January 1 and December 31). Theoretical articles and empirical articles are eligible, as are review articles that effectively redefine a problem. Selection criteria include coherence of argument, quality of conceptual development, and effective use of evidence. The selection committee prefers articles that promise to be influential over time, within particular field of communication and also across fields.

Young Scholar Award

The award honors a scholar no more than 7 years past receipt of the Ph.D. for a body of work that has contributed to knowledge of the field of communication and shows promise for continued development. The selection committee judges the contribution and promise of young scholars based on the strength of published work, including its conceptual foundation and argumentative clarity, on the scholar's productivity at a given career stage, on the rigor of the research produced so far, and on the promise of existing work serving as a springboard for continuing scholarship.

B. Aubrey Fisher Mentorship Award

Initiated in 1988 following the death of its namesake, this award honors outstanding scholars, teachers, and advisors who serve as role models in those capacities and who have had a major impact on the field of communication. Most importantly, recipients of this award have influenced the discipline through their former students, who themselves are important figures in the communication discipline.

ICA Fellows Book Award

Open to all ICA members, this award recognizes those books that have made a substantial contribution to the scholarship of the communication field as well as the broader rubric of the social sciences and have stood some test of time.

LINKS WITH OTHER COMMUNICATION ASSOCIATIONS

ICA fosters collaboration with other communication associations, including co-sponsoring conferences, and providing affiliate organizational status. Current relations include Asociacion de Comunicacion Politica; Bangladesh Center for Communication Programs; BBC Media Action; Binational Association of Schools of Comm of the Californias; Brazilian Society of Interdisciplinary Studies in Communication; Chinese Communication Association; Deutsche Gesellschaft fur Publizistik-und Kommunikationswissenschaft; Institute of Digital Media and Child Development, Inc.; International Association of Language & Social Psychology; International Association for Media and Communication Research; International Environmental Communication Association; Korean American Communication Association; Media Ecology Association; National Association of Mass Media Researchers; Polish Communication Association; and the Russian Communication Association.

PUBLICATIONS

The annual *Communication Yearbook* (begun in 1977) publishes state-of-the-art literature reviews and articles providing comprehensive syntheses of literature. *Communication Theory* (1991) publishes research articles, theoretical essays, and reviews on topics of broad theoretical interest from across the range of communication studies. *Human Communication Research* (1973) publishes the

best empirical research examining communication processes and effects. The *Journal of Communication* (1969) is a general forum for communication scholarship and publishes articles and book reviews examining a broad range of issues in communication theory and research. The *Journal of Computer-Mediated Communication* (acquired in 2003) is a Web-based journal that publishes scholarship on computer-mediated communication. ICA added a fifth journal, *Communication, Culture & Critique*, beginning 2008; it is an international forum for critical, feminist interpretive, and qualitative research examining the role of communication from a cultural and historical perspective. Beginning in January 2007, the abstracts of the articles of each of the journals are also provided through the publisher's databases, translated into Spanish, Korean, French, Chinese, and German.

IMPACT FACTORS AND LOCAL CITATION ENVIRONMENTS OF ICA JOURNALS

The underlying citations to and from journals, as reported in ISI's Journal Citation Report, are the basis for computing each journal's citation impact factor. Citation Impact Ratings are the ratio of number of citations received to articles in that journal, divided by number of articles published in that journal 2 years prior. Table 4 provides the 2011, 2013, and 2013 5-year ISI journal citation impact factors for the ICA journals.

The article citation data are also the basis for identifying clusters of shared concepts, journals, and authors—one widely used form of bibliometrics, or citation analysis. Leydesdorff[5] developed a reasonable way to extract what he calls "journal-citation environments" from the otherwise unwieldy matrix of possible citation relations (with over 1700 social science journals, based on data from the *Journal Citation Reports* from the Social Science Citation Index). Leydesdorff instead developed a procedure whereby one can choose any particular journal of interest; the program computes the distribution of citations to, and the distribution of citations from, that journal, and selects only those cited and citing journals that involve at least 1% of the total citations (from or to). Generally, 10–20 or so journals represent nearly all of the citations, so all remaining journals are ignored. The "cited" value represents the local impact in terms of citation volume, while the "citing" value represents "how the relevant journal environment is perceived by the collective authors of a given

Table 4 ICA journal citation impact ratings.

ICA journals	2011 impact factor	2013 impact factor	2013 5-year impact factor
Communication Theory	1.20	1.05	1.99
Human Communication Research	2.08	1.89	2.69
Journal of Communication	2.01	2.08	3.2
Journal of Computer-Mediated Communication	1.78	2.02	4.35

Source: 2013 Social Science Journal Citation Reports.

Informetrics–International Council

journal" (p. 25) (see www.leydesdorff.net). There are more detailed citation analyses of communication journals[6–12]

Based on 2004 data, *Communication Theory* is cited primarily by *Communication Research, Journal of Communication, Human Communication Research*, and *Communication Monographs*. It also has small (but greater than 1%) citations from *Health Communication, Media Psychology*, and *Journal of Health Communication*. However, nearly all of its citations go to *Communication Monographs*, with just a few in its local citation environment to *Journal of Personality and Social Psychology*. As *Communication Theory* was new at the time of the 2004 data collection, this network certainly has expanded since then.

Human Communication Research is embedded in a dense and diverse network of citing journals, including *Journal of Communication, Human Communication Research, Journal of Broadcasting and Electronic Media, Journalism and Mass Communication, Political Communication*, and, less frequently, *Critical Studies in Mediated Communication, International Journal of Public Opinion Research, European Journal of Communication, Media/Culture/Society, New Media & Society*, and *Harvard International Journal of Press and Politics*. Its citing environment (at least 1%) is far less dense, involving *Communication Research, Communication Monographs, Journal of Communication, Journal of Social & Personal Relations, European Journal of Social Psychology, Journal of Personality and Social Psychology, Psychology Bulletin*, and *Personality and Social Psychology Bulletin*.

The *Journal of Communication* is similar to *Human Communication Research* in being embedded in a dense and diverse journal citation environment. Most frequent citers of *Journal of Communication* articles include *Communication Research, Human Communication Research, Common Monographs, Journalism and Mass Communication, Journal of Broadcasting and Electronic Media, Critical Studies in Media Communication*, and *Political Communication*. Other direct but less frequent citers in the environment include *Journal of Public Opinion Research, Media Psychology, Harvard Journal of Press and Politics, New Media & Society, Media/Culture/Society*, and *European Journal of Communication*. Also like *HCR, JOC* cites a few primary journals, including *Communication Research, Communication Monographs, Political Communication, Journal of Broadcasting and Electronic Media, Journalism and Mass Communication, Human Communication Research*, and *Public Opinion Quarterly*.

CONCLUSION

The International Communication Association is a continually growing organization, in terms of research topics represented by divisions and interest groups, publications, size and internationality of its members, and relationships with other communication associations around the world. It provides the main academic association for primarily social-scientific approaches to the study, teaching, and application of communication research.

ACKNOWLEDGMENTS

I thank Michael Haley and Sam Luna of the International Communication Association for their support and provision of some information for this entry.

REFERENCES

1. Weaver, C.H. A history of the International Communication Association. In *Communication Yearbook*; Ruben, B.D., Ed.; Transaction Books: New Brunswick, NJ, 1977, 607–618.
2. Doerfel, M.L.; Barnett, G.A. A semantic network analysis of the International Communication Association. Hum. Commun. Res. **1999**, *25* (4), 589–603.
3. Barnett, G.A.; Danowski, J.A. The structure of communication. Hum. Commun. Res. **1992**, *19* (2), 264–285.
4. Meyen, M. International Communication Association fellows: a collective biography. Int. J. Commun. **2012**, *6*, 2378–2396.
5. Leydesdorff, L. Visualization of the citation impact environments of scientific journals: an online mapping exercise. J. Am. Soc. Inf. Sci. Technol. **2007**, *58* (1), 25–38.
6. Borgman, C.; Rice, R.E. The convergence of information science and communication: a bibliometric analysis. J. Am. Soc. Inf. Sci. **1992**, *43* (6), 397–411.
7. Funkhouser, E. The evaluative use of citation analysis for communication journals. Hum. Commun. Res. **1996**, *22* (4), 563–574.
8. Reeves, B.; Borgman, C. A bibliographic evaluation of core journals in communication research. Hum. Commun. Res. **1983**, *10*, 119–136.
9. Rice, R.E.; Crawford, G. Context and content of citations between communication and library & information science articles. In *Information and Behavior*; Schement, J., Ruben, B., Eds.; Transaction Press: New Brunswick, NJ, 1992; Vol. 4, 189–217.
10. Rice, R.E.; Borgman, C.; Reeves, B. Citation networks of communication journals, 1977–1985: Cliques and positions, citations made and citations received. Hum. Commun. Res. **1988**, *15* (2), 256–283.
11. Rice, R.E.; Chapin, J.; Pressman, R.; Park, S.; Funkhouser, E. What's in a name? Bibliometric analysis of 40 years of the *Journal of Broadcasting (and Electronic Media)*. J. Broadcast. Electron. Media, **1996**, *40*, 511–539.
12. So, C.Y. Citation patterns of core communication journals. Hum. Commun. Res. **1988**, *15* (2), 236–255.

Informetrics–International Council

International Council of Museums (ICOM)

Patrick J. Boylan
Department of Cultural Policy and Management, City University, London, U.K.

Abstract

The International Council of Museums (ICOM) is the global nongovernmental organization (NGO) representing the interests of museums, galleries, and related heritage institutions and services and their staff. Legally constituted in Paris as an *Association* in November 1946, ICOM is an independent NGO that represents both museum professionals and museums and related institutions and services, with a total of over 27,000 institutional and personal members in 151 countries. The ICOM's working languages are French, English, and Spanish, though national committees or individuals may use other languages in official meetings provided they arrange or pay for the necessary additional translation services.

ORIGIN AND DEVELOPMENT

The ICOM's history can be traced back to the International Museums Office established by the League of Nations, in Paris in 1927 under the League's International Institute of Intellectual Cooperation. Though legally constituted as an intergovernmental body of delegates appointed by Member States of the League, throughout its existence the International Museums Office operated with considerable freedom, acting very much as though it was a nongovernmental body. In particular, it drew on a very wide range of museum professionals and expertise in carrying out many cooperative studies of best practice and museum promotion and advisory programs, covering different museum and gallery activities, as well as work in other heritage areas, such as natural and historic monuments, sites and their conservation.

For example, its Athens Conference of 1931 examined the restoration of historic buildings, while between 1933 and 1939 the Office undertook a major international study of best modern practice relating to the conservation of paintings. Seven decades later these two are seen to have laid the foundations of modern approaches to conservation and restoration in the respective areas. In the case of the paintings study, the findings and recommendations, published in French and English editions in 1939 and 1940,[1,2] are still regarded as the foundation of scientific conservation and restoration of paintings, in contrast with the "cleaning" (often accompanied by heavy over-painting) of earlier times. Then, as war clouds gathered, and the devastating effect of the latest advances in warfare became clear from the Spanish Civil War, the Office carried out an urgent study of the protection of monuments and works of art in wartime, preparing a substantial practical manual of guidance,[3] which also included a proposed draft international treaty on cultural protection (much of which was finally to be adopted after World War II in the 1954 *Hague Convention on the Protection of Cultural Property in the Event of Armed Conflict.*)

The Office also published an international journal, *Mouseion*, which soon became a most important channel for international communication about museum developments and emerging practice. In addition, the Office launched a multivolume *Traité de Muséographie* covering best practice on all aspects of museum techniques, including the care and maintenance of collections, and many aspects of display and exhibition work. This series remained incomplete due to the outbreak of World War II. Although International Museums Office was in effect closed down in 1940 with the occupation of Paris, it was not formally abolished until after the war.

In October 1946, the new United Nations Educational, Scientific and Cultural Organization (UNESCO) was formally inaugurated in Paris, and started taking over relevant remaining functions and property of the League of Nations, including the library and other property of the International Museums Office. At the same time there were international consultations about establishing a world coordinating body for museums and museum organizations, and in November 1946 representatives of 14 countries met in the Musée du Louvre, Paris, supported by written representations from a further 13 countries, and resolved to create the International Council of Museums (ICOM) as a nongovernmental international *Association*.[4]

UNESCO, which had already welcomed the proposal, moved immediately to establish formal relations with the new nongovernmental organization (NGO), and in January 1947 the first contract between UNESCO and ICOM was agreed, providing for ICOM to take over responsibility for the museological library of the former International Museums Office as the UNESCO–ICOM Museum Documentation Centre, as well as much of the advisory and coordination role of the former body.

Encyclopedia of Library and Information Sciences, Fourth Edition DOI: 10.1081/E-ELIS4-120044714
Copyright © 2017 by Taylor & Francis. All rights reserved.

Informetrics–International
Council

ICOM quickly structured itself on the basis of the familiar NGO pattern. The membership was made up of small national committees of delegates appointed by the countries represented, typically by the national museums, national associations, or other national bodies (including national governments and ministries in the case of less democratic states). In addition to the officers and governing Council, who were elected from the membership, ICOM established international committees of appointed or invited experts (not necessarily members of ICOM itself). Soon these "museum subject" international committees that dealt with particular subjects, (typically different types of museums or collections) were joined by a growing number of interdisciplinary international committees, established to explore and develop best practice in subjects such as museum administration and training, educational services in museums, or the scientific conservation and restoration of collections and works of art.

When first created ICOM continued to cover the whole range of subjects and institutions for which the International Museums Office had been responsible, but over the next two decades or so areas of activity such as national parks, nature reserves, botanic and zoological gardens, and archaeological and historic monuments and sites came more and more within the scope of other international NGOs—particularly, the International Union for the Conservation of Nature (IUCN) in the case of the natural heritage, and the International Council on Monuments and Sites (ICOMOS) in the case of cultural heritage sites and monuments, a trend that was greatly reinforced when the IUCN and ICOMOS were given a special status in relation to these fields by the 1972 World Heritage Convention.

A much more far-reaching change of ICOM's structure began in the early 1970s. Though the official membership was restricted to those nominated at the national level (and with a maximum of 15 members in each national committee), ICOM's triennial General Conferences were open to, and increasingly popular with, the world's museum professionals generally on the payment of the appropriate "Associate" fee. By the time of the 1971 General Conference in Paris and Grenoble the official ICOM members present and entitled to vote were outnumbered several times over by nonvoting Conference participants, who were vocal in their protests about the membership structure. A joint review of the situation was carried out with the participation of representatives of the nonmembers, and at the next General Conference, held in Copenhagen in 1974, ICOM voted to turn itself into an international "membership" organization.

Consequently, from 1975 any museum professional in any country was entitled to join ICOM, becoming automatically a full member of the national committee. Similarly, the international committees, previously small bodies of no more than 30 appointed or elected experts, were reconstituted as unrestricted bodies open to all the members of ICOM, with each ICOM member entitled to register their membership in any international committee of their choice. Since this fundamental change in the democratic character of its membership, ICOM has grown very rapidly, from less than 1000 members in the early 1970s to 27,000 members today. At the same time, the ICOM's original list of eight international committees of no more than 30 members each has grown to 30 committees, some of which now have over 1000 members. As of 2008, ICOM also had 17 International Affiliated Organizations and 5 Regional Alliances.

MISSION

The ICOM's governing *Statutes* including the definition of a museum were also considerably updated as part of the 1974 reforms. In contrast with the long-standing narrow focus (on collection, research, and communication in relation to collections, specimens, and works of art), a museum was declared to have an explicitly social and developmental purpose. According to this new definition, http://icom.museum/definition.htm a museum is

> … a non-profit making, permanent institution in the service of the society and its development, and open to the public, which acquires, conserves, researches, communicates, and exhibits, for purposes of study, education and enjoyment, material evidence of man and his environment.

The current version of the Statutes of ICOM adopted in the 2007 General Conference describes the mission and purpose of ICOM as follows:[5]

> **Mission.** The ICOM is the international organization of museums and museum professionals, which is committed to the conservation, the continuation, and the communication to society of the world's natural and cultural heritage, present and future, tangible and intangible.
> **Purpose.** The ICOM establishes professional and ethical standards for museum activities, makes recommendations on such issues, promotes training, advances knowledge, and raises public cultural awareness through global networks and cooperation programmes. http://icom.museum/mission.html

CORE VALUES

Following the approval of the new *Statutes* the previous year, in 2008 ICOM has adopted and published a wide-ranging statement of core values and the vision for the future in the trilingual *Our Global Vision*.[6] Key provisions include:

Informetrics–International Council

Vision

For a world where the importance of the natural and cultural heritage is universally valued

Values

The ICOM values human creativity and its contribution to understanding the past, shaping the present, and planning the future.
The ICOM believes heritage has an innate humanistic value.
The ICOM values global dialogue based on intellectual, cultural, and social diversity.
The ICOM values transparent dialogue including the cross-cultural understanding of human rights.
The ICOM recognizes museums' social responsibility to engage with public issues of social change.

Following the very significant constitutional and policy developments of 2007–2008, ICOM is now recasting its central program, priorities, and budget to match the current objectives and the medium-term plan derived from them, and is urging its international and national committees to contribute very actively to the new approaches.

MEMBERSHIP

ICOM membership is open to all institutions and individuals approved by the appropriate National Committee as complying with the ICOM definitions of a museum or museum professional respectively in the ICOM *Statutes*, on payment of the appropriate annual subscription. (In countries without a National Committee, membership is regulated and managed by the ICOM Secretariat in Paris.)

In July 2008, ICOM had over 27,000 members, including over 1000 institutional members, organized through 118 National Committees, for which a minimum of five paid-up members are required. In addition, there were 100 members in 33 countries and territories that do not have a national committee, so in total ICOM has members in 151 countries. In order to encourage and assist membership development in less developed countries as indicated by appropriate UN and World Bank indexes, there is a 50% reduction in both institutional and individual subscriptions for such countries.

Although 65 of the 118 National Committees currently benefit from this membership subsidy, the percentage of members assisted in this way remains very low, because in most of these countries the ICOM committees are very small due to the limited number of museum professionals and due to the small number and size of museums. As for the Member States of UNESCO that do not currently have an ICOM National Committee, ICOM seeks to ensure that there is an official national correspondent, usually the national museum, the culture ministry or the UNESCO national commission, which receives regular information and publications from ICOM.

Each ICOM member in good standing is entitled to take a full part in the work of both their own national committee as well as one international committee of their choosing, and they can seek and hold office in either or both. Each is also eligible to be nominated by their national or international committee for the triennial election to serve as President of ICOM or one of the officers of ICOM, or as a member of its governing Executive Council. However, with great variations in the number of members in each country and region, ICOM uses an indirect franchise in order to try to achieve a much more balanced geographical representation at its governance level than would be possible with a one member—one vote system (under which Europe might well take most of the elected positions at each triennial election). Therefore, regardless of their size in terms of membership, in all elections each national and international committee exercises five votes, as determined by the committee's members in advance of the vote. (International Affiliated Organizations have three votes each.) In addition, the chairpersons of each national and international committee and international affiliated organization serve *ex officio* as members of ICOM's Advisory Committee.

National committees elect their own national officers and decide their own program of activities. In some countries, the ICOM National Committee serves as a national museums association, undertaking a wide range of programs, liaison with government on, for example, museum and heritage policy and financing, and activities such as meetings, conferences, and publishing. However, where there is a large, long-established, and well-developed national association, as in the United States or United Kingdom already undertaking much of this work, the ICOM National Committee will typically have a more limited role—for example, concentrating on international rather than domestic affairs and on membership promotion, recruitment, and management on behalf of ICOM internationally.

COOPERATIVE PARTNERSHIPS

The ICOM's key, and longest-established, partnership is with UNESCO; the first formal agreement between the two being adopted less than 3 months after the two organizations were formally established in the Autumn of 1946. For much of the following six decades, ICOM and its work was subsidized directly by UNESCO, and its Secretariat was housed within UNESCO offices. Over the past two decades or so UNESCO's policy toward its former Category A NGOs has changed, with a reduction and finally a withdrawal of operating subsidies and their replacement by opportunities to undertake contract work for UNESCO. More recently because of UNESCO's own office space problems, the ICOM Secretariat had to move out of the free accommodation in the *Maison de l'UNESCO* into rented accommodation nearby.

Informetrics–International
Council

Historically, ICOM has undertaken leading roles in the research and editing of UNESCO's cultural heritage publications programs, notably the quarterly journal *Museum* (now *Museum International*), and continues to run the UNESCO–ICOM Museum Information Centre (the successor to Documentation Centre, established in 1947). The ICOM has been a close partner in many UNESCO cultural heritage campaigns and initiatives, particularly museum development assistance and staff training programs in many parts of the world. For example, the world's first *Basic Syllabus for Museum Professional Training* was drawn up by ICOM for UNESCO in 1971, while the two bodies continue to work closely together in the new UNESCO/ICOM Museum Training Programme begun in 2004, initially as a part of the UN's proposed Iraq Reconstruction Programme, but later made available more generally with both printed and online resources centered around *Running a Museum: A Practical Handbook* (original editions in English, Arabic, and French, 2005), and a program of UNESCO training workshops run with ICOM participation. For details of the UNESCO/ICOM Museum Training Programme and links to its publications, etc., see UNESCO's Web site.[7]

ICOM has also been, and remains today, closely involved with a number of UNESCO's most important cultural heritage protection and promotion programs and international conventions, notably

- The 1954 *Convention on the Protection of Cultural Property in the Event of Armed Conflict ("Hague Convention")* of 1954 and its 1954 and 1999 *Protocols*.
- The UNESCO Convention on the Means of Prohibiting and Preventing the Illicit Import, Export and Transfer of Ownership of Cultural Property, 1970.
- The UNESCO Convention for the Safeguarding of the Intangible Cultural Heritage, 2003.

In each case, ICOM is accredited to an advisory body attending their related Intergovernmental Committees.

Other important links with international intergovernmental organizations include a long-standing partnership with the Rome-based International Centre for the Study of the Preservation and Restoration of Cultural Property (ICCROM) ever since its establishment in 1959, and ICOM's status as an NGO accredited to the Economic and Social Council of the United Nations (ECOSOC). Most recently, after several years of informal links and communications, in 2007 ICOM established a formal partnership with the World Intellectual Property Organization (WIPO), and is currently working closely with WIPO's Traditional Knowledge, Genetic Resources, and Traditional Cultural Expressions/Folklore studies in particular.

The ICOM also has close relations with many NGOs. At the national level, there are almost always close links and cooperation with any national museum associations and similar bodies, while a number of the International Committees similarly have links with other international academic and professional bodies in their various fields of interest.

At the international level, ICOM has always had close relations with the International Council on Monuments and Sites (ICOMOS) since its formation in 1965; the two organizations have mutual observer status representation at each other's conferences and executive councils. There have also been links for some years between some equivalent international committees of the two bodies. In June 2008, it was agreed that this kind of twinning cooperation should be established between all relevant ICOM and ICOMOS international committees.

From 1967 onward, ICOM welcomed and actively supported various initiatives toward international cooperation between the growing number of national federations of Friends of Museums organizations. Since the formalizing of this with the establishment of the World Federation of Friends of Museums (WFFM) as a new international NGO in 1975, ICOM has always been an active partner and enthusiastic supporter of the organization's work and its triennial Congresses. Today the WFFM brings together almost 50 national Friends organizations, and represents an estimated two million individual members of Friends organizations around the world.

In 1995, ICOM and ICOMOS entered into a formal cooperation agreement with two other UNESCO-linked NGOs: the International Federation of Library Associations and Institutions (IFLA) and the International Council on Archives through the establishment of the International Committee of the Blue Shield (ICBS) as a standing joint committee to facilitate professional and technical cooperation and coordination in relation to all kinds of emergencies affecting, or threatening, any kind of cultural property, whether building or site, library, archive, or a museum or art collection. More recently, the four ICBS organizations have been joined by a fifth: the Coordinating Council of Audiovisual Archives Associations (CCAAA).

GOVERNANCE

ICOM follows the fairly standard structure of an Association under the French *Loi des Associations de 1 juillet de 1901*. The ultimate authority is the annual General Assembly, which consists of all individual, student, supporting, and honorary members and the designated representatives of institutional members. However, only those individual members and representatives of institutional members who have been designated as voting delegates by National Committees, International Committee, and Affiliated Organization have the right to vote. The General Assembly adopts and amends the *Statutes*, its own Rules of Procedure, determines the overall policy and program of the organization and the location and themes of the Triennial General Conferences, and approves the budget, rates of subscription and the audited accounts. Once every three years, the General Assembly also elects the President, other Officers, and the Executive Council.

The President is elected for a 3-year term of office and can be reelected for a second term of the same duration. The President sets the strategic orientations for the activities of ICOM in its capacity as an international organization representing museums and museum professionals. The President represents ICOM in all civil acts and the signature of the President binds ICOM in contracts and agreements with third parties. The President convenes and chairs the meetings of the General Assembly and the Executive Council, and after consultation with the Executive Council as appropriate, also makes appointments to Standing Committees and representatives of ICOM to other bodies, conferences, meetings, etc.

The Executive Council is the decision-making body of ICOM, and consists of a total of 15 elected members: the President, 2 Vice-Presidents, Treasurer, and 11 other members, all elected once every 3 years in the General Assembly, together with the Chairperson of the Advisory Committee as an *ex officio* member.

The Council meets in ordinary session at least twice a year, one of these meetings being held in association with the annual Ordinary General Assembly, at the same time and place. The Executive Council ensures the good management of ICOM, overseeing the various resources of ICOM (financial, human, intellectual, and technical) and their development, safeguarding ICOM's reputation, international esteem, and public regard. The President, Vice-Presidents, and the Treasurer form the Bureau of the Executive Council, which has the power to resolve urgent issues, reporting on any action taken to the full Executive Council as soon as possible.

The Advisory Committee consists of the Chairpersons (or their appointed representatives) of every National and International Committee, Regional Alliance, and Affiliated Organization, and meets at least once a year in ordinary session, around the same date and at the same location as one of the Executive Council meetings. The Advisory Committee advises the Executive Council and the General Assembly on matters concerning the policies, programs, procedures, and finances of ICOM, and may propose amendments to the *Statutes*. It also advises on matters and activities in the general interest of ICOM referred to it by the Executive Council or the General Assembly.

The Chairperson and two Vice-Chairpersons of the Advisory Committee are elected by the membership of the Committee for a 3-year term of office, and may serve two consecutive terms. The Chairperson of the Advisory Committee convenes and chairs the meetings of the Committee, serves as an *ex officio* member of the Executive Council and as the Elections Officer of ICOM and finally, as an *ex officio* member of the Board of all Regional Alliances.

In addition to the Advisory Committee and the National and International Committees, ICOM has a small number of specialist Standing Committees, appointed for 3 year terms by the President after consultation with the Advisory Committee and Executive Council. Each has a specific remit and a membership of around 10 appointed members, with the President and Director General as *ex officio* members in addition.

The Chairperson and members of the Ethics Committee, first established in 1986, are eminent senior members of ICOM. The Committee's mission is to monitor the provisions and application of the ICOM Code of Ethics for Museums (first adopted in 1986 as the ICOM Code of Professional Ethics, and last revised by on the recommendation of the Committee in 2006)[8] and to advise the Executive Council in relation to the apparent or alleged serious violations of the Code. It also reviews other Codes of Ethics that may be developed by the International Committees concerning their special fields of interest and/or expertise, and reports to the Executive Council and General Assembly on any matters relating to the Code of Ethics or its application that the Committee thinks appropriate.

The Legal Affairs Committee was established in 2002 in the light of the increasingly complex legal and intellectual property matters that are seen to be affecting museums and the work of museum professional. In addition to ICOM members, the Committee is fortunate to have on it a number of distinguished specialist lawyers who volunteer their services to ICOM through the Committee. In addition to acting as an internal advisory body to ICOM, and in particular to the President, Director General, Executive Council, Advisory Committee and International Committees and its component bodies on legal questions relating to their governance and administration, the Committee is mandated to examine on its own initiative the broader environment of evolving legal issues affecting museums, museum professionals, and the wider cultural heritage sector today.

Two of the major issues currently being worked on by the Committee are a review of current trends in intellectual property law and its application so far as these relate to museums and related bodies, and the launching of a system of dispute resolution through mediation rather than court actions over disputes concerning museums, for example, over the ownership or the claim for a return of cultural objects in museum collections. The four Standing Committees each meet once or twice a year in plenary session, but nowadays carry out much of their business throughout the year by electronic communication.

Two other Standing Committees are particularly concerned with ICOM's internal affairs. The Finance and Resources Committee, established in 2002, reviews and advises on longer-term financial and investment policy and practice, while the Standing Committee on International Committees assists the Advisory Committee and

Informetrics–International Council

Informetrics–International
Council

Executive Council in reviewing policy and practice in relation to the establishment and operation of ICOM's International Committees.

The work of ICOM generally, and in particular that of the General Assembly, Executive Council, Bureau and Advisory Committee, is supported by a small Paris-based Operational Secretariat, consisting of the Director General and other staff members of ICOM, and which is the operational centre of ICOM. The Secretariat evaluates, initiates, and manages operational programs and contracts, manages membership, finances, the UNESCO–ICOM Information Centre and ICOM's publications, and promotes the identity of the Organization.

The Director General is the Chief Executive Officer, appointed by the Executive Council, is responsible to the Council for the efficient and effective management of ICOM, for the resources required for the functioning of ICOM and the daily operations of the Secretariat. The Director General also has important responsibilities for promoting the interests of ICOM and communication both externally, to partner organizations, other bodies and the media, and internally, to ICOM's members and committees. On a day-to-day basis, the Director General reports directly to the President of ICOM.

INTERNATIONAL COMMITTEES AND AFFILIATED ORGANIZATIONS

It is through its International Committees that ICOM achieves its major objectives and programs: the exchange of scientific information at an international level, the development of professional standards, and the adoption of rules and recommendations on best practice relating to their areas of specialization and expertise.

All individual members of ICOM (and representatives of institutional members) are entitled to register as full ("voting") members in any one International Committee of their choice, and to seek and hold office in their chosen Committee. In addition, a member may attend meetings of any other Committee (on payment of the required conference fee if applicable). Subject to the *Statutes of ICOM* and the *Model Rules for International Committees*, each is free to organize and run itself as its voting members decide in terms of meetings, research and other programs, committee publications, etc. However, each Committee is expected to hold a professional meeting at least once a year, and in the year of the Triennial General Conference of ICOM that meeting should be held within the overall program of the General Conference.

The 30 International Committees vary greatly in size. Some are small specialist groups with less than a 100 members focusing on a very specific area of museum collections or practices, while other are many times larger. The Conservation Committee (ICOMCC) is so big (with over a thousand members) and so wide in its scope, that in addition to its participation in the triennial General Conference it organizes a major international scientific conference of its own every 3 years (normally in the year following the ICOM Triennial Conference). Though there is no formal distinction between them, in practice the International Committees can be divided into two categories: those that focus on a specific type of museum or museum collection, and what may be termed as interdisciplinary committees that deal with a specific museum-related discipline relevant to most or all kinds of museum or similar institution.

The following are the 19 types of museum- or collection-based International Committees: CAMOC — Collections and Activities of Museums of Cities, CIMAM—Museums and Collections of Modern Art, CIMCIM–Museums and Collections of Musical Instruments, CIPEG—Egyptology, CIMUSET—Museums and Collections of Science and Technology, COSTUME—Museums and Collections of Costume, DEMHIST—Historic House Museums, GLASS—Museums and Collections of Glass, ICDAD—Museums and Collections of Decorative Arts and Design, ICFA—Museums and Collections of Fine Arts, ICLM—Literary Museums, ICME—Museums and Collections of Ethnography, ICOMAM—Museums of Arms and Military History, ICMEMO—Memorial Museums in Remembrance of the Victims of Public Crimes, ICOMON—Money and Banking Museums, ICMAH—Museums and Collections of Archaeology and History, ICR—Regional Museums, NATHIST—Museums and Collections of Natural History, and UMAC—University Museums and Collections.

The following are the 11 interdisciplinary subject International Committees: AVICOM—Audiovisual, Image and Sound Technologies, CECA—Education and Cultural Action, CIDOC—Documentation, ICAMT—Architecture and Museum Techniques, ICEE—Exhibition Exchange, ICOFOM—Museology, ICOM-CC—Conservation, ICMS—Security, ICTOP—Training of Personnel, INTERCOM—Management, and MPR—Marketing and Public Relations.

National Committees and their members in certain regions of the world are also grouped into a number of ICOM Regional Alliances as follows: ASPAC—Asia and Pacific, ICOM-ARAB (Middle East and North Africa), ICOM-EUROPE, ICOM-SEE (South-East Europe), and LAC—Latin America and Caribbean.

ICOM also has 17 International Affiliated Organizations: AEOM—Association of European Open-Air Museums, AFRICOM—International Council of African Museums, AIMA—International Association of Agricultural Museums, AMOI—Association of Museums of the Indian Ocean, CAM—Commonwealth Association of Museums, HO!E—Hands On! Europe Association of Children's Museums, IACM—International Association of Custom Museums, IAMFA—International Association of Museum Facility Administrators, IAMH—International

Association of Museums of History, IATM—International Association of Transport and Communication Museums, ICAM—International Confederation of Architectural Museums, ICMM—International Congress of Maritime Museums, MAC—Museums Association of Caribbean, MINOM—International Movement for a New Museology, PIMA—Pacific Islands Museums Association, SADCAMM—Southern Africa Development Community Association of Museums and Monuments, SIBMAS—International Association of Libraries and Museums of the Performing Arts.

In recent years, there has been a growing, and welcome, trend for two or more international committees to meet together to consider matters of mutual interest, and also to include other relevant organizations in their annual meetings. With the recent agreement to promote closer cooperation between the International Committees of ICOM and the International Scientific Committees of ICOMOS more joint meetings are anticipated.

ACTIVITIES

The highlight of ICOM's program is the General Conference, held once every 3 years in different parts of the world (most recently Melbourne 1998, Barcelona 2001, Seoul 2004, and Vienna 2007, with the next in Shanghai in 2010), and which typically attracts well over 2000 members.

Though the conference as such lasts 6 days, it is usually preceded the previous week by preparatory meetings of the Executive Council and Advisory Committee as well as meetings of the four Standing Committees, of any *ad hoc* working or project groups, and often of the Boards of the International Committees and Regional Alliances. The Conference begins with an opening ceremony involving the representatives of the host country and the leading partner organizations, including the Director-General of UNESCO or his personal representative. The rest of the opening day is devoted to plenary sessions and discussions on the chosen General Conference theme, led by invited distinguished keynote speakers and expert panels.

Days 2–4 are primarily devoted to sessions of the 30 International Committees, which are open to all registered Conference participants, and it is expected that at least some of these sessions will address the General Conference theme from the perspective of each Committee's specialization and field of expertise. Most Committees also arrange visits to museums or other institutions of particular interest to the Committee's specialist members. During the 3 days, the International Committees also set aside up to half a day for their triennial business meeting. At this all voting members of the Committee (including absent members represented by proxy) consider the administrative and financial reports of its Chairperson, Treasurer, and Board, adopt the forward program of

meetings and activities, elect Officers and Board for the following 3 years, and agree to the preparations for the ICOM General Assembly, including mandating the Committee's voting members on matters to be decided at the forthcoming ICOM General Assembly. In parallel with the 3 days of meetings of the International Committees there is always a large Trade Fair presenting museum and related supplies and services.

Day 5 of the Triennial General Conference is traditionally set aside for whole day study visits, while the final day is the meeting of the General Assembly of ICOM as a whole at which both reports on the past triennial period and proposals for the future policies, programs, and priorities are considered and adopted. Voting for the election of the President, Vice-Presidents, Treasurer, and Executive Council members for the following 3 years takes place throughout the week, and the results of the elections are announced in the General Assembly. Finally, but by no means least, the General Assembly debates, and if it thinks fit, adopts Resolutions setting out ICOM's policies and objectives, or responding to matters of concern. The full texts of the almost 400 General Assembly Resolutions from the founding meeting of 1946 to the most recent (Vienna 2007), available on line,[9] provide a comprehensive overview of the development of ICOM's policies and objectives, and indeed the changing focus of the principal concerns and priorities of ICOM over more than six decades.

ICOM also organizes important thematic conferences and seminars from time to time, most of which have played a significant role in developing policy and providing advice on professional practice over many areas through the production of conference or seminar publications. Examples have included the review of museum needs in Africa (in Benin, Ghana, and Togo), in Arab countries (in Amman, Jordan), on heritage protection and the struggle against illicit trafficking in cultural property (Tunis), on museums, heritage and tourism (in La Paz, Bolivia), and museum emergency planning and response (Hyderabad, India).

However, while the General Conference is very important, in terms of the total professional impact it is probably fair to say that the annual meetings of the 30 International Committees amount to ICOM's greatest impact on museums and the professional overall. The Committees aim to meet in all parts of the world, usually for a full week or more, with a program including lectures, discussions, and study visits to local museum of special interest. Many of these meetings have developed and promoted important advances in policy and practice.

ICOM has also undertaken many significant campaigns, most notably in relation to the protection of cultural property and the struggle against illicit trafficking in stolen, looted, or otherwise illegally transferred antiquities, works of art, and other cultural property. Recognizing that museums have often been the final destination of such material either directly through dealers or indirectly through

Informetrics–International Council

Informetrics–International
Council

collectors who eventually donate their collections to museums, as long ago as 1970 ICOM adopted a policy statement on the Ethics of Acquisition, and this was further developed in the 1986 ICOM Code of Professional Ethics. The ICOM also works closely with other international bodies, notably UNESCO, but also INTERPOL and the International Customs Union, in this work, and has published a number of *One Hundred Missing Objects...* books describing and illustrating typical missing items from particular countries or regions: so far these cover Angkor (Cambodia), Africa, Latin America, and South-East Europe, while "Red Lists" have been published for Afghanistan and Iraq.

PUBLICATIONS AND MEDIA

Since its establishment, ICOM has produced a regular newsletter for members and interested persons: *Nouvelles de l'ICOM/ICOM News* (with a Spanish edition as well since 1999). During its six decades of existence, ICOM has also published a very large number of books and reports, some produced centrally, but the majority have been published by the International and National Committees, most of which have also produced journals or newsletters. A complete catalog of ICOM publications from 1947 to date is available online on the ICOM Web site. For details of the online catalog of ICOM publications, see ICOM's Web site.[10]

ICOM also moved into new media at a relatively early date, with the launch of both its overall Internet policy and first Web site at the Stavanger General Conference in 1995. Most International Committees and many National Committees have since become very active in this field with their own Web sites (linked to the central ICOM Web site) and electronic publications. One of the long-term aims of the 1995 policy was to seek to establish "dot museum" as a top-level Internet domain controlled by the profession to ensure that only organizations deserving the title should be able to use the domain, and in 2000 Internet

Corporation for Assigned Names and Numbers (ICANN), the controlling body for the Internet, approved the establishment of the new domain.

REFERENCES

1. Office International des Musées. *Manuel de la Conservation et Restauration des Tableaux*, Institut International de Coopération Intellectuelle: Paris, 1939.

2. International Museums Office. *Manual on the Conservation of Paintings*, International Institute of Intellectual Cooperation: Paris, 1940 (Reprint of the English edition, with a new Foreword on the history of the International Museums Office and its work by P. J. Boylan, 1997, Archetype Publications, London).

3. Office International des Musées. *La Protection des Monuments et Oevres d'Art en Temps de Guerre*, Institut International de Coopération Intellectuelle: Paris, 1939.

4. Baghli, S.A.; Boylan, P.; Herreman, Y. *History of ICOM (1946–1996) [also French edition: Histoire de l'ICOM (1946–1996)]*, International Council of Museums: Paris, 1998.

5. ICOM. *Statutes of ICOM*, International Council of Museums: Paris, 2007 (also in French and Spanish editions). Available at http://icom.museum/statutes.html (accessed July 22, 2008).

6. ICOM. *Our Global Vision, Notre Vision Globale, Nuestra Vision Global*, International Council of Museums: Paris, 2008. Available at http://icom.museum/strat_plan.html (accessed July 22, 2008).

7. http://portal.unesco.org/culture/en/ev.phpURL_ID=35511&URL_DO=DO_TOPIC&URL_SECTION=201.html.

8. ICOM. *ICOM Code of Ethics for Museums*, International Council of Museums: Paris, 2006. Available at http://icom.museum/ethics.html (accessed August 16, 2008).

9. ICOM. *Resolutions Adopted by ICOM's General Conferences, 1946–2007*, International Council of Museums: Paris. Available at http://icom.museum/resolutions/ (accessed August 18, 2008).

10. http://icom.museum/ilca.html (accessed August 18, 2009).

International Council on Archives (ICA)

Perrine Canavaggio
International Council on Archives, Paris, France

Marcel Caya
Department of History, University of Quebec at Montreal (UQAM), Montreal, Quebec, Canada

Abstract

Founded in 1948, the International Council on Archives (ICA) is an international body representing the world community of records and archives managers. Its membership includes national archives administrations, professional associations, archival institutions of regional and local authorities, and private organizations, as well as individual archivists. An independent, nongovernmental, not-for-profit organization, the ICA is headquartered in Paris, France. As the leading international nongovernmental organization (NGO) for archives and archivists, ICA continues to work in cooperation with UNESCO and NGOs in related areas to realize shared objectives.

THE INTERNATIONAL COUNCIL ON ARCHIVES

The International Council on Archives (ICA) is a nongovernmental organization (NGO) bringing together national archive administrations, professional associations of archivists, regional and local archives, and archives of other organizations as well as individual archivists. As the professional organization for the world archival community, ICA has a global network of around 1500 institutional members in 195 countries and territories, and over 270 archivists and records managers as individual members. ICA has its registered office in Paris, France; it is a nonprofit organization set up under French law.

THE BEGINNINGS

The idea for an ICA had long been around. The Institute for Intellectual Cooperation, acting under the aegis of the League of Nations, made the first attempt after World War I by creating a Permanent Consultative Committee on archives in 1931. This committee published the first *International Guide on Archives* in 1934. Several factors contributed to the creation of the ICA in 1948. The first was the choice of Paris as the site of the headquarters of the United Nations Educational, Scientific, and Cultural Organization (UNESCO), which in the immediate postwar years was concerned with promoting NGOs in its field. In 1946, under the influence of an American conservator Chauncey J. Hamlin, an international council for museums (ICOM) had been set up. On a similar model, following the distribution of proposals at the international level in the autumn of 1947, and under the influence and tenacity of Dr. Solon J. Buck, then Archivist of the United States, a small group of experts met in Paris and agreed on June 9, 1948, to establish an "International Council on Archives," with the then Director-General of the Archives de France, Charles Samaran, as chairman. Charles Braibant succeeded him in 1950. The first assembly of the Council was held following a meeting of the group of experts in Paris, on August 21 and 22, 1950, at the UNESCO headquarters.

During its first 50 years, ICA functioned more or less as a centralized international organization, thanks to the support of UNESCO with leadership provided by the Paris Secretariat and the national archivists of member countries. (Thanks to the hospitality of the Archives de France, the Paris Secretariat has been housed since 1960 at the Archives nationales, 60 rue des Francs-Bourgeois in Paris.) Its various committees brought together experts in many fields to undertake study and research, prepare, and publish reports on various archival functions and issues as well as provide contents for various meetings including the quadrennial Congress and the International Conference of the Round Table on Archives (CITRA).

The first International Congress on Archives was held in Paris, from August 23 to 26, 1950; it brought together 360 archivists from 35 countries. The first Round Table on Archives was held in Paris in 1954 and, since then, meets every year except on the year a Congress is held.

Archivum, the first official journal of ICA, was created with the publication of the proceedings of the first Congress in 1950. It soon extended its contents to cover, in addition to the proceedings of congresses, the International Archival Bibliography, the International Directory of Archives, archival legislation around the world, and special issues on specific theme, such as notarial archives, municipal archives, etc.

Encyclopedia of Library and Information Sciences, Fourth Edition DOI: 10.1081/E-ELIS4-120044715
Copyright © 2017 by Taylor & Francis. All rights reserved.

Informetrics–International Council

Regional branches and sections were eventually created to allow the active participation of more countries sharing similar conditions: from 1968 to 1982, eight regional branches were created. With the creation in 1976 of the Section of Professional Archivists Associations (SPA) and the Section of International Organizations (SIO), sections brought together professionals sharing similar problems; the creation of the Section of Municipal Archives (SMA) inaugurated a trend away from central government archives which led to the creation of several other sections based on types of archives.

Since its creation, ICA has cooperated regularly with its sister organizations, particularly IFLA, ICOM, and ICOMOS. In this context, it has actively participated in the activities of the International Committee of the Blue Shield of which it is a founding member.

Created in 1996, the International Committee of the Blue Shield (ICBS) is formed by five NGOs: ICA, the Coordinating Council of Audiovisual Archives Associations (CCAAA), the International Council of Museums (ICOM), the International Council on Monuments and Sites (ICOMOS), and the International Federation of Library Associations and Institutions (IFLA) share the mission to work for the protection of the world's cultural heritage by coordinating preparations to meet and respond to emergency situations. Its main objectives are to facilitate international responses to threats or emergencies threatening cultural property and to encourage safeguarding and respect for cultural property especially by promoting risk preparedness. The Blue Shield is the symbol equivalent of the Red Cross used for marking cultural sites to be protected from attack in the event of armed conflict.

1948–1989 THE COLD WAR

Thanks to the ICA, the cold war did not prevail in the archives field. The Council played the unique role of establishing a forum for professional meeting and exchange between archivists from East and West as well as promoting discussion and cooperation beyond political divisions. These exchanges focused on issues of common interest, particularly in three technical areas dealing with microfilm, restoration of documents, and buildings. The ICA developed those exchanges largely with the intellectual and financial help of UNESCO during that period.

The main objective then was to open access to archives to allow historians to compare sources from diverse provenances; the archives of countries and institutions often convey significance beyond their own frontiers and activities: it is notably the case with diplomatic, military, university, and bank archives as much as it is the case with the records of international organizations which can inform on partners and users. In order to improve access, ICA has always promoted cooperation through two different while complementary means:

- *Microfilm reprography* (security, acquisition, and replacement) to complement existing archival holdings, reconstitute incomplete ones, settle or lessen legal dispute; the ICA has thus promoted bilateral agreements to microfilm in order to remedy the absence or the lack of complete textual resources.
- Publication of the *Guides to the Sources of the History of Nations* in three series from 1960 to 1970 to enable researchers to know the sources preserved outside their region by other countries, to identify them, and to promote their processing. Sixty volumes were thus published between 1958 and 1984; they provide an inventory of sources concerning Latin America, Africa, and Asia.

From 1960, during a period when many countries gained their independence and others put an end to their colonial power, priority was *given to the development of archives* in the new countries with a number of programs created for developing countries and the creation of regional branches to bring them together. A Committee on Archival Development (ICA/CAD) was formed in 1970. It operated the International Archival Development Fund (FIDA), which received major donations for some developing countries (Algeria, Iran, Nigeria, and Yugoslavia). While it enabled seminars and study missions to be held, it was not given the continuous support it needed. Since the beginning of the 1970s, almost all the developing countries have established archival services.

Thanks to its close cooperation with ICA, UNESCO has published a series of archival studies known as the Records and Archives Management Program (RAMP). More than 100 studies dealt with basic professional issues covering records and archives management in areas such as preservation, legislation, archival theory, and practices. They were authored by international experts and published in English, French, and Spanish. They have been valued a great deal, notably by professionals in developing countries. Many of these studies have been reissued on CD by UNESCO in 2008. Although some studies are now dated as a result of technological advances, others remain highly topical. The CD is intended as a working guide of selected RAMP studies and, as such, contains only a limited number of titles. The complete series can be accessed from UNESCO's Web site at: http://unesdoc.unesco.org/ulis/search_form.html.

At the same time, a long-term legal discussion was maintained within ICA to respond to the major and recurrent issue of the unresolved archival legal disputes, inherited from the past. While traditionally, articles dealing with archives were included in treaties during the seventeenth to the nineteenth centuries, no peace treaty was signed in 1945 with the defeated countries; therefore, many issues have never been settled and no systematic effort was made to return archival holdings seized during the hostilities. The archival question was not included in

Informetrics–International Council

the independence agreements with the new countries; new States found themselves without documentation for their historic rights.

The building and reconstitution of the archival heritage of those countries whose archives, in great part, are held in repositories of developed countries has been debated many times during meetings of the CITRA. The Declaration of the Executive Board at Guanzhou in 1995 on the settlement of archival claims has recommended to take a pragmatic approach; in cooperation with UNESCO, the ICA has provided a set of legal concepts and principles such as the inalienability and imprescriptibility of public records, provenance, and respect for the integrity of archival fonds, the right of access, and the right of reproduction. In order to make these rights effective and prevent the splitting of archival fonds, UNESCO has recommended the introduction of the concept of shared heritage since 1979.

The Council of Europe has published in 1997 a reference document prepared by the ICA Committee on Archival Legal Matters to facilitate the settlement of archival claims arising from war, military occupancy, and States succession.

With the end of the USSR and of several totalitarian (or repressive) regimes in the world, great masses of archives from police and security units of those regimes appeared and new legal problems emerged, particularly their access; it was urgent to help archivists work in a democratic environment and to reinforce the role and position of the National Archives. It is in that context that the issue of professional ethics was launched in 1992 within the Section of Professional Associations (SPA) generating the ICA Code of Ethics adopted in 1996. At the present time SPA is considering a revision to this Code in the light of a member survey.

The Council of Europe has helped ICA a great deal since 1993 to promote the modernization of archives in Europe through East–West seminars and financial support for expert missions. ICA has also invested greatly in promoting the accessibility of archives. This effort was reinforced in 2000 by Recommendation no. R 13 of the Council of Europe about a European Policy on access to archives and in 2001 on the teaching of history. The Council of Europe has adopted the first intergovernmental standard on the issue and recognized the right of people to know their history as a cultural human right.

ICA TODAY

From an association of directors of national institutions, the ICA has evolved toward a more complex organization bringing together professional associations and individual archivists interested in researching, developing, and sharing their full range of archival expertise. As a result, the ICA has become the professional organization for the world archival community, dedicated to promoting the preservation, development, and use of the world's archival heritage.

The activities of the ICA complement those of national associations and institutions and continue to be an exclusive source and channel of professional expertise in those regions where national associations do not yet exist.

As the leading international NGO for archives and archivists, ICA continues to work in cooperation with UNESCO and NGOs in related areas to realize shared objectives.

Mission and Values

ICA's current mission and core values were officially adopted in 2004 and 2008. While it continues to focus on the promotion of archives and the role of archivists in achieving high standards of governance and democracy, it makes room for the inclusion of improved records management as a precondition of the creation of authentic, accurate, and meaningful archives.

As stated in the ICA Constitution, the mission of the International Council on Archives is:

> to promote the preservation and use of archives around the world. In pursuing this mission, ICA works for the protection and enhancement of the memory of the world and to improve communication while respecting cultural diversity. (Preamble ICA Constitution)

To promote the preservation and use of archives around the world, ICA aims to support the management and use of current records as well as archives and the preservation of the archival heritage, by sharing experiences, research, and ideas on professional archival and records management matters, and on the management and organization of archival institutions. Its objectives are to:

- Encourage and support the development of archives in all countries, in cooperation with other organizations, including international agencies, governmental, and nongovernmental.
- Promote, organize, and coordinate best practice, the development of standards and other activities in the field of records and archives management.
- Establish, maintain, and strengthen relations between archivists of all countries and between all institutions, professional bodies, and other organizations, public and private, wherever located, which are concerned with the administration or preservation of records and archives, or with the professional training of archivists, especially through the exchange of information.
- Facilitate the interpretation and use of archives by making their content more widely known and by encouraging greater access to them.

Therefore, as expressed in its 2008 Strategic Directions, ICA promotes the central role of record-keeping and archives in protecting the rights of individuals and states, and in supporting democracy and good governance. It works for the effective management of archives from the moment of their creation, the permanent preservation of archives as the documented memory of nations and societies, and the widest possible public access to that memory. It advocates the importance of archives management to policy-makers.

It sees its role as providing opportunities for professional contact, information exchanges, research, and education, which support records and archives professionals and other partners throughout the world. It also endeavors to take a leading part in developing best practices and standards for the records and archives profession.

Its core values were also revised and stated in the 2008 Strategic Directions document. They are expressed in the following statement: "In fulfilling ICA's mission, we strive to uphold the values of equality, diversity, openness, and mutual respect across national boundaries and cultural traditions. We will be as transparent as possible to our members and provide them with full value in return for their contributions (whether monetary or in kind) to the organization."

Definition of Archives

The current evolution of ICA has followed quite closely the extraordinary developments of the profession in recent years. While the English definition of the word "archives" remains focused on materials of enduring value, most archivists, even in the English-speaking world, are also concerned with the management of current records. At the international level, this widening of the focus has never been a problem since the words "records" and "archives" are often used interchangeably; in French, the word "archives" means both current records and records of enduring value.

The Glossary of the Society of American Archivists defines archives as "Materials created or received by a person, family, or organization, public or private, in the conduct of their affairs and preserved because of the enduring value contained in the information they contain or as evidence of the functions and responsibilities of their creator, especially those materials maintained using the principles of provenance, original order, and collective control; permanent records." Other meanings also provide definitions of archives as organizations, buildings, professional discipline, and collection of papers.

More importantly, the archival community has traditionally been more concerned by the recognition of the special character of records and archives as the "Materials created or received by a person, family, or organization, public or private, in the conduct of their affairs" preserved because of the value (not only enduring) of the information they contain or as evidence of the functions and responsibilities of their creator.

Members

From 17 countries in 1949–1950, the membership had grown to 117 countries in 1984 and to 195 countries and territories in 2008.

ICA now has a global network of around 1500 institutional members and over 250 individual members. Its membership comprises public and private archival institutions, associations, and individual members:

- Central archives directorates or national archival institutions: 236 members.
- National associations of professionals: 81 members.
- International associations: 42 members.
- Institutions concerned with, or interested in, the administration or preservation of records and archives, or with archival training and education: 873 members.
- Individuals working in the field of the administration or preservation of records and archives, or of the archival training and education: 258 individual members.

In order to give its members increased opportunities to be involved in projects, the members of ICA can participate in two types of groupings: the regional branches and the sections.

Regional Branches

Through its 13 branches, ICA provides a basis for exchange and common initiatives at the regional level, more closely aligned to specific needs resulting from particular environments. Members of ICA wishing to further the aims of ICA and to strengthen cooperation within a particular geographical area may group themselves into regional branches. The global network comprises 12 regional branches and one regional network; their creation was developed over a period of almost 40 years.

1968 SARBICA (Southeast Asian Regional Branch).
1969 ESARBICA (Eastern and Southern Africa Regional Branch).
1972 ARBICA (Arab Regional Branch).
1975 CARBICA (Caribbean Regional Branch).
1976 SWARBICA (South and West Asian Regional Branch).
1976 ALA (Association of Latin American Archives).
1977 WARBICA (West African Regional Branch).
1981 PARBICA (Pacific Regional Branch).
1982 CENARBICA (Central African Regional Branch).
1993 EASTICA (East Asian Regional Branch).
2000 EURASICA (Eurasia Regional Branch).
2001 EURBICA (European Regional Branch).
2004 NAANICA (North American Archival Network).

Regional branches have separate leadership and programs. For example, PARBICA has its own Work Plan 2008–2010 which is in line with the ICA Strategic Direction. It is developing a good governance toolkit project which will be translated and adapted in other languages. EURBICA has three ongoing main projects: EURONOMOS, a database providing the European archival legislation online; a methodology to train the trainers in records management; and a European competency model.

Sections

Institutional or individual members of ICA sharing common professional interests or activities and wishing to further the aims of ICA and to strengthen cooperation within their professional competence may group themselves into sections. ICA members may join more than one section. ICA's sections are established along professional interests; they address other types of concerns and stimulate research and information exchange in more specific areas.

There are presently 11 full-fledged sections; two more are provisional until it is demonstrated that there is sufficient interest to give them a permanent status.

- SAE—Section for Archival Education and Training: 43 members.
- SAN—Section on Notarial Records: 8 members.
- SAR—Section on Architectural Records: 21 members.
- SBL—Section for Business and Labour Archives: 100 members.
- SIO—Section for Archivists of International Organizations: 42 members.
- SKR—Section for Archives of Churches and Religious Denominations: 53 members.
- SMA—Section for Municipal Archives: 152 members.
- SPA—Section of Records Management and Archival Professional Associations: 81 members.
- SPO—Section on Sports Archives: 14 members.
- SPP—Section for Archives of Parliaments and Political Parties: 94 members.
- SUV—Section on University and Research Institution Archives: 161 members.
- SLA—Provisional Section on Literature and Art Archives: 6 members.
- SSG—Provisional Section on Sigillography: 10 members.

Each section elects a bureau and draws up its program of activities in cooperation with the Programme Commission of ICA.

Project Committees and Working Groups

ICA also forms committees and groups at various levels to work on specific projects and activities in support of the objectives defined by its Strategic Direction. Expert committees on various specific archival issues created since 1959 were abolished in 2004. They

were replaced by project working groups or ad hoc committees with short and dedicated mandate under the Programme Commission. Only one committee [Committee on Best Practices and Standards (ICA/CBPS)] is currently active as the professional home for the maintenance and development of standards and best practices and related activity within ICA. Building on its strength in the area of archival description, this Committee is currently expanding its scope to cover more aspects of professional activity.

FIDA: International Archival Development Fund

FIDA was set up in 1975 as a means of attracting funds internationally. However, in recent years, difficult financial conditions have limited what has been raised. On a smaller scale, ICA used its own resources to assist small projects, such as expert missions and regional meetings, where matching funds were available locally. (Since 2000, 5% of the dues of all members are set aside for FIDA.) Thanks to the additional contribution by a number of countries, it is able to support new initiatives, particularly training programs in less-developed countries.

Governance

The highest decision-making body in ICA is the Annual General Meeting which meets once a year during the Congress or the CITRA; it consists of delegates from national institutions and associations. Between Annual General Meetings, the government of ICA is in the hands of the Executive Board, which includes chairs of all regional branches and most sections, thus ensuring broad representation internationally and professionally.

The work of the Executive Board is supported by three commissions:

- The Management Commission brings together the ICA President and Vice-President in addition to the President of a Regional Branch, the Secretary General, and the Deputy Secretary Generals; it is responsible for the preparation of Executive Board meetings and making management decisions between meetings of the Executive Board.
- The Programme Commission consists of the Vice-President Programme, who acts as chair, and of members appointed by the Management Commission. It is responsible for the preparation and execution of the professional and technical program; in that capacity, it also monitors the activities of regional branches, sections, and committees.
- The Audit Commission consists of a chair, known as the Internal Auditor, and four members elected by the members of the AGM. It is responsible for the evaluation of the performance of the ICA programs and of its

Informetrics–International Council

external and internal communications. It reports to the Executive Board and to the Annual General Meeting.

In addition to these three commissions, the work of the Executive Board is supported by a CITRA Bureau, composed of six elected members and a few ex-officio members to organize the annual International Conferences of the Round Table on Archives (CITRA) and to draw up the CITRA program.

The Secretariat is responsible for the day-to-day operation of ICA's organization, including communications with other ICA bodies and individual members, relations with partner organizations, and administration of ICA's governance meetings. It comprises a small staff based in Paris and is headed by the Secretary General, who acts as the organization's Executive Director.

Elected Officers

Since 2007, the top management of ICA is composed of a President and eight Vice-Presidents. Four Vice-Presidents are elected by the membership for Marketing and Promotion, Programme, CITRA, and Finances; the other four play that role by virtue of their particular function within ICA: host of the forthcoming congress, the chair of SPA, the representative of regional branches and the representative of sections. With the exception of the Vice-President of the CITRA, the elected officers are elected for a 2-year term, which may be renewed.

Budget

ICA has an annual budget of approximately €1,000,000, generated for the most part by dues from the members. The level of dues paid by national archival institutions is calculated on the basis of each country's gross national product as established by the International Monetary Fund. The dues of the associations are fixed according to the number of members. Part of the dues are allocated to the regional branches and the section; another portion provides the basis for the funding of projects approved by the Programme Commission. At the time of writing ICA has just started a review of the criteria used to calculate membership dues and the associated benefits.

ICA ACTIVITIES

Beyond the regular activities of ICA during the Congress, the CITRA and the publications, members are invited to submit projects which further the organization's objectives. The current Strategic Direction document includes six approved objectives, which provide the Programme Commission with a framework to make its decisions about projects submitted by members:

1. Raising awareness.
2. Influencing the development and use of new technologies.
3. Building capacity in the records and archives profession.
4. Strengthening the ICA network.
5. Improving the performance and accountability of ICA.
6. Building partnerships.

Congress

Every 4 years, in a different country, ICA holds an International Congress on Archives which can be attended by all archival professionals. The most recent congress was held in Kuala Lumpur in Malaysia in July 2008 on *Archives, Governance and Development*. The next one will take place in Brisbane, Australia, in 2012 on the theme of *Archives in a Digital Age*.

Previous Congresses presented a wide diversity of themes touching the multifaceted aspects of the profession.

- *1950 Paris:* Records management, micrography, private archives (mostly business archives), and bibliographies on archives.
- *1953 The Hague:* Terminology standardization, documentation, history of art and history museums, training, and public programs.
- *1956 Florence:* New buildings, archival appraisal, and private archives.
- *1960 Stockholm:* National archives, restoration, conservation, and photography; and economic and social history research.
- *1964 Brussels:* Modern methodology for the arrangement of archives.
- *1966 Washington, D.C. (Extraordinary Congress):* Opening archives to research.
- *1968 Madrid:* Improved access to archives and microfilm policy; history of archives; the Salvage and Restoration of the Italian Archival Heritage after the Inundation of November 1966; and records management.
- *1972 Moscow:* Records management and state archives; new techniques in archives; finding aids for research; and support for archives in developing countries.
- *1976 Washington, D.C.:* The pre-archival revolution; the technological revolution; the revolution in access and use; and the geo-archival revolution.
- *1980 London:* The academic, practical, and popular use of archives; the ICA: its achievement and its future.
- *1984 Bonn:* The challenge to archives: growing responsibilities and limited resources.
- *1988 Paris:* New archival material.
- *1992 Montreal:* The profession of the archivist in the information age.

Informetrics–International Council

- *1996 Beijing:* Archives at the end of the century: taking stock and looking ahead.
- *2000 Seville:* The archives of the new millennium in the information society.
- *2004 Vienna:* Archives, memory, and knowledge: http://www.wien2004.ica.org/fo/index.php.

While congresses before 2004 mostly consisted of a series of plenary sessions presenting wide-ranging reports on the evolution of the profession or the various aspects of a general theme, the Vienna 2004 Congress and the 2008 Kuala Lumpur meeting were organized along more dynamic lines presenting 10–15 parallel sessions attended by smaller audiences and allowing more direct discussion between the speakers and the audience. About 1200 participants came to the 2008 Congress in Kuala Lumpur to see 326 speakers presenting at 53 workshops and 169 sessions. Topics ranged from audiovisual archiving to indigenous knowledge, and "green archives buildings." ICA Commissions, Branches, and Sections used the opportunity to hold business meetings and the Annual General Assembly also took place. Many of the papers presented on that occasion are available on the Congress Web site (http://www.kualalumpur2008.ica.org/en). A selection of the papers will be published in the Congress *Proceedings*.

Conferences

In the intervening years of the Congresses, since 1954, there is an International Round Table Conference on Archives, also known as CITRA from the French acronym (Conférence Internationale de la Table Ronde des Archives). This is for representatives of national archive administrations, national professional associations, and the Chairs and secretaries of ICA sections. This Conference is accessible by invitation only and deals with strategic professional issues. The 41st CITRA was held in Quebec City in 2007. The papers are usually published in the *Proceedings*. The themes of the two more recent series of CITRA have been Archives and Society from 2001 to 2003 and Archives, Diversity, and Globalization for 2005–2008.

At the outset of Congresses and CITRA meetings, resolutions are usually adopted for the participants to implement in their respective countries.

Regional branches and sections regularly hold conferences and seminars.

Publications

The ICA Web site provides up-to-date information on the upcoming events and activities of ICA's bodies, branches, sections, and working groups (http://www.ica.org). It also offers a Resource Centre which contains hundreds of working documents, publications, and standards relevant to archival practice.

Comma, the ICA journal, is a merger of ICA publications *Archivum* (I–XLV), *Janus* (1983–1999), and *CITRA Proceedings*. It is edited in seven languages (Arabic, Chinese, English, French, German, Spanish, and Russian) and is usually published quarterly. Its main function is to disseminate research and discussion papers of interest to the membership of the organization, to the profession as a whole, and external readers. Printed on paper at the beginning, it moved in 2006 to a CD-ROM format. Three CD-ROMs have been published in 2006–2008. The 2008 Congress Proceedings will be published on paper as well as electronically, and it is possible that in the future paper publications will be reintroduced more generally.

Archivum was edited from 1951 to 2000 (no. 45) in five languages (English, French, German, Italian, and Spanish) and usually dealt with only one main subject. *Janus*, another ICA journal published between 1983 and 1999, was responsible for disseminating papers, reports, research work, and discussions of interest to the profession as a whole, mainly emanating from the activities of various ICA bodies. The *CITRA Proceedings* were printed as a separate publication from 1958 to 1999.

The newsletter *Flash* is published by ICA three times a year as a membership benefit. It conveys news on ICA activities and highlights current issues in archives. It can be downloaded from the ICA Web site.

The series *Studies* presents the works of ICA experts in a wide range of fields such as the management of electronic records, authenticity of electronic records, disaster prevention, control of radioactive waste information, and archival legal matters. The 19 *Studies* published are available on CD-ROM and can be downloaded from the ICA Web site.

Many sections and regional branches publish their own journal or a newsletter; most have their own Web site.

Projects

Since the 1990s, the emergence of information technologies has had a considerable impact on the archival profession, particularly for the creation, acquisition, processing, and dissemination of archives. The prevalence of computerized office work practices now requires the intervention of the archivist in the creation of records in the office. In order to ensure the preservation, authenticity, and integrity of records on a long-term basis, the archivist must be involved in all phases of the life of the record.

The new technological context has increased the needs for standardization and system interoperability, particularly in the area of *archival description*. Since the 1990s, ICA has adopted four professional standards (available on the ICA Web site):

- ICA-ISAD(G), the *International Standard for Archival Description* (General), provides guidance for the description of archival records.

Informetrics–International
Council

- ICA-ISAAR (CPF), the *International Standard Archival Authority Record for Corporate Bodies, Persons, and Families*, provides guidance for the creation of authority record information about creators of archival materials.
- ICA-ISDF, the *International Standard for Describing Functions*, provides guidance for the description of functions of records creators.
- ICA-ISDIAH, the *International Standard for Describing Institutions with Archival Holdings*, provides guidance for the description of holders of archives.

Other projects include the creation of dedicated open source software to facilitate the creation of databases for archival repositories and the exchange of the descriptive data they contain. The beta version 1.0 of *Access to Memory* (A to M) (available at http://ica-atom.org/) was launched in 2008, during the Kuala Lumpur Congress to cater for small archival institutions and allow them to publish their finding aids on the Web. It is based on freely available, multilingual open source software.

Terminology has been a long-time concern of ICA since the end of the 1950s. Special glossaries are available for several areas, such as sigillography and preservation. The first general Dictionary of Archival Terminology was published in 1984. A new approach to defining the language of the profession was recently adopted through discussion of the project Archipaedia, which proposed to prepare and publish a multifaceted, multilingual, and multimedia online tool to favor better understanding of archival terminology and practices in as many languages and cultural groups as possible.

The ICA *Code of Ethics* for archivists was adopted by ICA in 1996. It establishes high standards of professional conduct for the archival profession by providing an ethical framework for the guidance of members of the profession.

COOPERATION WITH OTHER ORGANIZATIONS

When other organizations have better expertise than ICA members, archives professionals are encouraged to join those specific organizations, instead of setting up their own group within ICA. For example, members interested in Audiovisual Archives are invited to contact the CCAAA of which ICA is a founding member.

ICA works closely with intergovernmental and NGOs. Most of these organizations are active mainly or partly in the cultural heritage field and/or in information management, business administration or in development of third world countries.

ICA maintains its status as an NGO recognized by UNESCO, with whom it has a Framework Agreement covering areas of joint interest; it regularly participates, as observer, in the meetings of the Information for All Program and has representatives in the various bodies of the memory of the world program. It has consultative status with the Economic and Social Council (ECOSOC of the UN), the International Federation of Library Associations and Institutions (IFLA) and the International Organization for Standardization (ISO) as well as observer status with the World Intellectual Property Organization (WIPO).

Throughout its 60 years of existence, ICA has constantly adapted to new environments and the information revolution. Its network of archival professionals is unique and encompasses the whole world and all facets of society. Facing a constant increase of the uses of archives and the expectations of society, it looks forward with confidence to new opportunities while continuing to work on the ever present problems of insufficient financial and human resources. In order to achieve significant results and encourage solidarity between its members, ICA must find additional allies and marshal energies and talents for the benefit of all its members and to further the cause of archives throughout the world.

BIBLIOGRAPHY

1. Access to archives. Council of Europe Publishing, 2005.
2. Council of Europe. *Reference Dossier on Archival Claims*, Strasbourg, January 1997.
3. Eckhart, G.F. Die Conseil internationale Archivrat: Vergangenheit, Gegenwart, Zukunft. Archivum **1980**, *XXIX*, 155–173.
4. Eckhart, G.F. Le Conseil international des archives: Ses réalisations et son avenir. Arch. Bibl. Belg. **1984**, *IV*, 3–24.
5. Kecskeméti, C. *Sovereignty, Disputed Claims, Professional Culture: Essays on Archival Policies*, Brussels, 2000. Archives et Bibliothèques de Belgique.
6. Robert, M.W. International archival adventures: A reminiscence. Am. Arch. Spring **1992**, *55*, 356–368.

International Council on Knowledge Management (ICKM)

Franz Barachini
Business Innovation Consulting—Austria, Langenzersdorf, Austria

Abstract

The objective of this entry is to explore the fundamental nature of knowledge management by examining relevant definitions, concepts, instruments, and strategies. It also reports on the development of the International Council on Knowledge Management (ICKM). ICKM is an association located in Vienna. The homonymous conference started in 2004 in Singapore with the launch of the first international conference on knowledge management. The tension between practitioners and academia is neither new nor limited to the field of knowledge management. The ability to bring these communities together will not only bridge the gap between the two worlds but also create the environment needed for the development of any discipline.

INTRODUCTION

Peter F. Drucker[1] was one of the first researchers to mention the term "knowledge worker." Since then, several approaches have focused on knowledge management initiatives, all of them pursuing one goal, to leverage the performance of individuals, groups, or companies. Knowledge management is regarded as an interdisciplinary field involving tasks such as learning, innovation, intellectual capital (IC) reporting (human, structure, relationships), and organizational optimization. The main challenge is how to discover, create, capture, share, and utilize knowledge via (social) networks. Knowledge management is not only an IT challenge, but mostly consists of motivating people to share valuable information so that IC of companies can be improved. Bontis,[2] Edvinsson and Malone,[3] as well as Sveiby[4] see IC as the "stock" of knowledge that exists in an organization at a particular point in time. A similar view is described by Nonaka and Takeuchi[5] who defined knowledge management as managing the stock of knowledge in an organization as it flows over time. Managing this stock remains a challenge, as there is the need to socialize and codify intangible (tacit) knowledge.

There are several various theories of knowledge management. Bonifacio et al.[6] characterize knowledge sharing and knowledge management as the process of creating, codifying, and disseminating knowledge. They claim that knowledge can be disseminated; however, this approach assumes the existence of an objective epistemology, so that all contextual, subjective, and social aspects of knowledge can be eliminated in favor of an objective and general codification. This is undoubtedly an interesting idea; however, individuals tend to interpret data immediately after acquiring it. It seems clear that different knowledge can be produced from the same chunk of information contained in different brains, no matter how this information is codified.

It would seem therefore that only information can be disseminated and exchanged and not knowledge. This view is also supported by the school of autopoietic epistemology which states that knowledge is a private, personal matter which is intuitively and strongly linked to a person's values and beliefs. Explicit knowledge is data and information that enable other people to create their own knowledge via a "structured coupling" process explained by Joia.[7] There are techniques existing such as sharing knowledge through common experience, through storytelling or microarticles—for all these techniques, the basis is information flow based on text, speech, smell, optics (behavior), or tangibles. This information is then interpreted by our brain according to our context knowledge, previous experiences, instincts, and intuitions. The usage of the terms "knowledge sharing" and "knowledge management" in this entry therefore refers to information exchange processes and various individual interpretations of transferred data. Thus, knowledge is created purely through information transfer and successful or unsuccessful knowledge sharing is a consequence thereof. This point of view has been explained in depth by Barachini[8] who asserts that knowledge management is performed in human brains only – all the rest is data and information management.

Scientists commonly recognize four types of knowledge:

1. Tangible and individual knowledge, characterized by fact knowledge
2. Tangible and collective knowledge, characterized by rules and written instructions

Encyclopedia of Library and Information Sciences, Fourth Edition DOI: 10.1081/E-ELIS4-120053443

Copyright © 2017 by Taylor & Francis. All rights reserved.

3. Intangible and individual knowledge, characterized by experience
4. Intangible and collective knowledge, characterized by hidden values and beliefs (society's unwritten laws)

As a result, there exists a distinct difference between tangible and intangible knowledge.

KNOWLEDGE MANAGEMENT CONCEPTS

Senge Approach

According to Peter Senge,[9] learning organizations are organizations where people continually expand their capacity to create the results they desire, new and expansive patterns of thought are nurtured, collective aspiration is generated, and where learning takes place on an individual as well as collective level.

Managers can detect organizational learning disabilities by utilizing the following five principles:

I. Personal Mastery: both life and work should be approached "as an artist would approach a work of art"
II. Mental Models: deeply ingrained assumptions or mental images "that influence how we understand the world and how we take action"
III. Building Shared Vision: when there is a genuine vision "people excel and learn, not because they are told to, but because they want to"
IV. Team Learning: team members engaging in true dialogue without assumptions
V. Systems Thinking: the integrative (fifth) discipline that fuses the other four into a coherent body of theory and practice

These five disciplines should be employed continuously in order to improve existing capacities. Since learning organization theories usually target the same approaches as that of knowledge management, there tends to be a close correlation between learning and managing knowledge.

Senge also mentions innovation management, which is the cornerstone of humankind. The success of innovation management heavily depends on the quality of IC. IC itself is characterized by human relationships, human knowledge, and structural aspects.

Nonaka/Takeuchi's Approach

Nonaka published the SECI model in 1991 (Fig. 1). His spiral model shows how to share tacit and individual knowledge with colleagues.[5]

The first step, socialization, transfers tacit knowledge between individuals through observation, imitation, and practice. In the next step, externalization is triggered by dialogue or collective reflection and relies on analogy or

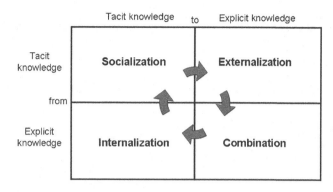

Fig. 1 The knowledge spiral.

metaphor to translate tacit knowledge into documents and procedures. In the third step, combination consequently reconfigures bodies of explicit knowledge through sorting, adding, combining, and categorizing processes and spreads it throughout an organization. Finally, internalization means the process of explicit knowledge transferred into individual tacit knowledge. Possibly, through a phenomenon that Nonaka calls the "knowledge spiral," knowledge creation and sharing becomes part of the culture of an organization.

In 1997/1998, Tsoukas[10] theorizes that tacit and explicit knowledge were not two separate forms of knowledge, but rather inseparable and necessary components of all knowledge. Nonaka followed with a slightly enhanced SECI model in 1998 called "Ba." "Ba" is a convenient place where knowledge can be exchanged. Nonaka pointed out that knowledge is not only produced from individuals, but from interaction between individuals and the surrounding environment. Therefore, the more inspiring the "Ba," the better the knowledge sharing results will be.

In 2011, Nonaka and Takeuich[11] coined the term phronetic leadership. For them, phronetic leadership means mastering the following management principles:

I. Ability to make judgment on goodness
II. Ability to create Ba
III. Ability to see the reality as it is
IV. Ability to articulate the essence
V. Ability to exercise political power
VI. Ability to foster phronesis on others

There is some parallelism between the observations of Senge, Drucker, and Nonaka. Phronetic leadership means pragmatic idealism that is not a contradiction in the eyes of Nonaka and Takeuichi. However, phronetic leadership might be harder to execute in western cultures than in the east because of cultural differences.

Probst/Raub/Romhardt's Approach

Probst[12] merged a set of connected activities into a framework called the "building blocks of knowledge" (Fig. 2).

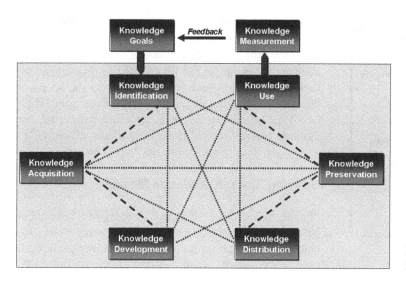

Fig. 2 Framework of the building blocks of knowledge.

This framework is often used to implement knowledge management initiatives in organizations. Senge's and Nonaka's approaches are more oriented toward sociology. Probst's approach is rather a technological one.

Knowledge goals point the way for strategic and operational knowledge management activities. The main focus is to improve competitiveness. Knowledge goals identify current skills and those which might be essential in the future.

Knowledge identification helps to establish whether internal and external knowledge is transparent. Knowledge acquisition has its focus on the external provision of knowledge. Knowledge development focuses on processes that generate new knowledge. Knowledge distribution deals with the transfer of knowledge inside a company.

Knowledge preservation memorizes valuable knowledge while ensuring suitable storage. Knowledge use is focused on the productive adoption of organizational knowledge.

The "knowledge measurement" building block is placed at the end of the process. In this block, the IC is analyzed and evaluated. This results in improvements such as better education, more intensive customer relations, or the need to invest into better infrastructure.

According to the feedback cycle, it is necessary to measure the "intellectual capital variables" in order to focus on target-oriented interventions. The problem is how to identify and measure these variables. Some variables such as fluctuation coefficients are easily measured while others such as tacit knowledge, which cannot be externalized by any of the methods mentioned, remain impossible to measure. Until recently, there was no commonly accepted standard for measuring IC.

INTELLECTUAL CAPITAL REPORTING

Intellectual capital consisting of structural, human, and relationship capital is part of each organization. Equipment,

infrastructure, intellectual property rights, procedures, and processes are regarded as structural capital. Skills and expertise of employees and management are parts of the human capital. The relationship between staff and external parties such as customers, business partners, friends, or teachers represents relationship capital.

Sveiby and Edvinsson[4] are considered the fathers of IC reporting. They identified methods and as a consequence variables characterizing structural, human, and relationship capital. Similar to accounting balance sheets, measured variables are reported once a year. Skandia and Celemi were one of the first companies in Europe to experiment with IC reports. It is not possible however to map all the different variables into one single value so that they can easily be compared between companies. Barachini[13] noted in his entry when he presented the business transaction theory that it is not possible to measure tacit individual knowledge since people do not offer knowledge (information) for free. He theorized that people employ "tit for tat" behavior during the information exchange process. This behavior is best explained by trading aspects of the modern portfolio theory. Taking the business transaction theory and the autopoiesis seriously, we can conclude that there will always be a part of knowledge which will remain undiscovered.

The main idea behind an IC report is that financial information reveals much about the past performance of an enterprise but says nothing about its future potential. An enterprise's future potential has much more to do with its IC. Creating transparency within the organization's IC will enable it to manage its intangible resources better, increase its staff's confidence and motivation, as well as impart greater certainty to investors and other stakeholders about its future earnings potential. Reflecting the importance of knowledge as an asset, the IC report outlines the knowledge goals of the company, its knowledge-based capital, its business processes, as well as its products and services.

Informetrics–International Council

Deductive Methods	Inductive Methods	
	Structural Model	Process Model
Tobin's Ratio	Skandia Navigator (Edvinsson)	Balanced Scorecard (Kaplan, Norton)
Return on Assets Methode-ROA	Intangible Asset Nonitor (Sveiby)	IC-Index (Roos)
Return on Management (Strassmann)	IC-Rating (Edvinsson)	Danish Guideline
Calculated Intangible Value		Intellectual Capital Report (ARCS)
Financial Method of Intangible Assets Measurement-FiMIAM (Rodov, Leliaert)		

Fig. 3 Selected methods for intellectual capital reports.

National and international accountancy rules increasingly regulate how IC is reported. There are more than 35 intangible asset-measuring models existing. These models basically differ in one aspect. One type of models use inductive methods, the others use deductive methods. Deductive methods evaluate IC by calculating functions expressing monetary values. Inductive methods are scorecard oriented. Inductive methods are subdivided into structure- and process-oriented models (see a selection of methods in Fig. 3). Structure-oriented models classify IC into categories and attempt to systematically measure an organization's knowledge assets. Process-oriented models focus on coverage and description of knowledge flows.

Although a wide range of methods for measuring and reporting IC have been developed during the last decade, especially for internal managerial purposes, companies have been reluctant to implement them. Investors are reluctant to invest in IC because of its inherent high-risk nature. Since IC is one of the main drivers of value creation and growth, this negative investment bias is seen as harmful, particularly for research-intensive and innovative enterprises.[14]

KNOWLEDGE MANAGEMENT INSTRUMENTS

On a formal level, instruments are tools, techniques, or methods. A complete list of all existing instruments of knowledge management would be beyond the scope of this entry. Following the popular framework from Probst (see Fig. 2), we can define at least one instrument per building block. Some of these instruments are supported by IT, web technologies, or social (soft)ware.

Building Block: Knowledge Measure

"Intellectual capital statement" represents coherences between organizational targets, business processes, IC, and organizational profit. One well-known framework used to measure IC is the Austrian Research Center's IC report. This report measures different indicators from structural, human, and relationship capital. Innovation indicators are also integrated (see Fig. 4).

The ARC IC report[15] is an inductive process-oriented model developed in 1999. Currently, these types of models form the most common representation of IC reports. The German approach provides a similar more practicable model.

The logic of this model combines goals, IC, knowledge processes, and intangible results. The process of acquiring, applying, and exploiting knowledge starts with the definition of specific knowledge goals, which can be derived from the corporate strategy. Knowledge goals define areas where specific skills, structures, and relationships should be established or increased in order to ensure the implementation of a corporate strategy. Derived from these goals, the IC consisting of structural, human, and relational capital is exploited. These intangible resources serve as input for the knowledge production process, which in turn is manifested in the different types of projects or processes carried out in an organization.

The model provides a framework for its adaptation and adoption by other organizations. When applying this

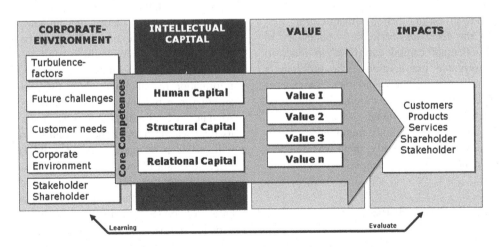

Fig. 4 Structure of the ARC intellectual capital report.

model, organizations have to formulate explicitly the organizational goals relevant for the resources and processes.[16]

Building Block: Knowledge Identification

Knowledge can be identified by knowledge or data miners. These are software programs that mine the web in order to identify useful chunks of information—a process known as "business intelligence." Knowledge can also be discovered by a "knowledge café" where people join different tables in order to discuss various topics with various partners.[16]

Building Block: Knowledge Acquisition

The simplest way to acquire knowledge is by reading a book, studying an encyclopedia, weblog, or communities of practice.

Building Block: Knowledge Development

Knowledge is developed through experience, trial, and error. This means that the practical application of acquired knowledge helps to develop further knowledge.

Building Block: Knowledge Distribution

Knowledge can be transferred by the telling of stories. Not only is the core message transmitted during this process but also all necessary background knowledge and semantics that are needed to understand the core message are relayed by dialogue.

Building Block: Knowledge Preservation

The brain is the body's primary repository of knowledge. Other sources such as databases on the web, data marts, MySpace, YouTube, Facebook, and blogs represent information stores.

Building Block: Knowledge Use

The techniques mentioned in the other blocks are combined and used in organizational processes so that the performance of individuals or groups is enhanced.

Information sharing is the cornerstone of knowledge management. Existing IT, referred to as social ware, helps people to share information and collaborate in an optimal fashion. Knowledge management is the management of this information flow, getting the right information to the people who need it so that they can act on it in due time.

Today many companies are using social ware to optimize collaboration and to improve results. Cultural and social problems however may occur during the collaboration process.

INTERNATIONAL COUNCIL ON KNOWLEDGE MANAGEMENT

For knowledge management as a discipline to succeed, a specialized body of knowledge, theory, hypotheses, observations, and problems must be formulated, tested, and applied. As the early activities in knowledge management were mainly dominated by practitioners and commercial activities, academicians and researchers saw the need for building the foundation for sustainable and solid research and development in this area. This effort started when a number of universities around the world started to offer graduate degrees in knowledge management. Given the interdisciplinary nature of knowledge management, it is also important to bring people from different but related disciplines to contribute to the development of the knowledge management profession. The absence of a scholarly professional body with the goal of advancing knowledge management as a discipline was the main motive for the formation of the International Council on Knowledge Management (ICKM). ICKM is an association that is based in Vienna.

The first ICKM conference started in 2004 in Singapore with the objectives of promoting knowledge management practices as well as bringing researchers, academics, and practitioners together to exchange ideas and share information. Since then, the conference became a great success and continues to move from one continent to another. Unfortunately, ICKM is not a trademarked word. Other organizations are using this name to arrange conferences with similar content.

ICKM council and ICKM series of conference came about as a result of one-person effort that started back in 1998. Dr. Suliman Hawamdeh who is currently a professor at the University of Texas founded the Information and Knowledge Management Society (iKMS), the organization behind the organization of the first ICKM conference in Singapore 2004. Dr. Hawamdeh was the founding director of the knowledge management program at Nanyang Technological University in Singapore and he is the editor in chief of the first refereed journal on knowledge management—the Journal of the Information and Knowledge Management. His vision is to create a scholarly and professional body with an international presence to promote and advance the iKMS profession.

While iKMS remained as a local Singapore-based KM association, it continues to support the ICKM council and the ICKM series of conferences. Professor Hawamdeh, the founding chair of the International Conference on Knowledge Management, continues the general chair duties and delegated the organization aspects to local organizers who manage the event as a nonprofit event with the objective of bridging the gap between academia and practitioners. ICKM is a platform for leading international forum for researchers and practitioners who come together to exchange ideas, share research findings, and network. Although all participants may openly and freely present

Informetrics–International Council

ideas and theories, the proceeding, which is published as a book and part of the book series Innovation and Knowledge Management and edited by professor Hawamdeh, is limited to peer-reviewed papers, an approach that should guarantee high scientific quality with practical implications. Key individuals who played an important role in the successful organization of ICKM conferences so far include Patrick Lambe, Martyn Laycok, Franz Barachini, Sam Chu, Waltraut Ritter, and Adeline du Toit.

CONCLUSION AND FUTURE TRENDS

We have presented three well-known concepts of knowledge management and discussed the different perspectives of knowledge management and IC reporting. Furthermore, we have presented instruments that are subject of investigation in conferences as the ICKM.

Knowledge management itself can be seen as bringing the right knowledge to the right people in due time so that IC can be improved. The problem is how to motivate people to share information. Appropriate rewarding schemas do exist, but they are not widely used in companies because it is too difficult to measure the value of information and the value of individual contributions. Much more research is needed in rewarding schemas.

Other obstacles for knowledge sharing are the divide between rich and poor and the divide between educated and uneducated. Cultural differences also hamper knowledge sharing. We are convinced that there is a need to develop performance measurements for corporate social responsibility and to combine this with shareholder value. Substantial research is needed in this area and we hope that the international conference on knowledge management will go a long way to stimulate such objectives.

If we accept knowledge as being a very private personal affair, then we recommend concentrating more research efforts toward neuroscience and neurobiology. In particular, the influence of emotions on knowledge sharing seems to be evident.

REFERENCES

1. Drucker, P.F. *The Effective Executive*; Butterworth Heinemann: Oxford, U.K., 2007.
2. Bontis, N.; Crossan, M.; J. Hulland; Managing an organizational learning system by aligning stocks and flows. J. Manage. Stud. **2002**, *39* (4), 437–469.
3. Edvinsson, L.; Malone, M. *Intellectual Capital*; Harper Business: New York, 1997.
4. Sveiby, K.E. *The New Organizational Wealth: Managing and Measuring Knowledge-Based Assets*; Berret-Koehler: New York, 1997.
5. Nonaka, I.; Takeuchi, H. *The Knowledge Creating Company*; Oxford University Press: New York, 1995.
6. Bonifacio, M.; Bouquet, P. Knowledge nodes: The building blocks of a distributed approach to knowledge management. Proceedings of I-Know, J. Univ. Comp. Sci. 2002.
7. Joia, L.A. A new model for workers retraining in Brazil. J. Workspace Learn. **1999**, *11* (4), 140–145.
8. Barachini, F. Frontiers for the codification of knowledge. J. Inform. Knowl. Manage. **2003**, *1*, 1–5.
9. Senge, P.M. *The Fifth Discipline*; Doubleday/Currency: New York, 1990.
10. Tsoukas, H.T. Forms of knowledge and forms of life in organized contexts. In *The Realms of Organizations*; Chia, R., Ed.; Routledge: London, U.K., 1997.
11. Nonaka, I.; Takeuchi, H. The wise leader. Harvard Business Rev. **2011**, Prod Nb. R1105B-PDF-ENG.
12. Probst, G.; Raub, S.; Romhardt, K. *Wissen Managen*; Gabler Verlag: Wiesbaden, Germany, 1997.
13. Barachini, F. Cultural and social issues for knowledge sharing. J. Knowl. Manage. **2008**, *12* (6), 2008.
14. RICARDIS, http://ec.europa.eu/invest-in-research/policy/capital_report_en.htm (accessed June 2008).
15. Austrian Research Center Seibersdorf, www.arcs.ac.at (accessed June 2008).
16. Brown, J. *The World Café: Shaping Our Futures through Conversations That Matter*; Berrett-Koehler: San Francisco, CA, 2005.

International Federation of Library Associations and Institutions (IFLA)

Ross Shimmon
Faversham, U.K.

Peter Johan Lor
School of Information Studies, University of Wisconsin-Milwaukee, Milwaukee, Wisconsin, U.S.A., and Department of Information Science, University of Pretoria, Pretoria, South Africa

Sofia Kapnisi
Sjoerd Koopman
Stuart Hamilton
International Federation of Library Associations and Institutions, The Hague, the Netherlands

Abstract
The International Federation of Library Associations and Institutions (IFLA) is the leading international body representing the interests of library and information services, their staffs, and users. The International Federation of Library Associations and Institutions is an independent, nongovernmental, not-for-profit organization, registered in The Hague as an association under the law of the Netherlands. Founded at an international congress in Edinburgh, Scotland, in 1927, it has become the global voice of the library and information profession.

International Federation—ISchools

INTRODUCTION

The International Federation of Library Associations and Institutions (IFLA) is the leading international body representing the interests of library and information services, their staffs, and users. The International Federation of Library Associations and Institutions is an independent, nongovernmental, not-for-profit organization. It was founded at an international congress in Edinburgh, Scotland, in 1927, as the International Federation of Library Associations, a federation of national library associations. Prior to World War II the orientation of the association was strongly European; eight of the nine presidents who served during IFLA's first 50 years were from Europe, and the majority of IFLA congresses were held in European cities. After the war, IFLA's membership expanded and in the 1970s special efforts were made to expand the membership to developing countries. The first of a series of presession seminars for librarians from developing countries was held in 1971. In 1976 a Division of Regional Activities, comprising three regional sections, for Africa, Asia and Oceania, and Latin America and the Caribbean, was established to serve members in the developing regions, where regional offices were subsequently set up. IFLA's first conference outside Europe and North America was held in Manila, the Philippines, in 1980. IFLA's first President from Africa, Kay Raseroka, from Botswana, served from 2003 to 2005;

the second, Ellen Tise, from South Africa, was elected to serve from 2009 to 2011.

In 1976 IFLA extended membership to libraries and related institutions and changed its name by adding "and Institutions," but left its well-known acronym unchanged. During the past three decades, IFLA has become the global voice of the library and information profession, and library leaders from many countries have served as president (see Appendix A).

MISSION

The statutes of IFLA (its constitution) state that the purposes of the federation shall be to: promote high standards of delivery of library and information services; encourage widespread understanding of the value and importance of high-quality library and information services in the private, public, and voluntary sectors; and represent the interests of members throughout the world. IFLA's mission, therefore, is to promote high standards of service by issuing guidelines to best practice and standards of provision, through international advocacy to persuade decision makers and opinion formers of the importance and relevance of libraries in the digital age, and to work for an estimated 690,000 librarians and information workers worldwide.

Encyclopedia of Library and Information Sciences, Fourth Edition DOI: 10.1081/E-ELIS4-120044963
Copyright © 2017 by Taylor & Francis. All rights reserved.

International Federation–
iSchools

CORE VALUES

The statutes also state IFLA's core values:

- The endorsement of the principles of freedom of access to information, ideas, and works of imagination, and freedom of expression embodied in Article 19 of the Universal Declaration of Human Rights.
- The belief that people, communities, and organizations need universal and equitable access to information, ideas, and works of imagination for their social, educational, cultural, democratic, and economic well-being.
- The conviction that delivery of high-quality library and information services helps guarantee that access.
- The commitment to enable all members of the federation to engage in, and benefit from, its activities without regard to citizenship, disability, ethnic origin, gender, geographical location, language, political philosophy, race, or religion.

These represent values and beliefs but also, especially in paragraph (d), ambitious aspirations. The mission and the core values form the basis of the federation's worldwide activities.

MEMBERSHIP

The federation is primarily an organization of members, relying upon them both for the bulk of its income and most of its professional input. There are two main categories of voting members: national association members and institutional members. National associations of library and information professionals, of library and information services, and of educational and research institutes within the broad field of library and information science, are enrolled as national association members. Institutional membership is designed for individual library and information services and all kinds of other organizations within the library and information sector. In addition, international organizations within the federation's sphere of interest may join as international association members. In 2008, there were 1224 voting members from 139 countries. Together, these associations and institutions represent the vast majority of the world's librarians and other library staff. Voting members are entitled to nominate and vote for candidates for the post of IFLA president and for places on the federation's governing board.

Individual practitioners and students in the field of library and information services may join as personal affiliates and student affiliates, respectively. They do not have voting rights, but they are able to nominate and vote for places on the standing committees of the professional sections. They provide invaluable contributions to the work of the federation, by serving on those committees and by contributing to the professional programs. In 2008 there were more than 300 personal and student affiliates in membership. National association members pay membership fees according to a graduated scale, based on the size of their operating expenditure. This helps ensure a reasonably equitable scale of fees.

For institutional members there is a system of differentiated fees based on the UNESCO scale of assessment. Personal affiliates pay a flat fee calculated so that it covers the expenses of administration and the benefits such as publications. For student affiliates there is a lower rate.

CORPORATE PARTNERS

The IFLA corporate partners' scheme enables a wide variety of companies in the library and information industry to have regular and direct contact in a variety of ways with the international library community. In return for financial and "in-kind" support, they receive a wide range of benefits, which may be negotiated on a flexible basis to suit individual needs. Corporate partners include publishers, subscription agents, software producers, and distributors of library furniture and equipment. Long-term relationships have been developed with a number of companies. For example, OCLC of Dublin, Ohio, U.S.A., offers the Jay Jordan IFLA/ OCLC Early Career Development Fellowship Program. Every year up to six fellows from countries with developing economies travel to OCLC headquarters for 4 weeks to participate in an intensive program of lectures, seminars, and mentoring. They also visit a number of libraries and relevant organizations in North America, the Netherlands (where they visit IFLA Headquarters), and Germany. Depending on the level of financial support, companies are listed as Gold, Silver, or Bronze Corporate Partners.

RELATIONS WITH OTHER BODIES

Over the years, IFLA has established good working relations with a variety of international organizations whose interests, at least partly, coincide with those of IFLA. This provides an opportunity for regular exchange of information, formal representation at meetings and, in some cases, the award of grants, the mutual approval of statements, and other initiatives. For example, IFLA holds

- Formal associate status with UNESCO.
- Observer status with the United Nations.
- Associate status with the International Council of Scientific Unions (ICSU).
- Observer status with the World Intellectual Property Organization (WIPO).
- Observer status with the International Organization for Standardization (ISO).
- Observer status with the World Trade Organization (WTO).

UNESCO formally approved

- The Public Library Manifesto, a document summarizing the aims and key missions of public libraries with the role to serve as a reference for anyone who can contribute to the progress of public libraries throughout the world,[1]
- The School Library Manifesto, which argues that school library services are so vital that they should be provided equally to all members of the school community, regardless of age, race, gender, religion, nationality, language, and professional or social status. The IFLA/UNESCO School Library Manifesto urges governments, through their ministries responsible for education, to develop strategies, policies, and plans that implement the principles of this Manifesto.[2]
- The Internet Manifesto, proclaiming that unhindered access to information is essential to freedom, equality, global understanding, and peace.[3]

All of these documents were drafted by IFLA sections. The common role of these manifestos is to advise and influence local, regional, and national governmental bodies in matters of library development. Funding has been received from UNESCO and other sources to distribute and promote the manifestos around the world. Guidelines for the provision of both public libraries and school libraries have been developed to supplement the manifestos and to help promote higher standards of service in these sectors. More recently the development of a set of IFLA/UNESCO Internet Manifesto Guidelines was funded by UNESCO and the Swedish International Development Cooperation Agency (Sida), and a series of workshops has been held in various parts of the world to promote their implementation.

The federation has offered consultative status to a number of nongovernmental organizations (NGOs), whose interests coincide with those of IFLA. This is often on the basis of mutual recognition. These arrangements include the International Publishers Association (IPA), the International Council on Archives (ICA), and the International Council for Scientific and Technical Information (ICSTI). This status facilitates the exchange of documents and mutual representation at each other's congresses. In some cases it has resulted in more tangible and practical outcomes. The IFLA and the IPA have, for example, set up the IFLA/IPA Steering Group to examine issues of mutual interest such as metadata, the legal deposit of electronic materials, and digital object identifiers.

In 1996 IFLA also collaborated with other NGOs to found the International Committee of the Blue Shield (ICBS) whose mission is to collect and disseminate information and to coordinate action in emergency situations where cultural heritage is threatened. The name was chosen because the 1954 Hague Convention for the Protection of Property in the Event of Armed Conflict specified use

of the blue shield for marking cultural sites to give them protection from attack in the event of war. In addition to IFLA, the NGOs within the ICBS are the International Council on Archives (ICA); the International Council of Museums (ICOM); and the International Council on Monuments and Sites (ICOMOS). In 2005 the Coordinating Committee of Audiovisual Archives Associations (CCAAA) joined ICBS. These international NGOs have joined together to provide the concerned authorities and professionals with expertise and guidance in cases of armed conflict and natural disasters that affect cultural heritage. They are also working together to organize risk preparedness at an international level and encourage its development at a local level. By 2008 national Blue Shield committees had been set up in 12 countries: Australia,Belgium, Benin, Brazil, Czech Republic, France, Italy, Former Yugoslav Republic of Macedonia, the Netherlands, Norway, Poland, and the United Kingdom; plans were afoot to set up such committees in a number of other countries.

THE IFLA WORLD LIBRARY AND INFORMATION CONGRESS

IFLA is clearly much more than just a congress. Nevertheless, IFLA's annual World Library and Information Congress (known until 2003 as the IFLA General Congress and Council) is its flagship event. At a gathering held in a different city each year, upward of 3000 delegates gather to exchange experience, debate professional issues, see the latest products of the information industry, conduct the business of IFLA, learn about the library and information infrastructure of the host country and to experience its culture. An important side benefit of attending the IFLA congress is the ability to renew and expand professional friendships from across the world. Every year IFLA's Governing Board selects the region in which the congress is to be held 3 years hence. A feasibility study is conducted by IFLA's professional conference organizer (PCO) and a shortlist of suitable venues in that region is drawn up. From these the Governing Board selects the winning city on the basis of criteria that include the geographic spread of the congress; the congress and exhibition facilities available; logistics, including ease of transportation and the availability of hotels in all price ranges; support from the local profession; and support from the government and other agencies. Each congress is arranged by a four-way partnership consisting of IFLA, an IFLA-controlled limited liability company based in the United Kingdom, the PCO, and a National Committee.

Each congress has a distinctive theme to which the various sessions, including plenary sessions, guest lectures open sessions, and workshops are expected to contribute. In recent years the IFLA congresses have been held in the following venues with the following congress themes:

- 2004, Buenos Aires, "Libraries: Tools for Education and Development."
- 2005, Oslo, "Libraries—A voyage of discovery."
- 2006, Seoul, "Libraries: Dynamic Engines for the Knowledge and Information Society."
- 2007, Durban, "Libraries for the future: Progress, Development and Partnerships."
- 2008, Québec City, "Libraries without borders: Navigating towards global understanding."

In 2009, the IFLA congress will take place in Milan with general theme "Libraries create futures: Building on cultural heritage" and in 2010 in Gothenburg with theme "Engaging, Embracing, Empowering." The 2011 congress will be held in San Juan, Puerto Rico, with a theme still to be announced.

A substantial trade and technical exhibition is arranged during the congress. The number of exhibiting companies and organizations usually exceeds 100. International Federation of Library Associations and Institutions Sections and other professional groups often arrange specialist workshops or seminars immediately preceding or following the congress. The venue for such satellite events is often in the same city as the congress itself or in some other location in the region.

Congress hosts sometimes link their own congress with the IFLA event in order to strengthen national participation. Other national, regional, or specialist professional groups often take the opportunity to economize on their members' travel costs by arranging their own regular meetings in connection with an IFLA congress, which many of their members could be expected to attend. The IFLA congress often tends to have an invigorating effect on the profession in that country.

The congress is usually held in the third or fourth week of August. The congress itself lasts 5 days, but it is preceded and followed by business meetings of the Governing Board, its committees, and the committees of IFLA's professional units. For members of these bodies the event may last up to 9 days. Starting on Sunday afternoon and continuing until Thursday morning there is a full program of guest lectures, professional sessions, and poster sessions. Around 400 papers on a wide spectrum of topics are presented in nearly 100 professional program sessions that are scheduled in six parallel slots, at two of which simultaneous interpretation is offered in IFLA's seven languages. Around 100 posters are also presented in seven languages. Library tours offer participants the opportunity to visit libraries in the host city and other cities nearby. Receptions and cultural performances are held during the evenings. Embassies often host receptions for their own nationals and invited guests. International Federation of Library Associations and Institutions has a close relationship with the Conference of Directors of National Libraries (CDNL), an independent body, which holds its annual meeting during the congress week.

Building on the initiative of Denmark in 1997, most of IFLA's congress hosts have established special funds to support participants from developing countries. A variety of congress participation grants, with varying eligibility requirements, are on offer. These are usually announced on IFLA's Web site 6–8 months before the relevant congress.

In addition to the annual congress a wide range of professional meetings, seminars, and workshops are held around the world by IFLA's professional units and core activities. Two other regular major international conferences are held under the auspices of IFLA: the five-yearly International Congress of Medical Librarians (ICML) will hold its 2009 congress in Brisbane in July 2009, and the biennial International Conference on Interlending and Document Supply (ILDS) will convene in Hanover, Germany, in October 2009.

GOVERNANCE

The governing structure of IFLA was revised in 2008, when revised Statutes and Rules of Procedure (regulations) were adopted. While the essential structure remained largely unchanged, greater flexibility was achieved by moving detailed provisions concerning professional units such as division and sections from the Statutes to the Rules of Procedure.

A description of the structure which will be in place from 2009 follows (see Fig. 1).

President

The president is the chief representative of IFLA and is expected to provide it with professional leadership. Among the formal duties of the president are the chairing of the meetings of the General Assembly and the Governing Board. The President is elected by the total voting membership by postal ballot and first serves a term of 2 years as president-elect, followed by 2 years as president. The president may serve for only one term. See Appendix A for a list of all past presidents.

General Assembly

The General Assembly, known until 2008 as the Council, is the highest organ of IFLA. It determines its policies and priorities. The voting members in good standing (that is, those who have paid their membership fees in full) constitute the General Assembly, which meets annually during the congress. Although voting in elections is by postal ballot, under Dutch laws decisions of the General Assembly have to be taken at these meetings. However, non-binding consultations are held by postal ballot on important issues. Voting members not able to be directly represented at a General Assembly meeting may arrange to have their vote

International Federation–
iSchools

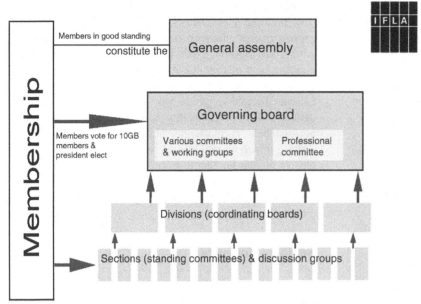

Fig. 1 IFLA organization chart.

International Federation–iSchools

exercised by proxy. Personal affiliates of the federation may attend the General Assembly as observers, but may not vote. Representatives of other organizations and other persons may be invited to attend as nonvoting observers. Observers may speak at General Assembly meetings at the invitation of the chair or with the permission of the chair. The International Federation of Library Associations and Institutions has a system of vote allocations which ensures that national association members have a majority vote in the General Assembly. At present, institutional members have one vote each, while international association members have five. National association members have an allocation ranging between 8 and 40, according to the membership fees they pay.

Governing Board

Over 1200 voting members are entitled to attend and vote at General Assembly meetings and to take part in postal ballots. The statutes, therefore, provide for a Governing Board of more manageable size to be responsible for the managerial and professional direction of the federation, within guidelines approved by the General Assembly. The Governing Board consists of: the president; the president-elect; ten members elected by postal and/or electronic ballot; the members of the Professional Committee, the chair of the Management of Library Associations Section and up to three co-opted board members. The Governing Board meets at least twice a year, once at the time and place of the annual congress. Other business may be conducted by post and electronic mail. The statutes provide for an Executive Committee with delegated executive responsibility to oversee the direction of the federation between meetings of the Governing Board. The Governing Board has the power to establish other committees.

Professional Committee

The Statutes provide for a Professional Committee that is responsible for coordinating the work of all the units within the federation responsible for professional activities, policies, and programs. This committee consists of a separately elected chair, a representative, usually the chair, of each of the five divisions of IFLA, together with three members of the Governing Board, elected by that board. The Professional Committee meets at least twice a year, once at the time and place of the general congress.

PROFESSIONAL UNITS

Much of the professional work of the federation is carried out by professional units known as sections and (from 2009) special interest groups, which replace the units formerly known as discussion groups. These are coordinated by divisions, which are in turn represented on the Professional Committee.

Divisions

The Governing Board is responsible for establishing a series of divisions, whose role is to promote and coordinate the work of IFLA in broad categories representing the aspects of the interests of the profession. Divisions coordinate the work of sections, special interest groups (SIGs) and core activities. However, the routine administrative work formerly carried out by divisions was reduced in 2008 and in terms of the new statutes their former coordinating boards, consisting of the chairs and secretaries of the sections belonging to the division, have been replaced by leadership forums. The chair of each division has a seat on the Professional Committee. As from 2008 there are five divisions: Library Types, Library Collections, Library Services, Support for the Profession, and Regions

Sections

Sections are the primary focus for the federation's work; they are grouped as follows in the five divisions:

- Library Types (for example, academic and research libraries, law libraries, biosciences libraries).
- Library Collections (for example, government information and official publications, rare books and manuscripts, newspapers).
- Library Services (for example, reference and information services, library services to multicultural populations).
- Support for the Profession (for example, management and marketing, education and training, library buildings, and equipment).
- Regions (Africa, Asia and Oceania, Latin America, and the Caribbean).

All IFLA members are entitled to register for sections of their own choice. Once registered, voting members have the right to nominate and elect specialists to the standing committee of the sections for which they are registered. The standing committee is the key group of professionals who develop and monitor the program of work of their section and prepare its sessions at the annual congress. Sections receive annual subventions from central funds with the approval of the Professional Committee. They are also able to apply for additional funds to carry out specific projects, such as the preparation of best practice guidelines, the compilation of a directory, or the conduct of a survey. Often such projects are published in the IFLA publications series. Each section publishes a newsletter for its members. They are usually published twice a year and may be made available to other interested persons. The contents are also usually published on IFLA's Web site. Some of the newsletters contain substantial professional articles. Most sections also have an electronic mailing list. There are, as of 2008, 45 sections. The Professional Committee has the power to approve a proposal to create a new section or to disband an existing section.

Special Interest Groups

In 2001 IFLA's Round Tables were disbanded, the relevant groups becoming either sections or discussion groups. Starting in 2009 the latter will be replaced by special interest groups (SIGs). SIGs are less formal groupings, which cater for aspects of library and information services that do not require the establishment of a section because they deal with matters that may be of highly specialized or potentially short-lived interest. SIGs are normally linked to a sponsoring section. To establish a SIG, interested members petition a relevant section. If sufficient members express interest, the sponsoring section agrees, and certain criteria are met, the Professional Committee approves the establishment of the SIG. As of 2008 IFLA had eight discussion groups that were expected to become SIGs. They include discussion groups on such topics as e-learning, agricultural libraries, quality issues in libraries, and new professionals. A substantial number of other groups was waiting to submit petitions as well. Although SIGs do not receive regular funding from central sources, they are eligible to apply for finance to carry out projects. They run sessions as part of the general congress. Most also have an e-mail discussion list.

Regional Activities

Three regional sections—Africa, Asia and Oceania, and Latin America and the Caribbean—make up the Division of Regional Activities. All IFLA members located in these regions are automatically registered for the respective regional sections free of charge, in addition to other sections for which they may choose to register. The three regional sections are concerned with all aspects of library and information services in their regions. They promote IFLA activities and work closely with all IFLA's professional units, IFLA core programs, and with the respective IFLA regional offices.

Core Activities

Between 1973 and 1997 IFLA established six core programs to provide leadership and a focal point for work on strategic issues of common concern to library and information services around the world. In the following decade financial pressures and management changes in several of the libraries hosting core programs forced a rethinking of these programs. They were renamed core activities, the new designation implying less permanence and a greater openness to change than before.

Several of the older programs had continued for some years and were thought to have achieved as much as they could. Consequently three were closed down during 2001–2003: Universal Dataflow and Telecommunications (UDT), Universal Bibliographic Control and International MARC (UBCIM), and Universal Availability of Publications (UAP), with the Office for International Lending. Responsibility for the international interlending vouchers scheme was taken over by IFLA Headquarters.

Universal Bibliographic Control and International MARC was replaced by a new group formed by a partnership between IFLA and the Conference of Directors of National Libraries (CDNL) to form an Alliance for Bibliographic Standards (ICABS), subsequently renamed IFLA-CDNL Alliance for Digital Strategies (ICADS).

International Federation– iSchools

The National Library of Portugal took over the UBCIM's UNIMARC activities.

With the exception of the **A**dvancement of **L**ibrarianship in the Third World **P**rogram (ALP), hosted in the University Library of the University of Uppsala, Sweden, the core programs were hosted and supported by major national libraries, which provide staff, accommodation, and support services. Such support in kind is supplemented by grants-in-aid from library associations, institutions, and aid agencies, particularly in the Nordic countries, as well as by project funding form foundations and aid agencies. The International Federation of Library Associations and Institutions itself provides on-going support from its Core Activities Fund, to which most major national libraries contribute. Since 2004 IFLA has had six core activities, which are described below.

Action for Development through Libraries (ALP) core activity

ALP was established in 1986 as the Advancement of Librarianship in the Third World Program. In 2004 it was renamed Action for Development through Libraries, but it retains its acronym and remains at the University Library of Uppsala, Sweden. The mission of ALP is to further the library profession, library institutions, and library and information services in the developing countries of Africa, Asia and Oceania, and Latin America and the Caribbean. Its goals are to assist in continuing education and training; to support the work of library associations; to promote the establishment and development of library and information services to the general public, including the promotion of literacy; and to introduce new technology into library services. ALP also acts as a catalyst within IFLA for the federation's activities in developing countries. Cooperation with a wide range of organizations within and outside the federation is a feature of ALP. ALP works through a planned program of activities in close cooperation between its office at Uppsala University, Sweden, IFLA's Regional Offices, the Division for Regional Activities, the three Regional Sections, and other partners. Activities include scholarships and attachment programs, conferences, seminars and training workshops, pilot projects, publications, and databases. ALP also administers grants from various foundations and aid agencies to enable librarians from developing countries to attend the IFLA general congress. During the period 2005–2009 ALP received substantial project funding from the Swedish International Development Cooperation Agency (Sida). A major contribution in-kind is made by Uppsala University, which hosts the ALP Office. Recent examples of projects undertaken by ALP are a Workshop entitled "Model of community information services in indigenous villages," held in Bolivia, Ecuador and Peru in May–June 2005, and an "International workshop on Information Literacy," held in Bangladesh in 2008.

Preservation and Conservation (PAC) core activity

PAC was established in 1986 with the mission to encourage best practice in preservation and conservation of library material internationally by publishing guidelines to good practice, running practical workshops, and persuading decision makers to give higher priority to preservation and conservation issues. Unlike the other IFLA Core Programs, PAC was established in a decentralized way with an international center and a series of regional centers responsible for their own policies and priorities.

The International Center has been hosted by the Bibliothèque nationale de France in Paris since 1992 and there are regional centers respectively located in Washington (Library of Congress), Caracas (Biblioteca Nacional de Venezuela), Rio de Janeiro (Fundaçao Biblioteca Nacional de Brasil), Santiago (Biblioteca Nacional de Chile), Port of Spain (National Library and Information System Authority of Trinidad and Tobago), Porto-Novo (National Library of Benin), Cape Town (UCT Libraries, South Africa), Tokyo (National Diet Library), Canberra (National Library of Australia), Moscow (Library for Foreign Literature) and Almaty (National Library of Kazakhstan). The International Center in Paris (Bibliothèque nationale de France) acts as the Regional Center for Western Europe, Middle East and Africa. Recent projects undertaken by PAC include an International Conference on "Newspapers Collection Management: Printed and Digital Challenges" held in Santiago, Chile, in April 2007 and the publication of "IFLA Disaster Preparedness and Planning: A Brief Manual" by John McIlwaine, in 2006.[4]

The roles of the centers are defined in a working agreement between IFLA and each center. Each center is, however, independent and acts according to the needs identified in its region. Together these centers form an international network. The directors meet annually for working sessions to coordinate the programs. Apart from the substantial contributions in-kind provided by the host libraries, funding is received from IFLA's Core Activities Fund, project finances from agencies such as UNESCO, and the sale of publications. PAC publishes *International Preservation News*, which appears three times a year.

Committee on Copyright and Other Legal Matters

The Committee on Copyright and Other Legal Matters (CLM) was established in 1996 to advise IFLA with respect to copyright and intellectual property, economic barriers to the acquisition and use of library materials, trade agreements affecting library services, disputed claims of ownership of library materials, authenticity of electronic texts, subscriptions and license agreements, and other legal matters of international significance to libraries and librarianship. The Committee operates through a committee which is representative of all regions of the world and includes invited resource persons. It cooperates with several important partner organizations with complementary missions: Electronic Information for Libraries (eIFL), the European Bureau of Library, Information and Documentation Associations (EBLIDA), the World Blind Union, and the (U.S.) Library Copyright Alliance.

The Committee's focus is on international activities and in recent years CLM has participated actively in meetings of the World Trade Organization (WTO) regarding the General Agreement on Trade in Services (GATS) and the Agreement on Trade Related Aspects of Intellectual Property Rights (TRIPS); at UNESCO, including meetings during 2001–2005 on the UNESCO Convention on the Protection and Promotion of the Diversity of Cultural Contents and Artistic Expressions (popularly known as the Convention on Cultural Diversity); and at the World Intellectual Property Organization (WIPO). Through written and oral interventions, collaboration with like-minded NGOs, and advocacy with representatives from member states, CLM achieved some notable successes for libraries in respect of such issues as the WIPO development agenda, traditional knowledge, and limitations and exceptions for libraries and for the visually impaired. The latter issue is an example of CLM's collaborative work: collaborating with IFLA's Libraries for the Blind Section, IFLA's national association members, and the World Blind Union (WBU) in persuading national governments to add to their national copyright laws provisions from WIPO's model copyright law that would improve access to information for print-disabled people. An important CLM activity has been raising awareness in the library community and providing guidance to the profession on issues with implications for library collections and services, for example, on copyright of digital resources.

Committee on Freedom of Access to Information and Freedom of Expression

The Committee on Freedom of Access to Information and Freedom of Expression (FAIFE) promotes freedom of information through libraries to improve the quality of life of individuals and groups. It tackles censorship of library materials; ideological, economic, political, or religious pressures resulting in limitations on access to information in libraries; and restrictions on librarians and other information specialists who provide reference and other information services. FAIFE empowers librarians and library users by promoting intercultural and interreligious tolerance, extending access to health information and combating corruption.

FAIFE attempts to monitor the state of intellectual freedom within the library community worldwide. In doing so it depends on networking and partnerships. For example, FAIFE is a member of various international intellectual freedom bodies such as the International Freedom of Expression Exchange (IFEX). In response to

violations of freedom of expression, and only once these have been confirmed from independent sources, IFLA may issue press statements, which can be found on the IFLA Web site.

Research and publications form an important part of FAIFE's advocacy work. Since 2001, FAIFE has annually published a unique *World Report* based on international data collection that provides an overview of how libraries around the world are tackling barriers to freedom of access to information and freedom of expression. Seven reports have appeared to date and the most recent, the IFLA/FAIFE World Report 2007, is entitled *Access to Libraries and Information: Towards a Fairer World*.[5]

FAIFE supports IFLA policy development by conducting research and drafting policy statements and guidelines on various aspects of intellectual freedom in libraries. A good example is the *Internet Manifesto*, which has thus far been translated into 19 languages, and the complementary *IFLA/UNESCO Internet Manifesto Guidelines* funded by UNESCO.[6] These have been workshopped and promoted in various parts of the world. This illustrates a recent shift in FAIFE's work: there is now more emphasis on raising the awareness of the library profession of freedom of information issues through educational seminars, workshops, and professional programs at IFLA's annual congresses and less on reacting to violations.

IFLA-CDNL Alliance for Digital Strategies

In 2003, when the UBCIM core activity was terminated, the National Library of Australia, the Library of Congress, the British Library, the Koninklijke Bibliotheek, and the Deutsche Nationalbibliothek agreed to participate in a joint alliance together with the Biblioteca Nacional de Portugal (responsible for the UNIMARC core activity), IFLA and the Conference of Directors of National Libraries (CDNL) to assure ongoing coordination, communication, and support for key activities in the areas of bibliographic and resource control for all types of resources and related format and protocol standards. This new alliance was known as the IFLA-CDNL Alliance for Bibliographic Standards (ICABS). In 2008 ICABS changed its name to ICADS, IFLA-CDNL Alliance for Digital Strategies, signaling a shift of emphasis away from "legacy systems" of bibliographic control such as the International Standard Bibliographic Descriptions (ISDN), toward digital library development and management, with three broad themes: creating and building digital collections (including digitization, Web archiving, and digital archiving); managing digital collections (including digital ingest, storage, and preservation); and accessing digital collections (digital resource discovery and digital rights management). IFLA-CDNL Alliance for Digital Strategies works through a coordinated Web presence based on the Preserving Access to Digital Information (PADI) site of the National Library of Australia, and though an annual program of events at the IFLA congress. The Secretariat of ICADS is currently maintained by the British Library.

UNIMARC

The Universal MARC (UNIMARC) standard format for machine-readable catalogs was originally created by IFLA to facilitate the international exchange of bibliographic data. It was developed and promoted by the former UBCIM core activity under the supervision of the Permanent UNIMARC Committee (PUC), which had been formed in 1991. When UBCIM was terminated in 2003, the IFLA UNIMARC Core Activity was established with the responsibility for the maintenance and development of the UNIMARC format.

The purpose of the UNIMARC core activity is to coordinate activities aimed at the development, maintenance, and promotion of the UNIMARC format, now a set of four formats, Bibliographic, Authorities, Classification. and Holdings and related documentation, through the Permanent UNIMARC Committee. In this connection it cooperates with relevant professional units of IFLA as well as with the International Organization for Standardization's Committee ISO TC46, the international agencies for standard numbers such as ISBN and ISSN, and various other international bodies. The IFLA UNIMARC core activity is hosted by the National Library of Portugal in Lisbon.

ADVOCACY

IFLA has a long history of advocacy in the field of library and information services with a focus on promoting the development of librarianship and library services worldwide through interlinked activities relating to international library cooperation, the development and dissemination of best professional practice and stimulating and assisting library development in developing countries. The emergence of the CLM and FAIFE core activities heralded a stronger advocacy focus, on the themes of Equity (fair and sustainable legal and economic relationships between the creators, intermediaries and users of information) and Freedom (freedom of access to information and freedom of expression), respectively. IFLA's advocacy became more prominent in the buildup to the World Summit on the Information Society (WSIS) in 2003–2005, with an emphasis on a third theme: Inclusion: the role of the library in the Information Society and the role of the library as an agency of social inclusion. The latter theme was emphasized in various events and actions, including a presummit Conference organized by IFLA and the Biblioteca Alexandrina just before the Tunis Summit in Alexandria, Egypt, on the theme "Libraries: the information society in action." Here IFLA showcased success stories illustrating the role of libraries in the Information Society. At the end of the presummit IFLA launched its *Alexandria Manifesto on Libraries, the Information Society in Action*.[7] Thanks to intensive and sustained advocacy work by IFLA and its allies the WSIS outcome documents contained some very favorable language concerning the role of libraries in the Information Society. Since 2005, IFLA has continued to follow up the WSIS advocacy work, by monitoring the Internet Governance Forum and participating in the WSIS action line facilitation and consultation meetings held annually in Geneva. In 2006 IFLA set up a working group, designated as the President-elect's Information Society Working Group (now the President's Information Society Working Group), to keep abreast of progress in respect of the action lines and other important issues (such as Internet governance) arising from WSIS, but not limited to it. The work of this Working Group is closely aligned to the presidential theme of IFLA's 2007–2009 President, Claudia Lux, "Libraries on the agenda!"

In its advocacy at international bodies such as UNESCO and WIPO, IFLA's internationally representative membership lends it a unique credibility when it states the concerns and interests of the library profession.

LANGUAGES

The IFLA has seven working languages: Arabic, Chinese, English, French, German, Russian, and Spanish. The federation's policy is to provide a simultaneous interpretation service in these languages for the major sessions at the annual general congress. For this purpose IFLA has built up a team of volunteer interpreters who are skilled in the language of librarianship and information work. At its congresses the language of the host country is sometimes also used, if it is not one of the official working languages. Congress papers are also translated into the working languages, subject to the resources being available. Other meetings and seminars may also require the use of some of the working languages for translation or interpretation. Many IFLA publications appear not only in the seven official languages, but also in other languages. For example, the IFLA/UNESCO public library guidelines are available on IFLA's Web site in 21 languages, and the IFLA/UNESCO school library guidelines in 17. For many of these translations IFLA gratefully relies on volunteer translators and, more recently, on the language centers referred to below.

HEADQUARTERS

The IFLA Headquarters is headed by a secretary general, appointed by the Governing Board, who is responsible for the strategic and operational direction and financial

International Federation–
iSchools

management of the federation, within the policies established by the General Assembly and the Governing Board. The secretary general has the right to attend and participate, in a nonvoting capacity, in all meetings of the General Assembly, the Governing Board, and the Professional Committee. The IFLA Headquarters consists of a small team of full- and part-time staff, based at in the Hague. It is hosted by the Koninklijke Bibliotheek (the Royal Library of the Netherlands), which provides the office space and the infrastructure.

Regional Offices

IFLA has established three regional offices: for Africa, Asia and Oceania, and Latin America and the Caribbean. Their regions correspond to those of the regional sections. The regional office for Africa is hosted by the University of South Africa in Pretoria, South Africa, the office for Asia and Oceania is hosted by the National Library Board of Singapore, while the office for Latin America and the Caribbean is hosted by the Biblioteca Pública do Estado do Rio de Janeiro, in Rio de Janeiro, Brazil. A regional manager heads each office. They receive modest funding from IFLA's central funds, but they also receive substantial support from their host organizations. They work closely with the regional sections and with the core activities to promote the work of IFLA in their region and to ensure that the needs of their region are reflected in the federation's policies and priorities. The International Federation of Library Associations and Institutions also has three language centers, for French (for Africa), Russian, and Arabic. The IFLA Center for Arabic Speaking Libraries and Information Institutions is hosted by the Bibliotheca Alexandrina, in Alexandria, Egypt; the IFLA French Language Center for Africa is hosted by the Central Library of Cheikh Anta Diop University, in Dakar, Senegal; and the IFLA Russian Language Center is hosted by the Russian State Library, in Moscow, Russian Federation. The regional offices are concerned with communication and recruitment tasks.

IFLA on the Internet

IFLA has had a presence on the Internet since 1993. It consists of a Web site, formerly called IFLANET (http://www.ifla.org), and a set of electronic mailing lists. It was initiated within the UDT core program in 1993 and hosted by the National Library of Canada (now Library and Archives Canada). From 2001 to 2008 it was hosted by the Institut de l'Information Scientifique et Technique (INIST), in Nancy, France. It is now administered by the IFLA Headquarters. As an essential tool for all those active in the work of the federation, it includes general information about IFLA, including all the professional units, details of future congresses, the papers presented at the general congress, lists of members and corporate

partners, complete publications and electronic collections, and reports on technologies and issues facing contemporary libraries. Use of the IFLA Web site has been increasing rapidly. In 2007 it logged an average of almost 290.000 visits per month. During 2008 the IFLA Web site was redeveloped and thoroughly updated, to convert it from a repository of documents to a multipurpose communication tool. The new site is based on a modern open-source content management system (Drupal). It provides clear and efficient navigation, an attractive Web presence for each of IFLA's professional units, and a range of Web 2.0 functionality, including blogs, wikis, and forums, to enable IFLA members to communicate, interact, and work together in innovative and flexible ways. Its design takes into account the seven official languages as well as the requirements of visually handicapped and bandwidth-challenged users. Because of the new site's higher demands on resources and hosting possibilities, it will be housed at another Web hosting company.

In 2008 there were 61 electronic mailing lists, including IFLA-L, a general electronic forum; LIBJOBS, a mailing list for librarians and information professionals seeking employment; IFLAPARL, the mailing list of the Section on Library and Research Services for Parliaments; and UNIMARC-DIS, a forum for those using or interested in the UNIMARC cataloging formats.

PUBLICATIONS

The results of the research, projects, and other activities of the federation's professional units are reflected in its publications. *IFLA Journal*, which covers the latest developments on the international library and information scene, is published quarterly by Sage Publications. Each issue provides current information on the federation, together with articles selected to reflect the many aspects of the international library and information profession.

The reports to the General Assembly of the President and the Secretary General are published annually in *IFLA Journal*, while a formal annual report is published separately. The *IFLA Directory* appears biennially. It provides information about the composition of IFLA's main steering bodies such as the Governing Board and the standing committees of all IFLA sections as well as other organizational information, including the Statutes and Rules of Procedure. The membership directory no longer appears in the *IFLA Directory*. Instead, it is now accessible online on the IFLA Web site.

IFLA produces a major series of monographs, *IFLA publications*, published on its behalf by K. G. Saur Verlag of Munich, Germany. Six titles are usually published each year, and they are available for separate purchase or by subscription as an optional addition to the membership fee. Recent titles include:

- Newspapers collection management: printed and digital challenges.[8]
- Information Literacy: International Perspectives.[9]
- Library Management and Marketing in a Multicultural World.[10]
- Networking for Digital Preservation—Current Practice in 15 National Libraries.[11]

The *IFLA Reports Series* consists of reports on congresses, surveys, and other studies, which do not warrant monograph publication. They are available for individual purchase. Recent titles include: Guidelines for Library Services for Young Adults[12] and Guidelines for Libraries of Government Departments.[13] In addition to this series, Saur also publishes the *IFLA Series on Bibliographic Control*.

Conclusion

From its modest beginning in 1927 as a kind of club of library associations and directors of major libraries in Europe and North America, IFLA has developed into a worldwide network of library associations, libraries, and librarians, exchanging information, developing guidelines to good practice, and influencing the world's decision-making bodies in the service of libraries and their users.

ACKNOWLEDGMENTS

This entry written by Ross Shimmon for the 2nd edition of the Encyclopedia, was extensively revised and updated by Peter Johan Lor with the assistance of IFLA staff Sofia Kapnisi, Ingeborg Verheul, Stuart Hamilton and Sjoerd Koopman.

APPENDIX

Tabe A.1　IFLA conferences, venues, and presidents.

Session	Year	Venue	President	Proceedings
			I. G. A. Collijn 1927–1931	
1	1928	Rome		I
2	1929	Rome, Florence, Venice		I
3	1930	Stockholm		II
4	1931	Cheltenham		III
			W. W. Bishop 1931–1936	
5	1932	Berne		IV
6	1933	Chicago and Avignon		V
7	1934	Madrid		VI

(Continued)

Tabe A.1　IFLA conferences, venues, and presidents. *(Continued)*

Session	Year	Venue	President	Proceedings
8	1935	Madrid and Barcelona		VII
			M. Godet 1936–1947	
9	1936	Warsaw		VIII
10	1937	Paris		IX
11	1938	Brussels		X
12	1939	The Hague and Amsterdam		XI
			W. Munthe 1947–1951	
13	1947	Oslo		XII
14	1948	London		XIII
15	1949	Basel		XIV
16	1950	London		XV
17	1951	Rome		XVI
			P. Bourgeois 1951–1958	
18	1952	Copenhagen		XVII
19	1953	Vienna		XVIII
20	1954	Zagreb		XIX
21	1955	Brussels		XX
22	1956	Munich		XXI
23	1957	Paris		XXII
24	1958	Madrid		XXIII
			G. Hofmann 1958–1963	
25	1959	Warsaw		XXIV
26	1960	Lund and Malmö		XXV
27	1961	Edinburgh		XXVI
28	1962	Berne		XXVII
29	1963	Sofia		XXVIII

Session	Year	Venue and theme	President	Proceedings/ Annual
			Sir Frank Francis 1963–1969	
30	1964	**Rome** *Index Cumulatif/ Cumulative Index, 1928–1964*		XXIX XXX
31	1965	Helsinki		XXXI
32	1966	**The Hague** *Libraries and Documentation*		XXXII
33	1967	**Toronto** *Library Service for a Nation Covering a Large Geographical Area*		XXXIII
34	1968	**Frankfurt am Main** *Books and Libraries in and Industrial Society*		XXXIV

(Continued)

International Federation– iSchools

Tabe A.1 IFLA conferences, venues, and presidents. *(Continued)*

Session	Year	Venue and theme	President	Proceedings/ Annual
35	1969	Copenhagen *Library Education and Research in Librarianship*		IFLA Annual 1969
			H. Liebaers 1969–1974	
36	1970	Moscow *Lenin and Libraries*		1970
37	1971	Liverpool *The Organization of the Library Profession*		1971
38	1972	Budapest *Reading in a Changing World*		1972
39	1973	Grenoble *Universal Bibliographic Control*		1973
40	1974	Washington *National and International Library Planning*		1974
			P. Kirkegaard 1974–1979	
41	1975	Oslo *The Future of International Library Cooperation*		1975
42	1976	Lausanne *IFLA*		1976
43	1977	Brussels *Libraries for All: One World of Information, Culture and Learning*		1977
44	1978	Strbské Pleso *Universal Availability of Publications*		1978
45	1979	Copenhagen *Library Legislation*		1979
			E. Granheim 1979–1985	
46	1980	Manila *Development of Libraries and Information Systems*		1980

(Continued)

Tabe A.1 IFLA conferences, venues, and presidents. *(Continued)*

Session	Year	Venue and theme	President	Proceedings/ Annual
47	1981	Leipzig *The Role of National Centres in National Library Development and in International Library Cooperation*		1981
48	1982	Montreal *Networks*		1982
49	1983	Munich *Libraries in a Technical World*		1983
50	1984	Nairobi *Basis of Information Services for National Development*		1984
51	1985	Chicago *Libraries and the Universal Availability of Information*		1985
			H.-P. Geh 1985–1991	
52	1986	Tokyo *New Horizons of Librarianship towards the 21st Century*		1986
53	1987	Brighton *Libraries and Information Services in a Changing World*		1987
54	1988	Sydney *Living together: People, Libraries, Information*		1988
55	1989	Paris *Les Bibliothèques et l'information dans l'économie hier, aujourd'hui et demain*		1989
56	1990	Stockholm *Libraries: Information for Knowledge*		1990
57	1991	Moscow *Libraries and Culture: Their Relationship*		1991

(Continued)

Tabe A.1 IFLA conferences, venues, and presidents. *(Continued)*

Session	Year	Venue and theme	President	Proceedings/ Annual
			R. Wedgeworth 1991–1997	
58	1992	New Delhi *Library and Information Policy Perspectives*		1992
59	1993	Barcelona *The Universal Library: Libraries as Centres for the Global Availability of Information*		1993
60	1994	Cuba *Libraries and Social Development*		1994
61	1995	Turkey *Libraries of the Future*		1995[a]
62	1996	Beijing *The Challenge of Change*		
63	1997	Copenhagen *Libraries and Information for Human Development*		
			C. Deschamps 1997–2003	
64	1998	Amsterdam *On Crossroads of Information and Culture*		
65	1999	Bangkok *On the Threshold of a New Century: Libraries as Gateways to an Enlightened World*		
66	2000	Jerusalem, Israel *Information for Cooperation: Creating the Global Library of the Future*		
67	2001	Boston, Massachusetts *Libraries and Librarians: Making a Difference in the Knowledge Age*		

(Continued)

Tabe A.1 IFLA conferences, venues, and presidents. *(Continued)*

Session	Year	Venue and theme	President	Proceedings/ Annual
68	2002	Glasgow/ Edinburgh, Scotland, United Kingdom *Libraries for Life: Democracy, Diversity, Delivery*		
69	2003	Berlin, Germany *Access Point Library: Media— Information— Culture*		
			H. K. Raseroka 2003–2005	
70	2004	Buenos Aires, Argentina *Libraries as Tools for Education and Development*		
71	2005	Oslo, Norway *Libraries—A voyage of discovery*		
			Alex Byrne 2005–2007	
72	2006	Seoul, Korea *Libraries: Dynamic Engines for the Knowledge and Information Society*		
73	2007	Durban, South Africa *Libraries for the future: Progress, Development and Partnerships*		
74	2008	Quebec, Canada *Libraries without borders: Navigating towards global understanding*	Claudia Lux 2007–2009	
Future Conferences				
75	2009	Milan, Italy *Libraries Create Futures: Building on Cultural Heritage*		
76	2010	Gotherburg, Sweden		
77	2011	San Juan, Puerto Rico		

[a]IFLA Annual was discontinued and replaced with the Biennial IFLA Council Report. IFLA Annual 1995 was the last issue published.

International Federation– iSchools

International Federation–
iSchools

REFERENCES

1. Public Library Manifesto. *IFLA/UNESCO Public Library Manifesto;* 1994. Available at http://www.ifla.org/VII/s8/unesco/manif.htm.
2. School Library Manifesto. *IFLA/UNESCO School Library Manifesto;* 1999. Available at http://www.ifla.org/VII/s11/pubs/schoolmanif.htm.
3. *IFLA/FAIFE Internet Manifesto;* 2002. Available at http://www.ifla.org/III/misc/internetmanif.htm.
4. McIlwaine, J. *IFLA Disaster Preparedness and Planning: A Brief Manual;* IFLA-PAC: Paris, 2006; (International Preservation Issues, no.6). Available at http://www.ifla.org/VI/4/news/ipi6-en.pdf.
5. Bothma, T.J.D., Ed. *Access to Libraries and Information: Towards a Fairer World;* IFLA/FAIFE world report 2007. World report series IFLA: The Hague, the Netherlands, 2008; Vol. 7, 468. Available at http://www.ifla.org/faife/report/world_report_2007.htm (accessed August 24, 2008).
6. Hamilton, S.; Seidelin, S., Eds. *IFLA /UNESCO Internet Manifesto Guidelines (September 2006);* IFLA/FAIFE: Copenhagen, Denmark, 2006; 37. Available at http://www.ifla.org/faife/policy/iflastat/Internet-ManifestoGuidelines.pdf (accessed August 24, 2008).
7. *Alexandria Manifesto on Libraries, the Information Society in Action.* Available at http://www.ifla.org/III/wsis/AlexandriaManifesto.html.
8. Walravens, H., Ed. *Newspapers Collection Management: Printed and Digital Challenges/La Gestión de las Colecciones de Periódicos: Desafíos en Impresos y Digitales;* IFLA Publications, K.G. Saur: Munich, Germany, 2008; Vol. 133, 396.
9. Lau, J., Ed. *Information Literacy: International Perspectives;* IFLA Publications, K.G. Saur: Munich, Germany, 2008; Vol. 132, 217.
10. Mullins, J.L., Ed. *Library Management and Marketing in a Multicultural World;* IFLA Publications, K.G. Saur: Munich, Germany, 2007; Vol. 125, 366.
11. Verheul, I. *Networking for Digital Preservation—Current Practice in 15 National Libraries;* IFLA Publications, K.G. Saur: Munich, Germany, 2006; Vol. 119, 269.
12. Muller, P.; Chew, I., Eds. *Guidelines for Library Services for Young Adults;* IFLA Professional Reports, IFLA Headquarters: The Hague, the Netherlands, 2008; Vol. 107, 20 Coordinators Eds. (Guidelines for Library Services for Young Adults).
13. Bolt, N.; Burge, S., Eds. *Guidelines for Libraries of Government Departments;* IFLA Headquarters: The Hague, the Netherlands, 2008; Vol. 106, 65 IFLA Professional Reports.

BIBLIOGRAPHY

1. Byrne, A. *The Politics of Promoting Freedom of Information and Expression in International Librarianship: the IFLA/FAIFE Project;* The Scarecrow Press: Lanham, MD, 2007.
2. Byrne, A.; Koren, M.; Shimmon, R.; Vitzansky, W. IFLA and the World Summit on the Information Society. IFLA J. **2004**, *30*(1), 71–72.
3. Campbell, H.C. IFLA: Library universality in a divided world. IFLA J. **2002**, *28*(3), 118–135.
4. *IFLA Directory 2007–2009;* IFLA: The Hague, the Netherlands, 2007; Compiled and edited by IFLA headquarters staff.
5. Koops, W.R.H.; Wieder, J., Eds. *IFLA's First Fifty years: Achievements and Challenges in International Librarianship;* Verlag Dokumentation: Munich, Germany, 1977.
6. Lor, P.J. IFLA: Looking to the future. Libr. Manage. **2006**, *27*(1–2), 38–47.
7. Lor, P.J. IFLA, the World Summit on the Information Society, and After. Alexandria **2008**, *20*(1), 11–21.
8. Shimmon, R. The International Committee of the Blue Shield 1998–2004: An overview. Alexandria **2004**, *16*(3), 133–141.
9. Wieder, J.; Campbell, H.C. IFLA's first fifty years: a reprise. Extracts from "An Outline of IFLA's History', by Joachim Wieder, Selected and Edited by Harry Campbell. IFLA J. **2002**, *28*(3), 107–117.

International Federation of Television Archives (FIAT/IFTA)

Steve Bryant
BFI National Archive, Herts, U.K.

Abstract

The International Federation of Television Archives (FIAT/IFTA) is an international association of archives holding television programs and production material. Formed in 1977, it was initially made up of the archives of major broadcasting organizations, but grew to encompass national archives, technology companies, academic institutions, and others. Its main aim is information exchange, which it achieves through annual conferences, regional and specialist seminars, publications and its Web site. It cooperates with other international associations in its field and with UNESCO and attempts to draw attention to the historic importance of the audiovisual heritage throughout the world and to the dangers to its continued preservation. The recent growth of digital technologies and outlets has revolutionized the possibilities for television archives and brought a host of new concerns to FIAT/IFTAs agenda.

INTRODUCTION

The International Federation of Television Archives (formally titled Fédération Internationale des Archives de Télévision—commonly abbreviated to FIAT/IFTA) is, in its own words, "an international professional association established to provide a means for cooperation amongst broadcast and national audiovisual archives and libraries concerned with the collection, preservation and exploitation of moving image, and recorded sound materials and associated documentation" (source: FIAT/IFTA Web site home page). The means for cooperation include an annual conference, regional seminars, publications, and an online forum. Full members are organizations holding archives of television programming, while other bodies with an interest in the field, including commercial, industrial, and academic interests, are affiliated.

FOUNDATION AND CONSTITUTION

The International Federation of Television Archives was founded in Rome in 1977 by the heads of the archives of four broadcasting or audiovisual organizations: INA (Institut National de l'Audiovisuel-France), RAI (Radiotelevisione Italiana), the BBC (British Broadcasting Corporation), and the first German public channel, ARD. Statutes governed by French law were drawn up and members sought from around the world, although the bulk of the membership was, at first, and has largely remained European. Part of the reason for the establishment of the new organization was the failure of these broadcasters, despite the extensive nature of their holdings, to be accepted as equal members of the only existing forum for moving image archives, the Fédération Internationale des Archives de Film (FIAF). This was, and remains, an organization of national film archives and cinematheques, dedicated to establishing and enforcing exacting preservation and usage standards, and the industrial and commercial nature of much of the work of television archives, even those run by state or semi-state broadcasters, did not meet their criteria.

Nonetheless, the establishment of an international professional body dealing with the concerns of the program archives of television companies was a need felt in many countries and its foundation in the late 1970s was timely and reflected a crucial development stage of these archives. As with the archives of cinema output, television archives were formally established only when the medium had developed to a stage where a need for repositories of its history was felt—unfortunately too late to avoid the loss of crucial material from its formative years. In television, much early broadcast material was transmitted live, so there was nothing to keep anyway, and this transitory feeling worked against the establishment of archives. The earliest material to be collected was that which had been shot specially on film, particularly news and magazine program material, and, although the technology existed to record live output on film (telerecording or kinescope) from the late 1940s onwards, it was expensive and sparingly used, especially as copyright restrictions meant that anything other than the strictly factual was unlikely to be needed for rebroadcast—the main reason for keeping it in a broadcaster's archive. When videotape was introduced in the late 1950s it revolutionized production but not archiving. It was expensive and, crucially, reusable. Most archive departments, which were actually really film libraries, did not even get control of it until the mid-1970s, as it required intricate machinery to replay, and thus remained the responsibility of engineering departments, whose priority was the next production rather than the last one.

Encyclopedia of Library and Information Sciences, Fourth Edition DOI: 10.1081/E-ELIS4-120044824

Copyright © 2017 by Taylor & Francis. All rights reserved.

International Federation–
iSchools

At least, this was the case in Europe, where FIAT/IFTA was formed, and where most state broadcasting institutions followed the lead of the oldest and most prestigious broadcaster, the BBC. In the United States, the home of the largest TV production sector, the situation was different. Much more material survived because of the needs of syndication and different time-zones, and because much of the production in entertainment and drama was on film, through established Hollywood production companies. It is significant that the earliest and longest established American members of FIAT/IFTA were the New York-based news divisions of the three main networks, CBS, NBC, and ABC, whose concerns were the nearest to those of the European broadcasters.

In its first decade, then, FIAT/IFTA was composed mainly of state broadcasters from European countries. In most cases, these were the only broadcasters in those countries, as commercial competition was not a full reality everywhere until the 1990s, even in many areas that were not part of the Communist bloc, such as the Scandinavian countries. The United States was represented by the network news companies and, apart from Japan, Korea, Canada, Australasia and a handful of intrepid South Americans (most notably, Brazil), there was little representation from the rest of the World. In many places, especially Africa and parts of Asia, television itself was barely established, let alone its archives.

The constitution of the organization set up an Executive Council of 12 to run the organization, plus a President, all to be elected by the General Assembly, which is held every 2 years. The Federation also has a General Secretary and a Treasurer, chosen from the ranks of the Executive Council. All these officers must be employees of Full Member organizations (there are also associate and individual member categories) and give their time for free, though the organization can, and has, employed individuals for specific tasks. The main funding comes from members' subscriptions, though industry sponsorship has played an increasing role since the early 1990s. All the presidents to date have been heads of major European broadcasting or national archives, and the post has been held by the BBC, RAI, NRK (Norway), ORF (Austria), INA, and the Netherlands Institute for Sound and Vision.

CONFERENCES

From the very beginning, the Federation's main focus has been its annual conference, held in a different country each year. The financing of these events has traditionally fallen to a combination of the host member organization or organizations and the Federation itself, though sponsorship from television technology manufacturers, most notably Sony, and income from exhibition stands has become increasingly important. Though there is no hard and fast rule, a tradition has been established that one conference

in every four should be held outside Europe. Paris and Lisbon have been the venue for three conferences each, as has Italy, where RAI has always hosted, but in different cities, while London and Madrid have each held two conferences to date and the emerging television nations in Eastern Europe have also been prominent, with conferences held in Sofia (Bulgaria), Bogensee (near Berlin), and Budapest in the 1990s. Venues outside Europe have included Rio de Janiero, Montreal, Tokyo, Washington, D.C., Santiago de Chile, New York and Beijing.

The annual conference is an opportunity for members to discuss mutual questions of interest, in formally structured plenary sessions with published papers, in workshop groups and, of course, in social gatherings. In the earliest years, the conference programs tended to be built around standing areas of concern, though later they came to be themed. It is fair to say that, in the first decade of FIAT/IFTAs existence, the main focus was on the members getting to know how others tackled similar problems to their own, whereas later the main focus became external pressures, particularly technological change and commercial opportunities. The main responsibility for the conference program falls to the Federation's commissions, established by the Executive Council to conduct research into specific areas of interest and to prepare the conference program. Like the Executive Council, the commissions are made up of volunteers with relevant experience from the membership, and chaired by a representative from the Council.

THE FIRST COMMISSIONS AND THEIR CONCERNS

The first three commissions to be established were the Documentation Commission, dealing mainly with issues of how to catalog moving image material; the Technical Commission, concerned with issues of broadcasting technology as they affected archives; and the Training Commission. Their reports made up a considerable volume of the early annual conferences and their documents, including the Documentation Commission's Minimum Data List (a standardized guide to what information must be documented about holdings—rather in the vein of later metadata standards like the Dublin Core) and the Glossary (a guide to useful television archive and technology terms in different languages) were regularly updated and distributed. One of the earliest technical issues to face FIAT/IFTA was the obsolescence of video formats, though this was a problem which emerged slowly.

The earliest focus for the Technical Commission was film preservation, but this was an issue already well covered by FIAF and the emphasis soon shifted to the greater problems posed by video. At the end of the 1970s, as FIAT/IFTA was being formed, the first broadcast video format, 2" Quadruplex, was being replaced by the 1" broadcast standard and portable camera formats, such as U-matic. Toward the end of the 1980s, manufacturers ceased to support the older technology, while large numbers of newer formats were about to be introduced, and it became clear that the central issue for television archives was how to ensure the preservation of material held on obsolete formats. This problem encompassed issues of standards for transfer, choice of new formats, maintenance of obsolete machinery and skill bases, making financial cases for transfer programs, selection on grounds of commercial value and cultural significance, and the particularly acute problems faced in developing countries—issues which stretched beyond the remit of the Technical Commission. Representatives of companies from the electronics manufacturing industry made up a panel at a FIAT/IFTA conference for the first time in Turin in 1991 and faced a hostile reception on this issue. It was, however, clear that their commercial imperatives demanded the regular introduction of newer formats and the phasing out of the old, and that what was needed was an ongoing dialog between the archives and the manufacturers, for which FIAT/IFTA has provided the main forum ever since.

MEMBERSHIP

In the early 1990s, membership of FIAT/IFTA spread more widely with the establishment of new commercial broadcasters in many countries and the growth of television around the world. The newer members were able to set up with the most recent (and increasingly cheaper) broadcast technologies and didn't (yet) face the problem of legacy collections on obsolete formats. Many of them didn't even know what a piece of film looked like. They had plenty to learn from other members about the establishment of archives, but their experiences of setting up from scratch also brought a fresh perspective to the organization.

Another area of membership growth was cultural organizations with responsibility for the preservation of television material. These followed either the model of the few national audiovisual archives with television operations, such as the British Film Institute or the Library of Congress, or that of the national organization with responsibility for the archives of the state broadcaster, such as INA. Some of them assumed preservation responsibilities, while others, like the Hungarian National Audiovisual Archives, offered a public access service. In the Netherlands, the creation of the Netherlands Institute for Sound and Vision (Beeldengeluid) from the merger of the archive of state broadcaster NOB and several government organizations, saw a new FIAT/IFTA member formed from several old ones. Some of these organizations were seen as a response to the economic problems of format obsolescence and the growing demand for public and academic access to historic material. Their growing significance in

FIAT/IFTA was reflected by the passing of the Presidency, traditionally held by a broadcasting organization, first to INA and then to Beeldengeluid.

INTERNATIONAL COOPERATION

The International Federation of Television Archives has been involved in international cooperation with other associations of audiovisual archives through the UNESCO Round Table of Audiovisual Archives, later renamed the Coordinating Council of Audiovisual Archive Associations, whose other members were initially FIAF, the International Association of Sound Archives (IASA) and the audiovisual sections of the International Council on Archives (ICA), and the International Federation of Library Associations. These have more recently been joined by the Association of Moving Image Archives and the Association of Recorded Sound Collections (ARSC), both mainly North American organizations, and the South East Asia-Pacific Audiovisual Archives Association. As well as information exchange and the coordination of training activities, the main practical outcome of this cooperation has been an irregular series of events under the banner of the Joint Technical Symposium, which have considered matters of audiovisual technology of common interest and which have been held in Paris, London, and Toronto. The International Federation of Television Archives also held some experimental joint conferences with IASA (Berlin, 1994) and IASA and ARSC (Washington, D.C., 1995).

Another outcome of this international cooperation has been some regional seminars which have been held in parts of the world where specific basic help has been required, particularly Africa, Latin America, South Asia, and Eastern Europe in the early 1990s. These have often been arranged in cooperation with the other associations, IASA being the most regular partner, and the venues have included Tunis, South Africa, the Caribbean, and Egypt. The International Federation of Television Archives has also aimed as far as possible to help archivists from distant or disadvantaged countries to attend its conferences, often using specially sought sponsorship, the most successful partnership being with the Organisation Internationale de la Francophonie, a French organization which has paid for delegates from French-speaking countries in Africa and elsewhere to attend conferences in Europe.

CHANGING EMPHASES

Changes in television structures and archive practices have been reflected over the years in changes to the FIAT/IFTA commission structure. In 1993, the first new Commission since the founding of the Federation was launched. This was the Programming and Production Commission, which was established to investigate issues

International Federation–iSchools

concerning the reuse of archival content and programs in the broadcast environment and public cultural spheres and to organize conference events considering program content. It was founded in the context of the expansion of the use of archive programming through repeat channels, public screenings, video releases, and an increasing number of programs about television history or using television archive material in a historical context. The commission produced two important documents: Selection Guidelines (for preservation purposes) and a video on misuses of archival material. The commission also organized the FIAT Award for the best use of archive material in a new program. The first award was given in 1994 (to Danmarks Radio) and thereafter became an annual highlight of the conference. Programs were nominated by members and screened at the conference, with members voting for the winner. This enabled delegates to consider different ways of reusing archival content in new programs and conference sessions and workshops were arranged featuring the producers of shortlisted programs.

Another growing aspect of the work of television archives considered by this commission was the sale of footage between broadcast companies. Strategies for publicizing these services ranged from presence at conferences to placing catalogs online, and FIAT/IFTA provided platforms for both furthering these developments and discussing the best strategies for success, often in collaboration with another international partner, the Federation of Commercial Audiovisual Libraries (FOCAL International).

Then, in the late 1990s, the Documentation Commission and the Technical Commission were merged, prompted by the convergence of recording and documentation technologies in the growing digital environment. From this merger came the Media Management Commission, considering all questions concerning of growing digitization and its effect on archives. The feeling grew that, with television production becoming tapeless, the broadcast company archivist needed to be involved with the documentation and preservation of material before transmission rather than after, or risk being cut out altogether. Rapidly digitizing companies such as Swedish Television (SVT) were at the forefront of this development and metadata issues were the key focus. A metadata guide by prominent FIAT/IFTA member, Annemieke de Jong of Beeldengeluid, became a key text and was translated into several languages with financial assistance from the Federation. However, many felt that traditional preservation issues were being overlooked because of the commission's emphasis on new technologies and, in 2007, a Preservation and Migration Commission was established to take over the role of the old Technical Commission and to reestablish the question of format problems on the FIAT/IFTA agenda. This problem had become particularly acute in developing countries, which lacked the resources for large-scale transfer programs, but was also still very much a live issue for even the most advanced organizations, as there were still question marks over the viability of certain formats and over the best future strategies.

DIGITAL DEVELOPMENTS

By this time, FIAT/IFTA had itself entered the digital age, with its Web site (http://www.fiatifta.org) containing the papers from all its conferences and regional seminars, as well as all other key documents, a list of members and a forum for the online discussion of television archive questions or for those seeking advice. This, however, relies, as FIAT/IFTA always has, on hosting by the key member organizations linked to the Presidency or General Secretaryship.

The Federation had also itself been at the forefront of developing digital technologies. One of the best examples of the sort of cooperation between members which could be fostered by providing a platform for meetings was the Euromedia project, a successful bid by several FIAT/IFTA members, including Sudwestrundfunk of Germany, ORF, SVT, and the BBC, plus some German and Austrian technology providers, for European Union funds to develop a prototype digital asset management system. The progress of the system was regularly demonstrated at FIAT/IFTA conferences in the late 1990s and one of the technology companies, Tecmath of Germany, became a sponsor of the FIAT/IFTA Award. Other EU-funded projects with FIAT input followed, including the BIRTH project, a Web site featuring clips of early television productions, and Presto Space, a film and video preservation project.

THE CULTURAL AND ACADEMIC APPROACH

Television and its history is now the subject of academic study in many schools and universities and this too has been reflected in the developing FIAT/IFTA commission structure. The Television Studies Commission was established in 1999 to consider aspects of the academic study of television, using archives, and in particular to address the question of access to archive holdings. This had previously been the domain of the national archives and bodies such as INA, which have a long tradition of making their holdings available for study and to as wide a public as possible, whereas broadcasters had maintained their archives for their own uses and, in many cases, resisted demands to make them available for study, while others were accessible only to those with good contacts within the company. The main argument against allowing academic access had been the expense of copying materials, but cheap digital technologies have opened up wider possibilities, and many major broadcasters now include making material publicly and academically available as part of their digitization programs. The Television Studies Commission has also sought to introduce the results of academic work to the FIAT/IFTA membership, mainly

International Federation– iSchools

through conference sessions, and the increasing academic awareness of the value of television archives was reflected by the fact that the 2006 conference in Madrid, Spain, was hosted by a university rather than a broadcaster.

Public access to television archive material for cultural purposes is now a major aspect of the work of television archives. DVD releases of popular titles can be a lucrative commercial prospect, public or academic viewing of archival material through digital technology is available at such venues as the Bibliotheque Nationale in Paris or the BFI's Mediatheque in London, and many broadcasters now have plans to make their archives available online, both commercially and as a public service. Television history is now of interest to both the public and the academic community, for both nostalgic and sociological reasons, and its practitioners require access to the archives in order to tell it.

CONCLUSION

Television archives have had to adapt to changing television production techniques and changing recording technologies throughout their relatively brief period of existence. Now that the medium is mature enough to have its own history, to be regarded as a cultural phenomenon and thus be the object of academic study, and to have ever increasing outlets and demands for its past product, the archives have never had greater opportunities. Digital technologies have increased the possibilities for exploitation, but bring with them familiar problems in terms of ensuring long-term preservation and dealing with format obsolescence, on a greater scale than before. The requirement for an international forum, provided by FIAT/IFTA, will continue to be felt and to grow.

International Organization for Standardization (ISO)

Alan Bryden
International Organization for Standardization, Geneva, Switzerland

Catherine Dhérent
National Library of France, Paris, France

Abstract

ISO (International Organization for Standardization, http://www.iso.org) is the leading organization for the production and dissemination of consensus-based and globally relevant standards which provide a growing support to companies for becoming and remaining competitive in world markets. It is the world's largest developer and publisher of International Standards. The organization is a network of the national standards institutes of 157 countries, one member per country, with a Central Secretariat in Geneva, Switzerland, that coordinates the system. As a nongovernmental organization it forms a bridge between the public and private sectors. On the one hand, many of its member institutes are part of the governmental structure of their countries, or are mandated by their government. On the other hand, other members have their roots uniquely in the private sector, having been set up by national partnerships of industry associations. Therefore, ISO enables a consensus to be reached on solutions that meet both the requirements of business and the broader needs of society. This entry comprises three main sections: a general introduction to ISO and standards; an overview of ISO technical committee ISO/TC 46, Information and documentation, and an article by the Chair of ISO/TC 46 on "Managing information in a changing age."

International Federation–
iSchools

DISCOVERING ISO

ISO (International Organization for Standardization, http://www.iso.org) is the leading organization for the production and dissemination of consensus-based and globally relevant standards which, in the context of globalization of trade and many other issues, such as the environment, security and health, provide a growing support to companies for becoming and remaining competitive in world markets. ISO is the world's largest developer and publisher of International Standards.

The organization is a network of the national standards institutes of 157 countries, one member per country, with a Central Secretariat in Geneva, Switzerland, that coordinates the system.

ISO is a nongovernmental organization that forms a bridge between the public and private sectors. On the one hand, many of its member institutes are part of the governmental structure of their countries, or are mandated by their government. On the other hand, other members have their roots uniquely in the private sector, having been set up by national partnerships of industry associations. Therefore, ISO enables a consensus to be reached on solutions that meet both the requirements of business and the broader needs of society.

ISO'S NAME

Because "International Organization for Standardization" would have different acronyms in different languages ("ISO" in English, "OIN" in French for *Organisation internationale de normalisation*), its founders decided to give it also a short, all-purpose name. They chose "ISO", derived from the Greek *isos*, meaning "equal". Whatever the country, whatever the language, the short form of the organization's name is always ISO.

Why Standards Matter

Standards make an enormous and positive contribution to most aspects of our lives. Standards ensure desirable characteristics of products and services such as quality, environmental friendliness, safety, reliability, efficiency and interoperability—and at an economical cost.

When products and services meet our expectations, we tend to take this for granted and be unaware of the role of standards. However, when standards are absent, we soon notice. We soon care when products turn out to be of poor quality, do not fit, are incompatible with equipment that we already have, are unreliable or dangerous. When products, systems, machinery and devices work

Encyclopedia of Library and Information Sciences, Fourth Edition DOI: 10.1081/E-ELIS4-120044716

Copyright © 2017 by Taylor & Francis. All rights reserved.

well and safely, it is often because they meet standards. And the organization responsible for many thousands of the standards which benefit the world is ISO.

What Standards Do

ISO standards:

- Make the development, manufacturing, and supply of products and services more efficient, safer, and cleaner.
- Facilitate trade between countries and make it fairer.
- Provide governments with a technical base for health, safety and environmental legislation, and conformity assessment.
- Share technological advances and good management practice.
- Disseminate innovation and accelerate the time-to-market of products and services derived from such innovation.
- Safeguard consumers, and users in general, of products and services.
- Make life simpler by providing solutions to common problems.

Who Standards Benefit

ISO standards provide technological, economic, and societal benefits.

- For businesses, the widespread adoption of International Standards means that suppliers can develop and offer products and services meeting specifications that have wide international acceptance in their sectors. Therefore, businesses using International Standards can compete on many more markets around the world.
- For innovators of new technologies, International Standards on aspects like terminology, compatibility, and safety speed up the dissemination of the innovations and their development into manufacturable and marketable products.
- For customers, the worldwide compatibility of technology which is achieved when products and services are based on International Standards gives them a broad choice of offers. They also benefit from the effects of competition among suppliers.
- For governments, International Standards provide the technological and scientific bases underpinning health, safety, and environmental legislation.
- For trade officials, International Standards create "a level playing field" for all competitors on those markets. The existence of divergent national or regional standards can create technical barriers to trade. International Standards are the technical means by which political trade agreements can be put into practice.

- For developing countries, International Standards that represent an international consensus on the state of the art are an important source of technological know-how. By defining the characteristics that products and services will be expected to meet on export markets, International Standards give developing countries a basis for making the right decisions when investing their scarce resources and thus avoid squandering them.
- For consumers, conformity of products and services to International Standards provides assurance about their quality, safety and reliability.
- For everyone, International Standards contribute to the quality of life in general by ensuring that the transport, machinery and tools we use are safe.
- For the planet we inhabit, International Standards on air, water, and soil quality, on emissions of gases and radiation and environmental aspects of products can contribute to efforts to preserve the environment.

The ISO Brand

- *Democratic*
  Every full member of ISO has the right to take part in the development of any standard which it judges to be important to its country's economy. No matter what the size or strength of that economy, each participating member in ISO has one vote. Each country is on an equal footing to influence the direction of ISO's work at the strategic level, as well as the technical content of its individual standards.
- *Voluntary*
  ISO standards are voluntary. As a nongovernmental organization, ISO has no legal authority to enforce the implementation of its standards. ISO does not regulate or legislate. However, countries may decide to adopt ISO standards—mainly those concerned with health, safety, or the environment—as regulations or refer to them in legislation, for which they provide the technical basis. In addition, although ISO standards are voluntary, they may become a market requirement, as has happened in the case of ISO 9001 quality management systems, or of dimensions of freight containers and bank cards. ISO itself does not regulate or legislate.
- *Market-driven*
  ISO only develops standards for which there is a market requirement. The work is mainly carried out by experts from the industrial, technical, and business sectors which have asked for the standards, and which subsequently put them to use.
- *Consensus*
  ISO standards are based on international consensus among the experts in the field. Consensus, like technology, evolves and ISO takes account both of evolving technology and of evolving interests by requiring a

International Federation–
iSchools

periodic review of its standards at least every 5 years to decide whether they should be maintained, updated or withdrawn. In this way, ISO standards retain their position as the state of the art.

- *Globally relevant*
  ISO standards are technical agreements which provide the framework for compatible technology worldwide. They are designed to be globally relevant—useful everywhere in the world.

HOW TO RECOGNIZE AN ISO STANDARD

In paper form, an ISO standard is published in A4 format, which is itself one of the ISO standard paper sizes. It may be anywhere between a four-page document and one several hundred pages' long. ISO standards are also available as electronic downloads and many are available as part of a collection on CD or in handbook. An ISO standard carries the ISO logo and the designation, "International Standard".

THE SCOPE OF ISO'S WORK

ISO has more than 17,000 International Standards in its current portfolio. ISO's work program ranges from standards for traditional activities, such as agriculture and construction, through mechanical engineering, manufacturing and distribution, to transport, medical devices, information and communication technologies, and to standards for good management practice and for services.

EXAMPLES OF THE BENEFITS STANDARDS PROVIDE

Standardization of screw threads helps to keep chairs, children's bicycles, and aircraft together and solves the repair and maintenance problems caused by a lack of standardization that were once a major headache for manufacturers and product users.

Standards establishing an international consensus on terminology make technology transfer easier and safer. They are an important stage in the advancement of new technologies and dissemination of innovation.

Without the standardized dimensions of freight containers, international trade would be slower and more expensive.

Without the standardization of telephone and banking cards, life would be more complicated.

A lack of standardization may even affect the quality of life itself: for the disabled, for example, when they are barred access to consumer products, public transport and buildings because the dimensions of wheelchairs and entrances are not standardized.

Standardized symbols provide danger warnings and information across linguistic frontiers.

Consensus on grades of various materials gives a common reference for suppliers and clients in business dealings.

Agreement on a sufficient number of variations of a product to meet most current applications allows economies of scale with cost benefits for both producers and consumers. An example is the standardization of paper sizes.

Standardization of performance or safety requirements of diverse equipment makes sure that users' needs are met while allowing individual manufacturers the freedom to design their own solution on how to meet those needs.

Standardized computer protocols allow products from different vendors to "talk" to each other.

Standardized documents speed up the transit of goods, or identify sensitive or dangerous cargoes that may be handled by people speaking different languages.

Standardization of connections and interfaces of all types ensures the compatibility of equipment of diverse origins and the interoperability of different technologies.

Agreement on test methods allows meaningful comparisons of products, or plays an important part in controlling pollution—whether by noise, vibration, or emissions.

Safety standards for machinery protect people at work, at play, at sea... and at the dentist's.

Without the international agreement contained in ISO standards on metric quantities and units, shopping and trade would be haphazard, science would be unscientific and technological development would be handicapped.

WHAT'S DIFFERENT ABOUT ISO 9001 AND ISO 14001

The vast majority of ISO standards are highly specific to a particular product, material, or process. However, ISO 9001 (quality) and ISO 14001 (environment) are "generic management system standards." "Generic" means that the same standard can be applied to any organization, large or small, whatever its product or service, in any sector of activity, and whether it is a business enterprise, a public administration, or a government department. ISO 9001 contains a generic set of requirements for implementing a quality management system and ISO 14001 for an environmental management system.

Generic standards can be applied to any organization. In recent years, new ISO management system standards have been developed and are now being rolled out worldwide. They include: ISO 22000 (food safety), ISO 28000 (supply chain security), and ISO/IEC 27001 (information security).

WHY CONFORMITY ASSESSMENT IS IMPORTANT

"Conformity assessment" means checking that products, materials, services, systems, processes, or people measure up to the specifications of a relevant standard or specification. Today, many products require testing for conformity with specifications or compliance with safety, or other regulations before they can be put on many markets. ISO guides and standards for conformity assessment represent an international consensus on best practice. Their use contributes to the consistency of conformity assessment worldwide and so facilitates trade.

WHAT "INTERNATIONAL STANDARDIZATION" MEANS

When the large majority of products or services in a particular business or industry sector conform to International Standards, a state of industry-wide standardization exists. The economic stakeholders concerned agree on specifications and criteria to be applied consistently in the classification of materials, in the manufacture and supply of products, in testing and analysis, in terminology and in the provision of services. In this way, International Standards provide a reference framework, or a common technological language, between suppliers and their customers. This facilitates trade and the transfer of technology.

ISO'S ORIGINS

In 1946, delegates from 25 countries met in London and decided to create a new international organization, of which the object would be "to facilitate the international coordination and unification of industrial standards." The new organization, ISO, officially began operations on February 23, 1947, in Geneva, Switzerland.

WHO CAN JOIN ISO

Membership of ISO is open to national standards institutes most representative of standardization in their country (one member in each country).

- Full members, known as member bodies, each have one vote, whatever the size or strength of the economy of the country concerned.
- Correspondent members pay reduced membership fees. They are entitled to participate in any policy or technical body as observers, with no voting rights.
- Subscriber members also pay reduced membership fees. They are institutes from countries with very small

economies that nevertheless wish to maintain contact with international standardization.

Although individuals or enterprises are not eligible for membership, both have a range of opportunities for taking part in ISO's work:

- Individuals may be selected by national member institutes to serve as experts on national delegations participating in ISO technical committees
- Individuals and enterprises may provide their input during the process of developing a national consensus for presentation by the delegation. This may done through national mirror committees to the corresponding ISO technical committee
- International organizations and associations, both nongovernmental and representing industry sectors, can apply for liaison status to a technical committee. They do not vote, but can participate in the debates and the development of consensus.

There is a range of opportunities for taking part in ISO's work.

How the ISO System Is Managed

All strategic decisions are referred to the ISO members, who meet for an annual General Assembly. The proposals put to the members are developed by the ISO Council, drawn from the membership as a whole, which resembles the board of directors of a business organization.

ISO Council meets twice a year and its membership is rotated to ensure that it is representative of ISO's membership.

ISO's operations are managed by a Secretary-General, which is a permanent appointment resembling the chief executive of a business enterprise. The Secretary-General reports to the ISO Council, the latter being chaired by the President who is a prominent figure in standardization or in business, elected for 2 years.

The Secretary-General is based at ISO Central Secretariat in Geneva, Switzerland, with a compact staff which provides administrative and technical support to the ISO members, coordinates the decentralized standards' development program, and publishes the output.

How the ISO System Is Financed

ISO's national members pay subscriptions that meet the operational cost of ISO's Central Secretariat. The subscription paid by each member is in proportion to the country's Gross National Income and trade figures. Another source of revenue is the sale of standards.

However, the operations of ISO Central Secretariat represent only about one-fifth of the cost of the system's

International Federation—iSchools

operation. The main costs are borne by the member bodies that manage the specific standards development projects and the business organizations that provide experts to participate in the technical work. These organizations are, in effect, subsidizing the technical work by paying the travel costs of the experts and allowing them time to work on their ISO assignments.

HOW ISO DECIDES TO DEVELOP A STANDARD

ISO launches the development of new standards in response to sectors and stakeholders that express a clearly established need for them.

An industry sector or other stakeholder group typically communicates its requirement for a standard to one of ISO's national members. The latter then proposes the new work item to the relevant ISO technical committee developing standards in that area. New work items may also be proposed by organizations in liaison (see below) with such committees. When work items do not relate to existing committees, proposals may also be made by ISO members to set up new technical committees to cover new fields of activity.

To be accepted for development, a proposed work item must receive the majority support of the participating members of the ISO technical committee which, amongst other criteria, verifies the "global relevance" of the proposed item—this means that it indeed responds to an international need and will eventually be suitable for implementation on as broad a basis as possible worldwide.

WHO DEVELOPS ISO STANDARDS?

ISO standards are developed by technical committees, (subcommittees or project committees) comprising experts from the industrial, technical, and business sectors which have asked for the standards, and which subsequently put them to use. These experts may be joined by representatives of government agencies, testing laboratories, consumer associations, nongovernmental organizations, and academic circles.

Proposals to establish new technical committees are submitted to all ISO national member bodies, who may opt to be participating (P), observer (O) or nonmembers of the committee. The secretariat (i.e., the body providing the administrative support to the work of the committee) is allocated by the Technical Management Board (which itself reports to the ISO Council), usually to the ISO member body which made the proposal. The secretariat is responsible for nominating an individual to act as chair of the technical committee. The chair is formally appointed by the Technical Management Board.

Experts participate as national delegations, chosen by the ISO national member body for the country concerned.

National delegations are required to represent not just the views of the organizations in which their participating experts work, but those of other stakeholders too. National delegations are usually based on and supported by national mirror committees to which the delegations report.

According to ISO rules, the national member body is expected to take account of the views of all parties interested in the standard under development. This enables them to present a consolidated, national consensus position to the technical committee.

International and regional organizations from both business and the public sector may apply for liaison status to participate in developing a standard, or to be informed about the work. Such "organizations in liaisons" are accepted through voting by the relevant ISO committee. They may comment on successive drafts, propose new work items or even propose documents for "fast tracking," but they have no voting rights.

At the end of 2007, there were 3093 technical bodies in the ISO system, including 201 ISO technical committees. The focus of the technical committees is specialized and specific. In addition, ISO has three general policy development committees that provide strategic guidance for the standards' development work on cross-sector aspects. These committees ensure that the specific technical work is aligned with broader market and stakeholder group interests. They are:

- CASCO (conformity assessment)
- COPOLCO (consumer policy)
- DEVCO (developing country matters)

These may recommend the development of new standards for their stakeholder groups, which are then submitted to the approval process described above, or in the case of CASCO, develop new standards itself.

HOW ISO STANDARDS ARE DEVELOPED

The national delegations of experts of a committee meet to discuss, debate and argue until they reach consensus on a draft agreement. The "organizations in liaison" also take part in this work. In some cases, advanced work within these organizations means that substantial technical development and debate has already occurred, leading to some international recognition and in this case, a document may be submitted for "fast-track" processing. In both cases, the resulting document is circulated as a Draft International Standard (DIS) to all ISO's member bodies for voting and comment.

If the voting is in favor, the document, with eventual modifications, is circulated to the ISO members as a Final Draft International Standard (FDIS). If that vote is positive, the document is then published as an International Standard.

International Federation–iSchools

Every working day of the year, an average of seven ISO technical meetings takes place around the world. In between meetings, the experts continue the standards' development work by correspondence. Increasingly, their work is carried out by electronic means, which speeds up the development of standards and cuts travel costs.

- *Public access*
  Most ISO members have some form of public review procedures for making proposed work items and draft standards known and available to interested parties. The ISO members then take account of any feedback they receive in formulating their position on the proposed work item or on the draft standard.

  Draft standards are also available for sale to interested members of the public who can provide input through the ISO member in their country. The public can purchase International Standards through the ISO or through ISO's national members.
- *Consensus*
  Because ISO standards are voluntary agreements, they need to be based on a solid consensus of international expert opinion. Consensus, which requires the resolution of substantial objections, is an essential procedural principle. Although it is necessary for the technical work to progress speedily, sufficient time is required before the approval stage for the discussion, negotiation and resolution of significant technical disagreements.

  "Consensus" is officially defined (in ISO/IEC Guide 2) as "general agreement, characterized by the absence of sustained opposition to substantial issues by any important part of the concerned interests and by a process that involves seeking to take into account the views of all parties concerned and to reconcile any conflicting arguments." The definition notes, "Consensus need not imply unanimity."
- *Voting*
  For a document to be accepted as an ISO International Standard, it must be approved by at least two-thirds of the ISO national members that participated in its development and not be disapproved by more than a quarter of all ISO members who vote on it.
- *Appeals*
  ISO national member bodies have the right of appeal to a parent technical committee on the decision of subcommittee, to the Technical Management Board on a decision of technical committee and to the ISO Council on a decision of the Technical Management Board. Appeals may relate to procedural, technical, or administrative matters.
- *Review of International Standards*
  All International Standards are reviewed at the least 3 years after publication and every 5 years after the first review by all the ISO member bodies. A majority of the P-members of the TC/SC decides whether an International Standard should be confirmed, revised or withdrawn.

ISO DELIVERABLES

In addition to International Standards, ISO can also offer other forms of normative agreements for situations where speedy publication is important, has developed a schematic representation of the different types of deliverable available. These include:

- ISO/PAS Publicly Available Specification
- ISO/TS Technical Specification
- ISO/TR Technical Report
- IWA International Workshop Agreement

ISO'S INTERNATIONAL PARTNERS

ISO collaborates with its partners in international standardization, the International Electrotechnical Commission (IEC) and International Telecommunication Union (ITU). The three organizations, all based in Geneva, Switzerland, have formed the World Standards Cooperation (WSC) to act as a strategic focus for collaboration and the promotion of international standardization.

ISO has a close relationship with the World Trade Organization (WTO) which particularly appreciates the contribution of ISO's standards to reducing technical barriers to trade.

ISO collaborates with the United Nations (UN) Organization and its specialized agencies and commissions, particularly those involved in the harmonization of regulations and public policies, such as:

- CODEX Alimentarius, on food safety measurement, management, and traceability.
- UN Economic Commission for Europe (UN/ECE), on the safety of motor vehicles and the transportation of dangerous goods.
- World Health Organization (WHO), on health technologies.
- International Maritime Organization (IMO), on transport security.
- World Tourism Organization (WTO-T), on the quality of services related to tourism.

In addition, ISO cooperates with UN organizations that provide assistance and support to developing countries, such as the United Nations Conference on Trade and Development (UNCTAD), the United Nations Industrial Development Organization (UNIDO), and the International Trade Centre (ITC).

ISO's technical committees have formal liaison relations with some 580 international and regional organizations.

ISO has reinforced its links too with international organizations representing different groups of stakeholders, including:

International Federation– iSchools

- World Economic Forum (WEF)
- Consumers International (CI)
- World Business Council for Sustainable Development (WBCSD)
- International Federation of Standards Users (IFAN)

Lastly, ISO also collaborates regularly with the major international organizations for metrology, quality and conformity assessment.

ISO'S REGIONAL PARTNERS

Many of ISO's members also belong to regional standardization organizations. ISO has recognized regional standards organizations representing Africa, the Arab countries, the area covered by the Commonwealth of Independent States, Europe, Latin America, the Pacific area, and the South-East Asia nations. The regional bodies commit themselves to adopt ISO standards as the national standards of their members.

ISO TECHNICAL COMMITTEE ISO/TC 46, INFORMATION AND DOCUMENTATION

Improving the production, classification and organization of documents and data is essential to avoid wasting human and financial resources.

—Catherine Dhérent
Chair, ISO/TC 46 (2006–2008)

Within ISO, technical committee ISO/ISO/TC 46, *Information and documentation*, has the responsibility for standardization of practices relating to libraries, documentation and information centers, publishing, archives, records management, museum documentation, indexing and abstracting services, and information science.

The Secretariat of the committee is held by AFNOR, the ISO member for France, and the national standards bodies of 34 countries participate in its work: Armenia (SARM), Australia (SA), Austria (ON), Bulgaria (BDS), Canada (SCC), China (SAC), Czech Republic (CNI), Denmark (DS), Egypt (EOS), Finland (SFS), Germany (DIN), Iran, Islamic Republic of (ISIRI), Ireland (NSAI), Italy (UNI), Japan (JISC), Kenya (KEBS), Korea, Republic of (KATS), the Netherlands (NEN), New Zealand (SNZ), Norway (SN), Poland (PKN), Portugal (IPQ), Russian Federation (GOST R), South Africa (SABS), Spain (AENOR), Sri Lanka (SLSI), Sweden (SIS), Switzerland (SNV), Thailand (TISI), the former Yugoslav Republic of Macedonia (ISRM), United States (ANSI), Ukraine (DSSU), and the United Kingdom (BSI). Another 39 countries have observer status.

In addition, the following organizations have liaison status with ISO/TC 46:

- International Documentation Committee, International Council of Museums (CIDOC)
- International Confederation of Societies of Authors and Composers (CISAC)
- International Digital Object Identifier System Foundation (DOI)
- European Association of Science Editors (EASE)
- European Commission (EC)
- International Atomic Energy Agency (IAEA)
- International Council on Archives (ICA)
- International Council for Scientific and Technical Information (ICSTI)
- International Federation of Library Associations and Institutions (IFLA)
- International Federation of Science Editors (IFSE)
- ISSN International Centre
- International Telecommunication Union (ITU)
- International Network for Terminology (TERMNET)
- United Nations (UN)
- United Nations Conference on Trade and Development (UNCTAD)
- United Nations Economic Commission for Europe (UN/ECE)
- Universal Postal Union (UPU)
- World Intellectual Property Organization (WIPO)

Established in 1947—the year that ISO began operating—ISO/ISO/TC 46 has 94 ISO International Standards in its current portfolio and 23 documents under development.

The following titles and short descriptions of the committee's subcommittees (CS) and working groups (WG) conveys a more detailed idea of the scope of its standardization work:

- WG 2, *Coding of country names and related entities*
- WG 3, *Conversion of written languages*
- WG 4, *Terminology of information and documentation*
- WG 5, *Archive boxes*
- SC 4, *Technical interoperability*
  Standardization of protocols, schemas, etc., and related models and metadata for processes used by information organizations and content providers, including libraries, archives, museums, publishers, and other content producers.
- SC 8, *Quality—Statistics and performance evaluation*
  Standardization of practices relating to the collection of statistics and performance indicators for information organizations and content providers, e.g., libraries, archives, museums, and publishers.
- SC 9, *Identification and description*
  Standardization of information identifiers, description and associated metadata and models for use in information organizations (including libraries, museums,

International Federation–
iSchools

and archives) and the content industries (including publishing and other content producers and providers).

- SC 11, *Archives/records management*
  Standardization of principles for the creation and management of documents, records, and archives as evidence of transactions and covering all media including digital multimedia and paper.

In addition, SC 11 participates in a joint working group on document management application issues related to PDF/A files with SC 2, *Application issues*, of ISO/TC 171, *Document management applications*, and ISO/TC 42, *Photography*.

Over the past few decades, numerous standard tools have been conceived in the professional area on an international scale for identifying, classifying, finding, and exchanging all types of documents. These standards have been conceived in a context where the stability of the form of the document in space and time was controlled and where the use of computerized systems was centralized and dedicated to one type of application.

The production of electronic documentation and the transformation of structured, paper based business practices into automated work processes can in many instances lead to a loss of control, accountability, and structure in the electronic business environment. Providing guidance to facilitate records and information management in this context is a significant area in which ISO/TC 46 can contribute in the framework of its market environment.

With the production of electronic documents and the possibilities of exchanging digitized multimedia information on telematic networks, the traditional reference points for document maintenance have been dimmed, obliging the profession to question certain practices. The exchange of information is becoming generalized and concerns all sectors of activity; it is no longer about producing individual standards for the single sector of libraries and documentation, but to integrate in a process of multisectorial standardization, or risk being marginalized.

Adoption of open and generic standards has become imperative under these circumstances. If there is little immediate general demand, the whole realm of organization and individuals involved in formation is concerned by the work of ISO/TC 46 (libraries, archives, museums, document centers, publishers, producers, rights managers...) and to this effect, the economic impacts are real.

In this context, the following objectives have priority in the work of ISO/TC 46:

- Optimize the interoperability of systems related to archives, libraries, and museums.
- Take into account in standardization all the stages constituting the life cycle of a document (production, encoding, identification, management, diffusion, preservation) to assure the compatibility and coherence of the standards among themselves.

- Promote records management as a means to establish control and accountability in business environment.

EMBLEMATIC ISO/ISO/TC 46 STANDARDS

As the means to present, to classify, to sort, to display, to contextualize, to manage, to preserve... and finally to use the information in all industrial and intellectual areas, ISO/ISO/TC 46 plays a very important political and economic role. This becomes obvious when considering the use of some standards developed within ISO/ISO/TC 46, such as:

- ISO 3166, *Codes for the representation of names of countries and their subdivisions*. This is an essential example: the standard is used for internationalization of information as well as legal and diplomatic questions, on the Internet, e-business, and in many other contexts.
- Other standards such as: ISO 639, *Codes for languages* (developed by a joint working group of ISO/TC 37 and ISO/ISO/TC 46/SC 4), or ISO 690, *Bibliographic references—content, form and structure*, are universally used. (This standard is developed in a joint working group of ISO/TC 37 and ISO/ISO/TC 46/SC 4).
- For identification numbering, especially for the management of the rights of authors, producers, publishers, and so on. Any book, audiovisual work, textual work, music, film video, or sound recording has to be identified. The relevant standards for international numbering, such as the International Standard Book Number (ISBN), are developed by ISO/TC 46.
- For records management, which is a discipline that needs to be practiced by every organization in the world. Without appropriately managed records and the information and accountabilities they bring, organizations would not survive. The standard that covers this essential management process was created in ISO/TC 46.

THE MARKET FOR ISO/TC 46'S STANDARDS

The market served by ISO/TC 46 is characterized by a high degree of interdependence. Market players include for-profit (such as commercial businesses, system vendors, and publishers) and nonprofit institutions (such as libraries, documentation centers, archives, and museums). Increasingly there is convergence between the for-profit and the non-for-profit players as organizations assume multiple roles—often both supplying services to another institution and also the end user or consumer. The market is also moving to encompass the broader business environment as organizations become increasingly aware of the need to control, manage and effectively utilize their records and other forms of information.

International Federation—
iSchools

International Federation–
iSchools

Information and documentation supports the following information supply chain:

1. Creators of information (e.g., individuals within business, authors, performers)
2. Producers, distributors, and managers of information (e.g., publishers, printers, film and recording producers, booksellers, bibliographic networks, records management professionals, and archivists)
3. Organizers and providers of information to end users (e.g., librarians, booksellers, record sellers, museums, records managers, and archivists)
4. Preservers of information (e.g., archives, libraries, and museums)

The organizations and institutional groups dependent on ISO/TC 46 standards have overlapping responsibilities in the supply chain, but taken together represent the creation, dissemination, management, preservation, and consumption of documented information in all media: print, audio, visual, digital, etc.

STRUCTURE OF THE MARKET: SUPPLIERS/ MANUFACTURERS

• *Creators of information*
Creators include all public and private organizations and especially public agencies, and also the authors, editors, writers, compilers, performers, musicians, and all others originating information content. Most often this constituency is represented through professional organizations, such as authors' collectives, rights organizations, professional societies, etc. It also includes both individuals within businesses and the business organizations themselves that are required to create and maintain records of their activities.
• *Producers, distributors, and managers of information*
Producers and distributors include publishers (primary and secondary), distributors and information aggregators, and information intermediaries of information. These businesses serve primarily the end user providers of information products, such as booksellers, record stores, and libraries. Included are publishers in the commercial trade book sector; publishers focusing on the scholarly and scientific markets; medical and reference publishers; corporate business information providers; and producers of sound recordings and videos for all markets.

The book publisher market alone is huge. Standards applied by suppliers and manufacturers are critical to the effective functioning of the consumer part of this market.

Managers of information include all business organizations that are required, often by law, to have adequate frameworks in place for the protection and management of their information resources. It also includes archival institutions with responsibility for ensuring the management through time of archival resources.

STRUCTURE OF THE MARKET: CUSTOMERS

• *Organizers and end user providers*
Organizers and end user providers describe a step in the information supply chain in which produced information "packages" are conveyed primarily to end users or consumers. The activities include organizing and providing access that enables end users to find information, then supplying the information products that satisfy their needs. The principal institutional groups that are the suppliers of organization of and access to information are libraries, archives, museums, and product sellers (on or off-line, for all media).

The customers for this information are the end users. The organization and supply process requires standards to enable services across institutions, including standards for data elements, protocols, search types, data formats, object descriptions, object classification, language codes, country codes, specification of access and security rules, and other forms of metadata. The organizers and suppliers may also need standards to acquire information objects such as product numbers, acquisition metadata. To enable various technologies to be used in organizing and delivering information, specialized software is created that follows the above standards.
• *Archives and preservation*
There is a large market segment that has responsibility for archiving and preserving information for use by future generations. These range from preservation and conservation laboratories housed in most large libraries and archives, to records management departments associated with many organizations, to sound and film archives maintained by associations and other organizations, to formal government and nongovernment archives. These groups have special needs for making information sustainable, be it printed, electronic, sound, or image media, and are dependent on a variety of suppliers for critical components in the archiving process. Standards are essential for trying to carry out the work in a cost effective and consistent manner.

MAJOR FACTORS IMPACTING THE MARKET

Some of the main evolutions and market trends that will have an impact on the development of the information and documentation field are the following:

• Major technical evolution from creation, distribution, and storage of information in paper form to electronic form, and transformation of business processes from controlled paper-based activities to uncontrolled electronic processes.

- Convergence of media into multimedia information objects, making the creation, manufacture, organization, dissemination, and storage of information objects more complex.
- Increase in distance-learning initiatives and computer-based training developments that require new standards and challenge the information distribution mechanisms used today.
- The increasing dependence on and intersection with Web standards that are developed outside the TC and even outside ISO.
- Need for best practice-type guidelines in place of formal standards where media are new and sound standards cannot yet be developed.
- Pressure for shorter time scales for development of standards with parallel pressure to s that they are globally accepted.
- Increasing dependence on outsourcing by various segments of the community, requiring standards to be in place to be able to outsource efficiently and confidently.
- Growing interest in ISO 9001 quality management and development of related standards tools to make it effective across the many facets of the information and documentation area.
- Increasing need for statistics methodologies and standards for use with this diverse and not easily quantified market, to be used to support budgets and growth.
- Multilingual research in a Web environment.
- Some aspects of knowledge management and information management in a shared environment.
- Definition of the best devices for preservation of the collections in archives, libraries and museums.

BENEFITS EXPECTED FROM THE WORK OF ISO/TC 46

The benefits of standards in the information community are enormous but not easy to quantify. They include especially:

- Interoperability of information systems and resource hosts
- Cost savings through increased competition
- Better delivery through more choice
- Increase of universal access to information
- Assurance of protection to rights holders
- Preservation of cultural heritage
- Better management of information
- Sound bases for development of enabling supporting systems

- More accountable business practices.

ISO/TC 46'S OBJECTIVES

Based on the above considerations and on the multidisciplinarity and the multiapplicability of standards developed by ISO/TC 46, the committee has defined the following objectives:

Scope

- To ensure the creation of timely and appropriate standards governing all facets of information and documentation.
- To ensure interoperability and harmonization among systems concerned with information and documentation.
- To adapt standards in a proactive way to emerging media or techniques, based on continuing observation of emerging market needs.
- To facilitate and encourage the effective and accountable operation of systems and processes associated with information and documentation.

Quality

- To ensure consistency among standards that deal with different facets of information and documentation and consistency with the other ISO standards.
- To encourage comprehensive input from all types of bodies concerned with information and documentation, including libraries, publishers, archives, business organizations, public sector bodies, museums, vendors, systems vendors, W3C, etc.
- To improve the worldwide representation of experts on the committee.
- To finalize and publish standards in a timely fashion to ensure focus and coordinated efforts, and avoid obsolescence.

Adoption

- To encourage the private and public sectors in the use of existing ISO standards and show the value of using ISO standards.
- To be responsive to the needs of potential standards users to ensure that standards are optimized in terms of usability and relevance.

(More information on ISO/TC 46, including its membership, contact details, business plan, work program and list of published standards can be accessed on the ISO Web site http://www.iso.org. Click on "Standards development" and then on "List of technical committees.")

International Federation—
iSchools

International Federation—
iSchools

MANAGING INFORMATION IN A CHANGING AGE

(This text was first published in the April 2008 issue of *ISO Focus* magazine http://www.iso.org/isofocus which featured various aspects of ISO's standardization work for information and document management.)

Information and document management is a crucial part of the daily functioning of any organization. It plays an important role in ensuring their performance and security, as well as promoting efficient relationships between them. However, creating, finding and communicating the most relevant information to the audiences who really need it through the most appropriate and simple means, is no easy feat. Which results in many people complaining that information is too widely spread, not easy to find, identify or criticize.

Several ISO technical committees are working to respond to these challenges, by addressing issues from the identification to the preservation of the content and of metadata, by way of their production and organization. This is especially true of course, for the electronic formats of information. Here the available support is often more fragile than the worst and most acid of papers. We need strong best practices to preserve electronic data and documents in the middle and long terms.

A widely recognized basic ISO standard which addresses this issue is OAIS (Open Archive Initiative Standard). It was originally proposed by the aerospace industry, anxious to maintain permanent access, understanding and reusability of the huge amounts of data it produces (and requires), which can span decades or even centuries.

The purpose of this general model is to establish a system for archiving information (both digitized and physical), with an organizational scheme composed of people who accept the responsibility of preserving information and making it available to a designated community.

This model must now be completed by other users, which explains why Web archiving experts recently launched a new standard project on the identification of data packets during their transfer to a virtual archive in the context of OAIS.

This identification is in fact crucial for exchanging data adequately, and for managing intellectual and economic rights. In fact, it is necessary to identify all elements of information in the greatest detail, so as to deal in the most appropriate manner with the rights of authors, producers, and publishers, while at the same time providing exactly what the public requires.

We are now able to identify even the smallest part of an author's work, which though it can be made available to all interested parties (on the Web for instance), still ensures a fair retribution and acknowledgement of its author. At the same time, there is also an ongoing attempt to identify authors, producers, publishers, and others, a more delicate task, as it involves the description of individuals rather than their work.

The improvement of the production, classification, and organization of the main documents and data is also essential to avoid wasting of human and financial resources. It is the aim of the records management standards to help institutions better produce the information needed to prove their rights and obligations towards their stakeholders.

It would be fruitful experience for ISO to first coordinate the management of its own documentation in relation with that of its national bodies. The great challenge is to identify what must be preserved, for what purpose and for how many years and where? We must not waste time nor money. It is crucial that we immediately provide the right information to the right person.

ACKNOWLEDGMENT

This entry is reproduced with the permission of the International Organization for Standardization, ISO, http://www.iso.org.

International Records Management Standards ISO 15489 and 23081

Barbara Reed
Recordkeeping Innovation, Sydney, New South Wales, Australia

Abstract

The first international standard on records management, ISO 15489, was issued in 2001, followed in 2006/2007 by standards on Metadata for Records, ISO 23081. This entry outlines the history of the development of these standards and provides an overview of their contents. The impact of the records management standards is discussed followed by an assessment of the strategic uses of such standardization work.

INTRODUCTION

The International Standard on Records Management ISO 15489: Information and Documentation, Records Management, was formally launched in Montreal in November 2001. It consists of two parts: Part 1: General and Part 2: Guidelines. The Standard has been endorsed for adoption for a further period of 5 years, and is now due for review in 2011. Following the publication of the Records Management Standard, the Committee charged with establishing and administering records management standards (ISO TC 46 SC11) has issued further standards, most notably ISO 23081 on Metadata for Records, and its accompanying Guidelines for Implementation. Other work on developing technical reports as ancillary documents to support the implementation of specific aspects of the standard is underway.

This entry discusses the ISO 15489, Records Management Standard in terms of its history, development, and contents. It then discusses the history, development, and content of ISO 23081, Metadata for Records. The entry concludes with an assessment of the impact of the standards and a consideration of the strategic uses of such standardization work.

Background to the Development of ISO 15489

Within the Australian recordkeeping community, the requirement for a standard on recordkeeping was identified in 1992 emerging from discussions on implementing quality systems in compliance with requirements in the ISO 9000 series of standards. What constituted good recordkeeping to support quality management? It is noteworthy that this question first arose from the private sector, rather than the government sector most commonly identified with formalized recordkeeping. Answering that question engaged the Australian recordkeeping community in 5 years of collaborative work between 1992 and 1997, a period of intense creativity and rethinking in the Australian recordkeeping community, culminating in the publication of AS 4390-1996, the Australian Standard on Records Management.[1] This Standard was issued in six parts, each covering a major functional area of recordkeeping.

In 1997, following a suggestion to the International Standards Organization to adopt the Australian standard as an international standard, a ballot was held internationally across the participating national standards organizations. The results were sufficient to adopt the Australian standard as an international standard in a fast track process, but because considerable interest in the document had been evidenced in the process of balloting and some divergent views raised, it was determined that a more appropriate outcome would be to form an international project to establish consensus in the content of a Records Management Standard.

Work commenced on internationalizing the Australian standard in 1998 using the existing Australian work as the base document for development. The existing six-part structure was merged into a single document for consideration. Considerable debate and discussion ensued in the next few years.

Some of the concepts and content of the Australian standard were thought to be specific to the national practice. Different methodologies for achieving specific recordkeeping outcomes were posited as equally valid. Initial attempts to create a set of appendices to the document outlining jurisdiction specific practices resulted in a document which was unmanageably large and cumbersome. The decision to separate the broad principles into Part 1: General and the more particular methodological approaches into Part 2: Guidelines overcame this impasse. As work progressed on Part 2, the more methodological approaches, consensus on approach was achieved as similarities were emphasized rather than differences.

Encyclopedia of Library and Information Sciences, Fourth Edition DOI: 10.1081/E-ELIS4-120044328
Copyright © 2017 by Taylor & Francis. All rights reserved.

International Federation–
iSchools

EVOLUTION FROM THE BASE AUSTRALIAN STANDARD

Of particular note in the formative discussions was the need to gain consensus on the definition of record, which was strongly articulated in the Australian work as "evidence of business activity." This articulation was the result of a number of years of extensive and introspective discussion in the Australian recordkeeping context, and was a view that was vigorously defended in the international sphere. The conceptual alignment of the Australian view to the European notions of a singular conception of record/archive created an interesting alignment of interests and something of a dichotomy in the international English-speaking records community, in which U.K.- and U.S.-based colleagues advocated a distinct difference between records and archives. The Australian view of recordkeeping, a very broad conceptual approach providing a framework consistent with the records continuum view, encompassed records in all contexts including their archival manifestations. This provided ground for much discussion. In the end, a compromise position on this was adopted which gave ground to the notion of a separate "records management" regime.

Other views were staunchly defended, including the strong emphasis on records being closely linked and aligned to the organizational functions and activities that resulted in their creation. The process of records classification was particularly controversial, but the close connection between functions and activities, the role of records and the importance of the central concept of provenance in interpreting records prevailed over alternative views which suggested that more library-oriented approaches to classification be adopted. Similarly controversial was the Australian concept of appraisal which expanded the traditional notion of appraisal from a process of evaluating the disposal and retention requirements for records into a broader notion encompassing defining what records were determined for creation/capture. This could not be reconciled. Appraisal therefore is not specifically mentioned as a process within the standard, but rather the two concepts—"determining documents to be captured into a records system" and "determining how long to retain records"—are independently addressed.

A tension in traditions of recordkeeping needed to be articulated and resolved. The traditional approach to records management in the United States supported primarily "post-action" controls. That is, records management controls were applied after the business action was completed. In contrast, the document being discussed for international adoption articulated a "pre-control" framework, where control of documents as records from the time they were received into an organizational framework, both prior to and during the conduct of the business action. This pre-action framework was more aligned to the European traditions of recordkeeping.

Work on the internationalization of the standard was taking place in the late 1990s in an environment where the management of electronic records as business enablers was really only beginning. Countries were at different stages in their attempts to control the proliferation of information in the workplace. Tensions were apparent between paper-based processes and the need to rethink those processes into an electronic world.

Much of the initial work in the development of the ISO 15489 came from establishing mutual understanding across language and cultural barriers and establishing a strong community respect for the views of diverse traditions and approaches to recordkeeping. The close alignment of records and archives in European countries with little distinction between the two created both an opportunity for knitting a closer conceptual bonding of records in all environments, but at the same time, a barrier to achieving the work in hand. It is possibly unfortunate in the longer term that the introduction of a new term "records management" into many non-English speaking countries seems to have undermined the conceptual unity in the European view. This conceptual unity was very present in the Australian notion of recordkeeping, but unable to be sustained at the time.

CONTENT OF THE STANDARD

ISO 15489 Part 1: General,[2] following introductory matters (Sections 1–3) contains:

- Statements outlining the organizational benefits of records management (Section 4).
- Clear requirements to locate and contextualize records management within the organizational and regulatory environment (Section 5).
- Concise statements of the responsibilities for records, including strong statements that recordkeeping roles are implicit in the activities of all employees, overall responsibility for programs and resources reside with management layers within organizations, while specific responsibility for establishing systems, frameworks and implementation reside with recordkeeping professionals (Section 6).
- Characteristics of records programs, records and records systems are outlined, including high level statements on their requirement to ensure that records survive as long as they are needed, which may be beyond the boundaries of specific technological applications implemented to manage records (Section 7).
- A high level statement of a methodology to achieve records management within an organization (Section 8).
- Records management processes including creation, retention, registration, classification, storage and handling, access and security, tracking, location, and implementing disposition (Section 9).

- Monitoring and auditing requirements (Section 10) and
- Training requirements (Section 11).

Perhaps the section of the standard of greatest strategic reach is that defining the characteristics of records. Section 7.2, which owes a debt to the InterPARES 1 research project,[3] clearly identifies the distinction between records and other types of information resources in terms of their defining characteristics of authenticity, integrity, reliability, and usability.

ISO 15489 Part 2: Guidelines,[4] broadly follows the structure of Part 1 of the Standard, providing greater detail on the methodological approach known as "Developing and Implementing Records Systems" (Section 3). It echoes the structure of Section 9 of Part 1 of the Standard in expanding on the specific processes of recordkeeping (Section 4), and in expanding on requirements for monitoring and auditing (Section 5), and training (Section 6). Part 2 contains two annexes which map between the Guidelines and the general requirements in Part 1.

ISO 23081, Metadata for Records

The second suite of standards to emerge from the international standards committee on Records Management is ISO 23081: Information and documentation, Records Management Processes, Metadata for Records. This standard also exists in two parts: Part 1 being "Principles" (published in 2006)[5] and Part 2 is "Conceptual and Implementation Issues" (published in 2007 as a technical specification but being proposed as an international standard).[6]

Recordkeeping metadata is of key importance in managing records in the electronic world. Articulating the recordkeeping requirements for metadata positions the recordkeeping community to contribute strongly to an emerging technical dialogue defining the behavior and characteristics of electronic information. The goal of articulating recordkeeping metadata is to ensure that particular resources can act as authoritative evidence of business action in the electronic world. This involves records being sustainable over application system boundaries in ways that render them able to be used and interpreted for as long as they are required. The conceptual stance of the metadata standard is to provide a unifying framework for the management of metadata about records regardless of their location, or age, or custody. Thus, it addresses records in all domains of action, including current operational systems, but stretching to records in archival repositories. Recordkeeping metadata, while by no means restricted to electronic records, none the less has a greater immediate and strategic impact in the electronic world.

BACKGROUND TO THE DEVELOPMENT OF THE STANDARD

Recordkeeping metadata was first addressed in research projects, that of the University of Pittsburgh (U.S.) project "Functional Requirements for Evidence in Recordkeeping," 1993–1996,[7,8] and following that Monash University's (Australia) project "Recordkeeping Metadata Standards for Managing and Accessing Information Resources in Networked Environments Over Time for Government, Commerce, Social, and Cultural Purposes," 1998–1999.[9] Using these projects as a basis, a number of recordkeeping metadata element sets were developed for specific jurisdictional purposes.[10–12] This was an area that was suited to an international standardization process seeking uniformity across requirements to enable vendor uptake and incorporation into application systems for records. In Australia, as various local jurisdictions adopted variations from the metadata standards established, forming a cohesive specification was seen as particularly desirable. There will always be a need for local and tailored implementation specific variables in recordkeeping metadata. The Australian Standards development community created generic models and high level guidance in these areas at the same time as the international community was working on the principles for recordkeeping metadata. The two sets of work were merged, with the Australian work being incorporated into Part 2 of the international standard.

CONTENT OF THE METADATA STANDARD

At the level of an international standard, the nature of the guidance provided to the implementing community is different from that applicable within a specific jurisdiction or domain. Thus the International Standard on Metadata for Records defines a framework and principles within which specific jurisdictions can further define their implementation guidelines. It positions recordkeeping metadata in relation to metadata from other closely related information disciplines and purposes—for example, information resource discovery, e-commerce, preservation and rights management (Section 7).

Part 1 of the Metadata for Records standards outlines the principles involved in defining records metadata. It adopts the following model of recordkeeping (Fig. 1) to illustrate the concepts:

The standard then outlines the requirements for recordkeeping metadata to fulfill the requirements outlined in the ISO 15489, International Standard on Records Management (Section 9.2). While the standard restricts its scope to the business environment implicit in the domain of records management, the models and principles it outlines applies to records regardless of their age,

International Federation–
iSchools

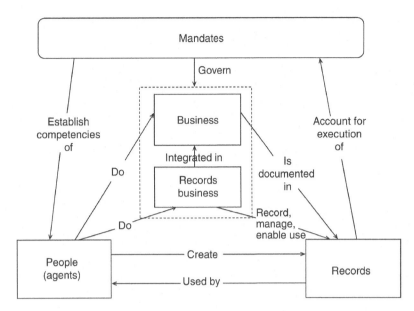

International Federation–
iSchools

Fig. 1 Main metadata types and their relationships. This model provides a conceptual approach to managing records in their context. Records are conceptualized as existing within a web of relationships to people (agents, structures), business (functions and activities), and mandates (legislation, authorizing competencies, policies, delegations). This view enables metadata to be identified for each of these separate entities and linked together via relationships, rather than having to be encompassed within the notion of the record itself. In metadata terms, this allows many different implementation options to be explored and articulated as suits the capacity and technological capability of the implementation site.
Source: From ISO 23081-1,[13] Derived from Figure 2: Recordkeeping and Figure 3: The Business Context, included in Mckemmish.[14]

format, or location, thus acting as a unified recordkeeping model for metadata in all environments.

One of the most important concepts outlined in the standard is the distinction between:

- Metadata assigned at the point of capture of a record into a management system which defines its context of creation and its structural and technical properties at a specific point in time.
- Recordkeeping process metadata which continues to accumulate as business and recordkeeping actions take place on the record (Section 5.2).

This notion is a powerful means of communicating the characteristics of records required to be addressed in the electronic world. It also distinguishes recordkeeping metadata from some other types of metadata in emphasizing the continual accumulation of metadata and requirements for automatic capture of this metadata as opposed to manual methods of "cataloging" or attributing user specified metadata.

Part 2 of the International Standard on Metadata for Records focuses on the conceptual and implementation issues involved in implementing recordkeeping metadata, covering issues such as developing schemas (Section 10), organizational variables in implementation and requirements for managing recordkeeping for metadata itself (Section 11). It provides guidance on implementing recordkeeping metadata in a relational way managing multiple entities and their continuing relationships over time or alternatively by "flattening" the multiple entities into fewer or even a single entity (Section 6.3). The notion of aggregation and aggregation levels required to manage records is discussed with a standardized scheme established to identify equivalence of aggregations across different implementations and to assist in implementing

recordkeeping interoperability (Section 7.1). A generic recordkeeping metadata model (Fig. 2) for defining specific types of elements required to manage records is introduced and elaborated (Sections 8 and 9).

Impact of Records Management Standards

A formal study of the impact of the ISO 15489 has been undertaken studying its uptake and impact in the United Kingdom[15,16] In that research, the organizational context, circumstances, and size of the organization were determined to be a key determinant in the uptake and influence of the Standard on organizational behavior.

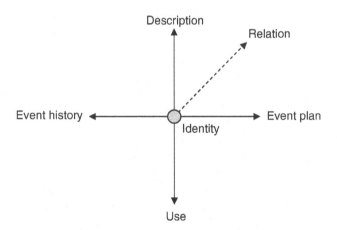

Fig. 2 Generic metadata model for managing records.
Source: From Figure 6 in *ISO/TS 23081-2: Information and Documentation, Records Management Processes, Metadata for Records, Part 2: Conceptual and Implementation Issues*; International Standards Organisation: Geneva, Switzerland, 2007, Section 8.1.[17]

However, other less precise measures exist to attest to the importance of records standard in the international context. The quantity of international sales of the ISO 15489 standard are reputed to rival the quantity of sales of the ISO 9000 suite.[16]

Every year, more countries join the community of developers actively participating in the Committee meetings to determine the scope, direction, and development of the Standards. In November 2007, over 120 active participants were registered within the international standards committee, representing over 26 individual countries, with a further 12 countries registered as "observers" to the Committee.[18] The Standard has been translated into over 10 languages, and representatives of each continent (with the exception of South America) are active participants. The Euro-Centric nature of ISO development and the English-speaking origins of the original ISO 15489 work has been superseded by a truly international community.

Role of Standards

Establishing standards is often a two-edged sword. On the one hand, codifying a body of practice to ensure it is carried out consistently vies with the other view that codifying practice means stifling innovation. The process nature of the ISO 15489 and the breadth of vision of the ISO 23081 standards attempt to mitigate against the evils of the latter. However, in aspiring to standards that enable rather than restrict, some frustration about lack of precision results.

Standards serve multiple purposes. In recordkeeping, our standards can be viewed from any one of the following perspectives:

- *As a place marker*: In this role, the standards setting work clearly articulates the concepts of recordkeeping, its importance and its specific characteristics. This acts as a clear delineator of recordkeeping from other methods of managing information. It stands in contrast to homogenizing views that everything is just information and that particular disciplines are merely guarding their professional domain in not accepting such a homogenized view. Similarly, it acts as a clear statement to others outside the recordkeeping profession who, for a variety of reasons, wish to restrict the scope of records practice to those areas applying only to paper-based records, to disposal and retention or to compliance issues.
- *As a set of facilitative tools*: The standards established in this domain have been adopted and adapted by a number of specific jurisdictions and by individual organizations seeking to achieve best practice. In adopting the frameworks and principles, the requirements for more and further definition and attention to specific aspects of recordkeeping have been identified,

creating an ongoing tide of development fuelling a process of continuing improvement.

- *As a means of profession building*: Providing international standards which set out clearly an area of specialized practice enables profession building. Once standards exist they can be cited by organizations and in other standards. They act as means of professionalizing the practice of recordkeeping. This is particularly important in the electronic environment where the homogenizing effect of generic information management has undermined the records' specific tasks in systems design and organizational consciousness. The standards act as strong statements from which individual practitioners can launch their claims to attention within organizations, as well as provide guidance on how to achieve the required outcomes.
- *As a means of improving practice*: The recordkeeping standards have been defined to be slightly ahead of practice. They have an agenda-setting role rather than just documenting the status quo. This is an important role of standards, but must be done knowingly and with a clear strategic vision.
- *As a means of achieving a significant mass*: The fact that these recordkeeping standards are international standards creates a worldwide community advocating and requiring the same outcomes. Records practitioners are a small group relative to other professional groupings in information management. Achieving international consensus increases the power of an individual disciplinary requirement, enabling a much greater degree of influence to be exerted. This can be seen in the impact in the vendor community developing software to manage records. The consolidated international market is big enough to have an effect in product direction and outcomes required, where individual fragmented smaller groups may never achieve sufficient strategic leverage.

CONTINUING WORK

The work of the ISO TC 46/SC11 Committee charged with developing international standards in recordkeeping is continuing. A further standard published is ISO 23310-2006, Information and Documentation: Guidelines for Standards Drafters for Stating Records Management in Standards, a standard geared to ensuring the appropriate inclusion of recordkeeping requirements into other standards.

Work is progressing on developing standard or technical reports on Work Process Analysis for Recordkeeping, Digitization, defining long-term retention requirements of electronic records, digital records conversion and migration. A recent strategic decision to move the Records Standards family into a Management Systems Structure is designed to enhance the status, impact, and coherence of the records standards.

International Federation–iSchools

CONCLUSION

The development of international standards for record-keeping has created a community of practitioners that extends worldwide, bridging language barriers. The impact of the work is evident in the adoption of the Standard into multiple jurisdictions and an increased international coherence in practice. Work continues within the standards development community to produce the next generation of standards and guidance to support implementations.

REFERENCES

1. AS 4390.1-6. *Australian Standard: Records Management*; Standards Australia: Homebush, 1996.
2. ISO 15489-1. *Information and Documentation: Records Management, Part 1: General*; International Standards Organisation: Geneva, 2001.
3. Duranti, L., Ed. *The Long Term Preservation of Authentic Electronic Records: Findings of the InterPARES Project*; Archilab: San Miniato, 2005. Available at http://www.interpares.org/book/index.cfm (accessed March 2008).
4. ISO 15489-2. *Information and Documentation: Records Management, Part 2: Guidelines*; International Standards Organisation: Geneva, 2001.
5. ISO 23081-1. *Information and Documentation, Records Management Processes, Metadata for Records, Part 1: Principles*; International Standards Organisation: Geneva, 2004.
6. ISO/TS 23081-2. *Information and Documentation, Records Management Processes, Metadata for Records, Part 2: Conceptual and Implementation Issues*; International Standards Organisation: Geneva, 2007.
7. Bearman, D. *Metadata Specifications Derived from Functional Requirements: A Reference Model for Business Acceptable Communications*, 1996. Available at http://www.archimuse.com/papers/nhprc/meta96.html (accessed March 2008).
8. Bearman, D. Sochats, K. Metadata requirements for evidence. In *Automating 21st Century Science—The Legal, Regulatory, Technical and Social Aspects of Electronic Laboratory Notebooks and Collaborative Computing in R&D*; Lysakowski, R., Schmidt, S., Eds.; TeamScience Publishing, 1996. Available at http://www.archimuse.com/papers/nhprc/BACartic.html (accessed March 2008).
9. McKemmish, S. *Report on the 1998–99 Strategic Partnerships with Industry—Research & Training (SPIRT) Project, Recordkeeping Metadata Standards for Managing and Accessing Information Resources in Networked Environments Over Time for Government, Commerce, Social and Cultural Purposes*. Available at http://www.sims.monash.edu.au/research/rcrg/research/spirt/spirtreport.html (accessed March 2008).
10. National Archives of Australia. *Recordkeeping Metadata Standard for Commonwealth Agencies*, 1999. Available at http://www.naa.gov.au/Images/rkms_pt1_2_tcm2-1036.pdf (accessed March 2007).
11. The National Archives (U.K.). *Records Management Metadata Standard*, 2002, Available at http://www.govtalk.gov.uk/documents/Records_management_metadata_standard_2002.pdf (accessed December 2007).
12. State Records South Australia, *South Australian Recordkeeping Metadata Standard*, 2008; (version 3, revised from 2003 original). Available at http://www.archives.sa.gov.au/files/management_standard_metadata.pdf (accessed March 2008).
13. Figure 1 in ISO 23081-1. *Information and Documentation, Records Management Processes, Metadata for Records, Part 1: Principles*, International Standards Organisation: Geneva, 2004.
14. Derived from Figure 2: Recordkeeping and Figure 3: The Business Context, included in Mckemmish S. Conceptual and Relationship models: Records in Business and Socio-Legal Contexts, in Recordkeeping Metadata Standards for Managing and Accessing Information Resources in Networked Environments Over Time for Government, Commerce, Social and Cultural Purposes. Available at http://www.sims.monash.edu.au/research/rcrg/research/spirt/reports.
15. McLeod, J. Childs, S. *Assessing the Impact of ISO 15489: The First International Standard for Records Management. Final Project Report, October 2005. Information Society Research & Consultancy Group, School of Computing, Engineering and Information Sciences*; Northumbria University: Newcastle upon Tyne, U.K., 2005. Available at http://northumbria.ac.uk/static/5007/isorep (accessed March 2008).
16. Moldrich, D. *La gestión de documentos en el entorno digital: La importancia de la norma ISO 15489*, San Diago de Compostela, May 10, 2007;as Jornadas Españolas de Documantación.
17. Figure 6 in ISO/TS 23081-2. *Information and Documentation, Records Management Processes, Metadata for Records, Part 2: Conceptual and Implementation Issues*; International Standards Organisation: Geneva, 2007, Section 8.1.
18. ISO/TC 46/SC11 N 787, *2007 Secretariat Report to the 19th Meeting, November 5–8, 2007*, Pretoria: South Africa, November 2007.

International Federation–iSchools

International Records Management Trust

Anne Thurston
International Records Management Trust, London, U.K.

Abstract

The significance of reliable and trustworthy records for public sector accountability and effectiveness, and the impact on citizens' rights when they are not managed, is far greater than is often realized. Records are the clearest and most durable evidence of the organization's operations, decisions, and activities. They are the underpinning factor in good governance. The International Records Management Trust (IRMT), a UK-registered charity governed by a board of trustees, exists for the sole purpose of supporting lower-resource countries in tackling the issues involved in managing public sector records as an essential national resource.

The IRMT was created in 1989 in response to a global study that documented widespread and progressive deterioration in the management of public sector records. It has always emphasized the significance of well-managed records for protecting and supporting citizens' interests as the evidence base for national and international development. It works with governments around the world to strengthen records systems as a basis for improved services for citizens; effective resource management; open, accountable, and transparent democracies; and national historical identity. From the time of its establishment, the IRMT has been committed to working with records professionals and their governments to find and apply new solutions for managing official records. In an environment of rapid administrative and technological change, it has become ever more important to find new solutions to protecting records as evidence.

INTRODUCTION

International efforts to reduce poverty, control corruption, strengthen democracy, and increase openness all depend on an evidence base of authentic records. In the rapidly evolving digital information environment, there are growing expectations for using information to support openness and digital development. However, information benefits are not automatic. The digital information created and held in IT systems is highly vulnerable; its value as evidence can easily be diminished or lost. An information governance/records management framework is essential to protect the availability and integrity of this evidence and to ensure that it provides a reliable evidence base for meeting development goals. The International Records Management Trust (IRMT) works with governments to help build this framework.

The IRMT is unique in its attention to the close relationship between records and good governance. A UK-registered charity governed by a board of trustees, the IRMT, was created in 1989 in response to a global study involving visits to several dozen lower-resource countries across the world where it was observed that records systems were weak and in many cases had decayed into informality. In some countries, information had become so difficult to retrieve that government operations relied increasingly on memory. In the paper environment, the loss of control of information integrity and of access to information resulting from weak record keeping had created an open door for corruption, misuse of resources, and abuse of citizens' rights.

Managing records efficiently will not, in itself, halt corruption, protect citizens' rights, and bring about good governance, but development goals cannot be achieved without trustworthy evidence. There are now great hopes that digital government will provide solutions, but the speed with which information technologies are being adopted around the world is not being matched by the skills and infrastructure needed to manage the records they generate, with the result that the accurate information needed to support economic growth, the rule of law, and initiatives aimed at supporting transparency and accountability are undermined.

Over the last two and a half decades, the IRMT has worked with governments around the world to strengthen paper and digital records systems as a basis for improved services for citizens, effective resource management, and increasingly accountable and transparent democracies. The IRMT's program of work is funded by grants and contracts from national and international development agencies that have included the World Bank, the UK Department for International Development, the Commonwealth Secretariat, the Canadian International Development Research Centre, and the United Nations Development Program.

The IRMT works continually to identify new ways of collaborating with governments, international agencies, and records professionals to articulate the requirements

Encyclopedia of Library and Information Sciences, Fourth Edition DOI: 10.1081/E-ELIS4-120053402
Copyright © 2017 by Taylor & Francis. All rights reserved.

International Federation–
iSchools

International Federation–iSchools

for managing records as evidence and to apply international good practice to meet local requirements in support of evidence-based governance. The IRMT employs core staff in London, works with a large team of international consultants, and liaises with a range of professional associations, consultancy firms, academic institutions, and NGOs to define strategies and deliver its portfolio of records and information management projects. It draws on its wide-ranging field experience and extensive international network of professional contacts to assist records professionals and government stakeholders from lower-resource countries in building awareness, capacity, and effective solutions. Its projects are described on its website: http://www.irmt.org. All of its products can be downloaded free of charge.

ORIGINS OF THE IRMT

Between 1984 and 1988, the University of London, through the Institute of Commonwealth Studies and the Department of Information Studies, and with funding from the Leverhulme Trust, carried out an extensive field study of the management of government records across 32 countries in Africa, the Caribbean, and Asia. The aim was to identify capacity requirements as a basis for developing a relevant program of studies for international records and archives students. The study revealed a largely unrecognized but internationally significant issue—an extensive breakdown in public record keeping across the several dozen countries visited. It resulted in a new approach to educating records and archives professionals at University College London. It also led to the establishment of the IRMT in 1989 as a nonprofit vehicle for addressing the conditions that were observed.

While specific conditions varied from country to country, the overall result was the loss of control of records, and the consequences for governments were broadly similar. The study made it clear that legal and organizational structures were not in place to manage official documents, that officials could not locate the information they needed to take decisions, that vast quantities of closed records with no ongoing value were being kept in government offices at great expense, and that national history and heritage were not being protected or preserved (Fig. 1).

The study considered the causes of this situation. It reported that the countries visited lacked national strategies, policies, frameworks, and systems for managing the official records needed to support national evidentiary requirements and that the status of the records profession was low or very low in virtually all of the countries visited. Although the national archives had statutory responsibility for official records, they were isolated from the management of public administration, often playing little or no role in managing the current records that were essential for delivering government functions and protecting citizens' rights and that would one day become historical archives. Because they focused almost exclusively on the historical archives created in earlier decades, the national archives were seen as largely irrelevant to the government operations, and governments allocated them very sparse resources for delivering their work. Records professionals were not trained to tackle these challenges. The breakdown of records systems that resulted from this situation had significant consequences for governments and for citizens in terms of opportunities for fraud, corruption in procurement, a lack of evidence for protecting civil and human rights, and difficulties in managing financial and human resources.

Fig. 1 Weak records systems meant that officials could not locate the information they needed to take decisions.

Much of the IRMT's early work was focused on developing practical approaches to bringing order to the vast backlogs of unmanaged records that had built up across government agencies due to the lack of controls. Offices and corridors were piled high with stacks of records, many of them inactive. The volume was so great that it was not uncommon to find staff surrounded by piles of files, sometimes even sitting on files, or with files filling the space under their desks. Whole offices were out of use because they were crammed with inactive files. The Head of Civil Service in one country described the situation as "walking on files." Not only did it become increasingly difficult to find information needed to deliver government functions, but the situation represented a serious security risk and an open door for corruption.

The IRMT developed a methodology for bringing order to this information through hands-on workshops, where records professionals and students began the task of sorting, assessing, structuring the records, and, where it was legally appropriate, destroying paper files with no ongoing value. It also developed assessment tools and training materials geared to defining the regulatory frameworks and control systems and building the practical skills needed to establish sustainable controls.

By the mid-1990s, the rapid growth of information technology was creating an awareness of the value of information and opportunities for its use. Governments and international development planners hoped that technology would solve the information problems that had become so widespread, and international investment in computerizing government functions and improving Internet connectivity began on a large scale. Crucially, virtually no attention was given to addressing the major new challenges of capturing and preserving fragile digital information created by computerized systems as reliable evidence. As technology had an increasing impact on the way that records were created, used, and stored, the IRMT committed itself to supporting the transition from paper to digital records as the basis for delivering government operations and enabling accountability.

Over the last two decades, the trend toward digital governance has expanded steadily, with government business and communications being routinely delivered electronically, personal computers becoming the norm, large-scale computerized systems being introduced to support the management of key state functions and resources, and scanned images being regarded as an effective alternative to paper copies. The crucial function of managing the fragile digital records that were created was not recognized as an essential component of this process, and this remains a largely unrecognized risk for the delivery of the digital development agenda. Finding new means of highlighting the issues and of integrating them into digital development planning remains a central focus of the IRMT's work.

SIGNIFICANCE OF DIGITAL RECORDS AS EVIDENCE FOR GLOBAL DEVELOPMENT GOALS

The unparalleled growth of information and communications technologies (ICTs) worldwide offers tremendous new possibilities for effective governance and social inclusion. There is a new level of global awareness of the value and power of information for economic development and for eradicating extreme poverty. The Open Government Partnership is committed to the goal of making information open to citizens as the foundation for empowering civil society, with an emphasis on Right to Information and Open Data. At the same time, the UN is preparing for the Post-2015 UN Development Agenda aimed at eradicating poverty and transforming economies. In May 2013, the Report of the High-Level Panel of Eminent Persons on the Post-2015 UN Development Agenda noted, "We need a transparency revolution so citizens can see exactly where their taxes, aid and revenues from extractive industries are spent. We need governments that tackle the causes of poverty, empower people, are transparent, and permit scrutiny of their affairs."

Delivering these goals will require reliable evidence of what governments plan, do, and spend. Just as in the paper environment, in the digital environment, achieving poverty reduction, controlling corruption, building accountability and transparency, and supporting citizen engagement will require authentic and reliable records. Digital records will be needed to provide the basis for defining and delivering day-to-day operations, including budgeting, planning, monitoring, and evaluating, as well as for management controls, including regulations, standards, audits, and investigations. In the new context of openness, digital records will be essential to efforts to make information available to citizens through Right to Information/Freedom of Information or Open Data Initiatives, which will be meaningful only if reliable evidence is available and can be accessed.

At present, in the digital environment, the requirements for protecting, preserving, and making this evidence available are not in place in many countries worldwide. There is a significant risk that the evidence needed to support development goals will not be available, authentic, and trustworthy unless these risks are mitigated.

VULNERABILITY OF DIGITAL RECORDS AS EVIDENCE

Electronic media deteriorate, software changes, and hardware becomes obsolete. Valuable records and data can be difficult to retrieve after a few years or even after a few months. Digital information can easily be manipulated, deleted, fragmented, or lost, leaving critical gaps and

International Federation– iSchools

International Federation–
iSchools

Fig. 2 Digital information can easily be manipulated, deleted, fragmented, or lost.

resulting in misguided policy, misdirected funding, cover-up of fraud, and weak data and statistics. Weak records systems can make it difficult if not impossible for citizens to prove unequal or unjust treatment or to challenge human rights violations. It can undermine their ability to make an informed contribution to the governance process. Laws that give citizens the right of access to government records are of little use if records are not created in the first place or cannot be found when needed (Fig. 2).

The ability to ensure that digital records are available and can be trusted depends upon having an effective records management strategy that defines the goals, principles, policies, processes, and roles needed to ensure effective and efficient use of records as evidence for governance. Records management is essentially a risk mitigation strategy that makes it possible to avoid or address gaps in the framework for managing records in relation to development goals. Defining a records management strategy is especially important for lower-resource countries, where governments continue to depend heavily on paper but are keen to introduce the benefits of information technology and open data as rapidly as possible, often with almost no capacity or resources for managing records systems. In the same way that it is vital that information security controls are in place, a records management framework is vital as a basis for achieving development goals.

The records profession, which is a coherent worldwide community of practice dedicated to protecting the availability and integrity of evidence through time and across technology change, has defined answers to the issues involved in establishing and maintaining control of records as reliable evidence. The community has reached a broad agreement on the continuum of controls required to support the capture, classification, disposition, preservation, access, and security of the records. These controls are defined in detail in international standards, which work together to provide evidence that records are reliable and accurate. The controls cannot be achieved piecemeal but require a unified records and information governance framework. Internationally accepted records standards tend to be applied differently in different countries, but the core requirements are universal and are relevant in all regions of the world.

Many governments have not yet recognized the importance of building the framework of laws, policies, structures, standards, systems, procedures, and skills needed to capture, preserve, and make digital records accessible in a reliable form through time. Development planners often do not realize that ICT systems contain digital records but lack the full functionality needed to protect and preserve them. The growing international body of standards and good practice is largely unknown to the ICT and development environments, and it has not been adapted to meet the requirements and circumstances of lower-resource environments. These gaps need to be bridged if fragile digital records are to survive and provide essential evidence.

THE IRMT'S WORK

The IRMT is unique in its commitment to strengthening public sector records management in relation to the governance process. Its three program areas (development research, education and training, and consultancy services) work together to support this purpose. The IRMT's long-term objective is to raise international awareness of the importance of managing evidence in the digital environment and to support countries in lower-resource environments in building capacity to introduce effective and appropriate strategies for managing digital records. Drawing on its track record of success, extensive field experience, network of globally recognized experts, and close

Fig. 3 The IRMT emphasizes the importance of teamwork and capacity building.

partnerships with records professionals across the world, the IRMT works to help facilitate and share new solutions to the global challenges of managing records as evidence in the transition to the electronic environment (Fig. 3).

The IRMT's work falls into three interrelated program areas. It studies the relationship between records management and public sector management in order to define means of strengthening effective government; it develops capacity building resources that it makes freely available internationally; and it provides consultancy support to help sustainable legal and regulatory frameworks, policies, systems, procedures, and facilities. Its programs and projects are, therefore, informed by a continuous cycle of research, education and training, and the application of its findings and products in practical situations.

The IRMT has identified key elements of success in building sustainable programs for managing records as evidence, and these feature in all its projects. They include the following: linking records management directly to governance functions; taking an integrated approach to the management of records across all media from creation to destruction or long-term preservation; ensuring that all projects are practical, relevant to local circumstances, and sustainable; emphasizing the importance of teamwork; and building ownership and awareness alongside capacity.

The IRMT also recognizes the importance of working closely with key government stakeholders and with partner organizations, including professional associations, consultancy firms, academic institutions, and NGOs to define strategies, structures, and programs for managing records in support of evidence-based governance and national and international development. It also works with national archives in many countries and with a range of international organizations, particularly the International Council on Archives and its regional branches, the Association of Records Managers and Administrators International, and national bodies, such as the UK Information

and Records Management Society. It also has worked in partnership with such international bodies as the International Federation of Accountants, Transparency International, and the Commonwealth Human Rights Initiative.

Development Research

Over the last 15 years, the IRMT carried out a series of research projects aimed at understanding the relationship between records management and governance, particularly in the transition to the digital environment. The premise has been that if digital information is to provide the basis for informed decision-making, effective service delivery, and tackling corruption through increased transparency, it must be reliable and trustworthy over time. The IRMT makes its research findings available internationally, uses them as the basis for developing education and training programs, and works with governments to apply the findings practically.

The IRMT's research projects have examined the practicalities of introducing records management to support international and national development priorities, focusing on key aspects of accountability, transparency, and openness, including the Right to Information and Open Data. Since the management of money and people is fundamental to all of these issues, the IRMT has given particular attention to financial and personnel records, in both the paper-based and electronic environments. The research projects, which have run almost continuously since 1998, have included the following: *From Accounting to Accountability: Managing Accounting Records as a Strategic Resource* (1999); *Evidence-Based Governance in the Electronic Age* (2001–2004); *Integrating Records Management Requirements into Financial Management Information Systems (FMIS)* (2005–2006); *Investigating and Addressing the Requirements for Building Integrity in Public Sector Information Systems in the ICT Environment* (2006–2008); and *Aligning Records Management*

International Federation–
iSchools

with E-Government/ICT, Freedom of Information, and Poverty Reduction in East Africa (2010–2011).

The IRMT also recognizes the need to monitor and measure records management frameworks, processes, and capacity in relation to the transition to the digital environment, and it draws on its research to produce assessment tools that include a gap analysis tool for assessing records management functionality in ICT systems, a high-level E-Records Readiness Tool for assessing capacity for managing electronic records and information, and a Records Management Capacity Assessment System for a more in-depth evaluation. The tools are linked to international records management standards. The IRMT is presently working to develop a Rapid Diagnostic Records Management Risk Assessment Tool.

All of the research reports and associated assessment tools can be downloaded from the IRMT's website free of charge.

Education and Training

The IRMT is committed to supporting education and training as a primary goal. Between 1996 and 2000, working with the International Council on Archives and other professional bodies, it developed the Management of Public Sector Records Study Program with the aim of helping to build core records management skills in countries where appropriate and relevant educational tools were hard to obtain. The material was intended to serve as an input to taught or distance learning courses, as a resource for conducting workshops, and as a tool for self-study. It also has provided the basis for strengthening staff capacity within local institutions. In fact, the material has been used more widely than originally expected, serving small communities across better-resourced countries, for instance, in Canada and Australia, and governments in transition, for instance, Estonia.

The study materials were distributed in hard copy to national archives and training institutions in 60 lower-resource countries with assistance from the Association of Records Managers and Administrators International. They also have been available on the IRMT's website since they were launched in 2000, with hundreds of thousands of downloads, free of charge, by educators, institutions, and individuals. The program has contributed to the development of new educational programs in countries including Uganda, Zimbabwe, Eritrea, and Tanzania. There is also a Spanish adaptation of some of the material, in two volumes, which was developed by the National Archives of Uruguay, and which also may be downloaded without charge.

The study program covers all phases of the records life cycle/continuum, as well as the application of records management principles and practices to financial, human resource, and legal and judicial records. There are about 4000 pages of training materials, including 18 teaching/study training modules, case studies, good practice procedure manuals, and an educators' resource kit. While the material addresses public sector record-keeping issues, it can also be used in the private sector.

In 2009, the IRMT released a second set of modules that aimed to begin the process of building records management capacity in the digital environment. The material included five modules, six case studies, and a set of good practice indicators for integrating records management in ICT systems.

In 2013 and 2014, at the request of UNESCO, the IRMT collaborated with the International Council on Archives to develop a digital preservation curriculum. It provided a draft outline of the contents of the curriculum and prepared two detailed modules: *Managing Metadata to Protect the Integrity of Records* and *Understanding Digital Records Preservation Initiatives*.

Although the core issues covered by the study material have not changed, the IRMT recognizes the urgent requirement to continue developing up-to-date study material to address evolving technological requirements and goals for openness.

Consultancy Services

For two and a half decades, working with dozens of governments and dozens of international institutions around the world, the IRMT has delivered numerous projects to improve records and information management in support of governance objectives. It works with governments to help build the effective laws, policies, systems, procedures, and capacity for creating and managing trustworthy and accessible records needed to protect citizens' rights, improve services for citizens, demonstrate accountability and transparency, and protect the national historical memory. The IRMT's projects are designed to strengthen local professional capacity and build awareness of the significance of records as evidence among government officials.

The IRMT's consultancy services support both paper and electronic records systems, particularly in relation to financial management, human resource management, legal and judicial management, healthcare management, land management, decentralization, and access to information. For instance, they seek to strengthen records control systems in public financial management to reduce opportunities for fraud, corrupt procurement, and money laundering; to strengthen controls in the areas of payroll management; and to eliminate ghost workers and the retention of workers past statutory retirement age. In this way, they strengthen the Financial Information Management Systems and Human Resource Information Systems, which are trustworthy only if the information they contain is accurate.

The projects can involve addressing government-wide requirements or sector-specific needs. Some last for only a few weeks, for instance, an analysis of records

International Federation–iSchools

management requirements. Others are delivered over a number of years where there is a need to build a sustainable infrastructure for records management across government. Longer-term projects can include establishing appropriate legal and institutional arrangements; developing clear management responsibilities and performance criteria; drafting policies, standards, and practices; implementing new systems; and building appropriate new skills.

CONCLUSION

For 25 years the IRMT has been committed to strengthening evidence-based governance to support the goals of improved services and resource management and to underpin accountable and transparent democracies. It has sought to build awareness of the significance of records as evidence among government officials and development planners; to support capacity building for records professionals; and to help develop innovative, appropriate, and practical solutions to records and information management problems. Most significantly, the IRMT has sought, in all of the countries where it has worked, to contribute to the well-being of citizens, whose rights and entitlements and ability to hold their governments accountable depend on the availability of accurate and reliable evidence.

International Federation–iSchools

International Society for Knowledge Organization (ISKO)

Ingetraut Dahlberg
Bad Koenig, Germany

Abstract

The aims, tasks, activities, and achievements of the International Society for Knowledge Organization (1989–) are presented. ISKO is that group of scholars and practitioners who feel responsible for questions pertaining to the conceptual organization and processing of knowledge, the scientific bases of which lie in knowledge drawn from the fields of logic, organization science, psychology, science theory, informatics, semiotics, linguistics, and philosophy. It aims at giving advice in the construction, perfection, and application of such organizational tools as classification systems, taxonomies, thesauri, terminologies, as well as their use for indexing purposes and thereby for the retrieval of information. Events leading up to the founding of ISKO in 1989 are described. The aims and objectives of ISKO according to its statutes are mentioned, as well as its organization, its biennial international conferences with their proceedings volumes, and the establishment of a further conference series and a textbook series. The drive and success of coordinators in establishing chapters in many countries is reviewed as well. The activities of the chapters (mainly by their own meetings and conferences) and subsequently their publications during the past years are also included. The idea and structure of ISKO's official journal—*Knowledge Organization*—is explained, and ISKO's Web site is given. Finally, the need for the Society is discussed, and its possible future is considered.

DEFINITIONS AND FORERUNNERS OF ISKO

One of the antecedents of ISKO was the establishment of the journal *International Classification* (IC) in 1974. It was edited by the entry author and published by K.G. Saur Verlag, Munich. With this journal, "classification" was understood as a multi-meaning word that includes the following concepts: 1) classification in the sense of "classification system" i.e., a system of classes arranged in hierarchical or faceted order; 2) classification in the sense of classifying, i.e., establishing a system of classes; 3) classification in the sense of classing, i.e., relating the classes of a classification system to objects or subjects of reality; and 4) classification in the sense of classification science, i.e., relating to this field of study and its activities. Another forerunner of ISKO was given by the founding of the German Classification Society on February 12, 1977, meant to study the philosophical and methodological foundations of classification and its application in many object- and subject-oriented fields of knowledge. It was chaired by the entry author from 1977 to 1986. This Society comprised members from library and information science, linguistics, philosophy, commodity science and some other sciences, and also statistics and mathematics. The non-mathematically oriented members based their understanding of knowledge on concepts as "units of knowledge" which means that any concept can be defined as a "synthesis of essential characteristics stated about any kind of a referent and needing a term or another kind of designator."[1,2] The mathematically oriented members of the Society which grew from a single representative (Prof. Dr. Hans-Hermann Bock) in 1977 to almost 100 members after 12 years, did not use the conceptual approach but a formal approach to their numerically or statistically oriented understanding of classification.[3] Thus it happened that the Society of some 200 members was dominated all in short order by the 100 mathematicians which were more strongly represented at the elections for the Executive Board in 1989. At this junction the conceptually oriented half—on the advice of Dr. Robert Fugmann—decided to leave and establish a new Society and thus, ISKO was founded on July 22, 1989. This decision had been supported by the members of the consulting editorial board of *International Classification*. In addition, it was intended to soar above the national level and to approach and include interested colleagues from other countries. At the founding meeting it was decided not to use any longer the term "classification" in the name of the new society but "Organization of Knowledge," as this had already been used in two publications on this field of classification as titles of books by H.E. Bliss (1932/1933). To simplify the name of the new society the direct translation from the German "Wissensorganisation." namely "Knowledge Organization" was preferred and accepted worldwide to the astonishment of its inventors. The founders of ISKO were (in alphabetical order) Dr. Ingetraut Dahlberg, Dr. Robert Fugmann, Dr. Alfred Gerstenkorn, Dipl.Bibl. Barbara Kelm, Prof. Dr. Norbert Meder, Mrs. Padmini Raj (India), Prof. Dr. Winfried Schmitz-Esser, Dipl. Vw. Ingeborg Stoltzenburg, Dipl.Ing. Rudolf Ungvary

Encyclopedia of Library and Information Sciences, Fourth Edition DOI: 10.1081/E-ELIS4-120044729
Copyright © 2017 by Taylor & Francis. All rights reserved.

International Federation–
iSchools

(Hungary). Therefore three nations were represented, a necessity for the founding of an international society in Germany. Thereafter the journal *IC* became the official organ of ISKO and was renamed into *Knowledge Organization* subsequently.

AIMS AND TASKS

ISKO was conceived to function both on a national and international level as the connecting link between any and all institutions concerned with conceptual questions pertaining to the organization and processing of knowledge. It is meant to serve in assembling all colleagues, mainly from the information science fields working on problems related to the conceptual organization of knowledge, the scientific bases of which lie in the methodical knowledge from the fields of logic, organization science, psychology, science theory, informatics, semiotics, linguistics, and philosophy (particularly epistemology). According to its Statutes, ISKO has set itself the following tasks:

> Awaken and support an understanding for the practical and heuristic usefulness of such an organization of knowledge, propose on a national and international level the exchange of information and experience of scientists and practitioners in this area, especially by giving advice in the construction, perfection, and application of such organization tools as classification systems, thesauri, terminologies, nomenclatures, as well as the syntactical tools going with them; observe internationally the progress made in this work; concentrate on major points of this knowledge field in special working groups, hold regular meetings in order to support these activities.[4]

It is also stated in the Statutes that the Society will collaborate with other groupings, associations, and institutions pursuing similar aims, if in line with its goals. It aims at promoting and carrying out studies, research work, conferences and other categories of scientific cooperation, as well as disseminating knowledge for research workers, scientists, and the general public through its publications. The last sentence of its Preamble says: "Thus, responsibility and initiative to make this society their worldwide forum lies in the hands of the personal members collaborating in their concern for knowledge organization in common efforts, refraining therefore from pursuing their subjective interests and respecting the postulates of integrity and truth, mutual recognition and assistance."

ORGANIZATION

ISKO's *Executive Board* (EB) consists of seven members and one ex-officio-member, the chair of the *Scientific Advisory Council*. This latter Council has up to 21

members and advises the EB. The necessary Secretarial work of the Society is accomplished by ISKO's *General Secretary* (this is at present Dipl.Vw. H. Peter Ohly, Bonn, Germany). *Membership Assemblies* take place every 2 years together with the biennial international conferences in even years. The *President* of ISKO and its EB is elected every 4 years. *National Chapters* are founded with the help of *National Coordinators* whenever there are at least 10 ISKO members in one country. Such chapters can establish their own statutes. Their conferences should take place every odd year. They receive a small part of the general membership fee for their own expenses. Here is the list of ISKO's presidents so far: Dr. Ingetraut Dahlberg, Frankfurt (1989–1996), Prof. Hanne Albrechtsen, Kopenhagen (1997–1998), Prof. Clare Beghtol, Toronto (1998–2002), Prof. Ia C. McIlwaine, London (2002–2006), Prof. Maria José Lopes Huertas, Granada (2006–). In the first years the sessions of the Executive Board were concerned among others also with the elaboration of *Bylaws to the Statutes*, such as one for the organization of Chapters and other ISKO Bodies.[5] One Bylaw for Conferences and one for the General Secretariat had been worked on but never published. Chair of *the Scientific Advisory Council* was Prof. Dr. Winfried Schmitz-Esser (1989–2006). He was succeeded in 2006 by Alexander Sigel.

ISKO'S INTERNATIONAL CONFERENCES

After one year of existence ISKO organized its first International Conference at the Technical University of Darmstadt, Germany, August 14–17 1990, entitled *Tools for Knowledge Organization and the Human Interface*. It assembled almost 200 participants from 25 countries, 60 papers were presented, edited by Robert Fugmann and published in the new series *Advances in Knowledge Organization*.[6] The conference in 1992 on *Cognitive Paradigms in Knowledge Organization* took place at Madras, India,[7] the next, in 1994, was held in Copenhagen, entitled *Knowledge Organization and Quality Management*,[8] in 1996 the fourth one, entitled *Knowledge Organization and Change*, took place at Washington, D.C.[9] Now back to Europe, the 1998 conference, entitled *Structures and Relations in Knowledge Organization*, took place at Lille, France.[10] The sixth conference, entitled *Dynamism and Stability in Knowledge Organization* took place at Toronto.[11] The next one, entitled *Challenges in Knowledge Representation and Organization for the 21st Century. Integration of Knowledge across Boundaries*, took place at Granada, Spain.[12] The eighth conference, entitled *Knowledge Organization and the Global Information Society*, took place at London, England[13] and the ninth international ISKO conference, entitled *Knowledge Organization for a Global Learning Society*, took place at Vienna, Austria.[14] In 2008, ISKO held its tenth conference on *Culture and Identity in Knowledge Organization* at Montreal, Canada, August 5–8, 2008. It will hold its 11th International Conference in Rome, Febr. 23–26, 2010, its topic: *Paradigms and Conceptual Systems in Knowledge Organization* http://www.iskoi.org/rome2010/

HISTORICAL DEVELOPMENTS AND EARLY CHAPTER ACTIVITIES

Version 2 of a 1992 leaflet of ISKO[15] (a version 4 was published in)[23] gives an account of the early development of ISKO. By that time a number of coordinators were already active in the following countries: Austria (Dr. G. Budin), Brazil (Prof. Dr. Ulf Baranow), Canada (Prof. Nancy Williamson), Denmark (Mrs. Hanne Albrechtsen), France (Dr. Jacques Maniez), Hungary (Dr. Maria Domokos), Italy (Dr. Giliola Negrini), Japan (Prof. Yukio Nakamura), Nigeria ((Mr. Emmanuel Adimorah), Portugal (Mrs. Ines Lopes), Russia (Dr. Eduard Sukiasyan), and Spain (Prof. Dr. Emilia Curras). International Society for Knowledge Organization Chapters have been established so far in Bulgaria (Mr. Peter Petrov), Germany (Prof. Winfried Goedert), India (Prof. Krishan Kumar), and Slovakia (Mrs. Pavla Stancikova). At this time, ISKO had about 400 members in over 40 countries. National conferences with international participation were held in 1991 in Bratislava, Slovakia (papers were published in a separate volume),[16] Varna, Bulgaria (18 papers were published in one-page form in Knowledge Organization 1992, except for the papers).[17,18] Russia's chapter held its three conferences: the first one on *Problems and Tendencies* 1993, and a second one in 1995 on *Linguistic Problems in KO*, both at Moscow. A third one was held in combination with the annual Crimean conference in 1997. Short versions of the 1993 papers were published in Knowledge Organization[19] together with two papers.[20,21] It should be mentioned, however, that the growth of ISKO in Eastern and developing countries was fostered in the years 1989–1996 by the fact that members from such countries with low incomes had to pay a rather reduced membership fee. The journal was sent to such countries in bulk and was distributed by the coordinators or chapter heads. In these years, there were about 50 ISKO members in India and some 30 members in China.

In 1993 a series of European conferences was planned on subject topics, such as Environment, Medicine, Agriculture, etc., but only one of them could be realized so far, it was the First European ISKO Conference at Bratislava, Slovakia, September 14–16, 1994 on *Environmental Knowledge Organization and Information Management*. Its 45 papers were edited by Pavla Stancikova and I. Dahlberg in another series *Knowledge Organization in Subject Areas*, Vol. 1, 1994.[22] A further international Research Seminar on a methodological problem took place at Warsaw, September 13–15, 1995 on *Compatibility*

and Integration of Order Systems. Its 20 papers were edited by I. Dahlberg and Krystyna Siwek.[23] The volume also contains an *Annotated Bibliography on Compatibility and Integration of Order Systems* by I. Dahlberg as well as the *Recommendations* of the participating ISKO members and the members of the Polish Society for Professional Information (TIP). In 1993, a series of *Textbooks for Knowledge Organization* was started with vol. 1 by Robert Fugmann: *Subject Analysis and Indexing. Theoretical Foundation and Practical Advice.*[24] A second volume followed in 1995 by Hemalata Iyer on *Classificatory structures: Concepts, Relations and Representations.*[25] A third volume was planned to be written by Eduard Sukiasyan on *Universal Classification Systems*. Unfortunately after 1996, these series were discontinued. From then on too—regrettably—the ISKO members of countries with low income had to discontinue their membership.

PRESENT CHAPTER ACTIVITIES

Three months after the founding of ISKO, a **German Chapter** was founded on October 6 in Frankfurt. It considers itself as successor of the non-numerical part of the *German Classification Society* (see above), although—ironically—most of the librarians stayed with the mathematicians as a section of their own, so far. Chairmen of the German Chapter since 1989 have been Prof. Winfried Goedert, Dr. Peter Jaenecke, Prof. Dr. Hans Czap, and Peter Ohly. At present there are 75 members including members from Austria, Switzerland, and the Netherlands as well as one Honorary Member, Dr. I. Dahlberg, since 2001. The proceedings volumes of the biennial conferences are available.[26–34] In addition there exists a discussion list (wiss-org), a Web site (wiss-org@gesis.org) and an irregularly appearing newsletter. Also in pursuance of the aims of the Society, working groups had been established from the very beginning with the aim to publish results in a series called *Recommendations for Knowledge Organization*. In the interim, the work was suspended. The first recommendation was published by the WG on Content Analysis, entitled *User Evaluation of Information Systems*.[35] Further WGs became active on University Education in KO, Cognition and KO and Universal Classification. At present new WGs are established ad hoc on demand.

Though the **Italian chapter** (chair Dr. Giliola Negrini) started its activities much earlier after the founding of ISKO, it was only in 1990 that G. Negrini arranged for a conference on *Documentary Languages and Databases* in Rome, December 1990. Although it was not co-organized by ISKO, but held in the spirit of ISKO, therefore its proceedings volume was included in the series *Advances in Knowledge Organization*.[36] In an e-mail of November 20, 2007, Claudio Gnoli reported: "On the initiative of Giliola

International Federation—iSchools

Negrini (National Research Council), who collaborated with Dahlberg applying her Systematifier model to documentation in various sectors and organized four scientific events in Rome with printed proceedings "(see bibliography[37–39]). In 2004, coordination was taken over by Claudio Gnoli (University of Pavia), and a national chapter was formed, currently including about 25 people and some institutions. The chapter organized annual meetings at Milan Bicocca University, as well as specialized events on the organization of local knowledge and of philosophical knowledge, all with online proceedings (http://www.iskoi. org). Several research projects are active within the chapter, including integrative level classification (http://www. iskoi.org/ilc/), relations between object and bibliographic classifications (http://www.iskoi.org/bagpipes/) and cooperation with GRIS (Subject Indexing Research Group)."

In **Spain**, Prof. Dr. Emilia Curras organized in 1992 the first ISKO Meeting in combination with a meeting of FID/CR, the Classification Research Committee of the Federation Internationale de Documentation. A year later, the Spanish Chapter was formed and a conference was held in November 1993 on *Knowledge Organization in Documentary Systems*, with the support of Profs. Javier Garcia Marco, Miguel Angel Esteban, and Rosa San Segundo. Subsequently, J. Garcia Marco started a journal called *Scire, Knowledge Representation and Organization*, appearing twice a year with a scientific board and peer-reviewed contributions. He published in it the papers from this and later conferences. A second ISKO-Spain national congress took place in 1995 and a third one in 1997, all these conferences took place in Madrid.[40–42] In 1998 the Chair of ISKO Spain went to Prof. M.J. Lopez-Huertas. The proceedings' volumes of the next four conferences are available.[43–46] From 2007 on, the Chair of ISKO Spain went to Prof. Rosa San Segundo.

The **Polish ISKO Chapter** started from the participation of Polish colleagues in the First European ISKO Conference on Subject Areas (see above), held at Bratislava 1994. A year later, the ISKO-TIP Research Seminar on Compatibility and Integration of Order Systems was held in Warsaw, which helped to bring the interested colleagues together from the whole country. It was, however, not until 2006 that a new Polish coordinator was elected, Prof. Wieslaw Babik from the Institute of Information and Library Science of the Jagiellonian University in Cracow, that the former Polish ISKO members were reassembled and newcomers added so that a group of 23 members was formed and the National ISKO Chapter could start its work in 2007. A plan for a number of activities for the years 2006–2010 is being proposed. It organized panels on *What is knowledge organization?* at Cracow and Katowice in June 2007 and also a Session during the 9th Forum of the Polish Society for Scientific Information in Zakopane (September 25–28, 2007) entitled: *The role of knowledge organization in information exchange and development of professional information services for education, science*

and culture for the knowledge society. Information on the Polish ISKO activities were published in two renowned Polish scientific journals and Web sites were designed and created. Twice a year an electronic bulletin *ISKO in Poland News* is issued.

The **French ISKO Chapter** was established after the Warsaw Research Seminar of 1995. Before that time, Prof. Jacques Maniez was ISKO Coordinator for France, however the participation of Mrs. Danièle Degez in Warsaw helped to assemble existing French ISKO members and to form the Chapter in 1996. Dr. Widad Mustafa el Hadi who had already attended the first International Conference of ISKO, Darmstadt 1990, was elected Chairperson, Danièle Degez as Deputy Chair, and Jacques Maniez as Treasurer. In November 2000, the French chapter was granted the nonprofit legal organization status. Since that time, ISKO France organized biennial conferences, known as Journées ISKO-France. The first one took place in Lille, 1997.[41] Until 2007, six biennial conferences have taken place. They are now called *ISKO-France Conferences*. Their topics and venues were as follows: *Indexing in the Era of the Internet* (Lyon): *Information Filtering and Automatic Summarization in Networks* (Paris); *Knowledge Organization Conceptual Approaches* (Grenoble); *Knowledge Organization and User-Oriented Strategic Watch Information Systems* (Nancy); *Knowledge Organization in the Information Society* (Toulouse). The proceedings volumes are available.[47–52] Chairpersons of ISKO-France were Dr. Widad Mustafa el Hadi (1996–1999), Prof. Dr. Jean-Paul Metzger, (1999–2005), and Prof. Dr. Stéphane Chaudiron, University of Lille (2005, reelected 2007). In June 2006 the French ISKO Chapter coorganized *La Semaine de la Connaissance*. This "*Knowledge Week*" gathered all French Societies concerned with knowledge and linguistic issues.

In **England**, Dr. Steve Pollitt had been active as coordinator ever since 1994, but unfortunately a serious illness lead to his early death. Much later, the **British ISKO Chapter** finally was planned in London, on February 7, 2007, in a preliminary meeting hosted by John Lindsay at Kingston University. A Web site was designed and an invitation to join ISKO UK was widely disseminated. Its inaugural meeting was held on March 26, 2007. Vanda Broughton, lecturer in the School of Library, Archive, and Information Studies (University College London) was voted chair, Bob Bater, a consultant in the field of knowledge organization was elected Vice-Chair, and Aida Slavic as Treasurer. Mrs. Broughton wrote:

> Starting with ten members, the chapter quadrupled its membership by December 2007, attracting an interesting mixture of academics, researchers, information consultants and practitioners in equal parts. Membership at the end of 2007 stands at 42, including two honorary members, Brian Vickery and Jean Aitchison, pioneers in knowledge organization in the United Kingdom. The

International Federation–iSchools

International Federation–
iSchools

popularization of ISKO in the United Kingdom was achieved through a series of London meetings organized around topics of interest. One type of meeting organized under the banner 'KOnnecting KOmmunities' was held in May with the expressed purpose of providing a forum for knowledge managers and taxonomists in nonacademic sectors. This gave us an opportunity to share experiences and interests in a formal discussion, followed by the opportunity for social networking. It was very apparent that KO practitioners in industry and government suffer from relative isolation and greatly welcomed the opportunity to meet and exchange views with others. The second, September meeting, entitled *Tools for knowledge organization today*, was a half-day themed conference, consisting of three talks on the subject of knowledge organization standards and was attended by an audience of over 50. The third was another KOnnecting KOmmunities meeting under the heading *Ranganathan revisited: Facets for the future* with two talks from the academic and research point of view on facet analysis, and three presentations of information organization and retrieval solutions based on facet analysis. This meeting was attended by more than 80 people. Further meetings are planned for 2008. The first ISKO U.K. biennial conference will be held in 2009.

The **Indian ISKO Chapter** was established right after the first ISKO Conference in Darmstadt at which a number of Indians were present, among them Dr. Mohinder Satija, GND University, Amritsar, who became India's ISKO Coordinator and Prof. Krishan Kumar, University of New Delhi, who took over the Chair of ISKO India. On January 7, 1994, an ISKO Seminar was held in Bangalore together with the DRTC and the Institute of Information Studies. A report by Mr. Sukhdev Singh and Dr. K.N. Prasad on the four papers given was published in ISKO News 16.[53] In 2005 coordinatorship went to Prof. K.S. Raghavan, DRTC Bangalore, and Prof. A. Neelameghan became its president. As of December 6, India has 21 ISKO members. Recently, in September 2007, DRTC in association with ISKO and some other institutions organized an international conference on *the Future of Knowledge Organization in the Networked Environment* (IKONE 2007). Papers were published in a preconference volume, edited by K.S. Raghavan.[54] He wrote that the biggest challenges in the next 5 years would be: to build KO schemes and hide them from the user; to design and implement education and development in KO; to understand "human needs" and what these needs are derived from; what are the factors that influence the mental reference model? And finally, to build methodologies for KO. At present the following three research projects are being pursued: Revision of Colon Classification; A bilingual thesaurus for classical Tamil Studies; and Work on defining, categorizing, and developing a taxonomy of lateral relationships, including multilingual multicultural contexts.

The **Brazilian ISKO Chapter** was officially created on October 31, 2007. It has now 34 members, all of them are PhDs and act as professors and researchers in the KO branch. It is officially located at the Department of Information Science of Sao Paulo State University (UNESP) in Marilia—Sao Paulo. Its President is José Augusto Chaves Guimaraes. He wrote that the first congress of the Brazilian ISKO Chapter will take place in Joao Pessoa, Brazil, in October 2009. He outlined the major research themes of his Chapter as follows: Epistemological foundations of KO; Interdisciplinary dimensions of KO; Terminological tools in KO; KO and cultural memory; KO and domain analysis; Technological background of KO; Social aspects of KO (education, professional acting, ethics, etc.) and he mentioned that the Brazilian ISKO Chapter is deeply attached to the Working Group 2—Knowledge Organization and Representation—of the Brazilian Information Science Research Society (http://www.anci.org).

ISKO's Nordic Chapter was founded on November 8, 2007 in Copenhagen. It covers Sweden, Denmark, Norway, Finland, Iceland, and the Faroe Islands. Its Chair is held by Mikkel Christoffersen with Birger Hjørland (DK), Hanne Albrechtsen (DK), and Per Nystroem (SWE) on the Board. So far, 22 people have expressed interest in the chapter. A Web presence will be established soon and a conference is being planned in Sweden in 2009.

ISKO's U.S. Chapter had been planned to be established in 1994 at a conference in Urbana Ill., organized by Prof. Pauline Atherton. Prof. Hemalata Iyer from the University of Albany had been the coordinator and had invited her colleagues in the United States. However, the strong voice of one person present at that meeting (which I attended too) sufficed to prevent the chapter from realization. Recently, Prof. Richard P. Smiraglia wrote[55] that at the 2007 *North American Symposium on Knowledge Organization* (convened at the University of Toronto, a general assembly voted for the creation of the **North American Chapter of ISKO**. A standing committee will bring forth bylaws and organize a second symposium for the summer of 2009. He also gave a survey on the papers of this Symposium and indicated that 13 of the papers can be found in the Web. It should be mentioned that Prof. Nancy Williamson of the University of Toronto had been active as ISKO Coordinator of Canada since the early 1990s and assembled around her the Canadian ISKO members, although an official Chapter had never been created there. She is well known to the ISKO community for her many excellent reports in our journal, also on the international ISKO conferences. At the ISKO Conference in Vienna, 2006, therefore, she was elected second Honorary ISKO member.

THE JOURNAL *KNOWLEDGE ORGANIZATION*

As stated above, this journal was started in 1974 as *International Classification*. It appeared in the first years only twice a year, later on three times and became a quarterly from 1980 onward. The journal is "devoted to Concept

Theory, Classification, Indexing, and Knowledge Representation." It contains a section for articles, for reports, for news in the field of classification/knowledge organization, book reviews, and a current bibliography in systematic order with an author index. From 1974 to 1996 all sections were edited and compiled by I. Dahlberg. From 1997 to 1998 it was edited by Charles Gilreath, Florida with Hanne Albrechtsen for ISKO News, Werner Bies for Book Reviews and Gerhard Riesthuis for the current bibliography. In 1999 it was edited by Clare Beghtol, from 2000 to 2004 by Hope Olson and from 2004 on by Richard Smiraglia. In the meantime, the ISKO News Section was dropped because of the ISKO Web site, but resumed by Hanne Albrechtsen in 2007. The book editor W. Bies was succeeded by Michèle Hudon and later-on by Clément Arsenault. The bibliography section of G. Riesthuis was—after his very helpful work from 1997 to 2006—succeeded by I.C. McIlwaine. The issue 1999/4 contains a systematically arranged bibliography of all ISKO publications of the past 10 years, compiled by Gerhard Riesthuis with the help of Winfried Schmitz-Esser. It comprises altogether 1148 titles from proceedings volumes, as well as from the journal. The Classification System for Knowledge Organization Literature, according to which the titles have been arranged, is placed on pages 192–201, followed by the outline of the Information Coding Classification. An author index has been added. Unfortunately there were severe backlogs during the years since 1999 due to the fact that the designated editor (after Ch. Gilreath) could not start his work immediately and gave up finally because of health reasons. Prof. Smiraglia's diligence succeeded in having it on schedule again by 2008. His own sincere interest in this field has given the journal a new attraction, especially by his editorial of the last issue of 2005 with his question: "What exactly is knowledge organization?"[56] A kind of an answer was meant to be provided by the article in the next issue (2006/1) *Knowledge Organization: A New Science?*[57] which also tries to outline future tasks of this new (old) science (see the section "An Age-Old Activity and Its Future Possibilities").

THE ISKO WEB SITE

The ISKO Web site is http://www.isko.org/contact.html. Under this address one will find the following entries: About ISKO, Join ISKO, *Knowledge Organization* journal, ISKO Events, ISKO Chapters, ISKO People, ISKO Publications, and Contact us.

AN AGE-OLD ACTIVITY AND ITS FUTURE POSSIBILITIES

The huge volume in which the Russian scholar, Eugen Shamurin[58] described the past 3000 years of attempts to develop instruments for the ordered collection of written material shows an interesting development from rather primitive lists of terms over elaborated schedules in the middle ages and the later centuries until the many classification schemes of the nineteenth century, of which some are still in use today, like the *Dewey Decimal Classification* and its younger offspring, the *Universal Decimal Classification* since in many revised editions. In the twentieth century, the Indian mathematician and librarian S. R. Ranganathan (1892–1972) enriched the field of classification with numerous new ideas, as well as practical advices especially by categorization of concepts—his so-called facet analysis—well described in his *Prolegomena to Library Classification* of 1967.[59] His ideas were taken up by the British Classification Research Group already in 1959 and used in the elaboration of many special classification systems, as well as for the revision of the *Bliss Classification*. In Germany, the biologist Martin Scheele used the same approach for the organization of knowledge in biology[60] and the author of this entry used it for the construction of an entirely new universal system, her fully faceted *Information Coding Classification,*[61] which is not based on disciplines, as all the other universal systems, but on general objects of reality, having by this an ontological basis as described in Dahlberg[62] and Dahlberg[63] The essential new aspect governing ISKO and its adherents are the possibilities lying in the more exact ways of system building by concept analysis. As it was said above, a concept is a knowledge unit because it refers with its concept elements (characteristics) to the necessary properties which can be stated on a referent. Thus, the characteristics resulting from such statements are the (knowledge) elements which create the relationships between concepts (identity, similarity) and can be used for system and structure building. Already Linné had known this who constructed his ingenious schemes for animals and plants on their anatomic properties. From all of this, it should also be understood, that knowledge organization differs essentially from knowledge management, see the critical remarks by J. Essers and J. Schreine.[64] See also work by Kasten.[65]

We are confronted today in the Internet search engines with the difficulty of retrieving information just by names and terms without considering their conceptual relationships. Any approach ignoring and failing to use the indispensable conceptually linked methodology will go astray and engross the jungle of "knowledge" in the Web or in his/her own files. But it is very hard to convince newcomers of the need for conceptual interrelationships. Millions of dollars have been wasted already for projects of people who think that computers can do automatic indexing. R. Fugmann has shown this very clearly[66] long ago. A paragon of systematic and definition-based organization of concepts is the UMLS, the Unified Medical Language System of the National Library of Medicine in Bethesda, Maryland. It should hopefully serve as a model for the elaboration of concept systems of other subject fields as well.

International Federation–iSchools

International Federation–
iSchools

Apart from this, the tasks of today, for which ISKO stands, should be seen in the collaboration of classificationists with terminologists and experts from the subject fields in question, in order to elaborate in possible future *Institutes for Knowledge Organization* the concept systems for each known subject field and area. This then would result in the necessary order of our concepts and their terms which can be visualized in adequate schemes and used to the benefit of all those who need to understand the relationships which link up human knowledge to a whole. Any single item in isolation, i.e., without its connection to other items cannot be understood, this has already been stated by the German theologian and philosopher Paul Tillich.[67] But the systematization of concepts is not an easy job, as Dagobert Soergel had stated in his first book of 1969 that "systematizing knowledge should occupy the same scientific rank as any original research work."[68] It is therefore hoped that such a new approach to our age-old science of classification should now be recognized and taken up as an absolute necessity for the organization of our knowledge and the subsequent understanding of what we actually know.

ACKNOWLEDGMENTS

I herewith thank the coordinators and chapter heads of the countries Italy, Russia, Spain, India, France, Poland, England, Brazil, and Scandinavia for their helpful answers included in this entry, as well as the ISKO General Secretary, Mr. H. Peter Ohly, who provided me with further information.

REFERENCES

1. Dahlberg, I. Zur Theorie des Begriffs. Intern. Classif. **1974**, *1*(1), 12–19 In English: On the theory of the concept. In *Ordering Systems for Global Information Networks*; Proceedings of 3rd International Conference on Classification Research, Bombay, India, January 6–11, 1975; Neelameghan, A., Ed.; FID/CR and Sarada Ranganathan Endowment for Library Science: Bangalore, India, 1979; 54–63.
2. Dahlberg, I. A referent-oriented, analytical concept theory for INTERCONCEPT. Int. Classif. **1978**, *5*(3), 142–151.
3. Bock, H.H. *Automatische Klassifikation*, Studia Mathematica; Vandenhoeck and Ruprecht: Göttingen, 1974; Vol. 24 (Automatic classification. Theoretical and practical methods for the grouping and structuring of data (cluster analysis)).
4. International Society for Knowledge Organization (ISKO), Charter and preamble. Int. Classif. **1989**, *16*(3), 165–167.
5. International Society for Knowledge Organization (ISKO), Bylaw for ISKO bodies. Int. Classif. **1994**, *21*(2), 101–102 (Part of ISKO News).
6. Tools for Knowledge Organization and the Human Interface Proceedings of 1st International ISKO Conference Darmstadt, Germany August, 14–17, 1990; Fugmann, R., Ed.; Advances in Knowledge Organization; INDEKS Verlag: Frankfurt/Main, Germany, 1990/1991; Vols.1 and 2, 279–280.
7. Cognitive Paradigms in Knowledge Organisation Proceedings of 2nd International ISKO Conference Madras August, 26–28, 1992; Neelameghan, A., Gopinath, M.A., Raghavan, K.S., Sankaralingam, P., Eds.; Sarada Ranganathan Endowment for Library Science: Bangalore, India, 1992.
8. Knowledge Organization and Quality Management Proceedings of 3rd International ISKO Conference Copenhagen, Denmark June, 20–24, 1994; Albrechtsen, H., Oernager, S., Eds.; Advances in Knowledge Organization; INDEKS Verlag: Frankfurt, Germany, 1994; Vol. 4.
9. Knowledge Organization and Change Proceedings of 4th International ISKO Conference Washington, DC July, 15–18, 1996; Green, R., Ed.; Advances in Knowledge Organization; INDEKS Verlag: Frankfurt, Germany, 1996; Vol. 5.
10. Structures and Relations in Knowledge Organization Proceedings of 5th International ISKO Conference Lille, France August, 25–29, 1998; Elhadi, M., Maniez, J., Pollitt, S., Eds.; Advances in Knowledge Organization; Ergon Verlag: Wuerzburg, Germany, 1998; Vol. 5.
11. Dynamism and Stability in Knowledge Organization Proceedings of 6th International ISKO Conference Toronto, Canada July, 10–13, 2000; Beghtol, C., Howarth, L.C., Williamson, N.J., Eds.; Advances in Knowledge Organization; Ergon Verlag: Wuerzburg, Germany, 2000; Vol. 7.
12. Challenges in Knowledge Representation and Organization for the 21st Century; Integration of Knowledge across Boundaries Proceedings of 7th International ISKO Conference Granada, Spain July, 10–13, 2002; Lopez-Huertas, M.J., Munoz-Fernandez, F.J., Eds.; Advances in Knowledge Organization; Ergon Verlag: Wuerzburg, Germany, 2002; Vol. 8.
13. Knowledge Organization and the Global Information Society Proceedings of 8th International ISKO Conference London, England July, 13–16, 2004; McIlwaine, I.C., Ed.; Advances in Knowledge Organization; Ergon Verlag: Wuerzburg, Germany, 2004; Vol. 9.
14. Knowledge Organization for a Global Learning Society Proceedings of 9th International ISKO Conference Vienna, Austria July, 4–7, 2006; Budin, G., Swertz, C., Mitgutsch, K., Eds.; Advances in Knowledge Organization; Ergon Verlag: Wuerzburg, Germany, 2006; Vol. 10.
15. *ISKO General Secretariat, ISKO-Brochure Nr.2*, 1992; December 31.
16. International Conference on Knowledge Organization, Terminology, and Information Access Management Proceedings of 1st NISKO Conference Bratislava, Slovakia May, 13–16, 1991 NISKO Scient.Techn.Society: Bratislava, Slovakia, 1991.
17. Dahlberg, I. Knowledge organization and terminology: Philosophical and linguistic issues. Int. Classif. **1992**, *19*(2), 65–71.
18. Iyer, H. Semantic interpretation of conjuncts: Boolean transformations. Int. Classif. **1992**, *19*(2), 72–76.

19. Knowledge Organization: Problems and Tendencies Papers and Summaries of the 1st Russian Regional ISKO Conference Moscow May, 10–14, 1993; Sukiasyan, E., Ed.; 189–222 Knowl. Org. **1993**, *20*(4).

20. Sukiasyan, E. Knowledge organization in Russia: Problem-related and historical aspects. Knowl. Org. **1993**, *20*(4), 189–191.

21. Dahlberg, I. Knowledge organization: Its scope and possibilities. Knowl. Org. **1993**, *2*(4), 211–222 (contains the Classification System for Knowl. Org. Literature).

22. Environmental Knowledge Organization and Information Management Proceedings of 1st European ISKO Conference Bratislava, Slovakia September, 14–16, 1994; Stancikova, P., Dahlberg, I., Eds.; Knowledge Organization in Subject Areas. INDEKS Verlag: Frankfurt/Main, Germany, 1994/1995; Vol. 1, 88 Supplement Vol. 216.

23. Compatibility and Integration of Order Systems Proceedings of Research Seminar of the TIP/ISKO Meeting Warsaw, Poland September, 13–15, 1995; Dahlberg, I., Siwek, K., Eds.; Wydawnistwo SBP: Warszawa, Germany, 1996.

24. Fugmann, R. *Subject Analysis and Indexing. Theoretical Foundation and Practical Advice*, Textbooks for Knowledge Organization; INDEKS Verlag: Frankfurt/Main, Germany, 1993; Vol. 1, 250.

25. Iyer, H. *Classificatory Structures. Concepts, Relations and Representations*, Textbooks for Knowledge Organization; INDEKS Verlag: Frankfurt/Main, Germany, 1995; Vol. 2, 230.

26. Kognitive Ansaetze zum Ordnen und Darstellen von Wissen 2.Tagung der Deutschen ISKO Sektion Weilburg, Okt 15–18, 1991; Gödert, W., Jaenceke, P., Schmitz-Esser, W., Eds.; Fortschritte in der Wissensorg; INDEKS Verlag: Frankfurt/Main, Germany, 1992; Bd. 2.

27. Konstruktion und Retrieval von Wissen 3.Tagung der Deutschen ISKO Sektion Weilburg, Okt 27–29, 1993; Meder, N., Jaenecke, P., Schmitz-Esser, W., Eds.; Fortschritte in der Wissensorg; INDEKS Verlag: Frankfurt/Main, Germany, 1993; Bd. 3.

28. Analogie in der Wissensrepräsentation: Case-Based Reasoning und räumliche Modelle 4.Tagung der deutschen ISKO Sektion Trier, Okt 17–20, 1995; Czap, H., Jaenecke, P., Ohly, H.P., Eds.; Fortschritte in der Wissensorg; INDEKS Verlag: Frankfurt/Main, Germany, 1996; Bd. 4.

29. Herausforderungen in der Wissensorganisation. Visualisierung, multimediale Dokumente, Internetstrukturen 5. Tagung der deutschen ISKO Sektion Berlin, Okt 7–10, 1997; Czap, H., Ohly, H.P., Pribbenow, S., Eds.; Fortschritte in der Wissensorg; Ergon Verlag: Wuerzburg, Germany, 1998; Bd. 5.

30. Globalisierung und Wissensorganisation: Neue Aspekte für Wissen, Wissenschaft und Informationssysteme 6. Tagung der deutschen ISKO Sektion Hamburg September, 23–25, 1999; Ohly, H.P., Rahmstorf, G., Sigel, A., Eds.; Fortschritte in der Wissensorg; Ergon Verlag: Wuerzburg, Germany, 2000; Bd. 6.

31. Wissensorganisation und Edutainment. Wissen im Spannungsfeld von Gesellschaft, Gestaltung und Industrie Proc. 7. Tagung der Deutschen ISKO Sektion Berlin, Maerz 21–23, 2001; Lehner, C., Ohly, H.P., Rahmstorf, G., Eds.; Fortschritte in der Wissensorg; Ergon Verlag: Wuerzburg, Germany, 2004; Bd. 7.

32. Wissensorganisation in kooperativen Lern- und Arbeitsumgebungen Proc. 8.Tagung der Deutschen ISKO Sektion Regensburg, Okt 9–11, 2002; Budin, G., Ohly, H.P., Eds.; Fortschritte in der Wissensorg; Ergon Verlag: Würzburg, Germany, 2004; Bd. 8.

33. Wissensorganisation und Verantwortung. Gesellschaftliche, ökonomische und technische Aspekte Proc. 9. Tagung der Deutschen ISKO Sektion Duisburg November, 5–7, 2004; Ohly, H.P., Sieglerschmidt, J., Swertz, C., Eds.; Fortschritte in der Wissensorg; Ergon Verlag: Wuerzburg, Germany, 2006; Bd. 9.

34. Kompatibilität, Medien und Ethik in der Wissensorganisation Proc. 10. Deutsche ISKO Tagung, Wien July, 3–6, 2006; Ohly, H.P., Netscher, S., Mitgutsch, K., Eds.; Fortschritte in der Wissensorg; Ergon Verlag: Wuerzburg, Germany, 2008; Bd. 10.

35. WG on Content Analysis, User evaluation of information systems. Recommendation for Knowledge Organization—R-01. October 1992. Int. Classif **1992**, *19*(3), 151–152.

36. Documentary Languages and Databases Papers from the Rome Conferecne December, 3–4, 1990; Negrini, G., Farnesi, T., Benediktsson, D., Eds.; Advances in Knowledge Organization; INDEKS Verlag: Frankfurt/Main, Germany, 1991; Vol. 3, 271.

37. Modelli e metodi di organizzazione della conoscenza organizzata dall'Istituto de studi sulla ricerca e documentazione scientifica del CNR. Lavori della Tavola rotonda Roma, February 2, 1994. L'indicizzazione **1993**, *8* (1–2), 25–176.

38. *Categorie, oggetti e struttura della conoscenza*, CNR, ISRDS: Roma, 1995; Atti del seminario organizzato dall'Istituto di studi sulla ricerca e documentazione scientifica, Roma, Dic. 1–2, 1994, a cura di Giliola Negrini.

39. *Modelli e modellizzazione*, CNR, ISRDS: Roma, 1997; Atti del seminario organizzato dall'Istituto di studi sulla ricerca e documentazione scientifica. Roma, Magio 17, 1996, a cura de Giliola Negrini.

40. Actas del 1 Encuentro de ISKO-Espana Madrid November, 4 y 5, 1993; Garcia Marco, F.J., Ed.; Universidad de Zaragoza: Zaragoza, Spain, 1995; Vol. 1, 290 Organisación del Conocimiento en Sistemas de Información y Documentación.

41. Actas del II Encuentro de ISKO-Espana Getafe November, 16 y 17, 1995; Garcia Marco, F.J., Ed.; Universidad de Zaragoza: Zaragoza, Spain, 1997; Vol. 2, 320 Organisación del Conocimiento en Sistemas de Información y Documentación.

42. Actas del III Encuentro de ISKO-Espana Getafe November, 19–21, 1997; Garcia Marco, F.J., Ed.; Universidad de Zaragoza: Zaragoza, Spain, 1999; Vol. 3, 470 Organización del Conocimiento en Sistemas de Información y Documentación.

43. La Representación y la Organización del Conocimiento en sus distintas perspectives; su influencia en la Recuperación de Información Granada Abril, 22–24, 1999; López-Huertas, M.J., Fernández-Molina, J.C., Eds.; Universidad de Granada: Granada, 1999; 447 Actas del IV Congreso ISKO-Espana EOCONSOD'99.

44. Tendencias de investigación en organisación del conocimiento Actas del vi Congreso del Capitulo Espanol de ISKO Salamanca, mayo 5–7, 2003; Placer, A.E., Ed.;

International Federation–iSchools

International Federation–
iSchools

Capitulo Espanol de ISKO: Alcalás de Henares, 2003; (Ed. on CD-ROM).

45. La dimensión humana de la organización del conocimiento Actas del VII Congresso del Capitulo Espanol de ISKO Barcelona Julio, 6–8, 2005; Gascon, J., Burguillos, F., Eds.; Universitat: Barcelona, Spain, 2005; 862.

46. La interdiscliniedad y la transdisciplinariedad en la organizacion del conocimiento cientifica Actas del VIII Congresso del Capitulo Espanol de ISKO Léon abril, 18–20, 2007; Bravo, R., Alvite Diaz, B., Luisa, M., Eds.; Universidad: Léon, Spain, 2007; 619.

47. La représentation des connaissances en vue de leur intégration dans les systèmes d'information Actes du premier colloque ISKO France, Lille 1997; Maniez, J., Mustafa el Hadi, W., Eds.; Editions Conseil Scientifique de l'Université Charles-De-Gaulle-Lille 3: Lille, France, 1997; 403.

48. L'indexation à l'ére d'internet Actes du 2e Colloque ISKO France, Lyon October, 21–22, 1999; Hassoun, M., Larouk, O., Metzger, J.-P., Eds.; Services d'impression de L'ENSSIB: Villeurbanne.

49. Résumé automatique et filtrage d'information dans les réseaux Actes du 3e Colloque ISKO France, Paris Juillet, 5–6, 2001; Chaudiron, S., Fluhr, Ch., Eds.; Université Paris X.

50. L'organistion des connaissances: approches conceptuelles Actes de la 4ème édition du Congrés du Chapitre francais d'ISKO Grenoble Juillet, 3–4, 2003; Polity, Y., Henneron, G., Palermiti, R., Eds.; L'Harmattan: Paris, 2005.

51. In *Organisation des connaissances dans les systèmes d'information orientés utilisation cntexte de veille et d'intelligence économique*; David, A., Ed.; Université de Nancy 2005; Presses universitaires de Nancy: Nancy, France, 2005.

52. Organisation des connaissances et société des savoirs: Concepts, usages, acteurs Actes du 6ème congrès du Chapitre francais de l'ISKO Toulouse Juin, 7–8, 2007; Regimbeau, G., Couzinet, V., Eds.; Université Paul Sabatier: Toulouse, France.

53. Indian ISKO Chapter: Seminar on Classification and Knowledge Representation. Int. Classif. **1994**, *21*(1), 37–38.

54. International Conference on Future of Knowledge Organization in the Networked Environment; Raghavan, K.S., Ed.; IKONE 2007; Indian Statistical Institute. DRTC: Bangalore, India, 2007.

55. Smiraglia, R. A glimpse at Knowledge Organization in North America. An Editorial. Knowl. Org. **2007**, *34*(2), 9–7.

56. Smiraglia, R. About Knowledge Organization: An Editorial. Knowl. Org. **2005**, *32*(4), 139–140.

57. Dahlberg, I. Knowledge Organization: A new science?. Knowl. Org. **2006**, *33*(1), 11–19.

58. Shamurin, E.I. *Geschichte der bibliothekarisch-bibliographischen Klassifikation*, K.G. Saur Verlag: Muenchen, Germany, 1967; 404–781 Bd.1 u.2.

59. Ranganathan, S.R. Gopinath, M.A. *Prolegomena to Library Classification*, 3rd Ed. Asia Publ. House: Bombay, India, 1967; 640.

60. Scheele, M. *Wissenschaftliche Dokumentation*, Grundzüge, Probleme, Notwendigkeiten. Verlag Dr. M. Scheele: Schlitz, Germany, 1967; Reprint K.G. Saur Verlag: Muenchen, Germany, 1970 (contains also his faceted classification for biology).

61. Dahlberg, I. ICC—Information Coding Classification. Principles, structures and application possibilities. Int. Classif. **1982**, *9*(2), 87–93 Also in *Classification Systems and Thesauri 1950–1982*; International Classification and Indexing Bibliography; INDEKS Verlag: Frankfurt/Main, Germany, 1983; ICIB-1, 107–132.

62. Dahlberg, I. *Grundlagen universaler Wissensordnung*, DGD-Schriftenreihe. K.G.Saur Verlag: Muenchen, Germany, 1974; Vol. 3, 384 Probleme und Moeglichkeiten eines universalen Klassifikationssystems des Wissens. (Fundamentals of universal organization of knowledge).

63. Dahlberg, I. *Ontical Structures and Universal Classification*, Sarada Ranganathan Lectures. Sarada Ranganathan Endowment for Library Science: Bangalore, India, 1978; Vol. 11, 74.

64. Essers, J. Schreinemakers, J. Critical notes on the use of knowledge in Knowledge Management*Knowledge Organization and Change*, Proceedings of 4th International ISKO Conference Washington, DC July, 15–18, 1996; Green, R., Ed.; Advances in Knowledge Organization; INDEKS Verlag: Frankfurt, Germany, 1996; 5, 213–215.

65. Kasten, J. Thoughts on the relationship of knowledge organization to knowledge management. Knowl. Org. **2007**, *34*(1), 9–15.

66. Fugmann, R. Illusory goals in information science research Proceedings of 5th International Study Conference on Classification Research Toronto, Canada June, 24–28, 1991; Williamson, N., Hudon, M., Eds.; Elsevier: Amsterdam, the Netherland, 1992; 61–68.

67. Tillich, P. *Das System der Wissenschaften nach Gegenstaenden und Methoden*, Ein Enwurf. Vandenhoek und Ruprecht: Göttingen, Germany, 1923; 167.

68. Soergel, D. *Klassifikationssysteme und Thesauri*, Deutsche Gesellschaft für Dokumentation: Frankfurt/Main, Germany, 1969; 224 Eine Anleitung zur Herstellung von Klassifikationssystemen und Thesauri im Bereich der Dokumentation.

Internet Genres

Kevin Crowston
School of Information Studies, Syracuse University, Syracuse, New York, U.S.A.

Abstract

Rhetoricians since Aristotle have attempted to classify communications or documents into categories or "genres" with similar form, topic, or purpose. This entry surveys research on genre as it relates to Internet documents. The entry briefly presents the concept of genre in general, and then reviews the evolution and emergence of genres on the Internet. It concludes with an examination of the possible use of genre for improving information access on the Internet, with specific discussion of the issues in developing taxonomies of genre and automatically recognizing document genre.

INTRODUCTION

Rhetoricians since Aristotle have attempted to classify documents into categories or "genres" with similar form, topic, or purpose. (In this entry, we adopt a broad definition of document as "signifying objects,"[1] meaning something that serves as evidence, regardless of the particular medium or form.) Numerous definitions of genre have been debated in the applied linguistics community,[2,3–7] while other groups have struggled with similar notions, such as discourse or document types, for example, in SGML.[8] This entry, for example, is an instance of the *encyclopedia article* genre, commonly used to communicate the state of knowledge in a field. Other common genres include *letters* and *memos*, *project team meetings*, and *TV sitcoms*, all immediately recognizable by their typical purpose and characteristic form. In this entry, we provide a brief review of the concept of genre in general, drawing primarily on the cultural perspective of the New Rhetoric school,[4,9] before addressing the theory and applications of genre for digital documents found on the Internet.

Genres define classes of similar documents. Such a categorization can be made on different bases and approaches to defining genre have focused on different aspects of documents (see Breure[10] for a review of the development of the concept). Some genres are defined primarily in terms of the physical form, such as a *booklet* or *brochure*; still others in terms of the document form, such as *lists* or *directories*; while other genres are defined by purpose or function, such as a *proposal* or *inquiry*. However, most genres imply a combination of purpose and form,[2] such as a *newsletter*, which communicates "the news of the day," including multiple short articles and is distributed periodically to subscribers or members of an organization.

There is a close relation between the terms "genre" and "text type." Lee[11] distinguished between them by suggesting that the term "genre" is often used for definitions based on external criteria, such as purpose, while "text type" is used for definitions based on internal criteria, such as form, but goes on to conclude that genre can be used "to describe most of the corpus categories we have seen." (Moessner[12] makes the same distinction.) For the purpose of this entry, we will use the term genre as including aspects of both form and purpose.

Campbell and Jamieson[2] suggested that genres arise as responses to recurrent communicative situations. Given a recognized need to communicate (i.e., a purpose[13]), individuals will typically express similar social motives, themes, and topics in a communication with similar physical and linguistic characteristics (i.e., form), that is, they will communicate in a recognized genre. Miller[6] argued that the situations that give rise to the use of genres are social situations and that the process of creating genre is one of typification, as similarities in situations are recognized. If the typification is useful, the use of the genre becomes routine. She further argued that genres must accomplish a recognized social function and criticized the labeling of *environmental impact statements* as a genre because they did not meet this criterion, but rather had multiple conflicting motives.

Swales[7] similarly viewed genres as "a system for accomplishing social purposes by verbal means." He suggested analyzing documents in terms of their exhibited characteristic moves, defined as "a functional unit, used for some identifiable rhetorical purpose."[14] For example, Swales[7] analyzed the *introduction, methods, results, discussion*, and *conclusion sections* of research articles as well as briefly touching on other research process genres, such as *abstracts, presentation, theses*, and *grant proposals*. Following Swales's[7] approach, researchers have described other scientific genres such as *research paper abstracts*[15] and *discussion sections*,[16] *grant proposals*,[14] *posters*,[17] and other *visual presentations at scientific meetings*[18] and *French thesis defences*.[19]

Encyclopedia of Library and Information Sciences, Fourth Edition DOI: 10.1081/E-ELIS4-120043520
Copyright © 2017 by Taylor & Francis. All rights reserved.

Researchers have examined as well as journalistic genres such as *news*,[20,21]*editorial letters*,[22] and *magazine covers*[23] and genres from the commercial world, such as *business letters of negotiation*,[24]*letters of application for jobs*,[25]*Chinese sales letters*,[26]*environmental impact statements*,[27]*building reviews*,[28] and *philanthropic direct mail*.[29]

THEORY: DOCUMENTS AND GENRE

Viewed from the perspective of the reader of a document, identification of a document's genre makes the document more easily recognizable and understandable, thus reducing the cognitive load of processing it.[30] Because we drew on the *encyclopedia article* genre in writing this entry, for example, a reader should be able to more quickly determine the purpose and content of our communication and begin to evaluate its contribution. The form of the article gives hints to its meaning and appropriate uses. Similarly, following the form of the genre of a *research article, letter of application, parking ticket*, or *bank statement* makes the corresponding documents easier to recognize, to assess, and to use. This effect has been demonstrated experimentally: Vaughan and Dillon[31] found that readers of a Web newspaper that followed genre conventions reported better comprehension, usability, and ease of navigation than readers of a purported newspaper that did not. Knowledge of genres can similarly help creators of documents by providing a known form for achieving a communicative purpose. Rather than having to innovate in all aspects of a document, a writer can reuse the form of a familiar genre to achieve their purpose. Teaching of genres is thus seen as an important aspect of teaching language and communication, for example, in elementary,[32] second language,[33] and English for Special Purposes[34] education.

In addition to helping senders and recipients singly, knowledge of genres can also facilitate interaction, since multiple communications may be performed in a recognizable pattern, what Bazerman[35] called a "genre system." In other words, recognizing that a communication is of a particular genre may suggest the form expected for the reply. Swales[36] similarly defined a "genre chain" as a sequence of documents of different genres on a given topic. Examples include the sequence of *examination* and *cross-examination* in a trial, or the cycle of *article* submission to a journal or conference, *reviews, final acceptance* or *rejection letters* and publication. In each case, knowledge of the genre system provides information about how to proceed with the interaction. For example, Tardy[37] examined the genre system of research funding, identifying an interlocking set of genres such as a *research agency's mission statement* and *program information*, informal *meetings with program officers, applications, panel reviews*, and *decisions*. Antunes, Costas, and

Dias[38] analyzed genres related to electronic meetings. Features of a genre may enable their use in a genre system: for example, page numbers in a *technical paper* make it possible to more precisely cite concepts or quotations from the paper, thus binding the paper into the literature.

For genres to be of aid in communication though, they must be shared across the members of particular discourse communities.[7] Thus, genres are socially situated. Teachers and rhetoricians have acknowledged that learning about genres, and through genres, is learning how to participate in a community (e.g., Chapman, M.L.[32]). On the other hand, a genre may be unfamiliar or hard to understand for someone outside of the community. In fact, recognition of a particular genre is one sign of membership in a particular community (one needs only to witness the uncritical citing habits of college students who are not able to distinguish a popular Web genre from a serious scholarly one). Indeed, Freedman and Medway[39] suggest that incomprehensible genres may even be used deliberately to defend positions of privilege. Thus genres are not only a type of discourse but are themselves embodiments of social or communicative events.[40]

Leveraging the situated character of genres, Yates and Orlikowski[41,42] proposed using them as a lens into organizational practices. Studying organizational discourse as examples of genres, anchors, and situates the investigation in a way that other approaches could not because each genre has within it the information for how it should be interpreted within a particular discourse community. For example, Yates, Orlikowski, and Okamura[43] contrasted the explicit and implicit structuring of genres in the introduction of a new communications system, and Schryer and Spoel[44] examined genres as a way to understand professional identity formation of medical students and of midwives.

To capture these social elements, Orlikowski and Yates[42] introduced the notion of a "genre repertoire," that is, the set of genres in use within a community. They noted that different communities use different genres in their communication, and use common genres with different frequencies. (Hengst and Miller[45] refer to this situation as the "pervasive heterogeneity" of genres). These differences provide one source of insight into the communicative (and other) practices of the community. For example, a community of social scientists and computer scientists can be distinguished by the frequency of use of different paper genres, as well as the paucity of computer programs and program documentation created in the former, reflecting different modes of research.

Of course, the reality of documents and genre is not as clear-cut as the theory above suggests. First, not all communications or documents are necessarily generic. For example, Swales[7] ruled out conversation as a genre, arguing that the concept only applies to completed texts. Pieces of text or unfinished texts may not be generic. As well, if genres are formed in response to recurrent

International Federation–iSchools

communicative needs, then communications in novel (or even relatively novel) situations may also not be generic. This circumstance may describe large portions of the communication taking place via the Internet (and so of the documents found there). Even in typified circumstances, an author may deliberately or inadvertently fail to reproduce the necessary form of a genre, again producing a non-generic document. Finally, the relation amongst genres in a genre system is rarely linear; in any given situation, there may be a set of appropriate responses.[34]

Furthermore, the boundaries between genres are often fuzzy and documents may show considerable variation in form even within a genre.[12,46] As a result, it may be helpful to think of genres defined by exemplars and documents as being more or less good examples of a genre rather than attempting to draw firm boundaries. As well, as Orlikowski and Yates[42] point out, some communications use multiple genres simultaneously, such as a *proposal* embedded in a *memo* or a *book chapter* in a *book*, along with *table of contents* or *index*. Other documents might have some mixed attributes, e.g., *bibliography* that is also an *index to a document collection*. As a result, the mapping of documents to genre may be one to many. This mixing of genres is likely to be particularly problematic for digital documents, which can have multiple forms of presentation.

Further complicating the study of genre is the fact that knowledge of genres tends to be quite tacit and situated in use. Being able to recognize or use a genre is typically knowing "how to go on"[47] in a particular situation rather than formal articulable knowledge. The genre analyses cited above are research contributions precisely because they required research to uncover the hidden regularities in the documents. In practice, an individual may recognize and be able to use a document, while being unable to articulate a name for its particular genre or to say how they know what it is or which particular features are important for defining the form. When tested out of context, users may find genre hard to apply. For example, Santini[48] had 135 users to classify the genre of 25 Web pages and found high levels of agreement on only a handful of documents, while others attracted as many as four equally popular labels. Similarly, in a study with 102 Web pages, Rosso[49] found a wide variety of genre terms[49] when three users were asked to pick their own labels. On the other hand, in a study with 257 users and 55 pages, he obtained a reasonable level of agreement (70%) when the choice was restricted to one of 18 terms, again suggesting that genre can be recognized more easily than produced.

INTERNET GENRES

We now turn our focus to genres of digital documents found on the Internet. The Internet and in particular the World Wide Web provides a particularly interesting setting in which to study the use and development of genres for several reasons. First, the capabilities of the new medium have led to the development of many new genres of communication. Space limitations preclude a comprehensive review of the development of the Internet from the Advanced Research Project Agency Network's (ARPAnet's) four computers in 1969 to the immense and nearly ubiquitous network of today, but we note that the increased functionality of the Internet has been paralleled by an explosion in Internet genres. In particular, the technology of the Web extends the notion of a document—and thus the notion of genre—because Web pages can provide functionality in addition to information. Indeed, some Web pages are more comparable to computer interfaces than to conventional paper documents. As a result, functionality may be important in understanding genres on the Internet. Furthermore, the rapid development of this medium suggests a high level of experimentation with potential genres. Bearman,[50] for examples, notes the rapid evolution in what he refers to as "forms of material" in electronic media in general.

Second, since many Web sites are open to the public, many examples of Web communication are easily available for study. Furthermore, because there is no central management of the Internet or the Web, there is no explicit management or enforcement of genres of communication, as might happen in the introduction of a communication system in a corporate environment.[51] Instead, individual Web developers individually choose how to present their information, drawing on their understanding as members of a community, what Orlikowski et al.[51] called implicit structuring (in this case, from the point of view of the Web page developer rather than the recipient of the communication). Yates and Sumner refer to the "democratization of genre production" as "communities evolve increasingly well-defined genres to better support their particular communicative needs and work practices."[52] However, even in this free-for-all, mutual acceptance of genre is important to enable communications. Yates and Sumner[52] argue that on the Web, genres help in both the production and consumption of documents because genre adds "fixity" in a medium that does not otherwise distinguish very well between text types (say, a *book* and a *post-it*).

Finally, there are many communities meeting on the Web, bringing experiences with different genres and using the Web for many different purposes. The Web is sometimes used for direct communication where someone with a Web server "delivers" a document to members of a known community by giving them a URL. For example, some academics use the Web to communicate with colleagues by publishing their own papers, and with students by publishing syllabi and assignments. Another example of communication within a predictable community is computer companies announcing new products, publishing catalogs, or providing troubleshooting tips online for

International Federation–iSchools

their customers. However, in many other cases the audience is unpredictable. Unlike the Usenet or electronic mail groups, there is no clear separation of communities into different channels of communication (as is the case for journals or talks given at conferences, for which the audience is likely to have shared interests).

Indeed, it seems a stretch to say that there is a single Web community at all. Instead, the genre repertoire reflected in a collection of Web pages will be the result of interactions within and among multiple communities. In some cases, a genre may act as a type of boundary object,[53] providing a common point of contact between different groups.[39] In others, this mixing may lead to genre confusion, meaning that there is a practical need to understand the way genres enable communication. For example, organizations have used the Web to publish information such as *product brochures*, *annual reports*, country, state, and city *home pages*, *government agency press releases*, etc. These organizations tend to use familiar genres when putting information on the Web. However, a person happening to reach a document on one of their Web sites has a good chance of being outside the community in which that genre evolved. As a result the document may be confusing and the communicative purpose lost.

Evolution of Genres

To understand the evolution of genres on the Web, we draw on studies of how predigital genres have evolved over time. Drawing on Giddens'[47] structuration theory, Orlikowski and Yates[42] argued that, "People produce, reproduce and change genres through a process of structuring." As members of the community draw on their knowledge of a genre repertoire to communicate, they reinforce the use of these genres, making them more appropriate or legitimate for use in the given situation. For example, by creating an order entry Web page that draws on the genre of a paper order form, a designer reinforces the appropriateness of the order form genre for this type of communication, making its use in future situations more likely. In other words, the set of genres in use (i.e., the genre repertoire) is both a product of and a shaper of the communicative practices of a community.

Orlikowski and Yates[42] suggested that in a new situation (such as in the introduction of a new medium such as the Internet) individuals will typically draw on their existing genre repertoires, reproducing genres they have experienced as members of other communities. For example, Görlach[46] notes the emergence of new genres, such as the *cooking recipe*, that draw on early genres, in this case the *medical recipe* (though he uses the term text type rather than genre). However, people are also free to modify a genre and communicate in a way that invokes only some of the expected aspects of a form. If these changes become repeatedly used (i.e., typified), they too may

become accepted and used together with or instead of existing genres, thus extending or altering the genre repertoire. Because the definition of genre relies on social acceptance, it is impossible to define the exact point at which a new genre emerges from the old one. Acceptance may take many years. However, after some period of coexistence, the new combination of form and purpose may become generally recognized and even named as a separate genre. As well, genres may be accepted in different communities at different rates. The emergence of distinctive new genres would be one sign of the formation of a new community with new communicative practices.

Take, for example, the *academic journal article*, a distinctive genre with the communicative goal of reporting research results and establishing a researcher's credentials and reputation. Journal articles have moved nearly intact to the Web and can be found in many online databases and on publishers' Web sites as well as, on the Web sites of individual authors. These documents are often identical to the paper versions, an example of a reproduced genre (literally reproduced, as in many cases, the Web versions are simple scans of the paper form). However, in a few cases, the form of the journal article has begun to change to take advantage of the possibilities of linking or embedding information. For example, citations in papers may be hyperlinks to the referenced articles. In part to enable easier searching of results, some journals now require *structured abstracts*, a particular genre of *abstract* with a distinctive form. Some publisher sites allow users to comment on papers, enabling more interactive follow-up discussion. Such documents are examples of adapted genres. Even more interesting is the emergence of forms other than journal articles for reporting research results, such as *datasets*, *software*, or other products of research, all examples of emergent genres. For example, researchers in genetics may publish *gene sequences* in a variety of specialized databases that can substitute in some case for a journal publication.[54] Similar efforts are underway in other disciplines, meaning that the eventual form used for reporting research may bear only passing resemblance to the self-contained 20- to 25- page articles of today.

Related changes are already visible at the level of *journals*. For example, while paper journals are often reproduced on a Web site, there are now journals that publish only online editions, which need not conform to typical page limits or even have volumes at all (an adapted genre). There are suggestions that the increased use of online databases for finding articles (either by topical search or citation indexing), as opposed to subscribing to a handful of specific journals, is blurring previously distinct publications into "the literature."[55] As a result, the need for individual journals with distinct missions and readerships may be reduced, as is the utility of the genre itself. Similarly, the widespread use of *working paper* archives and of general search engines that cover such "grey literature" (*working papers*, *conference papers*,

International Federation-
iSchools

etc.) may blur the boundary between these genres and journal articles and thus lead to hybrid or novel genres. (Indeed, such a shift may have already happened in disciplines that value *conference papers* on par with *journal articles*, reducing the distinction between the purposes of these genres).

These emergent genres may be immediately accepted or, more likely, there may be a transition period during which the limits of the genre are renegotiated. For example, the *electronically distributed journal article* is still in transition.[56,57] It is being used, but this adapted genre is not yet completely accepted or considered legitimate for all purposes (e.g., as evidence for a tenure case) by the academic community as a whole. As well, modifications of genres that are parts of genre systems may require corresponding changes to the rest of the system. For example, changes in citation habits will be necessary before page numbers can be dropped from the *technical paper* genre. Such interdependencies between genres will tend to slow the adoption of a new genre.

Internet Genres

While many genres have been reproduced more-or-less faithfully, as in the example of *journal articles*, the Internet has seen the rise of a few novel genres. In a study of 1000 Web documents, Crowston and Williams[58] were able to identify documents of many familiar genres and of a few genres that seemed to be new to the Web, such as the *hotlist*. A specific example of a novel genre is the *home page*. As early as 1996, Furuta and Marshall[59] noted the emergence of this genre as a result of the specific affordances of the Internet. While Bates and Lu in 1997 suggested that the *home page* genre was still inchoate,[60] soon after Dillon and Gushrowski[61] found that the features of *personal home pages* seemed to have stabilized rather quickly. The *Frequently Asked Questions* (*FAQ*) document emerged as a distinct genre on the Usenet and was then translated to the Web. An AltaVista search done by Crowston and Williams[58] indicated approximately 170,000 Web pages with FAQ in their title (a search in 2007 with Google finds more than 16 million such pages).

Other authors have identified a variety of Internet specific genres. Some have to do with particular communications media used on the Internet, such as *e-mail message* or *Weblogs*. Gains[62] analyzed small collections of *business* and *academic e-mail messages*. He suggested that e-mail as a whole has too many uses to be considered one genre and that the business e-mails analyzed "appear to follow the normal conventions for standard written business English," suggesting that they did not include new genres. On the other hand, he noted that *academic e-mail messages* had some conversational features and suggested that the collection might include new genres of communications. Gruber[63] analyzed contributions to two *academic mailing lists* as forming a single genre with

features of *academic letters* and *scholarly publication* as well as of oral communication. (It should be noted that these analyses were carried out when the medium was still novel to many users.) More recently, Barron[64] analyzed the properties of *unsolicited commercial e-mail* (UCE or "spam"). She noted similarities between *spam* and other promotional genres, with moves such as capturing attention, establishing credentials, introducing the offer, and multiple moves soliciting a response. She noted differences though, such as the need to capture attention to get the message opened and the inclusion of offers to unsubscribe the recipient.

A more recent innovation is the *Weblog* or *blog*. Based on an analysis of a random sample of 203 blogs, Herring et al.[65] characterized *blogs* as a "hybrid genre that draws from multiple sources" both off-line and Internet. They distinguished several types of *blogs* with different forms and purposes as well as distinct origins. They characterized most of their samples as *journal blogs*, which they suggested draw on the form and purpose of *diaries*, since they report the writer's feelings rather than other content. A few were *filter blogs*, providing pointers to other content of interest and perhaps deriving from the earlier Web genre of *hotlists* or, they suggest, from the off-line antecedent of *letters to the editor*. Other types of blogs identified include *community*, *travel*, *memory*, and *communications blogs*, though these were rare in their sample.

Other authors have analyzed particular genres of documents commonly appearing on the Internet, such as the *personal home pages* mentioned above,[59–61,66] *Web resumes*,[67] *Internet advertising* ("netvertising"),[68] and *online encyclopedias*.[69] Howard[70] went as far as to claim the existence of a "Web vernacular", a particular form of Web page that was expected and so copied by commercial developers.

Still others have examined non-textual documents, such as *audio loops* (short sound sample),[71] *multimedia*,[72] and *databases*,[73] as well as mixed media such as *PowerPoint presentations*.[74] Exploration of genres of digital documents therefore blends at some point into the study of non-textual genres. The discussion above can be extended to such documents. For example, we can see the recreation of genres of music (e.g., *pop song* or *concerto*), even as the medium shifts from LP to CD to MP3, as well as adaptation of the genres of *televisions shows* to take advantage of the increased functionality (and decreased screen size) as they move from broadcast TV to Web distribution.

Genre Classification

While we do not have a list of all of the genres on the Internet (nor is it clear that such a thing is even possible), there is a substantial body of work categorizing genre in printed documents and some work studying them on the

International Federation– iSchools

Internet. Many attempts to develop a categorization of genres have been top-down, that is, they analyzed a set of documents based on theoretical principles or according to a priori classifications. A key difference in these efforts is the number of genre categories distinguished. Many studies of Web pages have used fewer broader categories: for example, zu Eissen and Stein[75] used only eight genres (*help; article; discussion; shop; portrayal, non-private; portrayal, private; link collection;* and *download*). At the other extreme, Görlach[46] offered a catalog of some 2000 genre (or text type) terms, which is intended to be an exhaustive list of the terms used in English. Somewhere in between, Lee[11] categorized documents in the British National Corpus (BNC) into 70 genres or subgenres (with some document assigned more than one genre). However, he notes that the genre terms used were "meant to provide starting points, not a definitive taxonomy," for example, grouping *textbooks* and *journal articles* as *academic texts* that can be further distinguished by medium.

If the classification includes more than a handful of terms, it is useful to group together similar terms and necessary to deal with terms of different levels of generality.[11] For example, *social science papers* might be grouped with *computer science implementation papers*, *biology research papers*, and so on as examples of *academic papers*. These genres share some similarities, such as a title, abstract, and bibliography, but differ in other particulars, such as the expected section headings, types of arguments or evidence. Many organized lists of genres are structured as single hierarchies. Fig. 1 shows a small section of the hierarchy of genres of Web documents identified by Crowston and Williams.[58] *Advertisements* and *announcements* are both examples of *declaratory document* genres; *classified advertisements* are a special kind of *advertisement*, and so on. Similarly, *social science papers*, *computer science papers*, and *biology papers* might be seen as examples of a more general genre of *research papers*, which are in turn examples of *papers* or *articles*.

An advantage of a hierarchy is that it avoids the need to predetermine the level of detail needed in the classification. Depending on the circumstances, we can consider genres at any of these different levels and different levels might be more or less useful for different purposes. Of course, there is no guarantee that convenient and well-known terms will exist for all levels of the hierarchy. A second criticism of traditional hierarchies is that they rely on a single organizing principle, which may not be useful or appropriate for all cases. Harrell and Linkugel[5] note that there are multiple bases on which such a classification could be constructed. To overcome this problem, Kwaśnik and Crowston[76] suggested using the faceted-analysis approach, following the example of previous genre-identification studies such as Päivärinta,[77] Tyrväinen and Päivärinta,[78] and Karjalainen et al.[79] who looked at the management of enterprise documents, and Kessler, Nunberg, and Schuetze[80] who sought to identify a limited set of facets for communicative purposes. Crowston and Williams[58] based their classification of genres on the *Art and Architecture Thesaurus*,[81] which is also a faceted classification overall.

The previously discussed classification schemes can be described as top-down or *a priori*. Though this approach is quite common in conventional settings, given the communal nature of genres, a top-down approach to classification seems problematic. As genres are socially constructed, different social groups using documents with similar structural features may think about them and describe them differently (i.e., as different genres, though perhaps similar text types[11]). While many genres may be widely shared, even more will be local to particular groups. Documents may be of genres that are not necessarily vetted by traditional schemes, particularly documents that come out of domain-specific work. Furthermore, while genres have always been conceptualized as dynamic, Dillon and Gushrowski[61] point out that genres are no longer necessarily "slow-forming, often emerging only over generations of production and consumption. . . .." Thus, a static typology of genre or document forms may not be sufficient to describe the emerging and dynamic genres in use on the Internet. It seems important instead to capture users' own language and understanding of genres.

Some researchers have attempted to identify genres bottom-up through user studies. Dewe, Karlgren, and Bretan[82] asked users to provide lists of genres found on the Web and received 67 responses. They noted though

<declaratory document genres>	
Advertisements	
Classified advertisements	Short paid announcements appearing in a periodical sorted according to the good or service being offered or requested
Announcements	Printed or published statements or notices that inform the reader of an event or other news
Custom 404 page	A Web page announcing that the requested Web page could not be found on the server
News bulletins	
Press releases	Official or authoritative statements giving information for publication in newspapers or periodicals

Fig. 1 A section of a hierarchy of document genres.
Source: Crowston, and Williams.[[104]]

International Federation– iSchools

that users tended to conflate genre and topic. Nilan, Pomerantz, and Paling[83] surveyed 242 Web users in person and via the Web about their purpose in searching the Web, the genre of document expected and the actual document found, and collected 1335 example pages; genres could be assigned for 1076, giving a total of 116 genres. They then grouped the genres given, first following the plan of the *Art and Architecture Thesaurus* and second based bottom-up on the user responses. The second classification was much broader and shallower than the first, and some genres were classified in multiple locations, suggesting that there may be difference between genres in use and formal structured knowledge. Freund, Clarke, and Toms[84] developed a list of 16 genres based on interviews with users and analysis of document repositories in a particular organization. They found that the 16 genres covered about 75% of documents randomly sampled from the repositories.

APPLICATIONS OF GENRE IN INFORMATION SCIENCE

In this final section, we discuss how ideas about genre might be applied to system design. Researchers have addressed a variety of information systems design questions, such as the use of genre to design electronic meeting systems[38] or to guide assembly of output documents from a content management system, for example, creating training documents by reusing content from operations manuals.[79,85] We will focus on one particular question likely to be of interest and importance to information scientists, namely how genre metadata might be used to improve information access on the Internet.

A significant problem in information access is that topic alone is not enough to define an information problem. Different users may require different solutions for seemingly similar topics because the situation (or context) of the user determines not only what topics are requested and what strategies are invoked in searching and evaluating output, but also what types of resources are considered relevant and useful. For example, "methods for learning mathematics" (a topic) will be construed differently by a student, by a parent, and by a classroom teacher because of their different information-use situations. Indeed, even the same user may require different information at different times.

Although we know that it is important to understand the situation of the user, the actual representation of situations and then their implementation in a system remains a difficult problem. Our efforts to create user profiles, universal situation grammars, and so on suffer from limitations of scope to specific domains and lack of extensibility and flexibility. However, in a study using Text Retrieval Conference data, Karlgren[86] found significant differences in style between documents judged relevant and not relevant,

suggesting that non-topical metadata can be helpful. In particular, inclusion of genre information as non-topical characteristics of the documents might be useful as a signal to their purpose and so fit the user information need. For example, a university professor looking for information about computer database systems for the class that she teaches would most likely be interested in documents of educational genres (e.g., *syllabi, assignments, class notes*). On the other hand, when working on a research paper in the database area, the same professor would more likely appreciate scholarly work (e.g., *research papers, annotated biographies, calls for papers*). The relevant documents for these two searches would be quite different, even though the topic and query keywords might be nearly the same.

Explicit identification of genre seems likely to be particularly important for large digital collections (the Web being the largest) because—unlike earlier collections of documents comprising a limited set of genres (e.g., a document database containing primarily *journal articles*)—these collections contain documents addressing a diversity of discourse communities with a diversity of genres (e.g., *journal articles* but also *magazine articles, hot lists, memos, home pages, class syllabi*, etc.). A user searching such a diverse document collection by topic will likely receive some documents of relevant genres along with many documents of irrelevant genres—a low precision result—even if all retrieved documents conform to search specifications regarding the topical content of the document. This analysis suggests that one way to exploit genre information is to create specialized search engines that retrieve only documents of a particular genre. This approach has already been followed by several systems, such as Indeed for *job listings*, CiteSeer and Google Scholar for *academic articles* and various Google specialized searches for *blogs, books, business addresses, news articles, patents, product sales pages*, and *source code* (but excluding those specialized by media, e.g., searches for images or video).

A second way to use genre information is to enrich queries with information about expected genres of the results, for example, as a form of relevance feedback.[86,87] Because most genres are characterized by both form and purpose, identifying the genre of a document provides information as to the document's purpose and its fit to the user's situation, which can be difficult to assess otherwise. When medical information is sought, identical keywords might retrieve a *newsletter*, a *personal home page*, a *journal article*, or a hospital's *patient-information site*. A person searching for one of these genres is unlikely to be satisfied by the others.

Knowledge of the form of genres can also help in the process of matching documents to queries. For example, an *FAQ* document is divided into question and answer pairs (indeed, documents of many genres have a form with repeated subpieces). Requiring search terms to be found in

International Federation—iSchools

International Federation– iSchools

the same question–answer pair (or subpiece) may reduce spurious matches or false drops.

Once a search is completed, document genre may be useful to improve the accuracy of relevance judgments made to rank order search results. It has been noted that some genres are less likely to be relevant for the majority of search tasks. This implies that certain Web pages could be promoted or demoted in the ranked results if their genre were known. For example, it has been claimed that most searchers are not interested in retrieving *personal home pages*,[88] so the latter could be moved down the results list by request. Bretan[89] suggested using genre to group search results while Freund, Clarke, and Toms[84] suggest filtering results.

Finally, a one-size-fits-all approach to summarizing or evaluating Web documents is likely to misrepresent many documents when confronted with diverse genres. For example, a *newspaper article* can often be summarized by the first few paragraphs of the document, but such an approach will not work for a *home page* or *FAQ*.[90] Rehm[91] analyzed the necessary components for a document to be an *academic home page* as a prelude to extracting information for further processing.

Automatic Identification of Document Genre

For genre to be useful in large-scale systems, techniques will be needed to automatically assign genre to large collections of documents. Researchers have tried numerous approaches to automatic genre identification; a sampling of studies is shown in Table 1. This work has used statistical (e.g., regression or discriminant analysis) or machine learning techniques (e.g., decision trees or support vector machines) to classify documents into genres based on features in the documents (Sebastiani[92] has reviewed these techniques). Comparing the algorithm's assignment to the known genre measures the success of the classification. Table 1 presents accuracy, though the some authors compute both precision and recall. For example, Freund, Clarke, and Toms[84] suggest that for filtering, higher recall might be preferred even at the cost of lower precision, to ensure that all documents of a given genre are presented to the user.

Document features that have been suggested for use in genre recognition include counts of specific words or of closed-class words (e.g., days of the week), counts and ratios of parts of speech, word and sentence length, layout features,[93] punctuation,[94] URLs, and HTML tags,[95] and even the level of spelling and typing errors in the document.[96] There has been a trend toward the use of larger and more comprehensive feature sets, from which the machine learning techniques can pick useful subsets. Which features are useful and necessary is still a topic for research. For example, Dewdney et al.[93] suggested that presentation features alone were sufficient to recognize genre, while Ferizis and Bailey[97] found that POS tagging

was not needed for genre recognition; since it is computationally expensive, avoiding these features may be desirable. Dong et al.[98] found that more features increased recall but decreased precision, and that including more types of features improved both.

For statistical analysis or machine learning to be successful requires a large set of categorized documents to use as a training set. Creating such corpuses is time-consuming, so early studies used preexisting ones, such as the Brown corpus, which includes 500 samples (802 documents) in 15 text categories (*press reportage; press editorial; press reviews; religion; skill and hobbies; belles letters; miscellaneous U.S. government and house organs; learned; fiction general; mystery and detective fiction; science fiction; romance and love story;* and *humor*). However, this corpus is not very suitable for the purpose as the average of 30 samples per genre is small for training and the categories mix topics and genres. More recent studies have created corpuses that are more focused and often larger (as large as 5–10 thousand pages with hundreds of examples of each genre). A concern here is the diversity of the documents included. Techniques applied to a corpus that includes only particular genres will yield more precise results than would be obtained with a more diverse sample.

Another key issue is number of genres to be recognized. Most studies have used small number of categories (from 4 to a maximum of 32, with a median of 10 in the studies in Table 1), which is small compared to the hundreds found in the user studies and general Web surveys reviewed above. Experimenters have examined fewer genres because increasing the number to be detected reduces precision and demands a larger corpus for training. But as Boese[99] noted, definitions of broader categories have be "softer" to include more documents and so very broad categories may be less useful to users or for the information access systems discussed above. Another concern is that the design of classification interacts with the features chosen. Grouping together documents with similar purposes but dissimilar structural features (i.e., genres as opposed to text types) may be useful for users, but creates problems for automatic classification. With a faceted classification, different techniques could be used to recognize individual facets.[100] Researchers have experimented with recognizing speech acts in e-mail,[101] a document's degree of expertise, detail, and subjectivity,[102] or positive and negative tone in reviews.[103]

CONCLUSIONS AND OUTLOOK

The research reviewed in this entry suggests that genre provides a useful lens for examining Internet documents. First, knowing the set of genres in use by a target audience can help ensure that information presented is easily understood and used. As well, there seems to be good potential

Table 1 Studies of automated classification of documents by genre.

Study	Techniques	Features	Corpus	Typology	Results
Karlgren and Cutting[105]	Discriminant analysis	20 linguistic features, such as adverb count, character count, first person pronoun count, type/token ratio	Brown corpus	Brown corpus categories	52% accuracy overall; grouping all fiction together improved accuracy to 65%
Kessler, Nunberg, and Schütze[80]	Logistic regression and neural nets	55 features including structural, lexical, character-level, and derivative cues	Brown corpus	Three part classification of 6 genres: reportage; editorial; scitech; legal; nonfiction; and fiction; plus "brow" (popular, middle, upper-middle, and high) and narrative (yes or no)	"Good results" for reportage and fiction but not for other genres. Only small difference between using surface and structural cues
Dewe et al.[82]	Classification rules	40 features including lexical, textual, and genre specific features	Own corpus of 1358 Web pages	11 genres: informal/private; public/commercial; searchable indexes; journalistic material; reports; other running text; FAQs; link collections; asynchronous multiparty correspondence; and error messages	90% accuracy on first split; 66–75% on remaining decisions
Wolters and Kirsten[106]	k-nearest neighbor classification, Relational Instance-Based Learning (RIBL); learning vector quantization; Instance Based Learning (IBL)	100, 500, or 1000 lemma features and 54 part of speech tags	Limas corpus, a collection of 500 German documents modelled on the Brown corpus	33 categories taken from the Deutsche Bibliographie (not all genres); but experiments run with fewer: academic texts from humanities and from science and technology; press texts; fiction; politics; law; and economy	75–100% precision in assignment, but each genre done is separately that the corpus provided too little material for training
Stamatatos et al.[94]	Regression and discriminant analysis suggest that regression works better than other techniques with a small number of training instances	22 features: token-level measures (e.g., word counts) and outputs from NLP processing (e.g., number of noun phrases detected, average length of a noun phrase)	Own corpus of 250 modern Greek documents, 25 of each genre	10 genres: press editorial; press reportage; official documents; literature; recipes; curricula vitae; interviews; planned speeches; and broadcast news; scripted	82% accuracy overall. Press editorial and press reportage often confused
Dewdney et al.[93]	Support Vector Machine (SVM), decision tree and naïve Bayes	323 word features and 89 presentation features: closed-class words, parts of speech, word and sentence length, punctuation, layout features	CMU corpus of 9750 documents	7 genres: advertisement; bulletin board; frequently asked questions; message board; radio news; Reuters newswire; television news	89% accuracy. Presentation features alone were sufficient to classify genre
Lim et al.[95]	Tilburg Memory Based Learner (TiMBL)	329 features in five sets: URL, HTML tags, token information, lexical information, and structural information	Own corpus of 1224 Web pages	16 genres: Dewe et al.'s[82] taxonomy, plus product specifications and image collections, and splitting public and commercial homepages in two, and reports into research reports, official materials and informative materials	74% accuracy in assignment; improved slightly with optimal subset of features. Could not reliably determine genre for input pages and other
Bisant[107]	Neural network with hidden layer, decision trees, SVM	89 features including part of speech and characters. Analysis shows 25 are not useful	Own corpus of 5000 e-mails and Web pages	10 genres: advertisement, business correspondence, data entry forms, e-mail administration, e-zine, friend correspondence, Internet chat, news, notices, and technical data	86% overall accuracy using neural nets with considerable variation. Decision trees are 79% accurate. Notices confused with news

(Continued)

International Federation—iSchools

International Federation—
iSchools

Table 1 Studies of automated classification of documents by genre. (*Continued*)

Study	Techniques	Features	Corpus	Typology	Results
Boese[99]	Bayes Net, decision trees, logit boost, bagging	Considered 1600 features: style, form, content. Narrowed to a set of 78	Own corpus of 343 Web pages	Developed classification of 115 genres but used 10 for experiments: abstract; call for papers; FAQ; how-to; hub/sitemap; job description; resume/CV; statistics; syllabus; and technical paper	91% accuracy using logit boost and 78 features
Freund et al.[84]	SVM light	"Bag of words," but no structural features	Own corpus of 800 documents (about 50 per genre) drawn from repositories in a single organization	16 genres (manuals; presentations; product documents; technotes, tips; tutorials and labs; white papers; best practices; design patterns; discussions/forums; cookbooks and guides; engagement summaries; problem reports; technical articles) developed within a specific organization	81–97% recall, but lower precision
Stubbe et al.[96]	Decision trees	Hand selected sets of genre-specific features: form, vocabulary and parts of speech, complex patterns, level of typing errors	Own corpus of 1280 Web pages, 40 of each genre	32 genres in 8 broad classes: journalism, literature, information, documentation, directory, communication, nothing	78% accuracy at first level; 72% at second level with considerable variation
Dong et al.[98]	Naïve Bayesian	5, 20, or 100 features from form, content, and functionality	Corpus of 1280 Web pages; 170 of 4 genres (3 from Santini, M.[48]) plus 600 random pages	genres: FAQ; news; e-shopping; personal home pages	86–92% accuracy (precision). Precision improved by fewer features, but recall by more. More types of features improved both

to incorporate genre metadata in information access systems. However, to realize these benefits, more research is needed. First, we do not as yet have a fully articulated set of data that reveals what genres various target groups recognize nor for what tasks they find documents of specific genres useful. Second, while genre recognition has improved, it is still limited in the number of genres that can be detected reliably. These two research agendas interact, as better knowledge of the genres in use will inform our attempts to recognize and use them in future Internet systems.

ACKNOWLEDGMENT

This research was partially supported by NSF IIS Grant 04-14482.

REFERENCES

1. Buckland, M.K. What is a "document". J. Am. Soc. Inform. Sci. **1997**, *48* (9), 804–809.
2. Campbell, K.K., Jamieson, K.H., Eds.; *Form and Genre: Shaping Rhetorical Action*; Speech Communication Association: Fall Church, VA, 1978.
3. Johns, A.M.; Bawarshi, A.; Coe, R.M.; Hyland, K.; Paltridge, B.; Reiff, M.J.; Tardy, C. Crossing the boundaries of genre studies: Commentaries by experts. J. Sec. Lang. Writ. **2006**, *15* (3), 234–249.
4. Hyon, S. Genre in three traditions: Implications for ESL. TESOL Quart. **1996**, *30* (4), 693–722.
5. Harrell, J.; Linkugel, W.A. On rhetorical genre: An organizing perspective. Philos. Rhetor. **1978**, *11*, 262–281.
6. Miller, C.R. Genre as social action. Quart. J. Speech **1984**, *70*, 151–167.
7. Swales, J.M. *Genre Analysis: English in Academic and Research Settings*, Cambridge University Press: New York, 1990.
8. Dollar, C. Electronic objects circa 2001: Problems or opportunities? Yes. Paper Presented at the Conference on Electronic Records in the New Millennium, Vancouver, BC, 1994; 25–38.
9. Muntigl, P.; Gruber, H. Introduction: Approaches to genre. Folia Linguist. **2005**, *39* (1–2), 1–18.
10. Breure, L. *Information and Computing Sciences*, University of Utrecht: Utrecht, 2001; Vol. 2007.
11. Lee, D.Y.W. Genres, registers, text types, domains, and styles: Clarifying the concepts and navigating a path through the BNC jungle. Lang. Learn. Technol. **2001**, *5*(3), 37–72.
12. Moessner, L. Genre, text type, style, register: A terminological maze. Eur. J. English Stud. **2001**, *5* (2), 131–138.
13. Bitzer, L.F. The rhetorical situation. Philos. Rhetor. **1968**, *1*, 1–14.
14. Connor, U.; Mauranen, A. Linguistic analysis of grant proposals: European Union Research Grants. English Spec. Purp. **1999**, *18* (1), 47–62.
15. Martín, P.M. A genre analysis of English and Spanish research paper abstracts in experimental social sciences. English Spec. Purp. **2003**, *22* (1), 25–43.
16. Peacock, M. Communicative moves in the discussion section of research articles. System **2002**, *30* (4), 479–497.
17. MacIntosh-Murray, A. Poster presentations as a genre in knowledge communication: A case study of forms, norms and values. Sci. Commun. **2007**, *28* (3), 347–376.
18. Rowley-Jolivet, E. Visual discourse in scientific conference papers: A genre-based study. English Spec. Purp. **2002**, *21* (1), 19–40.
19. Maingueneau, D. Analysis of an academic genre. Discour. Stud. **2002**, *4* (3), 319–342.
20. Vestergaard, T. That's not news: Persuasive and expository genres in the press. In *Analysing Professional Genres*; Trosborg, A., Ed.; John Benjamins: Amsterdam, 2000; 97–119.
21. Ljung, M. Newspaper genres and newspaper English. In *English Media Texts-Past and Present. Language and Textual Structure*; Ungerer, F., Ed.; John Benjamins: Amsterdam, 2000; 131–149.
22. Flowerdew, J.; Dudley-Evans, T. Genre analysis of editorial letters to international journal contributors. Appl. Linguist. **2002**, *23* (4), 463–489.
23. Held, G. Magazine covers: A multimodal pretext-genre. Folia Linguist. **2005**, *39* (1–2), 173–196.
24. Pinto dos Santos, V.B.M. Genre analysis of business letters of negotiation. English Spec. Purp. **2002**, *21* (2), 167–199.
25. Henry, A.; Roseberry, R.L. A narrow-angled corpus analysis of moves and strategies of the genre: "Letter of application". English Spec. Purp. **2001**, *20* (2), 153–167.
26. Zhu, Y. Rhetorical moves in Chinese sales genres, 1949 to the present. J. Busin. Commun. **2000**, *37* (2), 156–172.
27. Bazerman, C.; Little, J.; Chavkin, T. The production of information for genred activity spaces: Informational motives and consequences of the environmental impact statement. Writ. Commun. **2003**, *20* (4), 455–477.
28. Caballero Rodriguez, R. Metaphor and genre: The presence and role of metaphor in the building review. Appl. Linguist. **2003**, *24* (2), 145–167.
29. Upton, T.A. Understanding direct mail letters as a genre. Intl. J. Corp. Linguist. **2002**, *7* (1), 65–85.
30. Bartlett, F. *Remembering: A Study in Experimental and Social Psychology*, University Press: Cambridge, 1932/1967.
31. Vaughan, M.W.; Dillon, A. Why structure and genre matter for users of digital information: A longitudinal experiment with readers of a web-based newspaper. Intl. J. Hum. Comput. Stud. **2006**, *64*, 502–526.
32. Chapman, M.L. Situated, social, active: Rewriting genre in the elementary classroom. Writ. Commun. **1999**, *16* (4), 469–490.
33. Hyland, K. Genre-based pedagogies: A social response to process. J. Sec. Lang. Writ. **2003**, *12* (1), 17–29.
34. Swales, J.M. Languages for specific purposes. Annu. Rev. Appl. Linguist. **2000**, *20*, 59–76.
35. Bazerman, C. Systems of genres and the enactment of social intentions. In *Genre and the New Rhetoric*; Freedman, A., Medway, P., Eds.; Taylor & Francis: London, 1995; 79–101.

International Federation–iSchools

International Federation–
iSchools

36. Swales, J.M. *Research Genres: Exploration and Applications*, Cambridge University Press: Cambridge, 2004.

37. Tardy, C.M. A genre system view of the funding of academic research. Writ. Commun. **2003**, *20* (1), 7–36.

38. Antunes, P.; Costa, C.J.; Pino, J.A. The use of genre analysis in the design of electronic meeting systems. Inform. Res. Intl. Electron. J. **2006**, *11* (3).

39. Freedman, A. Medway, P. Locating genre studies: Antecedents and prospects. In *Genre and the New Rhetoric*; Freedman, A., Medway, P., Eds.; Taylor & Francis: London, 1994; 1–22.

40. Askehave, I.; Swales, J.M. Genre identification and communicative purpose: A problem and a possible solution. Appl. Linguist. **2001**, *22* (2), 195–212.

41. Yates, J.; Orlikowski, W.J. Genres of organizational communication: A structurational approach to studying communications and media. Acad. Manag. Rev. **1992**, *17* (2), 299–326.

42. Orlikowski, W.J.; Yates, J. Genre repertoire: The structuring of communicative practices in organizations. Admin. Sci. Quart. **1994**, *33*, 541–574.

43. Yates, J.; Orlikowski, W.J.; Okamura, K. Explicit and implicit structuring of genres in electronic communication: Reinforcement and change of social interaction. Organ. Sci. **1999**, *10* (1), 83–103.

44. Schryer, C.F.; Spoel, P. Genre theory, health-care discourse, and professional identity formation. J. Bus. Tech. Commun. **2005**, *19*, 249–279.

45. Hengst, J.A.; Miller, P.J. The heterogeneity of discourse genres: Implications for development. World English **1999**, *18* (3), 325–341.

46. Görlach, M. *Text Types and the History of English*, Mouton de Gruyter: New York, 2004. Trends in Linguistics. Studies and Monographs 139.

47. Giddens, A. *The Constitution of Society: Outline of the Theory of Structuration*, University of California: Berkeley, CA, 1984.

48. Santini, M. Zero, single, or multi? Genre of web pages through the users' perspective. Inform. Process. Manag. **2007**, *44* (2), 702–737.

49. Rosso, M.A. What type of page is this? Genre as web descriptor Paper presented at the 5th ACM/IEEE-CS Joint Conference on Digital libraries Denver, CO, 2005.

50. Bearman, D. *Electronic Evidence: Strategies for Managing Records in Contemporary Organizations*, Archives and Museum Informatics: Pittsburgh, PA, 1994.

51. Orlikowski, W.J.; Yates, J.; Okamua, K.; Fujimoto, M. Shaping electronic communication: The metastructuring of technology in the context of use. Organ. Sci. **1995**, *6* (4), 423–444.

52. Yates, S.J. Sumner, T. Digital genres and the new burden of fixity Paper Presented at the Hawaiian International Conference on System Sciences (HICCS 30) Wailea, HA, 1997.

53. Star, S.L.; Griesemer, J.R. Institutional ecology, "translations" and boundary objects: Amateurs and professionals in Berkeley's Museum of Vertebrate Zoology, 1907-39. Soc. Stud. Sci. **1989**, *19*(3): 387–420.

54. Krawczak, M.; Ball, E.V.; Fenton, I.; Stenson, P.D.; Abeysinghe, S.; Thomas, N.; Cooper, D.N. Human gene mutation database: A biomedical information and research resource. Hum. Mutat. **2000**, *15* (1), 45–51.

55. Nunberg, G. The places of books in the age of electronic reproduction. Representations **1993**, *42* (Spring), 13–37.

56. Kling, R.; Covi, L. Electronic journals and legitimate media in the systems of scholarly communication. Inform. Soc. **1995**, *11* (4), 261–271.

57. Harter, S.P. Scholarly communication and electronic journals: An impact study. J. Am. Soc. Inform. Sci. **1998**, *49* (6), 507–516.

58. Crowston, K.; Williams, M. Reproduced and emergent genres of communication on the World Wide Web. Inform. Soc. **2000**, *16* (3), 201–215.

59. Furuta, R. Marshall, C.C. *Genre as Reflection of Technology in the World-Wide Web*, Hypermedia Research Lab: Texas A&M, 1996.

60. Bates, M.J.; Lu, S. An exploratory profile of personal home pages: Content, design, metaphors. Online CDROM Rev. **1997**, *21* (6), 331–340.

61. Dillon, A.; Gushrowski, B. Genres and the Web: Is the personal home page the first uniquely digital genre. J. Am. Soc. Inform. Sci. **2000**, *51* (2), 202–205.

62. Gains, J. Electronic mail–A new style of communication or just a new medium? An investigation into the text features of e-mail. English Spec. Purp. **1999**, *18* (1), 81–101.

63. Gruber, H. E-mail discussion lists: A new genre of scholarly communication. Wiener Linguistische Gazette **1997**, *60/61*, 24–43.

64. Barron, A. Understanding spam: A macro-textual analysis. J. Pragmat. **2006**, *38* (6), 880–904.

65. Herring, S.C. Scheidt, L.A. Bonus, S. Wright, E. Bridging the gap: A genre analysis of weblogs Paper Presented at the 37th Hawaii International Conference on System Sciences, Waikoloa, HI, 2004.

66. Killoran, J.B. The gnome in the front yard and other public figurations: Genres of self-presentation on personal home pages. Biogr. Interdiscip. Quart. **2003**, *26* (1), 66–83.

67. Killoran, J.B. Self-published Web resumes—Their purposes and their genre systems. J. Bus. Tech. Commun. **2006**, *20* (4), 425–459.

68. Fortanet, I.; Palmer, J.C.; Posteguillo, S. The emergence of a new genre: Advertising on the internet (netvertising). Hermes **1999**, *23*, 93–113.

69. Emigh, W. Herring, S.C. Collaborative authoring on the web: A genre analysis of online encyclopedias Paper Presented at the 38th Hawaii International Conference on System Sciences Waikoloa, HI, 2005.

70. Howard, R.G. Toward a theory of the world wide web vernacular: The case for pet cloning. J. Folkl. Res. **2005**, *42* (3), 323–367.

71. Stillar, G. Loops as genre resources. Folia Linguist. **2005**, *39* (1–2), 197–212.

72. Lemke, J.L. Multimedia genres and traversals. Folia Linguist. **2005**, *39* (1–2), 45–56.

73. Manovich, L. Database as a genre of new media. AI Soc. **2000**, *14*, 176–183.

74. Myers, G. Powerpoints: Technology, lectures, and changing genres. In *Analysing Professional Genres*; Trosborg, A., Ed.; John Benjamins: Amsterdam, 2000; 177–191.

75. zu Eissen, S.M. Stein, B. Genre classification of web pages: User study and feasibility analysis Paper Presented at the 27th Annual German Conference on Artificial Intelligence (KI 04) Ulm, 2004.

76. Kwasnik, B.H. Crowston, K. A framework for creating a facetted classification for genres: Addressing issues of multidimensionality Paper Presented at the Hawai'i International Conference on System Science (HICSS) January, 5–9 Big Island, HI, 2004. Waikoloa, HI.

77. Päivärinta, T. A genre approach to applying critical social theory to information systems development Paper Presented at the 1st Critical Management Studies Conference, Information Technology and Critical Theory Stream Manchester, 1999.

78. Tyrväinen, P. Päivärinta, T. On rethinking organizational document genres for electronic document management Paper Presented at the 32nd Annual Hawaii International Conference on System Sciences Los Alamitos, CA, 1999, Waikoloa, HI.

79. Karjalainen, A. Päivärinta, T. Tyrväinen, P. Rajala, J. Genre-based metadata for enterprise document management Paper Presented at the 33rd Annual Hawaii International Conference on System Sciences Los Alamos, CA, 2000, Wailea Maui, HI.

80. Kessler, B. Nunberg, G. Schuetze, H. Automatic detection of text genre Paper Presented at the 35th Annual Meeting of the Association for Computational Linguistics and the 8th Meeting of the European Chapter of the Association for Computational Linguistics Madrid, 1997.

81. Petersen, T. *Art and Architecture Thesaurus*, Oxford: New York, 1994.

82. Dewe, J. Karlgren, J. Bretan, I. Assembling a balanced corpus from the Internet. Paper Presented at the 11th Nordic Conference of Computational Linguistics Copenhagen, 1998.

83. Nilan, M.S. Pomerantz, J. Paling, S. Genres from the Bottom up: What has the web brought us? Paper Presented at the American Society for Information Science and Technology Conference Washington, DC 2001; 330–339.

84. Freund, L. Clarke, C.L.A. Toms, E.G. Towards genre classification for IR in the workplace ACM International Conference Proceeding Copenhagen, 2006; 30–36, 176.

85. Honkaranta, A. Evaluating the 'genre lens' for analyzing requirements for content assembly. Paper Presented at the Eighth CAiSE/IFIP8.1 International Workshop on Evaluation of Modeling Methods in Systems Analysis and Design, Velden, Austria, 2003.

86. Karlgren, J. Stylistic experiments in information retrieval. In *Natural Language Information Retrieval*; Stralkowski, T., Ed.; Kluwer: Dordrecht, 1998.

87. Roussinov, D. Crowston, K. Nilan, M. Kwasnik, B.H. Liu, X. Cai, J. Genre-based navigation on the web. 34th Hawaii International Conference on Systems Science (HICSS–34) Maui, HI, January 3–6, 2001.

88. Chen, H.; Schuffels, C.; Orwig, R. Internet categorization and search: A self-organizing approach. J. Vis. Commun. Image Represen. **1996**, *7* (1), 88–102.

89. Bretan, I. Dewe, J. Hallberg, A. Wolkert, N. Web-Specific genre visualization. Paper Presented at WebNet '98, Orlando, 1998.

90. Marcu, D. From discourse structures to text summaries. Paper Presented at the 14th National Conference on Artificial Intelligence (AAAI-97), Providence, RI, July 27–31, 1997.

91. Rehm, G. Towards automatic web genre identification: A corpus-based approach in the domain of academia by example of the academic's personal homepage Paper Presented at the 35th Annual Hawaii International Conference on System Sciences, Big Island, HI, Jan. 10, 2002, 101.

92. Sebastiani, F. Machine learning in automated text categorization. ACM Comput. Surv. **2002**, *34* (1), 1–47.

93. Dewdney, N. VanEss-Dykema, C. MacMillan, R. The form is the substance: Classification of genres in text Paper Presented at the Workshop on Human Language Technology and Knowledge Management, ACL 2001 Conference July, 6–7, 2001, Toulouse, 2001.

94. Stamatatos, E.; Fakotakis, N.; Kokkinakis, G. Automatic text categorization in terms of genre and author. Comput. Linguist. **2000**, *26* (4), 471–498.

95. Lim, C.S.; Lee, K.J.; Kim, G.C. Multiple sets of features for automatic genre classification of web documents. Inform. Process. Manag. **2005**, *41* (5), 1263–1276.

96. Stubbe, A. Ringlstetter, C. Schulz, K.U. Genre as noise – noise in genre. Paper Presented at the IJCAI-2007 Workshop on Analytics for Noisy Unstructured Text Data Hyderabad, 2007; 9–16 Genre as noise – noise in genre. Paper Presented at the.

97. Ferizis, G. Bailey, P. Towards practical genre classification of web documents. Paper Presented at the WWW 2006 Conference Edinburgh, 2006.

98. Dong, L. Watters, C. Duffy, J. Shepherd, M. An examination of genre attributes for web page classification. Paper Presented at the 41st Hawai'i International Conference on System System (HICSS-41) Waikola, HI, 2008.

99. Boese, E.S. *Stereotyping the Web: Genre Classification of Web documents*, Colorado State University: Boulder, CO, 2005, MS thesis.

100. Kim, Y. Ross, S. An examining variations of prominent features in genre classification. Paper Presented at the 41st Hawai'i International Conference on System System (HICSS-41) Kona, HI, 2008.

101. Carvalho, V.R.; Cohen, W.W. Improving email speech acts analysis via n-gram selection. HLT-NAACL 2006 Workshop on Analyzing Conversations in Text and Speech, New York, June 8–9, 2006, 35–41.

102. Dimitrova, M. Finn, A. Kushmerick, N. Smyth, B. Web genre visualization. Paper Presented at the Conference on Human Factors in Computing Systems (CHI 2002), Minneapolis, MN, 2002.

103. Finn, A.; Kushmerick, N. Learning to classify documents according to genre. J. Am. Soc. Inform. Sci. Technol. **2006**, *57* (11), 1506–1518.

104. Crowston, K.; Williams, M. Reproduced and emergent genres of communication on the World-Wide Web. Inform. Soc. **2000**, *16* (3), 201–216.

105. Karlgren, J. Cutting, D. Recognizing text genres with simple metrics using discriminant analysis Paper Presented at the 15th International Conference on Computational Linguistics Kyoto, 1994.

106. Wolters, M. Kirsten, M. Exploring the use of linguistic features in domain and genre classification Paper Presented at the 9th Conference of the European Chapter of the Association for Computational Linguistics Bergen, 1999.

107. Bisant, D. An application of neural networks to sequence analysis and genre identification. Intl. J. Pattern Recognit. Artif. Intel. **2005**, *19* (2), 199–215.

International Federation– iSchools

Internet Search Tools: History to 2000

Dale J. Vidmar
Connie J. Anderson-Cahoon
Southern Oregon University Library, Ashland, Oregon, U.S.A.

Abstract

The early history of Internet search systems was quite diverse, and went through several stages before settling into the more mature recent environment of a few major search engines. The authors note: "From the early beginnings of Telnet, File Transfer Protocol (FTP), Archie, Veronica, and Gopher to the current iterations of Web search engines and search directories that use graphical interfaces, spiders, worms, robots, complex algorithms, proprietary information, competing interfaces, and advertising, access to the vast store of materials that is the Internet has depended upon search tools."

International Federation–
iSchools

INTRODUCTION

Finding information on the Internet and the World Wide Web (WWW) has always been somewhat like trying to find a needle in a haystack. An added dimension to the haystack metaphor is that the Internet environment is a dynamic collection of information. Changes occur almost every second. New pages are added. Old pages are deleted or altered. From the very beginning of the World Wide Web (WWW), search tools were needed to create order and provide an interface that allowed users to retrieve current documents while at the same time deleting inactive sites. Search databases and indexes could not be static; neither could the interface that served as the public relations instrument for the product. The tools of Internet searching emerged from the simple and modest beginnings of research and graduate school projects to the highly competitive and highly secretive proprietary corporate environment. As search tools evolved, they changed not only how people find information, but also how they viewed the world of the twenty-first century.

The Internet grew out of a need to connect computers at one location to computers at other locations, thus creating a globalization of shared resources. The early iterations of shared data were basic but grew rapidly as more and more computers became connected. Connectivity led to an information base that multiplied and evolved exponentially. This information base ultimately became unwieldy, and some of the early Internet pioneers began to see the necessity for both an organizational scheme and a method for accessing what was available. Each new tool provided more order, and in general an improved searching mechanism. From the early beginnings of Telnet, File Transfer Protocol (FTP), Archie, Veronica, and Gopher to the current iterations of Web search engines and search directories that use graphical interfaces, spiders, worms, robots, complex algorithms, proprietary information, competing interfaces, and advertising, access to the vast store of materials that is the Internet has depended upon search tools.

THE BEGINNINGS

What we now know as the Internet had its origins in the early 1960s by several visionary thinkers who understood the value of having computers linked to one another and being able to share information. Most applications were in the scientific and military fields at that time. Early developers included J. C. R. Licklider from MIT, who proposed a global network of computers in 1962. Licklider moved to the Defense Advanced Research Projects Agency (DARPA) and became the head of the project in late 1962. Leonard Kleinrock from UCLA developed the theory of packet switching that later became the basis for Internet connections. An MIT professor, Lawrence Roberts, connected two computers via telephone lines in 1965. Roberts became part of DARPA in 1966 and developed the plan for ARPANET. In 1969, the U.S. Department of Defense changed the name of DARPA to the Advanced Research Projects Agency (ARPA).

The purpose of ARPA was to develop and maintain automated communication methods that would operate in an emergency. As a result, ARPANET, a distributed communications network capable of communicating with multiple computer platforms, was born in 1969. Ultimately, these multiplatform and multichannel methods became known as the transmission control protocol and Internet protocol (TCP/IP), which for the most part defines the Internet as it is now configured today. Data are encoded and transmitted between computers via the common format TCP/IP provides. TCP/IP protocol was first proposed by Bob Kahn at BBN Technologies, a division of GTE, and further developed by Kahn and Vint Cerf at Stanford.

Encyclopedia of Library and Information Sciences, Fourth Edition DOI: 10.1081/E-ELIS4-120044130

Copyright © 2017 by Taylor & Francis. All rights reserved.

The National Science Foundations (NSF) extended its network in the 1980s to increase international educational and research opportunities. This network used NSF computers for data storage, file transfer, and E-mail. NSFnet evolved into what is now known as the Internet. It incorporated the TCP/IP format. As the Internet grew, there became an increasing need for better tools to access and organize information. Using FTP information could be shared between computers. File transfer protocol enables a user to obtain files of text, executable programs, graphics, movies, sound files, and other information, but early restrictions of FTP sites allowed only short names with little description about content. Files were often named README, INDEX, NOTICE, ABOUT, and other variations. These file names were typically capitalized, so they appeared in a more prominent position in a list of entries. There were thousands of FTP sites across the world, but each site was a collection of files that were not searchable. A user would have to visit each FTP site and browse through the files to hopefully discover relevant information. Archie, Veronica, Gopher, Wide Area Information System (WAIS), and others were the early search tools of the Internet—the first attempts to provide more order and searchability. Although these early tools are still accessible today, they were developed prior to Web browsers and have generally been replaced by more popular Web search tools.

Archie

In 1990 Alan Emtage, Peter Deutsch, Bill Heelan, and others created the oldest search engine at McGill University in Montreal. At the time, there was no World Wide Web, and files were scattered over a vast network. These files were stored and retrieved via FTP. The transfer of publicly available information has been one of the most widespread uses of the file transfer capability on the Internet. Institutions and organizations throughout the world provide openly accessible file transfer sites with information that anyone can obtain. Archie short for "archives," was a manually indexed system for exchanging these types of files, particularly the very popular anonymous FTP sites, which were repositories of files that anyone could access. Archie was a search tool for finding things in FTP space based on keywords.

Prior to Archie, a system administrator set files up on a computer called an FTP server. Those files could then be retrieved by someone else by connecting to the files via an FTP client following specifications set forth in FTP protocol. These files were generally shared by sending an E-mail alerting others of the location of the files or by posting a message to a listserv or discussion forum. Archie used a script-based data gatherer to retrieve listings of anonymous FTP files. It then made these files accessible by indexing them. The result was a method of organizing files into accessible listings, but Archie servers generally contained only a small portion of available information.

Gopher

Gopher was developed at the University of Minnesota in 1991. It was named Gopher after the University's mascot—the Golden Gopher—suggesting a user "go for" information. Gopher was designed to be an easy, menu-driven way of finding online information. Mark MacCahill, project leader, described the program as "the first Internet application that my mom and dad could use." Gopher did not require any knowledge of computer architecture or UNIX to use. Gopher was like FTP except that it retrieved plain-text documents rather than files, having no images or hypertext. In a gopher system, typing or clicking on a number that represented the document on a menu accessed a hierarchically structured list of documents. Menu entries were more descriptive than FTP sites. Gopher searched through files and resources in a variety of formats—text, Telnet sites, WAIS databases, and a wide range of other data—in order to find online information.

Gopher was popular for several years, especially at universities, because it provided a way to share text files from all over the world. Gopher was a step toward the WWW hypertext transfer protocol (HTTP). Ultimately with the advent of hypertext links, hypertext markup language (HTML), and a graphical browser—Mosaic and later Netscape—the Web quickly transcended gopher. Most gopher text files were eventually transferred to Web documents, but many original file structures still exist on university servers. A gopher client program is needed to run gopher. Public gopher sites are available via Telnet without the client program, however. To explore an example of gopher information hierarchy, go to the gopher menu at the University of Minnesota at: gopher://gopher. tc.umn.edu:70/11/Other%20Gopher%20and%20 Information%20Serves. The major limitation of Gopher was burrowing through all the sites to find needed information. Like FTP files, Gopher needed keyword searching to access information more effectively.

Veronica

The usability of Gopher was further enhanced by the development of Veronica at the University of Nevada at Reno. Fred Barrie did most of the programming. Veronica stands for very easy rodent-oriented netwide index to computerized archives. Rodent-oriented refers to the way in which Veronica works with the Internet's gopher systems. Veronica searched public-access gopher menus using keywords in much the same way as Archie searched FTP sites. Veronica retrieved a list of entries from various gopher sites throughout the world and enabled a user to browse entries from a newly created single menu composed of entries related to the search query. Like Archie, however, the major drawback of Veronica was that it searched only file names, not the contents of files.

International Federation–iSchools

International Federation–
iSchools

Jughead

Jughead, an acronym for Jonzy's universal gopher hierarchy excavation and display, is another gopher search service that works in a way similar to Veronica. Rhett "Jonzy" Jones developed Jughead in 1993 at the University of Utah. Jughead allowed keyword searching throughout all levels of a gopher menu rather than moving from one menu level to another. Jughead did little to improve upon Veronica, which lends credence to the belief that it was invented primarily to round out the comic-strip characters rather than providing much new in terms of searching software. Jughead did, however, allow Boolean "and, or, not" searching and recognized truncations using an asterisk after the root of a term.

WAIS

The WAIS was developed by Brewster Kahle at Thinking Machines Corporation of Cambridge, Massachusetts, in collaboration with Apple Computer, Dow Jones, and KPMG Peat Marwick. It was developed at about the same time as Archie, in the early 1990s. WAIS was a system for organizing information into databases that could be searched using commands known as natural query language. The WAIS software performed keyword searches of databases and refined searches based on relevancy as determined by an algorithm—a series of steps or formulas designed to retrieve information by indexing data based on "weighting." The intent was to give more relevant documents a higher score or weight based on the search query. The WAIS search engine processed a search by retrieving a relevance-ranked list of documents. Each document was given a score from 1 to 1000 based on how well it matched the search expression. A search could be executed in the form of a question, through natural language, or by use of specified fields. To use WAIS effectively to find information, files and data in every site needed to be indexed, which was not the case. After the introduction of Mosaic and Netscape, WAIS was eventually used as a back end search engine for HTTP servers to find everything from relative hyperlinks to image references.

Search Tools: The World Wide Web and the Next Generation

When Tim Berners-Lee developed HTTP, the basis for graphical interface to the Internet, the WWW was born. The WWW changed the face of the Internet so much that the words Web and Internet became almost synonymous. HTML, the standard coding language for viewing and linking documents, allowed users to move from document to document by simply clicking a link. HTML also provided access to graphical representations and images. Telnet, FTP, Archie, and Gopher required knowledge of how to navigate nonintuitive interfaces.

A variety of databases that could be described as search tools were developed for the WWW. When the Web was in its infancy. Lynx was the browser of the day. Lynx was a text-based interface in which a user entered a specific address of a known page and began to "surf" through information by following links. It was possible at the time to navigate through the available information because the Web was relatively small. In 1992, the number of hosts or servers storing sites had just grown to over 1,000,000; in January 2000, that figure had grown to more than 72,000,000. With the introduction of Mosaic early in 1993 and its offshoot Netscape—graphical user interfaces or Web browsers—the Internet became more accessible, and individuals with personal computers took notice.

While Gopher was an improvement over the capabilities of Archie, it was essentially a table of contents that provided access to downloadable files. Veronica and Jughead advanced that technology, making gopher files searchable, but the Web offered users the ability to display text, graphics, illustrations, sound, video, voice, and other forms of information. Search tools depended on interfaces and the technology that created search engines, human-indexed subject directories, and other more user-friendly means of accessing information from the Internet. As search tools improved, easier, more intuitive modes of navigating the Internet and transferring information became readily available. With improved access to information, the WWW and Internet grew in staggering proportions.

Search Engine Technology: Robots, Spiders, Wanderers, Crawlers, and Indexers

Modern search engines are indexed databases of Web pages compiled by powerful programs called robots (also called bots, spiders, wanderers, or crawlers). Robots are a key component in Web search technology. They can perform a variety of tasks very quickly and efficiently, such as indexing, statistical analysis, maintenance, mirroring, and discovering new resources throughout the Internet. In addition, robots can be programmed to do one or several of these operations. In the early days of robots, bandwidth was at a premium and the seemingly tireless bots created a drain on server loads. During the minutes after the O. J. Simpson verdict, the CNN site was so overloaded it was virtually inaccessible.

Robots are basically software programs that work by retrieving documents using HTTP to request a specific Uniform Resource Locator (URL)—essentially the "address" to a Web page. Robots do not actually go anywhere. More accurately, they establish a connection with another server and compile the information about specific URLs or Web documents. The Internet search engine that uses a robot is essentially a program that searches documents for specified keywords and returns a list of the documents in which the keywords were found. A typical search engine works by sending out a request through a robot program that retrieves as many documents as possible. The robot moves through the Web surveying pages and indexing most of the words on publicly available sites. Most robots begin by searching an active page with a variety of links, following the links on the page to other pages and other links.

Another program, called an indexer, then reads these documents and creates an index based on the words contained in each document. By systematically exploring all links on a starter page and following those links, the spider tracks a large number of pages in the database and creates listings based on keywords. Every search engine uses different information from the Web sites to create its database. For example, some will use just the title and the first 20 words of the Web page. Others may go further, examining links and headers on a page. Consequently, the databases of search tools contain a variety of differing information, sometimes collected from the same sites. The spider will later return to sites to check for changes, adding and deleting content as necessary. A critical measure of a search engine is how often it refreshes its database to remove dead links and add revised pages.

When a query is sent to a search engine, the engine scans the database and matches keywords and phrases from the query with those in texts of collected Web sites. Every search engine has its own proprietary algorithm that ideally retrieves meaningful and relevant results for specific queries or searches. It is precisely these distinctly different and secretive programs for displaying a retrieval set that offer more variations and options to finding information on the Internet.

The Wanderer

The Wanderer, the first program to automatically traverse the Web, was created by Mathew Gray and is described by some as "the mother of all search engines." The Wanderer was the first autonomous robot program designed to search the Internet for Web pages to track the growth of the Web. At first, the Wanderer only counted Web servers, but before long it started capturing URLs. The resulting database of URLs was dubbed Wandex. The Wanderer was contentious when it was first introduced because the early version of the software created a noticeable slowness across the entire network. The Wanderer's bot program often accessed the same pages hundreds of times during the same day. The Web robot was a significant innovation, however, because it automatically combed through Web documents at a speed fast enough to maintain a current database that included new pages, updates, and revisions as well as renamed and relocated documents. While the Wanderer used a single bot program, search tools eventually began using multiple bots or spiders that perform different tasks. This was the beginning of the automated Web searcher.

ALIWEB

ALIWEB, created in October 1993 by Martijn Koster, was an early project designed to index the contents of Web servers. The name ALIWEB is derived from the name Archie-like indexing of the Web. It is unique because it is the hypertext equivalent of Archie. Unlike the Wanderer, ALIWEB does not have a Web-searching robot. Webmasters posted information for each page in order to have them included in the database. While this allowed the creators of Web pages to describe and index their own sites, it also required that they maintain a special ALIWEB file on their server. ALIWEB then used a robot to search for these special files, compiling them into an index. The disadvantage of this system is the most Web page developers either did not bother or did not understand how to create the special indexing file required, and therefore very few pages were submitted to the Internet utility. The major difference between ALIWEB and other search engines is that the typically proprietary information about how the robot worked was posted on the Internet by Koster. This allowed other programmers to modify future robots to perform additional tasks, such as finding additional Web pages and gathering information from the text of those pages. It even became possible for individual users to configure their own spiders to find sites about specific tops and automatically retrieve the information from those site.

THE UNIVERSITY CONNECTION

Jumpstation

Many Internet search tools had their origins at the graduate schools of various major universities. In 1993, after Mathew Gray's Wanderer unleashed the first bot program, three search engines powered by "robots" made their debut. Jumpstation was a weekend project created by Jonathan Fletcher at the University of Stirling in Scotland. Jumpstation gathered information about the title and header from Web pages, matching keywords in a linear fashion as it went. As the Web grew, the system slowed gradually before coming to a halt.

World Wide Web Worm

The WWW worm—started by Oliver McBryan at the University of Colorado—indexed only titles and URLs that it visited. The worm was first publicly available in February 1994. By following the hypertext links on Web sites, the worm took advantage of indexing sites that were "worthy" of a link by another site—an early system of referral using linking structures. On the downside, the worm also relied on the authors of Web pages for

International Federation—iSchools

descriptive titles and other information about a site. At the time, few authors were sophisticated enough to use metatags and other more current Web designs that provided titles or descriptions. Consequently, Web sites with little or no descriptive information could not be retrieved.

The Repository-Based Software Engineering (RBSE) Spider

The repository-based software engineering (RBSE) spider was developed and operated as part of the NASA-funded repository based software engineering program at the Research Institute for Computing and Information Systems, University of Houston, Clear Lake, by David Eichman. The search tool employed a robot that could go beyond the title and URL to index the text within Web pages. RSBE used two robots—one robot for finding and compiling URLs and a second for retrieving and indexing documents based on actual content. In addition, RBSE improved searching by implementing a primitive ranking system based on relevance. The search results for its predecessors, Jumpstation and the WWW worm, were posted in the order they were found, so often the results were often irrelevant.

EINet Galaxy

Another early search tool to emerge during this time was the Enterprise Integration Network—EINet Galaxy. EINet was the first Web search directory that could be browsed or searched. Launched in January of 1994, EINet Galaxy combined WWW and WAIS technologies, compiling information into a hierarchical list of sites organized by subject categories. The original prototype was associated with the DARPA-funded Manufacturing Automation and Design Engineering (MADE) program, intended to explore technologies for providing large-scale directory services in support of electronic commerce.

EINet's directory was created and maintained by humans, as opposed to the robots used by search engines. As one of the original "search directories," EINet originated categories that are fairly common in more modern search tools. The original Galaxy index arranged information under nine topics: arts and humanities, business administration and management, engineering and technology, general and interdisciplinary information, leisure and recreation, science, government, social sciences, and community. Each URL that was added to the site was submitted to EINet, then reviewed by editors specializing in subject areas. The search directory generally retrieved higher-quality Web sites that were more relevant, but also had a database of far fewer sites because they were cataloged by hand. EINet was purchased in 1998 by GoTo.com and merged with Fox/News Corporation in May 1999.

Yahoo!

In April of 1994, two electrical engineering Ph.D. candidates, David Filo and Jerry Yang from Stanford University, started a guide of personal interest Web pages that became quite popular. The guide began as a humble Web site named "Jerry's Guide to the World Wide Web." It was a student project that was a small collection of their favorite Web pages. When the collection began to become unwieldly, Filo and Yang broke the links into categories, then later subcategories. There was no business plan or calculated design to become a major publicly traded corporation. Filo and Yang were trying to create something that would make finding information on what was at the time a very small WWW. The guide became popular by word of mouth and E-mails to friends who then told others. As it continued to grow, Filo and Yang changed the name to Yahoo! which stood for "yet another hierarchical officious oracle." They chose the name as a reference to themselves as a couple of "yahoos," a term originating from Jonathan Swift's Gulliver's Travels that referred to a boorish, foolish class of people.

It was Filo and Yang's "foolishness" that led to one of the premier search services on the Internet. The database of categorized links first resided on Yang's computer, "akebono," a hierarchically organized list of 14 broad categories covering subjects such as business and economy, computers and the Internet, entertainment, and health. By following the hierarchy, a searcher could click down the subject areas from the main subject areas to thousands of deliberately chosen Web sites. As Yahoo! grew, a simple search engine was added, which was stored on Filo's computer, "konishiki." Filo and Yang developed customized software that allowed them to efficiently locate, identify, and edit documents stored on the Internet.

All of Yahoo's entries are categorized using human editors, so it is not really classified as a search engine, but as a searchable directory. Yahoo! discovers new Web pages primarily by submission by authors or others who submit a new URL for review. What sets Yahoo! apart from other search tools is its browsable hypertext classification structure combined with an editorial review of Web sites. It was originally designed to have intuitive paths to information. Yahoo! actually created only a brief description, title, and URL for each page it displays, then links to the actual page. As such, it is not possible to search the actual text of a Web page, but the classification system by which the sites are cataloged generally leads users to higher-quality documents.

Due to its popularity, Yahoo! executed more searches than many of the other search tools of its time. As such, it was in a better position than its competitors to gather information about what people were searching and what they were interested in. Yahoo! used this information to cater to emerging trends and launch affiliate sites based on interests, trends, and geography. Gathering information

International Federation–iSchools

about what users search and, more important, how they executed their searches was a key to designing better search tools from the very beginning, and it continues to guide development.

WebCrawler

In early 1994, students and faculty from the department of computer science and engineering at the University of Washington gathered at an informal seminar to talk about the Internet and the WWW. WebCrawler was an idea that emerged from one of these seminars. Brian Pinkerton created a single user application that found information on the Internet as a research project. Pinkerton was then persuaded by fellow students to develop a Web interface. WebCrawler was the first full-text search tool on the Internet. Not only did it capture URLs like other robots, but WebCrawler's robots could capture information and links from the entire text of Web pages. In addition, the robots indexed pages using past results to direct future results using both new URLs and old URLs that were already a part of the WebCrawler index. Pinkerton's search tool worked on the assumption that links would have information relevant to the subject matter of the original Web document.

WebCrawler was released to the public on April 20, 1994, with a database containing about 6000 servers on the Web. As WebCrawler became more popular, it began to overload the network at the university. By October 1994, Web Crawler was receiving an average of 15,000 queries per day. Although a number of companies had tried to ease the load on the servers by investing in server equipment, by March 1995 Web Crawler was so popular that it became unusable during the day. It became obvious that the University of Washington could not financially support the project on its server without additional funding by outside advertising. Due to the potential conflict of interest that soliciting advertising revenue might cause, WebCrawler was sold to America Online (AOL) on March 29, 1995. AOL began to run the service on its own network as AOL NetSearch. Excite Inc. bought WebCrawler from AOL in November 1996, adding the service to its other search products, Excite, WebCrawler, City.net, and Magellan. About a year after WebCrawler was first introduced, Lycos, Infoseek, and Opentext emerged. These three new competitors all improved on WebCrawler's basic functionality.

Lycos

John Leavitt's LongLegs program provided the basis of Lycos. Michael Mauldin led a team from the Center for Machine Transition at Carnegie Mellon University that began development work on Lycos in May 1994. Lycos's name was based on the Latin term *Lycosidae lycosa*, the family name of a ground spider that hunts at night by

chasing down prey rather than using a web. Similarly, Lycos's spider program gathered URLs at night. When it became available for public use on August 12, 1994, Lycos had a catalog of 54,000 documents. By January of 1995, the catalog expanded to 1.5 million documents. Lycos was licensed by Microsoft for its Microsoft Network in April 1995. The partnership was one of many by Carnegie Mellon that allowed use of Lycos but retained ownership of the search tool. In June 1995, however, CMG@Ventures purchased Lycos, forming a new company, Lycos, Inc. Mauldin received a minority take in the company that began providing advertising space to the emerging corporate market on the internet. By November of 1996, Lycos had indexed over 60 million documents.

Excite

Architext was started by six Stanford graduates, Joe Kraus, Graham Spencer, Mark Van Haren, Ben Lutch, Martin Reinfried, and Ryan McIntyre, in June 1993 in a garage in Cupertino, California. The six wanted to design a software product that would help mnanage the vast amount of information on the WWW. The original software combined search and retrieval with automatic hypertext linking, subject grouping, and automatic abstracting. Using statistical analysis of word relationships based on proximity and co-occurrence of terms, the team designed software that searched more sufficiently. It would not by publicly available until December of 1994. By that time, the original six members of the Architext team secured $500,000 in venture capital money from Kleiner Perkins Caufield & Byers and Institutional Venture Partners to launch the product. Architext evolved into the Excite search tool in October of 1995. The company quickly established itself, signing exclusive distribution agreements with Microsoft Network and Netscape. The company officially changed its name to Excite, Inc., and went public with an initial offering of 2 million shares of stock at $17 per share. By January of 1999, Excite, Inc. would have more than 700 employees worldwide.

Infoseek

Infoseek was founded by Steven Kirsh, founder of Frame Technology and Mouse Systems, and a team of high-tech industry professionals in January 1994. Infoseek's engine was based on Yahoo! and Lycos, and became available on March 26, 1995. Infoseek was a little more user friendly and had added features such as UPS tracking, news, and a directory. It searched the last four weeks of Usenet News and allowed natural language searching. Infoseek initially used a spider to index the full text of Web sites, but later added a human-organized directory. What launched Infoseek into the public market was the move it made with Netscape. Netscape first used Yahoo! as its default search engine, but in December of 1995, Infoseek paid Netscape

International Federation—iSchools

International Federation–
iSchools

to have Infoseek as the default search engine when the program starts.

Infoseek also signaled the beginning of commerce-based tools by taking advantage of advertising via the Web. At that time, Infoseek appointed Robin Johnson, the former senior vice president of corporate development at Time Inc. as the new president and CEO. Johnson's background in the advertising-supported publishing industry was a perfect mix for a popular Internet search tool with approximately 5 million hits per day. Infoseek became the first search tool to support itself through third-party advertising using the cost per thousand model (CPM). The pricing model was intended to apply an advertising rate that was similar to the pricing model used by print publications. Magazines base their ad rates on the number of subscriptions or the estimated number of people who will see the ad. Infoseek created a model that was similar in that it based its price on the number of viewings that a advertising banner would receive. Infoseek charged a set price for the assurance that an advertisement would be accessed or appear 1000 times. Infoseek was also the first search tool that allowed advertisers to target their audience by linking ads to specific search terms.

Infoseek attempted to combine electronic results and the editorial recommendations for Web sites with a third component, high-quality advertising and sponsorships. Four years after it was founded, Infoseek became a predominant force in the online information management industry, publicly traded on the NASDAQ and ranking as one of the most highly trafficked single Web domains. In 1999, Infoseek Corporation combined with Walt Disney's Buena Vista Internet Group to form a new Internet company, go.com.

AltaVista

AltaVista began as an experiment to test new server hardware and searching software by Digital Equipment Corporation (DEC) that could run programs about 100 times faster than other existing computers. Using a very fast spider to gather documents, developers created a full text index of the Web and Usenet. Alta-Vista also provided software to support high-volume access to the information. The name AltaVista was a juxtaposition of "alto" from Palo Alto and "vista." Ultimately, it became "AltaVista," meaning "the view from above." As a search tool, AltaVista became publicly available in December 1995. In the summer of 1996, it replaced Open Text as Yahoo!'s official search engine, and was soon one of the top search tools, using innovative features and, more important, speed. Run on the DEC network, AltaVista could handle millions of hits per day without slowing down.

One of the innovative features was natural language searching, allowing queries using phrases as well as keyword searches. AltaVista searched with words such as *what, the, as*, and *etc.*, and retrieved results without

getting all the pages containing those words. Advanced search features included both Boolean searching and a results ranking query box that retrieved results when the words appeared in the title of a Web page. AltaVista also allowed developers of Web sites to add and delete URLs from the index, and they could search for sites that linked to a particular URL. AltaVista included a tips section to help the user make a better, more efficient search. The tips periodically changed, so each time the user accessed tips, he or she could view a new tip. Other search tools soon implemented similar "help" and "tips to searching" menus. AltaVista was also one of the first search tools to offer multilanguage searching capabilities, and later introduced the translation feature, Babelfish.

Inktomi

Inktomi began as a research project at the University of California at Berkeley by Eric Brewer, assistant professor of computer science, and Paul Gauthier, a Ph.D. candidate in computer science. The name Inktomi is derived from a Plains Indians myth about a spider that brought culture to people. Brewer and Gauthier developed highly effective technologies during their research that were used to power search tools such as HotBot and Yahoo!. Using parallel processing consisting of 100 or more standard-issue workstations lashed together, Inktomi pioneered a fast search engine service that could search over 100 million Web documents in the space of 250 milliseconds. Each of the computers processed information from the Web independently before collating the information together as a single result. After posting their search engine on the Web, Brewer and Gauthier raised about $27 million in investment capital, including $2 million from Intel, before becoming a publicly traded corporation in June 1998. In July 1998, Yahoo! dropped AltaVista as its search engine in favor of Inktomi.

Northern Light

Like so many other search tools with humble beginnings. Northern Light began in the basement of an old mill building in Cambridge, Massachusetts. The search tool was released for public use in August 1997. Northern Light, named after the 1851 Clipper ship with a new design and technology that made it faster than its competitors, had two major innovations that were supposed to make it better than other search tools. Northern Light organizes query results into custom search folders by subject, type, source, and language specific to that search. The folders can be used to refine or give context to a search. For example, a search for lesson plans retrieves the first 20 relevant hits. It also retrieves various folders such as class notes and assignments, mathematics, teachers and teaching, middle school, and elementary school. The folders can be used to refine or give a context to a search to help retrieve highly relevant sites. The second innovation was the Northern Light's special collection, an online database of full-text journals, books, magazines, newswires, and reference sources that were accessible for a nominal fee of $1.00 to $4.00 per article.

Google

Google was developed in 1998 by two 26-year-old Stanford computer science graduate students. Sergey Brin and Larry Page. Google was named after a derivative of the word *googol*, a term coined by Milton Sirotta, a nephew of American mathematician Edward Kasner. It represents the number 1 followed by a 100 zeros. The commercial Google site was launched as http://www.google.com in September 1999 with the help of $25 million in funding from Sequoia Capital and Kleiner Perkins Caufield & Byers. Page and Brin pioneered the analysis of link structure as a determinate in the order of a retrieval set. Google's algorythm is based on the idea that a Web site that is linked to by others should hold a higher ranking than a site that has few referring pages. This means the quality or importance of a site is a determinant of the relevancy within a search query. Indexing a site is similar to citation indexing in that each page is assigned a value that is calculated by how many other pages refer to the page and how important the linking pages are. Even before Google was launched, it had 2 million views per day, largely by word of mouth.

METASEARCHERS

MetaSearchers, also called parallel or multiple search engines, are a group of search tools that produce a single integrated retrieval set from a query that is sent to several search engines and search directories simultaneously. A metasearch tool must contain three components: a dispatch mechanism, interface agents, and a display mechanism. Choosing search engines for a specific query is the function of the dispatch component. The interface agents then translate a query into the format required by a specific search engine or directory. When the results are retrieved from the various search tools, the display mechanism merges them. Sometimes the results are sorted or ordered either as a ranked list or as a site-by-site display. The more efficient metasearchers eliminate or reduce duplicate and inactive links.

SavvySearch

In March 1995, an ambitious student at Colorado State University (CSU), Daniel Drillinger, developed and launched SavvySearch as a public metasearch service. SavvySearch began as a project for the class "Introduction to Artificial Intelligence." The project evolved into Dreilinger's master's project and needed four dedicated workstation computer systems at the CSU computer science department to keep the program operational 24 hours a day. The original SavvySearch service directed queries to a subselection of 19 search tools and resources. Soon the service began adding more search tools and resources, such as Usenet, and access to software and shareware. In November 1998, the search service had expanded its user-selected metasearch service to include more than 200 search tools, including specialty collections such a Scour. net and image finders from Yahoo, Lycos, and AltaVista, SavvySearch also incorporated a topical or subject-based access to other collections as well as a capacity to employ Boolean search queries for advanced searching. The ability to select and customize the metasearch process distinguished SavvySearch from other later metasearchers. Savvy Search was acquired by CNET on October 14, 1999.

Metacrawler

In the spring of 1995, Eric Selburg, a student at the University of Washington, created Metacrawler as his master's degree project. Metacrawler takes the search query that it is given and forwards it to all the big search engines. AltaVista, Excite, Infoseek, Lycos, WebCrawler, and Yahoo! MetaCrawler gained so much popularity when it was publicly released that it was mentioned in a cover article by *Forbes* magazine. Other search engine companies didn't approve of Meta Crawler because it only showed the search results of each engine and left out the advertising banner that pops up when the engine is accessed, meaning not as many ads were reaching the intended audience. MetaCrawler was changed so that the intended ads would be shown above each engine's results.

AskJeeves

AskJeeves was the creation of a venture capitalist, Garret Gruener, and a chief technology officer, David Warthen. Using natural language technology combined with a knowledge database and human editors to find Web sites that answered commonly asked questions, AskJeeves maintained a site that provided answers instead of large retrieval sets of sites. In April 1997, AskJeeves was publicly available for searching. More recently, AskJeeves has purchased Direct Hit, a technology that accesses information based on sites that are popular in similar searches. What distinguishes AskJeeves in the evolution of search tools is the concentration on human evaluation to determine the relative worth of Web sites for particular queries.

THE FUTURE

Although many search tools began in universities and graduate institutions, eventually they moved to the now

International Federation– iSchools

International Federation–
iSchools

common advertiser-driven business model backed by venture capital. Within this business model, search tools provided free, unlimited access to their database while at the same time having a vested interest in maintaining a user/customer base that would increase ad revenues. Publicly owned companies selling stock and highly influenced by standard business and marketing practices have created a commercial environment in which search tools try to operate as a viable business model. Mergers and acquisitions have become common as the individual search tools group together to survive and attract more users.

Currently, the WWW is estimated at more than a billion publicly indexable sites. The "invisible" or "deep Web" contains as many as 550 billion additional sites. As of August 2000, the Open Directory Project listed 351 different search tools. That number will most likely continue to grow as more specialized search tools appear and new iterations of existing tools enhance access to information. One of the major weaknesses of the major search tools such as Yahoo!, AltaVista, Google, Northern Light, and FastSearch is that they do not index a large amount of the information available on the Web. The search tools of the next generation will require more and more integrated approaches to search technologies. Natural language, categorization, and meaning-based processing as well as information extraction, link analysis, multimedia and graphical retrieval systems, and additional value-added features will be integral to search tools designed to handle a variety of different queries. Visual, non-text-based representations of retrieval sets will allow users to graphically view relationships between documents and sites differently than the current text-based sets. Interfaces will continue to become easier to use as designs continue toward creating portals and one-stop searching to maintain a customer base that feeds the advertising stream.

More significant will be the ability for the searcher to interact with search tools to reformulate and refine queries. Metadata using the extensible markup language (XML) and resource description framework (RDF) will generate a more sophisticated and precise tagging system. The XML can provide contextual information, such as where the site was generated from, when, by whom, and other profile information. As this is further developed, searchers will have the ability to recall terms and information from previous queries. They will also be able to interact intuitively with the search interface to specify or eliminate specific kinds of contents. Queries will be customizable and have the ability to maintain criteria used in past searches. Searchers will also have the ability to add context to search terms similar to what can be done using Zapper's Intellizap, or they can choose a context term or phrase to refine a search, such as they can in Oingo. Link structure, made popular by Google, and traffic popularity, such as that from DirectHit, will continue to drive search tools toward better accuracy and precision searching. Other search tools will develop indexes based on referral

sites from the Web community at large, like that of the Open Directory Project.

Another future dimension of Internet searching is the invisible or deep Web—the information from sites that are not typically indexed by search tools. There are as many as 550 billion sites in the deep Web as compared to little over a billion indexed sites. The information in these sites is more refined and in-depth. Currently, approximately 85% of Internet users use search tools for finding information. The basic search methodology and technology will need to evolve further in order to retrieve the vast amount of information that is beneath the surface of the Web. One thing is certain in the history of search tools—they will change and evolve, especially as the Internet continues to expand toward higher-speed access. Multimedia is growing so rapidly that search tools are becoming conduits for providing information in a variety of formats. Also, as access to the Internet expands globally and internationally, multicultural/multilingual searching will become more than a feature; it will be a necessity. Internet search tools will be essential keys to the Internet's evolution to a truly "World" Wide Web.

BIBLIOGRAPHY

1. About Galaxy, 2000. Available at http://galaxy.einet.net/galaxy/Info/about.html.
2. Ackermann, E. Hartman, K. *The Information Specialist's Guide to Searching & Researching on the Internet & World Wide Web*, Fitzroy Dearborn: Chicago, IL, 1999.
3. AKST, D. What's my date line?. NetGuide May **1995**, *2*(5), 33.
4. Bergman, M.K. *The Deep Web: Surfacing Hidden Value*, August 2000. Available at http://www.completeplanet.com/Tutorials/DeepWeb/index.asp.
5. Carl, J. *Protocol gives sites way to keep out the 'bots*, November 1995. Available at http://www.internetworld.com/print/1995/11/01/news/nobots.html.
6. Cleland, K.; Cuneo, A.Z. Searching for a broader role on the Web. Ad. Age June 24, **1996**, *67*(26), 34.
7. December, J. Randall, N. *The World Wide Web Unleashed*, Sams.net Publishing: Indianapolis, IN, 1995.
8. Excite Company History. August 2000. Available at http://oldcorp.excite.com/Company/history.html.
9. Farrelly, G. *History of Search Engines—Evolution & Revolution*, July 2000. Available at http://webhome.indirect.com/glenjenn/search/history1.htm.
10. Gerwig, K. Archie, Veronica, and the Gang. NetGuide June **1996**, *3*(6), 83.
11. *Google Company Information*, August 2000. Available at http://www.google.com/company.html.
12. Griffiths, R.T. Internet for historians: History of the Internet search engines,. 1999. Available at http://www.let.leidenuniv.nl/history/ivh/zoeken.htm.
13. Head, A.J. *Design Wise: A Guide for Evaluating the Interface Design of Information Resources*, CyberAge Books: Medford, NJ, 1999.

14. Howe, W. *A Brief History of the Internet,* August 2000. Available at http://www0.delphi.com/navnet/history.html.

15. Inside architext. Red Herring, March **1995**. Available at http://www.redherring.com/mag/issue19/inside.html.

16. James-Catalano, C.N. *Researching on the World Wide Web: Spend More Time Learning, Not Searching*, Prima: Rocklin, CA, 1996.

17. Jasco, P. More search engine hype and reality. Info. Today **1999**, *16*(4), 30, April 1997.

18. Kassler, H. The search engines and beyond conference. Info. Today May **1998**, *15*(5), 66–74 26.

19. Kirkpatrick, D. What's a Google? A great search engine. That's what. Fortune November 8, **1999**, *140*(9), 298.

20. Koster, M. *Robots in the Web: Threat or Treat?*, 1995 April. Available at http://info.webcrawler.com/mak/projects/robots/threat-or-treat.html.

21. Maze, S. Moxley, D. Smith, D.J. *Authoritative Guide to Web Search Engines*, Neal-Schuman: New York, 1997.

22. Mand, A. WEB Search Engines: GOOGLE. MediaWeek July 1, **1999**, 29(28), 34.

23. Moukheiber, Z. Inktomi inside. Forbes **1998**, November 30. Available at http://www.forbes.com/forbes/98/1130/6212336a.htm.

24. Polly, J.A.; Cisler, S. Travels with *VERONICA*, part 1. Libr. J. January **1995**, *120*(1), 32.

25. Poulter, A. The design of World Wide Web search engines: A critical review. Program April **1997**, *31*(2), 131.

26. Reid, R.H. *Architects of the Web*, Wiley: New York, 1997.

27. Rioux, M. Tunneling through cyberspace in search of adventure: An introduction to Gopher. Ser. Libr. **1995**, *25*(3/4), 17.

28. Schwartz, C. Web search engines. JASIS September **1998**, *49*(11), 973.

29. Sonnenreich, W. Macinta, T. *Web Developer.com Guide to Search Engines*, Wiley: New York, 1998; *Whatis.com*, July 2000; Available at http://www.whatis.com/.

International Federation–iSchools

InterPARES

Luciana Duranti
School of Library, Archival and Information Studies, University of British Columbia,
Vancouver, British Columbia, Canada

Abstract

This entry presents the International research on Permanent Authentic Records in Electronic Systems (InterPARES) project, an international multidisciplinary research endeavor that, since 1998, has sought solutions to the issue of long-term preservation of the authenticity of digital records. The entry outlines the goals of the four phases of the project, its membership, methodology, principles, activities, and products, and discusses its conceptual findings—specifically, the concepts of record and of authenticity—and its methodological findings regarding archival appraisal, preservation, and description—specifically, requirements for trusted record-making, record-keeping and records preservation systems, development of systems for managing authentic digital records that meet those requirements, and their implementation in a scalable way in resource-limited organizations. The entry concludes by outlining the present direction of the project and providing a glimpse of its future.

International Federation–
iSchools

INTRODUCTION

InterPARES stands for International research on Permanent Authentic Records in Electronic Systems. It is a multinational collaborative research project pursuing the goal of developing the theory and methods necessary to ensure that digital records produced in databases and office systems, as well as in dynamic, experiential, and interactive systems, in the course of artistic, scientific, and e-government activities can be created in accurate and reliable form and maintained and preserved in authentic form for the use of those who created them and of society at large, regardless of technological obsolescence and media fragility.

With the financial support of the Social Sciences and Humanities Research Council of Canada, the University of British Columbia (UBC), the United States National Historical Publications and Records Commission and National Sciences Foundation, UNESCO's Memory of the World Program, and several other agencies and organizations around the world, the InterPARES project began in 1998 under the direction of Luciana Duranti, establishing its headquarter in Vancouver, Canada, at the UBC School of Library, Archival and Information Studies, and it has developed through four phases: 1998–2001, 2002–2006, 2007–2012, and 2013–2018. Over the years, it has involved investigators from numerous countries in five continents: Canada, the United States, Australia, New Zealand, the Netherlands, Belgium, the United Kingdom, Ireland, Sweden, Norway, Germany, France, Spain, Croatia, Russia, Ukraine, Italy, Turkey, China and Hong Kong, Japan, Singapore, Korea, Malaysia, Mexico, Brazil, Cuba, Argentina, Peru, Chile, South Africa, and many more.

INTERPARES METHODOLOGY

The research methodology has been based on the principles of "interdisciplinarity, transferability, open inquiry, and multimethod design." The project is interdisciplinary in the measure in which its goal and objectives can only be achieved through the contribution of several disciplines, among which are archival science, diplomatics and records management; computer science and engineering; jurisprudence and law; music theory, composition, and performance; film theory, production, and description; dance and theater theory; geography; chemistry; archaeology; and several other hard and social sciences. In fact, in order to analyze the nature, characteristics, behavior, relationships, and process of creation of the records produced in the course of artistic, scientific, business, and e-government activities, it is necessary to gather a deep understanding of not only those activities, their purpose, their phases and the component actions, their by-products and their structure, and their context but also their technological environment and their use. In addition, to analyze the results of the case studies, methodologies developed in the context of a variety of disciplines are needed. Among these are text analysis, diplomatic analysis, statistical analysis, visual analytics, digital forensics, etc.

The ultimate goal of InterPARES is archival in nature, in that the project is concerned with the development of trusted record-making and record-keeping systems, and of preservation systems that ensure the authenticity of the records under examination over the long term. This implies that the work carried out throughout the project in the various disciplinary areas must be constantly translated in archival terms and linked to archival concepts,

Encyclopedia of Library and Information Sciences, Fourth Edition DOI: 10.1081/E-ELIS4-120053297

Copyright © 2017 by Taylor & Francis. All rights reserved.

which are the foundation upon which the systems intended to protect the records are designed. However, upon completion of the research, the archival systems need to be made accessible and comprehensible to records creators, organizations and institutions, service providers, IT experts, and disciplinary researchers. In other words, the research outcomes must be translated back into the language and concepts of each discipline and profession that needs to make use of them. In light of these, it was essential at the outset of the research to examine the key archival concepts that are at the core of the InterPARES research so that each field could identify the corresponding entities within its own body of knowledge.

The InterPARES research questions have epistemological roots in the humanities, specifically in diplomatics and archival science. However, the investigators involved in each research activity identify the perspective(s), research design, and methods that they believe to be most appropriate to their specific inquiry. The reason for this openness is that InterPARES is conceived to work as a "layered knowledge" environment, in the sense that some research work will build upon knowledge developed in a variety of other research projects on similar and different issues, and some will explore new issues, study entities never examined before, and develop entirely new knowledge. Each case study, as well as each of the other research activities, is carried out using the methodology and the tools that the dedicated investigating team considers the most appropriate for it. The methods used are surveys, case studies, modeling, prototyping, diplomatic and archival analysis, visual analytics, and text analysis.

INTERPARES PRINCIPLES

A few principles have guided InterPARES research through the years. The first is that technology cannot determine the solution to the reliable and accurate creation of digital records or to their authentic preservation over the long term: "organizational needs" define the problem and "archival principles" must establish the correctness and adequacy of each technical solution. A corollary of this principle is the idea that solutions to the digital records challenges are inherently "dynamic," because of the continuing change of technology and therefore of the issues that it raises, and "specific" to the cultural, disciplinary, administrative, and legal situations in which digital records are generated, because of the contingent reasons why records are produced and kept. The second principle is that preservation is a "continuous process that begins with records creation." Accordingly, the development of solutions to the issue of long-term preservation is dependent upon the development of guidance for the proper creation and maintenance of records that can be preserved. The third principle is that, given the fact that we cannot

preserve digital records as physical entities, but only the ability to reproduce them, we cannot verify on the records at hand their authenticity; rather, we must develop methods of records creation, maintenance, and preservation that allow us either to presume the trustworthiness of the records till proof to the contrary is established or to infer it from the integrity of the system in which the records were created and kept overtime and the chain of their custody.

INTERPARES ACTIVITIES

In order to achieve the goal of developing a body of theory and methods for digital records, InterPARES, researchers focused their initial efforts on the identification of "what constitutes a record" in each type of system being examined and in each context, and of "what record in each system and context has the force of an original." They also studied large bodies of literature in a variety of disciplines for the purpose of defining "what a reliable, accurate, and authentic record" is in the arts, science, law, business, and administration. On this basis, they developed the requirements for the design of "a trusted record-making system," "a trusted record-keeping system," and "a trusted record preservation system," using primarily modeling and the diplomatic analysis of the results of several case studies. Then, they developed "methods and procedures for the creation, maintenance, appraisal, selection, and disposition, and long-term preservation of authentic digital records," as well as several products that could be and still are autonomously used.

At the end of the second phase of InterPARES, the need was felt to demonstrate that the findings and recommendations resulting from the research activities of the first two phases (1998–2006) were implementable in all kinds of organizations in a scalable way. Thus, the third phase of the project focused on enabling public and private archival organizations and programs with limited resources to preserve over the long-term authentic records that satisfy the requirements of their stakeholders and society's needs for an adequate record of its past. It did so by building on the products and conceptual and methodological findings of the first two phases.

INTERPARES PRODUCTS (1998–2006)

The products of the first two phases of InterPARES were a *Framework of Principles Guiding the Development of Policies* for records creating and preserving organizations; *Guidelines for Making and Maintaining Digital Materials* for individuals and small communities of practice; *Guidelines for Digital Preservation* for archival institutions; *Authenticity Requirements* for records systems; a *Template for Analysis* of digital records; principles and criteria for adoption of *File Formats, Wrappers, and Encoding*; a

International Federation–iSchools

International Federation iSchools

Model of the Chain of Preservation (COP) based on the lifecycle concept; a *Business-Driven Recordkeeping Model* based on the continuum concept; and a *Terminology Database*, including a glossary, a dictionary, and ontologies. These products are posted on the InterPARES website (http://www.interpares.org); and published in two books: Luciana Duranti ed., *The Long-term Preservation of Authentic Electronic Records: Findings of the InterPARES Project* (San Miniato: Archilab, 2005. Available online at http://www.interpares.org/book/index.cfm) and Luciana Duranti and Randy Preston eds., *InterPARES 2: Interactive, Dynamic and Experiential Records InterPARES 2: Interactive, Dynamic and Experiential Records* (Roma: ANAI, 2008. Available online at http://www.interpares.org/ip2/book.cfm). The products are also discussed in articles published in a dedicated space by the journal *Archivaria*;[1] and in writings published in a variety of venues, some of which are listed among the references and bibliography, while others can be found or cited on the project website: http://www.interpares.org/ip1/ip1_dissemination.cfm?proj=ip1 and http://www.interpares.org/ip2/ip2_dissemination.cfm?proj=ip2.

INTERPARES 1–2 CONCEPTUAL FINDINGS (1998–2006)

The InterPARES project does not study digital preservation in general, but it focuses its research on the long-term preservation of the "authenticity" of digital "records." Thus, among the key findings of the first two phases are the concept of record in the digital environment and the concept of authenticity.

The Concept of Record

In the digital environment, an entity captured as a record presents the following characteristics: 1) a stable content; 2) a fixed form; 3) explicit linkages to other records within or outside the digital system, through a classification code or a naming convention; 4) an identifiable context; 5) five persons (i.e., an author—the physical or organizational person issuing the record, a writer—the person responsible for the record content, an originator—the person responsible for the electronic account or space where the record is made and/or saved, an addressee—the person for whom the record is intended, and a creator—the person in whose records accumulation the record exists) involved with its creation; 6) an action, in which the record participates or which the record supports either procedurally or as part of the decision-making process; and 7) formal elements, attributes, and digital components. Three of these characteristics require further explanation, that is, stable content, fixed form, and the distinction among formal elements, attributes, and digital components.

Stable Content and Fixed Form

Stable content is defined as the fact that the data and the message in the record are unchanged and unchangeable, meaning that data cannot be overwritten, altered, deleted, or added to. Fixed form means that the binary content is stored so that the message it conveys can be rendered with the same presentation it had on the screen when first saved (even if the digital presentation is different, as is the case with a record received in Word and saved in PDF). In complex dynamic and interactive systems, fixed form is a more articulated concept and involves a distinction between the "stored record" and the "manifested record," the latter being the one we see on the computer screen. If the same content can be presented on the screen in several different ways in a limited series of possibilities, we may have either a different view of "the same stored record" having stable content and fixed form (i.e., different documentary presentations, as in the case of statistical information rendered as a pie chart, a bar chart, or a table), or "several manifested records" with stable content and fixed form derived from the same stored record. In addition, the concept of fixed form may be linked to that of "bounded variability," which exists when there is no stored record, but only stored content data, form data, and composition data that are quite separate and only connected by a query when a user searches the system. In these cases, changes to the form of the manifested record are limited and controlled by fixed rules, so that the same query or user interaction always generates the same result, and we have different views of different subsets of content, due to the intention of the author or to different operating systems or applications (pp. 47–52).[2]

Formal Elements, Attributes, and Digital Components

A "formal element" is a constituent part of the record's documentary form as shown on its face. Formal elements may be extrinsic, when they determine the appearance of the record and influence its capability of reaching its purposes; or intrinsic, when they convey the action in which the record participates or to which it is linked, and its context. Extrinsic and intrinsic elements of form are listed and described in the *Template for Analysis* mentioned among the InterPARES products (see http://www.interpares.org/book/interpares_book_j_app01.pdf).

Strictly related to the concept of formal elements is the concept of "records' attributes," which are the identifying characteristics of each given record or of a record element in it. An attribute may manifest itself as one or more elements of form. For example, the name of the author of a record is an attribute, which may be expressed as a letterhead or a signature, both of which are intrinsic elements of documentary form, that is, record's elements. In addition to attributes that manifest themselves in the form of the record, that is, on the face of the record, as record's elements, every record has attributes that are implicit in other parts of the record, such as the name of the creator or of the medium, but in digital records they are also expressed, albeit outside the documentary form. Because of this, they are mostly transparent to the user and manifest themselves as metadata included in either a record profile, a topic map, or other digital entity linked to the record.

In addition to all these, with electronic records, we also have to differentiate formal elements and attributes from the record's digital components. A "digital component" is a digital object that is part of one or more digital records, including any metadata necessary to order, structure, or manifest content, and that requires a given preservation action. For example, an e-mail that includes a picture and a digital signature will have at least four digital components (the header, the text, the picture, and the digital signature). Reports with attachments in different formats will consist of more than one digital component, whereas a report with its attachments saved in one PDF file will consist of only one digital component. Though digital components are each stored separately, each digital component exists in a specific relationship to the other digital components that make up the record. Each digital component requires one or more specific methods for decoding the bit stream and for presenting it for use over time. The bit stream can be altered, as a result of conversion for example, as long as it continues to be able to fulfill its original role in the reproduction of the record. All digital components must be able to work together after they are altered; therefore, all changes need to be assessed by the creator for the effects they may have on the record.

Record Trustworthiness

In the case of the concepts embedded in the record quality of trustworthiness, the definitions adopted by the InterPARES team were not derived from traditional archival theory. The team used the definitions developed by a previous research project, commonly known as the UBC-MAS project (pp. 23–30),[3] in the context of which "reliability" is the trustworthiness of a record as a statement of fact, that is, its ability to stand for the facts it is about, while "authenticity" is the trustworthiness of a record as a record, and refers to the fact that a record is what it purports to be and has not been tampered with or otherwise corrupted. Reliability is the exclusive responsibility of the record creator and is assessed on the basis of the completeness of the record, the authority and capacity of its author, and the degree of control exercised on the creation process. "Accuracy," a concern introduced in InterPARES research by science scholars, can sometimes be subsumed under the concept of reliability and refers to the exactness and correctness of content, mostly dependent on the competence of the author and the controls on the process by which data are recorded and transmitted through space (i.e., between persons, systems, or applications) and time (i.e., when stored offline or when the hardware or software used to process, communicate, or maintain it is upgraded or replaced). Different from reliability, authenticity and accuracy are the responsibility of both the creator and the preserver as these depend on the controls exercised on the processes of transmission of the record across space or time.

Finally, "authentication" was defined as a declaration of authenticity, resulting either by the insertion or the addition of an element or a statement to a record. To make a distinction between authenticity and authentication was considered important because governments have been legislating about the use of digital signatures and other similar devices as means of maintaining authenticity. The team wanted to emphasize the theoretical principle that authenticity is a property of the record that accompanies it for as long as it exists, while authentication is a means of proving that a record is what it purports to be at a given moment in time.

The researchers did not elaborate further the concept of reliability, but tried to elucidate the concept implied in the definition of authenticity by dividing it into two components: identity and integrity. "Identity" refers to the attributes of a record that, together, distinguish it from other records. These attributes include the names of the persons concurring in its formation (i.e., author, addressee, writer, originator, and creator); its date(s) of compilation, transmission, and filing; the naming of the matter or action in which it participates; the expression of its relationships with other records; its digital and documentary presentations; and an indication of any attachment(s). These attributes may be explicitly expressed in a formal element of the record or in metadata related to the record or may be implicit in its various contexts.

"Integrity" is the wholeness and soundness of a record. A record has integrity if it is intact and uncorrupted, that is, if the message that it is meant to communicate in order to achieve its purpose is unaltered. This means that a record's physical integrity, such as the proper number of bit strings, may be compromised, provided that the articulation of the content and its required elements of form remain the same. Integrity may be demonstrated by evidence found on the face of the record, in metadata attesting to the responsibility for the record over time and to its technological changes, or in one or more of the record's contexts.

While in traditional archival theory, following jurisprudence, records that are relied upon by their creator in the usual and ordinary course of business are presumed authentic, with records in digital systems, the presumption of authenticity must be supported by evidence that a record has not been modified or corrupted in essential respects during transmission and maintenance. To assess the authenticity of a record, the preserver must be able to

International Federation–iSchools

International Federation–
iSchools

establish its identity and demonstrate its integrity by observing the existence of certain conditions. These conditions are authenticity requirements and are used by the prospective preserver to guide the assessment of the authenticity of the records during the process of appraisal. The Authenticity Requirements developed by InterPARES can be found on the InterPARES website (http://www.interpares.org/book/interpares_book_k_app02.pdf) and in the first InterPARES book (pp. 204–219).[4]

Many of the concepts developed by InterPARES 1–2 were incorporated in the discipline of modern diplomatics, and these are discussed in detail in the entry "Diplomatics" of this Encyclopedia.

INTERPARES 1–2 METHODOLOGICAL FINDINGS (1998–2006)

It appeared quite clear to the InterPARES researchers that the team's understanding of the concepts of record and authenticity had a strong impact on the process of appraisal, which is inevitably influenced by the fact the objects to be selected for continuing preservation are not physical units but linked digital components whose continuing meaning is provided by attributes and whose trustworthiness relies on metadata and on unbroken control both on their transmission through time and space and on the processes of their creation, maintenance, and preservation.

Appraisal

Contrary to the archival tradition, with digital records, "authenticity" has to become one of the values assessed by the appraiser because, in the absence of an original, the future users of digital records will have only the word of the record preserver as the basis for trusting the records they will use as sources. Thus, the role of the appraiser becomes that of a neutral third party who acts as the inspector first and the warrantor later of the authenticity of the records that will be preserved.

In addition, the researchers found that several activities extraneous to traditional appraisal methodology have to be introduced in the appraisal process. Although it has been accepted for decades that archivists and records creators have to participate jointly in records scheduling for retention and disposition and that, with digital records, such an endeavor must occur as soon as possible in the life of the record, insufficient emphasis has been put by the archival community on the necessity of "monitoring" the records identified for permanent preservation on a regular basis in order to ensure that the inevitable ongoing changes of the technological environment of both the records and the creating office, and consequently of the business and documentary procedures of the creating office do not alter the records, their interrelationships, and their relationships

with the business processes to the point that a new appraisal is warranted. Monitoring is a key activity also with respect to a new concern for the appraiser: "feasibility of preservation."

Feasibility of preservation was never a preoccupation with records on traditional media, but preservation of digital records is a very complex activity, requiring technological competence and resources that sometimes are not accessible to archival programs and institutions. Thus, the appraiser must assess the records in light of the present and future capability of the archival program or institution to preserve them. As a consequence, the appraiser may advice the creator to make certain technological choices that make the records preservable or may postpone their acquisition till such a time when preservation is feasible.

In addition, in digital systems, a record may be created for one purpose, and then subsequently used for different purposes and by different persons. Any appraisal decision should consider all uses of the record, simultaneous and sequential, by different users and by the same users, and be aware of the business processes behind them. This is necessary in order to make an informed decision about what to preserve, as well as to be able to dispose effectively of all possible copies of the records that have not been selected for preservation.

The use of records or information within records by different business processes may be desirable from the creator's standpoint in terms of providing a degree of interoperability among the creator's information and record systems. In such situations, the preserver should advise the creator that metadata attached to records used by many business processes must identify each relevant business process. This is critical for the creator because it ensures the authenticity of the records by establishing their identity and integrity in each context. It is also critical for the preserver who must understand all contexts in which the records were used in order to effectively undertake appraisal and also to meet the requirements for maintaining authenticity for any records acquired into the preservation system.

Preservation

In light of the principle that it is not possible to preserve an electronic record, but only the ability to reproduce it, InterPARES established that preservation of electronic records involves creating authentic copies of the records of the creator. The authenticity of these copies is guaranteed by 1) a controlled process of migration of the records acquired from the creator to the archives technological environment; 2) the accurate documentation of any change that the records undergo during such process and every time that the archives technological environment is upgraded; 3) the implementation and monitoring of privileges concerning the access, use, and reproduction of the records within the archives; 4) the establishment of procedures to prevent, discover, and correct loss or corruption of records; 5) the establishment of procedures to guarantee the continuing identity and integrity of the records (i.e., their authenticity) against media deterioration and across technological changes; and 6) if authentication of individual records is required, the existence of rules determining responsibility for and means of authentication.

The person responsible for all these activities, the designated records preserver, has to take physical and legal custody of the records of the creators, protect them, and ensure continuous access to them. Be it an outside organization or an in-house unit, the role of the designated preserver should be that of a "trusted custodian" for a creator's records. To be considered as a trusted custodian, the preserver must

- Act as a neutral third party, that is, demonstrate that it has no stake in the content of the records and no reason to alter records under its custody, and that it will not allow anybody to alter the records either accidentally or on purpose
- Be equipped with the knowledge and skills necessary to fulfill its responsibilities, which should be acquired through formal education in records and archives administration
- Establish a trusted preservation system that is capable of ensuring that accurate and authentic copies of the creator's records are acquired and preserved

The authentic copies of the creator's records are kept by the trusted custodian in a trusted preservation system, which should include in its design a descriptive system and a retrieval system. This trusted preservation system must also have in place rules and procedures for the ongoing production of authentic copies as the existing system becomes obsolete and the technology is upgraded. It should be noted that the simple fact of reproducing records in the preserver's preservation system does not make the result an authentic copy. Such designation must be provided by the preserver's authority.

A sustainable preservation strategy requires close collaboration between a records creator and its designated trusted custodian. It is the preserver's responsibility to take the initiative in collaborating with the creator to establish acquisition and preservation procedures and in advising the creator in any records management activities essential to the preserver's acquisition and preservation activities.

Archival Description

The InterPARES researchers have agreed that, no matter how careful the preservation procedures and how trusted the records custodian, ultimately, to all future users, the most important source of the authenticity of the records is "archival description."

It has always been the function, either explicit or implicit of archival description, to authenticate the records by perpetuating their administrative and documentary relationships, but, with digital records, this function has moved to the forefront. In fact, as original digital records disappear and an interminable chain of nonidentical reproductions follows them, the researchers looking at the last of those reproductions cannot find in it any information regarding provenance, authority, context, or authenticity.

The authentication function of archival description is different from that of a certificate of authenticity because it is not simply an attestation of the authenticity of individual records, but a collective attestation of the authenticity of the records of an archival "fonds" (defined as the whole of the documents made or received by one creator and accumulated for action or reference) and of all their interrelationships as made explicit by their administrative, custodial, and technological history, the scope and content, and the hierarchical representation of the records aggregates. Also, it is different both from the identity and integrity metadata attached to individual records, which are part of the record itself and are reproduced time after time with it, and from the additional metadata attached to records aggregations (e.g., file, and series) identifying them and documenting their technological transformation. The unique function of archival description is to provide a historical view of the records and of their becoming while at the same time presenting them as a universality in which each member's individuality is subject to the bond of a common provenance and destination. Never before archival description has had such a key function in the preservation of records.

INTERPARES 1–2 CONCLUSIONS (1998–2006)

The InterPARES project began in 1999 to find a solution to the problem of the long-term preservation of the authenticity of digital records. In its first phase, it focused on the preservation function, but the findings of its research identified the need for a holistic approach that looked at preservation as an integral part of records creation, maintenance, use, and dissemination through time. For this reason, the second phase of the project began with the analysis of the entities being created in complex systems, while still live and often incomplete, in order to understand their nature, characteristics, behavior, and use. Among the results of this analysis, there is a new diplomatic theory for interactive and dynamic records and a new archival theory of preservation, along with methodologies supporting their application.

However, the second phase of the project made it clear that, although the body of concepts, principles, and methods developed through scientific research constitutes the essential foundation and framework of best practices, any solution to digital preservation problems is situation

International Federation— iSchools

International Federation— iSchools

specific and must be devised by preservers taking into account 1) the cultural, administrative, legal, and functional context in which they operate; 2) the nature and characteristics of the organizations producing the digital material to be preserved; 3) the typology of the material produced and its documentary and technological features; 4) the limitations imposed by the available financial and human resources; 5) the organizational culture of both the producer of the material and the preserver; and 6) access to educated professionals or educational programs and resources. Furthermore, while the conceptual and methodological findings of InterPARES are equally applicable to larger and smaller organizations and programs, archives with limited resources, which often have the greatest need for assistance, will find the outcomes of the research difficult to apply without specific directions on how to move forward. Thus, a third phase of InterPARES began in 2007.

INTERPARES 3 (2007–2012)

The third phase of InterPARES aimed to translate the theory and methods of digital preservation drawn from the previous research into concrete action plans for existing bodies of records that are to be kept over the long term by archives—and archival/records units within organization—endowed with limited resources. It developed detailed knowledge on 1) how general theory and methods can be implemented in small- and medium-sized archives and units and become effective practices; 2) what factors determine the type of implementation that is appropriate for each body of records in each context; and 3) what skills professionals will require to conduct such operations.

InterPARES 3 Activities

InterPARES 3 comprised a research component, involving short-term and long-term projects (including case studies and general studies); an education and training component that consisted of carrying out, in the context of the research projects, apprenticeships, activities credited as part of coursework, etc.; and a knowledge-mobilization component, in the form of workshops, seminars, colloquia, policy manuals and other publications, public lectures, etc., that met the needs of both academic and community partners.

InterPARES 3 Methodology

InterPARES 3 carried out "action research," that is, collaborative and pragmatic research directed toward producing solutions that were directly useful to a group of people. The research subjects were coparticipants and stakeholders in the process: jointly with academic researchers,

they defined research objectives and goals, co-constructed research questions, pooled knowledge, and developed solutions and performance tests that implemented specific strategies.

The two primary research methods were prototype development and ethnographic research. Prototype development was user-centered, collaborative prototyping exploring the interplay between theory and practice by using proof-by-demonstration through three major iterative stages: concept building, system building, and system evaluation. Ethnographic research was conducted by creators of records, their users, and archivists, who, together, formed a community of practice—the archival environment—for which social interaction created meaning and defined values. The researchers placed themselves within an archival environment to gain the cultural perspective of those responsible for records through observation of the environment with detailed description, extensive interviewing, and analysis of documentation. The researchers were divided in national teams because of their shared belief in the fundamental importance of juridical and cultural contexts in addressing each real situation. The research was structured in general studies and case studies.

The general studies were of four types: those carried out by one national team or a group of teams for the benefit of all teams (e.g., Annotated Bibliography of International Standards, E-mail Preservation); those in which all teams took part (e.g., Terminology Database); those conducted by a team that was useful for that team only (e.g., Annotated Canadian Standards); and those conducted by a group of teams sharing contextual characteristics for its own benefit (e.g., Electronic Protocol Register, procedurally required in Brazil, Italy, and Spain).

The case studies were of three types: those dealing with specific groups or types of records, those dealing with record/information systems, and those dealing with policies. The case study process was guided by a case study flow chart, which ensured that all steps were followed in the correct order, and was concluded by a final report. Each document produced in the course of a case study was structured as to form and content on the basis of a template used for all case studies. All the documents supporting the research can be found on the InterPARES 3 website: http://www.interpares.org/ip3/ip3_products. cfm?cat=2.

InterPARES 3 Key Findings

Among the many findings, the most important were management related. The case studies demonstrated that, if it is important to develop, learn, and teach how to use the structural features of an application or a system, it is even more important to understand the spirit behind those features; instead, in most cases, the training of users of acquired new applications and systems emphasizes details of use rather than general philosophy. Users who are not acquainted with archival principles and methodologies may—intentionally or unintentionally—appropriate an application or a system "unfaithfully" more easily than records professionals. Unfaithful appropriations are likely to happen frequently with digital tools that are developed by IT experts outside the organization that will use them and often without consulting archival professionals. Interpretive flexibility or lack of it may, therefore, determine acceptance or rejection.

The case studies also showed that, when the technology is tailored to the organization, it is common to design systems primarily focused on the codified, explicit organizational knowledge because managers favor the knowledge that is incorporated in organizational artifacts like processes, structures, documents, and technology. Thus, management reporting systems, decision support systems, and electronic records management systems, are all focused on the identification, collection, and dissemination of this knowledge type. Rather, managers should foster a more complex form of organizational capital, one where a core competency for implementers requires *know-how*, the particular ability to put know-what into practice.

InterPARES 3 Products

All case and general studies are available on the InterPARES 3 website: http://www.interpares.org/ip3/ip3_products.cfm?cat=1. On the basis of the findings of these studies, InterPARES 3 developed, in addition to a variety of annotated bibliographies and the *Terminology Database*, reports on *Keeping and Preserving E-mail*, *Open Source Records Management Software*, *Criteria for Open Standard File Formats*, *Acquiring and Preserving Digital Records in Small and Medium-sized Archives*, *Digital Preservation Cost-Benefit Models*, *File Viewers*, *Metadata Application Profiles*, *Organizational Culture*, *Organizational Policy*, *Public Sector Audit Reports*, *Guidelines and Recommendations for E-mail Records Management and Long-Term Preservation*, and *Guidelines for the Long-term Preservation of the Protocol Register* (http://www.interpares.org/ip3/ip3_products.cfm?cat=1).

However, the product that best embodies the findings and recommendation of InterPARES 3 is represented by the teaching modules for in-house training programs, continuing education workshops, and academic curricula meant to form archival professionals who are competent not only to preserve over the long term the documentary heritage in digital form but also to ensure the accountability of organizations and institutions through the protection of the accuracy and authenticity of the digital information they produce. The InterPARES education modules, called "Digital Records Pathways: Topics in Digital Preservation," were cosponsored by the Section on Archival

Education (SAE) of the International Council on Archives (ICA). Therefore, in addition to being accessible from the InterPARES website (ip3_canada_gs12_education-modules_digital-records-pathways.zip), they are also accessible on the ICA-SAE website, accompanied by a video that describes them and their use (http://www.ica-sae.org/).

By the time, the third phase of InterPARES was reaching its conclusions, new issues related to the authentic long-term preservation of electronic records were coming to the forefront, primarily related to the increase of records creation, maintenance, and/or preservation on the Internet and on the cloud, and to the trustworthiness of the online networked environment. Thus, a new phase of InterPARES began, called InterPARES Trust.

INTERPARES TRUST (2013–2018)

The goal of this research project is to generate the theoretical and methodological frameworks that will support the development of integrated and consistent local, national, and international networks of policies, procedures, regulations, standards, and legislation concerning digital records entrusted to the Internet, to ensure public trust grounded on evidence of good governance, a strong digital economy, and a persistent digital memory. The focus is on the relationship between organizations (both not-for-profit and for-profit) and given client groups (citizens, customers, readers, students, etc.), with client groups being concerned about the degree of "trust" they can place on records generated and/or stored and accessed on the Internet and organizations being concerned about establishing and maintaining that trust. The same themes are also addressed within the context of organization to organization and client group to client group relationships. This research will develop new knowledge on digital records kept on social media and in the cloud and on methods for identifying and protecting the balance between privacy and access, secrecy and transparency, the right to know, and the right to oblivion in globally connected networks. It will propose law reform, and other infrastructural reform, model policies, procedures, and practices, and functional requirements for the systems in which Internet providers store and manage digital records.

The partnership conducting this research comprises universities and organizations, national and multinational, public and private, in North America, Latin America, Europe, Africa, Australasia, and Asia. It also includes a "Transnational Team" comprising international organization like UNESCO and the World Bank. The list of the partners is available at http://interparestrust.org/trust/aboutus. The academic researchers have expertise in archival science, records management, diplomatics, law, information technology, communication and media, e-commerce, health informatics, cybersecurity, information

International Federation–iSchools

International Federation–
iSchools

governance and assurance, digital forensics, computer engineering, and information policy. The empirical knowledge for this research comes from the researchers who are members of the professions having the highest stake in the questions being asked, for example, law and law enforcement, journalism, records management, finances, health, etc.

InterPARES Trust Activities

The project is divided into five research domains and five research cross-domains. The research domains are as follows: 1) *Infrastructure*: this domain considers issues relating to system architecture and related infrastructure as they affect records held in online environments. Examples of areas to be investigated include types of cloud and their reliability; types of contractual agreements and their negotiation, coverage, flexibility, etc.; costs, upfront and hidden; etc. 2) *Security*: this domain considers records issues relating to online data security, including security methods (encryption, sharding, obfuscation, geographic location); data breaches; cybercrime; risks associated with shared servers; information assurance; governance; audits and auditability; forensic readiness; risk assessment; and backup. 3) *Control*: this domain differs from the security domain in its focus on the management of digital material in online environments. It addresses such issues as authenticity, reliability, and accuracy of data; integrity metadata; chain of custody; retention and disposition; transfer and acquisition; and intellectual control and access controls. 4) *Access*: this domain researches open access/open data; the right to know/duty to remember/right to be forgotten; privacy; accountability; and transparency. 5) *Legal*: this domain considers issues such as the application of legal privilege (including the issue of extra-territoriality); legal hold; chain of evidence; authentication of evidence offered at trial; certification; and soft laws (in particular, UN standard-setting instruments)—mapping, scope, potential impact, and constraints.[5]

The research cross-domains are as follows: 1) *Terminology*: this cross-domain is concerned with the ongoing production of a multilingual glossary; a multilingual dictionary with sources; ontologies as needed; and essays explaining the use of terms and concepts within the project. 2) *Resources*: this cross-domain is concerned with the ongoing production of annotated bibliographies, identifying relevant published articles, books, etc., case law, policies, statutes, standards, blogs, and similar gray literature. 3) *Policy*: this cross-domain considers policy-related issues emerging from the five research domains; for instance, it covers policy issues pertaining to the development and implementation of the "infrastructure" or "security" standards, or as the facilitator for the implementation of laws. In general, it addresses record-keeping issues associated with the development and implementation of policies having an impact on the management of records in an online environment. 4) *Social issues*: this cross-domain is concerned with the analysis of social change consequent to the use of the Internet, including but not limited to the use/misuse of social media of all types, trustworthiness of news, data leaks (intentional or accidental/force majeure) consequences, development issues (power balance in a global perspective), organizational culture issues, and individual behavior issues. 5) *Education*: this cross-domain is concerned with the development of different models of curricula for transmitting the new knowledge produced by the project.

Within each domain and cross-domain, studies are carried out by multidisciplinary teams. The entire list of studies can be found on the website of the research project: http://interparestrust.org/trust/about_research/studies. Examples of studies are contract terms for cloud-based record-keeping services; ensuring trust in storage in infrastructure-as-a-service; retention and disposition in a cloud environment; modeling preservation as a service for trust; metadata, mutatis mutandis: design requirements for authenticity in the cloud and across contexts; models for monitoring and auditing of compliance in the flow from registration to archives in e-register; evaluating metadata description schemas of cultural heritage organizations in electronic environments for interoperability; comparative analysis of implemented governmental e-services; standard of practice for trust in protection of authoritative records in archives; assessment of privacy-preserving and security techniques for records management in cloud computing; the use of cloud services for records management in international organizations; security classification of records in the cloud; open government, open data, and big data on the management of digital records online; comparative analysis of the role of the records manager in an open government environment in the United Kingdom, Scotland, and Sweden; social and ethical foundations of preservation of digital historical-cultural heritage; developing model cloud computing contracts; identifying privacy concerns and attendant issues in cloud computing; putting the "fun" back in "functional"; social media use in government; and plurality and policy: designing for trust in the digital age.

The findings of the many studies carried out in the first 4 years will be the foundation on which the research team, in the final year of the project, will build the international conceptual and legal framework for the long-term preservation of authentic records in a networked online environment.

CONCLUSION

The InterPARES Project began in 1998 and is scheduled to close in 2018. It is quite possible that InterPARES Trust will not be the last phase of the project as technological development will continue to challenge our ability to maintain and verify the trustworthiness of electronic records. Whatever the case will be, the theory, methods, and practices developed by InterPARES, which are already embedded in the disciplines of records and archival management and diplomatics, will continue to support digital record-keeping and preservation for many years to come.

REFERENCES

1. Duranti, L. The InterPARES 2 Project (2002–2007): an overview. Archivaria **2007**, *64*, 113–121. Lauriault, T.; Craig, B.; Taylor, D.R.F.; Pulsifer, P. Today's data are part of tomorrow's research: archival issues in the sciences. Ibid, 123–179; Dingwall, G.; Marciano, R.; Moore, R.; Peters McLellan, E. From data to records: preserving the Geographic Information System of the city of Vancouver. Ibid, 181–198; Bushey, J. He shoots, He stores: new photographic practice in the digital age. Archivaria **2008**, *65*, 125–149; Roeder, J. Art and digital records: paradoxes and problems of preservation. Ibid, 151–163; Luchow, R.; Turner, J. M. All singing, all talking, all digital: media windows and archiving practice in the motion picture studios. Ibid, 165–186; Hawkins, K. A pattern language for electronic records. Archivaria 2009, 67, 157–188.
2. Duranti, L. Thibodeau, K. The concept of record in interactive, experiential and dynamic environments: The view of InterPARES. Arch. Sci. **2006**, *6* (1), 13–68. http://dx.doi.org/10.1007/s10502-006-9021-7.
3. Duranti, L.; Eastwood, T.; MacNeil, H. *Preservation of the Integrity of Electronic Records*; Kluwer Academic Publishers Group: Dordrecht, the Netherlands, 2000.
4. Duranti, L. *The Long-term Preservation of Authentic Electronic Records: Findings of the InterPARES Project*. Archilab: San Miniato, Italy, 2005.
5. Duranti, L. Preservation in the cloud: towards an international framework for a balance of trust and trustworthiness. In *APA/C-DAC International Conference on Digital Preservation and Development of Trusted Digital Repositories, February 5–6, 2014. New Delhi, India*, Excel India Publishers: New Delhi, India, 2014; 23–38.

BIBLIOGRAPHY

1. Duranti, L. *The Long-term Preservation of Authentic Electronic Records: Findings of the InterPARES Project*; Archilab: San Miniato, Italy, 2005. http://www.interpares.org/book/index.cfm.
2. Duranti, L. La memòria històrica documental al núvol: un oxímoron o el futur indefugible? Revista D'arxius **2012–2014**, 19–60.
3. Duranti, L.; MacNeil, H. The preservation of the integrity of electronic records: an overview of the UBC-MAS research project. Archivaria **1997**, *42*, 46–67.
4. Duranti, L.; Preston, R. InterPARES 2: Interactive, Dynamic and Experiential Records InterPARES 2: Interactive, Dynamic and Experiential Records. ANAI: Roma, Italy, 2008. http://www.interpares.org/ip2/book.cfm.
5. Duranti, L.; Rogers, C. Trust in digital records: an increasingly cloudy legal area. Comput. Law Secur. Rev. **2012**, *28* (5), 522–531.
6. InterPARES Project, www.interpares.org.
7. InterPARES Trust Project, www.interparestrust.org.
8. MacNeil, H. Providing grounds for trust: developing conceptual requirements for the long-term preservation of authentic electronic records. Archivaria **2000**, *50*, 52–78.
9. MacNeil, H. Providing grounds for trust II: the findings of the authenticity task force of InterPARES. Archivaria **2002**, *54*, 24–58.
10. MacNeil, H. Contemporary archival diplomatics as a method of inquiry: lessons learned from two research projects. Arch. Sci. **2004**, *4* (3–4), 199–232.

International Federation–iSchools

iSchools

Ronald L. Larsen
School of Information Sciences, University of Pittsburgh, Pittsburgh, Pennsylvania, U.S.A.

Abstract
Information Schools ("iSchools") address the relationship between information, technology, and people. This is characterized by a commitment to learning and understanding the role of information in human endeavors. The iSchools take it as given that expertise in all forms of information is required for progress in science, business, education, and culture. This expertise must include understanding of the uses and users of information, as well as information technologies and their applications. As of 2008, twenty-one iSchools in the United States and Canada have joined the "iCaucus," a forum in which iSchools' deans collaborate to further their collective interests through focused events such as the "iConference" and resources of broader interest such as the iSchools Web site.

ORIGINS

In 1988, Toni Carbo, dean of the School of Library and Information Sciences (now the School of Information Sciences) at the University of Pittsburgh, formed the "Gang of Three," including her decanal colleagues at Syracuse University's School of Information Studies (Donald Marchand) and Drexel University's College of Information Science and Technology (Richard Lytle). Within the next couple of years, the dean of the School of Communication, Information, and Library Studies at Rutgers University (Richard Budd) joined the group, making it a "Gang of Four." The Gang grew out of informal conversations at a meeting of the Association for Library and Information Science Education (ALISE). Each of the schools offered graduate Library and Information Science (LIS) and a variety of "other" programs, including undergraduate information science (IS), telecommunications, journalism, etc. The objective was to share information and to foster the development of a community of colleagues addressing such questions as "How do you explain IS to your provost?" The Gang met informally into the mid-1990s.

In 2001, the group was reconstituted under Toni's leadership at a meeting in Pittsburgh. Participants included deans from Syracuse University (Raymond von Dran), Drexel University (David Fenske), the University of Washington's Information School (Michael Eisenberg), and the University of Michigan's School of Information (John King). With that meeting, the "Gang of Five" was formed.

Beginning in 2003, Gang membership grew with the addition of deans from the Graduate School of Library and Information Science at the University of Illinois, the School of Information and Library Science at the University of North Carolina, the College of Information at Florida State University, the School of Informatics at Indiana University, and the School of Information at the University of Texas, bringing it to the "Gang of Ten." By this point, the informal name was becoming unwieldy and a bit inappropriate, particularly as continued growth was anticipated. Through the leadership of deans John King, the late Raymond von Dran, and Michael Eisenberg, the group's agenda became more focused on building a sense of identity and community among the "information schools," or "iSchools."

Typically, the group met twice per year. Meetings, hosted by one of the deans, included private discussions among the deans as well as open conversations with faculty of the host school, and usually an informal reception or lunch. During the deans-only sessions, the agenda focused on challenging administrative, programmatic, and planning issues, in addition to the continuing interest in explaining IS better to our non-IS colleagues. The sessions also provided an opportunity to learn about the curriculum and research of each school. An early goal was to nurture the development of a critical mass of faculty across the schools to undertake collaborative research.

The group was formally named "the iSchools Caucus" (more casually referred to as the iCaucus), and its membership grew rapidly with the addition of:

- The School of Communication, Information, and Library Studies
  Rutgers University (rejoining)
- The School of Information
  University of California, Berkeley
- The Donald Bren School of Information and Computer Sciences
  University of California, Irvine
- The Graduate School of Education and Information Studies
  University of California, Los Angeles
- The College of Information Sciences and Technology
  Pennsylvania State University

Encyclopedia of Library and Information Sciences, Fourth Edition DOI: 10.1081/E-ELIS4-120043670

Copyright © 2017 by Taylor & Francis. All rights reserved.

- The College of Computing
  Georgia Institute of Technology
- The School of Library and Information Science
  Indiana University
- The College of Information Studies
  University of Maryland
- The Faculty of Information
  University of Toronto

And in 2008, two more institutions joined:

- The Heinz School
  Carnegie Mellon University
- The School of Information Systems
  Singapore Management University

As a board member of the Computing Research Association (CRA), King introduced the iSchools Caucus to the CRA IT Deans Group, founded in 2000 at the Snowbird meeting and chaired by Peter Freeman (Georgia Tech). In 2008, the name of the CRA group was shortened with majority approval to the "CRA Deans" group. The CRA Deans group provides a broad forum for leaders of IT schools, colleges, and institutes to share experiences, strategies, opportunities, and concerns. It illuminates issues and seeks common ground leading to a coherent and unified voice for the academic and research communities, and to the general public. A substantial majority of the iSchool deans have joined the CRA Deans group in order to assure that information-related issues are appropriately reflected in the group's evolving agenda.

MOTIVATION

The emergence and evolution of iSchools was triggered by the explosive growth in digital information. In a 2003 study,[1] Peter Lyman and Hal Varian estimated that about 5 exabytes (5×10^{18}) of new information was generated in 2002 worldwide, with a growth rate of about 30% per year. They note that 5 exabytes "is equivalent in size to the information contained in 37,000 new libraries the size of the Library of Congress book collections." A 2007 study by IDC[2] concluded that the worldwide production of information in 2006 exceeded 161 exabytes, increasing at a compound annual growth rate of 57%. While only a small fraction of this information is accessible online (<2% by some estimates), it still represents an enormous and increasing amount of information that presents major challenges (and opportunities) in information management, access, and preservation.

Marcia Bates defines "the *domain* of information science [as] the universe of recorded information that is selected and retained for later access," and posits that

applied IS is "primarily concerned with the form and organization of information, its underlying structure, and only secondarily with its content."[3] Add to this the study of human use of information and the design and development of the technological tools to utilize information, and an understanding of the domain of the iSchools emerges. Bates succinctly states these through three driving questions:

- What are the features and laws of the recorded-information universe? (physical question)
- How do people relate to, seek, and use information? (social question)
- How can access to recorded information be made most rapid and effective? (design question)

The iSchools are interested in the relationship between information, technology, and people. This is characterized by a commitment to learning and understanding the role of information in human endeavors. The iSchools take it as given that expertise in all forms of information is required for progress in science, business, education, and culture. This expertise must include understanding of the uses and users of information, as well as information technologies and their applications.

(From the iSchools Web site http://www.ischools.org, 2008.)

POSITIONING

The "identity debate" has a long tradition in information studies and it influenced the formation of the iSchools as a group. It takes on many forms and has multiple dimensions. Wanda Orlikowski and Suzanne Iacono[4] argued for a theoretical focus on IT artifacts and laid out five relevant conceptualizations:

- Tool view (e.g., a productivity enhancer).
- Proxy view (e.g., surrogate measures such as return on investment).
- Ensemble view (e.g., technology embedded in a socio-economic system).
- Computational view (e.g., models and algorithms).
- Nominal view (e.g., studies of broad impacts such as outsourcing).

Ron Weber[5] posited, "the identity of a discipline is established through the contributions it makes to theory." He went on to suggest that he could find "only one class of phenomena for which theories sourced from other disciplines seemed deficient—namely, phenomena associated with building conceptual models and designing databases."

International Federation–
iSchools

Another facet of the identity discussion has been the attempt to draw boundaries. Izak Benbasat and Robert Zmud[6] summarized some of this line of thought as placing claim on three necessary and sufficient criteria: a central character, distinctiveness, and temporal continuity. They argued that a dominant design for the information systems discipline "has yet to be realized" and that this hinders the field's legitimacy. They affirmed the centrality of the IT artifact, placing the notion in a broad context including understanding capabilities and practices, human behaviors, usage, and impacts.

Robert Galliers[7] pushed back on Benbasat and Zmud, arguing that boundaries and disciplinary cores emerge naturally as a field evolves. In IS, forces shaping this evolution include such topics as the digital divide, globalization, and IT in the developing world, resulting in a broadening of the locus of study to include societal, policy, and ethical issues. He suggested adopting a "transdisciplinary" perspective on the field of IS. Table 1 adapts Galliers' characterization for IS to the domain of the iSchools.

DeSanctis[8] reflected on the increasing pervasiveness of information technology, observing that "knowledge and creative use are no longer the sole domain of specialists." This has shifted the dominant functional role of information professionals from development to leadership and support, and put many in strategic business positions. As information professionals take on these new roles, technical skills must be supplemented with new competencies in human relations and organizational effectiveness. As DeSanctis observed, "the institutional paradox for IS is that the domain has become of interest to many faculty groups yet the sole purview of none." While, perhaps, not the *sole* purview, this is, most certainly, the *primary* purview of the iSchools. Rather than focusing on a bounded "domain," DeSanctis argued for a "focus on the questions" and observed that these have historically generated excitement and impact in IS.

Daniel Robey[9] continued the call for a "more flexible identity for IS" that avoids "the lure of a dominant research paradigm." He suggested a pursuit of "pragmatic legitimacy" that casts IS as a "valued partner in intellectual exchanges with our external constituents: the governing bodies, business executives, university officials, and scholars from other disciplines who are the key actors in IS's organizational field."

John King and Kalle Lyytinen[10] acknowledged that the IS field lacks a theoretic core and has been "haunted by feelings of inadequacy" for 30 years. They proposed an alternative model for establishing legitimacy, grounded in three drivers:

- Salience of issues studied.
- Production of strong results.
- Maintenance of plasticity.

They offered an alternative view of the core of the discipline as a "market of ideas" where the IS field is defined as "the study of the design and management of information and associated technologies in organized human enterprise." Rather than accepting the argument that theory should provide the foundation, they suggest, rather, that theory "to the extent that it has a role, is in the service of producing strong results."

King[11] sums up this discussion of identity, observing that iSchools

> straddle the academy's ancient engagement with information and the contemporary challenges of ubiquitous information affecting all aspects of society…. The [iSchool] movement is emergent; its equilibrium can only be found in an essential tension among competing visions in a world of rapid technical and social change. [iSchool] identity is elusive and will remain so for the foreseeable future.

EMPOWERMENT

Studying at an iSchool immerses students in this dynamic and emerging "iField," where they confront the issues, opportunities, and challenges of an information society in the twenty-first century, in all their richness, controversy, and ambiguity. The iField addresses the fundamental issue of harnessing the incredible flow of information for the betterment of humanity.

The iField also empowers people in other fields to create, find, store, manipulate, and share information in useful forms. It may be unique in that, despite its elusive core, its subject, information, is at the heart of what individuals, organizations, and societies need in order to advance human endeavors, from acting to zoology. The iField's most visible and viable outcome is the delivery of the right information at the right time to the right people in the right form.

ORGANIZATION

The iSchools were founded as a consortium to establish broad recognition of the iField and its importance to

Table 1 IS as a transdisciplinary domain.

	Disciplinarity	Trans-disciplinarity
Boundary	Organization	Society
Central artifact	IT	People/information
Focus	Inward	Outward
Scope	Narrow	Broad
Reference disciplines	Org-behavior, Computer science, etc.	IS, LIS, telecommunications
Properties	Defined	Emergent
Interdisciplinary	A threat	An opportunity

society. In this role, they sought to position a group of academic institutions to identify, clarify, and speak to the major issues, challenges, and driving questions at the nexus of information, technology, and society. While a relatively small number of universities took the lead in establishing an organization with this goal, those who share the goal and contribute to its achievement go far beyond the small collection of organizers. The defining characteristics of iSchools (whether iCaucus members or not) include:

- An interest in the relationship between information, technology, and people.
- A commitment to learning and understanding the role of information in human endeavors.
- A recognition that expertise in all forms of information is required for progress in science, business, education, and culture.
- A belief that this expertise must include understanding of the uses and users of information, as well as information technologies and their applications.

The collective efforts of the iSchools (e.g., the iConference, the Web site, and special projects) are managed by the iCaucus. Members of the iCaucus pay an annual fee and have one vote on iCaucus decisions. The iCaucus charter specifies its membership criteria. Candidate memberships are reviewed by a membership committee and voted on by the full iCaucus membership. While not rigid, iCaucus members are expected to have substantial sponsored research activity, to engage in the training of future researchers (usually through an active, research-oriented doctoral program), and a commitment to progress in the information field. Each iSchool's representative to the iCaucus (usually a dean) is expected to report to the chief academic officer of the parent institutions.

The iSchools sponsor the iConference as a forum for faculty, students, and researchers to share their work and to develop their extended network of colleagues. The conference runs 3–4 days and the program typically includes a doctoral colloquium, poster and paper sessions, panels, roundtables, and social events. The first iConference was held at Penn State in September 2005.[12] Subsequent iConferences were hosted by the University of Michigan and UCLA, with the 2009 iConference being hosted by UNC Chapel Hill.

VISION

As a relatively straightforward example, consider an iSchool's approach to information assurance, an issue of contemporary salience, for which we seek to produce strong results while adapting to changing conditions. When viewed as a technological issue, scientists and

engineers are likely to focus on topics such as cryptography, steganography, public key infrastructure, and intrusion detection, or, in other words, technical areas in which they are likely to have significant interest and expertise. The same set of issues viewed from the perspective of librarians may be more likely to draw attention to questions of identification, authentication, provenance, and access. A social scientist, on the other hand, may focus on issues of confidentiality, authentication, privacy, and integrity. So who is right? Clearly, they all are. Information assurance is a multidisciplinary problem with extraordinarily complex and interrelated technical, policy, and social challenges. An iSchool provides the venue that enables scholars from a variety of contributing disciplines to leverage their individual insights, perspectives, and interests, informed by a rich, "transdisciplinary" community.

But transdisciplinary collaboration is not a natural act. Not only does each discipline bring to the table a set of values, goals, models, economics, and ethics that have evolved slowly and in relative isolation over an extended period of time within their discipline, but also they must interact with and respond to the interests of external bodies. These are not always aligned in ways that foster rapid agreement.

- Values—some will argue that strength is derived from information access, while others contend that power is founded on information control.
- Goals—some argue for increasing safety and security by way of imposing limits and locks, while others opine that justice and accountability are advanced through dialogue and debate.
- Models—some see information access primarily as a societal responsibility, where others view it dominantly as a business opportunity.
- Economics—information is expensive to create and publish, but cheap to replicate and distribute.
- Ethics—some argue that ethics are trumped by the realities of the real world, while others rebut that they are motivated by that very same world.

The complex interaction among the disciplines, when allowed to play out in an iSchool, provides a rich environment for the education of information professionals. Exploiting the very tensions that arise among the various constituencies enriches the creative insight of each. Among the issues feeding such creative dialogue are topics such as:

- Intellectual property rights and its relation to fair use.
- Open, extensible systems as an alternative to proprietary, closed designs.
- Access to publicly funded information balanced against legitimate security requirements.
- Assuring ethical public policy when the need for expediency feels overwhelming.

International Federation–iSchools

International Federation–
iSchools

- Recognizing the need for both selective government secrecy and accountability through open records.

While the resolution of these issues is ultimately expressed in society's evolving social contract, the iSchools serve a vital role by:

- Preparing the next generation of information professionals.
- Informing the relevant social and political structures regarding the implications and use of information technologies.
- Assuring that debates surrounding the development of policy and law are properly informed by sound scholarship.
- Advising society of the potential consequences of policy alternatives.
- Interpreting opportunities and implications of policy alternatives.
- Remaining, themselves, engaged students of a highly dynamic landscape of change.

So what is an iSchool in the twenty-first century? Informed by decades of debate and responding to exceptionally rapid changes in technology and uncertainty in public policy, iSchools foster the development of an intellectual space where true interdisciplinarity plays out. In so doing, they introduce a range of challenges to traditional university structures and practices regarding organizational boundaries, promotion and tenure policies, doctoral education, research legitimacy, etc., as they create an environment where issues of information are addressed systematically, regardless of disciplinary heritage or presumed "ownership." In this way, iSchools respond to the salient issues of the time by stressing the production of strong results. They are in a constant state of adaptation within their core competencies, while building necessary bridges among disciplines. The iSchools recognize that the near-term future will be shaped largely by industry, so their applied research agenda is strongly influenced by these emerging needs and directions. But the iSchools lead industry and government in the study of timeless, recurring, theoretical questions, and educate the next generation of information professionals who will shape the future of a global information society.

RECOGNITION

Von Dran was a dynamic and powerful force in both the development of the School of Information Studies at Syracuse University and the formation of the iSchools movement. In his own words,

> Information schools are advancing a common notion that it's *information*, and not simply the technology, that is the

driver. The information field must harness a number of disciplines and approaches that critically affect the relevance, timeliness, accessibility, and quality of information. These schools bring together the various aspects of technology, management, policy, and usability, among others, for the benefit of people everywhere.

In his honor, the iSchools have established an award to recognize others who have demonstrated Ray's commitment to excellence and leadership. The award is presented at the iConference and includes a monetary award and an opportunity for the award winner to share his or her vision of the challenges and opportunities confronting the information profession to conference participants.

ACKNOWLEDGMENT

This entry is dedicated to the memory of Raymond von Dran, Dean of the School of Information Studies, Syracuse University, 1995–2007. The author gratefully acknowledges the assistance of Toni Carbo and Jonathan Grudin in reconstructing the historical timeline for the iSchools and of Maeve Reilly for improving the readability of this entry.

REFERENCES

1. Lyman, P. Varian, H. *How Much Information?* School of Information Management and Systems at the University of California at Berkeley: Berkeley, CA, 2003. Available at http://www2.sims.berkeley.edu/research/projects/how-much-info-2003/.
2. IDC. *A Forecast of Worldwide Information Growth Through 2010*, IDC: Framingham, MA, 2007. Available at http://www.emc.com/collateral/analyst-reports/expanding-digital-idc-white-paper.pdf.
3. Bates, M.J. The invisible substrate of information science. J. Am. Soc. Inform. Sci. Technol. **1999**, *50*(12), 1043–1050. Available at http://www.gseis.ucla.edu/faculty/bates/substrate.html.
4. Orlikowski, W.J.; Suzanne Iacono, C. Research commentary: Desperately seeking the 'IT' in IT research—A call to theorizing the IT artifact. Inform. Syst. Res. **2001**, *12*(2), 121–134. Available at http://isr.journal.informs.org/cgi/content/abstract/12/2/121.
5. Weber, R. Still desperately seeking the IT artifact. In *Information Systems, The State of the Field*; King, J.L., Lyytinen, K., Eds.; John Wiley & Sons, Ltd: West Sussex, England, 2006; 43–54 (Reprinted from *MIS Quarterly*. Available at http://www.misq.org/archivist/vol/no27/issue2/EdCommentsV27N2.pdf).
6. Benbasat, I. Zmud, R.W. The identity crisis within the IS discipline: Defining and communicating the discipline's core properties. In *Information Systems, The State of the Field*; King, J.L., Lyytinen, K., Eds.; John Wiley & Sons, Ltd.: West Sussex, England, 2006; 55–70.

7. Galliers, R.D. Change as crisis or growth? Toward a trans-disciplinary view of information systems as a field of study: A response to Benbasat and Zmud's call for returning to the IT artifact. In *Information Systems, The State of the Field*; King, J.L., Lyytinen, K., Eds.; John Wiley & Sons, Ltd.: West Sussex, England, 2006; 147–162.

8. DeSanctis, G. The social life of information systems research: A response to Benbasat and Zmud's call for returning to the IT artifact. In *Information Systems, The State of the Field*; King, J.L., Lyytinen, K., Eds.; John Wiley & Sons, Ltd.: West Sussex, England, 2006; 163–182.

9. Robey, D. Identity, legitimacy and the dominant research paradigm: An alternative prescription for the IS discipline. In *Information Systems, The State of the Field*; King, J.L., Lyytinen, K., Eds.; John Wiley & Sons, Ltd.: West Sussex, England, 2006; 183–190.

10. King, J.L. Lyytinen, K. Nothing at the center?: Academic legitimacy in the information systems field. In *Information Systems, The State of the Field*; King, J.L., Lyytinen, K., Eds.; John Wiley & Sons, Ltd.: West Sussex, England, 2006; 233–266.

11. King, J.L. Identity in the I-school movement. Bull. Am. Soc. Inform. Sci. Technol. April/May **2006**. Available at http://www.asis.org/Bulletin/Apr-06/king.html.

12. Harmon, G. The first I-conference of the i-school communities. Bull. Am. Soc. Inform. Sci. Technol. April/May **2006**. Available at http://www.asis.org./Bulletin/Apr-06/.

International Federation—iSchools

Israel: Libraries, Archives, and Museums

Snunith Shoham
Silvia Schenkolewski-Kroll
Department of Information Science, Bar-Ilan University, Ramat Gan, Israel

Abstract

This entry presents three cultural institutions—libraries, museums and archives—in Israel, against the backdrop of the international Jewish Diaspora and the establishment of the State of Israel in 1948, as an immigrant absorbing nation, where foreign powers previously ruled (the Ottoman Empire until 1917 and the British Mandate from 1917 to 1948). In this historical and governmental context (with its legislative, municipal, social and cultural ramifications), the entry traces the development of these three institutions and paints an up-to-date portrait of their current situation.

INTRODUCTION

After the failure of the rebellion against the Romans and the fall of Jerusalem in 70 C.E., many Jews were dispersed to foreign lands and only a few remained in *Eretz Yisrael* (The Land of Israel), living under rulers who changed several times over the centuries. From 1517 until 1917, Eretz Yisrael was part of the Ottoman Empire. Following World War I, the British received a mandate to rule in Eretz Yisrael, which continued until May 15, 1948 (as a result of a United Nations decision made in November 1947) (see Fig. 1).

Modern Israel is a country that absorbs Jewish immigrants. It developed primarily through five waves of pre-State immigration, which brought some 450,000 immigrants to Israel from 1882 to 1948 and a mass immigration from Eastern Europe and the Arab countries after the Holocaust and the establishment of the State of Israel. The Jewish population has grown from 649,000 in 1948 to 5,567,000 in December 2008.[1,2]

The Arab sector in Israel numbers 1,487,000 people, who are 20.2% of Israel's population. There are also 319,000 non-Jewish immigrants and 200,000 foreign workers, who are not citizens, living in Israel.

This entry will survey the development of libraries, archives, and museums in the State of Israel and present a current portrait of these cultural institutions.

LIBRARIES

Historical Perspective

During the years when there was no autonomous Jewish rule in Eretz Yisrael, libraries existed in synagogues and study houses (*Beitei Midrash*), as well as private collections. In the nineteenth century, non-Jewish communities also maintained libraries in Eretz Yisrael, mainly in Jerusalem. These were owned by foreign institutions and mainly contained books about Eretz Yisrael for the use of archeologists, historians, and tourists. There were also theological collections and devotional literature in monastery and church libraries.

The first library in Eretz Yisrael to include secular literature was the one established in the Jewish hospital in Jerusalem in 1854, which received a delivery of books in several languages, sent from Paris. In 1870, the first agricultural school, Mikve Israel, was founded, including a library that began with 300 volumes and grew to approximately 3000 by the end of the century.

The last quarter of the nineteenth century saw the opening of the first secular public libraries in Jerusalem (the Montefiore Book Collection in 1874), Rishon Lezion (1883), Jaffa (1886), Safed (1891), *Sha'ar Zion* Library in Jaffa (1891), the Abravanel House Library in Jerusalem in 1891 (which later became the National Library), Petah Tikva (1892), Zichron Yaacov (1895), Hadera (1899), and Sejera (1902).[3] During the period of the British Mandate, there was not one Jewish town or village in the Land of Israel that did not have a library of some type, although many were unable to maintain an uninterrupted existence.[4] These libraries were established, first and foremost, because the ideology of the Jewish national revival movement strove, among other things, to create a society with modern goals for education and cultural creativity.[4] Other contributing factors were the tradition of study and the unique status of books in Jewish culture. The Enlightenment Movement led to the development of cultural and educational institutions and the establishment of Hebrew newspapers. Indeed, the founders of many libraries in Israel were teachers and groups of educated people.

The nineteenth century also saw, for the first time, the establishment of libraries as part of *educational institutions*, though some of these also served the general public.

Encyclopedia of Library and Information Sciences, Fourth Edition DOI: 10.1081/E-ELIS4-120043746

Copyright © 2017 by Taylor & Francis. All rights reserved.

Israel–Knowledge Discovery

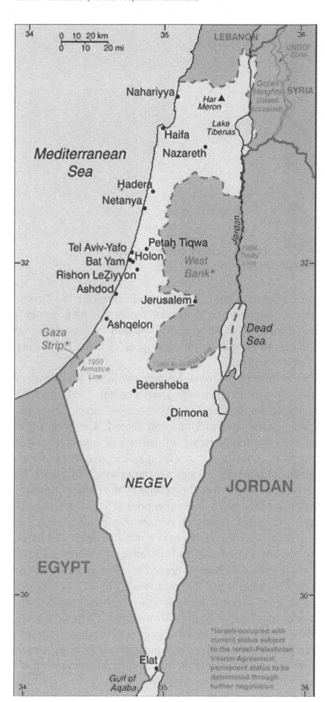

Fig. 1 Map of Israel.
Source: CIA *The World Factbook.*

During the 1890s, libraries were set up in schools for the first time, in Petah Tikva, Gedera, and Sejera. The collections in these school libraries reflected the education that the schools provided and educational trends at that time. They generally included religious literature and, sometimes, secular Hebrew literature. In some libraries, French literature was also included.

The General Federation of Labor of the Hebrew Workers in Eretz Yisrael, or *Histadrut* partially compensated for the lack of the autonomous municipal governments that were responsible for the establishment of public libraries throughout the Western world. The Histadrut concerned itself not only with workers' interests but also with the provision of culture, and regarded libraries as a basic component of social, educational, and cultural life. Among other things, the Histadrut set up workers' libraries in many urban communities, mainly beginning in the 1920s and 1930s. Earlier instances of this phenomenon involved small workers' associations that set up small "workers' clubs" and "reading rooms" in the late nineteenth and early twentieth centuries.

In 1892, the Jerusalem bureau of the B'nai B'rith organization set up the Abravanel House Library. This library initially contained *belles lettres* as well as theoretical and scientific literature and soon adopted the goal of amassing *all* Hebrew works and material pertaining to the Jews of Eretz Yisrael, some of which had also been published in foreign languages. Hence it gave priority to books on Judaism and rare books, and issued appeals to Diaspora Jewry to establish depositories for the books of the Jewish people.

It was thus, at the initiative of a few individuals, that the nucleus of the National Library of Israel was formed. The first to call for the creation of a national library that would amass books in the areas of Judaism and the Land of Israel came from Rabbi Yehoshua Heschel Levine of Volozhin, whose article on the topic appeared in the Jerusalem periodical *Havatzelet* in 1872. The Hibbat Zion movement in Odessa also advocated the creation of a national library. Among those active in this connection was a Hibbat Zion member Dr. Joseph Chazanowicz of Bialistok, who, after visiting Eretz Yisrael in 1890, decided to devote his life to the collecting of books. During 30 years of activity he collected 16,000 books, many of them rare, and transferred them to the Abravanel House Library.[5]

In 1920, the library was acquired by the World Zionist Organization and, for the first time, a professional librarian, Dr. Shmuel Hugo Bergmann, was appointed as its director.[6] In 1925 with the establishment of the Hebrew University, the first university in Eretz Yisrael, it was decided that the library would serve as a national and university library. The library also served as a public library, open to all, thus filling a void that had previously existed in Mandatory Eretz Yisrael.

The National Library

Since its establishment, *The Jewish National and University Library* has served a threefold purpose. It is the national library of the State of Israel, the national library of the Jewish people, and the central library of the Hebrew University. However, there are plans to change this and the process of reestablishing the national library as an organizationally and financially independent body has

Israel–Knowledge Discovery

Fig. 2 National Library of Israel.
Source: National Library of Israel.

Israel–Knowledge Discovery

begun. A law passed in November 2007 delineates the transition process and the goals of the National Library. In accordance with the law, the National Library has been as a public-service corporation since June 2008 but remains a subsidiary of the Hebrew University. When the transition process is complete, within 3 years, it will no longer be a subsidiary of the Hebrew University but rather an independent organization known as the National Library (Fig. 2).[7]

The library serves as a depository for all books published in Israel. In 1953, the first legislation was passed requiring that a copy of all publications be submitted to the National Archive, to the Knesset (parliament) Library, and to the National Library. In 2000, the law was expanded to include publications that are not printed on paper. The library also collects material about Israel, the Jewish people, and Judaism, as well as material written in Hebrew script and in other Jewish languages (Yiddish, Ladino, etc.) from every place and time. In addition, it has collections of rare Judaica and Hebraica, manuscripts and incunabula amassed from all corners of the world. The library also contains one of the largest and best-organized collections on Arab and Islamic subjects in the Middle East.

The library contains over 5 million books and periodicals, as well as many thousands of items in special collections, such as manuscripts and archives (see the section on Archives), maps, and music recordings. Most of the collections are in closed stacks. The library also has about 11,000 manuscripts, 9000 of them in Hebrew and the rest in Arabic. The library's Paleography Project is conducting research on the codicology and paleography of dated medieval Hebrew manuscripts. The library also houses the Institute of Microfilmed Hebrew Manuscripts, which has undertaken to collect microfilm copies of all Hebrew manuscripts extant in public and private collections. Over 60,000 items, representing 90% of known Hebrew manuscripts, are already available to scholars.

Among the library's special collections are the Depository Collection of the United Nations, which contains publications of the United Nations and documents of the League of Nations; the European Union Depository Collection.

The Jewish National Library publishes the *National Bibliography* (*Kiryat Sefer*), an annotated bibliography that contains entries for all works on Israel, Jews and Judaica, published in Israel and abroad. The library also publishes a bibliography of periodical literature called *Index of Articles on Jewish Studies (RAMBI)*, which covers journals and periodicals from all parts of the world.

Another research tool prepared by the library is a retrospective bibliography of books printed in Hebrew characters, *The Bibliography of Hebrew Books, 1472–1960*. It also provides online links to two other indexes: The Index to Hebrew Periodicals and the Index to Hebrew Israeli Newspapers, which are prepared by other Israeli libraries. The library has begun a digitalization project that includes making the library's collection of Jewish marriage certificates, manuscripts of the Mishna and Talmud, ancient maps of Jerusalem, official records of Jewish communities, the Einstein archive and historical Jewish and Israeli newspapers, etc. available to all on its Internet site: jnul. huji.ac.il.

Academic Libraries

When the State of Israel was proclaimed in 1948, it had two universities: the Technion Israel Institute of Technology, founded in Haifa in 1924, and the Hebrew University of Jerusalem, established in 1925, on Mount Scopus. Since then, six additional universities have been established: the Weizmann Institute of Science (1949), Tel Aviv University (1953), Bar-Ilan University (1955), the University of Haifa (1963), Ben-Gurion University of the Negev (1966), and the Open University (for distance education, 1976). Today there are also 30 academic and regional colleges, including some private institutions, and 25 teachers' training colleges. In recent years many colleges have been upgraded and have begun to grant academic degrees.

The Israeli universities do not use a uniform library model. Whereas the University of Haifa and Ben-Gurion University have one central library, other universities, for example, Bar-Ilan University and the Technion, have many departmental libraries. Others, like the Hebrew University, also have large division libraries.

Interuniversity cooperation

In 1969, the government established the Israeli Standing Committee of the National and University Libraries (SCONUL), a voluntary forum for discussing problems of policy and planning. SCONUL initiated an interlibrary loan system among the universities and set up a group of committees to deal with cataloging, acquisition, reference, periodicals, and circulation.

In 1979, the Hebrew University developed a library automation system (ALEPH) that was adopted as the software program of the university libraries in Israel. The Grants Committee of the Israel Council of Higher Education has also contributed to this by subsidizing the university libraries' participation in ALEPH. Today, all the catalogs of the universities and the majority of the colleges in Israel are on the ALEPH network. The *Israel National Catalog* currently lists over 8 million books, periodicals, and audiovisual items in 65 university, college, and specialty libraries. The catalog uses MARC format and ALEPH-500 software. All Unicode characters are supported.

In 1998, the university heads established a consortium framework, the Israel Center for Digital Information Services (MALMAD). MALMAD's main function is the acquisition, licensing, and operation of information services for all the Israeli universities. It makes databases, directories, and digital journals available to the universities.[8]

Public Libraries

In the 1960s, just 15 years after the establishment of the State of Israel, there was an attempt to change the educational system in order to promote social equality and integration in the new society, which included immigrants from various cultures. In this context, the government began to address the issue of public libraries.

In 1962, a Department of Libraries was created in the Ministry of Education for the purpose of encouraging public libraries, which more than half of the communities lacked. Furthermore, few of the existing libraries met the criteria for proper service in terms of collections, opening hours, and staffing.

In 1975, the Knesset passed the Libraries Law which did not mandate the establishment of a public library in every town but did set criteria for recognizing a library as

"public" and the resultant eligibility for some degree of funding from the national budget. The law also established the Council for Public Libraries, which advises the minister regarding implementation of the law and submits its own proposals to him.

When the development of the libraries began, there was a gradual but steady increase in the percentage of registered readers using public libraries. In 1985, 25% of all residents of the state were registered in libraries. Since that time, there has been an ongoing, gradual decline in the number of readers and in 2007 approximately 16% of residents are registered in public libraries.

In 2007, all Israeli public libraries together circulated 8.7 million items and 3 million users visited their reference rooms; of these, 900,000 were Internet users. (Information from the Department of Libraries, Ministry of Science, Culture and Sport.) As of today (2008), there are 212 administrative library units in Israel, which together encompass 862 service points (including all branches). The library units include 44 regional libraries and 50 urban units located in community centers. Another 120 have a double function, serving as both regional and school libraries; of these, 80 libraries operate in elementary schools and 40 in high schools. The regional libraries, which began in the 1960s, are now being transformed to conform to a new organizational conception, adopted in 2006. Instead of having a small library in every town or village, larger libraries are being formed to serve several communities, alongside central libraries that serve not only the public but also an educational institution.

A vast majority of the libraries' current collections are in Hebrew, even though Israel is an immigrant society. For many years, a melting-pot conception of immigration prevailed in Israel. A survey done in 1980, found that only 11% of all the collections in the public libraries included material in foreign languages, and most of it was not in dynamic collection.[9]

During the 1990s, a different concept of immigration developed in Israeli society and it came to be understood that immigrants have an inner need to preserve their mother tongue and cultural heritage. In the library field, this was manifested in a greater emphasis on materials in languages spoken by the immigrants living in a given community. To aid the libraries in this regard, a central library for Russian was set up in 1989 to provide libraries throughout the country with long-term loans of books in Russian. There are also central libraries for books in French, established in 1986, and Spanish, established in 2003.

Most libraries do not have nonbook collections. Only a few libraries have audio or video collections, but in the last decade libraries have begun to make computers available to the public, offering multimedia materials, games, and access to the Internet. Currently, computer stations are available in half of the libraries (see Figs. 3 and 4).

Fig. 3 Computers in Holon Mediatheque (Public Library).
Source: Central Library in Holon.

Israel–Knowledge Discovery

Funding of the Israeli public libraries is the responsibility of the local governments, which determine their budgets, and there are substantial differences in amounts allocated by the different local authorities. In addition, the libraries receive some support from the Ministry of Culture, though the proportion of its budget allocated to libraries has declined over the years and was about 10% of the total budget for libraries. On July 16, 2007, the Knesset passed a law that set a scale for the gradual increase in the State's budgetary allocation for the libraries, beginning in 2008. In 2008, the proportion of the libraries' budget allocated by the government rose to about 15%. By 2013, the State should be funding half of the libraries' budgets. Over the past 25 years, 70% of libraries in the urban communities have resorted to collecting fees for subscriptions to lending services. This source constitutes 5% of the libraries' budget. The new law makes receiving the higher allocation conditional on discontinuing the collection of subscription fees. Most libraries did indeed stop collecting fees as of January 2008. This is probably the reason for the increase of approximately 20% in the number of readers and circulation in 2008.

The Israeli Center for Libraries

In the 1960s, a decision was made to learn from the Scandinavian model of a public library system. This led, in 1965, to the creation of the Center for Libraries that

Fig. 4 Seating Area in Holon Mediatheque (Public Library).
Source: Central Library in Holon.

provides central services to the libraries. The Center provides central cataloging services to public and school libraries in Israel (now in electronic form), publishes professional literature and tools for librarianship. It also offers an array of courses, and training; organizes annual conferences; serves as the Israeli representative of ISBN; and provides consultancy services to libraries on the management, architecture, equipping, and furnishing of libraries, as well as supplying products and services for the encouragement of reading.

School Libraries

During the first years of its existence, Israel absorbed massive waves of immigration, and the focus in those years was on the establishment of a school system. For a long period, many schools had only a small number of books or small library collections. Only in the 1970s, with the increased awareness of the importance of school libraries, did the creation of school libraries begin.

In 1988, the Department of Libraries of the Ministry of Education and Culture assumed responsibility for dealing with school libraries and this led to the intensified cultivation of existing libraries and establishment of new libraries in the schools that still lacked them. The findings of a survey done by the department in 1993–1994 showed a substantial increase in the number of school libraries in Israel, with libraries functioning in 87% of the high schools and 83% of the elementary schools. During 1992–1994 an average of 66 new libraries were established each year.[10] Since the early 1990s, the concept of the library as a "resource center" has developed and there has been a countrywide effort to make the libraries into resource centers.

Today, there are a total of 2414 elementary schools in Israel (in the educational streams of all sectors, including small, private ultraorthodox schools) and 1941 high schools.[11] Currently, 20% of the elementary schools still lack libraries, as do 10% of the high schools. Undoubtedly, the situation of the high school libraries is better than that of the elementary school libraries, although more books are lent for free reading in the elementary schools reflecting the decline in reading as students get older and the greater emphasis that elementary schools place on encouraging reading.

The Ministry of Education's regulations require that there be a librarian in every high school but not in every elementary school. Therefore, elementary school principals can decide whether or not there will be a librarian in their school and what the scope of the librarian's activities will be.

Special Libraries

In Israel approximately 600 special libraries are operated by government agencies, institutes and research centers, hospitals, museums, banks, corporations, and enterprises.

One special library is the *Library of the Knesset*, which began to operate in 1950. Its main role is to serve the members of Knesset and support the legislative process. To this end, it includes an *Information Center*, which was set up in 1973, and prepares surveys on various subjects, at the request of members of Knesset and their aides or of the various Knesset committees and bureaus. In the framework of the *Freedom of Information Law* (1998), which stipulates that it is the right of every Israeli citizen or resident to receive information from a public authority and defines information as "any information that exists within a public authority and is written, recorded, filmed, photographed or computerized," the library provides citizens with information on the activities of the Knesset and its committees, on bills presented and laws enacted. The information is provided by means of telephone, mail, fax, and the Knesset's Internet site (http://www.knesset.gov.il), which is operated by the library.

Medical libraries are a prominent group of special libraries. At present, there are approximately 80 medical libraries in Israel of various kinds. Israel has four medical schools (at the Hebrew University, Tel Aviv University, the Technion, and Ben-Gurion University), each with its own large medical library. In addition, all hospitals have medical libraries, some are large but others employ only one person. Twenty-two of the medical libraries are organized into two regional networks, centered around university libraries. The network began its operation in 1975, aiming to promote interlibrary cooperation based not only on the sharing of resources but also on specialized biomedical information and professional skills. The academic medical school libraries are responsible for coordinating the work of all the medical libraries in their region.[12] The consortium of medical libraries fills the following functions: 1) joint purchase of online data bases and e-journals; 2) interlibrary loans—supplying documents and scientific publications to libraries, using the same software for transmitting documents; and 3) holding seminar days and training sessions.

Another special library is that of the Standards Institution of Israel, which has an extensive standards and technical documentation library (http://www.sii.org.il), where the Israeli standards and specifications are collected in both electronic and print formats. There is also a vast collection of foreign standardization documents, including international standards, as well as guidebooks and databases in the field.

The Arab Sector

The Arab sector accounts for 20% of the population. They live in 123 settlements and consist of five different groups: Moslem Arabs (58%), Moslem Bedouins (15.4%), Christian Arabs (15%), Druze (8.8%), and Circassians (2.8%). Eight mixed towns or cities are home to 35% of the Arab

Israel–Knowledge Discovery

population while the remainder live in exclusively minority towns (88) and villages (35).

Academic and research libraries

Five universities—the University of Haifa, Hebrew University, Tel Aviv University, Ben-Gurion University and Bar-Ilan University—offer studies in Middle Eastern and Islamic Studies and Arabic language and literature. Each of these universities maintains large academic collections of literature and books in Arabic to serve the academic departments.

The University of Haifa has a large Arab student population and its library is used by Arab teachers and high school students in the region. Therefore, it has a policy of building a more comprehensive collection of Arabic books on all subjects.[13] It also has a collection of children's literature in Arabic.

Israel also has three colleges for training Arab teachers: the Academic Center for Training Arab Teachers (part of Beit Berl College), the Arab College in Haifa, and the Islamic College in Baka al-Garbia. Each of these has a library that provides resources for instruction. Not many books in Arabic are published in Israel, a small amount of fiction and a few scholarly works. Therefore, the librarians have to travel to the annual book fair in Cairo, where they can order books that have been published in Egypt, Jordan, Saudi Arabia, Kuwait, Morocco, and Sudan.

There are also research institutes in related fields, among the better-known ones being the Harry S Truman Research Institute for the Advancement of Peace and the Moshe Dayan Center for Middle Eastern and African Studies, both of which maintain collections of books, periodicals, and daily newspapers from Israel, the West Bank, and Arab countries.

There are other institutions in Israel that, though not part of universities, conduct research on the Middle East and maintain collections in Arabic. These include the Givat Haviva Institute for Advanced Studies, which includes the Jewish–Arab Center for Peace that houses an information center includes several dozen items in the field of Middle East studies, including files of newspaper articles published in Israel and various Arab countries, etc. Use of this collection, which offers items in Arabic as well as Hebrew and English, is open to all, but it is used mostly by lecturers, doctoral candidates, college students and high school students working on term papers, including many students from the nearby settlements of Wadi Ara.

Public libraries

During the Mandatory period there were no public libraries for Arabs. Until Israeli educational patterns began to influence the Arab sector, religious organizations played an important role in promoting reading and libraries among the literate elite of this sector. The Moslem Religious Endowment (*waqf*) still maintains two libraries, in Jerusalem and Jaffa. Their collections consist mainly of Moslem religious and legal literature.[13]

In the Arab sector, too, the Histadrut played an important role during the pre-State era and the two first decades of statehood. The Arab Department of the Histadrut established 47 clubs in villages of the Galilee and central Israel, each containing 500–3000 library items.

After 1948, the Arab libraries were almost exclusively initiated and operated by Jewish authorities, mixed municipalities, the Histadrut, the Prime Minister's Office, the Department of Libraries of the Ministry of Education and Culture, and other Jewish and Arab organizations.[13]

The development of modern libraries by the Arab community itself began in the 1970s. This reflected social, political, and educational changes that encouraged the creation of library services in the Arab and Druze sectors. During the 1960s, the Ministry of Interior encouraged the development of municipal self-rule in Arab communities and they began to change. A vast improvement in Israeli communication and transportation systems gave Arab villages access to neighboring urban centers. The combination of high population growth and high unemployment impelled the younger generation to seek employment outside the villages. There was also a growth of light industry and commerce in the villages, in addition to agriculture. Young people went to the universities, and new political power centers began to develop in the villages.

Today, there are 56 independent public libraries in the Arab settlements, 12 libraries that are branches of regional libraries and 5 libraries in mixed settlements. Seventeen Arab towns still do not have libraries. About one-third of the libraries in the Arab sector are located in schools and serve as combined libraries. Indeed, most of the library users in the Arab sector are children and teenagers.

School libraries

Before the British Mandate, there were only a few Arab schools in Eretz Yisrael, supervised by the Turkish Ministry of Education. The British authorities regarded the educational advancement of the Arabs in Eretz Yisrael as an important goal. The public school system was designed mainly for the Moslems, while Christians had missionary schools. The British Mandate's efforts, however, lagged behind the Arab population's growth rate, so that many children still received no education.[14]

The Compulsory Education Act of 1949 obligated parents to enroll children in school and led to a great improvement in the Arab sector's educational level. In Israel today, there are 417 Arab elementary schools and 202 Arab high schools. Recent years have seen an impressive growth in the number of school libraries in the Arab sector, reflecting the encouragement of increased awareness among the school administrators, especially in the Druze sector. At present, 70% of the elementary schools

Israel–Knowledge Discovery

have a library and 84% of the high schools. Their collections are smaller than those in the Jewish sector because most Arab libraries were established more recently and have not yet acquired a large stock of books. In addition, they tend to limit their collections to material directly related to the curriculum and do not purchase many fiction books. Moreover, it is difficult to obtain material in Arabic, since it must be ordered from foreign countries. Most is ordered from Jordan (this is also affected by the political situation in the region). Most of the collections in these libraries are in Arabic (71–83%), with only a small proportion in Hebrew.

Professional Education

Until the first school of librarianship was established in Israel in 1956, an Israeli could only become a professional librarian by going to Europe or the United States for training. Under the directorship of Shmuel Hugo Bergmann (1920–1935), the National Library sent workers abroad for training and sometimes employed immigrant librarians who had been trained in their home countries. During 1936–1947, the library profession came to be regarded differently. Fewer people went abroad for training, instead receiving short courses at the workplace as well as on-the-job training.[15]

In 1956, the first library school was set up as an academic department at the Hebrew University of Jerusalem, the School of Library, Archive and Information Studies, which was closed 3 years ago.

In 1973, the Department of Library and Information Studies was inaugurated at the University of Haifa, where training courses had been provided since 1971. Today this is a small department that offers a postgraduate diploma as well as a librarianship track within the framework of a general B.A.

The following year (1974), Bar-Ilan University opened a department of librarianship, known since 1999 as the Department of Information Science, which has become the largest department in Israel, offering B.A., M.A., and Ph.D., degrees. The areas of specialization it offers are

For the M.A., degree: Organizational Information Services and Knowledge Management; Information Technology; Information Specialization in Cultural and Educational Institutions; and Social Information.

B.A.: Web Technologies; Information studies.

In addition, there are three teachers' colleges that offer nonacademic programs in Librarianship and Information Studies: Beit Berl College (Kfar Saba), Oranim College (Haifa), and David Yellin College (Jerusalem).

There are currently two relevant professional organizations: the Organization of Israeli Librarians was set up in 1952, and its members are mostly librarians of public and school libraries. The Association of Special Libraries and Information Centers in Israel (ASMI) was founded in 1966, and mainly encompasses academic libraries, special

libraries, and information centers. These two professional organizations have decided to merge into one organization and the merger will occur during 2009.

MUSEUMS

Historical Perspective

In Israel today, there are approximately 200 museums involved in the collection and display of art-objects in a wide range of cultural areas: archaeology, history and heritage, art, anthropology, folklore, and Judaica, as well as nature, science, and technology.

The first museums were established under the Ottoman regime. Between 1848, when the first museum was opened in Jerusalem, and 1917, 30 museums were opened in Eretz Yisrael. Most of the museums and collections established in the late Ottoman period where located in either monasteries and churches or schools and research institutes.

The establishment of the museums was influenced by eighteenth century Europeans' growing interest in Middle Eastern archaeology and the settlement of European subjects in Eretz Yisrael and the opening of foreign consulates, which opened educational and cultural institutions. These institutions began to collect archaeological findings and set up museums, although most were not open to the general public.

Meanwhile, the national movements in Europe, including the awakening of the Zionist movement, led to the establishment of Jewish museums in Europe and the United States. Although these expressed the desire to be integrated into the general community,[16] they also led to recognition of the importance of Jewish culture and efforts to establish national museums in Eretz Yisrael.[17]

In this spirit, Yosef Hazanovitz proposed establishing a Jewish national library, including a museum and, in 1895, he began collecting portraits of Jewish personalities.

In 1906, the *Bezalel National Museum* was established by Boris Shatz, as part of the Bezalel School of Art that also he founded, and began to collect works by Jewish artists, archaeological relics and local ethnographical artifacts of Jews from Middle Eastern countries. The 1930s marked a milestone in the development of museums, as result of German Jews' arrival in Eretz Yisrael, bringing with them artistic trends and collections that were not present previously. During that period, works by Jewish artists, Dutch paintings from the seventeenth century, and French paintings from the nineteenth and twentieth centuries were acquired and the museum collection of graphic arts was started. After World War II, it became a repository for many art objects belonging to people who had been killed during the war. These collections formed the foundation for the collections of the Israel Museum, which was founded in 1965.

Israel–Knowledge Discovery

The 1970s and 1980s were a vital period of growth during which new museums of many types were established.[18] During this period, more than 80 heritage museums and sites were established in *moshavot* (rural towns) and *kibbutzim* throughout the country, to commemorate the nation-building, pre-State era.[19] Many of them were established through local initiative and later gained public recognition and support.[20,21] This trend continued into the 1990s, when museums became progressively more interactive and began to rely less on collections of objects.

The interactive trend is evident in both science museums, such as Bloomfield Science Museum in Jerusalem, and historical museum, such as those in Ein Shemer and Yifat. In addition, art museums that are also based less on a collection and more on changing exhibits of contemporary art were founded in Herzliya, Tefen, and other places.

Museums in Jerusalem

A large concentration of museums is located in Jerusalem. Some of them were established during the Mandatory period (1917–1948), some in the period after the establishment of the State in 1948 and the rest in the 1970s.

During the British Mandate, the following, mostly archeological, museums were established or refurbished: *Greek Orthodox Patriarchate Museum* in the Old City of Jerusalem; The *Museum for Islamic Art* on the Temple Mount in the Old City (1923), which is dedicated to Islamic artistic traditions and craftsmanship and the *Franciscan Biblical Museum*, on the Via Dolorosa in the Old City (1902) which houses archeological artifacts that were excavated by Franciscan archeologists.

The Rockefeller Museum was founded outside of the Old City walls in 1938, with a donation from John D. Rockefeller, Jr. It was designed by the British architect Austen Harrison, who combined concepts of Western architecture with Eastern influences. The museum still exists and is now managed by the Israel Museum. Its archeological displays are arranged chronologically; most were unearthed during Mandatory period excavations, including those at Megiddo, Samaria, Beit Shean, Lachish, Jericho, Ha'i, Tel Beit Marsis, Beit Shemesh, and Gezer.

The largest and most important museum in Israel, *The Israel Museum, Jerusalem* was dedicated in 1965. The museum, which is currently (2009) undergoing extensive renovations, has important collections in the fields of archaeology, ethnography, and Judaica, in addition to Israeli and world art. The archeological displays are arranged chronologically, beginning with the pre-historic era and continuing until medieval times. It includes a hall display of the cultures of neighboring countries and the religion and ritual of the Biblical world.

The Judaica and Jewish Ethnography Wing preserves Jewish ritual objects from Jewish communities around the world, including two synagogues, one from Italy (seventeenth century) and one from Germany (eighteenth century) that were moved to the museum in their entirety. The museum's Judaica collection is one of the largest in the world and it includes important manuscripts, including the Rothschild Miscellany, the Birds Head Haggadah, and the Cassuto Pentateuch.

A separate building, The Shrine of the Book, houses the Dead Sea Scrolls, which were accidentally discovered in a cave at Qumran (near the Dead Sea) in 1947, and were written by the Essenes during the Second Temple period (second century B.C.E. to the first century C.E.) (see Figs. 5 and 6).

It is interesting to note that other than the Israel Museum's Judaica collection and several small collections in small museums (the Ein Harod Museum of Art and the Italian Synagogue in Jerusalem), most Judaica collections are located outside of Israel, in hundreds of Jewish museums around the world.[20]

Since the 1970s, Jerusalem is again seeing a period of growth and the construction of new museums. *Tower of David—Museum of the History of Jerusalem*, at the Jaffa Gate to the Old City, presents the story of Jerusalem throughout the 4000 years of its history and the central events of each period, with emphasis on the city's importance to the three major monotheistic religions. It is

Fig. 5 The Shrine of the Book, Israel Museum.
Source: The Israel Museum.

Israel–Knowledge Discovery

Israel–Knowledge Discovery

Fig. 6 The Shrine of the Book, Israel Museum.
Source: The Israel Museum.

housed in the Citadel and includes carefully tended, internal archaeological garden.

The L. A. Mayer Museum for Islamic Art was opened in 1974 and consists of nine galleries, staged in chronological order, displaying the beliefs and art of Islamic civilization. *The Bible Lands Museum*, Jerusalem, (1992) focuses on biblical history through ancient Near Eastern art, from the dawn of civilization through the early Christian era. The museum illustrates the culture of all the people mentioned in the Bible from Egypt eastward, across the Fertile Crescent to Afghanistan, and from Nubia, north to the Caucasian mountains.

Art Museums

In addition to the art collection of the Israel Museum, there are other art museums and many small galleries. The most prominent art museum is the *Tel Aviv Museum* that was founded in 1932 at the initiative of the city's mayor at the time. Meir Dizengoff, who acted to collect outstanding works by Jewish and non-Jewish artists. The museum's Israeli and international collection incorporates a wide range of the paintings, sculptures, drawings, and prints from the impressionist, postimpressionist, modern and contemporary periods. The collection of Israeli artists includes a representative cross-section from the earliest days of Israeli art up to the works of today's current artists. The museum's changing exhibits feature both group and individual shows of Israeli and international artists.

Other art museums include: *The Haim Attar Museum of Art Ein Harod*, which is one of the oldest and largest museums in an agricultural settlement, founded in 1938. The museum building is an architectonic creation that is adapted to the conditions of the local natural lighting and blends into its surroundings. The collections are representative of Israeli art, with emphasis on artists from the Kibbutz Movement, and Jewish folk art from many Jewish ethnic groups.

The Haifa Art Museum was founded in 1951 and primarily deals with Israeli art. *The Museum of Israeli Art* in Ramat Gan was founded in 1987 and is located in a former industrial building that was converted into a museum while preserving its former character. The display is based on changing exhibitions devoted solely to Israeli art of many genres, painting, sculpture, photography, cinema, design, and graphic arts. There is a sculpture garden next to the museum.

In addition to the many galleries, there are also museums that are dedicated to the work of a single artists, for example the *Nachum Gutman Art Museum*; the *Manne Katz Museum*, Haifa; the *Janco-Dada Museum*, Ein Hod devoted to the works of Marcel Janco; and the *Rubin Museum* located in the former Tel Aviv home of painter Reuven Rubin, one of Israel's pioneering modern artists, whose paintings give expression to the life and landscape of Israel.

Archaeological Museums

Many museums in Israel are devoted to local archaeology and most of them focus on findings from an adjacent excavation site. One example is the recently opened *Masada Museum* that displays findings from the rebellion against Rome and the fall of Masada.

Other Israeli museums feature broad archaeological collections. In addition to the *Israel Museum* and the *Rockefeller Museum* (see above), there is the *Eretz Yisrael Museum* with more than 100,000 artifacts and the *Museum of Prehistory of the Hula Valley* at Kibbutz Maayan Baruch in the Upper Galilee with a large collection of more than 120,000 prehistorical findings and ethnographical exhibits from around the world, which illustrate the lifestyle of early humankind.

There are also many artifacts in the collections of small museums in smaller towns throughout the country.

Historical Museums

Throughout Israel there are many historical museums devoted to telling local stories of the people, settlements and organizations which played a role in settling the land and establishing the State.

Many museums concerned with the history of Jewish settlement in Eretz Yisrael are found around the country, some located in the historical buildings where the activities represented actually occurred. In these museums, the emphasis is on the settlement's nascent period, as expressed in a historical collection of documents, photographs, and artifacts from the local material culture including agricultural implements, clothing, and toys. *The Tower and Stockade Museum* at Kibbutz Hanita in the Galilee displays not only to the history of the kibbutz but also the Zionist enterprise of the tower and stockade (*homa u'migdal*) settlements.

The largest historical museums are *Rishon Lezion History Museum* and *The K'han Museum* in Hadera, which has the largest collection of artifacts from the history of early Zionist settlement. Located in an agricultural building from the Ottoman period, the K'han Museum houses archival documents as well as objects, household utensils, furniture clothing, and decorative objects, as well as agricultural implements and medical instruments from different communities. Many cities, towns, and rural settlements have "Founders Rooms."

The Ministry of Defense Museums' Unit brings together a dozen museums that have a joint collection of many thousand artifacts representing the history of the Jewish defense forces in Eretz Yisrael and their development from the beginning of the *Hibbat Zion* movement (1880s) through the modern military development of the Israel Defense Forces. The Defense Ministry museums include *Beit Hashomer*, Kfar Giladi; *Beit Hagedudim*, Avihail; *Hapalmach Museum, Hagana Museum, Ha'etzel Museum*, and *Lechi Museum* in Tel Aviv; and the *Clandestine Immigration and Naval Museum* in Haifa.

The unique *Herzl Museum* in Jerusalem offers information about Theodor Herzl and his Zionist vision for the State of Israel.

Since Israel is a country that has absorbed immigrants from many countries, museums have been established to tell the story of these different communities. Examples include the *Babylonian Jewry Heritage Center* in Or Yehuda, the *Rabbi Shalom Shabazi Yemenite Jewish Heritage House* in Rosh Ha'ayin, and the *Memorial Museum of Hungarian Speaking Jewry* in Safed.

Holocaust heritage museums

Several museums have been established in Israel to document the memory and terrifying stories of the Holocaust perpetrated by the Nazis against the Jews during World War II. This category includes the *Yad Vashem Museum, The Ghetto Fighters' House—Itzhak Katzenelson Holocaust and Jewish Resistance Heritage Museum, Yad Mordechai Museum, Massuah Interactive Educational Museum* at Kibbutz Tel Yitzhak, and the *Diaspora Museum*.

Yad Vashem Museum in Jerusalem was established in 1953, in accordance with the provisions of Holocaust and Heroes' Remembrance–Yad Vashem Law. The Museum now resides in new building that was designed by architect Moshe Safdie and includes an impressive display using many different types of media to depict events during the Holocaust in chronological order, with emphasis placed on human-personal stories. Yad Vashem houses a documentary archive of the Holocaust (see the section on Archives). The museum includes the Hall of Names where the names of the individual victims are stored as well as

other unique memorial sites: the Valley of the Communities, the Children's Memorial, and The Hall of Remembrance.

Ghetto Fighters'House—Itzhak Katzenelson Jewish Resistance Heritage Museum at Kibbutz Lohamei Hagetaot in the Western Galilee was founded in 1949 by a community of Holocaust survivors, members of the Jewish underground in the ghettos of Poland and veteran of partisan units. The exhibitions include the background of the Jewish communities before the Holocaust and the Jewish resistance during the Holocaust.

Beit Hatefutsoth—The Nachum Goldman Museum of Jewish Diaspora in Tel Aviv was established in 1978 to convey the story of the Jewish people from the time of their expulsion from the Eretz Yisrael 2500 years ago to the present. The museum is unique because the exhibits are arranged by topic, rather than chronologically.

Science and Nature Museums

Israel has two relatively small science museums: one in Haifa, the *National Museum of Science, Technology and Space*, founded in 1984, and *the Bloomfield Science Museum* in Jerusalem. These museums emphasize understanding scientific principles rather than collections.

There are several small museums devoted to nature, agricultural, and local history at locations throughout Israel, including *Beit Ussishkin Nature Museum* at Kibbutz Dan in the Upper Galilee and *Yigal Alon Museum of Man in the Galilee* which focuses on the landscape of the Galilee during different historical periods. Among its exhibits is an ancient boat, dated from the first century C. E., known as the "Jesus Boat," which was discovered on the shores of the Sea of Galilee in 1986.

The Arab Sector

The Arab sector still lacks significant museums, despite several attempts that have been made, some in cooperation with the Ministry of Culture's Museum Department, to establish some. These attempts have been made in Uhm El-Fahm, Shefaram and the Druze Museum in Jat-Yanuch. There are also small, private exhibitions, which are not recognized as museums, in Ussifiya, Daliyat-El-Carmel, Shibli, and elsewhere.

Official Recognition of Museums

In Israel today, there are approximately 200 museum-like institutions but only 53 are officially recognized according to the Museums Law of 1983, which established a procedure for official recognition of museums. Recognition of a museum entitles it to financial support from the State, via the Ministry of Culture. A recognized museum is required to meet professional standards regarding the employment of professional staff members, proper preservation of displays, record keeping, descriptive and photographic records of the exhibits, and making information about them available to the public. This law states that a museum's management is to be granted freedom of action, as long as it complies with its bylaws and budget.

The Ministry of Culture, through its Museums Department, works to ensure that recognized museums comply with the law and regulations, guides museums through the process of receiving recognition and advises museums in the process of being established. By law, a 21-member public board of directors advises the heads of ministry's Museum Department on matters of policy and budgetary allocations to recognized museums. In addition, some museums receive funding from municipalities. The remainder of the budget is covered by independent income and contributions from the private sector.

In 2005, there were 3,110,393 visits to the 53 budgeted museums. Of these 21% were guided tours for pupils. In addition, 23,299 teachers took in-service training courses given by museums.[22]

Professional Education

Two Israeli universities have diploma programs in Museology. At Haifa University the program is part of humanities faculty and meets 2 days/week for 1 year while the Tel Aviv University program is in the arts faculty and meets 1 day/week for 2 years.

ARCHIVES

The Archives Law and the State Archives

The beginning of legislation regarding archival material dates to the period of the British Mandate and dealt with keeping court files (1935). After the establishment of the State (1948), the Antiquities Ordinance (1935) protected books and manuscripts produced before 1700. The preservation of newer materials was covered by the Archives Law in 1955. This law establishes arrangements for all archival material existing in Israel, with particular emphasis on official material (from government ministries, the Knesset, the judiciary, government corporations, and local authorities). According to this law, the system is headed by the State Archivist, who is appointed by the Prime Minister and manages the Israel State Archives, established in 1949. The State Archivist is responsible for implementation of the law. One function of the State Archive is to receive for deposit all archival material dating from before the establishment of the State, from government institutions and local authorities that have ceased to exist and from all government institutions and local authorities that are inactive and which have value for permanent preservation. An additional function, related to the first, is supervision of the archival arrangements in state institutions and local authorities. This is the source of the legal requirement that none of the aforementioned institutions may dispose any material, except in accordance with the guidelines and regulations. Any person may use material deposited in the State Archives, dependent on limitations related to its type and period of closure. In order to ensure the preservation of archival material in the possession of individuals, which has value for the study of the past, the people, the state, or society, the State Archivist manages a register, based on the declaration given by the person who owns or possesses it. In order to protect the individual's rights, the Archivist is not permitted to read this material without the agreement of the person who owns or possesses it. The law permits taking archival material out of the country only if the Archivist is permitted to read and copy it or if he waives this requirement.[23,24]

Regulations for the practical implementation of the Archives Law were added later: regulations regarding transferring archival material to storage; regulations regarding the management of public archives (see below); regulations regarding use of archival material deposited in the archive, including those with limited access rights; regulations usage fees and regarding the disposal of archival material by state institutions and local authorities.

The State Archives fulfills the functions enumerated in the law using a structure that includes the following departments: Research and Public Services, Supervision and Training Unit, Preservation and Restoration Laboratory, Audio-visual Department, Information and Registration Department, Computerization Department, Division for State Documents, Memorials and Official Publications and Repository. The archival material deposited in the National Archive includes 40,000 linear meters (43,744 linear yards) of shelves with 3,750,000 files; 1500 movies and videos; 150,000 photographs and negatives, and 10,000 audio recordings. One million documents have been digitalized and half of them can be accessed via the Internet. The aforementioned audiovisual material has also been digitalized. There is a computerized registry of all paper materials on the record group and subrecord group levels and of 70% on the file level. A portion of this computerized system is accessible to readers in the reading room. In 2004, the State Archives adopted the International Standard for Records Management (ISO 15489) and is preparing to develop a comprehensive program for managing and preserving electronic records. The program is being adapted to Israel's unique needs. (http://www. archives.gov.il/ArchiveGov Information received from Assaf Tractinsky, head of the Information and Records Department of the State Archives.)

Branch Archives

There are also archives that are branches of the State Archives. The most important of these is the *I.D.F. &*

Israel–Knowledge Discovery

Defense Establishment Archives, which was established in 1948 and includes, in addition to materials from these institutions, documentation on the underground organizations that preceded the establishment of the State, the Jewish volunteers who fought in the world wars and a collection on Jewish soldiers beginning in the nineteenth century. This archive includes approximately 9 million files; audiovisual documentation (approximately 10,000 videos recordings, approximately 65,000 audio recordings, and approximately 500,000 photographs and negatives), maps, drawings, and digital documentation. Approximately 5 million pages of declassified, scanned documents are accessible to readers in accordance with the Archives Law, 50 years after their creation. Since security, the military, and society in Israel are closely intertwined, information related to the fields of the education, culture, medicine, economics, religion, and the law can be found in this archive. (Information received from Mihal Tzur, Manager, *I.D.F.& Defense Establishment Archives*.)

Other branch archives of the National Archives are the *Ben Gurion Heritage Institute Archives* at Sde Boker, *The Yitzhak Rabin Center for Israeli Studies Archives*, and the *Menahem Begin Heritage Foundation Archives*.[25,26]

Municipal Archives

Although the Archives Law allows the depositing the archives of local authorities in the State Archives (see above), the State Archivist's policy was to develop special local archives in the older cities and towns, in order to develop local heritage. Not only administrative materials from the local authorities are deposited in these archives but also the archives of institutions, organizations, economic corporations, and individuals who were active there. The archives also house photographs, city publications, announcements, posters, and maps. Local authorities maintain 54 historical archives with the most important being in the three largest cities.[27]

The Jerusalem City Archives was established in 1963. The earliest material in the archive dates from the mid-eighteenth century and belongs to the Sephardic Community Committee record group. The municipality, itself, was established only in 1863 by the Ottoman authorities. There is a small amount of material remaining from that period, beginning from 1892 (records of city council decisions). From the British period (1917–1948), there remains continuous documentation of the city council and various municipal departments. This sequence continues after the establishment of the State of Israel, when Jerusalem became its capital. From the years following 1948, the archive also includes documentation of the city's mayors, deputy mayors, councilors, the bureaus of the city managers and their deputies, and various advisors to the mayor (a total of 502 subrecord groups and series). The archive also houses 53 record groups for various institutions that

have closed such as the Jerusalem Community Committee and the City Committee; 15 archives of neighborhood committees and 89 from schools that have ceased to exist. In addition, there are 93 economic archives and personal archives of professionals (architects, engineers, accountants), educators, artists, authors, and rabbis. The total size of the historical archive is 4000 linear meters (4374 linear yards) of shelves. There is a computerized archival management system. The municipal archive is also responsible for the city's records management. (Information received from Michael Mahler manager of the Jerusalem City Archives and Menahem Levin, the former manager of the city archive.)

The Municipal Archives Tel-Aviv—Yafo houses material beginning with the establishment of the Ahuzat Bayit Association in the 1906 and minutes of the Yafo Community Committee from 1896 to 1898. The historical archive was opened to the public in 1971. It was preceded by the municipal records center. Today there are two branches of the municipal archive department. There are 38 record groups in the archive for city departments, archives of the cultural, sports, and commercial organizations, etc., including the files of 28 mayors, deputy mayors, members of the city management and councilors and 11 record groups of personal archives and private documents. Furthermore, it houses collections of municipal publications, posters, and maps. The total shelf length is 1500 linear meters (1640 linear yards). There is a computerized system for recording and retrieving information. The photographic collection is digitalized.[28] (Information received from Ziona Raz, manager of the The Municipal Archives Tel-Aviv—Yafo.)

The Haifa City Archives was founded in 1977 and includes 2000 linear meters (2187 linear yards) of shelves. The earliest material is from the Hebrew Community Committee and neighborhood committees in 1920s, with city council records starting in 1926. Most of the material comes from the municipality and its institutions but there are also 45 private archives from individual and institutions that are valuable for the history of the city. The archive is also responsible for managing municipal records. (Information received from Mihal Hankin, manager of the Haifa City Archives.)

Public Archives

The Archives Law recognizes "public archives," which are defined as "an archive that is owned or managed by a non-profit organization and recognized by the government as a 'public archive,' in an announcement published in the Official Record."[29] There are 17 public archives that have been recognized on the basis of this definition. (Additional information on the most important may be found below.) According to the Regulations regarding Arrangements for Managing Public Archives, a public archive can be recognized if it has bylaws that define its purposes and missions; the conditions for permitting study and use of the material and if the archive has the organizational and financial necessary to develop its activity. The managers of public archives must submit an annual report to the State Archivist. The public archive category includes historical, administrative, and documentary archives, the archives of political movements and memorial organizations. Each of the public archives has a library to supplement the archival collection. In addition to books on the subject, they also include collections of newspapers and periodicals, which contain some unique and rare copies.[30]

The Central Archives for the History of the Jewish People, Jerusalem (CAHJP) was founded in 1939 by the Historical Society of Israel for the purpose of reconstructing an unbroken chain of historical documentation that reflects the collective past of the Jewish people. It was reorganized in 1969. The collection includes 6000 linear meters (6561 linear yards) of shelf space of material gathered from 1600 archives of communities, organizations, and individuals; 9 million frames of microfilmed documents; 2000 lists of documents and files concerning Jews held by in other archives; 12,000 photographs; 8000 publications; 1 million newspaper clippings; and 12,000 books and publications on Jewish history. The archive includes materials from the entire Jewish Diaspora.[31]

The Central Zionist Archives (CZA) (Fig. 7) was established in Berlin in 1919 and serves as an historical archive of the World Zionist Organization, the Jewish Agency, the National Funds, and the World Jewish Congress, documenting the growth of the Zionist movement around the world, from its beginnings in the 1880s. When the Nazi rose to power in 1933, the archive was moved to Jerusalem. Since then it has acquired the function of the being the historical archive of the new Jewish settlement in Eretz Yisrael. In parallel, it was decided to

systematically collect the personal archives of leaders of the Zionist movement and the pre-State Jewish settlements. It also continued to collect books, periodicals, and photographs. When the State was established in 1948, many files from the Jewish Agency and National Committee, whose functions were transferred to ministries of the new government, were deposited in the CZA. The rapid growth of the collections and the poor storage conditions led to the decision to build a special building for the CZA, the first of its kind in Israel. It was dedicated in 1987. In the 1990s, CZA undertook computerize its collections and a massive effort began to enter the titles of thousands of files and other collections into the computer. Since then the CZA has scanned over 14 million documents, 350,000 photographs, 90,000 maps and settlement plans, 26,000 posters, and 1,200,000 cards containing genealogical information, and 1600 sound recording. The CZA is currently adapting a Web-based document management system to manage its data- and image-base with the intention of making its records available to the wider public. The archive houses 10,000 linear meters (10,936 linear yards) of archival material divided into approximately 400 organizational record groups and 1200 personal archives. There are 500,000 photographs, 50,000 maps and plans, more than 18,000 posters and flyers, and 13,000 newspapers and periodicals. In cooperation with the Hebrew University, the archive manages the *Steven Spielberg Jewish Film Archive* that includes more than 3000 film and video titles. In addition to the customary services to scholars and other interested people, it is notable that CZA has developed a genealogy department and educational activities.[32,33] (Information received from Rochalle Rubinstein, deputy manager of the CZA.)

The Yad Vashem Archives was established in 1953, as part of the Holocaust Martyrs' and Heroes' Remembrance Authority. Its purpose to document the history of the

Israel–Knowledge Discovery

Fig. 7 The Central Zionist Archives.
Source: Central Zionist Archives.

Jewish people during the Holocaust period, preserving the life stories and memories of each one of the 6 million who perished and transmitting the heritage of the Holocaust to coming generations. Gathering materials for the archive began in 1946. It is the world's largest collection of materials related to the Holocaust, with 62 million documents, more than 268,000 photographs, tens of thousands of testimonies dictated, recorded or videotaped by Holocaust survivors in Israel and abroad. There are also several thousand original film titles including raw materials, cinema newsreels, amateur movies, propaganda films, and more. The Hall of Names is designed to remember the Jewish victims in the Holocaust as human beings and individuals. It currently includes more than 3 million names, gathered from more than 2 million Pages of Testimony and other lists of victims. Yad Vashem has scanned all of the Pages of Testimony and photographs, and has computerized systems to locate and retrieve information.[34]

The Labor Archives was founded in 1932 by the Histadrut. Since 1982, it has been part of the *Pinhas Lavon Institute for Labor Research*. It was founded for the purpose of gathering archival material from all Histadrut institutions and from individuals and organizations that were active in Eretz Yisrael from the beginning of the twentieth century. Its record groups include ones for material originating in the Histadrut, its institutions, organizations, and departments; political organizations related to the labor movement; youth movements from the labor sector; the Labor Movement overseas; archives of the Workers Councils and of individuals, for a total of 170,000 files. There are also departments of oral testimony, photographs (approximately 50,000), in addition to a collection of approximately 10,000 glass negatives taken by the photographer Avraham Suskin and a collection of photographs (approximately 500,000) from the newspaper *Davar*, videos, and posters.[35] (Information received from Alexandra Tumarinson, manager of the Labor Archives.)

The Jabotinsky Institute in Israel was established in 1933 for the purpose of gathering documents, publications, and photographs related to Ze'ev Jabotinsky and the Revisionist Zionist Movement. The archive holds 366 personal archives of leaders of the Revisionist Movement, including that of Ze'ev Jabotinsky and 188 archives relating to all branches of the movement and its institutions, in Israel and abroad, including the New Zionist Organization (N.Z.O), the Beitar Youth Movement, the National Labor Federation, etc. Additional collections include oral documentation (550 files of testimony and 1000 recordings), approximately 35,000 photographs, 150 films and videos, 300 flags, and several hundred stamps. There is a computerized system to search and retrieve the aforementioned information.[36] (Information received from Masha Zolotarevsky and Amira Stern, manager of the Archive.)

Kibbutz Movement Archives are a special type of public archive where materials originating in the central institutions of the five movements, each with its own ideology,

of economically and socially collective settlements in Eretz Yisrael and the State of Israel. Several of the movements merged and this process is evident in the organization of their archives: *Yad Tabenkin Archive* at Efal, *The Takam* (United Kibbutz Movement) *Archive* at Hulda and *The Hashomer Hatzair* (Young Gard) *Archive* at Givat Haviva, as distinguished from the *Kibbutz Hadati* (Religious Kibbutz Movement) *Archive* at Kvutzat Yavne.[37–41] (Information received from Milca Har-Tal, Yad Tabenkin Archive.)

The common denominator of these archives is that, in addition to administrative record groups, they include the archives of the movements' allied youth movements, in Israel and overseas, as well as the relevant political parties, educational institutions, personal archives, publications, and journals. Each of these archives has a computerized archive management system that includes work stations for employees and the public. Most of the collections are computerized.

The archive that has gathered the largest collection is that of Yad Tabenkin, because of its position in the merged movement. Founded in 1957 as the archive of *Hakibbutz Hameuhad* ("The United Kibbutz," 1927–1980), it was housed at Ein Harod. In 1975, it was moved to Hakibbutz Hameuhad's seminar center in Efal, where it is part of an educational-research complex. With merger of Hakibbutz Hameuhad and *Ihud HaKvutzot veHaKibbutzim* (Union of the Kvutzot and Kibbutzim, see below) and the establishment of the United Kibbutz Movement in 1980, material generated in the new movement was divided between Yad Tabenkin and the United Kibbutz Movement Archive at Hulda (see below). This arrangement continued until 2000, when *Hakibbutz Ha'artzi* (The National Kibbutz) joined the United Kibbutz Movement to form The Kibbutz Movement. Since then, all material created by the new organization has been deposited at Yad Tabenkin, which has 543 record groups and subrecord groups, 240 personal archives, and 2500 linear meters (2734 linear yards) of files. In addition, there are approximately 100,000 photographs, 1600 posters, and 2000 audio recordings. The archive is in the process of digitalizing its documents and photographs. *The Takam Archive* at Hulda was founded in 1963 and incorporated the archives of *Hever Hakvutzot* ("League of *Kvutzot*," 1925–1951) and the *Ihud HaKvutzot veHaKibbutzim* (1951–1980). Until 2000, materials from some departments of the United Kibbutz Movement were deposited here but since then, no new material has been added. The archive has 919 linear meters (1005 linear yards) of shelf space.

The Hashomer Hatzair Archive at Givat Haviva was founded in 1937 at Kibbutz Merhavia and belongs to *Hakibbutz Ha'artzi* of Hashomer Hatzair. In 1982, it was transferred to Givat Haviva and became part of the movement's *Yad Ya'ari* ideological and documentation center. It includes 2680 linear meters (2930 linear yards)

Israel–Knowledge Discovery

of shelf with approximately 200,000 photographs, approximately 1000 posters, 3220 audio and/or video recordings and the approximately 600 flags and other museum-type exhibits.

The Kibbutz Hadati Archive was founded in the 1976 and includes administrative material from the movement dating from 1931 and other materials related to religious Zionism, going back to 1917. In addition, to material from the movement offices, other affiliated institutions deposit material in this archive, which houses 7000 administrative files, 3200 files of collections, 16,800 photographs, and approximately 1500 audiovisual items.

The Jewish National and University Library (see above) includes five archival departments: The *Albert Einstein Archives*, which includes scientific, public, and personal material that was transferred from Princeton to the National Library in 1982 (also includes rare material on Sir Isaac Newton). *The Manuscripts and Archives Department* was founded in 1968 (previously, from 1923 to 1968, archives were cataloged as Judaica). In 2006, the manuscripts were separated from the archive, which became the Archives Department, which incorporates 450 personal archives of intellectual leaders of the Jewish world, including Martin Buber, S.Y. Agnon, and Else Lasker-Schüler. It also houses archives of living people including author A.B. Yehoshua and poet Haim Gouri, plus 40 archives from institutions and settlements and 300 collections of various types. (http://www.jnul.huji.ac.il/eng/col_special.html, Information received from Rachel Mashrati, Archives Department, The Jewish National and University Library.)

The Music Department began operations in the 1964 and its importance increased in 2000 when the law requiring mandatory deposit of publications was expanded to include audiovisual materials. It is divided into two sections: the department itself and the National Sound Archives. The Department houses collections of notated Jewish music from the sixteenth century to the current day; 225 personal archives of Jewish and Israeli composers from the last century; 25 archives from musical institutions, and other relevant research materials. Recordings of Jewish music of all types and of other ethnic groups in Eretz Yisrael (Arab Moslems, Christian communities, Circassians, and Druze) are deposited in the National Sound Archives. The collection began in the 1920s and includes 30,000 hr of recordings. In addition, there are 10,000 hr of the ethnographic documentation, 15,000 hr of commercial recordings, and 5000 that were deposited by the Israel Broadcast Authority. (Information received from Dr. Gila Flam, manager of the Music Department and National Sound Archives, The Jewish National and University Library)

The newest archive is *Israeli Internet Sites Archive*, an experimental attempt to preserve copies of Internet sites in their entirety.

Archival Science as a Discipline and Profession

Until the middle of the twentieth century, Israeli archival science inherited the traditions that the first archivists brought from Germany and was also strongly influenced by the British (H. Jenkinson) and American (T. Shellenberg) schools, which were accepted during that period. Only in the late twentieth century and the early twenty-first century were echoes of new streams of thought, such as the social value of archives and the influence of the macroappraisal theory and practice. Despite the existence of programs for educating archivists and the work of certified licensed archivists, the law does not require someone to have professional certification, in order to manage an archive. Either an academic diploma or 5 years of experience is considered sufficient.

Educating Archivists

During the 1950s, archivists were educated through on-the-job training. In 1960–1961, the Hebrew University held the first course for certified archivists. Beginning in the early 1970s, these courses became part of the Hebrew University School of Library, Archive and Information Studies. Until its closure in 2003, this was the only institution in the country that granted a diploma or master's degree in the profession.

The Information Science Department of Bar-Ilan University teaches several individual courses that deal with archival science.

Parallel to the university programs, the National Archives, the civil service commissioner, municipalities, the Israel Archivists Association, and the Kibbutz Movement also hold courses for archivists and records managers. Each course is designed for different sector working in the field of archives. These courses train people on a practical level. In the 1990s, at the initiative of the State Archives and the Israel Archivists Association, three colleges: Max Stern Academic College of Emek Yezreel, Beit Berl Academic College, and David Yellin College of Education began to offer programs at the bachelor's degree level toward a certified archivists diploma.[42]

PROFESSIONAL ASSOCIATIONS

The first attempt to organize an archives association was in 1951 but the Israel Archive Association (IAA) was not founded until 1956. Its members included both representatives of archives and individual members but only institutional members were permitted to sit on the Board of Directors until 1982 when permission was given for individual members to join the board. This trend gained strength as the number of individual members grew and in 1993, IAA became an organization consisting solely of individual members with elected institutions and the current name, Israel Archivists Association, was adopted. Throughout its existence, the Association's primary activity consisted of professional in-service training courses on various levels and professional ranking of its members. It is a member of the International Council on Archives and members of the IAA have served as officers and committee members of the international organization. The Association sponsors three publications: an annual professional journal *Arkhiyyon*, *Meida* ("Information") a quarterly review, and *Studies in Archives*, which publishes transcripts of lectures from seminar days. The IAA has an Internet site in Hebrew.[43] (Updated to 2007 by Zohar Alufi, Chairperson of the Israeli Archives Association.)

ACKNOWLEDGMENTS

We wish to thank the following people who kindly provided us with current information on agencies referred to in this entry:

Victor Ben Naim, Director, Department of Libraries, Ministry of Science, Culture and Sport.

Idit Amihai, Director, Department of Museums, Ministry of Science, Culture and Sport.

Shlomit Nemlih, Consultant, Department of Museums, Ministry of Science, Culture and Sport.

Israel–Knowledge Discovery

REFERENCES

1. Israel Central Bureau of Statistics, Press Release, 2007. Available at http://www1.cbs.gov.il/hodaot2007/11_07_07b.doc.

2. Israel Central Bureau of Statistics, Press Release, 2007. Available at http://www1.cbs.gov.il/www/hodaot2008n/01_08_275b.doc.

3. Schidorsky, D. *Library and Books in Late Ottoman Eretz Israel*; Magnes Press: Jerusalem, Israel, 1990; (Hebrew).

4. Schidorsky, D. The emergence of libraries in the Jewish community in Eretz Israel. In *The History of the Jewish Community in Eretz-Israel Since 1882: The Construction of Hebrew Culture in Eretz-Israel*; Shavit, Z., Ed.; The Israel Academy for Sciences and Humanities, The Bialik Institute: Jerusalem, Israel, 1998; 367–396 Part 1; (Hebrew).

5. Shidorsky, D. From the "Abarbanel" Library to the Jewish National and University Library—The years of the British Mandate. In *Libraries and Book Collections*; Kaplan, Y., Sluhovsky, M., Eds.; The Zalman Shazar Center for Jewish History: Jerusalem, Israel, 2006; 369–411.

6. Schidorsky, D. Samuel Hugo Bergman and his role in shaping the Jewish National and University Library. Cathedra Q. Hist. Eretz Yisrael its Yishuv **1995**, *76*, 116–146.

7. Committee for Changing the Status of the National Library, *Report*, The Committee: Jerusalem, Israel, 2004.

8. Adler, E. University library cooperation in Israel: The MALMAD consortium. Info. Technol. Libr. **1999**, *18*(3), 135–138.

9. Shoham, S. Public libraries adaptation to the environment. Public Libr. Q. **1988**, *9*(1), 25–33.

10. Israel Ministry of Education and Culture, Department of Libraries, *Survey on School Libraries*, Jerusalem, Israel, 1996; (Hebrew).

11. Israel Central Bureau of Statistics, Local Authorities in Israel, 2005 (Publication no. 1295) () (Hebrew). Available at http://www.cbs.gov.il/publications/local_authorities2005/pdf/080_081.pdf.

12. Frenkiel, L. Israel. *Medical Librarianship in the Eighties and Beyond*; Picken, F.M., Kahn, A.M.C., Eds.; Mansell: London, U.K., 1986.

13. Sever, S. The Arab library in Israel. Libr. Q. **1979**, *49*(2l), 163–181.

14. Nebenzahl, O. School libraries in the Israeli minority sector Paper presented at the IASL Conference Ramat Gan, Israel July, 5–10, 1998.

15. Sever, I.; Shmuel, S. *The Library in Society*; Israeli Center for Libraries: Jerusalem, Israel, 1997; (Hebrew).

16. Shay, O. *The Beginning of Museums and Collections in Late Ottoman Eretz Israel (1848–1917)*; Bar-Ilan University: Ramat Gan, Israel, 2006; Ph.D. Dissertation; (Hebrew).

17. Kol-Inbar, Y. *The History of Museums in Eretz Yisrael before the Establishment of the State as an Expression of the Zionist Vision*; Hebrew University of Jerusalem: Jerusalem, Israel, 1992; M.A. Thesis, (Hebrew).

18. Shalev, A. Introduction. In *Museums in Israel*; Inbar, J., Shiler, E., Eds.; Ariel: Jerusalem, Israel, 1995; (Hebrew).

19. Katriel, T. *Performing the Past: A Study of Israeli Settlement Museums*; Lawrence Belrraum Associates: Mahwah, NJ, 1997.

20. Inbar, Y. Towards a history and characterization of museums in Israel. Ariel **1990**, *12*, 17–28.

21. Katriel, T. Sites of memory: discourses of the past in Israel pioneering settlements. Q. J. Speech **1994**, *80*(1), 1–20.

22. Karmeli, A., Ed. *Museums in Israel: The Annual Activities 2005*; Ministry of Science, Culture and Sport, The Center for Information and Cultural Research: Tel Aviv, Israel, 2006; (Pilat Report) (Hebrew).

23. Alsberg, P.A. The Israeli Archives Law—A retrospect after 30 years. Miscellanea Carlos Wyffels, Archives et Bibliotheques the Belgique **1987**, *57*, 13–49.

24. Israeli Archives Law; State of Israel, Archives Law-5715–1955. Archivum. Conseil International des Archives **1961**, *XI*, 176–179.

25. http://bgarchives.bgu.ac.il/moreshet/English/index.html.

26. http://www.rabincenter.org.il/site/en/homepage.asp; http://www.begin.center.org.il.

27. Mossek, M. The Israeli State Archives and archives in local authorities. Arkhiyyon **1999**, *10–11*, 114–130.

28. Hebrew Website. Available at http://tel-aviv.millenium.org.il.

29. Israel Archives Law 5715-1955, Prime Minister Office. Jerusalem **2003**, *I*, 2 (Hebrew).

30. Israel Archives Law 5715-1955, Prime Minister Office. Jerusalem **2003**, *I*, 9–11 (Hebrew).

31. http://sites.huji.ac.il/archives/index1.html.

32. The World Zionist Organization, *The Future of our Past—The Central Zionist Archives and its Collections*, Bialik

Institute: Jerusalem, Israel, 1994; V–XXI. http://www.zionistarchives.org.il/ZA/pMain.aspx (accessed July 2007).

33. http://www.spielbergfilmarchive.org.il/about.htm.
34. http://www1.yadvashem.org.
35. http://yeda.amalnet.k12.il/LavonInstitute.
36. http://www.jabotinsky.org/archiv_h.htm.
37. Schenkolewski-Kroll, S. Training of "Kibbutz" Archivists: The transition from occupation to profession. Yad-Lakore **1994**, *29*, 19–26.
38. Schenkolewski-Kroll, S. El archivo del kibutz. In *El archivo, los archivos*; Gutiérrez Muñoz, C., Ed.; Instituto Panamericano de Geografía e Historia: Lima, Peru, 2001; 51–55.
39. http://www.givathaviva.org.il/english/.
40. http://www.yadtabenkin.org.il/ewelcome.htm.
41. Hebrew Web site. Available at http://www.kdati.org.il/info/archion/archion.htm.
42. Schenkolewski-Kroll, S. Archival education as part of Information Science Studies: The case of Israel. In *The Archival Science and Archival Education in the Electronic Age*, The 2nd Asia-Pacific Conference for Archival Educators and Trainers Tokyo, Japan October, 18–19, 2006 192–197.
43. Aloufi, Z. From Conference to Conference The Israeli Archives Association June 1950–February 1993, 1999 10–11, 131–169. Available at http://www.archives.org.il Arkhiyyon. (accessed January 2009).

BIBLIOGRAPHY

1. Cole, T. Nativation and nationalization: a comparative landscape study of holocaust museums in Israel, the US and the UK. J. Isr. Hist. **2004**, *23*(1), 130–145.
2. Fenichel, D. *Exhibiting Ourselves as Others: Jewish Museums in Israel*; Indiana University: Bloomington, IN, 2005; PhD Dissertation.
3. Golden, D. The Museum of the Jewish diaspora tells a story. In *The Tourist Image: Myths and Myth Making in Tourism*; Selwyn, T., Ed.; John Wiley & Sons: Chichester, U.K., 1996; 223–250.
4. Kedar, R. Bibliographic control in the State of Israel. Int. Cataloguing Bibliographic Control (IFLA) **2000**, *29*(2), 27–30.
5. Rosental, M.; Romm, D.; Getz, I. School libraries to media centers: Service to the children of Israel in the twenty-first century. Sch. Libr. Media Annu. **1995**, *13*, 150–156.
6. Rosovsky, N.; Ungerleider-Mayerson, J. *The Museums of Israel*; Harry N. Abrams, Publishers: New York, 1989.
7. Schenkolewski-Kroll, S.; Tractinsky, A. Archival description, information retrieval and the construction of thesauri in Israeli Archives. Archival Sci. **2006**, *6*(1), 69–107.
8. Shoham, S. Libraries and librarianship in Israel. IFLA J. **2000**, *26*(3), 165–176.
9. http://www.mod.gov.il/pages/heritage/welcome.asp (accessed January 2009).
10. http://www.ilmuseums.com (accessed January 2009).
11. http://www.icom.org.il (accessed July 2007).

Israel–Knowledge Discovery

Japan: Libraries, Archives, and Museums

Masaya Takayama
National Archives of Japan, Tokyo, Japan

Yoriko Miyabe
Rikkyo University, Tokyo, Japan

Toru Koizumi
Library, Rikkyo University, Tokyo, Japan

Hiroyuki Hatano
Surugadai University, Saitama, Japan

Abstract

This entry provides an overview of information services in Japan, with separate sections on libraries, archives, and museums. Libraries and collection of documents have a long history in Japan, based on a fundamental respect for written information and knowledge. Archives in Japan are divided into three main groups: public archives, university archives, and private archives including business archives. The history of modern museums in Japan dates back to the time of the Meiji Restoration. After examining the historical evolution of libraries, archives, and museums, the author discusses current trends and activities such as professional education, professional associations, digitization projects, and cooperative efforts.

GENERAL ORIENTATION

Consisting of over 3000 islands, Japan is an East Asian archipelago located in the north Pacific. It lies to the east of the People's Republic of China, North Korea, South Korea, and Russia. With over 127,704,000 residents, Japan is the 10th most populous country in the world and is a member of the United Nations, G8, and the OECD (Fig. 1).

HISTORICAL INTRODUCTION

It is difficult to say exactly when libraries first appeared in Japan. There must have been some collection of documents even before any library came into existence. In the sixth and seventh centuries A.D., the advent of Buddhism promoted an influx of Chinese classics and the arrival of scholars, as well as the growth of Japanese academic and publishing culture. With this, the importation of documents and the practice of archiving grew to significant proportions. The Bureau of Books and Drawings (*Zushoryo*), a government organization in charge of document storage in the ancient period, can be seen as early as 702, when it appeared in the *Taihoryo* (Taiho Code of Laws) that was promulgated in that year.

In addition to government repositories, it is generally known that, even in the ancient period, a number of institutions made their archival collections open for public consultation. These included the *Untei* library of Isonokami no Yakatsugu, thought to have existed at the end of the Nara era in the second half of the eighth century AD, and the Kobaiden of Sugawara no Michizane, at the end of the ninth century. Regrettably, neither of these collections has survived. In the medieval period, many repositories were created for temples or by samurai families. These include the Ashikaga School, known for its precious collections that still survive (there are various theories as to the date of its creation, but it was revived in the middle of the fifteenth century) and the *Kanazawa Bunko* repository, established in the mid-thirteenth century (Fig. 2).

Historians suggest that the development of Japan's modern libraries, archives, and museums emerged following the 1868 Meiji Restoration. The first museum was established in 1872, when the institutional system of the Meiji government was consolidated. In the same year, the *Shojakukan* Library was set up inside the Museum (*Hakubutsukan*). Hisanari Machida, the inaugural curator, envisioned a museum with a large-scale library on the model of the British Museum, which he saw while studying in Britain. The main collection of the *Shojakukan* Library consisted of works from the former *Shoheizaka Gakumonsho* school. The Museum and the *Shojakukan* Library were initially under the jurisdiction of the Ministry of Education, which had only been established the previous year. They were subsequently transferred to the Ministry of Home Affairs. Some museums were then transferred to the jurisdiction of the Ministry of

Copyright © 2017 by Taylor & Francis. All rights reserved.

Israel–Knowledge Discovery

Fig. 1 Map of Japan.
Source: CIA World Factbook.[1]

Fig. 2 *Ukiyoe* by Utamaro, copyright Keio University.

Agriculture and Commerce, the Imperial Household Agency, while others were transferred back to the Ministry of Education in 1874.[2] In the early years of the Meiji era, museums were divided into two types: those connected to the Ministry of Home Affairs, and those connected to the Ministry of Education, respectively. The first of these was initially known as the Imperial Household Museum, which later became the Tokyo National Museum, while the latter was the National Science Museum.

The collections of the *Shojakukan* Library, Japan's first governmental public library, remained under the jurisdiction of the Ministry of Internal Affairs but were moved first to the Asakusa Repository and then to the Cabinet Library. Meanwhile, the Tokyo *Shojakukan* Library, established by the Ministry of Education using the buildings of the former *Shojakukan* Library in Yushima, started to build a new collection from 1875. This then moved to the Imperial Library. After the Second World War, its jurisdiction was transferred from the Ministry of Education to the National Diet (Japan's Parliament), whereupon it became the National Diet Library (NDL). The books from the *Shoheizaka Gakumonsho* school that we find in the NDL today are books that were released to accompany the transfer of stacks during the Meiji years.[3]

In terms of maintaining public repositories, a "record compiling clerk" was appointed among the administrative officials in the *Dajokan* (Department of State) in 1868. The *Dajokan* system was reformed in August 1871, and a Records Bureau that would "oversee the work of documentary record compilation" was set up in the Main Office of the *Dajokan*. In the following year, 1872, a Records Division and a History Division were set up within the Records Bureau.[4] This marked the beginning of Japan's documentary administration. After subsequently passing through various different guises (such as the Records Department of the Clerical Bureau in the *Dajokan* and the Records Division of the Cabinet Clerical Bureau), in 1885 it became the Cabinet Records Bureau, and again in 1893 the Records Division of the Cabinet Clerical Office.

Thus, while it would appear that a system for central management of official documents was initially developed, this gradually shifted to a system of decentralized management. In July 1942, the Records Division of the Cabinet Secretariat passed its administrative work to the General Affairs Division of the Cabinet Secretariat, whereupon a document management institution with the word "Records" in its title disappeared from the state bureaucracy. Under the Constitution of Japan, the National Archives of Japan was finally launched in July 1971, having previously been the General Affairs Division of Prime Minister's Agency Secretariat and the General Affairs Division of the Prime Minister's Secretariat.[5]

The remainder of this entry will provide an introduction to contemporary Japanese libraries, public archives, and museums will be introduced individually.

Israel–Knowledge Discovery

Israel-Knowledge Discovery

LIBRARY AND INFORMATION PROFESSIONS, SYSTEMS, AND SERVICES

Legislation Concerning Libraries

The library is called "*toshokan*" in Japanese. The "*Toshokan-rei*" (the Library Decree) was issued for the first of the kind as an Imperial decree in 1899. This law was totally reformed to "*Toshokan-ho*" (the Library Law), enforced in 1950, after WWII. The basis of the new Library Law was the Social Education Law, and thus it stipulated that public libraries be tax-supported, free of charge and required, and the law required librarians adequate to meet the information needs of the community. In addition, the Library Law allows that a library can be established by anyone, not only by public organizations.

Under the Library Law, a public library is defined as a facility established by a municipal government or non-profit foundation. In 2007 there were approximately 3000 public libraries under local governments and 20 libraries under nonprofit foundations. The qualifications to become a professional librarian are regulated by law. Librarians must be college graduates who have taken certain accepted library science courses.

With respect to legislation regarding other kinds of libraries, the National Diet Library is regulated by the National Diet Library Law (enacted in 1948). University libraries are legally based on "*Daigaku Setchi Kijun*" (University Establishment Standards, enacted in 1956), under "*Gakko Kyoiku-ho*" (School Education Law, enacted in 1947). School libraries are based on the School Library Law (enacted in 1953), which is also under the School Education Law.

Copyright Law is another aspect of legislation concerning libraries. The origin of Copyright Law in Japan dates back to 1899, although the law was revised in 1970 and 1978 in response to the advent of new audiovisual materials. It allows libraries to provide photocopy service to a maximum of half of a book if more than 50 years have passed since the author has passed away. Along with the increase in quantity of library services, it is now controversial whether libraries should accept public lending rights in the face of complaints from the viewpoint of protecting authors' rights.

NDL and Information Services

The NDL is the national library belonging to the Diet (Japan's Parliament), established in 1948. As the legal depository library, the library acquires all kinds of materials published in Japan to preserve them for the national cultural heritage. Taking advantage of this library collection, NDL provides various services such as compiling the Japanese National Bibliography, reference service to the members of the Diet, providing a reading room for the public, interlibrary loan, and Internet services to

remote users. In addition, NDL offers a bibliographical database of digital talking books and Braille books and imperative services for visually disabled users. NDL has three facilities: the Tokyo Main Library, the Kansai-kan (a new facility in the Kansai region), and the ILCL (International Library of Children's Literature, also opened in 2002). The Tokyo Main Library comprises the Research and Legislative Reference Bureau, Administrative, Acquisitions, Bibliography, Public Services, Reference and Special Collections Departments, together with the Detached Library in the Diet. The *Toyo Bunko* (Oriental Library) and 26 branch libraries in the executive and judicial agencies also report to the NDL.

The origins of the NDL date back to the Imperial Library, established in 1872 under the Ministry of Education. The Lower House Library and House of Peers Library, established in 1891, were later incorporated, and the three libraries became the NDL during the Occupation era. The NDL was opened to the public in 1948, and later moved to the current Main Building adjacent to the National Diet in 1961. The NDL has 923 staff members, a 2.5-billion yen book budget (FY 2007), and a collection of 8.6 million books and 11 million serials items (FY 2005). The Library has also been acting as the Japanese National Centre for ISSN since 1976 and as the Asia Regional Center for the IFLA Preservation and Conservation since 1989.

The NDL promotes digital library projects as one of its priority areas (Fig. 3). Through the NDL Web site (http://www.ndl.go.jp), the following digital services are open to public: 1) Rare Books Image Database; 2) Digital Library from the Meiji era (1868–1912, 1912–1926); 3) Web Archiving Project (WARP) which collects and preserves Web sites and online periodicals on the Internet; and 4) Digital Archive Portal, which provides access to Japanese digital information; and cross database searching is now possible for NDL-OPAC, etc.

Academic and Research Libraries

Japan's first modern university was the University of Tokyo, which was founded in 1877. It became the foundation of the imperial system of higher education in pre-World War II Japan. Some faculty libraries were built in the same year. The UT main library was built in 1892 and rebuilt in 1928 after the Great Kanto Earthquake, with aid of the Rockefeller Foundation and others. In addition to other public universities, private universities, such as Waseda University and Keio University, were officially approved under the University Order, enacted in 1918. After World War II, the higher educational system was dramatically reformed. More and more citizens were able to pursue a higher education, unlike the pre-war situation, when universities existed only for the privileged elite. Today 50% of high school graduates go on to a university or junior college.

Fig. 3 Photo of NDL, Kansai-kan.

During the 1960s and 1970s, a number of universities (mostly private) expanded their enrollment with Japan's rapid economic growth. "*Daigaku Setchi Kijun*" (University Establishment Standards) by the Ministry of Education contributed to maintaining a certain quality among new university libraries. Many more universities built main libraries with open-shelves and free access for graduate students.

University libraries' catalogs were mostly automated and networked in the 1980s. The NACSIS (the National Center for Science Information Systems) was established by the Ministry of Education in 1986 to create the academic information network. The automation of libraries was accelerated by NACSIS, particularly from the perspective of technical services to OPAC preparation. NACSIS was reorganized in 2000 as the NII (National Institute of Informatics). NII provides the following services online for researchers and academic libraries:

1. NII is primarily a research laboratory with more than 80 information science researchers and 60 staff.
2. Webcat (http://webcat.nii.ac.jp/webcat_eng.html) is the online union catalog of the books held nationwide by university libraries. This system is linked to the national interlibrary loan system.
3. The GeNii (NII Scholarly and Academic Information Portal) offers databases in partnership with more than 270 academic associations, including some full-text information.

In terms of legislation, the National University Corporation Law was revised in 2003, and former national universities have now gained corporate status. Since 2004, all universities must be evaluated at least once every 7 years by a quality assurance agency certified by the agency now known as the Ministry of Education, Culture, Sports, Science and Technology (MEXT) (Table 1).

Public Libraries

Public libraries are quite common in Japan, being established in each city (local community with a population over 50,000) and in 50% of all towns and villages. The average public library holds 110,000 books, and lends 200,000 volumes per year. On average, each Japanese citizen borrows about five books in a year from a public library. Public libraries are especially popular with younger people, such as students preparing for college entrance exams, and with children accompanied by mothers who use the children's corner, situated conveniently near the entrance. Bunko, small voluntary libraries for children, usually run by parent groups, are quite popular at the neighborhood level. Meanwhile in larger cities, services providing business information, legal information, and medical information are popular (such as at the Tokyo Metropolitan Central Library or Chiyoda Public Library) (Fig. 4).

Although public library service was quite limited before WWII, the number of public libraries greatly increased during the 1960s and 1970s. *The Management*

Israel–Knowledge Discovery

Table 1 Statistics of university and junior college libraries (as of 2006).

	Number of libraries	Number of acquired books per year	Number of books borrowed	Number of students
National	297	1,559,000	6,854,000	628,945
Public	122	433,000	1,772,000	127,860
Private	919	4,775,000	19,938,000	2,102,402
Total	1,338	6,767,000	28,564,000	2,859,207
Junior College	256	328,000	1,236,000	202,197

Source: Statistics by JLA.

of Public Libraries in Medium and Small Libraries, published in 1963 by the Japan Library Association (JLA), emphasized the importance of services for smaller local libraries. Since then the network of prefectural libraries and small branch community libraries has grown steadily. Following the economic downturn in the 1990s many public libraries have been affected by legislation supporting a Designated Manager System (*Shitei Kanrisha Seido*) or PFI (Private Finance Initiatives). The private sector has become involved in libraries' services and operations. It is thought that the policy has caused a degradation of services, which goes against the spirit of the Library Law, however more and more local governments have adopted the policy as the central government has cut its budget for public facilities (Table 2).

School Libraries

The Japanese School Library Law, enacted in 1953, required every school (grades 1–12) to establish a school library as a reading and learning center, and to employ a teacher-librarian (*shisho-kyoyu*), with a supplementary provision that stated that "the placement of a teacher-

librarian is optional for the time being." Many schools did not have teacher-librarians for nearly 50 years until 1997 when the supplementary provision was revised to require all schools with 12 or more classes to employ a teacher-librarian by March 31, 2003. According to Article 5 of the School Library Law, a 10-credit training program for teacher-librarians can be administered by colleges, universities, or boards of education in compliance with the Minister of Education, Culture, Sports, Science and Technology (MEXT). Since 1997, many schools have started to employ teacher-librarians, however, in most cases schools have asked existing teachers to obtain the teacher-librarian certificate through intensive summer courses rather than appoint new teacher-librarians. In many cases, the teacher-librarian remains a full-time teacher and his or her teaching responsibilities are not reduced despite being appointed as a teacher-librarian.[6] However, an increasing number of schools employ clerical staff in school libraries (collectively called *gakko-shisho*) who generally manage collection development, circulation, and many other business practices. Computers were introduced into school libraries in the 1980s. According to a MEXT survey, nearly 40% of primary and

Fig. 4 Yamaguchi City Library, photo by Urushibara.

Table 2 Statistics of public libraries.

	Number of libraries	Number of full time staff	Number of books borrowed	Number of holding
2002	2,711	15,284	546,287,000	310,165,000
2003	2,759	14,928	571,064,000	321,811,000
2004	2,825	14,664	609,687,000	333,962,000
2005	2,953	14,302	616,957,000	344,856,000
2006	3,082	14,070	618,264,000	356,710,000

Source: Statistics by JLA, 2006.

lower secondary schools, and 70% of upper secondary school libraries have automated catalogs. Table 3 shows some statistics on school libraries in Japan.

Special Libraries

In 2007 the membership institutions of the Special Library Association consisted of 560 libraries belonging to local and central governments, private companies, and research institutes. Despite the fact that about a quarter of these libraries are small, one-person libraries, special libraries provide diverse and unique collections and services. Many of their services are accessed primarily online.

The followings are major special libraries in various fields.

Science and technology

The Japan Science and Technology Agency (JST, http://www.jst.go.jp/EN/index.html) was reorganized in 2003, absorbing a former organization known as JICST (1957–1996); it is now providing various services such as J-STAGE, an electronic journal support system, photocopying service, and translation services. JST services are used broadly by research libraries and natural science researchers both domestically and abroad.

Medical sciences

The IMIC (International Medical Information Center, http://www.imic.or.jp/about/outline_e.html) is located in Tokyo, and is the national document supply center of medical information. It succeeded the Kitasato Memorial Medical Library of Keio University in 1972, collecting and disseminating highly sophisticated medical information.

Table 3 Average holdings of public school libraries as of December 2005.

Primary school	7,312 volumes
Lower secondary school	9,040 volumes
Upper secondary school	21,771 volumes

Source: Statistics by MEXT.

Business

JETRO (Japan External Trade Organization) Business Library (http://www.jetro.go.jp/library/) used to be a government agency before it was reorganized as an independent administrative agency (IAA) in 2004. It has offices in Tokyo and Osaka, and provides business information on a country-by-country basis for the advancement of Japanese trade.

Another JETRO library is at the IDE (Institute of Developing Economics) Library (http://www.ide.go.jp/English/Library/), located near Tokyo, with collections on economics, politics, and social issues of regions in Asia, Middle East, Africa, Latin America, Oceania, and Eastern Europe.

Braille library

The Japan Braille Library (Nihon Tenji Toshokan, http://www.nittento.or.jp/) is a social welfare corporation, founded in 1940 by Kazuo Homma (1915–2003). It produces 3000 volumes of Braille and recorded books yearly, and provides a free recorded books service. In 2004, it started Internet service of DAISY contents. There are also more than 200 Braille libraries and public libraries that make Braille books available to the public in Japan.

Art and museum library

Following the 1986 IFLA conference in Tokyo, the Japan Art Documentation Society (http://wwwsoc.nii.ac.jp/jads/eng/index.html) was established by curators and librarians in 1989 to meet the needs of museum libraries. In 2004 the ALC (Art Libraries' Consortium) was founded by eight museums in Tokyo. They have a cross-searchable online-public access catalog.

Japanese studies

The Japan Foundation is a renowned foundation among Japanese studies scholars, offering various cultural exchange programs, Japanese language teaching, and library service. The JFIC (Japan Foundation Information Center, http://www.jpf.go.jp/e/jfic/lib/index.html) is in Tokyo and there are two other libraries in other parts of Japan. It also operates 18 JF libraries outside Japan, which function as gateways to Japanese language and culture.

Israel–Knowledge Discovery

Digital Library Collections and Services

The digital library dates back to the 1980s with the advent of CD-ROM. During the 1990s, the focus of discussion moved from electronic publishing to "digital library" or "electronic library" on the Internet. In the 2000s, some larger public, university, special libraries began offering rare book images, institutional academic documents, and books with expired copyright protection. In addition to the digital library created by the National Diet Library as mentioned above, the following libraries also offer digital library collections to public.

The University of Kyoto Library started its digital library (http://edb.kulib.kyoto-u.ac.jp/minds-eu.html) in 1998, and contains images of rare books registered as national property, some texts of the university's publisher, theses, and a repository of articles and reports published within the campus. EDMC (Great Hanshin-Awaji Earthquake Disaster Materials Collection, http://www.lib.kobe-u.ac.jp/eqb/e-gallery.html), created by Kobe University Library in 1995, is a one-of-a-kind digital gallery on its Web site, containing invaluable records and images with a risk management perspective.

IPDL (Industrial Property Digital Library, http://www.ipdl.inpit.go.jp/homepg_e.ipdl) was created in 2000 by The Japan Patent Office. Patents, utility models, trademarks, and design can be searched on the Internet, and the patent gazettes and other industrial property information can be accessed at the reference library of the National Center for Industrial Property Information and Training.

Aozora Bunko (Blue Sky Library, http://www.aozora.gr.jp/#main) is the digital library that is the best-known among the general public; it was created by Eiji Noguchi in 1997 and now contains thousands of copyright-expired Japanese books (mainly in literature).

Education for Library and Information Science

Currently, there are five types of library and information science (LIS) education offered at colleges and universities in Japan.

- Librarian (*shisho*) training provided by more than 250 colleges and universities, during the regular academic year and as an intensive summer program.
- Teacher-librarian (*shisho-kyoyu*) training provided by more than 100 colleges and universities, during the regular academic year or as intensive summer programs.
- Undergraduate LIS majors offered by fewer than 10 colleges and universities.
- Master-level LIS programs offered by eight colleges and universities.
- Doctoral level LIS programs offered by six colleges and universities.

These courses or programs produce approximately 12,000 qualified *shisho* and 12,500 qualified *shisho-kyoyu* every year. The majority are trained at an undergraduate level. The knowledge and skills held by graduates of these programs are quite diverse while, employment opportunities for full-time librarians in 2007 were quite limited.

The legal basis of Japanese LIS education was established by The Library Law (enacted in 1950) and The School Library Law (enacted in 1953). Formal LIS education programs are given mainly by colleges or universities in compliance with the MEXT, as training programs for librarians of public libraries and teacher-librarians of school libraries. Courses, credit units and other guidelines are specified by Ministry rules. There is no formal education system in place for information professionals in academic and special libraries. The certificate for *shisho*, which was intended for public library professionals, is considered the basic requirement for other types of library professionals in Japan.

The first comprehensive program for library education at the university level was established in 1951 at Japan Library School of Keio University, under the auspices of the American Library Association. According to MEXT, 13 colleges and universities offer Intensive Summer Courses of formal librarian training, while seven offer correspondence training courses.

In the area of continuing education in LIS, The Graduate School of Library and Information Science at Keio University established a new course for library workers in 2004, in order to give them opportunities for continuing education. Some other colleges and universities, such as Tsukuba University or the University of Tokyo are also establishing new tracks for continuing education at the graduate level, while the vast majority of librarians in Japan have a bachelor's degree, there will be more librarians with master's degrees in LIS in the future, especially in academic libraries. MEXT, National Diet Library, Tokyo Metropolitan Library, and some other major libraries also offer various staff training programs throughout the year.

One of the biggest issues in education and training for librarianship in Japan is how to strengthen the profession and to improve the status of librarians in society. Based on the shared understanding of current problems in LIS, the Library and Information Professionals and Education Renewal, a 3-year research project to study LIS education systems and curricula in Japan, proposed two areas for reform. They include: 1) The introduction of an independent LIS examination as a formal quality-assuring mechanism for overall education of information professionals; and 2) provision of an integrated curriculum for information professionals overall.[6–8]

Professional Associations

According to *Library Year Book* 2007, there are about 90 national associations, councils, or societies related to

Israel–Knowledge Discovery

libraries. Among them, the JLA is the largest and most comprehensive association in the field of libraries in Japan, representing all types of libraries and related organizations in Japan.

JLA (*Nihon Toshokan Kyokai*, JLA, http://www.jla.or.jp) was founded in 1892, and promotes the development of libraries and librarianship in Japan. Its activities have been supported by member librarians throughout Japan for over a century. JLA consisted of 5100 individual members and 2600 institutional members as of 2006. JLA has been a member of IFLA since 1929. The mission of JLA consists of four basic policies: 1) to be the national information center for all libraries and librarians in Japan; 2) to be an education, training, and career development center for librarians; 3) to cooperate with, and coordinate all kinds of libraries and library organizations; and 4) to promote and support international relations activities with libraries and librarians around the world.

The all-Japan Library Conference is held annually in different cities around the nation, and is hosted by a prefectural library and regional communities. There are six divisions (Public Libraries, University Libraries, Junior College Libraries, School Libraries, Special Libraries, and Education), and about 25 committees and working groups (Library Policies, Library Management, Copyright, Intellectual Freedom, Preservation and Conservation, International Relations, Services for the Handicapped, Library Services for Children, etc.). JLA started publishing its monthly organ, *Library Journal* (*Toshokan Zasshi*) in 1907. It also publishes an average of 20 new monographs each year, as well as *Libraries Today* (*Gendai no Toshokan*, a quarterly), *Basic Subject Headings*, *Guide to Japanese Reference Books*, *JLA Librarian's Glossary*, *JLA Librarians Handbook*, *Library Year Book*, and *Statistics on Libraries in Japan*.

The following is a list of some leading associations related to libraries in Japan:

1. Japan Medical Library Association: JMLA (*Nihon Igaku Toshokan Kyokai*). Founded in 1927, it became a nonprofit organization in 2003 (http://wwwsoc.nii.ac.jp/jmla/index.html).
2. Japan Association of Private Universities Libraries: JAPUL (*Shiritsu Daigaku Toshokan Kyokai*): Founded in 1938. Membership in 2006 was 496 private university libraries, covering approximately 91% of total number of private universities in Japan (http://www.jaspul.org/).
3. Japan School Library Association: JSLA (*Zenkoku Gakko Toshokan Kyogikai*). Founded in 1950, it is the most comprehensive institute in the field of school libraries (http://www.j-sla.org.jp).
4. Japan Special Libraries Association: JSLA (*Senmon Toshokan Kyougikai: Sentokyo*). Founded in 1952, it publishes the Directory of Special Libraries, Japan (http://www.jsla.or.jp/eng/index.html).

5. Japan Association of National University Libraries: JANUL (*Kokuritsu Daigaku Toshokan Kyokai*). Founded in 1954, it is a membership organization comprising mainly libraries of national universities in Japan, totaling 92 libraries and library facilities (http://wwwsoc.nii.ac.jp/anul/index-e.html).

ARCHIVES

Overview of Japan's Archives Today

In Japan today, a large number of archives exist as physical entities, irrespective of whether they are independent organizations or not. Not only do these contribute to affairs in a variety of sectors, including academia, culture, government administration, and business, but they also preserve precious historical materials. In Japan, however, there is no system of central management for working documents in record centers, archives, or the like, either in the public or the private sector. Instead, a system of decentralized management by each department creating documents is preferred. As a result, archives on an organized level have not developed on a scale commensurate with Japan's national strengths in culture or economy, and many remain quite small. A system of public archives for documents not in current use has been created in order to guarantee public access to information (a founding principle of democracy in Japan). This comes along with the Act on Access to Information Held by Administrative Organs (1999), which guarantees access to documents in current use. An overview of present situation in Japan will be introduced below with a focus on public archives that have been established and are broadly perceived by the public as centers for access to documents not in current use.

The National Archives of Japan

The National Archives of Japan were established in July 1971 as a body affiliated with the Prime Minister's Office. Later renamed the National Archives of Japan in April 2001, it functions as an Independent Administrative Institution with the mandate to ensure the appropriate preservation and use of public documents, which are regarded as important historical materials designated for deposit by government institutions.

The holdings of the National Archives of Japan are broadly divided into: 1) public documents of state institutions, starting with the *Dajokan* after the Meiji Restoration; and 2) the Cabinet Library, mainly consisting of ancient Japanese and Chinese classical books passed down since the archives of the Shogun during the Edo era. As of March 31, 2007, its holdings consisted of 625,996 public document files and 479,500 ancient and classical books. Of these, 99.7% have been cataloged in a database, which

Israel–Knowledge Discovery

can be accessed via the Internet (http://www.archives.go.jp/). In fiscal 2006, the Archives received 29,420 visitors. The institution employs a staff of 42 regular employees and about twice that number of nonregular employees. The main office is inside Kitanomaru Park (next to the Imperial Palace in Tokyo), while there is also a Tsukuba Annex in Ibaraki Prefecture and the Japan Center for Asian Historical Records in Chiyoda Ward, Tokyo. The total floor area of the three buildings is about 6900 m^2 (Figs. 5 and 6).

One of the branch facilities of the National Archives of Japan is the Japan Center for Asian Historical Records. This is Japan's first full-scale digital archive specializing in public documents on the relationship between Japan and surrounding countries in the modern and contemporary eras (http://www.jacar.go.jp/). It houses some 12.5 million images of public documents and documents archived by the Imperial Army and Navy, the Ministry of Foreign Affairs and the National Archives of Japan up to 1945. These are provided in digital form, in both English and Japanese. Over the past 5 years or so, the Center has received more than 3 million access requests from both Japan and abroad.

The main activities undertaken by the National Archives of Japan, including this Japan Center for Asian Historical Records, can be summarized under the following six headings:

- Promoting digital archiving.
- Strengthening training systems for national and local government personnel.
- Participating in and contributing to international public archive activities.
- Locating and providing information on the location of historical public documents, etc.
- Conducting surveys and research activities aimed at raising the level of public archive activities.

- Creating a database and providing data on Asian historical materials.

Meanwhile, in cooperation with the Cabinet Office (the body with jurisdiction over the National Archives), research aimed at introducing an intermediate repository system is being vigorously pursued, as well as research on the transfer of public documents created using electronic recording media. The aim in doing so is to promote smoother transfers of public documents from the various government ministries and agencies.

Public Archives of Local Authorities

As of April 2007, there were approximately 1800 local authorities in Japan, but of these, only 50 authorities maintain public archives. Specifically, public archives are maintained by just 30 out of 47 prefectures, 7 of the 15 cities designated by government ordinance and, of the other authorities, 13 municipalities. As for the others, in many cases, a division in charge of public documents manages public documents based on a predetermined number of storage years, as stipulated in file management ledgers, etc.

The first local authority to create public archives was Yamaguchi Prefecture in 1959. Public archives generally come under the jurisdiction of the General Affairs Department or the Board of Education, and the scale is invariably small, with a staff of fewer than 20 (including both regular and nonregular employees). Each local authority undertakes its own personnel management of archivists. Despite a somewhat difficult administrative and funding environment, local public archives are gradually increasing in number, at the rate of one or two a year.

Fig. 5 Photo of National Archives of Japan, Main office.

Fig. 6 Photo of Stacks of National Archives of Japan.

College and University Archives

At the start of the twenty-first century there were about 700 colleges and universities in Japan. Of these, mainly large colleges and universities with long histories vigorously moved to create college and university archives starting in the 1980s in connection with the publication of university histories. A survey of college and university archives conducted by the Japan Association of College and University Archives of Japan in 2003 attracted responses from 84 colleges and universities. From this, we may assume that at least 84 colleges and universities maintain college and university archives.

University archives in some cases have focused on the collection and classification of historical and other materials related to the personal archives of the founders—particularly in the case of private universities. Recently there has been a growing interest in the management and preservation of university management documents that are no longer current.

Corporate and Other Archives

In many cases, archives kept by private companies have been established in connection with the compilation of company histories and they have sometimes been part of special libraries. Since the 1970s, there has been a progressive trend in Japanese industry to compile and publish company histories. As a byproduct, business archives have been accumulated and archive organizations created. However, this creation of corporate and other private-sector archives is highly sensitive to the economic environment. After peaking about 1990 at about 140, business archives started to decline along with a decline in the compilation of company histories. Today the number has fallen to about 100. Moreover, there are hardly any private-sector organizations that hire business archivists as specialist professionals. The majority of these private-sector archives belong to the Business Archives Association (BAA), which was established in 1981.

Laws Governing Archives

Two laws directly related to archives have been enacted in Japan. The Public Archives Law was enacted in 1987 and came into force a year later, while the National Archives Law was enacted in 1999 and took effect in 2000. A brief overview of these two laws will be given below.

On the problem of information disclosure, which is closely related to archive activities, the Information Disclosure Law (or, to use its formal title, the "Act on Access to Information Held by Administrative Bodies") was enacted in 1999 and came into force in 2001. Some commentators have pointed out that this law is incomplete, in that it only deals with aspects of the disclosure of public documents. They are calling for the enactment of a Public Documents Management Law (tentative name) to address these problems.

The Public Archives Law

The purpose of the law is to stipulate necessary matters related to public archives, in awareness of the importance of archiving public documents and records as historical

Israel–Knowledge Discovery

materials and making them available for use. The law consists of seven articles, and is said to have a strong tone of moral guidance. Among these seven articles, there are rules to the effect that the government should strive to furnish or facilitate the funds needed by local authorities to set up public archives, and that, in addition to a president, special research officers, and other necessary officers should be appointed. As for the necessity of special research officers, however, Article 2 of the Supplementary Provisions states, as "Exceptions to the Provision regarding Special Research Officers" that special research officers do not need to be appointed to public archives for the time being.

The National Archives of Japan Law

This is an organizational law for the National Archives of Japan (established as a department of the Prime Minister's Office in 1971), enacted upon its conversion to an independent administrative institution. It consists of 16 articles, which provide for the title, purpose, and scope of operations of the National Archives of Japan as an independent administrative institution undertaking activities based on the regulations in the Public Archives Law. They also provide for the appropriate preservation and use, of public documents. In this law, the term "government documents and records" is used to mean government documents and other records excluding those in current use by organs of the state. As the scope of its operations, meanwhile, the law provides that the National Archives of Japan shall preserve and make available for public use governmental documents and records that are of importance as historical materials. To that end, the National Archives is mandated to gather, classify, and provide information, provide professional and technical advice, conduct research and give training.

Archive-Related Societies and Associations

Academic societies

There are two academic societies related to archive studies, namely the Records Management Society of Japan (established in 1989) and the Japan Society for Archival Science (JSAS) (established in 2004). The Records Management Society of Japan was established with the intention of diffusing and disseminating the concept of record management in Japan, mainly among librarians, archivists, filing consultants, and other people with interest in the management of documents in current use. Its present membership is around 300. It holds a Research Convention combined with its Annual Conference, and publishes the semi-annual *Record Management* (*Journal of the Records Management Society of Japan*) as a peer-reviewed journal. Besides this, it is currently lobbying hard for the enactment of a Public Documents

Management Law. Internationally, it enjoys a close relationship with the Tokyo branch of the American Records Management Association (ARMA).

The JSAS was formed by researchers in the archives field and in the field of historical studies. Some of its leading members have studied overseas and have expert knowledge of innovative trends in archival science around the world. As such, there are now increasing cases of research activities conducted jointly by JSAS, many of whose members are interested in documents not in current use (based on the theory of lifecycle of records) and the Records Management Society of Japan, which is principally concerned with documents in current use. The outcome of such research has occasionally been published. Besides holding research presentations twice a year, the JSAS also publishes the annual *Journal of the Japan Society for Archival Science* as a peer-reviewed journal. It, too, has about 300 members, the majority of whom are archive-related researchers and postgraduate students. The principal focus of its activities is on establishing and diffusing archival science in Japan. For the time being, this involves an effort by its core members to consolidate and develop the foundation for a course majoring in archival science at the Graduate School of Gakushuin University in Tokyo.

Associations and organizations

Japan Society of Archives Institutions (JSAI): This is a national organization of institutions for the preservation and use of archives, etc., established in 1976. It consists of institutional members and individual members who work for them. Initially, it had about 160 institutional members and 270 individual members, and was the only organization in Japan that promoted the archive movement. As a result, it has undertaken a broad range of survey and research activities, communication and coordination activities, and others fundamental to this movement. Now that archives have achieved a degree of diffusion and establishment in Japanese society, however, related academic associations have been formed while institutions and organizations for communication and coordination have also been established. Furthermore, the public archives of local authorities, which used to serve in promoting activities, have become somewhat passive owing to the constraints on local government finances. JSAI holds an annual convention, at which features research presentations and training programs, in addition to the general meeting for its operational management. It publishes the journal *Records and Archives* (annual), of which 17 had been issued by March 2007.

Business Archives Association (BAA): This is a national organization concerned with business archives, which was established in 1981. In recognition of the social and historical value of business archives, the association's purpose is to conduct surveys and research on the gathering,

Israel–Knowledge Discovery

preservation, and management of business archives, and to improve practice in these areas. According to BAA's regulations, its operations include publishing journals, holding research meetings, touring-related institutions, and nurturing business archivists (business archive managers). It also promotes international exchange between Japan and China. Its publications include the occasional research bulletin *Kigyo to Shiryo* (*Business and Archives*). Its membership initially consisted of 55 institutional members and 20 individual members, but today these have increased to about 100 institutional and 60 individual members.

Japan Association of College and University Archives: This association was formed in 2005, when existing liaison groups responsible for college and university history in East and West Japan merged. At the time, its membership consisted of 83 universities and 40 individual members. The purpose of its activities is to provide a forum for information exchange, to promote research on college and university history, and to work for improvement in practice among its members. Its day-to-day activities are still conducted separately by its predecessor organizations, i.e., the East Japan Branch and the West Japan Branch, and the association's only collective activity is its yearly national convention.

Systems of Education and Training

Systems of education and research in universities

It would be fair to say that the training of archivists in Japan is still in the process of being established. Many people who have worked as archivists are involved in managing archive materials in addition to their historical research, and the amount of this archival work has increased. Consequently, as of 2007, there were no faculties or departments of archival science in Japanese universities. The only course that exists on archival science is offered by the Faculty of Cultural Information Resources at Surugadai University. Starting in April 2008, Master's and Ph.D. courses majoring in archival science were to be set up in the Graduate School of Gakushuin University. However, there is no undergraduate course that allows students to major in archival science. In Japan, therefore, archival science is not taught as part of library information studies in the departments of undergraduate faculties or graduate schools, as is the case in other countries.

Systems of on-the-job training

To compensate for the lukewarm attitude of Japanese universities toward archival science, on-the-job training programs are essential. Training programs that are held on a regular basis every year and the programs that are considered authoritative are those of the National Archives of Japan and the National Institute of Japanese Literature. Besides these, there are isolated training programs offered

by public archives and others in various parts of the country.

Training programs of the National Archives of Japan: The National Archives of Japan is planning to offer five different training programs for employees and related personnel already working in archives. These training programs may be broadly divided into two types:

1. Training aimed at developing archive literacy, with 1 day of on-the-job observation and 3 days of training aimed at ordinary non-specialist personnel involved in records management work in public institutions; and
2. Programs designed to train as archivists selected staff who need greater expertise because they are working as specialists in records management in public institutions. The latter will be divided into elementary grade (1 week), intermediate grade (4 weeks), and advanced grade (3 days). The non-specialist training is to be given to about 60 trainees every year and the specialist training to about 70. Training will be delivered by lecturers selected from universities, administrative bodies and others, in addition to the archivists of the National Archives of Japan. The style of training basically is done through classroom sessions in the main office of the National Archives of Japan. The trainees of intermediate grade are required to complete a final paper equivalent to graduate or master thesis in universities.

Archives College programs: Workers in the field are familiar with the name of the "Archives College," a term applied to archives management seminars offered by the National Institute of Japanese Literature. This Institute is a part of the National Institute for the Humanities in the Inter-University Research Institute Corporation. This training consists of a long-term course and a short-term course, the former lasting for 6 weeks divided into two phases and held at the National Institute of Japanese Literature in Tokyo. The short-term course lasts for 2 weeks and is held in regional locations. The fixed capacity of trainees is 35 for both long-term and short-term courses, and lecturers are invited from other universities, etc., besides the full-time instructors of the National Institute of Japanese Literature. Graduate students majoring in archival science are permitted to take part in the long-term course.

MUSEUMS

Modern Museums in Japan

National museums *hakubutsukan* and *bijutsukan*

The history of modern museums in Japan dates back to the Meiji era. In 1872, an exhibition was organized under the name of the Museum of the Ministry of Education of the Meiji government. The exhibition was opened at the

Israel–Knowledge Discovery

Taiseiden Hall in *Yushima Seido* with a view to making preparations for the Vienna World Exposition to be held the following year. As a result, an identity was given to the museums as exhibition-oriented facilities housing and exhibiting *hakubutsu*, meaning in Japanese, a variety of domestic articles to encourage new industries. The Japanese word for museum, *hakubutsukan*, literally means a house collecting various objects. *Hakubutsukan* has come to have a meaning different from the original word in the European languages.

When the first National Industrial Exhibition was held in 1877, the arts and crafts products were displayed in what was called *bijutsukan*. Since then, the Japanese *hakubutsukan* together with *bijutsukan* has been used to refer to art museums. During the late nineteenth century the *hakubutsukan* museums began to collect and show traditional cultural artifacts, although initially other kinds of products were also displayed. The Tokyo National Museum has kept the name *hakubutsukan* in Japanese even though it is a museum of fine art. It is currently under the Agency for Cultural Affairs which reports to the ministries in charge of internal affairs (Fig. 7).

Another type of institution which was called the "educational *hakubutsukan*" museum was set up under the control of the Ministry of Education with the goal of presenting learning materials related to natural science, such as samples of plants, stones, or rocks. This museum has grown into the current National Museum of Nature and Science, Tokyo. In the meantime, museums with increased emphasis on research activities were established under the control of the Academic and International Affairs Bureau of the Ministry of Education. These museums are the National Museum of Ethnology, Osaka, and the National Museum of Japanese History. These state-run museums have been reorganized as independent corporations since 2001. As of 2007, the reorganization and consolidation of the museums were as follows:

The National Institutes for Cultural Heritage (Independent National Agencies) consist of the

- Tokyo National Museum,
- Nara National Museum,
- Kyoto National Museum,
- Kyushu National Museum,
- National Research Institutes for Cultural Properties, Tokyo and
- National Research Institutes for Cultural Properties, Nara.

The National Museums of Art (Independent National Agencies) include

- the National Museums of Modern Art, Tokyo, and Kyoto,
- the National Museum of Western Art,
- the National Museum of Art, Osaka, and
- the National Art Center, Tokyo.

National Institutes for the Humanities (Inter-University Research Institute Corporations) include

- the National Museum of Ethnology,
- the National Museum of Japanese History, and
- the National Institute of Japanese Literature.

Hakubutsukan and Bijutsukan Museums run by local governments, foundations, and private companies

After the first museums were founded by the Ministry of Internal Affairs, local governments founded various types

Fig. 7 Main Gallery of Tokyo National Museum, copyright, TNM Image Archives.

Israel–Knowledge Discovery

of museums and organized exhibitions and fairs showing both contemporary products and antiquities. Most of them, however, were exhibitions of articles or products with only a few that developed into full-scale museums. The Ministry of Education set up museums for educational purposes. This encouraged the foundation of such museums in regional cities, but this initiative was short lived. In the 1910s, "popular" museums were opened and in the latter half of the 1920s, many provincial museums were founded for the promotion of local education. Both types of museums were strongly supported by nationalist movements. Apart from these, it should be noted that there were also private initiatives to create museums, such as the Attic Museum founded in 1921 by Keizo Shibusawa (now the Institute of the Study of Japanese Folk Culture, Kanagawa University) and the Japan Folk Crafts Museum founded in 1936 by Muneyoshi Yanagi. In 1897, the Old Temples and Shrines Conservation Law was promulgated. Prompted by this law, temples and shrines preserved collections of ancient artifacts to show to the public.

In the field of fine art, the Tokyo Metropolitan Museum was founded in 1926 as the first local government-run *bijutsukan* museum. This museum is the predecessor of both the Tokyo Metropolitan Museum and the Museum of Contemporary Art, Tokyo. In 1917, a foundation-run museum was founded: Okura Shukokan Museum of Fine Arts, an institution that collected Asian fine artworks.

As for private museums, in 1930 the Ohara Museum of Art was opened as the first Japanese museum featuring Western art. In 1952, Bridgestone Museum of Art was opened to the public. These museums are now managed by foundations. Some private enterprises also run their own museums, an example being the Printing Museum in Tokyo (2000) established by Toppan Printing Co. A survey shows that there are a total of about 900 corporate museums in Japan.

Following the examples of the Library Decree (1899) and Revised Library Decree (1933), efforts arose to establish a museum decree. Such efforts were given added impetus when the Museum Promotion Society (renamed Japanese Association of Museums in 1931) was set up. However, it was not until 1951 that a museum law was promulgated. It came into force the next year, and was based the principle of the Fundamental Law of Education under the new constitution. Museums are now under the control of the Lifelong Learning Bureau of the MEXT.

The museums under the law are classified as below:

1. Registered museums meet specified requirements such as the employment of curators and storage of reference materials. The public museums of local governments are under the control of local education boards and are outside the control of MEXT. As for museums set up by corporations, the law covers only those established by special corporations such as the Japanese Red Cross Society and religious corporations.

2. The museum-equivalent institutions operate similar to museums. In the museums established by local governments, those authorized by heads of the local governments are included.

     Museums not covered by the law are:

3. Museum-like institutions. A 2005 survey showed that the total number of museums was 5614.

     *   Category (1): 865 museums (126 run by prefectures, 344 by wards and cities, and 263 by towns and villages).
     *   Category (2): 331 institutions (national two, prefectural 26, ward- and city-run 94, town- and village-run 12).
     *   Category (3): 4418 institutions (national 127, prefectural 266, ward- and city-run 1919, town- and village-run 1166).

Statistics show that the overwhelming majority of institutions are in Category (3) and the ones covered by the museum law, Categories (1) and (2), are about one-fifth of the total (source: Social Education Survey Report 2005 published by the MEXT).

University museums

As of 1999 there were 145 university-run museums around Japan, including facilities called reference rooms or historical materials rooms, and botanical gardens. The time-honored examples to note in this regard are the Agricultural Department Museum of Hokkaido University (founded in 1882), Tsubouchi-Memorial Theater Museum of Waseda University (1928), and Meiji University Museums including the Criminal Museum (1929). Various departments of the state-run universities including the imperial universities have been collecting samples and reference materials in many fields. In 1995, the Science Council, an advisory board to the Minister of Education, submitted a report encouraging the establishment of museums in the universities. Tokyo University, the first among the national universities, established a multidisciplinary museum in 1997, as the successor to a university museum opened in 1961 with 6.5 million items and reference materials). This was followed by Kyoto University (multidisciplinary museum in 1997, 2.5 million pieces) and Kyushu University (multidisciplinary museum in 2000, 6.5 million items).

Many arts universities also include museums. For example, Musashino Art University founded in 1966 an art reference materials library, which includes a museum. In 1999, Tokyo University of Fine Arts and Music opened a museum, which keeps art objects collected over a long period extending to before the foundation of Tokyo Art School, the predecessor of the university (founded in 1887). The art objects were once stored in a university

Israel-Knowledge Discovery

library and then in the art reference materials facility along with music-related reference materials.

Professional Staff and Museum Libraries

Professional staff

The Museum Law provides that registered museums must employ professional staff, *gakugei-in*. The Japanese term used for curator, *gakugei-in* literally means a person in charge of *gaku* or learning and *gei* or art. "*Gakugei-in*" do not have exactly the same significance of curators, keepers, or conservators in the European languages. The number of the curators totaled 2898 in 865 museums as of 2003, which is 3.4 curators per museum on average. Combined with the staff of the museum-equivalent institutions, the total number of them amounts to 3827 in 1196 museums (3.2 curators per museum on the average). The museum-like institutions are far more poorly staffed with 2397 curators in 4418 museums (0.5 curators per museum on the average).

The museums, in principle, must be provided with the professional staff other than the curators. However, the Japanese curators in the museums are commonly forced to perform various other functions as well. Most museums tend to employ librarians, educators, conservators, registrars, and other professional workers. At present, staff strength is slowly increasing, but remains far below the required level. A few of the museums, mostly national museums, are staffed with full-time workers specialized in library management and information system construction. In most cases, the library of the museums is managed by a part-time librarian.

Museum libraries or art libraries

In the area of museum libraries, development of those in fine art museums has been most remarkable.

The first full-fledged art library in Japan was founded in 1930 by the Imperial Fine Arts Academy (now National Research Institute for Cultural Properties, Tokyo). Then, the Library and Museum of Musashino Art University (1966) and the art library of Tokyo Metropolitan Art Museum (1976) followed suit. Tokyo National Museum built the independent Research and Information Center* in 1984. The establishment of these museum libraries was followed by

- Yokohama Museum of Art* (1989),
- Aichi Arts Center (1992),
- Tokyo Metropolitan Museum of Photography* (1995),
- Museum of Contemporary Art, Tokyo* (1995, which inheriting the reference materials collected by Tokyo Metropolitan Art Museum),
- Hyogo Prefectural Museum of Art (2002),
- National Museum of Modern Art, Tokyo* (2002),

- National Museum of Western Art* (2002),
- Museum of Modern Art, Hayama (2003) and
- National Art Center, Tokyo* (2007).

In spite of the different characters of these museums, the seven museum libraries* above have organized an art library consortium, presenting, via Internet, a cross-search service of their own books, magazines, etc. (http:llalc. opac.jp)

Museum-Related Societies and Associations, and Education and Training Systems

Societies and associations

The Japanese Association of Museums, a nationwide professional body (about 1900 institutions and individuals) was organized in 1928 initially as the Museum Service Promotion Society. This association aims at promoting lifelong learning activities, and at conducting investigation and research for the development of museums. It publishes a monthly journal *Museum Studies*. There is another association called the Japanese Association of Zoos and Aquariums (membership of 160 organizations). In the art-related field, the Japanese Council of Art Museums (membership: 350 museums) was founded in 1951, and the Japan Association of Art Museums started its activity in 1982 with membership of 120 museums. The former association has as its purpose the exchange of information and professional training; it is composed of the national, public, and private art museums. The latter has membership of the public art museums with the main purposes of coordinating traveling exhibitions and encouraging art-related activities.

As for societies, the Museological Society of Japan has about 360 members, and publishes the *Journal of the Museological Society of Japan* twice a year. In 1995, the Japan Museum Management Academy was set up, and had a membership of 400 individuals and 40 organizations. The academy publishes the *Annual Bulletin of Japan Museum Management Academy*. In this connection, the Japan Society for Exhibition Studies (about 500 members) was established in 1982. The society publishes a semi-annual journal *Tenjigaku*. Founded in 1989, the Japan Art Documentation Society (about 300 individual members) is engaged in library- and archive-related activities, with emphasis placed on promotion of museum documentation services. The society has an official annual journal, *The Bulletin of the Japan Art Documentation Society*.

Education and training systems

To become a curator requires completion of a number of credit units in university curatorship courses or successfully passing a national examination. In fact, 99% of the qualification is dependent on the credits obtained by university courses: 12 units from 8 subjects. The number of the units needed to become a curator is less than that for a librarian. The need for improvement of curator education has been pointed out repeatedly.

At present, more than 200 universities in Japan have curatorship courses. About 10,000 students receive the qualification annually. However, only about 400 have been employed per year in recent years. As mentioned above, museums, and museum-similar institutions in particular, are not staffed with the required number of curators. To solve this problem, it will be necessary to improve the basic abilities of curators. In this connection, there have not been university faculties or departments specializing in curatorship, as is the case with librarians. Improvement in the quality of curators is a serious problem, which should include programs at the graduate level.

With regard to training of museum workers, professional courses include a nationwide 3-week course for museum workers by the National Institute for Educational Policy Research; a 1- to 4- week (period variable with the fields) course for the archeologists offered by the National Research Institute for Cultural Properties, Nara; a training course (2-year course of 1 week a year) for historical and ethnological staff by the National Museum of Japanese History; and a 2-week training course for curators of the museums in charge of conservation by the National Research Institute for Cultural Properties, Tokyo.

Problems Concerning Museums

Computerization and evaluation of management

Since opening to the public in 1977, the National Museum of Ethnology, Osaka, has had an artifact catalog database system and video system "videotheque," which are well known around the world. From the mid-1990s, many museums built up in-house computer systems. Today, the museums provide data on their collections via Internet. However, a nationwide collection search system has not yet been realized. This may be because most of the museums tend to stress exhibitions and to think little of collection building and cataloging. According to a survey conducted by the Japanese Association of Museums, 53% of museums record nearly all the data in an accession register, and 22% of them keep a so-called "collection catalog," which covers all the data (source: "Comprehensive Survey Report of the Museums of 2004).

The administrative reform starting in the 1990s influenced and attracted considerable interest from museums. In response to this reform movement, the Japan Museum Management Academy was founded. Since 2001, the national *hakubutsukan* and *bijutsukan* museums have been reorganized as an independent national agency.

The revision of the Local Autonomy Law in 2003 provides for the use of a designated administrator in the services of local governments. According to this law, 93 museums (as of 2005) decided to consign part of their work to a private company or nonprofit organization. Some people say such changes may damage the regular service level that the museums have so far maintained. More museums are going to introduce evaluation systems by themselves or by third party to enhance the restructuring. For example, Asahiyama Zoo of Asahikawa City has for 10 years monitored the remarkable renovation of its unique animal viewing system. Opened in 2004, the Twenty-first Century Museum of Contemporary Art, Kanazawa, features contemporary art, which is considered hard to appreciate by many people. Both zoo and museum together these two have succeeded in attracting more than 1.5 million guests per year although they are in the less populated local cities. Paying close attention to users, the two institutions are highly evaluated for their management abilities.

Movements toward revision of the Museum Law

In 2007, MEXT published a report for the revision of the Museum Law, in which the Ministry points out advances in registered museums and enhancement of education for curators. As mentioned above, the registered museums and museum-equivalent institutions are now only about one-fifth of the total institutions. The Ministry seeks to create a legal framework to improve as many institutions as possible, raising their status to the registered-museum level. In the area of curatorship, MEXT will try to enhance the ability of curators. In this context, curators will be qualified in fundamental curatorship when finishing the essential courses in university, regular curatorship when achieving the training course in a graduate program, and superior curatorship after a period of work in museum.

When the museum law was enacted more than 50 years ago, there were about 200 museums. Now, the number of museums has reached more than 5600. Furthermore, the Fundamental Law of Education, revised in 2006, puts great value on the lifelong learning principle. The important role of museums is once again being discussed. The registration standard of museums will be based mainly on abilities required for "management," "collection," and "communication," with reduced emphasis on the period of open days per year, one of the former registration standards. With respect to the requirements for curators, more emphasis will be placed on communication-related ability than the conventional abilities of research and exhibition. In addition, the national museums (Independent National Agencies), university museums, and non-profit private museums, which are not covered by the Museum Law, will be taken into consideration to be treated like

Israel—Knowledge Discovery

registered museums. The cooperative network of museums in Japan is being realized.

CONCLUSION

Libraries and document collection have a long history in Japan, based on a fundamental respect for written information and knowledge. Today almost all cities have public libraries. Japanese university and college libraries have also seen substantial improvements in technology, networking, and new library construction in recent decades. Economic growth also brought development of special libraries. User interest is now mainly directed toward the Internet and electronic resources and this has spurred library development of digital searching and storage.

The history of modern museums in Japan dates back to the time of the Meiji Restoration. The museums were initially set up to organize exhibitions for display of various articles. For this reason, the activities of the museums focused mainly on "organizing exhibitions" rather than building and management of collections. This characterized Japanese museums (in particular museums of fine art), curators, and museum specialists. Against this background, librarians, conservators, educators, and other specialists have been progressively staffed for individual sectors. Furthermore, reforms are underway for making collection databases, opening data to the public, and introducing the IAA system and third party management evaluation.

Archives in Japan are divided into three main groups: public archives, university archives, and private archives, including business archives. It was not until the late twentieth century that archival legislation, academic societies on archival studies, and training systems for experts engaged in the operation of archives were developed in Japan, and new development is still underway. Interrelationships among archival institutions are based on the decentralized administration system and there is no unified base or central management organization for implementing archival policies. Digitized archival materials are provided online on a large scale by the Japan Center for Asian Historical Records.

In Japan today, the fruits of the progress in information technology is becoming increasingly widespread among libraries, museums, and archives. The pace of digitization is remarkable, and development of digital libraries, digital archives, and other digital projects have become common. Under these circumstances, professionals in this field in Japan also recognize the need for links between museums, libraries, and archives (otherwise known as "MLA partnership"). Nationwide networks that include the principal institutions are already being formed by the curators of museums, libraries, and archives. There are now plans to go further in forming and consolidating MLA partnership as a reciprocal relationship that will embrace all of these

and transcend boundaries between different types of institutions. In our opinion, the main issue to be resolved before this can be realized, however, is the problem of who should take leadership. Japan's library sector should take the initiative to bring about cooperation and coordination. But the JLA, which would normally be expected to take the lead in the MLA partnership, does has not have enough capacity to achieve this. The National Diet Library has its own institutional issues that prevent it from taking national leadership on this agenda. Resolving this issue is of immediate concern to everyone working in data storage and search services in Japan.

ACKNOWLEDGMENTS

We would like to express our appreciation to a librarian, Charles Laurier, librarian at Lakeland college in Tokyo.

REFERENCES

1. CIA World Factbook. Available at https://www.cia.gov/library/publications/the-world-factbook/geos/ja.html.
2. Shiina, N. *Zukai Hakubutsukanshi*; Yuzankaku Shuppan: Tokyo, Japan, 2000; 58 (Illustrated History of Museums) (revised and supplemented edition).
3. National Archives of Japan. *Naikaku Bunko Hyakunenshi*; National Archives of Japan: Tokyo, Japan, 1985; 30–32 (Hundred-year History of the Cabinet Library).
4. Nakanome, T. *Kindai Shiryogaku no Shatei: Meiji Dajokan Bunsho Kenkyu Josetsu*; Kobundo: Tokyo, Japan, 2000; 96, 232 (Range of Modern Historical Archive Studies: Introduction to Documentary Research on the Meiji Dajokan).
5. National Archives of Japan. *Naikaku Bunko Hyakunenshi*; National Archives of Japan: Tokyo, Japan, 1985; 429–434 (Hundred-year History of the Cabinet Library).
6. Ueda, S.; Nemoto, A.; Miwa, M.; Oda, M.; Nagata, H.; Teruyo, H. LIPER Project in Japan 71st IFLA General Conference and Council, Programme and Proceedings Oslo, Norway, 2005; Aug 14–18, 2005, Available at http://www.ifla.org/IV/ifla71/programme.htm (accessed August 6, 2007).
7. Makiko, M.; Shuichi, U.; Akira, N.; Mitsuhiro, O.; Haruki, N.; Teruyo, H. Final Results of the LIPER Project in Japan 72nd IFLA, Programme and Proceedings Seoul, Korea, 2006; Aug 20–24, 2006, Available at http://www.ifla.org/IV/ifla72/papers/107-Miwa-en.pdf (accessed August 6, 2007).
8. *Social Education Survey Report 2005*. Published by the Ministry of Education, Culture, Sports and Science and Technology (MEXT): Tokyo, Japan.

BIBLIOGRAPHY

1. Ando, M. A challenge to archival development and archival science in Japan. Archivum. J. Inter. Council Archiv **1999**, *XLIV*, 139–151 in Access to Archives: The Japanese and American Practices, 2007, Available at http://www.archivists.org/publications/proceedings/.

Israel–Knowledge Discovery

2. International Relations Committee of Japan Library Association. Ed. *Librarianship in Japan*; Rev. Ed.; Japan Library Association: Tokyo, Japan, 1994.

3. Japan's Local Government Archives: Standards for their Establishment, Functions, and Operations. East Asian Archiv **2007**, *13*, 59–81.

4. *Kodansha Encyclopedia of Japan*, 1st Ed. Kodansha: Tokyo, Japan; New York, 1983; 11–1986.

5. Present Status of Museum in Japan; Ministry of Education, Culture, Sports, Science and Technology: Tokyo, Japan.

6. Muta, S. Preservation and access to vital records of the National Archives of Japan: Endeavor of the National Archives of Japan Digital Archive. East Asian Archiv **2006**, *12*, 46–54.

7. Roberts, L.P. *Roberts' Guide to Japanese Museums of Art and Archaeology*, Simul Press: Tokyo, Japan, 1987; iv, 383 Rev. & updated.

8. Sugimoto, S. Ensuring the preservation and use of electronic archives. East Asian Archiv. **2008**, *14*, 56–67.

9. Welch, T.F. *Toshokan: Libraries in Japanese Society*, American Library Association: Chicago, IL, 1976.

10. Welch, T.F. *Libraries and Librarianship in Japan*, Greenwood Press: Westport, CT, 1997.

WEB SITES

1. The Japan Library Association, Available at http://www.jla.or.jp/index-e.html.

2. The Japan Society of Library and Information Science, Available at http://wwwsoc.nii.ac.jp/jslis/aboutjslis_1_en.html.

3. The National Diet Library, Available at http://www.ndl.go.jp/en/index.html.

4. The National Institute of Informatics, Available at http://www.nii.ac.jp/index.shtml.en.

5. The National Archives of Japan, Available at http://www.archives.go.jp/english/index.html.

6. Japan Center for Asian Historical Records, Available at http://www.jacar.go.jp/english/index.html.

7. Records Management Society of Japan, Available at http://wwwsoc.nii.ac.jp/rmsj/index_e.html.

8. The Tokyo National Museum, Available at http://www.tnm.jp/en/servlet/Con?pageId=X00&processId=00.

9. The National Museum of Nature and Science, Available at http://www.kahaku.go.jp/english/.

10. The National Art Center, Tokyo, Available at http://www.nact.jp/english/index.html.

11. The Japan Art Documentation Society, Available at http://www.jads.org/eng/index.html.

Israel–Knowledge Discovery

Kazakhstan: Libraries, Archives, and Museums

Leslie Champeny
Alaska Resources Library and Information Services (ARLIS), Anchorage, Alaska, U.S.A.

Joseph Luke
Anna Bergaliyeva
Olga Zaitseva
Kazakhstan Institute of Management, Economics and Strategic Research (KIMEP), Almaty, Kazakhstan

Abstract
This entry describes the development and present situation (as of 2007) of information institutions and practices in Kazakhstan, primarily the histories and cultural roles of libraries, archives, and museums, and the education, status, and activities of information workers.

INTRODUCTION

This entry describes the historical development and current conditions of libraries, archives, and museums in Kazakhstan. Early institutions and practices in the region were Islamic, and later Russian imperial and Soviet influence is also still evident in educational philosophy, scientific practice, and institutional structure. Today institutions face the challenge to modernize and globalize information practices in a multiethnic, multilingual state.

Kazakhstan is in the middle of the Eurasian land mass (Fig. 1). Bounded by China to the east, Russia to the north and northwest, the Caspian Sea to the southwest, and Turkmenistan, Uzbekistan, and Kyrgyzstan to the south, it is the ninth largest country in the world (2.7 million km^2). The desert, steppe, and mountain ecologies have supported nomadic pastoralists, trade cities of the Silk Road, and settled agriculturalists. At 15.3 million citizens, it is the least densely populated Central Asian state. The development of rich oil, gas, and mineral resources makes Kazakhstan the wealthiest Central Asian republic, second to Russia among the former Soviet republics.

History

By 1500 B.C.E. horse-herding nomads were inscribing petroglyphs at Tamgaly (Fig. 2). Several cultural traditions later marked the region's inhabitants: the Scythian or Saka presence from the eighth to the third centuries B.C.E., the spread of Islam from the seventh century C.E., the Mongol incursion in the thirteenth century, the Persian-influenced Timurid dynasty from the fourteenth century, the rise of the Turkic Uzbeks in the fifteenth century, and the entrance of Russia from the eighteenth century. The Muslim philosopher Al-Farabi (ca. 870–950) is said to have founded a library in his birthplace Otrar

that rivaled ancient Egypt's Alexandria. The Mongol forces of Chingiz (Genghis) Khan (ca. 1162–1227) later destroyed Otrar and other localities. Many of these places were rebuilt under Chingiz Khan's descendant Amur Timur (Tamerlane) (1336–1405), including the mausoleum of the Sufi poet Khoja Ahmed Yasavi (1106–1166) in Turkistan. In the fifteenth century the Kazakhs emerged as a distinct cultural and linguistic group from the Uzbek confederation of Timur's descendant Abu'l-Khayr Khan (ca. 1412–1468). The appellation *Kazakh* is most commonly translated as "free, independent." Other proposed etymologies include from Old Turkic *qazgac*, "to gain"[1] or from a Turkic term used to describe splinter groups.[2] In the early seventeenth century the Kazakh khanate split into three competing *zhus* or hordes. External threats from Mongol Oirats and Dzungars in the eighteenth century led Kazakhs under Ablai Khan (1711–1781) to turn to China and Russia for recognition and protection.

By the nineteenth century the Russian Empire had established settlements across the north including Uralsk (Oral), Semipalatinsk (Semey), and Ust-Kamenogorsk (Oskemen) and a frontier outpost in the south, Fort Vernyi (Almaty). Colonizing Russians disrupted Islamic influence in the region, in part by establishing Russian-language libraries adjunct to their military installations in the region, which served increasing numbers of immigrating Slavs.[3] Soviet-era historians describe this as a period of enlightenment when individuals such as Chokan Valikhanov (1835–1865) (descendant of Ablai Khan), Ibrai Altynsarin (1841–1889), and Abai Kunanbayev (1845–1904) (Fig. 3) aspired to spread the benefit of books and reading among Kazakh people. More recent histories note uprisings against the Russians during this time that suggest the beginnings of Kazakh nationalism.

Encyclopedia of Library and Information Sciences, Fourth Edition DOI: 10.1081/E-ELIS4-120043545
Copyright © 2017 by Taylor & Francis. All rights reserved.

Israel–Knowledge Discovery

Fig. 1 Republic of Kazakhstan.
Source: Adapted from *CIA World Factbook*, https://www.cia.gov/library/publications/the-world.factbook/geos/kz.html

Well into the nineteenth century Kazakhs were a people of oral tradition, and when imperial Russia required literacy from Kazakh elites it was in Russian.[4] In 1918, the new Soviet state found Central Asians to be largely illiterate and early literacy campaigns focused on primary education—the Kazakh region reached acceptable levels of literacy in the 1930s.[5] Russian was the main language and written Kazakh was converted from Arabic and Latin into a modified Cyrillic script. Authors who wrote on Kazakh themes or in the Kazakh language were sometimes exiled or executed, including poet Saken Seyfullin (1894–1938) and linguist Akhmet Baytursynuly (1873–1938).

During the Soviet era of the twentieth century (1918–1991), the region became increasingly collectivized and urbanized. The Communist government required nomads to adopt more sedentary animal husbandry and industrialized methods of agriculture. Cities developed into centers

Fig. 2 Petroglyphs at the Tamgaly World Heritage Site outside of Almaty.
Source: Photograph by Kristopher D. White.

Israel–Knowledge Discovery

Fig. 3 Abai Kunanbayev, seminal Kazakh author. Statue at the Republican Palace performance hall in Almaty.
Source: Photograph by Kristopher D. White.

Israel–Knowledge Discovery

of economic and cultural life, supporting urban institutions such as schools, hospitals, libraries, museums, and book and newspaper publishers. When the single Turkistan Autonomous Soviet Socialist Republic proved difficult to administer, Central Asia was divided into smaller republics in 1923 and 1924, and boundaries were redrawn again several times. Immigrants came from other Soviet Republics as internal exiles, war refugees, or developers of virgin lands, and forced migrations of Koreans, Crimean Tatars, Germans, and others also populated the area so that by the 1960s ethnic Kazakhs had become a minority group.

Present Day

Kazakhstan was the last state to declare independence from the Soviet Union on December 16, 1991. The country is organized into 14 administrative units known as *oblasts*, plus the two city units Astana and Almaty, the present and past capitals. The government recognizes over 130 ethnicities in the country; 2006 figures estimate

9 million Kazakhs, 4 million Russians, 450,000 Ukrainians, 433,000 Uzbeks and 250,000 each of Uighurs, Tatars, and Germans. Religions include varieties of Islam (60%), Christianity (30%), and others such as Judaism, Hinduism, and Buddhism. The monetary unit is the tenge (KZT), valued at roughly 120 tenge to the U.S. dollar in September 2007. President Nursultan Nazarbayev has led the country since 1989 and may run for re-election indefinitely: recent legislation limits future presidents to two consecutive 5 year terms. Power is concentrated in the executive branch of the government, and national companies manage physical infrastructure and much of banking and industry. In an effort to enter the top 50 of the world's most competitive nations,[6] President Nazarbayev has urged the development of an information society, supported by national research and development funds and manifested in projects such as the IT City recently established near Almaty.

The constitution identifies Kazakh as the state language (Article 7.1); authorizes government institutions to use Russian as equal to Kazakh (Article 7.2); and states that everyone should be able to enjoy their native language and culture (Article 19). Primary education may be in Kazakh or Russian, according to local circumstance, and in some urban areas parents may choose to enroll their children in either a Kazakh or Russian track. Government-mandated basic education curricula allot approximately 30% of teaching time to languages and literature.[7] The majority of Kazakhstanis are at least bilingual, in Russian or Kazakh and a second language—Kazakh, Russian, or one of the minority native languages (e.g., Uighur, Ukrainian, Uzbek), and many are also proficient in other languages that are increasingly part of required school curricula (e.g., English, Mandarin, Korean, and Japanese).[5,8] Literacy rates, which government statistics have reported as over 99% since independence, usually do not specify the language(s) in which literacy is assessed. The government's pursuit of a "sovereign (Kazakh) identity" may bring about a shift to the Latin alphabet for the Kazakh language within the next 15 years.[9]

Publishing is a highly controlled activity in Kazakhstan, regulated by the AIC, the Agency of the Republic of Kazakhstan for Informatization and Communication.[10] In 2006 the government recognized 314 sociopolitical, 1029 informational, 198 advertising, 172 science, 28 women's, 41 youth, 39 children's, and 37 religious media outlets in Kazakhstan. In 2007, 29 large book publishers reported operations in Kazakhstan, including specialty publishers of children's, legal, and reference works. At least in quantity, print publishing in Kazakhstan lags behind comparable EU states[11] and the demand for Kazakh language materials in particular exceeds supply.[12] As for booksellers, this entry's authors have observed that in cities, large chain-style bookstores are replacing book sales from corner kiosks and used dealers.

LIBRARY AND INFORMATION SCIENCE PROFESSIONS, SYSTEMS, AND SERVICES

History

Soviet-era libraries were organized in a hierarchy from the central research collections, down through regional university, college, institute and academy libraries, to public libraries in a variety of locations including factories, plants, trade unions, culture centers, and schools.[13] Research libraries maintained broad and deep collections for the restricted use of scientists; university libraries provided approved knowledge to students; and public libraries worked toward universal literacy and the transfer of party policy and practical knowledge to the working classes.[14] Following both Islamic and Russian-adopted European traditions, libraries emphasized preservation of key authoritative texts over dissemination of newer knowledge. Technologically, Soviet libraries fell behind their western counterparts beginning in the 1960s due to slow development of civilian telecommunications infrastructure and personal computers.[15]

Legislation Concerning Libraries

Two government ministries supervise libraries. The Ministry of Culture and Information[16] oversees more than 3500 national, regional and public libraries, and the Ministry of Education and Science[17] is responsible for approximately 7500 school, university, professional, academic, and scientific-technical libraries. Some government agencies and research institutes maintain separate libraries, such as agriculture, health, and physics. From the Soviet era Kazakhstan continues the National Book Chamber that is responsible for state bibliographic control and cataloging, statistics on print publications, and ISBN and ISSN assignment.[11]

Specific laws governing libraries and legal deposit have been drafted, but have not yet been adopted. In the meantime state libraries are regulated by standards approved in an order of the Ministry of Culture and Information from 2002.[18] Legal deposit is regulated by the 1991 Soviet-era Law On Print Media and Other Mass Media Outlets, amended by the Kazakhstani parliament in 1995.[11] Library legal deposit is entangled with regulations requiring deposit of all printed matter to "authorized agencies" that could be used to suspend publications and printers.[19] Other relevant laws include On Informatization (2003), On Science (2001), On Mass Media (1999), On Culture (1996), the Patent Law (1999, amended 2007), On Trademarks, Service Marks, and Apellations Of Origin (1999), and On Copyright and Neighboring Rights (1996, amended 2004, 2005). The copyright law, which does not address fair use, has been analyzed as more attuned to Kazakhstan's future international relations than its current

domestic situation,[20] and as detrimental to information dissemination efforts in education and publishing.[21] In practice, the unauthorized reproduction and translation of print and electronic works for nonprofit and commercial purposes is declining in situations where education about intellectual property issues is provided and laws are enforced.

National Library and Information Services

Kazakhstan has several national libraries. The predecessor of the oldest National Library[22] was conceived by the Vernyi Municipal Council in 1910, and has had a series of prominent directors,[23] from politician and statesman Uraz Dzhandosov (1908–1938) through Murat Auezov— Orientalist–philologist, diplomat, and descendant of Mukhtar Auezov (1897–1961), the author famous for his studies of the works of Abai. In 1931, this library became the State Public Library of the Kazakh SSR, with depository responsibility, and was renamed the National Library in 1991. In 2006 the library reported 280 employees and holdings of 5.8 million items. Collecting focuses on social studies, culture, art, literature, and linguistics. The library building, designed in 1971, is 30,000 m^2 and since 2006 is undergoing major renovation.

In 2004 the National Academic Library[24] opened in Astana under the direction of R. Berdigaliyeva, formerly director of the National Library in Almaty. The Astana facility combines traditional library service with new communication and information technologies, as in a virtual reference service. A variety of electronic and some print resources are available.

A third national facility opened recently in the new Presidential Center of the Culture of the Republic of Kazakhstan[25] in Astana. This library's mission is to bring together materials on Kazakh history and culture from around the world, and to organize and preserve the materials for serious scholarship.[26] The library is 15,000 m^2, with holdings of 700,000 items including the collections of the previous Saken Seyfullin Regional Universal Scientific Library and the first UN depository in Central Asia.

The National Libraries encourage the technological informatization of Kazakhstan's public regional libraries in various ways. Multimedia collections are beginning; CD-ROM and Web-based resources are being introduced, as well as electronic document delivery, and a domestic automated library system, the Republican Automated Library Information System (RABIS) is underway. Development is progressing as quickly as budgets can provide infrastructure installation and sustained staff training.

Public Libraries

Public libraries are organized into a hierarchy from national to village libraries, and by categories of children's, juvenile, special needs (blind and deaf), oblast

Israel–Knowledge Discovery

universal research, municipal, and rural libraries. The ministry estimates 9 million users annually, including 4 million reader accounts—public libraries operate on a subscription system in which a modest annual fee (300 tenge in 2006) secures privileges for facility use and borrowing. Service hours typically fall within the standard Monday to Friday 40 hr work week. Stacks may be open if space allows.

Public libraries continue to play an important role in supporting universal, lifelong education, and promoting national identity. Recent outreach programs have promoted the library as a center for ecological information and for village development. The "Library Capital" conference is held annually since 2001 at a regional library to advance regional innovation and develop local government support. Each conference produces a document of best policies and practices that is afterwards applied throughout the republican library network.

Kazakhstan also has a number of other institutions for general readers, sponsored by foreign embassies, multinational and nongovernmental organizations and cultural associations, and supported by membership fees, such as the British Council libraries.[27] Library materials typically promote the language or purpose of the supporting agency. Such collections may close and open with economic and political changes—for example, a "new" American Corner at the Central Scientific Library, opened in 2006, reinvigorates a collection of books donated in the early 1990s.

Academic and Research Libraries

The Ministry of Education and Science[17] exercises centralized control over all aspects of the educational process beginning from preschool. Higher education begins with undergraduate training or study at the 181 colleges and universities (51 public and 130 private) attended by nearly 1.3 million students in 2005–2006. In its education strategy for 2005–2010, the government is working out procedures for accreditation so as to harmonize the quality of grading with the terms of the Bologna process.[28] In efforts to bring Kazakhstan into line with international standards, many universities are in transition from 5-year *diplom* to 4-year baccalaureate programs, and from highly structured program requirements to a more flexible credit system.[29] Graduate departments exist in 72 universities and 70 research institutes, and were attended by 4700 postgraduates and 303 doctoral students in 2005. Graduate level education is also in flux, with Master's and Ph.D. programs offered alongside *aspirantura* and *candidatskaya* degrees. The terminal Soviet degree, the *Doktor Nauk*, once paved the way to positions in one of the approximately 30 academies of sciences, the premiere research institutions in the Kazakh SSR. Since independence, foreign aid has increased the status of universities

and their teaching professors vis-à-vis research academies and their members.[30,31]

Academic and research libraries are typically open only to members of their institutions (at national or oblast facilities, credentialed scholars) during the standard work week. Closed stacks and fee-for-service, on-site use of print and electronic resources are the norm. Electronic cataloging has been introduced, and institutions with large collections face generations of work to convert card catalogs, as well as the items they describe, to electronic formats.

Research libraries

The Central Scientific Library[32] is the main research library for scientists and scholars in the country. (In Russian, "scientific research" connotes the entire range of scholarly activity, from poetry to physics.) Founded in Almaty in 1932 as the Kazakh affiliate library of the Academy of Sciences of the USSR, it currently holds over 5.3 million volumes in its main facility and 16 affiliate libraries throughout Almaty and the republic. Collections span the arts and sciences, including the largest foreign languages collection (850,000 items) in Central Asia. The main facility of 37,000 m^2 is undergoing a major renovation from 2006. Director K. Abugalieva manages a staff of about 300.

The Republican Scientific-Technical Library (RNTB),[33] headquartered in Almaty, was created in 1960 to support scientists, engineers, innovators, and researchers. In 1966–1976 a centralized system of the country's regional scientific-technical libraries was developed, which now includes several Almaty locations and 12 regional libraries. Combined holdings of 23 million items include patents, dissertations, and standards. The total staff of 447 is headed by General Director-RNTB Director K. Urmurzina. RNTB uses IRBIS, a mid-1990s Russian automated library system inspired by UNESCO's CDS/ISIS package.[34] O. Kvochkina, head of RNTB's Center for the Development of Libraries, also manages the Information Consortium of Kazakhstan.[35]

University libraries

The Scientific Library[36] of Al-Farabi Kazakh National University (KazNU)[37] supports the leading higher educational institution of the republic (annual enrollment: 15,000). Established in 1934, this largest university library in the country holds over 2 million items at various campus facilities and in 1962 was designated the scientific-methodical center for libraries of educational institutions.

The Scientific-Technical Library[38] of the Kazakhstan National Technical University[39] (annual enrollment: 12,000) was also created in 1934, with the 8500 volume collection of the Semipalatinsk Geological Technicum Library. It has become the most important university

Israel–Knowledge Discovery

Fig. 4 The KIMEP Library.
Source: Photograph by Leslie Champeny.

technical library for the Almaty area with 1.3 million current holdings. In recent years the library has been able to add facilities, collections, and computing capacity with the support of the U.S. Agency for International Development (USAID).

Notable among private universities is the new library at the Kazakhstan Institute of Management, Economics and Strategic Research (KIMEP)[40] that was completed in 2006 (Fig. 4). KIMEP, an English-language university offering social science and business education to over 3000 students, has been fortunate to be able to combine its heritage as the former Communist High Party School with over a decade of strong international support to produce a four-floor facility with open stacks for 100,000 books and 7-days-a-week study space.

School Libraries

Public education is mandatory and free. Preschool for children aged 5 and 6 was recently reformed, and basic education is divided into three grade levels: 1–4, 5–9, and 10–11. School libraries are managed by an oblast administrator responsible for oversight of proper materials to support approved curricula throughout the region. The position of school librarian is a recognized degree specialty. Funding is at discretion of the school principal, and many schools encourage additional support from parents including the purchase of textbooks.

Special Libraries

Medicine and law (like library science) are undergraduate professional degrees. Law schools and law offices

maintain their own resource collections. Legislative decisions are first published in a government register, and commercial indexes can be purchased on CD or subscribed to online. The Ministry of Health[41] information resources focus on pharmaceuticals, and medical schools maintain their own libraries. Business does not yet appear to support corporate libraries, although there is a keen appreciation of information as a competitive advantage and a marketable product. More common is for well-established libraries to be offered specialized resources in exchange for providing space and staff to maintain services—for example, the National Library in Almaty hosts a collection of oil and gas information resources funded by an international petroleum company.

Digital Library Collections and Services

Libraries are eager to possess digital technologies and collections. International support for digital library development since the mid-1990s is beginning to show results. For example, UNESCO's 2004 training in Greenstone digital library software enabled the Human Rights Digital Library launched in 2006 at the National Academic Library. Collections of locally produced electronic documents are beginning to appear online at some of the larger libraries, including digitized rare manuscripts and musical recordings.

Librarianship and Information Science as a Discipline and Profession

Considering the relatively recent development of mass literacy in Kazakh society, and the decades of Soviet censorship that followed, it becomes apparent why jobs like

Israel–Knowledge Discovery

Israel–Knowledge Discovery

Fig. 5 Kazakhstani librarians continuing their education.
Source: Photograph by Leslie Champeny.

journalist, publisher, and librarian might be low in security and status. The librarian (and wife of Lenin) Nadezhda Krupskaya (1869–1939) is a model who represents the essential role of libraries in education and nation building. Those within the profession recognize the erudition, technical expertise, and multilingual abilities required. It is difficult to attract individuals with this skills set to entry-level positions at low wages, and equally difficult to retain their services after they develop the skills on the job. Library-flavored information science hardly exists, although there are excellent mathematicians, linguists, computer scientists, and business information systems experts.

Regarding professional education, in 1934 the first Regional Kazakh Library College was formed, and the undergraduate degree in library science and bibliography is currently offered at three institutions. Required courses cover the history of the book, bibliographical theory and description, user issues, library management, collections (*fond*) and information resources, and automated library systems; specialized disciplines include documentation, networks, bibliography of Kazakhstan, standardization, information culture, and library marketing. In 2001 a post-graduate course on Librarianship, Bibliography Science, and Book-Science was developed and in 2004 a graduate program opened at a state university. Continuing education for professional librarians is available through the major libraries, often in conjunction with international development support organizations (Fig. 5). In 2000 the Eurasia Foundation and the Open Society Institute funded

the Centre for Professional Development of Library Workers at the RNTB.[42]

As for professional associations, the Library Association of the Republic of Kazakhstan (LARK) (founded in 1997) brings together workers from a variety of libraries, offering occasional lectures and information on opportunities for participation in international organizations. National and scientific-technical libraries can join appropriate regional organizations. Major libraries regularly send participants to meetings sponsored by international organizations.

ARCHIVES AND ARCHIVAL SCIENCE

History

Archives were started by the Inner Bukeev horde around 1795. The present archival system derives from the USSR. In 1921 the first central archives was founded in Orenburg, the capital of Kazakhstan's predecessor state, the Kyrgyz Autonomous Socialist Republic. Aleksandr Mikhailov was its first director. The capital of Soviet Kazakhstan moved twice, to Kzyl Orda in the mid-1920s and to Almaty in 1929. Because of these moves, as well as several border realignments, some document collections remain in archives in Russia or other Central Asian countries, and others were lost. Nevertheless, Kazakhstan's archives include original documents from as early as 1733 on the khanates, on Kazakh accession to the Russian empire, and on other state activity prior to and during the Soviet period.

Kazakhstan followed the usual Soviet model for state archives. In addition to the Central State Historical Archives, there was a Central State Archive of the October Revolution and Socialist Development (founded 1931), and these were combined in 1957 into the Central State Historical Archives of the Kazakh SSR. Regional archives were also opened during the 1920s. The 1940s–1950s brought improvements in archival processing and storage including a laboratory devoted to microfilming, preservation, and restoration, despite sporadic funding and support for training. Central archives for film, photographs and audio recordings, and for technical and scientific documents opened in 1974. By 1989 there were 20 oblast archives, including regional branches.

The Communist Party had its own parallel network of archives in Kazakhstan. Before the Revolution, the Central Committee of the Russian Social Democratic Party maintained collections in various cities. In 1920, the Russian Council of the People's Commissars (SNK) created a special body for the collection and study of documents relating to the October Revolution. A year later the Party created a special office to archive material in the *gubernia* (forerunner of the oblast). In 1943, Kazakhstan's central Party archive in Almaty became part of the Institute of the Party's History of the Central Committee. By 1980 there were 20 Party archives throughout Kazakhstan with around 200 employees.

Legislation Concerning Archives

By treaty Kazakhstan became the successor to the Kazakh SSR archives in 1992 but it did not pass any law regarding state archives until 1998. Between 1992 and 1998 a number of Ministry decisions and Presidential edicts ensured that the existing archives survived, though with minimal support. The 1998 law (with amendments from 2001) provides the legal framework for the current organization of Kazakhstan's archives. This law states that the items in the national archives collections are an inimical part of the historical and cultural heritage of the people of Kazakhstan, and that the collections encompass all documents that have a bearing on the history and identity of the nation regardless of legal ownership. The law also created restricted archives for the security of the nation within the Ministry of Defense, the Interior Ministry's Committee of National Security, the Agency on Fighting Economic Crimes and Corruption, and the Agency for the Protection of the President. Most of the material in restricted archives is inaccessible but the Ministry of Defense archivists will process requests for information on persons who were politically repressed or regarding people in World War II. The 1998 law further authorizes the national archives to seek and retrieve originals or copies of items of national

significance to Kazakhstan from foreign archives, and the central- and oblast-level archives have retrieval agreements with Russian, Korean, German, Turkish, Egyptian, and other archives.

National Archive System

In 1992 the Communist Party archives became the Central State Archives of Recent History, and in 1994 the Presidential Archive. This archive remains in Almaty and is the most advanced in Kazakhstan with climate control and some electronic cataloging. The current director is V. Shtempel.

Archival activity is supervised by the Ministry of Culture and Information. On the national level the ministry's Committee of Information and Archives (originally the Committee for Managing Archives and Documentation) manages the National Center for Archeography and Source Identification; Central State Archive for Scientific and Technical Documentation; Central State Archives; Central State Archive of Film Documents and Audio Recordings; Science and Technical Center for Document Management and Archival Activity; State Repository Collection of Document Copies; and the National Archives of Kazakhstan. The current and fourteenth head of the Central Archives is B. Zhanaev.

Government archives are organized by *fond* (collection), *opis* (register), *delo* (file), and *list* (page). In 2003, the National Archives had approximately 13.6 million documents and was growing at a rate of half-a-million documents a year. The national archival collection included 1,090 fonds in the presidential archives, 144 fonds in the scientific-technical archives, 284,700 records in museums and libraries, and 10,900 audiovisual records.

Oblast and Municipal Archives

In 2006 Kazakhstan had 16 oblast-level departments of archives and documentation, 36 oblast filial archives, and 166 regional and municipal archives. Regional archives are subordinate to the national Committee of Information and Archives. Administratively, they are branches of the regional governments. The oblast archives include all media in one collection. They are tasked with being repositories of nationally important documents of local origin and inputting this information into Kazakhstan's unified document accounting system. All of these archives have published guides and aids to their collections; mount local exhibits of archival documents; and provide technical and organizational leadership in document retention to local organizations and government agencies. They are the repositories of employment and other business documents of the oblast.

Israel–Knowledge Discovery

Archival Work

All documents that have national value are part of the national archive system, no matter their origin, location, or format. Examples are legislation, construction project drafts, technological patent licensing, machine readable and audiovisual documentation, and historic and cultural documents. The state archives must maintain a catalog of this material, with the help of the sources of the items. The documents originating in private or other government agencies must be kept and cataloged for the national archival system. The Committee of Information and Archives has produced rules for the handling of documents and defining the length of retention. If a legal entity (e.g., corporation) ceases to exist, certain documents must be organized and delivered to the oblast or city archives (e.g., employment documents, records of board meetings).

The National Archives is actively pursuing document preservation and the retrospective conversion of paper documents into other media. The State Insured Collection of Document Copies of the National Archives Collection has prepared over 1.6 million frames of microfilm, restored over 12,000 pages of faded text and converted into digital format over 818 photographs, 172 films and 1,350 photographic documents.

In 2006 the government developed its 2007–2009 archival development plan. It announced that its archives would work to become ISO 15489-certified by the end of 2009. The plan notes that current conditions in some archives are not yet compliant with existing national requirements, due to lack of a single unified electronic information system and limitations of older infrastructure.

Kazakhstan initiated efforts in 2002 to develop electronic archives. The Presidential Archives became the first to introduce an electronic holding system and a program to digitize existing holdings. The archives' database shows partial holdings, and as of 2004 the archivists still operated the database for the client. Problems with the rate of digitization, storage, and integration of new document formats were reported in 2006. In the same year the government formed a working group towards creating an "electronic government" by 2009 that included archivists to examine issues regarding the introduction of a nationwide system of electronic archives.

Print and electronic publishing activity

Since 1987 the Center of Scientific and Technical Information on Document Handling and Archival Activity has published a national quarterly. The Central State and oblast-level archives publish periodically, including *The Archival Herald* (Karaganda Oblast, since 2000) and *The Archivist* (Kostenai Oblast, since 2002). An independent monthly covering document management and archives, *Deloproizvodstvo v Kazakhstane*, began publication in 2007. Under the auspices of UNESCO's HeritageNet program, several CDs of archival documents were produced, including *Kazakhstani Chronicle* (2000), a short history of Kazakhstan from the National Library's collection of newspaper articles 1913–1937, and *The Electronic Archive of Kazakhstan* (2002), 168 pages of archival documents from the seventeenth and eighteenth centuries.

The Central State Archives Internet site[43] published legislation and regulations pertaining to archives and their use, a list of the oblast-level archives and their publications and other basic information. Closed temporarily in June 2007 for lack of funding, the government's 2007–2009 plan includes a new or upgraded site. The Presidential Archives Web site[44] includes contact information, a small history, description, and rules on the use of the collections, and its semiannual bulletin. Archive Web sites of Eastern Kazakhstan Oblast[45] and Kostenai Oblast[46] include full texts of the laws and regulations governing archives, and descriptions of the collections and services offered.

Access and Use

Access and use of the archives are guaranteed to all. The Committee of Information and Archives has created detailed rules for access. Documents judged to contain state or commercial secrets or that would violate the privacy of an individual have restricted access. The managers of individual archives may judge original documents as too fragile or valuable to be given to a researcher and may substitute copies.

Committee rules state that researchers should present an official letter from their sponsoring organization. University students should present a letter from the rector of their school asserting the necessity of the archival documents for the student's research. Independent researchers must prove their identity and complete an application form to the proper archive. Permission is typically valid for 1 year or one stay in Kazakhstan. A change in the area of research requires a reapplication. There is a daily limit on the number of registers that may be used and an annual limit on photocopying. Visitors are provided free consultation, have access to any automated catalogs, may bring in their own documents and avail themselves of a translator's services.

Archival Science as a Discipline and Profession

In 2007, the Kazakhstan Central State Archives Web site listed 12 colleges and universities that offer programs appropriate for work in archives, sometimes combined with document management programs. Working archivists must be certified periodically by the Committee for Information and Archives. Government-mandated continuing education is frequent, and has recently focused on compliance with the changing labor code and the administration of documentation transition to the Kazakh language.

Israel–Knowledge Discovery

Archivists may belong to the Society of Archivists of the Republic of Kazakhstan. Kazakhstan is also a member of international organizations on archives including the International Council of Archives, the International Federation of Information and Documentation, the International Association of Sound Archives, and the International Federation of Television Archives.

In sum, the role of documentation in Soviet society cannot be overstated, and made archiving an essential profession. However, the resulting "document explosion" has made the archivist's task extremely difficult. The status of archiving as a profession also suffers from the Soviet reputation for altering documents. Similar to libraries, archives have difficulty attracting and retaining talented employees.

MUSEUMS AND MUSEOLOGY

The history of museums dates to 1832, when Vladimir Dal (1801–1872) (who would become Russia's first lexicographer) was sent to the Russian military outpost at Orenburg. Dal took an interest in the nature and culture of the region and reportedly opened a museum of zoology and botany, and some of his collections now reside with the Central State Museum in Almaty. Today the Ministry of Culture and Information reports more than 150 museums throughout Kazakhstan, primarily regional, historical, and ethnographic, fine arts, and biographical memorial institutions; unique topics including mining and rice cultivation. The ministry estimates that 20,000 exhibits and events have been presented in recent years with an attendance of approximately 1 million.

National Museums

There are six national museums. The Central State Museum[47] is one of the largest museums in Central Asia, with permanent and rotating exhibits on natural history and cultural heritage. The museum opened in 1931 in Almaty's Cathedral in Panfilov Park, incorporating collections of the Cossak Army and the Republic Anti-religious Museums. In 1985 it moved to its current facility of 17,577 m^2, where it can display about one-tenth of its 200,000 item collections. A journal *Kazakhstan Muzeileri* ("Kazakhstan Museums") has been published since 2002.

The Kasteyev Arts Museum[48] was named for the first major national artist Abylkhan Kasteyev (1904–1973) in 1984. The museum originally opened as the National Art Gallery in Almaty in 1935 with an exhibit celebrating 15 years of the Kazakh SSR. In 1936 the State Tretyakov Gallery and the A. Pushkin State Museum of Fine Arts in Moscow donated approximately 200 works. In 1939 the gallery was named after the Ukrainian writer Shevchenko on the 125th anniversary of his birth. In 1976 the gallery and the Museum of Applied Art moved to a new building

of 19,400 m^2 with ample storage space, photo laboratory, large exposition halls, and climate control. It owns about 22,000 Kazakh, Russian, European, and Asian fine art showpieces including paintings, graphic works, sculptures of popular arts and theatre, and decorative art.

Of special interest to librarians, the Republican Book Museum was opened in Almaty in 1978. It has six halls for exhibitions of the history of Kazakh writing and book printing as well as modern publications in Kazakhstan. Holdings include 5,123 rare original manuscripts, ancient books and drawings, and 45,000 other books, periodicals, booklets, emblems, and charts (Fig. 6).

The State Museum of Popular Musical Instruments was created in 1980 in a beautiful nineteenth-century wooden building in Almaty's central park. The collection displays instruments from Kazakhstan and around the world including the personal *dombras* (a long necked, two-stringed instrument similar to a lute) of famous Kazakh poets and composers such as Abai.

The State Gold and Precious Metals Museum was founded in 1990 as the main repository of Kazakh jewelry from the earliest time up to present. It annually replenishes its collection with unique showpieces.

The newly established State Museum of Archeology and Ethnography[49] is in the Presidential Centre in Astana. This museum is charged with the material and technical, managerial, scientific-methodical, and financial backing of studies of the country's national cultural heritage and current development. Its collections include the Berelskaya and Buzuk archeological items, and gifts given to the Head of State.

Other Museums, Galleries, Zoos, and Preserves

Each oblast has a museum that includes science and natural history-themed exhibits, and several academies of the natural and physical sciences operate small museums. Notable is the Geology Museum in Almaty, which offers an interactive computer show demonstrating different geological processes. KazNU reports museums for its departments of paleology, archeology, and biology. In Semipalatinsk, site of former Soviet nuclear testing grounds, the state medical academy maintains a teaching collection of malformed fetuses that is said to be unforgettable.[50]

Oblast museums present exhibits of regional history or ethnography. In addition to the World Heritage sites of Tamgaly and the Yasavi mausoleum, the Ministry of Culture and Information supports several other historical and cultural reserves, and large-scale digs at 32 sites of ancient settlements, burial grounds, and tumuli were performed in 2005. Biographical memorial museums are numerous, as are monuments, statues, and commemorative plaques on buildings associated with prominent persons.

Many oblasts also operate art museums for their regions, and there are numerous art galleries in urban centers. Four zoos (and three circuses) operate in

Israel–Knowledge Discovery

Israel–Knowledge Discovery

Fig. 6 The Republican Book Museum in Almaty. **Source:** Photograph by Leslie Champeny.

Kazakhstan. Nine national nature preserves protect over 70 plant and 129 animal endangered species.

Museology as a Discipline and Profession

Museums are valued primarily as cultural and historical centers, and are responsible for the organization of scientific research to elucidate and preserve Kazakhstan's national heritage. Archaeological and ethnographic work is especially important given the relatively recent development of written history. Perhaps even more than libraries, museums have become a tool for promoting national identity locally and internationally, as in the organization of exhibitions such as *Of Gold and Grass*: *Nomads of Kazakhstan*,[51] which recently toured the U.S. Professionals in the discipline may be found in research and consulting positions in museums, historical and cultural centers, specialized schools and colleges, governmental management bodies, and tourist organizations.

Regarding education for curators and museum administrators, museology was a certified undergraduate degree in the USSR, usually offered from a department of archaeology or history. Current educational paths to museum work are the designated specialities Culture Studies, Archaeology and Ethnic Studies, and Museums and Preservations of Artifacts, offered at three state universities. The curriculum includes organization of museums, conservation and reconstruction of historical artifacts and culture, regional studies and research, organization of regional studies museums in secondary schools and colleges, expertise and consultation on culture in government, and creation of historical sites tourist routes.

Regarding professional associations, the National Committee of the International Council of Museums assists the country's leading museums to enter into cooperation with international institutions such as the British Museum, Russian State Library, and Hamburg Ethnographic Museum.

CONCLUSION: TOWARDS THE FUTURE

Kazakhstani librarians of a certain age often reminisce about the old days of economic and job security, when they were part of the largest network of information institutions on earth, and the sharing of knowledge among the republics was well regulated and reliable. With the departure of Russian economic and administrative support, interorganizational cooperation declined for a time as each institution struggled to maintain its own resources. With the encouragement and support of the international community, information professionals are beginning to rebuild the network of relationships that will be required to support information sharing practices such as interlibrary loan.

Ambivalence remains about how to build on the Soviet legacy while at the same time acknowledging, and then solving its problems. The call to forge a new national identity is one proposed solution, and many information institutions have responded, as in recent library projects *Til Oneri* ("Language is the foundation of everything"), *Shanyrak* (history, cultural traditions, and customs), and *Atamura* (the revival and preservation of national musical heritage). Language issues already affect the daily decisions of information workers from catalogers to programmers and publishers, and policy changes will further complicate decision making at all stages of the information cycle, for example, regarding production formats, organizational schemes, and selection of items for preservation. The focus on informatization is another solution, perhaps less politically charged at present, but also more expensive.

Institutions will have to upgrade infrastructure, import technologies, retrain staff, and improve organizational operation to participate fully in the global information society. Given Kazakhstan's regional economic dominance, it is to be hoped that the political will exists to implement the necessary changes.

ACKNOWLEDGMENTS

We are deeply grateful to the staffs of the ministries and institutions described in this entry, especially A. Yusupova of the Central Scientific Library. We also appreciate the suggestions of two anonymous reviewers, which we have incorporated wherever possible. Special thanks to our colleagues at KIMEP, whose collective wisdom spans more than 40 years in information institutions across the former Soviet space.

APPENDIX 1

Table A.1 Timeline

Century	Event	Year
15th B.C.E.	Horse-herding nomads at Tamgaly	
8th–3rd B.C.E.	Scythian Saka in region	
8th C.E.	Islam introduced	
9th–10th	Al-Farabi (870–950) builds library in Otrar	
12th	Khoja Ahmed Yasavi (1106–1166) retires to underground cell in Turkistan	ca.1163
13th	Chingiz Khan (1162–1227) sacks Otrar	1219
15th	Amur Timur (1336–1405) dies in Otrar; Kazakh khanate later emerges from his descendants' rule	
17th	Kazakh khanate splits into three *zhus*	
18th	Ablai Khan (1711–1781) allies with Russia against Mongol threats	
19th	Fort Vernyi established	1854
	Abai Kunanbayev (1845–1904) writes Kazakh poetry	
20th	Kazakhs protest conscription into Russian army	1916
	Bolshevik Party takes control of Kazakh *Alash Orda*	1919
	Turkistan Autonomous SSR split into Central Asian republics	1923–1924
	Kazakhstan becomes full-fledged Soviet Socialist Republic	1936
	Great Patriotic War; Stalin deports undesirables to region	1941–1945
	Soviet nuclear tests begin near Semipalatinsk	1949
	Kruschev declares virgin lands campaign	1954
	First manned space launch from Baykonur	1961
	Republic of Kazakhstan becomes independent state	1991

REFERENCES

1. Yudin, V.P. *Tsentralnaya Aziya v 14–18 vekah glazami vostokoveda*; Dajk-Press: Almaty, Kazakhstan, 2001.
2. Olson, J.S.; Pappas, L.B.; Charles, N. *An Ethnohistorical Dictionary of the Russian and Soviet Empires*; Greenwood Press: Westport, CT, 1994; 355.
3. Allworth, E. Central Asian libraries. In *International Dictionary of Library Histories*; Stam, D., Ed.; Fitzroy Dearborn: Chicago, IL, 2001; 46.
4. Kuzhabekova, A. *Past, Present and Future of Language Policy in Kazakhstan*; University of North Dakota: Grand Forks, ND, 2003; M.A. thesis, Available at http://www.und.edu/dept/linguistics/theses/2003Kuzhabekova.PDF (accessed April 2006).
5. Kazakhstan—Education System; *Encyclopedia of Modern Asia*, Macmillan Reference (Gale Group): U.S.A., 2001–2006; Available at http://www.bookrags.com/research/kazakhstaneducation-system-ema-03/ (accessed January 2009).
6. Nazarbayev, N. *Presidential address to the nation*, 2006; Available at http://www.akorda.kz/www/www_akorda_kz.nsf/sections?OpenForm&id_doc=5D4D3D423A0AB331462572340019E627&lang=en&L1=L2&L2=L2-22 (accessed October 2007).
7. World Education Forum. *Education for all 2000 assessment*, Country reports: Kazakhstan. Available at http://www.unesco.org/education/wef/countryreports/kazakhstan/rapport_2_1.html (accessed January 2009).
8. Suleimenova, E.; Smagulova, J. Kazakhstan: Language situation. In *Encyclopedia of Language & Linguistics*, 2nd Ed. Elsevier: Boston, MA, 2006; 175–177.
9. Bartlett, P. Moving forward with plan to replace Cyrillic with Latin alphabet. *Eurasianet.org*, 2007; September 4, Available at http://www.eurasianet.org/departments/insight/articles/eav 090407.shtml (accessed September 2007).
10. Agency for Informatization and Communication website. Available at http://www.aic.gov.kz/.
11. Dzhigo, A.A.; Teplitskaya, A.V. Status of national bibliographies in the CIS countries of central Asia *Bibliography Meeting*, World Library and Information Congress: 72nd IFLA General Conference and Council Seoul, Korea August, 20–24, 2006 109. Available at http://www.ifla.org/IV/ifla72/papers/109-Dzhigo_Teplitskaya-en.pdf (accessed May 2007).
12. Federal Research Division, Library of Congress, *Country Studies: Kazakhstan*, Available at http://lcweb2.loc.gov/frd/cs/kztoc.html (accessed January 2009).
13. Zaitsev, V. Problems of Russian libraries in an age of social change. Daedalus **1996**, *125*(4), 293–306.
14. Richards, P.S. Soviet-American library relations in the 1920s and 1930s: a study in mutual fascination and distrust. Libr. Quart. **1998**, *68*(4), 390–405.
15. Shraiberg, Y. International experience and Russian reality: Library and information field *America and Russia on the Way to Global Information Society*, Seventh International Workshop Electronic Resources and International Information Exchange East–West, Washington, DC March, 12, 2004. Available at http://www.iliac.org/seminar/docs/shra1.html (accessed September 2005).

Israel–Knowledge Discovery

16. Ministry of Culture and Information website. Available at http://www.sana.gov.kz/.

17. Ministry of Education and Science website. Available at http://www.edu.gov.kz/.

18. Berdigaliyeva, R. Annual report to CDNL 2002–2003. Available at http://www-prod.nla.gov.au/initiatives/meetings/cdnl/2003/kazakhstan.rtf.

19. *Article XIX. Memorandum on the Draft Law of the Republic of Kazakhstan "On Publishing" (LAW/2007/0105)*, Article XIX: London, U.K., 2007; http://wwwsoc.nii.ac.jpwww.article19.org/pdfs/analysis/kazakhstan-media-la.pdf (accessed May 2007).

20. Massalina, S. The WCT and the Kazakhstan copyright law: Putting the cart in front of the horse?. UNESCO e-Copyright Bull. **2005**, October–December. Available at http://portal.unesco.org/culture/en/files/30525/11431980071 massalina_en.pdf/massalina_en.pdf (accessed January 2009).

21. Consumers International. *Copyright and Access to Knowledge: Policy Recommendations on Flexibilities in Copyright Laws*, Consumers International Asia Pacific Office: Kuala Lumpur, 2006; Available at http://www.soros.org/initiatives/information/focus/access/articles_publications/publications/copyright_20060602/copyright_access.pdf (accessed September 2007).

22. National Library of Kazakhstan website. Available at http://wwwsoc.nii.ac.jpwww.nlrk.kz.

23. http://www.nlrk.kz/index.php?modname=page&action=show&id=17&lang=1.

24. National Academic Library website. Available at http://nabrk.kz/.

25. Presidential Culture Center website, —English links nonfunctional. Available at http://prescentreculture.kz/.

26. Carlson, C. Central Asia: Libraries in a difficult bind following soviet collapse. *Eurasianet*, 2003; May 24, Available at http://www.eurasianet.org/departments/culture/articles/eav052403.shtml (accessed May 2007).

27. British Council Kazakhstan–Kyrgyzstan Information and Learning Center website. Available at http://www.britishcouncil.org/kazakhstan.htm.

28. State-Run Education Development Program to be implemented in the Republic of Kazakhstan in 2005–2010. Available at http://en.government.kz/resources/docs/doc8.

29. Matuszkiewicz, R. The credit system in Kazakhstan's higher education: Challenges and opportunities. In *Changing Society through Research and Practice*, Proceedings of the V Annual KIMEP International Research Conference (KIRC-2005) October, 6–8, 2005 KIMEP (Dike-Press LTD): Almaty, Kazakhstan, 2006; 116–121.

30. Graham, L. How willing are scientists to reform their own institutions?. In *Academia in Upheaval: Origins, Transfers, and Transformations of the Communist Academic Regime in Russia and East Central Europe*; David-Fox, M., Peteri, G., Eds.; Bergin & Garvey: Westport, CT, 2000.

31. Peteri, G. On the legacy of state socialism in academia. In *Academia in Upheaval: Origins, Transfers, and Transformations of the Communist Academic Regime in Russia and East Central Europe*; David-Fox, M., Peteri, G., Eds.; Bergin & Garvey: Westport, CT, 2000.

32. Central Scientific Library website. Available at http://www.library.kz/.

33. Republican Scientific-Technical Library website. Available at http://rntb.kz/engl.htm.

34. Zaitsev, V.N.; Marshak, B.I. *The Experience of Practical Activities of National and Other Professional Library Associations in Russia*, Management of Library Associations – workshop, 68th IFLA Council and General Conference Glasgow, Scotland August, 18–24, 2002 (041-148-E) 5, Available at http://www.ifla.org/IV/ifla68/papers/041-148e.pdf (accessed September 2007).

35. Information Consortium of Kazakhstan website. Available at http://www.rntb.kz/kkak/.

36. KazNU Library website. Available at http://lib.kazsu.kz/.

37. Kazakhstan National University website. Available at http://www.kazsu.kz/english.aspx.

38. KazNTU Library website, (Russian language links only). Available at http://www.ntu.kz/web_nb/gl_str.html.

39. Kazakhstan National Technical University website. Available at http://www.kazntu.kz/2/.

40. KIMEP Library website. Available at http://www.kimep.kz/academics/library.

41. Ministry of Health Information Resources website. Available at http://www.dari.kz/.

42. A recent wiki workshop at the Centre is described. Available at http://digcit.wordpress.com/.

43. Central State Archives website. Available at http://www.kazarchives.kz/.

44. Central State Archives website. Available at http://www.aprk.kz/.

45. Eastern Kazakhstan Oblast Archives website. Available at http://arhiv.vko.gov.kz/.

46. Kostenai Oblast Archives website. Available at http://kostarchiv.netfirms.com/.

47. Central State Museum website. Available at http://www.unesco.kz/heritagenet/kz/hn-english/csmrk/engl/index_en.htm.

48. Kasteyev Arts Museum website. Available at http://www.art.nursat.kz.

49. State Museum of Archeology and Ethnography website. Available at http://prescentreculture.kz/museum.shtml.

50. A photo of one specimen appears. Available at http://prosites-kazakhembus.homestead.com/Nuc_h.html.

51. *Of Gold and Grass: Nomads of Kazakhstan touring exhibition websites*, Available at http://www.mingei.org/exhibitions/detail.php?EID=29; http://www.hmns.org/exhibits/special_exhibits/goldandgrass.asp; http://www.fiae.org/onexhibit.html (accessed October 2007).

BIBLIOGRAPHY

1. M. Auezov Institute of Literature and Art website, Available at http://litart.academset.kz/?q=en (accessed January 2009).

2. Avtokratov, V.N.; Vaganov, F.M.; Andreeva, N.M.; Volkova, I.V. *Gosudarstvennye arkhivy SSSR: spravochnik*, Mysl: Moskva, 1989.

3. Beisembaeva, Z.A. Reading in Kazakhstan. Intl. Inform. Libr. Rev. **1995**, *27*, 37–46.

4. Faculty of Journalism, Kazakhstan National University (KazNU). Electronical course on journalism "Mass communications" website, Available at http://www.unesco.kz/massmedia/english.htm (accessed January 2009).

Israel–Knowledge Discovery

5. Gribanova, E.M. *'Arkhiv Prezidenta Respubliki Kazakhstan: putevoditel'*, Zheti zharghy: Almaty, Kazakhstan, 2001.

6. Khalid, A. *The Politics of Muslim Cultural Reform: Jadidism in Central Asia*, University of California: Berkeley, CA, 1998.

7. Olcott, M.B. *The Kazakhs (Studies of Nationalities)*, 2nd Ed. Hoover Institute Press: Stanford, CA, 1995.

8. Richardson, J. Developments in the Russian Far East: The state of education for librarianship. JELIS **2003**, *44*(2), 137–152.

9. Richardson, J. The origin of soviet education for librarianship: The role of Nadezhda Krupskaya (1869–1939), Lyubov' Borisovna Khavkina-Hamburger (1871–1949) and Genrietta K. Abele-Derman (1882–1954). JELIS **2000**, *41*, 106–128.

10. Sarieva, R.; Abdulina, A. *Ocherki po istorii organizatsii arkhivnogo dela v Kazakhstane (1918–1945)*, Arys: Almaty, 2006.

11. Shayakhmetov, M. *The Silent Steppe: The Story of a Kazakh Nomad under Stalin*, Stacey International: London, U.K., 2006.

12. Svanberg, I., Ed. *Contemporary Kazaks: Cultural and Social Perspectives*; Curzon Press: Richmond, Surrey, 1999.

13. Vaneev, A.; Minkina, B., Eds. *Spravochnik bibliografa*; Professiya: St. Petersburg, FL, 2003.

14. Vlachoutsicos, C. Russian communitarianism: An invisible fist in the transformation process of Russia. In *Managing Organizational Change in Transition Economies*; Denison, D.R., Ed.; Lawrence Earlbaum Associates: Mahwah, NJ, 2001; 149–206.

Israel–Knowledge Discovery

Kenya: Libraries, Museums, and Archives

Irene Muthoni Kibandi
Pancras Kimaru
Caroline Kayoro
Philomena Kagwiria Mwirigi
Sophie Ndegwa
Nelson Otieno Karilus
Charles Nzivo
Kenya National Library Service (KNLS), Nairobi, Kenya

Linda Mboya
National Museums of Kenya, Nairobi, Kenya

Lilian Gisesa
Kenya National Archives, Nairobi, Kenya

Abstract

This entry traces the evolution, development, and growth of information systems in Kenya, especially noting the importance of Information Communication Technology in propelling economic development. The authors provide a historical overview of libraries, archives, and museums, outlining patterns and trends through precolonial to post independence. Topics covered include: national, public, academic, special, and school libraries; Kenya National Archives and Documentation services and the regional record centers; National Museums of Kenya, regional museums; and sites and monuments of national and international importance. The legal framework upon which these institutions were established and operate is highlighted. The entry also identifies some key personalities who have made an impact in the fields of librarianship, archival services, and museology in Kenya and discusses the role of professional associations in the development and growth of these institutions.

Israel–Knowledge Discovery

INTRODUCTION

Kenya is an Eastern African country that is bordered by Ethiopia to the north, Somalia to the northeast, and Sudan to the northwest, Uganda to the west, and Tanzania to the south, with the Indian Ocean providing the southeast border. The Equator runs through the center of the country. The climate varies from the humid tropical areas in the coastal region to a cool Mediterranean climate in the highlands in the Southwest. The majority of the terrain is made up of low plains covering about three-fourths of the country. Kenya boasts of a spectacular variety of wildlife. These include elephants, lions, giraffes, zebras, buffalos, and other wild beasts, which attract tourists to Kenya (Fig. 1).

Kenya is comprised of people of all races and religions, and includes over 42 different tribes. A large percentage of the population lives in the rural areas in small settlements where they raise crops and livestock for a living. Many of these farmers also hold part-time jobs to add to their income. However, each year, many rural Kenyans move to towns to find jobs. Most of the urban population work in factories, stores, supermarkets, government offices, or carry out business. Kenyans, who move to cities, must adjust to the fast pace of life in the cities and regular work schedules.

The British colonial government ruled Kenya from 1895 until the country attained independence in 1963. During this time they influenced political, social, economic, and cultural life in Kenya. However since independence, the indigenous leaders have emphasized the African heritage of the nation. Politically, Kenya is a republic which adopted its constitution in 1963. The constitution grants its people the fundamental human rights such as freedom of speech, freedom of expression, freedom of association, intellectual freedom, and religion. Kenya is headed by a president elected by the people through democratic elections every 5 years.

While initially Kenyan children were not required by law to attend schools, the current trends dictate that the government be more forceful on school attendance. Although educational opportunities have continued to expand, the demand for education at all levels has outstripped the available educational institutions. Kenya has over 13,000 primary schools, over 4000 secondary schools, several middle-level colleges, 7 public universities,

Encyclopedia of Library and Information Sciences, Fourth Edition DOI: 10.1081/E-ELIS4-120045356
Copyright © 2017 by Taylor & Francis. All rights reserved.

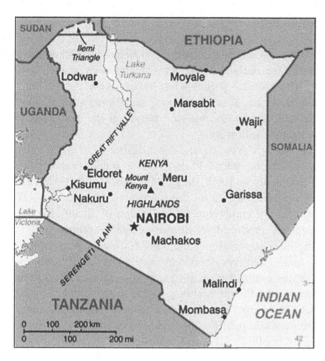

Fig. 1 Map of Kenya.
Source: *CIA World Factbook.* https://www.cia.gov/library/publications/the-world-factbook/geos/ke.html.

and over 10 private universities. As the literacy levels grow, albeit slowly, the need for information in the country has also grown.

The field of library and information is relatively young in the country. Most of the supporting legislation for libraries, archives, and museums were enacted in the 1960s. However there has been a significant growth in the number of libraries and information centers in the past decade and this can in part be attributed to the importance attached to education by individuals and the government. There has been an increase in the number of universities, middle-level colleges and schools. The publishing and book industry is still not fully developed and the reading culture in the country struggles to flourish. If well utilized, the National Archives should therefore become a very important basis for national planning and development. The Archives provides key linkages with the past, present, and future of Kenya.

LIBRARIES

Historical Background

The first library known in Kenya was established in 1887 by the European missionaries at Frere town near Mombasa. The establishment of modern libraries in Kenya can be traced to the early part of 1900s. At that time the creation of libraries was closely linked with the establishment of the British colonial rule and the subsequent arrival in Kenya of European settlers and Indian traders. In an effort to propel economic development in the newly colonized areas, the colonial government identified the need to have a literate society. Although the history of libraries in Kenya cannot be divorced from the establishment of colonial rule and subsequent settlement of Europeans and Indian traders, library development is also closely linked to the growing political awareness of Africans following World War II. The war awakened a spirit of nationalism that preceded the agitation for self-government by patriotic Africans. After World War II Africans realized that their development lay in the European type of education which in turn required access to information.

The libraries that existed before 1945 were mainly set up to serve the interest of the white settlers and the Indian traders. The literacy level among the foreigners was higher than that of the indigenous Kenyans. This entry traces development of libraries and the growth of library profession in Kenya from precolonial period to date. The history of libraries in Kenya can be approached from three historical periods namely: precolonial, colonial, and postcolonial.

Precolonial period: During this period, there were no records of libraries existing in Kenya. This was mainly due to the fact that information was passed from one person to the other through oral traditions and art. These practices inhibited the growth of libraries. The only library on record during this period is said to have existed at Kilwa on the east coast and it served a small literate class of the community.

Colonial period: This is the period when missionaries began to appear in the East coast of Africa and set up a mission at Frere town. In 1887 they established a small library which was meant to be used by the new converts. However, in 1902 the *East African Standard* newspaper, which had been established by Mr. Jeevanjee, set up a news library which stocked reference books and manuscripts for use by the staff.

The High Court of Kenya Library was also established in Mombasa in 1902, but it moved its headquarters to Nairobi in 1905. It had a rich collection of reading materials on law. Later in 1935, a new building was completed in Nairobi which to date houses an important library that serves the judges of the High Court, magistrates, and advocates.

Other libraries established between 1910 and 1932 included Kenya National Assembly library and National Museum library in 1910, and the National public health library (now located at Kenyatta National Hospital) in 1911. The Attorney General's library was established in 1914 and Kenya Agricultural Research Institute library in 1927.

Library development followed racial patterns prevailing at that time. In 1903 that the philanthropic Asians founded the Seif Bin Salim public library in Mombasa. The collection, which was biased toward

Israel–Knowledge Discovery

Indian literature, was later acquired by Kenya National Library Service (KNLS) in 1975. In 1928, Lady Macmillan established a lending library for the white settlers in Nairobi. This library, which was named in memory of her husband, opened its doors in 1931. The Desai Memorial library was established in 1942 by the Indians providing the third public library in Kenya. Nevertheless, none of the established public libraries served African interests.

It was during this period that the colonial government realized the importance of ensuring that the colony was financially self-sufficient. Which meant the involvement of the Africans in the governance of the colony and this required that Africans be educated and be provided with the relevant information resources.

As a result of this that two kinds of libraries developed. First were special libraries to assist in exploiting natural resources of the colony. These included the Departments of Forestry and Agriculture libraries established in 1905 and 1907, respectively, and the National Assembly Library formed immediately after the first sitting of the Kenya Legislative Council in 1907. The second were public libraries including the Seif Bin Salim, Desai Memorial, and the Macmillan Memorial library. In 1948 Elspeth Huxley proposed the establishment of the East African Literature Bureau to produce and distribute literature to African libraries.

After independence: The 1960s were a turning point in the development of libraries in Kenya. The Macmillan Library was handed over to Nairobi city council and opened to all Kenyans. It became the first ever free and open public library in Kenya. Following the recommendation by the East African Library Association and by the British council library consultant, Sydney Hockey, the parliament enacted the Kenya National Library Service Act in 1965 (Chapter 225), of the laws of Kenya. The KNLS became operational in 1967 inheriting the resources and programs of the East African Literature Bureau.

Several government departments and private companies have continued to maintain libraries to support their ministerial and organizational programs. The desire by the government to embrace information in development planning saw the establishment of District Information Documentation Centers (DIDCs) in all districts headquarters. As per District focus circular 1/86 and Provincial Administration circular Ref. OP 16/174/11/23 of September 1984. The objectives of the DIDCs were to provide information to the District planning unit, District Development committees, individuals, and organizations involved in planning; collect and preserve the local statistics; support the planning, monitoring, and evaluation of development projects in the districts; strengthen the district capacity in the management of its activities. However accessing information is still constrained by the Official Secrets Act.

Legislation

Library and information service in Kenya is influenced by several legislations. Some of these laws were enacted during the colonial period while others were passed after independence. These laws have undergone several revisions to cope with changing trends in the field. These include the following:

Books and Newspapers Act (Chapter 111): This legislation can be traced back to 1906 and has undergone amendments in 1960, 1962, 1980, 1987, and 2002. This act serves as the legal deposit law of Kenya. The Act provides for comprehensive collection of all information materials produced in Kenya to enable proper bibliographic control and preparation of National bibliography.

Public Archives Act (Chapter 19): The Public Archives Act was established in 1965 and later revised in 1990 to become the Public Archives and Documentation Service Act. The purpose of the act is to establish the National Archives as a public archive and provide for the preservation of public archives and records.

KNLS Board Act (Chapter 225): This Act was enacted in 1965 and revised in 1969, 1970, 1984, 1988, and 2008. Through this Act, the KNLS board was formed and given the responsibility to "promote, establish, equip, manage, maintain, and develop libraries in Kenya as a national library service." This Act empowers the board to advise the government, local authorities, and private sector on all matters regarding library development.

Science and Technology Act (Chapter 250): This law was enacted in 1977 and was revised in 1979, 1980, 1986, and 2000. The purpose of the Act is to promote scientific research and technological development in Kenya. Through this act, a mechanism was established to ensure that all matters of scientific and technological activities were available to the government. National Council of Science and Technology, which coordinates activities of all major research programs, was a product of this Act.

Industrial Property Act (Chapter 509): This Act was enacted in 1989. The goal of the act is to promote inventions and innovative activities in order to facilitate acquisition of technology through models and industrial designs. It also aims at protecting intellectual property through patenting.

Copyright Act (Chapter 130): This Act was established in 1966 and amended in 1989. It makes provision for copyright in literary artistic works, audiovisual works, sound recordings, broadcast, and for connected purposes.

The legislation discussed above covers the entire information field, from innovation and production (Copyright Law, Science and Technology, and Industrial property Act), to accessibility (Books and Newspapers Act, and Public Archives Act), to establishing and developing libraries (KNLS Act). The government of Kenya recognizes the need to develop an Information Communication Technology (ICT) legal framework that will act as a

Israel–Knowledge Discovery

catalyst for responsiveness and growth in the ICT sector for the benefit of all Kenyans.

Types of Libraries

National library

KNLS serves a dual role of public and national library. The National Library division was established in 1980 in recognition of the need for bibliographic control in Kenya. Some of the services provided include:

- Production of Kenya National Bibliography, Kenya Periodical Directory
- Legal depository center
- Centre for World Bank, UN publications, and IMF collections
- Issuance of International Standard Book Number to Kenyan publishers
- Interlibrary programs
- Rare collections (manuscripts and books out of print with research value)
- Online databases
- Government publications
- Africana and Kenyana publications

Public libraries

Libraries that provide public library service in Kenya include KNLS, Macmillan Library, and several cultural centers (embassy-sponsored libraries). The major public library service provider is KNLS, which has established 54 branches countrywide by 2008. Thirty-nine of these are community-based libraries developed in partnership with the local communities. The Macmillan library has four branches which are run by the city council of Nairobi.

Various embassies have cultural centers which are opened to the public, e.g., the American Cultural Centre, the Iran Library, and the British Council Library, among others.

Fig. 2 Camel library.

The KNLS has a wide network of libraries covering all the eight provinces in the country. Services provided include:

- Adult and junior lending.
- Advisory library services.
- Bulk lending of books to lending institutions.
- Technical assistance on library development to interested government and private institutions.
- Internet service in some of the branch libraries.
- Interlibrary lending, community information services, which include HIV/AIDS information service.
- Repackaging indigenous information.
- Service to the visually challenged persons.
- User education and outreach services including motorized (four mobile trucks and several motor bikes) and nonmotorized mobile library service (donkey and camel), book box service, and cupboard library service in schools (Figs. 2 and 3).
- The library also offers special services to children such as story telling, reading, and writing competitions, games, drama, and cultural activities among others.

Fig. 3 Donkey library.
Source: http://www.knls.or.ke.

Academic libraries

Academic libraries include university and college libraries. The demand for higher education in Kenya has resulted in the proliferation of institutions of higher learning. Currently, Kenya has over seven public universities with well-equipped libraries in the main campuses and in colleges spread in various parts of the country. These include Nairobi University, Kenyatta University, Jomo Kenyatta University of Agricultural Technology, Moi University, Egerton University, Maseno University, and Masinde Muliro University of Science and Technology. There are several private universities with sizeable libraries; among these are Baraton University, Daystar University, United States International University, Kenya Methodist University, Kabarak University, Kiriri Women University, and African Nazarene University among others.

The Kenya Commission for Higher Education requires all universities to establish a library managed by professionals before being awarded a charter. Universities therefore place libraries high in their development priorities. Many middle-level colleges and institutes offering certificate and diploma courses have continued to maintain admirable libraries to support their academic programs (Fig. 4).

Specialized research libraries

Research libraries have been developed in Kenya to support scholarly research in various fields. The oldest being Kenya Forestry research library, Kenya Agricultural Research Institute, an agri-based research institution, the high court library and Ministry of Agriculture library established in the 1900s. Others include:

• International Livestock Research Institute, which undertakes research on animal diseases.

• The Kenya Medical Research Institute, a human diseases research center.
• Kenya Industrial Research Development Institute.
• Kenya Institute of Public Policy Research Analysis, African Medical Research Foundation.

Other major centers for specialized research include international missions such as World Bank, UNESCO, UNICEF, UNEP, WHO, Bakhita documentation center, and Nongovernmental organizations resource and information centers among others. The Government Reference library housed at the Kenya National Archives and Documentation Service (KNA&DS) and the Museum library also serve as research libraries.

Other special libraries

Many businesses and public organizations such as hospitals, research laboratories, law firms, government departments and agencies maintain their own libraries for the use of their employees in doing specialized research related to their work. These libraries may or may not be accessible to members of the public. Some of these libraries in Kenya include the Central Bank of Kenya Library, Unilever library, Capital Market Authority library, National Assembly library, Kenya Bureaus of Standards, and Kenya National Bureau of Statistics. In addition, the Kenya Broadcasting Corporation has the richest collection of Audio-Visual Material of which a majority are gramophone records in East Africa. Most government departments and agencies also have libraries. Government libraries vary from ministry to ministry in terms of size, budgets, and personnel. While many ministries provide generous library support, others provide lukewarm support. For example, the ministries of agriculture, health, and planning have supported their libraries very well. However, inadequate government schemes of service and the lack of political goodwill from the political leadership have led to mass exodus of the professional librarians

Fig. 4 Margaret Thatcher library, Moi University.
Source: http://www.mu.ac.ke.

Israel–Knowledge Discovery

from many government libraries to better paying institutions especially the private sector libraries.

School libraries

Although some public and private primary and secondary schools have functional libraries, most public schools do not have adequate libraries. Only a handful of public schools can afford to employ professional librarians. Nevertheless, well-stocked school libraries are common features of private schools. These libraries also offer computer facilities for their learners. They remain accessible to the elite population who are able to afford the high tuition fee required. High performing secondary schools maintain well-equipped libraries. Mangu high school, Alliance girls and boy's high schools, Starehe boys and girl's centers, and Precious Blood School are good examples. Several have also employed qualified librarians to facilitate provision of efficient and effective library service to the school community.

With the introduction of Free Primary Education by the government in 2003 and free secondary education in 2008, respectively, public schools now receive a book budget. This might be a starting point toward school library development in both public primary and secondary schools in Kenya.

Education for Library and Information Science (LIS)

The need for trained manpower in Kenya can be traced to the 1950s when the Royal Technical College (now Nairobi University) was established. The college provided employees with in-service training in basic library skills. Later, the City and Guilds (a United Kingdom-based correspondence education program) started offering library courses through correspondence. These courses led to the award of certificates in librarianship. Library employees were encouraged to take these British correspondence courses organized by the Library Association of the United Kingdom. As libraries in East Africa developed, it became apparent that highly trained personnel at the senior professional levels were needed. In 1964, therefore, the East African School of Librarianship was established as a regional school located at the Makerere University in Uganda. The school offered non-professional library assistant courses. However, the curricula for the library training have changed tremendously over time.

In 1971, the United Nations Educational, Scientific, and Cultural Organization (UNESCO) developed the concept of harmonization as a basis for the training of information professionals. In the same year, the Kenya Library Association (KLA) appointed an education subcommittee to study the need for manpower in LISs in Kenya. In 1973, KLA facilitated the establishment of certificate programs in library and records management at the Kenya Polytechnic. This training began in 1974 through a partnership of the UNESCO and the KLA. This was a 1-year certificate course which ran for 3 years. Prior to this, the only institution that had the mandate to offer library education was the East African School of Librarianship at Makerere University in Uganda. It offered nonprofessional library assistant certificate and much later diploma and postgraduate courses.

Training in LIS in Kenya is presently in various levels namely certificate, diploma, higher national diploma, undergraduate degree, and postgraduate (Master's and Doctorate) degree.

Certificate and diploma: These are accredited by

- National polytechnics—Kenya Polytechnic University college, Mombasa Polytechnic and Eldoret Polytechnic.
- Technical training institutes—Kenya Technical Training College, Railway training Institute, Sigalagala training Institute, Siaya Institute of Technology, among others.
- Private colleges—Kenya School of Professional Studies, Nairobi North college, Technical Institute of Management, among others.
- Universities—Nairobi University, Egerton University.

Undergraduate and postgraduate degree

- Moi University was the pioneer in the establishment of undergraduate training in LIS in Kenya in 1988.
- Kenyatta University.
- Kenya Methodist University.
- Egerton University.

Professional Associations

Kenya Library Association remains the single professional body that advocates for library professional standards in Kenya. It is a neutral professional association whose origin dates back to 1956 when the East African Library Association was formed. It draws its membership from all stakeholders in the field of information including librarians, documentalists, archivists, information specialists, record managers, and other interested persons.

In 1971, the Standing Conference of African University Librarians of East African met in Addis Ababa where UNESCO developed the concept of harmonization as a basis for training of information professionals (UNESCO, 1994, 2). KLA has continued to agitate for professional standardization and is heavily involved in all matters of library development and participates in forums where library education curriculum is being discussed.

It collaborates and partners with other international bodies for the benefit of its members. It is a member of International Federation of Library Association (IFLA) and Commonwealth Libraries Association (COMLA).

Israel–Knowledge Discovery

KLA major achievements are

- Hosting IFLA conference in 1984. This was the first time for IFLA conference to be held on the African soil and was attended by over 2000 delegates.
- Holding successful annual conferences over the years.
- Hosting COMLA and International Association of Agricultural Librarians and Documentalists conferences in 1983.
- Hosting Standing Conference of East and Southern African Librarians conference in 1998.
- Setting up a Web site through the assistance of International Network for Availability of Scientific Publications.
- Promoting reading culture through Children Reading Tents where it targets marginalized communities, peri-urban poor, slums, and people of low economic status.

In 2006 KLA celebrated a Silver Jubilee where personnel in library and information profession were recognized and given awards. These were

- Ralp Opondo—the first African city librarian in Kenya.
- Nathan Fedha—the first African chief archivist in Kenya.
- John Ndegwa—the first professional in LIS and the first university librarian in Kenya.
- Dr. Wanja Thairu—the first female Ph.D. in LIS in Kenya.
- Professor Ojiambo—the first male Ph.D. in LIS in Kenya.
- Jacinta Were—the first lady chairperson of KLA and member of International Federation of Library Associations and Institutions Board.
- Ruth Thomas—pioneer indexer and committed supporter of KLA.
- Jafred Musisi—a committed supporter of KLA who successfully lobbied to bring the first IFLA conference to Kenya (the first IFLA meeting in Africa).
- Late William Umbima—longest serving editor of KLA.
- Ann-Marie Kinara—pioneer documentalist in agricultural information in Kenya.
- Late Francis Otieno Pala—first chief librarian in KNLS.

KENYA NATIONAL ARCHIVES AND DOCUMENTATION SERVICE

"A nation without a past is lost and a people without a past is a people without a soul"—*Sir Seretse Khama (1980)*

Archives serve not only contemporary (often transient) needs but also the possible needs of researchers in the far distant future. They preserve the past to enrich the future.

Preserving the past, documenting heritage, and making it accessible to the public are the core function of the KNA&DS, which is a department within the office of the Vice President and Ministry of State for National Heritage and Culture.

Historical Background

Archives service in Kenya is a relatively recent development. Throughout the colonial era, which lasted from 1895 to 1963, there was no major effort on the part of colonial administration to preserve public records in Kenya. Between 1903 and 1948, these records were vulnerable to climate and theft owing to the quality of accommodation and storage then available—i.e., early colonial offices buildings were of corrugated iron and wood, which offered neither protection nor security. Many government officials were more concerned with destruction of records that appeared to hinder their work by clogging and congesting registries; such "unneeded" records could conveniently provide scratch paper. Apart from accidental destruction of public records, it is possible that there was unauthorized massive destruction contrary to official local and Colonial Office instructions. In 1910, Governor Percy Giroudi stressed the importance of preservation of public records for posterity by issuing a *Confidential Memoranda* on local official instructions on the destruction *to Provincial and District Commissioners*.

Fires also accounted for some of the destruction of colonial records in Kenya. For example, in September 1905, a fire broke out and destroyed some Government offices and Indian shops in Nairobi. The fire of September 1939 is another case, which involved a fire that burned down government facilities. The 1939 fire mysteriously broke out at night and destroyed the Government Secretariat Offices on the site presently occupied by the Prisons Headquarters in Nairobi. This unfortunate event had very disastrous effects on the records of the Central Government, especially those relating to the earlier days of colonization of Kenya by Britain. Fortunately the government was able to function through the generous cooperation of members of the public and other government departments. As Sir Walter Harragin, the then Acting Governor, admitted in the Legislative Council of November 14, 1939 in the Legislative Council Debate:

> Since the war broke out, the government has had to cope with many and difficult problems. Its task has not been made easier by the fire at the old secretariat which resulted in the loss of the many valuable government records as well as most, though not all of the current files. The Secretary has however, been able to carry on reasonably efficiently, thanks to the cooperation of other government departments and of the members of the general public in supplying copies of correspondence with Government.

Israel–Knowledge Discovery

Following this calamity, no attempt was made to develop some "new records," which could conveniently supplement the partially destroyed archives. Furthermore, the administration persistently showed the same lack of concern as before. The continued unauthorized destruction of public records arose from sheer neglect; in fact such records had been allowed to deteriorate to the point where massive destruction was inevitable. In some instances, the shortage of paper in district offices resulted in earlier records being sacrificed. One case in point occurred on June 8, 1948 when the District Commissioner, Kitui petitioned the Provincial Commissioner, Central Province for permission to use earlier files for preparing rough drafts, adding that he would salvage file covers and fasteners for future use. But surely, saving file covers and fasteners at the expense of public records was absolutely indefensible.

Despite the setbacks described above, as early as 1948 there was clearly widespread concern and dismay among the highest echelons of the colonial administration in the East African territories (Kenya, Uganda, and Tanganyika) over the haphazard accumulation of public records and their inevitable fate if they were not properly cared for.

In the three territories, it had become apparent that overcrowded conditions were creating a pressing need for more storage. Construction of accommodation for public records would not, in the long run, provide an adequate solution. Meanwhile, the uncontrolled destruction of documents had become the inevitable option taken in the absence of a suitable archival agency to which public records could be transferred. With this realization in mind, the Governors of Uganda, Kenya, and Tanganyika and the Administrator of the newly created East African High Commission embarked on high-level discussions aimed at finding a common solution to the preservation of the public records in their respective territorial jurisdictions. This process began in March 1948, when the Governor of Uganda Sir John Hall, wrote to the Governor of Kenya proposing the establishment of an archive service, either as an offshoot of the Central African Archives Service (which had been established in Southern Rhodesia) or as a common service within the auspices of the East African High Commission.

However this recommendation was not immediately implemented due to procrastination and long bureaucratic delays within the service. Finally in May 1952, the Deputy Chief Secretary, C.H. Hartwell, issued a proposal entitled "Accommodation, Equipment, and Staff for Central Government Archives in the New Secretariat." In this document, he reviewed the progress made in the preservation of public records since the 1939 Secretariat fire. Hartwell asserted that following this fire, the problem of keeping closed files had not become acute. He warned that it would become a major problem within a few years unless early arrangements were made to address these issues. The thrust of Hartwell's proposal was focused on the accommodation of public records in Nairobi. He was much less concerned with preservation of those records in Provincial and District offices where they were stored in appalling accommodation. At a later meeting which was held on June 18, 1952, Bingley, the then government archivist, confirmed that "approximately 16,000 ft^2 was reserved for archives."

Following the June meeting, the Chief Secretary issued a circular to all heads of departments, first, informing them of government decision to establish an archives service. Secondly, inviting the Heads of Departments to state "whether they wished to store their records in the Central Archives and, if so, give approximate estimates of the area required." Before all Departmental Heads could adequately react to the Secretariat circular, political events intervened. On October 20, 1952, The *War of Liberation* prompted the colonial government to declare a state of emergency. Consequently, although the interdepartmental consultations were at an advanced stage with regard to planning for the allocation of accommodation for the housing of public records in the new secretariat office complex (the present Jogoo House "A"), these plans were shelved indefinitely.

The *War of Liberation* affected the development of archives services in various contradictory ways. From 1948 to 1953 (apart from the above-mentioned abortive interterritorial consultations and the cosmetic Kenyan government departmental proposals), virtually nothing meaningful was done to initiate suitable measures for the custody, care, and preservation of public archives, or to introduce proper records management programs within government offices. In 1954, at the height of the *War of Liberation*, however, the colonial administrators suddenly declared that emergency measures should be taken to preserve records of importance which had accumulated over a period of nearly 60 years of colonial domination.

In realizing the prevailing records management problems in public offices in Kenya, the government appointed the first archivist in 1956. The first consolidated plans for a uniform approach to records management in Kenya can be traced back from 1956 when an Archival Circular was issued. Before then, different departments approached their records keeping practices in their own way. Thus, the records management practices of the Provincial and District Commissioners and those of the attorney general and other departments of the colonial regime in Kenya differed from each other and from the practices of the local governments and private companies.

During the years 1975 and 1976, the Department of Kenya National Archives witnessed great changes particularly in its expanded activities. These included the collection, recording, preservation, and conservation of all valuable documents and data for national reconstruction, planning, and development. Some of the materials found in the National Archives of Kenya include many of central and local government records of both colonial and postindependence period. There is a wide collection of

Israel–Knowledge Discovery

private and public records concerning socioeconomic and cultural activities of national significance and importance.

In order to provide more comprehensive documentation of the social, economic, technological, political, and cultural aspects of African traditional ways of life, additional information has been collected through the recording of oral traditions. Today, this rich oral collection and a well-maintained archival department form the Kenya National Archive, which has become the central national memory system. It now provides valuable resources for planners and administrators, as well as serving the needs of researchers and educators from Kenya and from abroad. If well utilized, the National Archives should therefore become a very important basis for national planning and development. The Archives provides key linkages with the past, present, and future of Kenya.

Legal Framework

Circular No. 1 of 1956 on the implementation of the archival service was issued together with the Rules and Regulations under which the Archivist was to operate. Paragraph 10 of these rules and regulations provided that the government departments should prepare schedules for the disposal of "...files and documents existing or accruing in the department which are considered to be valueless..." In the same circular, the departments were asked to proceed with the scheduling of their records for the preservation and destruction with adherence to the general principles set out in the Archives Rules and Regulations.

The Kenya National Archives was established by an act of parliament, The Public Archives Act of 1965, which took effect on January 25, 1966.

> There shall be established, constituted, and maintained a public department to be known as the Public Archives Service for which there shall be appointed a Chief Archivist, and such other staff as may be necessary for the purposes of this Act.
> [*Section 3 (1)—Establishment of Public Archives Service*]

The Act was later revised in 1990 to become The Public Archives and Documentation Service Act, Chapter 19 of the Laws of Kenya. There was a slight amendment in this Section 3 (1) to rename the Public Archives Service to the KNA&DS. Besides the renaming, the position of the Director was created instead of that of Chief Archivist. Notable was also inclusion of Section 5A, that distinctly set up the National Documentation Service and outlined its major roles of which empowered the section to select, collect, process, house, control, and preserve all bound documents created by any government ministry or department.

Records Disposal Act, Chapter 14 of the Laws of Kenya

Circular No. 2 paragraph 6 "Disposal of Records" Section (i) stated that:

"In order to deal quickly with the accumulated backlog of non-current records, the Cabinet authorized the immediate transfer to the Archives of Records dated earlier than 31st December 1945."

This was later developed into The Records Disposal Act in 1962 to take control of the haphazard destruction of public records, in addition to giving guidelines on the kind of records that are to be destroyed.

Other legislation

The *Books and Newspapers Act Chapter 111* names the KNA&DS as a Legal Deposit, in addition to the KNLS and The University of Nairobi Library.

Composition of KNA&DS

The department has seven divisions:

1. Records Management Service.
2. Archives Management Service.
3. National Documentation Service.
4. The Conservation Section.
5. The Audiovisual Archives Section.
6. The Microfilming Section.
7. Support Division (General Administration).

The Records Management Service is decentralized with five provincial record centers:

- *Nairobi Records Centre*: Established in 1980 and serves four provinces Nairobi, Eastern, North Eastern, and Central Provinces.
- *Nakuru Records Centre*: Established also in 1980 to serve Rift Valley Province, right from the South to the North Rift.
- *Mombasa Records Centre*: Established in 1981 to serve Coast Province.
- *Kakamega Records Centre*: Set up in 1982 to serve Western Province.
- *Kisumu Records Centre*: Inaugurated in 1989 to serve Nyanza Province.

The main purpose of this service is to provide guidelines to public offices on proper records management practices. This is implemented through developing file classification schemes as well as file retention and disposal schedules. A Provincial Archivist is in charge of each of these activities.

Israel–Knowledge Discovery

The Archives Management Service is centralized at the department's headquarters in Nairobi. Its main purpose is to provide preservation of public archives (microfilming, storage, audiovisual, and conservation) and access facilities (search room) of the same materials. Efforts have been made to computerize archival lists and catalogs. Users are able to access both manual and online catalogs on archival holdings.

The department has embarked on a digitization project with the purpose of long-term preservation of archives as well as increased accessibility of archival holdings. *The Repository* houses the records within the department. *The Search Room* is the "heart" of KNA&DS as it is the central point from where all the other departments are linked. It has facilities for searching the databases. Any user of the holdings—be it the microfilms, the library books, the records in the repository, etc.—has to pass through this section for the materials to be recalled. Holdings must be used to justify being maintained and thus the strategic importance of the search room.

National Documentation Service (NDS) supplements archival materials with publications. In addition, it facilitates establishment of information resource centers/documentation link centers in public offices. The NDS has six distinct sections:

- The Government Publications Section.
- The Murumbi Africana Collection.
- The Staff Library.
- The Legal Deposit Library.
- The General Publications Section.
- The Periodicals Section.

The Conservation Section has state-of-the-art equipment for conservation purposes. The major role of the department is to restore damaged specimens. In order for information to be available, it has to be preserved and conserved. The department also offers advisory services on the best practices for preservation and conservation of information resources across formats—print, digital, microfilm, etc.

The Audiovisual Archives Section houses a rich collection of still photos on Kenya's heritage; it also houses audiotapes and tape reels about Kenya. All these have information about the rich Kenyan heritage.

The Microfilming Section concentrates on converting print documents to digital formats. Notable are the Kenyan Dailies—the Nation, the Standard, and the Kenya Times. The section has also started digitizing the Murumbi Africana Collection—the rich collection of the late Joseph Murumbi, onetime Kenyan vice president.

Support Division (*General Administration*): The KNA&DS is headed by a Director, who has two deputy directors; reporting to the deputy directors are the Provincial Archivists and the Heads of the various sections mentioned above.

In addition the KNA&DS maintains an Art Gallery which is one of the major attractions. It has artifacts from throughout Africa. The majority of this collection was bequeathed to the department by the late Joseph Murumbi.

Migrated Archives

When independence was attained on December 12, 1963, the former colonial masters left the country taking public records with them. They argued that these records were created in their tenure, so they were owned by British government. In the *Independence Instruments* (Great Britain, 1962) there was no mention that Britain should hand over to the new Kenya Government "all public archives and records." This very unfortunate omission could have been an oversight or it may have been a deliberate attempt to do away with the records that could provide evidence as to the extent of human rights abuses against Africans during colonial rule. Since independence there has been concerted effort to get those records from Britain. Some have already been received, but others have not and the process is ongoing.

Interministerial cooperation is of great importance to the success of the KNA&DS particularly in the reacquisition and repatriation of Kenya's migrated archives and also in the formation of national information policies and strategies for information collection, preservation, and dissemination. Some of the Ministries involved include: Ministry of Foreign Affairs, Office of the President, Ministries of Finance and Planning, Ministry of State for National Heritage, and the Office of the Attorney general.

Other Kinds of Repositories

Most institutions in Kenya manage their archival repositories privately. However, the Kenya Ports Authority's archives are managed with the help of the KNA&DS. Others like the National Museums of Kenya have their autonomously functioning archives.

Many companies and financial institutions also have archives, which are managed independently.

Finding AIDS

The National Archives has two kind of finding aids: manual catalogs and online databases. Each department has a database. For example, the library has an NDS database

Israel-Knowledge Discovery

running on CDS/ISIS Automation Software. Other databases include:

- An AV database.
- An archive database for records management.
- The JNL database for journals.
- The DOCA 9 for court records.
- A microfilm database.

Cooperation

The department is trying to cooperate with librarians, documentalists, and information specialists in other fields with an aim of adopting modern techniques of storage, retrieval, and conservation.

The department has ventured into partnership with several organizations such as:

1. The Kenya Anti-Corruption Commission, with the purpose of enhancing effective records management since records are the cornerstone to accountability and transparency, a factor underpinning good governance and ensuring corruption free nation.
2. The Murumbi Trust Foundation, which has assisted in the refurbishment of Murumbi Art Gallery Exhibition. Because of this renovation, the department has been able to attract many more viewers to the gallery.
3. The FORD foundation, with the purpose of improving the management of audiovisual records, in terms of capacity building and provision of equipment.
4. Professional bodies, both regional and international bodies such as:
   - International Council on Archives (ICA).
   - Eastern and Southern Africa Regional Branch of ICA (ESARBICA).
   - Association of Commonwealth Archivists and Records Managers (ACARM).

Through interaction with these bodies, the department is able to keep abreast with current trends in the profession.

Training Institutions

Most of the training of Kenyan archival professionals was initially done in India and the United Kingdom. University training of information professionals in Kenya and especially in the archival field is in its relatively "early" stages. Archival training was first offered at Moi University where the Faculty of Information Sciences was inaugurated in 1988; the first students in Archival studies graduated in 1992. However, due to the increased demand for information workers in this area, even private tertiary colleges are now taking the cue and are offering archival courses in their curriculum. The following is a brief summary of this training in Kenya.

Moi University was the pioneer institution in Kenya for archival training at the undergraduate degree level. It offers programs in Librarianship, Archival Studies, Publishing and Book Trade, and Information Technology. The students specialize in their chosen field during their final year(s) of study. There is also postgraduate training in these same fields and both M.Phil. (Master of Philosophy) and M.Sc. (Masters in Science) Programs in Records and Archives Management are offered. The former is for those students with a background in information science and the latter for those who are interested in an archives and records management career and already hold a graduate degree in another field.

Kenyatta University has a postgraduate program—M. Sc. in Records and Archives Management. Most of the staff members at the National Archives have completed, or are in the process of completing this program.

Egerton University trains graduates in information work and among the units is archives and records management.

Kenya Polytechnic is a public institution. It was the pioneer trainer of information workers in the country but at "lower" academic levels offering certificates and diplomas. Currently, it has a Higher National Diploma in Records Management, Ordinary Diploma, and Certificate in Records Management.

Sigalagala Training Institute is also a public institution training at both Diploma and Certificate levels.

Kenya School of Professional Studies—Inoorero Centre is a privately owned tertiary institution that trains archival and record management workers at Higher National Diploma, Diploma, and Certificate level. Its affiliate School of Professional Studies, Thika Road, trains at diploma and certificate levels. It also offers Degree training through distance learning in collaboration with UNISA—University of South Africa.

Railway Training Institute is a college that trains information workers at both diploma and certificate levels. Among the units is archives and records management.

Personalities who contributed to records management in Kenya

- *Sir Percy Girourd*, 1910—He issued the first circular toward streamlined records management in Kenya.
- *Derek Charman*—He was the first archivist.
- *Nathan Fedha*—The first African archivist.
- *Joseph Murumbi*—while in the archives council of 1977/1978 had good ideas for the running of the archival service. Apart from that his rich collection of manuscripts, books and, artifacts is still housed within the KNA&DS. He also requested Professor Bethwel Ogot of University of Nairobi to outline strategic projections, functions, and resources necessary to sustain and develop an archive service.

Israel–Knowledge Discovery

- *Professor Bethwel Ogot*—He consulted a number of leading authorities on the subject, particularly works of Sir Hillary Jenkinson and wrote a well-documented paper which was later used by Murumbi to gain support for the establishment and development of archives from the Kenyatta cabinet.

In conclusion, it is important to note that there is a general realization of the role of records for good governance. Despite the sorry state of the archival service in the "earlier" years, currently there have been concerted efforts to improve on the same.

MUSEUMS AND MUSEOLOGY: NATIONAL MUSEUMS OF KENYA

The concept of museums in Kenya (and Africa as a whole) is a foreign import. While sacred and ritual artifacts were kept in the courts and palaces and homes of Kings and Chiefs, in practice these were for ritual purposes only and each object had its meaning. Objects were never collected. The first museums in Africa started in the early nineteenth century and were colonial institutions created to display African cultural and natural heritage in order to entertain and amuse an elite group of Europeans. In addition, much of African heritage occupies large spaces in some of the biggest museums around the world.

Historical Background

The history of the National Museums of Kenya (NMK) dates back to 1910 when a museum was established in Nairobi by the then East Africa and Uganda Natural History Society (currently the East African Natural History Society). The membership consisted mainly of colonial settlers and naturalists who collected artifacts and specimens for their own enjoyment and study, but also with the goal of making a critical scientific examination of the East African environment. The Society needed a place to keep and preserve their collections of various specimens, and this necessitated the establishment of a museum. Its first site was at the present Nyayo House which soon became too small. A larger building was constructed in 1922 where the Nairobi Serena Hotel stands.

It was not until 1929 that the colonial government set aside land at the Museum Hill and construction work started at the current site. The new building was officially opened on September 22, 1930 and named Coryndon Museum in honor of Sir Robert Coryndon, onetime Governor of Kenya and a staunch supporter of Uganda Natural History Society. On the attainment of independence in 1963, it was renamed the National Museums of Kenya. Since the 1960s, NMK has expanded its services and assets to include regional museums, and has acquired

under its jurisdiction sites and monuments which the government has set aside as monuments of national heritage. Each of the Regional Museums has its own identity and develops its own programs. The museum has also established collaborations, research, and development programs, such as the Institute of Primate Research and Research Institute for Swahili Studies in East Africa.

Before the Museums Act 2006 became operational, it is important to note that from its humble beginnings, the Museum grew into a research institution of international repute, which boasted over 20 research departments, various museums, sites, and monuments open to the public; these are spread across the country's eight provinces.

NMK Legislation

The NMK was initially established as a corporate body under the Ministry of National Heritage, drawing its mandate from two Acts of Parliament: the National Museums of Kenya Act (Chapter 216) and the Antiquities and Monuments Act (Chapter 215) both passed in 1983. These Acts have been reviewed and have been merged into what is known as the Heritage Bill 2006, which was recently passed into law by Parliament.

In the early years of its development, the NMK established itself as a research institution of great international repute, especially in the field of paleontology where the search for human origins yielded some remarkable finds resulting in the famous collections of hominid and other fossils. However the period of the 1980s was characterized by a low level of activity in the public domain. Little was done to draw attention to the research carried out by the museum and its relevance to the public it served. At the time besides exhibitions and a modest school education service, little else was done to encourage the public to visit the museum. Public criticism emerged, centered on the fact that the results of scientific research, leading to many useful discoveries and breakthroughs, were hardly communicated to the public. The token activities in the area of public programming included activities such as guided tours, lectures, and slide talks, and these programs tended to dwell more on the objects than on the contexts which they represent. This resulted in the view of the museum as a boring stuffy place full of old relics.

Presently, the NMK is a state corporation established by an Act of Parliament, the Museums and Heritage Act 2006. NMK is a multidisciplinary institution whose role is to collect, preserve, study, document, and present Kenya's past and present cultural and natural heritage. This is for the purposes of enhancing knowledge, appreciation, respect, and sustainable utilization of these resources for the benefit of Kenya and the world, for now and posterity.

In addition, NMK as the custodian of heritage in Kenya manages Regional Museums, Sites, and Monuments of national and international importance alongside priceless collections of Kenya's living cultural and natural heritage.

Israel–Knowledge Discovery

Nairobi Museum

Nairobi Museum is the flagship Museum managed by the NMK. The newly expanded and refurbished museum opened recently with double the exhibition space, brand new exhibitions, and a new name: The Nairobi National Museum. It has as its slogan, *The Place of Discovery*.

The new museum reflects the repositioning of the NMK as the country's dynamic heritage management institution. In an effort to portray a vibrant and enjoyable place for experiencing cultural heritage, the NMK undertook a re-branding exercise that has seen the Nairobi Museum become a one-stop shop.

Through the years, the NMK has grown to become one of regional and international importance. The museum has become a leading center of excellence, housing some of the finest museum collections and exhibits on the continent. Over the years, the NMK was faced with the challenge of justifying its relevance to the public and the need to generate revenue. NMK begun to recognize the need to become more responsive to demands and the changing needs of its wider public without losing sight of its mission.

Thus these demands have required that the museum redefines its vision and become responsive to the current needs of society in order to remain relevant. NMK recognized that sustainable support depends on the museums' contribution to national development through addressing issues that affect its communities. NMK thus has attempted to change its image of "static exhibit showcases of the past" which it acquired from its Eurocentric history. Its goal has been to move toward a more dynamic contemporary image, departing from the outdated view that museums exhibit "old relics," and instead creating a place where people from all walks of life meet and have dialogue on various socioeconomic issues. In 2002, the NMK with support from the European Union (EU) embarked on a refurbishment and expansion effort known as the "Museum in Change" program. This program was funded by €8 million donated by the EU within the framework of National Museums of Kenya Support Program. These funds were used for the renovated and expanded exhibition space in Nairobi Museum which was completed at the end of 2007. The program work which begun in 2002 has resulted in the development of an institutional strategic plan for public programming 2005–2009, the basis upon which NMK is evaluating its policies.

With the expansion of its mandate and with the dynamic environment in which it operates, the NMK had to redefine its operations to become more responsive to the changing circumstances. In order to keep abreast with changes in the environment in which it is operating, the NMK has developed programs that promote cultural dynamism in order to build a sense of nationhood and belonging.

Regional Museums

In terms of the management of heritage within the country, the NMK continues to expand its regional Museums network and prepare many of its important sites for listing on the prestigious World Heritage List as well and the list of endangered sites. The regional museum network serves as a means for the NMK to reach a wider segment of the population. While most of the research and collections are concentrated at the NMK headquarters in Nairobi, the regional museum network also provides galleries and sites for interpretation of various aspects of the country's heritage. This regional concept was developed in the 1980s in accordance with UNESCO guidelines to bring museums to the people and it is meant to cater for the needs of the population in regions away from the Capital Nairobi. Two of the first purpose-built regional museums are located in the west of the country, in Kisumu and Kitale, and have exhibition on natural and cultural history of the region. Some of the regional museums established in historic buildings can be found in Lamu, Malindi, Mombasa, Meru, Karen, Kabarnet, and Kapenguria. Other museums opened their doors to the public in Gede, Narok, Gilgil, Nakuru, and Loiyangalani.

The main aim of all regional museums is the presentation of Kenya's natural and cultural heritage, with special programs to create awareness for the preservation and sustainable utilization of the country's heritage. The regional museums furthermore specialize in particular areas of interest relevant to the regions they serve. Some regional museums have live displays of reptiles and fish, while others have traditional homesteads of the communities in the region.

Apart from regional museums, the NMK has developed over the years a number of sites and monuments and equipped them with interpretation and visitor facilities. The coastal region has many of these sites located in ruined Swahili settlements that date from the thirteenth to seventeenth centuries A.D.; examples include the Takwa, Gede, Mnarani, and Jumba La Mtwana Ruins. Three military monuments are open to the public, Siyu Fort on Pate Island, Lamu Fort on Lamu Island, and the world famous Portuguese-built Fort Jesus on Mombasa Island.

Three religious monuments can be visited:

- The Portuguese chapel in Malindi from the time of the Portuguese supremacy over the Indian Ocean trade.
- The architecturally unique Kongo Mosque, on the beach in Diani, South Coast, which is still in use by the local community.
- Krapf Memorial Site, an interpretation of early Christianity in East Africa, is the first Christian church in Kenya, completed in 1848, when missionaries endeavored to ensure abolition of the slave trade. Related to the latter subject is Shimoni Cave on the South Coast, a community program in conservation of a historically important cave and in tourism development.

Numerous other sites are under the custodianship of NMK but are not yet open to the public. One of them is Mtwapa Ruins, a large ruined Swahili settlement that was included on the World Monuments List of most endangered sites in 2004.

Karen Blixen Museum

This museum was once the home owned by the Danish author Karen Blixen and her Swedish husband, Baron Bror von Blixen Finecke. Located 10 km from the city center, the museum belongs to a different time period in the history of Kenya, and its architecture is typical of the kind of homes built by European settlers in the early years of the twentieth century. The house and the farm at the foot of the Ngong Hills gained international fame with the release of the movie *Out of Africa* an Oscar-winning film based on Karen's autobiography by the same title. The popularity of the film prompted the opening of Nairobi's Karen Blixen Museum.

The house was sporadically occupied until purchased in 1964 by the Danish government and given to the Kenyan government as an independence gift. The museum was opened to the public in 1986. Many pieces of furniture that Karen Blixen sold to Lady McMillan on her departure were reacquired and constitute part of the exhibition in the museum. The museum house remains a serene environment that seems to belong to the past, surrounded by a tranquil garden and indigenous forest, with a splendid view of Karen Blixen's beloved Ngong Hills. Whereas most regional museums have a good proportion of both foreign and local visitors, the Karen Blixen Museum generates most of its revenue from international visitors.

Fort Jesus Museum

Fort Jesus was built in 1593 by the Portuguese to solidify their power on the East African Coast, but the fort changed hands several times between the Portuguese and the Omani Arabs. The British also used the fort as a prison during the colonial period. Today it is a national monument and a popular museum, which displays ancient artifacts of the coastal life. It also holds a conservation laboratory, a gift shop, and a cafeteria. Part of the museum is in the Old Law Court, which holds a research library, coastal archeology department, and a regional center for archeological study.

Lamu Museum

One of the oldest towns along the East African Coast is Lamu town, located on Lamu Island north of Malindi. This Swahili town is said to have been founded around the tenth century. It used to be a very busy port in the eighteenth and the nineteenth centuries. The Old Fort in the center of the town built in 1812 is today a cultural center. The town has numerous Museums such as the Swahili House Museum, the German Post Office Museum, the Lamu Fort Environment Museum, and the Lamu Museum. The Lamu Museum occupies what used to be the District commissioner's house, a house originally built for Queen Victoria's consul, Jack Haggard. This museum houses a rich collection of ethnographic material from the Swahili, Orma, and Pokomo ethnic groups. Also on display are the traditional Swahili crafts such as the Siwa (side-blown horn), furniture, and jewelry. The Island town of Lamu can only be approached by boat. It served as a prison from 1910 to 1984, and was used by both the British colonial regime and the Kenya government, before it was handed over to the NMK in 1984. Efforts to turn the Fort into a museum were started with technical and financial assistance from Swedish International Development Agency. From its inception, the museum had environmental conservation as its general theme; Lamu Fort is basically a community center for the people of Lamu old town.

Lamu World Heritage Site

However, the crown jewels of NMK's assets at the coast are:

* *Lamu World Heritage Site*: In December 2001, Lamu Old Town Conservation Area was inscribed on the UNESCO's World Heritage List to protect and conserve its rich and unique cultural and architectural heritage, as a major contribution to the development of humankind. NMK has six assets in Lamu Old Town, which is the oldest surviving Swahili town of the entire East African coast and Indian Ocean islands. The operation of Lamu Museums is—more than anywhere else—very much intertwined with the lives of the people and the activities of the local authorities.
* *The Miji-Kenda Kaya forests* which were listed on the World Heritage List at the 32nd Committee of the World Heritage Convention in Quebec, Canada, July 2008.
* *Fort Jesus* which has also been proposed for World Heritage listing. It is expected that Fort Jesus and Mombasa Old Town Conservation Area will soon be declared a World Heritage Site, because this important site represents the millennium-old human history of the East African coast. At various points in time, the Portuguese, Omani Arabs, the British, the Baluchis, and the Indians were present at one time or another in Fort Jesus.

Archeological and Paleontological Sites

Kariandusi, Olorgesailie, and Koobi Fora: Kenya is home to some of the most renowned paleontological/archeological sites in the Great Rift Valley. Both

Israel–Knowledge Discovery

Olorgesailie and Kariandusi sites represent the Acheulian Culture of the Early Stone Age. Koobi Fora in Sibiloi National Park is a mixed World Heritage Site and home to important early hominid finds. Visitor facilities in these Rift Valley sites include an interpretation gallery and accommodation facilities. All NMK sites are very strategically located and offer often breathtaking panoramic views of the surrounding landscape at the bottom of the Rift Valley.

Thimlich Ohinga: In Kenya's Lake Victoria region is Thimlich Ohinga Cultural Landscape, nominated by the World Monuments Watch into the list of the 100 most endangered sites for the period 2000/2001. Thimlich Ohinga is a fine example of a complex of dry stone wall enclosures and is sometimes referred to as the Great Zimbabwe of East Africa; it represents the same indigenous building technique in the form of circular interconnected defensive structures.

Historical sites

Kapenguria Museum: While some sites and monuments are reminders of the colonial period (old Provincial Commissioner or District Commissioner offices or residences), other sites evoke the country's political history and mainly the struggle for independence. Two sites (Kapenguria and Lokitaung) are prisons where the founding fathers of the nation were detained, while two other sites (Lodwar and Maralal) are residential houses where the first president, Mzee Jomo Kenyatta, was kept in isolation after his release from prison and before they signed the declaration of independence.

Uhuru Gardens: Uhuru Gardens in Nairobi is the park where the first flag was raised by the first president on the night of independence. Currently, a "Heroes and Heroines Square" is being developed there to commemorate all those who contributed to the liberation and nation building.

Education for Curators and Museum Administration

For continuous capacity building in the various fields in the museum, the NMK together with other stakeholders in the region started an international nongovernmental organization previously known as Program for Museum Development in Africa (PMDA) dedicated to the preservation, management, and promotion of cultural heritage in Africa through a program of training and development support services.

Since its inception in 2000, PMDA, now known as Centre for Heritage Development in Africa (CHDA), has become recognized for the quality and innovative character of its training and development support programs and activities that it provides to professionals and institutions responsible for movable and immovable heritage in English-speaking sub-Saharan Africa. CHDA works in close collaboration with the University of Nairobi and is supported in its programs and activities by funding and technical partners throughout the world.

For its future activities, CHDA intends to pay special attention to ensuring the better utilization of museum collections for public programs and to making museums play a positive role in the lives of children.

Because of its diverse and strategic roles, the NMK plays host to a number of regional and international programs as well as collaboration projects. Some of these are Africa 2009 Program, Koobi Fora Field School, a joint program with the Rutgers University in New Jersey.

Professional Associations

International Council of African Museums

Of special note, is the establishment of the International Council of African Museums (AFRICOM), a professional association that brings together museum and heritage professionals in Africa and is housed within the NMK. The AFRICOM Program was born as an outcome of the Encounters "What Museums for Africa? Heritage in the Future" organized by ICOM in Benin, Ghana, and Togo in November 1991. The aim of the encounters was to address the role and the relevance of the museum for the African continent. The African professionals drew up a program addressing issues considered as priorities. In September 1992, this program was adopted by the General Assembly of ICOM within its Triennial Programme of Activities for 1993–1995 at ICOM's General Conference in Quebec. Its major objective was to develop exchanges among professionals of the continent and outside of Africa, and to consolidate the regional professional networks.

AFRICOM was created to help the continent promote the development of museums and museum-related institutions in Africa in the context of global development and to promote the development of professions on which museum activities are built, strengthen collaboration and cooperation among museums and its professionals in Africa, promote participation of all components of the society in the protection and enhancement of cultural and natural heritage among other activities. Membership is mostly African but museum professionals and partners around the globe are encouraged to participate in its activities.

International Committee of Museums

Other museum professional bodies include the International Council of Museums (ICOM), which brings together museum professionals from all over the world. ICOM is different from AFRICOM and it is more committee-oriented depending on one's professional specialty. For example, those responsible for marketing and public

Israel–Knowledge Discovery

relations (MRP) within the museum would be members of the MPR committee of ICOM.

Societies

The NMK also plays host to various societies that work closely with the institution to either raise funds for projects within the various museums or to increase public awareness of the heritage of Kenya or bring together those with a particular field of interest. Some of these include:

- Kenya Museum Society
- Malindi Museum Society
- Friends of Fort Jesus
- Kenya Prehistory Club

Museology as a Discipline and Profession

From the discussion above, it is clearly evident that NMK is a diverse and complex organization with a broad mandate and a wide range of activities. However there is a need for continuous capacity building in the area of museum training which until recently was not seen as the kind of knowledge needed to manage a museum. It must be noted that African museums were largely founded during the colonial era to house artifacts that were collected out of curiosity by colonists, who often assembled these collections as a means of trying to understand African culture and customs which were believed to be "backward" and "primitive."

With museums burgeoning all over the world, there was need for the identification of a clear role for museums in society and there gradually developed a body of theory and practice which is known as museology. Museum professionals were nearly always trained in a discipline related to a particular collection, and therefore they had little understanding of the museum as a whole, its operation, and its role in society. As a result, the practical aspects of museum work, for example, conservation and exhibition development were achieved through borrowing from other disciplines and other techniques, whether or not they particularly met the requirements of the museum and its public. This is still the case in Kenya as there are no local universities or educational institutions offering Museology as a discipline. The only disciplines offered that may be closely related include anthropology and archeology. To study museology, African museum professionals have to apply to universities outside of the African continent thus making this a great challenge for museums in terms of capacity building. It is also difficult for museologists to work in isolation as they may need the expertise of other specialized disciplines in the development and curation of exhibitions.

On the other hand, through collaboration with other institutions and partners, Kenyan museums have been able to send some staff on exchange programs that culminated in extensive projects that brought together people from different disciplines to develop significant exhibitions and programs. For example, in 2006, the NMK in collaboration with the British Museum were able to host an exhibition of the Hazina (Treasures). For this exhibition, a huge collection of artifacts from the East African region that are held by the British Museum were brought to Kenya for the very first time. Other important collaborations include the Koobi Fora Field school which is organized in partnership with Rutgers University in New Jersey, United States. Students from the United States and local students come together to acquire skills in hominid collections. The University of the Western Cape and The University of Cape Town in South African saw a gap in museum training on the continent and designed a postgraduate course for African professions titled the African Programme for Museum and Heritage Studies in Africa.

Key Contemporary Issues, Access, Preservation, and Educational Role

On October 15, 2005, the museum was partially closed, launching a project for a major expansion supported by the EU. The year 2008 marked an extraordinary milestone for the NMK as the institution began a historic transformation with the opening of the New Nairobi Museum.

The end result was the opening on July 14, 2008 of a state-of-the-art facility with new exhibitions and larger exhibition galleries as well as a new visitor center. The museum also features an array of new visitor amenities including restaurants and shops that will make the museum a one-stop shop.

Essential to the transformation of the Nairobi Museum are the goals of increased accessibility to the collections for students, scholars, and the public and enhanced collaboration and interdisciplinary work across all departments and collaborators.

The new and renovated museum offers greatly enhanced flexibility for viewing, studying, and interacting with the collections while providing dynamic museum experiences for visitors and establishing an innovative new model for object-based learning.

Outstanding Personalities

1. Sir Arthur Loveridge—first paid museum curator in 1914
2. James Maikweki—first African curator
3. Louis and Mary Leakey—renowned paleontologists
4. Richard and Meave Leakey—renowned paleontologists
5. Dr. Mohamed Isahakia—first Black African Director General, NMK
6. Rev. Kenneth St. Aubyn Rogers—founder of the East African Natural History Society (Now Nature Kenya)

Israel–Knowledge Discovery

Museums the world over are reexamining their traditional responsibilities to society. New demands are constantly being placed on museums to be accountable and relevant to the communities that they serve. In Kenya, this process of "new" museology is heightened by the sociopolitical changes that are taking place. In order to survive, the NMK is working hard to shake off its former static, "don't touch" image to be more participatory, user friendly, and sensitive to its visitors.

The NMK remains committed to the development of arts and culture in the country and continues to work with the other stakeholders in the study of our modern and contemporary collections, in keeping with the transformation shaping museums around the world. NMK must be seen to endeavor to contribute to developing national consciousness by unifying the country using its collections to sensitize Kenyan people to economical, social, and political issues.

The NMK also continues to present diverse and enlightening programming that offer new opportunities and challenges to our curatorial, education, programming staff who must draw on their creative talents and utilize the great resources at NMK. At the same time, the prospect of working in partnership with institutions outside the NMK represents another exciting opportunity for the NMK.

CONCLUSION

Kenya is well aware of the fact that the world has changed to an information-driven economy. Major stakeholders have taken various steps to include information in every sector of development. In view of increased demand for library and information services, the KNLS has adopted the community-based library initiative which aimed at accelerating library development in the country. The major public, academic, and special libraries in Kenya are embracing ICT in their operations and service delivery.

There is a general realization of the role of records for good governance. Despite the sorry state of the archival service in the "earlier" years, currently there have been concerted efforts to improve on the same.

The NMK remains committed to the development of arts and culture in the country and continues to work with the other stakeholders in the study of our modern and contemporary collections, in keeping with the transformation of museums around the world. NMK must be seen to endeavor to contribute to developing national consciousness by unifying the country using its collections to sensitize Kenyan people on all fronts economical, social, and political.

The dissemination of information in Kenya relies too much on the printed word, which is not accessible to all Kenyans. The press, libraries, museums, archives, various information centers, and broadcasting services cannot really satisfy the information needs of Kenyans. The ICTs have become central to information dissemination. In the government's Vision 2030 development strategy, the country plans to introduce digital villages in both urban and rural areas by 2030. This will facilitate easy and faster information flow, thus propelling economic development. The government of Kenya must formulate favorable policies that would encourage the use of ICT. It is important to note that LIS schools in Kenya have embraced the use of ICTs and introduced them in the curriculum.

ARCHIVAL SOURCES CONSULTED

Kenya National Archives, June 8, 1948: File ARC.1.
Kenya Legislative Council Debates, Vol. VIII, 1939–1940.
Kenya Public Record Office, F.O. 533 Reel 9–10: 312.

BIBLIOGRAPHY

1. Abungu, G. ICOM Proceeding on Guidelines to Improve Museum Quality and Standards African Museums, 2002; 56–61 defining new roles.
2. Abungu, G.H.O. Museum 2000 Confirmation or Challenge?. Opening up new frontiers **2000**, 37–43.
3. Antiquities and Monuments Act, 1983 Government Printer Nairobi, Kenya, 1983 Chapter 215.
4. Atiti, B.A. The role of botanic gardens in the dissemination of ethnobotanical knowledge in Kenya, http://www.bgci. org/education/1769/.
5. Books and Newspapers Act, 1962 Government Printer Nairobi, Kenya, 1962 Chapter 111.
6. *Contextualizing teaching and learning ion rural primary schools*, UNESCO, 1994; (2). http://www.nzdl.sadl.uleth. ca/cgi-bin/library (accessed November 2008).
7. Copyright Act. 1989, Government Printer Nairobi, Kenya, 1989 Chapter.130.
8. Farah, I. The National Museums of Kenya. Museum Int. **2006**, *58* (1/2), 19–30.
9. Gathegi, J.N.; Mwathi, P.G. Creating a needs-responsive LIS curriculum in a developing country: A case study from Kenya. Int. Inf. Libr. Rev. **2007**, April *39* (2), 134–144.
10. IFLA/FAIFE World Report, *Libraries and intellectual freedom*, 1999; http://www.ifla.org/faife/report/kenya.htm (accessed November 2008).
11. IPR, *Institute of Primate Research Scientific Report 1998–2000*, 2001; 50–51.
12. *Issues in Library and Information Studies*, Jomo Kenyatta Foundation: Nairobi, 1993.
13. Industrial Property Act, 1989 Government Printer Nairobi, Kenya, 1989 Chapter 509.
14. Kenya Library Association, http://wwwsoc.nii.ac.jpwww. klas.or.ke.
15. Kenya National Archives Navigating the Kenya National Archives: Research and Its Role in Kenyan Society, http://muse.jhu.edu/demo/history_in_africa/v032/32.1 carotenuto.pdf.

Israel–Knowledge Discovery

16. Kenya National Archives, *The Role of the Kenya National Archives in National Reconstruction and Development*, KNA: Nairobi, Kenya, 1976.

17. Kenya National Library Services Board Act, 1965 Government Printer Nairobi, Kenya, 1965 Chapter 225.

18. *Kenya National Library Services Board Annual Report 2007/2008*, KNLS: Nairobi, Kenya.

19. Kenya National Library Service, http://www.knls.or.ke.

20. Kukubo, R.J. *The Kenya National Archives and the Post-independence Developments: Repercussions of Uncontrolled Paper-work Production: An Overview 1963–1974*, Kenya National Archives: Nairobi, Kenya, 1996.

21. Mansoor, F., 2001; Fort Jesus Museum Report.

22. Matwale, G.; Owano, A. Words of Wisdom. National Museums of Kenya: Horizons **1999**, 7–10.

23. Mboya, L. Museum highlights. Kenya Past and Present **2005**, 35.

24. Ministry of Planning and National Development, *Kenya Vision 2030*, Ministry of Planning and National Development: Nairobi, Kenya, 2007.

25. Monda, L.; Ombachi, G. IT in African Museums. National Museums of Kenya: Horizons **1998**, *Vol. 4*, 18–19.

26. Muchimuti, R. *Evaluation of Nairobi museum education program offered to school students Between 1980–1986*, 1986; Diploma Dissertation.

27. *Museums and Heritage Act, 2006*, Government Printer: Nairobi, Kenya, 2006; Chapter 216.

28. Mwangi, I. *Establishment of Records Management in Kenya up to 1984*, 1973.

29. National Museums of Kenya Act, 1983 Government Printer Nairobi, Kenya, 1983 Chapter 215.

30. National Museums of Kenya, *Proposed Long Term Development Program Strategic Plan 1995–2010*,.

31. National Museums of Kenya, http//www.museums.or.ke.

32. National Museums of Kenya, 1992; 28–29 The Annual Report 1991–1992.

33. National Museums of Kenya, *Saving a Nation's Finite Variety*, 1991; 75–76 Biennial Report (1989–1991).

34. *National Museums of Kenya Annual Report 1997/1998*, 31–33.

35. Ng'ang'a, J.M. *The Development of Public Libraries in Kenya: Past, Present and Future: A Dissertation Submitted in Partial Fulfillment for the Masters of Library Studies*, Loughbrough University: Loughbrough, U.K., 1979.

36. Nyika, E. Owano, A. New technologies and information handling in East Africa Proceeding of IAMSLIC Annual Conference Fort Pierce Publishers: FL, 2000; 77–83.

37. Ocholla, D.N. *Professional Development, Manpower Education and Training in Information Science in Kenya*, University Press: Nairobi, Kenya, 1995.

38. Office of the President. District Focus for Rural Development Government Printer Nairobi, Kenya, March 1987.

39. Ondari-Okemwa, E. Training needs for practicing professional librarians in the Kenyan public universities: a critical analysis. Libr. Manage. **2000**, *21*(5), 257–268.

40. Owano, A. Information management at national museums of Kenya library. Window Newsl. **1999**, *10*(4), 6.

41. Records Disposal Act, 1962 Government Printer Nairobi, Kenya, 1962 Chapter 14.

42. Science and Technology Act, 1989 Government Printer Nairobi, Kenya, 1977 Chapter 250.

43. Thang'wa, J. Museum highlights. Kenya Past and Present **2001**, 32.

44. The Public Archives Act Government Printer Nairobi, Kenya, 1965 Chapter 19.

45. The Public Archives and Documentation Service Act, 1991 Government Printer Nairobi, Kenya, 1991 Chapter 19.

46. The East African Standard, 1939; September 13.

Israel–Knowledge Discovery

Knowledge

Paul K. Moser
Arnold vander Nat
Department of Philosophy, Loyola University Chicago, Chicago, Illinois, U.S.A.

Abstract

Among Western philosophers, the study of knowledge emerged in ancient Greece, under the definitive influence of Plato and Aristotle. Plato's *Theaetetus* immortalized the view that knowledge consists of justified true belief, and this view has come to be called "the traditional analysis of knowledge." This entry outlines the traditional analysis, and presents a formidable threat to it: the Gettier problem.

INTRODUCTION

Human knowledge naturally falls into various categories: empirical (or, a posteriori) knowledge, nonempirical (or, a priori) knowledge, knowledge by description (a kind of propositional knowledge), knowledge by acquaintance (a kind of non-propositional knowledge), and knowledge of *how* to do something. Empirical knowledge depends for its evidence, or justification, component on sensory experience, whereas nonempirical knowledge depends for its evidence component solely on what Kant called "pure reason" or "pure understanding." Although current understanding of the distinction between a priori and a posteriori knowledge stems largely from Kant,[1] earlier variations on the distinction are found in Leibniz and Hume. Knowledge of physical objects serves as a standard example of empirical knowledge, whereas knowledge of logical and mathematical truths provides a typical instance of nonempirical knowledge. Knowledge of logical and mathematical truth seems not to depend on sensory experience for its evidence component.

Bertrand Russell[2,3] famously distinguished between propositional knowledge by description and non-propositional knowledge by acquaintance. Knowledge by description includes knowledge *that* something is the case, whereas knowledge by acquaintance includes direct non-propositional awareness of something, and does not necessarily include knowledge that something is the case. We shall focus on the traditionally required components of propositional knowledge that something is the case: belief, truth, and justification.

Belief

Propositional knowledge requires belief, but belief does not entail knowledge. We cannot know, for example, that pomegranates are red without believing that they are red. Propositional knowledge is belief that satisfies the *truth* condition and the *justification*, or evidence, condition for knowledge.

Philosophical controversy arises over what exactly beliefs are, and yields two prominent views: a *dispositional view* and a *state–object view*. The dispositional view implies that beliefs are just *dispositions to act in a certain way*, and receives support from Charles Peirce and Gilbert Ryle, among others. According to this view, believing that the food before me is deadly is just to be disposed to act toward it in a manner appropriate to its being deadly. Identifying beliefs with dispositions to act gives beliefs a practical function that they might otherwise lack. If beliefs are just dispositions to act, then beliefs will figure centrally in the motivating forces of actions; and they evidently do.

The view that beliefs are just dispositions to act must confront a serious problem. We often invoke beliefs, including their propositional objects indicated by a "that"—clause, to explain why we do what we do. We say, for instance, that I ate the pomegranate *because* I believed that I was hungry and that eating it would satisfy my hunger. The dispositional view implies that I ate the pomegranate because doing so was part of a disposition of mine to behave in certain ways. This view fails, however, to account for the role of the relevant propositional *content* in my behavior: namely, the belief-content that I was hungry and that my eating the pomegranate would satisfy my hunger. We typically explain actions in ways that rely on the propositional contents of beliefs, but the dispositional view of belief does not allow for this. It omits propositional contents, and thus precludes the central role of such contents in the explanation of actions.

The *state–object view* of belief seems more promising than the dispositional view. It implies that belief requires a special relation between a person and an *object of belief*. It thus distinguishes a person's *state* of believing and an object of belief, that is, what is believed. On this view, to believe that pomegranates are red is to be related in a special way to an object of belief. The objects of belief,

Encyclopedia of Library and Information Sciences, Fourth Edition DOI: 10.1081/E-ELIS4-120043462

Copyright © 2017 by Taylor & Francis. All rights reserved.

Israel–Knowledge Discovery

according to a prominent view from Frege, are *abstract propositions*, which are nonphysical entities that exist independently of anyone's thinking of them. They are similar to numbers and other mathematical objects as represented by Platonists. The special relation of believing, according to many philosophers, is a *propositional attitude* that involves some degree of confidence toward a propositional object of belief. Endorsed by Frege,[4,5] Russell,[6] and Moore,[7] among others, this view aims to make sense of how two persons can believe *the same thing*: for example, that pomegranates are red. Each person has *access* to one and the same abstract proposition, and each can have the attitude of believing that proposition.

A familiar problem concerns the supposed realm of abstract, nonphysical propositions, which many proponents regard as eternal, infinite in number, and accessible by an act of the human mind. Philosophers with physicalist inclinations have doubts about the existence of such a realm, and they regard the supposed special relation of believers to that Platonic realm as unacceptably mysterious. They demand a view of the intersubjectivity of belief that adds to its intelligibility and plausibility without increasing mystery.

Seeking to avoid mystery, some philosophers, including Rudolf Carnap[8] and Quine,[9] hold that the objects of belief are *sentences*. We need to distinguish between a sentence *token* and a sentence *type*. A sentence token is a physical sentence resulting from someone's speaking or writing, whereas a sentence type is the abstract class of all such sentence utterances or inscriptions that have the same form. Each utterance of "It is red," for instance, is a member of the abstract class of all such utterances, and is thus a token of that sentence type.

If the objects of belief are sentence tokens, the belief relation between a person and an object of belief is relatively straightforward, since physical occurrences can be intelligibly related to in various ways, for example, causally. There is, however, a difficulty for this view: if the objects of belief are inscriptions and utterances, a person not now related to such tokens does not now believe *anything*, since there is no object of belief for that person. This is a real problem, given the familiar position that there can be beliefs in the absence of physical inscriptions and utterances.

One might seek refuge in the view that the objects of belief are sentence· *types*. Even if a person is not now related to an inscription or utterance, an abstract sentence-type can still be the object of belief so long as the person has a belief relation to it. Still, many philosophers will wonder whether abstract sentence-types actually exist. If they do, can a person have a belief relation to such an abstract entity, and what kind of mechanism or process is at work between the two? In addition, can a person have a belief relation to an abstract type without having a similar relation to a physical token of that type? If not, why

should we hold that the presumed role of abstract sentence-*types* is ineliminable?

We should mention a traditional view on the objects of belief suggested by Aristotle, certain medieval scholastics, classical modern philosophers such as Descartes, Locke,[10] Hume, and Kant, and contemporary thinkers such as Noam Chomsky[11] and Jerry Fodor.[12] This view entails that the objects of belief are *mental, or psychological, propositions*, rather than abstract propositions. That is, they are the *thoughts* we think as we live our lives. Of course, we can *express* our thoughts in words or in some other manner, but typically our thoughts are not expressed at all. Mental propositions belong to the mental life of an individual and have no existence apart from that life. The mental-proposition view avoids problems involving a realm of Platonic objects that exist independently of us and our thoughts. Since mental propositions are psychological particulars in the mental life of a person, the belief relation between a person and an object of belief is not obviously troublesome. Improving on the sentence-object view, the mental-proposition view allows that the objects of belief can be expressed in various natural languages, and may even be altogether unexpressed.

Many philosophers will press the issue of what exactly mental propositions, or thoughts, are. In addition, they will ask how we can account for the evident fact that some people believe *the same thing*, if mental propositions are the private thoughts of an individual. They will also ask how there can be verbal communication between individuals if thoughts are private? Wittgenstein[13] may have had such a worry in his famous discussion of private languages.

We have contrasted dispositional and state-object views of belief, because belief is a necessary component of propositional knowledge. Two other necessary conditions for such knowledge merit comment: truth and justification.

Truth

I know that all pomegranates are red only if it is true that all pomegranates are red. If there are pomegranates that are not red, but are walnut black, then I do not know that all pomegranates are red. So, knowledge requires truth. It is false, then, that astronomers before Galileo *knew* that the sun moves around the earth. Since it is false that the sun moves around the earth, no one *at any time* knows that the sun moves around the earth. Of course, one might believe, even justifiably believe that the sun moves around the earth, since neither mere belief nor justifiable belief requires truth. Even so, propositional knowledge without truth is impossible, according to the traditional conception of such knowledge.

The question of what truth is does not ask what the standards are for discerning truth. Our standards for discerning truth concern our ways of *finding out* what is true

Israel–Knowledge Discovery

and what is not true. The question of what truth is, in contrast, concerns the nature of truth, or what constitutes truth. We might rephrase the question as: what does it mean to say that something is true? Someone could know what it means to say that something is true, but lack a standard for finding out whether a particular proposition is actually true. We shall note three approaches to truth that philosophers have proposed for capturing the truth condition of propositional knowledge: correspondence, coherence, and pragmatic theories.

Correspondence

Many philosophers, including Moore, Russell, and the early Wittgenstein, have held, in the tradition of Aristotle that truth consists in a *correspondence relation* between truth-bearers that state something and features of the actual world. According to a correspondence theory, true statements represent how the world is in virtue of their "corresponding" to some aspects of the actual world, that is, to some actually existing situation. This is an account of what constitutes truth, not of how we tell whether a statement is true.

A key issue concerns the exact sense in which a true statement, such as, "The earth orbits the sun," *corresponds* to reality. It is difficult to capture the pertinent sense of correspondence, and thus no exact account of correspondence has come to be shared by philosophers. Correspondence is not literal "picturing" of the world by true statements, because many true statements are not literal pictures of what they are true of. Consider true statements that are negative ("It is not the case that the sun orbits the earth"), or true statements that involve unrealized conditions ("If the sun explodes, life on earth will cease"), or true statements about nonempirical matters ("Nothing can be both a triangle and an octagon"). Such truths do not literally picture what they are true of, or what makes them true. It is unclear, in addition, how exactly they "correspond" to what they are true of. Proponents of a correspondence theory must identify the kind(s) of correspondence that obtains for true sentences, including those just mentioned.

Mackie[14] and others have endorsed the following "simple" view of truth, in the light of problems concerning the nature of correspondence: to say that a statement is true is to say that whatever in the making of the statement is stated to obtain does actually obtain. This view has affinities with Aristotle's position that truth is a statement of what is that it is or a statement of what is not that it is not. Mackie opposes Ramsey's[15] "redundancy" view of truth, which states that the predicate "is true" is eliminable because it adds nothing to a statement to which it is applied. On the basis of the simple view, Mackie denies that the statement that *P* is true is just a re-affirmation of the statement that *P*. According to the simple view, truth is a distinctive relation, as identified by the simple view,

between a statement and an actual situation. A statement that does not ascribe truth thus does not necessarily ascribe the truth relation in question. The simple view is a minimal correspondence theory in virtue of its characterizing truth as a relation between a statement and an actual situation.

Alfred Tarski's[16] "semantic approach" to truth is a correspondence theory, according to some philosophers. This approach offers the following principle not as a definition of truth but as a necessary condition that must be met by any acceptable definition of truth: *X* is true if and only if *P* (where "*P*" stands for a declarative sentence, and "*X*" stands for an expression that refers to *P*.) Accordingly, the sentence "All pomegranates are red" is true if and only if all pomegranates are red. What follows "if and only if" in Tarski's necessary condition connotes an existing situation to which the pertinent true sentence is appropriately related. Various philosophers have thus understood Tarski's necessary condition as specifying a correspondence requirement on truth.

Even if we had an adequate explanation of the correspondence definitive of truth, we would still face a difficult epistemological question in combining a correspondence approach with a claim to knowledge. How can a person *know* that a correspondence relation actually holds between a statement and the world? In particular, how can a person be *justified* in believing that such a relation holds? If truth is correspondence, then to know that a proposition is true, a person must know that a correspondence relation obtains. Are we thus required to compare a proposition with the way the world is and thereby determine that the proposition corresponds to the world? In that case, to show that we have the knowledge in question, we apparently need an independent means of access to the way the world is. Some philosophers contend that we lack such a means of access, and thus hold that a correspondence theory of truth raises insurmountable problems when joined with claims to knowledge. Even so, a correspondence theory of truth does *not* entail that a person must *know* that the correspondence relation obtains. It entails rather that a statement is true simply because the correspondence relation does obtain, even if no one knows that it obtains. The correspondence relation definitive of truth is not offered as a knowledge-dependent and relation.

Coherence

A coherence theory of truth aims to characterize truth without reliance on talk of correspondence relations. In short: to say that a statement is true is to say that it "coheres" with a specific comprehensive system of statements. The fact that a set of statements is suitably interconnected or systematic (i.e., "coherent") is thus offered as being definitive of truth. This approach to truth has been endorsed by Spinoza among others,[17] and it is

Israel–Knowledge Discovery

offered as capturing what is constitutive of truth, and not only as a test of truth. Logical implication is the strongest kind of coherence, and some proponents of the coherence theory appeal to it to illustrate the kind of coherence that characterizes truth. These proponents typically regard the system of mathematical truths as being a standard coherent system yielding truth.

Proponents of a coherence theory must explain what exactly coherence is and what kind of comprehensive system a true proposition must cohere with. Their key assumption is that truth is a comprehensive system of interconnected statements or propositions. Their position thus does not define truth in terms of a correspondence relation between propositions and the non-propositional world, but rather in terms of systematic interconnectedness of propositions. Even so, many philosophers deny that every person's set of beliefs constitutes a truth-making system in virtue of systematic coherence. Many people have logically inconsistent sets of beliefs, and it is not plausible to hold that all the members of an inconsistent set of beliefs are true. A similar problem arises for the view that a particular community's set of believed propositions qualifies as a true-making system. In addition, it would not help to restrict the view to propositions agreed on by all the members of a community. We can imagine another community all of whose members agree on numerous opposite propositions. Of course, both sets of accepted propositions cannot be true.

A defensible coherence theory seems to need the requirement that the relevant comprehensive set of propositions must be intimately connected in some way with actual states of affairs. Otherwise, truth and knowledge will neglect the way the world actually is. So, it appears that coherence among propositions or beliefs is inadequate by itself for the sort of truth required by knowledge. Such coherence by itself may have nothing to do with what is factual, as we can see from a case of obviously far-fetched but coherent science fiction. Proponents of a coherence theory of truth must explain, then, the essential connection between coherence and how things are. The formulation of this explanation is a serious problem facing coherentism about truth.

Pragmatic value

Pragmatism about truth entails that to say that a proposition is true is to say that it is useful in a certain way. Pragmatist theories of truth emerge from William James[18,19] and John Dewey,[20] although Charles Peirce[21] deserves credit for founding the philosophical movement called "pragmatism." James and Dewey emphasized that the kind of usefulness definitive of truth is not identical with what we ordinarily call "usefulness." The common theme of the pragmatist approaches of James, Peirce, and Dewey is that truth consists in a certain kind of validation of ideas, and that such validation determines the "pragmatic" value of an idea. Even so, the resulting notion of cognitive usefulness, or validation, is not satisfactorily explained by Peirce, James, or Dewey. They sometimes seem to identify truth with a kind of verification. Specifically, they seem to hold that any proposition suitably conducive to a unified, or coherent, account of our experience qualifies as true. They evidently assume that such conduciveness to a unified account is constitutive of truth.

Some philosophers fault pragmatism about truth for confusing matters of justification (or, warrant) and matters of truth. They challenge pragmatists to explain why *false* propositions cannot have pragmatic value in virtue of their being useful in unifying our experience and even being accepted by all inquirers. The challenge for pragmatists is to give an account of the alleged necessary connection between what is pragmatically valuable, in virtue of verification, and what is factual. We ordinarily allow for validated beliefs that are, unknown to inquirers, not actually true. The history of science offers cases illustrating this point. Many comprehensive theoretical systems, including the Ptolemaic model of the universe, in fact include false propositions. So, it's unclear how to defend the view that cognitive usefulness is definitive of truth. Pragmatists have not offered a convincing case for a necessary connection between what has pragmatic value and what is factual.

Justification

Some true beliefs result just from lucky guesses and thus fail to qualify as knowledge. A groundless guess might be true, and even be believed by a person, but still would not be knowledge. Knowledge requires not only that a belief condition and a truth condition be satisfied, but also that the satisfaction of the belief condition be "properly related" to the satisfaction of the truth condition. This is one general way to characterize the justification condition for knowledge. *Epistemic*, or *cognitive*, justification is the kind of justification appropriate to true beliefs that qualify as knowledge. More specifically, a knower must have an *adequate indication* that a known proposition is true. Such adequate indication may be understood as *evidence* indicating that a proposition is true; we then have a traditional view of justification as evidence, as suggested by Plato and Kant, among others. This view entails that true beliefs qualifying as knowledge must be based on justifying reasons, or evidence.

Justified beliefs can be false, and this view is *fallibilism* about justification. It allows, for instance, that astronomers before Galileo could be *justified* in holding that the sun moves around the earth, even though their position is *false*. Justifying support for a proposition need not be such that necessarily if the justifying proposition is true, then the justified proposition is true too. *Inductive* justification does not logically entail a proposition

Israel–Knowledge Discovery

thereby justified. It obtains when, if the justifying support is true, then the justified proposition is *probably* true to some extent. In addition, epistemic justification is typically *defeasible* in that justifying support for a proposition for a person can cease to be justifying for that person when that person acquires additional evidence. Your justification, for example, for thinking that there is a large flower display in the corner of the museum can be defeated by new evidence acquired upon your noticing that a holographic image of a flower display is being projected into the corner.

According to many epistemologists, our beliefs about the external world, including our beliefs about household physical objects, are justified nondeductively, probabilistically, fallibly, and defeasibly. There is, however, a skeptical problem that confronts such claims of justification. This problem takes the form of a regress argument that prompts the question of whether, and if so how, we are justified in holding any belief entailing the existence of an external world *on the basis of other beliefs*.

An example will help. While strolling along the Pacific Ocean, we decide that surfing would be refreshing, but that the risks of surfing are serious today. Our belief that surfing is dangerous today receives support from other beliefs we have. We believe, for instance, that: 1) local weather reports predict dangerous ocean waves in our area today; 2) there are formidable waves already in our sight; and 3) the local weather reports and the presence of the formidable waves are reliable indicators of dangerous waves in the very near future. Our belief that surfing now is dangerous gets support from our belief that (1), (2), and (3) are true. Other beliefs we have will provide support for (1), (2), and (3) for us, thus, continuing the chain of inferential justification. Part of the support for (1) might be that (4) we talked with our friends about today's weather reports. Part of the support for (2) might be our belief that (5) we apparently see formidable waves nearby. Our support for (4) and (5) might be likewise inferential; so, the chain of inferential justification continues.

Skeptics will ask how our allegedly justifying beliefs for a belief in an external object are themselves justified. If they are justified by still further beliefs, how are those beliefs justified? We seem faced with an endless regress of required justifying beliefs, and such a regress seems too complex to employ in our actual everyday reasoning. So, we have a couple of options: either to accept the skeptical conclusion that inferential justification is unavailable or to explain how to handle the threatening regress. Epistemologists have offered three prominent approaches to the regress problem: coherentism, foundationalism, and contextualism.

Coherentism

Epistemic coherentism implies that all justification is inferential in virtue of "coherence relations" among beliefs. Inferential justification, according to epistemic coherentism, ends in a system or network of beliefs with which the justified proposition coheres. Epistemic coherentism, being a coherence theory of justification, is not a coherence theory of *truth*. Coherentism about truth, as noted previously, aims to specify the meaning of "truth" or the essential nature of truth. A coherence theory of justification, in contrast, seeks to explain the kind of justification appropriate to knowledge.

Epistemic coherentists must explain, first, what kind of coherence is essential to justified belief, and, second, what kind of belief system a justified belief must cohere with. Many coherentists acknowledge logical entailment and explanation as typical coherence relations among beliefs. Explanatory coherence relations obtain when some of one's beliefs explain why some other of one's beliefs are true. My belief that it is thundering outside, for instance, might effectively explain the truth of my belief that my cat is running for cover. Of course, not just any belief system will confer epistemic justification, since some belief systems, such as those consisting of science-fiction propositions, are clearly erroneous and thus unable to confer epistemic justification.

According to the *isolation objection*, epistemic coherentism entails that one can be justified in believing empirical propositions that are incompatible with, or at least improbable given, one's total empirical evidence, includes one's non-propositional, sensory experiences. Such sensory experiences are non-propositional, and thus cannot be included in a belief system that confers justification. Epistemic coherence theories make justification depend just on coherence relations among propositions one believes or accepts, and therefore neglect the evidential significance of the non-propositional contents of nonbelief sensory states. Proponents of coherentism have not offered a cogent answer to the isolation objection.

Foundationalism

Epistemic foundationalism states that epistemic justification has a two-tier structure, given that some instances of justification are non-inferential, or foundational, and all other instances of justification are inferential, or non-foundational, in deriving ultimately from foundational justification. This structural view occurs in Aristotle's *Posterior Analytics* as a view about knowledge, and it receives an extreme statement in Descartes's *Meditations*, where it joins with the assumption that foundations of knowledge must be certain. Foundationalism is represented, in one form or another, by Russell,[22] Lewis,[23] and Roderick Chisholm,[24] among many others.

Versions of epistemic foundationalism differ on the explanation of non-inferential, foundational justification, and on the explanation of how justification is transmitted from foundational beliefs to non-foundational beliefs. Some foundationalists, following Descartes, have assumed

Israel–Knowledge Discovery

Israel-Knowledge Discovery

that foundational beliefs must be indubitable or infallible. They embrace *radical* foundationalism, the view that foundational beliefs must be certain and that such beliefs must guarantee the certainty or the truth of the non-foundational beliefs they support. Such foundationalism is now unpopular, because very few, if any, of our perceptual beliefs are certain, and the beliefs that might be candidates for certainty (e.g., the belief that I am now conscious) are insufficiently informative to guarantee the certainty or the truth of our highly specific inferential beliefs concerning the external world, including beliefs from physics, chemistry, and biology.

Modest foundationalism, favored by most contemporary foundationalists, implies that foundational beliefs need not possess or yield certainty and need not deductively support justified non-foundational beliefs. A *non-inferentially justified, foundational* belief is a belief whose epistemic justification does not derive from other beliefs, regardless of whether the *causal* basis of foundational beliefs includes other beliefs. Modest foundationalists have characterized non-inferential, foundational justification as: 1) self-justification; 2) justification by nonbelief, non-propositional experiences; or 3) justification by a reliable nonbelief origin of a belief. Recent proponents of self-justification have included Chisholm[24] and Ducasse,[25] who hold that a foundational belief can justify itself, apart from any evidential support from something else. In contrast, proponents of foundational justification by nonbelief experiences reject literal self-justification, and hold, following Lewis,[23] that foundational perceptual beliefs are justified by nonbelief sensory or perceptual experiences (e.g., my nonbelief experience involving seeming to see a pomegranate) that either make true, are best explained by, or otherwise support those foundational beliefs (e.g., the belief that there is, or at least appears to be, a pomegranate here). Proponents of foundational justification by reliable origins claim that non-inferential justification depends on nonbelief belief-forming processes (e.g., perception, memory, and introspection) that are truth-conducive to some extent, in virtue of tending to produce true rather than false beliefs. Such *reliabilism* invokes, as a justifier, the reliability of a belief's nonbelief origin, whereas the previous view invokes the particular sensory experiences underlying a foundational belief. Modest foundationalists typically agree that non-inferential justification can, at least in most cases, be defeated upon expansion of one's justified beliefs.

Foundationalists must explain the necessary and sufficient conditions for non-inferential justification and for the transmission of justification from foundational beliefs to inferentially justified, non-foundational beliefs. Modest foundationalists acknowledge nondeductive connections that transfer justification, but they have not reached agreement on the exact nature of such connections. Some modest foundationalists hold that a kind of "inference to a best available explanation" can account for transmission of

justification in many cases. The belief, for example, that there is a red pomegranate before me can, in my current circumstances, provide a best available explanation of various foundational beliefs about my perceptual inputs. This, however, is a controversial matter among contemporary foundationalists.

Contextualism

Wittgenstein[26] suggested a central thesis of contextualism with his claim that "at the foundation of well-founded belief lies belief that is not founded." If Wittgenstein is claiming that at the foundation of justified beliefs lie beliefs that are unjustified, we have an alternative to coherentism and foundationalism. According to contextualism, in any context of inquiry, people simply assume (the acceptability of) some propositions as starting points for inquiry.[27] These "contextually basic" propositions themselves lack evidential support, but can nonetheless support other propositions. Contextualists emphasize that contextually basic propositions can vary from social group to social group and from topical context to topical context, for example, from moral inquiry to physical inquiry. What functions as an unjustified justifier in one context need not in another context.

Contextualists must explain how epistemically unjustified beliefs can provide epistemic justification for other beliefs. They need to avoid the implausible view that just *any* unjustified belief, however obviously false or contradictory, can yield justification in certain contexts. If just any unjustified proposition can serve as a justifier, we shall be able to justify any proposition we want. Even if we typically take certain things for granted in certain contexts, this does not underwrite the view that there are unjustified justifiers. The things typically taken for granted may actually be supportable by good reasons. If they are not, we need some way to distinguish them from unjustified beliefs that cannot transmit justification to other beliefs. Contextualists must explain, then, how an unjustified belief, but not just any unjustified belief, can confer inferential justification on other beliefs, but they have not reached agreement on the needed explanation.

Some recent philosophers have rejected the traditional justification condition for knowledge. Some of these philosophers recommend a *causal theory of knowing* according to which you know that P if you believe that P, P is true, and your believing that P is *causally produced and sustained* by the fact that makes P true. One can develop such a causal theory in various ways, but one will need to give special attention to knowledge of universal propositions. Perhaps I know, for example, that all encyclopedia entries have been written by humans, but my believing this seems not to be causally supported by the fact that all encyclopedia entries have been written by humans. It is doubtful that the latter fact produces any of my beliefs. We need, in any case, a careful explanation of how a causal theory can account for knowledge of such universal propositions.

Fourth Condition

Contemporary epistemologists have no widespread agreement on what precisely the key components of knowledge are, even if there is a considerable agreement that knowledge requires justified true belief. Traditionally, many philosophers held that justified true belief is logically sufficient as well as necessary for knowledge. This is a minority position now, owing mainly to "Gettier counterexamples" to this view. Edmund Gettier[28] published a challenge to the view that if you have a justified true belief that *P*, then you know that *P*. One of Gettier's counterexamples is:

> Smith and Jones have applied for the same job. Smith is justified in believing that (a) Jones will get the job, and that (b) Jones has ten coins in his pocket. On the basis of (a) and (b) Smith infers, and thus is justified in believing, that (c) the person who will get the job has ten coins in his pocket. As it turns out, Smith himself actually gets the job, and he happens to have ten coins in his pocket. So, although Smith is justified in believing the true proposition (c), Smith does not know that (c).

Gettier-style counterexamples are cases where one has a justified true belief that *P* but lacks knowledge that *P*. The Gettier problem is the challenge of finding a modification of, or an alternative to, the traditional justified-true-belief analysis that avoids Gettier-style counterexamples. After four decades of vigorous research, contemporary epistemologists have not produced a widely accepted solution to the Gettier problem. Even so, many epistemologists take the main lesson of Gettier-style counterexamples to be that propositional knowledge requires a fourth condition, beyond the justification, belief, and truth conditions. The importance of the Gettier problem stems from the importance of our having a precise understanding of the nature, or the essential components, of propositional knowledge. A precise understanding of the nature of knowledge requires a Gettier-resistant account of knowledge.

CONCLUSION

Our familiar concept of knowledge resists easy analysis, but it does have some identifiable components. We do well, however, not to demand more precision of this concept than is available. Philosophers, in particular, will benefit from attention to that lesson.

Israel–Knowledge Discovery

REFERENCES

1. Kant, I. Critique of Pure Reason; Translated by Smith, N.K.; New York, 1965.
2. Russell, B. Knowledge by acquaintance and knowledge by description. In *Mysticism and Logic*; Doubleday: Garden City, NY, 1957.
3. Russell, B. *The Problems of Philosophy*; Oxford University Press: London, 1912.
4. Frege, Gottlob. On sense and reference. In *Translations from the Philosophical Writings of Gottlob Frege*; Geach, P., Black, M., Eds.; Basil Blackwell: Oxford, 1960.
5. Frege, G. Thoughts. In *Propositions and Attitudes*; Salmon, N., Soames, S., Eds.; Oxford University Press: Oxford, 1988.
6. Russell, B. On propositions: What they are and how they mean. In *Logic and Knowledge*; Marsh, R., Ed.; Allen and Unwin: London, 1956.
7. Moore, G.E. *Some Main Problems of Philosophy*; Allen and Unwin: London, 1953.
8. Carnap, R. *Meaning and Necessity*, 2nd Ed.; University of Chicago Press: Chicago, IL, 1956.
9. Quine, W.V.O. *Word and Object*; MIT Press: Cambridge, MA, 1960.
10. Locke, J. In *An Essay Concerning Human Understanding*; Nidditch, P.H., Ed.; Clarendon Press: Oxford, 1975.
11. Chomsky, N. *Aspects of the Theory of Syntax*; MIT Press: Cambridge, MA, 1965.
12. Fodor, J.A. *The Language of Thought*; Thomas Y. Crowell: New York, 1975.
13. Wittgenstein, L. *Philosophical Investigations*, 3rd Ed.; Anscombe, G.E.M., Ed.; Blackwell: Oxford, 1967; Translated by.
14. Mackie, J.L. *Truth, Probability, and Paradox*; Clarendon Press: Oxford, 1973.
15. Ramsey, F.P. Facts and propositions. *The Foundations of Mathematics*; Routledge & Kegan Paul: London, 1931.
16. Tarski, A. The semantic conception of truth and the foundations of semantics. Philos. Phenomenol. Res. **1944**, *4*.
17. Blanshard, B. *The Nature of Thought*; Allen & Unwin: London, 1939; Vol. 2.
18. James, W. *Pragmatism*; Harvard University Press: Cambridge, MA, 1979.
19. James, W. *The Meaning of Truth*; Harvard University Press: Cambridge, MA, 1975.
20. Dewey, J. *Logic: The Theory of Inquiry*; Holt, Rinehart, and Winston: New York, 1938.
21. Peirce, C.S. How to make our ideas clear. In *Philosophical Writings of Peirce*; Buchler, J., Ed.; Dover: New York, 1955.
22. Russell, B. *An Inquiry Into Meaning and Truth*; Allen & Unwin: London, 1940.
23. Lewis, C.I. *An Analysis of Knowledge and Valuation*; Open Court: LaSalle, IL, 1946.
24. Chisholm, R. Theory of knowledge in America. In *The Foundations of Knowing*; University of Minnesota Press: Minneapolis, MN, 1982.
25. Ducasse, C.J. Propositions, truth, and the ultimate criterion of truth; *Truth, Knowledge, and Causation*, Routledge & Kegan Paul: London, 1968.
26. Wittgenstein, L. *On Certainty*; Harper and Row: New York, 1969.

27. Gettier, E. Is justified true belief knowledge. Analysis **1963**, *23*, 121–23 Reprinted in *Empirical Knowledge*, 2nd Ed.; Moser, P., Ed.; Rowman & Littlefield: Lanham, MD, 1996.

28. Scheffler, I. *The Anatomy of Inquiry*; Knopf: New York, 1963.

BIBLIOGRAPHY

1. Alston, W. *Beyond "Justification" : Dimensions of Epistemic Evaluation*; Cornell University Press: Ithaca, NY, 2005.

2. Audi, R. *Epistemology: A Contemporary Introduction to the Theory of Knowledge*; 2nd Ed. Routledge: London, 2003.

3. BonJour, L. *Epistemology*; Rowman & Littlefield: Lanham, MD, 2002.

4. Moser, P.; Mulder, D.H.; Trout, J.D. *The Theory of Knowledge: A Thematic Introduction*; Oxford University Press: New York, 1998.

5. Moser, P., Ed. *The Oxford Handbook of Epistemology*; Oxford University Press: New York, 2002.

6. Moser, P.; vander Nat, A., Eds. In *Human Knowledge: Classical and Contemporary Approaches*; Oxford University Press: New York, 2003.

Knowledge Creation and Use in Organizations

Maija-Leena Aulikki Huotari
Anna Suorsa
University of Oulu, Oulu, Finland

Abstract

The entry provides an overview of knowledge creation and information use within the organizational context. It is claimed that research focusing on these issues has developed since the 1990s within library and information science (LIS). Research on information use within organizational settings belongs to the research field of information behavior and information seeking and has gained attention in research focusing on information needs and uses of different professions and tasks and recently on outcomes or effects of information. Research on knowledge creation, in turn, is related to the multidisciplinary field of knowledge management (KM) and has been more focused on within the field of organization theory and management studies. In this entry, first, the distinctive nature of the concepts of information and knowledge is highlighted, and the main types of organizational knowledge are presented. Information management (IM) and KM as the fields of LIS and their research traditions are discussed. Research on information use is reviewed by placing the emphasis on information use environments in particular. Moreover, a model of organizational information use that includes knowledge creation is examined, and the Japanese models of knowledge creation are presented. These models are compared to highlight their potential relationships. After that, an alternative framework will be presented as a theoretically consistent foundation to understand knowledge creation in organizational settings. Finally, future research trends are outlined.

Israel–Knowledge Discovery

INTRODUCTION

Knowledge creation and use within organizational settings is quite a recent phenomenon in library and information science (LIS) research but emphasized by multidisciplinary research on knowledge management (KM) since the mid-1990s. However, the conceptual base of KM research has caused quite a deal of debate about the legitimacy of KM as a research field of LIS. This debate is based on the terminological confusion related to the concepts of information and knowledge. For example, often the concepts of information use, knowledge use, and knowledge utilization are used as synonyms. It has even been argued that the phenomenon that is referred to as KM in other fields of science refers to information management (IM) in LIS.[1] To avoid the terminological confusion in this entry, the foci are on the creation of knowledge and the use of information within the organizational context. First, the differences of the concepts of information and knowledge are examined, and the main types of organizational knowledge are outlined. Second, the research traditions of IM and KM are discussed. Third, research on information use and the idea of information use environments and a model of organizational information use that includes knowledge creation are examined. Fourth, the Japanese models of knowledge creation are shortly reviewed. This is followed by a comparison of these models to indicate their main relationships. After that, an alternative framework is presented as a theoretically

consistent foundation to understand knowledge creation in organizational settings. In the "Conclusion," some future research trends are outlined as well.

CONCEPTIONS OF INFORMATION AND KNOWLEDGE

Information and knowledge are closely related concepts. However, they are not synonyms. Research on LIS has widely utilized Claude Shannon and Warren Weaver's[2] information transfer model, which treats information as a entity that can be transmitted through a channel. This is called an objective view of information. From the cognitive viewpoint, in turn, knowledge refers to something that resides in human mind. In this conception, knowledge is an outcome of information that is interpreted and internalized and thus becomes a part of the person's existing knowledge structure.[3] This implies that internalized information also gives a new shape or form to the person's knowledge structure. In fact, the etymology of the word information as "informatio" in Latin refers among other things to the act of giving a form to something (Capurro and Hjorland,[4] p. 351). From the cognitive viewpoint, this refers to learning, too. This is called the subjective view of information. Moreover, in LIS, information has been defined as information-as-thing (referring to, e.g., a document), information-as-process

Encyclopedia of Library and Information Sciences, Fourth Edition DOI: 10.1081/E-EISA-120053440
Copyright © 2017 by Taylor & Francis. All rights reserved.

(referring to becoming informed), and information-as-knowledge.[5]

Knowledge is often understood to consist of explicit, implicit, and tacit elements. In the mid-1990s, the Japanese researcher Ikujiro Nonaka and his colleagues' theory of knowledge creation, the so-called SECI model, popularized the Hungarian scientist Michael Polanyi's[6] identification of the tacit nature of knowledge.[7,8] Tacit knowledge is the most intangible and very personal form of knowledge in organizations and thus difficult to articulate and formalize. However, many authors argue that tacit knowledge is understood too superficially in the conceptions of KM[9] when actually referring to implicit knowledge.[10,11] It has even been claimed that Nonaka has misused the concept of tacit knowledge as Polanyi's idea of *tacit knowing* refers to the most personal knowledge that cannot be expressed verbally.[1]

The concept of organizational knowing and its management is based on the assumption that information and knowledge are something social by nature. For example, the constructionist viewpoint regards knowledge as a social construct assuming that tacit knowledge is manifest in organizational practices. Knowledge creation and innovation can be viewed as "a generative dance" and an outcome of the interplay of knowledge and knowing.[12] Moreover, it has been claimed that cognition and action are inseparable that makes articulation of tacit knowledge unnecessary.[11] Knowledge can also be viewed as a collection of processes that allow learning to occur and knowledge to be internalized within a social community.[13] This view relates to the idea of a community of practice as "groups of people informally bound together by shared expertise and passion for a joint enterprise— engineers engaged in deep-water drilling, for example, consultants who specialize in strategic marketing, or frontline managers in charge of check processing at a large commercial bank... Instead of being composed primarily of people working on their own, they often exist within larger organizations"(Wenger and Snyder,[14] pp. 139–140).

Even the five types of organizational knowledge, namely, embrained, embodied, encultured, embedded, and encoded, are claimed to be insufficient to account for knowledge as a social process.[15] Moreover, it has been suggested that the evolution of knowledge forms a social learning circle: through the codification of shared experience, personal knowledge can become proprietary knowledge or the intellectual capital of an organization. Once externally scrutinized, this knowledge becomes public, while widely internalized, it turns to common sense.[16] The assumption that knowledge exists in human minds makes it hard to manage causing much debate about the relevance of the concept of KM. Therefore, we can claim that the management of people is crucial when aiming at the management of knowledge and information as a resource. Thus the structure of an organization among

other enabling factors becomes the main focus of managerial activities when aiming at enhancing knowledge creation throughout the organization and beyond its borderlines.[17]

RESEARCH TRADITIONS OF IM AND KM

Research on IM and KM are quite recent phenomena in LIS. IM research has its roots in the beginning of industrialization,[18] though widely applied in practice as information resources management (IRM) since the 1970s as an outcome of introducing and utilizing computers and automatic data processing to manage paperwork in public enterprises. KM research has its roots in the visions of information society and knowledge-based economy[19], which strives for innovations. Innovations, in turn, are based on knowledge creation. The multidisciplinary field of KM research emphasizes the enhancement of an organization's innovative capability and the ability to create new knowledge and has gained wider interest since the mid-1990s. KM research can be viewed, for example, as four different discourses, namely, a neo-functionalist, a constructivist, a critical, and a dialogic discourse. The main argument in this view is that the nature of knowledge including its tacit dimension is understood differently in these four research traditions. The neo-functionalist discourse treats tacit knowledge in a separable form from explicit knowledge, and similarly does the critical discourse, which treats tacit knowledge as power. The constructivist discourse, in turn, does not separate tacit from explicit knowledge and comes close to Polanyi's idea of tacit knowing, and the dialogic discourse treats tacit knowledge as deeply internalized consisting of normalizing judgments.[20]

In LIS we can make a clear difference between research on IM and KM. Research on IM is most interested in the use of information technology (IT) and information systems (IS) to manage organizational information resources. Besides different discourses, we can identify multiple research traditions within the multidisciplinary field of KM, for example, IT and management information systems (MIS), organization theories, and education science and learning theories. The first research tradition refers to the use of IT and IS to manage organizational information and knowledge and, thus, comes very close to IM within LIS. The second KM research tradition understands information and knowledge as social phenomena by nature and aims at enhancing organizations and their environments to support knowledge creation, also often called as knowledge construction or generation. The second research tradition has its roots in organizational theory and social and educational sciences, whereas the first tradition is based more on the computer science's point of departure. Also LIS has two research traditions, that is, the social sciences and humanities–based library science, or

Israel–Knowledge Discovery

information studies, and information science that is more oriented toward computer and information processing and cognitive sciences. Therefore, we can view KM as a field of LIS from these two ontological and epistemological viewpoints too.

From the LIS viewpoint, it is important to increase understanding of information and knowledge as resources due to their partly intangible nature. This development is supported by the resource- and knowledge-based views of an enterprise (e.g., Barney[21], Grant[22], Penrose[23]) and the idea of organizational learning.[24] As the value of information and knowledge resources is difficult to estimate in economic, quantitative terms,[9] it is necessary to have a holistic view of how to combine human, technological, and structural factors in a unique manner to prolong strategic capability and sustainability. The core capabilities are created through activities consisting of values and norms, skills, and managerial and physical systems,[25,26] and knowledge creation occurs by combining people's distinct characteristics with a particular set of activities.

RESEARCH ON INFORMATION USE

With regard to LIS, rigorous research on information seeking and use focusing on library collections and users' interaction with them was initiated in the late 1930s.[27] Besides involving library users, these studies have later focused on information needs and uses of professionals such as scientists, engineers, managers, or civil servants. Quite often, these studies have been based on the positivist survey tradition typical in sociological research of the Chicago School in the United States. This system-oriented view is based on the conceptualization of information as an entity. An opposite, user-oriented view[28] is based on the conceptualization of information as a process and as knowledge. In other words, information is regarded as a construct that is subjectively created in the mind of its user (see, e.g., Todd[29], Savolainen[30]). Moreover, the phenomenon of information use can be viewed from the macro and micro perspective. In this entry, the focus is placed on the macro perspective by examining the ideas presented by Robert S. Taylor and further elaborated by Chun Wei Choo.

Information Use Environments

Within LIS, Robert S. Taylor's research on information use is perhaps the most well known. Taylor's[31] point of departure is complementary to the system-oriented, technology-driven, and content-driven views of IS design. Taylor states, "These conventional approaches need to be tempered and informed by a third approach that looks at the user and the uses of information, and the contexts within which those users make choices about what

information is useful to them at particular times. These choices are based, not only on subject matter, but on other elements of the context within which a user lives and works" (Taylor,[31] p. 218). This means that the environment where information is used impacts on information flows and uses and also determines the criteria used to assess the value of information.

Taylor defines information behavior as the sum of activities through which information becomes useful and states that information behavior differs in different groups. The elements of information use environments are the following: sets of people, which include professions (e.g., lawyers, engineers, social workers), entrepreneurs, special interest groups (e.g., hobbyists), and special socioeconomic groups (e.g., elderly); problem dimensions, which refer to typical problems for these groups; work settings and embedded factors that refer to influencing attitudes toward information, information flows, and types and structures of required information; and problem resolution assumptions. Taylor suggests that his model is applicable to a variety of contexts. He claims that the final determiner of information value is the user who is in a particular context and develops criteria on information value from that context.[32] Furthermore, he points out that it is important to take into account that different sets of people perceive information differently, which means that information may have different interpretations according to the context, and in the processes by which it becomes useful. Therefore, better understanding of the less rational factors affecting decision processes should be gained too.

General Model of Organizational Information Use

Chun Wei Choo[33] has applied Taylor's model of information use environments, Dervin's[30] situation-gap-model of sense making, and Kuhlthau's[34] information search process, which includes the affective dimension, to a general model of information use within organizational settings. Choo's idea of information use embraces information seeking covering the thoughts, feelings, actions, and the environment in which these are played out. He contends that organizations use information on three arenas: to make sense of the environment in which they operate, to create or generate new knowledge, and to make decisions. Choo's thesis is that these interconnected processes provide a holistic view of organizational information use and form the essence of a knowing organization. The three modes of information use of a knowing organization consist of sense making based on the idea of an enacting organization,[35] knowledge creating based on the idea of a learning organization,[36] and decision making based on the idea of a rational organization.[37]

Choo's model is concerned with information use at three stages: information needs, information seeking, and information use. For Choo, information seeking (as a part of information behavior) is a human and social process

Israel–Knowledge Discovery

through which information becomes useful. This assumption is based on Taylor's conception of information use as the individual making a choice or selecting messages from a larger pool to attend to or to act on. Information use implies the selection and processing of information in order to answer a question, solve a problem, make a decision, negotiate a position, or understand a situation. This also makes the relevance of information important and refers to the pertinence of information as a term used to describe the capability of information content to satisfy more personal information needs. Pertinence, a concept also incorporated in Kuhlthau's information search process model, integrates cognitive and affective needs and addresses demands of a particular situation in which the information need emerges.

In Choo's model, the definition of information uses is based on Taylor's[31] classification of the types of uses as follows: enlightenment referring to the development of a context or making sense of a situation; problem understanding; instrumental; factual; conformational; projective; motivational; and personal or political use. These different types of uses are generated by the need perceived by users in particular situations. The model also highlights constructed, situational, and dynamic properties of information use.

Moreover, Choo examines information use in organizational sense making, knowledge creation, and decision making. In sense making, information is used to reduce ambiguity and to develop shared meanings for taking collective actions. However, organizations also maintain a certain level of information equivocality and accommodate a diversity of interpretations. In knowledge creation, Choo draws on three types of organizational knowledge: explicit, tacit, and cultural, and on Nonaka's SECI model and its extension, as well as on Normann and his colleagues'[38,39] (see also Huotari and Iivonen[17]) ideas on knowledge processes as the basis for organizational knowledge creation. He describes information needs, seeking, and use on knowledge creation through cognitive needs, affective responses, and situational dimensions. For Choo, knowledge creation includes the modes of knowledge conversion (SECI; Nonaka and Takeuchi[8]), knowledge building,[25] and knowledge linking (e.g., Wikström et al.[39]).

KNOWLEDGE CREATION

It is widely accepted that knowledge creation is a social phenomenon, but theoretical research of this phenomenon is quite limited. The examination of Choo's model of organizational information use in the previous section also highlights phenomena related to knowledge creation. The Japanese models of knowledge creation provide further insights about knowledge creation within organizational settings. The most well-known among these models were

presented by Ikujiro Nonaka and his colleagues Hirotaka Takeuchi, Ryoko Toyama, and Noboru Konno during the 1990s and the beginning of this millennium.

Nonaka has criticized the notion of the organization as an information processing system and, instead, stressed a holistic and dynamic view of the organization that creates new knowledge through interaction. Nonaka and his colleagues' views are based on the idea of the social nature of information and knowledge and the dynamic nature of the organization, its activities, and the environment. They state that "Knowledge creation is a continuous, self-transcending process through which one transcends the boundary of the old self into a new self by acquiring a new context, a new view of the world, and new knowledge... knowledge is created through the interactions amongst individuals or between individuals and their environment... An individual (micro) influences and is influenced by the environment (macro) with which he or she interacts" (Nonaka et al.,[40] p. 8). With the organizational knowledge creation, they mean "...the capability of a company as a whole to create new knowledge, disseminate it throughout the organization, and embody it in products, services, and systems" (Nonaka and Takeuchi,[8] p. viii). Nonaka and his colleagues' models of organizational knowledge creation are shortly reviewed in the following sections.

SECI Model

One of the first models of knowledge creation is the so-called SECI model or the SECI process, which is based on the notion of conversion of knowledge between its tacit and explicit types through four phases: socialization, externalization, combination, and internationalization. Though the SECI model has been criticized, it is also widely used to describe the social aspects related to knowledge creation.

The SECI model implies spirals from one ontological level to the next, for example, from the level of an individual to the level of a group. Nonaka and Takeuchi drew on the ideas of tacit knowledge suggested by Polanyi and the idea of mental models. In addition, tacit knowledge consists of technical elements and know-how. In socialization, the members of a work community share and transfer their experiences in tacit form when working together in practice or when socializing in an informal manner and thus create new tacit knowledge. Interaction is crucial at this phase and face-to-face interaction enhances socialization, which can occur beyond organizational boundaries. In externalization tacit, personal knowledge is converted by articulating it to explicit form by using, for example, metaphors, analogies, mathematical formulas, or models. This is seen as a critical phase in the knowledge creation process because the externalized, conceptualized knowledge forms the basis for new knowledge to be created. Communication is essential and group work techniques

Israel–Knowledge Discovery

can be utilized. At the combination phase, new, externalized knowledge is combined with the existing explicit knowledge. Techniques, methods, and means, including modern ICT, of interaction can support communication. This phase can also be used to operationalize concepts, for example, a vision into business or product concepts. In the internalization phase created, new explicit knowledge is converted to tacit knowledge. At this phase, all people involved in the knowledge creation process reform what they have already known. This is related to learning by doing as they internalize the created new knowledge to become a part of their daily activities and embedded in organizational routines. Interaction and collaboration of the members of the work community are essential and, for example, self-organizing teams or work groups can enhance internalization.

Models of Organizational Knowledge Creation

The SECI model was further developed by Nonaka and Takeuchi toward a model of organizational knowledge creation involving a wider range of issues and ontological levels, that is, the individual, the team or group, the department or the division, the organization, and the networks, and the definition of the factors that enable knowledge creation. This model consists of five phases, namely, sharing tacit knowledge, creating concepts, justifying concepts, building an archetype, and cross-leveling knowledge. Nonaka and Takeuchi define the enabling factors as organizational intention, that is, "an organization's aspiration to its goals" (Nonaka and Takeuchi,[8] p. 74), autonomy, fluctuation and creative chaos, information redundancy, and requisite variety. Moreover, they stress flexibility in acquiring, interpreting, and relating information and claim that love, care, trust, and commitment enhance interaction, communication, and knowledge creation.[8]

As knowledge creation is essential to sustain an organization's innovative capability and strategic position in the marketplace, it must be in line with the strategic vision and goals set. The unified model of knowledge creation presented by Toyama, Konno, and Nonaka[40] incorporates into the knowledge vision the SECI process, the shared context of knowledge creation called Ba, and the knowledge assets. The knowledge vision directs the relations of these three main elements and defines what kind of knowledge should be created at different sectors of activity and also how the organization and its knowledge base are developed with time. The knowledge vision also defines the values and norms that are used to determine how created new knowledge is assessed and valued, that is, how important new knowledge is for gaining the strategic goals.

The idea of Ba is based on the concept of Basho introduced by the Japanese philosopher Kitaro Nishida in the 1920s. Ba refers to time, space, and place where information is interpreted to become knowledge. Locationality and simultaneous incorporation of space or place and time and mental state of mind are typical for Ba; in other words, Ba can be an office, a virtual space for working, and the state of mind. By localizing and activating organizational members to interaction, Ba enables knowledge conversion from tacit to explicit and from individual to collective. Moreover, by transcending the boundary between micro and macro for interactions at different levels, Ba can amplify the knowledge-creating process.

The SECI model and the four types of Ba, namely, originating, dialoguing, systemizing, and exercising, are linked, and they interact to create knowledge assets of four types. Experimental knowledge assets consist of shared tacit knowledge that is based on organizational members' and stakeholders' shared experience and thus are difficult to conceptualize, copy, or imitate. Conceptual knowledge assets are based on symbolic and conceptual models, for example, product and brand characteristics. Systemic knowledge assets consist of organized explicit knowledge that is easy to store and transfer in digital IS. These knowledge assets are most visible, and they can be protected by patents. Routine knowledge assets consist of tacit knowledge that is embedded in organizational activities and practices. These knowledge assets include daily organizational routines, working culture, and climate. These four types of knowledge assets form the basis for the knowledge-creating process.

COMPARISON OF THE MODELS OF ORGANIZATIONAL INFORMATION USE AND KNOWLEDGE CREATION

The strength of Choo's model is the holistic view provided by integrating in an interdisciplinary manner the previous research findings, theoretical models, and frameworks. The Japanese models provide a holistic and unique approach to knowledge creation within organizational setting. All models examined provide a macro perspective of organizational phenomena and pursue to incorporate information use to a wider context including the physical place and the mental state of the information user. In the Japanese models, the macro perspective is an extension of the micro perspective whose interaction is embedded in the processes of knowledge creation. Choo's model focuses on organizational knowledge creation as one of the three aspects of organizational information use. In Nonaka and his colleagues' model of organizational knowledge creation, in turn, the knowledge assets provide inputs for the knowledge creation processes and are their outcomes too. In the Japanese models, information use is related to interaction and communication through which information is interpreted into knowledge and embedded in practices. These models are based on the assumption of the collective and dynamic nature of organizational

Israel–Knowledge Discovery

knowledge creation and the transfer of individual knowledge to collective knowledge. These aspects are included in Choo's model through Robert S. Taylor's conception of the information use environments, as sets of people, work settings, problems dimensions, and their resolution assumptions, which are embedded in the context and provide a collective platform to interpret information. This context is very collective in nature and provides the criteria for judging the value and usefulness of information. In Nonaka and his colleagues' models, the essence of knowledge creation is based on the conversion of tacit and explicit knowledge through interaction between the individual, the organization, and its environment. This aspect is evident in the concept of Ba, which is the collective and shared context of knowledge creation where information is interpreted to become knowledge and create the four types of knowledge assets.

The strategic orientation of these models differs. In Choo's model, the strategic aspect is embedded in the idea of a knowing organization, which uses information through the interconnected processes of sense making and enacting the environment, creating knowledge through learning, and making decisions. In these processes, uses of information are characterized as constructed, situational, and dynamic. In Nonaka, Toyama, and Konno's model, the knowledge vision directs the three elements, namely, the SECI process, the Ba, and the knowledge assets, of organizational knowledge creation.

Alternative Framework to Understand Knowledge Creation

The model of organizational knowledge creation presented by Chun Wei Choo and the Japanese knowledge creation models reviewed in this entry have both their strengths and weaknesses. Nonaka's and his colleagues' models are the most well-known in the Western countries, but their work has been criticized, too. Besides critique toward the use of Polanyi's concept of tacit knowing, the fact that their ideas are culturally bound has been under scrutiny. Choo's idea of the knowing organization has not been under scrutiny to such an extent, though it is evident that it is demanding to indicate how consistent the model's conceptual basis is.

As an alternative to these models, a novel framework of knowledge creation is shortly presented by the authors of this entry. It is based on hermeneutic phenomenology, which provides a theoretically and conceptually consistent foundation for understanding the phenomenon of knowledge creation.[41] By introducing a novel way to conceptualize the collaborative nature of knowledge creation, the framework clarifies the conceptual vagueness of research on KM. Thus, it also contributes to the debate on the relevance of the concept of KM as a field of LIS. The point of departure is hermeneutic phenomenology and Hans-Georg Gadamer's idea of hermeneutic

conversation.[42,43] This allows examination of knowledge creation, which is started by defining the concept of a human being and focusing on the human existence in interaction—constantly creating and simultaneously being created when living in the world—and not on the concept of knowledge as such. In other words, the framework provides a definition of a human subject as a creator of knowledge, contrary to the models presented in this entry, in which the definition is taken for granted. Moreover, contrary to previous research on knowledge creation, this framework provides a thorough definition for the concept of interaction[41] (see also von Krogh[44]).

The thesis of this novel framework is that the conceptualization of interaction is dependent on the conceptualization of a human being. Knowledge creation is examined in the following three areas: structure of the interactive event as the hermeneutic cycle involving distanciation, anticipation, correction, and reassessment; construction of the human experience in interaction consisting of the temporal dimensions of past, present, and future; and modes of being in interaction, such as reflective, critical, and open ones (see also Suorsa[45]). In this framework, interaction is regarded as a communal and shared experience, which demands total presence in the course of events. It is claimed that the framework's hermeneutic circle and phenomenological conceptualization of a human being provide a defined and coherent structure for understanding the event of knowledge creation as a future-oriented, conscious act of interaction.[41]

CONCLUSION

This entry aimed at providing an overview of information use and knowledge creation within organizations. The examination was placed on the context of KM research in order to indicate how information use relates to knowledge creation within organizational settings. Choo's model of organizational information use and Nonaka and his colleagues' models of organizational knowledge creation were shortly reviewed and further compared to highlight their potential relationships. It can be concluded that these models are based on the ideas of the social and dynamic nature of knowledge and knowledge transfer from the individual to the collective through knowledge conversion between its tacit and explicit types. These models relate to the LIS and KM research traditions based on the social and educational sciences and organization theory, rather than to the computer and IS and cognitive sciences.

However, as the conceptual vagueness of research on KM has been a concern in LIS, a framework based on phenomenological hermeneutics is finally introduced by the authors of this entry as a theoretically consistent foundation to understand and clarify the conceptualization of the phenomenon of knowledge creation in organizational

Israel–Knowledge Discovery

settings. In this framework, the foci are on the conceptualization of a human being and interaction as the major elements of knowledge-creating events.

Future Trends

The phenomena addressed by research on KM seem to some extent emerge in the research agenda of LIS. As pointed out recently, research interests in information use and outcomes, effects, applications, or impacts of information have been increasing steadily.[27] These should be linked with the aspects of knowledge creation or construction. Research on collective practices of information use and knowledge construction could be increasingly emphasized. Furthermore, research on the use of new Internet-based technologies including applications of social media and web 3.0 may extend the scope of inquiry toward strategic knowledge creation and information use within networked organizational settings at the global level. Moreover, introducing novel, ontologically and epistemologically consistent interdisciplinary, or even cross-disciplinary models and frameworks would be fruitful for investigating and further understanding this multidimensional organizational phenomenon.

REFERENCES

1. Wilson, T.D. The "nonsense" of knowledge management. Inform. Res. **2002**, *8*. http://informationresearch.net/ir/8-1/paper144.html (accessed March 2007).
2. Shannon, C.; Weaver, W. *The Mathematical Theory of Communication*; University of Illinois Press: Urbana, IL, 1949.
3. Ingwersen, P. *Information Retrieval Interaction*; Taylor Graham: London, U.K., 1992.
4. Capurro, R.; Hjorland, B. The concept of information. In *Annual Review of Information Science and Technology (ARIST)*; Cronin, B., Ed.; Information Today Inc.: Medford, NJ, 2003; *37*, 343–411.
5. Buckland, M.K. *Information and Information Systems*; Praeger: New York, 1991.
6. Polanyi, M. *The Tacit Dimension*; Routledge & Keagan: London, U.K., 1966.
7. Nonaka, I. A dynamic theory of organizational knowledge creation. Organ. Sci. **1994**, *5* (1), 14–37.
8. Nonaka, I.; Takeuchi, H. *The Knowledge Creating Company: How Japanese Companies Create the Dynamics of Innovation*; Oxford University Press: New York, 1995.
9. Yates-Mercer, P.; Bawden, D. Managing the paradox: The valuation of knowledge and knowledge management. J. Inf. Sci. **2002**, *28* (1), 19–29.
10. Nahapiet, J.; Ghoshal, S. Social capital, intellectual capital and organizational advantage. Acad. Manage. Rev. **1998**, *23* (2), 242–266.
11. Orlikowski, W.J. Knowing in practice: Enacting a collective capability in distributed organization. Organ. Sci. **2002**, *13* (3), 249–273.

12. Cook, S.D.N.; Brown, J.S. Bridging epistemologies: The generative dance between organizational knowledge and organizational knowing. Organ. Sci. **1999**, *10* (4), 381–400.
13. McInerney, C. Knowledge management and the dynamic nature of knowledge. J. Am. Soc. Inf. Sci. Technol. **2002**, *53* (12), 1009–1018.
14. Wenger, E.C.; Snyder, W.M. Communities of practice: The organizational frontier. Harv. Bus. Rev. **January–February 2000**; 139–145.
15. Blackler, F. Knowledge, knowledge work and organizations: An overview and interpretation. In *The Strategic Management of Intellectual Capital and Organizational Knowledge*; Choo, C.W., Bontis, N., Eds.; Oxford University Press: New York, 2002; 47–64.
16. Boisot, M.H. *Knowledge Assets: Securing Competitive Advantage in the Knowledge Economy*; New York University Press: New York, 1998.
17. Huotari, M.-L.; Iivonen, M. Knowledge processes: A strategic foundation for the partnership between the university and its library. Libr. Manage. **2005**, *26* (6/7), 324–335.
18. Black, A.; Brunt, R. Information management in business, libraries and British military intelligence: Towards a history of information management. J. Doc. **1999**, *55*, 361–374.
19. Machlup, F. *The Production and Distribution of Knowledge in the United States*; Princeton University Press: Princeton, NJ, 1962.
20. Schultz, U.; Stabell, C. Knowing what you don't know? Discourses and contradictions in knowledge management research. J. Manage. Stud. **2004**, *41* (4), 549–573.
21. Barney, J. Firm resources and sustained competitive advantage. J. Manage. **1991**, *17* (1), 99–120.
22. Grant, R.M. Towards a knowledge-based theory of the firm. Strat. Manage. J. **1996**, *17* (Winter), 109–122.
23. Penrose, E.T. *The Theory of the Growth of the Firm*; Wiley: New York, 1959.
24. Argyris, C.; Schön, D.A. *Organizational Learning II: Theory, Method and Practice*; Addison-Wesley: Reading, MA, 1996.
25. Leonard-Barton, D. *Wellsprings of Knowledge: Building and Sustaining the Sources of Innovation*; Harvard Business School Press: Boston, MA, 1995.
26. Prahalad, C.K.; Hamel, G. The core competence of the corporation. Harv. Bus. Rev. **May–June 1990**, 79–91.
27. Case, D.; O'Connor, L. What's the use? Measuring the frequency of studies of information outcomes. J. Assoc. Inf. Sci. Technol. **2016**, *67* (3), 649–661.
28. Dervin, B.; Nilan, M. Information needs and uses. In *Annual Review of Information Science and Technology (ARIST)*; Williams, M.E., Ed.; Knowledge Industry Publications: New York, 1986; *21*, 3–33.
29. Todd, R. Utilization of heroin information by adolescent girls in Australia: A cognitive analysis. J. Am. Soc. Inf. Sci. Technol. **1999**, *50* (1), 10–23.
30. Savolainen, R. Information use as gap-bridging: the viewpoint of sense-making methodology. J. Am. Soc. Inf. Sci. Technol. **2006**, *57* (8), 1116–1125.
31. Taylor, R.S. Information use environments. In *Progress in Communication Sciences*; Dervin, B.; Voigt, M.J., Eds.; Ablex Publishing Corporation: Norwood, NJ, 1991; *10*, 217–255.

Israel–Knowledge Discovery

32. Taylor, R.S. *Value-Added Processes in Information Systems*; Ablex Publishing Corporation: Norwood, NJ, 1986.

33. Choo, C.W. *The Knowing Organization*; Oxford University Press Inc.: New York, 2006.

34. Kuhlthau, C. *Seeking Meaning: A Process Approach to Library and Information Services*; Ablex Publishing: Norwood, NJ, 1992.

35. Weick, K. *The Social Psychology of Organizations*; Random House: New York, 1979.

36. Senge, P.M. *The Fifth Discipline: The Art & Practice of the Learning Organization*; Doubleday Currency: New York, 1990.

37. Simon, H.A. *Models of Man: Social and Rational*; John Wiley: New York, 1957.

38. Normann, R.; Ramírez, R. *Designing Interactive Strategy: From Value Chain to Value Constellation*; John Wiley & Sons: Chichester, U.K., 1994.

39. Wikström, S.; Normann, R.; Anell, B.; Ekvall, G.; Forslin, J.; Skävad, P.-H. *Knowledge and Value: A New Perspective on Corporate Transformation*; Routledge: London, U.K., 1994.

40. Nonaka, I.; Toyama, R.; Konno, N. SECI, ba and leadership: A unified model of dynamic knowledge creation. Long Range Plann. **2000**, *30*, 5–34.

41. Suorsa, A.; Huotari, M.-L. Knowledge creation and the concept of human being: A phenomenological approach. J. Assoc. Inf. Sci. Technol. **2014**, *65* (5), 1042–1057.

42. Gadamer, H.-G. Vom Zirkel des Verstehens. In *Gesammelte Werke 2: Hermeneutik II*; J.C.B. Mohr: Tübingen, Germany, 1999; 57–65.

43. Gadamer, H.-G. *Truth and Method*; Continuum: London, U.K. and New York, 2004.

44. von Krogh, G. Individualist and collectivist perspectives on knowledge in organizations: Implications for information systems research. J. Strat. Inf. Syst. **2009**, *18*, 119–129.

45. Suorsa, A. Knowledge creation and play—A phenomenological approach. J. Doc. **2015**, *71* (3), 503–525.

Israel–Knowledge Discovery

Knowledge Discovery in Data Streams

Xuan Hong Dang
Computer Vision and Image Understanding, Institute for Infocomm, A STAR, Singapore,*

Kok-Leong Ong
School of Information Technology, Deakin University, Burwood, Victoria, Australia

Abstract
Knowing what to do with the massive amount of data collected has always been an ongoing issue for many organizations. While data mining has been touted to be the solution, it has failed to deliver the impact despite its successes in many areas. One reason is that data mining algorithms were not designed for the real world, i.e., they usually assume a static view of the data and a stable execution environment where resources are abundant. The reality however is that data are constantly changing and the execution environment is dynamic. Hence, it becomes difficult for data mining to truly deliver timely and relevant results. Recently, the processing of stream data has received many attention. What is interesting is that the methodology to design stream-based algorithms may well be the solution to the above problem. In this entry, we discuss this issue and present an overview of recent works.

INTRODUCTION

Knowing what to do with the massive amount of data collected has always been an ongoing issue for many organizations. Today, data are not just ingredients for churning out statistical reports, but are the basis of supporting efficient operations in many organizations. And to some extent, they provide the competitive intelligence needed to survive in today's economy. Since data can be potentially so important, it becomes increasingly difficult to refrain from collecting any data available. The effect of this is that organizations are overloaded with information.

Data mining has been touted to be the solution (or perhaps, the killer application) to the problem of information overloading. It is supposed to replace the human in performing the laborious task of sieving through data and to report only important results. In one sense, data mining technologies have created many successful stories and have in the recent years, gained research and industry interests. Yet, it does not seem to deliver the impact[1] in terms of penetrating every aspect of life or systems (compared to, for example, the Internet).

There are many reasons for a lack of impact—such as human factors, technical issues, or a combination of both. On the technical issue, we believe conventional data mining algorithms (and hence their products) were designed with two wrong assumptions. First, it assumes that the data are static in all aspects. Second, it assumes that the execution environment where the algorithm runs is stable with abundant resources (e.g., memory or computing power). The reality however is that both assumptions do not hold in the context of the problems that we are trying to address.

First, most conventional data mining algorithms operate on a snapshot of the data. The data may be collected and stored in a data warehouse where during data mining, is assumed to remain static even though new data could have arrived, or parts of the snapshot may no longer be valid. And throughout the lifetime of the algorithm's execution, this snapshot is assumed to be a reflection of the real-world situation. In addition, the data are assumed to be constantly available while the algorithm runs, i.e., there is some unbound or huge storage space for the snapshot where the algorithm can read as many times as it needs. While this may not appear to be an issue, real-world data are often many times larger. And we are not talking about scientific data here.

In a single day, Centrelink, Australia's welfare agency, has more than 11 million page requests in their Web logs; Telstra, Australia's largest telecommunications company, produces 15 million mobile call records; American supermarket chain WalMart records 20 million sales transactions; and Google handles 150 million searches. For such massive amount of data, it would be difficult, if not impossible, to generate any results in useful time by running off-the-shelves algorithms—even when unbounded memory, storage, and CPU time are available. This is because existing algorithms are simply not designed to do so.

The other problem with conventional data mining algorithms is that they all assumed an execution environment with all the resources they need, and that all resources are available until the execution terminates. Although such assumption is common in other applications, data mining algorithms cannot have such luxury by the sheer amount of time it needs to complete a task. In some cases, this may be ongoing as data keep arriving. Hence, data mining

Encyclopedia of Library and Information Sciences, Fourth Edition DOI: 10.1081/E-ELIS4-120043643

Copyright © 2017 by Taylor & Francis. All rights reserved.

algorithms must be aware of the conditions of the host environment (e.g., unavailability of host, reduced resources, etc).

This awareness is becoming very important in today's computing paradigm. Conventionally, data mining is considered a specialized technology available to a limited number of organizations. They were often operated in a controlled and centralized environment, where the analysis involved an expert user. The conventional process of knowledge discovery follows a strict sequence and algorithms ran in batch modes. Nevertheless, progress in other technologies changed the paradigm.

Advancements in data storage and acquisition technologies, wireless and mobile technologies, the Internet, and smaller computing devices all contributed to this change. Huge amount of data can now be collected from multiple sources; wireless and mobile technologies created pervasive computing; the Internet gave rise to connectivity; and as a result, users can work across different devices. Most important of all, these technologies generate enormous amount of data that demand ongoing and real-time analysis.

For a while, data mining researchers overcame the problem by developing faster algorithms and incorporating interactively into the knowledge discovery process. But the amount of data continues to grow exponentially compared to the efficiency of the algorithms. The gap between data mining and the real world enlarges. Very recently, the database community has recognized that the existing database approaches (including data mining) are no longer suitable for handling this class of data that arrives continuously at a very high rate. Because of its continuity, they are called data streams.[2] New algorithms for processing and mining streams were proposed.[3,4] In particular, the mining of stream data does not require a complete snapshot. All results are reflected as soon as possible when data arrive, and it can operate in host environments where resources are scarce. Despite the limited resources, the algorithm is able to compute very quickly using a small amount of CPU cycle. This speedup and lower resource consumption come at the price of lower accuracy in the results; but the error is maintained at a user-acceptable level.

To give a clearer picture of what we have discussed so far, Fig. 1 shows a timeline of a sequence of events occurring during data mining. The same data are analyzed by both conventional algorithms (in the upper half of the

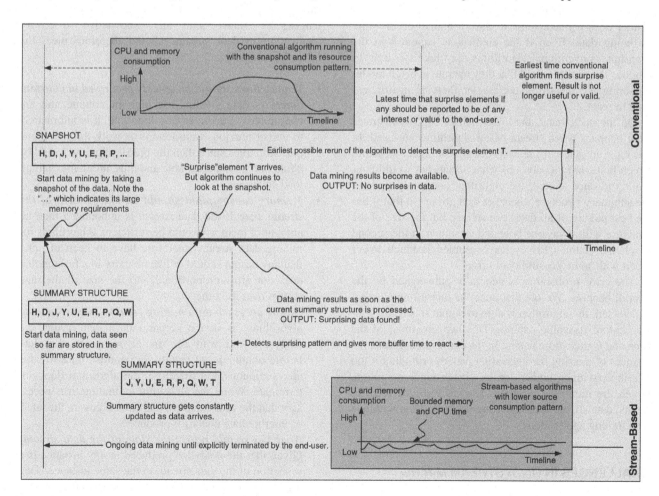

Fig. 1 A comparison between conventional data mining algorithms and the new stream-based algorithm by looking at the sequence of events happening in the data. Also shown are two graphs depicting their resource consumption pattern.

figure) and stream-based algorithms (lower half). We first illustrate the example for the case when the conventional algorithm is used. Our hypothetical problem here is that we are interested in looking for interesting patterns. An interesting pattern in this case is defined as the occurrence of a symbol which we denoted as **T** in the Fig. 1.

As in the conventional case, a snapshot of the data is taken when the user begins data mining. In our example, the snapshot contains the symbols {**H, D, J, Y, U, E, R, P**, . . .}. Once the snapshot is read, the algorithm begins processing using some sophisticated search technique which at some point in time, will usually consume a large amount of memory and CPU cycles as the graph at the top of the figure shows. During execution, data continue to arrive (usually at a rapid rate). In the snapshot approach, this newly arrived data may be stored somewhere until the next analysis is commissioned. As illustrated in our example, the interesting element was missed and the algorithm reported an outdated or invalid result.

To capture the interesting element, the next run of the algorithm can only start after it arrives and is captured in the snapshot. In real life, this would be impossible— because it is impractical to start instances of the algorithm at a regular intervals due to resource availability, and neither does it make sense to have a human observe the incoming data. Even if the element is captured in the snapshot, conventional algorithms may take too long to produce the results (recall that they operate in batch mode) rendering the discovery useless, or there is insufficient time to react.

On the other hand, the lower half of Fig. 1 illustrates what happens when stream-based algorithms are used. In this case, in place of the snapshot is a summary structure which holds only a subset of what a snapshot would contain. And once started, the algorithm constantly updates the summary structure whenever data arrive (so that it has the best picture of all data seen so far); but the size of the structure will always be bounded as shown in the second graph. Also, the CPU cycles consumed is much lower albeit with some possibility of error.

The error probability is generally outweighed by the overall benefits. We see that once the interesting element is detected, the algorithm is able to output this result usually before its value expires. This happens most of the time and is thus more useful. In the conventional case, the chances of missing the interesting pattern or finding it too late is very much higher due to a batch mode operation. Given the improved results and lower resource requirements, data stream techniques are popular in some unique data mining applications.

CHALLENGES IN DATA STREAM MINING

Applications that generate and/or consume data streams are found mainly in novel applications in the recent years.

This includes customer relationship management (CRM) applications,[5,6] Web click streams,[7,8] financial markets[9,10] that retailed products on the Internet, telecommunication systems,[9,11,12] and sensor networks.[13,14] The data records generated by these systems are usually referred to as *transactional data streams*, and its data objects are often referred to as *transactions* or *data instances*.

Compared to traditional data sets, data streams are characteristically unique. First, it is unbounded in size compared to traditional data sets that are saved on storage devices limited by their capacity. Consequently, the infinite amount of data that needs to be consumed by any analytical algorithm is also limited by the amount of physical memory on the computing device. Since there is no persistent storage facility in that sense, algorithms have to process the data streams in an online fashion and in the order in which it arrives. This is where the challenges lie when designing algorithms for data streams— the order in which data objects arrived can neither be controlled nor can the algorithm have random access to the data. This gave rise to the well-known "one pass" requirement concept that is virtually nonexistent in algorithms for mining traditional data sets. Given these challenges,[5,15] states that any knowledge discovery application in data streams should therefore meet the following criteria.

- *Transactions should be quickly processed in constant time:* As data streams are high in volume and are continuously generated at a high rate, it is impractical to revisit previous transactions or work through some data structures since then the processing time would be a function of some variable and thus, unreliable in high load situations.

- *Memory consumption should be independent of the stream size:* If the data stream is unbounded then no amount of memory would be sufficient. Algorithms for mining data streams therefore have to keep in mind that any design should utilize memory in a fashion that does not grow proportionally to the size of the data stream over the time.

- *Online access to data mining results:* In conventional algorithms, as in the scenario discussed earlier, the analyst would wait for the algorithm to complete before obtaining the results. In contrast, data streams are continuous and therefore, the algorithm does not terminate. While the algorithm is running, it is necessary that the user can have real-time access to the latest or intermediate analytics produced.

- *Analytics should reflect the state of the data stream:* Given that the analytics produced at any instance is a reflection of the data stream in the same instance, such a system should be capable of adapting to the changes in the data stream and produce the relevant analytics as discussed in the previous criterion. Preferably, the

Israel–Knowledge Discovery

system should also be capable of retrieving results at any instance of the data stream.

• *Analytics should be a good approximate to actual results:* In theory, the actual results would correspond to the results of conventional data mining algorithms been applied to a snapshot of the data stream been stored on a disk that is unbounded in size. While this exact result is often not necessary in data stream applications, the estimate produced under the above constraints should be a good reflection of the actual result. Otherwise, the analytics would be meaningless.

As a consequence of the above requirements, existing algorithms are no longer appropriate in the data stream setting. First, the assumption that data is available at anytime and that they can be read multiple times violates the "one pass" constraint. Second, the algorithms are not design to enable real-time queries. Therefore, changes in the underlying data stream could possibly invalidate the results. Unless human intervention takes place to rerun the analytics, existing algorithms do not have the means to automatically detect the changes and produce an updated set of results. These conventional algorithms include Apriori and FP-Tree in association analysis; k-means and k-centroid methods in clustering; and ID3 and C4.5 in classification.

Data Stream Management Systems

Of course, it would do injustice to the conventional data mining algorithms for not fulfilling the various data stream constraints since they exist in the context of a larger system such as a database management system (DBMS). When we take a system view to the problem, we see that the conventional algorithms were built on the legacy of DBMS design, where data queries are executed over a data store. On the other hand, data streams simply invalidated this mode of operation since it is infeasible to load the data stream into a data store, and have the queries executed in a similar fashion. This motivated the need for a data stream management system (DSMS),[7,16] where the query operations and the relevant analytics have to be redesigned accordingly. The uniqueness of a DSMS can be effectively characterized by the following attributes.

• In a DSMS, data appear in transient streams and may not be stored persistently. This is in contrast to conventional databases, where data are placed in some storage device and retrieved through the execution of a query. Data objects in a transient stream however are processed in memory and discarded as soon as it was processed.

• In conventional database systems, the execution of a query will produce the exact result and the operation does not have a real-time constraint. Data stream systems, however, have execution constraints such as processing cost and time. Hence, the results provided by the DSMS are usually an approximate.

• In data stream systems, a query is often not seen as a one-time operation. In other words, once executed, it runs continuously against the changing data stream and produces results (and updates) until the operation is cancelled by the analyst. In the current database environment, once the exact answer is obtained, the operation ceases. In the event that the data has changed, the operation is not executed until invoked by the analyst.

• In current database systems, data can be stored in any granularity and later retrieved for further operations. Again, this contrasts data stream systems, where data objects arrive at their finest granularity and only the summary of it is stored. With the DSMS, there is no way that the analyst can retrieve the original data objects in the data stream.

• In traditional database systems, performance can be optimized through a query plan that exploits the storage pattern of the physical database. This is not possible in data stream systems since the underlying stream is unpredictable. Therefore, query plans in DSMS are often hard to design in advance.

Suffice to say, these characteristics justified the need to reconsider how a data stream system is built. Unlike existing database systems, the DSMS requires a different set of techniques and operations. The essence of any data stream systems, given the difficult requirements, is the summary structure as discussed in our example. Therefore, the problem of designing a DSMS revolves around the techniques of summarizing the data to facilitate similar database queries on the data stream.[16–18] In the sections that follow, we shall review some of these techniques.

Histogram

Histograms has been one of the most popular data reduction techniques.[7,19] They use binning methods to approximate data distributions to minimize the information to be stored. The distribution of values in a bucket usually have a uniform spread assumption, i.e., the values are assumed to be at equal distance from one another. Hence, one only needs to store the minimum and maximum value, and the number of values in each bucket; and that provides a good summary about the original data values. For those values in the bucket, they can be easily approximated with good accuracy by the above arrangements.

We present some of the common histogram techniques[20,21] below. In all these variants, data is partitioned into a certain number of β disjoint buckets (or intervals) B_j ($1 \leq j \leq \beta$); and the data distribution is represented as $T = (v_1, f_1), (v_2, f_2), ., (v_d, f_d)$, where v_i denotes a distinct value in T and f_i denotes the corresponding frequency.

Israel–Knowledge Discovery

- *Equi-width histograms:* Partition the data distribution into buckets such that the number of data points v_i in each bucket B_j is approximately uniform to the other buckets.
- *Equi-height histograms:* Partition the data distribution into buckets based on the summation of the frequencies. Generally, this value is the same for every bucket.
- *Maxdiff (Max difference) histograms:* Partition the data distribution such that the differences in frequencies between adjacent bucket boundaries are maximized.
- *V-optimal histograms:* If n_j is the number of entries in the jth bucket, $\overline{f_j}$ is the average frequency of that bucket, and $f_{j,k}$ is the frequency of kth entry in the jth bucket, then this technique partitions T such that $\sum_{j=1}^{\beta} \sum_{k=1}^{n_j} (\overline{f_j} - f_{j,k})^2$ is minimized. In other words, $\sum_{k=1}^{n_j} (\overline{f_j} - f_{j,k})^2$ is the variance of the jth bucket, Hence, a V-optimal histogram is the one with the least (smallest) variance of all histograms with the same number (β) of buckets.
- *Compressed histograms:* First store the most $n(n < \beta)$ frequent values in n singleton buckets. The remaining values are then partitioned into ($\beta - n$) buckets using equi-width or equi-height histograms.

Wavelet Transformation

Another technique for data summarization stems from a linear signal processing technique called discrete wavelet transformation (DWT).[15,19] With DWT, one can transform a set of numerical values into a set of wavelet coefficients of the same length. The wavelet coefficients are then reduced by retaining only those values that are above a user-specified threshold. This creates a sparse representation that is well-suited for data reduction. The Haar wavelet is one of the simplest algorithms used in summarizing data streams.

Assume a data set $D = \{x_1, x_2, \ldots, x_n\}$ with the size of $n = 2^k$. Then, the wavelet tree can be obtained as follows:

1. Let the original data set (also called input signal) be at level 0 in a wavelet tree.
2. At level 0, each pair wise average and difference of adjacent data points (x_{2i}, x_{2i+1}) is computed to produce the coefficients for level 1. Thus, $s_{0,i} = C \times (x_{2i} + x_{2i+1})$ and $d_{0,i} = C \times (x_{2i} - x_{2i+1}); 0 \le i \le n/2$, where C is a predefined proportionality constant. The values $s_{0,i}$ constitutes a "smooth" (low-frequency) version of the signal, while the values $d_{0,i}$ represent the high-frequency content.
3. At level 1, the value of $s_{0,i}$ is used to compute the next level by repeating the previous step. This would give a smoother version of the signal, $s_{1,i}$ and $d_{1,i}; 0 \le i \le n/4$.

4. The above is performed repeatedly at each level i to get the averages and differences at level $i + 1$ until the top level is reached, which has only one average and difference.
5. Finally, the coefficients are represented in a hierarchical form, including the average value at the top level, and the different values at all remaining levels.

Because the compressed wavelet coefficients can be used to easily reconstruct the original data set, they are often used to approximate queries[22,23] and in data mining, for burst detection.[14]

Sampling

In statistics, the idea of sampling is that a set of random samples is often a reflection of the original data set and thus captures the underlying characteristics using less resources. Therefore, sampling is a good way to summarize the data in question, or to process large databases.[24,25]

Since most sampling techniques are applied on data sets with finite sizes, the unbounded stream makes sampling more challenging than it appears to be. In the data stream context, Viter's work becomes the fundamental solution to this problem. In Vitter,[26] Viter introduced a number of algorithms to sample N records (without replacement) from a pool of N records, where the value of N is unknown a priori. Viter's algorithms were used by others[27–29] with various degree of success.

To conclude our discussion of data stream systems, we briefly list some of the relevant projects undertaken in this area.

- *Aurora (Brown/Massachusetts Institute of Technology (MIT))* is a DSMS built for monitoring data streams. In Aurora (http://www.cs.brown.edu/research/aurora), the data streams are generated from sources such as sensors, satellites, or stock feeds. The DSMS tracks the data from numerous streams to detect abnormal activities and also produces summary (aggregation and reduction) and correlation reports.[30]
- *STREAM* (http://www-db.stanford.edu/stream) is a DSMS project at Stanford University that investigates memory management issues, query processing,[31] and algorithm design for mining data streams.[32]
- *Cougar* (http://www.cs.cornell.edu/database/cougar) is a project by Cornell University to investigate query operations in sensor networks.[33]
- *Hancock* is a project by AT&T. The project investigates the building of a domain-specific language, i.e., Hancok, to compute evolving profiles of their customers over telecommunication streams, stock market transaction streams, and credit card transaction streams.[9,11]

Israel–Knowledge Discovery

- *NiagaraCQ* is a project at OGI/Wisconsin (http://cs. wisc.edu/niagara) focused on studying continuous queries over Internet XML streams. The project was motivated by the observation that many Web queries shared similar structures. The project exploits this observation to group queries in an attempt to reduce computational and I/O cost.[34]
- *TelegraphCQ* is a Berkeley project (http://telegraph. cs.berkeley.edu) to develop a DSMS for querying in sensor networks. Much of the research issues investigated focuses on designing algorithms to run continuous adaptive queries over the data stream generated by the sensor network.[35]
- *Traderbot* is a Web-based financial search engine (http://www.traderbot.com) that evaluates (both one-time and continuous) queries over real-time streaming financial data such as stock ticks or news feeds.[7]

KNOWLEDGE DISCOVERY IN DATA STREAMS

So far, we have given an overview motivating the need for data stream applications; discussed the challenges that such applications face; and also the issues surrounding the design of data stream management systems, in which data mining facilities are a part of. In this section, we present some of the data mining algorithms designed for data streams. In doing so, we will provide the necessary background for the reader to compare the differences in the design of such algorithms against their conventional counterparts, and to appreciate how the data stream constraints are incorporated so as to develop other data stream algorithms in future data mining tasks.

Frequent Pattern Mining

Let $I = \{x_1, x_2, \ldots, x_n\}$ be a set of items where $X \subseteq I$ is an itemset or pattern. Further, let $D = \{t_1, t_2, \ldots, t_N\}$ be a database of transactions, where $t_i \subseteq I$ and N is the number of transactions in D. Given the minimum support $s \in (0,1)$, a pattern X is a frequent pattern (or frequent itemset) if the support of X, i.e., $supp(X) = |\{X \subseteq t_i \in D\}|/N$, satisfies $supp(X) \geq s$.

The problem of frequent pattern mining in a transactional database is to find all frequent itemsets in D with respect to the given minimum support threshold s. Apriori is one of the most famous algorithm that is often used to uncover all frequent itemsets from transactional databases. By using Apriori, the number of times to scan a database can reach k or $k + 1$ times, where k is the size of the largest frequent itemset. This approach quickly becomes a significant issue in mining very large databases where the cost to scan databases is very expensive and time-consuming. To reduce mining cost, feature selection,[36,37] parallel computing,[38,39] and sampling[25,40] has been used.

Among them, sampling is often the preferred technique by virtue of its simplicity.

Generally, once the load is shed to a manageable level where processing the incoming sampled stream is possible under the available processing resources, we can perform one of the three common frequent pattern mining activities.

Frequent item mining

Frequent item mining arose out of a variety of applications including network management systems, search engines, telephone call records, etc., where each generated instance corresponds to an item. In most of these applications, there are two issues to be addressed: 1) to find the top k frequent patterns; and 2) to optimize memory consumption during discovery. Most of the literature has solution in memory optimization through optimized counting techniques.

Let us consider an example of this problem in network management systems. In Demaine,[41] an Internet Service Provider may be interested in monitoring a data stream of Internet Protocol (IP) packets to find the top k user's IP addresses which consume the most bandwidth. Such a query changes over time and given the speed at which IP packets are potentially generated in a large multiuser setting, this is where a one-pass frequent item mining algorithm is needed. The Simple algorithm proposed in Demaine[41] (and also in Karp[42]) was designed for such problems. Each transaction is seen to contain one data object, which in this case is the IP address, and the objective is to find those IP addresses which consume a certain amount of bandwidth (i.e., the threshold).

In the Simple algorithm, an array K of size $\lceil 1/s \rceil$ is used to count the frequent IP addresses, where s is the minimum threshold. Each element in the array K contains two fields: the item label (IP address) and the frequency count. When a new item arrives in the stream, look for it in K and increments the frequency count by 1 if found or otherwise, insert the item into K and initializing the frequency count to 1. Since K stores much lesser items than N, the number of unique items seen in the stream so far, K can become full. When that happens, the algorithm decreases the frequency count of all items by 1 and for those whose frequency value is zero, they are removed from the array. Clearly, the items in k at any time would be the superset of those frequent items since K's size was determined by $\lceil 1/s \rceil$.

This straightforward algorithm is a good example of a design for data stream applications. The array size is bounded and fixed regardless of the size of the incoming data stream. In terms of memory consumption, the array size is very small compared to the memory utilization by conventional algorithms. Also, each incoming item in the stream only needs to be looked at once and the processing takes place on a fix time bounded by the maintenance of K against the incoming item. On the drawback, while the top

K frequent items are obtained at anytime against the latest state of the data stream, we observe that this algorithm is unable to accurately provide the actual frequency count from K. While the items in K is guaranteed to be the top K frequent items, the frequencies recorded is at best an approximation.

Frequent pattern (or itemsets) mining

Applications that generate transactional data streams are candidates for frequent pattern mining. These include Web click streams, e-commerce recommendation systems, and financial markets to name a few. Generally, the solutions for finding frequent patterns in data streams are extensions from algorithms for finding frequent items. Hence, most of these techniques are memory optimization methods. Needless to say, the memory issue is far more challenging in frequent pattern mining (compared to frequent item mining discussed in the previous section) due to the exponential increase of patterns to be tracked when the number of items increased linearly. As a result, it is difficult to determine the memory consumption in advance and thus force some research to estimate memory usage empirically.[29,43,44]

The Lossy Counting-based algorithm reported in Manku[29] was one of the first piece of work for frequent pattern mining in data streams. The algorithm uses a summary structure D containing a set of entries of the form (set, f, Δ), where set is an itemset, f is the approximate frequency, and Δ is the maximum error probability. The data stream is divided into buckets of equal size w and processed in batches. Suppose the main memory contains β buckets, then Manku and Motwani's[29] algorithm maintains D as follows.

For each entry in D, f is updated by counting the occurrences of set in the current batch. A new itemset is inserted into D if its frequency in the current batch of buckets satisfies $f \geq \beta$. An entry (set, f, $b_{\text{current}} - \beta$) for the new itemset is thus created in D. Periodically, the entries that satisfy $f + \Delta \leq b_{\text{current}}$ are deleted from D. To ensure that the transactional stream is efficiently processed, the algorithm uses a number of implementation techniques. Specifically, there are three modules—the buffer, the Trie, and SetGen. The buffer repeatedly reads a batch of transactions into the available main memory while the Trie is used as the physical representation for D. The SetGen module operates on the current batch of transactions to find frequent itemsets. To handle variable sized transactions and to avoid explicit enumeration of all subsets in a transaction (which is extremely expensive), the algorithm uses a rule that a subset will be enumerated if and only if it occurs in the Trie or its frequency in the current batch exceeds β. This is why the algorithm needs as much memory as possible to process the data stream in batches.

The inherited drawbacks of Lossy Counting aside, the first drawback of Manku and Motwani's[29] work is that to reduce the number entries in D, β must be large since a small β value results in a large increase in the number of entries placed into D. Secondly, all available memory is used for buffering the transactions and hence, D has to be made a disk-based data structure. As a result, there is a major impact on the performance. Consequently, the solution is suitable only in situations where queries and analysis of the data streams are pseudo real-time. Later works however, e.g., Yu[43] and Jin,[44] did make improvements to this limitation.

Time changing frequent pattern mining

Given that data streams are constantly changing the state of the database, the patterns discovered at one instance may no longer be the ones that are frequent in the next instance. Unfortunately, most algorithms find all frequent itemsets and hence, process the data stream in batches. In other words, the transactions are buffered and the discovery takes place on the buffered transactions. When the next set of transactions overflow the buffer, it triggers the algorithm to replace the existing frequent patterns with the ones recently discovered. In this mode of operation, real-time processing is absent and results are not timely. In situations where the patterns can change quickly over time, the buffer approach fails.

FP-Streaming[45] is an example of an algorithm that finds frequent patterns with respect to the time parameter. The frequent patterns obtained by a query is time-sensitive in the sense that the analyst can query for frequent patterns between arbitrary time intervals. Central to the algorithm is the maintenance of a data structure call FP-Stream which is an extension of the FP-tree structure.[46] FP-Stream includes two components: a pattern tree and a tiled-time window. Instead of representing transactions like FP-tree, the pattern tree stores patterns where each node in the pattern tree represents an itemset including all items from the root node to the current node. The tiled-time window at each node maintains the frequency count of the corresponding itemset at different periods of time. The FP-Stream structure is maintained over the lifetime of the data stream.

Over a period of time T, the frequency of a pattern is counted. Since the pattern may be frequent in one time period T_i but not in a longer period $T_j(T_i T_j)$, the logarithm tiled-time window is used to store the frequencies of a node at different granularities of time. For example, the frequency of a pattern X would be stored as $f(n, n)$; $f(n-1, n-1)$; $f(n-2, n-3)$; $f(n-4, n-7)$, and so on. Hence, the number of levels at each node is relatively small $(\log_2(n) + 1)$. Next, the data stream is divided into batches of transactions $B_1, B_2, \ldots, B_n, \ldots$, where B_n is the latest batch. Patterns are computed whenever a batch B_i arrives. Each pattern is used to find a node in the pattern tree and the frequency updated in the tiled-time window. At the node, the frequency counts are shifted to the next window to make space for the update or if all the windows are full, merging of the counts occur before saving the latest count.

Given that the above has to be done for all possible patterns, memory consumption is a concern and so the algorithm does housekeeping of the pattern tree from time to time. This is done by deleting the older tiled-time windows toward the tail end if a delete condition is satisfied. This delete condition is used in conjunction with the Apriori property to further limit the level of consumption in main memory.

The strength of this algorithm is its ability to answer queries about the frequent patterns between any two time instances. The answers to the queries are much more precise at the expense of a much higher processing cost and memory cost. As a result, it is difficult to consider FP-Streaming an online algorithm where real-time responses are required from high speed data streams. Nevertheless, this work forms the basis for mining patterns under time-changing conditions. Subsequent works addressed the various aspects of this issue include the use of sliding windows in Chang[47] and Chang[48] for better real-time analysis; finding the difference in patterns of two data streams;[49] and finding temporal patterns.[50]

Clustering

Clustering is the process of partitioning a group of records into subgroups (or clusters) such that the data points in each group are similar to the other points in the same group but are different to the data points in the other groups.[51] Clustering algorithms predominantly fall into two main techniques. The *partitioning* method, where k partitions are predefined and the objects are then placed, based on greedy heuristics, into a partition based on some objective function. The other approach is the *hierarchical* method, where the algorithm works either in a top-down or bottom-up approach. In the top-down approach, all data objects are initially in one cluster and in each iteration, the algorithm divides the clusters into smaller clusters. In the bottom-up approach, each data object started as a cluster and up iteratively merged until the desired number of clusters is reached.

The nature of data streams presents three key challenges clustering algorithms: 1) the compactness of the representation; 2) incremental process of new data objects; and 3) clear identification of outliers. The first challenge meant that the clusters must be representable in a form that is independent on the size of the growing data stream. The second challenge meant that clustering algorithms must be capable of placing a newly arrived data object quickly into a cluster. In other words, the similarity function must depend on the comparison of all data objects. Finally, the last challenge is the need to quickly identify outliers. This is more difficult than it appears to be due to the fact that an outlier at some point in time may form a new cluster in the future. In the sections that follow, we review some of the algorithms for clustering data streams.

CluStream and variants

Probably the most representative algorithm for clustering data streams is CluStream first reported in Aggarwal.[52] CluStream was designed to address the issue of discovery over evolving data streams. To address this problem, two novel concepts were proposed: 1) the use of microclusters which is an extension of the feature vector in BIRCH;[53] and 2) the pyramidal timeframe.

Essentially, the microcluster is some sort of summary structure for the atomic cluster obtained from the online component of CluStream. It maintains statistical information about the data points assigned to the cluster which is used to compute the centroid. A micro-cluster is defined as a $(2d + 3)$ tuple $(\overline{CF2^x}, \overline{CF1^x}, CF2^t, CF1^t, n)$, where d is the dimension of data points. $\overline{CF2^x}$ and $\overline{CF1^x}$ are the sum and squared sum of the data values for each dimension in the cluster respectively and both are vectors of d entries. Correspondingly, $CF2^t$ and $CF1^t$ are the sum and squared sum of the time stamps; and n is the number of data points assigned in the cluster.

The pyramidal timeframe is a table that stores snapshots (at different time instances) of the microclusters. Periodically, a snapshot is taken to capture the set of microclusters in existence. As the snapshot becomes "older" overtime, less space is allocated to store information about the microcluster at that time instance. That is, the longer the snapshot of the microclusters exist in the pyramidal timeframe, the more space is allocated and hence, the microclusters are further summarized by merging the information that two microclusters contain. The algorithm in CluStream that uses the above concepts is given below.

1. Initially, CluStream clusters off-line from an initial set of data points to create the initial q-clusters.
2. After that, the online component kicks in. When a new data point arrives, it will be clustered into one of q clusters and the corresponding microcluster updated. The new data point may end up as a new cluster to reflect the evolution in the data stream. In order to get more space for new clusters, the old ones may be deleted if they are identified as outliers, or two old clusters may be merged.
3. Periodically, a snapshot is taken to capture the set of q microclusters, and that is stored in the pyramidal timeframe. The old snapshot is deleted (if the pyramidal timeframe is full), or the latest snapshot is "aged" to the next slot before inserting the new snapshot in the latest slot.
4. The off-line component is used each time a query is made. The answer to the query will come from the

Israel—Knowledge Discovery

summary information held in the pyramidal time-frame and the q clusters.

The design in CluStream allows the algorithm to store the status of the data stream at different time instances and thus allow interesting queries to be issued. For example, given two different time instances, we can compare the differences in the clusters formed to understand how a particular cluster has evolved and potentially identify the data item(s) that caused the change.

The CluStream framework was later utilized in Ong[54] to cluster categorical data streams. Named SCLOPE, the algorithm was derived from three previous works namely, CLOPE,[55] CluStream, and FP-tree.[46] In SCLOPE, a categorical data stream is divided into windows. With each window, the online component is utilized to construct a FP-Tree for all transactions appearing in the window similar to the algorithm proposed in Han[46]] but with additional information about each branch of the data structure. From the constructed FP-Tree, SCLOPE groups the similar paths, i.e., those branches sharing the same prefix in the FP-Tree into microclusters. Since each branch represents a set of similar transactions and that overlapping branches are more similar than those that do not, the effect is similar to clustering as observed in CLOPE. Once the local microclusters are created, the off-line component is applied to cluster them into global clusters using the CLOPE algorithm.

Another variant of the CluStream algorithm is the StreamCluCD algorithm. This algorithm is designed based on the Lossy Counting algorithm discussed in Manku.[29] In this algorithm, each cluster is represented by a histogram (for all m attributes), which are used to compare the similarity of a new record to the cluster. When a new data object arrives, it is compared with the histogram to determine the best cluster for the data object. The cluster's histogram is then updated to reflect the new data object. If no cluster fits, the data object becomes a new cluster if the space constraint, controlled via the e and s parameter in the Lossy Counting algorithm, is not violated. The drawback of this algorithm is in the sensitivity of the objects chosen as the initial clusters.

k-Median

An alternative approach to CluStream is based on approximation algorithms to cluster the data points in metric space.[32,56–59] k-Median is one such notable algorithm, where the sum of the distance from each data point to its closest assigned median is expected to be minimized.

Let $\omega = (N, dist)$ be a metric space, where n is a ground set and $dist : N \times N \rightarrow \mathbb{R}^+ \cup \{0\}$ be a distance function. Further, let M be a median set and Y be the data set that we want to cluster into k clusters, where both are the subsets of N. Then for all data points $x \in Y$, we denote $ASG(x, M) = min_{m \in M} dist(x, m)$ as the closest member of M to x, and denote $AD(x, M) = dist(x, ASG(x, D))$ as the assignment distance of x under the set M. Using these notations, the cost function of k-median problem can be defined as

$$\phi^Y(M) = \sum_{x \in Y} AD(x, M) \qquad (1)$$

Thus, the objective of k-median is to find a set M that can minimize the cost function $\Phi^Y(M)$. The k-median problem can be further divided into two subproblems: continuous k-median and discrete k-median. We call continuous k-median if the set M is chosen from space N, which means it is not limited in Y. Otherwise, we call discrete k-median, i.e., M is chosen from Y.

To cluster stream data, bicriterion (a, b) approximation algorithms are often used. In this approach, the produced set M has at most $a \times k$ medians and the cost function for that M is no more than b times the cost of the optimal solution. An algorithm for k-median problems was introduced in Guha[32] and Guha,[56] where the algorithm builds clusters (using the bicriterion) incrementally and hierarchically. Like SCLOPE, the algorithm processes the stream in batches of data points, each fitting the primary memory. The algorithm is summarized below.

Let m be the size of memory, k be the given number of expected clusters. This algorithm can be summarized as follows:

1. Let m be the number of data points that can be held in primary memory. Upon receiving m data points, the algorithm clusters them into $2k$ points, i.e., $a = 2$. These points are called *intermediate medians* and are weighted by the number of data points assigned to it.
2. The algorithm reiterates the step above until it has $m^2/2k$ data points from the data stream, where it will cluster the m first-level medians into $2k$ second-level medians. Each median in the $2k$ new intermediate medians is also weighted by the total number of data points assigned to it.
3. Maintaining at most mi-level medians and on seeing m data points, the algorithm generates $2k(i + 1)^{th}$-level medians with the weight of each new median as the sum of the weights of all intermediate medians assigned to it.
4. When users request the result, the algorithm clusters all intermediate medians into k final medians.

This approach was later improved by Charikar[58] and Mishra,[59] where the accuracy of the approximation factor b is enhance and the memory is better utilized. Babcock et al.[57,60] later extend the solution to work in a window model rather than processing them in batches. The advantage of these algorithms is that they can process the data stream in limited space, and the clusters are represented in

Israel–Knowledge Discovery

a compact manner—it only requires the set of medians to be recorded. On the down side, these algorithms are extensions of the k-median and thus find hyper-spheres as clusters. Additionally, it is not clear how these approaches can be extended to categorical data streams.

Classification

In contrast to clustering, the objective of classification is to build a model that can be used to predict the class (or missing attribute value) of a future data object whose class (or the value of interest) is unknown. Generally, classification is a two-step process.

In the first step, as known as learning, the model is built from a set of training samples, where the class of each sample is known in advance. In the second step, the model constructed by the algorithm by learning from the samples are used to predict future objects.[61] Typically, the learning models are represented as classification rules, decision trees, or some mathematical function. Classification using decision trees has been well-studied and many algorithms were developed.[62] Classification using the Bayesian[63] network is a technique based on statistics. There are also techniques in machine learning and neural networks.[61,64–66] In the sections that follow, we review the data stream variants that were built on the foundations of these classic algorithms.

Very fast decision tree (VDFT) construction

VFDT[67] builds a decision tree for classification based on the Hoeffding bound. The initial state of the decision tree consists of only one single leaf node, i.e., the root node. As data points arrive, the tree is built iteratively (starting from the root) by replacing the leaf nodes with decision (or test) nodes. To do this, statistics about the data points are stored at each leaf node. The statistics include the counts n_{ijk} representing the number of data points of class label k reaching that leaf node when the attribute j receives the value i.

The decision on whether a node is to become a test node depends on two factors—whether there are enough data points at the leaf node, and whether the selected heuristic evaluation function, e.g., C4.5 or the Gini index, supports the split. If both criteria are met, the node is changed into a decision node and one of the available attributes is selected as the test condition. This is done throughout the lifetime in processing the data stream. The significant strength of VFDT is the time cost to evaluate the heuristic evaluation function each time a data point arrives at a leaf node. VFDT minimizes this cost by evaluating the function using only those data points since the last evaluation. This is further capped by using the minimal number of such points using the Hoeffding bound before deciding to split a leaf node.

One weakness of VDFT is that it assumes the underlying stream to have a stationary distribution.[67] And if the

datapoints are buffered on disk, performance takes a hit as the data points are read at random.

VFDT for continuous attributes

An extension of VFDT is reported in Gama[68] for continuous attributes. Named VFDTc, a decision node has only two descendent branches and the splitting test is a condition of the form attribute$_i$ ≤ cuttingpoint. Therefore, the two descendant branches correspond to the values of *true* and *false* as returned by an evaluation of the condition.

To identify the cutting point, a vector representing the distribution for the data points reaching a leaf node is maintained, and for each continuous attribute, a binary tree is maintained. Each node in the binary tree contains three fields. The first is the node identifier, which is also the value i of the attribute. The other two are vectors of k dimensions, where k corresponds to the number of classes. Each time a data point reaches the leaf, all its binary trees are updated. From these binary trees, the information gain of a given attribute can be computed. Hence, the best attribute with its best cutting point can be found.

On the drawback of this algorithm, this approach is computationally expensive due to the amount of work needed to create metadata for identifying the split. Also, VFDT does not work well on data streams where concept drifts occur.

Concept-adapting VFDT

Where concept drifts occur in the data streams, the decision tree constructed by VFDT quickly becomes outdated and so, the prediction accuracy on new data objects drops significantly over time. To address this problem, Hulten et al.[69] proposed an extension of the VFDT. Called concept-adapting VFDT (or CVFDT), the decision is built from at most n data points. And unlike VFDT where only leaf nodes are required to store sufficient statistics, the decision nodes in CVFDT must also maintain sufficient statistics.

To maintain concept drifts, the CVFDT algorithm periodically scans the decision nodes and for those nodes whose sufficient statistics suggest some new attribute that would be a better candidate for the test condition, an alternative subtree starting at that node is created. Over time, as the new subtree becomes more accurate than the older one, the old subtree is replaced. Hence, there can be more than one subtree rooted from the same internal node in CVFDT. In this case, there are instances when CVFDT actually maintains them simultaneously.

Ensemble classifiers

The classifiers that we have discussed thus far built a single model to predict every possible outcomes in the data stream. The issue with this approach is the implicit assumption that the training data and the testing data shared a similar distribution. While this assumption is arguably reasonable, it contradicted with the assertion that a data stream's distribution and its characteristics do evolve over time. Consequently, it was argued in Wang,[70] Fan[71,72] and Gao[73] that a better model is to have a number of classifiers working on the same data stream where the results among the classifiers are combined to give a prediction. This led to the development of a generic framework to discover concept drifting data streams using weighted ensemble classifiers.

In Wang et al.'s[70] framework, the set of classifiers may be a combination of models, e.g., decision trees, Naive networks, Ripper, etc., learnt using different techniques or algorithms. The ensemble of classifiers will build the top k-classifiers that can learn with the best accuracy. To do so, the data stream is processed in "chunks." When a chunk of data points arrives, a new classifier is created for that chunk. At the same time, the same chunk is used to update the weights of the older classifiers. The weight of each classifier is updated based on the expected error of that classifier in predicting the data points in the new chunk. Often, this weight is inversely proportional to the error value. The top k-classifiers that gave the most accurate prediction are chosen into the ensemble.

This approach has the advantage that it can produce a better prediction than the single classifier approach.[67] The disadvantage lies in the complexity of maintaining the set of k classifiers. Furthermore, the results are often sensitive to the size of the data chunk and the number of classifiers in the ensemble. Given that different types of classifiers are picked in the ensemble, trying to identify the proper parameter is often not easy—especially when the data stream is concept drifting.

StreamMiner

StreamMiner[71,72,74] is a classifier system that can detect and learn changing in data streams automatically. The system relies on the decision tree model. There are two types of changes that StreamMiner can learn: concept drift and distribution drift.

Different from other learning systems, StreamMiner does not need the labeled data in new data stream immediately. It only needs when the change is detected. To identify the change, it bases on statistically estimated loss measures. In detail, firstly, the model based on the decision tree is built from a training data set. When processing new stream data, the system compares the statistical value at each leaf in the tree to detect the change. Let dt be a decision tree constructing from training data set D; and S be a data stream. Each instance in S is classified by a unique path from the root to some leaf node. Assume that n is the number of instances classified by leaf ℓ; and N is

the size of the data stream seen so far. The statistics at leaf ℓ is defined as

$$P(\ell) = \frac{n_\ell}{N} \qquad (2)$$

Clearly, the sum of $P(\ell)$ overall leaf nodes in the tree dt is equal to 1, i.e., $\sum P(\ell) = 1$. The $P(\ell)$ describes how the instance space of the stream S is shattered among the leaf nodes solely based on attribute test results of the given decision tree dt. It does not consider either the true class labels or attributes that are not tested by dt. Now the statistical difference between the training data set D and the stream data S can be identified. This value will be reflected in $P(\ell)$ as follows

$$PS = \frac{\sum_{\ell \in dt} |P_S(\ell) - P_D(\ell)|}{2} \times 100 \qquad (3)$$

where

$PD(\ell)$ is statistics at leaf ℓ on the training data set D
$P_S(\ell)$ is statistics at leaf ℓ on the data stream S.

This PS is called the *error rate* or *guessed loss* of the model on the new stream data. Therefore, this approach does not need the labeled data in the data stream for identifying the change. Instead, it compares statistical difference at each leaf node in the model. If this PS value is much higher than an application-specific tolerable maximum value, a small number of data records in the new data stream is chosen to investigate their true class labels. This means, only after "guessing" there are some changes in the data stream that the model may not be suitable, the system needs to identify true labels of some samples in the new streaming data. With these true class labels, the true loss of current decision tree is statistically estimated. If this value is also higher than the tolerable maximum value, the decision tree should be reconstructed by using the same true class labels sampled in the previous step. This system has been tested and used for credit card fraud detection applications.

CONCLUSIONS

It might appear to some readers that data stream problems are very much restricted to a few application domain and thus, the solutions may not deliver an impact on a larger scale. For example, it is probably easier to see the value of a clustering algorithm on any data applications over a clustering algorithm in the data stream environment that is restricted to only a few specific applications. In our opinion, this view does not do justice to the solutions brought about by data stream problems.

Regardless of the application, we are witnessing an exponential growth in the amount of data to be processed. And that has kept the data mining and database

Israel–Knowledge Discovery

community working on better algorithms to process the larger volume of data. If we consider the bigger picture of data analytics, the larger data set affects not just analytical times but also the ease at which the analytics can be presented and interpreted by the analyst. Since it has been known that data mining is an iterative and interactive process, the analyst will require multiple runs of the algorithm with different parameters. Consequently, the exact results may not be paramount during analysis, and improvements in the level of interactivity between the algorithm and the analyst is often preferred.

In other words, the analysis of data usually begins with the analyst forming a hypothesis and so, the algorithms are run with parameters to obtain analytics that verifies that hypothesis. In most cases, this process would involve fine tuning of the algorithm's parameters as the analyst tries to zero in on the results. Therefore, the intermediate results during the process serve more to give directions to the analyst rather than giving the answer to the hypothesis. If so, the analysis would be more productive if the analyst's chain of thoughts are not broken, and that the analyst does not have to wait for the algorithm.

This is where the techniques brought about by data stream problems can be useful. Since data stream algorithms process data far more quickly than conventional algorithms and give an estimate in real time, the level of interactivity is much higher between the algorithm and the analyst within the same time period. Therefore, we argue that the analyst is likely to zoom in on the right results far more quickly than using conventional algorithms.

It is on this basis that we believe data streams algorithms might be the way future data mining algorithms are developed. The amount of data will continue to grow larger although they might not necessarily become data streams. However, when the data set is sufficiently large, the benefits of data stream techniques will no doubt become useful.

REFERENCES

1. Wu, X.; Yu, P.S.; Piatetsky-Shapiro, G.; Cercone, N.; Lin, T.Y.; Kotagiri, R.; Wah, B.W. Data mining: How research meets practical development. Knowl. Inform. Syst. **2003**, *5* (2), 248–261.

2. Carney, D. Cetintemel, U. Cherniack, M. Convey, C. Lee, S. Seidman, G. Stonebraker, M. Tatbul, N. Zdonik, S.B. Monitoring streams—A new class of data management applications Proceedings of International Conference on Very Large Databases (VLDB) August, 20–23, 2002.

3. Aggarwal, C. Han, J. Wang, J. Yu, P.S. A framework for clustering evolving data streams Proceedings of International Conference on Very Large Databases (VLDB) Berlin, Germany September, 2003.

4. Manku, G. Motwani, R. Approximate frequency counts over data streams Proceedings of International Conference on Very Large Databases (VLDB) Hong Kong 2002.

5. Domingos, P. Hulten, G. Catching up with the data: Research issues in mining data streams Proceedings of Workshop on Research Issues in Data Mining and Knowledge Discovery Santa Barbara, CA May, 20, 2001.

6. Shen, Y.D. Yang, Q. Zhang, Z. Lu, H. Mining the customer's up-to-moment preferences for e-commerce recommendation Proceedings of Pacific-Asia Conference on Knowledge Discovery and Data Mining (PAKDD) Seoul, Korea 2003.

7. Babcock, B. Babu, S. Datar, M. Motwani, R. Widom, J. Models and issues in data stream systems Proceedings of Principles of Database Systems (PODS) Madison, WI 2002.

8. Lee, S.Y. Li, H.F. Shan, M.K. On mining web click stream for path traversal patterns Proceedings of World-Wide Web Conference (WWW) New York 2004.

9. Cortes, C.; Fisher, K.; Pregibon, D.; Rogers, A.; Smith, F. Hancock: A language for analyzing transactional data streams. ACM Trans. Program. Lang. Syst. **2004**, *26* (2), 301–338.

10. Yang, J. Dynamic clustering of evolving streams with a single pass Proceedings of International Conference on Data Engineering (ICDE) Bangalore, India 2003.

11. Cortes, C. Fisher, K. Pregibon, D. Rogers, A. Hancock: A language for extracting signatures from data streams Proceedings of International Conference on Knowledge Discovery and Data Mining (SIGKDD) New York 2000.

12. Lambert, D. Pinheiro, J.C. Mining a stream of transactions for customer patterns Proceedings of International Conference on Knowledge Discovery and Data Mining New York 2001.

13. Madden, S. Franklin, M.J. Fjording the stream: An architecture for queries over streaming sensor data Proceedings of International Conference on Data Engineering (ICDE) San Jose, CA 2002.

14. Zhu, Y. Shasha, D. Efficient elastic burst detection in data streams Proceedings of International Conference on Knowledge discovery and Data Mining (SIGKDD) Washington, DC 2003.

15. Garofalakis, M. Gehrke, J. Rastogi, R. Querying and mining data streams: You only get one look (Tutorial) Proceedings of International Conference on Management of Data (SIGMOD) New York 2002.

16. Golab, L.; Tamer Ozsu, M. Isues in data stream management. SIGMOD Rec. **2003**, *32* (2), 5–14.

17. Gibbons, P.B. Matias, Y. Synopsis data structures for massive data sets Proceedings of Symposium on Discrete Algorithms Philadelphia, PA 1999.

18. Muthukrishnan, S. Data streams: Algorithms and applications Proceedings of Symposium on Discrete Algorithms Baltimore, MD 2003.

19. Barbara, D.; DuMouchel, W.; Faloutsos, C.; Haas, P.J.; Helerstein, J.M.; Ioannidis, Y.E.; Jagadish, H.V.; Johnson, T.; Ng, R.; Poosala, V.; Ross, K.A.; Sevcik, K.C. The New Jersey data reduction report. IEEE Data Eng. Bull. **1997**, *20* (4), 3–45.

20. Ioannidis, Y.E. The history of histograms (Abridged) Proceedings of International Conference on Very Large Databases (VLDB) Berlin, Germany 2003.

21. Ioannidis, Y.E. Poosala, V. Balancing histogram optimality and practicality for query result size estimation

Proceedings of International Conference on Management of Data New York 1995.

22. Gilbert, A.C.; Kotidis, Y.; Muthukrishnan, S.; Straus, M. One-pass wavelet decompositions of data streams. IEEE Trans. Knowl. Data Eng. **2003**, *15* (3), 541–554.

23. Muthukrishan, S.; Straus, M.J. Approximate histogram and wavelet summaries of streaming data. Technical report (DIMACS TR: 2004-52) **2004**, ftp://dimacs.rutgers.edu/pub/dimacs/TechnicalReports/TechReports/2004/2004-52.ps.gz (accessed September 22, 2008).

24. Mannila, H. Toivonen, H. Verkamo, A.I. Efficient algorithms for discovering association rules Proceedings of AAAI Workshop Knowledge Discovery in Databases Seattle, WA 1994.

25. Zaki, M. Parthasarathy, S. Li, W. Ogihara, M. Evaluation of sampling for data mining of association rules Proceedings of Workshop on Research Issues in Data Engineering Birmingham, U.K. 1997.

26. Vitter, J.S. Random sampling with a reservoir. ACM Trans. Math. Softw. **1985**, *11* (1), 37–57.

27. Babcock, B. Datar, M. Motwani, R. Sampling from a moving window over streaming data Proceedings of Symposium on Discrete Algorithms (SODA) San Francisco, CA 2002.

28. Park, B.H. Ostrouchov, G. Samatova, N.F. Geist, A. Reservoir-based random sampling with replacement from data stream Proceedings of SIAM International Conference on Data Mining (SDM) Florida 2004.

29. Manku, G.S. Motwani, R. Approximate frequency counts over streaming data Proceedings of International Conference on Very Large Databases (VLDB) Hong Kong, China 2002.

30. Cherniack, M. Balakrishnan, H. Balazinska, M. Carney, D. Cetintemel, U. Xing, Y. Zdonik, S.B. Scalable distributed stream processing Proceedings of Conference on Innovative Data Systems Research (CIDR) Asilomar, CA 2003.

31. Motwani, R. Widom, J. Arasu, A. Babcock, B. Babu, S. Datar, M. Manku, G.S. Olston, C. Rosenstein, J. Varma, R. Query processing, approximation, and resource management in adata stream management system Proceedings of Conference on Innovative Data Systems Research (CIDR) Asilomar, CA 2003.

32. Guha, S.; Meyerson, A.; Mishra, N.; Motwani, R.; O'Calaghan, L. Clustering data streams: Theory and practice. IEEE Trans. Knowl. Data Eng. **2003**, *15* (3), 515–528.

33. Yao, Y. Gehrke, J. Query processing in sensor networks Proceedings of Conference on Innovative Data Systems Research (CIDR) Asilomar, CA 2003.

34. Chen, J. DeWitt, D. Tian, F. Wang, Y. Niagaracq: A Scalable continuous query system for internet databases Proceedings of International Conference on the Management of Data (SIGMOD) Dallas, TX 2000.

35. Chandrasekaran, S. TelegraphCQ: Continuous data flow processing for an uncertain world Proceedings of Conference on Innovative Data Systems Research (CIDR) Asilomar, CA 2003.

36. Kohavi, R.; John, G. Wrappers for feature subset selection. Artif. Intell. **1997**, *97* (1–2), 273–324.

37. Liu, H.; Setiono, R. Incremental feature selection. Appl. Intell. **1998**, *9* (3), 217–230.

38. Cheung, D.; Ng, V.T.; Fu, A.W.; Fu, Y. Efficient mining of association rules in distributed databases. IEEE Trans. Knowl. Data Eng. **1996**, *8* (6), 911–922.

39. Parthasarathy, S. Zaki, M. Li, W. Memory placement techniques for parallel association mining Proceedings of International Conference on Knowledge Discovery and Data Mining (KDD) New York 1998.

40. Toivonen, H. Sampling large databases for association rules Proceedings of International Conference on Very Large Databases (VLDB) Bombay, India 1996.

41. Demaine, E. Lopez-Ortiz, A. Munro, J.I. Frequency estimation of internet packet streams with limited space Proceedings of Annual European Symposium on Algorithms London, U.K. 2002.

42. Karp, R.M.; Shenker, S.; Papadimitriou, C.H. A simple algorithm for finding frequent elements in streams and bags. ACM Trans. Database Syst. **2003**, *28* (1), 51–55.

43. Yu, J.X. Chong, Z. Lu, H. Zhou, A. False positive or false negative: Mining frequent itemsets from high speed transactional data streams Proceedings of International Conference on Very Large Databases (VLDB) Toronto, ON 2004.

44. Jin, R. Agrawal, G. An Algorithm for in-core frequent itemset mining on streaming data Proceedings of International Conference on Data Mining (ICDM) Houston, TX 2005.

45. Giannela, C. Han, J. Pei, J. Yan, X. Yu, P.S. Mining frequent patterns in data streams at multiple time granularities. In *Next Generation Data Mining*; Kargupta, H., Joshi, A., Sivakumar, K., Yesha, Y., Eds.; MIT Press: Cambridge, MA, 2004.

46. Han, J.; Pei, J.; Yin, Y. Mining frequent patterns without candidate generation. SIGMOD Rec. **2000**, *29* (2), 1–12.

47. Chang, J. Lee, W.S. EstWin: Adaptively monitoring the recent change of frequent itemsets over online data streams Proceedings of International Conference on Information and Knowledge Management New York 2003.

48. Chang, J.H.; Lee, W.S. A sliding window method for finding recently frequent itemsets over online data streams. J. Inform. Sci. Eng. **2004**, *20* (4), 753–762.

49. Li, H.F. Lee, S.Y. Single-pass algorithms for mining frequency change patterns with limited space in evolving append-only and dynamic transaction data streams Proceedings of International Conference on e-Technology, e-Commerce and e-Service (EEE) Taipei, Taiwan 2004.

50. Teng, W.G. Chen, M.S. Yu, P.S. A regression-based temporal pattern mining scheme for data streams Proceedings of International Conference on Very Large Databases (VLDB) Berlin, Germany 2003.

51. Mannila, H. Hand, D. Smyth, P. *Principles of Data Mining*, MIT Press: Cambridge, MA, 2001.

52. Aggarwal, C.C. Han, J. Wang, J. Yu, P.S. A framework for clustering evolving data streams Proceedings of International Conference on Very Large Databases (VLDB) Berlin, Germany 2003.

53. Zhang, T. Ramakrishnan, R. Livny, M. BIRCH: An efficient clustering method for very large databases Proceedings of International Conference on Management of Data (SIGMOD) Montreal, QC 1996.

54. Ong, K. Li, W. Ng, W. Lim, E. SCLOPE: An algorithm for clustering data streams of categorical attributes Proceedings of International Conference on Data Warehousing

Israel–Knowledge Discovery

and Knowledge Discovery (DaWaK) Zaragoza, Spain 2004.

55. Yang, Y. Guan, X. You, J. CLOPE: A fast and effective clustering algorithm for transactional data Proceedings of International Conference on Knowledge Discovery and Data Mining (SIGKDD) Edmonton, AB 2002.

56. Guha, S. Mishra, N. Motwani, R. O'Calaghan, L. Clustering data streams Proceedings of Symposium on Foundations of Computer Science Redondo Beach, CA 2000.

57. Babcock, B. Datar, M. Motwani, R. O'Calaghan, L. Maintaining variance and k-medians over data stream windows Proceedings of Symposium on Principles of Database Systems (PODS) San Diego, CA 2003.

58. Charikar, M. O'Calaghan, L. Panigrahy, R. Better streaming algorithms for clustering problems Proceedings of ACM Symposium on Theory of Computing New York 2003.

59. Mishra, N. Meyerson, A. Guha, S. Motwani, R. Streaming-data algorithms for high-quality clustering Proceedings of International Conference on Data Engineering (ICDE) Washington, DC 2002.

60. Babcock, B. Datar, M. O'Calaghan, L. Motwani, R., 2002; Sliding window computations over data streams. Technical report http://dbpubs.stanford.edu:8090/pub/2002-25 (accessed September 22, 2008).

61. Mitchel, T.M. *Machine Learning*, McGraw Hill: Columbus, OH, 1997.

62. Murthy, S.K. Automatic construction of decision trees from data: A multi-Disciplinary survey. J. Data Min. Knowl. Discov. **1998**, *2* (4), 345–389.

63. Duda, R.O. Hart, P.E. *Pattern Classification and Scene Analysis*, John Wiley & Sons Press: NewYork, 1973.

64. Han, J. Kamber, M. *Data Mining: Concepts and Techniques*, Morgan Kaufmann Publishers: San Francisco, CA, 2001.

65. Dunham, M.H. *Data Mining: Introductory and Advanced Topics*, Prentice Hall: Englewood Cliffs, NJ, 2003.

66. Kantardzic, M. *Data Mining: Concepts Models, and Algorithms*, IEEE Press and John Wiley: Piscataway, 2003.

67. Domingos, P. Hulten, G. Mining high-speed data streams Proceedings of International Conference on Knowledge Discovery and Data Mining (SIGKDD) New York, NJ 2000.

68. Gama, J. Rocha, R. Medas, P. Accurate decision trees for mining high-speed data streams Proceedings of International Conference on Knowledge Discovery and Data Mining New York 2003.

69. Hulten, G. Spencer, L. Domingos, P. Mining time-changing data streams Proceedings of International Conference on Knowledge Discovery and Data Mining (SIGKDD) San Francisco, CA 2001.

70. Wang, H. Fan, W. Yu, P.S. Han, J. Mining concept-drifting data streams using ensemble classifiers Proceedings of International Conference on Knowledge Discovery and Data Mining (SIGKDD) Washington, DC 2003.

71. Fan, W. StreamMiner: A classifier ensemble-based engine to mine concept-drifting data streams Proceedings of International Conference on Very Large Databases (VLDB) Toronto, ON 2004.

72. Fan, W. Huang, Y. Wang, H. Yu, P.S. Active mining of data streams Proceedings of SIAM International Conference on Data Mining (SDM) Florida 2004.

73. Gao, J. Fan, W. Han, J. On appropriate assumptions to mine data streams: Analysis and practice Proceedings of International Conference on Data Mining (ICDM) Omaha, NE 2007.

74. Fan, W. Systematic data selection to mine concept-drifting data streams Proceedings of International Conference on Knowledge Discovery and Data Mining (SIGKDD) Seattle, WA 2004.

Israel–Knowledge Discovery

Knowledge Management

Kimiz Dalkir
Graduate School of Library and Information Studies, McGill University, Montreal, Quebec, Canada

Abstract
Knowledge management (KM) is defined as a deliberate and systematic coordination of an organization's people, technology, processes, and organizational structure in order to add value through reuse and innovation. There is a lack of consensus on clearly defining KM partly due to the multidisciplinary origins of the concept, ranging from organizational science, to cognitive science, to library and information science. Core management concepts include the notion of difficult to articulate tacit knowledge, documented tangible or explicit knowledge, organizational learning as encapsulated in the form of best practices (successes) and lessons learned (failures), and preservation of this content in an organizational memory system. The knowledge processing life cycle then consists of creating new knowledge; capturing existing knowledge; contributing knowledge for reuse by others; documenting knowledge; reconstructing, refining, and sharing knowledge; and continually evaluating the value of each knowledge resource in order to decide whether to keep it in circulation or to retire it from "active duty." The Nonaka and Takeuchi knowledge spiral model is used to illustrate how knowledge is transformed from one form to the other. A brief historical overview of KM is presented to show the evolution from a management fad to a scholarly discipline of study and research. Finally, the emerging roles for information professionals in this field are briefly described, outlining some of the key roles such as chief knowledge officer, knowledge manager, content editor, and knowledge journalist.

INTRODUCTION

This chapter provides an overview of knowledge management (KM), both as a scholarly discipline and a professional field of practice. Key terms such as "knowledge" and "knowledge management" are defined. Core concepts such as intellectual capital, lessons learned, best practices, and value-added knowledge reuse are introduced and defined. Key stages in the knowledge processing cycle are defined and described. A brief historical chronology of KM is outlined to show the multidisciplinary roots and the evolution that has taken place to date. The emerging roles for information professionals in KM are presented, and the links to information studies are emphasized. The primary goal of this chapter is to illustrate how KM that rests on a solid foundation of information management emerges as a stronger and more rigorous field of study and practice.

DEFINITION OF KNOWLEDGE MANAGEMENT

There is no universally accepted definition of KM. Part of this stems from the fact that there is a lack of consensus in defining knowledge. A sample dictionary definition of knowledge is

"the fact or condition of knowing something with familiarity gained through experience or association; acquaintance with or understanding of a science, art, or technique; the fact or condition of being aware of something; the range of one's information or understanding (e.g., answered to the best of my *knowledge*); the circumstance or condition of apprehending truth or fact through reasoning; the sum of what is known: the body of truth, information, and principles acquired by humankind; cognizance, awareness, learning."[1]

It is useful to view the knowledge in KM as being composed primarily of experiential knowledge that is highly subjective in nature. This can be contrasted with information which, although subject to different interpretations, is typically thought of as having a more neutral and verifiable nature. The same dictionary defines information as

"knowledge obtained from investigation, study, or instruction; intelligence, news data or facts; the attribute inherent in and communicated by one of two or more alternative sequences or arrangements of something (as nucleotides in DNA or binary digits in a computer program) that produce specific effects **c** 1: a signal or character (as in a communication system or computer) representing data 2: something (as a message, experimental data, or a picture) which justifies change in a construct (as a plan or theory) that represents physical or mental experience or another construct."[1]

Other definitions from the KM literature include the following:

"Knowledge is a subset of information: it is subjective; it is linked to meaningful behaviour; and it has tacit

Encyclopedia of Library and Information Sciences, Fourth Edition DOI: 10.1081/E-ELIS4-120053698

Copyright © 2017 by Taylor & Francis. All rights reserved.

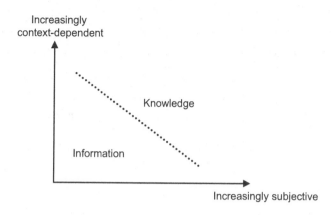

Fig. 1 Key attributes of knowledge assets.

elements born of experience"(Leonard and Sensiper,[2] p. 113).

Knowledge is always recreated in the present moment. Most of us cannot articulate what we know. It is largely invisible, and often comes to mind when we need it to answer a question or solve a problem.[3]

"Knowledge is a fluid mix of framed experience, values, contextual information, and expert insight that provides a framework for evaluating and incorporating new experiences and information. It originates and is applied in the minds of knowers. In organizations, it often becomes embedded not only in documents or repositories but also in organizational routines, processes, practices and norms" (Davenport and Prusak,[4] p. 5).

A typical example of information would be to read the listings of movies being shown on a given week, reading the reviews, and consulting the times and places the film will be showing at. An example of knowledge would be calling on a friend who has, in the past, demonstrated an uncanny inverse relationship with respect to likes and dislikes: if this person liked a movie, experience has shown that I would hate it and vice versa. Knowledge is also brought into play in making a decision to drive or take public transport, given the time of year, possibility of inclement weather, and the rapid trend analysis that concludes that it was never possible to find parking in time to see a movie being shown downtown.

A key point is that not all information is of value to a given individual, group, or organization. A knowledge asset is defined as knowledge that is of value, which is more context dependent and more subjective in nature, as illustrated in Fig. 1.

The Multidisciplinary Nature of Knowledge Management

There is a great diversity to be found in KM definitions. This is due to the multidisciplinary nature of the field. In fact,

Table 1 Diverse disciplines that contribute to knowledge management

1. Organizational development, organizational science, organizational learning
2. Cognitive science, individual learning, mental models
3. Linguistics and computational linguistics
4. Information technologies such as knowledge-based systems, document and information management, electronic performance support systems, and database technologies
5. Information and library science, classification, taxonomy
6. Technical writing and journalism
7. Anthropology and sociology, sociograms, social network analysis
8. Education and training
9. Storytelling and communication studies
10. Collaborative technologies such as CSCW and groupware, as well as intranets, extranets, portals, and other web technologies

most definitions appear to provide only one piece of the KM definition puzzle, as they are heavily influenced by their particular discipline. Table 1 lists some of the different disciplines that have contributed to and that make use of KM.

Here are a few sample definitions from the business perspective:

Knowledge management is a business activity with two primary aspects: treating the knowledge component of business activities as an explicit concern of business reflected in strategy, policy, and practice at all levels of the organization and making a direct connection between an organization's intellectual assets—both explicit (recorded) and tacit (personal know-how)—and positive business results.[5]

Knowledge management is a collaborative and integrated approach to the creation, capture, organization, access, and use of an enterprise's intellectual assets.[6]

"There is much more to knowledge management than technology alone. Management is a business process" (Sarvary,[7] p.95).

Some definitions from the cognitive science or knowledge science perspective are as follows:

Knowledge—the insights, understandings, and practical know-how that we all possess—is the fundamental resource that allows us to function intelligently. Over time, considerable knowledge is also transformed to other manifestations—such as books, technology, practices, and traditions—within organizations of all kinds and in society in general. These transformations result in cumulated (sic) expertise and, when used appropriately, increased effectiveness. Knowledge is one, if not *the*, principal factor that makes personal, organizational, and societal intelligent behavior possible.[8]

Some sample definitions from the process/technology perspective are the following:

Knowledge management (KM) was initially defined as the process of applying a systematic approach to the capture, structuring, management, and dissemination of knowledge throughout an organization to work faster, reuse best practices, and reduce costly rework from project to project.[9–11]

APQC[12] defines KM as systematic approaches to help information and knowledge emerge and flow to the right people at the right time to create value.

Some "people-oriented" definitions are as follows:

"Knowledge management is not seen as a matter of building up a large electronic library, but by connecting people so they can think together" (McDermott,[13] p.104).

"Most executives seem to understand that knowledge is highly people-based, but they are stuck with an investment model that is geared primarily toward technology implementations" (Ruggles and Holtshouse,[14] p. 86).

Wiig[13] also emphasizes that given the importance of knowledge in virtually all areas of daily and commercial life, two knowledge-related aspects are vital for viability and success at any level. These are knowledge *assets* that must be applied, nurtured, preserved, and used to the largest extent possible by both individuals and organizations and knowledge-related *processes* to create, build, compile, organize, transform, transfer, pool, apply, and safeguard knowledge—must be carefully and explicitly managed in all affected areas.

"Historically, knowledge has always been managed, at least implicitly. However, effective and active knowledge management requires new perspectives and techniques and touches on almost all facets of an organization. We need to develop a new discipline and prepare a cadre of knowledge professionals with a blend of expertise that we have not previously seen. This is our challenge!" (Wiig[8]).

The Intellectual Capital Perspective

The focus of Intellectual Capital Management (ICM), on the other hand, is on those pieces of knowledge that are of *business value* to the organization—referred to as intellectual capital or assets.[15] While some of these are more visible (e.g., patents, intellectual property), the majority consists of know-how, know-why, experience, and expertise that tend to reside within the head of one or a few employees.[16,17]

KM is often characterized by "pack rat" approach to content: "save it, it may prove useful some time in the future." Many documents tend to be warehoused, sophisticated search engines are then used to try to retrieve some of this content, and fairly large-scale and costly KM systems are built. KM solutions have proven to be most successful in the capture, storage, and subsequent dissemination of knowledge that has been rendered explicit—particularly lessons learned and best practices.

ICM is characterized by less content—because content is filtered and judged and only the best are inventoried (e.g., the "top ten"). ICM content tends to be more representative of peoples' real thinking (contextual information, opinions, stories) due to its focus on actionable knowledge and know-how, resulting in less costly endeavors and a focus on learning (at the individual, community, and organizational level), rather than on the building of systems.

It is essential to identify that knowledge is of value and is also at risk of being lost to the organization, through retirement, turnover, and competition. The best way to retain valuable knowledge is to identify intellectual assets and then ensure legacy materials are produced, and subsequently stored in such a way as to make their future retrieval and reuse as easy as possible.[18] These tangible by-products need to flow from individual to individual, between communities of practice (CoPs) members, and, of course, back to the organization itself, in the form of lessons learned, best practices, and corporate memory.

The knowledge capture and transfer approaches described here thus help to

- Facilitate a smooth transition from those retiring to their successors who are recruited to fill their positions
- Minimize loss of corporate memory due to attrition and retirement
- Identify critical resources and critical areas of knowledge so that the corporation "knows what it knows and does well—and why"
- Build up a toolkit of methods that can be used with individuals, with groups, and with the organization to stem the potential loss of intellectual capital

Knowledge management is often mistakenly perceived as a process of documenting knowledge held in people's minds, then storing or archiving this knowledge.[19] In fact, it is better to view KM in a broader context, one that encompasses all the processes used to generate value from knowledge-based assets. Knowledge management is facilitated by technology and by the culture of an organization. A good way of defining KM is

...the deliberate and systematic coordination of an organization's people, technology, processes and organizational structure in order to add value through reuse and innovation. This is achieved through the promotion of creating, sharing and applying knowledge as well as through the feeding of valuable lessons learned and best practices into corporate memory in order to foster continued organizational learning. (Dalkir,[20] p. 3)

CORE KNOWLEDGE MANAGEMENT CONCEPTS

Kransdorff[21] coined the term "corporate amnesia" to refer to the loss of accumulated expertise and know-how

Knowledge Management–
Law Librarianship

due to employee turnover as people take what they know with them when they leave. The costs of employee turnover to the organization have been well documented (e.g., separation costs, recruitment and selection costs, training of replacements, initial lack of productivity of new hire, and the loss of productivity of co-workers during the transition). Far less research attention has been paid to the cost to the firm of losing know-how that resides within the minds of individual employees who depart. In an era of knowledge workers, learning organizations and service economies individuals are increasingly responsible for value creation. Although many organizations have succession plans in place, the process usually involves transferring know-how from the departing employee to their successor, but the whole process has to be repeated again for the next departure. Organizations need to "capture" this know-how and transfer it to a stable, easily accessible, cumulative knowledge base—an organizational memory—to retain and make accessible valuable knowledge gained through the experiences of all knowledge in a continuous and uninterrupted manner.

Organizations need to effectively manage their organizational memory in order to prevent the loss of essential knowledge, particularly knowledge that resides predominantly in the heads of their knowledge workers ("tacit knowledge") and less in documents, procedures, and other tangible forms ("explicit knowledge").[22] More often than not, it is this difficult to articulate "know-how" that is of greatest value in organizational competitiveness and viability and which represents the vast majority of experiential know-how. Fig. 2 shows how the metaphor of an

Fig. 2 The iceberg metaphor used to show the respective proportions of tacit and explicit knowledge.

iceberg is often used to depict tacit and explicit knowledge forms.

The National Aeronautics and Space Administration (NASA), for example, has publicly admitted that the knowledge of how to put a man on the moon has been lost.[23] The lessons that were learned and the innovations that were sparked cannot be found in the collective organizational memory of NASA. This means that NASA's organizational memory cannot be used as a resource to plan a more effective mission to send another manned flight to the moon or to Mars. A well-designed and well-managed organizational memory does not only combat corporate amnesia, but it ensures knowledge continuity— the effective transfer of know-how among peers and to future generations of knowledge workers. A better understanding of the nature of organizational memory, what it should include (content), how it can best be retained (technological containers), and how the accumulated lessons learned and best practices can be used by newcomers (connections) will help mitigate the cost of lost, forgotten, or untransferred knowledge and know-how.

Organizations today face escalating risks of losing strategic knowledge and know-how and face incredible difficulties in recruiting and retaining skilled employees. Many industries face astounding rates of high and constant turnover. In addition, we are experiencing a demographic pressure as baby boomers are rapidly approaching the retirement age, which means that a "critical mass" of knowledge will literally walk out the door over the next 5–10 yrs. Approximately, 11,000 baby boomers are turning 50 yrs old every day.[24] In the Canadian federal government, for example, 15,000 civil servants are expected to retire within the next 5 yrs.[25] In the United States, more than 50% of the government workforce will be eligible for retirement by 2004.[28] Other vulnerable include organizations high technology companies with very high turnover rates and the military or banking, where constant turnover is the norm given rotational postings. Since 2007, "…the total, the number of people not in the labor force rose by 12.6 million (16%) from the fourth quarter of 2007 to the fourth quarter of 2013."[27] The aging of the workforce is a trend that does not show any signs of slowing down: "America is getting older, a trend that will undoubtedly continue to have a profound impact on the labor market going forward."[28]

The most successful organizations will state that their two greatest assets are the people who work for them and the knowledge they possess. The imminent turnover signals a potential for the loss of valuable accumulated knowledge and know-how in the form of the competence and expertise possessed by the departing individuals. This valuable knowledge and know-how exists in both formal and tangible forms, such as documents, but also in less visible forms—often referred to as tacit or difficult to articulate knowledge. Particular emphasis must be placed on the tacit form as this often resides within a given individual or group and is therefore more

Knowledge Management– Law Librarianship

easily and completely lost when the people leave the organization.[29]

The typical technological tools used in KM are some form of centralized database system, an intranet or web portal to access the database content, as well as other organizational knowledge, some type of messaging system (typically e-mail and discussion groups), some content management tools to organize the knowledge resources (e.g., content management software, taxonomy software), and some form of collaborative software (e.g., virtual meeting tools, groupware).

The essential elements that go into organizational memory include best practices, which are innovations or improved practices, processes and so forth; together with the flip side of the coin: lesson learned, outcomes that were not desirable, or errors that should not be repeated. By carefully capturing, documenting, organizing, and making available accumulated experiential knowledge in the form of best practices and lessons learned, KM can provide a framework within which we can process knowledge throughout its useful life cycle.

Knowledge management typically addresses three levels within an organization: the individual, the group, and the organization. Organizational memory resides at the level of the organization, and this is the preservation layer of KM. Innovation and knowledge creation occurs at the individual level, while knowledge dissemination and sharing occur at the group level. In KM, groups of a particular nature, called "communities of practice", are often a key element in ensuring that valuable knowledge flows or moves around appropriately. These CoPs are essentially thematic networks of like-minded individuals who share a common purpose, a common professional zeal, and agree to mutually help out one another to achieve some strategic goals for the organization.[30,31]

Szulanski[32] introduced the notion of knowledge "stickiness" to refer to knowledge that was difficult to move around and thus could provide little in the way of value to individuals, groups, or the organization as a whole. The knowledge processing cycle is used to describe the various stages a particular knowledge resource goes through during the course of its "life span" within an organization.

THE KNOWLEDGE PROCESSING CYCLE

Nonaka and Takeuchi described how knowledge was disseminated and transformed as it made its way around an organization in their knowledge spiral model.[9] Essentially, knowledge is created by an individual, who has an innovative idea, for example, but remains initially tacit. This innovation or idea is typically shared only with trusted friends and colleagues at first ("socialization"). With time, others may be aware of the innovation, and the knowledge may be transformed from its tacit state to

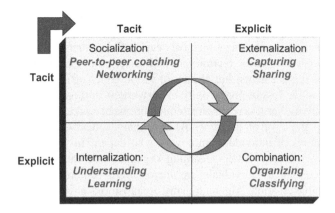

Fig. 3 The Nonaka and Takeuchi knowledge spiral model of KM.

an explicit one ("externalization"), by documenting it in the form of text, audio, or other formats. Once explicit, it is easier to disseminate more widely and to preserve in an organizational memory system. At this stage ("combination"), the content may be better organized and reworked (e.g., addition of an abstract or executive summary). In the final stage ("internalization"), explicit knowledge once again becomes tacit as an individual learns, understands, and "buys into" a knowledge resource (e.g., sees its value and decides to apply this new knowledge). The knowledge resource then continues cycling through the four quadrants in a "knowledge spiral." Fig. 3 outlines the major stages in the Nonaka and Takeuchi KM model, as knowledge is transformed, disseminated, and applied within an organization.

As knowledge resources circulate throughout an organization, value can be added at each step. A more detailed view of what happens to knowledge as it undergoes transformation from tacit to explicit and back again is provided in the form of a knowledge life cycle. The first stage is to either capture existing knowledge (e.g., already existing in tangible form such as project reports, conference reports, or other documents) or to create knowledge that does not yet exist in documented form (e.g., by interviewing subject matter experts to document a particular procedure). This knowledge resource can then be contributed or made available for reuse by others. Knowledge is then codified by the addition of sufficient descriptive information about both the content and the format it is in (e.g., metadata describing theme, whether it is a text or also available as a short video clip). At this point, knowledge is further refined by sanitizing (removing all sensitive information that may identify a person, place, or event or other confidential content) and reconstruction (e.g., recombining or synthesizing in a new version). Contributions that have been refined and reconstructed are then subjected to a selective filtering process, and those that are deemed to be valuable are made available for knowledge sharing.

Knowledge Management—
Law Librarianship

Table 2 Key steps in a knowledge processing cycle

Step number	Description
1.	Knowledge capture
2.	Knowledge creation
3.	Knowledge contribution
4.	Knowledge codification
5.	Knowledge refinement (including sanitize) and reconstruction (e.g., synthesis)
6.	Knowledge selection—filter contributions
7.	Knowledge sharing and pooling
8.	Knowledge organization and access
9.	Knowledge learning and application
10.	Knowledge evaluation and reuse or divest (e.g., destroy, archive)

Knowledge sharing involves the pooling and distribution of valuable content, either globally (e.g., a "broadcast" mode) or selectively (e.g., targeted to specific users, communities, or based on user profiles, and subscriptions). The knowledge is better organized (classified using a taxonomic scheme), and access is typically provided through an intranet or portal interface. These valuable knowledge resources are then learned and applied by knowledge workers. Each knowledge resource is evaluated periodically in order to ensure continued relevance and to decide whether to discard or to archive at the appropriate time. Table 2 lists the key phases in knowledge processing that occurs during the useful life cycle of a knowledge resource, such as a best practice or lesson learned.

A more recent review of existing KM life cycle models[33] compared and contrasted the different approaches. A number of different terms were found to be used for essentially the similar types of knowledge processing activities. The result of this analysis led to the formulation of a holistic KM life cycle model with seven core steps: *identify*, *store*, *share*, *use*, *learn*, *improve*, and *create*. One of the major advantages of this framework is that it builds upon existing frameworks and adds in the notion of double loop learning in order to capture the nonsequential or cyclical nature of knowledge processing. The key KM objectives of reuse for efficiency are also complemented by the goals of learning to continually improve, at the individual, group, and organizational levels.

HISTORY AND EVOLUTION OF KNOWLEDGE MANAGEMENT

Knowledge and management are concepts that have obviously been around for some—the combination, "knowledge management," however, is fairly recent. The emergence of communication technologies that create real-time networks such as the Internet, intranets, e-mail, and so forth has made KM easier to implement.[34]

A number of management theories have contributed to the definition of KM. Two KM gurus were responsible for establishing the field as a serious target for scholarly study: Peter Drucker,[35] who coined the term "knowledge worker" and who wrote about KM from a management perspective in the 1970s, and Nonaka and Takeuchi, who wrote the seminal book *The Knowledge Creating Company* in the 1990s.[9] Others such as Peter Senge[36] and Chris Argyris[37,38] have focused on the "learning organization" and cultural dimensions of managing knowledge. By the mid-1980s, the notion of knowledge as an asset became more widely adopted. Early pioneers in information technologies from artificial intelligence and expert systems at Carnegie Mellon University (CMU) and Digital Equipment Corporation (DEC) developed hypertext and groupware tools that allow information to be better shared and organized. Knowledge management–related articles began appearing in prestigious journals such as the *Harvard Business Review* and *Organization Science*, and a number of foundational books were published such as *The Fifth Discipline* and *The Knowledge-Creating Company*. Table 3 illustrates the major milestones in KM history.

In 1989, the International Knowledge Management Network (IKMN) was founded in Europe and was joined by the U.S.-based Knowledge Management Forum in 1994. Businesses began implementing KM solutions in earnest in the 1990s. At first, projects tended to be technological implementations, mostly portals and knowledge repositories. This was followed by a wave of "people-not-technology" emphasis that led to the popularity of thematic networks or CoPs. A third wave emerged as knowledge workers, much like information workers, found themselves faced with "content overload" that in turn led to a number of content management, knowledge organization, or taxonomic classification projects to make the knowledge more readily accessible to users.

Table 3 Major milestones in KM history

Year	Source	Event
1980	DEC, CMU	XCON Expert System
1986	Dr. K Wiig	Coined KM concept at UN
1989	Consulting firms	Start internal KM projects
1991	HBR article	Nonaka and Takeuchi
1993	Dr. K Wiig	First KM book published
1994	KM Network	First KM conference
Mid-1990s	Consulting firms	Start offering KM services
Late 1990s	Key vertical industries	Implement KM and start seeing benefits
2000–2003	Academia	KM courses/programs in universities with KM texts
2004–present	Professionalization of KM	Professional certification in KM, master's and PhD degrees in KM conferred by universities, and KM job titles in a broad range of sectors

Knowledge Management–
Law Librarianship

With the new millennium, KM faded a bit from public view, likely due to disappointment as expectations were raised too much by "KM hype" and focusing too much on technologies that were largely left untouched. Practitioners and researchers came to the realization that converting theory into practice was more challenging than previously thought. Some of the missing elements were ensuring that KM was not being done for KM's sake, but that there was a clear link to organizational objectives and that all participants saw value in KM (e.g., incentives for knowledge sharing). By 2004, the field had finally shaken its burden of being yet another management fad. Organizations appreciated the holistic nature of KM and paid attention not only to tools but to organizational culture requirements for successful KM solutions.

In parallel, the nature of work evolved, with collaboration becoming the default rather than the exception, not only for our professional lives but for social interactions and learning objectives. Knowledge sharing with a group of trusted peers has become the de facto way of working, learning, and living. Knowledge management found itself in tune with these changes, which greatly facilitated its adoption as a philosophy, a mindset, a strategic perspective, and a way of interacting to create, share, and use valuable content.

Knowledge management today is being taught in top universities around the world, typically in business, computer science, education, and information studies departments. Doctoral students are completing PhD theses on KM topics. International conferences are being held around the world, with both practitioner and researcher tracks. A number of consortia and KM professional organizations have been established. The number and type of KM journals has also changed. While at first publications were primarily authored by KM tool vendors and practitioners, there has been a significant shift to more scholarly venues and publications that represent KM research rather than KM project mandates. Along with the proliferation in the number of journals, there has also been increasing specialization (e.g., *International Journal of Nuclear Knowledge Management*), more interdisciplinary journals (e.g., *Interdisciplinary Journal of Information, Knowledge and Management*), and more emphasis on international KM (e.g., *International Journal of Knowledge Management*). Up until about the year 2000, only non-peer-reviewed journals were available (e.g., *KMWorld, Knowledge Management Review*). Some of the major peer-reviewed KM journals available today are shown in Table 4, ordered by the first year of publication.

KM is found in all vertical industry sectors (e.g., banking, pharmaceutical), in all sizes of organizations (including volunteer-run associations with less than ten full-time employees), profit and nonprofit organizations, and organizations with a strong hierarchical structure (e.g., the U.S. military was one of the early pioneers of KM). Organizations today are defined and staffing KM positions. KM

is increasingly perceived as an element that cuts across organizational structures, projects, and silos—it enjoys a status similar to that of "quality assurance" or "ethics" and it has become a critical element of organizational viability. KM is no longer something interesting to explore—it has become subsumed in the way in which individuals, groups, and organizations work, learn, and remember.

EMERGING ROLES FOR INFORMATION PROFESSIONALS

The KM field has transformed from one led primarily by consultants and other KM practitioners to a bona fide discipline, with a distinct body of knowledge. This has been paralleled by the growing number of academic programs that offer KM as compared to the predominately private sector training that had been the only way to learn about KM up until now.[39] TFPL[40] is a specialist recruitment, advisory, training, and research services company

Table 4   Major peer-reviewed knowledge management journals

Journal title	Year founded
IBM Systems Journal	1962
Journal of Managerial and Organizational Learning	1970
International Journal of Management Information Systems	1984
Journal of Organizational Change Management	1989
Knowledge and Process Management	1996
Journal of Knowledge Management	1997
Journal of Management Studies	1997
Journal of Knowledge Management Practice	1998
Journal of Intellectual Capital	2000
E-Journal of Organizational Learning and Leadership	2002
Journal of Information and Knowledge Management (JIKM)	2002
Electronic Journal of Knowledge Management	2003
International Journal of Knowledge, Culture and Change Management	2003
Knowledge Management Research and Practice	2003
An Interdisciplinary Journal of Storytelling Studies	2004
International Journal of Nuclear Knowledge Management (IJNKM)	2004
International Journal of Knowledge Management	2005
Knowledge Management for Development Journal	2005
International Journal of Knowledge Management Studies	2006
Interdisciplinary Journal of Information, Knowledge and Management (IJIKM)	2007
Knowledge Management and E-Learning: An International Journal	2009
International Journal of Knowledge Management and Information Technology	2012
The Online Journal of Applied Knowledge Management	2013

Knowledge Management–
Law Librarianship

with offices in London focusing on KM, library and information management, records management, and web and content management. Since 1987, TFPL has worked with organizations in both public and private sectors to help them develop and implement knowledge and information strategies and to recruit and train information and knowledge leaders and their teams. TFPL has drafted a KM skills and competencies guide to provide a clear and practical overview of KM skills and competencies that draws on the practical experience of organizations in a wide range of sectors and with varying approaches to KM.

In general, these KM skills include

- Time management to use their time and energy effectively for acquiring
- Knowledge (spending all day surfing the net is probably counterproductive)
- The use of different learning techniques to absorb key knowledge and learning quickly
- Effective skills of advocacy and inquiry to present knowledge to, and gather knowledge from, others
- Informal networking skills to build one's influence to gain access to people with knowledge
- Resource investigation skills
- Effective IT skills for recording and disseminating information
- Skills of cooperative problem solving
- Open dialog skills
- Flexibility and willingness to try new things and take educated risks
- Active review of learning from mistakes, risks, opportunities, and successes

The TFPL KM skills map[41] is based on an extensive international research. The project team contacted over 500 organizations involved in implementing KM and identified the roles that they had created, and the skills that were needed in those roles, and the additional skills that were required across the organization. These key skills included an understanding of the KM concept—the philosophy and theory—and an awareness of the experience of other organizations in developing KM solutions and approaches an understanding of, and the ability to, identify the business value of KM activities to the organization, an appreciation of the range of activities, initiatives, and labels that are employed to create an environment in which knowledge is effectively created, shared, and used to increase competitive advantage and customer satisfaction.

KM roles are quite diverse and include such categories as senior and middle management roles: chief knowledge officer who ensures that KM goals are in line with organizational strategies and objectives; chief learning officer who ensures that the organization acts like a learning organization, improving over time with the help of accumulated best practices and lessons learned; and knowledge managers who are typically responsible for the acquisition

and management of internal and external knowledge. Other roles include

- Knowledge navigators, responsible for knowing where knowledge can be located, also called knowledge brokers
- Knowledge synthesizers, responsible for facilitating the recording of significant knowledge to organizational memory, also called knowledge stewards
- Content editors, responsible for codifying and structuring content, also called content managers; researchers, writers, editors—roles involving capturing and documenting knowledge
- Web developers, electronic publishers, intranet managers, and content managers
- Learning-oriented roles such as trainers, facilitators, mentors, and coaches—including those with responsibility for developing information and knowledge skills
- Human resources roles with specific responsibility for developing programs and processes that encourage knowledge-oriented cultures and behaviors
- Knowledge publishers, responsible for internal publishing functions, usually on an intranet, also called webmasters, knowledge architects, knowledge editors
- Coaches and mentors, responsible for assisting individuals throughout the business unit or practice to develop and learn KM activities and disciplines
- Help desk activities, including the delivery of KM and information related to training, also called knowledge support office

KM professionals require a multidisciplinary skillset that consists of such competencies as finding, appraising, and using knowledge, being able to reformulate questions, navigate through content, evaluate the relevance of content, filter out what is not needed, and synthesize from diverse sources in order to apply the knowledge (e.g., to make a decision). Last but not the least, they must contribute to the recording of such valuable experiences to organizational memory systems.[42]

CONCLUSION

Knowledge management has assumed a greater priority due to the demographic pressures created by retiring baby boomers. Retirement en masse means a loss of valuable knowledge and know-how that has been accumulated by experience over the years. All organizations, regardless of type of industry, size, country, and so forth, will have to face the issue of knowledge continuity. Knowledge continuity is analogous to business continuity: while the latter targets data loss prevention due to disasters, the former targets knowledge loss due to turnover in personnel. Valuable knowledge must not only be preserved and transferred to future workers but also transferred across geographical and temporal boundaries due to the fact that work today is spread out over networks that may extend beyond organizational boundaries. Knowledge management is the discipline and field of practice that will equip us with the necessary tools, processes, and skillset to ensure that knowledge reaches all knowledge workers so that they can carry out their work more efficiently and more effectively.

REFERENCES

1. Definition of knowledge. Merriam-Webster Dictionary Online. Available at: https://www.merriam-webster.com/dictionary/knowledge. Retrieved May 26, 2017.
2. Leonard, D.; Sensiper, S. The role of tacit knowledge in group innovation. Calif. Manage. Rev. **1998**, *40* (3), 112–132.
3. McDermott, R. Why information technology inspired but cannot deliver knowledge management. Calif. Manage. Rev. **1999**, *41* (4), 103–117.
4. Davenport, T.; Prusak, L. *Working Knowledge*; Harvard Business School Press: Boston, MA, 1998.
5. Barclay, R.; Murray, P. What is knowledge management? Knowledge Praxis, 1997. Available at: http://www.providersedge.com/docs/km_articles/what_is_knowledge_management.pdf. Retrieved May 29, 2017.
6. Grey, D. What is knowledge management? Knowl. Manage. Forum March 1996. Retrieved May 29, 2017 from: http://www.km-forum.org/what_is.htm.
7. Sarvary, M. Knowledge management and competition in the consulting industry. Calif. Manage. Rev. **1999**, *41* (2), 95–107.
8. Wiig, K. *Knowledge Management Foundations*; Schema Press: Arlington, TX, 1993.
9. Nonaka, I.; Takeuchi, H. *The Knowledge-Creating Company: How Japanese Companies Create the Dynamics of Innovation*; Oxford University Press: New York, 1995.
10. Pasternack, B.; Viscio, A. *The Centerless Corporation*; Simon and Schuster: New York, 1998.
11. Pfeffer, J.; Sutton, R. *The Knowing-Doing Gap: How Smart Companies Turn Knowledge into Action*; Harvard Business School Press: New York, 1999.
12. APQC The American Productivity and Quality Centre. 1996, Available at: http://www.apqc.org.
13. McDermott, R. Why information technology inspired but cannot deliver knowledge management. Calif. Manage. Rev. **1999**, *41* (4), 103–117.
14. Ruggles, R.; Holtshouse, D. *The Knowledge Advantage*; Capstone Publishers: Dover, NH, 1999.
15. Bontis, N.; Nikitopoulos, D. Thought leadership on intellectual capital. J. Intell. Capit. **2001**, *2* (3), 183–191.
16. Klein, D. *The Strategic Management of Intellectual Capital*; Oxford, U.K.: Butterworth-Heineman, 1998.
17. Stewart, T. *Intellectual Capital*; Doubleday: New York, 1997.
18. Stewart, T.A. Software preserves knowledge, people pass it on. Fortune **2000**, *142* (5), 390–92.
19. Rothberg, H.; Erickson, G. *From Knowledge to Intelligence: Creating Competitive Advantage in the New Economy*; Butterworth-Heineman: Boston, MA, 2005.
20. Dalkir, K. *Knowledge Management Theory and Practice*, 2nd Ed.; MIT Press: Boston, MA, 2011.

21. Kransdorff, A. *Corporate Amnesia: Keeping Know-How in the Company*; Butterworth-Heineman: Oxford, U.K., 1998.
22. Polanyi, M. *The Tacit Dimension*; Peter Smith: Gloucester, MA, 1966.
23. Petch, G. The cost of lost knowledge. *Knowledge Management Magazine*, **Oct 1998**; 1–6.
24. Noble, F.P., Harper, E. Strategy and policy for phased retirement. Benefits Q. **2010**; *26* (3), 11.
25. Schetagne, S. Building bridges across generations in the workplace. A response to the ageing of the workforce.. Columbia Foundation: Vancouver, British Columbia, Canada, 2001.
26. Williams, T. Government knowledge management initiatives gain foothold. Post Newsweek, **2001**, *15*(12).
27. Terry, E. What accounts for the decrease in the labor force participation rate? Federal Reserve Bank of Atlanta. Retrieved May 29, 2017 from: http://macroblog.typepad.com/macroblog/2014/01/what-accounts-for-the-decrease-in-the-labor-force-participation-rate.html.
28. Boesler, M. Here's what's really going on with baby boomers and the labor force. Business Insider, 2014. Available at: http://www.businessinsider.com/baby-boomers-are-retiring-2014-2#ixzz3LWkpxoZB.
29. LaBarre, P. People go, knowledge stays. Fast Company **2001**, *17*(48), Available at: http://www.fastcompany.com. Retrieved Apr 20, 2007.
30. Wenger, E.; Snyder, W. Communities of practice: The organizational frontier. Harvard Business Rev. **2000**, *January–February*, 139–145.
31. Wenger, E.; McDermott, R.; Snyder, W. *Cultivating Communities of Practice: A Guide to Managing Knowledge*; Harvard Business School: Cambridge, MA, 2002.
32. Szulanski, G. *Sticky Knowledge—Barriers to Knowing in a Firm*; Sage: Thousand Oaks, CA, 2003.
33. Evans, M.; Dalkir, K.; Bidian, C. A holistic view of the knowledge life cycle: The knowledge management cycle (KMC) model. Electron. J. Knowl. Manage. **2014**, *12* (2), 85–97.
34. Alvesson, M.; Karreman, D. Odd couple: Making sense of the curious concept of knowledge management. J. Manage. Stud. **2001**, *38* (7), 995–1018.
35. Drucker, P. Knowledge worker: New target for management. Christian Sci. Monitor. **Nov 11, 1964**, *10*.
36. Senge, P. *The Fifth Discipline: The Art and Practice of the Learning Organization*; Doubleday: New York, 1990.
37. Argyris, M.; Schön, D. *Theory in Practice: Increasing Professional Effectiveness*; Jossey-Bass: San Francisco, CA, 1974.
38. Argyris, C. *Knowledge for Action: A Guide to Overcoming Barriers to Organizational Change*; Jossey Bass: San Francisco, CA, 1993.
39. Al-Hawamdeh, S. *Knowledge Management: Cultivating Knowledge Professionals*; Chandos Publishing: Rollinsford, NH, 2003.
40. Progility PLC website: http://www.tfpl.com.
41. TFPL website http://library.tmu.edu.tw/chiu/KMmap2000.pdf. Retrieved May 29, 2017.
42. Henczel, S. Supporting the KM environment: The roles, responsibilities, and rights of information Professionals. Inform. Outlook **2004**, *8* (1), 13–18.

Knowledge Management–
Law Librarianship

Knowledge Management Systems

Dick Stenmark
Department of Applied IT, IT University of Gothenburg, Gothenburg, Sweden

Abstract
Knowledge management systems (KMS) are loosely understood as a type of information technology (IT) to support organizational knowledge management (KM) work. The challenge here is to understand first what KM is and then figure out how it can be supported by IT. This entry first provides a review of KM work and the critique it received. Then KMS are defined and analyzed through various well-used theoretical frameworks. The major challenges KMS are facing today are discussed and the entry ends with some hints on what may lie ahead.

INTRODUCTION

Knowledge management systems (KMS) refers to a class of information systems (IS) that is used to enhance knowledge and information transfer within an organization and to manage organizational knowledge.[1] Although this statement seems straightforward, it is rather difficult to define what a KMS is, since it is still unclear exactly what should be included in the concept of knowledge management (KM). What is the difference between knowledge and information and can computer applications really deal with knowledge? Some have argued that computers can only process data, and certainly not knowledge.[2] What, then, is a KMS and what role does it play in KM work? Before we can talk about *systems* for KM, we need a shared view of KM itself.

Is KM an emerging new discipline of its own or is it a topic that runs across several existing scholarly discourses? Throughout the years, there have been advocates of both positions. There are also commentators arguing that organizations have always been practicing KM-related activities so there is essentially nothing new to KM. This is no uncommon phenomenon but something that happens whenever new terminology is introduced. In the 1980s, Cronin asked whether information management had something new to offer or if it was just a new label for librarianship.[3] Twenty or so years later, people ask the same thing about KM and KMS.

Whilst several voices claim that there is no consensus regarding what exactly knowledge management is or how it differs from information management, Davenport and Grover in their editorial comment on the 2001 Special KM issue of Journal of Management Information Systems (JMIS) concluded that KM as a *practical* phenomenon was here to stay but that *formal research* on the topic was lacking.[4] A couple of years have passed since Davenport and Grover made this observation and today it is fair to say that KM has established itself as a research topic, as

reported elsewhere in this encyclopedia. Davenport and Grover continued by observing that IT support for KM, i.e., KMS, was seen as a useful but far from required resource by practitioners and scholars alike.

In the following text, we shall first look briefly at the history of KM and KMS before turning to the various theories underpinning this field. Thereafter, some of the most well-cited frameworks for KMS found in the IS literature are introduced to help the reader see what *types* of KMS are available. The ontological aspects of KMS are touched upon before finally discussing the challenges KMS are facing today.

ROOTS OF KM

It can be debated when and where KM started, since it depends on what discipline you examine. A large number of fields have clearly influenced the emerging KM discourse—e.g., sociology, human resource management, organization science, and IS research to name but a few. Many commentators would probably hold organizational learning as the one discipline that has had the perhaps most profound effect on the KM field.[5,6] When it comes to KMS, though, the IS discipline has taken a leading role, since the development, implementation, and use of systems to informate and automate are central to the IS field.[7]

Tiwana[8] places the roots of KM in the 1950s management literature, whereas Maier[6] traces the first instances of KM back to the studies of societal application of knowledge in the late 1960s and early 1970s. However, it was not until the late 1980s, through the writings of, e.g., Sveiby and Lloyd[9] and Wiig,[10] that the phenomenon started to receive more widespread attention. Nonaka and Takeuchis's book "The Knowledge Creating Company"[11] is also an early landmark in organizational KM

Encyclopedia of Library and Information Sciences, Fourth Edition DOI: 10.1081/E-ELIS4-120043724
Copyright © 2017 by Taylor & Francis. All rights reserved.

literature and one of the most cited sources with almost 10,000 references in Google Scholar.

What propelled the development of KM as a new research discipline was the growing emphasis on knowledge work and knowledge workers as the primary source of productivity as opposed to assets such as land or capital.[11] This view paved way for the knowledge-based perspective of the firm[12] that suggests that the tangible resources of an organization generate value dependent on how they are combined and applied, which in turn depends on the organization's knowledge. This knowledge is deeply permeated in culture, procedures, routines, systems, and minds of the individual employees.

In the introduction of their 2001 paper, Alavi and Leidner note that it is not the existence of this knowledge per se that matters, but the ability to apply it and put it to use. To that end, advanced information technologies can be instrumental in effectuating the knowledge-based view of the firm by systemizing, enhancing, and expediting large-scale knowledge management.[13]

CRITIQUE OF KM

Knowledge management as a research discipline has also received critique. Some have argued that it is no more than yet another exemplar in a long list of management fads that have come and gone over the years.[2,14] In his critical analysis of KM, Wilson concludes:

> [Knowledge management] is, in large part, a management fad, promulgated mainly by certain consultancy companies, and the probability is that it will fade away like previous fads.[14]

Much of this skepticism stems from the fact that many consultancy firms and software vendors simply seemed to have renamed their old services and products, replacing the term "information" with the term "knowledge." Therefore, says Wilson:

> [T]he confusion of 'knowledge' as a synonym for 'information' is one of the most common effects of the 'knowledge management' fad.[14]

In addition to the fad debate, the KM discourse was also criticized for being "technology-driven." Comparing and contrasting the KM literature to that of organizational learning (OL), Swan et al. found that although the two disciplines are concerned with the improvement of organizational performance through knowledge development, i.e., human issues, only the OL literature focused on humans whereas the KM literature was predominantly occupied with tools and techniques.[5] The emphasis on information technology in the KM literature resulted in people being marginalized to either "inputs to KM [...]

or as constraints on its effectiveness [...]" (p. 673).[5] Swan and colleagues argue that much of the richness of human relations is lost when KM is reduced to merely technology.

This distinction between technology-oriented and human-oriented approaches has a long tradition in organization science and goes back to at least the early 1980s. However, a more holistic understanding of KM that encompasses both these stances has developed, and much of the turf wars from the late 1990s have now abated.

THEORETICAL FOUNDATION

Much of the epistemology used in KM literature has been influenced by the separation of knowledge in a tacit and an explicit component. The notion of tacit knowing is attributed to philosopher Michael Polanyi but was introduced to the KM discourse by Nonaka and Takeuchi.[11] Interestingly, the commonly used tacit–explicit distinction is not directly derived from Polanyi's work. Most commentators see explicit knowledge as knowledge that has been captured and codified into manuals, procedures, and rules, and is easy to disseminate. Tacit knowledge, on the other hand, is then knowledge that cannot be easily articulated and thus only exists in people's hands and minds, and manifests itself through their actions. In contrast, Polanyi does not make such a distinction. Instead, he envisions tacit knowing as the backdrop against which all understanding is distinguished.

While Polanyi speaks of tacit *knowing*, i.e., the verb, as a backdrop against which all actions are understood, Nonaka and Takeuchi use the term tacit *knowledge*, i.e., the noun, to denote particular type of knowledge that is difficult to express. This view has been criticized but due to the strong influence of Nonaka and Takeuchi's writings on the knowledge management discourse, this interpretation has been widely adopted. Amongst the critics are Tsoukas, who argues that tacit knowledge is *not* explicit knowledge internalized. Instead, tacit knowledge is inseparable from explicit knowledge since "[t]acit knowledge is the necessary component of all knowledge" (p. 14).[15] According to Tsoukas the two are so inseparately related that to even try to separate the two would be to "miss the point." There had perhaps been less confusion had Nonaka instead used the term "implicit knowledge."

Tsoukas recognizes that the dichotomy between tacit and explicit knowledge and the taxonomies derived from this duality have advanced our understanding of organizational knowledge by showing its multifaceted nature. However, such typologies also limit our understanding by the inherent formalism that accompanies them. "The conceptual categories along which the phenomena are classified must be assumed to be discrete, separate, and stable. The problem is that they hardly ever are" (p. 14).[15]

Knowledge Management–
Law Librarianship

The tacit–explicit dichotomy has also taken other expressions. Choo suggests a differentiation between tacit, explicit, and cultural knowledge,[16] and Spender suggests, in addition to tacit and explicit knowledge, individual and collective knowing.[12] Blackler speaks of embodied, embedded, embrained, encultured, and encoded knowledge.[17] Yet another derivative is the distinction between the community view and the commodity view. The community view sees knowledge as socially constructed and inseparable from the knower, whereas the commodity view holds knowledge as a universal truth, and as facts and collectable objects.[18] Though several other ways to classify knowledge exist and have been suggested, they all, more or less, build on the tacit–explicit dichotomy.

DEFINITION OF KM SYSTEMS

Whereas most people agree that data and information may exist outside humans, supporters of the community view of knowledge have argued that knowledge can never be separated from the knower and thus never stored digitally.[2,13] Computer support for knowledge management would thus be, in a sense, impossible. How can we then talk about KMS?

KMS is often employed as a catalyst or enabler of KM but such implementations should not be carried out without careful coordination with the required people-oriented activities needed. Alavi and Leidner note that while KM initiatives may not *require* tools, IT can certainly support KM in many ways, in particular in firms where the ratio of *knowledge workers* is high.[13] Schultze defines a knowledge worker as someone who interacts knowledgeable with information and sees information not only as something derived from knowledge but as something that changes knowledge.[19] There is thus a tight relationship between information and knowledge and it seems that any knowledge work needs to be supported by information technology.

As stated in the introduction, a KMS is an IS and IS and knowledge systems are thus not radically different; instead, there is a subtle yet important difference in the *attitude* towards and the *purpose* of the systems. Whereas an IS processes information without engaging the users, a KMS must be geared towards helping the users to understand and assign *meaning* to the information.[13] The value of any given piece of information resides in the relationship between the information and the user's knowledge. This means that design of KMS should be based on an understanding not only of the information per se, but also of the context where the user develops the information need, and the analysis of the usage of the same information once it has been obtained and interpreted by the user.[20]

Following Alavi and Leidner,[13] a KMS should thus be understood as *a particular class of information systems developed specifically to support organisations in their attempt to create, codify, collect, store, integrate, share, and apply knowledge.*

KMS THEORY

The theoretical foundation underpinning KMS vary considerably and are not easily detected but we can get a reasonably good picture by looking at Schultze and Leidner's classification of theoretical perspectives in KM-related IS research. Having reviewed six leading IS journals and thoroughly analyzed nearly 100 articles from 1990 to 2000, Schultze and Leidner showed that a vast majority or 70% belonged to the Normative Discourse, 25% could be labeled as Interpretative Discourse and only a handful of papers represented a Critical (or Dialogic) Discourse.[21]

According to Schultze and Leidner's analysis, the normative discourse, which is characterized by a strive towards consensus from an a priori understanding of what the research problems are, typically assumes progressive enlightenment and increasing rationalisation, management, and control. IS research representing the normative discourse are thus concerned with "codification, normalisation of experience and the search for law-like relationships" (pp. 216–217).[21] Much of the research focus on problem solving, and it creates "a problem space that can be decomposed in a logical, top-down fashion" (p. 221).[21] Although both the research topics and the way knowledge is operationalised show great diversity, a common metaphor used within the normative discourse is that of knowledge as an asset. Researchers in this category typically view knowledge as a key driver of organizational efficiency and performance. Amongst the theories underpinning normative research, Schultze and Leidner mention innovation diffusion theory, absorptive capacity theory, and management cognition theory (p. 222).[21]

The interpretative discourse, which also opts for consensus but from an emergent understanding of the organizational situation, emphasizes the social aspects of organizational life that has not been rationalized or systematized. IS research representing the interpretative discourse thus aims "to create a coherent, consensual, and unified representation of what the organisational reality is 'actually' like" (p. 217),[21] and is typically targeted on work situations and organizational practices. Knowledge is therefore studied indirectly via its role in organizational transformation and how it is supported by various types of KMS. In this discourse, knowledge, technology, and organisational practice are all seen as socially constructed and dynamic, and the theories upon which interpretative research rests include organisational learning, communities of practice, activity theory, and bricolage (pp. 224–225).[21]

It is evident that almost all KM-related IS research is consensus-oriented. There are, however, also those who apply a dissensus-oriented approach. Although Schultze and Leidner treat critical and dialogic as two separate discourses, I shall here use the critical discourse label to include both these perspectives, since both understand struggle, conflict, and tension as natural organizational states. Seen from this perspective, organizations are "sites of political struggle and fields of continuous conflict" (p. 217)[21] and the objective of the research is thus to show that there is no coherent reality but different forms of domination and distortions. KMS (and other IT tools) are thus not to be understood as neutral, according to this perspective, but should be seen as instruments to make invisible work visible or to actively change social conditions. Schultze and Leidner call for more research in the critical discourse since this perspective allows the highlighting of the social inequities underpinning the distinction between service and knowledge work and the examination of contradictions in managing knowledge.[21] The direct implications for KMS, however, are less obvious.

TYPES OF KMS AND ITS APPLICATIONS

As we saw earlier, many vendors tried to repackage their applications under the KM label at the end of the last millennium and a list of different KMS can therefore be made arbitrarily long. Instead of presenting a list of software that not all would agree upon, and, in addition, soon would be dated, it is more useful to examine three of the most referenced classification schemes for KMS and let them define the *various types of applications* that are possible. The frameworks are Hansen et al.'s *Codification vs. Personalization* from *Harvard Business Review* in 1999,[22] Hahn and Subramani's *Knowledge Residence and Level of Structure* from ICIS 2000,[23] and finally Alavi and Leidner's scheme from MISQ in 2001.[13]

Codification vs. Personalization

An early framework for KM work (and hence for KMS to support that work) is found in Hansen et al.'s well-referred article from *Harvard Business Review*. Based on their studies of management consultancy firms, and implicitly building on Nonaka's dichotomy of explicit and tacit knowledge, Hansen et al. divide knowledge management efforts into two different strategies; codification and personalization.[22]

Companies where the KM strategy centers on codifying and storing knowledge into databases for easy dissemination and retrieval is said to follow a codification strategy. In such companies, computers have a central role in the strategy, as carriers of knowledge. Hansen et al. point to Ernst and Young as a company following

a codification strategy. Knowledge is harvested and coded into documents or other "knowledge objects" as an informant called them (p. 108),[22] and these are thereafter stored in electronic repositories for later retrieval. Even though the codification process is laborious, Ernst and Young has dedicated staff members doing nothing else but codifying knowledge into documents—this approach allows for scaling up since the repositories are accessible for all employees worldwide and available around the clock. Once the object is put into the repository it can be used over and over again at a very low cost, provided it does not have to be modified. Companies using the codification strategy thus typically deal with problems where the same solution can be applied many times. The "economics of reuse" is what motivates the KM efforts in these companies, and the KMS used are typically document management systems and databases.[22]

In contrast, when knowledge is tied to the individual that developed it and thus cannot be stored in a database, it has to be shared through face-to-face interactions. The role of the computers is thus to facilitate communication between people. Companies with this approach are said to follow a personalization strategy, and Hansen et al. mention McKinsey as a company in this category. In their company, knowledge emerges out of dialogues between individuals and their IT focus is thus to enable interactions between employees. Part of McKinsey's KM strategy is to move people between offices to expand their networks. Even though face-to-face meetings are unequalled for sharing tacit knowledge, space and time distances may sometime prevent people from physical meetings. McKinsey thus engage e-mail and video conferencing equipment to communicate and allow employees tap into the expertise of their peers. Companies following a personalization strategy typically deal with unique problems that do not have clear solutions and where customized answers must be provided. In "experts economics" knowledge is tacit and cannot be systematized and made efficient. Instead, these companies charge much higher prices, and KMS used are expert finder systems and communications software.[22]

Hansen et al. stress that companies should not try to combine these two strategies but, based on their business strategy, select one as their main KM strategy and merely use the other as a complementary strategy.

Knowledge Residence and Level of Structure

Adding another dimension to the tacit–explicit dichotomy, Hahn and Subramani present a framework for KMS by looking on the one hand at where the knowledge is said to reside (i.e., in artifacts or in people) and on the other hand to the extent to which knowledge is said to impose or

Knowledge Management–
Law Librarianship

require an a priori structure. These axes form a two-by-two matrix hosting four different classes of KMS.[23]

- One is where the system manages knowledge artifacts that has an inherent structure or where the system imposes a structure on the artifacts. Formal document repositories and data warehouses belong to this class.
- A second class also requires an a priori structure but manages links to knowledgeable people. A competence database intended to let employees find colleagues with specific skills falls into this class.
- A third class does not impose any structure in particular and assumes that knowledge is codified into artifacts. Intranets where Web pages and documents are found through full-text indexing search engines belong to this class.
- Finally, a fourth class again requires no structure but provides means for employees to identify and communicate with local experts. Discussion forums and e-mail Listservs are systems in this class.

Hahn and Subramani identify three interesting challenges regarding KMS. First, balancing information overload and potential useful content involves the size and diversity of both the users and the content. When the knowledge resides in artifacts, more items means higher chances of being able to find what you need. Also when human resources are required, more users increase the possibilities of finding a knowledgeable coworker. The down side is that more information also means more unrelated or useless information, and more users typically generate more interactions and more e-mails, which blurs the picture. For the same reason is diversity useful, and no problem in highly structured environments, but when structures and shared vocabularies are lacking, diversity can easily get overwhelming.[23]

Second, balancing additional workload and accurate content addresses the issue of keeping KMS updated. Highly structured environments require considerable efforts to ensure the appropriateness of the structure, and this work often comes on top of the employees' ordinary work tasks. In more loosely structured systems motivation to share knowledge often comes in the form of higher social status. The downside is that those who contribute and earn a reputation may end up being occupied answering people's questions and helping colleagues instead of doing their jobs.[23]

Third, balancing exploitation and exploration means being aware of the fact that reliance on existing solutions only may result in a competency trap.[24] A system that supports the exploitation of existing knowledge may provide short-term benefits but in the long run be detrimental to the organization. At the same time, a system preoccupied with generating new knowledge may prevent organizational members from learning and adding to the collective experience that exists in the organization.

Hahn and Subramani suggest the KMS should consider including agent technology, collaborative filtering methods, advanced visualization tools, in order to address the above challenges.[23]

Alavi and Leidner's Scheme

Without suggesting an explicit framework, Alavi and Leidner in their review of the literature discussing applications of IT to knowledge management efforts, identify three common approaches: Coding and sharing of best practice, Creation of knowledge directories, and Creation of knowledge networks [[13], p. 114].

Coding and sharing of best practice is one of the most common applications of KMS, according to Alavi and Leidner. The term "best practice" is typically used to refer to a superior or exemplary practice that leads to superior performance. By collecting and codifying stories that mediate such practice, organizations can build KMS that stores and disseminates these experiences within the organization.

Creation of knowledge directories forms a second common class of KMS. Knowledge directories are also known as expert finder systems and aim at mapping the internal expertise of the organization. Alavi and Leidner report that 74% of the respondents in Gazeau's survey believed that their organization's most useful knowledge was not available in explicit form. When knowledge cannot be codified into artifacts, creating knowledge directories allows organizational members to benefit from the knowledge by being able to find and subsequently talk to the knowledgeable coworker.

Creation of knowledge networks is the third commonly used approach to KMS. Applications to first identify and then bring together (virtually or face-to-face) people from the same community of practice or those who share an interest has proven useful in many organizations. Ford Motor Company found that by sharing knowledge in networks the development time for cars was reduced by 33%. Online forums belong to the technology used in this approach.[13]

We have seen that KMS can either be used to support a commodity view of KM, where the explication of knowledge is assumed not only to be possible but also necessary, or a community view of KM, where the implicit nature of knowing puts people in focus. The success of KMS (as with most IS) depends on the extent of use, which in turn depends on a number of factors. In their concluding discussion, Alavi and Leidner point to a set of research questions concerning the application of IT to KM. In sum, they ask what effect an increased breadth and depth of knowledge via KMS would have on organizational performance; how to ensure that knowledge in an KMS can be modified (if necessary) prior to being used, and how these modifications too can be captured; how anonymized knowledge in a KMS can be trusted; and what are the quality and

Knowledge Management–
Law Librarianship

Knowledge Management–
Law Librarianship

usefulness factors of KMS.[13] The answers to many of these questions are still pending.

ONTOLOGICAL ASPECTS

It has often been argued that only individuals can think and act—not organizations. At the same time, as human beings we are social creatures and we tend to seek, and benefit from, each other's company. Inputs from colleagues and the surrounding context greatly affect our ability to create and use knowledge because the individual and the collective interact in fruitful ways. Focusing primarily on how new knowledge emerges, Nonaka and Takeuchi stress the fact that knowledge creation initiates from the individual but is a process that moves through expanding communities of interaction, crossing group, division, and, finally, organizational boundaries.[11] Other scholars have made similar comments about other KM processes.

Still, IT support for KM has traditionally focused on organizational-wide systems, possibly due to the acknowledged fact that the usefulness of a KMS grows exponentially with the size of the organization. Much of the IS research has thus had a macro-level focus, but also applications supporting organizational learning and organizational memory are common in the KMS repertoire. The challenge associated with organizational KMS is that individuals often have to provide input without getting much back in return. This problem, often referred to as the maintenance problem seriously threatens the quality and usefulness of these systems.

Another category of KMS are the groupware systems targeting smaller subsets of the organization, typically aiming for management. This category includes various types of Decision Support Systems (DSS). Many KMS in this category can also be related to the field of Computer-Supported Collaborative Work (CSCW). Typical applications here include Helpdesk applications and expert finder systems within specific subgroups. The maintenance problem continues to be a challenge also at this level.

When it comes to the individual, there has—until recently—not been equally much support. Some argue that this situation is about to change. One of the problems here is that not all of the applications used at an individual level are officially labeled KMS. For example, the information retrieval (IR) field has provided the knowledge worker with search engines and other tools to help locate information, but not all would agree that a search engine is a KMS. Another noticeable trend is the growth of social media. These applications exploit the individual–collective relationship and are able to provide the individual with added value through the actions of the collective relationship and vice versa. It will be interesting to follow this development to see whether social media will provide a means to avoid, if not solve, the maintenance problem.

THE KMS CHALLENGES

A number of KMS challenges can be identified in the KM literature. One issue is that of dispersion of work. It is argued that knowledge workers are increasingly dispersed—spatial as well as contractual.[25] Organizational members work outside the physical boundaries of the firm and/or change positions within the firm, often including geographical changes. This, it is argued, makes them less exposed to colleagues with similar functional skills.

There is also the contractual dispersion, i.e., the provisional nature of employment and the higher level of partial or temporary involvement in the firm that many knowledge workers experience. In addition, many are engaged in virtual teams that often reorganize and have high turnover rates. This dispersion of work requires KMS that allows for effective sharing of the latest knowledge.[25,26]

Another issue is the shorter product and process life cycles in today's organizations.[26] This compresses the time window for capturing the lessons learned and knowledge created in the process and leaves the knowledge workers with little time to document and save their experiences. At the same time knowledge becomes obsolete much quicker. KMS need to be able to deal effectively with these circumstances.

The above concerns can be seen as aspects of a larger and overarching challenge, i.e., how to keep KMS updated and current. While many of today's organizations expect KMS to become major catalysts for innovations in terms of the ways in which businesses can be organized and conducted, there is plenty of IS research that indicate that such systems often fail when implemented in everyday knowledge work. In response, a distinguishable issue in KMS research is how to support knowledge work with IS in a successful way. It has been found that although the systems work technically and should function well in theory, they remain unused by the organizational members.[27] Following this, the development of systems with the capacity to bridge the knowing-doing gap in organizations has been recognized as a significant area of KMS research.

However, the imbalance between the desire for accurate content and the workload required to achieve this still appears to be a critical problem, leading to systems of little use for organizations in their knowledge application processes. It has been suggested that the problem stems from the fact that the requirements for KMS are fundamentally different from those of other types of IT and are thus not covered by existing IS design theories.

Markus et al. have identified three primary differences.[28] First, knowledge work processes requires that expert knowledge is adapted and/or contextualized to specific local conditions. Decision support systems and executive IS do not provide system features that can handle expert knowledge or contextualize translation rules. Resulting from this, DSS and expert systems inhibit creative problem finding and solution generation. While expert systems manage general expert knowledge, they fail to support contextual knowledge and the flexibility needed for process emergence. Second, these types of systems are all specifically designed for a known type of user, e.g., managers. Being designed for a particular type of user community, these systems are not well adapted to emergent work processes characterized by shifting user types having varying knowledge requirements. Third, knowledge workers have access to many different types of systems but since these systems often are isolated and not integrated into work practice, knowledge workers tend to manage their systems rather than getting the job done.

To circumvent these problems, it has been suggested that KMS should be integrated with or build into already existing applications since key to a successful KMS is to facilitate usage.[29] As knowledge work requires creativity in order to produce idiosyncratic and esoteric knowledge, knowledge work practice is untidy compared to operational or administrative business processes. Hence, KMS must be able to go beyond written instructions and official task descriptions, thus appreciating exceptions not only as something inevitable but as a necessity. Consequently, KMS must not be isolated but should be integrated into work practice. For the purpose of avoiding situations where knowledge workers manage their systems rather than getting the job done, developers must recognize sociotechnical issues associated with disparity in work and benefit. In this way, KMS capable of attracting a critical mass of users can be developed. In addition, paying attention to unobtrusive accessibility and the adoption process may deepen developers' understanding of how support systems can be better integrated with both the day-to-day tasks of knowledge workers and their performance of the tasks.

CONCLUDING SUMMARY

In the 1990s there was a rather heated debate whether or not KM was a fad but this seems to have abated. Now, there is consensus that KM—at least as a pragmatic issue—is here to stay. With knowledge replacing economy of scale as business driver and with increasing portion of knowledge workers in today's organizations, knowledge management, and the need for IT support for it, is not likely to go away.

The strong focus on technology that we witnessed in early KM work has been compensated for and practitioners and researchers alike now have acknowledged that knowledge cannot exist outside the mind of a human being. Cultures that encourage and motivate individuals to share, combine, and reuse knowledge are recognized as equal, if not more, important as IT, even amongst technologists. IT

is still likely to continue to play an important part, not as driver and single success factor but as catalyst, facilitator and enabler of social networks, virtual meeting places, and new discussion forums. One of the general lessons learned is that technology is important and useful but it should not be the driving force in KM work.

Several commentators have pointed to the fact that KMS in the late 1990s were discrete, stand-alone systems not aligned with the organizations' business processes. Such systems had to be explicitly attended to on top of ordinary tasks, thus adding to—not facilitating—the work to be carried out.[29] Newer KMS appear to be better integrated with existing business infrastructure and enterprise applications, thereby allowing employees to seamlessly apply organizational knowledge in whatever work they are engaged. However, there is still a need for development and research in this area.

On the theoretical side, no core theory on knowledge management has yet been developed, and KM may still be understood as an "umbrella construct," i.e., a broad and somewhat unclear label that is used to contain a whole variety of loosely connected issues.[30] Without a clear theoretical focus, some commentators argue, the original concept risks being eroded until it has no value and collapses, as researchers explore divergent paths and build isolated islands of knowledge. Spender[31] has argued strongly that KM and KMS research need a core theory that distinguishes them from other fields but at the same time is narrow enough to allow laypeople to recognize and understand what is and what is not a KMS. Not much work is currently to be found along such lines.

In their editorial introduction to the 2003 special issue on KM and IT in *IT and People*, Gray and Meister argue that KMS researchers are facing a bigger problem than did researchers of earlier organizational phenomena, since knowledge is neither new nor physically present and there is thus nothing concrete to point to. An independent core theory of KM and KMS is therefore needed, they argue.[32]

However, several future scenarios are possible. If the development towards more knowledge work continues, we may end up in the scenario predicted by Davenport and Grover where "every industry will view itself as knowledge-intensive [[4], p. 4]. If everything is KM, will the concept then still be meaningful, and if every application is a KMS, will the term be useful? At the other end of the spectrum lies a scenario where KM becomes so diversified and scattered that for this reason is pointless to talk about KM and IT support for it. Where we will end up remains to be seen.

REFERENCES

1. Voelpel, S.; Dous, M.; Davenport, T. Five steps to creating a global knowledge-sharing system: Siemens' ShareNet. Acad. Manage. Execut. **2005**, *19* (2), 9–23.

Knowledge Management–
Law Librarianship

2. Galliers, R.; Newell, S. Back to the future: From knowledge management to data management. In *Proceedings of European Conference on Information Systems 2001*, Bled, Slovenia, June, 27–29, 2001; 609–615.

3. Cronin, B. Introduction. In *Information Management: From Strategies to Action*; Cronin, B., Ed.; Aslib: London, U.K., 1985; vii–ix.

4. Davenport, T.H.; Grover, V. Editorial: Special issue on knowledge management. J. Manage. Inform. Syst. **2001**, *18* (1), 3–4.

5. Swan, J.; Scarbrough, H.; Preston, J. Knowledge management—The next fad to forget people. In *Proceedings of European Conference on Information Systems 1999*, Copenhagen, Denmark, June, 23–25, 1999; 668–678.

6. Maier, R. *Knowledge Management Systems*, 2nd Ed.; Springer: Berlin, Germany, 2004.

7. Butler, T. From data to knowledge and back again: Understanding the limitations of KMS. Knowl. Process Manage. **2003**, *10* (3), 144–155.

8. Tiwana, A. *The Knowledge Management Toolkit: Practical Techniques for Building Knowledge Management Systems*; Pearson Education: Upper Saddle River, NJ, 1999.

9. Sveiby, K.E.; Lloyd, T. *Managing Know-How*; Bloomsbury: London, U.K., 1987.

10. Wiig, K.M. Management of knowledge: Perspectives of a new opportunity. In *User interfaces: Gateway or bottleneck?*; Bernold, T., Ed.; Gottlieb Duttweiler Institute: Zurich, Switzerland, 1988; 101–116.

11. Nonaka, I., Takeuchi, H. *The Knowledge-Creating Company: How Japanese Companies Create the Dynamics of Innovation*; Oxford University Press: Oxford, U.K., 1995.

12. Spender, J.-C. Making knowledge the basis of a dynamic theory of the firm. Strateg. Manage. J. Winter Special Issue, **1996**, *17*, 45–62.

13. Alavi, A.; Leidner, D. Review: Knowledge management and knowledge management systems: Conceptual foundations and research issues. MIS Q. **2001**, *25* (1), 107–136.

14. Wilson, T.D. The nonsense of knowledge management. Inform. Res. **2002**, *8*(1), paper no. 144. http://informationr.net/ir/8-1/paper144.html (accessed December. 2008).

15. Tsoukas, H. The firm as a distributed knowledge system: A constructionist approach. Strateg. Manage. J. Winter Special Issue **1996**, 17, 11–25.

16. Choo, C.W. *The Knowing Organization*; Oxford University Press: Oxford, U.K., 1998.

17. Blackler, F. Knowledge, knowledge work and organizations: an overview and interpretation. Organ. Stud. **1995**, *16* (6), 1021–1046.

18. Swan, J.; Scarbrough, H. Knowledge management: Concepts and controversies. J. Manage. Stud. **2001**, *38* (7), 913–921.

19. Schultze, U. A confessional account of an ethnography about knowledge work. Manage. Inform. Syst. Q. **2000**, *24* (1), 3–41.

20. Stenmark, D. Information vs. knowledge: The role of intranets in knowledge management. In *Proceedings of HICSS-35*, Hawaii, January, 7–10, 2002.

21. Schultze, U.; Leidner, D. Studying knowledge management in information systems research: Discourses and theoretical assumptions. Manage. Inform. Syst. Q. **2002**, *26* (3), 213–242.

22. Hansen, M.; Nohria, N.; Tierney, T. What's your strategy for managing knowledge? Harvard Bus. Rev. March–April **1999**, *77* (2), 106–116.

23. Hahn, J.; Subramani, M. A framework of knowledge management systems: Issues and challenges for theory and practice. In *Proceedings of International Conference on Information Systems 2000*, Brisbane, Victoria, Australia, December, 10–13, 2000; 302–312.

24. Levitt, B.; March, J.G. Organizational learning. Annu. Rev. Sociol. **1988**, *14*, 319–340.

25. Corso, M.; Martini, A.; Pellegrini, L.; Massa, S.; Testa, S. Managing dispersed workers: The new challenge in knowledge management. Technovation **2006**, *26* (5–6), 583–594.

26. Donnellan, B.; Fitzgerald, B. Developing systems to support organisational learning in product development organisations. Electron. J. Knowl. Manage. **2003**, *1* (2), 33–46.

27. Schultze, U.; Boland, R.J. Knowledge management technology and the reproduction of knowledge work practices. J. Strateg. Inform. Syst. **2000**, 9, 193–212.

28. Markus, L.M.; Majchrzak, A.; Gasser, L. A design theory for systems that support emergent knowledge processes. Manage. Inform. Syst. Q. **2002**, *26*, 179–212.

29. Stenmark, D.; Lindgren, R. System support for knowledge work: Bridging the knowing-doing gap. Intl. J. Knowl. Manage. **2006**, *2* (2), 46–68.

30. Hirsch, P.; Levin, D. Umbrella advocates versus validity police: A life-cycle model. Organ. Sci. **1999**, *10*, 199–212.

31. Spender, J.-C. Exploring uncertainty and emotion in the knowledge-based theory of the firm. Inform. Technol. People **2003**, *16* (3), 266–288.

32. Gray, P.H.; Meister, D.B. Introduction: Fragmentation and integration in knowledge management research. Inform. Technol. People **2003**, *16* (3), 259–265.

BIBLIOGRAPHY

General KM

1. Davenport and Prusak, *Working Knowledge: How Organizations Manage What They Know*; Harvard Business School Press: Boston, MA, 1997.

Knowledge Management Systems

2. Barnes, S., Ed.; *Knowledge Management Systems: Theory and Practice*; Thomson learning: London, U.K., 2002.

3. Malhotra, Y. Why knowledge management systems fail? Enablers and constraints of knowledge management in human enterprises. In *Handbook on Knowledge Management 1: Knowledge Matters*; Holsapple, Ed.; Springer-Verlag: Berlin, Germany, 2002; 577–599.

4. Rubenstein, A.H.; Geisler, E. *Installing and Managing Workable Knowledge Management Systems*; Greenwood Publishing Group Inc.: Westport, CT, 2003.

5. Ruggles, R.L., Eds.; *Knowledge Management Tools*; Butterworth Heinemann: Boston, MA, 1997.

Knowledge Management–
Law Librarianship

Knowledge Management: Early Development

Michael Koenig
Ken Neveroski
College of Information and Computer Science, Long Island University, Brookville,
New York, U.S.A.

Abstract

Knowledge management (KM) as a business concept, though it had earlier antecedents, evolved in the late 1980s. It sprang from the combination of the recognition of the importance to a firm of its information and knowledge assets, and from the appearance of the Internet and the recognition of the utility of the Internet as an information and knowledge sharing tool, particularly for geographically dispersed organizations. KM has gone through four stages:

1. An emphasis upon the new technology, the Internet, and upon the development of "best practices" or "lessons learned."
2. An increased recognition of human and cultural factors, and upon the development of "communities of practice" to facilitate the sharing of information.
3. An increased recognition of the importance of designing the systems for retrievability, and the importance of data design and taxonomies.
4. An emphasis upon extending KM systems beyond the parent organization to include, for example, vendors and suppliers, customers, users, alumni, etc.

KM has exhibited remarkable staying power and growth in a fashion that is dramatically different from other business enthusiasms of the late twentieth century.

INTRODUCTION

This entry is a discussion of the historical origin of the phrase/concept called "Knowledge management (KM)." While KM is a recent development of information and communication technology (ICT) becoming integrated with business practice and intellectual capital (IC), it should not be ignored that the capture and passing on of "knowledge" is an ancient practice. In that sense, KM could be traced at least as far back as the thirteenth century and the Dominican Order's development, manufacture, and promotion of concordances for organizing and accessing knowledge within the Bible.

The use of the term "knowledge management" is a surprisingly recent phenomenon, becoming common and part of the professional vocabulary only in the mid-1990s. The earliest print reference appears to have been used first in the context of library and information work. Marchand,[1] then Dean of the School of Information Studies at Syracuse University, coined it in the 1980s as a descriptor for the final level in his stage hypothesis of information systems development.[2] However, the term, as presently used, appears to have been re-coined more or less anonymously somewhere among the major accountancy and consulting firms. The earliest reports seem to be from McKinsey & Co. Brook Manville, the first Director of Knowledge Management at McKinsey, reports that

McKinsey launched an internal study whose title included the phrase knowledge management in 1987 (Manville, personal communication, 2007). Prusak, another acknowledged pioneers of the field, in a very corroborative and independent communication, reports that Ernst and Young started using the term in 1992, and that McKinsey & Co. was using it "a bit earlier - 1988?" (Prusak, personal communication, 2007).

In the article entitled "Where Did Knowledge Management Come From" written in 1999, Prusak described KM as originating "about 7 years ago," i.e., in 1992, and describes what appears to be the first conference organized specifically on the topic of KM, held in Boston in the spring of 1993, as "a good milestone to mark the beginning of the knowledge management time-line."[3] The conference, organized and sponsored by the Center for Business Strategy at Ernst and Young, was held at the Four Seasons Hotel (Prusak, personal communication, 2007).

BACKGROUND

While KM as it is known today came out of the consulting world, the concepts of managing knowledge can be traced back to earlier works in the fields of government intelligence and policy management. Early works often cite

Encyclopedia of Library and Information Sciences, Fourth Edition DOI: 10.1081/E-ELIS4-120043809
Copyright © 2017 by Taylor & Francis. All rights reserved.

Organizational Intelligence: Knowledge and Policy in Government and Industry by Wilensky.[4] In his book, Wilensky discussed the value of the "Knowledge Expert" as being the primary source of reliable information in the "Intelligence Field" of the government. So it should not be ignored that KM did have roots inside of other disciplines that are not directly related to the technology consulting firms.

KM, as the term is understood today however, did arise basically in the consulting world, and it was they that publicized it. The consulting firms quickly realized the potential of the intranet flavor of the Internet for linking together their own geographically dispersed knowledge-based organizations. They then quickly realized that the expertise they had gained was a product that could be marketed and sold to other organizations. That product needed a name, and the name chosen was knowledge management. In his article on where KM came from, Prusak in fact felt it appropriate to say "some skeptics may believe that consultants developed knowledge management to replace declining revenues from the waning re-engineering movement."[3] The two enthusiasms are related in that both were driven by increased ICT capabilities, but the timing, though convenient for the consulting firms was driven not by their convenience, but by the straightforward dynamics of ICT capability growth. The KM was dependent upon the Internet, while pre-Internet ICT already enabled the major restructuring of an organization's work flows and processes. In a sense, KM also has roots in the implementation of supply chain management (SCM) software and business process re-engineering (BPR) as well as the more recent development of enterprise resource planning (ERP). IT development has always had a pattern, an oft repeated pattern, of growth from addressing more structured data to addressing less tractable, less well structured, or comparatively unstructured data. Remember that text processing was at one time called "string handling," because to people brought up on handling numeric data, text was most conveniently thought of, not as words, but as a string of symbols to be manipulated. In that sense, SCM and BPR and ERP to KM, is simply a logical and predictable progression.

DEFINITION

A good functional and illustrative definition of KM and how it developed is the equestrian metaphor of "by the intranet out of intellectual capital."[5] By this definition, KM has two parents, the enthusiasm for and the appreciation of IC, and the development of the Internet and its offspring, intranets and extranets. The IC is essentially a name given to the recognition of the importance of information and knowledge. It represented the awareness that as Drucker (Hibbard (p. 46)[6]) put it:

We now know that the source of wealth is something, specifically human knowledge. If we apply knowledge to tasks that we obviously know how to do, we call it productivity. If we apply knowledge to tasks that are new and different, we call it innovation. Only knowledge allows us to achieve those two goals.

Indeed Drucker is clearly one of the intellectual fathers of KM. His *Post-Capitalist Society* which appeared in 1993, is about the shift from capitalism to the knowledge society. Almost one full page of an 11-page index is devoted to knowledge or knowledge phrases such as knowledge workers, yet the phrase knowledge management is surprisingly absent.[7] The early use of the phrase knowledge management is sometimes attributed to Drucker, but at this point it appears to be still unsubstantiated. Given Drucker's stature and his emphasis on knowledge and knowledge workers it is almost inevitable that such an attribution would arise. It may be noted however that while Drucker did, carefully, claim a first for the phrase "Knowledge Worker," he does not appear to have made any similar claim for the phrase "Knowledge Management," and he was certainly active and involved well into the time frame in which he might well have, and likely would have, made such a claim if he thought it warranted.

It is beyond the scope of this entry to pursue the development of the IC in detail, and that is covered elsewhere.[8–10] However, a brief review of the development of IC is vital to understanding the origins and development of KM.

A pioneer in the KM field was Sveiby.[11] His book *The Invisible Balance Sheet* (1989) was a key work in the development of thinking about IC. His principal point was precisely that the important assets of an organization did not show up on the balance sheet, and that in thinking about a company's assets one should think, as it were, in terms of an invisible balance sheet. From that starting point, his writings morphed smoothly and rapidly into KM. The work of Robert Buckman at Buckman Laboratories[12] and Hubert St. Onge at the Canadian Imperial Bank of Commerce[13] were key players in operationalizing the concept and in popularizing IC. Perhaps most important in bringing the concept of IC to the business community was Stewart's[14] article in *Fortune* magazine, "Intellectual Capital, Your Company's Most Valuable Asset."

The first blush of enthusiasm for IC centered on quantifying and measuring it.[15,16] Surely if it was so important, it needed to be measured. As the difficulty of measuring such an amorphous commodity as information, much less knowledge became apparent to the business community the enthusiasm for, or at least the publication of articles about, IC subsided. Then the Internet emerged. The business world realized that the Internet could be used to link an organization together. This was the take-off point for KM.[8,9] KM was first defined as having two components (Fig. 1).

Knowledge Management–
Law Librarianship

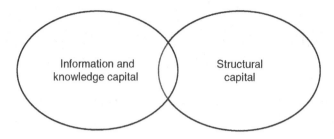

Fig. 1 Early conception of KM.

Information and knowledge capital was the organization's information and knowledge, but including the informal and unstructured, the implicit and tacit, as well as the formal.

The structural capital was the mechanisms in place to take advantage of the information and knowledge capital, the mechanisms to capture, store, retrieve, and communicate that information and knowledge. The phrase that has emerged that largely represents what was meant by KM's structural capital, is content management (CM), or its variant, ECM, electronic content management. As they are now used, these phrases are typically used in the context of the software packages used to facilitate CM or KM.

The transition from IC to KM is clearly seen in Peters 1992 book *Liberation Management*.[17] Peters has four chapters specifically entitled "Knowledge Management Structures (KMS)" (I–IV: Taking Knowledge Management Seriously; Getting Physical; Knowledge Bases, Expert Systems, Computer Augmented Collaboration; and Developing and Tapping Expert Power in the Hierarchy-less Organization), almost 10% of a very large book. The KMS phrase rapidly withered away in favor of the simpler KM, but Peters was clearly writing about KM as it was becoming to be understood.

Applications of Internet technology were soon extended beyond intranets, the use of the Internet within an organization, to extranets that would still be private, but were used to connect an organization with its suppliers and customers. The consequence of this development was an expanded definition of KM to include the customer's knowledge and input, customer capital (Fig. 2).

The inclusion of customer capital was also not unrelated to the popularity of TQM, total quality management, in which responding to customer need and demand was a key element.

Concurrent with IC, sharing the same etiology, and very much reinforcing IC was the notion of the "Balanced Score Card."[18] The idea behind the balanced score card was that traditional financial reporting was too narrow in its outlook, and that in effect Sveiby's "Invisible Balance Sheet" should be added to a company's "score card" to make it balanced. In particular the concern was that the traditional balance sheet focused only on the present and on the past, with no thought to the future. Using only traditional financial indicators, if the current balance sheet

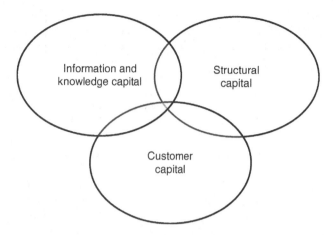

Fig. 2 Expanded conception of KM.

looks good, but for example customers have begun to defect to the competition, there is nothing to reveal that the situation is in fact not healthy. The exposition of the balanced score card recognized the difficulty of measuring IC per se, recognized its importance, but principally sought other non-financial indicators such as product quality, turnover or churn, or customer satisfaction, that would indicate an organization's health and sound positioning, and that were better indicators of likely future performance (Fig. 3).

It is very similar to the graphic above with the "customer capital" component replaced by "social capital." It is now assumed that customer capital is included in all of the above, the infrastructure extended to include the customer, the knowledge resources including the customer, and the social capital embracing the relationships not just within the organization, but with the customer (and the supplier to whom one is a customer) as well.

The concept of knowledge management continued to expand, most particularly by incorporating the notion of "the learning organization." Senge's[20] *The Fifth Discipline, the Art and Practice of the Learning Organization* appeared in 1990 and had established something of a cult following, but had not made a major impact in the business world, but with KM it meshed perfectly. The thesis of the learning organization is that what ultimately creates and distinguishes a successful organization is its success in creating and sharing information and knowledge; in short, its success at learning. The obvious corollary is that to be successful, an organization must create a culture that fosters learning.[21] One can say, in brief summary that the concept of the learning organization focuses on the creation of knowledge, while KM, as it was originally construed, focuses on the acquisition, structuring, retention, and dissemination of that knowledge. What then happened to KM is that the term was expanded to include the concept of the learning organization.

Similarly, a fit was quickly perceived with Nonaka and Takeuchi's[22] work on tacit knowledge and how to

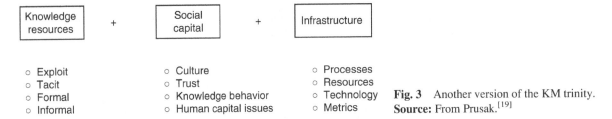

○ Exploit   ○ Culture   ○ Processes
○ Tacit   ○ Trust   ○ Resources
○ Formal   ○ Knowledge behavior   ○ Technology   **Fig. 3**   Another version of the KM trinity.
○ Informal   ○ Human capital issues   ○ Metrics   **Source:** From Prusak.[19]

Knowledge Management–
Law Librarianship

discover and cultivate it (*The Knowledge-Creating Company: How Japanese Companies Create the Dynamics of Innovation*, New York, Oxford University Press, 1995). Nonaka's work was an obvious way to point out that KM was not just about explicit and structured knowledge, but also about how to retain, find, and share knowledge that was difficult to make explicit and that resided in people's heads, tacit knowledge. Nonaka's name became the token for that recognition. While the KM literature generally speaks of explicit and tacit knowledge, it is in fact more useful, as Keen and Tan[23] point out, to think of three categories of knowledge, explicit, implicit, and tacit. Explicit knowledge is then that knowledge or information which has been captured in some explicit form, a procedures manual, or a database for example, implicit knowledge being that knowledge or information which has not been captured in some explicit form, but potentially could be, while tacit knowledge is that knowledge, like how to knead dough (the example Nonaka most famously used) or how to ride a bicycle, that cannot be fully captured in explicit form.

Both Senge's and Nonaka's work were not only about the human factors of KM implementation and use; they were also about knowledge creation as well as knowledge sharing and communication.

More recently,[24] KM is described as a structure supported now by five columns, i.e., with five major constituents (Fig. 4).

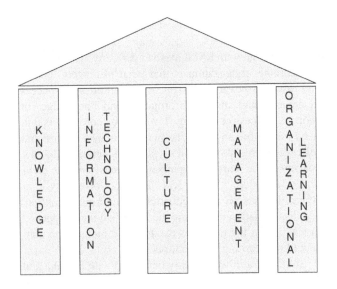

Fig. 4   KM with yet more components.

We can reflect briefly for a moment on whether the Parthenon-like image of the structure is an unintended homage to KM as the latest temple to which the consultants lead the faithful.

Another way to look at the origin and development of KM is to view it as a series of stages.

STAGE 1

The initial stage of KM was driven primarily by IT, information technology. That first stage is well described with an equestrian metaphor as "by the Internet out of IC." Organizations, particularly the large international consulting organizations, understood quite well that their stock in trade was information and knowledge, that often the left hand as it were had no idea what the right hand knew, and if they could share that knowledge—then they could avoid reinventing the wheel, underbid their competitors, and make more profit. When the Internet emerged, they realized that the intranet flavor of the Internet was an almost God given tool to accomplish that knowledge coordination and sharing. The first stage of KM was about how to deploy that new technology to accomplish those goals.

KM exploded in visibility in the business community because those large international consulting organizations, also realized quickly that many of their customers shared exactly the same problems, and that the expertise they were building for themselves could also be a product, an expertise, that they could purvey to those customers. A new product needs a name and a theme or rationale. The name for their new product was knowledge management, and the theme/rationale justifying it was *intellectual capital*, a theme which coincidentally had emerged as a hot topic in the business literature only a few years earlier, and which provided a wonderful rationale for the importance of KM. The first stage might be described as the "If only Texas Instruments knew what Texas Instruments knew." stage, to revisit a much quoted aphorism.[25] The hallmark phrase of Stage 1 was first "*best practices*," to be replaced by the more politic "*lessons learned*."

STAGE 2

The second stage of KM added recognition of the human and cultural dimensions. The second stage might be described as the "If you build it they will come is a fallacy" stage. It was soon recognized that "If you build it they will come" is a recipe that can easily lead to quick and embarrassing failure if human factors are not sufficiently taken into account. As this recognition unfolded, two major themes from the business literature were brought into the KM fold. The first was Senge's work on the learning organization, and the second was Nonaka and Takeuchi's[22] work on tacit knowledge and how to discover and cultivate it (both mentioned above). Both were not only about the human factors of KM implementation and use; they were also about knowledge creation as well as knowledge sharing and communication. The hallmark phrase of Stage 2 was "*communities of practice*."

Much attention in Stage 2 focused on the World Bank. Under Wolfensohn's administration the World Bank emphasized knowledge as their most important product, not the loans per se or the direct consequences of the projects supported, but rather the knowledge created by and shared from those projects.[26,27] The centerpiece of their emphasis on KM was their very deliberate development of communities of practice (COPs) specifically designed to encompass experts external to the bank.[28] At the same time, Denning's[29,30] work on storytelling as a technique to sell KM, focused on the intangibility of knowledge and the consequent frequent intangibility of KM results, and therefore the resulting need to justify KM by telling stories or anecdotes of results achieved, and then projecting "what if" consequences of further deployment of KM. Most of the storytelling examples centered on applications at the World Bank.

The Conference Board started organizing meetings on the subject of KM in 1997 (the first conference was entitled "Organizational Learning"). That first meeting was populated overwhelmingly by IT people. A good marker of the shift from the first to the second stage of KM, is that for the 1998 Conference Board conference (now called "Knowledge Management/Organizational Learning"), there was a noticeable contingent of attendees from HR, human resources, departments, and by 1999 HR was the largest single group. The year 1997 was also the first KMWorld conference, and can be seen as marking a certain coming of age of KM and its recognition as an important development to be paid attention to.

STAGE 3

The third stage is the awareness of the importance of content, and in particular an awareness of the importance of the retrievability and therefore of the importance of the arrangement, description, and structure of that content. Since a good alternate description for the second stage of KM is the "it's no good if they don't use it" stage, then in that vein, perhaps the best description for the third stage is the "it's no good if they can't find it" stage, or perhaps "it's no good if they try to use it but can't find it."

If one peruses the content of the 1999, 2000, and 2001 KMWorld conferences, one can see the

emergence of Stage 3 clearly. At KMWorld 2000 a track on content management appeared for the first time and at KMWorld 2001 in October/November content management was the dominant track, constituting the largest cluster of topics in the conference. That third stage that emerged is well described as the *taxonomy/content* stage.

Another bellwether is that TFPL, a major UK consulting group, in a report of their October 2001 CKO (Chief Knowledge Officer) Summit reported that for the first time taxonomies emerged as a topic, and it emerged full blown as a major topic.[31] The hallmark phrases emerging for the third stage are *content management* (or enterprise content management) and *taxonomies*.

STAGE 4

Starting roughly in 2003, a fourth stage of KM began to emerge. This stage is the awareness of the importance of information and knowledge external to the organization.

The inclusion of information and knowledge external to the organization is not new to KM, one need only think of the World Bank applications mentioned above. That being said however, the overwhelming emphasis of KM to date has been to mobilize and make accessible the organization's information and knowledge. The most basic mantra of KM, is still the stage one mantra, "if only Texas Instruments knew what Texas Instruments knew"; the classic metaphoric example of what KM is all about, making *an organization's* knowledge more useable and more productive.

The KM's traditional emphasis upon just an organization's internal knowledge can be best illustrated by quoting two of the most frequently quoted and used definitions of KM:

(Ponzi,[32] attributed to Ruggles[33]) Knowledge management is a newly emerging interdisciplinary business model dealing with all aspects of knowledge <u>within the context of the firm</u>, including knowledge creation, codification, sharing, learning, and innovation. Some aspects of this process are facilitated with information technologies, but knowledge management is to a greater degree, about organizational culture and practices.

(underlining added)

(Gartner Group[34]—now Gartner Inc.) A discipline that promotes an integrated approach to identifying, capturing, evaluating, retrieving, and sharing all of <u>an enterprise's information assets</u>. These assets may include databases, documents, policies, procedures, and previously uncaptured expertise and experience in individual workers.

(underlining added, Quoted in Malhotra[35])

The mainstream KM mindset up until now of focusing only on the firm's or the organization's or the enterprise's information and knowledge assets could hardly be clearer. Note that while Ruggles is an individual author, and may be expressing a more particular view, the Gartner Group is a major high profile consulting firm, and their definition is in effect a description of the product, KM consulting, that they are offering, and in this their product description they are limiting KM to "an enterprise's information assets."

Several threads have converged to drive this emphasis upon including or providing access to external information:[36]

- The extension of intranet-based KM systems to extranet-based systems. (Indeed a good name for Stage 4 might be the "Extranet stage of KM.") A logical extension of intranet-based KM is to build an "extranet" so that persons outside the organization, vendors, suppliers, dealers, major customers, etc. can be included. This has proceeded slowly however, as security, particularly for for-profit corporations is a major concern. It was precisely this lack of a need to be concerned about competitive information that allowed the World Bank to so quickly move into extranet-based COP. However as security techniques have improved, the willingness of corporations to extend COP onto extranets so as to incorporate the knowledge of "outsiders" has correspondingly increased.

- Concern about the knowledge about to be lost as postwar baby-boomers are beginning to hit retirement age. Corporations are beginning to realize that KM, in the form of retiree involvement in their COPs, is a powerful tool to address this issue.

- A repeat of the same broadening phenomenon that occurred with MIS, Management Information Systems, the realization that the information constituting the bulk of the information needed for managerial decisions lies near the top of the managerial decision making pyramid, and is typically external contextual information, not the organization's internal information. That same awareness is rapidly developing in the KM world, the

awareness that much of the key information needed for critical decisions lies outside the corporation or organization, and that the ideal KM system should provide appropriate links to the world outside the organization.

- *Globalization*: The increasing awareness that most organizations can no longer just think of themselves as a national company, and that they must compete globally or be overtaken by those who do, is now almost unquestioned received wisdom. The first corollary of this realization is that globalization requires knowledge about the external environment in spades. And furthermore, to avoid information overload, this external information should be gathered, organized, and made available in some coherent fashion.

- *Competitive intelligence*: Hard on the heels of the recognition of an increasingly global marketplace has come the awareness that you do not know where your competition will be coming from, and that to be adequately alert requires a conscious planned effort to acquire competitive intelligence on a global front, and that just attending the standard trade shows and chatting in the corridors will no longer suffice.

The result of these factors is a greatly increased emphasis upon external information. It should also be noted that another emphasis emerging simultaneously is that of the importance of situating information and knowledge in context. This is in fact another facet of the same evolution, the awareness that the importance, the usability, and the value of information is a function of how it relates to other information. New knowledge derives from the combination of information, either the juxtaposition of existing information, or the addition of new information to existing information.

SUMMARY OF THE FOUR STAGES OF KM

Stage 1: "by the Internet out of Intellectual Capital"

Information Technology
Intellectual Capital

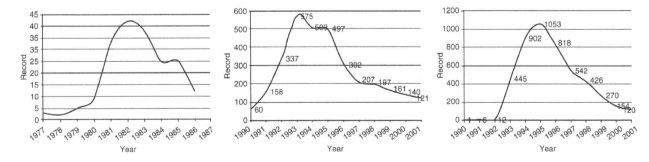

Fig. 5   Bibliometric representation of business hot topics. The Lifecycle of Quality Circles, 1977–1986;[37] Total Quality Management, 1990–2001;[38] Business Process Reengineering, 1990–2001.[38]
Source: From Abrahamson.[37]

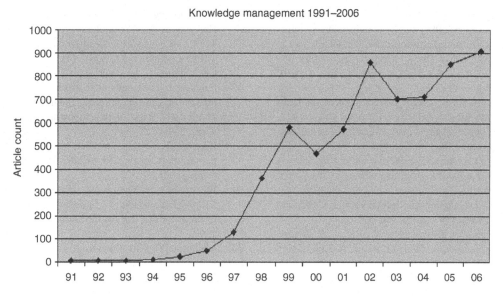

Fig. 6 Bibliometric representation of KM.

The Internet (including intranets, extranets, etc.)
Key phrases: "*best practices*," later replaced by the more politic "*lessons learned.*"

Stage 2: Human and cultural dimensions, the HR, Human Relations, stage

Communities of Practice
Organizational Culture
The Learning Organization (Senge), and
Tacit Knowledge (Nonaka) incorporated into KM
Key phrase: "*communities of practice.*"

Stage 3: Content and retrievability

Structuring content and assigning descriptors (index terms)
Key phrases: *content management* and *taxonomies.*

Stage 4: The Extranet stage

External information
Key phrases: *globalization and competitive intelligence.*

Note that new stages do not replace earlier stages, they merely add an emphasis to aspects of KM that though there were inadequately recognized previously.

The KM clearly appears to be uniquely different from other business enthusiasms and fads, to use a blunt term, of the late twentieth century. Above are simple bibliometric graphs (the number of occurrence of the term per year in the titles of articles in the business literature) for "Quality Circles," "Total Quality Management," and "Business Process Re-engineering."[37] Notice how similar the pattern is (Fig. 5).

The profile of KM however is dramatically and fundamentally different (Fig. 6).

It is clear that KM is now in a pattern uniquely its own, first the typical 4- or 5-year burst of explosive growth, but since then a pattern of stable mature growth – not a pattern of boom and bust, but a pattern of boom and continuity.

REFERENCES

1. Marchand, D.A. Information management: strategies and tools in transition. Inform. Manage. Rev **1985**, *1*(1), 27–37.
2. Koenig, M.E.D. Entering stage III—The convergence of the stage hypotheses. J. Am. Soc. Inform. Sci **1992**, *43*(3), 204–207.
3. Prusak, L. Where did knowledge management come from?. Knowl. Dir **1999**, Fall *1*(1), 90–96.
4. Wilensky, H. *Organizational Intelligence: Knowledge and Policy in Government and Industry*; Basic Books: New York, 1967.
5. Koenig, M.E.D. The evolution of knowledge management. In *Knowledge Management for the Information Professional*; Srikantaiah, T.K., Koenig, M.E.D., Eds.; Information Today for the American Society for Information Science: Medford, NJ, 2000; 23–36 Chapter 3.
6. Hibbard, J. Knowing what we know. Inform. Week **1997**, 653, October 20 46–64.
7. Drucker, P.F. *Post-Capitalist Society*; Harper Business Division of Harper Collins: New York, 1993.
8. Koenig, M.E.D. Intellectual capital and knowledge management. IFLA J. **1996**, *22*(4), 299–301.
9. Koenig, M.E.D. From intellectual capital to knowledge management: what are they talking about?. INSPEL **1998**, *32*(4), 222–233.
10. Sullivan, P.H. *Value-Driven Intellectual Capital: How to Convert Intangible Corporate Assets into Market Value*; Wiley: New York, 2000.

Knowledge Management– Law Librarianship

Knowledge Management–
Law Librarianship

11. Sveiby, K.-E. *The Invisible Balance Sheet*; Lederskap: Stockholm, Sweden, 1989; (English translation at http://www.sveiby.com/PublishedBooks/tabid/89/Default.aspx); published in Swedish as *Den Osynliga Balansräkningen*.

12. Liebowitz, J. *Knowledge Management Handbook*; CRC Press: Boca Raton, FL, 1999.

13. Allee, V. 12 Principles of knowledge management. Train. Dev. **1997**, November *51*(11), 71–74.

14. Stewart, T. Your company's most valuable asset: intellectual capital. Fortune **1994**, (3 October), 68–74.

15. Edvinsson, L. *Visualizing intellectual capital in Skandia. Skandia's 1994 Annual Report*; Skandia AFS: Stockholm, Sweden, 1995.

16. Edvinsson, L. Developing intellectual capital at Skandia. Long Range Plann. **1997**, *30*(3), 366–373.

17. Peters, T. *Liberation Management: Necessary Disorganization for the Nanosecond Nineties*; Alfred A. Knopf: New York, 1992.

18. Kaplan, R.S.; Norton, D.P. The balanced scorecard—Measures that drive performance. Harvard Bus. Rev **1992**, *70*(1), 71–91.

19. Prusak, L. Managing Principal, IBM Global Services, Consulting Group Presentation to the Conference Board Paper Presented at the 1998 Conference on Knowledge Management and Organizational Learning Chicago, IL April, 16, 1998.

20. Senge, P.M. *The Fifth Discipline: The Art and Practice of the Learning Organization*; Doubleday/Currency: New York, 1990.

21. Davenport, T.H.; Prusak, L. *Working Knowledge: How Organizations Manage What They Know*; Harvard Business School Press: Woborn, MA, 1998.

22. Nonaka, I.; Takeuchi, H. *The Knowledge—Creating Company: How Japanese Companies Create the Dynamics of Innovation*; Oxford University Press: New York, 1995.

23. Keen, P.G.W.; Tan, M. Knowledge fusion: a framework for extending the rigor and relevance of knowledge management. Int. J. Knowl. Manage. **2007**, October–December *3*(4), 1–17.

24. Fishkin, J. KM and OL from an IT perspective: A presentation to the 2001 Conference Board Conference The 2001 Knowledge Management/Organizational Learning Conference: Convergence, Application, and Infrastructure New York May, 3–4, 2000.

25. O'Dell, C.; Grayson, C.J. *If Only We Knew What We Know: The Transfer of Internal Knowledge and Best Practice*; American Productivity & Quality Center: Houston, TX, 1998.

26. Denning, S. *What is Knowledge Management? (A Background Paper to the World Development Report 1998)*, World Bank: Washington, DC, 1998; Available at http://www.stevedenning.com/Find_what_is_km.html.

27. Drew, S. Building knowledge management into strategy: making sense of a new perspective. Long Range Plann. **1999**, March *32*(1), 130–136.

28. Wenger, E.C.; Snyder, W.M. Communities of practice: The organizational frontier (a new business management aid). Harvard Bus. Rev. **2000**, January *78*(1), 139–146.

29. Denning, S. *The Springboard, How Storytelling Ignites Action in Knowledge-Era Organizations*; Elsevier: New York, 2001.

30. Brown, J.S.; Denning, S.; Groh, K.; Prusak, L. *Storytelling in Organizations: How Narrative and Storytelling are Transforming 21st Century Management*; Butterworth Heinemann: New York, 2004.

31. TFPL. *Knowledge Strategies—Corporate Strategies*, TFPL: London, U.K., 2001; [TFLPs Fourth International CKO Summit]; Available at http://www.tfpl.org.

32. Ponzi, L.J. The intellectual structure and interdisciplinary breadth of knowledge management: A bibliometric study of its early stage of development. Scientometrics **2002**, *55*(2), 259–272.

33. Ruggles, R.L., III. The State of the notion: knowledge management in practice. Calif. Manage. Rev. **1998**, *40* (Spring), 80–89.

34. *Wildermen, J. Knowledge Management: Moving from Academic Concepts to Fundamental Business Practice*; Conn. InfoEdge Inc. for the Gartner Group: Stamford, CT, 1999.

35. Malhotra, Y. Why knowledge management systems fail: Enablers and constraints of knowledge management in human enterprises. In *Knowledge Management: Lessons Learned: What Works and What Doesn't*; Koenig, M., Srikantaiah, T.K., Eds.; Information Today for the American Society for Information Science and Technology: Medford NJ, 2000; 91.

36. Koenig, M.E.D. KM moves beyond the organization. Inform. Serv. Use **2005**, *25*(2), 87–93.

37. Abrahamson, E. Managerial fashion. Acad. Manage. Rev. **1996**, *21*(1), 254–285.

38. Ponzi, L.J.; Koenig, M.E.D. Knowledge management: another management fad?. Inform. Res. **2002**, *8*(1), 8 (Online Journal). Available at http://informationr.net/ir/8–1/paper145.html.

BIBLIOGRAPHY

1. Davenport, T. Prusak, L. *What's the Big Idea?*, Harvard Business School Press: Boston, MA, 2003.

2. Davenport, T.H. Prusak, L. *Working Knowledge: How Organizations Manage What They Know*, Harvard Business School Press: Woborn, MA, 1992.

3. Davis, S.; Botkin, J. The coming of knowledge-based business. Harvard Bus. Rev. **1994**, (September/October) *72*(5), 165–170.

4. Fahey, L.; Prusak, L. The eleven deadliest sins of knowledge management. Calif. Manage. Rev. **1998**, *40*(3), 265–276.

5. Koenig, M.E.D.; Srikantaiah, K. The business world discovers the assets of librarianship. Inform. Outlook **2002**, *6*(4), 14–18.

6. In *Knowledge Management, Lessons Learned; What Works and What Doesn't*; Koenig, M.E.D., Srikantaiah, T.K., Eds.; Information Today Inc., for the American Society for Information Science and Technology: Medford, NJ, 2004.

7. Rumizen, M.C. *The Complete Idiot's Guide to Knowledge Management*, Prentice Hall: Indianapolis, IN, 2001.

8. Knowledge management. In *Practice: Connections and Context*; Srikantaiah, T.K., Koenig, M.E.D., Eds.; Information Today Inc., for the American Society for Information Science and Technology: Medford, NJ, 2007.

9. Tiwana, A. *The Knowledge Management Toolkit: Practical Techniques for Building a Knowledge Management System*, Prentice Hall: Upper Saddle River, NJ, 2000.

Knowledge Organization System Standards

Stella G. Dextre Clarke
Information Consultant, Oxfordshire, U.K.

Abstract

This entry presents an overview of the standards for different types of knowledge organization system (KOS). Their development history and the principles within them are described. Standards for thesauri receive most attention, since other types of KOS are less standardized. The arrival of the Internet, enabling simultaneous access to multiple disparate systems and resources, caused a major reorientation of standardization efforts in the last decade, towards interoperability goals. Current initiatives address two main needs: interoperability between KOSs, and data exchange between one vocabulary application and another. The prospects for bringing the standards together are discussed.

INTRODUCTION

After considering the basic definitions of knowledge organization systems (KOSs) and standards, this entry is structured chronologically. First it deals with thesaurus standards in the twentieth century, then standards for other types of KOS in the same century, after which it moves on to developments in the twenty-first century. The principles embodied in the standards are described, and the reasons for a change of emphasis at the turn of the century. The prospects for bringing the differing standards together are briefly discussed, before conclusions are drawn.

WHAT IS A KNOWLEDGE ORGANIZATION SYSTEM?

Gail Hodge's explanation (p. 1)[1] is widely quoted:

> The term *knowledge organization systems* is intended to encompass all types of schemes for organizing information and promoting knowledge management. Knowledge organization systems include classification and categorization schemes that organize materials at a general level, subject headings that provide more detailed access, and authority files that control variant versions of key information such as geographic names and personal names. Knowledge organization systems also include highly structured vocabularies, such as thesauri, and less traditional schemes, such as semantic networks and ontologies. Because KOS are mechanisms for organizing information, they are at the heart of every library, museum, and archive.

To this it is worth adding that the most common reason for organizing information is so that you can find it again. Thus information retrieval is a key motivation for the design and application of KOSs, and a driver for most of the relevant standards.

In this entry, most attention will be given to thesauri, because for them we have well-developed standards with a good user base. The standardization scenario for classification schemes, subject heading schemes, and name authority lists will be discussed in less detail. Semantic networks and ontology standards will be mentioned only in passing, partly because they are dealt with elsewhere in this encyclopedia, and partly because they may have functions other than knowledge organization or information retrieval.

WHY STANDARDIZE?

According to BS 0, *A standard for standards* [[2], Part 1 p. 4], a standard is a "document, established by consensus and approved by a recognized body, that provides, for common and repeated use, rules, guidelines, or characteristics for activities or their results, aimed at the achievement of the optimum degree of order in a given context." Important benefits are said by the same source to be "improvement of the suitability of products (including services) and processes for their intended purposes, prevention of barriers to trade and facilitation of technological cooperation."

But not everyone agrees on the need for standards. Ralph Waldo Emerson is usually credited with the famous line in support of innovation: "If a man write a better book, preach a better sermon, or make a better mousetrap than his neighbour, tho' he build his house in the woods, the world will make a beaten path to his door." Thus progress in all fields requires that innovators continually enhance and differentiate their products, sometimes in contravention of the norms. On the other hand, conformity with standards often makes it easier for a new component to plug into an existing assembly, where it will be understood and accepted by existing users. This tension between

Encyclopedia of Library and Information Sciences, Fourth Edition DOI: 10.1081/E-ELIS4-120044538
Copyright © 2017 by Taylor & Francis. All rights reserved.

Knowledge Management–
Law Librarianship

innovation and standardization can be seen throughout the history of KOS development, with no end in sight.

For KOS development and use, the potential advantages of standards compliance include

- Good practice guidance speeds up the development process.
- Off-the-shelf software may be available for building and maintaining KOSs.
- KOS-savvy users will understand the conventions used in format and display.
- Systems administrators and developers may find it easier to implement KOSs in applications such as search engines, cataloging, and content management systems.
- Searches across multiple systems, networks, and resources are much easier if the same indexing language applies to all of them.

The advantages of departing from the standards can include

- Opportunity to meet special user requirements in a particular domain.
- Opportunity to exploit a new technology that needs a different sort of vocabulary.
- Freedom to use existing vocabulary construction software that fails to comply with the standards.
- Untrained users may be more comfortable using a product that does not embody sophisticated conventions—even if performance is inferior.

Plainly there are pros and cons. This entry will show that in some respects the standards are widely taken up; in other respects diversity reigns.

THESAURUS STANDARDS IN THE TWENTIETH CENTURY

Prehistory

A standard rarely falls from a clear blue sky. The story usually starts with an exemplar of some new form of technology; then other specimens appear; then the need to standardize is perceived; then work begins to obtain consensus on the required features of future specimens. Sometimes one of the early exemplars is so widely received that it is adopted as an ad hoc standard. In all cases consensus is vital to ensure take-up of the eventual standard.

In the case of thesauri, original development was stimulated around the time of the Second World War by society's need (especially in the scientific and business arenas) to store and retrieve increasing volumes of documentary resources. While some researchers and

practitioners continued to pin their faith on classification, especially the emerging ideas for faceted classification, other pioneers were attempting term-based indexing approaches. Thus the systems of Uniterms and Zatocoding were developed by Mortimer Taube and Calvin Mooers respectively. N. Roberts[3] provides an excellent account of their work, together with that of Luhn, Bernier, Crane, Whelan, Joyce, Needham, and others in the late 1940s and through most of the 1950s. All used the term "thesaurus," but none had come up with a fully satisfactory working model.

The first fully operational thesaurus, according to Krooks and Lancaster[4] as well as Roberts,[3] was developed for the E. I. Du Pont Nemours and Co., Inc. in the United States. Stemming from this model a succession of vocabularies was developed in the ensuing decade, the most influential being the *Thesaurus of Engineering and Scientific Terms (TEST)*[5] in 1967. According to Aitchison and Dextre Clarke[6] *TEST* embodied most of the standard features visible in alphabetically organized thesauri for the next 30 years. Apart from the thesaurus itself, Appendix 1 of *TEST* gave a set of rules and conventions for thesauri that formed the basis of the first national and international standards, and are still traceable in today's versions of these. (For a synopsis of these, see "Principles embodied in the thesaurus standards" on page 4.) The rules have subsequently been augmented somewhat for techniques not used in *TEST*, such as facet analysis or classified displays.

Early Guidelines

But before the "official" standards were issued, several other sets of guidelines were published by bodies influential in the information management research community. According to Krooks and Lancaster,[4] these included

- Committee on Scientific and Technical Information (COSATI) *Guidelines for the development of information retrieval thesauri* (1967).[7]
- Educational Resources Information Center of the US Department of Education (ERIC) *Rules for thesaurus preparation* (1969).[8]
- United Nations Educational, Scientific and Cultural Organization (UNESCO) *Guidelines for the establishment and development of monolingual scientific and technical thesauri for information retrieval* (1970, revised 1971).[9]

Study of these guidelines suggests that the authors were often aware of each other's efforts. Commonly the examples used in one of them are borrowed in some of the others. (See Krooks and Lancaster[4] for an analysis of the sharing of examples.)

Notably absent from all of them is any guidance for multilingual situations.

Knowledge Management–
Law Librarianship

National and International Standards Emerge

In 1972, the German Standard 1463 was published, followed in 1974 by publication of both the international standard ISO 2788 *Documentation—Guidelines for the establishment and development of monolingual thesauri*[10] and the American national standard ANSI Z39.19 *American National Standard Guidelines for thesaurus structure, construction and use.*[11] All of these documents drew heavily on the already published guidelines and milestone thesauri described above. And all were broadly compatible with each other. ISO 2788 was then widely adopted as a national standard in countries such as Britain, Canada, France, Germany, and Spain. In some cases the national standard incorporated adaptations such as translation into the national language. For example the British Standard BS 5723 based on ISO 2788 and published in 1979 incorporated additional examples and procedures for dealing with compound terms (but when the 1985 editions of ISO 2788 and BS 5723 were published, they had become identical).

Interestingly, the 1974 edition of ISO 2788 acknowledged that a thesaurus could be defined either in terms of its structure or its function, as follows:

- In terms of function, a thesaurus is a terminological control device used in translating from the natural language of documents, indexers, or users into a more constrained "system language."
- In terms of structure, a thesaurus is a controlled and dynamic vocabulary of semantically and generically related terms which covers a specific domain of knowledge.

Although these definitions have been revised in later editions, and the house rules of most standards bodies nowadays frown on such a dual definition, most thesaurus practitioners today would recognise the validity of the basic principles behind the words, and the importance of clarifying what a thesaurus is *for* as well as what is in it.

It was not until 1985 that ISO 5964 *Documentation—Guidelines for the establishment and development of multilingual thesauri*[12] came out, the first standard to deal with cross-language issues. It followed the same principles and conventions as ISO 2788, but extended them and provided practical examples of how to deal with the complexities when exact matches between the scope of terms in different languages are hard to find. ISO 5964 too has been adopted as a national standard in several countries. BS 6723, for example, is identical to ISO 5964.

Sector Specific Standards

All of the national and international standards are of the "guide" type rather than the "specification" type. That is to say, they give broad and general information about a subject, rather than setting out detailed requirements with procedures for checking conformity to the requirements. (See BS 0[2] for more discussion of types of standards.) They are not backed by legislation that requires anyone to follow them in whole or in part. And they allow considerable room for discretion on the part of users, with no bar on optional extension. In practice, few published thesauri abide by the standards in every detail, and many have additional features compatible with the spirit of the standards. Sometimes one particular thesaurus enjoys such popularity in a given sector that its variant features become "standard" for all other thesauri in the same sector.

For example, the vocabulary *Medical Subject Headings (MeSH)*[13] has become a classic in the medical field. The first edition was published in 1960, well before *TEST* had established the thesaurus rules and conventions. Nowadays *MeSH* is often considered to be a thesaurus, even though it began life as a subject headings scheme and departs significantly from the thesaurus standards. One of its key features is a set of "Tree structures" with an elaborate expressive notation which is not required by the standards. (For example, the concept of Meningitis is represented by the notation C10.228.228.507, and that of Bacterial meningitis by C10.228.228.507.280). Later in the 1960s and 1970s Elsevier built its own medical vocabulary *Master List of Medical Terms (MALIMET)* in a completely different style. Such was the popularity of *MeSH* and the pressure from users that when *MALIMET* was overhauled in 1988, one of the major enhancements was incorporation of a notation comparable to that of *MeSH*, and the vocabulary was renamed *EMTREE: The Life Science Thesaurus.*[14]

Another trend-setter is the *Art & Architecture Thesaurus (AAT)*[15] first published in 1990 on behalf of the Getty Art History Information Program. Its distinctive features include the rigorous application of facets, and the use of "guide terms" (rather than node labels as advocated by the standards) to structure the extensive hierarchies. The *AAT* has been hugely influential in its sector, adopted and adapted by countless museums and galleries around the world, where facets and guide terms are accepted as the norm.

Popular vocabularies like *MeSH* and the *AAT*, perhaps also the *Thesaurus of ERIC Descriptors*[16] in the educational field and *Macrothesaurus*[17] for industrial and economic development are often considered in their particular sectors as standards in their own right.

Successive Updates

ISO 2788-1974 was updated in 1986. Some of the changes were cosmetic, such as collecting up all the definitions, abbreviations, and other conventions previously scattered through the text, into separate clauses at the start. Original content (not foreseen in *TEST*) was added on how to

Knowledge Management–
Law Librarianship

organize systematic displays, especially using facet analysis, and more examples of all kinds of displays were incorporated. Another significant substantive change was to adopt the rules for compound terms that first appeared in BS 5723:1979. Filling 32 pages rather than just 13, the 1986 edition[18] is altogether more helpfully laid out and more definitive in its recommendations.

Z39.19 was updated twice in the last century—in 1980 and again in 1993. The foreword to the 1993 edition[19] explicitly acknowledges that successive updates have built on the precursor guidelines mentioned above as well as the two editions of ISO 2788. This tendency towards convergence is reassuring for the user community of any of the standards.

Principles Embodied in the Thesaurus Standards

As explained above, the basic principles were set out in Appendix 1 of *TEST*. Over the decades they have been refined, augmented, and articulated in different ways, but the following essentials have survived:

- In a thesaurus, each concept is represented by a "preferred term" or "descriptor" (although optionally a language-independent code or notation may be used as the unique, unambiguous identifier of a concept). Each term may have only one meaning.
- Since in normal language several different terms may often be used to represent the same concept, each of these "non-preferred terms" or "nondescriptors" is provided as an entry point, guiding the user to the corresponding preferred term. A formal "equivalence relationship" is established between the preferred and non-preferred term.
- In a multilingual thesaurus, all the languages should have equal status and no language should be regarded as dominant. As ISO 5964 puts it in Clause 12.2, "every preferred term in one language should be matched by a corresponding term in the other language(s)."
- Since in normal language the same term may often take several different meanings, a means of disambiguation is necessary. A qualifier in parentheses should be added to the ambiguous term before it can be admitted as a preferred or non-preferred term. ISO 2788:1974 gives the example of thesaurus terms "beams (structural)" and "beams (electromagnetic)" to distinguish between two concepts that could be described by the same natural language term. The qualifier is treated as an integral part of the term.
- Where further clarification of the underlying concept is needed, a scope note may be provided. The scope note does not form part of the term. From ISO 2788:1974 a scope note example for "copper alloys" is "alloys in which copper is the principal constituent."

- As well as the equivalence relationships mentioned above, a thesaurus should explicitly recognize hierarchical and associative relationships between concepts.
- The hierarchical relationship is often called broader/narrower, and most commonly applies when the two concepts are generically related, for example "dogs" are generically related to "mammals," since every dog is a kind of mammal. The 1974 edition of ISO 2788 also admits some part–whole relations as hierarchical, for example between "botany" and "biology," where botany is a part rather than a kind of biology. The 1986 edition further admits as hierarchical the instance relationship, for example between "Himalayas" and "Mountain regions." (The Himalayas are neither a kind nor a part of a mountain region, but do represent an instance.)
- All of the standards show signs of difficulty in defining the associative relationship. Often it has a negative definition, as any relationship that does not qualify as hierarchical or equivalence. (For example, an associative relationship may be established between "teaching" and "training," or between "transportation" and vehicles.") But underlying this fuzziness is a clear understanding that the function of this relationship is to guide users to terms that could usefully supplement or replace the one they first thought of. The subjectivity of this function causes difficulties in setting hard and fast rules. Successive editions of the standards provide increasingly copious examples, and further elucidation is provided in Milstead[20] and Dextre Clarke.[21]
- Thesaurus displays should follow well-established conventions for scope note and relationship tags, the most widely used ones in English being SN (Scope Note), USE (Use), UF (Use For or Used For), BT (Broader Term), NT (Narrower Term) and RT (Related Term). Use of these conventions results in entries of the following form:

  Age discrimination
  SN: Unfair treatment of people on the basis of their age, especially where it concerns older people.
  UF: Ageism
  BT: Discrimination
  NT: Age discrimination at work
  RT: Older people

French and German equivalent tags are established in ISO 5964.

Differences between the Standards

It is hard to find great differences in principle, apart from the enhancements at each update. Successive editions of Z39.19 have more pages and are organized differently from ISO 2788 and its variants. But the most noticeable substantive differences are:

Knowledge Management–
Law Librarianship

- Z39.19 tends to be more prescriptive. For example, the 1993 edition gives rules for reciprocal scope notes, and for dealing with trademarks, neither of which are mentioned in ISO 2788.
- Unlike ISO 2788, Z39.19 has an index, a more elaborate table of contents, and a more extensive glossary.
- There are small differences in the definition and recommendations for handling compound terms.
- There is a difference of emphasis concerning the various forms of display recommended.
- Z39.19-1993 makes no mention of facet analysis or any form of classified display.
- Z39.19 has been updated more often.

Weaknesses in the Standards at the Turn of the Century

Inspired by the ground-breaking thesauri of the 1960s, the national and international standards were conceived in a print-oriented era and had barely adapted to exploit the opportunities of the electronic medium. Z39.19-1993 was the furthest ahead, incorporating a clause on computer-based thesaurus management systems. But all of them were written for a print-oriented audience and none of them had any advice on formats or protocols for data exchange. The only available standard applicable to data exchange formats was ISO 2709:1996 *Information and documentation. Format for information interchange*,[22] based on the MARC format developed and maintained by the U.S. Library of Congress.

The MARC format was commonly used by libraries, as its principal application was for exchange of bibliographic records. But the module for "authority records" (i.e., for thesauri and other types of authority list)[23] inherited features required for bibliographic data, making it cumbersome when applied to thesauri. MARC was (and still is) a sensible format to use when exchanging data with users of library management systems already adapted to the bibliographic format, but tends to impede exchanges with any other user community. Something else was needed for wider applicability.

A second form of weakness lay in the extent of implementation. Most respectable published thesauri in the 1990s claimed to follow one or other of the standards, but on close inspection most of them departed from the standards to some degree, for example in following the rules for compound terms. Comparison of almost any selection of published thesauri shows huge disparities in general layout and philosophy. In the 1990s, furthermore, a breed of vocabularies called "taxonomies" was emerging, a clear sign that the thesaurus model was proving either unsatisfactory or just not well enough understood for widespread adoption.

Plainly all of the national and international standards for thesauri needed to be overhauled.

STANDARDS FOR OTHER TYPES OF KOS IN THE TWENTIETH CENTURY

The reason is not entirely clear, but somehow the urge for national or international standards has barely extended to other types of KOS. Certainly there has been some standardization, but within the user communities of a particular KOS rather than across the boundaries. The situation with respect to ontologies is described in another entry of this encyclopedia, and the present discussion will be limited to classification schemes, subject heading schemes, and name authority lists.

Classification Schemes

The use of classification in organizing knowledge goes back to at least the third century BC, well before the establishment of the first national standards bodies. The *Dewey Decimal Classification* (*DDC*), probably the most widely used classification scheme today, was first published in 1876. By the end of the last century it had seen 21 printed editions in English, plus 13 abridged editions, plus many translations into other languages, plus regular electronic updates; and we should not forget the countless local adaptations made by libraries with special collections. Within its community, the *DDC* is often seen as a standard in its own right, despite the coexistence and potential conflicts of so many versions.

The *Universal Decimal Classification* (*UDC*) and the *Library of Congress Classification* (*LCC*) too have august histories, with multiple versions in diverse libraries. Both are discussed elsewhere in this encyclopedia. Suffice it for present purposes to note that some members of the consortium that maintains and publishes the *UDC* are national standards bodies, and so the *UDC* has the status of a national standard in countries such as Spain and the United Kingdom.

And there is no way of counting the diversity of other classification schemes in use today, each with its own adaptations for particular subject areas, contexts, and user communities. There are usually very good reasons for differentiation. While in the past some dreamt of a scheme so universal that it could be applied to every library, that dream is now largely discredited.

If we accept that there will always be a need for different ways of organizing subjects, could we at least agree on the principles of classification, to which all the schemes would conform? Even here there are difficulties, stemming from the diverse origins of the different schemes. For example, the ideas of faceted classification expounded by S. R. Ranganathan and H. E. Bliss, further developed by the Classification Research Group and embodied in today's *Colon Classification* and the second edition of the *Bliss Classification*, are widely accepted as very sound and full of promise for electronic applications. The

Knowledge Management–
Law Librarianship

maintenance agencies of the major schemes such as *DDC* and *UDC* have for years been adopting what they can of faceted principles into successive updates. But a practical problem stems from the huge volume of existing collections that have been indexed with earlier editions of the schemes. The user libraries face difficulties and much expense in switching to a new way of doing things, however superior in principle, because it becomes more cumbersome to retrieve items in their heritage collections. Hence much resistance to changes that are too sweeping, even when those changes bring convergence with other schemes.

Subject Heading Schemes

The scenario for subject heading schemes is dominated by the very widely used *Library of Congress Subject Headings (LCSH)*. Arguably *LCSH* is the standard, leaving nothing more to be said. However, few libraries use the whole of the *LCSH*; most add headings devised for their own audiences/collections; and not a few may be lax in applying the *LCSH* rules for combining headings in precoordinated strings. (For those unfamiliar with the different types of KOS, the provision of precoordinated strings is one of the key features distinguishing a subject heading scheme from the other types. Although in recent years LCSH has adopted some of the display conventions that apply to thesauri, its strength is still the provision of subject headings, whether uncoordinated or precoordinated.) In practice, diversity abounds. It is another illustration of the general observation that when a standard is not backed up by some legislation or monitoring authority, there is always a tendency to diverge in practice.

Name Authority Lists

Rather than national or international standards, again what we see are standardizing initiatives within particular communities. In some cases, such as the German National Library's *Personnamendatei (PND)*[24] the approach has simply been to build an authority list with such a wide scope that it becomes a standard in its own right, without needing accreditation by an external standards body. In other cases guidelines have been drawn up to serve common needs when an organization is developing its own authority lists. These include

- IFLA *guidelines for authority records and references*,[25] serving library associations worldwide.
- ICA/CDS *International Standard Archival Authority record for corporate bodies, persons, and families*,[26] for archivists.
- *NCA rules for the construction of personal, place, and corporate names*,[27] again for archivists but extending to place names as well as people and organizations.

All of them aim to combat the confusion that arises when one entity (a place, person, organization, etc.) is known by several different names. All support unique identification, usually by a single consistent name, and enable linkage of variant and alternative names to the appropriate entity.

THE TWENTY-FIRST CENTURY BRINGS CHANGE

The arrival of the desktop computer in the 1990s had exposed weaknesses in the standards, as well as opportunities for more effective exploitation of KOSs. The arrival of the Internet highlighted those opportunities and brought a step-change in the need for interoperability, both between one vocabulary and another, and between vocabularies and their applications. The scenario at the turn of the century was one in which new styles of vocabulary were bursting on the scene, new forms of technology inspired innovative applications, new user expectations were driving performance, and widespread budgetary restrictions imposed a new requirement for end-users to take on (or manage without) the tasks previously undertaken by trained intermediaries. Networking was the name of the game, driving the demand for interoperability.

Whereas the twentieth-century standards had addressed issues affecting the construction and use of any one KOS, interoperability was now needed to help us overcome the barriers between one KOS and another. A 2006 state-of-the-art review on *Terminology Services and Technology* from the Joint Information Systems Committee (JISC)[28] highlights two key requirements for KOSs (see pp. 7 and 8, respectively):

- Mapping is a key requirement for semantic interoperability in heterogeneous environments.
- Interoperability requires commonly agreed standards and protocols.

The challenge and the opportunity was recognised, not only by the committees responsible for the existing KOS standards, but by some new players in the standards world, notably the World Wide Web Consortium (W3C). The ensuing initiatives will be described in these two groups:

Emerging standards for data exchange	Evolution of existing KOS standards
ADL Thesaurus Protocol	IFLA Guidelines for multilingual thesauri
Zthes	ANSI/NISO Z39.19-2005
SKOS (Simple Knowledge Organization Systems)	BS 8723
	ISO NP 25964

Knowledge Management–
Law Librarianship

EMERGING STANDARDS FOR DATA EXCHANGE

ADL Thesaurus Protocol

The Alexandria Digital Library (ADL) was one of the first to take up the challenge of developing a protocol[29] to support navigating and live querying of online thesauri. It is a lightweight protocol for accessing monolingual thesauri, especially those modeled on ANSI/NISO Z39.19. It is based on XML and the Hypertext Transport Protocol (HTTP), the basic transport mechanism for the World Wide Web. The protocol defines XML structures for describing the thesaurus as a whole as well as "brief" and "fuller" term formats. The brief format consists of preferred or non-preferred term. The fuller format comprises term; notes (with a specification of type); hierarchical (BT/NT), associative (RT), and equivalence (USE/UF) relationships. A list element provides a wrapper for a list of terms, and a hierarchy element a wrapper for presenting a hierarchy of terms. Wrapper elements also exist for all interactions and an error element allows for the reporting of errors to the client. The following stateless services are defined

- Getting general information about the thesaurus.
- Downloading a list of all terms.
- Searching the thesaurus using full term, keyword, or regular expression matching.
- Getting terms higher or lower than the current term in the hierarchy, to a specified number of levels.

These provide convenient methods for getting information for hierarchical displays or for extending searches to include all narrower terms. HTTP bindings for the abstract protocol are explained and examples given, facilitating implementation as a Web service.

Zthes

Zthes[30] was originally developed as an application profile of Z39.50 *Application Service Definition and Protocol Specification*[31] to enable exchange of thesaurus data. At its heart is a model which represents a thesaurus as a database of interlinked terms (in contrast with the SKOS model, which is based on concepts rather than on terms). Thus each individual term in a thesaurus, whether preferred or non-preferred, is represented by a record in the database. Term records consist of an initial part describing the term itself (with information such as its unique identifier, scope note, etc.), together with subrecords (that is, named sections within the main record) briefly describing related terms. The primary means of navigation from one term to another is by searching for the unique identifiers of the terms related to the first one.

The Zthes abstract model can be represented in XML. A single Zthes document in XML format consists of a wrapper element plus a sequence of term elements, each of which represents a single thesaurus term composed of the elements described in the abstract model.

Additional specifications show how Zthes-compliant thesauri may be accessed using the Search and Retrieve by URL (SRU) protocol.[32] This is a Web-based information retrieval protocol designed as a successor to the older protocol, Z39.50. It provides a simple means for expressing search requests, encoding them in URLs, sending them to servers and getting back results in a well-defined XML format.

The Zthes Profile for SRU provides the set of specifications prescribing the use of SRU to navigate remote thesauri. An SRU server conforming to this profile can expose its thesaurus to any conforming client, enabling its use in many applications.

Development of the Zthes model and specifications has been heavily reliant on inputs from interested organizations and individuals, without the backing of a standards authority. The outputs are freely available on the Web.

SKOS

Since this section was written, the 2005 Working Drafts of the SKOS Core Vocabulary Specification have been superseded by 2008 versions. More information is available at http://www.w3.org/TR/skos-reference/. The name SKOS[33–36] refers to a program of work on developing specifications and standards to support KOS use within the framework of the Semantic Web. SKOS aims to work for a wide range of KOSs, such as thesauri, classification schemes, subject heading systems, and taxonomies. It does not deal with their construction, just with data sharing and exchange. As appropriate for the Semantic Web, the SKOS specifications are built upon the Resource Description Framework (RDF), which in turn is an application of XML.

Originally funded by the European Commission as part of its Semantic Web Advanced Development (SWAD) project in 2002–2004, SKOS is now backed by the Semantic Web Deployment Working Group of the W3C. As a standards organization with worldwide membership, W3C applies rigorous consultation and approval procedures, aiming to bring SKOS forward from a set of working drafts to the eventual status of W3C Recommendation. Unlike ISO and its family of national standards bodies, W3C makes its standards and other documentation freely available over the Web.

SKOS is designed as a modular and extensible family of languages. The main components are as follows:

- *SKOS Core* is the basic specification of a common data model for sharing and linking KOS. In contrast with Zthes, it is based on a concept-centric view of the vocabulary, where primitive objects are not terms, but abstract concepts represented by terms. Development work was substantially influenced by BS 8723-2,

Knowledge Management– Law Librarianship

resulting in a good level of compatibility between the underlying models for both of these. The first Public Working Draft of SKOS Reference[35] was published on January 25, 2008. It is accompanied by several guidance documents, lists of use cases, etc.

- *SKOS Mapping* will address interoperability by providing a vocabulary to express matching of concepts from one concept scheme to another. This part of SKOS was developed in the SWAD-Europe project and has not yet been adopted by W3C, but is maintained informally by SKOS editors.
- *SKOS Extensions* is intended to provide for features of KOSs beyond the most basic ones. For example it will support subclasses of the thesaurus hierarchical relationship (commonly known as BT/NT) such as generic, partitive, and instantial (commonly known as BTG/NTG, BTP/NTP, BTI/NTI, respectively). Like SKOS Mapping, active development of this part awaits completion of SKOS Core as a W3C Recommendation.
- *SKOS API* is a Web Service Application Programming Interface (API), designed to provide access to thesauri and other simple KOSs via the Web.[36] It defines a core set of operations for programmatically accessing and querying a thesaurus. While intended for Web service calls, the API itself remains independent of such concrete implementation details. It could also be capable of adaptation to formats other than SKOS Core.

A recurring question in discussions on SKOS development work is the depth to which SKOS should attempt to model the different vocabulary types. If the modeling is relatively superficial, it is easier to accommodate a wide range of KOS types and hence allow easy data exchange within a wide community. If the modeling goes deeper and imposes semantic constraints on encoded data, it will enable more powerful reasoning about the type of information indexed with or retrieved by the KOS. At present the weight of opinion seems to favor the former approach, in order to keep things as simple as possible.

EVOLUTION OF EXISTING KOS STANDARDS

IFLA Guidelines for Multilingual Thesauri

Although the International Federation of Library Associations (IFLA) had never published its own thesaurus standard, it has taken a long-standing interest in the international standards. In 2002 it set up a working group to update and enhance the content of ISO 5964. A draft report[37] was circulated for comment in April 2005, carrying a large number of up-to-date multilingual examples to supplement the existing ones. Largely the draft builds

on the long-established principles of ISO 2788 and ISO 5964, but one radical departure is to define a "nonsymmetrical thesaurus" as a "multilingual thesaurus in which the number of descriptors in each language is not necessarily the same and also the way descriptors are related to each other can be different for the different languages." This contrasts with the approach of BS 8723-4, which considers such a situation as a case of mapping between two or more different thesauri.

The target date for publication of the final version of the guidelines is 2009. There is every prospect the outcome will feed into the development process for ISO 25964.

ANSI/NISO Z39.19-2005

In November 1999 National Information Standards Organization (NISO) organized a workshop to investigate "the desirability and feasibility of developing a standard for electronic thesauri." Among its conclusions were that a new standard "should provide for a broader group of controlled vocabularies than those that fit the standard definition of 'thesaurus'," and that, "the primary concern is with shareability (interoperability), rather than with construction or display." (See full report at http://www.niso.org/news/events_workshops/thes99rprt.html).

Following the meeting an advisory group was assembled and the eventual outcome was publication of the 2005 edition of Z39.19, *Guidelines for the construction, format, and management of monolingual controlled vocabularies*.[38] The change of title reflects its extension to cover lists (such as drop-down lists), synonym rings, and taxonomies, as well as thesauri. Some other significant changes were:

- Make the text clearer for untrained users, giving the reasons behind the rules and more explanation of the basic principles of vocabulary control.
- Include display formats for electronic as well as print media.
- Cater for browsing and navigation applications as well as keyword searching.
- Consider Web applications as well as the traditional ones.

Despite the original aspiration to address interoperability concerns, however, the revised standard stops short of embarking on cross-database search issues, multilingual situations, or data exchange formats and protocols.

BS 8723: Structured Vocabularies for Information Retrieval

The international standards ISO 2788 and ISO 5964 (which are identical to BS 5723 and BS 6723) came up for their quinquennial review in 2000. Members of the BSI

Knowledge Management–
Law Librarianship

committee took the view that revision was long overdue. Rather than attempt to establish an international working group, they opted to work first on the British Standards, which would later be offered up to the international community. And so work began on BS 8723, requiring a complete overhaul of the monolingual and multilingual standards, bringing them together and addressing the interoperability needs discussed above.

Over the next 7 years, the standard was published progressively in five parts as follows:[38–43]

BS 8723: Structured vocabularies for information retrieval—Guide
Part 1: Definitions, symbols, and abbreviations (2005)
Part 2: Thesauri (2005)
Part 3: Vocabularies other than thesauri (2007)
Part 4: Interoperability between vocabularies (2007)
Part 5: Exchange formats and protocols for interoperability (2008)

Part 2 is effectively an update of ISO 2788 and BS 5723, covering monolingual thesauri and adding:

- Clearer guidance on applying facet analysis to thesauri.
- Some changes to the perennially challenging rules for compound terms.
- More guidance on managing thesaurus development and maintenance.
- A functional specification for software to manage thesauri.
- A general expectation that people will use the thesaurus electronically, as well as in print.

Apart from the rules for compound terms, the principles in the earlier standards remain intact, only they have been reexpressed to apply more intelligibly in the electronic era.

Part 3 covers completely new ground, for the following vocabulary types:

- Classification schemes
- Business classification schemes for records management
- Taxonomies
- Subject heading schemes
- Ontologies
- Authority lists

None of these is covered in the same depth as thesauri. The standard does not, for example, explain how to build a new classification scheme. With interoperability needs in mind, the thrust was to compare and contrast the essential elements of each of these vocabulary types. The aim was to provide enough description of these types of tool so that an information technology developer would be able to implement them interoperably with other vocabularies. An exception was made for the clause on taxonomies, which does also incorporate guidance on general good

practice, particularly on the issues around designing and using taxonomies for Web browsing and navigation.

Part 4 deals with mapping between vocabularies. It addresses the common scenario enabled by today's networks, where a query expressed in one vocabulary needs to be applied to multiple resources indexed with a variety of different vocabularies. By treating a multilingual thesaurus as a special case of mapping between vocabularies, it effectively updates ISO 5964 and BS 6723 as well as extending their scope considerably.

Part 5 establishes a data model for monolingual and multilingual thesauri, and also a format based on XML for exchanging data. The model and format provide for all the thesaural features described in Parts 2 and 4—not just the commonly used features but also sophistications such as classified arrangements with facet names and characteristics conveyed in node labels. So much original work had to be done on the model and schema that the final document has number DD 8723-5 and its status is Draft for Development. In line with good practice for XML, a namespace has been established for the XML schema at http://www.bsigroup.com/resources/standards/bs8723/. A development Web site at http://schemas.bs8723.org/ shows examples of encoding as well as providing a discussion forum to encourage user testing and feedback, and transformations between alternative formats.

ISO 25964

Following publication of BS 8723, a project named ISO NP 25964 has been established to adopt it as an International Standard.[44] The standards bodies of 11 member countries, including the United States, are participating in the work. The target date for completion is late 2010. There is every hope that the eventual standard, ISO 25964, will complete the development work begun in BS 8723, integrate inputs from the IFLA Guidelines, and generally bring the whole international community together.

PROSPECTS FOR RESOLVING THE DIFFERENCES BETWEEN STANDARDS

The differences between ISO 2788, ISO 5964, BS 8723, and the forthcoming ISO 25964 are irrelevant for this discussion, since the underlying set of principles is constant. The documents are simply evolving in step with the context in which they are applied. Backwards compatibility is rarely a problem. Comparing this family with ANSI/NISO Z39.19, the main differences are in scope and presentation. Each of them covers some aspects that the other does not, and the content is organized in different ways. Any differences of principle are quite hard to spot. The recommendations for applying facet analysis do differ, and to a lesser degree those for compound terms. In general, however, the areas of conflict are minor and there seems

Knowledge Management–
Law Librarianship

no harm in the coexistence of these standards. Perhaps there is even some benefit, as coexistence allows working groups in different geographical zones to learn from each other and build stepwise on each other's shoulders.

More serious are the differences between the data exchange formats expressed in MARC, Zthes, SKOS, and DD 8723-5. In theory there could be big interoperability gains if everyone would use the same format. But in practice this is very hard to achieve, since each of these corresponds to a different context and set of needs. The future probably lies in developing transformations between these formats, so that a vocabulary expressed in one of them can readily be converted to another.

The biggest challenge of all lies in the coexistence of a huge variety of individual KOSs and types of KOS. Some of these have been around for a very long time, without need of accreditation by any standardizing body, and have large user constituencies. There seems little prospect of bringing them all together under one set of principles and practices. The best hope of overcoming the barriers seems to lie with mapping.

CONCLUSIONS

- At the level of national and international standards bodies, thesauri have attracted more sustained attention than any other form of KOS.
- Several different national and international standards for thesauri coexist, without causing significant compatibility problems.
- For classification schemes, most standards work has been within the user communities of particular schemes, the major challenge being to accommodate successive updates without impeding retrieval of data classified using earlier versions.
- While thesaurus standards in the twentieth century have done much to encourage common approaches to construction, they have not addressed the major semantic interoperability problem inherent in the proliferation of hundreds (perhaps thousands) of different individual KOSs.
- Arrival of the Internet and other networks has highlighted the need for interoperability, both at the semantic level and at the data exchange level. To address these needs, the main approaches now being explored are mapping, for semantic interoperability, and standard formats and protocols for data exchange.
- Initiatives such as SKOS, Zthes, and ADL are now yielding a range of standard formats and protocols.
- The recently published British Standard BS 8723 addresses both the mapping challenge and the exchange format needs, but would benefit from more development work.
- The international project ISO NP 25964 offers the opportunity for participants from the major national standards bodies in 11 countries to take the BS 8723

work forward and integrate contributions in an enhanced international standard for KOS construction, management, and interoperability.

REFERENCES

1. Hodge, G. *Systems of Knowledge Organization for Digital Libraries: Beyond Traditional Authority Files;* Digital Library Federation: Washington, DC, 2000; Available at http://www.clir.org/pubs/reports/pub91/contents.html (accessed February 2008).
2. British Standards Institution. BS 0., *A Standard for Standards*; British Standards Institution: London, 2005; 2 vols.
3. Roberts, N. The pre-history of the information retrieval thesaurus. J. Doc. **1984**, *40*(4), 271–285.
4. Krooks, D.A.; Lancaster, F.W. The evolution of guidelines for thesaurus construction. Libri. **1993**, *43*(4), 326–342.
5. *Thesaurus of Engineering and Scientific Terms (TEST);* Engineers Joint Council and U.S. Department of Defense: New York, 1967.
6. Aitchison, J.; Dextre Clarke, S.G. The thesaurus: a historical viewpoint, with a look to the future. Catalog. Classif. Quart. **2004**, *37*(3/4), 5–21.
7. Sub-panel on Classification and Indexing of Committee on Scientific and Technical Information (COSATI), *Guidelines for the Development of Information Retrieval Thesauri;* COSATI: Washington, DC, 1967.
8. Office of Education. Panel on Educational terminology, *Rules for Thesaurus Preparation;* U.S. Government Printing Office: Washington, DC, 1969.
9. UNESCO, *Guidelines for the Establishment and Development of Monolingual Thesauri for Information Retrieval. CS/WS/500*, 1st revised Ed.; UNESCO: Paris, 1971.
10. International Organization for Standardization, *ISO 2788-1974 Documentation—Guidelines for the Establishment and Development of Monolingual Thesauri*, 1st Ed.; International Organization for Standardization: Geneva, 1974.
11. American National Standards Institute, *ANSI Z39.19-1974 American National Standard Guidelines for Thesaurus Structure, Construction and Use;* American National Standards Institute: New York, 1974.
12. International Organization for Standardization, *ISO 5964-1985. Documentation—Guidelines for the Establishment and Development of Multilingual Thesauri;* International Organization for Standardization: Geneva, 1985.
13. *Medical Subject Headings (MeSH)*, 1st Ed.; National Library of Medicine: Bethesda, MD, 1960.
14. *EMTREE: The Life Science Thesaurus;* Elsevier B.V.: Amsterdam, the Netherlands, 1988; first published.
15. Getty Art History Information Program, *Art & Architecture Thesaurus*, 2nd Ed.; Oxford University Press: Oxford and New York, 1994; 5 Vols. Available at http://www.getty.edu/research/tools/vocabulary/aat/index.html (accessed February 2008).
16. Houston, J.E. *Thesaurus of ERIC descriptors;* 13th Ed Oryx press: Phoenix, AR, 1995; 704. Available at http://www.eric.ed.gov/ERICWebPortal/Home.portal?_nfpb=true&_pageLabel=Thesaurus&_nfls=false (accessed February 2008).
17. Viet, J. *Macrothesaurus for Information Processing in the Field of Economic and Social Development*, 1st Ed.; OECD Development Centre: Paris, 1972.

Knowledge Management– Law Librarianship

18. International Organization for Standardization, *ISO 2788-1986 Documentation—Guidelines for the Establishment and Development of Monolingual Thesauri,* 2nd Ed.; International Organization for Standardization: Geneva, 1986.

19. National Information Standards Organization, *ANSI/NISO Z39.19-1993 Guidelines for the Construction, Format and Management of Monolingual Thesauri*; NISO Press: Bethesda, MD, 1993.

20. Milstead, J.L. Standards for relationships between subject indexing terms. In *Relationships in the Organization of Knowledge*; Bean, C.A., Green, Rebecca, Eds.; Kluwer: Dordrecht, 2001; 53–66.

21. Dextre Clarke, S.G. Thesaural relationships. In *Relationships in the Organization of Knowledge*; Bean, C. A., Green, R., Eds.; Kluwer: Dordrecht, 2001; 37–52.

22. International Organization for Standardization, *ISO 2709:1996 Information and Documentation. Format for Information Interchange;* International Organization for Standardization: Geneva, 1996.

23. US Library of Congress Network Development and MARC Standards Office, *MARC 21 Format for Authority Data;* Library of Congress: Washington, DC, 2000; (with subsequent updates online). Concise version available online at http://www.loc.gov/marc/authority/ (accessed February 2008).

24. German National Library, *Personnamendatei (PND)*, Available at http://de.wikipedia.org/wiki/Personennamendatei (accessed February 2008).

25. IFLA Working Group on GARE Revision, *Guidelines for Authority Records and References*, 2nd Ed.; UBCIM Publications: Munich, 2001; Available at http://www.ifla.org/VII/s13/garr/garr.pdf (accessed February 2008).

26. International Council on Archives, *ISAAR(CPF): International Standard Archival Authority Record for Corporate Bodies, Persons and Families*, 2nd Ed.; International Council of Archives Committee on Descriptive Standards (ICA/CDS): Canberra, 2004; Available at http://www.icacds.org.uk/eng/isaar2ndedn-e_3_1.pdf (accessed February 2008).

27. National Council on Archives, *Rules for the Construction of Personal, Place and Corporate Names;* National Council on Archives, 1997; available at http://www.ncaonline.org.uk/materials/namingrules.pdf (accessed February 2008).

28. Tudhope, D.; Koch, T.; Heery, R. *Terminology Services and Technology: JISC State of the Art Review*, 2006; Sep 15 Final draft for approval ed. JISC; Available at http://www.ukoln.ac.uk/terminology/JISC-review2006.html (accessed February 2008).

29. Janée, G.; Ikeda, S.; Hill, L.L. *The ADL Thesaurus Protocol—Version 1.0*, Available at http://www.alexandria.ucsb.edu/thesaurus/specification.html (accessed February 2008).

30. Taylor, M.; Hammer, S.; LeVan, R.; Lynch, D.; Place, T.; Stevens, P.; Tice, R. *The Zthes Specifications for Thesaurus Representation, Access and Navigation*, 2006; February. Available at http://zthes.z3950.org/ (accessed February 2008).

31. National Information Standards Organization, ANSI/NISO Z39.50-2003. *Information Retrieval: Application Service Definition & Protocol Specification;* NISO Press: Bethesda, MD Also available from the maintenance agency U.S. Library of Congress. Available at http://www.loc.gov/z3950/agency/ (accessed February 2008).

32. US Library of Congress, *SRU: Search/Retrieval via URL;* Library of Congress: Washington, DC Available at http://www.loc.gov/standards/sru/ (accessed February 2008).

33. World Wide Web Consortium, *SKOS Core Guide*, W3C Working Draft November 2005, Available at http://www.w3.org/TR/swbp-skos-core-guide/ (accessed February 2008).

34. World Wide Web Consortium, *SKOS Core Vocabulary Specification*, W3C Working Draft November 2005, Available at http://www.w3.org/TR/skos-reference/ (accessed February 2008).

35. World Wide Web Consortium, *SKOS Simple Knowledge Organization System Reference*, W3C Working Draft January 2008,Available at http://www.w3.org/TR/skos-reference/ (accessed February 2008).

36. World Wide Web Consortium, Information Society Technologies and SWAD Europe, *SKOS API (Simple Knowledge Organization Systems Application Programming Interface)*, Available at http://www.w3.org/2001/sw/Europe/reports/thes/skosapi.html (accessed February 2008).

37. Working Group on Guidelines for Multilingual Thesauri, Classification and Indexing Section, IFLA. *Guidelines for Multilingual Thesauri*, 2005; Available at http://www.ifla.org/VII/s29/pubs/Draft-multilingualthesauri.pdf (accessed February 2008).

38. National Information Standards Organization, *ANSI/NISO Z39.19-2005 Guidelines for the Construction, Format and Management of Monolingual Controlled Vocabularies;* NISO Press: Bethesda, MD, 2005; http://www.niso.org/standards/index.html (accessed February 2008).

39. British Standards Institution, *BS 8723-1:2005 Structured Vocabularies for Information Retrieval—Guide—Definitions, Symbols and Abbreviations*; British Standards Institution: London, 2005; 10.

40. British Standards Institution, *BS 8723-2:2005 Structured vocabularies for information retrieval—Guide—Thesauri;* British Standards Institution: London, 2005; 60.

41. British Standards Institution, *BS 8723-3:2007 Structured Vocabularies for Information Retrieval—Guide—Vocabularies other than Thesauri;* British Standards Institution: London, 2007; 52.

42. British Standards Institution, *BS 8723-4:2007 Structured Vocabularies for Information Retrieval—Guide—Interoperability between Vocabularies;* British Standards Institution: London, 2007; 62.

43. British Standards Institution, *DD 8723-5:2008 Structured Vocabularies for Information Retrieval—Guide—Formats and Protocols for Data Exchange;* British Standards Institution: London, 2008; 60.

44. Dextre Clarke, S.G. Evolution towards ISO 25964: an international standard with guidelines for thesauri and other types of controlled vocabulary. Inform. Wissensch. Prax. **2007**, *58*(8), 441–444.

BIBLIOGRAPHY

(a) KOS Basics

1. Aitchison, J.; Gilchrist, A.; Bawden, D. *Thesaurus Construction and Use: A Practical Manual*, 4th Ed.; Aslib: London, 2000.

Knowledge Management–
Law Librarianship

2. Broughton, V. *Essential Classification*; Facet publishing: London, 2004.

3. Broughton, V. *Essential Thesaurus Construction;* Facet publishing: London, 2006.

4. Will, L. Thesaurus principles and practice [Web Page] 1998. Available at http://www.willpower.demon.co.uk/thesprin. htm (accessed February 2008).

(b) KOS Mapping and Interoperability

1. Doerr, M. Semantic problems of thesaurus mapping. J. Dig. Inform. **2000**, *1*(8), Available at http://journals.tdl.org/jodi/ article/view/jodi-35/32 (accessed February 2008).

2. Landry, P. Multilingual subject access: the linking approach of MACS. Catalog. Classif. Quart. **2004**, *37*(3/4), 177–191.

3. McCulloch, E.; Shiri, A.; Nicholson, D. Challenges and issues in terminology mapping: a digital library perspective. Electron. Libr. **2005**, *23*(6), 671–677.

4. Shiri, A.A.; Revie, C. Thesauri on the Web: current developments and trends. Online Inform. Rev. **2000**, *24*(4), 273–279.

5. Vizine-Goetz, D.; Hickey, C.; Houghton, A.; Thompson, R. Vocabulary mapping for terminology services. J. Digit. Inform. **2004**, *4*(4), Article no. 272, Available at http://jodi. tamu.edu/Articles/v04/i04/Vizine-Goetz/ (accessed February 2008).

6. Zeng, M.L.; Chan, L.M. Metadata interoperability and standardization. a study of methodology. Part I: Achieving interoperability at the schema level. D-Lib. Mag. **2006**, *12*(6), Available at http://www.dlib.org/dlib/june06/chan/06chan. html (accessed February 2008).

7. Zeng, M.L.; Chan, L.M. Metadata interoperability and standardization. a study of methodology. Part II: Achieving interoperability at the record and repository levels. D-Lib. Mag. **2006**, *12*(6), Available at http://www.dlib.org/dlib/ june06/zeng/06zeng.html (accessed February 2008).

Knowledge: Tacit and Explicit

Philippe Baumard
School of Engineering, Stanford University, Stanford, California, U.S.A., and University Paul Cézanne, Aix-en-Provence, France

Abstract
This entry explores the differences between tacit and explicit knowledge. Tacit knowledge is defined as a form of knowing that cannot be expressed. Organizational theory has been particular concerned with tacit knowledge as a part of an effort to identify and utilize the unique knowledge that is distinctive to successful organizations.

The distinction between tacit and explicit knowledge was popularized by the works of Polanyi[1] on personal knowledge. Tacit knowledge is the knowledge that cannot be expressed; it is unknown to the knower, however actionable, either through automatisms (for swimming, in Polanyi's examples), or more or less deliberately. As codification is achieved by means of abstraction, tacit knowledge is usually opposed to explicit knowledge for being "not codified" or "escaping representation." Categorizing knowledge and the act of knowing into different forms is a practice as old as civilizations. The act itself, of declaring that there is a "knowledge" that is *not* embodied in the traits of a ruler, is *not* coming from a god or a mystical source, is an act of culturally forming a civilization. Archaic societies associated knowledge with either a gift of their gods, an unexplainable trait of a mystic ruler (sorcerer, priests, and the like), and in shamanic societies, knowledge was considered an independent realm, access to which was synonymous with loss of consciousness and abusive use of drugs.

As many rational myths accompanied mystical explanation(s) of the existence of knowledge in archaic societies, they also accompanied the formation of the role of knowledge in civilization. As we will see in this entry, the Greeks, circa 220 B.C., came up with extraordinary labels to differentiate between the practicality of the swordsman's know-how, which they labeled *métis*, and the wisdom of the city ruler, which they labeled *phronesis*. Were they trying to please both? Is it just that each stage of civilization is bringing its new categories of knowing, to please rulers, priests, artisans, slaves, and workers? Is engineering merely an adaptation of the Greek concept of *techne*? Or is there a real science in the art of knowing?

In the first section, we will investigate whether there is strong evidence in support of knowledge transformation. If tacit and explicit knowledge forms are anything else than a mere "social categorizing," then "implicit learning" must be supported by scientific evidence. In the second section, we investigate known knowledge transformation, between the tacit and the explicit, the individual and the collective. Building on propositions by Nonaka,[2] we propose an integrative framework showing the different forms that knowledge can pass through when being applied, used, and mobilized. In the two last sections of this entry, we end up questioning if knowledge can, *by any means*, be represented? Therefore, we suggest that as knowledge escapes representation, the production of an actionable model of knowledge transformation shows little evidence, and abundant mythology. This mythological questioning concludes our investigation, as we question knowledge as a mere artifact of behavior, or truly essential to survival; and if, ultimately, knowing—tacitly or explicitly—can be separated from being by means other than abstraction or social categorization.

WHEN GREEK PHILOSOPHERS WANTED TO GET RID OF THE ORACLES...

Many societies made distinctions between what is known and can be transcribed, and what is believed to be known, but impossible to transcribe, express, or qualify. In archaic societies, what was impossible to express or explain was usually considered an act of gods, oracles, or mystical artifacts. Ancient Greek scribes and philosophers were the first to elaborate a non-religious pragmatic distinction between the tacit and the explicit by opposing the hard-to-imitate practical knowledge of the astute fisherman or the cunning of the hunter with knowledge captured and stored in scriptures. Detienne and Vernant, in their 1974 study of cunning intelligence, identified four generic categories used in ancient Greece: the *phronesis*, a form of unarticulated social wisdom learned through experience, which we would call "tacit knowledge" today; the *techne*, the codified or non-codified procedural knowledge of craftsmen; the *episteme*, the art of abstraction and generalization, which corresponds to contemporary collective and explicit

Encyclopedia of Library and Information Sciences, Fourth Edition DOI: 10.1081/E-ELIS4-120043273
Copyright © 2017 by Taylor & Francis. All rights reserved.

knowledge; and finally, the *Métis*, the non-codified knowledge of short-cuts, cunning, and oblique strategies.

Episteme can be defined as universal knowledge that we share and circulate, that we teach and preserve, and that is commonly understood by firms as their "culture," recipes, rules of thumb, know-how, etc. *Episteme* is knowledge *about* things, the opposite of *phronesis*, which is the result of experience and social practice. *Phronesis* is singular, idiosyncratic, and assumed to be difficult to share. It is personal, and has profound meaning only for the individual who has lived the experience. This non-scientific, practical, contextual knowledge is generated in the intimacy of lived experience. It is acquired by trial and error, through organizational and environmental learning, and is generally very difficult to analyze or test. Its intuitive content renders it difficult for organizational science to grasp.

Greek society had an in-depth understanding of the precise societal roles that could be played by the three above forms of tacit knowledge: *phronesis* was built through councils, management of the cities, estates, and large organizations; experience and seniority was used to select organizational members who accumulated this form of social implicit learning over time. *Techne* was the tacit knowledge, the know-how, of the workforce, the builders, and the artisans. *Métis* was the know-how of the warriors, fishermen, and military commanders.

Little is known about the motivations of Socrates, Heraclitus, and contemporary philosophers and scribes in introducing such distinctions. Detienne and Vernant[3] see in this categorization the reflection of a Greek society that liked to ordinate and rule all matters of status, prerogatives, and social claims. Another hypothesis might well be that Greek philosophers, by making explicit the different categories of knowledge, and above all, knowing, might have fought the over-arching authorities of oracles and rulers. Stating that knowledge can be accessed by its simple production, by means of abstraction, social wisdom, or basic cunning, is not it already asserting that the way of oracles lacks of adequate grounding?

Information technologies could well be the modern "oracles" that trigger, twenty centuries later, a re-flourishing of studies of tacit knowledge. The rise of electronic data interchange, and its rapid globalization, generated optimistic expectations of a new era of a globally codified knowledge, moving assets, endless combinations of technological systems. Of course, the ease of knowledge codification with information systems has been since challenged. This codification of industry, craftsmanship, medical, or managerial practice has become the source of growth of the new capitalism. However, if knowledge is being codified in larger quantities on larger scales, most human learning remains implicit, hard to codify, to replicate or to digitalize.[4]

IN THE PURSUIT OF EVIDENCE OF KNOWLEDGE TRANSFORMATION

Implicit learning means learning without being aware of what is being learned.[5] Linguists carried out the first studies concerning the unconscious acquisition of complex information at the end of the 1960s. Other works in the field of perceptual learning have highlighted the existence of implicit rules and patterns of individual perception, of which people have no awareness. In other words, complex information is acquired with little awareness of the context in which it happens. Human learning can proceed with rare, infrequent, discrepant stimuli, and still deliver forms of valid learning from imperfect, scarce, and unstable knowledge. This characteristic of human learning was expressed 2000 years ago by the Latin proverb "*Intelligenti Pauca*"—intelligence (here the capacity to make sense of things and to learn) proceeds from the slightest of things.

The implicit nature of human learning is also ambiguously temporal. Most human sense-making is retrospective, i.e., people access and formalize perceptions after they have occurred; yet, it is impossible for a human being to determine which part of his or her learning was anterior or posterior to a single given event. In other words, learning is more analogically related to biological growth, than to systems, processes, and machines. As one cannot see the lawn grow, one cannot contemplate his or her own knowledge "growing." Accordingly, although they have consistently tried over several decades, both social and engineering sciences have been unable to establish any form of correlation between information and knowledge. The amount of information possessed by an individual is not a predictor of the validity, range, and depth of the knowledge that this individual will be able to produce. Reversibly, the amount of knowledge, wisdom, social experience that is possessed by an individual does not constitute a predictor of the quantity of valid information this individual will produce. There is, simply said, no correlation between information and knowledge. A little information can produce a very valuable knowledge. Large quantities of codified, refined, dispatched information can produce very poor knowledge. Hence, there are neither pyramids nor hierarchies between data, information, and knowledge. Several pieces of data put together *do not* systematically produce information. Interpreted information, senses attributed to information, and data do not systematically produce a chunk of knowledge.

This hierarchy between data, information, and knowledge is a powerful post-modern myth. Modernity was about advancing positive science in the service of general welfare, and human, social and technological progress. The core belief that a society could unilaterally advance its societal knowledge also belongs to the myth that societal progress is cumulative, predictable, and can be attained through layers or steps. Human, societal, and

Knowledge Management–
Law Librarianship

technological progressions are neither linear, nor fairly balanced on a positive scale along history timelines. Some ancient societies, for example pre-Socratic Greece or Qin China in 220 B.C., were more advanced and learned than many societies that followed them. As post-modern societies have become more and more dependent upon the processing of very large amounts of information, the belief that data and information are scalable into proportional advances in knowledge has become the new social contract, the veracity of which being rarely questioned.

Definitions of knowledge and information have followed different paths, until they collided in management studies. For Polanyi,[1] knowledge is an activity that he describes as the process of knowing. For Wiener,[6] information is a structure that precedes the activity of knowing, while Shannon[7] saw information as the original disorder from which knowledge is generated by discovering or crafting messages from the articulation of chaotic information. Wiener's perspective led to distinguishing information from rules, reasoning, and treatments that can be applied to it, and was the foundation stone of cybernetics.

KNOWING IS EXPERIENTIAL

One factor that could support the lack of correlation between information and knowledge lies in the fact that most human cognition is experiential; either we look forward, or we look backward. As Gavetti and Levinthal (p. 113)[8] put it, "cognition is a forward-looking form of intelligence that is premised on an actor's beliefs about the linkage between the choice of actions and the subsequent impact of those actions on outcome." Foreknowledge of potential outcomes develop with experience, not related with age, but more so related to similarities in patterns and design of the complexity of the situation being apprehended.[9,10] People naturally rate the outcomes of their predictions according to their results, either positively or negatively. This experiential wisdom generates itself "rules of thumb" and experiential memory that can be contrary to rational models or individual mental models.[11]

For Polanyi,[1] most of this experiential knowledge is unknown to the beholder. Polanyi differentiates knowledge that is explicit to us, that which is modifiable and transmittable in a formal and systematic language, from tacit knowledge, which is personal, difficult to convey, and which does not easily express itself in the formality of language. Polanyi's principal argument is that tacit knowledge demonstrates the lack of pertinence of Gestalt psychology. Whereas Gestalt psychology argues that all images are contained in nature, Polanyi wants to demonstrate that human beings acquire knowledge through their engagement in the creation and organization of their own experiences. Thus, by distinguishing knowledge that is

acquired and developed through behavior, and knowledge that is acquired, stored, and transformed through cognition, Polanyi opened a vivid debate, opposing the behaviorist and cognitive perspectives on knowing.

Founded in Kantian psychology,[12] the cognitive dimension of tacit knowledge refers to patterns that serve as a basis for the perception of, and interaction with, the external world. Thus, it is only on a selective basis that we accept information to which we are exposed, staying faithful to our own pre-established cognitive patterns. This phenomenon is known as "perceptual filtering."[13] This approach has been exhausted by managerial studies of knowledge in the workplace, noticeably by Nonaka[2] who introduced a dynamic perspective on knowledge creation, based on its explicit vs. tacit, collective vs. individual dimensions.

EXPLICIT AND COLLECTIVE KNOWLEDGE

Explicit and collective knowledge is all the knowledge a community can tell it knows. Several authors use the term "objectified knowledge" to suggest that this knowledge is considered as objective by the community that shares it. In a positivist understanding, science is a collective and explicit knowledge, though this conception has been challenged by Kuhn, in the *Structure of Scientific Revolutions* or by Feyerabend[14] in *Against Method*. For these authors, scientific knowledge is embedded in "paradigms" that are constituted by both scientific discoveries that are commonly acknowledged as valid, and beliefs on the state of the paradigm. Thus, for these authors, scientific researchers should challenge (scientific revolutions) existing paradigms in order to help science progress.

In the organizational body of knowledge, patents, corporate written rules and procedures, organizational charts, and management decisions that are produced, acquired or applied by an organization are all part of the explicit and collective body of knowledge. Patents, for example, are the articulation, embedded in written format, of the technical know-how of the firm. The purpose of making knowledge explicit and collective can be to disseminate this knowledge to others, to inform people about recent management decisions, to implement new programs and procedures within the organization, or to signal to the "external environment" the organizational purpose and positions, i.e., prices signal to the competitors and partners of the organization the market value of the services or products offered by the organization. All explicit and collective knowledge is not systematically explicit or collective in the first place. Rules that are informal and ephemera can become permanent and explicit through institutionalization.[15] Organizational ceremonies[16] can also become explicit rituals, and progressively stand for permanent rules.

Knowledge Management– Law Librarianship

Knowledge Management–
Law Librarianship

EXPLICIT AND INDIVIDUAL KNOWLEDGE

We can approach individual and explicit knowledge from two perspectives: the sociological and the technological. From an elementary sociological view, we would say that everything that becomes conscious to us becomes part of our individual explicit knowledge, i.e., we discover that we belong to a certain group of people in the organization, as commercial middle managers for example. As soon as we become aware of this belonging, we acknowledge explicitly in our behavior what has become a "fact." Spender[17] uses the term "conscious knowledge" to express this type of knowledge.

The other side of individual and explicit knowledge is what we will call our known-expertise, not to betray precedent findings on expertise that clearly state that the essence of expertise lies in the tacit understanding of rules that are unknown to the beginner or non-expert. The example of the chess masters used by De Groot[18] or Newell and Simon[19] clearly illustrate this point. However, some types of expertise have solely an explicit purpose. The diploma and the titles of doctors have the purpose of communicating the reliability of his or her services. It may as well have the purpose of stating a social and power position, as unveiled by Foucault[20] in his study of the "statutory knowledge" of doctors in the history of medicine. This type of explicit and individual knowledge, with the purpose of "declaring," has been termed "declarative knowledge" by Polanyi.[1] Positioning and social role-play consequently form a major part in the transformation and exposure of individual and explicit knowledge.

TACIT AND COLLECTIVE KNOWLEDGE

Managers elaborate informal task forces that work on critical issues in parallel to—not instead of—formal structures. These "collateral organizations"[21] often crystallize in the course of action. People gather to deal with a specific problem, and naturally gather again when a similar problem arises. "Web of complicities" allows organizations to deal obliquely with delicate tasks when formal and explicit processes seem to fail. In the *Challenger* disaster, NASA engineers progressively assimilated the Thiokol rubber joints defaults as acceptable. Although measures were explicitly showing unreliable performances, it became tacitly accepted that this imperfection was within the boundaries of "normal" and "acceptable" risks.[13] Studies in organizational crises and disasters underline the socially constructed nature of knowledge.[4] Knowledge, in this perspective, is the result of various social constructions,[22] and consequently adopting different forms and states according to its different points of observation. For Berger and Luckmann, individuals are born in a "social construction," from which we learned to assimilate, to articulate the stimuli around us to formulate our language. Likewise, Lave and Wenger[23] assert that people in organizations belong to "communities of practice" where they share a practical knowledge, learning collectively and tacitly their trade.

Many trades are thus learned tacitly and collectively. Masonry apprenticeship is a learning-by-doing and by-seeing-others-doing-it process. The tacit and collective know-how of cathedral builders has become legendary. As cathedrals were sometimes built over three or four centuries, generations of cathedral builders—many of whom were illiterate—transmitted from fathers to sons a know-how of achieving complex tasks, without the knowledge or reading and writing. Commitment and faith in supra-ordinal goals were part of the process. Tacit and collective knowledge can also be a guarantee of organizational operational safety. The "collective mind" of flight deck operators[24] permits highly complex organizational tasks to be achieved with very few accidents. This "organizational mentality" or "organization mind"[25] relies upon a tacit understanding that do not necessitate explication. Thus, technical knowledge is often acquired through repetitive tasks, the know-how of which is difficult to communicate. Scribner[26] explains how tacit knowledge is held collectively by workers in a commercial dairy (warehouse order packers, delivery drivers, inventory takers). This tacit and collective know-how is difficult to imitate, and can procure valuable technological rents, allowing the firm to develop an "appropriability regime." Many times we say "we know" to express assumptions that seem to be common sense, while in fact we only express the output of a tacit and collective learning[27] or things we have learned by traditions whose origins have been forgotten.[28] Many elements of our knowledge are gathered without awareness from others while we socialize.[2,29] We assimilate assumptions that are not ours, and personalize or rationalize them, so to give them our "signature." Then, we would eventually say, "It's common knowledge" or "it's common sense."[17]

TACIT AND INDIVIDUAL KNOWLEDGE

As Polanyi[30] put it, "We know more that we can tell." First, there are many stimuli that we notice without being aware of noticing them. We learn without the awareness of what is being learned.[31] We cannot communicate what we learn, thus, we are the only one to be the receiver of this "knowledge." Second, we do not always learn systematically or intentionally. There are many things that we have learned "incidentally,"[32] because we had the luck to encounter an unexpected learning experience, or because we were focusing on another task, and something else was to be learned in this task that we did not expect. In the routine of repetitive tasks, we may also acquire a

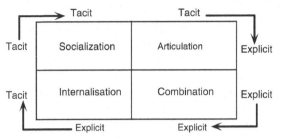

Adapted from Nonaka, I. (1990), "Managing innovation as a knowledge creation process". Paper presented at New York University, Stern School of Business, International Business Colloquium.

Fig. 1 Transitions from tacit to explicit and vice versa.

tacit knowledge concerning the improvement of our task. This "procedural knowledge"[26] is difficult to share, and when somebody replaces us at our task, the know-how is difficult to transmit. As termed by Spender,[17] a large part of our knowledge is "automatic knowledge." We do not know where it comes from, we cannot tell that we know, though "it's here" and "it works." We encode without awareness of encoding.[33] We act mindlessly and instinctively, relying on an "animal knowledge" made of erratic reactions, or impulsive, based on feelings, smells, guts, like animals do.[34] We often rely on a "practical knowledge,"[28] which we are not able to isolate, define, or describe, for we acquired it through mindless and automatic practice. Some elements of our knowledge were constructed unconsciously, by serendipity, that is to say by luck, by imagining a body of knowledge that does not rely upon the noticing of stimuli, but is solely the work of our mind. All this heterogeneous, and rather mysterious, body of knowledge is our "tacit and individual knowledge."

ARTICULATING THE TACIT WITH THE EXPLICIT

It would be misleading to state that the four above types of knowledge are independent of each other, and constitute separate and idiosyncratic bodies of knowledge. The dynamics of knowledge is a continuous, either deliberate or unconscious, movement, exchange, transformation of

one type of knowledge into another, and back and forth. To express the speed of these transformations and shifts, a suggestive analogy would certainly be close to the notion of electrical frequencies. We have, unfortunately, no clues to know if, in the human brain, these four types of knowledge are processed in parallel or sequentially. Researching the epistemological and ontological dimensions of knowledge, Nonaka[2] synthesized the four kinds of transitions between explicit and tacit dimensions of knowledge (Fig. 1). As Nonaka compiled it from different authors (Piaget, Teece, etc.), a specific mode of transition exists for each transformation. For example, tacit knowledge circulates through socialization, i.e., we learn tacit behaviors and rules, by interacting and observing other people. This tacit knowledge (i.e., the baker's know-how in preparing bread) can be articulated in more explicit rules (i.e., by using different sets of measure in all various conditions of the process to identify rules that are used tacitly by the baker) and then become explicit knowledge. This explicit knowledge can then be combined with other elements of explicit knowledge. For example, two software programs can be merged. The new set of instructions is a combination of formerly separated sets of instructions included in the software. When we face an explicit set of knowledge, we have then to integrate it into our behavior and practice. We achieved this task through practice of the explicit rules, techniques, scientific findings, etc. We internalized our tacit knowledge and made it ours, transforming it into the elements of explicit knowledge.

Using various precedent findings,[1,17,30] we developed the precedent matrix by integrating the individual and collective dimensions. We finally identified eight forms of transitions in an integrative framework to analyze the different shifts between knowledge types (see Fig. 2). We use these eight forms of transitions as to identify, describe, and explain when and how they occur in the studied organizations. For example, we would identify an "appropriability regime" between the knowledge of engineers—planning and executing the construction of the Guinean plant—and newcomers to the plant. In another example, managers would gather various uncertain or ambiguous stimuli and build a tacit understanding

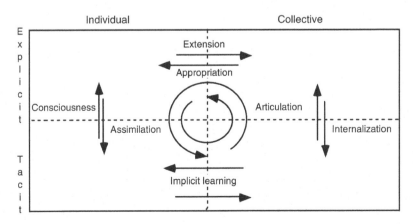

Fig. 2 An integrative framework to analyze transitions of knowledge types.

of the situation. They would share this understanding by socialization (tacit and collective knowledge) and would learn implicitly to organize this knowledge. Finally, by meeting together and "putting things on the table," they would articulate all their tacit knowledge in one explicit and collective form of knowledge. The elaboration of the following matrix involved extensive reviews of the literature, as to confirm by different sources the validity of each transition. The terms "extension," "appropriation," "internalization," and "assimilation" are used by Nonaka.[2] The term "implicit learning" seemed to be more adequate to

enclose the whole process of socialization, gathering tacit and implicit stimuli and automatic knowledge[17] that are involved in the process of transition from individual–tacit knowledge to collective–tacit knowledge. The term is used by Reber.[5]

The next step of the elaboration of the matrix was then to compile all precedent elements into one single matrix. This enlarged and completed matrix (see Fig. 3) contains both succinct descriptions of various types of knowledge *within* a specific knowledge type, and all the above eight transitions (see next page). The matrix is presented here as

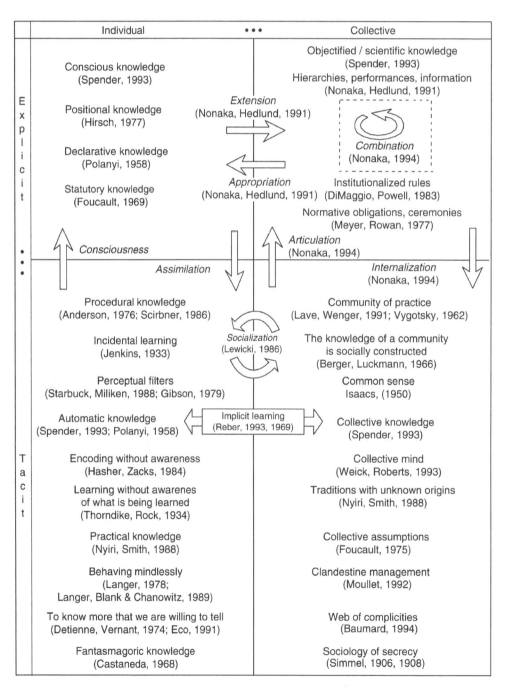

Fig. 3   An augmented and completed matrix of knowledge modes.
Source: From Baumard.[4]

a guideline to read the case descriptions. It was used accordingly in the data analysis process to verify the validity of findings with precedent works, and eventually come back to more empirical work to avoid bias.

CAN MODELS EXPLAIN THE TRANSFORMATION OF KNOWLEDGE?

Can we replicate this implicit learning with a mathematical model? How would it translate? Implicit learning, i.e., the production of tacit knowledge, is a process that applies unconscious schemata and interpretation schemes to an on-going flow of stimuli, either perceived with full awareness, or perceived automatically without the awareness of the perceiver. One can consider that a complex system, e.g., organizational or organic, mechanical or biological, digital or analogical, is also treating or interpreting various stimuli in its different parts or sub-systems, without necessarily informing the other components. In fact, the historical evolution of the architecture of computers has been driven by the growth of parallel-process design, which implies that some operations, such as graphical outputs, are taken care of by different processors.

Organizations, alike, are processing large amounts of information in their different sub-systems, without the awareness—mutual or asymmetric—of other components. Unlike machines, however, these interpretations are not archived, stored, or systematically accounted for in registers, although members of organizations try their best to develop routines that capture their experience and can be eventually revised when their learning becomes ineffective.[35] Learning in organizations is very dispersed; so dispersed, indeed, that several authors have challenged the idea that learning could fit in any fashion a category labeled as "organizational." Noteworthy was the effort of Sandelands and Stablein[25] who proposed that organizations ought to have a "mind" of themselves, for the results achieved by organizations out-measure individual achievements. However, because organizations comprise a category that is so varied and ambiguous, the extent to which human output can be attributed to an organization, or to an organized action, is difficult to assert. It is hence conceivable that organizations are merely temporary categories that exist in people's imagination, according to their purpose, their intended level of outreach or discretion, their expectations and the framing of events, contexts and people that create the most comfortable and actionable setting. In this perspective, Morgan[36] proposed that organizations are products of metaphors, which people use to explain their intended action, or lead other people to conform to an ideal-type of action that they wish will take form. Such metaphors can be machines, like Frederick Taylor's scientific management; organisms, like the neo-institutionalists' vision of organizations as biotopes of living organisms in symbiosis or adversity; brains like Wiener's cybernetics,[37] etc. Morgan coined the term "imaginisation" to suggest that the boundary between action and knowledge is nothing other than an academic one: action is knowledge, and knowledge is action.

Indeed, cognitive science has long identified knowledge as symbolic representations stored in the brain,[38] but Morgan suggested that what we label actions and what we label knowledge are the same reality, put in two differently imagined categories. Yet, imagination, as Morgan sees it, is still a representative form. Following Morgan, one can agree that knowledge is embodied into organizational structures, and that, accordingly, organizational structures might be projections of human knowledge. But following this path, if we admit that knowledge is partly embodied into people, we cannot assert that people are the exact projections of their knowledge. Von Krogh and Roos[39] noted that most academic and business evocations of knowledge are directed by an epistemology that sees knowledge as a representation. This "representationist" bias fails to capture two phenomenon: (1) knowledge's propensity for its autonomous development,[4] i.e., the fact that representation never captures exhaustively the knowledge it addresses combined with the fact that knowledge continues to grow, within individuals, within organizations and groups, without any form of control, and, eventually, awareness, of its beholders and (2) knowledge being transformed, and acted upon, outside of the realm of representation; swimming being a striking example of an action based on a knowledge that escapes representation while being applied.[40]

There are several examples of forms of knowledge that do not require any form of representation to be applied; and do not require a tight coupling between application and output to generate learning. Lave and Wenger[23] identified "communities of practice" as such a phenomenon. Representation may take place, but most of the learning is acquired by mimicking, listening, intuitively adapting to peers in sharing a practice. Apprentice masons and midwives are examples. Weick and Roberts[24] note that high reliability organizations depend upon a "collective mind" shared by operators, as they conduct perilous and complex tasks. Once again, this collective mind made of mindful interactions, of mutual awareness, of tacit and implicit behavioral coordination does not require a representation to be efficient. On the contrary, excessive efforts to represent and codify high reliability organizations through checklists and normative rules, may increase the risk of failures and accidents.

LITTLE EVIDENCE, ABUNDANT MYTHS

Hence, most theories about knowledge creation in organizations are merely fantasies, which reflect more the observers' rational myths and beliefs, than capturing how knowledge is produced and transformed in organizations. As Starbuck put it, "scientific rationality is a fantasy that appeals us aesthetically, but it violates its own rules,

Knowledge Management— Law Librarianship

Knowledge Management–
Law Librarianship

distorts our observations, and extrapolates incomplete knowledge to ridiculous extremes."[41] Among those fantasies, some are long lasting, displaying a strong congruence with widely shared practices. For example, it is assumed that learning is achieved through the application of knowledge; hence asserting that knowledge comes to human awareness through its application. This perspective on learning has led to the differentiation of information and knowledge, by stating that knowledge is produced through the application or experimentation of information to a given context, hence defining knowledge as "applied information." Unfortunately, experimental evidence is still lacking to demonstrate a linear causality between knowledge, its application and learning. While Argyris and Schön[42] stated that human beings improve awareness through "double-loop learning," i.e., learning about their learning through observing the gaps between the outputs of their "theory in use" and their on-going actions, Van de Ven et al.[43] provided evidence that disruptive innovations are not the outputs of an action–reaction chain of events. In other words, disruptive inventions are not the result of either single-loop or double-loop learning. They occur through the use of knowledge that clearly escapes scientific explanations. While one can agree that knowledge is both created and preserved through its application, it is impossible to observe a direct correlation between the application of knowledge and an increase in learning, and therefore, the continuation or improvement of knowing. A possible explanation for this lack of evidence may be found in the fact that most knowledge transformation is tacit, much alike a young swimmer who discovers the automatic coordination of his members in an indescribable "flowing" movement. In fact, the tenets of the autopoietic theory of knowledge maintain that "knowing is effective action, that is, operating effectively in the domain of existence of living beings" (p. 29).[44] Such a perspective defends the idea that knowledge creation is self-contained, and hence cannot be projected on any other dimensions than personal perception.

Fundamentally opposed to the idea that knowledge is a commodity, codified or not, Maturana and Varela (p. 74)[44] "admit knowledge whenever we observe an effective (or adequate) behavior in a given context, i.e., in a realm or domain which we define by a question (explicit or implicit)." Hence, inspired by Polanyi's automatic knowledge, defenders of this perspective reject the idea that knowledge pursues a purpose or an object. They sum it up nicely: "All doing is knowing and all knowing is doing." (p. 27)[44]

IS KNOWLEDGE MERELY A TEMPORARY ARTIFACT OF BEHAVIOR?

Hence, Maturana and Varela underline a phenomenon long known by behaviorists: the tendency of human beings to exaggerate their aware participation in the production of knowledge and learning. Behaviorists have asserted that such misperceptions are driven by the tendency of scientists to give exaggerated attention to consciousness, instead of making behavior the points of their attacks. When doing so, it is rather clear that the link between problems and solutions, knowledge and its application, acting and learning, is rather shallow, ambiguous, irrational and often, political. Starbuck[45] observed that people are mostly "action-generators." Captured in the flow of actions, escalating their deeds to emerging behaviors, people have sets of solutions and sets of problems; and they try to match the available solutions with the available problems, aiming at maintaining a satisfying congruence and consistency as an acceptable level. Organizational politics ask people to be "solutions providers," while organizational belief in rationality asks them to display themselves as "problem solvers." In such a dialectic tension, knowledge becomes alternatively a repertory of solutions to fix random flows of problems, or an invented solution to fix an unsolved problem.

Moreover, most learning is biased by the expectations of rewards and incentives that people know of, or imagine. People tend to adopt behaviors that they believe will trigger rewards, or eventually display those behaviors, even if not much learning is involved. Accordingly, people engaged in "placebo interactions";[33] engaging in behaviors, knowledge production and exchange, learning activities that pursue the goal of maintaining vital on-going social interactions, whatever the usefulness, meaningfulness, productivity of those behaviors and knowledge. Of course, organizations favor behavioral control over cognitive efficiency, because behaviors are observable, measurable, and therefore can be used as a sanction/reward platform. It is hard to imagine Tolman[46] rewarding his rats for their cognitive performance, congratulating them for the accuracy of their cognition; yet, Tolman by rewarding their behaviors learned much about their cognition. This is much the same as organizations that reward behavior, aiming at producing efficient cognition among their members. Tolman hence discovered that rats possess "cognitive maps," i.e., they register the most efficient path towards the promised reward, and reapply it when they recognize a similar situation. But only 36% of Tolman's rats had correct maps,[47] which beats a random choice between all the possible paths, but does not reassure scientists regarding whether a rat sense of smell would simply outbid its sense of orientation.

IS KNOWLEDGE REALLY ESSENTIAL TO SURVIVAL?

Another widespread fantasy states that human beings have progressed in society and survivability through their superior knowledge among all living species. The accumulation of knowledge is, indeed, a unique property of human beings; however, science has not reached a sufficient level of investigative power to demonstrate that other species do not accumulate knowledge in other forms than thoughts, representations, and physical embodiments.

The fact that human beings are fully aware of the importance of their procedural and abstract knowledge leads them to attribute to knowledge all kinds of sources of superiority. While, in fact, people survive in spite of gross errors of perception, repeated throughout their personal and collective history. Starbuck and Mezias[48] wondered if people in organizations had accurate knowledge of objective facts concerning their environment, and decided to investigate. They found that managers have erroneous perceptions that can range from 30% to 300% of objective values, on such common information as their company size, the volume of the sales, or what their company does. Hence, knowledge theorists have tended to attribute exaggerated causal and explanatory power to cognitive phenomena, often forgetting that the human ability to adapt, while being fully ignorant, may well be the main source of their resilience and organizational performance. Cognition follows behavior, as much as behavior follows cognition; but when they happen simultaneously, in such an intertwined organic relation, it is rather difficult to determine which one commands the other, and on which occasion. As Starbuck (p. 357)[47] put it: "Behaviorists have long maintained that cognition is only a subcategory of behavior and subject to the same laws as other behavior. (. . .) Certainly, behaviorists have had little success in demonstrating that behaviorist theories explain complex cognitive behavior, and behaviorist psychology has not subsumed cognitive psychology."

IS "KNOWING" TRULY SEPARABLE FROM "BEING"?

Indeed, the variability of preferences, and the volatility of aspirations over time and according to contexts, makes it difficult to generalize *ex ante* normative rules of cognition. Prior experiences influence how stimuli are selected and perceived, and in turn, new stimuli can revise previous experience. A new and scarce configuration of data may well become the new model, while all sets of previous models can no longer handle new stimuli. Hence, both models and stimuli are in real life interchangeable. A new stimulus can carry a whole model, and models in turn, turn into old and prior stimuli. The fallacy about explicit knowledge lies in the fact that data, information, knowledge, models, and stimuli belong to a configuration that is so unified, that any attempt to disaggregate them turns their properties into an artificial reduction. This integrated perspective on knowledge owes much to Gestalt psychology. In 1922, in his book *Nature and Human Conduct*, the American philosopher Dewey[49] identified two forms of knowledge: *knowing how* (that gleaned through habit and intuition) and *knowing about* (which implies reflection

and conscious appreciation)—practical knowledge and constructed knowledge. Dewey theorized that both learning through practice, and generalizing from practice, form a single, unique continuum. Disaggregating or sequencing the phenomenon of *knowing* from experiencing, acting, doing, or being, is empirically impossible. Such divisions or abstractions are indeed quite recent in the knowledge-studies literature. Early studies focused on understanding why such a disaggregation could not, or *should not*, be attempted.

For a better appreciation of the agonies of interpreting practical knowledge we have to return to the nature of experience, as expressed in the tenets of Gestalt psychology. For Christian von Ehrenfels, founder of the movement in the 1890s, actions of a complex order are carried out by being divided into relatively routine tasks, each of these able to be executed without recourse to thought or conscious reflection. Here we find the source of Taylorism, which turned human endeavor into a "division of chores" (chores that become automatism) and opened the way for assembly line production. The central idea of Gestalt psychology is that our perceptual experiences do not emerge as a result of the conscious or unconscious application of rules or concepts to data received from our sensory receptors, but that these experiences come from an immersion in a perceptual environment in which the information we perceive already carries meaning. Perception is then an indivisible holistic structure, uniting our lived experience and the experience we are in the process of living, and it is through continually looking back on our experience that we construct a repertory of perceptual structures.

Gestalt psychology raises the question of recognition, which is little studied in management. It explains how we can recognize a person instantaneously by their physiognomy even from some distance, even though we may not be able to precisely make out their features. Recent research on organizations' cognitive maps is not so far from this concept, while having little relation with Tolman's rats. This capacity for recognition would allow us to automatically take appropriate action in a given situation, without having to make an effort to analyze and decide what approach to apply. The Gestalt psychologists' argument is that our sense-making capacities are indivisible from a physiological–psychological whole, which embraces both thought and perception.

PUTTING KNOWLEDGE BACK WHERE IT BELONGS

It is in our everyday learning, in the development of our practical knowledge, that these automatisms are deployed. At least this was the central argument advanced by Merleau-Ponty[50] in 1941, in a veritable defense of practical knowledge. Through practice we acquire patterns of behavior—skills such as walking, running, and speech—

which we can then call up spontaneously. In 1966, Polanyi[30] continued this study of tacit knowledge by looking at similar kinetic phenomena. We learn how to swim, to co-ordinate our movements, to float, in the context of the experience itself, and "we know more than we can express." For Merleau-Ponty, these patterns become "a part of us." It was in the repetition of practice that Merleau-Ponty saw the true nature of human learning.

The valuation of cognition results is itself problematic, as people do not have absolute rules to value knowledge. In fact, most informational behavior of human beings is somehow "positional," in Hirsch's terms.[51] People seek to gain information that allows them to gain a positional perspective, i.e., to position their own past experience in relation to the new one, while asserting their own position towards the new situation. Information superiority is hence more a theoretical construct than an organizational reality. People do not see information as having absolute superior value, but rather an immediate, practical leverage for their ongoing programs. Rather than challenging the information being used and articulated in on-going programs, people favor collateral and *ad hoc* organizations, which would leave their main programs untouched, and their deeds unchallenged.[20] Programs emerge from action-generation, and in turn, learning follows the emergent paths of action. In essence, most human knowledge is therefore conjectural, and implicitly collated in the face of action dilemmas. As social researchers, we are all working under the assumption that our efforts at generalization, explanation, and rationalization of management are an urgent need for organizations. What the case tells us is not to forget the unsaid, the unreadable, the erratic, and the mutable in our genuine assumptions. It seems that we blind ourselves from conjectural knowledge and forms of intelligence that proceed obliquely. As Detienne and Vernant put it, "there has been a prolonged silence on the subject of the intelligence of cunning" and the powerful reason behind that silence may well be a "concept of Platonic Truth, which has overshadowed a whole area of intelligence with its own kind of understandings," and "has never really ceased to haunt Western metaphysical thought" (p. 318).[52]

REFERENCES

1. Polanyi, M. *Personal Knowledge: Toward a Post-critical Philosophy*, University of Chicago Press: Chicago, IL, 1958.
2. Nonaka, I. A dynamic theory of organizational knowledge creation. Organ. Sci. **1994**, *5* (1), 14–37.
3. Detienne, M. Vernant, J.P.In *Cunning Intelligence in Greek Culture and Society*; Lloyd, J., Ed.; University of Chicago Press: Chicago, IL, 1991. Trans. (The original work in French is from 1974.).
4. Baumard, P. *Tacit Knowledge in Organizations*, Sage Publications: London, 1999.
5. Reber, A.S. *Implicit Learning and Tacit Knowledge: An Essay on the Cognitive Unconscious*, Clarendon Press and Oxford University Press: New York, Oxford, 1993. Oxford Psychology Series No. 19.
6. Wiener, N. *Cybernetics: Or the Control and Communication in the Animal and the Machine*, MIT Press: Cambridge, MA, 1948.
7. Shannon, C.E. A mathematical theory of communication. Bell Syst. Tech. J. **1948**, *27*, 379–423, 623–656.
8. Gavetti, G.G.; Levinthal, D.D. Looking forward and looking backward: Cognitive and experiential search. Admin. Sci. Quart. **2000**, *45* (1), 113–137.
9. Freudenthal, D. The role of age, foreknowledge and complexity in learning to operate a complex device. Behav. Inform. Technol. **2001**, *20* (1), 23–135.
10. Kieras, D.E.; Bovair, S. The role of a mental model in learning to operate a device. Cognitive Sci. **1984**, *8*, 255–273.
11. Levitt, B.; March, J.G. Organizational learning. Annu. Rev. Sociol. **1998**, *14*, 319–340.
12. Piaget, J. *Recherches sur la contradiction*, Presses Universitaires de France: Paris, 1974.
13. Starbuck, W.H. Milliken, F.J. Executives' perceptual filters: What they notice and how they make sense. In *The Executive Effect: Concepts and Methods for Studying Top Managers*; Hambrick, D.C., Ed.; JAI Press: Greenwich, CT, 1988; 35–65.
14. Feyerabend, P.K. *Against Method. Outline of an Anarchistic Theory of Knowledge*, NLB Verso Humanities Press: London, 1975.
15. DiMaggio, P.J.; Powell, W.W. The iron cage revisited: Institutional isomorphism and collective rationality in organizational fields. Am. Sociol. Rev. **1983**, *48*, 147–160.
16. Meyer, J.W.; Rowan, B. Institutionalized organizations: Formal structure as myth and ceremony. Am. J. Sociol. **1977**, *83* (2), 340–363.
17. Spender, J.C. Competitive advantage from tacit knowledge: Unpacking the concept and its strategic implications. Acad. Manage. Proc. **1993**, *53*, 37–41.
18. De Groot, A.D. *Thought and Choice in Chess*, Mouton: The Hague, 1965.
19. Newell, A.; Simon, H.A. The logic theory machine: A complex information processing system. IEEE T. Inform. Theory **1956**, *2* (3), S-61–79.
20. Foucault, M. *L'Archéologie du savoir*, Gallimard: Paris, 1969.
21. Zand, D.E. *Information, Organization and Power: Effective Management in the Knowledge Society*, McGraw-Hill: New York, 1981; 57–88.
22. Berger, P.L. Luckmann, T. *The Social Construction of Reality*, Doubleday: Garden City, NY, 1966.
23. Lave, J. Wenger, E. *Situated Learning: Legitimate Peripheral Participation*, Cambridge University Press: Cambridge, 1991.
24. Weick, K.E.; Roberts, K.H. Collective mind in organizations heedful interrelating on flight decks. Admin. Sci. Quart. **1993**, *38*, 357–381.
25. Sandelands, L.E. Stablein, R.E. The concept of organization mind. In *Research in the Sociology of Organizations*; DiTomaso, N., Bachrach, S., Eds.; JAI Press: Greenwich, CT, 1987; Vol. 6, 135–162.

Knowledge Management– Law Librarianship

26. Scribner, S. Thinking in action: Some characteristics of practical thought. In *Practical Intelligence: Nature and Origins of Competence in Everyday World*; Sternberg, R., Wagner, R.K., Eds.; Cambridge University Press: Cambridge, 1986; 13–30.

27. Isaacs, N. *The Foundations of Common Sense*, Roy Publishers: New York, 1950.

28. Nyíri, J.K., Smith, B., Eds. *Practical Knowledge: Outlines of a Theory of Traditions and Skills*; Croom Helm: New York, 1988.

29. Lewicki, P. *Non-conscious Social Information Processing*, Academic Press: New York, 1986.

30. Polanyi, M. *The Tacit Dimension*, Doubleday: Garden City, NY, 1966.

31. Thorndike, E.L.; Rock, R.T., Jr. Learning without awareness of what is being learned or intent to learn it. J. Exp. Psychol. **1934**, *17*, 1–19.

32. Jenkins, J.G. Instruction as a factor of 'incidental' learning. Am. J. Psychol. **1933**, *45*, 471–477.

33. Langer, E.; Blank, A.; Chanowitz, B. The mindlessness of ostensibly thoughtful action: The role of 'placebic' information in interpersonal interaction. J. Pers. Soc. Psychol. **1978**, *36*, 635–642.

34. Griffin, D.R. *Animal Mind, Human Mind*, Springer-Verlag: New York, 1982.

35. Cyert, R.M. March, J.G. *A Behavioral Theory of the Firm*, Prentice Hall: Englewood Cliffs, NJ, 1963.

36. Morgan, G. *Images of Organisation*, Sage: Thousand Oaks, CA, 1986.

37. Wiener, N. *Cybernetics: Or the Control and Communication in the Animal and the Machine*, MIT Press: Cambridge, MA, 1948.

38. Newell, A. *Unified Theories of Cognition*, Harvard University Press: Cambridge, MA, 1990.

39. Von Krogh, G. Roos, J. *Organizational Epistemology*, Macmillan: London, 1995.

40. Polanyi, M. *The Tacit Dimension*, University of Chicago Press: Chicago, IL, 1967.

41. Starbuck, W.H. Surmounting our human limitations. InIn *Paradox and Transformation: Toward a Theory of Change in Organization and Management*; Quinn, R., Cameron, K., Eds.; Ballinger: Cambridge, MA, 1988; 65–80.

42. Argyris, C. Schön, D.A. *Theory in Practice: Increasing Professional Effectiveness*, Jossey-Bass: San Francisco, CA, 1974.

43. Van de Ven, A. Polley, D. Garud, R. Venkataraman, S. *The Innovation Journey*, Oxford University Press: New York, 1999.

44. Maturana, H. Varela, F. *The Tree of Knowledge: The Biological Roots of Human Understanding*, Shambhala: Boston, MA, 1992.

45. Starbuck, W.H. Organizations as action generators. Am. Soc. Rev. **1983**, *48*, 91–102.

46. Tolman, E.C. Cognitive maps in rats and men. Psychol. Rev. **1948**, *55*, 189–208.

47. Starbuck, W.H. Is Janus the god of understanding?. In *Managerial and Organizational Cognition*; Lant, T., Shapira, Z., Eds.; Erlbaum: Mahwah, NJ, 2000; 351–365.

48. Starbuck, W.H.; Mezias, J.M. Opening Pandora's box: Studying the accuracy of managers' perceptions. J. Organ. Behav. **1996**, *17* (2), 99–117.

49. Dewey, J. *Human Conduct and Nature: An Introduction to Social Psychology*, George Allen and Urwin: London, 1922.

50. Merleau-Ponty, M. *La structure du comportement*, Presses Universitaires de France: Paris, 1941.

51. Hirsch, F. *Social Limits to Growth*, Routledge & Kegan Paul: London, 1977.

52. Detienne, M. Vernant, J.P.In *Cunning Intelligence in Greek Culture and Society*; Lloyd, J., Ed.; Humanities Press: Atlantic Highlands, NJ, 1978.

Latent Semantic Indexing

Dian I. Martin
Small Bear Technical Consulting, LLC, Thorn Hill, Tennessee, U.S.A.

Michael W. Berry
Department of Electrical Engineering and Computer Science, University of Tennessee, Knoxville, Tennessee, U.S.A.

Abstract

Latent Semantic Indexing (LSI) is a proven successful indexing and retrieval method. This method is based on an automated, mathematical technique known as singular value decomposition (SVD). Given a large information database, LSI uses SVD to create a "semantic space" of the document collection where both terms and documents are represented. It does this by producing a reduced dimensional vector space in which the underlying or "latent" semantic structure in the pattern of word usage of the document collection emerges. Similarities between terms, terms and documents, or documents in the document collection are then based on semantic content not on individual terms. This ability to extract meaning of terms and documents has given LSI success in many different applications.

INTRODUCTION

This entry describes and explains the concepts and theories related to a well known and highly successful automatic information retrieval and analysis technique known as Latent Semantic Indexing (LSI). Given a large information database where the text is heterogeneous and the vocabulary varies, documents and terms in the database are indexed by an underlying or "latent" semantic structure in the pattern of word usage defining the documents. This characteristic of LSI is what gives the technique its name.

Prior to LSI, most information retrieval systems matched words in a user's query with words in documents contained in the collection being searched. This approach frequently returns irrelevant information while failing to retrieve other relevant documents because people use a tremendous diversity in words to express the same concept. LSI uses a mathematical approach known as the singular value decomposition (SVD) which produces a vector space with single vector representations for each unique term and document in a given document collection. Given the vector space, LSI then uses a dimension reduction technique to produce a "semantic space" that yields improved indexing of documents based on semantic content. Relationships among documents are based on the representation and meaning of the words they contain, and relationships among terms are based on their semantic effect on all the documents in which they occur. LSI uses this reduced dimensional vector space to induce similarities among documents that may or may not contain the same terms and among terms that may or may not occur together in a document. These similarities are based upon the meaning or semantics of word usage for the entire document collection.

This entry outlines the history of LSI and discusses the basic mechanics behind the algorithm. There is a high level description of the mathematical background for LSI, a short explanation of the computational technology, and a summary of current applications and issues involved with the use of this technique.

OVERVIEW OF LSI

History

There is an ever increasing flood of information generated by a growing number of sources. In order to make use of this information it must be organized into a manageable state where relevant and meaningful items can be accessed and correlated. The large volumes of data involved necessitate a technology that is capable of automatically indexing and retrieving desired information in a timely fashion.

Traditionally, lexical matching was used for retrieving information from a document database or collection. Lexical matching consists of matching words in a user's query with words in the documents contained in the collection. This technique proves to be inaccurate as it often times retrieves irrelevant results for a given query while failing to return other relevant documents that do not contain exact term matches. The problem is linked to variability in vocabulary and word usage. There is a tremendous amount of diversity in the language or words people use to describe a single concept. This is known as synonymy.

Encyclopedia of Library and Information Sciences, Fourth Edition DOI: 10.1081/E-ELIS4-120044505

Copyright © 2017 by Taylor & Francis. All rights reserved.

Research shows that two people will pick the same term for a given object less than 20% of the time.[1] Synonymy can lead to poor recall in queries where the ratio of the number of relevant documents retrieved to all the relevant documents that exist in a document collection is low.[2,3] Related information may not be retrieved because the concept in a given query is not expressed using the same words as in the documents. People may also use the same word to express several different concepts or meanings. This is known as polysemy and can lead to poor precision in queries where the ratio of the number of relevant documents in the set of documents retrieved is low.[2,3] Irrelevant information could be retrieved because a word might be used differently in a document than it is in a given query, essentially misunderstanding the context in which the word was used. An ideal retrieval system would have both high precision and recall for any given query.

In 1988, a group at Bell Communications Research (Dumais, Furnas, and Landauer) as well as Deerwester from the Center for Information and Language Studies at the University of Chicago and Harshman from the University of Western Ontario first published a new approach to indexing and retrieval known as "Latent Semantic Indexing" which used an automated technology to overcome term-matching retrieval problems.[2,4] They originally set about to develop a solution for helping people find desired services in the Bell System Yellow Pages. Users had trouble finding services due to the fact that their searches or queries used many more words (with similar meanings) than were used to index the information in the document collection.[1] This group chose to overcome the term-matching retrieval deficiencies by using a statistical approach to organize documents in a collection into a semantic structure better suited for retrieval. This approach developed into what is now LSI. Large document collections, consisting of large amounts of text, were automatically analyzed to induce knowledge about the relationships among terms and documents such that the retrieval system could identify when a user's query words meant about the same as the words the system used for indexing.[5] This approach exploited the concept that the content of a document is not based on its individual words, but rather that there exists some underlying or "latent" structure in the pattern of word usage. LSI attempts to estimate this latent structure and eliminate the noise that is present due to variability in word choice. Indexing of documents in the document collection is based on the estimated latent semantic structure. As a result, the similarity of documents is not determined by the exact words they contain but on the semantic content.[6]

LSI is considered a variant of the traditional vector space model (VSM). The vector space model was developed to handle text retrieval from a large information database with heterogeneous text and varied vocabulary. One of the first systems to use a traditional VSM was the System for the Mechanical Analysis and Retrieval of Text (SMART).[7] Among the notable characteristics of the VSM is the premise that the meaning of documents can be derived from its components. The underlying formal mathematical model of the VSM defines unique vectors for each term and document. Queries are performed by constructing a vector to represent the query and then compare this query representation to the representation of each document in the vector space.[8] LSI uses a reduced dimensional VSM. Query-document similarities are then based on concepts or similar semantic content.

Basic Mechanics of LSI

LSI is a fully automatic technique for extracting and inferring the meaning of terms and documents. Prior to the development of LSI, these tasks involved significant human intervention. To obtain the "latent" structure of the document collection, LSI processes a large collection of machine-readable text that consists of multiple documents. No human dictionaries, semantic networks, grammars, syntactic parsers, or morphologies are used; therefore, no preconceived knowledge about the physical word, word order, syntactic relations, or morphology is incorporated in the processing. Only raw text separated into documents is taken as input. Documents are a predetermined size of text such as paragraphs, collections of paragraphs, sentences, book chapters, books, etc. depending on the application. These documents are parsed into terms, which are the individual components that make up a document. Typically, terms are words, but they can be phrases or concepts, also depending on the application. The terms and documents are organized into a single large matrix which is then processed using the SVD matrix decomposition technique.

The SVD produces a vector space from the document collection, which is considered the "semantic space," where vector representations for both terms and documents are produced simultaneously. Within this "semantic space," the meaning of a term is represented as the average effect that it has on the meaning of documents in which it occurs.[5,9] Similarly, the meaning of a document is represented as the sum of all the words it contains. Each term and document is represented by a single vector, with each vector having a certain number of elements or dimensions in the vector space. The SVD allows for the adjustment of the representation of terms and documents in the vector space by choosing the number of dimensions. This controls the number of parameters by which a word or document is described. Usually the number of dimensions is much smaller than either the number of terms or documents, but still is considered a large number of dimensions (typically 200—500 dimensions). This reduction of dimensionality is the key to sufficiently capturing the underlying semantic structure of a document collection. It reduces the noise associated with the variability in word usage and causes minor differences in terminology to be ignored.[2]

Knowledge Management–
Law Librarianship

Selecting the optimal dimensionality is an important factor in the performance of LSI. The conceptual space for a large document collection needs more than a few underlying independent concepts to define it, but the semantic space is overly distorted by using too few dimensions.[4] Using full dimensionality regenerates the original data matrix and provides no semantic grouping of terms and documents, considering every term and document to be unique in meaning.[6] On the other hand, using a low number of dimensions is undesirable as it does not produce enough differentiation between terms and documents. Essentially too many terms and documents would be considered identical in meaning. Optimal dimensionality is what gives LSI its powerful retrieval effectiveness. For a pictorial representation of the effects of dimensionality in the semantic space and its relation to success of LSI in a word knowledge test, see Landauer.[15]

The difference between the traditional VSM and the reduced dimensional VSM used by LSI is that terms form the dimensions (the axes) of the vector space in the traditional VSM and documents are represented along those dimensions. Therefore, since the terms are the axes of the vector space in the traditional VSM, they are orthogonal (90°) to each other, causing documents that do not contain a term in a user's query to have a similarity of zero with the query. The result is that terms have their own unique independent meanings. In LSI, however, the dimensions are derived from the SVD not the terms themselves. These derived dimensions are orthogonal, but terms (as well as documents) are vectors in the reduced dimensional space. Terms no longer have unique meaning on their own, nor are they independent. Terms get their meanings from their mappings in the semantic space. The location of the term vectors reflects the correlation of the term's usage across documents in the collection, thus, it carries all of the term's senses (all the different ways is which the term has been used).[5,10]

In this reduced dimensional vector space produced by the SVD, the closeness of terms and documents can be determined by examining the position and proximity of term and document vectors. Terms close to one another in the reduced dimensional space will be considered to have similar meaning regardless of whether or not they appear in the same document. Terms could be considered dissimilar in meaning because they are far away from each other in the vector space even though they occur in the same document. The closeness of documents is determined by the overall pattern of term usage for the document. Documents can be similar to each other, having close proximity in the vector space, regardless of the specific words they contain.[6,9] The position of terms and documents in the vector space serves as a "semantic indexing." Users' queries are projected into the vector space, and documents in the neighborhood of the projected query are returned in ranked order, with the most similar document being first. The nearby documents need not share any terms with the user's query since the location of the query in the vector space is determined by the underlying semantic structure of the document collection, patterns of term usage across documents.[2]

MATHEMATICAL BACKGROUND

LSI consists of four basic steps.

Assembling the Term–Document Matrix

Given a large collection of text, documents are first preprocessed. Oftentimes, documents must be filtered to remove unwanted information. Documents might contain graphical images, tables, charts, etc. that may need to be removed. There are also unnecessary tags and features that help identify how the documents are organized or formatted which may need to be omitted because they add no semantic content to the document. Stemming and stoplisting might also need to be applied to the words in the documents. Stemming is the removing of suffixes to reduce a word to its root form. Stoplisting is simply the filtering of words that have little or no value to the semantic content of the documents, such as "the," "a," "of," "about," etc.[3] With stemming and stoplisting, there is always a risk of losing valuable information.

The cleaned documents are then processed to construct a term-by-document matrix. The columns of the matrix stand for the documents and the rows represent terms. Often, with smaller document collections the number of terms is greater than the number of documents. However, as the volume of information increases and the document collections become larger, the opposite (more documents than terms) is more frequently the case. Initially each column of the matrix contains zero and nonzero elements. Each nonzero element or cell of the matrix is the frequency with which the term occurs in a document. The term-by-document matrix is considered sparse because it contains many more zero elements than nonzero elements. Each document in the collection tends to only use a small subset of terms from the entire unique term set. Usually about 1% or less of the matrix entries is nonzero.[3]

Weighting Elements of the Term–Document Matrix

The second step of LSI is to apply a local and global weighting function to each nonzero, term–frequency entry, in the term-by-document matrix in order to increase or decrease the importance of terms within documents (local) and across the entire document collection (global). Terms that best distinguish particular documents from the rest of the documents in a collection are the most important; therefore, a weighting function should give a low weight to a high frequency term that occurs in many documents

Knowledge Management–
Law Librarianship

and a high weight to terms that occur in some documents but not all.[8] Applying a weighting function generally improves retrieval performance. The local and global weighting functions for each cell are usually directly related to how frequently a term occurs within a document and inversely related to how frequently a term occurs in documents across the collection, respectively. For a more detailed description on different types of local and global weighting functions, see Dumais.[6] A common local and global weighting function that dampens the effect of large differences in term frequencies within a document and that takes the distribution of terms over all documents is log-entropy. The local weighting function of log is defined as $\log(tf_{ij} + 1)$, and the global weighting function of entropy is defined as

$$1 + \sum_j \frac{p_{ij}\log_2(p_{ij})}{\log_2 n}$$

where $p_{ij} = tf_{ij}/gf_i$, tf_{ij} = term frequency of term i in document j, and gf_i = the total number of times that term i appears in the entire collection of n documents. It has been found that log-entropy gave the best retrieval results, 40% over raw term frequency, on several standard document collections.[6]

Producing the Reduced Dimension Vector Space

Given a rectangular term-by-document matrix A, A can be decomposed into the product of three other matrices using SVD.[11] Thus the SVD of matrix A is

$$A = T * S * D^{\mathrm{T}}$$

where T is an orthogonal matrix, D is an orthogonal matrix, and S is a diagonal matrix. The first r, where r is the rank of A, columns of the orthogonal matrix T contain r orthonormal eigenvectors associated with the r nonzero eigenvalues of $A*A^{\mathrm{T}}$, and the first r columns of the orthogonal matrix D contain r orthonormal eigenvectors associated with the r nonzero eigenvalues of $A^{\mathrm{T}}*A$. The first r diagonal entries of S are the nonnegative square roots of the r nonzero eigenvalues of $A*A^{\mathrm{T}}$ and $A^{\mathrm{T}}*A$, and are in decreasing order. The columns of matrix T are known as the left singular vectors, and the columns of matrix D are known as the right singular vectors. The nonzero diagonal elements of S are known as the singular values.[11,12] The rows of matrix T correspond to the term vectors, and the rows of matrix D correspond to the document vectors. The SVD simply rerepresents matrix A using orthogonal indexing dimensions.[10]

If only the k largest singular values and their associated singular vectors are kept then the SVD of A is truncated to

$$A_k = T_k * S_k * D_k^{\mathrm{T}}$$

which is the reduced dimension SVD. The matrix A_k is the best or closest (distance is minimized) rank k approximation to the original matrix A.[12,13] The matrix A_k is created by ignoring or setting equal to zero all but the first k elements or columns of the term vectors in T, the first k singular values in S, and the first k elements or columns of the document vectors in D. A pictorial representation of the SVD of term-by-document matrix A and the best rank-k approximation to A can be seen in Fig. 1.[12,14] The k-dimensional vector space, where the rows in T_k are the term vectors and the rows in D_k are the document vectors, is the foundation for the semantic structures LSI exploits. By reducing the dimension from r to k, extraneous information and variability in type usage (referred to as "noise") that is associated with the database or document collection is removed. Reducing the dimension is what captures the important underlying semantic structure of terms and documents. Terms similar in meaning are "near" each other in k-dimensional vector space even if they never co-occur in a document, and documents similar in conceptual meaning are near each other even if they share no terms in common.[12]

The best selection for the number of dimensions to use in the space remains an open question. In practice, the choice for k is much smaller than the number of terms or documents in the term-by-document matrix and usually depends on empirical testing. As described earlier, too few dimensions or too many dimensions result in poor performance. For large datasets, empirical testing shows that the optimal choice for the number of dimensions ranges between 200 and 500. Currently there exists no theory to explain this observation nor is there any method to accurately predict optimal dimensionality.[5,15] There are however a few techniques mentioned in Dumais[10] for estimating k.

Querying in the Reduced Dimension Vector Space

Since both term vectors and document vectors are represented in the reduced dimensional vector space, similarities between two terms or two documents or a term and a document can be computed. Most often the cosine

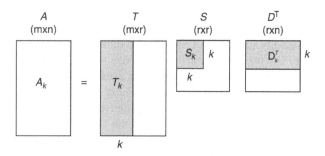

Fig. 1 Diagram of the reduced dimensional SVD for the term-by-document, $m \times n$, matrix A.

Knowledge Management–
Law Librarianship

(which is the angular distance between two vectors) is used as a measure of similarity because of its relation to the dot-product criterion and its effectiveness in many information retrieval applications.[4,10,15] The dot product of two vectors $\mathbf{u}$ and $\mathbf{v}$, where $\mathbf{u} = (u_1, u_2, \ldots, u_n)$ and $\mathbf{v} = (v_1, v_2, \ldots, v_n)$, is the sum of each element in $\mathbf{u}$ multiplied by the corresponding element in $\mathbf{v}$, so $\mathbf{u} \cdot \mathbf{v} = (u_1 v_1 + u_2 v_2 + \ldots + u_n v_n)$ Thus, term-term, document-document, and term-document similarities are easy to compute. New vectors for new terms and/or documents can be added to the existing space by a process called *folding-in*. This same process is used to project queries into the vector space. A query is treated as another "document," and the query vector is located at the weighted average of its component term vectors or at the centroid of the component term vectors in k-dimensional space. Then the query vector is compared to document vectors to find the most similar documents. The documents corresponding to cosines greater than a certain threshold are ordered by their nearness to the query vector and returned as the results of the querying process.[12]

For a thorough description on the mathematics supporting LSI refer to Deerwester,[4] Berry[12] and Martin.[14]

LSI Example

To illustrate the capability of LSI a very small example is presented here. A small document collection consisting of book titles and authors is shown in Table 1. There are 13 documents in the collection, and the terms are words appearing at least twice in the document collection. There are 13 terms, shown in boldface in Table 1. The corresponding term-by-document matrix is found in Table 2. The entries in the matrix are all zeros except for the cells corresponding to terms found in each document. Those cells are the frequency with which the term occurs in the documents. Even though this is a small example, the matrix is still sparse with approximately 22% of the matrix cells being nonzero. In this example, only the term frequency is used for the local weighting function, and no global weighting function is applied. If the term-by-document matrix is decomposed using the SVD and term and documents vectors are obtained, the dimensionality of the vector space can be reduced to two dimensions. Of course, two dimensions are never used in practice with large document collections, but for this small collection and for the sake of visually illustrating LSI only two dimensions are used here. The two-dimensional vector space for this document collection can be seen in Fig. 2. If a user wants to find documents related to the query "Henry Ford," a vector corresponding to the query can be projected into the vector space, as seen in Fig. 2, and then the query vector can be compared to the document vectors by computing the angle between it and all the document vectors. The cosines between the query vector and all the document vectors produce a list in decreasing order. The documents

Table 1 Book titles and authors found on Amazon.com (terms are in boldface).

Label	Titles and authors
D1	*A Guide To Style: A Manual for **Business** and Professional **Women*** by Iris P. McMillan
D2	***Art Models** 2: Life Nude Photos for the Visual **Arts*** by Maureen Johnson and Douglas Johnson
D3	***Open Business Models**: How to Thrive in the New Innovation Landscape* by **Henry** Chesbrough
D4	*Legendary **Model A Ford**: The Complete **History** of America's Favorite **Car*** by Peter Winnewisse
D5	*The **Automobile** (Inventions That Shaped the World)* by Robyn Conley
D6	*Legends of the **Open Road**: The **History**, Technology, and Future of **Automobile** Design* by Garbriella Belli
D7	*The House of Klein: **Fashion**, Controversy, and a **Business** Obsession* by Lisa Marsh
D8	*The **Art** of **Fashion** Draping* by Connie Amaden-Crawford
D9	*Costume and **Fashion**: A Concise **History** (World of **Art**)* by James Laver, Amy De LA Haye, and Andrew Tucker
D10	*The **Art** of the **Automobile**: The 100 Greatest **Cars*** by Dennis Adler
D11	*The **Lady** Mechanic's Total **Car** Care for the Clueless: A Manual for **Car** Owners* by Ren Volpe
D12	*Everything **Women** Always Wanted to Know about **Cars**; But Didn't Know Who to Ask* by Lesley Hazelton
D13	***Henry's Lady**: An Illustrated **History** of the **Model A Ford*** (The **Ford Road** Series, Vol. 2) by Ray Miller and Glenn Embree

corresponding to the highest cosines are deemed most relevant to the query "Henry Ford." The top five documents deemed relevant to the query, which are those documents with cosines greater than 0.95, can be seen in Table 3. Notice that the top document is about the Ford model A and that the top five documents are all about cars or automobiles even though the book titles for D11, D12, and D5 contained none of the query words. The document corresponding to D5, *The Automobile (Inventions That Shaped the World)* by Robyn Conley, is definitely relevant to "Henry Ford," one of the first to mass produce automobiles which shaped the world. Another observation is that of all the relevant documents returned only one contains both of the query terms. If the cosines are computed between the query vector and the document vectors based on a lexical matching then only cosines for D3, D4, and D13 are computed and returned. Of course, D13 is deemed the most relevant in lexical matching, but obviously some relevant documents are missed, such as D5 *The Automobile (Inventions That Shaped the World)* by Robyn Conley.

Using this small example, a new document can be added to the existing vector space by *folding-in*. If a new document, "Fashion (*Oxford History of Art*) by Christopher Breward," labeled D14 is to be added to the semantic space, the document vector is projected into the vector

Knowledge Management—
Law Librarianship

Table 2 Term-by-document matrix with the term frequencies corresponding to the book titles found in Table 1.

Terms	Documents												
	D1	D2	D3	D4	D5	D6	D7	D8	D9	D10	D11	D12	D13
Art(s)	0	2	0	0	0	0	0	1	1	1	0	0	0
Automobile	0	0	0	0	1	1	0	0	0	1	0	0	0
Business	1	0	1	0	0	0	1	0	0	0	0	0	0
Car(s)	0	0	0	1	0	0	0	0	0	1	2	1	0
Fashion	0	0	0	0	0	0	1	1	1	0	0	0	0
Ford	0	0	0	1	0	0	0	0	0	0	0	0	2
Henry	0	0	1	0	0	0	0	0	0	0	0	0	1
History	0	0	0	1	0	1	0	0	1	0	0	0	1
Lady	0	0	0	0	0	0	0	0	0	0	1	0	1
Model(s)	0	1	1	1	0	0	0	0	0	0	0	0	1
Open	0	0	1	0	0	1	0	0	0	0	0	0	0
Road	0	0	0	0	0	1	0	0	0	0	0	0	1
Women	1	0	0	0	0	0	0	0	0	0	0	1	0

space at the centroid, or weighted average, of its constituent term vectors, which are "art," "fashion," and "history" in this case. Fig. 3 shows the new document being placed in the existing vector space for this small book title example. Notice its placement, at the centroid of the vectors corresponding to "art," "fashion," and "history." The new document vector, D14, is near D2, D7, D9, and D8 which are all about artwork and fashion.

COMPUTATIONAL TECHNOLOGY

The automatic computation of the reduced dimensional vector space for a term-by-document matrix derived from a given document collection is a nontrivial calculation. Given a large term-by-document matrix A where there are more terms than documents, the SVD computation becomes a problem of finding the k largest eigenvalues

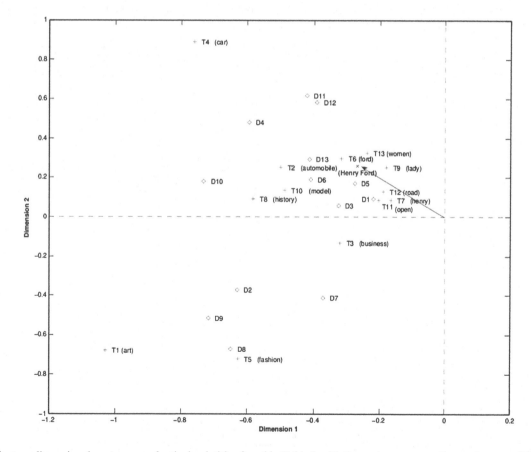

Fig. 2 The two-dimensional vector space for the book titles found in Table 1 with the vector corresponding to the query "Henry Ford." Legend: Diamonds are documents found in Tables 1 and 2 with the labels D1-D13. Crosses are terms found in Tables 1 and 2 with the labels T1-T13 along with the actual word.

Knowledge Management–
Law Librarianship

Table 3 Results for the query "Henry Ford" using a cosine threshold of 0.95.

Document	Cosine
D4: *Legendary Model A Ford: The Complete History of America's Favorite Car* by Peter Winnewisse	0.9960
D13: *Henry's Lady: An Illustrated History of the Model A Ford* (The Ford Road Series, Vol. 2) by Ray Miller and Glenn Embree	0.9882
D11: *The Lady Mechanic's Total Car Care for the Clueless: A Manual for Car Owners* by Ren Volpe	0.9795
D12: *Everything Women Always Wanted to Know about Cars; But Didn't Know Who to Ask* by Lesley Hazelton	0.9780
D5: *The Automobile (Inventions That Shaped the World)* by Robyn Conley	0.9768

and eigenvectors of the matrix $B = A^T * A$. Finding the eigenvectors and eigenvalues of B produces the document vectors and the singular values (the nonnegative square roots of the eigenvalues of B). Then the term vectors are produced by back multiplying. If there are more documents than terms, then computing the SVD is reduced to finding the k largest eigenvalues and eigenvectors of $B = A * A^T$. In this case, finding the eigenvectors and eigenvalues of B produces the term vectors and the singular

values, and the document vectors are produced by back multiplying. To summarize, given the symmetric matrix B, which is created from the sparse input matrix A, the objective is to find the k largest eigenvalues and eigenvectors of B. Thus, the SVD computation is based on solving a large, sparse symmetric eigenproblem.[11,16]

Currently the technology most often used to compute the SVD is based on the Lanczos algorithm. The Lanczos algorithm, which is an iterative method, is proven to be accurate and efficient in solving large, sparse symmetric eigenproblems where only a modest number of the largest or smallest eigenvalues of a matrix are desired.[11,17] The Lanczos algorithm, used to compute the k largest eigenvalues and eigenvectors of B (described in the previous paragraph), actually approximates the eigenvalues of B.[18] In using finite-precision arithmetic, the basic Lanczos procedure suffers from the loss of orthogonality among Lanczos vectors, which lead to the eigenvectors of B. Currently the best option for remedying the problems associated with finite arithmetic is to use selective reorthogonalization of the Lanczos vectors, which is known as the "Lanczos algorithm with selective reorthogonalization."[16,17] The Lanczos algorithm with selective reorthogonalization has made it computationally possible to produce a reduced dimensional vector space for a large document collection. With the growing amount of information available, the

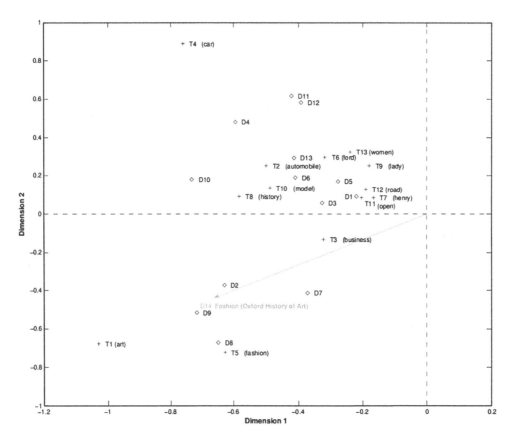

Fig. 3 The two-dimensional vector space for the book titles found in Table 1 with a new document, D14 "Fashion (*Oxford History of Art*) by Christopher Breward," *folded-in* the semantic space.

Knowledge Management–
Law Librarianship

computation of the SVD is manageable with current computer architectures (including clusters and symmetric multiprocessors) and the advent of a highly parallel Lanczos algorithm.[18]

ISSUES AND LIMITATIONS

There are some known issues and limitations with LSI, and a few of the most important ones are described here.

The Value of Word Order

Given a document collection, as documents are automatically read and terms parsed the implicit word order is ignored. The meaning of terms and documents is desired and achieved with LSI without concern for word order or syntactic structure. In some applications, this disregard of word order might result in incompleteness or error.[9] However, LSI performs amazingly well at characterizing the semantics of a given document in a document collection despite the fact that syntactic information is not considered.

Computational Challenges

There are computational challenges associated with calculation of the SVD. The time and storage required to compute the SVD of a document collection correspond to the overall size of the collection, the amount of information or raw text. Larger document collections require more computation time to create a vector space as well as more storage to store the vectors. As document collections grow these scalability issues increase. There are a few solutions available for handling document sets of increasing size. One solution can be found in Martin[19] where out-of-core capabilities for the SVD computation are explored. Another solution is the parallel SVD algorithm that is described in Berry.[18]

Updating

As information is constantly being generated there is often a need to add new documents and terms to an existing vector space. In the simple case, new items are projected into the vector space based on the relationships between the set of term and document vectors used in the vector space creation by a process called *folding-in* (described earlier). However, the addition of new documents can change the relation among terms, and this change is not reflected in the vector space when using the *folding-in* process. As new documents are added, there is a point at which the vector space needs to be recomputed, especially for large collections with rapidly changing content. It has been found that recomputing the vector space only changes the underlying semantic space significantly if

the document collection has changed by about 20% or more.[5] Recomputation of the SVD can be costly as described in the previous section, but the out-of-core and parallel capabilities described in Berry[18] and Martin[19] make recomputation more feasible. A computationally less expensive algorithm known as SVD-*Updating* has also been developed.[12,20] However, to date there is no optimal way to add information to an existing reduced dimensional vector space which directly and accurately affects the underlying latent semantic structure of the collection that is as accurate as recomputing the k-dimensional vector space with the added information.

APPLICATIONS

Over the past two decades, LSI has been tested and employed in a wide range of problems and applications. LSI has been successful as an automated, practical tool for constructing representation of meaning. The book *Handbook of Latent Semantic Analysis* describes and demonstrates an assortment of research and applications for LSI (also known as Latent Semantic Analysis or LSA). LSI has made it possible to build a computational model for many semantic problems.[21] There are three main categories of applications for LSI. They include information retrieval and analysis, cognitive psychology, and educational applications.

Information Retrieval and Analysis

LSI originated as a technique for improving information retrieval[4] and has been shown to improve retrieval performance by up to 30%, being able to match user's queries to documents of the same or similar meanings without having terms in common and rejecting irrelevant documents that have many terms in common with the query.[6] As an information retrieval technique, LSI's capabilities have been utilized to help users locate information, learn from the information, and use the learned information from online manuals. LSI-based tools can automatically present information that is adapted to an individual user's background knowledge and levels of expertise.[21] LSI has been extended to cross-language information retrieval where users can query in one language and retrieve documents in another. The classical cross-language information retrieval method creates a multilingual semantic space by using dual-language documents, where a dual-language document is the same version of a document in two different languages concatenated together. Then other documents from the two languages are folded-in, and queries in one language can find matching documents in another language. This method has shown promising results.[10,22] An extension to this cross-language LSI method has been developed and explored using a technique that maps a semantic space in one language into a

Knowledge Management–
Law Librarianship

semantic space of another to allow for multiple (more than two) languages to be represented in one semantic space.[23] This extension has allowed for creating of Hindi, Arabic, Swahili, and English multilingual space.[10]

Recent work[24] has applied LSI to the task of spam filtering. They compared the classification performance of the traditional VSM and LSI using text-based feature sets from the de-facto spam filtering system SpamAssassin.[25] In classifying e-mail messages as spam or not spam, they demonstrated that a surprisingly large amount of truncation (or low-rank) for the SVD is often possible without a significant loss in classification performance. Although performance can greatly depend on feature (text) extraction strategies, LSI-based spam filtering has been demonstrated to be significantly better than the standard approaches offered by SpamAssassin.

Cognitive Psychology

LSI has been used for research in the field of cognitive theory, testing theories of cognition and trying to better understand the development of the human mind. Landauer and Dumais were the first to attempt to use LSI to build a psychological theory of meaning. They tried to build a system that acquires something similar to human knowledge, which in their case was a human child. LSI was able to acquire English vocabulary at a comparable rate to the vocabulary growth of an American child.[15] This led to LSI being explored as a tool for assisting human vocabulary acquisition. Research in modeling a child's semantic memory with LSI has been explored with some success.[21] In research conducted by Kintsch, a comprehension model incorporating LSI has been shown to accurately represent word meanings despite the fact that a word might have multiple meanings and multiple senses (for example *horses run* and *colors run*).[21] Many more cognitive theories and processes have been explored and modeled using LSI and are described in Landauer.[21]

Educational Applications

LSI has been used in many educational applications. LSI has been used to help to develop educational, interactive Web-based applications. Intelligent tutoring systems need to be able to capture meaning in text. Some examples of tutoring applications using LSI are the following: 1) iSTART, which helps students to better self-explain by teaching them reading strategies; 2) AutoTutor, which helps students learn a certain subject by engaging with a computer tutor; 3) Knowledge Post, which supports online learning and collaboration; and 4) Summary Street, which helps teach children how to compose a written summary of a subject by having students write summaries and giving feedback, automatically coaching them.[21] One of the most successful educational applications using LSI is the Intelligent Essay Assessor (IEA).[26] IEA is a full-scale grading system that has been used commercially to score the adequacy of the content of millions of expository essays for important exams with as high a reliability as two human graders. Again please see *Handbook of Latent Semantic Analysis* for more on these applications.

CONCLUSION

Initially LSI was introduced as a technique to improve information retrieval. It makes use of a mathematical technique to create a semantic space for a document collection in a completely automatic fashion. LSI uses SVD to overcome vocabulary mismatch problems, the variability in word usage, by reducing the dimensionality of the vector space produced by SVD. The dimension reduction causes term and document vectors in the vector space to drop unimportant detail, thus, achieving optimum levels of similarity. Therefore, relevant documents can be identified and retrieved from a document collection even when the documents contain no words presented in the user's query. This dimension reduction step is what captures the underlying semantic structure of terms and documents and what has given LSI its success in many different applications.

While LSI has been used and tested in many different research and application areas with varied success, there still remain issues to be addressed or investigated. Computational issues are still a challenge for large and rapidly changing document collections, especially since the amount of information to be managed continues to grow.

Two decades after its conception, LSI is being used in many different areas other than informational retrieval with promising results. Its capabilities in information retrieval have increased. LSI has great potential for future applications and projects.

REFERENCES

1. Furnas, G.; Landauer, T.; Gomez, L.; Dumais, S. The vocabulary problem in human-system communication. Commun. ACM **1987**, *30*, 964–971.
2. Dumais, S.; Furnas, G.; Landauer, T.; Deerwester, S.; Harshman, R. Using Latent Semantic Analysis to Improve Access to Textual Information Proceedings of SIGCHI Conference on Human Factors in Computing Systems, Washington, DC; 1988; 281–285.
3. Berry, M.; Browne, M. *Understanding Search Engines: Mathematical Modeling and Text Retrieval*; SIAM: Philadelphia, PA, 1999.
4. Deerwester, S.; Dumais, S.; Furnas, G.; Landauer, T.; Harshman, R. Indexing by latent semantic analysis. J. Am. Soc. Inform. Sci. **1990**, *41*, 391–407.
5. Landauer, T. LSA as a theory of meaning. In *Handbook of Latent Semantic Analysis*; Landauer, T., McNamara, D., Dennis, S., Kintsch, W., Eds.; Lawrence Erlbaum Associates, Inc.: Mahwah, NJ, 2007; 3–34.

Knowledge Management–
Law Librarianship

6. Dumais, S. Improving the retrieval of information from external sources. Behav. Res. Meth. Instrum. Comput. **1991**, *23*, 229–236.

7. Salton, G. McGill, M. *Introduction to Modern Information Retrieval*; McGraw-Hill: New York, 1983.

8. Salton, G.; Buckley, C.; Allan, J. Automatic structuring of text files. Electronic Publish. **1992**, *5*, 1–17.

9. Landauer, T.; Foltz, P.; Laham, D. An introduction to latent semantic analysis. Discourse Process. **1998**, *25*, 259–284.

10. Dumais, S. LSA and information retrieval: Getting back to basics. In *Handbook of Latent Semantic Analysis*; Landauer, T., McNamara, D., Dennis, S., Kintsch, W., Eds.; Lawrence Erlbaum Associates, Inc.: Mahwah, NJ, 2007; 293–321.

11. Golub, G.; Van Loan, C. *Matrix Computations*, 2nd Ed.; Johns Hopkins University Press: Baltimore, MD, 1989.

12. Berry, M.; Dumais, S.; O'Brien, G. Using linear algebra for intelligent information retrieval. SIAM Rev. **1995**, *37*, 573–595.

13. Björck, Å. *Numerical Methods for Least Squares Problems*; Linköping University: Linköping, Sweden, 1996.

14. Martin, D.; Berry, M. Mathematical foundations behind latent semantic analysis. In *Handbook of Latent Semantic Analysis*; Landauer, T., McNamara, D., Dennis, S., Kintsch, W., Eds.; Lawrence Erlbaum Associates, Inc.: Mahwah, NJ, 2007; 35–55.

15. Landauer, T.; Dumais, S. A solution to Plato's problem: The latent semantic analysis theory of acquisition, induction, and representation of knowledge. Psychol. Rev. **1997**, *104*, 211–240.

16. Berry, M. Large sparse singular value computations. Int. J. Supercomput. Appl. **1992**, *6*, 13–49.

17. Parlett, B.; Scott, D. The Lanczos algorithm with selective reorthogonalization. Math. Comput. **1979**, *33*, 217–238.

18. Berry, M.; Martin, D. Principle component analysis for information retrieval. In *Statistics: A Series of Textbooks and Monographs: Handbook of Parallel Computing and Statistics*; Kontoghiorghes, E., Ed.; Chapman & Hall/ CRC: Boca Raton, FL, 2005; 399–413.

19. Martin, D.; Martin, J.; Berry, M.; Browne, M. Out-of-core SVD performance for document indexing. Appl. Numer. Math. **2007**, *14*(10), 1–10.

20. Zha, H.; Simon, H. On updating problems in latent semantic indexing. SIAM J. Sci. Comput. **1999**, *21*, 782–791.

21. Landauer, T., McNamara, D., Dennis, S., Kintsch, W., Eds. *Handbook of Latent Semantic Analysis*; Lawrence Erlbaum Associates, Inc.: Mahwah, NJ, 2007.

22. Dumais, S.; Littman, M.; Landauer, T. Automatic cross-linguistic information retrieval using latent semantic analysis. In *Cross Language Information Retrieval*; Grefenstette, G., Ed.; Kluwer Academix Publishers: Boston, MA, 1998; 51–62.

23. Littman, M.; Jiang, F.; Keim, G. *Learning a Language-Independent Representation for Terms from a Partially Aligned Corpus*, Proceedings of the 15th International Conference on Machine Learning Madison, WI July, 24–27, 1998.

24. Gansterer, W.; Janecek, A.; Neumayer, R. Spam filtering based on latent semantic indexing. In *Survey of Text Mining II: Clustering, Classification, and Retrieval*; Berry, M., Castellanos, M., Eds.; Springer-Verlag: London, 2008; 165–183.

25. Apache Software Foundation, *SpamAssassin Open-source Spam Filter*, 2006; Available from World Wide Web: Available at http://doi.acm.org/10.1145/345508.345569.

26. Landauer, T.; Laham, D.; Foltz, P. Automated essay assessment. Assess. Educ. Principle. Policy Pract. **2003**, *10*(3), 295–308.

BIBLIOGRAPHY

1. Deerwester, S.; Dumais, S.; Furnas, G.; Landauer, T.; Harshman, R. Indexing by latent semantic analysis. J. Am. Soc. Inform. Sci. **1990**, *41*, 391–407.

2. Dumais, S. Improving the retrieval of information from external sources. Behav. Res. Methods, Instrum. Comput. **1991**, *23*, 229–236.

3. Landauer, T., McNamara, D., Dennis, S., Kintsch, W., Eds. *Handbook of Latent Semantic Analysis*; Lawrence Erlbaum Associates, Inc.: Mahwah, NJ, 2007.

4. Landauer, T.; Foltz, P.; Laham, D. An introduction to latent semantic analysis. Discourse Process. **1998**, *25*, 259–284.

5. Landauer, T.; Dumais, S. A solution to Plato's problem: The latent semantic analysis theory of acquisition, induction, and representation of knowledge. Psychol. Rev. **1997**, *104*, 211–240.

Knowledge Management-
Law Librarianship

Latinos and U.S. Libraries: History

Romelia Salinas
California State University, Los Angeles, Los Angeles, California, U.S.A.

Abstract

A circumstance that has greatly impacted library services in the United States has been the increased presence of ethnically and linguistically diverse user populations. Central in this development is the Latino community, now the largest minority group in the nation. This entry provides a historical overview of the development of library and information services to the Latino community and the development of Latinos as library professionals. It highlights key policies, initiatives, organizations, and leaders who were instrumental in the development of services to this community and in the recruitment of Latinos to the profession.

INTRODUCTION

Libraries like other institutions are shaped by social, political, and cultural forces. Therefore, a history of library services must consider the social context of that time and how it fashioned its direction. A circumstance that has greatly impacted library services in the United States (U.S.) has been the increased presence of ethnically and linguistically diverse user populations. Central in this development is the Latino community, now the largest minority group in the nation. This entry provides a historical overview of the development of library and information services to the Latino community and the development of Latinos as library professionals.

The history of Latinos in the U.S. as library users and as library professionals prior to the late 1960s has not been well documented. Nevertheless, it is known that before the development of modern Latino library collections there were community libraries established by *mutualistas* (mutual aid societies) during the first part of the twentieth century for this community.[1] It is also known that Spanish-language newspapers, such as *El Clamor Publico*, *Regidor*, and *La Voz de la Mujer*, were important vehicles for the exchange of news, information, and opinions and that by 1939 there were over 400 Spanish-language newspapers in the southwest.[2] Finally, it has also been documented that Latino literary historiography is not a recent phenomenon, but has existed for several hundreds of years.[3] The work by Padilla (1971) is among the few that provides an extensive review of Latino bibliographic history extending back to 1848.[4] However, more on these early years needs to be investigated and recorded. It was not until the late 1980s that the Library and Information Science (LIS) literature began to document and to discuss issues related to information services for the Latino community.

The Civil Rights Movement of the 1960s, along with other political changes, created an environment where questions of library services to ethnic communities began to receive attention. Legislation such as the Federal Government's Library Services Construction Act (LSCA) of 1964, the Civil Rights and Economic Opportunity Acts of 1964, and the Elementary, Secondary, and Higher Education Acts of 1965 made funds available for programs and services aimed at underserved communities.[5,6] It was mainly during this time that library services targeting the Latino community were mainstreamed.

LATINOS IN THE UNITED STATES

The history of the Latino population in the United States is diverse, complicated, and important to know in order to better serve this community. In recent years the role of the Latino community in changing the demographic landscape of the United States has received much discussion. It is estimated that between 2005 and 2050, the Latino population will triple in size and will account for most of the nation's population growth. There were 42 million Latinos in the U.S. in 2005 and this number is expected to rise to 128 million by 2050.[7] These estimates do not count the number of undocumented Latinos who live and work in the United States. Clearly Latinos represent a key economic, political, and cultural force in the U.S., but they are also culturally, demographically, and geographically diverse. The largest group is people of Mexican origin (64%), followed by Puerto Rican (9%), Central American (7.6%), South Americans (5.5%), Cuban-American (3.4%), and then Dominican (2.8%).[8] They come from as many as 20 countries, speak various languages, and sometimes share very little in common with each other. Differences are apparent not only by country of origin, but also by generational status, language preferences, and socio-economic class. The information needs of a first-generation Spanish-speaking Latino will be very different

Encyclopedia of Library and Information Sciences, Fourth Edition DOI: 10.1081/E-ELIS4-120044911

Copyright © 2017 by Taylor & Francis. All rights reserved.

Knowledge Management–
Law Librarianship

than those of a third-generation monolingual English-speaking Latina.

In addition to being a growing and diverse population Latinos are also a young community. The average age of a Latino male is 27 compared to an overall average of 35. Contradictory to popular belief more Latinos are U.S. born (60%) than foreign-born (40%).[8] A final interesting demographic trend is that although Latinos have tended to reside in southern and western regions of the states most recently states such as Arkansas, Georgia, and South Carolina have seen a tremendous growth in their Latino populations. The geographic distribution of the Latino community is changing and expanding and libraries in impacted communities need to be prepared to meet the needs of these new members.

IDENTITY LABELS

The demographic profile of the Latino community highlights the diversity within the community. For this reason, it is important for libraries to learn as much as possible about the Latino community in their service area before making investments in collections, programming, services, publicity, and staffing.[9] Along with this task is the need to learn about the identity politics of that particular community. Terms such as "Latino" and "Hispanic" are often used interchangeably to generally refer to this population, but it is important to understand the semantics of such words. Latino is employed as a generic descriptor for people from Latin American descent. While the term Hispanic, instituted by the federal government, refers to Spanish-speaking people residing in the U.S., this term is often criticized for excluding those who are not Spanish-speaking, as well as for stressing Spanish ancestral origins over indigenous and other racial influences which make up the Latino heritage. Both terms (Latino and Hispanic) are somewhat problematic in that they group together people from many geographically and culturally diverse regions. A number of other labels have been applied to this ethnic group by the literature, such as Raza, Spanish-speaking, Spanish-surnamed, Latin, Spanish, Latin American, Hispano, and Chicano/a. Arguments have frequently been presented for the advantages of one over the other.[10,11] Libraries need to be sensitive to the identity politics that certain labels carry for sectors of this community as they provide services to them. Preferred terms usually reflect local preferences and may differ by generational status, age, class, as well as other variables.

LATINOS AND LIBRARY SERVICES

The Civil Rights Movement set in motion a process that brought ethnicity into the forefront of many societal discussions. Racial minority students across the United States began to demand courses and studies depicting their ethnic heritage and contributions to U.S. society. The growth of these programs stimulated the development of library collections in these areas, including collections reflective of the various Latino populations.[5] At that time the American Library Association (ALA) was not known to be a bastion of support for library services to Latinos.[12] Although ALA lagged behind mainstream America in efforts aimed at addressing the needs of Latinos it eventually established the Committee on Library Services to the Spanish-Speaking in the mid-1970s. In 1978 Library Journal, published the "Guidelines for Library Services to the Spanish-Speaking" by Yolanda Cuesta and Particia Tarin.[13] In 1988 ALA also adopted the policy, "Guidelines for Library Services to Hispanics" which was prepared by the Library Services to the Spanish-Speaking Committee of what was then called the Reference and Adult Services Division, now the Reference and User Services Association.[12]

The development of library and information services to the Latino community called not only for the creation of guidelines and targeted initiatives; it also necessitated the establishment of collections and access tools. The growth of collections would not have been possible without the founding of Latino focused publishers and book distributors such as Arte Publico Press (1979), the Hispanic Book Distributor (1980), and the creation of other collection development tools. For instance in 1973 REFORMA (The National Association to Promote Library and Information Services to Latinos and the Spanish-Speaking) began publishing its newsletter which included book reviews of interest to the Latino community.[14] By 1994 Library Journal started "En Espanol" a semi-annual review of Spanish-language books. A more recent event has been the partnering of ALA and the Guadalajara International Book Fair. For the last 10 years this partnership has awarded librarians who work in the area of Spanish-language acquisitions funds to attend the Fair. Finally in 2002 Criticas: An English Speaker's Guide to the Latest Spanish-Language Titles began to be published. Criticas is a monthly review of Spanish-language books produced by Publishers Weekly, Library Journal, and School Library Journal.

As the collections grew so did the need for access tools. There were certain tools like the Chicano Thesaurus and COMEXAZ (Comite de Mexico y Aztlan) that were useful across a variety of library settings. The Chicano Thesaurus, a subject-heading guide used to organize Latino collections and to make searching easier was first published in 1979. COMEXAZ, a newspaper monitoring and indexing service established in 1972, ceased service in 1980.[1] Both of these tools were instrumental in increasing access to Latino materials. There were other access tools, to be discussed, created to meet the needs of particular types of libraries as well.

Knowledge Management–
Law Librarianship

LATINOS AND PUBLIC LIBRARIES

Services to the Latino community within public libraries began mainly as services to the Spanish-speaking. There have been many initiatives targeting the various sectors of the Latino community throughout the United States since the late 1960s. An early effort aimed at the Puerto Rican community was the New York Public Library's South Bronx Project implemented in 1967 with federal funds under the direction of Lillian Lopez. In 1970, the Cleveland Public Library initiated Project Libros.[6] Project Libros was funded by a Library Services and Construction Act grant through the State Library of Ohio and ran until 1978. In Albuquerque, New Mexico, the Model Cities Neighborhood Library, also a federally funded project, was opened in 1973 to provide services to predominately Mexican American communities. In 1978, El Centro (The Center), a Brooklyn Public Library bilingual center was opened in the Williamsburg Branch Library. In New Jersey, the Newark Public Library inaugurated a model program in 1979 to reach New Jersey Latinas/os which lead to the founding of La Sala Hispanoamericana, a permanent program for the Latino community.[12] In Florida, La Rama Hispanica Branch was opened in the heart of Little Havana in 1978 to serve the Cuban community.[13] Also during the late 1970s in California the Los Angeles County Public Library established Project LIBRE (Libraries Involved in Bilingual Reading Education) and the San Francisco Public Library established the Latin American Library.[15] Although many of the outreach programs and services were launched during the height of the civil rights era there have also been recent programs. For example under the leadership of Martin Gomez, the Serra Cooperative Library System implemented the highly successful "Latino Services Project" from 1982 to 1984.[12] California's Partnerships for Change established in 1989 is credited for revitalizing library services to ethnic communities across the state and in 1996 the Library Service to Hispanic Immigrants of Forsyth County, North Carolina was established.[12] In 1993, Project Colorin-Colorado was started in Miami-Dade Public Library System to create and perform special programs in libraries to celebrate Hispanic Heritage Month. The San Antonio Public Library instituted the Lea Por Vida (Read for Life) program in 1995, a joint project with the WIC (Women, Infants, and Children) program to combine health education with an introduction to library services. These programs vary in focus, but all provided culturally relevant collections and programs and hired bilingual and/or bicultural staff. However, these projects in public libraries were developed with special funding, such as LSCA grants, and were never fully integrated into ongoing budgets, causing the projects to be weakened or eliminated over time.

In recent years public libraries have seen a dwindling in government funding causing them to seek out other sources of capital. A current example is WebJunction's Spanish-Language Outreach Program funded by the Bill and Melinda Gates Foundation. This program, piloted in 2004, helps equip local library staff with knowledge and resources to reach out to Spanish-speakers in their communities and to increase their access to technology.

Central to public library initiatives was the development of collections to meet the needs of the Latino community they served. In general, public libraries focused on the development of Spanish-language collections to serve the Spanish-speaking patron, which is different than developing collections with a focus on the Latino experience. Latino focused collections remained for the most part removed from the community located in institutions of higher education. It was not until the mid and late 1970s that a few of such collections began appearing in public libraries while such collections were created in academic libraries in the late 1960s.[1] One of the earliest resources established in a public library was the Chicano Resource Center of the Los Angeles County Public Library (1976) located in East Los Angeles, the heart of the Latino community.[1]

Although a wide range of models to improve public library services to Latinos were implemented during the late 1960s and early 1970s the development of an appropriate indexing system to ensure access to Spanish-language information or to information by or about the Latino community had been ignored. Libraries soon came to the realization that greater savings would be generated by the use of an appropriate bilingual, Spanish, or culturally relevant subject indexing system. Early on the Alameda County Library in northern California began the development of Spanish-language subject headings based on a scheme called *La Lista de Encabezamientos*.[16] Another effort to develop Spanish-language access to library materials was the California Spanish-Language Database, also known as Hispanex (Hispanic Information Exchange), which was initiated in 1977. It originated as a joint request by the East Bay Cooperative and the Oakland Public Library (now combined and known as the Bay Area Library and Information System) for LSCA funding to develop a union catalog of their Spanish-language books with subject headings in Spanish.[17] The English/Spanish subject headings created for this catalog were published in a publication entitled *Bilindex*: *A Bilingual Spanish–English Subject-Heading List*: *Spanish Equivalents to Library of Congress Subject Headings* in 1984.[18] The goal of this work was to provide authorized Spanish equivalents for English Library of Congress Subject Headings.

Although many efforts targeting the Latino community have occurred in the last few decades a study carried out in 1994 identified areas of weakness for public libraries. Reynaldo Ayala and Marta Steifel Ayala conducted a project sponsored by REFORMA and funded by the W.K. Kellogg Foundation to evaluate the then current state of public library services to the Latino community in the United States. The findings were published in a report

Knowledge Management–
Law Librarianship

entitled *The Report Card on Public Library Services to the Latino Community*: *Final Report*.[12] They highlighted that the demand for services, especially for Latino children, was growing, but lamented the fact that there were so few Latino librarians, only 1.8% of all librarians at that time.

LATINOS AND SCHOOL LIBRARIES

The advent of bilingual education legislation (Bilingual Education Act of 1968 and 1974) and program implementation changed the face of school library services. Bilingual education programs made funds available for the purchase of bilingual or Spanish-language materials for school libraries. However, what became evident was that traditional jobbers provided little assistance in locating bilingual and/or ethnic materials for schools. Therefore new distributors, such as Las Americas and Bilingual Education Services, came about to fill these particular needs.[19] Publishers like Arte Público Press, Piñata Press, Lectorum, and Children's Book Press have also been helpful in seeking out quality materials produced by non-mainstream publishers.

Advocates for services to Latino children and youth have stressed the importance for children to have access to reading materials that portray their cultural heritage in a positive manner. Dr. Isabel Schon, Director of the Barahona Center for the Study of Books in Spanish for Children and Adolescents, has been a leader of this campaign. She has led an active career dedicated to research in the area of materials for children and young adults and continues to provide reviews and recommended reading lists for children and adolescents.

As the availability of Latino themed children's books grew book awards were instituted to encourage creativity and quality works. The Pura Belpré Award was established in 1996 by REFORMA and the ALA Association of Library Services to Children. This award is presented to a Latino/a writer and an illustrator whose work best portrays, affirms, and celebrates the Latino cultural experience in an outstanding work of literature for children and youth. Awards are given for narrative and illustrations, with honored books in each category. This award is named after Pura Belpré, the first Latina librarian of the New York Public Library. Belpré was a children's librarian who enriched the lives of Puerto Rican children in the United States through her storytelling, writing, and dissemination of Puerto Rican folklore.[20] The Tomás Rivera Mexican American Children's Book Award was established in 1995 by the Southwest Texas State University to encourage authors, illustrators, and publishers to produce books that authentically reflect the lives of Mexican American children and young adults in the Southwestern regions of the United States.[9] In 1993, the National Consortium of Latin American Studies Programs bestowed the first Américas Award for Children's and Young Adult Literature. The Américas Award is given in recognition of U.S. works of fiction, poetry, folklore, or selected non-fiction published in the previous year in English or Spanish that authentically and engagingly portray Latin America, the Caribbean, or Latinos in the United States.[20]

An additional program that has furthered attention to library and information services to Latino children has been the instituting of El Día de los Niños/El Día de los Libros (Children's Day/Book Day). This is a celebration of children, families, and reading held annually on April 30th. The celebration emphasizes the importance of literacy for children of all linguistic and cultural backgrounds. This event is the brainchild of nationally acclaimed children's book author Pat Mora, who proposed it in 1996. This national event has been funded by a series of grants from the W.K. Kellogg Foundation, and most recently Target. The Association for Library Service for Children continues to increase public awareness of the event in libraries throughout the country in collaboration with REFORMA, a founding partner of the event.

The demise of funding for school libraries throughout the United States, particularly in low-income communities has weakened the momentum of developing strong collections to meet the needs of Latino children. Other legislations like California's 1998 Proposition 227, which ended bilingual education and Proposition 187 in 1994, which denied undocumented immigrants social services, health care, and public education, furthered damaged the quality and quantity of services available to Latino children in public schools.

LATINOS AND ACADEMIC LIBRARIES

The development of collections and services to meet the needs of Latinos began in the academic setting. Precursors to what is known today as "Chicano collections" were Latin American and Southwest collections, such as the Genaro Garcia Library and the Eugene Barker Texas History collection at the University of Texas.[3] Initiatives targeting the Latino student population had existed since the late 1960s, but the Ethnic Studies Heritage Act of 1972 provided funding for higher education institutions to increase their course offerings in ethnic studies.[13] This lead to a greater demand for Chicano/Latino studies collections and services. Often libraries were established as a result of student initiated efforts.[21] The development of Chicano/Latino library collections within academia was difficult because this area of study was not perceived as a legitimate discipline by some institutions.[1] The establishment of Chicano focused publishing houses, such as Quinto Sol, assisted in the production and availability of literature for and about the Latino community.[2] Although challenging, the work of pioneering academic librarians such as Richard Chabran, Francisco Garcia, Lillian Castillo-Speed, Nelida Perez, and Margo Gutierrez, to name a

Knowledge Management–
Law Librarianship

few, lead to what today are considered highly valuable Chicano/Latino primary source and reference collections and libraries.

The path towards instituting these special libraries was set by the Chicano Studies Library at the University of California, Berkeley and the Chicano Research Library at the University of California, Los Angeles, both established in 1969. In 1970, the Chicano Studies Collection, at Arizona State University, the Colección Chicano at California State University, San Diego and the Chicano Reference Library at Stanford University were soon after founded. Following the lead of these trailblazing institutions many universities across the United States introduced Chicano/Latino focused collections throughout the 1970s. For instance, the Centro de Estudios Puertorriqueños is an outstanding collection on the study and interpretation of the Puerto Rican experience in the United States. It was established in 1973 to support the Center for Puerto Rican Studies at the City University of New York.[6] Other collections established during this decade were the Colección Tloque Nahuaque, University of California, Santa Barbara, 1971; the Chicano Studies Collection, University of Texas, El Paso, 1971; the Mexico and Southwest Collection, California State University, Fullerton, 1972, now renamed the Chicana and Chicano Resource Center;[1] the Mexican American Library Program, University of Texas, Austin, 1974; and the National Chicano Research Network, University of Michigan, 1977.

Similar to public libraries academic libraries also encountered a need for appropriate and relevant access tools. However the problem of indexing in academic libraries was more complicated. It was assumed that Latino students within higher education institutions were fluent English speakers so the rational for special indexing system was harder to articulate. However, it was the development of Latino/Chicano Studies that required the organization of subjects according to proper concepts within the framework of the discipline.[16] In early 1977, a pilot project to index 17 Chicano serial titles was coordinated by Richard Chabran along with Francisco Garcia and Roberto Trujillo. Nine libraries in four Southwestern states cooperated in the indexing project. During the development of this indexing scheme for Chicano serials the Committee for the Development of Subject Access to Chicano Literature was formed. In 1979, the Committee published the *Chicano Thesaurus for Indexing Chicano Materials*.[15] It was the intention of the *Chicano Thesaurus* to provide more culturally sensitive and accurate descriptors than those from traditional controlled vocabularies. The *Thesaurus* used a combination of English, Spanish and Calo (slang) words or descriptors to approximate natural language.[18]

Another early tool created to provide access to serials was the *Chicano Studies Library Serials Collection* of 1978. This work included citations for over 400 serials available in the Chicano Studies Library at the University

of California, Berkeley. This was the beginning of *The Chicano Periodical Index*. The early volumes of this index covered only Latino journals, while more recent ones cover periodical literature beyond Chicano/Latino Studies and other types of works such as books and poetry. In 1989 it changed its name to the *Chicano Index*.[22] It eventually became available in machine readable format creating the *Chicano Database* and first released in 1990 on CD-ROM under the leadership of Lillian Castillo-Speed.[18] In 1996 the database went online as an RLG product and in 2007 it became available via OCLC First Search. It is to date the only electronic research tool that focuses solely on indexing Chicano/Latino related materials and includes most of the small publications that came out during the late 1960s and 1970s.

Another significant access tool is the *Hispanic American Periodical Index* established in 1977 by Barbara Valk at the UCLA Latin American Institute.[22] Although primarily an index of Latin American literature in more recent years it has included articles on the experience of Latinos in the United States. The *Spanish Speaking Mental Health Research Center Database* was established in 1975 and was the first searchable Latino focused database. This database ceased publication in 1990 and eventually its records became part of the *Chicano Database*.

LATINOS IN THE PROFESSION

The growth in collections and services for Latino library users created a need to prepare librarians to serve this community. The shortage of qualified librarians to serve this population can be attributed to both the small numbers of Latinos who enter the LIS profession and to the paucity of appropriate courses in library programs. The latest available statistical report of the Association of Library and Information Science Education (2004) stated that Latinos continue to be under represented in terms of earning a master's degree in Library Science. The report revealed that only 146 Latinos graduated with a master's degree in Library Science or in Information Science for the 2002–2003 academic year. This was from a total of 5762 graduates. Hence, Latinos continue to represent less than 3% of MLS degree recipients in the United States.

During the 1970s two programs were instituted to train qualified students to provide library services to Latinos. In 1968 Elizabeth Martinez, Jose Taylor, and David Barron formed a Los Angeles-based group called the Committee to Recruit Mexican American Librarians. A few years later in 1972 Patrick Sanchez worked with this group to establish the Mexican American Institute of Library Science at the California State University at Fullerton (1972–1975).[13,14] This program was funded by the California State Library's Minority Recruitment and Advancement Program. This was the first time a library school program was aimed at training Latina/o librarians with specialized course work and seminars and by providing financial aid to participants. The second program, established by Dr. Arnulfo Trejo, was the Tucson-based Graduate Library Institute for Spanish-Speaking Americans at the University of Arizona (1976–1979).[23] These programs produced an impressive number of Latino librarians, many who went on to become leaders within the profession such as Martin Gomez, Luis Herrera, Salvador Güereña, Liz Rodríguez Miller, José Aponte, and Margo Gutiérrez. These programs were funded by soft money and ended after a few years. Although programs like these have not been reproduced, in 2001 the University of Arizona School of Information Resources and Library Science received an Institute of Museum and Library Services grant to create the Knowledge River Institute, a master's degree program to attract Native Americans and Latinos into the LIS field.[13] Also, in 1997 the Spectrum Initiative, the brainchild of then ALA Director Elizabeth Martinez, was implemented to recruit applicants and award scholarships to minorities, including Latinos, for graduate programs in LIS.[24]

The development of such recruitment efforts would not have been possible without the perseverance and dedication of many librarians who believed that services to the Latino community needed to be improved. The work of these individuals was often carried out via various national and local organizations. Some of the earliest of such organizations were the California-based Asociación de Bibliotecarios Chicanos, established in 1975 and Bibliotecas Para La Gente, established in 1978 in the San Francisco Bay area. The American Library Association established the Chicano Task Force of the Social Responsibilities Roundtable, and the Committee on Services to the Spanish-Speaking of the Reference and Adult Services Division.[23] Many of the locally based organizations eventually became chapters of REFORMA, the first national association dedicated to the improvement of the full spectrum of library and information services for Spanish-speakers and Latinos in the United States.

REFORMA was established in 1971 by a group of Latino/a librarians at an ALA conference in Dallas, Texas. Leading the group were founding members Dr. Arnulfo Trejo and Elizabeth Martinez. Dr. Trejo served as president of the organization for the first 4 years.[14] REFORMA was established to pursue the ideals of reforming libraries' lack of outreach to Spanish-speaking people, to create better library services to that community, and to recruit bilingual/bicultural librarians.[12] At the time REFORMA was established it was called the National Association of Spanish-Speaking Librarians in the United States. It went on to change its subtitle to the National Association to Promote Library Services to the Spanish-Speaking and then to the National Association to Promote Library and Information Services to Latinos and Spanish Speaking in recognition that not all Latinos are Spanish speaking and not all Spanish speakers are Latinos. Over the years REFORMA has grown

to a national organization with 26 chapters located across the United States and Puerto Rico. Chapters function autonomously, working through their local library systems, state library associations, and local organizations to achieve local and national objectives.

In 1982 the REFORMA National Scholarship Program was instituted to be awarded annually to Latinos who are candidates for library school.[14] In addition, many of the chapters have also established scholarships given to local LIS students who have demonstrated an interest in serving the Latino community. As an indicator of REFORMA's maturity it held its first national conference in Austin, Texas in August 1996, its second conference in Tucson, Arizona August 2000 and the third in El Paso, Texas September 2008. Although struggling during its initial years REFORMA has blossomed into a sophisticated and vital organization.

In addition to recruitment, professional development has also been an issue for serving the Latino community. In an effort to address this weakness, Dr. Arnulfo Trejo established the Trejo Foster Foundation for Hispanic Library Education (TFF) in 1992. The TFF has sponsored bi-annual, educational institutes to bring together leaders, practitioners, and students in the library and information fields to discuss and advocate for issues, policies, and practices that affect Latino communities. The Foundation provides support to finance research, seminars, workshops, and other activities that promoted and enhanced library education for Latinos. It is best known for its various educational institutes such as, the "Status of Hispanic Library and Information Services: A National Institute for Educational Change" (July 1993), "Latino Populations and the Public Library" (November 1995), "Hispanic Leadership in Libraries" (August 1997), "Library Services to Youth of Hispanic Heritage" (March 1999), "Bridging Borders: Building Hispanic Library Education in a Global Perspective" (July 2001), "Memoria, Voz, y Patrimonio: The First Conference on Latino/Hispanic Film, Print, and Sound Archives" (August 2003) and "Salud Se Puede: Health Information for Hispanic/Latino Populations" (July 2007).[25] These institutes were funded through a variety of public and private sources as well as in partnership with other institutions.

CONCLUSION

The history of library services to the Latino community reveals advances in many areas. There have been vast improvements brought upon by the work of many dedicated individuals and organizations over the years. However, many of the issues that plagued librarians during the 1960s continue today. There is still a shortage of Latino librarians, a need for more curriculum development in library science programs to prepare future librarians to meet the needs of this community, and the need for more collections that reflect the Latino community. Nevertheless, the accomplishments of the last few decades should be applauded and recognized.

REFERENCES

1. Olvera, J. Escatiola, E. Mercado, M. Ocon, B. Tovar, A. Chicano collections of library resources. In *Ethnic Collections in Libraries*; Josey, E.J., DeLoach, M.L., Eds.; Neal-Schuman: New York, 1983; 75–100.
2. Chabran, R. The production of Chicano writing. In *Biblio-Politica: Chicano Perspectives on Library Service in the United States*; Chabran, R., Garcia, F., Eds.; Chicano Studies Library Publications: Berkeley, CA, 1984; 23–44.
3. Guerena, S. Archives and manuscripts: historical antecedents to contemporary Chicano collections. Collect. Build. **1988**, *8* (4), 3–11.
4. Padilla, R. Apuntes para la documentacion del al cultura Chicana. El Grito **1971**, *5* (2), 3–79.
5. Josey, E.J., DeLoach, M.L., Eds. *Ethnic Collections in Libraries*; Neal-Schuman: New York, 1983.
6. Verges, B. Developing collections on Puerto Rican heritage. In *Ethnic Collections in Libraries*; Josey, E.J., DeLoach, M.L., Eds.; Neal-Schuman: New York, 1983; 65–74.
7. http://pewhispanic.org/files/reports/85.pdf.
8. http://www.census.gov/population/www/socdemo/hispanic/hispanic_pop_presentation.html.
9. Byrd, S.M. *Bienvenidos Welcome: A Handy Resource Guide for Marketing Your Library to Latinos*, American Library Association: Chicago, IL, 2005.
10. Hayes-Bautista, D.E.; Chapa, J. Latino terminology: conceptual bases for standardized terminology. Am. J. Public Health. **1987**, *77*, 61–68.
11. Trevino, F.M. Standardized terminology for hispanic populations. Am. J. Public Health **1987**, *77*, 69–72.
12. Guerena, S.; Erazo, E. Latinos and librarianship. Libr. Trends **2000**, *49* (1), 138–181.
13. Jones, P.A. *Still Struggling for Equality: American Public Library Services with Minorities*, Libraries Unlimited: Westport, CT, 2004.
14. Dawson, P.J. The history and role of REFORMA. In *Latino Librarianship: A Handbook for Professionals*; Guerena, S., Ed.; McFarland: Jefferson, NC, 1990; 121–134.
15. Haro, R.P. *Developing Library and Information Services for Americans of Hispanic Origin*, Scarecrow Press: Metuchen, NJ, 1981.
16. Cabello-Aragandona, R. Haro, R. Library services for the Spanish-speaking: a systematic review and analysis. In *Library Services to Mexican Americans: Policies, Practices and Prospects*; Urzua, R., Cotera, M., Stupp, E.G., Eds.; Clearinghouse on Rural Education and Small Schools: Las Cruces, NM, 1978; 1–36.
17. Cabello-Argandona, R. Library services to the Spanish speaking and the data base development. In *Ethnic Collections in Libraries*; Josey, E.J., DeLoach, M.L., Eds.; Neal-Schuman: New York, 1983; 101–118.
18. Rodriguez, R. Latino databases. In *Latino Librarianship: A Handbook for Professionals*; Guerena, S., Ed.; McFarland: Jefferson, NC, 1990; 58–67.
19. Cotera, M. The impact of bilingual education on school libraries services: some problems and recommendations. In *Library Services to Mexican Americans: Policies, Practices and Prospects*; Urzua, R., Cotera, M., Stupp, E.G., Eds.; Clearinghouse on Rural Education and Small Schools: Las Cruces, NM, 1978; 100–118.
20. Dresang, E. Outstanding literature: Pura Belpre and Americas selections with special appeal in the digital age. In *Library Services to Youth of Hispanic Heritage*; Immroth, B., de la Peña McCook, K., Eds.; McFarland: Jefferson, NC, 2000; 69–87.
21. Chabran, R. Notes on the history and future of major academic Chicano libraries. In *Biblio-Politica. Chicano Perspectives on Library Service in the United States*; Chabran, R., Garcia, F., Eds.; Chicano Studies Library Publications: Berkeley, CA, 1984; 89–106.
22. Chabran, R. Latino reference sources: a bibliographic essay. In *Latino Librarianship: A Handbook for Professionals*; Guerena, S., Ed.; McFarland: Jefferson, NC, 1990; 35–57.
23. Baeza, G. The evolution of educational and public library services to Spanish-speaking children. In *Library Services for Hispanic Children: A Guide for Public and School Librarians*; Allen, A., Ed.; Oryx Press: Phoenix, AZ, 1987; 3–11.
24. Espinal, I. Wanted: Latino librarians. Criticas Mag. (November) **2003**, *19*, 19–24.
25. http://www.tffoundation.org/accomp.html.

Knowledge Management–Law Librarianship

Law Firm Librarianship

Brenda A. Burton
Mary B. Eggert
Clara C. Mosquera
Library, Kirkland & Ellis LLP, Chicago, IL, USA

Abstract
Law firm libraries differ from their municipal law library and academic law library counterparts in clients served, projects researched, and challenges faced. That law firms are profit-driven businesses influences the skills needed for a law firm librarian to succeed as well as how the library operates. As with all libraries, digitization continues to influence key aspects of law firm library practices.

INTRODUCTION

Law firm libraries vary from their law school library counterparts in that the stakes are much different at a law firm. Law firms are a business whose product is advice and counsel. Millions of dollars and hundreds of billable hours can ride upon discovering the missing piece of information or identifying the ideal expert who will help win a trial. Experienced law firm librarians work behind the scenes researching the facts and figures necessary for the attorney's practice and, ultimately, the client's success.

Law firm librarians provide these research services in the high-pressure environment that is a law firm. There are deadlines to meet for various trials, several corporate transactions taking place all at once, and additional nonresearch responsibilities to juggle, as well. A good law firm librarian has the ability and preparation necessary to meet these demands. Lawyers know the law, but law firm librarians support them with everything else. In many ways, the digital age has made research easier considering the vast amount of information now readily available online. However, analog skills are still necessary for a law firm librarian to perform well.

ORGANIZATION OF LAW FIRM LIBRARIES

Law firm libraries are organized in various ways depending on the size of the firm, the number of staff members, the number of offices, and the location of the offices. The libraries can range from having one solo librarian at a small firm to multiple librarians with a support staff at a large firm.

For firms with several offices, there can be a centralized library located in the firm's main office or library staff located within each office to provide onsite assistance. The staffing of a library in each office depends on the size of that office and perceived need of support. For firms with international offices, the domestic library can support the needs of the foreign offices. However, because of differences in time zones and languages, many international offices will have their own libraries and librarians who can be consulted during their normal working hours.

Within a large law firm library, there can be a mixture of professional, paraprofessional, and administrative positions. Described here are the possible positions at a large law firm library and their corresponding responsibilities:

- **Library Director** (also called Library Manager, Information Manager, or Chief Librarian): The library director oversees the operation of the firm-wide library system and is in charge of vendor contract negotiations, annual budgets, long-range planning, and staffing. The library director also serves as the liaison to the firm's executive committee and typically reports to the executive director of the firm. At some firms, the library director is also in charge of the departments that handle knowledge management, competitive intelligence, records management, conflicts, and docketing.
- **Research Manager** (also called Assistant Library Director): Research managers usually head one of the individual offices. Their responsibilities include supervising the research librarians and administrative staff at their location as well as managing their own budget. They also oversee collection development including the selection of materials for acquisition and cancellation. Research managers often conduct research in addition to their administrative duties.
- **Research Librarian** (also called Research Specialist or Reference Librarian): Research librarians focus on conducting high-quality and cost-effective research for the attorneys, legal assistants, and support staff of the firm. They often have additional nonresearch responsibilities such as maintaining various library guides, evaluating new products, and providing training. Gen-

Encyclopedia of Library and Information Sciences, Fourth Edition DOI: 10.1081/E-ELIS4-120053502
Copyright © 2017 by Taylor & Francis. All rights reserved.

Knowledge Management–
Law Librarianship

Knowledge Management–
Law Librarianship

erally, the research librarian does not have any supervisory responsibilities.

- **Electronic Services Librarian**: Electronic services librarians are in charge of database and password management, library intranets, attorney training, and evaluation of new online services.
- **Embedded Librarian**: An embedded librarian works for a specific practice group. The librarian is usually situated on the same floor as the practice group, provides targeted research, and attends practice group meetings. This role is becoming more common in larger law firms.
- **Legislative/Regulatory Librarian**: Legislative/regulatory librarians research governmental materials and agencies and often compile legislative and regulatory histories.
- **Research Assistant**: Research assistants typically handle document retrieval and interlibrary loan requests. They can also assist the librarians with research projects.
- **Library Assistant** (also called Library Technician): A library assistant can have a variety of responsibilities, including placing book orders, routing periodicals, shelving books, processing invoices, filing loose-leaf materials, and retrieving books and articles from outside libraries.
- **Filer/Shelver**: Filers keep library materials up-to-date by filing loose-leaf supplements and pocket parts. They also reshelve books and periodicals. Many large law firm libraries outsource the filing services.
- **Cataloger** (also called Technical Services Librarian): Catalogers manage the cataloging and classification of library materials. They can also oversee the circulation system of the library. Many firms outsource the cataloging services.

For midsize law firms, there is often a library manager, a research librarian, and one or two library assistants. The library manager will handle the administrative tasks such as contract negotiations and budgets but will most likely do research as well. Smaller firms often have a solo librarian without any support staff. Working in a small law firm library can be a challenging position as the librarian handles all administrative responsibilities related to the library and its collection in addition to conducting research.

SERVICES AND USERS

A law firm library is a department of the law firm. As with other private business libraries, the law firm library focuses on the business of the firm it serves. That business is providing legal services to clients. The law firm library serves the information needs of both lawyers and staff. In a large law firm setting, there are both legal and nonlegal staff. The legal staff consists of equity partners, junior or nonequity partners, and associates. The attorneys are supported by legal assistants or paralegals, project assistants, and case assistants.

A law firm's nonlegal staff includes the administrative personnel found in various departments such as accounting, human resources, and information technology. This is similar to any corporation. Departments that may be unique to a law firm include a business development department, conflicts department, and docketing department. Law firm librarians support the firm and all its departments by providing research, document retrieval, interlibrary loan, training, and maintenance of the library collection.

Research

Research librarians in a law firm library must provide research service in a cost-effective and timely manner. In many instances, the firm bills the client for the librarian's time and database charges.

Librarians have the ability to sort through a great deal of information, paring it down into a manageable amount, and ultimately providing only the most relevant documents to the requestor. They organize and summarize the results of their research. Research projects are usually wide-ranging and cover a variety of topics. The research librarian must be adept at switching gears because no two requests are quite the same. A typical day may have a law librarian doing background research on an expert witness, identifying intellectual property owned by a company for due diligence purposes, and finding Securities and Exchange Commission company filings precedent. Many projects are deadline sensitive in a law firm, and a librarian is often called upon to juggle multiple research projects at a time. It is usually a fast-paced work environment.

Examples of research projects in a law firm library include:

- Assembling a dossier on a particular company including biographical information on officers and directors, a listing of recent acquisitions or divestitures, major news stories, and stock quotes
- Cite checking a case to determine whether it is still "good law"
- Compiling a legislative history to discover the intent of specific law
- Creating media alerts to monitor current business of a client
- Determining state of incorporation and principal place of business for companies
- Identifying statutes or administrative agency regulations
- Looking for secondary source materials, such as legal treatises, law review, or bar journals

- Obtaining background on expert witnesses (biographical information, media, publications, and prior testimony) or identifying potential experts in a particular academic field
- Identifying all the intellectual property (copyrights, domain names, patents, and trademarks) owned by a company
- Searching for particular language in company Securities and Exchange Commission filings (e.g., how they disclose to investors that they are subject to pending litigation)
- Finding information to assist the business development department in preparing a bid for work from a new or existing client
- Assisting the conflicts department in determining whether an existing client may be on the other side of a legal matter
- Identifying case information for a lawsuit to aid the docketing department in obtaining pleadings from the court
- Researching the background of potential new vendors for the IT department

Research Desk/Triage System

A large law firm may have multiple research librarians who work on research and document requests. The workflow may be managed through a centralized research intake or triage system. The librarian managing the research desk assigns the projects, while keeping in mind deadlines and cost constraints. Reference interviews are conducted to determine the best and most cost-efficient manner to conduct the research. Good communication skills come into play as the librarian negotiates deadlines, discusses parameters of the research, and provides cost estimates. Other firms may use a decentralized or less formal intake system.

In addition to taking and assigning incoming research and document requests, the librarian also receives questions from patrons wishing to conduct their own research. The librarian will make suggestions on which sources the patron should consult and in what format.

Document Retrieval and Interlibrary Loan

The library can obtain copies of articles, patents and patent file histories, technical papers, dissertations, standards, and conference proceedings. Although technology and the Internet have made many documents, especially those from government agencies, readily available electronically, there is still a need for materials not online or owned by the law firm library. Firm librarians work with university, public, government, and other law firm libraries to obtain documents as well as legal and nonlegal books. Interlibrary loan in law firms is often done by e-mail and telephone as many requests must be filled quickly, often within hours.

Firm Intranet and Knowledge Management Systems

The library contributes to the firm intranet by maintaining a library services page. Attorneys and staff may access the library catalog, sign up to receive newsletters, and obtain pathfinders or library guides for particular areas of law. These pathfinders may address current developments or link to primary law materials, online treatises, and periodicals.

Law librarians often are advisors in creating the firm's knowledge management system. They create the organizational taxonomy of terms used in such systems allowing the attorney to search for internal work product and drafting tools for both litigation and transactional documents.

Training and Orientation

Law librarians provide library orientation for new associates as well as attorneys hired from other firms, known as lateral hires. They introduce the new attorneys to the firm's library and its services, focusing on the attorney's specific practice area. These sessions are often done one-on-one.

Newly admitted attorneys coming from law school are comfortable in the new digital era, but may not be aware of all the databases and sources the library can offer them. Lateral hires might want to be assured that they will have access to a source that they had at their prior firm. If the library does not currently own the resource, the librarian may offer alternatives. Orientation is a good time to let new hires know what the library can offer and to remind them of the informal yet practical "Google Rule" where if they are looking for something on the web or some other source and cannot find it after 10 minutes, they should contact the library. The librarians often have access to additional resources and can locate information in the quickest and most cost-effective manner.

Maintenance of Collection and Library Catalog

The library maintains an electronic catalog of its materials. In turn, the technical services or library operations staff manages the catalog. They are responsible for serials check-in, routing, and processing of new materials. The library routes a variety of print and electronic periodicals to support the firm's business and practice areas. Increasingly, current awareness is electronic-only via e-newsletters, RSS feeds, or e-zines that are pushed to the desktop or mobile device.

In today's environment, librarians must develop and maintain library collections keeping in mind not only what the best resources are, but also the optimal format for their users in this hybrid era of print and digital materials. Electronic subscriptions often involve license negotiation, determining whether a separate per user license will be needed or whether the firm will have IP authentication. Librarians also monitor billing and passwords/logins for each resource.

COLLECTIONS

For the most part, the digital age has made for an ever-shrinking library footprint. The traditional image of a law firm library with rows and rows of reporters, statute volumes, and treatises has evolved into the modern, digital universe with the same information only a keystroke, mouse-click, or touch-screen away. Some law firms have almost completely eliminated paper collections while others still have books, but fewer and fewer of them each year.

Current federal and state statutes, regulations, and case reporters are available via services such as Lexis-Nexis, Westlaw, and Bloomberg Law. These are the same materials that formerly occupied the most space in a law firm library. These vendors and others such as HeinOnline also provide access to collections of law reviews, law journals, newspapers, trade journals, etc.

Some items still found on library shelves are current awareness materials such as newspapers and journals. There are also specialized dictionaries (medical, scientific, technical) and practice guides meant to bring an attorney up to speed on the topic in question. However, many of these books and periodicals are also converting to digital media via the migration to e-books and online subscriptions.

Searching these materials online is more time- and space-efficient than hunting through indexes and book-shelves. However, many online services are moving from command language and Boolean searching to more nebulous, search engine type searching, or what can be described as changing from searching to browsing.[1]

While the accessibility of current materials is essential for a law practice, historical materials are also extremely important when researching precedent or legal intent. The extent to which historical materials are available online varies. This is where interlibrary loan comes in. Law school libraries at research institutions will have deep collections of historical materials unavailable digitally.

EDUCATION

Law firm librarians can have JDs or MBAs, but ideally have a master's degree in library science (MLS). A library science degree provides librarians with not only research skills, but more importantly the ability to interact with patrons who range from the highest ranking equity partners to case assistants. Knowing how to conduct a reference interview—identifying intent and pinning down what information the requestor truly needs—is an essential aspect of performing well in a law firm setting.

Depending on the practice areas or size of the firm, other areas of knowledge are useful. A science or technical background will be prized in an intellectual property practice. A background in finance is advantageous when working with a private equity/venture capital practice. Foreign languages are helpful at international firms with offices throughout the world. Because research projects are wide-ranging and diverse, the more knowledge and intellectual curiosity the law librarian has, the better.

PROFESSIONAL ASSOCIATIONS

There are several associations for librarians that support professional development at national, international, or local levels. The American Association of Law Libraries (AALL), the Special Libraries Association (SLA), and Strategic and Competitive Intelligence Professionals (SCIP) are the most relevant to law firm librarians. These organizations are useful not only for networking purposes, but also to keep up with best practices in research, to keep abreast of trends affecting libraries, and not least, to advocate for librarians.

Like other professional organizations, they publish trade journals, track membership, disseminate information via social media, and lobby government. Members gather at annual or semiannual meetings for workshops and seminars on topics such as copyright issues in libraries, technical services, or digital collections. They are essential for continued professional development.

TWENTY-FIRST CENTURY CHALLENGES

In the last 25 years, the law firm librarian profession has undergone dramatic changes primarily as a result of the rise of the Internet and a shift from a reliance on print resources to an ever-growing dependence on electronic resources. This trend will persist and will present numerous challenges to law firm librarians as well as librarians in academic, public, and special libraries.

One of the biggest challenges facing all librarians is how to best manage their library collections, which consist of both print and electronic resources. As more titles are made available in electronic formats, librarians have to decide which format best serves their attorneys. In some instances, the decision is made to obtain both the print and electronic versions of materials, but this can be expensive as a result of legal publishers bundling the print and electronic products together at a high cost. According to the 2015 AALL Biennial Salary Survey & Organizational Characteristics, law firms spend an average of 69.2% of their information budget on electronic resources.[2] While that percentage is already high, it will likely continue to rise in the near future as publishers offer less print material in favor of electronic resources.

Knowledge Management– Law Librarianship

Electronic resources pose their own challenges. While electronic databases provide users with the ability to do sophisticated searching of full-text materials, each product has its own platform and search syntax. Not only do librarians have to become experts in using each product, they have to be able to instruct the attorneys in how to best use the databases. Another challenge is determining whether the library should obtain an enterprise license or individual seat licenses for the electronic resource. Fortunately, there are electronic resource management tools that allow the library to track usage of databases to determine if there is sufficient use of the electronic databases to justify their costs.

The realm of e-books is also proving to be a challenge. More and more attorneys are asking for e-books that they can read on their mobile devices, tablets, e-readers, and desktop computers. There are some publishers providing access to e-book collections through subscriptions, but there are also ways to buy an individual e-book directly from a publisher. Unlike print books, once an e-book is purchased, it can be difficult to circulate to the end user due to license restrictions. E-books will continue to become more prevalent in the years ahead as librarians determine the best way to implement this technology.

Another challenge arising from the increase in electronic resources relates to attorney training. Law firms have attorneys with varying levels of comfort with technology. Training sessions have to be customized to accommodate differing degrees of skill. Many databases are being redesigned to be more Google-like in their search functionality, although this brings its own challenges for librarians and attorneys adept at doing more sophisticated searching.

Compliance with copyright laws has always been a challenge in the library world, and the increasing use of electronic resources has only magnified this issue. Many databases have strict license agreements for their electronic materials. The librarian is often asked to obtain an electronic copy of an article, standard, or book on behalf of an attorney. It is the librarian's responsibility to make sure that the license agreement is not violated once the material is shared with the attorney. However, once the item has been given to the attorney, it is difficult for the librarian to keep track of how the document is being used and/or distributed. Many law firms have document management systems that are designed to share materials internally. These document management systems can be especially problematic in terms of copyright compliance as users can unwittingly post copyrighted materials.

In addition, obtaining materials through interlibrary loan is becoming more difficult as libraries are replacing print materials with electronic versions. The license agreements for these electronic resources prohibit the lending library from sharing the materials with people outside of their organization. As a result, libraries will be limited in what they can share with other libraries, which will make it harder for libraries to obtain articles and books through traditional interlibrary loan methods.

Budgeting is a perpetual challenge for libraries including law firm libraries. The rise of electronic resources and the unpredictable nature of their costs have made it progressively more difficult to plan an annual budget and to stay within the budget from year to year. In addition, cost recovery in law firm libraries is becoming more problematic. According to the 2016 ALM Law Librarian Survey, 71% of the Am Law 200 firms reported recovering 40% or less of their online research costs.[3] A growing number of firms are beginning to consider database costs as overhead and are no longer attempting to recoup those expenses from clients.

Another challenge relates to outsourcing. Some library services, such as filing of loose-leaf treatises and cataloging, are often outsourced. However, the concern is that research services could also be outsourced. While this type of outsourcing has not yet spread throughout the law firm community, the threat is still an ongoing consideration.

CONCLUSION

Whether working in a small, midsize, or large law firm, the law firm librarian's main responsibility is to support the research needs of the firm's attorneys, legal assistants, and administrative staff. The librarian's knowledge of a wide variety of resources, both print and electronic, and ability to produce quality research in a timely and cost-effective way is a valuable asset to the firm. The library often cooperates with the other departments in the firm including the business development, information technology, conflicts, human resources, and accounting departments. These collaborations with the administrative and legal staff help the library maintain its status as a highly regarded and much used department in the firm.

Even though the law firm librarian profession is undergoing significant changes and is facing numerous challenges, it continues to be a dynamic and fulfilling career. The demanding deadlines and the stimulating research projects give law firm librarians a unique work environment not typically found in other types of libraries. It is important that law firm librarians strive to demonstrate to the attorneys and executive committees at their firms that the library is a vital contributor to the overall success of the firm. By doing this, law firm librarians can ensure the continued longevity of this type of librarianship.

REFERENCES

1. Vaidhyanathan, S. *The Googlization of Everything: (And Why We Should Worry)*; University of California Press: Berkeley, CA, 2011; 201.
2. American Association of Law Libraries. *The AALL Biennial Salary Survey & Organizational Characteristics*; American Association of Law Libraries: Chicago, IL, 2015; 19.
3. ALM Legal Intelligence. *2016 Law Librarian Survey*; ALM Media Properties, LLC: New York, NY, 2016.

Law Librarianship

Richard A. Danner
School of Law, Duke University, Durham, North Carolina, U.S.A.

Mark E. Estes
Alameda County Law Library, Oakland, California, U.S.A.

Judith Adams Meadows
State Law Library of Montana, Helena, Montana, U.S.A.

Abstract

This entry presents a current picture of law librarianship in the United States, with some international coverage, through discussion of three major types of law libraries: those supporting legal education, law firms, and the public. The primary mission of the law school library is to meet the information needs of the faculty and students of the institution it supports. Beyond support for the core functions of legal education and research, the specific missions of law school libraries vary depending on the size and missions of law schools of different types. Law firm libraries combine the atmosphere of research with the stimulations of big business. Law firm librarians help lawyers clarify and refine their research projects and provide timely and cost-effective solutions for those projects. The term "public law library" refers to all law libraries that are not affiliated with either law firms or law schools. In this category are found county public law libraries, court libraries, state law libraries, state and federal agency law libraries, and bar association and subscription law libraries.

INTRODUCTION

Law librarians work in various legal settings, including law schools, private law firms, and public law libraries of a variety of types. The profession is bound together by law librarians' expertise in working with legal materials, and for many law librarians by their work in direct support of legal professionals or students training to become lawyers. Many law librarians, especially in law school libraries, hold graduate degrees in law as well as in library science; some have graduated from library schools with specialized programs in law librarianship.

Law is a profession that is heavily dependent on ready access to the current texts of primary source legal materials—statutes, court decisions, and administrative regulations and decisions—issued by a variety of law-making authorities. The job of the law librarian has always been to obtain and organize the primary source materials, as well as published commentary on the law, and the indexes and other finding tools needed to use them. Because the primary sources of law have long been available in full-text electronic formats, law librarians are also highly skilled in working with electronic sources and in choosing appropriate information formats to meet the needs of users at specific types of libraries. This entry discusses the practice of law librarianship in three major types of law libraries: law school or academic law libraries; law firm or private law libraries; and public law libraries, which include court libraries, state law libraries, state and

federal agency law libraries, bar association and subscription law libraries, and other libraries open to the public.

LAW SCHOOL LIBRARIES

Introduction

The primary mission of the law school library is to meet the information needs of the faculty and students of the institution it supports. In addition to their role in educating future lawyers, law schools are the major producers of scholarly literature in law and rely on academic law libraries to provide the resources and support needed for research and publication. Beyond support for the core functions of legal education and research, the specific missions of law school libraries vary depending on the size and missions of law schools of different types. Differences among law schools result in differences among their libraries in collection size and composition, staffing and services offered, and additional clienteles served. In the United States, libraries at publicly supported law schools are likely to provide a fuller range of services to local or state attorneys than are libraries at privately funded law schools, while libraries at urban law schools are more likely than others to provide services to the general public. The range of services an academic law library provides to others than its own students and faculty depends also on its proximity to law firm libraries or public law libraries,

Encyclopedia of Library and Information Sciences, Fourth Edition DOI: 10.1081/E-ELIS4-120044120
Copyright © 2017 by Taylor & Francis. All rights reserved.

established to meet the needs of firms, courts, practicing attorneys, or the public. The presence of large numbers of a law school's own graduates in the area also normally results in greater library services for the local bar.

Organization and Administration

In the United States, the professional degree in law, the Juris Doctor, is attained after three years of study and training beyond the baccalaureate degree. Lawyers are educated in separate schools or colleges within the university, rather than in departments of graduate schools or other units. Law schools are normally housed in their own physical facilities and a law school's control over its physical plant is among the factors considered by the American Bar Association (ABA) in its accreditation processes.[1]

These factors, in addition to the specialized nature of legal collections, have contributed to U.S. law school libraries' traditional administrative autonomy from the larger library systems at their universities.[2,3] Only a handful of the libraries at the nearly 200 law schools accredited by the ABA are administered directly through their university library systems. The ABA standards require that the law library have sufficient autonomy to direct the growth and development of the library collections and that the dean of the law school and the library director determine law library policies in consultation with the faculty.[1] In practice, therefore, the budgets of most academic law libraries are administered as part of the law school's budget rather than as part of the overall budget of the university library. If the law library budget must be justified to a higher authority than the law school dean, it is typically the dean or the dean and law library director together who defend the budget at the university level. Similarly, the law library director normally hires and supervises law library staff without involvement by the university library and is responsible for all typical library operations and services, including selection, ordering, cataloging, and processing of library materials.

Although there are a number of variations in internal administrative structure among law school libraries, most U.S. law school libraries are organized traditionally in some form of division between technical and public services, with an administrative unit, often consisting of the law library director, an associate director, and administrative staff to provide support for the library's operations.[4] Variations on the basic organizational model depend on the size of the law school, the number of library staff, and the ratio of professional librarians to support staff members. Increasingly, organizational structures also depend on the role played by the library in supporting the law school's use of information technology and other media. Some law schools place significant overall responsibility for technology within the library's jurisdiction; others

maintain separate units for law school technology, which may support the specialized needs of the library as well.[5]

As a practical matter, the traditional autonomous administration of academic law libraries at U.S. universities is affected by a number of factors, including the widespread implementation of university-wide library information systems, and the need to develop new structures to share costs and access to common databases and other forms of networked information on university campuses.[6] As space tightens, law libraries also increasingly share remote storage facilities for less-used materials with other campus libraries. Law librarians at some universities are included in the shared ranking and job security systems for librarians at all campus libraries. As the forms of legal publication move from print to electronic formats, requiring less in the way of manual filing and other labor-intensive means to be kept current, some of the long-standing justifications for separate law library processing staffs are called into question.

In a number of countries outside the United States, law is taught as an undergraduate subject, and law libraries are likely to be less autonomous than in the United States. In the United Kingdom, for example, only about a third of law library collections are housed in locations separate from collections in other subjects, and the law faculty typically does not have direct control over budget and policy.[7]

History and Development

The history of academic law libraries is closely tied to the history of the development of formal legal education within the university setting. In the United States, the College of William and Mary lays claim to founding of the first professorship in law and the beginnings of a small collection of law books within the confines of the college library in 1779.[8] The Harvard Law Library, now the largest academic law library in the United States, was established in 1817. Yet, until the primary locus for legal education moved in the late nineteenth century to the university from the law office, where aspiring lawyers clerked and read the law under the tutelage of established practitioners, few law school libraries (other than Harvard's) compared in size and breadth of collections with bar association libraries or membership libraries developed to meet the needs of the practicing bar.[9,10]

With the changes in legal education that followed the appointment of Christopher C. Langdell (a former student librarian) as dean of the Harvard Law School in 1870, the perceived role and importance of the academic law library changed significantly. Under Langdell's case method of instruction (which was adopted at law schools throughout the United States), reading, analysis, and application of the law found in selected court opinions became the focus of the law school classroom, and the books containing the opinions took on new prominence as the sources of legal knowledge.[11] Langdell's focus on the importance of the judge-made law in published cases may have initially limited the breadth of academic law library collections, but in the twentieth century the importance of other sources of domestic, foreign, and international legal authority (statutes, administrative regulations and rulings, treaties, and other international agreements) broadened the scope of the law library's collections of primary source research materials. The entry of commercial publishers such as the West Publishing Company into the legal publishing market increased the amount of primary source material available for lawyers to use and for law libraries to collect, as well as the variety of finding tools needed to enable lawyers and other researchers to locate sources of legal authority and to evaluate their usefulness. The solidification of the university law school's role in educating lawyers also contributed to an expansion of the secondary literature in law. Spurred by the establishment of the *Harvard Law Review* in 1887, law professors and law students began writing and editing articles for publication in reviews and journals typically published at the law schools themselves. Although initially consisting primarily of doctrinal articles aimed in large part at the needs of practicing lawyers, the early law reviews became the locus of the most important scholarly literature in law, which would grow to be a significant component of academic law library collections. The increasingly scholarly emphasis of law school faculty writing (in journals, monographs, and treatises) also led to pressures on law school libraries to collect domestic materials beyond the strictly legal and to make at least selective forays into collecting materials of foreign jurisdictions.

The history of academic law libraries in the twentieth century was characterized by: growth in numbers of law schools (and law libraries) as the value of a legal education was seen to extend beyond traditional legal practice; the challenges posed in collecting and preserving growing amounts of primary source materials; the expansion of the scope of collections to include nonlegal materials; the effects of globalization on the need for access to foreign and international legal materials, and staff skilled in using them; the dramatic impacts of information technology on collections and services in the last quarter of the century; and the development of academic law librarianship as a professional specialty. These and other topics are treated briefly in the following sections of this entry and more exhaustively in the literature of the field. In addition, articles about the history and development of individual law school libraries can be found in the journals of law librarianship, which are noted below.

Standards and Statistics

The collections and services offered by the modern academic library, as well as other aspects of its operation, are influenced by the standards developed by legal education's external accrediting bodies and other

agencies. In the United States, nearly 200 law schools are accredited by the ABA through its Section of Legal Education and Admissions to the Bar. In nearly all states, graduation from an ABA-approved law school is a prerequisite for taking the bar examination and qualifying for a license to practice law. As part of its approval and ongoing review processes, the ABA promulgates standards for law school libraries and gathers extensive statistical data about libraries at approved schools. The law library standards speak to such matters as administrative structures, personnel and services, and collections.[1] Each approved law school (and its library) is visited and reevaluated at seven-year intervals. Library data from the ABA's annual questionnaires for law schools are compiled annually into comparative tables and made available to law school deans and library directors. Although distribution of the compiled questionnaire data is limited, some data appear in the annual *ABA/LSAC Official Guide to ABA— Approved Law Schools*.[12] Selected comparative data about law school libraries also appear in unofficial guides to law schools[13,14] and are available from 1998–1999 to date through the Association of Research Libraries.[15] Comparative data from the ABA questionnaires for the years 1969–1993 can be found in the 1970–1994 annual volumes of *Law Library Journal*.

The Association of American Law Schools (AALS) is a membership organization for law schools, which promulgates standards in the forms of bylaws and associated regulations for its members' libraries. The AALS library regulations are similar in coverage to the ABA standards.[16] The AALS reviews its member schools in conjunction with reaccreditation visits by the ABA. Standards for university law libraries in the United Kingdom have been promulgated by the Society of Legal Scholars.[17]

Law School Library Collections

The core collections of all law school libraries include the primary sources of legal authority produced by the major branches of government: reported court opinions (or cases), statutes enacted by legislatures, and executive or administrative materials (regulations and quasijudicial rulings). Academic law libraries in the United States typically include comprehensive collections of primary materials from the federal government and from each of the 50 states in print or electronic formats. Although the states each have their own legal systems, each is a "common law" legal system in which much of the law has developed historically through judicial decisions and written opinions. Under the common law, decisions from courts outside the jurisdiction where a case is being heard will not control the results in the case but can be cited and used as the basis for lawyers' arguments, and can influence the court's decision. As a result, U.S. law school libraries often collect materials from common law jurisdictions outside the United States, such as England, Canada, and

Australia, even if they do not generally collect foreign law materials. Because controlling judicial precedents for a current case may be found in cases as old as the jurisdiction itself, law school library collections of primary source materials are usually deep in their coverage, as well as broad.

Reported decisions, as well as legislation and administrative law materials (each of which grew in importance during the twentieth century) provide the raw materials for legal research and make the law library into the lawyer's laboratory that Dean Langdell emphasized at Harvard.[18] Finding the law applicable to a research problem, however, becomes increasingly difficult as the body of potential useful material grows in volume and complexity. In addition to primary materials, therefore, law library collections include large holdings of secondary materials— treatises, journals, encyclopedias, and a number of specialized publications written to guide the researcher through the law on a topic, as well as indexes, digests, and other more typical finding tools. Some secondary sources are designed primarily for practicing lawyers and serve to organize and provide access to the body of primary authorities on a topic, providing little in the way of detailed analysis or evaluation; others, including the journal articles and monographs produced by law professors and other legal scholars are more analytical, critical, and prescriptive in their approaches.

Because the legal researcher usually needs to have the most up-to-date version of the law, as well as to be certain that an apparently applicable case has not been overturned by a higher court, or that a statute has not been amended, repealed, or found to be unconstitutional, legal publications rely on a variety of means for regular supplementation and updating. Historically, new court opinions and statutes have been published as quickly as possible in pamphlets that are eventually compiled into bound volumes. Some materials have been published in loose-leaf formats so that pages with new information could be easily added as those with older information were replaced and discarded; other sets that require less frequent updating may provide supplemental materials in "pocket parts" inserted inside the back covers of the volumes. Although the bodies with the authority to make law (courts, legislatures, and agencies) have themselves published the materials they issue in official versions, official publication has always been slow and usually lacking in sophisticated finding tools. Beginning at least in the late 1800s, commercial publishers in the United States competed for lawyers' (and law libraries') dollars with their own versions of primary source materials, which were likely to be published before the official versions and linked to the publisher's own finding tools and other products. As a result, academic law libraries have typically offered several commercially published versions of court reports and other important publications, as well as the official versions. Most U.S. law school libraries also

have depository status for federal documents and maintain substantial selective collections of government documents, some of which also are duplicated in commercial publications.[19]

While the common image of a large library reading room surrounded by rows of book stacks packed with neatly arranged volumes is still accurate for most law school libraries, the impact of electronic databases and the Internet on legal research and the law library has transformed the ways in which lawyers and law students conduct research. As one observer noted in 2007: "The debate about whether print or electronic resources are better for legal research ended essentially because the consumers of the resources made a decision.... Faculty, attorneys, and law students voted with their feet, and their feet led them to the computer terminal."[20] The advantages of full-text electronic access to the materials of law for research are apparent, and large databases of primary source materials have long been commercially available to lawyers and law.[21] The potential size of the law market created significant competition between the two major database suppliers, which led to rapid expansion of the databases to the point where retrospective coverage of important U.S. primary sources is essentially complete. The major database vendors have also viewed law schools as important areas of competition for future users of their services, and have generally provided low-cost access to the databases for law school faculty and students, as well as training in the use of the products for research. The two major databases, LexisNexis and Westlaw, now provide law students and faculty 24 hr access using personal equipment within the law school building or from home. In addition, the World Wide Web has increased the direct availability of primary source U.S. legal materials over the Internet, both through new Web-based commercial services, on official sites offered by courts and government agencies, and through open access sites, such as Cornell Law School's Legal Information Institute.[22]

The growth in sources for accessible online legal information first allowed many law school libraries to reduce their holdings of duplicate copies of court reports and other heavily used sets of primary source materials in their print collections. Secondary legal materials, including large retrospective journal and treatise collections, and finding tools are also available in electronic formats, leaving law school librarians with ongoing decisions about choices of appropriate formats for their user communities and whether to bear the costs of providing information in multiple formats.[23]

As increasing accessibility of legal information in networked electronic formats continues to make local availability of large print collections less important to legal researchers, the distinctiveness of individual academic law library collections is increasingly dependent on their current and retrospective collections of secondary sources and foreign law materials.[24,25] Collection development in academic law libraries is normally based on a written plan, required by the ABA[1] that must take into account the importance of electronic formats, the needs of faculty researchers for specialized nonlegal materials, the extent to which the library serves constituencies beyond its own faculty and students, and the library's proximity to and ongoing relationships with other libraries on its campus and beyond.[26,27] Academic law libraries' interests in cooperative collection development have been major factors in the development of regional consortia of law libraries.[28]

Historically, major foreign and international law collections were developed only at the largest academic law libraries and were supported by lawyer–librarians who immigrated to the United States from foreign countries.[29] During the latter half of the twentieth century, U.S. legal scholars' increased interest in foreign and international law and the law schools' efforts to recruit visiting scholars and students from outside the United States led a broader range of law schools to devote significant resources to their foreign and international law collections. As interest in foreign and international law expanded, academic law libraries faced major challenges finding qualified staff to manage and support growing collections, and obtaining the financial resources to develop and maintain them.[30–32] In foreign and international law, as for domestic law, academic law librarians produced major bibliographic works and research texts to support the efforts of scholars.[33,34] To support research in foreign law, the American Association of Law Libraries (AALL) publishes the *Index to Foreign Legal Periodicals* (1960–). Greater access to legal information worldwide on the Internet has also been enhanced by the Free Access to Law Movement and the activities of legal information institutes throughout the world collaborating through the World Legal Information Institute (WorldLII).[35,36]

Many academic libraries maintain at least small rare books collections both to support research and to demonstrate the importance of the historical record to the development of the law. Morris L. Cohen is the major figure in American rare law books librarianship and is the author of the *Bibliography of Early American Law*[37] and other works in the field.[38,39] In most law school library collections, materials old enough to suggest their classification as rare books are shelved in open stacks, leading to academic law librarians' ongoing concerns with preservation of print materials.[40] As more primary legal research materials are issued primarily or exclusively in electronic formats, academic law libraries have been challenged to define their roles in both preserving and authenticating digital legal information.[41,42]

Because many of the core primary source materials of the law library (court reports, volumes of statutes, journals, etc.) have been published as serials, and are to some extent self-organizing by numbered volume and date, organization by subject classification was a relatively late development for law library collections. Subject organization became increasingly important with the growth of a significant secondary literature for law and the growing need to organize foreign and international legal materials. The first fully developed Library of Congress (LC) schedule for legal materials (KF for U.S. law) was published in 1969. Since that time, schedules have been completed for all foreign jurisdictions and international law. While many academic law libraries still do not classify all U.S. primary source materials, most use the LC schedules to organize their treatise and monograph collections, and collections in foreign law.[43] Because of the need for frequent supplementation and updating, as well as the nature of the materials themselves, primary sources, finding tools, and many secondary sources are noncirculating in most academic law libraries. The need for ready access to information housed in large, complicated collections makes sophisticated collection management systems essential to the successful operation of the academic law library.

Law School Librarians

Nearly all academic law librarians in the United States hold master's degrees in library or information sciences; reference librarians and administrators typically hold law degrees in addition to their credentials in librarianship. The ABA standards for law schools and the membership requirements of the AALS state that the law library director should have both law and library degrees, and the ABA standards require that the director hold an appointment on the law school faculty.[1,16] Depending on practices at individual law schools and, in part, on whether they teach in the law school, other law librarians may also have some kind of faculty status.[44]

Within the law school curriculum, law-trained librarians typically provide formal or informal instruction in legal research techniques and the literature of the law. Legal research courses take a variety of forms: most programs focus on introducing the sources of law and legal research to first-year law students; some law schools offer advanced legal research courses in either United States or foreign and international law as electives in the upper-class curriculum.[45] Law school librarians have also figured prominently in the writing of the standard legal research textbooks, a number of which have gone through several editions.[46–49] A listing of the major law librarian textbook writers—Robert C. Berring, Harry Bitner, Morris Cohen, Frederick C. Hicks, J. Myron Jacobstein, Roy M. Mersky, Miles O. Price, and William R. Roalfe—serves as well as a list of some of the major figures in modern academic law librarianship in the United States.

In part because of law library directors' usual status as members of law school faculties, academic law librarians as a group have been major contributors to the professional and scholarly literature of law librarianship.[50] Most of that literature is published in such specialized

Knowledge Management–
Law Librarianship

journals as *Law Library Journal* (1908–) and *Legal References Services Quarterly* (1981–) in the United States; *Legal Information Management* (1970–) and *Australian Law Librarian* (1993–); *Canadian Law Library Review/ Revue canadienne des bibliothèques de droit* (1970–) published abroad; and the *International Journal of Legal Information* (1973–), as well as in publications sponsored by the AALL and other law library organizations outside the United States. Some law library literature is published in more general journals of library and information science; and some is also published in scholarly journals of law, bar association journals, or other specialized legal periodicals. *Legal Information & Technology Abstracts* is a Web journal providing access to legal information scholarship.[51]

The importance of the law degree as a credential, the faculty status accorded to academic law library directors and other librarians, and the tendency to write for legal audiences all provide evidence of the strength and durability of the academic law librarian's connections with the legal profession. The history of the development of academic law librarianship in the twentieth century indicates that, through the 1950s, many head librarians at U.S. law schools did not hold library degrees and those who did have both law and library degrees thought of themselves primarily as lawyers and then as librarians. Because of the positions of influence that academic law librarians have traditionally held within the profession, it is possible that the emphasis on "law" in law librarianship hindered the overall development of law librarianship as a profession.[10,52] As noted above, however, the law school accreditation standards now emphasize the desirability for library directors to hold both degrees and the need for qualified staff in all positions; there are now few directors who do not hold advanced degrees in law and librarianship, and few law librarians who are not professionally educated in library and information science.

A number of U.S. schools of library and information science offer specialized courses for prospective law librarians in legal research, law library administration, and information policy. In recognition of the need for specialized law library training within the context of graduate education in librarianship, the AALL has established Guidelines for Graduate Programs in Law Librarianship[53] and maintains an online list of accredited graduate programs in library science that offer law library courses.[54] The University of Washington Information School has offered a specialized program in law librarianship since 1939.[55]

Like librarianship generally, both law librarianship and the academic law library specialty are overwhelmingly female in composition. Studies of the role and status of women in the profession have noted historical disparities in salaries between male and female law librarians, as well as the disproportionate numbers of males in academic library directorships.[56,57] Some studies have indicated a continuing trend toward gender balance between males and females in academic law library directorships but not a distribution proportionate to the numbers of women working in academic law libraries.[58,59]

Professional Associations

The primary professional association for U.S. law librarians is the AALL, which was founded in 1906 at the annual meeting of the American Library Association.[60–63] American Association of Law Libraries' stated purpose is to promote and enhance the value of law libraries to the legal and public communities, to foster the profession of law librarianship, and to provide leadership in the field of legal information. Its current membership of over 5000 includes law librarians and related professionals affiliated with law firms, corporate legal departments, courts, and government agencies, as well as with law schools.[64,65] The AALL provides law librarians opportunities for professional development through its annual meeting programs, educational workshops, and institutes; provides scholarships and grants for members requiring assistance to further their formal education or to attend AALL educational programs; supports an active publications program; and provides placement services.

Throughout its history, AALL and its members have been involved in public policy activities, focusing on issues of national information policy, copyright, and public access to legal information.[66] Since 1990, the association's Government Relations Office has monitored legislative, judicial, and regulatory activities, and represents the views of AALL through congressional testimony and legal briefs, frequently working in concert with other library associations and information policy groups.

Since 1976, AALL has encouraged the creation of special interest sections (SISs), organized by subject matter or professional specialty (e.g., foreign, comparative and international law, technical services), or by type of library. The Academic Law Libraries SIS was established in 1979 and serves as an umbrella organization for all law school librarians, sponsoring educational programs, providing discussion forums and workshops for directors and middle managers, and publishing a newsletter. The AALL also has a number of local and regional chapters in which academic law librarians are active participants.[67]

Academic law librarians have played significant roles in the development and activities of AALL. Over half of AALL's presidents were affiliated with law school libraries at the time they served, and all of the major figures in academic law librarianship in the United States have been heavily involved in AALL activities. Many prominent and historically significant academic law librarians have been profiled in AALL publications.[68–73] Biographical information about academic law librarians can also be found in occasional directories published by AALL;[74] information about academic law library directors can be found in the annual *Directory of Law Teachers* published by the AALS.[75] Memorials for deceased law librarians, which normally include biographical information and personal reminiscences, are published in *Law Library Journal*,[76,77] as well as in the publications of other law library organizations.

The International Association of Law Libraries (IALL)[78] was founded in 1959 through the efforts of a special committee of the AALL led by former AALL president William R. Roalfe, who became IALL's first president. Since its founding, IALL has provided a significant focus of professional activity for academic law librarians interested in substantive areas of international and comparative law and research, and a forum for cooperation among academic law schools and their libraries.[79,80] The IALL publishes the *International Journal of Legal Information* and sponsors annual educational conferences.

U.S. academic law librarians are also active in national legal organizations. The AALS includes a section on law libraries and maintains a standing committee on libraries and technology. The law libraries committee of the ABA Section of Legal Education and Admission to the Bar is charged with periodic review of the accreditation standards relating to law libraries and the law library sections of ABA questionnaires. Law school library directors frequently serve as members of ABA/AALS site evaluation teams established for law school accreditation reviews, and are usually represented on the ABA accreditation committee and on the AALS membership review committee, as well as on the committees devoted primarily to library matters.

Outside the United States, there are a number of other national and regional associations of law librarians, which provide venues for professional activity and continuing education for academic law librarians, as well as for their colleagues in other types of law libraries.[81,82] A list of known law library organizations (some of which may not be currently active) includes: Arbeitsgemeinschaft für Juristisches Bibliotheks-und Dokumentationswesen/ Association for Law Librarianship and Documentation in German-speaking countries; Association Belge des Bibliothecaires et des Documentalistes Juridiques (Belgium); the Association of Swiss Law Libraries/Association des bibliothèques juridiques suisses—Vereinigung der juristischen Bibliotheken der Schweiz; the Australian Law Librarians Association; the Bahamas Association of Law Libraries; the British and Irish Association of Law Librarians; the Canadian Association of Law Libraries/ Association canadienne des bibliothèques de droit; the Caribbean Association of Law Libraries; the Consortium of Legal Resource Centers and Legal Information Specialists (Central and Eastern Europe); the Law Librarians' Group of Malaysia; the New Zealand Law Librarians' Group; the Nigerian Association of Law Libraries; the Nordic Law Librarians' Group; the

Philippine Group of Law Librarians; the Organization of South African Law Libraries/Organisasie van Suid-Afrikaanse Regsbiblioteke; Red de Bibliotecas de Derecho y Ciencias Jurídicas (Argentina); the Russian Association of Law Libraries/Assotsiatsiia Iuridicheskikh Bibliotek; the Scottish Law Librarians' Group; and the Turkish Platform of Law Librarians/Türk Hukuk Kütüphanecileri Platformu.

Twenty-First Century Roles

In the twenty-first century, like other institutions, the law school library faces a variety of challenges from the impacts of technology and globalization, as well as from continuous change on all fronts. In many ways, the law library's long-standing mission remains similar to what it has been, while the means to accomplishing that mission have changed. The responses of academic law libraries to a changing environment can be seen both in the increased attention given to building stronger collections in foreign and international law and in non-law materials, and in efforts to improve access to digital information through electronic publication projects.[83,84] In addition, many academic law librarians have taken leadership roles for general technology development and implementation within their law schools.[5]

Yet, because technology-based solutions to information storage and technological advances in information access and retrieval serve to provide ubiquitous access to information, they can be characterized as challenging the future value of the library as a physical place. If books are less important to legal research, and if students (and faculty) prefer to work with online information sources, why should law schools devote significant areas of their physical plants to collections of books? If the Internet makes legal information readily available through any wired or wireless network, why should any space at all be used for a library? How important will an institution historically centered on the acquisition and preservation of print information be in an increasingly digital information environment in which less information is acquired in physical formats? Is the role of the law librarian so tied to the law book and to physical library collections that the profession itself is no longer relevant to the information needs of law faculty and students? What kinds of new skills will be needed?[85,86]

Conclusion

In light of these and similar questions, it will be essential for law librarians to think hard about core values and the services they and the law library itself provide.[87,88] Is the law library a place only for the storage of books for students to study and perform research, or does the law school library provide an important (or perhaps the only) shared space in the law school where students can

Knowledge Management– Law Librarianship

work and learn collaboratively with each other and with faculty, and to work with librarians to develop legal information literacy skills? What must the profession of law librarianship do to continue to grow, and to foster the new leadership it will need to meet the difficult challenges it faces?[89] It is likely that the future of the academic law library will be shaped in large part by law librarians' answers to questions like these, as well as on the library's ability to reshape its role in a new information environment.

LAW FIRM LIBRARIES

Introduction

"[A] law office library combines the student atmosphere of research with the stimulating activity of big business."[90] The business is a law firm, providing legal advice to clients. The library exists to meet the research needs of the law firm's lawyers. The librarians try to anticipate those research needs so they can: 1) help lawyers clarify and refine their research project; and 2) provide a timely and cost-effective solution for that research project. Historically, the firm used the library space and library collection to impress clients, opposing counsel, and potential hires; the leather bindings, full shelves, large writing surfaces, and comfortable chairs suggested success and wisdom to clients and opposing counsel. Today, the librarian solves information problems unconstrained by a physical library collection.

In 1956 a law librarian described her role as "to keep happy anywhere from 35 to 125 lawyers, whose diversified interests may cover anything from having '235 U.S.' delivered at once to ascertaining all the stops on the New York subway system and the Hudson Tubes to New Jersey or to producing a speech delivered in the Maritime Provinces...."[91] More than 60 years later the librarian's role still includes fact gathering and document retrieval from many time zones. Law librarians use hundreds of online sources to research legal topics unknown in 1956, gather information about companies engaged in global commerce and monitor activities of competitors. In addition, the librarian negotiates contracts and license agreements with information vendors, outsources some library tasks, and creates systems that let a less highly paid person find basic information that once required a professional librarian.

Customers, Users, and Owners

The law firm library serves two groups of customers: 1) the firm's lawyers; and 2) the employees supporting the lawyers—paralegals, law clerks, secretaries, records center, accounting department, etc. The first group includes partners or shareholders—the owners of the firm. The second group of employees often request information for the partner(s) and are the most direct users of the library. This means that often the heaviest users of the library are those with the least political clout or influence when it comes to spending money on the library. The customer base tends to be more homogenous than the clientele is in public libraries. Customers in the law library are part of the legal service industry—even if they are relatively new to it. Typically, all have college educations and over half of the customers have law degrees.

The primary customer of the law firm library is the individual attorney seeking a solution to an information problem. That attorney either contacts the librarian directly or through an intermediary—a secretary, a paralegal, or another attorney. These delegated reference/ research requests often pose the greatest challenge because the messenger is not the requester and may not have a full understanding of the problem. Often the requesting attorney is unavailable for clarification. So, the librarian seeks to discern the intent of the attorney through the messenger to first understand the information request and then to complete the request within the constraints defined by the attorney.

Often, the key decision makers in the firm seldom use the library directly, because they are too busy working directly with key clients. They delegate research work and receive synthesized research results in the form of memos of law. They often do not realize the extent to which the library supports their information needs and can easily feel like the library does nothing for them personally.

Some libraries provide service directly to the firm's clients:

- Document retrieval requests
- Monitoring legislative activity
- Researching case law
- Finding statutes on a particular topic
- Compiling a chart of state statutes on a particular topic
- Doing business research on a competitor, etc.

Sometimes the request comes through the responsible attorney and sometimes directly from the client. The library contributes directly to serving the client and thus building and maintaining the client relationship.

One customer type, the summer law clerk, or summer associate, hopes to work as an associate at the firm. The summer clerkship serves as an extended job interview— where the firm continues to evaluate the clerk and the clerk assesses the firm as a potential employer, rather than a job where work is produced.

The large law firm hires summer clerks with the expectation of offering them jobs. The firm has already invested significant amounts of money to find and entice the law student to come to work for the summer. A significant part of the clerk's job during the summer involves legal research. However, because most summer clerks have minimal research skills, they start their summer worrying about their ability to find the right answer. The librarian serves as bibliographic/research instructor and nonjudgmental resource for the frightened, stressed clerk. This role of research consultant enables the librarian to make the firm more attractive to the clerk by helping to improve the clerk's research skills. In addition, the librarian can also evaluate the overall effectiveness of the clerk and the likelihood of their success as an associate.

Services

Most libraries provide staffing during the firm's normal business hours, 8:00 A.M.–5:00 P.M., Monday–Friday. The global economy forces lawyers to extend their hours and librarians change their service hours accordingly: opening earlier and staying open later to provide assistance during the time when most lawyers are in their offices. Law firms with multiple offices and librarians in multiple time zones provide extended coverage to the entire firm through telephone and e-mail. Some firms are testing instant messaging to communicate with users and ways to best send documents to personal data assistant (PDAs).

Reference services include the traditional quick reference and bibliographic instruction services that answer questions such as: "Do we have?" "Where is it?" "How do I?"

In research, the librarian answers the question: "Can you find the statutes and/or the cases on the following issue(s)?" "I'm meeting this person tomorrow, what can you get me to inform me about their business?"

Research provides an opportunity for the librarian to add value to the basic answer by synthesizing from many sources the solution to the lawyer's information problem and by making personal/professional observations about implications and possible interpretations of the research.

Business briefing book preparation involves locating, selecting, compiling, and summarizing information about a company. This form of research has grown in importance because law firms face intense competition for quality clients. The briefing book enables the lawyer and the firm's marketing professional to identify the client's needs that the firm can best meet. It also gives crucial background information so that the lawyer can demonstrate the firm's understanding of the unique challenges facing a business owner.

Access to information

The Catalog. Catalogs began as a simple list of the books owned by the firm. As the collection grew, the catalog evolved, first to a card catalog and then to an online catalog. The quality of cataloging correlates with the resources available to the librarian. Namely, the better-funded the library the more effective the catalog access to

the material in the library's collection—both physical and virtual. As librarians worked through the process of cataloging their collections, they allocated significant resources to building a detailed inventory of their collections. This was done by either assigning a significant portion of a staff member's time to the project, or by contracting out the project to a third-party service. Law firm library catalogs continue to evolve to provide access to books on the library shelves, electronic subscriptions available online through the Web, or in CD-ROM towers and "free" resources on the Internet.

Law librarians use Web technology to provide access to information by building and maintaining the library page on the firm's intranet or building and maintaining the firm-wide intranet. The intranet includes links to answers to commonly asked questions such as "how do I . . . find a translation service, find a zip code, find a case." It also organizes online research resources, whether fee-based or at no additional costs, by the ways the library's customers think of them. The organization could be by practice area, by geography, etc.

Librarians apply their skills of collecting and organizing externally produced information to internally created information and build knowledge management systems. Lawyers use these systems to find prior work product so that they can customize a solution to a client's problem. "Work product" could be a research memorandum on a point of law, an agreement for a purchase or sale of a company, or a response to a request for proposal from a potential client.

Interlibrary Loan. As a way to provide access to materials not in their library—whether not owned or not on the shelf, law firm librarians built interlibrary loan (ILL) systems as soon as there were two librarians in the same city. These systems function more informally than academic and public systems. Law firm librarians use phone calls and e-mails to expedite requests that must be filled within hours, not days or weeks.

Current awareness

Current awareness services include paper-based services: clipping articles from newspapers, routing newsletters, routing photocopied tables of contents of periodicals, maintaining a vertical file of continuing legal education (CLE) opportunities, as well as electronic-based services: subscriptions to electronic newsletters, and creation of customized electronic newsletters that are either e-mailed or posted on the firm's intranet.

The physical routing of material uses route slips. Generally the priority on the route lists is by seniority in the firm. But, in some libraries it is adjusted to reflect the need to know, political clout, or circulated in straight alphabetical order. The alphabetical approach includes a periodic reversal of the list or randomizing it so that everyone is

Knowledge Management–
Law Librarianship

reminded of the need to promptly read the current-awareness material. This system saves subscription costs by sharing a subscription but increases lost opportunity costs if important information is delayed when one of the individuals does not promptly read their mail. In that instance a person further down the list may not get the weekly item for many months.

Increasingly, current awareness is electronic only—whether as e-newsletters, e-zines, RSS feeds, or customized regular searches of commercial databases that are pushed to the customer's desktop or PDA.

Cite checking

Cite checking validates citations in a brief or memo by looking up each cited source and comparing the proposition for which it is used or any quotations against the original source, and confirming that the case or statute has not been overturned or superseded.

CLE provider, credit tracker

Continuing legal education is mandatory in 43 states.[92] To keep their licenses active lawyers must complete a designated number of CLE hours within a specified time. Librarians organize events, teach courses, and maintain systems to track the credits earned and needed. Tracking CLE becomes an element of knowledge management systems when librarians track the subject matter of what was taken and by whom so that others can consult with the attendee.

Training includes the overview orientation to the library, its collection, and services. Training can also include the traditional bibliographic instruction of how to use available information. These sessions may be in small groups, but most often they are one-on-one, provided just in time, when the lawyer needs the training. New technologies expand the just-in-time training; enabling librarians to develop self-paced computer-based instruction, or to train remotely by viewing the user's computer screen.

Conflict checking

Conflict checking involves searching the firm's internal databases for clients who might be on the other side of a legal matter. The ethical code for lawyers precludes representing two sides in the same dispute. Further, without specific waiver from the client, the law firm may not represent a client in one proceeding and oppose the client in another matter. Librarians build the systems to search internal records for existing clients and external sources to identify the corporate structures to properly name all the affiliates of a company.

Impact on Other Units within the Firm

The library's research resources and skills aid the marketing department by finding the information for responding to requests for proposal. Current awareness services include alerting the human resources department to new developments; the accounting department for currency exchange rates and accounting standards; and the facilities department with comparisons on equipment, space allocation in other industries; and new standards for office equipment.

How Does the Library Achieve the Organization's Goals?

The library achieves the firm's goals by first understanding the goals of the firm; second by aligning the library activities with the firm's goals. Typically that means encouraging cost-effective research and applying ongoing and rigorous cost-control efforts—only buying information that is likely to be used and canceling and discarding that which is not used.

Recent Developments

Five recent developments impact law firm libraries. First, the information explosion and the Internet have increased the online availability of more cases, more statutes, more regulations, more news sources, and different search engines. These developments make clients wonder why, if everything is available for free on the Internet, they should have to pay extra for information. Clients often are not aware that online sources are purchased by the firm.

The second factor is the growth of branch, or other offices. In the 1980s and 1990s law firms expanded their markets by opening offices in other cities to better serve an existing client or to serve a developing area. With the branch office, came the need for a library and the challenges of managing remote services. Sometimes the solution was to staff the branch library, sometimes to depend on the central office.

Third, the changing and expanding roles of professional law firm staff impacts the law library. For example, the office manager evolved to a firm administrator and then to an executive director. With each change, the individual assumed greater responsibilities in governing the law firm. That role change demands that the librarian think and act in a more business-like manner. Librarians' roles also evolved to assume greater responsibility for information collection, organization, and reuse. About one-third of law librarians now have nontraditional roles: supervising the records center or the conflicts checking department, the firm intranet, CLE, or knowledge management.

The fourth factor is the increasing number of law firm mergers involving firms that already have librarians. While the merger increases the resources available for information problem solving it also may create overlapping skill sets in the library staff and displace some of the staff.

Fifth, the "google-ization" of research expectations. Not only the younger customers but also the older ones now believe they should be able to find the answer themselves by just typing words into a search box.

Principal Concepts—Alternative Interpretations

In the law firm, significant numbers of the library's customers are the partners or shareholders who own the firm—and the library. The law firm, while it exists to serve clients, must also make a profit by providing quality client services in cost-effective manner to clients who will pay their bills. The traditional law firm bill includes an hourly rate and disbursements, money the firm spent while doing the client's work, for example, court filing fees, long distance charges, etc. Hourly rates are calculated using the costs of having the firm open, using factors such as rent, utilities, salaries, benefits, etc. The two biggest factors are how much profit the partners want for a given level of work and what they think the market will bear. In recent years, clients have been asking for predictable pricing. Predictable pricing is where the client knows in advance what the work will cost.

In each of these two billing models, the librarian contributes to the firm's bottom line by promoting the most cost-effective research possible. In addition, law firm librarians record the time they spend on reference and research projects. By recording their time, the firm can bill the client for their time—just like lawyers' time. Even if the time is not billed to the client, it enables the firm to analyze the cost of servicing the client.

Time

Law firm work is always driven by deadlines: court filing deadlines, contract acceptance deadlines, etc. The Internet has compressed time and magnified its importance. Clients work in multiple time zones around the world. The firm itself may have offices in multiple time zones. When communication went at the speed of the mail, the client did not expect an immediate answer by return mail. While there was never enough time to research every possible nuance, there was time to reflect on the advice to be provided. Now, with clients expecting a call back from someone within 30 min and an answer within hours instead of days, time is in even shorter supply. The successful law firm uses the skills of law librarians to get higher quality answers faster and cheaper than lawyers themselves can supply.

Technology

Law firm libraries were one of the first departments in the firm to apply technology. While accounting first applied technology to crunch numbers for billing clients, the library used technology to solve information problems and thus led in introducing technology to the rest of the firm. The library first had stand-alone terminals for online research. Later, libraries used spreadsheets to manage budgets, word processors to summarize research results, and database programs to manage serials and create online catalogs. Now, the computers—but now desktops and laptops—include word processing, spreadsheets, Internet browsers, and access to CD-ROMs, access to subscription databases, and time-entry programs.

Budgeting and planning

For many years libraries operated without budgets or forecasted spending. They spent as much as they wanted or needed. As law firms continued to become more business-like, librarians adopted budgeting techniques to track and forecast their expenditures. The budgeting and planning reflect the business acumen of law firm management and the pressures facing law firms' profitability. Over 80% of law firm library budgets goes to electronic resources.[93] Almost 90% of the print budget is spent on keeping the library current and up-to-date. Some firms treat flat-priced online research contracts as part of overhead; others try to recover the cost through charge-backs to clients. Sometimes the income from charge-backs is treated as an offset to the library budget and other times it goes in a separate category.

As part of for-profit organizations, librarians must address tax and accounting issues like sales tax, property tax, and capitalizing versus expensing items, and then, if items are capitalized, track the depreciation. For multilocation libraries, sales and property taxes can mean that taxes are paid on an item when it is shipped to one location for processing and then taxed again as personal property at the ultimate location.

Physical Arrangement/Space

Design also communicates what activities matter. Firms that view their primary stock in trade as their knowledge and intellectual capacity like to show off their libraries and configure space so that clients can see lawyers at work.[94]

Constrained by the space available, law firm librarians seek to arrange the collection in an overall useful fashion. The traditional configuration used broad topical areas. Cataloged and classified collections are arranged in call number order. Some firms use satellite libraries (subsets of the collection or duplicates of selected subject matter titles on other floors near significant practice group members). A centralized or consolidated collection is easiest for the staff to maintain. Satellite libraries, because they put the books closer to the lawyers, are easiest for the customer.

Knowledge Management–
Law Librarianship

The satellite library does not encourage coming to the central library or asking a librarian to conduct a research project for the attorney.

Seating type

The number of study spaces ranges widely—from one per every ten attorneys to one to twenty or more. Lawyers tend to do research with several books open to different cases or statutes, so they can more easily compare the language in each. This means that each study space, whether a table or carrel, has a larger work surface than in other libraries. Many libraries have physically downsized, making extensive use of hybrid collections and compact shelving to house the physical collection. Instead of built-in carrels, they use modular furniture to permit using the space for other functions.

Collections

Collections range from less than 10,000 volumes to more than 70,000 volumes. Libraries collect both external and internal information sources. The external sources include hard copy and electronic materials. "Hard copy" includes the traditional hardbound texts, treatises, court reporters, statutes, etc. Most of the hard copy books are supplemented with a paperbound pamphlet inserted in the back of the book; others are loose-leaf—binders with loose pages that can be replaced with updated text. The collection may also include microforms, audio, video, CD-ROMs, and other electronic media via Web, dial-up, or leased line. Internal sources include memoranda of law files, brief banks, and opinion letters written to clients. Some libraries use podcasts or MP3 players to distribute CLE programs.

Libraries have a core collection of the primary and secondary materials in the jurisdiction(s) in which the firm practices. Primary materials are the law itself: statutes, regulations, and cases. Secondary materials explain the primary materials. Finding materials provide means to locate the primary and secondary materials.

Libraries physically expanded in the 1980s as many law firms moved to new space. New libraries were designed to double the size of the collection every five years. However, in the 1990s the collection growth rate slowed and even began to shrink. Causes for this reversal include: expensive real estate leases that made justifying housing books difficult when many of the primary sources of law are also available electronically; and the continuing codification of American law, namely, more reliance on statutes and regulations than on case law. This codification in turn enabled a new work, the handbook that compiled the most relevant statutes, regulations with minimal commentary into one or two volumes. This provided the perfect desk reference for the attorney to find a quick answer while on the phone with a client.

Serials

Serials comprise about 90% of the titles in a law firm library. Serials control systems range from manual ones, such as Kardex files, through specially adapted, created computer files such as word processing documents, spreadsheets, or databases to integrated serials, circulation, acquisition, and catalogs. Some libraries record invoice number and amount for each item, in addition to keeping a copy of the invoice and sending a copy of the invoice to accounting.

The nature of law, as an ever changing discipline, requires that the materials be updated constantly so that the most recent information is available to the lawyers. Publishers address this problem with different approaches, for example, pocket parts (pamphlets inserted in the back of books). The pocket part is arranged like the parent volume and includes new law, case analysis or commentary by chapter, and section or page number of the parent volume. The researcher reading the main volume must check the pocket part for newer information. When the size of the pocket part becomes too large to go into the back of the book it may become a freestanding supplement shelved after the book or the publisher may recompile the complete title into a new edition. Another approach is loose-leaf services. Binder volumes are updated by a package with instructions of which pages to remove and discard and which new pages to insert. Because the revised material is integrated into the text, the researcher saves time. Typically, loose-leaf services cost more than pocket parts both in dollars to the publisher and in the time to file the updates.

Many law firm librarians have stopped binding law journals and other legal periodicals. They reason that they are less likely to lose the entire volume—one issue may be off the shelf, but the other three issues are still on the shelf. In addition, the pressure for space savings and cost controls impels the decision not to bind materials that probably will be discarded in five years or less. The availability of electronic full-text and images of the journal further reduces the need to dedicate lineal feet to little used materials.

Collection development policies

Most collection development policies are informal and unwritten. They generally "support the immediate information needs of the practitioners" in that particular firm. Thus, one library that does extensive appellate work may have a historical collection of proposed regulations, extensive legislative histories, and old editions of significant treatises. Another firm will have a different collection with little historical material because of the nature of their work.

Knowledge Management–
Law Librarianship

Generally, the library seeks to have core materials to support the practice. The largest libraries define core materials to include multiple treatise titles on the same subject to give alternative views of the issues. Law firm libraries usually rely on academic and court law libraries to maintain extensive historical collection of earlier versions of statutes, regulations, or treatises. These materials are of interest to the legal scholar tracing the development of the law but are seldom used by the practitioner.

Demand drives the number of copies of works held in the collection. If a set is frequently used in a lawyer's office, the librarian acquires multiple copies of the title. In recent years as space constraints and budget limitations loomed, especially when coupled with the ability to retrieve documents from various electronic sources, the number of duplicate copies has shrunk.

The collection is primarily legal information. However, the trend is to include more nonlegal information because the practice of law now requires research in other areas. In addition, the nonlegal materials help the lawyers understand their clients better.

The reverse of acquiring, reviewing for continued supplementation, and/or discarding also varies widely. Decisions range from the librarian acting alone to heavy lawyer involvement in the process. The heavy involvement can vary from lawyers physically coming to the library to look at the materials, to lawyers reviewing compilations of the materials with notations indicating costs and frequency of use. In other scenarios, the librarian surveys when the renewal comes due and/or reviews the complete subject matter at one time.

The retention policy varies from keeping permanently to keeping only the most recent few years of newsletters or law journals. Librarians, limited by space, are cognizant of alternative sources for the information. Citation patterns indicate the heaviest use of most materials is within two years of publication.

Classification

Law firm libraries use many approaches to cataloging and classification. Most generally follow the LC classification with local variations to reflect the firm's practice. For example, the LC classification puts pension materials in the labor area, but for many firms the pension practice focuses on tax aspects so these materials are reclassified into the tax area. The degree to which the collection adheres to the LC scheme is often driven by the maturity of the library.

However, for smaller firms that have not had the money and people to manage their resources, the collection may lack an inventory, a catalog, or a classification scheme. Books are arranged in the manner that reflects the most vocal and important of the library users—probably by their practice preference. Thus, if one person takes the book off the shelf and another returns the book—especially if some additional books have been taken in the interim—the first book may not be reshelved in the same relative place.

Circulation Systems

Law firm libraries, unlike public or academic libraries, can show people in the firm who has the book checked out. This improves the use of the collection because the attorney is able to find who has the book at any hour and can call or go to their office to use the book. Circulation systems range from a notebook for the title, date, and initials of the attorney taking the book, to small cards and pockets with the cards completed and left in a box at the library entrance. Another method uses oversized cards in the book, which are to be left on the shelf in place of the book. A few of the largest libraries now have systems with bar code readers or radio frequency identification (RFID) tags that integrate the circulation records with the online catalog.

Unfortunately, there is no security in a law firm library, except within the office itself. In other words, any time the office is open, so is the library. This means it is easy to walk out of the library without properly signing out the book. These "not on shelf/not signed out books" slow the lawyer's response to the client. Efforts to find the needed information for the lawyer include office searches, contacting the likely users of the book by phone or e-mail, broadcasting e-mail to the entire firm, borrowing the book, or replacing it.

Staffing

Staff sizes range from one solo librarian to staffs of 20 to 50, reflecting the size of the firm, the nature of the practice, the location of the firm, and the ability of librarians to prove their worth to the firm's bottom line. On an average, there is one professional librarian for every 22 attorneys.[95] Many law librarians work in a solo shop with little or no clerical support. Most do not have the opportunity to bounce ideas off a peer during the normal workday. The solo librarian can achieve that professional interchange through participating in the local, regional, and national professional associations, and by regularly planned lunches with colleagues from other firms.

Positions in the law firm library include professional, paraprofessional, technical, clerical, and administrative. The title manager, director, supervisor, or simply librarian indicates who is responsible for managing the library. The title reference librarian denotes one who focuses on providing reference and research answers. This person may also have special expertise in one or more subjects, for example, tax, trademark, patents, immigration, labor, or business. Regardless of title, the actual responsibilities for each staff member cross the traditional functional activity lines because there is usually not enough work to keep a single function position busy for a 40 hr week.

Librarians report either to a library committee, usually comprised of partners or associates, or to a library partner, the firm managing partner, information services director or the executive director/chief operating officer. Increasingly, the librarian's performance review includes how closely aligned the library is with the firm's business objectives.

Education

A master's in library science (M.L.S.) is the entry-level professional degree. A significant number of law firm librarians also have law degrees. Law firms tend to be practical in orientation, so demonstrated skill and experience can substitute for the M.L.S. With more nonlegal research being done in the firm, an additional master's degree in business, science, or technology can increase the value of the librarian to the firm.

Clerical, technical, or paraprofessional positions typically require a Bachelor of Arts (B.A.) degree or, significant demonstrated experience. These nonprofessional positions may include library network support, such as maintaining the library's portion of the technology network, maintaining the firm's intranet page, etc.

Continuing education

Law firm librarians find opportunities for continuing their education in local, regional, and national programs. The AALL's annual meeting typically draws one-third to one-half of the law firm members of the Association. In addition, AALL offers workshops in different cities. Local or regional chapters supplement the offerings of the national / education opportunities as well: the Association of Legal Administrators has chapters in almost every city and also offers many telephone conference programs. The Special Libraries Association and general library associations also provide opportunities for continuing professional education.

Finally, each of the largest legal publishers presents programs on topics related to private law firm librarians.

Experience and skills

The AALL 2005 Salary Survey reported that, on average, law firm librarians have held their current positions for 7–8 years.[96]

History

Lawyers rely on information—statutes passed by legislatures, written opinions from judges, and commentaries or treatises written by scholars or practitioners. The solo practitioner in the 1800s, as now, might have survived with very few books. As lawyers joined together forming law firm partnerships, their book collections grew. As the number of lawyers in the firm increased, the book collection grew as well. At around 50 lawyers, the book collection—and the information needs—becomes so large and so complex the firm hires a librarian.

One of the earliest law firm librarians, Elizabeth Finley,[97] began her career in New York in 1921. In 1961 she was the first law firm librarian to serve as president of AALL. Through the 2007–2008, a total of five law firm librarians served as president: Jack S. Ellenberger 1976–1977, Carolyn P. Ahearn 1991–1992, Mark E. Estes 1992–1993, and Kay M. Todd 1993–1994.

Future

Law librarians will work more outside of traditional roles and the physical confines of the library in the future. They will pay greater attention to customer service by attending to what the customers value, not just what the customers say they want. They will translate their customers' needs to publishers to create customized information products. These customized information products will enable customers, to retrieve more quality information for themselves.

Challenges

A current trend in law firm recruiting is to hire more attorneys with three to five years of experience and fewer recent graduates. These attorneys come to the firm with expectations of library service from their old firms that differ from the services available in their new firm. This challenges librarians to create ways to break the habits and expectations of these experienced new attorneys and convert them into loyal customers.

The law firm librarian's customers range in age from mid-20s to 70-plus. Generally, each of these generations has vastly different levels of comfort and skills in using technology to solve information problems. The youngest attorneys tend to be the most comfortable with technology while the oldest tend to be the least adept with it. The youngest technologically savvy attorney expects Web-like searching and has poor legal research skills. The older attorney has better research skills, but limited computer skills. This challenges librarians to balance the demands for hard copy materials with the demand for desktop, Web-based research tools, etc. Librarians also need new technology skills to keep up with the younger attorneys.

Time constraints on getting/using information

The demands of clients require faster than ever turnaround times from attorneys. This challenges some tenets of traditional collection development practices. Namely, libraries do not need to own everything if a book can be borrowed quickly. Attorneys often do without the information because they cannot wait the one to two hours required to borrow the book. Librarians must revise collection development policies and ILL procedures to provide timely access to information within limited budgets.

Proving the return on investment value

The decision makers in law firms seldom use the library. Therefore, the librarian must build the case that money spent on information resources earns a significant return on investment. Librarians must track usage of library resources and the time spent on reference and research projects for clients and firm projects. These firm projects include preparing the business dossiers for business development and designing and maintaining information resource systems. The librarian must report these statistics in a concise and meaningful way that demonstrates that the library saves the lawyers' time, and makes them more productive and the firm more profitable.

Confidentiality

While some firms emphasize the confidentiality requirement by requiring employees to sign a confidentiality agreement, the employee is bound by the same ethical standards that apply to lawyers: namely, to not disclose confidential information to people outside the firm. Nondisclosure includes the seemingly innocent remark of what a client plans to do in a future transaction. With publicly traded companies, this sort of breach could subject the librarian to federal insider trading laws as well.

The firm, in order to protect itself against conflict of interests posed by one or more attorneys or staff who worked for another firm or company adverse to a client, erects ethical or confidentiality walls. These ethical walls are intended to keep the attorney from seeing any part of the client's file without prior clearance. The librarian, as knowledge manager, who knows when someone has researched a similar topic or issue, may inadvertently put two attorneys together to talk about a research result that could violate the ethical wall. The challenge then is to integrate the barriers of ethical walls into the knowledge management system.

PUBLIC LAW LIBRARIES

Introduction

The term "public law library" refers to all law libraries that are not affiliated with either law firms or law schools. In this category are found county public law libraries, court libraries, state law libraries, state and federal agency law libraries, and bar association/subscription law libraries. Clientele, funding, and governance are the main differentiating factors between these entities. Collections, staffing and credentials, facilities, teaching methods and responsibilities, national standards, and advocacy and public outreach are all important characteristics that make pubic law libraries quite different from those in law schools and law firms.

Public law libraries are a major component of the justice system, as they provide the information necessary for litigants to access the courts. In fact, they have been referred to as the first rung in the ladder to justice.[98] They generally differ from academic and law firm libraries in that they are funded by the public in order to serve the public. Although there are many variables and more than a few exceptions to this statement, the public's right to access the law that it is required to follow is the principle that supports the existence of public law libraries. The rapid growth in the number of self-represented litigants, the escalation of the costs of maintaining library collections at a time of decreasing resources, changing competencies required of staff and directors, and the harnessing of technology to accomplish the library's goals are all elements of the public law library in the first decade of the twenty-first century.

Customers

The public law library, by definition, is generally designed for use by the public. Courts have seen an astonishing growth in the number of people who are involved in some kind of litigation or court action and not represented by legal counsel. Statistics vary across the United States, with over 75% of divorce cases having at least one party proceeding "pro se" (without an attorney) known as "pro per" in California, and close to 85% in landlord/tenant matters.[99] A Legal Needs Study that was conducted in Montana in 2005 determined that there were over 207,000 unmet legal needs each year for a state with a population of less than 920,000 people.[100] The loss of funding for legal services resulting in fewer legal aide attorneys is one factor that is driving this trend. There also is the perception that disagreements previously settled by family, friends, and the parties simply talking out the issues are now better solved in court, fueled by the media and television shows like Judge Judy.[101]

As law librarians are committed to providing access to legal information, it quite naturally has fallen on them to take on an important role and growing responsibility to serve the unrepresented. Although the basic tools of legal research, such as statutes, opinions, and legal forms, have always been available, law librarians are finding themselves more involved both institutionally and individually in providing resources to assist this major portion of their customer base. Everything from collection development, staff training and retention, and Internet presence and other technologies has changed in order to accommodate the demands of these customers.

Most self-represented litigants have not studied the law, are not familiar with many of the Latin and archaic

Knowledge Management–
Law Librarianship

terms still used by courts (such as stare decisis and res ipsa loquitur), and have little experience with the judicial system. These clients come into the law library with significant disadvantages. It is difficult for them to understand the materials that have been developed for attorneys to navigate the legal system. They often do not have access to the Internet unless it is at their public law library. The mothers among them frequently cannot find affordable child care and therefore must bring their young children with them. These factors have driven significant changes in how public law libraries do their business. Self-Help book collections are being moved so that they are more available near the entrance to the library, Web information is being produced to include forms and explanations of court procedures, and reference and access services librarians are receiving special training on the difference between legal information and legal advice,[102] how to assist difficult and angry people, and how to assist those who do not speak English. Many law librarians are now partnering with public libraries to assist the courts with the significant increase in unrepresented litigants. The hope is that if reference staff at public libraries can be expert navigators on court and law library Web sites, they will become important community partners in our effort to provide access to justice systems and ease the burden on court staffs.

Public law libraries have frequently assumed the role of legal resource center for the practicing bar. Although large law firms may have their own in-house librarian, sole practitioners and firms of fewer than 100 attorneys (82% of all private practice in the United States according to the ABA)[103] do not have significant law libraries and rarely have librarians to provide legal research and reference service. When these legal professionals cannot find what they need through subscriptions to online databases, they rely on their public law library for research. Judges, law clerks, and judicial assistants use their county and state law libraries. Legal counsel to state and federal agencies and public defenders also rely on the resources of public law libraries.

Law firm libraries and law school libraries have defined user populations, for which they establish their policies, collection development, and staffing priorities. Public law libraries have challenges provided by an infinite variety of customers. In a one-hour time frame the library could be serving a high school debate student, an appellate judge, an angry father who is about to lose visitation rights, someone in state government who needs access to the federal regulations on water quality from 10 years ago, a bankruptcy attorney, and a visiting law professor from another state or country. This diversity makes the management of the public law library interesting and challenging, and it requires nimble administration.

Governance and Funding

Most public law libraries are governed by a board of trustees, similar to a general public library. Usually, the members of the board are stipulated by statute or ordinance, and are chosen to represent the constituent's interests for services and resources. However, it is not at all unusual for the trustees themselves to be infrequent users of the library. For example, many state and Supreme Court law libraries are governed by the state's supreme court justices. These officials rarely do their own research, as they have law clerks for that purpose; thus, they infrequently come into the library. Their most common need for assistance is when they need access to statistics, published humor, or quotations for teaching or addressing the public.

County law libraries are generally established by statutes or ordinances, where their funding mechanisms are laid out, but they can also be governed by local bar associations. In some instances, this has led to charges of conflicts and cronyism, since, although the library is supported by either filing fees or taxes paid by the pubic, only lawyers can decide what materials are to be purchased and what staff should be hired. Recently, county law libraries have been scrambling for funding, as formulae for the sharing of court filing fees have changed dramatically. In Florida, for example, funding dropped precipitously in 2004 when the state legislature reconfigured how filing fee revenues would be distributed.[104] This was a decision made by authorities far removed from the affected program, who generally can afford attorneys for personal and business use.

The exception to this scenario is the private, subscription law library. The oldest law library in the United States, Jenkins Memorial Law Library, is supported by the dues structure into which its members pay.[105] These libraries generally allow nonmembers (the public) on-site access for a nominal daily fee. Other prominent, historical law libraries of this character include the Social Law Library (Boston), the New York Law Institute (New York City), the Library Company of the Baltimore Bar, and the Cincinnati Law Library.

In searching for additional funding, many other public law libraries have taken on part of the character of the subscription law library. By offering special services to dues-paying members, the King County Law Library in Seattle and the Sacramento Public Law Library have generated both more revenue and a loyal customer base.[106]

Most state law libraries are funded through appropriations from their state's general fund. Usually they are not allowed to keep any revenue that is derived from activities such as photocopying and document delivery. When it is legislators who make the ultimate decision as to what funding will be available to the library, the user is even further removed from the process. For this reason, some law librarians ask especially sympathetic users, such as the self-represented, to testify at their appropriations hearings.

State and federal agency law librarians, including those who work for legislators and attorneys general, are also

Knowledge Management–
Law Librarianship

funded from appropriations made by legislative bodies. In most other respects, however, these libraries are organized and operated like law firm libraries. They rarely serve the public, and have a defined user base consisting of the attorneys and other employees of the agencies. They also tend to have small collections and only one librarian.

Services

Public law libraries provide most of the services that other kinds of law libraries offer. However, they rarely conduct in-depth research for customers, and the teaching they do is frequently more of the informal, "teachable moment" variety. They spend considerable time and resources developing finding guides and explanations to legal process and procedure which can be placed on their Web sites.[107,108] They work with public libraries and state library associations to train public librarians on how to use their Web sites and when to refer patrons to the law library.

The issue of legal information vs. legal advice, or the unauthorized practice of law, is a hot topic for many public law librarians.[109] There is considerable effort to make reference librarians more comfortable in teaching and working with pro ses.[110] Basically, the standard has been established that questions that begin with phrases such as "Can I? Where is?" and "What is?" can be answered, as they are fact based. Questions that begin with "Should I" cannot be answered, as they involve giving legal advice as to what action should be taken.

State, court, and county law libraries are frequently asked to host tours and informational sessions for students of high schools, trade schools, and colleges, for visiting librarians and scholars, and for other kinds of groups. Court librarians generally conduct in-depth orientation sessions for new law clerks and court employees. They offer brown bag, lunchtime classes on a variety of subjects such as legislative process and intent, state-specific tax resources, and using the library's electronic licenses.

County law libraries frequently have evening and weekend hours. Most court libraries are open only during standard, business hours. Many court and county law libraries also provide access at any time for attorneys who practice before the court. The attorneys generally sign in with a security guard. After hours, however, there is no staff present in the library, and therefore no reference assistance. This is controversial, and has been challenged by independent paralegals and self-represented litigants. Most federal court libraries only allow access to their libraries if the researcher has an active case before the court, no matter what time it is.

The "Ask the Librarian" button that many libraries provide on their Web sites[111] may feed into a 24/7 system in which other law libraries participate. The Los Angeles County Public Law Library's Web site has this information:

24/7 Chat Reference: Click on the 'Ask Now' icon to be connected to a reference librarian using real-time chat software. This is a service of the Metropolitan Cooperative Library System, so your question will not necessarily be answered by a Los Angeles County Law Librarian. Reference questions are answered by librarians from California's County Public Law Libraries, and LA County librarians provide some hours of coverage in answering law questions.[112]

Many court libraries will order multiple sets of the same title for all judges in their jurisdiction, and have them drop-shipped to the judges by the publisher. These libraries frequently purchase and maintain the collections that are held in judges' chambers. This can involve a significant commitment on the part of library management when the chambers' collections are located in other cities, because it requires a staff member to travel to another site. Maintaining chambers collections can be a significant matter, as law books generally have at least annual updates. Loose-leaf services may have to be updated as often as once a week, and court staffs rarely understand why the weekly releases cannot be ignored.

Some state law libraries design and manage the Web site for the entire judicial branch of government. Others take their court's opinions and appellate briefs, and place them on the Internet.[113] These services keep the library in the management loop of the branch, and contribute law librarians' hopes that others will have high opinions both of their competencies in the digital age and their commitment to serve the public.

Almost all public law libraries circulate their collections. Some allow any citizen in their jurisdiction to check out materials. Others check out items just to court staff and attorneys. Some will provide circulation to members who pay for the privilege. Public law libraries also provide ILL service for materials in their collection that circulate. Similar to other libraries, law libraries generally will not send titles that have been published out of state in the current year.

Document delivery is a major service of public law libraries, and is almost always fee-based. Many public law libraries derive significant income from providing such transactions. The King County Law Library (Seattle) charges $20 per citation for documents up to 20 pages long, with a $5 discount for subscribers. If the citation is incorrect and has to be researched there is an additional $10 charge.[106] The Jenkins Memorial Law Library (Philadelphia) charges $25 for rush deliveries, which does not include costs.[114] Although photocopying and then mailing, faxing, or sending via an overnight delivery provider were acceptable delivery systems until recently, more and more of the law library's clients now want their information delivered in a digital format. Judges and litigants like the convenience of taking something that comes to them electronically and merely cutting and pasting relevant text into the legal brief or opinion that is being

Knowledge Management—
Law Librarianship

written. This is easily done if the information is retrieved from a Web site or from an electronic product. If it is from a print source, the information can be easily digitized and e-mailed with most state-of-the-art copiers. Library management prefers this kind of delivery because it cuts back on envelope preparation and postage expenses. Most public law libraries want to provide and deliver requested information at the time and in the format that is required by the customer. Scanning technology has helped significantly with these libraries' missions.

Other services offered by many public law libraries include the rental of conference rooms, notary publics, free Internet access, custom cataloging for small law firms, and customized research, including expert witness background reports. Today's public law libraries are scrambling for revenues to support their operations. Unlike law schools, which must have law libraries for accreditation, public law libraries are increasingly under attack from those who make funding decisions. Lawmakers at local and state levels ask why the public should support a legal research facility that is used by one special interest group—the legal profession. They have to be shown and convinced not only that lawyers do serve the legislators' constituents, but that more than half of the libraries' users are nonlawyers. The other main purpose for providing such extensive services is to generate a loyal customer base. Public law libraries are run like businesses, and work on many of the same challenges as the commercial sector, including market analysis and client development.

Collections

Some of the largest law libraries in the United States are public law libraries, such as the Los Angeles County Public Law Library and the Social Law Library in Boston. Other county law libraries are very small, with only one or two staff members and collections of less than 50,000 volumes. Suffice to say, there is no average size or average collection. However, the AALL has approved Standards for both appellate court libraries[115] and county public law libraries.[116] These standards are annotated, which gives guidance and support to staff, directors, and library boards of trustees.

A strong core collection for a county public law library will have legal materials from its home state, including a complete collection of the published decisions of the state's courts and current and superseded state and local court rules. It will have a state digest, a citation service, and other significant state court publications such as annual reports, court commission findings, and statistical analyses. For legislative materials, it will have current (and if space permits older) statutory compilations, current session laws, the state constitution and its various historical versions, as well as published debates and proceedings of constitutional conventions. It will hold local, county, and municipal codes, charters, bylaws, and ordinances for

the area it serves. If available, the library will have the state's administrative code and published decisions of state agencies, as well as the opinions of the state's attorney general. If there is a state legal encyclopedia the library will hold it, as well as significant state-oriented legal treatises, practice materials, and legal periodicals and newspapers.

For federal law, the library should have at least one set of reporters for the decisions of the United States Supreme Court, as well as a digest for finding those opinions. It will have at least one version of the *United States Code* and the published decisions of the U.S. District Court, U.S. Court of Appeal, and U.S. Bankruptcy Court for its jurisdiction. The library will also have the *Federal Register* and the *Code of Federal Regulations*, and a citation service for these reports and codes. For general U.S. publications, it will have units of the National Reporter System and the digests to go with those reporters. It may have current statutory compilations for contiguous states, and will have a national legal encyclopedia. General legal forms will be available, as well as a broad selection of legal periodicals with an index for finding articles, and other reference tools such as legal dictionaries, legal quotations compilations, and the Martindale-Hubbell law directories. Restatements of the Law, *Uniform Laws Annotated* and *American Law Reports* will be held. A collection of general legal and self-help titles on subjects of interest to the public and the self-represented litigant must generally be held very near the reference desk and/or entrance to the library.

The titles above will be available in print or electronic format, and sometimes both. State, appellate court, and large urban law libraries will hold all the above materials as well, in addition to full runs of most legal periodicals, all major treatises and loose-leaf services, treaties with other countries, significant foreign and international law collections and a strong collection of secondary materials, in particular, see the Los Angeles County Law Library.[117] Public law libraries serve a broad client base, and their customers' comfort with digital media covers a wide spectrum. The AALL Standards make another point: "While online technology will provide a fundamental baseline for research platforms of future law libraries, certain print collections will always be needed and should be retained as part of the libraries holdings as a balance against countless deficiencies inherent in today's electronic media."[116]

Many public law libraries are selective U.S. Government depositories. Unlike academic libraries, which usually segregate their government documents in separate collections that are not integrated into their general subject matter collections, most public law libraries catalog their government publications using the standard LC classification system and integrate them into the rest of the collection. Thus, documents emanating from the Internal Revenue Service can be found with commercially published titles such as the *Standard Federal Tax Reporter* and the *Tax*

Knowledge Management– Law Librarianship

Knowledge Management–
Law Librarianship

Management Portfolios. Most state Supreme Court libraries also are depositories for the State Justice Institute. All publications that have been funded by the Institute are distributed to these libraries so that there is greater dispersion of the research for use by state judiciaries.

Public law libraries are running out of shelf space. Most have been in existence far longer that either law firm libraries or the majority of law schools. Many are in older courthouses which have no additional room for library growth. Actually, the court often is looking at the library to give up space for new judges and court staff. Fortunately, solutions are easier to come by now than they were 20 years ago. Public law libraries are turning to cost-effective digital solutions, such as HeinOnline[118] and Law Library Microform Consortium Digital[119] to replace long runs of legal materials. The preeminent legal databases, LexisNexis and Westlaw, provide access to most primary materials and many legal periodicals, but are too expensive for pubic law libraries to use for the purpose of replacing print. Each search carries a price tag. However, the vendors of these databases have begun offering public research subscriptions that are free to the public, by pairing public access to the databases with the contracts for print subscriptions that the library continues to retain. The public work stations are appreciated by the self-represented and solo practitioners, and their availability has been a marketing tool for the public law libraries.

Facilities

There is a wide spectrum to consider when discussing the physical plant of the public law library. The gamut runs from those libraries owning their own buildings to those having only one or two rooms in an old courthouse. In some states, notably California, the county is required to provide space, utilities, and janitorial service for operation of the library.[120] Some county law libraries have branches located throughout the county. Court and state law libraries are located in their courthouse, which is ideal for serving court employees and those customers who have business before the court. Many county law libraries have been forced out of the courthouse, both due to their escalating needs for shelf space and the increasing requirements for space for new judges. This makes the library harder to find and less convenient to use, as it is no longer near the clerk of court's office and may not have suitable parking.

Twenty years ago, public law libraries worried about having enough seating space. Many had as many tables and study carrels as law school libraries, as well as private briefing rooms for the use of visiting judges and those with long term research projects. Now, however, fewer people access the public law library physically and more use the library's resources from the Internet. The library's ability quickly to e-mail materials and have books delivered overnight has also changed the user dynamics. As a result, public libraries are not as anxious about having a certain number of desks and chairs available.

Collections for public law libraries do not have to be justified by the number of volumes held. Rather, it is access and ease of delivery that govern collection development decisions. The libraries have had to remodel to accommodate the public access computers now provided as well as special collections that should be shelved close to the reference desk. In the 1980s and 1990s, computers were difficult to install in older facilities constructed before anyone knew that wiring would eventually be required. Now, however, many of these libraries have gone wireless, which has solved many of the challenges posed by remodeling for technology in an historical building with granite walls that are a foot thick.

Staff and Education

Public law libraries tend to have fewer staff than law school libraries and more than firm libraries. There is a very wide range, however, and an average cannot be stated. More than two-thirds of public law library directors have at least an M.L.S., and 22% have a law degree.[121]

Public libraries are increasingly looking for employees who bring to the information center skills and experience beyond those needed in the traditional library setting. Automation, Web services, and networking specialists are in high demand. Unfortunately, like the rest of the pubic sector, the library can rarely afford to pay computer specialists what they would earn in the private sector. People with marketing, public relations, and adult education talents are also highly valued.

Employees of most public law libraries are bound by both the ethical standards adopted by the AALL[122] and whatever confidentiality policies have been adopted by their governing bodies. Court-based libraries have very strict rules concerning the absolute confidentiality of all matters that are before the court. These rules can involve which law clerks are checking out which books, which clerk is being trained on using specific libraries of electronic databases, and even conversations overheard in the elevator. This can indicate which judge is writing the majority opinion. Inadvertent divulgence, in turn, can affect financial markets, the well-being of corporations, and personal lives. Training all staff, not just those working in public services, must include these privacy issues.

Technology

Most public law libraries now have integrated library systems, public Internet stations that allow access to the Web, electronic licenses to legal materials, and copiers that allow for digitizing and e-mailing materials. Technology is no longer the extreme challenge it was a decade ago. After significant staff realignment, physical reconfigurations, and staff training in a plethora of digital competencies—from HTML mark-up to negotiating electronic licenses, the public law library now has folded technology into its business plan and daily operations.

Connections

Connections and networking in the larger legal community are critical for the public law library's image and continuing presence. Bar associations, legal services and legal aide groups, judicial entities, civic associations, and advocacy organizations all are valued partners for the library. Both print and broadcast media are cultivated to help the public know what services the library offers. Other libraries, such as public libraries and the information centers for other public agencies, are consulted and also joined for cooperative ventures.

Law Librarians usually belong to the AALL. Those in the public sector join AALL's State, Court, and County Law Libraries Special Interest Section. They also generally belong to the AALL chapter for their city or region of the country. It is from these groups that the librarians receive most of their continuing education, professional guidance and mentoring, and have opportunities for networking specific to law librarianship. They frequently also join their state library associations.

Challenges

All law libraries are challenged by the popular notion that everything is available on the Internet, for free. Even when it is the library that has created and posted the information, there is little appreciation by the general public, as well as those decision makers who hold the purse strings, of what it takes to make the available information on the Web site. Another concern of public law librarians is that, although much primary law (statutes, court opinions, and regulations) is available on the Web and consequently relied on by the public, it has neither the authority nor the authenticity attached or guaranteed. Secretaries of State are beginning to jettison their print versions of administrative rules and codes in favor of digital versions that can be accessed from the Web sites. There is little appreciation outside of the library world of what this can mean in the future.[123] The permanent preservation of born-digital legal materials is another concern of the profession.[124]

The continuing escalation of prices of legal materials has been a problem for all law libraries for years. Those book budgets that have not been routinely raised to accommodate book inflation have been decimated. The serial nature of the law collection, which is based on the continuation and updating of most of the items, means that those books that cannot be updated are no longer of worth and generally have to be removed from the collection.

Another concern of public law librarians is that, as more and more of their services are provided to customers who do not actually walk into the library, there could be a perception that fewer and fewer people are actually using the library. Statistics are somewhat more difficult to collect for validation purposes. It is known that clients without legal training, whether they are pro se litigants, students, or citizens who want to know what their rights are, require significantly more time to assist because of their unfamiliarity with legal materials.

Conclusion

Providing a balanced collection and competent staff to serve the wide variety of people who use the public law library is a significant challenge. Clients may be attorneys or judges, but they could just as likely be angry, confused or desperate lay people who have every right to access the law but just do not know how. The public law librarian is committed to providing access, but cannot interpret the law or suggest legal advice. Managing the pubic law library requires a delicate balancing act.

Public law libraries are challenged by trying to manage their facilities in an entrepreneurial fashion when they are significantly restricted by government barriers. Continuing price increases have forced many public law libraries to cut back on their collections. Subscribing to electronic databases does not help with budgeting, since they are as expensive as their print counterparts, if not more so. Nevertheless, the public law library with nimble management continues to be a vital and valued part of the judicial system.

REFERENCES

1. *Standards for Approval of Law Schools*, American Bar Association: Indianapolis, IN. Annual, http://www.abanet.org/legaled/standards/standards.html (accessed January 2009).
2. Price, M.O. The place of the law school library in library administration. J. Legal Educ. **1960**, *13*(2), 230–238.
3. Pollack, E.H. Autonomy versus integration in law library administration: A reply to Dr. Price. J. Legal Educ. **1961**, *14*(2), 229–239.
4. Dragich, M.J. Organizational structure in law libraries: A critique and models for change. Law Libr. J. **1989**, *81*(1), 69–96.
5. Danner, R.A. Facing the millennium: law schools, law librarians, and information technology. J. Legal Educ. **1996**, *46*(1), 43–58.
6. Milles, J.G. Leaky boundaries and the decline of the autonomous law school library. Law Libr. J. **2004**, *96*(3), 387–423.
7. Clinch, P. SLS/BIALL academic law library survey 2006/2007. Legal Info. Manage. **2008**, *8*(3), 188–204.
8. Heller, J.S. America's first law school library: a history of the College of William and Mary's Marshall–Wythe Law Library, 1779–1995. In *Law Librarianship: Historical Perspectives*; Gasaway, L.N., Chiorazzi, M.G., Eds.; Fred B. Rothman & Co.: Littleton, CO, 1996; 43–76.
9. Ellenberger, J.S. History and development of the modern law library in the United States. In *Law Librarianship: A*

Knowledge Management–
Law Librarianship

Handbook; Mueller, H.P., Kehoe, P.E., Eds.; Fred B. Rothman & Co.: Littleton, CO, 1983; 1–12.

10. Brock, C.A. Law libraries and law librarians: A revisionist history; or more than you ever wanted to know. Law Libr. J. **1974**, *67*(3), 325–361.

11. Martin, H.S. A world-class law library. Harv. Law Bull. **1992**, *43*(2), 5–10.

12. *ABA/LSAC Official Guide to ABA -Approved Law Schools*, Newtown, PA Annual.

13. *Barron's 2009 Guide to Law Schools*, 19th Ed. Barron's Educational Series: Woodbury, NY, 2008.

14. *The Princeton Review Best 170 Law Schools, 2007 Edition*, Random House: New York, 2007.

15. http://www.arl.org/stats/annualsurveys/law/index.shtml *Law Library Statistics*. Annual.

16. *Handbook*, Association of American Law Schools: Washington, DC Annual. http://www.aals.org/about_handbook_regulations.php (accessed January 2009).

17. http://www.legalscholars.ac.uk/documents/standards2003. pdf A library for the modern law school: A statement of standards for university law library provision in the United Kingdom, Prepared on behalf of the Society of Legal Scholars by a Consultative Group to the Libraries Committee, Convenor: Jules Winterton, 2003.

18. Harvard Law School (Remarks by Professor Langdell at the quarter-millennial celebration of Harvard University, November 5, 1887). Law Quart. Rev. **1887**, *3*(1), 118–125 at 124.

19. Morgan, J.B. The evolution of government documents. In *Law Librarianship in the Twenty-First Century*; Balleste, R., Luna Lamas, S., Smith-Butler, L., Eds.; Scarecrow Press: Lanham, MD, 2007; 165–199.

20. Bintliff, B. Context and legal research. Law Libr. J. **2007**, *99*(2), 249–266 249.

21. Harrington, W.G. A brief history of computer-assisted legal research. Law Libr. J. **1985**, *77*(3), 543–556.

22. http://www.law.cornell.edu/.

23. Svengalis, K.F. *The Legal Information Buyer's Guide and Reference Manual*, Rhode Island LawPress: Barrington, RI, 1996.

24. In *Law Library Collection Development in the Digital Age*; Chiorazzi, M., Russell, G., Eds.; Haworth Information Press: Binghamton, NY, 2002.

25. Prager, S.W. Law libraries and the scholarly mission. Law Libr. J. **2004**, *96*(3), 513–524.

26. Heller, J.S. Collection development, licensing, and acquisitions. In *Law Librarianship in the Twenty-First Century*; Balleste, R., Luna Lamas, S., Smith-Butler, L., Eds.; Scarecrow Press: Lanham, MD, 2007; 89–161.

27. http://www.aallnet.org/sis/allsis/secure/Colldev/policies. asp See *Academic Law Libraries' Collection Development Policies*.

28. http://www.aallnet.org/chapter/consortia.asp See *AALL Consortia*.

29. Kulpa, L. The contributions and unique role of foreign-born, foreign-educated law librarians. In *Law Librarianship: Historical Perspectives*; Gasaway, L.N., Chiorazzi, M.G., Eds.; Fred B. Rothman & Co.: Littleton, CO, 1996; 203–213.

30. Kearley, T. Foreign and international collections part 1: Foreign. In *Law Librarianship: A Handbook for the Electronic Age*; Kehoe, P.E., Lyman, L., McCann, G.L., Eds.; Fred B. Rothman & Co.: Littleton, CO., 1995; 257–312.

31. Strzynski, J. Foreign and international collections part 2: International. In *Law Librarianship: A Handbook for the Electronic Age*; Kehoe, P.E., Lyman, L., McCann, G.L., Eds.; Fred B. Rothman & Co.: Littleton, CO., 1995; 313–348.

32. Rumsey, M. Foreign, comparative, and international law librarianship. In *Law Librarianship in the Twenty-First Century*; Balleste, R., Luna Lamas, S., Smith-Butler, L., Eds.; Scarecrow Press: Lanham, MD, 2007; 129–145.

33. Reynolds, T.H. Flores, A.A. *Foreign Law: Current Sources of Codes and Basic Legislation in Jurisdictions of the World*, Fred B. Rothman: Littleton, CO, 1989.

34. Germain, C.M. *Germain's Transnational Law Research: A Guide for Attorneys*, Transnational Juris Publications, Inc.: Ardsley-on-Hudson, NY, 1991.

35. http://worldlii.org/.

36. Greenleaf, G. Chung, P. Mowbray, A. *Emerging Global Networks for Free Access to Law: WorldLII's Strategies*, 2007; http://papers.ssrn.com/sol3/papers.cfm?abstract_id=975614 (accessed January 2009).

37. Cohen, M.L. *Bibliography of Early American Law*, William S. Hein: Buffalo, NY, 1998; 6 Vol.

38. Cohen, M.L. Training law librarians in the use of rare legal materials. Legal Ref. Serv. Q. **2001**, *20*(1/2), 29–39.

39. Cohen, M.L. Researching legal history in the digital age. Law Libr. J. **2007**, *99*(2), 377 393.

40. *Special Committee on Preservation Needs of Law Libraries: Report and Recommendations*, American Association of Law Libraries: Chicago, IL, 1992.

41. Oakley, R.L. Preserving legal information for the twenty-first century: Toward a national agenda. Law Libr. J. **2004**, *96*(4), 570–668.

42. Matthews, R.J. Baish, M.A. *State-by-State Report on Authentication of Online Legal Resources*, American Association of Law Libraries: Chicago, IL, 2007.

43. Goldberg, J.A. Development of a universal law classification: A retrospective on Library of Congress Class K. Catalog. Classif. Q. **2003**, *35*(3/4), 355–436.

44. Blackburn, S.; Hu, R.H.; Patrum, M.; Scott, S.K. Status and tenure for academic law librarians: A survey. Law Libr. J. **2004**, *96*(1), 127–165.

45. Hemmons, A. Advanced legal research courses: A survey of ABA-accredited law schools. Law Libr. J. **2002**, *92*(2), 209–241.

46. Cohen, M.L. Berring, R.C. Olson, K.C. *How to Find the Law*, 9th Ed. West: St. Paul, MN, 1989.

47. Price, M.O. Bitner, H. *Effective Legal Research; A Practical Manual of Law Books and Their Use*, Little Brown: Boston, MA, 1953.

48. Hicks, F.C. *Materials and Methods of Legal Research with Bibliographical Manual*, Lawyers Co-operative Pub. Co.: Rochester, NY, 1923.

49. Mersky, R.M. Dunn, D.J. *Fundamentals of legal research*, 8th Ed. Foundation Press: New York, NY, 2002.

50. In *Legal Information and the Development of American Law*; Danner, R.A., Houdek, F.G., Eds.; Thomson-West: St. Paul, MN, 2007.

51. http://ssrn.com/isn/index.html.

52. Liivak, A. Academic law librarians in the United States of America: Lawyers or librarians?. Int. J. Law Libr. **1975**, *3* (2), 162–168.

53. http://www.aallnet.org/about/graduate_guidelines.asp.

54. http://www.aall.org/about/ala_accredited.asp.

55. Goldsmith, L.M. History of the University of Washington law librarianship program. Law Libr. J. **1990**, *82*(1), 239–279.

56. Gasaway, L.N. Women as directors of academic law libraries. In *Law Librarianship: Historical Perspectives*; Gasaway, L.N., Chiorazzi, M.G., Eds.; Fred B. Rothman & Co.: Littleton, CO, 1996; 497–553.

57. Carrick, K. Silk v. corduroy: The status of men and women in law librarianship. Law Libr. J. **1986**, *78*(3), 425–441.

58. Malmquist, K.E. Academic law librarians today: Survey of salary and position information. Law Libr. J. **1993**, *85*(1), 135–183.

59. Hoeppner, C.J. Trends in compensation of academic law librarians, 1971–91. Law Libr. J. **1993**, *85*(1), 185–203.

60. Gasaway, L.N. A brief history of the American Association of Law Libraries. In *Law Librarianship: Historical Perspectives*; Gasaway, L.N., Chiorazzi, M.G., Eds.; Fred B. Rothman & Co.: Littleton, CO, 1996; 289–307.

61. Houdek, F.G. AALL history and the law library professional. In *The Spirit of Law Librarianship: A Reader*; Mersky, R.M., Leiter, R.A., Eds.; Fred B. Rothman & Co.: Littleton, CO, 1991; 19–36.

62. Houdek, F.G. *AALL Reference Book: A Compendium of Facts, Figures, and Historical Information about the American Association of Law Libraries*, William S. Hein & Co.: Buffalo, NY, 1994.

63. Houdek, F.G. Frequently asked questions about AALL's first hundred years. Law Libr. J. **2006**, *98*(1), 157–167.

64. *AALL Directory and Handbook*, American Association of Law Libraries: Chicago, IL Annual.

65. http://www.aallnet.org/about/ *About AALL*.

66. Coggins, T.L. The American Association of Law Libraries and its government relations program, parts I and II. In *Law Librarianship: Historical Perspectives*; Gasaway, L.N., Chiorazzi, M.G., Eds.; Fred B. Rothman & Co.: Littleton, CO, 1996; 309–371 373–429.

67. http://www.aallnet.org/chapter/ *Chapters and Related Organizations*.

68. In *Reflections on Law Librarianship: A Collection of Interviews*; Garson, M.A., Dabirashtiani, S., Sherwin, R.L., Dattalo, E.F., Perrine, S.L., Eds.; Fred B. Rothman & Co.: Littleton, CO, 1988.

69. Berring, R.C. Reflections on mentors. In *Law Librarianship: Historical Perspectives*; Gasaway, L.N., Chiorazzi, M.G., Eds.; Fred B. Rothman & Co.: Littleton, CO, 1996; 185–202.

70. Chiorazzi, M.G. William R. Roalfe: Builder of libraries, scholar, association animal. In *Law Librarianship: Historical Perspectives*; Gasaway, L.N., Chiorazzi, M.G., Eds.; Fred B. Rothman & Co.: Littleton, CO, 1996; 215–260.

71. Anderson, M.R. The history of African–American law librarians: A research agenda. In *Law Librarianship: Historical Perspectives*; Gasaway, L.N., Chiorazzi, M.G., Eds.; Fred B. Rothman & Co.: Littleton, CO, 1996; 261–274.

72. Roalfe, W.R.; Frederick, C.H. Scholar-librarian. Law Libr. J. **1957**, *50*(2), 88–98 Reprinted In *Law Librarianship: Historical Perspectives*; Gasaway, L.N., Chiorazzi, M.G., Eds.; Fred B. Rothman & Co.: Littleton, CO, 1996; 275–285.

73. Houdek, F.G. "Meet my mentor": A collection of personal reminiscences. Law Libr. J. **1999**, *91*(1), 177–255.

74. *Biographical Directory*, 5th Ed. American Association of Law Libraries: Chicago, IL, 1992.

75. *AALS Directory of Law Teachers*, Association of American Law Schools: Washington, DC Annual.

76. Houdek, F.G. An index to memorials published in the *Law Library Journal*, 1916–92. Law Libr. J. **1992**, *84*(4), 769–786.

77. Houdek, F.G. An index to memorials published in the *Law Library Journal*: 1993–2005 Supplement. Law Libr. J. **2005**, *97*(4), 701–708.

78. http://www.iall.org/.

79. Sprudzs, A. The International Association of Law Libraries and its twenty-five years of activities. Law Libr. **1984**, *15*(3), 50–53.

80. Sprudzs, A. Thirty-five years of international cooperation: The case of the IALL. Law Libr. **1995**, *26*(2), 321–326.

81. National or legal law library organizations and their publications. Int. J. Leg. Inf. **1993**, *21*(2), 120–123.

82. http://www2.lib.uchicago.edu/~llou/iall.html.

83. http://avalon.law.yale.edu/default.asp *The Avalon Project at Yale Law School*.

84. http://library.lawschool.cornell.edu/WhatWeHave/SpecialCollections/Donovan/ *Donovan Nuremberg Trials Collection*.

85. Danner, R.A. Redefining a profession. Law Libr. J. **1998**, *90*(3), 315–356.

86. Danner, R.A.; Kauffman, S.B.; Palfrey, J.G. The 21st Century Law Library. Law Libr. J. **2009**, *101*(2), 143–156.

87. *Toward a Renaissance in Law Librarianship: The Report, Recommendations, and Materials of the American Association of Law Libraries Special Committee on the Renaissance of Law Librarianship in the Information Age*, American Association of Law Libraries: Chicago, IL, 1997.

88. *Beyond the Boundaries: Report of the Special Committee on the Future of Law Libraries in the Digital Age*, American Association of Law Libraries: Chicago, IL, 2002.

89. Bintliff, B.A.; Gasaway, L.; Hazelton, P.A.; Houdek, F.G.; Johnston, J.L.; Dragich, M.P.; Ten Brink, C.; Wu, M. Rebuilding the profession: Recommendations for librarians interested in becoming academic law library directors. Law Libr. J. **2007**, *99*(1), 102–132.

90. Finley, E. Law Office Libraries. Law Libr. J. **1947**, *40*(3), 179–182 182.

91. Proceedings of the Golden Jubilee Meeting of the American Association of Law Libraries, Philadelphia, Pennsylvania, June 25–28, 1956. Law Libr. J. **1956**, *49*(4), 375–511 419 (remarks of Beatrice S. McDermott). 235 U.S. is the citation for a volume from a multiple volume set of books containing the written opinions of the U.S. Supreme Court. Volume 235 has cases decided in 1914–1915.

92. http://www.abanet.org/cle/mcleview.html *Summary of State MCLE Requirements*.

93. *Library Survey 2007*, 2007; July/August Law Firm Inc.

94. Studley, J.S. Firm culture is reflected in design, space planning. Conn. Law Trib. **1992**, May 25 18 30.

95. *AALL Salary Survey & Organizational Characteristics*, American Association of Law Libraries: Chicago, IL, 2005; Table 32, at 23.

96. *AALL Salary Survey & Organizational Characteristics*, American Association of Law Libraries: Chicago, ILL, 2005; Table 16, at 16.

97. Ellenberger, J. Memorial: Elizabeth Finley. Law Libr. J. **1980**, *73*(3), 737–739.

98. http://www.lawlibrary.state.mn.us.

99. Administrative Office of the Courts, *Model Self-Help Pilot Program: a Report to the Legislature*, Judicial Council of California: San Francisco, CA, 2005; 1.

100. Dale, M. Montana study finds "profound level" of unmet legal needs. Mont. Law **2005**, *31*(2), 5–8.

101. http://www.tv.com/judge-judy/show/12762/summary.html.

102. http://www.selfhelpsupport.org/library.cfm?fa=detail&id=136884&appView=folder.

103. http://www.abanet.org/marketresearch/lawyer_demographics_2006.pdf.

104. http://www.mdcll.org/html/News.htm.

105. http://www.jenkinslaw.org/.

106. http://www.kcll.org/letushelp/kclldelivers/index.html.

107. http://wsll.state.wi.us/wisco.html.

108. http://www.montanacourts.org/library/law_by_top.asp.

109. Cannan, J. Are public law librarians immune from suite? Muddying the already murky waters of law librarian liability. Law Libr. J. **2007**, *99*(1), 7–32.

110. http://www.courtinfo.ca.gov/programs/cfcc/pdffiles/SH-tab3.pdf.

111. http://www.montanacourts.org/library/asklib.asp.

112. http://lalaw.lib.ca.us/asklib.html.

113. http://fnweb1.isd.doa.state.mt.us/idmws/custom/sll/sll_fn_home.htm.

114. http://www.jenkinslaw.org/services/document-rates.php.

115. http://www.aallnet.org/sis/sccll/pdfs/SCCLL%20Appellate%20Standards%20Mar%202005.pdf.

116. http://www.aallnet.org/sis/sccll/pdfs/stdfin02.pdf.

117. http://lalaw.lib.ca.us/services.html#foreign.

118. http://heinonline.org/.

119. http://ets.umdl.umich.edu/cgi/t/text/text-idx?g=llmc;page=home.

120. http://leginfo.public.ca.gov/cgi-bin/waisgate?WAISdocID=02286519601+2+0+0&WAISaction=retrieve.

121. http://www.aallnet.org/members/pub_salary05.asp.

122. http://www.aallnet.org/about/policy_ethics.asp.

123. http://www.aallnet.org/aallwash/authenreport.html.

124. http://www.aallnet.org/aallwash/PPAreport.html.

Law Literature and Its Users

Penny Hazelton
Gallagher Law Library, University of Washington, Seattle, Washington, U.S.A.

Abstract

This entry introduces the legal system of the United States by describing the branches of government that create the laws of a civilized society. These sources of law are interrelated and must be understood in order to find answers to legal questions. The law has characteristics that impact the work of the researcher, including the division of law into primary and secondary authority, the doctrine of precedent, the need for both stability and change in our laws, and the multiplicity of sources of the law. The types of legal materials are then described, along with examples followed by a section on legal publishing and the formats of legal information. Finally, the entry concludes with a description of various types of users of legal information.

INTRODUCTION

In a very real way, the law is nothing more than words. But it is really more than that; these words articulate the policies and rules that govern our behavior. These words are published in print and digital format, and they are accessible at libraries and through commercial and free sources on the Internet.

The diversity of sources of the law contributes to the complexity of answering even simple legal questions. Over time, sophisticated research and finding tools were created—first in print and then electronically—to help locate this vast body of legal information. An understanding of the interconnectedness of legal materials will aid in the use of these multiple sources of law.

This entry will describe our legal system in basic terms, followed by a discussion of the sources of law and the characteristics that influence its use. The next section covers some basic information about the publication of legal information and the various commercial and governmental entities that make legal information available. Although most people now access legal information in electronic form, we will also cover print sources.

Primary authority, secondary authority, and finding tools make up the legal literature. Each has a special role in legal research. And because everyone creates and/or is subject to our laws, we will address how citizens, lawyers and other legal professionals, law students, and the general public navigate the legal system.

THE LEGAL SYSTEM

The law comes from the legislative, executive, and judicial branches of government. The law is designed to shield citizens from both tyranny and lawlessness, to protect freedom, and to enable society to conduct its affairs. Our legal system is complex because in the eighteenth century the founders wanted to distribute the power of lawmaking in a balanced way so that no one part of government could take complete control. Our legal system in the broadest sense is composed of branches of government with powers to make, interpret, and enforce the law. It also includes a legal profession responsible for advising government and representing litigants in their conflicts with the government or others.

It is important to note that the U.S. Constitution[1] created a federal system. Some powers are centralized at the federal (national) level, and some powers in the hands of the states. And within individual states there are cities and counties that have lawmaking powers—some more than others. In the United States, we also have Indian tribes that have a certain amount of sovereignty due to both treaties and federal legislation. Thus, the law on any particular subject can come from one or more governmental units. As we will see in the following, this raises some special challenges for the legal researcher.

We use the word law in many senses. Some legal literature contains the law—the legislation, administrative regulations, and court decisions we live by. But we cannot understand the literature of the law until we understand how law is created, and by whom.

The legal system of the United States is called a common law system. In a pure common law system, the law is derived from the decisions of judges when specific cases come before courts. Under what we call "precedent" (or stare decisis), judges are to follow those earlier decisions so there is consistency among these decisions. Other countries, such as Germany and Japan, are called civil law countries; their legal systems rely on codes or constitutions. It should be noted, however, that in the United States, law is also created by the executive and the legislative branches of government as described in the following. Although we call the United States a "common law"

Encyclopedia of Library and Information Sciences, Fourth Edition DOI: 10.1081/E-ELIS4-120053425
Copyright © 2017 by Taylor & Francis. All rights reserved.

country, as we will see in the following, one begins his or her research not with cases, but with legislative and administrative codes. And one state, Louisiana, is based on civil law because of the influence of the French Napoleonic Code.[2]

SOURCES OF LAW

In the democratic form of government in the United States, the power to make law is not centralized. For example, copyright law is governed by federal law because of an explicit delegation in the U.S. Constitution, "To promote the progress of science and useful arts, by securing for limited times to authors and inventors the exclusive right to their respective writings and discoveries...," U.S. Constitution, Art. 1, Sec. 8. On the other hand, creation of laws to regulate families and domestic relations are historically a matter for the states. This is reinforced by the tenth amendment, which states that "[t]he powers not delegated to the United States by the Constitution, nor prohibited by it to the states, are reserved to the states respectively, or to the people." U.S. Constitution, Amend. X. As a general matter, legislative bodies pass laws with broad application to everyone. They do not decide disputes between individual parties; this is done by judges. This distributed model of lawmaking among various branches of government and at all levels of government makes it essential that the researcher understand all of the sources of law and their interrelationships.

Discussion of the sources of law in this entry is necessarily generalized, since different levels of government in the United States (federal, state, Indian tribe, city, county) may have slightly different specific relationships. For example, the state of Nebraska has a unicameral legislature, not a bicameral (house and senate) legislature like all other states. The Nebraska legislature's homepage includes an excellent explanation of their one-house legislative system.[3] So although we will use the federal government as an example of lawmaking in the United States, the concepts described in the following apply at every governmental level.

Constitutions and Charters

Our legal system was created by the Constitution of the United States as the supreme law of the land. The U.S. Constitution is a single document, but it is also the basis for the vast body of laws that make up the American legal system. As a legal document, a constitution or charter creates the form of government and allocates power to the various branches of that government. For example, the U.S. Constitution created three branches of government, each of which has specific duties and responsibilities. Some of these responsibilities involve making or interpreting the law.

All branches of government must be certain that their work does not violate the constitutional framework. In that sense, all lawmaking activities must conform to the requirements of the constitution. No branch of government can change its own lawmaking responsibilities unless such changes are constitutional. A reallocation of power among the branches of government can only happen if the charter or constitution is amended or changed. However, many legal disputes are between the branches of government (Congress vs. the executive branch, for example), or between the federal and state or local governments (federalism issues).

There are constitutions at all levels of government, but in cases where a state constitution conflicts with the U.S. Constitution, the latter is always supreme.[4]

Legislative Branch

The legislative branch of government has the authority to make, amend, and repeal laws of general application. This power is granted by a state or federal constitution or charter. Many legislatures meet once a year to consider new laws that should be enacted. Legislative bodies propose new or amending legislation, hold hearings before committees with jurisdiction over certain subjects, debate the merits of proposed laws, and vote to pass or reject those proposed laws. The constitutions in about one-half of the states provide for the people to make laws directly through the initiative and referendum processes. For an excellent book on this subject, see Williams,[5] also published as issues 3 and 4 of volume 26 of *Legal Reference Services Quarterly*.

As part of the checks and balances in our form of government, the president of the United States or a state governor has to agree to these new laws or veto the passed legislation. Administrative agencies, part of the executive branch, are often granted lawmaking powers by statute, which is called "enabling legislation." The laws passed by administrative agencies are called "rules" or "regulations." In some cases, courts void agency regulations when they conclude that the agency acted outside the boundaries of its delegated authority. Furthermore, the judiciary can limit application of legislation and regulations if the scope exceeds the powers granted by the Constitution or charter that formed the government.

Judicial Branch

The judicial branch of government includes the court system, which adjudicates disputes. Judges are either appointed or elected to serve in trial and appellate courts at all levels of government. Their job is to enforce legal rules by hearing cases from parties who cannot agree on the solution to their own conflicts (civil cases), or who are being charged with criminal activity that represents a violation of a federal or state statute.

Each court has jurisdiction,[6] or the "power, right, or authority" to take action over certain types of cases. Courts also have rules of procedure that must be followed. Normally there is a trial court level, usually an intermediate appellate court, and finally the highest appellate court (or court of last resort). An appellate court is a court having jurisdiction to hear appeals (a request to a higher court to overturn the legal ruling of a lower court) and to review the trial court procedure. Legal terms have been defined by the American Bar Association on their website.[7]

Judges decide cases at all levels, but in most jurisdictions, only appellate court decisions are published and made available to the public. Cases can be appealed from the trial court to an appellate court to review issues of law; an appellate court must accept the facts as determined at trial. Thus, trial courts handle the vast majority of disputes; only a small proportion of cases are reviewed by a higher court.

Judges can interpret legislative enactments, can declare legislation in violation of the constitution unconstitutional, can decide issues of law based on common law (non-statutory) principles, and may review administrative decisions and rules. Judicial decisions can have wide precedential impact, as the rule of the case may be applied in later similar circumstances involving different parties.

Executive Branch

The executive branch of government is charged with implementing and enforcing the law, as well as operating of the government. Chief executives—the president or a governor—actually have limited power to create law through executive orders. Administrative agencies—the primary lawmaking entities of the executive branch—are created either by the executive (often through "Reorganization Plans")[8] or by legislation to implement government policy).

The role of the executive branch of the federal government in lawmaking was quite limited until the 1930s when Congress, due to the Great Depression, created several new independent, regulatory agencies. Added to the more traditional executive agencies (i.e., the Department of State or the Treasury), the body of regulations that governs behavior of our citizens has grown tremendously in our complex society. Essentially, when Congress creates a law, say, to clean the air, some governmental agency is put in charge of making this happen. Every government with an executive branch (i.e., city, county, state, Indian tribe, or federal) has administrative agencies responsible for the implementation of its initiatives and priorities. The implementation of governmental policy will be through the issuance of rules (regulations), and often through interpretations of those rules.

Administrative agencies have broad powers, but when power is delegated by legislation, it is constrained by the legislative branch. And because the agencies are part of the executive branch, the president may restrain the power of agencies. For example, there usually is much less regulation of business by the Federal Trade Commission during Republican than Democratic administrations. Furthermore, in cases of arbitrary and capricious action on the part of an agency, its regulations can be reviewed by the judicial branch. Again, we see the checks and balances of lawmaking as outlined by the U.S. Constitution at work.

International Law

Public international law governs relations among nations and as such regulates a wide range of transnational activities. Agreements between and among nations, normally called treaties, can govern a nation's behavior in the international sphere. For example, the United States might sign a treaty about the treatment of prisoners taken during wartime (the Geneva Convention[9]) or governing the use of space for various purposes (the Outer Space Treaty[10]).

The executive has the power to sign treaties with the advice and consent of the Senate.[11] Again, we see the checks and balances that disperse power throughout the branches of government.

Common Law

Our system of law in the United States is based on the common law system of England. Before the American Revolution, the customary laws of England formed the basis of the laws in the United States. These customs were the rules that governed behavior, ordinarily determined by a judge hearing a specific case before the court. Once the U.S. Constitution was written, it took many years for the young federal and state governments to enact their own laws. During that time, when conflicts or disputes arose, they were often settled by courts that applied common law doctrine. Today things are much more complex: the legislative, executive, and judicial branches of our federal, state, and local governments create the laws that govern our rights, obligations, and behavior.

An example of a common law rule is the no-longer-held view that when a woman married a man she gave up her individual legal status.[12] Before judicial opinions and state legislation changed this common law doctrine in the early twentieth century, a married woman did not have individual legal standing and, for example, could not bring a lawsuit, hold property, nor sue her husband.

It is not unusual for a federal or state legislature to adopt judge-made law. At the same time, it is not uncommon for Congress or state legislatures to pass laws that have the effect of overturning judicial decisions, which is fine unless such legislation violates federal or state constitutional law.

Law Literature–Library Architecture

CHARACTERISTICS OF THE LAW

Several characteristics of the law influence the use and interpretation of legal information and profoundly affect the tasks of the legal researcher. An understanding of these factors will help researchers understand the complex nature of the law, and learn to effectively use legal research tools.

Primary and Secondary Authority

All law and law-related information is classified in one of two ways. Either the information is the law or it is not. Primary materials contain the law, which is found in legislative enactments, judicial decisions, administrative rules, regulations and decisions, and in international treaties or agreements. Because these materials are "the law," we say they must be followed and therefore represent primary authority. Researchers need to rely on the law when answering legal questions, so the researcher's main task is to locate relevant primary authority.

Secondary authority discusses, evaluates, criticizes, or otherwise comments on the law. They analyze and synthesize legal doctrine, analyze policy, refer extensively to primary authorities, operate as finding aids to locate legal information, and are a great source for summaries, special terminology, and context of specific legal subjects.

This classification of legal information drives the research process. Secondary sources can help lead the researcher to appropriate and relevant primary materials when the primary materials themselves may be hard to search or are otherwise elusive. Understanding what types of legal materials can be relied upon to answer legal questions is essential to understanding the function of law in our society. Here, the interrelationships among the law created by different branches of government also come into play. The researcher must know, for example, which primary authority to rely on when the holding of a court decision in Connecticut appears to conflict with a Connecticut statute.

Precedent

Another characteristic of the law is that the doctrine of precedent applies to judicial opinions.[13] *Stare decisis*, a Latin phrase, means let the decision stand. This doctrine of precedent requires a judge to apply the same reasoning in deciding a current case as that which was used in previous cases coming from higher courts in that jurisdiction involving the same facts and legal issues. Among the forms of primary materials, judicial opinions are issued from several levels of courts within the federal, state, city, county, and Indian tribal governmental structures. The theory underlying the doctrine of precedent is that society, through its legal rules, should treat people the same if they are similarly situated. Thus, legal researchers look to past court decisions to find out how similar cases would be decided today.

Judicial opinions are either mandatory (binding) or persuasive authority. The rules established in judicial opinions *must* be followed by courts when they are mandatory authority. The rule of the case is mandatory in courts in that same jurisdiction at a higher level. So, for example, in a current case dealing with the standard of review in the licensing of a limousine driver, the Oregon Court of Appeals must follow the rules established in earlier cases dealing with this same subject decided by the Oregon Supreme Court. But an Idaho Supreme Court does not have to follow a rule made by the Oregon Supreme Court. That is, Oregon Supreme Court cases are not mandatory authority in Idaho courts.

As a general matter, appellate courts at the same level, in the same jurisdiction, will say they follow earlier decisions from their court involving the same facts and issues. Using the same example as earlier, the Oregon Court of Appeals is likely to follow earlier decisions from that court involving the same facts and issues. However, because it is the *same* court—rather than a higher court—it really is not compelled to do so.

The rule of the case is clearly the linchpin to the determination of the authority of the case—whether it is mandatory or merely persuasive. The rule of the case is the legal rationale or reasoning used by the judge in making a determination of who wins and who loses in the dispute before the court. Lawyers often disagree about the rule in the same case, throwing into controversy whether that case is mandatory, and whether the rule must be followed by the current court.

Persuasive authority is just that—rules established in court opinions that *may* be used by lawyers to persuade a court to adopt a certain ruling in a case. Cases outside the line of mandatory authority are merely persuasive. For example, an Idaho court will never *have* to follow the rule of a case from Oregon, but the Idaho court might like the Oregon rule and decide to apply it in Idaho.

This theory of precedent is important because a researcher needs to cite the strongest possible authority for any proposition. The weight of authority of a court decision—that is, is it mandatory or persuasive authority—is relevant to the search for case law and to an evaluation of those research results. The doctrine of precedent guides our research and requires that the huge body of judicial opinions decided since the establishment of our country must be available to the researcher. We do not discard old court decisions because a 200-year-old opinion might still reflect the rule of law in a particular area of law.

Stability and Change

There is great tension in the legal system between the need for stability of law so that outcomes are predictable, and

Law Literature–Library
Architecture

the need to change in order to reflect the world we live in today. The doctrine of precedent, discussed earlier, makes it clear that the legal system looks to earlier court decisions to help determine how a case should be decided today.

But what if the world changes and the old rules no longer work? As we discussed earlier in this entry, in nineteenth-century America under common law rules, when a woman married, her legal status as an individual was merged with her husband. She could not bring a lawsuit because she was not considered an individual under the law.[12] Obviously, this rule is very out of balance with our current society. So, how did this rule change? The subject—the legal status of a married woman—is a matter of state law. The rule changed because legislatures (through new laws) and courts (through their opinions) reviewed the reasons for the rule, found that those reasons violated public policy, and created new rules that did not disable the legal rights of a woman who married.

The rules we live by in our society—the law—must be able to change. But if societal rules were in a constant state of flux, we would neither know how to act nor be able to predict the consequences of our behavior. A society without rules is anarchy.

This characteristic of the law—that it needs to be predictable, yet flexible—has important consequences for legal research. First, you must have access to the most current sources of law. Second, you must also have access to older sources of law. Third, you must understand that law exists within the context of current societal norms and values. Understanding research in economics, sociology, psychology, history, politics, medicine, technology, and natural science—in short, all disciplines—helps a legal researcher appreciate forces that might operate to change the laws.

Multiplicity of Sources

The final characteristic of the law that impacts legal research is the sheer number of sources. On the federal level, all three branches of government make laws. In addition, every state, Indian tribe, city, and county has lawmaking powers. And in most cases, states, Indian tribes, cities, and counties have a legislative branch, a court system, and an executive branch. All have lawmaking responsibilities and powers.

When a person wants to know what the law is on a certain subject, there is very rarely one source to look to for the answer. A researcher may have to research federal, state, and local law (at the city and county level we use the term "ordinances") to advise a client on, say, a land use question that involves federal and state wetland legislation and interpretative court decisions, and city/county ordinances. Furthermore, we are not likely to know whether a legislative act, a court decision, or an administrative rule will be dispositive. This means that a legal research

project must be planned carefully, and that the researcher must understand how all the sources of law fit together.

TYPES OF LEGAL MATERIALS

In order to understand the literature of the law, knowledge of the types of legal materials created is essential. Each type plays a role in solving legal problems. Many legal materials are available in print and electronic formats. Because many electronic legal materials are based on the original print sources, understanding the patterns of print publication of the different types of materials can aid in the use of these documents in electronic form.

All legal information can be divided into two types—primary and secondary sources. Primary sources contain the law—the rules we live by. Secondary sources are *about* the law. What follows is necessarily an abbreviated overview of legal materials. Legal research textbooks are a rich source for further investigation.[14–24]

Primary Sources

The law is contained in several different types of primary source material. Constitutions and charters, statutes, judicial opinions, administrative rules and decisions, and treaties are sources of the law. Each of these types of law derives their force from the powers delegated through the document that forms the government, such as the U.S. Constitution, a state constitution, or a city charter.

Constitutions and charters

As mentioned earlier, a constitution or charter creates the form of government and allocates power among the various branches of government. The checks and balances established in the federal constitution create complex interrelationships among the executive, judicial, and legislative branches of government. These relationships are important to remember when trying to solve legal research problems, since they affect the relative weight of the authority.

Statutes or codes

Once laws are passed, they are numbered sequentially by legislative session and made available as "slip laws." A slip law is, simply, a single legislative act. These laws are chronologically published, and eventually organized by date in a compilation called "session laws."

Because these session laws are not arranged by subject, they are time-consuming and awkward to use when a researcher wants to know the current law in a particular subject area. In order to make it easier to find the current law on any particular subject, the session laws are codified by the jurisdiction (i.e., federal, state, or local), which means they are arranged by subject. These "codes" or "statutes," as they are commonly called, are normally created by the government. They have excellent indexes and tables of contents to facilitate finding relevant laws. Most of these codes are published in both print and electronic formats by the government, but almost always also are published unofficially by commercial publishers. Whether published by the government or commercial publishers, the text of the code or statutes is identical, and both are considered reliable sources of the legislation.

Because the role of judicial opinions is often crucial to understanding how legislative enactments should be interpreted, commercial publishers created annotated codes. An annotated code includes the code itself, plus "annotations" that reference the history of the law, secondary materials that refer to the law, and cases that interpret the law. These annotated codes save the researcher a lot of time, since legislation, court opinions, and secondary sources on a particular subject are all gathered together in one resource.

Codes and annotated codes are updated by the session laws in order to be current. These updates occur at least once a year, but there is a trend to integrate the language of the session laws into the codes or statutes several times a year. Both Westlaw and LexisNexis update their digital versions within weeks after the passage of a new federal or state act.

The checks and balances incorporated into our form of government are evident as we look at the interrelationships between legislation, the constitution, the judiciary, and the executive. Legislation can be enacted on nearly any subject as long as it is within the grant of power by the Constitution. Legislation can change judicial interpretations of statutes or change a common law rule relied upon by a judge. Legislation can create or eliminate administrative agencies, as well as grant or eliminate power to implement the purposes of the legislation. At the same time, legislative enactments also are subject to the checks and balances of the Constitution so that no one branch of government would have all lawmaking power. In the famous decision *Marbury v. Madison*, 1 Cranch 137 (1803), the Supreme Court made it clear that the Court was the final arbiter as to whether a statute was constitutional.

Citation to codes or statutes is the shorthand reference lawyers use to refer to specific sections of a law. Citations to statutes or codes will ordinarily look like this: 28 U.S.C. § 1291 (2006). In this example, 28 is the title number of the law, U.S.C. is the abbreviation of the source of the law (*United States Code*), § 1291 refers to the section of the code containing your specific language, and 2006 refers to the year the USC was published. See the standard manual for citing legal materials for further explanation (*The Bluebook*, rules 12 and 13[25]).

Judicial opinions

Court opinions are issued directly by a judge or panel of judges through an official court website. The first appearance

of a court opinion is called a slip opinion. Eventually, the opinions from that court are gathered together and published in a court report, or reporter. At this point, the slip opinion will be given a permanent citation. On the state level, as a general matter only decisions from appellate courts are published. And of those, fewer than half of the states publish their appellate court opinions in print under government auspices. The rest have contracted out this distribution of court opinions (unofficial reports) to a commercial vendor.

Court opinions are organized by jurisdiction, so, for example, all the decisions of the Washington State Supreme Court will be found in the official government publication called Washington Reports. One commercial publisher—West Publishing Co.—gathers appellate court opinions from several different states into what they call regional reporters. For example, the opinions of the Washington State Supreme Court can also be found in the Pacific Reporter, a series that includes cases from Washington and 13 other western states.

Most series of court reports number hundreds or thousands of volumes. Subject access to court opinions is through full text word searching in databases containing court opinions (free from government websites, and for a fee from publishers such as Westlaw, LexisNexis, and Bloomberg Law). The West key number digest system (available in print and on Westlaw) provides a comprehensive subject index to all state and federal cases. In addition, virtually all secondary tools analyze and cite freely to judicial opinions.

Citation of court opinions follows this form: *Princeton University Press v. Michigan Document Services, Inc.*, 99 F.3d 1381 (6th Cir. 1996). The names of the parties come first in the citation, followed by the volume number of the reporter where the opinion can be found (99), the abbreviation of the reporter containing the opinion (F.3d for *Federal Reporter* 3rd series), and the first page of the opinion (1381). The parenthetical contains the abbreviation for the court that decided the case and the year the opinion was decided. In the aforementioned citation, this case was decided in 1996 by the United States Court of Appeals for the Sixth Circuit. More details and other examples can be found in the standard work on legal citation rules, *A Uniform System of Citation*, commonly known as *The Bluebook,* rule 10.[25]

Administrative decisions, rules, and regulations

An executive or administrative agency has two types of lawmaking power. One has characteristics of legislation, and the other has attributes of the way courts work. Writing rules and regulations to implement the mandate of the legislation to create clean air is one kind of lawmaking done by administrative agencies. The rule-making process is governed by the Administrative Procedure Act (5 U.S.C. §§500 et. seq. 2012), legislation that requires, among other things, an opportunity for public notice and comment before rules and regulations can be finalized.

In addition, some administrative agencies have what is called quasi-judicial power. That is, agencies can interpret their own rules and regulations in a specific conflict between the agency and a citizen or organization. The resulting determination in this specific conflict is called an administrative decision or opinion. It is enforceable, and in certain cases the opinion can be reviewed by a court of law in the judicial branch of government.

Citation to agency regulations and agency decisions can be found in *The Bluebook*, rule 14.[25]

International law

To solve legal problems with international issues requires consultation of treaties and other international agreements, as well as the relevant customary law. Decisions of international tribunals will also be relevant to many questions with international ramifications.

International legal research is unique and requires knowledge of many different sources of law than are used to research American legal issues. A good, current research guide will help the novice locate and use the needed materials.[26] A new book on this topic by Winer, Archer, and Louis-Jacques would also be a great place to start.[27]

Citation to international resources can be found by consulting *The Bluebook*, rule 21.[25]

Secondary Sources

Information resources that discuss, evaluate, or otherwise comment on the law are called secondary sources. In some cases, secondary sources such as treatises and law review articles are cited by attorneys to support their arguments, and by judges in their opinions. Secondary sources are particularly important to the process of research as they can help shape the sources consulted by the researcher and help make the research more efficient by citing relevant primary authority. The many types of secondary sources play different roles in the research process. The following section describes the major types of secondary sources and explains where they are most useful. Someone who is researching a topic he or she is unfamiliar with should begin with secondary sources.

Books

There are several types of books published for legal researchers. Many are still available only in print, but more and more are available in digital format from legal publishers like Thomson-Reuters, LexisNexis, and Bloomberg Law, or nonlegal publishers like Oxford University Press and Cambridge University Press. Few recently published books are available at low cost or free through the Internet. At this point, some historical legal works are being digitized by the Google Book Project. Gale's "Making of Modern Law" and HeinOnline's "Legal Classics" databases include many important eighteenth and nineteenth century legal works.

Citation to books and non-periodical literature is governed by *The Bluebook*, rule 15.[25]

Scholarly treatises. The scholarly treatise is one of the most useful types of law books. These works are often written by legal academics, and reflect years of research and expertise in an area of law. There are one volume and multivolume treatises. Most are updated at least once a year, but some titles may be updated several times per year. The object of these works is comprehensive analysis and synthesis of legal doctrine in the subject matter of the book. They cite heavily to primary legal materials and other relevant secondary materials. For the novice legal researcher, they can be overwhelming since they cover their topic in great depth. Examples of scholarly treatises are the multivolume work, *Environmental Law* by Professor William H. Rodgers and *Cohen's Handbook of Federal Indian Law*, a comprehensive one-volume work. Both were originally published several years ago and are supplemented on an annual basis.

Monographs. Single-volume legal works on a narrow topic are called monographs. They can have a historical or current focus. They are authored by law professors and often rely heavily on footnotes and citation to legal primary and secondary sources. Most of these works are not updated at all. *Most Humble Servants*: *The Advisory Role of Early Judges* written by Professor Stewart Jay is an example of a legal monograph.

Practice materials. As the generic name suggests, these books are primarily written by and for lawyers. They tend to be very practical, rather than scholarly treatments of the subject. The best ones are updated at least annually, and may include sample forms and checklists. They also cite heavily to primary materials and other useful sources. A two-volume work written for Washington State practitioners, *Creditors' Remedies—Debtors' Relief*, authored by Professor Marjorie D. Rombauer, is an excellent example of the type of a secondary source written especially for lawyers.

Student texts. There is a whole genre of books published to help law students succeed in law school. These works cover the spectrum from glorified outlines to substantive one-volume works covering a specific law school course, like contracts or property. The latter, called Hornbooks, regularly cite to primary and other secondary legal materials as they summarize and synthesize the law. *McCormick's Evidence*, 7th edition, was published in 2014 and would be a great resource not only for students but also for the researcher who has no background in the

Law Literature–Library Architecture

law of evidence. These works are usually updated with the publication of a new edition every few years. However, some have annual supplementation.

Books for the layperson. As is true in any specialized field, a wealth of publications can be found designed to fill the layperson's information needs. Do-it-yourself books in law abound as well. *How to Do Your Own Divorce*, *The Renter's Legal Guide*, and *Write Your Own Will* are examples of the types of books published to help the non-law-trained person with legal problems. Nolo Press specializes in law books for the layperson.[28] Many people act on their own behalf or become pro se litigants because meaningful access to the legal system is not available. Books about the law that explain legal rights in a clear way can be very useful to those who want a basic understanding of the law.

Legal periodicals

There is an abundance of legal periodical literature in law of four distinct types. Periodical literature has been added to Westlaw and LexisNexis since the early 1980s, but the vast majority of academic law review articles have been digitized and are available on HeinOnline, a subscription database. Since the digitization process scanned articles using the pdf format, the materials in the HeinOnline databases look exactly like the print volumes with the added enhancement of full text searchability.

Access to this vast body of literature is through full text searching of the digital files as well as use of legal indexes such as H.W. Wilson's *Index to Legal Periodicals*, EBSCOHost's *Legal Source*, and Gale/Cengage Learning's *LegalTrac*. These indexes may be available on Westlaw and/or LexisNexis, as well as directly from the publishers.

Citation to periodical literature in law can be found in *The Bluebook*, rule 16.[25]

Academic law reviews. Law is the only discipline in which articles written by law professors, attorneys, and other scholars or practitioners are selected, edited and published in student-run journals called law reviews. Every American law school has a general law review, and most have several specialized law reviews. For example, the University of Washington School of Law has a general law review called the *Washington Law Review* which publishes articles on all legal topics, and several specialized journals: the *Washington International Law Journal*, the *Washington Journal of Environmental Law & Policy*, and the *Washington Journal of Law, Technology & Arts*. Law schools subsidize their law reviews, so subscription rates are very low, at least compared to the journals published commercially for profit.

Published one to eight times per year, articles and student comments published in law reviews analyze and synthesize the law. These works are heavily footnoted with references to all types of legal information and can be very helpful in the early stages of a legal research problem. Most articles are in the 30–60 page range.

Today, some journals are published only in digital form and are available through institutional, open access, digital repositories. More and more law schools are making all of their journals available on the school's website, and one can expect this will be the rule, rather than the exception, in the not too distant future.

Bench and bar journals. Periodicals published by judges' and lawyers' associations are generically called bench and bar journals. They may be published as frequently as monthly, or only annually, Virtually all the content is written by legal practitioners and judges. *The Colorado Lawyer* is an example of a state bar association's publication. The articles tend to be short and practical. They cite to relevant primary and secondary legal materials, but not comprehensively.

Membership in the bar association or judge's organization is usually required in order to receive copies of these journals. Many current issues are available in electronic form on the organization's website. Some titles are available through Westlaw, LexisNexis, and HeinOnline.

Commercial journals and newsletters. By far the most common delivery of scholarship in most other disciplines, commercial journals are far more rare in the legal literature. There are some; but they tend to be directed toward the legal practitioner. The articles are not very long, but most include reference to primary legal authority. The journals (called commercial journals because they are published by for-profit publishers) usually cover very specialized subjects of law. They are expensive, often costing several hundred dollars for an annual subscription. The *Intellectual Property and Technology Law Journal* published by Aspen (Wolters Kluwer) is an example of a commercially published journal.

Legal newsletters are very common in law and are often published to notify legal practitioners about current cases, legislation, and administrative actions that impact a specific legal subject. Most of these are commercially published, although a few are written and distributed by non-profit legal organizations. Most newsletters are available online. Good examples of newsletters are those issued by Bloomberg BNA (formerly the Bureau of National Affairs, or BNA). A comprehensive list of all legal newsletters can be found in the annual *Legal Newsletters in Print*.

Legal newspapers. Of course, information about the law can be found in nearly any type of newspaper. However, legal newspapers that specialize in legal content regularly make specific reference to legal authority, including citations, so the references can be found by the researcher. There are two national legal newspapers, and several

Law Literature–Library Architecture

city/regional legal newspapers written for members of the legal profession. The *National Law Journal* and the *American Lawyer* cover legal issues nationwide, while the *Los Angeles Daily Journal* focuses on local and regional legal news. They cover very recent legal developments, analyzing various sources of law, policy, and other related disciplines. Most are published weekly or monthly. They are available through subscription in print, microform, and electronically.

Looseleaf services

As the law became more complex, practitioners needed access to all sources of law on a particular subject. Since most primary legal materials are published by jurisdiction and not by subject, a lawyer who practiced labor law needed to have access to federal and state legislation on labor law, federal and state cases on labor law, and all administrative activities related to labor law at the state and federal level—virtually thousands of volumes of law books.

In the 1940s, legal publishers created looseleaf services that included primary legal materials on one subject. An example is Bloomberg BNA's *Labor Relations Reporter*. This reporter includes all primary legal materials about labor law—statutes, court decision, administrative materials—along with checklists and analysis. Multivolume and updated on a weekly basis (and now available electronically by subscription), looseleaf services are some of the most sophisticated legal research tools published. Today, these "looseleaf services" are published online, and most users get the contents in digital, rather than print, format.

A comprehensive list of looseleaf services in law can be found in *Legal Looseleafs in Print*, published in a new revised edition annually.

Legal encyclopedias

Legal encyclopedias summarize and synthesize the law from judicial opinions and some federal statutes. The encyclopedias are organized by legal subject from A to Z and include analysis and citation to primary and secondary sources. There are two national encyclopedias, *American Jurisprudence 2d* (Am. Jur. 2d) and *Corpus Juris Secundum* (C.J.S.). These are a great source for an overview of a body of law, and they include references that cite cases, statutes, and other authority.

Commercial publishers have also created legal encyclopedias for some states. These can be very useful when dealing with issues of state law.

Legal encyclopedias are updated annually. In addition to print, they can be found in LexisNexis or Westlaw.

ALR

American Law Reports (ALR) include selected court/judicial opinions with an accompanying annotation or essay summarizing the case law in all state and federal jurisdictions. The analysis is comprehensive as to the very narrow point of law which is the topic of the annotation. Updated annually in print, this set is also available electronically through a subscription to Westlaw.

Restatements

The American Law Institute (ALI) meets regularly to offer, in the form of the Restatements, general principles—and sometimes *recommended* principles—of law that are primarily driven by judicial decisions. The Restatements themselves are secondary authority, that is, they do not come from any governmental unit. However, when a state court adopts a particular Restatement, that principle becomes part of the primary authority—the law—within that jurisdiction. If many states adopt the language of a Restatement—sometimes with modifications, we should add—the Restatements help understand the general rule among the states. The Restatements are updated once a year in print and are also available by subscription on Westlaw and LexisNexis.

Citators

One of the most interesting research tools created in law is a method that permits a researcher to find out whether the rule of a specific judicial opinion (case) is still good law. Since a court ruling can be appealed to a higher appellate court, over time the rule of the case can be eroded or solidified by later court decisions. The first citator was created by Frank Shepard in 1873. Eventually, his work allowed the lawyer to check the authority of every published case from all jurisdictions in his Shepard's Citations series. Frank Shepard's surname became a verb, as all lawyers were taught to "Shepardize" all cases before relying on them.

Shepards Citations are published by LexisNexis. Although still available in print, today Shepards is typically accessed as part of a subscription to LexisNexis. Not only is Shepards online easier to use than the print, but it is also much more current. To compete with Shepards, Westlaw created KeyCite in 1997. KeyCite is an electronic-only citator and available only on Westlaw by subscription.

KeyCite and Shepards Citations both operate also as integrated research finding tools. Once a legal citation to one relevant case or statute is known, these sophisticated electronic systems can lead the experienced legal researcher to many other relevant cases, statutes, regulations as well as many types of secondary authorities.

Case digests

The publication of court opinions chronologically by jurisdiction inspired the creation of another important secondary source in the late 1800s—the West Digest System (sometimes called the "Key Number") system. Subject access to court cases is facilitated by this gigantic outline of case law. Legal editors at West Publishing Company (now a Thomson Reuters affiliate) read each court decision and write a short summary of the various points of law made in the court's opinion. Each summary is called a headnote, and each headnote in every case is assigned to a topic and key number in the West outline of the law. The headnotes, organized by a subject of law and then keyed to a specific point of the outline of that body of law, were then compiled in digests. It is easiest to think of the West key number digest system as a subject index to court opinions. The digests are organized by jurisdiction (individual states, regional groups of states, and by levels of federal courts).

Now, available electronically by Westlaw subscription and in print, the digest system provides controlled vocabulary subject access to all federal and state court decisions.

LEGAL PUBLISHING

Since branches of governments make the laws through legislation, judicial opinions, and administrative rules and decisions, you might expect that the government would disseminate and publish them. But you would be wrong. Some governmental units published their court opinions and legislation, but until recently, many others did not. And even when governments published their law, the materials were often published with a long lag time. Of all the types of legal information sources, administrative regulations are the only type that has typically been published by the government at the federal level, and sometimes by many states, without resort to a commercial publisher.

The role that commercial (for-profit) publishers have played in the distribution of the law and the creation of legal research finding tools has been critical to the success of the legal system and the legal profession. For example, at the federal level only the decisions of one court—the U.S. Supreme Court—historically were published by the government. Until the digital revolution of the late twentieth century, all other federal court decisions were published only by commercial publishers.

Commercial publishers add value to the basic legal information they produce by including case summaries, annotations, indexes, and other finding aids. They also create new tools that assist the researcher in connecting different types of legal information on the same subject. Legal literature is rich in tools that synthesize and analyze legal information and reference other relevant materials.

In the United States, historically there were over three dozen publishers who produced a wide variety of legal research materials for law of all kinds. The consolidation of the legal publishing market in the mid-1990s that resulted in three international corporations controlling the

publication of virtually all American legal materials, both primary and secondary, changed the face of American legal publishing forever. For the most comprehensive history of the legal publishing industry in the United States, see Svengalis.[29] As of 2014, Thomson Reuters (Canadian), Reed-Elsevier (British-Dutch), and Wolters Kluwer (Dutch) accounted for the vast majority of the worldwide sales of legal information. In 2010, Bloomberg L.P., a New York mass media corporation, acquired the Bureau of National Affairs, the next to the last major, independent American publisher.

Issues in legal publishing today center around the consolidation of the market and the transition from print research tools to electronic databases. Inflation rates in legal literature have been three to four times the regular rate of inflation for the past 25 years. Stagnant budgets in law libraries of all kinds, combined with the availability of new research tools, have added to the stress all law libraries are under in this early part of the twenty-first century. Publishers' experimentation with economic models that create the profit needed for the vendor, but at prices law libraries can afford, has been the predominant feature of the past decade.

Vendors who had an historical print business in legal publishing have faced this century with different issues than those whose primary products were electronic only. Digitization of the law by the governments that make the law—and making the law free on the Internet—have led to a proliferation in the number of companies creating new information products for the legal marketplace.

At this point, legal publishing is widely dispersed, but the tools most commonly relied on by the legal profession are still published by the historically large commercial vendors—most notably LexisNexis and Westlaw—whose electronic databases and print publications have proven to be reliable, current, and authentic.

Will only the best of the legal research tools come to the surface after some years of experimentation? Or will legal researchers of the future continue to have an unlimited number of research tools from which to choose?

FORMATS OF LEGAL INFORMATION

Primary legal materials—court opinions, statutes, and administrative rules and decisions—have been available in the United States for over 100 years in print. Published both by government and commercial groups, a sophisticated group of legal research tools emerged to aid the lawyer in researching a legal problem for a client. When laws enacted by legislatures were organized solely by the date they were passed into law, governments and commercial publishers created codes—current legislation organized by topic, rather than by date. When court opinions were published in sets by jurisdiction (Washington State, federal, U.S. Supreme Court, for example) and then by

Law Literature–Library
Architecture

date, enterprising publishers created massive subject indexes to all published court reports. When there were so many cases published on a particular area of law that it was hard to understand what rule to apply, practitioners and law professors wrote articles and books synthesizing and analyzing the doctrines. Finding aids such as legal encyclopedias, periodical indexes, scholarly treatises, Shepard's Citations, and the West Digest system were created to help lawyers locate relevant authority quickly.

Methods were needed to keep these print materials up to date. The pocket part supplement was created to update the work in the main volume. It slipped inside the back cover to remind users to update the main work. If the supplemental materials were so large that the pocket part would not fit in the back of the book without breaking the book spine, a free-standing paperback pamphlet supplement was used. Later books were published in binders that allowed old, outdated material to be removed and new material to be added. Looseleaf services, comprehensive as to one subject, were published and updated on a weekly or monthly basis with new material filed and older material discarded.

However, digital information and the Internet have changed the world of legal research completely. Mead Data Central introduced the first database of legal information in 1973 called LEXIS.[30] For the first time, state court opinions were full-text searchable. No longer were lawyers limited to the indexes and tables of contents created by book editors to locate relevant information. Now a researcher could locate opinions written by a particular judge or find all cases on a specific topic. Revolutionary!

Within a few years, the major print publisher of American legal materials, West Publishing Company, introduced Westlaw to the legal profession. In the 1980s and 1990s, Westlaw and LexisNexis (as it is now called) worked to add content and sophisticated search features to their aggregated databases. The vendors urged buy-in from law firms by providing programs which allowed law firms to charge their clients specifically for computer-assisted legal research (CALR). And these vendors provided a significant discount to law schools who subscribed to their services for their students and faculty. Significant discounts were also negotiated with courts that contracted with Westlaw and LexisNexis.

A huge change occurred in the mid-1990s when governments started to publish their documents and other content on the Internet in digital form, free to all users.

By early in the twenty-first century, flat rate contracts for commercially published legal electronic content were standard in academic, law firm, court, and county law libraries. And most of this content was bundled at discounted prices, often taking into account the print subscriptions to the same material. E-book contracts to license the content of legal monographs were available from some publishers.

Today, most governments publish and distribute the law from courts, legislature, and executive agencies in digital form on the Internet—at all levels of government. Their collections of legal information are rarely historically comprehensive. Furthermore, the navigational tools and access to this information vary tremendously from one website to another. While these free government websites are often excellent for access to current legislation, and court opinions, and administrative agency regulations and decisions, they lack the sophistication (and of course cost) of the commercially available research databases such as Westlaw, LexisNexis, and the recent competitor, Bloomberg Law.

Not all print tools have transitioned comfortably into the electronic environment. Many legal materials are still not in electronic form[31] and even if they are, they often lack the functionality of the print materials. In particular, a legal research tool (i.e., treatise, monograph, code, or statute) with a hierarchical arrangement that relies on the context of the previous or following material can be very hard to read and understand when only in electronic form.[32]

It is small wonder that law libraries that have a lot of print have been pressured on the budget side when trying to provide legal information in both print and electronic formats. With regards to primary authority from the legislative, judicial, and executive branches, today most law libraries receive this in digital format. Treatises, on the other hand, are still primarily acquired in print. With law reviews now accessible on HeinOnline and an increasingly number of law schools making their journals available for free (with articles in .pdf), more and more law libraries are canceling their print subscriptions to law school journals.

Two other important issues stand out in this time of transition to electronic materials. The first is how to handle the preservation of legal information that is born digital—and never has a tangible, print equivalent. After nearly 20 years of born-digital information being published and disseminated on the Internet, the amount of this information that is no longer available at all is staggering. The problem is that no one knows how much legal information is really gone forever. Many organizations have identified this as an important problem, but only piecemeal solutions have been offered to date. The American Library Association's Government Documents Roundtable[33] and the Government Documents Special Interest Section of the American Association of Law Libraries[34] both have strong interests in fugitive and born-digital government publications. And many academic law libraries are creating permanent digital repositories of important materials, primarily their law reviews and articles published by their faculty.

The Legal Information Preservation Alliance (LIPA) is working on several projects to preserve print and born digital legal information.[35] Another consortium of law libraries and other legal agencies—perma.cc—is acting to preserve the content of links to the open web which are cited in legal documents.[36]

Law Literature–Library Architecture

The second problem relates to the authentication of legal information. Although most legal information is now published on the web by the issuing government agency, most official websites disclaim the legal authority of what they include on the website. Sometimes, the user is referred to a print product. In many cases, there is no print equivalent. The American Association of Law Libraries (AALL) took the lead in the concern about this topic and published a ground-breaking paper, State-by-State Report on Authentication of Online Legal Resources, in 2007.[37]

As a result of this advocacy, the National Conference of Commissioners on Uniform State Laws appointed a drafting committee and approved for enactment in all states a new uniform law called the Uniform Electronic Legal Material Act (UELMA). UELMA was approved by the Conference in 2011, and to date 12 states have enacted its provisions. This law has three purposes: 1) to guarantee the authenticity of legal documents produced by our governments, 2) to preserve this same legal material in perpetuity, and 3) to provide for permanent public access to these legal materials.[38]

USERS

Our society was founded on the principle that the rules we live by—the law—must be accessible in a real way to everyone. Branches of governments create the laws, but until recently have not consistently made these laws available. The very best legal research tools for locating primary and secondary legal authority historically were available through commercial publications and databases, and often at high cost. This is one of the reasons that law libraries—especially those open to the public—are important.

Many people are interested in the law. Lawyers, judges, paralegals, and law librarians use legal information to answer questions for clients and library users every day. Law students learn how to search for legal information and how to apply the rules they find to specific problems. Students of all kinds—K-12 to graduate students—have questions about the law that are raised in their classes or through what they learn from their friends, parents, news, TV shows, or the Internet. Members of the public care about how the law applies to their daily lives, and some attempt to represent themselves in family law, landlord-tenant, or other disputes.

Ideally, primary sources of law—court opinions, statutes, administrative agency regulations and decisions, and treaties—would be widely available, in both print and digital format. However, a person's interaction with just the primary material is likely to be quite unsatisfactory because of the complexity of our legal system and the different levels of governments involved in the most simple questions. Reading a single statute and several cases interpreting that statute will rarely answer a legal question.

And the publications that contain the law itself do not necessarily refer to all of the types of legal materials that might be relevant to a specific inquiry.

These factors make the process of legal research complex, even for sophisticated lawyers or judges. Thus, each group of people who use legal literature will interact with legal resources in different ways, potentially using very different research tools in the process.

Lawyers

Members of the legal profession arguably are the most intense users of legal information. Most legal research tools have been designed to be used by lawyers who need very current and comprehensive information. A lawyer needs to be able to locate and understand applicable sources of law to address clients' issues, and be aware of the research tools he or she can use to answer those issues.

Do all lawyers regularly do legal research? No. Law firms are no different than other organizations. There are different responsibilities for different levels in the hierarchy. Size of the law firm also matters. A lawyer in a solo or small firm is more likely to do legal research throughout her career than a more senior lawyer in a large multinational law firm. Newly hired lawyers, usually called associates, handle more of the research done in large law firms. The more senior the lawyer in a large firm, the more likely they are to be finding and keeping clients and advising clients based on the research done by more junior lawyers. A senior lawyer is also much more knowledgeable about what the law is in narrow, specialized areas of legal practice. While the more experienced lawyer must keep that knowledge current since the law is always in flux, their expertise means they do not resort to the use of legal research tools very often.

In a similar vein, law clerks hired to work for judges for 1- to 2-year terms perform most of the research to support the work of the judge. Over time, judges develop a wide expertise in the matters that come before the court. And lawyers who are advocates before a judge provide written briefs and other filings that contain the research on which their legal position is based.

Law school faculty are lawyers. Part of their job is to write and publish scholarship in areas of their expertise. Many do their own legal research. And many use law librarians and/or hire research assistants who are current law students.

In law practice, legal research is also performed regularly by law librarians and paralegals. These professionals often do research which is outside the expertise of a practicing lawyer. Perhaps information is needed for statistical or economic data or other nonlegal topics. Or a highly specialized database or resource that is not familiar to the lawyer may be consulted.

Law librarians in court, county, academic, and firm law libraries (many of whom have law degrees) work directly

Law Literature–Library Architecture

with lawyers to acquire and manage the legal resources needed to perform research, and to plan and arrange training on research tools for lawyers. The national professional association for law librarians, the American Association of Law Libraries, has an excellent website that includes information on education and careers in law librarianship.[39] For an example of a special program to train lawyers who want to be law librarians, see the University of Washington Information School's website.[40]

Successful legal research by lawyers and other professionals requires a research plan or design that takes into account the financial resources of both the client and the firm. Unless the area of law is very familiar to the researcher, secondary sources are very likely to be used early on in the research process. Research in books, periodicals, and/or encyclopedias will give an overview of the topic, help identify and clarify the issues, identify terminology that will help locate other relevant materials, and analyze and synthesize different sources of law over time on the topic.

The smart and efficient legal researcher will then select from a wide array of print and electronic research tools to begin the search for the primary materials that respond to the legal question. Many times, cases, statutes, and other relevant primary legal materials are identified initially from secondary sources. Armed with a more thorough understanding of the area of law and citations to specific primary materials can shorten the research project significantly.

The lawyer with expertise is more likely to consult comprehensive, current publications like online databases, looseleaf services, or government Web pages to be sure her knowledge is still current.

Every research project is different. If we knew the answer to the question, legal research would not be necessary! A few studies have been published that survey how lawyers actually do legal research. You will find a list with an abstract of each study in the appendix to this entry.

Overall, lawyers and other members of the legal profession use the widest possible array of legal information tools—from the large subscription databases (Bloomberg Law, LexisNexis, and Westlaw) to print treatises to the free and low-cost information found on the Internet. In recent years, in order to reduce the cost of research and even the playing field as between solo practitioners and large law firms, many state bar associations license a comprehensive legal database for all of their members. For example, the Casemaker database has been licensed for use by all members of the Washington State Bar Association, while Fastcase is the research database available to members of the Oregon State Bar.

Tools that permit lawyers to locate the most current statute on a particular subject, to easily determine if relevant judicial opinions are still good law, to have all important and current information on a particular subject, and to know the relevant law they have found is authentic and official are essential if lawyers are to carry out their ethical obligations to their clients.

Law Students

The legal literature created specifically for law students is that which is centered around the courses offered in most law schools. Outlines, Nutshells, and Hornbooks are published specifically to help law students learn the material for their classes. These works range from simple outlines to one-volume works like those in the West Hornbook series. These materials can also be useful for lawyers researching in an area of law with which they are unfamiliar, and, to a lesser extent, for members of the public who are trying to understand a body of law.

Law students for the most part read the law as it is published in casebooks for each of their courses. Many legal subjects taught in law school are based primarily on judicial opinions. Some courses, such as tax and commercial law, rely more heavily on statutes. So the first exposure law students have to the law is not to read relevant cases and statutes directly from the primary legal materials (i.e., court reporters and codes) themselves.

This practice of excerpting primary material and repackaging for law students is one of the main reasons why courses in legal research are taught in all law schools. Otherwise, students would not be exposed to the array of research tools they will need when they begin practicing. Student use of the legal research tools created for lawyers is pretty minimal unless the student takes a seminar course in which he or she must write a paper, writes an article as part of their membership on the law review, fulfills an analytical writing project required by many law schools, or works in a clinic or law firm while in law school. Even for students who must research and write a significant paper, limited exposure to the vast array of legal information resources available is the norm. Legal research courses offered in the first year, and advanced research courses during the second or third year of legal education, introduce students to many more of the available practitioner tools.

Access to LexisNexis, Westlaw, and Bloomberg Law for all students and other members of the law school community is negotiated in a flat-rate contract with the vendors and paid from the law library budget. The educational discount is significantly lower than commercial rates. The vendors provide professional staff from their offices and hire law student representatives to train and work with students, faculty, and librarians at each law school.

Several smaller legal databases such as Loislaw, VersusLaw, Fastcase, and Casemaker may also have educational contracts to which many academic law libraries subscribe.

There are several challenges in providing law students with the legal literature they need to succeed as a law student and then as a practicing attorney. Research tools

Law Literature–Library Architecture

are changing all the time, and proficiency using one tool today does not mean proficiency forever. Right now a bewildering array of legal research tools are available, making the choice of any specific tool more complex. Does the free government court website have the coverage I need, or do I need to use a large and comprehensive commercial database? Do I need to use sources other than LexisNexis or Westlaw? How can I evaluate the information found on the Internet?

The Google generation thinks it knows how to use electronic databases. But their LexisNexis, Westlaw, or Bloomberg Law searches must yield comprehensive yet precise results, and most law students find their generic Internet search skills are not adequate to the task. All of these challenges have as their backdrop the need for law students to understand the sources of law and the role that secondary legal literature plays in their research projects, as well as the need to critically evaluate what they find.

Public

Continuous and permanent access to legal information is at the heart of a democratic society. The Internet has made widespread distribution of the law a reality for anyone with an Internet connection. But lawyers and law librarians know that just adding judicial opinions or new statutes and administration regulations to the Internet does not create equal access to justice.

Members of the public who need to write papers or do presentations for class or other organizations have benefited tremendously from the large amount of legal material on the Internet. Together with libraries that provide access to books and journals on many law and law-related subjects, many people who wish to understand an area of law can do so. However, the lay person who decides to do their own legal research for their own legal problem can face many obstacles. The person who represents herself is called a pro se litigant.

While the wide array of primary legal information distributed for free through government websites is to be applauded, access to the *words* of the law is not enough for people who do not understand the sources of law, the types of materials published, and how the characteristics of law impact anyone trying to find an answer to a legal problem. A judicial opinion available on the Internet may have been overruled (i.e., changed) by a higher court. But the low-cost or free source on the Internet usually will not note this change. And if a person reads this case and thinks the rule of the case governs their problem because they do not know about the overruling decision, easy access to this judicial opinion is misleading, to say the least.

Many organizations are very concerned about the issue of the self-represented or pro se litigant and about the growing number of people who simply cannot afford the legal services they need. State bar associations, law libraries, publishers, and legal aid groups are widely involved in the Access to Justice movement. To address these concerns, many organizations have created in-depth resources to help the pro se litigant navigate through the legal system and perform the legal research necessary to answer for his or her problem. But such a person must work hard to locate and understand how to use relevant materials.

Websites and print resources abound that can assist the self-represented litigant. One of the best general sites is the Nolo Press website which includes definitions of legal terms, summaries of types of legal problems, forms, and books on common legal issues.[41] The Maryland State Law Library maintains a really excellent website for pro se litigants in Maryland that should serve as a model for other states.[42] The National Center for State Courts has a resource guide for self-represented litigants that links to various projects in all 50 states.[43]

The best advice to a member of the public who is interested in doing legal research is to direct them to secondary sources that explain the legal system, the interplay of the various sources of law, and the publications containing legal information. Critical evaluation of Internet sites that include legal materials is a very important skill to master.

Law libraries open to the public can be found in many counties and many law schools. Legal research texts, various websites, and even this entry can give members of the public the overview and background they need to successfully research a legal issue. A good example of a basic research guide was written by the Legal Information Services to the Public Special Interest Section of the American Association of Law Libraries.[44] While members of the public need access to the law itself (the primary legal materials), they also need resource guides that are specific to the subject matter or court they must understand. In particular, the many books written specifically for lay people about the law can be most helpful. And the texts written for students who are studying the law—nutshells, outlines, and West's Hornbook series—can be very useful as well.

CONCLUSION

Legal literature, once the domain of the commercial publisher, is now found in a vast array of different sources—free and expensive; print and electronic. Any one type of legal information, such as the current legislative code for the state of Washington, can be located in different print and electronic sources. Understanding the legal system, the sources of law, the interplay of those sources, the characteristics of legal information within our legal system, and the nature of legal publishing provide the essential knowledge needed to use and understand the legal literature of our time.

The law changes constantly, and the challenge for any legal researcher is to find the most recent rule of law

Law Literature–Library Architecture

affecting a specific problem. Since the research tools themselves are undergoing constant reinvention, the legal researcher also needs to be a lifelong learner who is willing to keep up with the new technology and the changes in favorite legal research tools. Methods of access to legal information will continue to change, but the underlying framework of our government and the decentralization of lawmaking are constants that will continue to bring stability to the process of legal research. Legal literature is shaped by these principles, and users must continue to demand high-quality, reliable legal research tools.

APPENDIX: HOW LAWYERS CONDUCT LEGAL RESEARCH

Research to Locate Studies and Descriptions Written by Carissa Vogel

Cohen, M.L. Research habits of lawyers. Jurimetr. J. **1968–1969**, *9*, 183, 189–192.

Abstract (focusing on the above cited pages): Cohen briefly discusses three surveys conducted from 1965 to 1968 on the research habits of lawyers. The first survey Cohen discusses is one he conducted in 1968 looking at 25 small law offices in Philadelphia. This survey was focused on the materials contained in the firms' law libraries. Next, Cohen discusses an interview survey of 100 lawyers undertaken by the Missouri Bar. Cohen notes the results and the Bar's interpretation of the data it collected. Lastly, Cohen reviews a survey of 500 lawyers that he conducted in Philadelphia in 1965. He discusses the resources most often used by lawyers and the kinds of law being researched.

Cole, C.; Kuhlthau, C. Information and information seeking of novice versus expert lawyers: how experts add value. New Rev. Inf. Behav. Res. Stud. **2000**, *1*, 103.

Abstract: This entry presents the results of a pilot study of 15 lawyers at various stages of their career. Concepts of task, information, and information seeking as viewed by novice and expert lawyers are examined in order to concentrate on adding value to information collected for a client or case. The authors develop a four-point arc related to value adding and suggest that it can be used by novice lawyers trying to understand and solve task-related problems. The entry was presented at the *Third International Conference on Information Needs, Seeking and Use in Different Contexts*, Goteborg, Sweden, 2000.

Estes, M. Law librarianship research needs survey. PLL Perspectives. November–December **1991**, *3* (2), 11–14.

Perspectives is a newsletter from the Private Law Library section of AALL. The table of contents for all the issues can be accessed through http://www.aallnet.org/sis/pllsis/newslett/newsletter.asp. Visit your nearest law library for articles which are not yet available online.

Gilliland, K. Abstract, the research habits of lawyers. Law Libr. J. **2003**, *95*, 719, 722–723.

Abstract: Gilliland describes her research grant project, which tabulated and analyzed the data collected in a 1995 survey by Morris Cohen, Penny Hazelton, and Patricia DeGeorges "to test some of the basic assumptions of librarians about how lawyers do research." Gilliland mentions findings regarding online usage, concerns about the quality of legal research, and how often lawyers sought out a librarian's assistance when facing unfamiliar legal issues.

Haruna, I.; Mabawonku, I. Information needs and seeking behavior of legal practitioners and the challenges to law libraries in Lagos, Nigeria. Int. Inf. Libr. Rev. **2001**, *33*, 69.

Abstract: Several findings are included in this entry which examines the information needs and information-seeking behavior of lawyers in Lagos, Nigeria. The need to know the latest decisions of superior courts is the greatest professional information need for many lawyers. Other lawyers say they need to find recent legislation and to learn about local and international legal conferences. In this study, the library was identified as the most heavily consulted information resource, but most lawyers claimed the library does not fill its role in meeting the information needs of lawyers. The entry includes recommendations made on the basis of these findings.

Hazelton, P.A. Compilation, surveys on how attorneys do legal research. Perspective. January **1993**, *1* (2), 53.

Abstract: This compilation of citations to journal articles is at the end of an article by Hazelton on advanced legal research courses. The compilation includes cites to articles on legal training, lawyering skills, and two articles on the research habits of lawyers.

Innes, H.J. The evolution of the traditional: novice lawyer information seeking in a CALR world, http://capping.slis.ualberta.ca/cap07/HeatherInnes/litreview.html (last visited October 4, 2007).

Abstract: This website contains a review of studies on the information behavior of lawyers. Innes examines studies performed in England, Nigeria, and Canada, specifically, a survey by the Canadian Department of Justice (Operation Complex) and a follow-up survey by Mark Vale published by the Canadian Legal Information Centre. Additionally, Innes discusses studies by Kuhlthau and Tama on novice versus expert researchers and by Wilkinson on lawyers' preferred sources of information. Lastly, Innes reviews the history and the trends in the use of computer-assisted legal research.

Kuhlthau, C.C.; Tama, S.L. Information search process of lawyers: a call for "just for me" information services. J. Doc. January **2001**, *57*, 25, 28–38.

Abstract: Prior studies by Kuhlthau based on the model of the Information Search Process (ISP) provide the basis

Law Literature–Library Architecture

for her ongoing research. This study reviews the information-seeking tasks of lawyers in order to learn how they use information and to understand the role of mediators in the process of information seeking and use. The authors conclude that lawyers are often involved in complex tasks that require a constructive process of interpreting, learning, and creating. The study participants preferred printed texts over computer databases to accomplish these complex tasks primarily because computer databases required specific requests. "Just for me" services are explored as a way to help lawyers deal with complex information needs.

Leary, M.A.; Cooper, W.L. Research needs of outstate Michigan lawyers. Mich. Bar J. **1981**, *60*, 641.

Abstract: This entry presents the results of a 1981 survey of 1592 Michigan lawyers whose offices were in counties without large public law libraries. The purpose of the survey was to find out the lawyers' requirements for 34 kinds of research material and to learn how they accessed the material. The goal of the survey was to discover the availability and the need for resources. The researchers found that Lexis and Westlaw were needed the least and that the Michigan Statutes Annotated was needed the most. Additionally, the respondents accessed their own libraries and other libraries (public, county, and university) for sources, like law reviews, court rules, and magazines. The authors make recommendations for improving access including improving funding for county libraries, increasing accessibility to resources in the State Law Library, and making use of technology for producing faster and cheaper documents.

Leckie G.J.; Pettigrew, K.E.; Sylvain, C. Modeling the information seeking of professionals: a general model derived from research on engineers, health care professionals, and lawyers. Lib. Q. **1996**, *66* (2), 161.

Abstract: This entry studies the information-seeking behavior of engineers, health care professionals, and lawyers. From their study, the authors create an original model of information seeking applicable to all professionals. The entry presents in detail the general model and its components. The entry concludes with suggestions as to the potential usefulness of the model.

Maine Bar Association. The survey: who we are, what we think. Me. B. J. **2007**, *22*, 78–83.

Abstract: This entry presents the highlights of a survey on the services offered by the Maine Bar Association. The entry did not cite how the survey was presented, who was given the survey, or how many bar members responded. Most of the information in the entry focuses on who uses Casemaker and how they use it.

Marke, J.J. New study: how lawyers use the library, N Y Law J. November 21, **1995**, *214* (98), 5.

Abstract: This entry presents highlights from a 1995 survey conducted to determine how lawyers perform research. The questionnaire was sent to 1500 randomly

chosen alumni from five law schools. Responses were received from more than 440 people. The researchers wanted to find out what resources were used, how often they were used, where information was accessed, and the purposes for the research. Marke relates 20 highlights of the findings.

Palmer S. If you can't beat 'em, train 'em: how lawyers conduct legal research. Leg. Inf. Alert. January **2006**, *25*, 1.

Abstract: This entry reviews the findings of the 2004–2005 American Bar Association Legal Technology Survey Report on lawyers in offices of 50 or more and suggests the uses of training to boost results. Palmer divides the entry into sections on survey results and training for legal sources and nonlegal sources. Palmer also suggests how to conduct effective training for lawyers in large firms.

Panel Discussion. Historical development of the American lawyer's library. Law Libr. J. **1968**, *61*, 440, 458–460 [discussing three surveys conducted in Missouri (1966) and Pennsylvania (1965, 1968)].

This panel discussion briefly mentions these studies. More complete coverage of the surveys can be found in The Research Habits of Lawyers by Morris Cohen.

Sanders Reach, C.; Ikens, L.; Palmer, S.; Stine, S. *2007 ABA Legal Technology Resource Center Survey Report Online Research*; American Bar Association: Chicago, IL, 2007.

Abstract: In 1990, the ABA started to survey law firms on their technology usage. Since 2001, the survey changed to look at lawyers exclusively. The survey was sent to 28,018 ABA members in private practice: the researchers received 1876 responses. The findings were published in the Online Research section report (this volume), which represents one in a series of five volumes published annually. The Online Research volume includes a short trend report describing the general information gathered from the surveys. The rest of the volume contains graphic representations of the survey questions, covering everything from electronic budgets to the use of fee-based online legal research resources.

Reusch, R.T. *Patterns of legal research in North Dakota: a Survey*. N. D. L. Rev. **1985**, *61*, 383.

Abstract: This entry explains the results of a 1984 survey conducted to determine how North Dakota attorneys use and acquire legal information and to figure out if North Dakota attorneys need a legal research assistance program. The survey was mailed to 1150 people, all members of the North Dakota State Bar Association who had addresses in North Dakota. A copy of the original questionnaire is included in the Appendix of the entry. The researchers received 505 responses. Reusch discusses the results of the survey, includes tables representing the results, and concludes that North Dakota needs an assistance program that provides services like affordable computer research services.

Law Literature–Library Architecture

Speer, L. Private law libraries survey. PLL Perspectives. November–December **1989**, *1* (2), 5.

Perspectives is a newsletter from the Private Law Library section of AALL. The table of contents for all the issues can be accessed through http://www.aallnet.org/sis/pllsis/newslett/newsletter.asp. Visit your nearest law library for articles which are not yet available online.

Wilkinson, M.A. Information sources used by lawyers in problem-solving: an empirical exploration. Libr. Inf. Sci. Res. **2001**, *23* (3), 257.

Abstract: More than 150 practicing lawyers were interviewed about their information-seeking behavior. The results demonstrated to the author that legal research should not be considered as the only information-seeking behavior of lawyers as has been assumed in past research. Administration of their law practices, for example, was identified as constituting a problem-solving, information-seeking activity. The study analyzes whether lawyers seek to solve problems through formal or informal means, whether they are likely to look to sources inside or outside their organization, and whether the lawyer's gender or size of practice influences the type of information resources sought. The model for information-seeking behavior of professionals as posited by others is analyzed and modifications are suggested that create a new model.

REFERENCES

1. Legal Information Institute, Cornell University Law School. U.S. Constitution. https://www.law.cornell.edu/constitution (accessed October 11, 2016).
2. Civil Law. *Britannica Concise Encyclopedia*; Encyclopedia Britannica, Inc.: Chicago, IL, 1997. Answers.com. http://www.answers.com/topic/civil-law (accessed October 23, 2014).
3. Nebraska Legislature. History of the Nebraska Unicameral. http://nebraskalegislature.gov/about/history_unicameral.php (accessed October 11, 2016).
4. U.S. Constitution. Art. VI. http://www.law.cornell.edu/constitution/constitution.articlevi.html (accessed October 11, 2016).
5. Williams, B. *Exploring Initiative and Referendum Law: Selected State Research Guides*; Haworth Press: Binghamton, New York, 2008.
6. *Merriam-Webster Online Dictionary*. http://www.merriam-webster.com/dictionary/jurisdiction (accessed October 11, 2016).
7. American Bar Association, Division for Legal Services. Consumers' Guide to Legal Help Legal Terms Glossary. http://apps.americanbar.org/legalservices/findlegalhelp/faq_legalterms.cfm (accessed October 11, 2016).
8. Government Publishing Office (GPO), 5 United States Code Sec. 903 *Reorganization plans*, 2012.
9. Peace Pledge Union. Geneva Convention. http://www.ppu.org.uk/learn/texts/doc_geneva_con.html (accessed October 11, 2016).
10. U.S. Department of State. Treaty on Principles Governing the Activities of States in the Exploration and Use of Outer Space. http://www.state.gov/t/isn/5181.htm (accessed October 11, 2016).
11. U.S. Constitution, http://www.law.cornell.edu/constitution/index.html.
12. Farlex. The Free Dictionary. http://encyclopedia2.thefreedictionary.com/husband+and+wife (accessed October 11, 2016).
13. Nolo. Nolo's Plain-English Law Dictionary. http://www.nolo.com/dictionary/precedent-term.html (accessed October 11, 2016).
14. Fine, T.M. *American Legal Systems: A Resource and Reference Guide*; Anderson Publishing: Southington, CT, 1997.
15. Sloan, A.E. *Basic Legal Research: Tools and Strategies*, 5th Ed.; Wolters Kluwer: New York, 2012.
16. Berring, R.C.; Edinger, E. *Finding the Law*, 12th Ed.; West: St. Paul, MN, 2005.
17. Algero, M.G. et al. Federal Legal Research, 1st Ed.; Carolina Academic Press: Durham, NC, 2012.
18. Roberts, B.K.; Schlueter, L.L. *Legal Research Guide: Patterns and Practice*, 6th Ed.; LexisNexis Matthew Bender: New Providence, NJ, 2011.
19. Elias, S. *Legal Research: How to Find & Understand the Law*, 16th Ed.; Nolo: Berkeley, CA, 2012.
20. Barkan, S.M.; Mersky, R.M.; Dunn, D.J. *Legal Research Illustrated: An Abridgment of Fundamentals of Legal Research*, 9th Ed.; Thomson Reuters/Foundation Press: New York, 2009.
21. Olson, K.C.; Cohen, M.L. *Legal Research in a Nutshell*, 11th Ed.; West Academic: St. Paul, MN, 2013.
22. Oates, L.C.; Enquist, A. *Just Research*, 4th Ed.; Wolters Kluwer: New York, 2014.
23. Kunz, C.L. et al. *The Process of Legal Research*, 8th Ed.; Wolters Kluwer: New York, 2012.
24. Armstrong, J.D.S.; Knott, C.A. *Where the Law Is: An Introduction to Advanced Legal Research*, 4th Ed.; West Academic: St. Paul, MN, 2012.
25. Harvard Law Review Association. *The Bluebook: A Uniform System of Citation*, 19th Ed.; Harvard Law Review Association: Cambridge, MA, 2010.
26. Vinopal, K. *Researching Public International Law, American Society of International Law*. http://www.asil.org/sites/default/files/ERG_PUBLIC_INT.pdf (accessed November 5, 2014).
27. Winer, A.S.; Archer, M.E.; Louis-Jacques, L. *International Law Legal Research*; Carolina Academic Press: Durham, North Carolina, 2013.
28. Nolo. Homepage. http://www.nolo.com/ (accessed October 11, 2016).
29. Svengalis, K.F. *Legal Information Buyer's Guide and Reference Manual*; New England LawPress: Guilford, CT, 2014, Chapter 2.
30. LexisNexis. The LexisNexis timeline. http://www.lexisnexis.com/anniversary/30th_timeline_fulltxt.pdf (accessed October 11, 2016).
31. Hazelton, P. How much of your print collection is really on WESTLAW or LEXIS-NEXIS? Leg. Ref. Serv. Q. **1999**, *18*(1), 3–22.

Law Literature–Library Architecture

32. Hazelton, P. An essay on integrating manual and computer legal research. In *The Spirit of Law Librarianship: A Reader*; Roy, M., Leiter, R., Eds.; Rothman & Co.; Littleton, CO, 1991.

33. American Library Association. Government Documents Round Table (GODORT). http://www.ala.org/godort/ (accessed October 11, 2016).

34. American Association of Law Libraries. Government Documents Special Interest Section. http://www.aallnet.org/sections/gd (accessed October 11, 2016).

35. Legal Information Preservation Alliance (LIPA). https://lipalliance.org/ (accessed October 11, 2016).

36. Perma.cc. https://perma.cc/ (accessed October 11, 2016).

37. American Association of Law Libraries. Government Relations, 2007 State-by-State Report on Authentication of Online Legal Resources. http://aallnet.org/Documents/Government-Relations/2007statereport.html (accessed October 11, 2016).

38. The AALL Government Relations Committee has created an excellent research guide of UELMA Resources, http://www.aallnet.org/Documents/Government-Relations/UELMA.

39. American Association of Law Libraries. http://aallnet.org/mm/Careers/lawlibrarycareers (accessed October 11, 2016).

40. University of Washington Information School. https://ischool.uw.edu/academics/mlis/degree-options/law-librarianship (accessed October 11, 2016).

41. Nolo. Homepage. http://www.nolo.com/ (accessed October 11, 2016).

42. Maryland State Law Library. The People's Law Library of Maryland. https://www.peoples-law.org/ (accessed October 11, 2016).

43. National Center for State Courts. Self-Representation Resource Guide. http://www.ncsc.org/Topics/Access-and-Fairness/Self-Representation/Resource-Guide.aspx (accessed October 11, 2016).

44. American Association of Law Libraries. Legal Information Services to the Public Special Interest Section. http://www.aallnet.org/sections/lisp (accessed October 11, 2016).

Learning and Information Seeking

Louise Limberg
Swedish School of Library and Information Science, University of Borås and University of Gothenburg, Borås, Sweden

Mikael Alexandersson
University of Gothenburg, Gothenberg, Sweden

Abstract

The purpose of this entry is to present and analyze the relationship between learning and information seeking. The analysis draws on research studies on information seeking set in educational contexts and is framed in theories of learning, mainly constructivism. Themes of the entry are based on five dimensions of the relationship between learning and information seeking: 1) seeking information for learning purposes; 2) learning information seeking; 3) teaching information seeking; 4) learning from information; and 5) reshaping conditions for information seeking and learning through information and communications technologies (ICTs). Conclusions are that the fields of learning and information seeking draw nearer to one another partly due to educational ideas based in constructivism and partly due to the development of digital tools that reshape conditions for learning in postmodern society. This development contributes to the transformation of the professional role of librarians, implying an emphasis on the pedagogical aspects of the profession. Future prospects for information seeking research and practice linked to learning may involve strengthened interests in the cognitive authority and expertise of information as well as information sharing through communicative interaction.

INTRODUCTION

The topic of this entry is the central relationship between learning and information seeking, where information seeking is seen as a condition for learning to take place. Our point of departure is that learning and information seeking are intimately intertwined in a constantly ongoing human activity. For purposes of research, education, and professional practice the fields of learning and information seeking have been divided into separate disciplines and occupational fields. As a human activity, learning and information seeking are inseparable and mutually shape each other.

A massive amount of empirical research on information seeking is set in learning contexts and is directed at students' information seeking for learning assignments. With few exceptions, the vast majority of such studies are restricted to an interest in information seeking and do not direct specific attention at the wider aspects of the learning processes or outcomes, which form the purpose as well as the result of the information seeking under study. During the last decades, societal developments in information and communication technologies as well as the globalization of economies have dramatically changed conditions for learning and information practices, with tools for online information seeking accessible worldwide. The Internet and other digital media have brought the world into classrooms and libraries implying immediate access to abundant amounts of information, and changing conditions for the ways and whats of teaching and learning. Traditional ways of teaching and learning are substituted by inquiry-based methods, involving students in independent information seeking and use. One consequence is an increased emphasis within librarianship on teaching information skills to all kinds of users, especially students at all educational levels, from elementary school to undergraduate education. Librarians' expertise in information seeking together with the expansion of their professional domain into teaching contributes to reshaping the view of librarianship, where an emphasis on the pedagogical aspects of the profession is emerging. This in turn has contributed to an increased interest in the relationship between learning and information seeking. In this entry the topic of learning and information seeking is viewed as a range of interconnected dimensions pertaining to

1. Seeking information for learning purposes—associated with the common practice of information seeking related to carrying out learning tasks in formal educational contexts as well as in work-life or everyday life. In this respect, information seeking is strongly linked to the notion of lifelong learning.
2. Learning information seeking—a notion closely connected to the concept of information literacy, implying learning how to critically seek, evaluate, and use information in purposeful ways for various problems or situations.
3. Teaching information seeking—reflects the perspective of learning information seeking, and is a matter of interest in the field of information literacy education.

Encyclopedia of Library and Information Sciences, Fourth Edition DOI: 10.1081/E-ELIS4-120044669
Copyright © 2017 by Taylor & Francis. All rights reserved.

Law Literature–Library Architecture

4. Learning from information—may be associated with information use rather than seeking, implying a range of various aspects such as understanding the contents of information sources, critically evaluating and relating sources to one another as well as to the topic of a task.

5. Development of information and communication technologies (ICTs)—changes in the conditions for information seeking and learning, reinforcing the connections, and interdependence between these two areas of human practice.

The aim of this entry is to present and analyze aspects of the relationship between learning and information seeking, taking into account the various dimensions listed above. The entry is based in theories of learning and in research on issues of learning and information seeking.

KEY CONCEPTS

Learning is nowadays one of the most frequent concepts used in more or less all social practices—both formal and informal. It is closely related to notions of communication and knowledge but also to meaning-making. Learning is generally seen as contextual and as an integration into a community of practice in which social actions are identified. It is a social activity in which the learner uses sensory input and constructs meaning out of it. Learning involves language, and language and learning are inextricably intertwined.

Information seeking—the concept of information seeking is well established in Library and Information Science (LIS). However, the term "information practices" is currently being used for including new perspectives on the concept, implying that information seeking can only be understood as embedded in the practices in which it takes place. In this entry, the terms "information seeking" and "information practice" will be used interchangeably to denote information seeking practices related to learning. It is worth underlining that related to learning information *use* is of particular interest, as an extension of information seeking.[1] Research of concepts, contexts, and practices of information seeking is the object of interest of ISIC: the Information Behaviour Conference where information seeking related to learning has lately gained ground.

STAKEHOLDERS, ASSOCIATIONS, AND INSTITUTIONS

It appears that until the early 2000s the interest in pedagogical issues was greater within the professional practice of librarianship than within the research communities of information seeking. One example of this is Donald Case's survey of information seeking research,[2] devoting very scarce space for studies of information seeking set in learning contexts. This may be contrasted to the abundant literature in professional journals, especially those targeted at academic and school librarianship, on the topic of students' information seeking, and often linked to interests in information seeking and learning.

School and academic librarians are central agents in the field of learning and information seeking. A range of professional organizations devote considerable interest to issues of teaching and learning information seeking and use. Two such organizations in the United States are the Association of College and Research Libraries (ACRL), the largest section of the American Library Association (ALA), which publishes the journal *College and Research Libraries*, and the American Association of School Librarians (AASL), also a section of the ALA. AASL, the most important professional association for school librarianship, publishes one print journal, *Knowledge Quest*, and an online research journal, *School Library Media Research*. In these publications, topics of learning and information seeking appear frequently. There are similar professional associations in other parts of the world, for instance, the Australian and New Zealand Institute for Information Literacy (ANZIIL), and, in the Nordic countries, the Nordic Forum for Information Literacy (NordINFOLIT), all with a common interest in advocating information literacy education. An informative Web log on information literacy is located at http://information-literacy.blogspot.com/. The International Association of School Librarianship with the research journal *School Libraries Worldwide* is yet another example. The mentioned associations and networks combine a strong interest in the relationship between learning and information seeking, and strive to link professional interests with research communities through conferences, seminars, and publications.

The Center for International Scholarship in School Librarianship (CISSL) at Rutgers University (http://cissl.scils.rutgers.edu/) is an international research and scholarly centre that examines the dynamics and impacts of school libraries on student learning, and has a strong interest in learning and information seeking.

FOCUSING LEARNING THEORIES FOR UNDERSTANDING "LEARNING AND INFORMATION SEEKING"

Studies of how and what individuals learn while seeking information either in an educational setting such as a classroom or a library, through books or through the Web, depend on theoretical assumptions about teaching and learning. These assumptions are based in epistemology and raise issues such as What is knowledge? Where is knowledge? How is knowledge created? What is knowledge about?

Law Literature–Library Architecture

Theories of Learning

Basically, three main theoretical assumptions—or waves—underpin the late history of learning. Before we outline constructivism which, in its different forms, is the most current in research today, we shall comment briefly on the other two waves. The first wave—*behaviorist theory*—corresponds to an empirical tradition founded in the assumption that learning is based on physical experience and that individuals tend to repeat behavior linked to positive experiences of satisfaction or reinforcement. B.F. Skinner[3] was a particularly influential scholar in this tradition, claiming that only behavior itself—not inner processes such as thinking or reflection is considered as available for study. Human learning is seen as a change in external, observable behavior, while cognitive activities are considered unavailable to scientific observation. Research based on behaviorist theory claims that reality is observable and that there is objectivity in all empirical data. The golden age of behaviorist theories of learning lasted until the end of the 1950s.

Cognitive theory—the second wave—challenged behaviorist theory as the dominant paradigm with its restricted application of scientific methods. The main argument was that people are not "programmed animals" that merely respond to environmental stimuli; people are rational beings who actively participate in learning, and whose actions are a consequence of thinking. During the 1960s cognitive-oriented researchers became interested in what takes place in the mind of the learner. Changes in behavior were still observed but only as indications of what occurs in the learner's mind. Cognitive theory focuses on inner mental activities—opening the "black box" of the human mind is therefore a valuable and necessary contribution to understanding how people learn. Research interests are directed at the exploration of mental processes such as thinking, memory, knowing, problem solving, and information processing. Knowledge is seen as schema or symbolic mental constructions and learning is defined as changes in a learner's schemata. Cognitivism was strongly inspired by the emerging computer technology, viewing humans as processors of information.[4]

Constructivism—The Third Wave to Understand Learning

Towards the end of the 1980s a third wave—Constructivism—partly replaced cognitive theory. Today constructivism represents one of the major ideas in education and has been characterized as the dominant philosophy of learning. It proposes that learners need to build their own understanding of new ideas, and that information emerges within these built constructs rather than exists in the external environment. John Dewey[5] is often cited as the philosophical founder of this approach. Its implications for how teachers teach and learn to teach are enormous. The constructivist approach to teaching and learning—and also to information seeking—is based on a combination of a subset of research within cognitive psychology and a subset of research within social psychology.

Constructivism embodies two major perspectives, cognitive constructivism, and social constructivism. These perspectives are different in emphasis, but they also share many common views about teaching and learning. Widespread interests in the theory of constructivism have led to a debate between those who emphasize the individual cognitive structuring process and those who emphasize the social context of learning. While Jean Piaget[6] is considered the major theorist among the cognitive constructivists, Lev Vygotsky[7,8] is the major theorist among the social constructivists. The core of different theories related to social constructivism goes back to Vygotsky's cultural historical theory of human development propounded in the 1920s and early 1930s. Standard discussions of the difference between Vygotsky and Piaget place a crucial distinction in the proximal locus of cognitive development. For Piaget, individual children construct knowledge through their actions in the world: to understand is to invent. In contrast, the Vygotskian claim is that understanding is social in origin (see further discussion in Wertsch[9]). According to Vygotsky,[8] "Every function in the child's cultural development appears twice: first, on the social level, and later, on the individual level; the first, between people (interpsychological), and then within the child (intrapsychological)." He claims that this development principally takes place through a form of apprenticeship learning.

Cognitive constructivism

Jean Piaget's theory of cognitive development suggests that humans cannot be "given" information which they automatically understand and use, they must "construct" their own knowledge. They have to build their knowledge through experience. The role of the teacher is to provide a classroom full of interesting things to encourage students to construct their own knowledge and to develop their ability to explore phenomena in the world. The classroom should offer students the opportunity to construct knowledge through their own experiences. There is less emphasis on directly teaching specific skills and more emphasis on learning in meaningful contexts. Piaget's ideas concerning active construction, structuring knowledge, and stages of development, have been drawn on for some time in education and especially, during the last decades in the ongoing integration of ICT in education.

Constructivist approach to information seeking research

Some major work has been done on information seeking and learning using constructivist approaches. Carol Kuhlthau's studies and her ISP model is a prominent example of

Law Literature–Library Architecture

information seeking research framed in a constructivist view of learning with an emphasis on individual learners. Kuhlthau articulates information seeking as a process of construction and she emphasizes that her research is directed at intellectual access to information and ideas, implying a close relationship to learning. The model adopts the user's perspective of the information seeking process, and thus places the user as the central actor, constructing meaning through the process.[10] Kuhlthau's model has been highly influential in LIS research as well as in professional practice.

Limberg studied the interaction between information seeking and learning in the context of upper secondary school using a phenomenographic approach.[11–13] Phenomenography has a linkage to cognitive constructivism and constitutes a theoretical strand for framing research on information seeking and learning. Similar to cognitive constructivism phenomenography has human experience as its object and investigates people's experiences of phenomena in the world.[14] From a phenomenographical standpoint the world exists and different people construe it in different ways. The main focus is on the qualitatively different ways in which people experience something or think about something, e.g., photosynthesis or information seeking. Besides Sweden, where a phenomenographic approach has been adopted for studying the interaction between information seeking and learning,[11–13] phenomenography is also being frequently used among information literacy researchers in Australia and the United Kingdom.[15–19]

Social constructivism

Lev Vygotsky's claim that social learning precedes development is linked to his focus on the connections between people and the context in which they act and interact through shared experiences. According to Vygotsky, humans use cultural tools, such as speech and writing, to mediate their social environments. Initially children develop such tools in order to function socially as ways of communicating needs. Vygotsky claims that the internalization of these tools leads to higher order thinking skills. For Vygotsky culture provides the child with the cognitive tools needed for development.[7] Today such tools also include electronic means of information access.

There are some general principles of learning that are derived from social constructivism. These principles are

- Learning is an active process in which the learner uses sensory input and constructs meaning out of it. In the learning process the learner compares new experience with knowledge constructed from previous experience, resulting in the reinforcement or adaptation of knowledge. Knowledge is not a fixed object; the individual constructs it through experience with the object of study.

- Learning is constructing meaning and systems of meaning. Shared meanings develop through negotiation in the learning environment, leading to the development of common or "taken-as-shared" knowledge. According to a constructivist view, knowledge is not "about" the world, but rather "constitutive" of the world.

- Learning involves language, and language and learning are inextricably intertwined.

- Learning is a social activity. It is intimately associated with our connection with other human beings. It takes place within some sociocultural setting. Social interactions within the learning environment are an essential part of this experience and contribute fundamentally to individual knowledge construction.

- Learning is contextual. We learn in relationship to what else we know, to our beliefs, our prejudices, and our fears.

Situated cognition and situated learning

Vygotsky's theories, and those of other developmental psychologists, form the foundation for the concepts of situated cognition and situated learning. Constructivists view cognition as situation-bound and socially distributed rather than as decontextualized tools and products of the mind. It is not possible to separate cognitive tasks from social tasks, because all cognitive tasks have a social component. Thinking is both physically and socially situated and problem tasks can be significantly shaped and changed by the available tools and the social interactions that take place during problem solving. Situated cognition emphasizes apprenticeship, coaching, collaboration, multiple practices, and articulation of learning skills, stories, and technology. Applied to information seeking, this means a variety of ways of seeking and using information linked to various practices. It further implies a wide variety of ways of learning how to seek and use information related to various tasks, tools, and situations.

The concept of situated learning means that knowledge is situated and is partly a product of the activity, context, and culture in which it is used. Situated learning occurs when students work on authentic tasks in real-world settings. Knowledge cannot be taught in the abstract; it can only be constructed in context. Jean Lave[20] states that learning is a function of the activity, context, and culture in which it occurs, in contrast with most classroom learning which tends to be abstracted from context. Toward the beginning of the 1990s Jean Lave[21] and Etienne Wenger[22] developed a model of situated learning proposing that learning involves a process of engagement in a "community of practice." Their basic argument is that communities of practice are everywhere; at work, at school, in the home, or

Law Literature–Library Architecture

associated with our civic and leisure interests. The sustained pursuit of a shared enterprise gives rise, over time, to these communities. The concept of "community of practice" has had a huge impact on both research and practices of learning—both formal and informal.

A sociocultural view of learning and information seeking

Parallel to the development of the concepts of situated cognition, situated learning, and community of practice, sociocultural theory has developed and has become a powerful and competitive paradigm in today's landscape of social and cultural sciences. The core of the sociocultural theory is rooted in Lev Vygotsky's view of learning as communicative interaction, and it has gained in significance in learning and information seeking research during the last decade. James Wertsch,[9] one of the main scholars in this research field developed Vygotsky's theory in relation to contemporary issues and argues, as Vygotsky did, that human mental functions are inextricably situated in social, cultural, institutional, and historical contexts. From a sociocultural standpoint language is seen as the most important cultural tool available to man. It is through communication that sociocultural resources are created, but it is also through communication that they are carried forth.

Sociocultural theorists view learning as integration into a community of practice in which social actions are identified. Learning is seen as the process by which individuals are introduced to a culture by more skilled members. As this happens they "appropriate" cultural tools through their involvement in the activities of this culture.[23] This implies that the contents of learning (e.g., subject matter of learning assignments), the contexts in which people act (e.g., school, undergraduate education, specific course or discipline, work-life), and the cultural tools (e.g., the Web, Google, databases, journals, textbooks) people have available, must be taken into account in the understanding of what characterizes productive learning. A sociocultural perspective has been increasingly applied in recent studies of information seeking and learning[24–26] as well as in information literacy research.[27–30]

Summary

The constructivist paradigm has led us to understand how learning and information seeking may be facilitated through certain types of engaging, constructive activities. This view of learning and information seeking emphasizes meaning-making through active participation in socially, culturally, historically, and politically situated contexts. A crucial element of active participation is dialogue in shared experiences. Situated collaborative activities, such as modeling, discourse, and decision-making,

are necessary to support the negotiation and creation of meaning and understanding.

Theories of Learning in Information Seeking Research and Practice

It is worth pointing out that very few studies on information seeking in learning, or in other contexts, have framed their research within a theoretical perspective of learning. Case's survey of research on information seeking[31] lists a number of theories applied in information seeking studies; among the disciplines most frequently used during the last 30 years are sociology, communication, and psychology. Exceptions to this statement have been mentioned above as examples of information seeking research framed in theories of learning.[10–13,24–26] In a wider perspective we see that constructivism has influenced information science, for instance in the theory of sense-making. However, sense-making has not been specifically linked to learning. Such wider theoretical applications of constructivism go beyond the scope of this entry. A qualified prediction is that constructivist theories of learning will be increasingly applied in future research on information practices, given the growing interplay between information seeking and learning in ICT environments.

While constructivist theory is only beginning to be utilized to frame research in information seeking, the experiences and observations of school and undergraduate education during the last decades, suggest that constructivist ideas have strongly influenced practices in education and librarianship during this period, shaping teaching and learning in ways that engage students in active information seeking for independent, inquiry-based learning. Constructivist views of learning have, thus, contributed to the increased interest in the relationship between learning and information seeking.

INFORMATION SEEKING FOR LEARNING PURPOSES

The issue of information seeking for learning purposes is tied to the context of students' carrying out learning assignments implying independent information seeking for finding, selecting, evaluating, and using a variety of information sources to construct meaning about some particular knowledge content. Research questions related to such practices concern how students seek, select, and use information for their tasks. How do task requirements interact with students' information seeking? How do students experience information seeking for learning assignments? Research studies have focused on students' *searching* behavior that is on their interaction with online information systems and digital tools, as well as on their information *seeking* behavior, that is the series of searches related to the same learning assignment.[32]

Law Literature–Library Architecture

Over the years, thousands of empirical studies have been carried out on students' information seeking in contexts of formal learning at all levels of education, from elementary school to undergraduate levels. Only a few of these take the learning context into close account. Vakkari[33] criticizes typical studies of university students searching for information without framing these activities within their contexts of learning assignments.

As pointed out above, information seeking for learning purposes characterizes ways and means of learning in classrooms throughout the world in contemporary society. Textbooks and library collections have been replaced by information accessible online, where the World Wide Web is the main resource for access to information, and is widely used in schools and universities all over the globe. Independent learning through active information seeking, however, has a longer history than the World Wide Web. Student-centered learning linked to information seeking is clearly influenced by the constructivist view of learning, which allocates great responsibility for knowledge construction to learners and their exploration of the world through various information resources. Before the breakthrough of the Internet when students were required to seek information independently for their school tasks, information resources were restricted to local collections, where teachers and librarians exerted control over what was available for students. In those days the crucial problem tended to be to find and retrieve any sources relevant for students' various tasks. Librarians and teachers would spend a lot of time building up collections suitable for school curricula and instructional units. In the Internet era corresponding activities of collection building take the form of collections of links to approved information resources or recommended Web sites, hosted by libraries or other knowledge institutions. It is hard to deny that the breakthrough of the Internet has brought dramatic qualitative changes to education and conditions for learning. It is not just a matter of quantities of information but of new ways of interacting with and communicating via digital tools, opening up the walls of classrooms, libraries, and school buildings.

Learning Tasks

A critical issue of information seeking related to learning is the character of the learning tasks that students work with. The concept of task is germane to information seeking in educational and learning contexts. Nevertheless, this area of research does not often present itself as task-based. It seems that the task is more or less implicit in information seeking studies set in learning contexts.

Particular conditions shape the practice of information seeking related to learning tasks in formal education. Two such conditions are that they are always imposed,[34] and that they are related to the intended learning outcomes of various contents as well as to abilities. The intended learning outcomes are formulated by teachers and ideally expressed in the goals of an assignment. A typical attribute of learning assignments is that students' work and their mastery of subject matter and various competences, such as information seeking, are subject to assessment by teachers. This indicates the importance of an ever-present norm in education, expressed in assessment and evaluation. This norm implies that there are poorer or better ways of understanding and managing a particular phenomenon, with reference to the cognitive authority[35] of teachers, curriculum, science, and academia. This necessarily is a critical feature of information seeking related to learning tasks.

Students' Information Seeking

One issue, discussed both in research and in teachers' and librarians' professional practices is that students tend to adopt a restricted fact-finding approach to information seeking for learning tasks. Students' intentions and ensuing approaches tend to be focused on finding enough information and then writing up a report for submission in due course. This is found to be typically linked to learning assignments and shaped within the discursive practice of school.

Since the mid-1990s intensive interest has been devoted to studies on students' information seeking in digital environments, especially the Web. Findings from such studies indicate that students exhibit great self confidence in their own ability to search the Web and find what they are looking for. In spite of this, according to the teachers and librarians as well as to the researchers involved, students' information seeking seems neither adequate nor effective for the purposes of their school-related assignment. Young people seem to be more successful in information seeking for their personal interests and for everyday life. This indicates differences between the cultural practices of school and of students' leisure time and may imply a gap between information practices developed inside and outside school, which in turn might complicate efforts of learning and teaching the critical abilities required for information seeking and use.

A British research group[36] recently studied the information expertise of the "Google generation," that is those born after 1993. Main questions were whether or not young people are searching for and researching content in new ways, different from the ways that existing scholars carry out their work, and whether this is likely to shape their future behavior as mature researchers. The study was commissioned by the British Library and Information Systems Committee (JISC, U.K.) with the aim to inform and stimulate discussion about the future of libraries in the Internet era. JISC's activities support education and research by promoting innovation in new technologies and by the central support of ICT services. Findings partly confirm previous studies of students' information seeking practices, indicating shortcomings among students both as regards their use of digital tools and search operators and

Law Literature–Library Architecture

particularly as regards students' ways of assessing and evaluating information—or rather their lack of conscious and systematic evaluation of information. Students' primary evaluation criterion is the topicality of content. Conclusions drawn from this study, as well as from similar studies, are that they highlight the importance of teaching and learning how to critically evaluate and assess information, related to various contexts and situations.

University students' information seeking has been investigated within a framework of learning theories about differences in learning styles[37,38] as well as differences between undergraduates' epistemological beliefs.[39] Findings indicate that different study approaches influence both search strategies and reflective judgment on information sources.

LEARNING AND TEACHING INFORMATION SEEKING

"All information-seeking behaviour is learnt, nothing is innate," according to Wilson.[40] Linked to constructivist theory of learning information seeking can be viewed as an object of learning, which may be constructed and reconstructed into various shapes or ways of understanding related to the different contexts and situations in which it is carried out.

A constructivist approach to learning emphasizes, as described above, authentic, challenging projects in professional practices that include students, teachers, librarians, and experts in the learning community. Its goal is to create learning communities that are more closely related to the collaborative practice of the real world. In an authentic environment, learners assume responsibility for their own learning, they have to develop metacognitive abilities to monitor and direct learning and performance. When people work collaboratively in an authentic activity, they bring their own framework and perspectives to the activity. They can see a problem from different perspectives, and are able to negotiate and generate meanings and solutions through the activity itself. From this viewpoint it is counterproductive for teachers to make all the vital decisions about what is to be learned and how it should be learned and to be the sole dispenser of information without involving students in the decision process. To then assess students' abilities in constructing knowledge seems to miss the point. In other words, guided instruction is suggested, placing students at the centre of the learning process, and providing guidance and concrete teaching whenever necessary.

Learning Information Seeking

The notion of fact-finding is a widespread way of understanding information seeking, implying searching for facts with the aim of finding correct answers to specific questions, such as: "How many casualties were caused by car traffic in Sweden in 2006?" or "What are the colors of the South African flag?" However, learning assignments in education as well as in work-life often concern highly complex issues, such as "How can we reduce global warming?" or "How does gender affect work-life in Germany?" Research as well as professional experience show that the notion of information seeking as fact-finding is too restricted in relation to complex questions.[12,24,41] Information seeking linked to inquiry-based assignments insists on information *use* rather than seeking and finding, and requires critical and conscious evaluation and analysis of sources for the purpose of constructing meaning through information. Forming an understanding of information seeking and use appropriate for complex learning assignments thus involves examining the way users interpret information for meaningful learning. Christine Bruce emphasizes the interdependence of information use and learning and proposes the term *informed learning* for "engaging in information practices in order to learn" or "engaging with the different ways of using information to learn."[16] Constructivist ideas about guided instruction in collaborative work on authentic learning tasks form an appropriate theoretical foundation for understanding this type of learning, and has implications for teaching.

Teaching Information Seeking

The idea of information seeking behavior as learned further suggests that education can support people in developing suitable ways and means of seeking and using information. This concerns teaching information seeking practices for learning purposes. Teaching information seeking has a long history with a background in library skills instruction (bibliographic instruction) from the first half of the 1900s, later to be succeeded by information skills instruction from the 1970s. Library skills (bibliographic instruction) tended to encompass knowledge about the use of libraries and its various tools such as catalogs, indexes, and various reference tools (bibliographies, abstracts). Library skills instruction corresponds to what is sometimes called the bibliographic paradigm in LIS, based on the structure and order of collections of documents. The concept of information skills implies less focus on documents, and encompasses instead a wide range of information resources, such as lectures, texts, pictures, field studies, interviews, etc. going beyond the walls of libraries or information centers. An influential model in this tradition is the Big6 Skills (http://www.big6.com/) model first presented in the 1980s and since then widely developed and marketed.[42] Models of information skills instruction tend to be framed in a cognitive view of learning, emphasizing ways of thinking, and mental models.

Since the early 1990s the concept of information literacy has replaced earlier concepts such as information skills or library skills for labeling the art of purposeful and adequate information seeking related to a task or a problem. There

Law Literature–Library Architecture

are large numbers of definitions of what constitutes information literacy, which will not be dwelt upon in this entry. Nevertheless, in the context of this entry we wish to draw attention to the links between, on the one hand, learning information seeking, and on the other, the concept of information literacy. The relationship between information seeking and information literacy is inherent in the notion of learning and teaching information seeking. Information literacy implies mastering appropriate ways of seeking and using information for various purposes, and as emphasized above, this ability is an object of learning. In this respect, the interest in the practice of teaching information seeking for information literacy is simultaneously related to a long-term interest in pedagogical issues within librarianship and to the specific condition that contemporary information and communication technologies provide (See the entry, "Information Literacy," p. 2421).

Constructivism has important implications for teaching and of course for scaffolding information seeking. Teaching is not viewed as the transmission of knowledge from the enlightened to the unenlightened; constructivist teachers do not take the role of the "sage on the stage." Instead, constructivist teachers create a context for learning in which students may become engaged in interesting activities that encourage and facilitate learning. The teacher may often guide students as they approach problems, may persuade them to work in groups to think about issues and questions, and support them with encouragement and advice as they tackle problems, adventures, and challenges rooted in real-life situations that are both interesting to the students and satisfying in terms of the result of their work. If learning is based on prior knowledge, then teachers must take that knowledge into account and provide learning environments that exploit inconsistencies between learners' current understandings and the new experiences before them. This challenges teachers, since they cannot assume that all students understand something in the same way. Further, students may need different experiences to advance to different levels of understanding. These constructivist ideas apply equally to different teaching areas, including information seeking.

LEARNING FROM INFORMATION

As mentioned above, the majority of research studies in the area of information seeking and learning restrict their interest to information seeking, not taking learning outcomes into account. However, since the mid-1990s there are examples of studies where the object of research is to explore the interaction between information seeking and learning, including an interest in studying students' learning outcomes related to their information seeking and use.[12,24,25,41,43] These studies have adopted either a cognitive constructivist or a social constructivist view of learning as a theoretical framework. The research object

of such studies concerns the major question about what characterizes the complex links between information seeking, information use, and knowledge formation, that is the transformation of information into knowledge.

Information Seeking and Learning Outcomes

Findings from such studies identify various approaches that students adopt in information practices for learning purposes. Related to complex learning tasks, a fact-finding approach is found to coincide with a poor learning outcome, characterized by fragmentary pieces of knowledge. Approaching information seeking as analyzing and scrutinizing information for understanding a complex issue, for finding different perspectives, and for identifying values and hidden motives in information sources corresponds with sophisticated learning outcomes. High-quality learning outcomes are characterized by students' abilities to argue coherently about an issue, to discuss matters from different perspectives, and to make consistent inferences based on substantial factual knowledge. Conclusions drawn from these studies are that there is a close relationship between the quality of information seeking and use and the quality of learning outcomes.

Information Use as Text Transport

Observations in practice as well as in various studies of students' information use related to ICT for learning assignments concern the issue of "copy and paste." Learning outcomes as represented in students' papers indicate the common practice of moving text from information sources to students' own texts, sometimes also slightly transforming the original texts through deleting or adding a few word, making the text "their own." Occasionally this text transport is seen as plagiarism by educators. However, studies on students' ways of using information sources to produce their own texts show that the transport and transformation of text may constitute practices developed among students in order to deal with their writing tasks as best they can. The studies also indicate that this practice is part of the discursive practice of school, where copying and memorizing text is a long-standing tradition. The findings indicate that the art of using other people's texts for producing one's own text is an ability that requires purposeful learning, and that teaching this ability needs to be better developed.[24,25,44] We conclude that this aspect of information use for producing new text is worthy of further research as well as considerations for ways of changing practice.

Critical Features for Meaningful Learning Outcomes

Studies of the relationship between the quality of information seeking and use and the quality of learning outcomes identify a range of critical features, that is qualities that

Law Literature–Library Architecture

make a difference, for meaningful learning. These features relate to various dimensions of learning tasks. It seems essential that learning assignments are based in researchable questions, meaning inquiry-based assignments built on questions that are appropriate for examining complex issues, neither simple fact-finding questions, nor very broad and unspecified topical questions. For meaningful learning it is further underlined that various aspects of information practices should be observed throughout the learning process, implying a shift from an emphasis on information skills instruction toward a stronger accent on the critical use of information. It is considered as vital that the interactions between teachers and librarians on the one hand and students on the other focus strongly on the knowledge contents of an assignment; researchers found that the interaction in information use for learning is often directed at order and procedure rather than at the process of understanding and constructing meaning through information use. Meaningful feedback through assessment on various dimensions of tasks, including aspects of information practices, is further underlined as necessary for supporting meaningful learning.

Learning and Information Seeking Shaped by School Practice

A sociocultural view of information seeking and learning sheds light on the interplay between the described practices of information seeking and learning. We may assume that authentic exploration of complex tasks in school settings is contrary to the tradition of schooling. The limitations and shortcomings of information practices and learning outcomes observed in a number of studies set in school contexts may be explained by the idea that information seeking and learning are shaped by the discursive practice of school, where the traditional mission has been to deliver "the right knowledge" and for students to learn "the right answers." Studies that take the entire process from task initiation to learning outcomes as their research object, observing information practices embedded in the learning task, contribute to multifaceted understandings of the intricately interwoven process of learning and information seeking. The different strands of information seeking and learning shed light on each other. Through the identification of important critical features required for meaningful learning to occur, these studies imply that the discursive practice of school may be reshaped through reflective and conscious ways of designing, shaping, and managing situations for authentic learning.

CONCLUSIONS

Our presentation of learning and information seeking is founded on the view that these strands of human activity are inextricably intertwined, mutually shaping each other.

The analysis has shown that current constructivist theories strongly influence learning and information practices, emphasizing the perspective of students or users. These changes of practice currently contribute to a gradual change within librarianship underscoring the pedagogical aspects of the profession. The analysis also suggests that there is a powerful potential in the use of learning theories for framing studies of information practices. This development strongly interacts with ICT technologies and practices.

Based on these conclusions we propose that ideas for future research will need to explore concepts such as the reshaping of the authority and expertise of information, information sharing, and the professional role of librarians. All three topics are related to further innovation in ICT, and the development of new digital tools for information use and learning.

In postmodern society individuals are allocated great responsibility for their own active choices. This means that public institutions, such as libraries and schools, are in a process of transformation from controlling knowledge processes to supporting people's own decision-making about where to find information and how and what to learn. One implication of this change concerns the view of expertise, the authority of knowledge, and the control of information constituted by the new digital tools and media, especially the Internet. Authority issues currently receive much attention not only in information science but also in other fields, including education, human–computer interaction, and computer science. The essence of cognitive authority[35] is that people primarily depend on others for ideas as well as for information outside the range of direct experience. The concept of cognitive authority provides an important framework for understanding the basis on which information users decide whether a particular information source is credible or not, and we anticipate further exploration in matters of the authority of information as essential for issues of knowledge, learning, and information at all levels of society.

It is obvious that new digital tools for information seeking and learning change the form, the content, and the infrastructure for learning in our society. New tools, such as those associated with the concept Web 2.0, which allow the production, interaction, and sharing of information, blur the boundaries between producers, mediators, and consumers of information and knowledge. Relevant research questions to investigate may concern how students handle the issue of formal expertise and control of information in Web 2.0 tools, and how people in current and future online environments—such as Web 3.0—create trust and reflect upon authority.

Another anticipated research area concerns *information sharing*. Our view is that research on collaborative information seeking and learning is of vital importance for further understanding of the essence of learning and information seeking in postmodern society. We see

Law Literature–Library Architecture

information seeking and learning as firmly embedded in work and other social practices. This view intertwines work practice with information practice and information technologies. The social and collective aspects of human knowledge and experiences involve both information seeking on a collective level, and the relationship between people and the sharing of other people's knowledge and experiences. From this perspective we see a mutually shaping relationship between information and collaboration practices and the tools developed for the purposes of communication and knowledge sharing. A central issue is how can learning by sharing information be developed and supported in the future?

It has been repeatedly pointed out in this entry that the intensified interest in the relationship between learning and information seeking, caused by constructivist theories as well as the development of ICT, has contributed to reshaping the occupational practice of librarianship, emphasizing the pedagogical aspects of the profession. The research topics suggested above about the shift from authority and control of information to sharing responsibilities of authority and expertise with users reinforce the changing professional role of librarians, and need further exploration through research. Web 2.0 tools constitute a heated issue in current librarianship. Research questions that need further exploration in relation to this topic concern the characteristics of librarians' expertise in relation to users' information seeking and learning in Web 2.0 environments, as well as the characteristics of the negotiation of the professional expertise of librarianship in relation to other knowledge professions such as teachers and journalists.

These are but a few ideas for future research in the dynamic field of learning and information seeking. We want to conclude by insisting on the potential for understanding information practices through further examination of the multifaceted and intricate relationship between learning and information seeking.

REFERENCES

1. Wilson, T.D. On user studies and information needs. J. Doc. **1981**, *37*(1), 3–15.
2. Case, D.O. *Looking for Information: A Survey of Research on Information Seeking, Needs, and Behavior*; 2nd Rev. Ed. Academic Press: Amsterdam, 2007.
3. Skinner, B.F. *Verbal Behavior*; Appleton-Century-Crofts: New York, 1957.
4. Norman, D. *Memory and Attention: An Introduction to Human Information Processing*; Wiley: New York, 1969.
5. Dewey, J. *How We Think*, Rev. Ed. Houghton Mifflin Company: Boston, MA, 1933/1998.
6. Piaget, J. *The Psychology of the Child*; Basic Books: New York, 1972.
7. Vygotsky, L. *Thought and Language*; MIT Press: Cambridge, MA, 1962.
8. Vygotsky, L. *Mind and Society*; Harvard University Press: Cambridge, MA, 1978; 57.
9. Wertsch, J.V. *Vygotsky and the Social Formation of Mind*; Harvard University Press: Cambridge, MA, 1985.
10. Kuhlthau, C.C. *Seeking Meaning: A Process Approach to Library and Information Services*, 2nd Rev. Ed.; Libraries Unlimited: Westport, CT, 2004.
11. Limberg, L. *Att söka information för att lära. En studie av samspel mellan informationssökning och lärande. [Experiencing information seeking and learning: A study of the interaction between two phenomena] Valfrid*, Borås: Sweden, 1998; Ph.D. thesis, University of Gothenburg.
12. Limberg, L. Three conceptions of information seeking and use Information Seeking in Context (ISIC'98) Conference Proceedings; Wilson, T.D., Allen, T.D., Eds.; Taylor Graham: London, 1999; 116–132.
13. Limberg, L.; Sundin, O. Teaching information seeking: relating information literacy education to theories of information behaviour. Inform. Res. **2006**, *12*(1), paper 280, Available at http://InformationR.net/ir/12-1/paper280.html.
14. Marton, F.; Booth, S. *Learning and Awareness*; Lawrence Erlbaum Associates: Mahwah, NJ, 1997.
15. Bruce, C.S. *The Seven Faces of Information Literacy*; Auslib Press: Adelaide, SA, 1997.
16. Bruce, C.S. *Informed Learning*; Association of College and Research Libraries: Chicago, IL, 2008.
17. Lupton, M. *Information literacy and learning*; Queensland University of Technology: Brisbane, QLD, 2008; Ph.D. thesis.
18. Boon, S.; Johnston, B.; Webber, S. A phenomenographic study of English faculty's conceptions of information literacy. J. Doc. **2007**, *63*(2), 204–228.
19. Williams, D.A.; Wavell, C. *Information Literacy in the Classroom: Secondary School Teachers' Conceptions*, Aberdeen Business School: Aberdeen, 2006; Research Report 15; Department of Information Management.
20. Lave, J. *Cognition in Practice: Mind, Mathematics, and Culture in Everyday Life*; Cambridge University Press: Cambridge, U.K., 1988.
21. Lave, J.; Wenger, E. *Situated Learning: Legitimate Peripheral Participation*; Cambridge University Press: Cambridge, U.K., 1991.
22. Wenger, E. *Communities of Practice: Learning, Meaning and Identity*; Cambridge University Press: Cambridge, U.K., 1999.
23. Driver, R.; Asoko, H.; Leach, J.; Scott, P.; Mortimer, E. Constructing scientific knowledge in the classroom. Educ. Res. **1994**, *23*(7), 5–12 7.
24. Alexandersson, M.; Limberg, L. Constructing meaning through information artefacts. New Rev. Inform. Behav. Res. **2003**, *4*, 17–30.
25. Limberg, L.; Alexandersson, M.; Lantz-Andersson, A. To be lost and to be a loser through the web. In *Handbook of Research on Digital Information Technologies: Innovations, Methods, and Ethical Issues*; Hansson, T., Ed.; Information Science Reference: Hershey, PA, 2008; 248–262.
26. Sundin, O. Nurses' information seeking and use as participation in occupational communities. New Rev. Inform. Behav. Res. **2002**, *3*, 187–202.
27. Lloyd, A. Information literacy landscapes: An emerging picture. J. Doc. **2006**, *62*(5), 570–583.

Law Literature–Library Architecture

28. Lundh, A.; Limberg, L. Information Practices in Elementary school. Libri **2008**, *58*(2), 92–101.

29. Sundin, O. Negotiations on information seeking expertise: A study of web-based tutorials for information literacy. J. Doc. **2008**, *64*(1), 24–44.

30. Tuominen, K.; Savolainen, R.; Talja, S. Information literacy as a socio-technical practice. Libr. Quart. **2005**, *75*(3), 329–345.

31. Case, D.O. *Looking for Information. A Survey of Research on Information Seeking, Needs, and Behavior*, 2nd Rev. Ed. Academic Press: Amsterdam, 2007; 148–169.

32. Wilson, T.D. Models in information behaviour research. J. Doc. **1999**, *55*(3), 249–270.

33. Vakkari, P. Task-based information searching. Annu. Rev. Inform. Sci. Technol. **2003**, *37*, 413–464.

34. Gross, M. The imposed query. In *Theories of Information Behaviour*; Fisher, K., Erdelez, S., McKechnie, L., Eds.; Information Today, Inc.: Medford, NJ, 2005; 164–168.

35. Wilson, P. *Second-Hand Knowledge. An Inquiry into Cognitive Authority*; Greenwood Press: Westport, CT, 1983.

36. CIBER, *Information Behaviour of the Researcher of the Future*, University College London, 2008; January 11 A ciber briefing paper, Available at http://www.bl.uk/news/pdf/googlegen.pdf (accessed November 2008).

37. Ford, N.; Miller, D.; Moss, N. Web search strategies and approaches to studying. J. Am. Soc. Inform. Sci. Technol. **2003**, *54*(6), 473–489.

38. Heinström, J. Fast surfing for availability or deep diving into quality: motivation and information seeking among middle and high school students. Inform. Res. **2006**, *11*(4), paper 265, Available at http://informationr.net/ir/11-4/paper265.html (accessed November 2008).

39. Whitmire, E. The relationship between undergraduates' epistemological beliefs, reflective judgment, and their information-seeking behaviour. Inform. Process. Manage. **2004**, *40*, 97–111.

40. Wilson, T.D. Information needs and uses: Fifty years of progress?. In *Fifty Years of Information Progress. A Journal of Documentation Review*; Vickery, B.C., Ed.; Aslib: London, 1994; 15–51 42.

41. Pitts, J. *Personal Understandings and Mental Models of Information: A Qualitative Study of Factors Associated with the Information Seeking and Use of Adolescents*; Florida State University, 1994; Ph.D. thesis.

42. Eisenberg, M.; Berkowitz, R. *The Definitive Big6 Workshop Handbook*; Linworth Publishing: Columbus, OH, 2003.

43. Todd, R.J. From information to knowledge: Charting and measuring changes in students' knowledge of a curriculum topic. Inform. Res. **2006**, *11*(4), paper 264, Available at http://informationr.net/ir/11-4/paper264.html (accessed November 2008).

44. Williamson, K.; McGregor, J. Information use and secondary school students: a model for understanding plagiarism. Inform. Res. **2006**, *12*(1), paper 288, http://InformationR.net/ir/12-1/paper288.html (accessed November 2008).

BIBLIOGRAPHY

1. Hansson, T., Ed. *Handbook of Research on Digital Information Technologies: Innovations, Methods, and Ethical Issues*; Information Science Reference: Hershey, PA, 2008.

2. Kuhlthau, C.C.; Maniotes, L.K.; Caspari, A.K. *Guided Inquiry. Learning in the 21st Century*; Libraries Unlimited: Westport, CT, 2007.

3. Streatfield, D.R.; Markless, S. *Invisible Learning? The Contribution of School Libraries to Teaching and Learning*, British Library Research and Development Department: London, 1994; Library and Information Research Report 98.

Libraries

Jennifer Weil Arns
*School of Library and Information Science, University of South Carolina, Columbia,
South Carolina, U.S.A.*

Abstract
People have recorded information in many ways for many centuries. The media used for these activities
have changed with social circumstances and technological developments, as have the opportunities and
means to collect and organize recorded knowledge. As a result, libraries have taken many forms over time,
moving most recently from primarily paper-based collections to collections that house a wide range of
media and experiment with new technologies. Library services have evolved also, and they now engage
multiple communities, including children, young adults, and a wide range of educational, governmental,
and corporate organizations. Library missions, however, have remained relatively constant: identifying,
collecting, organizing, and providing access to materials with personal or social value.

While generally defined as a collection of materials organized so that they may be easily identified and used by an individual or group, libraries have actually taken many forms over time, reflecting the cultures in which they are embedded and propelled by technological innovations and social currents. The commonalities that have survived these changes pertain to collection, organization, and mission, however, even these continue to produce lively discussion.

LIBRARIES OF THE ANCIENT WORLD

In ancient times, merchants and farmers recorded their activities, accounts, possessions, and experiences using materials that needed to be preserved and organized in order to record events and construct meaning. Examples of these include early Sumerian clay tablets dating from 3000 B.C. that contain pictorial representations and, eventually, more standardized symbols; http://www.upenn.edu/museum/Games/cuneiform.html).[1] Excavations conducted at Ugarit, Syria have unearthed deposits of tablets, thought to date close to 1200 B.C., that appear to have served palace and temple as well as personal record keeping purposes.[2] Another palace collection, the Royal Library of Ashurbanipal, included thousands of tablets dating from the seventh century B.C. The subjects presented in these, found in northern Mesopotamia, ranged widely, including religious texts, poetry, royal decrees, and incantations.[3] There is some evidence of purposeful collection and subject organization, and the collection is now housed at the British Museum (http://www.britishmuseum.org/research/research_projects/ashurbanipal_library_phase_1.aspx).

Historical records provide more information concerning the famous Royal Library of Alexandria. Assembled both thoughtfully and aggressively, the collection is believed to have been the largest of its time. The library's contents mirrored the subjects that characterized Greek literature during this period, and works in other languages were frequently copied and translated in order to broaden the scope of the collection. In addition to its unmatched size and scope, this library is notable for the presence of both a cataloging system that provided some degree of subject access and the presence of designated librarians.[3–5]

As the Roman Empire expanded, few libraries flourished. Those that did so relied on the interests of a small group of powerful leaders and wealthy individuals who moved parts of the plundered Greek collections that interested them to locations of their choosing. In some cases, these libraries appear to have been open to scholars and members of the literate public; however, with the sacking of Rome and decline of the empire most were destroyed or abandoned. The literature they contained, including materials once housed in the Greek libraries, was lost to those who did not live in the Byzantine and Moslem empires.[6]

MEDIEVAL LIBRARIES

Within the disordered society that followed, the preservation of information was often more explicitly linked to the power of memory than to the security of shelves and buildings. Common cognitive frameworks likened experiences and facts to objects that could be stored in imagined rooms containing categorical or symbolic pointers that facilitated recollection through visualization. Memory-making was a recognized craft, with tools and techniques that were specifically taught and particularly valued within the monastic culture for public use in sermons and personal meditations. Imaginative literature,

Encyclopedia of Library and Information Sciences, Fourth Edition DOI: 10.1081/E-ELIS4-120045507
Copyright © 2017 by Taylor & Francis. All rights reserved.

including stories, poems, and popular histories, were similarly stored and restored in memory as they evolved through retelling.[7]

The traditional libraries of this period were typically created and maintained by religious orders. Their collections, often mixtures of scrolls (rolled pieces of paper or papyrus) and codices (an early form of the book, with pages cut and bound together), were usually modest and stored in chests or cupboards with little need for special attention or finding aids. Larger collections accumulated in religious and commercial settings, and in these situations, physical subdivision was typically used to indicate variations in use or topic. Physical descriptions were also sometimes recorded, and a degree of subject classification occurred in some of the larger libraries, including the collections housed at Christchurch, Canterbury, and Durham Cathedral in England.[8] The value of the collections varied. Reading, and consequently, transcription, was emphasized within the Benedictine order. In some instances, the act of transcription was connected to religious experience.

RENAISSANCE AND EARLY MODERN LIBRARIES

The expansion of trade, the rediscovery of classical literature, and the formation of secular political states combined to contribute to a decline in the relevance of small monastic libraries and the emergence of more familiar modern models. The first, the extensive private library, was directly associated with the concentration of wealth that characterized the Renaissance period. These libraries housed collections created by the Renaissance rulers and commercial princes, including the Laurentian Library commissioned by the Medici pope Clement VII and the personal library of the Duke of Urbino. A royal library may be found today at Windsor Castle (http://www.royal collection.org.uk/default.asp?action=article&ID=21).

The intellectual and artistic awakening that characterized the Renaissance also propelled and transformed university education, almost doubling the number of universities functioning in Europe.[9] The curricula at the famous universities that were already in place, including the University of Bologna, the University of Paris, and Oxford and Cambridge Universities, were also developing rapidly; and these changes, as well as new pedagogical methods, increased the influence and size of university libraries. The growing availability of printed books also favored larger collections, the appointment of librarians, and the development of printed catalogs.

The national libraries that emerged toward the end of this period were typically created for custodial as well as educational purposes. In many cases, their contents were drawn from the private collections of monarchs, scholars, and statesmen, including Charles the V of France, whose

personal library is linked to the founding of the Bibliothèque Nationale, located in Paris. The Royal Danish Library was built similarly upon gifts from Frederick III of Denmark, and the Vatican Library benefited from the attention of popes Nicholas V and Sixtus IV in the fifteenth century. The British Museum Library was likewise partially assembled from collections owned by the family of Sir Robert Cotton and the Old Royal Library of the English sovereigns. The United States Library of Congress benefited similarly from the collections of President Thomas Jefferson and the scholar Peter Force. Many smaller libraries today benefit from contributions of time and funds from library benefactors. The Placitas Community Library in the U.S. state of New Mexico provides an example of a library that has been created by community members and is staffed primarily by volunteers.

Municipal and town reference libraries also offered limited collections for public use in European cities as early as the sixteenth and seventeenth centuries. However, their contents are reported to have been typically limited to materials of moderate interest. As in the case of the national libraries, the collections were often bequeathed, rather than purposely purchased, and not frequently tended by librarians. Private and circulating libraries were, in contrast, more stable and provided materials of considerable interest.[3]

NINETEENTH CENTURY LIBRARIES

By the midpoint of the nineteenth century, remnants of each of these models could be easily seen in the libraries that provided services in the United States. Proprietary and subscription libraries, such as the Library Company of Philadelphia, the Boston Athenaeum, and the Charleston Library Society were already well established and provided reading materials, including popular texts and fiction, to their members and subscribers. Mercantile and mechanic's libraries also housed collections intended for the use of young men entering business, commercial tradesmen, and aspiring artisans. In 1850, contemporary reports indicated these libraries numbered over 100, and their joint collections were thought to be in the range of 600,000 volumes.[10] Although fewer in number today, several of these libraries, including the Boston Athenaeum, continue to provide services on a subscription basis. Technical and business libraries are also a common feature and vital factor within the business and technical communities.

Writers also link Edward Everett and George Ticknor's continental education and familiarity with the great university libraries of Europe to the establishment of the first major public library in the United States in the city of Boston. The influence of the Boston Athenaeum is also evident. Of the members of the Joint City Council

Law Literature–Library Architecture

Committee appointed to consider this question and the five citizens appointed to the first Board of Trustees, the mayor, four of the appointed trustees, and five of the City Council members were Athenaeum proprietors. New perspectives concerning the value of workingmen, social and intellectual mobility, and the importance of social harmony and prosperity to an emerging nation provided additional contextual impetus.[11,12]

Education also figured prominently in the words of those who favored the establishment of public libraries in the United States.[13] By mid-century, the public school movement, led by Horace Mann, Henry Barnard, and others had gained substantial momentum, and the benefits of extending public education provided a persuasive argument for the establishment of equally public libraries. The growing prominence of an international scientific community based on the premise of collective advancement, acculturation issues related to an increasingly urban and immigrant population, and modern concepts related to the values of democracy and moral stewardship also pointed to a need to extend basic scholarship and educational opportunity. By the end of the nineteenth century, children's reading rooms had been opened in Brookline, Massachusetts, Minneapolis, and Denver. Publicly supported school libraries followed slowly, although in some states, including New York, funds were allocated for this purpose.

MODERN LIBRARIES

Although these categories sometimes overlap, modern libraries typically fall into one of four groupings: school, academic, public, and special.[6,14] School library media centers are usually located within primary and secondary schools. Their collections are diverse, including children's and young adult materials intended to support classroom activities and curriculum development. School library media centers are also often technology intensive. Their services are intended to be an integral part of their school's instructional process, and their programs contribute through reading guidance and technology instruction to the personal, social, and intellectual development of the students in their schools.

Academic libraries maintain collections and provide services that further the purpose and mission of the higher education institutions to which they belong. Their collections and services are geared to promote faculty research, teaching excellence, and student learning. In recent years, academic libraries have taken advantage of new technologies through contract arrangements that allow them to purchase and provide journals, books, and other materials in electronic format directly to dorms, faculty offices, and student's homes. They also teach technology courses that introduce students to electronic classroom resources, and they often participate in shared acquisition arrangements

through university library consortia that provide some relief from rapidly rising journal prices.

Public libraries in the United States are generally tax-supported institutions with service areas that usually coincide with city and county boundaries. In other cases, public libraries are operated as special district libraries. In both cases, public libraries play a crucial role in their communities, providing services intended to meet the social, educational, and recreational needs of the people residing in their service areas. Their collections typically span the interests of all age groups. Public libraries often produce educational programs, such as the National Endowment for the Humanities Picturing America programs that bring great American art directly to schools and libraries across the United States (http://www.neh.gov/news/archive/20080227.html). Public libraries also forge an important link between communities and local, state, and federal government agencies by assuring access to governmental documents and providing access to information about government rules and regulations. In the United States, public, academic and school libraries share a common professional association in the American Library Association (ALA), founded in 1876.

Special libraries vary considerably, but are generally defined by a special purpose and clientele. They are common in business and industry, government, nongovernmental organizations, and associations. Special libraries generally have deep coverage of narrow subject areas of interest to their parent organization, with restricted coverage of other subject areas. Common examples of special libraries are law libraries, medical and hospital libraries, corporate libraries, and museum and research institute libraries. Government agencies, especially at the Federal level, have many specialized libraries as well. Examples of special libraries in the United States include the American Medical Association Library, the Fashion Institute of Technology Gladys Marcus Library, the John F. Kennedy Museum and Library, the Newberry Library (an independent humanities research library), the National Air and Space Museum Library, and the Mayo Clinic Libraries. They are alternatively referred to as information and knowledge centers.

Special libraries are usually funded by their parent organization to meet the needs of that organization. In private industry, the staff and resources are evaluated on the basis of their contribution to the bottom line, as well as their contributions to research, development, and operations. In 1909, special librarians in the United States founded their own association apart from the ALA, and called it the Special Libraries Association.

LIBRARY FUNCTIONS

The tasks required to provide access and services in most of these libraries are generally organized around a set of

Law Literature–Library Architecture

core functions typically referred to as technical services, public services, and management. The first of these, technical services, is associated with the identification, assessment, procurement, cataloging, classification, preparation, and maintenance of the materials that constitute the collection. At this time, many of these activities are aided by automation systems and cataloging utilities. Public services include reference services, bibliographic instruction, reader's advisory assistance, community programming, and other services where library staff interact directly with those who use the library. Management functions include marketing, planning, financial management, and human resources development.

The size of these libraries and the content and complexity of their collections typically determine the size and stratification of the staff that performs these activities. However, in most cases there is at least one individual whose duties include some portion or combination of those listed under the heading of *Librarian* once developed for *Dictionary of Occupational Titles* as follows:

> Maintains library collections of books, serial publications, documents, audiovisual, and other materials, and assists groups and individuals in locating and obtaining materials: Furnishes information on library activities, facilities, rules, and services. Explains and assists in use of reference sources, such as card or book catalog or book and periodical indexes to locate information. Describes or demonstrates procedures for searching catalog files. Searches catalog files and shelves to locate information. Issues and receives materials for circulation or for use in library. Assembles and arranges displays of books and other library materials. Maintains reference and circulation materials. Answers correspondence on special reference subjects. May compile list of library materials according to subject or interests, using computer. May select, order, catalog, and classify materials. May prepare or assist in preparation of budget. May plan and direct or carry out special projects involving library promotion and outreach activity and be designated Outreach Librarian (library). May be designated according to specialized function as Circulation Librarian (library); Readers'-Advisory-Service Librarian (library); or Reference Librarian (library). –Source: http://www.occupationalinfo.org/10/100127014. html (accessed October 10, 2001)

In the United States, the title *Librarian* is generally reserved for individuals who hold a Masters degree from graduate programs accredited by the ALA. These programs also provide continuing education workshops that introduce new concepts and techniques to currently practicing librarians. Other staffing levels are paraprofessionals and library aids. These individuals perform many duties that are critical to library operations, including shelving, interlibrary loan, circulation, and basic reference activities.

Librarians and others who work in traditional libraries also receive support from a network of professional associations that represent their interests, facilitate the development of professional standards, create public forums, and provide continuing education materials and opportunities. Most countries have professional library associations, as do many states and provinces. The International Federation of Library Associations and Institutions (founded in 1927) attracts members from a wide range of nations and provides similar services at the international level.

LIBRARY BUILDINGS

Library buildings vary in design and construction. They generally include spaces for their collections, electronic work stations, meeting rooms, staff work rooms, and public reading areas. New building and renovation projects tend to be ongoing, and annual data places the number of public library projects completed in the United States between July 1, 2007 and June 30, 2008, at 183 and the number of new academic libraries at 30. In the case of academic libraries, project costs for new libraries ranged from $6,190,300 to $92,000,000. New public library project costs ranged more widely, including project costs close to $250,000 and $64,000,000.[15] Although many communities in the United States enjoy and are proud of libraries built with support from the Carnegie Foundation at the turn of the century,[16] new libraries and renovation allow libraries to create spaces for the electronic services, children's programs, and community activities, while making their facilities more accessible in terms of the design standards provided in the Americans with Disabilities Act at 28 CFR Part 36, as revised July 1, 1994 (http://www.ada.gov). New buildings also provide opportunities to experiment with designs and incorporate modern "green" building materials, often with striking and award-winning architectural results (http://www.oclc.org.pallas2.tcl.sc.edu/nextspace/010/advocacy. htm; http://www.ala.org/ala/mgrps/divs/llama/llamaawards/ aiaalalibrarybuildings.cfm).

LIBRARY NUMBERS

While it is difficult to determine the number of entities currently providing library services due to variations in reporting procedures, information related to library operations is typically collected and periodically reported. In the United States, these data are currently provided through a cooperative arrangement between the Institute of Museum and Library Services and the National Center for Education Statistics. The most recent information available places the number of academic libraries in the United States in 2006 at 3617 with holdings estimated at over 1 billion items.[17] The number of public libraries in 2006 exceeded 9000 with the number of library visits estimated at 1.4 billion and the number of circulation

Law Literature–Library Architecture

transactions at slightly over 2 billion.[18] Similar figures indicate that the number of public schools with library media centers in 2000 approached 77,000, representing 92% of U.S. public schools.[19]

Similar data are collected for European libraries by LIBECON, an organization funded by the Directorate General for the Information Society of the European Commission within the 5th Framework Programme for Research. Other sources include surveys administered by UNESCO and nationally available statistics. A 2003 synthesis of data collected from these sources by the International Federation of Library Associations provides the following estimates based on service points, which are defined as any library in which a service for users is provided in separate quarters, whether it is an independent library or part of a large administration unit (http://www.uis.unesco.org/ev.php?ID= 5622_201&ID2=DO_TOPIC). The data were developed using the numbers most recently reported by each country in the data set used for calculation (see Table 1).

RECENT DEVELOPMENTS AND THE TWENTY-FIRST CENTURY

As libraries developed over many centuries from a very small number to hundreds of thousands, the media they employed to record information also grew and changed significantly. In the early days and over a period of centuries, collected knowledge moved from clay tablets to papyrus to parchment to paper. More recently, over just a few decades, libraries have become homes for audio recordings, games, interactive educational materials, videos, and many other forms of digitized information that can be downloaded and accessed using computers, smart phones, and other devices. There have also been remarkable changes in library services, and many people are now using libraries differently, especially young people who have grown up surrounded by digital media.

Recently, the changes in media have focused on the concept of digital libraries, a term that became popularized

among librarians in 1993 with the publication of a special issue of the *Journal of the American Society for Information Science*. The digitized collections to which the term refers have grown in number for over a decade, and they include small projects such as the historic photographs in the South Carolina Georgetown County Library Digital Library (http://www.gcdigital.org/browse/index.php#brook green) and large collections, such as the award winning Valley of the Shadows digital library developed by the Institute for Advanced Technology in the Humanities at the University of Virginia (http://valley.vcdh.virginia.edu). Both of these collections are of general interest to students and adults who enjoy exploring historical documents. Personal music digital libraries are also popular, and collections of this type fold easily into and extend the traditional purposes of libraries: the identification, collection, and organization of materials in a way that makes information easily available.[20]

In some cases, the items in digital library collections are originally created in electronic format. In others, the accession of an item involves scanning a physical object into memory and editing the image as needed to produce the highest possible quality. Additional steps include describing the properties and content of the image (adding data about the information resource, known as metadata, for effective retrieval); creating backup copies; and planning for the preservation of the image as systems, software, and standards change over time.

Many traditional "brick and mortar" libraries have also been transformed by these developments, and most are actively adding digital content, including audiovisual material, electronic journals, Web pages, and databases, to their collections for use both on their premises and at remote locations. Downloadable digitized books, self-service functions (such as book renewals and interlibrary loans), and electronic reference services delivered through e-mail or instant messaging offer patrons new levels of convenience and effectively extend these libraries, too, beyond their physical confines.

Innovative libraries are also using a wide range of Web 2.0 technologies, including social networking platforms, podcasts, mashups, and gaming to maintain the centrality of their positions within their communities and foster interactive learning. Building on the popularity of MySpace, Flickr, Wikipedia, and YouTube, these libraries have developed new forms of library programming that extend the walls of traditional libraries and enrich their interiors with opportunities to create knowledge and foster digital learning in an environment that matches busy lifestyles and connects people to people around the world. Digital media and learning is of particular interest to the John D. and Catherine T. MacArthur Foundation (http://digitallearning. macfound.org/site/c.enJLKQNlFiG/b.2029199/k.94AC/ Latest_News.htm), and libraries such as the Kankakee Public Library in Illinois are exploring these new library technologies (http://www.kankakee.lib.il.us/).

Table 1 Libraries serving the public.

Region	Public	Education	School	National	Total
Library service points					
Africa	797	266	51	15	1,129
Asia	37,063	6,909	29,992	66	74,030
North America	20,081	11,460	78,773	50	110,364
South America	3942	17		32	3991
Oceania	–	–	2	–	2
Europe	205,336	10,161	164,436	178	380,111
Total	**267,219**	**28,813**	**273,254**	**341**	**569,627**

Source: Data from UNESCO and Libecon. See http://www.ifla.org/III/ wsis/wsis-stats4pub_v.pdf.

REFERENCES

1. Manguel, A. *A History of Reading*; Viking Press: New York, 1996.
2. Yon, M. *The City of Ugarit at Tell Ras Shamra*, Eisenbrauns: Winona Lake, IN, 2006.
3. Harris, M. *Libraries in the Western World*; Scarecrow Press: Metuchen, NJ, 1984.
4. Canfora, L. *The Vanished Library*; University of California Press: Berkeley, CA, 1990.
5. MacLeod, R., Ed. *The Library of Alexandria: Centre of Learning in the Ancient World*; St. Martin's Press: New York, 2000.
6. Rubin, R. *Foundations of Library and Information Science*; Neal-Schuman Publishers: New York, 2004.
7. Carruthers, M., Ziolkowski, J.M., Eds. *The Medieval Craft of Memory: An Anthology of Texts and Pictures*; University of Pennsylvania Press: PA, 2002.
8. Russell, B.M. Hidden wisdom and unseen treasure: revisiting cataloging in medieval libraries. Cataloging Classif. Quart. **1998**, *26*(3), 21–30.
9. Grendler, P.F. The universities of the renaissance and reformation. Renaissance Quart. **2004**, *57*(1), 1–42.
10. *Appendix to the Report of the Board of Regents of Smithsonian Institution Containing a Report of the Public Libraries of the United States of America*, U.S. Senate, 31st Cong, 1st sess. (S. Miscellaneous Prt. 120), 1850.
11. Garceau, O. *The Public Library in the Political Process: A Report of the Public Library Inquiry*; Columbia University Press: New York, 1949.
12. Shera, J. *Foundations of the Public Library; The Origins of the Public Library Movement in New England*; University of Chicago Press: Chicago, IL, 1949.
13. Trustees of the Public Library of the City of Boston, *Upon the Objects to Be Attained by the Establishment of a Public Library*, J.H. Eastburn, City Printer: Boston, MA, 1852; City Document - No. 37.
14. Martin, L. *Organizational Structure of Libraries*; Scarecrow Press: Metuchen, NJ, 1984.
15. Fox, B.L. Library buildings 2008: keeping the 'ECO' in economy: public and academic buildings combine for 213 projects in 2008. Libr. J. **2008**, *33*(20), 36–50.
16. Bobinski, G.S. *Carnegie Libraries: Their history and Impact on American Public Library Development*; American Library Association: Chicago, IL, 1969.
17. Holton, B.; Hardesty, L. O'Shea, P. *Academic Libraries: 2006 (NCES 2008–337)*, National Center for Education Statistics, Institute of Education Sciences, U.S. Department of Education: Washington, DC, 2008.
18. Miller, K. et al. *Public Libraries Survey: Fiscal Year 2006*; Institute of Museum and Library Services: Washington, DC, 2008; (IMLS-2008-PLS-02).
19. Michie, J.S.; Holton, B.A. *America's Public School Libraries: 1953–2000 (NCES 2005–324)*, U.S. Department of Education. National Center for Education Statistics. U.S. Government Printing Office: Washington, DC, 2005.
20. Pomerantz, J.; Marchionini, G. The Digital library as place. J. Doc. **2007**, *63*(4), 505–533.
21. Chute, A.; Kroe, P.E. *Public Libraries in the United States: Fiscal Year 2005 (NCES 2008–301)*, National Center for Education Statistics, Institute of Education Sciences, U.S. Department of Education: Washington, DC, 2007.

BIBLIOGRAPHY

1. Buckland, M.K. *Library Services in Theory and Context*; Pergamon Press: New York, 1988.
2. Ellsworth, J.E.; Stevens, N.D. *Landmarks of Library Literature, 1876–1976*, Scarecrow Press: Metuchen, NJ, 1976.
3. Moran, B.; Stueart, R. *Library and Information Center Management*, 7th Ed. Libraries Unlimited: Westport, CT, 2007.
4. OCLC Online Computer Library Center, Inc, Information content trends: Content, not containers. 2004; http://www.oclc.org/reports/2004format.htm.
5. OCLC Online Computer Library Center, Inc, From Awareness to funding: a Study of library support in America. 2008; http://www.oclc.org/reports/funding/fullreport.pdf.

Law Literature–Library Architecture

Library and Information Science

Miriam E. Sweeney
School of Library and Information Studies, University of Alabama, Tuscaloosa, Alabama, U.S.A.

Leigh S. Estabrook
Graduate School of Library and Information Science, University of Illinois at Urbana-Champaign, Champaign, Illinois, U.S.A.

Abstract

Library and information science (LIS) is an interdisciplinary domain concerned with the creation, management, and uses of information in all its forms. Emerging from parallel developments in libraries and in information science, the field now encompasses diverse activities that are part of the *information transfer cycle*—such as the creation, instantiation, communication, acquisition, organization, management, regulation, preservation, distribution, and use of information. This entry traces the development of LIS from its beginnings in thinking about libraries and the growth of library science as a field. It then explores the nature of *information science* and the interweaving paths of the two—which eventually encountered the field of *communications*. The entry concludes with current trends and emerging areas in the field that present both challenges and opportunities in terms of defining LIS as a vast, interdisciplinary area.

INTRODUCTION

Library and information science (LIS) is an interdisciplinary domain concerned with the creation, management, and uses of information in all its forms. Taught in colleges and universities at the undergraduate and graduate levels and a subject of research in both industry and academia, LIS brings together a variety of theoretical approaches. Its focus is on representations of information—the documentary evidence of civilization—as well as on the technologies and organizations through which information becomes accessible.

The research domain is young, beginning in the late 1960s and early 1970s, but its roots lie in the nineteenth century. As can be seen in Fig. 1, LIS represents the intersection of library science, information science (originally called documentation), and communications. The first, library science, has sought to solve the problems of organizing and providing access to collections of materials. The second, information science, seeks to understand the properties of information and how to manage it. Aspects of the field of communication, always a facet of the first two, became interwoven with both as library science and information science matured and increasingly intersected with one another.

The field of LIS can be characterized as "user-focused." The concern is not just for the isolated information artifact—for example, data, reports, books, video, and museum objects. Instead, the social, technical, and cultural systems that structure recorded knowledge, making it available and useful to the people who want or need it—or even happen upon it—are considered. Historically LIS has focused on technical systems, such as cataloging and classification, as well as organization systems such as the development and management of collections and user services. Legal systems that structure information access such as licensing, intellectual property rights, and information policy are central to the domain, particularly in the current information landscape that relies heavily on digital information and Internet technologies. LIS researchers also study ways in which the use of indexes, citations, and other bibliographic information can reveal such things as the relationship between disciplines, networks of scholarship, and the value of information in decision-making. LIS encompasses research on the social and cultural contexts of information, considering implications of race, ethnicity, class, gender, and sexuality for information creation, transfer, and use. Such questions lead beyond the initial concerns of the field, demonstrating the flexibility of LIS to meet the changing role of information in society.

The LIS domain extends to the structures of the institutions that make information available and usable—such as libraries, archives, and museums, whose primary purpose is collecting, preserving, organizing, and making useful information and cultural artifacts. The field also includes systems—such as information resource management—within business and organizations.

LIS grew out of philosophies of the Enlightenment. Its foundations were built in the United States in the late eighteenth and throughout the nineteenth century. Thomas Jefferson, James Madison, and other founders viewed both libraries and information as important to the new democracy. The Library of Congress was established in 1800

Encyclopedia of Library and Information Sciences, Fourth Edition DOI: 10.1081/E-ELIS4-120053401

Copyright © 2017 by Taylor & Francis. All rights reserved.

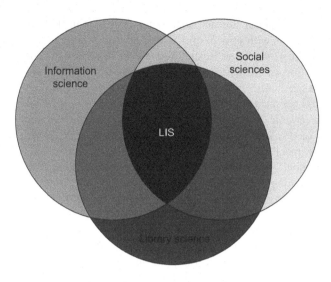

Fig. 1 The domain of LIS.

during the administration of John Adams; article 1, section 8 of the Constitution established copyright protection to "promote science and the useful arts." Government support for the U.S. mail system, including roads over which the mail was carried, and for national surveys (including the Lewis and Clark expedition) are among the ways in which the new federal government promoted the creation and dissemination of information.

During the nineteenth century, scientific discovery and exploration grew rapidly, fueled by government subsidies and industrial growth. The U.S. government published 100,000 different titles between 1774 and 1881,[1] and the Government Printing Office printed 41 million copies of their publications by 1894. Research universities and library collections grew exponentially. Between 1850 and 1875, local communities and philanthropists created 2240 public libraries.[2]

FOUNDATIONS: 1880–1960

Library Science

Libraries are collections of recorded knowledge, organized for use. Libraries may exist in buildings of bricks and mortar or as digital collections held in the memory of one or more connected computers. Whatever the form or format, libraries are intended to provide access to cultural and scientific materials for an audience—for users who will take that information for enjoyment, increased understanding, or as the basis for creating new information.

The nineteenth century was a productive period for the development of tools for organizing information. These included William Frederick Poole's (1821–1894) *Index to Periodical Literature*, begun in 1848, and several important indexing and abstracting services, among them *Index*

Medicus (1879) and *Engineering Index* (1896). The *Library of Congress Classification* and *Dewey Decimal Classification* systems were developed in the late nineteenth century to help manage the growth of library collections. By the early twentieth century, the Library of Congress published catalog records from their collections for use by other libraries, a practice that encouraged standardization in library practice and contributed to the possibilities of automating library work.

In 1887 library science took the first step from education by apprenticeship—the usual way one gained occupational competence in nineteenth century America—to an academic area within higher education. Melvil Dewey (1851–1931) created the School of Library Economy at Columbia University in 1887.[3–4] At its inception, library science focused on history and bibliography—the description and classification of recorded knowledge. (These areas remain the primary focus of library science in many countries, particularly those countries formerly associated with the Soviet Union.) The academic field did not begin to develop until the Carnegie Corporation funded two critical studies on the quality of library science education. The second of these , *Training for Library Service* (1923), by Charles C. Williamson (1877–1965)., is often credited with bringing about the changes necessary for library science to become a mature academic field.[5]

In 1926 the Carnegie Corporation provided funding to create the Graduate Library School (GLS) at the University of Chicago. It was the first such program to offer a doctoral program and played a significant role in opening the field to change during the 1930s. Library science became more interdisciplinary and began to develop deeper theoretical foundations and more substantive research. The GLS faculty included Pierce Butler (1884–1953), Douglas Waples (1893–1978) and, for a time, Bernard Berelson (1912–1979) who received his doctoral degree from the GLS in 1941. These three applied various methods from the social and behavioral sciences to the examination of libraries. Their differing views were widely influential, partly because of their doctoral students and partly because of their research, including *The Library's Public* (1949), of which Berelson was a principal author. The monograph was one of seven resulting from a significant social science investigation known as *The Public Library Inquiry*.

Two of those Chicago graduate students became faculty colleagues at Western Reserve University. Dean Jesse Shera (1903–1982) and Professor Margaret Egan (1905–1959) played a critical role in bringing the bibliographic history of library science together with communication. In a classic 1952 article,[6] they argue that bibliography has a social purpose: an approach they called "social epistemology." Bibliography does not exist for a small group of users, but is the way in which graphic communications move through society and contribute to shaping that society.

Law Literature–Library Architecture

Information Science

Information Science is concerned with information itself and its representations—what information is; how to represent it; how to understand its functions; how it is used; and how to design systems to organize, classify, and retrieve information. Noted information scientist Harold Borko stated, it "is that discipline that investigates the properties and behavior of information, the forces governing the flow of information, and the means of processing information for optimum accessibility and usability."[7]

The history of information science embodies technological developments, notably those in computing, theoretical advances in mathematics and finding ways to measure information, and innovations in retrieving information for research and scholarship. Historically, much of the work of information science was concerned with scientific, technical, and medical information.

Belgian lawyer Paul Otlet (1868–1944) is credited with identifying the field of documentation, a term more commonly used in Europe and the precursor to the phrase "information science." With his colleague Henri La Fontaine (1854–1943), Otlet founded the Institut International de Bibliographie in 1895 and created the multilingual *Universal Decimal Classification* (1905). Both were created to provide universal access to all recorded knowledge, to support Otlet's ambition to promote world peace.

It was not until the founding of the American Documentation Institute (ADI) in 1937 by Watson Davis (1896–1967) that the field began to coalesce in America. Prior to its founding, developments in information science were primarily the result of individual invention, such as the Hollerith punch cards for sorting data or independent organizations, and work of scholarly societies like the American Chemical Society. Originally a service organization with particular interest in microform technology, ADI's membership began with representatives from the government, professional societies, and foundations concerned about similar problems in information management. With a particular interest in scientific communication, ADI fostered collaboration among its members and sponsored research. In 1952, ADI also became a professional society by admitting individual members.

Most of the early developers of documentation and information science had a background in science and industry, and were involved in trying to solve problems of managing large amounts of data and information resources, often for the government. A driving force for their work was scientific research and development during and after World War II, with the attendant growth in the publication of scientific information. The military and defense industries provided significant funding not only for technical but also theoretical research in information storage and retrieval.

Information science historians often credit two researchers with post–World War II advances in their field. The first, Vannevar Bush (1890–1974), described his conception of the memex system, outlined in *As We May Think*.[8] The system, based on microform technology, was intended to make human knowledge easily and widely accessible. Contemporary scholars note that Otlet promoted many of Bush's ideas earlier, but it is Bush who has received most of the credit for anticipating the development of the World Wide Web and other contemporary technologies.

The second was Claude Shannon (1916–2001), whose 1948 paper *A Mathematical Theory of Communication*[9] provided the foundation for information scientists seeking to quantify information and to understand its properties. His book, written with communications researcher Warren Weaver (1894–1978), also entitled *A Mathematical Theory of Communication*,[10] became the basis for significant research and change in social science work in communication. The field of LIS expanded well beyond these original models as it embraced the field of communications in its broader forms.

Communications

Literacy, book history, reading—tools for communicating history, culture, and information—have always been inextricably connected to libraries. By the late nineteenth century, librarians were considering their role in communicating with users, not just conserving materials. At the first American Library Association conference in 1876, for example, Samuel Green (1837–1918), then director of the Worcester Free Public Library, presented a paper entitled "The Desireableness of Establishing Personal Intercourse and Relations between Librarian and Reader in Popular Libraries."[11] As early as 1910 librarians conducted studies of the types of books their users were reading; such studies became common in both the United States and Europe.

Both library science and documentation were historically thought to be related to communication, but communications research did not begin to mature until the 1940s. Histories of communication frequently mention the contributions of University of Chicago Professor Douglas Waples' studies of reading conducted in the 1930s and 1940s. One of the areas of research in The Public Library Inquiry was *The Effects of the Mass Media* (1949)—a study on what was happening to popular taste and its effects on book reading and other library-related matters.

In 1955, Western Reserve University created the Center for Documentation and Communication Research with an explicit intention to bring those two disciplines—information science and communications—together. Allen Kent (1921–) became associate director of the Center, performing important experiments in information

Law Literature–Library Architecture

retrieval before moving to the University of Pittsburgh (1963) where he established the Department of Information Science in 1970. It would not be until the 1960s and 1970s that researchers began significant research representing communication, library science, and information science linked together.

EMERGENCE OF LIS

LIS theory and research coalesced over the last 40 years of the twentieth century. It was a time of rapid technological development that made more complex both managing information and making it accessible. In the early 1960s, works like Marshall McLuhan's (1911–1980) *Gutenberg Galaxy* (1962) and Fritz Machlup's (1902–1983) *The Production and Distribution of Knowledge in the United States*, (1962) spurred public imagination about the role of information in society. The problems of classifying and organizing data, of creating tools for retrieval, and of designing them so they could be used became the concern of many other researchers disconnected from the LIS community. Responses by a number of the U.S. and European library schools to this implicit challenge became important to LIS development.

In the early 1960s, two U.S. LIS schools developed research centers: the Library Research Center at the University of Illinois (1961) and the Institute of Library Research at the University of California (1964). Each provided research opportunities for faculty and student. At the University of Sheffield, England, the Centre for Research in User Studies (CRUS) within the Postgraduate School of Librarianship and Information Studies (1976) provided a similar foundation.

Federal funding for doctoral studies in LIS and for research in both LIS increased dramatically beginning in the 1960s. Over less than a decade, the profile of LIS faculty shifted dramatically with an increasing number holding doctoral degrees and actively engaged in research.[12]

Some of the leading post–World War II information scientists left government, business, and industry for faculty positions in LIS. Besides Allen Kent's association with Case Western and Pittsburgh Universities, other examples are Robert Hayes (1926–), president of Advanced Information Systems joining the University of California at Los Angeles's faculty, Pauline Cochrane's (1929–) move from the American Institute of Physics to Syracuse University (1966), and F.W. Lancaster's (1933–) recruitment to the University of Illinois in 1970 after experience with the Cranfield Experiments (1962) and *the MEDLARS Evaluation Project of the National Library of Medicine* (1965–1968).

Cross-disciplinary faculty teaching was equally enriching to LIS programs. Stanford University communications professor William Paisley taught, for example, at Berkeley's School of Librarianship. Doctoral students from Syracuse University's newly named School of Information Studies took advantage of computer scientist Gerald Salton's lectures at Cornell University.

Most significant for what LIS has become today was not, however, the addition of information science to the library science curriculum, but LIS's shift away from a focus on libraries and scholarly communication to one on information. Research ranged from that on information retrieval to the accuracy of reference service. Throughout the 1970s many of the schools, formerly considered "library schools" added the word information to their name and broadened their curricula. In 1968, the American Documentation Institute became the American Society for Information Science. In 1970, a U.S. Government agency, The National Commission for Library and Information Science, was formally charged with research and policy regarding the two.

Robert S. Taylor (1919–2009), who in 1972 became dean of what is now the School of Information Studies at Syracuse University, led the evolution of LIS from a library-centered field to one that revolves around the cycle of information transfer (see Fig. 2). In this model, LIS is concerned with all of the processes and institutions that finally make recorded knowledge available and accessible. These include not only the publication of scholarship and creative works, but also information storage and retrieval and libraries as a medium of distribution. Information transfer depends, for example, on social policy, including copyright law and censorship activities; it depends on the design of buildings or websites and user education to make information easy to use, and on the coding and formatting of electronic materials so they might be retrieved. The adoption of this new model was not immediate and has not been adopted by all LIS schools, but it represents what LIS has become as a domain.

The use of information and its users has become a central concern of the domain in the process of this shift.

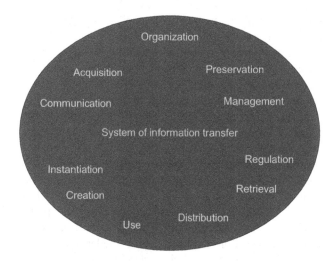

Fig. 2 The information transfer cycle.

Law Literature–Library Architecture

Research of communication scholars like Paisley and Brenda Dervin (1938–) and their students became increasingly important to LIS research. Dervin and Nilan's seminal 1986 article[13] identified the shift in LIS research, building on Taylor and Paisley, to widespread concern about information needs, seeking, and use. This more theoretically grounded research has led LIS education toward its user focus.

A particularly rich example of this change is the work of information behavior researchers who are both interdisciplinary in their theoretical approaches and also in the community of scholars with which they associate. Their work is presented at Information Seeking in Context (ISIC) conferences as well as in information science journals such as the *Journal of Documentation* and the *Journal of the American Society for Information Science and Technology*. This research stream has matured well beyond Shannon and Weaver through the work of such theorists as T.D. Wilson (models of information behavior), Brenda Dervin[13] (evolving sense-making theory), and Carol Kuhlthau[14] (information search process). Chun Wei Choo has provided one integrated model of information behavior research.[15]

As the field became more theoretically grounded, interdisciplinary ties among researchers were strengthened. One important way that these linkages have been expressed is through the institutional structuring of LIS education, with some LIS programs being housed in schools or colleges of education or communication. For example, in 1982 Rutgers Graduate School of Library and Information Studies merged with the School of Communication Studies and the Department of Urban Journalism to form a new School of Communication and Information. Currently, there are approximately 15 accredited LIS programs following similar institutional models as part of education or communication schools and colleges. These interdisciplinary mergers are often controversial from a domain perspective, though they can serve to highlight some of the shared values across LIS and sister disciplines. In terms of LIS and communication fields, there are particular synergies to be found between LIS and journalism, both of which share a mission of training professionals according to an ethical code; value access to information; and are highly responsive to a rapidly changing information technology landscape.

Equally important, as the field has become more theoretical, LIS research has become cumulative and deeper, utilizing a diversity of theories and methods that were not historically emphasized in the discipline. For instance, the inclusion of theoretical approaches from critical studies, cultural studies, ethnic studies, and gender studies has helped LIS researchers approach domain-specific problems from new perspectives. These perspectives serve important functions in privileging under-represented voices in the field, surfacing counter narratives, and revealing the ideological commitments undergirding LIS

technologies and practices as in Hope Olson's [16] work on gender and classification.

Shifting away from libraries as the center of LIS research and education did not remove libraries from the domain. Library and information science is built on such areas as cataloging, classification, and collection development that derive from library research, theory, and practice. Libraries, both virtual and concrete, are critical repositories of information in all forms. At the same time the shift in LIS programs starting in the 1970s has highlighted longstanding tensions between library science and information science. The signature for librarians is their code of ethics that emphasizes a commitment to intellectual freedom, resistance to censorship, user privacy, and equity of access to information. Information science, with its roots in business and industry, is without such a commitment. Some librarians express concerns that LIS has abandoned them by removing libraries from their center and, in the process, abandoning professional norms. Of particular concern is whether LIS programs adequately prepare students for practice in libraries.

LIS educators historically have sought to analyze and improve professional practice in libraries. That has not diminished today, although important developments of research in information retrieval, human–computer interaction, and other such areas may be invisible in day-to-day practice. Most visible and immediately important to librarians is work such as that of Kuhlthau (1937–)[14] on the information search process of users. Notable also are the strong contributions to the practice of reference, including the work of Dervin and Dewdney,[17] Durrance's many works on community information needs and services, and most recently analyses of the return on investment in public libraries carried out by Jose-Marie Griffiths and Donald W. King (1932–).

The growth of the Internet and of digital collections have reinforced the continued importance of libraries to LIS. They also made LIS an increasingly attractive target of opportunity for disciplines outside LIS. In 1996 the National Science Foundation (NSF) awarded the first round of four-year grants under its "digital library initiative." The purpose of NSF was to "dramatically advance the means to collect, store, and organize information in digital forms, and make it available for searching, retrieval, and processing via communication networks— all in user-friendly ways." The initiative, lasting eight years, along with a similar joint effort of NSF and the Joint Information Systems Committee in the United Kingdom, advanced research in LIS, stabilized the domain, and enhanced collaborations outside traditional LIS schools.

Federal funding for LIS in the 1960s and 1970s helped transform LIS in the United States by spurring research and doctoral study. Similarly, funding in the 1990s later contributed to expanding the domain of LIS and provided strong incentives for other disciplines to take up problems in LIS. Andrew Abbott's 1988 study, *The System of*

Professions,[18] remains one of the most cogent sociological analyses of the challenges LIS has faced.

In 2005 a group of university programs in LIS, informatics, computer science, communications, and public policy formed the "iSchools caucus" which governs the iSchools organization, currently over 55 member schools, internationally. The website of the caucus refers to their focus on "iField," an academic area of study and professional preparation in the intersection of technology, information, and people. Almost two-thirds of caucus members offer a program to prepare librarians that is accredited by the American Library Association. The focus of the iSchools, however, is on the broad domain knowledge of LIS. The iSchools reflect a movement to rebrand LIS as an "information" field, which remains widely debated in the field. Some librarians and library researchers fear that the rebranding represents a move toward higher status corporate partners, potentially marginalizing the position of libraries as a public good and threatening the core mission of service in the profession.

THE PRESENT

Throughout LIS's history of creating and establishing itself, scholars have debated such questions as how to define information and communication and whether there is evidence that the related fields are truly converging. These questions are beyond the scope of this entry. Despite the debates, LIS teaching and research continues to expand into newly developing areas of information organization and use. Among those areas of expansion are discipline-specific applications of informatics—for example, medical informatics, social informatics, and community informatics—the study of design, application, and use of information technology within specific domains. Another domain-specific area of development is data curation—the management of data through the information transfer cycle including data creation, management, preservation, and use. The fields of application are new, but essentially replicate in new disciplines approaches that historically were applied to libraries, and information retrieval research is now addressing issues in digital humanities that raise new questions about ontologies and retrieval of text.

CONCLUSION

The field of LIS began in the United States; it grew initially out of the interaction of library science and information science. Although the development of LIS in countries outside the United States has been constrained by different educational systems, scholars particularly in the Nordic countries and Britain have conducted significant LIS research, notably in the Department of Information Studies

at Sheffield University (England) and the Danish Royal School of Library and Information Science. Within the past two decades, both Finnish and Norwegian universities have created schools and departments apart from library education devoted to information science.

In the United States, a wide range of Federal agencies, foundations, and businesses now support LIS research. These reflect the new questions being raised in both teaching and research within the domain. In early 2015, a conference sponsored by the Institute of Museum and Library Services focused on "Re-visioning Library and Information Science Education." Bringing together leaders from the multiple domains of LIS, the conference considered trends shaping LIS and LIS education such as the growth of digital content, social media, search tools, big data, mobile technologies, diversity, and globalization. This conference reflects a strong commitment within LIS to "not only keep pace, but take the lead."[19]

REFERENCES

1. Spofford, A.R. *The Government as a Great Publisher*; The Forum: New York, 1895.
2. Willjam, A.M. *Dedicatory address at the Dedication of the Norton Public Library*; Issued by the board of directors, Press of Lane Brothers: Norton, MA, Wednesday, February 1, 1888, available at Internet Archive, http://www.archive.org/stream/dedicationofnort00nortiala/dedicationofnort00-nortiala_djvu.txt (accessed December 4, 2008).
3. Lynch, B. Library education: Its past, its present, its future. Libr. Trends **2008**, *56* (4), 931–953.
4. Markey, K. Current trends in the information and library science curriculum. J. Educ. Libr. Inf. Sci. **2004**, *45* (4), 317–339.
5. Williamson, C.C. *Training for Library Service*; Carnegie Corporation: New York, 1923.
6. Egan, M.E.; Shera, J.H. Foundations of a theory of bibliography. Libr. Q. **1952**, *22* (2), 125–137.
7. Bates, M.J. The invisible substrate of information science. J. Am. Soc. Inf. Sci. **1999**, *50* (12), 1044.
8. Bush, V. As we may think. Atlantic Mon. **1945**, *176* (1), 101–108.
9. Shannon, C. A mathematical theory of communication. Bell Syst. Tech. J. **(July and October) 1948**, *27*, 379–423. 623–656. [CrossRef].
10. Shannon, C.E.; Weaver, W. *The Mathematical Theory of Communication*; University of Illinois Press: Urbana, IL, 1963.
11. Rothstein, S. The development of the concept of reference service in American libraries, 1850–1900. Libr. Q. **January/October 1953**, *23* (1/4), 5.
12. Heim, K.M. The changing faculty mandate. Libr. Trends **1986, Spring**, *34* (4), 581–606.
13. Dervin, B.; Nilan, M. Information needs and uses. *Annual Review of Information Science and Technology (ARIST)*; Knowledge Industry Publications: White Plains, NY, 1986; *21*, 3–33.

Law Literature–Library Architecture

14. Kuhlthau, C.C. *Seeking Meaning: A Process Approach to Library and Information Services*, 2nd Ed.; Libraries Unlimited: Westport, CT, 2004.

15. Choo, C.W. *The Knowing Organization: How Organizations Use Information to Construct Meaning, Create Knowledge, and Make Decisions*, 2nd Ed.; Oxford University Press: London, U.K., 2006.

16. Olson, H.A. The power to name: Representation in library catalogs. Signs **2001**, *26* (3), 639–68.

17. Dervin, B.; Dewdney, P. Neutral questioning: A new approach to the reference interview. Ref. Quart. **1986**, *25* (4), 506–513.

18. Abbott, A.D. *The System of Professions: An Essay on the Division of Expert Labor*; University of Chicago Press: Chicago, IL, 1988.

19. Narrative, Envisioning Our Information Future and How to Educate For, https://slis.simmons.edu/blogs/ourinformation future/ (accessed January 15, 2015).

Library and Information Technology Association (LITA)

Rachel E. Vacek
University of Michigan, Ann Arbor, Michigan, U.S.A.

Abstract

The Library and Information Technology Association (LITA) is a division of the American Library Association (ALA), established in 1966. Through publishing, programs, training, national conferences, and strategic partnerships, LITA educates, serves, and reaches out to its members, ALA members and divisions, and the entire library and information technology community through the promotion and implementation of library automation and technology.

INTRODUCTION

The Library and Information Technology Association (LITA) is a division of the American Library Association (ALA). The division began in 1966 as the Information Science and Automation Division (ISAD) and became LITA in 1972. LITA's mission statement, adopted in May 1999, begins with its strategic mission "to educate, serve, and reach out" to the library community through the use and promotion of information technology. LITA celebrated its fiftieth anniversary in 2016.

LITA VISION

As the center of expertise about information technology, LITA leads in exploring and enabling new technologies to empower libraries. LITA members use the promise of technology to deliver dynamic library collections and services.

LITA MISSION

LITA educates, serves, and reaches out to its members, other ALA members and divisions, and the entire library and information community through its publications, programs, and other activities designed to promote, develop, and aid in the implementation of library and information technology.

FUNCTION STATEMENT

LITA is concerned with the planning, development, design, application, and integration of technologies within the library and information environment, with the impact of emerging technologies on library service, and with the effect of automated technologies on people. Its major focus is on interdisciplinary issues and emerging technologies. LITA disseminates information, provides educational opportunities for learning about information technologies and forums for the discussion of common concerns, monitors new technologies with potential applications in information science, encourages and fosters research, promotes the development of technical standards, and examines the effects of library systems and networks.

MEMBERSHIP

LITA membership (Table 1), like any organization, has increased and decreased over the course of its existence. Although LITA was established in 1966, members were not able to join until 1967. Initial membership started at 2334 people, and LITA membership peaked in 1993 with 5802 members. LITA's membership, like all the other ALA divisions, has been in decline since the early 2000s.

GOVERNING STRUCTURE

LITA is governed by a Board of Directors headed by the president (Table 2). In addition to the president, the Board includes the vice-president/president-elect, the immediate past president, the LITA/ALA councilor (representative of LITA on ALA's governing council), and seven directors at large. Ex officio members include the executive director (Table 3) of the division, the chair of the Bylaws and Organization Committee, and the chair of the Financial Advisory Committee.

The Executive Committee of the board is composed of the president, the vice-president, the past president, the LITA/ALA councilor, and one director chosen by the board each year, with the executive director being an ex officio member. The Board of Directors meets virtually and at every ALA Annual and Midwinter Conference, as

Encyclopedia of Library and Information Sciences, Fourth Edition DOI: 10.1081/E-ELIS4-120053447
Copyright © 2017 by Taylor & Francis. All rights reserved.

Law Literature–Library Architecture

Table 1 Information Science and Automation Division/ Library and Information Technology Association membership

Date	Total membership
2014	2,900
2013	3,116
2012	3,258
2011	3,444
2010	3,412
2009	3,587
2008	3,916
2007	4,338
2006	4,106
2005	4,054
2004	4,414
2003	4,611
2002	4,735
2001	4,910
2000	4,757

does the Executive Committee. In addition, the Executive Committee meets virtually every spring and in-person in the fall near the ALA headquarters in Chicago, IL. The functions of LITA are carried out by approximately 50 committees and interest groups, most of which conduct business and hold meetings virtually, as well as at every ALA Conference.

HISTORY

Early Years

LITA's history, through approximately 1973, was delineated in the first edition of the *Encyclopedia of Library and Information Sciences*; the entry was entitled "Information Science and Automation Division (ISAD)." Going back to its earliest incarnation as the autonomous and unaffiliated "Coalition on Library Automation (COLA)" in the early 1960s, the group that would lay the foundation for today's LITA grappled with an issue that is still with the division today, that is, interest in technology runs across existing ALA divisions and types of libraries. From its inception, LITA has maintained a balance of service to other divisions, the library technology, and vendor community, and the ALA membership as a whole. To that end, LITA has consistently worked to develop and maintain a flexible, adaptable structure that focuses on facilitating education and information exchange to help those interested in the use of computer technology in library and information-related organizations to better perform their work.

In the same year as the retirement of ISAD's first executive secretary, 1973, then division president Ralph Shoffner appointed an Objectives Committee chaired by Stephen Salmon, ISAD's first president, to determine whether the division should continue. Concluding that the division's functions warranted continuation, new

Table 2 Information Science and Automation Division/ Library and Information Technology Association presidents

Date	Name
1966–1967	Stephen R. Salmon
1967–1968	Joseph Becker
1968–1969	Russell Shank
1969–1970	Robert M. Hayes
1970–1971	Richard DeGennaro
1971–1972	Jesse H. Shera
1972–1973	Ralph M. Shoffner
1973–1975	Frederick G. Kilgour
1975–1976	Henriette B. Avram
1976–1977	Joseph A. Rosenthal
1977–1978	Maurice J. Freedman
1978–1979	Susan K. Martin
1979–1980	Barbara E. Markuson
1980–1981	S. Michael Malinconico
1981–1982	Brigitte L. Kenney
1982–1983	Carolyn M. Gray
1983–1984	Kenneth Dowlin
1984–1985	Nancy L. Eaton
1985–1986	Lois M. Kershner
1986–1987	Raymond DeBuse
1987–1988	William Gray Potter
1988–1989	Sherrie Schmidt
1989–1990	Carol A. Parkhurst
1990–1991	Jo-Ann Michalak
1991–1992	Paul Evan Peters
1992–1993	Walt Crawford
1993–1994	Tamara J. Miller
1994–1995	Nancy K. Roderer
1995–1996	Michele Dalehite (née Newberry)
1996–1997	Thomas W. Leonhardt
1997–1998	Linda D. Miller
1998–1999	Barbra B. Higginbotham
1999–2000	Michael J. Gorman
2000–2001	Sara L. Randall
2001–2002	Florence J. Wilson
2002–2003	Pat Ensor
2003–2004	Thomas Wilson
2004–2005	Colby Riggs
2005–2006	Patrick Mullin
2006–2007	Bonnie Postlethwaite
2007–2008	Mark Beatty
2008–2009	Andrew K. Pace
2009–2010	Michelle Frisque
2010–2011	Karen Starr
2011–2012	Colleen Cudy
2012–2013	Zoe Stewart-Marshall
2013–2014	Cindi Trainor Blyberg
2014–2015	Rachel E. Vacek
2015–2016	Thomas Dowling
2016–2017	Aimee Fifarek
2017–2018	Andromeda Yelton
2018–2019	Bohyun Kim

objectives were created that highlighted ISAD's programs, advisory services, publications, discussion groups, and standards promotion; the group's objectives were then revised accordingly.

Law Literature–Library Architecture

Table 3 Information Science and Automation Division/ Library and Information Technology Association executive directors

Date	Name
1967–1973	Don S. Culbertson
1973–1986	Donald P. Hammer
1987–1995	Linda J. Knutson
1996	Lillian Lewis (acting)
1996–2001	Jacqueline Mundell
2001–2015	Mary Taylor
2015–	Jenny Levine

Following the restatement of purpose, and with the approval of the membership, ISAD changed its name to the Library and Information Technology Association. Various early division periodical publications were subsumed in 1973 into the referred *Journal of Library Automation* (*JOLA*). In 1982, the journal's editors selected a new name more reflective of the name change of the division and *JOLA* became *Information Technology and Libraries* (*ITAL*; Table 4). A *LITA Newsletter* was published from 1979 to 2000. Issues from Spring 1995 to Summer 2000 were published electronically, with issues from Winter 1997 to Summer 2000 being available only in electronic format. An abbreviated supplement, *LITA Notes*, was published as part of *ITAL* from 1997 through March 2000. The *LITA Newsletter* editors included Pat Barkalow, Carol Parkhurst, Walt Crawford, Gail Junion-Metz, and Martin Kalfatovic. Since 2000, the LITA news function has been subsumed by the divisional website and blog, as well as periodic electronic mailings to the membership.

With the goal of greater member participation in the division, and with objectives and a name change firmly in place, LITA underwent a major reorganization in 1984– 1985. Many of the committees were restructured, and LITA went back to its COLA discussion group roots to encourage the creation of varied interest groups. Ten or more LITA members could petition to form an interest group in a library/information technology topic; if the

Table 4 *Journal of Library Automation/Information Technology and Libraries* editors

Date	Name
1968–1971	Frederick G. Kilgour
1972	A.J. Goldwyn
1973–1977, 1980	Susan K. Martin
1978–1979	William D. Mathews
1981–1983	Brian Aveney
1984–1989	William Gray Potter
1990–1995	Thomas W. Leonhardt
1996–1998	James J. Kopp
1999–2004	Dan K. Marmion
2004–2007	John Webb
2007–2011	Marc Truitt
2011–2017	Robert Gerrity

interest group's formation was approved—and the vast majority are to this day—by the LITA Board, the group can elect officers, organize discussions, put on programs, create publications, and perform other educational and information exchange functions. New interest groups are formed and disbanded on a regular basis; at any given time, 15–20 interest groups are active in the division. This model reflects the ever-changing landscape in information technology.

Another major initiative that began in the late 1970s/ early 1980s is the provision of sponsored awards and scholarships that support achievement and study in library and information technology. Stemming from this time period are the LITA/Gaylord Award for Achievement in Library and Information Technology, LITA participation in the multidivisional Hugh C. Atkinson Memorial Award, and the LITA/Computer Library Services, Inc. (later the LITA/GEAC) scholarship to encourage entry into the library automation field.

High demand for workshops and face-to-face discussions also led to the creation of National Conferences in the 1980s and 1990s. These large-scale multiple-day gatherings involved presentation of papers, vendor exhibits, workshops, and computer demonstrations. The national conferences in Baltimore (1983), Boston (1988), and Denver (1992) were well attended and financially successful.

The Internet Era

Trends within the LITA division can be tracked along with those throughout the other divisions, libraries, and even the world at large. These trends and influences include the decline of the spending power of libraries, an increasingly rapid pace of change in technology, the growing attention to empowering diverse population groups, the advent and spectacular growth of the Internet as a worldwide network, the rapid improvements in computing power, and a resulting exponential increase in the amount of available electronic content.

As it became clear that no area of libraries—and no type of library—would be untouched by information technology, and, therefore, that most library organizations became concerned by technology topics, LITA shifted its focus and identity to leadership in the more advanced use of technology in libraries and other related organizations. The 1990s also cemented the role of systems librarians— degreed professionals with added expertise in hardware, software, networks, and computing—establishing LITA as the logical division for these professionals' participation. LITA also emerged as a home for a growing number of information science and IT professionals who are not librarians.

In 1996, the supposed last LITA National Conference was cosponsored by the Library Administration and Management Association division and held in Pittsburgh,

Law Literature–Library Architecture

Table 5 LITA National conference/national forum venues

LITA National conference/national forum

Date	Place
1983	Baltimore, Maryland
1988	Boston, Massachusetts
1992	Denver, Colorado
1996	Pittsburgh, Pennsylvania
1998	Oakland, California
1999	Raleigh, North Carolina
2000	Portland, Oregon
2001	Milwaukee, Wisconsin
2002	Houston, Texas
2003	Norfolk, Virginia
2004	St. Louis, Missouri
2005	San Jose, California
2006	Nashville, Tennessee
2007	Denver, Colorado
2008	Cincinnati, Ohio
2009	Salt Lake City, Utah
2010	Atlanta, Georgia
2011	Columbus, Ohio
2012	Louisville, Kentucky
2013	St. Louis, Missouri
2014	Albuquerque, New Mexico
2015	Minneapolis, Minnesota
2016	Fort Worth, Texas
2017	Denver, Colorado

Pennsylvania. Despite good attendance and feedback from participants, the expenses and the 3-yr planning cycle of the endeavor led LITA to determine that this was not the best method for continuing its own major conference. In 1998, LITA had its first annual National Forum. Taking place in Oakland, California, the more focused format was an immediate success. Education opportunities, attendee satisfaction, divisional revenue, and the development of training opportunities through regional institutes and preconferences continue to make LITA Forum a popular annual event (Table 5).

LITA became an early supporter of the move to encourage diversity in the library profession by creating the LITA/OCLC and LITA/Library Systems and Services, Inc. minority scholarships in Library and Information Technology. Additional awards and scholarships created in the 1990s have included the LITA/Ex Libris Student Writing Award, the Frederick G. Kilgour Award for Research in Library and Information Technology (jointly sponsored by LITA and OCLC), and the LITA/Christian Larew Memorial Scholarship (sponsored by Baker & Taylor). The LITA/Library Hi Tech Award (sponsored by LITA and Emerald Press) rewards innovation and scholarship in library technology. Awarded each year, these competitive awards not only engage the partnership of sponsors, but give a meaningful leg up to new professionals and reward those most active in library technology. The LITA/Brett Butler Entrepreneurship Award (sponsored by LITA and Gale) was retired in 2009.

LITA was also a pioneer among library associations in the area of electronic communications. An electronic edition of the *LITA Newsletter* was first published in 1995. The first electronic-only serial publication by a division of ALA, Telecommunication Electronic Reviews (TER), appeared in 1994 and spawned many imitators. In 2009, LITA retired TER in favor of community-based blog and wiki communication platforms. LITA garnered the thanks of ALA members at large by originating Internet rooms at ALA conferences, setting up and managing the Internet rooms at seven ALA Annual and Midwinter conferences from 1993 through 1996.

In 1996, the LITA website, http://www.lita.org, was created, as was the LITA electronic discussion list, LITA-L. In 1998, LITA created an online jobs list—"Jobs in Library and Information Technology" that has been heavily used by job posters and job seekers since then.

Twenty-First Century

With the advent of weblogs, social software, and group-edited wiki sites, LITA established an online presence for open participation and discussion of library technology issues with its LITA Blog (litablog.org) in 2005 and LITA Wiki (wikis.ala.org/lita) in 2006. Many of the members instrumental in establishing a foothold with these technologies established the Blogs, Interactive Groupware Wikis Interest Group (BIGWIG). In 2008, BIGWIG launched Your BIGWIG (yourbigwig.com) and established itself as the leading social software discussion group within ALA. BIGWIG hosted the extremely well attended Social Software Showcase, an "unconference" that occurred both virtually and physically at every ALA Annual Conference. However, as more structure for social technology was needed within LITA, and as other divisions, roundtables, committees, and interest groups embraced social software, BIGWIG's purpose had been served, and in 2011, the interest group retired.

In 2009, ALA had also created a new tool called ALA Connect (connect.ala.org), which was intended to be the centralized space where both unofficial and official ALA groups are able to work together online. This content management system, built on the open-source Drupal platform, greatly impacted LITA. Having multiple web-based tools for different purposes can be helpful, but managing content and having working spaces across a blog, wiki, website, and within ALA Connect seemed to be a few too many places. It became unclear on each tool's purpose. It was decided in 2011 that the LITA Web Coordinating Committee would manage the Blog and Wiki. Then in 2012, the Wiki was retired and LITA members were encouraged to use ALA Connect as a workspace for all committee and interest group business.

ALA Connect has also served the LITA Board and Executive Committee as a place to organize and share meeting notes, vote on issues, and engage with the

Law Literature–Library Architecture

community in new ways. Posts can be marked as public or private, and users can add comments, attachments, create polls, make meeting time requests, or even chat, all within ALA Connect. It has significantly helped make more accessible the intuitional memory of LITA's digital presence.

During the mid-2000s, capturing and then immediately sharing the digital recordings of speakers, board meetings, and major events like the Top Technology Trends, the President's Program, or keynote speakers at the LITA Forum became extremely important to LITA. Travel to conferences was financially challenging for many people at this time due to library travel funds being reduced or cut completely. Consequently, the desire to participate virtually (such as watching a live stream while discussing the event through a Twitter backchannel) was increasing. Many of LITA's educational events were streamed live, or were recorded and made available at later times. Jason Griffey, LITA Board Member (2011–2014), was the primary source for audio and video equipment, provided the recording expertise and posted the digitized events for LITA for most of the past decade.

During the late 2000s, LITA's online presence continued to expand. LITA engaged and informed current and potential members on social media sites like YouTube, Twitter, and Facebook. Additionally, more educational opportunities were being created for virtual consumption. Perhaps the most significant online transition was that of LITA's peer-reviewed journal, *Information Technology and Libraries* (*ITAL*), which moved from a print format to a free journal with unrestricted online access. The transition to being an open-access journal took approximately 2 yrs, between 2010 and 2012. Embarking on an e-publishing model only has helped ensure the long-term viability of *ITAL* by making it more accessible, more current, more relevant, and more environmentally friendly. *ITAL* continues to feature high-quality articles that have undergone a rigorous peer-review process, but it also expanded content to include more case studies, commentary, and information about topics and trends of interest to the LITA community and beyond. Although many LITA members helped with the open-access transition, key people included Kristin Antelman, Bob Gerrity, Maurice York, and Michelle Frisque.

Over the past 15 yrs, almost all the divisions of ALA experienced financial challenges and saw a trend of flat or declining membership, and LITA was no exception. In 2012, the LITA Financial Strategies Task Force was established under President Zoe Stewart-Marshall (2012–2013) to reexamine existing financial strategies and revenue sources for the Division and identify strategies based upon a sustainable infrastructure to allow LITA to continue to provide valued networking and educational opportunities by and to its members. Their final report, full of short-term and long-term recommendations, was presented to the Board in early 2014. Later that year,

under President Cindi Blyberg (2013–2014), the Financial Advisory Committee was established. Many of the recommendations will continue to be reviewed and implemented in years to come.

In addition to creation of the Financial Advisory Committee, other changes were made to LITA committees in the 2000s and early part of the decade. In 2008, the Assessment and Research Committee was formed to work with other LITA groups to assess progress against the strategic goals through the collection and assessment of data and feedback. This committee, like many others, originally started out as a task force that was charged to conduct research and present a final report to the Board with future recommendations.

In 2012, a Metadata Standards Committee was established that has appointed membership from LITA, the Association for Library Collections & Technical Services, and the Reference & User Services Association. In 2014, the Board voted to disband both the International Relations Committee and the Technology and Access Committee because much of the work of these committees was being done at the ALA level, and these committees had been created at a time when there was not as much focus on these topics in libraries.

Later in 2014, president Rachel Vacek saw the need to help LITA streamline, improve branding, and more effectively communicate across LITA's virtual presence and proposed to the Board a committee to help with these efforts. In October 2014, the Communications and Marketing Committee was created. To compliment these communication efforts, the Web Coordinating Committee also hired a blog manager, Brianna Marshall, who along with a dozen dedicated blog writers, have a goal to revitalize LITA's blog and social media presence. In a short few months, organic reach and engagement had explosive growth and positive feedback from members and nonmembers alike.

STRATEGIC FUNCTIONS AND MAIN PROGRAMS

In 1998–1999, under the presidency of Barbra Buckner Higginbotham and the leadership of president-elect and future ALA president Michael Gorman, LITA went through a process of reexamining its strategic directions, resulting in a sharpened and renewed focus on educating, serving, and reaching out. Many LITA activities fulfill more than one of these objectives that help LITA maintain its status for IT leadership within ALA in particular and libraries in general.

Under the initial leadership of president Colby Riggs (2004–2005), the LITA Board of Directors approved its first detailed strategic plan for the years 2005–2008. Establishing the Mission, Vision, and Function of the division, the plan set a tactical objective to fulfill its strategy to educate, serve, and reach out, established in the late 1990s.

Law Literature–Library Architecture

President Michelle Frisque (2009–2010) and the LITA Board led the creation of LITA's second ambitious strategic plan for the years 2008–2011 that focused on the organization, innovation, training and continuing education, collaboration and outreach, and advocacy and policy. Input was gathered through surveys, open forums, and the LITA Town Meetings at ALA Midwinter conferences. From 2013 to 2015, the work of the LITA Board focused on four goal statements from the previous Strategic Plan. The division's principal focus on education, publishing, and networking remained the same, but other ideas including collaboration, advocacy, and infrastructure were incorporated. These concepts have been central to the Board's and the membership's work over the past several years and reflect the LITA gestalt.

EDUCATION

In the area of education, LITA presents 15–20 programs at every ALA Annual Conference on a wide variety of technology-related topics, such data management, linked data, web analytics, search engine optimization, user experience, digital libraries, graphical information systems, and languages like Python or XML. Popular programs, such as Top Technology Trends, the Ultimate Debate, and the President's Program draw large crowds and are immensely popular. In addition, two preconferences are scheduled along with every Annual Conference, allowing more in-depth presentations of specific topics. Such daylong workshops are also sometimes presented as regional institutes, as previously noted, often in partnership with other associations and agencies. The annual LITA National Forum is perhaps the most popular educational venue.

However, despite all success of the in-person educational offerings, the advent of new technologies has also given LITA the opportunity to create new strategies for virtual education, unconstrained by time and place. These strategies have created numerous opportunities for members and nonmembers alike. Webinars and online courses taught over the course of multiple weeks and utilizing Adobe Connect, a web conferencing platform, have become increasingly popular and have become a great revenue-generating avenue for LITA to explore more and expand.

LITA's publications have long served as a source of excellent education in library and information technology. In addition to the open-access periodical, *ITAL*, almost since its inception, LITA has published monographic works of great value to the library and information technology community, and many LITA members are active in library science publishing. A drop-off in the production and profitability of monographic publishing has led LITA to focus on the publication of brief, practical, useful handbooks—*LITA Guides*—for the use of technology in libraries and related institutions. *ITAL* continues to attract serious scholarly additions to the field of library automation, digital libraries, systems, and web technology.

SERVICE

Of course, the efforts listed under the function of education can also be considered part of LITA's service objective. The LITA website has become the focus of LITA's provision of services to the library and information technology community. In addition to the previously mentioned online "Jobs in Library and Information Technology" site, LITA has drawn on the expertise of individual members and subgroups of LITA to provide information and recommendations on a variety of subjects.

In addition to the resources available on the main LITA website, the library and information technology community continually benefits from virtual activities of LITA members. Most conference activities are actively blogged and tweeted by participants, not only creating a record of the activity, but a forum in which those not in attendance can be updated and participate in topical discussions.

LITA has sponsored one or two LITA members almost every year to participate in ALA Emerging Leaders program. The Emerging Leaders program is designed to develop the next generation of library leaders from across the country to participate in problem-solving workgroups, network with peers, gain an inside look into ALA structure, and have an opportunity to serve the profession in a leadership capacity. By sponsoring ALA Emerging Leaders, LITA has an opportunity to help create new leaders while benefiting from the participation of that new leader in the work of the division. Projects are approved by the Board and have focused on service to LITA through creating documentation, workflows, orientation materials, and new programs, as well as providing recommendations on branding, collaborations, and web tools. These emerging leaders have been instrumental to moving forward new ideas and needed change within the organization, and continuing to support this valuable initiative has been a priority of the LITA Board since the programs' inception in 2007.

OUTREACH

LITA's outreach objective is aimed at "a broad membership, new professionals, systems librarians, library administrators, and vendors." Of course, many of the projects mentioned above are also efforts to reach out. In addition, LITA works closely with ALA's Office for Information Technology Policy and is a member of other related organizations, such as the Coalition for Networked Information and EDUCAUSE.

Law Literature–Library Architecture

LITA is also involved with the creation, promotion, and endorsement of newly developed standards and maintains a close working relationship with the National Information Standards Organization. New initiatives aimed at more technical audiences, such as Code4Lib, and administered by groups such as the Digital Library Federation also include the participation of many LITA members and volunteers.

FUTURE DIRECTIONS

LITA will continue other efforts to make use of electronic communication practices, social software use, and online education and publication to support organization activities. "Virtual membership" and participation on committees continue to increase, and many groups within LITA conduct business between meetings via virtual methods. LITA's web presence—website, blog, ALA Connect, and social media channels—will continue to be the home of new educational efforts and useful material for LITA members. LITA is also an eager partner with ALA in its efforts to improve virtual membership and participation, including online communities, e-commerce functions, and social networking. LITA will also continue to partner with ALA in finding solutions to technology challenges such as net neutrality, E-Rate, broadband, copyright, and open access to digital content.

Moving forward with the development of a new strategic direction under the leadership of president Thomas Dowling (2015–2016), LITA will continue its theme of educating, serving, and advocating, even if the tactics in doing so change. Continued recruitment to the division of nonlibrarians, other divisional members, and professionals new to the field will be vital in moving forward. LITA is a division whose direction comes from its leaders and staff, but whose strength comes from its volunteer membership.

BIBLIOGRAPHY

1. Culbertson, D.S. Information Science and Automation Division (ISAD), ALA. In *Encyclopedia of Library and Information Science*; 1st Ed.; Kent, A., Lancour, H., Daily, J.E., Eds.; Marcel Dekker, Inc.: New York, 1968–1998; Vol. 11, 495–500.
2. Ensor, P. Library and information technology association. Encycloped. Libr. Inform. Sci. **2003**, *1* (1), 1653–1656.
3. LITA Strategic Plan. 2005–2008, Library and Information Technology Association Strategic Plan for 2005–2008, http://www.lita.org/ala/lita/aboutlita/org/plan.cfm (accessed May 23, 2017).
4. LITA Strategic Plan. 2008–2011, LITA Strategic Plan: Goals & Objectives, 2008–2011, http://www.ala.org/lita/sites/ala.org.lita/files/content/about/strategic/2010-strategic.pdf (accessed May 23, 2017).
5. Pace, A.K. Library and information technology association. Encyclopedia of Library and Information Science 2009.
6. Salmon, S.R. LITA's first twenty-five years: A brief history. Inform. Technol. Libr. **1993**, *12* (1), 15–35.

Library Anxiety

Diane Mizrachi
University Libraries, University of California–Los Angeles, Los Angeles, California, U.S.A.

Abstract

Library anxiety is the negative, overwhelming feelings and emotions often experienced when needing to use a library that was first studied by Constance Mellon in 1986. She identified four sources for the students' anxieties: 1) the relative size of the library; 2) not knowing where resources were located; 3) not knowing how to begin library research; and 4) not knowing how to proceed with library research. Earlier studies had begun to investigate library interactions from the users' viewpoint, and the widespread recognition of Mellon's findings invigorated further exploration of this particular phenomenon. The development of the Library Anxiety Scale enabled quantitative measurements among large groups of students in the United States and abroad. Researchers using the LAS found five factors of library anxiety and identified characteristics and antecedents most closely associated with this occurrence. Knowing which groups of users are most at risk and developing the most appropriate approaches for intervention and alleviation are important steps to efficient library service to all.

INTRODUCTION

"A former Olympic silver medalist, known to be fearless in her sport, was a college student in a library session I taught. Afterwards she confided to me, 'I really recognized myself when you spoke of library anxiety. I've always been scared of libraries.' She was unafraid to perform in front of the whole world but afraid of libraries, a perfect illustration of how fear can be an individual and very personal construct." (Personal experience of the author, January 2014.)

Library anxiety is the feeling of being overwhelmed, intimidated, nervous, uncertain, or confused when using or contemplating use of the library and its resources to satisfy an information need. It is a state-based anxiety that can result in misconceptions or misapplications of library resources, procrastination, and avoidance of library tasks. Public service librarians have long noticed this type of behavior, and pioneering studies of the reference interview process and users' perceptions of libraries and librarians provided impetus for theoretical development. In 1986, Constance Mellon published her seminal study in which she compared her own analysis to similarities found in the education and psychology fields on math and test anxiety, and coined the term "library anxiety." Librarians and researchers were quick to recognize it as a distinct phenomenon of library user behavior.

Development of the Library Anxiety Scale (LAS) by Sharon Bostick in 1992 enabled researchers to measure this phenomenon quantitatively and explore the factors and characteristics of library anxiety among a broad population. It was discovered that library anxiety and its debilitating effects are found among all levels of undergraduates, graduates, and doctoral students, as well as among students

in different countries. Some researchers have looked at library anxiety within the context of the information seeking process (ISP) and its respective cognitive and emotional aspects as defined by Carol Kuhlthau in her ISP model. Since the publication of Mellon's grounded theory, a knowledge base for understanding the characteristics of those affected by library anxiety, and its factors, antecedents, and outcomes has been developed, but there still remain many questions and areas for further research and exploration.

HISTORY AND THEORETICAL BASIS

Historically, the research of public service librarianship focused on measurements of system interactions, circulation statistics, patron demographics, and policy developments without much investigation into library user experiences. By the late 1960s, theoreticians began calling for librarians to think about services from their users' perspective. Issues raised for consideration included patron's cognitive state when thinking about an information need, the question-negotiation process of the reference interview, causes of user frustration when seeking information, and why patrons might decide not to seek assistance at all. A greater emphasis on communication and interpersonal skills training for librarians and attention to the social dynamics of the user community were suggested in order to increase understanding and lessen both librarian and user frustration. Many factors later recognized as components of library anxiety surfaced in pioneering studies of the 1970s. These included the perception of librarians as being preoccupied or rude, and patron reluctance to ask for help for fear of ridicule by librarians. One study

Encyclopedia of Library and Information Sciences, Fourth Edition DOI: 10.1081/E-EISA-120053504

Copyright © 2017 by Taylor & Francis. All rights reserved.

found that 65% of the students would not ask a librarian for assistance with their specific need because they did not want to disturb the librarian, felt their questions were too basic, or had experienced dissatisfaction with a previous librarian interaction.[1] Such findings help explain the conclusion of another study that up to half of all patrons leave the library without obtaining the book they are seeking.[2] Yet researchers continued to decry the significant lack of user studies among the literature, particularly behavioral research into how people interact with information and libraries. By the early 1980s, information increased in complexity and availability, and became more crucial in people's everyday lives. Libraries were employing new automated and computerized systems and patrons were faced with the challenges of learning to cope in this rapidly changing environment. New theories and methodologies were needed to research how people react with information, which was obviously more complicated than just "getting it" or "having it."[3]

Brenda Dervin and Michael Nilan reviewed the literature on research of information needs and uses from 1978 to 1986 and note a subtle but noticeable change in the epistemological approaches of library and information researchers. They perceive a gradual shift to the inclusion of more varieties of measurements and methods; from the strictly traditional scientific approach that measures user interaction with information through quantitative means, to more alternative approaches that recognize information as constructed by humans whose behavior can and should be measured through qualitative as well as quantitative methods. Calling this shift a "quantum and conceptual leap" in the field, they encouraged more researchers to take up their challenge to invent "new ways of looking at users and linking systems to them."[4]

MELLON'S GROUNDED THEORY OF LIBRARY ANXIETY

Like many public service librarians, Constance Mellon had long noticed the anxieties and hesitations many students displayed when using the library. She felt a more efficient library instruction program would help alleviate the problem, but had to convince skeptic faculty and administration of the need. For 2 years, she analyzed the journals of over 6000 first-year English composition students in which they recorded their process and emotions as they conducted research for their term papers. Entries from these journals were analyzed using the constant comparative method by which recurrent themes were discovered. Mellon found that 75%–85% of her student participants described their initial library encounters in terms of anxiety and fear.

Terms like *scary, overpowering, lost, helpless, overwhelming, confused,* and *fear of the unknown* were used repeatedly by the students. She noticed a striking similarity to research in math and test anxieties, and felt that this new phenomena should also be considered within the anxiety framework. Mellon called her grounded theory "library anxiety."[5]

Mellon identified four sources for the students' anxieties: 1) the relative size of the library; 2) not knowing where resources were located; 3) not knowing how to begin library research; and 4) not knowing how to proceed with library research. Embarrassment over their lack of competence drove their anxieties deeper; it seemed that all the other students knew what to do in the library and only they did not. They felt their lack of library skills was shameful and were afraid to reveal their inadequacies, or "look dumb," by asking a librarian for assistance. She states that students became so overwhelmed and "anxious about having to gather information in a library for their research paper that they are unable to approach the problem logically or effectively."[6]

Professionals in library and academic fields have successfully used libraries for many years and may not remember or realize how intimidating the institution can be for many people. Mellon stresses that librarians and educators must acknowledge library anxiety as a common, legitimate phenomenon, and create encouraging and successful experiences for the students in order to alleviate the anxiety. She notes that students' anxieties lessened after encounters with professional librarians and encourages more personal contact between librarians and students to help them see the library as truly relevant to their academic needs with friendly and helpful professionals to assist them.[5]

THE ISP

Two years after the publication of Mellon's seminal study, Carol Kuhlthau began publishing results of her groundbreaking investigations into the emotional aspects of research. The two studies do not indicate any influence of one on the other, but similar methodologies were used and parallel results were found. Kuhlthau based her epistemology primarily upon ideas of personal construct theory. She developed a model of six stages of the ISP and describes the emotions, thoughts, tasks, and actions typical of each. Kuhlthau identified stages 3 and 4 of the ISP, exploration and formulation, as critical from the seekers' emotional perspective. She found the exploration stage, when seekers are looking for general information about their topic in order to broaden their own understandings and construct new knowledge into their already existing knowledge, as fraught with increasing feelings of doubt, uncertainty, and confusion. The users often become discouraged and, especially at this stage, their sense of inadequacy may be so heightened that they abandon their task altogether. By the next stage, formulation, the users have succeeded in breaking through the threatening doubts of their earlier explorations and managed to focus their topic and the information they retrieve.[7] These anxious feelings found in the ISP, especially at the information exploration stage, strengthen Mellon's findings of the highly emotional experiences of many students when conducting library research.

Librarians had long observed behaviors of library anxiety and knew anecdotally that it existed, but no one before Mellon had so precisely studied and labeled it. Recognition of Mellon's theory generated numerous discussions and studies of the influence of library user behavior, library graphics, bibliographic instruction, and the ISP on library anxiety. By 1992, a reliable instrument was developed to measure library anxiety quantitatively.

BOSTICK'S LIBRARY ANXIETY SCALE

Influenced by Mellon's research identifying library anxiety, Sharon Bostick developed the LAS in order to discover whether the phenomena could be measured quantitatively. It is a questionnaire consisting of 43 Likert-type statements relying on self-reporting by the participants and tested an internal consistency of 0.80 using Cronbach's alpha coefficient. Through her study, Bostick identified five dimensions of library anxiety:

1. *Barriers with the staff*: Feelings by students that the librarians and library staff were preoccupied or unapproachable for assistance
2. *Affective barriers*: The "not knowing what to do in the library" situation first identified by Mellon
3. *Comfort with the library*: The physical comfort level students felt in the library building
4. *Knowledge of the library*: Knowing where things are located and how to find their way around in the building
5. *Mechanical barriers*: The perceived reliability and ease of using the library's printers, photocopiers, computers, etc.[8]

In subsequent studies, reliability measures of the complete LAS have been as high as Cronbach's alpha 0.92,[9] and independent measurements of each of the five dimensions all confirm the scale's reliability. Since the advent of more online, electronic and offsite library resources and services, there have been calls and attempts to modify the LAS to better reflect this new environment. The Multidimensional Library Anxiety Scale (MLAS) integrates online research attitudes and the principles of Kuhlthau's ISP into the original LAS, specifically for measuring library anxiety and perceptions among doctoral students.[10] Most subsequent quantitative studies use the LAS, MLAS, or modified versions of either.

JIAO AND ONWUEGBUZIE QUANTITATIVE STUDIES

Through their prolific studies using the LAS, Anthony J. Onwuegbuzie and Qun G. Jiao have identified many of the characteristics and situations of students most at risk for library anxiety; demographic patterns, learning preferences, personality traits, study habits and behavioral characteristics most closely associated with library anxiety; and the relationship between social interdependence and library anxiety. Participants in their studies include undergraduates, graduate and doctoral students, and results indicate that library anxiety is found among all segments of these populations—it is not a phenomenon limited to first-year students and novice researchers. Jiao and Onwuegbuzie conducted much of their research by surveying large groups of students using the LAS and one or more other instruments that measure behavioral or demographic characteristics. They were thus able to identify major factors associated with each of Bostick's five dimensions of library anxiety as well factors relating to library anxiety in general.[11]

Major factors associated with high levels of library anxiety include

- A non-English native language
- Working full- or part-time while studying
- Not being a frequent visitor to the library
- Being a high achiever
- Displaying high levels of perfectionism
- Not receiving library instruction
- Negative self-perception in scholastic competence, intellectual ability, creativity, and social acceptance
- Low cooperative attitudes in group tasks
- Poor study habits

Another important finding is that library anxiety is a state-based anxiety, an independent phenomenon from trait anxiety, meaning that being affected by library anxiety does not necessarily indicate having a high-anxiety personality.

Onwuegbuzie, Jiao, and Bostick gathered findings from several studies into three categories of antecedents that interact to determine the overall level of library anxiety:

- Dispositional—particular personality traits
- Situational—the environment of the particular stimulus
- Environmental—the demographic factors

This is illustrated in their model of conceptualization of antecedents of library anxiety in Fig. 1.[12]

INTERNATIONAL STUDENTS IN US INSTITUTIONS

Studies involving international students in American universities consistently show their levels of library anxiety to be much higher than their American peers. International

Law Literature–Library Architecture

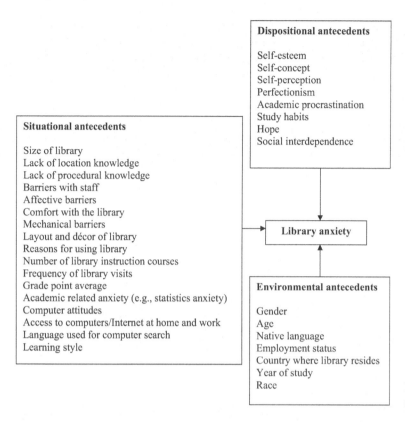

Situational antecedents

Size of library
Lack of location knowledge
Lack of procedural knowledge
Barriers with staff
Affective barriers
Comfort with the library
Mechanical barriers
Layout and décor of library
Reasons for using library
Number of library instruction courses
Frequency of library visits
Grade point average
Academic related anxiety (e.g., statistics anxiety)
Computer attitudes
Access to computers/Internet at home and work
Language used for computer search
Learning style

Dispositional antecedents

Self-esteem
Self-concept
Self-perception
Perfectionism
Academic procrastination
Study habits
Hope
Social interdependence

Library anxiety

Environmental antecedents

Gender
Age
Native language
Employment status
Country where library resides
Year of study
Race

Fig. 1 Conceptualization of antecedents of library anxiety.

students visit the library more frequently and are more likely to participate in library instruction sessions than American students, so their anxiety is not related to those factors nor do they result in avoidance behavior. But there are many cultural differences, communication barriers, and challenges using English-language resources and search strategies with which these students must cope in their new environment. They often arrive with erroneous beliefs about the functions of American academic libraries such as the purposes for using the library and types of services offered, which may be very different from what they are used to in their home countries. Multiple sessions of information literacy instruction were shown to help alleviate library anxiety in one study.[13] But while there are many studies of international students' library behavior, only a few focus on library anxiety among this population. More research is needed to further identify the specific antecedents and develop mechanisms to help alleviate their anxieties.[14]

INTERNATIONAL STUDIES

Academic libraries worldwide vary greatly in their organization, cultures, philosophies, function within their institutions, user expectations, and interaction styles with their patrons. Until the early 2000s, nearly all studies of library anxiety were performed in American universities and institutions. Based on the research of Mellon, Bostick, Jiao,

Onwuegbuzie and others, researchers began exploring library anxiety outside of the United States, and results indicate that it is indeed an international phenomenon. Studies performed in England, Israel, Kuwait, Malaysia, Sudan, Canada, Poland, and China[15–22] show that while cultural differences do exist, students worldwide are affected by similar anxieties when using their academic libraries. Researchers used translations and modifications of Bostick's LAS in order to better reflect local culture. Analysis in each study produced slightly different factor groupings than the American studies, and the findings suggest that although library anxiety may be an international phenomenon, cultural context must always be considered when studying and measuring it.

INTERVENTIONS

Libraries engage in many proactive strategies to help educate their users and bring in new ones. They may not consciously be seeking specific mechanisms for reducing library anxiety, but with enough careful thought and planning, each individual effort can make a difference. Onwuegbuzie, Jiao, and Bostick categorize procedures into three types of approaches: library facilities and resources management, library instruction, and mediated informational services. Within each category, they place specific intervention strategies that address the various dimensions of library anxiety.[23]

Law Literature–Library Architecture

Library facilities and resources: This category includes all the strategies that librarians and library managers employ to make their facility and resources as user friendly and welcoming as possible, ensuring a pleasant atmosphere within the physical compound that will encourage the patron to return often and without hesitation. It directly addresses the third factor of library anxiety identified by Bostick, "comfort with the library," and can help alleviate Bostick's fourth factor, "knowledge of the library," and the fifth, "mechanical barriers." Strategies in this category include effective library signage and graphics, logical space and furniture arrangements, library tours, in-library computing labs, laptop stations and wireless availability, laptop lending, small group workrooms, coffee bars and snack areas, efficient document delivery systems, and fully functioning library consortia.

Even in this age of electronic library collections that enable users the convenience of accessing many resources and materials online, students still value the library building as a learning and study space. Outreach efforts to bring them into the library and help them become comfortable with staff and the facilities often include methods not formally associated with academic libraries. Toward the end of the term and during final exams for example, many libraries offer extended hours as well as free healthy snacks and other study-break treats known as stress busters—therapy dogs, free massages, origami and crafts corners, meditation, etc. Throughout the academic year, libraries also hold events including concerts, dances, poetry readings, contests, displays of student research, and exhibits targeted to student interest, all designed to raise library awareness, interest, and comfort levels.[24–26]

Library instruction: This category includes all types of information literacy instruction—teaching users how to identify an information need, locate, evaluate, and use information effectively and ethically. It directly addresses the cognitive obstructions that Bostick termed "affective barriers." Most instructional strategies, however, involve professional library staff, and this librarian/patron interaction can also help alleviate Bostick's first factor, "barriers with staff." Academic libraries today see instruction as one of their primary tasks, and they perform this through numerous ways such as classroom instruction; online tutorials; drop-in workshops; print and online help guides, and through multimedia technologies such as television broadcasts, webcasts, streaming video, and podcasts. Targeted outreach and marketing campaigns to raise student awareness of library resources and services, "putting a familiar face with the place," are also being used. Studies on the impact of bibliographic instruction on library anxiety show that in-person instruction can significantly reduce library anxiety among college students.[27–29]

Mediated informational services: This category includes the traditional reference services such as mediated reference assistance at the reference or information desk, active reference roving, and individualized information consultation,

but also includes chat reference services, reference through instant messaging, email, and online social network services.[30] Successful interactions with staff will help alleviate the "barriers with staff" factor, but depending on the content of reference or information query, the interaction may help dissipate any of Bostick's five factors.

The best strategies and procedures are secondary, of course, to a friendly, patient, welcoming, and effective library staff. The most efficient services and instruction devoid of any warmth solidifies preconceived perceptions of the rude and uncaring librarian and an intimidating institution.[31]

CONCLUSION

"Of all forms of academic-related anxiety, library anxiety appears to be the most common."[32] When Constance Mellon published her breakthrough study in which she systematically identified library anxiety two decades ago, practicing librarians finally had a name for the behavioral phenomenon they had observed for years. The library environment has experienced rapid change during this time, but the hesitations, inhibitions, confusion, and lack of self-confidence students often display when using or contemplating use of the library for an academic need are still in evidence. Various epistemological approaches and theories have been used to explore and explain this area of library and information user behavior. Through the use of Bostick's LAS and other research methods, library anxiety has been studied quantitatively among large heterogeneous groups of students, and prominent characteristics and antecedents of students most at risk for library anxiety have been identified. Studies of international students in American universities and research conducted outside the United States indicate that while cultural variations exist library anxiety is a global phenomenon.

Research of college students in academic libraries dominates the literature. Library anxiety among other populations, including people with disabilities, who are homeless, have immigrant status, or are elderly, and among other institutions such as public and school library users still need to be explored. In an age demanding information literate citizens, library anxiety research and understanding can be integrated into current information literacy initiatives and help shape information policy decisions.

REFERENCES

1. Swope, M.J.; Katzer, J. Why don't they ask questions? RQ **1972**, *12* (2), 161–166.
2. Saracevic, T.; Shaw, W.M., Jr. Causes and dynamics of user frustration in an academic library. Coll. Res. Libr. **1977**, *38* (1), 7–18.

Law Literature–Library Architecture

3. Fine, S. Research and the psychology of information use. Libr. Trends **1984**, *32*, 441–460.

4. Dervin, B.; Nilan, M. Information needs and uses. In *Annual Review of Information Science and Technology*; Williams, M.E., York, N., Eds.; K.I. Publications and Inc. for American Society for Information Science, 1986; Vol. 21, 3–33.

5. Mellon, C. Library anxiety: a grounded theory and its development. Coll. Res. Libr. **1986**, *47*, 160–165.

6. Mellon, C. Attitudes: the forgotten dimension in library instruction. Libr. J. **1988**, *113*, 137–139.

7. Kuhlthau, C.C. Developing a model of the library search process: cognitive and affective aspects. RQ **1988**, *28*, 232–242.

8. Bostick, S.L. *The development and validation of the library anxiety scale*; Doctoral dissertation, Wayne State University: Detroit, MI, 1992.

9. Jiao, Q.G.; Onwuegbuzie, A.J.; Lichtenstein, A.A. Library anxiety: characteristics of at-risk college students. Libr. Inf. Sci. Res. **1996**, *18*, 151–163.

10. Van Kampen, D.J. *Library anxiety, information search process and doctoral use of the library*; Doctoral dissertation, University of Central Florida: Orlando, FL, 2003.

11. Cleveland, A. Library anxiety: a decade of empirical research. Libr. Rev. **2004**, *53* (3), 177–85.

12. Onwuegbuzie, A.J.; Jiao, Q.G.; Bostick, S.L. *Library Anxiety: Theory Research, and Applications*; Scarecrow Press: Lanham, MD, 2004; 41.

13. Battle, J.C. *The effect of information literacy instruction on library anxiety among international students*; Doctoral dissertation; University of North Texas: Denton, TX, 2004.

14. Onwuegbuzie, A.J.; Jiao, Q.G. Academic library usage: a comparison of native and non-native English speaking students. Aust. Libr. J. **1997**, 258–269.

15. Andrews, J. An exploration of students' library use problems. Libr. Rev. **1991**, *40* (1), 5–14.

16. Shoham, S.; Mizrachi, D. Library anxiety among undergraduates: a study of Israeli B.Ed. students. J. Acad. Librariansh. **2001**, *27*, 305–319.

17. Anwar, M.A.; Al-Kandari, N.; Al-Qallaf, C.L. Use of Bostick's library anxiety scale on undergraduate biological sciences students of Kuwait University. Libr. Inf. Sci. Res. **2004**, *26* (2), 266–283.

18. Karim, N.H.A.; Ansari, N.A. A cross-cultural evaluation of Bostick's (1992) library anxiety scale: investigating the scale's psychometric properties in a Malaysian University Library. Malays. J. Libr. Inf. Sci. **2010**, *15* (1), 115–134.

19. Abusin, K.A.; Zainab, A.N. Exploring library anxiety among Sudanese university students. Malays. J. Libr. Inf. Sci. **2010**, *15* (1), 55–81.

20. Lawless, L. An examination of library anxiety at Cape Breton University. Evid. Based Libr. Inf. Pract. **2011**, *6* (3), 16–27.

21. Swigon, M. Library anxiety among Polish students: development and validation of the Polish Library Anxiety Scale. Libr. Inf. Sci. Res. **2011**, *33* (2), 144–150.

22. Song, Z.; Zhang, S.; Clarke, C.P. Library anxiety among chinese students: modification and application of LAS in the context of Chinese Academic Libraries. J. Acad. Librariansh. **2014**, *40* (1), 55–61.

23. Onwuegbuzie, A.J.; Jiao, Q.G.; Bostick, S.L. *Library Anxiety: Theory Research, and Applications*; Scarecrow Press: Lanham, MD, 2004; 235–274.

24. Robbins, E.M. Breaking the ice: using non-traditional methods of student involvement to effect a welcoming college library environment. Southeast. Libr. **2014**, *62* (1), 19–23.

25. Bell, A. Paws for a study break: running an animal assisted therapy program at the gerstein science information centre. Partnersh. Can. J. Libr. Inf. Pract. Res. **2013**, *8* (1), 1–14.

26. Brown, C.M. Concerts and dances in a library? An undergraduate library as campus cultural space. Coll. Res. Libr. News **2014**, *75* (7), 387–391.

27. Cleveland, A.M. *Reducing library anxiety in first-year students: computer-assisted instruction vs. bibliographic instruction*; Masters thesis, University of North Carolina: Chapel Hill, NC, 2001.

28. Van Scoyoc, A.M. Reducing library anxiety in first-year students: the impact of computer-assisted instruction and bibliographic instruction. Ref. User Serv. Q. **2003**, *42* (4), 329–341.

29. Battle, J.C. *The effect of information literacy instruction on library anxiety among international students*; Doctoral dissertation, University of North Texas: Denton, TX, 2004.

30. Brown, L.J. Trending now-reference librarians: how reference librarians work to prevent library anxiety. J. Libr. Adm. **2011**, *51* (3), 309–317.

31. Westbrook, L.; De Decker, S. Supporting user needs and skills to minimize library anxiety. Ref. Libr. **1993**, *40*, 43–51.

32. Onwuegbuzie, A.J.; Jiao, Q.G. Information search performance and research achievement: an empirical test of the anxiety-expectation mediation model of library anxiety. J. Am. Soc. Inf. Sci. Technol. **2004**, *55* (1), 41–54.

Law Literature–Library Architecture

Library Architecture and Design

Charlene S. Hurt
University Library, Georgia State University, Atlanta, Georgia, U.S.A.

Thomas L. Findley
Leo A. Daly/Architects & Engineers, Omaha, Nebraska, U.S.A.

Abstract

A survey of the evolution of library architecture and interior design during the latter half of the twentieth and early twenty-first centuries focuses on the change from libraries primarily designed to hold paper collections, sometimes used only in the library, to libraries primarily designed to provide access to technology, digitally stored information, and research and learning spaces. The societal changes that led to the growing role of libraries as places for building community, collaborating, and engaging in independent learning are also discussed. The major components of the design process for libraries are discussed, and the design impacts on the core areas of the library are described.

The past several decades have brought about radical changes in all types of library buildings, driven primarily by technical and cultural/societal changes. Libraries have been changing over the centuries as the formats for inscribing and preserving the written record of human history have changed, and as the concept of public libraries developed alongside the earlier concept of private libraries. Seen from that perspective, the evolution of library design in the twentieth and early twenty-first century does not seem revolutionary, although the speed with which it has taken place may be unprecedented. The changes are the result of several factors: changes in the format of materials, changes in the audience for libraries, and changes in the role libraries play in the community at large.

The current transition is driven by the increasing dominance of various means of electronic storage of materials, the demand for easily accessible computers for library patrons, and a declining emphasis on physical collections as the primary purpose for the library building. The changes are deeper than that, however, and respond to a range of developments in the social and economic environment that would have required adjustment under any circumstances. It may well be that the advent of the digital age, contrary to the early fears that it would destroy the library, actually saved libraries from having to choose between their missions to store the world's knowledge and their need to provide their supportive communities with the services they demand.

IMPACT OF TECHNOLOGY

Design of library buildings during the nineteenth and much of the twentieth century tended to focus on the need to hold the growing physical collections that resulted from the mass production of books and periodicals. A thorough discussion of this type of library architecture can be found in Schell's "Buildings, Library," in the 1970 edition (volume 3) of *Encyclopedia of Library and Information Sciences*.[1] Beginning with the post-World War II era, that classic design, often referred to as the Carnegie rectangle, was challenged by the increased presence of various types of technology, each creating their own demands: microfilm, with its need for darkened space for viewing; various forms of media, each needing appropriate equipment to use; and copy machines, requiring spaces to store paper and handle financial transactions. Computers, which first appeared in the workrooms of libraries as tools for managing the paper resources, moved out to the public areas of the library, beginning with online catalogs, and the computers became sources of information for library staff and patrons. This change has escalated rapidly, requiring libraries to bring electrical and network connections to large public spaces, and putting pressure on spaces designed to hold stacks and readers that frequently had minimal power and network connections available. Meanwhile, the paper collections continued to grow, and in many libraries traditional reader space was sacrificed to make room for collection growth.

The changes required by technology had an impact on all types of libraries, but in many ways, the smaller public and school libraries were initially better able to adjust, not being burdened by the need for comprehensive archival collections. Many had moved toward providing more media equipment for patron use and encouraging more active patron engagement in various programs. The school libraries that became part of elementary and secondary school design were often viewed as teaching libraries, and frequently served as media centers. Public libraries built smaller branch libraries closer to their users than the

Encyclopedia of Library and Information Sciences, Fourth Edition DOI: 10.1081/E-ELIS4-120044656

Copyright © 2017 by Taylor & Francis. All rights reserved.

larger central libraries, and responded to the popularity of their children's collections and the growing demands of young adult patrons with specially designed spaces more suited to housing children's and young adults' books, media, and computer equipment. These newer buildings were more likely to incorporate better power and network connectivity in their design, although the breadth of need was not at first anticipated.

The growth of public computer installations in research libraries, both public and academic, continued alongside the growth of their collections, leading library planners to face decisions about how to develop new, flexible, highly wired space in buildings poorly suited to that purpose. For librarians, the choice sometimes seemed to be between their collections and the needs of their changing mission. The solutions varied according to the availability of other space, the resources of the libraries, and their missions. A variety of solutions developed, including the development of separate undergraduate libraries, much less focused on archival collections and often located in the older original libraries, allowing the large collections and technologically demanding resources to move to new facilities. Another trend has been the development of storage facilities for the less-heavily used collections, sometimes serving multiple institutions, such as the Washington Research Library Consortium's storage facility in the DC area. One technology that helped libraries with collection growth was the development of compact shelving for less-heavily used collections, which began in Europe and Japan before moving to the United States in the 1960s.[2] These movable stacks can compress collections into approximately one half of the space otherwise needed, but installation of compact shelving into many extant library buildings is impractical because of the need for heavy load-bearing floors.

The recent development of radio frequency identification technology for tagging books has enhanced the possibilities of storage of collections, including the use of robotized facilities, such as the stacks in the University of Nevada Las Vegas Library, where the automated book retrieval system is across from the Circulation Desk and can be viewed through a large glass window (see Fig. 1).

IMPACT OF CULTURAL CHANGES

Changes in the culture have also created new demands on libraries. The growth of the free public library and the impetus given to that by the large-scale construction of Carnegie libraries in the early twentieth century initiated those changes as the size and diversity of the population expecting access to libraries and the resources they provide began to grow. In the past 15 years, public libraries, often with significant support from foundations such as the Bill and Melinda Gates Foundation, have become primary

Fig. 1 Automated book retrieval system, library, University of Nevada, Las Vegas.
Source: Photograph by Paul Brokering, http://www. paulbrokering.com. Used with permission of photographer.

vehicles for providing public access to computing for those who do not have such access readily available. Libraries serving large immigrant populations have also begun providing books, periodicals, and services in languages frequently used in their service area, which creates new collections and service space requirements. For academic libraries, there has been a rapid growth in the student population and, in recent years, an increasing emphasis on international studies, resources, and students. Libraries which previously collected only in English are called upon to collect materials in other languages, and provide access to them. Changes in the methods of instruction have had a significant impact on what kinds of library space students desire, as the use of online courses and supplemental materials grew and the emphasis on group projects expanded.

An extremely important aspect of cultural change that is driving the evolution of library architecture is the

Law Literature–Library Architecture

emergence of the library as a place for community. This is most pronounced in public libraries, where library as a meeting place for various community groups and as a provider of information-related and special population programming has taken on a very important role. Public libraries devote considerable space and staff to serving children, usually in specially furnished areas designed to attract children and their parents (see Fig. 2), and to areas designed to appeal to their young adult users, often needing a place to study, do research, and be with friends in a safe space when not in school. In many ways, this population is much like the academic population of users in academic libraries.

The role of libraries as spaces for community is an increasing focus on academic campuses, where the end of the "quiet study only" library and the emergence of the library coffee shop have created a sense of the library as the place for "academic community," as opposed to the social community spaces in student centers or the recreational community spaces in gyms and recreation facilities. Since the Leavey Library opened at the University of Southern California in 1994, there has been a trend to build Information Commons or Learning Commons, each designed slightly differently but all having in common very large, technologically intensive space which seeks to meet the student need for computers and assistance in using those computers and the information they deliver in highly visible and social space.

Many students prefer to work in very public spaces, and want to be within view of someone who can help them, and they will congregate in heavily traveled areas where they can see and be seen. The degree to which these common areas include such things as paper collections, lounging areas, group study areas, and specialized technology environments varies from library to library, and the ultimate evolution of these spaces remains to be seen.

University campuses still may contain specialized libraries that are often quite different from the central library, although the effects of technology and differing expectations of students have similarly affected their design. The most common examples are law school libraries and music libraries.

A growing trend is to build multipurpose facilities that house more than the library. For many public libraries, this consists of a cluster of community spaces, including recreational space, municipal offices, performance space, and the public library. Examples include the Asker Public Library outside of Oslo, Norway, which combines an art gallery, theater, and restaurant, and the Largo Public Library in the heart of that Florida city's Central Park. Combined public and school libraries are also popular. Combined public and university libraries are also emerging, such as the libraries of San Jose State University and the City of San Jose and the combined Royal Library, National Library of Denmark and Copenhagen University Library (see Fig. 3).

Community college libraries are often colocated with other learning facilities, such as counseling and tutoring centers, and sometimes share their buildings with various student services like registration and financial aid. Academic libraries, such as the library of the University of Otago in New Zealand, are creating spaces to share with

Law Literature–Library Architecture

Fig. 2 Children's area storytime, Lexington public library northside branch.
Source: Photograph by Frank Doring. Used with permission of Lexington Public Library.

Fig. 3 The new building ("Black Diamond") of the Danish Royal Library, viewed from the south-east, taken in 2005.
Source: Wikipedia. Photograph by Thue. Image released into the public domain by its author, Thue. This applies worldwide: http://en.wikipedia.org/wiki/File:Den_Sorte_Diamant_1.jpg, accessed December 28, 2008.

the Instructional Technology Divisions, with Centers for Teaching and Learning, and with various student services such as Writing Centers and English as a Second Language (ESL) tutors. Some academic libraries are linked to student unions, such as the Johnson Center at George Mason University. In all cases, the mix of facilities is driven by the local needs of the environment, and ideally by the perception of librarians as to what services students need that can be best colocated in their libraries.

Whatever the combinations, the realities of different missions, user base, collection priorities, specialty areas, and hours and services present significant challenges and call for careful planning and a great deal of diplomacy and flexibility. The rewards can be substantial, both in cost savings and better services to library users and the communities.

Libraries have always emphasized security, but until recently the biggest concern was keeping collections safe from theft. The very concept of libraries as places where all the users have equal access to the information they provide has created another security requirement: keeping the patrons of the library secure. The growth of large homeless populations has made this a particularly difficult issue in large downtown libraries, but there are few libraries that have not had to deal with this issue. Locations of service desks and computer clusters are driven by the need for visibility, and small nooks and private spaces need to be in areas where traffic regularly passes.

Other impacts on libraries and therefore their buildings have been related to equal access and services for disabled patrons, which has been both enhanced and made more complex by the many technologies available to assist them. Power wheelchairs allow increased mobility, but

their size usually exceeds that of manual wheelchairs and should be taken into consideration in sizing of aisles.

A fairly recent trend in library architecture and interior design has been the emphasis on sustainable design, also known as greening the library. Librarians and architects share an interest in using building materials that emphasize recycled and environmentally friendly components, and design focused on energy conservation and effective use of materials that will not need frequent replacement. Meeting the challenge of greater natural light and showcasing the activities within a library to passers-by without energy loss is a particular challenge, and has led to some of the more creative design solutions, such as can be seen at the Phoenix Central Library.[3] Interior designers seek finishes and furniture that are made from recycled materials, such as old tires or seatbelts, and from renewable resources such as cork and bamboo. Construction companies are developing more environmentally friendly ways of excavating the site and reusing or disposing of materials used in the building process. Some campuses, such as Emory University in Atlanta, have committed to building all new structures and renovations using the guidelines of sustainable design. Libraries increasingly seek to be certified by the Leadership and Energy Environmental Design Green Building Rating System (LEED) at one of the four levels: certified, silver, gold, or platinum, and calls for proposals for designing and constructing their facilities where evidence of LEED-certified team members and methodology is a requirement.

The rise in popularity of coffee shops as parts of libraries began in the 1990s, and has become an expected part of almost all new or renovated academic library planning and many public libraries. This trend arose as librarians realized the futility of keeping food and drinks entirely out of their libraries, and tried instead to contain some of the possible damage by encouraging use of covered containers, providing adequate trash facilities, and specifying certain areas where a ban on food and beverages will be enforced—often around computers. The prevalence of food and beverages in the library has particular impact on the selection of interior finishes and furniture, as they must be able to handle beverage and food stains and be easily cleaned. Provision for waste disposal and recycling also needs to be made.[4]

MAJOR COMPONENTS OF THE DESIGN PROCESS

The architecture of the modern library is clearly evolving from the old Carnegie boxes of earlier centuries, and we see in recent library design a number of solutions to the changes outlined above. The keys to successful library planning in the twenty-first century are careful analysis of the needs of the population to be served and their expectations, a building program that is informed by an awareness of future trends and how they might impact on the building being designed, recognition that one cannot anticipate everything that the library will become, a firm commitment to flexibility of space and furnishings, and deep library staff involvement in the planning process. These qualities will be seen in each aspect of the final design, and take specific form in each aspect of the plan.

The Master Planning Process

Involvement of librarians in the architectural decisions of library buildings needs to begin early and continue throughout the process, culminating in the occupation of the new space. Often that planning process begins with a survey of the user community to determine their interests and needs. Under ideal circumstances, the library building is part of a master plan for related spaces around it, which recognizes the need for common traffic control, security, and parking facilities. For large libraries or library systems, there is often a master plan that considers their overall development, and anticipates changes in spaces of buildings that are not part of the original plan.

Developing the Building Program

The core document in a library's design process is the library building program. This may be developed by the library in conjunction with planning consultants or the architectural design team, or both. A well-prepared library staff begins preparation long before this process with internal discussions of what the library needs, where the library anticipates change, and what the library staff dreams of in their new facility. Imaging the future sessions are often used during this process.

The programmers will work closely with staff, asking them to describe their current space and think about how they would like their new space to work. Careful attention is given to adjacencies, which areas need to be next to which, importance of public access, and special furnishing, equipment, and security needs. This document is often described as the bible for what comes afterward, and it is essential that the final document is thorough and looks toward the future.

Consulting with External Experts

External experts are often employed to bring their perspectives and knowledge to the project. Most commonly consulted are library building consultants, structural engineers (often part of the design team), Audio-Visual (AV)/ Media Specialists, Acoustical Consultants, Security Consultants, Library Move Management Consultants, and Way-finding/Signage Consultants. The need for each of these varies with the library under design.

One specialized area of knowledge that cannot be neglected is knowledge of the building regulations related to access and safety. These tend to vary by geographic location, and failure to plan for them can be very expensive. In addition to the usual requirements for power, plumbing, and structural integrity, there are regulations related to emergency egress and disabled access.

Impact of Library Architecture on the Community

Although the usability of the building on the inside is the primary consideration, planners need to recognize and be sensitive to the importance of the appearance of the library in its environment. It is not uncommon for the library to be one of the largest buildings in the area, and a beautifully designed library can enhance the area around it, make a statement about the organization to which it belongs, provide a centerpiece for a larger cluster of buildings, and serve as a beacon to the community. Dramatic public libraries like the main library in Salt Lake City and the recently opened Seattle Public Library become destinations and objects of pride for the cities. On a smaller scale, public libraries seek to reflect their communities, such as the Spanish Spring Library in Nevada with its Native American design and interior treatments-based images in the nearby environment.

Aesthetics, Display Space, and Signs

Geoff Freeman, architect for many innovative library buildings, has talked about the increased expectations for "immeasurables that only a library can provide." These include how the spaces feel, "how they attract, and how they stimulate and inspire as well as give pause for reflection and focus." These immeasurables are considerations in all stages of the library's design, and are key to the interior design.[5] Good interior design will have a significant impact on the library's aesthetics and will impact the behavior, use, and security of library buildings. Library patrons will welcome opportunities to offer their opinions on the types of furniture that are used and the color palates that are chosen. It has become common to ask furniture companies to provide sample furniture that can demonstrate how well it holds up to use and gives patrons opportunities to comment on comfort and "look and feel." This can help create excitement about the new space, and assure the planners that they have correctly interpreted their patrons' needs.

The important consideration of traffic flow can be much enhanced by use of appropriate finishes that help identify and guide patrons through the various spaces of the library. Good signage is also essential, and use of technological methods for delivering information, such as video and computer screens, is becoming common.

In addition to the buildings and furnishings, libraries often have important display space and large empty walls inviting installation of art. The selection and purchase of art for libraries has the potential to develop good

Law Literature–Library Architecture

partnerships with art departments and the local arts community, and possibly attract financial support. There are also the practical aspects of design, such as budgeting for, and coordinating, receptacles for recycling and trash during the overall building design.

Construction

Newer methods of design and construction of buildings, such as design/build construction and guaranteed maximum price construction, have tended to blend the entire process, making it much more interactive between planners and builders. Working with such projects varies greatly from the earlier model of buildings planned and designed and then turned over to the contractors for bidding and construction. More than ever, it is essential that all members of the team remain informed, involved, and available during this process, although the involvement of librarians will lessen as the process continues, but iterative decision making continues throughout, and unexpected compromises or pleasant surprises can have a major impact on the final building.

DESIGN IMPACTS ON CORE AREAS OF LIBRARIES

This process will not result in a group of identical libraries because the strengths, expectations, and ambitions of each library vary in important ways. Nevertheless, there are specific factors that apply to the major areas of the library: public service areas; teaching, training, and meeting space; individual and group work space; collections space; specialized collections and services areas; staff space; technology support areas; and building support and security.

Public Service Areas

The increasing complexity of library resources and the concomitant education and training required by those providing assistance to library patrons have led to reorganizations of these services, a trend which continues to evolve. Factors, which impact on the architecture of the library, include a variety of solutions as to size and placement of service desks, increasing provision for small group work and individual consultation, and technologically sophisticated teaching and learning spaces. Some libraries have a variety of public service desks, often characterized by the type of assistance being given: security enforcement, general information, research assistance, technology assistance, and circulation of materials. Others have only one combined desk, and some have eliminated the traditional reference desk. The degree to which professional assistance is available at service counters varies considerably, with some libraries trending toward most professional

librarian assistance delivered in consultation rooms and offices, with service desks staffed with trained assistants who have various specializations, including technology. Some libraries are experimenting with roving assistance rather than centralized desk assistance, and self-check-out equipment is being provided for routine circulation transactions. The nature of the community of users and their service expectations need to be carefully and realistically analyzed to determine how public service areas should be designed. Desks that can be reconfigured as needs change will provide maximum flexibility.

Teaching, Training, and Meeting Space

Libraries have long recognized that there are substantial efficiencies in teaching groups of patrons rather than teaching the same thing to one patron at a time, but often lack dedicated and appropriate teaching space in which that instruction can be scheduled. There is also a growing need for training space for library staff, and spaces for offering training on various technologies to the library's patron groups. For many patrons, the first contact with a library may be through attendance at a class, training session, or public event in the library's space, and there is strong evidence to suggest that they are much more likely to return once they have seen the richness of the library's resources. Newer libraries are dedicating much more space to these functions, which is partially enabled by the lessening pressure of physical collection growth. These spaces vary according to their purposes and availability of technology, but common characteristics are provision of an installed computer base with presentation technology, multipurpose rooms that can be used with or without computers at each workstation, and attractive public meeting space for conferences, media presentations, performances, and various types of meetings. Recent improvements in wireless technology and the growing downsizing of computers make flexibility easier to achieve, and reliance on laptops, which can be installed in the furniture and made accessible on an as-needed basis, is becoming more common. The location of teaching space is ideally very visible and easily reached from outside of the library, but the large dimensions of that space and need for technology also must be considered.

Individual and Group Work Space

A substantial and outspoken group of library patrons still come to the library to find quiet spaces for reading and study. Planning in advance for areas designed to meet their needs is essential, and needs to be done in a way that does not discourage library use by patrons seeking other kinds of space. Libraries can designate specific areas for quiet study, sometimes creating special rooms for that purpose. They can also utilize furniture types and overall environments to encourage quiet, taking advantage of

Law Literature–Library Architecture

stacks that can act as sound buffers, specifying more remote areas for quiet study, using sound absorbing materials such as upholstery and carpet, and providing individual study carrels with high panels on both sides. Some libraries have installed white noise technology in their buildings to lessen the impact of various sources of noise.

For many library users, especially students, the library is seen as a place to meet with groups, work together on projects, and practice presentations of their work, almost always with technology near at hand and often with whiteboards or other space for posting their work in progress. Student demands are likely to include needs for multimedia creation, collaborative computer use, digitizing equipment, color printers, and places to plug in personal electronic devices. Information and Learning Commons are usually designed with these users in mind, as are the proliferation of group study rooms and various types of media-equipped rooms (see Fig. 4). Design of these spaces will continue to evolve as technology develops; the trend toward smaller devices with more connectivity will surely impact how those spaces are configured and furnished. For maximum flexibility, careful

Fig. 4 Georgia State University Learning Commons.
Source: Photograph by Visko Hatfield. Used with permission of Visko Hatfield and Leo A. Daly, Architects.

thought needs to be given to provision of raised floors, wiring channels, and dropped ceilings.

In general, libraries need to provide a variety of types and configurations of seating, including classic library tables and chairs, carrels of various types, computer pods, group study tables, lounge furniture, and possibly benches or booths. Patrons tend to adapt what is provided to their needs, and so furniture which can be moved and reconfigured should be considered. There is a large contingent of people who prefer working in a busy and very visible environment, preferably with lots of natural light. Taking advantage of windows and traffic patterns can help planners meet this need.

As a general rule, all of the library should be accessible to disabled patrons, but there may be a section of seating which provides various assistive technologies. Throughout the library consideration should be given to providing seating that can meet the needs of patrons with special needs.

Space for Collections

Libraries need a variety of shelving configurations for differing types of collections, including less-immediately accessible space for seldom-used materials and a mix of shelving for collections that need to be associated with equipment required to access the information they contain. Common shelving configurations include standard stacks, compact shelving units, folio stacks, reference stacks, atlases and maps, browsing materials, and media. Consideration should be given to the possibility that space now configured for a particular collection (reference, for example) may shrink, grow unexpectedly, or be relocated, or that the total amount of shelving will be reduced in order to create space for new needs.

Specialized Collections and Service Areas

Specialized collections include children's collections, media collections, maps, government documents, and archives and special collections. Each of these has unique requirements for storage and use of materials, and some of them may offer independent service points. Shelving which is appropriate for the children's collection is different from that for other book collections, and may include media storage. Seating in these areas is also unique to children's needs, as are many of the interior design features. Some of the other collections are primarily different in their shelving requirements, but media collections may be in unique space in order to meet the equipment, security, and assistance needs of those collections.

Archives and special collections have unique needs for security, service, and appearance, and are often in a space

Law Literature–Library Architecture

separated from the rest of the library. There is a trend toward greater visibility of these collections, as exemplified by the housing of the King's Library (King George III's collection) in a smoked glass tower at the British Library, visible from the main entrance hall and various areas of the library.[6] As archival and special collections make increasing use of digital technologies, it is reasonable to assume that users of the digitized materials in these collections may also migrate into the common public areas, creating additional service requirements and greater demand to see the original materials from which these images are derived.

Staff Areas

Staff spaces need to be highly configurable and flexible. The nature of library work has been evolving for many years, and that evolution probably has not been completed. The trend is to a more open architecture, with fewer private offices and more readily rearranged furniture and equipment. Shared small conference rooms for consultation are often provided. Space that can be repurposed for technology and/or individual or online patron assistance may supplant space now used for the decreasing traditional physical processing of materials. Staff spaces should also allow for the highly collaborative, teamwork approach to modern library work, and for the realities of today's workforce, which may include working parents, disabled employees, and staff working a large variety of schedules. Security of staff, their personal possessions, and library equipment and supplies must be an important consideration. Absolutely essential is a pleasant staff lounge with appropriate equipment for employee use. Some libraries provide a private space for nursing mothers.

Technology Support Areas

The growth of the use of technology in all areas of the library will likely continue to expand the staffing of these areas, and the need for various kinds of equipment for such activities as digitizing collections, designing Web pages, managing online systems, equipment repair and updating, and multimedia creation and viewing. Design of that space will need to allow for intense power and network connections, careful security, specialized spaces for any equipment needing constant environmental control, and collaborative work spaces, including room for groups to work on a common screen. The exact nature of this space continues to change as the technology changes, and more compact equipment may lead to differing space and heating, ventilating, and air conditioning needs. It is particularly important that these areas are built as flexibly as possible, with easy upgrading of power and connectivity needs.

Security and Building Support Spaces

The open nature of libraries creates unique needs for security, and heavy usage provides a substantial challenge to maintaining the facility. In addition to control gates at exits, planners may control entrance to the library. Workstations open to all users may be placed in locations close to staffing and security points. Building managers and custodians need accessible and strategically placed facilities.

CONCLUSION

Fortunately for library planners, there are many prominent and innovative architects and interior designers who are interested in designing library buildings and renovation projects, including a number of firms that have groups of library specialists. Libraries are one of a small group of public buildings that still offer the challenge of creating an important space for a large community, and their design is a matter of great interest to the communities in which they are built. Libraries today are characterized by large, light-filled spaces, showcasing their contents and services and featuring welcoming facades. Often their design needs to be part of an overall master plan for the area in which they are built, and which fits with the overall architectural vocabulary. There are so many notable new library buildings that it is difficult to provide a selected list; there are numerous lists of notable library buildings, including the annual Architecture issue of *Library Journal* and the Design Issue of *American Libraries* and a wide variety of articles on new buildings in library and higher education literature, as well as in local and campus newspapers. The Web pages of libraries in the process of new or renovated buildings also provide a wealth of information. A brief list of books that are valuable resources for understanding the evolution of library architecture and the continuing requirements of library buildings appears below.

Winston Churchill said: "We shape our buildings; thereafter they shape us." At the heart of the evolution of library buildings is the evolution of library services and staff, and library planners will often discover that by the time they occupy their new space, their needs would have already changed in various ways. The familiar admonition to think outside of the box applies especially to the process of designing libraries, as does the need to recognize that the perfect library has yet to be built.

REFERENCES

1. Schell, H.B. The library building: An overview. In *Reader on the Library Building*; Schell, H.B., Ed.; Microcard Editions Books: Englewood, CO, 1975; 3–29 Reprinted from 1970

Law Literature–Library Architecture

Edition of *Encyclopedia of Library and Information Sciences*, Vol. 3.

2. Muller, R.H. Economics of compact book shelving. In *Reader on the Library Building*; Schell, H.B., Ed.; Microcard Editions Books: Englewood, CO, 1975; 292–300.

3. Edwards, R.M. A new central library for phoenix. In *Building Libraries for the 21st Century—The Shape of Information*; Webb, T.D., Ed.; McFarland & Company: Jefferson, NC, 2000; 156–167.

4. http://www.usgbc.org/DisplayPage.aspx?CMSPageID=222.

5. Freeman, G.T. How do we inspire in the information age? Understanding the immeasurables of the library. In *Building Libraries for the 21st Century—The Shape of Information*; Webb, T.D., Ed.; McFarland & Company: Jefferson, NC, 2000; 168–175.

6. Carr, J. The British library. In *Building Libraries for the 21st Century—The Shape of Information*; Webb, T.D., Ed.; McFarland & Company: Jefferson, NC, 2000; 21–31.

BIBLIOGRAPHY

1. Kaser, D. *The Evolution of the American Library Building*; The Scarecrow Press, Inc.: Lanham, MD, 1997.

2. Leighton, P.D.; Weber, D.C. *Planning Academic and Research Library Buildings*, 3rd Ed.; American Library Association: Chicago, IL, 1999.

3. McCabe, G.B., Kennedy, J.R., Eds.. *Planning the Modern Public Library Building*; Libraries Unlimited: Westport, CT, 2003; The Libraries Unlimited Library Management Collection.

4. Oldenburg, R. *The Great Good Place: Cafés Coffee Shops, Community Centers, Beauty Parlors, General Stores, Bars, Hangouts, and How they Get You Through the Day*, 1st Ed.; Paragon House: New York, 1991.

5. Schell, H.B., Ed.. *Reader on the Library Building*; Microcard: Editions Books: Englewood, CO, 1975.

6. Webb, T.D., Ed.. *Building Libraries for the 21st Century—The Shape of Information*; McFarland & Company: Jefferson, NC, 2000.

Library Architecture: History

Nan Christian Ploug Dahlkild
Royal School of Library and Information Science, Copenhagen, Denmark

Abstract
The history of library architecture goes back to the third millennium before Christ. Library architecture has been closely related to the development of library collections and their materials: from the clay tablets and papyri of temple libraries to the stately interiors of noble and royal libraries and the rationally organized stacks of the twentieth century research libraries. However, in the twentieth century and around the millennium many libraries have also developed into multipurpose or multispace cultural and public centers. Important steps in the development of the modern library have been: Gabriel Naudé's Advice from 1627, the library visions of the Age of Enlightenment, the open access of the public libraries, and the opening of the library space of the twentieth century. Around the millennium physical library space is challenged by "the library without walls."

There is a close connection between the development of books and media and the development of library architecture and interiors. Existing library buildings, historical libraries, and library projects can be seen as expressions of the politics of culture, knowledge, and information of different societies and historical periods from the first written documents to the digital challenges to the physical library space.

CLASSICAL, MONASTIC, AND ROYAL LIBRARIES

The history of library buildings goes back to the third millennium before Christ, where clay tablets were kept in rooms in palace compounds in Mesopotamia. In Egypt, papyrus scrolls were kept in both palace and temple libraries. In China, bamboo slips, panels of silk, and paper scrolls were stored in libraries. In Greece and Rome, the standardization of simple alphabets leads to the growth of popular literacy, and along with the democratization of the reading process public library buildings occurred. Often these public libraries were constructed as parts of public meeting places in the communities such as public baths, stoas, forums, and basilicas. In the third century after Christ the codex form increasingly came into use. Examples of library buildings from this period are the great library in Alexandria, the library in Ephesus in The Middle East, and the library in Timgad in North Africa. The Trajan's Forum with Bibliotheca Ulpia was built as a twin library with colonnade facades around the Trajan Column, which could in itself be read as a library document. Here the library was connected to a coherent urban space.

In the middle ages libraries were related to monasteries and cathedrals. There was a close connection between the writing of documents in a scriptorium and the collection of documents in an armarium. In the ideal plan for the abbey of St. Gall from c. 820 there was a two-storeyed library building with a scriptorium below and a library above. Often the reading took place in stalls with chained books. Still existing libraries of this type are the Corpus Christi College in Oxford and The Hereford Cathedral Library. A more spacious example is the Bibliotheca Maletestiana in the city of Cesena in Northern Italy with lecterns in a row from 1452. Universities and university libraries were established in the thirteenth century along with the growth of commerce and towns and the beginning secularization of knowledge. At the University Library in Leiden (Fig. 1) readers were placed at lecterns with chained books that were divided into seven sciences: theology, literature, philosophy, mathematics, law, medicine, and history.

Typically collections from the Renaissance period included books, art, antiquities, religious relics, and objects of geology and natural history. Often these early encyclopedic collections with various categories had the character of a Cabinet of curiosities or Wunderkammer. The arrangement of objects could also be defined as a memory theater. Later collections were divided into more specialized archives, libraries, and different kinds of museums.

The art of printing gradually changed the amount of documents from the fifteenth century and influenced the selling, collecting, and lending of books. A few libraries were opened to the public, and the chaining of books became more seldom. The first comprehensive theory of library organization was formulated in 1627 by the Renaissance physician and librarian Gabriel Naudé in his *Advice* from 1627. Naudé was the librarian of the French Cardinal Mazarin and created his library. His theory was characterized by Renaissance humanism, emphasizing thorough and comprehensive studies. It presented all-round guidelines not only for arranging library collections,

Encyclopedia of Library and Information Sciences, Fourth Edition DOI: 10.1081/E-ELIS4-120044550
Copyright © 2017 by Taylor & Francis. All rights reserved.

Law Literature–Library Architecture

Fig. 1 The University Library in Leiden in 1610 with chained books, divided into seven sciences. **Source:** Carlssons.

but also for furnishing and equipping library premises and making them accessible to the public. He introduced modern principles such as open access, representing opposite viewpoints in the collection and professional order. He recommended a practical design of the library and preferred a quiet location, possibly near a beautiful garden. He praised contemporary libraries of Sir Thomas Bodley in Oxford, of Cardinal Borromeo in Milano and the Augustin brothers in Rome for their open access. The library of the Medici in Florence was "beautiful and admirable."

The long hall of the Medici Library, designed by Michelangelo 1523–1571, was a Renaissance library with rows of lecterns, flanking the central aisle. The architectural experience was shaped by the steady rhythm of corresponding lecterns and windows. The books were stored permanently at the lecterns. Therefore the reader had to move from one lectern to another to read different books. Another important Renaissance library of the same type was the Sansovino Library in Venice with its impressive façade at Piazza San Marco. The library building was begun by Sansovino in 1536 and completed in 1591 by Scamozzi.

The hall or Saal library developed together with the Baroque and Rococo styles in the seventeenth and eighteenth centuries in monastic, noble and royal libraries, with their stately interiors and distinguished collections. In these libraries both the collection and the interior served representative purposes of the owner or patron. Books were typically stored in shelves along the walls, impressing the viewer with the extent of the collection. Fine examples are the Hofbibliothek from 1726 in Vienna with its huge Prunksaal at the size of a cathedral with Baroque frescoes, showing Glory with a pyramid in the middle, the Monastic Library of Wiblingen in Germany from 1757 with its symbolic sculptures, and the

Benedictine Abbey Library at Admont in Austria with its collection and interior in white and gold. Experimental geometrical forms have the Wolfenbüttel Library from 1710 and the Radcliffe Camera in Oxford from 1749. The Herzogin Anna Amalia Library from 1766 in Weimar is interesting because of its almost oval library within the library.

Also in the oriental tradition, libraries represented places of learning and contemplation. The contemporary Tinayi Ge Library in China, built 1561–1566 by minister of the Ming dynasty Fan Quin, was placed in a garden with a small pool, connected to a lake, not only for recreation, but also to avoid fire. The building around a small yard has double eaves and gable roofs. The library was divided into six parts, corresponding to the idea, that the earth was formed in six parts. The collection of books had labels such as Gentle, Respectful, Modest, Sun, Moon, Time, Dragon and characters, referring to Chinese music.

THE ENLIGHTENMENT AND THE GRAND LIBRARY DESIGN

In the age of the enlightenment a new notion of public libraries arose against the background of an expanding readership and a growth in the number of published books and scientific, literary, and political journals. The ideas of the enlightenment were expressed in a series of grand utopian projects. The French enlightenment architect Étienne-Louis Boullée envisaged a universal library in a grand design in 1784. Boullée's library project was called the Bibliotheque du Roi (Fig. 2). Before the French revolution the king and the state were so closely intertwined that one could interpret the Bibliotheque du Roi as an institution in which the state began to assume responsibility for providing books to the people. Like the French

Law Literature–Library Architecture

Fig. 2 Étienne-Louis Boullée's utopian library project from around 1780.
Source: Arkitekturmuseet.

encyclopedia it should gather, order, and disseminate all available knowledge. Boullée's revolutionary library project was a manifesto for the kind of building that would promote access to knowledge and educated thinking—the prerequisites for an enlightened and critical public discourse. It acquired significance as the model for a series of grand library buildings of the nineteenth century, and gave libraries and other cultural institutions a new, hitherto undreamt centrality in the urban landscape.

At the same time educational parks were established such as the Woerlitz Park at Dessau in Germany with both examples of agricultural cultivating methods and a small library building with agricultural and horticultural literature. Visitors could bring the library's books with them to the park, both enjoying and being educated by the surroundings. In Beverwijk in the Netherlands, the female writer Bethje Wolff built a small hut with a library in her garden (Fig. 3). This decentralization of the dissemination

of knowledge was possible because of the easier access and transportation of smaller books.

The library visions of Étienne-Louis Boullée inspired the grand library design of the nineteenth century.

In 1850 Henry Labrouste finished his Bibliotheque St. Genevieve in Paris. He conceived the building as a monument over the history of civilization and knowledge. The exterior was covered with plates, showing inscriptions of names of 810 names of international authors, philosophers, and scientists from Moses to the Swedish chemist Berzelius in chronological order, almost like a catalog in stones. Thus the building itself became a document, a book. The interior of the building had iron columns and decorative iron arches over the vast reading room one story above ground level. In 1875 Labrouste finished a new building for the Bibliotheque Nationale. In the reading room, 16 iron columns carried 9 domes of faience and glass. Murals were painted with wooden motives with blue skies. In Copenhagen, J.D. Herholdt designed a new University Library in 1855–1861 with elegantly slim iron columns and a tunnel vault, painted in pastel colors. Fine examples of the library architecture of the industrial age are also the cupola of the British Library in London from 1857 by Panizzi/Smirke and the Library of Congress in Washington from 1897 by Smithmeyer and Pelz. The reading rooms were panoptically arranged, respectively radial and concentric. Many public institutions from this period were built as panopticons, where you could supervise the building from its center. The Library of Congress also had a monumental staircase, which was a new representative element in library architecture.

THE ANGLO-AMERICAN MODEL

In the course of the nineteenth century a more publicly oriented form of library developed in England and in the

Fig. 3 Bethje Wolff's library hut in natural surroundings also from around 1780.
Source: Carlssons.

Law Literature–Library Architecture

United States. The "free public library" had its roots in places that served simultaneously as bookshops, subscription libraries, readers' associations, and literary salons. In both countries the social background for the development of the new public library movement was the mass industrialization and urbanization of the nineteenth century. An important conception was the library's central role in education, enlightenment, and democracy. The ideal was that library materials should be available to all, regardless of class, race, origin, language, or education. These libraries were often founded and funded by private patrons of culture and education (Fig. 4).

In terms of architecture and interior design library buildings became steadily grander, more numerous and more prominent as features of the cityscape, with monumental facades in historical styles, often including classical elements that expressed the enlightenment tradition. Whereas the reading room had been the central feature of the classic European libraries, the lending department now became the most important room of the library. At the same time the introduction of new technology and the

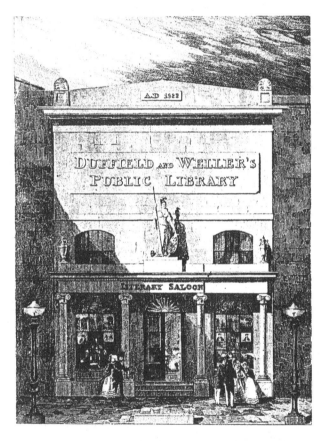

Fig. 4 Duffield's and Weller's Public Library and Literary Salon was founded in Cheltenham in 1822 as a bookshop, subscription library, and literary salon. It was not until the late nineteenth century that larger and more monumental public library buildings were erected in cities in England and America. Copperplate from circa 1850.
Source: Dr. Hauswedell & Co.

increase in the number of users, including women and children, led to greater specialization in the use of space.

Women and children were by no means unknown in the subscription libraries. Special women's reading associations were organized and special departments were established in the public libraries, which served as respectable public meeting places for women and reflected the Victorian segregation of the sexes in all sorts of contexts, from schools to public beaches. Women's reading rooms tended to be furnished in a more homely style, with carpets, polished furniture, curtains, fan palms, and fireplaces. By the end of the nineteenth century special library rooms with appropriate furniture were established for children in both England and the United States. Many large libraries had both academic and public sections.

Serving a larger public, libraries began to organize their space and their methods of distribution more strictly and professionally. Lending to larger numbers of people meant standardizing classification, arrangement and marking of books and routinizing library procedures, including those for borrowing and returning. Advanced systems were introduced for physical transport of books and information both inside and outside the new libraries. The big American public libraries developed all-purpose systems involving small carts for moving books around internally and horse-drawn vehicles, later superseded by cars, for external transport. At the same time extensive systems of branch libraries and deposit stations, mobile libraries, traveling libraries, and book distribution boxes were developed.

In several American cities, including Boston, Chicago, New York, Detroit, and Indianapolis, striking new freestanding buildings were erected to house the libraries. Boston Public Library was built between 1887 and 1895 as a "people's palace" by the architects McKim, Mead, and White. The facade and parts of the plan were clearly inspired by the Bibliotheque St. Genevieve, which in turn had been inspired by Boullée's projects. This inspiration was evident in both the exterior and the interior: in both the main facade and in the placing of the large reading room, Bates Hall, on the first floor. Divided into Bates Hall, with its scholarly literature and donated special collections, and Lower Hall, with its public book collection, the library integrated elements of both the scholarly libraries and the modern public libraries. Book ordering was automated, with the orders delivered by pneumatic post to the stacks, whence the books were transported in little wagons by miniature electric railway. The library moreover had 10 ancillary branches and a total of 17 lending facilities.

While these large library buildings were built as compact "boxes" in classical or renaissance style, or in the special style dubbed "renaissance classicism" that referred to the classical cultural tradition, the architect Henry Hobson Richardson built a number of libraries in free Mediaeval style, with especially Romanesque elements

Law Literature–Library Architecture

such as the Winn Memorial Library (1877–1878) and the Crane Memorial Library (1880–1883). The exteriors of these buildings were expressive and rustic, with rough-hewn stone, solid round arches, high gables, and asymmetrically placed turrets; inside, however, logic reigned, with the rooms all following in orderly sequence. Richardson's style was associated internationally with the Anglo-American library model and can be seen as the prototype for early Scandinavian public buildings, including the Dickson Public Library from 1897 in Gothenburg in Sweden and the Bergen Public Library from 1917 in Norway.

In addition, the Scottish–American steel magnate Andrew Carnegie funded no fewer than 2509 libraries throughout the English-speaking world. These libraries, built as miniature temples of knowledge, belong to a distinctive category of their own. To begin with Carnegie supported a plethora of charitable initiatives. In his essay *The Best Fields for Philanthropy* he listed seven fields: universities, libraries, hospitals, public parks, meeting and concert halls, public baths, and churches. But the best gift that could be made to a local community, he argued, was a public library.

In the first decades of the twentieth century some libraries were built as high-rise buildings as for example the John Crerar Library in Chicago (1920) and Yale's Sterling Memorial Library (1930), which provided an effective means of storing and transporting an ever-growing number of books. The John Crerar Library had a central location in Chicago next to the Chicago Public Library. It occupied premises from the 6th to the 14th floor, with reading rooms on the top two floors and each floor containing roughly 110,000 books.

In the interwar period library architecture and design were simplified and modernized. A good example can be seen in Los Angeles' all-white Art Deco main library, built by Bertram Goodhue in 1926. The exterior reflected both Indian and Mexican elements, which were combined with symbols of knowledge from Western cultural history. Inside, the cupola of the big central rotunda was decorated in 1927–1932 with murals depicting themes from California's history through the ages. Four different panels illustrated, respectively, the discovery of California, the Spanish mission, the Americanization of the state, and the founding of Los Angeles. At the top of the building's pyramid-shaped roof a gilded hand held a man-sized torch in turquoise terracotta—The Light of Learning—to express the library's mission of enlightenment.

OPEN ACCESS

The introduction of "open shelves" or "open access" around the turn of the last century was an important and much-discussed prerequisite for the development of modern public libraries. Open access heralded a whole new form of library space, but gave rise to great debate and was usually introduced in several phases.

In the United States, open shelves in the modern sense were introduced from 1890 onwards, with the libraries in Boston and Cleveland leading the way, while in England they appeared for the first time in 1894 at the Clerkenwell Public Library in north London. In Denmark, they were introduced in 1902 with the establishment of the State Library in Aarhus, where the reading room was equipped with a special lending department. In 1909, a 1:1 model library, that was presented at a national exhibition and was intended as a prototype for future library buildings, was equipped with open shelves. The library was built in conjunction with a public meeting hall and served as a working model during the exhibition period. In England, only 70 out of 550 public libraries had open shelves in 1910, but from 1916 onwards open access became the norm. Thus the development was almost synchronous in North America, England, and Scandinavia.

Internationally the introduction of open access gave rise to heated debate. Advocates of the new system emphasized that it was a democratic, public-minded initiative that allowed borrowers to choose books on a more informed basis. Opponents put forward a great many arguments: there was a greater risk of theft or of books being misplaced and becoming impossible to re-locate. They also criticized lazy librarians who were bound to stay at their desks and not bother to help borrowers. There was a danger indeed that librarians would become redundant and perhaps be paid lower wages. There was a debate as to whether open shelves were more educational, since they allowed borrowers to orient themselves (though only among books that were not lent out) or whether, on the contrary, the closed-stacks system was better, because it forced borrowers to search systematically in the catalogs.

This discussion was accompanied by a number of compromises between open and closed shelves, usually in the form of gates at the counter or shelves protected by wire netting. Special book "cages" with wire netting were developed, that allowed the borrowers to see the backs of the books displayed with the relevant number or short text. In the Deichman Library in Oslo a special "cage" was set up in the youth department, so that children and young people could point out to the librarian the books stacked behind the net (Fig. 5). The Town Hall library in Copenhagen (built 1905) with shelves protected by netting offers a good example of the transitional methods adopted at the time. The introduction of open shelves was accompanied by a panoptic organization of the library, in which the librarian was placed at a counter at the center of a fan-shaped arrangement of bookshelves. This enabled him to survey the entire room so that he could assist borrowers in their searches and counter any problems with misplaced books or theft. The panoptic arrangement of libraries culminated in the 1920s.

Fig. 5 Book cage in the Youth Department of the Deichman Library in Oslo from around 1900.
Source: Aschehoug.

To serve the growing library readership efficiently a modern counter was introduced that became the centerpiece of the panoptic arrangement of furniture. This type of counter incorporated a number of practical functions relating to lending and correspondence and could be used in many types of premises, serving the borrowers as they passed to and from the open shelves. Gradually it became necessary to extend the library's initially rather small office area, and some of the pressure on the many functions of the counter was relieved.

Open access was thus an important part of the creation of a new library space in which the borrowers could walk freely about the premises, browse among the shelves, and chat with one another. They could find and read the books they were looking for, but they could also stumble on something unexpected. These possibilities were important aspects of a new type of library and a new library identity that the room itself both expressed and helped to create. This new openness would later be related to the open, flowing, and transparent space of modernist architecture. Borrowers were no longer bound to present their wish lists to a librarian behind a closed counter. Borrowing was simplified by replacing long forms with the simple method of stamping a loan card.

THE LIBRARY AS A TEMPLE OF KNOWLEDGE

With the open-shelf system, new library technology and the standardization of library routines for cataloging, classifying, and lending books, an international model was created that had a crucial influence on the development of the physical design of pubic libraries in the first half of the twentieth century. An important aspect of this library model was the almost standard division into an adults' lending library, a reading room and a children's lending library/reading room.

Both in terms of architecture and interior design the many Carnegie Libraries—often quite small, yet monumental and temple-like in appearance—became highly influential internationally, offering model planning solutions for libraries of various types and sizes. Andrew Carnegie's secretary James Bertram drew up a set of guidelines in his *Notes on the Erection of Library Bildings.* Here he set out six practical planning solutions for libraries of various sizes, which with suitable advice could be freely adapted by local architects to meet local needs. A feature common to all these plans was a flight of steps at the center of the building, leading up to an elevated ground floor with a reading room on one side, an adult library with a centrally placed counter in the middle, and a children's library on the other side. Together, the steps and columns emphasized the loftiness of knowledge (Fig. 6).

The ideal form of the classical "temple of knowledge," "temple of enlightenment," or "temple of books" involved a symmetrical ground plan, shaped like a "butterfly" with the entrance and the adult lending library representing the body in the middle axis, and the adult reading room and children's library forming the "wings." The form could be compact like a basilica with a central nave, with the wings folded into the body, or the wings could be spread out to form a T-shape. Often the middle axis served to connect the library building with its surroundings. This classical monumentality was further underscored by the high steps that led up to the entrance, often with columns. The symmetrical design continued into the front hall and on into the adult lending library, culminating in the counter or librarian's desk, which commanded a view of the whole room.

The main catalog with its record of the library's holdings was likewise placed on the middle axis, and frequently a clock embellished the center of the end wall as well; these features symbolized order—in both time and

Law Literature–Library Architecture

Fig. 6 Carnegie Library in Decatur, Alabama, built 1903.
Source:http://www.plannersweb.com/publicbldgs/LIB-DecaturAL.html.

space—in the library's comprehensive collections. The ground plan of the building, its interior design and furnishings and the arrangement of the books all served to express objectivity, stability, and solidity.

The "trinity" formed by the division into adult lending library, reading room and children's library became the archetypal plan of the temple of knowledge. From the outside, the ground plan and the building itself could be read as forming a secularized temple of enlightenment and the interior a secularized basilica, based on the model of the mediaeval church with a nave and aisles. Thus the temple of knowledge was at the same time sacred and secular, both in terms of architecture and interior design. Moreover, the three types of library rooms were distinct in terms of function, codes of behavior, and the identity of the librarians who served in them. The distinction between the three types, however, was stronger in Europe than in America.

The adult lending library was the central room of the public library. It usually took the form of a symmetrical gallery with high windows or top lighting. This arrangement emphasized the loftiness of the room and the many meanings of light. With its open shelves the adult lending library represented the library's intention to reach out to the great reading public, to whom it offered professional guidance and modern methods of lending. The borrowers could search and browse freely among the shelves and it was possible to converse normally. The ideal librarian of the adult lending department was seen as an active communicator of culture, with special experience and skills in choosing the collection of books.

The reading room was the place for enlightenment, concentration, and reflection, and often included special rooms for study. It was also associated with reference work, which in its modern form was an important part of the identity of the library profession. With rules enjoining users to converse in low voices and move around quietly, it was also the room with the most regulated behavior. It

contained a collection of practical, informative reference books designed for purposeful study. Newspapers could also be read here if there was no special newspaper room. Newspaper reading harked back to the recreational reading rooms, often designed to be social places where the public could take shelter in the warmth. Although newspapers played an important role in the political arena, the perusal of newspapers did not enjoy the same high status in the library world at the time, with its lofty ideology of enlightenment, as did the use of reference books. Moreover, newspaper reading could disturb the peace and concentration of the reading room. Often newspapers were stored in tall reading stands, which precluded barely tolerated users from sitting down, getting comfortable, and wiling away the hours.

Finally, the children's library was oriented toward the reading, education, and enlightenment of the coming generation. Initially, libraries simply provided special shelves with books for children. Later, special children's rooms were introduced, which in larger libraries were further divided into a lending department and a reading room. Although the children's library was the liveliest and freest room, it was furnished in the same style as the adult library, albeit on a smaller scale. However, the children's library was often specially decorated and in some cases equipped with a story-telling space for reading aloud.

Among the qualities of the temples of knowledge were their recognizability, regularity, clear functional division, spaciousness, and airy premises with good high ceilings. It is somewhat paradoxical, however, that the public library as a supremely democratic institution should become associated with a relatively closed and pompous style of building.

The Stockholm City Library offers a good example of the way in which the temple of knowledge was architectonically refined. It was designed by the Swedish architect Gunnar Asplund and built between 1924 and 1928. The simple geometric ground plan consisted of a circle inscribed in a quadrangle, corresponding to the central cylindrical building which rises above the four wings. The monumentality of this cylinder corresponded to the cupola of the British Library and the cupola of the Library of Congress in Washington. The building had four virtually identical facades. From the entrance hall one ascended a long, narrow "scala regia" which lead like a dark passage to the great, light lending room, formed as a rotunda with two circular book galleries, containing Swedish and international fiction, poetry, and drama. Nonfiction, which was considered the highest form of educational literature, was placed in two halls in the side wings; here you could find reference books and borrow scholarly or technical works on different subjects. The division of books into different subject areas, and the amalgamation of reference and lending collections, were novelties in librarianship.

Law Literature–Library
Architecture

PUBLIC LIBRARIES IN CENTRAL EUROPE

In Central Europe the closed-stacks system remained the rule in public libraries right up to the decades after World War II. A German survey of library buildings in 1930, *Der Volksbüchereibau*, explained the reasoning behind the closed system and illustrated its use in German public libraries. It was alleged that the English "Freihandbibliothek" ("free-hand library") deprived readers of the opportunity for individual, qualitative, in-depth enlightenment that was the hallmark of the German public library's educative tradition. It was criticized that in the English open-access library the reader did not engage directly with a librarian. German public libraries in the Weimar period retained their closed stacks with sober dispatch rooms for ordering and borrowing books. Whereas the adult lending room was the main room in the Anglo-American and Scandinavian open-shelf libraries, the closed stacks, often with several dispatch rooms attached, were given pride of place in the German public library buildings of the time.

It is interesting to note that the first public libraries with open shelves in Germany were introduced in Bremen in 1939 and in Hamburg in 1940 under the Nazi regime. The Nazis were eager to have a public-minded and effective library service in which they fully controlled the contents, just as they recognized the benefit of using mass media such as film and radio for propaganda purposes. After World War II, the Amerika Gedenkbibliothek, established in West Berlin in 1954, was equipped with open shelves that served as a model for public libraries in post-war democratic Germany.

In Austria the social democratic workers movement introduced large-scale buildings of public housing in "Red Vienna." These great buildings consisted of numerous small apartments that were designed to solve the city's housing problems, but at the same time included a number of communal facilities such as kindergartens, public baths, and libraries that reflected the ideological emphasis on health and culture. The libraries in these Viennese apartment blocks were generally the same size as an ordinary apartment and furnished as reading rooms without direct access to the actual books. Reflecting the ideological and political significance of knowledge, the library in Sandleitenhof had the following inscription on the wall: "Bücher haben uns in die Sklaverei gebracht. Bücher werden uns wieder befreien." ("Books have enslaved us. Books should liberate us again"). The Viennese workers' libraries are interesting because they were conceived as part of an overall cultural–political plan that embraced all aspects of leisure: health, body culture, reading, adult education, enlightenment, and political activities. The Viennese apartment block libraries exemplified politicized institutions, as did, to an even greater extent, the Soviet workers' clubs, which were dominated by Communist Party propaganda, but which were also at the beginning an arena for experiment in architecture and interior design.

RUSSIAN EXPERIMENTS

After the Russian Revolution in 1917, libraries were seen as an important prerequisite for creating a new socialist society in the Soviet Union. The Russian constructivists contributed to a number of projects in this regard, ranging from utopian cultural centers built in soaring avant-garde style to practical proposals for the design of "workers' clubs" that were conceived as breeding grounds for the new culture. For the Soviet Union's exhibition pavilion at the World Exhibition in Paris in 1925 the artist and designer Alexander Rodchenko had set up a model of such a workers' club. The idea behind the project was that after a long day's work the worker could relax with some politically enlightening reading, chess and good fellowship in simple proletarian surroundings without bourgeois carpets, polished furniture, or curtains. The club was furnished extremely austerely with a long narrow table and chairs, shelves for journals and magazines, a chess table with seating for players, a blackboard and photographs of Lenin. One wall could be used for slide shows. Rodchenko's proposal was never put into practice and never exhibited in the Soviet Union.

One of the most experimental library projects in the 1920s was Ivan Leonidov's 1927 model for a Lenin Library or Lenin Institute of Librarianship in Moscow, which together with Tatlin's tower and El Lissitzky's Proun room became one of the icons of Russian constructivism. The Institute was conceived as the Soviet Union's collective information center with space for 15 million books, 5 reading rooms with seating capacity for 500–1000 people, and an institute of librarianship. The project also included a balloon-shaped planetarium and flexible auditoria. The library would be automated, with systems for transporting books horizontally and vertically. As a building complex, it was composed of various soaring geometrical shapes with plenty of potential for expansion. The materials to be used were glass, steel and concrete, and the library would be connected with the city via the metro and aerodrome, and with the world at large via a large-scale radio station. It was also an interesting novelty to conjoin a working library with an institute of librarianship. Leonidov's "information architecture" without doubt constituted the most advanced library project in the interwar period. Quite how advanced it was, can be seen if one compares it, for example, with the main libraries in Los Angeles and Stockholm from the same period. Leonidov's library, on the other hand, was never actually built.

Leonidov also developed open plans for cultural centers and "clubs of a new social type," in which film and radio would function as "living newspapers." His projects were criticized for being too utopian, and he was charged with "left deviationism." Leonidov's advanced projects, in which the library was seen as a universal communications center in an experimental information architecture of iron and glass constructions anticipated present challenges to the traditional library space.

In 1928–1939 the Lenin Library in Moscow, designed by Shcuko and Gelfreikh, was erected in Moscow as the national library of the Soviet Union. This was a far more traditional and classical building than that envisaged in Leonidov's project. The entrance was constructed with pillars in polished black granite bearing a frieze of workers and peasants. The library interior, which served traditional library functions, was designed in the same historic style as the Moscow metro stations of the same period, with polished stone floors, pillars, circular chandeliers, and coffered ceilings.

THE SCANDINAVIAN MODEL

During the interwar years a new type of Scandinavian library arose, that reflected the growth of the welfare state, the cultural movements and the modern architecture of the time. It was less monumental and more oriented toward ordinary everyday life than the temples of knowledge. The hallmark of the Scandinavian model was its combination of modernistic experiment with traditional library design.

International modernism was first introduced in library architecture by Alvar Aalto's library from 1935 in Viborg/ Viipuri in Finland, which at that time was Finland's second largest city. The building consisted of white cubic shapes with a large entrance in glass, but also had inner organic features. The library was set in a park, and Aalto envisaged the white walls being brought alive both in summer and winter by the shadows of the park's trees.

From the entrance one went up to the lending library, where the counter stood as the culminating point, modeled as a small mountain of the Finnish landscape, at the end of a symmetrical staircase. The sunken part of the lending library offered a new interpretation of the classic gallery library. Natural and traditional light wooden materials were used extensively, and the wooden ceiling in the lecture hall was organically folded. The idea was to distribute the sound in the long auditorium and thus make the room more democratic, with everyone being able to hear everyone else. Aalto later designed several libraries.

Nyborg Public Library was one of the last new libraries to be built in Denmark in the interwar period, and with its combination of tradition and modernity it represented in several ways a synthesis of Scandinavian cultural politics and library architecture of the period. The library was designed by Erik Møller and Flemming Lassen and was completed in 1939. It consisted of two red brick wings, joined by a low glass passage, which formed the entrance to the library and its garden, and like a greenhouse united the exterior with the interior. The simple entrance was markedly different from the grand steps and high doors that characterized the temple of knowledge.

The library's various functions were carefully designed with regard to both overall unity and the needs of the individual user. The interior was designed especially for Nyborg Public Library with the assistance of furniture designer Hans J. Wegner. Chairs, tables, bookshelves, and wall panels were made of sycamore wood. The freestanding shelves projected out from the walls, allowing a view through the windows to the town's houses and canals (Fig. 7).

This open, user-friendly architecture and design brought the library closer to everyday life. With its accommodating form, it was a break with the monumental tradition of the time and became an example of a new type of library architecture where easy access, freedom of movement, spacious rooms, and the use of light wooden furniture were expressions of democratization and public enlightenment. The Scandinavian model with its open, informal, and familiar-looking library buildings, often of high architectonic quality, became an inspiration for library architecture in the following decades.

FLEXIBILITY, FUNCTIONALITY, AND MODULARITY

After World War II library buildings expanded, influenced by the ideas of modernist architecture and rational planning of space and functions. Modernism influenced library architecture in the direction of the sober and down-to-earth: "No columns, no pillars, no arches, no ornament, no contrived monumentality" as the architectural historian Nikolaus Pevsner put it. After the war there was a movement toward library environments that were "light, spacious, and informal." Library space became even more open and transparent. In urban planning, these modern libraries became part of the new cultural centers of the suburban landscape.

Another aspect of modernism in library architecture, but also as a consequence of a new rationality in library planning, was the development of modular systems with structural columns. These systems made massive load-bearing walls unnecessary and at the same time they made flexible interior functions and furnishings possible. Walls were temporal and could be removed according to changing needs and functions. The idea of the module was twofold: to ensure that the bookshelves could be located anywhere in the library (providing flexibility) and to position the structural columns so they would not interfere with the spacing of bookshelves (providing functionality). The keywords of library planning in the decades after the war became flexibility, functionality, and modularity.

Much attention was paid to standards of space and furnishing. Needs of space for staff and users were defined. As seminar-style teaching became more common, it seemed important to merge study space with book storage space in libraries with educational purposes. The

Law Literature–Library Architecture

Fig. 7 The interior of Nyborg Public Library from 1939 with light sycamore panels and almost floating free-standing shelves.
Source: Folkebibliotekernes Bibliografiske Kontor.

ideals of library service and design were to create inviting and pleasant as well as efficient interiors, combined with well-organized and coordinated architectural elements. While the ideals were very attractive and progressive, the buildings themselves—with consistent ceiling heights, large floor-plates, and artificial lighting—tended to become monotonous. Rectangular buildings and furnishings became typical with the book as "the real library module."

An artistic and minimalistic version of the modular library in glass and steel is the Martin Luther King Jr. Memorial Library in Washington DC, designed by Ludwig Mies van der Rohe and completed in 1972. A special and elegant expression, that is only modular in its architectural expression, is The Beinecke Rare Book & Manuscript Library from 1963 at Yale, designed by Gordon Bunshaft from Skidmore, Owings, and Merill. A six-story above-ground tower of book stacks is surrounded by a rectangular windowless building with walls made of a translucent marble, which transmit subdued lighting and provide protection of the historical collections from direct light. The marble wall makes the building look quite different from the outside and from the inside.

An almost futuristic example of library architecture from this period is The Marin County Civic Centre in San Rafael in California from 1960, designed by Frank Lloyd Wright and containing public administration, library, and auditorium. The grand tunnel-like arches make the center look both classic and modern. Worth mentioning in this context is also the extension of The Boston Public Library from 1967 to 1971 by Philip Johnson, built in the same pink granite as the historical building and repeating the architectural elements in simple and abstract forms. The extension houses the circulating parts of the library. With its massive walls, it is often compared to a mausoleum. The "half-moon" windows and "rounded columns" are almost post-modern. The Exeter Library in New Hampshire by Louis I. Kahn from 1967 to 1972 has some of the

same monumentality with square form and brick piers. In the inner space, the reading room is a central hall encircled by balconies with books and study alcoves. The reading room is overlooked through giant circular openings in the interior screen walls. The light comes from above through a diagonal cross of concrete. All constructions and materials are visible.

In Berlin, the State Library from 1967 to 1978 by Hans Sharoun represents the period of late-modern architecture, but not the modular thinking. On the contrary the State Library like the nearby Berlin Philharmonic Hall, also by Sharoun, are examples of modern expressionistic architecture, going back to alpine and crystalline architectural visions from Sharoun's youth in the early decades of the century. The exterior of both buildings is covered with aluminium plates, colored yellow. Inside the State Library the reading room is located on the third floor, with triple floor height of 9 m. Hanging mezzanines with sharp edges are part of the inner complex constructions. Books are delivered from a closed-stack system by request.

SPECTACULAR LIBRARIES AS PUBLIC PLACES

Around the turn of the millennium new tendencies in library architecture and design have occurred. The development of new media and digital information technology has challenged the traditional library with different visions of "the library without walls," but it has not weakened, rather apparently heightened international interest in the library as a physical space.

Especially, a series of grand metropolitan libraries has been built around the millennium. Almost as "icons" these "new downtown libraries" as well as museums and other spectacular buildings have become a parameter in the competition between great cities of branding themselves and attracting the creative and wealthy classes. However, the intentions are also to revitalize the inner districts of the

Law Literature–Library Architecture

metropolitan areas. The post-modern architectural expressions, interiors, media collections, and organization of these highly visible buildings may vary. Typically libraries develop as multiuse public spaces, where collections of books and other materials are important, but in connexion with educational, cultural, and social activities. Often libraries are defined as "third places" in society between home and work. In some of these initiatives the experience economy plays an important role. In other contexts the significance of the library as a place of retreat and reflexion is emphasized. The concept of "open access" and "open space" has thus become even more important in library architecture.

Whereas the decades of modular libraries were dominated by ideals of systematic planning, also for the future, the millennium period is characterized by rapidly changing functions and experiments. The architectural styles go from classical symmetrical buildings with columns and decoration, almost like the historical Carnegie libraries, such as the new libraries in Chicago and Nashville, to the deconstructed colosseum of the library in Vancouver and the ice pack of glass and steel that marks the library in Seattle.

Especially the new public library of Seattle from 2004, designed by architect Rem Koolhaas of the Dutch firm OMA (Office for Metropolitan Architecture) has been discussed as example of the new iconic library architecture. The history of Seattle's main library is in itself a show-case of the development of twentieth century library architecture at the same site in downtown Seattle. A Central Carnegie Library was opened in 1906 as a typical temple of knowledge in Beaux-Arts design. It was replaced in 1960 by a modular library in five stories in international style that contained special facilities such as a drive-in service window, where patrons who ordered books in advance could pick them up without having to get out of their cars. The library from 2004 is an 11-story crystalline building with striking appearance among the high-rise office buildings of the area. The glass and steel net is the skin around the inner floating platforms. At ground level you find the Microsoft auditorium and on the third floor the open "living room" with several activities including reading. From here the escalator will take you to the "mixing chamber" with a computers and professional help, and you can continue to the four-story "book spiral," where the non-fiction collection is placed in a continuous series of shelves according to the Dewey Decimal System, without breaking the collection up onto different floors or sections. On Level 10 you find quiet areas of reading, local history, and administration. As an ideal the library design tries to combine fixed and flexible functions.

The iconic status is corresponding to other spectacular downtown library buildings such as Chicago, Denver, Las Vegas, Los Angeles, Nashville, Salt Lake City, and San Francisco, trying to be part of the experience economy, to create multiuse public spaces and to anchor community development of inner city areas.

In a smaller scale the public library of Cerritos, south of Los Angeles near Disneyland, is an example of an experience and learning library, where each room of the library tells a story. Already outside the library you are met by futuristic sounds, old films, or public announcements. Inside the ground floor is organized around a "Main Street" with palm trees. To your right you find "The Old World Reading Room" with soft carpet on the floor, a fireplace, chandeliers, and dark wooden shelves with old editions, inviting you to sit down and read. To your left is the spectacular children's library with an entrance of oversize children's books, saltwater aquarium, a dinosaur reconstruction, a lighthouse, and a changing sky. Moving through Art Deco-shelves of the central book collection or proceeding up the escalator you will reach the twenty-first century level in futuristic design with computer stations and study rooms. This postmodern library design represents the opposite of the modular library other more minimalistic tendencies around the millennium.

Also in Europe a series of spectacular libraries have been built. In Paris the Bibliothèque Nationale de France was erected 1988–1995, designed by Dominique Perrault. The library is situated in a former industrial wasteland at the banks of the Seine. The four corner towers of the building can be interpreted as open books with symbolic meaning, and the inner courtyard with trees can be experienced in relation to Naudé's thoughts about the importance of library gardens and Labrouste's painted artificial landscapes. Around the garden specialized libraries are arranged on mezzanine levels with deliverance from the towers, that are housing stacks and administration.

In London the British Library near St. Pancras Station was begun in 1982 and opened in 1997, designed by Sir Colin St. John Wilson. Red brick materials and colors are corresponding the old station, but the modernism of the new library building is contrasting the Neo-Gothical Hotel and Station. The library is situated in central London. The portico, the piazza, and the amphitheater connect the library with the surrounding urban space. The building has four floors below ground. The exhibition galleries with easy general access are located at two floors at ground level and the three top floors contain reading rooms with daylight. The library is crowned by a roof garden.

In Copenhagen "The Black Diamond" was built as an extension to The Royal Library as part of the creation of a new harbor promenade with several cultural activities and institutions. It was designed by the architects Schmidt, Hammer, and Lassen and opened in 1999. The name refers to the sharp prismatic edges and its surface of black granite and glass, reflecting the water of the harbor. The black surface is contrasting the inner open spaces with reading rooms in light wooden materials in Scandinavian style. From the wave-like balconies of the central foyer, that cuts into the building as a 24-m high atrium, there is a panoramic view over the harbor. The seven floors of the building contain not only traditional library functions such as the four reading rooms, but also a concert hall, exhibition galleries, bookshop, café and restaurant. A small Jewish Museum, designed by Daniel Libeskind, has been integrated in the old red brick library cathedral from 1906, designed by Hans J. Holm.

Other examples of metropolitan libraries are the Main Library of Amsterdam by Jo Coenen from 2007 with multimedia and multiuse space and the main Library of Vienna by Ernst Mayr from 2003, built over the underground system. A special experiment in library architecture is the Library of the Delft University of Tecnology by Mecanoo from 1993 to 1997, where the roof of the library is transformed into a green campus. The futuristic design makes the library look like a landed spaceship. The Madrid Regional Documentary Center by Mansilla +Tunón from 1994 to 2002 is an example of adapted reuse of historical industrial architecture, in this case a former brewery.

GLOBALIZATION

Another important issue of library architecture around the millennium is globalization, both of communication networks and access to information, but also of library architecture and design. Especially in Japan, China, and South East Asia new library buildings are expanding and experimenting with the possibilities of new information technologies. Some of these buildings are built in regional styles, but often they are representing the same "monumental futurism" as the library buildings of the west. In 2003, the international library organization IFLA published *New Library Buildings of the World*, that is an international survey of spectacular new library buildings, documenting this development, where library architecture is becoming increasingly international.

An interesting example of Japanese library architecture is the Sendai Mediatheque, designed by Toyo Ito and completed in 2000. This "mediatheque" complex combines a library, an art gallery, and a media center of visual images. The open space building is defined by three elements: "plate," "tube," and "skin." The "plates" are the six horizontal squares, representing the different media, connected by the 13 vertical "tubes" with flow of information, energy, water, light, and sound.

The "skin" is the outer layer, separating indoors and outdoors of the building. The glass façade is facing the main street, making visual contact possible both from the outside and the inside.

In China some of the new library buildings are reflecting regional architectural traditions such as the National Library from 1987 and the Peking University Library from 1998. The Shenzhen Library 1998–2003 is designed by the Japanese architect Arata Isozaki. It is a

Fig. 8 The Bibliotheca Alexandrina at the Mediterranean Sea. **Source:** webmaster@nile.co.za.

cultural center that also contains a concert hall. The large open spaces have visible constructions and hanging escalators.

One of the most ambitious cross-continental and cross-cultural library initiatives is the new library of Alexandria. The Bibliotheca Alexandrina was designed by the Norwegian drawing office Snøhetta and opened in 2002. The library is sited by the water front avenue in the same district, where Greco-Roman remains were uncovered in 1996, and overlooks the Mediterranean Sea. As the ancient Egyptian image of the sun the library concept is a circular building, inclined toward the sea and submerged into a pool of water. The wall is of Aswan granite with calligraphy, inscriptions and signs from alphabets and civilizations from all over the world. The ideals of the library are both to combine history with the present and to connect different cultures, languages and parts of the world (Fig. 8).

BIBLIOGRAPHY

1. Arenson, A. Libraries in public before the age of public libraries: Interpreting the furnishings and design of Athenaeums and other "social libraries," 1800–1860. In *The Library as a Place: History, Community and Culture*; Buschman, J.E.; Leckie, G., Eds.; Libraries Unlimited: Westport, CT and London, 2007; 41–60.

Law Literature–Library Architecture

2. Arnesen, A. *Bibliotekbygninger*; Norsk Bibliotekforening: Kristiania, 1919.

3. Black, A.; Pepper, S.; Bagshaw, K. *Books, Buildings and Social Engineering*; Ashgate: Aldershot, 2009.

4. Bobinski, G. *Carnegie Libraries: Their History and Impact on American Public Library Development*; American Library Association: Chicago, IL, 1969.

5. Bosser, J. *The Most Beautiful Libraries in the World*; Harry N. Abrams: New York, 2003.

6. Brawne, M. *Libraries: Architecture and Equipment*; Verlag Arthur Niggli: Teufen, 1970.

7. Breisch, A.B. *Henry Hobson Richardson and the Small Public Library in America*; The MIT Press: Cambridge, MA and London, 1997.

8. Burgoyne, F.J. *Library Construction: Architecture, Fittings and Furniture*; George Allen: London, 1897.

9. Buschman, J.E.; Leckie, G. *The Library as a Place: History, Community, and Culture*; Libraries Unlimited: Westport, CT and London, 2007.

10. Cooke, C. *Russian Avantgarde: Theories of Art, Architecture and the City*; Academy Editions: London, 1995.

11. Dahlkild, N. Architecture and design of Danish public libraries, 1909–1939: Between tradition and modernity. In *New Frontiers in Public Library Research*; Johannsen, C. G.; Kajberg, L.; Eds.; The Scarecrow Press: Lanham, MD, 2005; 211–227. Toronto, ON; Oxford.

12. Dickson, P. *The Library in America: A Celebration in Words and Pictures*; Facts on File Publications: New York and Oxford, 1986.

13. Edwards, B.; Fisher, B. *Libraries and Learning Resource Centres*; Architectural Press: Oxford, 2002.

14. Fenelonov, E.A. Soviet public libraries. In *Libraries in the USSR*; Francis, S.; Ed.; Clive Bingley: London, 1971.

15. Fröberg, V. *Tystnaden och ljuset: Om bibliotekens arkitektur*; Carlssons: Stockholm, 1998.

16. Futagava, Y., Ed. *Global Architecture 03; Library. A.D.A.*; EDITA: Tokyo, 2006.

17. Galvin, H.R.; van Buren, M. *The Small Public Library Building*; UNESCO: Nijmegen, 1959.

18. Gram, M.; Ed. *Bibliotek och arkitektur: Byggnader. Rum. Samlinger*; Arkitekturmuseet: Stockholm, 2002.

19. Greenhalgh, L.; Landry, C.; Worpole, K. *Libraries in a World of Cultural Change*; UCL Press: London, 1995.

20. *Libraries: New Concepts in Architecture and Design*; Meisei Publications: Tokyo, 1995.

21. Mattern, S. *The New Downtown Library: Designing with Communities*; University of Minnesota Press: Minneapolis, MN, 2007.

22. Naudé, G. *Advis pour dresser une bibliotheque*; Paris, 1627.

23. Petrosky, H. *The Book on the Bookshelf*; Alfred A. Knopf: New York, 1999.

24. Pevsner, N. *A History of Building Types*; Thames and Hudson: London, 1976.

25. Sherriff, C. But the empire cannot live by muscle alone: An architectural history of the Edwardian public library. Libr. Hist. **2005**, *21* (3), 195–211.

26. Stieg, M.F. *Public Libraries in Nazi Germany*; The University of Alabama Press: Tuscaloosa, AL and London, 1992.

27. Taubert, S. *Bibliopola: Bilder und Texte aus der Welt des Buchhandels*; Dr. Ernst Hauswedell & Co: Hamburg, 1966; Vols. 1–2.

28. Van Slyck, A.A. *Free to All: Carnegie Libraries and American Culture 1890–1920*; The University of Chicago Press: Chicago, IL and London, 1995.

29. Wiegand, W.A.; Davis, D.G.; Eds. *Encyclopedia of Library History*; Garland Publishing: New York and London, 1994.

30. Wieser, M.; Ackerknecht, E. *Der Volksbüchereibau*; Bücherei und Bildungspflege: Stettin, 1930.

31. Wu, J., Ed. *Classical Library Buildings of the World*; IFLA: Shanghai, 2006.

Law Literature–Library Architecture

Library Automation: History

Robert M. Hayes
Department of Information Studies, University of California, Los Angeles, Los Angeles, California, U.S.A.

Abstract

This entry provides a review of the history of developments in library automation in the United States. It discusses four contexts within which library automation should be seen, and does so within each of six time periods: 1) pre-1945; 2) 1945–1960; 3) 1960–1975; 4) 1975–1990; 5) 1990–2008; and (6) post-2008. In each time period, it reviews the societal context and the information technology context, and then two library contexts—technical services and information services.

INTRODUCTION

This entry provides a review of the history of developments in library automation in the United States (It is based in part on an earlier one: Hayes[1]). It discusses four contexts within which library automation should be seen, and does so within each of six time periods: 1) pre-1945; 2) 1945–1960; 3) 1960–1975; 4) 1975–1990; 5) 1990–2008; and 6) post-2008.

Two of the contexts are external to libraries. One is the societal context, including publishing and the perceived role of libraries. This context is important for understanding the development of library automation because it is the environment within which libraries function. The other is that of the information technologies, the hardware and software that are the tools used in library automation.

Two of the contexts are internal to libraries. They include its management and technical services, on the one hand, and information services, on the other. For the purposes of this entry, "technical services" include those library operations involved in management of the materials acquired by the library: the processes in acquisition itself, in cataloging and classifying, in preservation and conservation, in collection control, including circulation. "Information services" include reference services, instructional services and guidance in use of the library's collections, and access to databases and other electronic materials and services, both within the library and through the Internet.

The timelines for these contexts all interact and affect each other, and the discussion will highlight some of the interactions. Of special importance were developments in the commercial, industrial, and consumer sectors in society of parallels to those in the library and information science sectors. In many respects, though almost unheralded, developments of automation in libraries served as means for demonstrating the feasibility of their application in the larger arena. A specific example was the leadership of the National Library of Medicine in proving the feasibility of high quality typographic output from computers, thus demonstrating that computer-controlled photocomposition was feasible. The use of online reference data services was first demonstrated in libraries and then found great acceptance in industry. As we proceed through this history, those kinds of interactions should be evident.

Also of special importance has been the effect of technological capabilities upon not only what could be done but upon the very perception of how to do it. This was evident in the early years, when the limits of punched card technology as well as the means for logical processing it embodied largely determined how people thought about using technology.

PRECURSORS OF LIBRARY AUTOMATION: PRE-1945

Although automation in libraries, as one normally thinks of it, is a phenomenon of the last 50–60 years, it is of value to recognize that there are precursors. Three of them represent elements of continuing importance.

First, Charles Coffin Jewett, as Librarian and Assistant Secretary of the Smithsonian Institution visualized a union catalog of the libraries in the United States. In 1852, he proposed the use of "stereotype plates" as the means for maintenance and production of such a union catalog[2] (A stereotype plate is a metal plate containing a raised image of a page of type or engraving from which prints can be made). Clearly this represents an early stage in the development of automation, but it is more than that since it also represents the theme of cataloging as one of continuing importance that arises during each of the subsequent time periods.

Second, Dr. John Shaw Billings, head of the Library of the Surgeon General's Office (which in 1956 metamorphosed into the National Library of Medicine, as will be

Encyclopedia of Library and Information Sciences, Fourth Edition DOI: 10.1081/E-ELIS4-120044024
Copyright © 2017 by Taylor & Francis. All rights reserved.

Library Automation–Library Publishing

discussed later) was credited by Herman Hollerith with the basic idea of punched cards as means for data processing. According to Hollerith, Billings said to him, "There ought to be some mechanical way of doing this job (i.e., processing 1880 census data), something on the principle of the Jacquard loom, whereby holes in a card regulate the pattern to be woven."[3] And indeed, Hollerith developed such a punched card system which was then used for the data processing of the 1890 census. His company, Tabulating Machine Company, later became IBM, and the Hollerith card dominated data processing throughout the world for 50 years. The punched card represents one stage, perhaps the first stage, in the development of means for data processing as a theme in this review of the history of library automation.

Third, microphotography dates from 1839 and was seen, from at least the early 1850s, as a means for preservation of library materials.[4] In the ensuing 100 years and more, microforms (whether as microfilm, microcards or microfiche, aperture cards, or other forms) were increasingly used by libraries not only for preservation but as a means for acquisition and compact storage of materials, newspapers in particular. Microforms thus represent another continuing theme: developments of alternative means for publication and for acquisition and storage of library materials. In 1938, Eugene Power founded University Microfilms to serve as such a publisher.[5] In 1943, Power and Watson Davis established the National Microfilm Association as means for furthering development of microforms for publication and for managing and using document collections.

Even earlier, in 1937, Watson Davis was instrumental in establishing ADI (American Documentation Institute, in 1963 renamed American Society for Information Science, ASIS, and in 1999, ASIS & Technology, ASIS&T) which was one of the professional societies instrumental in the development of library automation.[6] Other professional societies key to that development were the Association for Computing Machinery, founded in 1947,[7] and the Library and Information Technology Association (LITA, but originally Information Science and Automation Division, ISAD, of the American Library Association), founded in 1966.[8]

EXPLORING THE POTENTIAL OF COMPUTERS: 1945–1960

Societal Context

During this entire 1945–1960 period, the United States was the dominant economic power in the world and the major producer of scientific research publications. The reason is evident: It was the only major country that had not suffered catastrophic losses during World War II. Its economic infrastructure was intact, as was its academic superstructure. Fortunately, it used its economic power

wisely, as best represented by the Marshall Plan that made U.S. resources available for the rebuilding of Europe and the Far East. From the standpoint of science information, at the beginning of this period (say 1948–1950), the United States produced more than 50% of the world's scientific publications.

From the time of Vannevar Bush, as the Science Advisor to the President, the needs for information in science and technology provided a continuing rationale for development of automated information management systems. Indeed, this period started with his frequently cited article, "As we may think."[9] In a very real sense, it foretold virtually everything we have since seen in the developments presented here. Much though that article has been cited, however, a far more important document is the earlier 1945 report of the Office of Scientific Research and Development (OSRD) of which he was chairman. It urged that there be continued support to scientific research after conclusion of World War II and by doing so led to what in 1950 became the National Science Foundation and the National Institutes of Health.[10]

Of specific relevance to this history, the OSRD report identified many of the continuing themes that have been important to library automation. It says, "It seems probable that use of cataloging and sorting devices now available in the form of business machines and microfilm technique might go far to improve present methods of searching the literature and making bibliographies."[11] Indeed, by the end of the period from 1945 to 1960 the realization of that conjecture was well underway.

This was the period of the cold war, reaching its peak in the Korean War and the Cuban Missile Crisis. So there was a continuing emphasis on the needs for information services to support U.S. national defense. As the Cold War became more intense, the intelligence community—CIA (Central Intelligence Agency), National Security Agency, the intelligence arms of each of the branches of the Armed Services—required means for assembling, storing and retrieving, and analyzing massive amounts of data; their needs, more than any others, supported the development of computer hardware and software.[12]

One of the most critical events came toward the end of this period—the launching of Sputnik by the Soviets in 1957—which shocked the military, industrial, and scientific establishment of the United States.[13] The demands for automated systems reached a crescendo as a result of Sputnik and led directly to some of the most crucial developments in automation of libraries. The National Science Foundation launched its Office of Science Information Service to support development and implementation of automated systems and to sponsor the necessary research; of special importance was its funding of the automation of indexing and abstracting services, such as Chemical Abstracts Services.[14–16]

It is also important to note that, consistent with the recommendations of the OSRD, health care and related

Library Automation–Library Publishing

research became a priority of the federal government. The National Institute of Health, established in 1930 by the Ransdell Act, was greatly expanded, becoming the National Institutes of Health and encompassing many individual institutes.[17]

During this period, publishing was much as it always had been. Composition was essentially manual. Though there were a few experiments with use of computer technology, they were completely outside the mainstream of commercial publishing.

The form of publication was simply print, using the traditional means for doing so. Xerographic means for duplication were just beginning to have an impact toward the end of this period. And the computer as means for publishing simply had not yet arrived.

Where then were libraries during this period? Indeed, there was increasing recognition of the importance of libraries, both as part of the activities referred to above and independent of them. Of great significance was the Library Services Act (later expanded into the Library Services and Construction Act) which, among other things, fostered the creation of library networks that have been of vital importance as automated systems became important to libraries.[18] By the Medical Library Act of 1956, (Miles;[19] Public Law 84-941, August 3, 1956:[20] An amendment to Title III of the Public Health Service Act, the National Library of Medicine Act, placed the Armed Forces Medical Library under the PHS, and renamed it the National Library of Medicine) the Surgeon General's Library (first created in 1840) became the National Library of Medicine. At the end of this period, the National Library of Medicine launched its efforts to automate the production of Index Medicus.[21]

In 1862, Congress had created the library of the Department of Agriculture, and in 1961 it too became a national library. (The "Organic Act of 1862", which established the Department of Agriculture, clearly identified the need for a library within it, and the first librarian was appointed in 1867. Over the years, the Department of Agriculture Library became, de facto, a national library but it was not officially designated as the National Agricultural Library until 1962, when "Memorandum No. 1496" of the Secretary of Agriculture did so).

All of these were clear recognition of the importance of libraries.

Information Technology Context

It is with a sense of shock that one compares the nature of the technology during that 15 year period with what we have today. At the beginning of it, data processing meant punched-cards and key-operated accounting machines (such as cash registers), with punched-tape (like teletype tape) as the "common language" for communication among such machines.[22] Computers were limited in capabilities, in numbers, and in applications. While computers were viewed as large and fast at the time, their capabilities were exceptionally limited.[23]

The first computers for application in business and similar operations (among which would be included libraries and information services) appeared in the early 1950s, and "main-frame" computers became widespread by the end of the period. But all of that equipment suffered from the lack of adequate means for input, storage, display, and output of data. Punched cards and punched tape were the only means for input, and they operated at data rates roughly equivalent to 10 characters per second—the speed of teletype! Vacuum tubes (cathode ray tubes or CRTs, as they were called) and then, later, magnetic cores were the means for storage of operating programs and data while immediately being processed; but both were exceptionally expensive and limited in capacity—60,000 bytes would be a big internal memory! For large-scale data storage, there were magnetic tapes and magnetic drums—each slow and with inherent limitations in the ways they could be used. For display, there were the most primitive CRT units, with low resolution and presenting only limited amounts of data. And the means for output were punched card tabulators, with uppercase only fonts and operating again at the equivalent of 10 characters per second. Thus, even though the computers were fast, there wasn't much they could do, given the limited internal memory; they were inherently limited by capabilities for storage of large files and the slow speed of input and output.

However, during this 1945–1960 period technological developments of profound importance were taking place. Specifically, at the beginning the electronic components were essentially vacuum tubes. But the invention of the transistor in 1948 led rapidly to supplant vacuum tubes in computers and then the integrated circuit, first created in 1958, would become the basis for central processing units and make microcomputers possible (For a history of the transistor, see PBS's Web site).[24]

There was one other event of immense importance to technological development at the end of this period. In a talk at Cal Tech in 1959, Richard P. Feynman, the great physicist of our times, said,

> I want to talk about the problem of manipulating and controlling things on a small scale ... all of the information that man has carefully accumulated in all the books in the world can be written in this form in a cube of material one two-hundredth of an inch wide ... Why can't we make (computers) very small ... For instance, the wires should be 10 or 100 atoms in diameter, and the circuits should be a few thousand angstroms across. ... If (computers) had millions of times as many elements, they could make judgments. ...They could select the method of analysis which, from their experience, is better than the one that we would give to them.[25]

Nanotechnology, based on that talk, is today the crucial basis for the future of computing technology.

Library Automation–Library Publishing

Library Technical Services Context

During this period, there was at best slow progress in development of automation for internal, technical processing in libraries. Of course, there were the highly successful uses of microfilm in management of circulation records, especially in public libraries, and there were efforts to use punched-card equipment for that purpose.[26] There were similar efforts to deal with serial records, again using punched-card equipment. For the core technical service functions—acquisition and cataloging—while there were efforts, the problems were great, especially with respect to the number of data entries involved and the overwhelming costs in converting them to machine-processable form.

Two among the experiments, each by Ralph Parker, were of historical interest. The first was his effort in 1930 at the University of Texas. He told the story about wanting to try using a punched-card system for circulation control. The then library director, Don Coney (later to become Director of Libraries at the University of California, Berkeley) said, "OK. Here's $300 but use it wisely."[27] The second was his effort, at the University of Missouri, to initiate an evolutionary approach to an integrated library records system.[28]

By the end of this period, the Council on Library Resources (since 1997, the Council on Library and Information Resources; The merger of the Commission on Preservation and Access and the Council on Library Resources (CLR)[29] became official on May 30, 1997 when the Board approved the new enterprise, the Council on Library and Information Resources, CLIR) had begun to play crucial roles in successive stages in development of library automation;[30] they were of special importance in providing support to the National Library of Medicine in its effort to automate the production of Index Medicus[31] and to the Library of Congress in its first explorations of the use of computer-based systems.[32] More generally, they were concerned with alternative means for producing catalogs and making catalog data available.

In that respect, one of the important attempts to apply computers for access to catalog data was the production of book-form catalogs, especially for union catalogs. It's worth noting again the historical efforts of Charles Jewett to use stereotypes for the production of a national union catalog, as referred to above.[33] In Los Angeles, the County Library system experimented with the use of punched-card equipment for its own union catalog,[34] and there was a similar effort in the 1950s in Seattle, Washington, at the King County Library System ("The King County Library System has embraced each new wave of technology over the years," said KCLS Director Bill Ptacek. "Our first catalog was produced from IBM punch cards in the 1950s..."[35]). While those efforts were essentially dead-ends in the context of later developments, they were important steps in the general progress.

Information Services Context

Given the requirements for information storage and access, focused especially in the intelligence community, computers were seen as a potential means for meeting them. Despite the limitations during this period, the expectations were that the technologies would steadily improve, so there were many efforts to solve the technical and theoretical problems in this field.

But at the beginning of this period, the methodologies for information retrieval were largely based on physical matching of search criteria with document data. In this vein, Calvin Mooers had developed Zatocoding as a means for using edge-notched cards, and Mortimor Taube had developed implementations of his Uniterm concept.[36,37] The Intellofax system at the CIA did much the same thing, using punched card equipment, and Hans Peter Luhn at IBM developed a set of similar approaches.[38] In a real sense, this focus on physical matching reflected the very nature of punched card logical processing which was based on direct connection by wires on a plugboard.

It is of interest to note that, at that time, even the attempts to apply computer technology to the tasks in retrieval started with physical matching of search criteria with document data, using optical coincidence. In particular, the Rapid Selector (the realization by Ralph Shaw, at the National Agricultural Library, of the Memex of Vannevar Bush) used optical matching; the Minicard system, developed by Eastman Kodak and the Magnavox Company for the intelligence community, similarly used optical matching; even the Western Reserve "Searching Selector," developed by James W. Perry and Allen Kent, used an electronic counterpart of such matching.[39]

The point is that those early developments had not yet recognized the capabilities of the computer for complex processing of recorded symbols, so it was not until the end of this period that the techniques of modern computer-based retrieval began to appear.

There was one development toward the end of this period, made operationally possible by use of computer technologies that deserves special recognition. That was the creation of the *Science Citation Index* by Eugene Garfield and his associates at the Institute for Scientific Information. It truly revolutionized the means for indexing of the literature of science, placing it in the hands of the users of that literature through their citations.[40]

BEGINNING TO BRING COMPUTERS INTO LIBRARIES: 1960–1975

Societal Context

In retrospect, although it was not evident at the time, there was a steady reduction in the cold war conflict between the United States and the Soviet Union. The tensions were still

Library Automation–Library Publishing

there, and the cold war conflict would periodically bubble up and then simmer down. But the focus moved into Vietnam and a real war.

The needs in the intelligence community continued, of course, but there was something else, more fundamental and ultimately revolutionary that had become the driving force for automation of information activities. That was the transition of the United States and, at a much slower pace, other industrialized countries, from being "industrial" economies to being "information" economies. Today that transition has impact on every component of our economy and our society, but it was during this period that the changes began to become evident. The report by Marc Porat on the information economy of the United States,[41] clearly identified what was happening and the fact that by the mid-1970s over 50% of the nation's workforce was engaged in information work.

It is important to note that, although many see the appearance of the information economy as something created by and driven by information technology, the cause is much more fundamental. It is the imperative in development of the society that has created it and the technology merely feeds and serves that imperative, making it possible, yes, but not causing it. In any event, the information economy, whatever the cause, was the driving force for developments in library and information science during this period.

Of course, the importance of science information continued to be recognized. The Department of Commerce established NTIS as one means to improve dissemination of scientific and technical information. The National Academy of Sciences repeatedly reviewed the status of developments and recommended increased efforts.[42,43]

During this period, the processes of publishing were revolutionized, as computer-based photocomposition completely replaced the former manual methods. And xerography became a fact of daily life in business of every kind. From the standpoint of this history, though, the important development in publishing was the onset of electronic formats, as represented by the creation of databases, initially as a result of efforts by the U.S. federal government.

Information Technology Context

During most of the 1960–1975 period, computing was centered on large main-frame computers. In fact, what was called "Grosch's Law" (named after Herbert R. J. Grosch) governed most of the decisions about computing installation.[44] It stated that "computing power goes up as the square of the cost," the implication of which is crystal clear: the bigger the better! During this period, the University of California developed the MELVYL system, initially visualized as a centralized university-wide library service in the spirit of Grosch's Law.

In parallel, there was extensive development of networks among computers, starting from the work of the University of California, Los Angeles (UCLA) Western Data Processing Center (literally the first such network)[45] and expanding into Advanced Research Project Agency Network (ARPANET), of the Department of Defense,[46] and National Science Foundation (NSF) super-computer network.[47] Together they became the backbone of today's Internet (now supplemented by all of the commercial communication networks).

In 1962, Dr. Leonard Kleinrock published the basic principles of packet switching, the technology underpinning the Internet. The birth of the Internet then occurred when his host computer at UCLA became the first node of the Internet in September 1969.[48] Of course, as we will see later, the impact of the Internet has been profound, not only on libraries but on the entire world.

Library Technical Services Context

It must be said that, even near the end of this period, there were at best mixed feelings in the library community about the use of the information technologies. Some librarians regarded it as a meaningless diversion of funds and efforts.

> "In sum, our experience with the computer in library operations has been one more replay of The Emperor's New Clothes, and what we were led to believe were distant mountains laden with gold, available merely by boring a drift in the slope, turn out, upon close inspection, to be the hairy buttocks of the well-fed computer industry. And from such a source we have gotten exactly what we should expect."[49]

But, during this period, despite such views by some librarians, there were increasing efforts to at least experiment with the use of library automation. A context of special importance in doing so were efforts to establish cooperative networks among libraries. Each of the states, under the stimulus of the Library Services and Construction Act, created its own state library network, intended to include public, academic, school, and special libraries together. Washington State, in particular, established the Washington Library Network (WLN) as an automated union catalog system for the northwest region of the United States.[50]

In parallel, OCLC (originally Ohio College Library Network, then Online Computer Library Network, later simply as the term OCLC itself) was established by Fred Kilgour in Dublin, Ohio.[51] And the Research Library Network (RLIN) was created as a part of the Research Library Group. Each was intended to serve on a national basis as means for dealing with the generic issue of retrospective conversion of catalog records, a dominant concern in the effort to introduce automation in academic libraries.

Library Automation–Library Publishing

Cooperation in the area of cataloging was made possible because of the crucial contribution of Henriette Avram, at the Library of Congress, in establishing the Machine Readable Cataloging (MARC) format as the de facto national standard for exchange of catalog data; without that, it would have been intolerably difficult. Avram[52–54] So, using the MARC format, WLN, OCLC, and RLIN could serve as economic solutions to the catalog conversion task, and automated systems to support cataloging and catalog access could be developed within institutions. At about the same time Stanford University developed the BALLOTS system; it later became the basis for the RLIN national bibliographic database system. IBM developed DOBIS for the University of Dortmund, in Germany, as an online catalog system.[55]

In parallel, modules began to be developed at individual libraries to support other aspects of internal, technical services—circulation and collection management, serials records, and support to acquisitions. An example was the Leuvens Integraal Bibliotheek Systeem (LIBIS) at the Catholic University of Leuven, Belgium. Although that was not in itself a United States development, IBM negotiated the right to market it with the DOBIS catalog system, as a quasi-integrated product.[56] In 1971, Béla Hatvany founded Computer Library Services, Inc. to provide a minicomputer based library application, focused on circulation control.[57]

Perhaps the first of the efforts to produce a truly integrated system was at Northwestern University and it became the basis for NOTIS, the commercial version.[58] Roughly in parallel, was the Southwest Academic Libraries Cooperative Mechanization Project and the University of Chicago Library Data Management System. Each started in the late 1960s.[59]

Information Services Context

As a result of all that had occurred during the 1945–1960 period, the production and distribution of bibliographic, indexing, and abstracting databases became a reality rather than merely a speculation. All of the research and technical development had come to fruition during the period 1960–1975, and with great success. Of special importance were the online services for access to the reference databases (such as Chemical Abstract Services, ERIC, and Medline). DIALOG was created by Roger K. Summit in 1966[60] and ORBIT by Carlos Cuadra in 1967–1968,[61] for example. Bibliographic Retrieval Services (BRS) was created in 1968 at State University of New York, Albany, and library OPACs (online public access catalogs) were developed by many individual libraries for access to catalog databases. Less dramatic but still important was the implementation of Interlibrary Lending (ILL) services by OCLC and RLIN.

COMPUTERS ARE ACCEPTED BY LIBRARIES: 1975–1990

Societal Context

This was a most remarkable 15 years! At the end of it, there was the end of the Cold War with the disintegration of the Soviet empire. The effects of these international events for library automation are less tangible, perhaps, but are very real. In particular, the separate republics of the former Soviet Union became independent countries each of which has needed to deal with the information revolution. And beyond them, other countries of Central and Eastern Europe which had functioned under the stultifying effects of Soviet-style communism faced similar needs. The Soros Foundation[62] and the Mellon Foundation[63] each saw library automation as a valuable tool for bringing the libraries of those countries into support of modern social and economic development. They each began their funding of such developments.

During this period, publishing continued essentially unchanged, though with steadily increasing concern about how best to deal with the impact of electronic formats (which, as will be seen, became virtually a crisis situation in the next period).

During this 1975–1990 period in the United States, funding problems for both public and academic libraries were real and in some cases catastrophic. University libraries experienced 10–20% budget reductions each year for 5 years and more. But the prices of materials sky-rocketed; journals, in particular, escalated in cost at 15–20% per year during this period. Yet, in the face of the economic travails, the use of both public and academic libraries grew dramatically. The information economy requires the kinds of resources and means for information access that libraries and only libraries provide.

Information Technology Context

During the first 30 years or so of this history, the decisions concerning computer acquisition, as said above, were based largely on Grosch's Law: Bigger is better! But something happened toward the end of the 1970s that was a fundamental revolution. The microcomputer—the PC and the Apple Computer Macintosh—totally reversed the law: Smaller is better! The new law was "Moore's law" (named after Dr. Gordon Moore, cofounder of Intel) which states that the capabilities of microprocessors double every 2 years.[64] The result is that today, one can hold in the palm of the hand more computing power than even the largest of main frames of two decades ago. The result has been a distribution of computing power that puts the PC, laptop, or palmtop in the plane seat, the police car, the fire engine, the personal auto, as well as in virtually every home and office.

The revolution in information technology is far greater than just the computer itself, though it indeed is the centerpiece. Increases in telecommunication capacity in some respects equal those in computer capacity. Whereas 50 years ago, we were limited to 10 characters per second (roughly the equivalent of 100 baud), today we have data rates 10,000 times greater for use in our own homes. Whereas 40 years ago we had CRTs with minimal capability, today we have displays with resolutions virtually the equivalent of the printed page and screen capacities that permit the most beautiful images imaginable and the ability to observe in real time the operation of the heart or the brain of a human being, in living color no less. Whereas 50 years ago we were happy to have 6000 bytes of internal memory, today we can have almost unlimited numbers of megabytes. And whereas 30 years ago the means for mass storage of data were limited in capacity and unbelievably slow, today we have gigabytes of capacity with rapid random access.

What a revolution it has been!

Library Technical Services Context

During this time period, the bits and pieces that were created by individual institutions were replaced by integrated library systems (i.e., systems including the full range of functions in both technical services and reader services), commercially available and with the support of highly qualified professional staffs. They were operational on both main frames and personal computers; they functioned in both stand-alone and "client-server" modes; they served every type and size of library; they functioned well in any country of the world.

The NOTIS and DOBIS/LIBIS systems were the first of the products of this kind, but during the 1975–1990 period, the number of integrated library systems steadily grew. An inventory of them for each year since the early 1980s is available online at Integrated Library Systems Report.[65] These commercial systems differ in their means for software implementation, in the hardware they will use, in the services they will provide, in their pricing. But, in essence, they each provide essentially the same coverage of the technical services operations.

Information Services Context

The effects on information services during this period were dramatic. The availability of OPACs in virtually every library made the resources of the library and, in most cases, of the world readily available. The availability of CD-ROMs brought a wealth of materials into the library, not only available but in processable form. The Internet and the World Wide Web began to provide means

for online communication and access that would change the entire information economy.

COMPUTERS AS INTEGRAL TO LIBRARIES: 1990–2008

Societal Context

And this also was a most remarkable period! In the United States, the continued progress in development of the Internet led the Clinton administration to identify the need for a national and then international "global information infrastructure." For the first time, "information" beyond simply science information had explicitly become an identified priority in national policy.[66,67]

This period has seen a virtual revolution in the extent to which information resources are used throughout the U.S. society. Today, massive amounts of data are generated, transmitted, and consumed. The cellular telephone is ubiquitous. The Internet is growing in use at a phenomenal rate—doubling in use every 3–6 months! The entertainment and amusement industries are exploding. The publishing of books and magazines has grown similarly. Indeed, the "super bookstores" proliferate at an almost unbelievable frequency, and one of the success stories of the Internet was "amazon.com" as an online bookstore.

During this period, there was almost a revolution in publishing. As a result of the transfer of advertising budgets to the Internet, newspapers found themselves in serious financial difficulties.[68] Journals increasingly moved into electronic distribution. Even electronic books began to appear, although print continued to be the overwhelming means for distribution of books.

The spectacular growth off the Internet during this period did lead to the "dot-com mania" of the mid-1990s which came to a resounding crash in March 2000. The investment frenzy created billionaires, literally over night, and the crash then wiped out many of them. In the 8 years since then, though, the Internet as an investment vehicle has essentially recovered. Google went public in 2004 and since then has sky-rocketed. And the shares of other Internet companies have also done well.[69]

One other societal event needs to be included here, since it has had dramatic and devastating effects upon libraries. The catastrophe of the September 11, 2001 attacks, the ensuing wars in Afghanistan and Iraq, the continuing and growing tension in the Middle East, all have led to the diversion of federal funds from domestic needs to military needs. The resulting deficits have cascaded into state and local economies, with one result being that funding for libraries, both public and academic, has been significantly curtailed. And there appears to be no end in sight.

Library Automation–Library Publishing

Information Technology Context

During this period, the information technologies continued to develop based on Moore's law. The capacities and speeds continue to double yet the costs stay the same or even decrease.

One development that could have significant impact on publishing, book distribution, and libraries is "print on demand," in which material is printed and bound at the time of delivery to the purchaser.[70–72] The value for the publisher and for book distribution is that large inventories are not needed, so storage costs, handling costs, and accounting costs are eliminated, and there is no loss from unsold copies. The value for the library is instant delivery.

Library Technical Services Context

The commercial integrated library systems continued to be the basis for library automation, essentially little changed from those developed and marketed during the prior period. The major impact of automation of libraries, though, was on the print journals, which are rapidly disappearing, and replacement of them by electronic access, via the Internet.

During this period, the fact that services provided by WLN, OCLC, and RLIN were duplicative, without any essential differences, led to OCLC becoming the surviving agency. The merger of WLN into OCLC occurred in 1998–1999;[73,74] that of RLIN into OCLC, in 2006.[75] The result is the effective realization of a union catalog for the United States as envisioned by Charles Jewett over 150 years ago.

Major research libraries began participating in joint efforts to digitize their collections of materials no longer in copyright.[76]

Information Services Context

The impact of the Internet search engines, Google especially, on information services was immense during this period. The first of the tools underlying the search engines, called Archie, appeared in 1990. It was followed by Gopher, Veronica, and Jughead, in 1991. They searched in file names and menus, but not in content. WebCrawler and Lycos, in 1994, were the first to provide for content searches. And then the number of content search engines exploded.[77] There were, as of April 24, 2008 over 130 organizations providing these generic Internet services.[78] Table 1 shows just a sample of the range of search engines now available, sequenced by date of their initiation and showing an Internet source for each date.

The database services continued but now as part of the Internet. A listing of database services providers includes 87 organizations. It is of more than passing interest to note the extent to which these organizations are now not based in the United States. This surely reflects the extent to which the information economy has become a global phenomenon. Just as an example, Dialog was acquired by Knight-Ridder in 1995; then, in 1997, Knight-Ridder merged with Marketing Analysis and Information Database and the new corporation became The Dialog Corporation; in 2000, the Thomson Corporation acquired the database service operations from The Dialog Corporation; in 2008, Thomson and Reuters merged.[79] In much the same vein, Wolter Kluwer, a Netherlands based company acquired Ovid in 1998[80] and then Silver Platter in 2001.[81] Beyond the Internet commercial search services and database access services, academic and public libraries throughout the United States developed Internet "online reference desks" and library-based research guides

Table 1 A sample of currently available search engines.

Lycos	1994	http://en.wikipedia.org/wiki/Lycos
Yahoo!	1994	http://en.wikipedia.org/wiki/Yahoo!
MetaCrawler	1994	http://en.wikipedia.org/wiki/Metacrawler
AltaVista	1995	http://en.wikipedia.org/wiki/AltaVista
MSN	1995	http://en.wikipedia.org/wiki/MSN
Ask Jeeves	1996	http://en.wikipedia.org/wiki/Ask.com
(now Ask.com)	1996	http://en.wikipedia.org/wiki/Ask.com
HotBot	1996	http://en.wikipedia.org/wiki/HotBot
Dogpile	1996	http://en.wikipedia.org/wiki/Yahoo!
Mamma	1996	http://en.wikipedia.org/wiki/Mamma.com
Google	1998	http://www.google.com/corporate/execs.html
Ixquick	1998	http://en.wikipedia.org/wiki/Ixquick
AllTheWeb	1999	http://en.wikipedia.org/wiki/AlltheWeb
Teoma	2000	http://en.wikipedia.org/wiki/Teoma
Turbo10	2000	http://en.wikipedia.org/wiki/Turbo10
Vivisimo	2000	http://en.wikipedia.org/wiki/Vivisimo
SearchHippo	2001	http://www.searchhippo.com/about.php
Wisenut	2001	http://en.wikipedia.org/wiki/WiseNut
A9.com	2004	http://en.wikipedia.org/wiki/A9.com
Gigablast	2004	http://www.forumpostersunion.com/showthread.php?t=355
Myriad Search	2005	http://en.wikipedia.org/wiki/Myriad_Search

for specific subject areas. The University of Illinois "online reference collection"[82] and the Internet Public Library (maintained by a consortium of information science academic programs)[83] are two specific examples, but there is a broad range of other libraries using a variety of software tools.[84]

THE FUTURE FOR COMPUTERS IN LIBRARIES: POST-2008

It is the year 2008, at the time of writing this. It is very difficult to make predictions, especially about the future, but the discussion of this sixth and last time period is about the coming years rather than past years.

Societal Context

The revolution that has resulted in the "information economy" will continue, and the pace will accelerate in other countries of the world as well as in the United States. The facts are that information products and services have become a world-wide phenomenon. It has been estimated that it is a trillion dollar market, and the United States today is the dominating supplier. The Internet is the means for access as well as a manifestation of the information economy.

What is the future of publishing, especially in the light of what is happening with the information technologies? In particular, what will happen to publication in print formats? While there is clear evidence for a shift in journal publication from printed issues to on-demand publication of articles, there is no evidence of comparable shift of monograph publication in the same way. Therefore, for libraries, it is necessary to plan for continued acquisition of book materials in print form See, for example: "...experts predict that elementary and high school textbook sales will jump by 35%, to $3.5 billion, from 1996 through 2001. College textbook sales are expected to zoom 40%, to $3.47 billion, over the same span."[85]

Digitized imaging is a form of publication that will be of increasing importance. It has become a powerful tool in research of all kinds. It is the basis for publishing of materials such as maps and will probably replace print as the means for publication of them. Academic libraries, especially, should plan not only for management of digitized images but for serving as significant sources for publication of them.

So, what will happen to libraries? There are persons who forecast their demise, in the perception that they will be replaced by the wealth of resources becoming available through the information technologies; such voices have been heard for at least the past three to four decades. It is a fact that during the past decade libraries have faced enormous economic pressures; they have had to operate within the constraints of reduced budgets even while the costs of acquisitions—especially of journals—have been escalating at exponential rates of 15–20% per annum. At the same time, they have needed to make continuing investments in automated systems and to deal with the array of computer-based forms of publication.

The likely picture, though, is very different from that of those who wish to get rid of libraries. Libraries are essential and will continue to be so in the foreseeable future. Instead of being overwhelmed by technologies, they have absorbed them, made them economic and effective, and served as the basis for testing and proving them. It is also a fact that the effect of electronic information resources was to increase not decrease the use of the library. The various forms of publication are complementary and mutually supportive rather than being substitutes for each other. The use of any of them leads to increased use of the others, and the library serves as the agency for access to all of them.

There is every expectation that the library will continue not only to exist but to thrive and to play its historic leadership role in the coming decades. Underlying that expectation is the view that, while electronic publication will be increasingly important, it will not replace print in the foreseeable future. And libraries will be the means of access to both print and electronic formats.

Information Technology Context

During the more than 60 years the computer business has continued to grow at a phenomenal rate. Each year the capabilities have increased, the effectiveness and even efficiency have increased, the pervasiveness in our society has increased.

Of that more than 60 year history, though, the most spectacular gains have been made within the past 30 when "microprocessors"—computers on chips—became the basis for the hardware. The first microprocessors were breathtaking innovations and they revolutionized not only the design of computers but their use throughout our world.

Will the process continue? In a recent book,[86] Michael Malone poses that question and concludes that the answer is Yes, saying that, while there are absolute barriers in the laws of physics, there are still means by which the process can continue. Most important among them are those that relate to the software, in which future developments may have even greater impact than we have seen to date from the hardware.

Library Technical Services Context

The integrated library systems operational and commercially available today surely meet the needs in technical services. They are well proven and there is now extensive experience in their use.

Library Automation–Library Publishing

Having said that, the role of technical services themselves in libraries for the coming future is problematic. Acquisition of journals is now a matter of negotiation with the publishers and consolidators, in which large numbers of electronic journals are dealt with as a package. Processing becomes nonexistent for those journals, since they are available, under the negotiated arrangements, directly online from the publisher or consolidator. Acquisition of books and special collections, on the other hand, is likely to continue if, as predicted above, printing continues to be the primary means for book distribution. Even given that, one can visualize the library with the equipment and online access necessary to use print on demand. The impact on technical processing in such cases could be profound.

With respect to cataloging, the situation already has had a significant impact. Increasingly, the national bibliographic database maintained by OCLC serves not only as the source for cataloging data but as the OPAC. Here the effect on technical processing is even greater.

Information Services Context

The implications are that library services to patrons will become increasingly important and that staff will be shifted from internal operations to direct services.

First among the direct information services is the Internet. Indeed, the pace in growth of the use of the Internet is likely to continue on into the future, though with likelihood of significant slowing in perhaps 5 years. Access to the Internet will continue to be important for academic roles. It is important to note, however, that while the Internet was highly academic in its origins and orientation, those uses, while growing, will do so at a substantially more limited rate and are already very small in comparison to the commercial uses.

The crucial point is that the widening scope of information resources increases the importance of the information services. In this respect, it is important to recognize that the library is more than simply a collection of materials, valuable though that is and will continue to be. It is also more than simply a means for access to those materials and the information contained in them, again valuable though that is and will continue to be. The library is the agency that serves as the means for selection. It does so when acquisition librarians make decisions about what materials are worth adding to the collection. It does so when reference librarians help patrons in locating and selecting from the wealth of resources those that will meet needs. It does so when library-based information specialists select from retrieved information and analyze the results.

The library is also a means for users to learn how to manage information resources. Library services in teaching are therefore of special significance, and the increasing wealth of resources adds greatly to their importance.

REFERENCES

1. Hayes, R.M. "History review: The development of information science in the United States" Proceedings of the 1998 Conference on the History and Heritage of Science Information Systems Pittsburgh, PA 23–25 October, 1998; Bowden, M.E., Hahn, T.B., Williams, R.V., Eds.; Information Today, Inc.: Medford, NJ, 1999; 223–236 for the American Society for Information Science and the Chemical Heritage Foundation. See also http://slim.emporia.edu/globenet/Warsaw/Notes.htm (accessed October 2, 2008).

2. Jewett, C.C. *On the Construction of Catalogues of Libraries, and Their Publication by Means of Separate, Stereotyped Titles. 2nd ed*, Smithsonian Institution: Washington, D.C., 1853.

3. Truesdell, L.D. *The Development of Punch Card Tabulation in the Bureau of the Census, GPO*, GPO: Washington, D.C., 1965.

4. http://en.wikipedia.org/wiki/Microfilm.

5. Power, P.H.; Eugene, B. Power (June 4, 1905–December 6, 1993). Proc. Am. Philos. Soc. **1995**, September *139*(3), 301–304 http://www.jstor.org/sici?sici=0003-049X(199509)139%3A3%3C300%3AEBP(J1%3E2.0.CO%3B2-Z (accessed October 2, 2008).

6. Heilprin, L.B. Annual Review of Information Science and Technology (ARIST): Early historical perspective. J. Am. Soc. Inform. Sci. **1988**, *39*(4), 273–280.

7. Snodgrass, R. *Our Past as a Prelude to our Future*, 2003; June http://www.cs.arizona.edu/~rts/initiatives/history/history.pdf (accessed October 2, 2008).

8. http://www.ala.org/ala/lita/lita40thanniversary/index.cfm LITA 40th Anniversary.

9. Bush, V. As we may think. Atl. Mon. **1945**, August *176*, 101–108.

10. Bush, V. *Science: The Endless Frontier. Report to the President on a Program for Postwar Scientific Research*, Government Printing Office: Washington, DC, 1945; July.

11. Bush, V. *Science: The Endless Frontier. Report to the President on a Program for Postwar Scientific Research*, Government Printing Office: Washington, DC, 1945; July 112–115.

12. *Documentation, Indexing, and Retrieval of Scientific Information: A Study of Federal and Non-Federal Science Information Processing and Retrieval Programs. Committee on Government Operations, United States Senate*, GPO: Washington, DC, 1961; March 9 (See especially pages 63–64, CIA Intellofax system, and page 65, Minicard system).

13. http://history.nasa.gov/sputnik/.

14. *Current Research and Development in Scientific Documentation*, National Science Foundation, Office of Science Information Service. No.: Washington, DC, 1957–1969; July 1–15.

15. *Nonconventional Scientific and Technical Information Systems in Current Use*, GPO for National Science Foundation (Office of Science Information Service): Washington, DC, 1958; No. 1, No. 2, 1960; No. 3, 1962; No. 4, December 1966.

16. *Specialized Science Information Services in the United States*, GPO for National Science Foundation (Office of Science Information Service): Washington, DC, 1961; November Washington, DC.

17. *A Short History of the National Institutes of Health*, http://history.nih.gov/exhibits/history/index.html (accessed October 2, 2008).

18. Holley, E.G. *The Library Services and Construction Act: An Historical Overview from the Viewpoint of Major Participants*, JAI Press: Greenwich, CT, 1983.

19. Miles, W.D. *A History of the National Library of Medicine*, GPO: Washington, DC, 1982; 353–355 (National Medical Library Act of 1956).

20. http://www.nlm.nih.gov/about/legislativechronology.html (accessed October 2, 2008). See also http://www.mlanet.org/government/gov_pdf/nlm_resolution_50th.pdf.

21. Miles, W.D. *A History of the National Library of Medicine*, GPO: Washington, DC, 1982; 365 (support grant from Council on Library Resources in 1958), 372–373. (GRACE graphic arts composing equipment in 1963), 378. (Medical Library Assistance Act of 1965).

22. Head, G.W. "What does automation mean to the marketing man?". J. Market **1960**, April *24*(4), 35–37 (published by: American Marketing Association). http://www.jstor.org/stable/view/1248402?seq=1 (accessed October 2, 2008).

23. Pugh, E.W.; Aspray, W. Creating the computer industry. IEEE Ann. Hist. Comput. **1996**, *18*(2), 7–17 http://ieeexplore.ieee.org/iel4/85/10525/00489720.pdf?arnumber=489720 (accessed October 2, 2008).

24. http://www.pbs.org/transistor/album1/index.html.

25. http://www.zyvex.com/nanotech/feynman.html.

26. Williams, R.V. "The use of punched cards in US libraries and documentation centers, 1936–1965". IEEE Ann. Hist. Comput. **2002**, April *24*(2), 16–33 http://ieeexplore.ieee.org/iel5/85/21773/01010067.pdf (accessed October 2, 2008).

27. Hayes, R.M. Becker, J. *Handbook of Data Processing for Libraries*, Wiley: New York, 1970; 3–4.

28. Parker, R. *Library Applications of Punched Cards*, American Library Association: Chicago, IL, 1952.

29. *Council on Library and Information Resources. Annual Report*, Washington, DC, 1996–1997; 1997.

30. Marcum, D.B. "Automating the library: The council on library resources". IEEE Ann. Hist. Comput. **2002**, July–September *24*(3), 2–13.

31. Miles, W.D. *A History of the National Library of Medicine*, GPO: Washington, DC, 1982; 365 (support grant to NLM from Council on Library Resources in 1958).

32. King, G.W. *Automation and the Library of Congress*, Library of Congress: Washington, DC, 1963.

33. *Fifth Annual Report of the Board of Regents of the Smithsonian Institution*, GPO: Washington, DC, 1851; 28–41 ("Report of the Assistant Secretary in Charge of the Library") and 81 ("Report of the Commissioners upon the General Catalogue").

34. MacQuarrie, C. The metamorphosis of book catalogs. Libr. Resour. Tech. Serv. **1964**, Fall *8*(4), 370–378.

35. King County Library System News. **2007**, Fall http://www.kels.org/foundation/newsletter/07%20Fall%20KCLSF%20News.pdf (accessed October 2, 2008). [King Count Library: Seattle, WA].

36. In *Information Storage and Retrieval: Theory, Systems, and Devices (Air Force Office of Scientific Research Symposium)*; Taube, M., Wooster, H., Eds.; Columbia University Press: New York, 1958; (Contains articles by Luhn, H.

P., Calvin, M., Ralph, S., and others as well as by M.T. himself).

37. In *Emerging Solutions for Mechanizing the Storage and Retrieval of Information (Studies in Coordinate Indexing, Vol. V)*; Taube, M., Ed.; Documentation, Inc: Washington, DC, 1959; (Contains a description by H.P. Luhn of the "IBM universal card scanner" that involved optical coincidence as the means for selection. Contain a variety of articles concerning coordinate indexing written by Mortimor Taube and his associates).

38. In *H.P. Luhn: Pioneer of Information Science, Selected Works*; Schultz, C., Ed.; Spartan Books: New York, 1968; 164–185 (See especially "The IBM electronic information searching system", 35–51 and "Information retrieval through row-by-row scanning on the IBM 101 electronic statistical machine".

39. Becker, J. Hayes, R.M. *Information Storage and Retrieval*, Wiley: New York, 1963; 148–149.

40. Garfield, E. *Essays of an Information Scientist*, ISI Press: Philadelphia, PA, 1977; [See especially Weinstock, M., "Citation indexes", 188–195. (reprinted from Encyclopedia Libr. Inform. Sci. Vol. 5, 16–40. Marcel Dekker: New York, 1971)].

41. Porat, M.U. *The Information Economy: Definition and Measurement*, U.S. Department of Commerce, Office of Telecommunications: Washington, DC, 1977; May.

42. *Science Information Activities*, National Academy of Sciences—National Research Council: Washington, DC, 1965; A Report of the Office of Documentation.

43. Committee on Scientific and Technical Communication National Academy of Sciences—National Research Council *Scientific and Technical Communication: A Pressing National Problem and Recommendation for its Solution*, National Academy of Sciences: Washington, DC, 1969; The SATCOM report.

44. Orr, W.D. *Conversational Computers*, John Wiley: New York, 1968; 152.

45. http://personal.anderson.ucla.edu/clay.sprowls/history/WDPC/wdpc.htm.

46. http://en.wikipedia.org/wiki/ARPANET#Initial_ARPA_deployment.

47. http://www.sri.com/policy/csted/reports/techin/inter2.html.

48. http://en.wikipedia.org/wiki/Leonard_Kleinrock.

49. Mason, E. The great gas bubble prick't; or, computers revealed—by a gentleman of quality. Coll. Res. Libr. **1971**, *32*(3), 183–196.

50. Pulsifer, J.S. *MARC Book Catalog Production in Washington State*, Graduate School of Library Science, University of Illinois: Urbana-Champaign, IL, 1970.

51. http://en.wikipedia.org/wiki/Fred_Kilgour.

52. Avram, H.D. Knapp, J.F. Rather, L.J. *The MARC II Format; A Communications Format for Bibliographic Data*, Library of Congress, Information Systems Office: Washington, DC, 1968.

53. Avram, H.D. *The MARC Pilot Project: Final Report on a Project Sponsored by the Council on Library Resources, Inc*, Library of Congress: Washington, DC, 1968.

54. Avram, H.D. *MARC, Its History and Implications*, Library of Congress: Washington, DC, 1975.

55. Grosch, A.N. *Library Information Technology and Networks*, CRC Press: New York, 1995; 27 28.

56. Grosch, A.N. *Library Information Technology and Networks*, CRC Press: New York, 1995; 27.

57. Hatvany, B. How to prosper in the era of the Internet 2000 Miles Conrad Memorial Lecture NFAIS Annual Conference Philadelphia, PA 2000 http://www.nfais.org/publications/mc_lecture_2000.htm (accessed October 2, 2008).

58. Hatvany, B. How to prosper in the era of the Internet 2000 Miles Conrad Memorial Lecture NFAIS Annual Conference Philadelphia, PA 2000 http://www.nfais.org/publications/mc_lecture_2000.htm (accessed October 2, 2008) 27.

59. http://www.librarytechnology.org/?SID=20080423200256347&Username=&timeout=1208973242.

60. Summit, R. Reflections on the beginnings of dialog: The birth of online information access. Chronolog **2002**, June The Dialog Corp. http://www.dialog.com/about/ (accessed October 2, 2008).

61. Bourne, C.P. Trudi, B.H. *A History of Online Information Services, 1963–1976*, MIT Press: Cambridge, MA, 2003.

62. http://en.wikipedia.org/wiki/Soros_Foundation.

63. Quandt, R.E. *The Foundation's Program in Eastern Europe, 1992*, Annual Report—The Mellon Foundation. http://www.mellon.org/news_publications/annual-reports-essays/presidents-essays/the-foundation-s-program-in-eastern-europe (accessed October 2, 2008).

64. Moore, G.E. Cramming more components into integrated circuits. Electronics **1965**, April *19*, 114ff.

65. http://www.goalexandria.com/solutions/uni_corp.html.

66. Clinton, W.J. Gore, A. *Putting People First: How We Can All Change America*, Times Books: New York, 1992.

67. The NTIA Infrastructure Report, *Telecommunications in the Age of Information*, U.S. Department of Commerce: Washington, DC, 1991; NTIA.

68. *"Weak ad market hurts newspapers. Many publications are seeing profits fall, which is leading to more employee cuts"*, Times Wire Services: Los Angeles, 2008; February 28.

69. La Monica, P.R. *Dot-com mania, part II? After a huge boom and painful bust during the past decade, the Internet is booming again*, 2005; June 13 CNN/Money, 12:11 PM EDT http://money.cnn.com/2005/06/13/technology/internet/index.htm (accessed October 2, 2008).

70. http://en.wikipedia.org/wiki/Print_on_demand.

71. http://www.sfwa.org/BEWARE/printondemand.html.

72. http://www.instabook.net/home.html.

73. Hane, P.J. OCLC and WLN Begin Negotiations to Merge. Inform. Today (Posted On November 16, 1998). http://newsbreaks.infotoday.com/nbreader.asp?ArticleID=17872 (accessed October 2, 2008).

74. *"OCLC and WLN agree to merge"*, *Business Wire*, 1999; January 4 http://www.highbeam.com/doc/1G1–53507696.html (accessed October 2, 2008).

75. Hane, P.J. *"RLG to Merge with OCLC"*, 2006; May 8 http://newsbreaks.infotoday.com/nbreader.asp?ArticleID=15851 (accessed October 2, 2008).

76. *Google Books Library Project—An Enhanced Card Catalog of the World's Books*, http://books.google.com/googlebooks/library.html (accessed October 2, 2008).

77. http://en.wikipedia.org/wiki/Search_engine Web search engine.

78. Tenopir, C.; Baker, G.; Grogg, J.E. Database marketplace 2007: Not your family farm the information industry added value with unique content and custom tools as large search engines entered the market. Libr. J 5/15/2007. http://www.libraryjournal.com/article/CA6440567.html (accessed October 2, 2008).

79. http://www.dialog.com/about/keydates/ Key Dates for Dialog.

80. Quint, B. *Ovid technologies bought by Wolters Kluwer for $200 million*, Posted on October 5, 1998. http://newsbreaks.infotoday.com/nbreader.asp?ArticleID=17998 (accessed October 2, 2008).

81. *Wolters Kluwer acquires SilverPlatter*, posted April 6, 2001. http://www.library.yale.edu/~llicense/ListArchives/0104/msg00020.html (accessed October 2, 2008).

82. http://www.library.uiuc.edu/rex/erefs/.

83. http://www.ipl.org/.

84. http://www.libsuccess.org/index.php?title=Online_Reference.

85. *"Textbook case: Publishers look to cash in on rising demand for books"*, 1998; Dec 7 Barron's.

86. Malone, M.S. *The Microprocessor: A Biography*, Springer-Verlag: New York, 1998.

Library Consortia in Europe

Tommaso Giordano
Library, European University Institute, Florence, Italy

Abstract

In the professional literature the term "consortium" covers a great diversity of cooperative situations and experiences according to the different contexts and times in which it was developed. In this entry the term "consortium" will accordingly be discussed with its meaning restricted to structured cooperative activities aimed at acquiring and administering electronic information resources in European countries. More exactly, this definition here includes consortium initiatives in which the main program is focused on activities related to the purchasing of electronic licenses (academic journals, databases, etc.) and handling access to, and archiving of, the collections acquired. Recently library consortium initiatives have shown increasing attention to new issues of major interest for future developments: among these, long-term preservation of electronic resources (including noncommercial publications and institutional repositories), digitalization programs, acquisition of backfiles, etc. Regarding types of libraries, it should be kept in mind that the development of consortia for electronic resource sharing has so far spread chiefly among university libraries, and research and higher education communities. There are also some cases of direct, active involvement of national libraries. One can, however, note almost everywhere the growing involvement of public libraries in consortial activities. This entry focuses on the territory that forms the European Union (currently 27 countries) and some countries which, while not officially a part of this organization, are found within its geopolitical area. The countries of the former Soviet Union have not been included in this study.

INTRODUCTION

In the professional literature the term "consortium" covers a great diversity of cooperative situations and experiences according to the different contexts and times in which it was developed. The ideals and practice of library cooperation were progressively affirmed during the last century, giving rise to a considerable variety of activities and organizational forms with various names, often related to the most fashionable cultural trends or suggested by new technologies and innovative models developed in business contexts. This explains the popularity in the past of such terms as system or network, used to refer to cooperation initiatives in the library sphere. Clearly, these terms denote fairly precise concepts, and were in most cases used to focus attention on organizational models, technologies, and services set at the center of a particular cooperation initiative.

Use of the term "consortium" became established in the North American library lexicon in the 1960s[1] and indicates forms of structured cooperation focused primarily on resource sharing and cost reduction. In some European countries use of the term in library contexts has very remote origins. In Italy, for instance, the word "consorzio" has, with changing fortunes, been used in the area of public libraries throughout the twentieth century. The "Consorzio delle biblioteche popolari milanesi" set up in Milan in 1903[2] under the impetus of the social reform movements of the times in order to promote literacy among the working classes is probably one of the oldest cooperation experiments to use this term in a library context.

In some European languages consortium has a fairly precise meaning in legal terms: it indicates a union of people, of public and private institutions (in Italian) or union of banks (in German),[3] with a specific legal structure. The reference to specific legal structures means that in Europe the word consortium takes on different meanings in different countries, engendering some misunderstandings in professional communication. With some approximation, we may say that the difference in use of the word among European librarians chiefly concerns the differing extent of legal formalization of the assemblage called a consortium.

However, more recently, under the influence of Anglo-American experience, the word consortium has tended to take on a broader meaning, no longer linked with particular legal formulas. It is, however, clear that the favor the term has met with on the international librarianship scene in the last 15 years is chiefly associated with its use in the area of cooperation initiatives pertaining to the acquisition and management of electronic information resources (i.e., e-journal collections, data bases, and full text access services). Indeed, currently in the language of European librarians the word consortium chiefly indicates cooperation initiatives born under the impulse of the "academic

Encyclopedia of Library and Information Sciences, Fourth Edition DOI: 10.1081/E-ELIS4-120044707

Copyright © 2017 by Taylor & Francis. All rights reserved.

Library Automation–Library Publishing

journals crisis" (a term indicating the continuing rise in subscription prices that is particularly impacting the university and research sector), and the greater availability of collections and publications in electronic format.[4,5] In this area, too, most consortia are actively engaged in or support broader-range actions, such as the search for alternative models of academic communication, or the action by library organizations to support nonrestrictive copyright provisions. Use of the term "consortium" in the sense we have here sought to clarify is attested by many conferences on the theme and by articles that have appeared in authoritative specialized journals.[6,7] See the European ICOLC annual conferences that have taken place regularly since 1999 in various countries. In this entry the term "consortium" will accordingly be discussed with its meaning restricted to structured cooperation activities aimed at acquiring and administering electronic information resources in European countries. More exactly, this definition here includes consortium initiatives in which the main program is focused on activities related to the acquisition of electronic licenses (e-journals, databases, etc.) and handling access to and archiving of the collections acquired. It should be noted that recently library cooperation initiatives have shown increasing attention to new issues of major interest for future developments: among these, long-term preservation of electronic resources (including noncommercial publications and institutional repositories), digitalization programs, and the acquisition of backfiles and important historical collections by commercial publishers.

Regarding types of libraries, it should be kept in mind that the development of consortia for electronic resource sharing has for the above-mentioned reasons so far spread chiefly among university libraries, and research and higher education communities. There are also some cases of direct active involvement by the national libraries. One can, however, note almost everywhere the growing involvement of public libraries in this type of consortial activities. Regarding the contents, we must keep in mind that attention is currently focused on international academic publishing (primarily in the scientific and medical disciplines) which, as is well known, is essentially in English. Publications in the fields of humanities and social sciences in the other, European languages, are seldom available in electronic format. In fact, with the exception of the United Kingdom, publishers in Europe are in general still reluctant to make the transition to e-format, among other reasons due to the limited dimensions of the market in the different linguistic areas.

THE CONTEXT

This entry focuses mainly on the territory that forms the European Union (currently 27 countries) (Initially, the European Union consisted of just six countries: Belgium,

Germany, France, Italy, Luxembourg, and the Netherlands. Denmark, Ireland, and the United Kingdom joined in 1973, Greece in 1981, Spain and Portugal in 1986, Austria, Finland, and Sweden in 1995. In 2004 the biggest-ever enlargement took place with 10 new countries joining: Cyprus, the Czech Republic, Estonia, Hungary, Latvia, Lithuania, Malta, Poland, Slovakia, and Slovenia, followed, in 2007, by Bulgaria and Romania.) and some countries which, while not officially a part of this organization, are found within its geopolitical area (Iceland, Norway, Switzerland, Serbia, Bosnia Herzegovina, Albania, and Montenegro and also the EU candidate countries: Croatia. Turkey, and the former Yugoslav Republic of Macedonia.). We are dealing, then, with a territory smaller than the United States but one with a much higher population and one that is characterized by an extreme cultural and linguistic diversity—there are 23 official languages just in the 27 countries of the European Union—as well as by very different socioeconomic situations. The countries of the former Soviet Union have not been included in this study, both because their context is not easily comparable due to the strong political and economic differences that are still evident in Europe and because the available documentation regarding the present topic appears rather scarce. Nevertheless, interesting developments are evident in most of these countries, particularly in Russia, where several initiatives are supported by EU programs (i.e., Russian Information Library Consortium [RILC]),[8] and by foreign foundations (i.e., National Electronic Information Consortium [NEICON]),[9] which involve a large number of state and university libraries, public libraries, and research and special libraries.

We cannot, however, allow to pass unobserved an important historic event which took place in Europe at the beginning of this new century: the enlargement of the European Union in 2004 and, subsequently, in 2007 which resulted in 12 new member states scattered throughout an area ranging from the Baltic Sea to the Mediterranean. This peaceful "geopolitical revolution" has enormously enriched the diversity of the cultural heritage of the European Union as well as posed new challenges for the future of the Old Continent. In the current transition phase we should note the effort made by the new member countries to overcome the economic and social gap that divides them from the rest of the European Union and the progress that they have made on various levels, including technological innovation and reform in their educational systems.

In general, we can say that in Europe the level of commitment to electronic resources in the libraries reflects the differing degrees of economic development mentioned above, since to the traditional gap between North and South Europe we now must add the disparity between East and West. In reality, the picture is more complex than it appears at first glance. Observing more carefully the current initiatives in the library field, it appears instead the

Library Automation–Library Publishing

case that this simplistic schematization does not always reflect the evidence; examples of advanced consortia for the management of electronic resources are visible in the South as well as the North, and in the East as well as the West, demonstrating once again the differences between different regions of the same country.

The cases of Spain, Italy, and Slovenia are fairly indicative in this regard. In Spain the Catalan consortium[10] is quite an advanced organization, but is also rather atypical of the general position of libraries in those countries; in Italy, on the other hand, consortium activities are chiefly concentrated in the center and north, confirming the existing gap between these areas and the south of the country.[11] In Slovenia, however, the development of programs for library cooperation is comparable to the situation of the most advanced European countries.

In fact the degree of progress and modes of implementation of consortium initiatives in the various countries depends on both current investment policies to develop the information society applied by the various countries and numerous factors of a social, historical and cultural nature that have brought the emergence and establishment of library cooperation practices specific to each context. It is clear that in countries where library cooperation is not well rooted, organizing consortium initiatives face a much harder (and especially more uncertain) task than in Britain or other countries of Northern Europe with more deeply rooted traditions in this field of activity.

Looking at the scene of cooperation initiatives in progress, one has the impression that the gap between the different countries has been shrinking in recent years. And indeed over the last 15 years there has been a considerable increase of cooperation in all European countries. Probably, as far as EU territory is concerned, the special programs launched by the European Commission to promote technological cooperation among libraries have not been entirely without influence in creating conditions favorable for this trend.[12] Over and above the concrete results for which they may have been responsible in terms of services and technological applications, these programs have over the years offered libraries in the various European countries the chance to collaborate on joint projects, promoting the exchange of experience and development of cooperation practice, also among archives and museums. Among the recent noteworthy developments is the *European Digital Library*, a long-term program, wide in scope, which involves national libraries and numerous important libraries, archives, and museums of many countries, in a joint efforts to promote access to Europe's cultural heritage. Another relevant initiative promoted by the European Commission deals with scientific and scholarly communication, aiming to support new approaches and economic models to foster better access to scientific information online (including academic journals) and to preserve research results digitally for future generations.

In addition to these factors, however, a decisive role is played by the policies pursued and administrative mechanisms and structures through which the resulting programs are activated. If, concerning policies for implementing an information society, some similarities of intentions and general objectives can be discerned, not just among EU member countries (which as we know move in concert in this area) but more generally in all European countries, there are instead considerable differences in terms of instruments and operational programs. Regarding the latter aspect, one of the main factors directly influencing library cooperation models is the structure of the political and administrative system in the individual countries. This factor relates to autonomies and the degree of decentralization of the different national models, which vary considerably in Europe. Obviously, the German federal order based on the autonomy of the Länder, which have specific powers in the sector of culture, education, and research, presents different opportunities and conditions for cooperation than more centralized systems, such as the French. A somewhat similar system is that of Switzerland, with a specific feature represented by the official languages of the various cantons on which the federal organization is based. In the case of Spain, founded on administrative devolution to the regions (*comunidades autónomas*), practical aspects of library cooperation (e.g., funding) are more reminiscent of Germany than of Italy, even though the system is closer to the latter country. Without dwelling further on this point, we may take it for granted that the political and administrative system has no little influence on the levels (and aims) of cooperation, and that developing a national consortium in Belgium—where the institutional pattern is based on representation of the two communities (French and Flemish)—is a much more complex matter than in France or United Kingdom, despite their greater size.

OVERVIEW

To provide an overview of the picture, we shall take a quick, panoramic look, moving from West to East, at the consortium experiences that in our view best represent the problems associated with the current stage of development of these initiatives. Thereafter we shall analyze and compare some components of consortium organization, with an eye to identifying features common to the various experiences.

The Nordic countries—Finland, Sweden, Norway, Iceland, and Denmark—represent one of the areas where library cooperation practice is most widespread. With common historical backgrounds and cultural roots (with the exception of Finnish, all the languages spoken in the area are from the same linguistic family), the five countries maintain solid collaboration relationships and have developed major library cooperation programs, some of which also gather together the Baltic countries. Among

Library Automation–Library Publishing

these the Nordic Council for Scientific Information (NORDINFO), closed in 2004, developed a broad range of projects and activities for 30 yr. One of the larger cooperation programs in the region is Northern/Baltic Union Catalogue of Serials (NOSP), in which 1300 libraries from Denmark, Iceland, Sweden, Finland, Estonia, Latvia, Lithuania, the Faroe Islands, and Norway, take part. This solid basis for common work and mutual exchange does not prevent the individual countries from displaying their own peculiarities in the development of consortium models. One common feature of the Nordic experience is the role that the national libraries play in organizing cooperation and the various degrees of centralization in solutions adopted. Among these consortia FINELIB, based at the Finnish National Library, is a model with a high degree of centralization but also a high level of participation in decisions, ensured by a fairly elaborate structure of governing bodies. This consortium currently comprises over 100 university, research, and public libraries. FINELIB's programs include the negotiation of electronic licenses and other activities in the sphere of electronic resources sharing. Among these should be mentioned the project NELLI, a national portal for access to licensed resources management based on a common user interface.[13]

In Sweden, the main consortium initiative has been pursued by BIBSAM, the department of the Royal Library that coordinates cooperation and development activities at national level.[14] BIBSAM carries out various programs of activities to support the Swedish university and research library network, underpinned by central funding. It also has a fund to support access by libraries to electronic resources. Though not a consortium, BIBSAM acts like one, and in recent years has negotiated many agreements with publishers and suppliers of electronic information on behalf of libraries, and supported the implementation of this program both financially and technically.

In Norway, a wide range of cooperation programs have been developed by BIBSYS, the major academic library network. Most of the consortium initiatives for electronic resource sharing are handled by the ABM, the Norwegian Archive, Library and Museum Authority, which negotiates licenses at a national level.[15]

In Denmark, consortium agreements were initially handled directly by the university libraries; subsequently, some agreements with major scientific publishers were amended into national agreements with support from the Denmark Electronic Research Library Project (DEF), a major cooperation program supported by the National Library Authority, which embraces a wide range of projects and activities, including creation of a high-speed network connecting the largest university libraries, the central purchase automated library systems, the digitization of relevant collections, license management, and portals.[16]

In Iceland, the cooperation programs are handled by Landskerfi bókasafna (the Iceland Library Consortium);[17] regarding e-licenses, agreements have been reached with a major supplier of electronic services by the Steering Committee on Access to Electronic Material, the consortium organization supported by the National and University Library of Iceland in Reykjavik.

On the European scene, Great Britain is regarded as the most advanced model in terms of innovation in library services and development of advanced forms of cooperation. Helped by a language which is by now almost universally known, experience from that country is often regarded as a reference point. Established practice in the area of cooperation and the activism of relevant bodies at the national level are yielding good results in the digital age too. On the other hand, we must keep in mind that there is a strong position of autonomy among both universities and territorial units, resulting in a path to cooperation that seeks to balance the various requirements of coordination and decentralization. Consortium initiatives in Britain are numerous at both the national and the regional level and in all library sectors. In the university research library sector, one of the most well-established consortia is Consortium of University Research Libraries (CURL) (Research libraries in the British Isles) which provides a wide range of projects and activities involving a large number of research and academic institutions. The main organization operating in the field we are considering, however, is Joint Information System Committee (JISC),[18] set up to promote the development of electronic information in U.K. universities. JISC supports many projects concerned with education and research based on information technologies, and has set up synergies and alliances with various organizations operating in the information sector. Among projects launched by JISC, we should mention JANET, the United Kingdom's education and research network; and NESLI2, which follow the original National Electronic Site License Initiative (NELSI),[19] founded in 1995, the consortium regarded as one of the main reference models beyond the United Kingdom as well. This consortium's operational structure is in the hands of two external bodies: the "managing agent"—a private company with the task of handling negotiations of electronic licenses—and a computer center in Manchester which provides technical support. A Journal Working Group membership provides advice and support on developing priorities and license negotiations according to the JISC collection strategy. JISC supports a wide range of initiatives in the academic information domain, among them cooperation projects on digital repositories (i.e., SHERPA) and the long-term preservation of digital publications.

In Ireland, on the other hand, consortium initiatives in the field of electronic resources, mainly between university libraries, are informal in character. Of these, the consortium for the acquisition of electronic periodicals, under the supervision of the Conference of Heads of Irish Universities (CHIU), involves most higher education institutions in the country.[20]

In Germany, as we already mentioned, the federal structure determines that cooperation is principally at Länder level, but there are also national programs funded by the Deutsche Forschungsgemeinschaft (the German National Research Council). Since the 1970s, various cooperation programs have been developed (some of them bringing several Länder together) to create union catalogs. Activities associated with acquiring electronic resources have given rise to a variety of cooperation forms. Only the Friedrich Althoff Consortium in Berlin-Brandenburg has the legal status enabling it to act as a corporate nonprofit body. In the other Länder, consortia "are represented by an individual library (e.g., Baden Württemberg) or a central institution such as the Bayerische Staatsbibliothek, or the Hochschulbibliotekszentrum NRW in North Rhine-Westphalia."[21] Ways of funding consortia also differ considerably, even if the main sources are the Länder governments within whose jurisdiction, as we have said, the libraries fall. In some cases the consortia are funded directly by participating libraries, but in the majority of cases they receive substantial subventions supplied by the Länder. There is an emerging need for programs to bring all the Länder together into a national strategy; since 2004 considerable attention has been focused on negotiating national licenses of important digital collections.[22] Further, there is a significant initiative by the leaders of the German consortia, who in 2000 founded an association subsequently joined also by the consortia from Austria (where a cooperation scheme at the national level has been developed as well, Konsortien in Österreich) and Switzerland: this body, German, Austrian and Swiss Consortia Organization (GASCO), is intended to develop joint strategies for acquiring and handling publications, creating the conditions for activating action plans at the supranational level.[23]

The tendency to converge toward a national strategy, or at least to create synergies with programs and instruments operating in different sectors, is emerging with various patterns and orientations in many countries in Central Europe. This is the case of the Dutch consortium—the UKB Association—in which 13 university libraries participate along with the Royal Library and the Library of the Royal Dutch Academy of Science.[24] UKB is supported by contributions from the participating libraries. Its activities are focused chiefly on negotiating electronic licenses with major publishing groups, with which it has reached numerous agreements. The UKB Association in recent years has enlarged its objectives and strategies within a broader vision including academic publishing output of the learned societies and digital repositories. These developments take advantage of a strong tradition in library cooperation, in which important programs like PICA, a library network very active in central Europe and now comprised in OCLC, have matured.

One interesting national library cooperation program has been developed in Switzerland, despite the intrinsic difficulty of achieving an objective of this type in a country structured in 26 states (cantons and sub-cantons) where three language communities (German, French, and Italian) coexist. The first consortium aggregates emerged at the local level, since the universities are financed by the cantons. Subsequently, in 1988, thanks to the commitment of the conference of university rectors, the Consortium of Swiss Academic Libraries (Konsortium der Schweizer Hochschulbibliotheken), partially funded by the federal government, was established. At present the consortium (with about 50 libraries, including the Swiss National Library), in addition to the acquisition of electronic licenses, is developing into other sectors, among which is a project for electronic archiving. The consortium's organizational structure—which also provides for potential members from among public and research libraries—is based on a central office and a fairly elaborate governing structure, at the top of which is the conference of university rectors.[25]

The linguistic and cultural barriers and the complications due to the political administrative system have to date still not been overcome in Belgium, where the libraries of the French and Flemish language communities organize separate consortium initiatives. The consortium program of the universities and research institutes of the Flemish area come under the Vlaams Overlegorgaan inzake Wetenschappelijk Bibliotheekwerk—WOWB (Flemish Research Libraries Council)[26]—and the Flemish Ministry of Education, which supports the e-resource acquisition project Elektron.

The e-resource-sharing initiative of Francophone university libraries come under a nonprofit body, the BICfB: la Bibliothéque Interuniversitaire de la Communauté Française de Belgique, established in 2000 under the auspices of the country's conference of Francophone university rectors.[27]

At the end of the 1990s various consortia programs were developed at the local level in France. A major example is COUPERIN, a consortium initially promoted by a group of six university libraries, including Strasbourg University Library. This initiative had a noteworthy success and, thanks also to the support of the presidents of the universities, has expanded rapidly to become national in its dimensions. In 2007, COUPERIN had 212 members among university, higher education, and research libraries. Supported by the group of universities that provided the resources in the initial stage of development, today COUPERIN enjoys ad hoc support from the French Ministry of Education. The success scored in the license negotiating sector is forcing this consortium to broaden its mission and its programs and to integrate its digital collection development and management policy within the framework of a national strategy. To meet these new challenges, COUPERIN recently reinforced its structures and established collaborations and alliances with other consortia and agencies, including ABES, the major library network of the country.[28]

Library Automation–Library Publishing

Consortium experience under way in the countries of southern Europe is highly diverse, even in more culturally homogeneous areas where Romance languages are spoken. In the Iberian Peninsula, much of consortium activity aimed at electronic resource sharing started with the new Millennium, though since the 1980s Portugal and Spain have secured remarkable growth of library services and also a considerable development of cooperation activities. The turning point in Spanish interlibrary cooperation came in 1996 with the creation of the consortium of university libraries of Catalonia CBC (Consorci de Biblioteques Universitaries de Catalunya), later followed by other initiatives in Galicia (Bugalicia), the Madrid region (Madroño) and Andalusia (CBUA). On the basis of the regional decentralization typical of the Spanish system, the consortia are financed by the universities and/or the local government (*comunidades autónomas*) to which they belong. Consortium activities concern acquisition of electronic resources and, in the case of Galicia and Catalonia, also the development of other bibliographical utilities.[29,30] The Catalan consortium represents one of the most advanced model in South Europe: it is a legal entity with solid institutional ties (the National Library of Catalonia is also a member), supported by a funding mechanism based on the contribution of the local government and equipped with dedicated infrastructures and staff. Thanks to the common technological platform used by participating libraries (the consortium was born as a library automation network), this organization shows great potential in terms of integration of resources and development of value-added services.[31]

In 2004, a national consortium has been established in Portugal with the support of the government. The program is called B-ON: Biblioteca do Conhecimento Online (Library of Knowledge Online). This initiative includes 50 participants—universities and research libraries—and provides access to several important e-journal collections which should expand significantly during the current year.[32]

In Italy initiatives to share electronic resources began to appear only in the late 1990s and are currently located chiefly in the center and north of the country. Of the three most important consortium activities, two are led by university computing consortia—CILEA in Milan and CASPUR in Rome—nonprofit organizations that supply computing services and, in the electronic information sector, act as intermediaries on behalf of the associated libraries. The third, Interuniversity Cooperation on Electronic Journals (CIPE), in the center and north, includes important universities, such as Padua, Bologna, Florence, and Pisa.[33] In Italy for a long time there was no real national strategy in the area of electronic information, though the three consortia mentioned come together in Italian National Forum on Electronic Information Resources (INFER)[34] a voluntary inter-

consortium forum that also undertakes awareness activity to develop cooperation in the area of access to digital information. Since 2007 a more consistent national approach has begun in the form of CARE, an interconsortium program established by the Conference of Italian University Rectors (CRUI).[35]

A country which differs in a number of ways, in terms of both historical experience and geographical location, from the Mediterranean European countries we have just covered—though sharing deep cultural roots with them, as well as EU membership—Greece today presents a very interesting experience of library consortia in Europe. Born on the initiative of a group of universities, including Thessaloniki, and with the support of European Commission technological library programs, Hellenic Academic Libraries (HEAL) Link currently includes more than 30 institutions of higher education plus the Athens Academy and the National Library. The sphere of activities of this program—which is supported by central government funds—is wider than the electronic licensing negotiation, including also other projects ranging from production of the union catalog to operational standards and staff training.[36]

In the transition phase toward a free market economy and a democratic government that characterizes their recent history, the countries of Central and Eastern Europe have made a considerable effort to reach the development of the West and to align their legislation with EU standards. In this context we can note the reforms realized in the field of library legislation and copyright and the current investments for a more extensive use of technology in the management of information—a fundamental condition today to develop the sharing of library resources. In this process (one not always free of obstacles) the countries of Eastern Europe have been able to rely on the support and encouragement of various governments and international organizations such as the Council of Europe, and above all specific programs designed by the European Union and by public and private nonprofit organizations. Regarding the development of the consortia in particular we should note the action carried out by the European Union through various programs including TEMPUS and the programs undertaken by the Open Society Institute (OSI), a branch of the Soros Foundations. Among the EU programs deserving of particular mention we should include Central and East European Licensing Information Platform (CELIP),[30] supported by the European Union and developed by European Bureau of Library, Documentation and Information Associations (EBLIDA),[37] an organization for the library associations of different European countries with the aim of raising awareness of the issues regarding copyright and the management of electronic licenses. The action of the Soros Foundations, carried out through eIFL. net (Electronic Information for Libraries) has been on a larger scale and more systematic. Created in 1999, eIFL is active in numerous countries throughout Europe, Asia,

Library Automation–Library Publishing

and Africa; its principle aim is to provide support and assistance for the access to electronic resources "by library users in transition and developing countries."[38] Its activity is concentrated on the organization of consortia in various countries, and in this context has realized an agreement with important aggregators and publishers for access to the collection of electronic periodicals made available by this provider. eIFL has been particularly active in the countries of Central and Eastern Europe, in the Balkans, and in the countries of the ex-Soviet Union, where thanks to this program access has been made available to the electronic resources in many university institutes in countries with economic difficulties; in several cases it has been possible to give considerable aid for the development of national consortia in the formative stages.

The Baltic countries in the last few years have made important progress in the field of library cooperation and automation. We should note that the three principal consortia founded in these countries have a legal basis and a relatively solid organizational structure. Perhaps also due to their limited geographical dimensions the Baltic countries have been able to work more easily toward a larger picture of national cooperation. Among these countries Estonia appears the most advanced from a technological point of view, as the data on the use of the internet and the availability of personal computers in the homes demonstrate. The activities of library cooperation based on the use of IT in Estonia refer mainly to the ELINET network,[39] which also includes a task force that collaborates with eIFL on programs for the acquisition of electronic licenses.

In Latvia, the cooperation activities on a national level are mainly concentrated in a central agency, Culture Information Systems (Kultūras informācijas sistēmas),[40] which also oversees the acquisition of electronic resources in collaboration with eIFL.

In Lithuania, too, eIFL collaborates with the principal national consortium (recently formed) for the acquisition of electronic resources, Lithuanian Research Library Consortium (LIMBA),[41] which began operating in 2001.

Poland, on the other hand—the largest in size and population among the ten most recent states to enter the European Union—does not have a strong tradition of library cooperation. Nevertheless, in line with recent trends in IT, a greater vitality is visible in this area as well, and several programs have arisen both in the cataloging sector (e.g., NUKAT, the central catalog of academic libraries, located at Warsaw University and of which 58 libraries are members) and in hardware/software acquisitions and electronic publishing. In the latter field we should mention the development of several consortia, such as the Poznan Foundation of Scientific Libraries, the Consortium of Worcław Libraries, and the Górnoslaskie Consortium of University Libraries. The Poznan Foundation—the only Polish consortium to have a legal basis—was founded in 1996 and includes today ten universities and two public libraries.

The Foundation, initially oriented toward the acquisition and management of library automation systems, since 1999 has overseen the eIFL project on the national level, specifically the acquisition of electronic resources; in addition, since 2001 it has participated in the Digital Library of Wielkopolska project, which provides access to the oldest Polish works held by different libraries.[42]

Launched in the early 1990s (i.e., before the division of Czechoslovakia) the Czeck and Slovak Library Information Network (CASLIN), has been[36] split into different library networks in the two countries, according to the new political situation. In the Czech Republic, the main program for electronic resources named Uniform Information Gateway (UIG),[43] currently attracts the largest number of libraries and provides simultaneous searching in different local and international bibliographic resources and full text information.

In Slovakia, too, access to electronic resources is provided by several different initiatives, among which the most important is LIBNET,[44] the consortium, managed by the National Library, realized in the context of eIFL.

Library cooperation in Hungary takes place in the environment of three main networks: Mokka (The Hungarian Shared Catalogue); VOCAL (Cooperative Cataloguing Program) and KozelKat (Common Electronic Catalogue). Electronic resources sharing initiatives are being carried out by the Hungarian Electronic Information Service (EISZ) a national electronic service consortium sponsored by the Ministry of Education.[45]

Slovenia can boast of a consolidated practice of interlibrary cooperation at the national level, the principal infrastructure of which is the national library network Co-operative Online Bibliographic System and Services (COBISS) which counts 240 libraries as members. Cooperation for acquisition and the management of electronic resources has been developed principally by Consortium of Slovenian Electronic Collections (COSEC),[46] with 210 libraries of various types as participants. Founded in 2003 in the context of the eIFL program, the consortium has developed as a program of the National and University Library, and has acquired several electronic licenses. In Croatia the principal cooperation initiatives in the field of electronic resources have as their reference point the Croatian Academic Research Network (CARNET)[47] university network and the eIFL program. Founded with the principal aim of providing support for the implementation of IT in libraries, CARNET has acquired the licenses of several important data bases, primarily in the scientific and medical fields. In addition to the programs for the acquisition of electronic collections, we should mention the formation of various buying clubs for specific disciplines.

In spite of the dramatic events that have shaken this region, a certain amount of activity is visible in the field of shared management of electronic collections in almost all the countries of ex-Yugoslavia, above all due to the

Library Automation–Library Publishing

initiatives supported by eIFL, which is quite involved in this area. There are several consortia currently operational or in the set-up phase in Bosnia and Herzegovina, Kosovo, Albania, and Macedonia. In Serbia, KOBSON (Serbian Library Consortium for Coordinated Acquisition)[48] at the National Library in Belgrade has operated since the end of the war.

In Romania, the relevant activity in the field of electronic resources sharing (which involves a number of university, research, and public libraries) has its main reference in the Biblioteca Centrale Universitara in Bucharest.[49] In Bulgaria, several initiatives have arisen in the domain of electronic resources, among which primarily Bulgarian Information Consortium (BIC),[50] a consortium with a legal basis supported by eIFL.

Turkey, on the other hand, has demonstrated significant capacity and initiative; since 2000, Anatolian University Library Consortium (ANKOS)[51] has been operational. It is a program at the national level which has rapidly gathered together 40 universities and research institutions, quite a large number considering that Turkish higher education consists of 49 state and 20 private universities. ANKOS is an open consortium to which one may adhere by subscribing to at least one of the current license contracts. Currently ANKOS provides access to a number of important collections of periodicals and data bases. Contracting and shared management of electronic licenses is the central aim of ANKOS, which is administered by a steering committee and secretariat located at the Middle West Technical University of Ankara.

CONCLUSION

After this rapid excursus through the most significant consortium experiences in the various European countries, we can briefly turn our attention to the main trends under way, and draw a few conclusions.

Currently, cooperative resource-sharing initiatives are concentrated in the area of university libraries, even though there is a slowly strengthening trend to involve other types of libraries as well. Many consortia are focusing their attention on negotiating electronic licenses, while other initiatives, chiefly in Northern Europe, are aimed at broader objectives and seek to integrate electronic resource-sharing activities into broader-scope national programs; in several cases (e.g., the Nordic and Baltic countries and some Eastern countries) national libraries and other central agencies are coming to play an important role.

In organizational terms, it should in the first place be noted that the bulk of the consortia operating in European countries have no real legal basis, and have structures that might be called "light." Frequently they are supported by a logistical structure provided by one of the partners, or else make use of an existing central structure (an example here

being the model of the Nordic countries). In other cases the services are outsourced (e.g., the NESLI model). On the other hand, the governing systems of these bodies seem fairly developed and often complex, although they still do not dispel the impression of being rather fragile and transitional structures.

The majority of the consortia can rely on substantial ad hoc government funds, or else receive incentives and logistical support from central bodies, whereas cases of entirely self-financed activities are fairly limited. The availability of central funds is certainly a determining factor for the success of a consortium; at least as much as the administrative political system in which the consortium is set in terms of dimension and strategies.

As regards objectives, a growing concern of most consortia is to extend their sphere of activities to cover other functions including portals and common user interfaces, archiving and repositories. One practically universal need is to move the initiatives toward a national strategy, in some cases including even a transnational dimension.

Among the programs that operate in this perspective eIFL—already mentioned above—is the one which can count the greatest quantity of means and partners. On a smaller scale and with more limited objectives there are also several initiatives of a regional character in operation. Among these we have already mentioned German, Austrian and Swiss Consortia Organization (GASCO), the alliance of library consortia of the German language area. Another is Southern European Libraries Link (SELL), which has been founded as an association that primarily carries out activities of monitoring and information exchange at the level of the library consortia of the southern area.[52] Regarding the exchange of experience, an important instrument of communication has been gradually developing in the last few years: the European meeting of ICOLC (the E-ICOLC Annual Conference), which periodically brings together consortium managers, academics, and operators in the sectors of electronic publishing in order to discuss issues of common interest.

In conclusion, albeit with a considerable variety of strategies and operational modalities, European consortium experiences show a number of affinities and, most recently, convergent approaches. These tendencies are bound to accelerate chiefly in the countries of the European Union in the near future. On the other hand, we must keep in mind that despite the differences that may exist, the European countries we have referred to in this entry share not just a common heritage of historical events and deeply rooted principles and values but also, as far as the member states of the European Union are concerned, common policies and rules covering a wide range of economic and social matters, associated in a single political project which in the short to medium term will be taking further, decisive steps forward.

REFERENCES

1. Kopp, J.J. Library consortia and information technology: the past the present, the promise. Inform. Technol. Libr. **1998**, *17*(1), 7–12.
2. Turati, F. Crescite et multiplicamini. Biblioteche oggi **2001**, *19*(4), 52–53.
3. Reinhardt, W.; Boekhorst, P. Library consortia in Germany. Lib. Q. **2001**, *11*(1), 67–79.
4. Giordano, T. Library consortium models in Europe: a comparative analysis. Alexandria **2002**, *14*(1), 41–52.
5. King, D.W.; Xu, H. *The Role of Library Consortia in Electronic Journal Services, the Consortia Site License: Is It a Sustainable Model?*, Ingenta Institute: Oxford, 2002; 9–68.
6. Inform. Technol. Libr. **2000**, *19*(2), Special issue: Library consortia around the world.
7. Lib. Q **2001**, *11*(1), Special issue on library consortia.
8. RILC. http://www.ribk.net/?i18n = en.
9. NEICON. http://www.neicon.ru/.
10. CBUC. http://www.cbuc.es.
11. Giordano, T. Consorzi per la condivisione di risorse informative elettroniche. Biblioteche Oggi. **2001**, *21*(7), 16–26.
12. European Commission, RTD Framework Programme, 5-Year Assessment Reports. http://www.cordis.lu/fp5/5yr_reports.htm.
13. FINELIB – The National Electronic Library. http://www.nationallibrary.fi/libraries/finelib/tietoafinelibista.html.
14. Kungl. Biblioteket. http://www.kb.se/.
15. ABM. http://www.abm-utvikling.no/?set_language = en.
16. DEF. Denmark Electronic Research Library Project. http://www.deflink.dk/eng/default.asp.
17. Landskerfi bókasafna. http://www.landskerfi.is/sja_uk.php?id = 53.
18. JISC (Joint Information Systems Committee) [United Kingdom]. http://www.jisc.ac.uk/.
19. NESLI. http://www.nesli2.ac.uk/.
20. CHIU (Conference of Head of Irish Universities). http://www.chiu.ie/.
21. Reinhardt, W.; Boekhorst, P. Library consortia in Germany. Lib. Q. **2001**, *11*(1), 67–79.
22. Cremer, M. National licenses in Germany: The new promotion of online products for study and research. ICOLC Fall 2006, 8th European Meeting, Rome. http://www.aepic.it/conf/index.php?cf=7.
23. GASCO (German, Austrian and Swiss Consortia Organization). http://www.hbz-nrw.de/angebote/digitale_inhalte/gasco/.
24. UKB. http://www.ukb.nl/english/index.html.
25. Consortium of Swiss Academic Libraries. http://lib.consortium.ch/index.php?lang = 0.
26. VOWB. http://www.vowb.be/.
27. BICfB. http://www.bicfb.be/.
28. COUPERIN. http://www.couperin.org/.
29. Duarte Barrionuevo, M. New strategies in library services organization: Consortia university libraries in Spain. Inform. Technol. Libr. **2000**, *19*(2), 96–102.
30. Anglada, L.M.; Comellas, N. Reti cataloghi collettivi e consorzi in Spagna: l'esperienza del Consorci de biblioteques universitaries de Catalunya. Bollettino AIB **2000**, *40*(3), 295–308.
31. CBUC. http://www.cbuc.es/.
32. BO-ON (Biblioteca do Conhecimento Online). http://www.b-on.pt/.
33. Giordano, T. Library cooperation on ICT in Italy: an overview. Program **2002**, *36*(3), 144–151.
34. INFER. http://www.infer.it/.
35. CARE. http://www.crui-care.it/.
36. HEAL Link (Hellenic Academic Libraries Link) [Greece]. http://www.heal-link.gr/journals/en/.
37. EBLIDA. http://www.eblida.org/.
38. eIFL.net (Electronic Information for Libraries). http://www.eifl.net/cps/sections/home.
39. ELINET Konsortsium. http://www.elnet.ee/.
40. Kultūras informācijas sistēmas (Culture Information Systems). http://www.kis.gov.lv/.
41. LIMBA (Lithuanian Research Library Consortium). http://www.lmba.lt/.
42. Poznan Foundation of Scientific Libraries. http://www.pfsl.poznan.pl/english/index.html.
43. Uniform Information Gateway (UIG). http://info.jib.cz/for-users/helps/basic-help?set_language = en.
44. LIBNET. http://www.eifl.net/cps/sections/country/slovakia.
45. EISZ. http://www.eisz.hu/main.php?folderID = 875.
46. COSEC (Consortium of Slovenian Electronic Collections). http://www.nuk.uni-lj.si/cosec.
47. CARNET (Croatian Academic Research Network). http://www.carnet.hr/english.
48. KOBSON (Serbian Library Consortium for coordinated acquisition). http://nainfo.nbs.bg.ac.yu/Kobson/page/.
49. Biblioteca Centrala Universitara Carol I. http://www.bcub.ro/index.htm.
50. BIC (Bulgarian Information Consortium). http://www.bic.bg/.
51. ANKOS (Anatolian University Library Consortium). http://www.ankos.gen.tr/indexe.html.
52. SELL (Southern European Libraries Link). http://www.heal-link.gr/SELL/about.htm.

BIBLIOGRAPHY

1. Anglada, L.M.; Comellas, N. What's fair? Pricing model in electronic era. Libr. Manag. **2002**, *23*(4/5), 227–233.
2. Berard, R. Les Consortia en France. Lib. Q. **2001**, *11*(1), 60–66.
3. Carbone, P. Consortium negotiations with publishers: Past and future. Lib. Q. **2007**, *17*(2), Available at http://0-liber.library.uu.nl.bibliosun.iue.it/ (accessed January 2008).
4. CURL (Consortium of University Research Libraries) [United Kingdom], http://www.curl.ac.uk/ (accessed January 2008).
5. Dobrzyńska-Lankosz, E. Co-operation amongst Polish research libraries. Lib. Q. **2007**, *17*(3/4), http://0-liber.library.uu.nl.bibliosun.iue.it/ (accessed January 2008).
6. EDINA [United Kingdom], http://edina.ed.ac.uk/index.shtml (accessed January 2008).
7. Estelle, L. NESLi2: A report on progress. Serials **2004**, *17*(2), 149–153.
8. European Commission, *Study on the Economic and Technical Evolution of the Scientific Publications Market in Europe—Final Report*, EC Directorate C: Brussels, 2006; January http://ec.europa.eu/research/science-society/

pdf/scientific-publication-study_en.pdf (accessed January 2008).

9. European Commission, Digital library Initiatives, http://ec.europa.eu/information_society/activities/digital_libraries/index_en.htm (accessed January 2008).

10. FAK (Friedrich Althoff Konsortium) [Germany], http://www.althoff-konsortium.de/ (accessed January 2008).

11. Friend, F.J. Library consortia in Electronic Age. Alexandria **2002**, *14*(1), 17–24.

12. Gargiulo, P. Electronic journal and users. The CIBER experience in Italy. Serials **2003**, *16*(3), 293–298.

13. Giordano, T. Digital resources sharing and library consortia in Italy. Inform. Technol. Lib. **2000**, *19*(2), 84–89.

14. Griebel, R.; Reinhardt, W. Grundung der Arebeitsgemeinschaft Konsortien. Bibliotheksdienst **2000**, *34*, 799–803.

15. Hakli, E. Libraries in Finland Establish Consortia. Lib. Q. **2001**, *11*(1), 53–59.

16. Hormia-Putanen, K.; Xenidou-Dervou, C.; Kupryte, R.; Stange, K.; Kuznetsov, A.; Woodward, H. Consortia in Europe: Describing the various solutions through four country examples. Libr. Trends **2006**, *54*(3), 359–381.

17. ICOLC (International Coalition of Library Consortia), Available at http://www.library.yale.edu/consortia/ (accessed January 2008).

18. ICOLC, *6th European ICOLC*(International Coalition of Library Consortia in Europe), Barcelona, 2004, 28–30, Available at http://www.cbuc.es/icolc04bcn/ (accessed January 2008).

19. ICOLC, Fall 2006 (8th European Meeting) Rome, Available at http://www.aepic.it/conf/index.php?cf=7 (accessed January 2008).

20. IFLA Library Consortium Pre-conference, Boston, MA, 2001; August 16–17, Available at http://www.nelinet.net/edserv/conf/special/ifla/ifla.htm (accessed January 2008).

21. Klugkist, A. Consortium building and licensing by university libraries in the Netherlands. Lib. Q. **2001**, *11*(1), 80–86.

22. Neubauer, W.; Piguet, A. The long road to becoming a Consortium of Swiss University Libraries. Lib. Q. **2001**, *11*(1), 87–97.

23. Potter, W.G. Recent trends in statewide academic library consortia. Libr. Trends **1997**, *45*(3), 416–434.

24. Reibel, I. La creation d'un consortium de bibliothèques universitaires: son impact sur la politique d'abonnements aux périodiques électroniques. Bulletin des Bibliothèques de France.

25. SHERPA, Available at http://www.sherpa.ac.uk/about.html (accessed January 2008).

26. Urbano, C.; Anglada, L.M.; Borrego, A.; Cantos, C.; Cosculluela, A.; Comellas, N. The use of consortially purchased electronic journals by the CBUC (2000–2003). D-Lib Mag. **2004**, *10*(6), Available at http://www.dlib.org/dlib/june04/anglada/06anglada.html (accessed January 2008).

27. Van Borm, J.; Dujardin, M. Consortia for electronic library provision in Belgium. Lib. Q. **2001**, *11*(1), 14–33.

28. Vitiello, G. *Alessandrie d'Europa. Storie e visioni di biblioteche nazionali*; Bonnard: Milano, 2002.

29. Xenidou-Dervou, C. Consortial journal licensing: experiences of Greek academic libraries. Interlend. Doc. Supply **2001**, *29*(3), 120–125.

Library Automation–Library Publishing

Library Fundraising and Development

Susan K. Martin
Lauinger Library, Georgetown University, Washington, District of Columbia, U.S.A.

Abstract

Fundraising and development are activities new to the academic library scene, although as this entry illustrates, certain kinds of charitable giving have existed in universities and public institutions for many decades, if not centuries. Although some of the largest private universities in the United States have endowments that date back two or more centuries, few institutions of higher education have been involved in fund-raising in a serious manner for more that two or three decades. The great fortunes made in the Industrial Revolution enabled the establishment of a culture of philanthropy toward social institutions unknown elsewhere, or at any other time. With the attention of Andrew Carnegie, libraries became the focus of giving for a segment of America's wealthy, although for a number of decades this giving remained relatively restricted to public libraries.

HISTORY OF DEVELOPMENT IN ACADEMIC LIBRARIES

U.S. Phenomenon

Although some significant fund-raising and development programs have been established elsewhere in the world, two factors have caused academic library development to be largely a phenomenon of the United States: most of the early universities in the United States were private, and in this century tax laws have favored charitable giving by private individuals, foundations, and corporations. One of the very early library donors was Thomas Jefferson, who gave his collection to the Library of Congress and also ensured that the University of Virginia was established with a proper library for its role and mission.

A more recent philanthropic gift that made a significant difference not only to its own institution but to academia throughout the nation was the gift of Harry Elkins Widener's collection to Harvard, after the young man became a casualty of the Titanic. His mother, determined that her son would be remembered at least at his alma mater, was persuaded by the Harvard administration that a building carrying her son's name would perpetuate his memory; she would surely be pleased today to know that her son's name continues to be known worldwide wherever there is scholarship.

Private universities and colleges in particular have taken advantage of the human desire for immortality by raising funds from wealthy alumni or friends to build buildings—and few things are more tantalizing than to have "your" building be the one that represents our cultural heritage, the place where all students congregate to meet and study, and where faculty pursue their research.

The History of the Literature

The first edition of the *Encyclopedia of Library and Information Science*, published nearly 30 years ago, reflected the issues of the profession at the time, most naturally. A perusal of the index of the work finds very little reference to the topics that occupy so much of the time of so many academic library directors these days—external funding, the donor base, and gifts of cash, books, or bequests. In the 1960s and 1970s, academic institutions were in a significant period of financial recovery, going from postwar poverty to the riches of the National Defense Education Act and the country's instinctive desire to outthwart the Soviet Union by producing better educated and qualified graduates. The trickledown effect shaped academic libraries, which saw incredible growth for several decades following the war. Massive buildings were constructed; suddenly everyone could have a college degree, and many new universities were created. Money was not an issue, but the effective growth, management, and operation of our libraries were concerns. More than a generation of library administrators grew up with values that reflected a culture of growth and wealth; friends' groups were fine, but they were a frill. Of more concern was the perceived information explosion, which was said to double the size of research libraries every 16 years—a statistic that was unrealistic even at the time and turned out to be without foundation.

Therefore, it is not surprising that in the first edition of this encyclopedia just two articles summarize the extent of coverage of development: William Vernon Jackson's "Funding: Library Endowments in the United States"[1] and Sarah L. Wallace's "Friends of Libraries";[2] both of these articles cover *all* types of libraries. As a result, although Jackson's description of the size and purpose of

Encyclopedia of Library and Information Sciences, Fourth Edition DOI: 10.1081/E-ELIS4-120008674
Copyright © 2017 by Taylor & Francis. All rights reserved.

Library Automation–Library Publishing

endowment funds in academic libraries is fairly extensive, in today's terms, there is little attention paid to the process of *acquiring* these funds (the development process).[1] Similarly, the discussion of the history of academic library friends' groups is quite helpful, but otherwise, does not touch on operational issues of major concern to university and college libraries of the twenty-first century.[2]

This limited view of academic library fund-raising is not surprising. The role of the academic library as the "heart of the university" has changed significantly in the past three decades. As the financial constraints on both libraries and universities grew after the 1970s, it became more inevitable that the libraries that were once held apart from the fray of seeking funding outside the university would have to face this new and sometimes unwelcome activity. "The view of the library as a special preserve, protected from the rough-and-tumble of the business world, is fast disappearing."[3] Two major new functions have been introduced in academic libraries in the past decades—systems/automation and development. In both cases, another unit of the university is considered to be the focus of the specialty, requiring the library to define its plans and policies according to standards set elsewhere in the institution and forcing the library director to take on a role not envisaged by librarians just a generation ago.[4,5]

Despite the very many changes that have affected our universities and colleges in the past 30 years or so, the character and functions of friends' groups have not changed significantly. What *has* changed is the number of libraries with friends' groups, despite the discussion of the negative aspects of these support groups. In 1990, more than 50% of university libraries had friends' groups, compared to 20% of comprehensive and college libraries and only 5% of community college libraries.[6] A survey of 196 college libraries one decade later showed that of the friends' groups that existed, half of them had been formed in the 1990s, suggesting that the need for external support had grown sufficiently pressing that even smaller institutions have by now been affected.[7] Their governance, programs, and missions remain relatively stable.

The areas that have changed most significantly in the past decade have been the establishment of the role of development director for libraries; the intrusion of the institutional capital campaign into the library's way of doing business; and the role of the university or college librarian in development.

The Development of Development

An examination of the progression of activity and sophistication of library development over the past three decades is useful in permitting an understanding of the current activities of academic libraries.

In the 1970s, relatively few libraries engaged in what was at that time typically termed "public relations." As noted above, general social policy and economic well-being placed libraries in a beneficial financial situation. In these years, prior to double-digit inflation, and with a significant influx of funding, librarians felt as though the world was their oyster. At Harvard, for example, a large portion of the materials budget came from the payout from its large endowments; when inflation began to eat into this payout, the Harvard library administrators were to be shocked to discover that they would need to depend more heavily on university funding, or raise more money, to support the materials budget to which the faculty had become accustomed.

Rather than engaging in the acquisition of external funds, librarians focused on the extent to which they could enlarge their resources (read "collections") by soliciting gifts of excellent collections from private collectors.[8] However, by the end of the decade, it had become clear that the halcyon days of the 1960s and 1970s were about to disappear and that academic librarians would have to use more ingenuity, as well as external resources, to maintain the kinds of collections and services that their users had come to rely on.[9] Lynden noted that several of the efforts to obtain outside monies included: appointing staff members whose specific duties were to seek funds from external sources; including the library in the capital campaigns of their parent institutions; turning away from federal funding toward alumni, corporation, or local foundation support; and increasing publicity about the library by printing special annual reports, creating friends of the library newsletters, and developing other annual fund literature.[9] It should be emphasized that these techniques are described as being novel and unusual means of addressing budgetary problems—only 21 years ago—because they are in such common use today.

The 1980s saw a significant increase in development activity in not-for-profit institutions. Development offices were created, and capital campaigns began to be the single most significant way that universities used to increase their endowments and build their infrastructures. In the library world, a review of the literature shows an increase in publishing material about development and fund-raising, although a book of interviews with library leaders, published in 1988, shows that almost without exception, these leaders did not yet consider development to be an important part of their role and of the library's activities. One exception was Eastman, who said "Put to the test, a lot of library directors indicate that public relations and fund-raising are "soft" areas, not real library functions. In the years ahead, they may pay quite a price for that attitude."[10] Although not targeting any specific type of library, another author wrote about donors and prospects for libraries in a blunt and outspoken manner that would have been unheard of 10 years earlier.[11]

With the 1990s came a sudden expansion of the literature on academic library development and a geometric increase of the number of libraries engaged in development efforts.

Library Automation–Library Publishing

The golden age for higher education in the United States was the 1950s and part of the 1960s. We began to see a downturn in funding in the 1970s that accelerated in the 1980s. True to form, we have seen an explosion of development activities in academic libraries since the early 1980s and in public universities during the 1990s.[12]

Hood continues by identifying the various development-oriented groups that were created since 1980 to assist librarians and directors of library development with fund-raising issues; among these are Friends of the Library U.S.A. (FOLUSA), Development Officers of Research Academic Libraries (DORAL), and the Academic Library Advancement and Development Network (ALADN). All these groups hold annual meetings and sponsor listservs.[12]

Although the literature discussing academic library development began to increase significantly in the 1990s, most of what was published remained in the "how I did it good at my institution" category. Despite some public complaint about a lack of research or theoretical structure, the literature tended to reflect the structure and problems of each author's institution.[13] The very newness of the field accounts for this lack of theory and reliance on practice. However, because each institution is unique and its advancement programs are designed to serve its own needs, the advice given in the literature should be regarded as examples, rather than as a prescription for every library to follow.

Recently published articles are building on the knowledge gained through the practice of a generation of librarians and development officers. Wedgeworth links fund-raising done by academic libraries to the better established field of professional public relations, indicating that despite differing organizational structures or goals, the process of identifying and developing constituencies is essentially the same.[14] Surveys of librarians have begun to be published, giving the field some quantitative and qualitative data on which to make decisions in this area. Particularly useful is the survey of academic libraries done by Hoffman, Smith, and DiBona; it is an excellent example of basic research into fundamental issues, identifying factors that allow libraries to succeed or fail in fund-raising.[15]

THE LAY OF THE LAND: THE ENVIRONMENT OF ACADEMIC LIBRARY DEVELOPMENT

As we enter the twenty-first century, the higher education sector is raising more money than ever before, and academic libraries are increasingly included in this effort, either because the library director aggressively forces the library to be inserted into the institutional effort, or because the academic administration expects it. At this writing, more than 20 universities are engaged in multiyear comprehensive or capital campaigns with goals of $1 billion or more; in most of these cases, the library is identified with specific goals and a dollar target.

In earlier years, libraries experienced some fluctuations in the numbers of support organizations; these structures grew during periods of financial constraint and shrank when there was ample funding.[12] However, the downturn in support for higher education in the 1980s and 1990s has seen an explosion of development activities and support groups, which appears to reflect a fundamental change in the way that many libraries are organized and supported. The growing body of literature on library development is a direct result of the establishment of library development offices, with the attendant organizational structures and changes in roles (see below).

The more wealthy and larger a library is, the more likely it is to be engaged in development activities.[14] As in so many areas, success breeds success; the larger and wealthier academic libraries seem to command the bulk of foundation and government grants.

The Library Within the Institution

The politics of the campus

As noted above, the view of the library as a special preserve, to be protected and shielded from the everyday concerns of the business world, is disappearing rapidly. Each institution handles this situation slightly differently, depending on its resources, goals, and priority of the library within the research and educational functions. Librarians must attempt to persuade university officers not only that libraries need external sources of funds but also that they are worthy of the effort required to find those funds in the same manner as do the schools and colleges of the university. At almost every institution, the library faces some barriers:

- No one ever graduated from the library.
- There is a perception that it is difficult to raise funds for libraries.
- The library is everyone's second priority (their first being their own office or academic program).

Centralized versus decentralized development

Of primary importance is the organizational structure of development within the university at large. Such structures can be centralized, decentralized, or hybrid; each model has its advantages and disadvantages. With a centralized structure, all development staff report to, and are usually located in, the central institutional development office. Often, every development officer is asked to keep the library's needs in mind when talking with potential donors. This approach is ineffective for the library; development officers tend to focus on the "sexier" academic

Library Automation–Library Publishing

programs unless the university administration has made the library a specific high priority—a rather unusual circumstance.

With the decentralized model, each unit of the university handles its own development process. The library would need to create its own development positions and would retain control of its entire fund-raising planning and structure. This sounds appealing, but a major disadvantage lies in the lack of communication with the central development structure and its typical special support of areas such as planned giving, corporate support, prospect research, and special events staff.

The hybrid model, in which the library development staff are responsible just for library fund-raising but also have a formal relationship with the central development office, is likely to achieve the best results for the institution. No matter where the development officer reports, whether to the library director or to central development, the communication links between the two departments are likely to be healthy and more productive. The relationship of the library with the development office is key to its ultimate success; if the development office is not supportive of library goals, the effort to gain resources for the library will be significantly impaired.[7]

The role of the library director

A rule of thumb is that people give to people, and the corollary for library development is that the library director plays a key role in ensuring the existence and success of the library's fund-raising efforts. A director who is uninterested in development, or who doesn't recognize the significance of external support, or who is reluctant to "schmooze" or to ask donors for gifts, is unlikely to be the leader of a successful fund-raising effort. At least one expert states that it is not necessary to hire a fund-raiser with a sizable track record because the success of fund-raising depends on the leader of the organization rather than on the fund-raiser.[13]

Whether this statement reflects reality may be subject to argument; however, there is no question that the role of the library director needs to be that of a leader—to define the library's goals and level of involvement in development, and to be the face of the library in meeting its supporters. Most library administrators entered their field without recognizing that they might at some point be required to ask people for money, a task that many people find extremely difficult. There is little solid tradition, and certainly no formal education in our degree programs, to allow librarians to approach development and marketing with comfort.[5] One suspects that in the next decade or two, library and information studies programs will incorporate fund-raising as part of administration courses. Current job listings for academic library directors are increasingly calling for

fund-raising responsibility, making it obvious to aspiring directors that this new function will take up some portion of their time.

Access to donors

A major issue on many campuses, and one that can be a considerable barrier to the library's fund-raising success, is the access that is provided to the donors. In most institutions of any size, a centralized database tracks alumni, friends, donors, and other supporters of the institution.

> Many institutional development professionals feel that the university library presents a real challenge in garnering support. They argue that the colleges have a ready-made constituency in their graduates, whereas the library offers no degree and has difficulty building a loyal base of support.[16]

It has already been pointed out that several institutional barriers exist for academic libraries wishing to raise external funds. Access to the institution's alumni and supporters is critically important to the library, yet in some instances these people, who potentially have more interest than any other group, are off limits to the library, usually unless they "self-identify," or come forward on their own as supporters of the library.

These barriers are foolish. No college or university is able to tap all of their alumni, neighbors, and other supporters, and finding in the library another possible attraction for the university's community should be regarded as a positive asset. At the very least, the library should be given access to those alumni who are nondonors, by presenting them with other options for supporting their alma mater.[17] Indeed, when several members of a family attended a university, they might be alumni of different schools or colleges and can, therefore, contemplate a family gift to the library rather than trying to determine which of their schools should be the beneficiary of a family donation. Similarly, alumni of a reunion class all used the library, no matter what their major or school was; they can all support a gift to the library. The University of Pennsylvania has had great success in appealing to fiftieth reunion classes to focus their reunion gift on the library.

In some cases, universities are unwilling or unable to change their mode of assigning responsibility for donors. But in those cases in which the library is able to gain access to the university's constituency, its development officer is also likely to be able to "manage" donors when a case has been made that the donor is appropriately the supporter of the library. Sometimes the donor self-identifies; in other cases, another supporter has led the library to the donor; in yet other circumstances, the membership of the friends of the library leads to managed prospects and major gifts.

Library Automation–Library Publishing

DEVELOPMENT TOOLS, SMALL TO LARGE

Successful library development involves a numbers of approaches, several of which are described here. These tools should be regarded as building blocks. It is not necessary for a library to participate in a capital campaign, but if it has not established a group of donors (friends of the library) and engaged in annual fund and major giving programs, any attempt to launch a capital campaign is unlikely to succeed. The small gifts and donors inevitably lead to larger gifts and more donors, and should not be ignored.

Friends of Libraries

Whether to have a friends' group or not is a question that has been under discussion for decades, for various reasons. The earliest such groups were formed in California in the 1890s, although they were not called by that name. The first "Friends of the Library" group was founded in Paris in 1913, as a support group for the Bibliothèque Nationale, with a branch of that group formed in Berkeley, California, in 1930. The first academic friends of the library was established at Harvard in 1925, followed within a few years by similar groups at Columbia, Yale, Princeton, and Johns Hopkins.[2] This author's experience at Johns Hopkins brought her into frequent contact with the three surviving charter members of that group, all of whom continued to be very supportive of the library and very proud to be charter members.

At their very best, friends' groups provide resources for the libraries with which they are associated, and form the basic building block of the library's constituency. Because the library has no natural constituency as do the academic schools, it should be able to use the friends to attract people who like libraries, enjoy books, and value the education they received. In its turn, the library staff and development officer can use the members of the friends to identify people who, with additional cultivation, may be prospects for major gifts, planned gifts, or bequests. The funds raised by the friends can be used to support special events, newsletter production, staff to coordinate and manage the friends' group, and resources for special collections or other library functions.

Much of the cultivation of the friends group is very long term. Considered in the time frame of the present, with its priorities and constraints, cultivating a friends' group could seem to be an unwise use of resources, bringing little return. The utility of a friends' group has been a topic of discussion because some librarians believe that friends, or volunteers, take up too much time and often have a tendency to micromanage.[2] There is no question that fostering a successful friends' group does take time, and given the wrong people in volunteer slots, micromanagement can be a problem. In a recent discussion, library directors within the Association of Research Libraries learned that some of their colleagues intend to eliminate their friends' groups to focus entirely on the smaller group of supporters that provides them with major gifts.[18]

However, this author's experience suggests that those people who are now major or planned giving donors often started out as $10 or $15 annual fund donors and members of the friends' group. With few other formal mechanisms available to the library to create its list of prospects, having a group of several hundred people as supporters is not at all unwelcome. Some of these friends can and should become members of the library's external advisory council or visiting committee (addressed below). The long-term benefits to be gained by attracting potential donors and obvious annual fund supporters to the library cannot be overemphasized.

Friends' groups are typically multifunctional, although which particular functions are the purview of any single group depends on local circumstance. Friends of libraries are usually (but not always) library supporters, and program events featuring books and authors are traditionally used to attract members. These groups also offer financial support, and as such constitute one of the elements of the library's fund-raising program. If the library's special collections are particularly strong, the group may focus its attention there, and the special collections staff may take on the role of managing the friends' activities. In a few universities (the University of Maryland is an excellent example), the friends group has one major meeting each year, but it is a black-tie affair with a distinguished speaker, and seats are available at a fairly high price.

According to Thompson and Smith,

> College friends' groups will continue to flourish where they are embraced by the library administration, supported by the development staff, and honored by the community in which they reside. College libraries fortunate enough to have strong friends' groups will find these organizations are a means to continue strengthening the research and service they are able to provide to their constituencies.[7]

Annual Fund

With or without a friends' group, academic libraries are increasingly involved in their institutions' annual fund drives. As with friends' groups, the annual fund drive carries with it both advantages and disadvantages. Like the friends' group, it is a high cost and relatively low contribution program, but also like the friends' group, it is likely to be very worthwhile over time. Libraries with long-standing friends' and/or annual fund programs can bring in considerable amounts of money each year, depending, of course, on the size of the alumni base, the dues assessed, and other factors. One observer suggests that revenues of $25,000 annually are a reasonable

Library Automation–Library Publishing

expectation; evidence suggests that larger libraries are typically able to bring in revenues of $250,000 or more annually.[6,13]

Most university or college annual funds allow donors to specify an area of the institution to which they wish their funds to be targeted. Even without a check-off box dedicated to the library, alumni and friends have the opportunity to give to the library, and many of them do so. Given the obstacles faced by the library as described above, the annual fund can provide access to the university's donor pool, permitting those who have an interest in the library to "self-identify" and, therefore, giving the library development officer a rationale for visiting them.

Annual funds are typically unrestricted, current-use funds. In some institutions, these gifts are taxed by the administration to fund unfunded priorities. Where possible, the library should attempt to retain the entirety of these gifts; if nothing else, the director is able to tell the donors that their gifts are fully supplemental to the library's budget. Donors like to feel that their dollars are making a real difference to the program that they are supporting. They rail at underwriting administrative costs and also dislike the notion that their monies are being used by the university for budgetary relief.

Libraries can carry on annual fund programs without having friends' groups; it is more difficult to define a friends' group without assuming that this group is an analog of the annual fund giving for the library, but it can be done. As we will see below, libraries are most likely to succeed in their fund-raising efforts when their friends' and annual fund programs are linked.

Major Gifts

The next step after the unrestricted, current-use giving programs for libraries is the major giving arena. Development professionals and librarians disagree in their definitions of major gifts, particularly as applied to libraries. When the development office defines a major gift as any six figure gift or more, it can be difficult for the librarian to argue that book fund endowments should be part of the library's major gifts program. However, unlike almost any other area of the university, the library can make excellent use of the payout from a $10,000 or $25,000 endowment. When that payout is $500 or $1250 annually, the library can purchase materials that are of benefit to the institution's students and faculty—and this can be very attractive to potential donors. An alumnus giving $1000 annually can often be persuaded to increase that gift to $2000, thereby creating a $10,000 endowment over a 5-year period.

Once it is determined that the library should embark on a major gifts program, the library administration will need to clearly identify and describe the library's needs and its fund-raising goals. The central development office is likely to require annual targets for each university unit, and the library's development officer should use this requirement as an occasion to plan the year—how many prospects will be visited? Which potential donors will be asked to consider a gift and at what level? What special events and programs will be held?

Armed with the list of names from the friends of the library and from annual fund giving, the library director and the director of development are then able to do the research necessary to determine which donors are capable of larger gifts and should be visited. Vast quantities of public data are available to give the fund-raisers guidelines regarding the possible size of gift that any particular donor might be able to consider.[11] For example, libraries have an unusually high proportion of "never married/no kids" supporters—one demographic element that ranks high in the list of interesting characteristics of suspects and prospects. Elderly couples with many children and grandchildren, on the other hand, may be loyal library supporters but are unlikely to have the wherewithal to make a major gift to the library.

Unlike other areas of the university, libraries tend to receive a large number of gifts in kind. Someone moving out of a house to an apartment is likely to give the library very nice books that are not worth more than $1 or $2 each and that the library does not need to add to its general collections. A gift in kind of this nature can not be called a major gift, and the library should probably take as little time to process and handle these gifts as possible. Not to be overlooked, however, are the gifts in kind that represent truly important additions to the collection, and perhaps even special collections. A single book worth over $100,000 can enhance the library's collection considerably and is just as valuable as a gift in cash of the same quantity to the library's fund-raising goals.

Planned Giving

"Estate planning, deferred giving and planned giving are the names commonly given [this] important area of fund raising."[19] After a decade of a bull market, with the increasing number of senior citizens, and in a country where charitable giving is still supported by tax incentives, planned giving is an ideal tool for library development. In many circumstances, people are able to consider significant gifts by using vehicles such as bequests or charitable remainder unitrusts. The library will not see the funds immediately in most cases, so shouldn't count on supporting positions or even accomplishing an immediate building project. However, in the short run, these gifts count toward annual and campaign goals, and in the long run, the library will benefit significantly from the generosity of these donors.

Planned giving is a complex area; many universities have central staffs of planned giving experts to ensure that these gifts are structured appropriately and that the university is taking advantage of all the tools available to it.

Library Automation–Library Publishing

A recent publication for librarians, although not totally focused on libraries, is very important in laying out all the options and considerations for not-for-profit institutions and their supporters.[20]

Capital Campaigns

Institutional capital or comprehensive campaigns were mentioned earlier as vehicles by which many libraries are drawn into fund-raising. Indeed, colleges and universities began to embrace the campaign as a fund-raising tool in the 1970s, and by the early twenty-first century many universities seem to be perpetually in "campaign mode." Given this environment, libraries tend to participate in campaigns, together with the friends of the library, annual fund, and major giving programs that have heretofore sustained it.

The library director's active engagement with the planning of the campaign is key to the success of the library within that campaign. It is not unusual for universities to hire consultants to assist them in planning a campaign, and these consultants usually do a feasibility study to determine the state of readiness of the university's community for a campaign. Ensuring that a community understands what philanthropy is, and is ready to engage in such an activity in support of the university, is an important element of this study.[21] Library participation at this stage in the development of a campaign can bring visibility to the library, so that the university administration and the consultants alike recognize the library's existence (not to be taken for granted!), needs, and potential donors.

Once it has been determined that a campaign is appropriate and likely to bear desirable results, the university/library will identify the institutional needs and priorities, associate dollar figures with these needs, and develop a pyramid chart that indicates how many gifts at each level the library requires to meet its goals. Matching the size and focus of the gift with the appropriate benefactor is a simple follow-up step if all the necessary research and planning has been accomplished. One expert says

> Giving is a habit. Has your annual support grown over the last three years? Are the numbers of volunteers at least stable? Does at least half of your support come from a few large donors? Are your contributors thanked and informed on what happens to their gift? If these questions cannot be answered in the affirmative, you need to review and take corrective action before launching a campaign.[21]

Because capital campaigns are more likely than the other tools to be run at the university level, much library activity will be dictated from above. What is the overall goal of the campaign and the goals for each university unit? How long will the campaign be? How many years will the campaign be in silent phase—it is usually thought that at least 50% of the goal needs to be in hand or

identified before the campaign goes public? What will the kickoff consist of? Will there be constituency (read 'library') kickoffs as well? At what level will the president of the institution participate and support the individual units of the university?

The appropriate goal for the library will be determined in much the same way as is the goal for the university at large. The consultants' feasibility study should take into consideration the number of library supporters and their capacity for giving. Some larger university libraries in the 1990s engaged in campaigns with goals of $20 million or more; Harvard University Library's goal was $76 million and was successfully reached.

Despite the doubts of librarians, campaigns do succeed, and they succeed in building a future for the library. This author, 5 years after the commencement of the campaign at Georgetown, suddenly found that payout from recently established endowments was making a real difference to the total library budgeting process. The campaign, even at that time, had worked to provide the library with the additional funds it so needed to appropriately support the teaching and research programs of the university.

FUTURE OF DEVELOPMENT

The future of development requires some consideration here. Technology is now able to insert itself into the development process and not only to provide lists and reports. It is now possible to use the Internet as a communications device with donors. Also, the previous narrative has identified some issues that clearly will need to be addressed by librarians involved in the areas of development and fund-raising.

Development on the Web

With the increased ability of universities and colleges to carry out transactions on the Web, libraries are beginning to use their home pages to publicize the opportunities for giving or for joining the friends of the library, and in some cases they are able to accept credit card numbers to pay for friends' dues. An advocate suggests that most nonprofit organizations should move to a Web-centric communications model, as being just an update of communication by telephone.[22] This approach clearly has tremendous implications for the future.

In considering the use of the Web, libraries need at first to determine where in their website there should be mention of giving, or of the Friends of the Library. A brief assessment of ARL libraries' home pages shows widely varying practices. About one third of the libraries have placed some reference to giving or the friends on their home pages; another large group (perhaps 50%, although this is a moving target) refer to library support, but not on

Library Automation–Library Publishing

the library's home page; and about 15% carry no reference to giving or support at all.[23]

Websites can be used to great advantage in various ways. Libraries can recognize major donors by devoting pages to the donors and their gifts. Electronic plaques, online pledges, e-mail to the friends of the library support staff, signing up to attend events, and remote access to the library's information structure are only a few of the possibilities that the Web presents.[22]

However, the future is not here yet. To design a total development program around the Web would assume that all our donors are online and that it is easy for colleges and universities to gain access to the e-mail addresses of their alumni and friends. Neither assumption is accurate at this date, and one should anticipate that traditional means of communication will gradually mingle increasingly with Web communications until a critical mass of our population is Web-familiar and our own systems for keeping up with e-mail addresses are more sophisticated than they are now.

Theoretical and Philosophical Bases for Fund-Raising

As mentioned above, the library field lacks literature on the theoretical and philosophical foundations of fund-raising. With additions to the literature such as that of Hoffman, Smith, and DiBona, this situation is gradually being rectified.[15] Typically, library literature begins to cover a specialty with pragmatic articles and treatises, moving only later to analytical and philosophical discussion. Library fund-raising is just now at the point where the doers and thinkers are starting to contribute to the philosophy of the profession, and that trend should continue in the future.

Institutionalization of Fund-Raising

Several experts have suggested that until fund-raising is seen as a "regular" part of library services, it will not be regarded as a part of a library's operating expenses.[6] Just as information technology was initially not considered a full part of the library organization, structure, and activity, neither is fund-raising in today's library world. Without the full incorporation of these functions within the library, either by assigning responsibility for development to existing staff or by hiring development staff, the fund-raising program will always be seen as separate, and perhaps only temporary. Experience shows that a development structure is not at all temporary, and to gain the most from this function, it needs to be perceived as a permanent partner within the library organization.

Surveys indicate that the factors of success for a library development program are the age of the program itself; the size of the donor pool; the level of involvement of the library director; the amount of time that is able to be devoted to development, by the library director, by the director of development, and by other library staff; the type of institution, because private colleges and universities still raise more money than do public institutions; having a friends group that is part of the annual fund process; adopting high monetary goals; and maintaining a strong and positive connection to the central development office.[15]

> The best protection the library can have...is the institutionalization of the fund-raising process...While research, cultivation, solicitation and recognition will still be the fundamentals of the fund-raising process, its incorporation into the broader efforts of library management to improve the library's visibility, tell the library story, set a vision for the library of the future, and gain support from key constituencies is likely to result not only in successful fund-raising campaigns but also in a more effective organization.[14]

CONCLUSION

Library fund-raising and development have become a part of many librarians' everyday lives. Once considered foreign territory, an area inappropriate for librarians to wander, development is now incorporated into the process of ensuring that our libraries have sufficient resources to provide necessary support to the students and faculty of our universities. Literature that once was sorely lacking is becoming a standard commodity of the tables of contents of journals and of the book lists of library publishers.

The changing world of higher education has made it almost imperative for librarians to be fully engaged in the process of fund-raising and development. Fighting the old adage that "it is impossible to raise money for libraries," an increasing number of academic libraries participate in their institutions' campaigns with impressive goals or conducting their own major gifts programs.

Libraries need to build constituencies and define directions that make it clear to those both inside and outside the university what payoff results from investments in the university's library. Each library director will have to work with his or her community, development office, potential and actual constituency, and administration to identify the best way in which to supplement increasingly scarce resources. Development, the library world's newest special function, serves as the means to insert the library's interests into the overall institutional goals.

REFERENCES

1. Jackson, W. V. Funding: Library endowments in the United States. In *Encyclopedia of Library and Information*

Library Automation–Library Publishing

Science; Kent, A., Ed.; Marcel Dekker: New York, 1972; 138–186.

2. Wallace, S. L. Friends of libraries. In *Encyclopedia of Library and Information Science*; Kent, A., Ed.; Marcel Dekker: New York, 1972; 111–131.

3. Veaner, A. B. *Academic Librarianship in a Transformational Age: Program, Politics, and Personnel*, G.K. Hall: Boston, MA, 1990; 442.

4. Martin, S. K. Academic library fund-raising: Organization, process, and politics. In *Development and Fund-Raising Initiatives*; Martin, S.K., Ed.; Library Trends, 2000; Vol. 48 (3), 560–578.

5. Martin, S. K. The changing role of the library director: Fund-raising and the academic library. J. Acad. Librariansh. **1998**, *24* (1), 3–10.

6. Lynch, M. J. *Alternative Sources of Revenue in Academic Libraries*, American Library Association: Chicago, IL, 1991; 7 15.

7. Thompson, R.K.H. Smith, A. M. *Friends of College Libraries*, 2nd Ed. American Library Association: Chicago, IL, 1999; 9–11 CLIP Note #27.

8. Magrill, R.M. East, M. Collection development in large university libraries. In *Advances in Librarianship*; Harris, M. H., Ed.; Academic Press: New York, 1978; Vol. 8, 26–27.

9. Lynden, F. C. Library materials budgeting in the private university library: Austerity and action. In *Advances in Librarianship*; Harris, M. H., Ed.; Academic Press: New York, 1980; Vol. 10, 106.

10. In *Libraries in the 90s: What the Leaders Expect*; Riggs, D. E., Sabine, G. A., Eds.; Oryx Press: Phoenix, AZ, 1988; 137.

11. Strand, B. J. Finding and researching major donor prospects. In *Library Development: A Future Imperative*; Burlingame, D. F., Ed.; Haworth Press: New York, 1990; 53–65.

12. Hood, J. M. Past, Present and future of library development (fund-raising). In *Advances in Librarianship*; Lynden, F.C., Chapman, E.A., Eds.; Academic Press: San Diego, CA, 1998; Vol. 22, 124–126.

13. Steele, V. Elder, S. D. *Becoming a Fundraiser: The Principles and Practice of Library Development*, 2nd Ed. American Library Association: Chicago, IL, 2000; ix 41, 86.

14. Wedgeworth, R. Donor relations as public relations: Toward a philosophy of fund-raising. In *Development and Fund-Raising Initiatives*; Martin, S.K., Ed.; Library Trends, 2000; Vol. 48 (3), 530–539.

15. Hoffman, I. M. Smith, A. DiBona, L. Factors for success: Academic library development survey results. In *Development and Fund-Raising Initiatives*; Martin, S.K., Ed.; Library Trends, 2000; Vol. 48 (3), 540–559.

16. Clark, C. K. Private support for public purposes: Library fund raising. Wilson Libr. Bull. **1986**, *60* (6), 20.

17. Paustenbaugh, J. Trojahn, L. Annual fund programs for academic libraries. In *Development and Fund-Raising Initiatives*; Martin, S.K., Ed.; Library Trends, 2000; Vol. 48(3), 586.

18. Association of Research Libraries. *ARL Directors' Listserv*, March 2001, personal communications.

19. Hodge, J.M. Richardson, D. B. The role of planned giving. In *Library Development: A Future Imperative*; Burlingame, D.F., Ed.; Haworth Press: New York, 1990; 121.

20. Smith, A.S. Lehrer, M. D. *Legacies for Libraries: A Practical Guide to Planned Giving*, American Library Association: Chicago, IL, 2000; 138.

21. Burlingame, D. F. Library capital campaigns. In *Library Development: A Future Imperative*; Burlingame, D. F., Ed.; Haworth Press: New York, 1990; 90–91.

22. Corson-Finnerty, A. Blanchard, L. *Fundraising and Friend-Raising on the Web*, American Library Association: Chicago, IL, 1998; 6 21–23.

23. *Author's Survey of Web Sites*, May 2001.

Library Leadership and Management Association (LLAMA)

Robert Allen Daugherty
University Library, University of Illinois at Chicago, Chicago, Illinois, U.S.A.

Abstract
This entry outlines the history of the Library Leadership and Management Association, a division of the American Library Association, from its establishment as the Library Administration Division in 1957 through the celebration of its 50th anniversary in 2007 when it was the Library Administration and Management Association to its recent name change in 2008. It includes details about its mission and vision, organizational structure, programs, publications, and awards.

INTRODUCTION

The Library Leadership and Management Association (LLAMA) is a national organization, one of 11 divisions of the American Library Association (ALA). The mission of LLAMA is to encourage and nurture current and future library leaders, and to develop and promote outstanding leadership and management practices. Personal, organization, and corporate members number more than 5000 and represent all types of libraries. Members include library workers at all levels as well as those who support libraries. Division-wide committees include Budget and Finance, Continuing Education, Financial Advancement, Leadership Development, Marketing Communication, Membership, Mentoring, Organization, Program, Publishing, and Strategic Plan Action Committee as well as committees devoted to Cultural Diversity Grants, Recognition of Achievement, and a Web site Advisory Board.

There are seven sections to address major areas of interest: Buildings and Equipment (BES); Fund Raising and Financial Development (FRFDS); Human Resources (HRS); Library Organization and Management (LOMS); Measurement, Assessment, and Evaluation (MAES); Public Relations and Marketing (PRMS); and Systems and Services (SASS). Several less formal discussion groups are comprised of Assistants to the Director, Diversity Officers, and Women Administrators; other groups are comprised of members who are interested in issues related to Dialog with Directors, Middle Management, Library Storage, Education, Government Affairs, and Research.

The Library Leadership and Management Association is well known for its conference and pre-conference programs at the ALA Annual Conference as well as for regional institutes. In addition to these continuing education events, the Division produces publications and awards related to its mission and goals.

ORIGINS AND HISTORY OF LLAMA

The ALA was organized in 1876 and incorporated in 1879. The American Library Association included such standing groups as the Large Libraries Section, the Library Administration Committee, the Library Architecture Committee, etc. Following several years of study, the ALA reorganized in 1956/1957. While some divisions continued, others were established and more clearly delineated as the type-of-library and type-of-activity or function structure characteristic of ALA today. The Library Administration Division (LAD) formed to focus on general personnel administration, library organization, buildings and equipment, financial administration, insurance, public relations, statistics, relations with library governing bodies, governmental relations, legislation, and friends groups.

The mission of LAD was the general improvement and development of all aspects library administration, at all levels of administration in libraries, and for all types and sizes of libraries. Preexisting ALA groups transferred to LAD included the Federal Relations Committee (created 1923), Library Legislation Committee (1923), Public Relations Committee (1923), Friends of Libraries Committee (1929), Insurance for Libraries Committee (1929), Buildings Committee (1932), Equipment Committee (1931), Statistics Committee (1936), and the Board on Personnel Administration (1936).

The Library Administration Division had specific responsibility for

1. Continuous study and review of the activities assigned to the division and of the changing developments in those activities.
2. Conduct of activities and projects within its areas of responsibility and stimulation of the development of these activities in libraries.
3. Synthesis of the activities of all units within ALA that have a bearing on the type of activity represented.

Encyclopedia of Library and Information Sciences, Fourth Edition DOI: 10.1081/E-ELIS4-120043640

Copyright © 2017 by Taylor & Francis. All rights reserved.

Library Automation–Library Publishing

4. Representation and interpretation of these activities of libraries in contacts outside the profession.
5. Stimulation of the development of librarians engaged in its type of activity and stimulation of participation in appropriate type-of-library divisions.
6. Planning and development of programs of study and research in those areas of activity for the total profession.[1]

The broad focus, along with the other major restructuring within ALA, provided something of a *tabula rasa* for the new type-of-activity division. In addition to reconciling and coordinating the activities of the other committees that had been cobbled together to form it, LAD needed to coordinate with other existing type-of-library divisions to clarify and refine their respective areas of responsibilities. Early on, there was a LAD Committee on Recruitment with subcommittees devoted to recruiting for children's librarians, for school librarians, and for college and university librarians, as well as for cataloging and classification. Similarly, the Division's LOMS Section had committees devoted to statistics for school libraries, for public libraries, and for college and university libraries, as well as a statistics coordinating committee. The BES Section also formed committees based on types-of-libraries, as did the Public Relations Section.

While these reflected the past, there were also committees being formed to deal with urgent and emergent issues. The LOMS Advisory Committee on USOE Statistics was formed even as the plans for the ALA reorganization were being finalized. (See also Appendices 1 and 2, listing the Division Presidents and Executive Directors.) In 1958, the Government Relations Section established a Copyright Revision Committee to deal with anticipated activities and actions occurring during the 1960s and 1970s; and, in 1961, that Section became ALA's Legislation Committee. In 1959, LAD formed its Advisory Committee for the Library Technology Project. This ALA project was announced that year and, although its initial interests were in such mundane items as supplies and machinery, automation developments and applications quickly came to the fore throughout ALA, its divisions, and the profession at large.

The Friends of Libraries Committee, established in 1929 as an ALA committee and a foundation committee of LAD in 1957, was active within PRMS for many years. At ALA Annual Conferences, audiences were delighted to hear such significant luncheon speakers as Sir Edmund Hillary, mountaineer and explorer (1962); Clifton Fadiman, author, editor, and radio/television celebrity (1967); Alex Haley, author of 'The Autobiography of Malcolm X" (1968); Helen Hayes, first lady of the theatre (1969); Rep. Julian Bond, State of Georgia (1970); Erich Segal, author of "Love Story" (1971); and William Blatty, author of "The Exorcist" (1972). In 1979, members formed Friends of Libraries USA(FOLUSA) and incorporated as an independent organization in 1984. It is a national leader in library support and advocacy.

Given the broad responsibilities from its inception, LAD encountered criticism as it sought to define itself through its interests and activities. In the early 1960s, there were concerns expressed that its growth and influence had extended beyond its proper sphere, encroaching upon the provinces of other divisions. These concerns were referred to the ALA Committee on Organization (COO).

The ALA COO report on the place of the LAD in the ALA structure conclusions:

1. Some assignments to LAD have dealt with matters other than purely administrative, and some have been limited to a single type of library.
2. While there may have been too broad a definition of LADs field of responsibility, there is evidence that some divisions have been giving too narrow and literal an interpretation of their own fields of responsibility.
3. The dual principle in the reorganization theory, i.e., type-of-library as against type-of-activity, has not been followed perfectly. Perfection may well be impossible, since the logic upon which the principle is based is not absolutely flawless.
4. Under the reorganization, the type-of-activity divisions seem to feel they are faring well. Since they are new, there is some reason to believe that where no fixed patterns of thought have existed, groups have been able to work well, but that where there were older fixed patterns of thought, it has been difficult for the group to adjust to the new pattern of organization. The new type-of-library divisions which emerged in the reorganization are as creatively active as type-of-activity divisions.
5. The reorganization principle stated thus: "Matters concerning one kind of library activity or service in two or more kinds of libraries are the responsibility of a type-of-activity division; and, conversely, matters concerning two or more kinds of activities in one type of library are the responsibility of that type-of-library division," is sound. This is the principle which has not altogether been followed in the assignment of projects.
6. Statements from the divisions seem to offer no evidence that such drastic action as the dissolution of LAD is required to resolve the dissatisfactions which have been expressed to COO.
7. Despite its complexity, the present organizational pattern of ALA is basically sound and deserves to be given at least 10–15 years of wholehearted support before a radical reorganization is considered. The framework exists within which to solve specific organizational problems, other than those of personality conflicts.

Library Automation–Library Publishing

RECOMMENDATIONS OF ALA COO

1. The LAD should be retained as a division of the ALA, subject to the conditions outlined in the recommendations which follow.
2. Certain modifications in the scope of LADs activities should be achieved by:
   a. Revision of LAD's statement of responsibility to clarify and limit the phrases "library administration in general" and "library organization."
   b. Greater care in the assignment of projects or programs to divisions, particularly those involving expenditure of a significant amount to money.
   c. Further study and reassessment of certain activities now being carried on in LAD about which question has arisen and which are possible candidates for reallocation to another division.
3. The committee urges the adoption of a policy within ALA which will encourage the individual divisions to conduct as many and as varied activities as they can, giving due consideration to monetary costs and the activities of other divisions or associations.
4. The committee recommends that the Executive Board and staff find some specific means of reviewing activities and assignments promptly and if possible before their inception, to assure as far as possible a judicious decision in making the assignment.
5. Some study should be given by the Membership Committee, the committee on Constitution and Bylaws, and other appropriate officers or agencies to proposals received from various sources that LAD membership be on a different basis that than in other type-of-activity divisions.[2]

ANNUAL CONFERENCES, PRE-CONFERENCES, AND INSTITUTES

At the ALA Annual Conferences, LLAMA typically offers both pre-conference and conference programs for continuing education. These address current administration, management, supervision, and leadership issues as well as current trends and "hot" topics. A review of programs can trace the changing emphases over the years. In the early years, particularly contemporary programs covered the Library Services Act (1957); Copyright Law Revisions and Libraries (1959); Standards in Library Technology (1959); Physical Requirements for Bookmobiles (1960); and Urban Renewal and the Library (1961).

In the 1960s, developments in a couple areas were the focus of programs as well as having an impact on the organization. Library automation, particularly of circulation functions, prompted such programs as An Administrative Look at Circulation (1963); Library Circulation Systems—from Hand Charging to IBM (1964); The Prospect and Hardware for Computerized Circulation Systems (1966); Circulation Automation—Anti-Blue Sky: Practical Thoughts About Systems Planning (1967); Library Equipment Institute: Charging Systems (1968); Architectural Requirements of Circulation Services (1968); and Criteria for Evaluating a Library Circulation System (1972). Throughout these attentions paid to circulation automation, libraries were concerned about getting books back to ensure initial thoroughness of the database and tighter inventory control, so there were programs like Rx for Book Recovery—Practices to Obtain the Return of Books (1962); Security Methods Used to Forestall Book Thefts (1965); and Circulation Security Systems (1973). Similarly, there was interest in The Essential Role of the Circulation Librarian (1969) and The Role of the Circulation Librarian in Book Selection, Public Services, and Book Preservation (1970). For LLAMA, along with RUSA STARS, the future of resource sharing is now of increasing importance: Circulation + : Redefining Access (1989). These developments and interests were similarly reflected in the Division's magazine, LA&M, over the years.

The interest in circulation was also reflected organizationally. As early as 1958, within ALA, an Ad Hoc Committee on Circulation Services was formed "to prepare a statement of field of interest, to suggest an organizational attachment, and to provide continuity for the group while it is considering organization."[3] There was an initial recommendation for a Circulation & Reserve Services group to become part of the Resources & Technical Services Division. Circulation roots grew quickly in LAD—a Circulation Discussion Group was established in 1961; a Circulation Controls Committee in LOMS (1962); and in 1966, the Division established its Circulation Services Section, renamed Systems and Services Section (SASS) in 1983 as it broadened its scope to cover management of other library systems.

Buildings and equipment issues have also been among the original interests of the Division. Selecting and working with architects, the library building process, space, remodeling, and retro-fitting are on-going concerns and the focus of various activities even beyond conferences, preconferences, and institutes—publications and awards are built around them, as well. Current regional institute curricula include various topics in building projects, administration and management, diversity, HRS, and PRMS. Topics and details, including presenters, are available at the LLAMA Web site

Long, over-arching interests in better statistics have also been reflected in programs, organization, and other activities of the Division. These interests have been the focus not only of ALA units but also of governmental agencies, particularly those dealing with educational institutions. The ALA Statistics Committee, established in 1936, was one of the original Association-wide committees incorporated in the foundation of the LAD in 1957.

Library Automation–Library Publishing

The section dealing with LOMS started with separate committees devoted to college and university library statistics, public library statistics, school library statistics, and a statistics coordinating committee. By 1975, there were additional LOMS committees for state libraries, for reference services, for technical services, and for nonprint media. Eventually, a separate Statistics Section was formed to pull together and coordinate activities related to statistics, their collection and use.

Outside the library profession, the National Center for Education Statistics (NCES), located within the U.S. Department of Education is the primary federal entity for collecting and analyzing data related to education. The Higher Education Act requires the completion of data surveys for institutions participating in any federal student financial assistance programs. The Higher Education General Information Survey Series was designed to provide comprehensive information on various aspects of postsecondary education in the United States and its territories. The Integrated Postsecondary Education Data Systems is now the core postsecondary education data collection program for NCES. There is a library component that includes library resources, physical facilities, staffing patterns, salaries and wages, number of employees, level of educational attainment, current expenditures, and learning resource centers.

The Division also offers national conferences and regional institutes for continuing education. Historically, its institutes have addressed both general and specific management and administration issues. Human Resources issues have always been central to the Division's mission and are prominent in continuing education offerings: recruitment, training, and retention; organizational culture and effectiveness; team building; leadership development and staff appreciation; diversity; group decision-making; and, conflict management.

Increasing attention was devoted to leadership development. The Personnel Administration Section (PAS, now HRS), formed a Staff Development Committee in 1975. In 1982, midwinter planning sessions were begun, with leadership development as one of their goals. By 1986, a mentor program was implemented; 2 years later, LOMS formed a Leadership Discussion Group. In 2003, with the support of a grant from World Book, Inc., Library Administration and Management Association (LAMA) designated 10 new members as Leaders of the Pack—part of a 3 year program to develop new leaders. Beginning in 2006, LAMA took advantage of the ALA-wide Emerging Leaders program. Given the recurrent attention to and discussion of the centrality of leadership issues, an amendment to change the name to the LLAMA was put on the 2008 Spring Ballot and won overwhelming membership approval.

There are other continuing education activities. Among these have been some courses designed to support the Certified Public Library Administrator program. In 1996,

the executive boards of LAMA and the Public Library Association approved development of this post-MLS program of professional development for public librarians. The Association of Specialized and Cooperative Library Agencies quickly approved the proposal as well. "The focus on identifying and certifying competencies in both professional and preprofessional staff dates back to LAD's earliest days." Most recently, many of ALAs divisions have been working to develop competencies for the Library Support Staff Certification Program. More information on both these programs is available at the Web site of the ALA Allied Professional Association.

PUBLICATIONS

The Library Leadership and Management Associations quarterly magazine, formerly known as *Library Administration and Management* (*LA&M*) and now as *Library Leadership and Management* (*LL&M*), is available to members online at the Division's Web site. The Division news blog, *Leads from LLAMA*, is also at that site. The Division has produced a number of monographs. Current titles include:

Outstanding Public Relations: 60 Years of the John Cotton Dana Award, by Amy Shaw and Peter Deekle.

New Supervisors in Technical Services: A Management Guide Using Checklists, by Emily Bergman and Andrea Kappler.

Growing Leaders from Within — A Practical Guide for Recognizing and Developing Leadership Skills in the Library, by the LAMA HRS Section.

Risk and Insurance Management Manual for Libraries, by Mary Breighner, CPCU, and William Payton; Jeanne M. Drewes, general editor.

Fundamentals of Library Supervision, by Joan Giesecke and Beth McNeil.

Checklist of Library Design Considerations, 4th Ed. by William W. Sannwald.

Powerful Public Relations, Ed. by Rashelle S. Karp

Building Blocks for Planning Functional Library Space, Ed. by the LAMA BES Facilities Committee

Practical Strategies for Library Managers, Ed. by Joan Giesecke

Scenario Planning for Libraries, Ed. by Joan Giesecke.

Staff Development: A Practical Guide, 3rd Ed., by Beth Avery, Terry Dahlin and Deborah A. Carver.

AWARDS

The Library Leadership and Management Association administers one of ALA's most prestigious awards, the John Cotton Dana Public Relations Award. Sponsored by H.W. Wilson since 1946, it honors outstanding library

Library Automation–Library Publishing

public relations efforts. In recognition of their achievement, John Cotton Dana award winners receive a cash development grant of $5000. The awards are presented at an elegant reception, hosted by H.W. Wilson, held during the ALA Annual Conference.

The Library Leadership and Management Association BES administers two biennial awards, given in alternate years. The American Institute of Architects Awards, cosponsored by ALA and the AIA, encourage excellence in the architectural design and planning of libraries. Awards for distinguished accomplishment in library architecture by an architect licensed in the United States are made for any library in the United States or abroad. The ALA/ International Interior Design Association (IIDA) Library Interior Design Award, cosponsored by ALA and the IIDA, honors excellence in library interior design and promotes examples of extraordinary design reflected through innovative concepts.

The Diana V. Braddom FRFDS Scholarship is available to library staff from all types of libraries to support learning new fundraising skills, enabling them to increase funding to their libraries from public, private, and corporate sources. The Scholarship was begun in 2001.

The Library Leadership and Management Association Cultural Diversity Committee's Cultural Diversity Grant is awarded to LLAMA members or units in support of the creation and dissemination of resources that will assist library administrators and managers in developing a vision and commitment to diversity, and in fostering and sustaining diversity throughout their institutions. The Committee, formed in 1991, established a Diversity Fund in 1994 and the grant in 1997.

The PRMS Section's first "Swap and Shop," a program that displays library public relations and promotional materials from hundreds of libraries of all sizes and types, was held in 1974. Judges select Best of Show winners based on content, originality, design, format, and effectiveness.

The LLAMA/YBP Student Writing and Development Award Contest, begun in 1998, is for students enrolled in a graduate program in library and information studies. Applicants submit essays on an announced theme. The winning submission is published in an issue of the Division's quarterly magazine. The author also receives a travel grant, funded by YBP, Inc., to be used to attend the ALA Annual Conference, where he/she is recognized at the LLAMA President's Program and the first meeting of the LLAMA Board of Directors.

CONCLUSION

Starting its existence as the LAD in 1957, to acknowledge the development of interests and activities that had taken place during its first two decades, the name changed to the Library Administration and Management Association.

The next three decades led to yet another name change, to the Library Leadership and Management Association, in 2008. The Division has targeted other professional organizations with which to establish partnerships in creating new leadership programs and opportunities. These programs reach out to staff at all levels and in all types of libraries to meet the needs of individual members as well as the organizations in which they serve.

ACKNOWLEDGMENTS

Colleagues at the ALA headquarters have been very helpful and supportive in this and other endeavors devoted to the history of LLAMA. In particular, I thank Karen Muller in the ALA Library and Lorraine Olley in the LLAMA office. Other LLAMA members working on aspects of the history who merit special mention are Robert F. Moran, Jr., and Gregg Sapp, with whom I worked on documenting and writing about the first 50 years of LLAMA.

APPENDIX 1

Table A.1 Division presidents.

1957	Louis M. Nouris, St. Louis (MO) Public Library
1958	Katherine Martin Stokes, Western Mich. University, Kalamazoo
1959	Margaret Mary Klausner, Public Library of Stockton & San Juaquin Cty, CA
1960	Archie L. McNeal, University of Miami, Coral Gables, FL
1961	Ralph Blasingame, Jr., Pennsylvania State Library, Harrisburg
1962	Louise F. Rees, Michigan State Library, Lansing
1963	Keith Doms, Carnegie Library, Pittsburgh, PA
1964	Herbert Goldhor, University of Illinois, Urbana-Champaign
1965	Hoyt R. Galvin, Charlotte (NC) Public Library
1966	Charles F. Gosnell, New York University Libraries, New York City
1967	Eileen Thornton, Oberlin (OH) College Library
1968	John F. Anderson, San Francisco (CA) Public Library
1969	Julius R. Chitwood, Rockford (IL) Public Library
1970	James H. Richards, Jr., University of Wyoming, Laramie
1971	Lester L. Stoffel, Suburban Library System, Western Springs, IL
1972	Grace P. Slocum, Enoch Pratt Public Library, Baltimore, MD
1973	W. Joseph Kimbrough, Denver (CO) Public Library
1974	Herbert F. Mutschler, King County Library System, Seattle, WA
1975	Paxton P. Price, St. Louis (MO) Public Library
1976	Ernest Di Mattia, Jr., Ferguson Library, Stamford, CT

(Continued)

Table A.1   Division presidents. *(Continued)*

1977	Richard L. Waters, Dallas (TX) Public Library

LAD becomes LAMA

1978	Donald E. Wright, Evanston (IL) Public Library
1979	Dale B. Canelas, Stanford (CA) University
1980	Mary A. Hall, Prince George's County Mem'l Lib, Hyattsville, MD
1981	Carolyn A. Snyder, Indiana University Libraries, Bloomington, IN
1982	David R. Smith, Hennepin County Library, Minnetonka, MN
1983	Nancy R. McAdams, University of Texas, Austin, TX
1984	Gary E. Strong, California State Library, Sacramento CA
1985	Ronald G. Leach, Indiana State University, Terre Haute, IN
1986	Betty W. Bender, Spokane (WA) Public Library
1987	Ann Heidbreder Eastman, Virginia Tech., Blacksburg, VA
1988	Maureen Sullivan, Yale University, New Haven, CT
1989	Dallas Y. Shaffer, Monterey County Public Library, Salinas, CA
1990	Susanne Henderson MacTavish, General Electric Company Lib. Gaithersburg, MD
1991	Susan E. Stroyan, Illinois Wesleyan University, Bloomington, IL
1992	James G. Neal, Indiana University, Bloomington, IN
1993	Carol F. L. Liu, Queens Borough Public Library, Jamaica, NY
1994	Donald E. Riggs, University of Michigan, Ann Arbor, MI
1995	John J. Vasi, University of California, Santa Barbara, CA
1996	William W. Sannwald, San Diego (CA) Public Library
1997	Charles E. Kratz, Jr. University of Scranton, Scranton, PA
1998	Thomas L. Wilding, University of Texas, Arlington, TX
1999	Carol L. Anderson, State University of New York, Albany, NY
2000	Jeanne Thorsen, King County Library System Foundation, Issaquah, WA
2001	Joan Giesecke, University of Nebraska-Lincoln, Lincoln, NE
2002	Linda Dobb, Bowling Green State University, Bowling Green, OH
2003	Paul Anderson, University of Delaware, Newark, DE
2004	Virginia Steel, Washington State University, Pullman, WA
2005	Catherine Murray-Rust, Colorado State University, Fort Collins, CO
2006	Andrea Lapsley, Colorado State University, Fort Collins, CO

(Continued)

Table A.1   Division presidents. *(Continued)*

2007	W. Bede Mitchell, Georgia Southern University, Statesboro, GA

LAMA becomes LLAMA

2008	Molly Raphael, Multnomah County Library, OR
2009	Gina J. Millsap, Topeka & Shawnee County Public Library, KS
2010	Gail A. Kennedy, University of Kentucky, Lexington, KY

APPENDIX 2

Table A.2   Division secretaries/ executive directors.

1957–1960	Hazel B. Timmerman
1960–1968	Alphonse F. Trezza
1968–1973	Ruth R. Frame
1973	Jordan M. Scepanski
1974–1979	Donald P. Hammer
1979–1985	Roger H. Parent
1985–1989	John W. Berry
1989–2001	Karen Muller
2001–2007	Lorraine H. Olley
2007	Kerry Ward

REFERENCES

1. ALA Organization and Information 1959–60 Type-of-Activity Divisions Library Administration Division. ALA Bull. **1959**, *53* (December), 918–919.
2. Highlights of the Midwinter Meeting Council, Executivse Board, and PEBCO. ALA Bull. **1964**, *58* (March), 196–205.
3. The American Library Association. Committees Ad Hoc on Circulation Services. ALA Bull. **1959**, *53* (January), 896.

Used with permission from the ALA.

BIBLIOGRAPHIC NOTES

1. Aspects of the history of LLAMA are detailed to a greater degree in the 50th anniversary issue of *Library Administration & Management* **2007**, 21(3), 109–123. Included there are titles of programs and articles, organizational structure and growth, timelines, staff, etc. The LLAMA Web site.
2. http://www.ala.org/ala/mgrps/divs/llama/llama.cfm, also includes significant information about the history of the Association. Various ALA newsletters and conference programs contain a wealth of detail that can be used to trace the development of this and other ALA divisions.

Library Automation–Library Publishing

Library of Congress Classification (LCC)

Lois Mai Chan
School of Library and Information Science, University of Kentucky, Lexington, Kentucky, U.S.A.

Theodora L. Hodges
Berkeley, California, U.S.A.

Abstract

The Library of Congress Classification (LCC), originally designed for classifying the Library's own collection, is now used in a wide range of libraries, both in the United States and abroad. This entry recounts its history and development from its genesis to the present time, leading up to an explanation of LCC structure, tables, and notation. It then considers the system's potential for wider application in the online age, through speculation on using LCC as a tool for (a) partitioning large files; (b) generating domain-specific taxonomies; and (c) integrating classification and controlled subject terms for improved retrieval in the online public access catalog (OPAC) and the Internet. Finally, analyzing both its strong and relatively weak features, it addresses the question of whether in its current state LCC is in all respects ready for playing such roles.

INTRODUCTION

The Library of Congress Classification (LCC), developed for the Library's own use, has been adopted by so many other libraries that it has become one of the most widely used classification systems, particularly among large academic and research libraries in the United States and around the world. Several major factors have contributed to its wide acceptance:

1. Its wide-ranging and thorough coverage.
2. Its continuous revision.
3. Its dependability (in respect to maintenance) through its support by the Library of Congress (LC).
4. Its flexible, very hospitable, and expandable notation (i.e., its book numbering or labeling system).
5. Its base in literary warrant (the term "literary warrant" in the context of library classification indicates that new topics are added to the schedules as they are needed to reflect the subject content of the literature or materials being cataloged or classified).
6. The wide accessibility of its schedules, in both electronic and print versions.
7. The fact that LCC class numbers, as well as *Library of Congress Subject Headings* (LCSH), appear on almost all LC cataloging records and many records in OCLC's (Online Computer Library Center's) WorldCat. Further considerations may be that the system holds promise as one of the important elements in new systems to improve retrieval on the Internet and in the online public access catalog (OPAC).

To date, LCC has been applied primarily in the library environment, where, traditionally, its notation has provided a sequence for the shelf-ordering of library materials. Even in this role, LCC has had an information retrieval function; generations of library users have relied on classification as a means of locating wanted material on shelves or have used shelf browsing as one of the ways to discover related resources. A major question posed by this entry is whether, given modern searching amenities, LCC can also play a significant role in the future information environment. Many believe that it can. We turn first to clues from LCC's history and development.

BACKGROUND

The history of what was eventually to be LCC can be said to have begun in April 1800, when the American legislature was preparing to move from Philadelphia to the new capital city of Washington, D.C. A congressional act passed at the time provided $5000 "for the purchase of... books... for the use of Congress and the said city of Washington." A second act, in January 1802, called for the appointment of a librarian by the nation's president; soon thereafter, President Jefferson appointed John Beckley, then Clerk of the House, as the first Librarian of Congress.[1]

For the next several years, the collection was not classified in the current sense of the term; rather, books were arranged by size and, within size groups by accession number. Such an arrangement was fairly common at the time; and was used in many libraries for much of the 1800s. However, before Congress moved to Washington, its members used Benjamin Franklin's Library Company of Philadelphia. That library, ever since 1789, had been using a subject-based classification system for its

Encyclopedia of Library and Information Sciences, Fourth Edition DOI: 10.1081/E-ELIS4-120043714
Copyright © 2017 by Taylor & Francis. All rights reserved.

holdings, a system based in part on a work by Francis Bacon published in 1605 and also on another work by Jean le Rond d'Alembert published in 1751.[2]

The first LC catalogs, published in 1802 and in 1804, reflected the collection's size and its accession order arrangement. The 1808 catalog, however, revealed added categories for some bibliographic forms, and the 1812 catalog showed that the Library had by that time moved toward arranging books by subject, following the system used by the Library Company of Philadelphia.[3]

The next change was dramatic. In August 1814, when the War of 1812 was still raging, British solders set fire to the Capitol, and most of the Library's collection, which by then had grown to about 3000 volumes, was destroyed. Subsequently, Thomas Jefferson offered to sell Congress his personal library of 6487 volumes. The books arrived already classified by a system Jefferson had devised himself, a system also based on the work of Bacon and d'Alembert. Jefferson's system provided for 44 main categories with many subcategories. His scheme, with many changes made for practical rather than theoretical reasons, remained in force almost until the turn of the next century.[4] By that time, in spite of another disastrous fire in 1851 that destroyed two-thirds of the collection,[5] the LC collection had grown to at least 800,000 items.[6]

However, despite the fact that there were only minor changes in the library's approach to classification from Jefferson's time until the end of the century, developments during that period were not without influence on the library's future role in both classification and subject cataloging. One was the gradual change in opinion on the role of the library. Early in the century, under the direction of librarians J. S. Meehan (1829–1861) and J. G. Stephenson (1861–1864) and under the oversight of the Congress's Joint Committee on the Library, the library was viewed as merely a service agency for Congress. Its collection was narrow in scope, and little used. That picture changed through the influence of Ainsworth Spofford, who was Librarian of Congress from 1864 to 1897 and who served the library in various positions from 1861 until 1908. Spofford believed that there should be a national comprehensive collection available not only to members of Congress but to the general public and directed both the library's acquisitions program and its lending policies to that end.[7,8]

Development of the Library of Congress Classification

The next chapter in LCC's history was again rooted in a move, this time, in 1897, to the magnificent building it still occupies. The move itself, plus the size and continuous rapid growth of the collection, demonstrated that the Jefferson-based classification was no longer adequate for the Library's needs. The collection by that time was approaching a million items. John Russell Young, then Librarian of Congress, was in agreement with J. C. M. Hanson and Charles Martel (head of the catalog division and chief classifier, respectively) that reclassification was necessary. After an investigation that found extant schemes unsuitable for the library's use for one reason or another, Hanson and Martel concluded that a new classification should be developed using Charles A. Cutter's *Expansive Classification*[9] as a guide to the order of classes but with a modified notation. Young, who died suddenly in January 1899, was succeeded by Herbert Putnam, who also strongly supported reclassification. After much consultation and deliberation, the decision was made in 1900 to proceed with the development of an entirely new classification scheme. Work on the new classification began in 1901. The notation question was resolved by the choice of capital letters for main classes, with numerical expansion for subtopics and with gaps in the sequence left for future development. Hanson's 1901 proposed outline shows the use of only single letters for main classes, but his 1903 outline shows that he had moved to using double letters for major subclasses. The latter change was significant, because it greatly increased the hospitality, i.e., the expansion potential and ability to accommodate new subjects, of the new LCC system.[10,11]

As work began on the classification, each subject class was developed by specialists in the subject at issue who worked under the general direction of Hanson and Martel.

For all the classes, Martel worked out a "common arrangement pattern" which he referred to as his "seven points." The first six points covered general materials; the seventh was for specific subdivisions of the topic at issue. Martel's seven points[12] included

1. General form divisions: periodicals, societies, collections, dictionaries, etc.
2. Theory. Philosophy.
3. History.
4. Treatises. General works.
5. Law. Regulation. State relations.
6. Study and teaching.
7. Special subjects and subdivisions.

This pattern, used whenever applicable, brought a degree of unity to the classification as a whole that would probably not have been achieved without it.

The separate schedules were published (in individual print volumes) as they were completed. Although some schedules took decades to be finished, all of them except Class K (law) had appeared by 1948. (The final Law schedule, Religious law, was published only recently, in 2004.)

Library Automation–Library Publishing

The separate development of individual schedules meant that, unlike most other classification systems, LCC was not the product of one mastermind. The schedules that make up the classification were (and are) developed, published, and maintained separately; indeed, LCC has been called "a coordinated series of special classes."[13] This aspect of the system, each separate schedule prepared by experts in the subject area of the class being developed, lessened the homogeneity and predictability of the system as a whole. On the other hand, to quote Richard Angell, former chief of the LC Subject Cataloging Division, the system was "praised for the freedom allowed in each schedule for development according to its subject field's own intrinsic structure."[14]

Once a schedule was published, work began almost immediately on its revision; this was necessary in order to accommodate new topics, new relationships, and terminological changes that are continually found in new material being cataloged. Additions and changes are communicated to the library community through *Library of Congress Classification (LCC) Weekly Lists*.[15] Another source of such information is the Gale Research Company's publication *SuperLCCS*;[16] the yearly issue of each schedule contains the entire class or subclass incorporating additions and changes for the past year.

It bears noting here that, until the mid-1990s, the LCC schedules existed mainly as print products. Maintenance and revision remained basically manual tasks that were extremely labor-intensive and therefore both costly and slow. The conversion of LCC to electronic form became imperative. Work began in 1993 and was completed in 1996. For several reasons, the conversion to electronic form, which was done using the *USMARC* (now called MARC 21) *Classification Format*,[17] was an especially important development for LCC. That the change greatly improves internal operating efficiency goes without saying. For one thing, it enables much more efficient production of the print schedules. More important, it not only enables LCC to be consulted online but allows it to be part of new and powerful search tools.

Print versions of the schedules are still being produced as the extent of revisions dictates. However, the electronic version, *Classification Web*,[18] which includes a full-text display of the entire LCC plus correlations between LCC and LCSH, is in essence up to date and is heavily used.

Because all classes—there are 21—are constantly being revised as the LCC editors strive to keep abreast of the times, by now (2008) most schedules have undergone thorough revision at least once, and for some schedules many times. In total, whether consulted electronically or through the 41 volumes of the print version, LCC functions as a general, well-maintained, and comprehensive library classification scheme.

LCC STRUCTURE AND NUMBERING SYSTEM

Because LCC is largely an enumerative system, i.e., a system that lists numbers for complex as well as single subjects, the classification as a whole requires little number building. The extensive author tables in Class P (literature) and the form tables in Class K (law) are the most noticeable exceptions.

As was the case at its beginning, LCC main classes are denoted by one capital letter, and subclasses are represented by two or three capital letters followed by the Arabic numbers 1–9999 treated as integers. To provide for expansion there are gaps left between integers, and the integers may be expanded decimally where needed. They can also be expanded by Cutter numbers, a system originally invented by Charles A. Cutter, which uses a combination of a capital letter and one or more Arabic numerals, read decimally. For general use, Cutter numbers are available in multiple versions with different levels of details, for example, the *Cutter-Sanborn Three-Figure Author Table*.[19] In its classification, both for item numbers and when further subdivision is needed under topics, the Library of Congress uses a much less elaborate table that is based on Cutter's scheme.[20] The resulting letter–number combinations are referred to as "Cutter numbers." The use of that table is indicated by instructions and/or tables appearing where applicable throughout the schedules.

Within individual schedules, there are many internal tables, using numerals or Cutter numbers that apply only to specific segments of the classification. The extensive tables for schedules K (law) and P (literature), however, appear in separately published volumes. In addition, a few tables, published in *classification and Shelflisting*,[21] are used throughout the system.

In sum, although LCC began as an enumerative rather than a faceted classification, over the years, it has moved gradually toward faceting, through the increasing use of tables. Furthermore, the system is not rigid: Its notational system can be expanded in more ways than one to accommodate new and developing subject matter. In other words, both LCC's notation, and the classification itself, are remarkably hospitable to changes in what is known and written about.

The following details, discussion, and examples give substance to the brief description just provided.

LCC MAIN CLASSES, SUBCLASSES, AND DIVISIONS

The following list shows LCC's main classes with their alphabetical designations. Discussions of main classes, subclasses, divisions of subclasses, and LCC's numbering system follow the list:

Library Automation–Library Publishing

A	General works
B	Philosophy. Psychology. Religion
C	Auxiliary sciences of history
D	History (general) and history of Europe, Asia, etc.
E–F	History: America (Western hemisphere)
G	Geography. Maps. Anthropology. Recreation
H	Social sciences
J	Political science
K	Law
L	Education
M	Music
N	Fine arts
P	Language and literature
Q	Science
R	Medicine
S	Agriculture
T	Technology
U	Military science
V	Naval science
Z	Bibliography. Library science. Information resources

Main Classes

The rationale for the arrangement of LCC's main classes was explained by Charles Martel, one of the persons responsible for the original planning and supervision of the development of the system. Class A, general works, not limited to any particular subject, leads the scheme. It is followed by Class B, containing philosophy and religion, which sets forth theories about human beings in relation to the universe. The next classes (C–G history and geography) in the sequence cover such concepts as the human abode and the source of humanity's means of subsistence, humans as affected by and affecting their physical milieu, and the mind and soul of humanity in transition from primitive to advanced culture. The next group, Classes H–L, deals with the economic and social evolution of human beings. Classes M–P (music, fine arts, and language and literature) concern human aesthetic and intellectual development. Viewed in large groups, it can be seen that Classes B–P taken together form the group of the philosophical–historical and philological sciences, while the second large group, Classes Q–V, embraces the mathematical–physical, natural, and applied sciences. Bibliography, which in many libraries may be distributed throughout different subject classes, shares the same class (Z) with librarianship and information resources.[22]

Subclasses

Each of the main classes, with the exception of E and F, is divided into subclasses that represent disciplines or major branches of the main class. Class Q, for example, is divided into the following subclasses:

Library Automation–Library Publishing

Q	Science (general)
QA	Mathematics
QB	Astronomy
QC	Physics
QD	Chemistry
QE	Geology
QH	Natural history (general)—Biology (general)
QK	Botany
QL	Zoology
QM	Human anatomy
QP	Physiology
QR	Microbiology

Divisions

Each subclass is further divided into divisions that represent components of the subclass. For example, the subclass chemistry has the following divisions:

QD	*Chemistry*
1–65	General Including alchemy
71–142	Analytical chemistry
146–197	Inorganic chemistry
241–441	Organic chemistry
415–436	Biochemistry
450d–801	Physical and theoretical chemistry
625–655	Radiation chemistry
701–731	Photochemistry
901–999	Crystallography

Each of the divisions, in turn, has subdivisions (often called Martel's seven points) that specify different aspects of the subject, such as form, time, place, and more detailed subject subdivisions. In many schedules, the progression of subject provisions still mirrors these seven points, which were described above. The exception is point 5 (Law. Regulation. State relations. Legal topics). Legal matters, which had been scattered in different classes in earlier schedules, were moved to the law (Class K) schedules at the time they were being completed.

NOTATION (NUMBERING SYSTEM)

As mentioned earlier, the LCC uses a mixed notation of letters and Arabic numerals to construct call numbers. Main classes are represented by a single letter, for instance, K (law), N (fine arts), and Q (science). Most subclasses are represented by double or triple letters, for instance, QD (chemistry), DJK (history of Eastern Europe), and KFF (law of Florida). Classes E and F, the earliest classes to be developed, have not been divided into subclasses.

Divisions within subclasses are represented by Arabic numbers from 1 to 9999 (as integers) with possible decimal extension, and/or with further subdivision indicated by Cutter numbers (as noted above, a system originally invented by Charles A. Cutter[23] and modified for use with LCC, using a combination of a capital letter and one or more Arabic numerals).

The call number is completed by an item number based on the main entry (author or title) in the form of a Cutter number plus, in most cases, the year of publication. There are two common patterns of LC call numbers; they differ in the fact that in the second pattern the class number includes a topical extension expressed by a Cutter number.

1. Class number:
   One, two, or three capital letters
   Whole number 1 through 9999
   Possible decimal extension
   Item number
   Cutter number based on main entry
   Year of publication, as required
2. Class number:
   One, two, or three capital letters
   Whole number 1 through 9999
   Possible decimal extension
   First Cutter number based on term for topic, place, or form
   Item number
   Second Cutter number based on main entry
   Year of publication, as required

The following examples show typical forms of LC call numbers:

1. SD131.S29 2005 *Forests in landscapes*: *ecosystem approaches to sustainability*, by Jeffrey Sayer and Stewart Maginnis; assisted by Michelle Laurie. 2005
   Class number
   SD (two capital letters) Forestry
   131 (whole number) General works
   Item number
   .S29 (Cutter number based on author's name Sayer)
   2005 (Year of publication)
2. DJK7.75.V57 2005 *Virtual Slavica*: *digital libraries, digital archives*, edited by Michael Neubert. 2005
   Class number
   DJK (three capital letters) History of Eastern Europe
   7.75 (whole number with decimal extension of whole number) Electronic information resources
   Item number
   .V57 (Cutter number based on the title: Virtual...)
   2005 (Year of publication)
3. HD9651.9.D8 N3513 2007 *Nylon and bombs*: *DuPont and the march of modern America*, by Pap A. Ndiaye; translated by Elborg Forster. 2007
   Class number
   HD (two capital letters) Industries. Land use. Labor
   9651(whole number) Chemical industries

   .9 (decimal extension of whole number) By firm
   .D8 (Cutter number expansion for further subdivision) DuPont
   Item number
   .N3515 (Cutter number based on author's name) Ndiaye
   2005 (Year of publication)
4. N6512.5.P6 D67 Pop art and the contest over American culture, by Sara Doris. 2007
   Class number
   N (one capital letter) Fine arts
   6512 (whole number) United States. Twentieth century
   .5 (decimal extension) Special aspects or movements
   .P6 (Cutter number for further subdivision) Pop art
   Item number
   .D67 (Cutter number based on author's name) Doris
   2007 (Year of publication)

An LC call number may contain no more than one or two Cutter numbers. Call numbers for certain types of maps and atlases, however, may contain an additional letter–number combination that appears to be a third Cutter number but is actually an extension of the class number.

An important characteristic of LCC notation is that it is not hierarchical beyond the class/subclass level. Thus, in contrast to the notation for Melvil Dewey's *Decimal Classification*, LCC notation does not reflect all the general/specific relationships that are inherent in the scheme itself. There has been some criticism of LCC's nonhierarchical notation on this basis.[24] However, in some respects, the absence of notational hierarchy can be viewed as an advantage for LCC. For one thing, most of its class numbers are thereby relatively brief and are thus easily manageable for shelving or other purposes. For another, in part because hierarchical relationships are largely ignored in the notation, LCC is remarkably "hospitable": provisions for new subject matter can be easily added to the system.[25] This is a most important consideration in light of the rapid increase in world literature, both in the number of "pieces" and the range of subject matter, disciplines, and genres that are represented. Further details and explanations of the LCC notation can be found in *Classification and Shelflisting Manual*.[26]

LCC'S POTENTIAL IN THE FUTURE ONLINE ENVIRONMENT

Early in this entry, it was stated that a major question facing those interested in LCC is whether it can play an important role in tomorrow's information environment.

Library Automation–Library Publishing

At this time, mid-2008, there is considerable debate on the matter even within the library sector of the information professions. Some claim that library classification has had its day. On the other hand, there are those who believe that, quite the contrary, there are many areas and operations in the current information environment in which the use of a classification scheme that is kept up to date—as are both the Dewey and the LC schemes as well as some others—could make a significant contribution. These beliefs spring from three sources: First, awareness of the huge size and amorphous nature of the world's current store of accessible information; second, the observation that there are many specialized interest areas that would benefit from custom-designed organization schemes; and third, doubts that, with currently available search options, retrieval from the Internet is as thorough and as efficient as it could be. Three areas in which classification could make a positive contribution are noted below.

Partitioning Large Files

In recent decades, the Internet has seen an extraordinarily rapid growth. It now contains an enormous, hardly imaginable, heterogeneous store of electronic resources. Increasingly, many libraries and research institutions, recognizing the richness and overwhelming quantity of information available on the Web, have incorporated selected Web resources into their local online systems or portals. As time passes, with the rapid growth and phenomenal proliferation of electronic resources, it is becoming more and more apparent that effective means are needed to organize what the Internet has to offer. In addition to providing keyword searching, major holders of online resources, as well as Web resource providers themselves, have turned to directory or hierarchical schemes as means of categorizing and organizing their resources for access (e.g., a library-based system that uses LCC for this purpose is Cyberstacks on the Iowa State University Web site).[27]

Furthermore, recent developments in taxonomy and ontology indicate an increasing interest in a directory or categorical approach to organizing Web resources. This is a logical development; after all, classification was devised in the beginning as a response to the need for organizing large bodies of material. If such interest should continue, database managers and system designers may find that existing schemes based on hierarchical structures are promising candidates for serving as organizational models. Where LCC could make a particular contribution is in its detailed and specific provisions, its broad range of coverage, and its ease of access. Those who turn to classification as a way to manage huge databases are likely to try broad subject divisions first. Thus, the broad main classes, in whatever scheme they choose, would be a logical and effective way to start. But, as time goes on, if and when database or Web managers see a role for finer and finer topical divisions, they will find they have already been worked out and are at hand.

Generation of Domain-Specific Taxonomies

The existence of topical collections—special libraries being a case in point—shows that people involved in different fields of work have long found it productive to use collections of materials narrowly focused on their domains. Knowledge, it seems clear, is becoming more and more specialized. The usefulness of such collections may be enhanced if they are categorized by a scheme that does justice to the areas at hand. LCC may be of considerable help in this respect. Because it has been developed and maintained by subject specialists, LCC has sometimes been viewed from a theoretical standpoint as a scheme lacking an overall coherent and logical structure. However, from another perspective, this apparent weakness is a source of strength. The specialists responsible for a given area in a classification scheme are in a better position than generalists to keep the schedules for that area in conformance with current notions of how topics within it are either interrelated or related to other areas previously thought to be outside that area's bounds. The result of the departmentalized approach of LCC is that individual classes or parts of the scheme—such as the classifications of law, religion, art, and cartographic materials—are fully and painstakingly developed to the point that they can either be adopted as stand-alone specialized schemes or can serve as models for developing such schemes. Classification modules or miniclassification schemes with special foci can also be built on the basis of LCC to meet the needs for effectively organizing Web resources and digital libraries in specific subject areas. Where more details are needed in a particular situation, say to represent multitopics or subtopics, the basic structure of LCC could be extended to suit special situations and purposes. Another advantage is that specialized schemes based on LCC could be interoperable among one another within the main LCC structure. The availability of tools such as *Classification Web*[28] greatly facilitates such operations.

LCC and LCSH as a Combined Retrieval Tool

Finally, there is promise in a vehicle that would map LCC captions against terms in LCSH.[29] The goal is to create a merged search term system that would serve as a hidden cross-reference chain. In such a system, when a user submitted a search term the system response would include all the items that matched his or her search term in either LCSH or LCC, as well as all the items that were linked to that term in either system's cross-reference structure. If the users wanted to refine the search, they could be offered options such as "associated topics?," "narrower topics?," or "broader topics?." Such a system for merging classification captions and controlled subject vocabulary mapped

Library Automation–Library Publishing

each against the other has great potential for improving information storage, discovery, and retrieval. One of its advantages would be that it would link synonyms through the already existing references from lead-in terms to the "preferred term." Another and more important advantage is that it would offer a searcher two approaches to his or her chosen topic. This duality is possible because classification and subject headings complement each other. A subject heading or descriptor, along with its cross-reference apparatus, represents a particular topic treated from all aspects. On the other hand, classification of a topic places it among related topics treated from the same perspective or within the same discipline. Traditionally, each approach has a specific function in information storage and retrieval. Used together, they can improve both effectiveness and efficiency. The Library of Congress has already taken steps toward such a system. In LCSH, many headings are editorially linked to specific LC class numbers. In addition, under each LC class number in *Classification Web*,[30] the user can find up to 10 LC subject heading strings that are closely associated in the LC catalog. Implemented in a search vehicle, the gain in discovery and retrieval power would be tremendous. Were such the case, LC access provisions could have an even wider retrieval role to play in the future than they have had in the past.[31]

Library of congress classification in the future

One of the aims of this entry was to consider the questions of whether, first, there are roles LCC might reasonably play in the wider information environment, and second, whether LCC in its current state (mid-2008) is ready to do so. The first question was addressed in particular above, under the heading "LCC's Potential in the Future Online Environment." It is the second question that is addressed now (mid-2008). To answer this question we propose to begin with taking a new look at some of the criticisms that have been levied against LCC in the past.

Criticisms and Problems

Guidelines

One aspect that caused concern in the past was how few official guidelines there were respecting subject analysis in general and the application of LCC in particular. With the publication of *Classification and Shelflisting Manual*, 2008 Ed[32] this concern has been largely addressed.

National bias

A more fundamental concern was that the classification reflected a national bias. Because the Library was founded as a library *for* members of U.S. Congress, its early concentration on U.S. materials during the 1800s was natural. Over the past century, however, the collection has become

more and more general because many outside libraries are now contributing new classification numbers through SACO (a subject authority cooperative program). As a result, the subject scope of LCC is continually expanding at the same time that its national bias is decreasing.

Multitopical works

Another concern, a problem LCC shares with many other classification schemes, is its paucity of provisions for multitopical works. The problem is rooted in the still-prevailing limit of one class number per work, a rule that was appropriate when a primary function of classification was to determine the order of volumes on shelves. In the online age, however, the one-number-per-work limit holds only in the sense of designating a prime class number to indicate where a work is best shelved. With a change in policy, this problem could be easily solved: Assigning a class number for every significant topic covered in a work could be as much taken for granted as assigning multiple subject headings.

Obsolescence

A serious issue common to all classification systems is combating obsolescence, in other words, keeping systems up to date. The Library of Congress has a firm policy of continuous revision of its classification, a process that often involves moving topical provisions from one part of the schedules to another. This fact puts the Library in an uncomfortable position: it must balance the need for timely revision of its classification with the contrary need to maintain the system's stability because relocations within the schedules entail an often overwhelming amount of work for participating libraries.

There is a particular factor bearing on reclassification that cannot be ignored. Creating new classes or subclasses or divisions, or revising existing provisions to any extent, is the most intellectually challenging and time-consuming work in all of librarianship. It is therefore the most costly and may thus be hindered for budgetary reasons. Should more use be made of LCC in the future, there remains the matter of the expense entailed in ensuring that revision of the classification keeps pace with the times, that, in a more timely way than was allowable when knowledge was not expanding so fast, it is able to reflect new knowledge without distortion and without burying the old.

LCC Strengths and Potential

Strengths

LCC has been hailed as a system that has proved to be practical and widely accepted. In Arthur Maltby's words,

Library Automation–Library Publishing

"It is a triumph for pragmatism."[33] Its merits were enumerated at the beginning of this entry and are repeated more briefly here: It is very widely used; its coverage is wide-ranging and thorough; it is continuously revised; it has the support of the Library of Congress; its notation is terse, flexible, and expandable, and it is widely accessible in both electronic and print versions. That it is time-tested should give prospective users the confidence that the bugs, so to speak, have had time to work out. And the fact that each schedule was developed and is maintained by subject specialists rather than by generalists ensures the validity of its coverage. Therefore, to the extent that LC's continuous maintenance policy is not behind schedule due to budgetary constraint, the system is kept up-to-date and additions and changes are communicated to the cataloging community in a timely fashion. Furthermore, the availability of the online version of LCC has improved both its accessibility and its ease of application.

On the purely practical side, because LCC is a largely enumerative system, there is little number building, making the scheme relatively easy to use. And because LCC notation is compact, there is less likelihood of error when LCC numbers are assigned or input as search keys.

In sum, LCC, originally designed specifically for the Library's own collection, has become a comprehensive and hospitable classification used by many other large libraries. Furthermore, in recent years the Library of Congress has made a great effort to communicate with those who use LCC. Both its records and information about its policies are made easily and widely available, a demonstration of LC's sense of responsibility toward its user community.

CONCLUSIONS

In 2008, we are now in a different information age from when classification was used primarily for shelf-ordering and for browsing: the Internet, information databases, and OPACs (online public access [library] catalogs) are currently the primary search vehicles for those searching for topical information. Thus, new questions are being asked about classification itself and about LCC in particular. Among them are:

Is classification dead as an approach to searching?

The answer is no, not, at least for broad partitioning. Witness Google's many subdivisions by type of material covered. There is now a Google Books, a Google Business, a Google Earth, a Google Health, and a Google Scholar among the 20 search choices offered for those who access Google's search system.

Does LCC have the potential for playing a wider retrieval role in the future than in the past?

The answer here is yes. Three possible and specific new applications were described in an earlier section of this entry.

Is LCC as it stands ready to play wider roles?

The answer is: there is considerable potential. An encouraging fact for LCC overall is that in recent times there seems to have been an increasing interest in a directory or categorical approach to organizing Web resources. If such interest should continue, database managers and system designers may find that existing schemes based on hierarchical structures are promising candidates for serving as organizational models. Where LCC, as well as other comprehensive classification schemes, such as the Dewey Decimal Classification and the Universal Decimal Classification, could make a particular contribution is in its detailed and specific provisions, its broad range of coverage, and its ease of access. The broad main classes, in whatever scheme is chosen, would be a logical way to start. But if, as time goes on, if and when database or Web managers see a role for finer and finer topical divisions, they will find they have already been worked out and are at hand.

REFERENCES

1. Cole, J.Y. *The Library of Congress in Perspective*; R.R. Bowker: New York, 1978; 5.
2. LaMontagne, L.E. *American Library Classification with Special Reference to the Library of Congress*; Shoe String Press: Hamden, CT, 1961; 44–45.
3. Johnston, W.D. *History of the Library of Congress, 1800–1864*; Government Printing Office: Washington DC, 1904; 49 and plate 29.
4. Johnston, W.D. *History of the Library of Congress, 1800–1864*; Government Printing Office: Washington DC, 1904; 145–146.
5. Miksa, F. *The Development of Classification at the Library of Congress*; Graduate School of Library and Information Science, University of Illinois at Urbana-Champaign: Champaign, IL, 1984; 4 Occasional Paper # 164 (Printout from the library's Large-scale Digitation Project, 2007).
6. LaMontagne, L.E. *American Library Classification with Special Reference to the Library of Congress*; Shoe String Press: Hamden, CT, 1961; 27, 234–236.
7. Miksa, F. *The Development of Classification at the Library of Congress*; Graduate School of Library and Information Science, University of Illinois at Urbana-Champaign: Champaign, IL, 1984; 10–15 Occasional Paper # 164; (Printout from the library's Large-scale Digitation Project, 2007).
8. Cole, J.Y., Ed. *Ainsworth Rand Spofford, Bookman and Librarian*; Libraries Unlimited: Littleton, CO, 1975; 25.
9. Cutter, C.A. *Expansive Classification. Part I: The First Six Classifications*; C A. Cutter: Boston, MA, 1891–1893.
10. LaMontagne, L.E. *American Library Classification with Special Reference to the Library of Congress*; Shoe String Press: Hamden, CT, 1961; 27, 234–236.
11. Chan, L.M. *A Guide to the Library of Congress Classification*, 5th Ed.; Libraries Unlimited: Englewood, CO, 1999; 11–12.

Library Automation–Library Publishing

12. Martel, C. Classification: A brief conspectus of present day library practice. Lib. J. **1911**, August *36*, 415 reprinted in *Theory of Subject Analysis, A Sourcebook*; Chan, L.M., Richmond, P.A., Svenonius, E., Eds.; Libraries Unlimited: Littleton CO, 1985; 74.

13. Maltby, A. *Sayers' Manual of Classification for Librarians*, 5th Ed.; Andre Deutsch: London, 1975; 175.

14. Angell, R.S. Development of class K at the Library of Congress. Law Libr. J. **1964**, November *57*, 353–354.

15. Library of Congress Classification (LCC) *Weekly Lists*. Available at http://www.loc.gov/aba/cataloging/classification/weeklylists/.

16. Droste, K.D.; Runchock, R.; Reade, M.T.; Spinelli, P. *Super LCCS: Gale's Library of Congress Classification Schedules Combined with Additions and Changes Through...* Gale: Farmington Hills, MI, 1994.

17. Library of Congress, Network Development and MARC Standards Office. *USMARC Format for Classification Data: Including Guidelines for Content Designation*, Cataloging Distribution Service, Library of Congress: Washington, DC, 1990–1995.

18. Classification Web. Available at http://classificationweb.net/.

19. Cutter, C.A. *Cutter-Sanborn Three-Figure Author Table*; Swanson-Swift Revision: Chicopee, MA, 1969; distributed by H R Hunting Company.

20. Chan, L.M. *A Guide to the Library of Congress Classification*, 5th Ed.; Libraries Unlimited: Englewood, CO, 1999; 69.

21. Library of Congress, Cataloging Policy and Support Office. *Subject Cataloging Manual: Shelflistiing*, 2nd Ed.; Library of Congress: Washington, DC, 1995.

22. LaMontagne, L.E. *American Library Classification with Special Reference to the Library of Congress*; Shoe String Press: Hamden, CT, 1961; 254 (based on typescript [1918] in the Library of Congress, Subject Cataloging Division).

23. Chan, L.M. *A Guide to the Library of Congress Classification*, 5th Ed.; Libraries Unlimited: Englewood, CO, 1999; 67–68.

24. Maltby, A. *Sayers' Manual of Classification for Librarians*, 5th Ed.; Andre Deutsch: London, 1975; 180.

25. Chan, L.M. *Cataloging and Classification: An Introduction*, 3rd Ed.; Scarecrow Press: Lanham, MD, Toronto, Plymouth, UK, 2007; 383–384.

26. Library of Congress, Cataloging Policy and Support Office. *Subject Cataloging Manual: Classification*, 1st Ed.; Library of Congress: Washington, DC, 1992.

27. Cyberstacks. Available at http://www2.iastate.edu/~CYBERSTACKS/.

28. Classification Web, 78. Available at http://classificationweb.net/.

29. Library of Congress, *Library of Congress Subject Headings*, Library of Congress: Washington DC, 1975-.

30. Classification Web. Available at http://classificationweb.net/.

31. Chan, L.M. *Cataloging and Classification: An Introduction*, 3rd Ed.; Scarecrow Press: Lanham, MD; Toronto, Plymouth, UK, 2007; 375–408.

32. U.S. Library of Congress. Classification and shelflisting manuals, 2008 Ed. LOC: Washington.

33. Maltby, A. *Sayers' Manual of Classification for Librarians*, 5th Ed.; Andre Deutsch: London, 1975; 187.

BIBLIOGRAPHY

1. Bead, C.C. The Library of Congress Classification: Development, characteristics, and structure. In *The Use of the Library of Congress Classification: Proceedings of the Institute on the Use of the Library of Congress Classification*; Schimmelpfeng, R.H., Donald Cook, C., Eds.; American Library Association: Chicago, IL, 1968; 18–32.

2. Chan, L.M. *A Guide to the Library of Congress Classification*, 5th Ed.; Libraries Unlimited: Englewood, CO, 1999.

3. LaMontagne, L.E. *American Library Classification with Special Reference to the Library of Congress*, Shoe String Press: Hamden, CT, 1961.

4. Martel, C. Classification: a brief conspectus of present day library practice. Libr. J. **1911**, August *36*, 415 reprinted in *Theory of Subject Analysis: A Sourcebook*; Chan, L.M., Richmond, P.A., Svenonius, E., Eds.; Libraries Unlimited: Littleton, CO, 1985; 73–74.

5. Miksa, F. *The Development of Classification at the Library of Congress*, University of Illinois, Graduate School of Library and Information Science: Urbana, IL, 1984; August Occasional Papers, No. 164.

6. Miksa, F. *The Subject in the Dictionary Catalog from Cutter to the Present*; American Library Association: Chicago, IL, 1983.

Library of Congress Genre/Form Terms for Library and Archival Materials

Janis L. Young
Library of Congress, Washington, District of Columbia, U.S.A.

Abstract

Library of Congress Genre/Form Terms for Library and Archival Materials (LCGFT) is a multidisciplinary thesaurus that provides indexing terminology to describe what works *are*, rather than what they are *about*. Traditionally, access to genres and forms of works has been provided with subject headings, which poses two problems: first, subject headings are by definition more properly restricted to the topic of a work, and second, the rules for application of subject headings often treat forms secondarily to the topic, thereby limiting access.

This article will explain the differences between subjects and genres and forms, and put LCGFT in the context of other vocabularies that provide genre/form access. The development of LCGFT is a large undertaking, and the project management will be described. The majority of the entry will elaborate on the principles upon which LCGFT is built (the choice of authorized terms and the syndetic structure) and the application of terms. Finally, the article will outline developments in the provision of access to characteristics of works and expressions that are closely related to genre and form: musical medium of performance, intended audience, characteristics of creators and contributors, and time period of creation.

INTRODUCTION

Library of Congress Genre/Form Terms for Library and Archival Materials (LCGFT) is a unified, cohesive, multidisciplinary, easy-to-use controlled vocabulary that is built on twenty-first century principles of thesaurus construction. Independent of *Library of Congress Subject Headings* (LCSH), LC's best-known vocabulary, LCGFT builds on some of the principles that have made LCSH so popular while seeking to provide access to what a work *is* instead of what it is *about*.

In development since 2007, LCGFT remains a work in progress. Fundamental decisions regarding the scope and structure of the vocabulary and the application of terms have been made, but are subject to policy shifts as the thesaurus grows and more experience is gained with assigning the terms. The project's background, context, and management are outlined below, followed by a discussion of the characteristics of LCGFT and its application.

BACKGROUND AND CONTEXT

Before explaining the characteristics of LCGFT, it is important to understand what genres and forms are, and how they differ from subjects. *American Heritage* defines genre as "a category of artistic composition, as in music or literature, marked by a distinctive style, form or content."[1] Traditionally, genre is most closely associated with works of the imagination, as is evident by the definition of genre supplied by Martha Yee in *Moving Image Materials: Genre Terms*: any recognized category of fictional works which is characterized by recognizable conventions, that is, a group of works all of which tend to explore the same themes and use the same plot formulae, character-types and icons.[1]

The major genres are often part of the collective consciousness of a society. When one thinks of Westerns, for instance, one thinks of the desert southwest, sagebrush, cowboys and Indians, cattle rustling, and shootouts. Other well-known genres include action, adventure, horror, romance, and thriller.

Form, on the other hand, is defined by Yee as "any recognized category of works characterized by a particular format or purpose."[2] The introduction to the *Moving Image Genre-Form Guide* further elucidates that form is "separate from [a work's] actual content, not necessarily implying a particular narrative construction."[3] Therefore, form relates to organization or format (e.g., atlases, poems), length (haiku, short films), original publication parameters (periodicals, television programs), technique (3-D films, animated television programs), and purpose (educational films, proclamations).

The subject of a work, on the other hand, is the topic being discussed or depicted. A work may be a war film (the genre) that is animated (the form), and be about World War II (the subject). In some ways, genre and form are closer to descriptive cataloging than to subject

Encyclopedia of Library and Information Sciences, Fourth Edition DOI: 10.1081/E-ELIS4-120049497
Copyright © 2017 by Taylor & Francis. All rights reserved.

Library Automation–Library Publishing

analysis, but access to them has traditionally been provided as part of controlled subject vocabularies.

Two major multidisciplinary English language vocabularies that provide both subject and genre/form access are *Sears List of Subject Headings*[4] and *Library of Congress Subject Headings*.[5] Both include main headings that describe genres and forms (e.g., **Directories**; **Pastoral poetry**; **Short stories**), but sometimes restrict those headings' use. In LCSH, for instance, form headings may not be assigned to individual works of fiction, although they may be assigned to collections. An individual play may be assigned a form heading only if it includes a topical aspect (e.g., **Detective and mystery plays, American**), or if the play is of a highly specific form (e.g., **Carnival plays**).[6]

The rules are slightly less stringent in *Sears*, wherein any literary form heading can be assigned to collections by multiple authors, but "Headings describing the major literary forms (such as **Drama**; **Fiction**; and **Poetry**) and the headings for the major forms of a national literature (such as **Irish drama**; **Russian fiction**; and **Italian poetry**) are never assigned to an individual work or to a collection by a single author." Scope notes indicate that some minor literary forms and genres such as **Ballads**; **Fables**; **Horror fiction**, etc., may be applied to individual works, but headings for these minor forms that are qualified by nationality or language are not eligible for assignment to individual works.[7]

These policies may make it difficult for users to find all of the literary works of interest to them (e.g., love stories by American authors), because most of the literary works in library collections are separately published.

In both LCSH and *Sears*, the primary means of indicating form is to append a form subdivision to the end of a topical subject heading instead of using a form heading. Using *Sears*, for example, an encyclopedia of the American Civil War would be assigned **United States—History—1861–1865, Civil War—Encyclopedias,** while in LCSH the heading would be **United States—History—Civil War, 1861–1865—Encyclopedias**. In both cases, the form of the work is **—Encyclopedias**, and is treated secondarily to the topic. This is opposed to the thought process of many users, who are more likely to think of the form first, as indicated by the common question, "Do you have any encyclopedias about the Civil War?"

Another issue with using general subject vocabularies that include headings for genres and forms is that the form headings are generally coded in the 150 and 650 fields of the MARC 21 formats for authority and bibliographic data, respectively. These fields are defined as being for topical terms, that is, for subjects, not genres or forms.[8] In libraries that follow the general practice and code form headings in the 650 field, users search for genres and forms by doing a subject search. The display mixes the two, as can be seen in this example using LCSH:

Horror stories.
Horror stories—Dictionaries.

Horror stories—History and criticism.
Horror stories—Themes, motives, etc.
Horror stories—United States—History and criticism.
Horror stories, American.
Horror stories, American—History and criticism.
Horror stories, German.

Users looking for works that *are* horror stories have to know to select the headings that are not subdivided, such as **Horror stories**, and **Horror stories** qualified by a nationality (e.g., **Horror stories, American**). The rest of the headings in this list denote works *about* horror stories, that is, horror stories as the subject matter.

In 1979, the Machine-Readable Bibliographic Information committee (MARBI) of the American Library Association ameliorated this situation by defining the 655 field for genre/form terms in the MARC 21 bibliographic format, and some libraries chose to use it for form headings authorized by general subject vocabularies.[9] However, the associated authority fields, 155 (for the heading) and 455, 555, and 755 (for references) were not defined until 1995.[10] These fields made it possible for computers to distinguish between subjects and genres and forms, thereby enabling separate searches for the two, once data was encoded in the 155/655 fields.

Many English language controlled vocabularies are devoted to providing genre/form access to materials in a specific discipline or to specific types of materials. Examples include *Guidelines on Access to Individual Works of Fiction, Drama, Etc.* (GSAFD), which primarily includes terms describing literary works, but also includes some terms for major genres of radio and television programs and films; the *Radio Form/Genre Guide*; the *Moving Image Genre-Form Guide* (MIGFG); *Moving Image Materials: Genre Terms*; and *Controlled Vocabularies for Use in Rare Book and Special Collections Cataloging*, a suite of vocabularies developed and maintained by the Bibliographic Standards Committee of the Association of College & Research Libraries' Rare Books and Manuscripts Section.

Some discipline-specific vocabularies include subject headings along with headings describing genres and forms. The *Thesaurus for Graphic Materials* (TGM) is used to describe still-image media and formats such as photographs, cartoons, and pictorial ephemera. Formerly published in two parts, one dedicated to subjects and the other to genres and formats, TGM was merged into a single vocabulary in 2007.[11] The *Art & Architecture Thesaurus* (AAT) is a comprehensive vocabulary that is used to describe all aspects of art, architecture, decorative arts, material culture, and archival materials.[12] The *AFS Ethnographic Thesaurus* includes terminology from folklore, ethnomusicology, cultural anthropology, and related fields.[13] Finally, *Medical Subject Headings* (MeSH) covers terminology in the area of the health sciences.[14]

Library Automation–Library Publishing

All of these discipline-specific vocabularies make important contributions to genre/form access. They generally are most useful to libraries, museums, and archives that have extensive nonbook or special collections because the vocabularies enable deep, granular analysis of the materials. The exceptions to the general rule are GSAFD and MIGFG, which have been adopted by many public and general academic libraries, and MeSH, which is used not only in specialized medical libraries but also in universities that offer degrees in the health sciences.

Unlike *Sears* and LCSH, specialized vocabularies generally do not distinguish between individual works and collections in their rules for application, making the cataloging treatment more even. However, each specialized vocabulary has its own syntax and rules for application, which can sometimes cause collocation problems within a catalog. Take for example an academic library that uses MIGFG for its film collections, GSAFD for literary works, and LCSH for nonfiction, including film and literary criticism. A user writing a thesis about the relationship between modern detective novels and films of the same genre would probably want to view a sampling of films, read a sampling of novels, and also read published criticisms and histories of each. They would have to know three different syntaxes to find relevant materials:

> *Detective and mystery films—History and criticism*
> [LCSH; film criticism]
> *Detective and mystery stories—History and criticism*
> [LCSH; literary criticism]
> *Mystery—Feature*
> *Mystery—Short*
> [MIGFG; films]
> *Mystery fiction*
> [GSAFD; novels]

When it comes to providing access to genres and forms, therefore, most libraries have been left with two choices. Use LCSH or *Sears*, which usually subordinate genre and form to the topic and also put restrictions on the assignment of headings, or use multiple specialized vocabularies for different types of media, which requires users (and catalogers) to master multiple syntaxes.

LCGFT seeks to address this problem by creating a multidisciplinary vocabulary with a standard syntax that allows for more consistency within catalogs while also bringing genre and form to the forefront. Both aims simplify search and discovery. Since it uses a modified form of LCSH syntax, users who are already familiar with LCSH (or *Sears*, which also employs a modified form of LCSH syntax)[4] do not have to learn a new way to search. Furthermore, terms from LCGFT may be applied to individual works as well as to collections. The overall impact of LCGFT is increased access to many categories of works that formerly were at best difficult to find, or at worst,

hidden from users despite the fact that they were fully cataloged.

PROJECT MANAGEMENT

Since 2007, the year in which the first genre/form terms were approved, the Policy and Standards Division (PSD) of the Library of Congress has collaborated with the library community to develop LCGFT.

To allow for an orderly rollout of terms, LCGFT is being developed discipline by discipline. As of this writing, the vocabulary includes terminology for cartographic materials, law materials, moving images (films and television programs), nonmusical sound recordings (primarily radio programs), literature, music, art, and religious materials, as well as "general" terms—those terms that do not fit into a specific discipline, such as dictionaries, encyclopedias, and handbooks. Other projects, including newspapers, and science, have also been suggested and may be undertaken after the current projects are completed.

There are three major benefits to the orderly rollout. First, it provides predictability. When the project for a specific discipline is finished, all of the major terms in that discipline are available for use, thereby ameliorating the confusion that would result if terms for poetry, for example, were available before terms for fiction. Second, it allows developers to adjust policies incrementally as issues are discovered and resolved, meaning that a policy shift might affect a few dozen terms instead of hundreds. This minimizes the negative impact of revisions on catalogs, librarians, and users. And finally, the orderly rollout allows for effective collaboration.

PSD is spearheading the development of the vocabulary, but relies heavily on three groups for assistance: LC's librarians, who provide their subject and format expertise; the general library community, which comments on public discussion papers that are posted on LC's website; and last but not least, organizations with an interest in particular disciplines.

To date, PSD has formally partnered with four organizations, each of which has developed a thesaurus in its area of interest with the goal of incorporating the thesaurus into LCGFT. PSD's first partner was the American Association of Law Libraries, which provided terms for legal materials. The Music Library Association and the American Theological Library Association also agreed to assist PSD in developing terms for music and for religious materials, respectively. In 2008, the Subject Analysis Committee (SAC) of the Association for Library Collections and Technical Services (ALCTS), a division of the American Library Association, formed the Subcommittee on Genre/Form Implementation (SAC-SGFI), which was charged with helping to facilitate two-way communication between PSD and the cataloging communities with an interest in genre/form terms. SAC-SGFI took on the task

Library Automation–Library Publishing

of developing vocabularies for literary works and for general terms Finally, the Art Libraries Society of North America partnered with LC to develop terms that describe works of art.

Each project is considered complete when the terms from that discipline are implemented at the LC. That does not mean, however, that the list of terms is closed. Proposals for new and revised genre/form terms, which appear on tentative lists and are vetted for inclusion in LCGFT, may be submitted by Library of Congress catalogers and participants in the Subject Authority Cooperative Program (SACO) of the Program for Cooperative Cataloging (PCC). Also, as noted above, the lessons learned in later projects may require that authorized terms, references, or scope notes from earlier projects be modified or cancelled from LCGFT.

AUTHORIZED TERMS

Library of Congress Genre/Form Terms for Library and Archival Materials includes terms for works and expressions as defined in *Functional Requirements for Bibliographic Records*.[15] That is, the authorized terms indicate the intellectual or artistic expression, not the manifestation—the physical characteristics—of the item. For instance, in LCGFT, the word "film" refers not to reel-to-reel motion picture film (a physical carrier) but to works that were originally recorded on motion picture film, on video, or digitally. This policy allows for collocation of all of the manifestations of a work under a single term, instead of requiring the user to search separately under every possible carrier type.

To be eligible for LCGFT, concepts must indicate the genre or form of a work or expression, and not refer explicitly to any other closely related characteristics: intended audience; ethnicity or nationality of the creator(s); setting, including the time period depicted; time period of creation; popularity of the work (e.g., best sellers); and, in the case of music, the medium of performance (e.g., flute, tenor voice). Also excluded from the thesaurus are terms that are already provided elsewhere in the bibliographic record, including language and date and place of publication or production. However, these characteristics may be included implicitly in the meaning of the term, such as in the term **Actualities (Motion pictures)**, which refers to a specific form of short, unedited, silent films from the early days of cinema.[16]

At the time of this writing, there are a few practical exceptions to these policies, particularly in relation to children and people with disabilities as intended audiences. However, the intent is to remove terms such as **Children's films** and **Films for the hearing impaired** from LCGFT when there is another place to code that information. For more information, see the Related Developments section, below.

Terms are based on literary warrant. This means that there are works or expressions to which the terms can be assigned, and also that the terms are included in reference sources appropriate to the term. Each authorized term consists of a word or phrase that represents a single concept, and is always presented in natural language order to facilitate searching (e.g., **Outtakes**; **Remote-sensing maps**). Parenthetical qualifiers are used occasionally to distinguish between and among homonyms when it is not reasonable to construct an adjectival phrase due to common usage (e.g., **Thrillers (Motion pictures)**; **Thrillers (Radio programs)**; and **Thrillers (Television programs)**).

While there are parallel terms in LCGFT—such as the three terms for thrillers—the preference is to avoid them within a single discipline wherever possible. For instance, there are terms for specific types of maps (e.g., **Topographic maps**; **Physical maps**), but similar terms for topographic atlases, physical globes, and the like do not exist. Since by definition an atlas is a collection of maps, and a globe is nothing more than a spherical map, the appropriate term **Atlases** or **Globes** is assigned (i.e., postcoordinated) with the genre/form term for the type of map. Therefore, a road atlas is assigned two postcoordinated terms: **Road maps** and **Atlases**. Likewise, in the area of literature, there will not be a term such as the term *Fantasy short stories* does not exist. Instead, there are two terms, **Fantasy fiction** and **Short stories**.

The preference is to establish terms in English, but terms from other languages are permitted under two circumstances: when no English term for the concept exists and the foreign-language term has been borrowed into English, and when the concept is unique to the language of the work being cataloged and cannot be found in English-language reference sources. For example, **Heimatfilme** are German films and are known by the German word in the English-speaking world.[16]

Although LCGFT includes some very specific terms (e.g., **Coutumes**, a form of French medieval customary law[16]), the policy is to prefer more general terms. The general terminology makes cataloging simpler, since most artistic and literary works provide only the broadest indication of genre and form. Overly specific terminology would in many cases require catalogers either to guess at the appropriate term or to read/view the entire work. Relatively general terms also serve users' needs, particularly with regard to artistic and literary works. General terms collocate more works and serve as a form of readers' advisory, while defining terms too narrowly would separate similar works from each other and require users to look in multiple places for works of interest to them.

In addition, subject matter is excluded from the terms to the extent possible, considering that genre can sometimes be inextricably linked to subject matter in literary and artistic works. Recall that *American Heritage* defines genre as "a category of artistic composition, as in music or

Library Automation–Library Publishing

literature, marked by a distinctive style, form or *content*" [emphasis added].[1] The line between genre and subject can be fuzzy, as indicated by the initial inclusion in LCGFT of sport-specific films (e.g., **Football films**). In 2012, PSD and LC's Motion Picture, Broadcasting, and Recorded Sound Division decided to remove those types of terms from LCGFT. They were originally included because they already existed in LCSH as form headings. However, further analysis made it clear that films focused on a particular sport may fall into one of many genres, including, but not limited to, suspense films, thrillers, comedies, or romances. A single plot element (i.e., the depiction of a sport) does not, therefore, constitute a genre. Instead, the sport is the subject.[17]

The distinction between form and subject is generally easier to codify than the distinction between genre and subject. By definition, form designates the format or purpose of the work, independent of the content.[3] Therefore, LCGFT will not include terms such as *Science periodicals*, preferring instead the term **Periodicals**. The topic, science, is indicated with a subject heading. There are some apparent exceptions to this, such as **Legal maxims**, but by definition legal maxims are quite different from general maxims. Legal maxims are statements of established principles of law,[16] while a general maxim is a "succinct formulation of a fundamental principle, general truth, or rule of conduct."[1]

STRUCTURE

The guiding principles for the structure of LCGFT are contained in ANSI/NISO standard Z39.19-2005, *Guidelines for the Construction, Format, and Management of Monolingual Controlled Vocabularies*,[18] which is followed as closely as is practical.

Equivalence Relationships

Synonyms of the authorized terms are provided in Used For (UF) references, as are alternate forms of the authorized term itself, including inverted forms. The UFs provide additional entry points into the vocabulary and lead users to the authorized terms. Some typical examples of UFs are as follow:

Film auditions
USE Screen tests

Laws, Session
USE Session laws

Hierarchical Relationships

The hallmark of a thesaurus is the use of hierarchical relationships.[19] In LCGFT, every discipline has a

"broadest" or "top" term that serves as the collocation point for all of the terms from each discpline (e.g., **Cartographic materials; Literature; Motion pictures**). Except for the broadest terms, every authorized term in LCGFT must have at least one broader term (BT). The terms exhibit the class/class member relationship: each narrower term (NT) must by definition be part of the group defined by the BT. The hierarchical relationships of the term **Comedy films** are illustrative.

Comedy films
BT Motion pictures
NT Dark comedy films
NT Parody films

Comedy films is the class and **Dark comedy films** and **Parody films** are the class members. All parody films are comedy films, as are all dark comedy films. On the other hand, only some comedy films are dark comedies or parodies. Likewise, all comedy films are motion pictures, the broadest term in the film hierarchy.

While most terms belong to only one hierarchy, terms may occasionally belong to multiple hierarchies if appropriate. A good example is **Oral histories**, which has the BTs **Discursive works, Filmed interviews** and **Interviews (Sound recordings)**.

The general preference is for flatter, rather than deeper, hierarchies, corresponding to the desire for more general terminology. As of this writing, the deepest hierarchy has four levels, as exemplified by the relationships for **Loran charts**.

Loran charts
BT Nautical charts

Nautical charts
BT Maps

Maps
BT Cartographic materials

Cartographic materials
[broadest term]

Associative Relationships

The ANSI/NISO standard defines associative, or Related Term (RT), relationships as "terms that are neither equivalent nor hierarchical, yet the terms are semantically or conceptually linked to such an extent that the link between them should be made explicit in the controlled vocabulary, on the grounds that it may suggest additional terms for use in indexing or retrieval." The standard goes on to say that terms exhibiting the

Library Automation–Library Publishing

associative relationship may be from the same hierarchy or from different hierarchies.[20]

A slightly more stringent approach is taken in LCGFT, where related terms are generally in the same discipline, and thus have the same "broadest term," but they should not be related to each other if they are in the same subhierarchy. For example, **Inspirational radio programs** and **Religious radio programs** share the same BT, **Radio programs**, the broadest term for the discipline, and may be RTs. **Christian radio programs** and **Radio sermons** also share a BT, **Religious radio programs**, but may not be RTs because the shared BT is not the broadest term for the discipline.

As a matter of practicality, terms may not display an associative relationship if they begin with the same word or word stem because the terms generally file near each other, making an explicit RT relationship superfluous. Although one might consider Western novels, films, radio programs, and television programs to be conceptually linked, they alphabetize one after the other and thus RTs are unnecessary.

Scope Notes

Scope notes (SN) are provided to assist users in knowing if the term covers the materials in which they are interested and also to help catalogers maintain consistency in the way that terms are assigned to works. Typically, scope notes are provided if users may be unfamiliar with the term, or if the term is defined in multiple ways in reference sources, making it necessary to explain how it is defined in LCGFT. Since most general users of libraries probably do not know what a concordat is, it is defined as follows:

Concordats
SN Agreements between a government and the Roman Catholic Church.

Scope notes are also included when it is necessary to define one term in contrast to another. These are called contrasting scope notes, and appear on both of the terms being defined. Since the difference between disaster films and survival films may not be immediately apparent, definitions are provided as follows:

Disaster films
SN Films that feature a man-made or natural calamity that places people in imminent danger. For films that feature individuals or groups struggling for their lives in a harsh setting see Survival films.

Survival films
SN Films that feature individuals or groups struggling for their lives in a harsh setting. For films that feature a

man-made or natural calamity that places people in imminent danger see Disaster films.

Most terms in LCGFT do not have scope notes because the meanings of the terms are self-evident. Sometimes terms are part of the collective consciousness, or their meanings are clear without a note (e.g., **Administrative regulations; Christmas films; Documentary television programs**). In some cases, notes are not provided because doing so could unduly limit the term's usefulness. Let's say, for example, that a scope note for the term **Detective and mystery films** listed five characteristics indicative of such a film but an individual film exhibited only three of those characteristics. The term could not be applied to that film, even if it would be obvious to anyone viewing it that it was in fact intended to be a film of that genre. Not including a scope note therefore allows the cataloger to apply the principle of "I know it when I see it," instead of having to apply case law to creative works.

APPLICATION

The rules for assigning terms from LCGFT are straightforward: one term is assigned to bring out each genre or form applicable to a work or expression; the terms are not subdivided; and other vocabularies are used to describe other aspects, such as subject matter.

As discussed earlier in the section on authorized terms, each LCGFT term represents a single concept. The significant genre/form aspects of a work or expression are brought out by assigning multiple terms in separate fields, not by combining terms through the use of subdivisions. An atlas that includes both topographic and physical maps is therefore assigned three terms: **Topographic maps; Physical maps;** and **Atlases**.

In the case of moving image works, where the manifestation being cataloged may differ dramatically from the original release parameters, the LCGFT policy states that the original parameters should be used if known. A DVD of a two-hour long three-dimensional adventure film originally released in theaters, for example, is assigned the terms **Action and adventure films** along with **Feature films** (defined as films at least 40 minutes in length)[16] and **3-D films**. In addition, the rules for the application of genre/form terms for moving images state that the term **Fiction films** should also be assigned.[21] The fact that the manifestation is a DVD is represented in the descriptive portions of the bibliographic record rather than through a term from LCGFT.

If that DVD also includes a fifteen-minute behind-the-scenes documentary on the making of the film, and the documentary is considered significant to the users of the library or archive, then the LCGFT terms **Documentary films** and **Short films** may also be included, along with

Library Automation–Library Publishing

Nonfiction films.[21] In the same way, interviews with the actors may be brought out with the term **Filmed interviews** and **Nonfiction films**.

DVDs are sometimes manifestations of television programs. According to LCGFT policy, the original release parameters should be observed, here, too. A DVD containing season 8 of a popular animated sitcom should be assigned **Situation comedies (Television programs)** and **Animated television programs**, along with **Fiction television programs**. Likewise, a DVD of a suspenseful made-for-TV movie should be assigned the terms **Made-for-TV movies; Thrillers (Television programs);** and **Fiction television programs** because the work was originally intended to be broadcast on television.

As of yet, there are no rules governing the number of genre/form terms that may be assigned to an individual resource. Generally speaking, the goal is to assign a term for each genre and form that is considered significant for the users. The preference is therefore to assign more specific LCGFT terms rather than fewer terms that are more general. Assuming that full access is considered necessary for the users being served, a compilation of legal instruments that includes contracts, affidavits, charters, and legal memorandums will generally be assigned a specific heading for each of those forms: **Affidavits; Charters and articles of incorporation; Contracts;** and **Legal memorandums**. The BT of each of those terms is **Legal instruments**, which, although valid, generally would not be assigned unless access to the specific forms in the compilation was not considered necessary.

The option to choose the level of access necessary for an individual user population—the scalability of the vocabulary—is made possible by the strict hierarchies in LCGFT. Librarians and archivists can choose how narrowly the genres and forms should be assigned. There is one exception to this principle, though: the broadest terms within a discipline should rarely—and perhaps never—be assigned to a resource. The exception is when a record is being created for a collection of disparate works of multiple genres and/or forms to which more specific terms cannot be assigned.[16] Therefore, narrower terms are preferred.

So far, all of the discussion of application has related only to genres and forms. Subjects are equally as important in leading users to resources that are of interest to them. LCGFT is intended to be used in conjunction with subjects, not as a replacement for them. Subject headings should continue to be assigned according to the rules for the subject vocabulary being used. To show how this is done, let's expand upon a few of the examples given earlier.

An atlas that includes topographic and physical maps of the states of the United States, with the purpose of comparing the states to each other, could be assigned the array:

650 #0 $a U.S. states $v Maps.
655 #7 $a Topographic maps. $2 lcgft
655 #7 $a Physical maps. $2 lcgft
655 #7 $a Atlases. $2 lcgft

A popular animated sitcom that depicts children's experiences in elementary school could be assigned these *Sears* subject headings and terms from LCGFT:

650 #7 $a School children. $2 sears
650 #7 $a Elementary education. $2 sears
655 #7 $a Situation comedies (Television programs) $2 lcgft
655 #7 $a Animated television programs. $2 lcgft
655 #7 $a Fiction television programs. $2 lcgft

The suspenseful made-for-TV movie that depicts a woman being stalked would be assigned this array of LC subject headings and LCGFT terms:

650 #0 $a Stalking $v Drama.
655 #7 $a Made-for-TV movies. $2 lcgft
655 #7 $a Thrillers (Television programs) $2 lcgft
655 #7 $a Fiction television programs. $2 lcgft

Finally, the compilation of legal instruments discussed above might have high-tech firms based in Virginia as its collocation point. The array, using LCSH and LCGFT, might be

650 #0 $a High technology industries $z Virginia.
655 #7 $a Affidavits. $2 lcgft
655 #7 $a Charters and articles of incorporation. $2 lcgft
655 #7 $a Contracts. $2 lcgft
655 #7 $a Legal memorandums. $2 lcgft

Or, if less specific genre/form access is determined to be adequate,

650 #0 $a High technology industries $z Virginia.
655 #7 $a Legal instruments. $2 lcgft

RELATED DEVELOPMENTS

The genre/form projects triggered a reexamination of other LC subject headings that provide access to what something is instead of what it is about. Treated as form headings in LCSH, these subject headings are neither genres nor forms and are thus excluded from LCGFT. However, they remain valuable access points that indicate intended audience (e.g., **Children's poetry**), ethnicity, nationality, or other characteristic of the creator(s) (**Short stories, Swazi; Italian fiction; Airline pilots' writings**),

Library Automation–Library Publishing

and time period of creation (**Renaissance drama**). In the case of music, the medium of performance is also vitally important, and in LCSH is sometimes provided in dedicated headings (**Flute and accordion music**) and other times is described with hybrid headings that contain both the genre or form and the medium(s) of performance (**Trios (Bagpipe, hurdy-gurdy, continuo)**).

There was a pressing need to determine how access to these characteristics will be provided going forward, since headings of this type are most prevalent in the disciplines of literature and music. Once the LCGFT terms for literature and music are fully implemented, none of the form subject headings should be used to describe what a work or expression *is*. In the discipline of literature, the form subject headings will continue to be valid, but will be assigned only to works about the "form." For music, subject headings such as **Trios (Bagpipe, hurdy-gurdy, continuo)** will be cancelled from LCSH since they exist solely as form headings, and are never used as subjects (i. e., for works *about* trios for bagpipe, hurdy-gurdy, and continuo).

The Music Library Association (MLA) and LC's Policy and Standards Division closely examined various options for provision of medium of performance and determined that the best approach was to create a separate thesaurus for those terms. MLA and PSD partnered to develop the *Library of Congress Medium of Performance Thesaurus for Music* (LCMPT), the initial terms for which were approved in 2014.

Since medium of performance is neither a subject nor a genre or form, it was determined that these terms should not be coded in the 6xx block of the bibliographic record. Instead, MARBI approved an MLA proposal requesting that the 382 field, which was originally defined for the *Resource Description and Access* (RDA) medium of performance element, be made repeatable and used for both RDA and LCMPT—for description and for access, respectively.[22] The hope is that in the future the RDA instructions and the rules for application of LCMPT can be coordinated so that one instance of the field can serve both purposes.

In 2013, MARBI also approved a separate proposal for MARC 21 authority fields for medium of performance vocabulary: field 162 for the authorized term and 462, 562, and 762 for references.[23]

The SAC Subcommittee on Genre/Form Implementation (SAC-SGFI) and PSD examined the necessity of access for intended audience creator/contributor characteristics, and made two MARBI proposals for new fields. The proposals were approved by MARBI in January 2013.

The first proposal provided for intended audience through the creation of field 385 in both the bibliographic and authority formats. In the authority format, the field will be available for use in work and expression records.[24] These fields will not only permit access to works for age- or educational-level groupings, but also to

disability, occupational, gender, and ethnic groups, among others, thereby providing much more specific access than is currently available in library catalogs.

The second proposal was very similar to the first. It requested field 386 for creator/contributor group categories. Now approved for use in bibliographic records and in authority records for works and expressions,[25] it will also provide more access than was traditionally available in library catalogs.

In early 2014, PSD was authorized to develop another new controlled vocabulary, entitled Library of Congress Demographic Group Terms (LCDGT). Terms from LCDGT will be assigned to bring out the creators/contributors and the intended audiences of works and expressions[27] and will be assigned in the 385 and 386 fields in bibliographic records and in authority records for works and expressions. The first 400 demographic group terms were approved in June, 2015.[28]

It can also be important to access resources by the time period in which they were created. To that end, SAC-SGFI submitted a proposal that requested new coding for the existing field 046 (Special Coded Dates) in both the bibliographic and authority formats and for field 648 (Subject Added Entry—Chronological Term) in the bibliographic format. In the case of the 046 field, subfields for the beginning and ending date of the original publication of an aggregate work were approved. In field 648, the first indicator was defined to enable the cataloger to indicate whether the field is being used to convey the time period depicted or the time period of creation. The 046 and 648 fields may both be provided in a single bibliographic record, or one may be preferred over the other.[26] In either case, the fact that the resource being cataloged is an anthology of works from the Renaissance can be brought out as an access point. The next step is to determine best practices for the use of the new coding, and that conversation has just begun.

CONCLUSION

Genres and forms are often part of the collective consciousness of a society, and it is essential to provide access to them. Traditionally, access has been provided through subject analysis, but that practice poses both intellectual and technical problems. *Library of Congress Genre/Form Terms for Library and Archival Materials* (LCGFT) is a discrete vocabulary dedicated to terminology for genres and forms of works and expressions, and is intended to work in conjunction with subject vocabularies and descriptive elements to provide users with a full understanding of those works and expressions. The discussions surrounding LCGFT have also led to further developments in the access to other pertinent data, including musical medium of performance, the

Library Automation–Library Publishing

characteristics of the creators and contributors and the intended audience, and the time period of creation of the work or expression.

ACKNOWLEDGMENTS

Special thanks to Yael Mandelstam, Fordham University School of Law, Leo T. Kissam Memorial Library, for reviewing and commenting on several drafts of this article.

REFERENCES

1. *The American Heritage Dictionary of the English Language*, 4th Ed.; Houghton Mifflin Company: Boston, MA, 2006.

2. Yee, M.M. *Moving Image Materials: Genre Terms*, 1st Ed.; Library of Congress Cataloging Distribution Service: Washington, DC, 1988; 11.

3. Taves, B.; Hoffman, J.; Lund, K. *Moving Image Genre-Form Guide*; Library of Congress Motion Picture and Television Reading Room: Washington, DC, 1998. http://www.loc.gov/rr/mopic/migintro.html (accessed February 2013).

4. Miller, J.; McCarthy, S. *Sears List of Subject Headings*, 20th Ed.; H.W. Wilson Company: New York, 2010 x.

5. *Library of Congress Subject Headings*, 35th Ed.; Library of Congress Cataloging Distribution Service: Washington, DC, 2013.

6. H 1780. Literature: Drama. *Subject Headings Manual*, 2008 Ed.Washington, DC: , Library of Congress Cataloging Policy and Support Office, updated through July 2013, 2008.

7. Miller, J.; McCarthy, S. *Sears List of Subject Headings*, 20th Ed.; H.W. Wilson Company: New York, 2010; Xxix–xxx.

8. *MARC 21 Format for Bibliographic Data*, 1999 Ed. updated through September 2012; Library of Congress Network Development and MARC Standards Office: Washington, DC, 2012. http://www.loc.gov/marc/bibliographic/ (accessed February 2013). *MARC 21 Format for Authority Data*, 1999 Ed. updated through September 2012; Library of Congress Network Development and MARC Standards Office: Washington, DC, 2012. http://www.loc.gov/marc/authority/ad150.html (accessed February 2013).

9. In *Proposed MARC Format Change: Define One Additional Added Entry Field for the Books, Maps, Music, and Serials Formats. LC-216*; Library of Congress: Washington, DC, 1979.

10. *Definition of X55 Fields for Genre/Form Terms in the USMARC Authority Format: Proposal No. 95-11*; Library of Congress Network Development and MARC Standards Office: Washington, DC, 1995. http://www.loc.gov/marc/marbi/1995/95-11.html (accessed February 2013).

11. *Thesaurus for Graphic Materials*; Library of Congress Prints and Photographs Division: Washington, DC, 1995. http://www.loc.gov/rr/print/tgm1/ia.html (accessed February 2013).

12. *Art & Architecture Thesaurus Online*; The Getty: Los Angeles, CA; Pacific Palisades, CA, 2013. http://www.getty.edu/research/tools/vocabularies/aat/about.html (accessed February 2013).

13. *The AFS Ethnographic Thesaurus*; American Folklore Society: Columbus, OH, 2010. http://www.afsnet.org/?page=AFSET (accessed February 2013).

14. *Fact Sheet: Medical Subject Headings (MeSH)*; U.S. National Library of Medicine, National Institutes of Health: Bethesda, MD, 2012. http://www.nlm.nih.gov/pubs/factsheets/mesh.html (accessed February 2013).

15. IFLA Study Group on the Functional Requirements for Bibliographic Records. *Functional Requirements for Bibliographic Records; IFLA Series on Bibliographic Control 19*; K.G. Saur Verlag: Munich, Germany, 1998 as amended and corrected through February 2009; 13. http://www.ifla.org/files/assets/cataloguing/frbr/frbr_2008.pdf/ (accessed February 2013).

16. *Library of Congress Genre/Form Terms for Library and Archival Materials*, Library of Congress Cataloging Distribution Service: Washington, DC, 2013.

17. *Library of Congress to Cancel LCGFT Sport-Specific Terms for Moving Images*; Library of Congress Policy and Standards Division: Washington, DC, 2012. http://www.loc.gov/catdir/cpso/genre_form_sports_terms_cancellation.pdf (accessed February 2013).

18. In *Guidelines for the Construction, Format, and Management of Monolingual Controlled Vocabularies*, National Information Standards Organization: Bethesda, MD, 1995.

19. In *Guidelines for the Construction, Format, and Management of Monolingual Controlled Vocabularies*; National Information Standards Organization: Bethesda, MD, 1995; 46.

20. In *Guidelines for the Construction, Format, and Management of Monolingual Controlled Vocabularies*, National Information Standards Organization: Bethesda, MD, 1995; 51.

21. H 1913. Moving image genre/form terms. *Subject Headings Manual*, 2008 Ed.; Library of Congress Cataloging Policy and Support Office: Washington, DC, 2008, updated through July 2013.

22. *New Data Elements in the MARC 21 Bibliographic and Authority Formats for Medium of Performance: MARC Proposal No. 2012-01*; Library of Congress Network Development and MARC Standards Office: Washington, DC, 2012. http://www.loc.gov/marc/marbi/2012/2012-01.html (accessed February 2013).

23. *New Fields to Accommodate Authority Records for Medium of Performance Vocabulary for Music in the MARC 21 Authority Format: MARC Proposal No. 2013-02*; Library of Congress Network Development and MARC Standards Office: Washington, DC, 2012. http://www.loc.gov/marc/marbi/2013/2013-02.html (accessed February 2013).

24. *Defining New Field 385 for Audience Characteristics in the MARC 21 Bibliographic and Authority Formats: MARC Proposal No. 2013-05*; Library of Congress Network Development and MARC Standards Office: Washington, DC, 2012. http://www.loc.gov/marc/marbi/2013/2013-05.html (accessed February 2013).

25. *Defining New Field 386 for Creator/Contributor Group Categorizations in the MARC 21 Bibliographic and*

Library Automation–Library Publishing

Authority Formats: MARC Proposal 2013-06; Library of Congress Network Development and MARC Standards Office: Washington, DC, 2012. http://www.loc.gov/marc/marbi/2013/2013-06.html (accessed February 2013).

26. *Defining Encoding Elements to Record Chronological Categories and Dates of Works and Expressions in the MARC 21 Bibliographic and Authority Formats: MARC Proposal 2013-07*; Library of Congress Network Development and MARC Standards Office: Washington, DC, 2012. http://www.loc.gov/marc/marbi/2013/2013-07.html (accessed February 2013).

27. *Library of Congress Requests Comments on Pilot Demographic Group Vocabulary*; Library of Congress Policy and Standards Division: Washington, DC, 2015. http://www.loc.gov/catdir/cpso/lcdgt-announcement.html (accessed August 2017).

28. Library of Congress Approves Initial Demographic Group Terms; Library of Congress Policy and Standards Division: Washington, DC, 2015. http://www.loc.gov/catdir/cpso/lcdgt-initial.html (accessed August 2017).

Library Automation–Library Publishing

Library of Congress Subject Headings (LCSH)

Janis L. Young
Library of Congress, Washington, District of Columbia, U.S.A.

Abstract
Development of *Library of Congress Subject Headings* (LCSH) began in 1898 and the first edition was published in parts between 1909 and 1914. LCSH has undergone many changes over the years, so today's vocabulary—the most widely used subject vocabulary in the world—is quite different from what its initial developers envisioned. This article provides overviews of the current features of LCSH and the application of headings. It then discusses and evaluates several policy revisions made since the 1970s to take advantage of technology and to simplify cataloging. A final section describes several adjustments to LCSH that are being planned and executed, including those intended to increase LCSH's viability as linked data.

INTRODUCTION

Library of Congress Subject Headings (LCSH) is the most widely used subject vocabulary in the world. It is the model for many other vocabularies in English and other languages, and has been translated numerous times.[1] As of the beginning of 2017, it included over 342,000 individually established headings,[2] but catalogers can create untold more by combining main headings and subdivisions in specific ways.

This article will explain LCSH's scope, heading syntax, and syndetic structure before exploring several major policy changes that have occurred since the 1970s. When taken as a whole, those changes are so dramatic that the LCSH that entered the twenty-first century is quite different from the vocabulary that the initial developers envisioned over 100 years ago. Finally, the article will discuss current initiatives to take advantage of twenty-first century technology, including the need to make LCSH more viable as linked data.

SCOPE

LCSH is a multidisciplinary vocabulary that includes headings in all subjects, from agriculture to history, to education, literature, and military science. Ethnic groups, historical events and movements, building names, geographic features, and scientific theories are just some of the categories of headings represented in LCSH. LCSH is not complete unto itself; however, names of persons and corporate bodies, jurisdictions and quasi-jurisdictional entities, and titles can generally be assigned as LC subject headings, but are established in the LC/NACO Name Authority File (NAF) according to instructions contained in *RDA: Resource Description and Access* (p. xv).[2]

There is no attempt at comprehensiveness. Subject headings are proposed as needed for new cataloging, due to literary warrant; a heading must be needed to describe a work before it can be proposed for inclusion. Every month, hundreds of proposals for new headings are vetted and approved by cataloging policy specialists in the Library of Congress' Policy and Standards Division. The specialists ensure that the proposals conform to the rules and structure of LCSH, including heading format, provision of references, and scope notes. The rules are contained in two sources: the introduction to LCSH[2] and the *Subject Headings Manual* (SHM).[3] An overview is provided below.

HEADINGS

LC subject headings may consist of a single word or a phrase. A one-word heading is usually a singular or plural noun. Singular nouns generally denote abstract concepts (e.g., *Philosophy*) while plural nouns typically indicate tangible objects that can be counted (*Restaurants*).

Phrase headings usually consist of an adjective and a noun and may appear in natural-language order (e.g., *Constitutional history*) or as an inverted phrase (*Literature, Modern*). Natural language is preferred with exceptions for certain categories of headings, such as those qualified by nationality (*Art, Swiss*) and some geographic headings (*Michigan, Lake*).

Other phrase headings include the conjunction "and," which may indicate topics that are almost always treated together (e.g., *Bolts and nuts*) or topics with a reciprocal relationship (*Culture and law*). Phrase headings may also consist of prepositional phrases (*Student evaluation of teachers*).

Headings sometimes include a parenthetical qualifier that clarifies the meaning of the heading. In the case of

Encyclopedia of Library and Information Sciences, Fourth Edition DOI: 10.1081/E-ELIS4-120051662
Copyright © 2017 by Taylor & Francis. All rights reserved.

Library Automation–Library Publishing

Plates (Engineering) and *Plates (Tableware)*, the qualifier distinguishes among homonyms, while the qualifier in *Cooking (Peanuts)* provides context.

REFERENCES

Cross-references guide users to authorized headings that are of interest to them and are provided in the authority records for the headings. LCSH includes five types of cross-references: broader/narrower terms; related terms; see references, see also references, and general see references.

Broader and narrower terms (BT and NT) are reciprocal, meaning that they work in both directions. One can find a list of all of the established narrower terms under the entry for the broader term, and also find the broader term listed in the entry for the narrower term. The references are hierarchical, and each NT is a part of the concept represented in the BT. BT/NT references exhibit three types of relationships.

In a class/class member (a.k.a. genus/species) relationship, each of the narrower terms (the class members) is a member of the larger group: geriatricians and pediatricians are members of the class called *Physicians*.

Geriatricians
BT Physicians

Pediatricians
BT Physicians

Physicians
NT Geriatricians
NT Pediatricians

In the whole/part relationship, the each of the narrower terms is part of the whole: the endocardium and heart valves are parts of the heart.

Endocardium
BT Heart

Heart
NT Endocardium
NT Heart valves

Heart valves
BT Heart

The instance relationship brings together under one concept (the broader term) the individually named exemplars of that concept: Borax Lake and Donner Lake are both lakes in California.

Borax Lake (Calif.)
BT Lakes—California

Donner Lake (Calif.)
BT Lakes—California

Lakes—California
NT Borax Lake (Calif.)
NT Donner Lake (Calif.)

Some LC subject headings do not have a broader term. These "orphans" fall into one of several defined categories, including headings that are the broadest topic within a hierarchy, family names, and headings for geographic regions.

Related terms (RTs) are associative references and link two headings that are related to each other, but not hierarchically. Instead, they are mentally associated to such an extent that the alternative heading might be of interest to the user. The references are reciprocal and therefore appear in both entries. When one thinks of boats and boating, one often thinks of sailing.

Boats and boating
RT Sailing

Sailing
RT Boats and boating

See references, indicated with the notations UF (Used For) and USE, provide links from synonyms and alternate forms of the heading to the authorized heading. Two of the most common alternate forms are inversions to bring a significant word into the initial position and variant phrasings or spellings of the heading. Like BT/NT and RT references, UF/USE references are reciprocal.

Callirhoe
UF Callirrhoe (Plants) [alternate spelling]
UF Mallows, Poppy [inversion]
UF Poppy mallows [common name synonym]

Callirhoe (Plants)
USE Callirhoe

Mallows, Poppy
USE Callirhoe

Poppy mallows
USE Callirhoe

Two other classes of cross-references alert users to whole categories of headings instead of to an individual heading.

Library Automation–Library Publishing

See also (SA) references appear under authorized headings, and point either to subdivisions that may be relevant to the user's needs, or to headings that employ different wording. The SA reference under *Bombing, Aerial* indicates that the subdivision —*Aerial operations* is assigned after headings for individual wars. The example provided, *World War, 1939-1945—Aerial operations*, helps users who search under *Bombing, Aerial* but who are specifically interested in bombing during the Falkland Islands War to understand that they may find materials of interest under the combination *Falkland Islands War, 1982—Aerial operations*.

Bombing, Aerial
SA subdivision —Aerial operations under individual wars, e.g., World War, 1939–1945—Aerial operations

The reference under *Heat* points to headings that begin with the word "thermal." *Thermal analysis*, *Thermal batteries*, etc., do not have a formal relationship to the heading *Heat*, but may nonetheless be of interest to the user.

Heat
SA headings beginning with the word Thermal

General see references are not headings but provide information on consistently used terminology and sometimes replace UF references to individual headings. The following example indicates that LC subject headings for mountains never include the abbreviation "Mt." Instead, the word "Mount" should be searched.

Mt. . . .
USE subject headings for place names that include the word "Mount," e.g., Fuji, Mount (Japan)

General see references may also provide information about subdivisions. The general see reference *Office, Resignation from* indicates that the subdivision —*Resignation from office* is used under personal names. Therefore, the heading *Nixon, Richard M. (Richard Milhous), 1913-1994—Resignation from office* may appear in the catalog. (For more information on subdivisions, see below.)

Office, Resignation from
USE subdivision Resignation from office under names of individual persons

SCOPE NOTES

Scope notes also appear in some records for LC subject headings. Scope notes (SN) help users understand the meaning of the heading, and help catalogers assign the heading consistently. Some scope notes, such as that for *Accessory apartments*, define only one heading.

Accessory apartments
SN Here are entered works on apartments that are subordinate in size, location, and appearance to their companion principal units.

Other scope notes contrast two or more closely related or somewhat overlapping headings and are reciprocal—they appear in all of the headings being defined. Here, there may be confusion over the difference between *Alpine regions* and *Alps Region*.

Alpine regions
SN here are entered works on higher regions of mountain systems that lie above the timberline and below the level of permanent snow. Works on the area that surrounds and includes the Alps are entered under Alps Region.

Alps Region
SN here are entered works on the area that surrounds and includes the Alps. Works on higher regions of mountain systems that lie above the timberline and below the level of permanent snow are entered under Alpine regions.

A third type of scope note provides instructions on application and are chiefly intended for cataloger use, but also assist users in finding materials of interest to them.

Depressions
SN Subdivided by date and, if worldwide, may be further subdivided by country, city, etc., for example, Depressions—1929—United States; Depressions—1929—Illinois—Chicago

SUBDIVISIONS

LCSH is a *pre-coordinated* system: catalogers combine main headings with subdivisions in order to include multiple concepts in a single heading, thereby "pre-coordinating" headings for the user. It is also *post-coordinated* because two or more subject headings are often assigned to an individual work. The headings within a single bibliographic record may exhibit both pre- and post-coordination: multiple headings may be assigned (post-coordination) and each heading may be subdivided (pre-coordination).

In traditional online catalogs, users generally browse the subdivided headings alphabetically, as was done in card catalogs. Users of those catalogs must have at least a basic understanding of the structure of LCSH so they can formulate effective left-anchored searches. In the new generation of online catalogs and discovery systems there is usually an option to treat each LCSH subdivision as a separately indexed and displayable facet, allowing users to combine pieces from various subject headings. Faceting precludes the need for users to understand LCSH's structure, but also removes the context that subdivisions provide. Regardless of whether a catalog provides traditional left-anchored browsing of subject headings or a faceted interface, it is important to understand the types of subdivisions and the role that each plays within a subject heading string.

There are four categories of subdivisions: topical, chronological, geographic, and form.

Topical subdivisions limit the main heading to a particular subtopic (e.g., *Religion in public schools—Law and legislation*; *Theaters—Stage-setting and scenery*; *Virginia—Antiquities*).

Chronological subdivisions limit the heading to a particular period of time and are often preceded by the topical subdivision *—History*. They usually consist of a date span, and may include a descriptive phrase (e.g., *Furniture—Japan—History—Edo period, 1600–1868*; *Libraries—History—To 400*; *Philosophy, American—20th century*; *United States—Foreign relations—2001–2009*).

Geographic subdivisions limit a heading to a particular place, and are derived from authorized headings for jurisdictions and quasi-jurisdictions established in the NAF as well as geographic features established in LCSH. Only headings representing topics that can exist in a particular place, or that can be discussed in relation to a place, may be subdivided geographically. They are indicated with the notation (May Subd Geog). For example, the heading *Hotels* may be subdivided geographically, as indicated by the entry:

Hotels (May Subd Geog)

The following combinations are therefore possible:

Hotels—Egypt—Cairo.
Hotels—Europe.
Hotels—Finland.
Hotels—United States.

The combinations in the above example demonstrate the principle of indirect subdivision. Regions larger than countries, including continents, are used directly after topics, as are names of countries. For places within a country, the name of the country is interposed before the name of the place. There are three exceptions to the general rule: Canada, the United States, and Great Britain. For those countries, the provinces, states, and constituent countries, respectively, are assigned without first assigning the country. The name of the province, state, or constituent country is interposed before the name of a local place.

Hotels—Alberta.
Hotels—Alberta—Edmonton.

Hotels—England.
Hotels—England—London.
Hotels—Florida.
Hotels—Florida—Miami.

Some topical subdivisions can also be subdivided geographically. Geographic subdivision is always provided as far to the end of the heading string as possible. If the main heading and the topical subdivision can both be geographically subdivided, the geographic subdivision is assigned after the topical subdivision; if only the main heading can, the subdivision is interposed. This can sometimes lead to random-looking orders of subdivisions, as shown in this example.

Authorized headings:

Automobiles (May Subd Geog)
Automobiles—Accounting
Automobiles—Batteries (May Subd Geog)

Headings with geographic subdivision:

Automobiles—Batteries—Wyoming.
Automobiles—Wyoming.
Automobiles—Wyoming—Accounting.

Topical, geographic, and chronological subdivisions indicate the topic of the material being cataloged. Form subdivisions are quite different and indicate what the material is: a dictionary or an encyclopedia, for example. They almost always appear as the last element of a subject heading string (e.g., *London (England)—Guidebooks*; *English language—Dictionaries*; *United States—History—War of 1812—Encyclopedias*).

Free-Floating and Pattern Subdivisions

Some subdivisions are specifically established for use under a particular heading and are printed in LCSH, but most *[heading]—[subdivision]* combinations are created by catalogers in building-block fashion according to rules provided in the SHM. The topical, form, and chronological subdivisions that can be added to headings are called free-floating subdivisions.

The SHM includes lists of free-floating subdivisions that may be assigned to particular categories of headings as needed. There are, for instance, lists of subdivisions that are used under names of persons, classes of persons, and bodies of water. Each list is self-contained and is prefaced with a statement indicating the types of headings to which the subdivisions in the list may be appended.

Free-floating subdivisions may be combined with headings fitting the category, as long as they are appropriate and there is not a conflict. For example, the subdivision *—Navigation* may be assigned under bodies of water so the

Library Automation–Library Publishing

heading *Mississippi River—Navigation* may be assigned, although it is not specifically established and thus does not appear in LCSH. The subdivision *—Psychology* may be used under classes of persons, so one would expect that it can be used under *Children*, a class of persons. However, the combination *Children—Psychology* is a UF reference to *Child psychology*, so there is a conflict and *Child psychology* is used instead. Finally, some free-floating subdivisions that are technically valid under a particular heading are intellectually inappropriate. For example, the subdivision *—Coronation* may be used under names of persons, but it would not be appropriate under *Washington, George, 1732–1799* because Washington was inaugurated, not coronated.

Pattern subdivisions are a special type of free-floating subdivision and are assigned in the same manner. The difference is in the way they are established. Free-floating subdivisions appear in lists but may not ever be established under particular headings. Pattern headings appear in lists, too, but are also established after the "pattern" heading, which is a heading that is representative of the category. *Corn* is the pattern heading for the category Plants and Crops, for instance, so all of the subdivisions authorized for use under headings for plants and crops are established under *Corn*. Because the subdivided heading *Corn–Harvesting* is established, the headings *Spinach—Harvesting*, *Tomatoes—Harvesting*, and numerous others can also be created. In this way, subdivisions are established only once but are used many times.

Multiple subdivisions are another type of free-floating subdivision. They appear in LCSH under individual headings and are indicated with square brackets and the abbreviation "etc." as in the example *Future life—Buddhism, [Christianity, etc.]*. The subdivision suggests the creation of analogous subdivisions, which are free-floating. Due to the multiple, *Future life* may be subdivided by any religion (e.g., Christianity, Islam, Judaism).

ASSIGNMENT OF HEADINGS

Headings are assigned to represent the overall contents of the work; LC practice is to assign headings only for topics that comprise at least 20% of the work.[4] Some works are adequately cataloged with only one subject heading. Others may be assigned a maximum of 10 in order to bring out complex or compound topics that cannot be expressed with a single heading.

Headings assigned to a work are as specific as the work itself. A general work on chemistry would be assigned the heading *Chemistry*, while a work on optical isomers, a concept in chemistry, would be assigned *Optical isomers* and not the broader heading. Likewise, an encyclopedia of the ethnic groups of Africa would be assigned the relatively general heading *Ethnology—Africa—*

Encyclopedias, while a work on the marriage customs of the Xhosa people from South Africa would be entered under the more specific *Xhosa (African people)—Marriage customs and rites—South Africa*.

More information on these general principles, and also the rules on heading assignment for specific types of materials, is provided in the SHM.[3]

LCSH'S PAST AND PRESENT

LC subject headings and the policies governing their application have developed over more than one hundred years. LCSH's core vocabulary was the 1895 American Library Association publication entitled *The List of Subject Headings for Use in Dictionary Catalogs*. LC acquired copies of the ALA publication and interleaved them with blank pages. Beginning in 1898, headings that were assigned by LC catalogers were checked off, and new or revised headings were written on the blank pages. Those headings became the first edition of *Subject Headings Used in the Dictionary Catalogues of the Library of Congress*, which was published in parts between 1909 and 1914 and was kept up to date by supplements and by new editions. The vocabulary acquired its current title in 1975, when the eighth edition was published as *Library of Congress Subject Headings*.[5]

Many generations of librarians have maintained LCSH as theories of vocabulary construction have come and gone, knowledge of users' information-seeking behavior has increased, and technology has changed. The vocabulary therefore reflects the varied philosophies of the times and of the catalogers who have contributed headings (p. viii).[5] Variations in the formulation of headings can usually be attributed to policies in force at the time the headings were created. As Richard S. Angell phrased it in the introduction to the 6th edition, "The list is the product of evolutionary forces, among them the growth of the Library's collections, semantic change, and varying theories of subject heading practice over the years. As a consequence the list is, at any point in time, an accurate reflection of practice but not a complete embodiment of theory."[6]

Some existing headings were revised to reflect new "theories of subject heading practice," but revisions were quite labor intensive in the days of the card catalog and had to be carefully considered. In many libraries, cancelled headings were erased from cards, new headings typed, and the cards refiled; at LC, new card sets were ordered and filed as superseded ones were pulled.[7]

Large changes were massive undertakings due to the sheer size of LC's main catalog. The cancellation of the outdated heading *European War, 1914-1918* in favor of *World War, 1914–1918*, for example, was postponed until the card catalog was closed in 1981, meaning that cards would not need to be revised, but—perhaps most importantly—tens of thousands of cards filed between European... and World... did not have to be shifted.[7]

Library Automation–Library Publishing

The adoption of an automated system for LCSH in 1985 dramatically changed LC's ability to revise the vocabulary. Headings and references could be updated more easily, making it feasible to adopt some elements of thesaural structure. The past three decades have been a time of significant change for LCSH as technological advances have impacted every aspect of vocabulary development and maintenance. The utilization of twenty-first-century technology promises to bring further notable alterations in the way that LCSH is maintained and assigned.

This section will explore the ways that LCSH has changed over time by highlighting several watershed policy decisions. Some of the revisions occurred in the 1970s, but the pace of change significantly increased after 1985.

Scope

For most of LCSH's first hundred years, its scope was determined by LC's collections, which are strong in the humanities and social sciences; coverage of those disciplines is therefore particularly deep in LCSH. On the other end of the spectrum, coverage of medicine and agriculture is less granular. LC maintains relatively superficial collections in those areas, because each has a U.S. national library dedicated to it: the National Agricultural Library and the National Library of Medicine, respectively.

During the 1980s, advances in technology made it feasible for LC to routinely accept proposals for new and revised headings from other libraries. As a result, the Cooperative Subject Cataloging Project was born in 1983.[8] It was renamed the Subject Authority Cooperative Program (SACO) in 1994,[9] and is now a formal arm of the Program for Cooperative Cataloging (PCC).[10] Any library able to meet the contribution requirements may join SACO and propose headings needed for their own cataloging, and there are dozens of active members. Since member libraries collect in areas that LC does not, they are able to add depth and breadth to LCSH.

The growth of SACO has helped to provide more balance in LCSH, which has been charged with having an American or Western bias. One of LCSH's most vocal critics is Sanford Berman, who opined in 1971:

"In the realm of headings that deal with people and cultures—in short, with humanity—the LC list can only 'satisfy' parochial, jingoistic Europeans and North Americans, white-hued, at least nominally Christian (and preferably Protestant) in faith, comfortably situated in the middle- and higher-income brackets, largely domiciled in suburbia, fundamentally loyal to the Established Order, and heavily imbued with the transcendent, incomparable glory of Western civilization."[11]

LC's collections have traditionally emphasized American and Western European topics, and LCSH reflected that focus. More recently, LC has stressed the acquisition of materials published in developing countries,[12] and that

has likewise influenced the types of headings entering LCSH. In addition, SACO members regularly propose headings for geographic features and topics that are significant in other parts of the world, including those for ethnic groups, languages, historical periods, etc.

While SACO proposals clearly benefit LCSH overall by removing some of the inherent bias caused by the collection policies of a single library, they bring a different type of unevenness to the vocabulary. Since most SACO members are in the United States, the American bias of LCSH is in some ways increasing with regard to locally significant headings (e.g., ethnic groups, geographic features), even as ever-growing numbers of headings that are locally relevant to other countries are added. In addition, since proposals are driven by literary warrant and thus by collection development policies, some American SACO members with large local-interest collections propose numerous headings of local significance, while other SACO members are not as active in that respect. This leads to unevenness in coverage, even within the United States.

Heading Currency

Headings in LCSH are based on the terminology used in the work being cataloged and on language employed by reference sources at the time the heading was proposed.[13] The assumption is that the terminology employed there will be most familiar to those who will look for materials on that subject. However, the English language and societal attitudes evolve constantly, so older headings need to be revised to the current terminology.

Some headings become outdated due to language shifts over time. For instance, the heading *Livestock factories*, which was added to LCSH in 1980, was revised to *Factory farms* in 2008. The heading *Cellular telephones* was approved in 1998 and revised in 2009 to the more common and informal *Cell phones*. While the traditional preference has been for scientific and formal terminology, as befits a large research library,[14] LCSH is used in all types of libraries and also on the Semantic Web. It therefore behooves LC to move toward less formality when possible. No example is clearer than the 2007 deprecation of the heading *Mensuration* in favor of its commonly used synonym, *Measurement*.

Some biased language results from contemporary scholarship. Reference sources from decades ago were often politically incorrect by today's standards, particularly when naming groups of people, including indigenous ethnic groups, and languages. In some cases, obviously pejorative headings have been cancelled from LCSH (e.g., *Yellow peril*). Others have been revised to reflect contemporary terminology. For instance, the heading *Cripples*, first included in 1919, was revised in 1957 to *Physically handicapped*, and then again in 2002 to *People with disabilities*, the latest iteration reflecting the preferred "people first language" that emphasizes the person and not the disability.[15]

Library Automation–Library Publishing

Not every situation is this cut-and-dried, though, and names of ethnic groups pose particular problems. Some members of a group may consider the term used in the heading to be pejorative because it is the "colonialist" or ethnocentric name. That same term may have been adopted by other members of the group, who use it with pride. In those cases, general encyclopedias are consulted and the heading is based on the terminology found there, on the principle that it is probably the terminology that most users will employ.

Because of such disagreements, and because it is impossible to comprehensively review LCSH, it is unlikely that all of the headings will ever be considered completely current and unbiased. However, LC's attempts to remedy the problems have not gone unnoticed. Stephen A. Knowlton analyzed actions taken on the 225 headings that Berman considered problematic in 1971. Knowlton found that by 2005, 88 had been changed as suggested and 54 were revised to partially reflect Berman's views. Knowlton concluded, "It appears that bias in subject headings, while a continuing source of concern, has been addressed in a serious manner by the compilers of LCSH. The main biases found in this study are the persistence of the assumption that unglossed religious headings refer to Christian topics, and [the continued existence of] unglossed terms related to United States history and geography, which may simply be confusing to users outside the U.S."[16]

Heading Syntax

Although natural-language headings are preferred, inverted topical headings (e.g., *Conjunctivitis, Infantile*) have always existed. Headings were inverted in three situations: when users were considered more likely to search under the noun instead of the adjective denoting language, ethnic group, or nationality; when it was desirable to bring the noun into the first position so the phrase heading would file with other headings beginning with the noun; and when the noun was also an independent heading and the adjective qualified it.[17] The result of the inversions can be seen in the following array of headings:

Bridges
Bridges, Aluminum
Bridges, Arched
Bridges, Long-span

In libraries with large card catalogs, users might have had to walk quite a distance to follow references, so proximity was a service. Inverted headings are not nearly as useful in modern online catalogs, in particular because they can hinder keyword phrase searching. A user who searches for the phrase "long-span bridges" will not retrieve any works with the subject heading *Bridges, Long-span* and may therefore remain unaware of many pertinent works.

In 1983, the policy on inversion was updated so that most new headings are established in natural-language order. There are now only nine categories in which inverted topical headings are established.[18] In terms of the number of new headings, the most common category is those that are qualified by ethnic group, language, or nationality (e.g., *Masks, Yoruba*; *Ballads, Hindi*; *Coins, Russian*).

Due to the policy revision, headings for similar concepts are sometimes formulated differently (e.g., *Toxicological chemistry* but *Chemistry, Forensic*). Existing inverted topical headings that do not fall into one of the nine categories are eligible for revision as time and workload permit.[18] In 2008 and 2009, for example, the inverted headings for types of bridges, including those above, were revised to natural-language order, as were inverted headings qualified by a religion.

Revision of the inverted headings causes some tension. Most librarians probably agree that inverted headings inhibit access to some extent, but there is lack of agreement over whether the headings should be revised. Some see such revisions as "change for change's sake." Furthermore, lack of a global update capability in some integrated library systems makes it difficult for libraries to revise the headings locally. This fact illustrates the point that LCSH is used in so many libraries that even small adjustments in headings or policies can lead to upheaval. It can therefore be politically difficult to make adjustments, even when there is consensus that the adjustments are desirable.

Reference Structure

Early editions of LCSH were chiefly lists of authorized headings, arranged alphabetically. There were *see* references to the heading from synonyms and from some other terms that were not precisely synonymous with the heading, but there were not any hierarchical references. There were *see also references*, however, which were made to more specific subjects or to an application of the subject, and to "subjects which suggest themselves as likely to be of interest to the user" (pp. 13–14).[17]

The second category of see also references involved very subjective judgments. Mary K. Pietris, a chief of the former Subject Cataloging Division when those guidelines were in force, put it this way: "If you were establishing the heading *Swimming*, should *Lakes* be a see also reference, because people often swim in them?"[7] Two examples from the 5th (1948) edition[19] are illustrative.

Irrigation
see also Alkali lands; Dams; Drainage; Dry farming; Reservoirs; Sewage irrigation; Water-storage; Windmills
refer from (see also) Agricultural engineering; Agriculture; Civil engineering; Drainage; Engineering; Hydraulic engineering; Reclamation of land; Reservoirs; Soils; Waste lands; Water-storage; Water-supply

Ocean currents
see also Bottle-charts; Guinea Current; Gulf Stream; Kuroshio
refer from (see also) Hydrography; Navigation; Ocean; Physical geography

Note that the references varied in specificity (e.g., *Engineering* in general and various specialties of engineering are all references for *Irrigation*). They also mixed types of entities, as can be seen in the see also references to both bottle-charts (a type of map) and individual named currents from *Ocean currents*.

The existing structure had become unworkable by the 1970s, leading LC staff to want to update it to a more thesaurus-like system.[7] Several LC staff members attended a meeting sponsored by the Council on Library Resources (CLR) in 1982, which recommended that LC "edit the LCSH see also structure so that true hierarchical relationships are made explicit and both broader terms and narrower terms can be distinguished and retrieved."[20]

Planning for the automated subject system was underway by then, so LC was finally able to make the change. Proposals for new headings first included BTs and RTs in 1985, and hierarchical references first appeared in the 11th (1988) edition.[21]

Although BTs, NTs, and RTs are characteristics of thesauri, their inclusion in LCSH did not make LCSH a true thesaurus. For instance, LCSH includes numerous synthetic headings (e.g., *Animals in motion pictures*), which are generally undesirable in thesauri.[22] LCSH is therefore best described as a controlled vocabulary—a list of terms, each of which has an unambiguous, unique, and nonredundant definition and has been explicitly enumerated (p. 5).[22] Since LCSH is not a thesaurus, the staff who developed its hierarchy did not consider themselves bound by the strict rules of thesaurus construction[7] and LCSH's structure is still imperfect when weighed against the ANSI/NISO standard for monolingual controlled vocabularies. An examination of three practical decisions made in the 1980s highlights the ways that LCSH differs from a thesaurus.

The first decision was to programmatically generate the BT and RT references from the references already present. When a heading appeared as both a *see also* and as a *refer from (see also)* reference in the same entry, as *Water-storage* does in the entry for *Irrigation* above, the heading became an RT. Other references were converted into BTs and NTs.[23] This was an imperfect but necessary approach—imperfect because the new structure was predicated on the previous arbitrary system; necessary because it was impractical to intellectually reevaluate every existing heading to assign references. There have been efforts over the years to evaluate the references that were generated, but many still have not been reviewed for accuracy.

The second practical decision was to allow some categories of "orphan" headings, including headings that represent the broadest topic in a given category (e.g., *Science*), headings for geographic regions (*Europe, Western*) and family names (*Myers family*). Since they do not have obvious BTs, these headings' lack of hierarchy is perhaps reasonable. Another category consists of inverted headings when the BT would match the first word or the entry phrase of the heading; the inversion allows for proximal browsing and the BT was therefore considered superfluous (*Painting, French* files after *Painting*, so the BT *Painting* is not made). Among other categories of orphans are certain ubiquitous prepositional phrase headings such as those in the form *[topic] in literature* (e.g., *Librarians in literature*), which were not provided with a BT in order to contain the size of printed editions of LCSH.

"Orphans" are generally not connected to any other heading in LCSH. This is detrimental in the linked data world, which is predicated on relationships. LC's cataloging policy specialists have therefore added BTs to categories of headings as time permits. For instance, in 2012 the BT *Newspapers* was added to headings of the type *[nationality or language] newspapers* (e.g., *Albanian newspapers*).

The third practical decision with far-reaching implications involves BTs for headings that combine two concepts with either a preposition or the conjunction "and." In each case, the BT reflects the second part of the heading. A BT reflecting the first part of the phrase heading was considered unnecessary because the phrase heading would be filed after the heading representing the first part. For example, *Art in education* and *Communication and education* each have the BT *Education*. Since the phrase headings are filed after *Art* and *Communication*, respectively, BTs from those two headings are not made.

This policy sometimes leads to references that violate the general policies for hierarchical references. For example, the BT for *Physicians as authors* is *Authors*, which follows the policy on prepositional phrases and accurately represents a class/class member relationship. On the other hand, the BT for *Children of celebrities* is *Celebrities*, which follows the policy on prepositional phrases but is intellectually invalid. Children of celebrities are not (necessarily) celebrities.

The LC staff who maintain LCSH continue to refine the syndetic structure of the existing headings. The structure of new headings conforms to thesaurus construction guidelines to the extent practical, given that new headings must be compatible with the legacy data.

Subdivisions

According to the ANSI/NISO standard on monolingual controlled vocabularies, pre-coordinated strings composed of a heading and one or more subdivisions exhibit three benefits. They provide a way to locate highly specific

Library Automation–Library Publishing

information without having to search each term separately, group closely related terms together, and describe complex topics (p. 37).[22]

The benefits of pre-coordination are clear, but the complexity and expense involved in assigning such headings cannot be denied. Since the 1970s, LC has made numerous policy changes in an effort to reduce the complexity and cost of subdivision practice. The 1990s were particularly active in this regard, due in large part to the implementation of recommendations made in 1991 by the LC-sponsored invitational Subject Subdivisions Conference (familiarly called Airlie House or the Airlie House Conference) and also the impact of automation.

This section briefly addresses three significant pre-Airlie House activities regarding subdivision policy, and then examines how the Airlie House recommendations were implemented by LC.

Pre-Airlie House Actions

Free-floating and pattern subdivisions: Every subdivision had to be specifically established with the heading for which it was intended to be assigned until 1974, when LC created lists of pattern and free-floating subdivisions.[24] There were two primary benefits to the new practice. It decreased the average time and expense of cataloging a work at LC because fewer proposals were necessary. Catalogers in other institutions were also able to provide original subject cataloging more readily because they could combine headings and applicable subdivisions without waiting for LC to establish a specific combination.

Geographic subdivision: LCSH originally employed two methods of geographic subdivision. Some topics were subdivided directly by city (e.g., *Art—Paris*) and others were subdivided indirectly through the country (*Reformation—France—Paris*) (p. 2-3).[17] To simplify practice and provide more predictability for users, in 1974 LC began to move toward always using indirect geographic subdivision. In November 1976, indirect geographic subdivision became standard for all topical headings.[25]

Subject Cataloging Manual: Subject Headings: The SCM:SH, which described policies for proposing and assigning headings, was originally an in-house manual for LC catalogers, but library school faculty who taught LCSH and catalogers who wanted to follow LC policy lobbied LC to publish it. LC agreed, and the preliminary edition was published in 1984.[26] The manual has gone through several editions and was retitled the *Subject Headings Manual* (SHM) in 2008. It is kept up to date with quarterly updates. In 2013, the Policy and Standards Division began to provide it freely on LC's website, and it is also available through Cataloger's Desktop, LC's subscription-based online documentation service.[27,28]

Publication of the SCM:SH was significant because "For the first time, 'outside' catalogers were able to read the same memoranda, or instruction sheets, available to LC catalogers, and thus acquire the opportunity to become more consistent and improve the quality of the LCSH strings that they assigned to original-cataloging records for the bibliographic utilities."[29]

Airlie House Recommendations

The first Airlie House recommendation was to standardize the order of subdivisions for topical (not name or geographic) headings to *[topical]—[geographic]—[chronological]—[form]*.[30] The suggested order was adopted in 1992, with some variations to permit the inclusion of a topical subdivision.[31,32] There was community disagreement, though, over whether the standard order would best serve the user in certain areas, such as art, literature, and history, so headings in those categories were not updated.[8] There is still progress being made, however; in 2008, for example, the placement of chronological subdivisions in architectural headings was revised to remove an exception to standard practice.[33]

The placement of the geographic subdivision had the most impact on the overall order of subdivisions, and policies were adjusted to improve consistency. Previously, if the work prompting a proposal for a topical heading did not have a geographic focus, there was no provision made for geographic subdivision. Another proposal to add geographic subdivision would be made when warranted. This meant that many headings for which geographic subdivision was intellectually reasonable could not be so subdivided. This led to unpredictable orders of subdivisions, so since 1992 all proposals for topical headings and topical subdivisions that could have a topical orientation do include provision for geographic subdivision.[31,34] In addition, existing headings have been marked (*May Subd Geog*) on a case-by-case basis.[8]

To enable more headings to follow the standard order of subdivisions, LC also cancelled 79 topical subdivisions used under names of places in favor of the more common *[topic]—[geographic]* formulation (e.g., *[place]—Industries* was revised to *Industries—[place]*).[8]

LC programmatically generated over 78,000 "validation records" between 2007 and 2012 in response to the Airlie House recommendation that the authority file should contain records for *[topical heading]—[topical subdivision]* combinations, although the combinations would remain free-floating. Validation records are based on headings used over 20 times in LC's bibliographic database, the assumption being that frequently-used headings are probably formatted correctly.[35] The records contain all of the subdivisions—topical, geographic, chronological, and form—used within a particular heading and are chiefly intended to enable computer validation of subdivided headings. They may also be searched in Classification Web, LC's subscription-based vocabulary service,[36] and are freely available through LC's authorities

Library Automation—Library Publishing

website.[37] They are also included in LC's Authorities & Vocabularies linked data service,[38] from which they may be freely downloaded in a variety of formats.

The conference also requested that relationships between headings and topical subdivisions be coded (pp. 7–8).[30] This goal was partially realized in 1999 when authority records for the free-floating and pattern subdivisions were created; each record includes a MARC 21 "subdivision usage" field 073,[39] which lists the SHM instruction sheet(s) in which each subdivision appears. The other half of the relationship is provided by 072 "subject category code" fields that appear in authority records for the headings and contain the number of the instruction sheet into which the heading falls.[40] In the following example, the 072 and 073 fields link the heading, *Greybull River (Wyo.)*, with an appropriate subdivision —*Water rights*.

072 #7 $a H 1145.5 $2 lcsh
151 ## $a Greybull River (Wyo.)
073 ## $a H 1145.5 $z lcsh
180 ## $x Water rights

Subject policy specialists began to experiment with adding 072 fields to select proposals for new headings in 2012, and it quickly became clear that there are several challenges to full implementation. They will be addressed below, in the section on future directions.

The conference also made three recommendations regarding chronological subdivisions. First, it suggested that chronological subdivisions should relate to the content of the work and not to its publication date. In response, LC cancelled almost 200 subdivisions that were established under specific headings and referred to publication date. The second recommendation was to remove phrases from chronological subdivisions (e.g., revise *United States—History—Civil War, 1861–1865* to *United States—History—1861–1865*). LC partially implemented the recommendation by removing phrases from over 100 chronological subdivisions.[8] Third, the conference recommended that the pros and cons of using free-form chronological subdivisions be considered (pp. 8–9).[30] LC decided not to move in that direction. As stated in a 2010 report,

> "LC has decided not to pursue the use of free-form date subdivisions, which would exactly correlate to the chronological focus of a work, instead of using general century subdivisions, which are generally much broader. Using free-form date subdivisions would inhibit collocation of like works since works on the same historical period may differ in the beginning and ending dates of coverage. In addition, free-form date subdivisions would be much more time consuming and difficult to apply since catalogers would have to closely examine each work to determine its exact chronological coverage, which might in fact be vague (e.g., the United States during the Progressive Era)" (p. 5).[33]

Airlie House also recommended that LC investigate implementing a separate subfield for form subdivisions (pp. 9–10).[30] LC consulted with the Subject Analysis Committee of the Association for Library Collections and Technical Services (part of the American Library Association), which agreed that it would be feasible to establish and assign a separate subfield code. Subfield $v was approved by the Machine-Readable Bibliographic Information Committee (MARBI) in 1995 and implemented by LC in 1999.[8]

To assist catalogers and provide for machine manipulation, Airlie House recommended that LC investigate including in authority records for geographic headings, the form in which the heading would be used as a geographic subdivision (p. 10).[30] Like the subfield $v used in the MARC 6XX fields, this recommendation required action by MARBI, which approved the 781 linking field in 1992.[8,41] LC implemented the field in 1996, and entered into a cooperative project with OCLC to programmatically add 781 fields to existing records for geographic names that were already established in the NAF. That project, in which over 83,000 name authority records were enhanced, was completed in 2006. A similar project to add 781 fields to geographic LC subject headings, undertaken in cooperation with Northwestern University, was completed in 2003 (p. 31).[1] (There are some geographic name and subject headings that by policy cannot be used as geographic subdivisions. In those cases, a 781 field is not added, but a 667 field is. The note reads, "This heading is not valid for use as a geographic subdivision.")

Finally, Airlie House recommended the simplification of subdivisions by removing "overly fine distinctions," combining lists of free-floating subdivisions, and increasing consistency in syntax. The conference considered the changes to be "of such importance that they should be made in spite of possible disruptions to existing databases" (p. 10).[30]

In response, the lists of subdivisions used under groups of Indians, domestic animals, and literary authors were merged into the lists for ethnic groups, animals, and personal names, respectively, and three other lists were discontinued outright. Finally, some lists were shortened by removing subdivisions that were specific to a particular heading and were therefore not actually free-floating.[8,42]

There were also many dozens of changes to individual subdivisions. By 1996, over 75 subdivisions with similar meanings but different syntaxes were merged or discontinued. For example, the subdivision —*Terms and phrases*, which was used under legal topics, was merged into the subdivision —*Terminology*, which was used elsewhere in LCSH. The wording used in over 60 subdivisions was updated (e.g., the subdivision —*Preventive inoculation* was revised to —*Vaccination*). Over 250 *[heading]—[subdivision]* combinations were replaced by phrase headings, and 35 subdivisions were cancelled altogether.[8] LC continues to examine subdivisions on a case-by-case basis

Library Automation–Library Publishing

and revisions are made as necessary regardless of their impact on existing databases (p. 5).[33]

FUTURE DIRECTIONS

LCSH is a living system that adapts (albeit slowly at times) to social and technological changes, so LCSH at the turn of the twenty-first century is quite different from that which was envisioned at the dawn of the twentieth. This section will address some additional adjustments that are being planned and executed to bring LCSH further into the twenty-first century's linked data world.

RDA: Resource Description and Access, which was implemented by LC in 2013, has already impacted the scope of LCSH. Until mid-2013, new headings for individual fictitious and legendary characters, mythological beings and deities, and named animals were established in LCSH; they are now established in the LC/NACO NAF because under RDA, those entities are considered to be persons.[43] As the RDA Steering Committee continues its work relating to concepts, objects, events, and places, additional adjustments to LCSH will probably be necessary.

Also already impacting LCSH is the development of three new vocabularies by LC and several partner organizations. One of them is *Library of Congress Genre/Form Terms for Library and Archival Materials* (LCGFT), a multi-disciplinary thesaurus of terms that represent what something *is* rather than what it is *about*.[44]

In some disciplines, most notably literature and music, LC subject headings have been used to describe both what something *is* and what it is *about*. For example, a collection of haiku would be assigned the subject heading *Haiku*, while criticism of haiku would be assigned the subject heading *Haiku—History and criticism*. In the future, a work that is haiku will be assigned a term from LCGFT, while criticism will continue to be assigned the subject heading. [For more information, see the article on LCGFT.] Some subject headings that are assigned only to works *of* a particular form are likely to be cancelled in the future.

An open question is whether LCGFT will eventually supplant LCSH form subdivisions, which could then be cancelled. Many of the form subdivisions previously used to describe cartographic materials (e.g., the subdivision —*Maps, Comparative*) have already been cancelled in favor of the corresponding genre/form term, but other form subdivisions remain valid.[45]

The *Library of Congress Medium of Performance Thesaurus for Music* (LCMPT), which consists of terminology to describe the instruments, voices, etc. used in the performance of musical works, was implemented in early 2014. Terms are assigned in MARC 21 bibliographic field 382 and in the 382 field in authority records for works and expressions.[46]

LCSH includes thousands of headings that describe the form and/or mediums of performance of musical works, such as *Bass clarinet and piano music* and *Sonatas (Trumpet and piano)*. Most of those headings are only used to describe works *of* music, not works *about* it, and will be cancelled after LCGFT terms for music are implemented alongside the medium of performance terms.

Some LCSH form headings describe the intended audience or creator of the work (e.g., *Children's stories; Airline pilots' writings*). Since they do not represent a form or genre, they are outside the scope of LCGFT, but they will no longer be assigned to works of literature after LCGFT terms for literature are implemented. The access they provide is nonetheless important, so in early 2014 LC's Policy and Standards Division was authorized to develop *Library of Congress Demographic Group Terms* (LCDGT). The terms in LCDGT are based primarily on LCSH's headings for classes of persons and ethnic groups, with some modifications, and are assigned to bring out the creators/contributors and the intended audiences of works. Terms are eligible for assignment in MARC 21 fields 385 (for audience) and 386 (for creators/contributors) in bibliographic records and in authority records for works and expressions.[47]

Traditionally, a cataloger describing a sonata for clarinet and cello that was composed by an American woman would assign only the subject heading *Sonatas (Clarinet and cello)*. Now, catalogers can use LCMPT to explicitly indicate the mediums of performance (clarinet and cello), LCGFT to indicate the form (sonata), and LCDGT to indicate the characteristics of the creator (an American woman).

When these three vocabularies are fully implemented, LCSH will be more true to its title and describe the topics of works, as opposed to describing both forms and topics.

The 072 project, which was briefly discussed as an outcome of the Airlie House recommendations, shows promise for simplifying the application of LCSH. Machine-matching the 072 fields in authority records for headings to 073 fields in the authority records for free-floating subdivisions will allow both the automatic suggestion of subdivisions appropriate to the heading that is being assigned and the dynamic validation of full heading strings. When combined with the coding that indicates whether a heading may be geographically subdivided and the 781 linking fields in records for geographic headings, it should also enable the automatic generation of full heading strings on the Semantic Web. This last outcome is essential to the success of LCSH in the linked data environment, and particularly in BIBFRAME, which is intended to replace MARC.

Adding 072 fields to subject authorities is not straightforward; with few exceptions, the lists include subdivisions that cannot in fact be assigned to every heading fitting the category. For example, H 1100, Classes of Persons, includes some subdivisions that apply only to headings for occupational groups and types of employees, and others that may be used only under sex and age groups. Since there are no headings under which all of the subdivisions in H 1100 may be used, records for the classes of persons headings cannot be enhanced.

This raises questions about the future of subdivision practice because the exceptions add complexity for catalogers and make reliable computer manipulation impossible. To rectify the situation, should some lists be cancelled? Each *[heading]—[subdivision]* combination that is currently free-floating would have to be individually established. Since some of the problematic lists are those that were merged, should they be split again? Should the lists remain essentially intact, but problematic subdivisions be removed and established under specific headings as needed? Or is there some other option?

Multiple subdivisions (e.g., *Asceticism—[Buddhism, Hinduism, etc.]*) must also be addressed. They are not headings but are coded as if they were, so in linked data they are treated as authorized headings. Should they be cancelled, requiring that all subdivisions that would formerly have been authorized by the multiple be individually established? Should MARC be modified to include coding indicating that the "heading" is in fact not a heading at all? Or should programming be developed that will allow computers to recognize multiple subdivisions based on their unique syntax?

CONCLUSION

Since the 1970s, LCSH has undergone numerous policy changes, many of them made possible by technological advances. To maintain LCSH's standing as the most widely used vocabulary in the world, LC staff and their constituents throughout the world not only must use technology as a tool to adapt to changing circumstances, but also must adapt LCSH to technology. Twenty-first-century questions and challenges need to be confronted head-on, while the work that was begun in the last century—adding headings for new concepts, updating existing terminology, and refining the syndetic structure—must also continue.

REFERENCES

1. *Library of Congress Subject Headings: Pre- versus Post-Coordination and Related Issues*. Library of Congress Cataloging Policy and Support Office: Washington, DC, 2007; 2. http://www.loc.gov/catdir/cpso/pre_vs_post.pdf (accessed March 2014).

2. *Library of Congress Subject Headings*, 39th Ed.; Library of Congress Cataloging Distribution Service: Washington, DC, 2017; vii.

3. *Subject Headings Manual*, 2008 Ed.; Library of Congress Cataloging Policy and Support Office: Washington, DC, 2008, as updated through January 2014.

4. H 180. Assigning and constructing subject headings. In *Subject Headings Manual*; 2008 Ed.; Library of Congress Cataloging Policy and Support Office: Washington, DC, 2008 as updated through June 2013. http://www.loc.gov/aba/publications/FreeSHM/H0180.pdf (accessed March 2014).

5. *Library of Congress Subject Headings*, 12th Ed.; Library of Congress Cataloging Distribution Service: Washington, DC, 1989; viii.

6. Quattlebaum, M.V. *Subject Headings used in the Dictionary Catalogs of the Library of Congress*, 6th Ed.; Library of Congress Subject Cataloging Division, Processing Department: Washington, DC, 1957; iii.

7. Pietris, M.K. (former chief of the Library of Congress Subject Cataloging Division), in discussion with the author, February 2014.

8. Five-Year Progress Report on Subject Subdivisions Conference Recommendations, Library of Congress Cataloging Policy and Support Office: Washington, DC, 1996. http://www.loc.gov/catdir/cpso/subdconf.html (accessed March 2014).

9. SACO operations. LC Cataloging Newsline **1994**, 2(6), http://www.loc.gov/catdir/lccn/lccn0206.html (accessed March 2014).

10. Schiff, A. *SACO Participants' Manual*, 2nd Ed.; Program for Cooperative Cataloging: Washington, DC, 2007; 1.

11. Berman, S. *Prejudices and Antipathies*; Scarecrow Press: Metuchen, NJ, 1971; ix.

12. *Library of Congress Collections Policy Statements*; Library of Congress Cataloging Distribution Service: Washington, DC, 1994; x.

13. H 306. Authority research for subject heading proposals. In *Subject Headings Manual*; 2008 Ed.; Library of Congress Cataloging Policy and Support Office: Washington, DC, 2008, as updated through June 2013.

14. Taylor, A.G. *Introduction to Cataloging and Classification*, 8th Ed.; Libraries Unlimited: Englewood, CO, 1992; 395.

15. Communicating with and about People with Disabilities Centers for Disease Control and Prevention: Atlanta, GA, n.d. http://www.cdc.gov/ncbddd/disabilityandhealth/pdf/DisabilityPoster_Photos.pdf (accessed March 2014).

16. Knowlton, S.A. Three decades since prejudices and antipathies: A study of changes in the Library of Congress Subject Headings. Cat. Classif. Q. **2005**, *40* (2), 127–128.

17. Haykin, D.J. *Subject Headings, a Practical Guide*; U.S Government Printing Office: Washington, DC, 1951; Vol. 11, 22–24.

18. H 306. Natural language in topical subject headings. In *Subject Headings Manual*, 2008 Ed.; Library of Congress Cataloging Policy and Support Office: Washington, DC, 2008, as updated through June 2013.

19. Martin, N.J. *Subject Headings used in the Dictionary Catalogs of the Library of Congress*, 5th Ed.; Library of Congress Subject Cataloging Division: Washington, DC, 1948.

20. Russell, K.W. (Ed.) *Subject Access: Report of a Meeting Sponsored by the Council on Library Resources*, Dublin, Ohio, June 7–9, 1982; Council on Library Resources: Washington, DC, 1982; Vol. 70, B1–B2.

21. *Library of Congress Subject Headings*, 11th Ed.; Library of Congress Cataloging Distribution Service: Washington, DC, 1988.

22. *Guidelines for the Construction, Format, and Management of Monolingual Controlled Vocabularies*; National Information Standards Organization: Bethesda, MD, 1995; 25.

23. Svevonious, E. LCSH semantics, syntax, and specificity. Cat. Classif. Q. **2000**, *29* (1–2), 22.

24. H 1146. Subdivisions controlled by pattern headings. In *Subject Headings Manual*; 2008 Ed.; Library of Congress Cataloging Policy and Support Office: Washington, DC, 2008, as updated through June 2013.

25. H 830. Geographic subdivision. In *Subject Headings Manual*; 2008 Ed.; Library of Congress Cataloging Policy and Support Office: Washington, DC, 2008, as updated through September 2013.

26. *Subject Headings Manual*, 2008 Ed.; Library of Congress Cataloging Policy and Support Office: Washington, DC, 2008, as updated through January 2014. Preface.

27. *List of the Subject Heading Manual PDF Files*; Library of Congress Cataloging Policy and Support Office: Washington, DC, 2014. http://www.loc.gov/aba/publications/FreeSHM/freeshm.html (accessed March 2014).

28. Cataloger's desktop; Library of Congress Cataloging Distribution Service: Washington, DC, n.d., http://www.loc.gov/cds/products/product.php?productID=162 (accessed March 2014).

29. Stone, A.T. The LCSH century: A brief history of the library of congress subject headings, and introduction to the centennial essays. Cat. Classif. Q. **2000**, *29* (1–2), 6.

30. Conway, M.O. The Future of Subdivisions in the Library of Congress Subject Headings System: Report from the Subject Subdivisions Conference Sponsored by the Library of Congress May 9–12, 1991; Library of Congress Cataloging Distribution Service: Washington, DC, 1992; 6–7.

31. H 870. Interposition of geographic subdivisions. In *Subject Headings Manual*; 2008 Ed.; Library of Congress Cataloging Policy and Support Office: Washington, DC, 2008 as updated through June 2013.

32. H 1075. Subdivisions. In *Subject Headings Manual*; 2008 Ed.; Library of Congress Cataloging Policy and Support Office: Washington, DC, 2008, as updated through June 2013.

33. *The Policy and Standards Division's Progress on the Recommendations made in Library of Congress Subject Headings Pre- vs. Post-Coordination and Related Issues*; Library of Congress Policy and Standards Division, 2010; 4–5. http://www.loc.gov/catdir/cpso/pre_vs_postupdate.pdf (accessed March 2014).

34. H 364. Authorization for geographic subdivision. In *Subject Headings Manual*; 2008 Ed.; Library of Congress Cataloging Policy and Support Office: Washington, DC, 2008, as updated through September 2013.

35. *Library of Congress CDS Announcement: Distribution of Subject Authority Records for Validation Purposes*; Library of Congress Cataloging Distribution Service, 2008. http://www.loc.gov/cds/notices/2008-02-19.pdf (accessed March 2014).

36. Classification web. Library of Congress Cataloging Distribution Service: Washington, DC, n.d., / http://www.loc.gov/cds/classweb/ (accessed March 2014).

37. Library of congress authorities. Library of Congress: Washington, DC, 2012. http://authorities.loc.gov/ (accessed March 2014).

38. *LC Linked Data Service: Authorities and Vocabularies*; Library of Congress: Washington, DC, n.d. (accessed March 2014) http://id.loc.gov/.

39. 073, Subdivision usage. In *MARC 21 Format for Authority Data*. 1999 Ed. updated through September 2013; Library of Congress Network Development and MARC Standards Office: Washington, DC, 2013. http://www.loc.gov/marc/authority/ad073.html (accessed March 2014).

40. 072, Subject category code. In *MARC 21 Format for Authority Data*. 1999 Ed. updated through September 2013; Library of Congress Network Development and MARC Standards Office: Washington, DC, 2013. http://www.loc.gov/marc/authority/ad072.html (accessed March 2014).

41. *MARC 21 Format for Bibliographic Data*. 1999 Ed. updated through September 2013; Library of Congress Network Development and MARC Standards Office: Washington, DC, 2013. http://www.loc.gov/marc/bibliographic/ecbdhome.html (accessed March 2014).

42. H 1110. Free-floating subdivisions: Names of persons. In *Subject Headings Manual*; 2008 Ed.; Library of Congress Cataloging Policy and Support Office: Washington, DC, 2008, as updated through January 2014.

43. *Summary of Decisions, Editorial Meeting Number 07*; Library of Congress Policy and Standards Division: Washington, DC, 2007. http://www.loc.gov/aba/pcc/saco/cpsoed/psd-130715.html (accessed March 2014); Summary of Decisions, Editorial Meeting Number 08; Library of Congress Policy and Standards Division: Washington, DC, 2007. http://www.loc.gov/aba/pcc/saco/cpsoed/psd-130819.html (accessed March 2014).

44. Introduction to library of congress genre/form terms for library and archival materials. *Library of Congress Subject Headings*; 35th Ed.; Library of Congress Cataloging Distribution Service, 2013; GF-i.

45. *Frequently Asked Questions about Library of Congress Genre/Form Terms for Library and Archival Materials (LCGFT)*; Library of Congress Policy and Standards Division: Washington, DC, 2011; Q21, Q22.

46. *Library of Congress Launches Medium of Performance Thesaurus for Music*; Library of Congress Policy and Standards Division: Washington, DC, 2014. http://www.loc.gov/catdir/cpso/medprf-list-launch.html (accessed March 2014).

47. Young, J.L. Library of Congress report on subject cataloging. Report presented to the ALA ALCTS CCS Subject Analysis Committee (SAC) at the ALA Midwinter Meeting, Philadelphia, PA, January 26, 2014. 2014.

BIBLIOGRAPHY

1. Chan, L.M. *Cataloging and Classification: An Introduction*, 3rd Ed.; Scarecrow Press: Lanham, MD, 2007.

2. Chan, L.M. *Library of Congress Subject Headings: Principles and Application*, 4th Ed.; Libraries Unlimited: Westport, CT, 2005.

3. Taylor, A.G. *Introduction to Cataloging and Classification*, 9th Ed. Library Science Text Series. Libraries Unlimited: Englewood, CO, 1992.

Library of Congress: History

John Y. Cole
Center for the Book, Library of Congress, Washington, District of Columbia, U.S.A.

Abstract
The Library of Congress occupies a unique place in American civilization. Established as a legislative library in 1800, it grew into a national institution in the nineteenth century. In the first decades of the twentieth century, soon after it moved from the U.S. Capitol into its own spacious building, it became a leader among national libraries and one of the largest libraries in the world. Since World War II, it has become an international resource of unparalleled dimension. With the creation of the National Digital Library in the mid-1990s, it began to assume a new educational role.

INTRODUCTION: THE LIBRARY OF CONGRESS TODAY

The Library of Congress has grown immensely in size and influence since its sesquincentennial year in 1950, when the eminent librarian S. R. Ranganathan noted both its good fortune to have the U.S. Congress as its "godfather" and its role as "perhaps the most influential of the national libraries of the world."[1] Since 1950, its collections and staff have tripled and its annual appropriation has soared from $9 million to $613 million in fiscal year 2008. With collections totaling more than 138 million items, a permanent staff of nearly 3700, and national and international services unmatched in scope by any other research library, the Library of Congress is one of the world's leading cultural institutions.[2]

The diversity of the Library of Congress is startling. Simultaneously it serves as a legislative library and the major research arm of the U.S. Congress; the copyright agency of the United States; a center for scholarship that collects research materials in many media and in most subjects from throughout the world, with 460 languages represented in its collections; a public institution that is open without charge or restriction to everyone over the age of 16 and serves readers in 20 reading rooms; a government library that is heavily used by the executive branch and the judiciary; a national library service for the blind and physically handicapped; an outstanding law library, international in scope and service; one of the world's largest providers of bibliographic data and products; a center for the commissioning and performance of chamber music; the home of the nation's poet laureate; a national folklife center and veteran's history project; a national center for promoting reading with affiliates in all 50 states and the District of Columbia; the organizer of the annual National Book Festival; the sponsor of exhibitions and of musical, literary, cultural, and educational outreach programs that reach across the nation and the world; a

major worldwide research center for the preservation and conservation of library materials; and, as its research base, more than 60 million manuscripts, 12 million photographs, and the world's largest collections of maps, atlases, printed music, recorded music, motion pictures, and television programs.

Yet another new and important function had emerged by 2000, when Librarian of Congress James H. Billington informed the U.S. Congress that during the past few years the library had become a world leader in providing high-quality, free educational material in the revolutionary new world of the Internet.[3]

More than 13 million items from the library's American history collections (and those of its institutional partners) are available on the library's Web site (http://www.loc.gov). The site also provides access to the library's exhibitions, catalog data, and legislative and copyright information. With more than 93 million visits and 614 million page views in 2007, the site is among the most visited of all U.S. government Web addresses.

The library occupies three massive structures on Capitol Hill, near the U.S. Capitol. The Jefferson Building, opened in 1897, is a grand monument to civilization, culture, and American achievement (see Fig. 1 for a photograph of the Jefferson Building). The handsome, functional Adams Building opened to the public in 1939. The modern Madison Building, completed in 1980, is by far the largest of the three structures. Construction of storage facilities for paper-based collections continues at Ft. Meade, Maryland, an hour north of the library; more than 2 million items are now located in the first two modules. In 2007, the library opened a $155 million, 45-acre state-of-the-art audiovisual conservation center and home for its massive motion picture collections in Culpepper, Virginia. About 2 million researchers, scholars, and tourists visit the Library of Congress each year, and millions more use its bibliographic records, collections, and services through the Internet.

Encyclopedia of Library and Information Sciences, Fourth Edition DOI: 10.1081/E-ELIS4-120044659
Copyright © 2017 by Taylor & Francis. All rights reserved.

Library Automation–Library Publishing

Fig. 1 Until 1897, when the Thomas Jefferson Building opened to the public, the Library of Congress was located in the U.S. Capitol. The monumental Jefferson Building evoked national pride and provided space for the development of national library services.
Photo credit: Lisa Whittle.

Since its creation, the Library of Congress has been part of the legislative branch of the American government. Although it is recognized as the de facto national library of the United States, it does not have that official designation. Nevertheless, it performs most functions carried out by national libraries elsewhere, and has become a symbol of American democracy and faith in the power of learning.

The broad nature of its goals and ambition are reflected in its recently adopted mission and vision statements.

The library's mission is to make its resources available and useful to the Congress and the American people and to sustain and preserve a universal collection of knowledge and creativity for future generations. We will foster a free and informed society by building, preserving, and providing resources for human creativity, wisdom, and achievement. We continually strive to place these resources at the fingertips of the American people, their elected representatives, and the world—for the mutual prosperity, enlightenment, and inspiration of all.[4]

THE GROWTH OF A NATIONAL INSTITUTION, 1800–2000

How did a library established by the legislature for its own use become such an ambitious, multipurpose institution? Two points are clear: 1) the expansion of the Library's functions derives from the expansion of its collections; and 2) the growth of the institution is tied to the growth and ambitions of the United States itself. The development of the Library of Congress cannot be separated from the history of the nation it serves. Nor can it be separated from the philosophy and ideals of Thomas Jefferson (1743–1826), its principal founder.

The Library of Congress was established as the legislature of the young Republic prepared to move from Philadelphia to the new capital city of Washington. On April 24, 1800, President John Adams approved legislation that appropriated $5000 to purchase "such books as may be necessary for the use of Congress." The first books, ordered from London, arrived in 1801 and were stored in the U.S. Capitol, the library's first home. The collection consisted of 740 volumes and three maps.

On January 26, 1802, President Thomas Jefferson approved the first law defining the role and functions of the new institution. This measure created the post of Librarian of Congress and gave Congress, through the Joint Committee on the Library, the authority to establish the library's budget and its rules and regulations. However the 1802 law made the institution more than just a legislative library; the appointment of the Librarian of Congress was to be a presidential responsibility. The law also permitted the president and vice president to borrow books, a privilege that, in the next three decades, was extended to most government agencies and to the judiciary.

Three developments in the library's early history permanently established the institution's national roots. First, the Library of Congress was created by the national legislature, which took direct responsibility for its operation. Second, the Library of Congress was not only the first library but also the first national cultural institution of the U.S. government. Finally, in 1815, the scope of the library's collection was permanently expanded. The ideals, intellectual curiosity, and pragmatism of Thomas Jefferson were the key to this transformation.

Jefferson believed that the power of the intellect could shape a free and democratic society. It is not surprising that he took a keen interest in the Library of Congress and its development while he was president of the United States from 1801 to 1809. Throughout his presidency, he personally recommended books for the Library, and he appointed the first two Librarians of Congress. In 1814,

Library Automation–Library Publishing

the British army invaded the city of Washington and burned the Capitol, including the 3000-volume Library of Congress. By then retired to Monticello, Jefferson offered to sell his personal library, the largest and finest in the country, to Congress to replace the destroyed collection. In 1815, Congress approved the purchase of Jefferson's 6487 volumes for $23,940.

The library that Jefferson sold to Congress not only included over twice the number of volumes that had been destroyed, but it also expanded the scope of the library far beyond the bounds of a legislative library devoted primarily to legal, economic, and historical works. Jefferson was a man of encyclopedic interests, and his library included works on architecture, the arts, science, literature, and geography. It contained books in many languages, including French, Spanish, German, Latin, Greek, and Russian. Jefferson believed that the national legislature needed ideas and information on all subjects and in many languages in order to govern a democracy. Anticipating the argument that his collection might be too comprehensive, he argued that there was "no subject to which a member of Congress may not have occasion to refer."[5]

The acquisition by Congress of Jefferson's library provided the rationale for the eventual expansion of the library's functions. The Jeffersonian concept of universality is also the rationale for the comprehensive collecting policies of today's Library of Congress. Jefferson and his friend and successor as president, James Madison (1809–1817) believed that democracy depended on the mutual support of "liberty and learning." The vast collections and varied services of the Library of Congress are founded on this belief.

The Library of Congress grew slowly but steadily after the purchase of Jefferson's books. A separate law department was approved in 1832, along with an appropriation to purchase law books under the guidance of the chief justice of the United States. Yet even as the library was beginning to grow, it appeared that the Smithsonian Institution might become the American national library. During the early 1850s, the Smithsonian's talented and aggressive librarian, Charles Coffin Jewett, tried to move the institution in that direction and turn it into a national bibliographical center. Jewett's efforts were opposed, however, by Smithsonian Secretary Joseph Henry, who insisted that the Smithsonian Institution focus on scientific research and publication. In fact, the secretary favored the eventual development of a national library at the Library of Congress, which he viewed as the appropriate foundation for such a government-wide institution. On July 10, 1854, Henry dismissed Jewett, ending any possibility that the Smithsonian might become the national library. Moreover, 12 years later, Henry readily agreed to the transfer of the entire 40,000-volume library of the Smithsonian Institution to the Library of Congress.

The Library of Congress suffered difficult times during the 1850s. The growing division between North and South hindered the growth of government institutions. Furthermore, a serious fire in the Capitol building destroyed about two-thirds of the library's 55,000 volumes, including two-thirds of Jefferson's library. Congress responded quickly and generously: in 1852 a total of $168,700 was appropriated to restore the library's rooms in the Capitol and to replace the lost books. However no plan was set forth for expanding the collection or the library's services. This philosophy was in keeping with the conservative views of Librarian of Congress John Silva Meehan (1829–1861) and Senator James A. Pearce of Maryland, chairman of the Joint Committee on the Library, who favored keeping strict limits on the institution's activities.

A few years later, the library lost several collection-building functions, further impeding its progress toward the comprehensive collection that Jefferson had favored. In the 1830s and 1840s, it had begun distributing public documents to institutions throughout the United States, and exchanging books and documents with foreign institutions on behalf of the U.S. government. A joint resolution of Congress in 1857 transferred responsibility for public document distribution to the Bureau of Interior and responsibility for international exchange of books and documents to the Department of State. Moreover, in 1859 all U.S. copyright activities were centralized at the Patent Office, which meant that the Library of Congress and the Smithsonian Institution no longer received the copies of books and pamphlets deposited for copyright that had been sent to each institution since 1846.

Ainsworth Rand Spofford and the National Library

The person responsible for transforming the library into an institution of national significance in the Jeffersonian spirit was Ainsworth Rand Spofford, a former Cincinnati bookseller and journalist who served as Librarian of Congress from December 31, 1864 to July 1, 1897 (see Fig. 2 for photographs of Spofford in the early and late stages of his Library of Congress long career). Spofford accomplished this task by permanently linking the legislative and national functions of the library, first in practice and then, through the reorganization of the library approved by Congress in 1897, by law. He provided his successors as Librarian of Congress with four essential prerequisites for the development of an American national library: 1) firm, bipartisan congressional support for the notion of the Library of Congress as both a legislative and a national library; 2) the beginning of a comprehensive collection of Americana; 3) a magnificent new building, itself a national monument; and 4) a strong and independent office of Librarian of Congress. Spofford had the vision, skill, and perseverance to capitalize on the Library of Congress's claim to a national role. Each Librarian of Congress since Spofford has built upon his accomplishments. Each has shaped the institution in different ways,

Library Automation–Library Publishing

(a)   (b)

Fig. 2 (a) Ainsworth Rand Spofford, Librarian of Congress from 1864 to 1897, transformed the Library of Congress into a national institution that served the American public as well as Congress. The centralization of copyright at the library and the construction of the Jefferson building were his two greatest achievements. (b) Librarian Spofford at his desk in the badly overcrowded Library of Congress room in the U.S. Capitol in 1896, a year before the Library moved into its own building across the street from the Capitol. Photo credit: Library of Congress.

but none has wavered from the Jeffersonian belief that the democratic form of government depended on a comprehensive base of knowledge and information.

The idea of an American national library that Spofford revived had been languishing since Jewett's departure from the Smithsonian in 1854. Spofford and Jewett both recognized the importance of copyright deposit in developing a comprehensive collection of a nation's literature, yet there was a major difference in their views relating to a national library. Spofford never envisioned the Library of Congress as the center of a network of American libraries, a focal point for providing other libraries with cataloging and bibliographic services. Instead, he viewed it, in the European model, as a unique, independent institution—a single, comprehensive collection of a nation's literature to be used both by Congress and the American people. Congress needed such a collection because, as Spofford paraphrased Jefferson, "there is almost no work, within the vast range of literature and science, which may not at some time prove useful to the legislature of a great nation." It was imperative, he believed, such a great national collection be shared with all citizens, for the United States was "a Republic which rests upon the popular intelligence."[6]

Immediately following the Civil War, American society began a rapid transformation that saw the expansion of the federal government. Spofford took full advantage of the favorable political and cultural climate and the increasing national confidence, to promote the library's expansion. He always believed that the Library of Congress was the national library and he used every

conceivable argument to convince others, particularly the Joint Committee on the Library and the rest of Congress.

In the first years of his administration Spofford obtained congressional approval of six laws or resolutions that ensured a national role for the Library of Congress. The legislative acts were: 1) an appropriation for the expansion of the Library in the Capitol building, approved in early 1865; 2) the copyright amendment of 1865, which once again brought copyright deposits into the library's collection; 3) the Smithsonian deposit of 1866, whereby the entire library of the Smithsonian Institution, a collection especially strong in scientific materials, was transferred to the library; 4) the 1867 purchase, for $100,000, of the private library of historian and archivist Peter Force, establishing the foundation of the library's Americana and incunabula collections; 5) the international exchange resolution of 1867, providing for the development of the library's collection of foreign public documents; and 6) the copyright act of 1870, which centralized all U.S. copyright registration and deposit activities at the library.

The centralization of copyright activities at the library was Spofford's most impressive collection-building feat. The first U.S. copyright law was approved in 1790, but the practice of depositing items registered for copyright protection in libraries for the use of the public was not enacted until 1846, when the newly established Smithsonian Institution and the Library of Congress obtained the privilege. The Library of Congress received single copies of deposits from 1846 until 1859, and, thanks to Spofford, the practice began again in 1865. Enforcement was a problem, however, and Spofford

Library Automation–Library Publishing

decided he needed the authority that would come from centralizing all registration and deposit activities at the library, consolidating functions then performed at the Patent Office and by the district courts. The copyright law of 1870 ensured the continuing development of the library's Americana collections, for it stipulated that two copies of every book, pamphlet, map, print, photograph, and piece of music registered for copyright be deposited in the library.

In its 1876 survey of the libraries of the United States, the U.S. Bureau of Education listed the rapidly growing Library of Congress and the Boston Public Library as the two largest libraries in the United States, with approximately 300,000 volumes apiece. By 1897, when the library moved from its overcrowded rooms in the Capitol into its spacious new building, its collections ranked first among American libraries in size and scope. Over 40% of its 840,000 volumes and at least 90% of its map, music, and graphic arts collections had been acquired through copyright deposit. Important items deposited through copyright included Civil War photographs by Mathew Brady and what today are considered the earliest motion pictures.

The copyright privilege not only built the library's collections, it also helped determine the direction of their growth. When the Library of Congress moved into its new building, separate custodial units were established for the special collections formed primarily through copyright deposit: maps, music, and graphic arts. Spofford's successors as Librarian of Congress hired subject specialists to develop these and other collections and persuaded Congress to begin appropriating substantial funds for the purchase of research materials for all collections. Today, copyright is still one of the Library's major acquisitions sources, but between the years 1865 and 1897, it played a crucial role in the development of the Library of Congress into a national institution.

The copyright law of 1870 had another major effect: it forced the construction of a building for the Library. Spofford foresaw this result almost immediately. In his 1871 *Annual Report*, he suggested that a separate building would be needed because of the increased receipts resulting from the new copyright law. The next year he presented a plan for such a building, initiating a task more challenging than he anticipated, and one that dominated the rest of his career as Librarian of Congress. In his 25-year struggle to make the building a reality, Spofford enlisted the support of many powerful public figures: congressmen, cultural leaders, journalists, and even presidents. The speeches and statements he elicited usually endorsed not only a separate building, but also the concept of the Library of Congress as a national library. In 1886, Congress finally authorized a new structure directly across the East Plaza from the Capitol. After further delays, construction began in earnest in 1889 and the new building, opened to the public in 1897, was immediately hailed as a

national monument. Now called the Thomas Jefferson Building, this imposing structure in the style of the Italian Renaissance, with its grand Main Reading Room at the center and exuberant interior decoration throughout, is an incomparable symbol of the importance of books and learning and their close relationship to democracy.

Spofford also deserves primary credit for creating the library's tradition of broad public service. In 1865, he extended the hours of service, so that the library was open every weekday all year long. In 1869, he began advocating evening hours, but this innovation was not approved by Congress until 1898. Finally, in the mid-1880s Spofford began lending books directly to the citizens of the District of Columbia if an appropriate sum was left on deposit, a procedure that ended in 1894, when preparations were started for the move into the new library building.

In 1896, just before the actual move, the Joint Committee held hearings about "the condition" of the library and its possible reorganization. The hearings provided an occasion for a detailed examination of the institution's history and functions and for a review of what new services the library might perform once it occupied the spacious new building. The American Library Association sent six witnesses, including future Librarian of Congress Herbert Putnam from the Boston Public Library and Melvil Dewey from New York State Library. Members of Congress listened with great interest to the testimony of Putnam and Dewey, who argued that the national services of the library should be greatly expanded. Dewey believed that the Library of Congress now had the opportunity to act as a true national library, which he defined as "a center to which the libraries of the whole country can turn for inspiration, guidance, and practical help, which can be rendered so economically and efficiently in no other possible way."[7] Testimony at the 1896 hearings greatly influenced the reorganization of the library, which was incorporated into the Legislative Appropriations Act approved February 19, 1897, and effective on July 1, 1897. All phases of the library's activities were expanded and new administrative units were established.

Growth of Library Services

President William McKinley appointed a new Librarian of Congress to supervise the move from the Capitol and implement the new reorganization. He was John Russell Young, who held office briefly, from July 1, 1897, until his death in January 1899. A journalist and former diplomat, Young worked hard to strengthen both the comprehensiveness of the collections and the scope of the services provided to Congress. He honored Jefferson's influence on the library, placing Jefferson's books in a special room and commissioning a report on the Jefferson library that was published in the library's 1898 *Annual Report*.

Young used his diplomatic ties and experience to enlarge the Library's collections. In February 1898, for

Library Automation–Library Publishing

example, he sent a letter to U.S. diplomatic and consular representatives throughout the world, asking them to send "to the national library" newspapers, journals, pamphlets, manuscripts, broadsides, and "documents illustrative of the history of those various nationalities now coming to our shores to blend into our national life." He also asked for other categories of research materials, broadly described as "whatever, in a word, would add to the sum of human knowledge."[8] By the end of 1898, books and other materials had been received from 11 legations and 7 consulates.

Young skillfully guided the administrative reorganization. He made many important professional appointments, including Thorvald Solberg, the first register of copyrights, and catalogers J. C. M. Hanson and Charles Martel, who began reclassifying the collections after nearly a century of reliance on the classification scheme Thomas Jefferson provided to the library along with his books. Young also inaugurated what today is one of the Library's best known national activities: library service for the blind and physically handicapped. In November 1897, the library began a program of daily readings for the blind in a special "pavilion for the blind" complete with its own library. In 1913, Congress stipulated the deposit in the library of the embossed books produced by the American Printing House for the Blind, and in 1931 a separate appropriation was authorized for providing books for the use of adult blind residents of the United States.

Herbert Putnam, Young's successor, was appointed by President McKinley in the spring of 1899 and served as Librarian of Congress for 40 years, until the autumn of 1939 (see Fig. 3 for a photograph of Putnam in 1900). Asked to characterize the Library as he neared the end of his long career, Putnam penned the phrase "Universal in Scope: National in Service." If Spofford's major contributions were the creation of a national collection and obtaining the building, Putnam was the librarian who did the most to extend the library to the American people. He created a systematic program of widespread public use that exists to this day, opening up the collections to scholars, the public, and other libraries. The first experienced librarian to serve as Librarian of Congress, Putnam established a working partnership between the Library of Congress and the American library movement. Rather than serving merely as a great national accumulation of books, a national library should, he believed, actively serve other libraries, as well as researchers and scholars.

In the quarter century before Putnam took office, a new structure of scientific and scholarly activity had evolved rapidly in the United States. Professional schools and new universities offering graduate work were established; numerous professional associations and societies came into existence; and the federal government became an active supporter of education, research, and scientific activity. By 1900, the age of the great library had arrived in America, characterized by huge book stacks, scientific cataloging and classification, and full-time professional staffs. The library's new building symbolized this age and, as the first American library to reach 1 million volumes, the Library of Congress became the leader among American libraries. Putnam's imaginative and decisive actions were approved by both the Joint Library Committee and the professional library community. Under his leadership, in 1901, the first volume of a completely new classification scheme, based on the Library's own collections, was published; access to the Library was extended to "scientific investigators and duly qualified individuals" throughout the United States; an interlibrary loan service

(a)   (b)

Fig. 3 (a) Herbert Putnam, Librarian of Congress from 1899 to 1939, organized the library's collections and services in the Jefferson Building and initiated bibliographic and loan services to libraries. This photographic portrait by Frances Benjamin Johnson was taken in 1900. (b) Librarian Putnam with young readers in the Main Reading Room of the Library of Congress about 1910.
Photo credit: Library of Congress.

Library Automation–Library Publishing

was inaugurated; and the sale and distribution of Library of Congress printed catalog cards began.

The interlibrary loan system was an especially radical step, for it signaled the institution's transition from a national storehouse of books to a national laboratory for promoting the use of its collections. It required special legislation by Congress and approval was by no means assured. When asked to defend his position that books should be sent outside the District of Columbia, the Librarian explained that the risk was justified because "a book used, is after all, fulfilling a higher mission than a book which is merely being preserved for possible future use."[9] It was a telling statement about the openness of American libraries and the spirit of cooperation that would weld them into a strong community. Moreover, Librarian Putnam's extension of the Library's classification and cataloging schemes to the rest of the nation helped "democratize" knowledge, nationally and internationally. It established bibliographic standards and encouraged cooperative endeavors among librarians and scholars. This sharing of the Library's "bibliographic apparatus," as Putnam called it, helped to systematize and communicate information about intellectual activity in America and propelled the Library of Congress into a position of international leadership among research institutions.

The development of the Library's collections into a nationally useful resource took many forms. To aid historical research, Putnam felt that the national library "should be able to offer original sources" about the national life. In 1903, he persuaded his friend and supporter, President Theodore Roosevelt, to issue an executive order that transferred the papers of many of the nation's founding fathers, including George Washington, Thomas Jefferson, and James Madison, from the State Department archives to the library's Manuscript Division. In 1904, the Library began publishing important historical texts from its collections, such as the *Journals of the Continental Congress*. Putnam felt the publication of such manuscripts was "not perhaps so much a service from us as a library as a duty from us as the custodians of original sources for American history."[10]

As American influence and interests continued to expand in the twentieth century, Putnam looked abroad to build the Library's collections, boldly applying Jefferson's dictum that no subject was beyond the possible concern of Congress or the American people. The librarian was especially farsighted in acquiring research materials about other countries and cultures. In 1904, he purchased a 4000-volume library of Indica, explaining in the library's annual report that he "could not ignore the opportunity to acquire a unique collection which scholarship thought worthy of prolonged, scientific, and enthusiastic research, even though the immediate use of such a collection may prove meager."[11] In 1906, he acquired the famous 80,000-volume private library of Russian literature owned by G. V. Yudin of Siberia, even sending a staff member to Russia to supervise the packing and shipping

of the books. The Schatz collection of early opera librettos was purchased from a German collector in 1908. Large and important collections of Hebraica, as well as Chinese and Japanese books, were also acquired. By 1926, the Library had obtained appropriated funds to send a permanent representative to Europe, stationed in Paris, to assist with acquisitions by developing contacts with dealers, collectors, scholars, and learned institutions.

In one notable instance, Congress took the initiative in building the Library's collections. In December 1929, despite the stock market crash 2 months earlier, Congressman Ross Collins of Mississippi proposed the purchase for $1.5 million of the 3000-volume collection of early books assembled by collector Otto F. Vollbehr, which included one of three perfect existing vellum copies of the Gutenberg Bible. Congressman Albert Johnson of Washington, in the debate in the House of Representatives, maintained that "even if times are hard," Congress should purchase the collection because "it is all for the United States of America which is going to live we hope for thousands of years." Testifying before the Senate Library Committee, Putnam added his endorsement to the enthusiasm expressed by the House of Representatives. He reminded the committee that in 1815, the government paid Thomas Jefferson nearly $24,000 for his library, and "in proportion to the resources of the country that sum was not much short of the million and a half" asked for the Vollbehr collection. Moreover, "what was true of that purchase is certainly true of the one before you. It would form "a most admirable substratum for a (greater) national library."[12] The purchase was approved in 1930.

The Library's foremost function—support for legislative activities—was strengthened in 1914 when the Legislative Reference Service was established as a separate administrative unit. Its creation was a natural development in the Progressive era, when many people in business and public life advocated the "scientific" (and Jeffersonian) use of information to solve problems. Specialized library units for legislative research were established in several states, notably Wisconsin, during the first decade of the 1900s. Putnam responded to this movement and to hearings held by Congress under the leadership of Representative John M. Nelson and Senator Robert M. LaFollette of Wisconsin by creating the library's own Legislative Reference Service in 1914. The next year, he reported that the new service was anticipating questions from Congress on conservation bills, the merchant marine, the government of the Philippines, immigration, convict-made goods, railroad securities, federal aid in road making, publicity in campaign contributions, and a national budget system.

The Library as a Cultural Institution

While enhancing established functions Putnam also moved the library in new directions. The Library of

Library Automation–Library Publishing

Congress Trust Fund Board Act of 1925, which enabled the institution to accept gifts and bequests from private citizens, was the major vehicle for the librarian's innovations. This legislation, which created a new cultural role for the library, was inspired by a proposal from private citizen, Elizabeth Sprague Coolidge. She offered an endowment to the library for promoting the appreciation and understanding of music, and to pay for a concert hall within the library building that would support the commissioning of new works of music and provide the chief of the Music Division with a generous honorarium. Prominent individuals such as James B. Wilbur, Archer Huntington, John D. Rockefeller, Gertrude Clarke Whittall, and many others soon joined Mrs. Coolidge as Library of Congress benefactors. In particular, Gertrude Clarke Whittall's donation of five Stradivari instruments and the funding for concerts at which they could be played helped establish the library as a patron of the arts. This new private funding through the Trust Fund allowed the Library to establish chairs and consultantships for scholars and a consultantship for poetry, which by 1986 had evolved into the Poet Laureate Consultant in Poetry.

Putnam was careful in defining the use of the support the library received through the Trust Fund. Private funds were to serve a limited role and were intended to supplement, not replace, the annual government appropriation. His vision for the Library's cultural and educational role and its development established the precedent for the valuable private sector support that the Library of Congress receives today.

Putnam embraced the library's symbolic role as a cradle of Jeffersonian democracy in 1921, when he arranged for the nation's two most precious documents—the Declaration of Independence and the Constitution—to be transferred to the library from the State Department. In 1924, the documents went on permanent public display in a specially designed "Shrine" in the library's Great Hall. The library transferred both documents to the National Archives in 1952. The Library of Congress still holds, as one of its greatest treasures, Jefferson's handwritten draft of the Declaration of Independence. In his book *The Epic of America*, published in 1931, historian James Truslow Adams paid tribute to the Library of Congress "as a symbol of what democracy can accomplish on its own behalf ... founded and built by the people, it is for the people."[13]

The rapid expansion of the Library's collections and services during Putnam's 40 years as Librarian naturally required increased space. Additional book stacks within the Jefferson Building were built in 1910 and 1927. Legislation to acquire land for a new structure was approved in 1928, and the Annex Building (today the Adams Building) was authorized in 1930. Construction was delayed during the Depression years, but the classically simple, rectangular structure, chiefly intended for book storage, was completed in 1938 and opened to the public in 1939.

The Library of Congress as a democratic institution and repository of American cultural traditions was a concept that captured the imagination of Putnam's successor, writer, lawyer, and poet Archibald MacLeish. Appointed by President Franklin Roosevelt in 1939, MacLeish served as Librarian of Congress until the end of 1944, when he became assistant secretary of state. An advocate of U.S. involvement in World War II, MacLeish used the office of Librarian of Congress imaginatively to speak out on behalf of democracy. He urged librarians to become "active agents" of the democratic process, and criticized his fellow intellectuals for their failure to defend American culture against the threat of totalitarianism. He became the most publicly visible Librarian of Congress in the history of the office.

Paying tribute to Jefferson's concept of liberty and self-government, in 1941 Librarian MacLeish dedicated the South Reading Room in the Adams Building to the library's principal founder. At MacLeish's request, artist Ezra Winter decorated the Jefferson Reading Room with four murals that drew their themes from quotations from Jefferson on the subjects of freedom, labor, the "living generation," education, and democratic government. MacLeish also established a "democracy alcove" in the Main Reading Room, where readers could find "the classic texts of the American tradition," including the Declaration of Independence, the Constitution, the Federalist Papers, and other writings of American statesmen. When in 1943, the Library commemorated the bicentennial of Jefferson's birth, MacLeish noted that "if ever a library had a single founder, Thomas Jefferson was the single founder of the Library of Congress."[14] An annotated catalog of the books in Jefferson's personal library by bibliographer E. Millicent Sowerby was undertaken (it was published in five volumes between 1952 and 1959), and the library started microfilming its collection of Jefferson papers in the same year.

Thanks to MacLeish's personal interests and contacts, during his librarianship the Library of Congress established new and enduring relationships with American writers and scholars. Other highlights of the fruitful MacLeish years were the development of Library-wide objectives; an administrative reorganization so thorough that it lasted for more than three decades; the creation of a rotating consultantship in poetry; and fellowship programs for young scholars. The librarian extended Jefferson's rationale to foreign materials, asserting, in his "Canons of Selection" in the 1940 *Annual Report*, that the library should acquire the "written records of those societies and peoples whose experience is of most immediate concern to the people of the United States."[15] Indeed, World War II's most important effect on the Library was to stimulate further development of its collections about other nations.

Library Automation–Library Publishing

Postwar Expansion

Librarian MacLeish resigned in 1944 and, in 1945, President Truman named assistant librarian Luther H. Evans, a political scientist, as Librarian of Congress. Evans served until 1953. To justify his ambitious proposals in fiscal year 1947 to expand the Library's collections and services, Evans emphasized Jefferson's "doctrine of completeness and inclusiveness." The challenges of the postwar years meant, to Evans, that "no spot on the earth's surface is any longer alien to the interest of the American people." He believed that the major lesson of World War II was that "however large our collections may now be, they are pitifully and tragically small in comparison with the demands of the nation." He described the need for larger collections of foreign research materials in practical, patriotic terms, noting that in the years leading up to the war "the want of early issues of the *Voelkische Boebachter* prevented the first auguries of Naziism," whereas during the war, weather data on the Himalayas from the Library's collections helped the Air Force.[16]

The acquisitions, cataloging, and bibliographic services of the Library grew during the Evans years, but not as rapidly as the librarian would have liked. He believed that the Library of Congress should actively serve all libraries, but an economy-minded postwar Congress balked at his expansionist plans. Evans's leadership and energy helped to compensate for the lack of large budget increases, however. His strong personal interest in issues such as copyright and intellectual freedom strengthened the Library's involvement in each of these areas.

A new Library of Congress commitment to international librarianship and cultural affairs was one of Evans's major contributions. The Library of Congress Mission in Europe, organized by Evans and director of acquisitions Verner W. Clapp in 1945, acquired European publications for the Library and for other American libraries. The library soon initiated automatic book purchase agreements with foreign dealers around the world and greatly expanded its agreements for the international exchange of official publications. It organized a reference library in San Francisco in 1945 to assist the participants in the meeting that established the United Nations. In 1947, a Library of Congress Mission to Japan provided advice for the establishment of the National Diet Library.

Evans's successor as Librarian of Congress was L. Quincy Mumford, who was director of the Cleveland Public Library in 1954, when President Eisenhower nominated him. During his 20 years in office, Mumford guided the Library through its most intensive period of national and international expansion. In the 1960s, the Library of Congress benefited from increased federal funding for education, libraries, and research. Most dramatic was the growth of the foreign acquisitions program, an expansion based on Evans's achievements a decade earlier. In 1958, the library was authorized by Congress to acquire books by using U.S.-owned foreign currency under the terms of the Agricultural Trade Development and Assistance Act of 1954 (PL 480). The first appropriation for this purpose was made in 1961. The next year the library established acquisitions centers in New Delhi and Cairo to purchase publications and distribute them to research libraries throughout the United States. This, however, was only the first step.

In 1965, President Lyndon B. Johnson approved a Higher Education Act, which, through its Title IIC, directed the Library of Congress to acquire, insofar as possible, all current library materials of value to scholarship published throughout the world, and to provide cataloging information for these materials promptly after they had been received. This law came closer than any other legislation to making Jefferson's concept of comprehensiveness part of the Library's official mandate. The new effort was christened the National Program for Acquisitions and Cataloging (NPAC). The first NPAC office was opened in London in 1966 and expanded rapidly. By the end of the twentieth century, the library had six overseas offices, as well as cooperative acquisitions arrangements with booksellers and libraries around the world.

Shared acquisitions and cataloging made international bibliographic standards imperative. The crucial development took place in the mid-1960s: the creation of the Library of Congress Machine-Readable Cataloging (MARC) format for communicating bibliographic data in machine-readable form. This new capability for converting, maintaining, and distributing bibliographic information soon became the standard format for sharing data about books and other research materials. The potential for worldwide application was immediately recognized, and the MARC format structure became an official national standard in 1971 and an international standard in 1973.

The preservation and conservation of library collections became an important concern of research libraries in the 1960s. In 1967, the Library of Congress inaugurated a pilot project to study techniques for the preservation of deteriorating or "brittle" books—volumes disintegrating because they were printed on acidic paper. Today, the Library's Preservation Office administers what has become the world's largest library research and conservation laboratory and shares techniques with the library community.

Amid the rapid growth of collections, computer and preservation methods, there took place the most recent serious public debate about the dual legislative and national roles of the Library of Congress. The Library of Congress has played a leadership role in the American library community since 1901; however, its first responsibility, as part of the legislative branch of the American government, always has been to support the reference and research needs of the American national legislature.

Library Automation–Library Publishing

The National Library Debate

In 1962, at the request of Senator Claiborne Pell of the Joint Library Committee, Douglas Bryant, associate director of the Harvard University Library, prepared a memorandum on "what the Library of Congress does and ought to do for the Government and the Nation generally." Bryant urged further expansion of the library's national activities and services, proposals endorsed by many professional librarians, and suggested several organizational changes. He also said it would be "desirable" to transfer the Library to the executive branch of government. Mumford replied to the Bryant memorandum in his 1962 annual report, strongly defending the Library's position in the legislative branch and stating his opposition to the suggestion that the Library's name might be altered to reflect its national role: "The Library of Congress is a venerable institution, with a proud history, and to change its name would do unspeakable violence to tradition."[17]

The debate continued in the professional library community. The fiscal retrenchments of the 1970s and Congressional reemphasis on the library's legislative services under the provisions of the Legislative Reorganization Act of 1970 made increased national library aspirations impractical. The new law changed the name of the Legislative Reference Service to the Congressional Research Service and expanded its functions, placing increased emphasis on policy research and analysis and on direct services to both individual members of Congress and congressional committees.

Before he retired in 1974, Librarian Mumford witnessed the authorization by Congress of the construction of a third Library of Congress Building and, in 1971, the beginning of its construction. In 1975, President Gerald R. Ford nominated historian Daniel J. Boorstin, previous director of the Smithsonian Institution's National Museum of History and Technology (now the National Museum of American History), to be the twelfth Librarian of Congress. Boorstin was confirmed by the Senate and took the oath of office on November 12, 1975, in a ceremony in the Library's Great Hall.

Reorganization and New Technology

Boorstin immediately faced two major challenges: the need to review the Library's organization and functions and, pending the forthcoming expansion into the James Madison Memorial Building, the lack of space for both collections and staff. In 1976, he created a Task Force on Goals, Organization, and Planning, a staff group that conducted, with help from outside advisers, a 1-year review of the Library and its role. Many of the task force's recommendations were incorporated into a subsequent reorganization. The move into the Madison Building, which began in 1980 and was completed in 1982, relieved administrative as well as physical pressures, and enabled

Librarian Boorstin to focus on what he deemed most important: the strengthening of the Library's ties to Congress, and the development of new relationships between the Library and scholars, authors, publishers, cultural leaders, and the business community.

The Library of Congress grew steadily during Boorstin's administration, with its annual appropriation increasing from $116 million in 1975 to more than $250 million in 1987, even though budget restrictions slowed growth severely in 1985 and 1986. Similar to MacLeish, Boorstin relied heavily on his professional staff in technical areas such as cataloging, automation, and preservation of library materials. However he took a keen personal interest in collection development, copyright, in book and reading promotion, in the role of the Library of Congress in American life, both in practical terms and symbolically, and in the library as "the world's greatest Multi-Media Encyclopedia." Boorstin's style and accomplishments increased the visibility of the library to a point where, in January 1987, a *New York Times* reporter, discussing Boorstin's decision to retire as librarian, called the post of Librarian of Congress "perhaps the leading intellectual public position in the nation."[18]

Boorstin's successor, historian James H. Billington, was nominated by President Reagan and took the oath of office as the thirteenth Librarian of Congress on September 14, 1987. Billington instituted his own 1-year review of the library's functions through an internal Management and Planning (MAP) Committee, a review that also included regional forums in nine cities. The result was a major administrative reorganization based on goals identified through the MAP study. Convinced that the Library of Congress needed to share its resources more widely throughout the nation, he instituted several projects to test new technologies that might provide for direct access by libraries and schools to the library's collections and data bases. The experimental American Memory project, for example, provided electronic copies of selected collections of American history and culture to schools and libraries. A 2-year pilot project providing online access to the library to the 50 state library agencies began in 1991.

Envisioning a new educational role for the Library, Billington began strengthening the library's cultural programs and established its first Educational Office. Recognition of the crucial importance of private funds in building and sustaining national outreach projects led to the creation of a Development Office in 1988, and the establishment, in 1990, of the James Madison Council, a private sector support body consisting mostly of business executives and entrepreneurs. In fiscal 1991, Billington obtained a 12% budget increase for the library to help make its collections more accessible. In 1992, however, in response to a series of thefts and discoveries of vandalism, the library was forced to undertake new security measures that restricted access to the collections.

Library Automation–Library Publishing

In his budget presentation to Congress for fiscal year 1993, Billington emphasized how the Library of Congress was becoming an important catalyst for the educational, competitive, and creative needs of our nation. The complexities of the information age were most apparent in the librarian's discussion of new electronic technology. This new technology should, Billington stated, be applied to a Jeffersonian purpose, enabling the library to "increase the knowledge available to Americans in their local communities—in schools, colleges, libraries, and private sector research enterprises, from Florida to Alaska." Thus, "even those Americans far from great universities and the most affluent schools and libraries can still have access to the best of the nation's heritage and the latest in up-to-date information." Technology makes this possible; the library's strategy envisions bringing an "electronic library rapidly from concept into initial operation."[19]

In 1994, the Library made its bibliographic records and selected items from its Americana collections available electronically, and the institution began establishing what is now a multitiered presence on the World Wide Web. The same year Congress approved the Library's 5-year National Digital Library (NDL) program. Through a combination of private and government funding, the NDL program began digitizing historical materials from more than 70 American history and culture collections in the Library and collecting them from 33 other research institutions. The program made those digital collections available, free of charge, on the library's American Memory Web site.

Thus began a new era in service and accessibility to the library's collections. The library increasingly became a leader among large institutions making collections freely available via the World Wide Web. Its Web site, with sections devoted to its own collections, catalogs, and online exhibitions, as well as to legislation from Congress and information from the U.S. Copyright Office, has become one of the most frequently used in the world.

The Library of Congress at 2000

In testimony before Congress in January 2000, Billington told the legislative branch appropriations subcommittee that the Library of Congress had become a leading—if not the leading—provider of high-quality, free educational material in the revolutionary new world of the Internet.[20] Moreover, a National Academy of Sciences report about the library's role in the electronic age, *LC21: A Digital Strategy for the Library of Congress*, commissioned by Billington in 1998 and released in July 2000, called on the library to greatly increase its resources and leadership capabilities to develop a digital strategy for the next century. The librarian accepted the report's conclusion and soon obtained additional appropriations for its implementation.

A historian of Russian culture, Librarian Billington took a special interest in using the library and its resources to encourage the development of democracy in Russia and in Central and Eastern Europe after the collapse of Communism in the early 1990s. Congressionally approved projects included a parliamentary assistance program for Central and Eastern Europe (1990–1996) and, beginning in 1999, the Russian Leadership Program to bring young Russian civic, political, and professional leaders to the United States to observe American democracy and business firsthand.

The Library of Congress commemorated its Bicentennial throughout 2000. The Bicentennial Steering Committee chose "Libraries-Creativity-Liberty" as the major theme because it encompassed the library's ambition to promote creativity in the preservation, organization, and sharing of recorded knowledge as well as the key role all libraries play in connecting knowledge and information to citizenship in a democracy.

Major bicentennial projects looked to the library's future. They included: 1) "Gifts to the Nation," a high-visibility, privately supported initiative to acquire for the library's collections significant items identified by its curators and specialists. Thanks in large measure to support from the library's James Madison Council, "Gifts to the Nation" resulted in 384 separate gifts totaling $109.8 million; 2) the launching, with a $1 million gift from Madison Council members, of a project to reconstruct Thomas Jefferson's personal library; 3) the honoring, as Library of Congress "Living Legends," of 84 individuals selected for their significant creative contributions to American life; 4) "Local Legacies," a grassroots initiative developed through congressional offices and local organizations that documented America's cultural heritage at the turn of the millennium; and 5) on April 24, 2000 (the library's 200th birthday), the launching of "America's Library," a new Web site for children and families. As 2000 came to a close, Librarian Billington made two additional announcements: the library had achieved its bicentennial goal of mounting 5 million digital items on its American Memory Web site, and the Madison Council chairman John W. Kluge's gift to the bicentennial was an unprecedented gift of $60 million to establish a Kluge Center for Scholars and a Kluge Prize in the Human Sciences.

PERSPECTIVES ON THE LIBRARY'S DEVELOPMENT, 1800–2000

The Library's Legislative and National Roles

The library's initial organization act of 1802 gave the president the authority to appoint the Librarian of Congress—even though the library was a legislative branch agency. The Congress did not vote itself the power to confirm the president's choice as Librarian of Congress

Library Automation–Library Publishing

until 1897, on the verge of the move into the library's first building. There is no fixed term for a Librarian of Congress, but when the Senate gained the power to confirm the president's choice in 1897, a "balance" was struck; since then—when the office of librarian also gained the considerable power and independence it holds today—in effect the job has become a lifetime appointment.

The legislative and national functions of the Library of Congress are truly "dual" only in the sense that direct services to Congress receive priority. In all other respects, the legislative and national functions are each inherent parts of the Library's fabric. In 1962, in his response to the Bryant memorandum, Librarian of Congress L. Quincy Mumford (1954–1974) observed, accurately, that Congress had "recognized the national responsibilities of the Library in a way that matters most—with understanding and consistent support."[21] Historically the pattern has been for the library to grow in stages, often with legislative and national functions alternating in emphasis. Naturally there also have been periods of retrenchment, but on the whole the expansion of the institution has been remarkably steady.

The Library of Congress and American Librarianship

The Library of Congress did not provide direct services to the library community until after its first building opened in 1897 and until the administration of Librarian of Congress Herbert Putnam (1899–1939). Under Putnam's leadership, however, libraries and librarians became a major Library of Congress constituency—second in importance only to Congress itself.

Through the years, the relationship between the library and the American library community—while close—has not been necessarily close-knit and at times both rocky and controversial. In the digital age, the relationship has changed radically since librarians across the country no longer need to rely on centralized technical services from the Library of Congress—as they did from the first decade of the twentieth century until near the end of the century. From the 1980s onwards, other libraries increasingly drew on other massive databases for bibliographic information and began to access collections directly on the World Wide Web; the Library of Congress remained an enormously important supplier of bibliographic data, but it was much less the acknowledged leader of the American library community than it was in the first half of the century.

The International Role of the Library of Congress

World War II not only stimulated the growth of the library's international collections, but also a new international role for the institution, one first fully envisioned by Luther H. Evans, Librarian of Congress,1945–1953. As

the twentieth century came to a close, it was clear that the Library's international activities were increasing, not only for the benefit of libraries but also for Congress, the nation, and institutions around the world. New electronic resources began to make it easier to share the institution's unparalleled international collections. Moreover, a world role for the Library of Congress was advocated by the two scholarly public servants who served as Librarian of Congress during the last 25 years of the century: historians Daniel J. Boorstin (1975–1987) and James H. Billington (1987–).

For Boorstin, the evolution of the Library's international role was natural:

> Our country has been peopled with immigrants from all over the world. How could we pretend to make a truly national library for our United States unless we collected in the languages that millions spoke when they arrived—and still arrive on our shores? In the United States, of all the nations on earth, our *national* library (like our people) must be *international*.[22]

Billington, in a booklet published to accompany a new exhibit, *World Treasures of the Library of Congress*, echoed the theme:

> We at the Library of Congress are as proud of our international collections as we are of our American collections ... The Library of Congress is the largest and most inclusive library in the world, and it is truly an international institution.[23]

The Library's Educational Role

In the mid-1990s, Librarian of Congress Billington began advocating a new educational role for the library, one that would take full advantage of the institution's new presence on the World Wide Web and the success of the Library's National Digital Library program—which Congress endorsed and supported.

At the beginning of a new century, when the interdependence and complementarity of all types of educational and cultural institutions is increasingly recognized, Billington's efforts to exploit new electronic technologies and educational partnerships, governmental and private, indeed pointed to a greatly enhanced educational role for the Library of Congress in the century ahead.

Librarian Billington's determination to extend the reach and influence of the Library of Congress is very much in the ambitious tradition of his predecessors. Alone among the world's great libraries, the Library of Congress still attempts to be a universal library, collecting materials of research value in almost all languages and media. It continues to be guided by Thomas Jefferson's belief that

Library Automation–Library Publishing

democracy depends on knowledge and that all topics are important to the library of the American national legislature and therefore to the American people and indeed to all people.

REFERENCES

1. Ranganathan, S.R. The Library of Congress among national libraries. ALA Bull. **1950**, *44*, 356.

2. *Annual Report of the Librarian of Congress for the Fiscal Year Ending September 30, 2007*; Library of Congress: Washington, DC, 2008, VIII.

3. Billington, J.H. Testimony before U.S. Congress, January 26, 2000. In *Annual Report of the Librarian of Congress for the Fiscal Year Ending September 30, 2000*; Library of Congress: Washington, DC, 2001; 241.

4. *Annual Report of the Librarian of Congress for the Fiscal Year Ending September 30, 2007*; Library of Congress: Washington, DC, 2008; VIII–IX.

5. Cole, J.Y. *For Congress and the Nation: A Chronological History of the Library of Congress*; Library of Congress: Washington, DC, 1993; 9.

6. Spofford, A.R. The Government Library at Washington. Int. Rev. **1878**, *5*, 769.

7. Cole, J.Y. LC and ALA, 1876–1901. Libr. J. **1973**, *98*, 2967.

8. Cole, J.Y. *For Congress and the Nation: A Chronological History of the Library of Congress*; Library of Congress: Washington, DC, 1979; 62–63.

9. Putnam, H. The Library of Congress as the national library. Libr. J. **1905**, *30*, C30.

10. Putnam, H. The relation of the national library to historical research in the U.S. In *American Historical Association Annual Report for 1901*; Government Printing Office: Washington, DC, 1902; 120.

11. *Report of the Librarian of Congress for the Fiscal Year Ending June 30, 1904*; Government Printing Office: Washington, DC, 1904; 30.

12. Cole, J.Y. *For Congress and the Nation: A Chronological History of the Library of Congress*; Library of Congress: Washington, DC, 1979; 97.

13. Adams, J.T. *The Epic of America*; Garden City Books: New York, 1931; 325.

14. MacLeish, A. *The Jefferson Bicentennial, 1743–1943: A Catalogue of the Exhibitions in the Library of Congress*; U.S. Government Printing House: Washington, DC, 1943; 1.

15. *Annual Report of the Librarian of Congress for Fiscal Year Ended June 30, 1940*; U.S. Government Printing Office: Washington, DC, 1941; 24–26.

16. Evans, L.H. *Library of Congress Records a New Era of World Progress*; The Sunday Star: Washington, DC, December 2, 1945.

17. *Annual Report of the Librarian of Congress for the Fiscal Year Ending June 30, 1962*; Library of Congress: Washington, DC, 1963; 95.

18. Cole, J.Y. *Jefferson's Legacy: A Brief History of the Library of Congress*; Library of Congress: Washington, DC, 1993; 40.

19. Billington, J.H. Libr. Congr. Inform. Bull. **1993**, *52*, 91.

20. *Annual Report of the Librarian of Congress for the Fiscal Year Ending September 30, 2000*; Library of Congress: Washington, DC, 2001; 241.

21. *Annual Report of the Librarian of Congress for the Fiscal year Ending June 30, 1962*; Library of Congress: Washington, DC, 1963; 96.

22. Boorstin, D.J. Foreword. In *Treasures of the Library of Congress*; Goodrum, C., Ed.; Harry N. Abrams, Publishers: New York, 1980; 18.

23. Billington, J.H. Foreword. In *Beginnings: World Treasures of the Library of Congress*; Library of Congress: Washington, DC, 2002; 8.

BIBLIOGRAPHY

1. Conaway, J. *America's Library: The Story of the Library of Congress*; Yale University Press: New Haven, CI, 2000.

2. *Encyclopedia of the Library of Congress: For Congress, the Nation, and the World*; Cole, J.Y., Aikin, J., Eds.; Bernan Press: Lanham, MD, 2004.

3. Johnston, W.D. *History of the Library of Congress, 1800–1864, Volume I, 1800–1864*; Government Printing Office: Washington, DC, 1904.

4. Ostrowski, C. *Books, Maps, and Politics: A Cultural History of the Library of Congress, 1783–1861*; University of Massachusetts Press: Amherst, MA, 2004.

5. Rosenberg, J.A. *The Nation's Great Library: Herbert Putnam and the Library of Congress, 1899–1939*; University of Illinois Press: Urbana, IL, 1993.

6. *Special Collections of the Library of Congress: A Selected Guide*; Melville, A., Eds.; Comp. Library of Congress-Washington, DC, 1980.

7. *The Library of Congress in Perspective: A Volume Based on the Reports of the 1976 Librarian's Task Force and Advisory Groups*; Cole, J.Y., Eds.; R.R. Bowker Co.New York, 1976.

8. *The Library of Congress: The Art and Architecture of the Thomas Jefferson Building*; Cole, J.Y.; Reed, H.H., Eds.; W.W. NortonNew York, 1997.

9. Wills, G. Introduction. In *American Treasures of the Library of Congress: Memory/Reason/Imagination*; Harry Abrams: New York, 1997.

Library Portals and Gateways

Frank Cervone
Purdue University Calumet, Hammond, Indiana, U.S.A.

Abstract

Libraries have had web presences since the introduction of the World Wide Web. Providing access to information provided by the library has been attempted through various means throughout the years but no method has been as popular or pervasive as the uses of library gateways and portals. Development of gateways and portals in libraries has been affected by many factors many of which have been outside the direct control of libraries or librarians. Both the history of library practice in this area and these external factors have had a substantial impact on the state of library portal and gateway development today.

INTRODUCTION

In standard English, the literal meaning of "gateway" is a passage that is or may be closed by a gate.[1] In architecture, a portal refers to a door or gateway usually of stately or elaborate construction. In the early- and mid-twentieth century, an obsolete meaning of portal[2] was rejuvenated by science fiction writers to describe the concept of transference from one place to another via technological, and sometimes mysterious, means. From the complex intersection of these various definitions, the use of both gateway and portal within the information professions has developed to signify some type of single point of entry to a world of information resources.

Ever since the introduction of library Web sites in the early 1990s, the understanding of what a gateway is has remained fairly constant. In contrast, what constitutes a portal has progressively evolved in the relatively short period of time that libraries have been providing services via the Internet. In the early days of the World Wide Web (1994–1998), portal and gateway were used interchangeably. Both were used to refer to any Web site that provided some type of organized access to resources on the web.

As technology has developed, the use of these terms has diverged and both terms have become more specific. Current usage of gateway refines the original meaning to specifically refer to a Web site that attempts to present an end user with a comprehensive and related set of resources associated with a distinct subject area. This is in contrast to a portal which is a Web site that presents an end user with a comprehensive and related set of resources associated with the specific interests of the individual. Further complicating matters, portal also has a specific, technological meaning derived from its use in computer science. Portal in technological contexts normally refers to the specific technologies used to implement the services which provide customized information to an end user. When used in this sense, the emphasis is on the underlying software that implements the retrieval of information for display rather than the specifics of the information content presented to the end user.

One of the drivers behind library adoption of portal technology has been the desire to build communication mechanisms that mirror the collaborative and interactive use of traditional libraries[3] in the context of Web-based delivery of services. To accomplish this, a portal must provide components that lead a user to a set of information which is customizable to the individual interests of the user while being sensitive to the role of the user within the organization.[4]

Library portals are able to accomplish this through several features and functions. These include:

1. Single user authentication and authorization to resources within the portal.
2. Providing access multiple sources of information.
3. Facilitating a basic level of automated personalization based on the characteristics of the user.
4. Personalizing the selection of resources displays as well as the look-and-feel of the interface.
5. Incorporating a consistent access interface to the diverse information resources available via the portal.[5]

TYPES OF PORTALS

Conceptually, gateways all tend to be similar. The major differentiating factor is their focus. Most gateways in academic libraries are focused on subject or discipline, but gateways in libraries can also be designed for specific user communities (undergrads, engineering students, tweens, seniors, etc.) or by an area of interest such as mystery book club members, community action counsel members, etc.

Library Automation–Library Publishing

Encyclopedia of Library and Information Sciences, Fourth Edition DOI: 10.1081/E-ELIS4-120044562

Copyright © 2017 by Taylor & Francis. All rights reserved.

Portals are much more difficult to classify mainly because portals can be used in a wide variety of contexts and types of organizations. Therefore, different types of portals technologies have developed and each tends to fulfill the information needs of the end users in a different way. Even so, a common thread found in all portal definitions is an understanding that the main goal of a portal is to gather, share, and disseminate information from disparate sources through an easy-to-use, integrated interface.

Sites that serve as a generalized entry point to the Internet for the public, such as Yahoo!®, MSN, and Lycos are often referred to as "horizontal portals" given the broad array of resources and services they provide.[6] While portals of this type may provide individual options for customization, their primary function is to offer generalized services from diverse sources in a single, consistent interface. In addition to search services, this type of portal usually provides an integrated set of standard services such as news feeds, stock market information, entertainment, as well as value-added services such as an e-mail account, chat, instant messaging, and personal calendaring. By combining unique information sources and distinctive sets of services, portals of this type hope to become "sticky" to their users. That is, these sites hope to have significant inherent appeal that promotes a desire in people to repeatedly return to the site. Because of this goal, horizontal portals are usually designed to be "destination sites" that deliberately attempt to keep users within the confines of the portal, interacting with its content, rather than providing "gateway services" that lead to content on other sites.

While most library portals are "public portals" their primary function is to connect people with information regardless of where that information may actually be located. Consequently, library portals often have more in common with "vertical portals," also known as "vortals,"[7] than with horizontal portals. Vortals differ from horizontal portals in that they provide focused content and gateway services for specific, and oftentimes niche, audiences. Given that the content and services of a library portal are typically aimed at a specific community, such as the population of a local governmental jurisdiction, a particular institution, or organization, library portals tend to model the design patterns associated with vortals more so than the models associated with horizontal portals.

Nevertheless regardless of orientation, all of the portal types identified so far can be classified as "information" or "content portals."[8] Portals of this nature have been called "first-generation portals"[9] in an effort to distinguish them from more sophisticated systems such as "knowledge portals" which support the full range of tasks a knowledge worker performs on a day-to-day basis. Many libraries and information agencies have internal portals in the form of a "corporate" or "enterprise portal." These portals are not available to the general public as they provide staff within the organization with operational information and assistance to perform their jobs more effectively.

Traditionally, corporate portals tended to focus on either collaboration support or knowledge work support and were classified as either a "collaboration portal" or "decision processing portal"[10] depending on their primary purpose, but this distinction is fading rapidly. Collaboration portals, not surprisingly, focus on providing groupware tools such as e-mail, threaded discussions, and instant messaging functions as well as access to traditional work products such as reports, meeting minutes, and memos. Decision processing portals focus on providing access and tools that allow for better decision making based on organizational information. In a library, a typical application in a decision processing portal would be data mining tools that could be used against a wide variety of data collected in the library. For example, data mining could be used to discover patterns within circulation data that could be used to inform collection development practices.

A further factor differentiating corporate portals from traditional library portals is that corporate portals often provide life cycle management of corporate records (similar to a repository), auditing tools to provide insight into how the portal is being used, expert directories which are generated based on inferred or explicit declarations of expertise, and other tools to locate knowledge and experts within an organization.[11]

Within this overall environment of portals, the gateways and portals libraries have provided for public use are generally differentiated into three general types:

1. Customizable e-resource portals, primarily focused on providing access to external resources such as commercial databases and full-text products.
2. Integrated web service portals, which also include features such as content alerting services and some collaboration tools, such as reference chat.
3. Metasearch systems that contain portal features.[12]

This differentiation of portal types is reflective of both the development of portal technology as well as the evolution of information gateways within libraries.

Most library portals before 2004 were of the first type, customizable e-resource portals. Although some libraries, such as Cornell University, provided nascent integrated web service portals, the web services were often narrowly focused. For example, the Cornell University's My Library system provided a convenient dashboard of limited services such as a new book request and a content awareness notification for new books in the catalog.[13]

Since 2004, much of the development of portals in libraries has been focused on building integrated resource discovery systems based on metasearching.

Library Automation–Library Publishing

TECHNOLOGY AND STANDARDS USED IN LIBRARY PORTALS

Several technological standards are used within library portals to deliver content and services. Some of these protocols are specific to portals (such as JSR—Java Specification Request—168 and Web Services for Remote Portlets [WSRP]) while others are used in a more broad technological arena. The most essential of these standards for portals include:

- Java Specification Request (JSR) 168—The Java Portlet Specification (JPS) defines a programming model for developing "portlets," the user selectable interface components that are used within a portal for accessing content or services, in the Java programming language. The JPS V1.0 (JSR 168) provides for a basic programming model that includes such things as:
  - *Package formats* for defining methods for combining portlets into a single application that is installed on the portal server.
  - *Portlet data models* which provide mechanisms to the portlet for storing information related to content rendering, session status information, and persistent data.
  - *Portlet modes* which provide a vehicle for a portal to communicate with the portlet and tell it what tasks should be performed to generate content.
  - *Window states* that define the amount of space on a web page that will be permitted for the content generated by the portlet.

Work on providing additional functionality, such as the ability to transform the content of portlet requests and responses on the fly, is ongoing in the development of the successor protocol, JSR 268.[14]

- LDAP—the Lightweight Directory Access Protocol is a protocol for accessing information in directory servers. Most often, these directory servers are used to provide authorization and authentication information for the portal. Information in LDAP is stored hierarchically, in a tree structure, with finer levels of granularity being achieved as one traverses down the tree.[15]
- NCIP—the Circulation Interchange Protocol (Z39.83) defines the transactions required to support circulation activities among library systems. Some of the services supported by the protocol include patron and item inquiry as well as the ability to check-in, check-out, renew, hold, and reserve materials.[16]
- OAI-PMH—the Open Archives Initiative Protocol for Metadata Harvesting is a mechanism for the widespread exchange of metadata between a content provider and a portal. Based on a client/server model, "data providers" are systems that expose the metadata

related to their content whereas "service providers (SPs)" (also known as "harvesters") make requests of the data providers to retrieve (harvest) the metadata related to their collections.[17]

- OpenURL—the OpenURL standard is a syntax for creating metadata and/or identifiers about an information object. OpenURLs are used in place of static URLs to provide the opportunity for the requesting service to provide additional metadata or contextual information at the time of the information request in order to locate the most appropriate resource, given the users' current environmental context. The primary use of this technology in libraries is to direct users to appropriate, accessible copies of materials, given their current patron status and location within the organization (i.e., student, faculty, remote borrower, etc.).[18]
- RSS—defined variously as "RDF Site Summary," "Really Simple Syndication," and "Rich Site Syndication" is an XML-based data format used to publish information about a provider's content. Primarily used to indicate the availability of new content from an information resource, a "feed" or "channel" typically contains either the full text of a data item or content summary information with a link to the full text.[19]
- Shibboleth—is an architecture for federated identity-based authentication and authorization. It provides a mechanism for the secure exchange of information about credentials for users within a group of systems linked together in a common federation. With Shibboleth, single point authentication and authorization can be provided for all users for all services within the federation without each SP having to maintain local user identification and password information for each member of the federation. Based on a client/server model, identity providers (IdPs) in a Shibboleth federation supply user information to SPs who are responsible for interpreting the credentials returned. The SPs use this information to provide access to content as appropriate for the credentials that have been presented.[20]
- SRW/U—The Search/Retrieve via the Web or URL Service protocol builds upon the Z39.50 framework by providing a streamlined, web-based mechanism for searching databases via a standard search and retrieve service. Based on the CQL query language, SRW provides both Simple Object Access Protocol (SOAP) and URL-based request mechanisms through three operations,
  - *Explain*—provides the mechanism for an SRW/U client to retrieve a description of the features and facilities available on an SRU/W server.
  - *Search/retrieve*—allows the client to submit a search request and retrieve the results from the server that match the request.
  - *Scan*—provides the ability of a client to browse an index of terms on a server.

SRU and SRW differ only in the way they are implemented. In SRU, the request to the server is transmitted via a URL using HTTP as the transport mechanism, an architecture known as representational state transfer (REST). The results returned are XML-based, but it is assumed they will be used for display purposes. SRW on the other hand is SOAP-based and both the initial query and the result set are returned as XML data streams. Any available transport mechanism can be used for the request and response. Furthermore, no assumptions are made about the use of the returned result set.[21]

- WSRP—is a protocol designed for interacting with presentation-oriented web services on remote portlets. JSR 168 and WSRP are complementary technologies. In a typical environment, JSR 168 is used to define a portlet application and WSRP is used to define the actual operations of the portlet. This division of labor promotes application portability and therefore is common in environments where Java is not the only language used for building portlets. With operations defined via WSRP, portlet functionality can be harmonized across a diverse application development environment including, e.g., Microsoft's .NET framework.[22]
- Z39.50—was introduced in 1988 as the first network-based transfer protocol for bibliographic information. Based on a client/server model, Z39.50 provides a rich set of operations (such as search, retrieve, sort, and browse) as well as extensive database schemas that cover a wide variety of bibliographic and other data. This extensive functionality allows for great flexibility in searching and retrieving results from remote databases, but it is also one of the major impediments to Z39.50 implementation. Because of the complexity of functionality within Z39.50, vendors offer varying levels of support for the full Z39.50 protocol and no vendor completely supports the entire specification. Nonetheless, use of the Z39.50 protocol is ubiquitous in library automation; however, it is slowly being replaced by newer technologies that are easier to implement, such as SRU/W.

HISTORY OF PORTALS AND GATEWAYS IN LIBRARIES

The conceptual basis of portal functionality can be traced back to the decision support systems (DSS) of the 1970s, which provided support for decision making by staff in specific situations where expert advice was required. In the 1980s, these DSS systems were expanded and enhanced to create executive support systems (ESS) which contained many of the functions now found in portals.[23] By the early 1990s, systems were being considered and prototyped in libraries that would extend ESS-like functionality to

scholarly work. As noted at the time, a "scholar's workstation" would benefit the end user substantially as "errors in transcription of bibliographic citations could be reduced, reference works consulted directly from the workstation, and literature searches conducted and recorded without a trip to the library in some cases" (p. 269).[24]

In 1994, David Filo and Jerry Yang brought Yahoo! online and made it available to a worldwide audience via the Internet.[25] Originally designed as a way to keep track of their personal interests on the Internet, at the time of its introduction it was the first major site to introduce the concept of a gateway by using categorization (and subcategorization) for linking to Internet-based resources. As such, it provided the model for subsequent development of gateway sites.

The quick success of Yahoo! demonstrated the utility of the gateway concept. In October 1994, the Berkeley Public Library Index to the Internet, known today as the Librarians' Internet Index (LII), made its debut on the web, having been migrated from an earlier life as a "gopher" bookmark site.[26] The LII was not originally intended to be a gateway for the general public but as a gateway for librarians who wanted to learn more about resources available on the web. As such, the LII was an important factor in focusing the attention of libraries and librarians on the potential for Internet-based services.

In 1995, an enterprising group of graduate students in the School of Information and Library Studies at the University of Michigan developed the Internet Public Library (IPL) as a mechanism for exploring issues related to libraries, librarians, and librarianship in the newly emerging environment of the Internet.[27] In a model similar to the effect Yahoo! had on Internet gateways in general, the IPL set the course for future development of library gateways.

At the time however, few of the scholarly resources libraries have traditionally collected, such as books and journals, were available via the Internet. Most of what were referred to as "electronic resources" were still delivered on CD-ROM. Consequently, until 1997 most library Web sites functioned more as informational sites describing the resources and services available in the library and less as gateways to scholarly resources.

In 1997, things changed significantly for two reasons. Yahoo! once again introduced a service that had an important effect on expectations about information dissemination. With the introduction of My Yahoo!, many Internet users were introduced to the idea that content could be customized to their particular areas of interest. With the number of Internet users rapidly expanding, customized portals were seen as an ideal technological solution to the problem of meeting the diverse needs of a broad audience. Concurrently, traditional print publishers began to see the great economic potential of providing vast quantities of electronic content, mainly derived from legacy printed materials, to libraries.

Library Automation–Library Publishing

By the end of 1998, with the explosion in the number of Internet sites and the greatly expanded inventory of scholarly databases and full-text resources online, it became increasingly evident that the use of gateways as the sole mechanism for providing guidance to appropriate information resources was being stretched to its limits. As noted in the January 1999 report of the Cornell University Library gateway focus group,

> the Gateway presents networked resources and services but it does nothing to simplify the complexity of today's information scene...users appreciate the richness that the gateway offers for all subjects, but they yearn to have a more personal space. If they cannot 'rearrange the furniture' in the entire system, at least they would like a little corner to themselves where they can dictate how important certain resources are based on their own needs.[28]

Portal technology specifically designed for libraries became available in late 1998 when developers at North Carolina State University (NCSU) released the first version of the "MyLibrary" software. The debut of a portal for library-specific use came at an opportune time. Within a short period of time, libraries at California State Polytechnic at San Luis Obispo, Charlotte Public Library, Cornell University, Los Alamos National Laboratory, Mississippi State University, University of Toronto, University of Utah, University of Washington, and Virginia Commonwealth University (VCU) had all introduced some level of customizable services for their library patrons under the rubric of a "My Library" service, some using the software developed at NCSU, but many developing their own.

However, after this initial flurry of activity, development of library portals floundered[29] due to three different factors. The first was that many libraries hesitated about adopting portal technology due to early reports of less than overwhelming success in capturing the attention of library patrons with portals. In detailing the status of the first-year review of VCU's My Library implementation, the authors of the report noted that only 12% of the active accounts in the system had logged in more than 21 times in the prior 6 months.[30] At the third-year review, VCU reported just slightly 4% of the potential user population was actively using the My Library portal functions.[31] A comparably low level of portal adoption was also report at NCSU[32],[33] and University of Washington.[34] Two of the recurring themes in these reports related to the difficulty people had with customizing the portal to their information needs and the difficulties subject-based categorization created for undergraduates who needed to search across a broad range of material. In 2006, researchers at the University of Illinois at Chicago noted that the difficulty in using discipline-specific portals had not gone away or been alleviated in a substantive manner.[35]

The second factor inhibiting the adoption of portals was linked to work that was being done to position the library catalog as a portal to the Internet. Much of the impetus for this movement can be traced to the "Bicentennial Conference for Bibliographic Control in the New Millennium," were there was a great interest expressed by some segments of the library community in reinvigorating and repurposing the library catalog as a portal to the Internet. Thomas[36] discussed the pros and cons of this approach at the conference, noting that a major issue in transforming the catalog to function as a portal is that while portals are deficient at providing the depth of information a library catalog does, a library catalog does not provide the immediate and extensive coverage a portal does. In effect, the two technologies work to achieve different end results.

The third, and perhaps most influential, factor that inhibited adoption of local portal technology was associated with activities by the Association of Research Libraries (ARL) on what would become known as the "Scholars Portal." In September 1999, ARL and Online Computer Library Center (OCLC) hosted a meeting on strategic issues in academic libraries. From this meeting arose a consensus that libraries were in danger and ran a very real risk of being circumvented by commercial information services. An issue highlighted by the group was that because libraries tend to focus on local solutions, their Web sites do not provide an effective entry point for accessing the broad array of web resources available.[37] Jerry Campbell, then Dean of Libraries at the University of Southern California, was one of the early proponents for the development of a collaborative research library web presence.

To put this idea into practice, a working group (the ARL Scholars Portal working Group) was established in late 2000 with two guiding principles directing the work of the group:

- "First, that access to disparate electronic resources and services can be improved through integration, both within a single institution and across multiple institutions,
- Second, that efforts to effect such integration should leverage work already being carried out in ARL libraries."[38]

To begin the process however, the group had to focus on an initial goal. After discussions, the decision was made to develop a "super discovery tool" that would incorporate results from licensed, commercial content, as well as open access material, drawn from a broad range of subject areas and institutions. In spring 2001, the working group conducted an environmental scan to see if the technology was available to develop the super discovery tool, and after reviewing over 30 products, they determined that it would be possible to implement the initial concept. In

Library Automation–Library Publishing

early 2002, the project made a significant move forward when a core group of libraries (University of Southern California; University of California, San Diego; Dartmouth College; University of Arizona; Arizona State University; Iowa State University; and University of Utah) signed on to the Scholars Portal Project (SPP) and began working with the selected vendor (Fretwell-Downing) to implement the project.

While the final results of the ARL Scholars Portal Project did not meet the initial goals, the importance of the project in terms of library portals was the momentum it gave to the newly emerging concept of "federated search" and the routine integration of services in the web presences of libraries. An example is the formation of the ARL Metalib Portal Implementation Group (ARMPIG) in 2003. This group of ARL libraries (including Boston College; Florida Center for Library Automation; Harvard University; Massachusetts Institute of Technology; Northwestern University; University of Iowa; University of Maryland; University of California, Berkeley; University of California, Davis; and Washington State University among others) had partnered with another vendor (Ex Libris) to implement goals similar to the SPP, but with different software. This diversity of approaches within the ARL community provided a catalyst for much of the creative thinking that emerged on how to further develop library portals using federated search technology as its base.

Additionally, the Library of Congress stepped into the picture through the formation of the Library of Congress Portals Applications Issues Group (LCPAIG). Released in late 2003, the report on portal application functionalities for the Library of Congress[39] was a significant signal to the library community that the concept of a portal based on federated search technology was a reality and something all libraries needed to seriously consider.

In approximately the same time frame, researchers at the Joint Information Systems Committee (JISC) in the United Kingdom were investigating methods for making discipline-based information more accessible in their Subject Portals Project (SPP). The goal of the SPP was to enhance resource discovery by developing a series of collaboratively developed, subject-specific portals focused specifically on the requirements of end users located within the higher education community.[40] By late 2001, the first phase of the project had provided a prototype for combining Z39.50 federated searching with traditional selection processes in three disciplinary areas: social sciences; science, engineering, and technology; and health and life sciences. In early 2004, the second phase of the project came to a close with the launch of the integrated research portal that also now included subject areas in the arts and humanities.[41] Of particular note in this project is its demonstration of the feasibility of collaborative selection across a diverse group of institutions as well as the possibility of combining traditional selection processes found in gateways with federated searching.

By 2005, portals based on federated searching were an accepted, if not universally appreciated, fact of life. Many in the library community were of the opinion that while "the online catalog will continue to function as the principle tool for access control of the library's physical collections, the federated searching portal will ultimately serve as the library's principal web gateway to digital resources."[42]

However, not all were convinced[43] of the viability of federated searching in the long run, noting the problems inherent in the Z39.50 protocol and many issues related to vendor cooperation or lack thereof.

This shift in focus, along with other environmental changes such as the rapid adoption of both Google and Google Scholar[44] for resource discovery as well as the increased adoption of campus-wide portals[45,46] has taken some attention away from library portals as ends unto themselves. Increasingly, libraries view the library web presence, whether a portal or gateway, as just one component of their strategy to meet information needs.[47]

CURRENT ISSUES

The impacts of portals in libraries, if one uses a review of the literature as a basis, reached its peak in the period from 2001 to 2004. Since then, discussion of portals as a distinct subject has declined and there are several factors that undoubtedly have influenced this trend.

One of the most persistent problems is that the library community has never come to an agreement on a single definition of what portal means in the library context. While a common understanding, at least in principle, of gateways has existed since the late 1990s, the same has not been true for portals. For example, when asked to define a portal in 2002, five separate ARL libraries responded with divergent definitions of a portal including

- An environment that fits specific needs.
- An interactive gateway to resources and services.
- A gateway to digital resources and services providing a high level of seamless integration including a feature-rich tool kit that enables use along the entire scholarly communications spectrum.
- Services and tools that facilitate the discovery, retrieval, and management of information from various resources in an integrated fashion while taking into account personalized needs in doing research and creating knowledge.
- A multidimensional scholarly environment.[48]

In the intervening time, no universally accepted, single definition has taken hold.

A further complicating factor is that a review of the literature makes it clear that most library portal efforts have not achieved wide-scale adoption rates. In part, this may be due to the relative lack of resource integration, which is a defining characteristic of a portal. As Detlor and Lewis have observed, "many would argue that most library gateways are not portals at all, but rather collections of irregularly-shaped windows facing out in the same general direction" (p. 89).[49] It has been argued that this perception has taken hold because many library portals have been implemented in such a way that they do not "shield the user from the differences of the target resources or link them together" (p. 113).[50] Detlor and Lewis[51] have argued that because of this, and other deficiencies, library Web sites should not be referred to as portals.

Even if these preceding issues were to be resolved, library portals have been criticized as having the potential to create service gaps among certain segments of patrons. These criticisms are somewhat paradoxical because while a lack of robust personalization and recommendation tools on library portals[52] have been noted as significant deficiencies, Crawford[53] has noted that features such as these can actually create problems and service gap issues for the library patron such as:

- Differential service—because many patrons will not take the time to customize their view of the library portal, they may inadvertently create an environment where they receive less than optimal service because they do not use the portal.
- Solipsism—where the patron receives a biased or otherwise unbalanced profile of the information landscape because their interests have been too narrowly focused or precisely defined.
- Irrelevance—because of low adoption rates, the library portal suffers from neglect and fails to deliver all of the information resources that it should for a particular user.

In spite of these issues and notwithstanding the low adoption rates of library portals, libraries continue to investigate new approaches to providing relevant library resources and services by taking advantage of portal-like features and services but adopting them to new service contexts and technological developments. This shift in focus is being driven by changing patterns of information resource use as well as the realization that some older approaches to information dissemination may no longer be relevant.

This last issue is demonstrated by recent research which indicates that one of the reasons that subject gateways and MyLibrary-like portals are not adopted by undergraduate students is because they do not find them useful. Undergraduate students find Web pages specifically constructed to highlight resources and services for individual courses far more useful than generic subject guides.[54]

Societal forces have affected trends in library science. The shift "to the user as the driving force behind library services, not the Platonic ideals of information organization" (p. 22)[55] has led some libraries to experiment with the integration of library services through portlets into external services such as Facebook and My Space.[56] This is not a surprising development as Strauss noted back in 2002 that "libraries would best serve their users by building portal pages, channels, and cameos rather than portals themselves" (p. 36).[57]

CONCLUSIONS

As has been the case with many other technological developments, a potential downside to further exploration of the possibilities of integrating portal technology into systems developed outside the library is whether libraries have the resources and ability to implement these new services on a wide-scale basis. It has been noted that with "the relative scarcity of professional literature on campus portals, it does not appear that library participation in campus web portals is a primary concern among academic librarians" (p. 156).[58] Yet there is not any conclusive research that explains why this is, so it is not clear if the issue is true lack of interest or some other reason that has not been articulated.

In either case, the long-term viability of extensive local development of portlets and other types of applications of this nature is debatable. Except for projects like the SPP at JISC and the LII, collaboration on portal development has not occurred on a wide-spread basis throughout the information professions. As Campbell has noted, "letting a thousand flowers bloom, it turns out, has always been easier than cultivating a garden" (p. 16).[37] He warned that failure to create collective web presences and services for research could well mean that research libraries would essentially become invisible in the glut of Internet sources. Some would say that this has already occurred with the ubiquitous use of Google and Google Scholar as mechanisms for locating scholarly and reference-level information.

But as Jascó has noted,[59] Google Scholar does not provide a comprehensive level of resource discovery, so there is still a place for developing portal and gateway functionality to meet many information-seeking needs. Because it is evident that the single box search strategy used by Google is popular with scholars, students, and librarians in addition to the general public, development of library-specific portals (as opposed to portlets for use in other applications) will increasingly focus on making finding items simpler by leveraging Web 2.0 technologies and features to provide patrons with functionality to tag items, retrieve items through tag clouds, discover items for additional and further reading, automatically correct spelling mistakes in search terms, suggest alternative search terms, and use more sophisticated mechanisms for serendipitous discovery such as dynamic facet-based browsing.

Library Automation–Library Publishing

REFERENCES

1. *The Oxford English Dictionary*; 2nd Ed.; Oxford University Press: Oxford, 1989; "gateway, *n.*". OED online: Available at http://dictionary.oed.com/cgi/entry/50092955 (accessed December 12, 2007).

2. OED Online. Oxford University Press "portal, *n.*" December 2007. Available at http://dictionary.oed.com/cgi/entry/50184478 (accessed December 12, 2007).

3. Tochtermann, K. A first step toward communication in virtual libraries. *Technical Report*; Center for the Study of Digital Libraries: Texas A&M University. Available at http://www.csdl.tamu.edu/csdl/pubs/klaus/TecRepKlaus.html.

4. Committee on Institutional Cooperation (CIC), *Library Survey on Portals*; 2001; November. Available at http://www.cic.net/groups/LibraryInfoTechDirectors/archive/Report/CICLibrarySurveyonPortals.pdf.

5. Carden, M. Library portals and enterprise portals: Why libraries need to be at the centre of enterprise portal projects. Inform. Serv. Use **2004**, *24*(2004), 171–177.

6. Zirpins, C.; Weinreich, H.; Bartelt, A.; Lamersdorf, W. Advanced concepts for next generation portals Proceedings of the 12th International Workshop on Database and Expert System Applications Munich, Germany September, 3–7, 2001 IEEE: New York, 2001; 501–506.

7. Peek, R. When is a Web site a 'vortal'?. Inform. Today **1999**, *16*(8), 36–37.

8. Dias, C. Corporate portals: A literature review of a new concept in information management. Int. J. Inform. Manage. **2001**, *21*(2001), 269–287.

9. Mack, R.; Ravin, Y.; Byrd, R.J. Knowledge portals and the emerging digital knowledge workplace. IBM Syst. J. **2001**, *40*(4), 925–955.

10. White, C. Using information portals in the enterprise. DM Review Magazine **1999**, [online] April 1999. Available at http://www.dmreview.com/issues/19990401/61–1.html (accessed December 14, 2007).

11. Watson, J.; Fenner, J. Understanding portals: At the core. Inform. Manage. J. **2000**, *34*(3), 18–22.

12. McDonald, R.H. Portals in libraries: An environmental landscape. Bull. Am. Soc. Inform. Sci. Technol. **2004**, *31*(1), 10–11.

13. Cohen, S.; Fereira, J.; Horne, A.; Kibbee, B.; Mistelbauer, H.; Smith, A. MyLibrary: Personalized electronic services in the Cornell University Library. D-Lib Magazine **2000**, *6*(4), [online] Available at http://www.dlib.org/dlib/april00/mistlebauer/04mistlebauer.html (accessed December 1, 2007).

14. http://developers.sun.com/portalserver/reference/techart/jsr 168 (accessed March 21, 2009).

15. http://www.ietf.org/rfc/rfc1777.txt (accessed March 21, 2009).

16. http://www.niso.org/committees/committee_at.html (accessed March 21, 2009).

17. http://www.openarchives.org/pmh/ (accessed March 21, 2009).

18. http://www.niso.org/committees/committee_ax.html (accessed March 21, 2009).

19. http://www.rssboard.org/rss-specification (accessed March 21, 2009).

20. http://shibboleth.internet2.edu/ (accessed March 21, 2009).

21. http://www.loc.gov/standards/sru/ (accessed March 21, 2009).

22. http://www.oasis-open.org/committees/tc_home.php?wg_abbrev=wsrp (accessed March 21, 2009).

23. Watson, H.J.; Rainer, R.K.; Jr.; Koh, C.E. Executive information systems: A framework for development and a survey of current practices. MIS Quart. **1991**, *15*(1), 13–30.

24. Phillips, G.L. Z39.50 and the Scholar's workstation concept. Inform. Technol. Libr. **1992**, *11*(3), 261–270.

25. http://docs.yahoo.com/info/misc/history.html (accessed March 21, 2009).

26. http://lii.org/pub/htdocs/about_history.htm (accessed March 21, 2009).

27. http://www.ipl.org/div/about/timeline2.html (accessed March 21, 2009).

28. Cornell University Library, Library gateway focus group report. 1999; January. Available at http://www.library.cornell.edu/staffweb/GateEval/contents.html (accessed December 15, 2007).

29. Zhou, J. A history of web portals and their development in libraries. Inform. Technol. Libr. **2003**, *22*(3), 119–128.

30. Ghasphery, J.; Ream, D. VCU's My Library: Librarians love it…users? Well, maybe. Inform. Technol. Libr. **2000**, *19*(4), 186–190.

31. Ghaphery, J. My Library at Virginia Commonwealth University: Third Year Evaluation. D-Lib. Magazine **2002**, *8* (7/8), doi:10.1045/july2002-ghaphery (accessed December 17, 2007).

32. Gibbons, S. Building upon the MyLibrary concept to better meet the information needs of college students. D-Lib Magazine **2003**, *9*(3), doi:10.1045/march2003-gibbons (accessed December 17, 2007).

33. Ciccone, K. MyLibrary@NCState: A library portal after five years. J. Libr. Admin. **2005**, *43*(1/2), 19–35.

34. Ward, J.; Hiller, S. Usability testing, interface design, and portals. J. Libr. Admin. **2005**, *43*(1/2), 155–171.

35. Brantley, S.; Armstrong, A.; Lewis, K.M. Usability testing of a customizable library web portal. Coll. Res. Libr. **2006**, *67*(2), 146–163.

36. Thomas, S.E. The catalog as portal to the Internet Proceedings of the Bicentennial Conference on Bibliographic Control in the New Millennium 2001. Available at [online] http://www.loc.gov/catdir/bibcontrol/thomas_paper.html (accessed November 29, 2007).

37. Campbell, J.D. The case for creating a scholars portal to the web: A white paper. Portal: Libraries and the Academy **2001**, *1*(1), 15–21.

38. ARL Scholars Portal Working Group, The association of research libraries ARL scholars portal working group final report, May 2002. J. Libr. Admin. **2005**, *43*(1/2), 189–204.

39. http://www.loc.gov/catdir/lcpaig/portalfunctionalitieslist4-publiccomment1st7–22–03revcomp.pdf (accessed March 21, 2009).

40. Clark, J. Subject portals. Ariadne **2001**, *29*, http://www.ariadne.ac.uk/issue29/clark/intro.html (accessed November 23, 2007).

41. http://www.intute.ac.uk/ (accessed March 21, 2009).

Library Automation–Library Publishing

42. Byrum, J.D. Jr. Online catalogs and library portals in today's information environment. J. Libr. Admin. **2005**, *43* (1/2), 135–154.

43. Phipps, S.E.; Maloney, K. Choices in the paradigm shift: Where next for libraries?. Internet Ref. Ser. Quart. **2005**, *10* (3/4), 103–115.

44. Taylor, S. Google scholar—Friend or foe?. Interlend. Doc. Supply **2007**, *35*(1), 4–6.

45. Sort, J. Campus global. Educ. Q. **2003**, *26*(4), 24–32.

46. Stoffel, B.; Cunningham, J. Library participation in campus web portals: An initial survey. Ref. Ser. Rev. **2005**, *33*(2), 144–160.

47. Farkas, M. Your stuff, their space. Am. Libr. **2007**, *38*(11), 36.

48. Jackson, M. Looking ahead: The future of portals. J. Libr. Admin. **2005**, *43*(1/2), 205–220.

49. Detlor, B.; Lewis, V. Library portals: The impact of the library information environment on information seeking success Proceedings of the American Society for Information Science and Technology 2003 Long Beach, CA October, 19–22, 2003 American Society for Information Science and Technology: Silver Spring, MD, 2004; 84–92.

50. Dempsey, L. The recombinant library: Portals and people. J. Libr. Admin. **2003**, *39*(4), 103–136.

51. Detlor, B.; Lewis, V. Academic library web sites: Current practice and future directions. J. Acad. Libr. **2006**, *32*(3), 251–258.

52. Michalko, J. For whom is the library an anchor? Observations on library portals. J. Libr. Admin. **2003**, *39*(4), 5–17.

53. Crawford, W. Talking 'bout MyLibrary. Am. Libr. **2002**, *33*(4), 91.

54. Nichols, J.; Mellinger, M. Portals for undergraduate subject searching: Are they worth it?. Portal: Libraries and the Academy **2007**, *7*(4), 481–490.

55. Morgan, E.L. Portals in libraries: Portal implementation issues and challenges. Bull. Am. Soc. Inform. Sci. Technol. **2004**, *31*(1), 22–23.

56. Farkas, M. Going where the patrons are. Am. Libr. **2007**, *38*(4), 27.

57. Strauss, H. Library portals: A minority report. Sch. Libr. J. NetConnect **2002**, *2002*(Fall), 34–36.

58. Stoffel, B.; Cunningham, J. Library participation in campus web portals: An initial survey. Ref. Ser. Rev. **2005**, *33*(2), 144–160.

59. Jascó, P. Google scholar: The pros and cons. Online Inf. Rev. **2005**, *29*(2), 208–214.

Library Publishing Initiatives: North America

Katherine Skinner
Sarah Lippincott
Educopia Institute, Atlanta, Georgia, U.S.A.

Abstract

Library publishing refers to the set of services provided by libraries to support the creation, dissemination, and preservation of original content such as eJournals, monographs, scholarly websites, and gray literature. It encompasses a rapidly evolving range of initiatives taking place in academic, research, and public libraries.

INTRODUCTION

"Library publishing" is a rapidly evolving subfield of publishing, concentrated largely in the academic and research sector. It has arisen and matured in response to demands for publishing platforms and service infrastructures to support the production and dissemination of scholarship in myriad forms, including websites and eJournals, conference proceedings and technical reports, databases and mapping interfaces, gray literature and electronic theses and dissertations. It has also emerged in the middle of a volatile marketplace where the concept of "information-as-commodity" is at war with the concept of "information-as-public-good". As such, it has entered contested terrain, as exemplified by the high level of attention it is receiving in the publishing realm today.

The stakes in the broader field of academic publishing are high, and debates concerning the viability and appropriateness of different models—commercial, non-profit, academic, collaborative—are unresolved. This entry will begin by briefly defining library publishing. It will then situate this emerging publishing subfield in its historical context, documenting the broader spectrum of academic publishing practices that have helped to inspire and shape its development to date. Building from this framework, it will describe the current range of library publishing programs and activities in North America, including the methodologies that characterize this domain and the debates and "hot topics" that surround this set of activities.

DEFINING "LIBRARY PUBLISHING" IN AND BEYOND THE ACADEMY

"Library Publishing" is a term increasingly applied to the activities libraries undertake as they work with authors to prepare, disseminate, and preserve content. Library publishing is largely digital in nature (though some libraries provide print-on-demand services for some works). The term is usually used to denote a library's attention to production processes (e.g., editing, copyediting, layout/design, certification/review, rights management, branding, distribution).

In 2013, as one of its initial projects, the Library Publishing Coalition collectively formalized a definition of "library publishing" in the academic sphere as follows:

The LPC defines library publishing as the set of activities led by college and university libraries to support the creation, dissemination, and curation of scholarly, creative, and/or educational works.

Generally, library publishing requires a production process, presents original work not previously made available, and applies a level of certification to the content published, whether through peer review or extension of the institutional brand.

Based on core library values and building on the traditional skills of librarians, it is distinguished from other publishing fields by a preference for Open Access dissemination and a willingness to embrace informal and experimental forms of scholarly communication and to challenge the status quo.[1]

Academic and public libraries, as well as a handful of historical societies and archives, report their interest and growing work in this area. Academic libraries have focused primarily on scholarly research products; public libraries generally work with local authors in their communities. Most research and documentation to date has focused on the work of academic libraries; where possible, we will provide information about the role public libraries are beginning to create in this emerging field as well.

Libraries focus on an identifiable core set of publications, as follows.

Electronic Journals

Most library publishing programs anecdotally cite eJournals among their first publishing service offerings.

Encyclopedia of Library and Information Sciences, Fourth Edition DOI: 10.1081/E-ELIS4-120050673
Copyright © 2017 by Taylor & Francis. All rights reserved.

Library Automation–Library Publishing

Academic libraries work with individuals, departments, and organizations on and beyond their campuses to produce eJournals. Usually these eJournals arise when a faculty member (or graduate/undergraduate students in collaboration with a faculty member) approaches the library for help in launching a new journal or to transition a print journal to digital form. The scholar typically provides the topical focus, editorial board, and handles solicitation, peer review, and copy editing of articles. The library partner often provides the technical infrastructure and production know-how: hosting the journal using (or building) platforms such as the Public Knowledge Project's (PKP) Open Journal Software (OJS) and bepress' Digital Commons; providing layout/design advice; managing the copyright process (often using Creative Commons licenses); and disseminating the journal (most often through some form of Open Access publication). eJournals have matured in a range of forms and formats, including text-based journals (e.g., the hundreds of journals published using OJS); journals emphasizing the use of the digital medium to transform scholarship (e.g., *Southern Spaces*); and journals that provide scientists with mechanisms for publishing their datasets and databases along with the research findings drawn from them (e.g., *Elementa*).[2–4]

Monographs

Libraries publish scholarly, literary, and educational monographs in digital and print (typically print on demand) versions. The disciplinary interests of the university, the library, and/or the publishing program's advisory board frequently drive the editorial program for monographs. Some focus on specific disciplines, or geographical areas. Others concentrate on publications created by faculty at their institutions. A range of publishing models has emerged in this area, from lightweight systems that eschew some traditional scholarly monograph publishing process like peer review (e.g., The University of Nebraska-Lincoln's Zea E-Books imprint) to more traditional programs, often in collaboration with a university press (e.g., the *Signale* series, a joint endeavor of Cornell University Press and Cornell University Library).[5,6] Public libraries have also become involved in monograph publishing, typically focusing on the creative output of their local communities (e.g., the Provincetown Public Library, which plans to publish novels, short fiction, poetry, and other works through its Provincetown Public Press).[7]

Scholarly Websites

Another core set of library publishing examples has derived from faculty/library partnerships on scholarly websites. These have often been grant-funded endeavors, and they include a wide range of publication types,

including archives of primary research materials with topical focus (e.g., Valley of the Shadow, D-Scribe); database-driven websites, often with GIS/mapping components (e.g., SlaveVoyages.org); and collections of websites (e.g., Human Rights Web Archive.)[8–11]

Electronic Theses and Dissertations (ETDs)

Libraries have been hosting and distributing ETDs through their institutional repositories for many years. ETDs represent an important component of the university's original research output. They are typically text-based documents, though they may include audio-visual elements, datasets, or other supplementary materials. Many institutions require deposit of ETDs, a subject that has received attention and criticism from some who claim that offering open access to students' research may make it difficult for them to secure book contracts with academic publishers.[12]

Gray Literature

Preprints, technical reports, teaching materials, and other unpublished or informally published works are often referred to as gray litcrature.[13] While gray literature often documents important and timely information, it typically falls outside the scope of traditional publishing channels. Libraries support its collection and distribution through institutional or disciplinary repositories. The eprint repository arXiv is an early and significant example of a library rising to the challenge of providing access to a large corpus of gray literature for a set of disciplines.[14]

Conference Proceedings

As part of their efforts to preserve and disseminate the research output of their campuses, some libraries offer conference publishing services. The level of service varies based on the needs and capabilities of the library, but may include hosting presentation recordings, preparing formal publications, and even facilitating the process of submission and review of papers. Some libraries use a full-service software such as Open Conference Systems (OCS), which manages everything from creating a conference website, to coordinating registration, to soliciting and reviewing papers.[15]

Data

New data management mandates, and the increasing recognition of data as a valuable scholarly product, have led many libraries to consider or implement data hosting as part of their institutional repository or as a standalone service. The Purdue University Research Repository (PURR), for example, provides metadata, DOI assignment, and storage for data such as "spreadsheets,

Library Automation–Library Publishing

instrument or sensor readings, software source code, surveys, interview transcripts, or images and audiovisual files."[16]

Textbooks

As part of a broader push to encourage adoption of Open Educational Resources (OERs) and ease financial burdens on students, some libraries support the publication of original textbooks developed by their faculty. The SUNY Open Textbook Initiative, for example, plans to publish fifteen open textbooks in a range of disciplines.[17]

Appendices and Supplemental Content

Libraries partner with content creators and publishers (such as university presses) to host supplemental content, often consisting of digitized archival material, audio and video files, and other media. Examples, cited by Raym Crow in his 2009 study of university press and library collaborations include the University of Nebraska's *Journals of the Lewis and Clark Expedition Online* and Pennsylvania State University's *Times of Sorrow and Hope*.[18]

Digitized Out-of-Print Books and Print on Demand of Out-of-Print Materials

In addition to publishing original monographs, libraries also provide print on demand or digitization services for out-of-print books. For example, the library at the University of North Carolina at Chapel Hill offers print on demand for books originally published by the UNC Press through the "DocSouth Books" project.[19]

HISTORY OF PUBLISHING IN ACADEMIC LIBRARIES

Over the last few decades, faculty and students across a variety of disciplines have explored the use of digital technologies to create and disseminate their research. From campus to campus, the details differ but the trend has been consistent—in many cases, these researchers have found strong support for their efforts by partnering with their campus libraries.

University and college libraries have provided the technical infrastructure and staffing necessary to facilitate many early experiments in digital scholarship, from hosting eJournals to collaborating with researchers to create digital archives, handcraft "one-off" Web creations, and produce frameworks for database- and GIS-oriented websites. In the process, libraries have also engaged in activities that mark an extension of the traditional library roles, including managing peer review processes, editing, providing design/layout services, and facilitating

discovery through search engine optimization. Some of this work has been funded through grants (campus, government, and foundation-based), but much of it has been offered as an extension of the Library's traditional mission of collecting, disseminating, and preserving content.

Very few talked about the earliest of these experiments and forays as "publishing"; more often, these projects were discussed under the term "scholarly communications." This nomenclature began to change around 2008, not least due to the publication of two key reports, one by Ithaka S&R and another by the Association of Research Libraries (ARL).[13,20] The Ithaka S&R report, *University Publishing In A Digital Age*, drew clear conclusions regarding the need for presses and libraries to collaborate in order to propel the scholarly communication field forward. And the ARL report, *Research Library Publishing Services: New Options for University Publishing*, provided the first in-depth analysis of publishing services offered by academic libraries and perhaps the first "official" definition of library-based publishing as "the organized production and dissemination of scholarly works in any format as a service provided by the library."[20]

Other studies reinforced both this definition and the importance of these emerging library-based publishing endeavors. In particular, the seminal, IMLS-funded "Library Publishing Services: Strategies for Success" project and report demonstrated the active development and implementation of publishing services in a range of academic libraries, from small liberal arts colleges to premier research institutions.[21] Among the key findings, more than half (55%) of those surveyed either already had or were developing library publishing services. Of these, almost all (90%) cited their desire to "contribute to change in the scholarly publishing system" as an impetus for their work in this area.[21] The study also showed that most programs were operating in relative isolation from one another, and it documented the need for a central space where librarian-publishers could meet, work together, share information, and confront common issues. The report encouraged the development of a framework that could help library publishing services mature into a cohesive field of practice.

The "Strategies for Success" project laid a strong foundation for further action. Prompted by the results of this project, Educopia hosted a conversation in May 2012 between three library Deans who shared an interest in advancing the emerging field of library publishing: James Mullins (Purdue University), Martin Halbert (University of North Texas), and Tyler Walters (Virginia Tech). As an outcome of that conversation, in June 2012, a proposal was drafted to create a community-driven organization— the Library Publishing Coalition (LPC). Representatives from 18 major libraries and consortia vetted the vision outlined in that proposal in July 2012, and the revised proposal was released to prospective participants in August 2012. More than 50 academic libraries formally joined the project team before the project kicked off in January 2013.

Through seed support from the Educopia Institute and participating libraries, the Library Publishing Coalition (LPC) project (2013–2014) is now engaging practitioners to design an organization to support an evolving, distributed, range of library publishing practices. The project is about studying, documenting, and evaluating how best to structure this community-led initiative to promote collaboration and knowledge sharing in the field. The project will result in an organization (launch date set for 2014) and a set of services that include an annual forum, a Directory of Library Publishing, training and education offerings, and a documentation hub.

The evolution of library publishing in universities and colleges is closely tied to the broader academic publishing environment and the seismic shifts and "crises" that have plagued it over the last thirty years.

ACADEMIC PUBLISHING AND THE "CRISES"

From roughly the late 1600s to the 1970s, there was an established order to academic publishing. Creators (the author-researchers, usually ensconced in tenure-track or tenured positions) worked with publishers (mostly University Presses and non-profit scholarly societies, who practiced "publishing" in a service-oriented manner) to produce two main forms of written scholarship: monographs and journals. Publishers served as gatekeepers, editors, and disseminators of scholarship, and they engaged networks of scholars to ensure the merit of each publication they issued. Academic libraries purchased these works, catalogued, organized, and provided access to them, and preserved them for future generations of researchers.

The unsettling of this relatively healthy system, and the resulting articulation of "crisis" can be traced back to at least the 1970s (notably, an economically volatile moment for Western markets). Conventional wisdom today cites two main culprits as the causal agents in this "crisis": the shift from print- to digital- modes of communication and the consolidation and infamous "bundling" practices in the journal publishing market. However, this rather narrow view neglects other interwoven and critical factors that contributed to what some theorists have referred to as a "living dead" academic publishing arena.[22] These other factors include the proliferation of publications and increase in research specialization, the popularization of ranking systems based on research output and citations, and a lack of ready public/subsidization funding to enable libraries (or enough researchers) to acquire the content.[23] We briefly describe some of these below as part of the historical context that has prompted the emergence of library publishing and helped to inform its service orientation over the past decade.

An early factor contributing to the atmosphere of "crisis" came in the form of mimeograph technologies. In particular, the availability of the Xerox machine (popularized in the 1960s) enabled researchers to make a copy of any portion of a journal for a fraction of its cost. This presented a challenge for societies, which depended upon subscription revenues from *both* libraries and individuals to cover their publication costs. Rather than subscribing to a full journal or purchasing a book, a researcher could now visit the library, make copies of the individual articles or segments he/she needed from any journal or book the library maintained, and take those copies home. For researchers, this marked a major improvement in their ability to gather diverse literatures; for University Presses and society publishers, this marked a pain point as units purchased decreased.[23]

This early challenge was compounded by an increase in disciplinary specialization in the 1960s–1970s (e.g., "physical geography" subdivided into five subdisciplines: geomorphology, climatology, biogeography, soil science, and Quaternary environmental change). With disciplinary specialization came new (competing) societies and journals, which fractured the subscription and membership base for longstanding societies. This also presented an early challenge to the collections budgets for academic libraries, which had to expand their journal collections to encompass the new titles demanded by their researchers.[24]

The crisis mentality continued to grow—along with scholarly output—as higher education rankings and citation impact measures grew in stature and popularity during the 1970s. Although promotion and tenure already encouraged publication through its inclusion as one key measure of an Assistant or Associate Professor's performance evaluation for tenure and promotion to full professor, the degree of attention given to publishing in higher education rankings—both for disciplinary departments and across the university—heightened the "publish or perish" pressure. With increased supply (journal articles), more journals rose to fill the increasingly specialized disciplinary spaces. And libraries' acquisitions expenditures continued to grow to keep pace with the increased academic output.

Another "crisis" snowball came in the form of industry consolidation and market concentration practices, as publishers bought out the weakened societies, and then applied a powerful new market strategy—journal "bundling"—to improve the return on their investments. Bundling practices began with the so-called "Big Deal," in which libraries promised to maintain their print subscriptions for a number of years in order to rent electronic access to digitized journals, and expanded over time to bundled eJournals. The major conglomerates—Elsevier, Taylor & Francis, Pearson, Wiley—all have their roots in early academic publishing (of the top 12 academic publishers, only Thomson was founded after 1900), and they largely control the journal industry.[25]

Library Automation–Library Publishing

The steep pricing increases for journals (e.g., 600% between 1984 and 2002 for science journals) forced academic libraries worldwide to struggle to meet local user demand for these increasingly expensive journals. Libraries responded by cutting other materials—especially books/monographs—which shifted the immediate crisis onto the shoulders of the University Presses, which primarily published scholarly monographs and edited volumes, and depended upon library-based purchases of those books to meet their basic production costs.[26]

Although there is much debate about these and other causes (and culprits), most players agree today that the established order of academic publishing has been shaken. In the emerging, increasingly digital, publishing landscape, there is a mix of old and new voices—both within the academy (faculty, students, administrators, university presses, libraries, IT divisions, research centers) and beyond it (societies, nonprofits, commercial publishers, consortia). The groundwork laid by these players today will provide the foundation for the next generation of scholarship—making this a critical moment for scholarly communications.

It is also a critical moment for the Library as an institution. As documented by Walters and Skinner in the 2011 ARL report "New Roles for New Times," academic libraries are demonstrating the value that information managers (librarians) bring to the full lifecycle of scholarly communications, including digital content production, dissemination, and preservation.[27] Academic libraries are uniquely positioned to help their parent institutions advance their core missions of producing, sharing, and preserving new knowledge in the digital realm and within this evolving publishing landscape.[27] Providing services that support scholars' growing needs in these areas is mission-critical for the Library. Arguably, it is also crucial for the health of the research communities it supports.

ACADEMIC LIBRARY PUBLISHING TODAY

Libraries have a core role on university and college campuses, where they often provide information services to every academic program and department on campus. They are viewed as sources of authoritative information, and they have staff members who are knowledgeable in many aspects of information management, including the creation and hosting of systems designed for its preservation and dissemination. In this context, library publishing services are emerging in a number of forms and in a range of institutional contexts, usually in direct response to faculty and student requests.[28]

As campus demands for publishing services increase, libraries are formalizing activities that they previously undertook as either grant-based projects or with seed funding from operations budgets.[28] Where a university press is present (which is now only in about 100 of the 2500 U.S.-based colleges and universities, as one measure), collaborations between the press and library are becoming more prominent, especially on digital publishing activities. In nearly a fifth of these institutions, the university press is being reframed as a formal partner of the library, including through the merging of the university press with the library (see, e.g., Purdue University, University of North Texas, Penn State, Utah State, Syracuse, and Oregon State). Despite the different forms library publishing activities have assumed to date, these programs share a growing commonality of philosophy and approach combining traditional library values and skills (such as a concern with long-term preservation, expertise in the organization of information, and commitment to widening access) with lightweight digital workflows to create a distinctive "field" of publishing activity. As attention to additional content types increases (e.g., "Big Data" and "small data" and everything in between), the value of information management skills in publishing and preserving this content will likewise increase.

Among the emergent focal areas of libraries is hosting a suite of digital publishing services for faculty, staff, and students in support of the research, learning, and engagement goals of the institution. The products disseminated are often (but not always) open access, and they generally include both peer-reviewed electronic publication types such as eJournals and scholarly monographs, and less formally reviewed materials such as technical reports and database-driven websites. Some library publishing programs also include a particular focus on experimental forms of scholarly communication, such as the products of digital humanities research. These new forms of scholarship often involve multimedia components and require innovation in software platforms. Publication of all of these content types requires the establishment of workflows that add value to the raw material.

Missions and Motivations

Publishing has emerged as a strategic service area as libraries identify unmet needs and dissatisfaction with existing processes. Karla Hahn's 2008 study noted that "library-based publishing programs are pragmatic responses to evident needs, not services in search of clients."[20] Libraries receive direct requests from faculty and students who lack sufficient resources within their home departments. Additionally, libraries recognize the value of content that is not published through traditional channels (e.g., gray literature, data, scholarly websites); the need for an alternative to traditional publishing models in response to problems with the current system (e.g., escalating journals prices, restrictive author agreements); and the opportunity to complement existing publishing services on campus, which may have different audiences, goals, and models. Finally, libraries are invested in supporting their stakeholders throughout the academic process.

Library Automation–Library Publishing

Methodology and Practices

The LPC project team launched a survey of library publishing practices in Spring 2013, focusing primarily on North America. More than 110 academic libraries provided responses regarding their publishing practices, ambitions, and collaborations. The responses were edited and compiled for publication in the 2014 "Library Publishing Directory," which provides the first comprehensive view of the publishing support and services offered today by a broad range of academic libraries. A number of important findings regarding current practices in the field emerged from the data collected. Some of that data is reported here, along with findings from previous surveys of the field.

Core Services

Libraries have decades of experience in building, implementing, and maintaining technical infrastructure for digital content. Maintaining the Institutional Repository or publishing platform used to host publications is the basic level of service provision for library publishers.

Other core publishing services build on libraries' traditional strengths, including facilitating access, discovery, and preservation. In a *Library Journal* interview, Charles Watkinson described libraries' "strong focus on enriched and standardized metadata, the leveraging of digital repository systems, and integration with other library services, especially those concerned with research data management and special collections."[29] The LPC survey supported this description. More than three quarters of respondents said that they provide metadata (85%) and digitization (78%) services, cataloging (67%), DOI assignment (42%), ISSN registration (40%), Open URL support (28%), and analytics (62%). Other services, such as author advisory on copyright (78%) and other subjects (32%), and other types of training (66%), build on librarians' strengths as educators and advocates.

A smaller, but still substantial number of libraries offer services that support the editorial and production processes that are hallmarks of traditional publishing. These include peer review management (29%), copyediting (23%), typesetting (20%), print-on-demand (16%), and graphic design (42%). Finally, some libraries support business model development (13%), budget preparation (6%), and contract and license preparation (28%).

Organization and Staffing

Library publishers range in size and stature from prominent, well-staffed, institutionally based groups (e.g., Michigan's MPublishing, Columbia's Center for Digital Research and Scholarship) to collaborative units across multiple campuses (e.g., the California Digital Library's eScholarship service) to small programs with great

impacts (e.g., programs at Pacific University and Illinois Wesleyan University). Currently, there is no dominant model for the organization of publishing services in libraries. In many institutions, services are distributed across multiple library units or even across campus. The lead unit varies dramatically (from Scholarly Communications, to Technical Services, to Special Collections). Staffing also varies widely, but the LPC survey demonstrated that operations remain lean. Libraries reported between .1 and 8 full-time equivalent in library staff who are directly involved in publishing services. Many libraries also employ graduate and undergraduate students to support their publishing activities.

Business Models

Libraries support publishing efforts primarily through their operating budgets, though, as Karla Hahn previously reported, libraries typically rely on at least two funding streams, which include "grants, charge-backs to units or organizations, royalties and licensing fees, print-on-demand revenue, and other forms of sales of some kind."[20] Because libraries show a strong preference for open access models—95% report being focused mostly (48%) or entirely (45%) on Open Access—most do not rely on subscription or sales revenue to support the bulk of their activities. Libraries are experimenting with a number of ways to make their publishing operations sustainable. Some libraries sell content (either at-cost or for a profit) through e-commerce sites like Amazon.com, through publishing platforms like Tizra and Bibliolabs that support payment, or through their own websites in digital and print-on-demand formats. Libraries are also establishing partnerships with other libraries, non-profits, scholarly societies, and others in order to effectively share resources and distribute costs.

Partnerships and Collaboration

Libraries collaborate with a range of internal and external partners in order to sustain, expand, and enhance their publishing services. Internally, libraries routinely work with individual faculty and students across campus, with specific departments or research centers, and university presses. Library and university press partnerships have been explored in detail, most notably in a 2009 Scholarly Publishing and Academic Resources Coalition (SPARC) report, which offered case studies and considerations for collaboration.[18] These partnerships range from libraries digitizing backfiles of university press titles to cooperating on the publication of original monograph series.

Externally, libraries work with scholarly societies, non-profits, faculty on other campuses, individual libraries and library consortia, and others. Notable examples of external partnerships include the eJournal *Elementa*, a collaborative endeavor of the non-profit BioOne and five academic

Library Automation–Library Publishing

institutions and the Open Folklore Project a collaboration of the American Folklore Society, the Indiana University Libraries, and the IU Digital Library Program.[30,31]

Maturity

While publishing services have recently attracted much attention, libraries report that they have been offering these services from as early as 1960. According to the recent LPC survey, 10 libraries began publishing in 1999 or before, 14 started between 2000 and 2004, 39 between 2005 and 2009, and 25 since 2010.

HOT TOPICS AND DEBATES

A range of experiments, frictions, and open questions has emerged as this young field defines its boundaries. A few of those are discussed here.

ESTABLISHING CREDIBILITY AND IDENTITY

While library publishing endeavors in some cases resemble traditional scholarly publishing operations, they frequently offer a distinct set of core services, embrace an expanded range of content types, and pursue a different set of goals. These differences prompt reflection on what publishing means in a new scholarly communications landscape. For example, libraries frequently disseminate original content such as ETDs, scholarly websites, and data sets, which do not undergo the processes of editing and review that remain the hallmarks of scholarly publishing. When publishing eJournals, monographs, and other traditional content types, operate with digital-only, Open Access models, and produce on a very small scale. Like other Open Access publishers, libraries are actively working to establish the credibility of their publications and encourage widespread uptake from both content creators and other publishers. Some have objected to the use of the term "library publishing" because it may be used "to ghettoize what's happening" in libraries, further hindering efforts to be taken seriously by other publishers and the academy.[32]

Scholarly Publishing and the Academy

The idea that the academy could or should reclaim ownership of the publishing process has generated significant debate in the scholarly and publishing communities. Debates have centered on both the desirability and feasibility of colleges and universities replacing or competing with commercial publishers.[33] Barriers to achieving significant change to the current scholarly publishing system include the relatively small scale of campus-based publishing operations and the reluctance of scholars to change

their publishing practices (often due to promotion and tenure considerations). A 2012 CLIR/DLF-funded report argued, "If libraries are searching for transformation in scholarly publishing, small, individual efforts will not meet that goal. Collaborative efforts between institutions and with their presses may actually build a critical mass."[34]

Relationships with University Presses

As more libraries and university presses explore collaboration, partnerships, and/or administrative ties, there has been discussion of the nature of these relationships and the benefits and challenges of bridging the gaps between the distinct strengths of each. In the 2009 report on library and university press collaborations, Raym Crow noted that, "As their roles continue to evolve, the boundaries separating the activities of the library and the press have become less distinct." [18] Libraries have adapted to meet changing scholarly practices and to demonstrate their value to the research enterprise, while presses have responded to changes in publishing, most notably the shift from print to digital. While many examples of successful collaborations exist, a range of tensions and obstacles make this a fraught area. Challenges include the different business models of libraries and presses (the former operates primarily through subsidies, while the latter relies substantially on sales revenue), and structural issues (e.g., reporting lines within universities, and evolving models of collaboration at both system- and campus-based levels).

Sustainability

Libraries operate with a different set of financial expectations from traditional commercial publishers and university presses. Financial support comes primarily from the library's operating budget. Library publishing services may not be required to turn a profit or even recoup their costs, and the majority does not directly charge content creators for services. Many libraries work with streamlined digital-only or digital and print on demand models that reduce some of the costs of traditional publishing (e.g., maintaining an inventory, investing heavily in marketing). But costs in staff time and technology remain substantial. Particularly given libraries' preference for Open Access publication, how will libraries ensure that publishing services remain viable in the long-term? Where does money come from to expand services, hire new staff, or invest in new technologies?

CONCLUSION

Over the last few decades, library publishing has evolved from involvement in Institutional Repositories and *ad hoc* digital projects to a full set of services that support the

Library Automation–Library Publishing

publication of a range of content types. It has gained traction as a response to the needs of authors and library users and as an outgrowth of libraries' traditional skills and their commitment to supporting scholarship. Today, it is clear that "library publishing" is a meaningful term, one that denotes a growing area of scholarly communication activity.

As this work continues to expand, libraries—like all "publishers—will continue to confront a difficult and rapidly changing publishing landscape. Libraries today are working to articulate clearly their value proposition and business model(s), and demonstrate how the services and models they offer can help stabilize the scholarly publishing ecosystem. As part of this work, they are also cultivating and strengthening their relationships with each other, as well as with other stakeholders in this space, including scholarly societies and university presses. These strategic alliances will help to ensure that the overall scholarly communication apparatus is able to continue evolving at pace with the research and knowledge produced across academia.

REFERENCES

1. http://librarypublishing.org/about-us (accessed July 2013).
2. http://pkp.sfu.ca/ojs-journals (accessed July 2013).
3. http://www.southernspaces.org/ (accessed July 2013).
4. http://elementascience.org/ (accessed July 2013).
5. http://digitalcommons.unl.edu/zeacollections/ (accessed July 2013).
6. http://signale.cornell.edu/ (accessed July 2013).
7. http://provincetownpublicpress.org/about/ (accessed July 2013).
8. http://valley.lib.virginia.edu/ (accessed July 2013).
9. http://www.library.pitt.edu/dscribe/ (accessed July 2013).
10. http://slavevoyages.org/tast/index.faces (accessed July 2013).
11. http://library.columbia.edu/locations/chrdr/hrwa.html (accessed July 2013).
12. http://blog.historians.org/2013/07/american-historical-association-statement-on-policies-regarding-the-embargoing-of-completed-history-phd-dissertations/ (accessed July 2013).
13. Brown, L.; Griffiths, R.J.; Rascoff, M. et al.; *University Publishing in a Digital Age*; Ithaka, S&R: New York, 2007, http://www.sr.ithaka.org/research-publications/university-publishing-digital-age (accessed July 2013).
14. http://arxiv.org/ (accessed July 2013).
15. http://pkp.sfu.ca/?q=ocs (accessed July 2013).
16. https://purr.purdue.edu/about (accessed July 2013).
17. http://opensuny.org/omp/index.php/SUNYOpenTextbooks (accessed July 2013).
18. Crow, R. *Campus-Based Publishing Partnerships: A Guide to Critical Issues*; SPARC: Washington, DC, 2009, http://sparc.arl.org/sites/default/files/pub_partnerships_v1.pdf (accessed July 2013).
19. http://docsouth.unc.edu/support/docsouth_books/ (accessed July 2013).
20. Hahn, K.L. *Research Library Publishing Services: New Options for University Publishing*; ARL: Washington, DC, 2012, http://www.arl.org/storage/documents/publications/research-library-publishing-services-mar08.pdf (accessed July 2013).
21. Mullins, J.L.; Murray-Rust, C.; Ogburn, J.L.; Crow, R. et al.; *Library Publishing Services: Strategies for Success: Final Research Report*; SPARC: Washington, DC, 2012, http://docs.lib.purdue.edu/purduepress_ebooks/24/ (accessed July 2013).
22. Fitzpatrick, K. *Planned Obsolescence: Publishing, Technology, and the Future of the Academy*; NYU Press: New York, 2011.
23. Rosenbluth, G. Publishing economics. Can. J. Econ. **1979**, *12* (4), 551–574, http://www.jstor.org/stable/134865 (accessed July 2013).
24. Peter Weingart (various) and ARL stats, etc).
25. http://www.ulib.niu.edu/publishers/ (accessed July 2013).
26. Edlin, A.S.; Rubinfeld, D.L. Exclusion or efficient pricing? The "Big Deal" bundling of academic journals. Antitrust Law J. **2004**, *1* (72), 119–157, www.law.berkeley.edu/faculty/.../Edlin-Rubinfeld%20ALJ%20Paper.pdf (accessed July 2013).
27. Walters, T.; Skinner, S. *New Roles for New Times: Digital Curation for Preservation*; ARL: Washington, DC, 2011, http://www.arl.org/storage/documents/publications/nrnt_digital_curation17mar11.pdf (accessed July 2013).
28. http://librarypublishing.org/sites/librarypublishing.org/files/documents/lpc_proposal_08142012.pdf (accessed July 2013).
29. http://lj.libraryjournal.com/2013/04/library-services/ten-questions-with-the-library-publishing-coalition/ (accessed July 2013).
30. http://elementascience.org/.
31. http://openfolklore.org/.
32. http://chronicle.com/article/Hot-Off-the-Library-Press/136973/ (accessed July 2013).
33. http://scholarlykitchen.sspnet.org/2013/06/27/on-the-likelihood-of-academia-taking-back-scholarly-publishing/ (accessed July 2013).
34. http://mediacommons.futureofthebook.org/mcpress/business cases/.

BIBLIOGRAPHY

1. Brown, A. *Library Publishing Toolkit*; IDS Project Press: Geneseo, NY, 2013, http://opensuny.org/omp/index.php/IDSProject/catalog/book/25 (accessed July 2013).
2. Walters, T. The future role of publishing services in university libraries: Portal. Libr. Acad. **2012**, *12* (4), 425–454, http://muse.jhu.edu/ (accessed July 2013).

Index

A

AALL, *see* American Association of Law Libraries

AAM, *see* American Association of Museums

Aarhus Art museum, 1226

Aarhus State and University Library, 1216–1217, 1219

AASL, *see* American Association of School Librarians

AASL Hotlinks, 61

Abandoned Shipwreck Act of 1987, 1775

The Aboriginal and Torres Strait Islander Library and Information Resource Network (ATSILIRN) Protocols, 2041

Abridged WebDewey, 1259–1260

Absorption, distribution, metabolism, excretion, and toxicity (ADMET) testing, 837

Abstracts, 418–419

Academic art libraries, 251

Academic dishonesty
  definition, 3665
  faculty attitudes, 3668–3669
  individual differences, 3668–3669
  social factors, 3668

Academic e-mail messages, 2507

Academic law reviews, 2740

Academic Librarians Status Committee, 342

Academic libraries, 97, 2764, 3471–3472
  acquisitions units, organization of, 2918–2919
  administration, 9
  in Arab sector, 2548
  Armenia, 230–231
  in Australia, 384–385
  buildings, 10–11
  in China
    Peking University Library, 896
    Tsinghua University Library, 896–898
  in Croatia, 1125
  database integrators, 3472
  digital humanities (*see* Digital humanities)
  Ethiopia, 1498–1499
  external influence, 2–3
  in France, 1602–1603
  fund-raising and development
    access to donors, 2835
    annual fund, 2836–2837
    capital campaigns, 2838
    centralized *vs.* decentralized development, 2834–2835
    development activities, 2833–2834
    friends of libraries, 2836
    institutional barriers, 2834–2835
    institutionalization, 2839
    library director, role of, 2835
    literature, history of, 2832–2833
    major gifts, 2837
    planned giving, 2837–2838
    theoretical and philosophical foundations, 2839
    U.S. phenomenon, 2832
    Web communications, 2838–2839

games and gaming, 1639–1640
in Germany, 1695–1696
governance and hierarchy, 3–4
Greece, 1731–1732
history, 1–2
Hungary, 1922
in Israel, 2544–2545
Japan, 2562–2564
in Kazakhstan, 2582–2583
Kenya, 2596
Latinos, 2701–2702
library anxiety, 2785
Lithuania, 2951–2953
Mexican libraries, 3083–3086
mission, 1
in Moldova, 3125
music libraries, 3275
New Zealand libraries, 3375–3376
organizational structure, 4–5
personnel, 10
in Peru, 3608
professional associations, 3
resources and services
  expertise, 5–6
  public service, 7–8
  reference desk, 6–7
  technical services, 8–9
in Saudi Arabia, 3974
science and engineering librarians, 4009
Senegal, 4106
in Serbia, 4129–4131
Slovakia, 4177–4178
South Korea, 4310–4311
strategic planning (*see* Strategic planning, academic libraries)
Tunisia, 4628–4629
in Ukraine, 4642
in United Kingdom, 4703–4705
user privileges, 5
Venezuelan libraries, 4889–4890

Academic Library Advancement and Development Network (ALADN), 2834

Academic publications, 2826

Academic writing, 4548–4549

Academy of Beaux-Arts, 1594

Academy of Health Information Professionals (AHIP), 3035, 4356

Access control, *see* Authorization

Accessed information, 4236

Accessibility
  adaptive hardware and software, adults
    audiobooks and Playaways, 16
    audio description, 16
    Benetech, 16
    closed-circuit television, 15
    mouse challenges, 15
    outreach efforts, 16
    public meetings, signing for, 15–16
    screen reading software, 15
    talking books, 16
    TDDS and TTYS, 16

typing and voice recognition software, 15
virtual reference, 17
web conferencing platform, 17
Web sites, 16–17
audio/recorded books, 15
books by mail service, 14
Braille books, 15
building accommodations, 14
deposit collections, 14
homebound book delivery, 14
large print books, 14–15
services, 14
symbols, 4961, 4963

Access management, *see* Authorization

Access services, 173, 373, 895, 1910, 2912, 3472, 4735

Access to Knowledge (A2K) movement, 3386

Access-to-Own model, 1211

Accountability, 2055

Accounting in England and Scotland: 1543 to 1800, 645

Accreditation
  ALA, LIS programs
    Accreditation Process, Policies, and Procedures, 18, 20
    ALISE, 19–20
    ASPA Code of Good Practice, 18–19
    BEL, 19
    COA, 18–20
    Committee on Library Training, 19
    future prospects, 20–21
    Land Grant College Act, 19
    of postsecondary education, 19
    purpose of, 18
    standards, 18, 20
  of Canadian institutions, 19, 21
  fundamental assumptions of, 18

Accreditation Board for Engineering and Technology (ABET), 1434

Accredited Standards Committee (ASC), 413

Achenwall, Gottfried, 495

ACLU v. Reno, 2396

ACM, *see* Association for Computing Machinery

Acquisitions
  in academic libraries, 2918–2919
  approval plan vendors, 2919
  automated and integrated library systems, 2919
  bibliographic networks, development of, 2921
  definition, 2918
  EDI, 2919
  in public libraries, 2919
  purchasing decisions, 2918
  shared cataloging, 2921
  in small libraries, 2919
  in special libraries, 2918

Acquisitions Institute at Timberline Lodge
  collection development, 22
  facility, 2
  history and evolution, 22–23

Acquisitions Institute at Timberline Lodge
(cont'd.)
library acquisitions, 22
planning committee, 23–24
previous conference programs, 24–32
technical services, 22
ACRL, *see* Association of College and Research
Libraries
Acropolis Museum, 1741–1742
Acta Mathematica, 3024
Acta Mathematica Sinica, 3027
Act for the Protection of Copyright, 656
Active learning, 679, 4463, 4834, 4859
Activities Committee on New Directions for
ALA (ACONDA), 71, 2393
1997 Act on Archival Material and Archives,
1127
Act on the Right to Information Access, 1126
Actor-network theory (ACN), 2282, 2287,
4022–4023
ADA, *see* Americans with Disabilities Act
Adaptive indexing, 1623
Addis Ababa Museum, 1503
Addis Ababa University (AAU), 1498
Additional improvement (AI) patents, 3565
Adelaide, 390, 393
Ad-hocracy, 3512
Ad hoc retrieval, 4555
Ad Hoc Task Force on Structure Revision
(SRTF), 72–73
Administrative decisions, 149, 2735, 2738–2739
Administrative Management Society, 651
Administrative Procedure Act of 1946, 2150
Administrative rules, 2729, 2737, 4349, 4746
Adobe Connect, 2780
Adolescent development, YA services
physical growth
cognitive, 5060
early bloomers, 5059
emotional, 5061
height, weight, and secondary sex charac-
teristics, 5059
late bloomers, 5060
psychological, 5060
social, 5060–5061
social characteristics, 5059
ADRIANA, 4318
Advanced Research Project Agency (ARPA),
1015, 2516
Advanced Research Project Agency Network
(ARPANET), 2505, 2516
The Advantages of the Kingdome of England,
1400
Adventure novels, 855, 3701
Advertisements, 639
Aesop's Fables, 852–853
Aëtius of Amida, 3044
Affective needs, 2115, 2119
Affective relevance judgments, 3944
AFLI, *see* Arab Federation for Libraries and
Information
African Journals Online (AJOL), 38
African librarianship
colonization, 33–34
consortiums and networks, 39–40
developing countries, 35–36, 38–39
European colonization, 34

ICT, 38
innovative outreach, 40
LIS education, 40
OA, 39
open source software, 39
pan-African responses, 37–38
privately funded public libraries, 40
scholarly information, 38
African Library and Information Association
and Institutions (AfLIA), 37–38
African Newspapers Union List (AFRINUL),
790
AgeLine database, 3407
Agency affordance, 1118
Agoge games, 1641
Agora Research Initiative, 679
Agricultural Extension Service, 1011
Agricultural libraries, Ukraine, 4646
AGRINET, 4631
A&HCI, *see Arts and Humanities Citation Index*
Ahmes Papyrus, 3019–3020
AIS, *see* Association for Information Systems
Aksum Archaeological Museum, 1501
ALA, *see* American Library Association
ALA Code of Ethics, 4365
Albert Scholarship, 81
Albucasis, 3044
ALCTS, *see* Association for Library Collections
and Technical Services
ALCTS Honors, 332
ALCTS Outstanding Publications Award, 331
ALEPH network, 2545
Alert Services, 1880
Alexander of Tralles, 3044
Alexander's curriculum, 3218
Alexander Turnbull Library, 3373
Alexandria Digital Library (ADL), 2671
Alexandria Library, 745
Alexandros Soutsos, 1744
Algorithmic relevance judgments, 3944
ALIA, *see* Australian Library and Information
Association
aliaNEWS, 400
Alien property custodian (APC) documents,
3566
ALISE, *see* Association for Library and Infor-
mation Science Education
ALIWEB, 2519
Alliance for Bibliographic Standards (ICABS),
2456
Alliance for Nursing Informatics, 86
Alliance of Library Service Networks, 3922
Allied Professional Association (APA), 74–75,
713
All India Educational Surveys (AIESs), 2001
Alphabetico-classed catalog, 754
Alpha-Numeric System for Classification of
Sound Recordings (ANSCR), 3283
ALSC, *see* Association for Library Service to
Children
ALTAFF, *see* Association of Library Trustees,
Advocates, Friends and Foundations
AltaVista, 2522, 4048, 4983, 4986
Alte Pinakothek, 3153–3154
Altes Museum, 3153
Altmetrics, 44–46, 924
Amazon, 3734–3735

Amazon Kindle, 4054–4055
Ambiguous chemical identifiers
chemical formulae, 823–824
chemical names, 823
Ambrosian Iliad, 1946
American Accounting Association, 651
American Alliance of Museums (AAM), 3233,
3758
American Antiquities Act, 1774
American Archive of Public Broadcasting, 1579
American Archivist, *Archival Issues*, 137
American Association for State and Local His-
tory (AASLH), 1782
American Association for the Advancement of
Science (AAAS), 558
American Association of Colleges (AAC), 341
American Association of Law Libraries
(AALL), 710, 1097, 2708, 2714–2716,
2744, 4356–4357, 4370
goals and objectives, 49
legal information environment, 52–53
member growth
CPE, 50–51
ethics and diversity, 51–52
new members, 51
scholarships and grants, 51
NET (AALLNET), 50
publications
AALL Biennial Salary Survey, 55
AALL Directory and Handbook, 55
AALL Price Index for Legal Publications,
55
AALL Spectrum, 54
Index to Foreign Legal Periodicals, 55
LLJ, 55
publisher relations, 53–54
special interest sections, 49–50
2005–2010 strategic directions, 48
universal citation guide, 53
valued partnerships, 54
American Association of Museums (AAM), 255,
3146–3147, 3200, 3215–3216, 3255,
4379, 4766, 4769; *see also* American
Alliance of Museums
activities and priorities, 57
services to members, 58
structure and governance, 56–57
American Association of School Librarians
(AASL), 68, 2752, 3775, 3991,
4001–4002, 5052, 5058
affiliate assembly, 60–61
awards, grants, and scholarships, 62–63
board of directors, 60
executive committee, 60
goals, 59
guidelines and standards
fall forum, 63
national guidelines and standards, 64
school library programs, 63–64
history, 60
Knapp School Library Manpower Project, 64
mission, 59
national conference and exhibition, 63
National Library Power Program, 64–65
publications, 61
regional institutes, 63
responsibility, 59

sections, 61
special committees, 61
Standards, 4859
standing committees, 61
task forces, 61
values, 60
vision, 59
American Association of University Professors
    (AAUP), 341
American Association of Zoological Parks and
    Aquariums (AAZPA), 5078
American Astronomical Society (AAS), 3640
American Bar Association (ABA), 2711–2712,
    2716
American Chemical Society (ACS), 3641–3642
American Civil Liberties Union (ACLU), 783,
    2402
American Committee for Devastated France
    (CARD), 1600
American Cooperative School of Tunis (ACST),
    4630
American Documentation Institute (ADI), 90,
    311, 2770
American Economic Review (AER), 3470
American Federation of Labor (AFL), 4689
American Federation of Labor-Congress of
    Industrial Organizations (AFL-CIO),
    4761
American Federation of State, County and
    Municipal Employees (AFSCME),
    4690–4691
American Federation of Teachers (AFT), 3997–
    3998, 4689
American Film Institute (AFI), 1586
American Health Information and Management
    Association (AHIMA), 1854
American Historical Association (AHA), 1788,
    3316, 4272, 4741
American Historical Review, 1791
American Indian Library Association, 334–335
American Institute for Certified Public Accoun-
    tants (AICPA), 2918–2919
American Institute for Conservation of Historic
    and Artistic Works (AIC), 1072, 3729,
    4953
American Institute of Accountants, 651
American Institute of Architects Awards,
    2845
American Institute of Certified Public Accoun-
    tants, 651
American Institute of Physics (AIP), 3639, 4763
American Journal of Mathematics, 3024, 3027
American Law Reports (ALR), 2741
American librarianship, 2890
American Library Association (ALA), 3, 60,
    229, 255, 706, 757, 1336, 1846–1847,
    2764, 2775, 2964–2965, 3728, 3775,
    3778, 4001, 4649, 4773–4774, 4777
    accreditation of LIS programs
        *Accreditation Process, Policies, and Pro-
            cedures*, 18, 20
        ALISE, 19–20
        ASPA Code of Good Practice, 18–19
        BEL, 19
        COA, 18–20, 709
        Committee on Library Training, 19
        future prospects, 20–21

purpose of, 18
standards, 18, 20
ACONDA/ANACONDA, 71
ACRL, 2752
affiliated organizations, 77
Allied Professional Association, 74–75, 713
ALSC, 333
awards and scholarships, 81
chapters, 77
children's literature, awards for, 852
Code of Ethics, 3917
conference
    change and controversy, 80–81
    growth and development, 79–80
    Midwinter Meeting, 80
controversy, 72–73
Council, 75
Cresap, McCormick and Paget, 70
divisions, 75–76
    self-study, 74
dues schedule transition document, 73
Executive Board, 75
GameRT, 1637
Holley Committee, OSSC, 71–72
intellectual freedom (*see* Intellectual
    freedom)
International connections, 77–78
Latinos and library services, 2699
library network, definition of, 3920
LLAMA, 2841–2845
membership and organizational change, 69
membership statistics (August 2008), 83
MIGs, 76–77
offices, 81–82
older adults, library services for, 3407
operating agreements, 73–74
organizational development
    ALA divisions and allied professional
        association, 73
    growth and democratization, 69–70
organizational self-study (1992–1995), 72
periodic scrutiny, 70
PIALA, 3548
publishing, 78–79
round tables, 76
RUSA, 3913
Science and Technology Section, 4016
standards and guidelines, 81
standing committees, 76
state library agencies, 4394
values, priorities and missions, 67–69
web-based networking, 78
American Library Association-Allied Profes-
    sional Association (ALA-APA), 3777
American Library Association conference,
    2770
*American Library Association v. U.S. Depart-
    ment of Justice*, 2396
American Library Directory, 249
American Management Association, 651
American Marketing Association, 651
American Mathematical Society, 324
American Medical Informatics Association
    (AMIA), 85–86
American Memory Project, 5027
American Museum of Natural History (AMNH),
    3252, 4944

American museums, 3234
American National Standards Institute (ANSI),
    221, 1857, 1981, 2343–2344
    conformity assessment, 88–89
    history, 87
    industry sectors and services, 87
    international standards activities, 88
    logo, 88
    NISO, 88
    process, 88
    standards panels, 89
    U.S. standardization system, 87
American National Trust for Historic Preserva-
    tion, 4169
American Psychological Association, 4246
American Radio Archives, 1565
American Records Management Association
    (ARMA), 175, 1853–1855
American Sign Language (ASL), 1184, 1187
American Society for Engineering Education,
    Engineering Libraries Division (ASEE/
    ELD), 4016
American Society for Indexing (ASI), 441
American Society for Information Science
    (ASIS), 1097, 1375
American Society for Information Science and
    Technology (ASIST), 482
    awards, 95
    chapters and SIGs, 92
    governance, 93
    history
        documentation, beginnings (1937), 90
        human/social perspective, (1990s and
            2000s), 91–92
        information explosion (1960s), 90
        modern information science transition
            (1950s), 90
        online information (1970s), 91
        personal computers (1980s), 91
    meetings, 94
    publications, 93–94
    purpose, 92
American Society for Quality National Accredi-
    tation Board (ANAB), 88
American Society of Information Science and
    Technology (ASIST), 3368
American Standard Code for Information Inter-
    change (ASCII), 5024
Americans with Disabilities Act (ADA), 10,
    377, 1530, 3575–3576, 3843
Americans with Disabilities Act Assembly, 3778
American Technology Pre-Eminence Act
    (ATPA) of 1991, 1552
American Theological Library Association
    (ATLA)
    Carver Policy Governance model, 4607
    Committee on Microphotography, 4606
    daunting problems, 4606
    Ethics index, 4607
    Executive Director, 4607–4608
    importance, 4606
    Library Development Program, 4606
    management structure, 4607
    premier professional association, 4608
    religion database, 4607
    Religion index two, 4606–4607
    Retrospective Indexing Project, 4607

America Online (AOL), 2521
Amigos, 3922, 3924
Ammonite, *see* Snake stones
Amos Tuck School of Administration and
  Finance, 650
Anacostia Community Museum, 4192
Analytical bibliography, 477–478
Analytico-synthetic classification, 967, 971,
  4786
Anastosi I, 644
Anatolian University Library Consortium
  (ANKOS), 2829
Ancien Régime, 182
Ancient Greece, 999, 1460–1461, 1742, 1744,
  1788, 2677, 3831
Andrew Mellon Foundation, 372, 988
Anglo-American Cataloging Rules (AACR),
  449, 727, 2920–2921, 3062, 4144
Anglo-American Cataloguing Rules, 2nd ed.
  (AACR2), 137, 253, 453, 670,
  1230–1231, 1982–1983, 2921, 2923,
  3131, 3178, 3294, 3396, 4140–4141,
  4144
Anglo-American Cataloguing Rules 3rd ed.
  (AACR3), 670
*An Inquiry into the Wealth of Nations and
  Causes of the Wealth of Nations*, 646
Annales de Mathématiques Pures et Appliquées,
  3024, 3026
*Annales typographici ab artis inventae origine
  ad annum MDCLXIV*, 1968
ANNs, *see* Artificial neural networks
Annual fund, 2836–2837
Annual Meeting of the Document Academy
  (DOCAM), 1379
*Annual Review of Information Science and
  Technology* (*ARIST*), 312, 489
Anomalous state of knowledge (ASK), 2076,
  2118–2119, 2225, 4526–4527, 4874,
  4879
ANSI, *see* American National Standards
  Institute
ANSI/NISO Z39.50, 2983
Answer Garden (AG), 3865–3866
Anthropogeographie, 1687
Anthropological museum, Hungary, 1929–1930
Antiquarian book, 3820
Antiquarian Booksellers' Association of Amer-
  ica (ABAA), 4344, 4576, 4578, 4585,
  4588
Antiquarian Booksellers database, 4576
Antiquities Act of 1906, 4169
Antiquities Act of 1964, 4511
Antiquities of the Jews, 644
Apache Lucene IR system, 2204
Apache Project, 5025
Apollonios of Citium, 3043
Apologie, 1400
Appeal factors, 3700, 3705, 3850, 3857
Apple's HyperCard, 5023
Application ontologies, 3457
Application programming interfaces (APIs)
  FAST, 1545
  ILSs, 409
  ORCID, 3506–3508
Application Service Definition and Protocol
  Specification, 2983

Application service providers (ASPs), 698
Application software, 1056, 1333, 2272–2273,
  3650, 4805, 5034
Appraisal and selection process, 131
Apprentices' libraries, 1842
*The Apprentice's time enterteiner accomptantly:
  or a methodical means to obtain the
  equisite art of accomptantship*, 645
Approval plan
  history, 96–97
  profiles, 97–98
  transformation, 97
  vendors, 98
Apriori, 2631
Aquaria, 3238
Aquariums and zoological parks, 5077
  archives, 5083
  libraries
    current status and services, 5081–5083
    early libraries, establishment of, 5081
    need for, 5080–5081
  professional development
    animal collections, 5077
    captive wildlife management, 5077
    European collections, 5077–5078
    exotic wild animals, 5078
    modern aquariums, 5078
    modern zoological park management, 5077
    professional associations, 5078
    public aquarium, 5078
  professional literature, growth in, 5078–5080
Aquisitions Section (AS), 328
Arab Federation for Libraries and Information
  (AFLI), 100–101, 3978
  finance, 102
  honors and awards, 103–104
  location, 102
  membership, 101
  objectives, 101
  organizational structures, 101–102
  publications, 103
  relationships and cooperation, 103
  seminars and conferences, 102–103
  training and workshops, 103
Arabian Nights Entertainment, 853
Arabic Union Catalog, 3978
Arab Libraries Association, 100
*Arbetisgemeinschaft der Kunst-und Museumsbi-
  bliotheken* (AKMB), 255
Arboreta, 3238
Archaeological collections, curation of, *see*
  Curation, archaeological artifacts
Archaeological Conservancy, 1777
Archaeological museums
  in Croatia, 1129
  Hungary, 1929–1930
  in Israel, 2551
Archaeological Resources Protection Act
  (ARPA), 1774
Archaeological site museum, 4167–4168
Archie, 2517
Architecture, museum
  eighteenth century
    American Museum in Philadelphia, 3153
    Baroque design, 3152
    Belvedere sculpture court, 3151–3152
    Corinthian loggia, 3151

    courtyard plan, 3151
    curiosity/art cabinets, 3150
    exhibition spaces and galleries, 3151
    Galleria degli Uffizi in Florence, 3152
    Grande Galerie, 3152
    Greek cross, pattern of, 3151
    Inscriptiones vel tituli teatri amplissimi,
      3150–3151
    Louvre in Paris, 3152
    multifunctional institution, 3151
    Musei Capitolini in Rome, 3152
    Museo Nacional del Prado, 3152
    Museo Pio-Clementino, 3151–3152
    Museum Fridericianum, 3152
    neoclassical design, 3152–3153
    Newby Hall's gallery, 3151
    Pennsylvania Academy of the Fine Arts in
      Philadelphia, 3153
  nineteenth century
    Alte Pinakothek, 3153–3154
    Altes Museum, 3153
    Beaux-Arts method, 3153, 3156
    Belvedere statue court, 3154
    courtyard model, 3153–3154
    Dulwich Picture Gallery, 3154
    educational and training, 3155
    Glyptothek, 3153
    growth, specialization, and spatial concen-
      tration, 3154
    instructive decorations, 3155
    iron and glass structure, 3154–3155
    Neo-Gothic brick building, 3155
    Oxford University Museum, 3155
    shallow buildings, 3154
    South Kensington Museum, 3154–3155
    top lighting, 3154
    Victoria and Albert Museum, 3154–3155
  pre-eighteenth century
    arcaded perambulatories, 3149–3150
    Belvedere statue court, 3149
    centrally planned rooms, 3150
    circular and top-lit building, 3150
    curiosity/art cabinets, 3150
    galleries, 3150
    pinacotheca, 3149
    purpose-designed public museum, 3150
  twentieth century and beyond
    Akron Art Museum, 3158
    American metropolitan architecture, 3156
    Beaux-Arts inspired plan, 3156
    central foyer spaces, 3158
    historic museum buildings, 3157
    industrial buildings, 3157–3158
    Milwaukee Art Museum, 3158
    Modernism, 3156
    modernist glass box, 3156–3157
    Museo Civico di Castelvecchio, 3157
    Museo Guggenheim, Bilbao, 3158
    Museumsufer, 3157
    National Gallery of Art, 3156
    New York Museum of Modern Art,
      3157
    open museum concept, 3157
    Quadracci Pavilion, 3158
    Solomon R. Guggenheim Museum, 3156
Architecture of integrated information systems
  (ARIS), 632

Archival and Manuscripts Control (MARC
    AMC), 136
Archival appraisal
    alternative approaches
        documentation strategies, 110
        documenting society, 109
        functions-based appraisal, 110–111
        macro appraisal, 110
        Minnesota method, 110
    American traditions, 107
    definition, 105–106
    digital recordkeeping, 112–113
    European traditions, 106–107
    practices, 108–109
    tools
        collecting/acquisition policies, 107
        disposal/retention schedules, 107–108
        sampling, 108
        systemic reviews, 108
    traditional appraisal methods, 111–112
Archival collection
    agencies, 195–196
    archival appraisal and, 200–201
    barriers, 202–203
    collectors and, 196–197
    complicated times, 203
    definition, 195–196
    early modern profession, 197
    institutional collections and individual collec-
        tors, 199–200
    marginalization, 198
    organizational repositories, 198
    psychology of, 200
    record-keeping technology, 198
    shifting notions of, 198
Archival description, 1425–1426
Archival documentation
    archival program
        appraisal and selection process, 131
        archival materials, 131
        description, housing and management,
            130–131
        establishment, 129
        main phases, 128–129
        survey, 129–130
        transfer and accession, 130
    digital and networked technologies, 131–132
    principles, 128
    strategies, 201
Archival finding aids
    as access tool, 133
    archival journals, 137
    arrangement and description, 134
    container list, 134–135
    definition, 133–134
    front matter, 134
    2005 Greene-Meisner study, 138
    Next Generation Finding Aids project, 138
    NIDS-US, 136
    online finding aids, development of, 137–138
    sample finding aid, 135–136
    standards, 136–137
Archival information packages (AIP), 1365
Archival management and administration
    leadership, 143–145
    managing information
        planning, 145

    policies and procedures, 146
    project management, 146–147
    managing money, facilities and relationships
        budgets, 147
        resource development and outreach, 147–148
    theory and practice
        building partnerships, 143
        manager, role of, 142–143
Archival records, 1424–1425
Archival repositories
    academic repositories and digital projects
        California Digital Library, 4748
        Cornell University, 4747
        Duke University, 4748
        Making of America project, 4747–4748
        MIT and DSpace, 4748
        Stanford University, 4748
        University of Chicago, 4748–4749
        University of Michigan, 4747
        University of North Carolina (Chapel Hill),
            4749
        Yale University, 4749
    audiovisual archives, 4755
    business archives
        Coca-Cola, 4752
        Ford Motor Company, 4753
        history associates, 4753
        History Factory, 4753
        Levi Strauss, 4753
    cultural heritage archives
        American Folklife Center, 4757
        American Heritage Center, 4757
        Amistad Center, 4757
        Balch Institute, 4757
        Center for Puerto Rican Studies, 4757
        Clark Atlanta University, 4757–4758
        Heard Museum Archives, 4758
        Japanese American History Archives, 4758
        Moorland-Spingarn Research Center, 4758
        Museum of Chinese in America,
            4758–4759
        Schomburg Center for Black Culture, 4759
    data and electronic records archives
        Electronic and Special Media Records Ser-
            vices Division, NARA, 4754
        ERA, 4754
        ICPSR, 4753–4754
        Minerva/Library of Congress Web
            Archives, 4754
    gender and sexuality archives
        Cornell Human Sexuality Project, 4760
        GBLT historical society, 4760
        Kinsey Institute, 4760
        Lesbian Herstory Archives, 4760
        National Gay & Lesbian Archives,
            4760–4761
    labor archives, 4761
    manuscript repositories and historical
        societies
        American Philosophical Society, 4750
        Chicago History Museum, 4750
        Library of Congress, 4749–4750
        urban archives (Temple University), 4750–
            4751
    military archives
        Air Force Historical Research Center, 4751
        American Jewish Archives, 4751

        American Jewish Historical Society, 4751
        Archdiocese of Chicago, 4751–4752
        Billy Graham Center Archives, 4752
        Center for Military History, 4751
        Episcopal Church U.S.A., 4752
        Family History Center, Church of Jesus
            Christ of Latter-Day Saints, 4752
        Naval Historical Center, 4751
        religious archives, 4751
        United Methodist Church, 4752
    museum archives
        Getty museum, 4755
        Smithsonian Institution, 4754–4755
        United States Holocaust museum, 4755
        Warhol Museum, 4755
    NARA, 4746
    performing arts archives
        Center for Black Music Research, 4755
        Folger Shakespeare Library, 4756
        New York Public Library, 4756
    popular culture archives, 4756
    science, technology, and health care archives
        Alan Mason Chesney Medical Archives,
            4761–4762
        California Academy of Science, 4762
        California Institute of Technology, 4762
        Charles Babbage Center, 4762
        Claude Moore Library, 4762
        David Sarnoff Library, 4762
        Linda Hall Library, 4762
        National Agricultural Library, 4762–4763
        National Library of Medicine, 4763
        Niels Bohr Library and Archives and Cen-
            ter for History of Physics, 4763
    state and local government archives
        Multnomah County (Oregon) Archives,
            4746
        New Orleans Notorial Archives, 4746
        San Antonio Municipal Archives Program,
            4746–4747
    women's history archives
        Iowa Women's Archives, 4760
        Sallie Bingham Center for Women's His-
            tory and Culture, 4760
        Schlesinger Library, 4759–4760
        Sophia Smith Collection, 4759
Archival science
    access and use, 173
    acquisition, 172
    appraisal, 171–172
    archive fever, 171
    arrangement and description, 172–173
    education and research, 176–177
    organizational activity, 171
    preservation, 172
    professional discipline, 173–174
    provenance and original order, 170–171
    western world, 174–176
Archival services
    access
        breach privacy, 1467
        exclusive access, 1466
        information security and freedom, 1463
        law protected data, 1466
        policy sealing, 1466
        privacy and confidentiality restriction,
            1466

Archival services (cont'd.)
  access (cont'd.)
    private/confidential document posting,
      1467
    rare materials, research libraries, 1465
    SAA Code of Ethics, 1466
    safeguard privacy, 1467
    Scrolls, 1466
    sealing material, 1466
    selective access, 1466
    sensitive material, 1466
    sensitive/proprietary information, 1463
  acquisitions
    appraisals, 1464
    auction houses, 1465
    basic elements, 1464
    deed of deposit, 1464
    deed of gift, 1464
    donation, 1464
    ethical aspects, 1463
    gift and purchase materials, 1463
    intellectual and historical context, 1463
    legal issues, 1463
    long-term safekeeping, 1463
    manuscript dealers, 1465
    material's fair market value, 1464
    online auction sites, 1464
    open-ended deposits, 1464
    private sellers, 1465
    right to transfer, 1463
    tax deduction, 1464–1465
  terms of use, 1467–1468
Archival Studies Education, 4912–4913
Archive Museum of ERT, 1739
Archives
  in Australia
    Australian Joint Copying Project, 386
    business archives, 188
    as discipline and profession, 388
    educational and religious archives,
      188–189
    national and state archives, 386–387
    nongovernmental archives, 387–388
  avocational user groups, 152
  in China
    archive management bureaus and reposito-
      ries, 905–906
    CAC, 905
    China People's University, 908
    education courses, 907–908
    legislation, 905
    national archives, 906–907
    professional associations, 908
    provinces, 906–907
    religious archives, 907
    State Archives Bureau, 905
  closed-ended questions, 151
  copies, 160
  in Croatia
    Croatian State Archives, 1127–1128
    historical overview, 1126–1127
    legislation, 1127
    National Film Archives, 1128
    publishing and professional associations,
      1128
    specialized archives, 1128
  definition, 1792

  in Denmark
    archivists and records managers, education
      for, 1224
    college and university archives, 1223–1224
    conservation and preservation, 1225
    Danish Archives Act, 1222
    Danish Emigration Archives in Aalborg,
      1224
    digital archival collections and finding aids,
      1224
    electronic records, 1224–1225
    Map and Land Registry Agency, 1224
    national, regional, and local archives,
      1222–1223
    professional associations, 1224
    repositories, 1224
  digital surrogates/electronic records, 160–161
  direct use, 151
  Dodecanese, prefecture of, 1737
  Ethiopia, 1500
  evidential use, 150–151
  experience and preparation, 151
  in France (*see* France, archives)
  French Revolution and nineteenth century,
    182–183
  in Germany
    archival pedagogic/user education, 1703
    corporate archives, 1701
    digital archival collections and finding aids,
      1702
    education, 1702
    electronic records, 1703
    film and audiovisual archives, 1701
    legislation, 1699
    literary archives, 1701
    local archives, 1700–1701
    national archives and services, 1699–1700
    preservation and conservation, 1703
    private archives, 1701–1702
    professional associations, 1702–1703
    religious archives, 1701
    school and university archives, 1701
    state archives, 1700
  and human impulses, 168–181
  Hungary
    archivists and records managers, education
      for, 1926–1927
    college and university archives, 1925–1926
    corporate and religious, 1926
    as discipline and profession, 1926
    electronic documents, 1927
    film and audiovisual archives, 1926
    historical societies, 1926
    legislation, 1925
    manuscript repositories, 1926
    national archives and services, 1925
    preservation of documents, 1927
    professional associations, 1927
  ICA (*see* International Council on Archives)
  India (*see* India)
  indirect use, 151
  informational use, 150
  information family tree, 150
  information seeking
    electronic resources, 153, 162
    information seekers, 152–153
    in institutional archives, 154

    libraries, 153
    in organizations, 153–154
    people, 152–153
    personal collections, 153
    records, 153
  institutional form and function, 181–182
  institutions
    collecting tradition, 186–188
    North America, 184–185
    postcolonial era, twentieth century,
      183–184
    public records, Australia, 185–186
  intended use, 151
  intrinsic use, 151
  Ionian Islands, 1737
  in Israel
    archival science as discipline and profes-
      sion, 2557
    archives law and state archives, 2553
    branch archives, 2553–2554
    municipal archives, 2554
    professional associations, 2557–2558
    professional education, 2557
    public archives, 2554–2557
  in Japan, 2576
    academic societies, 2570
    associations and organizations, 2570–2571
    college and university, 2569
    corporate, 2569
    decentralized management, 2567
    education and training, 2571
    local public archives, 2568
    National Archives Law, 2569–2570
    National Archives of Japan, 2567–2569
    private sector archives, 2569
    Public Archives Law, 2569–2570
  in Kazakhstan
    access and use, 2586
    archival development plan, 2586
    as discipline and profession, 2586–2587
    history, 2584–2585
    legislation, 2585
    national archive system, 2585
    oblast and municipal archives, 2585
  Kenya (*see* Kenya National Archives and
    Documentation Service)
  legal access, 158–160
  loans, 161
  in Moldova, 3118–3120
  National Archives of Armenia, 235–236
  open-ended questions, 151
  Pacific Islands (*see* Pacific Islands Associa-
    tion of Libraries and Archives)
  parent institution, personal network develop-
    ment, 161
  people with disabilities, 3575
  physical access, 159–160
  as a place and virtual archives, 189–190
  popular illusion, 162
  primary uses, 150
  public programs, 161
  and records management
    careers and education (*see* Educators and
      trainers)
    institutional records and archives (*see*
      Institutional records and archives)
  reference services

administrative components of, 161
continuing interaction, 156
educating users, 154–155
exit interview, 156–157
facilitating research, 154
fundamental elements, 154
intellectual access, 149
legal access, 149
management of, 161–162
person, reference interactions in, 157–158
physical access, 149
query abstraction, 155
query resolution, 155–156
question negotiation, 155–156
reference function, evaluation of, 162
remote users, reference interaction with, 158
repository performance, quantitative and qualitative measures, 162
staff qualifications, 161–162
undertaking research, 154
Web, 158
remote inquiries, 162
research purpose, 151
SAA (*see* Society of American Archivists)
Samos, 1737
in Saudi Arabia, 3978–3979
Senegal, 4109–4110
in Serbia, 4132–4133
Slovakia
access to archives, 4181
education, 4182
history, 4180
legislation, 4180–4181
magazine and awards, 4183
national archives, 4181
organizations and associations, 4182–4183
specialized public archives, 4182
state archives, 4181–4182
South Korea
as discipline, 4309
legislative history, 4308–4309
NARS, 4308
Spain (*see* Spain)
television (*see* International Federation of Television Archives)
United Kingdom
archival profession, 4738
archive services, 4735–4736
business archives, 4736–4737
community archives, 4738
film and audiovisual archives, 4737
higher education organizations, 4736
legislation, 4732–4735
professional societies and organizations, 4738–4739
rare manuscript libraries, 4738
religious archives, 4737–4738
vocational user groups, 151–152
zoo and aquariums, 5083
Archives Association, 1224
Archives Leadership Institute, 3319
Archives Nationales of France, 1792
Archives of the Serbian Academy of Science and Arts, 4133
Archives, Personal Papers, and Manuscripts (APPM), 136

ArchivesSpace, 137
Archivum, 2437
Archway Publishing, 4058
Aristotle's *scala natura* concept, 1813
Aristotle University of Thessaloniki, 1731–1733, 1738, 1742
Arken Museum of Modern Art, 1226
ARL, *see* Association of Research Libraries
ArLA, *see* Armenian Library Association
ARMA International
association
and profession, 222–223
structure, 223–224
competencies and certification, 225
creation of, 222
education, 225
history
business records management, 221–222
government records management, 222
information and records management, 225–227
membership, 224
publications, 224
standards, 224–225
Armed services museums, United Kingdom, 4718–4719
Armenia, 238–239
education, 238
government, 238
information infrastructure and institutions, 238
libraries
academic libraries, 230
American University of Armenia Papazian Library, 230–231
Armenian Book Chamber, 230
Armenian Library Association, 233–235, 238
children's and school libraries, 230
in Diaspora, 235
education courses, 233
history of, 228
Khnko-Aper National Children's Library, 230–232
NAS RA, 232
National Library of Armenia, 230–231
public libraries, 230
RSML, 232
during Soviet era, 228–230
special libraries, 230
Yerevan State University Library, 230, 232–233
map of, 228–229
museums
Children's Art Gallery and Aesthetic Center, 237
Genocide Museum and Institute, 236–237
Matenadaran, 236–237
National Archives of Armenia, 235–236
people and economy, 238
World Summit on the Information Society, 238
Armenian Book Chamber, 230
Armenian Library Association (ArLA), 229
continuing education, 233–235
goals, 233
inaugural conference participants, 233

initiators, 233
international and regional cooperation, 234–235
library programs, 234
mission statement, 233
National Library Day, 234, 238
and National Library of Armenia, 234
Armenian Museum of Children's Artwork, 237
Arrangement and description
context control systems, 118–120
definitions, 117
digital and networked environments, 120–124
practices, 117–118
principles, 115–117
record group traditions, 118
ARSC *Journal*, 3278, 4302
Art & Architecture Thesaurus® (AAT), 1076, 1079, 2667, 2857, 4411–4412
ARTbibliographies Modern, 250
Artefacts Canada, 678
Art Full Text and Art Index Retrospective, 250
Art gallery(ies)
art world, 243–244
in Australia
Bendigo Art Gallery, 391
Indigenous art, international recognition of, 393
national and state galleries, 388–390
rock art in Kakadu National Park, 391–392
specialist galleries, 391
customers, 246–247
definition, 241–242
elite *vs.* commercially-oriented galleries, 243
in Germany, 1704
Hungary, 1928
international art market, 246
in Kazakhstan, 2587–2588
locations, 247
operations, 242
patronage to market, 244–245
primary, secondary, and tertiary markets, 245
professional artists, 245
resources
blogs, galleries, and auctions online, 248
directories and archives, 247–248
fairs, festivals, and biennials, 248
magazines and journals, 247
professional associations, 247
role, 242–243
in Serbia, 4133–4134
Arthur M. Sackler Museum of Art and Archaeology, 909–910
Article-level metrics (ALMs), 46–47
Artificial intelligence (AI), 2217, 4082–4083
automated reasoning, 271–272
Checkers playing program, 269–270, 273, 276
Deep Blue Chess program, 270, 276
in diverse disciplines, 270
electronic computers, 270
engineering and manufacturing applications, 276
environment protection, 276
financial applications, 276
heuristic search and problem solving, 271
intelligent information systems, 276–277
knowledge representation, 271–272
machine learning, 272–274

Artificial intelligence (AI) (cont'd.)
  machine translation, 277
  medicine and health care, 276
  natural language processing, 274–275
  objective of, 277
  online information tools, 270
  online shopping tools, 270
  robotics, 275
  signal and image processing, 275
  space science explorations, 276
  speech processing, 274
  syllogism, 269
  Turing test, 270
Artificial neural networks (ANNs), 273–274,
    3270
  backpropagation learning algorithm, 279
  as biological models, 279
  as computational systems, 279
  natural language processing (see Natural lan-
    guage processing, ANN)
Art Indemnity Australia, 389
Artists' books, 3736, 4337
Artists Rights Society (ARS), 4946
Art librarianship
  ARLIS/NA, 249, 254
  ARLIS/UK and Ireland, 249, 254
  art and art history-related journals, 250
  art library settings
    academic art libraries, 251
    museum, 251
    public libraries, 251–252
    visual resources, 252
  art-related library and affinity organizations,
    255–256
  digitization, 250
  directories, 249–250
  educational requirements, 250–251
  IFLA, 255
  OPACs, 250
  print-based art periodical indexes, 250
  professional responsibilities
    cataloging, 253
    collection development, 252
    reference, bibliographic instruction and
      research, 253
    staff, budget, and library facilities, man-
      agement of, 253–254
  publications, 249
  role of, 250
  VRA, 252–253, 255
Art Libraries Section, 249
Art Libraries Society of North America (ARLIS/
    NA), 249, 254–256, 4933–4934
Art Libraries Society United Kingdom and Ire-
    land (ARLIS/UK and Ireland), 249, 254
The Art Library as Place, 254
Art library, Japan, 2574
The Art Library Manual: A Guide to Resources
    and Practice, 249
Art market, 244–246
Art Museum Image Consortium (AMICO),
    3178, 3228
Art Museum Libraries and Librarianship, 249,
    251
Art museums, 3236–3237
  architecture, 261
  England, 265

  ethics and governance, 264–265
  exhibitions, 265–266
  France, 264
  gallery, 259
  globalization, 266
  Hermitage, 1818
  history
    antiquity, 260
    Enlightenment, 261
    Middle Ages, 260
    modern period, 262–264
    nineteenth century, 261–262
    Renaissance, 260
    United States, 262
  in Israel, 2551
  modern art, 263–264
  money and other measurements, 265
  ownership, 266–267
  politics, power, and representation, 3689,
    3692–3693
  Switzerland, 4495
Arts administration, 4928
Arts and Humanities Citation Index (A&HCI),
    925, 2370, 3471
Arts and Humanities Research Council (AHRC),
    4718
Arts and Industries Building, 4192
Arts literatures
  artist occupations, 293–294
  arts, definition, 293
  information retrieval
    image retrieval, 297–298
    melodic retrieval, 298
    subject retrieval, 297
  user studies
    art historians, 295
    characteristic of, 294–295
    children, 293
    dance, film, theatre, 296
    fine artists, 296
    musicians, 296–297
    music scholars, 295–296
    national service organizations, 297
    retirees, 293
    serendipity, 295
ARTstor, 250, 297–298, 4941
Art theft, 4577
Art world, 243–244
arXiv, 3466, 4013
arXiv.org's mathematics archive, 3645
ASCLA, see Association of Specialized and
    Cooperative Library Agencies
ASCLA Exceptional Service Award, 377
ASCLA Leadership and Professional Achieve-
    ment Award, 377
ASCLA/National Organization on Disability
    Award, 377
Ashmolean Museum, 1817, 4716, 4718
Asian papermaking, 1826
as-if models, 2361
ASIST, see American Society for Information
    Science and Technology
ASIS&T, see Association for Information Sci-
    ence and Technology
AskJeeves, 2523
ASLIB, see Association of Special Libraries and
    Information Bureaux

ASLIB Cranfield Project, 3712
Asni Gallery, 1504
assignFAST service, 1544–1545
Assignment indexing, 1987
ASSO, 4631
Associate university librarians (AULs), 4
Association des Bibliothe'caires de France
    (ABF), 255
Association for College and Research Libraries
    (ACRL), 4338, 4850
Association for Computers and the Humanities,
    1288
Association for Computing Machinery (ACM),
    631–632, 701, 2178, 2276, 3863, 4115
Association for Health Information and Librar-
    ies in Africa (AHILA), 3039
Association for Information and Image Manage-
    ment (AIIM), 2342
Association for Information Management,
    308–309
Association for Information Science and Tech-
    nology (ASIS&T)
  awards, 316
  chapters and SIGS, 313–314
  governance, 314–315
  history
    digital world, boundaries in, 313
    documentation, beginnings in, 311
    human/social perspective, 312–313
    information explosion, 312
    modern information science, transition to,
      311
    online information, 312
  meetings, 315–316
  publications, 315
  purpose, 313
Association for Information Systems (AIS),
    631–632, 701, 2276
  in business schools, 318
  evolution of
    Bjorn-Andersen, Niels (1996), 320
    Davis, Gordon (1998), 321
    Ein-Dor, Phillip (2002), 321–322
    Galletta, Dennis (2007), 322–323
    Galliers, Bob (1999), 321
    Ives, Blake (2001), 321
    King, Bill (1995), 320
    Loebbecke, Claudia (2005), 322
    Myers, Michael (2006), 322
    SIGs, 319–320
    Vitale, Mike (2000), 321
    Watson, Richard (2004), 322
    Weber, Ron (1997), 321
    Wei, K.K. (2003), 322
  governance of, 319
  history of, 318–319
  objectives of, 318
Association for Library and Information Science
    Education (ALISE), 19–20, 708, 1475,
    2042, 2536, 3039
Association for Library Collections and Techni-
    cal Services (ALCTS)
  Aquisitions Section, 328
  awards
    ALCTS Honors, 332
    ALCTS Outstanding Publications Award,
      331

Edward Swanson Memorial Best of LRTS Award, 331
Esther J. Piercy Award, 331
First Step Award, Wiley Professional Development Grant, 331
George Cunha and Susan Swartzburg Award, 332
Jan Merrill-Oldham Professional Development Grant, 332
Library Acquisitions Award, 331
Margaret Mann Citation, 331
Outstanding Collaboration Citation, 332
Paul Banks and Carolyn Harris Preservation Award, 331
Presidential Citations, 332
ProQuest Coutts Award for Innovation, 332
Ross Atkinson Lifetime Achievement Award, 330–331
Ulrich's Serials Librarianship Award, 331
best practices, 325
CaMMS, 328–329
CMS, 329
continuing education, 325
CRS, 329
division
    Advisory Committees, 328
    operational committees, 327
    Revenue Committees, 327
governance
    Board of Directors, 326
    bylaws, 326
history, 325
information exchange, 325
interest groups, 328
mission, 324
PARS, 329
products, services and member benefits, 324
professional development, 325
publications, 325
publishing
    ALCTS News, 330
    Continuing Education and Programming, 330
    LRTS, 329–330
    membership, 330
    Monographs Collection, 330
    Sudden Selector's Guides, 330
    Z 687, 330
standards, 324–325
strategic plan
    ALCTS strategic plan 2015, 326
    financial plan, 326–327
    preamble, 326
vision, 324
Association for Library Service to Children (ALSC), 880
activities
    advocacy, 336
    awards, 334–335
    continuing education and professional development, 335–336
    practice, 335
governance, 333–334
history, 333
Association for Literary and Linguistic Computing, 1288

Association for Recorded Sound Collections (ARSC), 3278, 4301–4302
Association for Supervision and Curriculum Development (ASCD), 3998
Association of American Law Schools (AALS), 2712, 2716
Association of American Library Schools (AALS), see Association for Library and Information Science Education
Association of American Medical Colleges (AAMC), 1872
Association of American Publishers (AAP), 3655
Association of Architecture School Librarians (AASL), 255
Association of Archivists of Quebec (AAQ), 667
Association of Art Museum Directors (AAMD), 259, 3201
Association of Canadian Archivists (ACA), 174, 666–667
Association of Central Libraries of Serbia, 4127
Association of College and Research Libraries (ACRL), 2–3, 81, 255, 367, 989, 2752, 4012, 4576, 4582, 4587–4588, 4691, 4775–4776
academic libraries, value of, 344
awards, 343–344
division of
    ALA Council, 339, 340
    chapters, 340
    communities of practice, 340
    discussion groups, 340
    interest groups, 340
    sections, 340–341
higher education associations, working with, 342
library campaign and grassroots advocacy, 347–348
origin of, 338–339
professional development and growth, 356
    ACRL conferences, 349
    ACRL consulting services, 352
    ACRL Insider, 357
    ACRL nonserial publications, 355–356
    ACRL office, 339–340
    ACRLog, 357
    ACRL podcasts, 357–358
    ACRL social media, 358
    ACRL website, 357
    ambassador, academic libraries and librarians, 341
    annual conference programs, 352
    career and job services, 352
    CHOICE office, 354–355
    clearinghouse, 341
    CLIPP, 356
    coordination and oversight, 341
    e-learning, 349–350
    information literacy immersion program, 351
    Keeping Up With. . ., 357
    knowledge and intellectual technique, 353
    leadership, 350
    library statistics, 356–357
    mentoring and training programs, 350–351
    section newsletters, 357

strategic planning, 341–342
workshops and preconferences, 351–352
professional recruitment, 348
public policy advocacy, 347
research and scholarly environment, 344–346
standards and guidelines, 342–343
student learning, 346–347
summits, 348–349
Association of Computing Machinery (ACM), 2222
Association of Computing Machinery/Special Interest Group (ACM/SIG) Proceedings Templates, 3067
Association of Danish Museums, 1227
Association of German Librarians, 1699
Association of Independent Information Professionals (AIIP), 4356
Association of Independent Museums (AIM), 4721
Association of Information and Image Management (AIIM), 715, 1854
Association of Information and Library Professionals, 1699
Association of Jewish Libraries (AJL), 4608
Association of Learned and Professional Society Publishers (ALPSP), 4897–4900
Association of Library Collections and Technical Services, 1332
Association of Library Directors, 1222
Association of Library Trustees, Advocates, Friends and Foundations (ALTAFF)
governance and structure
    advocacy committees cluster, 362
    ALTA AND FOLUSA, 362–363
    business committees cluster, 362
    education committees cluster, 362
    publications committee cluster, 362
history, 361
membership, 361
mission of, 361
responsibilities, 361
Association of Local Archives, 1224
Association of Moving Image Archivists (AMIA), 1579, 1586–1587, 3131
Association of Public Library Managers (APLM), 3377
Association of Recorded Sound Collections (ARSC), 1579
Association of Records Executives and Administrators (AREA), 222, 1854
Association of Records Managers and Administrators (ARMA), 3870
Association of Research Libraries (ARL), 3, 344, 347, 355, 2903, 2963, 4449
CNI, 368, 375
collections and access
    global resources, 372
    resource sharing, 373–374
    special collections, 372–373
constitution, 364
copyright and intellectual property policies, 369
cyberinfrastructure, 370
diversity initiatives, 370–371
establishment of, 364

Association of Research Libraries (ARL)
   (cont'd.)
   Executive Director, 364
   federal funding, 370
   federal legislation, influence on, 368
   governance, 375
   guiding principles, 364–365
   leadership development, 371–372
   membership, 375
   preservation, 367–368
   privacy, security, and civil liberties, 369–370
   public access policies, 369
   RTL, 370
   scholarly communication
      Create Change Web site, 367
      IAA, 366–367
      Institute on Scholarly Communication, 367
      open access, 365–366
      OSC, 365
      scholarly publishing market, 366
      SPARC, 367
   secretariat, 364
   statistics and measurement program
      ARL Statistics, 374
      performance measures, 374–375
   strategic directions (2005–2009), 365
   survey, 97
   vision statement, 364
   Web site, 375
Association of School Librarians (AASL), 334,
   1222
Association of Specialized and Cooperative
   Library Agencies (ASCLA), 3576
   awards and scholarships, 377
   continuing education opportunities, 377
   definition, 376
   membership, 376
   organization, 376–377
   problems and issues, 377
   publications, 377
   standards, 377
Association of Specialized and Professional
   Accreditors (ASPA), 18–19
Association of Special Libraries and Information
   Bureaux (ASLIB), 301–309, 1374,
   4707–4708, 4711
Association of State Libraries Agencies
   (ASLA), 4394
Association of Ukrainian Libraries (ABU), 4644
Association of Zoos and Aquariums (AZA),
   5078
Associations of Recorded Sound Collections
   (ARSC), 2467
Association to Support the Development of
   Archives and Libraries (ADABI), 3097
Astor, Jacob, 1845
Astor Library, 1845
Atheneum archive, 4322
ATLA, see American Theological Library
   Association
Atomic Energy Act of 1954, 3564
Attitude, definition of, 3192
Attribute granularity, 1174
Auckland Free Public Library, 3372
Auction sales catalogs and dealers' catalogs,
   3770
Audiobooks, 872

Audio indexing techniques, 1058
Audiophiles, 3280
Audiovisual archives, 4755
   Hungary, 1926
   UNESCO, 4659–4660
Audiovisual cataloging resources, 1575
Audiovisual preservation
   analog audio and videotape materials,
      1568–1572
   digital formats, 1571
   film, 1567–1568
   funding, 1578–1579
Aurora, 2630
Australasia, 3373
Australasian Digital Recordkeeping Initiative,
   388
Australasian Public Libraries and Information
   Services, 3407
Australia, 393–394
   archives and archival science
      Australian Joint Copying Project, 386
      as discipline and profession, 388
      national and state archives, 386–387
      nongovernmental archives, 387–388
   business archives, 188
   Education Acts in Victoria, 380
   educational and religious archives, 188–189
   institutions, public records, 185–186
   library and information professions, systems
      and services
      academic and research libraries, 384–385
      Australian Subscription Library and Read-
         ing Room, 380
      free circulating library, 380
      free public reference library, 380
      international influences, 386
      legislation, 381
      lending branch, 380
      librarianship as discipline and profession,
         385–386
      mechanics' institute, 380
      Munn-Pitt Report, 381
      National Library, 381–382
      school and college libraries, 383–384
      special libraries, 384–385
      state and public libraries, 382–383
      State Library of Victoria, 381
   map of, 379–380
   museums and galleries
      Bendigo Art Gallery, 391
      courses, 393
      curatorial issues, 393
      national and state museums and galleries,
         388–391
      national parks, 391–392
      professional associations, 393
      specialist museums and galleries, 391
      von Mueller, Ferdinand Jakob Heinrich,
         392–393
      zoos and aquaria, 391
Australian Academic and Research Libraries,
   400
Australian and New Zealand Institute for Infor-
   mation Literacy (ANZIIL), 2752
Australian Broadcasting Company (ABC), 1567
Australian Earth Sciences Information System
   (AESIS), 385

Australian Library and Information Association
   (ALIA), 385
   advocacy, 398
   awards and scholarships, 399
   conferences, 400
   constitution, 397
   copyright advice service, 399
   core values, 397
   education and training, 398–399
   governance and structure, 398
   history of, 396–397
   industrial relations advice service, 399
   interlibrary loan voucher scheme, 400
   membership, 399
   publications, 400
Australian Library Journal, 400
Australian National Maritime Museum,
   389–390
Australian National University (ANU), 384
Australian recordkeeping, 119
Australian Recordkeeping Metadata Research
   Project, 1415
Australian School Library Association, 385
Australian Science and Technology Heritage
   Centre, 387
Australian Science Archives Project, 387
Australian Society of Archivists (ASA), 174,
   688
Australian SPIRT Recordkeeping Metadata Pro-
   ject, 123
Australian Standards for Records Management
   (AS-4390), 3871
Australian Subscription Library and Reading
   Room, 380
Austrian National Library, 3322
Authentication
   assertion of identity, 401
   biometric method, 403
   Certificate Authorities, 404
   digital signatures, 404–405
   initialization processes, 404
   intermediary authenticating service, 405
   IP addresses, 403
   one-time passwords, 402
   PGP, 404
   public key encryption, 402
   shared secrets, 402
   smart cards, 402–403
   traditional signatures, 405
Author cocitation analysis, 2218
Authority, 1116; see also Cognitive authority
Authority file, 1076
Authorization
   access rules, categories, 405
   discretionary, 406
   goal of, 405
   mandatory, 405–406
   RBAC, 406
   trust management approach, 406
Authorized access points (AAPs), 726
Authors Guild, 1760–1761
Authorship, 1860
Author Solutions, 4058
AutoCAD, 2297
Autodesk, 1676
AutoDewey, 1262
Autograph collection, 199

Automated acquisitions systems
  components, 410–412
  e-commerce, 414
  electronic interfaces
    book and serial industry, 412–413
    external accounting systems, 412
  evolution, 408–410
  Internet, 414
  standards, 413–414
  workflows and organization, 414–415
Automated discourse generation, *see* Natural
    language generation
Automated patent system (APS), 3563
Automated reasoning, 271–272
Automated Records and Techniques Curriculum
    Project, 1415
Automated Retroactive Minimal Moderation
    (ARMM), 785
Automated testing, 4798
Automatic abstracting and summarization
  components/techniques
    coherence/coreference enforcers, 424
    cohesion-based methods, 422
    compression/paraphrasing, 423–424
    cue-phrase method, 421
    discourse-based method, 422
    importance identifiers, 420–422
    paraphrasing components, 420
    position-based method, 420–421
    sentence simplifiers/compressors, 422–423
    title-based method, 421
    word-frequency method, 421–422
  F-value metric, 419–420
  genres and types of, 418–419
  headline generation, 424
  multidoc summarization, 425–426
  nontextual information, 426
  recall and precision, 419–420
  semantics, 424–425
  SUMMAC evaluation, 420
Automatic Direct Access to information with
    Online UDC System (AUDACIOUS),
    4788
Automatic indexing, 1987–1988, 2221
Automatic Language Processing Advisory
    Committee of the National Academy of
    Science–National Research Council
    (ALPAC) report, 3348
Autonomous University of the State of Mexico
    (UAEM), 3092
Avant-Garde Masters Grants, 1588
Avery Index to Architectural Periodicals, 250
Avicenna (Prince of Physicians), 3044
Award of Merit, 95
A Way to Get Wealth, 1400
Axumite Heritage Library, 40

B

BaBar high-energy physics project, 2997
Babylonian Talmud, 3042
Back-of-the-book index, *see* Book indexing
Backstage LibraryWorks, 1545
Backward citation retrieval/footnote chasing,
    925
Badier's bindings, 544
Bahir Dar University, 1499

Baidu, 4051
"Ba," knowledge transfer, 2446
Bangemann report, 2140–2141
Bankers's Magazine, 1405
Bank Secrecy Act, 1106
Bank Street College's program, 3218
Barbara Kyle's classification, 971
Bardo National Museum, 4636
Bare-bones system, 1490
Bar journals, 2740
Barker, Dale Lockard, 497–498
Barnum, Phineas T., 1819
Bartlane system, 1308
Basadre, Jorge, 3607
Baseball Hall of Fame, 4756
Base de donnee´s des ressources gratuites sur
    Internet (BDRGI), 4629
Bash Scholarship, 81
Basic Local Alignment Search Tool (BLAST),
    826–827
Basic Multilingual Plane (BMP), 4665–4666
Baska Tablet, 1122
BATAB, 409
Bates' berry-picking approach, 2244, 4529,
    4878
Bates, Marcia J., 2057–2058
Bateson, Gregory, 2051
Bauhaus biography text, 436–437
Bayes Belief Networks, 274
Bayesian networks (BNs), 1204, 2635
Bayes' rule, 2355
Bayes theorem, 2205
Bayt al-Hikmah, 3972
Bayte and Snare of Fortune, 1400
BC, *see* Bibliographic classification
The Beginnings of Systematic Bibliography, 493
Behavioral economics, 2357
Behaviorism, 4918
Behaviorist theory, 2753
Beijing History Museum, 909
Beijing Jingcheng Olympic Education Museum,
    909
Beijing Library, 889–890
Beijing Library Association, 890
Beijing Museum of Natural History, 909
Beijing World Art Museum, 909
Beilstein Handbook of Organic Chemistry, 820
*Beit Hatefutsoth–The Nachum Goldman
    Museum of Jewish Diaspora*, 2552
Belgian binders, 547
Belgrade City Library, 4129
Belkin's episode model, 1898, 2246–2247
Bell system, 1013
Belmont Report, 3146
Belvedere Gallery, 1504
Belvedère Park, 4638–4639
Belvedere statue court, 3149, 3151–3152, 3154
Benakeios Library, 1729
Benaki Museum, 1732, 1742
Benaki Phytopathological Institute, 1732
Bench journals, 2740
Bendigo Art Gallery, 391
Bentham, Jeremy, 646
Bentley Systems, Inc., 1676
Bepress' Digital Commons, 2902
Berkeley Art Museum, 3218
Berkeley Community Memory, 1029

Berkeley Systems Distribution of Unix, 3488
Berlin Medical Papyrus, 3041
Bernan Press, 1724
Berne Convention, 1316, 5009
Berners-Lee's vision for Web, 5019–5020,
    5024–5026
Berry-picking model, 3936–3937
  Bates' berry-picking model, 2076, 2244,
    4529, 4878
  of searching, 3588
Bessarabia
  archives, 3119–3120
  history, 3117–3118
  library, 3123
  museum, 3120–3123
Betacam, 1568–1569
Bethje Wolff's library, 2799
Better Assessment Science Integrating Point
    and Nonpoint Sources (BASINS),
    2155
Beynon-Davies, Paul, 2058–2059
Bezalel National Museum, 2549
BI, *see* Business informatics
BIBFRAME Scribe, 1545
Bible Lands Museum, 2551
Bibliographical access control, 2910
Bibliographical Center for Research (BCR),
    3920, 3922
Bibliographical presses, 3743
Bibliographical Society (London)
  compositor analysis, 459
  ESTC, 458
  Gold Medal, 461
  grants and bursaries, 461
  handwritten slips, 459
  The Library, 460–461
  meagre and scrappy, 457
  meetings, 460
  membership, 460
  objectives and achievements, 456
  The Society's library, 461
  Society's objectives, 460
  STC, 457
  study and research, 456
Bibliographical Society of America (BSA)
  electronic publications, 466–467
  fellowships and prizes, 465
  founding and objectives, 463–464
  meetings, 464–465
  monograph publications, 466
  organization, 464
  periodical publications, 465–466
Bibliographic classification (BC), 4205–4207,
    4475
  adaptability, 574–575
  collocation, 573–574
  consensus, 574
  extent of use, 573
  gradation, 574
  notation, 576–578
    alternative location, 576
    alternative treatments, 576
    A-Z index, 578
    classification, 575–576
  present edition of, 579
  principles, 573
  weakness, 578–579

Bibliographic Classification of Henry Evelyn
    Bliss (BC1), 581
Bibliographic control
    AACR, 449
    Bicentennial Conference on Bibliographic
        Control for the New Millennium, 454
    book catalogs, 448
    British Museum's catalog, 448
    Callimachus, 448
    card catalog, 448
    catalogers, 454
    cataloging in source, 450
    CIP program, 450
    Dublin Core, 454
    electronic catalog records, 450
    FRAD, 453
    FRBR, 452–453
    ICABS, 451
    individuals, 447
    institutions, 447
    inventory lists, 448
    ISBDs, 451
    ISBN, 450
    libraries and collectors, 447
    MARC format, 449–450
    metadata, 453–454
    OCLC, 451–452
    OPAC, 451
    Panizzi's formulation, 91 rules, 448
    Paris Principles, 449
    PCC, 454
    The Pinakes, 448
    printed union catalogs, 448
    publishers, 447
    RDA, 453
    resources, 447
    retailers, 447
    RLG, 451–452
    RLIN, 451–452
    scrolls/tablets, 447
    shelf arrangement systems, 447
    Statement of International Cataloguing Prin-
        ciples, 449
    UBC, 451
    UBCIM Core Activity, 451
    WLN, 451
    Working Group address and conclusion, 455
Bibliographic coupling, 503–504, 946
Bibliographic Database of the Conservation
    Information Network (BCIN), 676
Bibliographic databases, 942
Bibliographic framework (BIBFRAME), 1079
    model, 2924
    project, 2938, 2941
    Transitions Initiative, 3295
Bibliographic instruction (BI), 1878
Bibliographic library knowledge organization
    classification, 960
    enumerative classification, 962
    faceted classifications, 962
    facet structure, 966–968
    hierarchical structure, 965–966
    history and foundations, 961–962
    idea, verbal, and notational plane, 961
    integrative levels, 968–969
    literary warrant, 962–963
    notation, 969–971

phenomenon-based knowledge organization,
    964–965
    precoordinated classification, 962
    scientific and educational consensus, 963–964
Bibliographic verification, 3914
Bibliography
    bibliographical searching, 477
    compilation
        annotation, 477
        citation style, 476–477
        organization, 477
        scope, 476
    definition of, 492–493
    history
        library cataloging codes, 471
        modern bibliography, rise of, 469–471
        new writings, serial bibliographies of,
            471–472
        origins of, 468–469
    national imprint bibliographies
        current national bibliographies, 473
        current online subject bibliographies, 474
        Germany and adjacent areas, 473
        Great Britain, 472
        Romance-Language Nations, 472
        United States, 472
    physical bibliography, 468, 472
        analytical bibliography, 477–478
        descriptive bibliography, 478
        historical bibliography, 478–468
        textual bibliography, 478
    reference, 468
Bibliography of the History of Art, 250
Bibliometrics, 523–524, 2367
    ARIST, 489
    bibliography, definition of, 492–493
    Bradford's law
        distribution, 2226
        of scattering, 509–514
    Bradford-Zipf phenomena, 516–519
    chronological list, 498
    citation analysis, 519–520
        citation indexes, 521–523
        clustering, 523
        half-life and obsolescence, 520–521
        practical applications of, 524
    cocitation map, 485
    data sources, 2227
    definition, 497, 499
    descriptive and evaluative, 499
    domain analysis, 485
    Google boom, 483–485
    human–literature interface, 488
    information behavior, 489
    interpersonal communication, 489
    IS, map of, 485–488
    L&IS definition
        answers properties, 482
        literature properties, 481
        mediating systems properties, 481
        questioners' properties, 481
    literature-based answering, 481–482, 488
    Lotka's law of scientific productivity,
        506–509
    mediators and automation, 483
    Pareto distributions, 2226
    science of recorded discourse, 499

seminal bibliometric papers, 506
    Bibliographic Coupling between Scientific
        Papers, 503–504
    Citation Analysis as a Tool in Journal
        Evaluation, 503
    Citation Indexes for Science, 502–503
    Co-Citation in the Scientific Literature: A
        New Measure of the Relationship
        between Two Documents, 505
    criteria, 499
    Fundamental Science and War, 501
    Fussler, Herman H., 502
    Generalization of the Theory of Epidemics:
        An Application to the Transmission of
        Ideas, 504–505
    The History of Comparative Anatomy-A
        Statistical Analysis of the Literature,
        499–500
    Human Behavior and the Principle of Least
        Effort, 502
    The Influence and Dependence of Psycho-
        logical Journals on Each Other,
        500–501
    Number of Journals Indexed arranged by
        Countries, 500
    Psycho-Biology of Language, 502
    Sources of Information on Specific Sub-
        jects, 501–502
    Statistics-The Frequency Distribution of
        Scientific Productivity, 501
    statistical bibliography, definition of, 492,
        496–497
    statistics
        Achenwall's concept of, 495
        descriptive statistics, 494–495
        Gaussian distribution, 494
        inductive statistics, 494–495
        meaning of, 493–494
        official statistics, 495
        science of method, 495
        scientific investigation, method of, 495
        theory of probability, 494–496
    uses, 523–524
    Zipf's law of word occurrence, 514–516
BIBLIONET, 1734
Biblioteca do Conhecimento Online (B-ON),
    2827
Biblioteca Nazionale Centrale, 3323
Bibliotheca Alexandrina, 2808
Bibliotheca Universalis, 749
Bibliothèque et Archives du Quebec, 3791
Bibliothèque et Archives nationales du Québec
    (BAnQ), 660
Bibliothèque nationale (BN), 1599, 1604–1605
Bibliothèque Nationale de France, 3327–3328
    mission and organization, 533
    new national library project, 532–533
    nineteenth and twentieth century, 531–532
    public and collections, 533–534
    royal library, 531
    twenty-first century
        library's web site, 534–535
        national and international cooperation and
            partnership, 535–536
Bibliothèque Nationale du Québec (BNQ), 535
BIBSAM, 2825
Biculturalism, 3377–3378

Big data, 1487, 2107, 2112
Big Science, 3639
Big6 Skills model, 2757
Bill and Melinda Gates Foundation, 3087
Billy Graham Evangelistic Association (BGEA), 4752
Binary image, 1309
Binary indexing, 2200
Binding(s), 3768–3769, 4147
  blind tooling, 540
  bosses, 540
  butter stamp, 540
  chains and catenati, 540
  chemises, 542
  clasps and catches, 540
  collation, 538
  Cosway bindings, 541
  cover boards, preparation of, 539
  doublure, 539
  edge marbling, 539
  edge-painting and gauffering, 539
  embroidered covers, 540
  end papers, decoration types, 539
  equipment and tools, 538
  Etruscan bindings, 541
  fore-edge painting, 539
  gold tooling, 540–541
  hand binding, history of, 542–548
  headbands, 539
  hollow backs, 539
  illuminated bindings, 541
  incised leather, 540
  intarsia (inlay), 541
  jeweled bindings, 542
  knocked-up, 539
  landscapes, 541
  leather, 539–540
  lettering, 541
  materials, 541
  nonato, 541
  preservation and restoration, 542
  rice marbling, 539
  sewing methods, 538–539
  slip cases, 542
  smooth gilding, 541
  spring backs, 539
  Sutherland tooling process, 541
  techniques, 538
  tight backs, 539
  trimming of edges, 539
Bing, 4051
Bingham Library for Youth, 1843
Bingham Youth Library, 5058
Biocomplexity thesaurus, 3311
Biofuels Standards Panel (BSP), 89
Biography(ies)
  children's books, 867–868
  definition, 1652
  index series, 1652
  World Biographical Information System, 1654
Bioinformatics, 555, 3308
Biological Informatics Program (BRD), 3307–3308
Biological information
  challenges
    access problem, 560

data sharing, 559
  preservation and curation, 559
collaborations, 555–556
cyberinfrastructure, 555
digital data, 556
formats, 556
information and data repositories, 556–557
information infrastructures, development of, 555
paper-based laboratory notebooks, 554, 556
UNISIST model, 556
users of
  amateurs, 559
  biologists, 557–558
  educational community, 558
  organizations and individuals, 558–559
  researchers, 558
  scholarly communities, 558
Biological taxonomy, 4471
BioMed Central journals, 3468–3469
Biometric systems, 403
BioOne®, 3924, 4014
Biosemiotics, 4096, 4102
Biržiška, Vaclovas, 2954
Bit depth, 1309–1310
Bitmap image, 1308–1309
Bit preservation, 1334
BitTorrent technology, 3653
Blackboard Unions, 4691
Black Hat SEO, 4031
Black Pine Animal Park, 3247
Blacksburg Electronic Village, 1031
Blind tooling, 540, 542
Bliss Bibliographic Classification 2nd edition (BC2)
  background and context, 581–582
  classes, internal structure of, 582
  in digital world, 588–589
  disadvantages, 588
  facet analysis and information retrieval, 582–583
  influence on other schemes, 589
  special libraries, 588
  structural principles
    citation order and combination of concepts, 585–586
    filing order and schedule inversion, 586–587
    fundamental categories, 584–585
    main class order, 583–584
    notation, 587
    order in array, 585
    organization within facets, 585
    practical classification, 587–588
  thesaurus format for, 589
  vocabulary, 582
Bliss Classification, 2669; *see also* Bibliographic Classification
Bliss Classification Association (BCA), 582
Blobworld approach, 4421
Blogs, 2507
Blogs, Interactive Groupware Wikis Interest Group (BIGWIG), 2778
Bloomberg Law, 2708
Board of Education for Librarianship (BEL), 19
Board of Trade Journal, 647
BOBBY program, 16

Bodleian catalog, 750, 751
Bodleian Library, 4649, 4703–4704
Boksburg Historical Association (1993), 1782
Bologna Declaration, 630, 710
Bologna process, 2951
Book and journal publishing trade
  advanced countries, 3984
  book readership, growth in, 3983
  budgetary constraints, 3987
  cultural outcomes, 3986–3987
  electronic products, explosion of, 3984–3985
  ephemeral literature, 3987
  future of, 3988–3990
  intellectual property protection, 3987
  international publishing, 3983
  Internet bookselling, 3986
  minor-language countries, government subsidies, 3987
  new book titles, growth in, 3982–3983
  niche/small publishers, 3983–3984
  out-of-print book dealers, 3986
  POD, 3986
  religious publishing, 3987
  retail bookstores, 3985–3986
  specialized publications, 3984
  STM writing/publishing, 3983–3984, 3987
  textbooks, 3986–3987
  twigging effect, 3984
  U.S. book trade, 3982
Book and record depository (BARD), 663
Bookbinding, *see* Binding
Book history, 1859–1864, 4269–4270
Book indexing
  The Chicago Manual of Style, 442–443, 445
  editing tasks, time for, 443–444
  elements
    cross-reference, 441–442
    headings, 441
    letter-by-letter alphabetizing, 442
    locators, 441
    word-by-word alphabetizing, 442
  genre specialties, 444–445
  history of, 440–441
  indented and run-in formats, 442–443
  index, definitions of, 441
  The Oxford Guide to Style, 443
  professional associations, 445
  professional software, 443
  standards, 443
  subject specialties, 445
  term selection, 444
  training, 445
Book Industry Standards and Communications (BISAC), 413, 1261
BookLab, Inc., 3729
Bookline Alert: Missing Books and Manuscripts (BAMBAM), 4576, 4578, 4588
Book Monitoring Unit, 1734
The Book of Marco Polo, 1684
Book of the Dead, 1945–1946
Bookplates, 3768
Books and Newspapers Act (Chapter 111), 2594, 2600
Bookselling, 1861–1862
Books for layperson, 2740
Book theft, 4579

Boolean algebra, 2221
  axiomatization, 594–595
  examples
    finite algebra, 592
    propositions, 592–593
    sets, 593–594
  history, 591–592
  physical phenomenon, 591–592
  switching function, 595–596
Boolean logic, 4048
Boolean model, 2202–2203
Boolean retrieval model, 1621–1622
Boolean searching, 833
Boone Library, 889
Border security, 2399
Borlund model, 4876
Born-digital works, 1335–1336
Boston Athenaeum, 1844
Boston Mercantile Library, 1843
Boston Public Library, 563
Botanical gardens, 3238, 4952
  Hungary, 1930
  Switzerland, 4495
  in United Kingdom, 4724–4725
Boullée's revolutionary library project, 2799
Bourbachique terminology, 328
Bourbaki gadgetry, 328
Bowker®, 3734
Bowman, Isaiah, 1688
Bradford, Samuel Clement, 501–502, 506
Bradford's law, 488, 501, 509–514, 944, 2371
  distribution, 2226–2227
  of scattering, 925, 2210
Braille and Audio Reading Download (BARD),
    568–569
Braille Authority of North America (BANA),
    570
Braille books, 3576
Braille library
  Japan, 2565
  in Korea, 4313
Bray, Thomas, 1840
Brazil
  distance education
    Bachelor in Library Science, 605
    Brazilian Association of Education in
      Information Science, 607
    CAPES, 604, 607–608
    communication process, 607
    course content preparation, 609
    course material development, 608–609
    graduate-level courses, 606
    implementation process, 608
    IPES, 607
    Knowledge Society, 603
    legislation, 604
    librarianship training, 605
    model classroom teaching, 605–606
    Moodle, 606
    new quality of education, 603
    pedagogical design, 607
    RFP, 607
    technical and operational support, 608
    UAB, 604–605
    undergraduate and graduate studies, 604
    undergraduate degree, 607
    virtual learning environments, 606

    graduate courses, 612
    Industrial Revolution, 597
    job market, 612–614
    scientific infrastructure, 597
    undergraduate courses, 597–599
Brazilian Association of Education for Library
    Science and Documentation (ABEBD),
    612
Brazilian Association of Education in Informa-
    tion Science, 607
Brazilian Institute of Bibliography and Docu-
    mentation (IBBD), 612
Brazilian Institute of Science and Technical
    Information (IBICT), 612
Brazilian museum, 611–615
Brenda Dervin's sense-making, 4119–4121
Brett Butler Entrepreneurship Award, 2778
Bridge/jump page, 4035
BrightSparcs, 557
Brisbane City Library, 383
Britain and the British Seas, 1687–1688
Britain-based Institute of Physics (IOP), 3639
British Board of Trade, 646–647
British Broadcasting Company (BBC), 1566
British Film Archive, 4737
British ISKO Chapter, 2497
British Library (BL), 3328–3329, 3729, 4701
  audiences, 628
  collections
    division, 628
    and services, 621–628
    storage building, 618–619
  finance division, 628
  funding, 619
  headquarters, 618
  history, 616–617
  operations division, 628
  strategy, 619–620
  two-site estates strategy, 617–618
  user communities, 620–621
  vision and mission, 619–620
British Library Act 1972, 616
British Library Research and Development
    Department (BLRDD), 4712
British Museum, 1818, 3260, 3758
British Museum Act of 1753, 616
British Museum Catalogue of Books Printed in
    the Fifteenth Century, 1970
British National Bibliography, 583, 1537
British Open University Library, 3438
British Technology Index, 1537
Broader term (BT), 1986
Brontë Parsonage Museum, 4166
Brookes, B.C., 2051
Brooklyn Museum, 1072–1073, 3252
Brooks–Dingell bill, 1020
Brotherton Library, 4704
Brown Popular Culture Library, 4756
Browsing strategies, 2241
Brugsch Maior Papyrus, 3041
Brunhes, Jean, 1687
Brute-force filtering, 5047
Bryant memorandum, 2890
BSA, see Bibliographical Society of America
Buckland, Michael, 2057
Budapest Open Access Initiative (BOAI), 365
Buildings and Equipment (BES), 2842, 2845

Bulgarian Information Consortium (BIC), 2829
Bulletin of the American Mathematical Society,
    3027
Bureaucratic culture, 3521–3522
Bureau of Canadian Archivists' Planning Com-
    mittee on Archival Descriptive Stan-
    dards, 3749
Bureau of Labor Statistics (BLS), 699
Büsching, Anton Friedrich, 1685
Busia Community Library, 40
Business archives
  Coca-Cola Company, 4752
  Ford Motor Company, 4753
  history associates, 4753
  History Factory, 4753
  Levi Strauss, 4753
  United Kingdom, 4736–4737
Business Archives Association (BAA),
    2570–2571
Business Archives Council of Australia
    (BACA), 188
Business broadcasters, 641
Business Committee for the Arts (BCA), 1087
Business directories, 640
Business e-mails, 2507
Business entities, 5013
Business finance, 3005–3006
Business informatics (BI)
  architectural framework, 632
  characteristics of, 631
  IS 2002 undergraduate model curriculum,
    631–632
  MSIS 2000 model curriculum, 631–632
  recommendation for, 631–632
  as science discipline, 631
  study framework, 632–633
  study program, 632–634
Business information users
  advertisements, 639
  business books, 641
  business broadcasters, 641
  contact information, 638
  credit reports, 639
  financial information, 638–639
  general information sources, 637
  industry information, 637–638
  informal and formal sources, 636
  information gathering, 636
  information technologies, 637
  internal and external sources, 636
  legal information, 637
  magazines and journals, 641
  market data, 637
  market research reports and data, 639
  newsletters, 641
  newspapers, 640–641
  product information, 637
  products and services, 639
  reference tools, 640
  small business owners and entrepreneurs,
    636–637
  soft external information, 636
  specialized and technical nonbusiness infor-
    mation, 639–640
Business & Intellectual Property Centre (BIPC),
    620–621
Business intelligence, 2449

Business literature
  abstracting services, 652
  accounting, 651
  banking, finance, and investments, 651
  Code of Hammurabi, 643
  on computer operations, 652–653
  cuneiform clay tablets, 643
  in Egypt, 643–644
  in England, 645–648
  foreign trade, 652
  France and Germany, publications in, 648
  in Greece, 643–644
  in late seventeenth century, 645–646
  loose-leaf services, 652
  marketing, sales management, and advertis-
      ing, 651–652
  newspaper indexes, 652
  periodicals, 653
  personnel and industrial relations, 651
  professional associations, 651
  public relations, 652
  real estate and insurance, 651
  during Romans, 644
  schools of business, 650
  scientific management studies
    in Europe and United States, 650
    list of books, 650–651
  in sixteenth and seventeenth centuries, 645
  statistics, 648–649
  trade associations, publications of, 649–650
  in United States, 647–649
  in Venice and Florence, 644–645
Business magazines, 641
Business process reengineering (BPR), 2658,
    3511
Business productivity software, 3650
Business Reference and Services Section
    (BRASS), 3909
Business Software Alliance (BSA), 3650–3651
Business Statistics, 649
Business Week, 650
Business writing, 4547–4548
Butterfly effect, 1036
Butter stamp, 540
Byzantine illumination, 1946–1947

C

Cabinets of curiosities, 1814
Cable Communications Policy Act, 1017
Cable Television Consumer Protection and
    Competition Act, 1017
Calcutta Public Library, 3326
Caldecott Committee, 334
Caldecott Medal, 334
Calendars, 133, 153, 170, 4084
California Digital Library, 1760
California Public Records Act, 1105
California's Meyers-Milias-Brown Act, 4690
California State University (CSU), 6, 9
Caliper Corporation, 1676
The Cambridge Crystallographic Data Centre,
    822
Cambridge Structural Database (CSD), 822, 834
*Cambridge Tracts in Mathematics and Mathe-
    matical Physics*, 3028
Camel library, Kenya, 2595

Cameo binding, 543
CaMMS, *see* Cataloging and Metadata Manage-
    ment Section
Campbell Collaboration, 1519
Canada
  broadcast archives, 1567
  library and archives (*see* Library and Archives
      Canada)
Canada Institute for Scientific and Technical
    Information (CISTI), 660–661
Canadiana.org, 667
Canadian Association of Research Libraries
    (CARL), 659–660, 664–665
Canadian Broadcasting Company (CBC), 1567
Canadian Committee on Archival Description
    (CCAD), 670
Canadian Council of Archives (CCA), 666
Canadian Federation of Library Associations
    (CFLA), 665
Canadian Heritage Information Network
    (CHIN)
  Artefacts Canada, 678
  BCIN, 676
  CIN, 676
  international activities, 675–676, 679
  knowledge exchange, 678
  membership, 679–680
  mission, 676–678
  NIP, 676
  online resources, 675
  research, 679
  strategies, 675
  VMC Investment Program, 676, 678–679
  Web sites, 678
Canadian Journal of Mathematics, 3027
Canadian Library Association (CLA), 19
  early history, 682
  governance, 682
  LIS community, 681
  roles and activities, 681–682
  1970s–2000, 682–683
  from 2000 On, 683
Canadian Urban Libraries Council (CULC), 666
Canberra, 186, 389, 1392–1393, 3692
Cancelbot, 785, 786
Canevari bindings, 543
Canned text systems, 431
Canstantinopolitanus, see Vienna Dioscorides
Capen, Edward, 1844
*Capital and Finance in the Age of the Renais-
    sance: A Study of the Fuggers and their
    Connections*, 645
Capitalism, 891, 1790, 1859, 1861, 4198–4199
Caracas Declaration, 4887–4890
Card sort, 4797
Careers, 706
  ALA's Office on Human Resource Develop-
      ment and Recruitment, 711
  categorization analyst, 711
  digital services librarian (assistant professor),
      711
  knowledge systems librarian/taxonomist, law,
      711
  staff training and development coordinator,
      712
  Youth Services Department Head, 712
CARIST, 4631

CARL, *see* Canadian Association of Research
    Libraries
Carlos III University, 4321
Carnegie, Andrew, 1839, 1845–1846
Carnegie Corporation, 3216–3217
Carnegie Library, 2387, 2802–2803, 3325
Carnegie United Kingdom Trust (CUKT), 1839
Carnegie–Whitney endowment, 78
Carnivore project, 2070
Carolingian illumination, 1947–1948
Carolingian leather bindings, 542
Carpenter, Nathaniel, 1685
Carthage National Museum, 4637
Carus Mathematical Monographs, 3028
CAS, *see* Chemical Abstracts Service
Cascading style sheets (CSS) specification,
    5021, 5025
Case digests, 2741–2742
Case-study model, 3814–3815
Casinos, 1123
Cason, Hulsey, 500–501
CASREACT database, 818
CAS Registry Numbers®, 824
CASS, *see* Chinese Academy of the Social
    Sciences
Cassette tapes, 3280
Catalan consortium, 2824
Catalog cards, 3450
Cataloging
  bibliographic records, 730–731
  components, 726
  forms, 724–725
  functions, 725–726
Cataloging and Metadata Management Section
    (CaMMS), 328–329
Cataloging cultural objects (CCO), 3178, 3761,
    4935, 4937–4938
  assessment of, 740–742
  elements
    authorities, 739–740
    class element, 738
    creator information, 736
    description element, 738
    location and geography, 737–738
    object naming, 736
    physical characteristics, 737
    stylistic, cultural and chronological infor-
        mation, 737
    subject element, 738
  entity relationship diagram, 735
  general guidelines
    database design, 735
    display and indexing, 735
    related works, 735
    subjective interpretation, 735
    work and image records, 735
  historical context of, 733–734
Cataloging in Publication (CIP) program, 450,
    3395
Cataloging Rules and Principles, 2921
Catalogs and cataloging
  AACR, 2920–2921
  archaeological collections, 1149
  arrangement, 744
  audiovisual archives, 1574–1575
  authority control, 2920
  BIBFRAME model, 2924

Catalogs and cataloging (cont'd.)
  bibliographer, influence of, 744
  bibliographic records, 704–705
  Cataloging Rules and Principles, 2921
  Catalogue of Bretton Monastery Library,
    2920
  codes of cataloging rules, 774–776
  components, 700, 2920
  database maintenance, 2920
  DDC system, 2920
  definition, 743, 2918, 2920
  discovery interfaces, 2922–2923
  in eighteenth century, 751–752, 773
  ERMS, 2922
  format/physical form, 744
  forms, 698–699
  FRBR report, 2923
  functions, 699–700, 745
  inventory, age of
    fifteenth century, 748–749, 773
    fifth through eleventh centuries, 746–747
    fourteenth century, 747–748, 773
    Greeks, 745, 773
    primitive methods, 745
    Roman period, 745–746
    sixteenth century, 749–750, 773
    thirteenth century, 747, 773
    twelfth century, 747
  as inventory list, 744, 745
  LCC, 2920
  MARC, 2921, 2923
  mergers and acquisitions, 2921
  in nineteenth century, 773–774
    ALA, 757
    alphabetical author catalog, 754, 755
    alphabetico-classed catalog, 754, 757–758
    arrangements and indexes, combinations
      of, 755–756
    Bodleian Catalogue of 1674, 754
    Boston Athenaeum catalog, 757–758
    British Museum Rules, 759–760
    card catalog, 756–757
    centralized cataloging, 758
    classified catalog, 754–755
    combined catalog, 754–755
    Crestadoro, Andres, 761
    Cutter, Charles A., 761–763
    Dewey Decimal Classification, 757
    dictionary catalog, 754–757
    index-catalog, 758
    Jewett, Charles C., 760–761
    old inventory concept, 753
    photographic techniques, 758
    printed book catalog, 754
    printed card service, 758–759
    slip catalogs, 762
    supplementary alphabetical subject index,
      758–759
  official catalog, 744
  online catalog, 2922–2923
  original *vs.* copy cataloging, 2920
  periodical indexes, 744
  preparation of, 744
  process of, 744
  public catalog, 744
  purpose/objects of, 744
  RDA, 2923

Rules for a Printed Dictionary Catalog, 2920
Rules for the Compilation of the Catalogue,
  2920
serial publications, publication of, 743
in seventeenth century, 750–752, 773
subject catalog, 744
subject headings, 2920
in twentieth century, 774
  book catalog, 769–770
  card catalog, 765–766
  Cards-with-Books-Program, 768
  Cataloging-in-Source Program, 767–768
  cataloging policies, reevaluation/
    reappraisal of, 766–767
  centralized cataloging, 767–768, 772–773
  classified catalog, 764–765, 771
  commercial services, 767
  computer-produced catalog, 770–771
  cooperative cataloging, 764, 772–773
  depository catalogs, 769
  descriptive cataloging, 765–766
  dictionary catalog, 764
  divided catalogs, 765
  KWIC Index, 770
  linotype slugs method, 769
  local and regional union catalogs, 768–769
  microprint, 770
  photolithographic process, 769
  printed cards, 767
  selective and simplified cataloging, 765
  Shared Cataloging Program, 768
  shingled card technique, 769
  subject catalog, 762–763, 766, 771–773
  tabulating machine, use of, 769–770
union catalog, 744
Catalogue of Bretton Monastery Library, 2920
Catalogue of Printed Books, 755
Catastrophic terrorism, 2400
Categorical data, 4065
Categories for the Description of Works of Art
  (CDWA), 734, 3760–3761, 4413
Category membership, 4797
Cathleen Bourdon Service Award, 377
Catholicon, 1972
Catholic Primatial Archives of Esztergom, 1926
CBIR, *see* Content-based image retrieval
CCO, *see* Cataloging Cultural Objects
CCSDS, *see* Consultative Committee for Space
  Data Systems
CDNL, *see* Conference of Directors of National
  Libraries
CD-ROM, 2322–2326
CDSS, *see* Clinical decision-support systems
CDWA, *see* Categories for the Description of
  Works of Art
Cell phone technology, 4006
Celtic illumination, *see* Hiberno-Saxon
  illumination
Cemetery records, 1658
Censorship, Internet
  ccTLD system, 780
  definition, 780–781
  diffused packet-switching architecture, 780
  history
    1994 to 1997, 781–782
    1996 to 1999, 782
    from 2000, 782–783

ICANN, 780
methods
  access control, 784–785
  filtering, 786
  passing laws, 785
  technology, 785–786
problems
  Internet highlights, 784
  many-to-many spectrum, 784
  maximum freedom, 784
  Neo-Nazis frames, 784
  regulation process, 784
  regulatory paradigm, 784
  Relay Chat and voice-telephony, 784
  scanning GIF files, 784
  surfeit of information, 783
  Web-based newspaper, 784
trends, 786
Censorship, published materials, 2387–2389
Census records, 1658
Center for Democracy and Technology (CDT),
  783
Center for Distance Higher Education of Rio de
  Janeiro (CEDERJ), 608
Center for Documentation and Information
  (CDI), 900–901, 1601
Center for Electronic Records, 1414
Center for European Nuclear Research (CERN),
  4468
Center for International Scholarship in School
  Librarianship (CISSL), 2752
Center for Museum Research and Conservation
  in France, 1596
Center for Networked Information Discovery
  and Retrieval (CNIDR), 3563
Center for Planning and Economic Research
  (KEPE), 1732
Center for Research Libraries (CRL), 372
  application, 793
  collections, 791
  cooperative collection development, 791–793
  global resources collaborations
    global resources programs, 790–791
    partnerships, 790
  history, 789
  resource sharing, 791
Centernet classification, 1290
Center of Legal and Economic Sciences (CCJE),
  612
Center of Research and Education (CORE) pro-
  gram, 3034
Central and East European Licensing Informa-
  tion Platform (CELIP), 2827
Central archive, 3000
Central Archives for the History of the Jewish
  People (CAHJP), 2555
Central European Research Network (CERN),
  3640
Central Information Officer (CIO), 1551
Central Lending Libraries, 1600
Central Library of the Ukrainian Association of
  the Blind, 4647
Central Library System (CLS), 3400
Central Medical Library (CML), 1125
Central Public Library
  of Sparta, 1730
  of Veroia, 1730

Central Zionist Archives (CZA), 2555
Centre de documentation nationale (CDN), 4631
Centre for Continuing Training of Librarians, 1126
Centre for Heritage Development in Africa (CHDA), 2606
Centre national de documentation agricole (CNDA), 4631
Centre national universitaire de documentation scientifique et technique (CNUDST), 4629
Century Scholarship, 377
Certain Ancient Tracts Concerning the Management of Landed Property, 1402
Certificate Authorities (CA), 404
Certified Public Library Administrator (CPLA) program, 2844, 3777, 3804
Certified Records Manager (CRM), 174, 1855
Chained data grids, 3000
Chain of preservation (COP), 2528
Chamber of Commerce of the United States of America, 649–650
Champion Award, NASIG, 3390
Changeable electric sign, 4974–4975
Change management, 717, 3523, 3526
Chapter-level indexing, 3131
Charleston Conference
    administration, 798
    ATG issues, 794
    commercial exhibits, 795
    concurrent presentation sessions, 795
    hotels and venues, 796
    legacy and publications, 798–799
    mentors, 796
    online program, 795
    plenary talks, 794
    printed program, 795
    program, 796–798
    registration, 796
    speakers, 794, 795
    values, 799
    vendor showcase, 795
Charleston Library Society, 1840–1841
Chartbook on Financial and Business Statistics, 649
Chartered Institute of Library and Information Professionals (CILIP), 681–682, 4709, 4711
    action plan, 813
    branches and groups, 808–810
    Ethical Principles and Code of Professional Practice, 812
    goals, 806
    governance, 806–807
        Council, Executive Board and Committees, 807
        Enterprise Board, 808
        policy development committee, 807
        professional development committee, 808
        professional practice committee, 808
    membership, 810
    mission, 806
    professional education and qualifications
        Chartered Membership, 810–811
        Fellowship, 811
        Framework of Qualifications, 811
        overseas qualifications, 811–812

services
    conference management service, 813
    consultancy services, 813
    facet publishing, 813
    INFOmatch, 813
    information and advice, 812
    library and information update, 813
    LIS Jobnet, 813
    networking and further support, 812–813
    news and comment, 812
    qualifications and professional development, 812
    training and development, 813
Charter of Athens, 1070
Chat software, 1056, 3442–3443
Checkers playing program, 269–270, 273, 276
Check-in, 980, 2894, 2982, 4143
Check-out, 917, 921, 980, 1698, 2894
Checksums, 1366
CHEMCATS, 820
Chemical Abstracts Service (CAS), 817–818, 834
Chemical Abstracts Service Registry System, 830
Chemical database, 830, 832–833
Chemical information, 830
Chemical literature
    catalogs, 820
    chemistry and, 814
    handbooks, 820–822
    indexing and abstracting services, 817–820
    information retrieval
        ambiguous chemical identifiers, 823–824
        unambiguous chemical identifiers, 824–825
    primary literature, 814–815
        chemists, 814
        journal articles, 815
        patents, 815
        publication of primary data, 815
    review sources
        encyclopedias, 816
        treaties and review articles, 816–817
    secondary literature, 815–816
    specialized search techniques, 825–827
    tertiary literature, 816–817, 820–822
        handbooks, 820–822
        review sources, 816–817
Chemical similarity, 833
Chemical structure, 830–831, 837, 3570
Chemical substructure, 832–835, 837, 3570
Chemise, 542
Chemistry Preprint Server (CPS), 3643
Chemoinformatics
    computer-aided drug discovery
        ADMET prediction, 837
        molecular diversity analysis, 836–837
        QSAR, 836
    3D structures, database search of, 830
        Cambridge Structural Database, 834
        Chemical Abstracts Service, 834
        similarity searching and docking, 835–836
        structure generation programs, 834
        substructure search, 834–835
    2D structures, database search of, 830
        chemical graph, 831
        connection table, 831
        line notation, 831

patent and reaction searching, 833–834
    similarity searching, 833
    structure diagram, 831
    structure search, 831
    substructure search, 832–833
Cheshire information retrieval system, 1251–1254
Chester Beatty Papyrus, 3041
Chetham catalog of 1791, 753
Chetham Library, 1837
The Chicago Manual of Style, 442–443, 445
Chicago Public Library, 563
Chicanos, 2699, 2701–2702
Chicano Thesaurus, 2699
"Chick lit," 3705–3706
Chief information officer (CIO), 2276
Chief Knowledge Officer (CKO), 2647
Chief Learning Officer (CLO), 2647
Chief Officers of State Library Agencies, Inc, (COSLA), 4394–4395
Child Internet Protection Act, 882, 1472
Child Online Protection Act (COPA), 2396
Children and information technology
    areas of research, 840–844
    digital media, 846–847
    Internet use, 844–846
Children, library services
    Armenia, 230–232
    children's librarians, 880
    collection development, 878–879
    history, 876–877
    at Hjoerring Public Library, 1221
    international dimensions, 882–883
    issues, 880–882
    programming, 879–880
    public library, implementation in, 877–878
    services
        children's librarians, 815
        collection development, 813–814
        history, 811–812
        international dimensions, 817–818
        issues, 815–817
        programming, 814–815
        public library, implementation in, 812–813
        reference services, 815, 880
        storytelling, 814, 879
    in Ukraine, 4645
    in United Kingdom, 4706–4707
Children Online Privacy Protection Act, 782
Children's Art Gallery and Aesthetic Center, 237
Children's Book Week, 334
Children's Internet Protection Act (CIPA), 817, 2396
Children's librarians, 333–336, 2842, 4645, 5061
Children's Library Association (CLA), 333, 5052
Children's literature
    awards, 852, 872–23
    children with disabilities, 871
    definition of, 852
    gay, lesbian/trangendered characters, 871
    history of
        adventures and domestic novels, 855
        fables and books of prayer, 852–853

Children's literature (cont'd.)
  history of (cont'd.)
    fantasy, 854–855
    fiction, 855
    folk tales and fairy tales, 853–854
    grammars, books of manners, and religious
      tracts, 853
    hornbook, 853
    illustrated books, 855–856
    imaginative literature, 853–854
    Newbery's books, 854
    orally transmitted stories, 852
    informational books and biographies,
      867–868
    international books, 868–869
    modern fantasy, 865–867
    multicultural books, 869–871
    nonprint media, 871–872
    picture books
      alphabet books, 859
      concept books, 859
      counting books, 859
      definitions, 856–857
      engineered books, 860
      graphic novels, 860
      illustration, styles of, 857–859
      text of, 857
      trends in, 860–861
      wordless picture books, 858–859
    poetry, 861–862
    realistic fiction
      contemporary fiction, 864–865
      historical fiction, 865
    research collections, 872
    traditional literature, 862–864
Children's museums, 3219, 3237
CHIN, see Canadian Heritage Information
  Network
China, 912–913
  archives and archival science
    archive management bureaus and reposito-
      ries, 905–906
    CAC, 905
    China People's University, 908
    education courses, 907–908
    legislation, 905
    national archives, 906–907
    professional associations, 908
    provinces, 906–907
    religious archives, 907
    State Archives Bureau, 905
  libraries
    academic and research libraries, 895–898
    agreements, 911
    American influence, 889–890
    CNKI, 902
    CNNIC Survey, 902
    CNSDL, 902
    cultural revolution and recovery, 892
    history of, 886–887
    legislation, 892–893
    library and information science education,
      903–904
    library science, 888–889
    Modern Library Movement, 888
    National Library of China, 892–895
    NPDLP, 902

People's Republic of China and Cold War,
  890–892
professional associations, 904–905
public libraries, 898–900
Public Library Movement, 888
PUL, 896, 903
school libraries, 900
special libraries (see Chinese Academy of
  the Social Sciences)
WDL, 903
map of, 886–887
museums and museology, 908–911
population, 886
China Academic Library Information System
  (CALIS), 896
China Association for Science and Technology
  (CAST), 904
China Education and Research Network
  (CERNET), 897
China. Ergebnisse eigener Reisen und darauf
  gegründeter Studien, 1687
China Internet Network Information Center
  (CNNIC) Survey, 902
China National Knowledge Infrastructure
  (CNKI), 902
China People's University, 908
China Science & Technology Museum,
  909–910
China Society for Library Science (CSLS),
  904
China Society for Scientific and Technical
  Information (CSSTI), 905
Chinese Academy of the Social Sciences
  (CASS)
  Institute of Law Library, 901–902
  IWAASL, 902
  library CDI, 900–901
Chinese American Librarians Association
  (CALA), 905
Chinese Archival Classification (CAC), 905
Chinese Archives Association (CAA), 905
Chinese Association for the Advancement of
  Education (CAAE), 890
Chinese Mathematics-Acta, 3027
Chinese Modern Library Movement, 888–889
Chinese National Museum, 909
Chinese National Science Digital Library
  (CNSDL), 902
Chinese radical-phonetic compound character
  types, 3834
Chinese Si Ku classification, 889
Chişinău Municipal Library (CML), 3124
Chomsky's theories, 3348
Choo's model, 2089, 2091
Chorography, 1684
Christchurch catalog, 747
Chromolithographs, 1868
Chronicon Rusticum-Commerciale; or, Memoirs
  of Wool, 1402
Churches and synagogues, 3416
CI, see Competitive Intelligence
CICs, see Corporate information centers
CIDOC Conceptual Resource Model (CIDOC
  CRM), 3760–3761
CILEA, 2827
CILIP, see Chartered Institute of Library and
  Information Professionals

CINAHL database, 1765
CINDEX, 443
Circulating library, 1842, 4481–4484
Circulation Interchange Protocol (NCIP), 2894
Circulation services
  borrowing cycle, 916
  definition, 916
  desk, 917
  ethics, 917
  kinds, 918–919
  stack management, 920–921
  staffing, 919–920
  technology, 921–922
  user communities, 919
Circumvention, 784, 1272, 1316–1319, 1321,
  2142, 2955
CISTI, see Canada Institute for Scientific and
  Technical Information
Citation analysis; see also Citer motivations
  Bradford-ZIPF phenomena, 519–520
  "impact factor," 505
Citation index, 521–523
  bibliographic and bibliometric database,
    940
  creation and structure of, 941
  definition, 941
  functions, cited references
    cited reference capture, 942
    cited reference linking, 942–943
    cited reference searching, 943–944
  information retrieval, 941
  standardized/unified cited reference index,
    941
Citation networks, 1041–1042
Citation order, 585–586
Citation tracking, 2214
Citators, 2741
Cited references, 940–946, 953, 3569, 3640
  searching, 926, 942–945, 948, 3640
  strings, 926
Citer motivations, 519–520
  altmetrics, 924
  bibliography rules, 952
  categories
    Chubin and Moitra, 955
    Moravcsik and Murugesan, 955
  citation content analysis, 935, 952
  citation context analysis, 935, 952
  citation counts, 925
  citation indexes, 521–523
  clustering, 523
  currency, 952–953
  Frost's citation classification, 954–955
  Garfield's taxonomy, 953
  half-life and obsolescence, 520–521
  Hodges's taxonomy, 953–954
  homonyms and allonyms, 927
  interdocumentary relations
    bibliographic coupling, 930
    cocitation, 930–931
    documents, 933–934
    historiographs, 932
    images, identities and recitation, 932–933
    intercitation, 930
    PFNET algorithm, 931–932
  Lipetz's citation relationships, science litera-
    ture, 953

measures derived from counts
author statistics, 928–929
journal statistics, 927–928
organizational and national statistics, 929
microlevel data, 925–927
multivariate models, 953
Peritz's social science taxonomy, 954
persuasion hypothesis, 935
practical applications of, 524
prima facie validity, 951
reward hypothesis, 936
scientists, 952
self-citations, 935
social constructivists, 935
univariate model, 952
validation of, 955–956
verbal objects, 924–925
"CiteScore" metrics, 928
CiteSpace, 923
CITE system, 3428
Citizen science, 559, 4015
CityGML, 1677
Civil registration, 1657
Civil society, 5013–5014
Civil War Preservation Trust, 1774
CLA, *see* Canadian Library Association
Clandestine presses, 3741
Clarivate Analytics, 818, 925
Clasps, 540
Classification
BC, 4475
adaptability, 574–575
alternative location, 576
alternative treatments, 576
A-Z index, 578
classification, 575–576
collocation, 573–574
consensus, 574
extent of use, 573
gradation, 574
notation, 576–578
present edition of, 579
principles, 573
weakness, 578–579
data streams
Bayesian network, 2635
CVFDT, 2635
decision trees, 2635
ensemble classifiers, 2635–2636
learning models, 2635
StreamMiner, 2636
VFDT, 2635
DDC, 961, 966, 969–970, 1802, 2669–2670,
2920, 3283, 3397, 4205, 4466, 4472,
4783, 4788
applications and research, 1261–1263
in China, 889
classes, hierarchies, and relationships,
1257–1258
development, 1258, 1260
editions, 1259
electronic versions, 1259–1260
general rules, 1258
Manual and Relative Index, 1257
mappings, 1261
notational synthesis, 1258
schedules and tables, 1257

summaries, 1256–1257
translations, 1260–1261
value of, 1256
LCC, 963, 970, 992, 1261–1262, 2669, 3283,
3902, 4205, 4466, 4472, 4475
in current information environment,
2851–2852
development, 2848–2849
divisions, 2850
domain-specific taxonomies, 2852
factors for acceptance, 2847
file partitioning, 2852
guidelines, 2853
history of, 2847–2848
information retrieval function, 2847
Internet, information databases, and
OPACs, 2854
and LCSH, 2852–2853
library materials, shelf-ordering of, 2847
main classes, 2849–2850
multitopical works, 2853
national bias, 2853
notation (numbering system), 2849–2851
obsolescence, 2853
strengths, 2853–2854
subclasses, 2849–2850
principles, 4474
schemes, 743, 753–754, 756, 772, 1175,
1536–1537, 3029
social influences on
hierarchical structure, consequences of,
4208–4209
structure, 4207–4208
warrant, 4204–4205
systems, 509, 959–962, 3424, 3426
theory, 958–971
UDC, 574, 961, 970, 1261, 2669, 4466, 4471,
4475
automation and, 4788–4789
auxiliary tables, 4785–4786
BC2, influence of, 589
citation order, 4787
classification structure, 4784–4785
filing order, 4787
general classification schemes, 4783
history, 4783–4784
main classes, 4787–4788
notation, 4785
theoretical basis, 4786
Classification Act 1995, 381
Classification and Search Support Information
System (CASSIS), 3563
Classification Research Group (CRG), 582–583
Classify prototype, 1546
Classsical libraries, 1221, 1797
Clay tablets, 643
Clear and present danger test, 1015
Click-wrap agreement, 1271
Clinical decision-support systems (CDSS)
current best evidence, 974
EBM, 974
history of, 975
medical knowledge engineering, guideline
ontologies for
AHRQ's National Guideline Clearing-
house, 977
barriers, 978–979

contextual factors, 979
CRS, 979–980
influential guidelines, 977
MLM code, 977
patient data codification, 979
system interoperability, 979
new generation of guideline, 975–977
Clinical informatics, 85–86
Clinical medical librarians (CML), 1884
Clinical reminder system (CRS), 979–980
Clinical Text De-identification (CTD) system,
3342
Cloaking, 4035, 4042
CLOCKSS, 1213
CLOPE algorithm, 2634
Closed questions, reference interview, 3915
Closed-system indexing, 440
Cloud-based storage services, 4942
Cloud computing, 5028
Cluster analysis, 837
Clustering, 1040, 3294
data streams
challenges, 2633
CluStream and variants, 2633–2634
hierarchical method, 2633
k-median, 2634–2635
partitioning method, 2633
CluStream algorithm, 2633–2634
CMC, *see* Computer-mediated communication
CMSs, *see* Content management systems
Coalition for Networked Information (CNI),
368, 375, 1391–1392
Coalition on Library Automation (COLA),
2776
Cochrane, 1878
Cochrane Collaboration, 1519
Code4Lib, 2781
Code of ethics, 3197
Code of Ethics and Guidelines for Practice, 1071
Code of Federal Regulations (CFR), 640
Code of Hammurabi, 643
Codicology, 4336
CODiE Award Program, 4298
Codification, 1373
Codified knowledge, 4115
Cody Firearms Museum, 4382
Cognitive authority, 2759
bases for, 1116–1117
definition, 1116
process, 1117–1118
Cognitive constructivism, 2753
Cognitive knowledge, 3535
Cognitive map, wayfinding, 4959
Cognitive model, 281
Cognitive moves, 2241
Cognitive needs, 2115, 2119
Cognitive psychology, 3854, 4542
Cognitive relevance judgments, 3943
Cognitive Task Analysis (CTA), 4116
Cognitive theory, 2753
Cognitive walkthrough, 4798
Coherence theory, 2612–2613
Cohesion-based methods, summarization, 422
Cole, F.J., 499–500, 506
Collaboration portals, 2893
Collaborative Initiative for French Language
Collections (CIFNAL), 790

Collaborative IR (CIR), 4880
Collaborative recommender systems
    elicit preferences, 3861
    predictions, 3862
    recommendations, 3862
    schematic representation, 3861
Collaborative Web browsing, 3443
Collabra, 1062
Collection development, 2333–2335
Collection Development and Evaluation Section
    (CODES), 3909
*Collection Development Policies: for Libraries
    & Visual Collections in the Arts*, 252
Collection maintenance, *see* Stack management
Collection Management Section (CMS), 329
*Collection of Letters for the Improvement of
    Husbandry and Trade*, 1401
*Collection of Tracts, on the Subjects of Taxing
    the British Colonies in America, and
    Regulating their Trade*, 1402
Collections Australia Network (CAN), 3178
Collection-specific local vocabularies,
    1078–1079
College archives, Hungary, 1925–1926
College Art Association (CAA), 255,
    4933–4934
College Level Examination Program (CLEP),
    1847
College library
    in Australia, 384
    bibliographic instruction/information literacy,
        987–988
    challenges, 983, 985
    collection development, 985–986
    history of, 983
    information technology, development of,
        983–985
    interlibrary loan, 986–987
    management, structure, and staff changes, 990
    rare book collections, 3822
    resources for, 354–355
    standards, 988–990
    in United Kingdom, 4705
College Library Directors Mentor Program, 990
College & Research Libraries (C&RL), 353
Collexis, 1768
Colon Classification (CC), 961, 967, 1534, 1536,
    2669, 4466, 4475
Colonial Williamsburg, 3218, 4166–4167
Colon scheme, 574
Colorado Alliance of Research Libraries, 1209,
    1212
Color formats, 1177
Color histogram, 4422–4423
Color illustration, 1945
Color management, 4943
Columbia River Basin Ethnic History Archive
    (CRBEHA), 1783–1784
Comanaged libraries, 4160
COM cats, 2078–2079
COMEXAZ, 2699
Commemorative landscape, 4165
Commemorative site monuments, 4164–4165
Commercial and Financial Chronicle, 648, 1404
Commercial galleries, 243
Commercial journals, 2740
Commercial lending libraries, 4478

Commission for Accreditation of Law-Enforce-
    ment Agencies (CALEA), 4258
Commission for Science and Technology
    (COSTECH), 4508
Commission of Trade and Plantations, 646
Commission on Preservation and Access, 3725
Committee on Accreditation (COA), 18–20, 709
Committee on Archival Development (CAD),
    2438
Committee on Best Practices and Standards
    (ICA/CBPS), 2441
Committee on Copyright and Other Legal Mat-
    ters (CLM), 2457–2458
Committee on Development and Intellectual
    Property (CDIP), 5002
Committee on Freedom of Access to Informa-
    tion and Freedom of Expression
    (FAIFE), 2458
Committee on Institutional Cooperation (CIC),
    1757, 1759
Committee on Museum Professional Training
    (COMPT), 3219
Committee on Organization (COO), 76
Committee on Program Evaluation and Support
    (COPES), 72–74
Committee on Reorganization, 339
Common Business-Oriented Language
    (COBOL), 2272
Common Command Language (CML), 2345
Common communication format (CCF), 4627
Common Core State Standards (CCSS) Initia-
    tive, 4002
Common Music Notation (CMN), 3267
Commonsense epistemology, 1456
Commonsense knowledge, 272
Commonwealth Archives Office, 119
Commonwealth Government archives, 185
Commonwealth Library Association (COMLA),
    2597–2598
Commonwealth National Library, 381
Commonwealth Record Series (CRS), 3876
Commonwealth Scientific and Industrial
    Research Organisation (CSIRO), 382
Communication channels, 2297
Communication engineering, 2051
Communication policy
    administrative and judicial interpretation,
        1008
    competition, 1022–1023
    competitive environment
        cable, regulatory regime, 1016–1017
        deregulate broadcasting, 1018–1019
        hybrid technology, 1016
        telecom regime, 1017–1018
    cultural concerns
        electronic media, 1013
        radio, 1013
    decision makers, 1008
    goals
        democracy, 1009
        First Amendment, 1009–1010
        intellectual property, 1010
        policy mechanisms, 1008
        postal roads, 1010
        print technology, 1009
    market, 1023–1024
    market-oriented environment, 1007

national integration, mass media and
    education
    agricultural extension, 1011
    land grant colleges and industrial educa-
        tion, 1011
    mass media, 1010–1011
    post-Civil War decision makers, 1010
    public school movement, 1011
national security and defense
    free speech and free market, 1015
    limits on speech, 1015
networked information society, 1007
technological and socioeconomic develop-
    ments, 1007
Telecommunications Act of 1996
    Internet vision, 1019
    legislative outcome, 1021–1022
    103rd Congress, defeat in, 1020
    104th Congress, retreat in, 1020
transportation, 1008
universal efficient interconnection via
    regulation
    defense technology, 1015
    industrial economy, 1011
    infrastructure, 1015
    "must carry rules," 1014
    public broadcasting, 1014
    public service company, 1012
    railroads and interstate commerce commis-
        sion, 1012
    spectrum licensing, 1014
    telegraph, 1012
    telephone, 1012–1013
    voluntary censorship, 1013–1014
Communications, 144–145, 994–995,
    2770–2771
    and communication studies
        contradictions, 1004–1005
        IAMCR, profile of, 1001, 1004
        ICA, profile of, 1001, 1003
        institutionalization, phases of, 999–1001
        mass and speech communication, 997–998
        media, 998–999
        NCA, profile of, 1001–1002
    CSCW, 1055–1056
    definitions of, 995–996
    human communication, 2354
    and mutual information, 2352–2354
    organization, 4117–4118
    PIALA, 3543
Communications Decency Act (CDA), 2396
Communicative memories, 1140
Communism, 4401
Communities of practice (COP), 1668, 2644,
    2661–2662, 2754–2755, 3529, 4256
Community Access Program (CAP), 2039
Community archives, 4738
Community-based museums, 3237–3238
Community hospital library, 1872
Community informatics
    community definitions, 1027–1028
    emergence, 1031
    Kling's definition, 1027
    new directions, 1031
    practitioners, 1027
    researchers, 1027
    roots of field

within libraries, 1029–1031
outside library, 1028–1029
Community Informatics Institute, 1031
Community museums
    AAM's Museums and Communities Initia-
        tive, 3246–3247
    Civic Engagement Initiative, 3247
    community advisory groups, 3248
    District Six Museum, 3245–3246
    early American museums, 3243–3244
    education, 3244
    El Museo Shan-Dany, 3245
    ethnic museum, 3244–3245
    ICOM, 3246
    Internet, 3248
    Lower East Side Tenement Museum, 3245
    mainstream museum, 3249
    National Park Service, 3247
    neighborhood museum, 3245–3246
    oral history, 3247–3248
    visitor-generated content, 3248–3249
Community Networking Initiative, 1030
Community Technology Centers Network, 1029
Compact disc (CD), 3280
Comparative librarianship
    actual comparisons, 2406
    basic elements, 2407
    cross-societal, 2405
    hierarchical, 2406
    methodology, 2407
    study-activity, 2406
    subject-methodology, 2406
Comparative Molecular Field Analysis
        (CoMFA), 836
Compendieuse Hausshaltungs Bibliotheck, 1403
Competitive intelligence (CI), 2108, 2662, 4354
Complex adaptive systems, 1034
Complexity and self-organization
    agents, 1035–1036
    attractors, 1038
    coevolution and synergy, 1037
    complex networks, 1042
        abstract mathematical network, 1039
        clustering, 1040
        features, 1039
        links, 1039
        nodes, 1039
        random network, 1039
        scale-free networks, 1040–1041
        small-world network, 1039–1040
        social network, 1039
    computer simulations, 1036–1037, 1042
    definition, 1037
    dissipative structures, 1034
    edge of chaos, 1035
    emergence, 1038–1039
    history, 1034–1035
    knowledge networks, 1041–1042
    Kolmogorov complexity, 1035
    local coordination to global organization,
        1037–1038
    mean field effect, 1036
    natural selection, 1037
    nonlinearity, 1036, 1042
    openness, 1042
    in between order and disorder, 1035
    order from noise, 1038

order through fluctuations, 1038
philosophy of, 1034
remote agents, actions of, 1037
traditional deterministic models, 1036
Web possesses, 1034
Complutense University, 4321
Component-based architecture (CBA), 2154
Composite specification, 1535
Compressed histograms, 2630
Compression techniques, 1310–1311
Compulsory Education Act of 1949, 2548
Computed tomography (CT), 4429
Computer assisted instruction (CAI), 3444
    benefits, 3435
    computer-assisted demonstration, 3434
    independent learning tutorials, 3435
    live assistance and hand-on, computer-based
        learning, 3434–3435
Computer-assisted software engineering
        (CASE) tools, 2297, 2344
Computer credibility, 1115
Computer engineering, 694
Computer ethics, 3617
Computer Fraud and Abuse Act (CFAA), 1275
Computer games, 872
Computer–Human Interaction (CHI), 4115
Computer Interchange of Museum Information
        (CIMI), 677
Computer Matching and Privacy Protection Act,
        1555
Computer-mediated communication (CMC),
        2935–2936
    description of, 1044–1045
    groups
        chat systems, 1050
        electronic mailing lists, 1051
        groupware and collaboration, 1050
        multiple user dialog, 1050
        networked meeting software, 1050
        newsgroups and blogs, 1050
        real-time video, 1050
        social networking software, 1051
    interpersonal communication
        asynchronous voice and video, 1049
        E-mail, 1049
        text-based chat and messaging, 1049
        video conferencing, 1049
        voice communication, 1049
    mass communication
        audio, 1051
        text, 1051
        video, 1051
    primary functions
        computer-supported cooperative work, 1048
        conferencing and collaboration, 1046–1047
        dissemination and control of information,
            1047–1048
        informatics, 1048
        teaching and learning, 1045–1046
    research, 1051–1052
Computer output microfilm (COM), 1414, 1851
Computer science and engineering (CS&E),
        1249
Computer Security Act of 1987, 1555–1556
Computer-supported cooperative work (CSCW),
        1048, 1064–1065, 2075, 2274, 2654,
        3864

aim, 1053
challenges, 1060–1061
collaborative software development, 1062–
        1063
definitions, 1053–1054
design areas and features
    communication, 1055–1056
    configuration, 1056
    coordination, 1056–1057
    information access, 1057–1058
    interaction, 1058–1060
design space, key dimensions in, 1054–1055
electronic meetings, 1054
groupware, 1054
media spaces, 1054
productivity improvements, 1053
success factors, 1061–1062
team computing, 1054
technologies, 1063–1064
workflow, 1054
Computer technologies, 1472
Computing Research Association (CRA), 2537
CONACULTA museum, 3098
Concept-adapting very fast decision tree
        (CVFDT), 2635
Concept identifier (CUI), 4674
Conceptualist searcher, 4878
Conceptual knowledge, 2622, 3423
Conceptual model, 1606–1607, 1609–1610,
        1612, 1615–1616
Conceptual moves, 2241
Conceptual Reference Model (CRM), 3178
The Conference Board Management Record,
        650
The Conference Board Record, 650
Conference of African National Libraries
        (CANL), 38
Conference of Directors of National Libraries
        (CDNL), 2456, 2458–2459, 3330
Conference of Directors of National Libraries of
        Asia and Oceania (CDNLAO), 3330
Conference of European National Librarians
        (CENL), 536, 3330–3331
Conference of Heads of Irish Universities
        (CHIU), 2825
Conference of Italian University Rectors
        (CRUI), 2827
Conference on Fair Use (CONFU), 4935
Conferred credibility, 1115
CONFOTO, 4088
Congressional Documents, 1404
Congressional Record, 640
Congressional Research Services, 4361
Congress on Professional Education (COPE), 708
Congress's Cooperative Online Serials
        (CONSER) program, 4140
Connectedness-based method, 422
Connecticut State Library, 4397
Conner Prairie historical site, 1776
Connexion cataloging service, 1259,
        3396–3397, 3400
Connotative meanings, 4097
CONSER, 2921
Conservation Information Network (CIN), 676
Conservation museums
    cultural heritage, preservation of, 1068
    development of, 1068

Conservation museums (cont'd.)
  documentation and public access, 1069, 1071–1073
  ethics and guidelines, 1070–1071
  facilities, 1069
  laboratories, 1069–1070
  museum conservators, role of, 1068
  preparators, duties of, 1069
  restoration, 1068–1069
Conservation OnLine (CoOL), 1350
Conservation Plan for Canadian Archival Records (CPCAR), 666
Conservation science, 3769
Conservatory libraries, music libraries, 3276
Consortial DDA programs, 1212
Consortium for Computer Interchange of Museum Information (CIMI), 3227
Consortium of European Research Libraries (CERL), 3771
Consortium of Slovenian Electronic Collections (COSEC), 2828
Consortium of Swiss Academic Libraries, 2826
Consortium of the libraries in Serbia for Cooperative Acquisition (KOBSON), 4128
Consortium of University Research Libraries (CURL), 2825, 4703
Constitution of Athens, 644
Constructivist model, 2118–2119
Consuetudo, vel, Lex Mercatoria, 1400
Consultative Committee for Space Data Systems (CCSDS), 3477–3480, 3485–3486
Consulting services, 1099–1100
Consumer contracts, 1272
ContactFinder, 3865
Contact information, 638
Contemporary academic library planning statements, 4451–4452
Content attributes, 2294
Content-based image retrieval (CBIR)
  affective image retrieval, 4428–4429
  content representation and objects
    composite object, 4421
    simple objects and attributes, 4420–4421
  digital imagery, 4417
  image formats and data compression
    encoding, 4418
    scalar quantization, 4419
    signal representation, 4418
    spatial domain, predictive coding, 4418
    spatial redundancy, 4418–4419
    thresholding, 4419
    transform domain, 4418
    vector quantization, 4419
    wavelet transform, 4418–4419
  image repositories and digital libraries
    medical image databases, 4429–4430
    oil industry, 4431
    remote sensed image databases, 4430–4431
  image searching, semantic level
    progressive semantic retrieval, 4427
    semantic content characterization, 4425
    semantic content extraction, 4426–4427
  metadata, 4427
  multiple abstraction levels
    color features, 4422–4423
    image searching, raw data level, 4421–4422

image segmentation, 4422
  searching, 4428
  semantics, multiple attributes combining, 4427–4428
  shape features, 4425
  texture features, 4423–4425
  query specifications, 4420
Content-based recommender systems, 3862–3863
Content creators, 3066–3067
Content is king, 4034
Content licensing agreements, 1274
Content management (CM), 2659
Content management systems (CMSs), 716, 2108, 3066, 4945
Content modeling, 3112–3113
Content scrambling system (CSS), 1319–1320
Content value standards, 3061
Context control systems, 118–120
Context of Small World, 1509–1510
Contextual Query Language (CQL), 2187, 2189, 2347
Contingency theory, 3514–3515
Continuing Education Committee (CEC), 3035
Continuing education (CE) courses, 3034–3035
Continuing legal education (CLE), 2719
Continuing Professional Development and Workplace Learning (CPDWL), 713
Continuing professional education (CPE), 50–51, 4257
Continuing Resources Section (CRS), 329
Continuous Acquisition and Life-Cycle Support (CALS) initiative, 3075
Continuum concept, 2379
Controlled LOCKSS (CLOCKSS), 4147
Controlled vocabulary, 2857
  LOD, 1079
  search
    authority control, 4467
    consistent and current terminology, 4469
    convenience of the public, 4468–4469
    direct and specific entry, 4469
    enumeration *vs.* faceting, 4469–4470
    lists, 4466–4467
    precoordination *vs.* postcoordination, 4470
    provision of cross-references, 4469
    uniform and unique headings, 4469
  uses, 1077–1078
  vocabulary tools, 1079–1080
Convention on Contracts for the International Sale of Goods (CCISG), 1270–1271
Convention on International Trade in Endangered Species of Wild Fauna and Flora (CITES), 1164
Conversation analysis, 2930
Co-occurrence matrix, 4423
Cooperative Africana Materials Project (CAMP), 790
Cooperative Children's Book Center (CCBC), 870
Cooperative Information Retrieval Network for Scotland (CAIRNS), 250
Co-operative Online Bibliographic System and Services (COBISS), 2828
Cooperative Online Resource Catalog (CORC), 1259, 1539, 3454
Cooperative Online Serials (CONSER), 3395

Coordinate indexing, 2221
Coordinating Committee on Service to the Disadvantaged, 4222
Coordinating Council of Audiovisual Archives Associations (CCAAA), 691, 2453, 3304, 4660
Coordination of Improvement of Higher Education Personnel (CAPES), 604, 608
Copenhagen hand-binding, 547
Coptic bindings, 540, 542
Copy cataloging, 2920
Copyright, 570, 4056
Copyright Act, 381, 682–683, 1271–1272, 2594, 4681–4682
Copyright and software licenses
  national library amendment, 4683
  public policy, 4681–4683
  Virginia libraries amendment, 4683–4684
Copyright Clearance Center (CCC), 4145
Copyright infringement, 3664
Copyright Law of 1976, 1577
Copyright laws, 369
Copyright Ordinance of 1924, 4513
Copyright Society of Tanzania (COSOTA), 4513
Copyright Term Extension Act (CTEA), 1577
Cornelius, Ian, 2054
Corporate amnesia, 2642–2643, 4199
Corporate Antipiracy Program, 4298
Corporate archives
  archival blog, 1083
  business archives, 1085
  communications placement, 1082
  compensation packages, 1085
  digital technology, 1083
  documentation, 1081
  functional leadership, 1082
  human resources function, 1083
  information gap, 1081
  information sharing, 1083
  intellectual capital, 1084
  litigation support, 1081
  marketplace, 1083
  mission/policy statement, 1082
  organizational scheme, 1084
  outreach programming, 1082
  research and reference responsibilities, 1084
Corporate Archives Forum, 1085
Corporate art collections
  alternative modes of, 1089–1090
  artwork, 1088
  challenges and concerns, 1090–1091
  collection management, 1089
  corporate sponsorship and patronage, 1091
  history, 1086–1087
  as investment, 1088–1089
  promoting culture, 1087–1088
  workplace evolution, 1091–1092
Corporate information centers (CICs)
  areas of service
    collection management, 1099
    current awareness, 1099
    document delivery, 1099
    information consulting, 1099–1100
    information resource management, 1099
    reference, 1098
    research, 1098–1099

building competitive edge
   challenges, 1102–1103
   customer intimacy, 1102
   for-profit sector, 1102
communication, 1101–1102
general services, 1100
organization, impact and strategic positioning
   budgets, 1101
   costs and productive time, 1100
   placement, 1100
professional development, 1096–1097
service specialization
   alerting (current awareness) service, 1094
   Deutsche Bank (*see* Deutsche Bank, CIC)
   information technology company, 1095
   law firm, 1096
   public libraries, 1094
special libraries, 1096
staff qualifications, 1096–1097
strategic planning, 1102
subject specialization
   Nike Design Library, areas of, 1094–1095
   textile company, 1094
user, 1095
Corporate libraries, 4374
Corporate mentality, 1089–1090
Corporate portals, 2893
Corporate records management programs
active records management
   components, 1107
   document management systems, 1108
   ECM systems, 1108
   electronic records management, 1108–1109
   equipment costs and use office space, 1107
   filing system, 1107
   imaging program, 1108
audits, 1111–1112
California Public Records Act, 1105
"cradle-to-grave" management, 1104–1105
elements, 1105
external requirements, 1104
FOIA, 1105
good corporate citizen, 1104
government agencies, 1105
inactive records management, 1109–1110
internal requirements, 1104
mergers, acquisitions and divestitures,
   1110–1111
records management placement, 1111
records retention
   appraisal, 1105
   legal environment and compliance,
     1106–1107
   litigation, legal holds, and discovery, 1107
   records series, 1105
   risk management, 1105–1106
standards, 1111
storage formats, 1104
vital records protection program, 1110
Corporation Credit, 1403
Corporation for Public Broadcasting (CPB),
   1014, 1579
Correspondence approach, 2612
Cosijn model, 4875
Cosine correlation, 2203–2204
Cosmographia, 494
Cosmographia universalis, 1685

Cost and benefit attributes, 2294
Cost per thousand model (CPM), 2522
Cosway bindings, 541
Cougar, 2630
Council for Higher Education Accreditation
   (CHEA), 18–19
Council of Australian University Librarians
   (CAUL), 384
Council of Provincial and Territorial Archivists
   (CPTA), 666
Council of Scientific and Industrial Research
   (CSIR), 2002–2003
Council of State Archivists (CoSA), 3319
Council on Library and Information Resources
   (CLIR), 368
Council on Library Resources (CLR), 988, 2873,
   2963–2964
COUNTER, 413
Counting Online Usage of Networked Electronic
   Resources (COUNTER) Project, 4146
Country code top level domain (ccTLD) system,
   780
County Library Authority, 1839
COUPERIN, 2826
The Course of the Exchange, 1401
Covers common foreign and security policy
   (CFSP), 2140
CPLEX, 1196
CQL, *see* Contextual Query Language
Cranfield model of information retrieval (IR),
   4872
Cranfield paradigm, 4554
Cranfield tests, 2222–2223
Create Change Web site, 367
Credentialed librarians, 4777
Credibility
   definition
     expertise, 1113–1114
     trustworthiness, 1113–1114
   historical development, 1114
   process, 1117–1118
   typology of, 1115
Credit reports, 639
Crelle's Journal, 3024, 3026
Crestadoro, Andres, 761
CRG, *see* Classification Research Group
Crime fiction, 3701–3702
Crimestat, 1676
Criminal network analysis, 2402
Critical discourse analysis (CDA), 1664–1665
Critical incidence technique, 4531
*Criticas: An English Speaker's Guide to the
   Latest Spanish-Language Titles*, 2699
CRL, *see* Center for Research Libraries
Croatia
   archives
     Croatian State Archives, 1127–1128
     historical overview, 1126–1127
     legislation, 1127
     National Film Archives, 1128
     publishing and professional associations,
       1128
     specialized archives, 1128
   historical development, 1121
   literacy, books, and libraries
     academic, research, and special libraries,
       1125

Church libraries, 1126
   diocese libraries, 1122–1123
   in fifteenth and sixteenth centuries, 1123
   Glagolitic and Cyrillic alphabets,
     1121–1122
   Latin language, 1121
   legislation, 1124
   library and information science education,
     1126
   monastery libraries, 1122
   national and university library, 1124–1125
   professional associations, 1126
   public and school libraries, 1125–1126
   reading rooms, 1123
   in seventeenth century, 1123
   in twentieth century, 1123–1124
location, 1121
map of, 1121–1122
museums
   history, 1129
   legislation and organization, 1129–1130
   publishing, staff, and professional associa-
     tion, 1130
National Programme for the Digitisation of
   Archival, Library and Museum Records,
   1130
Croatian Academic Research Network
   (CARNET), 1125, 2828
Croatian Archival Council, 1127
Croatian Archivist Association, 1128
Croatian Library Association, 1126
Croatian Library Council, 1124
Croatian Museum Association, 1130
Croatian National and University Library,
   1124–1125
Croatian National Film Archives, 1128
Croatian State Archives, 1127–1128
CrossCheck, 1137
Cross-correlation, 4421
Cross-disciplinary faculty teaching, 2771
Cross-domain linking, 3294
Cross-genre phenomenon, 3706–3707
Cross-Language Evaluation Forum (CLEF),
   3143
Cross-lingual information retrieval (CLIR),
   2222, 2402, 3140
CrossRef publisher linking network
   cited-by linking, 1137
   CrossCheck, 1137
   CrossRef metadata services, 1137
   database, 1133
   distributed integration, 1138
   DOI, 1133–1134
   endeavor, 1133
   history, 1132–1133
   impacts
     on intermediaries, 1137
     on libraries, 1136–1137
     on publishers, 1136
     on researchers, 1137
   initiative, 1133
   interlinking, 1138
   metadata, 1133
   mission, 1132
   working process
     citation submission, 1134
     DOI registration, 1134

CrossRef publisher linking network (cont'd.)
  working process (cont'd.)
    DOI resolution, end-user perspective, 1135
    journal-level and article-level metadata
      record, 1134
    metadata records, depositing, 1134
    non-XML interfaces, 1134
    reference linking workflow, 1134–1135
CrossRef registration agency, 1326, 1330
Crossref Web site, 1330
Crowdsourcing, 3294
CRS, *see* Clinical reminder system
CS AKTive Space, 4087–4088
CSCW, *see* Computer-supported cooperative
    work
Cue-phrase method, 421
Cuirbouilli, 540
Cuir cisele, 540, 542
Cultural heritage, 4168–4169, 4171
  archives
    American Folklife Center, 4757
    American Heritage Center, 4757
    Amistad Center, 4757
    Balch Institute, 4757
    Center for Puerto Rican Studies, 4757
    Clark Atlanta University, 4757–4758
    Heard Museum Archives, 4758
    Japanese American History Archives, 4758
    Moorland-Spingarn Research Center, 4758
    Museum of Chinese in America,
      4758–4759
    Schomburg Center for Black Culture, 4759
Cultural history museums, 1226
Cultural institutions
  advocacy, 1961–1962
  economic impact, 1961
  impact assessment, 1962–1963
  impact, definition of, 1960
  quantitative evidence, 1960–1961
  raw data and evidence, relationship between,
    1960
  requirements, 1959–1960
Cultural knowledge, 3535
Cultural management, 3522
Cultural memory
  criticisms of, 1143–1144
  group definition
    anti-Semitism, 1142
    depression, 1140–1141
    Holocaust consciousness, 1141–1142
    John F. Kennedy's death, 1140–1141
    public memory, 1141
    U.S. historical events, 1141
  historical context and terminology,
    1098–1140
  representations, 1142
  social relevance, 1142–1143
Cultural national libraries, 3321
Cultural Objects Name Authority® (CONA), 1079
Cultural patrimony, site museums
  historical perspective, interpretation chal-
    lenges, 4170
  Monument to the Great Fire of London, 4165
  preservation laws, 4169
  preventative preservation, 4170
  UNESCO, 4169
  war targets and cultural casualties, 4168

Cultural peoperty, 3772
Culture Information Systems, 2828
Cumulated gain (CG), 1903
Cumulated gain with discount (DCG), 1903
Cumulated Index to Nursing and Allied Health
    Literature (CINAHL), 1873, 1877
Cumulative frequency distribution, 2211
Cuneiform clay tablets, 643
Curating natural history collections
  administrative point of view
    collection manager, 1160–1161
    collectors, preparators, archivists and con-
      servators, 1161
    curator, 1160
    students, interns and volunteers, 1161
  organismal collections, 1156
  paleontological collections, 1156
  specimens
    accessioning, cataloging and installing,
      1158–1159
    collection and preparation, 1157–1158
    data and database management, 1159–1160
    ecological niche, speciation, 1162
    genetic diversity, 1162
    long-term care, 1159
    population structure, 1162
    predator, trophic level of, 1162
    symmetry and ecological stress, 1162
    use of, 1159
Curation, archaeological artifacts
  access and use, 1151
  acquisitions and accessions, 1149
  archaeological sites, 1147–1148
  cataloging, 1149
  ethical issues, 1152–1153
  interpretation, 1151–1152
  metadata standards, 1149–1150
  project design and records, 1148
  standards, 1148
  storage and care, 1150–1151
Curation crisis, 1152
Curatorial files, 3202
Currency, 1176
Current awareness services, 1099
Current Mathematical Publications (CPS), 3644
Current Population Surveys (CPS), 1280
*Current Practice in Health Sciences Librarian-
    ship*, 3037
Current research information systems (CRIS),
    1219
Curriculum Guidelines for Undergraduate
    Degree Programs in Information Sys-
    tems, 630
Custody and chain of custody
  archives, 1167–1168
  CITES, 1164
  history and post-custodial approaches,
    1165–1166
  museums, 1166
  provenience, 1165
  repatriation requests, 1166–1167
  replevin requests, 1168–1169
Customer capital, 2659
Customer relationship management (CRM),
    2274–2275
Customizable e-resource portals, 2893
Customized model generation approach, 1205

Cutter, Charles A., 761–763
Cutter numbers, 2849, 2851
Cyber-competence, 2306
Cyber-crimes, 2401
Cyberinfrastructures, 555, 5028–5029
Cybermetrics, 2367–2368
Cybernetics, 2050
"Cybernetic space," 2125
Cyc, 3456–3457
Cynefin, 4118
Cyrillic alphabet, 1121–1122
Czech National Library, 1261
Czeck and Slovak Library Information Network
    (CASLIN), 2828

D

Daily use software, 3066
DAISY, 1223
Dallas Museum of Art, 4945
Dana, John Cotton, 3244
DanBib, 1218–1219
Daniel Russell's (et al.) sensemaking,
    4115–4116
Danish Agency for Libraries and Media,
    1218–1219
Danish Agriculture Museum, 1226
Danish Archives Act, 1222
Danish Association of Research Librarians,
    1222
Danish Bibliographic Center, 1219
Danish bookbinding, 547
Danish Defence Museum, 1226
Danish Library Association, 1222
Danish Library Authority, 3784–3785
Danish Museum Act, 1225
Danish Museum of Hunting and Forestry, 1226
Danish National Archive in Copenhagen,
    1222–1223
Danish National Business Archives, 1223
Danish National Gallery, 1215
Danish National Library Authority, 1218
Danish Royal Library, 2791
Danish Union of Librarians, 1222
Danmarks Folkebogsamlinger, 1222
Dar al-Ilm, 3972
DARPA Agent Markup Language (DAML),
    4085
Darwin Core, 3311
Das Buch der Chroniken or Liber Chronicarum,
    1973
Das Kapital, 647
*Das Magazin für Historiographie und
    Geographie*, 495
Data and data quality
  accuracy, 1176
  completeness and duplication, 1176
  conceptual model
    attributes, 1173
    business rules, 1174
    composition, 1175
    content, 1174
    datum/data item, 1173
    domain, 1173
    entities, 1173
    IRS's model, 1173
    level of detail, 1174–1175

reaction to change, 1175
scope, 1174
semantic and structural consistency, 1175
universe/enterprise, 1173
consistency and integrity, 1175
criteria, 1172
currency, 1176
data representation, 1174, 1177
definition, 1172–1173
first-generation
error detection and correction, 1178–1179
inspection and rework, 1177–1178
Internet, 1180–1181
life-cycle model, 1171–1172
management, 1177
quality and quality control, 1178–1180
second-generation
error prevention, 1179–1180
process quality management, 1178
third-generation, process design, 1178
Data and electronic records archives
Electronic and Special Media Records Ser-
vices Division, NARA, 4754
ERA, 4754
ICPSR, 4753–4754
Minerva/Library of Congress Web Archives,
4754
Data bank, 1171–1172
Database aesthetics, 2069
Database bashing, 1179
Database for Orientation and Research in the
Archives, 1592
Database management system (DBMS), 1203,
2272, 2629
Database of Archives of Non-Governmental
Organizations (DANGO), 3386
Data Citation Index, 815
Data communication standards, 3061–3062
Data editing, 1179
Data elements, 3291–3292
Data grids, 2998
data virtualization, 2998
management virtualization, 3000–3002
name spaces, 2999
trust virtualization, 2999–3000
Data-information-knowledge-wisdom (DIKW),
2049, 2059
Data Interchange Standards Association (DISA),
88
Data management, 2108
Data Management Plan (DMP), 4015
Data mining, 2401–2403
conventional algorithms, 2626–2627
data stream algorithms (*see* Data streams)
iterative and interactive process, 2637
Data Preservation Alliance for the Social Sciences (Data-PASS), 4753
Data recording, 1173
Data retrieval systems (DRS), 2193
Data streams
applications, 2628
challenges
criteria, 2628–2629
DBMS, 2629
DWT, 2630
histograms, 2629–2630
one pass requirement concept, 2628

sampling, 2630–2631
transactions/data instances, 2628
classification
Bayesian network, 2635
CVFDT, 2635
decision trees, 2635
ensemble classifiers, 2635–2636
learning models, 2635
StreamMiner, 2636
VFDT, 2635
clustering algorithms
challenges, 2633
CluStream and variants, 2633–2634
hierarchical method, 2633
k-median, 2634–2635
partitioning method, 2633
vs. conventional algorithms, 2627–2628
frequent pattern mining
Apriori, 2631
FP-Streaming, 2632–2633
frequent item mining, 2631–2632
Lossy Counting algorithm, 2632
Manku and Motwani's algorithm, 2632
Data structures, 4065
Data structure standards, 3060–3061
Data tracking, 1180
Data virtualization, 2998–2999
Date searching, 4049
David Adamany Undergraduate Library,
4653
David Snowden's sense-making, 4118
*Davis versus Freedom of Information Commis-
sion*, 2399
Davis, William Morris, 1688
Day, Ronald, 2059
DBMS, *see* Database management system
DC, *see* Dublin Core
DC-dot, 3063, 3066
DCMI, *see* Dublin Core Metadata Initiative
DCMI Abstract Model (DCAM), 1396–1397
DCMS, *see* Department for Culture, Media and
Sport
DDA, *see* Demand-driven acquisition
DDC, *see* Dewey decimal classification
Deaccessioning, 1152–1153
Deaf and hearing impaired
communication adaptment, 1188–1189
communication environment, 1188
communication modes, 1185
communication with deaf people
fingerspelling, 1187
sign language, 1186–1187
speaking and facial expression, 1186
speechreading, 1186
deafness and deaf people, 1184–1185
empathy with Listener, 1189
group communication, 1189
initiating communication, 1188
interactive communication, 1188
misconceptions, 1185–1186
NTID, 1183
RIT reference librarians, 1183
simultaneous communication and total
communication
learning sign language, 1187
writing, 1188
terminology, 1184

*Decatur Public Library v. The District
Attorney's Office of Wise County*,
2390
Decimal Classification, 574
Deciphering MedSpeak publications,
3036–3037
Decision analysis, 1203–1205
Decision making
information use for
ecological rationality, 2361–2365
PsycINFO, 2359–2360
rationality perspectives, 2360–2361
Decision processing portals, 2893
Decision rule, 2363
Decision sciences
deterministic model
advantage of, 1193
economic lot sizing model, 1196–1197
IP models, 1195–1196
LP model, 1194–1195
game theoretic models, 1198
MCDM, 1198
professional associations, 1193
quantitative modeling (OR/MS) perspective,
1192–1193
queuing, and simulation, 1198
stochastic models, 1197
Decision support system (DSS), 2193–2194,
2274, 2654
application areas of, 1200, 1202
architecture of, 1203
DBMS, 1203
decisions and decision modeling
decision options, 1202
decision problem, 1201–1202
good decisions *vs.* outcomes, 1202
judgmental heuristics, 1201
preference, 1202
types of, 1201
uncertainty, 1202
DGMS, 1203
goal of, 1203
MBMS, 1203
normative systems, 1201
decision analysis, 1203–1205
ESP, 1206
expert systems, 1203
heuristic methods and ad hoc reasoning
schemes, 1203
structural equation models, 1205–1206
user interfaces
decision variables, choice and optimization
of, 1206
graphical interface, 1207
graphical model, 1203
model construction and analysis, 1203
numerical calculations, 1203
Decision Tree learning algorithm, 273
Declaration of Principles, 5016
Deductive justification, 1457
Deep archives, 3000
Deep Blue Chess program, 270, 276
Deep Web, 5021
de facto phenomenon, 2144
Defence of Trade, 1400
Defence Research and Development Organization (DRDO), 2003

Defense Advanced Research Program Agency
    (DARPA), 2402, 2516
Delivery and Registration of Publications Act of
    Bombay Government, 1993
Delivery of Advanced Network Technology to
    Europe (DANTE), 4629
Delivery of Books (Public Libraries) Amend-
    ment Act, 1956, 1993
Delivery of Books and Newspapers (Public
    Libraries) Act, 1954, 1993
DELNET database, 2005
DeLone and McLean IT success model,
    2293–2294
Delphi approach, 3598
Demand-driven acquisition (DDA)
    collection development, 1209–1210
    consideration pool, 1212
    consortia, 1212
    ILL, 1213
    models, 1210–1211
    preservation, 1213
    print monographs, 1211–1212
    rationale, 1209
    risks, 1212–1213
    themes, 1210
    video, 1211
Demand Purchase Program, 792
Demangeon, Albert, 1687
Democratic Ideals and Reality, 1688
Demographics, 3168
*Demonstrating Results: Using Outcome Mea-
    surement in Your Library*, 3794
Denmark
    archives and archival science
        archivists and records managers, education
            for, 1224
        college and university archives, 1223–1224
        conservation and preservation, 1225
        Danish Archives Act, 1222
        Danish Emigration Archives in Aalborg,
            1224
        digital archival collections and finding aids,
            1224
        electronic records, 1224–1225
        Map and Land Registry Agency, 1224
        national, regional, and local archives,
            1222–1223
        professional associations, 1224
        repositories, 1224
    constitution, 1215
    library and information systems and services
        absolute monarchy, 1215
        associations, 1222
        cathedral schools, 1215
        digital library collections and services, 1220
        education, 1221–1222
        legislation, 1218
        in monasteries, 1215
        national library, 1218–1219
        public libraries, 1215–1218, 1220
        school libraries, 1220–1221
        special libraries, 1219–1220
        universities, 1219
    map of, 1215–1216
    museums and museology
        art museums, 1225–1226
        cultural history museums, 1226

curatorship and museum administration,
    training for, 1227
Danish museum sector, 1225
digital museum exhibits and services,
    1226–1227
education, 1227–1228
Heritage Agency, 1225
legal framework, 1225
natural history museums, 1226
preservation, 1227–1228
professional associations, 1227
Denmark Electronic Research Library Project
    (DEF), 2825
Denmark's Electronic Research Library
    (DEFF), 1220
Denmark's National Private Archive Database
    (DANPA), 1223
Denotative meaning, 4096–4097
Denver Natural History Museum, 3254
Deontic authority, 1116
Departmental retention schedules, 3893
Department for Culture, Media and Sport
    (DCMS), 1958–1959, 4702
    advocacy, 1961–1962
    economic impact, 1961
    impact
        assessment, 1962–1963
        definition, 1960
    quantitative evidence, 1960–1961
    raw data and evidence, relationship between,
        1960
    requirements, 1959–1960
Department of Commerce and Labor, 647–648
Department of Energy (DOE), 1555
Department of Homeland Security (DHS), 2402
Department of Library and Information Science
    (DLIS), 4179
Department of Scientific and Industrial Research
    (DSIR), 301
Department of State Foreign Affairs Network
    (DOSFAN), 1556
Depository libraries, 1717–1718
Depository library programs, 2156
Deposit Systems for Electronic Publications
    (DSEP), 1333
De Re Medicina, 3043
Derr, Richard, 2052–2053
Dervin, Brenda, 2056–2057
Dervin's sense-making approach, 4114, 4226
Derwent World Patents Index (DWPI), 3643
Der Zoologische Garten, 5078
Descrezzione de Paesi Basse, 645
Describing Archives: A Content Standard
    (DACS), 137, 740, 1423
Description des arts et métiers, 1401
Descriptive bibliography, 478
Descriptive cataloging, 727–729
Descriptive markup, 3074–3075
Descriptive statistics, 494–495
Designer model, 4807
Design for Experiments, 1410
Designing for Digital, 1422
Design of Information Systems in the Social
    Sciences (DISISS) projects, 4246
Design science
    benefits, 1254
    constraints, 1246

conversations with materials, 1246
definition, 1242
design research, 1242
    Cheshire information retrieval system,
        1251–1254
    computer science and engineering, 1249
    constraints, 1250
    corporation, strategic competency, 1249
    definition, 1249
    disciplinary value systems, 1249
    rigor *vs.* relevance, 1249–1250
domain independent, 1243
failure, 1247
information retrieval systems, 1242
as intellectual work, 1247–1249
local vocabularies for image collections,
    1250–1251
problem setting, 1245–1246
product/service, 1243
professions, 1243
research and development, 1242
as social science approach, 1242
tools, 1246–1247
uncertainty, 1243–1245
Desktop computing, 1289
Dessie Museum, 1503
Destructive information, 2095
Detailed retention schedule, *see* Departmental
    retention schedules
Deterministic model
    advantage of, 1193
    economic lot sizing model, 1196–1197
    IP models, 1195–1196
    LP model, 1194–1195
Deterministic-transformational approach,
    1295
Deterritorialization, 2124
Deutsche Bank, CIC, 1097
    alerting area, 1096
    book cabinets, 1094
    computer work area, 1094, 1096
    employee at work, 1098
    specially designed information cabinet, 1098
    storage units, 1096
    storage wall in Information Center, 1097
    work area, 1099
Deutsche Bibliothek, 1694
Deutsche Bücherei Leipzig, 1694
Deutsche Mathematiker-Vereinigung, 324
Developing and Implementing a Recordkeeping
    System (DIRKS) methodology, 111
Developing countries
    definition, 2130
    features of, 2130
    human information-seeking behavior
        barrier to information needs and seeking
            behaviors, 2135–2136
        inadequate information sources, 2133–
            2134
        individuals and individual information
            seeking, 2131–2132
        information and information resources,
            2132–2133
        two-step information-seeking approach,
            2134
Development Information Service Center, 1496
Development knowledge, 2275

Development Officers of Research Academic Libraries (DORAL), 2834
Dewey decimal classification (DDC), 757, 961, 966, 969–970, 1534–1535, 1802, 2499, 2669–2670, 2920, 3283, 3397, 3903, 4205, 4466, 4472, 4783, 4788
   applications and research, 1261–1263
   in China, 889
   classes, hierarchies, and relationships, 1257–1258
   development, 1260
   general rules, 1258
   history
      development, 1258
      editions, 1259
      electronic versions, 1259–1260
   mappings, 1261
   notational synthesis, 1258
   structure and notation
      DDC Summaries, 1256–1257
      Manual and Relative Index, 1257
      schedules and tables, 1257
   translations, 1260–1261
   value of, 1256
Dewey Decimal system, 1818
Dewey for Windows, 1259
Dewey Online Catalog (DOC), 1262
DH, see Digital humanities
Dialog, 2221
Dialog generation and management system (DGMS), 1203
Dialogue systems, 3353
Dial-up services, 2240
Diana V. Braddom FRFDS Scholarship, 2845
Diaries, 4531–4532
Diasporic communities, 1028
Diasporic Information Environment Model (DIEM), 2127
Diasporic populations
   immigrant information-seeking behavior research, 2125–2126
   information behavior, 2126–2127
   media studies, 2122, 2125
   research
      globalization and transnationalism, 2123
      hybridity, imagination and identity, 2123–2124
      nation-states, 2124–2125
   transnational information networks, 2123
   voluntary economic immigrants, 2122
Diasporization, 4208
Dickinson classification system, 3283
Dictionary-based techniques, 3143
Dictionnaire Universal de Commerce, 645
Die Deutsche Nationalbibliothek, see German national library
Die Erde und das Leben, 1687
Differential facet, 1536
DigiQUAL®, 374
Digital Archive, 3400
Digital asset management systems (DAMS), 4942, 4945–4946
Digital Betacam, 1568–1569
Digital books, 3472
Digital collection, 2826
Digital content, 4298

Digital content licensing
   commercial law
      choice of law and forum, 1272–1274
      contractual terms, enforceability of, 1271–1272
      electronic self-help and denial of access, 1275–1276
      UCC, 1270
      UCITA, 1270
      warranties, 1274–1275
      writing requirement and requirements of formation, 1270–1271
   copyright law, 1268
   definition, 1267
   e-rights, 1269
   moral rights, 1268–1269
   neighboring rights, 1268
Digital Cultural Content Forum (dCCF), 679
Digital divide
   Digital Inclusion Network, 1284
   educational divide, 1283–1284
   historical context, 1279–1280
   human capital development, 1284
   ICT access, 1280
   infrastructural level, programs, 1284
   international digital divide, assessments of, 1282–1283
   social support, 1284
   in United States
      age gap, 1282
      disability, 1282
      educational attainment, 1282
      gender gap, 1281
      geography, 1282
      income, 1282
      internet users, demographics of, 1281
      NTIA reports, 1280–1281
      race/ethnicity gap, 1281–1282
Digital humanities (DH), 1295–1296
   categories, 1299
   definitions, 1286–1288, 1298–1299
   history, 1288–1290
   Index Thomisticus, 1299
   institutional location, 1290–1292
   and libraries
      collections, 1303–1304
      consultation and collaboration, 1303
      instruction, 1302–1303
      intensive commitment, 1301
      low commitment, 1301
      moderate commitment, 1301
      theory, 1299–1301
   library community, perspective of, 1292–1293
   modularity, 1293
   pattern discovery and visualization, 1295
   representation, 1293–1295
Digital images
   create, display and share, 1307
   fundamentals
      binary image, 1309
      bit depth, 1309–1310
      bitmap image, 1308–1309
      digitization guidelines, 1309, 1311
      halftone printing, 1309
      interpolation, 1309
      lossless compression, 1310–1311

      lossy compression, 1310
      pixelation, 1309
      pixels, 1308–1310
      raster image, 1308
      resolution, 1309–1310
      vector graphics, 1308
   history of
      computing technologies, 1308
      digital fax, 1308
      image capture peripheral devices, 1308
      photographic images, 1307–1308
      visual imagery, 1307
      World Wide Web, 1308
   image file formats, 1311
   in library and archive sector
      crowdsourcing, 1313
      digitization, 1312
      technical digitization guidelines, 1312–1313
   memory institutions, surrogates for, 1307
   personal digital image collections and librarian, 1313–1314
   POD, 3733, 3735
   of provenance evidence, 3771
Digital imaging, 1414
Digital Inclusion Network, 1284
Digital library(ies), 1760, 2079, 2228–2229, 2240, 2766, 3727
   in Denmark, 1220
   in Germany, 1694, 1698
   Greece
      Anemi, 1732–1733
      digital collections and institutional repository, 1733
      e-fimeris, 1733
      National Documentation Center, 1733
      Psifiothiki, 1733
   Hungary, 1923–1924
   Japan, 2566
   in Kazakhstan, 2583
   Switzerland, 4489–4490
   Venezuelan libraries, 4890
Digital Library Federation, 1312
Digital Library Initiatives, 2228–2229
Digital Library of India (DLI), 2004
Digital Library of Wielkopolska project, 2828
Digital Library System (DLS), 4311
Digitally based information art projects, 2072
Digital Media Management (DiMeMa), 3400
Digital media piracy
   economic harm, 3650
   file sharing, 3650
   legislative framework
      Copyright Act, 3656
      DMCA, 3656–3657
      e-books, 3658
      Google Book Search, 3658
      intellectual property, 3656
      libraries, 3657
      NIH Public Access Policy, 3658–3659
      Pirate Bay, 3656
      Public Law 102-561, 3656
      RIAA, 3657
      SIAA, 3656
      Software Rental Amendments Act, 3656
      Sonny Bono Copyright Term Extension Act (1998), 3656
      Telefonica, 3657

Digital media piracy (cont'd.)
  means, prevalence, and costs
      audio files/music, 3651–3653
      published works, 3655–3656
      software, 3650–3651
      video sharing, 3654
  open access materials/license, 3649
  responses, 3659–3661
Digital Millennium Copyright Act (DMCA)
      of 1998, 369, 1472, 1577, 2142,
      3656–3657
  Bnetd case (*Davidson & Associates v. Jung*),
      1321
  computer maintenance and repair copyright
      exemption, 1322
  DeCSS case (*MPAA v. Corley*), 1319–1320
  DVDXCopy case (*321 Studios v. Metro-
      Goldwyn-Mayer Studios, Inc.*), 1321
  Felten case (*Felten v. RIAA*), 1320
  ISP liability, 1316
  Lexmark case (*Lexmark Int'l v. Static Control
      Components, Inc.*), 1321
  miscellaneous provisions, 1322
  online copyright infringement liability limita-
      tion, 1321–1322
  original designs, protection of, 1322
  Sklyarov case (*U.S. v. ElcomSoft*),
      1320–1321
  WIPO treaties
      access rights, 1317–1318
      anticircumvention, 1317
      civil and criminal penalties, 1316
      device trafficking, 1318
      enabling legislation, 1316
      particular class rule making, 1318
      Section 104 Report, 1318–1319
Digital museum, 3179–3180, 4495
Digital Object Identifier (DOI), 815, 943, 1365
  concepts
      content management of, 1325–1326
      interoperability, 1325
      persistence, 1325
      resolution, 1325
      scheme, 1325–1326
      specification, 1325
      string, 1325
      uniqueness, 1325
  content entities, 1326
  descriptive metadata, 1134
  digital content entity, 1133
  history, 1330
  International DOI Foundation, 1326, 1330
  metadata, 1326, 1329
  prefix and suffix, 1133
  registration, 1132, 1134, 1326
  resolution, 1327–1328
      component, 1326
      end-user perspective, 1135
  scope, 1326–1327
  social infrastructure, 1326, 1329–1330
  syntax, 1326–1327
  technical activities, 1330
Digital preservation
  born-digital works, 1335–1336
  definition, 1332
  digital curation, 1336
  digitization, 1334–1335

frameworks, 1332–1333
  methodologies, 1333–1334
Digital Preservation Management (DPM) Work-
      shop, 1333
Digital Preservation Network (DPN), 1760
Digital printing, 3733
Digital recordkeeping, 120–121
Digital Revolution, 3378
Digital rights management (DRM), 2277,
      4056–4057, 4778–4779
Digital rights management systems (DRMS),
      4945–4946
Digital services librarian, 711
Digital Solidarity Fund, 5016–5017
Digital stewardship, 1336
Digital storage, 4942
Digital video disc (DVD), 3280
Digitization, 1757, 1760–1761
DiMeMa, 3400
Dimension reduction vector space
  producing, 2691
  querying, 2691–2692
Dimensions in Advanced Computing (DIAC)
      conferences, 1031
Diplomatics
  acts, 1341
  approach and purpose of
      accuracy, 1340
      authentication, 1340
      authenticity, 1339–1340
      reliability, 1339
  archival bond, 1344
  building blocks of, 1340–1341
  criticism, 1344–1345
  documentary form
      extrinsic elements of form, 1343
      intrinsic elements of form, 1343–1344
  history of, 1338–1339
  meaning, 1338
  objects of, 1339
  persons, 1342
  procedure, 1342
  records creation, 1341
  transmission, status of, 1340
Diptychs, 542
Direct instructions, 3914
Directorate of Archives of France, 1590–1592
Directories, 640
Directory of Art Libraries, 249
*The Directory of Art Libraries and Visual
      Resource Collections in North America*,
      249–250
Directory of Open Access Journals (DOAJ),
      3645
Disability Discrimination Act 1992, 381
*The Disability Rights Movement: From Charity
      to Confrontation*, 3574
Disaster Information Management Research
      Center (DIMRC), 3343
Disaster planning and recovery, cultural
      institutions
  assessment of risks, 1350
  improvements
      civil unrest, armed conflicts, 1349–1350
      earthquakes, 1348
      fires, 1348–1349
      water damage, 1347–1348

preparation activities
  chain of command, communication and
      contact information, 1352–1353
  collections assets and setting priorities,
      1351
  finances, 1352
  floor maps, 1354
  insurance, 1352
  management issues, 1353
  pack-out instructions, 1351
  security, 1353–1354
  staff training, 1351–1352
  supplies, suppliers, service vendors and
      consultants, 1352
prevention/mitigation, 1351
recovery phase
  building concerns, 1356
  debriefing, revision and training, 1356
  returning collections, building, 1356
response actions
  damage assessment, 1355
  salvage, 1355–1356
responsibilities
  assessment and documentation, 1357
  building issues, 1358
  communications, 1357
  financial issues, 1358
  management, 1357
  personnel issues, 1357
  recovery operations, 1358
  salvage operations, 1358
  security, 1357
  supplies and equipment, 1358
  user issues, 1358
Disaster recovery test (DRT), 3359, 3362–3363
Disciplinary value systems, 1249
Discourse-based summarization systems, 422
*A Discourse of the Common Weal of Thys Realm
      of England*, 646
Discourse of Trade, 1400
Discovery services, 4980–4981
Discrete wavelet transformation (DWT), 2630
Discretionary access control (DAC), 406
Disintermediation, 483
DisplayWriter, 4994
Disposal/retention schedules, 108
Dissemination Information Package (DIP), 1365
Distance education
  CAPES, 604, 607–608
  GIS, 1674–1675
  Knowledge Society, 603
  legislation, 604
  library science
      Bachelor in Library Science, 605
      Brazilian Association of Education in
          Information Science, 607
      communication process, 607
      course content preparation, 609
      course material development, 608–609
      graduate-level courses, 606
      implementation process, 608
      IPES, 607
      librarianship training, 605
      model classroom teaching, 605–606
      Moodle, 606
      pedagogical design, 607
      RFP, 607

technical and operational support, 608
undergraduate degree, 607
virtual learning environments, 606
new quality of education, 603
UAB, 604–605
undergraduate and graduate studies, 604
Distinguished name space, 2999
Distributed data management
principles
authenticity and integrity, 2998
chain of custody, 2998
data virtualization, 2998–2999
infrastructure independence, 2998
management virtualization, 2998, 3000–3002
shared collections, 2998
trust virtualization, 2998–3000
virtualization mechanisms, 2998
technologies, 3002
Distributed Object Computation Testbed project, 1415
Distributive justice, 4219
District Information Documentation Centers (DIDCs), 2594
District Rural Development Agency (DRDA), 2000
Divinity binding, 540
DLF/CLIR + ER&L Cross-Pollinator Travel Award, 1422
DocBook, 3075
Docents, 3192
Docking search, 835–836
Docklands Campus Library and Business School, 254
DOCK program, 836
Documentary meaning, 1375
Documentary photography, 3206
Documentation Inc., 2221
Documentation strategy model, 201
Document delivery services, 1099
Document information systems
authenticity, 1363–1364
definition of, 1360
design methodology, 1371
advantages, 1367
definition, 1367
disadvantages, 1368
way of control, 1370
way of modeling, 1368
way of thinking, 1368
way of working, 1368–1370
digital longevity, 1364
document, definition of, 1360
information, 1360
interoperability, 1363
ISO standard 15489, 1362, 1370
practical cases, 1361–1362
records management software functions, 1362–1363
Sarbanes-Oxley Act, 1362, 1370
software applications, 1362
standards and standard components
checksums, 1366
content representation, 1366
data formats, 1367
metadata, 1364–1366
OAI-PMH and OAI-ORE, 1365

OAIS, 1365
ODMA, 1365
persistent identifier, 1365
query language, 1366–1367
software selection, 1364
storage media, 1364
XML syntactic data model family, 1365
Document input model, 3112
Document-like object (DLOs), 1391
Document management, 718–719, 2108
Document output model, 3110–3111
Document-role relationship table, 3113
Document surrogates, 4466
Document theory
complementary approach, 1378–1379
digital age, 1377–1378
LIS, materialistic critique of, 1376–1377
professional interest, 1373–1375
scientific interest, 1375–1376
Document type definition (DTD), 1365, 1424, 2343, 2986, 3075, 3460, 5024
advantages, 1388
attributes, 1383–1384
built-in general entities, 1384–1385
declarations, 1385–1387
disadvantages, 1388
entities, 1384–1385
limitations, 1383
parameter entities, 1385
readability, 1385
RELAX NG, 1388
syntax, 1381–1382
validating parsers, 1387
W3C XML Schema, 1387–1388
Document Understanding Conferences (DUC), 424, 426
DOI, see Digital Object Identifier
DOI-X prototype, 1132
Domain Name System (DNS), 1325, 5021
Domain ontologies, 3457
Domain precision, 1175
Domain searching, 4049
Domain-specific retrieval tasks, 4574
Domestic counterterrorism, 2399
Domiciliation, 180
Dominion Library, 657
Donkey library, Kenya, 2595
Donor-organized nongovernmental organizations (DONGO), 3380
Doorway page, 4035
Doublure, 539
Downward causation, 1039
DPN, see Digital Preservation Network
Dretske, Fred, 2053
Drivers Privacy Protection Act (DPPA), 2399
DRM, see Digital rights management
Dr. Martin Luther King, Jr., Library, 4161
Droit d'auteur, 2142
Drop dead software device, 1275–1276
Drug nomenclature, see RxNorm
Drypoint printing, 1867
Dry-preserved preparation, 1158
DSpace, 3467
DSS, see Decision support system
DTD, see Document type definition
Dual-use libraries, 4158

Dublin Core (DC), 1366, 1391, 1417, 3826, 4413, 4472–4473
bibliographic control, 454
FAST project, 1539
Dublin Core Abstract Model (DCAM), 3068–3069
Dublin Core Metadata Element Set (DCMES), 3059
Dublin Core Metadata Initiative (DCMI), 454, 3059, 3401
abstract model
FRSAD model, 1616
and interoperability, 1396–1397
Australia, 1392
conference series, 1395
data models, 1393
DC-Down Under, 1392–1393
Frankfurt, 1395
Helsinki, 1393–1394
INDECS project, 1394
OCLC-CNI workshop on image description, 1391–1392
OCLC-NCSA metadata workshop, 1390–1391
organizational structure, 1396
Ottawa, and LOM, 1395
standardization strategies, 1396
structure and procedures, 1395
voting, 1394–1395
Warwick Framework, 1391
Duke Mathematical Journal, 3026
Dumptown Game, 2155
Dun and Bradstreet Sales and Marketing Identification Service, 653
Dun & Bradstreet Reference Book, 647
Dun's Review and Modern Industry, 647
Durham Catalog of 1416, 749
Duyvis, Frits Donker, 4783–4784
Dynamed, 1878
Dynamic Adaptive Streaming over HTTP (DASH) standard, 5021–5022
Dynamic geography, 1688
Dyslexia, 3841, 3845–3846

E

EAD, see Encoded Archival Description
EAD Working Group (EADWG), 1430–1431
Eales, Nellie B., 499–500, 506
Earlham's developing program, 987–988
Early Detection and Rapid Response (EDRR), 3310
The Earth and Man, 1686
East African Library Association (EALA), 37, 4515
East African Literature Bureau (EALB), 4499–4500
East Asian Character Code (EACC), 4663
EASTICA, 688
eAuditorium™, 1057
EBLIP, see Evidence-based library and information practice
e-books, 920–921, 3472
Ebooks Library (EBL), 1210
EBSCO, 3471, 3473
Ecclesiastical binding, see Divinity binding
Ecclesiastical documents, 3303

Ecological Model of ELIS, 1510
Ecological rationality
 adaptive toolbox, 2361
 as-if optimization models, 2362
 fast and frugal decision making, 2362
 heuristics
  building blocks, 2362–2363
  two memory-based heuristics, 2363–2364
  usability, and environmental design,
   2364–2365
Ecomuseums, 1822, 3264
Economic Almanac, 650
Economic and business literature
 first period
  agriculture, books on, 1399–1400
  arithmetic, books of, 1400
  commercial law, 1400
  enterprises, 1400
  money, 1400
  retail selling, books on, 1400
  usury, treatises and tracts on, 1399
 fourth period
  bibliographical works, 1409
  business cycles, study of, 1409–1410
  business institutions, operation of, 1410–
   1411
  businessmen's biographies, 1411
  corporate research agencies, 1408
  economic bibliographies, 1410
  ephemeral literature, 1410
  financial foundations, 1408–1409
  governmental production, 1408
  individual business units, histories of, 1411
  manuscript material, publication of, 1410
  national economic and statistical associations, 1408
  private institutions, 1408
  publishing houses, creative activities, 1408
  schools of business, 1408
  scientific management, 1410–1411
 second period, 1400–1401
  cameralistic thought, growth of, 1401
  cameralistic writings, 1403
  census of population, 1402
  commodity prices, lists of, 1401
  company ventures, documents on, 1403
  economic literature, bibliographies of,
   1402–1403
  economic systems, 1402
  financial affairs and shipping, periodicals
   on, 1401
  historical studies, 1402
  mercantile journal, 1401
  merchants' price lists, 1401
  political arithmetic, 1401–1402
  vital statistics, 1402
 third period
  agricultural journals, 1405–1406
  agricultural surveys, 1404
  businessmen's biographies and autobiogra-
   phies, 1406
  business publication, 1405
  census of population, 1404
  company histories, 1406
  economic thought, 1407
  graphic presentation of statistical data,
   1407

  historical bibliographies, 1405
  ideas and materials, international movement of, 1406
  international congress, 1406–1407
  international exhibition, 1407
  political arithmetic, 1405–1406
  political economy, 1407
  private corporations, 1406
  probability theory, 1405
  professional publications, 1405
  railway periodicals, 1405
  statistical publications, 1404
  translation, 1406
Economic and Social Council of the United
 Nations (ECOSOC), 2432
Economic Census, 637–638
Economic Commission for Africa's (ECA)
 library, 1499
Economic lot sizing model, 1196–1197
Economic model, 1754
Economic order quantity (EOQ) model, 1196
Economics of information, 2256–2257
Economics of reuse, 2652
Economic utility, 2354–2357
eCONTENT, 3399
e-democracy, 2945
Edge marbling, 539
Edinburgh University Library, 4453
Editorial Support System (ESS), 1259
Education
 for librarianship, 3376–3377
 LIS, 706–707
  from within, 707–708
  ALA's Committee on Accreditation, 708
  Bologna declaration, 710
  competency, 710
  continuing education, 712–713
  core courses, 708
  English language publications, 710
  IFLA, 710, 713
  M.L.I.S., 707, 709–710
  from profession, 707
  SIIA, 4298
Educational Clearinghouse, 3035
Educational need, 2116
Educational press, 3739
Educational Resources Information Center
 (ERIC), 91
Education collections, 3165
Educators and trainers
 archival research programs, 686
 career opportunities, 690–691
 competency standards, 687–688
 developing strategies, 685
 ICA Section, 689
 professional associations, role of, 688–689
 providers of, 689–690
 records management, 686
 RIBEAU, 686
Edwards, Edward, 1838
Edward Swanson Memorial Best of LRTS
 Award, 331
EFnet, 1049
Egalitarianism/equity, 4219
E-government, 2945, 4087
Egyptian Library Association, 100
e-Health Capacity strategy, 86

eHistory website, 5027
Eigenfactor metrics, 928
EINet Galaxy, 2520
E-journal preservation, 1335
Electrical Engineering (EE), 275
Electronic books, *see* Electronic publishing
 children's books, 872
Electronic commerce (e-commerce), 693, 1993
Electronic communication, 1108–1109
Electronic content management (ECM), 225,
 2659
Electronic Data Gathering, Analysis and
 Retrieval (EDGAR), 638, 1555
Electronic data interchange (EDI), 2273, 2919,
 4143
Electronic data processing (EDP), 2272
Electronic Dewey, 1259
Electronic document management (EDM), 3105
 analysis process, 3108–3109
 characteristics, 3106
 components, 3106
Electronic document management systems
 (EDMSs), 716
Electronic Freedom of Information Act
 (EFOIA), 1551
Electronic funds transfer (EFT) systems, 2273
Electronic government (e-gov), 2147, 2153–
 2154, 2158–2159
Electronic health record (EHR), 1889, 3339
Electronic Information Delivery Online System
 (EIDOS), 3399
Electronic Information for Libraries (eIFL),
 2827–2829
Electronic information packages, 1366
Electronic Information Service (EISZ), 2828
Electronic ink, 4058
Electronic Journals Library, 1696
Electronic licenses, 2823
 ANKOS, 2829
 Consortium of Swiss Academic Libraries,
  2826
 COSEC, 2828
 EBLIDA, 2827
 ELINET network, 2828
 FINELIB's programs, 2825
 HEAL, 2827
 Iceland Library Consortium, 2825
 NELSI, 2825
 UKB Association, 2826
Electronic mail (e-mail), 1108–1109
Electronic meetings, 1054
Electronic Meeting Systems (EMS), 1050
Electronic publishing, 415–416, 1335
 advantages, 4056–4057
 disadvantages, 4057
 forms, 4054
 future trends, 4058
 libraries and librarians, impact on, 4057–4058
 publishers and publishing services, 4056
 tasks, 4055–4056
 technologies for, 4054–4055
Electronic record keeping system (ERS), 1851
Electronic records
 archives context, 2384–2385
 collaboration, 2385
 content and context, 1413
 definition, 1413

deterioration and loss, 2384
NHPRC, 3315, 3319
obsolescence, 2384
poor records management, 2383
preservation
administrative metadata, 1417
backups and snapshots, 1417
challenges of, 1415–1416
descriptive metadata, 1417–1418
history of, 1413–1415
human error and vandalism, 1417
software and document encoding issues, 1416–1417
storage media, 1415–1416
records management context, 2384
Electronic Records and Signatures in Global and National Commerce Act of 2000, 1415
Electronic records management (ERM), 408, 1108–1109
Electronic Resources & Libraries conference (ER&L)
awards and scholarships, 1422
2016 conference tracks, 1421
history and growth, 1419–1421
mission, 1419
planning committee, 1420
presentation tracks, 1419
purpose, 1419
Electronic resources management system (ERMS), 2922
Electronic resources sharing, 2823, 2829
FINELIB's programs, 2825
Francophone university libraries, 2826
in Hungary, 2828
in Iberian Peninsula, 2827
in Italy, 2827
legislation and copyright, 2827
Norway, 2825
in Romania, 2829
Electronic Scholarly Communication Forums (e-SCFs), 4022
Electronic Theses and Dissertations (ETDs), 2902
Electronic Theses Online Service (EThOS), 620
Element ordering, 3062
Elgin Marbles, 267, 3758
El Greco Museum, 4332
Eli M. Oboler Award, 2392
ELINET network, 2828
ELIS, see Everyday life information seeking
Elite galleries, 243
Ellis' model of information-seeking behaviors, 2226, 2243–2244
El Museo Shan-Dany, 3245
Elsevier, 3472, 5026–5027
Elsevier's Scopus, 923, 925
E-mail, 1414, 2507
Embedded information, 2058
Emergency preparedness, 89, 2153, 2400, 3343
Emergent credibility, 1115
e-Metrics, 2226
Emigration records, 1658
Empirical knowledge, 2610
Empiricism, 3625
Employee Retirement Income Security Act (ERISA), 1858
Emulation, 1334, 2072

Enacted information, 2058
Encoded Archival Context for Corporate Bodies, Persons, and Families (EAC-CPF), 137
Encoded archival description (EAD), 134, 136–137, 734, 1292, 1366, 3686, 3826, 4273
semantics and structure
hierarchal analysis, 1429–1430
top level, 1427–1429
technical foundation, 1426–1427
Encoded Archival Description Document Type Definition (EAD DTD), 1593
Encyclopedia of Reagents for Organic Synthesis (EROS), 816
Encyclopédie ou Dictionnaire des Sciences, des Arts et des Métiers, 645
End-user training, database searching, 1878
Energy facet, 1536
Engineering
aerospace knowledge diffusion research project, 1448–1450
Allen's study, 1445
community, 1437–1439
formal registration, 1434
Herner's work, 1443, 1445
information processors, 1446
information-seeking behavior, engineers, 1433, 1439, 1444
Kaufman's study, 1446
knowledge, 1435–1437
Kremer's study, 1445
research, 1446–1448
research agenda development, 1450–1451
Rosenbloom and Wolek, 1445
science and technology, 1439–1441
and scientists, 1441–1442
Shuchman's study, 1445–1446
social systems, 1442–1443
STI, 1433
work, 1434–1435
Engineering librarianship, see Science and engineering librarianship
Engineering library, 4009–4010
English Fairy Tales, 854
English hand binding, 545–546
English Heritage, 4723
English Heritage Thesauri, 1080
English illumination
Gothic period, 1950
Romanesque period, 1948
English Short-Title Catalogue (ESTC), 458
Enterprise application integration (EAI) systems, 3455
Enterprise content management (ECM), 1108, 1854
Enterprise Integration Network (EINet), 2520
Enterprise resource planning (ERP), 2274, 2658
Enterprise systems, 2274–2275
Entry pages, 4035
Environmental Protection Agency (EPA), 2155
Environmental scanning, 2108, 3196
Environmental Systems Research Institute (ESRI), 1671, 1673, 1675, 1678
Environment for Strategic Planning (ESP), 1206
Epidemic theory model, 504

Episteme, 2678
Epistemetrics, 4199
Epistemic authority, 1116
Epistemic coherentism, 1458
Epistemic paternalism, 4199
Epistemic reason, 1461
Epistemology, 4918
justification
coherentism, 1458, 1460
deductive, 1457
defeasible, 1457
fallibilism, 1457
foundationalism, 1459–1460
inductive, 1457
inferential, 1457–1458
knowledge, analysis of, 1455
modern empiricism
contemporary Anglo-American epistemology, 1455–1456
pragmatic rationale, 1457
purpose-independent correctness, 1457
Russell's epistemology, 1456
skepticism, 1460–1461
EPO, see European Patent Office
Equal Rights Amendment (ERA), 2394–2395
Equi-height histograms, 2630
Equi-width histograms, 2630
E-Rate Modernization Order, 1283
Eratosthenes, 1683–1684
E-referencer system, 3427–3429
Ergebnisse der Mathematik und ihrer Grenzgebiete, 3028
E-rights, 1269
ER&L, see Electronic Resources & Libraries conference
Escalation theory, 2283
E-Science, 555, 4015, 4086
eSerials Holdings Service, 3398
E-Sign, see Electronic Records and Signatures in Global and National Commerce Act of 2000
Espresso Book Machine (EBM), 3735
ESRI, see Environmental Systems Research Institute
Essay of Drapery, 1400
Essays on Husbandry, 1402
Esther J. Piercy Award, 331
Estonian State Library, 3326
Ethernet standard, 2342
Ethical actions
individual actions
employers/clients/system users, responsibility to, 1479
profession, responsibility to, 1479
society, responsibility to, 1479–1480
organizational actions
board and administration, 1478
ethical awareness, 1479
orientations, 1478
staff development and training programs, 1479
written ethics policy, 1478
professional actions, 1479
Ethical issues, information systems
access, 1491
accuracy, 1489–1490
individual rights, 1487

Ethical issues, information systems (cont'd.)
　privacy
　　big data aggregation and analysis, 1489
　　Bill of Rights, 1488
　　cocreation of value, 1489
　　databases, 1488
　　enforcement, 1488
　　harmonization, 1488
　　invasion, 1489
　　legislation, 1488
　　loss of autonomy, 1487
　　marketing and personalization, 1489
　　patterns, 1489
　　personal data dispersion, 1489
　　PII, 1489
　　Privacy Act, 1488
　　records collection, storage, and dissemina-
　　　tion, 1488
　　safeguards, 1488
　　systematic monitoring and surveillance,
　　　1489
　property, 1490–1491
　sources, 1487
Ethics
　access issues, 1472
　administrative issues, 1472
　conflicting loyalties, 1473
　copyright issues, 1471–1472
　ethical actions
　　individual actions, 1479–1480
　　organizational actions, 1478–1479
　　professional actions, 1479
　ethical dilemmas, 1480
　ethical dissonance, 1469
　factors
　　respect for individuality, 1475
　　social responsibility, 1474
　　social utility, 1474
　　survival, 1474
　limitations, 1470
　privacy issues, 1470–1471
　professional ethics, 1475–1476
　reference services, 1471, 3917
　selecting materials and censorship, 1470
　societal issues, 1473
　technology-related issues, 1472–1473
　values, information professions
　　beauty, 1478
　　individual liberty, 1477
　　justice, 1477–1478
　　tolerance, 1477
　　truth, 1476–1477
Ethiopia
　history of, 1494–1495
　languages, 1494
　libraries
　　academic libraries, 1498–1499
　　education, 1499
　　national library, 1495–1496
　　professional association, 1499–1500
　　public libraries, 1498
　　school libraries, 1499
　　special libraries, 1498–1499
　location, 1494
　museums and galleries, 1500–1501
　　Addis Ababa Museum, 1503
　　Asni Gallery, 1504

　　Belvedere Gallery, 1504
　　Dessie Museum, 1503
　　exhibition of 1958, 1501
　　Goshu Art Gallery, 1504
　　Harar National and Community Museum,
　　　1503–1504
　　Institute of Ethiopian Studies Museum,
　　　1501–1503
　　before Italian occupation, 1501
　　Jimma Museum, 1503
　　Mekelle Museum, 1503
　　National museum of Ethiopia, 1501–1502
　　OAU, 1502
　　SOFIES, 1503
　　St. George Interior Decoration and Art
　　　Gallery, 1504
　　UACC, 1501
　　Wollega Museum, 1503
　　National Archives, 1500
　　printing and publishing, development of, 1495
Ethiopian Community Development Council
　　(ECDC), 40
Ethiopian Institute of Agricultural Research
　　(EIAR) Library and Documentation
　　Center, 1499
Ethiopian Library Association (ELA), 1499
Ethiopian Library, Information Science and
　　Archives Professional Association, 1500
Ethiopian Orthodox Library-Museum, 1499
Ethnic and Multicultural Materials Information
　　Exchange Roundtable (EMIERT), 334
Ethnic museums, 3244–3245
Ethnographic museums, 1927–1928
　politics, power, and representation,
　　3694–3695
　in Serbia, 4135
*Ethnography, History, Archeology, and Natural
　　Sciences*, 4185
Ethnolinguistic gatekeepers, 2126
Ethnology museum, 1820
Ethnomethodology, 2055, 3815
Ethnoscapes, 2124
etoy, 2066, 2071
Etruscan bindings, 541
Etruscan calf, 541
EURBICA, 2441
EURONOMOS, 2441
EUROPEANA, 1708
Europeana Linked Open Data Project, 2941
European Association for Library and Informa-
　　tion Education and Research (EUCLID),
　　708
European Bureau of Library, Documentation
　　and Information Associations
　　(EBLIDA), 2827, 2956
European Classification (ECLA), 3566–3567
European Confederation of Conservator-
　　Restorers' Organization (ECCO), 1071
European Conference on Digital Libraries
　　(ECDL), 3367
European Digital Library (EDL), 2824, 3332,
　　3684
European Directive on Data Privacy of October,
　　1998, 1106
European Economic Community (EEC), 2312
The European Library, 250
European museums, 3234

European Patent Office (EPO)
　ECLA system, 3566–3567
　ESPACE EP, 3569
　esp@cenet, 3569
　Register Plus, 3569
European Space Agency (ESA), 1347
European Union (EU) information policy
　Bangemann report, 2140
　challenges, 2140
　data protection and privacy, 2143
　electronic commerce, 2142–2143
　European information society, 2140–2141
　Hernon and Relyea definition, 2139
　historical overview of, 2139–2140
　ICT, 2141–2142
　implications, 2144
　information society, 2140–2141
　intellectual property, 2142
　legal and regulatory issues, 2140
　normative ethics, 2139
　objectives, 2140
　pragmatic ethics, 2139
　utilitarian approach, 2139
　Weingarten definition, 2138
Eurostat survey, 1741
Evaluative Bibliometrics, 500
Everlasting match, 2913
Every Child Ready to Read (ECRR), 335
Everyday life information seeking (ELIS),
　　842–843, 2087–2088, 2118–2119, 5070
　concept, 1506–1507
　information sources, 1507–1508
　needs, 1507
　theories and models
　　ecological model, 1510
　　information grounds, 1511–1512
　　information practices, 1511
　　sense-making methodology, 1508–1509
　　small world, 1509–1510
　　Way of Life, 1510–1511
　in "Way of Life," 1510–1511
Every Man His Own Broker, 1401
Evidence-based acquisition (EBA) model, 1211
Evidence-based librarianship (EBL), 1887–1888
Evidence-based library and information practice
　　(EBLIP), 1516, 1520–1521
Evidence-based medicine (EBM), 1764, 1888
Evidence-based practice (EBP), 4255, 4259
　apply the results, 1519–1520
　components, 1517–1521
　effect evaluation, 1520–1521
　evidence appraisal, 1518–1519
　meta-analysis, 1519
　question formulation, 1517–1518
　search for evidence, 1518
　systematic review, 1518–1519
Evidence-based selection (EBS), 1211
Ewart, William, 1838
"ExaByte-Counter," 2102–2103
Excite, 2521
Executive information systems (EIS), 2274
Executive support systems (ESS), 2895
Exhibition design, 241
　accounting for sustainability, 1531
　content team, 1529
　design team, 1529
　elements

architectural elements, 1525
color, lighting and acoustics, 1526
construction and finishes materials, 1526
graphics, 1526
media, 1526
narrative, 1525
objects, artifacts and images, 1526
physical and cultural context, 1525
space, 1525
formative evaluation, 1528
front-end evaluations, 1528
history
contemporary vision, 1524–1525
European Roots, 1524
planned experiences, transition to, 1524
new narratives, 1531
new perspectives of interpretation, 1530
new technology, 1531
NLM, 3343–3344
process
concept, 1527
design development, 1527
fabrication and installation, 1528
fabrication documents, 1527
schematic phase, 1527
project management side, 1529–1530
prototype testing, 1528
special collections, 4339
summative evaluations, 1528
universal access, 1530
EXIT project, 3785
Ex Libris Student Writing Award, 2778
Exosomatic flow line, 2058
Exosomatic information, 2058, 2060
Expectancy theory, 3513
Expectation-Maximization (EM) algorithm, 4421
Experienced credibility, 1115
Experienced information, 2058
Experimental knowledge assets, 2622
Expertise Recommender (ER), 3866
Expert locator systems
automatic expertise finders, 3865
expert databases, 3864–3865
expertise recommenders, 3865–3866
expert referral systems, 3866–3867
research communities, 3864
Expert systems, 1203
ExPlain, 1768
Explicit knowledge, 2445, 2643
Expressed information, 2058
Extensible HyperText Markup Language
(XHTML), 3076
Extensible Markup Language (XML), 1058,
1063–1064, 1361, 1381, 1416, 1423,
2222, 2524, 2986–2987, 3459–3460,
3962–3963, 4082, 4561
document format, 3107
Document Type Definitions, 3077–3078
family of languages, 3079–3080
identification problem, 3078
logical structure, 3076–3077
markup techniques, 3076–3078
name collision problem, 3078–3079
physical structure, 3077
standardization, 3106
standardization levels, 3107–3108
Unicode Standard, 4667–4668

Extensible Stylesheet Language (XSL), 1365
Extensible stylesheet language transformations
(XSLT), 1365, 3079, 3965, 4084
EXTRACT, 2155
Extreme Programming (XP), 1370
Eye movements, in reading, 3838

F
Fabrication Laboratory (Fab Lab), 2991–2992
Facet analysis
classes, 1535
definition, 1534
differential facet, 1536
energy and matter facet, 1536
entity terms, 1535
general analysis of information, 1534
lattice system, 1538
personality facet
levels of, 1536
rounds of, 1536–1537
purpose of, 1535
space facet, 1536
subjects
education, 1536
Food Technology, 1536
occupational safety and health,
1535–1536
science and technology, 1537
thesaurus, 1537–1538
time facet, 1536
Faceted application of subject terminology
(FAST), 4468, 4472–4473
application rules, 1542–1543
authority files, 4473
authority records, 1539
development and maintenance, 1543
faceted subject heading vocabulary, 1539
facets
chronological headings, 1542
corporate names, 1541
event names, 1542
form headings, 1542
genre headings, 1542
geographic names, 1540–1541
personal names, 1541
title of work, 1541–1542
topical headings, 1540
history, 1539
implementations, 1545
influences, 1539–1540
and LCSH, 1539–1540
Linked Data, 1539, 1545–1546
name headings, 4473
research prototypes, 1546
schema, 4472–4473
tools, 1544–1545
Facets, 4470
Facsimile, 1307
Factory libraries, 1697
Factual data, 4065
Fair Credit Reporting Act, 1106, 2152
Fair Use Doctrine, 4946
Fairy tales, 853–854
FALCON, 3440–3441
Fallout (F), 3945
Family Online Safety Institute (FOSI), 783

Family Place Libraries, 878
Fantasy, 854–855, 865–867, 3702
Farmington Plan, 372
Farnese binding, 543
FAST, see Faceted application of subject
terminology
FASTConverter, 1544
FastTrack MLIS Web site, 3438–3439
Fax technology, 1307–1308
Fayetteville Free Library (FFL), 2992
FCC, see Federal Communications Commission
FDLP, see Federal Depository Library Program
Federal Advisory Committee Act of 1972,
2151
Federal Bureau of Investigation (FBI), 2148
Federal Communications Commission (FCC),
1013–1014, 1021
Federal Council of Education (CFE), 611
Federal Council of Library Science (CFB), 605
Federal Cylinder Project, 4299
Federal Depository Library Program (FDLP),
369, 1549, 1555–1557, 1715–1716, 2148
Federal Emergency Management Association
(FEMA), 1352, 2153
Federal Fluminense University (UFF), 612
Federal Office of Culture (OFC), 4495
Federal Property and Administrative Services
Act of 1949, 1851
Federal Records Act, 185, 1414, 1851
Federal Register, 640
Federal Reserve Bulletin, 649
Federal Reserve Open Market Committee, 3006
Federal Rules of Civil Procedure (FRCP), 1107,
1858
Federal University of Rio de Janeiro (UFRJ),
607–608, 612
Fédération Internationale de Documentation
(FID), 4783–4784
FEMA, see Federal Emergency Management
Association
Fiction, 855
contemporary fiction, 864–865
historical fiction, 865
Fidel's models, 4877–4878
Field (in)accuracy, 1176
Field-based ethnographic research, 3814
Field Museum of Natural History (FMNH),
3252
Field study, 4798
Fiji Library Association, 3548
File Index (FI) system, 3566–3567
FileMakerPro, 4942
File-sharing, 3650–3653
File transfer protocol (FTP), 2183, 2517, 2983
Film and audiovisual archives, 4737
Film and broadcast archives
academic collections, 1561, 1563
Australia, 1567
broadcasting stations, 1566
Canada, 1567
government, 1565–1566
issues and trends, 1576–1579
Japan, 1567
motion picture archives, 1561–1563
museums and libraries, 1563, 1565
scope of activities, 1567–1576
United Kingdom, 1566

Film archives
AMIA, 1587
FIAF, 1585
Hungary, 1926
moving image media, 1585
NFPF, 1587–1588
photographic raw stock, 1584
public-sector archives, 1586, 1588
"safety" film, 1585
"Silent Era" Web site, 1584
Yugoslavia, 4133
Filter blogs, 2507
Financescapes, 2124
Financial commentary, 4456
Financial information, 638–639
Fine art presses, 3743
Fine Arts Museums of San Francisco (FAMSF),
3225–3226
FINELIB, 2825
Fingerprinting, 478
Firearms Museum, 4382
First-generation portals, 2893
FirstGov, 1553, 1557
First-impressions hypothesis, 3590
First Nations, 2032
First Nations libraries, 2038
FirstSearch Electronic Collections Online
(ECO), 3399
Fisher Library, 384–385
Fishscale model of omniscience, 4201
Five star data model, 2940
Fixed content signs, 4973–4975
Fixity information, 1364
F. Kennedy Memorial Library, 1498
Fleet Library, 253, 4774
Flemish Research Libraries Council, 2826
Flexible querying, 1618, 1626–1628
Flexible scheduling, 111
FlexoWriter, 4993–4994
Flink, 4088
Floor maps, 1351, 1354
Floppy Disk Project, 1554
Florentin, Antonin, 4176
Florian Psalter, 3681
Floridi, Luciano, 2048–2049
Fluency with Information Technology (FIT),
2304, 2306
Fluid-preserved preparation, 1158
Focus group, 4798
Fogerty, 202
Fogg Art Museum, 1070
Fogg's prominence-interpretation theory, 1117
FOIA, see Freedom of Information Act
FOLIO, 1711
Folksonomy, 1078, 4089, 4209, 4551, 4987
Folktales, 853–854, 858, 862–863, 866, 870,
4440–4442
Food and Agricultural Organization (FAO), 3385
Forbes, Edward W., 1070
Fore-edge painting, 539
Foreign Corrupt Practices Act (FCPA), 1106
The Foreign Gifts and Decorations Act, 3716
Foreign librarianship, 2405
Forensics, 1334
Forest Physiography: Physiography of the
United States and Principles of Soils in
Relation to Forests, 1688

Formal usability testing, 4797
Format attributes, 2294
Formats, 1177
FORmula TRANslation (FORTRAN), 2272
Forster, Johann Georg, 1685
Forster, Johann Rheinhold, 1685
Fort Jesus Museum, 2605
Forum for Knowledge, Information, Documen-
tation, and Archives (VIDA), 1224
Forward citation retrieval, 925
Foundational justification, 1459–1460
Fourth ages theory, 3406–3407
Fox, Christopher, 2053
FP-Streaming, 2632–2633
Fragment-screening approach, 832–833
Frame-level indexing, 3132
Framingham Heart Study, 1767
France
archives
access to, 1591–1592
Ancien Régime, 1589–1590
definition, 1589
départemental archives, 1591
Directorate for Archives, role of,
1590–1591
National Archives, 1590–1591
National Audiovisual Institute, 1591
private archives, 1592
Superior Archives Council, 1591
transformations, 1593
libraries
BNF, 1599, 1604–1605
history of, 1599–1601
public libraries, 1601–1602
school, academic, and research libraries,
1602–1603
space planning and interior design, 1603
visitors, 1603–1604
map of, 1589–1590
museums
Academy of Beaux-Arts, 1594
anthropology museum, 1595
architecture, 1596
Center for Museum Research and Conservation in France, 1596
City for Science and Industry, 1597
classified museums, 1595
cultural heritage, 1594
curieux, 1593–1594
Directorate, responsibility of, 1595–1596
fine arts museum, 1594
immigration, 1597
International Council of Museums, 1595
local museum, 1594
Louvre, 1596–1597
lycées, 1594
Ministry of Culture, 1595
Museum of Monuments, 1594
national heritage, 1594
national museums, 1595
natural history museum, 1594
in nineteenth century, 1594
Orsay Museum, 1597
Pompidou Center, 1597
princely collections, 1593–1594
professions, 1597–1598
Quai Branly museum, 1597

regional/local museums, 1596
smaller museums, 1595
transformations, 1593
in twentieth century, 1594
visitors, 1598–1599
France de l'Est, 1687
Franciscan Biblical Museum, 2550
Francis Joseph Campbell Award, 377
FRBR, see Functional Requirements for Biblio-
graphic Records
Frederick G. Kilgour Award, 2778
Free and Open Source Software (FOSS), 4659
Free discovery, 1210
Freedman, Maurice J, 75, 4691
Freedom of Information Act (FOIA), 186, 1105,
1472, 1551, 2150–2152, 2390
Freedom of information legislation, 3890
Freedom to Read Foundation, 2391–2393
"Free-floating" subdivisions, 4470
Free For All Web sites (FFAs), 4036
Free Matter for the Blind and Handicapped
mailing, 570–571
Freenets, 1029
FreePatentsOnline, 3570
Free-text searcher, 4878
French bookbinding, 544
French ISKO Chapter, 2497
Frequency distribution, 2211
Frequently Asked Questions (FAQ), 2507
Frequent pattern mining
Apriori, 2631
FP-Streaming, 2632–2633
frequent item mining, 2631–2632
Lossy Counting algorithm, 2632
Manku and Motwani's algorithm, 2632
Friedrich Althoff Consortium, 2826
Friedrich Rathgen Laboratory, 1069
Friend-of-a-friend (FOAF) ontology, 4089
Friends of Libraries Committee, 2842
Friends of Libraries USA (FOLUSA), 2834,
2842
Frohmann, Bernd, 2059–2060
FRSAD, see Functional requirements for subject
authority data
Full mesh topology, 3360
Full text indexing, 1621, 2653
Full-text searching, 297, 1758, 3468, 4467, 4476
Functional illiteracy, 4282–4283
Functional Requirements for Authority Data
(FRAD), 3295
Functional Requirements for Bibliographic
Records (FRBR), 726–727, 1233,
1238–1239, 1606–1610, 1612–1616,
2923, 3068
Classify prototype, 1546
conceptual model, 452
entity-relationship database model, 452–453
MARC 21, 2987
RDA, 453
user tasks, 452–453
Functional requirements for subject authority
data (FRSAD), 1606–1616
applications, 1615–1616
conceptual model, 1606–1607, 1609–1610,
1612, 1615–1616
development timeline, 1607–1608
thema, 1615

Functional retention schedules, 3893
Fund-raising, academic libraries, *see* Academic
    libraries, fund-raising and development
Furner, Jonathan, 2060
Fussler, Herman H., 497–498, 502, 506
Fuzzy set theory, information retrieval
    associative retrieval mechanisms
        clustering techniques, 1622, 1633
        compatible purposes, 1631
        ontologies, 1622
        pseudothesauri, 1622, 1631–1632
        thesauri, 1631–1633
    Boolean retrieval model, 1621–1622
    cross language retrieval, 1619
    document indexing
        generalized Boolean indexing,
            1622–1623
        HTML document, weighted representation
            of, 1625–1626
        probabilistic models, 1622
        structured documents, representation of,
            1623–1624
        techniques for, 1621
        term significance, 1624–1625
        vector space model, 1622
    flexible query languages, 1618
        definition of, 1621–1622, 1627–1628
        linguistic query weights, 1629–1630
        query evaluation mechanism, 1027–1028
        query weights, 1628–1629
        selection conditions, linguistic quantifiers,
            1630–1631
    imprecision, vagueness, uncertainty, and
        inconsistency, 1619–1621
    knowledge-based models, 1621
    MCDM activity, 1618
    multicriteria decision-making activity, 1618
    multimedia document, 1619
    OCAT methodology, 1621
    relevance, concept of, 1619
    representation of documents, 1619
    research trends, 1619
    retrieval status value, 1633–1634
    semantic web, 1619
F-value, 419–420

G

Gabor-based features, 4424
Gallery of the Serbian Academy of Science and
    Arts, 4134
Gallica, 1604
Game Making Interes Group, 1641
Games and gaming
    game, definition of, 1636–1637
    in library
        academic libraries, 1639–1640
        ALA, GameRT, 1637
        benefits, 1637
        collections, 1637
        computer and console games, 1636–1637
        as cultural significance, 1637
        digital preservation, 1640
        for instructional purposes, 1641
        for outreach purposes, 1640–1641
        publc libraries, 1638
        school libraries, 1638–1639

tabletop games, 1637
    video games, 1637
Games and Gaming Round Table (GameRT),
    1637
Game theory, 1198
Garfield, Eugene, 502–503, 506
Gary Klein's sensemaking, 4116–4117
Gateway page, 4035
Gaussian distribution, 494
Gay, Lesbian, Bisexual Transgender (GLBT)
    Historical Society, 4760
Gaylord Award, 2777
Gender and sexuality archives
    Cornell Human Sexuality Project, 4760
    GBLT historical society, 4760
    Kinsey Institute, 4760
    Lesbian Herstory Archives, 4760
    National Gay & Lesbian Archives, 4760–4761
Genealogical Library, 1649
Genealogical literature
    compiled sources, 1651–1652
        biographies, 1652, 1654
        family histories and genealogies, 1654,
            1656
        local histories, 1656
        pedigree chart, 1656
        Query services, 1656
        society and association resources, 1656
    definitions, 1644
    genealogical research
        classification and evaluation of, 1650–1651
        steps in, 1650
    genealogy, interest in, 1644
    history
        antiquity, 1645
        genealogical research, 1646
        historical associations, 1645
        Internet and digitization, 1646–1648
        modern genealogy, 1646
        new genealogy, characteristics of, 1646
        record keeping, 1645
        scientific genealogy, 1645–1646
    library catalogs and classification, use of,
        1649
    news and networking sources, 1657, 1660
    original sources, 1653–1654, 1656–1659
    periodical sources, 1657
        non-society periodicals, 1659
        periodical indexes, 1660
        society periodicals, 1659
    reference tools, 1655–1656, 1659
    users of, 1648–1649
Gene ontology, 4087
General Archives of the Nation (AGN), 3096
General comparative research methodology,
    2407
General Information Program (PGI), 2312,
    4656–4657
General International Standard Archival
    Description (ISAD-G), 1366, 1593
Generality (G), 3945
Generalized Markup Language (GML)
    applications, 3075
    descriptive markup, 3074–3075
Generalized Retrieval and Information
    Processing for Humanities Oriented
    Studies (GRIPHOS), 3179

Generalized systems of order in museum, 1817
General Material Disignation (GMD), 1235
General Research Library, 1697
General-specific-sparse search strategy,
    2213–2214
General State Archives (GSA), 1736
General systems theory, 3514
*The General Theory of Employment, Interest
    and Money*, 647
Generic ontologies, 3457
Generic Record Syntax (GRS), 2186
Genesis, 2068
Genetic Algorithms (GA), 274
Genetic flow line, 2058
Genetic information, 2058
Genetic programming, 274
Gennadius library, 1732
Genocide, 4400
Genocide Institute and Museum, 236–237
Genre
    definition, 1662
*Genreflecting: A Guide to Reading Interests in
    Genre Fiction*, 3856
Genre/form terms, 2856–2864
Genre repertoire, 2504, 2506
Genres
    commercial, 2504
    definition, 1662, 2503
    documents, 2509–2510
        automated classification, 2510–2512
        communication, 2504–2505
        educational genres, 2509
        genre chain, 2504
    environmental impact statements, 2503
    Internet
        business and academic e-mail messages,
            2507
        classifications, 2507–2509
        evolution of, 2506–2507
        information access, 2509
        non-textual documents, 2507
        personal home pages, 2507
        unsolicited commercial e-mail, 2507
        Web communication, 2505–2506
        Weblog/blog, 2507
        World Wide Web, 2505
    journalistic genres, 2504
    learning theories, 1669
    popular literature
        adventure, 3701
        appeal characteristics, 3700
        "chick lit," 3705–3706
        collection arrangement, 3700
        crime fiction, 3701–3702
        cross-genre phenomenon, 3706–3707
        fantasy, 3702
        historical fiction, 3702–3703
        horror, 3703
        narrative nonfiction, 3705
        reading interests, 3706
        romance, 3703–3704
        science fiction, 3704–3705
        slipstream, 3706
        street lit/urban fiction, 3706
        westerns, 3705
    recurrent communicative situations, 2503
    research in linguistics, 1664–1665

Genres (cont'd.)
  research process, 2503
  RGS
    Bakhtin communication, 1663–1664
    Bakhtin's insights, 1664
    Bitzer's notion of "exigence," 1663
    deliberative performances, 1662
    epideictic speeches, 1662
    forensic discourse, 1662
    Miller's insights, 1663
    pragmatic function, 1663
    reconceptualization, 1663
    renovation source, 1663
    speech genre, 1663–1664
    utterance, 1663–1664
  scientific genres, 2503
  social context theories
    activity system theory, 1667–1668
    Bourdieu's insights, 1666–1667
    Engeström definition, 1667–1668
    Giddens' insights, 1666
    Levi-Straussian structuralism, 1666
    linguistic habitus, 1667
    rhetorical and structuration theories, 1666
    socialized subjectivity, 1666
    structure and agency relationship, 1665–1666
  vs. text type, 2503
"Gentleman's agreement," 90
GeoDA, 1676
Geodata Analysis and Display Systems (GADS), 2274
GEO-DATA Explorer (GEODE), 2155
Geoexploration systems, 1677–1678
GeoFusion, 1677
Geographia Generalis, 1685
Geographica, 1683–1684
Geographic information system (GIS), 555, 2155, 2274, 2402
  applications, 1677–1678
  bibliography and additional resources
    books, 1678–1679
    conferences, 1680–1681
    dictionaries, 1681
    GIS Day, 1678
    journals and magazines, 1679–1680
    organizations, 1680
  definitions, 1671–1672
  markup languages, 1677
  PPGIS and PGIS, 1672–1673
  professionals, certification of, 1678
  software packages
    Autodesk, 1676
    Bentley Systems, Inc., 1676
    Caliper Corporation, 1676
    ESRI, 1675
    free and open-source packages, 1676
    geoexploration systems, 1677–1678
    IDRISI, 1675–1676
    Intergraph, 1676
    Manifold, 1676
    MapInfo, 1676
  spatial autocorrelation, 1677
  spatial data, 1672, 1678
  spatial thinking
    colleges, 1674
    masters courses, 1674

    schools, 1673–1674
    universities, 1674
    virtual campuses, 1674–1675
  systems vs. science, 1671
  volunteered geographic information, 1673
  Web-based devices, 1672
Geographic resources analysis support system (GRASS), 1676
Geographike Syntaxis, 1684
Geographische Zeitschrift, 1687
Geography, 643–644
  definition of, 1683
  Eratosthenes, 1683–1684
  geographical serials, 1688–1689
  Hecataeus, 1683
  Herodotus, 1683
  Homer, 1683
  Mela, Pomponius, 1684
  modern geographers
    Bowman, Isaiah, 1688
    Brunhes, Jean, 1687
    Carpenter, Nathaniel, 1685
    Davis, William Morris, 1688
    Demangeon, Albert, 1687
    explorers, 1684–1685
    Guyot, Arnold Henry, 1686
    Hettner, Alfred, 1687
    Humboldt, Alexander von, 1686
    Huntington, Ellsworth, 1688
    LePlay, Pièrre Guillaume Frédéric, 1687
    Mackinder, Halford John, 1687–1688
    Peschel, Oscar, 1687
    Ratzel, Friedrich, 1687
    Ritter, Karl, 1686
    Varenius, 1685
    Vidal de la Blache, Paul, 1687
    von Richthofen, Baron Ferdinand, 1687
  Polo, Marco, 1684
  Ptolemy, 1684
  as science, 1685–1686
  Strabo, 1684
  Thales of Miletus, 1683
  Theophrastes, 1683
  Travels, 1684
Geography markup language, 1677
Geography Network, 1673
Geological Museum of Vietnam, 4915
Geoponica, 1400
George Cunha and Susan Swartzburg Award, 332
George Meany Memorial Archives, 4761
George Padmore Research Library, 3324
George Washington University (GWU)'s program, 3218
Georgia Archives Building, 4389
Georgia Historical Society (GHS), 1779
Georgia Library Association, 920
Georgia library learning online (GALILEO), 1877
Georgia Public Library Service (GPLS), 4397
Georgia State University (GSU), 3655
Georgia Virtual History Project, 5027
Geospatial interoperability framework, 3311
Geostationary satellites, 4430
GeoWeb, 1677
German Association of Factory Libraries, 1697

German, Austrian and Swiss Consortia Organization (GASCO), 2826, 2829
German hand binding, 545
German Harvest automated Retrieval and Directory (GERHARD), 4789
German illumination
  in fifteenth and sixteenth centuries, 1951
  Gothic period, 1950
  Romanesque period, 1948–1949
German ISKO Chapter, 2496
German Library Association, 1699
German National Library, 1262, 3329
German–North American Resources Partnership (GNARP), 790
German Popular Stories, 854
German Research Foundation, 1695
German Society of Information, 1699
Germany
  after World War II, 1693
  archives and archival science
    archival pedagogic/user education, 1703
    corporate archives, 1701
    digital archival collections and finding aids, 1702
    education, 1702
    electronic records, 1703
    film and audiovisual archives, 1701
    legislation, 1699
    literary archives, 1701
    local archives, 1700–1701
    national archives and services, 1699–1700
    preservation and conservation, 1703
    private archives, 1701–1702
    professional associations, 1702–1703
    religious archives, 1701
    school and university archives, 1701
    state archives, 1700
  EUROPEANA, 1708
  libraries
    academic and research libraries, 1695–1696
    BAM-Portal, 1708
    digital library collections and services, 1694, 1698
    factory libraries, 1697
    legislation, 1694
    levels of service, 1694
    LIS education, 1698–1699
    national library and information services, 1694–1695
    professional associations, 1699
    public libraries, 1696–1697
    research libraries, 1693
    school libraries, 1698
    special libraries, 1698
    special subject libraries, 1695
  map of, 1693–1694
  museums
    art museums and galleries, 1704
    digital museum exhibits and services, 1706
    education, 1707
    historical, anthropological, and archeological museums, 1705–1706
    museology as discipline and profession, 1706–1707
    national museums, 1703–1704
    professional associations, 1707

science and natural history museums, 1704–1705
standards and guidelines, 1707
visitor research, 1707
volunteers, 1707
zoos and botanical gardens, 1706
poets and thinkers, 1693
political systems, 1693
population, 1693
Provenance Research, 1708
Gestalt psychology, 2679, 2685
Gettier problem, 1455
knowledge, 2616
Getty End-User Online Searching Project, 296–298, 1911, 1914
Getty Research Institute Research Library Catalog, 250
Getty Thesaurus of Geographic Names® (TGN), 1079
Ghana Library Board, 3324
Ghetto Fighters'House-Itzhak Katzenelson Jewish Resistance Heritage Museum, 2552
Ghettoization, 2072, 4208
Giddens' structuration theory, 2506
GIF format, 1311
Gift books, 3824
Giles Scholarship, 81
g-index, 2370
Glagolitic script, 1121–1122
Glastonbury catalog, 747
Gleaning Resource Descriptions from Dialects of Languages (GRDDL), 4084
Glenerin Declaration, 2158
Global Biodiversity Information Facility (GBIF), 3308, 3313
Global Earth Observation System of Systems (GEOSS), 555
Global Open Knowledgebase (GOKb) project
core features, 1711
data model and elements, 1712
founding partners, 1710
governing body, 1710
initial planning phases, 1710
KB+, 1710–1711
Kuali OLE and Jisc, 1710–1711
method of access
API, 1713
co-reference service, 1713–1714
OpenRefine, 1713
Web application, 1712–1713
phase 1 grant funding period, 1710
preview period, 1710
title record in, 1712
Global Partnership Program (GPP), 86
Global Resources Agriculture Partnership–Project Ceres, 790
Global Resources Law Partnership, 790
Global Resources Network (GRN), 372
Global Resources Program (GRP), 372
Glyphs, 4664
Glyptothek, 3153
GML, see Generalized Markup Language
Goals, Operators, Methods, and Selections model (GOMS), 1897
GOBI Library Solutions, 343
Goblin Threat, 1641
Goeldi Museum, 614

Goguen, Joseph, 2054–2055
Golden Gamers Group, 1638
Gold-tooled bindings, 544
England, 546
France, 546
Italy, 543, 545
Good old-fashioned artificial intelligence (GOFAI), 4088
Google, 2368, 2523, 2854, 3471, 3655, 4047, 4050–4051, 4461, 5028
Google Books, 1760–1761
Google Library Project, 1757
Google PageRank, 4039–4040
Google Patents, 3570
"Google Rule," 2707
Google Scholar (GS), 489, 923, 925, 1878, 2368, 5027
Google SketchUp, 1678
Google Uncle Sam, 1553
Goolatilake, Susantha, 2058
Gopher, 2517
Gordon Scholarship, 81
Goshu Art Gallery, 1504
Gosnell, Charles F., 496, 498
Gothic bindings, 543
Göttliche Ordnung, 1402
Governmentally organized nongovernmental organization (GONGO), 3380
Government documents
federal publications, 1715–1718
international publications, 1721–1724
local documents, 1720–1721
state publications, 1718–1720
Government Documents Roundtable (GODORT), 1724
Government Information Locator Service (GILS), 1550, 1552
Government Information Security Reform Act, 1556
Government in the Sunshine Act of 1976, 2151
Government of Wales Act 1997, 4734
Government Paperwork Elimination Act (GPRA) of 1998, 1415, 1556
Government Performance and Results Act, 4771
Government Printing Office (GPO), 1549–1550, 2148, 2150, 2156
Government Printing Office Electronic Information Access Enhancement Act of 1993, 1551
GPX model, 5045
Grade 1-1/2 braille code, 563
Graduate Library Institute for Spanish-Speaking Americans, 2703
Graduate Library School (GLS), 2769, 2910–2913, 4280
Grammar syntax, 3062
GRAMMY Foundation, 1579
Grand Mosque's library, 4624
Grant-funded projects, 346–347
Grants
AFI, 1587
Carnegie and British Council, 396
NHPRC, 3315, 3318–3319
scholarship funds, 880
Granular computing, 2194
Graphical models, 2086–2088
Graphical networks, 2212

Graphical user interface, 1289
Graphic novels, 860
Graphics Communications Association Research Institute (GCARI), 4611
Grassroots organization (GRO), 3380
Grateful Med, 91
Graunt, John, 494
Gray Information Functional Plan, 1746–1747
Gray-level differences histogram, 4423
Great Barrier Reef Marine Park, 391
Great Depression, 3254
Greece
archival studies, 1739
audiovisual archives, 1738–1739
college and university archives, 1738
digital archival collections and electronic finding aids, 1739
individual state archives, 1737
libraries
academic libraries, 1731–1732
contemporary libraries, 1728–1729
digital libraries and institutional repositories, 1732–1733
history, 1728
library and information science studies, 1734
networks, consortia and union catalogs, 1733
NLG, 1729
Parliament Library, 1729–1730
public libraries, 1730
publishing activities and conferences, 1734
school libraries, 1730–1731
special libraries, 1732
map, 1729
museums
from ancient to modern times, 1741–1742
Benaki Museum, 1744–1745
Byzantine and Christian Museum, 1744
developments and concerns, 1742–1743
National Archaeological Museum, 1743–1744
National Gallery, 1744
national archives and services
Constitution of Greece, 1736
primary mission, 1736–1737
Processing of Personal Data, 1736
protection of personal data, 1736
professional associations, 1739
state/provincial and local archives, 1737–1738
Greek Orthodox Patriarchate Museum, 2550
Greek society, 2677–2678
Green archiving, 3473
Grew, Nehemiah, 646
Grey literature
access and dissemination, 1753–1754
bibliographic control, 1752–1753
five periods, 1748
Gray Information Functional Plan, 1746–1747
importance
citation analyses, 1748–1749
publications in LIS, 1749
information professionals, 1747
Luxembourg definition, 1746
national program, 1747
open archives, 1751–1752
research activities, 1754–1755
typology, 1749–1751

GreyLIT Network, 1553
Grigg Report framework, 111
Grisaille technique, 1949
Grolier's bindings, 543
Gross Domestic Product (GDP), 4497
Gross, E.M., 501, 506
Gross' imposed query model, 5070
Gross national product (GNP), 2256, 2312
Gross, Paul L.K., 501, 506
Group decision support systems (GDSS), 2274
GroupLens recommender system, 3863–3864
Group support systems, 2274
Groupthink, 2097
Grove Art Online, 250
GSLIS scholarships, 3034
Guangdong Science and Technology Museum, 909
Guggenheim Bilbao Museum, 4332
Guided inquiry approach, 2237
Guided Inquiry Design (GID), 2237
Guide to Canadian Museums and Galleries, 676
Guide to the Study and Use of Reference Books, 3913
Gulf of Evaluation, 4807
Gutenberg Bible, 1972
Gutenberg, Johannes, 1865–1866
Guyot, Arnold Henry, 1686
Gymnastic exercises, 4743

H

Haar wavelet, 2630
Hackerspaces, 2991–2992
Hague Convention for Choice of Court Agreements (CCCA), 1271
Hague Conventions, 1349
Haifa Art Museum, 2551
Haifa City Archives, 2554
Haim Attar Museum of Art Ein Harod, 2551
Halftone printing, 1309
Hallmark Art Collection, 1092
Hancock, 2630
Hand binding
  in America, 546–547
  Coptic binding, 542
  Danish bookbinding, 547
  in England, 543, 546
  in France, 544–546
  in Germany, 545
  Gothic styles, 543
  in Holland, 547
  in Italy, 543–545
  Norwegian bookbinders, 548
  romanesque bindings, 542–543
  Scandinavia styles, 547
  in Spain, 545
  in Sweden, 548
  Venetian style, 545
  Western European binding, 542
Handbook of Medical Library Practice, 3037
Handbooks
  Beilstein, 821
  categories, 820
  Gmelin, 821
  Reaxys, 821–822
  spectral atlases and crystallography collections, 822

Handle System, 1328, 1330
Handmade paper, 1828, 1834
Hansch analysis, 836
Hanson, J.C.M., 2848
Haramaya University, 1499
Harar Community Museum, 1503
Harar National Museum, 1503–1504
"Hard-of-hearing," 1184
Harmonic Mean (F), 3946
Harvard curriculum, 3217
Harvard Graduate School of Business Administration, 650
Harvard University Library, 1, 11, 2833
Hashomer Hatzair Archive, 2556–2557
HathiTrust
  vs. Authors Guild, 1761
  content, 1758–1759
  copyright review, 1760
  DPN, 1760
  Google, 1760–1761
  government documents, 1760
  long term objectives, 1758
  membership, 1759
  mPach, 1760
  preservation and access, 1758
  print monograph, 1760
  repository certification, 1759
  research center, 1760
  short term objectives, 1758
  Zephir, 1760
HathiTrust Research Center (HTRC), 1760
Hawaii Library Association (HLA), 3548
Hazardous Substances Data Bank (HSDB®), 3343
HCI, *see* Human–computer interaction
Headbands, 539
Headline, 418–419
Health Care Financing Administration (HCFA), 1873
Healthcare Information Technology Standards Panel (HITSP), 89
Health informatics, 85–86
Health information literacy, 3037
Health information seeking, 843
Health Information Technology for Economic and Clinical Health (HITECH) Act, 3339
Health Insurance Portability and Accountability Act (HIPAA), 1488, 1858, 3342
Health Sciences Librarianship, 3034
Health sciences professionals
  biomedical researchers, 1767–1768
  nurses, 1765–1766
  physicians, 1763–1765
  public health, 1766–1767
Health Services/Technology Assessment Text (HSTAT) database, 1767
Hearst Medical Papyrus, 3041
Hearst Museum of Anthropology, 3252
Heating, ventilation, air conditioning (HVAC) system, 1351
Hecataeus, 1683
HeinOnline, 2708
Heisei period, 3569
Heliopolitan Recension, 1945
Hellenic Academic Libraries (HEAL), 1733, 2827
Hellenic Audiovisual Institute Archive, 1738–1739

Hellenic Literary and Historical Archive, 1738
Hellenism, 1742, 1745
Helping Young People Exel (HYPE) Makerspace, 2992
Hembygdmuseum, 3263
Henkle, H.H., 497–498
Henriette Bathily Museum, 4110
Henry the Navigator, 1684–1685
Heraldry, 3768
Heritage Agency of Denmark, 1225
Heritage Forum, 677–678
Heritage Lottery Fund (HLF), 4727
Heritage network, 4329
Herodotus, 1683
Herzl Museum, 2552
Het Groote Tafereel der Dwaashied, 1403
Hettner, Alfred, 1687
Heuristic evaluation, 4798
Heuristic knowledge, 3535
Heuristic search, 271
Hey Diddle Diddle, 856–857
Hiberno-Saxon illumination, 1947
HIBs, *see* Human information behaviors
Hidden Markov Model (HMM), 3351
Hierarchical force, 4208
High Court of Kenya Library, 2593
Higher education, 4791, 4794
Higher Education Act, 2844
Higher Education General Information Survey Series, 2844
Higher Institute of Documentation in Tunisia in 1984, 100
High Level Thesaurus (HILT) projects, 1262, 4074
High Performance Computing Act of 1991, 1551–1552
High-Quality Interactive Question-Answering (HITIQA) system, 1903
High School Art Program (HSAP), 3244
HighWire Press, 3645
Hill Order formula, 823
H-index, 928–929, 2370
Hippocratic Corpus, 3042
Hirschsprungske Collection, 1226
Hispanics, 2699
HistCite, 933
Histograms, 2629–2630
Histoire du Commerce du Levant au Moyen Age, 645
Historia animalium, 1816
Historia Naturalis, 3043
Historic Adams House, 4166
Historical archives
  of Crete, 1737
  Epirus (Ioannina), 1737
  Macedonia, 1737
  National and Capodistrian University of Athens, 1738
Historical bibliography, 478–468
Historical fiction, 865, 3702–3703
Historical Library, 643
Historical Manuscripts Commission, 183
Historical manuscripts tradition, 184
Historical museum
  in Israel, 2551–2552
  of Serbia, 4135
  Switzerland, 4495

Historical scholarship
  Anabasis of Xenophon (431-355 B.C.), 1787
  diversification, 1789
  Einhard (c. 775-840), 1787
  foundational questions, 1794
  Froissart (c. 1337-1405), 1787
  Herodotus (c. 484-after 424 B.C.), 1787
  Ibn al-Athir (1160-1233), 1787
  Ibn Khaldun (1332-1406), 1787
  Middle Kingdom period of Egypt (21st-18th
      century B.C.), 1787
  nineteenth century, 1786–1788
  primary and secondary sources, 1786
  publications, 1793–1794
  renaissance and enlightenment period,
      1787
  Sallust (86-34 B.C.), 1787
  sources, 1791–1794
  spread of, 1788
  Ssu-ma Chien (145-90 B.C.), 1787
  technology, 1793
  theory, 1789–1791
  Whig theory of history, 1794
Historical societies
  as digital library, 1783–1784
  nationalism, 1780–1781
  organization and mission, 1779–1780
  professionalism and librarianship, 1781–1782
  public history and institutional growth,
      1782–1783
Historical Society of Pennsylvania (HSP),
    1781–1782
Historic and archaeological sites
  buried sites, 1772
  excavation, 1772
  forensic sciences, 1771
  human behavior, 1771
  large-scale excavations, 1773
  "living history" approach, 1778
  "museum exhibit," 1778
  noninvasive tools, 1773
  prehistoric sites, 1772
  saving important sites, 1773–1775
  site preservation, 1776–1777
  tourism, 1777–1778
  underwater sites, 1775–1776
Historic house museums, 1820, 3237
Historic New Orleans Collection, 199
History flow visualization technique, 4988
History museums, 3237
A History of Art Libraries in Canada, 249
History of Libraries
  ancient world, 1796–1797
  change agent, 1808–1809
  diverse populations, 1807
  educator, 1809
  female participation, 1805
  globalization, 1808
  ideology of reading, 1809–1810
  librarianship education, 1804–1805
  medieval era, 1797–1798
  politics and society, 1801–1802
  professionalization and growth, 1802–1807
  Reformation, 1799–1800
  Renaissance, 1798–1799
  repository, 1808
  resource sharing, 1806–1807

  seventeenth and eighteenth centuries, 1800–
      1801
  twentieth century expansion, 1805–1806
History of Rome, 644
History Section (HS), 3909
HITS algorithm, 484
Hjoerring Public Library, 1221
Hobbes, Thomas, 646
Hodges Library, virtual tour, 3440–3441
Hollings–Danforth bill, 1020
Hollow backs, 539
Holon Mediatheque, 2546
Homebound delivery services, 14, 3577
Homeland Security Standards Panel (HSSP), 89
Homer, 1683
Homestead National Monument of America,
    4165
Horizontal portals, 2893
Hornbook, 853
Horror, 3703
Hospital librarians, 3415–3416
Hospital libraries
  administrative and management
      assessment, 1882–1883
    fiscal management, 1881–1882
    human resources, 1882
    marketing, 1882
    planning, 1882
  clinical decisions, 1873
  consumer health trends, 1889–1890
  digital resources, 1888
  EBL, 1887–1888
  educational services, 1878
  EHR and LATCH, 1889
  electronic resources, 1886–1887
  health care organizations
    cooperative networks, participation in,
        1885
    Loansome Doc, 1885–1886
  historical overview, 1870–1871
  information services, 1879
  knowledge management, 1889
  library clientele, 1874–1875
  library staff
    educational requirements, hospital librar-
        ians, 1875–1876
    hospital librarian, role of, 1875
  library standards, 1873–1874
  MEDLINE
    current awareness services, 1880
    interlibrary loan and document delivery,
        1880
    library collections, online access to, 1881
    outsourcing, 1881
  mission of, 1871
  organizational contributions
    CML, 1884
    customized services, 1883
    decision makers, 1883–1884
    health literacy, 1884–1885
    Internet access, 1883
  outreach, educational role in, 1888
  reference, 1879
  role of, 1871–1872
  services
    bibliographic information, access to,
        1877–1878

    circulation, 1877
    collection development, 1876–1877
    library collection, access to, 1877
    technical service, 1876
  social networking technologies, 1887
  types
    community hospital library, 1872
    nursing libraries, 1873
    specialty hospital library, 1872–1873
    teaching hospital library, 1872
    value-added services, 1888–1889
HotBot, 2522
Hotline, 3652
House museums, 4165–4166
HTML, *see* Hypertext markup language
HTRC, *see* HathiTrust Research Center
Huang Ti Nei Ching, 3042
Hubert, Robert, 4716
Hugh C. Atkinson Memorial Award, 2777
Hulme, E. Wyndham, 496, 498, 500
*Human Behavior and the Principle of Least
    Effort*, 502
Human-Centered Design Processes for Interac-
    tive Systems, 4808
Human–computer interaction (HCI), 2079,
    2272, 4115–4116, 4804, 4851–4852
  information retrieval research
    applications, tools and techniques, 1902
    Bates's cascade of interaction model,
        1899–1900
    Belkin's episode model, 1897–1899
    conferences, 1904
    history, 1895–1897
    Ingwersen's cognitive IR theory, 1897
    institutions, 1904
    Lin's MISE model, 1900–1901
    methodologies, validity and reliability of,
        1903–1904
    non-performance measures, 1903
    organizations, 1904
    performance measures, 1902–1903
    user-centered studies, design implications,
        1901
    workshops, 1904
  sense-making, 4113–4121
Human development index (HDI), 2312
Human genome epidemiology (HuGE), 1767
Human information behaviors (HIBs), 3407,
    4114, 4121
Human intelligence, 269
Humanism libraries
  England, 3952
  Germanies, 3952–3954
  Italy, 3948–3950
Humanities
  definition, 1909–1910
  primary literature, 1910–1911
    access to, 1911–1912
    characteristics, 1911
    digital literature, 1911–1913
    extent of use, 1911
    sources, 1911
  scholar's workflow, information seeking and
      use, 1914–1915
  secondary literature
    age, 1913
    characteristics, 1913

Humanities (cont'd.)
  secondary literature (cont'd.)
    digital literature, 1914
    formats, 1913
    identification and location, 1914
    language, 1913–1914
  user studies, 1910
The Humanities, 1909
Humanities Advanced Technology and Information Institute (HATII), 4738
Humanities and Social Sciences Federation of Canada (HSSFC), 4896
Humanities computing, 1286, 1288–1291, 1293, 4565
Human-like language processing, 3346
Human needs theory, 2115–2116
Human relations approach, 3513
Human Rights Archives and Documentation Program (HRADP), 790
Humboldt, Alexander von, 1686
Hunefer Papyrus, 1946
Hungarian Electronic Library, 1923
Hungarian National Bibliography, 1921
Hungary, 1931–1932
  archives and archival science
    archivists and records managers, education for, 1926–1927
    college and university archives, 1925–1926
    corporate and religious, 1926
    as discipline and profession, 1926
    electronic documents, 1927
    film and audiovisual archives, 1926
    historical societies, 1926
    legislation, 1925
    manuscript repositories, 1926
    national archives and services, 1925
    preservation of documents, 1927
    professional associations, 1927
  library and information professions
    academic and research libraries, 1922
    digital library collections and services, 1923–1924
    education for LIS, 1925
    legislation, 1920–1921
    LIS as discipline and profession, 1924–1925
    National Library, 1921–1922
    professional associations, 1925
    public libraries, 1923
    school libraries, 1923
    special libraries, 1923
  literacy, history of, 1917–1920
  Map of, 1917–1918
  museums
    art museums and galleries, 1928
    current priorities, 1931
    digital museum exhibits and services, 1930
    as discipline and profession, 1930–1931
    education, 1931
    historical, anthropological, and archaeological museums, 1929–1930
    laws, 1927
    National Museum, 1927–1928
    professional associations, 1931
    religiously affiliated museums, 1929
    science and natural history museums, 1929
    zoos and botanical gardens, 1930

Huntington, Ellsworth, 1688
Hunt Library Makerspace, 2992
Husbandry and Trade Improved, 1403
Hybridization, 4293–4294
Hybrid-mobile robots, 275
Hyper-book, 5068
HyperCard; *see also* Hypertext and hypercard
  accessibility levels, 1942
  advanced features, 1943
  Atkinson, Bill, 1940–1941
  basics, 1941
  graphics, 1942–1943
  hypermedia interface, 1943
  HyperTalk, 1943
  Message box, 1942
  navigational AIDS, 1941–1942
  stack, 1941
  text editing, 1942
Hyperlink-based data discovery, 2940
Hypertext and hypercard, 1290
  academic and corporate projects
    BioQUEST, 1938
    hyperties, 1938
    intermedia, 1938
    Jefferson notebook, 1938
    NoteCards, 1938
    Project Emperor-1, 1938
    Project Perseus, 1938
    SuperBook, 1939
  Apple II Software, 1939
  definition, 1935–1936
  history
    Bush, Vannevar, 1936–1937
    Engelbart, Douglas, 1937
    Kay, Alan, 1937–1938
    Nelson, Theodor Holm, 1937
    Wells, H.G., 1936
  Macintosh software, 1940
  MS-DOS Software, 1939–1940
Hypertext markup language (HTML), 1367, 1416, 1677, 2343, 2986, 3072, 3075, 4041–4042, 5025, 5029–5030
  Unicode Standard, 4667
HyperText Transfer Protocol (HTTP), 2183
Hypnerotomachia Poliphili, 1973

I

IAS, *see* Interdisciplinary and area studies
iBooks, 4055
Iceland Library Consortium, 2825
Ichkeul National Park, 4638
ICONCLASS, 1079–1080
Iconclass, 4412
Icon formats, 1177
ICT Development Index (IDI), 1282
Ideal ethics, 1473
Identifiers, 3292–3293
Identity links, 2940
Identity Management Standards Panel (IDSP), 89
I.D.F. & Defense Establishment Archives, 2553–2554
IDRISI, 1675–1676
IFLA, *see* International Federation of Library Associations and institutions

IFLA-CDNL Alliance for Bibliographic Standards (ICABS), 451
IFLA FRSAR working group, 1606–1609
IFLA/UNESCO Public Library Manifesto and Guidelines, 3781–3783
Iliad, 644
Illuminated bindings, 541
Illumination
  ancient Egypt
    Book of the Dead, 1945–1946
    Heliopolitan Recension, 1945
    Hunefer Papyrus, 1946
    Papyrus of Ani, 1945
  Byzantine art, 1946–1947
  Carolingian art, 1947–1948
  in color, 1945
  definition, 1945
  England
    Gothic period, 1950
    Romanesque period, 1948
  France
    in fifteenth century, 1951
    Gothic period, 1949
    Romanesque period, 1948
  Germany
    in fifteenth and sixteenth centuries, 1951
    Gothic period, 1950
    Romanesque period, 1948–1949
  Greco-Roman period, 1946
  Hiberno-Saxon art, 1947
  Islam (*see* Islamic illumination)
  Italy
    in fifteenth century, 1951
    Gothic period, 1950
    Romanesque period, 1949
  Low Countries
    in fifteenth century, 1951
    Gothic period, 1949–1950
    Romanesque period, 1948
  meaning, 1945
  Mogul miniatures (1525-1707), 1956–1957
  Ottonian, 1948
  Persian illumination (1502-1736), 1955–1956
  Spain, Romanesque period, 1948
  Turkish illumination (1451-1900), 1956
Illustrated books, 855–856
Image indexing, *see* Still image indexing
Imageline project, 250
Image processing, 275
Imaginary audience, 5060
Immediacy index, 928
Immigrant child mediators (ICMs), 2126
Immigration, 2065
  museum, 3245
  records, 1658
Impact factor (IF), 2370
ImpactStory, 45
Imperial Library Act, 1993
Imperial Museum, Campo de Santana, 613–614
Imperial War Museum, 4719
Implicit learning, 2678
Imposed query, 5070
Improvisation, 3531
InChls™, 824–825
Incised leather, 540
inCite, 400

Incunabula, 3820
  American libraries, collections in, 1974
  Catholicon, 1972
  Das Buch der Chroniken or Liber Chronicarum, 1973
  De evangelica praeparatione, 1973
  definition, 1966–1968
  European libraries, collections in, 1973–1974
  extant incunabula, 1971
  Gutenberg Bible, 1972
  Hypnerotomachia Poliphili, 1973
  Mainz Psalter, 1972
  The Recuyell of the Histories of Troy, 1973
  reference works
    Annales typographici ab artis inventae origine ad annum MDCLXIV, 1968
    Appendices ad Hain-Copingeri Repertorium Bibliographicum, 1969–1970
    British Museum Catalogue of Books Printed in the Fifteenth Century, 1970
    The Printers and Publishers of the XVth Century With a List of Their Works, 1969
    Repterorium Bibliographicum, 1968–1969
    Supplement to Hain's Repertorium Bibliographicum, 1969
    Subiaco Lactantius, 1973
    typographical detectives, 1971–1972
Independent Librarians' Exchange Section, 376
Independent Media Arts Preservation (IMAP), 1568
Independent museums, in United Kingdom, 4721–4722
Independent Television Authority (ITA), 1566
Index, 3470–3471, 4978–4982
The Index-Catalogue of the Library of the Surgeon-General's Office, 758
Indexer, 2519
The Indexer: The International Journal of Indexing, 445
Indexing
  and abstracting services, 817–820
    chemical abstracts, 818
    Inspec and compendex, 819
    MEDLINE, 819–820
    Web of science, 818–819
  automatic indexing, 1987–1988
  back-of-the-book index (*see* Book indexing)
  consistency of, 1987
  cross-references, syndetic structure, 1980
  disciplines related to, 1982–1983
  elements, 1978–1979
  history of, 1983–1984
  literature, 1981
  locators, 1978–1982
  mission-oriented indexing, 1987
  occupational home economics, 1986–1987
  open *vs.* closed system, 440, 1979
  semantic web, 1988
  site indexes, 1978
  subheadings, 1979
  theory of, 1984–1985
  thesauri, 1985–1986
  vogue words, 1980
Indexing Books, 443
Index Medicus, 3471

India
  academic and research libraries
    college libraries, 1997–1998
    higher education sector, 1997
    public libraries, 1998–2001
    school libraries, 2001–2002
    special libraries, 2002–2004
    university libraries, 1998
  archives and archival science
    archival science, discipline and profession, 2015
    Association of Indian Archivists, 2016
    documents preservation, 2016
    education, archivists and records managers, 2015
    electronic records, archival documents, 2016
    national archives and services, 2012–2015
    professional associations, 2015–2016
  digital library collections and services, 2004–2006
  discipline and profession
    information science, 2006–2007
    librarianship, 2007
    museology, 2025
  education for LIS, 2007–2009
  emerging new India, 1993
  geography and population, 1992
  government, 1992
  history of, 1992–1993
  library legislation
    post-independence period (1947–2000), 1993–1994
    pre-independence period, 1993
    twenty-first century, 1994
  museums and museology
    contemporary issues, 2027–2028
    digital museum exhibits and services, 2025
    education, curatorship and museum administration, 2025–2027
    historical, anthropological and archaeological museums, 2022
    history, 2016–2017
    legislation, 2017–2018
    major art museums and galleries, 2019–2020
    National Museums, 2018–2019
    National Parks, 2024–2025
    science and natural history museums, 2020–2022
    strengthening and modernization of, 2019
    surveys, 2022–2023
    zoos, 2023–2024
  National Library and Information Services (*see* National Library and Information Services)
  professional associations, 2010–2011
Indian Association of Special Libraries and Information Centres (IASLIC), 2011
Indian Association of Teachers of Library and Information Science (IATLIS), 2008
Indiana University Digital Library Program, 3285
Indian Copyright Act, 1993
Indian Council of Medical Research (ICMR), 2002
Indian ISKO Chapter, 2498

Indian National Digital Library in Engineering Sciences and Technology (INDEST) Consortium, 2005
Indigenous cultural and intellectual property (ICIP), 2037
Indigenous Knowledge Centres (IKCs), 2035
Indigenous knowledge systems (IKS), 2133
Indigenous librarianship
  education, 2042
  methodology, 2031–2032
  peoples and libraries (*see* Indigenous peoples and libraries)
  professional associations, 2042–2043
  research, 2041–2042
  terminology, 2032
Indigenous museums, 3238
Indigenous Nations Library Program (INLP), 2033
Indigenous peoples and libraries
  Aotearoa/New Zealand, 2036
  Australia, 2035–2036
  Canada, 2033–2035
  cultures and communities, 2032
  digital divide, 2038–2039
  equitable access, 2037
  ICIP rights, 2040–2041
  ICTs, 2038
  indigenous knowledge organization, 2040
  literacy, 2039–2040
  perennial funding challenges, 2037
  protocols, 2041
  and their intersections, 2036–2037
  United States, 2032–2033
  universal access, 2039
  virtual repatriation, 2041
Indira Gandhi National Centre for the Arts (IGNCA), 2015
Indirect instructions, 3914
Individuals with Disabilities Education Act (IDEA), 3843
Inductive justification, 1457
Inductive statistics, 494–495
Industrial Property Act (Chapter 509), 2594
Industrial Revolution, 597
Industry information, 637–638
Inferential justification, 1457–1458
Influence diagrams, 1204–1205
InfoEyes, 17
Information, 3106
  aboutness and relevance, 3613
  communicatory/semiotic definitions of
    Bateson, Gregory, 2051
    Brookes, B.C., 2051
    Losee, Robert, 2052
    Madden, A.D., 2051
    Nauta, Doede, 2051–2052
  cybernetics, 2050
  deconstruction
    Day, Ronald, 2059
    Frohmann, Bernd, 2059–2060
    Furner, Jonathan, 2060
  definitions
    epistemic family, 3613
    semiotic family, 3612–3613
    sociocognitive family, 3613
  DIKW, 2049, 2059
  as event, 2052

Information (cont'd.)
  human–information interaction, 3613–3614
  information-as-message, 3613
  kinesthetic and visual feedback, 2050
  knowledge-as-message, 3613
  multi-type definitions
    Bates, Marcia J., 2057–2058
    Beynon-Davies, Paul, 2058–2059
    Buckland, Michael, 2057
    Dervin, Brenda, 2056–2057
    Goonatilake's flow lines, 2058
    MacKay, Donald, 2056
  philosophy of, 3610
  Popper, Karl, 2055–2056
  propositional definitions
    Derr, Richard, 2052–2053
    Dretske, Fred, 2053
    Fox, Christopher, 2053
  resources, 3613
  Shannon's ideas, impact of, 2049–2051
    communication engineering, 2051
    deracinated definition, 2049
    information transmission, calculation of,
      2050–2051
    mathematical and engineering theory, 2050
    technical revolution(s), 2049
  social definitions
    Cornelius, Ian, 2054
    Goguen, Joseph, 2054–2055
    idiographic approach, 2054
    nomothetic approach, 2054
  structural definitions, 2053–2054
Information Access Alliance (IAA), 345,
    366–367
Informational books, children, 867–868
Informational occupations, 2257–2260
Informational semantics, see Semantic
    information
Information and communication technologies
    (ICTs), 2038, 2132–2133, 2141–2142,
    2253, 2304, 4212–4216, 4497, 5016
  diasporic information sources, 2125
  learning and information seeking, 2752,
    2759–2760
Information and Intelligent Systems (IIS), 2217
Information and Knowledge Management Soci-
    ety (iKMS), 2449
Information and Learning Commons, 2794
Information and Library Network (INLIBNET),
    2005
Information and Misinformation, 2053
Information and referral (I&R) services,
    1029–1030
Information arts
  definition, 2064–2065
  flow diagram, 2067
  formalism vs. culturalism, 2071
  information society, 2065–2067
  in museums, 2071–2073
  practice and production cycle, 2067–2071
Information-as-action, 2060
Information-as-evidence, 3616
Information-as-knowledge, 2057
Information-as-particular, 2060
Information-as-process, 2057
Information-as-thing, 2057
Information-as-universal, 2060

Information behavior (IB), 842, 2162, 4848
  Choo's model of information needs, seeking
    and use, 2089, 2091
  definition, 2086, 4459
  Godbold's model, 2092
  graphical models, 2086–2087
  human models, 2086
  information search process, Kuhlthau's model
    of, 2088–2089
  information seeking, generic model, 2087–
    2088
  Ingwersen's cognitive model, 2089–2090
  Johnson's model, 2089–2091
  mathematical models, 2086
  model of trust in health care, 2090–2092
  Niedzwiedzka's model, 2092–2093
  physical models, 2086
  pseudo-mathematical models, 2086
  what happens, models of, 2088
  Wilson's expanded model, 2089–2090
  Wilson's problem-solving model, 2088–2089
Information behavior (IB) research
  history of
    five laws of librarianship, 2075
    Graduate Library School, 2075
    information practice, 2077
    information-related theories and models,
      2076–2077
    information seeking, 2075–2076
    ISIC conferences, 2077
    sensemaking, 2076–2077
    social constructivism, 2077
  information, 2074–2075
  information searching vs. information seek-
    ing, 2078
  technology, role of
    catalog innovation, 2078–2079
    digital libraries, 2079
    HCI research, 2079
    information retrieval, 2079
    MARC records, 2078
    online database searching, 2079
    World Wide Web, 2078–2079
  topics of
    children's information needs, 2081
    cognitive authority, 2080
    information genres, 2081
    information grounds concept, 2081
    information seeking, 2080
    information use, 2081
    personal and professional contexts, 2080
    principle of least effort, 2080
Information brokers, 3416
Information business
  advertising, 3007
  cash flow, 3005–3006
  competencies, 3004
  contracts, 3008–3009
  firing, 3008
  hiring, 3007–3008
  investments, 3006–3007
  marketing, 3007
  priorities, 3005
  selling, 3007
  time management, 3004–3005
Information Coding Classification, 2499
Information commons, 4653

Information communication technology (ICT)
  African librarianship, 38
Information crises and crisis information
  asymmetric campaigning, 2094
  auto-feeding, 2096
  destructive information, 2095
  imperfect, incomplete and unreliable inter-
    pretation, 2095
  knowledge, 2095
  machine-to-machine communications, 2094
  management, 2097–2099
  Plato perspective, 2094
  presumptions, 2096
  reductive analysis, 2095
  self-reinforcement, 2096–2097
  sense-making, 2094–2095
  spiraling, 2096
  uncertainty, 2095
Information culture, 3521–3522
Information discovery, 4978
Information dissemination, 4237
Information economy, 2256–2257
Information environments (IEs), 4848
Information ethics (infoethics), 3617, 4658
Information exchange, 2088
Information explosion
  "ExaByte-Counter," 2102
  information age, 2102
  information management and evaluation,
    2102
  information overload, 2103–2104
  information society, 2101–2103
  Lyman and Varian's report, 2101
Information extraction (IE), 3353
Information for All Programme (IFAP), 2308,
    4657
Information gateways, 4653
Information gathering, 3660
Information-generating behavior, 2096
"Information grounds," 2126
Information literacy (IL), 2757–2758, 4199,
    4859–4860
Information Literacy Competency Standards for
    Higher Education, 342
Information management (IM), 2618–2620,
    3521, 3523
  consolidated view
    Big Data, 2107, 2112
    digital convergence, 2107, 2111
    libraries content-creation role, 2107,
      2111–2112
  definition, 2106
  library perspective, 2106, 2110–2111
  organizational perspective
    information life cycle, 2106, 2109
    information resources, 2106–2108
    IT management, 2106, 2109
    organizational information processing,
      2109–2110
  personal perspective, 2106–2107, 2111
  process perspective, 2107
  subsystem, 2195
Information Management Journal, 1856
Information meta-studies, 3611
Information needs and LIS
  constructivist/cognitive view, 2118–2119
  educational need, 2116

historical evolution, 2116–2118
human needs
    Maslow's hierarchy of needs, 2115
    physiological, affective and cognitive, 2115
    political economy research, 2115–2116
information transfer model, 2118
people's personal situations, understanding
    of, 2116
research, 2120
social constructionist/social view, 2119
Information occupation, 2257–2260
Information policy, 1718
historical development
    Administrative Procedure Act of 1946,
      2150
    Articles of Confederation, 2148
    Bill of Rights, 2148–2149, 2152
    Code of Federal Regulations, 2150
    common law rights of Englishmen, 2148
    fair information practices, 2152
    Federal Advisory Committee Act of 1972,
      2151
    Federal Register, 2150
    FOI Act, 2150–2152
    Government in the Sunshine Act of 1976,
      2151
    Internet and web activity, monitoring of,
      2152–2153
    military secrecy directives/regulations,
      2151
    National Security Act of 1947, 2151
    NSC, 2151–2152
    Philadelphia convention of 1787, 2149
    Printing Act of 1895, 2150
    printing and publication policy, 2149–2150
    Privacy Act, 2151–2152
    Progressive Movement, 2150
    security classification system, 2151
    state constitutions, 2148
    superintendent, responsibility of, 2150
    Trade Secrets Act, 2152
internal and external policies, impact of,
    2148
Library Awareness Program, 2148
literature on, 2154
national information policy, 2158
policy framework, 2156–2157
stakeholders, 2157
in United States
    depository libraries, 2148
    depository library programs, 2156
    electronic government, 2147, 2153–2154,
      2158–2159
    FBI's justification, 2148
    government information, public access to,
      2154–2156
    government policies, 2147–2148
Information practice, 2077
evolving conceptualizations, 2163–2164
implementation, 2166–2167
information science, 2164–2166
opportunities and theoretical pathways,
    2167–2168
Information producers, 2259
Information professional (IP), 4377–4378
Information Requirements of the Social Sci-
    ences (INFROSS) studies, 4246

Information resources management (IRM),
    2108, 2619
Information retrieval, 843–844
Information retrieval (IR), 1242, 2239, 2243,
    3926
algorithms, 2221–2222
Boolean model, 2202–2203
components
    indexes and query matching, 2201
    text processing, 2200–2201
definition, 2220
experiment
    Boolean model, 2173
    experimental approach, 2178
    experimental design and analysis,
      2177–2178
    laboratory experiment, 2172
    major information retrieval experiments,
      2174–2176
    performance measures, 2173–2174
    research concerns, 2176–2177
    vector space model, 2173
fuzzy set theory (*see* Fuzzy set theory, infor-
    mation retrieval)
hybrid models, 2207
inference network models, 2207
IRSS (*see* Information Retrieval Support Sys-
    tems (IRSS))
language models, 2206–2207
logistic regression algorithm, 2206
NLP (*see* Natural language processing)
Okapi BM-25 algorithm, 2205–2206
probabilistic retrieval methods
    document retrieval problem, 2204
    higher-level Model 3, 2204
    lower-level Model 0, 2204–2205
    Model 1 system, 2204
    Model 2 system, 2204–2205
protocols (*see* Information retrieval (IR)
    protocols)
query expansion and relevance feedback,
    2207–2208
relevance, 2220–2221
searching aboutness, 2220
specification for search, 2220
systems (*see* Information retrieval (IR) systems)
testing, 2222–2223
vector model, 2203–2204
Information retrieval (IR) protocols
abstract model of, 2181–2182
access points and indexes, 2182
bibliographic databases, 2181–2182
communications protocols, 2182–2183
interoperability and intersystem, 2186
IR system, 2181–2182
query, 2181–2182
result set and retrieved records, 2181–2182
SRU
    CQL, 2189
    Editorial Board, 2187
    explain operation, 2187–2189
    HTTP GET request, 2187–2188
    projects and implementations, 2189–2190
    REST approach, 2187
    searchRetrieve operation, 2187–2189
    SOAP, 2187
    SRW and, 2187

Z39.50 protocol, 2983
    chronology of, 2183–2184
    client and server software, 2184
    Init service, 2184–2185
    present service, 2185–2186
    search service, 2185
    ZING project, 2186–2187
Information Retrieval Support Systems (IRSS)
characteristics of, 2193–2194
conceptual architecture, 2194–2195
document-space granulation, 2196
DRS, 2193
implementation of
    computer graphics and information visuali-
      zation, 2195–2196
    expert systems, 2195
    intelligent information agents, 2196
    machine learning and data mining, 2195
    related fields, 2195
information retrieval support, 2193
KRS, 2192
retrieval-result-space granulation, 2196
RSS, 2192
term-space granulation, 2196
user-space granulation, 2196
Information saturation model, 2213
Information scattering
bibliometric laws, 2210
Bradford's law of scattering, 2210
coverage analyses, 2211–2212
definition, 2210
explanations for, 2212–2213
frequency distributions, 2211
future research challenges, 2214
informetric laws, 2210
Lotka's Law, 2210–2211
network visualizations and analysis, 2212–2213
search strategies and design, implications for,
    2213–2214
types of, 2211
Zipf's Law, 2210
"Information school movement," 4114
Information schools (iSchools), 2230
characteristics of, 2539
iConference, 2539
iField, 2538
motivation, 2537
origins, 2536–2537
positioning, 2537–2538
recognition, 2540
as transdisciplinary domain, 2538
vision, 2539–2540
Information science, 2770, 3612
bibliometrics
    ARIST, 489
    Google boom, 483–485
    interpersonal communication, 489
    IS, map of, 485–488
    L&IS definition, 481–483
    mediators and automation, 483
characteristics, 2230
definition, 2216, 2537
design science (*see* Design science)
education
    i-Schools, 2230
    Salton model, 2229–2230
    Shera model, 2229

Information science (cont'd.)
  human information behavior
    definition, 2223
    information needs and use, 2223–2224
    information searching, 2225
    information seeking, 2224–2225
    models and theories, 2225–2226
    social and individual question, 2223
  information explosion, problems of,
    2217–2218
  intellectual structure
    author cocitation analysis, 2218–2219
    design question, 2218
    information theory, 2219
    knowledge domains, visualization of,
      2219
    library automation, 2219
    literature people, 2219
    OPACs, 2219
    physical question, 2218
    1959 Proceedings, 2218–2219
    retrieval people, 2219
    social question, 2218
    webometrics, 2219
  International Conference on Scientific Infor-
    mation, 2216
  Memex, 2217
  metric studies, 2226–2228
  National Science Foundation, 2217
  orientations, 2216
  philosophy of, 3611
  scope, 3614
  social and human function, 2218
  VINITI, 2217
Information Science and Automation Division
    (ISAD), 2776, 2966
Information searching, 2225
  vs. information seeking, 2078
  and search models
    Bates' berry-picking approach, 2244
    Belkin's episode model of interaction with
      texts, 2246–2247
    digital libraries, 2240
    domain knowledge, 2243
    Ellis' model of information-seeking behav-
      iors, 2243–2244
    information retrieval systems, 2239, 2243
    Ingwersen and Järvelin's cognitive model,
      2245–2246
    IR knowledge, 2243
    Kuhlthau's ISP model, 2244
    multidimensional model of user-Web inter-
      action, 2248–2249
    online bibliographic retrieval, conceptual
      framework for, 2245
    online databases, 2240
    OPACs, 2240
    Saracevic's stratified interaction model,
      2247
    search strategies, 2240–2242
    search tactics/moves, 2239–2241
    serendipitous information search,
      2244–2245
    system knowledge, 2243
    task complexity and stages, 2242–2243
    usage patterns, 2240, 2242
    Vakkari's task-based IR process, 2245

    Web search engines, 2240
    Xie's planned-situational interactive IR
      model, 2247–2248
    task-based approach (see Task-based infor-
      mation searching)
Information search process (ISP) model, 2076,
    2244, 4529, 5069–5070
  development of, 2232
  educaion, implication for, 2237
  information seeking
    focus formulation, 2235
    personal construct theory, 2234
    principle of uncertainty, corollaries,
      2235–2236
    uncertainty, increase in, 2235
    user's perspective, 2232–2234
    workplace, 2234
  information services and systems, 2236
  meaning, 2232
  students, 4460
Information seeking, 2075–2076, 2078, 2080,
    2224–2225
  strategies, 2241–2242
Information seeking and retrieval (IS&R),
    4880
Information Seeking in Context (ISIC), 2077,
    2163, 4118–4119
Information Seeking in Context (ISIC) confer-
    ences, 2117, 2772, 4856
Information seeking process (ISP) model,
    2783–2784
Information sharing, 2759–2760
Information society
  culture, 2262–2264
  economics, 2256–2257
  information, definition of, 2266–2267
  occupational definition, 2257–2260
  quantitative vs. qualitative measures,
    2264–2266
  spatial, 2260–2262
  technological definition
    computer cost, reduction in, 2253
    information grid, 2254
    ISDN systems, 2254
    microelectronics revolution, 2254
    neo-Schumpeterian approach, 2254
    objections, 2254–2255
    techno-economic paradigm, 2254
    telecommunications, computerization of,
      2253
  theoretical knowledge, 2267–2269
Information sources, 2088
Information systems (IS), 2619
  application knowledge, 2275
  and business informatics
    architectural framework, 632
    characteristics of, 631
    IS 2002 undergraduate model curriculum,
      631–632
    MSIS 2000 model curriculum, 631–632
    recommendation for, 631–632
    as science discipline, 631
    study framework, 632–633
    study program, 632–634
  careers
    certification, 701
    experience, 701

    job domains and titles, 699, 702
    jobs by keyword in Monster.com, 699, 703
    occupations, application areas and job title
      domains, 699, 703
  Carr's "IT Doesn't Matter" hypothesis, 704
  changing technology, effects of, 704
  computer engineering, 694
  computing science, 694
  definition, 694
  development knowledge, 2275
  education
    M.S. model curriculum, 694–697
    Ph.D. programs, 694
    Schools of Information and Informatics,
      694
    training and continuing education, 696
    undergraduate curriculum, 694
  ethical and social issues
    accountability and liability, 2277
    information rights and obligations, 2277
    property rights and obligations, 2277
    quality of life, 2278
    system quality, 2277–2278
  ethics
    codes of ethics, 1484–1485
    definition, 1484
    domain scenarios, 1486
    ethical decision making, 1492
    ethical issues, 1486–1487
    ethical theories, 1485–1486
  failure (see Information systems (IS) failure)
  future organization, 702–703
  industry, 696
    consultant organizations, 699
    equipment manufacturers, 697–698
    internal organizations, 698–699
    service providers and outsourcers, 698
    software firms, 698
  IT talent challenge, 703–704
  LIS, definition of, 693–694
  management knowledge, 2275–2276
  online library catalogs, 704
  origins, 2272–2273
  professional associations, 701, 2276
  publications, 2276–2277
  reference curricula, 630
  research firms and consultancies, 2277
  social softwares, 704
  specialization and job categories, 699–701
  strategic use of, 701–703
  study programs, 630–631
  technology knowledge, 2275
  UCD (see User-centered design)
  varieties
    decision support systems, 2274
    enterprise systems, 2274–2275
    group support systems, 2274
    management information systems,
      2273–2274
    transaction-processing systems, 2273
  Wi-Fi and telecommuting, 704
Information systems (IS) failure
  cognate literatures, 2282–2283
  evolution of, 2281–2282
  interactionist approaches
    exchange perspective, 2286
    sociotechnical perspective, 2286

practitioners, 2287–2288
process approaches, 2286–2287
scale of, 2280–2281
static approaches
organizational/cultural perspective, 2284–2285
political perspective, 2285
technological perspective, 2283–2284
Information technologies (IT), 2253–2255, 2678
competence
digital literacy, 2307
expertise, 2307
incompetence, 2307
social competence, 2306
socio-technological information (cyber) competence, 2306–2307
workplace competency, 2307
information behavior research, role in, 2078–2079
information management, role in, 2106, 2109
records management, 716–717
Information technology (IT) adoption
background
discontinuities, role of, 2291–2292
individual/organizational performance, 2290
information society, 2291
categories
individuals, 2298–2299
organizations, 2299
S-Curve, 2298
innovation decision, types of
authoritative decision, 2296
change agents' promotional efforts, 2297
collective decision, 2296
communication channels, 2297
social system, nature of, 2297
voluntary decision, 2296
perceived attributes of innovation (see Perceived attributes, IT adoption)
Information Technology and Libraries (ITAL), 2777, 2779–2780
Information Technology Association, 1641
Information technology innovation life cycle, 2291
Information technology (IT) literacy
assessment, 2310
connectivism, 2309
information culture literacy, 2308
knowledge sharing, 2309–2310
learning and inquiry, 2309
personal computer, 2303
stages and limitations of
advanced literacies, 2304
basic literacy, 2304
multiliteracies, 2305–2306
social and workplace literacies, 2305
visual and media literacies, 2305
technology and academic literacies, 2308–2309
terminology issues, 2308
Information Technology Management Reform Act of 1996, 1551
Information technology project implementation
development, 2313–2314
HDI, 2312

management issues
communication, 2314
cultural, organizational and barriers, 2319–2320
financial resources, 2317
hardware and software options, 2317–2319
human resource concerns, 2315–2317
IFLA general conference, 2315
IT projects, 2314
planning committee, 2314
socioeconomic and political underdevelopment, 2314
operational issues
CD-ROM, 2322–2326
collection development, 2333–2335
interlibrary loan and document delivery, 2331–2333
internet access, 2328–2329
local databases, development and access, 2329–2331
network resources, 2326–2328
online searching, 2320–2322
user sensitization and training issues, 2335–2337
Information technology standards
ANSI, 2343–2344
definition
by British Standards Institution, 2342
by ISO, 2341
future, 2349
ISO
harmonizing national standards, 2346
ISO/IEC Joint Technical Committee 1, 2346
library and information services, 2346–2347
membership categories, 2346
principal phases, 2346
NISO, 2341
Architecture Committee, 2343
current standards, 2345
expert technical advisory group, 2344
final approval, 2345
formulation and implementation of standards, 2345
Library Standards Alliance, 2345
supporting organizations, 2345
Topic Committee, 2343
work item, 2343
standards-making bodies, 2344–2346
technical standards
American National Standards Committee Z39, 2341
benefits of, 2343–2344
in librarianship, 2348
types
conceptual standards, 2342
implementation standard, 2342–2343
process standard, 2343
product standard, 2342
W3C, 2347–2348
Information-theoretic epistemology, 3613
Information theory
behavioral economics, 2357
communication
human communication, 2354
and mutual information, 2352–2354

compression of information, 2353
equally probable alternatives, 2350–2351
identification, 2357–2358
IEEE Society for Information Theory, 2353
library and information science, 2354
origin, 2350
random variables
mutual information, 2351–2353
unpredictability, 2350
varying probabilities and entropy measure, 2351
scholarly and scientific organizations, 2358
string of characters, entropy of, 2351
surprise, 2357
symbolic utility, 2357
utility theory, 2354–2357
Information transfer model, 2118
Information workers, 2258–2260
Informetrics, 2057, 2210, 2226
citation analysis, 2369–2370
citation databases, 2370–2371
co-citation analysis, 2371
cybermetrics and webometrics, 2372–2373
h-index, 2370
impact factor, 2370
journals, 2369
link analysis, 2369
mapping and visualization, 2372
open access, 2371
research evaluation, 2373
terminology and definition, 2367–2368
theoretical informetrics, 2371–2372
WOS index, 2369
Infoseek, 2521–2522
Ingenta, 3471
IngentaConnect, 3471
Ingwersen–Järvelin integrated cognitive model, 2089–2090, 2245–2246, 4880–4881
INISS Project, 2117
Initiative to Recruit a Diverse Workforce, 371
Inktomi, 2522
Innovation diffusion theory, 2292
Innovation Project, 4263
Innovative culture, 3521–3522
Innovative libraries, 2766
Inorganic Crystal Structure Database (ICSD), 822
INQUERY IR system, 2207
Inquiry-based learning, 558
Inscriptions, 3768
Instant Response Order System (IROS), 409
Institut de presse et des sciences de l'information (IPSI), 4632
Institute for Conservation (ICON), 4739
Institute for Information Literacy (IIL), 346
Institute for International Affairs, 4912
Institute for Museum and Library Services (IMLS), 2033
Institute for Operations Research and Management Science (INFORMS), 2276
Institute for Scientific Information (ISI), 487, 2227
Institute for the History of Contemporary Publishing, 1592
Institute of Accountants, 651
Institute of Certified Records Managers (ICRM), 224, 688, 1855

Institute of Communication Research, 1000
Institute of Developing Economics (IDE)
    Library, 2565
Institute of Electrical and Electronics Engineers
    (IEEE), 4263
Institute of Ethiopian Studies Museum,
    1501–1503
Institute of Information Scientists (IIS), 4710
Institute of Law Library (ILL), 901–902
Institute of Medicine (IOM), 559
Institute of Museum and Library Services
    (IMLS), 81, 250, 371, 911, 1030, 4120,
    4770
Institute of Nuclear Research (INEGI), 3091
Institute of Scientific and Technical Information
    of Shanghai (ISTIS), 898–899
Institute of Scientific and Technological Infor-
    mation of China (ISTIC), 892
Institute of West Asian and African Studies
    Library (IWAASL), 902
Institute on Scholarly Communication, 367
Institutes for Knowledge Organization, 2500
Institut International de Bibliographie (IIB),
    4783
Institutional logos, 4961, 4964
Institutional records and archives
    appraisal and selection
        archival, 2380–2381
        records management appraisal, 2380
    archival arrangement and description,
        2381–2382
    broader information environment, 2383
    categories, 2378–2379
    conceptual models
        continuum concept, 2379
        life-cycle concept, 2379
    electronic records, challenges
        archives context, 2384–2385
        collaboration, 2385
        deterioration and loss, 2384
        obsolescence, 2384
        poor records management, 2383
        records management context, 2384
    in-house records vs. repositories, 2377
    institutional context, 2377–2378
    integrated management, 2377
    integration, 2382–2383
    research access, 2382
    value of, 2378
Institutional repositories, 1335–1336
Instituto Cultural Peruano Norteamericano
    (ICPNA), 3608
Instituto Nacional de Antropologia e Historia
    (INAH), 3245
Institut supérieur de documentation (ISD),
    4632
Instructional systems design (ISD), 2307
Intaglio printing, 1867–1868
Intarsia, 541
Integer programming (IP) model
    Branch and Bound algorithms, 1195
    CPLEX, 1196
    product mix decision problem, 1195–1196
Integrated approaches to participatory develop-
    ment (IAPAD), 1672
Integrated library systems (ILS), 409, 725, 3451,
    3453, 4141

Integrated library systems report, 2816
Integrated online library systems, 5027
Integrated Postsecondary Education Data Sys-
    tems, 2844
Integrated services digital network (ISDN),
    2254
integrate Rule-Oriented Data System (iRODS),
    3000–3001, 3319
Intellectual capital, 2660
Intellectual Capital Management (ICM), 2642
Intellectual freedom
    ALA
        censorship of specific publications,
            2387–2389
        challenges and issues, 2395–2396
        free access to materials, 2389–2391
        librarians, 2391–2393
        and libraries, 2393–2395
        profession's response, 2395
    myths, 2387
Intellectual Freedom Action Network, 2392
Intellectual Freedom Committee (IFC),
    2387–2388, 2390–2392
Intellectual Freedom Round Table (IFRT),
    2392
Intellectual property (IP), 3, 1487, 1490–1491
    SIIA, 4297–4298
Intellectual Property Digital Library (IPDL),
    3569
Intellectual property rights (IPR), 1392, 1754
Intellectual technologies, 1472
Intelligence and Security Informatics (ISI)
    civil liberties, and data mining, 2402–2403
    goal of, 2400–2401
    information technology annd national secu-
        rity, 2399–2400
    objective, 2400
    privacy vs. information sharing, 2398–2399
    problems and challenges, 2400
    research framework
        crime types and security concerns, 2401
        KDD technologies, 2401–2402
Intelligent information systems, 276–277
Intelligent Systems, 4084
Interactive science centers, 3219
Interactivity affordance, 1118
Intercat, 3453–3454
Interdisciplinary and area studies (IAS)
    definitions, 209
    drivers, 210–211
    gray literature, 211–212
    humanities, 214–215
    informal information systems, 213–214
    knowledge domain maintenance, 214
    library services and collections, 213
    measures and artifacts, 210
    natural sciences, 215–216
    online searching, 212–213
    primary sources, 211–212
    publication formats, 211
    social sciences, 215
Interface, 4978–4982
Intergovernmental Conference on the Planning
    of National Documentation, Library and
    Archive Infrastructures, 4657
Intergovernmental Informatics Program (IIP),
    4657

Intergovernmental organizations (IGOs), 1721–
    1723, 3380
    depositories, 1721–1722
    digital MARC records, 1723
    finding, 1724
    publications offices, 1723
    subscription databases, 1723–1724
    third-party vendors, 1724
    Web information, 1722–1723
Intergraph, 1676
Interlibrary Cooperation and Networking Sec-
    tion (ICAN), 376
Interlibrary loan and document delivery (ILL/
    DD) services, 372–373, 2331–2333
Interlibrary loans (ILL), 7, 987, 1210, 1213,
    1220, 1880, 3914
    department, 416
    law firm librarians, 2718
    zoo and aquarium libraries, 5082
Intermediate medians, 2634
Internal Revenue Service (IRS), 1173,
    1464–1465
International Accreditation Forum (IAF),
    2344
International Archival Development Fund
    (FIDA)
    ICA, 2438, 2441
International Association for Professional Art
    Advisors (IAPAA), 1087
International Association of Law Libraries
    (IALL), 2716
International Association of Linguistic Sound
    Archive (IALSA), 2413
International Association of Media and Com-
    munication Research (IAMCR), 1001,
    1004
International Association of Music Information
    Centres (IAMIC), 3277
International Association of Music Libraries
    (IAML), 2413–2414, 3277
International Association of School Librarian-
    ship (IASL), 2752, 3999, 4006
International Association of Sound and
    Audioviual Archives (IASA), 187, 2467,
    3278, 4301, 4303
    committees, 2415–2417
    Executive Board, election of, 2414–2415
    foundation and constitution, 2413–2414
    founding meeting, 2414
    IAML/IASA joint annual conferences,
        2414
    international cooperation, 2415–2417
    membership, 2417
    mid-term meeting, 2415
    as organization, 2416–2417
    presidents and terms served, list of, 2417
    publications, 2415–2416
    Record Libraries' Commission, 2414
    solo conference, 2415
    stages, qualities and problems, 2413
International Association of Technological Uni-
    versity Libraries (IATUL)
    historical development, 2418–2419
    membership, 2419
    objective of, 2418
    organization and activities, 2419–2420
    publications, 2420

International Business Machines (IBM), 1086
The International Catalogue of Scientific Literature, 500
International Centre for the Study of the Preservation and Restoration of Cultural Property (ICCROM), 2432
International Children's Digital Library (ICDL), 4852, 5074
International Classification (IC), 2494
International Coalition of Library Consortia (ICOLC), 9, 2823, 2829
International Coalition on Newspapers (ICON), 790
International Committee for Documentation (CIDOC), 734, 1149
International Committee for Information Retrieval among Examining Offices (ICIREPAT), 3562
International Committee for the Training of Personnel (ICTOP), 3218
International Committee of the Blue Shield (ICBS), 2432, 2438, 2453
International Communication Association (ICA), 1001, 1003
  annual conferences, 2425
  awards
    Applied Research Award, 2426
    B. Aubrey Fisher Mentorship Award, 2426–2427
    ICA Fellows Book Award, 2427
    James W. Carey Urban Communication Grant, 2426
    Outstanding Article Award, 2426
    Outstanding Book Award, 2426
    Steven H. Chaffee Career Achievement Award, 2426
    Young Scholar Award, 2426
  communication associations, collaboration with, 2427
  defined, 2421
  division and interest groups, 2422–2424
  early days, 2421
  fellows, 2425
  governance and administration, 2421
  ICA journal journal citation impact factors, 2427–2428
  membership, 2422, 2425
  presidents, 2422
  publications, 2427
  purpose of, 2421
International Conference on Information Systems (ICIS), 2276
International Conference on Scientific Information, 2216, 2218
International Conference on the History of Records and Archives (I-CHORA), 1864
International Conferences of the Round Table on Archives (CITRA), 2442
International Congress of Medical Librarians (ICML), 2454
International Consumer Protection and Enforcement Network (ICPEN), 782
International Council for Scientific and Technical Information (ICSTI), 2453
International Council of African Museums (AFRICOM), 2606

International Council of Museums (ICOM), 910–911, 1164, 1595, 1821–1822, 2606–2607, 3217–3218, 3233
  activities, 2430, 2435–2436
  cooperative partnerships, 2429, 2431–2432
  core values and vision, 2430–2431
  governance, 2432–2434
  International Committees and Affiliated Organizations, 2430, 2434–2435
  International Museums Office, 2429
  membership, 2430–2431
  mission and purpose, 2430, 3246
  museum and community, 3246
  publications and media, 2436
International Council of Museums (ICOM) Code of Ethics, 4593
International Council of Museums-United States (ICOM-US), 56–57
International Council of Scientific Unions (ICSU), 2452
International Council on Archives (ICA), 222, 688–689, 1423, 1856–1857, 2453, 2467, 3746
  activities, 2442
  archives, definition of, 2440
  Archivum, 2437
  budget, 2442
  cold war (1948-1989), 2438–2439
  conferences, 2443
  Congress, 2442–2443
  cooperation, 2444
  elected officers, 2442
  FIDA, 2438, 2441
  governance, 2441–2442
  ICBS, 2438
  membership, 2440
  mission and values, 2439–2440
  origin, 2437
  project committees and working groups, 2441
  projects, 2443–2444
  publications, 2443
  regional branches and sections, 2438, 2440–2441
International Council on Knowledge Management (ICKM)
  acquisition, knowledge, 2449
  iKMS, 2449
  intellectual capital reporting, 2447–2448
  knowledge development and distribution, 2449
  knowledge identification, 2449
  knowledge measure, 2448–2449
  knowledge use, 2449
  Nonaka/Takeuchi's approach, 2446
  preservation, knowledge, 2449
  Probst/Raub/Romhardt's approach, 2446–2447
  Senge approach, 2446
  Vienna, 2449
International Council on Monuments and Sites (ICOMOS), 2432
International Council on Museums (ICOM), 1742
International Criminal Tribunal for Rwanda (ICTR), 4504
International Digital Publishing Forum, 4055
International Directory of Art Libraries, 250

International DOI Foundation (IDF), 1132, 1326, 1330
International Dunhuang Project (IDP), 627
International Economic Association, 1408
International Electrotechnical Commission (IEC), 88, 2344
International Federation for Documentation, 1535
International Federation for Information Processing (IFIP), 2276
International Federation of Film Archives (FIAF), 187, 1561, 1585
International Federation of Library Associations and Institutions (IFLA), 3, 234–235, 249, 255, 449, 817, 882, 1229–1230, 2040, 2308, 2408, 2672, 3386, 3774, 3998–3999, 4006, 4174, 4658, 5014
  advocacy, 2459
  China
    CSLS, 904
    General Conference in Beijing., 905
    LAC, 890
  conferences, venues, and presidents, 2461–2463
  core values, 2452
  corporate partners, 2452
  governance
    General Assembly, 2454–2455
    Governing Board, 2455
    president, 2454
    Professional Committee, 2455
  headquarters, 2459–2460
  IATUL, 2418
  Internet, 2460
  languages, 2459
  Library Services to People with Special Needs, 3576
  LIS education, 710, 713
  membership, 2451–2452
  mission, 2451
  organization chart, 2455
  PIALA, 3547–3548
  professional units, 2456–2457
    ALP core activities, 2457
    Committee on Copyright and Other Legal Matters, 2457–2458
    divisions, 2455–2456
    FAIFE, 2458
    IFLA-CDNL Alliance for Digital Strategies, 2458–2459
    PAC core activities, 2457
    regional activities, 2456
    sections, 2456
    special interest groups, 2456
  publications, 2460–2461
  regional offices, 2460
  relations with other bodies, 2452–2453
  Science and Technology Libraries Section, 4016
  Ukraine, public libraries in, 4644
  UNIMARC, 2459
  World Library and Information Congress, 2453–2454
International Federation of Television Archives (FIAT/IFTA)
  conferences, 2466
  cultural and academic approach, 2468–2469

International Federation of Television Archives
(FIAT/IFTA)
(cont'd.)

   digital developments, 2468
   Documentation Commission, 2466
   foundation and constitution, 2465–2466
   international cooperation, 2467
   Media Management Commission, 2468
   menbership, 2467
   Preservation and Migration Commission,
     2468
   Programming and Production Commission,
     2467–2468
   Technical Commission, 2466–2467
   Training Commission, 2466
International Francophone Archival Portal
   (PIAF), 4635
International Health Terminology Standards
   Development Organisation, 4673
International Indigenous Librarians' Forum
   (IILF), 2042
International Indigenous Librarians' Forum
   (IILF)Aboriginal and Torres Strait
   Islander Library and Information
   Resource Network (ATSILIRN), 2043
International Institute for the Conservation of
   Historic and Artistic Works (IIC), 1072
International Institute of Bibliography (IIB),
   1373
International Institute of Documentation (IID),
   4783
International Interior Design Association
   (IIDA), 2845
Internationalized Domain Names (IDNs), 4659
International Knowledge Management Network
   (IKMN), 2645
International librarianship
   definitions, 2404–2405
   foreign librarianship, 2405
   methodology
     interviews, 2407
     literature, 2407
     observation, 2407
     questionnaire surveys, 2407
   Parker's definition, 2404
International Livestock Research Institute
   (ILRI), 1499
Internationally Agreed Numbers for the Identifi-
   cation of Data (INID) codes, 3564
International Medical Informatics Association
   (IMIA), 86
International Medical Information Center
   (IMIC), 2565
International modernism, 2804
International Museums Office, 2429
International Music Information Retrieval Sys-
   tems Evaluation Laboratory (IMIRSEL),
   3272
International Network for the Availability of
   Scientific Publications (INASP), 4505
International Office of Sociological Bibliogra-
   phy, 1373
International oral history movement, 3502
International Organization for Standardization
   (ISO), 88, 441, 443, 1111, 1857, 2452,
   3356

   benefits, 2471–2472
   conformity assessment, 2473
   deliverables, 2475
   democratic, 2471
   as electronic downloads, 2472
   finance, 2473–2474
   functions, 2471
   globally relevant, 2472
   harmonizing national standards, 2346
   information and document management, 2480
   international consensus, 2471–2472
   international partners, 2475–2476
   international standardization, 2473
   ISO/IEC Joint Technical Committee 1, 2346
   ISO/ISO/TC 46 standards
     benefits, 2479
     information and documentation,
       2476–2477
     ISO 3166 and ISO 639, 2477
     market for, 2477–2478
     objectives, 2479
   ISO 9001 *vs.* ISO 14001, 2472
   library and information services, 2346–2347
   market
     customers, 2478
     impact on, 2478–2479
     suppliers/manufacturers, 2478
   market-driven, 2471
   membership, 2473
   membership categories, 2346
   name, 2470
   new standards, development of, 2474–2475
   nongovernmental organization, 2470
   operations, management of, 2473
   origin, 2473
   in paper form, 2472
   principal phases, 2346
   regional partners, 2476
   standards, need for, 2470–2471
   technical committees, 2474
   Unicode Standard
     Consortium and ISO 15924, 4667
     ISO/IEC 10646, 4663
     ISO/IEC 2022 technique, 4662–4663
   voluntary, 2471
   work program, 2472
International organizations, 2404–2405, 2409
International Partnership Among Museums
   (IPAM) program, 3247
International Patent Classification (IPC) codes
   ECLA, 3567
   EPO, 3566–3567
   hierarchy, 3567
   JPO, 3566–3567
   utility model, 3565
International Permanent Exhibition of Publica-
   tions (ISIP), 1125
International Publishers Association (IPA),
   1209, 2453
International Records Management Council
   (IRMC), 1856
International Records Management Trust
   (IRMT), 689–690
   consultancy services, 2492–2493
   development research, 2491–2492
   education and training, 2492
   origins, 2488–2489

   teamwork and capacity building, 2491
   work, 2490–2491
International Research on Permanent Authentic
   Records in Electronic Systems
   (InterPARES) Project, 122, 1363, 1414
International Semantic Web Conference
   (ISWC), 4087
International Society for Informetrics and
   Scientometrics (ISSI), 2369
International Society for Knowledge Organiza-
   tion (ISKO), 959
   aims and tasks, 2495
   anage-old activity, 2499–2500
   British Chapter, 2497
   French Chapter, 2497
   German Chapter, 2496
   histroical developments, 2496
   Indian Chapter, 2498
   international conferences, 2495–2496
   Italian Chapter, 2496–2497
   knowledge representation, 2499
   logiic, 2495
   methodical knowledge, 2495
   Nordic Chapter, 2498
   North American Chapter, 2498
   organization, 2495
   Polish Chapter, 2497
   science theory, 2495
   Spain Chapter, 2497
   U.S. Chapter, 2498
   Web site, 2499
International Society for Technology in Educa-
   tion (ISTE), 64, 3998
International Standard Archival Authority
   Record (ISAAR), 3751
International Standard Archival Authority
   Record for Corporate Bodies, persons,
   and Families (ISAAR(CPF)), 7
International Standard Bibliographic Descrip-
   tion (ISBD), 451, 2971, 3062
   general structure
     general material designation, 1233–1234
     other title information, 1234
     parallel title, 1234
     statement of responsibility, 1234–1236
     title proper, 1233
   history and recent development
     bibliographic control, 1236
     consolidated ISBD, 1239
     data elements, 1236
     first general review project, 1238
     second general review project, 1238–1239
     shared cataloging projects, 1236
     UBC program, 1237
   IFLA, 1229
   objectives and principles, 1231–1232
   purpose, 1229–1231
   sources of information, 1232–1233
International Standard Book Number (ISBN),
   450, 1235–1236, 1325, 4055
International Standard For Describing Functions, 3751–3752
International Standard for Records Manage-
   ment, 2553
International Standard for the Description of
   Institutions with Archival Holdings
   (ISDIAH), 1432

International Standard Industrial Classification (ISIC), 638
International Standard Name Identifier (ISNI), 3288
International Standard on Records Management ISO 15489
  Australian standard, 2481–2482
  content of, 2482–2483
  evolution of, 2482
  impact of, 2484–2485
  ISO 23310-2006, 2485
  ISO 23081, recordkeeping metadata
    Australian standards, 2483
    content of, 2483–2484
    goal of, 2483
    in research projects, 2483
  role of, 2485
  work process, 2485
International Standard Serial Number (ISSN), 1236, 4139
International Standard Text Code (ISTC) numbering system, 1330
International Telecommunications Union (ITU), 1282, 2344
International Union of Pure and Applied Chemistry (IUPAC), 3642
International Vital Records Handbook, 1658
International Zoo News, 5078–5079
International Zoo Yearbook, 5078
Internation Association of Aquatic and Marine Science Libraries and Information Centers (IAMSLIC), 4016
Internet, 999, 1039, 1180–1181, 2094, 2516, 2627, 5021, 5071–5072
  bookselling, 3986
  cataloging services, 2922
  diasporic communities, 2125
  digital imaging, 1308
  IFLA, 2460
  LCC, 2852, 2854
  museum communities, 3248
  national libraries, 3331–3332
  older adults, 3410
  reading, impact on, 4283–4284
  search tools (*see* Search engines)
Internet access, 2328–2329
Internet Antipiracy Program, 4298
Internet Architecture Board (IAB), 2344
Internet Archive, 1415
Internet art, 2072
Internet Content Rating Association (ICRA), 782–783
Internet Corporation for Assigned Names and Numbers (ICANN), 780
Internet Engineering Task Force (IETF), 1394, 2344
Internet protocol (IP), 403, 1015, 2631
Internet relay chat (IRC) systems, 1049
Internet service providers (ISPs), 698, 3659–3660
InterPARES
  activities, 2527
  1–2 phase, 2530–2532
  methodology, 2526–2527
  principles, 2527
  products, 2527–2528

  third phase, 2532–2533
  trust, 2533–2534
Interpolation, 1309
Interstate Commerce Act, 1012
Inter-University Consortium for Political and Social Research (ICPSR), 3484, 4753–4754
Interuniversity Cooperation on Electronic Journals (CIPE), 2827
Interviews, 4530–4531, 4798
An Introduction to the Theory of Statistics, 493
Introduction to Universal Geography, 1685
Invasive Species Information Node (ISIN), 3310
Inventories, 133
Inverted index, 3142
IPC codes, *see* International Patent Classification codes
IP-specific page delivery, 4035
Iraqi Libraries Association, 100
IRCnet, 1049
IRMT, *see* International Records Management Trust
iSchools Caucus (iCaucus), 2536–2537, 2539
iSchools organization, 2773
Isidore of Seville, 3044
ISI Web of Science, 2368
ISI Web of Science database, 3906
Islamic Civilisation Museum, 4381
Islamic illumination
  Abbaside period (750-1258)
    Baghdad School, 1953–1954
    Seljuk School (1055-1256), 1954
  early Islamic period, 1952
  Fatimides (909-1171), 1953
  Kufic script, 1952
  Maghribi School, 1952–1953
  Maghribi script, 1952
  Mamelukes, 1953
  miniature painting, 1951
  Mongol period (1258-1500), 1954
  Moorish School (756-1492), 1953
  Mozarabic art, 1953
  Naskh script, 1952
  Nastaliq script, 1952
  styles, 1952
  Taliq script, 1952
  Timuride School (1386-1500)
    Herat, 1954–1955
    Shiraz, 1955
ISO 23950, 2983
ISO/IEC international standard, 2342
Israel
  archives
    archival science as discipline and profession, 2557
    archives law and state archives, 2553
    branch archives, 2553–2554
    municipal archives, 2554
    professional associations, 2557–2558
    professional education, 2557
    public archives, 2554–2557
  libraries
    academic libraries, 2544–2545
    Arab sector, 2547–2549
    historical perspective, 2542–2543
    national library, 2543–2544
    professional education, 2549

    public libraries, 2545–2547
    school libraries, 2547
    special libraries, 2547
  map of, 2542–2543
  museums
    Arab sector, 2552
    archaeological museums, 2551
    art museums, 2551
    historical museums, 2551–2552
    historical perspective, 2549–2550
    holocaust heritage museums, 2552
    in Jerusalem, 2550–2551
    official recognition, 2552–2553
    professional education, 2553
    science and nature museums, 2552
Israel Archive Association (IAA), 2557–2558
Israel Center for Digital Information Services (MALMAD), 2545
Israeli Internet Sites Archive, 2557
Israel Museum, Jerusalem, 2550–2551
Italian binding, 543–545
Italian illumination
  in fifteenth century, 1951
  Gothic period, 1950
  Romanesque period, 1949
Italian ISKO Chapter, 2496–2497
Italian National Forum on Electronic Information Resources (INFER), 2827
ITARAT, 4631
Item-level indexing, 3131
Itinerarium, 4964
Itinerating libraries, 1837
ITN Archive, 1566
ITU-T international standard X.509 certificates, 404

J

Jabotinsky Institute in Israel, 2556
Jacksonville Public Library, 3785–3786
Jagiellonian Library, 3679
Janco-Dada Museum, 2551
JANET, 2825
Jan Merrill-Oldham Professional Development Grant, 332
Japan
  archives, 2576
    academic societies, 2570
    associations and organizations, 2570–2571
    college and university, 2569
    corporate, 2569
    decentralized management, 2567
    education and training, 2571
    local public archives, 2568
    National Archives Law, 2569–2570
    National Archives of Japan, 2567–2569
    private sector archives, 2569
    Public Archives Law, 2569–2570
  libraries
    academic and research libraries, 2562–2564
    digital library collections and services, 2566
    history of, 2560–2561
    legislation, 2562
    LIS education, 2566
    NDL and information services, 2562–2563

Japan (cont'd.)
   libraries (cont'd.)
      professional associations, 2566–2567
      public libraries, 2563–2564
      school libraries, 2564–2565
      special libraries, 2565
   map of, 2560–2561
   museums
      computerization and evaluation of management, 2575
      education and training systems, 2574–2575
      local governments, foundations, and private companies, 2572–2573
      museum law, revision of, 2575–2576
      museum libraries/art libraries, 2574
      national museums, 2571–2572
      organizing exhibitions, 2576
      professional staff, 2574
      societies and associations, 2574
      university museums, 2573–2574
Japan Art Documentation Society (JADS), 255, 2574
Japan Association of Art Museums, 2574
Japan Association of College and University Archives, 2571
Japan Association of National University Libraries (JANUL), 2567
Japan Association of Private Universities Libraries (JAPUL), 2567
Japanese Association of Museums, 2574
Japanese Association of Zoos and Aquariums, 2574
Japanese knowledge creation models, 2621–2622
Japan External Trade Organization (JETRO), 2565
Japan Foundation Information Center (JFIC), 2565
Japan Library Association (JLA), 2564, 2567
Japan Medical Library Association (JMLA), 2567
Japan Patent Office (JPO)
   FI/F-term classification search, 3570
   FI system, 3566–3567
   IPDL, 3569
   PAJ, 3569
Japan School Library Association (JSLA), 2567
Japan Society for Archival Science (JSAS), 2570
Japan Society of Archives Institutions (JSAI), 2570
Japan Special Libraries Association (JSLA), 2567
Java Specification Request (JSR), 2894
Jefferson, Thomas, 2832, 2847–2848
Jenkins Memorial Law Library, 2725–2726
Jeweled bindings, 540, 545
Jewett, Charles C., 760–761, 1844
Jewish National and University Library, 2557
The Jewish National Library, 2544
Jimma Museum, 1503
Jimma University Library, 1499
John Cotton Dana Public Relations Award, 2844–2845
John F. Kennedy University, 3218
John Philip Immroth Memorial Award for Intellectual Freedom, 2392

John Rylands Library, 3046
Johnson's information-seeking model, 2089–2091
John von Neumann Digital Library, 1924
Joint Commission on Accreditation of HealthCare Organizations (JCAHO), 1873
Joint Council of Library Associations of India (JOCLAI), 2007
Joint Information Systems Committee (JISC), 2825, 2897
Joint Technical Symposia (JTS), 4660
Joint-use libraries
   benefits and opportunities, 4159
   definition, 4158
   evaluation and assessment, 4161–4162
   management, organizational models of
      joint school/public libraries, 4160–4161
      university/public joint libraries, 4160
   operational issues, 4159–4160
   political and fiscal motivations, 4158–4159
   public policy, 4162
   replicable models, 4161
   types of, 4158
   world, 4161
Jordanian Library Association, 100
JORTAGRI, 4631
Joshua Roll, 1946
Journal Article Versions (JAV) Technical Working Group, 4897–4899
Journal blogs, 2507
Journal für die reine und angewandte Mathematik, 3026
Journal Impact Factor (IF), 44
Journalistic genres, 2504, 2506–2507
Journal of Archival Organization, 137
Journal of Communication, 2421
Journal of Differential Geometry, 3027
Journal officiel de la république tunisienne (JORT), 4629
Journal of Library Automation (JOLA), 2777
Journal of Library Science in China (JLSC), 904
Journal of Management Information Systems (JMIS), 2649
Journal of Symbolic Logic, 3027
Journal of the American Society for Information Science, 2766
Journal of the London Statistical Society, 1405
Journal of the Medical Library Association (JMLA), 3037
Journal publishing, see Book and journal publishing trade
JPEG format, 1311
JPO, see Japan Patent Office
JSTOR, 3472–3473, 3728
JSTOR: the Scholarly Journal Archive, 250
Jughead, 2518
Jumpstation, 2519
Justice-as-desert theory, 4219
Justice-as-fairness, 4219

K

Kahun Papyrus, 3041
Kakadu National Park, 391–392
Kansas City Public Library, 3726
Kant, Emmanuel, 1686

Kantian psychology, 2679
Kapenguria Museum, 2606
Karen Blixen Museum, 2605
Karlsruhe Virtual Catalog, 1695
Karl Weick's sensemaking, 4117–4118
Kasteyev Arts Museum, 2587
Kazakhstan, 2588–2589
   administrative units, 2580
   archives and archival science
      access and use, 2586
      archival development plan, 2586
      as discipline and profession, 2586–2587
      history, 2584–2585
      legislation, 2585
      national archive system, 2585
      oblast and municipal archives, 2585
   in early seventeenth century, 2578
   in fifteenth century, 2578
   languages, 2580
   library and information science
      digital library collections and services, 2583
      as discipline and profession, 2583–2584
      history, 2581
      legislation, 2581
      national library and information services, 2581
      public libraries, 2581–2582
      research libraries, 2582
      school libraries, 2583
      special libraries, 2583
      university libraries, 2582–2583
   map of, 2578–2579
   monetary unit, 2580
   museums and museology
      as discipline and profession, 2588
      galleries, zoos, and preserves, 2587–2588
      history of, 2587
      national museums, 2587–2588
   in nineteenth century, 2578–2579
   print publishing, 2580
   during twentieth century, 2579–2580
Kazakhstan Institute of Management, Economics and Strategic Research (KIMEP) Library, 2583
Keayne, Robert, 1839–1840
Keep Commission, 3316
Keeper, 3218
Kellogg-ALISE Information Professions and Education Reform (KALIPER), 708
Kenya
   KNA&DS
      composition, 2600–2601
      cooperation, 2602
      finding aids, 2601–2602
      history, 2598–2600
      legal framework, 2600
      legislation, 2600
      migrated archives, 2601
      personalities contributed to records management, 2602–2603
      repositories, 2601
      training institutions, 2602
   libraries
      academic libraries, 2596
      after independence, 2594
      in colonial period, 2593–2594

education, 2597
  High Court of Kenya Library, 2593
  legislation, 2594–2595
  national library, 2595
  in precolonial period, 2593
  professional associations, 2597–2598
  public libraries, 2595
  research libraries, 2596
  school libraries, 2597
  special libraries, 2596–2597
map of, 2592–2593
NMK
  access, preservation, and educational role,
    2607
  archeological and paleontological sites,
    2605–2606
  curators and museum administration, edu-
    cation for, 2606
  as discipline and profession, 2607
  Fort Jesus Museum, 2605
  history of, 2603
  Karen Blixen Museum, 2605
  Lamu Museum, 2605
  Lamu World Heritage Site, 2605
  legislation, 2603–2604
  Nairobi museum, 2604
  outstanding personalities, 2607–2608
  professional associations, 2606–2607
  regional museums, 2604–2605
Kenya Library Association (KLA),
  2597–2598
Kenya National Archives and Documentation
  Service (KNA&DS)
  composition, 2600–2601
  cooperation, 2602
  finding aids, 2601–2602
  history, 2598–2600
  legal framework, 2600
  legislation, 2600
  migrated archives, 2601
  personalities contributed to records manage-
    ment, 2602–2603
  repositories, 2601
  training institutions, 2602
Kenya National Library Service (KNLS), 2594–
  2595, 3324
Kerberos authentication service, 402
Kessler, M.M., 503–504, 506
Keyword
  consistency, 4034
  density, 4033–4034
  jacking, 4035
  loading, 4035
  meta tag, 4035
  placement, 4034
  spamming, 4034–4035
Keyword AAA Thesaurus, 3889
Keyword and full-text search, 4467
Key Words in Context (KWIC), 2221, 4788
K'han Museum, 2552
Kheel Center, 4761
Khnko-Aper Apor National Children's Library,
  230–232
Kibbutz Hadati Archive, 2557
Kibbutz Movement Archives, 2556
King Abd al-Aziz Public Library in Riyadh,
  3974, 3976

King Abdulaziz City for Science and Technology (KACST), 2312–2313
King Fahd National Library, 3973–3974
Kirk-Othmer Encyclopedia of Chemical Technology, 816
Klein's sensemaking, 4113
Knapp School Library Manpower Project, 64
KNLS Board Act (Chapter 225), 2594
Knowledge, 2623–2624, 2677
  abundant myths, 2683–2684
  assets, 2641
  behaviorists, 2684
  creation and organizational information use
    Ba, types of, 2619, 2622–2623
    Choo's model, 2620–2623
    hermeneutic phenomenology, 2623
    information management, 2618–2620
    information use environments, Taylor's
      model of, 2620
    Japanese models, 2621–2622
    knowledge assets, 2622
    knowledge management, 2618–2620
    SECI model, 2619, 2621–2622
  dissemination, 2445
  economy, 2256
  empirical knowledge, 2610
  experiential, 2679
  explicit and collective, 2679
  explicit and individual, 2680
  Gestalt psychology, 2685
  Gettier counterexamples, 2616
  Greek society, 2677–2678
  and information, 2618–2619
  and information, relationship between, 2051
  information searching, 2243
  Merleau-Ponty, 2685–2686
  modes, 2682–2683
  networks
    citation networks, 1041–1042
    heterogeneous network, 1041
    information network, 1042
  nonempirical knowledge, 2610
  portals, 2893
  production, 2256
  propositional (see Propositional knowledge)
  sharing, 3535–3537
  society, 603, 4198
  spiral model, 2644
  state, 2086
  structure, 2051
  subject searching, 3423–3424
  survival, 2684–2685
  tacit and collective, 2680
  tacit and individual, 2680–2681
  tacit with explicit, 2681–2683
  transformation, 2678–2679, 2683
  types, 2681–2682
  worker, 2645
Knowledge Base and Recommended Practice
  (KBART) project, 413
Knowledge-based information (KBI), 1875
Knowledge-based management subsystem,
  2195
Knowledge base plus (KB+), 1710–1711
Knowledge discovery from databases (KDD)
  technologies, 2401–2402
Knowledge interchange format (KIF), 3458

Knowledge management (KM), 1889, 2445,
  2618–2620, 2647–2649, 3521–3522
  bibliometric representation, 2662–2663
  core knowledge management
    centralized database system, 2644
    corporate amnesia, 2642–2643
    organizational memory, 2643–2644
    tacit and explicit knowledge, 2643
    valuable knowledge and know-how, 2643
  definition of, 2640–2641, 2658–2660
    business perspective, 2641
    cognitive science/knowledge science per-
      spective, 2641
    intellectual capital perspective, 2642
    knowledge assets, attributes of, 2641
    "people-oriented" definitions, 2642
    process/technology perspective,
      2641–2642
  disciplines, 2641
  history and evolution of, 2645–2646,
    2657–2658
  information professionals, role of, 2646–2647
  knowledge processing cycle, 2644–2645
  ontologies, 3463
  special librarianship, 4354
  stages, 2662–2663
    best practices, 2660
    communities of practice, 2661
    content management and taxonomies, 2661
    external information, 2662
    human and cultural dimensions, recogni-
      tion of, 2660–2661
    information technology, 2660
    intellectual capital, 2660
    learning organization, 2661
    lessons learned, 2660
    organization's internal knowledge,
      2661–2662
    tacit knowledge, 2661
Knowledge management structures (KMS),
  2659
Knowledge management systems (KMS)
  challenges, 2654–2655
  critique, 2650
  definition, 2649, 2651
  information systems (IS), 2649
  librarian, 711
  ontological aspects, 2654
  roots, 2649–2650
  theoretical foundation, 2650–2651
  theory, 2651–2652
  types
    Alavi and Leidner's scheme, 2653–2654
    codification vs. personalization, 2652
    knowledge residence and level of structure,
      2652–2653
  umbrella construct, 2655
Knowledge organization classification, 2110
  bibliographic library, 960
    enumerative classification, 962
    faceted classifications, 962
    facet structure, 966–968
    hierarchical structure, 965–966
    history and foundations, 961–962
    idea, verbal, and notational plane, 961
    integrative levels, 968–969
    literary warrant, 962–963

Knowledge organization classification (cont'd.)
 bibliographic library (cont'd.)
  notation, 969–971
   phenomenon-based knowledge organiza-
    tion, 694–695
   precoordinated classification, 962
   scientific and educational consensus,
    963–964
  cultural concerns and contexts, 958
  field of study, 958
  groups of things, 958–959
  indexing theories and methods, 960
  joint exhaustivity, criterion of, 959
  mutual exclusivity, criterion of, 959
  organizations, 959–960
  terminology, 960
Knowledge organization systems (KOS),
  4066–4067
 advantages, 2666
 ANSI/NISO Z39.19-2005, 2672
 BS 8723: structured vocabularies for information retrieval, 2672–2673
 classification schemes, 2669–2670
 data exchange, emerging standards for
  ADL thesaurus protocol, 2670–2671
  SKOS, 2671–2672
  Zthes, 2671
 definition, 2665
 IFLA guidelines for multilingual thesauri,
  2672
 ISO 25964, 2673
 name authority lists, 2670
 need for, 2665–2666
 requirements for, 2670
 standards, 2673–2674
 structures and services, 1615–1616
 subject heading schemes, 2670
 thesaurus standards
  guidelines, 2666
  ISO 2788 and Z39.19, differences between,
   2668–2669
  national and international standards, 2667
  prehistory, 2666
  principles, 2668
  sector specific standards, 2667
  successive updates, 2667–2668
  weaknesses in, 2669
Knowledge Quest (KQ), 61
Knowledge representation (KR), 271–272
Knowledge retrieval systems (KRS), 2192
Know Your Copy Rights® Web site, 369
Kolhapur Public Libraries Act, 1993
Kolmogorov complexity, 1035
Kongelige Bibliotek, Copenhagen, 3332
Koninklijke Bibliotheek of the Netherlands, 3322
Konstanz University library, 1696
Korea Institute of Science and Technology
  (KIST), 4311
Korean Committee for the Bookstart Movement,
  4312
Korean Library Association, 4312
Korean Medical Library Association (KMLA),
  3039
Korean War, 1144
Korolenko State Scientific Library in Kharkiv,
  4645
Kosmos, 1686

Kovacs Consulting Web site, 3439–3440
Kuali Open Library Environment (Kuali OLE),
  1710–1711
Kuhlthau information search model, 2225
Kuhlthau model of information seeking, 4880
Kuhlthau's information search process model,
  5069–5070
Kuhlthau's ISP model, 1901, 2118–2119
Kulback-Leibler measure, 2357
Kunstfaggruppen (Denmark), 255
Kyiv-Mohyla Academy, 4646

L
La Asociación de Bibliotecas Nacionales de
  Iberoamérica (ABINIA), 3330
Labor archives, 2556, 4761
Labor market, librarians
 Fontoura notes, 613
 segmentation, 613–614
 studies, 613
 transformations, 612
La Fontaine, Henri, 4783
La Géographie Humaine, 1687
*La Grande Industrie en France sous Règne de
  Louis xiv*, 645
L. A. Mayer Museum, 2551
Lambeth Palace Library (LLP), 457
Lamont Library, 4650
Lamu Museum, 2605
Lamu World Heritage Site, 2605
Land Grant College Act, 19
Landscape bindings, 541
Language searching, 4049
Large aggregation retention schedules,
  3893–3894
Large-scale digitization initiative (LSDI), 1335
Last.fm recommender system, 3860
Latent semantic indexing (LSI)
 applications, 2695–2696
 books titles and authors, 2692
 cognitive psychology, 2696
 computational challenges, 2695
 educational applications, 2696
 Henry Ford, 2692–2694
 information retrieval and analysis, 2695–2696
 issues and limitations, 2695
 lexical matching, 2688
 mechanics, 2689–2690
 reduced dimension vector space
  producing, 2691
  querying, 2691–2692
 semantic space, 2688–2689
 term-by-document matrix, 2692–2693
 term-document matrix
  assembling, 2690
  weighting elements, 2690–2691
 two-dimensional vector space, 2692–2694
 updating, 2695
 VSM, 2689–2690
 word order, 2695
La Terre, 1686–1687
Latin Americanist Research Resources Project
  (LARRP), 791
Latinos
 academic libraries, 2701–2702
 identity labels, 2699

 legislation, 2698
 library services, 2699
 LIS profession, 2702–2703
 public libraries, 2700–2701
 school libraries, 2701
 in United States, history of, 2698–2699
"Lattice-based" access control systems, *see*
  Mandatory access control
Law
 characteristics, 2736–2737
 librarians, 3415
 sources, 2734–2735
 users
  lawyers, 2744–2745
  public, 2746
  students, 2745–2746
Law firm libraries
 analog skills, 2705
 collections, 2708
 education, 2708
 organization of
  catalogers, 2706
  electronic services librarians, 2706
  embedded librarian, 2706
  filer/shelver, 2706
  legislative/regulatory librarians, 2706
  library assistant, 2706
  library director, 2705
  research assistants, 2706
  research librarians, 2705–2706
  research managers, 2705
 professional associations, 2708
 services and users
  collection and library catalog, maintenance
   of, 2707–2708
  document retrieval and interlibrary loan,
   2707
  firm intranet and knowledge management
   systems, 2707
  research desk/triage system, 2707
  research projects, 2706–2707
  training and orientation, 2707
  twenty-first-century challenges, 2708–2709
Law librarianship
 law firm libraries
  budgeting and planning, 2720
  business briefing book preparation, 2718
  catalogs, 2718
  challenges, 2723–2724
  circulation systems, 2722
  cite checking, 2719
  classification, 2722
  CLE provider, credit tracker, 2719
  collection development policies, 2721–
   2722
  collections, 2721
  conflict checking, 2719
  continuing education, 2723
  current awareness services, 2718–2719
  customers, users, and owners, 2717–2718
  education, 2723
  experience and skills, 2723
  history, 2723
  impact on other units, 2719
  interlibrary loan, 2718
  organization's goals, 2719
  physical arrangement/space, 2720–2721

recent developments, 2719–2720
  seating type, 2721
  serials, 2721
  staffing, 2722–2723
  technology, 2720
  time, 2720
law school library
  collections, 2712–2714
  history and development, 2711–2712
  librarians, 2714–2715
  mission of, 2710
  organization and administration, 2711
  professional association, 2715–2716
  standards and statistics, 2712
  twenty-first century roles, 2716
public law libraries
  challenges, 2729
  collections, 2727–2728
  connections and networking, 2729
  customers, 2724–2725
  facilities, 2728
  governance and funding, 2725–2726
  services, 2726–2727
  staff and education, 2728
  technology, 2728–2729
Law of Guidelines and Bases (LDB), 604
Law of Libraries, 4888
Layton, Jeanne, 2393
LC, se Library of Congress
LC/NACO certification, 3293
Leadership and Career Development Program
  (LCDP), 370–371
Leaf elements, 5045
Leahy, Emmett, 1851–1853, 1855
Learned society, 4268
Learning and information seeking
  behaviorist theory, 2753
  cognitive authority, 2759
  cognitive theory, 2753
  constructivism
    cognitive, 2753
    Kuhlthau's model, 2753–2754
    phenomenographic approach, 2754
    sense-making, 2755
    situated cognition and learning,
      2754–2755
    social, 2753–2754
    sociocultural perspective, 2755
  digital tools, 2759–2760
  ICT, 2752, 2759–2760
  information practices, 2752, 2755
  information sharing, 2759–2760
  interconnected dimensions, 2751–2752
  language, 2752
  learning from information, 2752
    information use as text transport, 2758
    learning outcomes, 2758
    meaningful learning outcomes, 2758–2759
  learning information seeking, 2751, 2757
  learning tasks, 2756
  pedagogical librarianship, 2760
  research, 2755
  school practice, 2759
  social practices, 2752
  stakeholders, associations, and institutions,
    2752
  students' information seeking, 2755–2757

teaching information seeking, 2751
  constructivism, 2758
  information/library skills, 2757
  information literacy, 2757–2758
Learning literacy, 2305
Learning management system (LMS), 6
Learning Object Metadata (LOM), 1395
Leather, 539–540
Lectures in Applied Mathematics, 3028
Lectures on Mathematics in the Life Sciences,
  3028
Legal encyclopedias, 2741
Legal Information Preservation Alliance
  (LIPA), 2743
Legal newspapers, 2740–2741
Legal periodicals, 2740
Legal system
  constitutions and charters, 2734
  executive branch, 2735
  formats, 2742–2744
  judicial branch, 2734–2735
  legislative branch, 2734
  publishing, 2742
Legisigns, 4098
Legislation, 3372
Leningrad method, 478
LePlay, Pièrre Guillaume Frédéric, 1687
LeRoy C. Merritt Humanitarian Fund,
  2392–2393
Letter-by-letter alphabetizing, 442
Lettering, 541
Levi-Straussian structuralism, 1666
Lexical chains, 422
Lexical matching, 2688
Lexical scattering, 2211
Lexicography, 1864
Lexington public library, 2790
Lexis-Nexis, 2708
Liber Chronicarum, 1978–1979
LIBINFO, 1924
LIBNET, 2828
LibQual, 9
LibQUAL+®, 374
Librarianship
  education events, 2914–2916
  music (see Music librarianship)
Librarianship education
  South Korea, 4312
Librarians' Internet Index (LII), 2895
Libraries and Knowledge Centre (LKC) model,
  2035
Libraries, Archives, and Museums of Pohnpei
  (LAMP) Library Association, 3546
Libraries Serving Special Populations Section
  (LSSPS), 376
Library 2.0, 4780
Library(ies)
  in ancient times, 2762
  Australia, 382
  buildings, 2765
  definition, 2762
  functions, 2764–2765
  India (see India)
  medieval libraries, 2762–2763
  modern libraries, 2764
  in nineteenth century, 2763–2764
  number of, 2765–2766

recent developments and twenty-first century,
  2766
renaissance and early modern libraries, 2763
Spain (see Spain)
zoological parks and aquariums
  current status and services, 5081–5083
  early libraries, establishment of, 5081
  need for, 5080–5081
Library Acquisitions Award, 331
Library Act of 1997, 1124
Library Administration and Management Asso-
  ciation (LAMA), 74–75, 2844
The Library Administration Division (LAD)
  Advisory Committee for the Library Technol-
    ogy Project, 2842
  ALA Annual Conferences, 2842
  ALA Committee on Organization
    recommendations, 2843
    report, 2842
  BES committees, 2842
  Committee on Recruitment, 2842
  Friends of Libraries Committee, 2842
  LOMS Advisory Committee on USOE Statis-
    tics, 2842
  mission of, 2841
  preexisting ALA groups, 2841
  responsibility, 2841–2842
Library Advocacy Now! (LAN!), 683
Library and Archives Canada (LAC), 3303,
  3324
  Archives of Ontario, 661–662
  associations and groups
    ACA, 667
    ASTED, 665
    CARL, 664–665
    CCA, 666
    CFLA/FCAB, 665
    CULC, 666
    PTPLC, 665
    SCCA, 666
  BAnQ, 660
  Bibliothèque de l'Université de Montréal, 662
  Bibliothèque de l'Université Laval, 662
  bibliothèque et archives, 658–660
  British North America (1763–1867), 655–656
  decentralized federations, 654
  development of, 667–668
  development, twenty-first century, 658
  First Nations, 654–655
  Hudson's Bay company (1670-1870), 655
  issues and challenges
    access, 670
    collaboration, 672–673
    convergence, 672
    copyright, 671
    description, 670
    digital, 669
    government information management,
      670–671
    human resources, 672
    indigenous services and collections, 673
    multilingual services, 673
    National Planning and Coordination, 671–
      672
    preservation, 669–670
    resource sharing, 671
    services for people, disabilities, 673

Library and Archives Canada (LAC) (cont'd.)
  Library of Parliament, 661
  McGill University Library, 662–663
  New France (1605–1763), 655
  NRC-CISTI, 660–661
  Toronto Public Library, 663
  UBC Library, 663–664
  University of Alberta Libraries, 663
  University of Toronto Library, 664
  VPL, 664
  World War II, 656–658
Library and Information Association of New
        Zealand Aotearoa (LIANZA), 2036,
        3372, 3374, 3377–3378
Library and Information Research, 3406
Library and information science (LIS), 1029,
        1372, 1516, 2162
  definition, 693–694
  domain, 2768–2769
  emergence, 2771–2773
  IM and KM, research on, 2618–2620
  United Kingdom, 4709, 4711–4713
Library and Information Service of Western
        Australia (LISWA), 2035
Library and information studies (LIS) programs
  ALA accreditation, 18–21
  Canadian institutions, accreditation of, 19, 21
Library and information system of the 3rd gen-
        eration (KIS3G) project, 4175–4176
Library and Information Technology Associa-
        tion (LITA)
  education, 2780
  function statement, 2775
  governing structure, 2775–2776
  history
    early years, 2776–2777
    Internet Era, 2777–2778
    twenty-first century, 2778–2779
  membership, 2775
  mission, 2775
  outreach, 2780–2781
  service, 2780
  strategic functions and main programs,
        2779–2780
  vision, 2775
Library anxiety
  antecedents, conceptualization of, 2784–2785
  Bostick's LAS, 2784
  definition, 2782
  history and theoretical basis, 2782–2783
  international students, in US institutions,
        2784–2785
  international studies, 2785
  intervention strategies, 2785–2786
  ISP model, 2783–2784
  Jiao and Onwuegbuzie quantitative studies,
        2784
  Mellon's grounded theory, 2783
  MLAS, 2784
Library Anxiety Scale (LAS), 2782, 2784
Library architecture
  Anglo-American model, 2799–2801
  and design
    aesthetics, display space, and signs,
        2792–2793
    building program, 2792
    construction, 2793

  consulting with external experts, 2792
  cultural changes, impact of, 2789–2791
enlightenment age, 2798–2799
globalization, 2808
grand library design, 2799
impact on
  community, 2792
  individual and group work space,
        2793–2794
  public service areas, 2793
  security and building support spaces, 2795
  shelving configurations, 2794
  specialized collections and service areas,
        2794–2795
  staff spaces, 2795
  teaching, training, and meeting space, 2793
  technology support areas, 2795
master planning process, 2792
Open access, 2801–2802
Russian experiments, 2803–2804
Scandinavian model, 2804
spectacular buildings, 2805–2808
technology, impact of, 2788–2789
temple of knowledge, 2802–2803
Library Assistants' Association (LAA),
        4709–4710
Library assistantship, 919
Library Association (LA), 4709–4711
  LAC, 890, 904
  LARK, 2584
  LARM, 3125
  LLA, 385
  PIALA (see Pacific Islands Association of
        Libraries and Archives)
  of Serbia, 4127–4128
Library Association of Armenia, see Armenian
        Library Association
Library Association of Australia (LAA), 385
Library Association of China (LAC), 890, 904
Library Association of Serbia, 4127–4128
Library Association of the Republic of Kazakh-
        stan (LARK), 2584
Library Association of the Republic of Moldova
        (LARM), 3125
Library automation
  information services context
    database services providers, 2817–2818
    information resources, 2819
    information retrieval, 2813
    Internet, 2819
    online services, 2815
  information technology context
    computing installation, 2814
    microprocessors, 2818
    Moore's law, 2815
    print on demand, 2817
    technological development, 2812
  library technical services context
    cataloging, 2813, 2815, 2819
    cooperative networks, 2814
    integrated library systems, 2816–2817
  precursors, 2810–2811
  societal context
    digitized imaging, 2818
    information economy, 2813–2815
    OSRD report, 2811
    virtual revolution, 2816

Library Awareness Program (LAP), 2148, 2390
Library Bill of Rights (LBR), 2387–2389, 3777
Library Binding Institute, 4147
Library Board of Western Australia Act 1951,
        381
Library-College concept, 987
Library Company of Philadelphia, 1841,
        2847–2848, 4338–4339
Library consortia, in Europe, 2823–2824
  in Balkans, 2828
  in Belgium, 2824
  in Britain, 2825
  in Bulgaria, 2829
  in Denmark, 2825
  in Dutch, 2826
  eIFL, 2827–2829
  in Estonia, 2828
  in Finland, 2824–2825
  Flemish language communities, 2826
  in France, 2826
  in Germany, 2826
  in Greece, 2827
  in Iberian Peninsula, 2827
  in Iceland, 2825
  in Ireland, 2825
  in Italy, 2824, 2827
  in Latvia, 2828
  in Lithuania, 2828
  meaning, 2822–2823
  in Norway, 2825
  in Poland, 2828
  policies and administrative mechanisms, 2824
  in Portugal, 2827
  in Romania, 2829
  in Slovakia, 2828
  in Slovenia, 2824
  in Spain, 2824, 2827
  special programs, 2824
  in Sweden, 2825
  in Switzerland, 2824, 2826
  in Turkey, 2829
Library Control System (LCS), of Ohio State
        University Libraries, 3451–3452
Library cooperation, 2404, 2408
  in Britain, 2825
  in Denmark, 2825
  in Finland, 2824–2825
  in Germany, 2826
  in Iceland, 2825
  in Norway, 2825
  in Portugal, 2827
  in Slovenia, 2824
  in Spain, 2827
  special programs, 2824
  in Sweden, 2825
  in Switzerland, 2826
Library cooperatives, 3920
Library Copyright Alliance (LCA), 345, 369
Library Day, Germany, 1696
Library development, 2405, 2407–2409
Library Electronic Access Project (LEAP),
        4644
Library Hi Tech Award, 2778
Library Idea Drop House, 1421
Library Journal, 2699
Library Leadership and Management (LL&M),
        2844

Library Leadership and Management Association (LLAMA)
  American Institute of Architects Awards, 2845
  annual conferences, pre-conferences, and institutes, 2841, 2843–2844
  committees, 2841
  Cultural Diversity Grant, 2845
  Diana V. Braddom FRFDS Scholarship, 2845
  discussion groups, 2841
  Diversity Fund, 2845
  division presidents, 2845–2846
  division secretaries/executive directors, 2846
  IIDA Library Interior Design Award, 2845
  John Cotton Dana Public Relations Award, 2844–2845
  LLAMA/YBP Student Writing and Development Award Contest, 2845
  members, 2841
  mission of, 2841
  publications, 2844
  sections, 2841
  Swap and Shop program, 2845
Library legislation
  post-independence period (1947–2000), 1993–1994
  pre-independence period, 1993
  twenty-first century, 1994
Library management systems (LMS), 3066
Library marks and stamps, 3768
Library networks
  definition of, 3920
  U.S. regional library networks (*see* Regional library networks)
Library of American Broadcasting (LAB), 1563
Library of Congress (LC), 574, 1415, 1818, 2181, 2714, 2768–2769, 2981–2983, 3321, 3329–3330, 3722
  ARL Committee on Automation conference, 2963
  CLR, 2963–2964
  desirability, 2963
  development (1800–2000)
    American librarianship, 2890
    international role, 2890
    library's educational role, 2890–2891
    library's legislative and national roles, 2889–2890
  diversity, 2879
  460 languages, 2879
  legislative library, 2879
  library's mission, 2880
  MARC (*see* Machine-Readable Cataloging)
  national institution growth
    at 2000, 2889
    acquisition, 2881
    difficult times, 2881
    government institutions, 2881
    liberty and learning, 2881
    library as cultural institution, 2885–2886
    library's early history, developments in, 2880
    library services, 2883–2885
    national library debate, 2888
    postwar expansion, 2887
    public document distribution, 2881

    reorganization and new technology, 2888–2889
    role and functions, 2880
    rules and regulations, 2880
    Spofford, Ainsworth Rand, 2881–2883
  produced and distributed records, 2963
  structures
    Adams Building, 2879
    Jefferson Building, 2879–2880
    Madison Building, 2879
  symbol of American democracy, 2880
  13 million items, 2879
  world leader, 2879
Library of Congress (LCC), 2920
  classification, 963, 970, 992, 1261–1262, 2669, 3283, 3902, 4205, 4466, 4472, 4475
    in current information environment, 2851–2852
    development, 2848–2849
    divisions, 2850
    domain-specific taxonomies, 2852
    factors for acceptance, 2847
    file partitioning, 2852
    guidelines, 2853
    history of, 2847–2848
    information retrieval function, 2847
    Internet, information databases, and OPACs, 2854
    and LCSH, 2852–2853
    library materials, shelf-ordering of, 2847
    main classes, 2849–2850
    multitopical works, 2853
    national bias, 2853
    notation (numbering system), 2849–2851
    obsolescence, 2853
    strengths, 2853–2854
    subclasses, 2849–2850
Library of Congress Demographic Group Terms (LCDGT), 2876
Library of Congress Genre/Form Terms (LCGFT) for Library and Archival Materials, 2876
  application, 2861–2862
  associative relationships, 2860–2861
  authorized terms, 2859–2860
  developments, 2862–2863
  equivalence relationships, 2860
  hierarchical relationships, 2860
  project management, 2858–2859
  scope notes, 2861
  structure, 2860–2861
Library of Congress Medium of Performance Thesaurus for Music (LCMPT), 2863, 2876
Library of Congress Name Authority, 1080
Library of Congress/Name Authority Cooperative Program (LC/NACO), 3291
Library of Congress subject headings (LCSH), 1080, 1259, 1261, 1539–1540, 1615, 2670, 2847, 2852–2853, 2856–2858, 2860, 2862–2863, 3899, 3902, 3904, 3929, 4466, 4472–4473
  assignment of headings, 2870
  cross-references
    see also (SA) references, 2867–2868
    see references, 2867

    broader and narrower terms, 2867
    general see references, 2868
    related terms, 2867
  headings, 2866–2867
  LCMPT, 2876
  multiple subdivisions, 2877
  new/revised headings
    Airlie House recommendation, 2874–2875
    heading currency, 2871–2872
    heading syntax, 2872
    pre-Airlie House actions, 2874
    reference structure, 2872–2873
    scope, 2871
    subdivisions, 2873–2874
  RDA, 2876
  scope, 2866
  scope notes, 2868
  subdivisions
    chronological subdivisions, 2869
    free-floating subdivisions, 2869–2870
    geographic subdivisions, 2869
    multiple subdivisions, 2870
    pattern subdivisions, 2870
    topical subdivisions, 2869
Library of Congress television preservation report, 1578
Library of Congress Web Archives (LCWA), 4754
Library of Knesset, 2547
Library of the Eghishe Charents State Museum of Literature and Art, 230
Library of Tomorrow Project, 1030
Library Organization and Management (LOMS), 2842, 2844
Library portals
  features and functions, 2892
  issues, 2897–2898
  technology and standards used, 2894–2895
  types, 2892–2893
Library Publishing Coalition (LPC), 2901, 2903–2904, 2906–2907
Library publishing initiatives (North America)
  academic library publishing
    appendices and supplemental content, 2903
    business models, 2906
    conference proceedings, 2902
    core services, 2906
    and "crises," 2904–2905
    data, 2902–2903
    definition, 2901
    electronic journals, 2901–2902
    ETDs, 2902
    gray literature, 2902
    history, 2903–2904
    maturity, 2907
    missions and motivations, 2905
    monographs, 2902
    organization and staffing, 2906
    partnerships and collaboration, 2906–2907
    print on demand/digitization services for out-of-print books, 2903
    scholarly websites, 2902
    textbooks, 2903
  credibility and identity establishment
    scholarly publishing and academy, 2907
    sustainability, 2907
    university presses, relationship with, 2907

Library Publishing Unconference, 1422
Library Quarterly (LQ), 2167, 2910
Library questions, classification of, 1518
Library science, 2410, 2769
  American exceptionalism, 2909
  apostles of culture, 2909
  bibliothekswissenschaft, 2909
  in Brazil
    graduate courses, 612
    Industrial Revolution, 597
    job market, 612–614
    scientific infrastructure, 597
    undergraduate courses, 597–599
  C. C. Williamson report, 1923, 2910
  German influence, 2909
  Graduate Library School, 2910–2913
  institutional infrastructures, 2911
  knowledge and skills, 2910–2911
  librarianship education events, 2914–2916
  library automation, 2914
  library economy, 2910
  Library Quarterly (LQ), 2910
  protohistory, 2909
  scientism, 2913
  Social Gospel movement, 2909
  values, 2912–2913
A Library's Contribution to Your Community,
  3794
Library Services Act (LSA), 1847, 3775
Library Services and Construction Act (LSCA),
  1847, 3541, 3775, 4393
Library Services and Technology Act (LSTA),
  377, 4392, 4395
Library services platforms, 4982
Library Society of China (LSC), 893
Library's scribes, 2404
Library Support Staff Certification Program,
  2844
Library Trends, 249
LibraryU, 3438
Libricide, 4400–4403
Life-cycle concept, 2379
Lightweight Directory Access Protocol (LDAP),
  2894
Linda Hall Library (LHL), 790, 4009, 4361
Linear programming (LP) model
  applications, 1194
  limitation of, 1195
  objective function, 1194
  product mix decision problem
    graphical solution of, 1194–1195
    input data for, 1194
Lingua franca, 2982
Linguistic press, 3739
Linguistics
  discourse analysis, 2930
  lexicon, 2929
  morphology, 2929
  phonetics, 2928–2929
  phonology, 2928–2929
  structural subfields, 2927–2928
  syntax, 2929–2930
Linked data, 3294
  application, 2941
  benefits, 2940
  creation process, 2941
  five star data model, 2940

  HTTPs, 2939
  identity links, 2940
  in libraries, 2941
  principles, 2938–2939
  relationship links, 2940
  standards, 2939
  vocabulary links, 2940
Linked Open Data (LOD), 1079
Linking, SEO
  content-inspired linking, 4037
  FFAs, 4036
  inbound links, 4036
  link building strategy, 4036
  link-weighting fundamentals, 4035–4036
  non-reciprocal links, 4036
  paid links, 4036
Link searching, 4049
Lister Hill National Center for Biomedical
  Communication (LHNCBC), 3341–3342
"List of Serials Indexed for Online Users"
  (LSIOU), 1877
"Literacy 2.0," 2305
Literal sources, 3109
Literary fund, 1839
Literary politics, 1864
Literary warrant, 992–963
Literature Attached to Chart (LATCH), 1889
*The Literature of Political Economy: a Classi-
  fied Catalogue*, 1405
Lithuania
  historical context, 2943–2945
  library network, 2943
  library sector, 2943
  library system
    academic and research libraries,
      2951–2953
    foundation and ownership, 2946
    functions and community, 2946
    legal foundations, 2943, 2945–2946
    Martynas Mazvydas National Library,
      2947–2948
    public library, 2948–2951
    school libraries, 2951
    special libraries, 2953
    types, 2946–2947
  map of, 2944
  professional associations and unions,
    2955–2956
  research and education, 2953–2955
Lithuanian Integrated Library Information Sys-
  tem (LIBIS), 2947–2948
Lithuanian Librarians' Association (LLA),
  2955–2956
Lithuanian Library for the Blind, 2953
Lithuanian Research Library Consortium
  (LIMBA), 2828
*The Little Library of Museum Science Litera-
  ture*, 4185
Little presses, 3743
A Little Pretty Pocketbook, 854
Little Women, 855
Liverpool University Centre for Archive Studies
  (LUCAS), 4738
Living history museums, 3237
Living Museum Online (LEMO), 1706
Livres d'artistes, 4337
Lloyd's List, 1401

Loansome Doc, 1885–1886
Local area networks (LANs), 2291, 3356
Local authority museums, in United Kingdom,
  4719–4721
Local databases, development and access,
  2329–2331
Local documents, 1720–1721
Local education authorities (LEAs), 4705–4706
Local Government (Wales) Act 1994, 4735
Local Government Act of 1972, 1839, 4734
Local Government and Planning (Scotland) Act
  1982, 4720
Local standardization, 3107
Lock-and-key theory, 836
Logical name space
  for files/digital entities, 2999
  for storage systems, 2999
Logical Observations Identifiers Names and
  Codes (LOINC), 4673
Logistical distribution network, 3002
Logons, 2056
London, 302–309
London and Country Brewer, 1402
London Mathematical Society, 324
London Price-Current, 1401
London Zoo, 4724
Long playing (LP) recordings, 3280
Loose-leaf services, 652, 2741
Los Angeles Times, 3254–3255
Losee, Robert, 2052
Lossy Counting algorithm, 2632
"Lossy"-type formats, 4942
Lotka, Alfred J., 501, 506
Lotkaian informetrics, 2372
Lotka's Law, 501, 506–509, 2210–2211, 2371
Lots of Copies Keeps Stuff Safe (LOCKSS),
  1335, 3002, 4147, 4748
Louisiana Museum of Modern Art, 1226
Louvre
  French Revolution, 2959–2960
  nineteenth-century developments, 2960
Louvre museum, 1596–1597
Lubotsky, Marcella, 500–501
Lubuto Project, 883
Lucas, Alfred, 1070
LUNAR, 3348
Lunder Conservation Center, 1073
Lviv Stefanyk Scientific Library, 4643,
  4645–4646
Lycos, 2521
Lyndon Baines Johnson Foundation, 3715
Lynx, 2518

M

MAC, *see* Mandatory access control
Machine Aided Indexer, 1987
Machine-Assisted Reference Section (MARS),
  3909
Machine learning, 272–274
Machine-lending agencies (MLAs), 565
Machine-Readable Bibliographic Information
  Committee (MARBI), 2875, 2966
Machine-readable cataloging (MARC), 2, 733,
  739, 1252, 2220, 2887, 2921, 2923,
  3396, 4468, 4472–4473
  background (1961–1965), 2963

bibliographic control, 449–450
bibliographic data, 3058
cataloging systems, 3450–3454
character set expansion, 2983
development period
    character encoding, 2981
    IBM 360, 2980
    pilot project, 2980–2981
distribution service, 2965–2966
FAST authority file, 1539
features, 2981–2982
format family, 2982
internationalization
    content designation, library functions, 2985
    convergence, 2985
    ISO 2709, 2984–2985
    maintenance, 2985
    national basis design, 2984
    umbrella formats, 2985
Internet and Web introduction
    electronic resources, 2984
    new interchange options, 2983–2984
    Unicode, 2984
MARC-8, 2984
MARC 21, 449–450, 3396
    convergence, 2985
    development period, 2980
    formats for Classification and Authority
        data, 1260
    FRBR model, 2987
    maintenance, 2985
    Unicode, 2984
OPAC database records, 3422
pilot project (1961–1965)
    card and book catalog production, 2964
    contents and content designators, 2965
    initial distribution, 2964
    MARC I, 2964
    MARC II, 2964–2965
    participants, 2964–2965
    planning, 2964
    roman alphabet languages, 2965
    structure, 2965
recent developments
    MARCXML, 2986–2988
    modeling, 2987
    MODS, 2987–2988
    syntax, 2986–2987
record, 2982–2983, 3283
retrospective conversion
    automatic identification, 2968
    format recognition process, 2968
    initial conversion method, 2967
    large-scale centralized conversion, 2967
    NCLIS, 2970
    pilot project, 2967–2968
    record types, 2970
    reverse chronological order, 2967
    special studies, 2969
    task force, 2967–2970
standardization
    bibliographic standards, 2970
    cataloging data availability, 2970
    content designators, 2971–2972
    expanded roman-alphabet character set,
        2972
    information interchange, 2970–2971

ISBD, 2971
    publication and language codes, 2972
system development, 2983
users
    book catalogs, 2972
    MDO, 2972
    printed cards, 2972–2973
    retriever, 2973
    subscribers, 2973–2974
Machine-repair volunteers, 569
Machine-to-machine communication,
    2182–2183
Machine translation (MT), 277, 3141–3144,
    3346–3347, 3353
Macintosh computers, 4997
MacKay, Donald, 2056
Mackinder, Halford John, 1687–1688
Macquarie University Library, 4452, 4454
Macrex, 443
Macro-appraisal approach, 2381
Macrocosmic bibliography, 4198
Macroplanning, 432
Madden, A.D., 2051
Made for ads (MFA) Web sites, 4039
Madras Public Libraries Act in 1948, 1993
Magnetic Card Executive Typewriter, 4994
Magnetic Card Selectric Typewriter, 4994
Magnetic tape, 3280
Magnetic Tape Selectric Typewriter (MT/ST),
    4993–4994
Mahieu binding, 545
Maimonides, Moses, 3044
Maine State Library, 4397–4398
Mainz Psalter, 1972
Maioli bindings, 543
Major Orchestral Librarians' Association
    (MOLA), 3277
Makerspace Playbook, 2993
Makerspaces in libraries
    core library rules, strategic allignment
        entities, 2994
        innovation and entrepreneurship, 2994
        K-12 and lifelong learning initiatives,
            2993–2994
        technology/activities, 2993
        traditional roles, 2994
        values, 2992–2993
    knowledge creation, 2990, 2994
    makers, maker movement and rise of
        makerspace
        do-it-yourself culture, 2990
        hackerspaces and Fab Lab, 2991–2992
        learning, 2991
        Maker Faires, 2990
    timeline, 2992
Making of Amercica-2 (MOA-2) project, 3068
Maksymovych Scientific Library, 4646
Management information base (MIB), 3361
Management information systems (MIS), 2273–
    2274, 2662
Management Information Systems Research
    Center (MISRC), 2276
Management knowledge, 2275–2276
Management virtualization, 2998
    authenticity and integrity, 3000
    logical name spaces, 3001
    management policy

assessment criteria, 3000
    automation, 3000
    characterization, 3000
    metarule, 3001
    microservices, 3001
    persistent state information, 3001
    recovery operations, 3000
    rule-based systems, 3001–3002
Managing Electronic Records (MER) confer-
    ence, 1415
Manchester Museum, 4718
Mandatory access control (MAC), 405–406
Manifold, 1676
Manipulators, 275
Manne Katz Museum, 2551
Manufacturing Automation and Design Engi-
    neering (MADE) program, 2520
Manufacturing Census, 637
Manuscripts, 4344; *see also* Special collections
    collections, 202, 4791–4792
        AIP, 4763
        American Folklife Center, 4749
        American Heritage Center, 4757
        American Jewish Archives, 4751
        Brown Popular Culture Library, 4756
        California Academy of Science, 4762
        California Institute of Technology, 4762
        Cornell University Archives, 4747
        Iowa Women's Archives, 4760
        John Crerar Library, 4748
        Museum of Chinese in America, 4758–
            4759
        National Agricultural Library, 4762–4763
        Performing Arts Reading Room, 4749
        Schomburg Center for Black Culture, 4759
        Tamiment Library and Wagner Archives,
            4761
    core professional requirements, 4340–4341
    definition, 4336
Map
    of Armenia, 228–229
    of Australia, 379–380
    bird's-eye-view, 4961–4962
    of China, 886–887
    cognitive map, 4959
    of Croatia, 1121–1122
    of Denmark, 1215–1216
    of France, 1589–1590
    of Germany, 1693–1694
    of Greece, 1729
    history of, 4963–4964
    of Hungary, 1917–1918
    of Israel, 2542–2543
    of Japan, 2560–2561
    of Kazakhstan, 2578–2579
    of Kenya, 2592–2593
    librarianship responsibilities, 4013
    of Lithuania, 2944
    of Moldova, 3117–3118
    of Peru, 3606–3607
    plan view, 4961–4962
    of Poland, 3675
    of Saudi Arabia, 3970–3971
    of Senegal, 4104–4105
    of Slovakia, 4173–4174
    of South Korea, 4307–4308
    of Spain, 4315

Map (cont'd.)
   of Switzerland, 4487–4488
   of Tanzania, 4498
   three-dimensional tactile map, 4961–4962
   of Tunisia, 4625
mapFAST, 1546
MapInfo, 1676
Map-It, 2155
MARC, *see* Machine-readable cataloging
MARC Development Office (MDO), 2966
MarcEdit, 1545
Margaret Mann Citation, 331
Margaret Thatcher library, 2596
Maria's Libraries, 40
Market information centers (MIC), 2133
Market information prints (MIP), 2133
Marketing
   associations, 3015–3016
   definition, 3011
   education, 3017
   efforts, 3012–3013
Market researchers, 3416–3417
Markey–Fields bill, 1020
Marking format, 1177
Markov Networks, 274
Markov random fields (MRF), 4424
Markup languages, 1677
   computer use, 3073–3074
   Google search, 3072
   human use, 3073
   SGML, 3074–3075
   types, taxonomy of, 3073
   XML, 3076–3080
Marshall, Alfred, 647
Martel, Charles, 764, 961, 1806, 2848, 2850,
   3902–3903
Martel's seven points, 2848, 2850
Martynas Mažvydas National Library of
   Lithuania
   LIBIS, 2948
   library statistics, 2948
   national bibliography, 2947–2948
Marx, Karl, 647
Maslow's hierarchy of needs, 2115, 5068
Massachusetts Historical Society (MHS), 196,
   1780
Massachusetts Institute of Technology (MIT),
   2991, 4748
Mass communication, 997–998
Mass-market agreement, 1272
Master List of Medical Terms (MALIMET),
   2667
Master of library science (MLS) degrees, 3033
Master Reference File (MRF), 4784
Master's degree in library science (M.L.I.S.),
   707, 709–710
Master–slave data grids, 3000
Matching, 3294
Matenadaran, 236–237
Mathematical geography, 1683
Mathematical models, 2086
Mathematical Reviews (MR), 3025–3027, 3644
A Mathematical Theory of Communication,
   2770
Mathematics literature
   A.D. 400 to 1400, 3020–3021
   600 B.C. to A.D. 400, 3020

   5000 B.C. to 600 B.C., 3019–3020
   chronological periods, 3019
   contemporary mathematics periods, 3019
   current literature
      awareness needs, 3029–3030
      day-to-day needs, 3030–3031
      graduate education, 3025
      mathematical games, 3025
      popularizations, 3025
      primary literature, 3025–3028
      recreations, 3025
      retrospective needs, 3030
      secondary literature, 3028–3029
   eighteenth century, 3022–3023
   fifteenth and sixteenth centuries, 3021
   prehistory, 3019
   seventeenth century, 3021–3022
   1800 to 1940
      abstract axiomatic approach, 3024
      algebra, 3023–3025
      analysis, 3023, 3025
      axiom system, Gödel, 3024–3025
      Disquisitiones Arithmeticae, 3023
      Euclid's *Elements*, 3025
      Gauss, Carl Friedrich, 3023
      geometry, 3023–3024
      Hilbert, David, 3024
      international congresses of mathematicians,
         3024
      mathematical journal, 3024
      national professional society, 3024
      non-Euclidean geometries, Boole, 3024
      phenomenal growth rate, 3024
      topology, 3025
Mathematics of the USSR-Izvestija, 3027
Mathematics Subject Classification (MSC), 3644
Mathematische Annalen, 3024
Matica Srpska Library, 4127, 4130–4131
Matrix structure, 3189–3190
Matter facet, 1536
Maxdiff (Max difference) histograms, 2630
McClain doctrine, 1153
McKinsey's KM strategy, 2652
MCN, *see* Museum Computer Network
MDA, *see* Museum Documentation Association
Mean average precision (MAP), 3946
Meaningful learning, 2758–2759
Measuring the Impact of Networked Electronic
   Services (MINES), 374
Mechanics' libraries, 1842
Mechanistic organizations, 3514
Media, 998–999, 3277
   credibility, 1114–1115
   overload, 2104
Mediascapes, 2124
MediaSentry, 3660
Medical imaging databases, 4429–4430
Medical libraries, 4010
   in Israel, 2547
   MeSH, 4363
   in Vietnam, 4908
Medical Library Assistance Act (MLAA) of
   1965, 3335
Medical Library Association (MLA), 710, 1097,
   1874, 4016, 4355–4358, 4370
   advocacy
      governmental relations, 3036

      professional recognition, 3036
      public relations, 3036–3037
   global partners network, 3038–3039
   knowledge creation and communication
      professional networking, 3038
      publications, 3037–3038
      research, 3037
   lifelong learning
      AHIP, 3035
      continuing education, 3034–3035
      credentialing program, 3035–3036
   not-for-profit educational association, 3033
   organizational structure, 3033–3034
   professional and membership recruitment,
      3033–3034
   programs and services, 3034
*The Medical Library Association Guide to Man-
   aging Health Care Libraries*, 3037
Medical literature
   Arabic writings, School of Salerno and late
      manuscripts, 3044–3045
   Babylonian Talmud, 3042
   Berlin Museum, 3041
   bibliographic control, 3055–3057
   British Museum, 3041
   Code of Hammurabi, 3041
   early Greece, India, and China, 3042–3043
   early printed works, 3045–3046
   eighteenth century, 3049–3052
   King Assurbanipal of Assyria collection, 3041
   Latin and Greek manuscripts, 3043–3044
   nineteenth century, 3052–3054
   Old Testament, 3042
   papyrus, 3041
   seventeenth century, 3047–3049
   sixteenth century, 3046–3047
   Sumerian clay tablet, 3041
   twentieth century, 3054–3055
Medical Literature Analysis and Retrieval System (MEDLARS®), 3336
Medical Research Library of Ethiopia, 1499
Medical Subject Headings (MeSH), 2667, 2857,
   3336, 3929, 4468
   cross-references, 4474
   National Library of Medicine, 3340
   qualifiers, 4474
   thesaurus, 819
   tree structures, 4474
MEDLARS program, 652
MEDLINE, 1764, 1767, 3339, 3471
   current awareness services, 1880
   database, 819–820
   interlibrary loan and document delivery, 1880
   library collections, online access to, 1881
   outsourcing, 1881
   PubMed database, 474
MedlinePlus Connect, 3339
MedPix™, 4430
Medvescak Public Library, 883
Meeting the Challenges of a Culturally Diverse
   Workforce project, 370
Mekelle Museum, 1503
Mela, Pomponius, 1684
Mel-Frequency Cepstral Coefficients (MFCCs),
   3270
Melina Project, 1742
Mellon Conservation Documentation Survey, 1072

Mellon's grounded theory, 2783

MELVYL, 3452

Members Council Executive Committee, 3393

Membership Initiative Groups (MIGs), 76–77

Meme Tags, 1059

Memex, 1057, 2217

Memorial museums
in Hungary, 1928
in Moldova, 3123
Nehru Memorial Museum and Library, New Delhi, 2022

Memoria Slovaciae, 4176

Memory difficulties, 3842

Memory of the World Program, 4660–4661

Mendeley, 45

Mentions, altmetrics, 44

Mercantile libraries, 1842

Mercator projection, 1685

Merchants Avizo, 1410

Merchants' Magazine, 1404

Merchants Mappe of Commerce, 1400

Merck Index, 820

MeSH, *see* Medical Subject Headings

Mesrop Mashtots Institute of Ancient Manuscripts, 236–237

Message credibility, 1115

Message Digest Algorithm 5 (MD-5), 1366

Messkataloge, 469

MESUR database, 45

Metacrawler, 2523

Metadata, 1294–1295, 1364–1366, 1390, 2524, 3106
content value standards, 3061
data communication standards, 3061–3062
data structure standards, 3060–3061
definitions, 3059–3060
editing tools, 1545
etymology, 3058–3059
FIAT/IFTA, 2468
generation, 3063–3067
historical reference, 3059
models, 3067–3069
standards, 3060–3063
syntax standards, 3062–3063

Metadata Authority Description Schema, 731

Metadata Encoding and Transmission Standard (METS), 705, 1290, 1294, 1574–1575, 3068, 4938

Metadata Encoding & Transmission Standard, 731

Metadata Object Description Schema (MODS), 705, 731, 1292, 1294, 2987–2988

Meta-field
philosophy of information, 3610
philosophy of information sciences, 3611
philosophy of philosophy, 3611

Meta-information, 4559

Meta keyword tags, 4039

Metallurgy collection, 1744

Metamarkup, 3074

MetamorphoSys, 4678

Metaphilosophy, 3611, 3615

Meta-questions
information sciences, 3611
meta-fields, 3610–3611
philosophy, 3614, 3619
second-order questions, 3610–3611

Metasearch engine, 4053

MetaSearchers, 2523

Metatag Extractor, 3066

Metathesaurus
attributes, 4675
challenges, 4677–4678
concept identifier, 4674
concepts and concept names, 4673
definition, 4673
genomics vocabularies, 4673
MetamorphoSys, 4678
organization of, 4673–4674
production and distribution, 4676–4677
relationships, 4674–4676
semantic type, 4675
source vocabularies, 4673
standard clinical terminologies, 4673
synonymous terms and sources, 4674

Metcalfe's Law, 4081

Metrical information, 2056

Metrics
bibliometrics, 2226
data sources, 2226–2227
e-metrics, 2226
evaluative applications, 2227–2228
goals of, 2226
informetrics, 2226
Lotka's and Bradford's laws, 2227
relational applications, 2227
scientometrics, 2226
webometrics, 2226

Metrons, 2056

Metropolitan area network (MAN), 2291, 3356

Metropolitan Library, 893

Metropolitan Museum of Art, 1072, 3253

METS, *see* Metadata Encoding and Transmission Standard

Mexican Association of Librarians (AMBAC), 3095

Mexican Association of Museum Professionals (AMProM), 3097

Mexican Social Security Institute (IMSS), 3091

Mexican Student Grant Award, NASIG, 3389

Mexico
archives, 3096–3097
libraries
academic libraries, 3083–3086
accreditation, 3093
book publishing, 3095
chronology, 3099–3100
conferences, 3102
education programs, 3092–3093
government libraries, 3091
history, 3082–3083
information vendors, 3095
library associations, 3095–3096
national library institutions, 3091
private libraries, 3091
private university libraries, 3086
public libraries, 3086–3089
research institute libraries, 3090
schools, 3089, 3100–3101
science and technology libraries, 3090
serials, 3094, 3101
state university libraries, 3083–3084
teacher's institutions, 3085–3086
technological institutes, 3084–3085

U. S. library principles, 3093–3094
virtual/digital libraries, 3092
museums, 3097–3099

Microfilming, 4585

Micronesia, 3541–3542

Microplanning, 432

Microsoft Academic, 923

Microsoft Access, 4942

Microsoft Disk Operating System (MS-DOS), 4995–4996

Microtheory, 282

Microwave Communications, Inc. (MCI), 1017

Mid-America College Art Association (MACAA), 255, 4934

Mid-Atlantic Information Node (MAIN), 3310

Middle East Materials Project (MEMP), 791

Migration, 1334, 2072

Mildred L. Batchelder Award, 334

Militarism, 4403

Military archives
Air Force Historical Research Center, 4751
American Jewish Archives, 4751
American Jewish Historical Society, 4751
Archdiocese of Chicago, 4751–4752
Billy Graham Center Archives, 4752
Center for Military History, 4751
Episcopal Church U.S.A., 4752
Family History Center, Church of Jesus Christ of Latter-Day Saints, 4752
Naval Historical Center, 4751
religious archives, 4751
United Methodist Church, 4752

Military library, 1807, 4908

Military records, 1658

Millennium Declaration, 3382

Mill, John Stuart, 647

Milwaukee Public Museum, 3164

Milynes, Gerald de, 646

MINES for Libraries®, 374

Ming-Qing Archives, 906

Ming's New York Price Current, 1401

Miniature, 1945

Minimum Curriculum, 611–612

Minimum Standards for Public Library Systems, 1966, 1846

Mining Journal and Commercial Gazette, 1405

MINISIS, 4627

Ministry of Culture, 1595

Ministry of Foreign Affairs Library, 1499

MINITEX, 3924

Minnesota method, 110

Minority Librarian Fellowship program, 3402

MIR, *see* Music information retrieval

MIR Evaluation eXchange (MIREX), 3272

MIS, *see* Management information systems

Misinformation, 2053

Misselden, Edward, 646

"Missing heritability paradox," 3846

Mission Operations and Information Management Services (MOIMS), 3486

Mission-oriented indexing, 1987

MITRE MII Expert Finder, 3865

Mixed Integer Programming (MIP) model, *see* Integer programming model

MLA, *see* Medical Library Association

MLIA, *see* Multilingual information access

Mobile information, 4236
Mobile museum, 1820
Mobile robots, 275–276
Mobile Web Initiative (MWI), 2348
Mob mentality/group think, 3529
Modality affordance, 1118
Model-base management system (MBMS), 1203
Model Curriculum and Guidelines for Graduate Degree Programs in Information Systems, 630
Model human processor, 4806
Model requirements for management of electronic records (MoReq), 1109, 1361–1362, 1370
Modern bibliography
  commercial lists, 469
  library catalogs, 470–471
  recommended and forbidden books, 470
  topical lists, 469–470
  universal bibliography, 471
Modern Language Association of America (MLA), 3728–3729
Modern Library Movement, 888
Modified final judgement (MFJ), 1018
MODS, see Metadata Object Description Schema
Moffitt Library, 4650
Mogul miniatures (1525–1707), 1956–1957
Moldova
  archives, 3118–3120
  history, 3117–3118
  libraries
    academic libraries, 3125
    bibliographies and publications, 3124
    CML, 3124
    Internet, 3125
    LARM, 3125
    law, 3125
    library science education, 3125
    National Library, 3124
    NBC, 3125
    NLC, 3124
    programs, 3125–3126
    public libraries, 3123–3124
    special libraries, 3124
    users, 3124
  map of, 3117–3118
  museums, 3120–3123
Molecular diversity analysis, 836–837
MoMA, see Museum of Modern Art
Monastery libraries
  in Croatia, 1122
  in Greece, 1728
MONK Project, 1295
Monographic publishing, 2780
Monographs, 2739
Monster.com, 699
MONSTRAT Model, 4879–4880
Monteith College project, 987
Monuments Preservation Ordinance, 4511
Monument to the Great Fire of London, 4164–4165
Moodle, 606
Moody, John, 647
Moral rights, 1268–1269, 2142
Morino Foundation, 1030
Morrill Act, 1011

Mosaic, 5024
Moscow Mathematical Society, 3024
Motion picture
  archives, 1561–1563
  picture film, 1575–1576
Motivation theory, 3513
Moving image collections (MIC), 3131
Moving image indexing
  chapter-level indexing, 3131
  frame-level indexing, 3132
  image tagging, 3136–3138
  item-level indexing, 3131
  multilingual indexing, 3134–3135
  scene-level indexing, 3131
  sequence-level indexing, 3131
  shot-level indexing, 3131–3132
  text and image, 3132–3134
  text recycling, 3134
Mozarabic illumination, 1948, 1953
mPach, 1760
MRI, 4430
MT/ST, see Magnetic Tape Selectric Typewriter
Multicriteria decision-making (MCDM) activity, 1618
Multidimensional Library Anxiety Scale (MLAS), 2784
Multidimensional model of user–Web interaction, 2248–2249
Multidocument summarization, 425–426
Multilayer perceptrons (MLPs), 285
Multilingual cyberspace, 4659
Multilingual indexing, 3134–3135
Multilingual information access (MLIA)
  CLEF, 3143
  CLIR, 3141–3143
  history of, 3141
  information-seeking behavior, 3144
  language-specific process, 3144
  polyglots, 3140
  technological innovation, 3140
  translation quality, 3143
  Web search engines, 3144
Multilingual thesauri, 1984
Multimedia, 2242, 2524
MultimediaN E-Culture Demonstrator, 4088
Multiple criteria decision making (MCDM), 1198
Multiple identities, 3289–3291
Multiple USE MARC System (MUMS), 2966
Multiple user dialogs (MUD), 1050
Multipurpose community telecenters (MCT), 2133
Multi-State Anti-Terrorism Information Exchange (MATRIX) system, 2402
Municipal Archives Tel-Aviv-Yafo, 2554
Municipalities Ordinance, 4500
Municipal library, 1803–1804
  in Belgrade, 4129
  in Bratislava, 4175, 4179
  CML, 3124
  in France, 1600–1601, 1603
  in Montreal, 660
  in Peru, 3608
  in Poland, 3674
  of Thessaloniki, 1730–1731
Municipal Library of Thessaloniki, 1730–1731
Municipal School Library Association, 1222
Munn-Barr report, 3372, 3375, 3378

Munn-Pitt report, 381, 384–385, 3372
Mun, Thomas, 646
Murphy's Law, 1350
Murray Pease report, 1070–1071
Musaeum Tradescantianum, 1817
Museographica, 1817
Museo Guggenheim, Bilbao, 3158
Museological Society of Japan, 2574
Museology, see Museum studies
Museum
  America (see United States, museums)
  archaeological collections, curation of (see Curation, archaeological artifacts)
  archives
    Getty museum, 4755
    Smithsonian Institution, 4754–4755
    United States Holocaust museum, 4755
    Warhol Museum, 4755
  of Armenia
    Children's Art Gallery, 237
    Genocide Museum and Institute, 236–237
    Matenadaran, 236–237
    National Aesthetic Education Center, 237
  in Australia
    Bendigo Art Gallery, 391
    courses, 393
    curatorial issues, 393
    national and state museums and galleries, 388–391
    national parks, 391–392
    professional associations, 393
    specialist museums and galleries, 391
    von Mueller, Ferdinand Jakob Heinrich, 392–393
    zoos and aquaria, 391
  Brazil, 611–615
  catalogs, 1816
  challenges
    funding, 3239–3240
    politics, 3239
  changing role of
    ecomuseums, 1822
    ethnology museum, 1820
    historic house museum, 1820
    ICOM, 1821–1822
    mobile museum, 1820
    national museums, 1821
    natural history museums, 1820
    open air museums, 1820–1821
    research and public education, 1820
    virtual museums, 1822
  in China, 908–911
  civic discourse, 3238–3239
  civic outreach, 3236
  collecting and collections
    age of collection, 3161–3162
    age of education, 3165–3166
    age of exhibition, 3162–3165
    anthropology and history museums, 3167
    archaeology, 3168
    art curator, 3167
    changing culture, 3166
    data, online access, 3166
    demographics, 3168
    ethnic and cultural diversity, 3168
    history, 3161
    natural history, 3167

psychographics, 3168–3169
research, 3167, 3234–3235
and community, relationship between (see
    Community museums)
in Croatia
    history, 1129
    legislation and organization, 1129–1130
    publishing, staff, and professional associa-
        tion, 1130
DCMS (see Department for Culture, Media
    and Sport)
definition of, 2430, 3233
in Denmark
    art museums, 1225–1226
    cultural history museums, 1226
    curatorship and museum administration,
        training for, 1227
    Danish museum sector, 1225
    digital museum exhibits and services,
        1226–1227
    education, 1227–1228
    Heritage Agency, 1225
    legal framework, 1225
    natural history museums, 1226
    preservation, 1227–1228
    professional associations, 1227
Ethiopia, 1500–1501
    Addis Ababa Museum, 1503
    Dessie Museum, 1503
    exhibition of 1958, 1501
    Harar National and Community Museum,
        1503–1504
    Institute of Ethiopian Studies Museum,
        1501–1503
    before Italian occupation, 1501
    Jimma Museum, 1503
    Mekelle Museum, 1503
    National museum of Ethiopia, 1501–1502
    OAU, 1502
    SOFIES, 1503
    UACC, 1501
    Wollega Museum, 1503
evolution of, 1813–1814
exhibits and education, 3235
in France (see France, museums)
in Germany
    art museums and galleries, 1704
    digital museum exhibits and services, 1706
    education, 1707
    historical, anthropological, and
        archeological museums, 1705–1706
    museology as discipline and profession,
        1706–1707
    national museums, 1703–1704
    professional associations, 1707
    science and natural history museums,
        1704–1705
    standards and guidelines, 1707
    visitor research, 1707
    volunteers, 1707
    zoos and botanical gardens, 1706
history, 3233–3234
Hungary
    art museums and galleries, 1928
    current priorities, 1931
    digital museum exhibits and services, 1930
    as discipline and profession, 1930–1931

education, 1931
historical, anthropological, and archaeolog-
    ical museums, 1929–1930
laws, 1927
national museum, 1927–1928
professional associations, 1931
religiously affiliated museums, 1929
science and natural history museums, 1929
zoos and botanical gardens, 1930
India (see India, museums and museology)
information arts, 2071–2073
institution, history of, 3148–3149
in Israel
    Arab sector, 2552
    archaeological museums, 2551
    art museums, 2551
    historical museums, 2551–2552
    historical perspective, 2549–2550
    holocaust heritage museums, 2552
    in Jerusalem, 2550–2551
    official recognition, 2552–2553
    professional education, 2553
    science and nature museums, 2552
in Japan
    computerization and evaluation of manage-
        ment, 2575
    education and training systems, 2574–2575
    local governments, foundations, and private
        companies, 2572–2573
    museum/art libraries, 2574
    museum law, revision of, 2575–2576
    national museums, 2571–2572
    organizing exhibitions, 2576
    professional staff, 2574
    societies and associations, 2574
    university museums, 2573–2574
in Kazakhstan
    as discipline and profession, 2588
    galleries, zoos, and preserves, 2587–2588
    history of, 2587
    national museums, 2587–2588
Kenya (see National Museums of Kenya)
leisure destination, 3235–3236
modern museum
    American Museum in New York, 1819
    art, history, and natural history, 1818
    Ashmolean Museum, 1817
    classification systems, 1817–1818
    collections, nature of, 1817
    founding dates of, 1818–1819
    Grimani collections, 1816
    Musaeum Tradescantianum, 1817
    Museographica, 1817
    ordering system, 1817
    Peale's museum, 1818
    Sloane's collections, 1817
in Moldova
    Church Museum, 3121
    during communist period, 3122
    during czarist Russian domination, 3120
    early twentieth century, 3121
    exhibition activities, 3122
    during interwar period, 3122
    legislation, 3122
    memorial museums, 3123
    Moorish style, 3121
    national museums, 3121

political museums, 3123
public museums, 3121
scientific atheism, museums of, 3122
during Soviet regime, 3122–3123
during transitional period, 3123
objects
    collection and classification of, 1812–1816
    and knowledge transmission, 1816
    power of, 1815–1816
    preservation, 1813
    provenance (see Provenance of museum
        objects)
opportunities, 3238–3239
people with disabilities, 3575
place, 3263–3265
politics, power, and representation
    architecture and position, 3689–3690
    art museum, 3689, 3692–3693
    cabinets of curiosities, 3688
    contact zones, 3695–3696
    cultural governance, 3688–3689
    Enola Gay, 3693–3694
    ethnographic museums, 3694–3695
    Foucaultian perspective, 3689
    national museum, 3690–3692
    objects and exhibitions, 3690, 3697
    regulation of conduct, 3690
    representation, definition of, 3690
    social power, 3689
    status and community, 3688
professionalization, 3240
registration
    history, 3199–3200
    records, protection of, 3212–3213
in Saudi Arabia, 3979–3980
Senegal, 4110
in Serbia
    art museums and galleries, 4134
    churches and monasteries, 4133
    historical and ethnographic museums, 4135
    national museum, 4133–4134
    professional association, 4133
    science museums and galleries, 4134–4135
Slovakia
    ecucation and professional associations,
        4185–4186
    gallery network, 4185
    history, 4183
    political and social life, documentation of,
        4184–4185
    SNM, 4183–4185
    specialized museums, 4184
Spain (see Spain, museums and museology)
Switzerland, 4494–4495
technology, 3238
Temple of the Muses, 1813
training, 3240
types, 3236–3238
in United Kingdom
    armed services, 4718–4719
    botanical gardens, 4724–4725
    English Heritage, 4723
    financial support, 4727
    history of, 4715–4717
    independent, 4721–4722
    local authority, 4719–4721
    national museums, 4717–4718, 4727–4728

Museum (cont'd.)
in United Kingdom (cont'd.)
National Trust, 4722–4723
profession, 4725–4727
social exclusion, 4727
university, 4718
zoos, 4723–4724
visitors
American *vs.* European museums, 3251
AMNH, 3252
anecdotal assumptions, 3256
anthropological collections, 3252
art museums, 3251, 3253, 3255
attendance, 3254
blockbuster exhibitions, 3255
Brooklyn Museum's annual report, 3252
Carnegie Museum's annual report, 3252
cultural patrimony, 3252
cutting-edge research, 3252
Denver Natural History Museum, 3254
educational programs, 3255
European human remains, 3255
Excellence and Equity, 3255
experience, United States *vs.* Europe, 3254
Field Museum, 3255–3256
FMNH, 3252
golden age, 3251
Goldstein's arguments, 3254
historic visitors, 3251
history of, 3251
Los Angeles Times report, 3254–3255
Lucas' remarks, 3252–3253
mode of learning, 3253
nonart museum visitor, 3255
objects, 3252
occupations, 3253
Pennsylvania Museum's survey, 3254
Philadelphia Museum, 3253
professionals' speculation, 3251
school groups and students, 3251
sculptor, 3253
Second World War, 3254, 3256
Smithsonian's National Museum of American History, 3255
"The Good Old Days," 3255
transportation, 3253
Victorian museum visitor, 3251
volunteerism in, 4951–4952
web sites
business models, 3228
collecting and preserving, 3226
cultural experiments, 3223
exhibitions, 3223–3224
issues, 3228–3229
outreach, 3227
programming, 3223
searchable collections, 3225–3226
sectoral identity, 3226–3227
social experiences, 3224–3225
staffing and resource allocation, 3227–3228
virtual experiences, 3225
Museum Accreditation Program, 3146–3147
Museum Act (1998), 1129
Museum and Library Services Act of 1996, 4770
Museum Assessment Program (MAP), 57
Museum Computer Network (MCN), 255, 3179
communications, 3174

conferences and collaborations, 3172, 3174
consortium, 3171–3172
governance, 3173
incorporation and growth, 3171
from institutions to individuals, 3171
interactive and online, 3173
origins, 3170–3171
professional association, 3170
publications, 3172–3173
SIGs, 3173–3174
strategic planning, 3173
U.S. Congress, 3172
The Museum Directory, 4380
Museum documentation
deaccessions
authority to, 3208
criteria, 3208
deaccessioned objects, disposal of, 3209
procedures, 3208–3209
verification of records, 3208
loan documentation
correspondence, 3212
duty to loan, 3210
incoming condition reports, 3211
insurance, 3212
loan agreements, 3210–3212
loan file creation, 3211
loan requests, 3210
notes, 3212
outgoing condition reports, 3212
publications, 3212
shipping, 3212
policies
code of ethics policy, 3201–3202
collections management policy, 3200–3201
records, protection of, 3212–3213
registration files
accession numbers, 3202
accessions file, 3202–3203
appraisals, 3203
bequests, 3205
condition reports, 3203–3204
correspondence, 3204
deeds of gift, 3204–3205
documentary files, 3202
incoming and outgoing receipts, 3205–3206
loan records, 3206
notes, 3207
photography, 3206–3207
publications, 3207
purchase information, 3205
Museum Documentation Association (MDA), 255–256, 3178
Museum Documentation Centre (MDC), 1129
Museum for Islamic Art, 2550
Museum informatics
data sharing initiatives, 3178
definition, 3176
events, 3182
information management, 3181
information professionals, 3181
information representation, 3177
information technology
digital museum, 3179–3180
mainframe systems, 3178–3179

personalization technologies, 3180–3181
Web, 3180
professional organizations, meetings, 3182
repositories, 3176
as research area, 3182
resources, 3176–3177
standards and metadata, 3177–3178
visitors, 3176
Museum management
administration, 3186
authorizing agency, 3188
budget and promulgate policies, 3188
chief executive officer, 3186
director/manager, 3186
ethics, 3196–3197
financial management, 3193–9134
functions of, 3187
funding sources, 3194
institutional attitude, 3187
leadership, 3190–3191
mission, 3192–3193
nonprofit and not-for-profit, 3186
organizational management, 3186
personnel management, 3191–3192
philosophical policies, 3193
planning methods, 3196
planning process, 3194–3195
public service and philosophical ownership, 3186
resource development policies, 3193
responsibilities, 3187
self-assessment, 3195–3196
structure
hierarchic structure, 3189
horizontal/flat structure, 3189–3191
manager/director abilities, 3189
matrix structure, 3189–3191
organizational structure, 3189
teamwork, 3187, 3192
types of museums, 3188
upper, middle and lower management, 3187
volunteers, 3192
working policies, 3193
Museum Network, 1129
Museum of Anthropology, Xalapa, 3098
Museum of Art in São Paulo (MASP), 614
Museum of Bad Art (MOBA), 4381
Museum of Broadcast Communications (MBC), 1563, 1565
Museum of Chinese History, 909
Museum of Croatian Archaeological Monuments, 1129
Museum of Cycladic Art, 1742
Museum of Israeli Art, 2551
Museum of Modern Art (MoMA), 263, 3224, 3249, 3692–3693
Museum of Natural History, 611–612
Museum of Online Museums (MOOM), 4382
Museums Act of 1845, 1837
Museums and Community Collaborations Abroad (MCCA), 58, 3247
Museum science, *see* Museum studies
Museum sense, 3215–3216
Museumshojskolen, 1227
Museums, Libraries and Archives Council (MLA), 4702
Museum studies

departments, 3214
history, 3215–3217
interdisciplinary, 3214
issues, 3215
master's degree/certificate, 3214
scholars, 3215
societal role, 3214
twentieth century second half, 3217–3219
Music Information Centres, 3276
Music information retrieval (MIR)
audio techniques
evaluation, 3272
query type, 3270
representations and extracted information, 3270–3271
specificity, 3271
user interfaces, 3272
query-by-example application, 3267, 3270
query-by-humming application, 3267, 3272
3SUM problem
indexing, 3269
note durations, 3269
translation and scaling invariance, 3270
symbolic techniques
choosing representation, 3267–3268
geometric framework, 3268–3269
string matching framework, 3268
Music Instrument Digital Interface (MIDI), 3267
Music librarianship
career in, 3278
cataloging
Anglo-American Cataloging Rules (AACR 2 rev), 3281
future of, 3282–3283
music subject headings, 3282
music uniform titles, 3282
sheet music, 3282
Western classical music, 3282
definition, 3275
future challenges, 3284–3285
literature, 3275
professional organizations
ARSC, 3278
IAMIC, 3277
IAML, 3277
IASA, 3278
MLA, 3277
MOLA, 3277
MOUG, 3277–3278
Music libraries
classifications, 3283
developing collections
audio and visual recordings, 3279–3281
Basic Music Library, 3278
Fling's Library Acquisition of Music, 3278
indexes and abstracts, 3281
printed music and sound recordings, 3278
reference tools, 3281
scores, 3279
ethnic and world music, 3284
preservation, 3283–3284
professional organizations, 3277–3278
services, 567
types
academic libraries, 3275
conservatory libraries, 3276
media and broadcast libraries, 3277

Music Information Centres, 3276
national libraries, 3276
performance libraries, 3276–3277
public libraries, 3276
research libraries, 3275–3276
Music Library Association (MLA), 2863, 3277–3278
Music Library of Greece "Lilian Voudouri," 1732
Music OCLC Users Group (MOUG), 3277–3278
Mütter Museum, Philadelphia, 4381
My Friend Rabbit, 858–859
MyiLibrary e-books, 1210–1211

N
Nacandros of Colophon in Ionia, 3042
Nachum Gutman Art Museum, 2551
NACO, 454, 1540–1543, 2921, 3291–3293, 4669
Nairobi museum, 2604
Name authority control
bibliographic and authority records, 3292
crowdsourcing, 3294
data elements, 3291–3292
encoding and models, 3294–3295
identifiers, 3292–3293
linked data, 3294
matching and clustering, 3294
names and name variants, 3289
organization names and hierarchies, 3291
pseudonyms and multiple identities, 3289–3291
purposes, 3288
record creation and reuse, 3293–3294
undifferentiated names, 3291
VIAF and ISNI, 3288–3289
Name Authority File (NAF), 1076, 1543, 2866, 2921
Name variants, 3289
Nan Ching, 3042
Nancy DeLaurier Award, 4936
Nanjing Museum of Jiangsu Province, 909–910
Nanotechnology Standards Panel (NSP), 89
Napster, 1322, 3654
NARA, see National Archives and Records Administration
NARA Electronic Records Archive, 3001
Narin, Francis, 500
Narrative nonfiction, 3705
Narrower terms (NTs), 1986
NARS, see National Archives and Records Service
NASIG, see North American Serials Interest Group
National-academic libraries, 3321
National Academy of Sciences of Armenia Library (NAS RA), 232
National Aeronautics and Space Administration (NASA), 2155, 3640
National Aesthetic Education Center, 237
National Air and Space Museum (NASM), 3693, 4193
National and Capodistrian University of Athens, 1731

National and State Libraries Australasia (NSLA), 382
National and University Library in Zagreb, 1124
National Anthropological Museum, 4333
National Archaeological Museum
Athens, 1743–1744, 3689, 3691
Spain, 4333
National Archival Information System (ARHiNET), 1128
National archives, 177, 1414, 1851, 3316, 3716
in China, 906
concept, 3298
of Ethiopia, 1500
France, 1590–1592
Germany, 1699–1700
government, 3300–3301
Greece, 1736–1737
of Hungary, 1925
India, 2012–2015
issues, 3300
of Japan, 2567–2568
Kazakhstan, 2585–2586
NHPRC (see National Historical Publications and Records Commission)
scope of activity, 3304–3305
scope of holdings, 3302–3304
Senegal, 4109–4110
Slovakia, 4181
of Tanzania, 4508–4509
Tunisia, 4633–4635
of United States, 1792
National Archives Act, 4741
National Archives and Library of Ethiopia (NALE), 1495–1496
National Archives and Records Administration (NARA), 1362, 1566, 1648, 1851, 1853, 2154, 3715, 4746, 4754
National Archives and Records Service (NARS), 1851, 4308–4309, 4746
National Archives of Armenia, 235–236
National Archives of Scotland (NAS), 4733–4734
National Archives of the Republic of Moldova (NARM), 3119
National Archives Trust Fund, 3715
National Army Museum, 4719
National Assembly Library, South Korea, 4310
National Assessment and Accreditation Council (NAAC), 2010
National Association of Accountants, 651
National Association of Broadcasters (NAB), 1013–1014
National Association of Government Archivists and Records Administrators (NAGARA), 1854
National Association of Manufacturers, 649
National Association of State Libraries (NASL), 4394
National Audio-Visual Conservation Center, 4305
National Audiovisual Institute (INA), 1591, 3132
National Autonomous University of Mexico, 3323–3324
National Bank of Greece Historical Archives (NBG), 1738

National Biological Information Infrastructure
(NBII)
biodiversity, 3306–3308, 3310
biological information, 3313
DiGIR protocols, 3313
digital system, 3306
ecological information, 3308
ecology, 3306
GBIF, 3313
history, 3307–3308
knowledge domains, 3308
knowledge integration
catalogs and collections, 3312
collaborative platforms, 3313
expert coordination, 3313
harvesting partner sites, 3312
hosting, 3313
information suppliers, 3311
sample NBII data and information partners,
3312
Web crawling, 3312–3313
national standards and technology, 3311
national themes, 3310–3311
organization, 3309
regional foci, 3310
USGS, 3306
National Book Center of Greece, 1733–1734
National Book Chamber (NBC), 3125
National Book Coordination Act of 1957, 893
National Braille Association (NBA), 570
National Center for Biomedical Information
(NCBI), 3341–3342
National Center for Biotechnology Information
(NCBI), 559, 1768, 3037
National Center for Education Statistics
(NCES), 2844
National Center for Geographic Information and
Analysis (NCGIA), 1674
National Center for Science Information Sys-
tems (NACSIS), 2563
National Center for Supercomputing Applica-
tions (NSCA), 1390–1391, 3396
National Central Library (NCL), 4498
National Chamber of the Mexican Publishing
Industry (CANIEM), 3095
National Civil Rights Museum, 4165
National Commission on Libraries and Informa-
tion Science (NCLIS), 2033, 2158, 2970,
3921, 4222
National Communication Association (NCA),
1001–1002, 2354
National Council of Science and Technology
(CONACYT), 3089–3090
National Council on Archives (NCA), 4739
National Defense Education Act (NDEA), 2832,
4000
National Diet Library (NDL), 2561–2563
National Diet Library of Japan, 3321, 3326
National Digital Heritage Archive (NDHA),
3378
National Digital Library (NDL), 2889, 3727
National Documentation Center, 4631
National Documentation Service (NDS), 2601
National Document Delivery System, 1923
National Drug Code (NDC), 979
National Educational Technology Standards, 64
National Education Association (NEA), 60

National Electronic Information Consortium
(NEICON), 2823
National electronic library, 3727
National Electronic Site License Initiative
(NELSI), 2825
National Endowment for the Arts (NEA), 293,
1586
National Endowment for the Humanities, 293,
1909
National Federation of Advanced Information
Services (NFAIS), 4978
National Film and Sound Archive (NFSA), 187,
388, 1567
National Film Preservation Foundation (NFPF),
1587–1588
National Fire Protection Association (NFPA),
1349, 1853
National Freedom Fund for Librarians (NFFL),
2393
National Gallery of Art, 3217
National Gallery of Victoria (NGV), 388
National Herbarium of Tanzania (NHT), 4512
National Historical Publications and Records
Commission (NHPRC), 1414, 4746
advisory board, 3315
funding categories, 3315–3316
grants, 3315, 3318–3319
history, 3316–3318
National Archives and Records Administration, 3315
National Historical Publications Commission
(NHPC), 3317
National Historic Preservation Act of 1966,
1774, 4169
National imprint bibliographies
bibliographical guides, 474–475
bio-bibliography, 475
commercial lists, 475
current national bibliographies, 473
current online subject bibliographies, 474
Germany and adjacent areas, 473
Great Britain, 472
incunabula, 476
library publications, 475–476
Romance-Language Nations, 472
subject lists, monographic and analytic, 475
United States, 472
National Index of Functional Literacy (INAF),
603
National Information Infrastructure (NII), 1551
National Information Standards Organization
(NISO), 3, 88, 441, 443, 1133, 1250,
1396, 2183–2184, 2341, 2672
Architecture Committee, 2343
current standards, 2345
expert technical advisory group, 2344
final approval, 2345
formulation and implementation of standards,
2345
Library Standards Alliance, 2345
Open Discovery Initiative working group,
4982
supporting organizations, 2345
Topic Committee, 2343
version control, 4897–4900
work item, 2343
National Information System (NATIS), 2312

National Information System in Science and
Technology (NISSAT), 2003
National Initiative for a Networked Cultural
Heritage (NINCH), 4935
National Institute for Information (NII), 1395
National Institute for the History of Art (INHA),
1598
National Institute of Anthropology and History
(INAH), 3097
National Institute of Child Health and Human
Development (NICHD), 335
National Institute of Informatics (NII), 2563
National Institute of Science Communication
and Information Resources (NISCAIR),
2005
National Institute of Standards and Technology
(NIST), 2344
National Institutes of Health (NIH), 369, 559,
3658–3659, 4146
National Inventory of Documentary Sources in
the United States (NIDS-US), 136
National Inventory Programme (NIP), 676
Nationalism, 4402–4403
National Knowledge Commission (NKC),
1997
National Labor Relations Act, 4689
National Librarian and Archivist's Day,
4888–4889
National libraries
ABINIA, 3330
in Australia, 381–382
in Belgrade, 2829
CDNL, 3330
CDNLAO, 3330
CENL, 3330–3331
classification of, 3321
definition, 3320
in Denmark, 1218–1219
desirable functions, 3320
digital libraries, 3322, 3331–3332
essential functions, 3320
*Guidelines for Legislation for National
Library Services*, 3321–3322
Guidelines for National Libraries, 3321
history and development of
Bibliothèque nationale de France (France
national library), 3327–3328
British Library, 3328–3329
Die Deutsche Nationalbibliothek (German
national library), 3329
Europe, 3322–3323
Latin America, 3323–3324
Library of Congress, 3329–3330
postcolonial world, 3324–3326
post-Soviet world, 3326–3327
Hungary, 1921–1922
inessential functions, 3320–3321
in Israel, 2543–2544
Japan, 2561–2563
in Kazakhstan, 2581
Kenya, 2595
legislative position of, 3322
music libraries, 3276
National Library and Information Needs,
3321
in Peru, 3606–3608
rare book collections, 3822

SCANUL-ECS, 3330
science and technology, 4009–4010
specific target audience, services to, 3322
subject libraries, 3321
Switzerland, 4488–4489
in Ukraine, 4642, 4645
in United Kingdom, 4701
National Library Act 1960, 381
National Library and Archives of Canada,
4338
National Library and Archives of Egypt,
3325
National Library and Information Services
Australia, 381–382
Denmark, 1218–1219
Germany, 1694–1695
India
Central Reference Library, Kolkata, 1995
DESIDOC, 1996
government, role of, 1994
IARI, 1996
inter-library cooperation, 1996–1997
NASSDOC, 1996
National Library, Kolkata, 1994–1995
National Medical Library, 1995
national planning, 1997
National Science Library, 1995–1996
NISCAIR, 1996
SENDOC, Hyderabad, 1996
UGC, 1994
Kazakhstan, 2581
Senegal, 4105–4106
Spain, 4316–4319
Switzerland, 4488–4489
Tunisia, 4626–4627
National Library Day, 234, 238
National Library for Children (NLC), 3124
National Library for Children and Youth
(NLCU), 4310
National Library
of Algeria, 3325
of Armenia (NLA), 230–231
of Australia, 1392, 3324
of Beijing, see National Library of China
of Brazil, 597–598, 3323
of Bulgaria, 3323
of Canada, 1395
of Chile, 3323
of China (NLC), 892–895, 3325
of Colombia, 3323
Czech Republic, 3323
of Ecuador, 3323
of Ethiopia, 1495–1496, 1499
of Finland, 3323
of Germany, 1694–1695
of Greece (NLG), 1729
of India, 3326
of Indonesia, 3326
of Ireland, 3322
of Jamaica, 3325
of Korea (NLK), 4309–4310
of Latvia, 3326
of Lithuania, 3326
of Malaysia, 3325–3326
Mexico, 3323
New Zealand, 3324, 3372–3373
Nigeria, 3324

North Africa, 3325
Norway, 3323
of Peiping (NLP), 890, 893
Peru, 3323
Poland, 3323
Portugal, 3323
Republic of Argentina, 3323
Russia, 3326–3327
in Sarajevo, 3323
Scotland, 3322–3323, 4701
Serbia, 4127–4129
Singapore, 3326
South Africa, 3325
of Spain, 4317
of Sri Lanka, 3326
of Sweden, 1261
of Thailand, 3325
Tobago, 3325
of Tunisia, 3325
of Uganda, 3324
of Vietnam (NLV), 4904–4905
of Wales (NLW), 4701
in Warsaw, 3680
National Library of Medicine (NLM), 819,
1872, 3034, 3036, 3471, 3640, 4010,
4672
administration, 3335–3336
clinical terminologies, coordination of,
3341
collection
digital collections, 3338
historical, 3337
preservation, 3337–3338
print, 3337–3338
PubMed Central, 3338
databases
ClinicalTrials.gov, 3339–3340
MedlinePlus, 3339
MedlinePlus Connect, 3339
MEDLINE/PubMed®, 3339
DIMRC, 3343
exhibitions, 3343–3344
extramural programs, 3342
history of, 3334–3335
legislation, 3335
LHNCBC, 3341–3342
MeSH, 3340
mission and long range plans, 3336–3337
NCBI, 3341–3342
NN/LM, 3342–3343
ORCID identifiers, 3508
organizational structure, 3336
RxNorm, 3340
SNOMED CT®, 3340–3341
training, 3344
UMLS®, 3340
VSAC, 3341
National Library Power Program, 64–65
National library service (NLS)
Anglophone countries, 3324
British Council, 2408
Ghanaian model, 4500
in Japan, 3326
New Zealand, 3372–3373
National Library Service for the Blind and
Physically Handicapped, 16, 563–564,
3576, 3778, 4395

National maritime and oceanography museum,
4639
National Moving Image Database (NAMID),
1586
National museum
in Belgrade, 4133–4134
Campo de Santana, 613–614
in Japan, 2571–2572
politics, power, and representation,
3690–3692
Switzerland, 4494–4495
in United Kingdom, 4717–4718, 4727–4728
National Museum of African American History
(NMAAH), 3245
National Museum of African-American History
and Culture, 4192
National Museum of American History, 4192
National Museum of Australia, 3692
National museum of Ethiopia, 1501–1502
National Museum of India, 3691
National Museum of Natural History,
4193–4195
National Museum of New Zealand, 3692
National Museum of Nigeria, 3691
National Museum of Pakistan, 3691
National Museum of Scotland, 3691–3692
National Museum of the American Indian
(NMAI), 2041, 4193
National Museum of the Prado, 4331–4332
National Museums of Kenya (NMK)
access, preservation, and educational role,
2607
archeological and paleontological sites,
2605–2606
curators and museum administration, educa-
tion for, 2606
as discipline and profession, 2607
Fort Jesus Museum, 2605
history of, 2603
Karen Blixen Museum, 2605
Lamu Museum, 2605
Lamu World Heritage Site, 2605
legislation, 2603–2604
Nairobi museum, 2604
outstanding personalities, 2607–2608
professional associations
AFRICOM, 2606
ICOM, 2606–2607
societies, 2607
regional museums, 2604–2605
National Network of Libraries of Medicine
(NN/LM), 3342–3343, 4010
National parks
Australia, 391–392
India, 2024–2025
Tunisia
cultural and arts centers, 4639
natural parks and sites, 4638–4639
National Park Service (NPS), 3247, 4165,
4169
National Park Service Act of 1916, 4169
National Parliamentary Library of Ukraine
(NPLU), 4644–4645
National Parliament Library, 4643
National patrimony, 611
National Pilot Digital Library Project (NPDLP),
902

National Policy on Library and Information
System (NAPLIS), 2001
National Program for Acquisitions and Catalog-
ing (NPAC), 2965
National Programme for the Digitisation of
Archival, Library and Museum Records,
1130
National Public Broadcasting Archives (NPBA),
1561, 1563
National-public libraries, 3321
National Register of Historic Places (NRHP),
1774
National Research and Education Network
(NREN), 1551
National Research Council (NRC), 559, 660–
661, 1673
National Sample Survey Organisation (NSSO),
1993
National Science Digital Library (NSDL), 2998,
3646, 4012, 4073
National Science Education Standards (NSES),
558
National Science Foundation (NSF), 555, 1029,
1392, 2217, 2517, 2772, 3646, 4263
National Science Foundation Act of 1950, 2217
National Scientific and Documentation Center
(CNDST), 4106
National security, *see* Intelligence and Security
Informatics
National Security Act of 1947, 2151
National Security Agency, 2151
National Security Archive (NSA), 2390
National Security Council (NSC), 2151–2152
National Security Laws, 785
National Serials Data Program (NDSP), 4139
National Society for the Study of Communica-
tion (NSSC), 2421
National Stolen Art File (NASF), 4577
National Stolen Property Act (NSPA) of 1934,
1153
National Storytelling Festival, Jonesborough,
4443
National Study of School Evaluation (NSSE), 64
National System of Public Libraries (NSPL),
4886
National System of Scientific, Technical and
Organizational Information (SINTO),
3676
National Technical Information Center and
Library, 1922
National Technical Information Service (NTIS),
1552, 1554
National Technical Institute for the Deaf
(NTID), 1183
National Telecommunications and Information
Administration (NTIA), 1279–1281,
2038
National Television and Video Preservation
Foundation (NTVPF), 1579
National Terrorism Advisory Board, 4579
National Training Center and Clearinghouse
(NTCC), 3035
National Training Information Service (NTIS),
687
National Trust, 4169, 4722–4723
National Union Catalog (NUC), 448, 769, 771
National War Museum of Scotland, 4719

National Zoological Park, 4194
Nation's Business, 650
Native American Graves Protection and Repa-
triation Act (NAGPRA) of 1990, 267,
1153, 1165–1166, 1169, 3167, 3245
Natural History, 644
Natural history museum, 1820, 3237, 4134
Denmark, 1226
Germany, 1704–1705
Hungary, 1929
India, 2021–2022
London, 3224
Madrid, 3152
Tanzania, 4510
United States, 5080
Natural language generation (NLG)
applications, 430–431
biography text, 432
components, 431–432
computational linguistics, 430
current developments and outlook, 437–438
dialogue situations, 431
formal and computational properties, 430
functional linguistics, 430
linguistic variation
aggregation, 435
characterizations, 433
discourse deixis, 435
ideational representations, 434
interpersonal control, 434–42
lexicogrammar, 434–435
linguistic abstraction, 434
Penman text generation system, 434
propositional content, 434
semantic control, 434
semantics, 434
Sentence Plan Language, 434
sentences, 435
stratification, 433
syntactic theory, 434
textual control, 434–435
macroplanning, 432
message/text personalization, 433
nonlinguistic material, 430
non-NLG-based text production system,
433
syntactic description, 430
text planning, 436–437
Natural language processing (NLP), 274–275,
2201
ANN
advantages, 279–280
cognitive models, 282
connectionist/subsymbolic paradigm,
281
disadvantages, 280
formalisms, 281
language-oriented disciplines, 281
local and distributed representational
schemes, 283
meaning representation, 287
physical symbol system, 281
research paradigms, 283
Rumelhart and McClelland model,
287–288
sequential processing, 284–287
symbolic paradigm, 281

applications, 3353
approaches
connectionist approach, 3351
hybrid approach, 3350
similarities and differences, 3351–3353
statistical approach, 3351
symbolic approach, 3350–3351
definition, 3346
divisions, 3347
goal, 3346–3347
history, 3347–3348
human-like language processing, 3346
introspection, 3348
levels
discourse, 3350
lexical, 3349
lower *vs.* higher levels, 3350
morphology, 3349
phonological analysis, 3349
pragmatic, 3350
semantic, 3350
syntactic, 3349
origins, 3347
synchronic *vs.* sequential model, 3348
Natural Resource Monitoring Partnership
(NRMP), 3312
Natural SEM, *see* Search engine marketing
Nauta, Doede, 2051–2052
Navigability affordance, 1118
Nazi memorabilia, 783
NBII, *see* National Biological Information
Infrastructure
Nebraska Library Association, 920
Negative feedback, 1036
Neighboring rights, 1268
NELINET, 3922, 3924
NELLI, 2825
NEMO, *see* Network of European Museum
Organisations
Neoclassicism, 1742
Neo-Schumpeterian approach, 2254
NESLI2, 2825
netLibrary e-books, 1209–1211
Netscape Collabra™, 1057
Networked European Deposit Library
(NEDLIB), 1333
Networked Knowledge Organization Systems/
Services (NKOS)
aims and participants, 3366–3367
special journal issues, 3368–3369
workshops and special sessions, 3367–3368
"Networked Talent Model," 143–144
Network management
activities, 3356
ancillary support systems, 3357
applications, 3356
components, 3356
dimensions, 3356
accounting management, 3358
configuration management, 3357–3358
distributed computing systems, 3357
fault management, 3357
performance management, 3358
security management, 3358–3359
information and activity, 3362–3363
LAN, 3356
MAN, 3356

operating parameters, 3357
SOPs, 3357, 3361–3363
vendor-provided software, 3357
WAN, 3356
work patterns
and dimensions, 3361–3362
distributed infrastructure management, 3361
network design, 3360–3361
RTSC work, 3359–3360
Network management organization (NMO)
ancillary support systems, 3357
design work, 3356
formal databases, 3361
information management tools, 3361
MIBs, 3361
monitoring, 3357
real-time supervisory control work, 3356
SOPs, 3357, 3361–3363
waterfall software development life cycle, 3356
Network neutrality (NN), 4778
Network of European Museum Organisations (NEMO), 3365
Network organization, 3516
Network resources, 2326–2328
Network visualizations and analysis, 2212–2213
Neue Erdbeschreibung, 1685
Neural-cultural flow line, 2058
Neural-cultural information, 2058
New Amsterdam Public Library, 3792
Newbery Medal, 334, 852
The New Downtown Library: Designing with Communities, 3788
New England Journal of Medicine, 3470
New Jersey State Library, 4398
New Library Buildings of the World, 2808
New Media Consortium (NMC), 2993
New museology, 614–615
Newsletters, 641
Newspaper indexes, 652
Newspapers, 640–641, 647, 998
Newsvendor model, 1197–1198
Newtonian mechanics, 282
The New World: Problems in Political Geography, 1688
New York Free Circulating Library, 1845
New York Historical Society (NYHS), 1780
New York Mathematical Society, 324
New York Museum of Modern Art, 3157
New York Public Library (NYPL), 1845, 3722, 5058
New York Society Library, 1841
New York Times, 3470, 3472
New Zealand Law Libraries Association (NZLLA), 3377
New Zealand libraries
academic libraries, 3375–3376
biculturalism, 3377–3378
digital revolution, 3378
education for librarianship, 3376–3377
history, 3371–3373, 3377
legislation, 3372
origins, 3372
professional associations, 3377
professional registration, 3377
public libraries, 3373–3374

school libraries, 3374–3375
special libraries, 3376
New Zealand Library and Information Association, 3548
New Zealand Library Association (NZLA), 3376–3377
NGOs, *see* Nongovernmental organizations
NiagaraCQ, 2631
Nicomachean Ethics, 644
Niedzwiedzka's information behavior model, 2092–2093
Nieuwe Instructie, 1400
Nikola Tesla Museum, 4135
Niles, Hezebiah, 647–648
Niles Weekly Register, 647–648
Nippon Hoso Kyokai (NHK), 1567
Nirvana fallacy, 783
NISO, *see* National Information Standards Organization
NLG, *see* Natural language generation
NLM, *see* National Library of Medicine
NLP, *see* Natural language processing
NLS, *see* National library service
NLS Collection Building Policy, 566
NMK, *see* National Museums of Kenya
NMO, *see* Network management organization
No Child Left Behind (NCLB) Public Law 107–110, 3992
Noel Butlin Archives Centre, 387
Noisy-channel approach, 422–423
Noll, Roger, 1016
Nonacademic link analysis, 4987
Nonato bindings, 541
Noncredentialed librarians, 4777
Nonempirical knowledge, 2610
Nongovernmental organizations (NGOs), 1721–1723, 5013
A2K movement, 3386
archives and collections, 3386
definition, 3380–3381
development and international assistance, 3384–3385
development of, 3381–3382
educational NGOs, 3385
global civil society, 3386–3387
human rights information, 3383–3384
ICT education, 3385
information dissemination, 3382–3383
information types, 3382–3383
library professional development, 3386
literacy education, 3385–3386
pros and cons of, 3382
Non-patent literature (NPL), 3566
Non-propositional knowledge, 2610
Non-webometrics research, 4989
Nordic Council for Scientific Information (NORDINFO), 2825
Nordic Forum for Information Literacy (NordINFOLIT), 2752
Nordic ISKO Chapter, 2498
Normalized Discounted Cumulative Gain (NDCG), 3946
North American binding, 546
North American Graves Protection and Repatriation Act (NAGPRA), 3234
North American Industry Classification System (NAICS), 638

North American Interlibrary Loan and Document Delivery (NAILDD) Project, 372
North American ISKO Chapter, 2498
North American Serials Interest Group (NASIG)
ad-hoc executive council, 3388
annual conference, 3391
awards and scholarships, 3389–3390
continuing education, 3390
membership, 3388–3389
organizational structure, 3389
partnerships and other outreach, 3390
permanent archives, 3388
publications, 3390–3391
site selection committee, 3388
North Carolina State University (NSCU), 1710
Northeast Document Conservation Center (NEDCC), 1350
Northern/Baltic Union Catalogue of Serials (NOSP), 2825
Northern Ireland
archives and archival science
archive services, 4736
legislation, 4734
broadcasting collections, 1566
museums, 3261
National Trust, 4722
Northern Light, 2522–2523
Northwestern Online Total Integrated System (NOTIS), 3452
Notices of the American Mathematical Society, 3027
Notre Dame Journal of Formal Logic, 3026
Nouvelle Géographie Universelle, 1687
Novel-item retrieval, 4555
Nuclear Information and Records Management Association (NIMRA), 1854
Numerical taxonomy, 4539
Nuremberg Chronicle, 1973
Nursing libraries, 1873
Nyborg Public Library, 2804–2805
Nylink, 3924

O

OAICat, 3401
OAIHarvester, 3401
Oakland Museum, 3218
OASIS Search Web Services Technical Committee, 2347
Object-as-sign, 1376
Object modeling, 3112
Object-oriented programming (OOP), 4540
Observations, 1685
Observations Touching on Trade and Commerce with Holland, 645
Obsolescence, 520–521
Occupational Outlook Handbook 2007-2008, 636
Occupational Safety and Health Act (OSHA), 1857–1858
Occupation, information society, 2257–2260
Occurrence identifiability, 1175
Oceania, 3547–3548
Odyssey, 644
Oeconomicus, 644
Office Document Architecture (ODA), 1365
Office for Accreditation (OA), 18

Office for Intellectual Freedom (OIF), 2387, 2391–2392
Office for Scientific and Technical Information (OSTI), 306
Office of Information and RegulatoryAffairs (OIRA), 1550–1551
Office of Management and Budget (OMB), 1550–1551, 2154
Office of Research and Development (ORD), 3562
Office of Scholarly Communication (OSC), 365
Office of Scientific and Academic Publishing (OSAP), 365
Office of Scientific and Technical Information (OSTI), 1553
Office of Scientific Research and Development (OSRD), 2811
Official Gazette, 3561–3562, 3566
The Official Museum Directory, 4379
Official statistics, 495
Off-line storage, 4942
Ohio College Library Center (OCLC), 451, 1847, 2981; *see also* Online Computer Library Center
  bibliographic network, 2981
  cataloging system, 729–730
  EMEA, 3400
  WorldShare Record Manager, 1545
OhioLink, 987
Okapi BM-25 algorithm, 2205–2206
Okapi system, 3427–3428
Older adults' information needs and behavior
  computers and Internet, 3410
  everyday life information seeking, 3408, 3411
  imperative for studying older age groups, 3407
  information literacy (Fourth Age), 3409
  information needs, 3408–3409
  information sources, 3409
  library-based research, 3407
  old, definitions of, 3406–3407
  residential communities, 3409–3410
Old Testament, 644
On2broker, 3458
OncologySTAT.com, 3472
On-demand books (ODB), 3735
One-clause-at-a time (OCAT) methodology, 1621
One Laptop Per Child (OLPC) program, 1283–1284
One-mode network, 4237
One-person librarian (OPL)
  churches and synagogues, 3416
  future, 3418–3420
  history, 3413–3414
  hospital librarians, 3415–3416
  information brokers, 3416
  law libraries, 3415
  market researchers, 3416–3417
  meaning, 3413
  nontraditional sector, 3417
  organization's goals, 3418
  prison librarians, 3415
  public librarians, 3416
  school librarians, 3416
  special libraries, 3414–3415
  tasks, categories, 3417–3418
  zoo librarians, 3416

One Thousand and One Nights, 853
One type, one printer theory, 1971
ONIX metadata upstream, 3395
Online Account Management Service, 683
Online bibliographic database, 4629
Online bibliographic retrieval, 2245
Online catalogs, 2079
Online Computer Library Center (OCLC), 2, 671, 733, 894, 984, 1390–1391, 1880, 2181, 2921, 3381, 3450–3452, 3454, 3916, 4472, 4578, 4774–4775, 4800
  advocate for libraries, 3401–3402
  Asia pacific, 3404
  Canada, 3404
  cataloging service, 3396–3397
  DDC
    Abridged WebDewey, 1259–1260
    BISAC subject headings, 1261
    Classify, 1262
    development, 1260
    Scorpion software, 1262
    Subject Headings for Children and People, Places & Things, 1261
    translations, 1260
    WebDewey, 1259
    WorldCat Collection Analysis service, 1258, 1262–1263
    XML representations, 1260
  digital collection services, 3400
  eCONTENT, 3399
  electronic books, 3399–3400
  eSerials Holdings Service, 3398
  Europe, Middle East and Africa, 3405
  finances, 3394
  Google, 3403–3404
  governance
    Board of Trustees, 3393–3394
    contribution, 3392–3393
    Global Council, 3394
    Members Council, 3392–3393
    membership, 3392
    membership participation levels, 3393
    WorldCat Principles of Cooperation, 3393
  history, 3392
  integrated library systems, 3400
  Latin American and Caribbean, 3404–3405
  outside United States, 3404
  programs and research, 3400–3401
  QuestionPoint, 3398–3399
  reference and resource sharing, 3398
  RLNs, 3921–3923
  U.S. activity, 3404
  WebJunction, 3402
  WorldCat
    bibliographic database, 3394
    collection analysis, 3398
    CONTENTdm collections, 3400
    enrichment and quality control, 3395–3396
    evolution, 3396
    FirstSearch service, 3395
    growth, 3396–3397
    and information standards, 3396
    Navigator, 3398
    Online Union Catalog, 3394
    Open WorldCat pilot program, 3402–3403
    selection, 3398
    statistics, 3395

    web services, 3403
    WorldCat Local, 3403
    WorldCat.org, 3403
Online databases, 2240–2241
Online information exchange (ONIX), 4056
Online library instruction
  assessment
    economic viability, 3444
    learner/instructor preferences, 3444
    learning outcomes, 3444
    usability, 3443
  CAI, 3444
    benefits, 3435
    computer-assisted demonstration, 3434
    independent learning tutorials, 3435
    live assistance and hand-on, computer-based learning, 3434–3435
  early days of distance education, 3434
  history
    emergence of distance education, 3432–3433
    need for teaching librarian, 3432
    online education as distance education, 3433
  instructional opportunities
    credit course, 3437–3438
    discipline-specific online library instruction, 3437
    intended audience, 3435
    librarian professional development, 3438–3440
    popular database and OPAC, 3436
    in schools of library and information studies, 3438–3439
    teaching information literacy skills, 3436–3437
    virtual tour, 3436
  internet, libraries and online learning
    assessment of, 3443–3444
    case for CAI, 3435
    instructional opportunities for online library instruction, 3435–3439
  predictors and predecessors, 3433
  technology
    chat, 3442–3443
    collaborative Web browsing, 3443
    conferencing software and courseware, 3442
    reaching online learner through electronic mail, 3440, 3442
    static Web pages, 3439
    web site interaction, 3439–3441
Online Programming for All Libraries (OPAL), 17
Online public access catalogs (OPAC), 1–2, 250, 451–452, 487, 841, 1878, 2219–2220, 2240, 2847, 2854, 2947, 3399, 3435–3436, 4159, 4467–4468, 4789, 4978–4982
  Boolean retrieval systems, 3422
  vs. card catalog, 3450
  database records, 3422
  design, improvements, 3429
    automated search heuristics, 3428
    best-match retrieval approaches, 3427–3428
    browse interface, 3426
    catalog records, enhancement of, 3427

E-referencer system, 3427–3429
  expert intermediary systems, 3428
  graphical and direct manipulation inter-
    faces, 3425–3426
  helpful and user-oriented interfaces,
    3425
  knowledge-based techniques, 3428
  query expansion and formulation support,
    3427
  relevance feedback capability, 3428
  search/decision trees, 3428–3429
  development, 3450–3452
  effective, 3453–3454
  functions, 3452–3453
  multicatalog and electronic database search,
    3429
  search strategies, 2241
  subject descriptors, 3422
  subject searching
    class number search, 3424
    initial and reformulation strategies, 3424
    knowledge, 3423–3424
    problems, 3424–3425
    proportion of, 3423
    vs. specific-item searching, 3423
    subject field, 3423–3424
  types, 3451–3452
  usage patterns, 2242
  users, 3422
  Web interfaces, 3422
Online searching, 2079, 2320–2322
Online self-publishing, *see* Self-publishing
  online
Online Service Provider Safe Harbors provision,
  3654
On Medical Experience, 3043
Ontolingua system, 3458
Ontology
  Cyc, 3456–3457
  definition, 3455
  expressiveness, 3457–3458
  formal semantics, 3455
  generality of, 3456–3457
  hierarchy, 3456
  information integration, 3455
  knowledge sharing and reuse, 3455, 3463
  languages
    KIF language, 3458
    KL-ONE, LOOM, and CLASSIC, 3458
    Ontobroker and On2broker, 3458
    OWL, 3461–3463
    problems, 3462–3463
    RDF schema, 3460–3462
    Semantic Web, 3458–3459
    XML document, 3459–3460
  metaphysics, 3616
  real-world semantics, 3455
  Semantic Web, 3456
  types of, 3456
Ontology Interference Language (OIL), 1366
OPACs, *see* Online Public Access Catalogs
Open access (OA)
  African librarianship, 39
  ARL, 365–366
  version control, 4898
"Open access advantage," 2371
Open Access publication, 2902, 2907

Open access scholarship and publishing
  advertising, 3472
  author-funded journals, 3468–3469
  books, 3472
  from conventional to digital publishing,
    3465–3466
  database integrators, 3471–3472
  from digital to open publishing, 3466
  e-print services, 3466
  frontiers, 3473–3474
  knowledge base, 3474
  long-term storage and retrieval, 3472–3473
  open journals, 3467–3469
  search and indexes, 3470–3471
  self-archiving, 3466–3467
  subscriptions, 3469–3470
  Wikipedia, 3467
Open Access Working Group (OAWG), 345
Open air museums, 1820–1821
Open Annotation Data Model, 5020
Open Archival Information System (OAIS),
    1332, 1361, 1364–1366, 1577
  content, 3481
  development process, 3478–3480
  functional model, 3482–3483
  information model, 3483–3484
  reference model, 3480–3481
Open Archive Initiative Standard (OAIS), 2480
Open Archives Initiative (OAI), 3063, 3227,
    3401, 3467, 4899
Open Archives Initiative-Object Reuse and
    Exchange (OAI-ORE) standard, 1365
Open Archives Initiative Protocol for Metadata
    Harvesting (OAI-PMH), 1362, 1365,
    2894, 2983
Open Conference Systems (OCS), 2902
Open Content Alliance, 3655
Open Directory Project (ODP), 2524,
    4031–4032
OpenDocument format (ODF), 2342–2343
Open Document Management API (ODMA),
    1361, 1365
Open Educational Resources (OERs), 2903,
    4659
Open Journal Software (OJS), 2902
Open Journal Systems (OJS), 39, 3468
Open Ontology Repository (OOR), 4074–4075
Open Polytechnic of New Zealand, 3376
Open Society Archives, 1926
Open Society Institute (OSI), 2827
Open Software Foundation (OSF), 2344
OpenSource Metadata Framework (OMF) Tem-
    plate, 3064–3065
Open source software (OSS)
  BSD Unix (*see* Berkeley Systems Distribution
    of Unix)
  consensus-based approach, 3489
  Cygnus Support, 3489
  Deming's work, 3491
  Free Software Foundation, 3489
  GNU, 3488
  IBM, 3490–3491
  origin, 3488
  Sun Microsystems, 3489
  tech-heavy disciplines, 3492
  text, 3489–3490
  World Wide Web, 3491

Open-system indexing, 440
Open Systems Interconnection model, 3356
Open systems theory, 3514–3515
Open Training Platform (OTP), 4659
Open University of Brazil (UAB), 604–605
OpenURL, 1136, 1330, 2894
OpenURL/link resolvers, 4899
Operationalist searcher, 4877–4878
Operational moves, 2241
Operational Selection Policies, 111
Operation Cathedral, 782
Operations research/management science (OR/
    MS) perspective, 1192–1193
Opinion poll, 4798
OPL, *see* One-person librarian
Optimized network topology, 3360
Oracle, 2272–2273
Oral history, 3247–3248, 4794
  associations, 3499–3450
  curating, 3497–3499
  definition, 3494
  history, 3494–3496
  methods, 3496–3497
  programs, 3500–3502
*Oram's New York Price Current and Marine
    Register*, 1401
ORCID
  an open effort, 3505
  APIs, 3506–3508
  community involvement and governance,
    3506
  data exchange standards, 3508
  data privacy and security, 3506–3507
  goal of, 3505
  mission activities, 3509
  ORCID iD, 3505
  participants, 3507
  record creation, 3506
  registry, 3505–3506
  revenues, 3507
  use cases, 3508
Ordered weighted averaging (OWA) operators,
    1624, 1630–1631
Ordrupgaard Collection, 1226
Oregon State Library, 4398
Organic organization, 3514
Organic search, *see* Search engine marketing
Organizational communication, 4117–4118
Organizational culture
  assessment of, 3522–3523
  influences on, 3520–3521
  information culture, 3521–3522
  library context, 3523
Organizational framework, 3110
Organizational learning (OL), 2650, 3515
  behavioral perspectives, 3528
  cognitive perspectives, 3528
  conceptual landscape of, 3533
  definition, 3526–3527
  deutero-learning, 3531
  double-loop learning, 3531
  history, 3527
  knowledge assets, 3526
  learning agents
    groups, 3529
    individuals, 3528–3529
    organizational level, 3529

Organizational learning (OL) (cont'd.)
  process
    institutionalization, 3530–3531
    integration, 3530
    interpretation, 3529–3530
    intuition, 3529
  single-loop learning, 3531
  social constructivist perspectives, 3528
  value of, 3531
Organizational memory (OM), 2643–2644,
    3538–3539
  and culture
    knowledge sharing, 3535–3537
    management task, 3535
    organization knowledge management pro-
      grams, 3536
  definition, 3534–3535
  knowledge-management system, 3537
  long term memory, 3534
  operational knowledge, types of, 3535
  organizational forgetting, 3537–3538
  short-and medium-term memory, 3534
  strategic forgetting, 3538
  tacit knowledge, 3534
Organizational Self-Study Committee (OSSC),
    67
Organizational sociology, 3520
Organization Danish Archives (ODA), 1224
Organization for the Advancement of Structured
    Information Standards (OΛSIS) Consor-
    tium, 2190
Organization life cycle models, 3515
Organization names, 3291–3292
Organization of African Unity (OAU), 1502
Organization of Juvenile and Adolescent Librar-
    ies, 1733
Organization theory
  administrative decision-making behavior,
    3513–3514
  authority and power relations, 3510–3511
  bureaucracy, 3510–3511
  business process reengineering, 3511
  classical organization theory, 3511–3512
  competing values framework, 3515
  contingency theory, 3514–3515
  cooperative contract, 3513
  cooperative participatory process, 3511
  differentiation and coordination, 3510
  Fayol's theory, 3511
  human relations approach, 3513
  leadership and group processes, 3513
  life-cycle approach, 3515
  line-staff principle, 3512
  motivation, 3513
  networked organizations, 3516–3517
  network theory, 3515
  open systems, 3514–3515
  organization, definition of, 3510
  population ecology, 3514
  public administration, 3510–3512
  public management, 3517
  resource dependence theory, 3515
  resource exchange, 3515
  scientific management approach, 3511
  span of control, 3512
  structural approach, 3512
  total quality management, 3511

Original cataloging, 703, 729
Original order, 105, 116
Orphaned collections, 1152
Orphans Film Symposium, 1577
Orsay Museum, 1597
Orthographic awareness, 3844
Ostraka, 3552–3553, 3557
Otlet, Paul, 4783
Ottonian illumination, 1948
Outdoor museum, 4166–4167
Out of vocabulary (OOV) words, 4573
Outstanding Collaboration Citation, 332
Ouvriers Européans, 1687
Overcasting, *see* Oversewing
Overdrive, 4058
Oversewing, 539
OWL DL, 3463
The Oxford Guide to Style, 443
Oxford University Museum, 3155

P

Pacifica Radio Archives, 1566
Pacific Islands Association of Libraries and
    Archives (PIALA)
  advocacy, 3546
  American Library Association, 3548
  board meetings, 3543
  conferences, 3545–3546, 3548
  Dakio Syne Memorial Fund, 3549
  Fiji Library Association, 3548
  financial organization, 3543
  Florence Nalezny Warpeha Memorial Books
    to Micronesian Libraries, 3549
  goals of, 3541
  governance, 3543
  Hawaii Library Association, 3548
  history of, 3541–3543
  human networks, 3549
  IFLA, 3547–3548
  lifetime achievement award, 3549
  membership, 3544
  Micronesia, 3541–3542
  PIALA Listserv, 3544
  PIALA Newsletter, 3544
  PIALA Web page, 3544
  PREL, 3548–3549
  proceedings, 3544–3545
  purpose of, 3543
  resource sharing, 3547
  Swedish Library Association, 3548
  training initiatives, 3546–3547
Pacific Islands Association of Libraries,
    Archives and Museums (PIALAM),
    3542
Pacific Northwest Information Node (PNWIN),
    3310
Pacific Press Professor of Literacy Technology,
    3468
Pacific Resources for Educational and Learning
    (PREL), 3548–3549
PageRank algorithm, 484, 1042
Palace Museum Archives, *see* Ming-Qing
    Archives
Palace Museum in the Forbidden City, 909
Palau Library Association, 3546
Paley Center for Media, 1577

PALINET, 3920, 3922
Palo Alto Research Campus (PARC), 4025
Palo Alto Research Center, Inc. (PARC), 4115
Pandora recommender system, 3863
Panel stamps, 543
Pan-Pacific Education and Communication
    Experiments by Satellite (PEACESAT),
    3542
Pantheologia, 4176–4177
Papazian Library of the American University of
    Armenia, 230–231
Paper
  antecedents to
    papyrus, 1824–1825
    parchment/vellum, 1825–1826
  decoration, 1832–1833
  fibers, 1829–1830
  grain of, 1831
  history, 1826
  manufacture
    Asian methods, 1826–1827
    western methods, 1827–1829
  modern hand papermaking, 1834
  modern papermaking, 1833–1834
  preservation, 1832
  sizes, 1830–1832
  watermarks, 1830
  weight, 1831
Paperwork Reduction Act (PRA), 1550–1551,
    1857
Papyri
  collections, 3553
  history
    culture, 3557
    language, 3557
    law and institutions, 3556
    political history, 3555–3556
    society and economy, 3556–3557
  literature
    greek authors, 3555
    history of book, 3554–3555
    religious literature, 3555
  and paper, 3552
  publications, 3554
  rediscovery of, 3552–3553
  research and research facilities, 3553–3554
  treatment of, 3553
Papyrology, 3552
Papyrus, 1824–1825
Papyrus Ebers, 3041
Papyrus of Ani, 1945
Paraprofessionals, 878–879, 919–920
PARBICA, 688, 2440–2441
Parchment/vellum, 1825–1826
Pareto distributions, 2226
Parish libraries
  in United Kingdom, 1837
  in United States, 1840
Paris Psalter, 1947
Parliamentary Online Information Service
    (POLIS), 4507
Parliament Library
  Greece, 1729–1730
  New Delhi, India, 2006
PARLMEDIA, 661
PARRY, 3348
Participatory GIS (PGIS), 1672–1673

Participatory three-dimensional modeling (P3DM), 1672–1673
Particle-induced X-ray emission (PIXE), 478
Partner institutions network, 535
Partnership libraries, 4160–4161
The Past as Prologue: The Evolution of Art Librarianship, 249
Patchwriting, 3664
Patent Abstracts of Japan (PAJ), 3569
Patent Act of 1790, 3560
Patent Act of 1793, 3561
Patent Act of 1836, 3561
Patent and Trademark Depository Libraries (PTDL), 3562
Patent and Trademark Depository Library Program (PTDLP), 640
Patent Application Information Retrieval (PAIR) system, 3566
Patent classification systems
 IPC, 3566–3567
 USPC, 3566–3567
Patent Cooperation Treaty (PCT), 815
Patent documents
 AI patents, 3565
 APC documents, 3566
 certificates of correction, 3566
 dedications, 3566
 defensive publications, 3565
 design/industrial designs, 3565
 disclaimers, 3566
 drawing, 3564
 front page, 3563–3564
 INID codes, 3564
 kind codes, 3564
 plant patents, 3565
 reexamination certificates, 3566
 reissue patents, 3565
 SIRs, 3565–3566
 specification, 3564
 TVPP publications, 3566
 utility models, 3565
 utility patents, 3564–3565
Patent information
 history
  1790–1870, 3560–3561
  1870–1970, 3561–3562
  1970–2008, 3562–3563
 monopoly right, 3560
 patentability search, 3560
 patent protection, 3560
 WIPO, 3560
Patent Lens, 3570–3571
Patent Map Guidance, 3570
Patent Office Fire of 1836, 3561
Patents, 639–640, 815, 833–834; *see also* Patent documents; Patent information
PatentScope, 3570
Patents Ordinance of 1924, 4513
PatFT patent database, 3566
Pathfinder Network (PFNET), 485, 931–932
PATRIOT Act, 2402–2403
Patron-driven acquisition (PDA), 415–416, 1209
Paul Banks and Carolyn Harris Preservation Award, 331
Paul of Aegina, 3044
Paulo Montenegro Institute (IPM), 603
Peale, Charles Willson, 1818, 4767

Pedigree chart, 1656
PeerEvaluation, 47
Peer review, version control, 4898–4899
Peer-to-peer data grids, 3000
Peer-to-peer networks, 3652
Peircean sign theory, 4098, 4101
Peking University Library (PUL), 896, 903
Penman text generation system, 434
Pennsylvania Academy of Fine Arts, 4767
Pension Protection Act of 2006, 639
People–place–information trichotomy, 1512
People with disabilities and libraries
 archives, 3575
 barriers, 3573
 cataloging and indexing, 3580–3581
 collection development, 3580
 disability
  categories of, 3574
  definition, 3573
 disability rights movement, 3574
 electronic resource accessibility
  assistive technology, 3579
  circulating equipment, 3579
  library websites, 3578–3579
  Tatomir Accessibility Checklist, 3578
  vendor database, 3578
  WCAG guidelines, 3578
 for-profit sector, 3575
 history, 3575–3576
 language, 3575
 legislation, 3575
 museums, 3575
 outreach, 3580
 physical resource accessibility
  physical books and media, 3577
  services and programming, 3577–3578
  space, 3576–3577
 print disabilities, 3574
 social model, 3573
 staff training, 3579–3580
Perceived attributes, IT adoption
 compatibility, 2296
 complexity, 2293, 2296
 observability, 2293, 2296
 relative advantage
  behavioral intention to use/actual usage, 2295
  information quality, 2293–2294
  IT quality, 2293
  service quality, 2294–2295
  user satisfaction, 2295
 triability, 2296
Performance libraries, 3276–3277
Performing arts; *see also* Visual and performing arts
 archives
  Center for Black Music Research, 4755
  Folger Shakespeare Library, 4756
  New York Public Library, 4756
 definition, 4925
 live and recorded elements, 4925
 live events, 4925
Performing Arts Data Service (PADS), 297
Perseus Project, 1290
Persian illumination (1502–1736), 1955–1956
Persistent uniform resource locator (PURL), 2155

Personal anticipated information need (PAIN) hypothesis, 2119
Personal construct theory, 2234
Personal health record (PHR), 86, 979, 3342
Personal information management, 2111
 analysis
  finding/refinding activities, 3588
  information item and form, 3586
  keeping activities map, 3588
  meta-level activities, 3588
  personal information collections, 3587
  PSI, 3587
 checkbox methodology, 3597
 convergence and integration, 3599
 e-mails, 3598–3599
 factors, 3598
 history, 3585–3586
 information fragmentation, 3585
 maintenance and organization, 3585
 observant participation, 3598
 PICs, 3584
 practical methodologies, 3597
 privacy, security and information, 3585, 3599
 research
  finding/refinding activity, 3588–3591
  GIM and PIM social fabric, 3596
  keeping activities, 3591–3593
  meta-level activity, 3593–3596
 search technology, 3599
 user-subjective approach, 3598
Personality facet
 levels of, 1536
 rounds of, 1536–1537
PERsonalized and Successive Information Search Tools (PERSIST), 1901
Personally identifiable information (PII), 1489
Personal space of information (PSI), 3587
Personnel Administration Section (PAS), 2844
Pertinence relevance judgments, 3943
Peru
 libraries
  academic libraries, 3608
  education and professional associations, 3608
  modern challenges, 3608–3609
  National Library, 3606–3608
  publications, 3607
  public libraries, 3606–3608
  school libraries, 3608
  during Spanish domination, 3606
 map of, 3606–3607
Pervasive information systems, 1488
Peschel, Oscar, 1687
Pests, 1150–1151
Peterborough library, 1839, 1843
Pew Global Attitudes project, 1061
Pew Research Center, 5028
Pew Research Institute's American Life Project, 841
PFNET algorithm, 485
Pharmacophore searching, 834–835
Phenomenography, 2754
Philadelphia Museum of Art, 1072, 3253
Philadelphia Peale Museum, 3243
Philosophical Transactions of the Royal Society, 646

Philosophy
branches, 3615, 3617–3618
definitions, 3614–3615
of information
epistemology, 3616–3617
ethics, 3617
as meta-field, 3610
metaphysics, 3616
meta-studies, 3611
of information sciences
approaches, 3618
Becher's model, 3618–3619
epistemological questions, 3618
goals, 3618
hard fields, 3618
as meta-field, 3611
nomothetic–idiographic spectrum, 3619
preparadigmatic communities, 3618
scientific–humanistic distinction, 3618
soft fields, 3618–3619
metaphilosophy, 3615
meta-questions, 3614, 3619
personal/professional, 3611–3612
of philosophy, 3611
Philosophy of science
library and information sciences, 3631–3632
organization, 3624–3625
scope, 3623
Phoenix Central Library, 2791
Phonetics, 2–3
Phonogramm-Archiv, 4299
Phonographs, 4055
Phonological awareness, 3842, 3844
Phonological processing hypothesis, 3842
Photographic images, 1307–1308
Photostat technology, 1782
Phrase headings, 2866
Phrase searching, 4048–4049
Phronesis, 2678
Phronetic leadership, 2446
Physical bibliography
analytical bibliography, 477–478
descriptive bibliography, 478
historical bibliography, 478–468
textual bibliography, 478
Physical Geography, 1686
Physical Symbol System Hypothesis (PSSH),
283
Physical wayfinding, 4958
Physiological needs, 2115, 2119
PIALA, *see* Pacific Islands Association of
Libraries and Archives
Picasso Museum, 1596, 4332
Picture Australia, 1363
Picture books
alphabet books, 859
concept books, 859
counting books, 859
definitions, 856–857
engineered books, 860
graphic novels, 860
illustration, styles of, 857–859
text of, 857
trends in, 860–861
wordless picture books, 858–859
Pinakes ("tablets"), 468–469
Pio Clemente Museum, 1818

Pipeline architecture, 431–432
Piracy, 4298
Pirate Bay, 3653, 3656
Pittsburgh Project, 1415
Pixelation, 1309
Pixel-level object, 4421
Pixels, 1308–1310
PLA, *see* Public Library Association
Place identity, 3262
Plagiarism of print and electronic resources
academic dishonesty
definition, 3665
faculty attitudes, 3668–3669
individual differences, 3668–3669
social factors, 3668
cheating, 3665
coping with
ethical reasoning, 3669–3670
online instruction, 3670
prevention techniques, 3670
software detection programs, 3670
teacher's role to translate moral ideology,
3669
definitions, 3664–3665
effective pedagogical approaches, 3666
fabrication, 3665
hidden curriculum, 3669
inadvertent/unconscious plagiarism, 3665
paraphrasing plagiarism, 3665
ProQuest Platinum database, 3665–3666
Planetarium, 3238
Planned-situational interactive IR model,
2247–2248, 4881–4883
Planning and Budget Assembly (PBA), 72
Planning, organizing, staffing, directing, coordinating, reporting, and budgeting
(POSDCORB), 3511
Planographic printing, 1868
Plaquette binding, 551
Platform for Internet content selection (PICS),
783, 1393
PLATO, 1029
The Pleasant Art of Money Catching, 1400
PLOS ALM Reports, 47
Plum Analytics, 45
Pluralism, 3811–3812
PMEST
energy, space, and time, 2135–2136
matter, 2132–2133
personality, 2131–2132
PNG format, 1311
POD, *see* Print-on-demand
Poetry, 861–862
Poland
archives, 3685–3687
historical background, 3674–3676
library legislation, 3676–3677
map of, 3675
museums, 3685
national bibliography
Bibliografia Wydawnictw Ciągłych,
3683
Bibliografia Zawartości Czasopism,
3683
digital libraries, 3683–3684
librarians and libraries, organizations support to, 3684–3685

Polonica Zagraniczne. Bibliografia, 3683
professional education and training, librar-
ians, 3684
Przewodnik Bibliograficzny, 3682–3683
public libraries, 3677–3678
research libraries
National Library, 3679–3682
NUKAT, 3679
school libraries, 3678
Policy and Standards Division (PSD),
2858–2859
Policy on Loyalty Programs, 2392–2393
Polish ISKO Chapter, 2497
Political Arithmetic, 1402
Political ideologies, 4404–4405
Politics, 644
Politische Discurs, 1401
Politische Geographie, 1687
Polo, Marco, 1684
Polyphonic music, 3267–3268, 3272
Polysemy, 2689
Pompidou Center, 1597
Poor's Manual of Railroads, 1404
Popper, Karl, 2055–2056
Population ecology, 3514
Portable document format (PDF), 1367, 2342
Portico, 1213
Positional formats, 1177
Positive feedback, 1036
Positivism, 3628–3629
Post-cancellation access (PCA), 1335
Postcoordinate indexing, 1985
Poughkeepsie principles, 4565–4566
Power law, 1040–1041
Poznan Foundation of Scientific Libraries, 2828
Practical working ethics, 1473
Practice materials, 2739
Pragmatism, 2613
Prairienet, 1030
Pratt, Allan, 2052
Pratt–Smoot Act, 563, 3576
Precision (P), 3945
Precoordinated index, 1985
Preferential attachment, 1041
Pre-Hellenic mathematics, 3020
Preliterate society, 3831–3832
PrepComs, 5012–5013
Presentational markup, 3073
Preservation, 2468
of audiovisual material
analog audio and videotape materials,
1568–1572
digital formats, 1571
film, 1567–1568, 2465, 2467
funding, 1578–1579
sound and audiovisual collections, 2413, 2416
UNESCO, 4660–4661
Preservation and Conservation (PAC), 2457
Preservation and Reformatting Section (PARS),
329
Preservation Description Information (PDI),
1366
Preservation Metadata: Implementation Strategies (PREMIS), 1366, 1575
Preserved context indexing system (PRECIS),
3137
Preserving Digital Information (PDI), 3484

Presidential libraries
  history
    Archivist report, 3715
    Claypoole, Richard, 3715
    Clinton Presidential Project, 3715
    Eisenhower Library, 3715
    George H.W. Bush Library, 3715
    Hoover, 3714
    John F. Kennedy Library, 3715
    Johnson, Lyndon B., 3715
    Lyndon Baines Johnson Foundation, 3715
    NARA, 3715
    public–private partnership, 3715
    Roosevelt, Franklin D., 3714
    Truman Grants program, 3714
  list, 3717–3718
  presidential materials
    audiovisual and photographic record, 3716
    Clinton Presidential Materials Project, 3716
    economic indicators and project, 3717
    The Foreign Gifts and Decorations Act, 3716
    library websites, 3717
    National Archives, 3716
    National Study Commission report, 3716
    Nixon Presidential Materials Staff, 3716
    personal papers and historical materials, 3716
    presidential papers, 3715
    PRMPA, 3716
    selective donation and selective destruction, 3716
  public and educational programs, 3717
Presidential Libraries Act of 1955, 3714–3715
Presidential Recordings and Materials Preservation Act (PRMPA), 3716
Presidential Records Act, 3716
Pressure ethics, 1473
Presumed credibility, 1115
Pretty Good Privacy (PGP), 404
Preventive censorship, 3676
Primary mathematics literature
  biological and behavioral sciences, 3025
  book series, 3027–3028
  journals, 3026–3027
  nonserial book, 3025
  publishers, 3026
Primary records
  card catalogs, conversions of, 3722
  definition, 3719–3721
  electronic forms, 3721
  survival and accessibility of
    artifacts, preservation of, 3728–3730
    collection-based institution, 3727
    dematerialization of information, 3726
    ownership and access, 3726
    paper facsimiles, 3727
    physical presentation of verbal texts, 3730
    primary texts, 3726
    print products, 3726
    rare books, 3726
    storage, conservation and preservation, 3727
  uses of, 3722–3725
Primos Library in Secane, Philadelphia, 1638
Principal component analysis (PCA), 3272
Principle of cumulative advantage, 4199

Print DDA programs, 1211–1212
Print disabilities, 3574
Printing
  in China, 1865
  histories, 1861
  intaglio, 1867–1868
  modern techniques, 1868
  planographic, 1868
  relief, 1865–1867
Printing Act of 1895, 2150
Printing press, 999, 3606
Print-on-demand (POD), 3736–3737, 3986, 4055–4056
  authors, opportunities for, 3736
  book publishing, impacts on, 3733–3734
    commercial and vanity publishers, 3735
    long tail, 3734
    nontraditional and traditional publishing, 3734–3735
    ODB, 3735
    suppliers, growth in, 3735
  book retailers, 3736
  digital printing
    art reproductions and artist books, 3736
    digital image, 3733, 3735
    vs. offset printing, 3733
  music publishing, 3736
Prison librarians, 3415
Pritchard, Alan, 497–499, 506
Privacy Act of 1974, 1857, 2151
Privacy Act of 1976, 1555
Privacy vs. information sharing, 2398–2399
Private bureaucracy, 2256
Private libraries, 748
  America, 1839
  Croatia, 1123
  Mexican libraries, 3091
  Peru, 3606
  Poland, 3674
  Saudi Arabia, 3973–3974
  Ukraine, 4642
Private press
  aristocratic plaything, 3739–3740
  author, 3740–3741
  bibliography, 3743
  clandestine, 3741
  educational press, 3739
  fine books, 3741–3742
  little, 3743
  origins, 3738
  quasi-official press, 3738–3739
  scholarly presses, 3739
Private presses, 4337
Probabilistic models, 422–423
Probabilistic Relational Models (PRM), 274
Probability, theory of, 494–496
Probate records, 1658
Problem, intervention, comparison, and outcome (PICO), 1517
Problem-solving model, 2088–2089
Procedural and descriptive markup, 4560
Procedural knowledge, 3535
Procedural markup, 3074
Proceedings of Symposia in Pure Mathematics, 3028
Proceedings of the American Mathematical Society, 3027

Proceedings of the National Academy of Sciences (PNAS), 3469
Proceedings of the Steklov Institute of Mathematics in the Academy of Sciences of the USSR, 3028
Process-based retention schedules, see Large aggregation retention schedules
Process knowledge, 3535
Process quality management, 1178
Producer–Archive Interface Methodology Abstract Standard (PAIMAS), 3485
Producer–Archive Interface Specification (PAIS), 3485
Product catalogs, 639
Professional associations, 303, 3377
Professional conference organizer (PCO), 2453
Professional machine bureaucracies, 3512
Professional metadata creators, 3066
Professional recognition, MLA, 3036
Professional Records and Information Management, International Association (PRISM), 1853
Professional registration, 3377
Program for Cooperative Cataloging (PCC), 454, 2871, 3395
Program for Museum Development in Africa (PMDA), see Centre for Heritage Development in Africa
Programme on Information and Communication Technologies (PICT), 2255
Progression of actions lifecycle model, 168
Prolegomena to Library Classification, 1534
PROLOG, 272
Promotion and Identification of Emerging Advanced Telecommunications Services (PISTA), 4322
Property rights, 2277
Prophetic Shrine Library, 3976
Propositional knowledge
  belief
    dispositional view, 2610
    state-object view, 2610–2611
  justification
    adequate indication, 2613
    contextualism, 2615–2616
    epistemic coherentism, 2614
    epistemic foundationalism, 2614–2615
    fallibilism, 2613
    inductive justification, 2613–2614
    inferential justification, 2614
    modest foundationalism, 2615
    radical foundationalism, 2615
  vs. non-propositional knowledge, 2610
  truth, 2611–2612
    coherence, 2612–2613
    correspondence, 2612
    pragmatic value, 2613
Propositions, 592–593
ProQuest Coutts Award for Innovation, 332
ProQuest Ebooks, 1211
Prospectus d'un nouveau dictionnaire de commerce, 1403
Protein Data Bank, 836
Prototypical task, 4555
Provenance, 116
Provenance information, 1364

Provenance of archival materials
definition, 3746
historic developments, 3750
modern thinking
archivalterity, 3753
archivist, role of, 3752
authority control, creation of, 3751
computer retrieval systems, 3750–3751
corporate and personal provenance, 3752
creator context, 3752
custodial context, 3752
electronic records, 3751
ISAAR (CPF), 3751
original order, 3752–3753
physical and theoretical organization of
records, 3751
provenance information, 3751
record-keeping context, 3752
secondary provenance, 3752
societal provenance, 3752
origins and development
archive group, 3748
in Australia, 3749–3750
in Canada, 3749
diplomatic manuals, 3747–3748
organization and functions, 3748
original order, 3748–3749, 3753
record group, 3749
respect des fonds, 3747–3749
subject classification, 3747
title deeds, arrangement of, 3747
Provenance of museum objects
custodial paths
art, 3757
interest in provenance, 3758–3759
ownership/possession, 3756–3757
rightful, clear and good title, 3757–3758
definition, 3756
museum policies, 3759
museum practices, 3759–3760
museum standards, 3760–3761
tempered sharing, 3762–3763
time, diligence and care
ascertaining provenance, 3761
finding favored sources, 3761–3762
Provenance of rare books
book history, 3772
cataloging provenance information, 3770–
3771
definition, 3766–3767
early printed books, 3767
external evidence
auctions and dealers' sales catalog, 3770
inventories and library catalogs, 3769–
3770
internal evidence
bindings, 3768–3769
bookplates, 3768
conservation science, 3769
heraldry, 3768
inscriptions, 3768
library marks and stamps, 3768
physical features and formats, 3767–3768
legal implications, 3771–3772
modern editions, 3767
uses and value of, 3770
Provenance Online Project (POP), 3771

Provincial and Territorial Public Library Coun-
cil (PTPLC), 665
Pseudonyms, 3289–3291
Psycho-Biology of Language, 502
Psychographics, 3168–3169
Ptolemy, 1684
Public Access to Court Electronic Records
(PACER), 1554
Public Affairs Information Service (PAIS), 4370
Public Archives Act of 1965, 2594, 2600
Public Archives of Canada, 3749
Public art librarians, 251–252
Publication-quality photography, 3206
Public bureaucracy, 2256
Public Company Accounting Oversight Board
(PCAOB), 639
Public entrepreneurs, 3517
Public institutions of higher education (IPES),
607
Public international law, 2735
Public Knowledge Project (PKP), 2902, 3468
Public Lending Right Commission, 683
Public Lending Right Remuneration, 1218
Public librarians, 3416
Public librarianship
certification, 3777
community-based, 3776–3777
education, 3777
human rights, 3777–3778
immigrants, 3779
people with disabilities, 3778
privacy, 3778–3779
ranges, 3779
United States, 3774–3776
working conditions, 3777
Public libraries
acquisitions units, organization of, 2919
adults, 3786
Armenia, 230
in Australia, 382–383
children, 3784–3785
children, services to, 877–878
in China
autonomous regions/provincial libraries,
898
municipal public libraries, 898
Shanghai Library, 898–900
township and village libraries, 898
in Croatia, 1123, 1125–1126
in Denmark
Aarhus State and University Library,
1216–1217
budget for, 1220–1221
Danish National Gallery, 1215
digital service, 1220
interlibrary loans, 1220
interwar and postwar periods, 1216
legislation, 1218
librarian training course, 1216
merging, 1220
OPAC, 1216
outreach library service, 1220
Royal Library in Copenhagen, 1216–1217
State Inspectorate of Public Libraries, 1216
twentieth century, 1216, 1218
Web-based National Union Catalog, 1216
diverse populations, 3787

elements, 3784–3792
Ethiopia, 1498
in France, 1601–1602, 1837
games and gaming, 1638
in Germany, 1696–1697, 1837
Greece, 1730
human resources, 3788–3789
Hungary, 1923
Israel, 2542
Arab sector, 2548
budgetary allocation, 2546
Center for Libraries, 2546–2547
collections, 2545
Department of Libraries, 2545
Libraries Law, 2545
nonbook collections, 2545–2546
users, 2545
Japan, 2563–2564
Kazakhstan, 2581–2582
Kenya, 2595
Latinos, 2700–2701
legal and financial framework, 3783–3784
legislation, 3783–3784
Lithuania, 2948–2951
marketing, 3789–3790
measurement and evaluation, 3792,
3794–3795
Mexican libraries, 3086–3089
in Moldova, 3123–3124
music libraries, 3276
newcomers, 3786–3787
performance measurement, 3792, 3794
in Peru, 3606–3608
Poland, 3677–3678
in pre-Christian era, 1836
purposes, 3781–3783
rare book collections, 3822
resource collections, 3787–3788
in Rome, 1836
in Saudi Arabia, 3974–3976
science and engineering librarians, 4009
Senegal, 4106–4107
in Serbia, 4129
service responses, 3783
in sixth century B.C., 1836
Slovakia, 4178–4179
South Korea, 4311
trends and challenges, 3795–3797
Tunisia, 4629
in Ukraine, 4642, 4644
unions (see Unions)
in United Kingdom, 4701–4703
authorities, populations of, 1839
Chetham Library in Manchester, 1837
combined museums and libraries,
1837–1838
County Library Authority, 1839
CUKT, 1839
gifts of individuals, 1836
itinerating libraries, 1837
Local Government Act of 1972, 1839
Museums Act of 1845, 1837
parish libraries, 1837
public and joint-stock contribution, 1836
Public Library Acts, 1838
social library, 1837
town libraries, 1836–1837

in United States (*see* United States, public
    libraries)
urban libraries, 1848
users needs, 3784
value, 3794–3795
Venezuelan libraries, 4890
Public Libraries and Museums Act 1964, 4720
Public Library Act of 1919, 1839
Public Library Association (PLA), 74–75, 335,
    3783
  ALA, 3801
  CPLA program, 3804
  eight special-interest sections, 3801
  grant projects, 3804
  mangement, publications, 3803
  member-driven organization, 3801
  membership, 3802
  National Conference, 3804
  new clusters, 3802
  organization, 3802–3803
  preconferences and workshops, 3803
  presidents, 3805
  priority concerns, 3802
  Public Libraries magazine, 3803
  Public Library Data Service, 3803
The Public Library Inquiry, 2769–2770,
    3775–3776
Public Library Manifesto, 3774
Public Library Movement, 888
Public Library of Science (PLoS), 557,
    3468–3469
*Public Library Service: A Guide to Evaluation
    with Minimum Standards*, 1846
Public machine bureaucracies, 3512
Public metadata creators, 3067
Public museums
  Milwaukee Public Museum, 3164
  in Moldova, 3121
  purpose-designed public museum, 3150
  in United Kingdom, 4716
Public Participation GIS (PPGIS), 1672–1673
Public patent databases on Internet
  CIPO, 3568
  EPO, 3569
  FreePatentsOnline, 3570
  Google Patents, 3570
  JPO, 3569–3570
  Patent Lens, 3570–3751
  proliferation, 3567
  USPTO, 3568–3569
  WIPO, 3570
Public policy advocacy, 347
Public portals, 2893
Public Record Office (PRO), 108
Public Record Office (PRO) Act 1838,
    4732–4733
Public Record Office of Great Britain, 1792
Public Record Office of Northern Ireland
    (PRONI), 4734
Public Records Act, 183, 2012, 4733–4734
Public Relations and Marketing (PRMS), 2842
Public services, academic libraries, 4–5, 7–8
Public service special collections professionals,
    4349
Published informational content, 1274
Publishing histories, 1861
PubMed, 819, 1878

PubMed Central® (PMC), 3338
PubMed database, 1765, 1767
PubScience, 1555
Pugillares, 542
Punctuational markup, 3073
Pura Belpre Award, 334
Purdue University Research Repository
    (PURR), 2902
Pythagorean theorem, 3020
Python spatial analysis library (PySal), 1676

Q

Qayrawan Grand Mosque, 4626
Quai Branly Museum, 1596–1597
QuakeNet, 1049
Qualified Dublin Core (DCQ), 1366
Qualisigns, 4098
Qualitative research, 3807–3810
  methods and tools, 3813–3816
  principles, 3810–3813
  semiotics, 3816
Quality improvement, 568, 1179–1180, 1517,
    1874, 1889
Quality of service (QoS), 1056
Quality Oversight Organizations (QOO), 1889
Quantitative models, 1192–1193
Quantitative structure-activity relationships
    (QSAR), 836
Quarterly of Applied Mathematics, 3027
Quasi nongovernmental organization
    (QUANGO), 3380
Quasi-official press, 3738–3739
Queensland Art Gallery, 389
Queen Sofia Center of Art National Museum,
    4332
Query languages, 1366–1367, 1621–1622
Questia service, 985
Question-answering, NLP, 3353
Question-answering (QA) systems, 1903, 4574
Questionnaires, 4530–4531, 4798–4799
QuestionPoint, 3398–3399
Quetelet, Adolph, 495

R

Radio, 1572–1573
Radio broadcast libraries, 3277
Radio Corporation of America (RCA), 1015
Radio frequency identification (RFID), 921,
    2924
Radio stations, 998–999
Raisig, L. Miles, 496, 498
Rajput School of painting, 1957
Randomized controlled trials (RCTs), 1519
Random network, 1039
Random variables, information theory
  mutual information, 2351–2353
  unpredictability, 2350
  varying probabilities and entropy measure,
    2351
Ranganathan, S.R., 1534, 1536
Ranked half-life (RHL), 1902
Rapid automatized naming (RAN), 3842, 3845
Rare book collections, 3726
  access points, 3825–3826
  colleges and universities, 3822

deaccessioning, 3825
  determination of, 3821–3822
  digitization, 3828
  donations, 3822–3823
  environmental issues, 3826
  exhibitions, 3828
  growth of
    gifts, 3824
    purchase of materials, 3823–3824
    transfers, 3824–3825
  independent rare book libraries, 3822
  institutional support, 3827–3828
  librarians, responsibilities of, 3823
  national libraries, 3822
  origins of, 3820
  public libraries, 3822
  public/quasi-public collections, 3823
  restrictions, 3823
  security, 3826–3827
Rare Books and Manuscripts Librarianship
    (RBML), 355
Rare Books and Manuscripts Section (RBMS),
    4336, 4338, 4344
Rare books, provenance of, *see* Provenance of
    rare books
Rare manuscript libraries, United Kingdom,
    4738
RASKE modeling, 3109
Raster images, 1308
Rathgen, Friedrich, 1069
Rationalism, 3625–3626
Ratzel, Friedrich, 1687
RDA, *see* Resource, Description and Access
RDF, *see* Resource Description Framework
rdfs:label property, 3964
rdfs:seeAlso property, 3964
Reaction searching, 825–826
Reactive strategies, 2241
A Reader in Art Librarianship, 249
ReaderMeter, 47
Readers' advisory, 3914
Readex United Nations Documents Collections,
    1724
Reading disorders
  adults, 3843
  causes of
    genetic factors, 3846
    language processes, 3845
    linguistic coding, 3844
    memory, 3845
    naming speed, 3845
    neurological basis, 3845–3846
    phonological coding, 3844
    semantic coding, 3844
    syntactic coding, 3844
    visual coding, 3844
    word recognition, 3844
  difficulties, 3841
  historical trends, 3842
  impairments, 3841
  intrinsic disorders, 3841
  learning disabilities, 3843–3844
  scientifically based interventions, 3846–3848
  subgroups of, 3842–3843
Reading interests
  advisory and appeal factors, 3857
  boredom, 3854–3855

Reading interests (cont'd.)
  comprehension, 3854–3855
  engagement, 3854–3855
  genres, 3856–3857
  high and low, 3855–3856
  intrinsic motivation, 3851
  research approaches
    bestseller lists and circulation statistics,
      3851
    "a central core/radix," 3853
    ethnographic research, 3852
    formats, 3854
    knowledge-based society, 3852
    large scale questionnaires, 3851
    marginalia, 3851–3852
    popular literary genres, 3853
    questionnaire/checklist, 3853
  voluntary reading, 3850
Reading rooms, 1123
Reading, sociology of
  bad reading, marginal readers, 4279–4280
  creative activity, 4281
  in developed countries, 4281–4283
  dominant readers/dominated reader, 4281
  emancipation, 4284
  history, 4280
  Internet, impact of, 4283–4284
  literary canon, 4283
  social issues, 4280–4281
  young people, 4283
Read_Me 1.2 software art festival, 2071
Ready reference, 3914
Realistic fiction
  contemporary fiction, 864–865
  historical fiction, 865
Realizers, 432
Really simple syndication (RSS), 637,
    1045, 2221, 2894, 3227, 3796, 4780,
    5020
Real-time Observatories, Applications, and
    Data management Network (ROADNet),
    2998
Real-time supervisory control (RTSC) work,
    3359–3362
Reasonable tendency test, 1015
Reaxys database, 821
Recall and precision
  cost factor, 3708–3709
  estimating method, 3711
  requirements, 3711–3712
  scatter diagram, 3709–3710
  table, 3709–3710, 3712
Recherche thematique pluridisciplinaire (RTP-
    doc), 1378
Recommender systems
  challenges, 3863
  collaborative systems, 3861–3862
  content-based systems, 3862–3863
  Internet, 3860–3861
  research, 3863–3864
RECON, see Retrospective conversion
Record (in)accuracy, 1176
Recorded information, 2058
Record group traditions, 118
Recording Industry Association of America
    (RIAA), 3281
Recordkeeping metadata models, 122–124

Records
  access
    access management systems, 3890
    electronic records, 3891
    physical records, 3890–3891
    security, and privacy, 3890
    tracking process, 3889
  attributes, 167–168
  business transaction, 3887
  definition, 167, 3887
  filing and arrangement, 3889
  lifecycle, 168–169
  organization, 3888
  series
    classification, 3888–3889
    indexing, 3889
    unit, 3888
Records and Archives Management Department
    (RAMD), 4508
Records and Archives Management Program
    (RAMP), 2438, 4659
Records and information management (RIM),
    221, 1857–1858
  archives management, 1850
  correspondence management, 1850
  electronic records keeping, 1851
  Federal Records Act of 1950, 1851
  filing and indexing system, 1850
  forms/reports management, 1850
  Hoover Commission Paperwork Task Force,
    1851
  ICA, 1856–1857
  image management, 1850
  information technology, 1850
  international standard, 1857
  Leahy, Emmett, 1851–1853
  literature, 1855–1856
  microfilm, application of, 1851
  NARS, 1851
  NFPA, 1853
  PRISM, 1853
  professional organization growth, 1853–1854
  professional status, 1855
  promotional programs, 1853
  records centers, 1850
  records protection, 1850
  retention scheduling, 1850
  training, 1854–1855
Records compliance
  accountability factors, 3870
  compliance requirements, 3870
  effective audit procedures, 3870
  and risk management
    AS-4390, 3871
    cost/benefit analysis, 3872
    qualitative approach, 3870
    quantitative approach, 3870
    records retention policy, 3871
    risk analysis, 3870
Records continuum model, 169
  archival framework, 3874
  Australia
    archival documents, 3875
    authenticity and reliability issues, 3876
    CRS system, 3876
    evidence-based decision making and public
      accountability, 3876

    Maclean's proto-continuum implementa-
      tion model, 3876
    reconstructible relationships, 3876
    recordkeeping-accountability nexus, 3875
    registry systems, 3877
  dimensions of, 3878–3879
  philosophical and sociological discourses,
    3880–3881
  points in, 3878–3880
  research instrument, 3882
  reshaping professional practice, 3882–3883
  seminal model form, 3877
  teaching tool, 3882
  transactionality, 3877
  uses of, 3881–3882
Records Disposal Act in 1962, 2600
Records inventory, 3895
Records management (RM), 715, 2108, 2490,
    4792–4793
  associated with risk, 716
  compliance requirements, 3870
  definition, 3869
  diversity, 716
  document/content management, 718–719
  education, 719–720
  historical and modern documents, 3869
  history of, 720–721
  information technology, 716–717
  litigation, 717–718
  purpose, 3869
  records retention audits, 3870
  titles, 719
Records Management Association of Australia
    (RMAA), 174, 388, 1856
Records Management Journal, 1856
Records management programs (RMP)
  corporations (*see* Corporate records manage-
    ment programs)
  establishment and administrative location,
    4390–4391
  NARA, 4746
  records retention, 3892
Records Management Society, 4739
  of Japan, 2570
  United Kingdom, 4739
Records retention schedule
  corporate culture, 3892
  definition, 3892
  development
    data collection types, 3895
    implementation, 3896
    inventory process, 3895
    legal research, 3895
    maintenance, 3896
    records inventory, 3895
    review and approval, 3895
    strategy, 3895
  dispositioning, 3892
  purpose, 3892–3893
  records series, 3892
  retention period, 3892, 3894–3895
  types
    departmental retention schedules, 3893
    functional retention schedules, 3893
    large aggregation retention schedules,
      3893–3894
Records Review, 1856

Recurrent networks (RANN), 285–287
Recursive auto associative memories (RAAM), 284
Redarte-SP (Sao Paulo, Brazil), 256
Red de Bibliotecas Universitarias (REBIUN), 4316, 4320–4321
Red Universitaria Española de Catálogs Absys (RUECA), 4316
Redwood Library, 1841
Reference and Adult Services Division (RASD), *see* Reference and User Services Association
Reference and informational genres
    almanacs, 3898
    atlases, 3898
    bibliographies, 3898
    biological sciences, 3901
    canonical texts, 3900
    catalogs, 3898
    chronologies, 3898
    concordances, 3898
    DDC, 3903, 3905
    dictionaries, 3898
    directories, 3898–3899
    document types, 3906
    encyclopedias, 3899
    formats, 3901
    gazetteers, 3899
    handbooks and manuals, 3899
    idiosyncratic order, 3900
    "index volume" bibliographies, 3904
    LCC system, 3902, 3904–3905
    Martel's structure, 3902
    monographs, 3904
    multidisciplinary sources of information, 3901
    newsletters, 3899
    personal bibliographies, 3904
    primary literature, 3900
    publication types, 3905–3906
    secondary literature, 3900
    sourcebooks, 3899
    subject bibliographies, 3904–3905
    subject groupings, 3897
    term weighting, 3902
    tertiary literature, 3900
    union lists, 3899
    yearbooks, 3899
Reference and User Services Association (RUSA), 2699, 3913
    award, 3909–3910
    education opportunities, 3910
    guidelines, 3910
    membership, 3908
    name change, 3908
    organization, 3909
    problems and issues, 3910–3911
    publications, 3909
    reference and information professionals, 3908
    2000 ALA midwinter meeting, value statement, 3908
Reference and User Services Quarterly (RUSQ), 3909
Reference desk, 6–7, 3914
Reference information, 1364
Reference interview, 3912
    communication techniques, 3915–3916
    purpose of, 3915

Reference services, 1098
    bibliographic verification, 3914
    changing context of, 3913
    components of, 3912
    definition, 3912
    direct and indirect instruction, 3914
    evaluation, 3917
    history of, 3912–3913
    instruction and guidance, responsibilities for, 3914
    interlibrary loan, 3914
    readers' advisory, 3914
    ready reference, 3914
    reference collection development and maintenance, 3916–3917
    reference desk, 3914
    reference ethics, 3912, 3917
    reference interview, 3912
        communication techniques, 3915–3916
        purpose of, 3915
    reference sources, 3912, 3916
    reference transactions, definition of, 3913–3914
    reference work, definition of, 3914
    research consulting, 3914
    roving method, 3914
    virtual reference, 3915
Reference Services Section (RSS), 3909
Reference tools, 1655–1656, 1659
Reference transactions, 3913–3914
Referential markup, 3074
ReferralWeb, 3866–3867
Reflexive meta-field, 3611
REFORMA, 2699, 2701, 2703
Reformation libraries, 3954–3956
Refreezing process, 2297
Refreshing, *see* Bit preservation
Regimen Sanitatis Salernitanum, 3044
Regional Bell holding companies (RBOCs), 1018, 1020–1021
Regional Library Associations, 4328
Regional library networks (RLNs)
    Alliance of Library Service Networks, 3922
    challenges, 3924
    consortia/consortium, 3920, 3924
    definition, 3920
    educational programs, 3923
    electronic resources, 3923–3924
    federal/state agencies, 3922
    governance, 3922
    history, 3920–3921
    OCLC, 3921–3923
    services, 3923
    support/help desks, 3922
    unique projects, 3924
    web sites of, 3922
Register of Australian Archives and Manuscripts, 388
Register Plus, 3569
Registry systems, 118–119
Rehabilitation Act, 3575
Reiter's pipeline architecture, 431–432
Related term (RT), 1986
Relational databases (RDBs), 4080–4082
Relationship links, 2940
Relative index, 1257, 1262

Relative relevance (RR), 1902
Relativism, 3811–3812
RELAX NG, 1388
Relevance assessment, 1902–1903, 2172, 2174, 3708–3709, 3711, 3944, 3946, 4876, 4880
Relevance feedback, 4420
Relevance judgments, 3941–3944
Relevance measurements, 3944–3947
Relevance theory
    "berrypicking" model of literature retrieval, 3933–3934
    and citation, 3936–3937
    cognitive effects, 3934
    definition, 3926–3927
    degrees of, 3931–3933
    evidentiary relevance, 3931
    historical precedents, 3928–3929
    intermediaries and disintermediation, 3928
    intersubjective agreement, 3935
    IR evaluation tests, 3934
    literature-based systems, 3927
    objectifying subjectivity, 3935–3936
    "objective system relevance," 3933
    question relevance, 3931
    systems evaluation, 3929–3931
    topical relevance, 3931
Relief printing, 1865–1867
Religious archives
    Australia, 188–189
    China, 907
    Germany, 1701
    United Kingdom, 4737–4738
Religious publishing, 3987
Religious storytelling, 4443
Renaissance libraries
    France, 3951–3952
    Italy, 3948–3950
    Spain, 3952
    Vatican Library, 3951
Renardus Service, 1262
Renouf Press, 1724
Repertoire Bibliographique Universel (RBU), 1373
Repository-based software engineering (RBSE) spider, 2520
Representational state transfer (REST), 2187, 2347, 2895
Repressive censorship, 3676
Repterorium Bibliographicum, 1968–1969
Republic, 644
Republican Book Museum in Almaty, 2587–2588
Republican Scientific-Medical Library (RSML), 232
Republican Scientific-Technical Library (RNTB), 230, 2582
Republic of Armenia, *see* Armenia
Reputed credibility, 1115
Request-for-proposal (RFP), 607
Research Assessment Exercise (RAE), 2373, 4712–4713
Research data services (RDS), 4015
Research Libraries Group (RLG), 451–452, 2181, 3400–3401
Research Libraries Information Network (RLIN), 450, 476, 2921

Research library
in Arab sector, 2548
in Australia, 384–385
in Germany, 1695–1696
Hungary, 1922
Japan, 2562–2563
in Kazakhstan, 2582
Kenya, 2596
Lithuania, 2951–2953
music libraries, 3275–3276
in Saudi Arabia, 3974
Senegal, 4106
Slovakia, 4178
Research methodology, 2407
Research Papers in Economics (RePEc),
3466
Research Scorecard, 47
Research services, 1098–1099
Research support system (RSS), 2192
Research Teaching and Learning (RTL), 370
Réseau national de santé (RNS), 4631
Residue, 2058
Resolution, digital images, 1309–1310
Resource Definition Framework (RDF), 1366
Resource dependence theory, 3515
Resource, Description and Access (RDA),
137, 453, 726–727, 1982–1983, 2923,
3283
Resource Description Framework (RDF), 1079,
1393, 2524, 2939–2941, 2986,
3067–3068, 3227, 3460–3462,
4082–4084
domain-neutral framework, 3961
FAST authority file, 1539
feature summary
ancillary properties, 3964
classes, 3963
containers and collections, 3963–3964
properties, 3963
reification, 3964
history, 3966
MCF, 3967
OWL, 3961
PICS, 3966–3967
semantics, 3965–3966
Semantic Web, 3961
1999 specifications, 3967
syntax, 3965
triple model, 3961–3962
vs. XML, 3962–363
Resources and Technical Services Division
(RTSD), 2966
Resource sharing
ARL, 373–374
Canada, 671
CRL, 766
hospital librarians, 1885
PIALA, 3547
Respect des fonds, 116, 170, 1425, 3301,
3746–3749, 4793
Response to intervention (RTI), 3843
Respublicae Elzevirianae, 494
Restatements, 2741
Retention period
based on event, 3894
definition, 3892
finite time period, 3894

in lower-cost storage area, 3895
Personnel Files, 3894–3895
termination, 3895
total retention time, 3895
in working environment, 3895
Retrieval status value (RSV), 1620, 1622, 1627,
1634
Retrieval subsystem, 2195
Retrieval task, 4555
Retrospective conversion (RECON)
automatic identification, 2968
format recognition process, 2968
initial conversion method, 2967
large-scale centralized conversion, 2967
NCLIS, 2970
pilot project, 2967–2968
record types, 2970
reverse chronological order, 2967
special studies, 2969
task force, 2967–2970
Return on investment (ROI), 1083, 3795
Reuther Library, 4761
Revised Braille code, 563
Revyu.com, 4088
RFID, *see* Radio-frequency identification
RGS, *see* Rhetorical genre studies
Rheingold's online/phone based communities,
1028
Rhetorical genre studies (RGS)
Bakhtin communication, 1663–1664
Bakhtin's insights, 1664
Bitzer's notion of "exigence," 1663
deliberative performances, 1662
epideictic speeches, 1662
forensic discourse, 1662
Miller's insights, 1663
pragmatic function, 1663
reconceptualization, 1663
renovation source, 1663
speech genre, 1663–1664
utterance, 1663–1664
Rhetorical Structure Theory (RST), 436–437
Rhind Papyrus, *see* Ahmes Papyrus
RIAA, 3649, 3651, 3652, 3657, 3660–3661
RIBEAU, 686
Ricardo, David, 647
Rice marbling, 539
Richelieu site, 532, 534
Rich-get-richer models, 2372
Rieh's Model of Judgment of Information Qual-
ity and Cognitive Authority, 1117
Riga Peace Treaty, 3675
RIM, *see* Records and information management
Ringo recommender system, 3864
Risk management and records compliance
AS-4390, 3871
cost/benefit analysis, 3872
qualitative approach, 3870
quantitative approach, 3870
records retention policy, 3871
risk analysis, 3870
Ritter, Karl, 1686
RLNs, *see* Regional library networks
Robert F. Sibert Informational Book Medal, 334
Roberts Commission, 3217
Robertson–Sparck Jones weights, 2206, 2208
Robotics, 275

Robots, 2518–2519
Robust networks, 4242
Rochester Institute of Technology (RIT), 1183
Rockefeller Family Foundations, 3216
Rockefeller Foundation, 77
Rockefeller Museum, 2550
Rocky Mountain Mathematical Journal, 3027
Rogers' S-Curve, 2292, 2298
Role-based access control (RBAC), 406
Role modeling, 3113
Romance, 3703–3704
Romanesque bindings, 542–543
Roman Virgil, 1946
Rosenberg, Gustav, 1069
Rose Robischon Scholarship Award, NASIG,
3390
Rostock Public Library, 1792
Round Table of Art Librarians, 249
R-O-U-N-D, wayfinding processes, 4959
Rousseau, Jean Jacques, 1685
Routine knowledge assets, 2622
Rowan Public Library, 1649
Royal Academy of Painting, 1594
Royal Air Force Museum, 4719
Royal Art Museum, 1215
Royal Botanic Gardens, Kew, 4333, 4725
Royal Charter, 655
Royal Library in Copenhagen, 1216–1217, 1219
Royal Library of Alexandria, 2762
Royal Library School, 1216
Royal Museum, Brazil, 612–613
Royal National Park, 391–392
Royal Ontario Museum (ROM), 3689
Rubin Museum, 2551
Rule interchange format (RIF), 4082
Rules for a Dictionary Catalog, 4468
Rules for a Printed Dictionary Catalog, 2920
Rules for Archival Description (RAD), 670
Rules for the Compilation of the Catalogue,
2920
"Rules of reading," 3855
Rural Free Delivery (RFD) Program, 1011
Rural knowledge centers (RKC), 2132–2133
RUSA, *see* Reference and User Services
Association
Russell's epistemology, 1456
Russell's sensemaking, 4113
Russian Geographical Society (RGS), 1780
Russian Information Library Consortium
(RILC), 2823
Russian State Library, 3326–3327
RxNorm, 4678

S

Sacred: Discover what we share, 624
Safe Harbor framework, 2143
Safety data sheets (SDS), 820
Salt Lake City new central library, 3793
Salton model, 2229–2230
Salton's SMART system, 2204
Sampson's writing systems, 3832
San Diego Supercomputer Center (SDSC), 3000
San Francisco Museum of Modern Art, 3218
San Francisco Public Library, 3729
Santa Monica's Public Electronic Network,
1028

Saracevic's stratified interaction model, 2247, 4875

Sarbanes-Oxley Act, 639, 1106, 1362, 1370, 1858

Saskatchewan Archives Act (1945), 658

Saudi Arabia
adult literacy rate, 3970
archives and archival institutions, 3978–3979
average temperature and rainfall, 3970
development plans, 3979–3980
history of, 3970–3971
libraries
academic and research libraries, 3974
AFLI, 3978
in Arabic and Islamic culture, 3971–3972
Arabic Union Catalog, 3978
education and training, 3977–3978
King Abd al-Aziz Public Library in Riyadh, 3974
King Fahd National Library, 3973–3974
planning/legislation, 3972–3973
public libraries, 3974–3976
school libraries, 3976
special libraries, 3976–3977
special library association, Gulf chapter of, 3978
Makkah and Madinah, 3970
map of, 3970–3971
museums, 3979–3980
religion, 3970

Saudi Arabian Center for Science and Technology (SANCST), 2312

Saussurean model, 4098, 4101

Savolainen's ELIS model, 2087–2088, 2118–2119

SavvySearch, 2523

Say, Jean-Baptiste, 647

Scaffold hopping, 835

Scale-free networks, 1040–1041

Scandinavian bookbinding, 548

Scene-level indexing, 3131

Schellenberg's seminal approach, 2380

Schlagwortnormdatei (SWD), 1261

Scholar, 3471

Scholarly and trade publishing, *see* Book and journal publishing trade

Scholarly communication
European Commission, 2824
webometrics
AltaVista, 4986
journals, 4984
link creation motiation, 4986
log analysis, 4984–4985
people, 4985
small world analysis, 4986
universities, 4985–4986
visualization, 4986–4987

Scholarly Communications Committee, 345

Scholarly presses, 3739, 3742

Scholarly publishing, 4512–4513

Scholarly Publishing and Academic Resources Coalition (SPARC), 345, 367, 2906, 3645, 4014

Scholarly treatises, 2739

Scholasticism, 4095

School librarianship
functions and skills, 3994–3998
global community, 3998–3999

history, 3991
preparation, 3992–3994

School libraries, 2764
advocacy, 4003
in Arab sector, 2548–2549
Armenia, 230
in Australia, 383
in China, 900
in Croatia, 1126
in Denmark, 1220–1221
education theory and practice, 4002
effectiveness, 4004–4005
Ethiopia, 1499
expansion, 4000
in France, 1601–1602
games and gaming, 1638–1639
in Germany, 1698
Greece, 1730–1731
Hungary, 1923
international perspective, 4005–4006
in Israel, 2543, 2547
Japan, 2564–2565
in Kazakhstan, 2583
Kenya, 2597
Latinos, 2701
Lithuania, 2951
OPLs, 3416
in Peru, 3608
Poland, 3678
public libraries, 4003–4004
in Saudi Arabia, 3976
Senegal, 4107
in Serbia, 4131–4132
South Korea, 4311
standards and guidelines, 4001–4002
technology, 4003
Tunisia, 4630–4631
in United Kingdom, 4705–4706
virtual school library, 4005

School Libraries Worldwide (journal), 4006

School Library Association (SLA), 4706

School Library Association of New Zealand (SLANZA), 3377

School Library Media Research, 61

School of Conservation, 1227

School of Industrial Arts, 3253

School of Information Science (SISA), 1499

School of Library, Archive, and Information Studies (SLAIS), 4738

School of Salerno, 3044–3045

School of the Louvre, 1598

Schools of business, 650

Science and engineering librarianship
continuing education, 4011
job requirements
education, 4010
skills, 4010–4011
need for, 4008
professional organizations, 4016–4017
professional responsibilities
citizen science, 4015
collections, 4012
conference proceedings, 4013
data-management plans and RDS, 4015
data sets, 4013
e-Science, 4015
handbooks and data sources, 4013

instruction, 4012
makerspaces, 4015
management, marketing and promotion, 4013–4014
maps, 4013
open access, 4014–4015
patents, 4013
preprints and e-prints, 4013
reference and consultation, 4011–4012
research and writing, 4014
scholarly communication, 4014
technical reports, 4013
translations, 4013
Web technologies, 4014
recruitment, 4011
science and engineering library settings, 4008–4009
academic, 4009
corporate organizations, 4009
government, 4009
medical libraries, 4010
museums, aquariums, and zoos, 4010
national libraries, 4009–4010
public, 4009
solo, 4010

Science and natural history museums
Croatia, 1129
Germany, 1704–1705
Hungary, 1929
India, 2020–2022
Switzerland, 4495

Science and Technology Act (Chapter 250), 2594

Science and Technology Museum, 4135

Science and Technology Museum Association of Serbia, 4135

Science and technology studies (STS)
ALA, 4016
ANT, 4022–4023
empirical programme of relativism, 4020–4021
gender and technology studies, 4024–4025
heterogeneous engineering, 4021
practice theory, 4025–4026
SCOT, 4024
social shaping of, 4021–4022
technological determinism, 4021
technology and information science theories, 4020
workplace studies, 4026

Science centers, 3237

Science citation index (SCI), 503, 522, 925, 942, 2227, 2370, 3471, 3640, 4198

Science library, 4009–4010

Science museums
gallery interpreters, 4952
Hungary, 1929
in Israel, 2552
in Serbia, 4134–4135

Science, technology, and health care archives
Alan Mason Chesney Medical Archives, 4761–4762
California Academy of Science, 4762
California Institute of Technology, 4762
Charles Babbage Center, 4762
Claude Moore Library, 4762
David Sarnoff Library, 4762

Science, technology, and health care archives
(cont'd.)
Linda Hall Library, 4762
National Agricultural Library, 4762–4763
National Library of Medicine, 4763
Niels Bohr Library and Archives and Center
for History of Physics, 4763
Scientific Agricultural Library, 4647
Scientific American, 4084–4085
Scientific and technical information (STI), 1433
Scientific communication models, 3637–3638
Scientific computing, 2272
Scientific data collections, 2997–2998
Scientific Electronic Library Online (SciELO),
614
Scientific genealogy, 1645–1646
Scientific genres, 2503
Scientific information system, 1125
Scientific knowledge, 2056
Scientific Medical Library (SML), 3124
Scientific, technical, and medical (STM) pub-
lishing, 1132, 2143, 3983–3984, 3987
Scientometrics journal, 2226, 2367–2368, 4984
Sci2 toolset, 923
SCLOPE, 2634
Scope note (SN), 1986, 2868
Scopus digital service, 2368, 3471
Scorpion software, 1262
Scotland
archives and archival science
archive services, 4735
legislation, 4733–4734
CUKT, 1839
parish libraries, 1837
social library, 1837
town library, 1837
Scott, Alexander, 1069
Scottish Higher Education Funding Council
(SHEFC), 4718
Scoville Memorial Library Association, 1843
Screening search, 832–833
Scriptores Rei Rusticae, 1400
Scrittori classici italiani di economia politica,
1405
Sculptures Collection, 1744
Search aids, 944
Search and retrieval system, 4978–4982
Search and retrieve via URL (SRU) protocol,
1253, 2347, 2671, 2983
CQL, 2189
Editorial Board, 2187
explain operation, 2187–2189
HTTP GET request, 2187–2188
projects and implementations, 2189–2190
REST approach, 2187
searchRetrieve operation, 2187–2189
SOAP, 2187
SRW and, 2187
Search engine marketing (SEM), 4029
Search engine optimization (SEO)
Black Hat *vs.* White Hat, 4031
definition, 4029
higher rankings, 4029–4030
methods
automated search engines *vs.* manually created directories, 4031–4032
content-focused approach, 4033–4034

content, technical, and linking combination, 4037
keywords selection to target, 4033
links, 4035–4037
technical strategy, 4034–4035
Web analytics, 4037
web page elements to be optimized,
4032–4033
Web site and Web page structure, 4037
origins and history, 4030
practitioners
current SEO industry, 4031
early promoters and reporters, 4030–4031
software, 4031
standards and regulation
certification, 4042
government regulation, 4042
HTML, 4041–4042
search engines, 4042
SEO industry, 4042
strategic issues
broad *vs.* narrow targeting and long-tail
terms, 4038
building downwards *vs.* outwards,
4037–4038
geographic targeting, 4039
increased competition, 4039
lead time and longevity, 4038–4039
only index words, 4039
source tracking, 4039
targeting and serendipity balance, 4038
trends
current trends, 4040
fading trends, 4039–4040
mobile communications devices, 4041
new search engine presentation methods,
4040–4041
SMO, 4041
specialized searches, 4041
user behaviors
basic behaviors, 4043
Boolean syntax, 4043
hardened/fixed, 4043
popular topical searches, 4043
search engine loyalty, 4043
SERP links, 4042
variables affecting, 4042–4043
worldwide, 4043
worldwide, 4031
Search engine results page (SERP), 4029–4030,
4042
Search engines
ALIWEB, 2519
AltaVista, 2522
Archie, 2517
Bing, 4051
Boolean logic, 4048
date searching, 4049
definition, 4046
EINet Galaxy, 2520
Excite, 2521
Google, 2523, 4050–4051
Gopher, 2517
identification and gathering of material,
4046–4047
index and indexing program, 4047
indexer, 2519

Infoseek, 2521–2522
Inktomi, 2522
invisible/deep Web, 2524
Jughead, 2518
Jumpstation, 2519
language searching, 4049
link searching, 4049
Lycos, 2521
metasearch engine, 4053
MetaSearchers, 2523
non-U.S. general search engines, 4051–4052
Northern Light, 2522–2523
Open Directory Project, 2524
phrase searching, 4048–4049
portal dilemma, 4048
retrieval and ranking algorithms, 4047
robots, 2518–2519
RSBE, 2520
searching by file type, 4049
search results pages, 4050
specialty search engines, 4052
spider, 2519
students, 4461
syntax, 4048
title searching, 4049
URL, site, and domain searching, 4049
user interface, 4046
Veronica, 2517
visualization engines, 4052–4053
WAIS, 2518
Wanderer, 2519
WebCrawler, 2521
worm, 2519–2520
WWW, 2518
XML, 2524
Yahoo!, 2520–2521, 4051
SearchFAST, 1545
Search moves, 2239–2241
Search/retrieve webservice (SRW), 1253, 2187
Search rule, 2363
Search strategies, 2240–2242
Search tactics, 2239–2241
Search trails, 4878–4879
Sears List of Subject Headings, 1261
Seattle Public Library, 2792, 3791
The Seattle Public Library Central Library:
Economic Benefits Assessment 2007,
3794
Second Historical Archives of China (SHAC),
906–907
Second Life, 1050
Secretariat General of Communication and
Information, 1738
Section elements, 5043
Section of International Organizations (SIO),
2438
Section of Municipal Archives (SMA), 2438
Section of Professional Associations (SPA),
2438
Sectoral standardization, 3107
Secure Digital Music Initiative (SDMI), 1320
Secure Hash Algorithm 1360 (SHA-1360), 1366
Securities Act of 1933, 638
Securities and Exchange Commission (SEC),
638, 1106
Securities Exchange Act of 1934, 638
Sedgwick Museum, 4718

Selected Translations in Mathematical Statistics and Probability, 3028
Select Essays on Husbandry, 1402
Selective dissemination of information (SDI), 1880, 2221
Selective indexing, 5045–5046
Selective information, 2056
Self-censorship, 1014
Self-descriptive data, 2940
Self Generating Master (SELGEM), 3179
Self-organization, *see* Complexity and self-organization
Self-organized maps (SOM), 3272
Self-publishing online
  advantages, 4056–4057
  definition, 4054
  disadvantages, 4057
  future trends, 4058
  libraries and librarians, impact on, 4057–4058
  publishers and publishing services, 4056
  tasks, 4055–4056
  technologies for, 4054–4055
  World Wide Web, 4054
Self-reinforcement, 2096–2097
Semantic-based summarization systems, 424–425
Semantic consistency, 1175
Semantic grids, 3002
Semantic information, 3613
Semantic interoperability
  absolute crosswalking, 4070–4071
  conceptualizing underlying models, 4065–4066
  co-occurrence mapping, 4072
  cross-switching, 4070–4071
  crosswalking services, 4072
  definition, 4062
  different levels, 4065
  different processes, 4064–4065
  dimensions, 4063–4064
  direct mapping, 4070–4071
  HILT, 4074
  KOS, 4066–4067
  localization and expansion
    application profiles, 4068–4069
    core/intermediate ontologies, 4069–4070
    DC metadata element, 4068
    domain ontologies, 4069–4070
    KOS, 4069
    leaf nodes, 4068–4069
    satellite vocabulary development, 4069
    upper ontologies, 4069–4070
  metadata, 4067–4068
  new vocabulary derivation, 4068
  NSDL registry, 4073
  OOR, 4074–4075
  records conversion, 4071
  relative crosswalking, 4071
  semantic conflicts and agreements, 4062–4063
  terminology services, 4073–4074
  Web services, 4073
Semantic knowledge, 3423
Semantic scattering, 2211
Semantic space, 2688–2696

Semantic web (SW), 277, 2938, 4212, 5020, 5029–5030
  academic work, 4087–4088
  aim of, 4080–4082
  application areas, 4086–4087
  bootstrapping, 4083–4084
  commercial activity, 4087
  components of, 4082–4083
  controversies
    arguments for and against ontologies, 4088–4089
    folksonomies, 4089
    GOFAI, 4088
    resolving, 4089
    symbol grounding, 4090
  history
    development progress, 4085–4086
    early layered view, 4085
    Intelligent Systems, 4084
    ontology-related information, 4085
    OWL, 4085
    Scientific American, 4084–4085
    SPARQL, 4085
    W3C recommendation, 4085
    WWW, 4084
  information standard, 4080
  infrastructure, 4083
  layered view of, 4081
  ontologies, 4080–4081
  properties of system, 4086
  reasoners, 4083
  semantic theory, 4080
  social context, 4084
  Web services, 4080
Semantic Web Advanced Development (SWAD), 2671
Semantic Web Challenge, 4087–4088
Semiotics
  history, 4094–4096
  and information, 4101–4102
  meanings, 4096–4098
  opposition theory, 4100
  poststructuralism, 4100–4101
  signs, 4098
  structure, text and code
    intellectual codes, 4099
    messages, 4099
    paradigmatic, 4098–4099
    representation, 4099
    social codes, 4099
    syntagmatic, 4098–4099
Semistructured messages, 1058
Sendai Mediatheque, 2808
Senefelder, Alois, 1868
Senegal
  archives and archival science
    laws, 4109
    National Archives and Services, 4109–4110
  language, 4104
  libraries
    academic and research libraries, 4106
    digital library collections and services, 4108
    education, 4108
    laws, 4104–4105
    professional associations, 4108–4109
    public libraries, 4106–4107

    school libraries, 4107
    special libraries, 4107–4108
  literacy rate, 4104
  map of, 4104–4105
  museums and museology, 4110
Sense-making
  approaches, 2117, 2119
    Cognitive Systems Engineering, 4116–4117
    HCI, 4115–4116
    LIS, 4118–4121
    organizational communication, 4117–4118
  clarion call, 4121
  spiraling, 2096
  user studies, 4113–4114
Sense-making methodology (SMM), 1508–1509
Sentence plan language, 434
Sentence-reordering algorithms, 424
SEO, *see* Search engine optimization
Sequence-level indexing, 3131
Sequence searching, 826–827
Serbia
  archives, 4132–4133
  economy, 4125
  history, 4125–4127, 4136–13
  libraries
    academic libraries, 4129–4131
    association, 4127–4128
    central libraries, 4127
    education, 4132
    laws, 4127
    National Library of Serbia, 4127–4129
    public libraries, 4129
    school libraries, 4131–4132
    special libraries, 4131
  location, 4125–4126
  museum
    art museums and galleries, 4134
    Churches and monasteries, 4133
    historical and ethnographic museums, 4135
    national museum, 4133–4134
    professional association, 4133
    science museums and galleries, 4134–4135
  population of, 4125
  provinces, 4125
  telecommunication infrastructure, 4125
Serbian Library Consortium for Coordinated Acquisition, 2829
Serbian Lyceum, 4129–4130
Serbian Museum Association, 4133
Serendipitous information search, 2244–2245
Serials collection and management
  acquisition, 4142–4143
  cataloging, 4143–4144
  check-in, 4143
  definitions, 4139–4140
  history, 4141
  maintenance, 4146
  preservation, 4147
  selection, 4141–4142
  weeding, 4147–4148
Serials Specialist Award of NASIG, 3390
Serials vendors
  claiming, 4154–4155
  EDI, 4156
  electronic journals, 4154, 4156–4157
  five year price analysis, 4151

Serials vendors (cont'd.)
  ILS, 4153–4154
  invoicing, 4154
  ordering, 4154
  publishers, 4155
  renewals, 4155
  reports, 4155
  research library, 4152
  subscription, 4152
Series systems, 119–120
SERP, *see* Search engine results page
Service level agreements (SLAs), 2295
SERVQUAL measurement attributes, 2295
Sets, algebra of, 593–594
Severe acute respiratory syndrome (SARS), 683
Sewing, 538–539
Shadowing, 4532–4533
Shakespeare Project, 1290
Shanghai Library, 3793
  collection, 899–900
  digital reference services, 900
  and ISTIS, merger of, 898–899
  mission, 899
  services, 899
Shanghai Science and Technology Museum, 909
Shannon and Weaver's communication theory, 4198
Shannon, Claude, 2049–2051
Shannon's information theory, 3613
Shannon's model, 4101
Shannon theory, *see* Information theory
Shared legal capability, *see* Library copyright alliance
Shared libraries, *See* Joint-use libraries
Sharing and Transforming Access to Resources (STARS), 3909
Sharjah Museum of Islamic Civilisation, 4381
SHARP News, 4269–4270
Shelf browsing, 4467
Shepard's Citation Index, 925
Shera model, 2229
Shibboleth, 2894
The Ship and Supercargo Bookkeeper, 645
Shipping and Commercial List and New York Price Current, 1401
Shneiderman's principles, 4807–4808
Shockwave, 2155
SHOE, 3458
Shojakukan Library, 2560–2561
Short-term loans (STLs), 1210–1211, 1213
Short-title catalog (STC), 457
Shot-level indexing, 3131–3132
Shrine Library, 3976
Shrine of the Book, Israel Museum, 2550–2551
Shrink-wrap agreement, 1271
SIAM-AMS Proceedings, 3028
Sichuan Provincial Archives, 906–907
SIGLE database, 1753–1754
Signage
  changeable content signs, 4974–4975
  definition, 4965
  design principals, 4965, 4972
  expected outcomes, 4965, 4972
  fixed content signs, 4973–4975
  history of, 4965, 4972–4973
  message groups, 4973–4974
  sign materials, 4965–4971

Signal detection theory (SDT), 3930
Signal processing, 275
Signed bindings, 543
Signs, 2263–2264
SIGUSE, 4118
Siloed information environment, 4979
Similarity searching
  2D chemical structures, 833
  3D chemical structures, 835–836
  paradigm, 4427
Simon's theory, 2194
Simple Knowledge Organization System (SKOS), 1260
Simple Mail Transport Protocol (SMTP), 2183
Simple Object Access Protocol (SOAP), 2187
Simple Recurrent Network (SRN), 285, 287
Simplified Molecular Input Line Entry Specification (SMILES), 831
Singapore National Library, 3791
Single-document summaries, 418
Singular value decomposition (SVD), 2688–2696
Sinsigns, 4098
Site museums and monuments
  archaeological site museum, 4167–4168
  commemorative landscape, 4165
  commemorative monuments, 4164–4165
  definition, 4164
  freezing time, 4170
  as heritage, 4168
  historical perspective, interpretation challenges, 4170
  historic site, 4164
  house museum, 4165–4166
  landscape freezing, 4170
  outdoor museum/living history site, 4166–4167
  preservation
    cultural factor, 4171
    private-sector groups and societies, 4169
    restoration *vs.* original controversy, 4170–4171
    UNESCO, 4169
    United States federal legislation, 4169
  traditional site museum, 4165
  as war targets and cultural casualties, 4168
Site usage log, 4798
Situational relevance judgments, 3943–3944
Skilled reading
  computer models, 3838–3839
  eye movements, 3838
  phonology, 3838
Skills knowledge, 3535
SKY Index, 443
Slavic and East European Materials Project (SEEMP), 791
Slip cases, 542
Slipstream, 3706
Slovakia
  archives and archival science
    access to archives, 4181
    education, 4182
    history, 4180
    legislation, 4180–4181
    magazine and awards, 4183
    national archives, 4181
    organizations and associations, 4182–4183

    specialized public archives, 4182
    state archives, 4181–4182
  digitization projects, 4186
  historical, geographic, economic and sociocultiral context, 4173–4174
  library and information professions, systems and service
    academic and research libraries, 4177–4178
    education, 4179
    history of, 4174
    informatization and digitization, 4179–4180
    legislation, 4174–4175
    public libraries, 4178–4179
    Slovak National Library, 4175–4177
    ULB, 4177–4178
  museums and museology
    ecucation and professional associations, 4185–4186
    gallery network, 4185
    history, 4183
    political and social life, documentation of, 4184–4185
    SNM, 4183–4185
    specialized museums, 4184
Slovak Librarians' Association (SLA), 4175
Slovak National Archives (SNA), 4180
Slovak National Library (SNL), 3322, 4175–4177, 4186
Slovak National Museum (SNM)
  collections, 4184
  history, 4183–4184
  political and social life, documentation of, 4184–4185
  publishing activities, 4185
  specialized museums, 4184
Sloval open-air museum, 4184
Small Business Administration (SBA), 636–637
Small businesses, 636–637, 3005
Small, Henry, 505–506
SMART project, 2222
Smashwords, 4058
Smith, Adam, 646
Smith-Lever Act, 1011
Smithsonian Center for Museum Studies, 3218
Smithsonian Institution, 4766–4767
  art museums, 4191–4192
  Building or Castle, 4191, 4193
  history and culture museums, 4192–4193
  legislation, 4188
  science museums, 4193–4195
Smithsonian Institution Information Retrieval System (SIIRS), 3178–3179
Smithsonian National Museum of American History, 1072–1073, 3255
Smooth gilding, 541
Snake stones, 1815
Snapshots, 1417
SNOMED Clinical Terms® (SNOMED CT®), 3340–3341
Social capital, 2126, 2659–2660
Social construction of technology (SCOT), 4020
Social constructivism, 2753–2754, 3528
Social epistemology, 2769, 3616
  epistemic justice, 4200–4202
  philosophical foundations and library and information science, 4197–4198

postmodernism, 4198–4200
Wikipedia, 4202
Social inclusion, 2127
Social informatics
assumptions, 4214
definitions, 4213
history, 4213–4214
ICTs, 4212
Kling's description, 4212
and library and information science, 4215–4216
research
approaches, 4214–4215
key insights, 4215
Semantic Web, 4212
Socialization, externalization, internalization and internationalization (SECI) model, 2619, 2621–2622
Social justice
Dervin's sense-making approach, 4226
distributive justice, 4219
egalitarianism/equity, 4219
etymological and conceptual origin, 4219
information behavior research, 4226–4227
inward-looking professional trends, 4223
justice-as-desert theory, 4219
justice-as-fairness, 4219
liberating roles, 4220
Library 2.0 efforts, 4222
library profession, 4224–4225
library's role, 4220
policy reports and guidelines, 4221
priveleged classes, tax-funded library for, 4223
public libraries, 4221–4222
socially-just society, 4218
Taparelli's concept, 4218
tensions, 4218
two-way learning outcomes, 4227
utilitarianism, 4219
Social learning theory, 3513
Social library
in United Kingdom, 1837
in United States, 1840–1842
Social literacy, 2305
Social media
altmetrics, 44
information searching, 2242
VRA, 4937
Social media optimization (SMO), 4041
Social networks, 844–846, 1039
actors, 4236
data collection, 4237–4238
graph theory, 4236
information networks
knowledge transfer, 4235
mobilized/accessible information, 4236
and information transfer
innovation, 4238
network structures, 4240–4242
roles and positions, 4240
small world hypothesis, 4239–4240
strong and weak ties, 4238–4239
knowledge, 3535
network clusters, 4237
personal and network outcomes, 4242
tie, 4236–4237

Social Network Sites (SNS), 844–845
Social Science Data Archives, 187
Social science literature, 4250–4251
academic communication, 4247–4248
electronic journals, 4249–4250
Ellis model, 4250–4251
Garvey and Griffith's studies, 4247–4249
Hogeweg-De Haart's discussion, 4246–4247
Janes' bibliography, 4246–4247
models, 4250–4252
refereeing process, 4247–4248
Rosenbaum's framework, 4246–4247
Tenopir analysis, 4251–4252
use, 4250–4252
Social science professions
code of ethics, 4255
information needs, 4259
journalists, 4259
librarians, 4256–4257
police officers, 4258
social workers, 4257–4258
teachers, 4255–4256
Social Science Research Network (SSRN) database, 3466
Social sciences citation index (SSCI), 925, 2370, 3471
Social shaping of technology (SST), 4020
Societe Mathematique de France, 324
Society for Industrial and Applied Mathematics (SIAM), 3026
Society for Information Management (SIM), 2276
Society for Promoting Christian Knowledge (SPCK), 1802, 1840
Society for Scholarly Publishing (SSP), 4266–4267
annual budget, 4262
committees, 4264–4265
educational purposes, 4262
funding, 4262
history, 4262–4263
logos of, 4262–4263
meetings and seminars, 4265–4266
mission of, 4262–4264
organizational membership category, 4262
organizational structure, 4264
publications, 4266
scholarly communication chain, 4262
scholarly publishers and producer, challenges to, 4264
strategic plans, 4265
Society for the Distribution of Useful Knowledge (SDUK), 1802
The Society for the History of Authorship, Reading and Publishing (SHARP), 4268–4269
book history, 1860
goal of, 4270
history of print culture, 4268
officers, 4268
publications, 4269–4270
scholarly and professional organizations, 4268
Society for the Propagation of the Gospel in Foreign Parts (SPG), 1840
Society of Accountants in Edinburgh, 651

Society of American Archivists (SAA), 174, 196, 256, 688, 1424, 1466, 4336, 4384, 4742
advocacy outreach and cooperation, 4276–4277
archival record formats, 4271
Diversity Committee, 4275–4276
governance and member services, 4276
history of, 4271–4273
membership interest groups, 4273
activities, 4273
roundtables, 4274–4275
sections, 4274
Mentoring Program, 4276
national and international leadership, 4271
publications, 4277
work, 4271
Society of Architectural Historians (SAH), 256
Society of Archivists, 4738–4739
Society of College, National and University Libraries (SCONUL), 4448, 4703–4705
Society of Competitive Intelligence Professionals (SCIP), 4354, 4356
Society of Friends of the Institute of Ethiopian Studies Museum (SOFIES), 1503
Society of Greek Archivists, 1739
Society of Indexers (SI), 445
Society periodicals, 1659
Socio-cognitive relevance judgments, 3944
Sociocultural theory, 2755
Sociology of the information disciplines
cultural record, 4292–4293
innovation and specialization, 4293–4294
knowledge and power, 4287–4288
modern university, 4289
scope and definition, 4288–4289
Sociotechnical interaction networks (STINs), 4022
Sociotechnical theory, 2286
SOFIA, 1223–1224
Software and Information Industry Association (SIIA), 3650
CODiE Award Program, 4298
departments, 4297–4298
global services, 4297
history of, 4297
membership, 4298
objective, 4297
Software art, 2071
Software Industry Association of America (SIAA), 3656
Software Publishers Association, 3650
Solander cases, 542
SOLINET, 3922, 3924
Solipsism, 2898
Solo librarians, 4352–4353
Somerset Archaeological and Natural History Society, 1794
Somerset Record Society, 1794
Sonny Bono Copyright Term Extension Act, 369
Sound and audio archives
challenges, 4304–4305
collection development policies, 4301–4302
content-centered approach, 4300
copyright, 4304
cylinder recordings, 4299
digital audio projects, 4305

Sound and audio archives (cont'd.)
  funding and support, 4304
  medium-centered archive, 4300
  music archives
    disc program, 4301
    Edison phonograph, 4300
    pulse code modulation (PCM), 4301
    rise of, 4301
  national efforts, 4305
  pay-as-you-go digital distribution, 4304
  Phonogramm-Archiv, 4299
  preservation and access, 4302–4304
  professional associations, 4302–4303
  sound recordings, 4299–4300
  supporting materials, 4302
  technical processing, 4302
  user needs, 4301
Source credibility, 1115
SourceForge, 1063
South Asia Materials Project (SAMP), 791
South Australian Literary Association, 391
South Central Region of National Network of
    Libraries of Medicine, 3034
South Dublin County Library Service, 3786
Southeast Asia Materials Project (SEAM), 791
Southeast Asia-Pacific Audiovisual Archive
    Association (SEAPAVAA), 1579
Southeastern College Art Conference (SECAC),
    4934
Southern Appalachian Information Node
    (SAIN), 3310
Southern California Earthquake Center (SCEC),
    2997
Southern European Libraries Link (SELL),
    2829
South Kensington Museum, 3154–3155
South Korea
  archives and archival science
    as discipline, 4309
    legislative history, 4308–4309
    NARS, 4308
  history, 4307–4308
  libraries
    academic libraries, 4310–4311
    administrative and legal systems,
      4309–4310
    Book Reading Seoul project, 4313
    Bookstart movement, 4312
    Children and Young Adult Services Pro-
      grams, 4312–4313
    education, 4312
    Enhancing Library Service for the Dis-
      abled, 4313
    Miracle Library project, 4312
    National Assembly Library, 4310
    NLK, 4309–4310
    One Book, One City movement, 4313
    professional association, 4312
    public libraries, 4311
    school libraries, 4311
    Small Library movement, 4313
    special libraries, 4311
    Supreme Court Library, 4310
    WLIC, 4313
  map of, 4307–4308
Soviet Mathematics-Doklady, 3027
Space facet, 1536

Spain
  archives and archival science
    administration, 4329–4330
    associations, 4330
    collections, 4330
    education, 4330
    expenditures, 4330
    representative archives profiles, 4330
    user services, 4330
  education, library and information science,
    4327–4328
  government libraries
    museum libraries, 4326
    religious libraries, 4327
    Royal Academies, 4326
  history, 4314–4315
  legislation, 4315–4316
  libraries
    in Peru, 3606
  library cooperation, 4329
  map of, 4315
  museums and museology
    administration, 4331
    associations, 4333
    collections, 4331
    education, 4333
    expenditures, 4331
    representative museum profiles, 4331–4333
    user services, 4331
  National Library
    CATMARC, 4316
    collections, 4317–4318
    cooperation, 4319
    databases and automation, 4318–4319
    digitization, 4319
    expenditures, 4317
    IBERMARC format, 4316
    LibEcon, 4316
    organization and structure, 4316–4317
    publications, 4318
    REBIUN, 4316
    RUECA, 4316
    special collections, 4318
    user services, 4319
  professional library associations, 4328
  public libraries
    administration and staff, 4322–4323
    automation, 4323–4324
    collections, 4323
    expenditures, 4323
    The Inform@tion Society for All, 4322
    Library of Catalonia, 4324
    Pedro Salinas Public Library, 4324
    PISTA Program, 4322
    user services, 4323
  school libraries
    administration, 4324
    automation, 4325
    collections, 4324
    expenditures, 4324
    staff, 4324
    user services, 4324–4325
  special libraries
    administration, 4325
    automation, 4325–4326
    collections, 4325
    expenditures, 4325

    staff, 4325
    user services, 4325
  university and research libraries
    administration and staffing, 4319–4320
    automation, 4320–4321
    collections, 4320
    CSIC libraries, 4321
    expenditures, 4320
    repesentative university library profiles, 4321
    Scientific and Literary Athenaeum of
      Madrid, 4322
    user services, 4320
  virtual and digital libraries, 4327
Spain ISKO Chapter, 2497
Spangler Library, 878
Spanish binding, 545
Spanish illumination, 1948
Spanish Spring Library, 2792
SPARQL, 2939–2941
Special auxiliaries, 4785
Special bulletins, 4937
Special collections, 3820–3821; *see also* Rare
    book collections
  age, 4336, 4344
  area studies collections, 4335
  care and security, 4335
  communication skills, 4348–4349
  condition, 4338, 4346
  core professional requirements, 4348–4349
  definition, 4335–4336
  definitions, 4343–4344
  digitization, 4341
  exhibitions, 4347
  foreign language skill, 4349
  format, 4345
  formats, 4335, 4337
  foundations, 4346
  fundraising, 4348
  future changes, 4349
  grant-writing, 4348
  and manuscripts
    core professional requirements, 4340–4341
    definition, 4336
  market value, 4336–4337, 4344
  modern special collections
    exhibitions and publications, 4339
    fund-raising and grant-writing, 4340
    public programs and performances, 4339
    security, preservation, and posterity, 4340
    teaching and research, 4339–4340
  noncirculating collections, 4335
  preservation, 4349
  provenance, 4337, 4345
  public programs, 4347
  rare book rooms, 4338
  scarcity, 4337–4338, 4345–4346
  securing posterity, 4349
  stand-alone research and independent librar-
    ies, 4336, 4338–4339
  subject matter, 4337, 4345
  teaching and research, 4347–4348
  treasure rooms, 4338
Special Collections in Mass Media & Culture
    (SCMMC), 1561
Special Committee to Review Program Assess-
    ment Processes and Procedures
    (SCRPAPP), 71

Special Interest Group for Classification Research (SIG/CR), 959–960
Special Interest Group on Computer–Human Interaction (SIGCHI), 1904, 4804
Special Interest Group on Information Retrieval (SIGIR), 482, 1904, 2222
Special Interest Group on Management Information Systems (SIGMIS), 2276
Special interest groups (SIGs), 91–92, 2007, 3173–3174
Special Interest Section on Aboriginal Archives (SISAA), 691
Special interest sections (SISs), 49–50
SPECIALIST lexicon, 4673
Special librarianship
    career opportunities, 4352–4353
    characteristics, 4354–4355
    competencies, 4357–4358
    education, 4358
    employability, 4358
    end user training, 4353–4354
    evolution, 4351
    global networks, 4357
    KM, 4354
    organizations, 4355–4357
    public image, 4353
    return on investment, 4353
    technology, 4353
    titles, 4355
    Web, 4351–4352
Special libraries, 301–303, 305, 307, 1096, 2764, 3414–3415
    acquisitions units, organization of, 2918
    Armenia, 230
    in Australia, 384–385
    in China, 900–902
    in Croatia, 1125
    definition, 4361–4362
    in Denmark, 1219–1220
    digital collections, 4368
    ethics, 4365
    Ethiopia, 1498–1499
    in Germany, 1698
    globalization, 4362–4363
    Greece, 1732
    Hungary, 1923
    information technology, 4367
    in Israel, 2547
    Japan, 2565
    in Kazakhstan, 2583
    Kenya, 2596–2597
    knowledge services, 4368
    learning organization, 4367
    library associations (see Special Libraries Association)
    Lithuania, 2953
    management
        marketing, 4366
        organizations, 4365–4366
        planning and budgeting, 4366
        value evaluation, 4366–4367
    in Moldova, 3124
    New Zealand libraries, 3376
    origin, 4362
    in Peru, 3608–3609
    physical and a virtual presence, 4368
    in Saudi Arabia, 3976–3977

Senegal, 4107–4108
    in Serbia, 4131
    services
        acquisitions and collection development, 4363
        competitive intelligence, 4364–4365
        knowledge management, 4365
        news updating, 4364
        organization of information, 4363
        reference and research center, 4363–4364
    South Korea, 4311
    Tunisia, 4631
    in Ukraine, 4646
    in United Kingdom, 4707–4708
    Venezuelan libraries, 4890
Special Libraries Association (SLA), 256, 652, 709–710, 1097, 2708, 4014, 4016, 4352, 4356–4357, 4362
    business and industry, advisory service to, 4374
    copyright legislation, 4374–4375
    core values, 4371
    corporate and technology libraries, 4374
    documentation, 4374
    Employment Committee, 4373
    Great Depression, challenges during, 4373
    information, knowledge and strategic learning, 4375–4376
    information/knowledge centers, 4370
    information professionals, 4377–4378
    knowledge services, 4372, 4376
    knowledge sharing, 4372–4373
    membership, growth of, 4374
    motto, 4373
    origin of, 4371–4372
    PAIS, creation of, 4373
    practical and utilitarian library services, 4373
    PREPS Commission, 4376
    professional knowledge workers, support to, 4370
    regional chapters, 4370
    research resources, analysis of, 4373
    research units, 4370
    responsibilities, 4374
    special libraries movement, 4374
    Vision Statement of 2004, 4370, 4377
Specialty hospital library, 1872–1873
Specialty Museums
    changing face, 4382
    examples, 4381–4382
    expertise, 4381
    number of, 4380
    organization, 4380
    types, 4379–4380
    United States, 4380
Spectrum scholarships, 81
Speculativism, 3628–3629
Speech communication, 997–998
Speech processing, 274
Speech recognition technology, 1058
SPICE (setting, perspective, intervention, comparison, and evaluation), 1517
Spiders, 2519
Spofford, Ainsworth, 2848
Spofford, Ainsworth Rand, 2881–2883
Spreading activation model, 3590
Spring backs, 539

SRW/U, 2894–2895
S-SRB, 3002
Stack management, 920–921
Standard citation order, 585
Standard Generalized Markup Language (SGML), 730–731
Standard generalized markup language (SGML), 1252, 1365, 1381, 1416, 2343, 2986, 3074–3075, 4560–4561, 5022
Standard industrial classification (SIC) system, 638, 653
Standardized Assessment of Information Literacy Skills (SAILS), 374
Standard operating procedures (SOPs), 3357, 3361–3363
Standards for Accreditation of Master's Programs in Library and Information Studies, 18, 20
Standards Institution of Israel, 2547
Standard Statistics Compustat Service, 652
Standing Committee of the National and University Libraries (SCONUL), 2545
Standing Conference of Eastern, Central and Southern African Library and Information Associations (SCECSAL), 37, 4515
Standing Conference of National and University Libraries of Eastern, Central and Southern Africa (SCANUL-ECS), 3330
Standish survey and analysis methodology, 2281
Stanford Graduate School of Business, 650
STARS, 1676
"Starvation policy," 4784
State and local government archives
    Multnomah County (Oregon) Archives, 4746
    New Orleans Notorial Archives, 4746
    San Antonio Municipal Archives Program, 4746–4747
State archives, 1222–1223
    in Dubrovnik, 1128
    establishment and administrative location, 4390–4391
    history, 4386–4389
    mission, 4384
    nature and functions, 4384–4386
    in Rijeka, 1128
    in Zadar, 1128
State Archives Bureau (SAB), 905
State Gold and Precious Metals Museum, 2587
State Historical Records Advisory Boards (SHRABs), 4743
State Historical Society of Wisconsin (SHSW), 1780–1781
State Historic Preservation Officer (SHPO), 1774
State Inspectorate of Public Libraries, 1216
State Library Agency Section (SLAS), 376
State library and state library agencies, 4392
    Arizona State Library, Archives and Public Records, 4397
    Connecticut State Library, 4397
    COSLA, 4394–4395
    definition, 4392–4393
    establishment dates, 4398–4399
    functions, 4394
    FY 2006, 4396
    GPLS, 4397
    history, 4393

State library and state library agencies (cont'd.)
librarian qualifications, 4396
Library of Virginia building, 4398
Maine State Library, 4397–4398
New Jersey State Library, 4398
Oregon State Library, 4398
personnel, education of, 4396
professional organizations, 4394
public library, federal aid to, 4393–4394
state government structure, 4395–4396
Texas State Library and Archives, 4398
trends and issues, 4396
State Library of Queensland, 383
State modeling, 3112
State Museum of Archeology and Ethnography,
2587
State Museum of Popular Musical Instruments,
2587
State Records Act 1997, 387
State Scientific Medical Library of Ukraine,
4646
State Scientific Technical Library of Ukraine,
4647
Static domain model, 1205
Statistical bibliography, 492, 496–497, 2911
Statistical control, 1178
Statistical Methods for Research Workers, 1410
Statistical View of the Number of Sheep, 1404
Statistical Yearbook of the League of Nations,
649
*Statistics of the Woollen Manufactories of the
United States*, 1404
StatsQUAL®, 374
STAT-USA, 1554–1555
Statutory invention registrations (SIRs),
3565–3566
Steering Committee on Canada's Archives
(SCCA), 666
Stemming/morphological analysis, 2201
Steven Spielberg Jewish Film Archive, 2555
Steve project, 3067
St. George Interior Decoration and Art Gallery,
1504
Still image indexing
collection level, 4408
concept-based indexing
data content tools, 4412–4413
data structure tools, 4413
data value tools, 4411–4412
history, 4410
theoretical basis, 4410–4411
content-based indexing
CBR, 4414–4415
cognitive processing, 4413–4414
context, 4409
controlled vocabulary, 4408–4409
Cranfield II experiments, 4408
features/attributes selection, 4407
image attribute, 4407–4408
image collection, 4407
image considerations, 4409
image retrieval, 4408
image tagging systems, 4415
subject indexing, 4407
user-centered indexing, 4408
visual perception, 4408
Stochastic decision models, 1197

Stone representation theorem, 595
Stone-tipped spear point, 1778
Stopping rule, 2363
Stopword processing, 2201
Storage, 2072
Storage Networking Industry Association
(SNIA), 715
Storage Resource Broker (SRB), 3000
Story Corps project, 1794
*The Story of John Winchcombe, commonly
called Jack of Newberry*, 647
Story slams, 4444
Storytelling
business, 4442
education, 4442
finding, 4440–4441
healing, 4442–4443
kinds, 4437–4438
learning, 4441
libraries, 4443
origins, 4438–4439
performing, 4441
religious, 4443
scope, 4437
Strabo, 1684
Strategic and Competitive Intelligence Professionals (SCIP), 2708
Strategic generation, 432
Strategic goals, 4455
Strategic long-range planning (SLRP), 68
Strategic planning, academic libraries
benefits, 4447
definition, 4447
elements
action planning, 4455–4456
financial commentary, 4456
goal statements, 4455
library missions, 4452–4453
scenario development, 4454–4455
service values, 4453
visioning, 4453–4454
environmental appraisal, 4448
functions, 4447
historical context, 4448–4449
planning processes, 4450–4451
presentation, 4448
program management, 4448
published literature
academic strategy, 4449
library planning, 4449–4450
strategic management, 4448
strategic profiling, 4448
strategy development, 4448
strategy documents, 4451–4452
terminology, 4447–4448
Strategy Hub, 2214
STREAM, 2630
StreamCluCD algorithm, 2634
StreamMiner, 2636
Street lit/urban fiction, 3706
Strengthening Public Health Research in Europe
(SPHERE), 1767
Strengths, weaknesses, opportunities and threats
(SWOT) analysis, 145, 1882, 3196
Stress/coping theory, 2089–2090
String formats, 1177
String indexing systems, 1985

String processing
feedforward ANN for, 285
RANN for, 285–287
TDNN for, 285–286
Structural consistency, 1175
Structural engineering, 1248
Structural equation model (SEM), 1205–1206
Structural information, 2056
Structured metadata, 4427
Students' information needs and behavior
developmental characteristics, 4459
information literacy, 4462–4463
information searching behavior, 4460–4461
library use, 4461–4462
net generation, 4460
specific student groups, 4463
Student texts, 2739–2740
Studies in the History of Statistical Method, 493
Subiaco Lactantius, 1973
Subject authority cooperative program (SACO),
2853, 2871, 2921
Subject authority data, 1612, 1615–1616
Subject authority record, 4467
Subject cataloging
approaches
classification numbers, 4467
controlled vocabulary search, 4466–4467
keyword and full-text search, 4467
library catalogs
early standard subject lists, 4467–4468
impact of automation, 4468
major classification systems
bibliographic classification, 4475
Colon Classification, 4475
DDC, 4474
LCC, 4474–4475
NLM classification, 4475
UDC, 4475
principles
classification theory, 4470
controlled vocabulary, 4468–4470
design and application principles, 4471
library classification, 4471
modern classification theory, 4470–4471
traditional classification theory, 4470
subject access systems
FAST, 4472–4473
LCSH, 4472
MeSH, 4474
Sears list of Subject Headings, 4473–4474
Subject Cataloging Manual (SCM), 2874
Subject classification (SC), 961, 964, 970
Subject headings, 2857, 2862–2863
*Subject Headings for Children and People,
Places & Things*, 1261
Subject Headings Manual (SHM), 2866
Subject Index for the Visual Arts, 1080
Subjective relevance, 3930, 3932–3933
Subject Portals Project (SPP), 2897
Subject scattering, 2211
Submission Information Package (SIP), 1365
Subscribing business, 1275
Subscription libraries, 916, 4478–4481
Substance identification for information retrieval
ambiguous chemical identifiers
chemical formulae, 823–824
chemical names, 823

unumbiguous chemical identifiers
  CAS Registry Numbers®, 824
  chemical structures, 824
  InChIs™, 824–825
  sequences, 824
Substructure searching, 825
  2D chemical structures, 832–833
  3D chemical structures, 834–835
Subversive ethics, 1473
Summa de Arithmetica, Geometrica et Proportionalta, 645
Summarization, *see* Automatic abstracting and summarization
  NLP, 3353
Summer Educational Institute (SEI), 4938
Sunderland Museum, 4716
Sunken Military Craft Act, 1776
SUNY Open Textbook Initiative, 2903
SuperCard, 1290
Supplement to Hain's Repertorium Bibliographicum, 1969
Supply chain management (SCM), 1180–1181, 2658
Supportive culture, 3521
Support vector machines (SVMs), 3270
Supralibros, 540
Supreme Court Library of Korea, 4310
Surface credibility, 1115
Surface Web, 5021
Survey of Current Business, 649
Survival ethics, 1473
Sutherland tooling process, 541
Šventupis secondary school library, 2951
Sveriges Allmanna Biblioteksförening (SAB), 1261
Swedish binding, 548
Swedish Library Association, 3548
Swiss Federal Archives (SFA), 4491
Swiss Library Association, 4490–4491
Switching function, 595–596
Switzerland
  archives and archival studies
    archivist education, 4494
    cantonal and local archives, 4491
    digital archival collections, 4493
    electronic records, 4494
    enterprise archives, 4493
    film and audiovisual archives, 4492
    international organizations, 4492
    legislation, 4491
    missionary societies, 4493
    national institutions, 4492
    preservation, 4494
    professional association, 4494
    SFA, 4491
    specialized archives, 4492–4493
    university archives, 4491–4492
    virtual archives, 4493
  Confederation, cantons, and communes, 4487–4488
  culture, 4487, 4495–4496
  economy, 4487
  libraries
    digital library, 4489–4490
    legislation and types, 4487–4488

national library and information services, 4488–4489
    professional associations, 4490–4491
  map of, 4487–4488
  museums and museology, 4494–4495
  official languages, 4487
  population of, 4487
SWOT analysis, *see* Strengths, weaknesses, opportunities and threats analysis
Sydney School, 1665
Syllogism, 269
Symbol grounding, 4090
Symbolic cultural theory, 3520
Symbolic interactionism, 3811
Symbolic learning approach, 273
Symbolic utility, 2357
Symbols, 4961, 4963–4964, 4972
Symposium on Computer Applications in Medical Care (SCAMC), 85
Synodontis acanthoperca, 1161
Synonymy, 2688–2689
Syntax
  search engines, 4048
  standards, 3062–3063
Systematized Nomenclature of Medicine-Clinical Terms (SNOMED-CT), 979, 4673
System for the Mechanical Analysis and Retrieval of Text (SMART), 2689
Systemic functional linguistic (SFL), 1664–1665
Systemic knowledge assets, 2622
System of Scientific and Technical Information project, 1125
Systems and Services Section (SASS), 2843
Systems knowledge, 3535

T
Tableau Geographique, 1687
Table of content services (TOC), 1880
Tabulated credibility, 1115
Tacit–explicit dichotomy, 2651–2652
Tacit knowledge
  and explicit knowledge, 2643, 2650
  organizational memory, 3534
Tactical generation, 432
Tagged Image File Format (TIFF), 1367
Take-the-best heuristics, 2362–2363
Taking Liberties: The struggle for Britain's freedoms and rights, 624
Talking-book machines (TBMs), 565, 567–568
Tallahassee FreeNet (TFN), 1030
Tamiment Library and Wagner Archives, 4761
Tamura's feature selection, 4423
TANIT, 4631
Tanzania
  academic libraries
    changing roles and challenges, 4505–4506
    policy shifts and higher learning institutions expansion, 1990s, 4504–4505
    UDSM and, 4504
  archives and archival system
    record management structures, 4508–4509
    status and downside, 4509–4510
  botanical gardens, 4511–4512
  challenges, 4517–4518
  characteristics and key ICT/development indicators, 4499

herbaria, 4512
higher learning institutions, 4521–4522
intellectual property regulations, 4513–4514
Internet users, 4498
LIS development, chronology of, 4518–4520
map of, 4498
museums
  antiquities, 4511
  National Museum System, 4510
  private art galleries, 4511
  private museums, 4510–4511
policy initiatives, 4517
professional associations, 4515–4516
professional development
  post-independence challenges and remedies, 4514–4515
  training institutions, 4515
public libraries
  bibliographic control, 4502
  cultural–educational relations and NGO libraries/ information centers, 4503–4504
  early pre-independence efforts, 4499–4500
  institutional structures and policies, 4502–4503
  libraries and literacy education, 4501–4502
  postindependence developments, 4500–4501
  pre-independence synopsis, 4499
school libraries
  information technology, teaching and learning, 4507
  library services for children, 4506–4507
  teacher–librarians associations, 4506
situation analysis, 4512–4513
special libraries
  emergence of, 4507
  specialized information services, 4507–4508
TLSB
  functions, 4520–4521
  powers of, 4521
zoos, 4512
Tanzania Library Services Board (TLSB), 4502
Tarlton Law Library, 4577
Task-based information interaction evaluation framework, 4883
Task-based information searching
  anomalous state of knowledge, 4526–4527
  contextual characteristics, 4526
  experimental and natural settings, 4527
  field studies
    critical incident technique, 4531
    diaries, 4531–4532
    ethical concerns, 4534
    interviews, 4530–4531
    multimethod approach, 4530
    questionnaires, 4530–4531
    shadowing, 4532–4533
    transaction log, 4533
    triangulation, 4533–4534
  information retrieval, 4527
  task performer's traits, 4526
tasks
  activity, 4527–4528
  process nature of searching, 4529
  task complexity, 4528–4529
  task granularity, 4528

Tasman, Abel, 1685
Tatomir Accessibility Checklist, 3578
"Taxidermy and Plastic Art" teaching lab and course, 3216
Taximetrics, *see* Numerical taxonomy
Taxonomic Databases Working Group (TDWG), 3311
Taxonomy
  classical taxonomy, 4538–4539
  classification, 4537
  contemporary taxonomy
    AI ontology, 4540
    classificatory structures, 4539
    information access systems, 4540–4541
    object-oriented programming, 4540
  definition, 4537
  history, 4538
  methodology and practices, 4543–4544
  numerical taxonomy, 4539
  organization, 4538
  theory and principles, 4541–4543
Taxpayer Return on Investment in Florida Public Libraries study, 3795
Tax-supported public libraries, 3774
Taylor and Fayol's scientific approach, 142
Taylor & Francis Group Student Travel Grant, 1422
Taylorism, 2065
Taylor's information need model, 2118–2119
Taylor Society, 651
Teach Act, 1472
Teaching hospital library, 1872
Team computing, 1054
TeamWare, 1062
Technical Center for Agricultural and Rural Cooperation (CTA), 2312
Technical Chamber of Greece (TEE), 1732
Technical Committee 8 (TC8), 2276
Technical libraries, 4009
Technical Library of Lithuania, 2953
Technical metadata creators, 3066
Technical Report Archive and Image Library (TRAIL), 791, 4012
Technical services (TS)
  academic libraries, 4–5, 8–9
  acquisitions, 2918–2919
  cataloging, 2918, 2920–2924
  collections management, 2918, 2924
Technical Subcommittee for Encoded Archival Description (TS-EAD), 1424, 1431
Technical writing
  audience analysis, 4547
  composition, 4548
  documentation, 4547–4550
  field of study
    early history, 4549
    new millennium, 4551–4552
    twentieth century, 4549–4551
  information architecture, 4552
  information design and architecture, 4548
  nonacademic writing, 4547
  professional communication, 4547
  professional writing, 4547, 4549
  research, 4548
  rhetoric and writing programs, 4548
  technical communication, 4547–4548, 4552
  writing studies, 4548, 4552

Techniques in Electronic Resource Management (TERMS), 414
Techno-economic paradigm, 2254
Technological Educational Institutions (TEIs), 1731
Technological Institute of Higher Education Studies in Monterrey (ITESM), 3086
Technological scarcity argument, 1017
Technology, 4978
  economy, 2308
  knowledge, 2275
Technology Opportunities Program (TOP), 1028–1029
Technoscapes, 2124
Teeple Scholarship, 81
TEI P1, 4566
TEI P2, 4566
TEI P3, 4566
TEI P4, 4566
TEI P5, 4567
Telecommunications and Information Infrasture Assistance Program (TIIAP), 1028
Telecoms Package, 2141–2142
TelegraphCQ, 2631
Television, 999, 1573–1574
Television archives, *see* International Federation of Television Archives
Television Studies Commission, 2468–2469
TEMPUS program, 2827, 2954
Term frequency–inverse document frequency (TFIDF) weights, 2204
Test collections
  available, 4557
  construction, 4556–4557
Texas State Archives, 4385
Text analysis, 2930
Text encoding initiative (TEI), 3075
  character encoding, 4559
  Consortium, 4559
  ground rules
    customization files, 4564
    guidelines, 4561–4562
    modules, 4562–4564
    structural grammars, 4564
    text structure, 4562
  Guidelines, 1289–1290
  history, 4565–4567
  humanities
    data representation, 4559
    flags, 4560
    markup languages, 4560–4561
Text generation, *see* Natural language generation
Text mining, 2401–2402
Text planning, 432
TExtract, 1987
Text retrieval conference (TREC), 482, 484, 1904, 2175–2176, 2223, 3932, 4557
  historical context, 4569–4570
  test collections, 4570–4571
  tracks, 4571–4572
Text schemas, 437
Textual bibliography, 478
Thales of Miletus, 1683
Theatrum Orbis Terrarum, 1685
The European Library (TEL), 3331, 3682

Theft, vandalism and security
  ABAA, 4578
  Antiquarian Booksellers database, 4576
  archival repositories, 4580
  BAMBAM, 4578
  basic security and preservation policies, 4580
  bomb threats, 4580
  book theft, 4579
  communication among librarians, 4587–4588
  communication, book dealers, 4581–4582
  digital recordings, 4579
  electronic articles, 4579
  ideological vandalism, 4580
  library crimes, 4578
  Library Proxy Server, 4580
  lobby state legislatures, 4586
  MARC format, 4578
  missing treasures, Library of Congress, 4582–4583
  in museums
    definitions, 4593–4594
    history, 4594
    prevention, 4598–4600
  OCLC database, 4578
  paging slips, 4580
  play vandalism, 4580
  preventions
    consistent security procedures, 4584–4585
    mark materials and use colored photocopy paper, 4585–4586
    microfilming, 4585
    security systems and trust no one, 4583–4584
  replevin, 4577, 4583
  security devices, 4586–4587
  stolen/mutilated library books, replacement of, 4577
  tactical vandalism, 4580
  vindictive vandalism, 4580
The information literacy tutorial (TILT), 3440
The Joint Commission on Accreditation of Healthcare Organizations (JCAHO), 1874
Thema–nomen conceptual model, 4066
Thematic wayfinding, 4958
The National Archives (TNA), 111, 4733, 4735
Theodor Seuss Geisel Award, 335
Theological librarianship
  ATLA, 4606–4608
  European library, 4605
  international association, 4608–4609
  North American experience, 4605–4606
  origins, 4604–4605
  professional associations support, 4608
  today, 4609–4610
Theophrastes, 1683
Theoretical Economics, 3468
Theoretical knowledge, 2267–2269
Theory of action, 4806–4807
Theory of forms, 2094
Recuyell of the Histories of Troy, 1973
Thesauri, 1984–1986
Thesaurofacet, 589
Thesaurus, 1076, 1537–1538
  BC2, 589
  definition, 4673

standards
  guidelines, 2666
  ISO 2788 and Z39.19, differences between, 2668–2669
  national and international standards, 2667
  prehistory, 2666
  principles, 2668
  sector specific standards, 2667
  successive updates, 2667–2668
  weaknesses in, 2669
Thesaurus for Graphic Materials (TGM), 1080, 2857, 4411–4412
Thesaurus Linguae Graecae (TLG), 1912
Thesaurus of Engineering and Scientific Terms (TEST), 2666
Thesaurus structure
  descriptors, selection of, 3423–3424
  knowledge of, 3423
Thessaloniki Historical Archives, 1738
The University Licensing Program (TULIP), 5026
ThinkLab makerspace, 2992
Thomas Register of American Manufacturers, 653
THOMAS system, 1552–1553, 4874
Thompson, Frederick, 2054
ThoughtMesh project, 1288
Three ages lifecycle model, 168–169
Thumb cases, *see* Slip cases
Thwaites, 1781
Thyssen-Bornemisza Museum, 4332
Tianjin Natural History Museum of Hebei Province, 909
Ticknor, George, 1843–1844
TIFF format, 1311, 1367, 3568
TIGER initiative, 86
Tilden Trust, 1845
Tilloch, Andrew, 1867
Time-delay neural network (TDNN), 285–286
Time facet, 1536
Title-based method, summarization, 421
Title instance package platform (TIPP), 1712
Title searching, 4049
TMark, 2066
Tokenization, 2201
Tokyo National Museum, 2572
Tolbiac site, 532–534
Topical relevance
  judgments, 3943
  subjectivity, 3933–3936
Topic Maps
  application areas, 4621–4622
  associative graph-based model, 4620
  bibliographic records, 4619–4620
  constraint language, 4618
  digital libraries, 4621
  e-learning, 4621
  enterprise information integration, 4621
  entity–relation (ER) model, 4620
  faceted classification, 4619
  family of standards, 4617
  glossaries, 4619
  indexes, 4618–4619
  key strengths, 4622
  KM perspective, 4621
  query language, 4617–4618
  TAO model, 4614–4616

thesaurus, 4619
  Web publishing, 4622
Top Management Roundtable (TMR), 4265–4266
Topography, 1684
Toronto Public Library, 3786
Toronto Virtual Enterprise (TOVE), 3458
Total Information Awareness (TIA) program, 2402
Total quality management (TQM), 3511
Tower and Stockade Museum, 2551–2552
Town library
  in England, 1836–1837
  in France, 1837
  in Germany, 1837
  in Scotland, 1837
Trace information, 2058
Trade associations
  magazines, 650
  official publications, 649–650
  SIIA, 4297–4298
Trade Marks Ordinance of 1922, 4513
Traderbot, 2631
Tradescant, John, 4715–4716
Trade Secrets Act, 2152
Traditional site museum, 4165
Transactional data streams, 2628
Transaction log, 4533
Transaction-processing systems, 2273
Transactions of the American Mathematical Society, 3027
Transactions of the Moscow Mathematical Society, 3028
Translation probability, 3142–3143
Translations of Mathematical Monographs, 3028
Translations Series I and II, 3028
Transmission–absorption model, 4918
Transmission control protocol (TCP), 1015
Transmission control protocol and Internet protocol (TCP/IP), 2516–2517
Transnationalism, 2123
Transportation security, 2399
Travels, 1684
Treaties and review articles, 816–817
Treatise of Commerce, 1400
Treaty of Waitangi, 2036
TREC, *see* Text retrieval conference
Tree calf, 541
Trial voluntary protest program (TVPP) publications, 3566
Triangulation, 4533–4534
Tribal Libraries Program (TLP), 2033
Tribal museums, 3245
Trinidad Public Library, 3325
Triptychs, 542
Tropical Pesticides Research Institute (TPRI), 4512
True Interest of Holland, 645
Truman Grants program, 3714
Trust management approach, 406
Trust virtualization, 2998–3000
Trustworthiness, 2529–2530
Trustworthy repositories, 1333
Truth and Reconciliation commission, 2034
Tsinghua University Library, 896–897
  automation and networking, 897
  collection development, 897
  subject librarian system, 898

Tübingen System of Text Processing Programs (TUSTEP), 1293
TUNAGRI, 4631
TUNIDOC, 4629
TUNIPER, 4629
Tunisia
  academic libraries, 4628–4629
  archives and archival science
    legislation, 4633
    National Archives, 4633–4635
  EUMEDCONNECT, 4629
  historic background
    independent Tunisia, 4625–4626
    preindependent Tunisia, libraries and books in, 4624–4625
  legislation, libraries
    legal deposit and copyright, 4627–4628
    statutes and legislation, 4628
  library, information science and archival education and training, 4631–4632
  map of, 4625
  museums and museology
    cultural heritage, 4636
    historic preservation, 4635–4636
    Musée archéologique de Chimtou, 4637
    Musée archéologique de Chimtou', 4637
    Musée Dar Cherait 4638
    Musée des arts et traditions populaires 4638
    Musée des arts islamiques de Rakkada, 4637
    Musée de Sidi Kasim al-Jalizi, 4637–4638
    Musée national de Carthage, 4637
    Musée national du Bardo, 4636–4637
    Musée national d'Utique, 4637
    Musée Sidi Zitouni, 4638
    National Parks, 4638–4639
  National Library and Information Services, 4626–4627
  public libraries, 4629
  school libraries, 4630–4631
  special libraries, 4631
Tunis summit meeting, 5016
Turing test, 270
Turkish illumination (1451-1900), 1956
Turock Scholarship, 81
Two-mode networks, 4237
Two-sheets-on sewing method, 539
Two-step information-seeking approach, 2134
Tycho Brahe's press, 3739
Typenrepertorium der Wiegendrucke, 1971–1972
Typographical detectives, 1971–1972
Typographic presses, 3742

U
UCD, *see* User-centered design
UCLA Film & Television Archive, 1563
UCS Transformation Format 8 (UTF-8), 2984
UDC Consortium (UDCC), 4784
UFRJ, *see* Federal University of Rio de Janeiro
UKB Association, 2826
Ukiyoe, 2561
Ukraine
  culture and history, 4642
  geopolitical location of, 4642–4643

Ukraine (cont'd.)
  libraries
    agricultural libraries, 4646
    Central Library of the Ukrainian Associa-
      tion of the Blind, 4647
    documents, 4643–4644
    goals, 4643
    history of, 4642
    information technologies, 4643
    international library society, 4644
    Korolenko State Scientific Library in Khar-
      kiv, 4645
    Lviv Stefanyk Scientific Library, 4643,
      4645–4646
    NPLU, 4644–4645
    problems, 4644
    professional associations, 4644
    professional education, 4644
    publications, 4643
    public libraries, 4644
    Scientific Agricultural Library, 4647
    special libraries, 4646
    State Library of Ukraine for Children,
      4645
    State Scientific Medical Library, 4646
    State Scientific Technical Library, 4647
    Ukrainica, 4643
    university libraries, 4646
    Vernadsky National Library, 4643, 4645
Ukrainian Library Association (UBA), 4644
Ukrainica, 4643
U.K. Research Assessment Exercise (RAE),
    2373
UK Research Reserve (UKRR), 620
Ulrich's Serials Librarianship Award, 331
Unambiguous chemical identifiers
  CAS Registry Numbers®, 824
  chemical structures, 824
  InChls™, 824–825
  sequences, 824
UNCITRAL Model Law on Electronic Com-
    merce, 1270
Unconscionable contracts, 1272
Uncontrolled vocabularies, 1078
Undergraduate Librarians Discussion Group
    (UGLI), 4653
Undergraduate libraries
  architecture, 4650–4651
  collection development, 4651–4652
  current libraries, 4653–4654
  organizations, 4653
  vs. research libraries, 4652
Undernet, 1049
U.N. Development Program (UNDP), 2312
Undifferentiated names, 3291
Undiscovered public knowledge, 4201
U.N. Educational Scientific and Cultural Orga-
    nization (UNESCO), 2312, 3217
UNESCO Convention on the Means of
    Prohibiting and Preventing the Illicit
    Import, Export and Transfer of Owner-
    ship of Cultural Property, 3759
Unfreezing process, 2297
Unicode, 2984
Unicode Character Database (UCD), 4662
Unicode Standard
  BMP, allocation on, 4665–4666

character sets, 4662–4663
  ISO/IEC 2022 technique, 4662–4663
  MARC 21 and UNIMARC, 4663
  multilingual software applications, prob-
    lems, 4662
codespace, 4665
Consortium, 4667
design principles
  characters vs. glyphs, 4663–4664
  convertibility, 4665
  dynamic composition, 4664–4665
  efficiency, 4663
  logical order, 4664
  plain text, 4664
  semantics, 4664
  stability, 4665
  unification, 4664
  universality, 4663
goal, 4663
ISO/IEC 10646, development of, 4663
and libraries
  MARC 21, 4668–4669
  systems and services, 4669
  UNIMARC, 4669
  Z39.50, 4669
UAXs, 4662
UCD, 4662
The Unicode Standard, 4662
UTF-16, 4665–4667
UTF-32, 4665–4667
UTF-4669, 4665–4667
versions, 4663
World Wide Web and XML, 4667–4668
Unicode Standard Annexes (UAXs), 4662
Unified medical language system (UMLS), 979,
    3340, 4672
  Information Sources Map, 4673
  Metathesaurus
    attributes, 4675
    challenges, 4677–4678
    concept identifier, 4674
    concepts and concept names, 4673
    definition, 4673
    genomics vocabularies, 4673
    MetamorphoSys, 4678
    organization of, 4673–4674
    production and distribution, 4676–4677
    relationships, 4674–4676
    semantic type, 4675
    source vocabularies, 4673
    standard clinical terminologies, 4673
    synonymous terms and sources, 4674
  RxNorm, 4678
  semantic network, 4673
    nodes, 4675–4676
    portion of, 4675, 4677
    semantic links, 4675
    semantic types, 4676
  SPECIALIST lexicon, 4673
Uniform Computer Information Transactions
    Act (UCITA)
  concerns
    consumer protection and warranties,
      4684–4685
    copyright and software licenses,
      4681–4684
    First Amendment principles, 4685

forum/choice of law, 4685
    scope, 4681
    unreasonable standard amendment,
      4685–4686
  courts and related legislation, 4686
  history, 4680–4681
Uniform Electronic Legal Material Act
    (UELMA), 2744
Uniform Information Gateway (UIG), 2828
Uniform Resource Identifiers (URIs), 3962
Uniform resource locator (URL), 1365, 2518,
    4049, 5023–5024
  addressing scheme, 2984
  definition, 5025
UNIMARC format, 1733, 4627, 4629
Union Catalog of Greek Academic Libraries,
    1733
Union List of Artist Names® (ULAN), 1080
Unions
  academic unions
    ACRL, 4691, 4694–4697
    ALA, 4691–4692
    collective bargaining agreement, 4691
    faculty unionism, 4691
    human rights, 4692
    Web sites, 4692
  public libraries, 4689–4690, 4692–4694
UNISIST model, 556, 2326, 2408, 4657
United Kibbutz Movement, 2556
United Kingdom, 302, 306, 308
  archives and archival science
    archival profession, 4738
    archive services, 4735–4736
    business archives, 4736–4737
    community archives, 4738
    film and audiovisual archives, 4737
    higher education organizations, 4736
    legislation, 4732–4735
    professional societies and organizations,
      4738–4739
    rare manuscript libraries, 4738
    religious archives, 4737–4738
  broadcasting collections, 1566
  history of, 4699
  libraries and librarianship
    academic libraries, 4703–4705
    children's libraries, 4706–4707
    colleges, 4705
    history of, 4699–4701
    library and information professions,
      4708–4711
    LIS education, training, and research,
      4711–4713
    national libraries, 4701
    public libraries, 4701–4703
    schools, 4705–4706
    special libraries, 4707–4708
  library consortia, 2825
  museums
    armed services, 4718–4719
    botanical gardens, 4724–4725
    English Heritage, 4723
    financial support, 4727
    history of, 4715–4717
    independent, 4721–4722
    local authority, 4719–4721
    national museums, 4717–4718, 4727–4728

National Trust, 4722–4723
profession, 4725–4727
social exclusion, 4727
university, 4718
zoos, 4723–4724
National Museum of Computing, 4381
public library
authorities, populations of, 1839
Chetham Library in Manchester, 1837
combined museums and libraries,
1837–1838
County Library Authority, 1839
CUKT, 1839
gifts of individuals, 1836
itinerating libraries, 1837
Local Government Act of 1972, 1839
Museums Act of 1845, 1837
parish libraries, 1837
public and joint-stock contribution, 1836
Public Library Acts, 1838
social library, 1837
town libraries, 1836–1837
United Kingdom Serials Group (UKSG), 3390
United Nations Convention on the Rights of
Persons with Disabilities, 3575
United Nations Educational, Scientific and Cultural Organization (UNESCO), 1164,
3201, 4500
Action Plan, 4657
audiovisual archives, 4659–4660
CCAAA and SEAPAVAA, 4660
Communication and Information Sector,
4656–4657
Declaration of Principles, 4657
Department of Documentation, Libraries and
Archives, 4657
digital preservation, 4660–4661
documentary heritage program, 4659
goal, 4656
ICOM, 2429, 2431–2432
IDNs, 4659
IFAP, 4657
information accessibility, 4659
information ethics, 4658
information for development, 4658
information literacy, 4658
information portals, 4659
information preservation, 4659
Information Society Division, 4656–4658
infostructures, 4660
international directory database, 4658
Joint Technical Symposia, 4660
libraries, construction/reconstitution of, 4659
Memory of the World Programme,
4660–4661
multilingual cyberspace, 4659
national information policies and laws, formulation of, 4658
RAMP, 4659
site museums and monuments, 4169
strategic actions, 4660
United Nations Millennium Development
Goals, 4656
World Digital Library, 4661
WSIS, 4657
*United States Government Publications Monthly
Catalog*, 649

United States of America
academic libraries and librarians, 4775–4776
advocacy and marketing strategies, 4781
ALA, 4773–4774
American libraries
blogs and blogging, 4780
DRM, 4778–4779
gaming and libraries, 4779
Library 2.0 debates, 4781
network neutrality, 4778
podcasts, 4780
Web 2.0 and Library 2.0, 4779–4780
wikis, 4780–4781
archival repositories (*see* Archival
repositories)
from awareness to funding, 4774–4775
book trade, 3982
communication policy
see Communication policy
digital divide, 1280–1282
early history, 4740–4741
federal electronic information
citizen-centered electronic government,
1549
economics, 1554–1555
EFOIA, 1551
electronic government (e-gov) bills, 1549
FDLP, 1549, 1551, 1557
GILS, 1552
GPO Access Act, 1551
GPO Access system, 1552
High Performance Computing Act of 1991,
1551–1552
media and formats, variation and obsolescence of, 1554
NTIS, 1552
permanent public access, 1556
PRA, 1550–1551
principles, 1557
privacy, security, and authenticity,
1555–1556
safety net, 1555
subject portals, 1552–1553
tangible products, 1549
Title 44 of the U.S. Code, 1550
Web search engines, 1553–1554
information policy (*see* Information policy, in
United States)
librarians and library salaries, 4776–4777
library networks (*see* Regional library
networks)
modern era, 4741–4743
museums
accountability, 4771
affiliate organizations, 4769–4770
collections, stewardship of, 4770–4771
curators, responsibilities of, 4768–4769
definition, 4766
departments, 4769
director's role, 4768
educators, role of, 4769
federal funding, criteria for, 4766–4767
grant support, 4770
history of, 4767–4768
IMLS, leadership roles, 4770
nongovernmental organizations, 4766
professional association, 4769

and publics, relationships between, 4771–
4772
registrars and conservators, responsibilities
of, 4768
social value, 4772
staff positions, 4768
standards, 4769
urban institutions, 4766
professional societies and professionalism,
4743–4745
public libraries
Anthology Reading Room and Library,
1844
Astor Library, 1845
Bingham Library for Youth, 1843
in Boston, 1843–1844
Bray libraries, 1840
Charleston library, 1840
circulating library, 1842
continuing education, 1847–1848
early seventeenth century, 1839
gifts and grants, 1845–1846
Harris's criticism, 1844–1845
in Indiana, 1843
Keayne, Robert, 1839–1840
Library Service Act, 1847
Library Services and Construction Act,
1847
mechanics and apprentices, 1842
mercantile libraries, 1842
New York Public Library, 1845
OCLC, 1847
parish and provincial libraries, 1840
Peterborough library, 1839, 1843
Publick Library, 1840
Public Library Inquiry, 1846
social library, 1840–1842
standards, 1846
system concept, 1846–1847
Tilden Trust, 1845
YMCA Library, 1842–1843
recruitment and diversity, 4777–4778
State of America's Libraries, 4773–4774
Uniterms, 2221
Universal Access to Publications (UAP), 2408
Universal automatic computer, 2066
Universal Availability of Publications (UAP),
2456
Universal Bibliographic Control (UBC), 451,
1229, 1237
Universal Bibliographic Control and International MARC (UBCIM) Programme,
451, 2456–2457
Universal Dataflow and Telecommunications
(UDT), 2456
Universal decimal classification (UDC), 574,
961, 970, 1261, 1373, 1818, 2499, 2669,
4466, 4471, 4475
automation and, 4788–4789
auxiliary tables, 4785–4786
BC2, influence of, 589
citation order, 4787
classification structure, 4784–4785
filing order, 4787
general classification schemes, 4783
history, 4783–4784
main classes, 4787–4788

Universal decimal classification (UDC) (cont'd.)
notation, 4785
theoretical basis, 4786
Universal Declaration of Human Rights
(UDHR), 2395, 4692
Universal Dictionary of Trade and Commerce,
646
Universal MARC (UNIMARC), 2459
Universal Multi-Octet Coded Character Set
(UCS), 2984
The Universal Photographic Digital Imaging
Guidelines, 4943
Universal resource identifier (URI),
4081–4082
Universal standardization, 3107
Universal Virtual Computer (UVC), 1364,
1370
Universidad Nacional Mayor de San Marcos
(UNMSM), 3606, 3608
Universidad Veracruzana Library, 3085
University archives
archival domains, 4793
archival holdings, 4793
archivist's characteristics and professional
background, 4795
constituencies, 4795
core functions, 4794
definitions, 4791–4792
emergence and development of, 4791
environmental variables, 4792
Hungary, 1925–1926
nature of, 4793
programmatic activities of, 4794–4795
Switzerland, 4491–4492
University College of Addis Ababa (UCAA)
library, 1498–1499
museums and galleries, 1501
University Grants Commission (UGC), 1998,
2007, 2010, 4704
University librarian (UL), 4–5
University libraries, 1498–1499
in Australia, 384
in Denmark, 1219
in France, 1602–1603
in Germany, 1696
in Israel, 2544–2545
Japan, 2562–2564
in Kazakhstan, 2582–2583
in Moldova, 3125
in Peru, 3608
rare book collections, 3822
in Saudi Arabia, 3974
in Ukraine, 4646
in United Kingdom, 4703–4704
University Library in Bratislava (ULB),
4177–4178
University Library in Warsaw, 3677
University Library, Leiden, 2798
University library Nikola Tesla, 4131
University Library of Prague, 3323
University Library Svetozar Marković, 4130
University museums
in Japan, 2573–2574
in United Kingdom, 4718
University of Belgrade Libraries Association,
4131
University of Botswana, 1, 2325

University of British Columbia (UBC) Library,
663–664
University of British Columbia (UBC) Project,
1414
University of Copenhagen, 1215
University of Crete, 1731–1732
University of Gondar Library, 1499
University of Illinois at Urbana-Champaign
(UIUC), 3272
University of Kragujevac Svetozar Marković,
4131
University of Macedonia of Economics and
Social Sciences, 1731
University of Michigan Community Networking
Initiative (UM-CNI), 1030
University of Patras, 1732
University of Salamanca, 4321
University of Southern California (USC), 10,
1641
University of Tasmania (UTAS), 9
University of the South Pacific, 1, 688, 3547
Unstructured information, 2108
Unstructured metadata, 4427
Up-front editorial costs, 3466
Upto-Date, 1878
Uptown, 858–859
Urban and Regional Information Systems Asso-
ciation (URISA), 1673, 1678
Urban libraries, 1848
Urban Library Council (ULC), 1848, 4781
Usability testing, user interfaces
vs. beta testing, 4797–4798
definition, 4797
materials, 4798–4799
need, 4797
outcomes, 4801
participants, 4799–4800
post-test activities, 4800–4801
preparation, 4798
process, 4798
session, 4800
Usage, in altmetrics, 44
USA Patriot Act, 369, 2143
U.S. Department of Agriculture (USDA), 1553
U.S. Department of Education (USDE), 18–19
Usenet, 1059
User-agent-specific page delivery, 4035
User-based evaluations, 4554
User-centered design (UCD)
definition, 4803
foundations, 4803–4805
philosophy
conceptual foundation, 4806–4807
design, 4805–4806
information system, 4805
user, 4806
principles, 4809
process
context of use, 4808
design evaluation against user requirements, 4809
human centered process plan, 4808
potential designs, 4809
Shneiderman's principles, 4807–4808
user and organizational requirements,
4808–4809
rationale, 4803

rules, 4809
scope, 4803
standards, 4809
style guides, 4809
use and value, 4809–4810
User-centered revolution, 4847–4865
Boolean pitfalls, 4817–4818
customer service, 4819–4820
education, 4820–4821
errors, 4815
futures planning, 4819
human-centered design, 4814–4815
information traits, 4822–4823
instructions, 4816
legislation, 4820
online design, 4815–4816
reformulations, 4826
search behavior, 4824–4825
self-efficacy, 4817
sense-making research, 4821–4822
vs. system-centered approaches, 4812–4813
technology, 4818
user categories, 4822
userfriendly features, 4814
User education, 4
User-generated content (UGC), 1508,
4861–4862
User interfaces
subsystem, 2195
usability testing (*see* Usability testing, user
interfaces)
User-oriented and cognitive information
retrieval (IR)
cognitive structures and actors, 4879–4880
conceptual models, 4873–4874
domain of, 4873
generic models
Ingwersen–Wormell model, 4874
Wilson's model, 4874–4875
online interaction–process models,
4876–4879
relevance models, 4875–4876
task-based models, 4880–4883
User-oriented evaluation (UOE), 4820
User sensitization and training issues,
2335–2337
Use studies, *see* Information behavior research
U.S. Geological Survey (USGS), 1671, 2155
U.S. Government Printing Office (GPO), 1725,
4896
Usgovsearch, 1553
U.S. ISKO Chapter, 2498
U.S. National Archives and Records Adminis-
tration (NARA), 111, 3748
U.S. News and World Report, 650
U.S. Patent and Trademark Office (USPTO),
640, 3562
AI patents, 3565
APS, 3563
assignment database, 3568
bibliographic data, 3563
CD-ROM-based patent search tool, 3563
certificate of correction, 3566
defensive publication, 3565
International AIDS Patent Database, 3563
patent databases, 3568
Public PAIR, 3563

reexamination certificates, 3566
  Web site, 3568
  WEST and EAST search tools, 3563
U.S. Patent Classification (USPC), 3563,
  3566–3567
USPTO, *see* U.S. Patent and Trademark Office
U.S. Technical Advisory Groups (TAGs), 88
Usury Condemned, 1400
Utah Academic Library Consortium's Internet
  Navigator Tutorial, 3437–3438
Utah Library Association, 2393
Utilitarianism, 4219
Utility theory, 2354–2357
UWired, 4653
UX Day, 1421–1422

V

Vakkari's task-based information search model,
  2245, 4529, 4880
Vallerti Agreement, 3384
Value Set Authority Center (VSAC), 3341
Value structuring, 3062
Valun Tablet, 1121
Vancouver Public Library (VPL), 664, 3793
Vandalism in museums
  history, 4596–4597
  museum responses, 4598
  prevention, 4598–4600
Vanderbilt Television News Archive, 1563,
  1577
Varenius, 1685
Variable Media Network project, 2072
Variable Media Questionnaire tools, 2073
Vatican Library, 2763, 3046, 3951, 3956
Vatican Psalter, 1947
Vatican Virgil, 1946
Vector graphics, 1308
Vector space model (VSM), 2203–2204,
  2689–2690, 2696
Vellum bindings, 542, 545–546
Venezuela
  academic libraries, 4889–4890
  digital libraries and repositories, 4890
  financial issues, 4892–4893
  legal issues, 4894
  librarianship and professional education,
    4891–4892
  public libraries, 4890
  special libraries, 4890
Venice Charter, 1070–1071
Verbal working memory, 3842
Verband Deutscher Zoodirektoren, 5078
Vernadsky National Library of Ukraine, 3326,
  4643, 4645
Veronica tool, 2517
Version control
  copyright, 4897
  open access (OA), 4898
  OpenURL framework, 4899
  peer review, 4898–4899
  Sally Morris versions list, 4897–4898
  self-archiving, 4897, 4899
  Technical Working Group, 4899–4900
Version of record (VoR), 4898, 4900
Very fast decision tree (VDFT), 2635
Very large corpus (VLC) track, 4573–4574

Victorian Electronic Records Strategy (VERS),
  190, 3883
Victoria University of Wellington, 3376
Vidal de la Blache, Paul, 1687
Videoconferencing systems, 1062
Videotape, 1568, 2465
Vienna Dioscorides, 1946
Vienna Genesis, 1947
Vietnamese Women's Museum, 4915
Vietnam Military History Museum, 4915
Vilnius University Library, 2952
Virginia Historical Society (VHS), 1783, 3280
Virginia Institute of Technology, 1414
Virginia Tech Libraries, 4454
Virtual International Authority File (VIAF),
  3288
Virtual interviews, 3915
Virtual library, 1880, 1886, 4454
Virtual Museum of Canada (VMC), 676, 678–679
Virtual Museum of Canada Investment Program,
  679
Virtual museums, 1822
Virtual reference (VR), 17
Virtual reference desk, 3442–3443
Virtual school library, 4005
Virtual volunteerism, 4955
Visitor studies
  audience, 4917
  evaluation, 4918
  free-choice learning, 4918
  goals and objectives of, 4919–4920
  hypothesis-driven (deductive)/emergent
    (inductive) research, 4918
  identity-related motivations, 4923
  informal learning, 4918
  intrinsic motivation, 4922
  leisure-time learning, 4922
  longitudinal studies, 4922–4923
  mixed method research designs, 4921
  museum visitors, 4921
  outcomes, 4922
  profession, 4920
  qualitative research designs, 4921
  quantitative research designs, 4921
  self-determination, 4922
  self-fulfillment, 4922
  theoretical foundations of
    behaviorism, 4918
    constructivism, 4919
    epistemology, 4918
    logic/program modeling process, 4919
    positive youth development, 4919
    socioculturalism, 4919
Visual and performing arts
  archives, 4925
  archiving and managing
    copyright, intellectual property and privacy
      issues, 4930
    documentation, 4929–4930
    ethical issues, 4930
    professional associations, 4930–4931
    understanding of practice, 4929
    understanding the materials, 4929
  film, 4925
  materials
    advertising materials, 4927
    collaboration, 4926

  creation process, 4926
  creative and technical processes, 4926
  dedicated repositories, 4928–4929
  digital performances, 4926
  examples, 4926
  film and broadcasts, 4926
  final outcome, 4926
  live performances, 4926
  local and international relevance, 4927
  national repositories, 4927–4928
  origin, 4926
  painting, 4926–4927
  SIBMAS Web site, 4929
  theatrical production, 4927
Visual arts
  definition, 4925
  performance art, 4925 (*see also* Visual and
    performing arts)
Visual imagery, 1307
Visualization search engines, 4052–4053
Visual perception, 4408, 4410, 4414
Visual resources, 252
Visual Resources Association (VRA), 252–253,
  255, 3178, 4413
  affiliates, 4938
  annual conference, 4938
  appointments, 4937
  Core, 734
  data standards
    CCO, 4937–4938
    core categories, 4938
  foundation, 4936
  history, 4933–4936
  international membership, 4933
  organizational structure, 4936
  publications and communications, 4937
  regional chapters, 4936–4937
  SEI, 4938
  standing committees, 4937
Visual resources management, cultural
    institutions
  authorities, 4949
  building collections
    archival images, 4943–4944
    best practices, 4942–4943
    content sources, 4941–4942
    landscape, 4942
  cataloging, 4949
  collection access
    cataloging and standards, 4945
    copyright, 4946
    DAMS and DRMS, 4945–4946
    preservation and dispersal, 4944–4945
    rights and reproductions, 4946
    user services, 4944
    virtual organization, 4944
  collections, 4950
  content, 4949
  copyright status assess, 4948
  data standards and guidelines, 4949
  digital formats, 4948
  historic context, 4940–4941
  project reports and white papers, 4948–4949
  software selection, 4950
  staff
    and advocacy, 4949
    competencies, 4946–4947

Visual resources management, cultural
    institutions (cont'd.)
    staff (cont'd.)
        planning and administration, 4947–4948
        professional organizations, 4947
    vocabularies, 4949
Vital records, 1657–1658
Vladimirovas, Levas, 2954
Vocabulary links, 2940
Vocabulary switching, 1984
Voice of Youth Advocates (VOYA), 5062
Voice over Internet Providers (VoIP), 1049,
    1052, 1888, 3443
Volos Municipality archive, 1738
Voluntary product accessibility template
    (VPAT), 3578
Volunteered geographic information, 1673
Volunteerism
    adolescents, 4953–4954
    civic engagement, 4953
    community access, 4954–4955
    institutional advancement, 4952–4953
    Internet, impact of, 4955
    midlife adults, 4954
    museums and related institutions, 4951
        community service, 4952
        docents, 4952
        gallery interpreters, 4952
        historical societies, 4952
        museum professionals, 4953
    older adults, 4954
    orientation, 4951
    resources, 4955–4956
    smile desks, 4951–4952
    studies of, 4953
    volunteer management, 4955
von Mueller, Ferdinand Jakob Heinrich, 392–393
von Richthofen, Baron Ferdinand, 1687
V-optimal histograms, 2630
Vortals, 2893
VOSviewer, 923
Voyage around the world, 1685
VRA Bulletin, 4935, 4937
VRA Listserv, 4937
VRAweb.org, 4937

W

Wagner Act, 4689
Waitangi Tribunal, 2036, 3378
Walk-up kiosk, 4798
The Wanderer, 864, 1500, 2519
Wang–Soergel model, 4875–4876
Waples' graduate courses, 2910
Warez, 3650
Warhol, Andy, 2066
Warhol Museum, 4755
Warranties, 1274–1275
Washington Affairs Office, 52–53
Washington Conference on Scientific Informa-
    tion, 1534
Washington Library Network (WLN), 451
Waterfall software development life cycle,
    3356, 3360
Wathen and Burkell's model of credibility
    assessment, 1117
Watson Davis Award, 95

Watsonline, 250
Watts–Strogatz model, 4239
Wavelet transform, 4418–4419, 4423–4424
Wayfinding
    coordinated program, 4958
    devices, 4964–4965
    expected outcomes, 4965, 4972
    map, 4961–4964
    mental processes, 4958–4959
    physical elements
        content, 4961–4964
        legibility, 4959
        objects, 4961
        positive attributes of, 4959–4960
        spaces, 4960–4961
        structures, 4961
    physical wayfinding, 4958
    professionals, designing, 4961–4963
    and signage program (*see* Signage)
    thematic, 4958
    visitability, 4958
    visitors, needs of, 4961
W3C, *see* World Wide Web Consortium
Wealth of Nations, 1402–1403
Web 2.0, 4779, 5020
    designs, 4040
    features, 4780
Web Accessibility Initiative (WAI), 2348
Web Archiving Project (WARP), 2562
Web-based communities (WBCs), 214
Web-based Information Science Education
    (WISE), 707
Web-based recommender systems, 3860–3861
Webcasting, 2155
Web conferencing, 17
Web Content Accessibility Guidelines
    (WCAG), 3578
WebCrawler, 2521
Web credibility, 1115
WebDewey, 1259
Web Impact Factor (WIF), 2372
WebJunction, 3402
Weblogs, 2507
WebMeeting^(TM), 1057
Web of data, 2938–2941
The Web of Science, 474, 489, 923, 925–926
    additional features and services, 948
    bibliographic full record, 946–949
    chemistry literature, 818–819
    cited reference searching, 944–945
    content, 944
    search results and results navigation, 945–946
    source records and searching, 944
Webometrics, 2219, 2226–2227, 2367–2368
    data collection, 4988
    definition, 4983
    evolutionary studies, 4988–4989
    nonacademic link analysis, 4983, 4987
    scholarly communication
        AltaVista, 4986
        journals, 4984
        link creation motiation, 4986
        log analysis of journal usage, 4984–4985
        people, 4985
        small world analysis, 4986
        universities, 4985–4986
        visualization, 4986–4987

search engine evaluation, 4983, 4988
    Web 2.0, 4987–4988
Web ontology language (OWL), 1366,
    3461–3463, 3961, 3965–3966,
    4082–4083, 5028
Web scale discovery services
    challenges, 4981–4982
    content, 4979–4980
    interface, 4980
    OPAC, 4978–4982
    potential development, 4982
    precedents, 4979
    technical infrastructure, 4980–4981
Web Science, 4084
Web science research initiative (WSRI), 4084
Web search engines, *see* Search engines
    emergemce of, 2240
    search strategies, 2241
    usage patterns, 2242
Weick's sensemaking, 4113
Weighted indexing, 2200
Weizenbaum's ELIZA, 3348
Wendell H. Ford Government Publications
    Reform Act of 1998, 1550
Western European illumination
    Carolingian, 1947–1948
    Hiberno-Saxon, 1947
    Ottonian, 1948
Western knowledge systems (WKS), 2133
Western novels, 3705
Westlaw, 2708, 2713, 2728, 2741–2743, 2748
Westport Public Library Makerspace, 2992
WGBH Media Archives and Preservation Cen-
    ter, 1566
Wharton School of Business, 650
Whipstitching, *see* Oversewing
White Hat SEO, 4031
White House Conference on Library and Infor-
    mation Services II (WHCLIS), 5054
Who-Knows, 3865
Wicked problems, 1244–1245
Wide area information system (WAIS), 2518
Wide area networks (WANs), 2291, 3356
Widener Library, 4650
Wiener, Norbert, 2049–2050
Wi-Fi, 704
Wikipedia, 277, 3467, 4461, 5029
Wildlife husbandry, 5077
Wilson's information need model, 2116, 2119
Winnipeg Public Library, 3792
Winograd's SHRDLU, 3348
Winsor, Justin, 1844
WIPO, *see* World Intellectual Property
    Organization
WIPO Copyright Treaty (WCT), 1316
WIPO Performances and Phonographs Treaty
    (WPPT), 1316
Wireless Information System for Emergency
    Responders (WISER®), 3343
Wiswesser line notation, 831
Wollega Museum, 1503
Women's history archives
    Iowa Women's Archives, 4760
    Sallie Bingham Center for Women's History
        and Culture, 4760
    Schlesinger Library, 4759–4760
    Sophia Smith Collection, 4759

Women Writers Project, 1291
Word-by-word alphabetizing, 442
Word-frequency method, 421–422
Wordless picture books, 858–859
WordNet, 3457
Word processor
definition, 4993
IBM, 4994
Macintosh computers, 4997
microcomputers, 4995
Microsoft Word, 4996
MS-DOS, 4995–4996
MT/ST, 4993–4994
multipurpose computers, 4994–4995
predecessors, 4993
simpler version, 4997
typesetting, 4997–4998
WordPerfect, 4996–4997
WordStar, 4995
Workers' libraries
in Israel, 2543
in Vienna, 2804
Working Group on Internet Governance
(WGIG), 780
Workplace literacy, 2305
Workplace studies, 4026
Works of art, 262, 1090, 4579
World bibliography, 492
World Blind Union (WBU), 5008
WorldCat, 2, 820, 924, 3067
and FAST, 1545
Identities, 1546
OCLC
bibliographic database, 3394
collection analysis, 3398
CONTENTdm collections, 3400
enrichment and quality control, 3395–3396
evolution, 3396
FirstSearch service, 3395
growth, 3396–3397
and information standards, 3396
Navigator, 3398
Online Union Catalog, 3394
Open WorldCat pilot program, 3402–3403
selection, 3398
statistics, 3395
web services, 3403
WorldCat Local, 3403
WorldCat.org, 3403
WorldCat Collection Analysis service, 1258,
1262–1263
World Cultures Gallery, 3691, 3694–3695
World Digital Library (WDL), 903, 3332,
4661
World Economic Survey, 649
World economy, 2260
World Federation of Friends of Museums
(WFFM), 2432
World Intellectual Property Organization
(WIPO), 815, 2432, 2452, 3386, 3560,
3564, 3570, 4514
Copyright Treaty, 2142
governance, 5001
history, 5001
international copyright norms, 5004–5005
libraries, archives, and international copy-
right, 5005

library advocates
copyright limitations and exceptions,
5005–5007
development agenda, 5008–5009
digital preservation and copyright, 5007
traditional cultural expression, 5009
membership, 5001
organizational structure
activity, 5002
committees, 5002–5003
decision-making bodies, 5001–5002
Secretariat, 5003
treaty administration, 1472, 5003–5004
World Library and Information Conference
(WLIC), 4313
World of Warcraft (WOW), 1050
World Summit on the Information Society
(WSIS), 780, 3386, 4492, 4517, 4657
civil society role, 5013–5014
information society for all, 5017
issues, 5014
library and information sector interventions,
5014–5015
outcomes, 5015–5016
process, 5012–5013
resolution, 5012
unfinished business, 5016–5017
World Trade Organization (WTO), 783, 1024,
1722, 2409, 2452, 2475, 3381, 5002,
5005
World Wide Web (WWW), 298, 1034, 1059,
1061, 1290, 2367, 2372, 2505, 2516,
2518, 2524, 2892, 2938–2939, 3075,
3995, 4054, 4084, 4468
digital image, 1308
information behavior research, 2078–2079
libraries, 5026–5027
social and cultural effects, 5028–5029
technological impact, 5028
worm, 2519–2520
World Wide Web Consortium (W3C),
1366–1367, 1393, 3060, 3072, 3076,
3578, 4082–4083, 5020, 5026
achievements, 2348
activities, 2348, 5036–5037
historical highlights, 5035–5036
membership, 5036
Modern Paradigm for Standards, 5026
MWI, 2348
nonproprietary standards, 2347
recommendation, 5037
Unicode Standard, 4667–4668
vision, 5034
Web, 5035
Web interoperability, 2347
WWW, 2348
XML Schema, 1387–1388
Wove paper, 1828–1830
Writing; *see also* Technical writing
children books, 334, 867–868
communication, 1188
electronic technology, 3985
emergence, 3832–3833
Writing studies programs, 4548, 4552
Writing surfaces, 1824, 1826, 2717, 3552
Wunderkammern, 1524, 3150
Würzburg library, 1697

X
Xenocrates of Aphrodisias, 3043
XML, *see* Extensible Markup Language
XML information retrieval
INEX, 5039
query languages
clause-based queries, 5041–5042
content-only queries, 5040
IEEE test collection, INEX, 5040
path-based queries, 5041
tag-based queries, 5040
ranking strategies
aggregation, 5045
merging, 5045–5046
overlaps removal, 5047
propagation, 5045
scoring, 5044–5045
structural constraints, 5046–5047
representation strategies, 5042–5043
XPath query, 1365, 5041
XQuery Full-Text, 5042, 5048
X-ray radiography, 4429
XSLT, *see* Extensible stylesheet language
transformations

Y
Yad Vashem Archives, 2555–2556
Yad Vashem Museum, 2552
Yahoo!, 2368, 2520–2521, 4048, 4051
YALSA, *see* Young Adult Library Services
Association
Yamaguchi City Library, 2563–2564
Yandex search engine, 4051
YBP Library Services, 342, 413, 1210
Year-round schooling, 4002
Yerevan Centralized Children's Library System,
230
Yerevan State University Library, 230, 232–233
Young Adult Library Services Association
(YALSA), 334, 3998, 5052–5059
Young adult (YA) services
AASL, 5058
adolescent development
physical growth, 5059–5061
social characteristics, 5059
advisory groups, 5061
Caleb Bingham's gift, 5058
definitions, 5059
group programs, 5062
issues
censorship, 5062–5063
preference, 5064
reference queries, 5063–5064
technology usage, 5064
YA congregate, 5063
personal reading, 5061–5062
public *vs.* school library services, 5058
specific information-seeking, 5062
staff, 5061
Teen Read Week, 5058
theoretical foundations, 5059
YALSA, 5052–5054, 5058
Young Adult Services Division (YASD),
5052–5054
Young Men's Christian Association (YMCA)
Library, 1842–1843

YouSendIt service, 3653
Youth information
  health information behavior studies, 843
  needs, 5067–5069
  research and practice, 5073–5074
  seeking behaviors
    reference services, 5073
    resource preferences, 5071–5072
    searching for information, 5072–5073
YouTube, 3227, 3654, 3862, 4551, 5064
Yo! Yes? (art), 858
Yugoslav Film Archives, 4133

Z

Zagreb Diocese Metropolitan Library, 1122
Zambia Library Services, 3324
Załuski Library, 3675
Zaytūnah's al-Abdalīyah Library, 4625
Zentralblatt MATH (Zbl) tool, 3644
Zephir system, 1760
Zephyr, 1733
Z39.50 Implementors Group (ZIG),
  2183–2184

Zincographic printing process, 1868
Z39.50 information retrieval protocols
  bibliographic information, 2895
  chronology, 2183–2184
  client and server software, 2184
  Init service, 2184–2185
  present service, 2185–2186
  search service, 2185
  ZING project, 2186–2187
Z39.50 International Next Generation (ZING)
  project, 2186–2187, 2347
Zipf, George Kingsley, 502, 506
Zipf's law, 502, 506, 514–516, 2210, 2371
Zoologica (publications), 5078
Zoological parks and aquariums
  archives, 5083
  libraries
    current status and services, 5081–5083
    early libraries, establishment of, 5081
    need for, 5080–5081
  professional development
    animal collections, 5077
    captive wildlife management, 5077
    European collections, 5077–5078

    exotic wild animals, 5078
    modern aquariums, 5078
    modern zoological park management, 5077
    professional associations, 5078
    public aquarium, 5078
    professional literature, growth in, 5078–5080
Zoological research, 1705
Zoological Society of London, 4723, 5077, 5081
Zoology, 575, 1534, 4723
Zoos
  Hungary, 1930
  in Kazakhstan, 2588–2589
  in museums, 3238
  OPLs, 3416
  Switzerland, 4495
  in United Kingdom, 4723–4724
  and botanical gardens
    Germany, 1706
    India, 2023–2025
    Switzerland, 4495
Zoosemiotics, 4096
Zthes specifications, 2671, 4074
The Z Was Zapped: A Play in Twenty-Six Acts,
  859–860